UNIVERSITY CASEBOOK SERIES®

THE CONSTITUTION OF THE UNITED STATES

THIRD EDITION

MICHAEL STOKES PAULSEN
Distinguished University Chair and Professor of Law
The University of St. Thomas

STEVEN GOW CALABRESI
Clayton J. and Henry R. Barber Professor of Law, Northwestern University
Visiting Professor of Law, Fall 2013–2016, Yale University
Visiting Professor of Political Theory, Brown University

MICHAEL W. MCCONNELL
Richard and Frances Mallery Professor of Law
Stanford University

SAMUEL L. BRAY
Professor of Law
University of California, Los Angeles

WILLIAM BAUDE
Neubauer Family Assistant Professor of Law
The University of Chicago Law School

FOUNDATION
PRESS

University Casebook Series is a trademark registered in the U.S. Patent and Trademark Office.

Printed in the United States of America

ISBN: 978-1-63459-938-2

To close readers of the Constitution

To Kristen, love of my life (MSP)
To Mimi, whose love is patient and kind (SGC)
To Mary (MWM)
To Abigail (SLB)
To Judith (WPB)

PREFACE

The third edition of this casebook continues the themes and organizing principles of previous editions. As we said in the preface to the first edition,

Why another casebook in the field of constitutional law? The existing casebooks are valuable. They offer a diverse array of approaches, and they are excellent compendia of cases. They tend, though, to focus *only* on cases—and almost exclusively U.S. Supreme Court decisions—as the source of constitutional law. They also emphasize present doctrine more than constitutional history. And they offer more attention to judicial discourse about the Constitution than to the document's own words and phrases and organization.

On each of these points, this casebook offers a different emphasis. It considers how the Constitution is interpreted and applied not only by the Court but also by Congress, the executive branch, lower federal courts, and all branches of state governments. It offers more detail on the history of the formation of the Constitution and more treatment of its principles in our nation's first 150 years. And in keeping with the premise that the document itself is the source of constitutional law, this book will emphasize the Constitution's text and structure. . . .

Our aim is that students should learn how to think about constitutional issues, rather than learn every fine detail of what the Court's most recent thinking is. We should not be in the business of producing law school graduates whose constitutional sophistication has a built-in obsolescence. We should be in the business of training future lawyer-citizens to be able to think about their Constitution, to deal with the constitutional law issues that will arise during their lifetimes, and to be able to place those issues in a broader context.

As in the previous editions, four features are especially prominent. First, the organization largely tracks the Constitution's own structure. Second, emphasis is placed on constitutional history. This history is not mere background. Rather, it reveals other paths for addressing enduring questions and it offers students a chance to interpret the Constitution a few steps away from contemporary politics. Third, the focus is on "Great Cases." These include not only the great good cases but also the great tragic ones (such as *Dred Scott*), and they include great "cases" of constitutional interpretation outside the courts (such as President Lincoln's First Inaugural Address). Fourth, the casebook lays stress on questions of interpretive methodology. Throughout the book, attention is given to five types of constitutional argument: text, historical context, structure, practice and precedent, and policy. The relative merits of these types of constitutional argument, and their inevitable conflicts, are considered in many scenarios.

Along with this continuity of design, there is some touching up. The organization is more linear, and the pace begins more quickly. In the chapter on separation of powers, new attention is given to the power of the purse and executive discretion, as well as the prerogative powers. In the federalism chapter, there is additional coverage of the taxing and spending powers, and of the Necessary and Proper Clause. In the chapter on the Reconstruction Amendments, there is new attention to slavery, the drafting of the Fourteenth Amendment, affirmative action, and incorporation.

Throughout these additions, we have continued to emphasize interpretation by the political branches, and the additions include congressional debates about the spending power, speeches in Congress about the Civil Rights Act of 1866 and the Fourteenth Amendment, a signing statement by President Barack Obama, a radio address by President Franklin Delano Roosevelt, and drafts of the Equal Rights Amendment. These additions mean that the casebook is now suitable not only for a survey course on structure or rights, but also for a course more specifically on federalism or the Fourteenth Amendment. But casebook revision giveth and taketh away, and there are painful cuts. The omitted materials—from *In re Neagle* and *Summers v. Earth Island Institute* to *Erie* and *Eisenstadt*—are all included in the supplemental materials for adopters of this book.

Finally, we are delighted to welcome a new coauthor, Will Baude. Will is a distinguished constitutional law professor at the University of Chicago, and he has already made major contributions to this edition.

We are grateful to all those who helped make this book possible. Thank you to the professors who gave invaluable criticisms and suggestions: Josh Blackman, Nathan Chapman, Peter Conti-Brown, Marc DeGirolami, Tessa Dysart, Rick Garnett, Christopher Green, Philip Hamburger, Kurt Lash, Zachary Price, Sai Prakash, and Ryan Williams. Thank you as well to Mark Burnside and Dottie Lee, for their meticulous proofreading. Thank you to the reference librarians of the UCLA School of Law for for their ever-skillful assistance. And thank you to the production team at Foundation Press. Due to these combined efforts this is, we hope, a good book made better.

MSP

SGC

MWM

SLB

WPB

September 2016

SUMMARY OF CONTENTS

TABLE OF CONTENTS

PART 1. STRUCTURE AND POWERS OF THE NATIONAL GOVERNMENT

PART 2. RIGHTS AGAINST THE GOVERNMENT

TABLE OF CASES

The principal cases are in bold type.

UNIVERSITY CASEBOOK SERIES®

THE CONSTITUTION OF THE UNITED STATES

THIRD EDITION

THE CONSTITUTION OF THE UNITED STATES

Preamble

We the People of the United States, in Order to form a more perfect Union, establish Justice, insure domestic Tranquility, provide for the common defence, promote the general Welfare, and secure the Blessings of Liberty to ourselves and our Posterity, do ordain and establish this Constitution for the United States of America.

Article I

§ 1. All legislative Powers herein granted shall be vested in a Congress of the United States, which shall consist of a Senate and House of Representatives.

§ 2. The House of Representatives shall be composed of Members chosen every second Year by the People of the several States, and the Electors in each State shall have the Qualifications requisite for Electors of the most numerous Branch of the State Legislature.

No Person shall be a Representative who shall not have attained to the age of twenty five Years, and been seven Years a Citizen of the United States, and who shall not, when elected, be an Inhabitant of that State in which he shall be chosen.

Representatives and direct Taxes shall be apportioned among the several States which may be included within this Union, according to their respective Numbers, which shall be determined by adding to the whole Number of free Persons, including those bound to Service for a Term of Years, and excluding Indians not taxed, three fifths of all other Persons. The actual Enumeration shall be made within three Years after the first Meeting of the Congress of the United States, and within every subsequent Term of ten Years, in such Manner as they shall by Law direct. The Number of Representatives shall not exceed one for every thirty Thousand, but each State shall have at Least one Representative; and until such enumeration shall be made, the State of New Hampshire shall be entitled to chuse three, Massachusetts eight, Rhode Island and Providence Plantations one, Connecticut five, New York six, New Jersey four, Pennsylvania eight, Delaware one, Maryland six, Virginia ten, North Carolina five, South Carolina five, and Georgia three.

When vacancies happen in the Representation from any State, the Executive Authority thereof shall issue Writs of Election to fill such Vacancies.

The House of Representatives shall chuse their Speaker and other Officers; and shall have the sole Power of Impeachment.

§ 3. The Senate of the United States shall be composed of two Senators from each State, chosen by the Legislature thereof, for six Years; and each Senator shall have one Vote.

Immediately after they shall be assembled in Consequence of the first Election, they shall be divided as equally as may be into three Classes. The Seats of the Senators of the first Class shall be vacated at the Expiration of the second Year, of the second Class at the Expiration of the fourth Year, and of the third Class at the Expiration of the sixth Year, so that one third may be chosen every second Year; and if Vacancies happen by Resignation, or otherwise, during the Recess of the

Legislature of any State, the Executive thereof may make temporary Appointments until the next Meeting of the Legislature, which shall then fill such Vacancies.

No Person shall be a Senator who shall not have attained to the Age of thirty Years, and been nine Years a Citizen of the United States, and who shall not, when elected, be an Inhabitant of that State for which he shall be chosen.

The Vice President of the United States shall be President of the Senate but shall have no Vote, unless they be equally divided.

The Senate shall chuse their other Officers, and also a President pro tempore, in the Absence of the Vice President, or when he shall exercise the Office of President of the United States.

The Senate shall have the sole Power to try all Impeachments. When sitting for that Purpose, they shall be on Oath or Affirmation. When the President of the United States is tried the Chief Justice shall preside: And no Person shall be convicted without the Concurrence of two thirds of the Members present.

Judgment in Cases of Impeachment shall not extend further than to removal from Office, and disqualification to hold and enjoy any Office of honor, Trust or Profit under the United States: but the Party convicted shall nevertheless be liable and subject to Indictment, Trial, Judgment and Punishment, according to Law.

§ 4. The Times, Places and Manner of holding Elections for Senators and Representatives, shall be prescribed in each State by the Legislature thereof; but the Congress may at any time by Law make or alter such Regulations, except as to the Places of chusing Senators.

The Congress shall assemble at least once in every Year, and such Meeting shall be on the first Monday in December, unless they shall by Law appoint a different Day.

§ 5. Each House shall be the Judge of the Elections, Returns and Qualifications of its own Members, and a Majority of each shall constitute a Quorum to do Business; but a smaller Number may adjourn from day to day, and may be authorized to compel the Attendance of absent Members, in such Manner, and under such Penalties as each House may provide.

Each House may determine the Rules of its Proceedings, punish its Members for disorderly Behaviour, and, with the Concurrence of two thirds, expel a Member.

Each House shall keep a Journal of its Proceedings, and from time to time publish the same, excepting such Parts as may in their Judgment require Secrecy; and the Yeas and Nays of the Members of either House on any question shall, at the Desire of one fifth of those Present, be entered on the Journal.

Neither House, during the Session of Congress, shall, without the Consent of the other, adjourn for more than three days, nor to any other Place than that in which the two Houses shall be sitting.

§ 6. The Senators and Representatives shall receive a Compensation for their Services, to be ascertained by Law, and paid out of the Treasury of the United States. They shall in all Cases, except Treason, Felony and Breach of the Peace, be privileged from Arrest during their Attendance at the Session of their respective Houses, and in going to and returning from the same; and for any Speech or Debate in either House, they shall not be questioned in any other Place.

No Senator or Representative shall, during the Time for which he was elected, be appointed to any civil Office under the Authority of the United States, which shall have been created, or the Emoluments whereof shall have been encreased during such time; and no Person holding any Office under the United States, shall be a Member of either House during his Continuance in Office.

§ 7. All Bills for raising Revenue shall originate in the House of Representatives; but the Senate may propose or concur with amendments as on other Bills.

Every Bill which shall have passed the House of Representatives and the Senate, shall, before it become a law, be presented to the President of the United States: If he approve he shall sign it, but if not he shall return it, with his Objections to that House in which it shall have originated, who shall enter the Objections at large on their Journal, and proceed to reconsider it. If after such Reconsideration two thirds of that House shall agree to pass the Bill, it shall be sent, together with the Objections, to the other House, by which it shall likewise be reconsidered, and if approved by two thirds of that House, it shall become a Law. But in all such Cases the Votes of both Houses shall be determined by Yeas and Nays, and the Names of the Persons voting for and against the Bill shall be entered on the Journal of each House respectively. If any Bill shall not be returned by the President within ten Days (Sundays excepted) after it shall have been presented to him, the Same shall be a Law, in like Manner as if he had signed it, unless the Congress by their Adjournment prevent its Return, in which Case it shall not be a Law.

Every Order, Resolution, or Vote to which the Concurrence of the Senate and House of Representatives may be necessary (except on a question of Adjournment) shall be presented to the President of the United States; and before the Same shall take Effect, shall be approved by him, or being disapproved by him, shall be repassed by two thirds of the Senate and House of Representatives, according to the Rules and Limitations prescribed in the Case of a Bill.

§ 8. The Congress shall have Power

To lay and collect Taxes, Duties, Imposts and Excises, to pay the Debts and provide for the common Defence and general Welfare of the United States; but all Duties, Imposts and Excises shall be uniform throughout the United States;

To borrow Money on the credit of the United States;

To regulate Commerce with foreign Nations, and among the several States, and with the Indian Tribes;

To establish an uniform Rule of Naturalization, and uniform Laws on the subject of Bankruptcies throughout the United States;

To coin Money, regulate the Value thereof, and of foreign Coin, and fix the Standard of Weights and Measures;

To provide for the Punishment of counterfeiting the Securities and current Coin of the United States;

To establish Post Offices and post Roads;

To promote the Progress of Science and useful Arts, by securing for limited Times to Authors and Inventors the exclusive Right to their respective Writings and Discoveries;

To constitute Tribunals inferior to the supreme Court;

To define and punish Piracies and Felonies committed on the high Seas, and Offences against the Law of Nations;

To declare War, grant Letters of Marque and Reprisal, and make Rules concerning Captures on Land and Water;

To raise and support Armies, but no Appropriation of Money to that Use shall be for a longer Term than two Years;

To provide and maintain a Navy;

To make Rules for the Government and Regulation of the land and naval Forces;

To provide for calling forth the Militia to execute the Laws of the Union, suppress Insurrections and repel Invasions;

To provide for organizing, arming, and disciplining, the Militia, and for governing such Part of them as may be employed in the Service of the United States, reserving to the States respectively, the Appointment of the Officers, and the Authority of training the Militia according to the discipline prescribed by Congress;

To exercise exclusive Legislation in all Cases whatsoever, over such District (not exceeding ten Miles square) as may, by Cession of Particular States, and the Acceptance of Congress, become the Seat of the Government of the United States, and to exercise like Authority over all Places purchased by the Consent of the Legislature of the State in which the Same shall be, for the Erection of Forts, Magazines, Arsenals, dock Yards and other needful Buildings;—And

To make all Laws which shall be necessary and proper for carrying into Execution the foregoing Powers and all other Powers vested by this Constitution in the Government of the United States, or in any Department or Officer thereof.

§ 9. The Migration or Importation of such Persons as any of the States now existing shall think proper to admit, shall not be prohibited by the Congress prior to the Year one thousand eight hundred and eight, but a Tax or duty may be imposed on such Importation, not exceeding ten dollars for each Person.

The Privilege of the Writ of Habeas Corpus shall not be suspended, unless when in Cases of Rebellion or Invasion the public Safety may require it.

No Bill of Attainder or ex post facto Law shall be passed.

No Capitation, or other direct, Tax shall be laid, unless in Proportion to the Census of Enumeration herein before directed to be taken.

No Tax or Duty shall be laid on Articles exported from any State.

No Preference shall be given by any Regulation of Commerce or Revenue to the Ports of one State over those of another: nor shall Vessels bound to, or from, one State, be obliged to enter, clear or pay Duties in another.

No Money shall be drawn from the Treasury, but in Consequence of Appropriations made by Law; and a regular Statement and Account of the Receipts and Expenditures of all public Money shall be published from time to time.

No Title of Nobility shall be granted by the United States: And no Person holding any Office of Profit or Trust under them, shall, without the Consent of the Congress, accept of any present, Emolument, Office, or Title, of any kind whatever, from any King, Prince or foreign State.

§ 10. No State shall enter into any Treaty, Alliance, or Confederation; grant Letters of Marque and Reprisal; coin Money; emit Bills of Credit; make any Thing but gold and silver Coin a Tender in Payment of Debts; pass any Bill of Attainder, ex post facto Law, or Law impairing the Obligation of Contracts, or grant any Title of Nobility.

No State shall, without the Consent of the Congress, lay any Imposts or Duties on Imports or Exports, except what may be absolutely necessary for executing it's inspection Laws: and the net Produce of all Duties and Imposts, laid by any State on Imports or Exports, shall be for the Use of the Treasury of the United States; and all such Laws shall be subject to the Revision and Controul of the Congress.

No State shall, without the Consent of Congress, lay any Duty of Tonnage, keep Troops, or Ships of War in time of Peace, enter into any Agreement or Compact with another State, or with a foreign Power, or engage in War, unless actually invaded, or in such imminent Danger as will not admit of delay.

[handwritten margin note: things states can't do w/o congress consent]

Article II

§ 1. The executive Power shall be vested in a President of the United States of America. He shall hold his Office during the Term of four Years, and, together with the Vice President, chosen for the same Term, be elected, as follows:

Each State shall appoint, in such Manner as the Legislature thereof may direct, a Number of Electors, equal to the whole Number of Senators and Representatives to which the State may be entitled in the Congress: but no Senator or Representative, or Person holding an Office of Trust or Profit under the United States, shall be appointed an Elector.

The Electors shall meet in their respective States, and vote by Ballot for two Persons, of whom one at least shall not be an Inhabitant of the same State with themselves. And they shall make a List of all the Persons voted for, and of the Number of Votes for each; which List they shall sign and certify, and transmit sealed to the Seat of the Government of the United States, directed to the President of the Senate. The President of the Senate shall, in the Presence of the Senate and House of Representatives, open all the Certificates, and the Votes shall then be counted. The Person having the greatest Number of Votes shall be the President, if such Number be a Majority of the whole Number of Electors appointed; and if there be more than one who have such Majority, and have an equal Number of Votes, then the House of Representatives shall immediately chuse by Ballot one of them for President; and if no Person have a Majority, then from the five highest on the List the said House shall in like Manner chuse the President. But in chusing the President, the Votes shall be taken by States, the Representatives from each State having one Vote; a quorum for this Purpose shall consist of a Member or Members from two thirds of the States, and a Majority of all the States shall be necessary to a Choice. In every Case, after the Choice of the President, the Person having the greatest Number of Votes of the Electors shall be the Vice President. But if there should remain two or more who have equal Votes, the Senate shall chuse from them by Ballot the Vice President.

The Congress may determine the Time of chusing the Electors, and the Day on which they shall give their Votes; which Day shall be the same throughout the United States.

No Person except a natural born Citizen, or a Citizen of the United States, at the time of the Adoption of this Constitution, shall be eligible to the Office of President; neither shall any person be eligible to that Office who shall not have attained to the Age of thirty five Years, and been fourteen Years a Resident within the United States.

In Case of the Removal of the President from Office, or of his Death, Resignation, or Inability to discharge the Powers and Duties of the said Office, the Same shall devolve on the Vice President, and the Congress may by Law provide for the Case of Removal, Death, Resignation or Inability, both of the President and Vice President, declaring what Officer shall then act as President, and such Officer shall act accordingly, until the Disability be removed, or a President shall be elected.

The President shall, at stated Times, receive for his Services, a Compensation, which shall neither be encreased nor diminished during the Period for which he shall have been elected, and he shall not receive within that Period any other Emolument from the United States, or any of them.

Before he enter on the Execution of his Office, he shall take the following Oath or Affirmation:—"I do solemnly swear (or affirm) that I will faithfully execute the Office of President of the United States, and will to the best of my Ability, preserve, protect and defend the Constitution of the United States."

§ 2. The President shall be Commander in Chief of the Army and Navy of the United States, and of the Militia of the several States, when called into the actual Service of the United States; he may require the Opinion, in writing, of the principal Officer in each of the executive Departments, upon any Subject relating to the Duties of their respective Offices, and he shall have Power to Grant Reprieves and Pardons for Offences against the United States, except in Cases of Impeachment.

He shall have Power, by and with the Advice and Consent of the Senate, to make Treaties, provided two thirds of the Senators present concur; and he shall nominate, and by and with the Advice and Consent of the Senate, shall appoint Ambassadors, other public Ministers and Consuls, Judges of the supreme Court, and all other Officers of the United States, whose Appointments are not herein otherwise provided for, and which shall be established by Law: but the Congress may by Law vest the Appointment of such inferior Officers, as they think proper, in the President alone, in the Courts of Law, or in the Heads of Departments.

The President shall have Power to fill up all Vacancies that may happen during the Recess of the Senate, by granting Commissions which shall expire at the End of their next Session.

§ 3. He shall from time to time give to the Congress Information on the State of the Union, and recommend to their Consideration such Measures as he shall judge necessary and expedient; he may, on extraordinary Occasions, convene both Houses, or either of them, and in Case of Disagreement between them, with Respect to the Time of Adjournment, he may adjourn them to such Time as he shall think proper; he shall receive Ambassadors and other public Ministers; he shall take Care that the Laws be faithfully executed, and shall Commission all the Officers of the United States.

§ 4. The President, Vice President and all Civil Officers of the United States, shall be removed from Office on Impeachment for and Conviction of, Treason, Bribery, or other high Crimes and Misdemeanors.

Article III

§ 1. The judicial Power of the United States, shall be vested in one supreme Court, and in such inferior Courts as the Congress may from time to time ordain and establish. The Judges, both of the supreme and inferior Courts, shall hold their Offices during good Behaviour, and shall, at stated Times, receive for their Services, a Compensation, which shall not be diminished during their Continuance in Office.

§ 2. The judicial Power shall extend to all Cases, in Law and Equity, arising under this Constitution, the Laws of the United States, and Treaties made, or which shall be made, under their Authority;—to all Cases affecting Ambassadors, other public ministers and Consuls;—to all Cases of admiralty and maritime Jurisdiction;—to Controversies to which the United States shall be a Party;—to Controversies between two or more States;—between a State and Citizens of another State;—between Citizens of different States;—between Citizens of the same State claiming Lands under Grants of different States, and between a State, or the Citizens thereof, and foreign States, Citizens or Subjects.

In all Cases affecting Ambassadors, other public Ministers and Consuls, and those in which a State shall be Party, the supreme Court shall have original Jurisdiction. In all the other Cases before mentioned, the supreme Court shall have appellate Jurisdiction, both as to Law and Fact, with such Exceptions, and under such Regulations as the Congress shall make.

The Trial of all Crimes, except in Cases of Impeachment, shall be by Jury; and such Trial shall be held in the State where the said Crimes shall have been committed; but when not committed within any State, the Trial shall be at such Place or Places as the Congress may by Law have directed.

§ 3. Treason against the United States, shall consist only in levying War against them, or in adhering to their Enemies, giving them Aid and Comfort. No Person shall be convicted of Treason unless on the Testimony of two Witnesses to the same overt Act, or on Confession in open Court.

The Congress shall have Power to declare the Punishment of Treason, but no Attainder of Treason shall work Corruption of Blood, or Forfeiture except during the Life of the Person attainted.

Article IV

§ 1. Full Faith and Credit shall be given in each State to the public Acts, Records, and judicial Proceedings of every other State. And the Congress may by general Laws prescribe the Manner in which such Acts, Records and Proceedings shall be proved, and the Effect thereof.

§ 2. The Citizens of each State shall be entitled to all Privileges and Immunities of Citizens in the several States.

A Person charged in any State with Treason, Felony, or other Crime, who shall flee from Justice, and be found in another State, shall on Demand of the executive Authority of the State from which he fled, be delivered up, to be removed to the State having Jurisdiction of the Crime.

No Person held to Service or Labour in one State, under the Laws thereof, escaping into another, shall, in Consequence of any Law or Regulation therein, be discharged from such Service or Labour, but shall be delivered up on Claim of the Party to whom such Service or Labour may be due.

§ 3. New States may be admitted by the Congress into this Union; but no new State shall be formed or erected within the Jurisdiction of any other State; nor any State be formed by the Junction of two or more States, or Parts of States, without the Consent of the Legislatures of the States concerned as well as of the Congress.

The Congress shall have Power to dispose of and make all needful Rules and Regulations respecting the Territory or other Property belonging to the United States; and nothing in this Constitution shall be so construed as to Prejudice any Claims of the United States, or of any particular State.

§ 4. The United States shall guarantee to every State in this Union a Republican Form of Government, and shall protect each of them against Invasion; and on Application of the Legislature, or of the Executive (when the Legislature cannot be convened) against domestic Violence.

Article V

The Congress, whenever two thirds of both Houses shall deem it necessary, shall propose Amendments to this Constitution, or, on the Application of the Legislatures of two thirds of the several States, shall call a Convention for proposing Amendments, which, in either Case, shall be valid to all Intents and Purposes, as Part of this Constitution, when ratified by the Legislatures of three fourths of the several States, or by Conventions in three fourths thereof, as the one or the other Mode of Ratification may be proposed by the Congress; Provided that no Amendment which may be made prior to the Year One thousand eight hundred and eight shall in any Manner affect the first and fourth Clauses in the Ninth Section of the first Article; and that no State, without its Consent, shall be deprived of its equal Suffrage in the Senate.

Article VI

All Debts contracted and Engagements entered into, before the Adoption of this Constitution, shall be as valid against the United States under this Constitution, as under the Confederation.

This Constitution, and the Laws of the United States which shall be made in Pursuance thereof; and all Treaties made, or which shall be made, under the Authority of the United States, shall be the supreme Law of the Land; and the Judges in every State shall be bound thereby, any Thing in the Constitution or Laws of any state to the Contrary notwithstanding.

The Senators and Representatives before mentioned, and the Members of the several State Legislatures, and all executive and judicial Officers, both of the United States and of the several States, shall be bound by Oath or Affirmation, to support this Constitution; but no religious Test shall ever be required as a Qualification to any Office or public Trust under the United States.

Article VII

The Ratification of the Conventions of nine States, shall be sufficient for the Establishment of this Constitution between the States so ratifying the same.

Amendment I

Congress shall make no law respecting an establishment of religion, or prohibiting the free exercise thereof; or abridging the freedom of speech, or of the press; or the right of the people peaceably to assemble, and to petition the Government for a redress of grievances.

Amendment II

A well regulated Militia, being necessary to the security of a free State, the right of the people to keep and bear Arms, shall not be infringed.

Amendment III

No Soldier shall, in time of peace be quartered in any house, without the consent of the Owner, nor in time of war, but in a manner to be prescribed by law.

Amendment IV

The right of the people to be secure in their persons, houses, papers, and effects, against unreasonable searches and seizures, shall not be violated, and no Warrants shall issue, but upon probable cause, supported by Oath or affirmation, and particularly describing the place to be searched, and the persons or things to be seized.

Amendment V

No person shall be held to answer for a capital, or otherwise infamous crime, unless on a presentment or indictment of a Grand Jury, except in cases arising in the land or naval forces, or in the Militia, when in actual service in time of War or public danger; nor shall any person be subject for the same offence to be twice put in jeopardy of life or limb; nor shall be compelled in any criminal case to be a witness against himself, nor be deprived of life, liberty, or property, without due process of law; nor shall private property be taken for public use, without just compensation.

Amendment VI

In all criminal prosecutions, the accused shall enjoy the right to a speedy and public trial, by an impartial jury of the State and district wherein the crime shall have been committed, which district shall have been previously ascertained by law, and to be informed of the nature and cause of the accusation; to be confronted with the witnesses against him; to have compulsory process for obtaining witnesses in his favor, and to have the Assistance of Counsel for his defence.

Amendment VII

In Suits at common law, where the value in controversy shall exceed twenty dollars, the right of trial by jury shall be preserved, and no fact tried by a jury, shall be otherwise re-examined in any Court of the United States, than according to the rules of the common law.

Amendment VIII

Excessive bail shall not be required, nor excessive fines imposed, nor cruel and unusual punishments inflicted.

Amendment IX

The enumeration in the Constitution, of certain rights, shall not be construed to deny or disparage others retained by the people.

Amendment X

The powers not delegated to the United States by the Constitution, nor prohibited by it to the States, are reserved to the States respectively, or to the people.

Amendment XI

The Judicial power of the United States shall not be construed to extend to any suit in law or equity, commenced or prosecuted against one of the United States by Citizens of another State, or by Citizens or Subjects of any Foreign State.

Amendment XII

The Electors shall meet in their respective states, and vote by ballot for President and Vice President, one of whom, at least, shall not be an inhabitant of the same state with themselves; they shall name in their ballots the person voted for as President, and in distinct ballots the person voted for as Vice-President, and they shall make distinct lists of all persons voted for as President, and of all persons voted for as Vice-President, and of the number of votes for each, which lists they shall sign and certify, and transmit sealed to the seat of the government of the United States, directed to the President of the Senate;—The President of the Senate shall, in the presence of the Senate and House of Representatives, open all the certificates and the votes shall then be counted;—The person having the greatest number of votes for President, shall be the President, if such number be a majority of the whole number of Electors appointed; and if no person have such majority, then from the persons having the highest numbers not exceeding three on the list of those voted for as President, the House of Representatives shall choose immediately, by ballot, the President. But in choosing the President, the votes shall be taken by states, the representation from each state having one vote; a quorum for this purpose shall consist of a member or members from two-thirds of the states, and a majority of all the states shall be necessary to a choice. And if the House of Representatives shall not choose a President whenever the right of choice shall devolve upon them, before the fourth day of March next following, then the Vice-President shall act as President, as in the case of the death or other constitutional disability of the President.—The person having the greatest number of votes as Vice-President, shall be the Vice-President, if such number be a majority of the whole number of Electors appointed, and if no person have a majority, then from the two highest numbers on the list, the Senate shall choose the Vice-President; a quorum for the purpose shall consist of two-thirds of the whole number of Senators, and a majority of the whole number shall be necessary to a choice. But no person constitutionally ineligible to the office of President shall be eligible to that of Vice-President of the United States.

Amendment XIII

§ 1. Neither slavery nor involuntary servitude, except as a punishment for crime whereof the party shall have been duly convicted, shall exist within the United States, or any place subject to their jurisdiction.

§ 2. Congress shall have power to enforce this article by appropriate legislation.

Amendment XIV

§ 1. All persons born or naturalized in the United States, and subject to the jurisdiction thereof, are citizens of the United States and of the State wherein they reside. No State shall make or enforce any law which shall abridge the privileges or immunities of citizens of the United States; nor shall any State deprive any person of life, liberty, or property, without due process of law; nor deny to any person within its jurisdiction the equal protection of the laws.

§ 2. Representatives shall be apportioned among the several States according to their respective numbers, counting the whole number of persons in each State, excluding Indians not taxed. But when the right to vote at any election for the choice of electors for President and Vice President of the United States, Representatives in Congress, the Executive and Judicial officers of a State, or the members of the Legislature thereof, is denied to any of the male inhabitants of such State, being twenty-one years of age, and citizens of the United States, or in any way abridged, except for participation in rebellion, or other crime, the basis of representation therein shall be reduced in the proportion which the number of such male citizens shall bear to the whole number of male citizens twenty-one years of age in such State.

§ 3. No person shall be a Senator or Representative in Congress, or elector of President and Vice President, or hold any office, civil or military, under the United States, or under any State, who, having previously taken an oath, as a member of Congress, or as an officer of the United States, or as a member of any State legislature, or as an executive or judicial officer of any State, to support the Constitution of the United States, shall have engaged in insurrection or rebellion against the same, or given aid or comfort to the enemies thereof. But Congress may by a vote of two-thirds of each House, remove such disability.

§ 4. The validity of the public debt of the United States, authorized by law, including debts incurred for payment of pensions and bounties for services in suppressing insurrection or rebellion, shall not be questioned. But neither the United States nor any State shall assume or pay any debt or obligation incurred in aid of insurrection or rebellion against the United States, or any claim for the loss or emancipation of any slave; but all such debts, obligations and claims shall be held illegal and void.

§ 5. The Congress shall have power to enforce, by appropriate legislation, the provisions of this article.

Amendment XV

§ 1. The right of citizens of the United States to vote shall not be denied or abridged by the United States or by any State on account of race, color, or previous condition of servitude.

§ 2. The Congress shall have power to enforce this article by appropriate legislation.

Amendment XVI

The Congress shall have power to lay and collect taxes on incomes, from whatever source derived, without apportionment among the several States, and without regard to any census or enumeration.

Amendment XVII

The Senate of the United States shall be composed of two Senators from each State, elected by the people thereof, for six years; and each Senator shall have one vote. The electors in each State shall have the qualifications requisite for electors of the most numerous branch of the State legislatures.

When vacancies happen in the representation of any State in the Senate, the executive authority of such State shall issue writs of election to fill such vacancies: Provided, That the legislature of any State may empower the executive thereof to make temporary appointments until the people fill the vacancies by election as the legislature may direct.

This amendment shall not be so construed as to affect the election or term of any Senator chosen before it becomes valid as part of the Constitution.

Amendment XVIII

§ 1. After one year from the ratification of this article the manufacture, sale, or transportation of intoxicating liquors within, the importation thereof into, or the exportation thereof from the United States and all territory subject to the jurisdiction thereof for beverage purposes is hereby prohibited.

§ 2. The Congress and the several States shall have concurrent power to enforce this article by appropriate legislation.

§ 3. This article shall be inoperative unless it shall have been ratified as an amendment to the Constitution by the legislatures of the several States, as provided in the Constitution, within seven years from the date of the submission hereof to the States by the Congress.

Amendment XIX

The right of citizens of the United States to vote shall not be denied or abridged by the United States or by any State on account of sex.

Congress shall have power to enforce this article by appropriate legislation.

Amendment XX

§ 1. The terms of the President and Vice President shall end at noon on the 20th day of January, and the terms of Senators and Representatives at noon on the 3d day of January, of the years in which such terms would have ended if this article had not been ratified; and the terms of their successors shall then begin.

§ 2. The Congress shall assemble at least once in every year, and such meeting shall begin at noon on the 3d day of January, unless they shall by law appoint a different day.

§ 3. If, at the time fixed for the beginning of the term of the President, the President elect shall have died, the Vice President elect shall become President. If a President shall not have been chosen before the time fixed for the beginning of his term, or if the President elect shall have failed to qualify, then the Vice President elect shall act as President until a President shall have qualified; and the Congress may by law provide for the case wherein neither a President elect nor a Vice President elect shall have qualified, declaring who shall then act as President, or the manner in which one who is to act shall be selected, and such person shall act accordingly until a President or Vice President shall have qualified.

§ 4. The Congress may by law provide for the case of the death of any of the persons from whom the House of Representatives may choose a President whenever the right of choice shall have devolved upon them, and for the case of the death of any of the persons from whom the Senate may choose a Vice President whenever the right of choice shall have devolved upon them.

§ 5. Sections 1 and 2 shall take effect on the 15th day of October following the ratification of this article.

§ 6. This article shall be inoperative unless it shall have been ratified as an amendment to the Constitution by the legislatures of three-fourths of the several States within seven years from the date of its submission.

Amendment XXI

§ 1. The eighteenth article of amendment to the Constitution of the United States is hereby repealed.

§ 2. The transportation or importation into any State, Territory, or possession of the United States for delivery or use therein of intoxicating liquors, in violation of the laws thereof, is hereby prohibited.

§ 3. This article shall be inoperative unless it shall have been ratified as an amendment to the Constitution by conventions in the several States, as provided in the Constitution, within seven years from the date of the submission hereof to the States by the Congress.

Amendment XXII

§ 1. No person shall be elected to the office of the President more than twice, and no person who has held the office of President, or acted as President, for more than two years of a term to which some other person was elected President shall be elected to the office of the President more than once. But this article shall not apply to any person holding the office of President when this article was proposed by the Congress, and shall not prevent any person who may be holding the office of President, or acting as President, during the term within which this article becomes operative from holding the office of President or acting as President during the remainder of such term.

§ 2. This article shall be inoperative unless it shall have been ratified as an amendment to the Constitution by the legislatures of three-fourths of the several states within seven years from the date of its submission to the states by the Congress.

Amendment XXIII

§ 1. The District constituting the seat of government of the United States shall appoint in such manner as the Congress may direct:

A number of electors of President and Vice President equal to the whole number of Senators and Representatives in Congress to which the District would be entitled if it were a state, but in no event more than the least populous state; they shall be in addition to those appointed by the states, but they shall be considered, for the purposes of the election of President and Vice President, to be electors appointed by a state; and they shall meet in the District and perform such duties as provided by the twelfth article of amendment.

§ 2. The Congress shall have power to enforce this article by appropriate legislation.

Amendment XXIV

§ 1. The right of citizens of the United States to vote in any primary or other election for President or Vice President, for electors for President or Vice President, or for Senator or Representative in Congress, shall not be denied or abridged by the United States or any state by reason of failure to pay any poll tax or other tax.

§ 2. The Congress shall have power to enforce this article by appropriate legislation.

Amendment XXV

§ 1. In case of the removal of the President from office or of his death or resignation, the Vice President shall become President.

§ 2. Whenever there is a vacancy in the office of the Vice President, the President shall nominate a Vice President who shall take office upon confirmation by a majority vote of both Houses of Congress.

§ 3. Whenever the President transmits to the President pro tempore of the Senate and the Speaker of the House of Representatives his written declaration that he is unable to discharge the powers and duties of his office, and until he transmits to them a written declaration to the contrary, such powers and duties shall be discharged by the Vice President as Acting President.

§ 4. Whenever the Vice President and a majority of either the principal officers of the executive departments or of such other body as Congress may by law provide, transmit to the President pro tempore of the Senate and the Speaker of the House of Representatives their written declaration that the President is unable to discharge the powers and duties of his office, the Vice President shall immediately assume the powers and duties of the office as Acting President.

Thereafter, when the President transmits to the President pro tempore of the Senate and the Speaker of the House of Representatives his written declaration that no inability exists, he shall resume the powers and duties of his office unless the Vice President and a majority of either the principal officers of the executive department or of such other body as Congress may by law provide, transmit within four days to the President pro tempore of the Senate and the Speaker of the House of Representatives their written declaration that the President is unable to discharge the powers and duties of his office. Thereupon Congress shall decide the issue, assembling within forty-eight hours for that purpose if not in session. If the Congress, within twenty-one days after receipt of the latter written declaration, or, if Congress is not in session, within twenty-one days after Congress is required to assemble, determines by two-thirds vote of both Houses that the President is unable to discharge the powers and duties of his office, the Vice President shall continue to discharge the same as Acting President; otherwise, the President shall resume the powers and duties of his office.

Amendment XXVI

§ 1. The right of citizens of the United States, who are 18 years of age or older, to vote, shall not be denied or abridged by the United States or any state on account of age.

§ 2. The Congress shall have the power to enforce this article by appropriate legislation.

Amendment XXVII

No law varying the compensation for the services of the Senators and Representatives shall take effect until an election of Representatives shall have intervened.

PART 1

STRUCTURE AND POWERS OF THE NATIONAL GOVERNMENT

CHAPTER 1

INTRODUCTION TO THE CONSTITUTION

[Assignment 1]

I. BEFORE THE CONSTITUTION

The Constitution of the United States is a distinctively American innovation and achievement. In the famous case of *Marbury v. Madison*, Chief Justice John Marshall commented approvingly on what he deemed to be "the greatest improvement on political institutions—a written constitution." 5 U.S. (1 Cranch) 137, 178 (1803). Indeed, the Constitution of the United States was the first written constitution to have three features: it created a national government; it was deliberately considered and adopted by the people; and it was designed to be binding as supreme law on all who would exercise governmental power under it.

The structure of government created by the Constitution was also distinctive. Its features include: the separation of powers among independent, co-equal branches of government, each being able to "check and balance" the others; federalism, in the sense of a division of power between a central government and the governments of several states; a written Bill of Rights to protect certain fundamental liberties against government interference; and popular sovereignty expressed through representative, republican government. The Constitution combined all four of these into a single supreme law.

Yet the Constitution did not spring to life out of nothing. Its arrangements of powers and rights had many sources. The immediate sources from the American experience included the corporate charters that were governing documents for the colonies, the ideological upheavals of the American War for Independence, the experiments of the first state constitutions, and the largely failed government under the Articles of Confederation. The Articles were actually the first national "constitution," proposed by the Continental Congress in 1777 and ratified in 1781. The defects of the Articles led to the call for a constitutional convention. That convention, held in Philadelphia in 1787, proposed an entirely new governing document. That document is the Constitution we have today (with twenty-seven amendments). The debate in 1787 and 1788 over ratification of the Constitution was heated, and the vote to ratify was very close in many states. Ratification ultimately depended on promises to propose the Bill of Rights, which was adopted as part of the Constitution in 1791, two years after the new national government had come into existence under the Constitution.

Thus the Constitution was the culmination of this nation-making process, from the start of the American War for Independence in 1776 until the ratification of the Bill of Rights in 1791. And the roots of the Constitution lie deeper still, in events of the century and a half between the Jamestown settlement in 1607 and the Declaration of Independence in 1776. Before 1776 the colonists were Englishmen, and so, to understand the Constitution they drafted, the place to begin is the English constitutional tradition.

English and American Constitutionalism

Americans were heirs to an English constitutional tradition that had emerged over centuries. In that tradition, a central "constitutional" event—one that at the time of the founding of the United States had happened only a century before—was the Glorious Revolution of 1688. In that revolution, the English overthrew the Stuart dynasty of King James II and established the supremacy of Parliament. The following year, Parliament enacted a statute that recognized a set of individual rights against the king, a statute known as the English Bill of Rights of 1689.

To compress drastically, the Glorious Revolution thus restored fundamental individual rights against executive authority, established the supremacy of representative government, and proclaimed that legitimate government must ultimately depend on the consent of the governed. This last principle was understood in 1688 (and again by the Americans in 1776) as implying a constitutional right of the people to alter or abolish their form of government and to create a new social contract. The chief defender of the Glorious Revolution was English political philosopher John Locke, especially in his TWO TREATISES OF GOVERNMENT (1690). Locke argued that freedom, not monarchy, was the natural condition of man. Yet people, wanting more security than they had in the state of nature, were willing to trade away some of their natural rights (to a government) in order to preserve all their other rights. That argument—that the true basis of government is not the divine right of kings, or force, but rather a social contract—was taken to heart by the American colonists. The rights that had been secured by the Glorious Revolution—including not only individual rights like those protected by the English Bill of Rights, but even the right of revolution to preserve those individual rights—were all features of the English constitutional tradition as it was known to American Englishmen in the late eighteenth century.

Although that tradition was largely unwritten, it did contain several important documents. These included (1) the Charter of Liberties of King Henry I of 1100, establishing that there was no Norman royal power to suspend the preexisting Anglo-Saxon laws; (2) Magna Carta ("Great Charter") of 1215, declaring among other things that the king had no royal power to deprive freeholders of life, liberty, or property except by "the law of the land"; (3) the Petition of Right of 1628, holding that there was no royal power of taxation without action by Parliament and no royal power to imprison subjects without trial by jury; (4) the Habeas Corpus Act of 1679, declaring that there was no royal power to imprison without trial by jury; (5) the English Bill of Rights of 1689, protecting rights to be governed by law, to be tried by a jury, to petition for a writ of habeas corpus, and to be represented in any legislative body that possessed the power to enact taxes; and (6) the Act of Settlement of 1701, providing life tenure for English judges.

As important as these documents were as elements of the English "constitution" (understood as a collection of written and unwritten traditions and practices), none of these documents purported to establish a comprehensive, supreme written constitution as the definitive instrument of government. None of them recognized the sovereignty of the people. The earlier documents were agreements by the king to limit or restrain his own sovereignty, and the later ones were agreements embodying a division of sovereignty between the king and Parliament. None purported to be the one supreme law of the land, and it is even doubtful that all of them were enforceable in court.

Nor did these documents limit the power of Parliament. Parliament consisted of two houses, the House of Lords and the House of Commons, and together with the king these were said to represent the three great estates of the realm: the monarchy (king), the aristocracy (Lords), and the people (Commons). When the king and Parliament acted together, they embodied the entire sovereignty of the English nation, and they were not limited by the English constitutional tradition. They could alter that tradition even by passing an ordinary law—as they did in passing the English Bill of Rights of 1689.

The premises of the U.S. Constitution are quite different. First, the preamble to the Constitution says, "We the People . . . do ordain and establish this Constitution." Thus sovereignty rests not in a king or legislative body but in the people. The Constitution is a delegation of power from the people, and all government actions must find their root in some grant of power it contains. Second, the Constitution is "the supreme Law of the land" (Article VI) and it can be amended only through the processes that it lays out (Article V). It cannot be changed merely by the agreement of Congress, the president, and the courts.

One consequence is a change in the relative importance of text and tradition. Both constitutional systems rely on text and on tradition. In England, the written constitutional documents are islands of text in a sea of unwritten tradition. In the United States, the written constitutional text—of the original Constitution and the twenty-seven amendments—is like a great continent, a land mass with scattered lakes and ponds and rivers of tradition. The relative importance of text in the United States means that two questions are central: "What does the written Constitution mean?" and "Who gets to interpret it?"

American Antecedents to the Constitution

On the American side of the Atlantic, the antecedents to the Constitution included the corporate charters that established various colonies, the Declaration of Independence, the Articles of Confederation, and the early state constitutions.

The English colonies in North America were governed by corporate charters. A charter defined the powers of the colonial governor and proprietors, and also the rights of colonists. In a sense, they were like ordinary contracts. But they were also prototypes for written constitutions. Some of these charters were issued by the king of England and functioned like articles of incorporation for the societies that colonized certain settlements. Other charters, like the Mayflower Compact, were drafted by the settlers themselves as they disembarked and as colonial life unfolded.

These charters were antecedents of the Constitution in at least two respects. First, they divided power horizontally between royal governors and the popularly elected lower houses of colonial legislatures—a proto-separation of powers. Second, they divided power vertically between the imperial government in London and the colonial governments in the thirteen original colonies—a proto-federalism, with London making decisions about foreign policy, defense, and the regulation of colonial trade while more local powers were devolved to the colonies. As grants from the king, however, colonial charters did not recognize the sovereignty of the people.

In the 1760s, tensions rose between the thirteen colonies and England. In the French and Indian War, England had conquered French Canada, adding the province of Quebec to the empire. But the war was costly. The new king, George III, sought to tax the American colonies in part to pay for the costs of defending them. But the colonists had largely avoided English taxation until the 1760s. They were determined not to acquiesce.

By 1776, the American colonists were outraged about what they perceived as imperial and royal tyranny. They thought it improper for the English government to tax them as long as they were not represented in Parliament. And they accused King George III of being a tyrant, insinuating that he resembled the Stuart dynasty that had been overthrown in the Glorious Revolution. That resemblance suggested another one: the colonists were the defenders of English liberty. History, they thought, was repeating itself.

The grievances of the colonists, and their claims to be defending their English rights, culminated in the Declaration of Independence (1776). Drawing on the ideas expounded a century earlier by Locke, the Declaration proclaimed not only the existence of "self-evident" natural rights to "life, liberty, and the pursuit of happiness" bestowed by the Creator, but also the right of the people to abolish a government that became abusive and tyrannical. To prove that the English government was in fact tyrannical, the Declaration recites a long train of abuses committed by King George III. (Strikingly, the Declaration never mentions abuses of power by Parliament. The omission reflected the colonists' greater concern with royal tyranny, and also the fact that the colonists denied that Parliament had any power over them since they were not represented in it.) It was widely thought that the right to alter and abolish old governments could be accomplished only through a solemn public act—and that is what the Declaration held itself out to be. In the words of its conclusion, the "Representatives of the united States of America" were undertaking to "solemnly publish and declare, That these United Colonies are, and of Right ought to be, Free and Independent States."

The Declaration asserted the powers of these "Independent States" to "levy War, conclude Peace, contract Alliances, establish Commerce, and to do all other Acts and Things which Independent States may of right do." What this apparently meant in practice was that these powers could be exercised by *each* of the newly independent states. But there was not yet any framework for a common government that would, at least on some questions, unite the colonies.

In the meantime, the states—that term is now appropriate—were drafting their own constitutions. Between 1776 and the writing of the Constitution in 1787, eleven of the thirteen newly independent states drew up constitutions, and all of them did so while keeping in mind the 1776 problem of executive tyranny. In many of these constitutions, governors lost their veto, appointment, and pardon powers, and they often served only short terms. Power was concentrated in the state legislatures, which were seen as closer to the people. Many of these constitutions included a declaration of rights or bill of rights. For example, the 1776 constitution for Pennsylvania declared that "all men are born equally free and independent, and have certain natural, inherent and inalienable rights." It also declared a number of the specific rights of the people of Pennsylvania. For example, "that all men have a natural and unalienable right to worship Almighty God according to the dictates of their own consciences and understanding"; that the government is "instituted for the common benefit, protection and security of the people, nation or community; and not for the particular emolument or advantage of any single man, family, or sett of men, who are a part only of that community"; "that all elections ought to be free"; "that the people have a right to hold themselves, their houses, papers, and possessions free from search or seizure"; "that the people have a right to freedom of speech, and of writing, and publishing their sentiments"; and "that the people have a right to bear arms for the defence of themselves and the state; and as standing armies in the time of peace are dangerous to liberty, they ought not to be kept up."

Finally, there was a first experiment in drafting a constitution for all of the states. This experiment in common government was "the Act of Confederation of the United States of America," commonly referred to as the Articles of Confederation. The Articles were proposed in 1777. But it was not until 1781—after General Cornwallis had surrendered the British army to General Washington at Yorktown, Virginia—that the Articles were approved by all thirteen states. You should now read the Articles of Confederation (p. 1673). As you read, ask yourself how the government it established differs from the government of the United States today. List the ways. Are there features of the government under the Articles of Confederation that you think the Constitution should have kept but did not? What defects can you detect in the government set up by the Articles of Confederation? Are you surprised that the Articles were eventually replaced?

———

In reading the Articles of Confederation, you probably noticed that the text begins as if it were a treaty among thirteen sovereigns. Indeed, it explicitly states that "[e]ach state retains its sovereignty, freedom, and independence, and every Power, Jurisdiction and right, which is not by this confederation *expressly* delegated to the United States, in Congress assembled" (Article II), and that the states "hereby severally enter into a firm league of friendship with each other" (III). The Articles provided for travel and trade between states (IV). The Articles also established a framework for a general government consisting of a unicameral Congress in which each of the thirteen states received one vote, no matter how large the state and no matter how large its congressional delegation (V). Members of Congress were paid by, and could be recalled by, the state governments they represented. The Articles also regulated treaties, duties, and war expenses (VI, VII, VIII)—but revenue was raised through the collection of taxes by the states, an arrangement that proved greatly problematic as it made the "common treasury" of the nation dependent on the separate action, authority, and good faith of each of the states. The Articles also described the powers of the "united states in congress assembled" (IX). And the Articles concluded by declaring that "the union shall be perpetual" and providing for amendments (XIII).

In the fight for independence, the deficiencies of the central government, first under the Continental Congress and then under the Articles of Confederation, became evident. The rule that each state had a single vote made Congress more like an assembly of independent nations—an eighteenth-century United Nations—than a representative legislature for the nation. Combined with the requirement that nine out of thirteen states had to agree on significant matters, this rule meant that Congress could be at the mercy of a small minority. Congress even struggled with the quorum requirement for ordinary business; it usually lacked representatives from a bare majority of the states.

Moreover, even when Congress could agree, it had little practical authority to enforce its enactments. The central government was completely dependent on the states, which had all of the real power. As Chief Justice John Marshall would later recall, "The confederation was, essentially, a league; and congress was a corps of ambassadors, to be recalled at the will of their masters. . . . They had a right to propose certain things to their sovereigns, and to require a compliance with their resolution; but they could, by their own power, execute nothing." Marshall's "A Friend of the Constitution" Essays, No. 7 (July 9, 1819), *reprinted in* JOHN MARSHALL'S DEFENSE OF MCCULLOCH V. MARYLAND 196, 199 (Gerald Gunther ed., 1969). This failure of execution soon became evident. The commands of the Articles of Confederation were not "inviolably observed by every state" but were in fact frequently disregarded. No state paid all that it owed for keeping up the government under the Articles, and one state, Georgia, never paid a cent.

Nor could the defects of the Articles of Confederation be easily remedied. As provided in Article XIII, changes to the Articles required the approval not only of Congress, but also of every one of the state legislatures.

Thus it was <u>unsurprising</u> that there were many striking failures of government under the Articles of Confederation. General Washington had trouble fighting the Revolutionary War because <u>Congress</u> second-guessed his decisions on troop movements and strategy. Congress, unable to tax the states or the people directly, was always short of funds and even failed to pay Washington's soldiers. And Congress lacked the power to regulate trade between the thirteen states or with foreign powers. Declining trade in the war and its aftermath led to an economic crisis. In this crisis, many debtors faced foreclosure and utter economic ruin (not to mention very high court costs). Outbursts of violence against debt collection, such as Shays' Rebellion in Massachusetts, frightened property owners. One response by Congress and the states—printing paper money—led to severe inflation, which worsened the economic situation still further. Many merchants found themselves ruined, while some debtors were effectively absolved of their debts by the inflation. And state legislatures threatened to abuse their nearly absolute powers by cancelling debts and further inflating the currency, dashing the hopes of those who thought that legislatures would always be friendly to liberty. Many feared that the bankrupt, incompetent central government under the Articles of Confederation would even be too weak to prevent invasion by a foreign power. Nor was this an idle fear. The army fielded by Congress "had shrunk to some 625 unpaid, poorly equipped men, mostly in western Pennsylvania. . . . The United States was becoming 'the sport of transatlantic politicians of all denominations.' " Pauline Maier, RATIFICATION: THE PEOPLE DEBATE THE CONSTITUTION, 1787–1788 13 (2010) (quoting John Adams).

By 1786—a mere decade after the Declaration of Independence—it seemed that the experiment of American independence was on the verge of failure. At last Congress agreed to call for a special convention of representatives from each state to consider revisions to the Articles of Confederation. The call produced a convention that met in Philadelphia in 1787.

The Convention and Ratification

The Constitution of the United States was drafted by a convention of fifty-five distinguished citizens assembled in Philadelphia during the hot summer of 1787. The Philadelphia Convention was chaired by (retired) General George Washington. The delegates agreed to keep their proceedings secret—something almost inconceivable today—to enable more vigorous debate and to conceal their disagreements. Accordingly, what we know about the proceedings comes from a few journals kept by those present, especially the notes of James Madison (called NOTES OF DEBATES IN THE FEDERAL CONVENTION OF 1787), which were published after his death, nearly forty years later. The authoritative collection of these journals and records is THE RECORDS OF THE FEDERAL CONVENTION OF 1787 (Max Farrand ed., 1911).

The Philadelphia Convention was called for the seemingly narrow purpose of proposing revisions to the Articles of Confederation. But what it produced was dramatically different: a proposal for an entirely new "Constitution of the United States." The document proposed by the Philadelphia Convention stated in its concluding Article that "[t]he Ratification of the Conventions of nine States, shall be sufficient for the Establishment of this Constitution between the States so ratifying the same." The document thus proposed a different form of national government than had existed under the Articles of Confederation and specified that it would take effect in a manner different from what the Articles of Confederation required for amendment—the *unanimous* concurrence of the *legislatures* of each state.

In many ways the Constitution was a compromise. In the eleven years between 1776 and 1787, attitudes had changed enormously. Where Americans once feared executive and national tyranny, many now feared legislative and local tyranny, and the solution seemed to be a strengthened national government and greater executive power. The Constitution was shaped by these cross-cutting fears. It created a powerful national government, yet that government was given only limited and enumerated powers; it created an executive more powerful than any executive under the state constitutions or the Articles of Confederation, yet that executive was not nearly as powerful as King George III.

At Philadelphia the framers made at least five major decisions. First, they greatly expanded national power. For example, they gave the proposed government the power to regulate commerce and the power to tax and spend to promote the general welfare. The framers decided that members of Congress under the new Constitution would be officers of the national government, with fixed terms and salaries paid by the national treasury. And Congress could legislate upon and directly tax citizens.

Second, in a decision called The Great Compromise, the framers agreed that the new government would have a bicameral legislature with each state having equal representation in the Senate and with representation in the House of Representatives based on each state's population. This was a deal between the more populous states, such as Virginia, which wanted representation based on population; and the less populous ones, such as New Jersey, which wanted a rule of "one state, one vote" as under the Articles of Confederation.

Third, the framers voted to create separate executive and judicial branches of the national government. It was decided that the executive branch would be led by a single president of the United States who was to be selected independently of Congress and guaranteed a four-year term. The president was even given a veto, which English monarchs effectively lacked. With respect to the judiciary, the framers voted to create a national Supreme Court, and Congress was given the power to create inferior courts. (No permanent national courts had existed in the government under the Articles of Confederation.)

Fourth, the framers wrangled over and finally reached an unhappy compromise with respect to slavery. Southern states disenfranchised their large slave populations but nonetheless wanted the slaves to count for apportioning seats in the House of Representatives and for votes for the president in the Electoral College. Northern states objected. The compromise adopted was that a slave would be counted as three-fifths of a person, and a clause would be added that imposed a duty to return fugitive slaves. The appeasement of slaveholders was the great tragedy in the work of the framers at Philadelphia.

Fifth, as mentioned above, the framers wrote the Constitution so that it would go into effect upon ratification by only nine of the thirteen states. This provision in Article VII was explicitly contrary to the Articles of Confederation, which could be amended only by unanimous agreement. Article V specified that the Constitution would be amendable by a two-thirds vote of both houses of Congress coupled with ratification by three-quarters of the states. Even though this was a step toward easier amendment, it is today regarded as one of the most difficult amendment processes of any constitution in the world.

The Convention began on May 25, 1787. It adjourned on September 17. The final text incorporating these five fundamental decisions was drafted by a Committee of Detail and by a Committee of Style and Arrangement which included among others Gouverneur Morris, Alexander Hamilton, and James Madison. Given the amount of work accomplished by the fifty-five delegates in this short time and the impact it would have on the United States and the world, the Convention has been called the Miracle at Philadelphia. It bears remembering, though, that the framers were building on a centuries-old constitutional tradition in England and the colonies, and also on the experience since 1776.

The Convention's proposal of the Constitution spurred debate in the thirteen states over whether it should be adopted. The most famous contribution to this debate was *The Federalist*, a series of eighty-five newspaper articles written by Alexander Hamilton, James Madison, and John Jay, all under the name "Publius." These articles urged the people of the state of New York to ratify the Constitution. (They were then collected in rough book form and sent to Virginia for that critical state's ratification debates.) Written in a rush of time and as explicit advocacy documents, *The Federalist* has nonetheless come to be regarded as one of the most important and influential treatises on the meaning of the Constitution. Below are excerpts from *The Federalist No. 1*, which is Hamilton's famous call for careful deliberation about the defects of the Articles of Confederation and the need for the new constitution; and *The Federalist Nos. 40* and *43*, which are Madison's defense of the Convention's proposal of a document that went beyond mere revision of the Articles and departed from the unanimity rule for amendment.

As you read these passages, consider the legality of the Constitution's adoption. Did it violate the rules for amendment specified by the Articles? Was it an exercise of the right of the people to abolish their government, like the Glorious Revolution of 1688 and the American Revolution of 1776? If so, was the Constitution an act of revolution? Or was it like states withdrawing from a treaty and forming a new nation? Thankfully, these are no longer live questions. The Constitution was eventually ratified by all the states and is now accepted by all as the United States' fundamental governing document. Still, understanding the change from the Articles to the Constitution may help us understand whether and how we can change the Constitution.

The Federalist No. 1

Alexander Hamilton, Oct. 27, 1787

To the People of the State of New York.

AFTER an unequivocal experience of the inefficacy of the subsisting Fœderal Government, you are called upon to deliberate on a new Constitution for the United States of America. The subject speaks its own importance; comprehending in its consequences, nothing less than the existence of the UNION, the safety and welfare of the parts of which it is composed, the fate of an empire, in many respects, the most interesting in the world. It has been frequently remarked, that it seems to have been reserved to the people of this country, by their conduct and example, to decide the important question, whether societies of men are really capable or not, of establishing good government from reflection and choice, or whether they are forever destined to depend, for their political constitutions, on accident and force. If there be any truth in the remark, the crisis, at which we are arrived, may with propriety be regarded as the æra in which that decision is to be made; and a wrong election of the part we shall act, may, in this view, deserve to be considered as the general misfortune of mankind. . . .

Among the most formidable of the obstacles which the new Constitution will have to encounter, may readily be distinguished the obvious interest of a certain class of men in every State to resist all changes which may hazard a diminution of the power, emolument and consequence of the offices they hold under the State establishments—and the perverted ambition of another class of men, who will either hope to aggrandise themselves by the confusions of their country, or will flatter themselves with fairer prospects of elevation from the subdivision of the empire into several partial confederacies, than from its union under one government. . . .

I propose, in a series of papers, to discuss the following interesting particulars— *The utility of the* UNION *to your political prosperity—The insufficiency of the present Confederation to preserve that Union—The necessity of a government at least equally energetic with the one proposed to the attainment of this object—The conformity of the proposed constitution to the true principles of republican government—Its analogy to your own state constitution—*and lastly, *The additional security, which its adoption will afford to the preservation of that species of government, to liberty and to property.*

In the progress of this discussion I shall endeavor to give a satisfactory answer to all the objections which shall have made their appearance that may seem to have any claim to your attention.

It may perhaps be thought superfluous to offer arguments to prove the utility of the UNION, a point, no doubt, deeply engraved on the hearts of the great body of the people in every state, and one, which it may be imagined has no adversaries. But the fact is, that we already hear it whispered in the private circles of those who oppose the new constitution, that the Thirteen States are of too great extent for any general system, and that we must of necessity resort to separate confederacies of distinct portions of the whole. This doctrine will, in all probability, be gradually propagated, till it has votaries enough to countenance an open avowal of it. For nothing can be more evident, to those who are able to take an enlarged view of the subject, than the alternative of an adoption of the new Constitution, or a dismemberment of the Union. It will therefore be of use to begin by examining the advantages of that Union, the certain evils and the probable dangers, to which every State will be exposed from its dissolution. This shall accordingly constitute the subject of my next address.

The Federalist No. 40
James Madison, Jan. 18, 1788

To the People of the State of New York.

THE *second* point to be examined is, whether the convention were authorised to frame and propose this mixed Constitution.

The powers of the Convention ought in strictness to be determined, by an inspection of the commissions given to the members by their respective constituents. As all of these however had reference, either to the recommendation from the meeting at Annapolis in September 1786, or to that from Congress in February, 1787, it will be sufficient to recur to these particular acts. *[The Annapolis meeting had been held to discuss the need for uniform regulations of commerce. Five states were represented. Its one accomplishment was calling for a convention, to be held the following year in Philadelphia, that would propose revisions to the Articles of Confederation.—Editors]*

The act from Annapolis recommends the "appointment of commissioners to take into consideration, the situation of the United States, to devise *such further provisions* as shall appear to them necessary to render the Constitution of the Fœderal Government *adequate to the exigencies of the Union*; and to report such an act for that purpose, to the United States in Congress assembled, as when agreed to by them, and afterwards confirmed by the Legislature of every State, will effectually provide for the same."

The recommendatory act of Congress is in the words following: "Whereas there is provision in the articles of confederation and perpetual Union, for making alterations therein, by the assent of a Congress of the United States, and of the Legislatures of the several States: And whereas experience hath evinced, that there are defects in the present confederation, as a mean to remedy which, several of the States, and *particularly the State of New-York*, by express instructions to their delegates in Congress, have suggested a Convention for the purposes expressed in the following resolution; and such Convention appearing to be the most probable mean of establishing in these States, *a firm national government.*

"Resolved, That in the opinion of Congress, it is expedient, that on the 2d Monday in May next, a Convention of delegates, who shall have been appointed by the several States, be held at Philadelphia, for the sole and express purpose *of revising the articles of confederation*, and reporting to Congress and the several

Legislatures, such *alterations and provisions therein*, as shall, when agreed to in Congress, and confirmed by the States, render the Fœderal Constitution *adequate to the exigencies of government and the preservation of the Union*."

From these two acts, it appears, 1st. that the object of the Convention was to establish in these States, *a firm national government*; 2d. that this Government was to be such as would be *adequate to the exigencies of government* and *the preservation of the Union*; 3d. that these purposes were to be effected by *alterations and provisions in the articles of confederation*, as it is expressed in the act of Congress, or by *such further provisions as should appear necessary*, as it stands in the recommendatory act from Annapolis; 4th. that the alterations and provisions were to be reported to Congress, and to the States, in order to be agreed to by the former, and confirmed by the latter.

From a comparison and fair construction of these several modes of expression, is to be deduced the authority, under which the Convention acted. They were to frame a *national government*, adequate to the *exigencies of government*, and *of the Union*, and to reduce the articles of confederation into such form as to accomplish these purposes. . . .

We have seen that in the new government, as in the old, the general powers are limited; and that the States, in all unenumerated cases, are left in the enjoyment of their sovereign and independent jurisdiction.

The truth is, that the great principles of the Constitution proposed by the Convention, may be considered less as absolutely new, than as the expansion of principles which are found in the articles of Confederation. The misfortune under the latter system has been, that these principles are so feeble and confined as to justify all the charges of inefficiency which have been urged against it; and to require a degree of enlargement which gives to the new system, the aspect of an entire transformation of the old.

In one particular it is admitted that the Convention have departed from the tenor of their commission. Instead of reporting a plan requiring the confirmation *of the Legislatures of all the States*, they have reported a plan which is to be confirmed by the *people*, and may be carried into effect by *nine States only*. It is worthy of remark, that this objection, though the most plausible, has been the least urged in the publications which have swarmed against the Convention. The forbearance can only have proceeded from an irresistible conviction of the absurdity of subjecting the fate of 12 States, to the perverseness or corruption of a thirteenth; from the example of inflexible opposition given by *a majority* of 1-60th of the people of America *[i.e., Rhode Island—Editors]*, to a measure approved and called for by the voice of twelve States, comprising 59-60ths of the people; an example still fresh in the memory and indignation of every citizen who has felt for the wounded honor and prosperity of his country. As this objection, therefore, has been in a manner waived by those who have criticised the powers of the Convention, I dismiss it without further observation. . . .

The *third* point to be enquired into is, how far considerations of duty arising out of the case itself, could have supplied any defect of regular authority. . . .

Let us view the ground on which the Convention stood. It may be collected from their proceedings, that they were deeply and unanimously impressed with the crisis which had led their country almost with one voice to make so singular and solemn an experiment, for correcting the errors of a system by which this crisis had been produced; that they were no less deeply and unanimously convinced, that such a reform as they have proposed, was absolutely necessary to effect the purposes of their appointment. . . . They must have borne in mind, that as the plan to be framed and proposed, was to be submitted *to the people themselves*, the disapprobation of this supreme authority would destroy it forever; its approbation blot out antecedent errors and irregularities. . . .

But that the objectors may be disarmed of every pretext, it shall be granted for a moment, that the Convention were neither authorised by their commission, nor justified by circumstances, in proposing a Constitution for their country: Does it follow that the Constitution ought for that reason alone to be rejected? If according to the noble precept it be lawful to accept good advice even from an enemy, shall we set the ignoble example of refusing such advice even when it is offered by our friends? The prudent enquiry in all cases, ought surely to be not so much *from whom* the advice comes, as whether the advice be *good*.

The sum of what has been here advanced and proved, is that the charge against the Convention of exceeding their powers, except in one instance little urged by the objectors, has no foundation to support it; that if they had exceeded their powers, they were not only warranted but required, as the confidential servants of their country, by the circumstances in which they were placed, to exercise the liberty which they assumed, and that finally, if they had violated both their powers, and their obligations in proposing a Constitution, this ought nevertheless to be embraced, if it be calculated to accomplish the views and happiness of the people of America. How far this character is due to the Constitution, is the subject under investigation.

The Federalist No. 43
James Madison, Jan. 23, 1788

. . . The express authority of the people alone could give due validity to the Constitution. To have required the unanimous ratification of the thirteen States, would have subjected the essential interests of the whole to the caprice or corruption of a single member. It would have marked a want of foresight in the Convention, which our own experience would have rendered inexcusable.

Two questions of a very delicate nature present themselves on this occasion: 1. On what principle the confederation, which stands in the solemn form of a compact among the States, can be superceded without the unanimous consent of the parties to it? 2. What relation is to subsist between the nine or more States ratifying the Constitution, and the remaining few who do not become parties to it.

The first question is answered at once by recurring to the absolute necessity of the case; to the great principle of self-preservation; to the transcendent law of nature and of nature's God, which declares that the safety and happiness of society are the objects at which all political institutions aim, and to which all such institutions must be sacrificed. PERHAPS also an answer may be found without searching beyond the principles of the compact itself. It has been heretofore noted among the defects of the Confederation, that in many of the States, it had received no higher sanction than a mere legislative ratification. The principle of reciprocality seems to require, that its obligation on the other States should be reduced to the same standard. A compact between independent sovereigns, founded on ordinary acts of legislative authority, can pretend to no higher validity than a league or treaty between the parties. It is an established doctrine on the subject of treaties, that all the articles are mutually conditions of each other; that a breach of any one article is a breach of the whole treaty; and that a breach committed by either of the parties absolves the others; and authorises them, if they please, to pronounce the treaty violated and void. Should it unhappily be necessary to appeal to these delicate truths for a justification for dispensing with the consent of particular States to a dissolution of the federal pact, will not the complaining parties find it a difficult task to answer the MULTIPLIED and IMPORTANT infractions with which they may be confronted? The time has been when it was incumbent on us all to veil the ideas which this paragraph exhibits. The scene is now changed, and with it, the part which the same motives dictate.

The second question is not less delicate; and the flattering prospect of its being merely hypothetical, forbids an overcurious discussion of it. It is one of those cases which must be left to provide for itself. . . .

NOTES

1.   Using legal arguments, evaluate James Madison's claim that the Convention did not exceed its mandate. Consider the argument that the nature of the "government" under the Articles of Confederation was more like a "league" of sovereignties than a government proper, so that the violation of its requirements on all sides left it with essentially the status of a breached treaty, no longer binding on anyone. What do you think? And what do you think of the quite different argument that if the Convention did go too far, subsequent ratification by the people cures the irregularity?

2.   What difference does it make whether the Constitution was adopted legally? Could anyone seriously argue that we are still governed by the Articles of Confederation rather than the Constitution of 1787? Does it matter in any way today whether or not the Constitution was legally adopted in the 1780s?

3.   Think about the Constitution's legitimacy more broadly. Suppose one did regard the Constitution as illegitimate because it was adopted by a mild-mannered *coup d'état*. Or suppose one regards it as illegitimate because it was adopted by undemocratic or unrepresentative bodies. Or suppose one simply regards it as a very bad constitution, full of foolish or unjust provisions. Or suppose one thinks it illegitimate as a matter of principle for one generation to bind another—for the work of dead, white, male, propertied slave-holders to govern us from the grave after more than two centuries. Do these suppositions affect what the Constitution, as a legal document, means? In other words, does its legitimacy or illegitimacy affect its interpretation?

Ratification and the Bill of Rights

One of the most contentious issues surrounding the ratification of the Constitution was the absence in the document of a statement of the rights that the people held against the government—in other words, a "Bill of Rights." Those who championed the new Constitution denied that one was necessary or even desirable. Federalists such as Alexander Hamilton, James Madison, and James Wilson argued that the Constitution would create a federal government of only limited, enumerated powers. To include a Bill of Rights, they maintained, would wrongly imply that the government had more powers than were intended and that all of the many individual rights that were not enumerated could be invaded at will by the national government. It would flip the presumption of the Constitution, because now everything the federal government did would be presumptively constitutional unless it contravened the Bill of Rights. The Anti-Federalist opponents of the Constitution, such as George Mason and Richard Henry Lee, replied that the powers of the federal government, even though enumerated, might still be construed broadly. In particular, the Anti-Federalists called the Necessary and Proper Clause "the Sweeping Clause," and they said that without a Bill of Rights it would sweep away all of the people's liberties.

The Anti-Federalists won the political argument, and the Federalists agreed to propose amendments in the First Congress—after ratification of the Constitution. Based in part on these assurances, the critical states of Massachusetts, New Hampshire, Virginia, and New York ratified the Constitution while also calling for amendments in the nature of a Bill of Rights. Representative James Madison of Virginia took the lead in drafting a series of proposed amendments. Eventually, Congress sent to the states twelve proposed amendments. Ten of these were promptly ratified, and it is these ten amendments that are called the Bill of Rights.

As you read the following passages from an essay called "What the Anti-Federalists Were *For*," evaluate the contending positions. What insights do you draw about the powers granted to the federal government?

Herbert Storing, What the Anti-Federalists Were *For*

1 THE COMPLETE ANTI-FEDERALIST 64–70 (1981)

It is often said that the major legacy of the Anti-Federalists is the Bill of Rights. Many of their suggestions found their way into the proposals for amendments made by state ratifying conventions and thence into the first ten amendments adopted in 1791. Three kinds of rights were stressed: the usual common law procedural rights in criminal prosecutions, liberty of conscience, and liberty of the press. The Anti-Federalists insisted that the Constitution should explicitly recognize the traditional procedural rights: to be safe from general search and seizure, to be indicted by grand jury, to trial by jury, to confront witnesses, and to be protected against cruel and unusual punishments. The most important of these was the trial by jury, and one of the most widely uttered objections against the Constitution was that it did not provide for (and therefore effectively abolished) trial by jury in civil cases. The Federalists' claim that practice among the states in this respect varied too much to provide a general rule was either denied by the Anti-Federalists or used as a further argument against the feasibility of consolidation. Regarding liberty of conscience, the Anti-Federalists' position was complex. Typically they favored both governmental encouragement of religion and liberty of individual conscience. The first proposal of the minority of the Pennsylvania convention was that rights of conscience shall be held inviolable and that no state provision regarding liberty of conscience shall be abridged by the federal government. Some Anti-Federalists professed to see in the prohibition against a religious test for officers of the United States a power to regulate religious beliefs in general, to which this prohibition was an exception. The rights of conscience should be secured, even though there was no immediate threat. Times change, and "the seeds of superstition, bigotry and enthusiasm, are too deeply implanted in our minds, ever to be eradicated. . . ." The third area of concern was liberty of the press, often declaimed by the Anti-Federalists as the palladium of American liberties. "It is the opinion of some great writers," Centinel argued, "that if the liberty of the press, by an institution of religion, or otherwise, could be rendered sacred, even in *Turkey*, that despotism would fly before it." "I say," another Anti-Federalist insisted, "that a declaration of those inherent and political rights ought to be made in a BILL OF RIGHTS, that the people may never lose their liberties by construction. If the liberty of the press by an inherent political right, let it be so declared, that no despot however great shall *dare to gain say it*." All of these concerns were pressed with enough vigor so that the Constitution was adopted only on the understanding that one of the first items of business in the new government would be the framing of amendments.

While the Federalists gave us the Constitution, then, the legacy of the Anti-Federalists was the Bill of Rights. But it is an ambiguous legacy, as can be seen by studying the debate. Indeed, in one sense, the success of the Bill of Rights reflects the failure of the Anti-Federalists. The whole emphasis on reservations of rights of individuals implied a fundamental acceptance of the "consolidated" character of the new government. A truly federal government needs no bill of rights. Indeed, there were some Federalists who tried to use the Anti-Federalists' federalism to destroy the Anti-Federalists argument for a bill of rights (incidentally undermining their own position). One Alfredus contended, for example, that a bill of rights was not necessary because the Constitution was a compact not between individuals but between sovereign and independent societies. This argument is easy enough to answer, and the Anti-Federalists often answered it: the government under the Constitution was not a mere compact of sovereign states—at least not in its operation—and it was not exempt from the need for a bill of rights on that account. But in making this reply the Anti-Federalists decisively abandoned the doctrine of strict federalism.

A more substantial "federal" argument against a bill of rights was made by James Wilson in his famous "State house speech" on 4 October 1787. Wilson acknowledge that maxim often put forward by the Anti-Federalists that in establishing governments all powers not expressly reserved are presumed to be granted, but he denied that it applied to the proposed general government, because that was to be a government of specifically enumerated powers. Whereas in the state constitutions the people "invested their representatives with every right and authority which they did not in explicit terms reserve," under the proposed Constitution "the congressional power is to be collected, not from tacit implication, but from the positive grant expressed in the instrument of the union. Hence, it is evident, that in the former case, everything which is not reserved is given; but in the latter the reverse of the proposition prevails, and everything which is not given is reserved." Thus, Wilson concluded, "it would have been superfluous and absurd to have stipulated with a federal body of our own creation, that we should enjoy those privileges of which we are not divested, either by the intention or the act that has brought the body into existent." This is a substantial argument; it was heavily relied on by defenders of the Constitution; and the basis theory on which it rests has become a part of American constitutional orthodoxy. Yet it has some serious difficulties, especially when applied to the question of a bill of rights.

Wilson's position depends on the assumption that the "powers" delegated to the government are fairly easily identifiable and unambiguous. Thus, for example, he contended that there is no "power" granted to the federal government "to regulate literary publications" and therefore no need for a reservation in favor of the liberty of the press. If Congress should enact such a law, the judges would declare it null and void because "inconsistent with those powers vested by this instrument in Congress. . . ." But (even leaving aside the question of libel and seditious libel) the general government is given authority to lay and collect taxes and to regulate commerce, for example, and could not either of these be used to stifle the press? More generally, does not the general government, in the pursuit of its delegated powers, have implied powers that need to be limited for the sake of individual liberties? Cannot the federal government define crimes and criminal procedures, in connection with federal postal regulations, for example; and is there not therefore a need for procedural restraints of the traditional kind? Brutus made the argument thus: "The powers, rights, and authority, granted to the general government by this constitution, are as complete, with respect to every object to which they extend, as that of any state government—It reaches to every thing which concerns human happiness—Life, liberty, and property, are under its controul. There is the same reason, therefore, that the exercise of power, in this case, should be restrained within proper limits, as in that of the state governments."

The constitutional grant of power to Congress—so laconic and broad—is an argument in favor of a bill of rights, not against it. . . . The inadequacy of Wilson's argument is further demonstrated by the presence in the Constitution of a truncated bill of rights. Why was there any need to restrict the suspension of the writ of habeas corpus or to prohibit granting titles of nobility? Where were such powers granted? The very few Federalists who made any attempt to meet this objection sought to show that these were exceptions to implied powers, but this only reinforced the contention that the "powers" granted are anything but simple and unambiguous— that they are in fact complex and doubtful and capable of great extension. . . .

Even if it were granted that a bill of rights was, strictly speaking, unnecessary, the Anti-Federalists asked, why not be safe? What is the harm? Would it, Patrick Henry asked, have taken too much paper? One answer was that a bill of rights would be positively dangerous, because, as Wilson explained, "it would imply that whatever is not expressed was given, which is not the principle of the proposed constitution." There is some basis for this view. Yet the Anti-Federalists could forcefully contend that any harm of this kind had already been done by the reservations in behalf of individual rights included in the Constitution. And, all things considered, this Federalist argument seemed a bit sophistical.

NOTES

1.   Who was right in this struggle over the interpretation of the original Constitution? Were the Anti-Federalists' fears exaggerated? Were the Federalists' assurances too confident? Does it make a difference, for the protection of the freedom of speech, that there is a First Amendment? Why?

2.   The preceding pages have passed quickly over a lot of history—the ideas and conflicts that sparked the American Revolution, the course of that Revolution, the failure of the government under the Articles of Confederation, the Philadelphia Convention, and the debate over ratification. If this is unfamiliar territory, two introductions to the major ideas and debates at the founding are Forrest McDonald, NOVUS ORDO SECLORUM: THE INTELLECTUAL ORIGINS OF THE CONSTITUTION (1985); and Jack N. Rakove, ORIGINAL MEANINGS: POLITICS AND IDEAS IN THE MAKING OF THE CONSTITUTION (1996).

[Assignment 2]

II. THE CONSTITUTION

You should now carefully read the text of the Constitution and its twenty-seven amendments. (It begins on p. 1 of this book.) As you read the Constitution, as well as the following selection from James Madison, ask what type of political order is being established. Is it a democracy in the style of ancient Athens, or an oligarchy of a few wealthy leaders, or a tyranny of a single executive? Or, as Madison argues, is it a republic? How did the framers distinguish a republic from other forms of political order?

The Federalist No. 39

James Madison, Jan. 16, 1788

. . . The first question that offers itself is, whether the general form and aspect of the government be strictly republican. It is evident that no other form would be reconcilable with the genius of the people of America; with the fundamental principles of the Revolution; or with that honorable determination which animates every votary of freedom, to rest all our political experiments on the capacity of mankind for self-government. If the plan of the convention, therefore, be found to depart from the republican character, its advocates must abandon it as no longer defensible.

What, then, are the distinctive characters of the republican form . . . ?

If we resort for a criterion to the different principles on which different forms of government are established, we may define a republic to be, or at least may bestow that name on, a government which derives all its powers directly or indirectly from the great body of the people, and is administered by persons holding their offices during pleasure, for a limited period, or during good behavior. It is *essential* to such a government that it be derived from the great body of the society, not from an inconsiderable proportion, or a favored class of it; otherwise a handful of tyrannical nobles, exercising their oppressions by a delegation of their powers, might aspire to the rank of republicans, and claim for their government the honorable title of republic. It is *sufficient* for such a government that the persons administering it be appointed, either directly or indirectly, by the people; and that they hold their appointments by either of the tenures just specified; otherwise every government in the United States, as well as every other popular government that has been or can be well organized or well executed, would be degraded from the republican character. . . .

"[I]t was not sufficient," say the adversaries of the proposed Constitution, "for the convention to adhere to the republican form. They ought, with equal care, to have preserved the *federal* form, which regards the Union as a *confederacy* of sovereign states; instead of which, they have framed a *national* government, which regards the Union as a *consolidation* of the States." And it is asked by what authority this bold and radical innovation was undertaken? The handle which has been made of this objection requires that it should be examined with some precision.

Without inquiring into the accuracy of the distinction on which the objection is founded, it will be necessary to a just estimate of its force, first, to ascertain the real character of the government in question; secondly, to inquire how far the convention were authorized to propose such a government; and thirdly, how far the duty they owed to their country could supply any defect of regular authority.

First. In order to ascertain the real character of the government, it may be considered in relation to the foundation on which it is to be established; to the sources from which its ordinary powers are to be drawn; to the operation of those powers; to the extent of them; and to the authority by which future changes in the government are to be introduced.

On examining the first relation, it appears, on one hand, that the Constitution is to be founded on the assent and ratification of the people of America, given by deputies elected for the special purpose; but, on the other, that this assent and ratification is to be given by the people, not as individuals composing one entire nation, but as composing the distinct and independent States to which they respectively belong. It is to be the assent and ratification of the several States, derived from the supreme authority in each State—the authority of the people themselves. The act, therefore, establishing the Constitution, will not be a national, but a federal act.

That it will be a federal and not a national act, as these terms are understood by the objectors; the act of the people, as forming so many independent States, not as forming one aggregate nation, is obvious from this single consideration, that it is to result neither from the decision of a *majority* of the people of the Union, nor from that of a *majority* of the States. It must result from the *unanimous* assent of the several States that are parties to it, differing no otherwise from their ordinary assent than in its being expressed, not by the legislative authority, but by that of the people themselves. Were the people regarded in this transaction as forming one nation, the will of the majority of the whole people of the United States would bind the minority, in the same manner as the majority in each State must bind the minority; and the will of the majority must be determined either by a comparison of the individual votes, or by considering the will of the majority of the States as evidence of the will of a majority of the people of the United States. Neither of these rules have been adopted. Each State, in ratifying the Constitution, is considered as a sovereign body, independent of all others, and only to be bound by its own voluntary act. In this relation, then, the new Constitution will, if established, be a *federal*, and not a *national* constitution. . . .

The difference between a federal and national government, as it relates to the *operation of the Government*, is supposed to consist in this, that in the former the powers operate on the political bodies composing the Confederacy, in their political capacities; in the latter, on the individual citizens composing the nation, in their individual capacities. On trying the Constitution by this criterion, it falls under the national, not the federal character; though perhaps not so completely as has been understood. In several cases, and particularly in the trial of controversies to which States may be parties, they must be viewed and proceeded against in their collective and political capacities only. So far the national countenance of the government on this side seems to be disfigured by a few federal features. But this blemish is perhaps unavoidable in any plan; and the operation of the government on the people, in their individual capacities, in its ordinary and most essential proceedings, may, on the whole, designate it, in this relation, a national government.

But if the government be national with regard to the *operation* of its powers, it changes its aspect again when we contemplate it in relation to the *extent* of its powers. The idea of a national government involves in it, not only an authority over the individual citizens, but an indefinite supremacy over all persons and things, so far as they are objects of lawful government. Among a people consolidated into one nation, this supremacy is completely vested in the national legislature. Among communities united for particular purposes, it is vested partly in the general and partly in the municipal legislatures. In the former case, all local authorities are subordinate to the supreme; and may be controlled, directed, or abolished by it at pleasure. In the latter, the local or municipal authorities form distinct and independent portions of the supremacy, no more subject, within their respective spheres, to the general authority, than the general authority is subject to them, within its own sphere. In this relation, then, the proposed government cannot be deemed a *national* one; since its jurisdiction extends to certain enumerated objects only, and leaves to the several States a residuary and inviolable sovereignty over all other objects. It is true that in controversies relating to the boundary between the two jurisdictions, the tribunal which is ultimately to decide, is to be established under the general government. But this does not change the principle of the case. The decision is to be impartially made, according to the rules of the Constitution; and all the usual and most effectual precautions are taken to secure this impartiality. Some such tribunal is clearly essential to prevent an appeal to the sword and a dissolution of the compact; and that it ought to be established under the general rather than under the local governments, or, to speak more properly, that it could be safely established under the first alone, is a position not likely to be combated.

If we try the Constitution by its last relation to the authority by which amendments are to be made, we find it neither wholly *national* nor wholly *federal*. Were it wholly national, the supreme and ultimate authority would reside in the *majority* of the people of the Union; and this authority would be competent at all times, like that of a majority of every national society, to alter or abolish its established government. Were it wholly federal, on the other hand, the concurrence of each State in the Union would be essential to every alteration that would be binding on all. The mode provided by the plan of the convention is not founded on either of these principles. In requiring more than a majority, and particularly in computing the proportion by *States*, not by *citizens*, it departs from the *national* and advances towards the *federal* character; in rendering the concurrence of less than the whole number of States sufficient, it loses again the *federal* and partakes of the *national* character.

The proposed Constitution, therefore, is, in strictness, neither a national nor a federal Constitution, but a composition of both. In its foundation it is federal, not national; in the sources from which the ordinary powers of the government are drawn, it is partly federal and partly national; in the operation of these powers, it is national, not federal; in the extent of them, again, it is federal, not national; and, finally, in the authoritative mode of introducing amendments, it is neither wholly federal, nor wholly national.

Six Broad Themes of the Constitution

In his argument that the government created by the Constitution is partly national and partly federal, Madison identifies several prominent features of the

Constitution. Stepping back from that discussion and viewing the Constitution at an even more general level, one can discern six broad themes, and they recur throughout this book.

1.   *A Written Constitution.* The first thing to notice about the Constitution is that it is a written text. As already discussed, it was the first time a nation took its governing structure and put it into writing, giving that written document the status of "supreme Law." (The phrase "supreme Law" is found in Article VI, Section 2, in what is called the Supremacy Clause.) Closely linked, then, to the idea of a written constitution was constitutional supremacy: the Constitution prevails over any contrary law or action by a state or federal government. This supremacy is the foundation for judicial review of legislative and executive action.

2.   *Republicanism and Popular Sovereignty.* From its first three words, the Constitution proclaims that it is an act of and for "We the People of the United States." In contrast to the Articles of Confederation, the states are not sovereign (though this point would remain disputed for decades, and ultimately lead to attempted secession and the Civil War). Nor is the national government sovereign. The people are sovereign.

To be sure, the people of the United States ordinarily exercise their sovereignty through representative institutions. Madison notes this fact in *The Federalist No. 39* when defending the "strictly republican" character of the government under the Constitution. Yet all government power proceeds, ultimately if sometimes indirectly, from the great body of the people, acting either through their national institutions or through their state institutions. Thus, the government is "partly national" and "partly federal."

As Madison notes, the Constitution was adopted by the collective decision of the people of the United States, acting through the separate decisions of the people in three-fourths of the states. Likewise, constitutional change—the adoption of amendments, pursuant to Article V—ultimately requires the ratification of the sovereign "people of the United States," also acting through the separate decision-making processes of three-fourths of the states.

Thus popular sovereignty, achieved through representative, republican institutions, pervades the Constitution, though imperfectly. In the original Constitution, it is present in the schemes of representation in Congress and in the system for election of the president (though both arrangements were tainted by accommodation of slavery). It is also present indirectly in the role of elected officials in the selection of the judiciary, as well as in Article IV's guarantee by the nation as a whole that each state will always have "a Republican Form of Government." Later amendments protected the right to vote and increased the representativeness and accountability of national institutions. This is true of the Fifteenth, Seventeenth, Nineteenth, Twenty-third, Twenty-fourth, Twenty-sixth, and Twenty-seventh Amendments, all of which are discussed below in "A Map of the Constitution."

3.   *Separation of Powers.* Another feature of the Constitution is its division and separation of powers among three branches of the national government—the legislative, executive, and judicial—represented by Congress, the president, and the federal courts. Each branch is, to a substantial degree, independent of the others, and each possesses powers to check or balance the powers of the others.

In America the government would not be a "mixed regime" divided among a king, an aristocracy, and the people (as in the English model of king, House of Lords, and House of Commons). A different division was necessary. The division the framers employed was functional. Subject to certain exceptions, the legislative function is for Congress, the executive function is for the president, and the judicial function is for the federal courts. The functional separation of powers had been endorsed by John Locke and William Blackstone, and especially by Montesquieu in THE SPIRIT OF THE LAWS (1748, first published in English in 1750).[1] The idea of a functional separation of powers influenced even the critics of the Constitution, who were pejoratively called Anti-Federalists. They argued that the Constitution's system of checks and balances actually intermingled the legislative, executive, and judicial powers that Montesquieu had said should be kept separate. And some supporters of the new Constitution, such as John Adams, never accepted the idea of a functional separation of powers. Adams would have preferred a democratic variation of the "mixed regime" where there were three components—the One (the president or governor), the Few (the upper house and the courts), and the many (the lower house)—but all were elected directly or indirectly by the people.

In this confused mass of different views about what kind of separation of powers was desirable, and what kind would actually be effected by the Constitution, the defense of the new proposed government for the United States fell to James Madison. Today the system of checks and balances in the Constitution is often called "Madisonian" because of his work in devising and defending it. In *The Federalist Nos. 47 to 51*, Madison discusses the separation of powers and argues that the Constitution of the United States is consistent with Montesquieu's insights.

Madison explains that under the Constitution each branch is given different responsibilities and only a partial role in the selection of the members of the others. The president, senators, and representatives are chosen in different ways by different electorates. A rolling six-year electoral cycle is set up before all the elected officers of the government can be replaced in three staggered elections. Political movements must usually sweep at least two national elections in a row, held two years apart, before they can accomplish much. Even then it may be years before the courts are transformed. Moreover, each branch is made as independent of the others as possible and is given a "will" of its own so that it does not become subject to one of the others. And vitally important powers—such as the power of war-making—are divided, requiring joint action by separate branches. The framers insisted on a separation of powers for the national government at the same time they were greatly expanding its strength.

4. *Federalism.* A fourth broad theme of the Constitution lies in its division of power between the national government and the governments of the states. The Constitution itself is the supreme law. The Supremacy Clause of Article VI makes any constitutionally valid actions of the national government prevail over actions of the states. But the national government remains, in theory at least, a government of limited, enumerated powers, with the people and the states retaining all the powers

---

[1] Montesquieu thought a functional separation of powers had been achieved in England after the Glorious Revolution of 1688, but he was almost certainly wrong. On his counsel, continental Europe and Latin America tended to adopt a rigid functional separation of powers. Even down to 1945 most civil law countries made no provision for judicial review of legislation, thinking it would give the judiciary a share in the legislative power. On Enlightenment thinking about separation of powers, see M.J.C. Vile, CONSTITUTIONALISM AND THE SEPARATION OF POWERS (1998).

not delegated to the national government. Of course, there remains plenty of room for argument over how broadly or narrowly to construe the enumerated powers of the national government, especially the power to "regulate Commerce . . . among the several States," the taxing power, the spending power, and the power to pass laws "necessary and proper" for carrying into execution the other enumerated powers.

Federalism is a division of labor. Ideally, a central government can solve the collective-action problems of the states. For example, it might be in the interest of all the states to maintain a navy for trade and protection. But each state, on its own, might have an incentive to do nothing. If a state were to maintain a navy on its own, it would bear all of the costs of the action but it might gain only some of the benefits— it could be that most of the benefits would go to neighboring states (depending on the states' locations and trading patterns). Thus each state might have an incentive to do nothing and "free-ride" on the actions of the other states. That kind of free-rider problem can be solved with coordinated action, which is easier for the states to engage in if there is a central government. In addition, a central government may benefit from economies of scale. And—again, ideally—the central government can step in whenever a state is trampling the rights of a minority.

At the same time, a federal system is supposed to allow local governments to address situations for which they are better suited. These include questions for which there is geographic variation in tastes and preferences, where competition can spur a race to the top, or where economic or social experimentation is valuable. And it may be easier for the people to control a local government than a distant one. In practice, however, this division is complicated, and the local governments will often think a question is best resolved at the local level while the central government will disagree. As a result, in the United States and the nations influenced by its federal system,[2] written constitutional federalism tends to lead to some form of judicial review, because a court will be needed to play umpire in disputes between the central and local governments.

5.   *Individual Rights.* The Constitution is also designed to promote liberty. The original Constitution of 1787 had some provisions protecting individual rights (e.g., Article I, Sections 9 and 10), but most of the explicit guarantees of such rights have come in subsequent amendments. The increasing protection of individual rights is a major theme in America's constitutional history.

As a general matter, the Bill of Rights, ratified in 1791, protected individual rights from abridgement by the *national* government, and the Reconstruction Amendments (the Thirteenth, Fourteenth, and Fifteenth Amendments, ratified after the Civil War) protected rights from abridgement by *state* governments. Indeed, the Reconstruction Amendments so radically transformed our Constitution that they have been described as a Second Founding of the Republic. The Bill of Rights and the Reconstruction Amendments together protect rights such as the freedom of speech and the freedom of religion, and they impose important constraints on the federal and state governments, such as a prohibition on the government taking life, liberty, or property without due process of law. The Thirteenth Amendment reaches

---

[2]   Since the adoption of the first written constitution embodying federalism—the U.S. Constitution— federal constitutions have been adopted in Australia, Austria, Argentina, Brazil, Canada, Germany, India, Mexico, and Switzerland. Similarly, the European Union has a federal system (though in its case the governing law is not a constitution but treaties).

even more broadly than government action, for it commands that slavery shall not "exist within the United States."

A related theme of the amendments to the Constitution is the steady expansion of national power to protect these rights. Each of the Reconstruction Amendments authorized Congress to pass enforcing legislation. And two constitutional amendments in the early twentieth century made the national government much more powerful. The Sixteenth Amendment (1913), allowing for the taxation of income, gave the federal government an enormous increase in revenue—revenue which it could itself use or return to the states with strings attached. The Seventeenth Amendment (1913), providing for the direct election of U.S. senators (who had previously been elected by the state legislatures), also made the federal government more independent from the states. And, as noted above, a number of amendments have expanded voting rights. Taken together, and read in light of the Declaration of Independence's statement that "All men are created equal," these amendments commit the nation to recognition of equal political and civil rights.

6. *The Imperfect Congruence of the Constitution with Justice.* A final feature of the Constitution is imperfection. It does not forbid all bad things; nor does it require all good things (even assuming there could be complete agreement on what these are). Much of the Constitution offers a framework in which different political choices can be made. Yet even the framework itself—its basic elements, like the separation of powers and federalism—is subject to criticism. Similarly, from the point of view of various theories of political morality, the substantive rights in the Constitution are likely to be both overinclusive and underinclusive.

Although the Constitution is in many ways a magnificent triumph, one cannot be blind to its shortcomings—including the atrocities that it originally permitted and rewarded (especially slavery), and the injustices that have been done since then in its name. Indeed, the imperfection of the Constitution was recognized from the beginning. Almost a third of the representatives at the Philadelphia convention either left before its conclusion or refused to sign the final document. Those who did sign it and support it in the ratification debates—including Madison, Hamilton, and Washington—were dissatisfied with various parts of it, but what they feared more was the alternative of disunion and collapse. As Washington wrote in a letter shortly after the end of the convention, "I wish the Constitution which is offered had been made more perfect, but I sincerely believe it the best that could be obtained at this time—and as a constitutional door is op[e]ned for amendment hereafter—the adoption of it under present circumstances of the Union is in my opinion desirable." 5 THE PAPERS OF GEORGE WASHINGTON 339 (W. W. Abbot ed., 1997).

When studying the Constitution and its interpretation by judges, presidents, and members of Congress, do not ignore the ways the document and its interpretation have produced grave wrongs. Consider, also, who has, or should have, the power to fix those imperfections. Judges? Elected officials? The people? Imperfection should not be celebrated like the other themes—written constitutionalism, popular sovereignty, separation of powers, federalism, and the promotion of individual rights—but it is just as essential to understanding the Constitution.

The Dead-Hand Problem

In addition to these themes of the Constitution, there is an even more basic question to consider. Why have a Constitution at all? Why allow a document, most of which was ratified in 1789 and 1791, to still bind us today? What these questions raise has been called "the dead-hand problem." Debate over it is hardly new. In a letter to James Madison, Thomas Jefferson wrote: "The earth belongs always to the living generation." Because no generation could bind the next one, "Every constitution, . . . and every law, naturally expires at the end of 19 years." 15 THE PAPERS OF THOMAS JEFFERSON 396 (Barbara B. Oberg & J. Jefferson Looney eds., 2008–16) (Sept. 6, 1789). In his reply to Jefferson, Madison warned of a weakened government beset by "pernicious factions." And he added: "Would not a Government so often revised become too mutable to retain those prejudices in its favor which antiquity inspires, and which are perhaps a salutary aid to the most rational Government in the most enlightened age?" 16 THE PAPERS OF THOMAS JEFFERSON 148 (Feb. 4, 1790).

The debate continues. One answer is the Jeffersonian one, that each generation should start anew, deciding for itself what its laws are, including its Constitution. And as the founding generation is further and further removed from the present, is the case stronger for starting again? Another answer would be that each generation is in fact free to decide whether to submit to the dead hand of the past, but our generation, like every preceding one, has accepted this old Constitution as our own. Yet another answer is that if we wish to use the institutions created by the Constitution, we are obligated to accept the limits it imposes: the children who inherit a house must accept its mortgage and its covenants. Still another answer is that of course individuals and groups can act in a way that is binding on their future selves. When the present shareholders of a corporation make a decision, it binds later shareholders, and any time a person makes a contract today it is binding tomorrow. If we are a nation, and not just a collection of people at different moments in time, then we can make plans and commit ourselves to values that will bind the next generation—and then it can do the same.

Types of Constitutional Argument

If we do accept the Constitution as binding—and it presents itself as "the supreme Law of the land"—there remains disagreement over how to interpret it. How should judges, other officials, or any of us decide exactly what it means? Throughout this book, you will notice the recurrence of five types of constitutional argument, or methods of interpretation. (The following list is adapted from Philip Bobbitt's work on modalities of constitutional interpretation. See Philip Bobbitt, CONSTITUTIONAL FATE 3–92 (1982).)

First, there are arguments based on the text of the Constitution—that is, the meaning of the words, in context, to informed readers. The Constitution's text can seem simple enough—you, like any member of the public, can read it for yourself— but it may not always be what it seems. Arguments based on the meaning of the text *as it was enacted* might draw on evidence from contemporaneous writings (including dictionaries), and from other legal texts the drafters might have borrowed from. Previous legal usage is especially important where the Constitution contains a "term of art," that is, a word or phrase with an established technical meaning in the law.

Second, there are arguments from historical context. These draw on the historical background for a provision, emphasizing not the particular words of the text but the intentions behind them and the goal they were supposed to accomplish or the problem they were supposed to solve. Evidence for these arguments will often be drawn from statements made by the drafters or ratifiers. These might be found, for example, in *The Federalist* or in the records of the debates at the Constitutional Convention. Evidence may also be drawn from the broader historical setting in which the document was adopted, such as the experience of the American Revolution and the desperate struggle under the Continental Congress.

Third, there are arguments based on the structure of the document. Some structural arguments draw inferences from the relationship of provisions to each other. Other structural arguments emphasize the location of a provision in the Constitution (e.g., whether a provision is located with powers, or with constraints on powers). Still other structural arguments emphasize the institutional arrangements created by the Constitution as a whole.

Fourth, there are arguments from precedent and practice. Here the focus is on previous interpretations, whether by the judiciary or by other branches of government, that have become sufficiently settled to "fix" or "liquidate" the meaning of an ambiguous constitutional provision. Arguments from practice are based not only on what happened in the past, but also on the rationale given. That rationale might be found, for example, in judicial opinions, in congressional debates or in presidential statements.

Fifth, there are arguments based on policy. These arguments look to consequences, and they ask which interpretation produces the best results according to a specific notion of what is best. One might, for example, ask which interpretation would maximize egalitarian justice, individual autonomy, or economic efficiency, or which interpretation would best comport with natural law. In constitutional law, policy arguments are often not about the narrow question of whether a particular statute or executive action is good. Rather, the question is usually at a higher level of abstraction—about whether it is desirable for the Congress to have the power to pass this kind of statute, or for the president to take this kind of action, or for this kind of decision to be made by the national government or the states.

Are all five types of argument legitimate? How should they relate to one another? Which arguments should be given the most force? Are all of the arguments in play in every case, or do some of them come into play only when certain other arguments are ambiguous or inconclusive?

A Map of the Constitution

In studying the Constitution, it is useful to start with an overview. As you read this section, flip back and forth to the text of the Constitution at p. 1.

The Preamble states the purposes of the Constitution, and the authority from which it claims to emanate—an exercise of popular sovereignty by "We the People of the United States."

Article I of the Constitution concerns the legislative powers of Congress. It says that Congress consists of a House of Representatives and a Senate, specifies how members are chosen, prescribes their qualifications, and provides rules for lawmaking. Article I vests in Congress "all legislative powers herein granted," which creates a national government of limited and enumerated powers. These legislative powers are listed in Section 8. Section 9 lists things Congress may not do, and Section 10 lists things states may not do.

Article II vests "the executive Power" in "a President of the United States." It thus creates a single, independent chief executive rather than a plural executive or a prime minister, and it describes the procedure for election. (What now seems like an unusual backup procedure—selection of the president by the House of Representatives—was expected by some of the founders to be used most of the time.) Article II also details certain presidential powers. Some are shared with the Senate, such as the power to make treaties or appoint high-ranking members of the administration. Other powers, such as the power to pardon, are held by the president alone. Finally, Article II makes clear that the president and vice president, unlike the English king, are subject to impeachment by Congress, as are all officers in the executive and judicial branches.

Article III vests "the judicial Power" of the United States in a Supreme Court and any inferior courts that Congress creates. Each judge is appointed by the president with the Senate's advice and consent, and the appointment is for life (which is the accepted meaning of holding office "during good behaviour"). The judicial power is not defined, but it extends only to specified kinds of "cases" and "controversies." Congress has some control over the courts' jurisdiction, but the extent of that control remains a matter of dispute. "Judicial review" is not referred to explicitly, but it can be inferred from the supremacy of the Constitution and the duty of judges to follow that supreme law as they decide cases and controversies.

Article IV defines certain relationships among the states. The states must recognize each other's legal proceedings. Each must accord citizens of other states the same "Privileges and Immunities" it gives to its own citizens. Fugitives—and originally fugitive slaves—escaping to another state must be returned. And Congress governs the "Territory" of the United States and may admit new states into the Union. (Disputes over these Article IV duties and powers led to the infamous *Dred Scott* case and contributed to the Civil War.) Finally, Article IV provides that the national government shall "guarantee" to every state "a Republican Form of Government" and protect each from invasion and insurrection.

Article V prescribes the procedures for amending the Constitution, the only way the Constitution itself authorizes constitutional change. Amendment was deliberately made difficult. It requires (1) a proposal, either by a two-thirds vote of both houses of Congress or by a special constitutional convention requested by two-thirds of the states, and (2) ratification by three-fourths of the states. Article V purports to make unamendable two provisions that were critical to ratification: equal representation of small and large states in the Senate, and the restriction on Congress's ability to outlaw the importation of slaves before 1808.

Article VI specifies the authority of the Constitution. It is "the supreme Law of the Land," and it binds the judges of every state, "notwithstanding" anything to the contrary in state law. Furthermore, all federal officers—and even all state officers—are required to swear an oath "to support this Constitution."

Article VII declared that the Constitution would go into effect when ratified by nine of the thirteen original states.

The original Constitution lacked a Bill of Rights, an omission that became a source of extensive opposition (see p. 31). In response, supporters of the Constitution promised to propose a Bill of Rights—*after* ratification. The First Congress proposed twelve amendments, ten of which were soon ratified. The First Amendment protects rights of religion and expression: the free exercise of religion, the freedoms of speech and of the press, and the rights of assembly and petition. It also prohibits Congress from making any law respecting an establishment of religion. The Second Amendment protects the right of the people to "keep and bear arms" to have a "well-regulated militia." The Third Amendment limits the quartering of soldiers in private homes. The Fourth, Fifth, Sixth, Seventh, and Eighth Amendments protect a variety of rights against the government, especially the abuse of the government's powers to investigate and prosecute crimes. These rights include the jury trial right in criminal and civil trials and the guarantee of "due process of law." There are also prohibitions on "unreasonable searches and seizures," uncompensated takings of private property, and "cruel and unusual punishments." The Ninth and Tenth Amendments appear to be clarifying provisions made necessary by the Federalists' initial argument that having a Bill of Rights would imply that all rights and powers were assigned into the hands of the national government. The Ninth says that the enumeration of rights in the Bill of Rights should not be construed to impair other rights. The Tenth confirms that the federal government is one of limited, enumerated powers. (Another of the twelve amendments proposed by the First Congress is now the Twenty-seventh Amendment.)

The Eleventh Amendment, ratified in 1798, reversed an early U.S. Supreme Court decision and removed a category of jurisdiction from the federal courts: suits against a state by citizens of another state.

The Twelfth Amendment, ratified in 1804 was designed to solve an unforeseen problem with presidential elections: the rise of political parties. In 1800 Thomas Jefferson and Aaron Burr ran as a ticket, with Jefferson expected to be the president—but they received the same number of electoral votes, a tie result. This amendment ensures that the president and vice president are voted for separately.

After the Civil War, the nation ratified the Reconstruction Amendments. The Thirteenth (1865) abolishes slavery, except as a punishment for a crime. The Fourteenth (1868) grants citizenship to those born in the United States. It also protects persons—including especially the newly freed slaves—from state mistreatment by guaranteeing them "due process of law" and "the equal protection of the laws," and by securing "the privileges and immunities of citizens of the United States." It is now widely accepted that these provisions of the Fourteenth Amendment make most of the Bill of Rights apply to state governments. The Fifteenth Amendment (1870) forbids denial of the right to vote based on race or slavery. Each of these amendments also gave enforcement power to Congress.

Another burst of amendments came in the early twentieth century. In 1913, the Progressives succeeded in ratifying the Sixteenth Amendment, giving Congress the power to tax individual incomes; and the Seventeenth, ending the indirect election of senators. And two other sometimes overlapping social movements that had toiled for decades finally achieved their aims. The temperance movement won the Eighteenth Amendment (1919), creating Prohibition; and the women's suffrage movement won the Nineteenth Amendment (1920), giving women the right to vote.

The first year of President Franklin Delano Roosevelt's presidency, 1933, saw the ratification of two more amendments. The Twentieth shortened the "lame duck" period for an outgoing president, and the Twenty-first repealed Prohibition.

In the second half of the twentieth century several amendments were ratified that affect elections. The Twenty-second (1951) limits presidents to two terms. The Twenty-third (1961) gives the District of Columbia votes in the Electoral College. The Twenty-fourth (1964) forbids imposing a tax on voting. The Twenty-fifth (1967) provides an elaborate scheme for a temporary presidential disability. The Twenty-sixth (1971) gives those over eighteen the right to vote.

Finally, the Twenty-seventh Amendment forbids alterations in congressional pay from taking effect without an intervening election for the House of Representatives. It was proposed in 1789 as part of the Bill of Rights, but was not ratified until 1992. (Its ratification raises constitutional questions considered on p. 800.)

[Assignment 3]

III. INTERPRETING THE CONSTITUTION: THE ALIEN AND SEDITION ACTS

Shortly after the ratification of the Constitution, there were many important debates about its meaning. One was over whether Congress had power under Article I to create a "Bank of the United States" (see p. 470). Another was over the extent of federal power regarding slavery and the slave trade (see p. 696). Another was about foreign affairs, and whether President Washington's powers under Article II allowed him to commit the nation to a policy of strict neutrality in a war between England and France (see p. 270). Finally, there were the Alien and Sedition Acts, which are presented here. This controversy is presented as a case study in how to argue about what the Constitution means—and about who gets to say what it means. It brings together all of the major parts of constitutional law: separation of powers, federalism, and individual rights.

The continuing conflict between France and England put the fledgling United States in great peril. In 1795, Chief Justice John Jay (an author of *The Federalist* along with Hamilton and Madison) had succeeded in negotiating a treaty with England on behalf of President Washington. But the Jay Treaty further strained relations with France. By 1797, when President Washington was succeeded by John Adams, France was interfering with the United States' shipping rights as a neutral country. There was an outrageous French demand for bribes or tribute (the "XYZ Affair"). By 1798, the United States and France were on the brink of war.

Congress, narrowly controlled by a Federalist Party majority supporting President Adams, enacted a series of measures known as the Alien and Sedition Acts. These were designed to prepare the nation for war with France, its former ally, and to guard against suspected subversion by aliens and those critical of President Adams. The first bill proposed (but the second one to be passed) was the Alien Enemies Act, which authorized the president to deport French citizens in the event of war with France. The next bill, the Alien Friends Act, gave the president wider authority—to deport any aliens he judged "dangerous to the peace and safety of the United States." The congressional debate over the constitutionality of the Alien Acts was intense. (The arguments are summarized in David P. Currie, THE CONSTITUTION IN CONGRESS: THE FEDERALIST PERIOD 1789–1791, at 254–259 (1997).) Next the Federalist majority passed the Sedition Act, again over the objections of the minority Democratic-Republican Party. In the House the vote was exceedingly close: 44–41. The Sedition Act authorized criminal penalties against "any person" who wrote, printed, uttered, or published seditious writings against the government.

As you read the following materials, ask yourself these questions: Does Congress have the power under Article I to enact these laws? May Congress delegate sweeping powers of deportation of aliens to the president acting without a judge or jury? Is the Sedition Act consistent with the First Amendment? And who gets to answer these questions?

The Alien Enemies Act
1 Stat. 577 (July 6, 1798)

SECTION 1. *Be it enacted by the Senate and House of Representatives of the United States of America in Congress assembled*, That whenever there shall be a declared war between the United States and any foreign nation or government, or any invasion or predatory incursion shall be perpetrated, attempted, or threatened against the territory of the United States, by any foreign nation or government, and the President of the United States shall make public proclamation of the event, all natives, citizens, denizens, or subjects of the hostile nation or government, being males of the age of fourteen years and upwards, who shall be within the United States, and not actually naturalized, shall be liable to be apprehended, restrained, secured and removed, as alien enemies. And the President of the United States shall be, and he is hereby authorized, in any event, as aforesaid, by his proclamation thereof, or other public act, to direct the conduct to be observed, on the part of the United States, towards the aliens who shall become liable, as aforesaid; the manner and degree of the restraint to which they shall be subject, and in what cases, and upon what security their residence shall be permitted, and to provide for the removal of those, who, not being permitted to reside within the United States, shall refuse or neglect to depart therefrom; and to establish any other regulations which shall be found necessary in the premises and for the public safety: Provided, that aliens resident within the United States, who shall become liable as enemies, in the manner aforesaid, and who shall not be chargeable with actual hostility, or other crime against the public safety, shall be allowed, for the recovery, disposal, and removal of their goods and effects, and for their departure, the full time which is, or shall be stipulated by any treaty, where any shall have been between the United States, and the hostile nation or government, of which they shall be natives, citizens, denizens or subjects: and where no such treaty shall have existed, the President of the United States may ascertain and declare such reasonable time as may be consistent with the public safety, and according to the dictates of humanity and national hospitality. . . .

The Alien Friends Act
1 Stat. 570 (June 25, 1798)

SECTION 1. *Be it enacted by the Senate and House of Representatives of the United States of America in Congress assembled*, That it shall be lawful for the President of the United States at any time during the continuance of this act, to *order* all such *aliens* as he shall judge dangerous to the peace and safety of the United States, or shall have reasonable grounds to suspect are concerned in any treasonable or secret machinations against the government thereof, to depart out of the territory of the United States, within such time as shall be expressed in such order. . . . And in case any alien, so ordered to depart, shall be found at large within the United States after the time limited in such order for his departure, and not having obtained a *license* shall not have conformed thereto, every such alien shall, on conviction thereof, be imprisoned for a term not exceeding three years, and shall never after be admitted to become a citizen of the United States. *Provided always, and be it further enacted*, that if any alien so ordered to depart shall prove to the satisfaction of the President, by evidence to be taken before such person or persons as the President shall direct, who are for that purpose hereby authorized to administer oaths, that no injury or danger to the United States will arise from suffering such alien to reside therein, the President may grant a *license* to such alien to remain within the United States for such time as he shall judge proper, and at such place as he may designate. . . .

SEC. 2. *And be it further enacted*, That it shall be lawful for the President of the United States, whenever he may deem it necessary for the public safety, to order to be removed out of the territory thereof, any alien who may or shall be in prison in pursuance of this act; and to cause to be arrested and sent out of the United States such of those aliens as shall have been ordered to depart therefrom and shall not have obtained a license as aforesaid, in all cases where, in the opinion of the President, the public safety requires a speedy removal. And if any alien so removed or sent out of the United States by the President shall voluntarily return thereto, unless by permission of the President of the United States, such alien on conviction thereof, shall be imprisoned so long as, in the opinion of the President, the public safety may require. . . .

The Sedition Act
1 Stat. 596 (July 14, 1798)

SECTION 1. *Be it enacted by the Senate and House of Representatives of the United States of America, in Congress assembled*, That if any persons shall unlawfully combine or conspire together, with intent to oppose any measure or measures of the government of the United States, which are or shall be directed by proper authority, or to impede the operation of any law of the United States, or to intimidate or prevent any person holding a place or office in or under the government of the United States, from undertaking, performing or executing his trust or duty, and if any person or persons, with intent as aforesaid, shall counsel, advise or attempt to procure any insurrection, riot, unlawful assembly, or combination, whether such conspiracy, threatening, counsel, advice, or attempt shall have the proposed effect or not, he or they shall be deemed guilty of a high misdemeanor, and on conviction, before any court of the United States having jurisdiction thereof, shall be punished by a fine not exceeding five thousand dollars, and by imprisonment during a term not less than six months nor exceeding five years; and further, at the discretion of the court may be holden to find sureties for his good behaviour in such sum, and for such time, as the said court may direct.

SEC. 2. *And be it further enacted*, That if any person shall write, print, utter or publish, or shall cause or procure to be written, printed, uttered or published, or shall knowingly and willingly assist or aid in writing, printing, uttering or publishing any false, scandalous and malicious writing or writings against the government of the United States, or either house of the Congress of the United States, or the President of the United States, with intent to defame the said government, or either house of the said Congress, or the said President, or to bring them, or either of them, into contempt or disrepute; or to excite against them, or either or any of them, the hatred of the good people of the United States, or to stir up sedition within the United States, or to excite any unlawful combinations therein, for opposing or resisting any law of the United States, or any act of the President of the United States, done in pursuance of any such law, or of the powers in him vested by the constitution of the United States, or to resist, oppose, or defeat any such law or act, or to aid, encourage or abet any hostile designs of any foreign nation against the United States, their people or government, then such person, being thereof convicted before any court of the United States having jurisdiction thereof, shall be punished by a fine not exceeding two thousand dollars, and by imprisonment not exceeding two years.

SEC. 3. *And be it further enacted and declared*, That if any person shall be prosecuted under this act, for the writing or publishing any libel aforesaid, it shall be lawful for the defendant, upon the trial of the cause, to give in evidence in his defence, the truth of the matter contained in the publication charged as a libel. . . .

NOTES

1.   Are Sections 1 and 2 of the Alien Friends Act constitutional? Does Congress have an enumerated power to legislate with respect to aliens and their presence in, or exclusion from, the United States? What enumerated power might justify the Act? Congress's power to naturalize aliens and make them citizens? Its power to declare war? Its power to make laws "necessary and proper" for carrying into execution the president's constitutional powers?

If the power to exclude aliens is not given to the national government, is it retained by the states? A little history: It was not until Congress enacted the Chinese Exclusion Act in 1882 (with openly racist motives) that the federal government began to seriously regulate the admission of aliens into the United States. In the 1920s, Congress passed new and more sweeping immigration acts designed to keep immigrants from Southern and Eastern Europe out of the United States while favoring admission of immigrants from Northern Europe. Again the reasons given were explicitly racist. It was not until President Lyndon Johnson's administration in the 1960s that immigration law was significantly reformed. More recently, the Supreme Court has viewed immigration as an area primarily reserved for federal regulation. See, e.g., *Arizona v. United States*, 132 S.Ct. 2492 (2012) (holding that several provisions of an Arizona immigration statute, including one making it a crime for a person to be in the state without valid immigration papers, were preempted by federal law).

2.   The Alien Acts assigned broad discretion to the president to exclude or expel certain aliens from the United States. If Congress does possess legislative power in this

area, may it *delegate* that power to the president? Does it matter how detailed Congress's instructions to the president are?

3.   Next think about the constitutionality of Section 2 of the Sedition Act. Was it within the enumerated powers of Congress to pass such an act? What about the Necessary and Proper Clause? If "necessary and proper" means "convenient," would it be convenient for carrying out the president's foreign policy to have a ban on public criticism? Recall the Federalists' argument that a Bill of Rights was unnecessary, because no power to regulate the press was granted to Congress in its enumerated powers—and recall the Anti-Federalists' response. How does that debate look in light of the Federalists' subsequent support for the Sedition Act?

4.   Even if the Sedition Act would otherwise fall within Congress's enumerated legislative powers, does it violate the First Amendment? Is it enough that under Section 3 truth is a defense?

5.   Should a jury be permitted to acquit a defendant charged with violating the Sedition Act on the ground that it is unconstitutional? If Congress, the president, and the federal courts all have a duty to follow the Constitution, why not also a jury?

Judicial Enforcement of the Sedition Act

The United States government brought a number of criminal proceedings under the Sedition Act—fourteen in all. The following is the report of the trial proceedings in the federal prosecution of Matthew Lyon, an irascible Democratic-Republican congressman from Vermont.

Lyon's Case
15 F.Cas. 1183 (D. Vt. 1798)

The indictment which was found on October 5, 1798, contained three counts, the first of which, after averring the intent to be "to stir up sedition, and to bring the President and the government of the United States into contempt," laid the following libellous matter: "As to the Executive, when I shall see the efforts of that power bent on the promotion of the comfort, the happiness, and accommodation of the people, that executive shall have my zealous and uniformed support: but whenever I shall, on the part of the Executive, see every consideration of the public welfare swallowed up in a continual grasp for power, in an unbounded thirst for ridiculous pomp, foolish adulation, and selfish avarice; when I shall behold men of real merit daily turned out of office, for no other cause but independency of sentiment; when I shall see men of firmness, merit, years, abilities, and experience, discarded in their applications for office, for fear they possess that independence, and men of meanness preferred for the case with which they know but little of—when I shall see the sacred name of religion employed as a state engine to make mankind hate and persecute one another, I shall not be their humble advocate."

The second count consisted of having maliciously, &c., and with intent, &c., published a letter, said to be a letter from a diplomatic character in France, containing two paragraphs, in the words following: "The misunderstanding between the two governments (France and the United States), has become extremely alarming; confidence is completely destroyed, mistrusts, jealousy, and a disposition to a wrong attribution of motives, are so apparent, as to require the utmost caution in every word and action that are to come from your Executive. I mean, if your object is to avoid hostilities. Had this truth been understood with you before the recall of Monroe, before the coming and second coming of Pinckney; had it guided the pens that wrote the bullying speech of your President, and stupid answer of your Senate, at the opening of Congress in November last, I should probably had no occasion to address you this letter.—But when we found him borrowing the language of Edmund Burke, and telling the world that although he should succeed in treating with the French, there was no dependence to be placed on any of their engagements, that their religion and morality were at an end, that they would turn pirates and plunderers; and it would be necessary to be perpetually armed against them, though you were at peace: we wondered that the answer of both Houses had not been an order to send him to a mad house. Instead of this the Senate have echoed the speech with more servility than ever George III. experienced from either house of parliament."

The third count was for assisting, counseling, aiding, and abetting the publication of the same.

Monday, Oct. 9. . . . The district attorney having opened the case, produced a letter from the same defendant, dated Philadelphia, July 7, 1798, and post marked on the same day, which was printed in Vermont on July 23. The authorship of the letter and the fact of the publication were admitted by the defendant. It was further proved that the defendant had several times read at public meetings in Vermont the letter (known at the time as the "Barlow" letter) from which the libellous matter in the second count was taken.

Several witnesses were called to show that the defendant, both in public and in private, had extensively used the letter for political purposes, and in doing so had frequently made use of language highly disrespectful to the administration. On cross examination, it appeared that on one occasion he had endeavored to prevent it from being printed.

The prosecution having closed its case, the defendant stated his defence to consist of three points: first, that the court had no jurisdiction of the offence, the act of Congress being unconstitutional and void, if not so generally, at least, as to writings composed before its passage; second, that the publication was innocent; and third, that the contents were true. . . .

Paterson, Circuit Justice (charging jury)[:] "You have nothing whatsoever to do with the constitutionality or unconstitutionality of the sedition law. Congress has said that the author and publisher of seditious libels is to be punished: and until this law is declared null and void by a tribunal competent for the purpose, its validity cannot be disputed. Great would be the abuses were the constitutionality of every statute to be submitted to a jury, in each case where the statute is to be applied. The only question you are to determine is, that which the record submits to you. Did Mr. Lyon publish the writing given in the indictment? Did he do so seditiously? On the first point, the evidence is undisputed, and in fact, he himself concedes the fact of publication as to a large portion of libellous matter. As to the second point, you will have to consider whether language such as that here complained of could have been uttered with any other intent that that of making odious or contemptible the President and government, and bringing them both into disrepute. If you find such is the case, the offence is made out, and you must render a verdict of guilty. Nor should the political rank of the defendant, his past services, or the dependent condition of his family, deter you from this duty. Such considerations are for the court alone in adjusting the penalty they will bestow. The fact of guilt is for you, for the court, the grade of punishment. As to yourselves, one point, in addition, in exercising the functions allotted to you, you must keep in mind: and that is, that in order to render a verdict of guilty, you must be satisfied beyond all reasonable substantial doubt that the hypothesis of innocence is unsustainable. Keeping these instructions in your mind, you will proceed to deliberate on your verdict."

At about eight o'clock in the evening of the same day, after about an hour's absence, the jury returned with a verdict of guilty.

The defendant being called up for sentence, a postponement was obtained till the next morning, when, after a representation of his circumstances, it appearing that he was almost insolvent, Judge Paterson addressed him as follows: "Matthew Lyon, as a member of the federal legislature, you must be well acquainted with the mischiefs which flow from an unlicensed abuse of government, and of the motives which led to the passage of the act under which this indictment is framed. No one, also, can be better acquainted than yourself with the existence and nature of the act. Your position, so far from making the case one which might slip with a nominal fine through the hands of the court, would make impunity conspicuous should such a fine alone be imposed. What however, has tended to mitigate the sentence which would otherwise have been imposed, is, what I am sorry to hear of, the reduced condition of your estate. The judgment of the court is, that you stand imprisoned four months, pay the costs of prosecution, and a fine of one thousand dollars, and stand committed until this sentence be complied with."

NOTES

1.   If you thought the Sedition Act was unconstitutional, does the fact that the federal courts upheld the convictions of Lyon and others change your mind? There were no judicial rulings holding the Sedition Act unconstitutional as it was being enforced.

2.   Lyon was not a reputable character. He was court-martialed for cowardice during the Revolutionary War. A perennial candidate for Congress, he was finally elected in 1797 and immediately made a pest of himself, developing a reputation as a demagogue. The House once moved (unsuccessfully) to expel him for spitting in the face of another member of Congress. When he was convicted and served time in prison for violating the Sedition Act, he became something of a martyr to his constituents: he ran for re-election from prison and won by a larger margin. After his conviction, a majority of the House voted to expel him, but again the vote fell short of the two-thirds required for expulsion under Article I, Section 5.

3.   James Callender, a Democratic-Republican journalist with a nose for scandal, was also convicted under the Sedition Act. He had published the following statement: "The reign of Mr. Adams has been one continued tempest of malignant passion. As President, he has never opened his lips, or lifted his pen without threatening and scolding; the grand object of his administration has been to exasperate the rage of contending parties, to calumniate and destroy every man who differs from his opinions. Mr. Adams has laboured, and with melancholy success, to break up the bonds of social affection, and under the ruins of confidence and friendship, to extinguish the only gleam of happiness that glimmers through the dark and despicable farce of life." Callender was forced to pay a fine of $200 and was sentenced to nine months in prison, a portion of which he served before being pardoned by Jefferson after his ascent to the presidency. Callender would later turn his scandal-mongering against Jefferson, and it was Callender

who exposed that Jefferson had a relationship with his slave Sally Hemmings and that together they had several children. That accusation, hotly disputed then, has been proved by DNA evidence. Joseph Ellis, AMERICAN SPHINX: THE CHARACTER OF THOMAS JEFFERSON 363–367 (1998). Callender ended up hated by all sides. As Ellis puts it, Callender's "only consistency was a perverse flair for treachery." *Id.* at 260.

The Virginia and Kentucky Resolutions

Opposition to the Alien and Sedition Acts was swift and vigorous. The Virginia and Kentucky legislatures adopted resolutions arguing that the statutes were unconstitutional. The Virginia Resolutions were drafted by James Madison, and the Kentucky Resolutions, by Thomas Jefferson. The legislatures of several Northern states responded, defending the laws and arguing that the constitutionality of an Act of Congress was a question reserved for the courts. Virginia then offered an elaborate defense of its resolutions, the Report of 1800, again written by Madison.

Four selections from this debate are printed here. First, there is Jefferson's draft of the Kentucky Resolutions. This draft was subsequently revised by the Kentucky legislature for brevity and also to delete the explosive reference to "nullification" as a "rightful remedy." Second, there is the response to the Virginia Resolutions by the Rhode Island legislature. Third, there is the Minority Report to the Virginia Resolutions. It has been variously attributed, including to Henry Lee and John Marshall. Finally, there is Madison's Report of 1800, which responds to criticism of the Virginia Resolutions.

As you read these documents, consider again the constitutionality of the Alien and Sedition Acts, and join the debate over who may and must interpret the Constitution. Are the Northern states right that only courts should decide whether federal laws are unconstitutional? Is the Report of 1800 right in defending the propriety of states' interpreting the Constitution? If so, what are the implications of that position? How far do Jefferson and Madison press the argument? And do "We the People" possess the power of constitutional interpretation?

Thomas Jefferson, Draft of the Kentucky Resolutions

Jefferson's Fair Copy, written before Oct. 4, 1798

1.   Resolved that the several states composing the US. of America are not united on the principle of unlimited submission to their general government; but that by a compact under the style and title of a Constitution for the US. and of amendments thereto, they constituted a general government for special purposes, delegated to that government certain definite powers, reserving, each state to itself, the residuary mass of right to their own self-government; & that whensoever the General government assumes undelegated powers, it's acts are unauthoritative, void, & of no force: that to this compact each state acceded as a state, and is an integral party, it's co-states forming, as to itself, the other party: that the government created by this compact was not made the exclusive or final judge of the extent of the powers delegated to itself; since that would have made it's discretion, & not the constitution, the measure of it's powers; but that, as in all other cases of compact among powers having no common judge, each party has an equal right to judge for itself, as well of infractions, as of the mode & measure of redress.

2.   Resolved that the constitution of the US. having delegated to Congress a power to punish treason, counterfieting the securities & current coin of the US. Piracies & felonies committed on the high seas, & offences against the law of Nations, & no other crimes whatsoever, and it being true as a general principle, and one of the Amendments to the constitution having also declared, that "the powers not delegated to the US. by the constitution, nor prohibited by it to the states, are reserved to the states respectively, or to the people" therefore the act of Congress passed on the 14th. day of July 1798. . . . *[i.e., the Sedition Act]* as also the act passed by them on the ___ day of June 1798. intituled "an Act to punish frauds committed on the bank of the US." [and all other their acts which assume to create, define or punish crimes, other than those so enumerated in the constitution] are altogether void & of no force, & that the power to create, define & punish such other crimes is reserved, & of right appurtains solely & exclusively to the respective states, each within it's own territory.

3.   Resolved that it is true as a general principle, and is also expressly declared by one of the Amendments to the Constitution that "the powers not delegated to the US. by the constitution, nor prohibited by it to the states, are reserved to the states respectively or to the people"; and that no power over the freedom of religion, freedom of speech, or freedom of the press being delegated to the US. by the constitution, nor prohibited by it to the states, all lawful powers respecting the same did of right remain, & were reserved, to the states or the people: that thus was manifested their determination to retain to themselves the right of judging how far the licentiousness of speech & of the press may be abridged without lessening their useful freedom, and how far those abuses which cannot be separated from their use should be tolerated rather than the use be destroyed. . . . And that in addition to this general principle and express declaration, another & more special provision has been made by one of the amendments to the constitution which expressly declares that "Congress shall make no law respecting an establishment of religion, or prohibiting the free exercise thereof or abridging the freedom of speech or of the press," thereby guarding in the same sentence, & under the same words, the freedom of religion of speech & of the press: insomuch that whatever violates either throws down the sanctuary which covers the others, and that libels, falsehood & defamation, equally with heresy & false religion, are withheld from the cognisance of federal tribunals: that therefore the act of Congress of the US. passed on the 14th. day of July 1798 . . . *[i.e., the Sedition Act]*, which does abridge the freedom of the press, is not law, but is altogether void & of no force.

4.   Resolved that ALIEN friends are under the jurisdiction and protection of the laws of the state wherein they are; that no power over them has been delegated to the US. nor prohibited to the individual states distinct from their power over citizens: and it being true as a general principle, & one of the amendments to the constitution having also declared that "the powers not delegated to the US. by the constitution, nor prohibited by it to the States, are reserved to the states respectively, or to the people," the act of Congress of the US. passed on the ___ day of July 1798 . . . *[i.e., the Alien Friends Act]*, which assumes powers over Alien-friends not delegated by the constitution, is not law, but is altogether void & of no force. . . .

6.   Resolved that the imprisonment of a person under the protection of the laws of this commonwealth on his failure to obey the simple *order* of the President to depart out of the US. as is undertaken by said act. . . . *[i.e., the Alien Friends Act]*, is

contrary to the constitution, one Amendment to which has provided that "no person shall be deprived of liberty without due process of law." and that another having provided that "in all criminal prosecutions the accused shall enjoy the right to public trial, by an impartial jury, to be informed of the nature and cause of the accusation, to be confronted with the witnesses against him, to have compulsory process for obtaining witnesses in his favor, & to have the assistance of counsel for his defence," the same act, undertaking to authorize the President to remove a person out of the US. who is under the protection of the law, on his own suspicion, without accusation, without jury, without public trial, without confrontation of the witnesses against him, without hearing witnesses in his favor, without defence, without counsel, is contrary to these provisions also of the constitution, is therefore not law, but utterly void & of no force. . . .

8.   Resolved that a committee of conference & correspondence be appointed, who shall have in charge to communicate the preceding resolutions to the legislatures of the several states, to assure them that this commonwealth continues in the same esteem for their friendship and union which it has manifested from that moment at which a common danger first suggested a common union: that it considers union, for specified national purposes, & particularly for those specified in their late federal compact, to be friendly to the peace, happiness & prosperity of all the states; that faithful to that compact, according to the plain intent & meaning in which it was understood & acceded to by the several parties, it is sincerely anxious for it's preservation: . . . & that therefore this commonwealth is determined, as it doubts not it's co-states are, to submit to undelegated, & consequently unlimited powers in no man, or body of men, on earth: that in cases of an abuse of the delegated powers the members of the general government, being chosen by the people, a change by the people would be the constitutional remedy; but, where powers are assumed which have not been delegated, a nullification of the act is the rightful remedy: that every state has a natural right, in cases not within the compact [casus non foederis] to nullify of their own authority all assumptions of power by others within their limits: that without this right, they would be under the dominion, absolute and unlimited, of whosoever might exercise this right of judgment for them: that nevertheless this commonwealth, from motives of regard & respect for it's co-states, has wished to communicate with them on the subject; that with them alone it is proper to communicate, they alone being parties to the compact, & solely authorized to judge in the last resort of the powers exercised under it, Congress being not a party, but merely the creature of the compact, & subject, as to it's assumptions of power, to the final judgment of those by whom, & for whose use, itself, & it's powers, were all created & modified. . . .

Rhode Island's Answer to the Virginia Resolutions
State of Rhode Island and Providence Plantations General Assembly, Feb. 1799

Certain resolutions of the legislature of Virginia, passed on 21st of December last, being communicated to this Assembly,—

1.   *Resolved,* That, in the opinion of this legislature, the second section of third article of the Constitution of the United States, in these words, to wit,—"The judicial power shall extend to all cases arising under the laws of the United States,"—vests in the federal courts, exclusively, and in the Supreme Court of the United States,

ultimately, the authority of deciding on the constitutionality of an act or law of the Congress of the United States.

2. *Resolved*, That for any state legislature to assume that authority would be—

1st. Blending together legislative and judicial powers;

2d. Hazarding an interruption of the peace of the states by civil discord, in case of a diversity of opinions among the state legislatures; each state having, in that case, no resort, for vindicating its own opinions, but the strength of its own arm;—

3d. Submitting most important questions of law to less competent tribunals; and,

4th. An infraction of the Constitution of the United States, expressed in plain terms.

3. *Resolved*, That, although, for the above reasons, this legislature, in their public capacity, do not feel themselves authorized to consider and decide on the constitutionality of the Sedition and Alien laws, (so called,) yet they are called upon, by the exigency of this occasion, to declare that, in their private opinions, these laws are within the powers delegated to Congress, and promotive of the welfare of the United States.

4. *Resolved*, That the governor communicate these resolutions to the supreme executive of the state of Virginia, and at the same time express to him that this legislature cannot contemplate, without extreme concern and regret, the many evil and fatal consequences which may flow from the very unwarrantable resolutions aforesaid of the legislature of Virginia, passed on the twenty-first day of December last.

The Minority Report to the Virginia Resolutions
Virginia House of Delegates, Jan. 22, 1799

. . . To constitute the crime, the writing must be false, scandalous, and malicious, and the intent must be to effect some of the ill purposes described in the act.

To contend that there does not exist a power to punish writings coming within the description of this law, would be to assert the inability of our nation to preserve its own peace, and to protect themselves from the attempts of wicked citizens, who, incapable of quiet themselves, are incessantly employed in devising means to disturb the public repose.

Government is instituted and preserved for the general happiness and safety— the people therefore are interested in its preservation, and have a right to adopt measures for its security, as well against secret plots as open hostility. But government cannot be thus secured, if by falsehood and malicious slander, it is to be deprived of the confidence and affection of the people. It is vain to urge that truth will prevail, and that slander, when detected, recoils on the calumniator. The experience of the world, and our own experience, prove that a continued course of defamation will at length sully the fairest reputation, and will throw suspicion on the purest conduct. Although the calumnies of the factious and discontented may not poison the minds of the majority of the citizens, yet they will infect a very considerable number, and prompt them to deeds destructive of the public peace and dangerous to the general safety.

This, the people have a right to prevent: and therefore, in all the nations of the earth, where presses are known, some corrective of their licentiousness has been deemed indispensable. But it is contended that though this may be theoretically true, such is the peculiar structure of our government, that this power has either never been confided to, or has been withdrawn from the legislature of this union.—We will examine these positions. The power of making all laws which shall be necessary and proper for carrying into execution all powers vested by the constitution in the government of the United States, or in any department or officer thereof, is by the concluding clause of the eighth section of the first article, expressly delegated to congress. This clause is admitted to authorize congress to pass any act for the punishment of those who would resist the execution of the laws, because such an act would be incontestably necessary and proper for carrying into execution the powers vested in the government. If it authorizes the punishment of actual resistance, does it not also authorize the punishment of those acts, which are criminal in themselves, and which obviously lead to and prepare resistance? Would it not be strange, if, for the purpose of executing the legitimate powers of the government, a clause like that which has been cited should be so construed as to permit the passage of laws punishing open resistance, and yet to forbid the passage of laws punishing acts which constitute the germ from which resistance springs? That the government must look on, and see preparations for resistance which it shall be unable to control, until they shall break out in open force? This would be an unreasonable and improvident construction of the article under consideration. That continued calumnies against the government have this tendency, is demonstrated by uninterrupted experience. They will, if unrestrained, produce in any society convulsions, which if not totally destructive of, will yet be very injurious to, its prosperity and welfare. It is not to be believed that the people of the western parts of Pennsylvania could have been deluded into that unprovoked and wanton insurrection, which called forth the militia of the neighbouring states, if they had not been at the same time irritated and seduced by calumnies with which certain presses incessantly teemed into the opinion that the people of America, instead of supporting their government and their laws, would join in their subversion. Those calumnies then, tended to prevent the execution of the laws of the union, and such seems to be their obvious and necessary tendency. . . .

That such was the contemporaneous construction of the constitution, is obvious from one of the amendments which have been made to it. The 3d amendment which declares, that Congress shall make no law abridging the liberty of the press, is a general construction made by all America on the original instrument admitting its application to the subject. *[The amendment proposed as the third was ratified as the First Amendment.—Editors]* It would have been certainly unnecessary thus to have modified the legislative powers of Congress concerning the press, if the power itself does not exist.

But altho' the original constitution may be supposed to have enabled the government to defend itself against false and malicious libels, endangering the peace, and threatening the tranquility of the American people, yet it is contended that the 3d amendment to that instrument, has deprived it of this power.

The amendment is in these words,—"Congress shall make no law respecting an establishment of religion, or prohibiting the free exercise thereof, or ABRIDGING the freedom of speech or of the press."

In a solemn instrument, as is a constitution, words are well weighed and considered before they are adopted. A remarkable diversity of expression is not used, unless it be designed to manifest a difference of intention. Congress is prohibited from making any law RESPECTING a religious establishment, but not from making any law RESPECTING the press. When the power of Congress relative to the press is to be limited, the word RESPECTING is dropt, and Congress is only restrained from the passing any law ABRIDGING its liberty. This difference of expression with respect to religion and the press, manifests a difference of intention with respect to the power of the national legislature over those subjects, both in the person who drew, and in those who adopted this amendment.

All ABRIDGEMENT of the freedom of the press is forbidden, but it is only an ABRIDGEMENT of that freedom which is forbidden. It becomes then necessary in order to determine whether the act in question be unconstitutional or not, to inquire whether it does in fact ABRIDGE the freedom of the press.

The act is believed not to have that operation, for two reasons.

1st. A punishment of the licentiousness is not considered as a restriction of the freedom of the press,

2d. The act complained of does not punish any writing not before punishable, nor does it inflict a more severe penalty than that to which the same writing was before liable.

1st. If by freedom of the press is meant a perfect exemption from all punishment for whatever may be published, that freedom never has, and most probably never will exist. It is known to all, that the person who writes or publishes a libel, may be both sued and indicted, and must bear the penalty which the judgment of his country inflicts upon him. It is also known to all that the person who shall libel the government of the state, is for that offence, punishable in the like manner. Yet this liability to punishment for slanderous and malicious publications has never been considered as detracting from the liberty of the press. In fact the liberty of the press is a term which has a definite and appropriate signification, completely understood. It signifies a liberty to publish, free from previous restraint, any thing and every thing at the discretion of the printer only, but not the liberty of spreading with impunity false and scandalous slanders which may destroy the peace and mangle the reputation of an individual or of a community.

If this definition of the term be correct, and it is presumed that its correctness is not to be questioned, then a law punishing the authors and publishers of false, malicious and scandalous libels can be no attack on the liberty of the press.

But the act complained of is no abridgment of the liberty of the press, for another reason.

2d. It does not punish any writing not before punishable, nor does it inflict a heavier penalty than the same writing was before liable to.

No man will deny, that at common law, the author and publisher of a false, scandalous and malicious libel against the government or an individual, were subject to fine and imprisonment, at the discretion of the judge. Nor will it be denied, that previous to our revolution, the common law was the law of the land throughout the now United States. . . .

[T]he common law continued to be the law of the land after the revolution . . . The only question is, whether the doctrines of the common law are applicable to libels against the government of the United States, as well as to libels against the governments of particular states. For such a distinction there seems to be no sufficient reason. . . .

If then it were even true that the punishment of the printer of malicious falsehoods affected the liberty of the press, yet the act does not abridge that liberty, since it does not substitute a harsher or severer rule of punishment than that which before existed.

The legislature of Virginia has itself passed more than one unconstitutional law, but they have not been passed with an intention to violate the constitution. On being decided to be unconstitutional by the legitimate authority, they have been permitted to fall. Had the judges deemed them constitutional, they should have been maintained. The same check, nor is it a less efficient one, exists in the government of the union. The judges of the United States are as independent as the judges of the state of Virginia, nor is there any reason to believe them less wise and less virtuous. It is their province, and their duty to construe the constitution and the laws, and it cannot be doubted, but that they will perform this duty faithfully and truly. They will perform it unwarmed by political debate, uninfluenced by party zeal. Let us in the mean time seek a repeal of any acts we may disapprove, by means authorized by our happy constitution, but let us not endeavor to disseminate among our fellow citizens the most deadly hate against the government of their own creation, against the government, on the preservation of which we firmly believe the peace and liberty of America to depend, because in some respects its judgment has differed from our own.

James Madison, Report of 1800
Virginia House of Delegates, Jan. 7, 1800

. . . It appears to your committee to be a plain principle, founded in common sense, illustrated by common practice, and essential to the nature of compacts; that where resort can be had to no tribunal superior to the authority of the parties, the parties themselves must be the rightful judges in the last resort, whether the bargain made, has been pursued or violated. The constitution of the United States was formed by the sanction of the states, given by each in its sovereign capacity. It adds to the stability and dignity, as well as to the authority of the constitution, that it rests on this legitimate and solid foundation. The states then being the parties to the constitutional compact, and in their sovereign capacity, it follows of necessity, that there can be no tribunal above their authority, to decide in the last resort, whether the compact made by them be violated; and consequently that as the parties to it, they must themselves decide in the last resort, such questions as may be of sufficient magnitude to require their interposition. . . .

But it is objected that the judicial authority is to be regarded as the sole expositor of the constitution, in the last resort; and it may be asked for what reason, the declaration by the General Assembly, supposing it to be theoretically true, could be required at the present day and in so solemn a manner.

On this objection it might be observed *first*, that there may be instances of usurped power, which the forms of the constitution would never draw within the controul of the judicial department: secondly, that if the decision of the judiciary be raised above the authority of the sovereign parties to the constitution, the decisions of the other departments, not carried by the forms of the constitution before the judiciary, must be equally authoritative and final with the decisions of that department. But the proper answer to the objection is, that the resolution of the General Assembly relates to those great and extraordinary cases, in which all the forms of the constitution may prove ineffectual against infractions dangerous to the essential rights of the parties to it. The resolution supposes that dangerous powers not delegated, may not only be usurped and executed by the other departments, but that the Judicial Department also may exercise or sanction dangerous powers beyond the grant of the constitution; and consequently that the ultimate right of the parties to the constitution, to judge whether the compact has been dangerously violated, must extend to violations by one delegated authority, as well as by another; by the judiciary, as well as by the executive, or the legislature.

However true therefore it may be that the Judicial Department, is, in all questions submitted to it by the forms of the constitution, to decide in the last resort, this resort must necessarily be deemed the last in relation to the authorities of the other departments of the government; not in relation to the rights of the parties to the constitutional compact, from which the judicial as well as the other departments hold their delegated trusts. On any other hypothesis, the delegation of judicial power, would annul the authority delegating it; and the concurrence of this department with the others in usurped powers, might subvert forever, and beyond the possible reach of any rightful remedy, the very constitution, which all were instituted to preserve. . . .

It is next affirmed of the alien act, that it unites legislative, judicial and executive powers in the hands of the President.

However difficult it maybe to mark, in every case, with clearness and certainty, the line which divides legislative power, from the other departments of power; all will agree, that the powers referred to these departments may be so general and undefined, as to be of a legislative, not of an executive or judicial nature; and may for that reason be unconstitutional. Details, to a certain degree, are essential to the nature and character of law; and, on criminal subjects, it is proper, that details should leave as little as possible to the discretion of those who are to apply and execute the law. If nothing more were required, in exercising a legislative trust, than a general conveyance of authority, without laying down any precise rules, by which the authority conveyed, should be carried into effect; it would follow, that the whole power of legislation might be transferred by the legislature from itself, and proclamations might become substitutes for laws. A delegation of power in this latitude, would not be denied to be a union of the different powers.

To determine then, whether the appropriate powers of the distinct departments are united by the act authorising the executive to remove aliens, it must be enquired whether it contains such details, definitions, and rules, as appertain to the true character of a law; especially, a law by which personal liberty is invaded, property deprived of its value to the owner, and life itself indirectly exposed to danger.

The alien act, declares, "that it shall be lawful for the president to order all such aliens as he shall judge *dangerous* to the peace and safety of the United States, or shall have reasonable ground to *suspect*, are concerned in any treasonable, *or secret machinations*, against the government thereof, to depart," &c.

Could a power be well given in terms less definite, less particular, and less precise? To be *dangerous to the public safety*; to be *suspected of secret machinations* against the government: these can never be mistaken for legal rules or certain definitions. They leave every thing to the President. His will is the law.

But it is not a legislative power only that is given to the President. He is to stand in the place of the judiciary also. His suspicion is the only evidence which is to convict; his order the only judgment which is to be executed.

Thus it is the President whose will is to designate the offensive conduct; it is his will that is to ascertain the individuals on whom it is charged; and it is his will, that is to cause the sentence to be executed. It is rightly affirmed therefore, that the act unites legislative and judicial powers to those of the executive. . . .

The next point which the resolution requires to be proved, is, that the power over the press exercised by the sedition act, is positively forbidden by one of the amendments to the constitution.

The amendment stands in these words—"Congress shall make no law respecting an establishment of religion, or prohibiting the free exercise thereof, *or abridging the freedom of speech or of the press*; or the right of the people peaceably to assemble, and to petition the government for a redress of grievances."

In the attempts to vindicate the "Sedition act," it has been contended, 1. That the "freedom of the press" is to be determined by the meaning of these terms in the common law. 2. That the article supposes the power over the press to be in Congress, and prohibits them only from *abridging* the freedom allowed to it by the common law.

Although it will be shewn, in examining the second of these positions, that the amendment is a denial to Congress of all power over the press; it may not be useless to make the following observations on the first of them.

It is deemed to be a sound opinion, that the sedition act, in its definition of some of the crimes created, is an abridgment of the freedom of publication, recognized by principles of the common law in England.

The freedom of the press under the common law, is, in the defences of the sedition act, made to consist in an exemption from all *previous* restraint on printed publications, by persons authorized to inspect and prohibit them. It appears to the committee, that this idea of the freedom of the press, can never be admitted to be the American idea of it: since a law inflicting penalties on printed publications, would have a similar effect with a law authorizing a previous restraint on them. It would seem a mockery to say, that no law should be passed, preventing publications from being made, but that laws might be passed for punishing them in case they should be made.

The essential difference between the British government, and the American constitutions, will place this subject in the clearest light.

In the British government, the danger of encroachments on the rights of the people, is understood to be confined to the executive magistrate. The representatives of the people in the legislature, are not only exempt themselves, from distrust, but are considered as sufficient guardians of the rights of their constituents against the danger from the executive. Hence it is a principle, that the parliament is unlimited in its power; or in their own language, is omnipotent. Hence too, all the ramparts for protecting the rights of the people, such as their magna charta, their bill of rights, &c. are not reared against the parliament, but against the royal prerogative. They are merely legislative precautions against executive usurpations. Under such a government as this, an exemption of the press from previous restraint by licensers appointed by the king, is all the freedom that can be secured to it.

In the United States, the case is altogether different. The people, not the government, possess the absolute sovereignty. The legislature, no less than the executive, is under limitations of power. Encroachments are regarded as possible from the one, as well as from the other. Hence in the United States, the great and essential rights of the people are secured against legislative, as well as against executive ambition. They are secured, not by laws paramount to prerogative; but by constitutions paramount to laws. This security of the freedom of the press, requires that it should be exempt, not only from previous restraint by the executive, as in Great Britain; but from legislative restraint also; and this exemption, to be effectual, must be an exemption, not only from the previous inspection of licensers, but from the subsequent penalty of laws.

The state of the press, therefore, under the common law, can not in this point of view, be the standard of its freedom, in the United States. . . . Notwithstanding the general doctrine of the common law, on the subject of the press, and the occasional punishment of those, who use it with a freedom offensive to the government; it is well known, that with respect to the responsible members of the government, where the reasons operating here, become applicable there; the freedom exercised by the press, and protected by the public opinion, far exceeds the limits prescribed by the ordinary rules of law. The ministry, who are responsible to impeachment, are at all times, animadverted on, by the press, with peculiar freedom; and during the elections for the House of Commons, the other responsible part of the government, the press is employed with as little reserve towards the candidates.

The practice in America must be entitled to much more respect. In every state, probably, in the union, the press has exerted a freedom in canvassing the merits and measures of public men, of every description, which has not been confined to the strict limits of the common law. On this footing, the freedom of the press has stood; on this footing it yet stands. And it will not be a breach, either of truth or of candour, to say, that no persons or presses are in the habit of more unrestrained animadversions on the proceedings and functionaries of the state governments, than the persons and presses most zealous, in vindicating the act of Congress for punishing similar animadversions on the government of the United States.

The last remark will not be understood, as claiming for the state governments, an immunity greater than they have heretofore enjoyed. Some degree of abuse is inseparable from the proper use of every thing; and in no instance is this more true, than in that of the press. It has accordingly been decided by the practice of the states, that it is better to leave a few of its noxious branches, to their luxuriant growth, than by pruning them away, to injure the vigor of those yielding the proper fruits. And can the wisdom of this policy be doubted by any who reflect, that to the press alone, chequered as it is with abuses, the world is indebted for all the triumphs which have been gained by reason and humanity, over error and oppression; who reflect that to the same beneficent source, the United States owe much of the lights which conducted them to the rank of a free and independent nation; and which have improved their political system, into a shape so auspicious to their happiness. Had "Sedition acts," forbidding every publication that might bring the constituted agents into contempt or disrepute, or that might excite the hatred of the people against the authors of unjust or pernicious measures, been uniformly enforced against the press; might not the United States have been languishing at this day, under the infirmities of a sickly confederation? Might they not possibly be miserable colonies, groaning under a foreign yoke?

To these observations, one fact will be added, which demonstrates that the common law cannot be admitted as the *universal* expositor of American terms, which may be the same with those contained in that law. The freedom of conscience, and of religion, are found in the same instruments which assert the freedom of the press. It will never be admitted, that the meaning of the former, in the common law of England, is to limit their meaning in the United States.

Whatever weight may be allowed to these considerations, the committee do not, however, by any means, intend to rest the question on them. They contend that the article of amendment, instead of supposing in Congress, a power that might be exercised over the press, provided its freedom be not abridged, was meant as a positive denial to Congress, of any power whatever on the subject.

To demonstrate that this was the true object of the article, it will be sufficient to recall the circumstances which led to it, and to refer to the explanation accompanying the article.

When the constitution was under the discussions which preceded its ratification, it is well known, that great apprehensions were expressed by many, lest the omission of some positive exception from the powers delegated, of certain rights, and of the freedom of the press particularly, might expose them to the danger of being drawn by construction within some of the powers vested in Congress; more especially of the power to make all laws necessary and proper, for carrying their other powers into execution. In reply to this objection, it was invariably urged to be a fundamental and characteristic principle of the constitution; that all powers not given by it, were reserved; that no powers were given beyond those enumerated in the constitution, and such as were fairly incident to them; that the power over the rights in question, and particularly over the press, was neither among the enumerated powers, nor incident to any of them; and consequently that an exercise of any such power, would be a manifest usurpation. It is painful to remark, how much the arguments now employed in behalf of the sedition act, are at variance with the reasoning which then justified the constitution, and invited its ratification. . . .

Without scrutinising minutely into all the provisions of the "sedition act," it will be sufficient to cite . . . section 2. . . . On this part of the act, the following observations present themselves. . . .

5. As the act was passed on July 14, 1798, and is to be in force until March 3, 1801, it was of course, that during its continuance, two elections of the entire House of Representatives, an election of a part of the Senate, and an election of a President, were to take place.

6. That consequently, during all these elections, intended by the constitution to preserve the purity, or to purge the faults of the administration, the great remedial rights of the people were to be exercised, and the responsibility of their public agents to be skreened, under the penalties of this act.

May it not be asked of every intelligent friend to the liberties of his country whether, the power exercised in such an act as this, ought not to produce great and universal alarm? Whether a rigid execution of such an act, in time past, would not have repressed that information and communication among the people, which is indispensable to the just exercise of their electoral rights? And whether such an act, if made perpetual, and enforced with rigor, would not, in time to come, either destroy our free system of government, or prepare a convulsion that might prove equally fatal to it?

In answer to such questions, it has been pleaded that the writings and publications forbidden by the act, are those only which are false and malicious, and intended to defame; and merit is claimed for the privilege allowed to authors to justify, by proving the truth of their publications, and for the limitations to which the sentence of fine and imprisonment is subjected. . . .

In the first place, where simple and naked facts alone are in question, there is sufficient difficulty in some cases, and sufficient trouble and vexation in all, of meeting a prosecution from the government, with the full and formal proof, necessary in a court of law.

But in the next place, it must be obvious to the plainest minds, that opinions, and inferences, and conjectural observations, are not only in many cases inseparable from the facts, but may often be more the objects of the prosecution than the facts themselves; or may even be altogether abstracted from particular facts; and that opinions and inferences, and conjectural observations, cannot be subjects of that kind of proof which appertains to facts, before a court of law.

Again, it is no less obvious, that the *intent* to defame or bring into contempt or disrepute, or hatred, which is made a condition of the offence created by the act; cannot prevent its pernicious influence, on the freedom of the press. For omitting the enquiry, how far the malice of the intent is an inference of the law from the mere publication; it is manifestly impossible to punish the intent to bring those who administer the government into disrepute or contempt, without striking at the right of freely discussing public characters and measures: because those who engage in such discussions, must expect and *intend* to excite these unfavorable sentiments, so far as they may be thought to be deserved. To prohibit therefore the intent to excite those unfavorable sentiments against those who administer the government, is equivalent to a prohibition of the actual excitement of them; and to prohibit the actual excitement of them, is equivalent to a prohibition of discussions having that tendency and effect; which, again, is equivalent to a protection of those who administer the government, if they should at any time deserve the contempt or hatred of the people, against being exposed to it, by free animadversions on their characters and conduct. Nor can there be a doubt, if those in public trust be shielded by penal laws from such strictures of the press, as may expose them to contempt or disrepute, or hatred, where they may deserve it, that in exact proportion as they may deserve to be exposed, will be the certainty and criminality of the intent to expose them, and the vigilance of prosecuting and punishing it; nor a doubt, that a government thus intrenched in penal statutes, against the just and natural effects of a culpable administration, will easily evade the responsibility, which is essential to a faithful discharge of its duty.

Let it be recollected, lastly, that the right of electing the members of the government, constitutes more particularly the essence of a free and responsible government. The value and efficacy of this right, depends on the knowledge of the comparative merits and demerits of the candidates for public trust; and on the equal freedom, consequently, of examining and discussing these merits and demerits of the candidates respectively. It has been seen that a number of important elections will take place whilst the act is in force; although it should not be continued beyond the term to which it is limited. Should there happen, then, as is extremely probable in relation to some or other of the branches of the government, to be competitions between those who are, and those who are not, members of the government; what will be the situations of the competitors? Not equal; because the characters of the former will be covered by the "sedition act" from animadversions exposing them to disrepute among the people; whilst the latter may be exposed to the contempt and hatred of the people, without a violation of the act. What will be the situation of the people? Not free; because they will be compelled to make their election between competitors, whose pretensions they are not permitted, by the act, equally to examine, to discuss, and to ascertain. And from both these situations, will not those in power derive an undue advantage for continuing themselves in it; which by impairing the right of election, endangers the blessings of the government founded on it.

It is with justice, therefore, that the General Assembly hath affirmed in the resolution, as well that the right of freely examining public characters and measures, and of free communication thereon, is the only effectual guardian of every other right; as that this particular right is leveled at, by the power exercised in the "sedition act." . . .

Resolved, That the General Assembly, . . . do hereby renew, their protest against "the alien and sedition acts," as palpable and alarming infractions of the constitution.

NOTES

1.   Evaluate the arguments in the Kentucky Resolutions and the Report of 1800 regarding the constitutionality of the Alien and Sedition Acts. Do these arguments cause you to revise your original views? If they make a persuasive case that the Sedition Act was unconstitutional, on what ground do they do so? The lack of an enumerated federal legislative power? An improper delegation to the executive? A violation of the First Amendment's freedom of speech and freedom of the press?

2.   Both sides in this debate agreed that the common law of seditious libel in force in Britain was harsher than the terms of the Sedition Act. To supporters of the Act, that proved that the Act did not "abridge"—that is, reduce in scope or importance—the freedom of the press. What are Madison's answers to that argument? Identify his answers based on (1) the difference between a monarchy and a republic, (2) the practice in American courts, and (3) the significance of popular sovereignty. Are those answers sound?

3.   Why might the First Amendment use the verb "abridge" with regard to the freedoms of speech and press, while using the verbs "respect" and "prohibit" with regard to establishment and free exercise of religion? Hint: What, exactly, was the extent of a

British subject's rights of speech and of the press? And of nonestablishment and free exercise?

4.   Who was right about the power to interpret the Constitution—the legislatures of Virginia and Kentucky or the legislatures of the Northern states? Is it legitimate for a state to resist what it considers unconstitutional enactments of the national government? How far may it go in such resistance? May a state purport to "nullify" those acts, treating them as having no force? May it "interpose" state power—including force—to resist any enforcement of what it regards as an unconstitutional enactment? Do the arguments of Jefferson and Madison lead inexorably to a constitutional right of states to *secede*, at least for a sufficiently serious breach of the Constitution by the national government? Are states the *supreme* interpreters of the Constitution? Is there a difference between Jefferson's arguments and Madison's in this regard? Were the Northern states right that the federal judicial branch has the *sole* power to decide that an Act of Congress is invalid and that every other political actor must adhere to its rulings?

5.   The idea that states may use their powers to guard against federal violations of the Constitution has some support in early defenses of the Constitution. In *Federalist No. 33*, Alexander Hamilton said: "the laws of the Union are to be the *supreme law* of the land. . . . But it will not follow from this doctrine that acts of the large society which are *not pursuant* to its constitutional powers, but which are invasions of the residuary authorities of the smaller societies, will become the supreme law of the land. These will be merely acts of usurpation, and will deserve to be treated as such." And Madison, in *Federalist No. 46*, had predicted:

> ambitious encroachments of the Federal Government, on the authority of the State governments, would not excite the opposition of a single State or of a few States only. They would be signals of general alarm. Every Government would espouse the common cause. A correspondence would be opened. Plans of resistance would be concerted. One spirit would animate and conduct the whole. The same combination in short would result from an apprehensive of the federal, as was produced by the dread of a foreign yoke; and unless the projected innovations should be voluntarily renounced, the same appeal to a trial of force would be made in the one case, as was made in the other. But what degree of madness could ever drive the Federal Government to such an extremity?

6.   If a state could nullify a federal law within its own borders, would the country be back to the regime under the Articles of Confederation, where the unanimous agreement of the states was necessary to do anything? Would that create a hold-up problem, where one state could try to extract major concessions before it would agree to new legislation?

The Election of 1800 and President Jefferson's Pardons

The Alien and Sedition Acts were a central issue in the election of 1800. President Adams was defeated by Thomas Jefferson, his vice-president, his political foe, and the author of the Kentucky Resolutions. When Jefferson took the oath of office on March 4, 1801, the Sedition Act had expired. But prosecutions could still be brought for violations before the Act expired. And one such prosecution was underway when Jefferson took office, the prosecution of William Duane, the editor of a Philadelphia newspaper. Jefferson ordered the U.S. attorney who had brought the case, Edward Livingston, to cease the prosecution of Duane under the Act. Jefferson explained his action this way:

the President is to have the laws executed. he may order an offence then to be prosecuted. if he sees a prosecution put into a train which is not lawful, he may order it to be discontinued and put into legal train. I found a prosecution going on against Duane for an offence against the Senate, founded on the Sedition act. I affirm that act to be no law, because in opposition to the Constitution; and I shall treat it as a nullity wherever it comes in the way of my functions.

35 THE PAPERS OF THOMAS JEFFERSON 544 (Nov. 1, 1801). Was Jefferson right to order the Sedition Act prosecution of Duane dropped? In doing so, was Jefferson in effect suspending an act of Congress? If so, did that violate the Take Care Clause of Article II, Section 3—which imposes on the president the duty to "take care that the laws be faithfully executed"? But what is the relevant law that Jefferson had sworn to follow: the Sedition Act or the Constitution?

President Jefferson also granted pardons to those already convicted under the Sedition Act. He did so on the grounds that the Sedition Act was unconstitutional. Jefferson justified his pardons in a letter in September 1804 to Abigail Adams, wife of former President Adams. For authority he relied once again on the president's duty of constitutional interpretation in the course of performing duties committed to him, including the pardon power. Jefferson further argued that judicial decisions contrary to the Constitution could not control the president in the exercise of his constitutional responsibilities. He said:

You seem to think it devolved on the judges to decide on the validity of the sedition law. But nothing in the Constitution has given them a right to decide for the Executive, more than to the Executive to decide for them. Both magistracies are equally independent in the sphere of action assigned to them. The judges, believing the law constitutional, had a right to pass a sentence of fine and imprisonment; because that power was placed in their hands by the Constitution. But the Executive, believing the law to be unconstitutional, was bound to remit the execution of it; because that power has been confided to him by the Constitution. That instrument meant that its co-ordinate branches should be checks on each other. But the opinion which gives to the judges the right to decide what laws are constitutional, and what not, not only for themselves in their own sphere of action, but for the Legislature & Executive also, in their spheres, would make the judiciary a despotic branch.

10 THE WORKS OF THOMAS JEFFERSON 89 (Paul Leicester Ford ed., 1905).

NOTES

1.   Were President Jefferson's pardons constitutionally appropriate? Even though the federal courts had found the Sedition Act constitutional? Press the point one step further: What if the courts were to hold that it is unconstitutional for the president to grant pardons on the basis of a constitutional argument that has been rejected by the courts themselves? May the president refuse to obey decisions of the courts if they rest on unfaithful interpretations of the Constitution?

2.   If the president may decline to enforce statutes, even though the courts have upheld them, what about the reverse? May the president *enforce* a statute, even if the courts have invalidated it?

3.   In *The Federalist No. 49*, James Madison stated that "[t]he several departments being perfectly co-ordinate by the terms of their common commission, neither of them, it is evident, can pretend to an exclusive or superior right of settling the boundaries between their respective powers." Do President Jefferson's actions suggest this view as well? This view was embraced by President Andrew Jackson in his veto of the bill to reauthorize the Second Bank of the United States and in other actions, and by President Abraham Lincoln on many occasions. What dangers can you foresee from these positions?

4.   If all three branches of the national government do possess an independent power to interpret the Constitution within the operation of their respective powers, does it follow that the states likewise may interpret the Constitution independently and are not bound by the interpretations of the national government (as argued in the Virginia and Kentucky Resolutions)? Are there principled distinctions between the two situations? How would a dispute about the Constitution between the national government and some state governments be resolved? By force of arms? President Jackson thought so. When South Carolina sought to "nullify" a federal tariff law in 1832, President Jackson, backed by Congress, threatened coercion and prevailed. And when states of the South attempted to secede in 1861, President Lincoln ordered the use of force—and eventually prevailed. Have fundamental questions of constitutional interpretation been resolved on the battlefield?

5.   After the passage in *The Federalist No. 49* quoted above, Madison went on to ask: "and how are the encroachments of the stronger to be prevented, or the wrongs of the weaker to be redressed, without an appeal to the people themselves, who, as the grantors of the commissions, can alone declare its true meaning, and enforce its observance?" Is Madison right about the role of "the people themselves" in interpreting the Constitution? How can they "enforce its observance"?

Similarly, was Jefferson right to "appeal" to the people, in the election of 1800, the judicial decisions upholding the convictions under the Sedition Act? Was the election of 1800 an act of constitutional interpretation, one by which the electorate sided with the Democratic-Republicans on the constitutionality of the Alien and Sedition Acts and overruled the Federalist-dominated federal courts?

As a practical matter, the largest and most important constitutional controversies in American history have eventually been settled by the American people acting through the medium of their presidents, their senators, and the judges selected by those presidents and senators. The Madisonian system of checks and balances guarantees that in the long run the people are the interpreters and enforcers of the Constitution. Is this a good thing? Would it be better to have a strict rule that only judges could interpret the Constitution, with judicial independence fortified by letting judges pick their own successors? If "We the People" are the ultimate interpreters of the Constitution, and if the very reason to have a constitution is to restrain the people, then is our effort to establish constitutional government bound to fail? Or is constitutional government aided rather than subverted by letting the people, acting through multiple agents, interpret *their* Constitution?

CHAPTER 2

THE SEPARATION OF THE NATIONAL POWERS

[Assignment 4]

The Constitution begins with a declaration of popular sovereignty: the Constitution is established by "We the People of the United States." The Preamble is also a statement of the broad purposes for which this new government was created. Then the Constitution proceeds in its first three Articles to lay out the structure and powers of three branches of government: the Congress, the president, and the courts. Each branch is substantially independent of the others, and has separate functions. Yet each branch checks, and is checked by, the others. None is superior. All derive their authority to act from the same constitutional grant of power by the people.

This chapter considers the structure, nature, and functions of the three branches of the national government, which are considered in the order of their appearance within the Constitution. This chapter is therefore addressed primarily to the *separation of powers*: the distribution of power among the branches of the national government. The next chapter considers *federalism*: the distribution of power between the national government and the states.

An Introduction to the Separation of Powers

Art. I, § 1: All legislative Powers herein granted shall be vested in a Congress of the United States, which shall consist of a Senate and House of Representatives. . . .

Art. II, § 1: The executive Power shall be vested in a President of the United States of America. . . .

Art. III, § 1: The judicial Power of the United States, shall be vested in one supreme Court, and in such inferior Courts as the Congress may from time to time ordain and establish.

Here in a nutshell is the separation of powers. We the People—remember the Preamble—have granted limited and enumerated powers to three branches of the federal government. Each branch may exercise only the powers given to it, not the powers given to the other branches. Note that this separation of powers is not absolutely pure, for the Constitution actually allocates some powers to *two* branches working in coordination. (This intermingling of powers was inspired by how the framers understood the largely unwritten English constitution and leading political theorists of the Enlightenment.) But even these shared allocations of power serve the purpose of ensuring that each branch is checked by the others. Consider a few of the checks and balances established by the Constitution:

Congress can check the president with its most formidable power—the power to raise revenues, called "the power of the purse." It can, for example, shut down a war by refusing to fund it. The Senate can hobble the executive branch by refusing to confirm the president's nominees. It can refuse to ratify the treaties the president signs. Congress can check the judiciary by altering its size or jurisdiction. It can hamper the judiciary by constraining its funding. And with the cooperation of the states, Congress can enact a constitutional amendment that would overturn the Supreme Court's construction of the Constitution, something it has done several times in American history (see Amendments XI, XIV, XVI, XXVI). Congress can impeach and remove officers, including the president and the justices.

The president can check Congress by vetoing its bills, and by setting priorities in law enforcement and execution that are different than those of Congress. The president also has ample powers to check Congress in the conduct of foreign affairs. As for the judiciary, the president has a measure of control through the appointment of judges. The executive branch also influences the issues that the courts are able to decide; the president can evade judicial resolution of a suit against the executive branch by choosing to settle it.

The federal courts check Congress and the president in only one way, but it is a check that constrains every action those branches can take: the courts may decide that the legislative or executive branch has violated the Constitution.

The checks each branch has on the others can be seen in one of the most important cases ever decided by the Supreme Court: *Youngstown Sheet & Tube Co. v. Sawyer*, 343 U.S. 579 (1952), also known as *The Steel Seizure Case*. At the height of the Korean War, the steel industry and the steel workers could not agree on wages and working conditions. The steel workers threatened to strike, and President Harry Truman feared that a strike would cripple the war effort. He issued an executive order that instructed the secretary of Commerce to seize the nation's steel mills and prescribe terms and conditions of employment as he saw fit.

President Truman's action was unilateral. Congress had not authorized it by legislation. Thus the steel seizure raised a question as to whether the president possesses either an inherent legislative power or a power to act in emergencies. *Youngstown* went to the Supreme Court in a tremendous rush, yet it produced enduring opinions by several Supreme Court justices.

The opinions in *Youngstown* illustrate the five types of constitutional argument (p. 42): text, historical context, structure, precedent and practice, and policy. As you read each opinion, look for its primary type or types of constitutional argument.

Youngstown Sheet & Tube Co. v. Sawyer
343 U.S. 579 (1952)

■ MR. JUSTICE BLACK delivered the opinion of the Court.

We are asked to decide whether the President was acting within his constitutional power when he issued an order directing the Secretary of Commerce to take possession of and operate most of the Nation's steel mills. The mill owners argue that the President's order amounts to lawmaking, a legislative function which the Constitution has expressly confided to the Congress and not to the President. The Government's position is that the order was made on findings of the President that his action was necessary to avert a national catastrophe which would inevitably result from a stoppage of steel production, and that in meeting this grave emergency the President was acting within the aggregate of his constitutional powers as the

Nation's Chief Executive and the Commander in Chief of the Armed Forces of the United States. The issue emerges here from the following series of events:

In the latter part of 1951, a dispute arose between the steel companies and their employees over terms and conditions that should be included in new collective bargaining agreements. Long-continued conferences failed to resolve the dispute. . . . On April 4, 1952, the Union gave notice of a nation-wide strike called to begin at 12:01 a. m. April 9. The indispensability of steel as a component of substantially all weapons and other war materials led the President to believe that the proposed work stoppage would immediately jeopardize our national defense and that governmental seizure of the steel mills was necessary in order to assure the continued availability of steel. Reciting these considerations for his action, the President, a few hours before the strike was to begin, issued Executive Order 10340. The order directed the Secretary of Commerce to take possession of most of the steel mills and keep them running. The Secretary immediately issued his own possessory orders, calling upon the presidents of the various seized companies to serve as operating managers for the United States. They were directed to carry on their activities in accordance with regulations and directions of the Secretary. The next morning the President sent a message to Congress reporting his action. Twelve days later he sent a second message. Congress has taken no action.

Obeying the Secretary's orders under protest, the companies brought proceedings against him in the District Court. Their complaints charged that the seizure was not authorized by an act of Congress or by any constitutional provisions. The District Court was asked to declare the orders of the President and the Secretary invalid and to issue preliminary and permanent injunctions restraining their enforcement. Opposing the motion for preliminary injunction, the United States asserted that a strike disrupting steel production for even a brief period would so endanger the well-being and safety of the Nation that the President had "inherent power" to do what he had done—power "supported by the Constitution, by historical precedent, and by court decisions." The Government also contended that in any event no preliminary injunction should be issued because the companies had made no showing that their available legal remedies were inadequate or that their injuries from seizure would be irreparable. Holding against the Government on all points, the District Court on April 30 issued a preliminary injunction restraining the Secretary from "continuing the seizure and possession of the plants . . . and from acting under the purported authority of Executive Order No. 10340." On the same day the Court of Appeals stayed the District Court's injunction. Deeming it best that the issues raised be promptly decided by this Court, we granted certiorari on May 3 and set the cause for argument on May 12. . . .

[The Court first considered the government's argument that the preliminary injunction was inappropriate because the companies were not suffering "irreparable injury," that is, the companies' losses could always be recovered later in a suit for damages if the seizure were held to be unconstitutional. The Court rejected that argument for several reasons, including the fact that the injuries suffered by the companies from the seizure would "be difficult, if not incapable, of measurement."—Editors]

The President's power, if any, to issue the order must stem either from an act of Congress or from the Constitution itself. There is no statute that expressly authorizes the President to take possession of property as he did here. Nor is there any act of Congress to which our attention has been directed from which such a power can fairly be implied. Indeed, we do not understand the Government to rely on statutory authorization for this seizure. There are two statutes which do authorize the President to take both personal and real property under certain conditions. However, the Government admits that these conditions were not met and that the President's order was not rooted in either of the statutes. The Government refers to the seizure provisions of one of these statutes (§ 201(b) of the Defense Production Act) as "much too cumbersome, involved, and time-consuming for the crisis which was at hand."

Moreover, the use of the seizure technique to solve labor disputes in order to prevent work stoppages was not only unauthorized by any congressional enactment; prior to this controversy, Congress had refused to adopt that method of settling labor disputes. When the Taft-Hartley Act was under consideration in 1947, Congress rejected an amendment which would have authorized such governmental seizures in cases of emergency. Apparently it was thought that the technique of seizure, like that of compulsory arbitration, would interfere with the process of collective bargaining. Consequently, the plan Congress adopted in that Act did not provide for seizure under any circumstances. Instead, the plan sought to bring about settlements by use of the customary devices of mediation, conciliation, investigation by boards of inquiry, and public reports. In some instances temporary injunctions were authorized to provide cooling-off periods. All this failing, unions were left free to strike after a secret vote by employees as to whether they wished to accept their employers' final settlement offer.

It is clear that if the President had authority to issue the order he did, it must be found in some provision of the Constitution. And it is not claimed that express constitutional language grants this power to the President. The contention is that presidential power should be implied from the aggregate of his powers under the Constitution. Particular reliance is placed on provisions in Article II which say that "The executive Power shall be vested in a President . . ."; that "he shall take Care that the Laws be faithfully executed"; and that he "shall be Commander in Chief of the Army and Navy of the United States."

The order cannot properly be sustained as an exercise of the President's military power as Commander in Chief of the Armed Forces. The Government attempts to do so by citing a number of cases upholding broad powers in military commanders engaged in day-to-day fighting in a theater of war. Such cases need not concern us here. Even though "theater of war" be an expanding concept, we cannot with faithfulness to our constitutional system hold that the Commander in Chief of the Armed Forces has the ultimate power as such to take possession of private property in order to keep labor disputes from stopping production. This is a job for the Nation's lawmakers, not for its military authorities.

Nor can the seizure order be sustained because of the several constitutional provisions that grant executive power to the President. In the framework of our Constitution, the President's power to see that the laws are faithfully executed refutes the idea that he is to be a lawmaker. The Constitution limits his functions in the lawmaking process to the recommending of laws he thinks wise and the vetoing of laws he thinks bad. And the Constitution is neither silent nor equivocal about who shall make laws which the President is to execute. The first section of the first article says that "All legislative Powers herein granted shall be vested in a Congress of the

United States. . . ." After granting many powers to the Congress, Article I goes on to provide that Congress may "make all Laws which shall be necessary and proper for carrying into Execution the foregoing Powers and all other Powers vested by this Constitution in the Government of the United States, or any Department or Officer thereof."

The President's order does not direct that a congressional policy be executed in a manner prescribed by Congress—it directs that a presidential policy be executed in a manner prescribed by the President. The preamble of the order itself, like that of many statutes, sets out reasons why the President believes certain policies should be adopted, proclaims these policies as rules of conduct to be followed, and again, like a statute, authorizes a government official to promulgate additional rules and regulations consistent with the policy proclaimed and needed to carry that policy into execution. The power of Congress to adopt such public policies as those proclaimed by the order is beyond question. It can authorize the taking of private property for public use. It can make laws regulating the relationships between employers and employees, prescribing rules designed to settle labor disputes, and fixing wages and working conditions in certain fields of our economy. The Constitution did not subject this law-making power of Congress to presidential or military supervision or control.

It is said that other Presidents without congressional authority have taken possession of private business enterprises in order to settle labor disputes. But even if this be true, Congress has not thereby lost its exclusive constitutional authority to make laws necessary and proper to carry out the powers vested by the Constitution "in the Government of the United States, or in any Department or Officer thereof."

The Founders of this Nation entrusted the law making power to the Congress alone in both good and bad times. It would do no good to recall the historical events, the fears of power and the hopes for freedom that lay behind their choice. Such a review would but confirm our holding that this seizure order cannot stand.

■ MR. JUSTICE FRANKFURTER, concurring.

. . . The issue before us can be met, and therefore should be, without attempting to define the President's powers comprehensively. . . . We must therefore put to one side consideration of what powers the President would have had if there had been no legislation whatever bearing on the authority asserted by the seizure, or if the seizure had been only for a short, explicitly temporary period, to be terminated automatically unless Congressional approval were given. These and other questions, like or unlike, are not now here. I would exceed my authority were I to say anything about them.

The question before the Court comes in this setting. Congress has frequently—at least 16 times since 1916—specifically provided for executive seizure of production, transportation, communications, or storage facilities. In every case it has qualified this grant of power with limitations and safeguards. . . . The power to seize has uniformly been given only for a limited period or for a defined emergency, or has been repealed after a short period. . . . Congress also has not left to implication that just compensation be paid: it has usually legislated in detail regarding enforcement of this litigation-breeding general requirement. . . .

In adopting the provisions which it did, by the Labor Management Relations Act of 1947, for dealing with a "national emergency" arising out of a breakdown in peaceful industrial relations, Congress was very familiar with Governmental seizure as a protective measure. On a balance of considerations, Congress chose not to lodge this power in the President. It chose not to make available in advance a remedy to which both industry and labor were fiercely hostile. . . . [N]othing can be plainer than that Congress made a conscious choice of policy in a field full of perplexity and peculiarly within legislative responsibility for choice. In formulating legislation for dealing with industrial conflicts, Congress could not more clearly and emphatically have withheld authority than it did in 1947. . . .

It cannot be contended that the President would have had power to issue this order had Congress explicitly negated such authority in formal legislation. Congress has expressed its will to withhold this power from the President as though it had said so in so many words. . . . By the Labor Management Relations Act of 1947, Congress said to the President, "You may not seize. Please report to us and ask for seizure power if you think it is needed in a specific situation." . . .

It is one thing to draw an intention of Congress from general language and to say that Congress would have explicitly written what is inferred, where Congress has not addressed itself to a specific situation. It is quite impossible, however, when Congress did specifically address itself to a problem, as Congress did to that of seizure, to find secreted in the interstices of legislation the very grant of power which Congress consciously withheld. To find authority so explicitly withheld is not merely to disregard in a particular instance the clear will of Congress. It is to disrespect the whole legislative process and the constitutional division of authority between President and Congress. . . .

Apart from his vast share of responsibility for the conduct of our foreign relations, the embracing function of the President is that "he shall take Care that the Laws be faithfully executed. . . ." Art. II, § 3. The nature of that authority has for me been comprehensively indicated by Mr. Justice Holmes. "The duty of the President to see that the laws be executed is a duty that does not go beyond the laws or require him to achieve more than Congress sees fit to leave within his power." *Myers v. United States*, 272 U.S. 52, 177 (1926). The powers of the President are not as particularized as are those of Congress. But unenumerated powers do not mean undefined powers. The separation of powers built into our Constitution gives essential content to undefined provisions in the frame of our government.

To be sure, the content of the three authorities of government is not to be derived from an abstract analysis. The areas are partly interacting, not wholly disjointed. The Constitution is a framework for government. Therefore the way the framework has consistently operated fairly establishes that it has operated according to its true nature. Deeply embedded traditional ways of conducting government cannot supplant the Constitution or legislation, but they give meaning to the words of a text or supply them. It is an inadmissibly narrow conception of American constitutional law to confine it to the words of the Constitution and to disregard the gloss which life has written upon them. In short, a systematic, unbroken, executive practice, long pursued to the knowledge of the Congress and never before questioned, engaged in by Presidents who have also sworn to uphold the Constitution, making as it were such exercise of power part of the structure of our government, may be treated as a gloss on "executive Power" vested in the President by § 1 of Art. II.

Such was the case of *United States v. Midwest Oil Co.*, 236 U.S. 459 (1915). . . . In the *Midwest Oil* case, lands which Congress had opened for entry were, over a period of 80 years and in 252 instances, and by Presidents learned and unlearned in the law, temporarily withdrawn from entry so as to enable Congress to deal with such withdrawals. No remotely comparable practice can be vouched for executive seizure of property at a time when this country was not at war, in the only constitutional way in which it can be at war. It would pursue the irrelevant to reopen the controversy over the constitutionality of some acts of Lincoln during the Civil War. Suffice it to say that he seized railroads in territory where armed hostilities had already interrupted the movement of troops to the beleaguered Capital, and his order was ratified by the Congress. . . .

[T]he list of executive assertions of the power of seizure in circumstances comparable to the present reduces to three in the six-month period from June to December of 1941. We need not split hairs in comparing those actions to the one before us, though much might be said by way of differentiation. Without passing on their validity, as we are not called upon to do, it suffices to say that these three isolated instances do not add up, either in number, scope, duration or contemporaneous legal justification, to the kind of executive construction of the Constitution revealed in the *Midwest Oil* case. Nor do they come to us sanctioned by long-continued acquiescence of Congress giving decisive weight to a construction by the Executive of its powers.

A scheme of government like ours no doubt at times feels the lack of power to act with complete, all-embracing, swiftly moving authority. No doubt a government with distributed authority, subject to be challenged in the courts of law, at least long enough to consider and adjudicate the challenge, labors under restrictions from which other governments are free. It has not been our tradition to envy such governments. . . . I know no more impressive words on this subject than those of Mr. Justice Brandeis:

> "The doctrine of the separation of powers was adopted by the Convention of 1787, not to promote efficiency but to preclude the exercise of arbitrary power. The purpose was, not to avoid friction, but, by means of the inevitable friction incident to the distribution of the governmental powers among three departments, to save the people from autocracy." *Myers*, at 240, 293. . . .

■ MR. JUSTICE DOUGLAS, concurring.

There can be no doubt that the emergency which caused the President to seize these steel plants was one that bore heavily on the country. But the emergency did not create power; it merely marked an occasion when power should be exercised. And the fact that it was necessary that measures be taken to keep steel in production does not mean that the President, rather than the Congress, had the constitutional authority to act. . . .

The legislative nature of the action taken by the President seems to me to be clear. When the United States takes over an industrial plant to settle a labor controversy, it is condemning property. The seizure of the plant is a taking in the constitutional sense. A permanent taking would amount to the nationalization of the industry. A temporary taking falls short of that goal. But though the seizure is only for a week or a month, the condemnation is complete and the United States must pay compensation for the temporary possession.

The power of the Federal Government to condemn property is well established. It can condemn for any public purpose; and I have no doubt but that condemnation of a plant, factory, or industry in order to promote industrial peace would be constitutional. But there is a duty to pay for all property taken by the Government. The command of the Fifth Amendment is that no "private property be taken for public use, without just compensation." That constitutional requirement has an important bearing on the present case.

The President has no power to raise revenues. That power is in the Congress by Article I, Section 8 of the Constitution. The President might seize and the Congress by subsequent action might ratify the seizure. But until and unless Congress acted, no condemnation would be lawful. The branch of government that has the power to pay compensation for a seizure is the only one able to authorize a seizure or make lawful one that the President had effected. . . .

We pay a price for our system of checks and balances, for the distribution of power among the three branches of government. It is a price that today may seem exorbitant to many. Today a kindly President uses the seizure power to effect a wage increase and to keep the steel furnaces in production. Yet tomorrow another President might use the same power to prevent a wage increase, to curb trade-unionists, to regiment labor as oppressively as industry thinks it has been regimented by this seizure.

■ Mr. Justice Jackson, concurring in the judgment and opinion of the Court.

That comprehensive and undefined presidential powers hold both practical advantages and grave dangers for the country will impress anyone who has served as legal adviser to a President in time of transition and public anxiety. While an interval of detached reflection may temper teachings of that experience, they probably are a more realistic influence on my views than the conventional materials of judicial decision which seem unduly to accentuate doctrine and legal fiction. . . .

A judge, like an executive adviser, may be surprised at the poverty of really useful and unambiguous authority applicable to concrete problems of executive power as they actually present themselves. Just what our forefathers did envision, or would have envisioned had they foreseen modern conditions, must be divined from materials almost as enigmatic as the dreams Joseph was called upon to interpret for Pharaoh. A century and a half of partisan debate and scholarly speculation yields no net result but only supplies more or less apt quotations from respected sources on each side of any question. They largely cancel each other. And court decisions are indecisive because of the judicial practice of dealing with the largest questions in the most narrow way.

The actual art of governing under our Constitution does not and cannot conform to judicial definitions of the power of any of its branches based on isolated clauses or even single Articles torn from context. While the Constitution diffuses power the better to secure liberty, it also contemplates that practice will integrate the dispersed powers into a workable government. It enjoins upon its branches separateness but interdependence, autonomy but reciprocity. Presidential powers are not fixed but fluctuate, depending upon their disjunction or conjunction with those of Congress. We may well begin by a somewhat over-simplified grouping of practical situations in which a President may doubt, or others may challenge, his powers, and by distinguishing roughly the legal consequences of this factor of relativity.

1.   When the President acts pursuant to an express or implied authorization of Congress, his authority is at its maximum, for it includes all that he possesses in his own right plus all that Congress can delegate. In these circumstances, and in these only, may he be said (for what it may be worth), to personify the federal sovereignty. If his act is held unconstitutional under these circumstances, it usually means that the Federal Government as an undivided whole lacks power. A seizure executed by the President pursuant to an Act of Congress would be supported by the strongest of presumptions and the widest latitude of judicial interpretation, and the burden of persuasion would rest heavily upon any who might attack it.

2.   When the President acts in absence of either a congressional grant or denial of authority, he can only rely upon his own independent powers, but there is a zone of twilight in which he and Congress may have concurrent authority, or in which its distribution is uncertain. Therefore, congressional inertia, indifference or quiescence may sometimes, at least as a practical matter, enable, if not invite, measures on independent presidential responsibility. In this area, any actual test of power is likely to depend on the imperatives of events and contemporary imponderables rather than on abstract theories of law.

3.   When the President takes measures incompatible with the expressed or implied will of Congress, his power is at its lowest ebb, for then he can rely only upon his own constitutional powers minus any constitutional powers of Congress over the matter. Courts can sustain exclusive presidential control in such a case only by disabling the Congress from acting upon the subject. Presidential claim to a power at once so conclusive and preclusive must be scrutinized with caution, for what is at stake is the equilibrium established by our constitutional system.

Into which of these classifications does this executive seizure of the steel industry fit? It is eliminated from the first by admission, for it is conceded that no congressional authorization exists for this seizure. That takes away also the support of the many precedents and declarations which were made in relation, and must be confined, to this category.

Can it then be defended under flexible tests available to the second category? It seems clearly eliminated from that class because Congress has not left seizure of private property an open field but has covered it by three statutory policies inconsistent with this seizure. . . .

This leaves the current seizure to be justified only by the severe tests under the third grouping, where it can be supported only by any remainder of executive power after subtraction of such powers as Congress may have over the subject. In short, we can sustain the President only by holding that seizure of such strike-bound industries is within his domain and beyond control by Congress. Thus, this Court's first review of such seizures occurs under circumstances which leave presidential power most vulnerable to attack and in the least favorable of possible constitutional postures.

I did not suppose, and I am not persuaded, that history leaves it open to question, at least in the courts, that the executive branch, like the Federal Government as a whole, possesses only delegated powers. The purpose of the Constitution was not only to grant power, but to keep it from getting out of hand. However, because the President does not enjoy unmentioned powers does not mean that the mentioned ones should be narrowed by a niggardly construction. Some clauses could be made almost unworkable, as well as immutable, by refusal to indulge some latitude of interpretation for changing times. I have heretofore, and do now, give to the enumerated powers the scope and elasticity afforded by what seem to be reasonable practical implications instead of the rigidity dictated by a doctrinaire textualism.

The Solicitor General seeks the power of seizure in three clauses of the Executive Article, the first reading, "The executive Power shall be vested in a President of the United States of America." Lest I be thought to exaggerate, I quote the interpretation which his brief puts upon it: "In our view, this clause constitutes a grant of all the executive powers of which the Government is capable." If that be true, it is difficult to see why the forefathers bothered to add several specific items, including some trifling ones.

The example of such unlimited executive power that must have most impressed the forefathers was the prerogative exercised by George III, and the description of its evils in the Declaration of Independence leads me to doubt that they were creating their new Executive in his image. Continental European examples were no more appealing. And if we seek instruction from our own times, we can match it only from the executive powers in those governments we disparagingly describe as totalitarian. I cannot accept the view that this clause is a grant in bulk of all conceivable executive power but regard it as an allocation to the presidential office of the generic powers thereafter stated.

The clause on which the Government next relies is that "The President shall be Commander in Chief of the Army and Navy of the United States. . . ." These cryptic words have given rise to some of the most persistent controversies in our constitutional history. Of course, they imply something more than an empty title. But just what authority goes with the name has plagued presidential advisers who would not waive or narrow it by nonassertion yet cannot say where it begins or ends. It undoubtedly puts the Nation's armed forces under presidential command. Hence, this loose appellation is sometimes advanced as support for any presidential action, internal or external, involving use of force, the idea being that it vests power to do anything, anywhere, that can be done with an army or navy.

That seems to be the logic of an argument tendered at our bar—that the President having, on his own responsibility, sent American troops abroad derives from that act "affirmative power" to seize the means of producing a supply of steel for them. To quote, "Perhaps the most forceful illustrations of the scope of Presidential power in this connection is the fact that American troops in Korea, whose safety and effectiveness are so directly involved here, were sent to the field by an exercise of the President's constitutional powers." Thus, it is said, he has invested himself with "war powers."

I cannot foresee all that it might entail if the Court should indorse this argument. Nothing in our Constitution is plainer than that declaration of a war is entrusted only to Congress. Of course, a state of war may in fact exist without a formal declaration. But no doctrine that the Court could promulgate would seem to me more sinister and alarming than that a President whose conduct of foreign affairs is so largely uncontrolled, and often even is unknown, can vastly enlarge his mastery over the internal affairs of the country by his own commitment of the Nation's armed forces to some foreign venture. I do not, however, find it necessary or appropriate to consider the legal status of the Korean enterprise to discountenance argument based on it.

Assuming that we are in a war *de facto*, whether it is or is not a war *de jure*, does that empower the Commander in Chief to seize industries he thinks necessary to supply our army? The Constitution expressly places in Congress power "to raise and *support* Armies" and "to *provide* and *maintain* a Navy." (Emphasis supplied.) This certainly lays upon Congress primary responsibility for supplying the armed forces. Congress alone controls the raising of revenues and their appropriation and may determine in what manner and by what means they shall be spent for military and naval procurement. I suppose no one would doubt that Congress can take over war supply as a Government enterprise. On the other hand, if Congress sees fit to rely on free private enterprise collectively bargaining with free labor for support and maintenance of our armed forces can the Executive because of lawful disagreements incidental to that process, seize the facility for operation upon Government-imposed terms?

There are indications that the Constitution did not contemplate that the title Commander in Chief *of the Army and Navy* will constitute him also Commander in Chief of the country, its industries and its inhabitants. He has no monopoly of "war powers," whatever they are. While Congress cannot deprive the President of the command of the army and navy, only Congress can provide him an army or navy to command. It is also empowered to make rules for the "Government and Regulation of land and naval Forces," by which it may to some unknown extent impinge upon even command functions.

That military powers of the Commander in Chief were not to supersede representative government of internal affairs seems obvious from the Constitution and from elementary American history. Time out of mind, and even now in many parts of the world, a military commander can seize private housing to shelter his troops. Not so, however, in the United States, for the Third Amendment says, "No Soldier shall, in time of peace be quartered in any house, without the consent of the Owner, nor in time of war, but in a manner to be prescribed by law." Thus, even in war time, his seizure of needed military housing must be authorized by Congress. . . .

We should not use this occasion to circumscribe, much less to contract, the lawful role of the President as Commander in Chief. I should indulge the widest latitude of interpretation to sustain his exclusive function to command the instruments of national force, at least when turned against the outside world for the security of our society. But, when it is turned inward, not because of rebellion but because of a lawful economic struggle between industry and labor, it should have no such indulgence. . . .

The third clause in which the Solicitor General finds seizure powers is that "he shall take Care that the Laws be faithfully executed. . . ." That authority must be matched against words of the Fifth Amendment that "No person shall be . . . deprived of life, liberty or property, without due process of law. . . ." One gives a governmental authority that reaches so far as there is law, the other gives a private right that authority shall go no farther. These signify about all there is of the principle that ours is a government of laws, not of men, and that we submit ourselves to rulers only if under rules.

The Solicitor General lastly grounds support of the seizure upon nebulous, inherent powers never expressly granted but said to have accrued to the office from the customs and claims of preceding administrations. The plea is for a resulting power to deal with a crisis or an emergency according to the necessities of the case, the unarticulated assumption being that necessity knows no law.

Loose and irresponsible use of adjectives colors all non-legal and much legal discussion of presidential powers. "Inherent" powers, "implied" powers, "incidental" powers, "plenary" powers, "war" powers and "emergency" powers are used, often interchangeably and without fixed or ascertainable meanings.

The vagueness and generality of the clauses that set forth presidential powers afford a plausible basis for pressures within and without an administration for presidential action beyond that supported by those whose responsibility it is to defend his actions in court. The claim of inherent and unrestricted presidential powers has long been a persuasive dialectical weapon in political controversy. . . .

The appeal, however, that we declare the existence of inherent powers *ex necessitate* to meet an emergency asks us to do what many think would be wise, although it is something the forefathers omitted. They knew what emergencies were, knew the pressures they engender for authoritative action, knew, too, how they afford a ready pretext for usurpation. We may also suspect that they suspected that emergency powers would tend to kindle emergencies. Aside from suspension of the privilege of the writ of habeas corpus in time of rebellion or invasion, when the public safety may require it, they made no express provision for exercise of extraordinary authority because of a crisis. I do not think we rightfully may so amend their work, and, if we could, I am not convinced it would be wise to do so, although many modern nations have forthrightly recognized that war and economic crises may upset the normal balance between liberty and authority. Their experience with emergency powers may not be irrelevant to the argument here that we should say that the Executive, of his own volition, can invest himself with undefined emergency powers.

Germany, after the First World War, framed the Weimar Constitution, designed to secure her liberties in the Western tradition. However, the President of the Republic, without concurrence of the Reichstag, was empowered temporarily to suspend any or all individual rights if public safety and order were seriously disturbed or endangered. This proved a temptation to every government, whatever its shade of opinion, and in 13 years suspension of rights was invoked on more than 250 occasions. Finally, Hitler persuaded President Von Hindenberg to suspend all such rights, and they were never restored. . . .

In view of the ease, expedition and safety with which Congress can grant and has granted large emergency powers, certainly ample to embrace this crisis, I am quite unimpressed with the argument that we should affirm possession of them without statute. Such power either has no beginning or it has no end. If it exists, it need submit to no legal restraint. I am not alarmed that it would plunge us straightway into dictatorship, but it is at least a step in that wrong direction. . . .

Executive power has the advantage of concentration in a single head in whose choice the whole Nation has a part, making him the focus of public hopes and expectations. In drama, magnitude and finality his decisions so far overshadow any others that almost alone he fills the public eye and ear. No other personality in public life can begin to compete with him in access to the public mind through modern methods of communications. By his prestige as head of state and his influence upon public opinion he exerts a leverage upon those who are supposed to check and balance his power which often cancels their effectiveness. . . .

I have no illusion that any decision by this Court can keep power in the hands of Congress if it is not wise and timely in meeting its problems. A crisis that challenges the President equally, or perhaps primarily, challenges Congress. If not good law, there was worldly wisdom in the maxim attributed to Napoleon that "The tools belong to the man who can use them." We may say that power to legislate for emergencies belongs in the hands of Congress, but only Congress itself can prevent power from slipping through its fingers. . . .

The Executive, except for recommendation and veto, has no legislative power. The executive action we have here originates in the individual will of the President and represents an exercise of authority without law. No one, perhaps not even the President, knows the limits of the power he may seek to exert in this instance and the parties affected cannot learn the limit of their rights. We do not know today what powers over labor or property would be claimed to flow from Government possession if we should legalize it, what rights to compensation would be claimed or recognized, or on what contingency it would end. With all its defects, delays and inconveniences, men have discovered no technique for long preserving free government except that the Executive be under the law, and that the law be made by parliamentary deliberations.

Such institutions may be destined to pass away. But it is the duty of the Court to be last, not first, to give them up.

■ [JUSTICE BURTON's concurring opinion is omitted.]

■ MR. JUSTICE CLARK, concurring in the judgment of the Court.

One of this Court's first pronouncements upon the powers of the President under the Constitution was made by Mr. Chief Justice John Marshall some one hundred and fifty years ago. In *Little v. Barreme*, 6 U.S. (2 Cranch) 170 (1804), he used this characteristically clear language in discussing the power of the President to instruct the seizure of the *Flying Fish*, a vessel bound from a French port:

> It is by no means clear that the president of the United States whose high duty it is to "take care that the laws be faithfully executed" and who is commander in chief of the armies and navies of the United States, might not, without any special authority for that purpose, in the then existing state of things, have empowered the officers commanding the armed vessels of the United States, to seize and send into port for adjudication, American vessels which were forfeited by being engaged in this illicit commerce. But when it is observed that [an act of Congress] gives a special authority to seize on the high seas, and limits that authority to the seizure of vessels bound or sailing *to* a French port, the legislature seem to have prescribed that the manner in which this law shall be carried into execution, was to exclude a seizure of any vessel *not* bound to a French port.

Accordingly, a unanimous Court held that the President's instructions had been issued without authority and that they could not "legalize an act which, without those instructions would have been a plain trespass." I know of no subsequent holding of this Court to the contrary.[3] . . .

In my view—taught me not only by the decision of Mr. Chief Justice Marshall in *Little v. Barreme*, but also by a score of other pronouncements of distinguished members of this bench—the Constitution does grant to the President extensive authority in times of grave and imperative national emergency. . . .

I conclude that where Congress has laid down specific procedures to deal with the type of crisis confronting the President, he must follow those procedures in meeting the crisis; but that in the absence of such action by Congress, the President's independent power to act depends upon the gravity of the situation confronting the nation. I cannot sustain the seizure in question because here, as in *Little v. Barreme*, Congress had prescribed methods to be followed by the President in meeting the emergency at hand. . . .

■ MR. CHIEF JUSTICE VINSON, with whom MR. JUSTICE REED and MR. JUSTICE MINTON join, dissenting.

. . . In passing upon the question of Presidential powers in this case, we must first consider the context in which those powers were exercised.

Those who suggest that this is a case involving extraordinary powers should be mindful that these are extraordinary times. A world not yet recovered from the devastation of World War II has been forced to face the threat of another and more terrifying global conflict.

Accepting in full measure its responsibility in the world community, the United States was instrumental in securing adoption of the United Nations Charter, approved by the Senate by a vote of 89 to 2. The first purpose of the United Nations is to "maintain international peace and security, and to that end: to take effective collective measures for the prevention and removal of threats to the peace, and for the suppression of acts of aggression or other breaches of the peace. . . ." In 1950, when the United Nations called upon member nations "to render every assistance" to repel aggression in Korea, the United States furnished its vigorous support. For almost two full years, our armed forces have been fighting in Korea, suffering casualties of over 108,000 men. Hostilities have not abated. . . . Congressional support of the action in Korea has been manifested by provisions for increased military manpower and equipment and for economic stabilization, as hereinafter described. . . .

Congress also directed the President to build up our own defenses. Congress, recognizing the "grim fact . . . that the United States is now engaged in a struggle for

---

[3]   Decisions of this Court which have upheld the exercise of presidential power include the following: *Prize Cases*, 67 U.S. (2 Black) 635 (1863) (subsequent ratification of President's acts by Congress); *In re Neagle*, 135 U.S. 1 (1890) (protection of federal officials from personal violence while performing official duties); *In re Debs*, 158 U.S. 564 (1895) (injunction to prevent forcible obstruction of interstate commerce and the mails); *United States v. Midwest Oil Co.*, 236 U.S. 459 (1915) (acquiescence by Congress in more than 250 instances of exercise of same power by various Presidents over period of 80 years); *Myers v. United States*, 272 U.S. 52 (1926) (control over subordinate officials in executive department) [but see *Humphrey's Executor v. United States*, 295 U.S. 602, 626–628 (1935)]; *Hirabayashi v. United States*, 320 U.S. 81 (1943), and *Korematsu v. United States*, 323 U.S. 214 (1944) (express congressional authorization); cf. *United States v. Russell*, 80 U.S. (13 Wall.) 623 (1871) (imperative military necessity in area of combat during war); *United States v. Curtiss-Wright Export Corp.*, 299 U.S. 304 (1936) (power to negotiate with foreign governments); *United States v. United Mine Workers*, 330 U.S. 258 (1947) (seizure under specific statutory authorization).

survival" and that "it is imperative that we now take those necessary steps to make our strength equal to the peril of the hour," granted authority to draft men into the armed forces. As a result, we now have over 3,500,000 men in our armed forces. . . .

The President has the duty to execute the foregoing legislative programs. Their successful execution depends upon continued production of steel and stabilized prices for steel. Accordingly, when the collective bargaining agreements between the Nation's steel producers and their employees, represented by the United Steel Workers, were due to expire on December 31, 1951, and a strike shutting down the entire basic steel industry was threatened, the President acted to avert a complete shutdown of steel production. . . .

After bargaining had failed to avert the threatened shutdown of steel production, the President issued [an] Executive Order [describing the emergency the country faced as he directed seizure of the steel mills.] . . . The next morning, April 9, 1952, the President addressed [a] Message to Congress[. It concluded]:

> On the basis of the facts that are known to me at this time, I do not believe that immediate congressional action is essential; but I would, of course, be glad to cooperate in developing any legislative proposals which the Congress may wish to consider.
>
> If the Congress does not deem it necessary to act at this time, I shall continue to do all that is within my power to keep the steel industry operating and at the same time make every effort to bring about a settlement of the dispute so the mills can be returned to their private owners as soon as possible.

Twelve days passed without action by Congress. On April 21, 1952, the President sent a letter to the President of the Senate in which he again described the purpose and need for his action and again stated his position that "The Congress can, if it wishes, reject the course of action I have followed in this matter." Congress has not so acted to this date. . . .

Secretary of Defense Lovett swore that "a work stoppage in the steel industry will result immediately in serious curtailment of production of essential weapons and munitions of all kinds." He illustrated by showing that 84% of the national production of certain alloy steel is currently used for production of military-end items and that 35% of total production of another form of steel goes into ammunition, 80% of such ammunition now going to Korea. The Secretary of Defense stated that: "We are holding the line [in Korea] with ammunition and not with the lives of our troops." . . . Even ignoring for the moment whatever confidential information the President may possess as "the Nation's organ for foreign affairs," the uncontroverted affidavits in this record amply support the finding that "a work stoppage would immediately jeopardize and imperil our national defense." . . .

A review of executive action demonstrates that our Presidents have on many occasions exhibited the leadership contemplated by the Framers when they made the President Commander in Chief, and imposed upon him the trust to "take Care that the Laws be faithfully executed." With or without explicit statutory authorization, Presidents have at such times dealt with national emergencies by acting promptly and resolutely to enforce legislative programs, at least to save those programs until Congress could act. Congress and the courts have responded to such executive initiative with consistent approval. . . .

[Chief Justice Vinson then invoked presidential precedents, such as President Washington's Neutrality Proclamation, President Jefferson's Louisiana Purchase, the Monroe Doctrine, actions by President Lincoln including the seizure of rail and telegraph lines around the capital, President Hayes's use of federal troops to suppress the Railroad Strike of 1877, President Wilson's establishment of a War Labor Board to prevent strikes, and actions by President Franklin Roosevelt including the seizure of an aviation plant in California six months before Pearl Harbor and the seizure of coal mines in 1943.—Editors]

This is but a cursory summary of executive leadership. But it amply demonstrates that Presidents have taken prompt action to enforce the laws and protect the country whether or not Congress happened to provide in advance for the particular method of execution. At the minimum, the executive actions reviewed herein sustain the action of the President in this case. And many of the cited examples of Presidential practice go far beyond the extent of power necessary to sustain the President's order to seize the steel mills. The fact that temporary executive seizures of industrial plants to meet an emergency have not been directly tested in this Court furnishes not the slightest suggestion that such actions have been illegal. Rather, the fact that Congress and the courts have consistently recognized and given their support to such executive action indicates that such a power of seizure has been accepted throughout our history.

History bears out the genius of the Founding Fathers, who created a Government subject to law but not left subject to inertia when vigor and initiative are required.

Focusing now on the situation confronting the President on the night of April 8, 1952, we cannot but conclude that the President was performing his duty under the Constitution to "take Care that the Laws be faithfully executed"—a duty described by President Benjamin Harrison as "the central idea of the office." . . .

Whatever the extent of Presidential power on more tranquil occasions, and whatever the right of the President to execute legislative programs as he sees fit without reporting the mode of execution to Congress, the single Presidential purpose disclosed on this record is to faithfully execute the laws by acting in an emergency to maintain the status quo, thereby preventing collapse of the legislative programs until Congress could act. The President's action served the same purposes as a judicial stay entered to maintain the status quo in order to preserve the jurisdiction of a court. In his Message to Congress immediately following the seizure, the President explained the necessity of his action in executing the military procurement and anti-inflation legislative programs and expressed his desire to cooperate with any legislative proposals approving, regulating or rejecting the seizure of the steel mills. Consequently, there is no evidence whatever of any Presidential purpose to defy Congress or act in any way inconsistent with the legislative will. . . .

The Framers knew, as we should know in these times of peril, that there is real danger in Executive weakness. There is no cause to fear Executive tyranny so long as the laws of Congress are being faithfully executed. Certainly there is no basis for fear of dictatorship when the Executive acts, as he did in this case, only to save the situation until Congress could act. . . .

The broad executive power granted by Article II to an officer on duty 365 days a year cannot, it is said, be invoked to avert disaster. Instead, the President must confine himself to sending a message to Congress recommending action. Under this messenger-boy concept of the Office, the President cannot even act to preserve legislative programs from destruction so that Congress will have something left to act upon. . . .

Seizure of plaintiffs' property is not a pleasant undertaking. Similarly unpleasant to a free country are the draft which disrupts the home and military procurement which causes economic dislocation and compels adoption of price controls, wage stabilization and allocation of materials. The President informed Congress that even a temporary Government operation of plaintiffs' properties was "thoroughly distasteful" to him, but was necessary to prevent immediate paralysis of the mobilization program. . . . A sturdy judiciary should not be swayed by the unpleasantness or unpopularity of necessary executive action, but must independently determine for itself whether the President was acting, as required by the Constitution, to "take Care that the Laws be faithfully executed."

. . . No basis for claims of arbitrary action, unlimited powers or dictatorial usurpation of congressional power appears from the facts of this case. On the contrary, judicial, legislative and executive precedents throughout our history demonstrate that in this case the President acted in full conformity with his duties under the Constitution. Accordingly, we would reverse the order of the District Court.

NOTES

1.   What is the dominant type of constitutional argument in each opinion? Which opinions are more flexible and which are more categorical? (In their own ways the opinions of Justice Black and Justice Jackson are categorical—the former categorizing powers as executive or legislative, and the latter categorizing situations as ones in which the president acts with Congress's support, in the face of Congress's silence, or over Congress's disapproval.) Which opinion is most persuasive to you? Why?

2.   Justice Black reads the three vesting clauses more literally. He thinks the grant of the executive power to the president and of all legislative power to Congress means that the president has no inherent power to respond to emergencies or to deal with foreign affairs. There is no presidential prerogative power. Is Justice Black's reading of the text plausible?

3.   Both Justice Frankfurter and Chief Justice Vinson cite past practice, but it leads them to different conclusions. Who has the better argument? How useful was practice as a guide when humanity seemed on the brink of another world war or even a nuclear apocalypse? Every emergency is unique, and the president who had access to all our military and intelligence secrets thought this one was really bad. Should the Court have deferred to the president because he had more information?

4.   If the Constitution had a clause granting the executive "emergency powers," would that make the nation more secure in a crisis, or would it be inimical to the very idea of constitutional governance? (The constitution of the Weimar Republic actually had an emergency-powers clause, and its abuse helped bring Adolf Hitler to power.) Would such a clause be less dangerous if there had to be a resolution by two-thirds of both houses of Congress declaring a state of emergency? Is the U.S. Constitution's studied ambiguity on emergency power a good thing? Is the threat of eventual impeachment and removal from office a sufficient check on the executive?

The Constitution creates the separation of powers. But from the beginning, James Madison recognized that the success of the system of separated powers depends on more than a piece of paper. In *The Federalist No. 48*, he asked: "Will it be sufficient to mark, with precision, the boundaries of these departments, in the constitution of the government, and to trust to these parchment barriers against the encroaching spirit of power?" He was troubled: "experience assures us, that the efficacy of the provision has been greatly overrated; and that some more adequate defense is indispensably necessary for the more feeble, against the more powerful, members of the government."

In *The Federalist No. 51*, Madison sketched out his solution. To endure over time, the separation of powers had to be made to protect itself: "the great security against a gradual concentration of the several powers in the same department, consists in giving to those who administer each department the necessary constitutional means and personal motives to resist encroachments of the others." How could this be done? "Ambition must be made to counteract ambition. The interest of the man must be connected with the constitutional rights of the place."

Does this sound unduly pessimistic? Here is Madison, again from *The Federalist No. 51*: "It may be a reflection on human nature, that such devices should be necessary to control the abuses of government. But what is government itself, but the greatest of all reflections on human nature? If men were angels, no government would be necessary. If angels were to govern men, neither external nor internal controls on government would be necessary. In framing a government which is to be administered by men over men, the great difficulty lies in this: you must first enable the government to control the governed; and in the next place oblige it to control itself."

As you read on and learn about the separation of powers in the U.S. Constitution, keep in mind Madison's vision. The public officials and judges you will encounter on these pages were not angels. Look for their ambition. Look for the ambition of each branch counteracting the ambition of the others. Keep thinking about the system of checks and balances. Is this an ingenious way to maintain the rule of law? Is it an inefficient waste of time and effort? Is it an invitation to dangerous brinksmanship? Is there, ultimately, any better way?

[Assignment 5]

I.   ARTICLE I: THE LEGISLATIVE POWER

A Map of Article I

> *§ 1: All legislative Powers herein granted shall be vested in a Congress of the United States, which shall consist of a Senate and House of Representatives.*

The first section of Article I is an introduction and a statement of substantive principles.

First, Congress is not granted a general legislative power over every subject, but is instead granted only certain legislative powers—the ones "herein granted." Most of those enumerated legislative powers are specified in Article I, Section 8.

Second, the fact that these powers are vested in Congress raises the question of whether Congress can give away those powers. This question is about the delegation of legislative powers. In other words, through the Constitution the people have delegated certain powers to Congress, and the question is whether Congress can then delegate (or "subdelegate") those powers to other actors.

Third, this section introduces the bicameral (or "two-house") structure of Congress. As described in Section 7, to become law a bill must pass both houses.

§ 2: The House of Representatives. . . .

This section describes the House: its mode of election, the qualifications of its members, the method for apportioning representation among the states, and the power of the House to select its officers. It also gives to the House "the sole power of impeachment."

§ 3: The Senate of the United States. . . .

This section describes the Senate: its composition, terms of office, mode of selection (until changed by the Seventeenth Amendment), qualifications, officers, and power to "try all Impeachments."

§ 4: The Times, Places and Manner of holding Elections for Senators and Representatives. . . .

This section provides that each state will prescribe the procedures for the election of its own representatives and senators, but subject to Congress's alterations.

§ 5: Each House shall. . . .

This section provides that each house judges the elections and qualifications of its members, determines its own rules of proceedings, and may punish and expel its members. Each house must keep a journal of its proceedings, and neither can adjourn for more than three days without the consent of the other.

§ 6: The Senators and Representatives shall receive a Compensation. . . .

This section provides that senators and representatives receive a salary "ascertained by law." (The Twenty-seventh Amendment provides that no law varying compensation may take effect without an intervening election.) They may not be arrested while going back and forth to Congress, except for "Treason, Felony and Breach of the Peace." Nor may they be appointed to any executive or judicial office that was created (or which had its "Emoluments" increased) during the term for which they were elected. No executive or judicial officer may be a member of Congress.

§ 7: All Bills. . . .

This section prescribes how Congress may enact laws. Bills for raising revenue must originate in the House of Representatives. Every bill must pass both houses and be approved or vetoed by the president. A veto may be overridden by a two-thirds vote of both houses.

§ 8: The Congress shall have Power. . . .

This section contains the famous enumeration of Congress's legislative powers in eighteen separate paragraphs. (These powers often raise questions of federalism, and are considered in detail in Chapter 3.) Although these eighteen clauses define, and thus limit, federal power, some of the enumerations are very broad.

> *§ 9: No Bill. . . . No Preference . . . No Title of Nobility. . . .*

This section lists things that Congress may *not* do with its enumerated legislative powers, including prohibition of the slave trade before 1808, suspension of the writ of habeas corpus outside of certain emergencies, and the enactment of bills of attainder and ex post facto laws. Nor may Congress enact certain commercial regulations, such as export taxes or discriminatory treatment of state ports. Finally, and anticlimactically, Congress may not grant a "Title of Nobility."

> *§ 10: No State shall. . . .*

This section lists things that the states may not do, or that they may do only with congressional consent. This section's placement in Article I can perhaps be explained by the fact that many of the things this section forbids the states to do are the very things that Congress is authorized to do by Article I, Section 8 (e.g., coin money).

A. LEGISLATIVE SPECIFICITY AND DELEGATION: "SHALL BE VESTED IN A CONGRESS OF THE UNITED STATES"

Art. I, § 1: All legislative Powers herein granted shall be vested in a Congress of the United States, which shall consist of a Senate and House of Representatives.

Does Article I's assignment to Congress of the enumerated legislative powers preclude it from delegating the exercise of those powers to someone else? The body of law answering this question is sometimes referred to as the "non-delegation doctrine."

Consider this question for yourself, using the following two case studies. The first is a debate from 1791 in the second session of Congress. The debate concerned whether Congress, in implementing its power under Article I, Section 8 to "establish Post Offices and post Roads," could assign to the president the task of specifying the particular post offices and roads to be built. The second case study is *Mistretta v. United States*, 488 U.S. 361 (1989), which represents the modern retreat from the non-delegation doctrine. *Mistretta* upheld a broad delegation by Congress to the U.S. Sentencing Commission under the modern rule: Congress may delegate its legislative powers as long as it provides an "intelligible principle" to guide the discretion of the delegatee. As you read the positions in the Post Roads Debate and the opinions in *Mistretta*, ask yourself which (if any) of these views makes sense. Is there a better one?

The Post Roads Debate

House of Representatives, December 6–8, 1791 (3 Annals of Cong. 229–41)

The House resolved itself into a Committee of the Whole House on the bill for establishing the Post Office and Post Roads within the United States.

Mr. SEDGWICK moved to strike out all that clause of the bill which designated the roads, and to insert, instead thereof, these words, *"by such route as the President of the United States shall, from time to time, cause to be established."*

It had appeared, he said, to be the sense of the House, when this subject was formerly under consideration, that the demarkation of the particular roads should be intrusted to the Executive; the only difference had been with respect to the mode of expression—but the effect was still to have been the same—some gentlemen thinking it best to leave the details of this business entirely to the supreme Executive, others wishing to name the Postmaster General. The members of the House could not be supposed to possess every information that might be requisite on this subject, and their opinions were liable to be biassed by local interests. He had ever considered it as highly incumbent on the House to give the people every possible information on public concerns; but in this, as in every other subject, he thought it sufficient that the House should establish the principle, and then leave it to the Executive to carry it into effect.

Mr. LIVERMORE observed that the Legislative body being empowered by the Constitution "to establish post offices and post roads," it is as clearly their duty to designate the roads as to establish the offices; and he did not think they could with propriety delegate that power, which they were themselves appointed to exercise. Some gentlemen, he knew, were of opinion that the business of the United States could be better transacted by a single person than by many; but this was not the intention of the Constitution. It was provided that the Government should be administered by Representatives, of the people's choice; so that every man, who has the right of voting, shall be in some measure concerned in making every law for the United States. The establishment of post roads he considered as a very important object. . . . If the post office were to be regulated by the will of a single person, the dissemination of intelligence might be impeded, and the people kept entirely in the dark with respect to the transactions of Government; or the Postmaster, if vested with the whole power, might branch out the offices to such a degree as to make them prove a heavy burden to the United States. . . . The most material point, in his opinion, was to determine the road itself; if the House gave up that, they might as well leave all the rest of the business to the discretion of the Postmaster, and permit him to settle the rates of postage, and every other particular relative to the post office, by saying, at once, "there shall be a Postmaster General, who shall have the whole government of the post office, under such regulations as he from time to time shall be pleased to enact."

Mr. SEDGWICK felt himself by no means disposed to resign all the business of the House to the President, or to any one else; but he thought that the Executive part of the business ought to be left to Executive officers. He did not, for his part, know the particular circumstances of population, geography, &c., which had been taken into the calculation by the select committee, when they pointed out the roads delineated in the bill; but he would ask, whether they understood the subject so thoroughly as the Executive officer would, who being responsible to the people for the proper discharge of the trust reposed in him, must use his utmost diligence in order to a satisfactory execution of the delegated power? As to the constitutionality of this delegation, it was admitted by the committee themselves who brought in the bill. . . .

Congress, he observed, are authorized not only to establish post offices and post roads, but also to borrow money; but is it understood that Congress are to go in a body to borrow every sum that may he requisite? Is it not rather their office to determine the principle on which the business is to be conducted, and then delegate the power of carrying their resolves into execution? They are also empowered to coin money, and if no part of their power be delegable, he did not know but they might be obliged to turn coiners, and work in the Mint themselves. Nay, they must even act the part of executioners, in punishing piracies committed on the high seas. In the delegation of power, the whole purpose, in his opinion, is answered, when the rules by which the business is to be conducted are pointed out by law; nor could he discover anything in the Constitution to restrict the House from adopting this mode of conducting business.

Mr. HARTLEY.—I cannot agree with the gentleman from Massachusetts, that as often as this business had been agitated, there had been a majority in the House in favor of leaving it to the Executive to designate the post roads. Nay, so far as my recollection (which is perhaps not so good as that gentleman's) serves me, we uniformly have had a majority for Congress to point out the post roads.

The Constitution seems to have intended that we should exercise all the powers respecting the establishing [of] post roads we are capable of; but the gentleman says we are not competent to this duty, that it must be intrusted to the Executive.

Sir, in many questions concerning the property or geography of the United States, we had full information on this floor from every quarter. The people's interests and circumstances have been known, however distinctly or differently situated. . . .

We represent the people[;] we are constitutionally vested with the power of determining upon the establishment of post roads; and, as I understand at present, ought not to delegate the power to any other person.

A General Post Office is intended to be established by the bill, and the collection of the revenue is put under the superintendence of a Postmaster General; the minutiae is submitted to him. I should imagine there ought to be a limitation of the law in point of time, say three, four, or five years; when we come to the proper place, a motion to that purpose may be made. No one in the United States has a greater respect for the President than myself, and I hold that the several Departments are filled with gentlemen of the first abilities and fitness, but we are not to confine ourselves to a view of the moment. This bill has the complexion of a perpetual law; we must have some regard to consequences. If the amendment takes place, the office as well as revenue will be thrown into the power of the Executive, who may increase the roads and offices as far as the revenues go. The revenue of the post office is at present not great, but if proper seeds are now sown, it may hereafter be productive. In Great Britain, much has been obtained from the post office, and most of the European nations count upon it as a considerable branch of revenue. Will it be prudent for us to grant this power to the Executive, in the latitude contended for? We must not suppose that this country will always remain incorrupt; we shall share the fate of other nations. Through the medium of the post office a weighty influence may be obtained by the Executive; this is guarded against in England by prohibiting officers in the Post Office Department from interfering at elections. There is no such guard or caution in the present bill. . . . This is a law of experiment, let us try it a few years. If, upon experience, we find ourselves incompetent to the duty, we must (if the Constitution will admit) grant the power to the Executive; or, if the Constitution will not allow such a delegation, submit the article for amendment in a constitutional way. I am against the amendment.

Mr. B. BOURNE was in favor of the amendment, which he thought both expedient and constitutional. In speaking of *post offices and post roads* the Constitution, he observed, speaks in general terms, as it does of *a mint, excises,* &c. In passing the excise law, the House, not thinking themselves possessed of sufficient information, empowered the President to mark out the districts and surveys; and if they had a right to delegate such power to the Executive, the further delegation of the power of marking out the roads for the conveyance of the mail, could hardly be thought dangerous. The Constitution meant no more than that Congress should possess the exclusive right of doing that, by themselves or by any other person, which amounts to the same thing. The business he thought much more likely to be well executed by the President, or the Postmaster General, than by Congress. He had himself been of the committee who framed the bill, but could not tell whether the roads marked out in it were better than any other, except so far as relates to the State which he represents; and he imagined the other members of the committee were in a similar predicament. The President having opportunities of obtaining information from the different members of the House, from the Postmaster General, and from others, will be more competent to determine the proper road. It will be occasionally necessary to change the route, and lay out new roads, and he could see no inconvenience from intrusting either the President or the Postmaster General with the necessary powers for these purposes. At all events, the House could guard against any apprehended danger, by the insertion of such a clause as had been proposed, [by Mr. HARTLEY,] limiting the operation of the bill to three, four, or five years. At the expiration of that term, the power would revert to Congress, and they might then retain the exercise of it in their own hands, if they found that any improper use had been made of it.

Mr. WHITE made several observations on the expediency and constitutionality of the measure. No individual could possess an equal share of information with that House on the subject of the geography of the United States. He disapproved of the amendment for many other reasons, and particularly its approximation to the custom of England. Such advances towards Monarchy, if not checked in season, he was apprehensive would tend to unhinge the present Government. If this Government retains its present Republican form, it will be owing to the members of this House. It is easy to see what hand could be made of the post offices, if ever they are under the direction of an improper person. At the time of a general election, for instance, how easy would it be for this man to dictate to particular towns and villages, "If you do not send such a man to Congress, you shall have no post office; but if you elect my friend, you shall have a post office, and the roads shall be run agreeably to your wishes." Another improper use may be made of this power by the interception of letters, and checking the regular channel of information throughout the country. Upon the whole, he was clearly for rejecting the motion for striking out the words in the bill. . . .

Mr. PAGE.—If the motion before the committee succeeds, I shall make one which will save a deal of time and money, by making a short session of it; for if this House can, with propriety, leave the business of the post office to the President, it may leave to him any other business of legislation; and I may move to adjourn and leave all the objects of legislation to his sole consideration and direction. But how the President should be better acquainted with the proper places for post offices and post roads than the Representatives of the people, I cannot conceive. In Virginia, for instance, cannot the ten Representatives say, with more certainty, what post roads would be proper in that State than any one man? I look upon the motion as unconstitutional, and if it were not so, as having a mischievous tendency, which I am willing to believe the member who made it is not aware of. . . .

Mr. VINING said[:] . . . With regard to the regulation being given to the President, two things should be considered; to a good President it would be a burden; to a bad President, a dangerous power of esstablishing [sic] offices and roads in those places only where his interest would be promoted, and removing others of long standing, in order to harrass [sic] those he might suppose inimical to his ambitious views. The Constitution has certainly given us the power of establishing posts and roads, and it is not even implied that it should be transferred to the President; his powers are well defined; we create offices, and he fills them with such persons as he approves of, with the advice of the Senate. . . .

Mr. BARNWELL was not surprised that a diversity of opinions should prevail on such a subject; but that there should be any question respecting the constitutionality of the amendment astonished him. It was very natural to suppose members from the same State would differ in opinion, and this showed the greater degree of necessity there was to vest the power in the hands of a high responsible officer to determine upon it; for, by doing so, there would be less partiality exhibited in the delineation of the roads, & c. But, if left to the House, it would be almost impossible to reconcile any line to all parties; for the members from each State would probably be guided more by the principle of domestic convenience than by a sense of general good. In reply to Mr. V.'s argument, that it would be a burden to a good President, he thought it would be a pleasure to him to render service to his country. Upon the whole, he was in favor of Mr. SEDGWICK'S motion. . . .

Mr. BENSON observed, that the constitutionality of the amendment is denied, and it is said that the Legislature alone is competent to establish post offices and post roads; notwithstanding this, there is not a single post office designated by the bill. Much has been observed respecting the Legislative and Executive powers, and the committee are cautioned against delegating the powers of the Legislature to the Supreme Executive. Without attempting a definition of their powers, or determining their respective limits, which he conceived it was extremely difficult to do, he would only observe that much must necessarily be left to the discretion of the Legislature. He was very doubtful whether it would ever be in the power of the House to form any bill that would give satisfaction. This he spoke from experience; for it had been often tried in the old Congress, and was as often defeated by the partial and local clauses proposed by the different members. For these reasons, he believed it would be better to delegate the power, and let the regulations be made by the President, than to be enacting supplementary laws year after year, at the instance of individual members.

The Committee now rose, and obtained leave to sit again. . . .

Wednesday, December 7. . . .

The House again resolved itself into a Committee of the Whole House on the bill establishing the Post Office and Post Roads, within the United States. Mr. SEDGWICK'S motion being under consideration. . . .

Mr. MADISON said, that the arguments which are offered by the gentleman who are in favor of the amendment, appear to be drawn rather from theory than any line of practice which had hitherto governed the House. However difficult it may be to determine with precision the exact boundaries of the Legislative and Executive powers, he was of opinion that those arguments were not well founded, for they admit of such construction as will lead to blending those powers so as to leave no line of separation whatever. The greatest obstacle to the due exercise of the powers vested in the Legislature by the bill, which has been mentioned, is the difficulty of accommodating the regulations to the various interests of the different parts of the Union; and this is said to be almost impracticable. But it may be remembered, that similar embarrassments appeared when the impost and tonnage bills were under consideration; on those subjects, the members were obliged to be governed, in a great degree, by mutual information and reciprocal confidence. In respect to the establishment and arrangements of the different ports of entry and clearance, and other objects, that was a business of much greater importance and difficulty than this; but it was accomplished. . . . Where is the necessity of departing from the principles of the Constitution in respect to the post office and post roads, more than in all other cases? The subject is expressly committed to Legislative determination by the Constitution. If the second section of the bill requires amendment, it can be rectified when it comes before us; and with respect to future cases, should there be a necessity for additional post roads, they can be provided for by supplementary laws; and therefore no reason on that account can be urged for delaying the provision proposed by the bill. He concluded by saying, that there did not appear to be any necessity for alienating the powers of the House; and that if this should take place, it would be a violation of the Constitution.

Mr. SEDGWICK would make a few observations, which he felt himself obliged to submit to the consideration of the Committee as well to defend himself as his motion from the unwarrantable attacks which gentlemen had made on both.

The powers of the Constitution, he was sorry to say, were made in debate to extend or contract, as seemed, for the time being, to suit the convenience of the arguments of gentlemen. . . . It was true, as had been observed by his friend from New York, [Mr. BENSON] that it was impossible precisely to define a boundary line between the business of Legislative and Executive; but from his own experience, as a public man, and from reflection, he was induced to believe, that as a general rule, the establishment of principles was the peculiar province of the former, and the execution of them, that of the latter. He would, therefore, at least, generally, as much, as possible, avoid going into detail. . . . From the nature of the business to be transacted, he had drawn his conclusion; he thought an Executive officer, responsible to the public for the performance of an important and interesting trust, would inquire with more scrupulous caution, and decide with more justice, than could be expected from a popular assembly, who, from the nature of things, would be more remiss than consisted with a just determination; and he appealed to those gentlemen who were members of the last House, for a recollection of that apathy and torpor which prevailed on a former attempt to demark the post roads. . . . Gentlemen had spoken in strong terms of the disinterestedness, information, and respectability of the members of the House, and of the popular confidence which resulted therefrom. No man had a more respectable opinion of the Representatives of the people than himself; he need not, however, observe to them, that they were men, subject to like passions and imperfections with their fellow-citizens. It could not have escaped the reflection of the committee, that the gentlemen who composed it, had a very important interest in establishing the directions of the post; that on the declarations of men thus interested, we must rely for the justness of our ultimate conclusions; on evidence of interested individuals, individuals who are, by their relation to the subject of inquiry, excluded, on principles of law, from all credit, must we rely for a knowledge of those facts which are to direct our judgment.

Mr. BOUDINOT and Mr. GERRY made some remarks, and then the question being taken, Mr. SEDGWICK'S motion was negatived.

NOTES

1.   What was Representative Sedgwick's theory of delegation? (Recall that "in this, as in every other subject, he thought it sufficient that the House should establish the principle, and then leave it to the Executive to carry it into effect.") Did Sedgwick think that Congress could delegate its legislative power, or did he think that the post roads bill was *not* a delegation?

2.   Because Sedgwick's motion to amend the bill was voted down, that means that Representative Madison and other opponents of the delegation "won" the debate, in a sense. What kind of precedent should that set for future controversies over the delegation of legislative power?

A NOTE ON *SCHECHTER POULTRY*

In two cases in 1935 the Supreme Court found that a delegation of legislative power was unconstitutional: *Panama Refining Co. v. Ryan*, 293 U.S. 388 (1935), and *A.L.A. Schechter Poultry Corp v. United States*, 295 U.S. 495 (1935). This is the first—and last—year in which the Supreme Court has found a non-delegation violation, giving rise to the quip that the "doctrine has had one good year, and 211 bad ones (and counting)." Cass R. Sunstein, *Nondelegation Canons*, 67 U. Chi. L. Rev. 315, 322 (2000). In cases before and after 1935, the Supreme Court would uniformly conclude that statutes were not forbidden delegations to the executive because they contained an "intelligible principle"—that is, a standard by which the executive's conduct could be judged. But the two statutes it considered in 1935 did not satisfy that requirement.

In the second of these two cases, *Schechter Poultry*, the Court heard challenges to the "Live Poultry Code," promulgated under Section 3 of the National Industrial Recovery Act, which was part of the New Deal. Under Section 3, trade groups could propose "codes of fair competition" to the president, who could choose to render them legally binding if he found that the group was "truly representative" of the industry and the code was "not designed to promote monopolies or to eliminate or oppress small enterprises." The president was given further discretion to "impose such conditions . . . for the protection of consumers, competitors, employees, and others, and in furtherance of the public interest, and . . . provide such exceptions to and exemptions from the provisions of such code, as the President in his discretion deems necessary to effectuate the policy herein declared." President Roosevelt had made binding the poultry industry's code, and when the Schechters violated that code, they and their company were convicted of nineteen violations of the National Industrial Recovery Act, which provided a fine of up to $500 per violation.

In a unanimous opinion, written by Chief Justice Hughes, the Court found this delegation invalid and overturned their convictions and fines. He wrote:

> Section 3 of the Recovery Act is without precedent. It supplies no standards for any trade, industry, or activity. It does not undertake to prescribe rules of conduct to be applied to particular states of fact determined by appropriate administrative procedure. Instead of prescribing rules of conduct, it authorizes

the making of codes to prescribe them. . . . [T]he discretion of the President in approving or prescribing codes, and thus enacting laws for the government of trade and industry throughout the country, is virtually unfettered. We think that the code-making authority thus conferred is an unconstitutional delegation of legislative power.

Some regard *Schechter Poultry* as a landmark victory for civil liberties and a vindication of limited government. Others regard it as a sign of an activist court run amok and a demonstration that the non-delegation doctrine is difficult to apply consistently. Consider those views as you turn to the next case.

Mistretta v. United States

488 U.S. 361 (1989)

■ JUSTICE BLACKMUN delivered the opinion of the Court.

In this litigation, we granted certiorari . . . to consider the constitutionality of the Sentencing Guidelines promulgated by the United States Sentencing Commission. The Commission is a body created under the Sentencing Reform Act of 1984 . . .

[The Act attempted to eliminate inequalities in the sentencing of criminal defendants. It did so by requiring the promulgation of new "Sentencing Guidelines" which fixed the sentences for federal crimes. The Guidelines contain hundreds of pages of rules for different offenses and different offenders. Numbers would be calculated based on the circumstances of each case, and then run through a matrix that yielded the appropriate sentencing range. In Mistretta's case, the range was 15–21 months, and he was given a sentence of 18 months.

The Sentencing Commission was in charge of promulgating these rules and amending them under the criteria discussed below. A later decision under the Sixth Amendment, United States v. Booker, *543 U.S. 220 (2005), held that the Guidelines are merely "advisory," but to this day they remain an important part of calculating every federal criminal sentence.—Editors]*

The Commission is established "as an independent commission in the judicial branch of the United States." It has seven voting members (one of whom is the Chairman) appointed by the President "by and with the advice and consent of the Senate." "At least three of the members shall be Federal judges selected after considering a list of six judges recommended to the President by the Judicial Conference of the United States." No more than four members of the Commission shall be members of the same political party. The Attorney General, or his designee, is an ex officio nonvoting member. The Chairman and other members of the Commission are subject to removal by the President "only for neglect of duty or malfeasance in office or for other good cause shown." Except for initial staggering of terms, a voting member serves for six years and may not serve more than two full terms. . . .

Petitioner argues that in delegating the power to promulgate sentencing guidelines for every federal criminal offense to an independent Sentencing Commission, Congress has granted the Commission excessive legislative discretion in violation of the constitutionally based nondelegation doctrine. We do not agree.

The nondelegation doctrine is rooted in the principle of separation of powers that underlies our tripartite system of Government. The Constitution provides that "[a]ll legislative Powers herein granted shall be vested in a Congress of the United States," U.S. Const., Art. I, § 1, and we long have insisted that "the integrity and maintenance of the system of government ordained by the Constitution" mandate that Congress generally cannot delegate its legislative power to another Branch. *Field v. Clark*, 143 U.S. 649, 692 (1892). We also have recognized, however, that the separation-of-powers principle, and the nondelegation doctrine in particular, do not prevent Congress from obtaining the assistance of its coordinate Branches. In a passage now enshrined in our jurisprudence, Chief Justice Taft, writing for the Court, explained our approach to such cooperative ventures: "In determining what [Congress] may do in seeking assistance from another branch, the extent and character of that assistance must be fixed according to common sense and the inherent necessities of the government co-ordination." *J. W. Hampton, Jr., & Co. v. United States*, 276 U.S. 394, 406 (1928). So long as Congress "shall lay down by legislative act an intelligible principle to which the person or body authorized to [exercise the delegated authority] is directed to conform, such legislative action is not a forbidden delegation of legislative power." *Id.*, at 409.

Applying this "intelligible principle" test to congressional delegations, our jurisprudence has been driven by a practical understanding that in our increasingly complex society, replete with ever changing and more technical problems, Congress simply cannot do its job absent an ability to delegate power under broad general directives. . . .

Until 1935, this Court never struck down a challenged statute on delegation grounds. After invalidating in 1935 two statutes as excessive delegations, see *A.L.A. Schechter Poultry Corp. v. United States*, 295 U.S. 495, and *Panama Refining Co. v. Ryan*, 293 U.S. 388, we have upheld, again without deviation, Congress' ability to delegate power under broad standards.

In light of our approval of these broad delegations, we harbor no doubt that Congress' delegation of authority to the Sentencing Commission is sufficiently specific and detailed to meet constitutional requirements. Congress charged the Commission with three goals: to "assure the meeting of the purposes of sentencing as set forth" in the Act; to "provide certainty and fairness in meeting the purposes of sentencing, avoiding unwarranted sentencing disparities among defendants with similar records . . . while maintaining sufficient flexibility to permit individualized sentences," where appropriate; and to "reflect, to the extent practicable, advancement in knowledge of human behavior as it relates to the criminal justice process." Congress further specified four "purposes" of sentencing that the Commission must pursue in carrying out its mandate: "to reflect the seriousness of the offense, to promote respect for the law, and to provide just punishment for the offense"; "to afford adequate deterrence to criminal conduct"; "to protect the public from further crimes of the defendant"; and "to provide the defendant with needed . . . correctional treatment."

In addition, Congress prescribed the specific tool—the guidelines system—for the Commission to use in regulating sentencing. More particularly, Congress directed the Commission to develop a system of "sentencing ranges" applicable "for each category of offense involving each category of defendant." Congress instructed the Commission that these sentencing ranges must be consistent with pertinent provisions of Title 18 of the United States Code and could not include sentences in excess of the statutory maxima. Congress also required that for sentences of imprisonment, "the maximum of the range established for such a term shall not exceed the minimum of that range by more than the greater of 25 percent or 6 months, except that, if the minimum term of the range is 30 years or more, the maximum may be life imprisonment." Moreover, Congress directed the Commission to use current average sentences "as a starting point" for its structuring of the sentencing ranges.

To guide the Commission in its formulation of offense categories, Congress directed it to consider seven factors: the grade of the offense; the aggravating and mitigating circumstances of the crime; the nature and degree of the harm caused by the crime; the community view of the gravity of the offense; the public concern generated by the crime; the deterrent effect that a particular sentence may have on others; and the current incidence of the offense. Congress set forth 11 factors for the Commission to consider in establishing categories of defendants. These include the offender's age, education, vocational skills, mental and emotional condition, physical condition (including drug dependence), previous employment record, family ties and responsibilities, community ties, role in the offense, criminal history, and degree of dependence upon crime for a livelihood. Congress also prohibited the Commission from considering the "race, sex, national origin, creed, and socioeconomic status of offenders," and instructed that the guidelines should reflect the "general inappropriateness" of considering certain other factors, such as current unemployment, that might serve as proxies for forbidden factors.

In addition to these overarching constraints, Congress provided even more detailed guidance to the Commission about categories of offenses and offender characteristics. . . .

We cannot dispute petitioner's contention that the Commission enjoys significant discretion in formulating guidelines. The Commission does have discretionary authority to determine the relative severity of federal crimes and to assess the relative weight of the offender characteristics that Congress listed for the Commission to consider. See §§ 994(c) and (d) (Commission instructed to consider enumerated factors as it deems them to be relevant). The Commission also has significant discretion to determine which crimes have been punished too leniently, and which too severely. Congress has called upon the Commission to exercise its judgment about which types of crimes and which types of criminals are to be considered similar for the purposes of sentencing.

But our cases do not at all suggest that delegations of this type may not carry with them the need to exercise judgment on matters of policy. In *Yakus v. United States*, 321 U.S. 414 (1944), the Court upheld a delegation to the Price Administrator to fix commodity prices that "in his judgment will be generally fair and equitable and will effectuate the purposes of this Act" to stabilize prices and avert speculation. In *National Broadcasting Co. v. United States*, 319 U.S. 190 (1943), we upheld a delegation to the Federal Communications Commission granting it the authority to promulgate regulations in accordance with its view of the "public interest." . . .

Congress has met [the applicable] standard here. The Act sets forth more than merely an "intelligible principle" or minimal standards. One court has aptly put it: "The statute outlines the policies which prompted establishment of the Commission, explains what the Commission should do and how it should do it, and sets out specific directives to govern particular situations." *United States v. Chambless*, 680 F.Supp.793, 796 (E.D. La. 1988).

Developing proportionate penalties for hundreds of different crimes by a virtually limitless array of offenders is precisely the sort of intricate, labor-intensive task for which delegation to an expert body is especially appropriate. Although Congress has delegated significant discretion to the Commission to draw judgments from its analysis of existing sentencing practice and alternative sentencing models, "Congress is not confined to that method of executing its policy which involves the least possible delegation of discretion to administrative officers." *Yakus v. United States*, at 425–426. We have no doubt that in the hands of the Commission "the criteria which Congress has supplied are wholly adequate for carrying out the general policy and purpose" of the Act. *Sunshine Coal Co. v. Adkins*, 310 U.S. 381, 398 (1940). . . .

■ JUSTICE SCALIA, dissenting.

While the products of the Sentencing Commission's labors have been given the modest name "Guidelines," they have the force and effect of laws, prescribing the sentences criminal defendants are to receive. A judge who disregards them will be reversed. I dissent from today's decision because I can find no place within our constitutional system for an agency created by Congress to exercise no governmental power other than the making of laws.

There is no doubt that the Sentencing Commission has established significant, legally binding prescriptions governing application of governmental power against private individuals—indeed, application of the ultimate governmental power, short of capital punishment. Statutorily permissible sentences for particular crimes cover as broad a range as zero years to life, see, *e.g.*, 18 U.S.C. § 1201 (1982 ed. and Supp. IV) (kidnaping), and within those ranges the Commission was given broad discretion to prescribe the "correct" sentence. . . .

The Commission also determined when probation was permissible, imposing a strict system of controls because of its judgment that probation had been used for an "inappropriately high percentage of offenders guilty of certain economic crimes." . . . Congress also gave the Commission discretion to determine whether 7 specified characteristics of offenses, and 11 specified characteristics of offenders, "have any relevance," and should be included among the factors varying the sentence. Of the latter, it included only three among the factors required to be considered, and declared the remainder not ordinarily relevant.

It should be apparent from the above that the decisions made by the Commission are far from technical, but are heavily laden (or ought to be) with value judgments and policy assessments. This fact is sharply reflected in the Commission's product, as described by the dissenting Commissioner:

> Under the guidelines, the judge could give the same sentence for abusive sexual contact that puts the child in fear as for unlawfully entering or remaining in the United States. Similarly, the guidelines permit equivalent sentences for the following pairs of offenses: drug trafficking and a violation of the Wild Free-Roaming Horses and Burros Act; arson with a destructive device and failure to surrender a cancelled naturalization certificate; operation of a common carrier under the influence of drugs that causes

injury and alteration of one motor vehicle identification number; illegal trafficking in explosives and trespass; interference with a flight attendant and unlawful conduct relating to contraband cigarettes; aggravated assault and smuggling $11,000 worth of fish.

Dissenting View of Commissioner Paul H. Robinson on the Promulgation of the Sentencing Guidelines by the United States Sentencing Commission 6–7 (May 1, 1987).

Petitioner's most fundamental and far-reaching challenge to the Commission is that Congress' commitment of such broad policy responsibility to any institution is an unconstitutional delegation of legislative power. It is difficult to imagine a principle more essential to democratic government than that upon which the doctrine of unconstitutional delegation is founded: Except in a few areas constitutionally committed to the Executive Branch, the basic policy decisions governing society are to be made by the Legislature. Our members of Congress could not, even if they wished, vote all power to the President and adjourn *sine die.*

But while the doctrine of unconstitutional delegation is unquestionably a fundamental element of our constitutional system, it is not an element readily enforceable by the courts. Once it is conceded, as it must be, that no statute can be entirely precise, and that some judgments, even some judgments involving policy considerations, must be left to the officers executing the law and to the judges applying it, the debate over unconstitutional delegation becomes a debate not over a point of principle but over a question of degree. As Chief Justice Taft expressed the point for the Court in the landmark case of *J. W. Hampton, Jr., & Co. v. United States,* at 406, the limits of delegation "must be fixed according to common sense and the inherent necessities of the governmental co-ordination." Since Congress is no less endowed with common sense than we are, and better equipped to inform itself of the "necessities" of government; and since the factors bearing upon those necessities are both multifarious and (in the nonpartisan sense) highly political—including, for example, whether the Nation is at war, see *Yakus v. United States,* or whether for other reasons "emergency is instinct in the situation"—it is small wonder that we have almost never felt qualified to second-guess Congress regarding the permissible degree of policy judgment that can be left to those executing or applying the law. As the Court points out, we have invoked the doctrine of unconstitutional delegation to invalidate a law only twice in our history, over half a century ago. See *Panama Refining Co. v. Ryan; A.L.A. Schechter Poultry Corp. v. United States.* What legislated standard, one must wonder, can possibly be too vague to survive judicial scrutiny, when we have repeatedly upheld, in various contexts, a "public interest" standard?

In short, I fully agree with the Court's rejection of petitioner's contention that the doctrine of unconstitutional delegation of legislative authority has been violated because of the lack of intelligible, congressionally prescribed standards to guide the Commission.

Precisely because the scope of delegation is largely uncontrollable by the courts, we must be particularly rigorous in preserving the Constitution's structural restrictions that deter excessive delegation. The major one, it seems to me, is that the power to make law cannot be exercised by anyone other than Congress, except in conjunction with the lawful exercise of executive or judicial power.

The whole theory of *lawful* congressional "delegation" is not that Congress is sometimes too busy or too divided and can therefore assign its responsibility of making law to someone else; but rather that a certain degree of discretion, and thus of lawmaking, *inheres* in most executive or judicial action, and it is up to Congress, by the relative specificity or generality of its statutory commands, to determine—up to a point—how small or how large that degree shall be. Thus, the courts could be given the power to say precisely what constitutes a "restraint of trade" or to adopt rules of procedure, or to prescribe by rule the manner in which their officers shall execute their judgments, because that "lawmaking" was ancillary to their exercise of judicial powers. And the Executive could be given the power to adopt policies and rules specifying in detail what radio and television licenses will be in the "public interest, convenience or necessity," because that was ancillary to the exercise of its executive powers in granting and policing licenses and making a "fair and equitable allocation" of the electromagnetic spectrum. Or to take examples closer to the case before us: Trial judges could be given the power to determine what factors justify a greater or lesser sentence within the statutorily prescribed limits because that was ancillary to their exercise of the judicial power of pronouncing sentence upon individual defendants. And the President, through the Parole Commission subject to his appointment and removal, could be given the power to issue Guidelines specifying when parole would be available, because that was ancillary to the President's exercise of the executive power to hold and release federal prisoners. . . .

The focus of controversy, in the long line of our so-called excessive delegation cases, has been whether the *degree* of generality contained in the authorization for exercise of executive or judicial powers in a particular field is so unacceptably high as to *amount to* a delegation of legislative powers. I say "so-called excessive delegation" because although that convenient terminology is often used, what is really at issue is whether there has been *any* delegation of legislative power, which occurs (rarely) when Congress authorizes the exercise of executive or judicial power without adequate standards. Strictly speaking, there is *no* acceptable delegation of legislative power. As John Locke put it almost 300 years ago, "[t]he power of the *legislative* being derived from the people by a positive voluntary grant and institution, can be no other, than what the positive grant conveyed, which being only to make *laws*, and not to make *legislators*, the *legislative* can have no power to transfer their authority of making laws, and place it in other hands." J. Locke, Second Treatise of Government 87 (R. Cox ed. 1982) (emphasis added). Or as we have less epigrammatically said: "That Congress cannot delegate legislative power to the President is a principle universally recognized as vital to the integrity and maintenance of the system of government ordained by the Constitution." *Field v. Clark*, at 692. In the present case, however, a pure delegation of legislative power is precisely what we have before us. It is irrelevant whether the standards are adequate, because they are not standards related to the exercise of executive or judicial powers; they are, plainly and simply, standards for further legislation.

The lawmaking function of the Sentencing Commission is completely divorced from any responsibility for execution of the law or adjudication of private rights under the law. It is divorced from responsibility for execution of the law not only because the Commission is not said to be "located in the Executive Branch" (as I shall discuss presently, I doubt whether Congress can "locate" an entity within one Branch or another for constitutional purposes by merely saying so); but, more importantly, because the Commission neither exercises any executive power on its own, nor is subject to the control of the President who does. The only functions it performs, apart from prescribing the law, conducting the investigations useful and necessary for prescribing the law, and clarifying the intended application of the law that it prescribes, are data collection and intragovernmental advice giving and education. These latter activities—similar to functions performed by congressional agencies and even congressional staff—neither determine nor affect private rights, and do not constitute an exercise of governmental power. See *Humphrey's Executor v. United States*, 295 U.S. 602, 628 (1935). And the Commission's lawmaking is completely divorced from the exercise of judicial powers since, not being a court, it has no judicial powers itself, nor is it subject to the control of any other body with judicial powers. The power to make law at issue here, in other words, is not ancillary but quite naked. The situation is no different in principle from what would exist if Congress gave the same power of writing sentencing laws to a congressional agency such as the General Accounting Office, or to members of its staff.

The delegation of lawmaking authority to the Commission is, in short, unsupported by any legitimating theory to explain why it is not a delegation of legislative power. To disregard structural legitimacy is wrong in itself—but since structure has purpose, the disregard also has adverse practical consequences. In this case, as suggested earlier, the consequence is to facilitate and encourage judicially uncontrollable delegation. Until our decision last Term in *Morrison v. Olson*, 487 U.S. 654 (1988), it could have been said that Congress could delegate lawmaking authority only at the expense of increasing the power of either the President or the courts. Most often, as a practical matter, it would be the President, since the judicial process is unable to conduct the investigations and make the political assessments essential for most policymaking. Thus, the need for delegation would have to be important enough to induce Congress to aggrandize its primary competitor for political power, and the recipient of the policymaking authority, while not Congress itself, would at least be politically accountable. But even after it has been accepted, pursuant to *Morrison*, that those exercising executive power need not be subject to the control of the President, Congress would still be more reluctant to augment the power of even an independent executive agency than to create an otherwise powerless repository for its delegation. Moreover, assembling the full-time senior personnel for an agency exercising executive powers is more difficult than borrowing other officials (or employing new officers on a short-term basis) to head an organization such as the Sentencing Commission.

By reason of today's decision, I anticipate that Congress will find delegation of its lawmaking powers much more attractive in the future. If rulemaking can be entirely unrelated to the exercise of judicial or executive powers, I foresee all manner of "expert" bodies, insulated from the political process, to which Congress will delegate various portions of its lawmaking responsibility. How tempting to create an expert Medical Commission (mostly M.D.'s, with perhaps a few Ph.D.'s in moral philosophy) to dispose of such thorny, "no win" political issues as the withholding of life-support systems in federally funded hospitals, or the use of fetal tissue for research. This is an undemocratic precedent that we set—not because of the scope of the delegated power, but because its recipient is not one of the three Branches of Government. The only governmental power the Commission possesses is the power to make law; and it is not the Congress. . . .

Today's decision follows the regrettable tendency of our recent separation-of-powers jurisprudence to treat the Constitution as though it were no more than a generalized prescription that the functions of the Branches should not be commingled too much—how much is too much to be determined, case-by-case, by this Court. The Constitution is not that. Rather, as its name suggests, it is a prescribed structure, a framework, for the conduct of government. In designing that structure, the Framers *themselves* considered how much commingling was, in the generality of things, acceptable, and set forth their conclusions in the document. That is the meaning of the statements concerning acceptable commingling made by Madison in defense of the proposed Constitution, and now routinely used as an excuse for disregarding it. When he said . . . that separation of powers "d[oes] not mean that these [three] departments ought to have no *partial agency* in, or no *controul* over the acts of each other," The Federalist No. 47, his point was that the commingling specifically provided for in the structure that he and his colleagues had designed— the Presidential veto over legislation, the Senate's confirmation of executive and judicial officers, the Senate's ratification of treaties, the Congress' power to impeach and remove executive and judicial officers—did not violate a proper understanding of separation of powers. He would be aghast, I think, to hear those words used as justification for ignoring that carefully designed structure so long as, in the changing view of the Supreme Court from time to time, "too much commingling" does not occur. Consideration of the degree of commingling that a particular disposition produces may be appropriate at the margins, where the outline of the framework itself is not clear; but it seems to me far from a marginal question whether our constitutional structure allows for a body which is not the Congress, and yet exercises no governmental powers except the making of rules that have the effect of laws.

I think the Court errs, in other words, not so much because it mistakes the degree of commingling, but because it fails to recognize that this case is not about commingling, but about the creation of a new Branch altogether, a sort of junior varsity Congress. It may well be that in some circumstances such a Branch would be desirable; perhaps the agency before us here will prove to be so. But there are many desirable dispositions that do not accord with the constitutional structure we live under. And in the long run the improvisation of a constitutional structure on the basis of currently perceived utility will be disastrous.

NOTES

1.   Does the Constitution limit the ability of Congress to delegate its legislative powers? On one hand consider the hypothetical invoked in both the Post Roads Debate and in *Mistretta*: Congress passes a one-line statute that gives the president power to do anything within the scope of national authority, and then adjourns and goes home. Doesn't that *have* to be unconstitutional? On the other hand, why shouldn't Congress be allowed to legislate by announcing general standards and letting the executive branch carry them into effect, even by making more specific regulations? And if Congress can do that, who is to say when the standards have become too general?

2.   Justice Scalia's dissent in *Mistretta* agreed that the non-delegation doctrine's requirement of an "intelligible principle" is "not . . . readily enforceable by the courts." Does that imply that the doctrine is enforceable outside of the courts? By whom? And how?

3.   If Congress makes a delegation of authority, must it delegate to the president or another officer in the executive branch? Despite the sources cited by Justice Scalia's dissent, *Mistretta* says that the answer is "not necessarily." If *Mistretta* is right, are there *any* limits on who can receive a delegation of authority? Could Congress delegate authority to purely private parties (e.g., a corporation, labor union, professional association, or church)? Could it delegate authority to a foreign head of state? Could it delegate all of its legislative authority to the Speaker of the House of Representatives, or to a congressional committee? Consider this last question again when you get to *INS v. Chadha*, p. 141.

4.   A leading constitutional law scholar of the late nineteenth century, James Bradley Thayer, famously argued that the federal courts should never hold an act of the political branches unconstitutional unless it was "a clear mistake." James Bradley Thayer, *The Origin and Scope of the American Doctrine of Constitutional Law*, 7 Harv. L. Rev. 129, 144 (1893). In other words, when a party challenges a legislative or executive act as unconstitutional, the burden of persuasion on the challenger is very high. Does that principle follow from the Constitution? What problem is it meant to avoid? What problems might it lead to? What are the practical conditions needed for it to work—for example, can the courts be Thayerian if the legislative and executive branches do not take seriously the constitutional limits on their power? How would Thayer have decided *Mistretta*?

[*Assignment 6*]

B.   THE COMPOSITION OF CONGRESS: "THE HOUSE OF REPRESENTATIVES . . . AND THE SENATE OF THE UNITED STATES SHALL BE COMPOSED . . . "

Art. I, § 2: . . . No Person shall be a Representative who shall not have attained to the Age of twenty-five years, and been seven Years a Citizen of the United States, and who shall not, when elected, be an Inhabitant of that State in which he shall be chosen. . . .

§ 3: . . . No Person shall be a Senator who shall not have attained to the Age of thirty Years, and been nine Years a Citizen of the United States, and who shall not, when elected, be an Inhabitant of that State for which he shall be chosen. . . .

§ 5: Each House shall be the Judge of the Elections, Returns and Qualifications of its own Members. . . . Each House may . . . punish its Members for disorderly behaviour, and, with the Concurrence of two thirds, expel a Member. . . .

After vesting the enumerated legislative powers in Congress, the next question that Article I addresses is the length of terms and eligibility requirements for members of its two bodies. The text is clear on the first question: a fixed term of two years for representatives and six years for senators. Once selected, representatives and senators cannot be recalled. They become officers of the national government and are paid a fixed salary out of the national treasury as prescribed in Article I, Section 6. In this respect, representatives and senators are radically different from the members of the Continental Congress who served under the Articles of Confederation government. The members of that body were almost like ambassadors from their home states: they were paid by their states and were subject to recall at any time. Notice how under the Constitution the fixed terms of representatives and senators make them independent not only of the states but also of the president. They can be fired only by their constituents.

Read carefully the constitutional text printed above. Article I, Sections 2 and 3 state the only qualifications for being a representative or a senator. Section 5 goes on to say, in what has been called the Exclusion Clause, that each house is the judge of whether individuals elected to that house have the required qualifications. Section 5 adds, in what has been called the Expulsion Clause, that each house may by a two-thirds vote expel a member for misconduct. These two provisions may seem clear, but in the 1960s they became the subject of a famous case, which appears below. As you read it, consider why the issues it addresses are fundamental to the existence of democracy. Was the Supreme Court right to decide the case, or should it have treated the case as a non-justiciable political question? Is intervention by the judiciary in cases like this one essential to protect the republic, or a dangerous threat to the republic? Or both?

Powell v. McCormack

395 U.S. 486 (1969)

■ MR. CHIEF JUSTICE WARREN delivered the opinion of the Court.

In November 1966, petitioner Adam Clayton Powell, Jr., was duly elected from the 18th Congressional District of New York to serve in the United States House of Representatives for the 90th Congress. However, pursuant to a House resolution, he was not permitted to take his seat. Powell (and some of the voters in his district) then filed suit in Federal District Court, claiming that the House could exclude him only if it found he failed to meet the standing requirements of age, citizenship, and residence contained in Art. I, § 2, of the Constitution—requirements the House specifically found Powell met—and thus had excluded him unconstitutionally. . . . Powell is entitled to a declaratory judgment that he was unlawfully excluded from the 90th Congress.

During the 89th Congress, a Special Subcommittee on Contracts of the Committee on House Administration conducted an investigation into the expenditures of the Committee on Education and Labor, of which petitioner Adam Clayton Powell, Jr., was chairman. The Special Subcommittee issued a report concluding that Powell and certain staff employees had deceived the House authorities as to travel expenses. The report also indicated there was strong evidence that certain illegal salary payments had been made to Powell's wife at his direction. No formal action was taken during the 89th Congress. However, prior to the organization of the 90th Congress, the Democratic members-elect met in caucus and voted to remove Powell as chairman of the Committee on Education and Labor.

When the 90th Congress met to organize in January 1967, Powell was asked to step aside while the oath was administered to the other members-elect. Following the administration of the oath to the remaining members, the House discussed the procedure to be followed in determining whether Powell was eligible to take his seat. After some debate, by a vote of 363 to 65 the House adopted House Resolution No. 1, which provided that the Speaker appoint a Select Committee to determine Powell's eligibility. Although the resolution prohibited Powell from taking his seat until the

House acted on the Select Committee's report, it did provide that he should receive all the pay and allowances due a member during the period.

The Select Committee, composed of nine lawyer-members, . . . [held hearings with testimony from Powell and others.] The Committee recommended that Powell be sworn and seated as a member of the 90th Congress but that he be censured by the House, fined $40,000 and be deprived of his seniority.

The report was presented to the House on March 1, 1967, and the House debated the Select Committee's proposed resolution. At the conclusion of the debate, by a vote of 222 to 202 the House rejected a motion to bring the resolution to a vote. An amendment to the resolution was then offered; it called for the exclusion of Powell and a declaration that his seat was vacant. The Speaker ruled that a majority vote of the House would be sufficient to pass the resolution if it were so amended. After further debate, the amendment was adopted by a vote of 248 to 176. Then the House adopted by a vote of 307 to 116 House Resolution No. 278 in its amended form, thereby excluding Powell and directing that the Speaker notify the Governor of New York that the seat was vacant.

Powell and 13 voters of the 18th Congressional District of New York subsequently instituted this suit in the United States District Court for the District of Columbia. Five members of the House of Representatives were named as defendants individually and "as representatives of a class of citizens who are presently serving . . . as members of the House of Representatives." John W. McCormack was named in his official capacity as Speaker, and the Clerk of the House of Representatives, the Sergeant at Arms and the Doorkeeper were named individually and in their official capacities. The complaint alleged that House Resolution No. 278 violated the Constitution, specifically Art. I, § 2, cl. 1, because the resolution was inconsistent with the mandate that the members of the House shall be elected by the people of each state, and Art. I, § 2, cl. 2, which, petitioners alleged, sets forth the exclusive qualifications for membership. . . . The complaint further alleged that the Clerk of the House threatened to refuse to perform the service for Powell to which a duly elected Congressman is entitled, that the Sergeant at Arms refused to pay Powell his salary, and that the Doorkeeper threatened to deny Powell admission to the House chamber.

. . . [Powell] requested that the District Court grant a permanent injunction restraining respondents from executing the House Resolution, and enjoining the Speaker from refusing to administer the oath, the Clerk from refusing to perform the duties due a Representative, the Sergeant at Arms from refusing to pay Powell his salary, and the Doorkeeper from refusing to admit Powell to the Chamber. The complaint also requested a declaratory judgment that Powell's exclusion was unconstitutional.

The District Court granted respondents' motion to dismiss the complaint "for want of jurisdiction of the subject matter." The Court of Appeals for the District of Columbia Circuit affirmed on somewhat different grounds, with each judge of the panel filing a separate opinion. We granted certiorari. While the case was pending on our docket, the 90th Congress officially terminated and the 91st Congress was seated. In November 1968, Powell was again elected as the representative of the 18th Congressional District of New York, and he was seated by the 91st Congress. The resolution seating Powell also fined him $25,000. Respondents then filed a suggestion of mootness. We postponed further consideration of this suggestion to a hearing on the merits. . . .

The resolution excluding petitioner Powell was adopted by a vote in excess of two-thirds of the 434 Members of Congress—307 to 116. Article I, § 5, grants the House authority to expel a member "with the Concurrence of two thirds." Respondents assert that the House may expel a member for any reason whatsoever and that, since a two-thirds vote was obtained, the procedure by which Powell was denied his seat in the 90th Congress should be regarded as an expulsion, not an exclusion. . . .

Although respondents repeatedly urge this Court not to speculate as to the reasons for Powell's exclusion, their attempt to equate exclusion with expulsion would require a similar speculation that the House would have voted to expel Powell had it been faced with that question. Powell had not been seated at the time House Resolution No. 278 was debated and passed. After a motion to bring the Select Committee's proposed resolution to an immediate vote had been defeated, an amendment was offered which mandated Powell's exclusion. Mr. Celler, chairman of the Select Committee, then posed a parliamentary inquiry to determine whether a two-thirds vote was necessary to pass the resolution if so amended "in the sense that it might amount to an expulsion." The Speaker replied that "action by a majority vote would be in accordance with the rules." Had the amendment been regarded as an attempt to expel Powell, a two-thirds vote would have been constitutionally required. The Speaker ruled that the House was voting to exclude Powell, and we will not speculate what the result might have been if Powell had been seated and expulsion proceedings subsequently instituted.

Nor is the distinction between exclusion and expulsion merely one of form. The misconduct for which Powell was charged occurred prior to the convening of the 90th Congress. On several occasions the House has debated whether a member can be expelled for actions taken during a prior Congress and the House's own manual of procedure applicable in the 90th Congress states that "both Houses have distrusted their power to punish in such cases." The House rules manual reflects positions taken by prior Congresses. . . . Members of the House having expressed a belief that such strictures apply to its own power to expel, we will not assume that two-thirds of its members would have expelled Powell for his prior conduct had the Speaker announced that House Resolution No. 278 was for expulsion rather than exclusion.

Finally, the proceedings which culminated in Powell's exclusion cast considerable doubt upon respondents' assumption that the two-thirds vote necessary to expel would have been mustered. . . .

[W]e turn to the question whether the case is justiciable. Two determinations must be made in this regard. First, we must decide whether the claim presented and the relief sought are of the type which admit of judicial resolution. Second, we must determine whether the structure of the Federal Government renders the issue presented a "political question"—that is, a question which is not justiciable in federal court because of the separation of powers provided by the Constitution.

In deciding generally whether a claim is justiciable, a court must determine whether "the duty asserted can be judicially identified and its breach judicially determined, and whether protection for the right asserted can be judicially molded." Respondents do not seriously contend that the duty asserted and its alleged breach cannot be judicially determined. If petitioners are correct, the House had a duty to seat Powell once it determined he met the standing requirements set forth in the Constitution. It is undisputed that he met those requirements and that he was nevertheless excluded.

Respondents do maintain, however, that this case is not justiciable because, they assert, it is impossible for a federal court to "mold effective relief for resolving this case." Respondents emphasize that petitioners asked for coercive relief against the officers of the House, and, they contend, federal courts cannot issue mandamus or injunctions compelling officers or employees of the House to perform specific official acts. Respondents rely primarily on the Speech or Debate Clause to support this contention.

We need express no opinion about the appropriateness of coercive relief in this case, for petitioners sought a declaratory judgment, a form of relief the District Court could have issued. The Declaratory Judgment Act, 28 U.S.C. § 2201, provides that a district court may "declare the rights . . . of any interested party . . . whether or not further relief is or could be sought." The availability of declaratory relief depends on whether there is a live dispute between the parties, and a request for declaratory relief may be considered independently of whether other forms of relief are appropriate. We thus conclude that in terms of the general criteria of justiciability, this case is justiciable.

Respondents maintain that even if this case is otherwise justiciable, it presents only a political question. It is well established that the federal courts will not adjudicate political questions. In *Baker v. Carr*, 369 U.S. 186 (1962), we noted that political questions are not justiciable primarily because of the separation of powers within the Federal Government. After reviewing our decisions in this area, we concluded that on the surface of any case held to involve a political question was at least one of the following formulations:

> a textually demonstrable constitutional commitment of the issue to a co-ordinate political department; or a lack of judicially discoverable and manageable standards for resolving it; or the impossibility of deciding without an initial policy determination of a kind clearly for nonjudicial discretion; or the impossibility of a court's undertaking independent resolution without expressing lack of the respect due co-ordinate branches of government; or an unusual need for unquestioning adherence to a political decision already made; or the potentiality of embarrassment from multifarious pronouncements by various departments on one question.

Respondents' first contention is that this case presents a political question because under Art. I, § 5, there has been a "textually demonstrable constitutional commitment" to the House of the "adjudicatory power" to determine Powell's qualifications. Thus it is argued that the House, and the House alone, has power to determine who is qualified to be a member.

In order to determine whether there has been a textual commitment to a coordinate department of the Government, we must interpret the Constitution. . . . In other words, whether there is a "textually demonstrable constitutional commitment of the issue to a coordinate political department" of government and what is the scope of such commitment are questions we must resolve for the first time in this case. For, as we pointed out in *Baker v. Carr*, "[d]eciding whether a matter has in any measure been committed by the Constitution to another branch of government, or whether the action of that branch exceeds whatever authority has been committed, is itself a delicate exercise in constitutional interpretation, and is a responsibility of this Court as ultimate interpreter of the Constitution."

In order to determine the scope of any "textual commitment" under Art. I, § 5, we necessarily must determine the meaning of the phrase to "be the Judge of the Qualifications of its own Members." . . . Our examination of the relevant historical materials leads us to the conclusion that petitioners are correct and that the Constitution leaves the House without authority to *exclude* any person, duly elected by his constituents, who meets all the requirements for membership expressly prescribed in the Constitution. . . .

[The Court then reviewed and discussed the eighteenth-century English experience with qualifications for membership in Parliament, focusing in particular on the case of John Wilkes. While serving as a member of Parliament, Wilkes publicly attacked a peace treaty with France, was convicted of seditious libel, received a 22–month prison sentence, and was expelled from Parliament. He was reelected several times, but Parliament refused to seat him. Wilkes's exclusion from Parliament eventually came to be seen as having been highly improper, and so his case came to stand for the proposition that Parliament had no authority to exclude properly elected members for misconduct. See 16 Parl. Hist. Eng. 589, 590 (1769).—Editors]

Relying heavily on Charles Warren's analysis of the Convention debates, petitioners argue that the proceedings manifest the Framers' unequivocal intention to deny either branch of Congress the authority to add to or otherwise vary the membership qualifications expressly set forth in the Constitution. . . . [W]e have concluded that the records of the debates, viewed in the context of the bitter struggle for the right to freely choose representatives which had recently concluded in England and in light of the distinction the Framers made between the power to expel and the power to exclude, indicate that petitioners' ultimate conclusion is correct. . . .

The debates at the state [ratification] conventions also demonstrate the Framers' understanding that the qualifications for members of Congress had been fixed in the Constitution. Before the New York convention, for example, Hamilton emphasized: "[T]he true principle of a republic is, that the people should choose whom they please to govern them. Representation is imperfect in proportion as the current of popular favor is checked. This great source of free government, popular election, should be perfectly pure, and the most unbounded liberty allowed." 2 Debates on the Federal Constitution 257 (J. Elliot ed. 1876). . . .

As clear as these statements appear, respondents dismiss them as "general statements . . . directed to other issues." They suggest that far more relevant is Congress' own understanding of its power to judge qualifications as manifested in post-ratification exclusion cases. Unquestionably, both the House and the Senate have excluded members-elect for reasons other than their failure to meet the Constitution's standing qualifications. For almost the first 100 years of its existence, however, Congress strictly limited its power to judge the qualifications of its members to those enumerated in the Constitution. . . .

There was no significant challenge to these principles for . . . several decades. They came under heavy attack, however, "during the stress of civil war [but initially] the House of Representatives declined to exercise the power [to exclude], even under circumstances of great provocation." The abandonment of such restraint, however, was among the casualties of the general upheaval produced in war's wake. In 1868, the House voted for the first time in its history to exclude a member-elect. It refused to seat two duly elected representatives for giving aid and comfort to the Confederacy. "This change was produced by the North's bitter enmity toward those who failed to support the Union cause during the war, and was effected by the Radical Republican domination of Congress. It was a shift brought about by the naked urgency of power and was given little doctrinal support." From that time until the present, congressional practice has been erratic; and on the few occasions when a member-elect was excluded although he met all the qualifications set forth in the Constitution, there were frequently vigorous dissents. Even the annotations to the official manual of procedure for the 90th Congress manifest doubt as to the House's power to exclude a member-elect who has met the constitutionally prescribed qualifications.

Had these congressional exclusion precedents been more consistent, their precedential value still would be quite limited. That an unconstitutional action has been taken before surely does not render that same action any less unconstitutional at a later date. . . . [W]hat evidence we have of Congress' early understanding confirms our conclusion that the House is without power to exclude any member-elect who meets the Constitution's requirements for membership.

Had the intent of the Framers emerged from these materials with less clarity, we would nevertheless have been compelled to resolve any ambiguity in favor of a narrow construction of the scope of Congress' power to exclude members-elect. A fundamental principle of our representative democracy is, in Hamilton's words, "that the people should choose whom they please to govern them." 2 Elliot's Debates 257. As Madison pointed out at the Convention, this principle is undermined as much by limiting whom the people can select as by limiting the franchise itself. In apparent agreement with this basic philosophy, the Convention adopted his suggestion limiting the power to expel. To allow essentially that same power to be exercised under the guise of judging qualifications, would be to ignore Madison's warning, borne out in the Wilkes case and some of Congress' own post-Civil War exclusion cases, against "vesting an improper & dangerous power in the Legislature." 2 Records of the Federal Convention of 1787, p. 249 (M. Farrand rev. ed. 1966). Moreover, it would effectively nullify the Convention's decision to require a two-thirds vote for expulsion. Unquestionably, Congress has an interest in preserving its institutional integrity, but in most cases that interest can be sufficiently safeguarded by the exercise of its power to punish its members for disorderly behavior and, in extreme cases, to expel a member with the concurrence of two-thirds. In short, both the intention of the Framers, to the extent it can be determined, and an examination of the basic principles of our democratic system persuade us that the Constitution does not vest in the Congress a discretionary power to deny membership by a majority vote.

For these reasons, we have concluded that Art. I, § 5, is at most a "textually demonstrable commitment" to Congress to judge only the qualifications expressly set forth in the Constitution. Therefore, the "textual commitment" formulation of the political question doctrine does not bar federal courts from adjudicating petitioners' claims. . . .

Petitioners seek additional forms of equitable relief, including mandamus for the release of petitioner Powell's back pay. The propriety of such remedies, however, is more appropriately considered in the first instance by the courts below. . . . [T]he judgment of the Court of Appeals for the District of Columbia Circuit is reversed and the case is remanded to the United States District Court for the District of Columbia with instructions to enter a declaratory judgment and for further proceedings consistent with this opinion.

■ [The concurring opinion of JUSTICE DOUGLAS and the dissenting opinion of JUSTICE STEWART are omitted.]

NOTES

1.   Was *Powell v. McCormack* right about the meaning of the Constitution? Sections 2 and 3 of Article I lay out three qualifications for members of Congress. But Article I, Section 5 gives each house of Congress the power to judge the qualifications of its members. How do these two provisions fit together?

2.   Does the text of the Constitution clearly speak to the issues raised by this case? If not, what other types of constitutional argument are helpful? Does the structure of the document answer the question? Does practice since the Founding "liquidate" any ambiguity in the text? In which direction does the practice cut? And what policy concerns are implicated here, and how much weight would you give them?

3.   What should the role of the Supreme Court be in cases like these? Does Article I, Section 5, commit this decision to the House of Representatives rather than to the Supreme Court? The Court in *Powell* says "no." But what about the reverse scenario? Suppose that the House had decided to *seat* a member after a debate about his or her qualifications. Would the Supreme Court have the power to force that person out of Congress against the House's wishes?

4.   As *Powell* notes, during and after the Civil War the House and Senate frequently exercised their respective powers to judge the qualifications of their members. Perhaps most importantly, both houses refused to seat officials elected from the rebelling states. Indeed, Congress ultimately decided to seat representatives and senators from the formerly Confederate states only if those states met certain conditions, including ratifying the proposed Fourteenth Amendment to the Constitution. Does *Powell* imply that this was unlawful? Did the Supreme Court have the power to intervene?

5.   Assume that the Court was right to decide *Powell* (i.e., the case was justiciable), and that the Court correctly decided the case on the merits (i.e., it correctly held that Powell was unlawfully excluded). What remedy should the Court have been willing to give? The Court gave a declaratory judgment, which is typically a remedy that resolves legal uncertainty about future conduct. See, e.g., *N.H. Hemp Council v. Marshall*, 203 F.3d 1 (1st Cir. 2000) (resolving uncertainty about whether growing industrial hemp would violate federal law). It is not typically used for retrospective adjudication, for decisions about whether past actions were legal. Why do you think the Court gave a declaratory judgment in this case? Based on the Court's reasoning about justiciability and the merits, do you think it would have been willing to award any other remedies— such as damages or an injunction—if the House of Representatives had ignored the declaratory judgment? Would awarding any other remedies have been constitutional?

Now that you have read *Powell v. McCormack*'s discussion of congressional power to enforce the Qualifications Clauses, consider a case, a quarter century later, that addresses the issue of state power relative to those clauses. Before reading this case, review the Qualifications Clauses and examine the Tenth Amendment.

Do the states have a reserved power under the Tenth Amendment to add qualifications to federal office? To what extent are members of Congress the representatives of their states and of their congressional district, and to what extent are they officers of the entire nation? Does it matter here that the Constitution specifically provides that members of Congress shall be paid their salaries out of the national treasury and that they serve a fixed term without the possibility of recall? Remember how the framers of the Constitution deliberately departed from the practice under the Articles of Confederation, according to which members of the Continental Congress were paid and subject to recall by their states. Remember also that the Articles of Confederation provided for congressional term limits, and the Constitution did not. These issues are at the core of this fascinating and hard case.

U.S. Term Limits, Inc. v. Thornton
514 U.S. 779 (1995)

■ JUSTICE STEVENS delivered the opinion of the Court.

The Constitution sets forth qualifications for membership in the Congress of the United States. Article I, § 2, cl. 2, which applies to the House of Representatives, provides:

> No Person shall be a Representative who shall not have attained to the Age of twenty five Years, and been seven Years a Citizen of the United States, and who shall not, when elected, be an Inhabitant of that State in which he shall be chosen.

Article I, § 3, cl. 3, which applies to the Senate, similarly provides:

> No Person shall be a Senator who shall not have attained to the Age of thirty Years, and been nine Years a Citizen of the United States, and who shall not, when elected, be an Inhabitant of that State for which he shall be chosen.

Today's cases present a challenge to an amendment to the Arkansas State Constitution that prohibits the name of an otherwise-eligible candidate for Congress from appearing on the general election ballot if that candidate has already served three terms in the House of Representatives or two terms in the Senate. The Arkansas Supreme Court held that the amendment violates the Federal Constitution. We agree with that holding. Such a state-imposed restriction is contrary to the "fundamental principle of our representative democracy," embodied in the Constitution, that "the people should choose whom they please to govern them." *Powell v. McCormack,* 395 U.S. 486, 547 (1969). Allowing individual States to adopt their own qualifications for congressional service would be inconsistent with the Framers' vision of a uniform National Legislature representing the people of the United States. If the qualifications set forth in the text of the Constitution are to be changed, that text must be amended.

I

At the general election on November 3, 1992, the voters of Arkansas adopted Amendment 73 to their State Constitution. Proposed as a "Term Limitation Amendment," its preamble stated:

> The people of Arkansas find and declare that elected officials who remain in office too long become preoccupied with reelection and ignore their duties as representatives of the people. Entrenched incumbency has reduced voter participation and has led to an electoral system that is less free, less competitive, and less representative than the system established by the Founding Fathers. Therefore, the people of Arkansas, exercising their reserved powers, herein limit the terms of elected officials.

. . . Section 3, the provision at issue in these cases, applies to the Arkansas Congressional Delegation. It provides:

> (a) Any person having been elected to three or more terms as a member of the United States House of Representatives from Arkansas shall not be certified as a candidate and shall not be eligible to have his/her name placed on the ballot for election to the United States House of Representatives from Arkansas.

> (b) Any person having been elected to two or more terms as a member of the United States Senate from Arkansas shall not be certified as a candidate and shall not be eligible to have his/her name placed on the ballot for election to the United States Senate from Arkansas. . . .

On November 13, 1992, respondent Bobbie Hill, on behalf of herself, similarly situated Arkansas "citizens, residents, taxpayers and registered voters," and the League of Women Voters of Arkansas, filed a complaint in the Circuit Court for Pulaski County, Arkansas, seeking a declaratory judgment that § 3 of Amendment 73 is "unconstitutional and void." . . .

II

As the opinions of the Arkansas Supreme Court suggest, the constitutionality of Amendment 73 depends critically on the resolution of two distinct issues. The first is whether the Constitution forbids States to add to or alter the qualifications specifically enumerated in the Constitution. The second is, if the Constitution does so forbid, whether the fact that Amendment 73 is formulated as a ballot access restriction rather than as an outright disqualification is of constitutional significance. Our resolution of these issues draws upon our prior resolution of a related but distinct issue: whether Congress has the power to add to or alter the qualifications of its Members.

Twenty-six years ago, in *Powell v. McCormack,* we reviewed the history and text of the Qualifications Clauses in a case involving an attempted exclusion of a duly elected Member of Congress. . . . [*Powell*] establishes two important propositions: first, that the "relevant historical materials" compel the conclusion that, at least with respect to qualifications imposed by Congress, the Framers intended the qualifications listed in the Constitution to be exclusive; and second, that that conclusion is equally compelled by an understanding of the "fundamental principle of our representative democracy . . . that the people should choose whom they please to govern them." . . .

III

... [P]etitioners argue that whatever the constitutionality of additional qualifications for membership imposed by Congress, the historical and textual materials discussed in *Powell* do not support the conclusion that the Constitution prohibits additional qualifications imposed by States. In the absence of such a constitutional prohibition, petitioners argue, the Tenth Amendment and the principle of reserved powers require that States be allowed to add such qualifications.

Before addressing these arguments, we find it appropriate to take note of the striking unanimity among the courts that have considered the issue. . . . Courts have struck down state-imposed qualifications in the form of term limits, district residency requirements, loyalty oath requirements, and restrictions on those convicted of felonies. Prior to *Powell,* the commentators were similarly unanimous. This impressive and uniform body of judicial decisions and learned commentary indicates that the obstacles confronting petitioners are formidable indeed.

Petitioners argue that the Constitution contains no express prohibition against state-added qualifications, and that Amendment 73 is therefore an appropriate exercise of a State's reserved power to place additional restrictions on the choices that its own voters may make. We disagree for two independent reasons. First, we conclude that the power to add qualifications is not within the "original powers" of the States, and thus is not reserved to the States by the Tenth Amendment. Second, even if States possessed some original power in this area, we conclude that the Framers intended the Constitution to be the exclusive source of qualifications for Members of Congress, and that the Framers thereby "divested" States of any power to add qualifications.

The "plan of the convention" as illuminated by the historical materials, our opinions, and the text of the Tenth Amendment draws a basic distinction between the powers of the newly created Federal Government and the powers retained by the pre-existing sovereign States. As Chief Justice Marshall explained, "it was neither necessary nor proper to define the powers retained by the States. These powers proceed, not from the people of America, but from the people of the several States; and remain, after the adoption of the constitution, what they were before, except so far as they may be abridged by that instrument." *Sturges v. Crowninshield*, 17 U.S. (4 Wheat.) 122, 193 (1819).

This classic statement by the Chief Justice endorsed Hamilton's reasoning in *The Federalist No. 32* that the plan of the Constitutional Convention did not contemplate "[a]n entire consolidation of the States into one complete national sovereignty," but only a partial consolidation in which "the State governments would clearly retain all the rights of sovereignty which they before had, and which were not, by that act, *exclusively* delegated to the United States." *The Federalist No. 32*, at 198. The text of the Tenth Amendment unambiguously confirms this principle:

> The powers not delegated to the United States by the Constitution, nor prohibited by it to the States, are reserved to the States respectively, or to the people.

As we have frequently noted, "[t]he States unquestionably do retain a significant measure of sovereign authority. They do so, however, *only to the extent that the*

Constitution has not divested them of their original powers and transferred those powers to the Federal Government."

Contrary to petitioners' assertions, the power to add qualifications is not part of the original powers of sovereignty that the Tenth Amendment reserved to the States. Petitioners' Tenth Amendment argument misconceives the nature of the right at issue because that Amendment could only "reserve" that which existed before. As Justice Story recognized, "the states can exercise no powers whatsoever, which exclusively spring out of the existence of the national government, which the constitution does not delegate to them. . . . No state can say, that it has reserved, what it never possessed." 1 Story § 627.

Justice Story's position thus echoes that of Chief Justice Marshall in *McCulloch v. Maryland*, 17 U.S. (4 Wheat.) 316 (1819). In *McCulloch,* the Court rejected the argument that the Constitution's silence on the subject of state power to tax corporations chartered by Congress implies that the States have "reserved" power to tax such federal instrumentalities. As Chief Justice Marshall pointed out, an "original right to tax" such federal entities "never existed, and the question whether it has been surrendered, cannot arise." In language that presaged Justice Story's argument, Chief Justice Marshall concluded: "This opinion does not deprive the States of any resources which they originally possessed."

With respect to setting qualifications for service in Congress, no such right existed before the Constitution was ratified. The contrary argument overlooks the revolutionary character of the Government that the Framers conceived. Prior to the adoption of the Constitution, the States had joined together under the Articles of Confederation. In that system, "the States retained most of their sovereignty, like independent nations bound together only by treaties." After the Constitutional Convention convened, the Framers were presented with, and eventually adopted a variation of, "a plan not merely to amend the Articles of Confederation but to create an entirely new National Government with a National Executive, National Judiciary, and a National Legislature." In adopting that plan, the Framers envisioned a uniform national system, rejecting the notion that the Nation was a collection of States, and instead creating a direct link between the National Government and the people of the United States. . . . In that National Government, representatives owe primary allegiance not to the people of a State, but to the people of the Nation. As Justice Story observed, each Member of Congress is "an officer of the union, deriving his powers and qualifications from the constitution, and neither created by, dependent upon, nor controllable by, the states. . . . Those officers owe their existence and functions to the united voice of the whole, not of a portion, of the people." 1 Story § 627. Representatives and Senators are as much officers of the entire Union as is the President. States thus "have just as much right, and no more, to prescribe new qualifications for a representative, as they have for a president. . . . It is no original prerogative of state power to appoint a representative, a senator, or president for the union." *Ibid.* . . .

Two other sections of the Constitution further support our view of the Framers' vision. First, consistent with Story's view, the Constitution provides that the salaries of representatives should "be ascertained by Law, and paid out of the Treasury of the United States," Art. I, § 6, rather than by individual States. The salary provisions reflect the view that representatives owe their allegiance to the people, and not to the States. Second, the provisions governing elections reveal the Framers' understanding that powers over the election of federal officers had to be delegated to, rather than reserved by, the States. It is surely no coincidence that the context of federal elections provides one of the few areas in which the Constitution expressly requires action by the States, namely that "[t]he Times, Places and Manner of holding Elections for Senators and Representatives, shall be prescribed in each State by the Legislature thereof." Art. I, § 4, cl. 1. This duty parallels the duty under Article II that "Each State shall appoint, in such Manner as the Legislature thereof may direct, a Number of Electors." Art. II, § 1, cl. 2. These Clauses are express delegations of power to the States to act with respect to federal elections.

This conclusion is consistent with our previous recognition that, in certain limited contexts, the power to regulate the incidents of the federal system is not a reserved power of the States, but rather is delegated by the Constitution. Thus, we have noted that "[w]hile, in a loose sense, the right to vote for representatives in Congress is sometimes spoken of as a right derived from the states, ... this statement is true only in the sense that the states are authorized by the Constitution, to legislate on the subject as provided by § 2 of Art. I."

In short, as the Framers recognized, electing representatives to the National Legislature was a new right, arising from the Constitution itself. . . . In the absence of any constitutional delegation to the States of power to add qualifications to those enumerated in the Constitution, such a power does not exist. . . .

We find further evidence of the Framers' intent in Art. I, § 5, cl. 1, which provides: "Each House shall be the Judge of the Elections, Returns and Qualifications of its own Members." That Art. I, § 5, vests a federal tribunal with ultimate authority to judge a Member's qualifications is fully consistent with the understanding that those qualifications are fixed in the Federal Constitution, but not with the understanding that they can be altered by the States. If the States had the right to prescribe additional qualifications—such as property, educational, or professional qualifications—for their own representatives, state law would provide the standard for judging a Member's eligibility. . . .

We also find compelling the complete absence in the ratification debates of any assertion that States had the power to add qualifications. In those debates, the question whether to require term limits, or "rotation," was a major source of controversy. The draft of the Constitution that was submitted for ratification contained no provision for rotation.[22] In arguments that echo in the preamble to Arkansas' Amendment 73, opponents of ratification condemned the absence of a rotation requirement, noting that "there is no doubt that senators will hold their office perpetually; and in this situation, they must of necessity lose their dependence, and their attachments to the people." Even proponents of ratification expressed concern about the "abandonment in every instance of the necessity of rotation in office." At several ratification conventions, participants proposed amendments that would have required rotation.

The Federalists' responses to those criticisms and proposals addressed the merits of the issue, arguing that rotation was incompatible with the people's right to choose. . . .

---

[22] A proposal requiring rotation for Members of the House was proposed at the Convention, but was defeated unanimously.

Regardless of which side has the better of the debate over rotation, it is most striking that nowhere in the extensive ratification debates have we found any statement by either a proponent or an opponent of rotation that the draft constitution would permit States to require rotation for the representatives of their own citizens. If the participants in the debate had believed that the States retained the authority to impose term limits, it is inconceivable that the Federalists would not have made this obvious response to the arguments of the pro-rotation forces. The absence in an otherwise freewheeling debate of any suggestion that States had the power to impose additional qualifications unquestionably reflects the Framers' common understanding that States lacked that power. . . .

Congress' subsequent experience with state-imposed qualifications provides further evidence of the general consensus on the lack of state power in this area. . . . Congress first confronted the issue in 1807 when it faced a challenge to the qualifications of William McCreery, a Representative from Maryland who allegedly did not satisfy a residency requirement imposed by that State. In recommending that McCreery be seated, the Report of the House Committee on Elections noted:

> "The committee proceeded to examine the Constitution, with relation to the case submitted to them, and find that *qualifications of members are therein determined, without reserving any authority to the State Legislatures to change, add to, or diminish those qualifications;* and that, by that instrument, Congress is constituted the sole judge of the qualifications prescribed by it, and are obliged to decide agreeably to the Constitutional rules." *Powell,* at 542, quoting 17 Annals of Cong. 871 (1807) (emphasis added).

. . . Though the House Debate may be inconclusive, commentators at the time apparently viewed the seating of McCreery as confirmation of the States' lack of power to add qualifications. . . . The Senate experience with state-imposed qualifications further supports our conclusions. In 1887, for example, the Senate seated Charles Faulkner of West Virginia, despite the fact that a provision of the West Virginia Constitution purported to render him ineligible to serve. The Senate Committee on Privileges and Elections unanimously concluded that "no State can prescribe any qualification to the office of United States Senator in addition to those declared in the Constitution of the United States." . . . We recognize, as we did in *Powell,* that "congressional practice has been erratic" and that the precedential value of congressional exclusion cases is "quite limited." Nevertheless, those incidents lend support to the result we reach today.

Our conclusion that States lack the power to impose qualifications vindicates the same "fundamental principle of our representative democracy" that we recognized in *Powell,* namely, that "the people should choose whom they please to govern them."

. . . [T]he *Powell* Court recognized that an egalitarian ideal—that election to the National Legislature should be open to all people of merit—provided a critical foundation for the constitutional structure. This egalitarian theme echoes throughout the constitutional debates. . . .

Finally, state-imposed restrictions, unlike the congressionally imposed restrictions at issue in *Powell,* violate a third idea central to this basic principle: that the right to choose representatives belongs not to the States, but to the people. From the start, the Framers recognized that the "great and radical vice" of the Articles of Confederation was "the principle of LEGISLATION for STATES or GOVERNMENTS, in their CORPORATE or COLLECTIVE CAPACITIES, and as contradistinguished from the INDIVIDUALS of whom they consist." The Federalist No. 15, at 108 (Hamilton). Thus the Framers, in perhaps their most important contribution, conceived of a Federal Government directly responsible to the people, possessed of direct power over the people, and chosen directly, not by States, but by the people. . . .

Permitting individual States to formulate diverse qualifications for their representatives would result in a patchwork of state qualifications, undermining the uniformity and the national character that the Framers envisioned and sought to ensure. Such a patchwork would also sever the direct link that the Framers found so critical between the National Government and the people of the United States.

Petitioners attempt to overcome this formidable array of evidence against the States' power to impose qualifications by arguing that the practice of the States immediately after the adoption of the Constitution demonstrates their understanding that they possessed such power. One may properly question the extent to which the States' own practice is a reliable indicator of the contours of restrictions that the Constitution imposed on States, especially when no court has ever upheld a state-imposed qualification of any sort. But petitioners' argument is unpersuasive even on its own terms. At the time of the Convention, "[a]lmost all the State Constitutions required members of their Legislatures to possess considerable property." Despite this near uniformity, only one State, Virginia, placed similar restrictions on Members of Congress, requiring that a representative be, *inter alia,* a "freeholder." Just 15 years after imposing a property qualification, Virginia replaced that requirement with a provision requiring that representatives be only "qualified according to the constitution of the United States." Moreover, several States, including New Hampshire, Georgia, Delaware, and South Carolina, revised their Constitutions at around the time of the Federal Constitution. In the revised Constitutions, each State retained property qualifications for its own state elected officials yet placed no property qualification on its congressional representatives.

The contemporaneous state practice with respect to term limits is similar. At the time of the Convention, States widely supported term limits in at least some circumstances. The Articles of Confederation contained a provision for term limits. As we have noted, some members of the Convention had sought to impose term limits for Members of Congress. In addition, many States imposed term limits on state officers, four placed limits on delegates to the Continental Congress, and several States voiced support for term limits for Members of Congress. Despite this widespread support, no State sought to impose any term limits on its own federal representatives. Thus, a proper assessment of contemporaneous state practice provides further persuasive evidence of a general understanding that the qualifications in the Constitution were unalterable by the States.[41]

---

[41] . . . Nor are we persuaded by the more recent state practice involving qualifications such as those that bar felons from being elected. As we have noted, the practice of States is a poor indicator of the effect of restraints on the States, and no court has ever upheld one of these restrictions. Moreover, as one moves away from 1789, it seems to us that state practice is even less indicative of the Framers' understanding of state power. Finally, it is important to reemphasize that the dissent simply has no credible explanation as to why almost every State imposed property qualifications on state representatives but not on federal representatives. . . .

In sum, the available historical and textual evidence, read in light of the basic principles of democracy underlying the Constitution and recognized by this Court in *Powell*, reveal the Framers' intent that neither Congress nor the States should possess the power to supplement the exclusive qualifications set forth in the text of the Constitution. . . .

IV

Petitioners argue that, even if States may not add qualifications, Amendment 73 is constitutional because it is not such a qualification, and because Amendment 73 is a permissible exercise of state power to regulate the "Times, Places and Manner of holding Elections." We reject these contentions.

Unlike §§ 1 and 2 of Amendment 73, which create absolute bars to service for long-term incumbents running for state office, § 3 merely provides that certain Senators and Representatives shall not be certified as candidates and shall not have their names appear on the ballot. They may run as write-in candidates and, if elected, they may serve. . . . In our view, Amendment 73 is an indirect attempt to accomplish what the Constitution prohibits Arkansas from accomplishing directly. . . .

Petitioners make the related argument that Amendment 73 merely regulates the "Manner" of elections, and that the amendment is therefore a permissible exercise of state power under Article I, § 4, cl. 1 (the Elections Clause). . . . A necessary consequence of petitioners' argument is that Congress itself would have the power to "make or alter" a measure such as Amendment 73. Art. I, § 4, cl. 1. That the Framers would have approved of such a result is unfathomable. As our decision in *Powell* and our discussion above make clear, the Framers were particularly concerned that a grant to Congress of the authority to set its own qualifications would lead inevitably to congressional self-aggrandizement and the upsetting of the delicate constitutional balance. . . .

V

The merits of term limits, or "rotation," have been the subject of debate since the formation of our Constitution, when the Framers unanimously rejected a proposal to add such limits to the Constitution. The cogent arguments on both sides of the question that were articulated during the process of ratification largely retain their force today. Over half the States have adopted measures that impose such limits on some offices either directly or indirectly, and the Nation as a whole, notably by constitutional amendment, has imposed a limit on the number of terms that the President may serve. Term limits, like any other qualification for office, unquestionably restrict the ability of voters to vote for whom they wish. On the other hand, such limits may provide for the infusion of fresh ideas and new perspectives, and may decrease the likelihood that representatives will lose touch with their constituents. It is not our province to resolve this longstanding debate.

We are, however, firmly convinced that allowing the several States to adopt term limits for congressional service would effect a fundamental change in the constitutional framework. Any such change must come not by legislation adopted either by Congress or by an individual State, but rather—as have other important changes in the electoral process—through the amendment procedures set forth in Article V. . . .

■ JUSTICE KENNEDY, concurring.

I join the opinion of the Court[,] . . . and it seems appropriate to add these few remarks to explain why that course of argumentation runs counter to fundamental principles of federalism.

Federalism was our Nation's own discovery. The Framers split the atom of sovereignty. It was the genius of their idea that our citizens would have two political capacities, one state and one federal, each protected from incursion by the other. The resulting Constitution created a legal system unprecedented in form and design, establishing two orders of government, each with its own direct relationship, its own privity, its own set of mutual rights and obligations to the people who sustain it and are governed by it. It is appropriate to recall these origins, which instruct us as to the nature of the two different governments created and confirmed by the Constitution.

A distinctive character of the National Government, the mark of its legitimacy, is that it owes its existence to the act of the whole people who created it. It must be remembered that the National Government, too, is republican in essence and in theory. . . .

In one sense it is true that "the people of each State retained their separate political identities," for the Constitution takes care both to preserve the States and to make use of their identities and structures at various points in organizing the federal union. It does not at all follow from this that the sole political identity of an American is with the State of his or her residence. It denies the dual character of the Federal Government which is its very foundation to assert that the people of the United States do not have a political identity as well, one independent of, though consistent with, their identity as citizens of the State of their residence. It must be recognized that "[f]or all the great purposes for which the Federal government was formed, we are one people, with one common country." *Shapiro v. Thompson,* 394 U.S. 618, 630 (1969) (quoting *Passenger Cases,* 48 U.S. (7 How.) 283, 492 (1849) (Taney, C.J., dissenting)).

It might be objected that because the States ratified the Constitution, the people can delegate power only through the States or by acting in their capacities as citizens of particular States. But in *McCulloch v. Maryland,* the Court set forth its authoritative rejection of this idea:

> The Convention which framed the constitution was indeed elected by the State legislatures. But the instrument . . . was submitted to the people. . . . It is true, they assembled in their several States—and where else should they have assembled? No political dreamer was ever wild enough to think of breaking down the lines which separate the States, and of compounding the American people into one common mass. Of consequence, when they act, they act in their States. But the measures they adopt do not, on that account, cease to be the measures of the people themselves, or become the measures of the State governments. *McCulloch,* at 403.

. . . It is maintained by our dissenting colleagues that the State of Arkansas seeks nothing more than to grant its people surer control over the National Government, a control, it is said, that will be enhanced by the law at issue here. The arguments for term limitations (or ballot restrictions having the same effect) are not lacking in force; but the issue, as all of us must acknowledge, is not the efficacy of those measures but whether they have a legitimate source, given their origin in the enactments of a single State. There can be no doubt, if we are to respect the republican origins of the Nation and preserve its federal character, that there exists a federal right of citizenship, a relationship between the people of the Nation and their National Government, with which the States may not interfere. Because the Arkansas enactment intrudes upon this federal domain, it exceeds the boundaries of the Constitution.

■ JUSTICE THOMAS, with whom THE CHIEF JUSTICE, JUSTICE O'CONNOR, and JUSTICE SCALIA join, dissenting.

It is ironic that the Court bases today's decision on the right of the people to "choose whom they please to govern them." Under our Constitution, there is only one State whose people have the right to "choose whom they please" to represent Arkansas in Congress. The Court holds, however, that neither the elected legislature of that State nor the people themselves (acting by ballot initiative) may prescribe any qualifications for those representatives. The majority therefore defends the right of the people of Arkansas to "choose whom they please to govern them" by invalidating a provision that won nearly 60% of the votes cast in a direct election and that carried every congressional district in the State.

I dissent. Nothing in the Constitution deprives the people of each State of the power to prescribe eligibility requirements for the candidates who seek to represent them in Congress. The Constitution is simply silent on this question. And where the Constitution is silent, it raises no bar to action by the States or the people.

I

Because the majority fundamentally misunderstands the notion of "reserved" powers, I start with some first principles. Contrary to the majority's suggestion, the people of the States need not point to any affirmative grant of power in the Constitution in order to prescribe qualifications for their representatives in Congress, or to authorize their elected state legislators to do so.

Our system of government rests on one overriding principle: All power stems from the consent of the people. To phrase the principle in this way, however, is to be imprecise about something important to the notion of "reserved" powers. The ultimate source of the Constitution's authority is the consent of the people of each individual State, not the consent of the undifferentiated people of the Nation as a whole.

The ratification procedure erected by Article VII makes this point clear. The Constitution took effect once it had been ratified by the people gathered in convention in nine different States. But the Constitution went into effect only "between the States so ratifying the same," Art. VII; it did not bind the people of North Carolina until they had accepted it. In Madison's words, the popular consent upon which the Constitution's authority rests was "given by the people, not as individuals composing one entire nation, but as composing the distinct and independent States to which they respectively belong." The Federalist No. 39. . . .

In each State, the remainder of the people's powers—"[t]he powers not delegated to the United States by the Constitution, nor prohibited by it to the States," Amdt. 10—are either delegated to the state government or retained by the people. . . . As far as the Federal Constitution is concerned, then, the States can exercise all powers that the Constitution does not withhold from them. The Federal Government and the States thus face different default rules: Where the Constitution is silent about the exercise of a particular power—that is, where the Constitution does not speak either expressly or by necessary implication—the Federal Government lacks that power and the States enjoy it.

These basic principles are enshrined in the Tenth Amendment, which declares that all powers neither delegated to the Federal Government nor prohibited to the States "are reserved to the States respectively, or to the people." With this careful last phrase, the Amendment avoids taking any position on the division of power between the state governments and the people of the States: It is up to the people of each State to determine which "reserved" powers their state government may exercise. . . .

The Constitution simply does not recognize any mechanism for action by the undifferentiated people of the Nation. Thus, the amendment provision of Article V calls for amendments to be ratified not by a convention of the national people, but by conventions of the people in each State or by the state legislatures elected by those people. Likewise, the Constitution calls for Members of Congress to be chosen State by State, rather than in nationwide elections. Even the selection of the President— surely the most national of national figures—is accomplished by an electoral college made up of delegates chosen by the various States, and candidates can lose a Presidential election despite winning a majority of the votes cast in the Nation as a whole.

In short, the notion of popular sovereignty that undergirds the Constitution does not erase state boundaries, but rather tracks them. . . .

Any ambiguity in the Tenth Amendment's use of the phrase "the people" is cleared up by the body of the Constitution itself. Article I begins by providing that the Congress of the United States enjoys "[a]ll legislative Powers herein granted," § 1, and goes on to give a careful enumeration of Congress' powers, § 8. It then concludes by enumerating certain powers that are *prohibited* to the States. The import of this structure is the same as the import of the Tenth Amendment: If we are to invalidate Arkansas' Amendment 73, we must point to something in the Federal Constitution that deprives the people of Arkansas of the power to enact such measures.

The majority disagrees that it bears this burden, . . . and begins by announcing an enormous and untenable limitation on the principle expressed by the Tenth Amendment. According to the majority, the States possess only those powers that the Constitution affirmatively grants to them or that they enjoyed before the Constitution was adopted; the Tenth Amendment "could only 'reserve' that which existed before." . . .

But it was not the state governments that were doing the reserving. The Constitution derives its authority instead from the consent of *the people* of the States. Given the fundamental principle that all governmental powers stem from the people of the States, it would simply be incoherent to assert that the people of the States could not reserve any powers that they had not previously controlled.

The Tenth Amendment's use of the word "reserved" does not help the majority's position. If someone says that the power to use a particular facility is reserved to some group, he is not saying anything about whether that group has previously used the facility. He is merely saying that the people who control the facility have designated that group as the entity with authority to use it. . . .

The majority also seeks support for its view of the Tenth Amendment in *McCulloch v. Maryland*. But this effort is misplaced. *McCulloch* did make clear that a power need not be "expressly" delegated to the United States or prohibited to the States in order to fall outside the Tenth Amendment's reservation; delegations and prohibitions can also arise by necessary implication. True to the text of the Tenth Amendment, however, *McCulloch* indicated that all powers as to which the Constitution does not speak (whether expressly or by necessary implication) are "reserved" to the state level. Thus, in its only discussion of the Tenth Amendment, *McCulloch* observed that the Amendment "leav[es] the question, whether the particular power which may become the subject of contest has been delegated to the one government, or prohibited to the other, to depend on a fair construction of the whole [Constitution]." *McCulloch*, at 406. *McCulloch* did not qualify this observation by indicating that the question also turned on whether the States had enjoyed the power before the framing. To the contrary, *McCulloch* seemed to assume that the people had "conferred on the general government the power contained in the constitution, and on the States the whole residuum of power." *McCulloch*, at 410. . . .

For the past 175 years, *McCulloch* has been understood to rest on the proposition that the Constitution affirmatively barred Maryland from imposing its tax on the bank's operations. See, *e.g., Osborn v. Bank of United States*, 22 U.S. (9 Wheat.) 738, 859–868 (1824) (reaffirming *McCulloch*'s conclusion that by operation of the Supremacy Clause, the federal statute incorporating the bank impliedly pre-empted state laws attempting to tax the bank's operations); *Maryland v. Louisiana*, 451 U.S. 725, 746 (1981) (citing *McCulloch* for the proposition that the Supremacy Clause deprives the States of the power to pass laws that conflict with federal statutes). For the majority, however, *McCulloch* apparently turned on the fact that before the Constitution was adopted, the States had possessed no power to tax the instrumentalities of the governmental institutions that the Constitution created. This understanding of *McCulloch* makes most of Chief Justice Marshall's opinion irrelevant; according to the majority, there was no need to inquire into whether federal law deprived Maryland of the power in question, because the power could not fall into the category of "reserved" powers anyway.[6]

. . . [T]he only true support for [the majority's] view of the Tenth Amendment comes from Joseph Story's 1833 treatise on constitutional law. Justice Story was a brilliant and accomplished man, and one cannot casually dismiss his views. On the other hand, he was not a member of the Founding generation, and . . . they represent only his own understanding. In a range of cases concerning the federal/state relation, moreover, this Court has deemed positions taken in Story's commentaries to be more nationalist than the Constitution warrants. . . .

---

[6]   . . . Marshall did go on to argue that the power to tax the operations of the Bank of the United States simply was not susceptible to control by the people of a single State. But that theory is perfectly consistent with my position. Marshall reasoned that the people of a single State may not tax the instrumentalities employed by the people of all the States through the National Government, because such taxation would effectively subject the people of the several States to the taxing power of a single State. This sort of argument proves that the people of a single State may not prescribe qualifications for the President of the United States; the selection of the President, like the operation of the Bank of the United States, is not up to the people of any single State. It does not follow, however, that the people of a single State may not prescribe qualifications for their own representatives in Congress. . . .

The majority also sketches out what may be an alternative (and narrower) argument. Again citing Story, the majority suggests that it would be inconsistent with the notion of "national sovereignty" for the States or the people of the States to have any reserved powers over the selection of Members of Congress. The majority apparently reaches this conclusion in two steps. First, it asserts that because Congress as a whole is an institution of the National Government, the individual Members of Congress "owe primary allegiance not to the people of a State, but to the people of the Nation." Second, it concludes that because each Member of Congress has a nationwide constituency once he takes office, it would be inconsistent with the Framers' scheme to let a single State prescribe qualifications for him.

Political scientists can debate about who commands the "primary allegiance" of Members of Congress once they reach Washington. From the framing to the present, however, the *selection* of the Representatives and Senators from each State has been left entirely to the people of that State or to their state legislature. See Art. I, § 2, cl. 1 (providing that Members of the House of Representatives are chosen "by the People of the several States"); Art. I, § 3, cl. 1 (originally providing that the Senators from each State are "chosen by the Legislature thereof"); Amdt. 17 (amending § 3 to provide that the Senators from each State are "elected by the people thereof"). The very name "congress" suggests a coming together of representatives from distinct entities.[7] In keeping with the complexity of our federal system, once the representatives chosen by the people of each State assemble in Congress, they form a national body and are beyond the control of the individual States until the next election. But the selection of representatives in Congress is indisputably an act of the people of each State, not some abstract people of the Nation as a whole. . . .

In a final effort to deny that the people of the States enjoy "reserved" powers over the selection of their representatives in Congress, the majority suggests that the Constitution expressly delegates to the States certain powers over congressional elections. Such delegations of power, the majority argues, would be superfluous if the people of the States enjoyed reserved powers in this area.

Only one constitutional provision—the Times, Places and Manner Clause of Article I, § 4—even arguably supports the majority's suggestion. It reads:

> The Times, Places and Manner of holding Elections for Senators and Representatives, shall be prescribed in each State by the Legislature thereof; but the Congress may at any time by Law make or alter such Regulations, except as to the Places of chusing Senators.

Contrary to the majority's assumption, however, this Clause does not delegate any authority to the States. Instead, it simply imposes a duty upon them. . . . Constitutional provisions that impose affirmative duties on the States are hardly inconsistent with the notion of reserved powers.

Of course, the second part of the Times, Places and Manner Clause does grant a power rather than impose a duty. . . . [H]owever, the Clause grants power exclusively to Congress, not to the States. If the Clause did not exist at all, the States would still be able to prescribe the times, places, and manner of holding

---

[7] See 1 Samuel Johnson, A Dictionary of the English Language 393 (4th ed. 1773) (defining "congress" as "[a]n appointed meeting for settlement of affairs between different nations: as, the *congress* of Cambray").

congressional elections; the deletion of the provision would simply deprive Congress of the power to override these state regulations. . . .

II

. . . Whatever one might think of the wisdom of [the Arkansas] arrangement, we may not override the decision of the people of Arkansas unless something in the Federal Constitution deprives them of the power to enact such measures.

The majority settles on "the Qualifications Clauses" as the constitutional provisions that Amendment 73 violates. Because I do not read those provisions to impose any unstated prohibitions on the States, it is unnecessary for me to decide whether the majority is correct to identify Arkansas' ballot-access restriction with laws fixing true term limits or otherwise prescribing "qualifications" for congressional office. . . . [T]he Qualifications Clauses are merely straightforward recitations of the minimum eligibility requirements that the Framers thought it essential for every Member of Congress to meet. They restrict state power only in that they prevent the States from *abolishing* all eligibility requirements for membership in Congress. . . .

III

It is radical enough for the majority to hold that the Constitution implicitly precludes the people of the States from prescribing any eligibility requirements for the congressional candidates who seek their votes. This holding, after all, does not stop with negating the term limits that many States have seen fit to impose on their Senators and Representatives. . . . Today's decision also means that no State may disqualify congressional candidates whom a court has found to be mentally incompetent, see, *e.g.*, Fla. Stat. § 97.041(2) (1991), who are currently in prison, see, *e.g.*, Ill. Comp. Stat. Ann., ch. 10, §§ 5/3–5 (1993), or who have past vote-fraud convictions, see, *e.g.*, Ga. Code Ann. § 21–2–2(25) (1993). Likewise, after today's decision, the people of each State must leave open the possibility that they will trust someone with their vote in Congress even though they do not trust him with *a* vote in the election for Congress. See, *e.g.*, R.I. Gen. Laws § 17–14–1.2 (1988) (restricting candidacy to people "qualified to vote").

. . . Current federal law (enacted, of course, by congressional incumbents) confers numerous advantages on incumbents, and these advantages are widely thought to make it "significantly more difficult" for challengers to defeat them. For instance, federal law gives incumbents enormous advantages in building name recognition and good will in their home districts. See, *e.g.*, 39 U.S.C. § 3210 (permitting Members of Congress to send "franked" mail free of charge); 2 U.S.C. §§ 61–1, 72a, 332 (permitting Members to have sizable taxpayer-funded staffs); 2 U.S.C. § 123b (establishing the House Recording Studio and the Senate Recording and Photographic Studios). At the same time that incumbent Members of Congress enjoy these in-kind benefits, Congress imposes spending and contribution limits in congressional campaigns that "can prevent challengers from spending more . . . to overcome their disadvantage in name recognition." Many observers believe that the campaign-finance laws also give incumbents an "enormous fund-raising edge" over their challengers by giving a large financing role to entities with incentives to curry favor with incumbents. In addition, the internal rules of Congress put a substantial premium on seniority, with the result that each Member's already plentiful opportunities to distribute benefits to his constituents increase with the length of his tenure. In this manner, Congress effectively "fines" the electorate for voting against incumbents. . . .

The voters of Arkansas evidently believe that incumbents would not enjoy such overwhelming success if electoral contests were truly fair—that is, if the government did not put its thumb on either side of the scale. The majority offers no reason to question the accuracy of this belief. Given this context, petitioners portray § 3 of Amendment 73 as an effort at the state level to offset the electoral advantages that congressional incumbents have conferred upon themselves at the federal level. . . .

For me, this suggests only two possibilities. Either the majority's holding is wrong and Amendment 73 does not violate the Qualifications Clauses, or (assuming the accuracy of petitioners' factual claims) the electoral system that exists without Amendment 73 is no less unconstitutional than the electoral system that exists with Amendment 73.

. . . [T]oday's decision reads the Qualifications Clauses to impose substantial implicit prohibitions on the States and the people of the States. I would not draw such an expansive negative inference from the fact that the Constitution requires Members of Congress to be a certain age, to be inhabitants of the States that they represent, and to have been United States citizens for a specified period. Rather, I would read the Qualifications Clauses to do no more than what they say.

NOTES

1.   Are you persuaded by the majority or by the dissent? Which side has the stronger argument about the text? About the historical context of the Qualifications Clauses? What structural arguments do you think are most persuasive? Does the history recounted in this case and in *Powell v. McCormack* affect your view of the correct outcome? To what extent do the last two centuries of practice settle this question? Is it dispositive that we have not had state-imposed term limits on federal office? Or, to the contrary, is it dispositive that many states have, for example, disqualified felons from voting or running for office? Do policy concerns cause you to side with the majority or the dissent? Or do you think they are irrelevant?

2.   Is it just as appropriate for the Court to decide the constitutional question presented in *Thornton* as it was for the Court to decide the question presented in *Powell*? Or should the Court have a different role when a constitutional provision is being construed by the states rather than by Congress? If so, should the Court's role in a *Thornton* situation be more deferential or less?

3.   In the wake of *Thornton*, can the states constitutionally disqualify felons from being elected to and serving in Congress? What if a felon is serving a lengthy prison term and cannot perform the duties of a member of Congress?

[Assignment 7]

C. LEGISLATIVE PROCEDURE AND PREROGATIVES: "EACH HOUSE MAY DETERMINE THE RULES OF ITS PROCEEDINGS"

Art. I, § 5: . . . Each House may determine the Rules of its Proceedings, punish its Members for disorderly Behaviour, and, with the Concurrence of two thirds, expel a Member. . . .

Article I, Section 5 grants to each house the power to determine the rules of its own proceedings. Consider two cases involving this provision. The first, *McGrain v. Daugherty*, grew out of the scandals that engulfed the presidency of Warren Harding in the 1920s. *McGrain* broadened Congress's ability to conduct investigations and hold oversight hearings. The second, *Committee on the Judiciary v. Miers*, grew out of a controversy during the presidency of George W. Bush. After the administration dismissed a group of United States attorneys in December 2006, the House and Senate Judiciary Committees began to investigate the motivation and attempted to force Harriet Miers, the former White House counsel, to testify.

Investigations and oversight hearings have become potent congressional weapons, and they have been used both famously and infamously—contrast the House Judiciary Committee's famous investigation of the Nixon administration with the infamous era of Senator Joseph McCarthy and the House Committee on Un-American Activities. As you read these cases, think about what constitutional arguments are at issue. Does the text establish the scope of Congress's power to investigate, oversee, and punish, and if not, what does?

McGrain v. Daugherty

273 U.S. 135 (1927)

■ MR. JUSTICE VAN DEVANTER delivered the opinion of the court.

This is an appeal from the final order in a proceeding in *habeas corpus* discharging a recusant witness held in custody under process of attachment issued from the United States Senate in the course of an investigation which it was making of the administration of the Department of Justice. A full statement of the case is necessary.

The Department of Justice is one of the great executive departments established by congressional enactment. . . . Harry M. Daugherty became the Attorney General March 5, 1921, and held that office until March 28, 1924, when he resigned. Late in that period various charges of misfeasance and nonfeasance in the Department of Justice after he became its supervising head were brought to the attention of the Senate by individual senators and made the basis of an insistent demand that the department be investigated to the end that the practices and deficiencies which, according to the charges, were operating to prevent or impair its right administration might be definitely ascertained and that appropriate and effective measures might be taken to remedy or eliminate the evil. The Senate . . . [and House passed] two measures taking important litigation then in immediate contemplation out of the control of the Department of Justice and placing the same in charge of a special counsel to be appointed by the President; and also adopted a resolution authorizing and directing a select committee of five senators "to investigate . . . the alleged failure of Harry M. Daugherty, Attorney General of the United States, to prosecute properly violators of the Sherman Anti-trust Act[.]" . . .

In the course of the investigation the committee issued and caused to be duly served on Mally S. Daugherty—who was a brother of Harry M. Daugherty and president of the Midland National Bank of Washington Court House, Ohio—a subpoena commanding him to appear before the committee. . . . The witness failed to appear. . . .

The committee then made a report to the Senate stating that the subpoenas had been issued, that . . . the witness was personally served; and that he had failed and refused to appear. After a reading of the report, the Senate adopted a resolution reciting these facts and proceeding as follows:

> . . . Resolved, That the President of the Senate pro tempore issue his warrant commanding the Sergeant at Arms or his deputy to take into custody the body of the said M. S. Daugherty wherever found, and to bring the said M. S. Daugherty before the bar of the Senate, then and there to answer such questions pertinent to the matter under inquiry as the Senate may order the President of the Senate pro tempore to propound; and to keep the said M. S. Daugherty in custody to await the further order of the Senate.

It will be observed from the terms of the resolution that the warrant was to be issued in furtherance of the effort be obtain the personal testimony of the witness. . . . The warrant was issued agreeably to the resolution and was addressed simply to the Sergeant at Arms. That officer, on receiving the warrant, endorsed thereon a direction that it be executed by John J. McGrain, already his deputy, and delivered it to him for execution.

The deputy, proceeding under the warrant, took the witness into custody at Cincinnati, Ohio, with the purpose of bringing him before the bar of the Senate as commanded; whereupon the witness petitioned the federal District Court in Cincinnati for a writ of *habeas corpus*. . . .

We have given the case earnest and prolonged consideration because the principal questions involved are of unusual importance and delicacy. They are (a) whether the Senate—or the House of Representatives, both being on the same plane in this regard—has power, through its own process, to compel a private individual to appear before it or one of its committees and give testimony needed to enable it efficiently to exercise a legislative function belonging to it under the Constitution; and (b) whether it sufficiently appears that the process was being employed in this instance to obtain testimony for that purpose. . . .

The Constitution provides for a Congress consisting of a Senate and House of Representatives and invests it with "all legislative powers" granted to the United States, and with power "to make all laws which shall be necessary and proper" for carrying into execution these powers and "all other powers" vested by the Constitution in the United States or in any department or officer thereof. Article 1, §§ 1, 8. Other provisions show that, while bills can become laws only after being considered and passed by both houses of Congress, each house is to be distinct from the other, to have its own officers and rules, and to exercise its legislative function independently. But there is no provision expressly investing either house with power to make investigations and exact testimony to the end that it may exercise its legislative function advisedly and effectively. So the question arises whether this power is so far incidental to the legislative function as to be implied.

In actual legislative practice power to secure needed information by such means has long been treated as an attribute of the power to legislate. It was so regarded in the British Parliament and in the Colonial legislatures before the American Revolution, and a like view has prevailed and been carried into effect in both houses of Congress and in most of the state legislatures.

This power was both asserted and exerted by the House of Representatives in 1792, when it appointed a select committee to inquire into the St. Clair expedition and authorized the committee to send for necessary persons, papers and records. Mr. Madison, who had taken an important part in framing the Constitution only five years before, and four of his associates in that work, were members of the House of Representatives at the time, and all voted for the inquiry. Other exertions of the power by the House of Representatives, as also by the Senate, are shown. . . .

The state courts quite generally have held that the power to legislate carries with it by necessary implication ample authority to obtain information needed in the rightful exercise of that power, and to employ compulsory process for the purpose. . . .

We have referred to the practice of the two houses of Congress; and we now shall notice some significant congressional enactments. . . .

While [our] cases are not decisive of the question we are considering, they definitely settle two propositions which we recognize as entirely sound and having a bearing on its solution: One, that the two houses of Congress, in their separate relations, possess not only such powers as are expressly granted to them by the Constitution, but such auxiliary powers as are necessary and appropriate to make the express powers effective; and, the other, that neither house is invested with "general" power to inquire into private affairs and compel disclosures, but only with such limited power of inquiry as is shown to exist when the rule of constitutional interpretation just stated is rightly applied. . . .

We are of opinion that the power of inquiry—with process to enforce it—is an essential and appropriate auxiliary to the legislative function. It was so regarded and employed in American Legislatures before the Constitution was framed and ratified. Both houses of Congress took this view of it early in their history—the House of Representatives with the approving votes of Mr. Madison and other members whose service in the convention which framed the Constitution gives special significance to their action—and both houses have employed the power accordingly up to the present time. . . . So, when their practice in the matter is appraised according to the circumstances in which it was begun and to those in which it has been continued, it falls nothing short of a practical construction, long continued, of the constitutional provisions respecting their powers, and therefore should be taken as fixing the meaning of those provisions, if otherwise doubtful.

. . . A legislative body cannot legislate wisely or effectively in the absence of information respecting the conditions which the legislation is intended to affect or change; and where the legislative body does not itself possess the requisite information—which not infrequently is true—recourse must be had to others who do possess it. Experience has taught that mere requests for such information often are unavailing, and also that information which is volunteered is not always accurate or complete; so some means of compulsion are essential to obtain what is needed. All this was true before and when the Constitution was framed and adopted. In that period the power of inquiry—with enforcing process—was regarded and employed as a necessary and appropriate attribute of the power to legislate—indeed, was treated as inhering in it. Thus there is ample warrant for thinking, as we do, that the constitutional provisions which commit the legislative function to the two houses are intended to include this attribute to the end that the function may be effectively exercised.

The contention is earnestly made on behalf of the witness that this power of inquiry, if sustained, may be abusively and oppressively exerted. If this be so, it affords no ground for denying the power. The same contention might be directed against the power to legislate, and of course would be unavailing. We must assume, for present purposes, that neither house will be disposed to exert the power beyond its proper bounds, or without due regard to the rights of witnesses. But if, contrary to this assumption, controlling limitations or restrictions are disregarded, the decisions in *Kilbourn v. Thompson* and *Marshall v. Gordon* point to admissible measures of relief. And it is a necessary deduction from the decisions in *Kilbourn v. Thompson* and *In re Chapman* that a witness rightfully may refuse to answer where the bounds of the power are exceeded or the questions are not pertinent to the matter under inquiry. . . .

We are of opinion that the court's ruling on this question was wrong, and that it sufficiently appears, when the proceedings are rightly interpreted, that the object of the investigation and of the effort to secure the witness' testimony was to obtain information for legislative purposes.

It is quite true that the resolution directing the investigation does not in terms avow that it is intended to be in aid of legislation; but it does show that the subject to be investigated was the administration of the Department of Justice—whether its functions were being properly discharged or were being neglected or misdirected, and particularly whether the Attorney General and his assistants were performing or neglecting their duties in respect of the institution and prosecution of proceedings to punish crimes and enforce appropriate remedies against the wrongdoers—specific instances of alleged neglect being recited. Plainly the subject was one on which legislation could be had and would be materially aided by the information which the investigation was calculated to elicit. This becomes manifest when it is reflected that the functions of the Department of Justice, the powers and duties of the Attorney General, and the duties of his assistants, are all subject to regulation by congressional legislation, and that the department is maintained and its activities are carried on under such appropriations as in the judgment of Congress are needed from year to year. . . .

NOTES

1.   What enumerated power is Congress relying on in *McGrain*? Is it Congress's power to adopt rules to govern its own proceedings? Is there any other enumerated power Congress could be exercising? Is there any enumerated power for which compelling the appearance of a witness might be "necessary and proper"?

2.   In *Watkins v. United States*, 354 U.S. 178 (1957), John Watkins was prosecuted and convicted in federal court for contempt of Congress in violation of 2 U.S.C. § 192. Watkins had refused, in 1954, to answer several questions posed to him by a subcommittee of the House Un-American Activities Committee (HUAC). Although Watkins testified before the subcommittee at length, he nonetheless refused to answer a few questions about the possible Communist Party membership of people he had associated with in the past but did not know to be Communist Party members. Chief Justice Earl Warren's opinion for the Court said:

> The power of the Congress to conduct investigations is inherent in the legislative process. That power is broad. It encompasses inquiries concerning the administration of existing laws as well as proposed or possibly needed statutes. It includes surveys of defects in our social, economic or political system for the purpose of enabling the Congress to remedy them. It comprehends probes into departments of the Federal Government to expose corruption, inefficiency or waste. But, broad as is this power of inquiry, it is not unlimited. There is no general authority to expose the private affairs of individuals without justification in terms of the functions of the Congress. . . . Nor is the Congress a law enforcement or trial agency. These are functions of the executive and judicial departments of government. No inquiry is an end in itself; it must be related to, and in furtherance of, a legitimate task of the Congress. Investigations conducted solely for the personal aggrandizement of the investigators or to "punish" those investigated are indefensible.

Chief Justice Warren concluded that the committee's questions were not pertinent to its mandate. Justice Clark dissented.

Two years later, in *Barenblatt v. United States,* 360 U.S. 109 (1959), the Supreme Court reversed course and by a 5–4 vote upheld broad congressional investigatory powers in the pursuit of alleged communists. Lloyd Barenblatt had been indicted and convicted under 2 U.S.C. § 192 for refusing to answer HUAC subcommittee questions about whether he was a member of the Communist Party or knew of Communist Party activities in U.S. educational institutions. Justice Harlan wrote for the Court that the resolution of the House of Representatives setting up HUAC had authorized the subcommittee to ask the particular questions it did, that the subcommittee's questions were pertinent to its investigation, and that it was not attempting to punish Barenblatt. Justices Black, Warren, Douglas, and Brennan dissented, arguing that the subcommittee was in fact trying to punish Barenblatt by making him unemployable. Justice Black's dissent was a blistering attack on the activities and purposes of HUAC:

> [T]he Court today fails to see what is here for all to see—that exposure and punishment is the aim of this Committee and the reason for its existence. To deny this is to ignore the Committee's own claims and the reports it has issued ever since it was established. I cannot believe that the nature of our judicial office requires us to be so blind, and must conclude that the Un-American Activities Committee's "identification" and "exposure" of Communists and suspected Communists . . . amount to an encroachment on the judiciary which bodes ill for the liberties of the people of this land. . . . Ultimately, all the questions in this case really boil down to one—whether we as a people will try fearfully and futilely to preserve democracy by adopting totalitarian methods, or whether in accordance with our traditions and our Constitution we will have the confidence and courage to be free.

Is there an enumerated power under which the House of Representatives could establish the House Committee on Un-American Activities?

3.   The division of the Senate and the House of Representatives into many committees and sub-committees has become an important part of the operation of our constitutional system. Committee membership is determined by a mix of seniority, party loyalty, fundraising ability, and member preference. The last of these considerations means that members of Congress will gravitate toward the committees that allow them to protect the interests of their constituents and local industries. The congressional committees serve as gatekeepers for new bills in their respective areas, and they can investigate and hold oversight hearings for their respective sections of the executive branch. The rise and proliferation of congressional committees and subcommittees—like the rise of political parties—is not explicitly addressed in the Constitution but has become a dominant feature of our system of government.

Committee on the Judiciary, U.S. House of Representatives v. Miers

558 F.Supp.2d 53 (D.D.C. 2008)

■ JOHN D. BATES, DISTRICT JUDGE.

This dispute pits the political branches of the federal government against one another in a case all agree presents issues of extraordinary constitutional significance. The heart of the controversy is whether senior presidential aides are absolutely immune from compelled congressional process. But as is often true of lawsuits that raise important separation of powers concerns, there are many obstacles to the invocation of the jurisdiction of the federal courts that must first be addressed.

The Committee on the Judiciary, acting on behalf of the entire House of Representatives, asks the Court to declare that former White House Counsel Harriet Miers must comply with a subpoena and appear before the Committee to testify regarding an investigation into the forced resignation of nine United States Attorneys in late 2006, and that current White House Chief of Staff Joshua Bolten must produce a privilege log in response to a congressional subpoena. Ms. Miers and Mr. Bolten have moved to dismiss this action in its entirety on the grounds that the Committee lacks standing and a proper cause of action, that disputes of this kind are non-justiciable, and that the Court should exercise its discretion to decline jurisdiction. On the merits, the Executive argues that sound principles of separation of powers and presidential autonomy dictate that the President's closest advisors must be absolutely immune from compelled testimony before Congress, and that the Committee has no authority to demand a privilege log from the White House.

Notwithstanding that the opposing litigants in this case are co-equal branches of the federal government, at bottom this lawsuit involves a basic judicial task—subpoena enforcement—with which federal courts are very familiar. The executive privilege claims that form the foundation of the Executive's resistance to the Committee's subpoenas are not foreign to federal courts either. After all, from *Marbury v. Madison*, 5 U.S. (1 Cranch) 137, 177 (1803) ("[i]t is emphatically the province and duty of the judicial department to say what the law is"), through *United States v. Nixon*, 418 U.S. 683, 705 (1974) (the judiciary is the ultimate arbiter of claims of executive privilege), to *Boumediene v. Bush*, 553 U.S. 723 (2008) (rejecting regime in which the political branches may "switch the Constitution on or off at will" and, rather than the judiciary, "say 'what the law is' "), the Supreme Court has confirmed the fundamental role of the federal courts to resolve the most sensitive issues of separation of powers. In the thirty-four years since *United States v. Nixon* was decided, the courts have routinely considered questions of executive privilege or immunity, and those issues are now "of a type that are traditionally justiciable" in federal courts, *Nixon*, at 697, and certainly not unprecedented, as the Executive contends. . . .

It is important to note that the decision today is very limited. To be sure, most of this lengthy opinion addresses, and ultimately rejects, the Executive's several reasons why the Court should not entertain the Committee's lawsuit, but on the merits of the Committee's present claims the Court only resolves, and again rejects, the claim by the Executive to absolute immunity from compelled congressional process for senior presidential aides. The specific claims of executive privilege that Ms. Miers and Mr. Bolten may assert are not addressed—and the Court expresses no view on such claims. Nor should this decision discourage the process of negotiation and accommodation that most often leads to resolution of disputes between the political branches. Although standing ready to fulfill the essential judicial role to "say what the law is" on specific assertions of executive privilege that may be presented, the Court strongly encourages the political branches to resume their discourse and negotiations in an effort to resolve their differences constructively, while recognizing each branch's essential role. To that end, the Court is reminded of Justice Jackson's observations in his concurring opinion in *Youngstown Sheet & Tube Co. v. Sawyer*, 343 U.S. 579, 635 (1952):

> While the Constitution diffuses power the better to secure liberty, it also contemplates that practice will integrate the dispersed powers into a workable government. It enjoins upon its branches separateness but interdependence, autonomy but reciprocity. Presidential powers are not fixed but fluctuate, depending upon their disjunction or conjunction with those of Congress. . . .

BACKGROUND

. . . [T]he Committee on the Judiciary—a standing Committee of the House of Representatives—commenced an investigation into the forced resignations in early 2007. . . . the Committee declared that it aimed to:

> (1) investigat[e] and expos[e] any possible malfeasance, abuse of authority, or violation of existing laws on the part of the Executive Branch related to these concerns, and (2) consider[ ] whether the conduct uncovered may warrant additions or modifications to existing Federal Law, such as more clearly prohibiting the kinds of improper political interference with prosecutorial decisions as have been alleged here.

[The House Judiciary Committee requested that Miers provide various documents and testify about the decision to terminate the U.S. attorneys. The White House would agree to no more than an unsworn interview of limited scope, a position the committee found unacceptable. The committee ultimately issued subpoenas to Miers and to White House Chief of Staff Joshua Bolten.—Editors]

The undisputed factual record, then, establishes the following. Notwithstanding a prolonged period of negotiation, the parties reached a self-declared impasse with respect to the document production and testimony at issue here. Faced with that reality, the full House of Representatives voted to hold Ms. Miers and Mr. Bolten in contempt of Congress and certified the Contempt Report to the U.S. Attorney for the District of Columbia to pursue criminal enforcement of the contempt citations. The Attorney General then directed the U.S. Attorney not to proceed against Ms. Miers and Mr. Bolten. The Committee, then, filed this suit seeking civil enforcement of its subpoena authority by way of declaratory and injunctive relief. . . .

DISCUSSION

[The court first discussed several procedural issues, including an argument that the case was nonjusticiable.—Editors]

. . . The Executive . . . steadfastly maintains that this dispute is not one traditionally thought to be amenable to judicial resolution. Instead, historical experience demonstrates that the Article III judiciary has been concerned primarily with adjudication concerning individual rights rather than " 'some amorphous general supervision of the operations of government.' " The type of direct judicial intervention in a dispute between the two political branches requested by the Committee in this case, the Executive argues, "has been virtually unknown in American jurisprudence." As the Executive would have it, this controversy is "perhaps the paradigmatic example of [a] dispute that ha[s] been resolved without resort to judicial process." The political branches have instead traditionally resolved their differences by the process of negotiation and accommodation. To the Executive, this "200-plus years of constitutional tradition," strongly suggests that the Committee's case is not the type normally amenable to judicial resolution, which in turn implies that the Committee lacks standing to bring the action. . . .

The Court disagrees for two primary reasons: (1) in essence, this lawsuit merely seeks enforcement of a subpoena, which is a routine and quintessential judicial task; and (2) the Supreme Court has held that the judiciary is the final arbiter of executive privilege, and the grounds asserted for the Executive's refusal to comply with the subpoena are ultimately rooted in executive privilege. Whatever merit there once was to the contention that questions of executive privilege are inherently non-justiciable, it can no longer be maintained in light of *United States v. Nixon* and its progeny.

Courts, as the Committee points out, routinely enforce subpoenas, whether they are grand jury subpoenas, deposition or trial subpoenas to compel testimony or produce documents pursuant to Fed. R. Civ. P. 45, or subpoenas issued by administrative agencies of the United States pursuant to Fed. R. Civ. P. 81(a)(5). That enforcement authority is deeply rooted in the common law tradition, as first explained by Chief Justice Marshall in *United States v. Burr*, 25 F.Cas. 30 (C.C.D. Va. 1807). Moreover, courts have entertained subpoena enforcement actions (or motions to quash subpoenas) where the political branches have clashed over congressional subpoenas. . . .

The Committee correctly points out that "courts have decided countless cases that involve the allocation of power between the political branches (not to mention between the political branches and the judiciary)." The Committee cites a litany of cases in support of that proposition, all of which deal with important separation of powers concerns in their own right. See, e.g., *Morrison v. Olson*, 487 U.S. 654 (1988) (removal); *Bowsher v. Synar*, 478 U.S. 714 (1986) (execution of laws); *INS v. Chadha*, 462 U.S. 919 (legislative veto); *Humphrey's Executor v. United States*, 295 U.S. 602 (1935) (removal); *Myers v. United States*, 272 U.S. 52 (1926) (removal). Hence, in the

Committee's view, federal courts have a long history of resolving cases that involve significant (and often contentious) separation of powers disputes between the branches of the federal government, thus refuting the Executive's assertion that this dispute is non-justiciable because it is not amenable to judicial resolution. . . .

[The court then discussed whether the committee had "a judicially remediable right" to enforce its subpoenas.—Editors]

. . . [T]he Supreme Court has already spoken to whether Article I provides Congress with an implied right to issue subpoenas and enforce them judicially. To be sure, "there is no [constitutional] provision expressly investing either house with power to make investigations and exact testimony, to the end that it may exercise its legislative function advisedly and effectively." *McGrain*, at 161. The question, then, is "whether this power is so far incidental to the legislative function as to be implied." *Id.* In *McGrain*, the Supreme Court answered that question in the affirmative, noting that the power of inquiry was well-established at the time of the founding:

> We are of the opinion that the power of inquiry—with process to enforce it—is an essential and appropriate auxiliary to the legislative function. It was so regarded and employed in American Legislatures before the Constitution was framed and ratified. Both houses of Congress took this view of it early in their history.

Indeed, the Necessary and Proper Clause gives rise to Congress's implied right to issue and enforce subpoenas found in Article I: Congress must have "auxiliary powers as are necessary and appropriate to [the legislative] end." *Id.*, at 175. "A legislative body cannot legislate wisely or effectively in the absence of information respecting the conditions which the legislation is intended to affect or change; and where the legislative body does not itself possess the requisite information . . . recourse must be had to others who do possess it." *Id.* Moreover, when "mere requests for such information . . . are unavailing . . . some means of compulsion are essential to obtain what is needed." *Id.*

In short, there can be no question that Congress has a right—derived from its Article I legislative function—to issue and enforce subpoenas, and a corresponding right to the information that is the subject of such subpoenas. . . .

[Finally, the court turned the to the executive branch's argument that "senior presidential advisors" were absolutely immune from subpoena.—Editors]

The Executive cannot identify a single judicial opinion that recognizes absolute immunity for senior presidential advisors in this or any other context. That simple yet critical fact bears repeating: the asserted absolute immunity claim here is entirely unsupported by existing case law. In fact, there is Supreme Court authority that is all but conclusive on this question and that powerfully suggests that such advisors do not enjoy absolute immunity. The Court therefore rejects the Executive's claim of absolute immunity for senior presidential aides. . . .

The Committee's primary argument on this point is incredibly straight-forward. Ms. Miers was the recipient of a duly issued congressional subpoena. Hence, she was legally obligated to appear to testify before the Committee on this matter, at which time she could assert legitimate privilege claims to specific questions or subjects. The Supreme Court has made it abundantly clear that compliance with a congressional subpoena is a legal requirement. *United States v. Bryan*, 339 U.S. 323, 331 (1950). Indeed, the Court noted:

A subpoena has never been treated as an invitation to a game of hare and hounds, in which the witness must testify only if cornered at the end of the chase. If that were the case, then, indeed, the great power of testimonial compulsion, *so necessary to the effective functioning of courts and legislatures*, would be a nullity. We have often iterated the importance of this public duty, which every person within the jurisdiction of the Government is bound to perform when properly summoned. . . .

The Executive maintains that absolute immunity shields Ms. Miers from compelled testimony before Congress. Although the exact reach of this proposed doctrine is not clear, the Executive insists that it applies only to "a very small cadre of senior advisors." The argument starts with the assertion that the President himself is absolutely immune from compelled congressional testimony. There is no case that stands for that exact proposition, but the Executive maintains that the conclusion flows logically from *Nixon v. Fitzgerald*, 457 U.S. 731 (1982), where the Supreme Court held that the President "is entitled to absolute immunity from damages liability predicated on his official acts." . . . In a similar context, the Supreme Court has extended Speech or Debate Clause immunity to legislative aides who work closely with Members of Congress. *See Gravel v. United States*, 408 U.S. 606, 616–17 (1972). Accordingly, forcing close presidential advisors to testify before Congress would be tantamount to compelling the President himself to do so, a plainly untenable result in the Executive's view. Indeed, as the Executive would have it, "[w]ere the President's closest advisers subject to compelled testimony there would be no end to the demands that effectively could be placed upon the President himself."

Unfortunately for the Executive, this line of argument has been virtually foreclosed by the Supreme Court. In *Harlow v. Fitzgerald*, 457 U.S. 800 (1982), the plaintiff sued "senior White House aides" for civil damages arising out of the defendants' official actions. The defendants argued that they were "entitled to a blanket protection of absolute immunity as an incident of their offices as Presidential aides." The Supreme Court rejected that position. . . .

In *Harlow* the Supreme Court rejected the analogy to legislative aides that the Executive now invokes here. There, the defendants "contend[ed] that the rationale of *Gravel* mandates a similar 'derivative' immunity for the chief aides of the President of the United States." The Court brushed that argument aside, explaining that it "sweeps too far." Even Members of the Cabinet, the Court reasoned, "whose essential roles are acknowledged by the Constitution itself," are not entitled to absolute immunity. There is no reason to extend greater protection to senior aides based solely on their proximity to the President, the Court concluded.

The defendants in *Harlow* also attempted to rely upon the "special functions" of White House aides, as distinct from the formality of their title. The Court explained that such an inquiry "accords with the analytical approach of our cases" but then indicated that the "burden of justifying absolute immunity rests on the official asserting the claim." Sensitive matters of "discretionary authority" such as "national security or foreign policy" may warrant absolute immunity in certain circumstances, but they do not justify a "blanket recognition of absolute immunity for all Presidential aides in the performance of all of their duties." *Id.* at 812. . . .

There is nothing left to the Executive's primary argument in light of *Harlow*. This case, of course, does not involve national security or foreign policy, and the Executive does not invoke that mantra. The derivative, "alter ego" immunity that the Executive requests here due to Ms. Miers's and Mr. Bolten's close proximity to and association with the President has been explicitly and definitively rejected, and there is no basis for reaching a different conclusion here. Indeed, the Executive asks this Court to recognize precisely the type of blanket derivative absolute immunity that the Supreme Court declined to acknowledge in Harlow. . . .

The Executive's concern that "[a]bsent immunity . . . there would be no effective brake on Congress's discretion to compel the testimony of the President's advisers at the highest level of government" is also unfounded. To begin with, the process of negotiation and accommodation will ensure that most disputes over information and testimony are settled informally. Moreover, political considerations—including situations where Congress or one House of Congress is controlled by the same political party that holds the Presidency—will surely factor into Congress's decision whether to deploy its compulsory process over the President's objection. In any event, the historical record produced by the Committee reveals that senior advisors to the President have often testified before Congress subject to various subpoenas dating back to 1973. Thus, it would hardly be unprecedented for Ms. Miers to appear before Congress to testify and assert executive privilege where appropriate. Still, it is noteworthy that in an environment where there is no judicial support whatsoever for the Executive's claim of absolute immunity, the historical record also does not reflect the wholesale compulsion by Congress of testimony from senior presidential advisors that the Executive fears.

Significantly, although the Supreme Court has established that the President is absolutely immune from civil suits arising out of his official actions, even the President may not be absolutely immune from compulsory process more generally. In *United States v. Nixon*, the Supreme Court held that the President is entitled only to a presumptive privilege that can be overcome by the requisite demonstration of need. There, the Supreme Court indicated that "an absolute, unqualified privilege would place [an impediment] in the way of the primary constitutional duty of the Judicial Branch to do justice in criminal prosecutions . . . [and] would plainly conflict with the function of the courts under Art. III." *Nixon*, at 707. Seizing on that passage, the Executive insists that this case is distinguishable because it does not involve a core function of another constituent branch but rather a peripheral exercise of Congress's power. That is mistaken. As discussed above, Congress's power of inquiry is as broad as its power to legislate and lies at the very heart of Congress's constitutional role. Indeed, the former is necessary to the proper exercise of the latter: according to the Supreme Court, the ability to compel testimony is "*necessary to the effective functioning of courts and legislatures.*" *Bryan*, at 331 (emphasis added). Thus, Congress's use of (and need for vindication of) its subpoena power in this case is no less legitimate or important than was the grand jury's in *United States v. Nixon*. Both involve core functions of a co-equal branch of the federal government, and for the reasons identified in *Nixon*, the President may only be entitled to a presumptive, rather than an absolute, privilege here. And it is certainly the case that if the President is entitled only to a presumptive privilege, his close advisors cannot hold the superior card of absolute immunity. . . .

The Court once again emphasizes the narrow scope of today's decision. The Court holds only that Ms. Miers (and other senior presidential advisors) do not have absolute immunity from compelled congressional process in the context of this particular subpoena dispute. There may be some instances where absolute (or qualified) immunity is appropriate for such advisors, but this is not one of them. For instance, where national security or foreign affairs form the basis for the Executive's assertion of privilege, it may be that absolute immunity is appropriate. Similarly, this decision applies only to advisors, not to the President. The Court has no occasion to address whether the President can be subject to compelled congressional process— the Supreme Court held in *Harlow* that the immunity inquiries for the President and senior advisors are analytically distinct. Similarly, there is no need to address here whether the Vice President could be subject to compelled congressional process. Most importantly, Ms. Miers may assert executive privilege in response to any specific questions posed by the Committee. The Court does not at this time pass judgment on any specific assertion of executive privilege.

There are powerful reasons supporting the rejection of absolute immunity as asserted by the Executive here. If the Court held otherwise, the presumptive presidential privilege could be transformed into an absolute privilege and Congress's legitimate interest in inquiry could be easily thwarted. . . .

. . . [I]f the Executive's absolute immunity argument were to prevail, Congress could be left with no recourse to obtain information that is plainly not subject to any colorable claim of executive privilege. For instance, surely at least some of the questions that the Committee intends to ask Ms. Miers would not elicit a response subject to an assertion of privilege; so, too, for responsive documents, many of which may even have been produced already. The Executive's proposed absolute immunity would thus deprive Congress of even non-privileged information. That is an unacceptable result.

Clear precedent and persuasive policy reasons confirm that the Executive cannot be the judge of its own privilege and hence Ms. Miers is not entitled to absolute immunity from compelled congressional process. Ms. Miers is not excused from compliance with the Committee's subpoena by virtue of a claim of executive privilege that may ultimately be made. Instead, she must appear before the Committee to provide testimony, and invoke executive privilege where appropriate. And as the Supreme Court has directed, the judiciary remains the ultimate arbiter of an executive privilege claim, since it is the duty of the courts to declare what the law is. See *Nixon*; *Marbury*. . . .

NOTES

1.　After the district court decision you have just read, Miers convinced the D.C. Circuit to stay the lower court's order. Then, "[o]n March 4, 2009—a month and a half into the Obama administration and two months into the 111th Congress—an agreement was reached under which Miers . . . would testify under oath in closed proceedings and a number of documents would be turned over to the committee." Josh Chafetz, *Executive Branch Contempt of Congress*, 76 U. Chi. L. Rev. 1083, 1092–93 (2009). After that, Miers agreed to dismiss her appeal.

The agreement was said to be driven by "the desire of the White House to 'avert a federal court showdown that could have restricted the authority of the president in future disputes with other branches of government.'" Chafetz, 76 U. Chi. L. Rev. at 1093 n.49

(quoting Carrie Johnson, *Deal Clears Rove, Miers to Discuss Prosecutor Firings*, Wash. Post A8 (Mar. 5, 2009)). What was the White House afraid of? Is it a good thing, or a bad thing, that the D.C. Circuit and the Supreme Court were deprived of an opportunity to rule in the case?

2.   The statute Congress passed in 1857 giving each house the power to subpoena witnesses is today codified as 2 U.S.C. § 192:

> Every person who having been summoned as a witness by the authority of either House of Congress to give testimony or to produce papers upon any matter under inquiry before either House, or any joint committee established by a joint or concurrent resolution of the two Houses of Congress, or any committee of either House of Congress, willfully makes default, or who, having appeared, refuses to answer any question pertinent to the question under inquiry, shall be deemed guilty of a misdemeanor, punishable by a fine of not more than $1,000 nor less than $100 and imprisonment in a common jail for not less than one month nor more than twelve months.

Since World War II, Congress has abandoned its efforts to prosecute contempt of Congress itself and has instead referred such cases to federal prosecutors pursuant to this statute. In *Miers*, the House took the unusual step of suing in court on its own behalf to enforce the subpoena. What is the best way for Congress to enforce its subpoenas? Does calling for the help of the executive branch or the courts alleviate separation of powers concerns, or does it aggravate them?

Illustrating Congressional Procedure: The Filibuster

Both the Senate and the House of Representatives have adopted rules to govern their proceedings that are of constitutional magnitude. An obvious example is Senate Rule 22, which provides that debates (and thus filibusters) can be stopped only by a three-fifths majority of the Senate, which today means sixty votes.

The most famous use of the filibuster came in the 1960s when Southern segregationists sought to stop the adoption of the Civil Rights of Act of 1964. The segregationists were defeated, and the threshold to get "cloture" (i.e., to stop debate) was lowered from two-thirds of those voting to three-fifths of the Senate (at least for Senate actions other than rules changes). This liberalization of cloture rules, however, did not lead to a reduction in the number of filibusters. Instead, filibusters have become more common, due in part to the fact that Senate leaders no longer make filibustering senators stay up and talk all night. The practice today is that once a filibuster is threatened and the leadership fails to end it with sixty votes on a cloture motion, the Senate simply discards the filibustered bill and goes on to other business. There is thus no practical cost to threatening to filibuster because one does not actually need to follow through on the threat to stop a bill.

During the presidencies of George W. Bush and Barack Obama, it became routine for the president's nominees, including judicial nominees, to be filibustered by the senators of the opposing party. Some observers criticized these filibusters as unwise and unconstitutional. Consider the following argument:

> The U.S. Constitution was written to establish majority rule. The historical reasons for this are clear. A major defect with the Constitution's precursor, the Articles of Confederation, was that it required super majorities for making many important decisions. The Framers deliberately set out to remedy this defect by empowering Congress to make most decisions by a

simple majority. The only exceptions to this principle are in seven express situations where a two-thirds vote is required. Each house of Congress does have the power by majority vote to establish the rules of its proceedings but there's no evidence this clause was originally meant to authorize filibusters. . . .

Now for the first time in 214 years a minority of senators are seeking to extend filibustering from legislation to the whole new area of judicial nominees—nominees who they know enjoy the support of a majority of the Senate.

This is a bad idea for three reasons. First, such filibusters weaken the power of the president, who is one of only two officers of government who is elected to represent all of the American people. Second, filibusters of judges undermine judicial independence by giving a minority of senators led by special interest groups a veto over who can become a judge. It's already hard enough for talented and capable individuals to be appointed judges without a minority of senators imposing a litmus test. Third, the filibuster of legislation can at least be defended on the ground that federal legislation ought to be considered with extraordinary care. In contrast, the confirmation of one out of one hundred and seventy-five appellate judges is a much less momentous matter. . . .

The Senate can always change its rules by majority vote. To the extent that Senate Rule Twenty-Two purports to require a two-thirds majority for rules changes, Rule Twenty-Two is unconstitutional. It is an ancient principle of Anglo-American constitutional law that one session of a legislature cannot bind a succeeding session of the same legislature. This principle goes back to the great William Blackstone, who said in his commentaries "Acts of Parliament derogatory from the power of subsequent parliaments be naught." Three vice presidents of the United States presiding over the Senate, Richard Nixon, Hubert Humphrey, and Nelson Rockefeller, have all ruled that the Senate rules can be changed by a simple majority of the Senate. Lloyd Cutler, White House Counsel to Presidents Jimmy Carter and Bill Clinton, has written in the Washington Post that Senate Rule Twenty-Two is plainly unconstitutional. The Senate can and should now amend Rule Twenty-Two by simple majority vote to ban filibusters of judicial nominations.

Testimony of Professor Steven G. Calabresi, Senate Judiciary Committee Hearing on Judicial Nominations and Filibusters, May 6, 2003.

In November, 2013, the Senate appeared to accept a version of this argument. By a 52–48 vote, the Senate upheld a point of order "that the vote on cloture under Rule 22 for all nominations other than that for Supreme Court of the United States is by majority vote." In practical terms this abolished the filibuster for all executive branch nominees and all judicial nominees (except nominees for the Supreme Court).

The Senate ruled this way despite two rules that the Senate had also adopted: Rule 22 itself, which says that "on a measure or motion to amend the Senate rules . . . the necessary affirmative vote shall be two-thirds of the Senators present and voting," and Rule 5, which says "[n]o motion to suspend, modify, or amend any rule, or any part thereof, shall be in order, except on one day's notice in writing, specifying precisely the rule or part proposed to be suspended, modified, or amended, and the purpose thereof."

NOTES

1.   The text of the Constitution requires a two-thirds majority for seven actions: passing constitutional amendments, overriding presidential vetoes, ratifying treaties (Senate only), convicting impeached officials (Senate only), expelling a member of either house, lifting by either house of the ineligibility for service of an individual who "engaged in insurrection or rebellion," and joint action by the House and Senate to remove from office a president who is disabled (upon petition by the vice president and a majority of the cabinet). A majority voting rule is expressly required by the Constitution for some other actions: law-making, admitting new states into the Union, and calling a new constitutional convention. What structural inferences can we draw from these voting rules? Is a majority voting rule the default? May each house of Congress decide whether and when to use a different voting rule?

2.   Can the Senate ignore its own rules? Professor Calabresi argues that Rule 22 was unconstitutional because the Senate has the inherent power to modify its rules by majority vote. What about Rule 5? Did the Senate have the inherent power to ignore the one day's notice requirement as well?

3.   Is there any principled basis for retaining the filibuster for Supreme Court nominees, but not for other judges? Is there a principled basis for retaining the filibuster for legislation but not for most nominations? Why do you think the Senate drew the distinction?

[Assignment 8]

D.   BICAMERALISM AND PRESENTMENT: "EVERY BILL WHICH SHALL HAVE PASSED THE HOUSE OF REPRESENTATIVES AND THE SENATE, SHALL . . . BE PRESENTED TO THE PRESIDENT"

Art. I, § 7: . . . Every Bill which shall have passed the House of Representatives and the Senate, shall, before it become a law, be presented to the President of the United States: If he approve he shall sign it. . . .

The modern era of broad delegations to executive branch agencies spawned a new development: the so-called "legislative veto." Congress sought to control, or check, its own delegations to the executive by adding the condition that one house or both houses could veto any actions that the executive branch took pursuant to the delegation. Was this a constitutional (and sensible) way to address the problems created by the need to delegate in sometimes sweeping terms? Or was this a case of "two wrongs do not make a right"? If legislative vetoes are unconstitutional, why? Is it because they interfere with *executive* power, on the theory that once broad statutory authority is conferred, the power to execute, or carry out that authority, should be the president's alone (under Article II's grant to the president of the "executive Power")? Or are legislative-veto provisions unconstitutional because they are congressional lawmaking that does not comply with Article I, Section 7's rules for how a bill becomes law? The latter theory was the ground on which the Supreme Court eventually held legislative vetoes unconstitutional in *INS v. Chadha*, presented below.

Chadha is a good opportunity to think about Article I's provisions governing the lawmaking procedure. As you just saw, Section 5 provides that each house acting unilaterally has the power to adopt rules for its own proceedings. Section 7 provides a different and more onerous requirement for how a bill becomes law: action by both houses of Congress and presentment to the president for signature or veto. A veto may be overridden, but only by a two-thirds majority of both houses. *Chadha* holds that Congress may not accomplish a change in the law other than through the Article I, Section 7 procedures.

But why couldn't Congress—each house using its Article I, Section 5 power to make its own rules of proceedings—formally satisfy but practically circumvent the rule of *Chadha* by providing for "bicameral" passage of a bill under certain expedited procedures? Could Congress delegate broad authority to executive agencies, but specify that the agencies' actions be treated merely as proposals for further legislative action—and then deem those proposals "passed" by both houses and presented to the president (pursuant to the rules-making power) unless affirmatively rejected? Such fast-track legislative procedures are used in other contexts, most commonly international trade and tariff legislation, where the president is delegated broad negotiating authority and Congress commits itself to a straight up or down vote on whatever the president has negotiated pursuant to that authority. Consider these questions as you read *Chadha* and the case that follows it, *Clinton v. City of New York*, where Congress attempted to give the president a form of line-item-veto authority.

INS v. Chadha

462 U.S. 919 (1983)

■ CHIEF JUSTICE BURGER delivered the opinion of the Court.

We granted certiorari . . . [to consider] a challenge to the constitutionality of the provision in § 244(c)(2) of the Immigration and Nationality Act, authorizing one House of Congress, by resolution, to invalidate the decision of the Executive Branch, pursuant to authority delegated by Congress to the Attorney General of the United States, to allow a particular deportable alien to remain in the United States.

Chadha is an East Indian who was born in Kenya and holds a British passport. He was lawfully admitted to the United States in 1966 on a nonimmigrant student visa. His visa expired on June 30, 1972. On October 11, 1973, the District Director of the Immigration and Naturalization Service ordered Chadha to show cause why he should not be deported for having "remained in the United States for a longer time than permitted." . . . Chadha conceded that he was deportable . . . [and filed] an application for suspension of deportation under § 244(a)(1) of the Act. . . . *[The application was granted through an immigration judge subject to veto by one house of Congress.—Editors]*

On December 12, 1975, Representative Eilberg, Chairman of the Judiciary Subcommittee on Immigration, Citizenship, and International Law, introduced a resolution opposing "the granting of permanent residence in the United States to [six] aliens," including Chadha. . . . The resolution was passed without debate or recorded vote. Since the House action was pursuant to § 244(c)(2), the resolution was not treated as an Art. I legislative act; it was not submitted to the Senate or presented to the President for his action.

After the House veto of the Attorney General's decision to allow Chadha to remain in the United States, the Immigration Judge reopened the deportation proceedings to implement the House order deporting Chadha. Chadha moved to terminate the proceedings on the ground that § 244(c)(2) is unconstitutional. . . .

[A deportation order resulted, which Chadha eventually appealed to] the United States Court of Appeals for the Ninth Circuit. The Immigration and Naturalization Service agreed with Chadha's position before the Court of Appeals and joined him in arguing that § 244(c)(2) is unconstitutional. In light of the importance of the question, the Court of Appeals invited both the Senate and the House of Representatives to file briefs *amici curiae*. . . . [The Ninth Circuit ruled for Chadha.] . . .

[The Court first held that it had appellate jurisdiction to hear the case, and then turned to severability.—Editors]

Congress . . . contends that the provision for the one-House veto in § 244(c)(2) cannot be severed from [the delegation of power to suspend deportations in] § 244. Congress argues that if the provision for the one-House veto is held unconstitutional, [then] all of § 244 [including the delegation of power to suspend deportations] must fall. If § 244 in its entirety is violative of the Constitution, it follows that the Attorney General has no authority to suspend Chadha's deportation under § 244(a)(1), and Chadha would be deported. From this, Congress argues that Chadha lacks standing to challenge the constitutionality of the one-House veto provision because he could receive no relief even if his constitutional challenge proves successful.

. . . [W]e need not [inquire into legislative intent here, however,] since Congress itself has provided the answer to the question of severability in § 406 of the Immigration and Nationality Act, note following 8 U.S.C. § 1101, which provides:

> If *any* particular provision of this Act, or the application thereof to *any* person or circumstance, is held invalid, *the remainder of the Act and the application of such provision to other persons or circumstances shall not be affected thereby.* (Emphasis added.)

This language is unambiguous and gives rise to a presumption that Congress did not intend the validity of the Act as a whole, or of any part of the Act, to depend upon whether the veto clause of § 244(c)(2) was invalid. . . . Congress could not have more plainly authorized the presumption that the provision for a one-House veto in § 244(c)(2) is severable from the remainder of § 244 and the Act of which it is a part. . . .

We turn now to the question whether action of one House of Congress under § 244(c)(2) violates strictures of the Constitution. We begin, of course, with the presumption that the challenged statute is valid. Its wisdom is not the concern of the courts; if a challenged action does not violate the Constitution, it must be sustained. . . .

By the same token, the fact that a given law or procedure is efficient, convenient, and useful in facilitating functions of government, standing alone, will not save it if it is contrary to the Constitution. Convenience and efficiency are not the primary objectives—or the hallmarks—of democratic government and our inquiry is sharpened rather than blunted by the fact that congressional veto provisions are appearing with increasing frequency in statutes which delegate authority to executive and independent agencies:

Since 1932, when the first veto provision was enacted into law, 295 congressional veto-type procedures have been inserted in 196 different statutes as follows: from 1932 to 1939, five statutes were affected; from 1940–49, nineteen statutes; between 1950–59, thirty-four statutes; and from 1960–69, forty-nine. From the year 1970 through 1975, at least one hundred sixty-three such provisions were included in eighty-nine laws.

Abourezk, *The Congressional Veto: A Contemporary Response to Executive Encroachment on Legislative Prerogatives*, 52 Ind. L. Rev. 323, 324 (1977).

JUSTICE WHITE undertakes to make a case for the proposition that the one-House veto is a useful "political invention," and we need not challenge that assertion. We can even concede this utilitarian argument although the long-range political wisdom of this "invention" is arguable. It has been vigorously debated, and it is instructive to compare the views of the protagonists. But policy arguments supporting even useful "political inventions" are subject to the demands of the Constitution which defines powers and, with respect to this subject, sets out just how those powers are to be exercised.

Explicit and unambiguous provisions of the Constitution prescribe and define the respective functions of the Congress and of the Executive in the legislative process. Since the precise terms of those familiar provisions are critical to the resolution of these cases, we set them out verbatim. Article I provides:

All legislative Powers herein granted shall be vested in a Congress of the United States, which shall consist of a Senate *and* House of Representatives. Art. I, § 1. (Emphasis added.)

Every Bill which shall have passed the House of Representatives *and* the Senate, *shall,* before it become a law, be presented to the President of the United States. Art. I, § 7, cl. 2. (Emphasis added.)

Every Order, Resolution, or Vote to which the Concurrence of the Senate and House of Representatives may be necessary (except on a question of Adjournment) *shall be* presented to the President of the United States; and before the Same shall take Effect, *shall be* approved by him, or being disapproved by him, *shall be* repassed by two thirds of the Senate and House of Representatives, according to the Rules and Limitations prescribed in the Case of a Bill. Art. I, § 7, cl. 3. (Emphasis added.)

These provisions of Art. I are integral parts of the constitutional design for the separation of powers. We have recently noted that "[t]he principle of separation of powers was not simply an abstract generalization in the minds of the Framers: it was woven into the document that they drafted in Philadelphia in the summer of 1787." *Buckley v. Valeo*, 424 U.S. 1, 124 (1976). Just as we relied on the textual provision of Art. II, § 2, cl. 2, to vindicate the principle of separation of powers in *Buckley*, we see that the purposes underlying the Presentment Clauses, Art. I, § 7, cls. 2, 3 and the bicameral requirement of Art. I, § 1, and § 7, cl. 2, guide our resolution of the important question presented in these cases. The very structure of the Articles delegating and separating powers under Arts. I, II, and III exemplifies the concept of separation of powers, and we now turn to Art. I.

The records of the Constitutional Convention reveal that the requirement that all legislation be presented to the President before becoming law was uniformly accepted by the Framers. Presentment to the President and the Presidential veto were considered so imperative that the draftsmen took special pains to assure that these requirements could not be circumvented. During the final debate on Art. I, § 7, cl. 2, James Madison expressed concern that it might easily be evaded by the simple expedient of calling a proposed law a "resolution" or "vote," rather than a "bill." 2 M. Farrand, The Records of the Federal Convention of 1787, 301–302. As a consequence, Art. I, § 7, cl. 3 was added.

The decision to provide the President with a limited and qualified power to nullify proposed legislation by veto was based on the profound conviction of the Framers that the powers conferred on Congress were the powers to be most carefully circumscribed. It is beyond doubt that lawmaking was a power to be shared by both Houses and the President . . .

The bicameral requirement of Art. I, §§ 1, 7, was of scarcely less concern to the Framers than was the Presidential veto and indeed the two concepts are interdependent. By providing that no law could take effect without the concurrence of the prescribed majority of the Members of both Houses, the Framers reemphasized their belief, already remarked upon in connection with the Presentment Clauses, that legislation should not be enacted unless it has been carefully and fully considered by the Nation's elected officials. . . .

We see therefore that the Framers were acutely conscious that the bicameral requirement and the Presentment Clauses would serve essential constitutional functions. The President's participation in the legislative process was to protect the Executive Branch from Congress and to protect the whole people from improvident laws. The division of the Congress into two distinctive bodies assures that the legislative power would be exercised only after opportunity for full study and debate in separate settings. The President's unilateral veto power, in turn, was limited by the power of two-thirds of both Houses of Congress to overrule a veto thereby precluding final arbitrary action of one person. It emerges clearly that the prescription for legislative action in Art. I, §§ 1, 7, represents the Framers' decision that the legislative power of the Federal Government be exercised in accord with a single, finely wrought and exhaustively considered, procedure.

The Constitution sought to divide the delegated powers of the new Federal Government into three defined categories, Legislative, Executive, and Judicial, to assure, as nearly as possible, that each branch of government would confine itself to its assigned responsibility. The hydraulic pressure inherent within each of the separate Branches to exceed the outer limits of its power, even to accomplish desirable objectives, must be resisted.

Although not "hermetically" sealed from one another, the powers delegated to the three Branches are functionally identifiable. When any Branch acts, it is presumptively exercising the power the Constitution has delegated to it. When the Executive acts, he presumptively acts in an executive or administrative capacity as defined in Art. II. And when, as here, one House of Congress purports to act, it is presumptively acting within its assigned sphere.

Beginning with this presumption, we must nevertheless establish that the challenged action under § 244(c)(2) is of the kind to which the procedural requirements of Art. I, § 7, apply. Not every action taken by either House is subject to the bicameralism and presentment requirements of Art. I. Whether actions taken by either House are, in law and fact, an exercise of legislative power depends not on their form but upon "whether they contain matter which is properly to be regarded as legislative in its character and effect."

Examination of the action taken here by one House pursuant to § 244(c)(2) reveals that it was essentially legislative in purpose and effect. In purporting to exercise power defined in Art. I, § 8, cl. 4, to "establish an uniform Rule of Naturalization," the House took action that had the purpose and effect of altering the legal rights, duties, and relations of persons, including the Attorney General, Executive Branch officials and Chadha, all outside the Legislative Branch. . . .

The legislative character of the one-House veto in these cases is confirmed by the character of the congressional action it supplants. Neither the House of Representatives nor the Senate contends that, absent the veto provision in § 244(c)(2), either of them, or both of them acting together, could effectively require the Attorney General to deport an alien once the Attorney General, in the exercise of legislatively delegated authority, had determined the alien should remain in the United States. Without the challenged provision in § 244(c)(2), this could have been achieved, if at all, only by legislation requiring deportation. Similarly, a veto by one House of Congress under § 244(c)(2) cannot be justified as an attempt at amending the standards set out in § 244(a)(1), or as a repeal of § 244 as applied to Chadha. Amendment and repeal of statutes, no less than enactment, must conform with Art. I. . . .

Finally, we see that when the Framers intended to authorize either House of Congress to act alone and outside of its prescribed bicameral legislative role, they narrowly and precisely defined the procedure for such action. There are four provisions in the Constitution, explicit and unambiguous, by which one House may act alone with the unreviewable force of law, not subject to the President's veto:

(a) The House of Representatives alone was given the power to initiate impeachments. Art. I, § 2, cl. 5;

(b) The Senate alone was given the power to conduct trials following impeachment on charges initiated by the House and to convict following trial. Art. I, § 3, cl. 6;

(c) The Senate alone was given final unreviewable power to approve or to disapprove Presidential appointments. Art. II, § 2, cl. 2;

(d) The Senate alone was given unreviewable power to ratify treaties negotiated by the President. Art. II, § 2, cl. 2.

Clearly, when the Draftsmen sought to confer special powers on one House, independent of the other House, or of the President, they did so in explicit, unambiguous terms. . . .

Since it is clear that the action by the House under § 244(c)(2) was not within any of the express constitutional exceptions authorizing one House to act alone, and equally clear that it was an exercise of legislative power, that action was subject to the standards prescribed in Art. I. . . . To accomplish what has been attempted by one House of Congress in this case requires action in conformity with the express procedures of the Constitution's prescription for legislative action: passage by a majority of both Houses and presentment to the President.

The veto authorized by § 244(c)(2) doubtless has been in many respects a convenient shortcut; the "sharing" with the Executive by Congress of its authority over aliens in this manner is, on its face, an appealing compromise. In purely practical terms, it is obviously easier for action to be taken by one House without submission to the President; but it is crystal clear from the records of the Convention, contemporaneous writings and debates, that the Framers ranked other values higher than efficiency. The records of the Convention and debates in the states preceding ratification underscore the common desire to define and limit the exercise of the newly created federal powers affecting the states and the people. There is unmistakable expression of a determination that legislation by the national Congress be a step-by-step, deliberate and deliberative process.

The choices we discern as having been made in the Constitutional Convention impose burdens on governmental processes that often seem clumsy, inefficient, even unworkable, but those hard choices were consciously made by men who had lived under a form of government that permitted arbitrary governmental acts to go unchecked. There is no support in the Constitution or decisions of this Court for the proposition that the cumbersomeness and delays often encountered in complying with explicit constitutional standards may be avoided, either by the Congress or by the President. See *Youngstown Sheet & Tube Co. v. Sawyer*, 343 U.S. 579 (1952). With all the obvious flaws of delay, untidiness, and potential for abuse, we have not yet found a better way to preserve freedom than by making the exercise of power subject to the carefully crafted restraints spelled out in the Constitution.

We hold that the congressional veto provision in § 244(c)(2) is severable from the Act and that it is unconstitutional.

■ JUSTICE POWELL, concurring in the judgment.

The Court's decision, based on the Presentment Clauses, Art. I, § 7, cls. 2 and 3, apparently will invalidate every use of the legislative veto. The breadth of this holding gives one pause. Congress has included the veto in literally hundreds of statutes, dating back to the 1930's. Congress clearly views this procedure as essential to controlling the delegation of power to administrative agencies. One reasonably may disagree with Congress' assessment of the veto's utility, but the respect due its judgment as a coordinate branch of Government cautions that our holding should be no more extensive than necessary to decide these cases. In my view, the cases may be decided on a narrower ground. When Congress finds that a particular person does not satisfy the statutory criteria for permanent residence in this country it has assumed a judicial function in violation of the principle of separation of powers. Accordingly, I concur only in the judgment. . . .

■ JUSTICE WHITE, dissenting.

Today the Court not only invalidates § 244(c)(2) of the Immigration and Nationality Act, but also sounds the death knell for nearly 200 other statutory provisions in which Congress has reserved a "legislative veto." For this reason, the Court's decision is of surpassing importance. And it is for this reason that the Court would have been well advised to decide the cases, if possible, on the narrower grounds of separation of powers, leaving for full consideration the constitutionality of other congressional review statutes operating on such varied matters as war powers and agency rulemaking, some of which concern the independent regulatory agencies.

The prominence of the legislative veto mechanism in our contemporary political system and its importance to Congress can hardly be overstated. It has become a central means by which Congress secures the accountability of executive and independent agencies. Without the legislative veto, Congress is faced with a Hobson's choice: either to refrain from delegating the necessary authority, leaving itself with a hopeless task of writing laws with the requisite specificity to cover endless special circumstances across the entire policy landscape, or in the alternative, to abdicate its law-making function to the Executive Branch and independent agencies. To choose the former leaves major national problems unresolved; to opt for the latter risks unaccountable policymaking by those not elected to fill that role. Accordingly, over the past five decades, the legislative veto has been placed in nearly 200 statutes. The device is known in every field of governmental concern: reorganization, budgets, foreign affairs, war powers, and regulation of trade, safety, energy, the environment, and the economy. . . . *[Justice White proceeds to recount the history of the legislative veto, beginning with the Hoover administration.—Editors]*

Even this brief review suffices to demonstrate that the legislative veto is more than "efficient, convenient, and useful." It is an important if not indispensable political invention that allows the President and Congress to resolve major constitutional and policy differences, assures the accountability of independent regulatory agencies, and preserves Congress' control over lawmaking. Perhaps there are other means of accommodation and accountability, but the increasing reliance of Congress upon the legislative veto suggests that the alternatives to which Congress must now turn are not entirely satisfactory.

The history of the legislative veto also makes clear that it has not been a sword with which Congress has struck out to aggrandize itself at the expense of the other branches—the concerns of Madison and Hamilton. Rather, the veto has been a means of defense, a reservation of ultimate authority necessary if Congress is to fulfill its designated role under Art. I as the Nation's lawmaker. While the President has often objected to particular legislative vetoes, generally those left in the hands of congressional Committees, the Executive has more often agreed to legislative review as the price for a broad delegation of authority. To be sure, the President may have preferred unrestricted power, but that could be precisely why Congress thought it essential to retain a check on the exercise of delegated authority.

. . . [T]he constitutionality of the legislative veto is anything but clear-cut. The issue divides scholars, courts, Attorneys General, and the two other branches of the National Government. If the veto devices so flagrantly disregarded the requirements of Art. I as the Court today suggests, I find it incomprehensible that Congress, whose Members are bound by oath to uphold the Constitution, would have placed these mechanisms in nearly 200 separate laws over a period of 50 years.

. . . We should not find the lack of a specific constitutional authorization for the legislative veto surprising, and I would not infer disapproval of the mechanism from its absence. From the summer of 1787 to the present the Government of the United States has become an endeavor far beyond the contemplation of the Framers. Only within the last half century has the complexity and size of the Federal Government's responsibilities grown so greatly that the Congress must rely on the legislative veto as the most effective if not the only means to insure its role as the Nation's lawmaker. But the wisdom of the Framers was to anticipate that the Nation would grow and new problems of governance would require different solutions. Accordingly, our Federal Government was intentionally chartered with the flexibility to respond to contemporary needs without losing sight of fundamental democratic principles. This was the spirit in which Justice Jackson penned his influential concurrence in the *Steel Seizure Case.* . . .

When the Convention did turn its attention to the scope of Congress' lawmaking power, the Framers were expansive. The Necessary and Proper Clause, Art. I, § 8, cl. 18, vests Congress with the power "[t]o make all Laws which shall be necessary and proper for carrying into Execution the foregoing Powers [the enumerated powers of § 8] and all other Powers vested by this Constitution in the Government of the United States, or in any Department or Officer thereof." It is long settled that Congress may "exercise its best judgment in the selection of measures, to carry into execution the constitutional powers of the government," and "avail itself of experience, to exercise its reason, and to accommodate its legislation to circumstances." *McCulloch v. Maryland,* 17 U.S. (4 Wheat.) 316, 415–416, 420 (1819).

The Court heeded this counsel in approving the modern administrative state. The Court's holding today that all legislative-type action must be enacted through the lawmaking process ignores that legislative authority is routinely delegated to the Executive Branch, to the independent regulatory agencies, and to private individuals and groups:

> The rise of administrative bodies probably has been the most significant legal trend of the last century. . . . They have become a veritable fourth branch of the Government, which has deranged our three-branch legal theories. . . .

FTC v. Ruberoid Co., 343 U.S. 470, 487 (1952) (Jackson, J. dissenting). This Court's decisions sanctioning such delegations make clear that Art. I does not require all action with the effect of legislation to be passed as a law.

Theoretically, agencies and officials were asked only to "fill up the details," and the rule was that "Congress cannot delegate any part of its legislative power except under the limitation of a prescribed standard." . . . In practice, however, restrictions on the scope of the power that could be delegated diminished and all but disappeared. In only two instances did the Court find an unconstitutional delegation. *Panama Refining Co. v. Ryan,* 293 U.S. 388 (1935); *A.L.A. Schechter Poultry Corp. v. United States,* 295 U.S. 495 (1935). . . .

If Congress may delegate lawmaking power to independent and Executive agencies, it is most difficult to understand Art. I as prohibiting Congress from also reserving a check on legislative power for itself. . . .

The Court also takes no account of perhaps the most relevant consideration: However resolutions of disapproval under § 244(c)(2) are formally characterized, in reality, a departure from the status quo occurs only upon the concurrence of opinion among the House, Senate, and President. . . .

The central concern of the presentment and bicameralism requirements of Art. I is that when a departure from the legal status quo is undertaken, it is done with the approval of the President and both Houses of Congress—or, in the event of a Presidential veto, a two-thirds majority in both Houses. This interest is fully satisfied by the operation of § 244(c)(2). The President's approval is found in the Attorney General's action in recommending to Congress that the deportation order for a given alien be suspended. The House and the Senate indicate their approval of the Executive's action by not passing a resolution of disapproval within the statutory period. Thus, a change in the legal status quo—the deportability of the alien—is consummated only with the approval of each of the three relevant actors. . . . Thus understood, § 244(c)(2) fully effectuates the purposes of the bicameralism and presentment requirements. . . .

I do not suggest that all legislative vetoes are necessarily consistent with separation-of-powers principles. A legislative check on an inherently executive function, for example, that of initiating prosecutions, poses an entirely different question. But the legislative veto device here—and in many other settings—is far from an instance of legislative tyranny over the Executive. It is a necessary check on the unavoidably expanding power of the agencies, both Executive and independent, as they engage in exercising authority delegated by Congress. . . .

Today's decision strikes down in one fell swoop provisions in more laws enacted by Congress than the Court has cumulatively invalidated in its history. I fear it will now be more difficult to "insur[e] that the fundamental policy decisions in our society will be made not by an appointed official but by the body immediately responsible to the people." I must dissent.

■ JUSTICE REHNQUIST, with whom JUSTICE WHITE joins, dissenting.

A severability clause creates a presumption that Congress intended the valid portion of the statute to remain in force when one part is found to be invalid. A severability clause does not, however, conclusively resolve the issue. "[T]he determination, in the end, is reached by" asking "[w]hat was the intent of the lawmakers," and "will rarely turn on the presence or absence of such a clause." Because I believe that Congress did not intend the one-House veto provision of § 244(c)(2) to be severable, I dissent. . . .

The Court finds that the legislative history of § 244 shows that Congress intended § 244(c)(2) to be severable because Congress wanted to relieve itself of the burden of private bills. But the history elucidated by the Court shows that Congress was unwilling to give the Executive Branch permission to suspend deportation on its own. Over the years, Congress consistently rejected requests from the Executive for complete discretion in this area. Congress always insisted on retaining ultimate control, whether by concurrent resolution . . . or by [the] one-House veto, as in the present Act. Congress has never indicated that it would be willing to permit suspensions of deportation unless it could retain some sort of veto.

. . . Congress' continued insistence on retaining control of the suspension process indicates that it has never been disposed to give the Executive Branch a free hand. . . .

Because I do not believe that § 244(c)(2) is severable, I would reverse the judgment of the Court of Appeals.

NOTES

1.   The majority opinion in *Chadha* asks which of the three powers of government Congress is exercising when it adopts a legislative veto. It reasons that Congress cannot be exercising executive power, because the Constitution gives all of the executive power to the president; nor can it be exercising judicial power, because the Constitution vests that in the federal courts. It thus concludes that Congress is trying to exercise its legislative power, which it may exercise only through bicameralism and presentment. Does the reasoning work? What power is Congress trying to exercise in this case? Hasn't Congress, in essence, delegated legislative power to a portion of itself here? That is,

instead of sweepingly delegating the ultimate power to suspend deportations to the INS, Congress has delegated that power to either one of the two houses, should they choose to act. Why can't it do that?

2.   The executive branch has long regarded legislative vetoes as unconstitutional. When a private party challenged the legislative veto in *Chadha*, the Department of Justice agreed with the challenge. But if the government and Chadha are on the same side—agreeing that the legislative veto is unconstitutional—why is this case in court? The unusual procedural answer is that the Senate and House of Representatives were allowed to "intervene" as parties in the court of appeals in order to defend their respective interests in having the legislative veto upheld. In the Supreme Court, the solicitor general (the officer in the Department of Justice who usually argues cases before the Supreme Court) argued that the statute was unconstitutional, and attorneys for the Senate and House of Representatives argued that it was constitutional. Does this make sense? Or should the Department of Justice be required to defend the constitutionality of Congress's acts whenever they are challenged by a private party? And if the president believes a law is unconstitutional, and instructs executive branch attorneys to make that argument in court, should the executive branch also decline to enforce the law? The Supreme Court confronted this situation again in *United States v. Windsor*, p. 420.

3.   Now consider the severability issue. Would Congress have intended to delegate to the attorney general the authority to make determinations that would "suspend deportation" of an otherwise deportable alien, *without* the string attached that one house of Congress could override that determination? Maybe. Maybe not. But if not, is it a problem that *Chadha* results in a statutory authority that Congress would never have enacted?

How should the courts handle these severability problems? How can one tell what Congress would have chosen to do, if it knew it could not have the unconstitutional part of the statute? Is Justice Rehnquist's reading of that hypothetical congressional intent persuasive? Or should severability doctrine completely ignore any counterfactuals about what Congress would have wanted? See Kevin C. Walsh, *Partial Unconstitutionality*, 85 N.Y.U. L. Rev. 738 (2010).

4.   A hypothetical: Congress passes a statute delegating to the attorney general the power to propose all laws and rules governing immigration policy in the United States and provides, pursuant to each house's rules power (Article I, Section 5), that such proposals shall automatically be deemed "passed" thirty days after submission, unless a member calls for a vote and the proposal is defeated by a simple majority of each house. The measure provides for presentment to the president of any immigration law or rule thus "passed." Constitutional? Does it get around the rule of *Chadha* in a way that satisfies the requirements of bicameralism and presentment? If the answer to the last question is *yes*, how different is this hypothetical situation from the scheme struck down in *Chadha*?

5.   Article I, Section 7 provides the president with veto authority, subject to a congressional override if two-thirds of the members of each house vote to pass the bill again. What is a "bill" as that word is used in Article I, Section 7? As illustrated by the severability issue in *INS v. Chadha*, a single legislative enactment can contain many provisions, both related and unrelated. Does anything in the Constitution restrict Congress's authority to "bundle" enactments? Is such bundling permitted by each house's Article I, Section 5 authority to enact rules to govern its own proceedings? What if the effect of such bundling is to present the president with one enormous "bill" with all of the government's appropriations in it—leaving a dreadful all-or-nothing decision as to whether to veto the bill? Is that unconstitutional? May the president veto *a provision* and

sign the rest of the bill? Does Congress get to define what is a "bill" for Article I, Section 7 purposes? Why?

Clinton v. City of New York
524 U.S. 417 (1998)

■ JUSTICE STEVENS delivered the opinion of the Court.

The Line Item Veto Act was enacted in April 1996 and became effective on January 1, 1997. . . . [Later that year] the President exercised his authority to cancel one [spending] provision in the Balanced Budget Act of 1997, and two [limited tax relief benefit] provisions in the Taxpayer Relief Act of 1997. Appellees, claiming that they had been injured by two of those cancellations, filed these cases in the District Court. That Court . . . held the statute invalid, and we . . . expedited our review. We now hold that these appellees have standing to challenge the constitutionality of the Act and, reaching the merits, we agree that the cancellation procedures set forth in the Act violate the Presentment Clause, Art. I, § 7, cl. 2, of the Constitution. . . .

[The Court began by concluding that it had jurisdiction and the parties had standing.—Editors]

The Line Item Veto Act gives the President the power to "cancel in whole" three types of provisions that have been signed into law: "(1) any dollar amount of discretionary budget authority; (2) any item of new direct spending; or (3) any limited tax benefit." It is undisputed that the New York case involves an "item of new direct spending" and that the Snake River case involves a "limited tax benefit" as those terms are defined in the Act. It is also undisputed that each of those provisions had been signed into law pursuant to Article I, § 7, of the Constitution before it was canceled.

The Act requires the President to adhere to precise procedures whenever he exercises his cancellation authority. In identifying items for cancellation he must consider the legislative history, the purposes, and other relevant information about the items. He must determine, with respect to each cancellation, that it will "(i) reduce the Federal budget deficit; (ii) not impair any essential Government functions; and (iii) not harm the national interest." Moreover, he must transmit a special message to Congress notifying it of each cancellation within five calendar days (excluding Sundays) after the enactment of the canceled provision. It is undisputed that the President meticulously followed these procedures in these cases.

A cancellation takes effect upon receipt by Congress of the special message from the President. If, however, a "disapproval bill" pertaining to a special message is enacted into law, the cancellations set forth in that message become "null and void." The Act sets forth a detailed expedited procedure for the consideration of a "disapproval bill," . . . but no such bill was passed for either of the cancellations involved in these cases. A majority vote of both Houses is sufficient to enact a disapproval bill. The Act does not grant the President the authority to cancel a disapproval bill, but he does, of course, retain his constitutional authority to veto such a bill.

The effect of a cancellation is . . . [that it] prevents the item "from having legal force or effect." Thus, under the plain text of the statute, the two actions of the President that are challenged in these cases prevented one section of the Balanced

Budget Act of 1997 and one section of the Taxpayer Relief Act of 1997 "from having legal force or effect." The remaining provisions of those statutes, with the exception of the second canceled item in the latter, continue to have the same force and effect as they had when signed into law.

In both legal and practical effect, the President has amended two Acts of Congress by repealing a portion of each. "[R]epeal of statutes, no less than enactment, must conform with Art. I." *INS v. Chadha*, 462 U.S. 919, 954 (1983). There is no provision in the Constitution that authorizes the President to enact, to amend, or to repeal statutes. Both Article I and Article II assign responsibilities to the President that directly relate to the lawmaking process, but neither addresses the issue presented by these cases. . . .

There are important differences between the President's "return" of a bill pursuant to Article I, § 7, and the exercise of the President's cancellation authority pursuant to the Line Item Veto Act. The constitutional return takes place *before* the bill becomes law; the statutory cancellation occurs *after* the bill becomes law. The constitutional return is of the entire bill; the statutory cancellation is of only a part. Although the Constitution expressly authorizes the President to play a role in the process of enacting statutes, it is silent on the subject of unilateral Presidential action that either repeals or amends parts of duly enacted statutes.

There are powerful reasons for construing constitutional silence on this profoundly important issue as equivalent to an express prohibition. The procedures governing the enactment of statutes set forth in the text of Article I were the product of the great debates and compromises that produced the Constitution itself. Familiar historical materials provide abundant support for the conclusion that the power to enact statutes may only "be exercised in accord with a single, finely wrought and exhaustively considered, procedure." *Chadha*, at 951. Our first President understood the text of the Presentment Clause as requiring that he either "approve all the parts of a Bill, or reject it in toto." What has emerged in these cases from the President's exercise of his statutory cancellation powers, however, are truncated versions of two bills that passed both Houses of Congress. They are not the product of the "finely wrought" procedure that the Framers designed. . . .

The Line Item Veto Act authorizes the President himself to effect the repeal of laws, for his own policy reasons, without observing the procedures set out in Article I, § 7. The fact that Congress intended such a result is of no moment. . . . Congress cannot alter the procedures set out in Article I, § 7, without amending the Constitution.

Neither are we persuaded by the Government's contention that the President's authority to cancel new direct spending and tax benefit items is no greater than his traditional authority to decline to spend appropriated funds. The Government has reviewed in some detail the series of statutes in which Congress has given the Executive broad discretion over the expenditure of appropriated funds. For example, the First Congress appropriated "sum[s] not exceeding" specified amounts to be spent on various Government operations. In those statutes, as in later years, the President was given wide discretion with respect to both the amounts to be spent and how the money would be allocated among different functions. It is argued that the Line Item Veto Act merely confers comparable discretionary authority over the expenditure of appropriated funds. The critical difference between this statute and all of its predecessors, however, is that unlike any of them, this Act gives the President the unilateral power to change the text of duly enacted statutes. None of the Act's predecessors could even arguably have been construed to authorize such a change.

. . . [A]lthough appellees challenge the validity of the Act on alternative grounds, the only issue we address concerns the "finely wrought" procedure commanded by the Constitution. *Chadha*, at 951. We have been favored with extensive debate about the scope of Congress' power to delegate law-making authority, or its functional equivalent, to the President. The excellent briefs filed by the parties and their *amici curiae* have provided us with valuable historical information that illuminates the delegation issue but does not really bear on the narrow issue that is dispositive of these cases. Thus, because we conclude that the Act's cancellation provisions violate Article I, § 7, of the Constitution, we find it unnecessary to consider the District Court's alternative holding that the Act "impermissibly disrupts the balance of powers among the three branches of government."

[O]ur decision rests on the narrow ground that the procedures authorized by the Line Item Veto Act are not authorized by the Constitution. The Balanced Budget Act of 1997 is a 500-page document that became "Public Law 105–33" after three procedural steps were taken: (1) a bill containing its exact text was approved by a majority of the Members of the House of Representatives; (2) the Senate approved precisely the same text; and (3) that text was signed into law by the President. The Constitution explicitly requires that each of those three steps be taken before a bill may "become a law." Art. I, § 7. If one paragraph of that text had been omitted at any one of those three stages, Public Law 105–33 would not have been validly enacted. If the Line Item Veto Act were valid, it would authorize the President to create a different law—one whose text was not voted on by either House of Congress or presented to the President for signature. . . .

If there is to be a new procedure in which the President will play a different role in determining the final text of what may "become a law," such change must come not by legislation but through the amendment procedures set forth in Article V of the Constitution. Cf. *U.S. Term Limits, Inc. v. Thornton*, 514 U.S. 779, 837 (1995). . . .

■ JUSTICE KENNEDY, concurring.

. . . [M]y colleague JUSTICE BREYER . . . observes that the statute does not threaten the liberties of individual citizens, a point on which I disagree. The argument is related to his earlier suggestion that our role is lessened here because the two political branches are adjusting their own powers between themselves. To say the political branches have a somewhat free hand to reallocate their own authority would seem to require acceptance of two premises: first, that the public good demands it, and second, that liberty is not at risk. The former premise is inadmissible. The Constitution's structure requires a stability which transcends the convenience of the moment. The latter premise, too, is flawed. Liberty is always at stake when one or more of the branches seek to transgress the separation of powers.

Separation of powers was designed to implement a fundamental insight: Concentration of power in the hands of a single branch is a threat to liberty. The Federalist states the axiom in these explicit terms: "The accumulation of all powers, legislative, executive, and judiciary, in the same hands . . . may justly be pronounced the very definition of tyranny." The Federalist No. 47. So convinced were the Framers that liberty of the person inheres in structure that at first they did not consider a

Bill of Rights necessary. The Federalist No. 84; G. Wood, The Creation of the American Republic 1776–1787, pp. 536–543 (1969). It was at Madison's insistence that the First Congress enacted the Bill of Rights. It would be a grave mistake, however, to think a Bill of Rights in Madison's scheme then or in sound constitutional theory now renders separation of powers of lesser importance.

In recent years, perhaps, we have come to think of liberty as defined by that word in the Fifth and Fourteenth Amendments and as illuminated by the other provisions of the Bill of Rights. The conception of liberty embraced by the Framers was not so confined. They used the principles of separation of powers and federalism to secure liberty in the fundamental political sense of the term, quite in addition to the idea of freedom from intrusive governmental acts. . . .

The principal object of the statute, it is true, was not to enhance the President's power to reward one group and punish another, to help one set of taxpayers and hurt another, to favor one State and ignore another. Yet these are its undeniable effects. The law establishes a new mechanism which gives the President the sole ability to hurt a group that is a visible target, in order to disfavor the group or to extract further concessions from Congress. The law is the functional equivalent of a line item veto and enhances the President's powers beyond what the Framers would have endorsed.

It is no answer, of course, to say that Congress surrendered its authority by its own hand; nor does it suffice to point out that a new statute, signed by the President or enacted over his veto, could restore to Congress the power it now seeks to relinquish. That a congressional cession of power is voluntary does not make it innocuous. The Constitution is a compact enduring for more than our time, and one Congress cannot yield up its own powers, much less those of other Congresses to follow. Abdication of responsibility is not part of the constitutional design. . . .

The citizen has a vital interest in the regularity of the exercise of governmental power. If this point was not clear before *Chadha*, it should have been so afterwards. . . . By increasing the power of the President beyond what the Framers envisioned, the statute compromises the political liberty of our citizens, liberty which the separation of powers seeks to secure. . . .

■ JUSTICE BREYER, with whom JUSTICE O'CONNOR and JUSTICE SCALIA join as to Part III, dissenting.

I agree with the Court that the parties have standing, but I do not agree with its ultimate conclusion. In my view the Line Item Veto Act does not violate any specific textual constitutional command, nor does it violate any implicit separation-of-powers principle. Consequently, I believe that the Act is constitutional.

I approach the constitutional question before us with three general considerations in mind. *First*, the Act represents a legislative effort to provide the President with the power to give effect to some, but not to all, of the expenditure and revenue-diminishing provisions contained in a single massive appropriations bill. And this objective is constitutionally proper.

When our Nation was founded, Congress could easily have provided the President with this kind of power. In that time period, our population was less than 4 million, federal employees numbered fewer than 5,000, annual federal budget outlays totaled approximately $4 million, and the entire operative text of Congress's first general appropriations law read as follows:

Be it enacted . . . [t]hat there be appropriated for the service of the present year, to be paid out of the monies which arise, either from the requisitions heretofore made upon the several states, or from the duties on import and tonnage, the following sums, viz. A sum not exceeding two hundred and sixteen thousand dollars for defraying the expenses of the civil list, under the late and present government; a sum not exceeding one hundred and thirty-seven thousand dollars for defraying the expenses of the department of war; a sum not exceeding one hundred and ninety thousand dollars for discharging the warrants issued by the late board of treasury, and remaining unsatisfied; and a sum not exceeding ninety-six thousand dollars for paying the pensions to invalids.

Act of Sept. 29, 1789, ch. 23, § 1, 1 Stat. 95.

At that time, a Congress, wishing to give a President the power to select among appropriations, could simply have embodied each appropriation in a separate bill, each bill subject to a separate Presidential veto.

Today, however, our population is about 250 million, the Federal Government employs more than 4 million people, the annual federal budget is $1.5 trillion, and a typical budget appropriations bill may have a dozen titles, hundreds of sections, and spread across more than 500 pages of the Statutes at Large. Congress cannot divide such a bill into thousands, or tens of thousands, of separate appropriations bills, each one of which the President would have to sign, or to veto, separately. Thus, the question is whether the Constitution permits Congress to choose a particular novel *means* to achieve this same, constitutionally legitimate, *end*.

Second, the case in part requires us to focus upon the Constitution's generally phrased structural provisions, provisions that delegate all "legislative" power to Congress and vest all "executive" power in the President. The Court, when applying these provisions, has interpreted them generously in terms of the institutional arrangements that they permit. . . . *McCulloch v. Maryland*, 17 U.S. (4 Wheat.) 316, 415 (1819). . . .

Third, we need not here referee a dispute among the other two branches. . . .

These three background circumstances mean that, when one measures the *literal* words of the Act against the Constitution's *literal* commands, the fact that the Act may closely resemble a different, literally unconstitutional, arrangement is beside the point. To drive exactly 65 miles per hour on an interstate highway closely resembles an act that violates the speed limit. But it does not violate that limit, for small differences matter when the question is one of literal violation of law. No more does this Act literally violate the Constitution's words. . . .

When the President "canceled" the two appropriation measures now before us, he did not *repeal* any law nor did he *amend* any law. He simply *followed* the law, leaving the statutes, as they are literally written, intact. . . .

Because I disagree with the Court's holding of literal violation, I must consider whether the Act nonetheless violates Separation of Powers principles—principles that arise out of the Constitution's vesting of the "executive Power" in "a President," U.S. Const., Art. II, § 1, and "[a]ll legislative Powers" in "a Congress," Art. I, § 1. There are three relevant separation-of-powers questions here: (1) Has Congress given the President the wrong kind of power, i.e., "non-Executive" power? (2) Has Congress given the President the power to "encroach" upon Congress' own constitutionally reserved territory? (3) Has Congress given the President too much power, violating the doctrine of "nondelegation?" These three limitations help assure "adequate control by the citizen's representatives in Congress," upon which JUSTICE KENNEDY properly insists. And with respect to *this* Act, the answer to all these questions is "no."

Viewed conceptually, the power the Act conveys is the right kind of power. It is "executive." As explained above, an exercise of that power "executes" the Act. Conceptually speaking, it closely resembles the kind of delegated authority—to spend or not to spend appropriations, to change or not to change tariff rates—that Congress has frequently granted the President, any differences being differences in degree, not kind.

The fact that one could also characterize this kind of power as "legislative," say, if Congress itself (by amending the appropriations bill) prevented a provision from taking effect, is beside the point. This Court has frequently found that the exercise of a particular power, such as the power to make rules of broad applicability, . . . can fall within the constitutional purview of more than one branch of Government. . . .

The Act does not undermine what this Court has often described as the principal function of the separation of powers, which is to maintain the tripartite structure of the Federal Government—and thereby protect individual liberty—by providing a "safeguard against the encroachment or aggrandizement of one branch at the expense of the other." See The Federalist No. 51 (J. Madison) (separation of powers confers on each branch the means "to resist encroachments of the others").

. . . [O]ne cannot say that the Act "encroaches" upon Congress' power, when Congress retained the power to insert, by simple majority, into any future appropriations bill, into any section of any such bill, or into any phrase of any section, a provision that says the Act will not apply. . . . And it is Congress that drafts and enacts the appropriations statutes that are subject to the Act in the first place—and thereby defines the outer limits of the President's cancellation authority. Thus *this* Act is not the sort of delegation "without . . . sufficient check" that concerns JUSTICE KENNEDY. . . .

Nor can one say the Act's grant of power "aggrandizes" the Presidential office. The grant is limited to the context of the budget. It is limited to the power to spend, or not to spend, particular appropriated items, and the power to permit, or not to permit, specific limited exemptions from generally applicable tax law from taking effect. These powers . . . resemble those the President has exercised in the past on other occasions. The delegation of those powers to the President may strengthen the Presidency, but any such change in Executive Branch authority seems minute when compared with the changes worked by delegations of other kinds of authority that the Court in the past has upheld. . . .

In sum, I recognize that the Act before us is novel. In a sense, it skirts a constitutional edge. But that edge has to do with means, not ends. The means chosen do not amount literally to the enactment, repeal, or amendment of a law. Nor, for that matter, do they amount literally to the "line item veto" that the Act's title announces. Those means do not violate any basic separation-of-powers principle. They do not improperly shift the constitutionally foreseen balance of power from Congress to the President. Nor, since they comply with separation-of-powers principles, do they threaten the liberties of individual citizens. They represent an experiment that may, or may not, help representative government work better. The Constitution, in my view, authorizes Congress and the President to try novel methods in this way. Consequently, with respect, I dissent.

■ JUSTICE SCALIA, with whom JUSTICE O'CONNOR joins, and with whom JUSTICE BREYER joins as to Part III, concurring in part and dissenting in part.

III

. . . The Presentment Clause requires, in relevant part, that "[e]very Bill which shall have passed the House of Representatives and the Senate, shall, before it becomes a Law, be presented to the President of the United States; If he approve he shall sign it, but if not he shall return it," U.S. Const., Art. I, § 7, cl. 2. There is no question that enactment of the Balanced Budget Act complied with these requirements: the House and Senate passed the bill, and the President signed it into law. It was only *after* the requirements of the Presentment Clause had been satisfied that the President exercised his authority under the Line Item Veto Act to cancel the spending item. Thus, the Court's problem with the Act is not that it authorizes the President to veto parts of a bill and sign others into law, but rather that it authorizes him to "cancel"—prevent from "having legal force or effect"—certain parts of duly enacted statutes.

Article I, § 7, of the Constitution obviously prevents the President from cancelling a law that Congress has not authorized him to cancel. Such action cannot possibly be considered part of his execution of the law, and if it is legislative action, as the Court observes, "repeal of statutes, no less than enactment, must conform with Art. I." But that is not this case. It was certainly arguable, as an original matter, that Art. I, § 7, also prevents the President from cancelling a law which itself *authorizes* the President to cancel it. But as the Court acknowledges, that argument has long since been made and rejected. In 1809, Congress passed a law authorizing the President to cancel trade restrictions against Great Britain and France if either revoked edicts directed at the United States. Joseph Story regarded the conferral of that authority as entirely unremarkable in *The Orono*, 18 F.Cas. 830 (No. 10,585) (CCD Mass. 1812). The Tariff Act of 1890 authorized the President to "suspend, by proclamation to that effect" certain of its provisions if he determined that other countries were imposing "reciprocally unequal and unreasonable" duties. This Court upheld the constitutionality of that Act in *Field v. Clark*, 143 U.S. 649 (1892). . . .

As much as the Court goes on about Art. I, § 7, therefore, that provision does not demand the result the Court reaches. It no more categorically prohibits the Executive *reduction* of congressional dispositions in the course of implementing statutes that authorize such reduction, than it categorically prohibits the Executive *augmentation* of congressional dispositions in the course of implementing statutes that authorize such augmentation—generally known as substantive rulemaking. There are, to be sure, limits upon the former just as there are limits upon the latter—and I am prepared to acknowledge that the limits upon the former may be much more severe. Those limits are established, however, not by some categorical prohibition of Art. I, § 7, which our cases conclusively disprove, but by what has come to be known as the doctrine of unconstitutional delegation of legislative authority: When authorized Executive reduction or augmentation is allowed to go too far, it usurps the nondelegable function of Congress and violates the separation of powers.

It is this doctrine, and not the Presentment Clause, that was discussed in the *Field* opinion, and it is this doctrine, and not the Presentment Clause, that is the issue presented by the statute before us here. . . . [The issue here has] nothing to do with whether the details of Art. I, § 7, have been complied with, but everything to do with whether the authorizations went too far by transferring to the Executive a degree of political, lawmaking power that our traditions demand be retained by the Legislative Branch.

I turn, then, to the crux of the matter: whether Congress's authorizing the President to cancel an item of spending gives him a power that our history and traditions show must reside exclusively in the Legislative Branch. I may note, to begin with, that the Line Item Veto Act is not the first statute to authorize the President to "cancel" spending items. . . .

Insofar as the degree of political, "lawmaking" power conferred upon the Executive is concerned, there is not a dime's worth of difference between Congress's authorizing the President to *cancel* a spending item, and Congress's authorizing money to be spent on a particular item at the President's discretion. And the latter has been done since the founding of the Nation. From 1789–1791, the First Congress made lump-sum appropriations for the entire Government—"sum[s] not exceeding" specified amounts for broad purposes. From a very early date Congress also made permissive individual appropriations, leaving the decision whether to spend the money to the President's unfettered discretion. In 1803, it appropriated $50,000 for the President to build "not exceeding fifteen gun boats, to be armed, manned and fitted out, and employed for such purposes as in his opinion the public service may require." President Jefferson reported that "[t]he sum of fifty thousand dollars appropriated by Congress for providing gun boats remains unexpended. The favorable and peaceable turn of affairs on the Mississippi rendered an immediate execution of that law unnecessary." Examples of appropriations committed to the discretion of the President abound in our history. During the Civil War, an Act appropriated over $76 million to be divided among various items "as the exigencies of the service may require." During the Great Depression, Congress appropriated $950 million "for such projects and/or purposes and under such rules and regulations as the President in his discretion may prescribe," and $4 billion for general classes of projects, the money to be spent "in the discretion and under the direction of the President." The constitutionality of such appropriations has never seriously been questioned. Rather, "[t]hat Congress has wide discretion in the matter of prescribing details of expenditures for which it appropriates must, of course, be plain. Appropriations and other acts of Congress are replete with instances of general appropriations of large amounts, to be allotted and expended as directed by designated government agencies." *Cincinnati Soap Co. v. United States*, 301 U.S. 308, 321–322 (1937).

Certain Presidents have claimed Executive authority to withhold appropriated funds even *absent* an express conferral of discretion to do so. In 1876, for example, President Grant reported to Congress that he would not spend money appropriated for certain harbor and river improvements, because "[u]nder no circumstances [would he] allow expenditures upon works not clearly national," and in his view, the appropriations were for "works of purely private or local interest, in no sense national." President Franklin D. Roosevelt impounded funds appropriated for a flood control reservoir and levee in Oklahoma. President Truman ordered the impoundment of hundreds of millions of dollars that had been appropriated for military aircraft. President Nixon, the Mahatma Gandhi of all impounders, asserted at a press conference in 1973 that his "constitutional right" to impound appropriated funds was "absolutely clear." Our decision two years later in *Train v. City of New York*, 420 U.S. 35 (1975), proved him wrong, but it implicitly confirmed that Congress may confer discretion upon the Executive to withhold appropriated funds, even funds appropriated for a specific purpose. The statute at issue in *Train* authorized spending "not to exceed" specified sums for certain projects, and directed that such "[s]ums authorized to be appropriated . . . shall be allotted" by the Administrator of the Environmental Protection Agency, 33 U.S.C. §§ 1285, 1287 (1970 ed., Supp. III). Upon enactment of this statute, the President directed the Administrator to allot no more than a certain part of the amount authorized. This Court held, as a matter of statutory interpretation, that the statute *did not grant* the Executive discretion to withhold the funds, but required allotment of the full amount authorized.

The short of the matter is this: Had the Line Item Veto Act authorized the President to "decline to spend" any item of spending contained in the Balanced Budget Act of 1997, there is not the slightest doubt that authorization would have been constitutional. What the Line Item Veto Act does instead—authorizing the President to "cancel" an item of spending—is technically different. But the technical difference does *not* relate to the technicalities of the Presentment Clause, which have been fully complied with; and the doctrine of unconstitutional delegation, which *is* at issue here, is preeminently *not* a doctrine of technicalities. The title of the Line Item Veto Act, which was perhaps designed to simplify for public comprehension, or perhaps merely to comply with the terms of a campaign pledge, has succeeded in faking out the Supreme Court. The President's action it authorizes in fact is not a line-item veto and thus does not offend Art. I, § 7; and insofar as the substance of that action is concerned, it is no different from what Congress has permitted the President to do since the formation of the Union. . . .

NOTES

1.   Does the result in *Clinton v. City of New York* follow inexorably from the holding of *INS v. Chadha*? Why exactly is the line-item veto unconstitutional given that there is nothing to stop Congress from inserting boilerplate language in a statute authorizing the president to, for example, spend between $300 billion and $0.00 on national defense in any given year? As the dissents point out, the first budget of the United States for the Washington administration read like this. Is the delegation of spending-power control to the president more problematic when the federal government spends almost 25% of the Gross Domestic Product rather than 1% or 2%? Is this a non-delegation doctrine case masquerading as a bicameralism and presentment case?

2.   Note Justice Kennedy's observation in his concurrence that a president armed with a line-item veto will have a powerful tool when negotiating with senators or representatives about other matters. Is this the real alteration in the balance of power that the Court fears in *Clinton v. City of New York*? Is Justice Kennedy too cynical about the log-rolling and horse-trading that he thinks go on between the president and Congress? What weight, if any, should the Court give to this concern in deciding whether the delegation of power went too far?

3.   You are advising Congress, which wants to enact a statute as close as possible to the substance the Line Item Veto Act. What changes would you recommend? What exactly did the Court find wrong with the statute?

[Assignment 9]

E. THE POWER OF THE PURSE: "NO MONEY SHALL BE DRAWN FROM THE TREASURY, BUT IN CONSEQUENCE OF APPROPRIATIONS MADE BY LAW"

Art. I, § 9: No bill of attainder or ex post facto Law shall be passed. . . . No Money shall be drawn from the Treasury, but in Consequence of Appropriations made by Law; and a regular Statement and Account of the Receipts and Expenditures of all public Money shall be published from time to time. . . .

Not much of the text of Article I is about control of the federal budget, but this is one of Congress's most important powers and responsibilities. In Chapter 3, at p. 609, we will examine the scope of the spending power as a matter of federalism. Here consider its implications for the separation of powers. We will especially consider two questions: (1) How much can Congress use its power of the purse to impose limits on the executive branch, and (2) if the executive branch tries to ignore those limits how can Congress enforce them?

The first of these questions is raised in *United States v. Lovett* and in a signing statement by President Obama. (*Lovett* also considers the clause of Article I that prohibits Congress from enacting a "bill of attainder.") The second question, about how Congress can enforce the limits it imposes on executive branch spending, is discussed in *U.S. House of Representatives v. Burwell.*

United States v. Lovett

328 U.S. 303 (1946)

■ MR. JUSTICE BLACK delivered the opinion of the Court.

In 1943 the respondents, Lovett, Watson, and Dodd, were and had been for several years working for the Government. The government agencies which had lawfully employed them were fully satisfied with the quality of their work and wished to keep them employed on their jobs. Over the protest of those employing agencies, Congress provided in Section 304 of the Urgent Deficiency Appropriation Act of 1943, by way of an amendment attached to the House bill, that after November 15, 1943, no salary or compensation should be paid respondents out of any monies then or thereafter appropriated . . . unless they were prior to November 15, 1943 again appointed to jobs by the President with the advice and consent of the Senate. Notwithstanding the Congressional enactment, and the failure of the President to reappoint respondents, the agencies kept all the respondents at work on their jobs for varying periods after November 15, 1943; but their compensation was discontinued after that date. *[The respondents argued that the statute (1) violated the separation of powers, (2) was a bill of attainder, and (3) violated due process.—Editors]* The Solicitor General, appearing for the Government, joined in the first two of respondents' contentions but took no position on the third. . . . [A] special counsel [was authorized] to appear on behalf of the Congress. This counsel denied all three of respondents' contentions. He urged that Section 304 . . . involved simply an exercise of congressional powers over appropriations, which according to the argument, are plenary and not subject to judicial review. . . . The Court of Claims entered judgments in favor of respondents. . . . We granted certiorari because of the manifest importance of the questions involved.

. . . According to the view we take we need not decide whether Section 304 is an unconstitutional encroachment on executive power or a denial of due process of law, and the section is not challenged on the ground that it violates the First Amendment. Our inquiry is thus confined to whether the actions in the light of a proper construction of the Act present justiciable controversies; and, if so, whether Section 304 is a bill of attainder against these respondents, involving a use of power which the Constitution unequivocally declares Congress can never exercise. These questions require an interpretation of the meaning and purpose of the section, which in turn requires an understanding of the circumstances leading to its passage. We, consequently, find it necessary to set out these circumstances somewhat in detail.

In the background of the statute here challenged lies the House of Representatives' feeling in the late thirties that many "subversives" were occupying influential positions in the Government and elsewhere and that their influence must not remain unchallenged. As part of its program against "subversive" activities the House in May 1938 created a Committee on Un-American Activities, which became known as the Dies Committee after its Chairman, Congressman Martin Dies. This Committee conducted a series of investigations and made lists of people and organizations it thought "subversive." The creation of the Dies Committee was followed by provisions such as Section 9A of the Hatch Act, and Sections 15(f) and 17(b) of the Emergency Relief Appropriations Act of 1941, which forbade the holding of a federal job by anyone who was a member of a political party or organization that advocated the overthrow of our constitutional form of Government in the United States. It became the practice to include a similar prohibition in all appropriations acts, together with criminal penalties for its violation. Under these provisions the Federal Bureau of Investigation began wholesale investigations of federal employees, which investigations were financed by special congressional appropriations. Thousands were investigated.

While all this was happening, Mr. Dies on February 1, 1943, in a long speech on the floor of the House attacked thirty-nine named Government employees as "irresponsible, unrepresentative, crackpot, radical bureaucrats" and affiliates of "Communist front organizations." Among these named individuals were the three respondents. Congressman Dies told the House that respondents, as well as the other thirty-six individuals he named, were because of their beliefs and past associations unfit to "hold a Government position" and urged Congress to refuse "to appropriate money for their salaries." In this connection he proposed that the Committee on Appropriations "take immediate and vigorous steps to eliminate these people from public office." Four days later an amendment was offered to the Treasury-Post Office Appropriation Bill which provided that "no part of any appropriation contained in this act shall be used to pay the compensation of" the thirty-nine individuals Dies had attacked. The Congressional Record shows that this amendment precipitated a debate that continued for several days. All of those participating agreed that the "charges" against the thirty-nine individuals were serious. Some wanted to accept Congressman Dies' statements as sufficient proof of "guilt," while others referred to such proposed action as "legislative lynching," smacking "of the procedure in the French Chamber of Deputies, during in Reign of Terror." The Dies charges were referred to as "indictments," and many claimed this made it necessary that the named federal employees be given a hearing and a chance to prove themselves innocent. Congressman Dies then suggested that the Appropriations Committee "weigh the evidence and take immediate steps to dismiss these people from the federal service." Eventually a resolution was proposed to defer action until the Appropriations Committee could investigate, so that accused federal employees would get a chance to prove themselves "innocent" of communism or disloyalty, and so that each "man would have his day in court," and "There would be no star chamber proceedings." The resolution which was finally passed authorized the Appropriations Committee acting through a special subcommittee "to examine into any and all allegations or charges that certain persons in the employ of the several executive departments and other executive agencies are unfit to continue in such employment by reason of their present association or membership or past association or membership in or with organizations whose aims or purposes are or have been subversive to the Government of the United States." The Committee was to have full plenary powers, including the right to summon witnesses and papers, and was to report its "findings and determination" to the House. It was authorized to attach legislation recommended by it to any general or special appropriation measure, notwithstanding general House rules against such practice. The purpose of the resolution was thus described by the Chairman of the Committee on Appropriations in his closing remarks in favor of its passage: "The third and the really important effect is that we will expedite adjudication and disposition of these cases and thereby serve both the accused and the Government. These men against whom charges are pending are faced with a serious situation. If they are not guilty they are entitled to prompt exoneration; on the other hand, if they are guilty, then the quicker the Government removes them the sooner and the more certainly will we protect the Nation against sabotage and fifth-column activity."

After the resolution was passed, a special subcommittee of the Appropriations Committee held hearings in secret executive session. Those charged with "subversive" beliefs and "subversive" associations were permitted to testify, but lawyers including those representing the agencies by which the accused were employed, were not permitted to be present. At the hearings, committee members, the committee staff, and whatever witness was under examination were the only ones present. The evidence, aside from that given by the accused employees, appears to have been largely that of reports made by the Dies Committee, its investigators, and Federal Bureau of Investigation reports, the latter being treated as too confidential to be made public.

After this hearing the subcommittee's reports and recommendations were submitted to the House as part of the Appropriation Committee's report. The subcommittee stated that it had regarded the investigations "as in the nature of an inquest of office" with the ultimate purpose of purging the public service of anyone found guilty of "subversive activity." The committee, stating that "subversive activity" had not before been defined by Congress or by the courts, formulated its own definition of "subversive activity" which we set out in the margin. Respondents Watson, Dodd, and Lovett were, according to the subcommittee guilty of having engaged in "subversive activity within the definition adopted by the Committee."

H. Rep. No. 448, 78th Cong., 1st Sess. 5–7, 9. The ultimate finding and recommendation as to respondent Watson, which was substantially similar to the findings with respect to Lovett and Dodd, read as follows: "Upon consideration of all the evidence, your committee finds that the membership and association of Dr. Goodwin B. Watson with the organizations mentioned and his views and philosophies as expressed in various statements and writings, constitute subversive activity within the definition adopted by your committee, and that he is, therefore, unfit for the present to continue in Government employment." House Report No. 448, 78th Congress, 1st Session, 6. As to Lovett the Committee further reported that it had rejected a "strong appeal" from the Secretary of the Interior for permission to retain Lovett in government service, because as the Committee stated, it could not "escape the conviction that this official is unfit to hold a position of trust with the Government by reason of his membership, association, and affiliation with organizations whose aims and purposes are subversive to the Government of the United States." *Id.* at 12.

Section 304 was submitted to the House along with the Committee Report. . . . Finally Section 304 was passed by the House.

The Senate Appropriation Committee eliminated Section 304 and its action was sustained by the Senate. 89 Cong. Rec. 5024. After the first conference report which left the matter still in disagreement the Senate voted 69 to 0 against the conference report which left Section 304 in the bill. The House, however, insisted on the amendment and indicated that it would not approve any appropriation bill without Section 304. Finally, after the fifth conference report showed that the House would not yield, the Senate adopted Section 304. When the President signed the bill he stated: "The Senate yielded, as I have been forced to yield, to avoid delaying our conduct of the war. But I cannot so yield without placing on record my view that this provision is not only unwise and discriminatory, but unconstitutional." H. Doc. 264, 78th Cong., 1st Sess.

I

In view of the facts just set out, we cannot agree with the two judges of the Court of Claims who held that Section 304 required "a mere stoppage of disbursing routine, nothing more," and left the employer governmental agencies free to continue employing respondents and to incur contractual obligations by virtue of such continued work which respondents could enforce in the Court of Claims. Nor can we agree with counsel for Congress that the section did not provide for the dismissal of respondents but merely forbade governmental agencies to compensate respondents for their work or to incur obligations for such compensation at any and all times. We therefore cannot conclude, as he urges, that Section 304 is a mere appropriation measure, and that since Congress under the Constitution has complete control over appropriations, a challenge to the measure's constitutionality does not present a justiciable question in the courts, but is merely a political issue over which Congress has final say.

We hold that the purpose of Section 304 was not merely to cut off respondents' compensation through regular disbursing channels but permanently to bar them from government service, and that the issue of whether it is constitutional is justiciable. The section's language as well as the circumstances of its passage which we have just described show that no mere question of compensation procedure or of appropriations was involved, but that it was designed to force the employing agencies to discharge respondents and to bar their being hired by any other governmental agency. Any other interpretation of the section would completely frustrate the purpose of all who sponsored Section 304, which clearly was to "purge" the then existing and all future lists of Government employees of those whom Congress deemed guilty of "subversive activities" and therefore "unfit" to hold a federal job. What was challenged, therefore, is a statute which, because of what Congress thought to be their political beliefs, prohibited respondents from ever engaging in any government work, except as jurors or soldiers. Respondents claimed that their discharge was unconstitutional; that they consequently rightfully continued to work for the Government and that the Government owes them compensation for services performed under contracts of employment. Congress has established the Court of Claims to try just such controversies. What is involved here is a Congressional proscription of Lovett, Watson, and Dodd, prohibiting their ever holding a Government job. Were this case to be not justiciable, congressional action, aimed at three named individuals, which stigmatized their reputation and seriously impaired their chance to earn a living, could never be challenged in any court. Our Constitution did not contemplate such a result. . . .

II

We hold that Section 304 falls precisely within the category of congressional actions which the Constitution barred by providing that "No Bill of Attainder or ex post facto Law shall be passed." In *Cummings v. State of Missouri*, 71 U.S. (4 Wall.) 277, 323 (1867), this Court said, "A bill of attainder is a legislative act which inflicts punishment without a judicial trial." . . . On the same day the *Cummings* case was decided, the Court, in *Ex parte Garland*, 71 U.S. (4 Wall.) 333 (1867), also held invalid on the same grounds an Act of Congress which required attorneys practicing before this Court to take a similar oath. Neither of these cases has ever been overruled. They stand for the proposition that legislative acts, no matter what their form, that apply either to named individuals or to easily ascertainable members of a group in such a way as to inflict punishment on them without a judicial trial are bills of attainder prohibited by the Constitution. Adherence to this principle requires invalidation of Section 304. We do adhere to it.

Section 304 was designed to apply to particular individuals. Just as the statute in the two cases mentioned it "operates as a legislative decree of perpetual exclusion" from a chosen vocation. This permanent proscription from any opportunity to serve the Government is punishment, and of a most severe type. It is a type of punishment which Congress has only invoked for special types of odious and dangerous crimes, such as treason, acceptance of bribes by members of Congress, or by other government officials, and interference with elections by Army and Navy officers.

Section 304, thus, clearly accomplishes the punishment of named individuals without a judicial trial. The fact that the punishment is inflicted through the instrumentality of an Act specifically cutting off the pay of certain named individuals found guilty of disloyalty, makes it no less galling or effective than if it had been done by an Act which designated the conduct as criminal. . . .

Section 304 therefore does not stand as an obstacle to payment of compensation to Lovett, Watson, and Dodd. The judgment in their favor is affirmed.

■ MR. JUSTICE JACKSON took no part in the consideration or decision of these cases.

■ MR. JUSTICE FRANKFURTER, whom MR. JUSTICE REED joins, concurring.

Nothing would be easier than personal condemnation of the provision of the Urgency Deficiency Appropriation Act of 1943 here challenged.

But the judicial function exacts considerations very different from those which may determine a vote in Congress for or against a measure. And what may be decisive for a Presidential disapproval may not at all satisfy the established criteria which alone justify this Court's striking down an act of Congress.

It is not for us to find unconstitutionality in what Congress enacted although it may imply notions that are abhorrent to us as individuals or policies we deem harmful to the country's well-being. Although it was proposed at the Constitutional Convention to have this Court share in the legislative process, the Framers saw fit to exclude it. And so "it must be remembered that legislatures are ultimate guardians of the liberties and welfare of the people in quite as great a degree as the courts." *Missouri, Kansas & Texas Ry. Co. of Texas v. May*, 194 U.S. 267, 270 (1904). This admonition was uttered by Mr. Justice Holmes in one of his earliest opinions and it needs to be recalled whenever an exceptionally offensive enactment tempts the Court beyond its strict confinements. . . .

The inclusion of Section 304 in the Appropriation Bill undoubtedly raises serious constitutional questions. But the most fundamental principle of constitutional adjudication is not to face constitutional questions but to avoid them, if at all possible. . . . Some of these rules may well appear over-refined or evasive to the laity. But they have the support not only of the profoundest wisdom. They have been vindicated, in conspicuous instances of disregard, by the most painful lessons of our constitutional history. . . .

The Court reads Section 304 as though it expressly discharged respondents from office which they held and prohibited them from holding any office under the Government in the future. On the basis of this reading the Court holds that the provision is a bill of attainder in that it "inflicts punishment without a judicial trial", *Cummings*, at 323, and is therefore forbidden by Article I, Section 9 of the Constitution. . . . As I see it, our duty precludes reading Section 304 as the Court reads it. But even if it were to be so read the provision is not within the constitutional conception of a bill of attainder.

Broadly speaking, two types of constitutional claims come before this Court. Most constitutional issues derive from the broad standards of fairness written into the Constitution (e.g. "due process," "equal protection of the laws," "just compensation"), and the division of power as between States and Nation. Such questions, by their very nature, allow a relatively wide play for individual legal judgment. The other class gives no such scope. For this second class of constitutional issues derives from very specific provisions of the Constitution. These had their source in definite grievances and led the Fathers to proscribe against recurrence of their experience. These specific grievances and the safeguards against their recurrence were not defined by the Constitution. They were defined by history. Their meaning was so settled by history that definition was superfluous. Judicial enforcement of the Constitution must respect these historic limits.

The prohibition of bills of attainder falls of course among these very specific constitutional provisions. The distinguishing characteristic of a bill of attainder is the substitution of legislative determination of guilt and legislative imposition of punishment for judicial finding and sentence. "A bill of attainder, by the common law, as our fathers imported it from England and practiced it themselves, before the adoption of the Constitution, was an act of sovereign power in the form of a special statute . . . by which a man was pronounced guilty or attainted of some crime, and punished by deprivation of his vested rights, without trial or judgment *per legem terrae.*" Farrar, *Manual of the Constitution* (1867) 419. . . . It was this very special, narrowly restricted, intervention by the legislature, in matters for which a decent regard for men's interests indicated a judicial trial, that the Constitution prohibited. . . . Section 304 lacks the characteristics of the enactments in the Statutes of the Realm and the Colonial Laws that bear the hallmarks of bills of attainder.

All bills of attainder specify the offense for which the attainted person was deemed guilty and for which the punishment was imposed. There was always a declaration of guilt either of the individual or the class to which he belonged. . . .

Not only does Section 304 lack the essential declaration of guilt. It likewise lacks the imposition of punishment in the sense appropriate for bills of attainder. The punishment imposed by the most dreaded bill of attainder was of course death; lesser punishments were imposed by similar bills more technically called bills of pains and penalties. . . . Punishment presupposes an offense, not necessarily an act previously declared criminal, but an act for which retribution is exacted. The fact that harm is inflicted by governmental authority does not make it punishment. Figuratively speaking all discomforting action may be deemed punishment because it deprives of what otherwise would be enjoyed. But there may be reasons other than punitive for such deprivation. A man may be forbidden to practice medicine because he has been convicted of a felony, or because he is no longer qualified. . . .

Is it clear then that the respondents were removed from office, still accepting the Court's reading of the statute, as a punishment for past acts? Is it clear, that is, to that degree of certitude which is required before this Court declares legislation by Congress unconstitutional? The disputed section does not say so. . . .

If Congress adopted, as it did, a form of statute so lacking in any pretension to the very quality which gave a bill of attainder its significance, that of a declaration of guilt under circumstances which made its determination grossly unfair, it simply passed an act which this Court ought not to denounce as a bill of attainder. . . .

While Section 304 is not a bill of attainder, as the gloss of history defines that phrase in the Constitution, acceptance of the Court's reading of Section 304 would raise other serious constitutional questions. The first in magnitude and difficulty derives from the constitutional distribution of power over removal. For about a century this Court astutely avoided adjudication of the power of control as between Congress and the Executive of those serving in the Executive branch of the Government "until it should be inevitably presented." *Myers v. United States,* 272 U.S. 52, 173 (1926). The Court then gave the fullest consideration to the problem. The case was twice argued and was under consideration for nearly three years. So far as the issues could be foreseen they were elaborately dealt with in opinions aggregating nearly two hundred pages. Within less than a decade an opinion of fifteen pages largely qualified what the *Myers* case had apparently so voluminously settled. *Humphreys Executor v. United States,* 295 U.S. 602 (1935). This experience serves as a powerful reminder of the Court's duty so to deal with Congressional enactments as to avoid their invalidation unless a road to any other decision is barred.

The other serious problem the Court's interpretation of Section 304 raises is that of due process. In one aspect this is another phase of the constitutional issue of the removal power. For, if Section 304 is to be construed as a removal from office, it cannot be determined whether singling out three government employees for removal violated the Fifth Amendment until it is decided whether Congress has a removal power at all over such employees and how extensive it is. Even if the statute be read as a mere stoppage of disbursement the question arises whether Congress can treat three employees of the Government differently from all others. But that question we do not have to answer. In any event respondents are entitled to recover in this suit and their remedy—a suit in the Court of Claims—is the same whatever view one takes of the legal significance of Section 304. . . .

Since it is apparent that grave constitutional doubts will arise if we adopt the construction the Court puts on Section 304, we ought to follow the practice which this Court has established from the time of Chief Justice Marshall. . . . "When the validity of an act of the Congress is drawn in question, and even if a serious doubt of constitutionality is raised, it is a cardinal principle that this Court will first ascertain whether a construction of the statute is fairly possible by which the question may be avoided." *Ashwander v. Tennessee Valley Authority*, 297 U.S. 288, 341 (1936) (Brandeis, J., concurring).

We are not faced inescapably with the necessity of adjudicating these serious constitutional questions. The obvious or, at the least, the one certain construction of Section 304 is that it forbids the disbursing agents of the Treasury to pay out of specifically appropriated moneys sums to compensate respondents for their services. We have noted the cloud cast upon this interpretation by manifestations by committees and members of the House of Representatives before the passage of this section. On the other hand, there is also much in the debates not only in the Senate but also in the House which supports the mere fiscal scope to be given to the statute. That such a construction is tenable settles our duty to adopt it and to avoid determination of constitutional questions of great seriousness.

Accordingly, I feel compelled to construe Section 304 as did Mr. Chief Justice Whaley below, whereby it merely prevented the ordinary disbursal of money to pay respondents' salaries. It did not cut off the obligation of the Government to pay for services rendered and the respondents are, therefore, entitled to recover the judgment which they obtained from the Court of Claims.

Barack Obama, Statement on H.R. 1473

Apr. 15, 2011

Today I have signed into law H.R. 1473, the "Department of Defense and Full-Year Continuing Appropriations Act, 2011."

Section 1112 of the Act bars the use of funds for the remainder of fiscal year 2011 to transfer Guantanamo detainees into the United States, and section 1113 bars the use of funds for the remainder of fiscal year 2011 to transfer detainees to the custody or effective control of foreign countries unless specified conditions are met. Section 1112 represents the continuation of a dangerous and unprecedented challenge to critical executive branch authority to determine when and where to prosecute Guantanamo detainees, based on the facts and the circumstances of each case and our national security interests. The prosecution of terrorists in Federal court is a powerful tool in our efforts to protect the Nation and must be among the options available to us. Any attempt to deprive the executive branch of that tool undermines our Nation's counterterrorism efforts and has the potential to harm our national security.

With respect to section 1113 of the Act, the restrictions on the transfer of detainees to the custody or effective control of foreign countries interfere with the authority of the executive branch to make important and consequential foreign policy and national security determinations regarding whether and under what circumstances such transfers should occur in the context of an ongoing armed conflict. We must have the ability to act swiftly and to have broad flexibility in conducting our negotiations with foreign countries. The executive branch has sought and obtained from countries that are prospective recipients of Guantanamo detainees assurances that they will take or have taken measures reasonably designed to be effective in preventing, or ensuring against, returned detainees taking action to threaten the United States or engage in terrorist activities. Consistent with existing statutes, the executive branch has kept the Congress informed about these assurances and notified the Congress prior to transfers. Requiring the executive branch to certify to additional conditions would hinder the conduct of delicate negotiations with foreign countries and therefore the effort to conclude detainee transfers in accord with our national security.

Despite my continued strong objection to these provisions, I have signed this Act because of the importance of avoiding a lapse in appropriations for the Federal Government, including our military activities, for the remainder of fiscal year 2011.

Nevertheless, my Administration will work with the Congress to seek repeal of these restrictions, will seek to mitigate their effects, and will oppose any attempt to extend or expand them in the future.

Section 2262 of the Act would prohibit the use of funds for several positions that involve providing advice directly to the President. The President has well-established authority to supervise and oversee the executive branch, and to obtain advice in furtherance of this supervisory authority. The President also has the prerogative to obtain advice that will assist him in carrying out his constitutional responsibilities, and do so not only from executive branch officials and employees outside the White House, but also from advisers within it.

Legislative efforts that significantly impede the President's ability to exercise his supervisory and coordinating authorities or to obtain the views of the appropriate senior advisers violate the separation of powers by undermining the President's ability to exercise his constitutional responsibilities and take care that the laws be faithfully executed. Therefore, the executive branch will construe section 2262 not to abrogate these Presidential prerogatives.

NOTES

1.   Is Congress constitutionally required to fund executive branch operations with which it disagrees, or may it withhold funds? If there are limits, what are they?

2.   If a court believes a funding bill has an unconstitutional restriction, what should be the remedy? To invalidate the whole bill? If the president believes a funding bill contains an unconstitutional restriction, what should be the remedy? To veto the whole bill? Or to spend money that Congress didn't authorize? Is it relevant that the Constitution says that "No Money shall be drawn from the Treasury, but in Consequence of Appropriations made by Law"?

3.   President Obama's statement on H.R. 1473 is what is known as a "signing statement," which presidents sometimes use when signing bills they believe contain unconstitutional provisions. In this way, a president may sign a bill but announce that the executive branch will not enforce its unconstitutional provisions. Is there a difference between this kind of signing statement and the "line item veto" forbidden in *Clinton v. City of New York* (p. 151)?

U.S. House of Representatives v. Burwell

130 F.Supp.3d 53 (D.D.C. 2015)

■ ROSEMARY M. COLLYER, UNITED STATES DISTRICT JUDGE

Article I of the United States Constitution established the Congress, which comprises a House of Representatives and a Senate. U.S. Const. art. I, § 1. Only these two bodies, acting together, can pass laws—including the laws necessary to spend public money. In this respect, Article I is very clear: "No Money shall be drawn from the Treasury, but in Consequence of Appropriations made by Law. . . ." U.S. Const. art. I, § 9, cl. 7.

Through this lawsuit, the House of Representatives complains that Sylvia Burwell, the Secretary of Health and Human Services, Jacob Lew, the Secretary of the Treasury, and their respective departments (collectively the Secretaries) have spent billions of unappropriated dollars to support the Patient Protection and Affordable Care Act. The House further alleges that Secretary Lew and Treasury have, under the guise of implementing regulations, effectively amended the Affordable Care Act's employer mandate by delaying its effect and narrowing its scope.

The Secretaries move to dismiss, arguing that the House lacks standing to sue. They argue that only the Executive has authority to implement the laws, and urge this Court to stay out of a quintessentially political fight in which the House is already well armed. The House opposes, adamant that it has been injured in several concrete ways, none of which can be ameliorated through the usual political processes.

The only issue before the Court is whether the House can sue the Secretaries; the merits of this lawsuit await another day. Although no precedent dictates the outcome, the case implicates the constitutionality of another Branch's actions and thus merits an "especially rigorous" standing analysis. *Ariz. State Legislature v. Ariz. Indep. Redistricting Comm'n*, 135 S.Ct. 2652, 2665 n. 12 (2015). The House sues, as an institutional plaintiff, to preserve its power of the purse and to maintain constitutional equilibrium between the Executive and the Legislature. If its non-appropriation claims have merit, which the Secretaries deny, the House has been injured in a concrete and particular way that is traceable to the Secretaries and remediable in court. The Court concludes that the House has standing to pursue those constitutional claims.

In contrast, the House's claims that Secretary Lew improperly amended the Affordable Care Act concern only the implementation of a statute, not adherence to any specific constitutional requirement. The House does not have standing to pursue those claims. The Secretaries' motion to dismiss will be denied as to the former and granted as to the latter.

I. FACTS

. . . Congress passes all federal laws in this country. U.S. Const. art. I, § 1 ("All legislative Powers herein granted shall be vested in a Congress of the United States[.]"). That includes both laws that authorize the expenditure of public monies and laws that ultimately appropriate those monies. Authorization and appropriation by Congress are nonnegotiable prerequisites to government spending: "No Money shall be drawn from the Treasury, but in Consequence of Appropriations made by Law. . . ." U.S. Const. art. I, § 9, cl. 7. The distinction between authorizing legislation and appropriating legislation is relevant here and bears some discussion.

Authorizing legislation establishes or continues the operation of a federal program or agency, either indefinitely or for a specific period. Such an authorization may be part of an agency or program's organic legislation, or it may be entirely separate. No money can be appropriated until an agency or program is authorized, although authorization may sometimes be inferred from an appropriation itself.

Appropriation legislation "provides legal authority for federal agencies to incur obligations and to make payments out of the Treasury for specified purposes." Appropriations legislation has "the limited and specific purpose of providing funds for authorized programs." *Andrus v. Sierra Club*, 442 U.S. 347, 361 (1979). An appropriation must be expressly stated; it cannot be inferred or implied. . . .

Appropriations come in many forms. A "permanent" or "continuing" appropriation, once enacted, makes funds available indefinitely for their specified purpose; no further action is needed from Congress. A "current appropriation," by contrast, allows an agency to obligate funds only in the year or years for which they are appropriated. Current appropriations often give a particular agency, program or function its spending cap and thus constrain what that agency, program, or function may do in the relevant year(s). Most current appropriations are adopted on an annual basis and must be re-authorized in each fiscal year. Such appropriations are an integral part of our constitutional checks and balances, insofar as they tie the Executive Branch to the Legislative Branch via purse string. . . .

The 111th Congress enacted the Patient Protection and Affordable Care Act, "to increase the number of Americans covered by health insurance and decrease the cost of health care." *Nat'l Fed'n of Indep. Bus. v. Sebelius*, 132 S.Ct. 2566, 2580 (2012). No party disputes here whether the ACA was validly adopted by both houses of Congress and signed into law by the President. . . .

The ACA provides monetary subsidies in several forms; two are relevant here. First, in order to assist certain individuals with the cost of insurance on the newly-established exchanges, Congress enacted a "premium tax credit" under the Internal Revenue Code for coverage of statutory beneficiaries with household incomes from 100% to 400% of the federal poverty level. These premium tax credits were enacted in Section 1401 of the ACA, and the Court will therefore refer to this subsidy as the "Section 1401 Premium Tax Credit."

Second, Section 1402 of the ACA requires insurers to reduce the cost of insurance to certain, eligible statutory beneficiaries. Specifically, these "cost-sharing" provisions require insurance companies that offer qualified health plans through the ACA to reduce the out-of-pocket cost of insurance coverage for policyholders who qualify. The federal government then offsets the added costs to insurance companies by reimbursing them with funds from the Treasury. The Court will refer to this subsidy as the "Section 1402 Cost-Sharing Offset." . . .

The House alleges that there is a marked, and constitutionally significant, difference in the way these two subsidies are funded. Essentially, the House contends that Section 1401 Premium Tax Credits are funded by a permanent appropriation in the Internal Revenue Code, whereas Section 1402 Cost-Sharing Offsets must be funded and re-funded by annual, current appropriations. The House alleges further that "Congress has not, and never has, appropriated any funds (whether through temporary appropriations or permanent appropriations) to make any Section 1402 Offset Program payments to Insurers."

2.   The Affordable Care Act's Employer Mandate

Apart from its monetary subsidies, the ACA provides incentives for employers to offer health insurance coverage to their employees. Under the title "Shared Responsibility for Employers Regarding Health Coverage," Section 1513 of the ACA adds a new chapter to the Internal Revenue Code that subjects every non-conforming employer to an "assessable payment," i.e., a tax. See 26 U.S.C. § 4980H(a). Cf. id. § 4980H(d)(7) ("For denial of deduction for the *tax* imposed by this section. . . .") (emphasis added); *Independent Business*, 132 S.Ct. at 2580, 2601 (concluding that the "[s]hared responsibility payment" in the ACA's individual mandate, 26 U.S.C. § 5000A(b)(1), could "reasonably be read as a tax"). The substance of Section 1513 is only relevant here insofar as it requires any "applicable large employer" to "offer its full-time employees (and their dependents) the opportunity to enroll in minimum essential coverage under an eligible employer-sponsored plan" or else to pay the tax. 26 U.S.C. § 4980H(a)–(b). Section 1513 concludes: "The amendments made by this section shall apply to months beginning after December 31, 2013." *Id.* § 4980H(d). . . .

The House alleges that the Secretaries, despite Congress's refusal to fund the Section 1402 Cost-Sharing Offsets through a current appropriation, nonetheless drew and spent public monies on that program beginning in January 2014. The House also alleges that Secretary Lew has effectively "legislate[d] changes" to Section 1513, both by delaying the employer mandate beyond December 31, 2013 and by altering the percentage of employees that must be offered coverage. *Id.* ¶¶ 45, 46. These changes to the mandate are said by the House to have "usurp[ed] its Article I legislative authority." *Id.* ¶ 50.

To right these perceived wrongs, the House took legal action. . . .

III. ANALYSIS

Under these long-established principles of law, and accepting the facts as alleged in the Complaint, the Court must decide whether it *can* hear this case (jurisdiction) and whether it *should* hear this case (justiciability).

A.   Standing. . . .

The instant Complaint presents two theories of legal harm. First, the House alleges that the Executive has spent billions of dollars without a valid appropriation, in direct contravention of Article I, § 9, cl. 7. . . .

Second, the House alleges that Secretary Lew has not abided by the employer mandate as it was enacted in the ACA, thereby "nullifying" the law. . . . The gist of this theory is that Secretary Lew stepped into congressional shoes by effectively amending a congressionally-adopted law through regulation. But as discussed below, the heart of the alleged violation remains statutory, not constitutional: the House alleges not that Secretary Lew has disobeyed the Constitution, but that he disobeyed the ACA as enacted.

Distilled to their essences, the Non-Appropriation Theory alleges that the Executive was unfaithful to the Constitution, while the Employer-Mandate Theory alleges that the Executive was unfaithful to a statute, the ACA. That is a critical distinction, inasmuch as the Court finds that the House has standing to assert the first but not the second.

a.   The Non-Appropriation Theory (Counts I–V)

The Secretaries argue that the House lacks standing to sue and stop expenditures for which no annual appropriation was enacted. The House rejoins that it has standing to sue on several grounds, not least of which is that it has been "divested utterly and completely of its most defining constitutional function." The Court agrees: the constitutional trespass alleged in this case would inflict a concrete, particular harm upon the House for which it has standing to seek redress in this Court.

i.   Nature of the Theory

The persistent refrain in the Secretaries' memorandum is that the House has no standing to "maintain an action against the Executive Branch concerning its *implementation* of a statute." Mem. at 1 (emphasis added). The Secretaries use the word "implement," or a derivative thereof, no fewer than forty times in their twenty-six page memorandum. They also cast this case as "concerning the proper *interpretation* of federal law," *id.* at 2 (emphasis added), and about "the *execution* of federal law," *id.* at 3 (emphasis added).

Properly understood, however, the Non-Appropriation Theory is not about the implementation, interpretation, or execution of any federal statute. It is a complaint that the Executive has drawn funds from the Treasury without a congressional appropriation—not in violation of any statute, but in violation of Article I, § 9, cl. 7 of the Constitution. The Non-Appropriation Theory, in other words, is not about how Section 1402 is being applied, but rather how it is funded.

This clarification renders most of the Secretaries' precedent inapposite. They argue, for example, that our "Constitution does not contemplate an active role for Congress in the supervision of officers charged with the execution of the laws it enacts," and that Congress does not "have standing anytime a President allegedly acts in excess of statutory authority." But again, the Non-Appropriation Theory is not about executing congressionally-enacted laws or staying within their bounds. Nor is it "a generalized grievance about the conduct of government." Mem. at 25 n.12.

It alleges a specific, constitutional violation that is wholly irrespective of the ACA's implementation.

ii.   Injury in Fact

Once the nature of the Non-Appropriation Theory is appreciated, it becomes clear that the House has suffered a concrete, particularized injury that gives it standing to sue. The Congress (of which the House and Senate are equal) is the only body empowered by the Constitution to adopt laws directing monies to be spent from the U.S. Treasury. Yet this constitutional structure would collapse, and the role of the House would be meaningless, if the Executive could circumvent the appropriations process and spend funds however it pleases. If such actions are taken, in contravention of the specific proscription in Article I, § 9, cl. 7, the House as an institution has standing to sue. . . .

The Secretaries . . . argue that the House is not injured by the lack of an appropriation because it can remedy or prevent that injury through means outside this lawsuit. Chief among those means, they contend, is "the elimination of funding." As the House points out, the Secretaries are "apparently oblivious to the irony" of their argument. Eliminating funding for Section 1402 is *exactly* what the House tried to do. But as the House argues, Congress cannot fulfill its constitutional role if it specifically denies funding and the Executive simply finds money elsewhere without consequence. Indeed, the harm alleged in this case is particularly insidious *because*, if proved, it would eliminate Congress's role via-a-vis the Executive. The political tug of war anticipated by the Constitution depends upon Article I, § 9, cl. 7 having some force; otherwise the purse strings would be cut. . . .

The House of Representatives as an institution would suffer a concrete, particularized injury if the Executive were able to draw funds from the Treasury without a valid appropriation. The House therefore has standing to sue on its Non-Appropriation Theory, to the extent that it seeks to remedy constitutional violations. That conclusion does not end the analysis, however.

Some of the counts under the Non-Appropriation Theory do not seek redress for *constitutional* violations. Count III alleges a violation of 31 U.S.C. § 1324, which appropriates funds for Section 1401 Premium Tax Credits but not, allegedly, the Section 1402 Cost-Sharing Offsets. Because that question is statutory and not constitutional, it falls within the sphere of cases . . . that concern the implementation, interpretation, or execution of federal statutory law. The Court will therefore grant the Secretaries' motion as to Count III and dismiss it. The Court will also dismiss Count IV, which similarly alleges a violation of the ACA's "statutory scheme." . . .

The Employer-Mandate Theory stands on very different footing than the Non-Appropriation Theory. The House alleges that Secretary Lew and Treasury have disregarded the congressionally-adopted employer mandate in two ways. First, Secretary Lew delayed the effective date of the mandate beyond the statutory prescription of January 1, 2014. Second, he reduced the percentage of employees or full-time equivalents (FTEs) who must be offered insurance, thereby decreasing the burden on employers. Both of these regulatory actions are said to "injure the House by, among other things, usurping its Article I legislative authority." Complaint ¶ 50. Specifically, the House assails two parts of a Treasury Rule preamble (Counts VI and VII) and another part of the substantive Rule (Count VIII).

Despite its formulation as a constitutional claim, the Employer-Mandate Theory is fundamentally a statutory argument. The House cites only Article I, § 1 and Article I, § 7, cl. 2 in its Complaint. Those provisions, taken together, establish that Congress has sole legislative authority and that laws cannot be adopted without its approval. The House extrapolates from this that any member of the Executive who exceeds his statutory authority is unconstitutionally legislating.

The argument proves too much. If it were accepted, every instance of an extra-statutory action by an Executive officer might constitute a cognizable constitutional violation, redressable by Congress through a lawsuit. Such a conclusion would contradict decades of administrative law and precedent, in which courts have guarded against "the specter of 'general legislative standing' based upon claims that the Executive Branch is misinterpreting a statute or the Constitution." *U.S. House of Representatives v. U.S. Dep't of Commerce*, 11 F.Supp.2d 76, 89–90 (D.D.C. 1998); cf. *United States v. Windsor*, 133 S.Ct. 2675, 2689 (2013) ("The integrity of the political process would be at risk if difficult constitutional issues were simply referred to the Court as a routine exercise."). In sum, Article I is not a talisman; citing its most general provisions does not transform a statutory violation into a constitutional case or controversy. . . .

The Court concludes that the House of Representatives has alleged an injury in fact under its Non-Appropriation Theory—that is, an invasion of a legally protected interest that is concrete and particularized. Article I could not be more clear: "No Money shall be drawn from the Treasury, but in Consequence of Appropriations made by Law. . . ." U.S. Const. art. I, § 9, cl. 7. Neither the President nor his officers can authorize appropriations; the assent of the House of Representatives is required before *any* public monies are spent. Congress's power of the purse is the ultimate check on the otherwise unbounded power of the Executive. See *U.S. Dep't of the Navy v. Fed. Labor Relations Auth.*, 665 F.3d 1339, 1347 (D.C. Cir. 2012) ("[If not for the Appropriations Clause,] the executive would possess an unbounded power over the public purse of the nation; and might apply all its monied resources at his pleasure.") (quoting 2 Joseph Story, *Commentaries on the Constitution of the United States* § 1342, at 213–14 (1833)). The genius of our Framers was to limit the Executive's power "by a valid reservation of congressional control over funds in the Treasury." *OPM v. Richmond*, 496 U.S. 414, 425 (1990). Disregard for that reservation works a grievous harm on the House, which is deprived of its rightful and necessary place under our Constitution. The House has standing to redress that injury in federal court. . . .

That the Court has jurisdiction over this case does not end the inquiry. It must also consider whether there is any reason it should not hear the case, i.e., whether the case is justiciable. That, in turn, presents two questions: (1) whether the claim presented and the relief sought are of the type which admit of judicial resolution; and (2) whether the structure of the federal government renders the issue presented a "political question," that is, not justiciable because of the separation of powers among the Legislative, Executive and Judicial Branches established by the Constitution. *Powell v. McCormack*, 395 U.S. 486, 516–17 (1969).

The first question is easily answered: the claims for which the House has standing involve pure questions of constitutional interpretation, amenable to resolution by this Court. "It would be difficult to say that there are no 'manageable standards' for adjudicating the issues raised. Familiar judicial techniques are available to construe the meaning" of the Constitution. . . . In short, centuries of precedent demonstrate the Judiciary's ability to adjudicate the Secretaries' compliance with the Constitution. *See, e.g., Marbury v. Madison*, 5 U.S. (1 Cranch) 137 (1803).

The Secretaries pin their hopes on the second question, arguing that to allow this suit to proceed would "upset the finely wrought balance" among the branches and that the case presents issues not "suitable for resolution by an Article III court." The argument is not persuasive. Whatever the merits of the parties' interpretations of the differing appropriation legislation—an issue not to be addressed at this stage of litigation—the Complaint makes clear that this is not a dispute over statutory semantics. To the contrary, the constitutional violation alleged is that, despite an intentional refusal by Congress to appropriate funds for Section 1402, the Secretaries freely ignored Article I, § 9, cl. 7 of the Constitution and sought other sources of public money. The Complaint's Non-Appropriation Theory presents a question of constitutional interpretation for the Judiciary, which provides "the primary means through which [constitutional] rights may be enforced." *Davis v. Passman*, 442 U.S. 228, 241 (1979).

The Secretaries' separation-of-powers argument, properly addressed here, is unavailing. It consists of two principal parts: (1) the history of non-litigiousness between the political branches, recounted in *Raines*, and (2) a page-long series of quotes from Justice Scalia's dissent in *Windsor*. The first part is unconvincing: the refusal by several presidents to sue Congress over the Tenure of Office Act hardly answers the question presented by the pending motion. The refrain by either branch from exercising one of its options does not mean that the option was unavailable; there will never be a history of litigation until the first lawsuit is filed. The second part is not precedential: for all of its eloquence, Justice Scalia's opinion remains a dissent joined by only two other Justices. It does not convince the Court to dismiss this case.

The Court concludes that prudential considerations do not counsel avoidance of this dispute. The Court is familiar with the standards for constitutional review of Executive actions, and the mere fact that the House of Representatives is the plaintiff does not turn this suit into a non-justiciable "political" dispute. See *Powell*, at 549 ("Our system of government requires that federal courts on occasion interpret the Constitution at variance with the construction given the document by another branch. The alleged conflict that such an adjudication may cause cannot justify the courts' avoiding their constitutional responsibility.") (collecting cases). Despite its potential political ramifications, this suit remains a plain dispute over a constitutional command, of which the Judiciary has long been the ultimate interpreter. See *Marbury*.

The Court is also assured that this decision will open no floodgates, as it is inherently limited by the extraordinary facts of which it was born. The Secretaries note that this case is a "novel tactic" by the House and "entirely without precedent." The House agrees that this "case is the result of an historic vote by plaintiff House of Representatives." The rarity of these circumstances itself militates against dismissing the case as non-justiciable. See *Windsor*, at 2689 ("The integrity of the political process would be at risk if difficult constitutional issues were simply referred to the Court as a routine exercise. But this case is not routine.").

IV. CONCLUSION

The House of Representatives has standing to pursue its allegations that the Secretaries of Health and Human Services and of the Treasury violated Article I, § 9, cl. 7 of the Constitution when they spent public monies that were not appropriated by the Congress. The Secretaries hotly dispute that any violation has occurred, maintaining that the Section 1402 "cost sharing reduction payments are being made as part of a mandatory payment program that Congress has fully appropriated." Mem. at 6 (citing 42 U.S.C. § 18082). The Court stresses that the merits have not been briefed or decided; only the question of standing has been determined. . . .

NOTES

1.   You will learn more about standing when we get to Article III (p. 413). But for now, what is the court's fundamental concern here? What value would be served by denying the House the ability to sue? What value is served by allowing it to sue?

2.   Much of the dispute in this case is about the scope of a federal statute, the Affordable Care Act. But the dispute also has a constitutional dimension. Does the court's decision suggest that every misinterpretation of a spending statute is a violation of the Constitution? If so, is that rule too broad? If not, where does the court draw the line?

3.   In a subsequent opinion on May 12, 2016, the district court reached the merits and concluded that the secretaries of Health and Human Services and of the Treasury had indeed violated Article I, Section 9. The court announced that it would enjoin all further reimbursements under Section 1402 until a valid appropriation was in place, but it agreed to stay its injunction pending appeal. The government is almost certain to appeal the decision to the D.C. Circuit. What should the D.C. Circuit do?

[*Assignment 10*]

II. ARTICLE II: THE EXECUTIVE POWER

As the framers deliberated in Philadelphia, they had a number of good models to choose from. For the legislative branch, those models included Parliament, the Continental Congress, and the colonial legislatures. They also had good models for the judicial branch, including the Court of King's Bench and the Chancery in England. But they lacked a good model for the executive. In 1776, the Declaration of Independence had laid out the case for the colonies separating from England, and the central argument was the tyrannical behavior of King George III. Surely he could not be the model for the new "president" established by the Constitution. But thirteen years had passed between the Declaration of Independence and the Convention in Philadelphia, and most of the colonies had swung wildly in the opposite direction. Opposed to King George's executive tyranny, they had hobbled and constrained their executives. Predictably, the colonies had run headlong into legislative tyranny. And there was no separate executive branch for the government under the Articles of Confederation. This, then, was one of the great challenges faced by the framers in Philadelphia: how to specify the powers of the executive without a good model, and all while avoiding the danger of tyranny on the one hand and weakness on the other.

The framers' difficulty in specifying the executive power can be seen by contrasting Article II with Articles I and III. Article I enumerates all of the powers of Congress. That enumeration is, and has to be, carefully done—after all, Congress is given only the legislative powers "herein granted." Article III grants "the judicial Power" and then carefully details the cases and controversies in which that power may be exercised. But Article II seems different. The president is given all of "the executive Power." But the contents of that power are not enumerated as the contents of the legislative power are in Article I. Nor are the boundaries of the executive power demarcated as the boundaries of the judicial power are through the list of cases and controversies in Article III. Instead the Vesting Clause of Article II is followed, after a lengthy description of the Electoral College, by a seemingly random assortment of executive powers, such as granting pardons and appointing ambassadors. Are these all of the executive powers? If so, why not say the president has only the executive powers "herein granted," as in Article I? But if there are other executive powers, then what are they, and why did some of them need to be expressly stated? Is there any rhyme or reason to what is in Article II? This is one of the great challenges faced by the interpreter of what the framers did in Philadelphia.

As you begin thinking about these questions, there is one important piece of background that you need to know. In English constitutional history, there were many controversies over royal power. In the medieval conflicts the king was sometimes opposed by the nobles and the bishops of the Church (e.g., the controversy leading to Magna Carta); in the sixteenth century and especially the seventeenth century the opponents of royal power were often found in Parliament and the common law courts. In the course of these conflicts, kings often claimed to have powers that they could exercise on their own, without the approval or contradiction of anyone else. John Locke defined "prerogative power" as the executive's "power to act according to discretion, for the public good, without the prescription of the law, and sometimes even against it." John Locke, TWO TREATISES ON GOVERNMENT 340, § 160 (sixth reprint 1764). The scope of the prerogative powers, and in some cases even their very legitimacy, was hotly debated. But specific instances of the prerogative power became well-known on both sides of the Atlantic. The Stuart monarchs had asserted all of the following prerogative powers, often leading to resistance in the form of rebellion, judicial decision, or parliamentary action:

Prerogative powers related to finance: powers to tax, to spend, and to borrow.

Prerogative powers related to lawmaking: a power of speaking to Parliament (i.e., giving the King's Speech); a power to veto legislation passed by Parliament; a power to "prorogue" (i.e., discontinue) a session of Parliament; a power to make law through royal proclamations; a power to "dispense" with the application of law in a particular case; a power to "suspend" the application of the law across all cases; the power to pardon individuals convicted of crime.

Prerogative powers related to war and foreign affairs: a power to create, equip, and control an army and navy, using tax money appropriated by Parliament plus other revenues of the Crown; a power to summon and command the militia, which is the armed citizenry; a power to initiate, conduct, and terminate wars; a power to send and receive ambassadors; a power to make treaties with foreign states; a power to carry on commerce with foreign states.

Other prerogative powers: a power to be the supreme governor of the Church of England; a power to correct the deficiencies of the law through equity; a power to create offices and make appointments to those offices; a power to grant titles of nobility; a power to grant patents, charters, and monopolies; a power to suspend habeas corpus.

The course of English constitutional history in the two centuries prior to American Independence can be seen as a series of largely successful, if often violent, struggles by Parliament and the courts to whittle down and defeat some of these claims of royal prerogative—primarily those that included the exercise of either judicial power or lawmaking power (including *law-unmaking* power). The attempt by James I (reigned 1603–1625) to impose law through proclamation was declared unlawful by Sir Edward Coke, Chief Justice of the Court of King's Bench. The attempt by Charles I (reigned 1625–1649) to impose taxes without Parliament led to the English Civil War and his execution. And the attempt by James II (reigned 1685–1688) to nullify parliamentary laws through the dispensing and suspending powers led to the Glorious Revolution and his removal from the throne, which in turn led to further curtailment of the royal prerogative. By 1789, however, the monarch still retained significant prerogative powers, including the powers of "peace and war," the pardon, the power of appointment, and (in theory) the veto. Without Parliament, he could no longer tax, spend, borrow, make or dispense with laws, or suspend habeas corpus.

Despite this curtailment, the prerogative powers were not eliminated. And it may not be possible to eliminate executive prerogative altogether. Locke also wrote: "since in some governments the law-making power is not always in being, and is usually too numerous, and so too slow, for the dispatch requisite to execution; and because also it is impossible to foresee, and so by laws to provide for, all accidents and necessities that may concern the public, or to make such laws as will do no harm, if they are executed with an inflexible rigour, on all occasions, and upon all persons that may come in their way; therefore there is a latitude left to the executive power, to do many things of choice which the laws do not prescribe." Locke, TWO TREATISES, at 340–41, § 160. But consider whether there is an ideal of executive power—one that includes the physical force of the government but not its lawmaking power—that might explain the framers' goals in Article II.

A Map of Article II

Article II of the Constitution contains four sections. Section 1 grants "the executive Power" of the new national government to one "President of the United States." It goes on to explain how the president is to be chosen, the length of term, and the oath of office. Section 2 specifies, describes, and limits certain presidential powers, and some of the powers mentioned in this section are prerogative powers from the English constitutional tradition. Section 3 further describes and limits executive power. The president has the following duties or powers: (1) giving a State of the Union address, (2) recommending new laws to Congress, (3) receiving ambassadors from foreign countries, (4) taking care that the laws are faithfully executed, and (5) commissioning all officers of the United States. These provisions further inform the grant of "the executive Power" in Section 1, and some of these, too, are prerogative powers. Section 4 concludes by providing that the president and vice president, unlike the king, are subject to impeachment.

Some of the prerogative powers, then, are explicitly mentioned in Article II. But not all of them. Which ones are mentioned? Are some explicitly given to Congress in Article I? Are some of these powers shared, with the Constitution prescribing a rule by which both the president and Congress (or the Senate) have some say in how the power is exercised? Are there certain prerogative powers that the Constitution denies to the executive? And what about the Constitution's silence—the prerogative powers that are not expressly assigned or denied? Who, if anyone, has those powers? And are there any prerogative powers that the Constitution eliminates entirely? These are hard questions. But they are fundamental to thinking about the scope of executive power, both in 1789 and today.

Taken together, the provisions of Article II also suggest certain themes about the role of the executive. One is *energy*, for the president retains a number of prerogative powers needed for vigorous leadership of the nation, especially in war. Another is *independence*, in particular independence from Congress. In parliamentary systems, the prime minister is a member of parliament and is dependent on his or her party's success in the legislature for continuance in office. By contrast, the president is elected for a four-year term and cannot be removed by Congress on a vote of no confidence. (The president may be selected by Congress, but only if no candidate secures a majority in the Electoral College.) Article II also creates *one* executive. The framers of the Constitution made a deliberate choice to vest the executive power in a single individual, rejecting the options of a plural executive or an executive council or cabinet. Fourth, the presidential powers are defined in ways that emphasize *law-executing, not law-making*. A number of the prerogative powers allowed an English king to circumvent Parliament, either by enacting laws (through proclamations) or by undoing laws that had already been enacted (dispensing, suspending, and pardoning). Except for the pardon power, none of these lawmaking prerogative powers are expressly given to the president, and to the contrary the president is expressly given the duty to "take Care that the Laws be faithfully executed."

Keep these themes in mind—as well as the twin problems of the weak colonial executives and the tyrannical English king—as you read Alexander Hamilton's essay that follows.

The Federalist No. 70

Alexander Hamilton, March 15, 1788

THERE is an idea, which is not without its advocates, that a vigorous Executive is inconsistent with the genius of republican government. The enlightened well-wishers to this species of government must at least hope that the supposition is destitute of foundation; since they can never admit its truth, without at the same time admitting the condemnation of their own principles. Energy in the Executive is a leading character in the definition of good government. It is essential to the protection of the community against foreign attacks; it is not less essential to the steady administration of the laws; to the protection of property against those irregular and high-handed combinations which sometimes interrupt the ordinary course of justice; to the security of liberty against the enterprises and assaults of ambition, of faction, and of anarchy. Every man the least conversant in Roman story, knows how often that republic was obliged to take refuge in the absolute power of a single man, under the formidable title of Dictator, as well against the intrigues of ambitious individuals who aspired to the tyranny, and the seditions of whole classes of the community whose conduct threatened the existence of all government, as against the invasions of external enemies who menaced the conquest and destruction of Rome.

There can be no need, however, to multiply arguments or examples on this head. A feeble Executive implies a feeble execution of the government. A feeble execution is but another phrase for a bad execution; and a government ill executed, whatever it may be in theory, must be, in practice, a bad government.

Taking it for granted, therefore, that all men of sense will agree in the necessity of an energetic Executive, it will only remain to inquire, what are the ingredients which constitute this energy? How far can they be combined with those other ingredients which constitute safety in the republican sense? And how far does this combination characterize the plan which has been reported by the convention?

The ingredients which constitute energy in the Executive are, first, unity; secondly, duration; thirdly, an adequate provision for its support; fourthly, competent powers.

The ingredients which constitute safety in the republican sense are, first, a due dependence on the people, secondly, a due responsibility.

Those politicians and statesmen who have been the most celebrated for the soundness of their principles and for the justice of their views, have declared in favor of a single Executive and a numerous legislature. They have with great propriety, considered energy as the most necessary qualification of the former, and have regarded this as most applicable to power in a single hand, while they have, with equal propriety, considered the latter as best adapted to deliberation and wisdom, and best calculated to conciliate the confidence of the people and to secure their privileges and interests.

That unity is conducive to energy will not be disputed. Decision, activity, secrecy, and despatch will generally characterize the proceedings of one man in a much more eminent degree than the proceedings of any greater number; and in proportion as the number is increased, these qualities will be diminished.

This unity may be destroyed in two ways: either by vesting the power in two or more magistrates of equal dignity and authority; or by vesting it ostensibly in one man, subject, in whole or in part, to the control and co-operation of others, in the capacity of counsellors to him. Of the first, the two Consuls of Rome may serve as an example; of the last, we shall find examples in the constitutions of several of the States. New York and New Jersey, if I recollect right, are the only States which have intrusted the executive authority wholly to single men. Both these methods of destroying the unity of the Executive have their partisans; but the votaries of an executive council are the most numerous. They are both liable, if not to equal, to similar objections, and may in most lights be examined in conjunction. . . .

Wherever two or more persons are engaged in any common enterprise or pursuit, there is always danger of difference of opinion. If it be a public trust or office, in which they are clothed with equal dignity and authority, there is peculiar danger of personal emulation and even animosity. From either, and especially from all these causes, the most bitter dissensions are apt to spring. Whenever these happen, they lessen the respectability, weaken the authority, and distract the plans and operation of those whom they divide. If they should unfortunately assail the supreme executive magistracy of a country, consisting of a plurality of persons, they might impede or frustrate the most important measures of the government, in the most critical emergencies of the state. And what is still worse, they might split the community into the most violent and irreconcilable factions, adhering differently to the different individuals who composed the magistracy.

Men often oppose a thing, merely because they have had no agency in planning it, or because it may have been planned by those whom they dislike. But if they have been consulted, and have happened to disapprove, opposition then becomes, in their estimation, an indispensable duty of self-love. They seem to think themselves bound in honor, and by all the motives of personal infallibility, to defeat the success of what has been resolved upon contrary to their sentiments. . . .

Upon the principles of a free government, inconveniences from the source just mentioned must necessarily be submitted to in the formation of the legislature; but it is unnecessary, and therefore unwise, to introduce them into the constitution of the Executive. It is here too that they may be most pernicious. In the legislature, promptitude of decision is oftener an evil than a benefit. The differences of opinion, and the jarrings of parties in that department of the government, though they may sometimes obstruct salutary plans, yet often promote deliberation and circumspection, and serve to check excesses in the majority. When a resolution too is once taken, the opposition must be at an end. That resolution is a law, and resistance to it punishable. But no favorable circumstances palliate or atone for the disadvantages of dissension in the executive department. Here, they are pure and unmixed. There is no point at which they cease to operate. They serve to embarrass and weaken the execution of the plan or measure to which they relate, from the first step to the final conclusion of it. They constantly counteract those qualities in the Executive which are the most necessary ingredients in its composition—vigor and expedition, and this without any counterbalancing good. In the conduct of war, in which the energy of the Executive is the bulwark of the national security, every thing would be to be apprehended from its plurality.

It must be confessed that these observations apply with principal weight to the first case supposed—that is, to a plurality of magistrates of equal dignity and authority a scheme, the advocates for which are not likely to form a numerous sect; but they apply, though not with equal, yet with considerable weight to the project of a council, whose concurrence is made constitutionally necessary to the operations of the ostensible Executive. An artful cabal in that council would be able to distract and to enervate the whole system of administration. If no such cabal should exist, the mere diversity of views and opinions would alone be sufficient to tincture the exercise of the executive authority with a spirit of habitual feebleness and dilatoriness.

But one of the weightiest objections to a plurality in the Executive, and which lies as much against the last as the first plan, is, that it tends to conceal faults and destroy responsibility. Responsibility is of two kinds—to censure and to punishment. The first is the more important of the two, especially in an elective office. Man, in public trust, will much oftener act in such a manner as to render him unworthy of being any longer trusted, than in such a manner as to make him obnoxious to legal punishment. But the multiplication of the Executive adds to the difficulty of detection in either case. It often becomes impossible, amidst mutual accusations, to determine on whom the blame or the punishment of a pernicious measure, or series of pernicious measures, ought really to fall. It is shifted from one to another with so much dexterity, and under such plausible appearances, that the public opinion is left in suspense about the real author. The circumstances which may have led to any national miscarriage or misfortune are sometimes so complicated that, where there are a number of actors who may have had different degrees and kinds of agency, though we may clearly see upon the whole that there has been mismanagement, yet it may be impracticable to pronounce to whose account the evil which may have been incurred is truly chargeable. "I was overruled by my council. The council were so divided in their opinions that it was impossible to obtain any better resolution on the point." These and similar pretexts are constantly at hand, whether true or false. And who is there that will either take the trouble or incur the odium, of a strict scrutiny into the secret springs of the transaction? Should there be found a citizen zealous enough to undertake the unpromising task, if there happen to be collusion between the parties concerned, how easy it is to clothe the circumstances with so much ambiguity, as to render it uncertain what was the precise conduct of any of those parties? . . .

It is evident from these considerations, that the plurality of the Executive tends to deprive the people of the two greatest securities they can have for the faithful exercise of any delegated power, *first*, the restraints of public opinion, which lose their efficacy, as well on account of the division of the censure attendant on bad measures among a number, as on account of the uncertainty on whom it ought to fall; and, *second*, the opportunity of discovering with facility and clearness the misconduct of the persons they trust, in order either to their removal from office or to their actual punishment in cases which admit of it. . . . I clearly concur in opinion, in this particular, with a writer whom the celebrated Junius pronounces to be "deep, solid, and ingenious," that "the executive power is more easily confined when it is ONE"; . . . that it is far more safe there should be a single object for the jealousy and watchfulness of the people; and, in a word, that all multiplication of the Executive is rather dangerous than friendly to liberty. . . . I will only add that, prior to the appearance of the Constitution, I rarely met with an intelligent man from any of the States, who did not admit, as the result of experience, that the UNITY of the executive of this State was one of the best of the distinguishing features of our constitution.

————

The next three assignments will consider three basic elements of executive power—the president's power to staff the executive branch (and the judiciary) through appointments; the power to supervise and remove those executive appointees; and the duty or power to take care that the laws are faithfully executed. As you consider these elements of the executive power, think about how they interrelate. Think, as well, about whether the types of constitutional argument are consistent across these elements—are some elements more textual than others? More policy-based than others? These three elements will be brought together in *Morrison v. Olson* (p. 249).

A. THE APPOINTMENT POWER: "HE . . . SHALL APPOINT"

Art. II, § 2: . . . [The President] shall nominate, and by and with the Advice and Consent of the Senate, shall appoint Ambassadors, other public Ministers and Consuls, Judges of the Supreme Court, and all other Officers of the United States, whose Appointments are not herein otherwise provided for, and which shall be established by Law: but the Congress may by Law vest the Appointment of such inferior Officers, as they think proper, in the President alone, in the Courts of Law, or in the Heads of Departments.

Under Article II, Section 2, the president has the general power to appoint officers with the Senate's consent. In addition, Congress can regulate some of these appointments, by eliminating the Senate's role and giving the power to the president alone, or by taking away both the Senate's and the president's role and giving the power to the heads of departments, or the courts. Why did the framers settle on this system?

Remember that one prerogative power of the king of England was creating offices, some of them highly profitable, and unilaterally appointing individuals to those offices. The king was called the "fountain of honors." English kings could thus raise up someone from nothing and make him rich and prominent. Indeed, when royal power was limited after the English Revolution of 1688—limited by the principle of parliamentary supremacy, for Parliament could pass laws that would bind the king, laws which the king could not suspend or dispense with—English kings responded by creating lucrative offices and appointing members of Parliament to them, in order to obtain their favor and sway their votes.

The American Revolutionaries were repulsed by this practice, which they denounced as an instrument of corruption. The first American state constitutions after 1776 took the appointment power away from governors and vested it either in an executive council or in the legislature. This led to weak governors and dominant legislatures. By 1787, many Americans thought their governors were too feeble to keep the peace or to enforce the law. They saw that making appointments could also corrupt a legislature.

The Philadelphia Convention wrestled at length with the problem of the appointment power. The framers considered vesting the power in Congress, the Senate, or the president alone, before settling on a compromise: presidential nomination and senatorial advice and consent. Consider Alexander Hamilton's defense of that compromise:

The Federalist No. 76

Alexander Hamilton, April 1, 1788

. . . It is not easy to conceive a plan better calculated than this to promote a judicious choice of men for filling the offices of the Union; and it will not need proof, that on this point must essentially depend the character of its administration.

It will be agreed on all hands, that the power of appointment, in ordinary cases, ought to be modified in one of three ways. It ought either to be vested in a single man, or in a *select* assembly of a moderate number; or in a single man, with the concurrence of such an assembly. The exercise of it by the people at large will be readily admitted to be impracticable; as waiving every other consideration, it would leave them little time to do anything else. . . .

Those who have themselves reflected upon the subject, or who have attended to the observations made in other parts of these papers, in relation to the appointment of the President, will, I presume, agree to the position, that there would always be great probability of having the place supplied by a man of abilities, at least respectable. Premising this, I proceed to lay it down as a rule, that one man of discernment is better fitted to analyze and estimate the peculiar qualities adapted to particular offices, than a body of men of equal or perhaps even of superior discernment.

The sole and undivided responsibility of one man will naturally beget a livelier sense of duty and a more exact regard to reputation. He will, on this account, feel himself under stronger obligations, and more interested to investigate with care the qualities requisite to the stations to be filled, and to prefer with impartiality the persons who may have the fairest pretensions to them. He will have *fewer* personal attachments to gratify, than a body of men who may each be supposed to have an equal number; and will be so much the less liable to be misled by the sentiments of friendship and of affection. A single well-directed man, by a single understanding, cannot be distracted and warped by that diversity of views, feelings, and interests, which frequently distract and warp the resolutions of a collective body. There is nothing so apt to agitate the passions of mankind as personal considerations whether they relate to ourselves or to others, who are to be the objects of our choice or preference. Hence, in every exercise of the power of appointing to offices, by an assembly of men, we must expect to see a full display of all the private and party likings and dislikes, partialities and antipathies, attachments and animosities, which are felt by those who compose the assembly. . . . "Give us the man we wish for this office, and you shall have the one you wish for that." This will be the usual condition of the bargain. And it will rarely happen that the advancement of the public service will be the primary object either of party victories or of party negotiations.

The truth of the principles here advanced seems to have been felt by the most intelligent of those who have found fault with the provision made, in this respect, by the convention. They contend that the President ought solely to have been authorized to make the appointments under the federal government. But it is easy to show, that every advantage to be expected from such an arrangement would, in substance, be derived from the power of *nomination*, which is proposed to be conferred upon him; while several disadvantages which might attend the absolute power of appointment in the hands of that officer would be avoided. In the act of nomination, his judgment alone would be exercised; and as it would be his sole duty to point out the man who, with the approbation of the Senate, should fill an office, his responsibility would be as complete as if he were to make the final appointment. . . .

There can, in this view, be no difference between nominating and appointing. The same motives which would influence a proper discharge of his duty in one case, would exist in the other. And as no man could be appointed but on his previous nomination, every man who might be appointed would be, in fact, his choice.

But might not his nomination be overruled? I grant it might, yet this could only be to make place for another nomination by himself. The person ultimately appointed must be the object of his preference, though perhaps not in the first degree. It is also not very probable that his nomination would often be overruled. The Senate could not be tempted, by the preference they might feel to another, to reject the one proposed; because they could not assure themselves, that the person they might wish would be brought forward by a second or by any subsequent nomination. They could not even be certain, that a future nomination would present a candidate in any degree more acceptable to them; and as their dissent might cast a kind of stigma upon the individual rejected, and might have the appearance of a reflection upon the judgment of the chief magistrate, it is not likely that their sanction would often be refused, where there were not special and strong reasons for the refusal.

To what purpose then require the co-operation of the Senate? I answer, that the necessity of their concurrence would have a powerful, though, in general, a silent operation. It would be an excellent check upon a spirit of favoritism in the President, and would tend greatly to prevent the appointment of unfit characters from State prejudice, from family connection, from personal attachment, or from a view to popularity. In addition to this, it would be an efficacious source of stability in the administration.

It will readily be comprehended, that a man who had himself the sole disposition of offices, would be governed much more by his private inclinations and interests, than when he was bound to submit the propriety of his choice to the discussion and determination of a different and independent body, and that body an entire branch of the legislature. The possibility of rejection would be a strong motive to care in proposing. . . . He would be both ashamed and afraid to bring forward, for the most distinguished or lucrative stations, candidates who had no other merit than that of coming from the same State to which he particularly belonged, or of being in some way or other personally allied to him, or of possessing the necessary insignificance and pliancy to render them the obsequious instruments of his pleasure. . . .

NOTES

1.   In *The Federalist No. 76*, Hamilton makes the case for appointment by presidential nomination and senatorial confirmation. Is Hamilton right that if the appointment power were given to the president alone there would likely be abuse? Is Hamilton right that giving the appointment power to a legislative body would result in log-rolling and capture by special interests? Is executive nomination with senatorial confirmation an ingenious solution to the appointments dilemma—or a recipe for gridlock and dysfunction?

2.   The appointment power was at issue in the case presented next, *Buckley v. Valeo*. It involved the constitutionality of the Federal Election Campaign Act, which regulates and publicizes contributions to political campaigns for federal office. The act created the Federal Election Commission, with the power to make rules and to enforce the statute. The commission was described as being in the legislative branch of the government and the statute setting it up provided that two members would be nominated by the president pro tempore of the Senate; another two members would be nominated by the Speaker of the House of Representatives; and two members would be nominated by the president. All six nominations required confirmation by a majority of both houses of Congress.

Buckley v. Valeo

424 U.S. 1 (1976)

■ PER CURIAM. . . .

Appellants urge that since Congress has given the [Federal Election] Commission wide-ranging rulemaking and enforcement powers with respect to the substantive provisions of the Act, Congress is precluded under the principle of separation of powers from vesting in itself the authority to appoint those who will exercise such authority. Their argument is based on the language of Art. II, § 2, cl. 2, of the Constitution, which provides in pertinent part as follows:

> [The President] shall nominate, and by and with the Advice and Consent of the Senate, shall appoint . . . all other Officers of the United States, whose Appointments are not herein otherwise provided for, and which shall be established by Law: but the Congress may by Law vest the Appointment of such inferior Officers, as they think proper, in the President alone, in the Courts of Law, or in the Heads of Departments.

Appellants' argument is that this provision is the exclusive method by which those charged with executing the laws of the United States may be chosen. Congress, they assert, cannot have it both ways. If the Legislature wishes the Commission to exercise all of the conferred powers, then its members are in fact "Officers of the United States" and must be appointed under the Appointments Clause. But if Congress insists upon retaining the power to appoint, then the members of the Commission may not discharge those many functions of the Commission which can be performed only by "Officers of the United States," as that term must be construed within the doctrine of separation of powers. . . .

We do not think appellants' arguments based upon Art. II, § 2, cl. 2, of the Constitution may be . . . easily dismissed. . . . Our inquiry of necessity touches upon the fundamental principles of the Government established by the Framers of the Constitution, and all litigants and all of the courts which have addressed themselves to the matter start on common ground in the recognition of the intent of the Framers that the powers of the three great branches of the National Government be largely separate from one another. . . .

The Framers regarded the checks and balances that they had built into the tripartite Federal Government as a self-executing safeguard against the encroachment or aggrandizement of one branch at the expense of the other. . . . This Court has not hesitated to enforce the principle of separation of powers embodied in the Constitution when its application has proved necessary for the decisions of cases or controversies properly before it. . . .

The principle of separation of powers was not simply an abstract generalization in the minds of the Framers: it was woven into the document that they drafted in Philadelphia in the summer of 1787. . . . The Appointments Clause could . . . be read as merely dealing with etiquette or protocol in describing "Officers of the United States," but the drafters had a less frivolous purpose in mind. . . .

We think that the term "Officers of the United States" as used in Art. II, defined to include "all persons who can be said to hold an office under the government" in *United States v. Germaine*, 99 U.S. 508, 510 (1878), is a term intended to have substantive meaning. We think its fair import is that any appointee exercising significant authority pursuant to the laws of the United States is an "Officer of the United States," and must, therefore, be appointed in the manner prescribed by § 2, cl. 2, of that Article. . . .

Although two members of the Commission are initially selected by the President, his nominations are subject to confirmation not merely by the Senate, but by the House of Representatives as well. The remaining four voting members of the Commission are appointed by the President *pro tempore* of the Senate and by the Speaker of the House. While the second part of the Clause authorizes Congress to vest the appointment of the officers described in that part in "the Courts of Law, or in the Heads of Departments," neither the Speaker of the House nor the President *pro tempore* of the Senate comes within this language. . . .

The Appointments Clause specifies the method of appointment only for "Officers of the United States" whose appointment is not "otherwise provided for" in the Constitution. But there is no provision of the Constitution remotely providing any alternative means for the selection of the members of the Commission or for anybody like them. . . .

An interim version of the draft Constitution had vested in the Senate the authority to appoint Ambassadors, public Ministers, and Judges of the Supreme Court, and the language of Art. II as finally adopted is a distinct change in this regard. We believe that it was a deliberate change made by the Framers with the intent to deny Congress any authority itself to appoint those who were "Officers of the United States." The debates on the floor of the Convention reflect at least in part the way the change came about.

On Monday, August 6, 1787, the Committee on Detail to which had been referred the entire draft of the Constitution reported its draft to the Convention, including the following two articles that bear on the question before us: . . .

Article IX, § 1: "The Senate of the United States shall have power . . . to appoint Ambassadors, and Judges of the Supreme Court."

Article X, § 2: "[The President] shall commission all the officers of the United States; and shall appoint officers in all cases not otherwise provided for by this Constitution."

It will be seen from a comparison of these two articles that the appointment of Ambassadors and Judges of the Supreme Court was confided to the Senate, and that the authority to *appoint*—not merely nominate, but to actually appoint—all other officers was reposed in the President.

During a discussion of a provision in the same draft from the Committee on Detail which provided that the "Treasurer" of the United States should be chosen by both Houses of Congress, Mr. Read moved to strike out that clause, "leaving the appointment of the Treasurer *as of other officers* to the Executive." Opposition to Read's motion was based, not on objection to the principle of executive appointment, but on the particular nature of the office of the "Treasurer." . . .

Meanwhile, on Friday, August 31, a motion had been carried without opposition to refer such parts of the Constitution as had been postponed or not acted upon to a Committee of Eleven. Such reference carried with it both Arts. IX and X. The following week the Committee of Eleven made its report to the Convention, in which the present language of Art. II, § 2, cl. 2, dealing with the authority of the President to nominate is found, virtually word for word, as § 4 of Art. X. The same Committee also reported a revised article concerning the Legislative Branch to the Convention. The changes are obvious. In the final version, the Senate is shorn of its power to appoint Ambassadors and Judges of the Supreme Court. The President is given, not the power to *appoint* public officers of the United States, but only the right to *nominate* them, and a provision is inserted by virtue of which Congress may require Senate confirmation of his nominees.

It would seem a fair surmise that a compromise had been made. But no change was made in the concept of the term "Officers of the United States," which since it had first appeared in Art. X had been taken by all concerned to embrace all appointed officials exercising responsibility under the public laws of the Nation. . . .

[The Federal Elections Commission] contend[s], and the majority of the Court of Appeals agreed . . . , that whatever shortcomings the provisions for the appointment of members of the Commission might have under Art. II, Congress had ample authority under the Necessary and Proper Clause of Art. I to effectuate this result. We do not agree. The proper inquiry when considering the Necessary and Proper Clause is not the authority of Congress to create an office or a commission, which is broad indeed, but rather its authority to [specify] that its own officers may make appointments to such office or commission.

So framed, the claim that Congress may provide for this manner of appointment under the Necessary and Proper Clause of Art. I stands on [a weak] footing. . . . Congress could not, merely because it concluded that such a measure was "necessary and proper" to the discharge of its substantive legislative authority, pass a bill of attainder or *ex post facto* law contrary to the prohibitions contained in § 9 of Art. I. No more may it vest in itself, or in its officers, the authority to appoint officers of the United States when the Appointments Clause by clear implication prohibits it from doing so. . . .

We hold that these provisions of the Act, vesting in the Commission primary responsibility for conducting civil litigation in the courts of the United States for vindicating public rights, violate Art. II, § 2, cl. 2, of the Constitution. Such functions may be discharged only by persons who are "Officers of the United States" within the language of that section. . . .

■ MR. JUSTICE WHITE, concurring in part and dissenting in part. . . .

[T]he FEC, in defending the legality of its members' appointments, does not deny that they are "officers of the United States" as that term is used in the Appointments Clause of Art. II. Instead, for reasons the Court outlines, its position appears to be that even if its members are officers of the United States, Congress may nevertheless appoint a majority of the FEC without participation by the President. . . .

The language of the Appointments Clause was . . . debated by the Framers [at length]. . . . The decision to give the President the exclusive power to initiate appointments was thoughtful and deliberate. . . . Under Art. II as finally adopted, law enforcement authority was not to be lodged in elected legislative officials subject to political pressures. Neither was the Legislative Branch to have the power to appoint those who were to enforce and administer the law. . . .

Congress clearly has the power to create federal offices and to define the powers and duties of those offices, *Myers v. United States*, 272 U.S. 52, 128–129 (1926), but no case in this Court even remotely supports the power of Congress to appoint an officer of the United States aside from those officers each House is authorized by Art. I to appoint to assist in the legislative processes. . . .

There is no doubt that the development of the administrative agency in response to modern legislative and administrative need has placed severe strain on the separation-of-powers principle in its pristine formulation. See *Kilbourn v. Thompson*, 103 U.S. 168, 191 (1881). Any notion that the Constitution bans any admixture of powers that might be deemed legislative, executive, and judicial has had to give way. The independent agency has survived attacks from various directions: that it exercises invalidly delegated legislative power, *Sunshine Coal Co. v. Adkins*, 310 U.S. 381 (1940); that it invalidly exercises judicial power, *ibid.*; and that its functions are so executive in nature that its members must be subject to Presidential control, *Humphrey's Executor v. United States*, 295 U.S. 602 (1935). Until now, however, it has not been insisted that the commands of the Appointments Clause must also yield to permit congressional appointments of members of a major agency. With the Court, I am not convinced that we should create a broad exception to the requirements of that Clause that all officers of the United States be appointed in accordance with its terms. . . .

NOTES

1.   The Court was unanimous in rejecting the appointments scheme in *Buckley*, but the bill was passed by Congress and signed by the president, who must have known that the law was likely to face legal challenges. What could they have been thinking? What are the best arguments in favor of the constitutionality of the statute?

2.   One key question in determining the applicability of the Appointments Clause is whether a given person is an "Officer of the United States," which in *Buckley* the Court defines to be "any appointee exercising significant authority pursuant to the laws of the United States." What do you think of this definition? What does it mean? Is there a better one?

3.   The Appointments Clause also refers to "inferior Officers," which are further discussed and defined in *Morrison v. Olson*, p. 249. Would it have made any difference in *Buckley* if the FEC commissioners had been "inferior Officers"? Why or why not?

Art. II, § 2: . . . The President shall have Power to fill up all Vacancies that may happen during the Recess of the Senate, by granting Commissions which shall expire at the End of their next Session.

The Appointments Clause is the primary method of appointing executive-branch officers, but it is not the only one. The Constitution also provides for temporary "recess appointments" in some circumstances, and every president back to George Washington has made some. But the Supreme Court went 225 years without considering the scope of the Recess Appointments Clause—until 2014.

National Labor Relations Board v. Noel Canning
134 S.Ct. 2550 (2014)

■ JUSTICE BREYER delivered the opinion of the Court.

Ordinarily the President must obtain "the Advice and Consent of the Senate" before appointing an "Office[r] of the United States." U.S. Const., Art. II, § 2, cl. 2. But the Recess Appointments Clause creates an exception. It gives the President alone the power "to fill up all Vacancies that may happen during the Recess of the Senate, by granting Commissions which shall expire at the End of their next Session." Art. II, § 2, cl. 3. We here consider three questions about the application of this Clause.

The first concerns the scope of the words "recess of the Senate." Does that phrase refer only to an inter-session recess (*i.e.,* a break between formal sessions of Congress), or does it also include an intra-session recess, such as a summer recess in the midst of a session? We conclude that the Clause applies to both kinds of recess.

The second question concerns the scope of the words "vacancies that may happen." Does that phrase refer only to vacancies that first come into existence during a recess, or does it also include vacancies that arise prior to a recess but continue to exist during the recess? We conclude that the Clause applies to both kinds of vacancy.

The third question concerns calculation of the length of a "recess." The President made the appointments here at issue on January 4, 2012. At that time the Senate was in recess pursuant to a December 17, 2011, resolution providing for a series of brief recesses punctuated by "*pro forma* session[s]," with "no business . . . transacted," every Tuesday and Friday through January 20, 2012. S. J., 112th Cong., 1st Sess., 923 (2011) (hereinafter 2011 S. J.). In calculating the length of a recess are we to ignore the *pro forma* sessions, thereby treating the series of brief recesses as a single, month-long recess? We conclude that we cannot ignore these *pro forma* sessions.

Our answer to the third question means that, when the appointments before us took place, the Senate was in the midst of a 3-day recess. Three days is too short a time to bring a recess within the scope of the Clause. Thus we conclude that the President lacked the power to make the recess appointments here at issue.

I

The case before us arises out of a labor dispute. . . . *[Noel Canning, a Pepsi-Cola distributor, lost before the National Labor Relations Board and challenged the decision on the ground that three members of the board had been invalidly recess appointed.—Editors]*

II

Before turning to the specific questions presented, we shall mention two background considerations that we find relevant to all three. First, *the Recess Appointments Clause sets forth a subsidiary, not a primary, method for appointing officers of the United States.* The immediately preceding Clause—Article II, Section 2, Clause 2—provides the primary method of appointment. It says that the President "shall nominate, *and by and with the Advice and Consent of the Senate,* shall appoint

Ambassadors, other public Ministers and Consuls, Judges of the supreme Court, and all other Officers of the United States" (emphasis added).

The Federalist Papers make clear that the Founders intended this method of appointment, requiring Senate approval, to be the norm (at least for principal officers). . . . Thus the Recess Appointments Clause reflects the tension between, on the one hand, the President's continuous need for "the assistance of subordinates," *Myers v. United States*, 272 U.S. 52, 117 (1926), and, on the other, the Senate's practice, particularly during the Republic's early years, of meeting for a single brief session each year, see Art. I, § 4, cl. 2; Amdt. 20, § 2 (requiring the Senate to "assemble" only "once in every year"); 3 J. Story, Commentaries on the Constitution of the United States § 1551, p. 410 (1833) (it would be "burthensome to the senate, and expensive to the public" to require the Senate to be "perpetually in session"). We seek to interpret the Clause as granting the President the power to make appointments during a recess but not offering the President the authority routinely to avoid the need for Senate confirmation.

Second, *in interpreting the Clause, we put significant weight upon historical practice.* . . .

We recognize, of course, that the separation of powers can serve to safeguard individual liberty, *Clinton v. City of New York*, 524 U.S. 417, 449–450 (1998) (KENNEDY, J., concurring), and that it is the "duty of the judicial department"—in a separation-of-powers case as in any other—"to say what the law is," *Marbury v. Madison*, 5 U.S. (1 Cranch) 137, 177 (1803). But it is equally true that the longstanding "practice of the government," *McCulloch v. Maryland,* 17 U.S. (4 Wheat.) 316, 401 (1819), can inform our determination of "what the law is," *Marbury*, at 177.

That principle is neither new nor controversial. As James Madison wrote, it "was foreseen at the birth of the Constitution, that difficulties and differences of opinion might occasionally arise in expounding terms & phrases necessarily used in such a charter . . . and that it might require a regular course of practice to liquidate & settle the meaning of some of them." Letter to Spencer Roane (Sept. 2, 1819), in 8 Writings of James Madison 450 (G. Hunt ed. 1908). And our cases have continually confirmed Madison's view. *E.g., Mistretta v. United States*, 488 U.S. 361, 401 (1989); *Dames & Moore v. Regan*, 453 U.S. 654, 686 (1981); *Youngstown Sheet & Tube Co. v. Sawyer*, 343 U.S. 579, 610–611 (1952) (Frankfurter, J., concurring); *The Pocket Veto Case*, 279 U.S. 655, 689–690 (1929); *Ex parte Grossman*, 267 U.S. 87, 118–119 (1925); *United States v. Midwest Oil Co.*, 236 U.S. 459, 472–474 (1915); *McPherson v. Blacker*, 146 U.S. 1, 27 (1892); *McCulloch*; *Stuart v. Laird*, 5 U.S. (1 Cranch) 299 (1803). . . .

We have not previously interpreted the Clause, and, when doing so for the first time in more than 200 years, we must hesitate to upset the compromises and working arrangements that the elected branches of Government themselves have reached.

III

The first question concerns the scope of the phrase *"the recess* of the Senate." Art. II, § 2, cl. 3 (emphasis added). The Constitution provides for congressional elections every two years. And the 2-year life of each elected Congress typically consists of two formal 1-year sessions, each separated from the next by an "inter-session recess." The Senate or the House of Representatives announces an inter-session recess by approving a resolution stating that it will "adjourn *sine die*," *i.e.,* without specifying a date to return (in which case Congress will reconvene when the next formal session is scheduled to begin).

The Senate and the House also take breaks in the midst of a session. The Senate or the House announces any such "intra-session recess" by adopting a resolution stating that it will "adjourn" to a fixed date, a few days or weeks or even months later. All agree that the phrase "the recess of the Senate" covers inter-session recesses. The question is whether it includes intra-session recesses as well.

In our view, the phrase "the recess" includes an intra-session recess of substantial length. Its words taken literally can refer to both types of recess. Founding-era dictionaries define the word "recess," much as we do today, simply as "a period of cessation from usual work." 13 The Oxford English Dictionary 322–323 (2d ed. 1989) (hereinafter OED) (citing 18th- and 19th-century sources for that definition of "recess"); 2 N. Webster, An American Dictionary of the English Language (1828) ("[r]emission or suspension of business or procedure"); 2 Samuel Johnson, A Dictionary of the English Language 1602–1603 (4th ed. 1773) (hereinafter Johnson) (same). The Founders themselves used the word to refer to intra-session, as well as to inter-session, breaks. See, *e.g.,* 3 Records of the Federal Convention of 1787, p. 76 (M. Farrand rev. 1966) (hereinafter Farrand) (letter from George Washington to John Jay using "the recess" to refer to an intra-session break of the Constitutional Convention); *id.,* at 191 (speech of Luther Martin with a similar usage); 1 T. Jefferson, A Manual of Parliamentary Practice §LI, p. 165 (2d ed. 1812) (describing a "recess by adjournment" which did *not* end a session).

We recognize that the word "the" in "*the* recess" might suggest that the phrase refers to the single break separating formal sessions of Congress. That is because the word "the" frequently (but not always) indicates "a particular thing." 2 Johnson 2003. But the word can also refer "to a term used generically or universally." 17 OED 879. The Constitution, for example, directs the Senate to choose a President *pro tempore* "in *the* Absence of the Vice-President." Art. I, § 3, cl. 5 (emphasis added). And the Federalist Papers refer to the chief magistrate of an ancient Achaean league who "administered the government in *the* recess of the Senate." The Federalist No. 18, at 113 (J. Madison) (emphasis added). Reading "the" generically in this way, there is no linguistic problem applying the Clause's phrase to both kinds of recess. And, in fact, the phrase "the recess" was used to refer to intra-session recesses at the time of the founding. See, *e.g.,* 3 Farrand 76 (letter from Washington to Jay); New Jersey Legislative-Council Journal, 5th Sess., 1st Sitting 70, 2d Sitting 9 (1781) (twice referring to a 4-month, intra-session break as "the Recess").

The constitutional text is thus ambiguous. And we believe the Clause's purpose demands the broader interpretation. The Clause gives the President authority to make appointments during "the recess of the Senate" so that the President can ensure the continued functioning of the Federal Government when the Senate is away. The Senate is equally away during both an inter-session and an intra-session recess, and its capacity to participate in the appointments process has nothing to do with the words it uses to signal its departure.

History also offers strong support for the broad interpretation. We concede that pre-Civil War history is not helpful. But it shows only that Congress generally took long breaks between sessions, while taking no significant intra-session breaks at all (five times it took a break of a week or so at Christmas). Obviously, if there are no significant intra-session recesses, there will be no intra-session recess appointments. . . .

In all, between the founding and the Great Depression, Congress took substantial intra-session breaks (other than holiday breaks) in four years: 1867, 1868, 1921, and 1929. And in each of those years the President made intra-session recess appointments.

Since 1929, and particularly since the end of World War II, Congress has shortened its inter-session breaks as it has taken longer and more frequent intra-session breaks; Presidents have correspondingly made more intra-session recess appointments. Indeed, if we include military appointments, Presidents have made thousands of intra-session recess appointments. . . .

Not surprisingly, the publicly available opinions of Presidential legal advisers that we have found are nearly unanimous in determining that the Clause authorizes these appointments. . . .

What about the Senate? Since Presidents began making intra-session recess appointments, individual Senators have taken differing views about the proper definition of "the recess." . . . But neither the Senate considered as a body nor its committees, despite opportunities to express opposition to the practice of intra-session recess appointments, has done so. Rather, to the extent that the Senate or a Senate committee has expressed a view, that view has favored a functional definition of "recess," and a functional definition encompasses intra-session recesses. . . . *[The Court discussed a 1905 Senate Judiciary Report and a 1948 statutory amendment that, it thought, supported the broader, "functional" reading.—Editors]*

We recognize that the Senate cannot easily register opposition as a body to every governmental action that many, perhaps most, Senators oppose. But the Senate has not been silent or passive regarding the meaning of the Clause: A Senate Committee did register opposition to President Theodore Roosevelt's use of the Clause, and the Senate as a whole has legislated in an effort to discourage certain kinds of recess appointments. And yet we are not aware of any formal action it has taken to call into question the broad and functional definition of "recess" first set out in the 1905 Senate Report and followed by the Executive Branch since at least 1921. Nor has JUSTICE SCALIA identified any. All the while, the President has made countless recess appointments during intra-session recesses.

The upshot is that restricting the Clause to inter-session recesses would frustrate its purpose. It would make the President's recess-appointment power dependent on a formalistic distinction of Senate procedure. Moreover, the President has consistently and frequently interpreted the word "recess" to apply to intra-session recesses, and has acted on that interpretation. The Senate as a body has done nothing to deny the validity of this practice for at least three-quarters of a century. And three-quarters of a century of settled practice is long enough to entitle a practice to "great weight in a proper interpretation" of the constitutional provision. *The Pocket Veto Case*, at 689. . . .

[The Court went on to hold that a 3-day recess was too short to fall within the clause, and that "a recess of more than 3 days but less than 10 days is presumptively too short to fall within the Clause," noting that it had "not found a single example of

a recess appointment made during an intra-session recess that was shorter than 10 days."—Editors]

IV

The second question concerns the scope of the phrase "vacancies *that may happen* during the recess of the Senate." Art. II, § 2, cl. 3 (emphasis added). All agree that the phrase applies to vacancies that initially occur during a recess. But does it also apply to vacancies that initially occur before a recess and continue to exist during the recess? In our view the phrase applies to both kinds of vacancy.

We believe that the Clause's language, read literally, permits, though it does not naturally favor, our broader interpretation. We concede that the most natural meaning of "happens" as applied to a "vacancy" (at least to a modern ear) is that the vacancy "happens" when it initially occurs. See 1 Johnson 913 (defining "happen" in relevant part as meaning "[t]o fall out; to chance; to come to pass"). But that is not the only possible way to use the word. . . .

[W]hen Attorney General William Wirt advised President Monroe to follow the broader interpretation, he wrote that the "expression seems not perfectly clear. It may mean 'happen to take place:' that is, '*to originate,*'" or it "may mean, also, without violence to the sense, 'happen to exist.'" 1 Op. Atty. Gen. 631, 631–632 (1823). The broader interpretation, he added, is "most accordant with" the Constitution's "reason and spirit."

We can still understand this earlier use of "happen" if we think of it used together with another word that, like "vacancy," can refer to a continuing state, say, a financial crisis. A statute that gives the President authority to act in respect to "any financial crisis that may happen during his term" can easily be interpreted to include crises that arise before, and continue during, that term. Perhaps that is why the Oxford English Dictionary defines "happen" in part as "chance *to be*," rather than "chance to occur." 6 OED 1096 (emphasis added); see also 19 OED 383 (defining "vacancy" as the "condition of an office or post being . . . vacant").

In any event, the linguistic question here is not whether the phrase can be, but whether it must be, read more narrowly. The question is whether the Clause is ambiguous. And the broader reading, we believe, is at least a permissible reading of a "doubtful" phrase. We consequently go on to consider the Clause's purpose and historical practice.

The Clause's purpose strongly supports the broader interpretation. That purpose is to permit the President to obtain the assistance of subordinate officers when the Senate, due to its recess, cannot confirm them. Attorney General Wirt clearly described how the narrower interpretation would undermine this purpose:

> "Put the case of a vacancy occurring in an office, held in a distant part of the country, on the last day of the Senate's session. Before the vacancy is made known to the President, the Senate rises. The office may be an important one; the vacancy may paralyze a whole line of action in some essential branch of our internal police; the public interests may imperiously demand that it shall be immediately filled. But the vacancy happened to occur during the session of the Senate; and if the President's power is to be limited to such vacancies only as happen to occur during the recess of the Senate, the vacancy in the case put must continue, however ruinous the consequences may be to the public." 1 Op. Atty. Gen., at 632.

Examples are not difficult to imagine: An ambassadorial post falls vacant too soon before the recess begins for the President to appoint a replacement; the Senate rejects a President's nominee just before a recess, too late to select another. Wirt explained that the "substantial purpose of the constitution was to keep these offices filled," and "if the President shall not have the power to fill a vacancy thus circumstanced, . . . the substance of the constitution will be sacrificed to a dubious construction of its letter." Thus the broader construction, encompassing vacancies that initially occur before the beginning of a recess, is the "only construction of the constitution which is compatible with its spirit, reason, and purposes; while, at the same time, it offers no violence to its language." *Id.*, at 633.

We do not agree with JUSTICE SCALIA's suggestion that the Framers would have accepted the catastrophe envisioned by Wirt because Congress can always provide for acting officers, see 5 U.S.C. § 3345, and the President can always convene a special session of Congress, see U.S. Const., Art. II, § 3. Acting officers may have less authority than Presidential appointments. 6 Op. OLC 119, 121 (1982). Moreover, to rely on acting officers would lessen the President's ability to staff the Executive Branch with people of his own choosing, and thereby limit the President's control and political accountability. Cf. *Free Enterprise Fund v. Public Company Accounting Oversight Bd.*, 561 U.S. 477, 497–498 (2010). Special sessions are burdensome (and would have been especially so at the time of the founding). The point of the Recess Appointments Clause was to *avoid* reliance on these inadequate expedients.

At the same time, we recognize one important purpose-related consideration that argues in the opposite direction. A broad interpretation might permit a President to avoid Senate confirmations as a matter of course. If the Clause gives the President the power to "fill up all vacancies" that occur before, and continue to exist during, the Senate's recess, a President might not submit any nominations to the Senate. He might simply wait for a recess and then provide all potential nominees with recess appointments. He might thereby routinely avoid the constitutional need to obtain the Senate's "advice and consent."

Wirt thought considerations of character and politics would prevent Presidents from abusing the Clause in this way. 1 Op. Atty. Gen., at 634. He might have added that such temptations should not often arise. It is often less desirable for a President to make a recess appointment. A recess appointee only serves a limited term. That, combined with the lack of Senate approval, may diminish the recess appointee's ability, as a practical matter, to get a controversial job done. . . .

Historical practice over the past 200 years strongly favors the broader interpretation. The tradition of applying the Clause to pre-recess vacancies dates at least to President James Madison. There is no undisputed record of Presidents George Washington, John Adams, or Thomas Jefferson making such an appointment, though the Solicitor General believes he has found records showing that Presidents Washington and Jefferson did so. . . .

President Adams seemed to endorse the broader view of the Clause in writing, though we are not aware of any appointments he made in keeping with that view. . . . We know that President Jefferson thought that the broad interpretation was linguistically supportable, though his actual practice is not clear. But the evidence suggests that James Madison—as familiar as anyone with the workings of the Constitutional Convention—appointed Theodore Gaillard to replace a district judge who had left office before a recess began. It also appears that in 1815 Madison signed a bill that created two new offices prior to a recess which he then filled later during the recess. He also made recess appointments to "territorial" United States attorney and marshal positions, both of which had been created when the Senate was in session more than two years before. JUSTICE SCALIA refers to "written evidence of Madison's own beliefs," but in fact we have no direct evidence of what President Madison believed. We only know that he declined to make one appointment to a pre-recess vacancy after his Secretary of War advised him that he lacked the power. On the other hand, he *did* apparently make at least five other appointments to pre-recess vacancies, as JUSTICE SCALIA does not dispute.

The next President, James Monroe, received and presumably acted upon Attorney General Wirt's advice, namely that "all vacancies which, from any casualty, happen to exist at a time when the Senate cannot be consulted as to filling them, may be temporarily filled by the President." 1 Op. Atty. Gen., at 633. Nearly every subsequent Attorney General to consider the question throughout the Nation's history has thought the same. . . . Indeed, as early as 1862, Attorney General Bates advised President Lincoln that his power to fill pre-recess vacancies was "settled . . . as far . . . as a constitutional question can be settled," 10 Op. Atty. Gen., at 356. . . .

Did the Senate object? Early on, there was some sporadic disagreement with the broad interpretation. . . . [But,] by 1862 Attorney General Bates could still refer to "the unbroken acquiescence of the Senate" in support of the broad interpretation.

Then in 1863 the Senate Judiciary Committee disagreed with the broad interpretation. It issued a report concluding that a vacancy "must have its inceptive point after one session has closed and before another session has begun." S. Rep. No. 80, 37th Cong., 3d Sess., p. 3. And the Senate then passed the Pay Act, which provided that "no money shall be paid . . . as a salary, to any person appointed during the recess of the Senate, to fill a vacancy . . . which . . . existed while the Senate was in session." Act of Feb. 9, 1863, § 2, 12 Stat. 646. Relying upon the floor statement of a single Senator, JUSTICE SCALIA suggests that the passage of the Pay Act indicates that the Senate as a whole endorsed the position in the 1863 Report. But the circumstances are more equivocal. During the floor debate on the bill, not a single Senator referred to the Report. Indeed, Senator Trumbull, who introduced the Pay Act, acknowledged that there was disagreement about the underlying constitutional question. Further, if a majority of the Senate had believed appointments to pre-recess vacancies were unconstitutional, it could have attempted to do far more than temporarily dock the appointees' pay. Cf. Tenure of Office Act of 1867, § 5, 14 Stat. 431 (making it a federal crime for "any person" to "accept any appointment" in certain circumstances).

In any event, the Senate subsequently abandoned its hostility. . . .

The upshot is that the President has consistently and frequently interpreted the Recess Appointments Clause to apply to vacancies that initially occur before, but continue to exist during, a recess of the Senate. The Senate as a body has not countered this practice for nearly three-quarters of a century, perhaps longer. See A. Amar, The Unwritten Constitution 576–577, n. 16 (2012) (for nearly 200 years "the overwhelming mass of actual practice" supports the President's interpretation). The tradition is long enough to entitle the practice "to great regard in determining the true construction" of the constitutional provision. *The Pocket Veto Case*, at 690. And we are reluctant to upset this traditional practice where doing so would seriously shrink the authority that Presidents have believed existed and have exercised for so long.

In light of some linguistic ambiguity, the basic purpose of the Clause, and the historical practice we have described, we conclude that the phrase "all vacancies" includes vacancies that come into existence while the Senate is in session.

V

The third question concerns the calculation of the length of the Senate's "recess." On December 17, 2011, the Senate by unanimous consent adopted a resolution to convene "*pro forma* session[s]" only, with "no business . . . transacted," on every Tuesday and Friday from December 20, 2011, through January 20, 2012. . . . *[Relying in part on the Senate's authority to "determine the Rules of its Proceedings," Art. I, § 5, cl. 2, the Court concluded that "the Senate is in session when it says it is, provided that, under its own rules, it retains the capacity to transact Senate business." The pro forma sessions met that standard. As a consequence, the recess was only three days long.—Editors]*

VI

The Recess Appointments Clause responds to a structural difference between the Executive and Legislative Branches: The Executive Branch is perpetually in operation, while the Legislature only acts in intervals separated by recesses. The purpose of the Clause is to allow the Executive to continue operating while the Senate is unavailable. We believe that the Clause's text, standing alone, is ambiguous. It does not resolve whether the President may make appointments during intra-session recesses, or whether he may fill pre-recess vacancies. But the broader reading better serves the Clause's structural function. Moreover, that broader reading is reinforced by centuries of history, which we are hesitant to disturb. We thus hold that the Constitution empowers the President to fill any existing vacancy during any recess—intra-session or inter-session—of sufficient length.

JUSTICE SCALIA would render illegitimate thousands of recess appointments reaching all the way back to the founding era. More than that: Calling the Clause an "anachronism," he would basically read it out of the Constitution. He performs this act of judicial excision in the name of liberty. We fail to see how excising the Recess Appointments Clause preserves freedom. In fact, Alexander Hamilton observed in the very first Federalist Paper that "the vigour of government is essential to the security of liberty." The Federalist No. 1. And the Framers included the Recess Appointments Clause to preserve the "vigour of government" at times when an important organ of Government, the United States Senate, is in recess. JUSTICE SCALIA's interpretation of the Clause would defeat the power of the Clause to achieve that objective.

The foregoing discussion should refute JUSTICE SCALIA's claim that we have "embrace[d]" an "adverse-possession theory of executive power." Instead, as in all cases, we interpret the Constitution in light of its text, purposes, and "our whole experience" as a Nation. *Missouri v. Holland*, 252 U.S. 416, 433 (1920). And we look to the actual practice of Government to inform our interpretation.

Given our answer to the last question before us, we conclude that the Recess Appointments Clause does not give the President the constitutional authority to make the appointments here at issue. Because the Court of Appeals reached the same ultimate conclusion (though for reasons we reject), its judgment is affirmed.

■ JUSTICE SCALIA, with whom THE CHIEF JUSTICE, JUSTICE THOMAS, and JUSTICE ALITO join, concurring in the judgment.

. . . To prevent the President's recess-appointment power from nullifying the Senate's role in the appointment process, the Constitution cabins that power in two significant ways. First, it may be exercised only in "the Recess of the Senate," that is, the intermission between two formal legislative sessions. Second, it may be used to fill only those vacancies that "happen during the Recess," that is, offices that become vacant during that intermission. Both conditions are clear from the Constitution's text and structure, and both were well understood at the founding. The Court of Appeals correctly held that the appointments here at issue are invalid because they did not meet either condition.

Today's Court agrees that the appointments were invalid, but for the far narrower reason that they were made during a 3-day break in the Senate's session. On its way to that result, the majority sweeps away the key textual limitations on the recess-appointment power. It holds, first, that the President can make appointments without the Senate's participation even during short breaks in the middle of the Senate's session, and second, that those appointments can fill offices that became vacant long before the break in which they were filled. The majority justifies those atextual results on an adverse-possession theory of executive authority: Presidents have long claimed the powers in question, and the Senate has not disputed those claims with sufficient vigor, so the Court should not "upset the compromises and working arrangements that the elected branches of Government themselves have reached."

The Court's decision transforms the recess-appointment power from a tool carefully designed to fill a narrow and specific need into a weapon to be wielded by future Presidents against future Senates. To reach that result, the majority casts aside the plain, original meaning of the constitutional text in deference to late-arising historical practices that are ambiguous at best. The majority's insistence on deferring to the Executive's untenably broad interpretation of the power is in clear conflict with our precedent and forebodes a diminution of this Court's role in controversies involving the separation of powers and the structure of government. I concur in the judgment only.

I.   Our Responsibility

Today's majority disregards two overarching principles that ought to guide our consideration of the questions presented here.

First, the Constitution's core, government-structuring provisions are no less critical to preserving liberty than are the later adopted provisions of the Bill of Rights. . . .

Second and relatedly, when questions involving the Constitution's government-structuring provisions are presented in a justiciable case, it is the solemn responsibility of the Judicial Branch " 'to say what the law is.' " *Zivotofsky v. Clinton,* 132 S.Ct. 1421, 1428 (2012) (quoting *Marbury,* at 177). . . .

Of course, where a governmental practice has been open, widespread, and unchallenged since the early days of the Republic, the practice should guide our interpretation of an ambiguous constitutional provision. But " '[p]ast practice does not, by itself, create power.' " *Medellín v. Texas*, 552 U.S. 491, 532 (2008) (quoting *Dames & Moore*, at 686). That is a necessary corollary of the principle that the political branches cannot by agreement alter the constitutional structure. Plainly, then, a self-aggrandizing practice adopted by one branch well after the founding, often challenged, and never before blessed by this Court—in other words, the sort of practice on which the majority relies in this case—does not relieve us of our duty to interpret the Constitution in light of its text, structure, and original understanding. . . .

II.   Intra-Session Breaks

A.   Plain Meaning

A sensible interpretation of the Recess Appointments Clause should start by recognizing that the Clause uses the term "Recess" in contradistinction to the term "Session." As Alexander Hamilton wrote: "The time within which the power is to operate 'during the recess of the Senate' and the duration of the appointments 'to the end of the next session' of that body, conspire to elucidate the sense of the provision." The Federalist No. 67.

In the founding era, the terms "recess" and "session" had well-understood meanings in the marking-out of legislative time. The life of each elected Congress typically consisted (as it still does) of two or more formal sessions separated by adjournments "*sine die*," that is, without a specified return date. The period *between* two sessions was known as "the recess." See 26 Annals of Cong. 748 (1814) (Sen. Gore) ("The time of the Senate consists of two periods, viz: their session and their recess"). As one scholar has thoroughly demonstrated, "in government practice the phrase 'the Recess' *always* referred to the gap between sessions." Natelson, *The Origins and Meaning of "Vacancies that May Happen During the Recess" in the Constitution's Recess Appointments Clause*, 37 Harv. J. L. & Pub. Pol'y 199, 213 (2014) (hereinafter Natelson). By contrast, other provisions of the Constitution use the verb "adjourn" rather than "recess" to refer to the commencement of breaks *during* a formal legislative session. See, *e.g.*, Art. I, § 5, cl. 1; *id.*, § 5, cl. 4.

To be sure, in colloquial usage both words, "recess" and "session," could take on alternative, less precise meanings. . . . But as even the majority acknowledges, the Constitution's use of "the word 'the' in '*the* [R]ecess' " tends to suggest "that the phrase refers to the single break separating formal sessions."

More importantly, neither the Solicitor General nor the majority argues that the Clause uses "session" in its loose, colloquial sense. And if "the next Session" denotes a *formal* session, then "the Recess" must mean the break *between* formal sessions. As every commentator on the Clause until the 20th century seems to have understood, the "Recess" and the "Session" to which the Clause refers are mutually exclusive, alternating states. *[Various citations omitted.—Editors]* It is linguistically implausible to suppose—as the majority does—that the Clause uses one of those terms ("Recess") informally and the other ("Session") formally in a single sentence, with the result that an event can occur during *both* the "Recess" *and* the "Session." . . .

Relatedly, the majority contends that the Clause's supposed purpose of keeping the wheels of government turning demands that we interpret the Clause to maintain its relevance in light of the "new circumstance" of the Senate's taking an increasing number of intra-session breaks that exceed three days. Even if I accepted the canard that courts can alter the Constitution's meaning to accommodate changed circumstances, I would be hard pressed to see the relevance of that notion here. The rise of intra-session adjournments has occurred in tandem with the development of modern forms of communication and transportation that mean the Senate "is always available" to consider nominations, even when its Members are temporarily dispersed for an intra-session break. Tr. Of Oral Arg. 21 (GINSBURG, J.). The Recess Appointments Clause therefore is, or rather, should be, an anachronism— "essentially an historic relic, something whose original purpose has disappeared." *Id.*, at 19 (KAGAN, J.). The need it was designed to fill no longer exists, and its only remaining use is the ignoble one of enabling the President to circumvent the Senate's role in the appointment process. That does not justify "read[ing] it out of the Constitution" and, contra the majority, I would not do so; but neither would I distort the Clause's original meaning, as the majority does, to ensure a prominent role for the recess-appointment power in an era when its influence is far more pernicious than beneficial. . . .

B. Historical Practice

. . . The first intra-session recess appointments in our history almost certainly were made by President Andrew Johnson in 1867 and 1868. That was, of course, a period of dramatic conflict between the Executive and Congress that saw the first-ever impeachment of a sitting President. The Solicitor General counts 57 intra-session recess appointments during those two years. But the precise nature and historical understanding of many of those appointments is subject to debate. It seems likely that at least 36 of the 57 appointments were made with the understanding that they took place during a recess *between sessions.*

As for the remainder, the historical record reveals nothing about how they were justified, if at all. There is no indication that Johnson's Attorney General or anyone else considered at the time whether those appointments were made between or during formal legislative sessions or, if the latter, how they could be squared with the constitutional text. . . . Thus, the relevance of those appointments to our constitutional inquiry is severely limited. . . .

More than half a century went by before any other President made an intra-session recess appointment, and there is strong reason to think that during that period neither the Executive nor the Senate believed such a power existed. . . .

It is necessary to skip over the first 13 decades of our Nation's history in order to find a Presidential legal adviser arguably embracing the majority's interpretation of "the Recess." In 1921 President Harding's Attorney General, Harry Daugherty, advised Harding that he could make recess appointments while the Senate stood adjourned for 28 days during the session because "the term 'recess' must be given a practical construction." 33 Op. Atty. Gen. 20, 25. . . .

Only after Daugherty's opinion did the flow of intra-session recess appointments start, and for several years it was little more than a trickle. . . .

The majority is correct that during this period, the Senate "as a body" did not formally repudiate the emerging executive practice. . . . But the rise of intra-session recess appointments in the latter half of the 20th century drew sharp criticism from a number of Senators on both sides of the aisle. At first, their objections focused on the length of the intra-session breaks at issue. . . .

Later, many Senators sought to end intra-session recess appointments altogether. In 1993, the Senate Legal Counsel prepared a brief to be filed on behalf of the Senate in *Mackie v. Clinton*, 827 F.Supp.56 (DC 1993), vacated in part as moot, 1994 WL 163761 (CADC 1994) (*per curiam*), but "Republican opposition" blocked the filing. The brief argued that "the recess[-appointment] power is limited to Congress' annual recess between sessions," that no contrary executive practice "of any appreciable magnitude" had existed before "the past fifty years," and that the Senate had not "acquiesced in this steady expansion of presidential power." It explained that some Senators had limited their objections to shorter intra-session breaks out of a desire "to coexist with the Executive" but that "the Executive's subsequent, steady chipping away at the length of recess sufficient for making recess appointments ha[d] demonstrated the need to return to the Framers' original intent and limit the power to intersession adjournments." Senator Kennedy reiterated that position in a brief to this Court in 2004. Today the partisan tables are turned, and that position is urged on us by the Senate's Republican Members. See Brief for Sen. McConnell et al. as *Amici Curiae* 26.

* * *

What does all this amount to? In short: Intra-session recess appointments were virtually unheard of for the first 130 years of the Republic, were deemed unconstitutional by the first Attorney General to address them, were not openly defended by the Executive until 1921, were not made in significant numbers until after World War II, and have been repeatedly criticized as unconstitutional by Senators of both parties. It is astonishing for the majority to assert that this history lends "strong support" to its interpretation of the Recess Appointments Clause. And the majority's contention that recent executive practice in this area merits deference because the Senate has not done more to oppose it is utterly divorced from our precedent. "The structural interests protected by the Appointments Clause are not those of any one branch of Government but of the entire Republic," *Freytag v. Commissioner*, 501 U.S. 868, 880 (1991), and the Senate could not give away those protections even if it wanted to. See *INS v. Chadha*, 462 U.S. 919, 957–958 (1983); *Clinton v. City of New York*, at 451–452 (KENNEDY, J., concurring).

Moreover, the majority's insistence that the Senate gainsay an executive practice "as a body" in order to prevent the Executive from acquiring power by adverse possession will systematically favor the expansion of executive power at the expense of Congress. In any controversy between the political branches over a separation-of-powers question, staking out a position and defending it over time is far easier for the Executive Branch than for the Legislative Branch. See generally Bradley and Morrison, *Historical Gloss and the Separation of Powers*, 126 Harv. L. Rev. 411, 439–447 (2012). All Presidents have a high interest in expanding the powers of their office, since the more power the President can wield, the more effectively he can implement his political agenda; whereas individual Senators may have little interest in opposing Presidential encroachment on legislative prerogatives, especially when the encroacher is a President who is the leader of their own party. (The majority would not be able to point to a lack of "formal action" by the Senate "as a body" challenging intra-session recess appointments had the appointing President's party in the Senate not blocked such action on multiple occasions.) And when the President wants to assert a power and establish a precedent, he faces neither the collective-action problems nor the procedural inertia inherent in the legislative process. The majority's methodology thus all but guarantees the continuing aggrandizement of the Executive Branch.

III. Pre-Recess Vacancies

. . .

A.   Plain Meaning

As the majority concedes, "the most natural meaning of 'happens' as applied to a 'vacancy' . . . is that the vacancy 'happens' when it initially occurs." The majority adds that this meaning is most natural "to a modern ear," but it fails to show that founding-era ears heard it differently. "Happen" meant then, as it does now, "[t]o fall out; to chance; to come to pass." 1 Johnson 913. Thus, a vacancy that *happened* during the Recess was most reasonably understood as one that *arose* during the recess. It was, of course, possible in certain contexts for the word "happen" to mean "happen to be" rather than "happen to occur," as in the idiom "it so happens." But that meaning is not at all natural when the subject is a vacancy, a state of affairs that comes into existence at a particular moment in time.[8]

In any event, no reasonable reader would have understood the Recess Appointments Clause to use the word "happen" in the majority's "happen to be" sense, and thus to empower the President to fill all vacancies that might *exist* during a recess, regardless of when they arose. For one thing, the Clause's language would have been a surpassingly odd way of giving the President that power. The Clause easily could have been written to convey that meaning clearly: It could have referred to "all Vacancies that may exist during the Recess," or it could have omitted the qualifying phrase entirely and simply authorized the President to "fill up all Vacancies during the Recess." Given those readily available alternative phrasings, the reasonable reader might have wondered, why would any intelligent drafter intending the majority's reading have inserted the words "that may happen"—words that, as the majority admits, make the majority's desired reading awkward and unnatural, and that must be effectively read out of the Clause to achieve that reading?

For another thing, the majority's reading not only strains the Clause's language but distorts its constitutional role, which was meant to be subordinate. As Hamilton explained, appointment with the advice and consent of the Senate was to be "the general mode of appointing officers of the United States." The Federalist No. 67. The Senate's check on the President's appointment power was seen as vital because " 'manipulation of official appointments' had long been one of the American revolutionary generation's greatest grievances against executive power." *Freytag*, at 883. The unilateral power conferred on the President by the Recess Appointments Clause was therefore understood to be "nothing more than a supplement" to the "general method" of advice and consent. The Federalist No. 67.

If, however, the Clause had allowed the President to fill *all* pre-existing vacancies during the recess by granting commissions that would last throughout the

---

[8]   Despite initially admitting that the text "does not naturally favor" its interpretation, the majority halfheartedly suggests that the "happen to be" reading may be admissible when the subject, like "vacancy," denotes a "continuing state." That suggestion distorts ordinary English usage. It is indeed natural to say that an ongoing activity or event, like a war, a parade, or a financial crisis, is "happening" for as long as it continues. But the same is not true when the subject is a settled state of affairs, like death, marriage, or vacancy, all of which "happen" when they come into being.

following session, it would have been impossible to regard it—as the Framers plainly did—as a mere codicil to the Constitution's principal, power-sharing scheme for filling federal offices. . . .

The original understanding of the Clause was consistent with what the majority concedes is the text's "most natural meaning." In 1792, Attorney General Edmund Randolph, who had been a leading member of the Constitutional Convention, provided the Executive Branch's first formal interpretation of the Clause. He advised President Washington that the Constitution did not authorize a recess appointment to fill the office of Chief Coiner of the United States Mint, which had been created by Congress on April 2, 1792, during the Senate's session. Randolph wrote: "[I]s it a vacancy which has *happened* during the recess of the Senate? It is now the same and no other vacancy, than that, which existed on the 2nd. Of April 1792. It commenced therefore on that day or may be said to have *happened* on that day." Opinion on Recess Appointments (July 7, 1792), in 24 Papers of Thomas Jefferson 165–166 (J. Catanzariti ed. 1990). Randolph added that his interpretation was the most congruent with the Constitution's structure, which made the recess-appointment power "an exception to the general participation of the Senate."

President John Adams' Attorney General, Charles Lee, was in agreement. See Letter to George Washington (July 7, 1796) (the President may "fill for a limited time an old office *become vacant* during [the] recess" (emphasis added)); Letter from James McHenry to John Adams (May 7, 1799) (conveying Lee's advice that certain offices were "vacanc[ies] happening during the session, which the President cannot fill, during the recess, by the powers vested in him by the constitution"). . . .

Early Congresses seem to have shared Randolph's and Lee's view. A statute passed by the First Congress authorized the President to appoint customs inspectors "with the advice and consent of the Senate" and provided that "if the appointment . . . shall not be made during the present session of Congress, the President . . . is hereby empowered to make such appointments during the recess of the Senate, by granting commissions which shall expire at the end of their next session." Act of Mar. 3, 1791, § 4, 1 Stat. 200. That authorization would have been superfluous if the Recess Appointments Clause had been understood to apply to pre-existing vacancies. We have recognized that an action taken by the First Congress "provides 'contemporaneous and weighty evidence' of the Constitution's meaning." *Bowsher v. Synar*, 478 U.S. 714, 723–724 (1986). And other statutes passed in the early years of the Republic contained similar authorizations. . . .

The majority, however, relies heavily on a contrary account of the Clause given by Attorney General William Wirt in 1823. See 1 Op. Atty. Gen. 631. Wirt notably began—as does the majority—by acknowledging that his predecessors' reading was "most accordant with the letter of the constitution." But he thought the "most natural" reading had to be rejected because it would interfere with the "substantial purpose of the constitution," namely, "keep[ing] . . . offices filled." He was chiefly concerned that giving the Clause its plain meaning would produce "embarrassing inconveniences" if a distant office were to become vacant during the Senate's session, but news of the vacancy were not to reach the President until the recess. The majority fully embraces Wirt's reasoning.

Wirt's argument is doubly flawed. To begin, the Constitution provides ample means, short of rewriting its text, for dealing with the hypothetical dilemma Wirt posed. Congress can authorize "acting" officers to perform the duties associated with a temporarily vacant office—and has done that, in one form or another, since 1792. And on "extraordinary Occasions" the President can call the Senate back into session to consider a nomination. Art. II, § 3. . . .

More fundamentally, Wirt and the majority are mistaken to say that the Constitution's "'substantial purpose'" is to "'keep . . . offices filled.'" The Constitution is not a road map for maximally efficient government, but a system of "carefully crafted restraints" designed to "protect the people from the improvident exercise of power." *Chadha*, at 957, 959. Wirt's and the majority's *argumentum ab inconvenienti* thus proves far too much. There are many circumstances other than a vacancy that can produce similar inconveniences if they arise late in the session: For example, a natural disaster might occur to which the Executive cannot respond effectively without a supplemental appropriation. But in those circumstances, the Constitution would not permit the President to appropriate funds himself. See Art. I, § 9, cl. 7. Congress must either anticipate such eventualities or be prepared to be haled back into session. The troublesome need to do so is not a bug to be fixed by this Court, but a calculated feature of the constitutional framework. As we have recognized, while the Constitution's government-structuring provisions can seem "clumsy" and "inefficient," they reflect "hard choices . . . consciously made by men who had lived under a form of government that permitted arbitrary governmental acts to go unchecked." *Chadha*, at 959.

B.   Historical Practice

For the reasons just given, it is clear that the Constitution authorizes the President to fill unilaterally only those vacancies that arise during a recess, not every vacancy that happens to exist during a recess. Again, however, the majority says "[h]istorical practice" requires the broader interpretation. And again the majority is mistaken. Even if the Constitution were wrongly thought to be ambiguous on this point, a fair recounting of the relevant history does not support the majority's interpretation. . . .

[Justice Scalia traced at length the antebellum practice.—Editors] [During the Civil War] the Senate directed the Judiciary Committee "to inquire whether the practice . . . of appointing officers to fill vacancies which have not occurred during the recess of Congress, but which existed at the preceding session of Congress, is in accordance with the Constitution; and if not, what remedy shall be applied." Cong. Globe, 37th Cong., 3d Sess., 100 (1862). The committee responded with a report denouncing Wirt's interpretation of the Clause as "artificial," "forced and unnatural," "unfounded," and a "perversion of language." S. Rep. No. 80, 37th Cong., 3d Sess. (1863). Because the majority all but ignores this evidence of the Senate's views, it is worth quoting the report at some length:

> "When must the vacancy . . . accrue or spring into existence? May it begin during the session of the Senate, or must it have its beginning during the recess? We think the language too clear to admit of reasonable doubt, and that, upon principles of just construction, this period must have its inceptive point after one session has closed and before another session has begun. . . .

> "We . . . dissent from the construction implied by the substituted reading, 'happened to exist,' for the word 'happen' in the clause. . . . [I]f a

vacancy once exists, it has in law happened; for it is in itself an instantaneous event. It implies no continuance of the act that produces it, but takes effect, and is complete and perfect at an indivisible point of time, like the beginning or end of a recess. Once in existence, it has *happened*, and the mere continuance of the condition of things which the occurrence produces, cannot, without confounding the most obvious distinctions, be taken or treated as the occurrence itself, as Mr. Wirt seems to have done. . . .

"Again, we see no propriety in forcing the language from its popular meaning in order to meet and fulfill one confessedly great purpose, (the keeping the office filled,) while there is plainly another purpose of equal magnitude and importance (fitting qualifications) attached to and inseparable from the former."

The Committee acknowledged that the broad reading "ha[d] been, from time to time, sanctioned by Attorneys General . . . and that the Executive ha[d], from time to time, practiced upon it," but it said the Executive's practice was entitled to no weight because the Constitution's text was "too plain to admit of a doubt or to need interpretation."

On the same day the Committee published its scathing report, its chairman, Senator Trumbull, proposed a law barring the payment of any officer appointed during the recess to fill a pre-recess vacancy. Senator Fessenden spoke in support of the proposal:

It ought to be understood distinctly, that when an officer does not come within the rules of law, and is appointed in that way in defiance of the wishes of the Senate, he shall not be paid. It may not be in our power to prevent the appointment, but it is in our power to prevent the payment; and when payment is prevented, I think that will probably put an end to the habit of making such appointments.

The amendment was adopted by the Senate, and after passing the House became the Pay Act, which provided that "no money shall be paid . . . out of the Treasury, as salary, to any person appointed during the recess of the Senate, to fill a vacancy . . . which . . . existed while the Senate was in session." Act of Feb. 9, 1863, § 2, 12 Stat. 646 (codified at Rev. Stat. § 1761; subsequently codified as amended at 5 U.S.C. § 56 (1925–1926 ed.)).

The Pay Act would remain in force without significant modification for nearly eight decades. The Executive Branch, however, refused to acknowledge that the Act embodied the Senate's rejection of the broad reading of "happen." . . .

The majority is not that bold. Instead, it relegates the 1863 Judiciary Committee report to a pair of anodyne sentences in which it says only that the committee "disagreed with" Wirt's interpretation. (With like understatement, one could say that Shakespeare's Mark Antony "disagreed with" Caesar's detractors.) Even more remarkably, the majority goes on to claim that the Senate's passage of the Pay Act on the same day the committee issued its report was not a strong enough statement to impede the constitutionalization-by-adverse-possession of the power asserted by the Executive. Why not? Because, the majority says, some Senators may have disagreed with the report, and because the Senate did not go so far as to make acceptance of a recess appointment that filled a pre-recess vacancy "a federal crime."

That reasoning starkly illustrates the excessive burden the majority places on the Legislative Branch in contests with the Executive over the separation of powers. . . . *[Justice Scalia went on to contest the majority's view of post-Civil War practice as well.—Editors]*

Consequently, there is no reason to assume that the majority's sampling—even if it accurately reflects practices during the last three decades—is at all typical of practices that prevailed throughout "the history of the Nation."

* * *

In sum: Washington's and Adams' Attorneys General read the Constitution to restrict recess appointments to vacancies arising during the recess, and there is no evidence that any of the first four Presidents consciously departed from that reading. The contrary reading was first defended by an executive official in 1823, was vehemently rejected by the Senate in 1863, was vigorously resisted by legislation in place from 1863 until 1940, and is arguably inconsistent with legislation in place from 1940 to the present. . . . I can conceive of no sane constitutional theory under which this evidence of "historical practice"—which is actually evidence of a long-simmering inter-branch conflict—would require us to defer to the views of the Executive Branch.

IV. Conclusion

What the majority needs to sustain its judgment is an ambiguous text and a clear historical practice. What it has is a clear text and an at-best-ambiguous historical practice. . . . There is thus no ground for the majority's deference to the unconstitutional recess-appointment practices of the Executive Branch. . . .

The real tragedy of today's decision is not simply the abolition of the Constitution's limits on the recess-appointment power and the substitution of a novel framework invented by this Court. It is the damage done to our separation-of-powers jurisprudence more generally. It is not every day that we encounter a proper case or controversy requiring interpretation of the Constitution's structural provisions. Most of the time, the interpretation of those provisions is left to the political branches—which, in deciding how much respect to afford the constitutional text, often take their cues from this Court. We should therefore take every opportunity to affirm the primacy of the Constitution's enduring principles over the politics of the moment. Our failure to do so today will resonate well beyond the particular dispute at hand. Sad, but true: The Court's embrace of the adverse-possession theory of executive power (a characterization the majority resists but does not refute) will be cited in diverse contexts, including those presently unimagined, and will have the effect of aggrandizing the Presidency beyond its constitutional bounds and undermining respect for the separation of powers.

I concur in the judgment only.

NOTES

1. What types of constitutional argument do the majority opinion and Justice Scalia's opinion use? What do the two disagree about? Do they disagree about the types of constitutional argument that are appropriate—or just about the facts?

2. The Recess Appointments Clause was originally intended to deal with circumstances in which the Senate was not immediately available because of travel time,

emergency, or the like. Today, it is much more likely to be invoked to deal with a Senate that is politically opposed to the administration or gridlocked. How should we think about this kind of change? Is it okay for a power intended for one purpose to be used for a different one as circumstances change? Should those changes affect how we interpret the clause today?

3.   There is one longstanding question about the Recess Appointments Clause that *Noel Canning* did not resolve. According to Article III, federal judges "shall hold their Offices during good Behavior," effectively for life. U.S. Const. art. III, § 1. May they nonetheless receive a recess appointment, which "shall expire at the end of [the Senate's] next session"? U.S. Const. art. II., § 2, cl.3. Does it affect your answer to know that George Washington made such an appointment, recess appointing *the second chief justice of the Supreme Court*—John Rutledge? Does it affect your answer to know that the Senate eventually rejected Rutledge for a permanent seat on the Court partly for political reasons?

[Assignment 11]

B.   SUPERVISING THE EXECUTIVE BRANCH: "IN A PRESIDENT . . . "

> *Art. II, § 1: The executive Power shall be vested in a President of the United States of America.*
>
> *§ 3: . . . he shall take Care that the Laws be faithfully executed. . . .*

A recurring question throughout American history is the existence and scope of a presidential power to remove non-congressional and non-Article III officers of the federal government. As considered above, Article II makes rules for the *appointment* of executive branch officers. But it says nothing expressly about their *removal* (except via impeachment). How should this silence be resolved? Is the right inference that the president may remove any executive branch officer for malfeasance, incompetence, or even mere policy disagreement? Do any provisions of Article II imply a need for unfettered presidential removal power? The Vesting Clause, or perhaps the Take Care Clause? Or does the role of the Senate in the appointment process suggest that it has a role in removal, too? Or should all of these decisions be up to Congress?

These questions about removal relate to some broader aspects of executive power: Is the power to remove subordinate officers the only constitutional tool the president has to supervise the executive branch, or are there others? For instance, may the president simply tell other members of the executive branch how to do their jobs? (Or should we think of every executive branch job as really the president's job?)

The Removal Power and the Decision of 1789

There was a heated debate in the First Congress over where the Constitution placed the removal power, and it culminated in what has been called the Decision of 1789. In creating the first cabinet departments, Representative James Madison proposed language that would have allowed the president, acting alone, to remove the cabinet secretaries from office. Some representatives thought the Constitution required this. Some thought it forbidden. And some thought Congress could allow it, but did not have to.

William Smith, for example, "[s]aid he had doubts whether the officer could be removed by the president; he apprehended he could only be removed by an impeachment before the senate, and that being once in office, he must remain there until convicted upon impeachment." 10 THE DOCUMENTARY HISTORY OF THE FIRST FEDERAL CONGRESS 727 (Charlene Bangs Bickford, Kenneth R. Bowling, & Helen E. Veit eds., 1992).

Madison responded that the impeachment power "[w]as intended as a supplemental security for the good behavior of the public officers," but that it was also "absolutely necessary that the president should have the power of removing from office; it will make him, in a peculiar manner, responsible for their conduct, and subject him to impeachment himself, if he suffers them to perpetrate with impunity high crimes or misdemeanours against the United States, or neglects to superintend their conduct, so as to check their excesses." *Id.*

Meanwhile Theodorick Bland proposed a third approach. He "[t]hought the power given by the constitution to the senate, respecting the appointment to office, would be rendered almost nugatory if the president had the power of removal. . . . He thought it consistent with the nature of things, that the power which appointed should remove; and would not object to a declaration in the resolution, if the words were added, that the president shall remove from office, by and with the advice and consent of the senate." *Id.* at 729.

And John Laurance suggested a fourth possibility—that Congress could decide: "as the constitution was silent with respect to the time the secretary of foreign affairs should remain in office, that it therefore depended upon the will of the legislature, to say how the department should be constituted and established by law, the conditions upon which he shall enjoy the office; we can say he shall hold it for three years from his appointment or during good behavior, and we may declare unfitness and incapacity, causes of removal and make the president alone judge of this case; we may authorize the president to remove him for any cause he thinks proper." *Id.* at 733.

The debate went on for weeks, and Madison eventually tied the asserted removal power directly to the Vesting Clause:

> The constitution affirms, that the executive power shall be vested in the president: Are there exceptions to this proposition? Yes there are. The constitution says that, in appointing to office, the senate shall be associated with the president, unless in the case of inferior officers, when the law shall otherwise direct. Have we a right to extend this exception? I believe not. If the constitution has invested all executive power in the president, I venture to assert, that the legislature has no right to diminish or modify his executive authority.
>
> The question now resolves itself into this. Is the power of displacing an executive power? I conceive that if any power whatsoever is in its nature executive it is the power of appointing, overseeing, and controling those who execute the laws. . . . Should we be authorized, in defiance of that clause in the constitution, "The executive power shall be vested in a president," to unite the senate with the president in the appointment to office? I conceive not.

11 THE DOCUMENTARY HISTORY OF THE FIRST FEDERAL CONGRESS 868–869 (Charlene Bangs Bickford, Kenneth R. Bowling, & Helen E. Veit eds., 1992).

Meanwhile, Fisher Ames made a more structural argument: "The constitution places all executive power in the hands of the president, and could he personally execute all the laws, there would be no occasion for establishing auxiliaries; but the circumscribed powers of human nature in one man, demands the aid of others. When the objects are widely stretched out, or greatly diversified, meandering through such an extent of territory as what the United States possess, a minister cannot see with his own eyes every transaction, or feel with his hands the minutiae that passes through his department; he must therefore have assistants: But in order that he may be responsible to his country, he must have a choice in selecting his assistants, a control over them, with power to remove them when he finds the qualifications which induced their appointment cease to exist." *Id.* at 880.

And Ames also invoked the Take Care Clause: "In the constitution the president is required to see the laws faithfully executed. He cannot do this without he has a control over officers appointed to aid him in the performance of his duty. Take this power out of his hands, and you virtually strip him of his authority; you virtually destroy his responsibility, the great security which this constitution holds out to the people of America." *Id.* at 979.

After some amendments, the final statute did indeed contain language about presidential removal, so Madison's side won the immediate debate. But it is not so clear whether that reflected widespread endorsement of Madison's constitutional theory, or a mixed coalition of those who believed in executive power and those who thought Congress could decide. (As you will see shortly, the Supreme Court eventually decided that Congress had endorsed the position of Madison and Ames. See Saikrishna Prakash, *New Light on the Decision of 1789*, 91 Cornell L. Rev. 1021 (2006).) But it is clear that the result was a rejection of the other two positions—that the Senate must be involved in removal, and that impeachment is the only method of removal.

During the debates, Madison had predicted that "[t]he decision that is at this time made will become the permanent exposition of the constitution; and on a permanent exposition of the constitution will depend the genius and character of the whole government." 11 THE DOCUMENTARY HISTORY OF THE FIRST FEDERAL CONGRESS at 921. Indeed, within decades the debate came to be known as "the Decision of 1789." But it did not end all debates about the removal power.

In the 1830s, for example, President Andrew Jackson fired a secretary of the treasury who refused to obey a presidential order to remove government deposits from the Bank of the United States. The Senate censured President Jackson for misconduct, and he responded with a document he called a "Protest": It argued that the grant of the executive power to the president gave him unlimited power to remove executive branch subordinates. When Jackson's party won the next election, the Senate voted to expunge its resolution of censure.

The issue of presidential removal power arose again in the 1860s when President Andrew Johnson attempted to derail Reconstruction by firing executive officials he had inherited from the Lincoln administration. Congress responded by passing a statute called the Tenure of Office Act, which required senatorial consent before removals could be made permanent. The president denounced this statute as unconstitutional, and in violation of the statute he tried to fire Secretary of War Edwin Stanton (another Lincoln holdover). The House of Representatives impeached President Johnson for doing this, and the Senate came within one vote of removing him from office. See p. 350. The act was subsequently diluted in the Grant administration and repealed in the first Cleveland administration.

The following two cases take stock of the removal power after the Decision of 1789 and the Jackson and Johnson controversies. In 1926, the Supreme Court endorsed the Decision of 1789 in *Myers v. United States*, 272 U.S. 52 (1926). *Myers* established the general principle that the president has a constitutional power of removal. Nine years later, in *Humphrey's Executor v. United States*, 295 U.S. 602 (1935), the Court announced an important exception to the removal power—that Congress could limit presidential removal power by creating "independent agencies," such as the Federal Trade Commission. Congress subsequently conferred independence on the Federal Reserve Board and the Securities Exchange Commission, and it has created other independent agencies, such as the National Labor Relations Board.

Myers v. United States
272 U.S. 52 (1926)

■ MR. CHIEF JUSTICE TAFT delivered the opinion of the Court.

This case presents the question whether under the Constitution the President has the exclusive power of removing executive officers of the United States whom he has appointed by and with the advice and consent of the Senate.

Myers . . . was on July 21, 1917, appointed by the President, by and with the advice and consent of the Senate, to be a postmaster of the first class at Portland, Oregon, for a term of four years. On January 20, 1920, Myers' resignation was demanded. He refused the demand. On February 2, 1920, he was removed from office by order of the Postmaster General, acting by direction of the President. On . . . February 10th, Myers sent a petition to the President and another to the Senate committee on post offices, asking to be heard, if any charges were filed. He protested to the department against his removal, and continued to do so until the end of his term. He pursued no other occupation and drew compensation for no other service during the interval. On April 21, 1921, he brought this suit in the Court of Claims for his salary from the date of his removal, which, as claimed by supplemental petition filed after July 21, 1921, the end of his term, amounted to $8,838.71. In August, 1920, the President made a recess appointment of one Jones, who took office September 19, 1920. . . . *[The Court of Claims ruled against Myers, and he appealed to the Supreme Court.—Editors]*

By the 6th section of the Act of Congress of July 12, 1876, under which Myers was appointed with the advice and consent of the Senate as a first-class postmaster, it is provided that

> Postmasters of the first, second, and third classes shall be appointed and may be removed by the President by and with the advice and consent of the Senate, and shall hold their offices for four years unless sooner removed or suspended according to law.

The Senate did not consent to the President's removal of Myers during his term. If this statute in its requirement that his term should be four years unless sooner removed by the President by and with the consent of the Senate is valid, the appellant, Myers' administratrix, is entitled to recover his unpaid salary for his full term and the judgment of the Court of Claims must be reversed. The Government maintains that the [statute is unconstitutional because] under Article II of the Constitution the President's power of removal of executive officers appointed by him with the advice and consent of the Senate is full and complete without consent of the Senate. . . . We are therefore confronted by the constitutional question and cannot avoid it. . . .

The question where the power of removal of executive officers appointed by the President by and with the advice and consent of the Senate was vested, was presented early in the first session of the First Congress. . . .

[The Court then discussed, at great length, the Decision of 1789.—Editors] [T]here is not the slightest doubt, after an examination of the record, that the vote was, and was intended to be, a legislative declaration that the power to remove officers appointed by the President and the Senate vested in the President alone, and until the Johnson impeachment trial in 1868 its meaning was not doubted, even by those who questioned its soundness. . . .

We have devoted much space to this discussion and decision of the question of the Presidential power of removal in the First Congress, not because a Congressional conclusion on a constitutional issue is conclusive, but, first, because of our agreement with the reasons upon which it was avowedly based; second, because this was the decision of the First Congress, on a question of primary importance in the organization of the Government, made within two years after the Constitutional Convention and within a much shorter time after its ratification; and, third, because that Congress numbered among its leaders those who had been members of the convention. It must necessarily constitute a precedent upon which many future laws supplying the machinery of the new government would be based and, if erroneous, would be likely to evoke dissent and departure in future Congresses. . . .

Congress in a number of acts, followed and enforced the legislative decision of 1789 for seventy-four years. . . . The acquiescence in the legislative decision of 1789 for nearly three-quarters of a century by all branches of the Government has been affirmed by this Court in unmistakable terms. . . . *[The Court adduced quotations from Chancellor Kent and Justice Story, as well as from attorneys general in the Tyler, Polk, Fillmore, and Buchanan administrations.—Editors]*

We come now to consider an argument, advanced and strongly pressed on behalf of the complainant, that this case concerns only the removal of a postmaster; that a postmaster is an inferior officer; and that such an office was not included within the legislative decision of 1789, which related only to superior officers to be appointed by the President by and with the advice and consent of the Senate. . . .

The very heated discussions during General Jackson's administration, except as to the removal of Secretary Duane, related to the distribution of offices, which were most of them inferior offices, and it was the operation of the legislative decision of 1789 upon the power of removal of incumbents of such offices that led the General to refuse to comply with the request of the Senate that he give his reasons for the removals therefrom. . . .

Section 2 of Article II, after providing that the President shall nominate and with the consent of the Senate appoint ambassadors, other public ministers, consuls, judges of the Supreme Court and all other officers of the United States whose appointments are not herein otherwise provided for, and which shall be established by law, contains the proviso "but the Congress may be law vest the appointment of such inferior officers, as they think proper, in the President alone, in the courts of law or in the heads of departments." ...

The power to remove inferior executive officers, like that to remove superior executive officers, in an incident of the power to appoint them, and is in its nature an executive power. The authority of Congress given by the excepting clause to vest the appointment of such inferior officers in the heads of departments carries with it authority incidentally to invest the heads of departments with power to remove. It has been the practice of Congress to do so and this Court has recognized that power. The Court also has recognized in the *Perkins* case that Congress, in committing the appointment of such inferior officers to the heads of departments, may prescribe incidental regulations controlling and restricting the latter in the exercise of the power of removal. But the court never has held, nor reasonably could hold, ... that the excepting clause enables Congress to draw to itself, or to either branch of it, the power to remove or the right to participate in the exercise of that power. To do this would be to go beyond the words and implications of that clause, and to infringe the constitutional principle of the separation of governmental powers. ...

Summing up, then, the facts as to acquiescence by all branches of the government in the legislative decision of 1789 as to executive officers, whether superior or inferior, we find that from 1789 until 1863, a period of seventy-four years, there was no act of Congress, no executive act, and no decision of this court at variance with the declaration of the First Congress; but there was, as we have seen, clear affirmative recognition of it by each branch of the Government.

Our conclusion on the merits, sustained by the arguments before stated, is that Article II grants to the President the executive power of the Government—i.e., the general administrative control of those executing the laws, including the power of appointment and removal of executive officers—a conclusion confirmed by his obligation to take care that the laws be faithfully executed. ...

We come now to a period in the history of the Government when both Houses of Congress attempted to reverse this constitutional construction, and to subject the power of removing executive officers appointed by the President and confirmed by the Senate to the control of the Senate—indeed, finally, to the assumed power in Congress to place the removal of such officers anywhere in the Government.

This reversal grew out of the serious political difference between the two Houses of Congress and President Johnson. There was a two-thirds majority of the Republican party, in control of each House of Congress, which resented what it feared would be Mr. Johnson's obstructive course in the enforcement of the reconstruction measures, in respect of the States whose people had lately been at war against the National Government. This led the two Houses to enact legislation to curtail the then acknowledged powers of the President. ... [T]he Tenure of Office Act of March 2, 1867, provid[ed] that all officers appointed by and with the consent of the Senate should hold their offices until their successors should have in like manner been appointed and qualified, and that certain heads of departments, including the

Secretary of War, should hold their offices during the term of the President by whom appointed and one month thereafter subject to removal by consent of the Senate. The Tenure of Office Act was vetoed, but it was passed over the veto. The House of Representatives preferred articles of impeachment against President Johnson for refusal to comply with, and for conspiracy to defeat, the legislation above referred to, but he was acquitted for lack of a two-thirds vote for conviction in the Senate. . . .

The extreme provisions of all this legislation were a full justification for the considerations so strongly advanced by Mr. Madison and his associates in the First Congress for insisting that the power of removal of executive officers by the President alone was essential in the division of powers between the executive and the legislative bodies. It exhibited in a clear degree the paralysis to which a partisan Senate and Congress could subject the executive arm and destroy the principle of executive responsibility and separation of powers, sought for by the framers of our Government, if the President had no power of removal save by consent of the Senate. It was an attempt to redistribute the powers and minimize those of the President.

After President Johnson's term ended, the injury and invalidity of the Tenure of Office Act in its radical innovation were immediately recognized by the executive and objected to. General Grant, succeeding Mr. Johnson in the presidency, earnestly recommended in his first message the total repeal of the act. . . .

While in response to this a bill for repeal of that act passed the House, it failed in the Senate, and, though the law was changed, it still limited the presidential power of removal . . . until 1887, when it was repealed. . . . In 1876 the act here under discussion was passed, making the consent of the Senate necessary both to the appointment and removal of first, second, and third class postmasters.

[I]n March, 1886, President Cleveland, in discussing the requests which the Senate had made for his reasons for removing officials, and the assumption that the Senate had the right to pass upon those removals and thus to limit the power of the President, said:

> "I believe the power to remove or suspend such officials is vested in the President alone by the Constitution, which in express terms provides that "the executive power shall be vested in a President of the United States of America," and that 'he shall take care that the laws be faithfully executed.
>
> "The Senate belongs to the legislative branch of the government. When the Constitution by express provision superadded to its legislative duties the right to advise and consent to appointments to office and to sit as a court of impeachment, it conferred upon that body all the control and regulation of Executive action supposed to be necessary for the safety of the people; and this express and special grant of such extraordinary powers, not in any way related to or growing out of general senatorial duties, and in itself a departure from the general plan of our government, should be held, under a familiar maxim of construction, to exclude every other right of interference with Executive functions." 11 Messages and Papers of the Presidents, 4964.

The attitude of the Presidents on this subject has been unchanged and uniform to the present day whenever an issue has clearly been raised. . . .

In spite of the foregoing Presidential declarations, it is contended that, since the passage of the Tenure of Office Act, there has been general acquiescence by the executive in the power of Congress to forbid the President alone to remove executive officers, an acquiescence which has changed any formerly accepted constitutional construction to the contrary. Instances are cited of the signed approval by President Grant and other Presidents of legislation in derogation of such construction. We think these are all to be explained, not by acquiescence therein, but by reason of the otherwise valuable effect of the legislation approved. Such is doubtless the explanation of the executive approval of the act of 1876, which we are considering, for it was an appropriation act on which the section here in question was imposed as a rider. . . .

Other acts of Congress are referred to which contain provisions said to be inconsistent with the 1789 decision. Since the provision for an Interstate Commerce Commission in 1887, many administrative boards have been created whose members are appointed by the President, by and with the advice and consent of the Senate, and in the statutes creating them have been provisions for the removal of the members for specified causes. Such provisions are claimed to be inconsistent with the independent power of removal by the President. This, however, is shown to be unfounded by the case of *Shurtleff v. United States*, 189 U.S. 311 (1903) *[which construed those removal provisions not to exclude the president's constitutional power to remove—Editors]*. . . .

There are other later acts pointed out in which doubtless the inconsistency with the independent power of the President to remove is clearer, but these cannot be said to have really received the acquiescence of the executive branch of the Government. Whenever there has been a real issue made in respect to the question of presidential removals, the attitude of the executive in Congressional message has been clear and positive against the validity of such legislation. The language of Mr. Cleveland in 1886, twenty years after the Tenure of Office Act, in his controversy with the Senate in respect to his independence of that body in the matter of removing inferior officers appointed by him and confirmed by the Senate, was quite as pronounced as that of General Jackson in a similar controversy in 1835. Mr. Wilson in 1920 and Mr. Coolidge in 1924 were quite as all-embracing in their views of the power of removal as General Grant in 1869, and as Mr. Madison and Mr. John Adams in 1789. . . .

An argument *ab inconvenienti [i.e., from inconvenience or hardship—Editors]* has been made against our conclusion in favor of the executive power of removal by the President, without the consent of the Senate, that it will open the door to a reintroduction of the spoils system. The evil of the spoils system aimed at in the Civil Service Law and its amendments is in respect to inferior offices. It has never been attempted to extend that law beyond them. Indeed Congress forbids its extension to appointments confirmed by the Senate, except with the consent of the Senate. . . .

What, then, are the elements that enter into our decision of this case? We have, first, a construction of the Constitution made by a Congress which was to provide by legislation for the organization of the government in accord with the Constitution which had just then been adopted, and in which there were, as Representatives and Senators, a considerable number of those who had been members of the convention that framed the Constitution and presented it for ratification. . . . This Court has repeatedly laid down the principle that a contemporaneous legislative exposition of the Constitution, when the founders of our government and framers of our Constitution were actively participating in public affairs, acquiesced in for a long term of years, fixes the construction to be given its provisions.

We are now asked to set aside this construction, thus buttressed, and adopt an adverse view, because the Congress of the United States did so during a heated political difference of opinion between the then President and the majority leaders of Congress over the reconstruction measures ... at the time of the Civil War. ... Without animadverting on the character of the measures taken, we are certainly justified in saying that they should not be given the weight affecting proper constitutional construction to be accorded to that reached by the First Congress of the United States during a political calm and acquiesced in by the whole Government for three-quarters of a century, especially when the new construction contended for has never been acquiesced in by either the executive or the judicial departments. ... When, on the merits, we find our conclusion strongly favoring the view which prevailed in the First Congress, we have no hesitation in holding that conclusion to be correct; and it therefore follows that the Tenure of Office Act of 1867, in so far as it attempted to prevent the President from removing executive officers who had been appointed by him by and with the advice and consent of the Senate, was invalid, and that subsequent legislation of the same effect was equally so.

For the reasons given, we must therefore hold that the provision of the law of 1876 by which the unrestricted power of removal of first-class postmasters is denied to the President is in violation of the Constitution and invalid. ...

■ MR. JUSTICE HOLMES, dissenting.

My Brothers McREYNOLDS and BRANDEIS have discussed the question before us with exhaustive research and I say a few words merely to emphasize my agreement with their conclusion.

The arguments drawn from the executive power of the President, and from his duty to appoint officers of the United States (when Congress does not vest the appointment elsewhere), to take care that the laws be faithfully executed, and to commission all officers of the United States, seem to me spiders' webs inadequate to control the dominant facts.

We have to deal with an office that owes its existence to Congress and that Congress may abolish to-morrow. Its duration and the pay attached to it while it lasts depend on Congress alone. Congress alone confers on the President the power to appoint to it and at any time may transfer the power to other hands. With such power over its own creation, I have no more trouble in believing that Congress has power to prescribe a term of life for it free from any interference than I have in accepting the undoubted power of Congress to decree its end. I have equally little trouble in accepting its power to prolong the tenure of an incumbent until Congress or the Senate shall have assented to his removal. The duty of the President to see that the laws be executed is a duty that does not go beyond the laws or require him to achieve more than Congress sees fit to leave within his power.

■ [The dissenting opinion of JUSTICE McREYNOLDS is omitted.]

■ MR. JUSTICE BRANDEIS, dissenting.

In 1833 Mr. Justice Story, after discussing in his Commentaries on the Constitution the much debated question concerning the President's power of removal, said:

If there has been any aberration from the true constitutional exposition of the power of removal (which the reader must decide for himself), it will be difficult, and perhaps impracticable, after forty years' experience, to recall the practice to the correct theory. But, at all events, it will be a consolation to those who love the Union, and honor a devotion to the patriotic discharge of duty, that in regard to "inferior officers" (which appellation probably includes ninety-nine out of a hundred of the lucrative offices in the government), the remedy for any permanent abuse is still within the power of Congress, by the simple expedient of requiring the consent of the Senate to removals in such cases.

Postmasters are inferior officer. Congress might have vested their appointment in the head of the department. . . .

[The challenged] statute has been in force unmodified for half a century. Throughout the period, it has governed a large majority of all civil officers to which appointments are made by and with the advice and consent of the Senate. May the President, having acted under the statute in so far as it creates the office and authorizes the appointment, ignore, while the Senate is in session, the provision which prescribes the condition under which a removal may take place?

It is this narrow question, and this only. which we are required to decide. We need not consider what power the President, being Commander-in-Chief, has over officers in the Army and the Navy. We need not determine whether the President, acting alone, may remove high political officers. We need not even determine whether, acting alone, he may remove inferior civil officers when the Senate is not in session. It was in session when the President purported to remove Myers, and for a long time thereafter. . . .

The contention that Congress is powerless to make consent of the Senate a condition of removal by the President from an executive office rests mainly upon the clause in § 1 of Article II which declares that "the executive Power shall be vested in a President." The argument is that appointment and removal of officials are executive prerogatives; that the grant to the President of "the executive power" confers upon him, as inherent in the office, the power to exercise these two functions without restriction by Congress, except in so far as the power to restrict his exercise of then is expressly conferred upon Congress by the Constitution; that in respect to appointment certain restrictions of the executive power are so provided for; but that in respect to removal there is no express grant to Congress of any power to limit the President's prerogative. The simple answer to the argument is this: The ability to remove a subordinate executive officer, being an essential of effective government, will, in the absence of express constitutional provision to the contrary, be deemed to have been vested in some person or body. But it is not a power inherent in a chief executive. The President's power of removal from statutory civil inferior offices, like the power of appointment to them, comes immediately from Congress. It is true that the exercise of the power of removal is said to be an executive act, and that when the Senate grants or withholds consent to a removal by the President, it participates in an executive act. But the Constitution has confessedly granted to Congress the legislative power to create offices, and to prescribe the tenure thereof; and it has not in terms denied to Congress the power to control removals. . . .

It is also argued that the clauses in Article II, § 3, of the Constitution, which declare that the President "shall take Care that the Laws be faithfully executed, and shall Commission all the Officers of the United States" imply a grant to the President of the alleged uncontrollable power of removal. I do not find in either clause anything which supports this claim. The provision that the President "shall Commission all the Officers of the United States" clearly bears no such implication. Nor can it be spelled out of the direction that "he shall take Care that the Laws be faithfully executed." There is no express grant to the President of incidental powers resembling those conferred upon Congress by clause 18 of Article I, § 8. . . . A power essential to protection against pressing dangers incident to disloyalty in the civil service may well be deemed inherent in the executive office. But that need, and also insubordination and neglect of duty, are adequately provided against by implying in the President the constitutional power of suspension. . . . Power to remove, as well as to suspend, a high political officer, might conceivably be deemed indispensable to democratic government and, hence, inherent in the President. But power to remove an inferior administrative officer appointed for a fixed term cannot conceivably be deemed an essential of government.

To imply a grant to the President of the uncontrollable power of removal from statutory inferior executive offices involves an unnecessary and indefensible limitation upon the constitutional power of Congress to fix the tenure of the inferior statutory offices. That such a limitation cannot be justified on the ground of necessity is demonstrated by the practice of our governments, state and national. In none of the original 13 states did the chief executive possess such power at the time of the adoption of the federal Constitution. In none of the 48 states has such power been conferred at any time since by a state constitution, with a single possible exception. In a few states the Legislature has granted to the Governor, or other appointing power, the absolute power of removal. The legislative practice of most states reveals a decided tendency to limit, rather than to extend, the Governor's power of removal. The practice of the Federal Government will be set forth in detail.

Over removal from inferior civil offices, Congress has, from the foundation of our Government, exercised continuously some measure of control by legislation. The instances of such laws are many. Some of the statutes were directory in character. Usually, they were mandatory. Some of them, comprehensive in scope, have endured for generations. During the first 40 years of our Government, there was no occasion to curb removals. Then, the power of Congress was exerted to ensure removals. . . .

In the later period, which began after the spoils system had prevailed for a generation, the control of Congress over inferior offices was exerted to prevent removals. The removal clause here in question was first introduced by the Currency Act of February 25, 1863, which was approved by President Lincoln. That statute provided for the appointment of the Comptroller, and that he "shall hold his office for the term of five years unless sooner removed by the President, by and with the advice and consent of the Senate." In 1867 this provision was inserted in the Tenure of Office Act of March 2, 1867, which applied, in substance, to all presidential offices. It was passed over President Johnson's veto. . . .

By Act of June 8, 1872, a consolidation and revision of the postal laws was made. The removal clause was inserted in section 63 in the precise form in which it had first appeared in the Currency Act of 1863. . . . [This] postal statute [was] approved by President Grant. When President Cleveland secured, by Act of March 3, 1887, the repeal of the [Tenure of Office Act], he made no attempt to apply the repeal to postmasters, although postmasters constituted then, as they have ever since, a large majority of all presidential appointees. The removal clause, which had become operative as to them by specific legislation, was continued in force. For more than half a century this postal law has stood unmodified. No President has recommended to Congress that it be repealed. A few proposals for repeal have been made by bills introduced in the House. Not one of them has been considered by it. . . .

The assertion that the mere grant by the Constitution of executive power confers upon the President as a prerogative the unrestricted power of appointment and of removal from executive offices, except so far as otherwise expressly provided by the Constitution, is clearly inconsistent also with those statutes which restrict the exercise by the President of the power of nomination. . . . [A] multitude of laws have been enacted which limit the President's power to make nominations, and which through the restrictions imposed, may prevent the selection of the person deemed by him best fitted. . . .

Thus Congress has, from time to time, restricted the President's selection by the requirement of citizenship. It has limited the power of nomination by providing that the office may be held only by a resident of the United States; of a state; of a particular state; of a particular district; of a particular territory; of the District of Columbia; of a particular foreign country. It has limited the power of nomination further by prescribing specific professional attainments, or occupational experience. It has, in other cases, prescribed the test of examinations. It has imposed the requirement of age; of sex; of races; of property; and of habitual temperance in the use of intoxicating liquors. Congress has imposed like restrictions on the power of nomination by requiring political representation; or that the selection be made on a nonpartisan basis. It has required, in some cases, that the representation be industrial; in others, that it be geographic. It has at times required that the President's nominees be taken from, or include representatives from, particular branches or departments of the government. By still other statutes, Congress has confined the President's selection to a small number of persons to be named by others. . . .

The historical data submitted present a legislative practice, established by concurrent affirmative action of Congress and the President, to make consent of the Senate a condition of removal from statutory inferior, civil, executive offices to which the appointment is made for a fixed term by the President with such consent. They show that the practice has existed, without interruption, continuously for the last fifty-eight years; that throughout this period, it has governed a great majority of all such offices; that the legislation applying the removal clause specifically to the office of postmaster was enacted more than half a century ago; and that recently the practice has, with the President's approval, been extended to several newly created offices. . . . A persistent legislative practice which involves a delimitation of the respective powers of Congress and the President, and which has been so established and maintained, should be deemed tantamount to judicial construction, in the absence of any decision by any court to the contrary. *United States v. Midwest Oil Co.*, 236 U.S. 459, 469 (1915). . . .

[The dissent disputed the majority's characterization of the 1789 debate, and also argued that it was applicable only to "high political office, not to inferior ones."—Editors]

It is true that several Presidents have asserted that the Constitution conferred a power of removal uncontrollable by Congress. But of the many statutes enacted since the foundation of our government which in express terms controlled the power of removal, either by the clause here in question or otherwise, only two were met with a veto: The Tenure of Office Act of 1867, which related to high political officers among others, and the Budget Act of 1921, which denied to the President any participation in the removal of the Comptroller and Assistant Comptroller. One was passed over the President's veto; the other was approved by the succeeding President. It is true also that several Presidents have at times insisted that for the exercise of their power they were not accountable to the Senate. But even these Presidents have at other times complied with requests that the ground of removal of inferior officers be stated. Many of the Presidents have furnished the desired information without questioning the right to request it. And neither the Senate nor the House has at any time receded from the claim that Congress has power both to control by legislation removal from inferior offices and to require the President to report to it the reasons for removals made therefrom. . . . A construction given to the Constitution by the concurrent affirmative action of Congress and the President continued throughout a long period without interruption should be followed despite the isolated utterances, made in the heat of political controversies not involving the question here in issue by individual Presidents supported only by the advice of the Attorney General. . . .

Checks and balances were established in order that this should be "a government of laws and not of men." As White said in the House in 1789, an uncontrollable power of removal in the Chief Executive "is a doctrine not to be learned in American governments." . . . In order to prevent arbitrary executive action, the Constitution provided in terms that presidential appointments be made with the consent of the Senate, unless Congress should otherwise provide; and this clause was construed by Alexander Hamilton in The Federalist, No. 77, as requiring like consent to removals. Limiting further executive prerogatives customary in monarchies, the Constitution empowered Congress to vest the appointment of inferior officers, "as we think proper, in the President alone, in the Courts of Law, or in the Heads of Departments." Nothing in support of the claim of uncontrollable power can be inferred from the silence of the convention of 1787 on the subject of removal. For the outstanding fact remains that every specific proposal to confer such uncontrollable power upon the President was rejected. In America, as in England, the conviction prevailed then that the people must look to representative assemblies for the protection of their liberties. And protection of the individual, even if he be an official, from the arbitrary or capricious exercise of power was then believed to be an essential of free government.

NOTES

1.　If there is a removal power, where in the Constitution does it come from? The Vesting Clause? The Take Care Clause? Somewhere else? Does your answer to that question have implications for other debates about executive power?

2.　Myers was appointed a postmaster after being nominated by the president and confirmed by the Senate. Does this mean he was a principal officer of the United States under the Appointments Clause and not an inferior officer? Is Justice Brandeis right that the president has less power to remove inferior officers than principal officers?

3.　The opinions in *Myers* focus heavily on practice from the Decision of 1789 to the Tenure of Office Act on down to the present day. How much weight should be given to constitutional arguments from practice? Should they be given more weight or less weight on questions of the separation of powers?

4.   How broad is the holding of *Myers* as opposed to its dicta? May the president fire not only a postmaster but also a federal trade commissioner or a special prosecutor? Also, could the Court have decided the case on narrower grounds? Could it have ignored the issue of executive removal power and instead held that the Senate's role was a one-house veto inconsistent with the principles that would later be recognized in *INS v. Chadha*, p. 141?

Humphrey's Executor v. United States
295 U.S. 602 (1935)

■ MR. JUSTICE SUTHERLAND delivered the opinion of the Court.

Plaintiff brought suit in the Court of Claims against the United States to recover a sum of money alleged to be due the deceased for salary as a Federal Trade Commissioner from October 8, 1933, when the President undertook to remove him from office, to the time of his death on February 14, 1934. The court below has certified to this court two questions in respect of the power of the President to make the removal. . . .

William E. Humphrey, the decedent, on December 10, 1931, was nominated by President Hoover to succeed himself as a member of the Federal Trade Commission, and was confirmed by the United States Senate. He was duly commissioned for a term of seven years, expiring September 25, 1938; and, after taking the required oath of office, entered upon his duties. On July 25, 1933, President Roosevelt addressed a letter to the commissioner asking for his resignation, on the ground "that the aims and purposes of the Administration with respect to the work of the Commission can be carried out most effectively with personnel of my own selection," but disclaiming any reflection upon the commissioner personally or upon his services. The commissioner replied, asking time to consult his friends. After some further correspondence upon the subject, the President on August 31, 1933, wrote the commissioner expressing the hope that the resignation would be forthcoming, and saying: "You will, I know, realize that I do not feel that your mind and my mind go along together on either the policies or the administering of the Federal Trade Commission, and, frankly, I think it is best for the people of this country that I should have a full confidence."

The commissioner declined to resign; and on October 7, 1933, the President wrote him: "Effective as of this date you are hereby removed from the office of Commissioner of the Federal Trade Commission."

Humphrey never acquiesced in this action, but continued thereafter to insist that he was still a member of the commission, entitled to perform its duties and receive the compensation provided by law at the rate of $10,000 per annum. . . .

[The Court first construed Section 1 of the Federal Trade Commission Act— which states that "any commissioner may be removed by the President for: (1) inefficiency, (2) neglect of duty, or (3) malfeasance in office"—as if it allowed the president to remove a commissioner only for those three reasons.—Editors]

We conclude that the intent of the act is to limit the executive power of removal to the causes enumerated, the existence of none of which is claimed here; and we pass to the [constitutional] question.

[T]o support its contention that the removal provision of section 1, as we have just construed it, is an unconstitutional interference with the executive power of the President, the government's chief reliance is *Myers v. United States,* 272 U.S. 52 (1926). That case has been so recently decided, and the prevailing and dissenting opinions so fully review the general subject of the power of executive removal, that further discussion would add little of value to the wealth of material there collected. These opinions examine at length the historical, legislative, and judicial data bearing upon the question, beginning with what is called "the decision of 1789" in the first Congress and coming down almost to the day when the opinions were delivered. They occupy 243 pages of the volume in which they are printed. Nevertheless, the narrow point actually decided was only that the President had power to remove a postmaster of the first class, without the advice and consent of the Senate as required by act of Congress. In the course of the opinion of the court, expressions occur which tend to sustain the government's contention, but these are beyond the point involved and, therefore, do not come within the rule of *stare decisis.* In so far as they are out of harmony with the views here set forth, these expressions are disapproved. . . .

The office of a postmaster is so essentially unlike the office now involved that the decision in the *Myers* case cannot be accepted as controlling our decision here. A postmaster is an executive officer restricted to the performance of executive functions. He is charged with no duty at all related to either the legislative or judicial power. The actual decision in the *Myers* case finds support in the theory that such an officer is merely one of the units in the executive department and, hence, inherently subject to the exclusive and illimitable power of removal by the Chief Executive, whose subordinate and aid he is. Putting aside *dicta,* which may be followed if sufficiently persuasive but which are not controlling, the necessary reach of the decision goes far enough to include all purely executive officers. It goes no farther; much less does it include an officer who occupies no place in the executive department and who exercises no part of the executive power vested by the Constitution in the President.

The Federal Trade Commission is an administrative body created by Congress to carry into effect legislative policies embodied in the statute in accordance with the legislative standard therein prescribed, and to perform other specified duties as a legislative or as a judicial aid. Such a body cannot in any proper sense be characterized as an arm or an eye of the executive. Its duties are performed without executive leave and, in the contemplation of the statute, must be free from executive control. In administering the provisions of the statute in respect of "unfair methods of competition," that is to say, in filling in and administering the details embodied by that general standard, the commission acts in part quasi legislatively and in part quasi judicially. In making investigations and reports thereon for the information of Congress under section 6, in aid of the legislative power, it acts as a legislative agency. Under section 7, which authorizes the commission to act as a master in chancery under rules prescribed by the court, it acts as an agency of the judiciary. To the extent that it exercises any executive function, as distinguished from executive power in the constitutional sense, it does so in the discharge and effectuation of its quasi legislative or quasi judicial powers, or as an agency of the legislative or judicial departments of the government.

If Congress is without authority to prescribe causes for removal of members of the trade commission and limit executive power of removal accordingly, that power at once becomes practically all-inclusive in respect of civil officers with the exception of the judiciary provided for by the Constitution. The Solicitor General, at the bar, apparently recognizing this to be true, with commendable candor, agreed that his view in respect of the removability of members of the Federal Trade Commission necessitated a like view in respect of the Interstate Commerce Commission and the Court of Claims. We are thus confronted with the serious question whether not only the members of these quasi legislative and quasi judicial bodies, but the judges of the legislative Court of Claims, exercising judicial power (*Williams v. United States,* 289 U.S. 553, 565–567 (1933)), continue in office only at the pleasure of the President.

We think it plain under the Constitution that illimitable power of removal is not possessed by the President in respect of officers of the character of those just named. The authority of Congress, in creating quasi legislative or quasi judicial agencies, to require them to act in discharge of their duties independently of executive control cannot well be doubted; and that authority includes, as an appropriate incident, power to fix the period during which they shall continue, and to forbid their removal except for cause in the meantime. For it is quite evident that one who holds his office only during the pleasure of another cannot be depended upon to maintain an attitude of independence against the latter's will. . . .

The power of removal here claimed for the President . . . threatens the independence of a commission, which is not only wholly disconnected from the executive department, but which, as already fully appears, was created by Congress as a means of carrying into operation legislative and judicial powers, and as an agency of the legislative and judicial departments.

In the light of the question now under consideration, we have re-examined the precedents referred to in the *Myers* case, and find nothing in them to justify a conclusion contrary to that which we have reached. The so-called "decision of 1789" had relation to a bill proposed by Mr. Madison to establish an executive Department of Foreign Affairs. . . . We shall not discuss the subject further, since it is so fully covered by the opinions in the *Myers* case, except to say that the office under consideration by Congress was not only purely executive, but the officer one who was responsible to the President, and to him alone, in a very definite sense. A reading of the debates shows that the President's illimitable power of removal was not considered in respect of other than executive officers. And it is pertinent to observe that when, at a later time, the tenure of office for the Comptroller of the Treasury was under consideration, Mr. Madison quite evidently thought that, since the duties of that office were not purely of an executive nature but partook of the judiciary quality as well, a different rule in respect of executive removal might well apply.

In *Marbury v. Madison,* 5 U.S. (1 Cranch) 137 (1803), it is made clear that Chief Justice Marshall was of opinion that a justice of the peace for the District of Columbia was not removable at the will of the President; and that there was a distinction between such an officer and officers appointed to aid the President in the performance of his constitutional duties. In the latter case, the distinction he saw was that "their acts are his acts" and his will, therefore, controls; and, by way of illustration, he adverted to the act establishing the Department of Foreign Affairs, which was the subject of the "decision of 1789."

The result of what we now have said is this: Whether the power of the President to remove an officer shall prevail over the authority of Congress to condition the power by fixing a definite term and precluding a removal except for cause will depend upon the character of the office; the *Myers* decision, affirming the power of the President alone to make the removal, is confined to purely executive officers; and as to officers of the kind here under consideration, we hold that no removal can be made during the prescribed term for which the officer is appointed, except for one or more of the causes named in the applicable statute.

To the extent that, between the decision in the *Myers* case, which sustains the unrestrictable power of the President to remove purely executive officers, and our present decision that such power does not extend to an office such as that here involved, there shall remain a field of doubt, we leave such cases as may fall within it for future consideration and determination as they may arise.

■ MR. JUSTICE MCREYNOLDS agrees [for reasons stated in his dissent] in *Myers v. United States*. . . .

NOTES

1. What kind of power did Humphrey exercise as an FTC commissioner: legislative power, judicial power, or executive power? Could it have been legislative power, since the Constitution vests all the granted legislative powers in Congress? Could it have been judicial power, since the Constitution vests all the judicial power in Article III judges? Is the conclusion inescapable that Humphrey exercised executive power? If so, does the Constitution require that he be under presidential control?

2. Can *Humphrey's Executor* be reconciled with *Myers*? If the president may remove a postmaster, does it follow that the president should be able to remove a policy-making official like Humphrey?

3. *Humphrey's Executor* spawned the category of so-called "independent agencies," which include many important institutions such as the Federal Reserve Board and the Securities and Exchange Commission. A new president therefore inherits the previous president's Federal Reserve Board and Securities and Exchange Commission, even while picking a new cabinet. As a policy matter, is that sensible? Or should a new president be able to choose an entirely new financial regulatory team?

The Power to Direct Subordinates

One of the practical and structural arguments for the removal power is the president's need to be able to control the executive branch. But the removal power is not the only way to accomplish this. Does the president have a power to directly control subordinates in addition to the removal power (or could it be *instead* of the removal power)?

President George Washington took office on April 30, 1789, and he immediately asserted control over all the executive entities of the government under the Articles of Confederation, even though Congress had not yet given him any statutory authority over those entities. President Washington issued directives to the acting secretary of war, the board of treasury, the acting postmaster general, and the acting secretaries of war and of foreign affairs. He continued throughout his presidency to issue hundreds of written communications approving plans and actions, conveying directions about administrative operations, and making requests. For instance, President Washington started and ended criminal prosecutions by federal district attorneys (the forerunners of today's U.S. attorneys). And his Neutrality Proclamation was a major exercise of presidential power, guiding foreign policy and ordering prosecutions.

President Washington's immediate successors, John Adams and Thomas Jefferson, also started and ended prosecutions. President Adams personally directed that a prosecution be brought against newspaper editor William Duane even though no statute purported to give the president the power to do that. On two other occasions he specifically ordered that prosecutions be dropped. So too did President Jefferson—indeed, he stopped the prosecution against Duane (see p. 66). For extensive discussion of more than two centuries of presidential practice, see Steven G. Calabresi & Christopher S. Yoo, THE UNITARY EXECUTIVE: PRESIDENTIAL POWER FROM WASHINGTON TO BUSH (2008).

By the time of the Monroe administration it was an established practice that presidents could control subordinates in the executive branch. Nonetheless, it was at this time that the first suggestions arose of limits on presidential power to direct and control. Consider two attorney general opinions from the first half of the nineteenth century. In the first, an opinion for President Monroe, Attorney General William Wirt expressed some hesitance about whether the president could direct and control lower-level executive employees. In the second, Attorney General Roger Taney (later Chief Justice Taney) advised President Andrew Jackson about his authority to control a federal prosecutor.

William Wirt, Opinion on the Accounting Officers
October 20, 1823

[Accounting officers in the Department of the Treasury made a decision that displeased Major Joseph Wheaton. He sought presidential review, and President James Monroe referred the matter to the attorney general.—Editors]

SIR: I have examined the case of Major Joseph Wheaton, submitted by you for my opinion; and would proceed at once to the expression of an opinion on the merits of his claims, but that there is a preliminary inquiry which must be first made, and as to which I beg leave to ask your direction; and that is, whether it is proper for you to interfere in this case at all? I will suggest the considerations which strike me as rendering it improper.

  I.   It appears to me that you have no power to interfere.

The constitution of the United States requires the President, in general terms, to take care that the laws be faithfully executed; that is, it places the officers engaged in the execution of the laws under his general superintendence: he is to see that they do their duty faithfully; and on their failure, to cause them to be displaced, prosecuted, or impeached, according to the nature of the case. In case of forcible resistance to the laws, too, [so] as to require the interposition of the power of the government to overcome the illegal resistance, he is to see that that power be furnished. But it could never have been the intention of the constitution, in assigning this general power to the President to take care that the laws be executed, that he should in person execute the laws himself. For example: if a marshal should either refuse to serve process altogether, or serve it irregularly, that the President should correct the irregularity, or supply the omission, by executing the process in person. To interpret this clause of the constitution so as to throw upon the President the duty of a personal interference in every specific case of an alleged or defective execution of the laws, and to call upon him to perform such duties himself, would be not only to require him to perform an impossibility himself, but to take upon himself the responsibility of all the subordinate executive officers of the government—a construction too absurd to be seriously contended for. But the requisition of the constitution is, that he shall take care that the laws be executed. If the laws, then, require a particular officer by name to perform a duty, not only is that officer bound to perform it, but no other officer can perform it without a violation of the law; and were the President to perform it, he would not only be not taking care that the laws were faithfully executed, but he would be violating them himself. The constitution assigns to Congress the power of designating the duties of particular officers: the President is only required to take care that they execute them faithfully. . . .

Let us carry this principle to the laws which regulate the settlement of public accounts. In the original organization of the Treasury Department . . . the duties of the officers are designated specifically. There was one Auditor and one Comptroller. The duty of the Auditor is declared to be to receive all public accounts; and, after examination, to certify the balance, and transmit the accounts, with the vouchers and certificate, to the Comptroller, for his decision thereon; with this proviso: that if any person be dissatisfied therewith, he may within six months appeal to the Comptroller against such settlement. Here the right of appeal stops; there is no proviso for an appeal to the President. . . .

So also the act of 3d March, 1817, which introduces the present organization of the Treasury Department, and under which Major Wheaton's accounts have been settled, assigns to [specific Treasury Department personnel the settling of Major Wheaton's accounts with no statutory right of appeal to the president]. . . . Were it the intention of Congress to subject these accounts to the farther revision and decision of the President, that intention would have been expressed. The truth of this position is illustrated by the act of the last session, "to provide for the settlement of the accounts of Daniel D. Tompkins, late governor of the State of New York." This act expressly provides that the proper accounting officers of the Treasury be authorized to adjust and settle the accounts and claims of Daniel D. Tompkins on principles of equity and justice, "subject to the revision and final decision of the President of the United States." Where was the necessity of this express provision, if all the accounts settled by those officers were already subject to the revision and final decision of the President of the United States? . . . The authority is confined to the accounting officers of the Treasury Department. . . . [T]he President has no authority to interfere.

It would be strange, indeed, if it were otherwise. The office of President is ordained for very different purposes than that of settling individual accounts. The constitution has committed to him the care of the great interests of the nation, in all its foreign and domestic relations. . . . How will it be possible for the President to perform these great duties, if he is also to exercise the appellate power of revising and correcting the settlement of all the individual accounts which pass through the hands of the accounting officers? Let it be remembered that, out of the vest multitude of these accounts which are annually settled by these officers, there are very few which are settled to the entire satisfaction of the claimants; and if every dissatisfied claimant has a right to appeal to the President, and call upon him to revise and correct the settlement, the President would be constrained to abandon the great national objects which are committed to his peculiar care, and become the accountant general of the government. . . .

My opinion is, that the settlement made of the accounts of individuals by the accounting officers appointed by law is final and conclusive, so far as the executive department of the government is concerned. If an individual conceives himself injured by such settlement, his recourse must be one of the other two branches of government—the legislative or judicial. . . .

II.   If you do possess the power of revising and correcting the settlements made by the accounting officers of the government, this is not a proper case for the exercise of that power. . . .

I have the honor to remain, sir, very respectfully, your obedient servant.

Roger Taney, Opinion on the Jewels of the Princess of Orange

December 28, 1831

To the SECRETARY OF STATE.

I have, according to your request, read your argument on the questions which have grown out of the seizure of the jewels said to have been stolen from the Princess of Orange; and I concur with you in the conclusion to which you have come, although I do not place my opinion on precisely the same grounds.

The main question, and the only one about which there seems to be much difficulty, is, whether the President may lawfully direct the district attorney to discontinue the libel now pending against these jewels in the district court of New York. The libel is in the name of the United States; it was filed by their attorney, in their behalf, and claims to have the property condemned as forfeited to the United States, for an offence alleged to have been committed against their revenue laws.

Having been absent from Washington when this subject was under consideration, I have seen none of the papers or documents in the case, and I take the facts as I find them set forth (no doubt correctly) in your argument. I understand them to be as follows:

The jewels were brought to New York by Polari, and the violation of the revenue laws was committed by him; and, as soon as they were known to be in this country, the minister of the King of the Netherlands, acting under the direction of his government, claimed them as the property of the Princess of Orange, who is one of the family of the King.

Polari does not pretend that the property seized belongs to him. On the contrary, his confessions show that he was either concerned in the theft, or obtained the jewels, knowing them to be stolen; and there is no claimant but the Princess of Orange; and a friendly sovereign, through his minister here, asserts that they belong to her. . . .

The fact that jewels of this description were stolen some time ago from the Princess of Orange, is notorious, and may now be regarded as a matter of history.

The jewels which have been seized at New York are of very great value. The seizure of this property has been publicly known for several months; and it is in a high degree improbable that any one who supposed himself entitled to it would neglect, for so long a time, to put in his claim. And as none is made, except that on behalf of the Princess of Orange, the circumstances above stated furnish sufficient evidence to conclude that the jewels in question belong to her, and will justify the President in treating them as her property. . . .

Taking this to be the true state of the case, it is, I think, very clear that the jewels are not liable to condemnation under the laws of the United States. The real owner has done no act that can rightfully subject the property to forfeiture. The party who imported them into this country obtained the possession fraudulently, and without her knowledge, and brought them here against her will. It was not in her power to prevent it; for she did not know who had the possession of them, or where they were to be found, until they were seized. And property thus obtained, and thus introduced against the consent of the owner, stands on the same footing with that which is cast upon our shores by the violence of the winds and waves, and is entitled to the same protection. It is not liable to forfeiture in either case; and the innocent owner will not be visited with that penalty for an act which it was out of his power to prevent.

There being, then, sufficient evidence to show that these jewels are the property of the Princess of Orange, and therefore not liable to forfeiture,—are the officers of the government, from the nature of our institutions, bound to carry on a prosecution against them, and endeavor to have them condemned, when they are fully convinced that they are not justly liable to condemnation? Must the distant owner be put to the trouble and expense of proving her title, according to the strict and technical rules of evidence which prevail in judicial proceedings?

. . . [W]here an offence has been actually committed, and the penalty of the law unquestionably incurred, no doubt can be entertained of the power of the President to absolve the party from the penalty or forfeiture to which he is liable. And if a prosecution is pending in court, the President may, by his pardon, enable the party to stop the proceedings, without going to trial. And the power to grant a *nolle prosequi* in such a case, is necessarily embraced in the power to pardon an offender.

It would be a singular anomaly in our law, if the power is given thus to put an end to a prosecution against one admitted to be guilty, and yet there should be no power vested anywhere to save a party admitted to be innocent, from a harassing and expensive litigation with the United States, and which, from the distance of its witnesses and the difficulty of collecting his proofs, may often be oppressive and ruinous to him. The men who framed the constitution have not, however, committed this oversight. And in cases of the latter description, the power to interpose appears to me to be evidently embraced by that clause of the constitution which makes it his duty "to take care that the laws be faithfully executed." I proceed to show how that power applies to the case in hand. . . .

[The attorney general proceeds to show that federal district attorneys had discretion not to prosecute cases like this one. The attorney general then considers whether the president can direct and control the exercise of that discretion.—Editors]

I think the President does possess the power. The interest of the country and the purposes of justice manifestly require that he should possess it; and its existence is necessarily implied by the duties imposed upon him in that clause of the constitution before referred to, which enjoins him to take care that the laws be faithfully executed. Cases readily suggest themselves which show the necessity of such a power to enable him to discharge this duty. . . .

If it should be said that, the district attorney having the power to discontinue the prosecution, there is no necessity for inferring a right in the President to direct him to exercise it,—I answer, that the direction of the President is not required to communicate any new authority to the district attorney, but to direct him or aid him in the execution of the power he is admitted to possess. It might, indeed, happen that a district attorney was prosecuting a suit in the name of the United States, against their interest and against justice, and for the purpose of oppressing an individual: such a prosecution would not be a faithful execution of the law; and upon the President being satisfied that the forms of law were abused for such a purpose, and being bound to take care that the law was faithfully executed, it would become his duty to take measures to correct the procedure. And the most natural and proper measure to accomplish that object would be, to order the district attorney to discontinue the prosecution. . . .

I have put the case of a district attorney who wilfully violates his duty, in order to show the necessity of the power in the President for which I am contending. But another class of cases frequently occur, in which the district attorney himself may believe that the prosecution ought to be discontinued, but feels that it would be indiscreet and rash in him to incur the whole responsibility of dismissing it. And no case would better illustrate this class of cases than the one which has given rise to this discussion. The amount of property claimed to be forfeited to the United States is very large. The collector insists that a great part of it is liable to condemnation. It is known to have attracted the attention of the President, and to have become the subject of a correspondence with the minister of a foreign power. It would be indiscreet in the highest degree in Mr. Hamilton, the district attorney, to dismiss such a prosecution on his own responsibility, without first obtaining the approbation of the President; . . .

. . . Upon the whole, I consider the district attorney as under the control and direction of the President, in the institution and prosecution of suits in the name and on behalf of the United States; and that it is within the legitimate power of the President to direct him to institute or to discontinue a pending suit, and to point out to him, his duty, whenever the interest of the United States is directly or indirectly concerned. And I find, on examination, that the practice of the government has conformed to this opinion; and that, in many instances where the interference of the Executive was asked for, the cases have been referred to the Attorney General, and, in every case, the right to interfere and direct the district attorney is assumed or asserted. . . . If the President possesses this power, the remaining inquiry is, whether this is a fit case for its exercise. My opinion on this point is sufficiently indicated by the remarks I have already made. . . .

NOTES

1.   What kind of power are the accounting officers exercising? Can it be legislative power, given the absence of bicameralism and presentment? Can it be judicial power, given that the officers are not Article III judges? If not, must it be executive power? But

if the accounting officers are exercising executive power, how is that consistent with the Vesting Clause, which gives that power to the president?

2.   Attorney General Taney argued in The Jewels of the Princess of Orange that the president can always stop a prosecution by a federal prosecutor. But, unlike with the accounting officers, there was no federal statute rendering the prosecutor's decision final. What if there were? Can Congress by statute give a special prosecutor the final decision to prosecute in a case the way it gave accounting officers the final decision?

3.   How are the power of removal and the power of directing related? Must the president have both of them? Either of them? Consider this argument:

> Even if the President has a constitutionally unlimited power to remove certain executive officials, that power alone does not satisfy the Article II Vesting Clause. If an official exercises power contrary to the President's directives and is then removed, one must still determine whether the official's exercise of power is legally valid. If the answer is "no," then the President necessarily has the power to nullify discretionary actions of subordinates, and removal is therefore not the President's sole power of control. If the answer is "yes," then the insubordinate ex-official will have effectively exercised executive power contrary to the President's wishes, which contravenes the vesting of that power in the President. A presidential removal power, even an unlimited removal power, is thus either constitutionally superfluous or constitutionally inadequate. . . . It is therefore constitutionally non-existent as well.

Gary Lawson, *The Rise and Rise of the Administrative State*, 107 Harv. L. Rev. 1231, 1244 & n.74 (1994). Is this argument persuasive? If not, what is it missing?

[Assignment 12]

C. SUSPENDING AND DISPENSING POWERS?: "HE SHALL TAKE CARE THAT THE LAWS BE FAITHFULLY EXECUTED"

Art. II, § 3: . . . he shall take Care that the Laws be faithfully executed. . . .

Article II places the president in charge of executing, i.e. enforcing, the law. But what does it tell the president about *how* to enforce it? Must the president enforce every law on the books, in every circumstance? Or does the president have discretion to decide when enforcement is wise? And if so, are there limits to that discretion? May the president decide that an entire legal regime is unwise and simply ignore it?

Two of the prerogative powers claimed by English monarchs were the power to suspend the operation of statutes entirely and the power to grant dispensations, excusing individuals from complying with the law. In England, shortly before the Glorious Revolution of 1688, King James II claimed powers to dispense with and to suspend the laws. (In particular, he used these powers to circumvent an act of Parliament that forbade Roman Catholics from holding office and participating in public life.) When King James II was ousted, and replaced by William and Mary, part of the settlement the English revolutionaries insisted on was that no future monarch would claim the powers of suspending or dispensing.

The Constitution does not address the suspending and dispensing powers in those terms. But the Constitutional Convention unanimously rejected a proposal to give the president a suspending power. And the text does state that the president "shall take Care that the Laws be faithfully executed." U.S. Const. Art. II, § 3. The historical context suggests that the clause was intended to impose upon the president a duty to enforce the law. Perhaps that duty went so far as to categorically reject both suspending and dispensing powers—but the word "faithfully" leaves ambiguous how far that duty extends. Moreover, some subsequent interpreters have argued that the Take Care Clause should be read as a *power* rather than (or in addition to) a duty.

We next present three episodes of enforcement discretion. There are two cases about an executive refusal to enforce the law. In one, *United States v. Cox*, the court did not interfere with the executive decision. In the other, *Adams v. Richardson*, the court ordered a series of enforcement actions. After these, we present a recent memorandum from the Office of Legal Counsel defending the president's discretion not to enforce the immigration laws. This non-enforcement policy caused a major political controversy—as well as extensive federal litigation—during the second term of the Obama administration. As you read these materials, continue to consider whether the Take Care Clause contains a power or a duty, and of what sort. And consider whether these enforcement decisions are distinguishable from, or might ever amount to, the old prerogative powers of suspending and dispensing.

United States v. Cox
342 F.2d 167 (5th Cir. 1965) (en banc)

■ Before TUTTLE, CHIEF JUDGE, and RIVES, JONES, BROWN, WISDOM, GEWIN and BELL, CIRCUIT JUDGES.

■ JONES, CIRCUIT JUDGE:

On October 22, 1964, an order of the United States District Court for the Southern District of Mississippi, signed by Harold Cox, a judge of that Court, was entered. The order, with caption and formal closing omitted, is as follows:

> THE GRAND JURY, duly elected, impaneled and organized, for the Southern District of Mississippi, reconvened on order of the Court at 9:00 A.M., October 21, 1964, in Court Room Number 2 in Jackson, Mississippi, for the general dispatch of its business. The grand jury was fully instructed as to their duties, powers and responsibilities and retired to the grand jury room number 538 in the Federal Building at Jackson to do its work. The United States Attorney (and one of his assistants) sat with the grand jury throughout the day on October 21 and explained in detail to the grand jury the perjury laws and the Court's construction of such laws for their information. The grand jury heard witnesses throughout the day on October 21, 1964. On the morning of October 22, 1964, the grand jury, through its foreman, made known to the Court in open court that they had requested Robert E. Hauberg, United States Attorney, to prepare certain indictments which they desired to bring against some of the persons under consideration and about which they had heard testimony, and the United States Attorney refused to draft or sign any such indictments on instructions of the Acting Attorney General of the United States; whereupon the Court ordered and directed said United States Attorney to draft such true bills or no bills as the grand jury may have duly voted and desired to report and to sign such instruments as required by law under penalty of contempt. The United States Attorney was afforded one hour

within which to decide as to whether or not he would abide by the instructions and order of the Court in such respect. At the end of such time, the Court re-convened and the United States Attorney was specifically asked in open court as to whether or not he intended to conform with the order and direction of the Court in said respects whereupon the United States Attorney answered that he respectfully declined to do so on instructions from Nicholas deB. Katzenbach, Acting Attorney General. He was thereupon duly adjudged by the Court to be in civil contempt of the Court and was afforded an opportunity to make any statement which he desired to make to the Court before sentence; whereupon the United States Attorney reiterated his inability to comply with the order of the Court upon express and direct instructions from Nicholas deB. Katzenbach, Acting Attorney General of the United States.

WHEREFORE, IT IS ORDERED AND ADJUDGED by the Court that Robert E. Hauberg, United States Attorney, is guilty of civil contempt of this Court and in the presence of the Court for his said refusal to obey its said order and he is ordered into custody of the United States Marshal to be confined by him in the Hinds County, Mississippi, jail, there to remain until he purges himself of this contempt by agreeing to conform to said order by performing his official duty for the grand jury as requested in the several (about five) pending cases before them on October 21 and October 22, 1964.

IT IS FURTHER ORDERED by the Court that a citation issue to Nicholas deB. Katzenbach, Acting Attorney General of the United States, directing him to appear before this Court and show cause why he should not be adjudged guilty of contempt of this Court for his instructions and directions to the United States Attorney to disregard and disobey the orders of this Court in the respects stated.

The United States Attorney requested a stay of enforcement of this order and further proceedings herein for five days after this date to enable him to apply to the United States Court of Appeals for the Fifth Circuit for a writ of prohibition and such request is granted; and these proceedings and enforcement of this order in its entirety is stayed for five days, subject to the further orders of the United States Court of Appeals on said application; and for the enforcement of all of which, let proper process issue.

The United States Attorney, Robert E. Hauberg, and the Acting Attorney General, Nicholas deB. Katzenbach, have appealed from the order and they, joined by the United States, seek a writ of prohibition against the District Judge from enforcing the Court's order, and from asserting jurisdiction to require the Attorney General or the United States Attorney "to institute criminal prosecutions or to take any steps in regard thereto." . . .

The judicial power of the United States is vested in the federal courts, and extends to prosecutions for violations of the criminal laws of the United States. The executive power is vested in the President of the United States, who is required to take care that the laws be faithfully executed. The Attorney General is the hand of the President in taking care that the laws of the United States in legal proceedings and in the prosecution of offenses, be faithfully executed. The role of the grand jury is restricted to a finding as to whether or not there is probable cause to believe that an offense has been committed. The discretionary power of the attorney for the United States in determining whether a prosecution shall be commenced or maintained may well depend upon matters of policy wholly apart from any question of probable cause. Although as a member of the bar, the attorney for the United States is an officer of the court, he is nevertheless an executive official of the Government, and it is as an officer of the executive department that he exercises a discretion as to whether or not there shall be a prosecution in a particular case. It follows, as an incident of the constitutional separation of powers, that the courts are not to interfere with the free exercise of the discretionary powers of the attorneys of the United States in their control over criminal prosecutions. . . . If the attorney refuses to sign, as he has the discretionary power of doing, we conclude that there is no valid indictment. . . .

Because, as we conclude, the signature of the Government attorney is necessary to the validity of the indictment and the affixing or withholding of the signature is a matter of executive discretion which cannot be coerced or reviewed by the courts, the contempt order must be reversed. It seems that, since the United States Attorney cannot be required to give validity to an indictment by affixing his signature, he should not be required to indulge in an exercise of futility by the preparation of the form of an indictment which he is unwilling to vitalize with his signature. Therefore he should not be required to prepare indictments which he is unwilling and under no duty to sign.

Judges Tuttle, Jones, Brown and Wisdom join in the conclusion that the signature of the United States Attorney is essential to the validity of an indictment. Judge Brown, as appears in his separate opinion, is of the view that the United States Attorney is required, upon the request of the grand jury, to draft forms of indictments in accordance with its desires. The order before us for review is in the conjunctive; it requires the United States Attorney to prepare and sign. A majority of the court, having decided that the direction to sign is erroneous, the order on appeal will be reversed.

So much of the order of the district court as adjudges the United States Attorney for the Southern District of Mississippi to be in contempt is a final order, appealable as such, and for the reasons here assigned, is reversed. . . .

■ RIVES, GEWIN, and GRIFFIN B. BELL, CIRCUIT JUDGES (concurring in part and dissenting in part):

. . . [T]he basic issue before this Court is whether the controlling discretion as to the institution of a felony prosecution rests with the Attorney General[2] or with the grand jury. . . .

The Attorney General insists that the prosecution of offenses against the United States is an executive function of the Attorney General deraigned from the executive power vested in the President to "take care that the laws be faithfully executed." U.S. Const. art. II, § 3. The short answer is that one of the most fundamental and important of the laws so to be faithfully executed is the clear and explicit provision of the Fifth Amendment to the Constitution that "No person shall be held to answer for a capital, or otherwise infamous crime, unless on a presentment or indictment of

---

[2] The United States Attorney has acted at the direction of the Attorney General, and the record does not disclose his independent views.

a Grand Jury." . . . *[The opinion then discussed the importance of the grand jury as a matter of history and structure—Editors.]*

The grand jury may be permitted to function in its traditional sphere, while at the same time enforcing the separation of powers doctrine as between the executive and judicial branches of the government. This can best be done, indeed, it is mandatory, by requiring the United States Attorney to assist the grand jury in preparing indictments which they wish to consider or return, and by requiring the United States Attorney to sign any indictment that is to be returned. Then, once the indictment is returned, the Attorney General or the United States Attorney can refuse to go forward. That refusal will, of course, be in open court and not in the secret confines of the grand jury room. To permit the district court to compel the United States Attorney to proceed beyond this point would invest prosecutorial power in the judiciary, power which under the Constitution is reserved to the executive branch of the government. It may be that the court, in the interest of justice, may require a showing of good faith, and a statement of some rational basis for dismissal. In the unlikely event of bad faith or irrational action, not here present, it may be that the court could appoint counsel to prosecute the case. In brief, the court may have the same inherent power to administer justice to the government as it does to the defendant. That question is not now before us and may never arise. Except for a very limited discretion, however, the court's power to withhold leave to dismiss an indictment is solely for the protection of the defendant. . . .

By way of precaution, let us state that nothing here said is intended to reflect upon the present Acting Attorney General, in whose integrity we have the utmost confidence. Memory goes back, however, to days when we had an Attorney General suspected of being corrupt. There is no assurance that that will never again happen. We are establishing a precedent for other cases; we are construing a Constitution; we should retain intact that great constitutional bulwark, the institution of the grand jury.

On the cases before the Court, we agree with Judge Brown that the United States Attorney is required, upon the request of the grand jury, to draft forms of indictment in accordance with its desires. There is thus a majority of the Court in favor of that holding. We go further, and think that the United States Attorney is required to sign any indictment that may be found by the grand jury. We concur with the majority as to the dismissal of the appeal of the Acting Attorney General and as to the denial of the petition for writ of prohibition. We would, however, affirm the judgment of civil contempt against the United States Attorney.

■ JOHN R. BROWN, CIRCUIT JUDGE (concurring specially):

Mine is a middle course. I agree with the opinion written by Judge Jones that the District Attorney may not be compelled to sign the formal indictment which the Grand Jury has voted to return. . . . But I do not agree that the District Attorney may ignore the efforts of the Grand Jury to the point of declining to prepare in proper legal form the indictment they have voted to return. On the contrary, I am of the view that the Court may properly compel the District Attorney to act as legal scrivener to the Grand Jury. The Court may, therefore, order the District Attorney to prepare the indictment in legal form. . . .

Responsibility for determining whether a prosecution is to be commenced or maintained must be clearly fixed. The power not to initiate is indeed awesome. But it has to reside somewhere. And the more clearly pinpointed it is, the more the public interest is served through the focus of relentless publicity upon that decision. It may not, with safety, be left to a body whose great virtue is the combination of anonymity, transitory authority, and political unresponsibility.

All must be aware now that there are times when the interests of the nation require that a prosecution be foregone. These instances will most often be in the area of state secrets and national security. With stakes so high, the safety of our country, and hence the security of the world, ought not to be imperiled by leaving the important decision to a body having no definitive political responsibility. And it is hardly realistic to suggest, as do the dissenters, that these factors may be evaluated by the Grand Jury. What will be the source of their information? How extensive will it be? How close will a Grand Jury session approach a presidential cabinet meeting? How will essential government secrets be kept when disclosed to persons none of whom as Grand Jurors will have been subjected to customary security clearance checks?

And even in less sensitive areas, the practical operation of the prosecutorial function makes imperative the need for executive determination. The familiar example is the deliberate choice between those to be prosecuted and those who, often equally guilty, are named as co-conspirators but not as defendants, or others not named who are used as star government witnesses. And in other situations, of which the instant case may well be typical, the executive's purpose to effectuate specific policies thought to be of major importance would be frustrated or encumbered were a Grand Jury given the sole prerogative of determining when a prosecution is to be effectively commenced. . . .

But while I am firm that signature is a vital and significant act which reflects the exercise of an executive discretion to initiate prosecution—a thing here lacking— I am equally positive that the District Attorney has the duty to prepare the indictment when requested to do so by the Grand Jury. If this lacks logical consistency, I can only urge that an institution as old as the Grand Jury, implanted in the structure as idealistic as the Constitution, is one born, not out of logic, but out of the needs of history's rich experience. . . .

The powers of the Executive are so awesome in determining those whom it will not prosecute, that where there is a difference between the Grand Jury and the Executive, this determination and the resulting conflict of views should be revealed in open court. With great power comes great responsibility. Disclosure of this difference of view and the resulting impasse would subject this decision of the Executive to the scrutiny of an informed electorate. . . .

■ WISDOM, CIRCUIT JUDGE (concurring specially):

. . . The prosecution of offenses against the United States is an executive function within the exclusive prerogative of the Attorney General. "There shall be at the seat of government an executive department to be known as the Department of Justice, and an Attorney General, who shall be the head thereof." 5 U.S.C. § 291. That official, the chief law-enforcement officer of the Federal Government is "the hand of the president in taking care that the laws of the United States in protection of the interests of the United States in legal proceedings and in the prosecution of offenses be faithfully executed." *Ponzi v. Fassenden*, 258 U.S. 254 (1922). He "has the authority, and it is made his duty, to supervise the conduct of all suits brought by or against the United States", including the authority "to begin criminal prosecution". *United States v. San Jacinto Tin Co.*, 125 U.S. 273, 278–279 (1888). He "is invested with the general superintendence of all such suits, and all the district attorneys who do bring them in the various courts in the country are placed under his immediate direction and control." *Id.*, p. 279 and see *In re Neagle*, 135 U.S. 1, 66 (1890). . . .

The reason for vesting discretion to prosecute in the Executive, acting through the Attorney General is two-fold. First, in the interests of justice and the orderly, efficient administration of the law, some person or agency should be able to prevent an unjust prosecution. The freedom of the petit jury to bring in a verdict of not guilty and the progressive development of the law in the direction of making more meaningful the guarantees of an accused person's constitutional rights give considerable protection to the individual before and after trial. They do not protect against a baseless prosecution. This is a harassment to the accused and an expensive strain on the machinery of justice. The appropriate repository for authority to prevent a baseless prosecution is the chief law-enforcement officer whose duty, *unlike the grand jury's duty, is to collect evidence on both sides of a case.*

Second, when, within the context of law-enforcement, national policy is involved, because of national security, conduct of foreign policy, or a conflict between two branches of government, the appropriate branch to decide the matter is the executive branch. The executive is charged with carrying out national policy on law-enforcement and, generally speaking, is informed on more levels than the more specialized judicial and legislative branches. In such a situation, a decision not to prosecute is analogous to the exercise of executive privilege. The executive's absolute and exclusive discretion to prosecute may be rationalized as an illustration of the doctrine of separation of powers, but it would have evolved without the doctrine and exists in countries that do not purport to accept this doctrine.

This brings me to the facts. They demonstrate, better than abstract principles or legal dicta, the imperative necessity that the United States, through its Attorney General, have uncontrollable discretion to prosecute.

The crucial fact here is that Goff and Kendrick, two Negroes, testified in a suit by the United States against the Registrar of Clarke County, Mississippi, and the State of Mississippi, to enforce the voting rights of Negroes under the Fourteenth Amendment and the Civil Rights Act.

Goff and Kendrick testified that some seven years earlier at Stonewall, Mississippi, the registrar had refused to register them or give them application forms. They said that they had seen white persons registering, one of whom was a B. Floyd Jones. Ramsey, the registrar, testified that Jones had not registered at that time or place, but had registered the year before in Enterprise, Mississippi. He testified also that he had never discriminated against Negro applicants for registration. Jones testified that he was near the registration table in Stonewall in 1955, had talked with the registrar, and had shaken hands with him. The presiding judge, Judge W. Harold Cox, stated from the bench that Goff and Kendrick should be "bound over to await the action of the grand jury for perjury". . . . *[Judge Wisdom then discussed at length the federal investigation and grand jury proceedings.—Editors.]*

Against the backdrop of Mississippi versus the Nation in the field of civil rights, we have a heated but bona fide difference of opinion between Judge Cox and the

Attorney General as to whether two Negroes, Goff and Kendrick, should be prosecuted for perjury. Taking a narrow view of the case, we would be justified in holding that the Attorney General's implied powers, by analogy to the express powers of Rule 48(a), give him discretion to prosecute. Here there was a bona fide, reasonable exercise of discretion made after a full investigation and long consideration of the case—both sides of the case, not just the evidence tending to show guilt. If the grand jury is dissatisfied with that administrative decision, it may exercise its inquisitorial power and make a presentment in open court. It could be said, that is all there is to the case. But there is more to the case.

This Court, along with everyone else, knows that Goff and Kendrick, if prosecuted, run the risk of being tried in a climate of community hostility. They run the risk of a punishment that may not fit the crime. The Registrar, who provoked the original litigation, runs no risk, notwithstanding the fact that the district court, in effect, found that Ramsay did not tell the truth on the witness stand. In these circumstances, the very least demands of justice require that the discretion to prosecute be lodged with a person or agency insulated from local prejudices and parochial pressures. This is not the hard case that makes bad law. This is the type of case that comes up, in one way or another, whenever the customs, beliefs, or interests of a region collide with national policy as fixed by the Constitution or by Congress. It is not likely that the men who devised diversity jurisdiction expected to turn over to local juries the discretionary power to bring federal prosecutions. This case is unusual only for the clarity with which the facts, speaking for themselves, illuminate the imperative necessity in American Federalism that the discretion to prosecute be lodged in the Attorney General of United States.

The decision not to prosecute represents the exercise of a discretion analogous to the exercise of executive privilege. As a matter of law, the Attorney General has concluded that there is not sufficient evidence to prove perjury. As a matter of fact, the Attorney General has concluded . . . that trial for perjury would have the effect of inhibiting not only Goff and Kendrick but other Negroes in Mississippi from registering to vote. There is a conflict, therefore, between society's interest in law enforcement (diluted in this case by the Attorney General's conclusion that the evidence does not support the charge of guilt) and the national policy, set forth in the Constitution and the Civil Rights Acts, of outlawing racial discrimination. It is unthinkable that resolution of this important conflict affecting the whole Nation should lie with a majority of twenty-three members of a jury chosen from the Southern District of Mississippi. The nature of American Federalism, looking to the differences between the Constitution and the Articles of Confederation, requires that the power to resolve this question lie in the unfettered discretion of the President of United States or his deputy for law enforcement, the Attorney General.

My memory, too, goes back to the days, pointedly referred to by the dissenters, when we had "an Attorney General suspected of being corrupt." But I am not aware that we have had more lawless Attorneys General than lawless juries.

NOTES

1.   What do you think of *United States v. Cox*? What are the constitutional arguments in favor of prosecutorial discretion? What are the arguments against it? What provisions of the text speak to this question?

2.   Judge Wisdom writes that "the facts . . . demonstrate, better than abstract principles or legal dicta, the imperative necessity that the United States, through its Attorney General, have uncontrollable discretion to prosecute." Is he right about the power of the facts of this case? But if so, should his logic extend to future cases, with different facts?

3.   Judge Brown adopts a compromise position. He would hold that a U.S. attorney must write up an indictment if a grand jury requests it but that the U.S. attorney has sole discretion as to actually whether to launch the prosecution by signing it. Does this make sense? What does an unsigned indictment accomplish?

4.   Even the dissenters, who thought that a court *could* order the prosecutor to sign an indictment, acknowledged that the executive branch could then stop the proceedings. Why is that? Is it a principle limited to criminal cases? Is the pardon power from Article II, Section 2, relevant?

5.   *Cox* seems to fall into Category 2 from Justice Jackson's *Youngstown* concurrence: Congress has neither expressly granted, nor expressly forbidden, enforcement discretion here. Does its logic extend to cases where Congress has expressly instructed the president to enforce? That question, among others, is addressed in the next case.

Adams v. Richardson

480 F.2d 1159 (D.C. Cir. 1973) (en banc)

■ Before BAZELON, CHIEF JUDGE, and WRIGHT, MCGOWAN, TAMM, LEVENTHAL, ROBINSON, MACKINNON,* ROBB, and WILKEY, CIRCUIT JUDGES sitting en banc.

■ PER CURIAM:

This action was brought to secure declaratory and injunctive relief against the Secretary of Health, Education, and Welfare, and the Director of HEW's Office of Civil Rights. Appellees, certain black students, citizens, and taxpayers, allege in their complaint that appellants have been derelict in their duty to enforce Title VI of the Civil Rights Act of 1964 because they have not taken appropriate action to end segregation in public educational institutions receiving federal funds. . . .

The District Court found appellants' performance to fall below that required of them under Title VI and ordered them to *[institute seven specific measures against a range of primary and secondary schools and systems of higher education.—Editors]* . . .

We modify the injunction concerning higher education and affirm the remainder of the order.

I

Appellants insist that the enforcement of Title VI is committed to agency discretion, and that review of such action is therefore not within the jurisdiction of the courts. But the agency discretion exception to the general rule that agency action is reviewable under the Administrative Procedure Act, 5 U.S.C. §§ 701–02, is a narrow one, and is only "applicable in those rare instances where 'statutes are drawn in such broad terms that in a given case there is no law to apply.' S. Rep. No. 752, 79th Cong., 1st Sess., 26 (1945)." *Citizens to Preserve Overton Park v. Volpe*, 401 U.S.

---

*   Judge MacKinnon, Circuit Judge, did not participate in the decision of this case.

402, 410 (1971). The terms of Title VI are not so broad as to preclude judicial review. A substantial and authoritative body of case law provides the criteria by which noncompliance can be determined, and the statute indicates with precision the measures available to enforce the Act.

Appellants rely almost entirely on cases in which courts have declined to disturb the exercise of prosecutorial discretion by the Attorney General or by United States Attorneys. Those cases do not support a claim to absolute discretion and are, in any event, distinguishable from the case at bar. Title VI not only requires the agency to enforce the Act, but also sets forth specific enforcement procedures. The absence of similar specific legislation requiring particular action by the Attorney General was one factor upon which this court relied in *Powell v. Katzenbach*, 359 F.2d 234, 235 (1965), to uphold the exercise of discretion in that case.

More significantly, this suit is not brought to challenge HEW's decisions with regard to a few school districts in the course of a generally effective enforcement program. To the contrary, appellants allege that HEW has consciously and expressly adopted a general policy which is in effect an abdication of its statutory duty. We are asked to interpret the statute and determine whether HEW has correctly construed its enforcement obligations.

A final important factor distinguishing this case from the prosecutorial discretion cases cited by HEW is the nature of the relationship between the agency and the institutions in question. HEW is actively supplying segregated institutions with federal funds, contrary to the expressed purposes of Congress. It is one thing to say the Justice Department lacks the resources necessary to locate and prosecute every civil rights violator; it is quite another to say HEW may affirmatively continue to channel federal funds to defaulting schools. The anomaly of this latter assertion fully supports the conclusion that Congress's clear statement of an affirmative enforcement duty should not be discounted.

Appellants attempt to avoid the force of this argument by saying that, although enforcement is required, the means of enforcement is a matter of absolute agency discretion, and that they have chosen to seek voluntary compliance in most cases. This position is untenable in light of the plain language of the statute:

> Each Federal department and agency which is empowered to extend Federal financial assistance to any program or activity . . . is authorized and directed to effectuate the provisions of section 2000d of this title with respect to such program or activity by issuing rules, regulations, or orders of general applicability. . . . Compliance with any requirement adopted pursuant to this section may be effected (1) by the termination of or refusal to grant or to continue assistance under such program or activity to any recipient as to whom there has been an express finding on the record, after opportunity for hearing, of a failure to comply with such requirement . . . or (2) by any other means authorized by law: Provided, however, That no such action shall be taken until the department or agency concerned has advised the appropriate person or persons of the failure to comply with the requirement and has determined that compliance cannot be secured by voluntary means. . . . 42 U.S.C. § 2000d–1.

The Act sets forth two alternative courses of action by which enforcement may be effected. In order to avoid unnecessary invocation of formal enforcement procedures, it includes the proviso that the institution must first be notified and given a chance to comply voluntarily. Although the Act does not provide a specific limit to the time period within which voluntary compliance may be sought, it is clear that a request for voluntary compliance, if not followed by responsive action on the part of the institution within a reasonable time, does not relieve the agency of the responsibility to enforce Title VI by one of the two alternative means contemplated by the statute. A consistent failure to do so is a dereliction of duty reviewable in the courts. . . .

[The court then turned to the substance of the district court's injunction and affirmed it in all but one minor respect.—Editors]

NOTES

1.   *Adams* was litigated as a statutory case under the Administrative Procedure Act, but it has constitutional implications. The D.C. Circuit, at least implicitly, concluded that the Article II did not give the executive branch the power to ignore a specific congressional enforcement mandate. What are the best arguments for such a power? What are the best arguments against?

2.   How does the court distinguish exercises of prosecutorial discretion like *Cox*? Is this distinction persuasive?

3.   Among its reasons for requiring enforcement, the court mentions the fact that the executive branch "is actively supplying segregated institutions with federal funds, contrary to the expressed purposes of Congress." Is *Adams* really a case about Congress's power of the purse? (See p. 237.) Should the court's reasoning be limited to funding?

4.   Twelve years later, the Supreme Court decided *Heckler v. Chaney*, 470 U.S. 821 (1985), an important case on the same question—judicial review under the Administrative Procedure Act of agency *failure to act*. The D.C. Circuit had ordered the Food and Drug Administration to bring enforcement actions against the possibly illegal uses of various drugs in capital punishment by lethal injection. The Supreme Court reversed, holding that "an agency's decision not to prosecute or enforce, whether through civil or criminal process, is a decision generally committed to an agency's absolute discretion." It gave practical reasons for this presumption, as well as reasons related to constitutional structure:

> First, an agency decision not to enforce often involves a complicated balancing of a number of factors which are peculiarly within its expertise. Thus, the agency must not only assess whether a violation has occurred, but whether agency resources are best spent on this violation or another, whether the agency is likely to succeed if it acts, whether the particular enforcement action requested best fits the agency's overall policies, and, indeed, whether the agency has enough resources to undertake the action at all. An agency generally cannot act against each technical violation of the statute it is charged with enforcing. The agency is far better equipped than the courts to deal with the many variables involved in the proper ordering of its priorities. Similar concerns animate the principles of administrative law that courts generally will defer to an agency's construction of the statute it is charged with implementing, and to the procedures it adopts for implementing that statute.

> In addition to these administrative concerns, we note that when an agency refuses to act it generally does not exercise its coercive power over an individual's liberty or property rights, and thus does not infringe upon areas

that courts often are called upon to protect. Similarly, when an agency does act to enforce, that action itself provides a focus for judicial review, inasmuch as the agency must have exercised its power in some manner. The action at least can be reviewed to determine whether the agency exceeded its statutory powers. Finally, we recognize that an agency's refusal to institute proceedings shares to some extent the characteristics of the decision of a prosecutor in the Executive Branch not to indict—a decision which has long been regarded as the special province of the Executive Branch, inasmuch as it is the Executive who is charged by the Constitution to "take Care that the Laws be faithfully executed." U.S. Const., Art. II, § 3.

But the Court also emphasized that the presumption of unreviewability could be rebutted, and in a footnote, specifically reserved judgment on the *Adams* decision:

> We do not have in this case a refusal by the agency to institute proceedings based solely on the belief that it lacks jurisdiction. Nor do we have a situation where it could justifiably be found that the agency has "consciously and expressly adopted a general policy" that is so extreme as to amount to an abdication of its statutory responsibilities. *See, e.g., Adams v. Richardson,* 480 F.2d 1159 (1973) (en banc). Although we express no opinion on whether such decisions would be unreviewable under § 701(a)(2), we note that in those situations the statute conferring authority on the agency might indicate that such decisions were not "committed to agency discretion."

Karl R. Thompson, The Department of Homeland Security's Authority to Prioritize Removal of Certain Aliens Unlawfully Present in the United States and to Defer Removal of Others

Office of Legal Counsel (Nov. 19, 2014)

MEMORANDUM OPINION FOR THE SECRETARY OF HOMELAND
SECURITY AND THE COUNSEL TO THE PRESIDENT

You have asked two questions concerning the scope of the Department of Homeland Security's discretion to enforce the immigration laws. First, you have asked whether, in light of the limited resources available to the Department ("DHS") to remove aliens unlawfully present in the United States, it would be legally permissible for the Department to implement a policy prioritizing the removal of certain categories of aliens over others. DHS has explained that although there are approximately 11.3 million undocumented aliens in the country, it has the resources to remove fewer than 400,000 such aliens each year. DHS's proposed policy would prioritize the removal of aliens who present threats to national security, public safety, or border security. Under the proposed policy, DHS officials could remove an alien who did not fall into one of these categories provided that an Immigration and Customs Enforcement ("ICE") Field Office Director determined that "removing such an alien would serve an important federal interest."

Second, you have asked whether it would be permissible for DHS to extend deferred action, a form of temporary administrative relief from removal, to certain aliens who are the parents of children who are present in the United States. . . .

As has historically been true of deferred action, these proposed deferred action programs would not "legalize" any aliens who are unlawfully present in the United

States: Deferred action does not confer any lawful immigration status, nor does it provide a path to obtaining permanent residence or citizenship. Grants of deferred action under the proposed programs would, rather, represent DHS's decision not to seek an alien's removal for a prescribed period of time. Under decades-old regulations promulgated pursuant to authority delegated by Congress, aliens who are granted deferred action—like certain other categories of aliens who do not have lawful immigration status, such as asylum applicants—may apply for authorization to work in the United States in certain circumstances. Under DHS policy guidance, a grant of deferred action also suspends an alien's accrual of unlawful presence for purposes of 8 U.S.C. § 1182(a)(9)(B)(i) and (a)(9)(C)(i)(I), provisions that restrict the admission of aliens who have departed the United States after having been unlawfully present for specified periods of time. A grant of deferred action under the proposed programs would remain in effect for three years, subject to renewal, and could be terminated at any time at DHS's discretion. . . .

I

We first address DHS's authority to prioritize the removal of certain categories of aliens over others. We begin by discussing some of the sources and limits of DHS's enforcement discretion under the immigration laws, and then analyze DHS's proposed prioritization policy in light of these considerations.

A

. . . As a general rule, when Congress vests enforcement authority in an executive agency, that agency has the discretion to decide whether a particular violation of the law warrants prosecution or other enforcement action. This discretion is rooted in the President's constitutional duty to "take Care that the Laws be faithfully executed," U.S. Const. art. II, § 3, and it reflects a recognition that the "faithful[ ]" execution of the law does not necessarily entail "act[ing] against each technical violation of the statute" that an agency is charged with enforcing. *Heckler v. Chaney*, 470 U.S. 821, 831 (1985). Rather, as the Supreme Court explained in *Chaney*, the decision whether to initiate enforcement proceedings is a complex judgment that calls on the agency to "balanc[e] . . . a number of factors which are peculiarly within its expertise." These factors include "whether agency resources are best spent on this violation or another, whether the agency is likely to succeed if it acts, whether the particular enforcement action requested best fits the agency's overall policies, and . . . whether the agency has enough resources to undertake the action at all." *Id.* at 831. . . .

The principles of enforcement discretion discussed in *Chaney* apply with particular force in the context of immigration. Congress enacted the INA against a background understanding that immigration is "a field where flexibility and the adaptation of the congressional policy to infinitely variable conditions constitute the essence of the program." *United States ex rel. Knauff v. Shaughnessy*, 338 U.S. 537, 543 (1950). Consistent with this understanding, the INA vested the Attorney General (now the Secretary of Homeland Security) with broad authority to "establish such regulations; . . . issue such instructions; and perform such other acts as he deems necessary for carrying out his authority" under the statute. 8 U.S.C. § 1103(a)(3). . . .

With respect to removal decisions in particular, the Supreme Court has recognized that "the broad discretion exercised by immigration officials" is a ""principal feature of the removal system" under the INA. *Arizona v. United States*, 132 S.Ct. 2492, 2499 (2012). . . .

Immigration officials' discretion in enforcing the laws is not, however, unlimited. Limits on enforcement discretion are both implicit in, and fundamental to, the Constitution's allocation of governmental powers between the two political branches. *See, e.g., Youngstown Sheet & Tube Co. v. Sawyer*, 343 U.S. 579, 587–88 (1952). These limits, however, are not clearly defined. The open-ended nature of the inquiry under the Take Care Clause— whether a particular exercise of discretion is "faithful[ ]" to the law enacted by Congress—does not lend itself easily to the application of set formulas or bright-line rules. And because the exercise of enforcement discretion generally is not subject to judicial review, see *Chaney*, at 831–33, neither the Supreme Court nor the lower federal courts have squarely addressed its constitutional bounds. Rather, the political branches have addressed the proper allocation of enforcement authority through the political process. As the Court noted in *Chaney*, Congress "may limit an agency's exercise of enforcement power if it wishes, either by setting substantive priorities, or by otherwise circumscribing an agency's power to discriminate among issues or cases it will pursue." The history of immigration policy illustrates this principle: Since the INA was enacted, the Executive Branch has on numerous occasions exercised discretion to extend various forms of immigration relief to categories of aliens for humanitarian, foreign policy, and other reasons. When Congress has been dissatisfied with Executive action, it has responded, as *Chaney* suggests, by enacting legislation to limit the Executive's discretion in enforcing the immigration laws.

Nonetheless, the nature of the Take Care duty does point to at least four general (and closely related) principles governing the permissible scope of enforcement discretion that we believe are particularly relevant here. First, enforcement decisions should reflect "factors which are peculiarly within [the enforcing agency's] expertise." *Chaney*, at 831. Those factors may include considerations related to agency resources, such as "whether the agency has enough resources to undertake the action," or "whether agency resources are best spent on this violation or another." *Id.* Other relevant considerations may include "the proper ordering of [the agency's] priorities," *id.* at 832, and the agency's assessment of "whether the particular enforcement action [at issue] best fits the agency's overall policies," *id.* at 831.

Second, the Executive cannot, under the guise of exercising enforcement discretion, attempt to effectively rewrite the laws to match its policy preferences. *See id.* at 833 (an agency may not "disregard legislative direction in the statutory scheme that [it] administers"). In other words, an agency's enforcement decisions should be consonant with, rather than contrary to, the congressional policy underlying the statutes the agency is charged with administering. *Cf. Youngstown*, 343 U.S. at 637 (Jackson, J., concurring) ("When the President takes measures incompatible with the expressed or implied will of Congress, his power is at its lowest ebb.").

Third, the Executive Branch ordinarily cannot, as the Court put it in *Chaney*, " 'consciously and expressly adopt[ ] a general policy' that is so extreme as to amount to an abdication of its statutory responsibilities." 470 U.S. at 833 n.4 (quoting *Adams v. Richardson*, 480 F.2d 1159, 1162 (D.C. Cir. 1973) (en banc)); see *id.* (noting that in situations where an agency had adopted such an extreme policy, "the statute conferring authority on the agency might indicate that such decisions were not 'committed to agency discretion'"). Abdication of the duties assigned to the agency by statute is ordinarily incompatible with the constitutional obligation to faithfully execute the laws. *But see, e.g.*, Presidential Authority to Decline to Execute Unconstitutional Statutes, 18 Op. O.L.C. 199, 200 (1994) (noting that under the Take Care Clause, "the President is required to act in accordance with the laws—including the Constitution, which takes precedence over other forms of law").

Finally, lower courts, following *Chaney*, have indicated that non-enforcement decisions are most comfortably characterized as judicially unreviewable exercises of enforcement discretion when they are made on a case-by-case basis. That reading of *Chaney* reflects a conclusion that case-by-case enforcement decisions generally avoid the concerns mentioned above. . . . That does not mean that all "general policies" respecting non-enforcement are categorically forbidden: Some "general policies" may, for example, merely provide a framework for making individualized, discretionary assessments about whether to initiate enforcement actions in particular cases. But a general policy of non-enforcement that forecloses the exercise of case-by-case discretion poses "special risks" that the agency has exceeded the bounds of its enforcement discretion.

B

We now turn, against this backdrop, to DHS's proposed prioritization policy. In their exercise of enforcement discretion, DHS and its predecessor, INS, have long employed guidance instructing immigration officers to prioritize the enforcement of the immigration laws against certain categories of aliens and to deprioritize their enforcement against others. . . .

Under the proposed policy, DHS would identify three categories of undocumented aliens who would be priorities for removal from the United States. The highest priority category would include aliens who pose particularly serious threats to national security, border security, or public safety, including aliens engaged in or suspected of espionage or terrorism, aliens convicted of offenses related to participation in criminal street gangs, aliens convicted of certain felony offenses, and aliens apprehended at the border while attempting to enter the United States unlawfully. The second-highest priority would include aliens convicted of multiple or significant misdemeanor offenses; aliens who are apprehended after unlawfully entering the United States who cannot establish that they have been continuously present in the United States since January 1, 2014; and aliens determined to have significantly abused the visa or visa waiver programs. The third priority category would include other aliens who have been issued a final order of removal on or after January 1, 2014. . . .

In our view, DHS's proposed prioritization policy falls within the scope of its lawful discretion to enforce the immigration laws. . . .

. . . although the proposed policy is not a "single-shot non-enforcement decision," neither does it amount to an abdication of DHS's statutory responsibilities, or constitute a legislative rule overriding the commands of the substantive statute. The proposed policy provides a general framework for exercising enforcement discretion in individual cases, rather than establishing an absolute, inflexible policy of not enforcing the immigration laws in certain categories of cases. Given that the resources Congress has allocated to DHS are sufficient to remove only a small fraction of the total population of undocumented aliens in the United States, setting forth written guidance about how resources should presumptively be allocated in particular cases is a reasonable means of ensuring that DHS's severely limited resources are systematically directed to its highest priorities across a large and diverse agency, as well as ensuring consistency in the administration of the removal system. . . .

. . . For these reasons, the proposed policy avoids the difficulties that might be raised by a more inflexible prioritization policy and dispels any concern that DHS has either undertaken to rewrite the immigration laws or abdicated its statutory responsibilities with respect to non-priority aliens.

II

We turn next to the permissibility of DHS's proposed deferred action programs for certain aliens. . . .

A

In immigration law, the term "deferred action" refers to an exercise of administrative discretion in which immigration officials temporarily defer the removal of an alien unlawfully present in the United States. It is one of a number of forms of discretionary relief—in addition to such statutory and non-statutory measures as parole, temporary protected status, deferred enforced departure, and extended voluntary departure—that immigration officials have used over the years to temporarily prevent the removal of undocumented aliens.

The practice of granting deferred action dates back several decades. For many years after the INA was enacted, INS exercised prosecutorial discretion to grant "non-priority" status to removable aliens who presented "appealing humanitarian factors." Letter for Leon Wildes, from E. A. Loughran, Associate Commissioner, INS at 2 (July 16, 1973). This form of administrative discretion was later termed "deferred action."

Although the practice of granting deferred action "developed without express statutory authorization," it has become a regular feature of the immigration removal system that has been acknowledged by both Congress and the Supreme Court. *Reno v. Am.-Arab Anti-Discrim. Comm.*, 525 U.S. 471, 484 (1999). Deferred action "does not confer any immigration status"—*i.e.*, it does not establish any enforceable legal right to remain in the United States— and it may be revoked by immigration authorities at their discretion. USCIS, Standard Operating Procedures for Handling Deferred Action Requests at USCIS Field Offices at 3, 7 (2012). Assuming it is not revoked, however, it represents DHS's decision not to seek the alien's removal for a specified period of time.

Under longstanding regulations and policy guidance promulgated pursuant to statutory authority in the INA, deferred action recipients may receive two additional benefits. First, relying on DHS's statutory authority to authorize certain aliens to work in the United States, DHS regulations permit recipients of deferred action to apply for work authorization if they can demonstrate an "economic necessity for employment." 8 C.F.R. § 274a.12(c)(14). Second, DHS has promulgated regulations and issued policy guidance providing that aliens who receive deferred action will temporarily cease accruing "unlawful presence" for purposes of 8 U.S.C. § 1182(a)(9)(B)(i) and (a)(9)(C)(i)(I). 8 C.F.R. § 214.14(d)(3). . . .

B

The practice of granting deferred action, like the practice of setting enforcement priorities, is an exercise of enforcement discretion rooted in DHS's authority to enforce the immigration laws and the President's duty to take care that the laws are faithfully executed. It is one of several mechanisms by which immigration officials, against a backdrop of limited enforcement resources, exercise their "broad discretion" to administer the removal system—and, more specifically, their discretion to determine whether "it makes sense to pursue removal" in particular circumstances. *Arizona*, 132 S.Ct. at 2499.

Deferred action, however, differs in at least three respects from more familiar and widespread exercises of enforcement discretion. First, unlike (for example) the paradigmatic exercise of prosecutorial discretion in a criminal case, the conferral of deferred action does not represent a decision not to prosecute an individual for past unlawful conduct; it instead represents a decision to openly tolerate an undocumented alien's continued presence in the United States for a fixed period (subject to revocation at the agency's discretion). Second, unlike most exercises of enforcement discretion, deferred action carries with it benefits in addition to non-enforcement itself; specifically, the ability to seek employment authorization and suspension of unlawful presence for purposes of 8 U.S.C. § 1182(a)(9)(B)(i) and (a)(9)(C)(i)(I). Third, class-based deferred action programs, like those for VAWA recipients and victims of Hurricane Katrina, do not merely enable individual immigration officials to select deserving beneficiaries from among those aliens who have been identified or apprehended for possible removal—as is the case with ad hoc deferred action—but rather set forth certain threshold eligibility criteria and then invite individuals who satisfy these criteria to apply for deferred action status.

While these features of deferred action are somewhat unusual among exercises of enforcement discretion, the differences between deferred action and other exercises of enforcement discretion are less significant than they might initially appear. The first feature—the toleration of an alien's continued unlawful presence—is an inevitable element of almost any exercise of discretion in immigration enforcement. Any decision not to remove an unlawfully present alien—even through an exercise of routine enforcement discretion— necessarily carries with it a tacit acknowledgment that the alien will continue to be present in the United States without legal status. Deferred action arguably goes beyond such tacit acknowledgment by expressly communicating to the alien that his or her unlawful presence will be tolerated for a prescribed period of time. This difference is not, in our view, insignificant. But neither does it fundamentally transform deferred action into something other than an exercise of enforcement discretion: As we have previously noted, deferred action confers no lawful immigration status, provides no path to lawful permanent residence or citizenship, and is revocable at any time in the agency's discretion.

With respect to the second feature, the additional benefits deferred action confers—the ability to apply for work authorization and the tolling of unlawful presence—do not depend on background principles of agency discretion under DHS's general immigration authorities or the Take Care Clause at all, but rather depend on independent and more specific statutory authority rooted in the text of the INA. *[The opinion then argued that Congress had granted specific statutory authority to confer these additional benefits.—Editors]*

The final unusual feature of deferred action programs is particular to class-based programs. The breadth of such programs, in combination with the first two features of deferred action, may raise particular concerns about whether immigration officials have undertaken to substantively change the statutory removal system rather than simply adapting its application to individual circumstances. But the salient feature of class-based programs—the establishment of an affirmative application process with threshold eligibility criteria—does not in and of itself cross the line between executing the law and rewriting it. Although every class-wide deferred action program that has been implemented to date has established certain threshold eligibility criteria, each program has also left room for case-by-case determinations, giving immigration officials discretion to deny applications even if the applicant fulfills all of the program criteria. Like the establishment of enforcement priorities discussed in Part I, the establishment of threshold eligibility criteria can serve to avoid arbitrary enforcement decisions by individual officers, thereby furthering the goal of ensuring consistency across a large agency. The guarantee of individualized, case-by-case review helps avoid potential concerns that, in establishing such eligibility criteria, the Executive is attempting to rewrite the law by defining new categories of aliens who are automatically entitled to particular immigration relief. *See Chaney*, at 833 n.4. Furthermore, while permitting potentially eligible individuals to apply for an exercise of enforcement discretion is not especially common, many law enforcement agencies have developed programs that invite violators of the law to identify themselves to the authorities in exchange for leniency. Much as is the case with those programs, inviting eligible aliens to identify themselves through an application process may serve the agency's law enforcement interests by encouraging lower-priority individuals to identify themselves to the agency. In so doing, the process may enable the agency to better focus its scarce resources on higher enforcement priorities. . . .

[The opinion then looked at the specific proposed programs and applied the above principles. It concluded that one of them—deferred action for the parents of U.S. citizens and lawful permanent residents—was legally permissible. It concluded that another proposed program—deferred action for parents of recipients of a previous deferred action program—was not permissible.—Editors]

NOTES

1.   The Office of Legal Counsel memorandum distinguishes between prioritizing enforcement and "deferred action." Why the distinction? What is the difference?

2.   What is the role of Congress here? Do prioritization and deferred action both need to be authorized by Congress? Can both be forbidden by Congress? The opinion concludes that there is "specific statutory authority" to grant benefits such as work-authorization and tolling to deferred action recipients. But what if there were no specific authority? Would that matter?

3.   How far could the logic of the memo be extended? Can the executive branch decide that it doesn't want to enforce any of the drug laws? Can it pick specific drug prohibitions to enforce and others not to? Can the IRS decide to collect some taxes and not others?

4.   The memo claims that non-enforcement presents a different issue if the president believes that the statute is unconstitutional—an issue not presented here. In such cases the president is arguably not ignoring the law but rather following a higher

law—the Constitution. See Presidential Authority to Decline to Execute Unconstitutional Statutes, 18 Op. Off. Legal Counsel 199 (Nov. 2, 1994). Does this distinction make sense?

5.   The deferred action program authorized by the memo was challenged in a federal lawsuit brought by 26 states. A federal judge in the Southern District of Texas granted a preliminary injunction against the program, and that preliminary injunction was affirmed by the Fifth Circuit in a 2–1 decision. *Texas v. United States*, 809 F.3d 134 (2015). The Fifth Circuit distinguished between enforcement discretion and "deferred action," noting that "the states have not challenged the priority levels [the administration] has established, and neither the preliminary injunction nor compliance with the APA requires the Secretary to remove any alien." It went on: "Deferred action, however, is much more than nonenforcement: It would affirmatively confer 'lawful presence' and associated benefits on a class of unlawfully present aliens. Though revocable, that change in designation would trigger . . . eligibility for federal benefits . . . that would not otherwise be available to illegal aliens." The court also concluded that those benefits were inconsistent with federal law: "Even with 'special deference' to the Secretary, the [Immigration and National Act] flatly does not permit the reclassification of millions of illegal aliens as lawfully present and thereby make them newly eligible for a host of federal and state benefits, including work authorization." The dissenting judge argued that the program was not inconsistent with the law and was simply an instance of enforcement discretion. She concluded: "Because federal courts should not inject themselves into such matters of prosecutorial discretion, I would dismiss this case as non-justiciable."

The Supreme Court granted certiorari to review the case, but then split 4–4. This tie meant that the injunction was affirmed with no opinion and without creating a precedent.

6.   A scholarly study of executive enforcement discretion has examined "the Constitution's text, structure, and normative underpinnings, as well as relevant historical practice," and it concludes that

> constitutional authority for enforcement discretion exists—but it is both limited and defeasible. Presidents may properly decline to enforce civil and criminal prohibitions in particular cases, notwithstanding their obligation under the Take Care Clause to ensure that "the Laws be faithfully executed." Congress also may expand the scope of executive enforcement discretion by authorizing broader nonenforcement. But absent such congressional authorization, the President's nonenforcement authority extends neither to prospective licensing of prohibited conduct nor to policy-based nonenforcement of federal laws for entire categories of offenders. Presuming such forms of executive discretion would collide with another deeply rooted constitutional tradition: the principle that American Presidents, unlike English kings, lack authority to suspend statutes or grant dispensations that prospectively excuse legal violations.

Zachary S. Price, *Enforcement Discretion and Executive Duty*, 67 Vand. L. Rev. 671, 671–672 (2014). Suppose this conclusion is correct. Are *Cox*, *Adams*, and the OLC memo all consistent with it? Are only some of them consistent with it? Is the conclusion correct?

[*Assignment 13*]

D. SYNTHESIS: APPOINTMENT, REMOVAL, AND ENFORCEMENT DISCRETION

Now consider one case that shows how all of these principles of executive power interact—*Morrison v. Olson*, in which the Supreme Court upheld, over a vigorous lone dissent, the independent counsel provisions of the Ethics in Government Act (EIGA).

In the 1970s, in the Nixon administration, the attorney general hired a special prosecutor, Archibald Cox, to investigate the break-in at the Watergate Hotel. When Cox's investigation began to get too close, President Nixon demanded that the attorney general fire Cox. In what came to be known as the "Saturday Night Massacre," the attorney general resigned rather than obey the president's order, and the deputy attorney general was removed by the president when he too refused to fire Cox. The third-ranking official in the Department of Justice, Solicitor General Robert Bork, fired Cox. In the ensuing uproar it was clear that unless a new and fiercely independent special prosecutor was appointed, President Nixon would be immediately impeached. Such a prosecutor was appointed, and nine months later he uncovered the evidence (thanks to *United States v. Nixon*, p. 356) that forced President Nixon to resign from office.

Eager to prevent any future Saturday Night Massacres, Congress proposed turning the entire Department of Justice into an independent agency, but Griffin Bell, the attorney general in the Carter administration, argued that this would be unconstitutional under *Myers*. (Bell had served as a court of appeals judge, and you might recall that he was one of the judges in *Cox*.) Congress settled for a system of temporary independent special prosecutors set up by the EIGA.

President Carter signed the EIGA. Its constitutionality was challenged, however, by the Reagan administration, on the grounds that it vested a core executive power—the power over prosecutions—in an unremovable official. During the Reagan administration, there were two major cases that challenged congressional power to create independent agencies and counsels. The first, *Bowsher v. Synar*, 478 U.S. 714 (1986), involved the constitutionality of the Gramm-Rudman-Hollings Deficit Reduction Act, which gave executive powers to an official who was not removable at will by the president but who was removable by Congress. The Court held the act unconstitutional. The Court's opinion was careful, however, not to call into question the constitutionality of all independent agencies. The second case, *Morrison v. Olson*, 487 U.S. 654 (1988), arose when Assistant Attorney General Theodore Olson was accused of wrongfully withholding documents from Congress. The attorney general referred the investigation to the three-judge special court, which appointed Alexia Morrison as an independent counsel. Olson objected that he was being prosecuted unconstitutionally because the independent prosecutor was unaccountable to the president or to anyone else. His case went up to the Supreme Court.

Morrison v. Olson

487 U.S. 654 (1988)

■ CHIEF JUSTICE REHNQUIST delivered the opinion of the Court.

This case presents us with a challenge to the independent counsel provisions of the Ethics in Government Act of 1978. We hold today that these provisions of the Act do not violate the Appointments Clause of the Constitution, Art. II, § 2, cl. 2, or the limitations of Article III, nor do they impermissibly interfere with the President's authority under Article II in violation of the constitutional principle of separation of powers.

I

Briefly stated, Title VI of the Ethics in Government Act (the Act) allows for the appointment of an "independent counsel" to investigate and, if appropriate, prosecute certain high-ranking Government officials for violations of federal criminal laws. The Act requires the Attorney General, upon receipt of information that he determines is "sufficient to constitute grounds to investigate whether any person [covered by the Act] may have violated any Federal criminal law," to conduct a preliminary investigation of the matter. When the Attorney General has completed this investigation, or 90 days has elapsed, he is required to report to a special court (the Special Division) created by the Act "for the purpose of appointing independent counsels." ... The Attorney General's application to the court "shall contain sufficient information to assist the [court] in selecting an independent counsel and in defining that independent counsel's prosecutorial jurisdiction." Upon receiving this application, the Special Division "shall appoint an appropriate independent counsel and shall define that independent counsel's prosecutorial jurisdiction."

With respect to all matters within the independent counsel's jurisdiction, the Act grants the counsel "full power and independent authority to exercise all investigative and prosecutorial functions and powers of the Department of Justice, the Attorney General, and any other officer or employee of the Department of Justice." The functions of the independent counsel include conducting grand jury proceedings and other investigations, participating in civil and criminal court proceedings and litigation, and appealing any decision in any case in which the counsel participates in an official capacity. Under [the Act], the counsel's powers include "initiating and conducting prosecutions in any court of competent jurisdiction, framing and signing indictments, filing informations, and handling all aspects of any case, in the name of the United States." The counsel may appoint employees, may request and obtain assistance from the Department of Justice, and may accept referral of matters from the Attorney General if the matter falls within the counsel's jurisdiction as defined by the Special Division. The Act also states that an independent counsel "shall, except where not possible, comply with the written or other established policies of the Department of Justice respecting enforcement of the criminal laws." In addition, whenever a matter has been referred to an independent counsel under the Act, the Attorney General and the Justice Department are required to suspend all investigations and proceedings regarding the matter. An independent counsel has "full authority to dismiss matters within [his or her] prosecutorial jurisdiction without conducting an investigation or at any subsequent time before prosecution, if to do so would be consistent" with Department of Justice policy.

Two statutory provisions govern the length of an independent counsel's tenure in office. The first defines the procedure for removing an independent counsel. Section 596(a)(1) provides:

> An independent counsel appointed under this chapter may be removed from office, other than by impeachment and conviction, only by the personal action of the Attorney General and only for good cause, physical disability, mental incapacity, or any other condition that substantially impairs the performance of such independent counsel's duties.

. . . [The attorney general's decision to terminate under this provision is subject to judicial review.—Editors]

The other provision governing the tenure of the independent counsel defines the procedures for "terminating" the counsel's office. Under § 596(b)(1), the office of an independent counsel terminates when he or she notifies the Attorney General that he or she has completed or substantially completed any investigations or prosecutions undertaken pursuant to the Act. In addition, the Special Division, acting either on its own or on the suggestion of the Attorney General, may terminate the office of an independent counsel at any time if it finds that "the investigation of all matters within the prosecutorial jurisdiction of such independent counsel . . . have been completed or so substantially completed that it would be appropriate for the Department of Justice to complete such investigations and prosecutions." . . .

[The Court then discussed the facts at some length, as well as a jurisdictional issue.—Editors]

III

The Appointments Clause of Article II reads as follows:

> "[The President] shall nominate, and by and with the Advice and Consent of the Senate, shall appoint Ambassadors, other public Ministers and Consuls, Judges of the Supreme Court, and all other Officers of the United States, whose Appointments are not herein otherwise provided for, and which shall be established by Law: but the Congress may by Law vest the Appointment of such inferior Officers, as they think proper, in the President alone, in the Courts of Law, or in the Heads of Departments."
> U.S. Const., Art. II, § 2, cl. 2.

. . . The parties do not dispute that "[t]he Constitution for purposes of appointment . . . divides all its officers into two classes." *United States v. Germaine*, 99 U.S. (9 Otto) 508, 509 (1879). As we stated in *Buckley v. Valeo*, 424 U.S. 1, 132 (1976): "[P]rincipal officers are selected by the President with the advice and consent of the Senate. Inferior officers Congress may allow to be appointed by the President alone, by the heads of departments, or by the Judiciary." The initial question is, accordingly, whether appellant is an "inferior" or a "principal" officer. If she is the latter, as the Court of Appeals concluded, then the Act is in violation of the Appointments Clause.

The line between "inferior" and "principal" officers is one that is far from clear, and the Framers provided little guidance into where it should be drawn. We need not attempt here to decide exactly where the line falls between the two types of officers, because in our view appellant clearly falls on the "inferior officer" side of that line. Several factors lead to this conclusion.

First, appellant is subject to removal by a higher Executive Branch official. Although appellant may not be "subordinate" to the Attorney General (and the President) insofar as she possesses a degree of independent discretion to exercise the powers delegated to her under the Act, the fact that she can be removed by the Attorney General indicates that she is to some degree "inferior" in rank and authority. Second, appellant is empowered by the Act to perform only certain, limited duties. An independent counsel's role is restricted primarily to investigation and, if appropriate, prosecution for certain federal crimes. Admittedly, the Act delegates to appellant "full power and independent authority to exercise all investigative and prosecutorial functions and powers of the Department of Justice," but this grant of authority does not include any authority to formulate policy for the Government or the Executive Branch, nor does it give appellant any administrative duties outside of those necessary to operate her office. The Act specifically provides that in policy matters appellant is to comply to the extent possible with the policies of the Department.

Third, appellant's office is limited in jurisdiction. Not only is the Act itself restricted in applicability to certain federal officials suspected of certain serious federal crimes, but an independent counsel can only act within the scope of the jurisdiction that has been granted by the Special Division pursuant to a request by the Attorney General. Finally, appellant's office is limited in tenure. There is concededly no time limit on the appointment of a particular counsel. Nonetheless, the office of independent counsel is "temporary" in the sense that an independent counsel is appointed essentially to accomplish a single task, and when that task is over the office is terminated, either by the counsel herself or by action of the Special Division. Unlike other prosecutors, appellant has no ongoing responsibilities that extend beyond the accomplishment of the mission that she was appointed for and authorized by the Special Division to undertake. In our view, these factors relating to the "ideas of tenure, duration ... and duties" of the independent counsel, *Germaine*, at 511, are sufficient to establish that appellant is an "inferior" officer in the constitutional sense. . . .

This does not, however, end our inquiry under the Appointments Clause. Appellees argue that even if appellant is an "inferior" officer, the Clause does not empower Congress to place the power to appoint such an officer outside the Executive Branch. They contend that the Clause does not contemplate congressional authorization of "interbranch appointments," in which an officer of one branch is appointed by officers of another branch. The relevant language of the Appointments Clause is worth repeating. It reads: ". . . but the Congress may by Law vest the Appointment of such inferior Officers, as they think proper, in the President alone, in the courts of Law, or in the Heads of Departments." On its face, the language of this "excepting clause" admits of no limitation on interbranch appointments. Indeed, the inclusion of "as they think proper" seems clearly to give Congress significant discretion to determine whether it is "proper" to vest the appointment of, for example, executive officials in the "courts of Law." . . . *[The Court went on to argue that this interpretation was supported by precedent and that "the history of the [Appointments] Clause provides no support for appellees' position."—Editors]*

We do not mean to say that Congress' power to provide for interbranch appointments of "inferior officers" is unlimited. In addition to separation-of-powers concerns, which would arise if such provisions for appointment had the potential to impair the constitutional functions assigned to one of the branches, [a prior decision—*Ex parte Siebold*, 100 U.S. 371 (1880)] suggested that Congress' decision to vest the appointment power in the courts would be improper if there was some "incongruity" between the functions normally performed by the courts and the performance of their duty to appoint. *Siebold*, at 398. ("[T]he duty to appoint inferior officers, when required thereto by law, is a constitutional duty of the courts; and in the present case there is no such incongruity in the duty required as to excuse the courts from its performance, or to render their acts void"). In this case, however, we do not think it impermissible for Congress to vest the power to appoint independent counsel in a specially created federal court. We thus disagree with the Court of Appeals' conclusion that there is an inherent incongruity about a court having the power to appoint prosecutorial officers. . . . Congress, of course, was concerned when it created the office of independent counsel with the conflicts of interest that could arise in situations when the Executive Branch is called upon to investigate its own high-ranking officers. If it were to remove the appointing authority from the Executive Branch, the most logical place to put it was in the Judicial Branch. . . .

[The Court then held that the power given to federal judges under the Act did not exceed their powers under Article III.—Editors]

V

We now turn to consider whether the Act is invalid under the constitutional principle of separation of powers. Two related issues must be addressed: The first is whether the provision of the Act restricting the Attorney General's power to remove the independent counsel to only those instances in which he can show "good cause," taken by itself, impermissibly interferes with the President's exercise of his constitutionally appointed functions. The second is whether, taken as a whole, the Act violates the separation of powers by reducing the President's ability to control the prosecutorial powers wielded by the independent counsel.

A

Two Terms ago we had occasion to consider whether it was consistent with the separation of powers for Congress to pass a statute that authorized a Government official who is removable only by Congress to participate in what we found to be "executive powers." *Bowsher v. Synar,* 478 U.S. 714, 730 (1986). We held in *Bowsher* that "Congress cannot reserve for itself the power of removal of an officer charged with the execution of the laws except by impeachment." *Id.,* at 726. A primary antecedent for this ruling was our 1926 decision in *Myers v. United States,* 272 U.S. 52 (1926). . . .

Unlike both *Bowsher* and *Myers,* this case does not involve an attempt by Congress itself to gain a role in the removal of executive officials other than its established powers of impeachment and conviction. The Act instead puts the removal power squarely in the hands of the Executive Branch; an independent counsel may be removed from office, "only by the personal action of the Attorney General, and only for good cause." There is no requirement of congressional approval of the Attorney General's removal decision, though the decision is subject to judicial review. In our view, the removal provisions of the Act make this case more analogous to *Humphrey's Executor,* 295 U.S. 602 (1935), and *Wiener v. United States,* 357 U.S. 349 (1958), than to *Myers* or *Bowsher.* . . .

Appellees contend that *Humphrey's Executor* and *Wiener* are distinguishable from this case because they did not involve officials who performed a "core executive function." They argue that our decision in *Humphrey's Executor* rests on a distinction between "purely executive" officials and officials who exercise "quasi-legislative" and "quasi-judicial" powers. In their view, when a "purely executive" official is involved, the governing precedent is *Myers,* not *Humphrey's Executor.* See *Humphrey's Executor,* at 628. And, under *Myers,* the President must have absolute discretion to discharge "purely" executive officials at will. See *Myers,* at 132–134.

We undoubtedly did rely on the terms "quasi-legislative" and "quasi-judicial" to distinguish the officials involved in *Humphrey's Executor* and *Wiener* from those in *Myers,* but our present considered view is that the determination of whether the Constitution allows Congress to impose a "good cause"-type restriction on the President's power to remove an official cannot be made to turn on whether or not that official is classified as "purely executive." The analysis contained in our removal cases is designed not to define rigid categories of those officials who may or may not be removed at will by the President, but to ensure that Congress does not interfere with the President's exercise of the "executive power" and his constitutionally appointed duty to "take care that the laws be faithfully executed" under Article II. *Myers* was undoubtedly correct in its holding, and in its broader suggestion that there are some "purely executive" officials who must be removable by the President at will if he is to be able to accomplish his constitutional role.[29] See 272 U.S., at 132–134. But as the Court noted in *Wiener*:

> The assumption was short-lived that the *Myers* case recognized the President's inherent constitutional power to remove officials no matter what the relation of the executive to the discharge of their duties and no matter what restrictions Congress may have imposed regarding the nature of their tenure. . . . 357 U.S., at 352.

At the other end of the spectrum from *Myers,* the characterization of the agencies in *Humphrey's Executor* and *Wiener* as "quasi-legislative" or "quasi-judicial" in large part reflected our judgment that it was not essential to the President's proper execution of his Article II powers that these agencies be headed up by individuals who were removable at will. We do not mean to suggest that an analysis of the functions served by the officials at issue is irrelevant. But the real question is whether the removal restrictions are of such a nature that they impede the President's ability to perform his constitutional duty, and the functions of the officials in question must be analyzed in that light.

Considering for the moment the "good cause" removal provision in isolation from the other parts of the Act at issue in this case, we cannot say that the imposition of a "good cause" standard for removal by itself unduly trammels on executive authority. There is no real dispute that the functions performed by the independent counsel are "executive" in the sense that they are law enforcement functions that typically have been undertaken by officials within the Executive Branch. As we

---

[29] The dissent says that the language of Article II vesting the executive power of the United States in the President requires that every officer of the United States exercising any part of that power must serve at the pleasure of the President and be removable by him at will. This rigid demarcation—a demarcation incapable of being altered by law in the slightest degree, and applicable to tens of thousands of holders of offices neither known nor foreseen by the Framers—depends upon an extrapolation from general constitutional language which we think is more than the text will bear. . . .

noted above, however, the independent counsel is an inferior officer under the Appointments Clause, with limited jurisdiction and tenure and lacking policymaking or significant administrative authority. Although the counsel exercises no small amount of discretion and judgment in deciding how to carry out his or her duties under the Act, we simply do not see how the President's need to control the exercise of that discretion is so central to the functioning of the Executive Branch as to require as a matter of constitutional law that the counsel be terminable at will by the President.

Nor do we think that the "good cause" removal provision at issue here impermissibly burdens the President's power to control or supervise the independent counsel, as an executive official, in the execution of his or her duties under the Act. This is not a case in which the power to remove an executive official has been completely stripped from the President, thus providing no means for the President to ensure the "faithful execution" of the laws. Rather, because the independent counsel may be terminated for "good cause," the Executive, through the Attorney General, retains ample authority to assure that the counsel is competently performing his or her statutory responsibilities in a manner that comports with the provisions of the Act. Although we need not decide in this case exactly what is encompassed within the term "good cause" under the Act, the legislative history of the removal provision also makes clear that the Attorney General may remove an independent counsel for "misconduct." See H.R. Conf. Rep. No. 100–452, p. 37 (1987). . . . We do not think that this limitation as it presently stands sufficiently deprives the President of control over the independent counsel to interfere impermissibly with his constitutional obligation to ensure the faithful execution of the laws. . . .

B

The final question to be addressed is whether the Act, taken as a whole, violates the principle of separation of powers by unduly interfering with the role of the Executive Branch. . . .

We observe first that this case does not involve an attempt by Congress to increase its own powers at the expense of the Executive Branch. Unlike some of our previous cases, most recently *Bowsher v. Synar,* this case simply does not pose a "dange[r] of congressional usurpation of Executive Branch functions." 478 U.S. at 727. Indeed, with the exception of the power of impeachment—which applies to all officers of the United States-Congress retained for itself no powers of control or supervision over an independent counsel. The Act does empower certain Members of Congress to request the Attorney General to apply for the appointment of an independent counsel, but the Attorney General has no duty to comply with the request, although he must respond within a certain time limit. Other than that, Congress' role under the Act is limited to receiving reports or other information and oversight of the independent counsel's activities, functions that we have recognized generally as being incidental to the legislative function of Congress. See *McGrain v. Daugherty,* 273 U.S. 135, 174 (1927).

Similarly, we do not think that the Act works any judicial usurpation of properly executive functions. As should be apparent from our discussion of the Appointments Clause above, the power to appoint inferior officers such as independent counsel is not in itself an "executive" function in the constitutional sense, at least when

Congress has exercised its power to vest the appointment of an inferior office in the "courts of Law." . . .

Finally, we do not think that the Act "impermissibly undermine[s]" the powers of the Executive Branch, *Commodity Futures Trading Comm'n v. Schor*, 478 U.S. 833, 856 (1986), or "disrupts the proper balance between the coordinate branches [by] prevent [ing] the Executive Branch from accomplishing its constitutionally assigned functions," *Nixon v. Administrator of General Services*, 433 U.S. 425, 442 (1977). It is undeniable that the Act reduces the amount of control or supervision that the Attorney General and, through him, the President exercises over the investigation and prosecution of a certain class of alleged criminal activity. The Attorney General is not allowed to appoint the individual of his choice; he does not determine the counsel's jurisdiction; and his power to remove a counsel is limited. Nonetheless, the Act does give the Attorney General several means of supervising or controlling the prosecutorial powers that may be wielded by an independent counsel. Most importantly, the Attorney General retains the power to remove the counsel for "good cause," a power that we have already concluded provides the Executive with substantial ability to ensure that the laws are "faithfully executed" by an independent counsel. No independent counsel may be appointed without a specific request by the Attorney General, and the Attorney General's decision not to request appointment if he finds "no reasonable grounds to believe that further investigation is warranted" is committed to his unreviewable discretion. The Act thus gives the Executive a degree of control over the power to initiate an investigation by the independent counsel. In addition, the jurisdiction of the independent counsel is defined with reference to the facts submitted by the Attorney General, and once a counsel is appointed, the Act requires that the counsel abide by Justice Department policy unless it is not "possible" to do so. Notwithstanding the fact that the counsel is to some degree "independent" and free from executive supervision to a greater extent than other federal prosecutors, in our view these features of the Act give the Executive Branch sufficient control over the independent counsel to ensure that the President is able to perform his constitutionally assigned duties. . . .

■ JUSTICE SCALIA, dissenting.

It is the proud boast of our democracy that we have "a government of laws and not of men." Many Americans are familiar with that phrase; not many know its derivation. It comes from Part the First, Article XXX, of the Massachusetts Constitution of 1780, which reads in full as follows:

> In the government of this Commonwealth, the legislative department shall never exercise the executive and judicial powers, or either of them: The executive shall never exercise the legislative and judicial powers, or either of them: The judicial shall never exercise the legislative and executive powers, or either of them: to the end it may be a government of laws and not of men.

The framers of the Federal Constitution similarly viewed the principle of separation of powers as the absolutely central guarantee of a just Government. In *No. 47* of *The Federalist*, Madison wrote that "[n]o political truth is certainly of greater intrinsic value, or is stamped with the authority of more enlightened patrons of liberty." *The Federalist No. 47*. Without a secure structure of separated powers, our Bill of Rights would be worthless, as are the bills of rights of many nations of the world that have adopted, or even improved upon, the mere words of ours.

The principle of separation of powers is expressed in our Constitution in the first section of each of the first three Articles. . . .

But just as the mere words of a Bill of Rights are not self-effectuating, the Framers recognized "[t]he insufficiency of a mere parchment delineation of the boundaries" to achieve the separation of powers. Federalist No. 73 (Hamilton). "[T]he great security," wrote Madison, "against a gradual concentration of the several powers in the same department consists in giving to those who administer each department the necessary constitutional means and personal motives to resist encroachments of the others. The provision for defense must in this, as in all other cases, be made commensurate to the danger of attack." Federalist No. 51. Madison continued:

> But it is not possible to give to each department an equal power of self-defense. In republican government, the legislative authority necessarily predominates. The remedy for this inconveniency is to divide the legislature into different branches; and to render them, by different modes of election and different principles of action, as little connected with each other as the nature of their common functions and their common dependence on the society will admit. . . . As the weight of the legislative authority requires that it should be thus divided, the weakness of the executive may require, on the other hand, that it should be fortified.

The major "fortification" provided, of course, was the veto power. But in addition to providing fortification, the Founders conspicuously and very consciously declined to sap the Executive's strength in the same way they had weakened the Legislature: by dividing the executive power. Proposals to have multiple executives, or a council of advisers with separate authority were rejected. Thus, while "[a]ll legislative Powers herein granted shall be vested in a Congress of the United States, which shall consist of a Senate *and* House of Representatives," U.S. Const., Art. I, § 1 (emphasis added), "[t]he executive Power shall be vested in *a President of the United States*," Art. II, § 1, cl. 1 (emphasis added).

That is what this suit is about. Power. The allocation of power among Congress, the President, and the courts in such fashion as to preserve the equilibrium the Constitution sought to establish—so that "a gradual concentration of the several powers in the same department," Federalist No. 51 (Madison), can effectively be resisted. Frequently an issue of this sort will come before the Court clad, so to speak, in sheep's clothing: the potential of the asserted principle to effect important change in the equilibrium of power is not immediately evident, and must be discerned by a careful and perceptive analysis. But this wolf comes as a wolf.

I

. . . The Court devotes most of its attention to such relatively technical details as the Appointments Clause and the removal power, addressing briefly and only at the end of its opinion the separation of powers. As my prologue suggests, I think that has it backwards. Our opinions are full of the recognition that it is the principle of separation of powers, and the inseparable corollary that each department's "defense must . . . be made commensurate to the danger of attack," Federalist No. 51 (J. Madison), which gives comprehensible content to . . . and determines the appropriate scope of the removal power. Thus, while I will subsequently discuss why our appointments and removal jurisprudence does not support today's holding, I begin with a consideration of the fountainhead of that jurisprudence, the separation and equilibration of powers. . . .

Article II, § 1, cl. 1, of the Constitution provides:

The executive Power shall be vested in a President of the United States.

As I described at the outset of this opinion, this does not mean *some of* the executive power, but *all of* the executive power. It seems to me, therefore, that the decision of the Court of Appeals invalidating the present statute must be upheld on fundamental separation-of-powers principles if the following two questions are answered affirmatively: (1) Is the conduct of a criminal prosecution (and of an investigation to decide whether to prosecute) the exercise of purely executive power? (2) Does the statute deprive the President of the United States of exclusive control over the exercise of that power? Surprising to say, the Court appears to concede an affirmative answer to both questions, but seeks to avoid the inevitable conclusion that since the statute vests some purely executive power in a person who is not the President of the United States it is void.

The Court concedes that "[t]here is no real dispute that the functions performed by the independent counsel are 'executive,' " though it qualifies that concession by adding "in the sense that they are law enforcement functions that typically have been undertaken by officials within the Executive Branch." The qualifier adds nothing but atmosphere. In what *other* sense can one identify "the executive Power" that is supposed to be vested in the President (unless it includes everything the Executive Branch is given to do) *except* by reference to what has always and everywhere—if conducted by government at all—been conducted never by the legislature, never by the courts, and always by the executive. There is no possible doubt that the independent counsel's functions fit this description. She is vested with the "full power and independent authority to exercise all *investigative and prosecutorial* functions and powers of the Department of Justice [and] the Attorney General." Governmental investigation and prosecution of crimes is a quintessentially executive function.

As for the second question, whether the statute before us deprives the President of exclusive control over that quintessentially executive activity: The Court does not, and could not possibly, assert that it does not. That is indeed the whole object of the statute. Instead, the Court points out that the President, through his Attorney General, has at least *some* control. That concession is alone enough to invalidate the statute, but I cannot refrain from pointing out that the Court greatly exaggerates the extent of that "some" Presidential control. "Most importan[t]" among these controls, the Court asserts, is the Attorney General's "power to remove the counsel for good cause." This is somewhat like referring to shackles as an effective means of locomotion. As we recognized in *Humphrey's Executor v. United States*—indeed, what *Humphrey's Executor* was all about—limiting removal power to "good cause" is an impediment to, not an effective grant of, Presidential control. . . . What we in *Humphrey's Executor* found to be a means of eliminating Presidential control, the Court today considers the "most importan[t]" means of assuring Presidential control. Congress, of course, operated under no such illusion when it enacted this statute, describing the "good cause" limitation as "protecting the independent counsel's ability to act independently of the President's direct control" since it permits removal only for "misconduct."

Moving on to the presumably "less important" controls that the President retains, the Court notes that no independent counsel may be appointed without a specific request from the Attorney General. . . . [T]he condition that renders such a request mandatory (inability to find "no reasonable grounds to believe" that further investigation is warranted) is so insubstantial that the Attorney General's discretion is severely confined. And once the referral is made, it is for the Special Division to determine the scope and duration of the investigation. And in any event, the limited power over referral is irrelevant to the question whether, *once appointed,* the independent counsel exercises executive power free from the President's control. Finally, the Court points out that the Act directs the independent counsel to abide by general Justice Department policy, except when not "possible." The exception alone shows this to be an empty promise. Even without that, however, one would be hard put to come up with many investigative or prosecutorial "policies" (other than those imposed by the Constitution or by Congress through law) that are absolute. Almost all investigative and prosecutorial decisions including the ultimate decision whether, after a technical violation of the law has been found, prosecution is warranted—involve the balancing of innumerable legal and practical considerations. Indeed, even political considerations (in the nonpartisan sense) must be considered, as exemplified by the recent decision of an independent counsel to subpoena the former Ambassador of Canada, producing considerable tension in our relations with that country. Another pre-eminently political decision is whether getting a conviction in a particular case is worth the disclosure of national security information that would be necessary. The Justice Department and our intelligence agencies are often in disagreement on this point, and the Justice Department does not always win. The present Act even goes so far as specifically to take the resolution of that dispute away from the President and give it to the independent counsel. In sum, the balancing of various legal, practical, and political considerations, none of which is absolute, is the very essence of prosecutorial discretion. To take this away is to remove the core of the prosecutorial function, and not merely "some" Presidential control.

As I have said, however, it is ultimately irrelevant *how much* the statute reduces Presidential control. The case is over when the Court acknowledges, as it must, that "[i]t is undeniable that the Act reduces the amount of control or supervision that the Attorney General and, through him, the President exercises over the investigation and prosecution of a certain class of alleged criminal activity." It effects a revolution in our constitutional jurisprudence for the Court, once it has determined that (1) purely executive functions are at issue here, and (2) those functions have been given to a person whose actions are not fully within the supervision and control of the President, nonetheless to proceed further to sit in judgment of whether "the President's need to control the exercise of [the independent counsel's] discretion is *so central* to the functioning of the Executive Branch" as to require complete control (emphasis added), whether the conferral of his powers upon someone else "*sufficiently* deprives the President of control over the independent counsel to interfere impermissibly with [his] constitutional obligation to ensure the faithful execution of the laws," (emphasis added), and whether "the Act give[s] the Executive Branch *sufficient* control over the independent counsel to ensure that the President is able to perform his constitutionally assigned duties" (emphasis added). It is not for us to determine, and we have never presumed to determine, how much of the purely executive powers of government must be within the full control of the President. The Constitution prescribes that they *all* are. . . .

Is it unthinkable that the President should have such exclusive power, even when alleged crimes by him or his close associates are at issue? No more so than that Congress should have the exclusive power of legislation, even when what is at issue is its own exemption from the burdens of certain laws. See Civil Rights Act of 1964, Title VII, 42 U.S.C. § 2000e et seq. (prohibiting "employers," not defined to include the United States, from discriminating on the basis of race, color, religion, sex, or national origin). No more so than that this Court should have the exclusive power to pronounce the final decision on justiciable cases and controversies, even those pertaining to the constitutionality of a statute reducing the salaries of the Justices. A system of separate and coordinate powers necessarily involves an acceptance of exclusive power that can theoretically be abused. . . . The checks against any branch's abuse of its exclusive powers are twofold: First, retaliation by one of the other branch's use of *its* exclusive powers: Congress, for example, can impeach the executive who willfully fails to enforce the laws; the executive can decline to prosecute under unconstitutional statutes, *cf. United States v. Lovett*, 328 U.S. 303 (1946); and the courts can dismiss malicious prosecutions. Second, and ultimately, there is the political check that the people will replace those in the political branches (the branches more "dangerous to the political rights of the Constitution," Federalist No. 78) who are guilty of abuse. Political pressures produced special prosecutors— for Teapot Dome and for Watergate, for example—long before this statute created the independent counsel.

The Court has, nonetheless, replaced the clear constitutional prescription that the executive power belongs to the President with a "balancing test." What are the standards to determine how the balance is to be struck, that is, how much removal of Presidential power is too much? Many countries of the world get along with an executive that is much weaker than ours—in fact, entirely dependent upon the continued support of the legislature. Once we depart from the text of the Constitution, just where short of that do we stop? The most amazing feature of the Court's opinion is that it does not even purport to give an answer. It simply *announces,* with no analysis, that the ability to control the decision whether to investigate and prosecute the President's closest advisers, and indeed the President himself, is not "so central to the functioning of the Executive Branch" as to be constitutionally required to be within the President's control. Apparently that is so because we say it is so. Having abandoned as the basis for our decision-making the text of Article II that "the executive Power" must be vested in the President, the Court does not even attempt to craft a *substitute* criterion—a "justiciable standard," *see, e.g., Baker v. Carr*, 369 U.S. 186, 210 (1962), however remote from the Constitution—that today governs, and in the future will govern, the decision of such questions. Evidently, the governing standard is to be what might be called the unfettered wisdom of a majority of this Court, revealed to an obedient people on a case-by-case basis. This is not only not the government of laws that the Constitution established; it is not a government of laws at all.

In my view, moreover, even as an ad hoc, standardless judgment the Court's conclusion must be wrong. Before this statute was passed, the President, in taking action disagreeable to the Congress, or an executive officer giving advice to the

President or testifying before Congress concerning one of those many matters on which the two branches are from time to time at odds, could be assured that his acts and motives would be adjudged—insofar as the decision whether to conduct a criminal investigation and to prosecute is concerned—in the Executive Branch, that is, in a forum attuned to the interests and the policies of the Presidency. That was one of the natural advantages the Constitution gave to the Presidency, just as it gave Members of Congress (and their staffs) the advantage of not being prosecutable for anything said or done in their legislative capacities. See U.S. Const., Art. I, § 6, cl. 1; *Gravel v. United States,* 408 U.S. 606 (1972). It is the very object of this legislation to eliminate that assurance of a sympathetic forum. Unless it can honestly be said that there are "no reasonable grounds to believe" that further investigation is warranted, further investigation must ensue; and the conduct of the investigation, and determination of whether to prosecute, will be given to a person neither selected by nor subject to the control of the President—who will in turn assemble a staff by finding out, presumably, who is willing to put aside whatever else they are doing, for an indeterminate period of time, in order to investigate and prosecute the President or a particular named individual in his administration. The prospect is frightening . . . even outside the context of a bitter, interbranch political dispute. Perhaps the boldness of the President himself will not be affected—though I am not even sure of that. (How much easier it is for Congress, instead of accepting the political damage attendant to the commencement of impeachment proceedings against the President on trivial grounds—or, for that matter, how easy it is for one of the President's political foes outside of Congress—simply to trigger a debilitating criminal investigation of the Chief Executive under this law.) But as for the President's high-level assistants, who typically have no political base of support, it is as utterly unrealistic to think that they will not be intimidated by this prospect, and that their advice to him and their advocacy of his interests before a hostile Congress will not be affected, as it would be to think that the Members of Congress and their staffs would be unaffected by replacing the Speech or Debate Clause with a similar provision. It deeply wounds the President, by substantially reducing the President's ability to protect himself and his staff. That is the whole object of the law, of course, and I cannot imagine why the Court believes it does not succeed.

Besides weakening the Presidency by reducing the zeal of his staff, it must also be obvious that the institution of the independent counsel enfeebles him more directly in his constant confrontations with Congress, by eroding his public support. Nothing is so politically effective as the ability to charge that one's opponent and his associates are not merely wrongheaded, naive, ineffective, but, in all probability, "crooks." And nothing so effectively gives an appearance of validity to such charges as a Justice Department investigation and, even better, prosecution. The present statute provides ample means for that sort of attack, assuring that massive and lengthy investigations will occur, not merely when the Justice Department in the application of its usual standards believes they are called for, but whenever it cannot be said that there are "no reasonable grounds to believe" they are called for. The statute's highly visible procedures assure, moreover, that unlike most investigations these will be widely known and prominently displayed. Thus, in the 10 years since the institution of the independent counsel was established by law, there have been nine highly publicized investigations, a source of constant political damage to two administrations. That they could not remotely be described as merely the application of "normal" investigatory and prosecutory standards is demonstrated by, in addition to the language of the statute ("no reasonable grounds to believe"), the following facts: Congress appropriates approximately $50 million annually for general legal activities, salaries, and expenses of the Criminal Division of the Department of Justice. This money is used to support "[f]ederal appellate activity," "[o]rganized crime prosecution," "[p]ublic integrity" and "[f]raud" matters, "[n]arcotic & dangerous drug prosecution," "[i]nternal security," "[g]eneral litigation and legal advice," "special investigations," "[p]rosecution support," "[o]rganized crime drug enforcement," and "[m]anagement & administration." *Id.,* at 284. By comparison, between May 1986 and August 1987, four independent counsel (not all of whom were operating for that entire period of time) spent almost $5 million (1/10th of the amount annually appropriated to the entire Criminal Division), spending almost $1 million in the month of August 1987 alone. For fiscal year 1989, the Department of Justice has requested $52 million for the entire Criminal Division, DOJ Budget Request 285, and $7 million to support the activities of independent counsel, *id.,* at 25.

In sum, this statute does deprive the President of substantial control over the prosecutory functions performed by the independent counsel, and it does substantially affect the balance of powers. That the Court could possibly conclude otherwise demonstrates both the wisdom of our former constitutional system, in which the degree of reduced control and political impairment were irrelevant, since *all* purely executive power had to be in the President; and the folly of the new system of standardless judicial allocation of powers we adopt today.

III

As I indicated earlier, the basic separation-of-powers principles I have discussed are what give life and content to our jurisprudence concerning the President's power to appoint and remove officers. The same result of unconstitutionality is therefore plainly indicated by our case law in these areas. . . .

Because appellant (who all parties and the Court agree is an officer of the United States) was not appointed by the President with the advice and consent of the Senate, but rather by the Special Division of the United States Court of Appeals, her appointment is constitutional only if (1) she is an "inferior" officer within the meaning of the above Clause, and (2) Congress may vest her appointment in a court of law.

As to the first of these inquiries, the Court does not attempt to "decide exactly" what establishes the line between principal and "inferior" officers, but is confident that, whatever the line may be, appellant "clearly falls on the 'inferior officer' side" of it. The Court gives three reasons: *First,* she "is subject to removal by a higher Executive Branch official," namely, the Attorney General. *Second,* she is "empowered by the Act to perform only certain, limited duties." *Third,* her office is "limited in jurisdiction" and "limited in tenure."

The first of these lends no support to the view that appellant is an inferior officer. Appellant is removable only for "good cause" or physical or mental incapacity. By contrast, most (if not all) *principal* officers in the Executive Branch may be removed by the President *at will.* I fail to see how the fact that appellant is more difficult to remove than most principal officers helps to establish that she is an inferior officer. And I do not see how it could possibly make any difference to her superior or inferior status that the President's limited power to remove her must be exercised through the Attorney General. If she were removable at will by the

Attorney General, then she would be subordinate to him and thus properly designated as inferior; but the Court essentially admits that she is not subordinate. If it were common usage to refer to someone as "inferior" who is subject to removal for cause by another, then one would say that the President is "inferior" to Congress.

The second reason offered by the Court—that appellant performs only certain, limited duties—may be relevant to whether she is an inferior officer, but it mischaracterizes the extent of her powers. As the Court states: "Admittedly, the Act delegates to appellant [the] *'full power and independent authority to exercise all investigative and prosecutorial functions and powers of the Department of Justice'* (emphasis added)." Moreover, in addition to this general grant of power she is given a broad range of specifically enumerated powers, including a power not even the Attorney General possesses: to "contes[t] in court . . . any claim of privilege or attempt to withhold evidence on grounds of national security." Once all of this is "admitted," it seems to me impossible to maintain that appellant's authority is so "limited" as to render her an inferior officer. The Court seeks to brush this away by asserting that the independent counsel's power does not include any authority to "formulate policy for the Government or the Executive Branch." But the same could be said for all officers of the Government, with the single exception of the President. All of them only formulate policy within their respective spheres of responsibility— as does the independent counsel, who must comply with the policies of the Department of Justice only to the extent possible.

The final set of reasons given by the Court for why the independent counsel clearly is an inferior officer emphasizes the limited nature of her jurisdiction and tenure. Taking the latter first, I find nothing unusually limited about the independent counsel's tenure. To the contrary, unlike most high-ranking Executive Branch officials, she continues to serve until she (or the Special Division) decides that her work is substantially completed. This particular independent prosecutor has already served more than two years, which is at least as long as many Cabinet officials. As to the scope of her jurisdiction, there can be no doubt that is small (though far from unimportant). But within it she exercises more than the full power of the Attorney General. The Ambassador to Luxembourg is not anything less than a principal officer, simply because Luxembourg is small. And the federal judge who sits in a small district is not for that reason "inferior in rank and authority." If the mere fragmentation of executive responsibilities into small compartments suffices to render the heads of each of those compartments inferior officers, then Congress could deprive the President of the right to appoint his chief law enforcement officer by dividing up the Attorney General's responsibilities among a number of "lesser" functionaries.

. . . I think it preferable to look to the text of the Constitution and the division of power that it establishes. These demonstrate, I think, that the independent counsel is not an inferior officer because she is not *subordinate* to any officer in the Executive Branch (indeed, not even to the President). Dictionaries in use at the time of the Constitutional Convention gave the word "inferiour" two meanings which it still bears today: (1) "[l]ower in place, . . . station, . . . rank of life, . . . value or excellency," and (2) "[s]ubordinate." Samuel Johnson, Dictionary of the English Language (6th ed. 1785). In a document dealing with the structure (the constitution) of a government, one would naturally expect the word to bear the latter meaning— indeed, in such a context it would be unpardonably careless to use the word *unless* a relationship of subordination was intended. If what was meant was merely "lower in station or rank," one would use instead a term such as "lesser officers." At the only other point in the Constitution at which the word "inferior" appears, it plainly connotes a relationship of subordination. Article III vests the judicial power of the United States in "one supreme Court, and in such *inferior* Courts as the Congress may from time to time ordain and establish." U.S. Const., Art. III, § 1 (emphasis added). In Federalist No. 81, Hamilton pauses to describe the "inferior" courts authorized by Article III as inferior in the sense that they are "subordinate" to the Supreme Court.

That "inferior" means "subordinate" is also consistent with what little we know about the evolution of the Appointments Clause. *[Justice Scalia then discusses the drafting history of the Appointments Clause as well as "our admittedly sketchy precedent in this area."—Editors]*

To be sure, it is not a *sufficient* condition for "inferior" officer status that one be subordinate to a principal officer. Even an officer who is subordinate to a department head can be a principal officer. . . . But it is surely a *necessary* condition for inferior officer status that the officer be subordinate to another officer.

The independent counsel is not even subordinate to the President. The Court essentially admits as much, noting that "appellant may not be 'subordinate' to the Attorney General (and the President) insofar as she possesses a degree of independent discretion to exercise the powers delegated to her under the Act." In fact, there is no doubt about it. As noted earlier, the Act specifically grants her the "*full* power and *independent* authority to exercise *all* investigative and prosecutorial functions of the Department of Justice," and makes her removable only for "good cause," a limitation specifically intended to ensure that she be *independent* of, not *subordinate* to, the President and the Attorney General.

Because appellant is not subordinate to another officer, she is not an "inferior" officer and her appointment other than by the President with the advice and consent of the Senate is unconstitutional.

IV

I will not discuss at any length why the restrictions upon the removal of the independent counsel also violate our established precedent dealing with that specific subject. For most of it, I simply refer the reader to the scholarly opinion of Judge Silberman for the Court of Appeals below. *See In re Sealed Case,* 838 F.2d 476 (D.C. Cir. 1988). I cannot avoid commenting, however, about the essence of what the Court has done to our removal jurisprudence today.

There is, of course, no provision in the Constitution stating who may remove executive officers, except the provisions for removal by impeachment. Before the present decision it was established, however, . . . that the President's power to remove principal officers who exercise purely executive powers could not be restricted, see *Myers,* at 127. . . .

Since our 1935 decision in *Humphrey's Executor*—which was considered by many at the time the product of an activist, anti-New Deal Court bent on reducing the power of President Franklin Roosevelt—it has been established that the line of permissible restriction upon removal of principal officers lies at the point at which the powers exercised by those officers are no longer purely executive. Thus, removal restrictions have been generally regarded as lawful for so-called "independent regulatory agencies," such as the Federal Trade Commission, the Interstate Commerce Commission, and the Consumer Product Safety Commission, which engage substantially in what has been called the "quasi-legislative activity" of rulemaking, and for members of Article I courts, such as the Court of Military Appeals, who engage in the "quasi-judicial" function of adjudication. It has often been observed, correctly in my view, that the line between "purely executive" functions and "quasi-legislative" or "quasi-judicial" functions is not a clear one or even a rational one. But at least it permitted the identification of certain officers, and certain agencies, whose functions were entirely within the control of the President. Congress had to be aware of that restriction in its legislation. Today, however, *Humphrey's Executor* is swept into the dustbin of repudiated constitutional principles. . . .

One can hardly grieve for the shoddy treatment given today to *Humphrey's Executor,* which, after all, accorded the same indignity (with much less justification) to Chief Justice Taft's opinion 10 years earlier in *Myers*—gutting, in six quick pages devoid of textual or historical precedent for the novel principle it set forth, a carefully researched and reasoned 70-page opinion. It is in fact comforting to witness the reality that he who lives by the *ipse dixit* dies by the *ipse dixit.* But one must grieve for the Constitution. *Humphrey's Executor* at least had the decency formally to observe the constitutional principle that the President had to be the repository of *all* executive power, see 295 U.S., at 627–628, which, as *Myers* carefully explained, necessarily means that he must be able to discharge those who do not perform executive functions according to his liking. . . . By contrast, "our present considered view" is simply that *any* executive officer's removal can be restricted, so long as the President remains "able to accomplish his constitutional role." . . . There are now no lines. If the removal of a prosecutor, the virtual embodiment of the power to "take care that the laws be faithfully executed," can be restricted, what officer's removal cannot? This is an open invitation for Congress to experiment. What about a special Assistant Secretary of State, with responsibility for one very narrow area of foreign policy, who would not only have to be confirmed by the Senate but could also be removed only pursuant to certain carefully designed restrictions? Could this possibly render the President "[un]able to accomplish his constitutional role"? Or a special Assistant Secretary of Defense for Procurement? The possibilities are endless, and the Court does not understand what the separation of powers, what "[a]mbition . . . counteract [ing] ambition," Federalist No. 51 (Madison), is all about, if it does not expect Congress to try them. As far as I can discern from the Court's opinion, it is now open season upon the President's removal power for all executive officers, with not even the superficially principled restriction of *Humphrey's Executor* as cover. The Court essentially says to the President: "Trust us. We will make sure that you are able to accomplish your constitutional role." I think the Constitution gives the President—and the people—more protection than that.

V

The purpose of the separation and equilibration of powers in general, and of the unitary Executive in particular, was not merely to assure effective government but to preserve individual freedom. Those who hold or have held offices covered by the Ethics in Government Act are entitled to that protection as much as the rest of us, and I conclude my discussion by considering the effect of the Act upon the fairness of the process they receive. . . .

Under our system of government, the primary check against prosecutorial abuse is a political one. The prosecutors who exercise this awesome discretion are selected and can be removed by a President, whom the people have trusted enough to elect. Moreover, when crimes are not investigated and prosecuted fairly, nonselectively, with a reasonable sense of proportion, the President pays the cost in political damage to his administration. If federal prosecutors "pick people that [they] thin[k] [they] should get, rather than cases that need to be prosecuted," if they amass many more resources against a particular prominent individual, or against a particular class of political protesters, or against members of a particular political party, than the gravity of the alleged offenses or the record of successful prosecutions seems to warrant, the unfairness will come home to roost in the Oval Office. . . .

That is the system of justice the rest of us are entitled to, but what of that select class consisting of present or former high-level Executive Branch officials? . . . An independent counsel is selected, and the scope of his or her authority prescribed, by a panel of judges. What if they are politically partisan, as judges have been known to be, and select a prosecutor antagonistic to the administration, or even to the particular individual who has been selected for this special treatment? There is no remedy for that, not even a political one. Judges, after all, have life tenure, and appointing a surefire enthusiastic prosecutor could hardly be considered an impeachable offense. So if there is anything wrong with the selection, there is effectively no one to blame. The independent counsel thus selected proceeds to assemble a staff. As I observed earlier, in the nature of things this has to be done by finding lawyers who are willing to lay aside their current careers for an indeterminate amount of time, to take on a job that has no prospect of permanence and little prospect for promotion. One thing is certain, however: it involves investigating and perhaps prosecuting a particular individual. Can one imagine a less equitable manner of fulfilling the executive responsibility to investigate and prosecute? What would be the reaction if, in an area not covered by this statute, the Justice Department posted a public notice inviting applicants to assist in an investigation and possible prosecution of a certain prominent person? . . . [And] even if it were entirely evident that unfairness was in fact the result—the judges hostile to the administration, the independent counsel an old foe of the President, the staff refugees from the recently defeated administration—*there would be no one accountable to the public to whom the blame could be assigned.* . . .

[A]n additional advantage of the unitary Executive [is] that it can achieve a more uniform application of the law. Perhaps that is not always achieved, but the mechanism to achieve it is there. The mini-Executive that is the independent counsel, however, operating in an area where so little is law and so much is discretion, is intentionally cut off from the unifying influence of the Justice Department, and from the perspective that multiple responsibilities provide. What would normally be regarded as a technical violation (there are no rules defining such things), may in his or her small world assume the proportions of an indictable offense. What would normally be regarded as an investigation that has reached the level of pursuing such picayune matters that it should be concluded, may to him or her be an investigation that ought to go on for another year. How frightening it must be to have your own independent counsel and staff appointed, with nothing else to do but to investigate you until investigation is no longer worthwhile—with whether it is worthwhile not depending upon what such judgments usually hinge on, competing responsibilities. And to have that counsel and staff decide, with no basis for comparison, whether what you have done is bad enough, willful enough, and provable enough, to warrant an indictment. How admirable the constitutional system that provides the means to avoid such a distortion. And how unfortunate the judicial decision that has permitted it. . . .

The notion that every violation of law should be prosecuted, including—indeed, *especially*—every violation by those in high places, is an attractive one, and it would be risky to argue in an election campaign that that is not an absolutely overriding value. *Fiat justitia, ruat coelum.* Let justice be done, though the heavens may fall. The reality is, however, that it is not an absolutely overriding value, and it was with the hope that we would be able to acknowledge and apply such realities that the Constitution spared us, by life tenure, the necessity of election campaigns. . . . By its shortsighted action today, I fear the Court has permanently encumbered the Republic with an institution that will do it great harm.

Worse than what it has done, however, is the manner in which it has done it. A government of laws means a government of rules. Today's decision on the basic issue of fragmentation of executive power is ungoverned by rule, and hence ungoverned by law. It extends into the very heart of our most significant constitutional function the "totality of the circumstances" mode of analysis that this Court has in recent years become fond of. Taking all things into account, we conclude that the power taken away from the President here is not really *too* much. The next time executive power is assigned to someone other than the President we may conclude, taking all things into account, that it *is* too much. That opinion, like this one, will not be confined by any rule. We will describe, as we have today (though I hope more accurately) the effects of the provision in question, and will authoritatively announce: "The President's need to control the exercise of the [subject officer's] discretion is so central to the functioning of the Executive Branch as to require complete control." This is not analysis; it is ad hoc judgment. And it fails to explain why it is not true that—as the text of the Constitution seems to require, as the Founders seemed to expect, and as our past cases have uniformly assumed—all purely executive power must be under the control of the President.

The ad hoc approach to constitutional adjudication has real attraction, even apart from its work-saving potential. It is guaranteed to produce a result, in every case, that will make a majority of the Court happy with the law. The law is, by definition, precisely what the majority thinks, taking all things into account, it *ought* to be. I prefer to rely upon the judgment of the wise men who constructed our system, and of the people who approved it, and of two centuries of history that have shown it to be sound. Like it or not, that judgment says, quite plainly, that "[t]he executive Power shall be vested in a President of the United States."

■ JUSTICE KENNEDY took no part in the consideration or decision of this case.

NOTES

1.   The majority and the dissent here disagree about a lot—among other things, they disagree about how to even frame the question. The majority starts with specific textual provisions and then finishes with a (cursory?) discussion of the structural principles of separation of powers. Justice Scalia starts by emphasizing the structural principles. Does the framing affect the outcome? Which framing is better? Forest or trees?

2.   Aside from authorizing an independent counsel, does Congress have other options for addressing executive branch malfeasance? What about the impeachment power? Even though two presidents and over a dozen federal judges have been impeached, none of the various cabinet officers who have eventually been convicted of felonies committed while they were in office were ever impeached. Why not? Are the barriers legal? Practical? Political?

3.   In Justice Scalia's dissent on the appointments clause issue, he says "it not a sufficient condition for 'inferior' officer status that one be subordinate to a principal officer." But he also relies on a founding-era dictionary that defines "inferior" as meaning "subordinate." Are his two arguments inconsistent? Does Justice Scalia have a clear rule for the definition of *inferior*?

4.   There have been two important legal developments since *Morrison*.

a.   One development has been about the definition of "inferior officer" under the Appointments Clause. In *Edmond v. United States,* 520 U.S. 651 (1997), the Court considered whether Congress had authorized the secretary of transportation to appoint civilian members of the Coast Guard Court of Criminal Appeals; and if so, whether this authorization was constitutional under the Appointments Clause. The Appointments Clause question turned on whether the judges were inferior officers. Justice Scalia wrote the majority opinion in *Edmond* and set forth the following test:

> Generally speaking, the term "inferior officer" connotes a relationship with some higher ranking officer or officers below the President: Whether one is an "inferior" officer depends on whether he has a superior. It is not enough that other officers may be identified who formally maintain a higher rank, or possess responsibilities of a greater magnitude. If that were the intention, the Constitution might have used the phrase "lesser officer." Rather, in the context of a Clause designed to preserve political accountability relative to important Government assignments, we think it evident that "inferior officers" are officers whose work is directed and supervised at some level by others who were appointed by Presidential nomination with the advice and consent of the Senate.

Applying that test, the Court held that the judicial appointments were valid. The work of the judges on the Court of Criminal Appeals is supervised by the judge advocate general (who is subordinate to the secretary of transportation) as well as the Court of the Appeals for the Armed Forces. Although seven justices joined Justice Scalia's opinion in *Edmond,* Justice Souter wrote separately, saying: "Because the term 'inferior officer' implies an official superior, one who has no superior is not an inferior officer. . . . It does not follow, however, that if one is subject to some supervision and control, one is an inferior officer. Having a superior officer is necessary for inferior officer status, but not sufficient to establish it." Justice Souter was unwilling to join Justice Scalia in saying that an officer with tremendous power would be an inferior officer so long as he or she had a supervisor. *Edmond* did not overrule *Morrison*. Are there now two tests for determining whether someone is an inferior officer—*Morrison*'s test of importance, and *Edmond*'s test of supervision and control?

b.   The most recent major case on the removal power is *Free Enterprise Fund v. Public Co. Accounting Oversight Bd.,* 561 U.S. 477 (2010), in which the Court considered the constitutionality of the removal limitation in the statute establishing the Public Company Accounting Oversight Board. The PCAOB was created in the wake of accounting scandals at major public companies such as Enron and WorldCom. Its board was subject to two layers of protection against presidential removal: the Securities and

Exchange Commission is an independent agency whose commissioners can be removed by the president only for cause; the members of the PCAOB could be removed by the Securities and Exchange Commission, again only for cause. Writing for the majority, Chief Justice Roberts summed up the Court's jurisprudence on the removal power this way. *Myers* states the principle that the president may remove executive branch officers, but *Humphrey's Executor* and *Morrison* limit this principle: *Humphrey's Executor* by allowing Congress to create independent agencies with principal officers the president can remove only for cause, and *Morrison* by allowing Congress to restrict the power of principal officers to remove *their* subordinates. The question in *Free Enterprise Fund*, Chief Justice Roberts said, was whether the "separate layers of protection" in *Humphrey's Executor* and *Morrison* "may be combined." In other words, "[m]ay the President be restricted in his ability to remove a principal officer, who is in turn restricted in his ability to remove an inferior officer, even though that inferior officer determines the policy and enforces the laws of the United States?" The Court held that this kind of double-layer insulation from removal violated Article II's assignment to the president of the executive power, because it could prevent the president from "tak[ing] Care that the Laws be faithfully executed." The Court severed the for-cause removal provision from the rest of the statute, leaving the PCAOB in place (and not invalidating all of its earlier acts). Although the Court chose not to extend *Humphrey's Executor* and *Morrison*, it did not reconsider them (noting pointedly that it had not been asked to by the parties).

Writing in dissent for himself and three other justices, Justice Breyer emphasized that both the president and Congress wanted the PCAOB structured in this way. And he argued that the double-layer insulation was not in practical effect any more of a limitation on presidential powers than a single layer of insulation from removal. Like the majority in *Morrison*, the dissenting justices in *PCAOB* were convinced that Congress had not limited presidential removal power in order to aggrandize its own power—and in their view only self-aggrandizing congressional restrictions on presidential removal were unconstitutional. Does double-layer insulation from presidential removal seem any different to you, as a constitutional matter, than single-layer insulation? How should the Court decide a question like that? Which of the types of constitutional argument are most useful? Does it matter whether the limitation on presidential removal is an aggrandizement of congressional power? Is *every* decrease in presidential power over an agency automatically an increase in congressional power over the same agency? And what does this line of cases—*Myers, Humphrey's Executor, Morrison*, and *Free Enterprise Fund*—suggest about the constitutional status of political accountability? Under the Constitution, must every government official be subject to control by an elected representative of the people? If so, how tight must this control be? Is this kind of accountability to the people always a good thing? If it can be a bad thing, is it a necessary evil?

5.   The Supreme Court may have upheld the Ethics in Government Act, but it did not have the last word. During President Bill Clinton's administration, Kenneth Starr was appointed by the three-judge special court to investigate the Whitewater investment scandal. Starr's investigation expanded to cover more and more allegations, including that officials in the White House travel office were illegally fired and even that a deputy White House counsel who committed suicide had in fact been murdered. Starr continuously expanded his investigation. Eventually, the investigation collided with a lawsuit brought against President Clinton by Paula Jones, who alleged that he had sexually harassed her when he was governor of Arkansas. In a deposition in that civil suit, President Clinton denied that he had ever had sexual relations with White House intern Monica Lewinsky. Starr concluded that the president had committed perjury and obstruction of justice. President Clinton was impeached by the Republican majority in

the House of Representatives, but he was overwhelmingly acquitted by the Senate. The EIGA came up for renewal a year later, and by this point Republicans and Democrats alike were willing to let it expire, on both policy and constitutional grounds.

Does this episode suggest that *Morrison* was wrongly decided? Or that it was right to leave the issue to the political branches?

[Assignment 14]

E. FOREIGN AFFAIRS: "HE SHALL RECEIVE AMBASSADORS"

Art. II, § 2: The President shall be Commander in Chief of the Army and Navy of the United States, and of the Militia of the several States, when called into the actual Service of the United States. . . . He shall have Power, by and with the Advice and Consent of the Senate, to make Treaties, provided two thirds of the Senators present concur; and he shall nominate, and by and with the Advice and Consent of the Senate, shall appoint Ambassadors, other public Ministers and Consuls, Judges of the supreme Court, and all other Officers of the United States, whose Appointments are not herein otherwise provided for. . . .

§ 3: . . . he shall receive Ambassadors and other public Ministers. . . .

Where does the Constitution allocate federal power over foreign affairs? As discussed at p. 177, in England, most foreign affairs powers were part of the king's "prerogative powers." Under the United States Constitution, some of those prerogative powers are given to Congress while others remain with the executive.

Article I vests important powers related to foreign affairs in Congress, which is given the powers "to declare war," to "define and punish Piracies" and "Offences against the Law of Nations," to "regulate commerce with foreign Nations," and to "establish an uniform Rule of Naturalization." Indeed, fully one-third of Congress's enumerated powers involve foreign affairs in some respect. In addition, the Senate is given a significant role in treaty-making.

Article II begins with the Vesting Clause's grant of "the executive Power" to the president. Then Sections 2 and 3 mention specific presidential foreign relations powers: the power to make treaties (with the Senate); the power of being the commander in chief of the nation's armed forces; the power to appoint ambassadors; and the duty to receive ambassadors and other public ministers.

But who has the remaining foreign affairs powers that are not specified? Do they inhere in the general grant of "the executive Power" to the president? (On that view, the foreign-affairs-related powers given to Congress would be exceptions, or carve-outs, from the general power given to the executive.) Or are unspecified foreign-affairs powers to be allocated between the legislative and executive branch by analogy to the powers that are specified? Or are the unspecified powers reserved to the states?

We postpone until the next assignments the perennial issues of the Constitution's allocation of war powers between Congress and the president. What follows here are two major controversies on the scope of and justification for the president's presumed constitutional foreign affairs power, one very old and one very new. The first is the Neutrality Controversy of 1793, which tested President Washington's power to respond to a crisis after the French Revolution. The second,

Zivotofsky v. Kerry, is a 2015 decision of the Supreme Court, decided 5–4, about a statute requiring the executive branch to allow those born in Jerusalem to have passports identifying them as having been born in "Israel." We conclude with a discussion of agreements made by the president without Senate ratification. The shared, enumerated power to make and enforce treaties will be addressed elsewhere, at p. 680.

The Neutrality Controversy

One of the first major tests of the Constitution's allocation of foreign affairs powers came in 1793, during the Washington administration. France and England were again at war with one another. During the American Revolution, France had come to the aid of the colonies. Benjamin Franklin had negotiated treaties of alliance and of commerce with France, and these had been absolutely critical to the colonists' victory. But then the French Revolution happened. Did those treaties with Royalist France now oblige the United States to join Republican France in its war against England? Or was neutrality permissible?

Americans divided sharply in their opinions about the French Revolution. Throughout the 1790s, the United States was sharply divided between pro-English elements (which became the "Federalist" party) and pro-French elements (which became Jefferson's "Democratic-Republican" party). President George Washington stood squarely between these factions. He faced an immediate legal and political dilemma: deciding whether the United States was bound by its treaty of alliance from the 1770s to give military aid to Revolutionary France. Washington thought that such action would be disastrous for America, which had little to add to France's power and much to lose by entangling itself in a European war.

After consulting his cabinet, President Washington settled on a policy of neutrality and issued a proclamation to that effect. The Neutrality Proclamation of 1793 went further than a mere declaration of neutrality, however, for Washington also claimed the power to prosecute Americans who violated the neutrality: "I have given instructions to those officers, to whom it belongs, to cause prosecutions to be instituted against all persons, who shall, within the cognizance of the courts of the United States, violate the law of nations, with respect to the Powers at war, or any of them."

The proclamation was challenged by some American defenders of France, such as Representative James Madison, as being beyond the president's power. Below are printed President Washington's proclamation, Alexander Hamilton's pseudonymous defense of it as "Pacificus," and James Madison's pseudonymous objections to it as "Helvidius." Also included is the Neutrality Act of 1794. The Neutrality Controversy raises fascinating questions of constitutional law concerning foreign affairs and executive power. These questions, and the answers ventured by the various parties involved, have proven to be of enduring importance to the life of the nation and they remain as much debated in the twenty-first century as they were in the eighteenth.

George Washington,
The Proclamation of Neutrality
Apr. 22, 1793

Whereas it appears that a state of war exists between Austria, Prussia, Sardinia, Great Britain, and the United Netherlands, on the one part, and France on the other; and the duty and interest of the United States require, that they should with sincerity and good faith adopt and pursue a conduct friendly and impartial toward the belligerent Powers;

I have therefore thought fit by these presents to declare the disposition of the United States to observe the conduct aforesaid towards those Powers respectfully; and to exhort and warn the citizens of the United States carefully to avoid all acts and proceedings whatsoever, which may in any manner tend to contravene such disposition.

And I do hereby also make known, that whatsoever of the citizens of the United States shall render himself liable to punishment or forfeiture under the law of nations, by committing, aiding, or abetting hostilities against any of the said Powers, or by carrying to any of them those articles which are deemed contraband by the modern usage of nations, will not receive the protection of the United States, against such punishment or forfeiture; and further, that I have given instructions to those officers, to whom it belongs, to cause prosecutions to be instituted against all persons, who shall, within the cognizance of the courts of the United States, violate the law of nations, with respect to the Powers at war, or any of them.

In testimony whereof, I have caused the seal of the United States of America to be affixed to these presents, and signed the same with my hand. Done at the city of Philadelphia, the twenty-second day of April, one thousand seven hundred and ninety-three, and of the Independence of the United States of America the seventeenth.

Pacificus, No. 1
Alexander Hamilton, June 29, 1793

... The objections which have been raised against the Proclamation of Neutrality lately issued by the President have been urged in a spirit of acrimony and invective, which demonstrates, that more was in view than merely a free discussion of an important public measure; that the discussion covers a design of weakening the confidence of the People in the author of the measure; in order to remove or lessen a powerful obstacle to the success of an opposition to the Government, which however it may change its form, according to circumstances, seems still to be adhered to and pursued with persevering Industry. ...

The objections in question fall under these heads—

1   That the Proclamation was without authority

2   That it was contrary to our treaties with France

3   That it was contrary to the gratitude, which is due from this to that country; for the succours rendered us in our own Revolution.

4   That it was out of time & unnecessary.

In order to judge of the solidity of the first of these objection[s], it is necessary to examine what is the nature and design of a proclamation of neutrality.

The true nature & design of such an act is—to *make known* to the powers at War and to the Citizens of the Country, whose Government does the Act that such country is in the condition of a Nation at Peace with the belligerent parties, and under no obligations of Treaty, to become an *associate in the war* with either of them; that this being its situation its intention is to observe a conduct conformable with it and to perform towards each the duties of neutrality; and as a consequence of this state of things, to give warning to all within its jurisdiction to abstain from acts that shall contravene those duties, under the penalties which the laws of the land (of which the law of Nations is a part) annexes to acts of contravention. . . .

It will not be disputed that the management of the affairs of this country with foreign nations is confided to the Government of the U[nited] States.

It can as little be disputed, that a Proclamation of Neutrality, where a Nation is at liberty to keep out of a War in which other Nations are engaged and means so to do, is a *usual* and a *proper* measure. *Its main object and effect are to prevent the Nation being immediately responsible for acts done by its citizens, without the privity or connivance of the Government, in contravention of the principles of neutrality.*

An object this of the greatest importance to a Country whose true interest lies in the preservation of peace.

The inquiry then is—what department of the Government of the U[nited] States is the proper one to make a declaration of Neutrality in the cases in which the engagements of the Nation permit and its interests require such a declaration.

A correct and well informed mind will discern at once that it can belong neither to the Legislative nor Judicial Department and of course must belong to the Executive.

The Legislative Department is not the *organ* of intercourse between the U[nited] States and foreign Nations. It is charged neither with *making* nor *interpreting* Treaties. It is therefore not naturally that Organ of the Government which is to pronounce the existing condition of the Nation, with regard to foreign Powers, or to admonish the Citizens of their obligations and duties as founded upon that condition of things. Still less is it charged with enforcing the execution and observance of these obligations and those duties.

It is equally obvious that the act in question is foreign to the Judiciary Department of the Government. The province of that Department is to decide litigations in particular cases. It is indeed charged with the interpretation of treaties; but it exercises this function only in the litigated cases; that is where contending parties bring before it a specific controversy. It has no concern with pronouncing upon the external political relations of Treaties between Government and Government. This position is too plain to need being insisted upon.

It must then of necessity belong to the Executive Department to exercise the function in Question—when a proper case for the exercise of it occurs.

It appears to be connected with that department in various capacities, as the *organ* of intercourse between the Nation and foreign Nations—as the interpreter of the National Treaties in those cases in which the Judiciary is not competent, that is in the cases between Government and Government—as that Power, which is charged with the Execution of the Laws, of which Treaties form a part—as that Power which is charged with the command and application of the Public Force.

This view of the subject is so natural and obvious—so analogous to general theory and practice—that no doubt can be entertained of its justness, unless such doubt can be deduced from particular provisions of the Constitution of the United States.

Let us see then if cause for such doubt is to be found in that constitution.

The second Article of the Constitution of the U[nited] States, section 1st, establishes this general Proposition, That "The Executive Power shall be vested in a President of the United States of America."

The same article in a succeeding Section proceeds to designate particular cases of Executive Power. It declares among other things that the President shall be Commander in Chief of the army and navy of the U[nited] States and of the Militia of the several states when called into the actual service of the U[nited] States, that he shall have power by and with the advice of the senate to make treaties; that it shall be his duty to receive ambassadors and other public Ministers and to take care that the laws be faithfully executed. . . .

The general doctrine then of our constitution is, that the Executive Power of the Nation is vested in the President; subject only to the *exceptions* and *qualifications* which are expressed in the instrument.

Two of these have been already noticed—the participation of the Senate in the appointment of Officers and the making of Treaties. A third remains to be mentioned the right of the Legislature "to declare war and grant letters of marque and reprisal."

With these exceptions the Executive Power of the Union is completely lodged in the President. This mode of construing the Constitution has indeed been recognized by Congress in formal acts, upon full consideration and debate. The power of removal from office is an important instance.

And since upon general principles for reasons already given, the issuing of a proclamation of neutrality is merely an Executive Act; since also the general Executive Power of the Union is vested in the President, the conclusion is, that the step, which has been taken by him, is liable to no just exception on the score of authority.

It may be observed that this Inference would be just if the power of declaring war had not been vested in the Legislature, but that this power naturally includes the right of judging whether the Nation is under obligations to make war or not.

The answer to this is, that however true it may be, that the right of the Legislature to declare war includes the right of judging whether the Nation be under obligations to make War or not—it will not follow that the Executive is in any case excluded from a similar right of Judgment, in the execution of its own functions.

If the Legislature have a right to make war on the one hand—it is on the other the duty of the Executive to preserve Peace till war is declared; and in fulfilling that duty, it must necessarily possess a right of judging what is the nature of the obligations which the treaties of the Country impose on the Government; and when in pursuance of this right it has concluded that there is nothing in them inconsistent with a *state* of neutrality, it becomes both its province and its duty to enforce the laws incident to that state of the Nation. The Executive is charged with the execution of all laws, the laws of Nations as well as the Municipal law, which recognises and adopts those laws. It is consequently bound, by faithfully executing the laws of neutrality, when that is the state of the Nation, to avoid giving a cause of war to foreign Powers. . . .

In this distribution of powers the wisdom of our constitution is manifested. It is the province and duty of the Executive to preserve to the Nation the blessings of peace. The Legislature alone can interrupt those blessings, by placing the Nation in a state of War. . . .

The President is the constitutional Executor of the laws. Our Treaties and the laws of Nations form a part of the law of the land. He who is to execute the laws must first judge for himself of their meaning. In order to the observance of that conduct, which the laws of nations combined with our treaties prescribed to this country, in reference to the present War in Europe, it was necessary for the President to judge for himself whether there was any thing in our treaties incompatible with an adherence to neutrality. Having judged that there was not, he had a right, and if in his opinion the interests of the Nation required it, it was his duty, as Executor of the laws, to proclaim the neutrality of the Nation, to exhort all persons to observe it, and to warn them of the penalties which would attend its non observance.

The Proclamation has been represented as enacting some new law. This is a view of it entirely erroneous. It only proclaims a *fact* with regard to the *existing state* of the Nation, informs the citizens of what the laws previously established require of them in that state, & warns them that these laws will be put in execution against the Infractors of them.

Helvidius, Nos. 1 & 2
James Madison, Aug. 24, 28, & 31, 1793

No. 1

Several pieces with the signature of Pacificus were lately published, which have been read with singular pleasure and applause, by the foreigners and degenerate citizens among us, who hate our republican government, and the French revolution; whilst the publication seems to have been too little regarded, or too much despised by the steady friends to both.

Had the doctrines inculcated by the writer, with the natural consequences from them, been nakedly presented to the public, this treatment might have been proper. Their true character would then have struck every eye, and been rejected by the feelings of every heart. But they offer themselves to the reader in the dress of an elaborate dissertation; they are mingled with a few truths that may serve them as a passport to credulity; and they are introduced with professions of anxiety for the preservation of peace, for the welfare of the government, and for the respect due to the present head of the executive, that may prove a snare to patriotism. . . .

The basis of the reasoning is, we perceive, the extraordinary doctrine, that the powers of making war, and treaties, are in their nature executive; and therefore comprehended in the general grant of executive power, where not especially and strictly excepted out of the grant.

Let us examine this doctrine: and that we may avoid the possibility of mistaking the writer, it shall be laid down in his own words; a precaution the more necessary, as scarce any thing else could outweigh the improbability, that so extravagant a tenet should be hazarded at so early a day, in the face of the public.

His words are—"Two of these [exceptions and qualifications to the executive powers] have been already noticed—the participation of the senate in the *appointment of officers,* and the *making of treaties.* A *third* remains to be mentioned—the right of the legislature to *declare war, and grant letters of marque and reprisal.*"

Again—"It deserves to be remarked, that as the participation of the senate in the *making of treaties,* and the power of the legislature to *declare war,* are *exceptions* out of the general *executive power,* vested in the president; they are to be construed *strictly,* and ought to be extended no further than is *essential* to their execution. . . ."

If we consult, for a moment, the nature and operation of the two powers to declare war and to make treaties, it will be impossible not to see, that they can never fall within a proper definition of executive powers. The natural province of the executive magistrate is to execute laws, as that of the legislature is to make laws. All his acts, therefore, properly executive, must presuppose the existence of the laws to be executed. A treaty is not an execution of laws: it does not presuppose the existence of laws. It is, on the contrary, to have itself the force of a *law,* and to be carried into *execution,* like all *other laws,* by the *executive magistrate.* To say then that the power of making treaties, which are confessedly laws, belongs naturally to the department which is to execute laws, is to say, that the executive department naturally includes a legislative power. In theory this is an absurdity—in practice a tyranny.

The power to declare war is subject to similar reasoning. A declaration that there shall be war, is not an execution of laws: it does not suppose pre-existing laws to be executed: it is not, in any respect, an act merely executive. It is, on the contrary, one of the most deliberate acts that can be performed; and when performed, has the effect of *repealing* all the *laws* operating in a state of peace, so far as they are inconsistent with a state of war; and of *enacting,* as a *rule for the executive, a new code* adapted to the relation between the society and its foreign enemy. In like manner, a conclusion of peace *annuls* all the *laws* peculiar to a state of war, and *revives* the general *laws* incident to a state of peace.

These remarks will be strengthened by adding, that treaties, particularly treaties of peace, have sometimes the effect of changing not only the external laws of the society, but operate also on the internal code, which is purely municipal, and to which the legislative authority of the country is of itself competent and complete.

From this view of the subject it must be evident, that although the executive may be a convenient organ of preliminary communications with foreign governments, on the subjects of treaty or war; and the proper agent for carrying into execution the final determinations of the competent authority; yet it can have no pretensions, from the nature of the powers in question compared with the nature of the executive trust, to that essential agency which gives validity to such determinations. . . .

3. It remains to be inquired, whether there be any thing in the constitution itself, which shows, that the powers of making war and peace are considered as of an executive nature, and as comprehended within a general grant of executive power.

It will not be pretended, that this appears from any *direct* position to be found in the instrument.

If it were *deducible* from any particular expressions, it may be presumed, that the publication would have saved us the trouble of the research.

Does the doctrine, then, result from the actual distribution of powers among the several branches of the government? or from any fair analogy between the powers of war and treaty, and the enumerated powers vested in the executive alone?

Let us examine:

In the general distribution of powers, we find that of declaring war expressly vested in the congress, where every other legislative power is declared to be vested; and without any other qualification than what is common to every other legislative act. The constitutional idea of this power would seem then clearly to be, that it is of a legislative and not an executive nature.

This conclusion becomes irresistible, when it is recollected, that the constitution cannot be supposed to have placed either any power legislative in its nature, entirely among executive powers, or any power executive in its nature, entirely among legislative powers, without charging the constitution, with that kind of intermixture and consolidation of different powers, which would violate a fundamental principle in the organization of free governments. If it were not unnecessary to enlarge on this topic here, it could be shown, that the constitution was originally vindicated, and has been constantly expounded, with a disavowal of any such intermixture.

The power of treaties is vested jointly in the president and in the senate, which is a branch of the legislature. From this arrangement merely, there can be no inference that would necessarily exclude the power from the executive class: since the senate is joined with the president in another power, that of appointing to offices, which, as far as relate to executive offices at least, is considered as of an executive nature. Yet on the other hand, there are sufficient indications that the power of treaties is regarded by the constitution as materially different from mere executive power, and as having more affinity to the legislative than to the executive character.

One circumstance indicating this, is the constitutional regulation under which the senate give their consent in the case of treaties. In all other cases, the consent of the body is expressed by a majority of voices. In this particular case, a concurrence of two-thirds at least is made necessary, as a substitute or compensation for the other branch of the legislature, which, on certain occasions, could not be conveniently a party to the transaction.

But the conclusive circumstance is, that treaties, when formed according to the constitutional mode, are confessedly to have force and operation of *laws,* and are to be a rule for the courts in controversies between man and man, as much as any *other laws*. They are even emphatically declared by the constitution to be "the supreme law of the land."

So far the argument from the constitution is precisely in opposition to the doctrine. As little will be gained in its favour from a comparison of the two powers, with those particularly vested in the president alone.

As there are but few, it will be most satisfactory to review them one by one.

"The president shall be commander in chief of the army and navy of the United States, and of the militia when called into the actual service of the United States."

There can be no relation worth examining between this power and the general power of making treaties. And instead of being analogous to the power of declaring war, it affords a striking illustration of the incompatibility of the two powers in the same hands. Those who are to *conduct a war* cannot in the nature of things, be proper or safe judges, whether *a war ought* to be *commenced, continued,* or *concluded.* They are barred from the latter functions by a great principle in free government, analogous to that which separates the sword from the purse, or the power of executing from the power of enacting laws. . . .

"He shall take care that the laws shall be faithfully executed, and shall commission all officers of the United States." To see the laws faithfully executed constitutes the essence of the executive authority. But what relation has it to the power of making treaties and war, that is, of determining what the *laws shall be* with regard to other nations? No other certainly than what subsists between the powers of executing and enacting laws; no other, consequently, than what forbids a coalition of the powers in the same department. . . .

Thus it appears that by whatever standard we try this doctrine, it must be condemned as no less vicious in theory than it would be dangerous in practice. It is countenanced neither by the writers on law; nor by the nature of the powers themselves; nor by any general arrangements, or particular expressions, or plausible analogies, to be found in the constitution. . . .

No. 2

. . . The declaring of war is expressly made a legislative function. The judging of the obligations to make war, is admitted to be included as a legislative function. Whenever, then, a question occurs, whether war shall be declared, or whether public stipulations require it, the question necessarily belongs to the department to which those functions belong—and no other department can be *in the execution of its proper functions,* if it should undertake to decide such a question.

There can be no refuge against this conclusion, but in the pretext of a *concurrent* right in both departments to judge of the obligations to declare war; and this must be intended by the writer, when he says, "It will not follow, that the executive is excluded *in any case* from a *similar right* of judging," & c. . . .

It has been seen, that the idea of a *concurrent* right is at variance with other ideas, advanced or admitted by the writer. Laying aside, for the present, that consideration, it seems impossible to avoid concluding, that if the executive, as such, has a concurrent right with the legislature to judge of obligations to declare war, and the right to judge be essentially included in the right to declare, it must have the same concurrent right to declare, as it has to judge; and, by another analogy, the same right to judge of other causes of war, as of the particular cause found in a public stipulation. So that whenever the executive, *in the course of its functions,* shall meet with these cases, it must either infer an equal authority in all, or acknowledge its want of authority in any.

If any doubt can remain, or rather if any doubt could ever have arisen, which side of the alternative ought to be embraced, it can be with those only who overlook or reject some of the most obvious and essential truths in political science.

The power to judge of the causes of war, as involved in the power to declare war, is expressly vested, where all other legislative powers are vested, that is, in the congress of the United States. It is consequently determined by the constitution to be a *legislative power.* Now, omitting the inquiry here, in what respects a compound power may be partly legislative, and partly executive, and accordingly vested *partly* in the one, and *partly* in the other department, or *jointly* in both; a remark used on another occasion is equally conclusive on this, that the same power cannot belong, *in the whole* to *both* departments, or be properly so vested as to operate *separately* in *each*. Still more evident is it, that the same *specific function or act*, cannot possibly belong to the *two* departments, and be *separately* exerciseable by *each*.

Legislative power may be *concurrently* vested in different legislative bodies. Executive powers may be concurrently vested in different executive magistrates. In legislative acts the executive may have a participation, as in the qualified negative on the laws. In executive acts, the legislature, or at least a branch of it, may participate, as in the appointment to offices. Arrangements of this sort are familiar in theory, as well as in practice. But an independent exercise of an *executive act* by the legislature *alone,* or of a *legislative* act by the executive *alone,* one or other of which must happen in every case where the same act is exerciseable by each, and the latter of which would happen in the case urged by the writer, is contrary to one of the first and best maxims of a well-organized government, and ought never to be founded in a forced construction, much less in opposition to a fair one. Instances, it is true, may be discovered among ourselves, where this maxim has not been faithfully pursued; but being generally acknowledged to be errors, they confirm, rather than impeach the truth and value of the maxim.

It may happen also, that different independent departments, the legislative and executive, for example, may, in the exercise of their functions, interpret the constitution differently, and thence lay claim to the same power. This difference of opinion is an inconvenience not entirely to be avoided. It results from what may be called, if it be thought fit, a *concurrent* right to expound the constitution. But this *species* of concurrence is obviously and radically different from that in question. The former supposes the constitution to have given the power to one department only; and the doubt to be, to which it has been given. The latter supposes it to belong to both; and that it may be exercised by either or both, according to the course of exigencies.

A concurrent authority in two independent departments, to perform the same function with respect to the same thing, would be as awkward in practice, as it is unnatural in theory.

If the legislature and executive have both a right to judge of the obligations to make war or not, it must sometimes happen, though not at present, that they will judge differently. The executive may proceed to consider the question to-day; may determine that the United States are not bound to take part in a war, and, *in the execution of its functions,* proclaim that determination to all the world. Tomorrow, the legislature may follow in the consideration of the same subject; may determine that the obligations impose war on the United States, and, *in the execution of its functions* enter into a *constitutional declaration,* expressly contradicting the *constitutional proclamation.*

In what light does this present the constitution to the people who established it? In what light would it present to the world a nation, thus speaking, through two different organs, equally constitutional and authentic, two opposite languages, on the same subject, and under the same existing circumstances?

The Neutrality Act of 1794

June 5, 1794

CHAP. L.—*An Act in addition to the act for the punishment of certain crimes against the United States.*

SEC. 1. *Be it enacted and declared by the Senate and House of Representatives of the United States of America in Congress assembled*, That if any citizen of the United States shall, within the territory or jurisdiction of the same, accept and exercise a commission to serve a foreign prince or state in war by land or sea, the person so offending shall be deemed guilty of a high misdemeanor, and shall be fined no more than two thousand dollars, and shall be imprisoned not exceeding three years. . . .

SEC. 3. *And be it further enacted and declared*, That if any person shall within any of the ports, harbors, bays, rivers or other waters of the United States, fit out and arm or attempt to fit out and arm or procure to be fitted out and armed . . . with intent that such ship or vessel shall be employed in the service of any foreign prince or state to cruise or commit hostilities upon the subjects, citizens or property of another foreign prince or state with whom the United States are at peace . . . shall upon conviction be adjudged guilty of a high misdemeanor, and shall be fined and imprisoned at the discretion of the court. . . .

SEC. 8. *And be it further enacted and declared*, That it shall be lawful for the President of the United States, or such other person as he shall have empowered for that purpose, to employ such part of the land or naval forces of the United States or of the militia thereof, as shall be necessary to compel any foreign ship or vessel to depart the United States, in all cases in which, by the laws of nations or the treaties of the United States, they ought not to remain within the United States. . . .

NOTES

1.   Consider some of the questions raised by the Hamilton-Madison debate over the Neutrality Proclamation. If the grant of "the executive Power" to the president in Article II, Section 1 means what Hamilton says, why isn't Article II only one sentence long? Aside from the election provisions, why list additional powers? Does the reference in Article II, Sections 2 and 3 to the president's commander-in-chief power, treaty-making power, and power to receive ambassadors suggest that the Vesting Clause is not as sweeping as Hamilton claims? Is there a different way of understanding *why* the specific provisions of Sections 2 and 3 might have been included in Article II that is reconcilable with the idea that the Vesting Clause's grant of "the executive Power" is an actual grant of the executive power? Can the provisions of Sections 2 and 3 be understood as clarifications or elaborations? Can they be explained as having been made necessary by grants of powers to Congress that touch on foreign affairs?

2.   Is Madison's skepticism about a broad, residual foreign affairs power inconsistent with the position he took during the removal debate in 1789? (See p. 207). Or are the two topics unrelated?

3.   Is it possible to justify Washington's actions without reference to a broad constitutional power under Article II? Could Washington be said to be following "the law of nations," which might be binding on him under the Take Care Clause? See Robert J. Reinstein, *Executive Power and the Law of Nations in the Washington Administration*, 46 U. Rich. L. Rev. 373 (2012).

4.   What do you think of President Washington's statement that it is a prosecutable crime for a U.S. citizen to violate his Neutrality Proclamation? Even if the Washington had the power to declare neutrality as a matter of foreign policy, does that extend to the power to punish private citizens who violate that neutrality?

5.   The Neutrality Controversy also raises the question of a president's power over a treaty once it has been made and ratified by the Senate. Specifically can the president (or a successor) terminate that treaty unilaterally? Why or why not? That issue has never been decided by the Supreme Court, and other courts have divided on the question. Consider three positions:

a.   The power to unmake is part of the power to make. Thus, the president can terminate a treaty only with Senate consent (or perhaps through legislation passed by Congress). Otherwise, the treaty is the "supreme Law of the Land." U.S. Const., Art. VI. This was the position taken by the district court in *Goldwater v. Carter*, 481 F.Supp.949, 965 (D.D.C.), a lawsuit by members of Congress trying to stop President Carter from withdrawing from a mutual-defense treaty with Taiwan.

b.   Treaty termination is executive power. Thus, the president's power over foreign affairs includes the power to decide whether to adhere to our international agreements or to break them. This was the position taken by Justice Brennan in a later dissent in *Goldwater v. Carter*, 444 U.S. 996, 1007 (1979) ("Our cases firmly establish that the Constitution commits to the President alone the power to recognize, and withdraw recognition from, foreign regimes.").

c.   It depends on what the treaty says. If the treaty itself has a termination clause, the president may activate it. On this view the executive power is to terminate a treaty *in accordance with its terms*. This was the position suggested by the D.C. Circuit when it reversed the district court decision in *Goldwater v. Carter*, 617 F.2d 697, 708 (D.C. Cir. 1979) (finding it "of central significance" that "the treaty here at issue contains a termination clause," with the president had used).

In the end, the Supreme Court granted review in *Goldwater v. Carter*, then ordered the case dismissed on justiciability grounds in a fractured mess of opinions. 444 U.S. 996, 1007 (1979). So the issue remains unresolved. How would you resolve it?

6.   One more treaty question for now: Perhaps the most consequential use of the treaty power in America's history was the Louisiana Purchase of 1803. See p. 730. Does the Louisiana Purchase example suggest that some treaties cannot be unilaterally terminated by the president? Which ones?

7.   Before going on to read the next case, you should know about *United States v. Curtiss-Wright Export Corporation*, 299 U.S. 304 (1936). *Curtiss-Wright* was a non-delegation challenge to President Roosevelt's embargo against the international arms trade. It was not clear whether the embargo would have violated the normal non-delegation doctrine at the time, but the Court concluded that domestic non-delegation principles did not apply in the sphere of foreign affairs. Along the way, perhaps in dicta, the Court made sweeping comments about federal power (e.g., "the investment of the federal government with the powers of external sovereignty did not depend upon the affirmative grants of the Constitution") and about executive power (e.g., "[i]n this vast external realm, with its important, complicated, delicate and manifold problems, the President alone has the power to speak or listen as a representative of the nation"). Look for those claims as you read the competing opinions in the next case.

Zivotofsky v. Kerry

135 S.Ct. 2076 (2015)

■ JUSTICE KENNEDY delivered the opinion of the Court.

A delicate subject lies in the background of this case. That subject is Jerusalem. Questions touching upon the history of the ancient city and its present legal and international status are among the most difficult and complex in international affairs. In our constitutional system these matters are committed to the Legislature and the Executive, not the Judiciary. As a result, in this opinion the Court does no more, and must do no more, than note the existence of international debate and tensions respecting Jerusalem. Those matters are for Congress and the President to discuss and consider as they seek to shape the Nation's foreign policies.

The Court addresses two questions to resolve the interbranch dispute now before it. First, it must determine whether the President has the exclusive power to grant formal recognition to a foreign sovereign. Second, if he has that power, the Court must determine whether Congress can command the President and his Secretary of State to issue a formal statement that contradicts the earlier recognition. The statement in question here is a congressional mandate that allows a United States citizen born in Jerusalem to direct the President and Secretary of State, when issuing his passport, to state that his place of birth is "Israel."

I–A

Jerusalem's political standing has long been, and remains, one of the most sensitive issues in American foreign policy, and indeed it is one of the most delicate issues in current international affairs. In 1948, President Truman formally recognized Israel in a signed statement of "recognition." That statement did not recognize Israeli sovereignty over Jerusalem. Over the last 60 years, various actors have sought to assert full or partial sovereignty over the city, including Israel, Jordan, and the Palestinians. Yet, in contrast to a consistent policy of formal recognition of Israel, neither President Truman nor any later United States President has issued an official statement or declaration acknowledging any country's sovereignty over Jerusalem. Instead, the Executive Branch has maintained that " 'the status of Jerusalem . . . should be decided not unilaterally but in consultation with all concerned.' " United Nations Gen. Assembly Official Records, 5th Emergency Sess., 1554th Plenary Meetings, United Nations Doc. No. 1 A/PV.1554, p. 10 (July 14, 1967). . . .

The President's position on Jerusalem is reflected in State Department policy regarding passports and consular reports of birth abroad. Understanding that passports will be construed as reflections of American policy, the State Department's Foreign Affairs Manual instructs its employees, in general, to record the place of birth on a passport as the "country [having] present sovereignty over the actual area of birth." Dept. of State, 7 Foreign Affairs Manual (FAM) § 1383.4 (1987). If a citizen objects to the country listed as sovereign by the State Department, he or she may list the city or town of birth rather than the country. The FAM, however, does not allow citizens to list a sovereign that conflicts with Executive Branch policy. Because the United States does not recognize any country as having sovereignty over Jerusalem, the FAM instructs employees to record the place of birth for citizens born there as "Jerusalem."

In 2002, Congress passed the Act at issue here, the Foreign Relations Authorization Act, Fiscal Year 2003. Section 214 of the Act is titled "United States Policy with Respect to Jerusalem as the Capital of Israel." The subsection that lies at the heart of this case, § 214(d), addresses passports. That subsection seeks to override the FAM by allowing citizens born in Jerusalem to list their place of birth as "Israel." Titled "Record of Place of Birth as Israel for Passport Purposes," § 214(d) states "[f]or purposes of the registration of birth, certification of nationality, or issuance of a passport of a United States citizen born in the city of Jerusalem, the Secretary shall, upon the request of the citizen or the citizen's legal guardian, record the place of birth as Israel."

When he signed the Act into law, President George W. Bush issued a statement declaring his position that § 214 would, "if construed as mandatory rather than advisory, impermissibly interfere with the President's constitutional authority to formulate the position of the United States, speak for the Nation in international affairs, and determine the terms on which recognition is given to foreign states." Statement on Signing the Foreign Relations Authorization Act, Fiscal Year 2003, Public Papers of the Presidents, George W. Bush, Vol. 2, Sept. 30, 2002, p. 1698 (2005). The President concluded, "U.S. policy regarding Jerusalem has not changed.". . . .

B

In 2002, petitioner Menachem Binyamin Zivotofsky was born to United States citizens living in Jerusalem. In December 2002, Zivotofsky's mother visited the American Embassy in Tel Aviv to request both a passport and a consular report of birth abroad for her son. She asked that his place of birth be listed as " 'Jerusalem, Israel.' " The Embassy clerks explained that, pursuant to State Department policy, the passport would list only "Jerusalem." Zivotofsky's parents objected and, as his guardians, brought suit on his behalf in the United States District Court for the District of Columbia, seeking to enforce § 214(d).

Pursuant to § 214(d), Zivotofsky claims the right to have "Israel" recorded as his place of birth in his passport. . . . *[The Court next traced the procedural history of the case, including its own earlier decision in* Zivotofsky v. Clinton, *which held that the case did not present a non-justiciable political question.—Editors]*

II

In considering claims of Presidential power this Court refers to Justice Jackson's familiar tripartite framework from *Youngstown Sheet & Tube Co. v. Sawyer*, 343 U.S. 579, 638 (1952) (concurring opinion). . . . In this case the Secretary contends that § 214(d) infringes on the President's exclusive recognition power by "requiring the President to contradict his recognition position regarding Jerusalem in official communications with foreign sovereigns." In so doing the Secretary acknowledges the President's power is "at its lowest ebb." Because the President's refusal to implement § 214(d) falls into Justice Jackson's third category, his claim must be "scrutinized with caution," and he may rely solely on powers the Constitution grants to him alone.

To determine whether the President possesses the exclusive power of recognition the Court examines the Constitution's text and structure, as well as precedent and history bearing on the question.

A

Recognition is a "formal acknowledgement" that a particular "entity possesses the qualifications for statehood" or "that a particular regime is the effective government of a state." Restatement (Third) of Foreign Relations Law of the United States § 203, Comment a, p. 84 (1986). . . .

Despite the importance of the recognition power in foreign relations, the Constitution does not use the term "recognition," either in Article II or elsewhere. The Secretary asserts that the President exercises the recognition power based on the Reception Clause, which directs that the President "shall receive Ambassadors and other public Ministers." Art. II, § 3. As Zivotofsky notes, the Reception Clause received little attention at the Constitutional Convention. In fact, during the ratification debates, Alexander Hamilton claimed that the power to receive ambassadors was "more a matter of dignity than of authority," a ministerial duty largely "without consequence." The Federalist No. 69.

At the time of the founding, however, prominent international scholars suggested that receiving an ambassador was tantamount to recognizing the sovereignty of the sending state. It is a logical and proper inference, then, that a Clause directing the President alone to receive ambassadors would be understood to acknowledge his power to recognize other nations.

This in fact occurred early in the Nation's history when President Washington recognized the French Revolutionary Government by receiving its ambassador. See A. Hamilton, Pacificus No. 1 (President "acknowledged the republic of France, by the reception of its minister"). After this incident the import of the Reception Clause became clear—causing Hamilton to change his earlier view. He wrote that the Reception Clause "includes th[e power] of judging, in the case of a revolution of government in a foreign country, whether the new rulers are competent organs of the national will, and ought to be recognised, or not." See *id.*; see also 3 J. Story, Commentaries on the Constitution of the United States § 1560, p. 416 (1833) ("If the executive receives an ambassador, or other minister, as the representative of a new nation . . . it is an acknowledgment of the sovereign authority *de facto* of such new nation, or party"). As a result, the Reception Clause provides support, although not the sole authority, for the President's power to recognize other nations.

The inference that the President exercises the recognition power is further supported by his additional Article II powers. It is for the President, "by and with the Advice and Consent of the Senate," to "make Treaties, provided two thirds of the Senators present concur." Art. II, § 2, cl. 2. In addition, "he shall nominate, and by and with the Advice and Consent of the Senate, shall appoint Ambassadors" as well as "other public Ministers and Consuls." *Ibid.*

As a matter of constitutional structure, these additional powers give the President control over recognition decisions. At international law, recognition may be effected by different means, but each means is dependent upon Presidential power. In addition to receiving an ambassador, recognition may occur on "the conclusion of a bilateral treaty," or the "formal initiation of diplomatic relations," including the dispatch of an ambassador. The President has the sole power to negotiate treaties, see *United States v. Curtiss-Wright Export Corp.*, 299 U.S. 304, 319 (1936), and the Senate may not conclude or ratify a treaty without Presidential action. The President, too, nominates the Nation's ambassadors and dispatches other diplomatic agents. Congress may not send an ambassador without his involvement. Beyond that, the President himself has the power to open diplomatic channels simply by engaging in direct diplomacy with foreign heads of state and their ministers. The Constitution thus assigns the President means to effect recognition on his own initiative. Congress, by contrast, has no constitutional power that would enable it to initiate diplomatic relations with a foreign nation. Because these specific Clauses confer the recognition power on the President, the Court need not consider whether or to what extent the Vesting Clause, which provides that the "executive Power" shall be vested in the President, provides further support for the President's action here. Art. II, § 1, cl. 1.

The text and structure of the Constitution grant the President the power to recognize foreign nations and governments. The question then becomes whether that power is exclusive. The various ways in which the President may unilaterally effect recognition—and the lack of any similar power vested in Congress—suggest that it is. So, too, do functional considerations. Put simply, the Nation must have a single policy regarding which governments are legitimate in the eyes of the United States and which are not. Foreign countries need to know, before entering into diplomatic relations or commerce with the United States, whether their ambassadors will be received; whether their officials will be immune from suit in federal court; and whether they may initiate lawsuits here to vindicate their rights. These assurances cannot be equivocal.

Recognition is a topic on which the Nation must "speak . . . with one voice." *American Ins. Assn. v. Garamendi*, 539 U.S. 396, 424 (2003). That voice must be the President's. Between the two political branches, only the Executive has the characteristic of unity at all times. And with unity comes the ability to exercise, to a greater degree, "[d]ecision, activity, secrecy, and dispatch." The Federalist No. 70 (A. Hamilton). The President is capable, in ways Congress is not, of engaging in the delicate and often secret diplomatic contacts that may lead to a decision on recognition. See, *e.g.*, *United States v. Pink*, 315 U.S. 203, 229 (1942). He is also better positioned to take the decisive, unequivocal action necessary to recognize other states at international law. These qualities explain why the Framers listed the traditional avenues of recognition—receiving ambassadors, making treaties, and sending ambassadors—as among the President's Article II powers. . . .

It remains true, of course, that many decisions affecting foreign relations—including decisions that may determine the course of our relations with recognized countries—require congressional action. Congress may "regulate Commerce with foreign Nations," "establish an uniform Rule of Naturalization," "define and punish Piracies and Felonies committed on the high Seas, and Offences against the Law of Nations," "declare War," "grant Letters of Marque and Reprisal," and "make Rules for the Government and Regulation of the land and naval Forces." U.S. Const., Art. I, § 8. In addition, the President cannot make a treaty or appoint an ambassador without the approval of the Senate. Art. II, § 2, cl. 2. The President, furthermore, could not build an American Embassy abroad without congressional appropriation of the necessary funds. Art. I, § 8, cl. 1. Under basic separation-of-powers principles, it is for the Congress to enact the laws, including "all Laws which shall be necessary and proper for carrying into Execution" the powers of the Federal Government. § 8, cl. 18.

In foreign affairs, as in the domestic realm, the Constitution "enjoins upon its branches separateness but interdependence, autonomy but reciprocity." *Youngstown*, at 635 (Jackson, J., concurring). Although the President alone effects the formal act of recognition, Congress' powers, and its central role in making laws, give it substantial authority regarding many of the policy determinations that precede and follow the act of recognition itself. If Congress disagrees with the President's recognition policy, there may be consequences. Formal recognition may seem a hollow act if it is not accompanied by the dispatch of an ambassador, the easing of trade restrictions, and the conclusion of treaties. And those decisions require action by the Senate or the whole Congress.

In practice, then, the President's recognition determination is just one part of a political process that may require Congress to make laws. The President's exclusive recognition power encompasses the authority to acknowledge, in a formal sense, the legitimacy of other states and governments, including their territorial bounds. Albeit limited, the exclusive recognition power is essential to the conduct of Presidential duties. The formal act of recognition is an executive power that Congress may not qualify. If the President is to be effective in negotiations over a formal recognition determination, it must be evident to his counterparts abroad that he speaks for the Nation on that precise question.

A clear rule that the formal power to recognize a foreign government subsists in the President therefore serves a necessary purpose in diplomatic relations. All this, of course, underscores that Congress has an important role in other aspects of foreign policy, and the President may be bound by any number of laws Congress enacts. In this way ambition counters ambition, ensuring that the democratic will of the people is observed and respected in foreign affairs as in the domestic realm. See The Federalist No. 51 (J. Madison).

B

No single precedent resolves the question whether the President has exclusive recognition authority and, if so, how far that power extends. In part that is because, until today, the political branches have resolved their disputes over questions of recognition. The relevant cases, though providing important instruction, address the division of recognition power between the Federal Government and the States, or between the courts and the political branches—not between the President and Congress. As the parties acknowledge, some isolated statements in those cases lend support to the position that Congress has a role in the recognition process. In the end, however, a fair reading of the cases shows that the President's role in the recognition process is both central and exclusive.

[Next the Court described a series of judicial precedents: a nineteenth-century case involving the Falkland Islands, and twentieth-century cases about recognition of Soviet Russia and Cuba. The Court concluded that these precedents provided "strong support" for exclusive executive authority, though it acknowledged that in previous cases the president "did not contradict an Act of Congress."—Editors]

The Secretary now urges the Court to define the executive power over foreign relations in even broader terms. He contends that under the Court's precedent the President has "exclusive authority to conduct diplomatic relations," along with "the bulk of foreign-affairs powers." In support of his submission that the President has broad, undefined powers over foreign affairs, the Secretary quotes *United States v.*

Curtiss-Wright Export Corp., which described the President as "the sole organ of the federal government in the field of international relations." This Court declines to acknowledge that unbounded power. A formulation broader than the rule that the President alone determines what nations to formally recognize as legitimate—and that he consequently controls his statements on matters of recognition—presents different issues and is unnecessary to the resolution of this case.

The *Curtiss-Wright* case does not extend so far as the Secretary suggests. . . .

[*Curtiss-Wright's*] description of the President's exclusive power was not necessary to the holding of *Curtiss-Wright*—which, after all, dealt with congressionally authorized action, not a unilateral Presidential determination. Indeed, *Curtiss-Wright* did not hold that the President is free from Congress' lawmaking power in the field of international relations. The President does have a unique role in communicating with foreign governments, as then-Congressman John Marshall acknowledged. See 10 Annals of Cong. 613 (1800) (cited in *Curtiss-Wright*, at 319). But whether the realm is foreign or domestic, it is still the Legislative Branch, not the Executive Branch, that makes the law.

In a world that is ever more compressed and interdependent, it is essential the congressional role in foreign affairs be understood and respected. For it is Congress that makes laws, and in countless ways its laws will and should shape the Nation's course. The Executive is not free from the ordinary controls and checks of Congress merely because foreign affairs are at issue. See, *e.g.*, *Medellín v. Texas*, 552 U.S. 491, 532 (2008); *Youngstown*, at 589; *Little v. Barreme*, 6 U.S. (2 Cranch) 170, 177–179 (1804). It is not for the President alone to determine the whole content of the Nation's foreign policy.

That said, judicial precedent and historical practice teach that it is for the President alone to make the specific decision of what foreign power he will recognize as legitimate, both for the Nation as a whole and for the purpose of making his own position clear within the context of recognition in discussions and negotiations with foreign nations. Recognition is an act with immediate and powerful significance for international relations, so the President's position must be clear. Congress cannot require him to contradict his own statement regarding a determination of formal recognition.

Zivotofsky's contrary arguments are unconvincing. The decisions he relies upon are largely inapposite. This Court's cases do not hold that the recognition power is shared. *Jones v. United States*, 137 U.S. 202 (1890), and *Boumediene v. Bush*, 553 U.S. 723 (2008), each addressed the status of territories controlled or acquired by the United States—not whether a province ought to be recognized as part of a foreign country. And no one disputes that Congress has a role in determining the status of United States territories. See U.S. Const., Art. IV, § 3, cl. 2 (Congress may "dispose of and make all needful Rules and Regulations respecting the Territory or other Property belonging to the United States"). Other cases describing a shared power address the recognition of Indian tribes—which is, similarly, a distinct issue from the recognition of foreign countries.

To be sure, the Court has mentioned both of the political branches in discussing international recognition, but it has done so primarily in affirming that the Judiciary is not responsible for recognizing foreign nations. This is consistent with the fact that Congress, in the ordinary course, does support the President's recognition policy, for instance by confirming an ambassador to the recognized foreign government. Those cases do not cast doubt on the view that the Executive Branch determines whether the United States will recognize foreign states and governments and their territorial bounds.

C

Having examined the Constitution's text and this Court's precedent, it is appropriate to turn to accepted understandings and practice. In separation-of-powers cases this Court has often "put significant weight upon historical practice." *NLRB v. Noel Canning*, 134 S.Ct. 2550, 2559 (2014) (emphasis deleted). Here, history is not all on one side, but on balance it provides strong support for the conclusion that the recognition power is the President's alone. As Zivotofsky argues, certain historical incidents can be interpreted to support the position that recognition is a shared power. But the weight of historical evidence supports the opposite view, which is that the formal determination of recognition is a power to be exercised only by the President.

[Next the Court described a series of recognition incidents that occurred outside the courts: France, South American republics, Texas, Liberia, Haiti, Cuba, and China. These incidents, the Court said, "establis[h] no more than that some Presidents have chosen to cooperate with Congress, not that Congress itself has exercised the recognition power."—Editors]

This history confirms the Court's conclusion in the instant case that the power to recognize or decline to recognize a foreign state and its territorial bounds resides in the President alone. For the most part, Congress has respected the Executive's policies and positions as to formal recognition. At times, Congress itself has defended the President's constitutional prerogative. Over the last 100 years, there has been scarcely any debate over the President's power to recognize foreign states. In this respect the Legislature, in the narrow context of recognition, on balance has acknowledged the importance of speaking "with one voice." *Crosby v. National Foreign Trade Council*, 530 U.S. 363, 381 (2000). The weight of historical evidence indicates Congress has accepted that the power to recognize foreign states and governments and their territorial bounds is exclusive to the Presidency.

III

As the power to recognize foreign states resides in the President alone, the question becomes whether § 214(d) infringes on the Executive's consistent decision to withhold recognition with respect to Jerusalem. If the power over recognition is to mean anything, it must mean that the President not only makes the initial, formal recognition determination but also that he may maintain that determination in his and his agent's statements. . . . [I]f Congress could alter the President's statements on matters of recognition or force him to contradict them, Congress in effect would exercise the recognition power.

As Justice Jackson wrote in *Youngstown*, when a Presidential power is "exclusive," it "disabl[es] the Congress from acting upon the subject." Here, the subject is quite narrow: The Executive's exclusive power extends no further than his formal recognition determination. But as to that determination, Congress may not enact a law that directly contradicts it. This is not to say Congress may not express its disagreement with the President in myriad ways. For example, it may enact an embargo, decline to confirm an ambassador, or even declare war. But none of these acts would alter the President's recognition decision.

If Congress may not pass a law, speaking in its own voice, that effects formal recognition, then it follows that it may not force the President himself to contradict his earlier statement. That congressional command would not only prevent the Nation from speaking with one voice but also prevent the Executive itself from doing so in conducting foreign relations.

Although the statement required by § 214(d) would not itself constitute a formal act of recognition, it is a mandate that the Executive contradict his prior recognition determination in an official document issued by the Secretary of State. As a result, it is unconstitutional. . . .

The flaw in § 214(d) is further underscored by the undoubted fact that that the purpose of the statute was to infringe on the recognition power—a power the Court now holds is the sole prerogative of the President. The statute is titled "United States Policy with Respect to Jerusalem as the Capital of Israel." . . . .

It is true, as Zivotofsky notes, that Congress has substantial authority over passports. The Court does not question the power of Congress to enact passport legislation of wide scope. . . . The problem with § 214(d), however, lies in how Congress exercised its authority over passports. It was an improper act for Congress to "aggrandiz[e] its power at the expense of another branch" by requiring the President to contradict an earlier recognition determination in an official document issued by the Executive Branch. *Freytag v. Commissioner*, 501 U.S. 868, 878 (1991). To allow Congress to control the President's communication in the context of a formal recognition determination is to allow Congress to exercise that exclusive power itself. As a result, the statute is unconstitutional.

* * *

In holding § 214(d) invalid the Court does not question the substantial powers of Congress over foreign affairs in general or passports in particular. This case is confined solely to the exclusive power of the President to control recognition determinations, including formal statements by the Executive Branch acknowledging the legitimacy of a state or government and its territorial bounds. Congress cannot command the President to contradict an earlier recognition determination in the issuance of passports.

■ JUSTICE BREYER, concurring.

I continue to believe that this case presents a political question inappropriate for judicial resolution. See *Zivotofsky v. Clinton*, 132 S.Ct. 1421 (2012) (BREYER, J., dissenting). But because precedent precludes resolving this case on political question grounds, I join the Court's opinion.

■ JUSTICE THOMAS, concurring in the judgment in part and dissenting in part.

Our Constitution allocates the powers of the Federal Government over foreign affairs in two ways. First, it expressly identifies certain foreign affairs powers and vests them in particular branches, either individually or jointly. Second, it vests the residual foreign affairs powers of the Federal Government—i.e., those not specifically enumerated in the Constitution—in the President by way of Article II's Vesting Clause.

Section 214(d) of the Foreign Relations Authorization Act, Fiscal Year 2003, ignores that constitutional allocation of power insofar as it directs the President, contrary to his wishes, to list "Israel" as the place of birth of Jerusalem-born citizens on their passports. The President has long regulated passports under his residual foreign affairs power, and this portion of § 214(d) does not fall within any of Congress' enumerated powers. . . .

I–A

The Constitution specifies a number of foreign affairs powers and divides them between the political branches. Among others, Article I allocates to Congress the powers "[t]o regulate Commerce with foreign Nations," "[t]o establish an uniform Rule of Naturalization," "[t]o define and punish Piracies and Felonies committed on the high Seas, and Offenses against the Law of Nations," and "[t]o declare War, grant Letters of Marque and Reprisal, and make Rules concerning Captures on Land and Water." Art. I, § 8. For his part, the President has certain express powers relating to foreign affairs, including the powers, "by and with the Advice and Consent of the Senate," to "appoint Ambassadors," and "to make Treaties, provided two thirds of the Senators present concur." Art. II, § 2. He is also assigned certain duties with respect to foreign affairs, including serving as "Commander in Chief of the Army and Navy of the United States," *ibid.*, and "receiv[ing] Ambassadors and other public Ministers," Art. II, § 3.

These specific allocations, however, cannot account for the entirety of the foreign affairs powers exercised by the Federal Government. Neither of the political branches is expressly authorized, for instance, to communicate with foreign ministers, to issue passports, or to repel sudden attacks. Yet the President has engaged in such conduct, with the support of Congress, since the earliest days of the Republic.

The President's longstanding practice of exercising unenumerated foreign affairs powers reflects a constitutional directive that "the President ha[s] primary responsibility—along with the necessary power—to protect the national security and to conduct the Nation's foreign relations." *Hamdi v. Rumsfeld*, 542 U.S. 507, 580 (2004) (THOMAS, J., dissenting). Specifically, the Vesting Clause of Article II provides that "[t]he executive Power shall be vested in a President of the United States." Art. II, § 1. This Clause is notably different from the Vesting Clause of Article I, which provides only that "[a]ll legislative Powers *herein granted* shall be vested in a Congress of the United States," Art. I, § 1 (emphasis added). By omitting the words "herein granted" in Article II, the Constitution indicates that the "executive Power" vested in the President is not confined to those powers expressly identified in the document. Instead, it includes all powers originally understood as falling within the "executive Power" of the Federal Government. . . .

[Justice Thomas next surveyed founding-era sources, concluding that "the practices of the Washington administration and First Congress confirm that Article II's Vesting Clause was originally understood to include a grant of residual foreign affairs power to the Executive."—Editors]

II

The statutory provision at issue implicates the President's residual foreign affairs power. Section 214(d) instructs the Secretary of State, upon request of a citizen born in Jerusalem (or that citizen's legal guardian), to list that citizen's place of birth as Israel on his passport and consular report of birth abroad, even though it is the undisputed position of the United States that Jerusalem is not a part of Israel. The President argues that this provision violates his foreign affairs powers generally and his recognition power specifically. Zivotofsky rejoins that Congress passed § 214(d) pursuant to its enumerated powers and its action must therefore take precedence.

Neither has it quite right. The President is not constitutionally compelled to implement § 214(d) as it applies to passports because passport regulation falls squarely within his residual foreign affairs power and Zivotofsky has identified no source of congressional power to require the President to list Israel as the place of birth for a citizen born in Jerusalem on that citizen's passport. Section 214(d) can, however, be constitutionally applied to consular reports of birth abroad because those documents do not fall within the President's foreign affairs authority but do fall within Congress' enumerated powers over naturalization. . . .

[Justice Thomas concluded that § 214(d) was constitutional inasmuch as it regulated consular reports of birth abroad. The majority did not reach that question, because it found Zivotofsky's challenge to that aspect of the statute to have been waived. Justice Thomas next argued that Congress had no power that justified the application of the statute to passports. He then responded to Justice Scalia's dissent, criticizing it for failing to offer a competing interpretation of the Article II Vesting Clause and the Necessary and Proper Clause. And he faulted Justice Scalia for describing "a supreme legislative body more reminiscent of the Parliament in England than the Congress in America."—Editors]

Because the President has residual foreign affairs authority to regulate passports and because there appears to be no congressional power that justifies § 214(d)'s application to passports, Zivotofsky's challenge to the Executive's designation of his place of birth on his passport must fail.

III

The majority does not perform this analysis, but instead relies on a variation of the recognition power. That power is among the foreign affairs powers vested in the President by Article II's Vesting Clause, as is confirmed by Article II's express assignment to the President of the duty of receiving foreign Ambassadors, Art. II, § 3. But I cannot join the majority's analysis because no act of recognition is implicated here. . . . Listing a Jerusalem-born citizen's place of birth as "Israel" cannot amount to recognition because the United States already recognizes Israel as an international person. Rather than adopt a novel definition of the recognition power, the majority should have looked to other foreign affairs powers in the Constitution to resolve this dispute. . . .

■ CHIEF JUSTICE ROBERTS, with whom JUSTICE ALITO joins, dissenting.

Today's decision is a first: Never before has this Court accepted a President's direct defiance of an Act of Congress in the field of foreign affairs. We have instead stressed that the President's power reaches "its lowest ebb" when he contravenes the express will of Congress, "for what is at stake is the equilibrium established by our constitutional system." *Youngstown*, at 638 (Jackson, J., concurring).

JUSTICE SCALIA's principal dissent, which I join in full, refutes the majority's unprecedented holding in detail. I write separately to underscore the stark nature of the Court's error on a basic question of separation of powers.

The first principles in this area are firmly established. The Constitution allocates some foreign policy powers to the Executive, grants some to the Legislature, and enjoins the President to "take Care that the Laws be faithfully executed." Art. II, § 3. The Executive may disregard "the expressed or implied will of Congress" only if the Constitution grants him a power "at once so conclusive and preclusive" as to "disabl[e] the Congress from acting upon the subject." *Youngstown*, at 637–638 (Jackson, J., concurring).

Assertions of exclusive and preclusive power leave the Executive "in the least favorable of possible constitutional postures," and such claims have been "scrutinized with caution" throughout this Court's history. For our first 225 years, no President prevailed when contradicting a statute in the field of foreign affairs. See *Medellín*, at 532; *Hamdan v. Rumsfeld*, 548 U.S. 557–595, 613–625 (2006); *Youngstown*, at 587–589 (majority opinion); *Little v. Barreme*, at 177–179.

In this case, the President claims the exclusive and preclusive power to recognize foreign sovereigns. The Court devotes much of its analysis to accepting the Executive's contention. I have serious doubts about that position. The majority places great weight on the Reception Clause, which directs that the Executive "shall receive Ambassadors and other public Ministers." Art. II, § 3. But that provision, framed as an obligation rather than an authorization, appears alongside the *duties* imposed on the President by Article II, Section 3, not the *powers* granted to him by Article II, Section 2. Indeed, the People ratified the Constitution with Alexander Hamilton's assurance that executive reception of ambassadors "is more a matter of dignity than of authority" and "will be without consequence in the administration of the government." The Federalist No. 69. In short, at the time of the founding, "there was no reason to view the reception clause as a source of discretionary authority for the president." Adler, The President's Recognition Power: Ministerial or Discretionary? 25 Presidential Studies Q. 267, 269 (1995).

The majority's other asserted textual bases are even more tenuous. The President does have power to make treaties and appoint ambassadors. Art. II, § 2. But those authorities are *shared* with Congress, so they hardly support an inference that the recognition power is *exclusive*.

Precedent and history lend no more weight to the Court's position. The majority cites dicta suggesting an exclusive executive recognition power, but acknowledges contrary dicta suggesting that the power is shared. See, *e.g.*, *United States v. Palmer*, 3 Wheat. 610, 643 (1818) ("the courts of the union must view [a] newly constituted government as it is viewed by *the legislative and executive departments* of the government of the United States" (emphasis added)). When the best you can muster is conflicting dicta, precedent can hardly be said to support your side.

As for history, the majority admits that it too points in both directions. Some Presidents have claimed an exclusive recognition power, but others have expressed uncertainty about whether such preclusive authority exists. Those in the skeptical camp include Andrew Jackson and Abraham Lincoln, leaders not generally known for their cramped conceptions of Presidential power. Congress has also asserted its authority over recognition determinations at numerous points in history. The majority therefore falls short of demonstrating that "Congress has accepted" the President's exclusive recognition power. In any event, we have held that congressional acquiescence is only "pertinent" when the President acts in the absence of express congressional authorization, not when he asserts power to disregard a statute, as the Executive does here.

In sum, although the President has authority over recognition, I am not convinced that the Constitution provides the "conclusive and preclusive" power required to justify defiance of an express legislative mandate. *Youngstown*, at 638 (Jackson, J., concurring). . . .

But even if the President does have exclusive recognition power, he still cannot prevail in this case, because the statute at issue *does not implicate recognition*. The relevant provision, § 214(d), simply gives an American citizen born in Jerusalem the option to designate his place of birth as Israel "[f]or purposes of" passports and other documents. The State Department itself has explained that "identification"—not recognition—"is the principal reason that U.S. passports require 'place of birth.' " Congress has not disputed the Executive's assurances that § 214(d) does not alter the longstanding United States position on Jerusalem. And the annals of diplomatic history record no examples of official recognition accomplished via optional passport designation. . . .

Resolving the status of Jerusalem may be vexing, but resolving this case is not. Whatever recognition power the President may have, exclusive or otherwise, is not implicated by § 214(d). It has not been necessary over the past 225 years to definitively resolve a dispute between Congress and the President over the recognition power. Perhaps we could have waited another 225 years. But instead the majority strains to reach the question based on the mere possibility that observers overseas might misperceive the significance of the birthplace designation at issue in this case. And in the process, the Court takes the perilous step—for the first time in our history—of allowing the President to defy an Act of Congress in the field of foreign affairs.

■ JUSTICE SCALIA, with whom THE CHIEF JUSTICE and JUSTICE ALITO join, dissenting.

Before this country declared independence, the law of England entrusted the King with the exclusive care of his kingdom's foreign affairs. The royal prerogative included the "sole power of sending ambassadors to foreign states, and receiving them at home," the sole authority to "make treaties, leagues, and alliances with foreign states and princes," "the sole prerogative of making war and peace," and the "sole power of raising and regulating fleets and armies." 1 W. Blackstone, Commentaries *253, *257, *262. The People of the United States had other ideas when they organized our Government. They considered a sound structure of balanced powers essential to the preservation of just government, and international relations formed no exception to that principle.

The People therefore adopted a Constitution that divides responsibility for the Nation's foreign concerns between the legislative and executive departments. The Constitution gave the President the "executive Power," authority to send and responsibility to receive ambassadors, power to make treaties, and command of the Army and Navy—though they qualified some of these powers by requiring consent of the Senate. Art. II, §§ 1–3. At the same time, they gave Congress powers over war, foreign commerce, naturalization, and more. Art. I, § 8. "Fully eleven of the powers that Article I, § 8 grants Congress deal in some way with foreign affairs." L. Tribe, American Constitutional Law, § 5–18, p. 965.

This case arises out of a dispute between the Executive and Legislative Branches about whether the United States should treat Jerusalem as a part of Israel. The Constitution contemplates that the political branches will make policy about the territorial claims of foreign nations the same way they make policy about other international matters: The President will exercise his powers on the basis of his views, Congress its powers on the basis of its views. That is just what has happened here.

I

The political branches of our Government agree on the real-world fact that Israel controls the city of Jerusalem. They disagree, however, about how official documents should record the birthplace of an American citizen born in Jerusalem. The Executive does not accept any state's claim to sovereignty over Jerusalem, and it maintains that the birthplace designation "Israel" would clash with this stance of neutrality. But the National Legislature has enacted a statute that provides: "For purposes of the registration of birth, certification of nationality, or issuance of a passport of a United States citizen born in the city of Jerusalem, the Secretary [of State] shall, upon the request of the citizen or the citizen's legal guardian, record the place of birth as Israel." Menachem Zivotofsky's parents seek enforcement of this statutory right in the issuance of their son's passport and consular report of birth abroad. They regard their son's birthplace as a part of Israel and insist as "a matter of conscience" that his Israeli nativity "not be erased" from his identity documents.

Before turning to Presidential power under Article II, I think it well to establish the statute's basis in congressional power under Article I. Congress's power to "establish an uniform Rule of Naturalization," Art. I, § 8, cl. 4, enables it to grant American citizenship to someone born abroad. *United States v. Wong Kim Ark*, 169 U.S. 649–703 (1898). The naturalization power also enables Congress to furnish the people it makes citizens with papers verifying their citizenship—say a consular report of birth abroad (which certifies citizenship of an American born outside the United States) or a passport (which certifies citizenship for purposes of international travel). As the Necessary and Proper Clause confirms, every congressional power "carries with it all those incidental powers which are necessary to its complete and effectual execution." *Cohens v. Virginia*, 19 U.S. (6 Wheat.) 264, 429 (1821). Even on a miserly understanding of Congress's incidental authority, Congress may make grants of citizenship "effectual" by providing for the issuance of certificates authenticating them.

One would think that if Congress may grant Zivotofsky a passport and a birth report, it may also require these papers to record his birthplace as "Israel." The birthplace specification promotes the document's citizenship-authenticating function by identifying the bearer, distinguishing people with similar names but different birthplaces from each other, helping authorities uncover identity fraud, and facilitating retrieval of the Government's citizenship records. To be sure, recording Zivotofsky's birthplace as "Jerusalem" rather than "Israel" would fulfill these objectives, but when faced with alternative ways to carry its powers into execution, Congress has the "discretion" to choose the one it deems "most beneficial to the people." *McCulloch v. Maryland*, 17 U.S. (4 Wheat.) 316, 421 (1819). It thus has the right to decide that recording birthplaces as "Israel" makes for better foreign policy. Or that regardless of international politics, a passport or birth report should respect its bearer's conscientious belief that Jerusalem belongs to Israel.

No doubt congressional discretion in executing legislative powers has its limits; Congress's chosen approach must be not only "necessary" to carrying its powers into execution, but also "proper." Congress thus may not transcend boundaries upon legislative authority stated or implied elsewhere in the Constitution. But as we shall see, § 214(d) does not transgress any such restriction.

II

The Court frames this case as a debate about recognition. Recognition is a sovereign's official acceptance of a status under international law. A sovereign might recognize a foreign entity as a state, a regime as the other state's government, a place as part of the other state's territory, rebel forces in the other state as a belligerent power, and so on. 2 M. Whiteman, Digest of International Law § 1 (1963). President Truman recognized Israel as a state in 1948, but Presidents have consistently declined to recognize Jerusalem as a part of Israel's (or any other state's) sovereign territory.

The Court holds that the Constitution makes the President alone responsible for recognition and that § 214(d) invades this exclusive power. I agree that the Constitution *empowers* the President to extend recognition on behalf of the United States, but I find it a much harder question whether it makes that power exclusive. The Court tells us that "the weight of historical evidence" supports exclusive executive authority over "the formal determination of recognition." But even with its attention confined to formal recognition, the Court is forced to admit that "history is not all on one side." To take a stark example, Congress legislated in 1934 to grant independence to the Philippines, which were then an American colony. In the course of doing so, Congress directed the President to "recognize the independence of the Philippine Islands as a separate and self-governing nation" and to "acknowledge the authority and control over the same of the government instituted by the people thereof." § 10, *id.*, at 463. Constitutional? And if Congress may control recognition when exercising its power "to dispose of . . . the Territory or other Property belonging to the United States," Art. IV, § 3, cl. 2, why not when exercising other enumerated powers? Neither text nor history nor precedent yields a clear answer to these questions. Fortunately, I have no need to confront these matters today—nor does the Court—because § 214(d) plainly does not concern recognition.

Recognition is more than an announcement of a policy. Like the ratification of an international agreement or the termination of a treaty, it is a formal legal act with effects under international law. It signifies acceptance of an international status, and it makes a commitment to continued acceptance of that status and respect for any attendant rights. . . . In order to extend recognition, a state must perform an act that unequivocally manifests that intention. That act can consist of an express conferral of recognition, or one of a handful of acts that by international custom imply recognition—chiefly, entering into a bilateral treaty, and sending or receiving an ambassador.

To know all this is to realize at once that § 214(d) has nothing to do with recognition. Section 214(d) does not require the Secretary to make a formal declaration about Israel's sovereignty over Jerusalem. And nobody suggests that international custom infers acceptance of sovereignty from the birthplace designation on a passport or birth report, as it does from bilateral treaties or exchanges of ambassadors. Recognition would preclude the United States (as a matter of international law) from later contesting Israeli sovereignty over Jerusalem. But making a notation in a passport or birth report does not encumber the Republic with any international obligations. It leaves the Nation free (so far as international law is concerned) to change its mind in the future. . . .

Section 214(d) performs a more prosaic function than extending recognition. . . . Since birthplace specifications in citizenship documents are matters within Congress's control, Congress may treat Jerusalem as a part of Israel when regulating the recording of birthplaces, even if the President does not do so when extending recognition. Section 214(d), by the way, expressly directs the Secretary to "record the place of birth as Israel" "*[f]or purposes of* the registration of birth, certification of nationality, or issuance of a passport." (Emphasis added.) And the law bears the caption, "Record of Place of Birth as Israel *for Passport Purposes*." (Emphasis added.) Finding recognition in this provision is rather like finding admission to the Union in a provision that treats American Samoa as a State for purposes of a federal highway safety program.

III

The Court complains that § 214(d) requires the Secretary of State to issue official documents implying that Jerusalem is a part of Israel; that it appears in a section of the statute bearing the title "United States Policy with Respect to Jerusalem as the Capital of Israel"; and that foreign "observers interpreted [it] as altering United States policy regarding Jerusalem." But these features do not show that § 214(d) recognizes Israel's sovereignty over Jerusalem. They show only that the law displays symbolic support for Israel's territorial claim. That symbolism may have tremendous significance as a matter of international diplomacy, but it makes no difference as a matter of constitutional law.

Even if the Constitution gives the President sole power to extend recognition, it does not give him sole power to make all decisions relating to foreign disputes over sovereignty. To the contrary, a fair reading of Article I allows Congress to decide for itself how its laws should handle these controversies. Read naturally, power to "regulate Commerce with foreign Nations," § 8, cl. 3, includes power to regulate imports from Gibraltar as British goods or as Spanish goods. Read naturally, power to "regulate the Value . . . of foreign Coin," § 8, cl. 5, includes power to honor (or not) currency issued by Taiwan. And so on for the other enumerated powers. . . .

The Constitution likewise does not give the President exclusive power to determine which claims to statehood and territory "are legitimate in the eyes of the United States," [majority opinion]. Congress may express its own views about these matters by declaring war, restricting trade, denying foreign aid, and much else besides. To take just one example, in 1991, Congress responded to Iraq's invasion of Kuwait by enacting a resolution authorizing use of military force. No doubt the resolution reflected Congress's views about the legitimacy of Iraq's territorial claim. The preamble referred to Iraq's "illegal occupation" and stated that "the international community has demanded . . . that Kuwait's independence and legitimate government be restored." These statements are far more categorical than the caption "United States Policy with Respect to Jerusalem as the Capital of Israel." Does it follow that the authorization of the use of military force invaded the President's exclusive powers? Or that it would have done so had the President recognized Iraqi sovereignty over Kuwait?

History does not even support an exclusive Presidential power to make what the Court calls "formal statements" about "the legitimacy of a state or government and its territorial bounds," [majority opinion]. For a long time, the Houses of Congress have made formal statements announcing their own positions on these issues, again without provoking constitutional objections. *[The Court cited congressional statements asserting support for "the independent Government" of Texas (1837); the "occupied country" of Tibet (1991); and "the legitimate, democratically-elected Government of Lebanon" (2008).—Editors]*

In the final analysis, the Constitution may well deny Congress power to recognize—the power to make an international commitment accepting a foreign entity as a state, a regime as its government, a place as a part of its territory, and so on. But whatever else § 214(d) may do, it plainly does not make (or require the President to make) a commitment accepting Israel's sovereignty over Jerusalem.

IV

. . . No consistent or coherent theory supports the Court's decision. At times, the Court seems concerned with the possibility of congressional interference with the President's ability to extend or withhold legal recognition. The Court concedes, as it must, that the notation required by § 214(d) "would not itself constitute a formal act of recognition." It still frets, however, that Congress *could* try to regulate the President's "statements" in a way that "override[s] the President's recognition determination." But "[t]he circumstance, that . . . [a] power may be abused, is no answer. All powers may be abused." 2 J. Story, Commentaries on the Constitution of the United States § 921, p. 386 (1833). What matters is whether *this* law interferes with the President's ability to withhold recognition. It would be comical to claim that it does. The Court identifies no reason to believe that the United States—or indeed any other country—uses the place-of-birth field in passports and birth reports as a forum for performing the act of recognition. That is why nobody thinks the United States withdraws recognition from Canada when it accommodates a Quebec nationalist's request to have his birthplace recorded as "Montreal."

To the extent doubts linger about whether the United States recognizes Israel's sovereignty over Jerusalem, § 214(d) leaves the President free to dispel them by issuing a disclaimer of intent to recognize. A disclaimer always suffices to prevent an act from effecting recognition. Restatement (Second) of Foreign Relations Law of the United States § 104(1) (1962). . . .

At other times, the Court seems concerned with Congress's failure to give effect to a recognition decision that the President has already made. The Court protests, for instance, that § 214(d) "directly contradicts" the President's refusal to recognize Israel's sovereignty over Jerusalem. But even if the Constitution empowers the President alone to extend recognition, it nowhere obliges Congress to align its laws with the President's recognition decisions. Because the President and Congress are "perfectly co-ordinate by the terms of their common commission," The Federalist No. 49 (Madison), the President's use of the recognition power does not constrain Congress's use of its legislative powers. . . .

The Court elsewhere objects that § 214(d) interferes with the autonomy and unity of the Executive Branch, setting the branch against itself. The Court suggests, for instance, that the law prevents the President from maintaining his neutrality about Jerusalem in "his and his agent's statements." That is of no constitutional significance. As just shown, Congress has power to legislate without regard to recognition, and where Congress has the power to legislate, the President has a duty to "take Care" that its legislation "be faithfully executed," Art. II, § 3. It is likewise "the duty of the secretary of state to conform to the law"; where Congress imposes a responsibility on him, "he is so far the officer of the law; is amenable to the laws for his conduct; and cannot at his discretion sport away the vested rights of others." *Marbury v. Madison*, 5 U.S. (1 Cranch) 137, 158, 166 (1803). The Executive's involvement in carrying out this law does not affect its constitutionality; the Executive carries out every law.

The Court's error could be made more apparent by applying its reasoning to the President's power "to make Treaties," Art. II, § 2, cl. 2. There is no question that Congress may, if it wishes, pass laws that openly flout treaties made by the President. *Head Money Cases*, 112 U.S. 580, 597 (1884). Would anyone have dreamt that the President may refuse to carry out such laws—or, to bring the point closer to home, refuse to execute federal courts' judgments under such laws—so that the Executive may "speak with one voice" about the country's international obligations? To ask is to answer. Today's holding puts the implied power to recognize territorial claims (which the Court infers from the power to recognize states, which it infers from the responsibility to receive ambassadors) on a higher footing than the express power to make treaties. And this, even though the Federalist describes the making of treaties as a "delicate and important prerogative," but the reception of ambassadors as "more a matter of dignity than of authority," "a circumstance which will be without consequence in the administration of the government." The Federalist No. 69 (Hamilton).

In the end, the Court's decision does not rest on text or history or precedent. It instead comes down to "functional considerations"—principally the Court's perception that the Nation "must speak with one voice" about the status of Jerusalem. The vices of this mode of analysis go beyond mere lack of footing in the Constitution. Functionalism of the sort the Court practices today will *systematically* favor the unitary President over the plural Congress in disputes involving foreign affairs. It is possible that this approach will make for more effective foreign policy, perhaps as effective as that of a monarchy. It is certain that, in the long run, it will erode the structure of separated powers that the People established for the protection of their liberty.

[Justice Scalia next critiqued Justice Thomas's concurrence for, among other things, a "stingy interpretation of the enumerated powers" and a view of executive powers that yields "a presidency more reminiscent of George III than George Washington."—Editors]

* * *

International disputes about statehood and territory are neither rare nor obscure. Leading foreign debates during the 19th century concerned how the United States should respond to revolutions in Latin America, Texas, Mexico, Hawaii, Cuba. During the 20th century, attitudes toward Communist governments in Russia and China became conspicuous subjects of agitation. Disagreements about Taiwan, Kashmir, and Crimea remain prominent today. A President empowered to decide all questions relating to these matters, immune from laws embodying congressional disagreement with his position, would have uncontrolled mastery of a vast share of the Nation's foreign affairs.

That is not the chief magistrate under which the American People agreed to live when they adopted the national charter. They believed that "[t]he accumulation of all powers, legislative, executive, and judiciary, in the same hands, . . . may justly be pronounced the very definition of tyranny." The Federalist No. 47 (Madison). For this reason, they did not entrust either the President or Congress with sole power to adopt uncontradictable policies about *any* subject—foreign-sovereignty disputes included. They instead gave each political department its own powers, and with that the freedom to contradict the other's policies. Under the Constitution they approved, Congress may require Zivotofsky's passport and birth report to record his birthplace as Israel, even if that requirement clashes with the President's preference for neutrality about the status of Jerusalem.

NOTES

1. What types of constitutional argument (p. 42) are used by the different opinions in *Zivotofsky*? Which opinion do you find most persuasive? Is there a good argument not made by any of the opinions?

2. Do you recognize any arguments from the Neutrality Controversy in the *Zivotofsky* opinions? Does anybody take Hamilton's side? Does anybody take Madison's?

3. The majority points out that many presidents have made recognition decisions in the absence of any congressional direction. Is that tradition instructive about whether the president is *bound* by congressional direction?

4. Does *Zivotofsky* ultimately turn on Congress's powers under Article I, or on the president's powers under Article II? Is it both? Which one should a court address first?

5. What is the majority's stance towards the claims made in *Curtiss-Wright*, that the president has a nearly comprehensive foreign affairs power? What *should* its stance have been?

6. The majority opinion notes that when George W. Bush signed Section 214 into law, he issued a "signing statement" that it could not be constitutionally enforced. (For another example of a constitutional signing statement, see p. 167) Should that fact have any relevance to the Court's decision on the constitutional issue? And in any event, is there something wrong with what President Bush did? Does the president have a duty to veto unconstitutional laws?

A NOTE ON EXECUTIVE AGREEMENTS

As mentioned above, Article II allows the president to make treaties with foreign nations with the consent of two third of the Senate. But can the president also make foreign agreements outside of the treaty power? Throughout the twentieth century, presidents have claimed the authority to make "executive agreements" with foreign nations. These agreements may have legal status as a matter of international law, but their status as domestic law is trickier. (Look at the text of the Supremacy Clause in Article VI. Do you see why?) Insofar as an executive agreement consists of the president's promise to exercise pre-existing powers, in exchange for undertakings by the foreign government, there is little doubt that the agreements are lawful. But may a president promise, on behalf of the United States, to do things that otherwise lie outside of unilateral presidential authority—such as preempting state law?

In 1933, President Roosevelt officially recognized the government of the Soviet Union in an exchange known as the Litvinov Agreement, which settled various claims between the two countries. In subsequent litigation, lower courts questioned whether the agreement could displace state property law and other commercial law. In two cases, *United States v. Belmont*, 301 U.S. 324 (1937), and *United States v. Pink*, 315 U.S. 203 (1942), the Supreme Court held that the agreements were lawful and displaced state law. The Court noted that even though treaties, unlike executive agreements were covered by "the express language" of the Supremacy Clause, "the same rule would result in the case of all international compacts and agreements from the very fact that complete power over international affairs is in the national government and is not and cannot be subject to any curtailment or interference on the part of the several states." *Belmont*, at 331. This language seemed to bless executive agreements as a substitute for the treaty power.

In a later case, *Dames & Moore v. Regan*, 453 U.S. 654 (1981), the Court again upheld an executive agreement that suspended state law, this time as part of the resolution of the Iranian hostage crisis of 1979. This time, the Court placed much more emphasis on Congress's authorization of the agreements. It concluded that some of the president's actions—those nullifying attachments and ordering the transfer of Iranian assets—were taken pursuant to "specific congressional authorization." Other actions—the suspension of claims in U.S. courts—were not "directly" authorized, but were supported by the "tenor of Congress' legislation in this area" and "a history of congressional acquiescence in conduct of the sort engaged in by the President." Not technically authorized by Congress, but kind of close.

Dames & Moore's implicitly cut back on *Belmont* and *Pink*. If executive agreements are authorized by Congress, then they can more easily displace state law because they are executing a statute, which is explicitly covered by the Supremacy Clause.

More recent cases are not uniform. Two cases have found state law to be displaced. See *Crosby v. National Foreign Trade Council*, 530 U.S. 363 (2000) (finding Massachusetts law forbidding state agencies from buying goods or services from companies that do business with the government of Burma [Myanmar] preempted because the state law was an obstacle to achieving the purposes of a congressional enactment designed to put pressure on the Burmese regime by authorizing the president to reduce sanctions); and *American Insurance Ass'n v. Garamendi*, 539 U.S. 396 (2003) (finding implied preemption of a California law requiring European affiliates of insurance companies doing business in California to divulge information related to unpaid Holocaust-era insurance policies for the purpose of facilitating lawsuits in California, on the grounds that the law was inconsistent with the president's foreign affairs powers even though not in conflict with any extant treaty or executive agreement). But another case has denied the president's power to invoke a non-self-executing treaty and various international obligations to set aside Texas death penalty proceedings. That case, *Medellín v. Texas*, 552 U.S. 491 (2008), is presented at p. 684.

A NOTE ON THE IRANIAN NUCLEAR AGREEMENT

In 2015, President Obama concluded negotiations with the Republic of Iran regarding its nuclear program, leading to an agreement, called the Joint Comprehensive Plan of Action. Under the Plan, Iran agreed to certain restrictions on the development of nuclear weapons in return for immediate lifting of economic sanctions, including the return of Iranian assets now frozen in Western banks, which probably amount to about $100 billion. In addition, the agreement called for lifting a U.N. prohibition on arms sales to Iran in five years and on Iranian development of a nuclear-capable ballistic missile in eight years.

The executive branch did not submit the Plan to the Senate for ratification as a treaty, so it has the status of an executive agreement. Congress responded in the same year by passing the Iran Nuclear Agreement Review Act, which required the administration to submit the terms of the agreement to Congress for approval or disapproval, subject to presidential veto. This meant, in effect, that the Plan could go into effect as an executive agreement with the support of one third of one of the two Houses of Congress. A motion of disapproval was filibustered in the Senate; the opponents could not muster 60 votes for cloture; and the measure died, allowing the Plan to go into effect.

During the final stages of negotiations, Senator Tom Cotton of Arkansas drafted an open letter to the leaders of Iran, signed by 41 senators. It warned that because the Plan had not been ratified by the Senate, "[t]he next president could revoke such an executive agreement with the stroke of a pen and future Congresses could modify the terms of the agreement at any time." Is that correct? Was it in any way improper for a group of Senators to publish such a letter? If so, why?

[Assignment 15]

F.   WAR: "CONGRESS SHALL HAVE POWER . . . TO DECLARE WAR" BUT "THE PRESIDENT SHALL BE COMMANDER IN CHIEF"

Starting War

How does the Constitution allocate the enormously important powers of war and peace? From the beginning, this has been a controversial question, with different views prevailing at different times. While there have been noteworthy judicial decisions in this area, the primary interpretive battleground has been in the political sphere, with Congress and the president advancing their own constitutional views and struggling for primacy.

We begin with a survey of the text of the Constitution's provisions concerning war powers, the history of their drafting, and a summary of modern practice. We then proceed to explore these issues by examining, roughly chronologically, a series of illustrative situations involving the exercise of war powers throughout America's history: the Civil War; World War II; the Korean War; the Vietnam War; the First Gulf War; the Kosovo War; the "War on Terror" following the attacks of September 11, 2001; and the 2011 military intervention in Libya.

As to each situation, consider the recurring constitutional questions: What is the scope of Congress's power "to declare War"? What is the scope of the president's power as "Commander in Chief"? Who has the power to initiate a war? What about defensive actions in immediate response to attacks? Who has the power to *conduct* war (and what does this include)? What happens where the several war powers of Congress and the president may intersect and overlap? What is "war"—is it any use of military force? And finally: Has America's actual constitutional practice with respect to war been consistent with the Constitution's allocation of war powers?

Text

The Constitution appears to vest both Congress and the president with a share of the war power of the nation. Congress has a number of quite specific Article I, Section 8 powers relevant to declaring and waging war. Here are the most relevant provisions:

The Congress shall have power . . .

[10] To define and punish Piracies and Felonies committed on the high Seas, and Offences against the Law of Nations;

[11] To declare War, grant Letters of Marque and Reprisal, and make Rules concerning Captures on Land and Water;

[12] To raise and support Armies, but no Appropriation of Money to that Use shall be for a longer Term than two Years;

[13] To provide and maintain a Navy;

[14] To make Rules for the Government and Regulation of the land and naval Forces;

[15] To provide for calling forth the Militia to execute the Laws of the Union, suppress Insurrections and repel Invasions;

[16] To provide for organizing, arming, and disciplining, the Militia, and for governing such Part of them as may be employed in the Service of the United States, reserving to the States respectively, the Appointment of the Officers, and the Authority of training the Militia according to the discipline prescribed by Congress. . . .

In addition, Congress possesses the taxing and spending powers (Art. I, Sec. 8, cl. 1) and the Necessary and Proper Clause power "[t]o make all Laws which shall be necessary and proper for carrying into Execution the foregoing Powers, and all other Powers vested by this Constitution in the Government of the United States, or in any Department or Officer thereof" (Art. I, Sec. 8, cl. 18).

At the same time, however, the president is given several general and specific powers with respect to war. The president possesses "[t]he executive Power" of the United States (Art. II, Sec. 1), and is specifically made "Commander in Chief of the Army and Navy of the United States, and of the Militia of the several States, when called into the actual Service of the United States" (Art. II, Sec. 2, cl. 1). The president "shall take Care that the Laws be faithfully executed" (Art. II, Sec. 3). And the president is charged by oath to "preserve, protect, and defend the Constitution of the United States."

These powers have formed the basis for the claimed authority of the president to send the nation's armed forces into combat even when Congress has not declared or authorized war.

Another section of the Constitution limits the war-making powers of *states*. Article I, Section 10, Clause 3 reads: "No State shall, without the Consent of Congress, . . . keep Troops, or ships of War in time of Peace, . . . or engage in War, unless actually invaded, or in such imminent Danger as will not admit of delay."

Historical Context

The Constitution's provisions were written against a background understanding of "executive power" as including prerogative powers over war and peace. See generally Saikrishna B. Prakash & Michael D. Ramsey, *The Executive Power Over Foreign Affairs*, 111 Yale L.J. 231 (2001). Obviously, the Constitution departs from this understanding in part. Specifically, it relocates to the legislative branch the power "to declare War" and to raise and support armies and navies, while retaining for the president the role of Commander-in-Chief and whatever else remains of the "executive power." Hence, understanding the war power in historical context requires us to understand the specific clauses mentioned above against the background understanding of executive power.

An account of a debate at the Constitutional Convention at Philadelphia may be illuminating. The debate, recorded in Madison's Notes, focused on a proposal to change the language from a grant of power to Congress to "*make* War" to a power to "*declare* War." What is printed below is the entire debate on this provision. As you read it, ask yourself what inferences can be drawn for interpreting the Constitution.

James Madison's Notes from the Constitutional Convention: "To Make War"

August 17, 1787

Mr. Pinkney opposed the vesting this power in the Legislature. Its proceedings were too slow. It wd. meet but once a year. The Hs. of Reps. would be too numerous for such deliberations. The Senate would be the best depositary, being more acquainted with foreign affairs, and most capable of proper resolutions. If the States are equally represented in Senate, so as to give no advantage to large States, the power will notwithstanding be safe, as the small have their all at stake in such cases as well as the large States. It would be singular for one authority to make war, and another peace.

Mr. Butler. The objections agst the Legislature lie in great degree agst the Senate. He was for vesting the power in the President, who will have all the requisite qualities, and will not make war but when the Nation will support it.

Mr. Madison and Mr. Gerry moved to insert "*declare*," striking out "*make*" war; leaving to the Executive the power to repel sudden attacks.

Mr. Sharman thought it stood very well. The executive shd be able to repel and not to commence war. "Make" better than "declare" the latter narrowing the power too much.

Mr. Gerry never expected to hear in a republic a motion to empower the Executive alone to declare war.

Mr. Elseworth. there is a material difference between the cases of making *war* and making *peace*. It shd be more easy to get out of war, than into it. War also is a simple and overt declaration. peace attended with intricate & secret negociations.

Mr. Mason was agst giving the power of war to the Executive, because not safely to be trusted with it; or to the Senate, because not so constructed as to be entitled to it. He was for clogging rather than facilitating war; but for facilitating peace. He preferred "*declare*" to "*make*."

On the motion to insert *declare*—in place of *make*, it was agreed to.

N.H. no. Mas. abst. Cont. no. * Pa. ay. Del. ay. Md. ay. Va. ay. N.C. ay. S.C. ay. Geo. ay.

[* On the remark by Mr. King that "*make*" war might be understood to "*conduct*" it which was an Executive function, Mr. Elseworth gave up his objection, and the vote of Cont. was changed to—ay.]

Mr. Pinkney's motion to strike out whole clause, disagd to without call of States.

Mr. Butler moved to give the Legislature power of peace, as they were to have that of war.

Mr. Gerry 2d him. 8 Senators may possibly exercise the power if vested in that body, and 14 if all should be present; and may consequently give up part of the U. States. The Senate are more liable to be corrupted by an Enemy than the whole Legislature.

On the motion for adding "and peace" after "war"

N. H. no. Mas. no. Ct. no. Pa. no. Del. no. Md. no. Va. No. N.C. no S.C. no. Geo. no.

NOTES

1. What (if anything) does this exchange tell us about the meaning of the phrase "declare war" in historical context? Looking at a broader set of historical materials, most scholars have concluded that Congress (and not the president) had the power to decide to take the nation into a condition of war. See Michael D. Ramsey, *Textualism and War Powers*, 69 U. Chi. L. Rev. 1543 (2002); Charles A. Lofgren, *War-Making Under the Constitution: The Original Understanding*, 81 Yale L.J. 672 (1972). But some others think the Declare War Clause was limited to providing formal recognition to such a state of affairs and triggering certain national and international legal relationships that come with a formal state of war. On that view, the executive retained the power to wage war, limited only by Congress's other powers such as the power of the purse. See John C. Yoo, *The Continuation of Politics by Other Means: The Original Understanding of War Powers*, 84 Cal. L. Rev. 167 (1996).

2. What about the president's power to use military force *defensively*—to "repel sudden attacks," in Madison's words? What (if anything) does this historical exchange tell us about that power? And what relevance does that history have today, in a world where technology permits "sudden attacks" that are increasingly quick and devastating?

Practice and Precedent

It should not be surprising that war powers have been an area of conflict between the political branches. Predictably, the executive branch has tended to take a pro-executive view while the legislative branch has adopted a pro-legislative view. Often, though, the two branches are in agreement. One obvious case was their agreement to go to war with Japan after the attack on Pearl Harbor. And yet the two branches frequently disagree as well, as in the later stages of the Vietnam War. They disagree about the meaning of congressional resolutions that can be taken as endorsements or quasi-authorizations of presidential authority to wage war, and they disagree about the still more ambiguous implications of congressional appropriations for support of military operations already underway.

In general, since the end of World War II, more of the initiative in the use of the war powers has been seized by the president. President Truman sent troops to Korea on his own authority. He quickly obtained both international support (from the United Nations) and congressional support through funding for the war effort, but the four-year Korean War was never authorized by Congress (unless funding decisions count). The Vietnam War was waged on the authority of the Gulf of Tonkin Resolution (see p. 312), a less than crystalline authorization for war. Numerous other military engagements in the second half of the twentieth century were the result of essentially unilateral presidential action. In recent practice the president has been the primary decision-maker on the question of use of military force and Congress has been reduced to the role of providing an uncertain check on presidential military action.

Many of the major armed conflicts involving the United States were not authorized by a formal declaration of war. Indeed, there have been only five formal declarations of war in U.S. history: The War of 1812, the Mexican-American War, the Spanish-American War, World War I, and World War II. (Six, if one counts the American Declaration of Independence, which was in part an attempt to clothe American forces with the status of legitimate armed belligerents entitled to the protections of the law of war.) Must Congress formally "declare" "war"—using those magic words—in order to exercise its war-initiating power under the Declare War Clause? And what kind of activities rise to the level that they have to be authorized by Congress? Rescue operations? Humanitarian actions? Deployment of troops for peacekeeping? Limited armed interventions to arrest a war criminal? Hacking the servers of a foreign army? How should a court decide? Should courts decide at all?

Many disputes about the war powers never reach the federal courts, though there are exceptions, such as *The Prize Cases*. What does that mean for the weight given to practice as a constitutional argument? Does practice "liquidate" the meaning of the Constitution, as Madison said in *The Federalist No. 37*? Or must we conclude, if practice is inconsistent with the Constitution, that a great deal of the nation's practice with respect to war powers has been unconstitutional? Consider these questions as you read the following case studies.

The Brig Amy Warwick (The Prize Cases)

67 U.S. (2 Black) 635 (1863)

[In 1861, after the South attacked Fort Sumter, President Lincoln proclaimed a blockade of Southern ports. Under the terms of the blockade, and in accordance with the law of nations at the time, vessels violating the blockade were subject to being captured and seized as "prizes." The legality of the blockade was challenged by the owners of four seized ships: the AMY WARWICK, *a merchant vessel carrying coffee from Rio de Janeiro, Brazil, to Hampton Roads, Virginia (she was "sailing under American colors, and her commander was ignorant of the war"); the* CRENSHAW, *sailing from Virginia to Liverpool, England with tobacco; the* HIAWATHA, *a British ship also carrying tobacco from Virginia to Liverpool; and the* BRILLIANTE, *a Mexican schooner carrying flour from New Orleans to the Yucatán peninsula in Mexico.*

Congress had not declared war on the states of the Confederacy. And while it did eventually authorize the blockade and other actions, it never made a declaration of war.—Editors]

■ MR. JUSTICE GRIER.

There are certain propositions of law which must necessarily affect the ultimate decision of these cases, and many others, which it will be proper to discuss and decide before we notice the special facts peculiar to each.

They are, 1st. Had the President a right to institute a blockade of ports in possession of persons in armed rebellion against the Government, on the principles of international law, as known and acknowledged among civilized States?

2d. Was the property of persons domiciled or residing within those States a proper subject of capture on the sea as "enemies' property?"

I. Neutrals have a right to challenge the existence of a blockade *de facto*, and also the authority of the party exercising the right to institute it. They have a right to enter the ports of a friendly nation for the purposes of trade and commerce, but are bound to recognize the rights of a belligerent engaged in actual war, to use this mode of coercion, for the purpose of subduing the enemy. . . . To legitimate the capture of a neutral vessel or property on the high seas, a war must exist *de facto*, and the neutral must have a knowledge or notice of the intention of one of the parties belligerent to use this mode of coercion against a port, city, or territory, in possession of the other.

Let us enquire whether, at the time this blockade was instituted, a state of war existed which would justify a resort to these means of subduing the hostile force.

War has been well defined to be, "That state in which a nation prosecutes its right by force."

The parties belligerent in a public war are independent nations. But it is not necessary to constitute war, that both parties should be acknowledged as independent nations or sovereign States. A war may exist where one of the belligerents, claims sovereign rights as against the other.

Insurrection against a government may or may not culminate in an organized rebellion, but a civil war always begins by insurrection against the lawful authority of the Government. A civil war is never solemnly declared; it becomes such by its accidents—the number, power, and organization of the persons who originate and carry it on. When the party in rebellion occupy and hold in a hostile manner a certain portion of territory; have declared their independence; have cast off their allegiance; have organized armies; have commenced hostilities against their former sovereign, the world acknowledges them as belligerents, and the contest a *war*. *They* claim to be in arms to establish their liberty and independence, in order to become a sovereign State, while the sovereign party treats them as insurgents and rebels who owe allegiance, and who should be punished with death for their treason.

The laws of war, as established among nations, have their foundation in reason, and all tend to mitigate the cruelties and misery produced by the scourge of war. Hence the parties to a civil war usually concede to each other belligerent rights. They exchange prisoners, and adopt the other courtesies and rules common to public or national wars. . . .

By the Constitution, Congress alone has the power to declare a national or foreign war. It cannot declare war against a State, or any number of States, by virtue of any clause in the Constitution. The Constitution confers on the President the whole Executive power. He is bound to take care that the laws be faithfully executed.

He is Commander-in-chief of the Army and Navy of the United States, and of the militia of the several States when called into the actual service of the United States. He has no power to initiate or declare a war either against a foreign nation or a domestic State. But by the Acts of Congress of February 28th, 1795, and 3d of March, 1807, he is authorized to called out the militia and use the military and naval forces of the United States in case of invasion by foreign nations, and to suppress insurrection against the government of a State or of the United States.

If a war be made by invasion of a foreign nation, the President is not only authorized but bound to resist force by force. He does not initiate the war, but is bound to accept the challenge without waiting for any special legislative authority. And whether the hostile party be a foreign invader, or States organized in rebellion, it is none the less a war, although the declaration of it be "*unilateral*." Lord Stowell (1 Dodson, 247) observes, "It is not the less a war on *that account*, for war may exist without a declaration on either side. It is so laid down by the best writers on the law of nations. A declaration of war by one country only, is not a mere challenge to be accepted or refused at pleasure by the other."

The battles of Palo Alto and Resaca de la Palma had been fought before the passage of the Act of Congress of May 13th, 1846, which recognized "*a state of war as existing by the act of the Republic of Mexico.*" This act not only provided for the future prosecution of the war, but was itself a vindication and ratification of the Act of the President in accepting the challenge without a previous formal declaration of war by Congress.

This greatest of civil wars was not gradually developed by popular commotion, tumultuous assemblies, or local unorganized insurrections. However long may have been its previous conception, it nevertheless sprung forth suddenly from the parent brain, a Minerva in the full panoply of *war*. The President was bound to meet it in the shape it presented itself, without waiting for Congress to baptize it with a name; and no name given to it by him or them could change the fact.

It is not the less a civil war, with belligerent parties in hostile array, because it may be called an "insurrection" by one side, and the insurgents be considered as rebels or traitors. It is not necessary that the independence of the revolted province or State be acknowledged in order to constitute it a party belligerent in a war according to the law of nations. Foreign nations acknowledge it as war by a declaration of neutrality. . . .

The law of nations is also called the law of nature; it is founded on the common consent as well as the common sense of the world. It contains no such anomalous doctrine as that which this Court are now for the first time desired to pronounce, to wit: That insurgents who have risen in rebellion against their sovereign, expelled her Courts, established a revolutionary government, organized armies, and commenced hostilities, are not *enemies* because they are *traitors*; and a war levied on the Government by traitors, in order to dismember and destroy it, is not a *war* because it is an "insurrection."

Whether the President in fulfilling his duties, as Commander in-chief, in suppressing an insurrection, has met with such armed hostile resistance, and a civil war of such alarming proportions as will compel him to accord to them the character of belligerents, is a question to be decided *by him*, and this Court must be governed by the decisions and acts of the political department of the Government to which this power was entrusted. "He must determine what degree of force the crisis demands." The proclamation of blockade is itself official and conclusive evidence to the Court that a state of war existed which demanded and authorized a recourse to such a measure, under the circumstances peculiar to the case. . . .

If it were necessary to the technical existence of a war, that it should have a legislative sanction, we find it in almost every act passed at the extraordinary session of the Legislature of 1861, which was wholly employed in enacting laws to enable the Government to prosecute the war with vigor and efficiency. And finally, in 1861, we find Congress "*ex major cautela*" and in anticipation of such astute objections, passing an act "approving, legalizing, and making valid all the acts, proclamations, and orders of the President, &c., as if they had been *issued and done under the previous express authority* and direction of the Congress of the United States." . . .

On this first question therefore we are of the opinion that the President had a right, *jure belli*, to institute a blockade of ports in possession of the States in rebellion, which neutrals are bound to regard.

II. We come now to the consideration of the second question. What is included in the term "*enemies' property?*" . . . The appellants contend that the term "enemy" is properly applicable to those only who are subjects or citizens of a foreign State at war with our own. . . .

They insist, moreover, that the President himself, in his proclamation, admits that great numbers of the persons residing within the territories in possession of the insurgent government, are loyal in their feelings, and forced by compulsion and the violence of the rebellious and revolutionary party and its "*de facto* government" to submit to their laws and assist in their scheme of revolution; that the acts of the usurping government cannot legally sever the bond of their allegiance; they have, therefore, a co-relative right to claim the protection of the government for their persons and property, and to be treated as loyal citizens, till legally convicted of having renounced their allegiance and made war against the Government by treasonably resisting its laws.

They contend, also, that insurrection is the act of individuals and not of a government or sovereignty; that the individuals engaged are subjects of law. That confiscation of their property can be effected only under a municipal law. That by the law of the land such confiscation cannot take place without the conviction of the owner of some offence, and finally that the secession ordinances are nullities and ineffectual to release any citizen from his allegiance to the national Government, and consequently that the Constitution and Laws of the United States are still operative over persons in all the States for punishment as well as protection.

This argument rests on the assumption of two propositions, each of which is without foundation on the established law of nations. It assumes that where a civil war exists, the party belligerent claiming to be sovereign, cannot, for some unknown reason, exercise the rights of belligerents, although the revolutionary party may. Being sovereign, he can exercise only sovereign rights over the other party. The insurgent may be killed on the battle-field or by the executioner; his property on land may be confiscated under the municipal law; but the commerce on the ocean, which supplies the rebels with means to support the war, cannot be made the subject of capture under the laws of war, because it is "*unconstitutional!!!*" Now, it is a proposition never doubted, that the belligerent party who claims to be sovereign, may exercise both belligerent and sovereign rights. Treating the other party as a belligerent and using only the milder modes of coercion which the law of nations has introduced to mitigate the rigors of war, cannot be a subject of complaint by the party to whom it is accorded as a grace or granted as a necessity. We have shown that a civil war such as that now waged between the Northern and Southern States is properly conducted according to the humane regulations of public law as regards capture on the ocean.

Under the very peculiar Constitution of this Government, although the citizens owe supreme allegiance to the Federal Government, they owe also a qualified allegiance to the State in which they are domiciled. Their persons and property are subject to its laws.

Hence, in organizing this rebellion, they have *acted as States* claiming to be sovereign over all persons and property within their respective limits, and asserting a right to absolve their citizens from their allegiance to the Federal Government. Several of these States have combined to form a new confederacy, claiming to be acknowledged by the world as a sovereign State. Their right to do so is now being decided by wager of battle. The ports and territory of each of these States are held in hostility to the General Government. It is no loose, unorganized insurrection, having no defined boundary or possession. It has a boundary marked by lines of bayonets, and which can be crossed only by force—south of this line is enemies' territory, because it is claimed and held in possession by an organized, hostile and belligerent power.

All persons residing within this territory whose property may be used to increase the revenues of the hostile power are, in this contest, liable to be treated as enemies, though not foreigners. They have cast off their allegiance and made war on their Government, and are none the less enemies because they are traitors. . . .

Whether property be liable to capture as "enemies' property" does not in any manner depend on the personal allegiance of the owner. "It is the illegal traffic that stamps it as 'enemies' property.' It is of no consequence whether it belongs to an ally or a citizen. The owner, *pro hac vice*, is an enemy."

The produce of the soil of the hostile territory, as well as other property engaged in the commerce of the hostile power, as the source of its wealth and strength, are always regarded as legitimate prize, without regard to the domicil of the owner, and much more so if he reside and trade within their territory.

III. We now proceed to notice the facts peculiar to the several cases submitted for our consideration. The principles which have just been stated apply alike to all of them. . . .

■ MR. JUSTICE NELSON, dissenting.

. . . Another objection taken to the seizure of this vessel and cargo is, that there was no existing war between the United States and the States in insurrection within the meaning of the law of nations, which drew after it the consequences of a public or civil war. A contest by force between independent sovereign States is called a public war; and, when duly commenced by proclamation or otherwise, it entitles both of the belligerent parties to all the rights of war against each other, and as respects neutral nations. Chancellor Kent observes, "Though a solemn declaration, or previous notice to the enemy, be now laid aside, it is essential that some formal public act, proceeding directly from the competent source, should announce to the people at home their new relations and duties growing out of a state of war, and which should equally apprize neutral nations of the fact, to enable them to conform their conduct to the rights belonging to the new state of things." "Such an official act operates from its date to legalize all hostile acts, in like manner as a treaty of peace operates from its date to annul the." He further observes, "as war cannot lawfully be commenced on the part of the United States without an act of Congress, such act is, of course, a formal notice to all the world, and equivalent to the most solemn declaration."

The legal consequences resulting from a state of war between two countries at this day are well understood, and will be found described in every approved work on the subject of international law. The people of the two countries become immediately the enemies of each other—all intercourse commercial or otherwise between then unlawful—all contracts existing at the commencement of the war suspended, and all made during its existence utterly void. . . . All the property of the people of the two countries on land or sea are subject to capture and confiscation by the adverse party as enemies' property, with certain qualifications as it respects property on land, all treaties between the belligerent parties are annulled, The ports of the respective countries may be blockaded, and letters of marque and reprisal granted as rights of war, and the law of prizes as defined by the law of nations comes into full and complete operation, resulting from maritime captures, *jur belli*. War also effects a change in the mutual relations of all States or countries, not directly, as in the case of the belligerents, but immediately and indirectly, though they take no part in the contest, but remain neutral.

This great and pervading change in the existing condition of a country, and in the relations of all her citizens or subjects, external and internal, from a state of peace, is the immediate effect and result of a state of war: and hence the same code which has annexed to the existence of a war all these disturbing consequences has declared that the right of making war belongs exclusively to the supreme or sovereign power of the State.

This power in all civilized nations is regulated by the fundamental laws or municipal constitution of the country.

By our Constitution this power is lodged in Congress. Congress shall have power "to declare war, grant letters of marque and reprisal, and make rules concerning captures on land and water."

We have thus far been considering the status of the citizens or subjects of a country at the breaking out of a public war when recognized or declared by the competent power.

In the case of a rebellion or resistance of a portion of the people of a country against the established government, there is no doubt, if in its progress and enlargement the government thus sought to be overthrown sees fit, it may by the competent power recognize, or declare the existence of a state of civil war, which will draw after it all the consequences and rights of war between the contending parties as in the case of a public war. . . . But before this insurrection against the established Government can be dealt with on the footing of a civil war, within the meaning of the law of nations and the Constitution of the United States, and which will draw after it belligerent rights, it must be recognized or declared by the war-making power of the Government. No power short of this can change the legal status of the Government or the relations of its citizens from that of peace to a state of war, or bring into existence all those duties and obligations to neutral third parties growing out of a state of war. The war power of the Government must be exercised before this changed condition of the Government and people and of neutral third parties can be admitted. There is no difference in this respect between a civil or a public war. . . .

The [Militia] Acts of 1795 and 1807 did not, and could not under the Constitution, confer on the President the power of declaring war against a State of this Union, or of deciding that war existed, and upon that ground authorize the capture and confiscation of the property of every citizen of the State whenever it was found on the waters. The laws of war, whether the war be civil or *inter gentes*, as we have seen, convert every citizen of the hostile State into a public enemy, and treat him accordingly, whatever may have been his previous conduct. This great power over the business and property of the citizen is reserved to the legislative department by the express words of the Constitution. It cannot be delegated or surrendered to the Executive. Congress alone can determine whether war exists or should be declared; and until they have acted, no citizen of the State can be punished in his person or property, unless he had committed some offence against a law of Congress passed before the act was committed, which made it a crime, and defined the punishment. The penalty of confiscation for the acts of others with which he had no concern cannot lawfully be inflicted. . . .

Congress assembled on the call for an extra session the 4th of July, 1861, and among the first acts passed was one in which the President was authorized by proclamation to interdict all trade and intercourse between all the inhabitants of States in insurrection and the rest of the United States, subjecting vessel and cargo to capture and condemnation as prize, and also to direct the capture of any ship or vessel belonging in whole or in part to any inhabitant of a State whose inhabitants are declared by the proclamation to be in a state of insurrection, found at sea or in any part of the rest of the United States. Act of Congress of 13th of July, 1861, secs. 5, 6. The 4th section also authorized the President to close any port in a Collection District obstructed so that the revenue could not be collected, and provided for the capture and condemnation of any vessel attempting to enter. . . .

This Act of Congress, we think, recognized a state of civil war between the Government and the Confederate States, and made it territorial. The Act of Parliament of 1776, which converted the rebellion of the Colonies into a civil territorial war, resembles, in its leading features, the act to which we have referred. . . .

Upon the whole, after the most careful consideration of this case which the pressure of other duties has admitted, I am compelled to the conclusion that no civil war existed between this Government and the States in insurrection till recognized by the Act of Congress 13th of July, 1861; that the President does not possess the power under the Constitution to declare war or recognize its existence within the meaning of the law of nations, which carries with it belligerent rights, and thus change the country and all its citizens from a state of peace to a state of war; that this power belongs exclusively to the Congress of the United States, and, consequently, that the President had no power to set on foot a blockade under the law of nations, and that the capture of the vessel and cargo in this case, and in all cases before us in which the capture occurred before the 13th of July, 1861, for breach of blockade, or as enemies' property, are illegal and void, and that the decrees of condemnation should be reversed and the vessel and cargo restored.

■ MR. CHIEF JUSTICE TANEY, MR. JUSTICE CATRON and MR. JUSTICE CLIFFORD, concurred in the dissenting opinion of MR. JUSTICE NELSON.

NOTES

1.   The key issue that divides the majority and the dissent is whether congressional authorization is required for Lincoln's actions. What does the majority say? What does the dissent say? What are their arguments? Notice that there is a third logically possible position: That Lincoln's actions are forbidden *even if* Congress authorizes them. Nobody on the Court makes that argument, but many in the Confederacy did. How would that argument go?

2.   The Civil War was not a formally declared "war." President Lincoln's view was that the use of force against the Southern states was not a *war* within the meaning of the Constitution, because it was not against a foreign enemy but was rather the suppression by force of a rebellion. Indeed, for one part of the United States to "declare war" against another would have been regarded as improper. Nor was President Lincoln prepared to recognize the "Confederate States of America" as a legitimate sovereign entity, let alone a foreign nation—that would have been inconsistent with the constitutional theory underlying the Union's prosecution of the war. Nevertheless, in practical terms the suppression of the rebellion plainly involved the application of the war power of the United States. Is that a problem? Was Lincoln being inconsistent? Was the Civil War unconstitutional?

3.   If the president can sometimes use force without congressional authorization, when? To respond to sudden attacks? In other circumstances? What do *The Prize Cases* say?

4.   *The Prize Cases* was a pivotal judicial decision concerning the Constitution's allocation of war powers, but it was not the only early judicial decision concerning these issues. The Court's earliest decisions on war powers emphasized congressional control over the use of force rather than presidential power to respond to the use of force by others. Several of these cases involved (like *The Prize Cases*) issues concerning the capture of vessels and claimed property rights, some of which arose in the ambiguous situation created by the so-called "Quasi-War" with France in the late 1790s (when Congress passed several statutes essentially putting the nation on a war footing without formally declaring war). For an early judicial statement embracing Congress's complete power over the decision to go to war and the extent of a war, but also noting that authorization of war brings into play the laws of war, see *Talbot v. Seeman*, 5 U.S. (1 Cranch) 1, 28 (1801) ("The whole powers of war being, by the constitution of the United States, vested in congress, the acts of that body can alone be resorted to as our guides in this enquiry. It is not denied, nor in the course of the argument has it been denied, that congress may authorize general hostilities, in which case the general laws of war apply to our situation; or partial hostilities, in which case the laws of war, so far as they actually apply to our situation, must be noticed."). See also *Bas v. Tingy*, 4 U.S. (4 Dall.) 37 (1800) (discussing the legal status of the "Quasi-War" with France as governed by Congress's enactments); *Little v. Barreme*, 6 U.S. (2 Cranch) 170 (1804) (Marshall, C.J.) (rules of "capture" and seizure of ships in prize cases governed by congressional enactment, not presidential military orders); *Brown v. United States*, 12 U.S. (8 Cranch) 110 (1814) (Marshall, C.J.) (authority of president to confiscate enemy property in United States during War of 1812 governed by Congress's statutes, not executive action); cf. *Durand v. Hollins*, 8 F.Cas. 111 (Circuit Court S.D.N.Y 1860) (sustaining unilateral presidential

military order of bombardment of Greytown, Nicaragua, in response to attacks on U.S. property and persons, against damages action for destruction of property).

———

If the power "to declare War" vests in Congress control over the decision to initiate sustained military action against an enemy force or nation, what counts as a legally effective authorization of such action? Does Congress need to formally and literally "declare" war, or is it sufficient that it enact legislation authorizing the use of military force? (Why might Congress choose the latter rather than the former?) May Congress enact a limited authorization—for example, authorizing a naval bombardment of ports but not an invasion by ground troops? May Congress enact a statute prospectively limiting the use of force that it has not specifically authorized, or specifying situations in which its laws should *not* be construed as authorizing the use of force?

What follows are four enactments of Congress in the modern era, for comparison and constitutional analysis: the explicit Declaration of War against Japan, marking America's formal entry into World War II; the more ambiguous Gulf of Tonkin Resolution of 1964, cited as authorization for the Vietnam War; the War Powers Resolution of 1973, passed over President Nixon's veto and purporting to regulate the use of force in a variety of situations; and the Authorization for Use of Military Force of September 18, 2001, conferring sweeping authority for the War on Terror.

Declaration of War Against Japan
Dec. 8, 1941

Joint Resolution. Declaring that a state of war exists between the Imperial Government of Japan and the Government and the people of the United States and making provisions to prosecute the same.

Whereas the Imperial Government of Japan has committed unprovoked acts of war against the Government and the people of the United States of America: Therefore be it Resolved by the Senate and House of Representatives of the United States of America in Congress assembled,

That the state of war between the United States and the Imperial Government of Japan which has thus been thrust upon the United States is hereby formally declared; and the President is hereby authorized and directed to employ the entire naval and military forces of the United States and the resources of the Government to carry on war against the Imperial Government of Japan; and, to bring the conflict to a successful termination, all of the resources of the country are hereby pledged by the Congress of the United States.

The Gulf of Tonkin Resolution
Aug. 7, 1964

Resolved by the Senate and House of Representatives of the United States of America in Congress assembled,

[Section 1.] That the Congress approves and supports the determination of the President, as Commander in Chief, to take all necessary measures to repel any armed attack against the forces of the United States and to prevent further aggression.

Section 2. The United States regards as vital to its national interest and to world peace the maintenance of international peace and security in southeast Asia. Consonant with the Constitution of the United States and the Charter of the United Nations and in accordance with its obligations under the Southeast Asia Collective Defense Treaty, the United States is, therefore, prepared, as the President determines, to take all necessary steps, including the use of armed force, to assist any member or protocol state of the Southeast Asia Collective Defense Treaty requesting assistance in defense of its freedom.

Section 3. This resolution shall expire when the President shall determine that the peace and security of the area is reasonably assured by international conditions created by action of the United Nations or otherwise, except that it may be terminated earlier by concurrent resolution of the Congress.

NOTES

1.   The Declaration of War Against Japan is a classic instance of a direct, unequivocal, and formal declaration of war. (Germany then declared war on the United States, and the United States declared war on Germany.) Was a declaration of war legally necessary for the president to deploy military force against Japan following the attacks on Pearl Harbor? If not, what additional legal force does a declaration of war permit?

2.   After World War II, Korea was partitioned into two zones of allied occupation: the northern zone, under Soviet forces; and the southern zone, under U.S. forces. (Eventually those occupation zones became North Korea and South Korea.) In 1950, North Korea attacked South Korea. President Truman unilaterally sent in U.S. forces. The United Nations Security Council approved President Truman's actions and called on U.N. members to support the collective defense of South Korea. (The Soviet Union was boycotting the Security Council; otherwise it would have vetoed the action.) Congress never declared war and never specifically authorized it, but it nonetheless continued to appropriate funds for the military. The United States, by treaty, was a member of the United Nations. The U.N. treaty does not itself commit member nations to use military force when requested to assist in enforcement of Security Council actions. (Would a treaty obligation committing the United States to war be consistent with the U.S. Constitution?) Did President Truman possess independent constitutional authority to commit U.S. troops to war in South Korea? Was it part of his executive power over foreign affairs? Was it his duty to faithfully execute U.S. treaty obligations? Does U.N. support dispense with the necessity of a congressional declaration of war? Was the Korean War constitutional?

3.   Was the Vietnam War constitutional? Did the Gulf of Tonkin Resolution constitute sufficient constitutional authorization for the president to wage war in Southeast Asia? (Was authorization needed?) Congress eventually voted to repeal the resolution, but it was the decision to withhold funds for military operations in Southeast Asia past a defined date that ultimately led to the U.S. military's withdrawal from, and the fall of, South Vietnam. Is control of funding the real constitutional power of Congress with respect to war? May Congress implicitly authorize war-making by its funding of the military? How specific must such funding decisions be in order to constitute authorization? Or is control over funding simply an ancillary way of *enforcing* Congress's power to authorize (or not to authorize) war-making?

The Vietnam War generated numerous legal challenges and lower court decisions. See, e.g., *Orlando v. Laird*, 443 F.2d 1039 (2d Cir. 1971) (finding the question properly justiciable but rejecting a constitutional challenge, noting that "[t]he Congress and the Executive have taken mutual and joint action in the prosecution and support of military operations in Southeast Asia from the beginning of those operations" and noting, among other things, the Gulf of Tonkin Resolution). The constitutionality of the war was never decided on the merits by the Supreme Court, though many opportunities were presented for such decision. Are constitutional issues of war and peace nonjusticiable political questions best left to the executive and legislative branches to decide? As long as a proper case with proper parties exists, where resolution of the dispute turns on an interpretation of the respective war powers of Congress and the president, is there any constitutional bar to a judicial decision?

4.   Consider the following military actions:

a.   When the Soviet Union attempted to set up short- and intermediate-range missiles in Cuba, President Kennedy ordered a military "quarantine" (essentially a blockade) of Cuba. Congress did not authorize the action. Constitutional?

b.   President Carter ordered a military commando raid (ultimately unsuccessful) to attempt to rescue U.S. hostages held in Iran following the Iranian seizure of the U.S. Embassy in Tehran in 1979. Congress did not authorize the action. Constitutional?

c.   In 1989, President George H. W. Bush ordered a military invasion of Panama in order to seize the country's dictator, General Manuel Noriega, and protect U.S. citizens in the Canal Zone. Congress did not authorize the action. Constitutional?

5.   What about "covert operations" that involve spying, sabotage, or the use of lethal force? Does Congress need to authorize them? Are they part of the war power? The "Intelligence Authorization Act of 1991" permits covert operations in the form of "activities of the United States Government to influence political, economic, or military conditions abroad, where it is intended that the role of the United States Government will not be apparent or acknowledged publicly." The president must determine that "such an action is necessary to support identifiable foreign policy objectives of the United States and is important to the national security of the United States," set forth this determination in writing within 48 hours, and report this information to the intelligence committees of each house of Congress (or, if the president thinks it necessary to withhold such information, report it only to eight designated high-ranking members of Congress).

6.   As the Vietnam War became increasingly unpopular politically, concern over the drift of war-making power toward the president led Congress in 1973 to pass the War Powers Resolution (WPR) over President Nixon's veto. The WPR purports to presents Congress's constitutional views concerning the respective war powers of Congress and the president, along with a framework for enforcing those views. As you read the materials on the WPR, ask yourself whether it is constitutional and whether it can be given meaningful enforcement by either Congress or the courts. Subsequent presidents have taken the position that the WPR is an unconstitutional attempt by Congress to limit the presidential authority as commander in chief. Even so, presidents have consistently reported military actions to Congress in a manner consistent with the WPR's requirements, seeking to avoid confrontation.

The War Powers Resolution of 1973

Initially passed by Congress in Oct. 1973;
repassed over President Nixon's veto in Nov. 1973

Resolved by the Senate and House of Representatives of the United States of America in Congress assembled,

Section 1. *Short Title.* This joint resolution may be cited as the "War Powers Resolution."

Section 2. *Purpose and Policy.*

(a) It is the purpose of this joint resolution to fulfill the intent of the framers of the Constitution of the United States and insure that the collective judgment of both the Congress and the President will apply to the introduction of United States Armed Forces into hostilities, or into situations where imminent involvement in hostilities is clearly indicated by the circumstances, and to the continued use of such forces . . .

(c) The constitutional powers of the President as Commander-in-Chief to introduce United States Armed Forces into hostilities, or into situations where imminent involvement in hostilities is clearly indicated by the circumstances, are exercised only pursuant to (1) a declaration of war, (2) specific statutory authorization, or (3) a national emergency created by attack upon the United States, its territories or possessions, or its armed forces.

Section 3. *Consultation* [President required to consult Congress "in every possible instance"]

Section 4. *Reporting* [President required to report military action to Congress within 48 hours]

Section 5. *Congressional Action. . . .*

(b) Within sixty calendar days after a report is submitted or is required to be submitted pursuant to section 4(a)(1), whichever is earlier, the President shall terminate any use of United States Armed Forces with respect to which such report was submitted . . . unless the Congress (1) has declared war or enacted a specific authorization for such use of the United States Armed Forces, (2) has extended by law such sixty-day period, or (3) is physically unable to meet as a result of an armed attack upon the United States. Such sixty-day period shall be extended for not more than an additional thirty days if the President determines and certifies to the Congress in writing that unavoidable military necessity respecting the safety of United States Armed Forces requires the continued use of such armed forces in the course of bringing about a prompt removal of such forces.

(c) Notwithstanding subsection (b), at any time that United States Armed Forces are engaged in hostilities outside the territory of the United States, its possessions and territories without a declaration of war or specific statutory authorization, such forces shall be removed by the President if the Congress so directs by concurrent resolution. . . .

Section 8. *Interpretation of Joint Resolution*

(a)   Authority to introduce United States Armed Forces into hostilities or into situations wherein involvement in hostilities is clearly indicated by the circumstances shall not be inferred—

(1)   from any provision of law . . . , including any provision contained in an appropriation Act, unless such provision specifically authorizes the introduction of United States Armed Forces into hostilities or into such situations and states that it is intended to constitute specific statutory authorization within the meaning of this joint resolution; or

(2)   from any treaty heretofore or hereafter ratified unless such treaty is implemented by legislation specifically authorizing the introduction of United States Armed Forces into hostilities or into such situations and stating that it is intended to constitute specific statutory authorization within the meaning of this joint resolution.

* * *

(c)   Nothing in this joint resolution—

(1)   is intended to alter the constitutional authority of the Congress or of the President, or the provisions of existing treaties; or

(2)   shall be construed as granting any authority to the President with respect to the introduction of United States Armed Forces . . . which authority he would not have had in the absence of this joint resolution. . . .

Richard Nixon, Statement Vetoing the War Powers Resolution

Oct. 24, 1973

To the House of Representatives:

I hereby return without my approval House Joint Resolution 542—the War Powers Resolution. While I am in accord with the desire of the Congress to assert its proper role in the conduct of our foreign affairs, the restrictions which this resolution would impose upon the authority of the President are both unconstitutional and dangerous to the best interests of our Nation.

The proper roles of the Congress and the Executive in the conduct of foreign affairs have been debated since the founding of our country. Only recently, however, has there been a serious challenge to the wisdom of the Founding Fathers in choosing not to draw a precise and detailed line of demarcation between the foreign policy powers of the two branches.

The Founding Fathers understood the impossibility of foreseeing every contingency that might arise in this complex area. They acknowledged the need for flexibility in responding to changing circumstances. They recognized that foreign policy decisions must be made through close cooperation between the two branches and not through rigidly codified procedures.

These principles remain as valid today as they were when our Constitution was written. Yet House Joint Resolution 542 would violate those principles by defining the President's powers in ways which would strictly limit his constitutional authority.

Clearly Unconstitutional

House Joint Resolution 542 would attempt to take away, by a mere legislative act, authorities which the President has properly exercised under the Constitution for almost 200 years. One of its provisions would automatically cut off certain authorities after sixty days unless the Congress extended them. Another would allow the Congress to eliminate certain authorities merely by the passage of a concurrent resolution—an action which does not normally have the force of law, since it denies the President his constitutional role in approving legislation.

I believe that both these provisions are unconstitutional. The only way in which the constitutional powers of a branch of the Government can be altered is by amending the Constitution—and any attempt to make such alterations by legislation alone is clearly without force.

Undermining Our Foreign Policy

While I firmly believe that a veto of House Joint Resolution 542 is warranted solely on constitutional grounds, I am also deeply disturbed by the practical consequences of this resolution. For it would seriously undermine this Nation's ability to act decisively and convincingly in times of international crisis. As a result, the confidence of our allies in our ability to assist them could be diminished and the respect of our adversaries for our deterrent posture could decline. A permanent and substantial element of unpredictability would be injected into the world's assessment of American behavior, further increasing the likelihood of miscalculation and war.

If this resolution had been in operation, America's effective response to a variety of challenges in recent years would have been vastly complicated or even made impossible. We may well have been unable to respond in the way we did during the Berlin crisis of 1961, the Cuban missile crisis of 1962, the Congo rescue operation in 1964, and the Jordanian crisis of 1970—to mention just a few examples. In addition, our recent actions to bring about a peaceful settlement of the hostilities in the Middle East would have been seriously impaired if this resolution had been in force.

While all the specific consequences of House Joint Resolution 542 cannot yet be predicted, it is clear that it would undercut the ability of the United States to act as an effective influence for peace. For example, the provision automatically cutting off certain authorities after 60 days unless they are extended by the Congress could work to prolong or intensify a crisis. Until the Congress suspended the deadline, there would be at least a chance of United States withdrawal and an adversary would be tempted therefore to postpone serious negotiations until the 60 days were up. Only after the Congress acted would there be a strong incentive for an adversary to negotiate. In addition, the very existence of a deadline could lead to an escalation of hostilities in order to achieve certain objectives before the 60 days expired.

The measure would jeopardize our role as a force for peace in other ways as well. It would, for example, strike from the President's hand a wide range of important peace-keeping tools by eliminating his ability to exercise quiet diplomacy backed by subtle shifts in our military deployments. It would also cast into doubt authorities which Presidents have used to undertake certain humanitarian relief missions in conflict areas, to protect fishing boats from seizure, to deal with ship or aircraft hijackings, and to respond to threats of attack. Not the least of the adverse consequences of this resolution would be the prohibition contained in section 8 against fulfilling our obligations under the NATO treaty as ratified by the Senate. Finally, since the bill is somewhat vague as to when the 60 day rule would apply, it could lead to extreme confusion and dangerous disagreements concerning the prerogatives of the two branches, seriously damaging our ability to respond to international crises.

Failure to Require Positive Congressional Action

I am particularly disturbed by the fact that certain of the President's constitutional powers as Commander in Chief of the Armed Forces would terminate automatically under this resolution. 60 days after they were invoked. No overt Congressional action would be required to cut off these powers—they would disappear automatically unless the Congress extended them. In effect, the Congress is here attempting to increase its policy-making role through a provision which requires it to take absolutely no action at all.

In my view, the proper way for the Congress to make known its will on such foreign policy questions is through a positive action, with full debate on the merits of the issue and with each member taking the responsibility of casting a yes or no vote after considering those merits. The authorization and appropriations process represents one of the ways in which such influence can be exercised. I do not, however, believe that the Congress can responsibly contribute its considered, collective judgment on such grave questions without full debate and without a yes or no vote. Yet this is precisely what the joint resolution would allow. It would give every future Congress the ability to handcuff every future President merely by doing nothing and sitting still. In my view, one cannot become a responsible partner unless one is prepared to take responsible action.

Strengthening Cooperation between The Congress and the Executive Branches

The responsible and effective exercise of the war powers requires the fullest cooperation between the Congress and the Executive and the prudent fulfillment by each branch of its constitutional responsibilities. House Joint Resolution 542 includes certain constructive measures which would foster this process by enhancing the flow of information from the executive branch to the Congress. Section 3, for example, calls for consultations with the Congress before and during the involvement of the United States forces in hostilities abroad. This provision is consistent with the desire of this Administration for regularized consultations with the Congress in an even wider range of circumstances.

I believe that full and cooperative participation in foreign policy matters by both the executive and the legislative branches could be enhanced by a careful and dispassionate study of their constitutional roles. Helpful proposals for such a study have already been made in the Congress. I would welcome the establishment of a non-partisan commission on the constitutional roles of the Congress and the President in the conduct of foreign affairs. This commission could make a thorough review of the principal constitutional issues in Executive-Congressional relations, including the war powers, the international agreement powers, and the question of Executive privilege, and then submit its recommendations to the President and the Congress. The members of such a commission could be drawn from both parties—and could represent many perspectives including those of the Congress, the executive branch, the legal profession, and the academic community.

This Administration is dedicated to strengthening cooperation between the Congress and the President in the conduct of foreign affairs and to preserving the constitutional prerogatives of both branches of our Government. I know that the Congress shares that goal. A commission on the constitutional roles of the Congress and the President would provide a useful opportunity for both branches to work together toward that common objective.

NOTES

1. Is the War Powers Resolution constitutional? Read it carefully: Does it authorize use of force? Does it implicitly invite unilateral presidential action in certain circumstances? Are its "legislative veto" provisions constitutional? Is its interpretation of the Constitution's allocation of war powers correct? Are its rules of interpretation for applying statutes (and treaties) within Congress's constitutional powers? Subsequent presidents have construed it narrowly, refused to concede its constitutionality, and sometimes have asserted it to be unconstitutional. The issue has never been addressed by the Supreme Court.

2. A case study: In late 1990, Iraq's leader, Saddam Hussein, invaded the nation of Kuwait, a nation friendly to the United States. In an operation known as Operation Desert Shield, President George H. W. Bush sent American troops to protect Saudi Arabia against invasion. A first set of questions: Did that action fall within the president's constitutional military power as commander in chief? Did it require a declaration of war or its legal equivalent? Was it subject to the requirements of the War Powers Resolution? The United Nations then authorized the use of force to expel Iraqi forces from Kuwait. President Bush enlarged the U.S. troop presence in the Persian Gulf region, explicitly stating that he was preparing an *offensive* military option. There followed a period of constitutional debate between Congress and President Bush, with many in Congress insisting that President Bush could not launch an attack against Iraqi forces without congressional authorization, and with President Bush insisting that he needed no further authorization in light of U.N. approval and his own constitutional power as commander in chief. Who was right? Did it matter that Congress approved funding specifically for Operation Desert Shield?

Two U.S. district court opinions in the District of Columbia found the issue nonjusticiable, but for different reasons. In *Dellums v. Bush*, 752 F.Supp.1141 (D.D.C. 1990), the court found that the issue was not "ripe" because Congress had not acted one way or the other and because there was no certainty of an attack; however, the court did not think the issue was a "political question" outside of judicial purview because the Constitution provided a clear standard requiring congressional authorization. In *Ange v. Bush,* 752 F.Supp.509 (D.D.C. 1990), a different district judge of the same district found the case nonjusticiable, concluding that the Constitution failed to provide a basis for resolving the dispute between Congress's and the president's war powers and thus that the issue was a political question to be worked out by those two branches. Which view do you think is right? In the end, Congress *did* authorize the use of force, mooting the constitutional and War Powers Resolution questions.

3. Another case study: In 1999, America was involved in armed conflict in Kosovo and other states of the former nation of Yugoslavia. The facts in brief: in March 1999, President Bill Clinton involved the United States in the NATO bombing of Yugoslavia without prior congressional authorization. The Senate quickly voted a resolution of support. In April 1999, all on the same day, the House of Representatives (a) failed, on a tie vote, to join the Senate's resolution; (b) rejected overwhelmingly a resolution to declare

war; (c) defeated a resolution pursuant to section 5(c) of the War Powers Act to "veto" the president's action; and (d) passed a resolution stating that the president must get Congress's authorization before sending any ground troops to Yugoslavia. Subsequently, Congress voted a supplemental appropriation for the military action. The Senate tabled a resolution that would have authorized the president to use "all necessary force" in Yugoslavia. What do you make of these conflicting actions by Congress? Was the Kosovo engagement constitutional? Was it consistent with the War Powers Resolution? Did it need to be?

4.   With the attacks on September 11, 2001, the war powers pendulum swung once again. Consider the Authorization for Use of Military Force of September 18, 2001, which follows. Is it the functional equivalent of a declaration of war? Does it repudiate (or revise) Congress's view of the Constitution's allocation of war powers?

Authorization for Use of Military Force
Pub. L. No. 107–40, 115 Stat. 224 (Sep. 18, 2001)

JOINT RESOLUTION

To authorize the use of United States Armed Forces against those responsible for the recent attacks launched against the United States.

Whereas, on September 11, 2001, acts of treacherous violence were committed against the United States and its citizens; and

Whereas, such acts render it both necessary and appropriate that the United States exercise its rights to self-defense and to protect United States citizens both at home and abroad; and

Whereas, in light of the threat to the national security and foreign policy of the United States posed by these grave acts of violence; and

Whereas, such acts continue to pose an unusual and extraordinary threat to the national security and foreign policy of the United States; and

Whereas, the President has authority under the Constitution to take action to deter and prevent acts of international terrorism against the United States: Now, therefore, be it

Resolved by the Senate and House of Representatives of the United States of America in Congress assembled,

SECTION 1.   SHORT TITLE.

. . . "Authorization for Use of Military Force."

SECTION 2.   AUTHORIZATION FOR USE OF UNITED STATES ARMED FORCES.

(a) IN GENERAL—That the President is authorized to use all necessary and appropriate force against those nations, organizations, or persons he determines planned, authorized, committed or aided the terrorist attacks that occurred on September 11, 2001, or harbored such organizations or persons, in order to prevent any future acts of international terrorism against the United States by such nations, organizations, or persons.

(b) WAR POWERS RESOLUTION REQUIREMENTS—

(1) SPECIFIC STATUTORY AUTHORIZATION.—Consistent with section 8(a)(1) of the War Powers Resolution, the Congress declares that this section is

intended to constitute specific statutory authorization within the meaning of section 5(b) of the War Powers Resolution.

(2) APPLICABILITY OF OTHER REQUIREMENTS.—Nothing in this resolution supercedes any requirement of the War Powers Resolution.

NOTES

1.   Was the AUMF the legal equivalent of a declaration of war? If so, what exactly did it authorize? What was its duration? Was it legally necessary in order for the president to wage war against al Qaeda and its affiliates? Was it legally sufficient to justify the subsequent war against Iraq? (The Iraq War was supported by a later, specific authorization for the use of force.) Does the president, under the AUMF, possess lawful authority to use military force against any nation that "harbors" or fails to expel known terrorists? And what if the persons are only suspected to be terrorists (or potential terrorists)? Is there any limitation on the persons or nations against whom U.S. military force may be employed pursuant to this authorization?

2.   What role does the phrase "he determines" play in the AUMF? Does it delegate to the president the power to decide where to go to war? Can Congress delegate the war power?

The War Powers Debate Continues: Libya

A recent development in the constitutional debate over war powers was President Obama's decision to employ military force against Libya to prevent Libyan dictator Colonel Muammar Qaddafi from massacring rebel forces. The U.S. Department of Justice's Office of Legal Counsel produced a legal opinion justifying unilateral presidential authority to use armed force. See Memorandum for the Attorney General Re Authority to Use Military Force in Libya (April 1, 2011) ("OLC Memorandum").

The OLC Memorandum said that the president had "constitutional authority to direct the use of force in Libya because he could reasonably determine that such use of force was in the national interest." The president had determined "that the use of military force in Libya serves important U.S. interests in preventing instability in the Middle East and preserving the credibility and effectiveness of the United Nations Security Council." Although "not required to direct the use of military force simply because the [U.N. Security Council] has authorized it," the president could use such authorization to justify military action on the ground that it served " 'a substantial national foreign policy objective.' " *Id.* at 12 (quoting *Military Forces in Somalia*, 16 Op. O.L.C. at 12). Because the goal of military action was to implement a U.N. Security Council resolution by enforcing a "no-fly zone" with military action, and because "no U.S. ground forces would be deployed," "the use of military force in Libya was supported by sufficiently important national interests to fall within the President's constitutional power." Thus, "the President had constitutional authority, as Commander in Chief and Chief Executive and pursuant to his foreign affairs powers, to direct such limited military operations abroad, even without prior specific congressional approval."

The Declare War Clause did not limit this unilateral presidential military action, the OLC Memorandum continued: "We have acknowledged one possible constitutionally-based limit on this presidential authority to employ military force in defense of important national interests—a planned military engagement that constitutes a 'war' within the meaning of the Declaration of War Clause may require prior congressional authorization." Nevertheless, "[t]he historical practice of presidential military action without congressional approval precludes any suggestion that Congress's authority to declare war covers every military engagement, however limited, that the President initiates." "In our view," the OLC Memorandum continued, "determining whether a particular planned engagement constitutes a 'war' for constitutional purposes instead requires a fact-specific assessment of the 'anticipated nature, scope, and duration' of the planned military operations. This standard generally will be satisfied only by prolonged and substantial military engagements, typically involving exposure of U.S. military personnel to significant risk over a substantial period." *Id.* (quoting *Haiti Deployment*, 18 Op. O.L.C. at 179). Since, at the time President Obama decided to use armed force, the "anticipated nature, scope and duration" of the military engagement was "limited," the use of force by the U.S. in Libya did not "r[i]se to the level of a 'war' in the constitutional sense, requiring the President to seek a declaration of war or other prior authorization from Congress."

At several points in its analysis, the OLC Memorandum relied on earlier OLC opinions defending the lawfulness of presidential military interventions, ranging from rescue operations and goodwill missions to sustained bombing campaigns or commitments of thousands of ground troops. The memorandum specifically cited an earlier bombing of Libya (1986); an intervention in Panama (1989); troop deployments to Somalia (1992), Bosnia (1995), and Haiti (1994 and 2004); air strikes in Bosnia (1993–95); and the bombing campaign in Yugoslavia (1999). "This historical practice is an important indication of constitutional meaning, because it reflects the two political branches' practical understanding, developed since the founding of the Republic, of their respective roles with respect to national defense." Quoting its earlier opinions, OLC concluded that the "pattern of executive conduct, made under claim of right, extended over many decades and engaged in by Presidents of both parties, evidences the existence of broad constitutional power."

The OLC Memorandum also argued that the War Powers Resolution of 1973 "implicitly recognized" unilateral presidential military authority, even though it "does not itself provide affirmative statutory authority for military operations." Quoting earlier OLC opinions, the Memorandum concluded that, notwithstanding section 1547(d)(2)'s directive that nothing in the War Powers Resolution be construed as authorizing military action, the "structure" of the Resolution, by purporting to impose length-of-time cut-offs for any unilateral presidential use of armed force, "recognizes and presupposes the existence of unilateral presidential authority to deploy armed forces into hostilities."

The OLC Memorandum with respect to Libya presents the following questions about the Constitution's allocation of war powers:

1.   Note how broad the April 1, 2011 OLC Memorandum's position is on unilateral presidential war powers: The president, acting alone, may initiate offensive military action against an enemy force or nation whenever it is "in the national interest." What provision of the Constitution confers that power? The Commander-in-Chief Clause? The foreign affairs power (flowing from the "executive Power" generally)? What are the practical limits on what presidents may identify as the "national interest"?

There is little direct precedent for the memorandum's position. In the past, presidential administrations typically defended unilateral presidential military action, where not authorized by Congress, as falling either within (1) a sometimes-aggressive understanding of the residual executive war power to "repel sudden attacks" (even preemptively or preventively) or to respond to attacks upon the nation or its citizens; or (2) a power to rescue or protect U.S. citizens abroad, derived from some understanding of the general duty of the president as chief executive of the nation to provide such protection to U.S. nationals. But it is not clear that any prior administration has asserted a presidential war power to advance national interests.

2.   Note that there are historical precedents of presidential war-making that appear to extend beyond these exceptional categories, as discussed above. The Korean War and the bombing of Kosovo might well be examples of presidential wars not authorized by Congress's exercise of the power to declare war. The Libyan intervention raises again the question of the relationship between the constitutional text and historical practice. In addition, it raises the question of whether the Constitution's allocation of war powers can be affected by institutional acquiescence or waiver. Does it matter whether Congress has acquiesced in the historical practice of the executive branch? (Note that the OLC Memorandum cites both Justice Frankfurter's concurrence in *Youngstown*, referring to history's "gloss" on the executive power; and Justice Jackson's concurrence in the same case, referring to his second category, congressional "quiescence.") And what constitutes such acquiescence? Did Congress, by enacting the War Powers Resolution (unwittingly) acquiesce to a unilateral presidential war-making power for sixty days, even though the Resolution itself states that nothing in it should be construed as granting the president any additional authority? When the sixty days runs out, does the acquiescence expire?

3.   The OLC Memorandum acknowledges that Congress's power under the Declare War Clause might limit unilateral presidential war-making—that this clause was a "possible" limitation. However, the Memorandum argued that the Declare War Clause applied only to military actions fitting the meaning of the word "war."

The issue is thus raised once again: What is the constitutional meaning of the word "war"? In the Libyan military engagement, the United States attacked the forces and targets of an enemy nation with whom it was not already engaged in hostilities and which had engaged in no attack on American forces or citizens. Is this not a "war"? But might not the same question be asked of other military actions that never received congressional authorization? Consider two factors emphasized in the OLC Memorandum: First, is the *absence of ground troops* controlling? In other words, does it matter to the constitutional understanding of "war" whether the object of an attack is bombed from the air or invaded with ground forces? Second, is the expected *duration* of hostilities controlling? If a military engagement is short and discrete, does it fall outside the category of "war" that Congress must authorize? A brief and tidy operation can grow into something big (as in the case of the Vietnam War). Does that mean that a "non-war" military action can *become* a "war"? When would congressional authorization be required?

4.   What is the effect of a U.N. Security Council resolution on the Constitution's allocation of war powers? May a treaty commitment substitute for a declaration of war? May a decision of an ally or an international body, pursuant to a

U.S. treaty, trigger a presidential power or duty to use armed force? (The question recalls the situation of the Korean War in certain respects.)

5.   Does it matter to the constitutional analysis whether an armed military intervention is for humanitarian purposes, such as preventing a massacre in a civil war?

Terminating War

The Constitution gives Congress the power to declare war, but how is war terminated? May a state of war be ended by a presidential proclamation, legislation, or a treaty? The question of how to terminate a war was considered during the Constitutional Convention, where the delegates debated the requirements for concluding a "treaty of peace." Madison argued that a treaty of peace should be easier to approve than other kinds of treaties: a two-thirds majority in the Senate should not be required, and even presidential concurrence was unnecessary. In the end, though, the Convention decided that treaties of peace should be subject to the same requirements as other treaties.

The Supreme Court addressed the question of war termination in *Ludecke v. Watkins*, 335 U.S. 160 (1948). The Court held:

> War does not cease with a cease-fire order, and power to be exercised by the President such as that conferred by the Act of 1798 is a process which begins when war is declared but is not exhausted when the shooting stops. "The state of war" may be terminated by treaty or legislation or Presidential proclamation. Whatever the modes, its termination is a political act.

In January of 1971, Congress, in response to growing public resistance to the Vietnam War, repealed the Gulf of Tonkin Resolution of 1964. However, President Nixon continued the war effort based on his authority as commander in chief, and Congress continued to fund the war effort for several more years. Is congressional legislation really an effective means to terminate a war that the executive is determined to pursue? Congress, empowered by the Constitution with the spending power (Art. I, Sec. 8), has the authority to "defund" a war, effectively forcing the United States to withdraw. Is this Congress's most effective tool for ending a war? Is this a politically viable option? Will a president determined to carry on the war effort, even without continued funding from Congress, always win the inter-branch showdown? If so, are there any effective checks on the president?

[*Assignment 16*]

Conducting War

Where the war power has been constitutionally invoked, what powers does the president have? What powers are still left to Congress, and what are forbidden to both of them? Does the Commander in Chief Clause give the president unfettered power over enemy combatants and enemy property? Or is the president subject to Congress's power to direct and control? And do the courts have a role in restraining the conduct of war as well? And against whom can such war-related powers be brought to bear?

These questions have arisen many times in America's history. We present here three key episodes. First, from the Civil War: the Emancipation Proclamation, a pair of executive orders by which President Lincoln freed Confederate slaves, as well the Order of Retaliation on the treatment of Confederate prisoners. Second, from World War II: *Korematsu v. United States*, 323 U.S. 214 (1944), which upheld a military order removing Japanese-Americans from their homes and relocating them in detention camps. Third, from the War on Terror: *Hamdi v. Rumsfeld,* 542 U.S. 507 (2004), which upheld the president's power to capture and detain enemy combatants, including American citizens, as part of the war power, but subject to some due process limitations. As you read through the materials, try to sort out what you think are the correct constitutional rules for each situation, and especially the role of each of the three branches. What can the president do unilaterally? What powers belong to Congress? When should the courts intervene?

Abraham Lincoln, The Preliminary Emancipation Proclamation

Draft released to the public on Sep. 22, 1862

I, ABRAHAM LINCOLN, President of the United States of America, and Commander-in-Chief of the Army and Navy thereof, etc., hereby proclaim and declare, that hereafter, as heretofore, the war will be prosecuted for the object of practically restoring the constitutional relation between the United States and the people thereof in which States that relation is or may be suspended or disturbed. . . .

That on the first day of January in the year of our Lord, one thousand eight hundred and sixty-three, all persons held as slaves within any state, or designated part of a state, the people whereof shall then be in rebellion against the United States shall be then, thenceforward, and forever free; and the executive government of the United States, including the military and naval authority thereof, will recognize and maintain the freedom of such persons, and will do no act or acts to repress such persons, or any of them, in any efforts they make for their actual freedom.

That the executive will, on the first day of January aforesaid, by proclamation, designate the States, and parts of states, if any, in which the people thereof respectively, shall than be in rebellion against the United States; . . .

That attention is hereby called to an act of Congress entitled "An act to make an additional Article of War" approved March 13, 1862 . . . *[prohibiting use of the military to return fugitive slaves.—Editors]* Also to the ninth and tenth sections of an act entitled "An Act to suppress Insurrection, to punish Treason and Rebellion, to seize and confiscate property of rebels, and for other purposes," approved July 17, 1862 . . . *[proclaiming that slaves of persons engaged in rebellion who escape and take refuge within the lines of the Union army would be free, and further requiring that fugitive slaves not be returned except upon an oath that their owner "has not borne arms against the United States in the present rebellion, nor in any way given aid and comfort thereto."—Editors]*

And I do hereby enjoin upon and order all persons engaged in the military and naval service of the United States, to observe, obey, and enforce, within their respective spheres of service, the act and sections above recited. . . .

Abraham Lincoln, The Final Emancipation Proclamation

Jan. 1, 1863

Whereas, on the twentysecond day of September, in the year of our Lord one thousand eight hundred and sixty two, a proclamation was issued by the President of the United States ... *[President Lincoln then quoted at length from the Preliminary Emancipation Proclamation.—Editors]*

Now, therefore I, Abraham Lincoln, President of the United States, by virtue of the power in me vested as Commander-in-Chief, of the Army and Navy of the United States in time of actual armed rebellion against the authority and government of the United States, and as a fit and necessary war measure for suppressing said rebellion, do, on this first day of January, in the year of our Lord one thousand eight hundred and sixty-three, and in accordance with my purpose so to do publicly proclaimed for the full period of one hundred days, from the day first above mentioned, order and designate as the States and parts of States wherein the people thereof respectively, are this day in rebellion against the United States, the following, to wit:

Arkansas, Texas, Louisiana, (except the Parishes of St. Bernard, Plaquemines, Jefferson, St. John, St. Charles, St. James Ascension, Assumption, Terrebonne, Lafourche, St. Mary, St. Martin, and Orleans, including the City of New Orleans) Mississippi, Alabama, Florida, Georgia, South Carolina, North Carolina, and Virginia, (except the forty-eight counties designated as West Virginia, and also the counties of Berkley, Accomac, Northampton, Elizabeth City, York, Princess Ann, and Norfolk, including the cities of Norfolk and Portsmouth[)], and which excepted parts, are for the present, left precisely as if this proclamation were not issued.

And by virtue of the power, and for the purpose aforesaid, I do order and declare that all persons held as slaves within said designated States, and parts of States, are, and henceforward shall be free; and that the Executive government of the United States, including the military and naval authorities thereof, will recognize and maintain the freedom of said persons.

And I hereby enjoin upon the people so declared to be free to abstain from all violence, unless in necessary self-defence; and I recommend to them that, in all cases when allowed, they labor faithfully for reasonable wages.

And I further declare and make known, that such persons of suitable condition, will be received into the armed service of the United States to garrison forts, positions, stations, and other places, and to man vessels of all sorts in said service.

And upon this act, sincerely believed to be an act of justice, warranted by the Constitution, upon military necessity, I invoke the considerate judgment of mankind, and the gracious favor of Almighty God. . . .

NOTES

1.   The Emancipation Proclamation was surely the most significant executive order ever. But was it constitutional? What was President Lincoln's constitutional justification? Remember that this was before the ratification of the Thirteenth Amendment, and so—offensive as it is—in a legal sense this might be seen as a taking of property without consent. Isn't that the legal issue presented a century later in *Youngstown*, p. 70, or can the two situations be distinguished?

2.   The Emancipation Proclamation applied only to areas in rebellion and controlled at the time by Confederate forces. It freed no slaves in the border slave states that remained in the Union (Kentucky, Maryland, Delaware, and Missouri) or in areas of the South already under the control of the Union army. Does this matter?

3.   President Lincoln issued the proclamation on his own authority. What would have, or should have, happened if the other branches had tried to intervene? Could Congress pass a law countermanding the proclamation? Would that require the new freedmen to be sent back to slavery in the rebelling states? And what if the Supreme Court held the proclamation unconstitutional? Would the president have to comply with that decision?

Abraham Lincoln, Order of Retaliation
July 30, 1863

It is the duty of every government to give protection to its citizens, of whatever class, color, or condition, and especially to those who are duly organized as soldiers in the public service. The law of nations and the usages and customs of war as carried on by civilized powers, permit no distinction as to color in the treatment of prisoners of war as public enemies. To sell or enslave any captured person, on account of his color, and for no offence against the laws of war, is a relapse into barbarism and a crime against the civilization of the age.

The government of the United States will give the same protection to all its soldiers, and if the enemy shall sell or enslave anyone because of his color, the offense shall be punished by retaliation upon the enemy's prisoners in our possession.

It is therefore ordered that for every soldier of the United States killed in violation of the laws of war, a rebel soldier shall be executed; and for every one enslaved by the enemy or sold into slavery, a rebel soldier shall be placed at hard labor on the public works and continued at such labor until the other shall be released and receive the treatment due to a prisoner of war.

NOTES

1.   When the Order of Retaliation was issued, there was no Thirteenth Amendment, which generally abolished slavery, and no Fourteenth Amendment, guaranteeing "the equal protection of the laws." So what kind of legal authority is Lincoln relying on here?

2.   As with the Emancipation Proclamation, consider whether Congress would have had the power to countermand the Order of Retaliation. Could it have banned the execution of prisoners or the use of "hard labor"? Under what power? The power to "make Rules concerning Captures on Land and Water"? "To make Rules for the Government and Regulation of the land and naval Forces"? The Necessary and Proper Clause? Or are all of these trumped by the Commander-in-Chief Clause? Analogous questions came up in a more recent controversy over the so-called "Torture Memos" issued by the Office of Legal Counsel during the administration of George W. Bush.

Korematsu v. United States

323 U.S. 214 (1944)

■ MR. JUSTICE BLACK delivered the opinion of the Court.

The petitioner, an American citizen of Japanese descent, was convicted in a federal district court for remaining in San Leandro, California, a "Military Area", contrary to Civilian Exclusion Order No. 34 of the Commanding General of the Western Command, U.S. Army, which directed that after May 9, 1942, all persons of Japanese ancestry should be excluded from that area. No question was raised as to petitioner's loyalty to the United States. The Circuit Court of Appeals affirmed, and the importance of the constitutional question involved caused us to grant certiorari.

It should be noted, to begin with, that all legal restrictions which curtail the civil rights of a single racial group are immediately suspect. That is not to say that all such restrictions are unconstitutional. It is to say that courts must subject them to the most rigid scrutiny. Pressing public necessity may sometimes justify the existence of such restrictions; racial antagonism never can.

In the instant case prosecution of the petitioner was begun by information charging violation of an Act of Congress, of March 21, 1942, 56 Stat. 173, which provides that "... whoever shall enter, remain in, leave, or commit any act in any military area or military zone prescribed, under the authority of an Executive order of the President, by the Secretary of War, or by any military commander designated by the Secretary of War, contrary to the restrictions applicable to any such area or zone or contrary to the order of the Secretary of War or any such military commander, shall, if it appears that he knew or should have known of the existence and extent of the restrictions or order and that his act was in violation thereof, be guilty of a misdemeanor and upon conviction shall be liable to a fine of not to exceed $5,000 or to imprisonment for not more than one year, or both, for each offense."

Exclusion Order No. 34, which the petitioner knowingly and admittedly violated was one of a number of military orders and proclamations, all of which were substantially based upon Executive Order No. 9066, 7 Fed. Reg. 1407. That order, issued after we were at war with Japan, declared that "the successful prosecution of the war requires every possible protection against espionage and against sabotage to national-defense material, national-defense premises, and national-defense utilities. . . ."

One of the series of orders and proclamations, a curfew order, which like the exclusion order here was promulgated pursuant to Executive Order 9066, subjected all persons of Japanese ancestry in prescribed West Coast military areas to remain in their residences from 8 p.m. to 6 a.m. As is the case with the exclusion order here, that prior curfew order was designed as a "protection against espionage and against sabotage." In *Kiyoshi Hirabayashi v. United States*, 320 U.S. 81 (1943), we sustained a conviction obtained for violation of the curfew order. The *Hirabayashi* conviction and this one thus rest on the same 1942 Congressional Act and the same basic executive and military orders, all of which orders were aimed at the twin dangers of espionage and sabotage.

The 1942 Act was attacked in the *Hirabayashi* case as an unconstitutional delegation of power; it was contended that the curfew order and other orders on which it rested were beyond the war powers of the Congress, the military authorities and of the President, as Commander in Chief of the Army; and finally that to apply the curfew order against none but citizens of Japanese ancestry amounted to a constitutionally prohibited discrimination solely on account of race. To these questions, we gave the serious consideration which their importance justified. We upheld the curfew order as an exercise of the power of the government to take steps necessary to prevent espionage and sabotage in an area threatened by Japanese attack.

In the light of the principles we announced in the *Hirabayashi* case, we are unable to conclude that it was beyond the war power of Congress and the Executive to exclude those of Japanese ancestry from the West Coast war area at the time they did. True, exclusion from the area in which one's home is located is a far greater deprivation than constant confinement to the home from 8 p.m. to 6 a.m. Nothing short of apprehension by the proper military authorities of the gravest imminent danger to the public safety can constitutionally justify either. But exclusion from a threatened area, no less than curfew, has a definite and close relationship to the prevention of espionage and sabotage. The military authorities, charged with the primary responsibility of defending our shores, concluded that curfew provided inadequate protection and ordered exclusion. They did so, as pointed out in our *Hirabayashi* opinion, in accordance with Congressional authority to the military to say who should, and who should not, remain in the threatened areas.

In this case the petitioner challenges the assumptions upon which we rested our conclusions in the *Hirabayashi* case. He also urges that by May 1942, when Order No. 34 was promulgated, all danger of Japanese invasion of the West Coast had disappeared. After careful consideration of these contentions we are compelled to reject them.

Here, as in the *Hirabayashi* case, ". . . we cannot reject as unfounded the judgment of the military authorities and of Congress that there were disloyal members of that population, whose number and strength could not be precisely and quickly ascertained. We cannot say that the war-making branches of the Government did not have ground for believing that in a critical hour such persons could not readily be isolated and separately dealt with, and constituted a menace to the national defense and safety, which demanded that prompt and adequate measures be taken to guard against it."

Like curfew, exclusion of those of Japanese origin was deemed necessary because of the presence of an unascertained number of disloyal members of the group, most of whom we have no doubt were loyal to this country. It was because we could not reject the finding of the military authorities that it was impossible to bring about an immediate segregation of the disloyal from the loyal that we sustained the validity of the curfew order as applying to the whole group. In the instant case, temporary exclusion of the entire group was rested by the military on the same ground. The judgment that exclusion of the whole group was for the same reason a military imperative answers the contention that the exclusion was in the nature of group punishment based on antagonism to those of Japanese origin. That there were members of the group who retained loyalties to Japan has been confirmed by investigations made subsequent to the exclusion. Approximately five thousand American citizens of Japanese ancestry refused to swear unqualified allegiance to the United States and to renounce allegiance to the Japanese Emperor, and several thousand evacuees requested repatriation to Japan.

We uphold the exclusion order as of the time it was made and when the petitioner violated it. In doing so, we are not unmindful of the hardships imposed by it upon a large group of American citizens. But hardships are part of war, and war is an aggregation of hardships. All citizens alike, both in and out of uniform, feel the impact of war in greater or lesser measure. Citizenship has its responsibilities as well as its privileges, and in time of war the burden is always heavier. Compulsory exclusion of large groups of citizens from their homes, except under circumstances of direst emergency and peril, is inconsistent with our basic governmental institutions. But when under conditions of modern warfare our shores are threatened by hostile forces, the power to protect must be commensurate with the threatened danger.

It is argued that on May 30, 1942, the date the petitioner was charged with remaining in the prohibited area, there were conflicting orders outstanding, forbidding him both to leave the area and to remain there. Of course, a person cannot be convicted for doing the very thing which it is a crime to fail to do. But the outstanding orders here contained no such contradictory commands.

There was an order issued March 27, 1942, which prohibited petitioner and others of Japanese ancestry from leaving the area, but its effect was specifically limited in time "until and to the extent that a future proclamation or order should so permit or direct." 7 Fed. Reg. 2601. That "future order," the one for violation of which petitioner was convicted, was issued May 3, 1942, and it did "direct" exclusion from the area of all persons of Japanese ancestry, before 12 o'clock noon, May 9; furthermore it contained a warning that all such persons found in the prohibited area would be liable to punishment under the March 21, 1942 Act of Congress. Consequently, the only order in effect touching the petitioner's being in the area on May 30, 1942, the date specified in the information against him, was the May 3 order which prohibited his remaining there, and it was that same order, which he stipulated in his trial that he had violated, knowing of its existence. There is therefore no basis for the argument that on May 30, 1942, he was subject to punishment, under the March 27 and May 3 orders, whether he remained in or left the area.

It does appear, however, that on May 9, the effective date of the exclusion order, the military authorities had already determined that the evacuation should be effected by assembling together and placing under guard all those of Japanese ancestry, at central points, designated as "assembly centers," in order "to insure the orderly evacuation and resettlement of Japanese voluntarily migrating from military area No. 1 to restrict and regulate such migration." Public Proclamation No. 4, 7 Fed. Reg. 2601. And on May 19, 1942, eleven days before the time petitioner was charged with unlawfully remaining in the area, Civilian Restrictive Order No. 1, 8 Fed. Reg. 982, provided for detention of those of Japanese ancestry in assembly or relocation centers. It is now argued that the validity of the exclusion order cannot be considered apart from the orders requiring him, after departure from the area, to report and to remain in an assembly or relocation center. The contention is that we must treat these separate orders as one and inseparable; that, for this reason, if detention in the assembly or relocation center would have illegally deprived the petitioner of his liberty, the exclusion order and his conviction under it cannot stand.

We are thus being asked to pass at this time upon the whole subsequent detention program in both assembly and relocation centers, although the only issues framed at the trial related to petitioner's remaining in the prohibited area in violation of the exclusion order. Had petitioner here left the prohibited area and gone to an assembly center we cannot say either as a matter of fact or law that his presence in that center would have resulted in his detention in a relocation center. Some who did report to the assembly center were not sent to relocation centers, but were released upon condition that they remain outside the prohibited zone until the military orders were modified or lifted. This illustrates that they pose different problems and may be governed by different principles. The lawfulness of one does not necessarily determine the lawfulness of the others. This is made clear when we analyze the requirements of the separate provisions of the separate orders. These separate requirements were that those of Japanese ancestry (1) depart from the area; (2) report to and temporarily remain in an assembly center; (3) go under military control to a relocation center there to remain for an indeterminate period until released conditionally or unconditionally by the military authorities. Each of these requirements, it will be noted, imposed distinct duties in connection with the separate steps in a complete evacuation program. Had Congress directly incorporated into one Act the language of these separate orders, and provided sanctions for their violations, disobedience of any one would have constituted a separate offense. There is no reason why violations of these orders, insofar as they were promulgated pursuant to congressional enactment, should not be treated as separate offenses. . . .

It is sufficient here for us to pass upon the order which petitioner violated. . . .

The Assembly Center was conceived as a part of the machinery for group evacuation. The power to exclude includes the power to do it by force if necessary. And any forcible measure must necessarily entail some degree of detention or restraint whatever method of removal is selected. But whichever view is taken, it results in holding that the order under which petitioner was convicted was valid.

It is said that we are dealing here with the case of imprisonment of a citizen in a concentration camp solely because of his ancestry, without evidence or inquiry concerning his loyalty and good disposition towards the United States. Our task would be simple, our duty clear, were this a case involving the imprisonment of a loyal citizen in a concentration camp because of racial prejudice. Regardless of the true nature of the assembly and relocation centers—and we deem it unjustifiable to call them concentration camps with all the ugly connotations that term implies—we are dealing specifically with nothing but an exclusion order. To cast this case into outlines of racial prejudice, without reference to the real military dangers which were presented, merely confuses the issue. Korematsu was not excluded from the Military Area because of hostility to him or his race. He was excluded because we are at war with the Japanese Empire, because the properly constituted military authorities feared an invasion of our West Coast and felt constrained to take proper security measures, because they decided that the military urgency of the situation demanded that all citizens of Japanese ancestry be segregated from the West Coast temporarily, and finally, because Congress, reposing its confidence in this time of war in our military leaders—as inevitably it must—determined that they should have the power to do just this. There was evidence of disloyalty on the part of some, the military authorities considered that the need for action was great, and time was short. We cannot—by availing ourselves of the calm perspective of hindsight—now say that at that time these actions were unjustified.

■ MR. JUSTICE FRANKFURTER, concurring.

According to my reading of Civilian Exclusion Order No. 34, it was an offense for Korematsu to be found in Military Area No. 1, the territory wherein he was previously living, except within the bounds of the established Assembly Center of that area. Even though the various orders issued by General DeWitt be deemed a comprehensive code of instructions, their tenor is clear and not contradictory. They put upon Korematsu the obligation to leave Military Area No. 1, but only by the method prescribed in the instructions, i.e., by reporting to the Assembly Center. I am unable to see how the legal considerations that led to the decision in *Hirabayashi v. United States* fail to sustain the military order which made the conduct now in controversy a crime. And so I join in the opinion of the Court, but should like to add a few words of my own.

The provisions of the Constitution which confer on the Congress and the President powers to enable this country to wage war are as much part of the Constitution as provisions looking to a nation at peace. And we have had recent occasion to quote approvingly the statement of former Chief Justice Hughes that the war power of the Government is "the power to wage war successfully." Therefore, the validity of action under the war power must be judged wholly in the context of war. That action is not to be stigmatized as lawless because like action in times of peace would be lawless. To talk about a military order that expresses an allowable judgment of war needs by those entrusted with the duty of conducting war as "an unconstitutional order" is to suffuse a part of the Constitution with an atmosphere of unconstitutionality. The respective spheres of action of military authorities and of judges are of course very different. But within their sphere, military authorities are no more outside the bounds of obedience to the Constitution than are judges within theirs. "The war power of the United States, like its other powers . . . is subject to applicable constitutional limitations." To recognize that military orders are "reasonably expedient military precautions" in time of war and yet to deny them constitutional legitimacy makes of the Constitution an instrument for dialectic subtleties not reasonably to be attributed to the hard-headed Framers, of whom a majority had had actual participation in war. If a military order such as that under review does not transcend the means appropriate for conducting war, such action by the military is as constitutional as would be any authorized action by the Interstate Commerce Commission within the limits of the constitutional power to regulate commerce. And being an exercise of the war power explicitly granted by the Constitution for safeguarding the national life by prosecuting war effectively, I find nothing in the Constitution which denies to Congress the power to enforce such a valid military order by making its violation an offense triable in the civil courts. To find that the Constitution does not forbid the military measures now complained of does not carry with it approval of that which Congress and the Executive did. That is their business, not ours.

■ MR. JUSTICE ROBERTS, dissenting.

I dissent, because I think the indisputable facts exhibit a clear violation of Constitutional rights.

This is not a case of keeping people off the streets at night as was *Hirabayashi v. United States*, nor a case of temporary exclusion of a citizen from an area for his own safety or that of the community, nor a case of offering him an opportunity to go temporarily out of an area where his presence might cause danger to himself or to his fellows. On the contrary, it is the case of convicting a citizen as a punishment for not submitting to imprisonment in a concentration camp, based on his ancestry, and solely because of his ancestry, without evidence or inquiry concerning his loyalty and good disposition towards the United States. If this be a correct statement of the facts disclosed by this record, and facts of which we take judicial notice, I need hardly labor the conclusion that Constitutional rights have been violated.

The Government's argument, and the opinion of the court, in my judgment, erroneously divide that which is single and indivisible and thus make the case appear as if the petitioner violated a Military Order, sanctioned by Act of Congress, which excluded him from his home, by refusing voluntarily to leave and, so, knowingly and intentionally, defying the order and the Act of Congress. . . .

The predicament in which the petitioner thus found himself was this: He was forbidden, by Military Order, to leave the zone in which he lived; he was forbidden, by Military Order, after a date fixed, to be found within that zone unless he were in an Assembly Center located in that zone. General DeWitt's report to the Secretary of War concerning the programme of evacuation and relocation of Japanese makes it entirely clear . . . that an Assembly Center was a euphemism for a prison. No person within such a center was permitted to leave except by Military Order.

In the dilemma that he dare not remain in his home, or voluntarily leave the area, without incurring criminal penalties, and that the only way he could avoid punishment was to go to an Assembly Center and submit himself to military imprisonment, the petitioner did nothing. . . .

I had supposed that if a citizen was constrained by two laws, or two orders having the force of law, and obedience to one would violate the other, to punish him for violation of either would deny him due process of law. And I had supposed that under these circumstances a conviction for violating one of the orders could not stand.

We cannot shut our eyes to the fact that had the petitioner attempted to violate Proclamation No. 4 and leave the military area in which he lived he would have been arrested and tried and convicted for violation of Proclamation No. 4. The two conflicting orders, one which commanded him to stay and the other which commanded him to go, were nothing but a cleverly devised trap to accomplish the real purpose of the military authority, which was to lock him up in a concentration camp. . . .

These stark realities are met by the suggestion that it is lawful to compel an American citizen to submit to illegal imprisonment on the assumption that he might, after going to the Assembly Center, apply for his discharge by suing out a writ of habeas corpus. . . . The answer, of course, is that where he was subject to two conflicting laws he was not bound, in order to escape violation of one or the other, to surrender his liberty for any period. Nor will it do to say that the detention was a necessary part of the process of evacuation, and so we are here concerned only with the validity of the latter.

Again it is a new doctrine of constitutional law that one indicted for disobedience to an unconstitutional statute may not defend on the ground of the invalidity of the statute but must obey it though he knows it is no law and, after he has suffered the disgrace of conviction and lost his liberty by sentence, then, and not before, seek, from within prison walls, to test the validity of the law. . . .

I would reverse the judgment of conviction.

■ Mr. Justice Murphy, dissenting.

This exclusion of "all persons of Japanese ancestry, both alien and non-alien," from the Pacific Coast area on a plea of military necessity in the absence of martial law ought not to be approved. Such exclusion goes over "the very brink of constitutional power" and falls into the ugly abyss of racism.

In dealing with matters relating to the prosecution and progress of a war, we must accord great respect and consideration to the judgments of the military authorities who are on the scene and who have full knowledge of the military facts. The scope of their discretion must, as a matter of necessity and common sense, be wide. And their judgments ought not to be overruled lightly by those whose training and duties ill-equip them to deal intelligently with matters so vital to the physical security of the nation.

At the same time, however, it is essential that there be definite limits to military discretion, especially where martial law has not been declared. Individuals must not be left impoverished of their constitutional rights on a plea of military necessity that has neither substance nor support. Thus, like other claims conflicting with the asserted constitutional rights of the individual, the military claim must subject itself to the judicial process of having its reasonableness determined and its conflicts with other interests reconciled. "What are the allowable limits of military discretion, and whether or not they have been overstepped in a particular case, are judicial questions."

The judicial test of whether the Government, on a plea of military necessity, can validly deprive an individual of any of his constitutional rights is whether the deprivation is reasonably related to a public danger that is so "immediate, imminent, and impending" as not to admit of delay and not to permit the intervention of ordinary constitutional processes to alleviate the danger. Civilian Exclusion Order No. 34, banishing from a prescribed area of the Pacific Coast "all persons of Japanese ancestry, both alien and non-alien," clearly does not meet that test. Being an obvious racial discrimination, the order deprives all those within its scope of the equal protection of the laws as guaranteed by the Fifth Amendment. It further deprives these individuals of their constitutional rights to live and work where they will, to establish a home where they choose and to move about freely. In excommunicating them without benefit of hearings, this order also deprives them of all their constitutional rights to procedural due process. Yet no reasonable relation to an "immediate, imminent, and impending" public danger is evident to support this racial restriction which is one of the most sweeping and complete deprivations of constitutional rights in the history of this nation in the absence of martial law.

It must be conceded that the military and naval situation in the spring of 1942 was such as to generate a very real fear of invasion of the Pacific Coast, accompanied by fears of sabotage and espionage in that area. The military command was therefore justified in adopting all reasonable means necessary to combat these dangers. In adjudging the military action taken in light of the then apparent dangers, we must not erect too high or too meticulous standards; it is necessary only that the action have some reasonable relation to the removal of the dangers of invasion, sabotage and espionage. But the exclusion, either temporarily or permanently, of *all* persons with Japanese blood in their veins has no such reasonable relation. And that relation is lacking because the exclusion order necessarily must rely for its reasonableness upon the assumption that all persons of Japanese ancestry may have a dangerous tendency to commit sabotage and espionage and to aid our Japanese enemy in other ways. It is difficult to believe that reason, logic or experience could be marshalled in support of such an assumption.

That this forced exclusion was the result in good measure of this erroneous assumption of racial guilt rather than bona fide military necessity is evidenced by the Commanding General's Final Report on the evacuation from the Pacific Coast area. In it he refers to all individuals of Japanese descent as "subversive," as belonging to "an enemy race" whose "racial strains are undiluted," and as constituting "over 112,000 potential enemies . . . at large today" along the Pacific Coast. In support of this blanket condemnation of all persons of Japanese descent, however, no reliable evidence is cited to show that such individuals were generally disloyal, or had generally so conducted themselves in this area as to constitute a special menace to defense installations or war industries, or had otherwise by their behavior furnished reasonable ground for their exclusion as a group.

Justification for the exclusion is sought, instead, mainly upon questionable racial and sociological grounds not ordinarily within the realm of expert military judgment, supplemented by certain semi-military conclusions drawn from an unwarranted use of circumstantial evidence. Individuals of Japanese ancestry are condemned because they are said to be "a large, unassimilated, tightly knit racial group, bound to an enemy nation by strong ties of race, culture, custom and religion." They are claimed to be given to "emperor worshipping ceremonies" and to "dual citizenship." Japanese language schools and allegedly pro-Japanese organizations are cited as evidence of possible group disloyalty, together with facts as to certain persons being educated and residing at length in Japan. It is intimated that many of these individuals deliberately resided "adjacent to strategic points," thus enabling them "to carry into execution a tremendous program of sabotage on a mass scale should any considerable number of them have been inclined to do so." The need for protective custody is also asserted. The report refers without identity to "numerous incidents of violence" as well as to other admittedly unverified or cumulative incidents. From this, plus certain other events not shown to have been connected with the Japanese Americans, it is concluded that the "situation was fraught with danger to the Japanese population itself" and that the general public "was ready to take matters into its own hands." Finally, it is intimated, though not directly charged or proved, that persons of Japanese ancestry were responsible for three minor isolated shellings and bombings of the Pacific Coast area, as well as for unidentified radio transmissions and night signaling.

The main reasons relied upon by those responsible for the forced evacuation, therefore, do not prove a reasonable relation between the group characteristics of Japanese Americans and the dangers of invasion, sabotage and espionage. The reasons appear, instead, to be largely an accumulation of much of the misinformation, half-truths and insinuations that for years have been directed against Japanese Americans by people with racial and economic prejudices—the same people who have been among the foremost advocates of the evacuation. A military judgment based upon such racial and sociological considerations is not entitled to the great weight ordinarily given the judgments based upon strictly military considerations. . . .

No adequate reason is given for the failure to treat these Japanese Americans on an individual basis by holding investigations and hearings to separate the loyal from the disloyal, as was done in the case of persons of German and Italian ancestry. It is asserted merely that the loyalties of this group "were unknown and time was of the essence." Yet nearly four months elapsed after Pearl Harbor before the first exclusion order was issued; nearly eight months went by until the last order was issued; and the last of these "subversive" persons was not actually removed until almost eleven months had elapsed. Leisure and deliberation seem to have been more of the essence than speed. And the fact that conditions were not such as to warrant a declaration of martial law adds strength to the belief that the factors of time and military necessity were not as urgent as they have been represented to be.

Moreover, . . . not one person of Japanese ancestry was accused or convicted of espionage or sabotage after Pearl Harbor while they were still free, a fact which is some evidence of the loyalty of the vast majority of these individuals and of the effectiveness of the established methods of combatting these evils. It seems incredible that under these circumstances it would have been impossible to hold loyalty hearings for the mere 112,000 persons involved—or at least for the 70,000 American citizens—especially when a large part of this number represented children and elderly men and women. Any inconvenience that may have accompanied an attempt to conform to procedural due process cannot be said to justify violations of constitutional rights of individuals.

I dissent, therefore, from this legalization of racism. Racial discrimination in any form and in any degree has no justifiable part whatever in our democratic way of life. It is unattractive in any setting but it is utterly revolting among a free people who have embraced the principles set forth in the Constitution of the United States. All residents of this nation are kin in some way by blood or culture to a foreign land. Yet they are primarily and necessarily a part of the new and distinct civilization of the United States. They must accordingly be treated at all times as the heirs of the American experiment and as entitled to all the rights and freedoms guaranteed by the Constitution.

■ MR. JUSTICE JACKSON, dissenting.

Korematsu was born on our soil, of parents born in Japan. The Constitution makes him a citizen of the United States by nativity and a citizen of California by residence. No claim is made that he is not loyal to this country. There is no suggestion that apart from the matter involved here he is not law-abiding and well disposed. Korematsu, however, has been convicted of an act not commonly a crime. It consists merely of being present in the state whereof he is a citizen, near the place where he was born, and where all his life he has lived.

Even more unusual is the series of military orders which made this conduct a crime. They forbid such a one to remain, and they also forbid him to leave. They were so drawn that the only way Korematsu could avoid violation was to give himself up to the military authority. This meant submission to custody, examination, and transportation out of the territory, to be followed by indeterminate confinement in detention camps.

A citizen's presence in the locality, however, was made a crime only if his parents were of Japanese birth. Had Korematsu been one of four—the others being, say, a German alien enemy, an Italian alien enemy, and a citizen of American-born ancestors, convicted of treason but out on parole—only Korematsu's presence would have violated the order. The difference between their innocence and his crime would result, not from anything he did, said, or thought, different than they, but only in that he was born of different racial stock.

Now, if any fundamental assumption underlies our system, it is that guilt is personal and not inheritable. Even if all of one's antecedents had been convicted of treason, the Constitution forbids its penalties to be visited upon him, for it provides that "no Attainder of Treason shall work Corruption of Blood, or Forfeiture except during the Life of the Person attainted." But here is an attempt to make an otherwise innocent act a crime merely because this prisoner is the son of parents as to whom he had no choice, and belongs to a race from which there is no way to resign. If Congress in peace-time legislation should enact such a criminal law, I should suppose this Court would refuse to enforce it.

But the "law" which this prisoner is convicted of disregarding is not found in an act of Congress, but in a military order. Neither the Act of Congress nor the Executive Order of the President, nor both together, would afford a basis for this conviction. It rests on the orders of General DeWitt. And it is said that if the military commander had reasonable military grounds for promulgating the orders, they are constitutional and become law, and the Court is required to enforce them. There are several reasons why I cannot subscribe to this doctrine.

It would be impracticable and dangerous idealism to expect or insist that each specific military command in an area of probable operations will conform to conventional tests of constitutionality. When an area is so beset that it must be put under military control at all, the paramount consideration is that its measures be successful, rather than legal. The armed services must protect a society, not merely its Constitution. The very essence of the military job is to marshal physical force, to remove every obstacle to its effectiveness, to give it every strategic advantage. Defense measures will not, and often should not, be held within the limits that bind civil authority in peace. No court can require such a commander in such circumstances to act as a reasonable man; he may be unreasonably cautious and exacting. Perhaps he should be. But a commander in temporarily focusing the life of a community on defense is carrying out a military program; he is not making law in the sense the courts know the term. He issues orders, and they may have a certain authority as military commands, although they may be very bad as constitutional law.

But if we cannot confine military expedients by the Constitution, neither would I distort the Constitution to approve all that the military may deem expedient. That is what the Court appears to be doing, whether consciously or not. I cannot say, from any evidence before me, that the orders of General DeWitt were not reasonably expedient military precautions, nor could I say that they were. But even if they were permissible military procedures, I deny that it follows that they are constitutional. If, as the Court holds, it does follow, then we may as well say that any military order will be constitutional and have done with it.

The limitation under which courts always will labor in examining the necessity for a military order are illustrated by this case. How does the Court know that these orders have a reasonable basis in necessity? No evidence whatever on that subject has been taken by this or any other court. There is sharp controversy as to the credibility of the DeWitt report. So the Court, having no real evidence before it, has no choice but to accept General DeWitt's own unsworn, self-serving statement, untested by any cross-examination, that what he did was reasonable. And thus it will always be when courts try to look into the reasonableness of a military order.

In the very nature of things, military decisions are not susceptible of intelligent judicial appraisal. They do not pretend to rest on evidence, but are made on information that often would not be admissible and on assumptions that could not be proved. Information in support of an order could not be disclosed to courts without danger that it would reach the enemy. Neither can courts act on communications made in confidence. Hence courts can never have any real alternative to accepting the mere declaration of the authority that issued the order that it was reasonably necessary from a military viewpoint.

Much is said of the danger to liberty from the Army program for deporting and detaining these citizens of Japanese extraction. But a judicial construction of the due process clause that will sustain this order is a far more subtle blow to liberty than the promulgation of the order itself. A military order, however unconstitutional, is not apt to last longer than the military emergency. Even during that period a succeeding commander may revoke it all. But once a judicial opinion rationalizes such an order to show that it conforms to the Constitution, or rather rationalizes the Constitution to show that the Constitution sanctions such an order, the Court for all time has validated the principle of racial discrimination in criminal procedure and of transplanting American citizens. The principle then lies about like a loaded weapon ready for the hand of any authority that can bring forward a plausible claim of an urgent need. Every repetition imbeds that principle more deeply in our law and thinking and expands it to new purposes. All who observe the work of courts are familiar with what Judge Cardozo described as "the tendency of a principle to expand itself to the limit of its logic." A military commander may overstep the bounds of constitutionality, and it is an incident. But if we review and approve, that passing incident becomes the doctrine of the Constitution. There it has a generative power of its own, and all that it creates will be in its own image. Nothing better illustrates this danger than does the Court's opinion in this case.

It argues that we are bound to uphold the conviction of Korematsu because we upheld one in *Hirabayashi v. United States*, when we sustained these orders in so far as they applied a curfew requirement to a citizen of Japanese ancestry. I think we should learn something from that experience.

In that case we were urged to consider only the curfew feature, that being all that technically was involved, because it was the only count necessary to sustain Hirabayashi's conviction and sentence. We yielded, and the Chief Justice guarded the opinion as carefully as language will do. . . . However, in spite of our limiting words we did validate a discrimination on the basis of ancestry for mild and temporary deprivation of liberty. Now the principle of racial discrimination is pushed from support of mild measures to very harsh ones, and from temporary deprivations to indeterminate ones. And the precedent which it is said requires us to do so is

Hirabayashi. The Court is now saying that in *Hirabayashi* we did decide the very things we there said we were not deciding. . . .

I should hold that a civil court cannot be made to enforce an order which violates constitutional limitations even if it is a reasonable exercise of military authority. The courts can exercise only the judicial power, can apply only law, and must abide by the Constitution, or they cease to be civil courts and become instruments of military policy.

Of course the existence of a military power resting on force, so vagrant, so centralized, so necessarily heedless of the individual, is an inherent threat to liberty. But I would not lead people to rely on this Court for a review that seems to me wholly delusive. The military reasonableness of these orders can only be determined by military superiors. If the people ever let command of the war power fall into irresponsible and unscrupulous hands, the courts wield no power equal to its restraint. The chief restraint upon those who command the physical forces of the country, in the future as in the past, must be their responsibility to the political judgments of their contemporaries and to the moral judgments of history.

My duties as a justice as I see them do not require me to make a military judgment as to whether General DeWitt's evacuation and detention program was a reasonable military necessity. I do not suggest that the courts should have attempted to interfere with the Army in carrying out its task. But I do not think they may be asked to execute a military expedient that has no place in law under the Constitution. I would reverse the judgment and discharge the prisoner.

NOTES

1.   What constitutional provisions does *Korematsu* actually involve? Article I? Article II? The Due Process Clause of the Fifth Amendment? Other provisions? What does the majority opinion say? What do the other opinions say? And to the extent that the Due Process Clause is involved, what kind of rights do the dissenters think it protects? A right to specific procedures? A substantive right not to be locked up? Or a right to be free from— or, perhaps more precisely, an equality rule that prohibits—racial discrimination?

2.   The United States' internment of Japanese-Americans is widely regarded as one of the great injustices in America's constitutional history. Four decades after the Supreme Court upheld Fred Korematsu's conviction, a federal district court, with the government's consent, granted a writ of *coram nobis* vacating his conviction. *Korematsu v. United States*, 584 F.Supp.1406 (N.D. Cal. 1984). The ground for vacating the conviction was that evidence the government had submitted, in the form of military officers' evaluation of the dangers from sabotage and espionage, had misrepresented the true known facts. In 1988, Congress appropriated funds for reparations.

The *Korematsu* decision is said to be part of the Supreme Court's "anticanon," that is, a decision widely and publicly repudiated by lawyers today. Jamal Greene, *The Anticanon*, 125 Harv. L. Rev. 379, 387–404 (2011). (Professor Greene says the three other cases in this category are *Dred Scott v. Sandford*, p. 733; *Plessy v. Ferguson*, p. 1338; and *Lochner v. New York*, p. 1521.) But *Korematsu* has never been formally overruled, and some of the doctrines discussed in *Korematsu* remain an important part of modern law— for instance, the rule that racial classifications are subject to "strict scrutiny" and the rule that discrimination by the federal government is unconstitutional. In contemporary cases, these questions tend to be discussed under the heading of "equal protection" rather than "due process." See p. 1366 and p. 1369.

3.   The *Hirabayashi* case, discussed in the *Korematsu* opinions, had been decided by the Supreme Court just the year before. It unanimously upheld an 8 pm to 6 am curfew on Japanese nationals and Japanese-American citizens within the military district. The Court did so on the basis of the need to defer to military authorities' judgment about the demands of military necessity in time of war or threatened invasion. Is there a principled basis for distinguishing *Hirabayashi* and *Korematsu*? Is it the magnitude of the intrusion on individual liberty ("stay in your house after dark" versus "leave your house and be relocated to a detention camp")? Is the question of deference to military judgment about matters of asserted military necessity any different? If the two cases are not distinguishable, should the Court have followed or overruled *Hirabayashi*?

4.   There were, on a much smaller scale, also internments of German-Americans and Italian-Americans during World War II, a story told in Jan Jarboe Russell, *The Train to Crystal City* (2015). Would the constitutional case for the internment have been stronger or weaker if the same rules had been applied to Americans of German, Italian, and Japanese ancestry?

5.   Would it really have been possible for the Court to rule against the military and invalidate its judgments during World War II? Would the president or the military have listened to an adverse ruling? Consider Justice Jackson's dissent in this regard. He argues that law cannot, as a practical matter, prevail over perceptions of military necessity and perhaps should not even try, but that the Court should not validate the military's action. Is this position principled? Is it wise? What would have been the consequence for Korematsu himself? Would it make a difference if the case had been before the Court on a motion for an *injunction* ordering the military to close the internment camps?

6.   On the same day the Court decided *Korematsu*, it decided *Ex parte Endo*, 323 U.S. 283 (1944). *Endo* was a habeas corpus challenge, not to the initial exclusion order but to continued detention once time had allowed for the determination that an internee was loyal and not a threat. The Court held that continued detention under such circumstances was not authorized by statute. The case has a strong aura of quasi-constitutional considerations. See Patrick O. Gudridge, *Remember* Endo?, 116 Harv. L. Rev. 1933 (2003). *Endo* effectively required the closing of the internment camps. Does that affect how you think about *Korematsu*? Was the Court trying to "split the difference" by simultaneously upholding the principle of military authority even while ending the internment program?

7.   The law about military detentions has continued to develop. Indeed, it is fair to say that, since September 11, 2001, the Supreme Court has been extraordinarily active in this area, issuing a large number of significant decisions concerning presidential and congressional military authority. A full treatment of these decisions is impossible in a general constitutional law survey course. Three recent cases, however, stand out as being especially important.

a.   In *Hamdi v. Rumsfeld*, presented next, the Court, by a divided vote and without a controlling opinion (and dividing differently on different questions), held that (1) the war power generally (and the AUMF of September 18, 2001, specifically) authorizes the president as commander in chief to capture and hold enemy combatants as war prisoners, including American citizens fighting for enemy forces and captured in the course of waging an authorized war; and (2) that American citizens nonetheless possess the right, under the Fifth Amendment's Due Process Clause, to contest the propriety of their classification as war prisoners through some form of hearing, perhaps including an informal military hearing.

b.   In *Hamdan v. Rumsfeld,* 548 U.S. 557 (2006), the Court, by a vote of 5–3, held that neither the AUMF nor the president's power as commander in chief authorized the use of a military tribunal to try an alleged enemy war criminal captured in Afghanistan and held at Guantanamo Bay, Cuba. Justice Stevens' wide-ranging opinion suggested a narrow reading of the Commander in Chief Clause powers (in considerable tension with prior decisions) and a broad reading of international law as constraining such power. A one-paragraph concurrence by Justice Breyer, joined by four of the five justices comprising the majority (all except Justice Stevens) embraced a more focused rationale, emphasizing that all that was required was congressional action in support of the president's position. Congress indeed responded quickly, with the Military Commissions Act of 2006 ("MCA"), Pub. L. No. 109–366, 120 Stat. 2600, which comprehensively defined punishable war crimes and specified the jurisdiction and procedures of military commissions.

c.   The MCA provided that challenges to detention and military punishment must proceed through the procedures prescribed for military tribunals, with only modest judicial review. In *Boumediene v. Bush,* 553 U.S. 723 (2008), the Court held 5–4 that this procedure unconstitutionally deprived enemy alien combatants of their constitutional right to the writ of habeas corpus to challenge their military detentions abroad and that judicial review of military determinations was an inadequate legal substitute for the writ of habeas corpus. This enormously significant decision addressed the scope of Congress's powers to prescribe the jurisdiction of federal courts and to suspend the writ of habeas corpus.

Hamdi v. Rumsfeld

542 U.S. 507 (2004)

■ JUSTICE O'CONNOR announced the judgment of the Court and delivered an opinion, in which THE CHIEF JUSTICE, JUSTICE KENNEDY, and JUSTICE BREYER join.

At this difficult time in our Nation's history, we are called upon to consider the legality of the Government's detention of a United States citizen on United States soil as an "enemy combatant" and to address the process that is constitutionally owed to one who seeks to challenge his classification as such. The United States Court of Appeals for the Fourth Circuit held that petitioner Yaser Hamdi's detention was legally authorized and that he was entitled to no further opportunity to challenge his enemy-combatant label. We now vacate and remand. We hold that although Congress authorized the detention of combatants in the narrow circumstances alleged here, due process demands that a citizen held in the United States as an enemy combatant be given a meaningful opportunity to contest the factual basis for that detention before a neutral decisionmaker.

I

On September 11, 2001, the al Qaeda terrorist network used hijacked commercial airliners to attack prominent targets in the United States. Approximately 3,000 people were killed in those attacks. One week later, in response to these "acts of treacherous violence," Congress passed a resolution [the "Authorization for Use of Military Force" (AUMF)] authorizing the President to "use all necessary and appropriate force against those nations, organizations, or persons he determines planned, authorized, committed, or aided the terrorist attacks" or "harbored such organizations or persons, in order to prevent any future acts of international terrorism against the United States by such nations, organizations or persons." . . .

This case arises out of the detention of a man whom the Government alleges took up arms with the Taliban during this conflict. . . . Born in Louisiana in 1980, Hamdi moved with his family to Saudi Arabia as a child. By 2001, the parties agree, he resided in Afghanistan. At some point that year, he was seized by members of the Northern Alliance, a coalition of military groups opposed to the Taliban government, and eventually was turned over to the United States military. . . . The Government contends that Hamdi is an "enemy combatant," and that this status justifies holding him in the United States indefinitely—without formal charges or proceedings—unless and until it makes the determination that access to counsel or further process is warranted. . . .

II

The threshold question before us is whether the Executive has the authority to detain citizens who qualify as "enemy combatants." . . . [W]e agree with the Government's position, that Congress has in fact authorized Hamdi's detention, through the AUMF. . . .

There can be no doubt that individuals who fought against the United States in Afghanistan as part of the Taliban, an organization known to have supported the al Qaeda terrorist network responsible for those attacks, are individuals Congress sought to target in passing the AUMF. We conclude that detention of individuals falling into the limited category we are considering, for the duration of the particular conflict in which they were captured, is so fundamental and accepted an incident to war as to be an exercise of the "necessary and appropriate force" Congress has authorized the President to use.

The capture and detention of lawful combatants and the capture, detention, and trial of unlawful combatants, by "universal agreement and practice," are "important incident[s] of war." *Ex Parte Quirin*, 317 U.S. 1, 28 (1942). The purpose of detention is to prevent captured individuals from returning to the field of battle and taking up arms once again.

There is no bar to this Nation's holding one of its own citizens as an enemy combatant. In *Quirin,* one of the detainees, Haupt, alleged that he was a naturalized United States citizen. We held that "[c]itizens who associate themselves with the military arm of the enemy government, and with its aid, guidance and direction enter this country bent on hostile acts, are enemy belligerents within the meaning of . . . the law of war." While Haupt was tried for violations of the law of war, nothing in *Quirin* suggests that his citizenship would have precluded his mere detention for the duration of the relevant hostilities. . . .

It is a clearly established principle of the law of war that detention may last no longer than active hostilities. . . . The United States may detain, for the duration of these hostilities, individuals legitimately determined to be Taliban combatants who "engaged in an armed conflict against the United States." If the record establishes that United States troops are still involved in active combat in Afghanistan, those detentions are part of the exercise of "necessary and appropriate force," and therefore are authorized by the AUMF. . . .

[O]ur opinion only finds legislative authority to detain under the AUMF once it is sufficiently clear that the individual is, in fact, an enemy combatant; whether that is established by concession or by some other process that verifies this fact with sufficient certainty seems beside the point. . . .

III

Even in cases in which the detention of enemy combatants is legally authorized, there remains the question of what process is constitutionally due to a citizen who disputes his enemy-combatant status. . . .

The ordinary mechanism that we use for balancing such serious competing interests, and for determining the procedures that are necessary to ensure that a citizen is not "deprived of life, liberty, or property, without due process of law," U.S. Const., Amdt. 5, is the test that we articulated in *Mathews v. Eldridge*, 424 U.S. 319 (1976). *Mathews* dictates that the process due in any given instance is determined by weighing "the private interest that will be affected by the official action" against the Government's asserted interest, "including the function involved" and the burdens the Government would face in providing greater process. The *Mathews* calculus then contemplates a judicious balancing of these concerns, through an analysis of "the risk of an erroneous deprivation" of the private interest if the process were reduced and the "probable value, if any, of additional or substitute procedural safeguards." We take each of these steps in turn.

It is beyond question that substantial interests lie on both sides of the scale in this case. . . . [A]s critical as the Government's interest may be in detaining those who actually pose an immediate threat to the national security of the United States during ongoing international conflict, history and common sense teach us that an unchecked system of detention carries the potential to become a means for oppression and abuse of others who do not present that sort of threat. . . . We reaffirm today the fundamental nature of a citizen's right to be free from involuntary confinement by his own government without due process of law, and we weigh the opposing governmental interests against the curtailment of liberty that such confinement entails. . . .

Striking the proper constitutional balance here is of great importance to the Nation during this period of ongoing combat. But it is equally vital that our calculus not give short shrift to the values that this country holds dear or to the privilege that is American citizenship. . . . We therefore hold that a citizen-detainee seeking to challenge his classification as an enemy combatant must receive notice of the factual basis for his classification, and a fair opportunity to rebut the Government's factual assertions before a neutral decisionmaker. "For more than a century the central meaning of procedural due process has been clear: 'Parties whose rights are to be affected are entitled to be heard; and in order that they may enjoy that right they must first be notified.' It is equally fundamental that the right to notice and an opportunity to be heard 'must be granted at a meaningful time and in a meaningful manner.'" *Fuentes v. Shevin*, 407 U.S. 67, 80 (1972) (quoting *Baldwin v. Hale*, 68 U.S. (1 Wall.) 223, 233 (1864). These essential constitutional promises may not be eroded.

At the same time, the exigencies of the circumstances may demand that, aside from these core elements, enemy-combatant proceedings may be tailored to alleviate their uncommon potential to burden the Executive at a time of ongoing military conflict. Hearsay, for example, may need to be accepted as the most reliable available evidence from the Government in such a proceeding. Likewise, the Constitution would not be offended by a presumption in favor of the Government's evidence, so long as that presumption remained a rebuttable one and fair opportunity for rebuttal were provided. . . .

We think it unlikely that this basic process will have the dire impact on the central functions of warmaking that the Government forecasts. The parties agree that initial captures on the battlefield need not receive the process we have discussed here; that process is due only when the determination is made to *continue* to hold those who have been seized. . . . While we accord the greatest respect and consideration to the judgments of military authorities in matters relating to the actual prosecution of a war, and recognize that the scope of that discretion necessarily is wide, it does not infringe on the core role of the military for the courts to exercise their own time-honored and constitutionally mandated roles of reviewing and resolving claims like those presented here.

In sum, while the full protections that accompany challenges to detentions in other settings may prove unworkable and inappropriate in the enemy-combatant setting, the threats to military operations posed by a basic system of independent review are not so weighty as to trump a citizen's core rights to challenge meaningfully the Government's case and to be heard by an impartial adjudicator.

In so holding, we necessarily reject the Government's assertion that separation of powers principles mandate a heavily circumscribed role for the courts in such circumstances. Indeed, the position that the courts must forgo any examination of the individual case and focus exclusively on the legality of the broader detention scheme cannot be mandated by any reasonable view of separation of powers, as this approach serves only to *condense* power into a single branch of government. We have long since made clear that a state of war is not a blank check for the President when it comes to the rights of the Nation's citizens. *Youngstown Sheet & Tube Co. v. Sawyer*, 343 U.S. 579, 587 (1952). Whatever power the United States Constitution envisions for the Executive in its exchanges with other nations or with enemy organizations in times of conflict, it most assuredly envisions a role for all three branches when individual liberties are at stake. . . .

There remains the possibility that the standards we have articulated could be met by an appropriately authorized and properly constituted military tribunal. Indeed, it is notable that military regulations already provide for such process in related instances, dictating that tribunals be made available to determine the status of enemy detainees who assert prisoner-of-war status under the Geneva Convention. In the absence of such process, however, a court that receives a petition for a writ of habeas corpus from an alleged enemy combatant must itself ensure that the minimum requirements of due process are achieved. . . .

■ JUSTICE SOUTER, with whom JUSTICE GINSBURG joins, concurring in part, dissenting in part, and concurring in the judgment.

[Justice Souter would have found Hamdi's detention forbidden by the "Non-Detention Act," 18 U.S.C. § 4001(a), which bars imprisonment or detention of U.S. citizens "except pursuant to an Act of Congress." Justice Souter did not believe that the Authorization for Use of Military Force (AUMF) was an act authorizing detention. Justices Souter and Ginsburg thus joined neither the plurality's holding that the AUMF authorized detention nor the plurality's due process analysis. Nonetheless, because of "the need to give practical effect to the conclusions of eight members of the

Court rejecting the Government's position," they joined in the order of remand for a hearing.—Editors]

■ JUSTICE SCALIA, with whom JUSTICE STEVENS joins, dissenting.

Petitioner Yaser Hamdi, a presumed American citizen, has been imprisoned without charge or hearing in the Norfolk and Charleston Naval Brigs for more than two years, on the allegation that he is an enemy combatant who bore arms against his country for the Taliban. His father claims to the contrary, that he is an inexperienced aid worker caught in the wrong place at the wrong time. . . .

Where the Government accuses a citizen of waging war against it, our constitutional tradition has been to prosecute him in federal court for treason or some other crime. Where the exigencies of war prevent that, the Constitution's Suspension Clause, Art. I, § 9, cl. 2, allows Congress to relax the usual protections temporarily. Absent suspension, however, the Executive's assertion of military exigency has not been thought sufficient to permit detention without charge. No one contends that the congressional Authorization for Use of Military Force, on which the Government relies to justify its actions here, is an implementation of the Suspension Clause. Accordingly, I would reverse the judgment below. . . .

The gist of the Due Process Clause, as understood at the founding and since, was to force the Government to follow those common-law procedures traditionally deemed necessary before depriving a person of life, liberty, or property. When a citizen was deprived of liberty because of alleged criminal conduct, those procedures typically required committal by a magistrate followed by indictment and trial. See, *e.g.*, 2 & 3 Philip & Mary, ch. 10 (1555). The Due Process Clause "in effect affirms the right of trial according to the process and proceedings of the common law." 3 J. Story, Commentaries on the Constitution of the United States § 1783, p. 661 (1833). . . .

These due process rights have historically been vindicated by the writ of habeas corpus. In England before the founding, the writ developed into a tool for challenging executive confinement. . . . The writ of habeas corpus was preserved in the Constitution—the only common-law writ to be explicitly mentioned. See Art. I, § 9, cl. 2. Hamilton lauded "the establishment of the writ of *habeas corpus*" in his Federalist defense as a means to protect against "the practice of arbitrary imprisonments . . . in all ages, [one of] the favourite and most formidable instruments of tyranny." The Federalist No. 84. . . .

The allegations here, of course, are no ordinary accusations of criminal activity. Yaser Esam Hamdi has been imprisoned because the Government believes he participated in the waging of war against the United States. The relevant question, then, is whether there is a different, special procedure for imprisonment of a citizen accused of wrongdoing *by aiding the enemy in wartime.* . . .

There are times when military exigency renders resort to the traditional criminal process impracticable. English law accommodated such exigencies by allowing legislative suspension of the writ of habeas corpus for brief periods. . . .

Our Federal Constitution contains a provision explicitly permitting suspension, but limiting the situations in which it may be invoked: "The Privilege of the Writ of Habeas Corpus shall not be suspended, unless when in Cases of Rebellion or Invasion the public Safety may require it." Art. I, § 9, cl. 2. Although this provision does not state that suspension must be effected by, or authorized by, a legislative act, it has been so understood, consistent with English practice and the Clause's placement in Article I. See *Ex parte Merryman*, 17 F.Cas. 144, 151–152 (CD Md. 1861) (Taney, C.J., rejecting Lincoln's unauthorized suspension).

The Suspension Clause was by design a safety valve, the Constitution's only "express provision for exercise of extraordinary authority because of a crisis," *Youngstown*, at 650 (Jackson, J., concurring). . . . Writings from the founding generation also suggest that, without exception, the only constitutional alternatives are to charge the crime or suspend the writ. . . .

The Government argues that our more recent jurisprudence ratifies its indefinite imprisonment of a citizen within the territorial jurisdiction of federal courts. It places primary reliance upon *Ex parte Quirin*, a World War II case upholding the trial by military commission of eight German saboteurs, one of whom, Herbert Haupt, was a U.S. citizen. The case was not this Court's finest hour. The Court upheld the commission and denied relief in a brief per curiam issued the day after oral argument concluded, see *Quirin*, at 18–19, unnumbered note; a week later the Government carried out the commission's death sentence upon six saboteurs, including Haupt. The Court eventually explained its reasoning in a written opinion issued several months later. . . .

But even . . . *Quirin* would still not justify denial of the writ here. In *Quirin* it was uncontested that the petitioners were members of enemy forces. They were "*admitted* enemy invaders," *Id.* at 47 (emphasis added), and it was "undisputed" that they had landed in the United States in service of German forces, *id.*, at 20. . . .

It follows from what I have said that Hamdi is entitled to a habeas decree requiring his release unless (1) criminal proceedings are promptly brought, or (2) Congress has suspended the writ of habeas corpus. A suspension of the writ could, of course, lay down conditions for continued detention, similar to those that today's opinion prescribes under the Due Process Clause. But there is a world of difference between the people's representatives determining the need for that suspension (and prescribing the conditions for it), and this Court's doing so. . . .

Having found a congressional authorization for detention of citizens where none clearly exists; and having discarded the categorical procedural protection of the Suspension Clause; the plurality then proceeds, under the guise of the Due Process Clause, to prescribe what procedural protections *it* thinks appropriate. It "weigh[s] the private interest . . . against the Government's asserted interest," and—just as though writing a new Constitution—comes up with an unheard-of system in which the citizen rather than the Government bears the burden of proof, testimony is by hearsay rather than live witnesses, and the presiding officer may well be a "neutral" military officer rather than judge and jury. It claims authority to engage in this sort of "judicious balancing" from *Mathews v. Eldridge*, a case involving . . . *the withdrawal of disability benefits!* Whatever the merits of this technique when newly recognized property rights are at issue (and even there they are questionable), it has no place where the Constitution and the common law already supply an answer. . . .

The Founders well understood the difficult tradeoff between safety and freedom. "Safety from external danger," Hamilton declared,

> "is the most powerful director of national conduct. Even the ardent love of liberty will, after a time, give way to its dictates. The violent destruction of life and property incident to war; the continual effort and alarm attendant

on a state of continual danger, will compel nations the most attached to liberty, to resort for repose and security to institutions which have a tendency to destroy their civil and political rights. To be more safe, they, at length, become willing to run the risk of being less free." The Federalist No. 8.

Many think it not only inevitable but entirely proper that liberty give way to security in times of national crisis—that, at the extremes of military exigency, *inter arma silent leges [i.e., among arms, the laws fall silent—Editors]*. Whatever the general merits of the view that war silences law or modulates its voice, that view has no place in the interpretation and application of a Constitution designed precisely to confront war and, in a manner that accords with democratic principles, to accommodate it. Because the Court has proceeded to meet the current emergency in a manner the Constitution does not envision, I respectfully dissent.

■ JUSTICE THOMAS, dissenting.

The Executive Branch, acting pursuant to the powers vested in the President by the Constitution and with explicit congressional approval, has determined that Yaser Hamdi is an enemy combatant and should be detained. This detention falls squarely within the Federal Government's war powers, and we lack the expertise and capacity to second-guess that decision. As such, petitioners' habeas challenge should fail, and there is no reason to remand the case. . . .

The Founders intended that the President have primary responsibility—along with the necessary power—to protect the national security and to conduct the Nation's foreign relations. They did so principally because the structural advantages of a unitary Executive are essential in these domains. "Energy in the executive is a leading character in the definition of good government. It is essential to the protection of the community against foreign attacks." The Federalist, No. 70 (A. Hamilton). The principle "ingredien[t]" for "energy in the executive" is "unity." This is because "[d]ecision, activity, secrecy, and dispatch will generally characterise the proceedings of one man, in a much more eminent degree, than the proceedings of any greater number."

These structural advantages are most important in the national-security and foreign-affairs contexts. "Of all the cares or concerns of government, the direction of war most peculiarly demands those qualities which distinguish the exercise of power by a single hand." The Federalist, No. 74 (A. Hamilton). . . .

This Court has long recognized these features and has accordingly held that the President has *constitutional* authority to protect the national security and that this authority carries with it broad discretion. . . .

I agree with the plurality that the Federal Government has power to detain those that the Executive Branch determines to be enemy combatants. But I do not think that the plurality has adequately explained the breadth of the President's authority to detain enemy combatants, an authority that includes making virtually conclusive factual findings. . . .

In this context, due process requires nothing more than a good-faith executive determination. To be clear: The Court has held that an Executive, acting pursuant to statutory and constitutional authority, may, consistent with the Due Process Clause, unilaterally decide to detain an individual if the Executive deems this necessary for the public safety *even if he is mistaken*. . . .

The Government's asserted authority to detain an individual that the President has determined to be an enemy combatant, at least while hostilities continue, comports with the Due Process Clause. . . . I therefore cannot agree with JUSTICE SCALIA's conclusion that the Government must choose between using standard criminal processes and suspending the writ. . . .

By detaining Hamdi, the President, in the prosecution of a war and authorized by Congress, has acted well within his authority. Hamdi thereby received all the process to which he was due under the circumstances. I therefore believe that this is no occasion to balance the competing interests, as the plurality unconvincingly attempts to do. . . .

NOTES

1.   First, sort out the holdings and the alignment of the justices. On the power to capture and hold a U.S. citizen pursuant to the war power: Five justices—Justice O'Connor, the three justices joining plurality opinion, and Justice Thomas in dissent— agreed that the government had authority to hold Hamdi, a U.S. citizen, pursuant to war powers triggered by the AUMF and the president's power as Commander in Chief. In what ways does Justice Thomas's legal position on this issue differ from that of the plurality? Why did he not join the plurality opinion on this point? Note that Justice Thomas's dissent is a dissent because he disagrees with the ultimate disposition of the case: he would uphold the president's power to detain Hamdi without a remand. Justices Souter and Ginsburg disagreed with this holding on the ground that Hamdi's detention was not authorized by congressional act—the AUMF was not sufficient. Justices Scalia and Stevens disagreed with this holding on the ground that a U.S. citizen may never be held by military authorities, unless Congress has exercised the power to suspend the privilege of the writ of habeas corpus. Which view on this point—the authority of the president to detain Hamdi—is right?

2.   Should we think of *Hamdi* as a wartime case or a peacetime case? The AUMF has been in force for fifteen years. Have we been at war the whole time? When does the War on Terror stop?

3.   On the requirement of a hearing: The plurality finds that, notwithstanding the president's authority to capture and hold enemy prisoners, a U.S. citizen has a due process right to some sort of hearing to challenge the validity of his detention as a war prisoner. What kind of procedures does the plurality envision? What is the alternative offered by Justice Scalia? (*Mathews v. Eldridge* is presented at p. 1490.)

4.   Both *Korematsu* and *Hamdi* raise the question, how much should the Supreme Court get involved in major questions of war and national security? Is that where we need the Court most? Or where we want it least?

[*Assignment 17*]

G. IMPEACHMENT: "THE PRESIDENT . . . SHALL BE REMOVED FROM OFFICE ON IMPEACHMENT . . . AND CONVICTION"

Art. II, § 4: The President, Vice President and all civil Officers of the United States, shall be removed from Office on Impeachment for, and Conviction of, Treason, Bribery, or other high Crimes and Misdemeanors.

The Impeachment Clause makes clear that the president, unlike the king of England, is removable from office by impeachment. The only methods for getting rid of the English king were to kill him, force him to abdicate, or drive him into exile. Each method was used from time to time, but none was free of inconvenience.

Indeed, at the convention in Philadelphia, Benjamin Franklin expressly compared impeachment to alternatives rather more violent:

> History furnishes one example only of a first Magistrate being formally brought to public Justice. Every body cried out agst this as unconstitutional. What was the practice before this in cases where the chief Magistrate rendered himself obnoxious? Why recourse was had to assassination in wch. he was not only deprived of his life but of the opportunity of vindicating his character. It wd. be the best way therefore to provide in the Constitution for the regular punishment of the Executive when his misconduct should deserve it, and for his honorable acquittal when he should be unjustly accused.

2 THE RECORDS OF THE FEDERAL CONVENTION OF 1787, at 65 (Max Farrand ed., 1911); see also Josh Chafetz, *Impeachment and Assassination*, 95 Minn. L. Rev. 347 (2010).

Three presidents in American history have faced a serious challenge from the impeachment power. Two of them, Andrew Johnson and Bill Clinton, were impeached by the House of Representatives but then acquitted by the Senate. The other one, Richard Nixon, was never actually impeached by the House; he resigned when it was clear that if he did not, he would be impeached.

The following sources consider each of these episodes. On the impeachment of President Johnson, there is an excerpt from Professor David Currie narrating the indictment and trial, and showing the constitutional arguments used on both sides. On the impeachment of President Nixon, there is *United States v. Nixon*, 418 U.S. 683 (1974), a decision which required the president to turn over evidence, an act that would quickly lead to his resignation. On the impeachment of President Clinton, we present two competing statements about the standard for impeachment and the House's proper constitutional role. As you read these materials, ask yourself what the circumstances are in which a president should be impeached and removed from office. Can the impeachment power be used to preserve the balance of power between the branches, by disciplining and constraining the president? Or can it be used to undermine the balance of power between the branches, allowing Congress to dominate the president? Or both? Can we have the sweet without the bitter?

David Currie on the Impeachment of Andrew Johnson

The Reconstruction Congress, 75 U. Chi. L. Rev. 383, 437–452 (2008)

Andrew Johnson was not a temperate man. Nor was he the least bit sympathetic toward congressional plans for Reconstruction. It was not long before influential members of Congress decided it would be best if he returned to private life.

Unfortunately for them, the United States did not have a parliamentary system in which a president could be deposed by a simple majority vote of no confidence. The only available weapon was impeachment for and conviction of "treason, bribery, or other high crimes and misdemeanors," which required an accusation by the House of Representatives and a two-thirds vote in the Senate. It was accordingly to the impeachment provisions that Johnson's enemies turned.

1.   *Failure in the House.*

As early as January 1867, before the first Reconstruction Act was adopted, no fewer than three resolutions were introduced in the House urging that President Johnson be impeached. The most detailed of the three was that submitted by Representative James Ashley of Ohio, which specified the crimes and misdemeanors he attributed to the President:

> I do impeach Andrew Johnson, Vice President and acting President of the United States, of high crimes and misdemeanors.
>
> I charge him with a usurpation of power and violation of law:
>
> In that he has corruptly used the appointing power;
>
> In that he has corruptly used the pardoning power;
>
> In that he has corruptly used the veto power;
>
> In that he has corruptly disposed of public property of the United States;
>
> In that he has corruptly interfered in elections, and committed acts which, in contemplation of the Constitution, are high crimes and misdemeanors.

This resolution was shipped off to the Judiciary Committee, which heard reams of evidence and took until November to report. When it did it recommended that the President be impeached—but only by a vote of 5–4.

The crux of Ashley's indictment, the majority declared, was "usurpation of power, which involves, of course, a violation of law." . . . President Johnson had had the gall to attempt to reconstruct the former Confederate states on his own.

The remainder of the report was a bill of particulars nearly sixty pages long. It accused the President, among other things, of having set up new governments in the former Confederate states; of having created offices, filled them, and paid those who held them, all without senatorial or congressional approval; of having returned to their original owners certain railroads seized by the government; of having granted indiscriminate pardons, employed the veto excessively, obstructed the execution of laws, and abused the appointing power by removing officers on political grounds and reappointing nominees after the Senate had rejected them; of having employed federal workers for electioneering purposes while they were being paid a government salary; of having tried to dissuade the people of the rebellious states from accepting the terms of congressional reconstruction; of having encouraged a bloody riot in New Orleans; and of having endeavored to bring Congress itself "into odium and contempt."

It may well be doubted whether any impeachable acts were shown. The dissenting members of the committee thought not. Among other things, they insisted, crimes were violations of penal laws; both crimes and misdemeanors meant indictable offenses. This conclusion, they argued, followed from the words of the Constitution itself: "[c]rimes" and "[m]isdemeanors" were "terms of art, and we have no authority for expounding them beyond their true technical limits." Other constitutional provisions, the dissenters contended, confirmed this interpretation. Article I provided that a party impeached and convicted would still be subject to indictment and punishment in the ordinary courts; "[h]ow can this be if his offence be not an indictable crime?" Article II empowered the president to pardon offenses against the United States "except in cases of impeachment"; Article III, with the same exception, required a jury trial of all crimes. Both of these clauses, the dissenters suggested, implied that impeachable offenses were indeed crimes in the narrow technical sense—as in their view the term "high crimes and misdemeanors" already made clear. The principal dissent went on to maintain that (with the exception of Judge Pickering's case, which it described as "disreputable") previous impeachments had invariably charged the respondents with indictable crimes, and that (although not all the precedents could be reconciled) the better English cases had recognized the necessity of an indictable offense before the Constitution was adopted. Along the way the dissent quoted Blackstone for good measure: "[A]n impeachment before the lords by the commons of Great Britain, in parliament, is a prosecution of the already known and established law."

The reader may have perceived that the above summary says nothing about the views of American commentators. In fact the dissenters barely mentioned them, and then in an effort to show they were not so opposed to the dissenters' own position as might at first glance appear. Not surprisingly, the majority report made considerable hay out of the American observers. In most prominent place stands no less an authority than Alexander Hamilton, who explained to the people of New York when the Constitution was being considered that "[t]he subjects of [a court of impeachment's] jurisdiction are those offenses which proceed from the misconduct of public men, or in other words from the abuse or violation of some public trust." Not a word was said about indictable offenses; the crux of impeachment was abuse of the public trust. . . .

[Then] the report turns to Justice Joseph Story, whose writings explicitly repudiate the minority's position:

> The offences to which the power of impeachment has been, and is ordinarily applied as a remedy, are of a political character. Not but that crimes of a strictly legal character fall within the scope of the power, but that it has a more enlarged operation, and reaches what are aptly termed political offences, growing out of personal misconduct, or gross neglect, or usurpation, or habitual disregard of the public interests in the discharge of the duties of political office. . . . [N]o one has as yet been bold enough to assert that the power of impeachment is limited to offences positively

defined in the statute book of the Union as impeachable high crimes and misdemeanors. . . .

The issue whether an indictable offense was necessary for impeachment would arise again in President Nixon's case a century later. I agree with the prosecution in both cases that it was not. The text of the Constitution does not answer the question; "high crimes and misdemeanors" is a term of art. British precedents are in disarray. The virtual unanimity of early American commentators, beginning with the knowledgeable Hamilton, goes a long way to demonstrate what the Framers must have had in mind. Congressional practice is equally probative of the original understanding, for in none of the earlier impeachments did the House allege the infraction of particular statutory provisions, even when it could easily have done so. Finally, the narrow interpretation urged by President Johnson's defenders left so much heinous conduct outside the pale of impeachment that the constitutional provisions could not serve their intended purpose—such as Judge Humphreys's abandonment of his duties or a president's deliberate usurpation of congressional power.

More important for present purposes than what I think constitute high crimes and misdemeanors is what the House thought in 1867, and significantly not all Republicans agreed at the time that no crime in the technical sense had to be alleged. The dissenters from the Judiciary Committee's report included two Republicans, James Wilson of Iowa and Frederick Woodbridge of Vermont. We must allege specific crimes, said Wilson on the floor of the House; "a bundle of generalities" would not suffice. Indeed, Wilson added, it really didn't matter whether indictable crimes had to be charged; even on the majority's test no impeachable offense had been shown The Constitutional Convention, as Ohio Democrat Philadelph Van Trump pointed out, had at Madison's suggestion rejected a proposal to provide for impeachment on grounds of mere "maladministration"; "[s]o vague a term," Madison had argued, "will be equivalent to a tenure during pleasure of the Senate." The majority's recommendation was roundly defeated; the House found no cause for impeachment.

2. Defeat in the Senate.

That was in December 1867. Then, on February 21, 1868, President Johnson sent the following message to his Secretary of War, Edwin M. Stanton:

> Sir: By virtue of the power and authority vested in me as President by the Constitution and laws of the United States, you are hereby removed from office as Secretary for the Department of War, and your functions as such will terminate upon the receipt of this communication. . . .

Johnson had played right into the House's hands, giving it the smoking gun it had been looking for. The President, crowed Representative Rufus Spalding of Ohio, had violated the Tenure of Office Act, which requires Senate consent to discharge a member of the Cabinet; and the statute makes violation of its provisions a misdemeanor punishable by law. Wilson and Woodbridge, who had dissented when impeachment was first proposed, were convinced: now the President had willfully offended the law of the land.

New York Democrat James Brooks had three answers for the committee: the Tenure Act was inapplicable to Stanton, who had been appointed not by Johnson but by his predecessor, Abraham Lincoln; Congress could not limit the president's authority to discharge a member of his Cabinet, as Congress had decided in 1789;

and in any event the president could not be impeached for an honest difference of opinion as to the validity or interpretation of the law.

After an ample measure of repetition of the arguments on both sides the House voted 126–47 that President Johnson should be impeached. Articles of impeachment were duly drafted and approved.

There were eleven articles in all. As Representative Boutwell informed the House when he offered the committee's draft, most of them were based upon the firing of Stanton. . . . The ninth article alleged that Johnson had told a certain General Emory that the appropriations rider requiring the president to issue orders through the general of the army was unconstitutional, with the intent of inducing Emory to accept orders directly from the president in violation of law. The tenth charged Johnson in a series of "intemperate, inflammatory, and scandalous harangues" had "attempt[ed] to bring into disgrace, ridicule, hatred, contempt, and reproach the Congress of the United States" and in so doing had "brought the high office of the President of the United States into contempt, ridicule, and disgrace." The final article in essence accused the President of attempting to obstruct the execution of the Tenure of Office Act, the Reconstruction Act, and the rider concerning the general of the army.

The President's answer admitted that he had removed Stanton . . . but denied that he had broken the law. It conceded he had told Emory the rider was unconstitutional but denied he had asked him to disobey it. It denied that in his addresses he had meant to bring Congress into disrespect or to call its legitimacy into question and invoked his constitutional freedom of speech. And it denied that he had sought to impede the enforcement of the laws.

The trial began on March 30 with the opening statement of Massachusetts Representative Benjamin Butler, one of the managers for the House. Butler was at pains to insist once more that no indictable crime had to be proved . . .

It was not necessary, he said again, that the act be in violation of some positive law.

The crucial question, said Butler, was whether the president had the right to remove and replace his secretary of war. If he had, then the first eight articles would collapse. But he had no such authority. The precedents were conflicting: if the First Congress had decided that Cabinet officers served at the president's pleasure, the Congress that enacted the Tenure of Office Act had decided they did not. The constitutional clause vesting executive power in the president did not give him all powers that could be classified as executive; it was more plausible to conclude that removal followed the power of appointment, which in relevant cases required Senate consent. And even if the president possessed the power of removal, Congress could regulate it under the Necessary and Proper Clause—as it had done by requiring Senate approval in the case of the comptroller of the currency in 1863 and a court-martial for military or naval officers in 1866.

The Tenure of Office Act, Butler continued, was yet another exercise of that congressional power, and it applied to the case at hand. What it said was that Cabinet officers should remain in office "for and during the term of the President by whom they may have been appointed and for one month thereafter, subject to removal by and with the advice and consent of the Senate." Secretary Stanton, said Butler, had been appointed by President Lincoln, whose term ran until 1869; he was thus still in office and could be removed only with the Senate's blessing. . . . Finally, the President had no right to disobey the Tenure of Office Act even if it was unconstitutional, for his authority to pass on its validity was "exhausted" when Congress passed it over his veto.

Former Supreme Court Justice Benjamin R. Curtis, author of the principal dissent in the *Dred Scott* case, made the opening statement for the defense. The Tenure of Office Act, he argued, was inapplicable to Stanton. The Secretary had been appointed by President Lincoln, not by his successor; and Lincoln's first and second terms had both expired. The reason for providing that a Cabinet officer held office only during the term of the president who appointed him was to allow a new president to choose his own Cabinet; and both the House and the Senate had been told when the statute was being debated that it would not require Johnson to keep his predecessor's advisers. Besides, Congress in 1789 had recognized the president's constitutional right to remove the secretary of war; and if he thought a law unconstitutional it was his duty to disobey it—as any ordinary citizen would be free to do—in order to provoke a judicial test of its validity. . . .

The Senate decided to vote separately on each article without debate, with leave to file written opinions within the next two days.

Presumably because it was thought to pose the strongest case for conviction, the Senate began with Article XI, which dealt largely with alleged efforts to impede execution of the laws. . . . The Senate acquitted President Johnson of this charge by a vote of 35–19. The shift of a single vote would have meant conviction.

The Senate then suspended the impeachment proceedings for ten days to reconnoiter. When it returned it voted on Articles II and III, which turned on the assignment of [Stanton's replacement]; the results were exactly the same. Recognizing that there was no point in proceeding further, the Senate adjourned the trial *sine die*. The attempt to remove President Johnson had failed.

Edmund Ross, Republican of Kansas, is commonly credited with having courageously rescued Johnson from conviction and removal. But Ross was not alone; at least seven Republicans joined opposition senators in voting not guilty on all three counts. Those seven included not only such predictable dissenters as Dixon of Connecticut and Doolittle of Wisconsin but, more dramatically, the influential mainstream Republicans Lyman Trumbull and William Pitt Fessenden.

Both Trumbull and Fessenden wrote opinions explaining their vote and how they would have ruled on the remaining articles. Both concluded that the Tenure of Office Act left the President free to discharge Stanton, for reasons that had been urged by lawyers for the defense. Even if Johnson had been mistaken, Trumbull added, it would have been wrong to convict him for mere misconstruction of a doubtful law. . . . Both Trumbull and Fessenden concluded that the evidence did not support the allegation that Johnson had attempted to induce General Emory to violate the law; that the President's speeches, while discreditable, were not grounds for impeachment; that the effort to keep Stanton from resuming his office was lawful because Johnson had the right to remove him; and that the other charges of obstructing the enforcement of statutes had not been proved.

Each of these opinions closed with an admonition not to be overzealous in wielding the fearsome weapon of impeachment. It was an instrument, wrote Fessenden, that "might be liable to very great abuse, especially in times of high party excitement." It was "a power to be exercised with extreme caution [if at all] when you once get beyond the line of specific criminal offenses." . . .

Wise words. Those of Senator Trumbull were even better:

Once set the example of impeaching a President for what, when the excitement of the hour has subsided, will be regarded as insufficient causes and no future President will be safe who happens to differ with a majority of the House and two thirds of the Senate on any measure deemed by them important, particularly if of a political character. Blinded by partisan zeal, with such an example before them, they will not scruple to remove out of the way any obstacle to the accomplishment of their purposes, and what then becomes of the checks and balances of the Constitution, so carefully devised and so vital to its perpetuity? They are all gone. In view of the consequences likely to flow from this day's proceedings, should they result in conviction on what my judgment tells me are insufficient charges and proofs, I tremble for the future of my country. I cannot be an instrument to produce such a result.

Other senators who voted for acquittal went beyond the purely statutory arguments of Fessenden and Trumbull to find constitutional grounds for their conclusion. Old Reverdy Johnson, the best of the congressional Democrats and a former Attorney General, concluded that the Tenure of Office Act was unconstitutional and that Article II, by vesting executive power in the president and constraining him to ensure execution of the laws, empowered him to assign someone to a vacant office to prevent a void in enforcement. . . .

What then do we learn about the Constitution from the disreputable effort to remove Andrew Johnson from the presidency? With respect to the meaning of the impeachment provisions themselves the bottom line is equivocal. For although the House's rejection of the original "bundle of generalities" suggests that a majority thought it necessary to allege some violation of law, its later approval of a count based exclusively on the President's irascible speeches suggests the contrary; and in the Senate the issue turned in the end on substantive questions of presidential power, not on the definition of an impeachable act. There was a reprise of constitutional arguments about the president's right of removal, but that was all old hat and nothing novel was added. The argument that the Constitution itself authorized the president to avoid a vacuum in office may have been new, and I find it persuasive. But the real lesson of the Johnson impeachment was the result, for it established for all time the salubrious constitutional principle that no one should be impeached because he disagrees with the congressional will.

NOTES

1.   The charges against President Johnson included arguments that he had wrongly exercised or abused many powers discussed in this chapter, such as the suspending power, the removal power, the directing power, the appointment power, and the war power. Which of these powers is most liable to abuse? (Are all of them presidential powers?) Should members of Congress be allowed to remove the president from office whenever they disagree about the scope of those powers? When they disagree really strongly? When the stakes are high?

2.   If impeachment is not an appropriate remedy for a constitutional disagreement between Congress and the president, what else is Congress supposed to do? What else can it do?

United States v. Nixon
418 U.S. 683 (1974)

■ MR. CHIEF JUSTICE BURGER delivered the opinion of the Court.

This litigation presents for review the denial of a motion, filed in the District Court on behalf of the President of the United States . . . to quash a third-party subpoena duces tecum issued by the United States District Court for the District of Columbia, pursuant to Fed. Rule Crim. Proc. 17(c). The subpoena directed the President to produce certain tape recordings and documents relating to his conversations with aides and advisers. The court rejected the President's claims of absolute executive privilege, of lack of jurisdiction, and of failure to satisfy the requirements of Rule 17(c). The President appealed to the Court of Appeals. We granted both the United States' petition for certiorari before judgment, and also the President's cross-petition for certiorari before judgment, because of the public importance of the issues presented and the need for their prompt resolution.

On March 1, 1974, a grand jury of the United States District Court for the District of Columbia returned an indictment charging seven named individuals[3] with various offenses, including conspiracy to defraud the United States and to obstruct justice. Although he was not designated as such in the indictment, the grand jury named the President, among others, as an unindicted coconspirator. On April 18, 1974, upon motion of the Special Prosecutor, a subpoena duces tecum was issued pursuant to Rule 17(c) to the President by the United States District Court and made returnable on May 2, 1974. This subpoena required the production, in advance of the September 9 trial date, of certain tapes, memoranda, papers, transcripts or other writings relating to certain precisely identified meetings between the President and others. . . . *[The Court then recounted the procedural history of the case, which culminated in the district court ordering the president to produce the documents, which the president appealed.—Editors]*

I

JURISDICTION

The threshold question presented is whether the May 20, 1974, order of the District Court was an appealable order . . . Since the appeal was timely filed and all other procedural requirements were met, the petition is properly before this Court for consideration if the District Court order was final. . . .

In applying this principle *[of finality—Editors]* to an order denying a motion to quash and requiring the production of evidence pursuant to a subpoena duces tecum, it has been repeatedly held that the order is not final and hence not appealable. This Court has

---

[3]   The seven defendants were John N. Mitchell, H. R. Haldeman, John D. Ehrlichman, Charles W. Colson, Robert C. Mardian, Kenneth W. Parkinson, and Gordon Strachan. Each had occupied either a position of responsibility on the White House staff or the Committee for the Re-election of the President. Colson entered a guilty plea on another charge and is no longer a defendant.

consistently held that the necessity for expedition in the administration of the criminal law justifies putting one who seeks to resist the production of desired information to a choice between compliance with a trial court's order to produce prior to any review of that order, and resistance to that order with the concomitant possibility of an adjudication of contempt if his claims are rejected on appeal. *United States v. Ryan*, 402 U.S., 530, 533 (1971).

The requirement of submitting to contempt, however, is not without exception and in some instances the purposes underlying the finality rule require a different result. . . .

Here too, the traditional contempt avenue to immediate appeal is peculiarly inappropriate due to the unique setting in which the question arises. To require a President of the United States to place himself in the posture of disobeying an order of a court merely to trigger the procedural mechanism for review of the ruling would be unseemly, and would present an unnecessary occasion for constitutional confrontation between two branches of the Government. Similarly, a federal judge should not be placed in the posture of issuing a citation to a President simply in order to invoke review. The issue whether a President can be cited for contempt could itself engender protracted litigation, and would further delay both review on the merits of his claim of privilege and the ultimate termination of the underlying criminal action for which his evidence is sought. These considerations lead us to conclude that the order of the District Court was an appealable order. . . .

II

JUSTICIABILITY

In the District Court, the President's counsel argued that the court lacked jurisdiction to issue the subpoena because the matter was an intra-branch dispute between a subordinate and superior officer of the Executive Branch and hence not subject to judicial resolution. That argument has been renewed in this Court with emphasis on the contention that the dispute does not present a "case" or "controversy" which can be adjudicated in the federal courts. The President's counsel argues that the federal courts should not intrude into areas committed to the other branches of Government. He views the present dispute as essentially a "jurisdictional" dispute within the Executive Branch which he analogizes to a dispute between two congressional committees. Since the Executive Branch has exclusive authority and absolute discretion to decide whether to prosecute a case, *Confiscation Cases*, 74 U.S. (7 Wall.) 454 (1869); *United States v. Cox*, 342 F.2d 167, 171 (5th Cir. 1965), it is contended that a President's decision is final in determining what evidence is to be used in a given criminal case. Although his counsel concedes that the President has delegated certain specific powers to the Special Prosecutor, he has not "waived nor delegated to the Special Prosecutor the President's duty to claim privilege as to all materials . . . which fall within the President's inherent authority to refuse to disclose to any executive officer." Brief for the President 42. The Special Prosecutor's demand for the items therefore presents, in the view of the President's counsel, a political question under *Baker v. Carr*, 369 U.S. 186 (1962), since it involves a "textually demonstrable" grant of power under Art. II.

The mere assertion of a claim of an "intra-branch dispute," without more, has never operated to defeat federal jurisdiction; justiciability does not depend on such a surface inquiry. In *United States v. ICC*, 337 U.S. 426 (1949), the Court observed, "courts must look behind names that symbolize the parties to determine whether a justiciable case or controversy is presented."

Our starting point is the nature of the proceeding for which the evidence is sought—here a pending criminal prosecution. It is a judicial proceeding in a federal court alleging violation of federal laws and is brought in the name of the United States as sovereign. Under the authority of Art. II, § 2, Congress has vested in the Attorney General the power to conduct the criminal litigation of the United States Government. 28 U.S.C. § 516. It has also vested in him the power to appoint subordinate officers to assist him in the discharge of his duties. 28 U.S.C. §§ 509, 510, 515, 533. Acting pursuant to those statutes, the Attorney General has delegated the authority to represent the United States in these particular matters to a Special Prosecutor with unique authority and tenure.[8] The regulation gives the Special Prosecutor explicit power to contest the invocation of executive privilege in the process of seeking evidence deemed relevant to the performance of these specially delegated duties.

So long as this regulation is extant it has the force of law. In *United States ex rel. Accardi v. Shaughnessy*, 347 U.S. 260 (1954), regulations of the Attorney General delegated certain of his discretionary powers to the Board of Immigration Appeals and required that Board to exercise its own discretion on appeals in deportation cases. The Court held that so long as the Attorney General's regulations remained operative, he denied himself the authority to exercise the discretion delegated to the Board even though the original authority was his and he could reassert it by amending the regulations. . . .

Here, as in *Accardi*, it is theoretically possible for the Attorney General to amend or revoke the regulation defining the Special Prosecutor's authority. But he has not done so. So long as this regulation remains in force the Executive Branch is bound by it, and indeed the United States as the sovereign composed of the three branches is bound to respect and to enforce it. Moreover, the delegation of authority to the Special Prosecutor in this case is not an ordinary delegation by the Attorney

---

[8]   The regulation issued by the Attorney General pursuant to his statutory authority, vests in the Special Prosecutor plenary authority to control the course of investigations and litigation related to "all offenses arising out of the 1972 Presidential Election for which the Special Prosecutor deems it necessary and appropriate to assume responsibility, allegations involving the President, members of the White House staff, or Presidential appointees, and any other matters which he consents to have assigned to him by the Attorney General." 38 Fed.Reg. 30739, as amended by 38 Fed.Reg. 32805. In particular, the Special Prosecutor was given full authority, inter alia, "to contest the assertion of 'Executive Privilege' . . . and handl(e) all aspects of any cases within his jurisdiction." *Id.*, at 30739. The regulations then go on the provide:

'In exercising this authority, the Special Prosecutor will have the greatest degree of independence that is consistent with the Attorney General's statutory accountability for all matters falling within the jurisdiction of the Department of Justice. The Attorney General will not countermand or interfere with the Special Prosecutor's decisions or actions. The Special Prosecutor will determine whether and to what extent he will inform or consult with the Attorney General about the conduct of his duties and responsibilities. In accordance with assurances given by the President to the Attorney General that the President will not exercise his Constitutional powers to effect the discharge of the Special Prosecutor or to limit the independence that he is hereby given, the Special Prosecutor will not be removed from his duties except for extraordinary improprieties on his part and without the President's first consulting the Majority and the Minority Leaders and Chairmen and ranking Minority Members of the Judiciary Committees of the Senate and House of Representatives and ascertaining that their consensus is in accord with his proposed action.'

General to a subordinate officer: with the authorization of the President, the Acting Attorney General provided in the regulation that the Special Prosecutor was not to be removed without the "consensus" of eight designated leaders of Congress. . . .

In light of the uniqueness of the setting in which the conflict arises, the fact that both parties are officers of the Executive Branch cannot be viewed as a barrier to justiciability. It would be inconsistent with the applicable law and regulation, and the unique facts of this case to conclude other than that the Special Prosecutor has standing to bring this action and that a justiciable controversy is presented for decision.

III

RULE 17(c)

[The Court concluded that the special prosecutor had satisfied the requirements of Rule 17(c) to get a subpoena.—Editors]

IV

THE CLAIM OF PRIVILEGE

A

Having determined that the requirements of Rule 17(c) were satisfied, we turn to the claim that the subpoena should be quashed because it demands "confidential conversations between a President and his close advisors that it would be inconsistent with the public interest to produce." App. 48a. The first contention is a broad claim that the separation of powers doctrine precludes judicial review of a President's claim of privilege. The second contention is that if he does not prevail on the claim of absolute privilege, the court should hold as a matter of constitutional law that the privilege prevails over the subpoena duces tecum.

In the performance of assigned constitutional duties each branch of the Government must initially interpret the Constitution, and the interpretation of its powers by any branch is due great respect from the others. The President's counsel, as we have noted, reads the Constitution as providing an absolute privilege of confidentiality for all Presidential communications. Many decisions of this Court, however, have unequivocally reaffirmed the holding of *Marbury v. Madison*, 5 U.S. (1 Cranch) 137 (1803), that "(i)t is emphatically the province and duty of the judicial department to say what the law is." *Id.*, at 177.

No holding of the Court has defined the scope of judicial power specifically relating to the enforcement of a subpoena for confidential Presidential communications for use in a criminal prosecution, but other exercises of power by the Executive Branch and the Legislative Branch have been found invalid as in conflict with the Constitution. *Powell v. McCormack*, 395 U.S. 486 (1969); *Youngstown, Sheet & Tube Co. v. Sawyer*, 343 U.S. 579 (1952). In a series of cases, the Court interpreted the explicit immunity conferred by express provisions of the Constitution on Members of the House and Senate by the Speech or Debate Clause, U.S. Const. Art. I, § 6. [E.g.,] *Gravel v. United States*, 408 U.S. 606 (1972). Since this Court has consistently exercised the power to construe and delineate claims arising under express powers, it must follow that the Court has authority to interpret claims with respect to powers alleged to derive from enumerated powers. . . .

Notwithstanding the deference each branch must accord the others, the "judicial Power of the United States" vested in the federal courts by Art. III, § 1, of the

Constitution can no more be shared with the Executive Branch than the Chief Executive, for example, can share with the Judiciary the veto power, or the Congress share with the Judiciary the power to override a Presidential veto. Any other conclusion would be contrary to the basic concept of separation of powers and the checks and balances that flow from the scheme of a tripartite government. The Federalist, No. 47. We therefore reaffirm that it is the province and duty of this Court "to say what the law is" with respect to the claim of privilege presented in this case. *Marbury v. Madison*, at 177.

B

In support of his claim of absolute privilege, the President's counsel urges two grounds, one of which is common to all governments and one of which is peculiar to our system of separation of powers. The first ground is the valid need for protection of communications between high Government officials and those who advise and assist them in the performance of their manifold duties; the importance of this confidentiality is too plain to require further discussion. Human experience teaches that those who expect public dissemination of their remarks may well temper candor with a concern for appearances and for their own interests to the detriment of the decisionmaking process. Whatever the nature of the privilege of confidentiality of Presidential communications in the exercise of Art. II powers, the privilege can be said to derive from the supremacy of each branch within its own assigned area of constitutional duties. Certain powers and privileges flow from the nature of enumerated powers; the protection of the confidentiality of Presidential communications has similar constitutional underpinnings.

The second ground asserted by the President's counsel in support of the claim of absolute privilege rests on the doctrine of separation of powers. Here it is argued that the independence of the Executive Branch within its own sphere, *Humphrey's Executor v. United States*, 295 U.S. 602, 629–630 (1935); *Kilbourn v. Thompson*, 103 U.S. 168, 190–191 (1881), insulates a President from a judicial subpoena in an ongoing criminal prosecution, and thereby protects confidential Presidential communications.

However, neither the doctrine of separation of powers, nor the need for confidentiality of high-level communications, without more, can sustain an absolute, unqualified Presidential privilege of immunity from judicial process under all circumstances. The President's need for complete candor and objectivity from advisers calls for great deference from the courts. However, when the privilege depends solely on the broad, undifferentiated claim of public interest in the confidentiality of such conversations, a confrontation with other values arises. Absent a claim of need to protect military, diplomatic, or sensitive national security secrets, we find it difficult to accept the argument that even the very important interest in confidentiality of Presidential communications is significantly diminished by production of such material for in camera inspection with all the protection that a district court will be obliged to provide.

The impediment that an absolute, unqualified privilege would place in the way of the primary constitutional duty of the Judicial Branch to do justice in criminal prosecutions would plainly conflict with the function of the courts under Art. III. In designing the structure of our Government and dividing and allocating the sovereign power among three co-equal branches, the Framers of the Constitution sought to provide a comprehensive system, but the separate powers were not intended to operate with absolute independence. . . .

C

Since we conclude that the legitimate needs of the judicial process may outweigh Presidential privilege, it is necessary to resolve those competing interests in a manner that preserves the essential functions of each branch. The right and indeed the duty to resolve that question does not free the Judiciary from according high respect to the representations made on behalf of the President. *United States v. Burr*, 25 F.Cas. 187, 190, 191–192 (C.C. Va. 1807).

The expectation of a President to the confidentiality of his conversations and correspondence, like the claim of confidentiality of judicial deliberations, for example, has all the values to which we accord deference for the privacy of all citizens and, added to those values, is the necessity for protection of the public interest in candid, objective, and even blunt or harsh opinions in Presidential decisionmaking. A President and those who assist him must be free to explore alternatives in the process of shaping policies and making decisions and to do so in a way many would be unwilling to express except privately. These are the considerations justifying a presumptive privilege for Presidential communications. The privilege is fundamental to the operation of Government and inextricably rooted in the separation of powers under the Constitution. . . .

But this presumptive privilege must be considered in light of our historic commitment to the rule of law. . . . *[The Court proceeded to "weigh the importance of the general privilege of confidentiality of Presidential communications in performance of the President's responsibilities against the inroads of such a privilege on the fair administration of criminal justice" and concluded that the materials should be produced to the district court and examined* in camera.*—Editors]*

Since this matter came before the Court during the pendency of a criminal prosecution, and on representations that time is of the essence, the mandate shall issue forthwith.

■ MR. JUSTICE REHNQUIST took no part in the consideration or decision of these cases.

NOTES

1.   *United States v. Nixon* presents a number of separation of powers questions, starting with the title. How can the United States litigate against the president, who is the head of the executive branch that represents the United States in court? How far could a suit against the president go? If the president disobeys an injunction or another court order, could the president be held in contempt and ordered to prison, like ordinary litigants?

2.   Then there are the issues of justiciability and judicial power. Are the Court's arguments for why it can and must adjudicate the claims of privilege persuasive? What would happen if the issue were left to the political branches? Would the process be better or worse?

3.   The Court doesn't address this issue as squarely, but what view does it seem to take about the president's control over the executive branch? Does the president control the attorney general? Does the attorney general control the special prosecutor? What is the legal status of the regulation that created the special prosecutor? Is it a law?

4.   At the time *Nixon* was decided, it was not clear whether President Nixon would obey an adverse court decision. Indeed, at oral argument, Justice Thurgood Marshall spent considerable time pressing Nixon's lawyer on this point. But Nixon did obey. Why? Did he have to? For further discussion of the president's obligation to obey court orders, see 403.

5.   Professor Paulsen argues:

> The *Nixon* case . . . suggests a corollary to the maxim that great cases make bad law: bad Presidents make bad law. . . . By "bad law" I mean here constitutional decisions of the courts harmful to the institution of the Presidency and destructive of its proper constitutional powers. President Nixon was a bad President—Richard Nixon was a crook—and it is therefore not surprising that *United States v. Nixon* is bad law.

Michael Stokes Paulsen, *Nixon Now: The Courts and the Presidency After Twenty-Five Years*, 83 Minn. L. Rev. 1337, 1343 (1999). Do you agree?

Law Professors' Letter on the
Clinton Impeachment
Nov. 6, 1998

Dear Mr. Speaker, Mr. Gephardt, Mr. Hyde and Mr. Conyers:

Did President Clinton commit "high Crimes and Misdemeanors" warranting impeachment under the Constitution? We, the undersigned professors of law, believe that the misconduct alleged in the report of the Independent Counsel, and in the statement of Investigative Counsel David Schippers, does not cross that threshold.

We write neither as Democrats nor as Republicans. Some of us believe that the President has acted disgracefully, some that the Independent Counsel has. This letter has nothing to do with any such judgments. Rather, it expresses the one judgment on which we all agree: that the allegations detailed in the Independent Counsel's referral and summarized in Counsel Schippers's statement do not justify presidential impeachment under the Constitution.

No existing judicial precedents bind Congress's determination of the meaning of "high Crimes and Misdemeanors." But it is clear that Members of Congress would violate their constitutional responsibilities if they sought to impeach and remove the President for misconduct, even criminal misconduct, that fell short of the high constitutional standard required for impeachment.

The President's independence from Congress is fundamental to the American structure of government. It is essential to the separation of powers. It is essential to the President's ability to discharge such constitutional duties as vetoing legislation that he considers contrary to the nation's interests. And it is essential to governance whenever the White House belongs to a party different from that which controls the Capitol. The lower the threshold for impeachment, the weaker the President. If the President could be removed for any conduct of which Congress disapproved, this fundamental element of our democracy—the President's independence from Congress—would be destroyed. It is not enough, therefore, that Congress strongly disapprove of the President's conduct. Under the Constitution, the President cannot be impeached unless he has committed "Treason, Bribery, or other high Crimes and Misdemeanors."

Some of the charges raised against the President fall so far short of this high standard that they strain good sense: for example, the charge that the President repeatedly declined to testify voluntarily or pressed a debatable privilege claim that was later judicially rejected. Such litigation "offenses" are not remotely impeachable. With respect, however, to other allegations, careful consideration must be given to the kind of misconduct that renders a President constitutionally unfit to remain in office.

Neither history nor legal definitions provide a precise list of high crimes and misdemeanors. Reasonable people have differed in interpreting these words. We believe that the proper interpretation of the Impeachment Clause must begin by recognizing treason and bribery as core or paradigmatic instances, from which the meaning of "other high Crimes and Misdemeanors" is to be extrapolated. The constitutional standard for impeachment would be very different if different offenses had been specified. The clause does not read, "Treason, Felony, or other Crime" (as does Article IV, Section 2 of the Constitution), so that any violation of a criminal statute would be impeachable. Nor does it read, "Arson, Larceny, or other high Crimes and Misdemeanors," implying that any serious crime, of whatever nature, would be impeachable. Nor does it read, "Adultery, Fornication, or other high Crimes and Misdemeanors," implying that any conduct deemed to reveal serious moral lapses might be an impeachable offense.

When a President commits treason, he exercises his *executive powers*, or uses information obtained by virtue of his *executive powers*, deliberately to aid an enemy. When a President is bribed, he exercises or offers to exercise his *executive powers* in exchange for corrupt gain. Both acts involve the criminal exercise of presidential powers, converting those awful powers into an instrument either of enemy interests or of purely personal gain. We believe that the critical, distinctive feature of treason and bribery is grossly derelict exercise of official power (or, in the case of bribery to obtain or retain office, gross criminality in the pursuit of official power). Non-indictable conduct might rise to this level. For example, a President might be properly impeached if, as a result of drunkenness, he recklessly and repeatedly misused executive authority.

Much of the misconduct of which the President is accused does not involve the exercise of executive powers at all. *If* the President committed perjury regarding his sexual conduct, this perjury involved no exercise of presidential power as such. *If* he concealed evidence, this misdeed too involved no exercise of executive authority. By contrast, *if* he sought wrongfully to place someone in a job at the Pentagon, or lied to subordinates hoping they would repeat his false statements, these acts could have involved a wrongful use of presidential influence, but we cannot believe that the President's alleged conduct of this nature amounts to the grossly derelict exercise of executive power sufficient for impeachment.

Perjury and obstructing justice can without doubt be impeachable offenses. A President who corruptly used the Federal Bureau of Investigation to obstruct an investigation would have criminally exercised his presidential powers. Moreover, covering up a crime furthers or aids the underlying crime. Thus a President who committed perjury to cover up his subordinates' criminal exercise of executive authority would also have committed an impeachable offense. But making false statements about sexual improprieties is not a sufficient constitutional basis to justify the trial and removal from office of the President of the United States.

It goes without saying that lying under oath is a very serious offense. But even if the House of Representatives had the constitutional authority to impeach for any instance of perjury or obstruction of justice, a responsible House would not exercise this awesome power on the facts alleged in this case. The House's power to impeach, like a prosecutor's power to indict, is discretionary. This power must be exercised not for partisan advantage, but only when circumstances genuinely justify the enormous price the nation will pay in governance and stature if its President is put through a long, public, voyeuristic trial. The American people understand this price. They demonstrate the political wisdom that has held the Constitution in place for two centuries when, even after the publication of Mr. Starr's report, with all its extraordinary revelations, they oppose impeachment for the offenses alleged therein.

We do not say that a "private" crime could never be so heinous as to warrant impeachment. Congress might responsibly take the position that an individual who by the law of the land cannot be permitted to remain at large, need not be permitted to remain President. But if certain crimes such as murder warrant removal of a President from office because of their unspeakable heinousness, the offenses alleged in the Independent Counsel's report or the Investigative Counsel's statement are not among them. Short of heinous criminality, impeachment demands convincing evidence of grossly derelict exercise of official authority. In our judgment, Mr. Starr's report contains no such evidence.

Sincerely,

[Signatures of 430 law professors]

Charles Canady, Statement on Impeachment of President Clinton

House of Representatives, Dec. 19, 1998

. . . The argument has been made that in essence, we in the House should, in carrying out our responsibility, look to the Senate, and make a guess about how the proceedings would turn out in the Senate, to determine how we exercise our responsibility under the Constitution.

I would suggest to you, I don't think that's a proper way for us to proceed. I believe that we have an independent responsibility, under the Constitution, to make a judgment concerning the conduct of the president, and whether he should be impeached or not. And it would be in derogation of our constitutional responsibility to attempt to count noses in the Senate. I will have to say that it's a very difficult thing to count noses in the Senate anyway, and in a proceeding like this, it's hard to predict the outcome.

But aside from that, I just don't think that's a proper undertaking for us to be involved in. And I'd also point out that the very structure of the Constitution indicates that. In the Constitution, the framers provided that the House could impeach with a simple majority. They provided that conviction in the Senate would have to be by a two-thirds majority.

Now, I would suggest to you that that structural feature of the Constitution suggests that the framers would have contemplated circumstances in which the House might very well impeach, but the Senate would not convict. Now, I think that's obvious on the face of the documents. Some of these arguments I think have to be brought back to the text of the Constitution and evaluated in that light.

But on this issue of prosecutorial discretion, let me pose a scenario here, which I think is very analogous to what we have before us. Suppose the chief executive of a Fortune 500 corporation, a major national corporation in the United States, was accused of sexual harassment, and the corporation had been sued—sexual harassment or any other civil rights offense. And in the course of the discovery in that case, the chief executive of that major national corporation lied under oath to impede that civil rights action.

Now, I believe that the fact that the chief executive of a major national corporation was engaged in that type of conduct, would be a relevant consideration for the prosecutors who were evaluating the case and whether to bring it, because of the impact of that conduct.

Now, I do believe that bringing prosecutions have a deterrent impact. And that is one of the considerations that has to be factored into prosecutorial discretion.

So, I think if we step back from this situation—and again, we can argue about the weight of the facts, and I understand you disagree with the evaluation some of us may have made about the weight of the facts here. But if the president of the United States did engage in obstruction of justice, and committed multiple acts of lying under oath, I think that we have to look at that conduct, in light of the consequences that it has, and the message it sends, just as we would look at the conduct of the chief executive of a major national corporation who was the defendant in a civil rights case brought against that corporation.

NOTES

1.   Do you find the arguments in the law professors' letter persuasive? If so, why do they concede that some private crimes could still be "high Crimes and Misdemeanors"?

2.   If the president cannot be impeached for private crimes, can the president be prosecuted for them? Who would do the prosecuting? Federal prosecutors, controlled by the president? An independent counsel? State prosecutors? Do any of these seem like good options?

3.   What do you make of Representative Canady's theory of the House's responsibility? What would happen in the long run if more of our presidents were impeached, but acquitted?

[*Assignment 18*]

III. ARTICLE III: THE JUDICIAL POWER

We turn next to Article III of the Constitution, the article vesting "the judicial Power" of the United States in the federal courts. This article describes the structure of the federal judiciary, and enumerates the categories of "Cases" and "Controversies" to which the federal judicial power extends.

A Map of Article III

§ 1: The judicial Power of the United States, shall be vested. . . .

Article III (like Article I and Article II) begins with a Vesting Clause that locates power in a department of the national government. Section 1 vests "[t]he judicial Power of the United States" in a system of federal courts. The first and most fundamental question of Article III is this: Exactly what is "the judicial Power" vested by Article III?

That large question entails a series of propositions and issues. Historically, the judicial power was simply the authority to decide cases of a judicial character in accordance with pre-existing governing law. In the United States, that governing law would be set forth in the Constitution, federal laws and treaties, the laws of the states, or some other source (such as the common law, the principles of equity, admiralty law, or the law of nations). In this sense, the judicial power was thought of as a law-applying power, not a law-making power. Of course, this distinction can hide an inevitable reality (one known to us, and also known to late-eighteenth-century judges): the reality that when courts apply a legal rule to new facts, they will be determining what the scope of the rule is, and will to that extent be making the rule as well as applying it. Nonetheless, as a historical matter, the starting point for the judicial power was the idea of deciding cases in accordance with existing law. (This understanding of the judicial power is reinforced by Article III, Section 2's specification of federal judicial jurisdiction as extending to "Cases" and "Controversies" of certain descriptions, which we will discuss in a moment.)

But what are the outer boundaries of "the judicial Power"? Are there limitations inherent in the notion of what "the judicial Power" is? Over the years the federal courts have developed a series of sub-doctrines attempting to mark the boundaries of the legitimate exercise of judicial authority. First, courts will not render "advisory opinions" outside the context of an actual dispute between parties with something at issue. Second, and building on the rule against advisory opinions, the parties in a case must have a real legal interest at stake, giving them "standing" to sue. In other words, something must turn on the court's decision. Third, the dispute must be sufficiently immediate, not remote and distant—in legal parlance, the case must be "ripe." Fourth, the dispute must remain a live one at all stages of the proceeding; if the conflict between the parties ever disappears, the case is "moot." The ripeness and mootness requirements also flow out of the rule against advisory opinions: if a court were speculating about a question that was entirely in the future or the past, it would merely be giving advice. Finally, the parties' legal interests must be genuinely in conflict, or "adverse," and the legal dispute must not be contrived, feigned, or collusive.

A further long-standing restriction on "the judicial Power" of Article III is that it does not extend to "political questions"—that is, matters that the Constitution appears to leave to political judgment or discretion, either by assigning policy discretion or final constitutional judgment concerning a topic to Congress or the president, or simply by not supplying any rule of law that would provide judges a principled basis for invalidating what a political actor has done. The precise scope and content—and even the legitimacy—of the "political question doctrine" has long been disputed. Is it a principled doctrine of judicial restraint, commanded by the

Constitution's separation of powers? Or is it an unprincipled, ad hoc doctrine of strategic non-decision, in effect a form of "activist judicial restraint"?

Another enduring question concerning the meaning of "the judicial Power" concerns its relationship to and authority vis-à-vis the other branches of government. Does the power to interpret and apply the law, in specific cases, make the judiciary the supreme branch of the national government? In *The Federalist No. 49*, Madison denied that this was the case: "The several departments being perfectly co-ordinate by the terms of their commission, neither of them, it is evident, can pretend to an exclusive or superior right of settling the boundaries between their respective powers." Similarly, Hamilton wrote in *The Federalist No. 78*: "Whoever attentively considers the different departments of power must perceive that, in a government in which they are separate from each other, the judiciary, from the nature of its functions, will always be the least dangerous to the political rights of the Constitution; because it will be least in a capacity to annoy or injure them. . . . It may truly be said to have neither FORCE nor WILL but merely judgment; and must ultimately depend upon the aid of the executive arm even for the efficacy of its judgments." Yet judicial supremacy—the idea that the federal courts are supreme in expounding the Constitution and the other branches must obey their interpretations—has become a widespread view. This debate remains a recurrent issue in understanding the scope of "the judicial Power."

> *. . . in one supreme Court, and in such inferior Courts as the Congress may from time to time ordain and establish. . . .*

Article III leaves to Congress the decision whether to have any lower federal courts *at all* and, if so, the decisions about what jurisdiction those courts will have. This was part of a compromise—commonly called the "Madisonian Compromise," for James Madison, who proposed it at the Constitutional Convention—between those who favored a complete system of national courts and those who wished to have only a Supreme Court, with the rest of the judicial power left to existing state court systems.

Article I, Section 8 specifically names Congress's power "To constitute Tribunals inferior to the supreme Court." From the beginning, Congress has exercised this power to create at least some lower federal courts. The Judiciary Act of 1789 created sixteen district court judgeships. Today, we have about a thousand lower federal trial and appellate judges. Congress could change that number again in the future.

A consequence of the Madisonian Compromise is that some potentially federal cases will instead be decided by *state* courts. In those cases, the Supreme Court is usually the only federal forum for reviewing state court decisions about federal law. An early, important decision held that when state supreme courts decide cases falling within Article III's menu of cases, these decisions can still be reviewed by the U.S. Supreme Court. *Martin v. Hunter's Lessee,* 14 U.S. (1 Wheat.) 304 (1816); see also *Cohens v. Virginia*, 19 U.S. (6 Wheat.) 264 (1821).

Note that Article III also does not specify the size of the Supreme Court, implicitly leaving that decision to Congress, too. The Supreme Court initially had six justices. Congress has adjusted the size of the Court several times, and the number of justices has ranged from six to ten. For much of the past century the number of justices has stood steady at nine. (In 1937, President Franklin D. Roosevelt proposed enlarging the Supreme Court to as many as fifteen justices, but his effort to thus "pack" the Court produced a political backlash, and no president or Congress has sought to adjust the size of the Court since that time. On the court-packing plan, see p. 521.)

> ... *The Judges, both of the supreme and inferior Courts, shall hold their Offices during good Behaviour, and shall, at stated Times, receive for their Services, a Compensation, which shall not be diminished during their Continuance in Office.*

A singular feature of Article III, Section 1 is that all federal judges—Supreme Court justices and lower federal court judges—serve "during good Behaviour," which generally means they serve for life unless they are impeached or otherwise found guilty of misbehavior. Further, Article III provides that the judges can never have their salaries reduced. These provisions were considered essential to the independence of federal judges in the exercise of their constitutional duties.

At the same time, the framers appear to have contemplated the possibility of impeachment of judges, including Supreme Court justices, for perceived abuse of the judicial power. Referring to the judiciary's "total incapacity to support its usurpations by force," Hamilton stated in *The Federalist No. 81* that this inference

> is greatly fortified by the consideration of the important constitutional check which the power of instituting impeachments in one part of the legislative body and determining them in the other, would give to that body upon the members of the judicial department. This is alone a complete security.

> *§ 2: The judicial Power shall extend to all Cases, in Law and Equity, arising under this Constitution, the Laws of the United States, and Treaties made, or which shall be made, under their Authority;—to all Cases affecting Ambassadors, other public ministers and Consuls;—to all Cases of admiralty and maritime Jurisdiction;—to Controversies to which the United States shall be a Party;—to Controversies between two or more States;—between a State and Citizens of another State;—between Citizens of different States;—between Citizens of the same State claiming Lands under Grants of different States, and between a State, or the Citizens thereof, and foreign States, Citizens or Subjects. ...*

Article III, Section 2 lists nine categories of "Cases" and "Controversies" to which the federal judicial power extends. The first three categories, denominated "Cases," consist of lawsuits concerning *national law or national authority*—presenting issues of federal statutory, treaty, or constitutional law; cases affecting ambassadors; and matters of "admiralty and maritime Jurisdiction." The next six categories, denominated "Controversies," are defined not by the legal issues presented but by *the parties to the suit*. These controversies all have some interstate aspect, such as suits between citizens of different states, or an international aspect, such as suits involving "foreign States."

Is Article III, Section 2's listing of cases and controversies within federal jurisdiction a command that federal courts must hear all such cases? Or is it a menu of cases in which federal courts can be permitted to exercise jurisdiction, if Congress so decides? Is it some of each? This question has engaged the attention of lawyers, judges, and scholars since the Constitution's creation.

The answer would seem to depend on two related features of Article III's design. First, the Madisonian Compromise, reflected in Article III, Section 1: If Congress need not create lower federal courts in the first place, it is plausible that it may create lower federal courts with limited jurisdiction—with some portion of the Article III "menu," or with different lower federal courts having different portions. (There is contrary dicta, though, in *Martin v. Hunter's Lessee,* 14 U.S. (1 Wheat.) 304 (1816).) And until 1875 there was no jurisdiction in lower federal courts to hear cases simply because they presented issues of federal law. For the lower federal courts, most of the statutory jurisdiction consisted of diversity-of-state-citizenship controversies— and even these were limited to suits involving a minimum amount in controversy. The Supreme Court eventually concluded that lower federal courts' jurisdiction is within Congress's discretion to grant, withhold, or limit as it sees fit. See *Sheldon v. Sill,* 49 U.S. (8 How.) 441 (1850).

The second feature of Article III bearing on the extent to which the jurisdiction of the federal courts is subject to Congress's control is this passage describing the Supreme Court's jurisdiction:

> . . . *In all Cases affecting Ambassadors, other public Ministers and Consuls, and those in which a State shall be Party, the supreme Court shall have original Jurisdiction. In all the other Cases before mentioned, the supreme Court shall have appellate Jurisdiction, both as to Law and Fact, with such Exceptions, and under such Regulations as the Congress shall make.*

The apparent import of this passage is that Congress could withdraw entirely some types of cases from the Supreme Court's appellate jurisdiction. This conclusion is controversial, but seems to have been accepted by the Court in the landmark Reconstruction-era case of *Ex parte McCardle,* 74 U.S. (7 Wall.) 506 (1868). If this is correct, would it mean that some cases might receive their final resolution by *state* courts—with the attendant possibility of different "final" resolutions for different states? Some have found that prospect so implausible that they have argued that Congress can withdraw appellate jurisdiction from the Supreme Court *only* if it also creates, and vests final jurisdiction in, some other federal court. In other words, Congress has the power to limit the Supreme Court's appellate jurisdiction, *or* to limit the existence and jurisdiction of lower federal courts, but not both.

Where authorized by the Constitution and as regulated by Congress in accordance with Article III's provisions, *jurisdiction* creates a power of federal courts to hear and decide cases. A grant of jurisdiction, however, does not ordinarily confer a power to create the substantive law governing those cases. Some federal jurisdiction is explicitly based on the source of substantive law—cases "arising under this Constitution, the Laws of the United States, and Treaties . . . ". But where federal courts have jurisdiction on the basis of party-identity—"diversity of citizenship" jurisdiction being the classic example—what is the governing source of law? Do the federal courts have power themselves to create the governing substantive rules, a kind of federal common law? For most of the first hundred and fifty years of the United States the answer was a qualified *yes.* But since *Erie Railroad Co. v. Tompkins,* 304 U.S. 64 (1938), the answer has been a qualified *no:* the federal courts do not have power to create their own body of substantive law simply because they possess jurisdiction to resolve a particular type of dispute, and so diversity cases are governed by *state* common law.

. . . The Trial of all Crimes, except in Cases of Impeachment, shall be by Jury; and such Trial shall be held in the State where the said Crimes shall have been committed; but when not committed within any State, the Trial shall be at such Place or Places as the Congress may by Law have directed.

§ 3: Treason against the United States, shall consist only in levying War against them, or in adhering to their Enemies, giving them Aid and Comfort. No Person shall be convicted of Treason unless on the Testimony of two Witnesses to the same overt Act, or on Confession in open Court.

The Congress shall have Power to declare the Punishment of Treason, but no Attainder of Treason shall work Corruption of Blood, or Forfeiture except during the Life of the Person attainted.

Article III closes with a number of procedural protections—requiring jury trials, limiting venue, requiring certain kinds of evidence, and limiting certain kinds of punishments. Several of these protections are quite narrow, but they are echoed and expanded in the Bill of Rights added to the Constitution two years later. Their inclusion in Article III can nonetheless be important in particular cases, and it emphasizes the connection between the separation of powers and the protection of individual rights.

In summary, Article III empowers the federal judiciary to apply law in deciding particular cases. It also ensures the independence and energy of the judiciary through a protected tenure and salary. The primary checks possessed by the other branches of the national government consist of the front-end check supplied by the political process of appointment; Congress's control over the creation of lower courts and the size of the Supreme Court; Congress's partial control of those courts' jurisdiction; and the blunt, difficult, rarely used, and controversial last resort of impeachment.

A. JUDICIAL REVIEW

The most famous exposition of judicial review is the Supreme Court's decision in *Marbury v. Madison*, 5 U.S. (1 Cranch) 137 (1803). But before *Marbury* the Supreme Court had already taken a stand on constitutional principle against another branch: it had declined to give advice to President Washington about constitutional questions that were not before it in a case, on the ground that doing so would violate the judiciary's proper role under Article III of the Constitution. (This exchange, called the Correspondence of the Justices, is presented at p. 413) Even before that, the justices, in circuit court opinions collected in *Hayburn's Case*, 2 U.S. (2 Dall.) 408 (1792), had objected, on constitutional grounds, to a statute requiring them to adjudicate veterans' pension claims but making those judicial determinations subject to revision by executive branch officers. And in *Hylton v. United States*, 3 U.S. (3 Dall.) 171 (1796), p. 598, the Court had *upheld* an act of Congress—a tax on carriages—against a serious constitutional challenge. In that case, no one questioned judicial review.

Indeed, judicial review was explicitly discussed in both Federalist and Anti-Federalist writings, even before the Constitution was ratified. (For an introduction to some of the points of contention, see p. 31.) The Anti-Federalist writer "Brutus" (probably Melancton Smith) was a strong New York critic of the proposed Constitution, who saw in the proposed federal judiciary the seeds of despotism and judicial oligarchy. Alexander Hamilton then tried to dispel some of Brutus's fears in *The Federalist No. 78*. Read their exchange and consider: what should a reader of this exchange have expected the judicial power to be?

Brutus, No. 11
Jan. 31, 1788

The nature and extent of the judicial power of the United States, proposed to be granted by this constitution, claims our particular attention. . . . Much has been said and written upon the subject of this new system on both sides, but I have not met with any writer, who has discussed the judicial powers with any degree of accuracy. And yet it is obvious, that we can form but very imperfect ideas of the manner in which this government will work, or the effect it will have in changing the internal police and mode of distributing justice at present subsisting in the respective states, without a thorough investigation of the powers of the judiciary and of the manner in which they will operate. This government is a complete system, not only for making, but for executing laws. And the courts of law, which will be constituted by it, are not only to decide upon the constitution and the laws made in pursuance of it, but by officers subordinate to them to execute all their decisions. The real effect of this system of government, will therefore be brought home to the feelings of the people, through the medium of the judicial power. It is, moreover, of great importance, to examine with care the nature and extent of the judicial power, because those who are to be vested with it, are to be placed in a situation altogether unprecedented in a free country. They are to be rendered totally independent, both of the people and the legislature, both with respect to their offices and salaries. No errors they may commit can be corrected by any power above them, if any such power there be, nor can they be removed from office for making ever so many erroneous adjudications.

. . . That we may be enabled to form a just opinion on this subject, [let us] 1st. Examine the nature and extent of the judicial powers—and 2d. Enquire, whether the courts who are to exercise them, are so constituted as to afford reasonable ground of confidence, that they will exercise them for the general good. . . .

In article 3d, sect. 2d, it is said, "The judicial power shall extend to all cases in law and equity arising under this constitution, the laws of the United States, and treaties made, or which shall be made, under their authority, & c." . . . The first article to which this power extends, is, all cases in law and equity arising under this constitution. . . . What latitude of construction this clause should receive, it is not easy to say. At first view, one would suppose, that it meant no more than this, that the courts under the general government should exercise, not only the powers of courts of law, but also that of courts of equity, in the manner in which those powers are usually exercised in the different states. But this cannot be the meaning, because the next clause authorises the courts to take cognizance of all cases in law and equity arising under the laws of the United States; this last article, I conceive, conveys as much power to the general judicial as any of the state courts possess. . . . The cases arising under the constitution must be different from those arising under the laws, or else the two clauses mean exactly the same thing. . . . The cases arising under the constitution must include such, as bring into question its meaning, and will require an explanation of the nature and extent of the powers of the different departments under it. . . . This article, therefore, vests the judicial with a power to resolve all questions that may arise on any case on the construction of the constitution, either in law or in equity.

1st. . . . This article vests the courts with authority to give the constitution a legal construction, or to explain it according to the rules laid down for construing a law.—These rules give a certain degree of latitude of explanation. According to this mode of construction, the courts are to give such meaning to the constitution as comports best with the common, and generally received acceptation of the words in which it is expressed, regarding their ordinary and popular use, rather than their grammatical propriety. Where words are dubious, they will be explained by the context. The end of the clause will be attended to, and the words will be understood, as having a view to it; and the words will not be so understood as to bear no meaning or a very absurd one. . . .

From these remarks, the authority and business of the courts of law, under this clause, may be understood. . . . They will give the sense of every article of the constitution, that may from time to time come before them. And in their decisions they will not confine themselves to any fixed or established rules, but will determine, according to what appears to them, the reason and spirit of the constitution. The opinions of the supreme court, whatever they may be, will have the force of law; because there is no power provided in the constitution, that can correct their errors, or controul their adjudications. From this court there is no appeal. And I conceive the legislature themselves, cannot set aside a judgment of this court, because they are authorised by the constitution to decide in the last resort. The legislature must be controuled by the constitution, and not the constitution by them. They have therefore no more right to set aside any judgment pronounced upon the construction of the constitution, than they have to take from the president, the chief command of the army and navy, and commit it to some other person. The reason is plain; the judicial and executive derive their authority from the same source, that the legislature do theirs; and therefore in all cases, where the constitution does not make the one responsible to, or controulable by the other, they are altogether independent of each other.

The judicial power will operate to effect, in the most certain, but yet silent and imperceptible manner, what is evidently the tendency of the constitution:—I mean, an entire subversion of the legislative, executive and judicial powers of the individual states. Every adjudication of the supreme court, on any question that may arise upon the nature and extent of the general government, will affect the limits of the state jurisdiction. In proportion as the former enlarge the exercise of their powers, will that of the latter be restricted. . . .

Not only will the constitution justify the courts in inclining to this mode of explaining it, but they will be interested in using this latitude of interpretation. Every body of men invested with office are tenacious of power; they feel interested, and hence it has become a kind of maxim, to hand down their offices, with all its rights and privileges, unimpared to their successors; the same principle will influence them to extend their power, and increase their rights; this of itself will operate strongly upon the courts to give such a meaning to the constitution in all cases where it can possibly be done, as will enlarge the sphere of their own authority. Every extension of the power of the general legislature, as well as of the judicial powers, will increase the powers of the courts; and the dignity and importance of the judges, will be in proportion to the extent and magnitude of the powers they exercise.

I add, it is highly probable the emolument of the judges will be increased, with the increase of the business they will have to transact and its importance. From these considerations the judges will be interested to extend the powers of the courts, and to construe the constitution as much as possible, in such a way as to favour it; and that they will do it, appears probable. . . .

The Federalist No. 78

Alexander Hamilton, May 28, 1788

To the People of the State of New York:

WE PROCEED now to an examination of the judiciary department of the proposed government. . . .

Whoever attentively considers the different departments of power must perceive, that, in a government in which they are separated from each other, the judiciary, from the nature of its functions, will always be the least dangerous to the political rights of the Constitution; because it will be least in a capacity to annoy or injure them. The Executive not only dispenses the honors, but holds the sword of the community. The legislature not only commands the purse, but prescribes the rules by which the duties and rights of every citizen are to be regulated. The judiciary, on the contrary, has no influence over either the sword or the purse; no direction either of the strength or of the wealth of the society; and can take no active resolution whatever. It may truly be said to have neither FORCE nor WILL, but merely judgment; and must ultimately depend upon the aid of the executive arm even for the efficacy of its judgments.

This simple view of the matter suggests several important consequences. It proves incontestably, that the judiciary is beyond comparison the weakest of the three departments of power; that it can never attack with success either of the other two; and that all possible care is requisite to enable it to defend itself against their attacks. It equally proves, that though individual oppression may now and then proceed from the courts of justice, the general liberty of the people can never be endangered from that quarter; I mean so long as the judiciary remains truly distinct from both the legislature and the Executive. For I agree, that "there is no liberty, if the power of judging be not separated from the legislative and executive powers." . . .

The complete independence of the courts of justice is peculiarly essential in a limited Constitution. By a limited Constitution, I understand one which contains certain specified exceptions to the legislative authority; such, for instance, as that it shall pass no bills of attainder, no ex-post-facto laws, and the like. Limitations of this kind can be preserved in practice no other way than through the medium of courts of justice, whose duty it must be to declare all acts contrary to the manifest tenor of the Constitution void. Without this, all the reservations of particular rights or privileges would amount to nothing.

Some perplexity respecting the rights of the courts to pronounce legislative acts void, because contrary to the Constitution, has arisen from an imagination that the doctrine would imply a superiority of the judiciary to the legislative power. It is urged that the authority which can declare the acts of another void, must necessarily be superior to the one whose acts may be declared void. As this doctrine is of great importance in all the American constitutions, a brief discussion of the ground on which it rests cannot be unacceptable.

There is no position which depends on clearer principles, than that every act of a delegated authority, contrary to the tenor of the commission under which it is exercised, is void. No legislative act, therefore, contrary to the Constitution, can be valid. To deny this, would be to affirm, that the deputy is greater than his principal; that the servant is above his master; that the representatives of the people are superior to the people themselves; that men acting by virtue of powers, may do not only what their powers do not authorize, but what they forbid.

If it be said that the legislative body are themselves the constitutional judges of their own powers, and that the construction they put upon them is conclusive upon the other departments, it may be answered, that this cannot be the natural presumption, where it is not to be collected from any particular provisions in the Constitution. It is not otherwise to be supposed, that the Constitution could intend to enable the representatives of the people to substitute their WILL to that of their constituents. It is far more rational to suppose, that the courts were designed to be an intermediate body between the people and the legislature, in order, among other things, to keep the latter within the limits assigned to their authority. The interpretation of the laws is the proper and peculiar province of the courts. A constitution is, in fact, and must be regarded by the judges, as a fundamental law. It therefore belongs to them to ascertain its meaning, as well as the meaning of any particular act proceeding from the legislative body. If there should happen to be an irreconcilable variance between the two, that which has the superior obligation and validity ought, of course, to be preferred; or, in other words, the Constitution ought to be preferred to the statute, the intention of the people to the intention of their agents.

Nor does this conclusion by any means suppose a superiority of the judicial to the legislative power. It only supposes that the power of the people is superior to both; and that where the will of the legislature, declared in its statutes, stands in opposition to that of the people, declared in the Constitution, the judges ought to be governed by the latter rather than the former. They ought to regulate their decisions by the fundamental laws, rather than by those which are not fundamental.

This exercise of judicial discretion, in determining between two contradictory laws, is exemplified in a familiar instance. It not uncommonly happens, that there are two statutes existing at one time, clashing in whole or in part with each other, and neither of them containing any repealing clause or expression. In such a case, it is the province of the courts to liquidate and fix their meaning and operation. So far as they can, by any fair construction, be reconciled to each other, reason and law conspire to dictate that this should be done; where this is impracticable, it becomes a matter of necessity to give effect to one, in exclusion of the other. The rule which has obtained in the courts for determining their relative validity is, that the last in order of time shall be preferred to the first. But this is a mere rule of construction, not derived from any positive law, but from the nature and reason of the thing. It is a rule not enjoined upon the courts by legislative provision, but adopted by themselves, as consonant to truth and propriety, for the direction of their conduct as interpreters of the law. They thought it reasonable, that between the interfering acts of an EQUAL authority, that which was the last indication of its will should have the preference.

But in regard to the interfering acts of a superior and subordinate authority, of an original and derivative power, the nature and reason of the thing indicate the converse of that rule as proper to be followed. They teach us that the prior act of a superior ought to be preferred to the subsequent act of an inferior and subordinate authority; and that accordingly, whenever a particular statute contravenes the Constitution, it will be the duty of the judicial tribunals to adhere to the latter and disregard the former.

It can be of no weight to say that the courts, on the pretense of a repugnancy, may substitute their own pleasure to the constitutional intentions of the legislature. This might as well happen in the case of two contradictory statutes; or it might as well happen in every adjudication upon any single statute. The courts must declare the sense of the law; and if they should be disposed to exercise WILL instead of JUDGMENT, the consequence would equally be the substitution of their pleasure to that of the legislative body. The observation, if it prove any thing, would prove that there ought to be no judges distinct from that body. . . .

Background to *Marbury*

Fifteen years after this exchange came *Marbury v. Madison*. It was the first time that the entire Court wrote an opinion holding an act of Congress unconstitutional.

Before you read the case itself, some background information may be helpful. *Marbury* had its roots in the hotly contested election of 1800, which matched President John Adams and his Federalist supporters against Vice President Thomas Jefferson and the new Democratic-Republican opposition party. Jefferson narrowly defeated Adams, with his margin of victory being supplied by the "slavery bonus" in the Electoral College afforded to the Southern states by the Three-Fifths Clause. Jefferson and Aaron Burr, who was intended to have been his vice president, tied in the Electoral College, and the choice between them was made by the lame-duck House of Representatives, with Jefferson being elected on the thirty-sixth ballot.

Meanwhile, the lame-duck Congress, which was dominated by defeated Federalists, passed the Judiciary Act of 1801, which replaced the antiquated system of having Supreme Court justices "ride circuit" and sit as members, with district judges, of a "circuit court." In its place, the statute created a new system of circuit courts—and of course new judgeships—and it greatly extended the statutory scope of federal jurisdiction. The abolition of circuit riding was of intense interest to the Federalist Supreme Court justices because it required them to spend as much as six months of the year away from their families travelling through the United States on horseback. (The rigors of circuit riding may have contributed to the health problems, and death at age forty-eight, of Justice James Iredell in 1799.) Some of these judicial reforms were probably good ideas, but the Democratic-Republicans could not help seeing the whole package as a Federalist attempt to ensconce themselves in the life-tenured judiciary. Jefferson wrote of the Federalists: "they have retired into the judiciary as a stronghold. There the remains of federalism are to be preserved and fed from the treasury, and from that battery all the works of republicanism are to be beaten down and erased." To John Dickinson (Dec. 19, 1801), in THE WRITINGS OF THOMAS JEFFERSON 301, 302 (Andrew A. Lipscomb ed., 1905). Indeed, in February 1801 President John Adams nominated and the lame-duck Federalist Senate confirmed sixteen new federal—and, of course, Federalist—circuit court judges.

Of more lasting importance, President Adams also nominated John Marshall to be the fourth chief justice of the United States. He was nominated on January 20, 1801, and was confirmed by the lame-duck Senate fourteen days later. (Prior to the adoption of the Twentieth Amendment, presidential and congressional terms did not begin until March 4th—a full four months after the November election.) The vacancy in the office had been created when former Chief Justice Oliver Ellsworth resigned because of poor health. But Ellsworth's resignation had also been timed to give the outgoing president the ability to pick a new chief justice. President Adams initially wanted John Jay, one author of *The Federalist* and the first chief justice, to again serve in that office. But Jay refused, thinking the job irksome and unimportant. Reluctantly, Adams turned to Marshall, who was his trusted forty-five-year-old secretary of state (as well as a friend and biographer of George Washington). Marshall would become one of the greatest, if not the greatest, of all the chief justices of the Supreme Court.

Finally, on February 27, 1801—only a week before Jefferson would take office—Congress passed the Organic Act for the District of Columbia. Among other things, this act created more than forty justices of the peace for the new district. This was not a petty office, but neither were the justices "judges" in the Article III sense of the term. They were more like local government officials, partly judicial but also partly administrative, and they had five-year terms. President Adams quickly nominated persons to fill the offices, but this time the nominees were a more bipartisan group. One was William Marbury.

On March 3, 1801—the day before Jefferson and the new Congress took office—the lame-duck Federalist Senate confirmed President Adams's nominees. On the night of March 3, 1801, Secretary of State John Marshall affixed the Great Seal of the United States to the commissions of the newly appointed justices of the peace in his office at the State Department. (By this time, Marshall had already been appointed chief justice, but he had not yet resigned as secretary of state, and he actually held both offices for almost a month. The Constitution forbids any member of Congress from also holding an executive or judicial office, but it does not prohibit joint executive and judicial office-holding.) President Adams signed the commissions before going to bed. He woke early on March 4, and made a speedy exit from the capital at 3 AM so as not to "witness the awful event of Jefferson's inauguration," but in the confusion of the transition

> [p]recisely what happened to the commissions is not clear. Some were delivered. Marshall's younger brother James—himself a newly commissioned Circuit Judge for the District of Columbia—delivered a few to appointees in Alexandria, where there were concerns about the possibility of disruptive political celebrations. Other commissions lay undelivered. Later, John Marshall explained that he was short-handed that night because two State Department aides were assisting the President. Besides, he considered delivery legally inconsequential, once they had been signed and sealed. That was a fateful error.

Michael W. McConnell, "The Story of *Marbury v. Madison*: Making Defeat Look Like Victory," in CONSTITUTIONAL LAW STORIES 17 (Michael Dorf ed., 2004). William Marbury's commission to be a justice of the peace was not delivered. When President Jefferson took office on March 4, he directed his new secretary of state, James

Madison, not to deliver any commissions still in the possession of the State Department.

Marbury eventually filed a suit in the Supreme Court to compel Madison to deliver his commission as a justice of the peace. Marbury's lawyer was Charles Lee, who had served as attorney general under Presidents Washington and Adams. Lee requested a writ of mandamus from the Supreme Court—essentially, an order directing Madison to appear before the Court and defend his non-delivery of the commissions. That was on December 16, 1801. The suit was filed in the Court's original rather than appellate jurisdiction. This means that the case originated in the Supreme Court itself, not in a lower federal court or state court.

As the developments surrounding Marbury's lawsuit against Madison were unfolding, the Jeffersonians were rapidly setting about to dismantle the new judicial structure enacted by the Federalists. They voted to repeal the Judiciary Act of 1801, thus abolishing the newly created circuit courts (and with them the judgeships of the newly confirmed judges). This statute again imposed on the justices the onerous duty of circuit riding. Both the abolition of sixteen life-tenured circuit-court judgeships and the reimposition of circuit riding were acts of dubious constitutionality. The nation waited to see how the Federalist-dominated Supreme Court would respond. The Jeffersonians even took the extraordinary step of abolishing by statute the Supreme Court's 1802 session, so Marbury's case was not heard until 1803. By doing this, they ensured that any Supreme Court ruling on the constitutionality of their various actions would not occur until after the 1802 midterm elections.

The constitutional debate over repeal of the Judiciary Act of 1801 was intense. See David P. Currie, THE CONSTITUTION IN CONGRESS: THE JEFFERSONIANS, 1801–1829, at 10–22 (2001). But at the time no one thought that the case about William Marbury's commission would be of much consequence. Instead, attention was fixed on *Stuart v. Laird*, another case pending before the Supreme Court and one in which the constitutionality of the Repeal Act was indirectly at issue. Could Congress constitutionally abolish federal judgeships and re-impose the duty of circuit riding? Would the Supreme Court defy the Jeffersonians—who had already begun impeachment proceedings against some Federalist judges—by actually holding that the Repeal Act was unconstitutional? That was the issue of the day. To give away the ending: one week after deciding *Marbury*, the Court upheld the Repeal Act in *Stuart*. In fact, one could even say that "*Marbury* must be understood as the product of a defeated and demoralized Court." McConnell, "The Story of *Marbury v. Madison*," at 22.

As you read *Marbury* and *Stuart*, consider the constitutional arguments made by the Court. In particular, how does the Court see its role in the constitutional structure?

Marbury v. Madison

5 U.S. (1 Cranch) 137 (1803)

■ The following opinion of the court was delivered by [CHIEF JUSTICE MARSHALL].

. . . In the order in which the court has viewed this subject, the following questions have been considered and decided.

1st. Has the applicant a right to the commission he demands?

2dly. If he has a right, and that right has been violated, do the laws of his country afford him a remedy?

3dly. If they do afford him a remedy, is it a *mandamus* issuing from this court?

The first object of inquiry is,

1st. Has the applicant a right to the commission he demands?

His right originates in an act of congress passed in February, 1801, concerning the district of Columbia.

After dividing the district into two counties, the 11th section of this law, enacts, "that there shall be appointed in and for each of the said counties, such number of discreet persons to be justices of the peace as the president of the United States shall, from time to time, think expedient, to continue in office for five years."

It appears, from the affidavits, that in compliance with this law, a commission for William Marbury as a justice of the peace for the county of Washington, was signed by John Adams, then president of the United States; after which the seal of the United States was affixed to it; but the commission has never reached the person for whom it was made out.

In order to determine whether he is entitled to this commission, it becomes necessary to inquire whether he has been appointed to the office. For if he has been appointed, the law continues him in office for five years, and he is entitled to the possession of those evidences of office, which, being completed, become his property.

The 2d section of the 2d article of the constitution, declares that "the president shall nominate, and, by and with the advice and consent of the senate, shall appoint ambassadors, other public ministers and consuls, and all other officers of the United States, whose appointments are not otherwise provided for."

The third section declares, that "he shall commission all the officers of the United States."

An act of congress directs the secretary of state to keep the seal of the United States, "to make out and record, and affix the said seal to all civil commissions to officers of the United States, to be appointed by the President, by and with the consent of the senate, or by the President alone; provided, that the said seal shall not be affixed to any commission before the same shall have been signed by the President of the United States." . . .

The acts of appointing to office, and commissioning the person appointed, can scarcely be considered as one and the same; since the power to perform them is given in two separate and distinct sections of the constitution. . . . This is an appointment made by the President, by and with the advice and consent of the senate, and is evidenced by no act but the commission itself. In such a case therefore the commission and the appointment seem inseparable; it being almost impossible to shew an appointment otherwise than by proving the existence of a commission; still the commission is not necessarily the appointment, though conclusive evidence of it. . . .

The last act to be done by the President, is the signature of the commission. He has then acted on the advice and consent of the senate to his own nomination. The time for deliberation has then passed. He has decided. His judgment, on the advice and consent of the senate concurring with his nomination, has been made, and the officer is appointed. This appointment is evidenced by an open, unequivocal act; and being the last act required from the person making it, necessarily excludes the idea of its being, so far as respects the appointment, an inchoate and incomplete transaction.

Some point of time must be taken when the power of the executive over an officer, not removable at his will, must cease. That point of time must be when the constitutional power of appointment has been exercised. And this power has been exercised when the last act, required from the person possessing the power, has been performed. This last act is the signature of the commission. . . .

The signature is a warrant for affixing the great seal to the commission; and the great seal is only to be affixed to an instrument which is complete. It attests, by an act supposed to be of public notoriety, the verity of the presidential signature.

It is never to be affixed till the commission is signed, because the signature, which gives force and effect to the commission, is conclusive evidence that the appointment is made.

The commission being signed, the subsequent duty of the secretary of state is prescribed by law, and not to be guided by the will of the President. He is to affix the seal of the United States to the commission, and is to record it.

This is not a proceeding which may be varied, if the judgment of the executive shall suggest one more eligible; but is a precise course as accurately marked out by law, and is to be strictly pursued. It is the duty of the secretary of state to conform to the law, and in this he is an officer of the United States, bound to obey the laws. He acts, in this respect, as has been very properly stated at the bar, under the authority of law, and not by the instructions of the President. It is a ministerial act which the law enjoins on a particular officer for a particular purpose. . . .

It has also occurred as possible, and barely possible, that the transmission of the commission, and the acceptance thereof, might be deemed necessary to complete the right of the plaintiff.

The transmission of the commission is a practice directed by convenience, but not by law. . . . It may have some tendency to elucidate this point, to enquire whether the possession of the original commission be indispensably necessary to authorize a person, appointed to any office, to perform the duties of that office. If it was necessary, then a loss of the commission would lose the office. Not only negligence, but accident or fraud, fire or theft, might deprive an individual of his office. In such a case, I presume it could not be doubted but that a copy from the record of the office of the secretary of state would be, to every intent and purpose, equal to the original. The act of congress has expressly made it so. . . .

In the case of commissions, the law orders the secretary of state to record them. When therefore they are signed and sealed, the order for their being recorded is given; and whether inserted in the book or not, they are in law recorded. . . .

It is therefore decidedly the opinion of the court, that when a commission has been signed by the President, the appointment is made; and that the commission is complete, when the seal of the United States has been affixed to it by the Secretary of State.

Where an officer is removable at the will of the executive, the circumstance which completes his appointment is of no concern; because the act is at any time revocable; and the commission may be arrested, if still in the office. But when the officer is not removable at the will of the executive, the appointment is not revocable, and cannot be annulled. It has conferred legal rights which cannot be resumed.

The discretion of the executive is to be exercised until the appointment has been made. But having once made the appointment, his power over the office is terminated in all cases where by law the officer is not removable by him. The right to the office is *then* in the person appointed, and he has the absolute, unconditional, power of accepting or rejecting it.

Mr. Marbury, then, since his commission was signed by the President, and sealed by the secretary of state, was appointed; and as the law creating the office, gave the officer a right to hold for five years, independent of the executive, the appointment was not revocable; but vested in the officer legal rights, which are protected by the laws of his country.

To withhold his commission, therefore, is an act deemed by the court not warranted by law, but violative of a vested legal right.

This brings us to the second inquiry; which is,

2dly. If he has a right, and that right has been violated, do the laws of this country afford him a remedy?

The very essence of civil liberty certainly consists in the right of every individual to claim the protection of the laws, whenever he receives an injury. One of the first duties of government is to afford that protection. In Great Britain the king himself is sued in the respectful form of a petition, and he never fails to comply with the judgment of his court. . . .

The government of the United States has been emphatically termed a government of laws, and not of men. It will certainly cease to deserve this high appellation, if the laws furnish no remedy for the violation of a vested legal right.

If this obloquy is to be cast on the jurisprudence of our country, it must arise from the peculiar character of the case.

It behooves us, then, to inquire whether there be in its composition any ingredient which shall exempt it from legal investigations or exclude the injured party from legal redress. In pursuing this enquiry the first question which presents itself, is, whether this can be arranged with that class of cases which come under the description of *damnum absque injuria*—a loss without an injury.

This description of cases never has been considered, and it is believed never can be considered, as comprehending offices of trust, of honor or of profit. The office of justice of peace in the district of Columbia is such an office; it is therefore worthy of the attention and guardianship of the laws. It has received that attention and guardianship. It has been created by special act of congress, and has been secured, so far as the laws can give security to the person appointed to fill it, for five years. It is not, then, on account of the worthlessness of the thing pursued, that the injured party can be alleged to be without remedy.

Is it in the nature of the transaction? Is the act of delivering or withholding a commission to be considered as a mere political act, belonging to the executive department alone, for the performance of which entire confidence is placed by our constitution in the supreme executive; and for any misconduct respecting which, the injured individual has no remedy?

That there may be such cases is not to be questioned; but that every act of duty, to be performed in any of the great departments of government, constitutes such a case, is not to be admitted. . . .

It follows then that the question, whether the legality of an act of the head of a department be examinable in a court of justice or not, must always depend on the nature of that act.

If some acts be examinable, and others not, there must be some rule of law to guide the court in the exercise of its jurisdiction. . . .

By the constitution of the United States, the President is invested with certain important political powers in the exercise of which he is to use his own discretion, and is accountable only to his country in his political character, and to his own conscience. To aid him in the performance of these duties, he is authorized to appoint certain officers, who act by his authority, and in conformity with his orders.

In such cases, their acts are his acts; and whatever opinion may be entertained of the manner in which executive discretion may be used, still there exists, and can exist, no power to control that discretion. The subjects are political. They respect the nation, not individual rights, and being entrusted to the executive, the decision of the executive is conclusive. . . .

But when the legislature proceeds to impose on that officer other duties; when he is directed peremptorily to perform certain acts; when the rights of individuals are dependent on the performance of those acts; he is so far the officer of the law; is amenable to the laws for his conduct; and cannot at his discretion sport away the vested rights of others.

The conclusion from this reasoning is, that where the heads of departments are the political or confidential agents of the executive, merely to execute the will of the President, or rather to act in cases in which the executive possesses a constitutional or legal discretion, nothing can be more perfectly clear than that their acts are only politically examinable. But where a specific duty is assigned by law, and individual rights depend upon the performance of that duty, it seems equally clear that the individual who considers himself injured, has a right to resort to the laws of his country for a remedy.

If this be the rule, let us inquire how it applies to the case under the consideration of the court.

The power of nominating to the senate, and the power of appointing the person nominated, are political powers, to be exercised by the President according to his own discretion. When he has made an appointment, he has exercised his whole power, and his discretion has been completely applied to the case. If, by law, the officer be removable at the will of the President, then a new appointment may be immediately made, and the rights of the officer are terminated. But as a fact which has existed cannot be made never to have existed, the appointment cannot be annihilated; and consequently, if the officer is by law not removable at the will of the President, the rights he has acquired are protected by the law, and are not resumable by the President. They cannot be extinguished by executive authority, and he has the privilege of asserting them in like manner as if they had been derived from any other source.

The question whether a right has vested or not, is, on its nature, judicial, and must be tried by the judicial authority. If, for example, Mr. Marbury had taken the oaths of a magistrate, and proceeded to act as one; in consequence of which a suit had been instituted against him, in which his defence had depended on his being a magistrate; the validity of his appointment must have been determined by judicial authority.

So, if he conceives that, by virtue of his appointment, he has a legal right, either to the commission which has been made out for him, or to a copy of that commission, it is equally a question examinable in a court, and the decision of the court upon it must depend on the opinion entertained of his appointment.

That question has been discussed, and the opinion is, that the latest point of time which can be taken as that at which the appointment was complete, and evidenced, was when, after the signature of the president, the seal of the United States was affixed to the commission.

It is, then, the opinion of the court,

1st. That by signing the commission of Mr. Marbury, the president of the United States appointed him a justice of peace for the county of Washington in the district of Columbia; and that the seal of the United States, affixed thereto by the secretary of state, is conclusive testimony of the verity of the signature, and of the completion of the appointment, and that the appointment conferred on him a legal right to the office for the space of five years.

2dly. That, having this legal title to the office, he has a consequent right to the commission; a refusal to deliver which, is a plain violation of that right, for which the laws of his country afford him a remedy.

It remains to be inquired whether,

3dly. He is entitled to the remedy for which he applies. This depends on,

1st. The nature of the writ applied for, and,

2dly. The power of this court.

1st. The nature of the writ.

Blackstone, in the 3d volume of his commentaries, page 110, defines a mandamus to be "a command issuing in the king's name from the court of king's bench, and directed to any person, corporation, or inferior court of judicature within the king's dominions, requiring them to do some particular thing therein specified, which appertains to their office and duty, and which the court of king's bench has previously determined, or at least supposes, to be consonant to right and justice." . . .

This writ, if awarded, would be directed to an officer of government, and its mandate to him would be, to use the words of Blackstone, "to do a particular thing therein specified, which appertains to his office and duty, and which the court has previously determined, or at least supposes, to be consonant to right and justice." . . .

These circumstances certainly concur in this case.

Still, to render the mandamus a proper remedy, the other to whom it is to be directed, must be one to whom, on legal principles, such writ may be directed; and the person applying for it must be without any other specific and legal remedy.

... The intimate political relation subsisting between the president of the United States and the heads of departments, necessarily renders any legal investigation of the acts of one of those high officers peculiarly irksome, as well as delicate; and excites some hesitation with respect to the propriety of entering into such investigation. Impressions are often received without much reflection or examination, and it is not wonderful that in such a case as this, the assertion, by an individual, of his legal claims in a court of justice; to which claims it is the duty of that court to attend; should at first view be considered by some, as an attempt to intrude into the cabinet, and to intermeddle with the prerogatives of the executive.

It is scarcely necessary for the court to disclaim all pretensions to such a jurisdiction. An extravagance, so absurd and excessive, could not have been entertained for a moment. The province of the court is, solely, to decide on the rights of individuals, not to enquire how the executive, or executive officers, perform duties in which they have a discretion. Questions, in their nature political, or which are, by the constitution and laws, submitted to the executive, can never be made in this court.

But, if this be not such a question; if, so far from being an intrusion into the secrets of the cabinet, it respects a paper, which, according to law, is upon record, and to a copy of which the law gives a right, on the payment of ten cents; if it be no intermeddling with a subject over which the executive can be considered as having exercised any control; what is there in the exalted station of the officer, which shall bar a citizen from asserting, in a court of justice, his legal rights, or shall forbid a court to listen to the claim; or to issue a mandamus, directing the performance of a duty, not depending on executive discretion, but on particular acts of congress and the general principles of law?

If one of the heads of departments commits any illegal act, under color of his office, by which an individual sustains an injury, it cannot be pretended that his office alone exempts him from being sued in the ordinary mode of proceeding, and being compelled to obey the judgment of the law. How, then, can his office exempt him from this particular mode of deciding on the legality of his conduct, if the case be such a case as would, were any other individual the party complained of, authorize the process?

... Where the head of a department ... is directed by law to do a certain act affecting the absolute rights of individuals, in the performance of which he is not placed under the particular direction of the President, and the performance of which the President cannot lawfully forbid, and therefore is never presumed to have forbidden; ... it is not perceived on what ground the courts of the country are farther excused from the duty of giving judgment, that right be done to an injured individual, then if the same services were to be performed by a person not the head of a department. ...

It is true that the mandamus, now moved for, is not for the performance of an act expressly enjoined by statute.

It is to deliver a commission; on which subject the acts of Congress are silent. This difference is not considered as affecting the case. It has already been stated that the applicant has, to that commission, a vested legal right, of which the executive cannot deprive him. He has been appointed to an office, from which he is not removable at the will of the executive; and being so appointed, he has a right to the commission which the secretary has received from the president for his use. . . .

This, then, is a plain case for a mandamus, either to deliver the commission, or a copy of it from the record; and it only remains to be enquired,

Whether it can issue from this court.

The act to establish the judicial courts of the United States authorizes the Supreme Court "to issue writs of mandamus in cases warranted by the principles and usages of law, to any courts appointed, or persons holding office, under the authority of the United States."

The secretary of state, being a person holding an office under the authority of the United States, is precisely within the letter of the description; and if this court is not authorized to issue a writ of mandamus to such an officer, it must be because the law is unconstitutional, and therefore absolutely incapable of conferring the authority, and assigning the duties which its words purport to confer and assign.

The constitution vests the whole judicial power of the United States in one supreme court, and such inferior courts as congress shall, from time to time, ordain and establish. This power is expressly extended to all cases arising under the laws of the United States; and, consequently, in some form, may be exercised over the present case; because the right claimed is given by a law of the United States.

In the distribution of this power it is declared that "the supreme court shall have original jurisdiction in all cases affecting ambassadors, other public ministers and consuls, and those in which a state shall be a party. In all other cases, the supreme court shall have appellate jurisdiction."

It has been insisted, at the bar, that if the original grant of jurisdiction, to the supreme and inferior courts, is general, and the clause, assigning original jurisdiction to the supreme court, contains no negative or restrictive words; the power remains to the legislature, to assign original jurisdiction to that court in other cases than those specified in the article which has been recited; provided those cases belong to the judicial power of the United States.

If it had been intended to leave it in the discretion of the legislature to apportion the judicial power between the supreme and inferior courts according to the will of that body, it would certainly have been useless to have proceeded further than to have defined the judicial power, and the tribunals in which it should be vested. The subsequent part of the section is mere surplusage, is entirely without meaning, if such is to be the construction. If congress remains at liberty to give this court appellate jurisdiction, where the constitution has declared their jurisdiction shall be original; and original jurisdiction where the constitution has declared it shall be appellate; the distribution of jurisdiction, made in the constitution, is form without substance.

Affirmative words are often, in their operation, negative of other objects than those affirmed; and in this case, a negative or exclusive sense must be given to them, or they have no operation at all.

It cannot be presumed that any clause in the constitution is intended to be without effect; and, therefore, such a construction is inadmissible unless the words require it. . . .

When an instrument organizing fundamentally a judicial system, divides it into one supreme, and so many inferior courts as the legislature may ordain and establish; then enumerates its powers, and proceeds so far to distribute them, as to define the jurisdiction of the supreme court by declaring the cases in which it shall take original jurisdiction, and that in others it shall take appellate jurisdiction; the plain import of the words seems to be, that in one class of cases its jurisdiction is original, and not appellate; in the other it is appellate, and not original. If any other construction would render the clause inoperative, that is an additional reason for rejecting such other construction, and for adhering to their obvious meaning.

To enable this court then to issue a mandamus, it must be shewn to be an exercise of appellate jurisdiction, or to be necessary to enable them to exercise appellate jurisdiction. . . .

It is the essential criterion of appellate jurisdiction, that it revises and corrects the proceedings in a cause already instituted, and does not create that cause. Although, therefore, a mandamus may be directed to courts, yet to issue such a writ to an officer for the delivery of a paper, is in effect the same as to sustain an original action for that paper, and therefore seems not to belong to appellate, but to original jurisdiction. Neither is it necessary in such a case as this to enable the court to exercise its appellate jurisdiction.

The authority, therefore, given to the supreme court, by the act establishing the judicial courts of the United States, to issue writs of mandamus to public officers, appears not to be warranted by the constitution; and it becomes necessary to enquire whether a jurisdiction, so conferred, can be exercised.

The question, whether an act, repugnant to the constitution, can become the law of the land, is a question deeply interesting to the United States; but, happily, not of an intricacy proportioned to its interest. It seems only necessary to recognize certain principles, supposed to have been long and well established, to decide it.

That the people have an original right to establish, for their future government, such principles as, in their opinion, shall most conduce to their own happiness, is the basis, on which the whole American fabric has been erected. The exercise of this original right is a very great exertion; nor can it, nor ought it to be frequently repeated. The principles, therefore, so established, are deemed fundamental. And as the authority, from which they proceed, is supreme, and can seldom act, they are designed to be permanent.

This original and supreme will organizes the government, and assigns, to different departments, their respective powers. It may either stop here; or establish certain limits not to be transcended by those departments.

The government of the United States is of the latter description. The powers of the legislature are defined, and limited; and that those limits may not be mistaken, or forgotten, the constitution is written. To what purpose are powers limited, and to what purpose is that limitation committed to writing, if these limits may, at any time, be passed by those intended to be restrained? The distinction, between a government with limited and unlimited powers, is abolished, if those limits do not confine the persons on whom they are imposed, and if acts prohibited and acts allowed, are of equal obligation. It is a proposition too plain to be contested, that the constitution controls any legislative act repugnant to it; or, that the legislature may alter the constitution by an ordinary act.

Between these alternatives there is no middle ground. The constitution is either a superior, paramount law, unchangeable by ordinary means, or it is on a level with ordinary legislative acts, and, like other acts, is alterable when the legislature shall please to alter it.

If the former part of the alternative be true, then a legislative act contrary to the constitution is not law: if the latter part be true, then written constitutions are absurd attempts, on the part of the people, to limit a power, in its own nature illimitable.

Certainly all those who have framed written constitutions contemplate them as forming the fundamental and paramount law of the nation, and consequently the theory of every such government must be, that an act of the legislature, repugnant to the constitution, is void.

This theory is essentially attached to a written constitution, and is consequently to be considered, by this court, as one of the fundamental principles of our society. It is not therefore to be lost sight of in the further consideration of this subject.

If an act of the legislature, repugnant to the constitution, is void, does it, notwithstanding its invalidity, bind the courts, and oblige them to give it effect? Or, in other words, though it be not law, does it constitute a rule as operative as if it was a law? This would be to overthrow in fact what was established in theory; and would seem, at first view, an absurdity too gross to be insisted on. It shall, however, receive a more attentive consideration.

It is emphatically the province and duty of the judicial department to say what the law is. Those who apply the rule to particular cases, must of necessity expound and interpret that rule. If two laws conflict with each other, the courts must decide on the operation of each.

So if a law be in opposition to the constitution; if both the law and the constitution apply to a particular case, so that the court must either decide that case conformably to the law, disregarding the constitution; or conformably to the constitution, disregarding the law; the court must determine which of these conflicting rules governs the case. This is of the very essence of judicial duty.

If then the courts are to regard the constitution; and the constitution is superior to any ordinary act of the legislature; the constitution, and not such ordinary act, must govern the case to which they both apply.

Those then who controvert the principle that the constitution is to be considered, in court, as a paramount law, are reduced to the necessity of maintaining that courts must close their eyes on the constitution, and see only the law.

This doctrine would subvert the very foundation of all written constitutions. It would declare that an act, which, according to the principles and theory of our government is entirely void; is yet, in practice, completely obligatory. It would declare that if the legislature shall do what is expressly forbidden, such act, notwithstanding the express prohibition, is in reality effectual. It would be giving to the legislature a practical and real omnipotence, with the same breath which professes to restrict their powers within narrow limits. It is prescribing limits, and declaring that those limits may be passed at pleasure.

That it thus reduces to nothing what we have deemed the greatest improvement on political institutions—a written constitution—would of itself be sufficient, in America, where written constitutions have been viewed with so much reverence, for rejecting the construction. But the peculiar expressions of the constitution of the United States furnish additional arguments in favour of its rejection.

The judicial power of the United States is extended to all cases arising under the constitution.

Could it be the intention of those who gave this power, to say that, in using it, the constitution should not be looked into? That a case arising under the constitution should be decided without examining the instrument under which it arises?

This is too extravagant to be maintained.

In some cases then, the constitution must be looked into by the judges. And it they can open it at all, what part of it are they forbidden to read, or to obey?

There are many other parts of the constitution which serve to illustrate this subject.

It is declared that "no tax or duty shall be laid on articles exported from any state." Suppose a duty on the export of cotton, of tobacco, or of flour; and a suit instituted to recover it. Ought judgment to be rendered in such a case? ought the judges to close their eyes on the constitution, and only see the law?

The constitution declares "that no bill of attainder or *ex post facto* law shall be passed."

If, however, such a bill should be passed and a person should be prosecuted under it; must the court condemn to death those victims whom the constitution endeavours to preserve?

"No person," says the constitution, "shall be convicted of treason unless on the testimony of two witnesses to the same overt act, or on confession in open court."

Here the language of the constitution is addressed especially to the courts. It prescribes, directly for them, a rule of evidence not to be departed from. If the legislature should change that rule, and declare *one* witness, or a confession *out* of court, sufficient for conviction, must the constitutional principle yield to the legislative act?

From these, and many other selections which might be made, it is apparent, that the framers of the constitution contemplated that instrument, as a rule for the government of *courts*, as well as of the legislature.

Why otherwise does it direct the judges to take an oath to support it? This oath certainly applies, in an especial manner, to their conduct in their official character. How immoral to impose it on them, if they were to be used as the instruments, and the knowing instruments, for violating what they swear to support!

The oath of office, too, imposed by the legislature, is completely demonstrative of the legislative opinion on this subject. It is in these words, "I do solemnly swear that I will administer justice without respect to persons, and do equal right to the poor and to the rich; and that I will faithfully and impartially discharge all the duties incumbent on me as _____, according to the best of my abilities and understanding, agreeably to *the constitution*, and laws of the United States."

Why does a judge swear to discharge his duties agreeably to the constitution of the United States, if that constitution forms no rule for his government? if it is closed upon him, and cannot be inspected by him?

If such be the real state of things, this is worse than solemn mockery. To prescribe, or to take this oath, becomes equally a crime.

It is also not entirely unworthy of observation, that in declaring what shall be the *supreme* law of the land, the *constitution* itself is first mentioned; and not the laws of the United States generally, but those only which shall be made in *pursuance* of the constitution, have that rank.

Thus, the particular phraseology of the constitution of the United States confirms and strengthens the principle, supposed to be essential to all written constitutions, that a law repugnant to the constitution is void; and that *courts*, as well as other departments, are bound by that instrument.

The rule must be discharged.

NOTES

1.   What are the Court's arguments for judicial review? Are they persuasive? Are its arguments closer to the views expressed by Brutus, or by Hamilton?

2.   What does *Marbury* actually *hold*, and which parts of the opinion are dicta? Chief Justice Marshall's decision is often described as being politically ingenious. It is sometimes said that Chief Justice Marshall went out of his way in the first half of the opinion to provoke President Jefferson, and that he then went out of his way in the second half of the opinion to decline to issue any order that Jefferson could resist. Is that a fair characterization?

3.   What does Chief Justice Marshall say about whether Congress had sought to add to the original jurisdiction of the Supreme Court? Here is Section 13 of the Judiciary Act of 1789:

> And be it further enacted, That the Supreme court shall have exclusive jurisdiction of all controversies of a civil nature, where a state is a party, except between a state and its citizens; and except also between a state and citizens of other states, or aliens, in which latter case it shall have original but not exclusive jurisdiction. And shall have exclusively all such jurisdiction of suits or proceedings against ambassadors, or other public minister, or their domestics, or domestic servants, as a court of law can have or exercise consistently with the law of nations; and original, but not exclusive jurisdiction of all suits brought by ambassadors, or other public ministers, or in which a consul, or vice consul, shall be a party. And the trial of issues of fact in the Supreme Court, in all actions at law against citizens of the United States, shall be by jury. The Supreme Court shall also have appellate jurisdiction from the circuit courts and courts of the several states, in the cases herein after specially provided for; and shall have power to issue writs of prohibition to the district courts, when proceeding as courts of admiralty and maritime jurisdiction, and writs of mandamus, in cases warranted by the principles and usages of law, to any courts appointed, or persons holding office, under the authority of the United States.

Judiciary Act of 1789, 1 Stat. 73, Sec. 13. Did the Act actually purport to confer "original jurisdiction" on the Supreme Court whenever someone seeks a writ of mandamus? Or did it provide that, whenever the Supreme Court already has appellate jurisdiction, mandamus is a writ the Court may grant as a remedy? Why does this question matter?

4.   Article III, Section 2, clause 2, says: "In all Cases affecting Ambassadors, other public Ministers and Consuls, and those in which a State shall be Party, the supreme Court shall have original Jurisdiction. In all the other Cases before mentioned, the supreme Court shall have appellate Jurisdiction, both as to Law and Fact, with such Exceptions, and under such Regulations as the Congress shall make." How does Chief Justice Marshall interpret this language? Is he right that Congress may not increase the Supreme Court's original jurisdiction? Is there any other plausible reading? What reading seems best?

5.   Consider this logic from Chief Justice Marshall's argument for judicial review. The major premise is constitutional supremacy—the Constitution prevails over any contrary action of government. The minor premise is interpretive independence—the judiciary, as an independent branch of government, cannot be bound by the constitutional views of another branch. The conclusion, of course, is that an Act of Congress that is unconstitutional (in the judiciary's view) cannot be enforced as law by the courts.

Now, consider whether this same logic applies in other, possibly parallel situations.

a.   Is this logic limited to reviewing acts of Congress? What if the president commits an act in violation of the Constitution? Does this logic suggest similar judicial treatment of an unconstitutional act of the president?

b.   Is this logic limited to interpretation by the judiciary? Or does the president have the same duty to disregard statutes that are unconstitutional (in his view) as the courts do? Imagine a situation where an Act of Congress purports to do something flagrantly unconstitutional. Must the president execute the unconstitutional act? Recall President Jefferson's pardons of persons convicted under the Sedition Act and his further decision not to bring any further prosecutions to enforce the Act. See p. 66. Were these decisions permitted by the Constitution? Required?

c.   A harder question: What if the president thinks that the judiciary has committed an unconstitutional action—for example, issued a decision or opinion the president thinks flagrantly contrary to the Constitution. (Invent your own hypothetical, or perhaps you have encountered one in this book.) Must the president abide by the decision of the judiciary? We will consider this at length in the next assignment.

d.   Does Congress likewise possess an independent power or duty to review the actions of the president for constitutionality? Of the courts? How might that play out? Again, imagine a situation where the president (or the judiciary) has acted in flagrant violation of the Constitution. What can Congress do? What should it do? Is *Marbury*'s argument one of judicial supremacy over the other branches, or of the Constitution's supremacy over all of them? Is *Marbury*'s argument for the judiciary's independent power of decision one that applies to the other branches as well?

e.   What about states? Does this logic give state governmental officials the power (or duty?) to resist what they believe to be unconstitutional actions of the national government? Again, recall the Alien and Sedition Acts. Did Virginia and Kentucky act properly or improperly in declaring the laws unconstitutional?

6.   As noted above, part of the political context of *Marbury* involved the Repeal of the Judiciary Act of 1801 and the Democratic-Republicans' attack on the Federalist-appointed judiciary. At the time, the case that looked like it would be the big

confrontation was *Stuart v. Laird*, which concerned the constitutionality of re-imposing circuit riding and abolishing federal judgeships. It was decided just a week after *Marbury*.

Stuart v. Laird

5 U.S. (1 Cranch) 299 (1803)

■ PATERSON, JUSTICE, (Judge Cushing being absent on account of ill health,) delivered the opinion of the court.

On an action instituted by John Laird against Hugh Stuart, a judgment was entered in a court for the fourth circuit in the eastern district of Virginia, in December term 1801. On this judgment, an execution was issued, returnable to April term 1802, in the same court. In the term of December 1802, John Laird obtained judgment at a court for the fifth circuit in the Virginia district, against Hugh Stuart and Charles L. Carter, upon their bond for the forthcoming and delivery of certain property therein mentioned, which had been levied upon by virtue of the above execution against the said Hugh Stuart.

Two reasons have been assigned by counsel for reversing the judgment on the forthcoming bond. 1. That as the bond was given for the delivery of property levied on by virtue of an execution issuing out of, and returnable to a court for the fourth circuit, no other court could legally proceed upon the said bond. This is true, if there be no statutable provision to direct and authorize such proceeding. Congress have constitutional authority to establish from time to time such inferior tribunals as they may think proper; and to transfer a cause from one such tribunal to another. In this last particular, there are no words in the constitution to prohibit or restrain the exercise of legislative power.

The present is a case of this kind. It is nothing more than the removal of the suit brought by Stuart against Laird from the court of the fourth circuit to the court of the fifth circuit, which is authorized to proceed upon and carry it into full effect. This is apparent from the ninth section of the act entitled, "an act to amend the judicial system of the United States," passed the 29th of April, 1802. The forthcoming bond is an appendage to the cause, or rather a component part of the proceedings.

2d. Another reason for reversal is, that the judges of the supreme court have no right to sit as circuit judges, not being appointed as such, or in other words, that they ought to have distinct commissions for that purpose. To this objection, which is of recent date, it is sufficient to observe, that practice and acquiescence under it for a period of several years, commencing with the organization of the judicial system, affords an irresistible answer, and has indeed fixed the construction. It is a contemporary interpretation of the most forcible nature. This practical exposition is too strong and obstinate to be shaken or controlled. Of course, the question is at rest, and ought not now to be disturbed.

NOTES

1.   What do you think of the constitutional analysis in *Stuart*? (What *is* the analysis?)

2.   Was the Court's decision a capitulation? A wise tactical retreat? When deciding whether to confront another branch, should the Court consider the risk to its institutional standing and authority? Or is that an improper consideration?

[*Assignment 19*]

B. THE CONSTITUTIONAL DILEMMA OF JUDICIAL SUPREMACY

Does judicial review imply judicial supremacy? When the courts independently judge the constitutionality of actions of the political branches—defended by Alexander Hamilton in *The Federalist No. 78*, and done by Chief Justice Marshall in *Marbury v. Madison*—does that practice imply a superiority of the judiciary over the other branches as to any question of interpretation of the Constitution? Would that be consistent with the vision of separation of powers created by the framers and defended in *The Federalist*? Or would it be the nightmare envisioned by Brutus? Is it essential to the maintenance of the constitutional order that the courts have the final say on the constitutionality of government action? These questions are explored in the following readings.

1858: *Lincoln v. Douglas*

The first great debate over the supremacy of Supreme Court opinions came in response to the Court's decision in *Dred Scott v. Sandford*, 60 U.S. (19 How.) 393 (1857). (The decision is presented later at p. 733.) In an aggressive and willful opinion, Chief Justice Taney concluded that no black person, slave or free, could ever be a federal "citizen." And he further concluded that Congress was constitutionally *forbidden* from banning slavery in federal territories, an egregious act of judicial activism invalidating a previous compromise that had divided the territories between slave and free. The Court went out of its way to protect slavery, and tried to entrench those protections in constitutional law.

The decision provoked furious controversy. Justices Benjamin Curtis and John McLean dissented passionately, and Curtis even resigned from the Court. *Dred Scott*'s critics attacked not just the merits of the Court's decision but also its *authority*. An editorial condemned the decision as entitled to "just so much moral weight as would be the judgment of a majority of those congregated in any Washington bar-room." Editorial, *New York Tribune* (Mar. 7, 1857). Abraham Lincoln attacked it too, starting with an 1857 speech in Springfield, Illinois. In that speech, Lincoln responded to a defense of the *Dred Scott* decision by Stephen Douglas, a U.S. senator for Illinois and a former judge on the Illinois Supreme Court. Lincoln challenged Douglas for his Senate seat, and in 1858 they publicly debated the Court's authority.

Abraham Lincoln, Speech at Springfield, Illinois

June 26, 1857

. . . Two weeks ago Judge Douglas spoke here on . . . the Dred Scott decision . . .

That decision declares two propositions—first, that a negro cannot sue in the U.S. Courts; and secondly, that Congress cannot prohibit slavery in the Territories. It was made by a divided court—dividing differently on the different points. Judge Douglas does not discuss the merits of the decision; and, in that respect, I shall follow his example, believing I could no more improve on McLean and Curtis, than he could on Taney.

He denounces all who question the correctness of that decision, as offering violent resistance to it. But who resists it? Who has, in spite of the decision, declared Dred Scott free, and resisted the authority of his master over him?

Judicial decisions have two uses—first, to absolutely determine the case decided, and secondly, to indicate to the public how other similar cases will be decided when they arise. For the latter use, they are called "precedents" and "authorities."

We believe, as much as Judge Douglas, (perhaps more) in obedience to, and respect for the judicial department of government. We think its decisions on Constitutional questions, when fully settled, should control, not only the particular cases decided, but the general policy of the country, subject to be disturbed only by amendments of the Constitution as provided in that instrument itself. More than this would be revolution. But we think the Dred Scott decision is erroneous. We know the court that made it, has often over-ruled its own decisions, and we shall do what we can to have it to over-rule this. We offer no resistance to it.

Judicial decisions are of greater or less authority as precedents, according to circumstances. That this should be so, accords both with common sense, and the customary understanding of the legal profession.

►If this important decision had been made by the unanimous concurrence of the judges, and without any apparent partisan bias, and in accordance with legal public expectation, and with the steady practice of the departments throughout our history, and had been in no part, based on assumed historical facts which are not really true; or, if wanting in some of these, it had been before the court more than once, and had there been affirmed and re-affirmed through a course of years, it then might be, perhaps would be, factious, nay, even revolutionary, to not acquiesce in it as a precedent.

But when, as it is true we find it wanting in all these claims to the public confidence, it is not resistance, it is not factious, it is not even disrespectful, to treat it as not having yet quite established a settled doctrine for the country . . .

Abraham Lincoln, Speech at the
First Lincoln-Douglas Debate
Aug. 21, 1858

. . . what is necessary for the nationalization of slavery? It is simply the next Dred Scott decision. It is merely for the Supreme Court to decide that no State under the Constitution can exclude it, just as they have already decided that under the Constitution neither Congress nor the Territorial Legislature can do it. When that is decided and acquiesced in, the whole thing is done. *[Lincoln is alluding to a case like* Lemmon v. The People, *see p. 712.—Editors]* This being true, and this being the way, as I think, that slavery is to be made national, let us consider what Judge Douglas is doing every day to that end. In the first place, let us see what influence he is exerting on public sentiment. In this and like communities, public sentiment is everything. With public sentiment, nothing can fail; without it nothing can succeed. Consequently he who moulds public sentiment, goes deeper than he who enacts statutes or pronounces decisions. He makes statutes and decisions possible or impossible to be executed. This must be borne in mind, as also the additional fact that Judge Douglas is a man of vast influence, so great that it is enough for many men to profess to believe anything, when they once find out that Judge Douglas professes to believe it. Consider also the attitude he occupies at the head of a large party—a party which he claims has a majority of all the voters in the country. This man sticks to a decision which forbids the people of a Territory from excluding slavery, and he does so not because he says it is right in itself—he does not give any opinion on that—but because it has been decided by the court, and being decided by court, he is, and you are bound to take it in your political action as law—not that he judges at all of its merits, but because a decision of the court is to him a "Thus saith the Lord." He places it on that ground alone, and you will bear in mind that, thus committing himself unreservedly to this decision, commits him to the next one just as firmly as to this. He did not commit himself on account of the merit or demerit of the decision, but it is a Thus saith the Lord. The next decision, as much as this, will be a Thus saith the Lord. There is nothing that can divert or turn him away from this decision. . . . I cannot shake Judge Douglas's teeth loose from the Dred Scott decision. Like some obstinate animal (I mean no disrespect), that will hang on when he has once got his teeth fixed; you may cut off a leg, or you may tear away an arm, still he will not relax his hold. . . . [T]here is a purpose strong as death and eternity for which he adheres to this decision, and for which he will adhere to all other decisions of the same court.

Stephen Douglas, Speech at the Third Lincoln-Douglas Debate

Sep. 15, 1858

. . . He makes war on the decision of the Supreme Court, in the case known as the Dred Scott case. I wish to say to you, fellow-citizens, that I have no war to make on that decision, or any other ever rendered by the Supreme Court. I am content to take that decision as it stands delivered by the highest judicial tribunal on earth, a tribunal established by the Constitution of the United States for that purpose, and hence that decision becomes the law of the land, binding on you, on me, and on every other good citizen whether we like it or not. Hence I do not choose to go into an argument to prove, before this audience, whether or not Chief Justice Taney understood the law better than Abraham Lincoln.

Mr. Lincoln objects to that decision, first and mainly because it deprives the negro of the rights of citizenship. I am as much opposed to his reason for that objection as I am to the objection itself. I hold that a negro is not and never ought to be a citizen of the United States. I hold that this Government was made on the white basis, by white men, for the benefit of white men and their posterity forever, and should be administered by white men and none others. I do not believe that the Almighty made the negro capable of self-government. . . .

I want to know whether he is not bound to a decision which is contrary to his opinions just as much as to one in accordance with his opinions. If the decision of the Supreme Court, the tribunal created by the Constitution to decide the question, is final and binding, is he not bound by it just as strongly as if he was for it instead of against it originally? Is every man in this land allowed to resist decisions he does not like, and only support those that meet his approval? What are important courts worth unless their decisions are binding on all good citizens? It is the fundamental principles of the judiciary that its decisions are final. It is created for that purpose, so that when you cannot agree among yourselves on a disputed point you appeal to the judicial tribunal which steps in and decides for you, and that decision is then binding on every good citizen. It is the law of the land just as much with Mr. Lincoln against it as for it. . . . I am willing to take the decision of the Supreme Court as it was pronounced by that august tribunal without stopping to inquire whether I would have decided that way or not. I have had many a decision made against me on questions of law which I did not like, but I was bound by them just as much as if I had had a hand in making them, and approved them. Did you ever see a lawyer or a client lose his case that he approved the decision of the court? They always think the decision unjust when it is given against them. In a Government of laws like ours we must sustain the Constitutions as our fathers made it, and maintain the rights of the States as they are guarantied under the Constitution, and then we will have peace and harmony between the different States and sections of this glorious Union.

Abraham Lincoln, Speech at the Fifth Lincoln-Douglas Debate
Oct. 7, 1858

. . . [Douglas] swells himself up and says, "All of us who stand by the decision of the Supreme Court are the friends of the Constitution; all you fellows that dare question it in any way, are the enemies of the Constitution." Now, in this very devoted adherence to this decision, in opposition to all the great political leaders whom he has recognized as leaders—in opposition to his former self and history, there is something very marked. And the manner in which he adheres to it—not as being right upon the merits, as he conceives (because he did not discuss that at all), but as being absolutely obligatory upon every one simply because of the source from whence it comes—as that which no man can gainsay, whatever it may be—this is another marked feature of his adherence to that decision. It marks it in this respect, that it commits him to the next decision, whenever it comes, as being as obligatory as this one, since he does not investigate it, and won't inquire whether this opinion is right or wrong. So he takes the next one without inquiring whether it is right or wrong. He teaches men this doctrine, and in so doing prepares the public mind to take the next decision when it comes, without any inquiry. In this I think I argue fairly (without questioning motives at all), that Judge Douglas is more ingeniously and powerfully preparing the public mind to take that decision when it comes. . . .

Stephen Douglas, Speech at the Fifth Lincoln-Douglas Debate
Oct. 7, 1858

I have a few words to say upon the Dred Scott decision, which has troubled the brain of Mr. Lincoln so much. He insists that that decision would carry slavery into the free States, notwithstanding that the decision says directly the opposite; and goes into a long argument to make you believe that I am in favor of, and would sanction the doctrine that would allow slaves to be brought here and held as slaves contrary to our Constitution and laws. Mr. Lincoln knew better when he asserted this. . . . Mr. Lincoln knows that there is not a member of the Supreme Court who holds that doctrine; he knows that every one of them, as shown by their opinions, holds the reverse. Why this attempt, then, to bring the Supreme Court into disrepute among the people? It looks as if there was an effort being made to destroy public confidence in the highest judicial tribunal on earth. Suppose he succeeds in destroying public confidence in the court, so that the people will not respect its decisions, but will feel at liberty to disregard them, and resist the laws of the land, what will he have gained? He will have changed the Government from one of laws into that of a mob, in which the strong arm of violence will be substituted for the decisions of the courts of justice. He complains because I did not go into an argument reviewing Chief Justice Taney's opinion, and the other opinions of the different judges, to determine whether their reasoning is right or wrong on the questions of law. What use would that be? He wants to take an appeal from the Supreme Court to this meeting to determine whether the questions of law were decided properly. He is going to appeal from the Supreme Court of the United States to every town meeting in the hope that he can excite a prejudice against that court, and on the wave of that prejudice ride into the Senate of the United States, when he could not get there on his own principles, or his own merits. Suppose he should succeed in getting into the Senate of the United States, what then will he have to do with the decision of the Supreme Court in the Dred Scott case? Can he reverse that decision when he gets there? Can he act upon it? Has the Senate any right to reverse it or revise it? He will not pretend that it has. Then why drag the matter into this contest, unless for the purpose of making a false issue, by which he can direct public attention from the real issue.

He has cited General Jackson in justification of the war he is making on the decision of the court. *[Douglas is referring to President Andrew Jackson's veto of the Second Bank of the United States, which stated that the Bank was unconstitutional even though it had been upheld by the Supreme Court, see p. 505.—Editors]* Mr. Lincoln misunderstands the history of the country, if he believes there is any parallel in the two cases. It is true that the Supreme Court once decided that if a Bank of the United States was a necessary fiscal agent of the Government, it was Constitutional, and if not, that it was unconstitutional, and also, that whether or not it was necessary for that purpose, was a political question for Congress and not a judicial one for the courts to determine. Hence the court would not determine the bank unconstitutional. Jackson respected the decision, obeyed the law, executed it and carried it into effect during its existence; but after the charter of the bank expired and a proposition was made to create a new bank, General Jackson said, "it is unnecessary and improper, and, therefore, I am against it on Constitutional grounds as well as those of expediency." Is Congress bound to pass every act that is Constitutional? Why, there are a thousand things that are Constitutional, but yet are inexpedient and unnecessary, and you surely would not vote for them merely because you had the right to? And because General Jackson would not do a thing which he had a right to do, but did not deem expedient or proper, Mr. Lincoln is going to justify himself in doing that which he has no right to do. I ask him, whether he is not bound to respect and obey the decisions of the Supreme Court as well as me? The Constitution has created that court to decide all Constitutional questions in the last resort, and when such decisions have been made, they become the law of the land, and you, and he, and myself, and every other good citizen are bound by them. Yet, he argues that I am bound by their decisions and he is not. He says that their decisions are binding on Democrats, but not on Republicans. Are not Republicans bound by the laws of the land as well as Democrats? And when the court has fixed the construction of the

Constitution on the validity of a given law, is not their decision binding upon Republicans as well as upon Democrats? Is it possible that you Republicans have the right to raise your mobs and oppose the laws of the land and the constituted authorities, and yet hold us Democrats bound to obey them? My time is within half a minute of expiring, and all I have to say is, that I stand by the laws of the land. I stand by the Constitution as our fathers made it, by the laws as they are enacted, and by the decisions of the court upon all points within their jurisdiction as they are pronounced by the highest tribunal on earth; and any man who resists these must resort to mob law and violence to overturn the government of laws.

Abraham Lincoln, Speech at the Sixth Lincoln-Douglas Debate

Oct. 13, 1858

. . . Speaking of me the Judge says: "He goes on and insists that the Dred Scott decision would carry slavery into the free States, notwithstanding the decision itself says the contrary." And he adds: "Mr. Lincoln knows that there is no member of the Supreme Court that holds that doctrine. He knows that every one of them in their opinions held the reverse."

I especially introduce this subject again for the purpose of saying that I have the Dred Scott decision here, and I will thank Judge Douglas to lay his finger upon the place in the entire opinions of the court where any one of them "says the contrary." It is very hard to affirm a negative with entire confidence. I say, however, that I have examined that decision with a good deal of care, as a lawyer examines a decision, and so far as I have been able to do so, the court has no where in its opinions said that the States have the power to exclude slavery, nor have they used other language substantially that. . . .

We oppose the Dred Scott decision in a certain way, upon which I ought perhaps to address you a few words. We do not propose that when Dred Scott has been decided to be a slave by the court, we, as a mob, will decide him to be free. We do not propose that, when any other one, or one thousand, shall be decided by that court to be slaves, we will in any violent way disturb the rights of property thus settled, but we nevertheless do oppose that decision as a political rule, which shall be binding on the voter to vote for nobody who thinks it wrong, which shall be binding on the members of Congress or the President to favor no measure that does not actually concur with the principles of that decision. We do not propose to be bound by it as a political rule in that way, because we think it lays the foundation not merely of enlarging and spreading out what we consider an evil, but it lays the foundation for spreading that evil into the States themselves. We propose so resisting it as to have it reversed if we can, and a new judicial rule established upon this subject. . . .

Stephen Douglas, Speech at the Sixth Lincoln-Douglas Debate

Oct. 13, 1858

. . . He wishes to discuss the merits of the Dred Scott decision when, under the Constitution, a Senator has no right to interfere with the decision of judicial tribunals. He wants your exclusive attention to two questions that he has no power to act upon; to two questions that he could not vote upon if he was in Congress, to two questions that are not practical, in order to conceal your attention from other questions which he might be required to vote upon should he ever become a member of Congress. He tells you that he does not like the Dred Scott decision. Suppose he does not, how is he going to help himself? He says that he will reverse it. How will he reverse it? I know of but one mode of reversing judicial decisions, and that is by appealing from the inferior to the superior court. But I have never yet learned how or where an appeal could be taken from the Supreme Court of the United States! The Dred Scott decision was pronounced by the highest tribunal on earth. From that decision there is no appeal this side of Heaven. Yet, Mr. Lincoln says he is going to reverse that decision. By what tribunal will he reverse it? Will he appeal to a mob? Does he intend to appeal to violence, to Lynch law? Will he stir up strife and rebellion in the land and overthrow the court by violence? He does not deign to tell you how he will reverse the Dred Scott decision, but keeps appealing each day from the Supreme Court of the United States to political meetings in the country. He wants me to argue with you the merits of each point of that decision before this political meeting. I say to you, with all due respect, that I choose to abide by the decisions of the Supreme Court as they are pronounced. It is not for me to inquire after a decision is made whether I like it in all the points or not. When I used to practice law with Lincoln, I never knew him to be beat in a case that he did not get mad at the judge and talk about appealing; and when I got beat I generally thought the court was wrong, but I never dreamed of going out of the court-house and making a stump speech to the people against the judge, merely because I had found out that I did not know the law as well as he did. If the decision did not suit me, I appealed until I got to the Supreme Court, and then if that court, the highest tribunal in the world, decided against me, I was satisfied, because it is the duty of every law-abiding man to obey the constitutions, the laws, and the constituted authorities. He who attempts to stir up odium and rebellion in the country against the constituted authorities, is stimulating the passions of men to resort to violence and to mobs instead of to the law. Hence, I tell you that I take the decisions of the Supreme Court as the law of the land, and I intend to obey them as such.

But Mr. Lincoln says that I will not answer his question as to what I would do in the event of the court making so ridiculous a decision as he imagines they would by deciding that the free State of Illinois could not prohibit slavery within her own limits. I told him at Freeport why I would not answer such a question. I told him that there was not a man possessing any brains in America, lawyer or not, who ever dreamed that such a thing could be done. I told him then, as I do now, that by all the principles set forth in the Dred Scott decision, it is impossible. I told him then, as I do now, that it is an insult to men's understanding, and a gross calumny on the court, to presume in advance that it was going to degrade itself so low as to make a decision known to be in direct violation of the Constitution.

[A voice interjects: "The same thing was said about the Dred Scott decision before it passed."]

[Douglas replies] Perhaps you think that the court did the same thing in reference to the Dred Scott decision: I have heard a man talk that way before. The principles contained in the Dred Scott decision had been affirmed previously in various other decisions. What court or judge ever held that a negro was a citizen?

The State courts had decided that question over and over again, and the Dred Scott decision on that point only affirmed what every court in the land knew to be the law.

But, I will not be drawn off into an argument upon the merits of the Dred Scott decision. It is enough for me to know that the Constitution of the United States created the Supreme Court for the purpose of deciding all disputed questions touching the true construction of that instrument, and when such decisions are pronounced, they are the law of the land, binding on every good citizen. Mr. Lincoln has a very convenient mode of arguing upon the subject. He holds that because he is a Republican that he is not bound by the decisions of the court, but that I being a Democrat am so bound. It may be that Republicans do not hold themselves bound by the laws of the land and the Constitution of the country as expounded by the courts; it may be an article in the Republican creed that men who do not like a decision, have a right to rebel against it; but when Mr. Lincoln preaches that doctrine, I think he will find some honest Republican—some lawabiding man in that party—who will repudiate such a monstrous doctrine. The decision in the Dred Scott case is binding on every American citizen alike; and yet Mr. Lincoln argues that the Republicans are not bound by it, because they are opposed to it, whilst Democrats are bound by it, because we will not resist it. A Democrat cannot resist the constituted authorities of this country. A Democrat is a law-abiding man, a Democrat stands by the Constitution and the laws, and relies upon liberty as protected by law, and not upon mob or political violence. . . .

Abraham Lincoln, Speech at the
Sixth Lincoln-Douglas Debate
Oct. 13, 1858

. . . Now, in regard to this matter of the Dred Scott decision, I wish to say a word or two. After all, the Judge will not say whether, if a decision is made, holding that the people of the States cannot exclude slavery, he will support it or not. He obstinately refuses to say what he will do in that case. The Judges of the Supreme Court as obstinately refused to say what they would do on this subject. Before this I reminded him that at Galesburgh he said the Judges had expressly declared the contrary, and you remember that in my opening speech I told him I had the book containing that decision here, and I would thank him to lay his finger on the place where any such thing was said. He has occupied his hour and a half, and he has not ventured to try to sustain his assertion. He never will. But he is desirous of knowing how we are going to reverse the Dred Scott decision. Judge Douglas ought to know how. Did not he and his political friends find a way to reverse the decision of that same court in favor the Constitutionality of the National Bank? Didn't they find a way to do it so effectually that they have reversed it as completely as any decision ever was reversed, so far as its practical operation is concerned? . . .

Judge Douglas also makes the declaration that I say the Democrats are bound by the Dred Scott decision, while the Republicans are not. In the sense in which he argues, I never said it; but I will tell you what I have said and what I do not hesitate to repeat today. I have said that, as the Democrats believe that decision to be correct, and that the extension of slavery is affirmed in the National Constitution, they are bound to support it as such; and I will tell you here that General Jackson once said each man was bound to support the Constitution "as he understood it." Now, Judge

Douglas understands the Constitution according to the Dred Scott decision, and he is bound to support it as he understands it. I understand it another way, and therefore I am bound to support it in the way in which I understand it. . . .

NOTES

1.   The position that each of the three departments of government can independently interpret and enforce the Constitution as it performs its own distinctive functions is often called "departmentalism." Lincoln appears to hold a version of that position. The position that all other government officials (or perhaps all citizens) must treat judicial opinions about the Constitution as if they were the Constitution itself is often called "judicial supremacy." Douglas appears to hold a version of that position. Who makes the better case? It can be hard to separate the views of Lincoln and Douglas on slavery from their views on interpretive authority, but it is important to try: the issues will change, but the question of interpretive authority will remain. After reading this initial clash of opinions, which view do you hold?

2.   Lincoln repeatedly warns that the Supreme Court might issue another decision—"the next Dred Scott"—holding that *all* states must allow slavery within their borders. Suppose it did. Is Lincoln right that such a decision would have the same force as the first *Dred Scott*? What is Douglas's answer? Is it convincing?

3.   Lincoln's opposition to the authority of *Dred Scott* was "an essential part of the platform on which Lincoln rose to national prominence and was elected President." Michael Stokes Paulsen, *Lincoln and Judicial Authority*, 83 Notre Dame L. Rev. 1227, 1230 (2008). That stance, "and Lincoln's election on such a platform, was featured among prominent Southerners' purported constitutional justifications for secession: the nation had just elected a lawless, anticonstitutional President who would invade the South's constitutional rights, as duly determined by the United States Supreme Court, with respect to slavery." *Id.*

Paulsen argues: "The decision by Lincoln and the Union to fight secession thus depends, for *its* legitimacy, on a rejection of the Southern position on the legitimacy of Lincoln's constitutional views." *Id.* If Stephen Douglas's view was right, "then Lincoln was wrong in nearly everything he stood for. Indeed, Lincoln's election as President rested on fundamentally anticonstitutional premises. If judicial supremacists are correct, the South was not only within its rights in seceding, but did so for [a] just constitutional cause—rebelling against an administration and government premised on a grave breach of the Constitution." *Id.* Do you agree with this logic? Is it really impossible both to believe in judicial supremacy and to think secession was unconstitutional?

4.   Does the attractiveness of departmentalism depend on which branch of the government you trust most? Are the branches likely to differ in how much weight they give to each of the types of constitutional argument? Are the branches likely to differ in how skillfully they use each type of argument?

1958: *Cooper v. Aaron*

Fast-forward one hundred years, to 1958. The Court's position on race has come around dramatically, but the dilemma of judicial supremacy remains.

In *Brown v. Board of Education*, 347 U.S. 483 (1954), the Supreme Court held that racial segregation in public schools violated the Equal Protection Clause of the Fourteenth Amendment. (See p. 1356) Throughout the South, many officials resisted the Court's decision. The governor of Arkansas, Orville Faubus, refused to comply with a federal court's desegregation decree and even called out the National Guard to block integration. The school district then sought a postponement of integration, because of the turmoil and the potential for violence. The case reached the Supreme Court, which offered its first clear-cut claim to judicial supremacy in constitutional interpretation in *Cooper v. Aaron*, 358 U.S. 1 (1958). The Court's *per curiam* decision was unanimous. It reaffirmed the principles of *Brown* and the obligation of state and local officials to abide by it. Appealing to *Marbury*, the Court claimed for its decisions the status of "supreme law of the land" under Article VI. Here is its reasoning:

Cooper v. Aaron

358 U.S. 1 (1958)

■ Opinion of the Court by THE CHIEF JUSTICE, MR. JUSTICE BLACK, MR. JUSTICE FRANKFURTER, MR. JUSTICE DOUGLAS, MR. JUSTICE BURTON, MR. JUSTICE CLARK, MR. JUSTICE HARLAN, MR. JUSTICE BRENNAN, and MR. JUSTICE WHITTAKER.

As this case reaches us it raises questions of the highest importance to the maintenance of our federal system of government. It necessarily involves a claim by the Governor and Legislature of a State that there is no duty on state officials to obey federal court orders resting on this Court's considered interpretation of the United States Constitution. Specifically it involves actions by the Governor and Legislature of Arkansas upon the premise that they are not bound by our holding in *Brown v. Board of Education*, 347 U.S. 483 (1954). That holding was that the Fourteenth Amendment forbids States to use their governmental powers to bar children on racial grounds from attending schools where there is state participation through any arrangement, management, funds or property. We are urged to uphold a suspension of the Little Rock School Board's plan to do away with segregated public schools in Little Rock until state laws and efforts to upset and nullify our holding in *Brown v. Board of Education* have been further challenged and tested in the courts. We reject these contentions. . . .

On . . . September 4, 1957, the Negro children attempted to enter the high school but, as the District Court later found, units of the Arkansas National Guard "acting pursuant to the Governor's order, stood shoulder to shoulder at the school grounds and thereby forcibly prevented the 9 Negro students . . . from entering," as they continued to do every school day during the following three weeks. *[The United States then obtained a federal injunction forbidding Arkansas officials from resisting the desegregation order.—Editors]*

The next school day was Monday, September 23, 1957. The Negro children entered the high school that morning under the protection of the Little Rock Police Department and members of the Arkansas State Police. But the officers caused the children to be removed from the school during the morning because they had difficulty controlling a large and demonstrating crowd which had gathered at the high school. On September 25, however, the President of the United States dispatched federal troops to Central High School and admission of the Negro students to the school was thereby effected. Regular army troops continued at the high school until November 27, 1957. They were then replaced by federalized National Guardsmen who remained throughout the balance of the school year. Eight of the Negro students remained in attendance at the school throughout the school year.

We come now to the aspect of the proceedings presently before us. On February 20, 1958, the School Board and the Superintendent of Schools filed a petition in the District Court seeking a postponement of their program for desegregation. Their position in essence was that because of extreme public hostility, which they stated had been engendered largely by the official attitudes and actions of the Governor and the Legislature, the maintenance of a sound educational program at Central High School, with the Negro students in attendance, would be impossible. The Board therefore proposed that the Negro students already admitted to the school be withdrawn and sent to segregated schools, and that all further steps to carry out the Board's desegregation program be postponed for a period later suggested by the Board to be two and one-half years.

After a hearing the District Court granted the relief requested by the Board. Among other things the court found that the past year at Central High School had been attended by conditions of "chaos, bedlam and turmoil"; that there were "repeated incidents of more or less serious violence directed against the Negro students and their property"; that there was "tension and unrest among the school administrators, the class-room teachers, the pupils, and the latters' parents, which inevitably had an adverse effect upon the educational program"; that a school official was threatened with violence; that a "serious financial burden" had been cast on the School District; that the education of the students had suffered "and under existing conditions will continue to suffer"; that the Board would continue to need "military assistance or its equivalent"; that the local police department would not be able "to detail enough men to afford the necessary protection"; and that the situation was "intolerable." . . . *[The court of appeals reversed the district court, thus refusing the postponement, and the Supreme Court affirmed.—Editors]*

In affirming the judgment of the Court of Appeals which reversed the District Court we have accepted without reservation the position of the School Board, the Superintendent of Schools, and their counsel that they displayed entire good faith in the conduct of these proceedings and in dealing with the unfortunate and distressing sequence of events which has been outlined. We likewise have accepted the findings of the District Court as to the conditions at Central High School during the 1957–1958 school year, and also the findings that the educational progress of all the students, white and colored, of that school has suffered and will continue to suffer if the conditions which prevailed last year are permitted to continue.

The significance of these findings, however, is to be considered in light of the fact, indisputably revealed by the record before us, that the conditions they depict are directly traceable to the actions of legislators and executive officials of the State of Arkansas, taken in their official capacities, which reflect their own determination to resist this Court's decision in the *Brown* case and which have brought about violent resistance to that decision in Arkansas. In its petition for certiorari filed in this Court, the School Board itself describes the situation in this language: "The legislative, executive, and judicial departments of the state government opposed the desegregation of Little Rock schools by enacting laws, calling out troops, making statements villifying federal law and federal courts, and failing to utilize state law enforcement agencies and judicial processes to maintain public peace."

One may well sympathize with the position of the Board in the face of the frustrating conditions which have confronted it, but, regardless of the Board's good faith, the actions of the other state agencies responsible for those conditions compel us to reject the Board's legal position. Had Central High School been under the direct management of the State itself, it could hardly be suggested that those immediately in charge of the school should be heard to assert their own good faith as a legal excuse for delay in implementing the constitutional rights of these respondents, when vindication of those rights was rendered difficult of impossible by the actions of other state officials. The situation here is in no different posture because the members of the School Board and the Superintendent of Schools are local officials; from the point of view of the Fourteenth Amendment, they stand in this litigation as the agents of the State.

The constitutional rights of respondents are not to be sacrificed or yielded to the violence and disorder which have followed upon the actions of the Governor and Legislature. . . .

The controlling legal principles are plain. The command of the Fourteenth Amendment is that no "State" shall deny to any person within its jurisdiction the equal protection of the laws. "A State acts by its legislative, its executive, or its judicial authorities. It can act in no other way. The constitutional provision, therefore, must mean that no agency of the State, or of the officers or agents by whom its powers are exerted, shall deny to any person within its jurisdiction the equal protection of the laws." *Ex Parte Virginia*, 100 U.S. 339, 347 (1879). . . . In short, the constitutional rights of children not to be discriminated against in school admission on grounds of race or color declared by this Court in the *Brown* case can neither be nullified indirectly by them through evasive schemes for segregation whether attempted "ingeniously or ingenuously."

What has been said, in the light of the facts developed, is enough to dispose of the case. However, we should answer the premise of the actions of the Governor and Legislature that they are not bound by our holding in the *Brown* case. It is necessary only to recall some basic constitutional propositions which are settled doctrine.

Article VI of the Constitution makes the Constitution the "supreme Law of the Land." In 1803, Chief Justice Marshall, speaking for a unanimous Court, referring to the Constitution as "the fundamental and paramount law of the nation," declared in the notable case of *Marbury v. Madison*, 5 U.S. (1 Cranch) 137, 177, that "It is emphatically the province and duty of the judicial department to say what the law is." This decision declared the basic principle that the federal judiciary is supreme in the exposition of the law of the Constitution, and that principle has ever since been respected by this Court and the Country as a permanent and indispensable feature of our constitutional system. It follows that the interpretation of the Fourteenth Amendment enunciated by this Court in the *Brown* case is the supreme law of the land, and Art. VI of the Constitution makes it of binding effect on the States "any Thing in the Constitution or Laws of any State to the Contrary notwithstanding." Every state legislator and executive and judicial officer is solemnly committed by oath taken pursuant to Art. VI, cl. 3 "to support this Constitution." Chief Justice Taney, speaking for a unanimous Court in 1859, said that this requirement reflected the framers' "anxiety to preserve it [the Constitution] in full force, in all its powers, and to guard against resistance to or evasion of its authority, on the part of a State." *Abelman v. Booth*, 62 U.S. (21 How.) 506, 524 (1858).

No state legislator or executive or judicial officer can war against the Constitution without violating his undertaking to support it. Chief Justice Marshall spoke for unanimous Court in saying that: "If the legislatures of the several states may, at will, annul the judgments of the courts of the United States, and destroy the rights acquired under those judgments, the constitution itself becomes a solemn mockery." *United States v. Peters*, 9 U.S. (5 Cranch) 115, 136 (1809). A Governor who asserts a power to nullify a federal court order is similarly restrained. If he had such power, said Chief Justice Hughes, in 1932, also for a unanimous Court, "it is manifest that the fiat of a state Governor, and not the Constitution of the United States, would be the supreme law of the land; that the restrictions of the Federal Constitution upon the exercise of state power would be but impotent phrases." *Sterling v. Constantin*, 287 U.S. 378, 397–398 (1932).

. . . The basic decision in *Brown* was unanimously reached by this Court only after the case had been briefed and twice argued and the issues had been given the most serious consideration. Since the first *Brown* opinion three new Justices have come to the Court. They are at one with the Justices still on the Court who participated in that basic decision as to its correctness, and that decision is now unanimously reaffirmed. The principles announced in that decision and the obedience of the States to them according to the command of the Constitution, are indispensable for the protection of the freedoms guaranteed by our fundamental charter for all of us. Our constitutional ideal of equal justice under law is thus made a living truth.

■ [The concurring opinion of JUSTICE FRANKFURTER is omitted.]

NOTES

1.   How did views of judicial supremacy and race shift from 1858 to 1958? Is Douglas's view the same as the Court's in *Cooper*? Is Lincoln's view that of Governor Faubus? Is it possible to have a *consistent* position on the Court's authority, one that will last you through good decisions and bad ones?

2.   Does the "chaos, bedlam, and turmoil" at Central High School cast new light on Douglas's warning that Lincoln would "change[ ] the Government from one of laws into that of a mob, in which the strong arm of violence will be substituted for the decisions of the courts of justice"?

3.   As the Court's opinion notes, President Eisenhower sent federal troops to Little Rock to quell unrest and ensure that the black students were actually allowed to attend school. What if he hadn't? Would the Supreme Court have had any power to enforce its rulings on its own? Would it have just hoped that the Arkansas officials would listen? Or would the Supreme Court itself have ruled differently if it knew that its rulings would not be supported by the president?

Ex parte Merryman and Specific Judgments

Now consider the dramatic case of *Ex parte Merryman*, 17 F.Cas. 144 (D. Md., April Term 1861), in which Chief Justice Roger Taney declared that President Abraham Lincoln's suspension of the writ of habeas corpus was unconstitutional and that the detention of a suspected rebel was illegal. Do the courts have the power to bind the president? Was President Lincoln required to release Merryman? For a thorough review of these complex proceedings, see Seth Barrett Tillman, Ex Parte Merryman*: Myth, History, and Scholarship*, 224 Mil. L. Rev. 481 (2016). But here is an abbreviated version.

In response to Lincoln's election as president in 1860, several Southern states purported to secede from the Union. In April 1861, secessionist forces fired on and captured a federal fort in the harbor of Charleston, South Carolina—Fort Sumter. In response, President Lincoln by executive decree called for troops to suppress the rebellion, and he imposed a blockade on shipping directed toward the ports of the seceding states. While his decree was largely supported in the North, it led to the secession of states in the Upper South, including the important state of Virginia. Secessionist activity was also pervasive in several "border slave states," including Maryland, Kentucky, Missouri, and Delaware. Virginia had seceded, and Maryland was poised to join her. Thus the capital of the United States, Washington, D.C., was essentially surrounded by secessionist sympathizers. When federal troops attempted to pass through Baltimore to defend the capital, they were attacked by a mob. On April 27, in a private order, President Lincoln authorized General Winfield Scott to suspend the privilege of the writ of habeas corpus for the "public safety" if he deemed it necessary to permit troops to travel through Maryland or to suppress secessionist violence. It was impossible at this time to convene Congress safely in Washington, D.C., in order to ask it to vote on the suspension of the writ of habeas corpus. Yet convening Congress outside of the capital would have been humiliating to the national government and might have strengthened the rebel cause.

Pursuant to President Lincoln's suspension of the writ, U.S. Army officers arrested a number of secessionist sympathizers. One was John Merryman, a prominent farmer and county commissioner, who was suspected of sabotaging bridges and railway lines. Merryman was held in Fort McHenry, Baltimore, yet (somehow) obtained access to legal counsel, who presented a petition for a writ of habeas corpus to Chief Justice Roger Taney. Chief Justice Taney issued a writ to the commanding officer at Fort McHenry, General Cadwalader, directing him to produce Merryman in court in Baltimore the next day, so the lawfulness of Merryman's detention could be determined. General Cadwalader declined to produce Merryman, instead sending a subordinate to appear and inform Chief Justice Taney of President Lincoln's order and request a postponement pending further instructions from the president. The chief justice was displeased, and he issued an attachment against General Cadwalader for contempt, returnable the next day. Service of the writ was refused at Fort McHenry, and the next day, May 28, 1861, Chief Justice Taney issued the following ruling from the bench, declaring Lincoln's suspension of the writ unconstitutional.

Ex parte Merryman
17 F.Cas. 144 (D. Md., April Term 1861)

■ TANEY, CIRCUIT JUSTICE.

. . . The case, then, is simply this: a military officer, residing in Pennsylvania, issues an order to arrest a citizen of Maryland, upon vague and indefinite charges, without any proof, so far as appears; under this order, his house is entered in the night, he is seized as a prisoner, and conveyed to Fort McHenry, and there kept in close confinement; and when a habeas corpus is served on the commanding officer, requiring him to produce the prisoner before a justice of the supreme court, in order that he may examine into the legality of the imprisonment, the answer of the officer, is that he is authorized by the president to suspend the writ of habeas corpus at his discretion, and in the exercise of that discretion, suspends it in this case, and on that ground refuses obedience to the writ.

As the case comes before me, therefore, I understand that the president not only claims the right to suspend the writ of habeas corpus himself, at his discretion, but to delegate that discretionary power to a military officer, and to leave it to him to determine whether he will or will not obey judicial process that may be served upon him. No official notice has been given to the courts of justice, or to the public, by proclamation or otherwise, that the president claimed this power, and had exercised it in the manner stated in the return. And I certainly listened to it with some surprise, for I had supposed it to be one of those points of constitutional law upon which there was no difference of opinion, and that it was admitted on all hands, that the privilege of the writ could not be suspended, except by act of congress. . . .

[B]eing thus officially notified that the privilege of the writ has been suspended, under the orders, and by the authority of the president, and believing, as I do, that the president has exercised a power which he does not possess under the constitution, a proper respect for the high office he fills, requires me to state plainly and fully the grounds of my opinion, in order to show that I have not ventured to question the legality of his act, without a careful and deliberate examination of the whole subject. . . .

The constitution provides, as I have before said, that "no person shall be deprived of life, liberty or property, without due process of law." It declares that "the right of the people to be secure in their persons, houses, papers and effects, against unreasonable searches and seizures, shall not be violated; and no warrant shall issue, but upon probable cause, supported by oath or affirmation, and particularly describing the place to be searched, and the persons or things to be seized." It provides that the party accused shall be entitled to a speedy trial in a court of justice.

These great and fundamental laws, which congress itself could not suspend, have been disregarded and suspended, like the writ of habeas corpus, by a military order, supported by force of arms. Such is the case now before me, and I can only say that if the authority which the constitution has confided to the judiciary department and judicial officers, may thus, upon any pretext or under any circumstances, be usurped by the military power, at its discretion, the people of the United States are no longer living under a government of laws, but every citizen holds life, liberty and property at the will and pleasure of the army officer in whose military district he may happen to be found.

In such a case, my duty was too plain to be mistaken. I have exercised all the power which the constitution and laws confer upon me, but that power has been resisted by a force too strong for me to overcome. It is possible that the officer who has incurred this grave responsibility may have misunderstood his instructions, and exceeded the authority intended to be given him; I shall, therefore, order all the proceedings in this case, with my opinion, to be filed and recorded in the circuit court of the United States for the district of Maryland, and direct the clerk to transmit a copy, under seal, to the president of the United States. It will then remain for that high officer, in fulfilment of his constitutional obligation to "take care that the laws be faithfully executed," to determine what measures he will take to cause the civil process of the United States to be respected and enforced.

———

Consider the implications: must the president obey a court order, no matter how mistaken? When President Lincoln addressed the issue, in a speech before Congress, he defended his actions as constitutional without ever mentioning Chief Justice Taney or any court order:

> Soon after the first call for militia, it was considered a duty to authorize the Commanding General, in proper cases, according to his discretion, to suspend the privilege of the writ of habeas corpus; or, in other words, to arrest, and detain, without resort to the ordinary processes and forms of law, such individuals as he might deem dangerous to the public safety. This authority has purposely been exercised but very sparingly. Nevertheless, the legality and propriety of what has been done under it, are questioned; and the attention of the country has been called to the proposition that one who is sworn to "take care that the laws be faithfully executed," should not himself violate them. Of course some consideration was given to the questions of power, and propriety, before this matter was acted upon. The whole of the laws which were required to be faithfully executed, were being resisted, and failing of execution, in nearly one-third of the States. Must they be allowed to finally fail of execution, even had it been perfectly clear, that by the use of the means necessary to their execution, some single law, made in such extreme tenderness of the citizen's liberty, that practically, it relieves more of the guilty, than of the innocent, should, to a very limited extent, be violated? To state the question more directly, are all the laws, but one, to go unexecuted, and the government itself go to pieces, lest that one be violated? Even in such a case, would not the official oath be broken, if the government should be overthrown, when it was believed that disregarding the single law, would tend to preserve it? But it was not believed that this question was presented. It was not believed that any law was violated. . . .

No more extended argument is now offered; as an opinion, at some length, will probably be presented by the Attorney General. . . .

President Lincoln, Message to Congress (July 4, 1861).

Attorney General Edward Bates addressed the question of judicial power in an opinion dated the next day.

Edward Bates, Opinion on the Suspension of the Privilege of the Writ of Habeas Corpus

10 Op. Att'y Gen. 74 (July 5, 1861)

[To the President:]

SIR: You have required my opinion in writing upon the following questions:

1.   In the present time of a great and dangerous insurrection, has the President the discretionary power to cause to be arrested and held in custody, persons known to have criminal intercourse with the insurgents, or persons against whom there is probable cause for suspicion of such criminal complicity?

2.   In such cases of arrest, is the President justified in refusing to obey a writ of *habeas corpus* issued by a court or a judge, requiring him or his agent to produce

the body of the prisoner, and show the cause of his caption and detention, to be adjudged and disposed of by such court or judge?

. . . In the formation of our national government, our fathers were surrounded with peculiar difficulties arising out of their novel, I may say unexampled, condition. In resolving to break their ties which had bound them to the British empire, their complaints were levelled chiefly at the King, not the Parliament nor the people. They seem to have been actuated by a special dread of the unity of power. . . .

Hence, keeping the sovereignty always out of sight, they adopted the plan of "checks and balances," forming separate departments of Government, and giving to each department separate and limited powers. These departments are co-ordinate and coequal—that is, neither being sovereign, each is independent in its sphere, and not subordinate to the others, either of them or both of them together. We have three of these co-ordinate departments. Now, if we allow one of the three to determine the extent of its own powers, and also the extent of the powers of the other two, that one can control the whole government, and has in fact achieved the sovereignty.

. . . Our fathers, having divided the government into co-ordinate departments, did not even try (and if they tried would probably have failed) to create an arbiter among them to adjudge their conflicts and keep them within their respective bounds. They were left, by design, I suppose, each independent and free, to act out its own granted powers, without any ordained or legal superior possessing the power to revise and reverse its action. And this with the hope that the three departments, mutually coequal and independent, would keep each other within their proper spheres by their mutual antagonism—that is, by the system of checks and balances, to which our fathers were driven at the beginning by their fear of the unity of power.

In this view of the subject it is quite possible for the same identical *question* (not *case*) to come up legitimately before each one of the three departments, and be determined in three different ways, and each decision stand irrevocable, binding upon the parties to each case; and that, for the simple reason that the departments *are* co-ordinate, and there is no ordained legal superior, with power to revise and reverse their decisions.

To say that the departments of our government are co-ordinate, is to say that the judgment of one of them is not binding upon the other two, as to the arguments and principles involved in the judgment. It binds only the parties to the case decided. But if, admitting that the departments of government are co-ordinate, it be still contended that the principles adopted by one department, in deciding a case properly before it, are binding upon another department, that obligation must of necessity be reciprocal—that is, if the President be bound by the principles laid down by the judiciary, so also is the judiciary bound by the principles laid down by the President. And thus we shall have a theory of constitutional government flatly contradicting itself. Departments co-ordinate and coequal, and yet reciprocally subordinate to each other! That cannot be. The several departments, though far from sovereign, are free and independent, in the exercise of the limited powers granted to them respectively by the Constitution. . . .

Indeed, [the judiciary] is not itself bound by its own decisions, for it can and often does overrule and disregard them, as, in common honesty, it ought to do, whenever it finds, by its after and better lights, that its former judgments were wrong. . . .

[W]hatever skilful soldier may lead our armies to victory against a foreign foe, or may quell a domestic insurrection; however high he may raise his professional renown, and whatever martial glory he may win, still he is subject to the orders of the *civil magistrate*, and he and his army are always "subordinate to the civil power."

And hence it follows, that whenever the President, (the *civil magistrate*,) in the discharge of his constitutional duty to "take care that the laws be faithfully executed," has occasion to use the army to aid him in the performance of that duty, he does not thereby lose his civil character and become a soldier, subject to military law and liable to be tried by a court-martial, any more than does a civil court lose its legal and pacific nature and become military and belligerent, by calling out the power of the country to enforce its decrees. The civil magistrates, whether judicial or executive, must of necessity employ physical power to aid them in enforcing the laws, whenever they have to deal with disobedient or refractory subjects; and their legal power and right to do so is unquestionable. The right of the courts to call out the whole power of the county to enforce their judgments, is as old as the common law; and the right of the President to use force in the performance of his legal duties is not only inherent in his office, but has been frequently recognized and aided by Congress. . . . To call, as is sometimes done, the judiciary the *civil power*, and the President the *military power*, seems to me at once a mistake of fact and an abuse of language.

While the judiciary and the President, as departments of the general government, are co-ordinate, equal in dignity and power, and equally trusted by the law, in their respective spheres, there is, nevertheless, a marked diversity in the character of their functions and their modes of action. The judiciary is, for the most part, passive. It rarely, if ever, takes the initiative; it seldom or never begins an operation. Its great function is *judgment*, and, in the exercise of that function, it is confined almost exclusively to cases not selected by itself, but made and submitted by others. The President, on the contrary, by the very nature of his office, is active; he must often take the initiative; he must begin operations. His great function is *execution*, for he is required by the Constitution, (and he is the only department that is so required,) to "take care that the laws (all the laws) be faithfully executed;" and in the exercise of that function, his duties are coextensive with the laws of the land.

Often, he comes to the aid of the judiciary, in the execution of its judgments; and this is only a part, and a small part, of his constitutional duty, to take care that the laws be faithfully executed. . . .

As to the first question: I am clearly of opinion that, in a time like the present, when the very existence of the nation is assailed, by a great and dangerous insurrection, the President has the lawful discretionary power to arrest and hold in custody persons known to have criminal intercourse with the insurgents, or persons against whom there is probable cause for suspicion of such criminal complicity. . . .

The Constitution requires the President, before he enters upon the execution of his office, to take an oath that he "will faithfully execute the office of President of the United States, and will, to the best of his ability, preserve, protect and defend the Constitution of the United States." . . .

And then follows the broad and compendious injunction to "take care that the laws be faithfully executed." And this injunction, embracing as it does all the laws— Constitution treaties, statutes—is addressed to the President alone, and not to any other department or officer of the Government. And this constitutes him, in a peculiar manner, and above all other officers, the guardian of the Constitution—its *preserver, protector*, and *defender*. . . .

As to the second question: . . .

If it be true, as I have assumed, that the President and the judiciary are co-ordinate departments of government, and the one not subordinate to the other, I do not understand how it can be legally possible for a judge to issue a command to the President to come before him *ad subjiciendum*—that is, to submit implicitly to his judgment—and, in case of disobedience, treat him as a criminal, in contempt of a superior authority, and punish him as for a misdemeanor, by fine and imprisonment. . . . [T]he whole subject-matter is political and not judicial. The insurrection itself is purely political. Its object is to destroy the political government of this nation and to establish another political government upon its ruins. And the President, as the chief civil magistrate of the nation, and the most active department of the Government, is eminently and exclusively political, in all his principal functions. As the political chief of the nation, the Constitution charges him with its preservation, protection, and defence, and requires him to take care that the laws be faithfully executed. And in that character, and by the aid of the acts of Congress of 1795 and 1807, he wages open war against armed rebellion, and arrests and holds in safe custody those whom, in the exercise of his political discretion, he believes to be friends of, and accomplices in, the armed insurrection, which it is his especial political duty to suppress. He has no judicial powers. And the judiciary department has no political powers, and claims none, and therefore (as well as for other reasons already assigned) no court or judge can take cognizance of the political acts of the President, or undertake to revise and reverse his political decisions.

The jurisdiction exercised under the writ of *habeas corpus* is in the nature of an appeal, for as far as concerns the right of the prisoner, the whole object of the process is to re-examine and reverse or affirm the acts of the person who imprisoned him. And I think it will hardly be seriously affirmed, that a judge, at chambers, can entertain an appeal, in any form, from a decision of the President of the United States—and especially in a case purely political.

. . . [The President's power to suspend the writ of *habeas corpus*] is no part of his ordinary duty in time of peace; it is temporary and exceptional, and was intended only to meet a pressing emergency, when the judiciary is found to be too weak to insure the public safety. . . . [S]hall it be said that when he has fought and captured the insurgent army, and has seized their secret spies and emissaries, he is bound to bring their bodies before any judge who may send him a writ of *habeas corpus*, "to do, submit to, and receive whatever the said judge shall consider in that behalf?

I deny that he is under any obligation to obey such a writ, issued under such circumstances. And in making this denial, I do but follow the highest judicial authority of the nation. *[Bates then discussed* Luther v. Borden, *48 U.S. (7 How.) 1 (1849), p. 431, and argued that it required the courts to defer to the president's determination of wartime emergency.—Editors]* "If (says that learned Court) the judicial power extends so far, the guarantee contained in the Constitution of the United States (meaning, of course, protection against insurrection) is a guarantee of anarchy and not of order." . . .

The power to do these things is in the hand of the President, placed there by the Constitution and the statute law, as a sacred trust, to be used by him, in his best discretion, in the performance of his great first duty—to preserve, protect, and defend the Constitution. And for any breach of that trust he is responsible before the high court of impeachment, and before no other human tribunal. . . .

NOTES

1. First, consider the merits. Does the president have the power to suspend habeas? Taney's arguments were (in brief): that the location of the Suspension Clause in Article I, Section 9 clearly signaled that it was a limitation on Congress's legislative power, and that by implication the power to suspend the writ was a purely *legislative* power (presumably flowing from the Necessary and Proper Clause of Article I, Section 8); and further, that the historical origin of the writ of habeas corpus and its function in English law had traditionally been to *limit executive power*—the power of the king arbitrarily to restrict personal liberty by holding prisoners (and that it would therefore be absurd to permit the executive to suspend the writ). Lincoln's arguments were (in brief): that the Suspension Clause as written does not specify who is to exercise the power; that the power was plainly designed for emergency situations, implying the executive branch could exercise it; that writ suspension was in the circumstances necessary to the executive's duty to execute the laws; and that logically only the president could exercise such a power when Congress was out of session. Who is right? Is it clear, or is it fairly debatable?

2. In thinking about whether the president must obey judicial judgments, does it matter if the question on the merits is fairly debatable? Would it matter if the judiciary's judgment in a case was flagrantly and horribly wrong? Would the president have to accept such a judgment? What if, for example, the Supreme Court ordered Lincoln to cease fighting the Civil War entirely, on the (not-entirely-implausible) premise that the war power does not permit the national government to use military force against the states? What if the Supreme Court ordered Lincoln to leave the White House, turn Maryland over to secessionists, and relocate the national government north of the Mason-Dixon line? Or, to choose another pointed example (again not entirely implausible as a historical matter), what if the Supreme Court, later in the Civil War, had declared the Emancipation Proclamation unconstitutional? Would Lincoln have been obliged to return the newly freed slaves? Reconsider *Merryman* itself: Does the chief justice of the United States have the power to release enemy soldiers and saboteurs? What is the president supposed to do if he suspects the Supreme Court is acting as a "fifth column"?

3. Should Congress have a role here? Could the House of Representatives have decided that President Lincoln committed an impeachable offense, in violation of the Take Care Clause? Or could they have decided that Chief Justice Taney had committed an impeachable offense by misinterpreting the Constitution and aiding the enemy? If not, why not?

4. Bottom line: In a showdown between Chief Justice Taney and President Lincoln over *authority* to interpret the Constitution, who is right? Is the president's sole power to execute the laws as expounded by the judiciary and in subordination to judicial authority (as Taney asserts)? Or does the Constitution's separation of powers mean that the president possesses a co-equal power or duty of constitutional interpretation with the judiciary (as Lincoln asserts, by implication, and Attorney General Bates asserts explicitly)?

5.   Recall that in his defense of judicial review in *The Federalist No. 78*, Alexander Hamilton argued that the judicial branch was the "least dangerous" to liberty because it has "neither FORCE not WILL, but merely judgment; *and must ultimately depend upon the aid of the executive arm even for the efficacy of its judgments*" (emphasis added). Does that imply, at least in extreme situations, that the president's power to execute (or not execute) judicial judgments was consciously thought a check on the judiciary? Is that an implied limitation on the power of judicial review? By contrast, what does Attorney General Bates mean by the judicial power of "calling out the power of the country to enforce its decrees." Is he disagreeing with Hamilton, or agreeing?

6.   Consider the dangers and implications of the Lincoln-Bates position: Would a power of the president to decline, on constitutional grounds, to enforce the final judgments of the federal judiciary render the federal courts powerless? Would it imply that every judicial decision was a mere advisory opinion, for the president to decide at leisure whether to obey? Wouldn't that pose an equally severe separation-of-powers problem? Alternatively, does the argument of *Cooper* and *Merryman* imply that the president and Congress can be forced to take actions that they think are violations of the Constitution? How could that be squared with the Supremacy Clause, Oath Clause, and Take Care Clause?

7.   Is there an intermediate position? Attorney General Bates's decision focuses on several reasons Chief Justice Taney might not have had *jurisdiction* to hear *Merryman*. If so, does lack of jurisdiction provide a more limited, or more principled, basis for disobeying a court order? Or is jurisdiction just one more place for a fight about the merits?

8.   Consider the contrasting views of two of your casebook's co-authors on the question of whether judicial judgments in specific cases are binding on the president in the exercise of the executive power. In *The* Merryman *Power and the Dilemma of Autonomous Executive Branch Interpretation*, 15 Cardozo L. Rev. 81 (1993), Professor Paulsen advanced the proposition that there is "no defensible middle ground" between the position of complete judicial supremacy (in all its implications) and the position of complete executive coordinacy (in all its implications, including what he called the "*Merryman* Power" of non-execution of judicial decrees). If the president must carry out judicial judgments no matter what, this could eviscerate presidential interpretive autonomy and erase the fundamental premise of separation of powers. All areas of supposed presidential interpretive autonomy—like President Jefferson's pardons of persons convicted under the Alien and Sedition Acts—would exist merely as a matter of grace. On the other hand, if the president rightfully may grant pardons or veto laws on the basis of independently exercised constitutional judgment, there is no basis (Paulsen argues) for distinguishing these presidential powers from any of the president's other powers, including law-execution. The inevitable slippery slope leads to the right and power of the president not to execute judicial decrees that the president concludes are contrary to the Constitution and existing laws. In *The Most Dangerous Branch: Executive Power to Say What the Law Is*, 83 Geo. L. J. 217 (1994), Professor Paulsen adopts the complete-presidential-autonomy horn of the dilemma. He argues that this follows from the logic of constitutional supremacy and separation of powers, and is indeed supported by the reasoning of *Marbury*.

Professor Baude takes a contrary view. In *The Judgment Power*, 96 Geo. L. J. 1807 (2008), he argues that the original understanding of the judicial power distinguished the specific *judgments* of courts over the parties from broader notions of judicial supremacy. Thus even if the executive is largely free to ignore the judiciary's views in most contexts, he must obey judicial judgments, *as long as the judiciary properly possessed jurisdiction*.

Baude argues that this is the best explanation of Bates's opinion in *Merryman*, and that Alexander Hamilton's statement in *Federalist No. 78* can be read consistently with this narrower view:

> Under an anti-judgment-supremacy theory, the President can ignore any judgment he thinks is incorrect, modified by whatever degree of deference he thinks appropriate. Under my theory, the President can ignore any judgment that exceeds the power and jurisdiction of the issuing court. Both theories are consistent with Hamilton's comment, and he gave no reason to prefer the former interpretation to the latter. The more plausible reading, in light of the other evidence, is that the President would fight against judicial oppression by ignoring judgments when the Judiciary lacked power to issue them, that is, lacked jurisdiction.

Id. at 1834.

Professor Paulsen argues in a recent article that the Baude concession of the power of the president to refuse to execute judgments rendered without jurisdiction "gives away the game." Michael Stokes Paulsen, *Checking the Court,* 10 N.Y.U. J. Law & Liberty 18, 110 (2016). Paulsen concedes the "enormous intuitive appeal" of the Baude position, *id.* at 107, but argues that it ultimately collapses into either judicial supremacy or the full-blown "*Merryman* Power" claimed by Lincoln and Bates:

> Here's the problem: *Who decides whether a particular judgment falls within the scope of judicial "jurisdiction"?* The courts? If so, we are back to pure, unadulterated judicial supremacy. . . . The executive? If so, we are back to the power of executive review of judgments, at least as to questions of "jurisdiction." [Quoting his earlier *Merryman Power* article, Paulsen then notes that this "only relocates the problem."]
>
> And while we're at it: Who decides the proper scope of the judiciary's "judgment"? Is that a matter of "jurisdiction"—the scope of a court's legitimate authority—or is it something else? Who decides *that*? If the executive must enforce a *judgment* rendered by a court with jurisdiction, but is otherwise not bound in its actions by judicial opinions, what is to keep a court from deciding, and making part of its "judgment," that the executive must enforce the judiciary's understanding of the law generally . . . ?

Id. at 112 (citations and footnotes omitted). Paulsen concludes:

> One is forced, eventually, down one slippery slope or another. The duty to enforce judicial "judgments" supplies no ledge or even much of a toehold against the inevitable avalanche of logic. The "judgment supremacy" position, with the slightest push, slides straightaway into complete judicial supremacy. Or, if it doesn't, the only principled conclusion is that the President retains the ultimate power to check the Court by refusing to carry into execution judicial judgments that he in good faith determines to be *beyond the scope of the judiciary's legitimate constitutional authority*—exactly as Hamilton appears to have said. . . .

Id. at 112–113.

Is the "slippery slope" described by Paulsen really inevitable, or is this just an unlikely doomsday scenario? Are history and tradition instructive here? More generally, what does Paulsen's slippery slope assume about the good faith of the judiciary and the executive? Does it assume that the executive branch will dishonestly recharacterize their views in terms of "jurisdiction"? Or does it assume that "jurisdiction" is an empty concept?

Is the slippery slope something that Paulsen fears—or hopes for? More generally, Paulsen complains that Baude's view only "relocates the problem," but isn't all of constitutional law about relocating problems?

Who is right in this duel, Baude or Paulsen? (Neither?) Swords or pistols?

[Assignment 20]

C. ADJUDICATION OF GENUINE DISPUTES: "CASES [AND] CONTROVERSIES"

The first paragraph of Article III, Section 2 says that the judicial power granted by Section 1's Vesting Clause "shall extend to" nine categories of "Cases" or "Controversies." What is a case or a controversy for purposes of this language? Over time the Court has tried to answer this question by articulating two related rules: First, a prohibition on the issuance of "advisory opinions," and later, the doctrine of "standing" to sue.

As a matter of background, Madison's notes taken at the Philadelphia Convention show that proposals were made to give the courts power to issue advisory opinions and they were rejected. Also rejected was a proposal to vest the veto power jointly in the president and the justices in what was called a Council of Revision. The first dispute in this assignment, "The Correspondence of the Justices," demonstrates the consequences of these decisions. As you will see, the justices of the Supreme Court concluded in the early 1790s that they did not have the power to issue advisory opinions. Rather, Article III was thought to require an actual dispute between adverse litigants before the judicial power could be invoked. This requirement and its connection to the justifications for judicial review is then discussed in a passage from Alexis de Tocqueville.

Over time, these constitutional requirements have developed into the modern doctrine about who has standing to sue. While there are many complications to this doctrine, at a bare minimum standing requires an actual dispute, between adverse litigants, and a substantial likelihood that a federal court decision will have an effect in the real world.

Finally, there are two twentieth-century cases on standing doctrine. The first, *Ex parte Levitt*, 302 U.S. 633 (1937), is spare and simple. It is a one-paragraph Supreme Court opinion rejecting a lawyer's claim that the appointment of Justice Hugo Black to the Court should be declared a violation of the Emoluments Clause of the Constitution. The second, *United States v. Windsor*, 133 S.Ct. 2675 (2013), is more complex. It considers standing to challenge the Defense of Marriage Act in a case with an unusual posture: the executive branch argued that the statute was invalid, while part of the legislative branch attempted to defend it. *Windsor* therefore considers the interaction of standing with the separation of powers.

The Correspondence of the Justices

In the Neutrality Controversy of 1793, President Washington sought to keep the United States out of any involvement in the war between France and England. (The Neutrality Controversy is discussed at p. 270.) The controversy gave rise to another important separation of powers precedent concerning the judicial power under Article III of the Constitution. Secretary of State Thomas Jefferson wrote to Chief

Justice John Jay asking the Supreme Court twenty-nine legal questions arising out of America's relationship with France. The precedent was not the justices' answers to the questions, but rather the justices' *refusal to answer them* and their declaration that the judicial power was constitutionally limited to deciding cases and controversies between actual parties in litigation. Consider the following exchange of letters.

Thomas Jefferson, Letter to the Justices of the Supreme Court
July 18, 1793

The war which has taken place among the powers of Europe produces frequent transactions within our ports and limits, on which questions arise of considerable difficulty, and of greater importance to the peace of the US. These questions depend on their solution on the construction of our treaties, on the laws of nature and nations, and on the laws of the land; and are often presented under circumstances which do not give cognisance of them to the tribunals of the country. Yet their decision is so little analogous to the ordinary functions of the Executive as to occasion much embarrassment and difficulty to them. The president would be much relieved if he found himself free to refer to questions of this description to the opinions of the Judges of the Supreme Court of the US whose knowledge of the subject would secure us against errors dangerous to the peace of the US and their authority insure the respect of all parties. He has therefore asked the attendance of such of the judges as could be collected in time for the occasion, to know, in the first place, their opinion, Whether the public may, without propriety, be availed of their advice on these questions? and if they may, to present for their advice, the abstract questions which have already occurred, or may soon occur, from which they will themselves strike out such as any circumstances might, in their opinion, forbid them to pronounce on.

The Letter of the Supreme Court Justices to President Washington
Aug. 8, 1793

Sir: We have considered the previous question stated in a letter written by your direction to us by the Secretary of State in the 18th of last month, [regarding] the lines of separation drawn by the Constitution between the three departments of the government. These being in certain respects checks upon each other, and our being judges of a court in the last resort, are considerations which afford strong arguments against the propriety of our extra-judicially deciding the question alluded to, especially as the power given by the Constitution to the president, of calling on the heads of the departments for opinions, seems to have been *purposely* as well as expressly united to the *executive* departments.

We exceedingly regret every event that may cause embarrassment to your administration, but we derive consolation from the reflection that your judgment will discern what is right, and that your usual prudence, decision, and firmness will surmount every obstacle to the preservation of the rights, peace, and dignity of the United States.

We have the honour to be, with perfect respect, sir, your most obedient and most humble servants.

NOTES

1. Why did the justices refuse to answer the administration's request for legal advice? Do you think they were right to refuse? What types of constitutional argument did they invoke? The Correspondence of the Justices has become a paradigm case of what is forbidden by Article III. But what exactly is the lesson to take from it?

2. Under Article III, Section 2, the federal courts may exercise "the judicial Power of the United States" when a matter falls within one of nine enumerated kinds of "Cases" or "Controversies." Can the Correspondence of the Justices be understood to tell us something about the meaning of any of these terms—"judicial Power" and "Cases" and "Controversies"?

3. How meaningful is it to say that federal judges cannot render advisory opinions in light of the expansive dicta in some opinions? Indeed, is there a sense in which *all* opinions are advisory, since they go beyond the bare judgment that "A wins and B loses"?

4. Is it ironic that the justices were in effect offering an advisory opinion to the president on the inadvisability, or outright unconstitutionality, of the justices offering advisory opinions to the president? Or did the administration's request for legal advice from the justices essentially present a "case" that at least raised the question of the Court's jurisdiction to answer such requests? Is the rendering of this opinion, in the form of a letter, merely an illustration of the proposition that every court properly has jurisdiction to determine whether it has jurisdiction?

Alexis de Tocqueville on the American Judiciary

1 DEMOCRACY IN AMERICA 92 (3d American ed. trans. Henry Reeve, 1839)

I have thought it essential to devote a separate chapter to the judicial authorities of the United States, lest their great political importance should be lessened in the reader's eyes by a merely incidental mention of them. Confederations have existed in other countries beside America, and republics have not been established upon the shores of the New World alone; the representative system of government has been adopted in several States of Europe, but I am not aware that any nation of the globe has hitherto organized a judicial power on the principle now adopted by the Americans. The judicial organization of the United States is the institution which a stranger has the greatest difficulty in understanding. He hears the authority of a judge invoked in the political occurrences of every day, and he naturally concludes that in the United States the judges are important political functionaries; nevertheless, when he examines the nature of the tribunals, they offer nothing which is contrary to the usual habits and privileges of those bodies, and the magistrates seem to him to interfere in public affairs of chance, but by a chance which recurs every day.

When the Parliament of Paris remonstrated, or refused to enregister an edict, or when it summoned a functionary accused of malversation to its bar, its political influence as a judicial body was clearly visible; but nothing of the kind is to be seen in the United States. The Americans have retained all the ordinary characteristics of judicial authority, and have carefully restricted its action to the ordinary circle of its functions.

The first characteristic of judicial power in all nations is the duty of arbitration. But rights must be contested in order to warrant the interference of a tribunal; and an action must be brought to obtain the decision of a judge. As long, therefore, as the law is uncontested, the judicial authority is not called upon to discuss it, and it may exist without being perceived. When a judge in a given case attacks a law relating to that case, he extends the circle of his customary duties, without however stepping beyond it; since he is in some measure obliged to decide upon the law in order to decide the case. But if he pronounces upon a law without resting upon a case, he clearly steps beyond his sphere, and invades that of the legislative authority.

The second characteristic of judicial power is that it pronounces on special cases, and not upon general principles. If a judge in deciding a particular point destroys a general principle, by passing a judgment which tends to reject all the inferences from that principle, and consequently to annul it, he remains within the ordinary limits of his functions. But if he directly attacks a general principle without having a particular case in view, he leaves the circle in which all nations have agreed to confine his authority, he assumes a more important, and perhaps a more useful, influence than that of the magistrate, but he ceases to be a representative of the judicial power.

The third characteristic of the judicial power is its inability to act unless it is appealed to, or until it has taken cognizance of an affair. This characteristic is less general than the other two; but, notwithstanding the exceptions, I think it may be regarded as essential. The judicial power is by its nature devoid of action; it must be put in motion in order to produce a result. When it is called upon to repress a crime, it punishes the criminal; when a wrong is to be redressed, it is ready to redress it; when an act requires interpretation, it is prepared to interpret it; but it does not pursue criminals, hunt out wrongs, or examine into evidence of its own accord. A judicial functionary who should open proceedings, and usurp the censorship of the laws, would in some measure do violence to the passive nature of his authority.

The Americans have retained these three distinguishing characteristics of the judicial power; an American judge can only pronounce a decision when litigation has arisen, he is only conversant with special cases, and he cannot act until the cause has been duly brought before the court. His position is therefore perfectly similar to that of the magistrate of other nations; and he is nevertheless invested with immense political power. If the sphere of his authority and his means of action are the same as those of other judges, it may be asked whence he derives a power which they do not possess. The cause of this difference lies in the simple fact that the Americans have acknowledged the right of the judges to found their decisions on the constitution rather than on the laws. In other words, they have left them at liberty not to apply such laws as may appear to them to be unconstitutional.

I am aware that a similar right has been claimed—but claimed in vain—by courts of justice in other countries; but in America it is recognized by all authorities; and not a party, nor so much as an individual, is found to contest it. This fact can only be explained by the principles of the American constitution. In France the constitution is (or at least is supposed to be) immutable; and the received theory is that no power has the right of changing any part of it. In England the Parliament has an acknowledged right to modify the constitution; as, therefore, the constitution may undergo perpetual changes, it does not in reality exist; the Parliament is at once a legislative and a constituent assembly. The political theories of America are more simple and more rational. An American constitution is not supposed to be immutable as in France, nor is it susceptible of modification by the ordinary powers of society as in England. It constitutes a detached whole, which, as it represents the determination of the whole people, is no less binding on the legislator than on the private citizen, but which may be altered by the will of the people in predetermined cases, according to established rules. In America the constitution may therefore vary, but as long as it exists it is the origin of all authority, and the sole vehicle of the predominating force. . . .

In the United States the constitution governs the legislator as much as the private citizen; as it is the first of laws it cannot be modified by a law, and it is therefore just that the tribunals should obey the constitution in preference to any law. This condition is essential to the power of the judicature, for to select that legal obligation by which he is most strictly bound is the natural right of every magistrate. . . .

Whenever a law which the judge holds to be unconstitutional is argued in a tribunal of the United States he may refuse to admit it as a rule; this power is the only one which is peculiar to the American magistrate, but it gives rise to immense political influence. Few laws can escape the searching analysis of the judicial power for any length of time, for there are few which are not prejudicial to some private interest or other, and none which may not be brought before a court of justice by the choice of parties, or by the necessity of the case. But from the time that a judge has refused to apply any given law in a case, that law loses a portion of its moral cogency. The persons to whose interests it is prejudicial learn that means exist of evading its authority, and similar suits are multiplied, until it becomes powerless. One of two alternatives must then be resorted to: the people must alter the constitution, or the legislature must repeal the law. The political power which the Americans have entrusted to their courts of justice is therefore immense, but the evils of this power are considerably diminished by the obligation which has been imposed of attacking the laws through the courts of justice alone. If the judge had been empowered to contest the laws on the ground of theoretical generalities, if he had been enabled to open an attack or to pass a censure on the legislator, he would have played a prominent part in the political sphere; and as the champion or the antagonist of a party, he would have arrayed the hostile passions of the nation in the conflict. But when a judge contests a law applied to some particular case in an obscure proceeding, the importance of his attack is concealed from the public gaze, his decision bears upon the interest of an individual, and if the law is slighted it is only collaterally. Moreover, although it is censured, it is not abolished; its moral force may be diminished, but its cogency is by no means suspended, and its final destruction can only be accomplished by the reiterated attacks of judicial functionaries. It will readily be understood that by connecting the censorship of the laws with the private interests of members of the community, and by intimately uniting the prosecution of the law with the prosecution of an individual, legislation is protected from wanton assailants, and from the daily aggressions of party spirit. The errors of the legislator are exposed whenever their evil consequences are most felt, and it is always a positive and appreciable fact which serves as the basis of a prosecution.

I am inclined to believe this practice of the American courts to be at once the most favorable to liberty as well as to public order. . . . [T]he American judge is brought into the political arena independently of his own will. He only judges the law because he is obliged to judge a case. The political question which he is called upon to resolve is connected with the interest of the suitors, and he cannot refuse to decide it without abdicating the duties of his post. He performs his functions as a citizen by fulfilling the precise duties which belong to his profession as a magistrate. It is true that upon this system the judicial censorship which is exercised by the courts of justice over the legislation cannot extend to all laws indiscriminately, inasmuch as some of them can never give rise to that exact species of contestation which is termed a lawsuit; and even when such a contestation is possible, it may happen that no one cares to bring it before a court of justice. The Americans have often felt this disadvantage, but they have left the remedy incomplete, lest they should give it an efficacy which might in some cases prove dangerous. Within these limits the power vested in the American courts of justice of pronouncing a statute to be unconstitutional forms one of the most powerful barriers which has ever been devised against the tyranny of political assemblies. . . .

Ex parte Levitt

302 U.S. 633 (1937)

■ PER CURIAM.

[This was an original motion in the Supreme Court brought by Albert Levitt for leave to file a petition for an order requiring Mr. Justice Black to show cause why he should be permitted to serve as a justice of the Court.—Editors]

The grounds of this motion are that the appointment of Mr. Justice Black by the President and the confirmation thereof by the Senate of the United States were null and void by reason of his ineligibility under article 1, § 6, cl. 2, of the Constitution of the United States, and because there was no vacancy for which the appointment could lawfully be made. The motion papers disclose no interest upon the part of the petitioner other than that of a citizen and a member of the bar of this Court. That is insufficient. It is an established principle that to entitle a private individual to invoke the judicial power to determine the validity of executive or legislative action he must show that he has sustained, or is immediately in danger of sustaining, a direct injury as the result of that action and it is not sufficient that he has merely a general interest common to all members of the public. . . . *Fairchild v. Hughes*, 258 U.S. 126 (1922); *Massachusetts v. Mellon*, 262 U.S. 447, 488 (1923).

NOTES

1.   First consider the merits of the constitutional challenge avoided by the Court in *Ex parte Levitt*. Article I, Section 6 of the Constitution says: "No Senator or Representative shall, during the Time for which he was elected, be appointed to any civil Office under the Authority of the United States, which shall have been created, or the Emoluments whereof shall have been increased during such time." (Noah Webster's 1828 dictionary defines "Emolument" as "The profit arising from office or employment. . . .")

On March 1, 1937, while Hugo Black was a U.S. senator for Alabama, Congress passed a statute which allowed Supreme Court justices to "retir[e] from active service on the bench" and continue to receive their full salary. 50 Stat. 24 (1937). While the statute did not *directly* increase the salary of the justices, it did so indirectly by giving them the option of a lucrative pension if they retired. Did Black's appointment to the Court obviously violate the Emoluments Clause? Is there anything that could be said to defend it?

2.   The Court rejected Levitt's challenge without reaching this question, saying he had "no interest" aside from being a citizen and member of the Supreme Court bar. Why is that not enough? What would be enough?

Think back to some of the cases earlier in this chapter on appointment and removal. What "interest" did Senator Buckley have to challenge the appointment of the FEC commissioners? (See p. 186) What "interest" did Noel Canning have to challenge the appointment of the NLRB commissioners? (See p. 190) What "interest" did Olson have to challenge the appointment, and tenure, of Morrison? (See p. 249) Who would be in an equivalent position toward Justice Black? A Supreme Court litigant? A lawyer threatened with discipline by the Court?

3.   What do you think happened next? After *Ex parte Levitt*, Hugo Black sat on the Court for 34 years, but no one ever again litigated the Emoluments Clause question. Why not?

4.   Even if nobody with standing ever challenged Justice Black's appointment, does that mean that it was lawful, or just that it was unchallenged? When he became a justice, Hugo Black took an oath to uphold the Constitution: shouldn't he have been required to immediately consider, on his own, the constitutionality of his own appointment? See generally Richard M. Re, *Promising the Constitution*, 110 Nw. U. L. Rev. 299 (2016). For that matter, shouldn't the president have considered the constitutional problem before appointing Justice Black?

5.   *Fairchild v. Hughes,* 258 U.S. 126 (1922), cited by the Court in *Ex parte Levitt*, was a suit by "taxpayers and members of the American Constitutional League," a private group interested in constitutional issues, alleging that the Nineteenth Amendment, granting women the right to vote, was not properly ratified and seeking to enjoin the secretary of state from enforcing it. The group's members claimed an interest in not having "the effectiveness of their votes" diminished and in the government not incurring election expenses. The Court said that the group lacked standing: "Plaintiff has only the right, possessed by every citizen, to require that the government be administered according to law and that the public moneys be not wasted. Obviously this general right does not entitle a private citizen to institute in the federal courts a suit to secure by indirection a determination whether a statute, if passed, or a constitutional amendment, about to be adopted, will be valid." Do you agree?

6.   *Massachusetts v. Mellon,* 262 U.S. 447 (1923), also cited by the Court, was a suit challenging a federal program as being beyond the powers of the national government to enact and thus in violation of the Tenth Amendment. Who should have standing to raise a judicial challenge on such grounds? Taxpayers? Everyone? No one?

7.   In the decades since *Levitt*, the doctrine of standing has hardened into a three-part test. To satisfy Article III standing, plaintiffs must show or allege: First, that they have suffered or will suffer a concrete injury; second, that the injury is fairly traceable to the defendant; and third, that the injury is redressable by a favorable ruling. For a bit of a sense of what these three parts mean, consider two brief examples.

In *Clapper v. Amnesty International*, 133 S.Ct. 1128 (2013), a group of attorneys and organizations challenged a provision of the Foreign Intelligence Surveillance Act that authorized warrantless wiretapping of some overseas communications. They claimed that the surveillance violated their rights under the Fourth Amendment, compromised their ability to communicate with clients and sources overseas, and forced them to undertake costly measures to protect confidentiality. In a 5–4 decision, the Supreme

Court held the plaintiffs lacked standing. It concluded that plaintiffs had failed to satisfy the "injury" part of the test, because any threatened injury was too speculative. It was not clear whose communications were targeted by the government or under what circumstances. It also concluded that any injury was not "fairly traceable" to the legal provision that the plaintiffs challenged, because it was not clear whether the government would rely on that statute or some other legal authority to conduct the surveillance.

In *Steel Co. v. Citizens for a Better Environment*, 523 U.S. 83 (1998), an environmental protection organization sought an injunction against a manufacturing company because of that company's *past* violations of federal law. The Court held that there was no standing because the organization failed to satisfy the "redressability" prong. It alleged "only *past* infractions . . . and not a continuing violation or the likelihood of a future violation," so the requested "injunctive relief [would] not redress its injury."

It appears that these three factors—injury, traceability, and redressability—must be satisfied in every single federal case. In most cases these inquiries are relatively straightforward, but we will next consider a trickier case that also raises broader questions about the separation of powers.

United States v. Windsor

133 S.Ct. 2675 (2013)

■ JUSTICE KENNEDY delivered the opinion of the Court.

Two women then resident in New York were married in a lawful ceremony in Ontario, Canada, in 2007. Edith Windsor and Thea Spyer returned to their home in New York City. When Spyer died in 2009, she left her entire estate to Windsor. Windsor sought to claim the estate tax exemption for surviving spouses. She was barred from doing so, however, by a federal law, the Defense of Marriage Act [DOMA], which excludes a same-sex partner from the definition of "spouse" as that term is used in federal statutes. Windsor paid the taxes but filed suit to challenge the constitutionality of this provision. The United States District Court and the Court of Appeals ruled that this portion of the statute is unconstitutional and ordered the United States to pay Windsor a refund. This Court granted certiorari and now affirms the judgment in Windsor's favor.

I

. . . Spyer died in February 2009, and left her entire estate to Windsor. Because DOMA denies federal recognition to same-sex spouses, Windsor did not qualify for the marital exemption from the federal estate tax, which excludes from taxation "any interest in property which passes or has passed from the decedent to his surviving spouse." 26 U.S.C. § 2056(a). Windsor paid $363,053 in estate taxes and sought a refund. The Internal Revenue Service denied the refund, concluding that, under DOMA, Windsor was not a "surviving spouse." Windsor commenced this refund suit in the United States District Court for the Southern District of New York. She contended that DOMA violates the guarantee of equal protection, as applied to the Federal Government through the Fifth Amendment.

While the tax refund suit was pending, the Attorney General of the United States notified the Speaker of the House of Representatives that the Department of Justice would no longer defend the constitutionality of DOMA's § 3. Noting that "the Department has previously defended DOMA against . . . challenges involving legally married same-sex couples," the Attorney General informed Congress that "the

President has concluded that given a number of factors, including a documented history of discrimination, classifications based on sexual orientation should be subject to a heightened standard of scrutiny." The Department of Justice has submitted many § 530D letters over the years refusing to defend laws it deems unconstitutional, when, for instance, a federal court has rejected the Government's defense of a statute and has issued a judgment against it. This case is unusual, however, because the § 530D letter was not preceded by an adverse judgment. The letter instead reflected the Executive's own conclusion, relying on a definition still being debated and considered in the courts, that heightened equal protection scrutiny should apply to laws that classify on the basis of sexual orientation.

Although "the President . . . instructed the Department not to defend the statute in *Windsor*," he also decided "that Section 3 will continue to be enforced by the Executive Branch" and that the United States had an "interest in providing Congress a full and fair opportunity to participate in the litigation of those cases." The stated rationale for this dual-track procedure (determination of unconstitutionality coupled with ongoing enforcement) was to "recogniz[e] the judiciary as the final arbiter of the constitutional claims raised."

In response to the notice from the Attorney General, the Bipartisan Legal Advisory Group (BLAG) of the House of Representatives voted to intervene in the litigation to defend the constitutionality of § 3 of DOMA. . . .

II

It is appropriate to begin by addressing whether either the Government or BLAG, or both of them, were entitled to appeal to the Court of Appeals and later to seek certiorari and appear as parties here.

There is no dispute that when this case was in the District Court it presented a concrete disagreement between opposing parties, a dispute suitable for judicial resolution. "[A] taxpayer has standing to challenge the collection of a specific tax assessment as unconstitutional; being forced to pay such a tax causes a real and immediate economic injury to the individual taxpayer." *Hein v. Freedom From Religion Foundation, Inc.*, 551 U.S. 587, 599 (2007) (plurality opinion). Windsor suffered a redressable injury when she was required to pay estate taxes from which, in her view, she was exempt but for the alleged invalidity of § 3 of DOMA.

The decision of the Executive not to defend the constitutionality of § 3 in court while continuing to deny refunds and to assess deficiencies does introduce a complication. . . .

[The position of the Court-appointed *amicus* arguing that there was no standing] . . . is that, given the Government's concession that § 3 is unconstitutional, once the District Court ordered the refund the case should have ended; and the *amicus* argues the Court of Appeals should have dismissed the appeal. The *amicus* submits that once the President agreed with Windsor's legal position and the District Court issued its judgment, the parties were no longer adverse. . . .

This position, however, elides the distinction between two principles: the jurisdictional requirements of Article III and the prudential limits on its exercise. The latter are "essentially matters of judicial self-governance." The Court has kept these two strands separate: "Article III standing, which enforces the Constitution's case-or-controversy requirement; and prudential standing, which embodies judicially self-imposed limits on the exercise of federal jurisdiction." *Elk Grove Unified School Dist. v. Newdow*, 542 U.S. 1–12 (2004).

The requirements of Article III standing are familiar:

"First, the plaintiff must have suffered an 'injury in fact'—an invasion of a legally protected interest which is (a) concrete and particularized, and (b) 'actual or imminent, not "conjectural or hypothetical." ' Second, there must be a causal connection between the injury and the conduct complained of— the injury has to be 'fairly . . . trace[able] to the challenged action of the defendant, and not . . . th[e] result [of] the independent action of some third party not before the court.' Third, it must be 'likely,' as opposed to merely 'speculative,' that the injury will be 'redressed by a favorable decision.' " *Lujan v. Defenders of Wildlife*, 504 U.S. 555, 560–561 (1992).

Rules of prudential standing, by contrast, are more flexible "rule[s] . . . of federal appellate practice," *Deposit Guaranty Nat. Bank v. Roper*, 445 U.S. 326, 333 (1980), designed to protect the courts from "decid[ing] abstract questions of wide public significance even [when] other governmental institutions may be more competent to address the questions and even though judicial intervention may be unnecessary to protect individual rights." *Warth v. Seldin*, 422 U.S. 490, 500 (1975).

In this case the United States retains a stake sufficient to support Article III jurisdiction on appeal and in proceedings before this Court. The judgment in question orders the United States to pay Windsor the refund she seeks. An order directing the Treasury to pay money is "a real and immediate economic injury," *Hein*, at 599, indeed as real and immediate as an order directing an individual to pay a tax. That the Executive may welcome this order to pay the refund if it is accompanied by the constitutional ruling it wants does not eliminate the injury to the national Treasury if payment is made, or to the taxpayer if it is not. . . .

While these principles suffice to show that this case presents a justiciable controversy under Article III, the prudential problems inherent in the Executive's unusual position require some further discussion. The Executive's agreement with Windsor's legal argument raises the risk that instead of a "real, earnest and vital controversy," the Court faces a "friendly, non-adversary, proceeding . . . [in which] a party beaten in the legislature [seeks to] transfer to the courts an inquiry as to the constitutionality of the legislative act." *Ashwander v. TVA*, 297 U.S. 288, 346 (1936) (Brandeis, J., concurring). Even when Article III permits the exercise of federal jurisdiction, prudential considerations demand that the Court insist upon "that concrete adverseness which sharpens the presentation of issues upon which the court so largely depends for illumination of difficult constitutional questions." *Baker v. Carr*, 369 U.S. 186, 204 (1962).

There are, of course, reasons to hear a case and issue a ruling even when one party is reluctant to prevail in its position. Unlike Article III requirements—which must be satisfied by the parties before judicial consideration is appropriate—the relevant prudential factors that counsel against hearing this case are subject to "countervailing considerations [that] may outweigh the concerns underlying the usual reluctance to exert judicial power." One consideration is the extent to which adversarial presentation of the issues is assured by the participation of *amici curiae* prepared to defend with vigor the constitutionality of the legislative act. . . .

In the case now before the Court the attorneys for BLAG present a substantial argument for the constitutionality of § 3 of DOMA. BLAG's sharp adversarial presentation of the issues satisfies the prudential concerns that otherwise might counsel against hearing an appeal from a decision with which the principal parties agree. Were this Court to hold that prudential rules require it to dismiss the case, and, in consequence, that the Court of Appeals erred in failing to dismiss it as well, extensive litigation would ensue. The district courts in 94 districts throughout the Nation would be without precedential guidance not only in tax refund suits but also in cases involving the whole of DOMA's sweep involving over 1,000 federal statutes and a myriad of federal regulations. . . . For these reasons, the prudential and Article III requirements are met here; and, as a consequence, the Court need not decide whether BLAG would have standing to challenge the District Court's ruling and its affirmance in the Court of Appeals on BLAG's own authority.

The Court's conclusion that this petition may be heard on the merits does not imply that no difficulties would ensue if this were a common practice in ordinary cases. The Executive's failure to defend the constitutionality of an Act of Congress based on a constitutional theory not yet established in judicial decisions has created a procedural dilemma. On the one hand, as noted, the Government's agreement with Windsor raises questions about the propriety of entertaining a suit in which it seeks affirmance of an order invalidating a federal law and ordering the United States to pay money. On the other hand, if the Executive's agreement with a plaintiff that a law is unconstitutional is enough to preclude judicial review, then the Supreme Court's primary role in determining the constitutionality of a law that has inflicted real injury on a plaintiff who has brought a justiciable legal claim would become only secondary to the President's. This would undermine the clear dictate of the separation-of-powers principle that "when an Act of Congress is alleged to conflict with the Constitution, '[i]t is emphatically the province and duty of the judicial department to say what the law is.'" *Zivotofsky v. Clinton*, 132 S.Ct. 1421, 1427–1428 (2012) (quoting *Marbury v. Madison*, 5 U.S. (1 Cranch) 137, 177 (1803)). Similarly, with respect to the legislative power, when Congress has passed a statute and a President has signed it, it poses grave challenges to the separation of powers for the Executive at a particular moment to be able to nullify Congress' enactment solely on its own initiative and without any determination from the Court.

The Court's jurisdictional holding, it must be underscored, does not mean the arguments for dismissing this dispute on prudential grounds lack substance. Yet the difficulty the Executive faces should be acknowledged. When the Executive makes a principled determination that a statute is unconstitutional, it faces a difficult choice. Still, there is no suggestion here that it is appropriate for the Executive as a matter of course to challenge statutes in the judicial forum rather than making the case to Congress for their amendment or repeal. The integrity of the political process would be at risk if difficult constitutional issues were simply referred to the Court as a routine exercise. But this case is not routine. And the capable defense of the law by BLAG ensures that these prudential issues do not cloud the merits question, which is one of immediate importance to the Federal Government and to hundreds of thousands of persons. These circumstances support the Court's decision to proceed to the merits. . . .

[In the remainder of its opinion, the Court struck down Section 3 of the Defense of Marriage Act on grounds that were a blend of federalism, individual rights, and equality. See p. 1632.—Editors]

■ JUSTICE SCALIA, with whom JUSTICE THOMAS joins, and with whom THE CHIEF JUSTICE joins as to Part I, dissenting.

This case is about power in several respects. It is about the power of our people to govern themselves, and the power of this Court to pronounce the law. Today's opinion aggrandizes the latter, with the predictable consequence of diminishing the former. We have no power to decide this case. And even if we did, we have no power under the Constitution to invalidate this democratically adopted legislation. The Court's errors on both points spring forth from the same diseased root: an exalted conception of the role of this institution in America.

I–A

The Court is eager—*hungry*—to tell everyone its view of the legal question at the heart of this case. Standing in the way is an obstacle, a technicality of little interest to anyone but the people of We the People, who created it as a barrier against judges' intrusion into their lives. They gave judges, in Article III, only the "judicial Power," a power to decide not abstract questions but real, concrete "Cases" and "Controversies." Yet the plaintiff and the Government agree entirely on what should happen in this lawsuit. They agree that the court below got it right; and they agreed in the court below that the court below that one got it right as well. What, then, are we *doing* here?

The answer lies at the heart of the jurisdictional portion of today's opinion, where a single sentence lays bare the majority's vision of our role. The Court says that we have the power to decide this case because if we did not, then our "primary role in determining the constitutionality of a law" (at least one that "has inflicted real injury on a plaintiff") would "become only secondary to the President's." But wait, the reader wonders—Windsor won below, and so *cured* her injury, and the President was glad to see it. True, says the majority, but judicial review must march on regardless, lest we "undermine the clear dictate of the separation-of-powers principle that when an Act of Congress is alleged to conflict with the Constitution, it is emphatically the province and duty of the judicial department to say what the law is."

That is jaw-dropping. It is an assertion of judicial supremacy over the people's Representatives in Congress and the Executive. It envisions a Supreme Court standing (or rather enthroned) at the apex of government, empowered to decide all constitutional questions, always and everywhere "primary" in its role.

This image of the Court would have been unrecognizable to those who wrote and ratified our national charter. They knew well the dangers of "primary" power, and so created branches of government that would be "perfectly co-ordinate by the terms of their common commission," none of which branches could "pretend to an exclusive or superior right of settling the boundaries between their respective powers." The Federalist, No. 49 (J. Madison). The people did this to protect themselves. They did it to guard their right to self-rule against the black-robed supremacy that today's majority finds so attractive. So it was that Madison could confidently state, with no fear of contradiction, that there was nothing of "greater intrinsic value" or "stamped with the authority of more enlightened patrons of liberty" than a government of separate and coordinate powers. The Federalist, No. 47 (J. Madison).

For this reason we are quite forbidden to say what the law is whenever (as today's opinion asserts) "an Act of Congress is alleged to conflict with the Constitution." We can do so only when that allegation will determine the outcome of a lawsuit, and is contradicted by the other party. The "judicial Power" is not, as the majority believes, the power "to say what the law is," giving the Supreme Court the "primary role in determining the constitutionality of laws." The majority must have in mind one of the foreign constitutions that pronounces such primacy for its constitutional court and allows that primacy to be exercised in contexts other than a lawsuit. See, e.g., Basic Law for the Federal Republic of Germany, Art. 93. The judicial power as Americans have understood it (and their English ancestors before them) is the power to adjudicate, with conclusive effect, disputed government claims (civil or criminal) against private persons, and disputed claims by private persons against the government or other private persons. Sometimes (though not always) the parties before the court disagree not with regard to the facts of their case (or not *only* with regard to the facts) but with regard to the applicable law—in which event (and *only* in which event) it becomes the "province and duty of the judicial department to say what the law is."

In other words, declaring the compatibility of state or federal laws with the Constitution is not only not the "primary role" of this Court, it is not a separate, free-standing role *at all*. We perform that role incidentally—by accident, as it were—when that is necessary to resolve the dispute before us. Then, and only then, does it become " 'the province and duty of the judicial department to say what the law is.' " That is why, in 1793, we politely declined the Washington Administration's request to "say what the law is" on a particular treaty matter that was not the subject of a concrete legal controversy. 3 Correspondence and Public Papers of John Jay 486–489 (H. Johnston ed. 1893). And that is why, as our opinions have said, some questions of law will *never* be presented to this Court, because there will never be anyone with standing to bring a lawsuit. See *Schlesinger v. Reservists Comm. to Stop the War*, 418 U.S. 208, 227 (1974); *United States v. Richardson*, 418 U.S. 166, 179 (1974). As Justice Brandeis put it, we cannot "pass upon the constitutionality of legislation in a friendly, non-adversary, proceeding"; absent a "real, earnest and vital controversy between individuals," we have neither any work to do nor any power to do it. *Ashwander*, at 346 (concurring opinion). Our authority begins and ends with the need to adjudge the rights of an injured party who stands before us seeking redress. *Lujan*, at 560.

That is completely absent here. Windsor's injury was cured by the judgment in her favor. And while, in ordinary circumstances, the United States is injured by a directive to pay a tax refund, this suit is far from ordinary. Whatever injury the United States has suffered will surely not be redressed by the action that it, as a litigant, asks us to take. The final sentence of the Solicitor General's brief on the merits reads: "For the foregoing reasons, the judgment of the court of appeals *should be affirmed*." Brief for United States (merits) 54 (emphasis added). That will not cure the Government's injury, but carve it into stone. One could spend many fruitless afternoons ransacking our library for any other petitioner's brief seeking an affirmance of the judgment against it. What the petitioner United States asks us to do in the case before us is exactly what the respondent Windsor asks us to do: not to provide relief from the judgment below but to say that that judgment was correct. And the same was true in the Court of Appeals: Neither party sought to undo the judgment for Windsor, and so that court should have dismissed the appeal (just as we should dismiss) for lack of jurisdiction. Since both parties agreed with the judgment of the District Court for the Southern District of New York, the suit should have ended there. The further proceedings have been a contrivance, having no object in mind except to elevate a District Court judgment that has no precedential effect in other courts, to one that has precedential effect throughout the Second Circuit, and then (in this Court) precedential effect throughout the United States.

We have never before agreed to speak—to "say what the law is"—where there is no controversy before us. In the more than two centuries that this Court has existed as an institution, we have never suggested that we have the power to decide a question when every party agrees with both its nominal opponent *and the court below* on that question's answer. The United States reluctantly conceded that at oral argument. . . .[2]

The majority's discussion of the requirements of Article III bears no resemblance to our jurisprudence. It accuses the *amicus* (appointed to argue against our jurisdiction) of "elid[ing] the distinction between . . . the jurisdictional requirements of Article III and the prudential limits on its exercise." It then proceeds to call the requirement of adverseness a "prudential" aspect of standing. *Of standing.* That is incomprehensible. A plaintiff (or appellant) can have all the standing in the world—satisfying all three standing requirements of *Lujan* that the majority so carefully quotes—and yet no Article III controversy may be before the court. Article III requires not just a plaintiff (or appellant) who has standing to complain but *an opposing party* who denies the validity of the complaint. It is not the *amicus* that has done the eliding of distinctions, but the majority, calling the quite separate Article III requirement of adverseness between the parties an element (which it then pronounces a "prudential" element) of standing. The question here is not whether, as the majority puts it, "the United States retains a stake sufficient to support Article III jurisdiction," the question is whether there is any controversy (which requires *contradiction*) between the United States and Ms. Windsor. There is not.

I find it wryly amusing that the majority seeks to dismiss the requirement of party-adverseness as nothing more than a "prudential" aspect of the sole Article III requirement of standing. (Relegating a jurisdictional requirement to "prudential" status is a wondrous device, enabling courts to ignore the requirement whenever they believe it "prudent"—which is to say, a good idea.) Half a century ago, a Court similarly bent upon announcing its view regarding the constitutionality of a federal statute achieved that goal by effecting a remarkably similar *but completely opposite* distortion of the principles limiting our jurisdiction. The Court's notorious opinion in *Flast v. Cohen,* 392 U.S. 83–101 (1968), held that *standing* was merely an element (which it pronounced to be a "prudential" element) of the sole Article III requirement of *adverseness.* We have been living with the chaos created by that power-grabbing

---

[2]   . . . There is no justification for the Justice Department's abandoning the law in the present case. The majority opinion makes a point of scolding the President for his "failure to defend the constitutionality of an Act of Congress based on a constitutional theory not yet established in judicial decisions." But the rebuke is tongue-in-cheek, for the majority gladly gives the President what he wants. Contrary to all precedent, it decides this case (and even decides it the way the President wishes) *despite* his abandonment of the defense and the consequent absence of a case or controversy.

decision ever since, see *Hein*, as we will have to live with the chaos created by this one.

The authorities the majority cites fall miles short of supporting the counterintuitive notion that an Article III "controversy" can exist without disagreement between the parties. In *Deposit Guaranty Nat. Bank v. Roper*, 445 U.S. 326 (1980), the District Court had entered judgment in the individual plaintiff's favor based on the defendant bank's offer to pay the full amount claimed. The plaintiff, however, sought to appeal the District Court's denial of class certification under Federal Rule of Civil Procedure 23. There was a continuing dispute between the parties concerning the issue raised on appeal. . . . The "prudential" discretion to which [this case refers] was the discretion to *deny* an appeal even when a live controversy exists—not the discretion to *grant* one when it does not. The majority can cite no case in which this Court entertained an appeal in which both parties urged us to affirm the judgment below. And that is because the existence of a controversy is not a "prudential" requirement that we have invented, but an essential element of an Article III case or controversy. The majority's notion that a case between friendly parties can be entertained so long as "adversarial presentation of the issues is assured by the participation of *amici curiae* prepared to defend with vigor" the other side of the issue effects a breathtaking revolution in our Article III jurisprudence.

It may be argued that if what we say is true some Presidential determinations that statutes are unconstitutional will not be subject to our review. That is as it should be, when both the President and the plaintiff agree that the statute is unconstitutional. Where the Executive is enforcing an unconstitutional law, suit will of course lie; but if, in that suit, the Executive admits the unconstitutionality of the law, the litigation should end in an order or a consent decree enjoining enforcement. This suit saw the light of day only because the President enforced the Act (and thus gave Windsor standing to sue) even though he believed it unconstitutional. He could have equally chosen (more appropriately, some would say) neither to enforce nor to defend the statute he believed to be unconstitutional, see Presidential Authority to Decline to Execute Unconstitutional Statutes, 18 Op. Off. Legal Counsel 199 (Nov. 2, 1994)—in which event Windsor would not have been injured, the District Court could not have refereed this friendly scrimmage, and the Executive's determination of unconstitutionality would have escaped this Court's desire to blurt out its view of the law. The matter would have been left, as so many matters ought to be left, to a tug of war between the President and the Congress, which has innumerable means (up to and including impeachment) of compelling the President to enforce the laws it has written. Or the President could have evaded presentation of the constitutional issue to this Court simply by declining to appeal the District Court and Court of Appeals dispositions he agreed with. Be sure of this much: If a President wants to insulate his judgment of unconstitutionality from our review, he can. What the views urged in this dissent produce is not insulation from judicial review but insulation from Executive contrivance.

The majority brandishes the famous sentence from *Marbury v. Madison* that "[i]t is emphatically the province and duty of the judicial department to say what the law is." But that sentence neither says nor implies that it is *always* the province and duty of the Court to say what the law is—much less that its responsibility in that regard is a "primary" one. The very next sentence of Chief Justice Marshall's opinion makes the crucial qualification that today's majority ignores: *"Those who apply the rule to particular cases,* must of necessity expound and interpret that rule." *Id.,* at 177 (emphasis added). Only when a "particular case" is before us—that is, a controversy that it is our business to resolve under Article III—do we have the province and duty to pronounce the law. For the views of our early Court more precisely addressing the question before us here, the majority ought instead to have consulted the opinion of Chief Justice Taney in *Lord v. Veazie,* 49 U.S. (8 How.) 251 (1850):

> "The objection in the case before us is . . . that the plaintiff and defendant have the same interest, and that interest adverse and in conflict with the interest of third persons, whose rights would be seriously affected if the question of law was decided in the manner that both of the parties to this suit desire it to be.

> "A judgment entered under such circumstances, and for such purposes, is a mere form. The whole proceeding was in contempt of the court, and highly reprehensible. . . . A judgment in form, thus procured, in the eye of the law is no judgment of the court. It is a nullity, and no writ of error will lie upon it. This writ is, therefore, dismissed." *Id.,* at 255–256.

There is, in the words of *Marbury,* no "necessity [to] expound and interpret" the law in this case; just a desire to place this Court at the center of the Nation's life. . . .

[Justice Scalia went on to argue that the majority's resolution of the merits was also wrong.—Editors]

■ JUSTICE ALITO, dissenting.

. . . I turn first to the question of standing. In my view, the United States clearly is not a proper petitioner in this case. The United States does not ask us to overturn the judgment of the court below or to alter that judgment in any way. Quite to the contrary, the United States argues emphatically in favor of the correctness of that judgment. We have never before reviewed a decision at the sole behest of a party that took such a position, and to do so would be to render an advisory opinion, in violation of Article III's dictates. For the reasons given in JUSTICE SCALIA's dissent, I do not find the Court's arguments to the contrary to be persuasive.

Whether the Bipartisan Legal Advisory Group of the House of Representatives (BLAG) has standing to petition is a much more difficult question. . . . In my view . . . BLAG ha[s] standing.

A party invoking the Court's authority has a sufficient stake to permit it to appeal when it has " 'suffered an injury in fact' that is caused by 'the conduct complained of' and that 'will be redressed by a favorable decision.' " *Camreta v. Greene,* 563 U.S. 692, 701 (2011) (quoting *Lujan,* at 560–561). In the present case, the House of Representatives, which has authorized BLAG to represent its interests in this matter, suffered just such an injury.

In *INS v. Chadha,* 462 U.S. 919 (1983), the Court held that the two Houses of Congress were "proper parties" to file a petition in defense of the constitutionality of the one-house veto statute. Accordingly, the Court granted and decided petitions by both the Senate and the House, in addition to the Executive's petition. That the two Houses had standing to petition is not surprising: The Court of Appeals' decision in *Chadha,* by holding the one-house veto to be unconstitutional, had limited Congress' power to legislate. In discussing Article III standing, the Court suggested that Congress suffered a similar injury whenever federal legislation it had passed was struck down, noting that it had "long held that Congress is the proper party to defend the validity of a statute when an agency of government, as a defendant charged with enforcing the statute, agrees with plaintiffs that the statute is inapplicable or unconstitutional."

The United States attempts to distinguish *Chadha* on the ground that it "involved an unusual statute that vested the House and the Senate themselves each with special procedural rights—namely, the right effectively to veto Executive action." Brief for United States (jurisdiction) 36. But that is a distinction without a difference: just as the Court of Appeals decision that the *Chadha* Court affirmed impaired Congress' power by striking down the one-house veto, so the Second Circuit's decision here impairs Congress' legislative power by striking down an Act of Congress. The United States has not explained why the fact that the impairment at issue in *Chadha* was "special" or "procedural" has any relevance to whether Congress suffered an injury. Indeed, because legislating is Congress' central function, any impairment of that function is a more grievous injury than the impairment of a procedural add-on. . . .

I appreciate the argument that the Constitution confers on the President alone the authority to defend federal law in litigation, but in my view, as I have explained, that argument is contrary to the Court's holding in *Chadha*, and it is certainly contrary to the *Chadha* Court's endorsement of the principle that "Congress is the proper party to defend the validity of a statute" when the Executive refuses to do so on constitutional grounds. See also 2 U.S.C. § 288h(7) (Senate Legal Counsel shall defend the constitutionality of Acts of Congress when placed in issue). Accordingly, in the narrow category of cases in which a court strikes down an Act of Congress and the Executive declines to defend the Act, Congress both has standing to defend the undefended statute and is a proper party to do so. . . .

[Justice Alito went on to argue that the majority's resolution of the merits was also wrong, and Justice Thomas joined that part (but only that part) of his dissent.—Editors]

■ [The dissenting opinion of CHIEF JUSTICE ROBERTS is omitted.]

NOTES

1.   The majority opinion notes: "There is no dispute that when this case was in the District Court it presented a concrete disagreement between opposing parties, a dispute suitable for judicial resolution. . . . Windsor suffered a redressable injury when she was required to pay estate taxes from which, in her view, she was exempt but for the alleged invalidity of § 3 of DOMA." This is an important point. Do not let the hard cases that find no standing distract you from the easy cases where standing is present.

2.   What exactly was the executive branch's interest in appealing *Windsor* to the Supreme Court? To avoid having to spend money out of the Treasury, or to secure a Supreme Court precedent on the Defense of Marriage Act? Which of those interests can support standing?

3.   Consider the relationship between defending a statute and enforcing it. In most cases, the executive branch does both. In some cases, it might neither defend the statute nor enforce it—think of President Jefferson and the Alien and Sedition Acts (p. 66). In

what circumstances would it make sense for the executive to do one and not the other? To defend, but not enforce? To enforce, but not defend? What does the majority think? What does Justice Scalia think?

4.   Justice Scalia suggests that the assertion of jurisdiction in *Windsor* was unprecedented. But we have already seen two other cases where the Supreme Court held a statute unconstitutional even though the executive branch declined to defend it— *United States v. Lovett*, p. 160, and *INS v. Chadha*, p. 141. Are those cases distinguishable? If so, how?

5.   Is defending the constitutionality of a statute an "executive power" or "legislative power"? What does Justice Alito think?

Mootness and Ripeness

As you have seen, the doctrine of standing asks whether a particular person is a proper party to raise an issue in federal court for adjudication. In order to have standing, plaintiffs must show that they have a concrete injury, fairly traceable to the defendant, that will be redressed by a successful suit. Standing thus deals with the "who" question in litigation.

The Court has also articulated two related doctrines, mootness and ripeness, that instead deal with the "when" of litigation. A case is moot when the requisite personal injury that gave rise to the case or controversy ceases for some reason to exist. Ripeness doctrine is concerned with the other end of timing, when the case is being brought too early for judicial decision, because the alleged legal injury is remote and speculative. Here are a few key points about these doctrines:

Mootness Doctrine: A change in the facts giving rise to a case that ends the immediate actual controversy will moot a case. The death of a party, the settlement of a case, or the repeal or expiration of a governmental action that is being challenged could each under some circumstances render a case moot. Recall that in *Powell v. McCormack* (p. 104) it was argued that the case was moot because the session of Congress in which Adam Clayton Powell was not seated was already over, Powell had already been re-elected to a new Congress, and the new Congress had seated him. The Supreme Court said the case was not moot because Powell was still entitled to sue for his salary and backpay for the session of Congress from which he had allegedly been unconstitutionally excluded. Another illustrative mootness case is *DeFunis v. Odegaard*, 416 U.S. 312 (1974), involving a lawsuit challenging affirmative action in state law school admissions. The plaintiff, Marco DeFunis, had been denied admission to the University of Washington School of Law allegedly on the basis of race—a real, concrete injury—and had won a preliminary injunction in the lower courts. He was provisionally admitted, and by the time the case was argued before the U.S. Supreme Court, he was in his last semester of law school and scheduled to graduate. The Court decided that the case was moot because nothing concrete turned on resolving the constitutional issue. (The dissenters argued that something might still go wrong—failing a final, perhaps?—and that the issue of DeFunis's legal entitlement to finish law school remained live.) There are exceptions to the mootness doctrine: where collateral consequences to an injury remain (the back-pay situation in *Powell*); where the legal injury is capable of repetition as to that party, but likely to evade final judicial review; and where a defendant has voluntarily ceased its alleged wrongful conduct but remains free to resume it later.

But there is no exception to mootness simply because the case is especially interesting or important (as in *DeFunis*).

Ripeness Doctrine: A case is considered "unripe" where the claimed injury has not occurred and its occurrence is thought too speculative or contingent to constitute a real, present dispute. The Supreme Court has announced a two-part test for determining whether a case is ripe under the Constitution. First, federal courts should look to the hardship to the parties from withholding court consideration. This element is usually satisfied when (a) there is a likelihood of prosecution with substantial consequences unless a plaintiff forgoes engaging in allegedly lawful behavior; (b) the enforcement of a statute is certain but enforcement proceedings have not yet begun; or (c) there is substantial hardship from collateral injuries. The second element of the ripeness test is establishing the fitness of the issues and of the record for judicial review. The more a question is purely legal, and the less development of a factual record matters, the more likely it is that a case will be deemed ripe for review.

[*Assignment 21*]

D. THE POLITICAL QUESTION DOCTRINE

Even where Article III's prerequisites for a "Case" or "Controversy" are satisfied—i.e., there is a genuine controversy and not a request for an advisory opinion, the case is adversarial, the parties have legal interests conferring standing, and the dispute is ripe and not moot—there may remain a further question. Is the *legal issue presented appropriate for judicial resolution* or is it instead a matter left to the resolution of the political branches of government? This is referred to as the "political question doctrine."

The content, and even the legitimacy, of the political question doctrine remains hotly disputed. We present here two cases bookending its creation and its modern application. *Luther v. Borden*, 48 U.S. (7 How.) 1 (1849), predates the modern doctrine, but has influenced its development. *Nixon v. United States*, 506 U.S. 224 (1993), is a modern case presenting, distilling, and debating the application of the political question doctrine in the context of a judicial impeachment proceeding. As you study these cases, identify the various strands of the political question doctrine and evaluate them. Should the doctrine exist at all? Are there cases involving constitutional issues that courts just should not decide? If so, what are they: Matters involving war and foreign affairs? Matters involving impeachment? Matters involving national authority to assure that the states maintain "a Republican Form of Government"? What else? Is it only the substance of the question that matters, or does it also matter whether the plaintiff is seeking a legal or equitable remedy? How should we decide the scope of the political question doctrine?

Luther v. Borden
48 U.S. (7 How.) 1 (1849)

■ MR. CHIEF JUSTICE TANEY delivered the opinion of the court.

This case has arisen out of the unfortunate political differences which agitated the people of Rhode Island in 1841 and 1842.

It is an action of trespass brought by Martin Luther, the plaintiff in error, against Luther M. Borden and others, the defendants, in the Circuit Court of the United States for the District of Rhode Island, for breaking and entering the plaintiff's house. The defendants justify upon the ground that large numbers of men were assembled in different parts of the State for the purpose of overthrowing the government by military force, and were actually levying war upon the State; that, in order to defend itself from this insurrection, the State was declared by competent authority to be under martial law; that the plaintiff was engaged in the insurrection; and that the defendants, being in the military service of the State, by command of their superior officer, broke and entered the house and searched the rooms for the plaintiff, who was supposed to be there concealed, in order to arrest him, doing as little damage as possible. . . .

The existence and authority of the government under which the defendants acted was called in question; and the plaintiff insists, that, before the acts complained of were committed, that government had been displaced and annulled by the people of Rhode Island, and that the plaintiff was engaged in supporting the lawful authority of the State, and the defendants themselves were in arms against it.

This is a new question in this court, and certainly a very grave one; and at the time when the trespass is alleged to have been committed it had produced a general and painful excitement in the State, and threatened to end in bloodshed and civil war. . . .

[Borden and the other defendants arrested Luther under the authority of Rhode Island's "charter government," which had existed since before Independence and was created by British royal charter. Under the charter government, voting was restricted to landowners. A large group of Rhode Islanders thought the charter government was illegitimate, and they wrote their own constitution, which extended the vote broadly to adult male citizens. They then submitted their constitution to a popular vote and declared that it had been ratified. This began what was called the Dorr Rebellion, in which Luther was a participant.—Editors]

The charter government did not, however, admit the validity of these proceedings, nor acquiesce in them. On the contrary, in January, 1842, when this new constitution was communicated to the governor, and by him laid before the legislature, it passed resolutions declaring all acts done for the purpose of imposing that constitution upon the State to be an assumption of the powers of government, in violation of the rights of the existing government and of the people at large; and that it would maintain its authority and defend the legal and constitutional rights of the people.

In adopting this measure, as well as in all others taken by the charter government to assert its authority, it was supported by a large number of the citizens of the State, claiming to be a majority, who regarded the proceedings of the adverse party as unlawful and disorganizing, and maintained that, as the existing government had been established by the people of the State, no convention to frame a new constitution could be called without its sanction; and that the times and places of taking the votes, and the officers to receive them, and the qualification of voters, must be previously regulated and appointed by law.

But, notwithstanding the determination of the charter government, and of those who adhered to it, to maintain its authority, Thomas W. Dorr, who had been elected governor under the new constitution, prepared to assert the authority of that government by force, and many citizens assembled in arms to support him. The charter government thereupon passed an act declaring the State under martial law, and at the same time proceeded to call out the militia, to repel the threatened attack and to subdue those who were engaged in it. In this state of the contest, the house of the plaintiff, who was engaged in supporting the authority of the new government, was broken and entered in order to arrest him. The defendants were, at the time, in the military service of the old government, and in arms to support its authority. . . .

[The charter government eventually agreed to a new state constitution, which went into force in 1843. At the time of the Luther v. Borden *decision, the charter government had "continued ever since to be the admitted and established government of Rhode Island."—Editors]*

The difficulties with the government of which Mr. Dorr was the head were soon over. They had ceased before the constitution was framed by the convention elected by the authority of the charter government. For after an unsuccessful attempt made by Mr. Dorr in May, 1842, at the head of a military force, to get possession of the State arsenal at Providence, in which he was repulsed, and an assemblage of some hundreds of armed men under his command at Chepatchet in the June following, which dispersed upon the approach of the troops of the old government, no further effort was made to establish it; and until the constitution of 1843 went into operation the charter government continued to assert its authority and exercise its powers, and to enforce obedience, throughout the State, arresting and imprisoning, and punishing in its judicial tribunals, those who had appeared in arms against it.

We do not understand from the argument that the constitution under which the plaintiff acted is supposed to have been in force after the constitution of May, 1843, went into operation. The contest is confined to the year preceding. The plaintiff contends that the charter government was displaced, and ceased to have any lawful power, after the organization, in May, 1842, of the government which he supported, and although that government never was able to exercise any authority in the State, nor to command obedience to its laws or to its officers, yet he insists that it was the lawful and established government, upon the ground that it was ratified by a large majority of the male people of the State of the age of twenty-one and upwards, and also by a majority of those who were entitled to vote for general officers under the then existing laws of the State. The fact that it was so ratified was not admitted; and at the trial in the Circuit Court he offered to prove it by the production of the original ballots, and the original registers of the persons voting, verified by the oaths of the several moderators and clerks of the meetings, and by the testimony of all the persons so voting, and by the said constitution; and also offered in evidence, for the same purpose, that part of the census of the United States for the year 1840 which applies to Rhode Island; and a certificate of the secretary of state of the charter government, showing the number of votes polled by the freemen of the State for the ten years then last past.

The Circuit Court rejected this evidence, and instructed the jury that the charter government and laws under which the defendants acted were, at the time the trespass is alleged to have been committed, in full force and effect as the form of government and paramount law of the State, and constituted a justification of the acts of the defendants as set forth in their pleas.

It is this opinion of the Circuit Court that we are now called upon to review. It is set forth more at large in the exception, but is in substance as above stated; and the question presented is certainly a very serious one: For, if this court is authorized to enter upon this inquiry as proposed by the plaintiff, and it should be decided that the charter government had no legal existence during the period of time above mentioned,—if it had been annulled by the adoption of the opposing government,—then the laws passed by its legislature during that time were nullities; its taxes wrongfully collected; its salaries and compensation to its officers illegally paid; its public accounts improperly settled; and the judgments and sentences of its courts in civil and criminal cases null and void, and the officers who carried their decisions into operation answerable as trespassers, if not in some cases as criminals.

When the decision of this court might lead to such results, it becomes its duty to examine very carefully its own powers before it undertakes to exercise jurisdiction.

Certainly, the question which the plaintiff proposed to raise by the testimony he offered has not heretofore been recognized as a judicial one in any of the State courts. In forming the constitutions of the different States, after the Declaration of Independence, and in the various changes and alterations which have since been made, the political department has always determined whether the proposed constitution or amendment was ratified or not by the people of the State, and the judicial power has followed its decision. In Rhode Island, the question has been directly decided. Prosecutions were there instituted against some of the persons who had been active in the forcible opposition to the old government. And in more than one of the cases evidence was offered on the part of the defence similar to the testimony offered in the Circuit Court, and for the same purpose; that is, for the purpose of showing that the proposed constitution had been adopted by the people of Rhode Island, and had, therefore, become the established government, and consequently that the parties accused were doing nothing more than their duty in endeavouring to support it.

But the courts uniformly held that the inquiry proposed to be made belonged to the political power and not to the judicial; that it rested with the political power to decide whether the charter government had been displaced or not; and when that decision was made, the judicial department would be bound to take notice of it as the paramount law of the State, without the aid of oral evidence or the examination of witnesses; that, according to the laws and institutions of Rhode Island, no such change had been recognized by the political power; and that the charter government was the lawful and established government of the State during the period in contest, and that those who were in arms against it were insurgents, and liable to punishment. This doctrine is clearly and forcibly stated in the opinion of the Supreme Court of the State in the trial of Thomas W. Dorr, who was the governor elected under the opposing constitution, and headed the armed force which endeavoured to maintain its authority.

Indeed, we do not see how the question could be tried and judicially decided in a State court. Judicial power presupposes an established government capable of enacting laws and enforcing their execution, and of appointing judges to expound and administer them. The acceptance of the judicial office is a recognition of the authority of the government from which it is derived. And if the authority of that government is annulled and overthrown, the power of its courts and other officers is annulled with it. And if a State court should enter upon the inquiry proposed in this case, and should come to the conclusion that the government under which it acted had been put aside and displaced by an opposing government, it would cease to be a court, and be incapable of pronouncing a judicial decision upon the question it undertook to try. If it decides at all as a court, it necessarily affirms the existence and authority of the government under which it is exercising judicial power.

It is worthy of remark, however, when we are referring to the authority of State decisions, that the trial of Thomas W. Dorr took place after the constitution of 1843 went into operation. The judges who decided that case held their authority under that constitution; and it is admitted on all hands that it was adopted by the people of the State, and is the lawful and established government. It is the decision, therefore, of a State court, whose judicial authority to decide upon the constitution and laws of Rhode Island is not questioned by either party to this controversy, although the government under which it acted was framed and adopted under the sanction and laws of the charter government.

The point, then, raised here has been already decided by the courts of Rhode Island. The question relates, altogether, to the constitution and laws of that State; and the well settled rule in this court is, that the courts of the United States adopt and follow the decisions of the State courts in questions which concern merely the constitution and laws of the State.

Upon what ground could the Circuit Court of the United States which tried this case have departed from this rule, and disregarded and overruled the decisions of the courts of Rhode Island? Undoubtedly the courts of the United States have certain powers under the Constitution and laws of the United States which do not belong to the State courts. But the power of determining that a State government has been lawfully established, which the courts of the State disown and repudiate, is not one of them. Upon such a question the courts of the United States are bound to follow the decisions of the State tribunals, and must therefore regard the charter government as the lawful established government during the time of this contest.

Besides, if the Circuit Court had entered upon this inquiry, by what rule could it have determined the qualification of voters upon the adoption or rejection of the proposed constitution, unless there was some previous law of the State to guide it? It is the province of a court to expound the law, not to make it. And certainly it is no part of the judicial functions of any court of the United States to prescribe the qualification of voters in a State, giving the right to those to whom it is denied by the written and established constitution and laws of the State, or taking it away from those to whom it is given; nor has it the right to determine what political privileges the citizens of a State are entitled to, unless there is an established constitution or law to govern its decision. . . .

Moreover, the Constitution of the United States, as far as it has provided for an emergency of this kind, and authorized the general government to interfere in the domestic concerns of a State, has treated the subject as political in its nature, and placed the power in the hands of that department.

The fourth section of the fourth article of the Constitution of the United States provides that the United States shall guarantee to every State in the Union a republican form of government, and shall protect each of them against invasion; and on the application of the legislature or of the executive (when the legislature cannot be convened) against domestic violence.

Under this article of the Constitution it rests with Congress to decide what government is the established one in a State. For as the United States guarantee to each State a republican government, Congress must necessarily decide what government is established in the State before it can determine whether it is republican or not. And when the senators and representatives of a State are admitted into the councils of the Union, the authority of the government under which they are appointed, as well as its republican character, is recognized by the proper constitutional authority. And its decision is binding on every other department of the government, and could not be questioned in a judicial tribunal. It is true that the contest in this case did not last long enough to bring the matter to this issue; and as no senators or representatives were elected under the authority of the government of which Mr. Dorr was the head, Congress was not called upon to decide the controversy. Yet the right to decide is placed there, and not in the courts.

So, too, as relates to the clause in the above-mentioned article of the Constitution, providing for cases of domestic violence. It rested with Congress, too, to determine upon the means proper to be adopted to fulfil this guarantee. They might, if they had deemed it most advisable to do so, have placed it in the power of a court to decide when the contingency had happened which required the federal government to interfere. But Congress thought otherwise, and no doubt wisely; and by the act of February 28, 1795, provided, that, "in case of an insurrection in any State against the government thereof, it shall be lawful for the President of the United States, on application of the legislature of such State or of the executive (when the legislature cannot be convened), to call forth such number of the militia of any other State or States, as may be applied for, as he may judge sufficient to sufficient to suppress such insurrection."

By this act, the power of deciding whether the exigency had arisen upon which the government of the United States is bound to interfere, is given to the President. He is to act upon the application of the legislature or of the executive, and consequently he must determine what body of men constitute the legislature, and who is the governor, before he can act. The fact that both parties claim the right to the government cannot alter the case, for both cannot be entitled to it. If there is an armed conflict, like the one of which we are speaking, it is a case of domestic violence, and one of the parties must be in insurrection against the lawful government. And the President must, of necessity, decide which is the government, and which party is unlawfully arrayed against it, before he can perform the duty imposed upon him by the act of Congress.

After the President has acted and called out the militia, is a Circuit Court of the United States authorized to inquire whether his decision was right? Could the court, while the parties were actually contending in arms for the possession of the government, call witnesses before it and inquire which party represented a majority of the people? If it could, then it would become the duty of the court (provided it came to the conclusion that the President had decided incorrectly) to discharge those who were arrested or detained by the troops in the service of the United States or the government which the President was endeavouring to maintain. If the judicial power extends so far, the guarantee contained in the Constitution of the United States is a guarantee of anarchy, and not of order. Yet if this right does not reside in the courts when the conflict is raging, if the judicial power is at that time bound to follow the decision of the political, it must be equally bound when the contest is over. It cannot, when peace is restored, punish as offences and crimes the acts which it before recognized, and was bound to recognize, as lawful.

It is true that in this case the militia were not called out by the President. But upon the application of the governor under the charter government, the President recognized him as the executive power of the State, and took measures to call out the militia to support his authority if it should be found necessary for the general government to interfere; and it is admitted in the argument, that it was the knowledge of this decision that put an end to the armed opposition to the charter government, and prevented any further efforts to establish by force the proposed constitution. The interference of the President, therefore, by announcing his determination, was as effectual as if the militia had been assembled under his orders. And it should be equally authoritative. For certainly no court of the United States, with a knowledge of this decision, would have been justified in recognizing the opposing party as the lawful government; or in treating as wrongdoers or insurgents the officers of the government which the President had recognized, and was prepared to support by an armed force. In the case of foreign nations, the government acknowledged by the President is always recognized in the courts of justice. And this principle has been applied by the act of Congress to the sovereign States of the Union.

It is said that this power in the President is dangerous to liberty, and may be abused. All power may be abused if placed in unworthy hands. But it would be difficult, we think, to point out any other hands in which this power would be more safe, and at the same time equally effectual. When citizens of the same State are in arms against each other, and the constituted authorities unable to execute the laws, the interposition of the United States must be prompt, or it is of little value. The ordinary course of proceedings in courts of justice would be utterly unfit for the crisis. And the elevated office of the President, chosen as he is by the people of the United States, and the high responsibility he could not fail to feel when acting in a case of so much moment, appear to furnish as strong safeguards against a wilful abuse of power as human prudence and foresight could well provide. At all events, it is conferred upon him by the Constitution and laws of the United States, and must therefore be respected and enforced in its judicial tribunals. . . .

Upon the whole, we see no reason for disturbing the judgment of the Circuit Court. . . . Much of the argument on the part of the plaintiff turned upon political rights and political questions, upon which the court has been urged to express an opinion. We decline doing so. The high power has been conferred on this court of passing judgment upon the acts of the State sovereignties, and of the legislative and executive branches of the federal government, and of determining whether they are beyond the limits of power marked out for them respectively by the Constitution of the United States. This tribunal, therefore, should be the last to overstep the boundaries which limit its own jurisdiction. And while it should always be ready to meet any question confided to it by the Constitution, it is equally its duty not to pass beyond its appropriate sphere of action, and to take care not to involve itself in discussions which properly belong to other forums. No one, we believe, has ever doubted the proposition, that, according to the institutions of this country, the sovereignty in every State resides in the people of the State, and that they may alter and change their form of government at their own pleasure. But whether they have changed it or not by abolishing an old government, and establishing a new one in its place, is a question to be settled by the political power. And when that power has decided, the courts are bound to take notice of its decision, and to follow it.

■ [JUSTICE WOODBURY's dissent is omitted.]

NOTES

1.   Article IV, Section 4 of the Constitution is often called the Guarantee Clause. It provides:

> The United States shall guarantee to every state in this union a republican form of government, and shall protect each of them against invasion; and on application of the legislature, or of the executive (when the legislature cannot be convened) against domestic violence.

In *Luther*, the Court concludes that under this section "it rests with Congress to decide what government is the established one in a State." Why Congress, rather than the federal courts? What arguments does the Court make? What arguments should it have made?

2.   In addition to this textual argument, *Luther* says that the "inquiry" into the lawful government of Rhode Island does not have a "judicial" character. Why not? What type of constitutional argument is the Court making?

3.   While *Luther* predates the modern political question doctrine, its specific holding that the Guarantee Clause is non-justiciable has been important throughout history and remains so today.

a.   Members of the Reconstruction Congress repeatedly invoked *Luther* to support their authority to impose military reconstruction on the South. (This episode is discussed at p. 1283.) Apparently, "during the Fortieth Congress, Republicans spent much more time endorsing *Luther v. Borden* than they did denouncing *Dred Scott*." John Harrison, *The Lawfulness of the Reconstruction Amendments*, 68 U. CHI. L. REV. 375, 424 (2001).

b.   At the start of the twentieth century, popular referenda and initiatives were introduced in many states, and some opponents argued that this popular democracy was not "Republican" because it lacked the filter provided by representative democracy. But the Supreme Court found the Guarantee Clause challenges barred by the political question doctrine. See, e.g., *Pacific States Telephone & Telegraph Co. v. Oregon*, 223 U.S. 118 (1912).

c.   In the late 1940s many states had failed to reapportion their congressional and state legislative districts for decades, with the result that some districts had far more constituents than others. This malapportionment was challenged under the Guarantee Clause and again the Supreme Court forbade the federal courts from hearing the challenge because of the political question doctrine.

A decade and a half later, the Supreme Court permitted a challenge to malapportionment under a different constitutional provision, the Equal Protection Clause. The case allowing the challenge to go forward was *Baker v. Carr*, 369 U.S. 186 (1962), which is presented at p. 776. It has become one of the most cited cases on the modern formulation of the political question doctrine, as you will see in the next case.

(Walter) Nixon v. United States

506 U.S. 224 (1993)

■ CHIEF JUSTICE REHNQUIST delivered the opinion of the Court.

Petitioner Walter L. Nixon, Jr., asks this Court to decide whether Senate Rule XI, which allows a committee of Senators to hear evidence against an individual who has been impeached and to report that evidence to the full Senate, violates the Impeachment Trial Clause, Art. I, § 3, cl. 6. That Clause provides that the "Senate shall have the sole Power to try all Impeachments." But before we reach the merits of such a claim, we must decide whether it is "justiciable," that is, whether it is a claim that may be resolved by the courts. We conclude that it is not.

Nixon, a former Chief Judge of the United States District Court for the Southern District of Mississippi, was convicted by a jury of two counts of making false statements before a federal grand jury and sentenced to prison. The grand jury investigation stemmed from reports that Nixon had accepted a gratuity from a Mississippi businessman in exchange for asking a local district attorney to halt the prosecution of the businessman's son. Because Nixon refused to resign from his office as a United States District Judge, he continued to collect his judicial salary while serving out his prison sentence.

On May 10, 1989, the House of Representatives adopted three articles of impeachment for high crimes and misdemeanors. The first two articles charged Nixon with giving false testimony before the grand jury and the third article charged him with bringing disrepute on the Federal Judiciary.

After the House presented the articles to the Senate, the Senate voted to invoke its own Impeachment Rule XI, under which the presiding officer appoints a committee of Senators to "receive evidence and take testimony." Senate Impeachment Rule XI. The Senate committee held four days of hearings, during which 10 witnesses, including Nixon, testified. Pursuant to Rule XI, the committee presented the full Senate with a complete transcript of the proceeding and a Report stating the uncontested facts and summarizing the evidence on the contested facts. Nixon and the House impeachment managers submitted extensive final briefs to the full Senate and delivered arguments from the Senate floor during the three hours set aside for oral argument in front of that body. Nixon himself gave a personal appeal, and several Senators posed questions directly to both parties. The Senate voted by more than the constitutionally required two-thirds majority to convict Nixon on the first two articles. The presiding officer then entered judgment removing Nixon from his office as United States District Judge.

Nixon thereafter commenced the present suit, arguing that Senate Rule XI violates the constitutional grant of authority to the Senate to "try" all impeachments because it prohibits the whole Senate from taking part in the evidentiary hearings. See Art. I, § 3, cl. 6. Nixon sought a declaratory judgment that his impeachment conviction was void and that his judicial salary and privileges should be reinstated. The District Court held that his claim was nonjusticiable, and the Court of Appeals for the District of Columbia Circuit agreed. We granted certiorari.

A controversy is nonjusticiable—*i.e.,* involves a political question—where there is "a textually demonstrable constitutional commitment of the issue to a coordinate political department; or a lack of judicially discoverable and manageable standards for resolving it. . . ." *Baker v. Carr,* 369 U.S. 186, 217 (1962). But the courts must, in the first instance, interpret the text in question and determine whether and to what extent the issue is textually committed. As the discussion that follows makes clear, the concept of a textual commitment to a coordinate political department is not completely separate from the concept of a lack of judicially discoverable and manageable standards for resolving it; the lack of judicially manageable standards may strengthen the conclusion that there is a textually demonstrable commitment to a coordinate branch.

In this case, we must examine Art. I, § 3, cl. 6, to determine the scope of authority conferred upon the Senate by the Framers regarding impeachment. It provides:

> The Senate shall have the sole Power to try all Impeachments. When sitting for that Purpose, they shall be on Oath or Affirmation. When the President of the United States is tried, the Chief Justice shall preside: And no Person shall be convicted without the Concurrence of two thirds of the Members present.

The language and structure of this Clause are revealing. The first sentence is a grant of authority to the Senate, and the word "sole" indicates that this authority is reposed in the Senate and nowhere else. The next two sentences specify requirements to which the Senate proceedings shall conform: The Senate shall be on oath or affirmation, a two-thirds vote is required to convict, and when the President is tried the Chief Justice shall preside.

Petitioner argues that the word "try" in the first sentence imposes by implication an additional requirement on the Senate in that the proceedings must be in the nature of a judicial trial. From there petitioner goes on to argue that this limitation precludes the Senate from delegating to a select committee the task of hearing the testimony of witnesses, as was done pursuant to Senate Rule XI. " '[T]ry' means more than simply 'vote on' or 'review' or 'judge.' In 1787 and today, trying a case means hearing the evidence, not scanning a cold record." Petitioner concludes from this that courts may review whether or not the Senate "tried" him before convicting him.

There are several difficulties with this position which lead us ultimately to reject it. The word "try," both in 1787 and later, has considerably broader meanings than those to which petitioner would limit it. Older dictionaries define try as "[t]o examine" or "[t]o examine as a judge." See 2 Samuel Johnson, A Dictionary of the English Language (1785). In more modern usage the term has various meanings. For example, try can mean "to examine or investigate judicially," "to conduct the trial of," or "to put to the test by experiment, investigation, or trial." Webster's Third New International Dictionary 2457 (1971). Petitioner submits that "try," as contained in T. Sheridan, Dictionary of the English Language (1796), means "to examine as a judge; to bring before a judicial tribunal." Based on the variety of definitions, however, we cannot say that the Framers used the word "try" as an implied limitation on the method by which the Senate might proceed in trying impeachments. . . .

The conclusion that the use of the word "try" in the first sentence of the Impeachment Trial Clause lacks sufficient precision to afford any judicially manageable standard of review of the Senate's actions is fortified by the existence of the three very specific requirements that the Constitution does impose on the Senate when trying impeachments: The Members must be under oath, a two-thirds vote is required to convict, and the Chief Justice presides when the President is tried. These limitations are quite precise, and their nature suggests that the Framers did not intend to impose additional limitations on the form of the Senate proceedings by the use of the word "try" in the first sentence.

Petitioner devotes only two pages in his brief to negating the significance of the word "sole" in the first sentence of Clause 6. As noted above, that sentence provides that "[t]he Senate shall have the sole Power to try all Impeachments." We think that the word "sole" is of considerable significance. Indeed, the word "sole" appears only one other time in the Constitution—with respect to the House of Representatives' "*sole* Power of Impeachment." Art. I, § 2, cl. 5 (emphasis added). The commonsense meaning of the word "sole" is that the Senate alone shall have authority to determine whether an individual should be acquitted or convicted. The dictionary definition bears this out. "Sole" is defined as "having no companion," "solitary," "being the only one," and "functioning . . . independently and without assistance or interference." Webster's Third New International Dictionary 2168 (1971). If the courts may review the actions of the Senate in order to determine whether that body "tried" an impeached official, it is difficult to see how the Senate would be "functioning . . . independently and without assistance or interference."

Nixon asserts that the word "sole" has no substantive meaning. To support this contention, he argues that the word is nothing more than a mere "cosmetic edit" added by the Committee of Style after the delegates had approved the substance of the Impeachment Trial Clause. There are two difficulties with this argument. First, accepting as we must the proposition that the Committee of Style had no authority from the Convention to alter the meaning of the Clause, we must presume that the Committee's reorganization or rephrasing accurately captured what the Framers meant in their unadorned language. See *Powell v. McCormack*, 395 U.S. 486, 538–539 (1969). That is, we must presume that the Committee did its job. This presumption is buttressed by the fact that the Constitutional Convention voted on, and accepted, the Committee of Style's linguistic version. We agree with the Government that "the word 'sole' is entitled to no less weight than any other word of the text, because the Committee revision perfected what 'had been agreed to.'" Second, carrying Nixon's argument to its logical conclusion would constrain us to say that the *second to last draft* would govern in every instance where the Committee of Style added an arguably substantive word. Such a result is at odds with the fact that the Convention passed the Committee's version, and with the well-established rule that the plain language of the enacted text is the best indicator of intent. . . .

Petitioner finally argues that even if significance be attributed to the word "sole" in the first sentence of the Clause, the authority granted is to the Senate, and this means that "the Senate—not the courts, not a lay jury, not a Senate Committee—shall try impeachments." It would be possible to read the first sentence of the Clause this way, but it is not a natural reading. Petitioner's interpretation would bring into judicial purview not merely the sort of claim made by petitioner, but other similar claims based on the conclusion that the word "Senate" has imposed by implication limitations on procedures which the Senate might adopt. . . .

The history and contemporary understanding of the impeachment provisions support our reading of the constitutional language. The parties do not offer evidence of a single word in the history of the Constitutional Convention or in contemporary commentary that even alludes to the possibility of judicial review in the context of the impeachment powers. This silence is quite meaningful in light of the several explicit references to the availability of judicial review as a check on the Legislature's power with respect to bills of attainder, *ex post facto* laws, and statutes. See The Federalist No. 78.

The Framers labored over the question of where the impeachment power should lie. Significantly, in at least two considered scenarios the power was placed with the Federal Judiciary. See 1 Records of the Federal Convention of 1787, pp. 21–22 (M. Farrand ed. 1966) (Virginia Plan); *id.*, at 244 (New Jersey Plan). Indeed, James Madison and the Committee of Detail proposed that the Supreme Court should have the power to determine impeachments. Despite these proposals, the Convention ultimately decided that the Senate would have "the sole Power to try all Impeachments." Article I, § 3, cl. 6. According to Alexander Hamilton, the Senate was the "most fit depositary of this important trust" because its Members are representatives of the people. See The Federalist No. 65. The Supreme Court was not the proper body because the Framers "doubted whether the members of that tribunal would, at all times, be endowed with so eminent a portion of fortitude as would be called for in the execution of so difficult a task" or whether the Court "would possess the degree of credit and authority" to carry out its judgment if it conflicted with the accusation brought by the Legislature—the people's representative. See *id.* In addition, the Framers believed the Court was too small in number: "The awful discretion, which a court of impeachments must necessarily have, to doom to honor or to infamy the most confidential and the most distinguished characters of the community, forbids the commitment of the trust to a small number of persons." *Id.*

There are two additional reasons why the Judiciary, and the Supreme Court in particular, were not chosen to have any role in impeachments. First, the Framers recognized that most likely there would be two sets of proceedings for individuals who commit impeachable offenses—the impeachment trial and a separate criminal trial. In fact, the Constitution explicitly provides for two separate proceedings. See Art. I, § 3, cl. 7. The Framers deliberately separated the two forums to avoid raising the specter of bias and to ensure independent judgments. . . .

Second, judicial review would be inconsistent with the Framers' insistence that our system be one of checks and balances. In our constitutional system, impeachment was designed to be the *only* check on the Judicial Branch by the Legislature. . . . Judicial involvement in impeachment proceedings, even if only for purposes of judicial review, is counterintuitive because it would eviscerate the "important constitutional check" placed on the Judiciary by the Framers. Nixon's argument would place final reviewing authority with respect to impeachments in the hands of the same body that the impeachment process is meant to regulate.

Nevertheless, Nixon argues that judicial review is necessary in order to place a check on the Legislature. Nixon fears that if the Senate is given unreviewable authority to interpret the Impeachment Trial Clause, there is a grave risk that the Senate will usurp judicial power. The Framers anticipated this objection and created two constitutional safeguards to keep the Senate in check. The first safeguard is that the whole of the impeachment power is divided between the two legislative bodies, with the House given the right to accuse and the Senate given the right to judge. This split of authority "avoids the inconvenience of making the same persons both accusers and judges; and guards against the danger of persecution from the prevalency of a factious spirit in either of those branches." The second safeguard is the two-thirds supermajority vote requirement. Hamilton explained that "[a]s the concurrence of two-thirds of the senate will be requisite to a condemnation, the security to innocence, from this additional circumstance, will be as complete as itself can desire."

In addition to the textual commitment argument, we are persuaded that the lack of finality and the difficulty of fashioning relief counsel against justiciability. See *Baker v. Carr*, at 210. We agree with the Court of Appeals that opening the door of judicial review to the procedures used by the Senate in trying impeachments would "expose the political life of the country to months, or perhaps years, of chaos." This lack of finality would manifest itself most dramatically if the President were impeached. The legitimacy of any successor, and hence his effectiveness, would be impaired severely, not merely while the judicial process was running its course, but during any retrial that a differently constituted Senate might conduct if its first judgment of conviction were invalidated. Equally uncertain is the question of what relief a court may give other than simply setting aside the judgment of conviction. Could it order the reinstatement of a convicted federal judge, or order Congress to create an additional judgeship if the seat had been filled in the interim?

Petitioner finally contends that a holding of nonjusticiability cannot be reconciled with our opinion in Powell v. McCormack. The relevant issue in *Powell* was whether courts could review the House of Representatives' conclusion that Powell was "unqualified" to sit as a Member because he had been accused of misappropriating public funds and abusing the process of the New York courts. We stated that the question of justiciability turned on whether the Constitution committed authority to the House to judge its Members' qualifications, and if so, the extent of that commitment. Article I, § 5, provides that "Each House shall be the Judge of the Elections, Returns and Qualifications of its own Members." In turn, Art. I, § 2, specifies three requirements for membership in the House: The candidate must be at least 25 years of age, a citizen of the United States for no less than seven years, and an inhabitant of the State he is chosen to represent. We held that, in light of the three requirements specified in the Constitution, the word "qualifications"—of which the House was to be the Judge—was of a precise, limited nature. . . .

In the case before us, there is no separate provision of the Constitution that could be defeated by allowing the Senate final authority to determine the meaning of the word "try" in the Impeachment Trial Clause. We agree with Nixon that courts possess power to review either legislative or executive action that transgresses identifiable textual limits. As we have made clear, "whether the action of [either the Legislative or Executive Branch] exceeds whatever authority has been committed, is itself a delicate exercise in constitutional interpretation, and is a responsibility of this Court as ultimate interpreter of the Constitution." Baker v. Carr, at 211. But we conclude, after exercising that delicate responsibility, that the word "try" in the Impeachment Trial Clause does not provide an identifiable textual limit on the authority which is committed to the Senate.

■ JUSTICE STEVENS, concurring.

For me, the debate about the strength of the inferences to be drawn from the use of the words "sole" and "try" is far less significant than the central fact that the Framers decided to assign the impeachment power to the Legislative Branch. The disposition of the impeachment of Samuel Chase in 1805 demonstrated that the Senate is fully conscious of the profound importance of that assignment, and nothing in the subsequent history of the Senate's exercise of this extraordinary power suggests otherwise. See generally 3 A. Beveridge, The Life of John Marshall 169–222 (1919); W. Rehnquist, Grand Inquests 275–278 (1992). Respect for a coordinate branch of the Government forecloses any assumption that improbable hypotheticals like those mentioned by JUSTICE WHITE and JUSTICE SOUTER will ever occur. Accordingly, the wise policy of judicial restraint, coupled with the potential anomalies associated with a contrary view, provide a sufficient justification for my agreement with the views of THE CHIEF JUSTICE.

■ JUSTICE WHITE, with whom JUSTICE BLACKMUN joins, concurring in the judgment.

Petitioner contends that the method by which the Senate convicted him on two articles of impeachment violates Art. I, § 3, cl. 6, of the Constitution, which mandates that the Senate "try" impeachments. The Court is of the view that the Constitution forbids us even to consider his contention. I find no such prohibition and would therefore reach the merits of the claim. I concur in the judgment because the Senate fulfilled its constitutional obligation to "try" petitioner.

It should be said at the outset that, as a practical matter, it will likely make little difference whether the Court's or my view controls this case. This is so because the Senate has very wide discretion in specifying impeachment trial procedures and because it is extremely unlikely that the Senate would abuse its discretion and insist on a procedure that could not be deemed a trial by reasonable judges. Even taking a wholly practical approach, I would prefer not to announce an unreviewable discretion in the Senate to ignore completely the constitutional direction to "try" impeachment cases. When asked at oral argument whether that direction would be satisfied if, after a House vote to impeach, the Senate, without any procedure whatsoever, unanimously found the accused guilty of being "a bad guy," counsel for the United States answered that the Government's theory "leads me to answer that question yes." Especially in light of this advice from the Solicitor General, I would not issue an invitation to the Senate to find an excuse, in the name of other pressing business, to be dismissive of its critical role in the impeachment process. . . .

[T]he issue in the political question doctrine is *not* whether the constitutional text commits exclusive responsibility for a particular governmental function to one of the political branches. There are numerous instances of this sort of textual commitment, *e.g.*, Art. I, § 8, and it is not thought that disputes implicating these provisions are nonjusticiable. Rather, the issue is whether the Constitution has given one of the political branches final responsibility for interpreting the scope and nature of such a power. . . .

The courts therefore are usually left to infer the presence of a political question from the text and structure of the Constitution. In drawing the inference that the Constitution has committed final interpretive authority to one of the political branches, courts are sometimes aided by textual evidence that the Judiciary was not meant to exercise judicial review—a coordinate inquiry expressed in *Baker*'s "lack of judicially discoverable and manageable standards" criterion.

The majority finds a clear textual commitment in the Constitution's use of the word "sole" in the phrase "[t]he Senate shall have the sole Power to try all Impeachments." It attributes "considerable significance" to the fact that this term appears in only one other passage in the Constitution. The Framers' sparing use of "sole" is thought to indicate that its employment in the Impeachment Trial Clause demonstrates a concern to give the Senate exclusive interpretive authority over the Clause.

. . . The significance of the Constitution's use of the term "sole" lies not in the infrequency with which the term appears, but in the fact that it appears exactly twice, in parallel provisions concerning impeachment. That the word "sole" is found only in the House and Senate Impeachment Clauses demonstrates that its purpose is to emphasize the distinct role of each in the impeachment process. As the majority notes, the Framers, following English practice, were very much concerned to separate the prosecutorial from the adjudicative aspects of impeachment. Giving each House "sole" power with respect to its role in impeachments effected this division of labor. . . .

The majority's review of the historical record . . . explains why the power to try impeachments properly resides with the Senate. It does not explain, however, the sweeping statement that the Judiciary was "not chosen to have any role in impeachments." Not a single word in the historical materials cited by the majority addresses judicial review of the Impeachment Trial Clause. . . .

What the relevant history mainly reveals is deep ambivalence among many of the Framers over the very institution of impeachment, which, by its nature, is not easily reconciled with our system of checks and balances. As they clearly recognized, the branch of the Federal Government which is possessed of the authority to try impeachments, by having final say over the membership of each branch, holds a potentially unanswerable power over the others. In addition, that branch, insofar as it is called upon to try not only members of other branches, but also its own, will have the advantage of being the judge of its own members' causes. . . .

The historical evidence reveals above all else that the Framers were deeply concerned about placing in any branch the "awful discretion, which a court of impeachments must necessarily have." The Federalist No. 65. . . .

The majority also contends that the term "try" does not present a judicially manageable standard. It notes that in 1787, as today, the word "try" may refer to an inquiry in the nature of a judicial proceeding, or, more generally, to experimentation or investigation. In light of the term's multiple senses, the Court finds itself unable to conclude that the Framers used the word "try" as "an implied limitation on the method by which the Senate might proceed in trying impeachments." . . .

To begin with, one would intuitively expect that, in defining the power of a political body to conduct an inquiry into official wrongdoing, the Framers used "try" in its legal sense. That intuition is borne out by reflection on the alternatives. The third Clause of Art. I, § 3, cannot seriously be read to mean that the Senate shall "attempt" or "experiment with" impeachments. It is equally implausible to say that the Senate is charged with "investigating" impeachments given that this description would substantially overlap with the House of Representatives' "sole" power to draw up articles of impeachment. That these alternatives are not realistic possibilities is finally evidenced by the use of "tried" in the third sentence of the Impeachment Trial Clause ("[w]hen the President of the United States is tried . . . "), and by Art. III, § 2, cl. 3 ("[t]he Trial of all Crimes, except in Cases of Impeachment . . . ").

The other variant of the majority position focuses not on which sense of "try" is employed in the Impeachment Trial Clause, but on whether the legal sense of that term creates a judicially manageable standard. The majority concludes that the term provides no "identifiable textual limit." Yet, as the Government itself conceded at oral argument, the term "try" is hardly so elusive as the majority would have it. Were the Senate, for example, to adopt the practice of automatically entering a judgment of conviction whenever articles of impeachment were delivered from the House, it is quite clear that the Senate will have failed to "try" impeachments.[2] Indeed in this respect, "try" presents no greater, and perhaps fewer, interpretive difficulties than some other constitutional standards that have been found amenable to familiar techniques of judicial construction, including, for example, "Commerce . . . among the several States."

The majority's conclusion that "try" is incapable of meaningful judicial construction is not without irony. One might think that if any class of concepts would fall within the definitional abilities of the Judiciary, it would be that class having to do with procedural justice. . . .

■ JUSTICE SOUTER, concurring in the judgment.

I agree with the Court that this case presents a nonjusticiable political question. Because my analysis differs somewhat from the Court's, however, I concur in its judgment by this separate opinion.

As we cautioned in Baker v. Carr, at 210–211, "the 'political question' label" tends "to obscure the need for case-by-case inquiry." The need for such close examination is nevertheless clear from our precedents, which demonstrate that the functional nature of the political question doctrine requires analysis of "the precise facts and posture of the particular case," and precludes "resolution by any semantic cataloguing":

> Prominent on the surface of any case held to involve a political question is found a textually demonstrable constitutional commitment of the issue to a coordinate political department; or a lack of judicially discoverable and manageable standards for resolving it; or the impossibility of deciding without an initial policy determination of a kind clearly for nonjudicial discretion; or the impossibility of a court's undertaking independent resolution without expressing lack of the respect due coordinate branches of government; or an unusual need for unquestioning adherence to a political decision already made; or the potentiality of embarrassment from multifarious pronouncements by various departments on one question.

Whatever considerations feature most prominently in a particular case, the political question doctrine is "essentially a function of the separation of powers," *ibid.*, existing to restrain courts "from inappropriate interference in the business of the other branches of Government," and deriving in large part from prudential concerns about the respect we owe the political departments. Not all interference is inappropriate or disrespectful, however, and application of the doctrine ultimately

---

[2]   It is not a sufficient rejoinder to this example to say, with one of the Court of Appeals judges below, that it postulates a "monstrous hypothetical abuse." The unlikelihood of the example being realized does not undermine the point that "try" has a definable meaning and thus ought to be regarded as judicially manageable.

turns, as Learned Hand put it, on "how importunately the occasion demands an answer." L. Hand, The Bill of Rights 15 (1958).

This occasion does not demand an answer. . . . It seems fair to conclude that the Clause contemplates that the Senate may determine, within broad boundaries, such subsidiary issues as the procedures for receipt and consideration of evidence necessary to satisfy its duty to "try" impeachments. . . . As the Court observes, judicial review of an impeachment trial would under the best of circumstances entail significant disruption of government.

One can, nevertheless, envision different and unusual circumstances that might justify a more searching review of impeachment proceedings. If the Senate were to act in a manner seriously threatening the integrity of its results, convicting, say, upon a coin toss, or upon a summary determination that an officer of the United States was simply "a bad guy," judicial interference might well be appropriate. In such circumstances, the Senate's action might be so far beyond the scope of its constitutional authority, and the consequent impact on the Republic so great, as to merit a judicial response despite the prudential concerns that would ordinarily counsel silence. . . .

NOTES

1.   Which of the opinions above is most persuasive? Is the answer that practice has established that Congress has the last word on impeachments? It is true that whoever has the last word can do something monstrous? Is there any more reason to fear the Court having the last word on impeachments, given that this is one of the few constitutional checks that the Constitution gives the political branches against the federal courts?

2.   What is the practical difference between the holding of the majority in *Nixon* that the case presents a "nonjusticiable" political question and a holding "on the merits" that the Senate's action was within the scope of its constitutional powers? Is there any? Are political question holdings really just merits holdings in disguise?

Consider in this regard the first two aspects of the political question doctrine. How is a holding that an issue is "textually committed" to a political branch any different from a straightforward holding, on the merits, that the action of the political branch was not unconstitutional, being within the sphere of its discretion to act? How is a holding that there are no "judicially discoverable and manageable standards" for resolving an issue any different from a straightforward holding, on the merits, that the Constitution does not supply a rule invalidating the action of the political branches and thus that the action was not unconstitutional?

3.   Consider other factors listed in standard formulations of the political question doctrine: "the impossibility of a court's undertaking independent resolution without expressing lack of the respect due coordinate branches of government; or an unusual need for unquestioning adherence to a political decision already made; or the potentiality of embarrassment from multifarious pronouncements by various departments on one question." *Baker v. Carr*, 369 U.S. 186, 217 (1962). Are these appropriate grounds for refusal to decide a case on the merits, where the issue is (by hypothesis) *not* textually committed to the judgment of the political branches and where the Constitution *does* supply a rule or standard that the political branches action violates?

Note that the fact that a case is politically important does not make it a political question. As you may have already seen, the courts rejected the application of the political question doctrine in *Powell v. McCormack*, p. 104; in *House of Representatives v. Burwell*,

p. 169; and in *United States v. Nixon*, p. 356. The Supreme Court also rejected the applicability of the doctrine in *Zivotofsky v. Clinton*, 132 S.Ct. 1428 (2012), which set the stage for the Court's decision three years later in *Zivotofsky v. Kerry*, p. 281.

4.   The political question doctrine may have some applicability in litigation over partisan gerrymandering—that is, a claim that one party had drawn district lines in order to disadvantage the other party. A case on that issue, *Vieth v. Jubelirer*, 541 U.S. 267 (2004), is presented at p. 786.

[Assignment 22]

E.   THE ELEVENTH AMENDMENT AND SOVEREIGN IMMUNITY: "THE JUDICIAL POWER . . . SHALL NOT . . . EXTEND TO"

Art. III, § 2: The judicial Power shall extend to all Cases, in Law and Equity, arising under this Constitution, the Laws of the United States, and Treaties made, or which shall be made, under their Authority; . . . to Controversies between two or more States;—between a State and Citizens of another State;—between Citizens of different States; . . . and between a State, or the Citizens thereof, and foreign States, Citizens or Subjects.

Amend. XI: The Judicial power of the United States shall not be construed to extend to any suit in law or equity, commenced or prosecuted against one of the United States by Citizens of another State, or by Citizens or Subjects of any Foreign State.

Before the Founding, it was a general principle of the common law that no sovereign government, which in America included the states, could be sued without its consent. It might be thought that the ratification of the Constitution changed that state "sovereign immunity" in two respects. First, the Constitution created a national government in which the states were arguably no longer sovereign. Second, it specifically authorized the establishment of federal courts with power over "Controversies . . . between a State and Citizens of another State" and "all Cases, in Law and Equity, arising under this Constitution," and "the Laws of the United States." Art. III, Sec. 2.

The impact of the Constitution on state sovereign immunity was a matter of intense constitutional controversy in the first decade of the United States. It was much-discussed during the ratification debates. It was the subject of one of the Court's most controversial early cases, *Chisholm v. Georgia*, 2 U.S. (2 Dall.) 419 (1793). And it was the subject of the first constitutional amendment after the Bill of Rights.

Before we dive into those early debates, it is worth noting that this issue, and these debates, remain of great importance today. In a series of controversial cases over the past twenty years (mostly decided 5–4), the Supreme Court has reaffirmed the sovereign immunity of the states, relying heavily on some of the arguments you will see below. Those modern decisions limit the enforcement of federal rights against states in areas ranging from employment law to patent law to shipping regulations. These decisions sometimes mean that the victims of a constitutional violation will have no remedy at all.

Now back to the Founding. At the Virginia ratification convention, George Mason criticized the proposed Constitution because it seemed to eliminate state sovereign immunity:

"To controversies between a State, and the citizens of another State."—How will their jurisdiction in this case do? Let Gentlemen look at the Westward. Claims respecting those lands, every liquidated account, or other claim against this State, will be tried before the Federal Court. Is not this disgraceful?—Is this State to be brought to the bar of justice like a delinquent individual?—Is the sovereignty of the State to be arraigned like a culprit, or private offender?—Will the States undergo this mortification? I think this power perfectly unnecessary.

Debates of the Virginia Convention (June 19, 1788), in 10 THE DOCUMENTARY HISTORY OF THE RATIFICATION OF THE CONSTITUTION 1387, 1406 (John P. Kaminski & Gaspare J. Saladino eds., 1993). The next day, James Madison attempted to dispel Mason's fears:

Its jurisdiction in controversies between a State and citizens of another State, is much objected to, and perhaps without reason. It is not in the power of individuals to call any State into Court. The only operation it can have, is, that if a State should wish to bring suit against a citizen, it must be brought before the Federal Court. . . . This may be illustrated by other cases. It is provided, that citizens of different States may be carried to the Federal Court.—But this will not go beyond the cases where they may be parties. A feme covert may be a citizen of another State, but cannot be a party in this Court. A subject of a foreign power having a dispute with a citizen of this State, may carry it to the Federal Court; but an alien enemy cannot bring suit at all. It appears to me, that this can have no operation but this—to give a citizen a right to be heard in the Federal Court; and if a State should condescend to be a party, this Court may take cognizance of it.

Debates of the Virginia Convention (June 20, 1788), in 10 DOCUMENTARY HISTORY OF RATIFICATION at 1414. Patrick Henry continued the debate by replying to Madison:

As to controversies between a State and the citizens of another State, his [James Madison] construction of it is to me perfectly incomprehensible. . . . [H]e says, that the State may be plaintiff only. If Gentlemen pervert the most clear expressions, and the usual meaning of the language of the people, there is an end of all argument. What says the paper? That it shall have cognizance of controversies between a State, and citizens of another State, without discriminating between plaintiff or defendant. What says the Honorable Gentleman?—The contrary—That the State can only be plaintiff. When the State is debtor, there is no reciprocity. It seems to me that Gentlemen may put what construction they please on it. What!—Is justice to be done to one party, and not to the other!—If Gentlemen take this liberty now, what will they not do when our rights and liberties are in their power?

Id. at 1422–1423. And John Marshall replied to Henry:

With respect to disputes between a State, and the citizens of another State, its jurisdiction has been decried with unusual vehemence. I hope no Gentleman will think that a State will be called at the bar of the Federal Court. . . . It is not rational to suppose, that the sovereign power shall be dragged before a Court. The intent is, to enable States to recover claims of individuals residing in other States. I contend this construction is warranted by the words. But, say they, there will be partiality in it if a State cannot be defendant—if an individual cannot proceed to obtain judgment against a State, though he may be sued by a State. It is necessary to be so, and cannot be avoided. I see a difficulty in making a State defendant, which does not prevent its being plaintiff. If this be only what cannot be avoided, why object to the system on that account?

Id. at 1433. Similar debates occurred in other states. See generally Caleb Nelson, *Sovereign Immunity As A Doctrine of Personal Jurisdiction*, 115 Harv. L. Rev. 1559, 1593–1594 (2002).

As it happens, almost immediately after the Constitution went into effect, a lawsuit was brought that required a decision on this very issue. The case of *Chisholm v. Georgia* was brought by South Carolinian Alexander Chisholm, the executor of the estate of Robert Farquhar, who sued the state of Georgia over a debt that dated back to the Revolutionary War. (The claim was for *assumpsit*, a claim at law, not equity, for restitution of money held by the defendant.) Chisholm filed suit in a lower federal court in Georgia. But Georgia denied the court's authority, claiming that as a sovereign state it was immune from suit without its consent. The lower court ruled in favor of Georgia and Chisholm appealed to the Supreme Court. Chisholm was represented in the Supreme Court by Edmund Randolph (who happened to have a side job as U.S. Attorney General). Jared Ingersoll and Alexander Dallas represented the state of Georgia; they submitted a protest against the Supreme Court's jurisdiction, but refused to participate in oral argument.

The *Chisholm* case excited great interest because many out-of-state citizens, including some foreigners, had claims against various state governments arising out of Revolutionary War debts. The Supreme Court ruled 4–1 that Georgia's sovereign immunity had been abrogated by the Diversity Clause in Article III. Accordingly, sovereign immunity did not bar Chisholm's lawsuit and it could go forward. The lone dissent was filed by Justice Iredell (who had sat on the lower federal court that already ruled in Georgia's favor). At the time the justices delivered *seriatim* opinions, each justice stating his individual views, with no "Opinion of the Court." Justice Iredell's opinion, which appears first in the U.S. Reports, is actually the dissent.

Chisholm v. Georgia

2 U.S. (2 Dall.) 419 (1793)

■ IREDELL, JUSTICE.

. . . The question . . . is,—will an action of *assumpsit* lie against a State? If it will, it must be in virtue of the Constitution of the *United States*, and of some law of *Congress* conformable thereto. The part of the Constitution concerning the Judicial Power, is as follows, viz: *Art. 3. sect. 2.* The Judicial Power shall extend, (1.) To all cases, in law and equity, arising under the Constitution, the laws of the *United States*, and treaties made, or which shall be made, under their authority. (2) To all cases affecting Ambassadors, or other public Ministers, and Consuls; (3) To all cases of Admiralty and Maritime Jurisdiction; (4) To controversies to which the *United States* shall be a party; (5) To controversies between two or more States; between a State and citizens of another State; between citizens of different States; between citizens of the same State, claiming lands under grants of different States; and, between a State or the citizens thereof, and foreign States, citizens or subjects. The Constitution, therefore, provides for the jurisdiction wherein a State is a party, in the following instances:—*1st.* Controversies between two or more States. *2d.* Controversies between a State and citizens of another State. *3d.* Controversies between a State, and foreign States, citizens, or subjects. And it also provides, that in all cases in which a State shall be a party, the Supreme Court shall have original jurisdiction.

The words of the general judicial act, conveying the authority of the Supreme Court, under the Constitution, so far as they concern this question, are as follow:— *Sect.* 13. "That the Supreme Court shall have exclusive jurisdiction of all controversies of a civil nature, where a State is a party, except between . . . a State and citizens of other States, or aliens, in which latter case it shall have original, but not exclusive jurisdiction. . . ." The suit now before the Court (if maintainable at all) comes within the latter description, it being a suit against a State by a citizen of another State.

The Constitution is particular in expressing the *parties* who may be the objects of the jurisdiction in any of these cases, but in respect to the subject-matter upon which such jurisdiction is to be exercised, uses the word "controversies" only. The act of *Congress* more particularly mentions *civil* controversies, a qualification of the general word in the Constitution, which I do not doubt every reasonable man will think well warranted, for it cannot be presumed that the general word "controversies" was intended to include any proceedings that relate to criminal cases, which in all instances that respect the same Government, only, are uniformly considered of a local nature, and to be decided by its particular laws. The word "controversy" indeed, would not naturally justify any such construction, but nevertheless it was perhaps a proper instance of caution in *Congress* to guard against the possibility of it.

A general question of great importance here occurs. What controversy of a civil nature can be maintained against a State by an individual? The framers of the Constitution, I presume, must have meant one of two things: Either 1. In the conveyance of that part of the judicial power which did not relate to the execution of the other authorities of the general Government (which it must be admitted are full and discretionary, within the restrictions of the Constitution itself), to refer to antecedent laws for the construction of the general words they use: Or, 2. To enable *Congress* in all such cases to pass all such laws, as they might deem necessary and proper to carry the purposes of this Constitution into full effect, either absolutely at their discretion, or at least in cases where prior laws were deficient for such purposes, if any such deficiency existed.

. . . I conceive, that all the Courts of the *United States* must receive, not merely their *organization* as to the number of Judges of which they are to consist; but all their authority, as to the manner of their proceeding, from the Legislature only. This appears to me to be one of those cases, with many others, in which an article of the Constitution cannot be effectuated without the intervention of the Legislative authority. There being many such, at the end of the special enumeration of the powers of *Congress* in the Constitution, is this general one: "To make all laws which shall be necessary and proper for carrying into execution the foregoing Powers, and all other powers vested by this Constitution in the Government of the *United States*, or in any department or officer thereof." None will deny, that an act of Legislation is necessary to say, at least of what number the Judges are to consist; the *President* with the consent of the *Senate* could not nominate a number at their discretion. The Constitution intended this article so far at least to be the subject of a Legislative act. Having a right thus to establish the Court, and it being capable of being established in no other manner, I conceive it necessary follows, that they are also to direct the manner of its proceedings. Upon this authority, there is, that I know, but one limit; that is, "that they shall not exceed their authority." If they do, I have no hesitation to say, that any act to that effect would be utterly void, because it would be inconsistent with the Constitution, which is a fundamental law paramount to all others, which we are not only bound to consult, but sworn to observe; and, therefore, where there is an interference, being superior in obligation to the other, we must unquestionably obey that in preference. Subject to this restriction, the whole business of organizing the Courts, and directing the methods of their proceeding where necessary, I conceive to be in the discretion of *Congress*. If it shall be found on this occasion, or on any other, that the remedies now in being are defective, for any purpose it is their duty to provide for, they no doubt will provide others. It is their duty to *legislate* so far as is necessary to carry the Constitution into effect. It is *ours* only to *judge*. We have no reason, nor any more right to distrust their doing their duty, than they have to distrust that we all do ours. There is no part of the Constitution that I know of, that authorises this Court to take up any business where they left it, and, in order that the powers given in the Constitution may be in full activity, supply their omission by making *new laws* for *new cases*; or, which I take to be the same thing, applying *old principles* to *new cases* materially different from those to which they were applied before. . . .

But the act of *Congress* has not been altogether silent upon this subject. . . . *[Justice Iredell next pointed to the Judiciary Act of 1789, which gave the federal courts power to issue writs "which may be necessary for the exercise of their respective jurisdictions, and agreeable to the principles and usages of law." Those principles of law, Justice Iredell said, must be either the particular laws of the state being sued, or the principles of law common to all the states. Under either, a sovereign is immune from suit.—Editors]*

Whatever be the true construction of the Constitution in this particular; whether it is to be construed as intending merely a transfer of jurisdiction from one tribunal to another, or as authorizing the Legislature to provide laws for the decision of all possible controversies in which a State may be involved with an individual, without regard to any prior exemption; yet it is certain that the Legislature has in fact proceeded upon the former supposition, and not upon the latter. For, besides what I noticed before as to an express reference to principles and usages of law as the guide of our proceeding, it is observable that in instances like this before the Court, this Court hath a *concurrent jurisdiction* only; the present being one of those cases where by the judicial act this Court hath *original* but not *exclusive* jurisdiction. This Court, therefore, under that act, can exercise no authority in such instances, but such authority as from the subject matter of it may be exercised in some other

Court. . . . [Its jurisdiction must be] concurrent with the Courts of the several States. It follows, therefore, unquestionably, I think, that looking at the act of *Congress*, which I consider is on this occasion the limit of our authority (whatever further might be constitutiona[l]ly, enacted) we can exercise no authority in the present instance consistently with the clear intention of the act, but such as a proper State Court would have been at least competent to exercise at the time the act was passed.

If therefore, no new remedy be provided (as plainly is the case), and consequently we have no other rule to govern us but the principles of the pre-existent laws, which must remain in force till superceded by others, then it is incumbent upon us to enquire, whether previous to the adoption of the Constitution . . . an action of the nature like this before the Court could have been maintained against one of the States in the *Union* upon the principles of the common law, which I have shown to be alone applicable. If it could, I think it is now maintainable here; If it could not, I think, as the law stands at present, it is not maintainable; whatever opinion may be entertained; upon the construction of the Constitution, as to the power of *Congress* to authorize such a one. Now I presume it will not be denied, that in every State in the *Union*, previous to the adoption of the Constitution, the only common law principles in regard to suits that were in any manner admissible in respect to claims against the State, were those which in *England* apply to claims against the crown; there being certainly no other principles of the common law which, previous to the adoption of this Constitution could, in any manner, or upon any colour apply to the case of a claim against a State in its own Courts, where it was solely and completely sovereign in respect to such cases at least. Whether that remedy was strictly applicable or not, still I apprehend there was no other. The only remedy in a case like that before the Court, by which, by any possibility, a suit can be maintained against the crown in *England*, or could be at any period from which the common law, as in force in *America*, could be derived, I believe is that which is called a *Petition of right*. . . . *[Here Justice Iredell discussed many English cases, as well as Blackstone.—Editors]*

Thus, it appears, that in *England* even in case of a private debt contracted by the *King*, in his own person, there is no remedy but by petition, which must receive his express sanction, otherwise there can be no proceeding upon it. If the debt contracted be avowedly for the public uses of Government, it is at least doubtful whether that remedy will lie, and if it will, it remains afterwards in the power of Parliament to provide for it or not among the current supplies of the year. . . .

I have now, I think, established the following particulars.—*1st.* That the Constitution, so far as it respects the judicial authority, can only be carried into effect by acts of the Legislature appointing Courts, and prescribing their methods of proceeding. *2d.* That *Congress* has provided no new law in regard to this case, but expressly referred us to the old. *3d.* That there are no principles of the old law, to which, we must have recourse, that in any manner authorise the present suit, either by precedent or by analogy. The consequence of which, in my opinion, clearly is, that the suit in question cannot be maintained. . . .

[U]nquestionably the people of the *United States* had a right to form what kind of union, and upon what terms they pleased, without reference to any former examples. If upon a fair construction of the Constitution of the *United States*, the power contended for really exists, it undoubtedly may be exercised, though it be a power of the first impression. If it does not exist, upon that authority, ten thousand examples of similar powers would not warrant its assumption. So far as this great question affects the Constitution itself, if the present afforded, consistently with the particular grounds of my opinion, a proper occasion for a decision upon it, I would not shrink from its discussion. But it is of extreme moment that no Judge should rashly commit himself upon important questions, which it is unnecessary for him to decide. My opinion being, that even if the Constitution would admit of the exercise of such a power, a new law is necessary for the purpose, since no part of the existing law applies, this alone is sufficient to justify my determination in the present case. So much, however, has been said on the Constitution, that it may not be improper to intimate that my present opinion is strongly against any construction of it, which will admit, under any circumstances, a compulsive suit against a State for the recovery of money. I think every word in the Constitution may have its full effect without involving this consequence, and that nothing but express words, or an insurmountable implication (neither of which I consider, can be found in this case) would authorise the deduction of so high a power. This opinion I hold, however, with all the reserve proper for one, which, according to my sentiments in this case, may be deemed in some measure extra-judicial. With regard to the policy of maintaining such suits, that is not for this Court to consider, unless the point in all other respects was very doubtful. Policy might then be argued from with a view to preponderate the judgment. Upon the question before us, I have no doubt. I have therefore nothing to do with the policy. But I confess, if I was at liberty to speak on that subject, my opinion on the policy of the case would also differ from that of the Attorney General. . . .

■ BLAIR, JUSTICE.

In considering this important case, I have thought it best to pass over all the strictures which have been made on the various European confederations; because, as, on the one hand, their likeness to our own is not sufficiently close to justify any analogical application; so, on the other, they are utterly destitute of any binding authority here. The Constitution of the *United States* is the only fountain from which I shall draw; the only authority to which I shall appeal. Whatever be the true language of that, it is obligatory upon every member of the *Union*; for, no State could have become a member, but by an adoption of it by the people of that State. What then do we find there requiring the submission of individual States to the judicial authority of the *United States*? This is expressly extended, among other things, to controversies between a State and citizens of another State. Is then the case before us one of that description? Undoubtedly it is. . . . It seems to me, that if this Court should refuse to hold jurisdiction of a case where a State is Defendant, it would renounce part of the authority conferred, and, consequently, part of the duty imposed on it by the Constitution; because it would be a refusal to take cognizance of a case where *a State is a party*. Nor does the jurisdiction of this Court, in relation to a State, seem to me to be questionable, on the ground that *Congress* has not provided any form of execution, or pointed out any mode of making the judgment against a State effectual; the argument *ab in utili [i.e., from that which is useless—Editors]* may weigh much in cases depending upon the construction of doubtful Legislative acts, but can have no force, I think, against the clear and positive directions of an act of *Congress* and of the Constitution. . . . When sovereigns are sued in their own Courts, [a petition of right] may have been established as the most respectful form of demand; but we are not now in State-Court; and if sovereignty be an exemption from suit in any other than the sovereign's own Courts, it follows that when a State, by adopting the Constitution, has agreed to be amenable to the judicial power of the *United States*, she has, in that respect, given up her right of sovereignty. . . .

■ WILSON, JUSTICE.

This is a case of uncommon magnitude. One of the parties to it is a STATE; certainly respectable, claiming to be *sovereign*. The question to be determined is, whether this State, so respectable, and whose claim soars so high, is amenable to the jurisdiction of the Supreme Court of the *United States*? This question, important in itself, will depend on others, more important still; and, may, perhaps, be ultimately resolved into one, no less radical than this "do the people of the *United States* form a NATION?" . . .

To the Constitution of the *United States* the term SOVEREIGN, is totally unknown. There is but one place where it could have been used with propriety. But, even in that place it would not, perhaps, have comported with the delicacy of those, who *ordained* and *established* that Constitution. They *might* have announced themselves "SOVEREIGN" people of the *United States*: But serenely conscious of the *fact*, they avoided the *ostentatious declaration*. . . .

MAN, fearfully and wonderfully made, is the workmanship of his all perfect CREATOR: A *State*; useful and valuable as the contrivance is, is the *inferior* contrivance of *man*; and from his *native* dignity derives all its *acquired* importance. . . .

I am, . . . chiefly, to examine the important question now before us, by the Constitution of the *United States*, and the legitimate result of that valuable instrument. Under this view, the question is naturally subdivided into two others. 1. *Could* the Constitution of the *United States* vest a jurisdiction over the State of *Georgia*? 2. Has that Constitution vested such jurisdiction in this Court? . . .

Concerning the prerogative of *Kings*, and concerning the sovereignty of States, much has been said and written; but little has been said and written concerning a subject much more dignified and important, the majesty of the people. . . . In order, therefore, to form a more perfect union, *to establish justice*, to ensure domestic tranquillity, to provide for common defence, and to secure the blessings of liberty, *those people*, among whom were the people of *Georgia*, ordained and established the present Constitution. By that Constitution Legislative power is vested, Executive power is vested, *Judicial* power is vested.

The question now opens fairly to our view, *could* the *people* of those States, among whom were those of *Georgia*, bind those *States*, and *Georgia* among the others, by the Legislative, Executive, and Judicial power so vested? If the principles, on which I have founded myself, are just and true; this question must unavoidably receive an affirmative answer. If those *States* were the *work* of those *people*; those people, and, that I may apply the case closely, the people of *Georgia*, in particular, could alter, as they pleased, their former work: To any given degree, they could *diminish* as well as enlarge it. Any or all of the former State-powers, they could *extinguish* or *transfer*. The inference, which necessarily results, is, that the Constitution ordained and established by *those* people; and, still closely to apply the case, in particular by the people of Georgia, *could* vest jurisdiction or judicial power over those States and over the State of *Georgia* in particular.

The next question under this head, is,—*Has* the Constitution done so? . . . Whoever considers, in a combined and comprehensive view, the *general texture* of the Constitution, will be satisfied, that the people of the *United States* intended to form themselves into a nation for *national purposes*. They instituted, for *such* purposes, a national Government, complete in all its parts, with powers Legislative, Executive and Judiciary; and, in all those powers, extending over the whole nation. Is it congruous, that, with regard to *such* purposes, any man or body of men, any person natural or artificial, should be permitted to claim successfully an entire exemption from the jurisdiction of the national Government? Would not such claims, crowned with success, be repugnant to our very existence as a nation? . . .

But, in my opinion, this doctrine rests not upon the legitimate result of fair and conclusive deduction from the Constitution: It is confirmed, beyond all doubt, by the *direct* and *explicit declaration* of the Constitution itself. "The judicial power of the *United States* shall extend, to controversies between *two* States." *Two* States are supposed to have a controversy between them: This controversy is supposed to be brought before those vested with the judicial power of the *United States*: Can the most consummate degree of professional ingenuity devise a mode by which this "controversy between two States" can be brought before a Court of law; and yet neither of those States be a Defendant? "The judicial power of the *United States* shall extend to controversies, between a *state* and *citizens* of *another* State." Could the strictest legal language . . . describe, with more precise accuracy, the cause now depending before the tribunal? *Causes*, and not *parties* to causes, are weighed by justice, in her equal scales: On the former *solely*, her attention is fixed: To the latter, she is, as she is painted, blind. . . .

■ CUSHING, JUSTICE.

The grand and principal question in this case is, whether a State can, by the Fœderal Constitution, be sued by an individual citizen of another State?

The point turns not upon the law or practice of *England*, although perhaps it may be in some measure elucidated thereby, nor upon the law of any other country whatever; but upon the Constitution established by the people of the *United States*; and particularly upon the extent of powers given to the Fœderal Judicial in the 2d section of the 3d article of the Constitution. . . . The judicial power, then, is expressly extended to "*controversies between a State and citizens of another State.*" When a citizen makes a demand against a State, of which he is not a citizen, it is as really a controversy between a State and a citizen of another State, as if such State made a demand against such citizen. The case, then, seems clearly to fall within the letter of the Constitution. It may be suggested that it could not be intended to subject a State to be a Defendant, because it would effect the sovereignty of States. If that be the case, what shall we do with the immediate preceding clause; "*controversies between two or more States,*" where a State must of necessity be Defendant? If it was not the intent, in the very next clause also, that a State might be made Defendant, why was it so expressed as naturally to lead to and comprehend that idea? Why was not an exception made if one was intended? . . .

■ JAY, CHIEF JUSTICE.

The question we are now to decide has been accurately stated, viz. Is a State suable by individual citizens of another State?

It is said, that *Georgia* refuses to appear and answer to the Plaintiff in this action, because she is a *sovereign* State, and therefore not *liable* to such actions. In order to ascertain the merits of this objection, let us enquire, 1st. In what sense *Georgia* is a sovereign State. 2d. Whether suability is incompatable with such sovereignty. 3d. Whether the Constitution (to which *Georgia* is a party) authorises such an action against her. . . .

1st. . . . The Revolution, or rather the Declaration of Independence, found the people *already* united for general purposes, and at the same time providing for their more domestic concerns by State conventions, and other temporary arrangements. . . . [A]fterwards, in the hurry of the war, and in the warmth of mutual confidence, they made a confederation of the States, the basis of a general Government. Experience disappointed the expectations they had formed from it; and then the people, in their collective and national capacity, established the present Constitution. It is remarkable that in establishing it, the people exercised their own rights, and their own proper sovereignty, and conscious of the plenitude of it, they declared with becoming dignity, "We the *people* of the *United States*, do ordain and establish this Constitution." Here we see the people acting as sovereigns of the whole country; and in the language of sovereignty, establishing a Constitution by which it was their will, that the State Governments should be bound, and to which the State Constitutions should be made to conform. . . .

Sover[e]ignty is the right to govern; a nation or State-sovereign is the person or persons in whom that resides. In *Europe* the sovereignty is generally ascribed to the *Prince*; here it rests with the people; there, the sovereign actually administers the Government; here, never in a single instance; our Governors are the agents of the people, and at most stand in the same relation to their sovereign, in which regents in *Europe* stand to their sovereigns. Their *Princes* have *personal* powers, dignities, and pre-eminences, our rulers have none but *official*; nor do they partake in the sovereignty otherwise, or in any other capacity, than as private citizens.

2d. The second object of enquiry now presents itself, viz. whether suability is compatible with State sovereignty. . . .

There is at least one strong undeniable fact against this incompatibility, and that is this, any one State in the *Union* may sue another State, in this Court, that is, all the people of one State may sue all the people of another State. It is plain then, that a State may be *sued*, and hence it plainly follows, that *suability* and *state sovereignty* are not incompatible. As one State may sue another State in this *Court*, it is plain that no degradation to a State is thought to accompany her appearance in this *Court*. . . .

Let us now turn to the Constitution. . . . The question now before us renders it necessary to pay particular attention to that part of the 2d section [of Article III], which extends the judicial power *"to controversies between a state and citizens of another state."* It is contended, that this ought to be construed to reach none of these controversies, excepting those in which a State may be *Plaintiff*. The ordinary rules for construction will easily decide whether those words are to be understood in that limited sense. . . .

If we attend to the *words*, we find them to be express, positive, free from ambiguity, and without room for such implied expressions: *"The judicial power of the United States shall extend to controversies between a state and citizens of another state.*" If the Constitution really meant to extend these powers only to those controversies in which a State might be *Plaintiff,* to the exclusion of those in which citizens had demands against a State, it is inconceivable that it should have attempted to convey that meaning in words, not only so incompetent, but also repugnant to it; if it meant to exclude a certain class of these controversies, why were they not expressly excepted; on the contrary, not even an intimation of such intention appears in any part of the Constitution. It cannot be pretended that where citizens urge and insist upon demands against a State, which the State refuses to admit and comply with, that there is no *controversy* between them. If it is a *controversy* between them, then it clearly falls not only within the spirit, but the very words of the Constitution. What is it to the cause of justice, and how can it effect the definition of the word *controversy,* whether the demands which cause the dispute, are made by a State against citizens of another State, or by the latter against the former? When power is thus extended to a *controversy,* it necessarily, as to all judicial purposes, is also extended to those, between whom it subsists.

The exception contended for, would contradict and do violence to the great and leading principles of a free and equal national government, one of the great objects of which is, to ensure justice to all: To the few against the many, as well as to the many against the few. . . .

I perceive, and therefore candor urges me to mention, a circumstance, which seems to favor the opposite side of the question. It is this: the same section of the Constitution which extends the judicial power to *controversies* "between a State and the citizens of another State," does also extend that power to *controversies to which the United States are a party.* Now, it may be said, if the word *party* comprehends both Plaintiff and Defendant, it follows, that the *United States* may be sued by any citizen, between whom and them there may be a *controversy.* This appears to me to be fair reasoning; but the same principles of candour which urge me to mention this objection, also urge me to suggest an important difference between the two cases. It is this: in all cases of actions against States or individual citizens, the National Courts are supported in all their legal and Constitutional proceedings and judgments, by the arm of the Executive power of the *United States;* but in cases of actions against the *United States,* there is no power which the Courts can call to their aid. From this distinction important conclusions are deducible, and they place the case of a State, and the case of the *United States,* in very different points of view. . . .

For my own part, I am convinced that the sense in which I understand and have explained the words "controversies between States and citizens of another State," is the true sense. The extension of the judiciary power of the United States to such controversies, appears to me to be *wise,* because it is *honest,* and because it is *useful.* It is *honest,* because it provides for doing justice without respect of persons, and by securing individual citizens as well as States, in their respective rights, performs the promise which every free Government makes to every free citizen, of equal justice and protection. It is *useful,* because it is honest, because it leaves not even the most obscure and friendless citizen without means of obtaining justice from a neighbouring State; because it obviates occasions of quarrels between States on account of the claims of their respective citizens; because it recognizes and strongly rests on this great moral truth, that justice is the same whether due from one man or a million, or from a million to one man; because it teaches and greatly appreciates the value of our free republican national Government, which places all our citizens on an equal footing, and enables each and every of them to obtain justice without any danger of being overborne by the weight and number of their opponents; and, because it brings into action, and enforces this great and glorious principle, that the people are the sovereign of this country, and consequently that fellow citizens and joint sovereigns cannot be degraded by appearing with each other in their own Courts to have their controversies determined. The people have reason to prize and rejoice in such valuable privileges; and they ought not to forget, that nothing but the free course of Constitutional law and Government can ensure the continuance and enjoyment of them. . . .

NOTES

1. Who is right—the majority or Justice Iredell? Was the case within the jurisdiction contemplated by Article III? Was South Carolina's sovereign immunity abrogated by the Constitution? Are those two ways of asking the same question, or is there a difference?

2. How powerful is the argument by Justice Wilson and Chief Justice Jay that it is unrepublican to think of states as sovereign—that only the People are sovereign? If Georgia is sued and has to pay, who would ultimately have to foot the bill? If the officials of the state violate their oath of office in the course of their duties, inflict injury, and are successfully sued, who should pay? Why should the sovereign People have to pay through taxes for the misconduct of their agents? Note that even skeptics of state sovereign immunity usually believe that *the United States* has sovereign immunity. But why is federal sovereign immunity not equally inconsistent with republicanism? (Note that Chief Justice Jay tries to answer this point. Is his answer persuasive?)

3. With the benefit of hindsight, think about the pre-*Chisholm* ratification debates. What do you make of the debate between George Mason and Patrick Henry on the one hand, and James Madison and John Marshall on the other? Were Mason and Henry paranoid? Were Madison and Marshall disingenuous? And what relevance should their debate have had to the *Chisholm* Court, if any? Do Madison's or Marshall's views deserve special weight?

4. One can also think of *Chisholm* as raising the question of what kind of power the federal courts acquire once they are given jurisdiction over a case. Defenders of state sovereign immunity might be said to think that a grant of *jurisdiction* over certain types of suits—including suits where states are a party—does not itself alter common law rules of *substantive law* concerning principles of sovereign immunity. Does this seem right?

This is a question that has implications far beyond sovereign immunity. What should federal courts do when deciding a case governed by common law? In such a case, should a federal court apply the judge-made common law of the state in which the case arises, or should it instead apply the general principles of the common law as the judge understands them? Does the grant to federal courts of diversity jurisdiction, or admiralty jurisdiction, or jurisdiction to resolve disputes between two states over their boundary carry with it a power to "discover" or "make" federal common law? In *Erie Railroad Co. v. Tompkins*, 304 U.S. 64 (1938), the Court held that in diversity cases the federal courts are bound to apply state substantive law, including applicable state common law. But the Court once reached the opposite conclusion, in *Swift v. Tyson*, 41 U.S. 1 (1842), which held that federal courts were not bound to apply the common law decisions of state courts. *Erie* overruled *Swift*.

5.   The reaction to *Chisholm* was immediate. The next day, a U.S. senator from Massachusetts made a motion to amend the Constitution, in order to erase the decision. But the congressional session was nearly over, and Congress soon adjourned without approving an amendment. Several state legislatures endorsed a constitutional amendment or instructed their senators to support an amendment. (Remember that before the Seventeenth Amendment, U.S senators were chosen by state legislatures.) The states complained that the Supreme Court had changed the deal. For example, the North Carolina General Assembly passed the following resolution on January 11, 1794:

> . . . Whereas it hath been determined in the Supreme Fœderal Court of the United States that a state may be sued by an individual or individuals in said Court.
>
> Resolved that such a power however it might have been contemplated by some was not generally conceived by the representatives of this State in the Convention which adopted the Fœderal Constitution as a power to be vested in the Judiciary of the General Government and that this General Assembly view the same as derogatory of the reserved rights and sovereignty of this State
>
> Resolved that the Senators from this State in the Senate of the United States be and they are hereby instructed and the representatives requested to take the most speedy and effectual measures to obtain such amendments to the Constitution of the United States as will remove or explain any clause or article of the said Constitution which can be construed to imply or justify a decision that a State is compellable to answer in any suit by an individual or individuals in any Court of the United States. . . .

5 THE DOCUMENTARY HISTORY OF THE SUPREME COURT OF THE UNITED STATES, 1789–1800: SUITS AGAINST STATES 615 (Maeva Marcus ed., 1994). Not content with supporting an amendment, the Georgia House of Representatives even passed a bill that, had it also been approved by the state senate, would have made executing the judgment in *Chisholm* a capital crime.

In early 1794, roughly a year after *Chisholm*, the U.S. Congress voted by overwhelming margins to approve an amendment—in the Senate the vote was 23–2, and in the House, 77–8. The proposed amendment read:

> The Judicial power of the United States shall not be construed to extend to any suit in law or equity, commenced or prosecuted against one of the United States by citizens of another State, or by citizens or subjects of any foreign State.

It was sent to each of the states, and within a year the amendment had been ratified by three-quarters of them (i.e., twelve of the then fifteen states). Which might seem to be the end of the story. "There was, however, a problem: not all of the states that had assented to the amendment had notified Congress, so therefore it was not officially known that the requisite number had ratified. Close to two years would pass, during which the Supreme Court would continue to entertain suits against states, before any effort was made to take an account of the progress of the ratification process and determine the amendment's status." *Id.* at 601. Finally, in January 1798, almost five years after the decision in *Chisholm*, President Adams declared that three-fourths of the states had ratified what was now the Eleventh Amendment. The white-hot anger at *Chisholm* had cooled, but the Constitution had changed. It was the first of many successful efforts to amend the Constitution.

As you ponder the Eleventh Amendment, think of what it means for *Chisholm*. Does the amendment show that the Court's interpretation was mistaken? Or is the sequence of *Chisholm* and the Eleventh Amendment a story of success, of the process working as it should, with judges following the Constitution no matter what the consequences and the people amending it as they see fit?

6. The Eleventh Amendment produces its own interpretive difficulties. Does it withdraw a sub-category of diversity jurisdiction only, or does it confer (or restore) state sovereign immunity?

Note that the words of the Eleventh Amendment do not say anything at all about whether a citizen of a state could sue that citizen's *own state*, under the so-called "federal question" jurisdiction of Article III ("all Cases, in Law and Equity, arising under this Constitution, the Laws of the United States, and Treaties made, or which shall be made under their Authority"). This question came before the Supreme Court in the 1890 case of *Hans v. Louisiana*. The case involved a citizen of Louisiana suing his own state for a violation of the Contracts Clause of Article I, § 9, because the state refused to pay some promised interest on its state bonds.

The Supreme Court rejected Hans's suit. It discussed the text and context of the Eleventh Amendment in the following passage:

> In the present case the plaintiff in error contends that he, being a citizen of Louisiana, is not embarrassed by the obstacle of the eleventh amendment, inasmuch as that amendment only prohibits suits against a state which are brought by the citizens of another state, or by citizens or subjects of a foreign state. It is true the amendment does so read, and, if there were no other reason or ground for abating his suit, it might be maintainable; and then we should have this anomalous result, that, in cases arising under the constitution or laws of the United States, a state may be sued in the federal courts by its own citizens, though it cannot be sued for a like cause of action by the citizens of other states, or of a foreign state; and may be thus sued in the federal courts, although not allowing itself to be sued in its own courts. If this is the necessary consequence of the language of the constitution and the law, the result is no less startling and unexpected than was the original decision of this court, that, under the language of the constitution and of the judiciary act of 1789, a state was liable to be sued by a citizen of another state or of a foreign country. That decision was made in the case of *Chisholm v. Georgia*, and created such a shock of surprise throughout the country that, at the first meeting of congress thereafter, the eleventh amendment to the constitution was almost unanimously proposed, and was in due course adopted by the legislatures of the states. This amendment, expressing the will of the ultimate sovereignty of the whole country, superior to all legislatures and all courts, actually reversed the decision of the supreme court.

But the Court also suggested that even without the Eleventh Amendment, Justice Iredell's dissent had been right all along:

> The truth is that the cognizance of suits and actions unknown to the law, and forbidden by the law, was not contemplated by the constitution when establishing the judicial power of the United States.

Is any of this reasoning persuasive? How *should* the Court think about state sovereign immunity after *Chisholm* and the Eleventh Amendment?

7. The question of state sovereign immunity continues to be hotly contested and vigorously litigated. In recent years, the Supreme Court has reaffirmed *Hans* and ruled that Congress lacks the power to abrogate state sovereign immunity in federal courts. See *Seminole Tribe of Florida v. Florida*, 517 U.S. 44 (1996). It has extended this holding

to forbid Congress from subjecting states to suit without their consent in *state* courts. See *Alden v. Maine*, 527 U.S. 706 (1999). But the Court has also held that Congress *does* have power to abrogate state sovereignty if it is using its power to enforce the Fourteenth Amendment. See *Fitzpatrick v. Bitzer*, 427 U.S. 445 (1976). (Congress's power to enforce the Fourteenth Amendment is discussed at p. 1309) Does this combination make sense?

8. The significance of *Hans* and more generally of sovereign immunity is limited as a practical matter by the doctrine associated with *Ex parte Young*, 209 U.S. 123 (1908), which allows plaintiffs to sue state officials, rather than the state, to obtain an injunction against official state action.

In *Young* itself, the Court allowed a railroad to sue a state official and obtain an injunction forbidding that official from enforcing an unconstitutional rate regulation. The case seems to have been a somewhat conventional suit for an anti-suit injunction, a kind of suit in equity that allows a person who might imminently be a *defendant* to instead start the legal process and raise as claims what the person would otherwise have raised as defenses. See generally John C. Harrison, *Ex parte* Young, 60 Stan. L. Rev. 989 (2008). The modern Court has read *Ex parte Young* more broadly as the foundation of a constitutional cause of action and an exception to sovereign immunity for suits seeking prospective relief against state officers.

CHAPTER 3

FEDERALISM

[Assignment 23]

There were republics before the United States, among them ancient Athens and Sparta; Rome before Julius Caesar; Italian city states such as Venice, Florence, Siena, Pisa, and Urbino; and the Netherlands. But they were small. Before the United States there had never been an *extended* republic. As republics grew into empires, power tended to be consolidated in the hands of an unelected leader. At the time of the American Revolution, many assumed it was impossible to sustain an extended republic. They believed that representative government would flourish only in small homogeneous states, perhaps allied in a confederation that would handle external affairs. If the thirteen American colonies formed a strong central government, these skeptics thought its representative character could not last long.

The framers' answer was a republic that would be federal, with a division of powers between the autonomous governments of the states and a collective government for the whole. The state and national governments would check each other, with more freedom and effective government at both levels. The framers thus sought to *exploit* geographical extent to create a pluralistic structure. This constitutional invention was the child of political necessity. The framers had little choice but to devise some kind of a working federal system. States were a given. Yet the need for a strong national government was also clear. The Constitution was thus designed to form a "more perfect Union"—distinct states, but together a new nation.

A Map of the Constitution's Federalism Provisions

The Constitution has no "Federalism Clause." Instead, *federalism* is the term for a pattern of structural features in the Constitution.

First, the states continue to exist and function as states, with their own powers and sphere of authority. While they are states within a larger union, governed by a single Constitution that in important respects limits their powers, the states are not merely subordinate administrative districts of the national government. Much of Article IV of the Constitution governs the relationship of the states to the national government, and to each other.

Second, the powers of the national government are specifically enumerated, and thus limited. All the remaining powers are "reserved" to the states. The division of powers between the national government and the states is the major theme of the first half of this chapter. The focus will often be on Article I, Section 8, which lists the enumerated legislative powers of the national government. In addition, Article I, Section 10 excludes or limits a number of state powers. Where the exercise of a state power conflicts with the exercise of a national power, Article VI makes clear which prevails. The Tenth Amendment confirms the reserved authority of the states in all matters in which the Constitution does not grant power to the national government. A number of amendments, especially the Reconstruction Amendments, grant additional power to the national government, and specifically to Congress.

Third, <u>federalism</u> is built into the structure of the national government. The Senate explicitly represents the states as states, with each state entitled to two senators irrespective of population. (The representation of the states in the Senate was reinforced by the original mode of selecting senators, as discussed in the next paragraph.) The House of Representatives, while apportioned on the basis of population, is nonetheless structured along state lines and provides that each state is entitled to at least one representative regardless of population. Finally, it is the state legislature that determines how each state's electors for the Electoral College are chosen, and the number of those electors is based on a state's combined representation in the House and Senate, a formula that builds on the federalism embodied in those provisions.

One way <u>federalism</u> pervaded the national government's structure has been emphatically changed from the original design. The Constitution originally provided for selection of a state's senators by its state legislature. This arrangement was seen by the framers as an important check on the power of the national government. Writing to John Adams in 1789, Roger Sherman put it this way: "The senators being eligible by the legislatures of the several states, and dependent on them for re-election, will be vigilant in supporting their rights against infringement by the legislative or executive of the United States." 6 THE WORKS OF JOHN ADAMS 440 (Charles Francis Adams ed., 1851). That arrangement persisted until the Seventeenth Amendment, ratified in 1913. That amendment reduced the senators' incentives to protect their state governments, because their reelection was no longer in the hands of the state legislature. The amendment also undermined the state legislatures' practice of "instruction" of senators on how they should vote on important questions. (Previously, state legislatures had instructed senators about their votes on major pending legislation, on the ratification of treaties, and even, though less frequently, on major nominations to executive and judicial offices.) The effects of the Seventeenth Amendment are hard to measure precisely, but what is certain is that it removed what the framers had expected would be a check on the exercise of national power.

The Political Theory of American Federalism

The starting point for thinking about America's constitutional federalism is *The Federalist No. 10*, by James Madison.

The Federalist No. 10

James Madison, Nov. 22, 1787

To the People of the State of New York.

AMONG the numerous advantages promised by a well constructed Union, none deserves to be more accurately developed than its tendency to break and control the violence of faction. The friend of popular governments, never finds himself so much alarmed for their character and fate, as when he contemplates their propensity to this dangerous vice. He will not fail therefore to set a due value on any plan which, without violating the principles to which he is attached, provides a proper cure for it. The instability, injustice and confusion introduced into the public councils, have in truth been the mortal diseases under which popular governments have everywhere perished; as they continue to be the favorite and fruitful topics from which the adversaries to liberty derive their most specious declamations. The valuable improvements made by the American Constitutions on the popular models, both ancient and modern, cannot certainly be too much admired; but it would be an unwarrantable partiality, to contend that they have as effectually obviated the danger on this side as was wished and expected. Complaints are every where heard from our most considerate and virtuous citizens, equally the friends of public and private faith, and of public and personal liberty; that our governments are too unstable; that the public good is disregarded in the conflicts of rival parties; and that measures are too often decided, not according to the rules of justice, and the rights of the minor party; but by the superior force of an interested and over-bearing majority. However anxiously we may wish that these complaints had no foundation, the evidence of known facts will not permit us to deny that they are in some degree true. It will be found indeed, on a candid review of our situation, that some of the distresses under which we labor, have been erroneously charged on the operation of our governments; but it will be found, at the same time, that other causes will not alone account for many of our heaviest misfortunes; and particularly, for that prevailing and increasing distrust of public engagements, and alarm for private rights, which are echoed from one end of the continent to the other. These must be chiefly, if not wholly, effects of the unsteadiness and injustice, with which a factious spirit has tainted our public administrations.

By a faction I understand a number of citizens, whether amounting to a majority or minority of the whole, who are united and actuated by some common impulse of passion, or of interest, adverse to the rights of other citizens, or to the permanent and aggregate interests of the community.

There are two methods of curing the mischiefs of faction: the one, by removing its causes; the other, by controling its effects.

There are again two methods of removing the causes of faction: the one by destroying the liberty which is essential to its existence; the other, by giving to every citizen the same opinions, the same passions, and the same interests.

It could never be more truly said than of the first remedy, that it is worse than the disease. Liberty is to faction, what air is to fire, an aliment without which it instantly expires. But it could not be a less folly to abolish liberty, which is essential to political life, because it nourishes faction, than it would be to wish the annihilation of air, which is essential to animal life, because it imparts to fire its destructive agency.

The second expedient is as impracticable, as the first would be unwise. As long as the reason of man continues fallible, and he is at liberty to exercise it, different opinions will be formed. As long as the connection subsists between his reason and his self-love, his opinions and his passions will have a reciprocal influence on each other; and the former will be objects to which the latter will attach themselves. The diversity in the faculties of men from which the rights of property originate, is not less an insuperable obstacle to a uniformity of interests. The protection of these faculties is the first object of Government. From the protection of different and unequal faculties of acquiring property, the possession of different degrees and kinds of property immediately results; and from the influence of these on the sentiments and views of the respective proprietors, ensues a division of the society into different interests and parties.

The latent causes of faction are thus sown in the nature of man; and we see them every where brought into different degrees of activity, according to the different circumstances of civil society. A zeal for different opinions concerning religion, concerning Government and many other points, as well of speculation as of practice; an attachment to different leaders ambitiously contending for pre-eminence and power; or to persons of other descriptions whose fortunes have been interesting to the human passions, have in turn divided mankind into parties, inflamed them with mutual animosity, and rendered them much more disposed to vex and oppress each other than to co-operate for their common good. So strong is this propensity of mankind to fall into mutual animosities, that where no substantial occasion presents itself, the most frivolous and fanciful distinctions have been sufficient to kindle their unfriendly passions and excite their most violent conflicts. But the most common and durable source of factions, has been the various and unequal distribution of property. Those who hold, and those who are without property, have ever formed distinct interests in society. Those who are creditors, and those who are debtors, fall under a like discrimination. A landed interest, a manufacturing interest, a mercantile interest, a monied interest, with many lesser interests, grow up of necessity in civilized nations, and divide them into different classes, actuated by different sentiments and views. The regulation of these various and interfering interests forms the principal task of modern Legislation, and involves the spirit of party and faction in the necessary and ordinary operations of Government.

No man is allowed to be a judge in his own cause; because his interest would certainly bias his judgment, and, not improbably, corrupt his integrity. With equal, nay with greater reason, a body of men, are unfit to be both judges and parties, at the same time; yet, what are many of the most important acts of legislation, but so many judicial determinations, not indeed concerning the rights of single persons, but concerning the rights of large bodies of citizens; and what are the different classes of legislators, but advocates and parties to the causes which they determine? Is a law proposed concerning private debts? It is a question to which the creditors are parties on one side, and the debtors on the other. Justice ought to hold the balance between them. Yet the parties are and must be themselves the judges; and the most numerous party, or, in other words, the most powerful faction must be expected to prevail. Shall domestic manufactures be encouraged, and in what degree, by restrictions on foreign manufactures? are questions which would be differently decided by the landed and the manufacturing classes; and probably by neither, with a sole regard to justice and the public good. The apportionment of taxes on the various descriptions of property, is an act which seems to require the most exact impartiality; yet, there is perhaps no legislative act in which greater opportunity and temptation are given to a predominant party, to trample on the rules of justice. Every shilling with which they over-burden the inferior number, is a shilling saved to their own pockets.

It is in vain to say, that enlightened statesmen will be able to adjust these clashing interests, and render them all subservient to the public good. Enlightened statesmen will not always be at the helm: Nor, in many cases, can such an adjustment be made at all, without taking into view indirect and remote considerations, which will rarely prevail over the immediate interest which one party may find in disregarding the rights of another, or the good of the whole.

The inference to which we are brought, is, that the *causes* of faction cannot be removed; and that relief is only to be sought in the means of controling its *effects*.

If a faction consists of less than a majority, relief is supplied by the republican principle, which enables the majority to defeat its sinister views by regular vote: It may clog the administration, it may convulse the society; but it will be unable to execute and mask its violence under the forms of the Constitution. When a majority is included in a faction, the form of popular government on the other hand enables it to sacrifice to its ruling passion or interest, both the public good and the rights of other citizens. To secure the public good, and private rights, against the danger of such a faction, and at the same time to preserve the spirit and the form of popular government, is then the great object to which our enquiries are directed. Let me add that it is the great desideratum, by which alone this form of government can be rescued from the opprobrium under which it has so long labored, and be recommended to the esteem and adoption of mankind.

By what means is this object attainable? Evidently by one of two only. Either the existence of the same passion or interest in a majority at the same time, must be prevented; or the majority, having such co-existent passion or interest, must be rendered, by their number and local situation, unable to concert and carry into effect schemes of oppression. If the impulse and the opportunity be suffered to coincide, we well know that neither moral nor religious motives can be relied on as an adequate control. They are not found to be such on the injustice and violence of individuals, and lose their efficacy in proportion to the number combined together; that is, in proportion as their efficacy becomes needful.

From this view of the subject, it may be concluded, that a pure Democracy, by which I mean, a Society, consisting of a small number of citizens, who assemble and administer the Government in person, can admit of no cure for the mischiefs of faction. A common passion or interest will, in almost every case, be felt by a majority of the whole; a communication and concert results from the form of Government itself; and there is nothing to check the inducements to sacrifice the weaker party, or an obnoxious individual. Hence it is, that such Democracies have ever been spectacles of turbulence and contention; have ever been found incompatible with personal security, or the rights of property; and have in general been as short in their lives, as they have been violent in their deaths. Theoretic politicians, who have patronized this species of Government, have erroneously supposed, that by reducing mankind to a perfect equality in their political rights, they would, at the same time, be perfectly equalized and assimilated in their possessions, their opinions, and their passions.

A Republic, by which I mean a Government in which the scheme of representation takes place, opens a different prospect, and promises the cure for which we are seeking. Let us examine the points in which it varies from pure Democracy, and we shall comprehend both the nature of the cure, and the efficacy which it must derive from the Union.

The two great points of difference between a Democracy and a Republic are, first, the delegation of the Government, in the latter, to a small number of citizens elected by the rest: secondly, the greater number of citizens, and greater sphere of country, over which the latter may be extended.

The effect of the first difference is, on the one hand to refine and enlarge the public views, by passing them through the medium of a chosen body of citizens, whose wisdom may best discern the true interest of their country, and whose patriotism and love of justice, will be least likely to sacrifice it to temporary or partial considerations. Under such a regulation, it may well happen that the public voice pronounced by the representatives of the people, will be more consonant to the public good, than if pronounced by the people themselves convened for the purpose. On the other hand, the effect may be inverted. Men of factious tempers, of local prejudices, or of sinister designs, may by intrigue, by corruption or by other means, first obtain the suffrages, and then betray the interests of the people. The question resulting is, whether small or extensive Republics are most favorable to the election of proper guardians of the public weal: and it is clearly decided in favor of the latter by two obvious considerations:

In the first place it is to be remarked that however small the Republic may be, the Representatives must be raised to a certain number, in order to guard against the cabals of a few; and that, however large it may be, they must be limited to a certain number, in order to guard against the confusion of a multitude. Hence the number of Representatives in the two cases, not being in proportion to that of the Constituents, and being proportionally greatest in the small Republic, it follows, that if the proportion of fit characters, be not less, in the large than in the small Republic, the former will present a greater option, and consequently a greater probability of a fit choice.

In the next place, as each Representative will be chosen by a greater number of citizens in the large than in the small Republic, it will be more difficult for unworthy candidates to practice with success the vicious arts, by which elections are too often carried; and the suffrages of the people being more free, will be more likely to centre on men who possess the most attractive merit, and the most diffusive and established characters.

It must be confessed, that in this, as in most other cases, there is a mean, on both sides of which inconveniencies will be found to lie. By enlarging too much the number of electors, you render the representative too little acquainted with all their local circumstances and lesser interests; as by reducing it too much, you render him unduly attached to these, and too little fit to comprehend and pursue great and national objects. The Federal Constitution forms a happy combination in this respect; the great and aggregate interests being referred to the national, the local and particular, to the state legislatures.

The other point of difference is, the greater number of citizens and extent of territory which may be brought within the compass of Republican, than of Democratic Government; and it is this circumstance principally which renders factious combinations less to be dreaded in the former, than in the latter. The smaller the society, the fewer probably will be the distinct parties and interests composing it; the fewer the distinct parties and interests, the more frequently will a majority be found of the same party; and the smaller the number of individuals composing a majority, and the smaller the compass within which they are placed, the more easily will they concert and execute their plans of oppression. Extend the sphere, and you take in a greater variety of parties and interests; you make it less probable that a majority of the whole will have a common motive to invade the rights of other citizens; or if such a common motive exists, it will be more difficult for all who feel it to discover their own strength, and to act in unison with each other. Besides other impediments, it may be remarked, that where there is a consciousness of unjust or dishonorable purposes, communication is always checked by distrust, in proportion to the number whose concurrence is necessary.

Hence it clearly appears, that the same advantage, which a Republic has over a Democracy, in controling the effects of faction, is enjoyed by a large over a small Republic—is enjoyed by the Union over the States composing it. Does this advantage consist in the substitution of Representatives, whose enlightened views and virtuous sentiments render them superior to local prejudices, and to schemes of injustice? It will not be denied, that the Representation of the Union will be most likely to possess these requisite endowments. Does it consist in the greater security afforded by a greater variety of parties, against the event of any one party being able to outnumber and oppress the rest? In an equal degree does the encreased variety of parties, comprised within the Union, encrease this security. Does it, in fine, consist in the greater obstacles opposed to the concert and accomplishment of the secret wishes of an unjust and interested majority? Here, again, the extent of the Union gives it the most palpable advantage.

The influence of factious leaders may kindle a flame within their particular States, but will be unable to spread a general conflagration through the other States: a religious sect, may degenerate into a political faction in a part of the Confederacy; but the variety of sects dispersed over the entire face of it, must secure the national Councils against any danger from that source: a rage for paper money, for an abolition of debts, for an equal division of property, or for any other improper or wicked project, will be less apt to pervade the whole body of the Union, than a particular member of it; in the same proportion as such a malady is more likely to taint a particular county or district, than an entire State.

In the extent and proper structure of the Union, therefore, we behold a Republican remedy for the diseases most incident to Republican government. And according to the degree of pleasure and pride, we feel in being Republicans, ought to be our zeal in cherishing the spirit, and supporting the character of Federalists.

NOTES

1.   Is Madison right in saying that the causes of faction are sown in human nature, or is he overly pessimistic? Are human beings inherently good, so that if private property were abolished everyone would behave like angels and factions would disappear? Are human beings so prone to wage a Hobbesian war of all against all that only a dictatorship can prevent disaster? Is the truth about human nature somewhere between utopianism and unrelenting despair? What ground does Madison occupy?

2.   What are the possible solutions to the problem of faction that Madison raises but then rejects? Is he right to reject them?

3.   Today, the Electoral College has the effect of requiring a successful candidate to appeal to multiple constituencies throughout the nation; overwhelming support that is concentrated in a few large states or a particular region will usually not translate into an Electoral College majority. (The counter-example is of course the election in 1860 of Abraham Lincoln, whose supporters were concentrated in Northern and Western states. But what made that exception possible was a four-way presidential race.) Does this arrangement fit the theory of federalism offered in *The Federalist No. 10*?

4.   Did Madison think the thirteen original states would constitute a small republic or a large one? What would he think of the size of the United States now? Would a federal system for the world be likely to succeed?

I.   ARTICLE I, SECTIONS 8 AND 10: FEDERALISM AND NATIONAL POWERS

A.   INTRODUCTION TO THE SCOPE OF NATIONAL POWERS: THE BANK OF THE UNITED STATES

In the early republic, the most lasting constitutional controversy concerned the "Bank of the United States." Did Congress have authority under the Constitution to incorporate a national bank, or would such an act intrude on the powers reserved to the states? The fight over this question began in 1791 and went on for more than four decades. Before the Civil War, it was one of the two or three central questions about the scope of federal powers.

The First Bank of the United States

To an eighteenth-century legislature that needed money, a national bank was an irresistible proposition. It could be chartered as a corporation, which would give the advantage of limited liability for shareholders. To further attract investment, the legislature might give the bank a monopoly. Once it was running, the bank would accept deposits of "specie" (i.e., coined money), both from the government and from the private sector. In return for deposits it would give depositors bank notes, which were like IOUs for the gold and silver deposited with the bank. Those bank notes would circulate throughout the country, and if lenders were willing to take them as payment for debts, then they would serve as a kind of paper currency. Finally, the bank could make money by lending—lending not only to the public but also to the government. By keeping some control over a national bank, a legislature could ensure that it had a secure source of financing, especially in times of economic crisis.

But national banks also raised fears. They were seen as corrupt—a collusion between capital and the capitol. The bank might receive government funds and secure favorable laws. In return, it might give favors to lawmakers and make sure their private investments in the bank received ample returns. And a national bank would answer to the moneyed elite, not to the small farmers and merchants who might turn to local banks, the very institutions who would be hurt by any monopoly given to the national bank.

In the early republic, the conflict between these two ideas of a national bank— fuel for the economic engine of the nation, or a corrupt alliance between bankers and legislators—was not only economic but also cultural. The first treasury secretary, Alexander Hamilton, had ambitious plans to transform the United States from a nation of farmers into a commercial power, and central to those plans was a national bank. Hamilton drew inspiration from the first national bank, the Bank of England, which had been created in 1694 and which over the next century made England the world's financial leader. But others in the new United States—including Thomas Jefferson—wanted America to remain an agrarian society and were suspicious, and even contemptuous, of commerce. A career in business, producing goods for consumers, was considered unworthy of gentlemen. Jefferson thought land ownership, not speculation in bank stocks, would promote civic virtue and concern for the public good. Thus the conflict over the Bank, at least in the minds of those involved, was about what kind of nation America would become.

In 1791, at Hamilton's urging, Congress deliberated about a bill to charter a Bank of the United States. The proposed Bank would have ten million dollars in capital (by comparison, two million dollars was the total capital of the state banks at the time). President Washington would be authorized to invest two million dollars of public money in the Bank. The government would be not only a depositor but also an owner, holding twenty percent of the shares in the corporation. The Bank would accept deposits, make loans, and issue notes that could circulate throughout the economy and be used as money (especially needed, given the scarcity at the time of gold and silver coins—see p. 660). The board of directors of the Bank would elect one of their number to be president. And the Bank would have a monopoly: no other banks could be chartered by the national government during its twenty-year term.

There were sharp debates in Congress and in the cabinet of President Washington over whether the new Constitution gave the national government the power to charter a bank. Before you read the conflicting opinions that follow, think through the question on your own. Begin by reading the enumeration of Congress's legislative powers in Article I, Section 8 of the Constitution. Does Congress have power to charter a "Bank of the United States"? To charter any corporations at all? Which of the enumerated powers most plausibly supports a national bank? As you are engaging in this exercise, ask yourself: How should the Constitution be interpreted?

As you think about the constitutionality of the Bank of the United States, two pieces of background information may be helpful. First, the Constitutional Convention of 1787 considered giving Congress an enumerated power to charter corporations. But an incorporation power would have raised opposition to ratification from New York and Philadelphia commercial interests who feared federally chartered competitors. No enumerated power was written into the Constitution. There was a narrower proposal at the Convention to give Congress power to charter corporations for the construction of canals, but it was voted down eight to three. Should these facts affect your interpretation?

Second, at the Founding there was a widely accepted principle of "implied powers" or "incidental powers." This principle was understood to mean that the grant of a power included powers that were "incident" to it, what might be the means needed to carry out the granted power. One illustration came from real property: imagine a tenant at will who had a right to grow crops, and who did grow crops, but then was evicted. Would that former tenant have the right to go back onto the land to carry away the crops? The principle of incidental powers supplied the answer: *yes*, because the right to carry away the crops was "incident" to the right to grow the crops. It was a smaller right that was related to the greater right and included with it—even though there were no express words in the lease saying that there was a right to carry away the crops. This was thought to be a background principle that could be found in the common law, the law of nations, and reason itself.

There were a number of considerations involved in deciding what counted as a "principal" and what counted as an "incident" that could be fairly implied. One was proximity or relation: how close was the claimed incidental power to the principal power? Another was size: was the claimed incidental power really subordinate to the principal power, or was it such a significant power that we should expect it to have been stated explicitly?

Behind the incidental-powers principle is a bit of common sense, and it can be given a contemporary illustration. Imagine that you give a friend a bookcase, and you tell your friend that you will leave the door of your apartment unlocked so she can take away the bookcase. She comes into your apartment, and decides to repaint and remodel it. Did she have a right to do that? The incidental-powers answer is *no*—repainting and remodeling is not an incident of going into your apartment to retrieve a bookcase, because it is just not related. But what if she went to retrieve the bookcase, and she noticed that there was a stack of books on top of the bookcase. Does she have a right to move the books off in order to take the bookcase away? Yes, moving off whatever is on the bookcase would be an incident of the power to retrieve the bookcase (it is both related to and smaller than that power). Now what if, she finds that it is difficult or impossible to maneuver the bookcase out of the room. Can she knock out a wall or enlarge the doorway? Surely not. It's true that knocking out the wall would be related to moving the bookcase, just as related as moving the books was, but it would not be a small power that one would expect to be included in a grant of authority to move the bookcase. If you wanted your friend to have permission to knock out your walls, you would have said that expressly. The illustration is contemporary, but it shows the intuitions behind the principle of incidental powers at the Founding.

————

When the bill to incorporate a Bank of the United States was introduced in the House of Representatives, there were several days of debate on its constitutionality. The most important speech against the Bank was delivered by Representative James Madison.

James Madison, Speech on the Bank Bill
House of Representatives, Feb. 2, 1791

Mr. Madison began with a general review of the advantages and disadvantages of banks. . . .

In making these remarks on the merits of the bill, he had reserved to himself, he said, the right to deny the authority of Congress to pass it. He had entertained this opinion from the date of the constitution. His impression might perhaps be the stronger, because he well recollected that a power to grant charters of incorporation had been proposed in the general convention and rejected.

Is the power of establishing an *incorporated bank* among the powers vested by the constitution in the legislature of the United States? This is the question to be examined.

After some general remarks on the limitations of all political power, he took notice of the peculiar manner in which the federal government is limited. It is not a general grant, out of which particular powers are excepted—it is a grant of particular powers only, leaving the general mass in other hands. So it had been understood by its friends and its foes, and so it was to be interpreted.

As preliminaries to a right interpretation, he laid down the following rules:

An interpretation that destroys the very characteristic of the government cannot be just.

Where a meaning is clear, the consequences, whatever they may be, are to be admitted—where doubtful, it is fairly triable by its consequences.

In controverted cases, the meaning of the parties to the instrument, if to be collected by reasonable evidence, is a proper guide.

Cotemporary and concurrent expositions are reasonable evidence of the meaning of the parties.

In admitting or rejecting a constructive authority, not only the degree of its incidentality to an express authority, is to be regarded, but the degree of its importance also; since on this will depend the probability or improbability of its being left to construction.

Reviewing the constitution with an eye to these positions, it was not possible to discover in it the power to incorporate a Bank. The only clauses under which such a power could be pretended, are either—

1. The power to lay and collect taxes to pay the debts, and provide for the common defence and general welfare: Or,

2. The power to borrow money on the credit of the United States: Or,

3. The power to pass all laws necessary and proper to carry into execution those powers.

The bill did not come within the first power. It laid no tax to pay the debts, or provide for the general welfare. It laid no tax whatever. It was altogether foreign to the subject.

No argument could be drawn from the terms "common defence, and general welfare." The power as to these general purposes, was limited to acts laying taxes for them; and the general purposes themselves were limited and explained by the particular enumeration subjoined. To understand these terms in any sense, that would justify the power in question, would give to Congress an unlimited power; would render nugatory the enumeration of particular powers; would supercede all the powers reserved to the state governments. These terms are copied from the articles of confederation; had it ever been pretended, that they were to be understood otherwise than as here explained?

It had been said that "general welfare" meant cases in which a general power might be exercised by Congress, without interfering with the powers of the States; and that the establishment of a National Bank was of this sort. There were, he said, several answers to this novel doctrine.

1. The proposed Bank would interfere so as indirectly to defeat a State Bank at the same place. 2. It would directly interfere with the rights of the States, *to prohibit* as well as to establish Banks, and the circulation of Bank Notes. He mentioned a law of Virginia, actually prohibiting the circulation of notes payable to bearer. 3. Interference with the power of the States was no constitutional criterion of the power of Congress. If the power was not given, Congress could not exercise it; if given, they might exercise it, altho it should interfere with the laws, or even the constitution of the States. 4. If Congress could incorporate a Bank, merely because the act would

leave the States free to establish Banks also; any other incorporations might be made by Congress. They could incorporate companies of manufacturers, or companies for cutting canals, or even religious societies, leaving similar incorporations by the States, like State Banks to themselves: Congress might even establish religious teachers in every parish, and pay them out of the Treasury of the United States, leaving other teachers unmolested in their functions. These inadmissible consequences condemned the controverted principle.

The case of the Bank established by the former Congress, had been cited as a precedent. This was known, he said, to have been the child of necessity. It never could be justified by the regular powers of the articles of confederation. Congress betrayed a consciousness of this in recommending to the States to incorporate the Bank also. They did not attempt to protect the Bank Notes by penalties against counterfeiters. These were reserved wholly to the authority of the States.

The second clause to be examined is that, which empowers Congress to borrow money.

Is this a bill to borrow money? It does not borrow a shilling. Is there any fair construction by which the bill can be deemed an exercise of the power to borrow money? The obvious meaning of the power to borrow money, is that of accepting it from, and stipulating payment to those who are *able* and *willing* to lend.

To say that the power to borrow involves a power of creating the ability, where there may be the will, to lend, is not only establishing a dangerous principle, as will be immediately shewn, but is as forced a construction, as to say that it involves the power of compelling the will, where there may be the ability, to lend.

The *third* clause is that which gives the power to pass all laws necessary and proper to execute the specified powers.

Whatever meaning this clause may have, none can be admitted, that would give an unlimited discretion to Congress.

Its meaning must, according to the natural and obvious force of the terms and the context, be limited to means *necessary* to the *end*, and *incident* to the *nature* of the specified powers.

The clause is in fact merely declaratory of what would have resulted by unavoidable implication, as the appropriate, and as it were, technical means of executing those powers. In this sense it had been explained by the friends of the constitution, and ratified by the state conventions.

The essential characteristic of the government, as composed of limited and enumerated powers, would be destroyed: If instead of direct and incidental means, any means could be used, which in the language of the preamble to the bill, "might be conceived to be conducive to the successful conducting of the finances; or might be *conceived* to *tend* to give *facility* to the obtaining of loans." He urged an attention to the diffuse and ductile terms which had been found requisite to cover the stretch of power contained in the bill. He compared them with the terms *necessary* and *proper,* used in the Constitution, and asked whether it was possible to view the two descriptions as synonymous, or the one as a fair and safe commentary on the other.

If, proceeded he, Congress, by virtue of the power to borrow, can create the means of lending, and in pursuance of these means, can incorporate a Bank, they may do any thing whatever creative of like means.

The East-India company has been a lender to the British government, as well as the Bank, and the South-Sea company is a greater creditor than either. Congress then may incorporate similar companies in the United States, and that too not under the idea of regulating trade, but under that of borrowing money.

Private capitals are the chief resources for loans to the British government. Whatever then may be conceived to favor the accumulation of capitals may be done by Congress. They may incorporate manufactures. They may give monopolies in every branch of domestic industry.

If, again, Congress by virtue of the power to borrow money, can create the ability to lend, they may by virtue of the power to levy money, create the ability to pay it. The ability to pay taxes depends on the general wealth of the society, and this on the general prosperity of agriculture, manufactures and commerce. Congress then may give bounties and make regulations on all of these objects.

The States have, it is allowed on all hands, a concurrent right to lay and collect taxes. This power is secured to them not by its being expressly reserved, but by its not being ceded by the constitution. The reasons for the bill cannot be admitted, because they would invalidate that right; why may it not be *conceived* by Congress, that an uniform and exclusive imposition of taxes, would not less than the proposed Banks "be *conducive* to the successful conducting of the national finances, and *tend* to *give facility* to the obtaining of revenue, for the use of the government"?

The doctrine of implication is always a tender one. The danger of it has been felt in other governments. The delicacy was felt in the adoption of our own; the danger may also be felt, if we do not keep close to our chartered authorities.

Mark the reasoning on which the validity of the bill depends. To borrow money is made the *end* and the accumulation of capitals, *implied* as the *means*. The accumulation of capitals is then the *end*, and a bank *implied* as the *means*. The bank is then the *end*, and a charter of incorporation, a monopoly, capital punishments, &c. *implied* as the *means*.

If implications, thus remote and thus multiplied, can be linked together, a chain may be formed that will reach every object of legislation, every object within the whole compass of political economy.

The latitude of interpretation required by the bill is condemned by the rule furnished by the constitution itself.

Congress have power "to regulate the value of money"; yet it is expressly added, not left to be implied, that counterfeitors may be punished.

They have the power "to declare war," to which armies are more incident, than incorporated Banks, to borrowing; yet is expressly added, the power "to raise and support armies"; and to this again, the express power "to make rules and regulations for the government of armies"; a like remark is applicable to the powers as to a navy.

The regulation and calling out of the militia are more appurtenant to war, than the proposed bank, to borrowing; yet the former is not left to construction.

The very power to borrow money is a less remote implication from the power of war, than an incorporated monopoly bank, from the power of borrowing—yet the power to borrow is not left to implication.

It is not pretended that every insertion or omission in the constitution is the effect of systematic attention. This is not the character of any human work, particularly the work of a body of men. The examples cited, with others that might be added, sufficiently inculcate nevertheless a rule of interpretation, very different from that on which the bill rests. They condemn the exercise of any power, particularly a great and important power, which is not evidently and necessarily involved in an express power.

It cannot be denied that the power proposed to be exercised is an important power.

As a charter of incorporation the bill creates an artificial person previously not existing in law. It confers important civil rights and attributes, which could not otherwise be claimed. It is, though not precisely similar, at least equivalent, to the naturalization of an alien, by which certain new civil characters are acquired by him. Would Congress have had the power to naturalize, if it had not been expressly given?

In the power to make bye laws, the bill delegated a sort of legislative power, which is unquestionably an act of a high and important nature. He took notice of the only restraint on the bye laws, that they were not to be contrary to the law and the constitution of the bank; and asked what law was intended; if the law of the United States, the scantiness of their code would give a power, never before given to a corporation—and obnoxious to the States, whose laws would then be superceded not only by the laws of Congress, but by the bye laws of a corporation within their own jurisdiction. If the law intended, was the law of the State, then the State might make laws that would destroy an institution of the United States.

The bill gives a power to purchase and hold lands; Congress themselves could not purchase lands within a State "without the consent of its legislature." How could they delegate a power to others which they did not possess themselves?

It takes from our successors, who have equal rights with ourselves, and with the aid of experience will be more capable of deciding on the subject, an opportunity of exercising that right, for an immoderate term.

It takes from our constituents the opportunity of deliberating on the untried measure, although their hands are also to be tied by it for the same term.

It involves a monopoly, which affects the equal rights of every citizen.

It leads to a penal regulation, perhaps capital punishments, one of the most solemn acts of sovereign authority.

From this view of the power of incorporation exercised in the bill, it could never be deemed an accessary or subaltern power, to be deduced by implication, as a means of executing another power; it was in its nature a distinct, an independent and substantive prerogative, which not being enumerated in the constitution could never have been meant to be included in it, and not being included could never be rightfully exercised.

He here adverted to a distinction, which he said had not been sufficiently kept in view, between a power necessary and proper for the government or union, and a power necessary and proper for executing the enumerated powers. In the latter case, the powers included in each of the enumerated powers were not expressed, but to be drawn from the nature of each. In the former, the powers composing the government were expressly enumerated. This constituted the peculiar nature of the government, no power therefore not enumerated, could be inferred from the general nature of government. Had the power of making treaties, for example, been omitted, however necessary it might have been, the defect could only have been lamented, or supplied by an amendment of the constitution.

But the proposed bank could not even be called necessary to the government; at most it could be but convenient. Its uses to the government could be supplied by keeping the taxes a little in advance—by loans from individuals—by the other banks, over which the government would have equal command; nay greater, as it may grant or refuse to these the privilege, made a free and irrevocable gift to the proposed bank, of using their notes in the federal revenue.

He proceeded next to the cotemporary expositions given to the constitution.

The defence against the charge founded on the want of a bill of rights, presupposed, he said, that the powers not given were retained; and that those given were not to be extended by remote implications. On any other supposition, the power of Congress to abridge the freedom of the press, or the rights of conscience, &c. could not have been disproved.

The explanations in the state conventions all turned on the same fundamental principle, and on the principle that the terms necessary and proper gave no additional powers to those enumerated. (Here he read sundry passages from the debates of the Pennsylvania, Virginia and North-Carolina conventions, shewing the grounds on which the constitution had been vindicated by its principal advocates, against a dangerous latitude of its powers, charged on it by its opponents.) He did not undertake to vouch for the accuracy or authenticity of the publications which he quoted—he thought it probable that the sentiments delivered might in many instances have been mistaken, or imperfectly noted; but the complexion of the whole, with what he himself and many others must recollect, fully justified the use he had made of them.

The explanatory declarations and amendments accompanying the ratifications of the several states formed a striking evidence, wearing the same complexion. He referred those who might doubt on the subject to the several acts of ratification.

The explanatory amendments proposed by Congress themselves, at least, would be good authority with them; all these renunciations of power proceeded on a rule of construction, excluding the latitude now contended for. These explanations were the more to be respected, as they had not only been proposed by Congress, but ratified by nearly three-fourths of the states. He read several of the articles proposed, remarking particularly on the 11th. and 12th. *[ratified as the Ninth and Tenth Amendments—Editors]* the former, as guarding against a latitude of interpretation—the latter, as excluding every source of power not within the constitution itself.

With all this evidence of the sense in which the constitution was understood and adopted, will it not be said, if the bill should pass, that its adoption was brought about by one set of arguments, and that it is now administered under the influence of another set; and this reproach will have the keener sting, because it is applicable to so many individuals concerned in both the adoption and administration.

In fine, if the power were in the constitution, the immediate exercise of it cannot be essential—if not there, the exercise of it involves the guilt of usurpation, and establishes a precedent of interpretation, leveling all the barriers which limit the powers of the general government, and protect those of the state governments. If the point be doubtful only, respect for ourselves, who ought to shun the appearance of precipitancy and ambition; respect for our successors, who ought not lightly to be deprived of the opportunity of exercising the rights of legislation; respect for our constituents who have had no opportunity of making known their sentiments, and who are themselves to be bound down to the measure for so long a period; all these considerations require that the irrevocable decision should at least be suspended until another session.

It appeared on the whole, he concluded, that the power exercised by the bill was condemned by the silence of the constitution; was condemned by the rule of interpretation arising out of the constitution; was condemned by its tendency to destroy the main characteristic of the constitution; was condemned by the expositions of the friends of the constitution, whilst depending before the public; was condemned by the apparent intention of the parties which ratified the constitution; was condemned by the explanatory amendments proposed by Congress themselves to the Constitution; and he hoped it would receive its final condemnation, by the vote of this house.

————

Despite Madison's protestations, the Bank bill passed Congress and was sent to the president for his signature or veto. President Washington asked the attorney general, Edmund Randolph, and the secretary of state, Thomas Jefferson, for their opinions on the constitutional question. Both sent opinions concluding that the Bank bill was unconstitutional, and Jefferson enclosed with his opinion a copy of Madison's speech in the House. Then President Washington asked for the opinion of Alexander Hamilton, the secretary of the treasury, who defended its constitutionality. Below are selections from the opinions of Jefferson and Hamilton. What constitutional arguments does each one make? Whose arguments are more persuasive?

Thomas Jefferson, Opinion on the Bank Bill

Feb. 15, 1791

. . . I consider the foundation of the Constitution as laid on this ground that "all powers not delegated to the U.S. by the Constitution, nor prohibited by it to the states, are reserved to the states or to the people." [XIIth. Amendment] *[ratified as the Tenth Amendment.—Editors]*. To take a single step beyond the boundaries thus specially drawn around the powers of Congress, is to take possession of a boundless f[ie]ld of power, no longer susceptible of any definition.

The incorporation of a bank, and the powers assumed by this bill have not, in my opinion, been delegated to the U.S. by the Constitution.

I.   They are not among the powers specially enumerated, for these are

1.   A power to *lay taxes* for the purpose of paying the debts of the U.S. But no debt is paid by this bill, nor any tax laid. Were it a bill to raise money, it's origination in the Senate would condemn it by the constitution.

2.   "to borrow money." But this bill neither borrows money, nor ensures the borrowing it. The proprietors of the bank will be just as free as any other money holders, to lend or not to lend their money to the public. The operation proposed in the bill, first to lend them two millions, and then borrow them back again, cannot

change the nature of the latter act, which will still be a payment, and not a loan, call it by what name you please.

3.   To "regulate commerce with foreign nations, and among the states, and with the Indian tribes." To erect a bank, and to regulate commerce, are very different acts. He who erects a bank creates a subject of commerce in it's bills: so does he who makes a bushel of wheat, or digs a dollar out of the mines. Yet neither of these persons regulates commerce thereby. To erect a thing which may be bought and sold, is not to prescribe regulations for buying and selling. Besides; if this was an exercise of the power of regulating commerce, it would be void, as extending as much to the internal commerce of every state, as to it's external. For the power given to Congress by the Constitution, does not extend to the internal regulation of the commerce of a state, (that is to say of the commerce between citizen and citizen) which remain exclusively with it's own legislature; but to it's external commerce only, that is to say, it's commerce with another state, or with foreign nations or with the Indian tribes. Accordingly the bill does not propose the measure as a "regulation of trade," but as "productive of considerable advantages to trade."

Still less are these powers covered by any other of the special enumerations.

II.   Nor are they within either of the general phrases, which are the two following.

1.   "To lay taxes to provide for the general welfare of the U.S." that is to say "to lay taxes *for the purpose* of providing for the general welfare". For the laying of taxes is the *power* and the general welfare the *purpose* for which the power is to be exercised. They are not to lay taxes ad libitum *for any purpose they please*; but only to *pay the debts or provide for the welfare of the Union*. In like manner they are not *to do anything they please* to provide for the general welfare, but only *to lay taxes* for that purpose. To consider the latter phrase, not as describing the purpose of the first, but as giving a distinct and independent power to do any act they please, which might be for the good of the Union, would render all the preceding and subsequent enumerations of power completely useless. It would reduce the whole instrument to a single phrase, that of instituting a Congress with power to do whatever would be for the good of the U.S. and as they would be the sole judges of the good or evil, it would be also a power to do whatever evil they pleased. It is an established rule of construction, where a phrase will bear either of two meanings, to give it that which will allow some meaning to the other parts of the instrument, and not that which would render all the others useless. Certainly no such universal power was meant to be given them. It was intended to lace them up straitly within the enumerated powers, and those without which, as means, these powers could not be carried into effect. It is known that the very power now proposed *as a means*, was rejected *as an end*, by the Convention which formed the constitution. A proposition was made to them to authorize Congress to open canals, and an amendatory one to empower them to incorporate. But the whole was rejected, and one of the reasons for rejection urged in debate was that then they would have a power to erect a bank, which would render the great cities, where there were prejudices and jealousies on the subject adverse to the reception of the constitution.

2. The second general phrase is "to make all laws *necessary* and proper for carrying into execution the enumerated powers." But they can all be carried into

execution without a bank. A bank therefore is not *necessary*, and consequently not authorised by this phrase.

It has been much urged that a bank will give great facility, or convenience in the collection of taxes, Suppose this were true: yet the constitution allows only the means which are "*necessary*" not those which are merely "convenient" for effecting the enumerated powers. If such a latitude of construction be allowed to this phrase as to give any non-enumerated power, it will go to every one, for [among] these is no one which ingenuity may not torture into a *convenience, in some way or other*, to *some one* of so long a list of enumerated powers. It would swallow up all the delegated powers, and reduce the whole to one phrase as before observed. Therefore it was that the constitution restrained them to the *necessary* means, that is to say, to those means without which the grant of the power would be nugatory. . . .

The Negative of the President *[i.e., the veto]* is the shield provided by the constitution to protect against the invasions of the legislature [regarding] 1. the rights of the Executive 2. of the Judiciary 3. of the states and state legislatures. The present is the case of a right remaining exclusively with the states and is consequently one of those intended by the constitution to be placed under his protection.

It must be added however, that unless the President's mind on a view of every thing which is urged for and against this bill, is tolerably clear that it is unauthorised by the constitution, if the pro and the con hang so even as to balance his judgment, a just respect for the wisdom of the legislature would naturally decide the balance in favour of their opinion. It is chiefly for cases where they are clearly misled by error, ambition, or interest, that the constitution has placed a check in the negative of the President.

Alexander Hamilton, Opinion on the Bank Bill

Feb. 23, 1791

The Secretary of the Treasury having perused with attention the papers containing the opinions of the Secretary of State and Attorney General, concerning the constitutionality of the bill for establishing a National Bank proceeds according to the order of the President to submit the reasons which have induced him to entertain a different opinion.

It will naturally have been anticipated that, in performing this task he would feel uncommon solicitude. Personal considerations alone, arising from the reflection that the measure originated with him would be sufficient to produce it: The sense which he has manifested of the great importance of such an institution to the successful administration of the department under his particular care; and an expectation of serious ill consequences to result from a failure of the measure, do not permit him to be without anxiety on public accounts. But the chief solicitude arises from a firm persuasion, that principles of construction like those espoused by the Secretary of State and the Attorney General would be fatal to the just & indispensable authority of the United States.

In entering upon the argument it ought to be premised, that the objections of the Secretary of State and Attorney General are founded on a general denial of the authority of the United States to erect corporations. The latter indeed expressly admits, that if there be anything in the bill which is not warranted by the constitution, it is the clause of incorporation.

Now it appears to the Secretary of the Treasury, that this *general principle* is *inherent* in the very *definition* of *Government* and *essential* to every step of progress to be made by that of the United States; namely—that every power vested in a Government is in its nature *sovereign*, and includes, by *force* of the *term*, a right to employ all the *means* requisite, and fairly *applicable* to the attainment of the *ends* of such power; and which are not precluded by restrictions & exceptions specified in the constitution; or not immoral, or not contrary to the essential ends of political society.

This principle in its application to Government in general would be admitted as an axiom. And it will be incumbent upon those, who may incline to deny it, to *prove* a distinction; and to shew that a rule which in the general system of things is essential to the preservation of the social order is inapplicable to the United States.

The circumstance that the powers of sovereignty are in this country divided between the National and State Governments, does not afford the distinction required. It does not follow from this, that each of the *portions* of powers delegated to the one or to the other is not sovereign *with regard to its proper objects*. It will only *follow* from it, that each has sovereign power as to *certain things*, and not as to *other things*. To deny that the Government of the United States has sovereign power as to its declared purposes & trusts, because its power does not extend to all cases, would be equally to deny, that the State Governments have sovereign power in any case; because their power does not extend to every case. The tenth section of the first article of the constitution exhibits a long list of very important things which they may not do. And thus the United States would furnish the singular spectacle of a *political society* without *sovereignty*, or of a people *governed* without *government*.

If it would be necessary to bring proof to a proposition so clear as that which affirms that the powers of the federal government, *as to its objects*, are sovereign, there is a clause of its constitution which would be decisive. It is that which declares, that the constitution, and the laws of the United States made in pursuance of it, and all treaties made or which shall be made under their authority shall be the supreme law of the land. The power which can create the *Supreme law* of the land, in any case, is doubtless sovereign *as to such case*.

This general & indisputable principle puts at once an end to the *abstract* question—Whether the United States have power to *erect a corporation?* that is to say, to give a *legal* or *artificial capacity* to one or more persons, distinct from the natural. For it is unquestionably incident to *sovereign power* to erect corporations, and consequently to *that* of the United States, in *relation to the objects* intrusted to the management of the government. The difference is this—where the authority of the government is general, it can create corporations in *all cases*; where it is confined to certain branches of legislation, it can create corporations only in those cases. . . .

To return—It is conceded that implied powers are to be considered as delegated equally with express ones.

Then it follows, that as a power of erecting a corporation may as well be *implied* as any other thing, it may as well be employed as an *instrument* or *mean* of carrying into execution any of the specified powers, as any other instrument or mean whatever. The only question must be, in this as in every other case, whether the mean to be employed, or in this instance the corporation to be erected, has a natural relation to any of the acknowledged objects or lawful ends of the government. Thus a corporation may not be erected by congress, for superintending the police of the city of Philadelphia, because they are not authorised to *regulate* the *police* of that city; but one may be erected in relation to the collection of taxes, or to the trade with foreign countries, or to the trade between the States, or with the Indian Tribes, because it is the province of the fœderal government to regulate those objects & because it is incident to a general *sovereign* or *legislative power* to *regulate* a thing, to employ all the means which relate to its regulation to the *best & greatest advantage.*

A strange fallacy seems to have crept into the manner of thinking & reasoning upon the subject. Imagination appears to have been unusually busy concerning it. An incorporation seems to have been regarded as some great, independent, substantive thing—as a political end of peculiar magnitude & moment; whereas it is truly to be considered as a *quality, capacity,* or *mean* to an end. Thus a mercantile company is formed with a certain capital for the purpose of carrying on a particular branch of business. Here the business to be prosecuted is the *end*; the association, in order to form the requisite capital, is the primary mean. Suppose that an incorporation were added to this; it would only be to add a new *quality* to that association; to give it an artificial capacity by which it would be enabled to prosecute the business with more safety & convenience.

That the importance of the power of incorporation has been exaggerated, leading to erroneous conclusions, will further appear from tracing it to its origin. The roman law is the source of it, according to which a *voluntary* association of individuals, at *any time* or *for any purpose* was capable of producing it. In England, whence our notions of it are immediately borrowed, it forms part of the executive authority, & the exercise of it has been often *delegated* by that authority. Whence therefore the ground of the supposition, that it lies beyond the reach of all those very important portions of sovereign power, legislative as well as executive, which belong to the government of the United States?

To this mode of reasoning respecting the right of employing all the means requisite to the execution of the specified powers of the Government, it is objected that none but *necessary* & proper means are to be employed, & the Secretary of State maintains, that no means are to be considered as *necessary*, but those without which the grant of the power would be *nugatory*. Nay so far does he go in his restrictive interpretation of the word, as even to make the case of *necessity* which shall warrant the constitutional exercise of the power to depend on *casual* & *temporary* circumstances, an idea which alone refutes the construction. The *expediency* of exercising a particular power, at a particular time, must indeed depend on *circumstances;* but the constitutional right of exercising it must be uniform & invariable—the same to day as to morrow. . . .

It is certain that neither the grammatical, nor popular sense of the term requires that construction. According to both, *necessary* often means no more than *needful, requisite, incidental, useful,* or *conducive to*. It is a common mode of expression to say, that it is *necessary* for a government or a person to do this or that thing, when nothing more is intended or understood, than that the interests of the government or person require, or will be promoted by, the doing of this or that thing. The imagination can be at no loss for exemplifications of the use of the word in this sense.

And it is the true one in which it is to be understood as used in the constitution. The whole turn of the clause containing it, indicates, that it was the intent of the convention, by that clause, to give a liberal latitude to the exercise of the specified powers. The expressions have peculiar comprehensiveness. They are—"to make *all laws*, necessary & proper for *carrying into execution* the foregoing powers & all *other powers* vested by the constitution in the *government* of the United States, or in any *department* or *officer* thereof." To understand the word as the Secretary of State does, would be to depart from its obvious & popular sense, and to give it a *restrictive* operation; an idea never before entertained. It would be to give it the same force as if the word *absolutely* or *indispensably* had been prefixed to it.

Such a construction would beget endless uncertainty & embarrassment. The cases must be palpable & extreme in which it could be pronounced with certainty, that a measure was absolutely necessary, or one without which the exercise of a given power would be nugatory. There are few measures of any government, which would stand so severe a test. To insist upon it, would be to make the criterion of the exercise of any implied power, a *case of extreme necessity;* which is rather a rule to justify the overleaping of the bounds of constitutional authority, than to govern the ordinary exercise of it. . . .

The *degree* in which a measure is necessary, can never be a test of the *legal* right to adopt it. That must ever be a matter of opinion; and can only be a test of expediency. The *relation* between the *measure* and the *end*, between the *nature* of the *mean* employed toward the execution of a power and the object of that power, must be the criterion of constitutionality not the more or less of *necessity* or *utility*.

The practice of the government is against the rule of construction advocated by the Secretary of State. Of this the act concerning light houses, beacons, buoys & public piers, is a decisive example. *[Hamilton refers to 1 Stat. 53–54 (Aug. 7, 1789).—Editors]* This doubtless must be referred to the power of regulating trade, and is fairly relative to it. But it cannot be affirmed, that the exercise of that power, in this instance, was strictly necessary; or that the power itself would be *nugatory* without that of regulating establishments of this nature.

This restrictive interpretation of the word *necessary* is also contrary to this sound maxim of construction namely, that the powers contained in a constitution of government, especially those which concern the general administration of the affairs of a country, its finances, trade, defence &c ought to be construed liberally, in advancement of the public good. This rule does not depend on the particular form of a government or on the particular demarkation of the boundaries of its powers, but on the nature and objects of government itself. The means by which national exigencies are to be provided for, national inconveniencies obviated, national prosperity promoted, are of such infinite variety, extent and complexity, that there must, of necessity, be great latitude of discretion in the selection & application of those means. Hence consequently, the necessity & propriety of exercising the authorities intrusted to a government on principles of liberal construction. . . .

It is no valid objection to the doctrine to say, that it is calculated to extend the powers of the general government throughout the entire sphere of State legislation. The same thing has been said, and may be said with regard to every exercise of power by *implication* or *construction*. The moment the literal meaning is departed from, there is a chance of error and abuse. And yet an adherence to the letter of its powers would at once arrest the motions of government. It is not only agreed, on all hands, that the exercise of constructive powers is indispensible, but every act which has been passed is more or less an exemplification of it. One has been already mentioned, that relating to light houses &c. That which declares the power of the President to remove officers at pleasure, acknowlidges the same truth in another, and a signal instance.

The truth is that difficulties on this point are inherent in the nature of the fœderal constitution. They result inevitably from a division of the legislative power. The consequence of this division is, that there will be cases clearly within the power of the National Government; others clearly without its power; and a third class, which will leave room for controversy & difference of opinion, & concerning which a reasonable latitude of judgment must be allowed.

But the doctrine which is contended for is not chargeable with the consequences imputed to it. It does not affirm that the National government is sovereign in all respects, but that it is sovereign to a certain extent; that is, to the extent of the objects of its specified powers.

It leaves therefore a criterion of what is constitutional, and of what is not so. This criterion is the *end* to which the measure relates as a *mean*. If the end be clearly comprehended within any of the specified powers, & if the measure have an obvious relation to that end, and is not forbidden by any particular provision of the constitution—it may safely be deemed to come within the compass of the national authority. There is also this further criterion which may materially assist the decision. Does the proposed measure abridge a preexisting right of any State, or of any individual? If it does not, there is a strong presumption in favour of its constitutionality; & slighter relations to any declared object of the constitution may be permitted to turn the scale. . . .

Another argument made use of by the Secretary of State, is, the rejection of a proposition by the convention to empower Congress to make corporations, either generally, or for some special purpose. . . .

But whatever may have been the nature of the proposition or the reasons for rejecting it concludes nothing in respect to the real merits of the question. The Secretary of State will not deny, that whatever may have been the intention of the framers of a constitution, or of a law, that intention is to be sought for in the instrument itself, according to the usual & established rules of construction. Nothing is more common than for laws to *express* and *effect* more or less than was intended. If then a power to erect a corporation, in any case, be deducible by fair inference from the whole or any part of the numerous provisions of the constitution of the United States, arguments drawn from extrinsic circumstances, regarding the intention of the convention, must be rejected. . . .

It shall now be endeavoured to be shewn that there is a power to erect [a corporation] of the kind proposed by the bill. This will be done, by tracing a natural & obvious relation between the institution of a bank, and the objects of several of the enumerated powers of the government; and by shewing that, *politically* speaking, it is necessary to the effectual execution of one or more of those powers. . . .

The proposed bank is to consist of an association of persons for the purpose of creating a joint capital to be employed, chiefly and essentially, in loans. So far the object is not only lawful, but it is the mere exercise of a right, which the law allows to every individual. The bank of New York which is not incorporated, is an example of such an association. The bill proposed in addition, that the government shall become a joint proprietor in this undertaking, and that it shall permit the bills of the company payable on demand to be receivable in its revenues & stipulates that it shall not grant privileges similar to those which are to be allowed to this company to any others. All this is incontrovertibly within the compass of the discretion of the government. The only question is, whether it has a right to incorporate this company, in order to enable it the more effectually to accomplish *ends*, which are in themselves lawful.

To establish such a right, it remains to shew the relation of such an institution to one or more of the specified powers of the government.

Accordingly it is affirmed, that it has a relation more or less direct to the power of collecting taxes; to that of borrowing money; to that of regulating trade between the states; and to those of raising, supporting & maintaining fleets & armies. To the two former, the relation may be said to be *immediate*. . . .

A Bank relates to the collection of taxes in two ways: *indirectly*, by increasing the quantity of circulating medium & quickening circulation, which facilitates the means of paying—*directly*, by creating a *convenient species* of *medium* in which they are to be paid. . . .

A Bank has a direct relation to the power of borrowing money, because it is an usual and in sudden emergencies an essential instrument in the obtaining of loans to Government. . . .

The institution of a bank has also a natural relation to the regulation of trade between the States: in so far as it is conducive to the creation of a convenient medium of *exchange* between them, and to the keeping up a full circulation by preventing the frequent displacement of the metals in reciprocal remittances. Money is the very hinge on which commerce turns. And this does not merely mean gold & silver, many other things have served the purpose with different degrees of utility. Paper has been extensively employed. . . .

The relation of a bank to the execution of the powers, that concern the common defence, has been anticipated. It has been noted, that at this very moment the aid of such an institution is essential to the measures to be pursued for the protection of our frontier. . . .

A hope is entertained, that it has by this time been made to appear, to the satisfaction of the President, that a bank has a natural relation to the power of collecting taxes; to that of borrowing money; to that of regulating trade; to that of providing for the common defence: and that as the bill under consideration contemplates the government in the light of a joint proprietor of the stock of the bank, it brings the case within the provision of the clause of the constitution which immediately respects the property of the United States.

Under a conviction that such a relation subsists, the Secretary of the Treasury, with all deference conceives, that it will result as a necessary consequence from the position, that all the specified powers of government are sovereign, as to the proper objects; that the incorporation of a bank is a constitutional measure; and that the objections taken to the bill, in this respect, are ill-founded. . . .

President Washington sided with Hamilton, and he signed the bill chartering the first Bank of the United States for twenty years. But the debate over the Bank and its constitutionality had only just begun.

[*Assignment 24*]

The Second Bank of the United States

The First Bank of the United States was chartered for twenty years, from 1791 to 1811, and by the end of its charter the political scene had changed markedly. George Washington and Alexander Hamilton were dead. The party of the opponents of the First Bank, the Democratic-Republicans, was riding high. The president was James Madison. A bill was proposed in 1811 to charter another Bank of the United States, again for a twenty-year term, but it was voted down. Some thought that the practice begun by President Washington and the First Congress had not yet settled the constitutional question.

But soon the United States was at war with England. The War of 1812 plunged the young nation into economic crisis. In 1815, Congress voted to charter a Second Bank, but President Madison vetoed the bill. Twenty-five years earlier, in the House of Representatives, he had opposed the constitutionality of the Bank; now he based his veto on policy grounds. The constitutional question, Madison said, had been settled in favor of the Bank by the intervening practice: he was "[w]aiving the question of the constitutional authority of the Legislature to establish an incorporated bank as being precluded in my judgment by repeated recognition under varied circumstances of the validity of such an institution in acts of the legislative, executive, and judicial branches of the Government, accompanied by indications, in different modes, of a concurrence of the general will of the nation." James Madison, Veto Message, in 1 A COMPILATION OF THE MESSAGES AND PAPERS OF THE PRESIDENTS, 1789–1897, at 555, 555 (James D. Richardson ed., 1897).

Within a year, another Bank bill was presented to President Madison, and this time he signed it. It created the Second Bank of the United States, which had a twenty-year term, from 1816 to 1836.

It is worth pausing here to think about the implications of these events for the project of constitutional interpretation. If Congress considers and vigorously debates the constitutionality of a bill, and decides that the bill is constitutional and passes it, does that settle the constitutional issue for a future Congress? Did the acceptance of the Bank's constitutionality by President Washington oblige President Madison to accept it, despite his prior views? Did the existence of the Bank for twenty years settle the question of its constitutionality? As a general proposition, if the Constitution says one thing but practice under the Constitution is different, which one is controlling?

Several states responded to the Second Bank with opposition. Maryland imposed a special tax of between one and two percent on banks it had not authorized—in effect, a tax that applied only to the Bank of the United States. Five other states moved to tax the Bank, and two of them, Kentucky and Ohio, went so far as to impose annual taxes of $60,000 and $50,000 respectively on branches of the Bank in their states. Yet economic elites tended to support the Bank, as did "the Washington establishment," not only for reasons of national policy but also, it seems, because the Bank had proved a reliable lender for members of Congress when they found that they "had gotten into economic difficulties." Richard E. Ellis, AGGRESSIVE NATIONALISM: *MCCULLOCH V. MARYLAND* AND THE FOUNDATION OF FEDERAL AUTHORITY IN THE YOUNG REPUBLIC 64 (2007).

In 1819 the Supreme Court finally added its voice to the constitutional debate with *McCulloch v. Maryland*. *McCulloch* has become a foundational decision on national legislative powers. It is one of the few constitutional decisions that every attorney—in the nineteenth century or the twenty-first century—would be expected to know. Consider carefully Chief Justice Marshall's arguments about the scope of the Necessary and Proper Clause. What are the positions that Marshall rejects? What, exactly, is the position he accepts? (Is he clearer sometimes about what he is rejecting?) In the end, what principles does Marshall lay down for the scope of the enumerated powers of the national government?

McCulloch v. Maryland

17 U.S. (4 Wheat.) 316 (1819)

■ MR. CHIEF JUSTICE MARSHALL delivered the opinion of the Court.

In the case now to be determined, the defendant, a sovereign State, denies the obligation of a law enacted by the legislature of the Union, and the plaintiff, on his part, contests the validity of an act which has been passed by the legislature of that State. The constitution of our country, in its most interesting and vital parts, is to be considered; the conflicting powers of the government of the Union and of its members, as marked in that constitution, are to be discussed; and an opinion given, which may essentially influence the great operations of the government. No tribunal can approach such a question without a deep sense of its importance, and of the awful responsibility involved in its decision. But it must be decided peacefully, or remain a source of hostile legislation, perhaps, of hostility of a still more serious nature; and if it is to be so decided, by this tribunal alone can the decision be made. On the Supreme Court of the United States has the constitution of our country devolved this important duty.

The first question made in the cause is, has Congress power to incorporate a bank?

It has been truly said, that this can scarcely be considered as an open question, entirely unprejudiced by the former proceedings of the nation respecting it. The principle now contested was introduced at a very early period of our history, has been recognised by many successive legislatures, and has been acted upon by the judicial department, in cases of peculiar delicacy, as a law of undoubted obligation.

It will not be denied, that a bold and daring usurpation might be resisted, after an acquiescence still longer and more complete than this. But it is conceived, that a doubtful question, one on which human reason may pause, and the human judgment be suspended, in the decision of which the great principles of liberty are not concerned, but the respective powers of those who are equally the representatives of the people, are to be adjusted; if not put at rest by the practice of the government, ought to receive a considerable impression from that practice. An exposition of the constitution, deliberately established by legislative acts, on the faith of which an immense property has been advanced, ought not to be lightly disregarded.

The power now contested was exercised by the first Congress elected under the present constitution. The bill for incorporating the bank of the United States did not steal upon an unsuspecting legislature, and pass unobserved. Its principle was completely understood, and was opposed with equal zeal and ability. After being resisted, first, in the fair and open field of debate, and afterwards, in the executive cabinet, with as much persevering talent as any measure has ever experienced, and being supported by arguments which convinced minds as pure and as intelligent as this country can boast, it became a law. The original act was permitted to expire; but a short experience of the embarrassments to which the refusal to revive it exposed the government, convinced those who were most prejudiced against the measure of its necessity, and induced the passage of the present law. It would require no ordinary share of intrepidity, to assert that a measure adopted under these circumstances, was a bold and plain usurpation, to which the constitution gave no countenance.

These observations belong to the cause; but they are not made under the impression, that, were the question entirely new, the law would be found irreconcilable with the constitution.

In discussing this question, the counsel for the State of Maryland have deemed it of some importance, in the construction of the constitution, to consider that instrument, not as emanating from the people, but as the act of sovereign and independent States. The powers of the general government, it has been said, are delegated by the States, who alone are truly sovereign; and must be exercised in subordination to the States, who alone possess supreme dominion.

It would be difficult to sustain this proposition. The Convention which framed the constitution was indeed elected by the State legislatures. But the instrument, when it came from their hands, was a mere proposal, without obligation, or pretensions to it. It was reported to the then existing Congress of the United States, with a request that it might be "submitted to a Convention of Delegates, chosen in each State by the people thereof, under the recommendation of its Legislature, for their assent and ratification." This mode of proceeding was adopted; and by the Convention, by Congress, and by the State Legislatures, the instrument was submitted to the people. They acted upon it in the only manner in which they can act safely, effectively and wisely, on such a subject, by assembling in Convention. It is true, they assembled in their several States—and where else should they have assembled? No political dreamer was wild enough to think of breaking down the lines which separate the States, and of compounding the American people into one common mass. Of consequence, when they act, they act in their States. But the measures they adopt do not, on that account, cease to be the measures of the people themselves, or become the measures of the State governments.

From these Conventions, the constitution derives its whole authority. The government proceeds directly from the people; is "ordained and established" in the name of the people; and is declared to be ordained, "in order to form a more perfect union, establish justice, insure domestic tranquility, and secure the blessings of liberty to themselves and to their posterity." The assent of the States, in their sovereign capacity, is implied, in calling a Convention, and thus submitting that instrument to the people. But the people were at perfect liberty to accept or reject it; and their act was final. It required not the affirmance, and could not be negatived, by the State governments. The constitution, when thus adopted, was of complete obligation, and bound the State sovereignties.

It has been said, that the people had already surrendered all their powers to the State sovereignties, and had nothing more to give. But, surely, the question whether they may resume and modify the powers granted to government, does not remain to be settled in this country. Much more might the legitimacy of the general government be doubted, had it been created by the States. The powers delegated to the State sovereignties were to be exercised by themselves, not by a distinct and independent sovereignty, created by themselves. To the formation of a league, such as was the confederation, the State sovereignties were certainly competent. But when, "in order to form a more perfect union," it was deemed necessary to change this alliance into an effective government, possessing great and sovereign powers, and acting directly on the people, the necessity of referring it to the people, and of deriving its powers directly from them, was felt and acknowledged by all.

The government of the Union, then (whatever may be the influence of this fact on the case), is, emphatically, and truly, a government of the people. In form, and in substance, it emanates from them. Its powers are granted by them, and are to be exercised directly on them, and for their benefit.

This government is acknowledged by all to be one of enumerated powers. The principle, that it can exercise only the powers granted to it, would seem too apparent to have required to be enforced by all those arguments which its enlightened friends, while it was depending before the people, found it necessary to urge. That principle is now universally admitted. But the question respecting the extent of the powers actually granted, is perpetually arising, and will probably continue to arise, so long as our system shall exist.

In discussing these questions, the conflicting powers of the general and State governments must be brought into view, and the supremacy of their respective laws, when they are in opposition, must be settled.

If any one proposition could command the universal assent of mankind, we might expect it would be this—that the government of the Union, though limited in its powers, is supreme within its sphere of action. This would seem to result necessarily from its nature. It is the government of all; its powers are delegated by all; it represents all, and acts for all. Though any one State may be willing to control its operations, no State is willing to allow others to control them. The nation, on those subjects on which it can act, must necessarily bind its component parts. But this question is not left to mere reason: the people have, in express terms, decided it, by saying, "this constitution, and the laws of the United States, which shall be made in pursuance thereof," "shall be the supreme law of the land," and by requiring that the members of the State legislatures, and the officers of the executive and judicial departments of the States, shall take the oath of fidelity to it.

The government of the United States, then, though limited in its powers, is supreme; and its laws, when made in pursuance of the constitution, form the supreme law of the land, "anything in the constitution or laws of any State to the contrary notwithstanding."

Among the enumerated powers, we do not find that of establishing a bank or creating a corporation. But there is no phrase in the instrument which, like the articles of confederation, excludes incidental or implied powers; and which requires that everything granted shall be expressly and minutely described. Even the 10th amendment, which was framed for the purpose of quieting the excessive jealousies which had been excited, omits the word "expressly," and declares only, that the powers "not delegated to the United States, nor prohibited to the States, are reserved to the States or to the people;" thus leaving the question, whether the particular power which may become the subject of contest, has been delegated to the one government, or prohibited to the other, to depend on a fair construction of the whole instrument. The men who drew and adopted this amendment had experienced the embarrassments resulting from the insertion of this word in the articles of confederation, and probably omitted it to avoid those embarrassments. A constitution, to contain an accurate detail of all the subdivisions of which its great powers will admit, and of all the means by which they may be carried into execution, would partake of the prolixity of a legal code, and could scarcely be embraced by the human mind. It would, probably, never be understood by the public. Its nature, therefore, requires, that only its great outlines should be marked, its important objects designated, and the minor ingredients which compose those objects, be deduced from the nature of the objects themselves. That this idea was entertained by the framers of the American constitution, is not only to be inferred from the nature of the instrument, but from the language. Why else were some of the limitations, found in the ninth section of the 1st article, introduced? It is also, in some degree, warranted, by their having omitted to use any restrictive term which might prevent its receiving a fair and just interpretation. In considering this question, then, we must never forget that it is *a constitution* we are expounding.

Although, among the enumerated powers of government, we do not find the word "bank" or "incorporation," we find the great powers to lay and collect taxes; to borrow money; to regulate commerce; to declare and conduct a war; and to raise and support armies and navies. The sword and the purse, all the external relations, and no inconsiderable portion of the industry of the nation, are entrusted to its government. It can never be pretended, that these vast powers draw after them others of inferior importance, merely because they are inferior. Such an idea can never be advanced. But it may with great reason be contended, that a government, entrusted with such ample powers, on the due execution of which the happiness and prosperity of the nation so vitally depends, must also be entrusted with ample means for their execution. The power being given, it is the interest of the nation to facilitate its execution. It can never be their interest, and cannot be presumed to have been their intention, to clog and embarrass its execution by withholding the most appropriate means. Throughout this vast republic, from the St. Croix to the Gulph of Mexico, from the Atlantic to the Pacific, revenue is to be collected and expended, armies are to be marched and supported. The exigencies of the nation may require, that the treasure raised in the north should be transported to the south, *that* raised in the east conveyed to the west, or that this order should be reversed. Is that construction of the constitution to be preferred which would render these operations difficult, hazardous, and expensive? Can we adopt that construction (unless the words imperiously require it), which would impute to the framers of that instrument, when granting these powers for the public good, the intention of impeding their exercise by withholding a choice of means? If, indeed, such be the mandate of the constitution, we have only to obey; but that instrument does not profess to enumerate the means by which the powers it confers may be executed; nor does it prohibit the creation of a corporation, if the existence of such a being be essential to the beneficial exercise of those powers. It is, then, the subject of fair inquiry, how far such means may be employed.

It is not denied, that the powers given to the government imply the ordinary means of execution. That, for example, of raising revenue, and applying it to national purposes, is admitted to imply the power of conveying money from place to place, as the exigencies of the nation may require, and of employing the usual means of conveyance. But it is denied that the government has its choice of means; or, that it may employ the most convenient means, if, to employ them, it be necessary to erect a corporation.

On what foundation does this argument rest? On this alone: The power of creating a corporation, is one appertaining to sovereignty, and is not expressly conferred on Congress. This is true. But all legislative powers appertain to sovereignty. The original power of giving the law on any subject whatever, is a sovereign power; and if the government of the Union is restrained from creating a corporation, as a means for performing its functions, on the single reason that the creation of a corporation is an act of sovereignty; if the sufficiency of this reason be acknowledged, there would be some difficulty in sustaining the authority of Congress to pass other laws for the accomplishment of the same objects.

The government which has a right to do an act, and has imposed on it the duty of performing that act, must, according to the dictates of reason, be allowed to select the means; and those who contend that it may not select any appropriate means, that one particular mode of effecting the object is excepted, take upon themselves the burden of establishing that exception.

The creation of a corporation, it is said, appertains to sovereignty. This is admitted. But to what portion of sovereignty does it appertain? Does it belong to one more than to another? In America, the powers of sovereignty are divided between the government of the Union, and those of the States. They are each sovereign, with respect to the objects committed to it, and neither sovereign, with respect to the objects committed to the other. We cannot comprehend that train of reasoning which would maintain, that the extent of power granted by the people is to be ascertained, not by the nature and terms of the grant, but by its date. Some State constitutions were formed *before*, some *since* that of the United States. We cannot believe that their relation to each other is in any degree dependent upon this circumstance. Their respective powers must, we think, be precisely the same as if they had been formed at the same time. Had they been formed at the same time, and had the people conferred on the general government the power contained in the constitution, and on the States the whole residuum of power, would it have been asserted that the government of the Union was not sovereign with respect to those objects which were entrusted to it, in relation to which its laws were declared to be supreme? If this could not have been asserted, we cannot well comprehend the process of reasoning which maintains, that a power appertaining to sovereignty cannot be connected with that vast portion of it which is granted to the general government, so far as it is calculated to subserve the legitimate objects of that government. The power of creating a corporation, though appertaining to sovereignty, is not, like the power of making war, or levying taxes, or of regulating commerce, a great substantive and independent power, which cannot be implied as incidental to other powers, or used as a means of executing them. It is never the end for which other powers are exercised, but a means by which other objects are accomplished. No contributions are made to charity for the sake of an incorporation, but a corporation is created to administer the charity; no seminary of learning is instituted in order to be incorporated, but the corporate character is conferred to subserve the purposes of education. No city was ever built with the sole object of being incorporated, but is incorporated as affording the best means of being well governed. The power of creating a corporation is never used for its own sake, but for the purpose of effecting something else. No sufficient reason is, therefore, perceived, why it may not pass as incidental to those powers which are expressly given, if it be a direct mode of executing them.

But the constitution of the United States has not left the right of Congress to employ the necessary means, for the execution of the powers conferred on the government, to general reasoning. To its enumeration of powers is added that of making "all laws which shall be necessary and proper, for carrying into execution the foregoing powers, and all other powers vested by this constitution, in the government of the United States, or in any department thereof."

The counsel for the State of Maryland have urged various arguments, to prove that this clause, though in terms a grant of power, is not so in effect; but is really restrictive of the general right, which might otherwise be implied, of selecting means for executing the enumerated powers.

In support of this proposition, they have found it necessary to contend, that this clause was inserted for the purpose of conferring on Congress the power of making laws. That, without it, doubts might be entertained, whether Congress could exercise its powers in the form of legislation.

But could this be the object for which it was inserted? A government is created by the people, having legislative, executive, and judicial powers. Its legislative powers are vested in a Congress, which is to consist of a Senate and House of Representatives. Each house may determine the rule of its proceedings; and it is declared that every bill which shall have passed both houses, shall, before it becomes a law, be presented to the President of the United States. The 7th section describes the course of proceedings, by which a bill shall become a law; and, then, the 8th section enumerates the powers of Congress. Could it be necessary to say, that a legislature should exercise legislative powers, in the shape of legislation? After allowing each house to prescribe its own course of proceeding, after describing the manner in which a bill should become a law, would it have entered into the mind of a single member of the Convention, that an express power to make laws was necessary to enable the legislature to make them? That a legislature, endowed with legislative powers, can legislate, is a proposition too self-evident to have been questioned.

But the argument on which most reliance is placed, is drawn from that peculiar language of this clause. Congress is not empowered by it to make all laws, which may have relation to the powers conferred on the government, but such only as may be *"necessary and proper"* for carrying them into execution. The word *"necessary,"* is considered as controlling the whole sentence, and as limiting the right to pass laws for the execution of the granted powers, to such as are indispensable, and without which the power would be nugatory. That it excludes the choice of means, and leaves to Congress, in each case, that only which is most direct and simple.

Is it true, that this is the sense in which the word "necessary" is always used? Does it always import an absolute physical necessity, so strong, that one thing, to which another may be termed necessary, cannot exist without that other? We think it does not. If reference be had to its use, in the common affairs of the world, or in approved authors, we find that it frequently imports no more than that one thing is convenient, or useful, or essential to another. To employ the means necessary to an end, is generally understood as employing any means calculated to produce the end, and not as being confined to those single means, without which the end would be entirely unattainable. Such is the character of human language, that no word conveys to the mind, in all situations, one single definite idea; and nothing is more common than to use words in a figurative sense. Almost all compositions contain words, which, taken in their rigorous sense, would convey a meaning different from that which is obviously intended. It is essential to just construction, that many words which import something excessive, should be understood in a more mitigated sense— in that sense which common usage justifies. The word "necessary" is of this description. It has not a fixed character peculiar to itself. It admits of all degrees of comparison; and is often connected with other words, which increase or diminish the impression the mind receives of the urgency it imports. A thing may be necessary, very necessary, absolutely or indispensably necessary. To no mind would the same idea be conveyed, by these several phrases. This comment on the word is well illustrated, by the passage cited at the bar, from the 10th section of the 1st article of the constitution. It is, we think, impossible to compare the sentence which prohibits a State from laying "imposts, or duties on imports or exports, except what may be *absolutely* necessary for executing its inspection laws," with that which authorizes Congress "to make all laws which shall be necessary and proper for carrying into execution" the powers of the general government, without feeling a conviction that the convention understood itself to change materially the meaning of the word "necessary," by prefixing the word "absolutely." This word, then, like others, is used in various senses; and, in its construction, the subject, the context, the intention of the person using them, are all to be taken into view.

Let this be done in the case under consideration. The subject is the execution of those great powers on which the welfare of a nation essentially depends. It must have been the intention of those who gave these powers, to insure, so far as human prudence could insure, their beneficial execution. This could not be done by confiding the choice of means to such narrow limits as not to leave it in the power of Congress to adopt any which might be appropriate, and which were conducive to the end. This provision is made in a constitution intended to endure for ages to come, and, consequently, to be adapted to the various *crises* of human affairs. To have prescribed the means by which government should, in all future time, execute its powers, would have been to change, entirely, the character of the instrument, and give it the properties of a legal code. It would have been an unwise attempt to provide, by immutable rules, for exigencies which, if foreseen at all, must have been seen dimly, and which can be best provided for as they occur. To have declared that the best means shall not be used, but those alone without which the power given would be nugatory, would have been to deprive the legislature of the capacity to avail itself of experience, to exercise its reason, and to accommodate its legislation to circumstances. If we apply this principle of construction to any of the powers of the government, we shall find it so pernicious in its operation that we shall be compelled to discard it. The powers vested in Congress may certainly be carried into execution, without prescribing an oath of office. The power to exact this security for the faithful performance of duty, is not given, nor is it indispensably necessary. The different departments may be established; taxes may be imposed and collected; armies and navies may be raised and maintained; and money may be borrowed, without requiring an oath of office. It might be argued, with as much plausibility as other incidental powers have been assailed, that the Convention was not unmindful of this subject. The oath which might be exacted—that of fidelity to the constitution—is prescribed, and no other can be required. Yet, he would be charged with insanity who should contend, that the legislature might not superadd, to the oath directed by the constitution, such other oath of office as its wisdom might suggest.

So, with respect to the whole penal code of the United States: whence arises the power to punish in cases not prescribed by the constitution? All admit, that the government may, legitimately, punish any violation of its laws; and yet, this is not among the enumerated powers of Congress. The right to enforce the observance of law, by punishing its infraction, might be denied with the more plausibility, because it is expressly given in some cases. Congress is empowered "to provide for the punishment of counterfeiting the securities and current coin of the United States," and "to define and punish piracies and felonies committed on the high seas, and offences against the law of nations." The several powers of Congress may exist, in a very imperfect state to be sure, but they may exist and be carried into execution, although no punishment should be inflicted in cases where the right to punish is not expressly given.

Take, for example, the power "to establish post offices and post roads." This power is executed by the single act of making the establishment. But, from this has been inferred the power and duty of carrying the mail along the post road, from one post office to another. And from this implied power, has again been inferred the right to punish those who steal letters from the post office, or rob the mail. It may be said, with some plausibility, that the right to carry the mail, and to punish those who rob it, is not indispensably necessary to the establishment of a post office and post road. This right is indeed essential to the beneficial exercise of the power, but not indispensably necessary to its existence. So, of the punishment of the crimes of stealing or falsifying a record or process of a Court of the United States, or of perjury in such Court. To punish these offences is certainly conducive to the due administration of justice. But courts may exist, and may decide the causes brought before them, though such crimes escape punishment.

The baneful influence of this narrow construction on all the operations of the government, and the absolute impracticability of maintaining it without rendering the government incompetent to its great objects, might be illustrated by numerous examples drawn from the constitution, and from our laws. The good sense of the public has pronounced, without hesitation, that the power of punishment appertains to sovereignty, and may be exercised, whenever the sovereign has a right to act, as incidental to his constitutional powers. It is a means for carrying into execution all sovereign powers, and may be used, although not indispensably necessary. It is a right incidental to the power, and conducive to its beneficial exercise.

If this limited construction of the word "necessary" must be abandoned in order to punish, whence is derived the rule which would reinstate it, when the government would carry its powers into execution by means not vindictive in their nature? If the word "necessary" means "needful," "requisite," "essential," "conducive to," in order to let in the power of punishment for the infraction of law; why is it not equally comprehensive when required to authorize the use of means which facilitate the execution of the powers of government without the infliction of punishment?

In ascertaining the sense in which the word "necessary" is used in this clause of the constitution, we may derive some aid from that with which it is associated. Congress shall have power "to make all laws which shall be necessary and *proper* to carry into execution" the powers of the government. If the word "necessary" was used in that strict and rigorous sense for which the counsel for the State of Maryland contend, it would be an extraordinary departure from the usual course of the human mind, as exhibited in composition, to add a word, the only possible effect of which is to qualify that strict and rigorous meaning; to present to the mind the idea of some choice of means of legislation not straitened and compressed within the narrow limits for which gentlemen contend.

But the argument which most conclusively demonstrates the error of the construction contended for by the counsel for the State of Maryland, is founded on the intention of the Convention, as manifested in the whole clause. To waste time and argument in proving that, without it, Congress might carry its powers into execution, would be not much less idle than to hold a lighted taper to the sun. As little can it be required to prove, that in the absence of this clause, Congress would have some choice of means. That it might employ those which, in its judgment, would most advantageously effect the object to be accomplished. That any means adapted to the end, any means which tended directly to the execution of the constitutional powers of the government, were in themselves constitutional. This clause, as construed by the State of Maryland, would abridge, and almost annihilate this useful and necessary right of the legislature to select its means. That this could not be intended, is, we should think, had it not been already controverted, too apparent for controversy. We think so for the following reasons:

1st. The clause is placed among the powers of Congress, not among the limitations on those powers.

2d. Its terms purport to enlarge, not to diminish the powers vested in the government. It purports to be an additional power, not a restriction on those already granted. No reason has been, or can be assigned for thus concealing an intention to narrow the discretion of the national legislature, under words which purport to enlarge it. The framers of the constitution wished its adoption, and well knew that it would be endangered by its strength, not by its weakness. Had they been capable of using language which would convey to the eye one idea, and, after deep reflection, impress on the mind, another, they would rather have disguised the grant of power, than its limitation. If, then, their intention had been, by this clause, to restrain the free use of means which might otherwise have been implied, that intention would have been inserted in another place, and would have been expressed in terms resembling these. "In carrying into execution the foregoing powers, and all others," &c. "no laws shall be passed but such as are necessary and proper." Had the intention been to make this clause restrictive, it would unquestionably have been so in form as well as in effect.

The result of the most careful and attentive consideration bestowed upon this clause is, that if it does not enlarge, it cannot be construed to restrain the powers of Congress, or to impair the right of the legislature to exercise its best judgment in the selection of measures to carry into execution the constitutional powers of the government. If no other motive for its insertion can be suggested, a sufficient one is found in the desire to remove all doubts respecting the right to legislate on that vast mass of incidental powers which must be involved in the constitution, if that instrument be not a splendid bauble.

We admit, as all must admit, that the powers of the government are limited, and that its limits are not to be transcended. But we think the sound construction of the constitution must allow to the national legislature that discretion, with respect to the means by which the powers it confers are to be carried into execution, which will enable that body to perform the high duties assigned to it, in the manner most beneficial to the people. Let the end be legitimate, let it be within the scope of the constitution, and all means which are appropriate, which are plainly adapted to that end, which are not prohibited, but consist with the letter and spirit of the constitution, are constitutional.

That a corporation must be considered as a means not less usual, not of higher dignity, not more requiring a particular specification than other means, has been sufficiently proved. If we look to the origin of corporations, to the manner in which they have been framed in that government from which we have derived most of our legal principles and ideas, or to the uses to which they have been applied, we find no reason to suppose that a constitution, omitting, and wisely omitting, to enumerate all the means for carrying into execution the great powers vested in government, ought to have specified this. Had it been intended to grant this power as one which should be distinct and independent, to be exercised in any case whatever, it would have found a place among the enumerated powers of the government. But being considered merely as a means, to be employed only for the purpose of carrying into execution the given powers, there could be no motive for particularly mentioning it.

The propriety of this remark would seem to be generally acknowledged by the universal acquiescence in the construction which has been uniformly put on the 3rd section of the 4th article of the constitution. The power to "make all needful rules and regulations respecting the territory or other property belonging to the United States," is not more comprehensive, than the power "to make all laws which shall be necessary and proper for carrying into execution" the powers of the government. Yet all admit the constitutionality of a territorial government, which is a corporate body.

If a corporation may be employed, indiscriminately with other means, to carry into execution the powers of the government, no particular reason can be assigned for excluding the use of a bank, if required for its fiscal operations. To use one, must be within the discretion of Congress, if it be an appropriate mode of executing the powers of government. That it is a convenient, a useful, and essential instrument in the prosecution of its fiscal operations, is not now a subject of controversy. All those who have been concerned in the administration of our finances, have concurred in representing its importance and necessity; and so strongly have they been felt, that statesmen of the first class, whose previous opinions against it had been confirmed by every circumstance which can fix the human judgment, have yielded those opinions to the exigencies of the nation. Under the confederation, Congress, justifying the measure by its necessity, transcended perhaps its powers to obtain the advantage of a bank; and our own legislation attests the universal conviction of the utility of this measure. The time has passed away when it can be necessary to enter into any discussion in order to prove the importance of this instrument, as a means to effect the legitimate objects of the government.

But, were its necessity less apparent, none can deny its being an appropriate measure; and if it is, the degree of its necessity, as has been very justly observed, is to be discussed in another place. Should Congress, in the execution of its powers, adopt measures which are prohibited by the constitution; or should Congress, under the pretext of executing its powers, pass laws for the accomplishment of objects not entrusted to the government; it would become the painful duty of this tribunal, should a case requiring such a decision come before it, to say that such an act was not the law of the land. But where the law is not prohibited, and is really calculated to effect any of the objects entrusted to the government, to undertake here to inquire into the decree of its necessity, would be to pass the line which circumscribes the judicial department, and to tread on legislative ground. This court disclaims all pretensions to such a power.

After this declaration, it can scarcely be necessary to say, that the existence of State banks can have no possible influence on the question. No trace is to be found in the constitution of an intention to create a dependence of the government of the Union on those of the States, for the execution of the great powers assigned to it. Its means are adequate to its ends; and on those means alone was it expected to rely for the accomplishment of its ends. To impose on it the necessity of resorting to means which it cannot control, which another government may furnish or withhold, would render its course precarious, the result of its measures uncertain, and create a dependence on other governments, which might disappoint its most important designs, and is incompatible with the language of the constitution. But were it otherwise, the choice of means implies a right to choose a national bank in preference to State banks, and Congress alone can make the election.

After the most deliberate consideration, it is the unanimous and decided opinion of this Court, that the act to incorporate the Bank of the United States is a law made in pursuance of the constitution, and is a part of the supreme law of the land.

The branches, proceeding from the same stock, and being conducive to the complete accomplishment of the object, are equally constitutional. It would have been unwise to locate them in the charter, and it would be unnecessarily inconvenient to employ the legislative power in making those subordinate arrangements. The great duties of the bank are prescribed; those duties require branches; and the bank itself may, we think, be safely trusted with the selection of places where those branches shall be fixed; reserving always to the government the right to require that a branch shall be located where it may be deemed necessary.

It being the opinion of the Court, that the act incorporating the bank is constitutional; and that the power of establishing a branch in the State of Maryland might be properly exercised by the bank itself, we proceed to inquire—

2.   Whether the State of Maryland may, without violating the constitution, tax that branch?

That the power of taxation is one of vital importance; that it is retained by the States; that it is not abridged by the grant of a similar power to the government of the Union; that it is to be concurrently exercised by the two governments: are truths which have never been denied. But, such is the paramount character of the constitution, that its capacity to withdraw any subject from the action of even this power, is admitted. The States are expressly forbidden to lay any duties on imports or exports, except what may be absolutely necessary for executing their inspection laws. If the obligation of this prohibition must be conceded—if it may restrain a State from the exercise of its taxing power on imports and exports; the same paramount character would seem to restrain, as it certainly may restrain, a State from such other exercise of this power, as is in its nature incompatible with, and repugnant to, the constitutional laws of the Union. A law, absolutely repugnant to another, as entirely repeals that other as if express terms of repeal were used.

On this ground the counsel for the bank place its claim to be exempted from the power of a State to tax its operations. There is no express provision for the case, but the claim has been sustained on a principle which so entirely pervades the constitution, is so intermixed with the materials which compose it, so interwoven with its web, so blended with its texture, as to be incapable of being separated from it, without rending it into shreds.

This great principle is, that the constitution and the laws made in pursuance thereof are supreme; that they control the constitution and laws of the respective States, and cannot be controlled by them. From this, which may be almost termed an axiom, other propositions are deduced as corollaries, on the truth or error of which, and on their application to this case, the cause has been supposed to depend. These are, 1st. that a power to create implies a power to preserve. 2nd. That a power to destroy, if wielded by a different hand, is hostile to, and incompatible with these powers to create and to preserve. 3d. That where this repugnancy exists, that authority which is supreme must control, not yield to that over which it is supreme.

These propositions, as abstract truths, would, perhaps, never be controverted. Their application to this case, however, has been denied; and, both in maintaining the affirmative and the negative, a splendor of eloquence, and strength of argument, seldom, if ever, surpassed, have been displayed.

The power of Congress to create, and of course to continue, the bank, was the subject of the preceding part of this opinion; and is no longer to be considered as questionable.

That the power of taxing it by the States may be exercised so as to destroy it, is too obvious to be denied. But taxation is said to be an absolute power, which acknowledges no other limits than those expressly prescribed in the constitution, and like sovereign power of every other description, is trusted to the discretion of those who use it. But the very terms of this argument admit that the sovereignty of the State, in the article of taxation itself, is subordinate to, and may be controlled by the constitution of the United States. How far it has been controlled by that instrument must be a question of construction. In making this construction, no principle not declared, can be admissible, which would defeat the legitimate operations of a supreme government. It is of the very essence of supremacy to remove all obstacles to its action within its own sphere, and so to modify every power vested in subordinate governments, as to exempt its own operations from their own influence. This effect need not be stated in terms. It is so involved in the declaration of supremacy, so necessarily implied in it, that the expression of it could not make it more certain. We must, therefore, keep it in view while construing the constitution.

The argument on the part of the State of Maryland, is, not that the States may directly resist a law of Congress, but that they may exercise their acknowledged powers upon it, and that the constitution leaves them this right in the confidence that they will not abuse it.

Before we proceed to examine this argument, and to subject it to test of the constitution, we must be permitted to bestow a few considerations on the nature and extent of this original right of taxation, which is acknowledged to remain with the States. It is admitted that the power of taxing the people and their property is essential to the very existence of government, and may be legitimately exercised on the objects to which it is applicable, to the utmost extent to which the government may chuse to carry it. The only security against the abuse of this power, is found in the structure of the government itself. In imposing a tax the legislature acts upon its constituents. This is in general a sufficient security against erroneous and oppressive taxation.

The people of a State, therefore, give to their government a right of taxing themselves and their property, and as the exigencies of government cannot be limited, they prescribe no limits to the exercise of this right, resting confidently on the interest of the legislator, and on the influence of the constituent over their representative, to guard them against its abuse. But the means employed by the government of the Union have no such security, nor is the right of a State to tax them sustained by the same theory. Those means are not given by the people of a particular State, not given by the constituents of the legislature, which claim the right to tax them, but by the people of all the States. They are given by all, for the benefit of all— and upon theory, should be subjected to that government only which belongs to all.

It may be objected to this definition, that the power of taxation is not confined to the people and property of a State. It may be exercised upon every object brought within its jurisdiction.

This is true. But to what source do we trace this right? It is obvious, that it is an incident of sovereignty, and is co-extensive with that to which it is an incident. All subjects over which the sovereign power of a State extends, are objects of taxation; but those over which it does not extend, are, upon the soundest principles, exempt from taxation. This proposition may almost be pronounced self-evident.

The sovereignty of a State extends to every thing which exists by its own authority, or is introduced by its permission; but does it extend to those means which are employed by Congress to carry into execution powers conferred on that body by the people of the United States? We think it demonstrable that it does not. Those powers are not given by the people of a single State. They are given by the people of the United States, to a government whose laws, made in pursuance of the constitution, are declared to be supreme. Consequently, the people of a single State cannot confer a sovereignty which will extend over them.

If we measure the power of taxation residing in a State, by the extent of sovereignty which the people of a single State possess, and can confer on its government, we have an intelligible standard, applicable to every case to which the power may be applied. We have a principle which leaves the power of taxing the people and property of a State unimpaired; which leaves to a State the command of all its resources, and which places beyond its reach, all those powers which are conferred by the people of the United States on the government of the Union, and all those means which are given for the purpose of carrying those powers into execution. We have a principle which is safe for the States, and safe for the Union. We are relieved, as we ought to be, from clashing sovereignty; from interfering powers; from a repugnancy between a right in one government to pull down what there is an acknowledged right in another to build up; from the incompatibility of a right in one government to destroy what there is a right in another to preserve. We are not driven to the perplexing inquiry, so unfit for the judicial department, what degree of taxation is the legitimate use, and what degree may amount to the abuse of the power. The attempt to use it on the means employed by the government of the Union, in pursuance of the constitution, is itself an abuse, because it is the usurpation of a power which the people of a single State cannot give.

We find, then, on just theory, a total failure of this original right to tax the means employed by the government of the Union, for the execution of its powers. The right never existed, and the question whether it has been surrendered, cannot arise.

But, waiving this theory for the present, let us resume the inquiry, whether this power can be exercised by the respective States, consistently with a fair construction of the constitution?

That the power to tax involves the power to destroy; that the power to destroy may defeat and render useless the power to create; that there is a plain repugnance, in conferring on one government a power to control the constitutional measures of another, which other, with respect to those very measures, is declared to be supreme over that which exerts the control, are propositions not to be denied. But all inconsistencies are to be reconciled by the magic of the word CONFIDENCE. Taxation, it is said, does not necessarily and unavoidably destroy. To carry it to the excess of destruction would be an abuse, to presume which, would banish that confidence which is essential to all government.

But is this a case of confidence? Would the people of any one State trust those of another with a power to control the most insignificant operations of their State government? We know they would not. Why, then, should we suppose that the people of any one State should be willing to trust those of another with a power to control the operations of a government to which they have confided their most important and most valuable interests? In the legislature of the Union alone, are all represented. The legislature of the Union alone, therefore, can be trusted by the people with the power of controlling measures which concern all, in the confidence that it will not be abused. This, then, is not a case of confidence, and we must consider it is as it really is.

If we apply the principle for which the State of Maryland contends, to the constitution generally, we shall find it capable of changing totally the character of that instrument. We shall find it capable of arresting all the measures of the government, and of prostrating it at the foot of the States. The American people have declared their constitution, and the laws made in pursuance thereof, to be supreme; but this principle would transfer the supremacy, in fact, to the States.

If the States may tax one instrument, employed by the government in the execution of its powers, they may tax any and every other instrument. They may tax the mail; they may tax the mint; they may tax patent rights; they may tax the papers of the custom-house; they may tax judicial process; they may tax all the means employed by the government, to an excess which would defeat all the ends of government. This was not intended by the American people. They did not design to make their government dependent on the States.

Gentlemen say, they do not claim the right to extend State taxation to these objects. They limit their pretensions to property. But on what principle is this distinction made? Those who make it have furnished no reason for it, and the principle for which they contend denies it. They contend that the power of taxation has no other limit than is found in the 10th section of the 1st article of the constitution; that, with respect to every thing else, the power of the States is supreme, and admits of no control. If this be true, the distinction between property and other subjects to which the power of taxation is applicable, is merely arbitrary, and can never be sustained. This is not all. If the controlling power of the States be established; if their supremacy as to taxation be acknowledged; what is to restrain their exercising this control in any shape they may please to give it? Their sovereignty is not confined to taxation. That is not the only mode in which it might be displayed. The question is, in truth, a question of supremacy; and if the right of the States to tax the means employed by the general government be conceded, the declaration that the constitution, and the laws made in pursuance thereof, shall be the supreme law of the land, is empty and unmeaning declamation.

In the course of the argument, the *Federalist* has been quoted; and the opinions expressed by the authors of that work have been justly supposed to be entitled to great respect in expounding the constitution. No tribute can be paid to them which exceeds their merit; but in applying their opinions to the cases which may arise in the progress of our government, a right to judge of their correctness must be retained; and, to understand the argument, we must examine the proposition it maintains, and the objections against which it is directed. The subject of those numbers, from which passages have been cited, is the unlimited power of taxation which is vested in the general government. The objection to this unlimited power, which the argument seeks to remove, is stated with fullness and clearness. It is, "that an indefinite power of taxation in the latter (the government of the Union) might, and probably would, in time, deprive the former (the government of the States) of the means of providing for their own necessities; and would subject them entirely to the mercy of the national legislature. As the laws of the Union are to become the supreme law of the land; as it is to have power to pass all laws that may be necessary for carrying into execution the authorities with which it is proposed to vest it; the national government might at any time abolish the taxes imposed for State objects, upon the pretence of an interference with its own. It might allege a necessity for doing this, in order to give efficacy to the national revenues; and thus, all the resources of taxation might, by degrees, become the subjects of federal monopoly, to the entire exclusion and destruction of the State governments."

The objections to the constitution which are noticed in these numbers, were to the undefined power of the government to tax, not to the incidental privilege of exempting its own measures from State taxation. The consequences apprehended from this undefined power were, that it would absorb all the objects of taxation, "to the exclusion and destruction of the State governments." The arguments of the *Federalist* are intended to prove the fallacy of these apprehensions; not to prove that the government was incapable of executing any of its powers, without exposing the means it employed to the embarrassments of State taxation. Arguments urged against these objections, and these apprehensions, are to be understood as relating to the points they mean to prove. Had the authors of those excellent essays been asked, whether they contended for that construction of the constitution, which would place within the reach of the States those measures which the government might adopt for the execution of its powers; no man, who has read their instructive pages, will hesitate to admit, that their answer must have been in the negative.

It has also been insisted, that, as the power of taxation in the general and State governments is acknowledged to be concurrent, every argument which would sustain the right of the general government to tax banks chartered by the States, will equally sustain the right of the States to tax banks chartered by the general government.

But the two cases are not on the same reason. The people of all the States have created the general government, and have conferred upon it the general power of taxation. The people of all the States, and the States themselves, are represented in Congress, and, by their representatives, exercise this power. When they tax the chartered institutions of the States, they tax their constituents; and these taxes must be uniform. But, when a State taxes the operations of the government of the United States, it acts upon institutions created, not by their own constituents, but by people over whom they claim no control. It acts upon the measures of a government created by others as well as themselves, for the benefit of others in common with themselves. The difference is that which always exists, and always must exist, between the action of the whole on a part, and the action of a part on the whole—between the laws of a government declared to be supreme, and those of a government which, when in opposition to those laws, is not supreme.

But if the full application of this argument could be admitted, it might bring into question the right of Congress to tax the State banks, and could not prove the rights of the States to tax the Bank of the United States.

The Court has bestowed on this subject its most deliberate consideration. The result is a conviction that the States have no power, by taxation or otherwise, to retard, impede, burden, or in any manner control, the operations of the constitutional laws enacted by Congress to carry into execution the powers vested in the general government. This is, we think, the unavoidable consequence of that supremacy which the constitution has declared.

We are unanimously of opinion, that the law passed by the legislature of Maryland, imposing a tax on the Bank of the United States, is unconstitutional and void.

This opinion does not deprive the States of any resources which they originally possessed. It does not extend to a tax paid by the real property of the bank, in common with the other real property within the State, nor to a tax imposed on the interest which the citizens of Maryland may hold in this institution, in common with other property of the same description throughout the State. But this is a tax on the operations of the bank, and is, consequently, a tax on the operation of an instrument employed by the government of the Union to carry its powers into execution. Such a tax must be unconstitutional. . . .

NOTES

1.   Below the surface of *McCulloch*—and sometimes on the surface—are many of the arguments made in the debates in the First Congress and President Washington's cabinet about the constitutionality of the first Bank. What does Chief Justice Marshall say about Jefferson's arguments? About Hamilton's? About Madison's?

2.   *McCulloch* was decided in 1819, twenty-eight years after the first Bank was chartered. Marshall begins his opinion by acknowledging that practice supports the Bank's constitutionality. Does he consider the practice dispositive? What kinds of questions does Marshall think can and cannot be settled by practice?

Which of the remaining types of constitutional argument does Marshall emphasize—text, historical purpose, structure, or policy? See if you can outline the arguments he made, first, for the scope of federal legislative power, and, second, for the proposition that a state law may not interfere with the operation of a federal instrumentality (the two principal holdings of the case). Which of Marshall's structural arguments strike you as most clever? As most correct?

3.   Does Marshall think the Necessary and Proper Clause *restricts* the powers of the national government? If he does not think it restricts those powers, does it follow that Marshall thinks the clause *adds* to the powers of the national government? Or does he think the clause confirms something that was already true, i.e., that the national government has the incidental powers that belong to its enumerated powers?

4.   What, exactly, does Marshall say that "necessary" means in the Necessary and Proper Clause? What work does he think "proper" does in the clause? Does he treat "necessary" and "proper" as two separate requirements for congressional action under the clause? Or does he treat the phrase as a unity, with "proper" perhaps suggesting that "necessary" should not be taken in its strictest Jeffersonian sense? See Samuel L. Bray, *"Necessary AND Proper" and "Cruel AND Unusual": Hendiadys in the Constitution*, 102 Va. L. Rev. 687 (2016). Is the famous sentence in *McCulloch* that begins "Let the end be legitimate," a good paraphrase of "necessary and proper"?

5.   Does Marshall say which enumerated powers the incorporation of the Bank would be "necessary and proper" to carry into execution? Did Hamilton?

6.   Consider as well the second part of Chief Justice Marshall's opinion, addressing Maryland's legislation imposing a special tax on the operation of the Bank. What, exactly, was the problem with the tax? Was it that states cannot tax (or regulate?) the federal government at all? That Maryland was singling out the federal government for disfavored treatment? That members of Congress probably would have disapproved of the tax, if they had thought about it?

Consider an extension of the second holding of *McCulloch*. Suppose a federal mail carrier drives on public roads to deliver the mail. Must the mail carrier comply with state traffic laws? In *Johnson v. Maryland*, 254 U.S. 51 (1920), the Court held that federal mail carriers could *not* be required to get a state driver's license, though they might be required to obey "a statute or ordinance regulating the mode of turning at the corners of streets."

Should these questions about the preemption of state laws be resolved by constitutional interpretation? Or should the courts let Congress decide which state laws to preempt?

After *McCulloch*

The reaction in the country to *McCulloch* was sharply divided. Some supported it, while others were critical. The Pennsylvania legislature proposed a constitutional amendment that would allow the Bank to operate only in the District of Columbia. In Ohio the reaction was especially dramatic. As noted, the state had laid a $50,000 annual tax on each branch of the Bank of the United States. Undeterred by *McCulloch*, the state auditor decided to collect. He sent his agents to raid one of the branches, and they carried away coins and notes worth $100,000. (The money was later returned, but only after much legal wrangling and another decision of the U.S. Supreme Court.) In addition, there were serious proposals to amend the jurisdictional statute governing the Supreme Court; these would have taken away the Court's jurisdiction to review appeals from state supreme courts on questions of federal law. But none of these post-*McCulloch* jurisdiction-stripping bills passed.

Among the critics of *McCulloch* were two Virginians who wrote essays against the decision under the names "Amphictyon" and "Hampden." (Hampden was Spencer Roane, a leading justice on the Virginia Supreme Court.) Their essays drew a response from Chief Justice Marshall himself, who wrote pseudonymous essays under the names "A Friend of the Constitution" and "A Friend of the Union." In his responses, Marshall found much to disagree with in the charges of his critics. On some points they disagreed about first principles: e.g., Marshall did not accept his critics' view that the Constitution was a compact between sovereign states. On other points, he disagreed with the critics' reading of *McCulloch*. For example, Marshall argued that the opinion did not say Congress could do anything "convenient" to federal power. But he agreed with Hampden that the Necessary and Proper Clause did not augment national power but merely stated that Congress had the incidental powers it would have had anyway. These essays can be found in JOHN MARSHALL'S DEFENSE OF *McCULLOCH V. MARYLAND* (Gerald Gunther ed., 1969).

McCulloch spared the life of the Second Bank, but in a decade the pendulum would swing again. In 1929, a man became president who was an implacable foe of the Bank and an ardent supporter of federalism: Andrew Jackson. The Second Bank's charter was not set to expire until 1836, but the Bank sought renewal for another twenty years in the election year of 1832. This time, more than forty years after the creation of the Bank during the Washington administration, President Jackson vetoed the Bank bill, and he did so *on the grounds that the Bank was unconstitutional.* This veto—on constitutional grounds that had been previously rejected by all three branches of the national government—is worth considering for its implications for constitutional interpretation. What do you think of President Jackson's analysis? Should he have accepted that the Bank was constitutional because Presidents Washington and Madison had? Because the Supreme Court had in *McCulloch v. Maryland*? Or was he right to stick to his convictions about the Constitution?

Here is the veto message from President Jackson explaining his position on the Bank, preceded by a letter from former President Madison explaining his.

James Madison, Letter to Lafayette
Nov. 1826

Dear Friend:

. . . As I have been charged with inconsistency, in not putting a veto on the last act of Congress establishing a Bank, a power to do which was denied in the Report, a word of explanation may not be improper. My construction of the Constitution on this point is not changed. But I regarded the reiterated sanctions given to the power by the exercise of it, thro' a long period of time, in every variety of form, and in some form or other, under every administration preceding mine, with the general concurrence of the State authorities, and acquiescence of the people at large, and without a glimpse of change in the public opinion, but evidently with a growing confirmation of it; all this I regarded as a construction put on the Constitution by the Nation, which having made it had the supreme right to declare its meaning, and regarding moreover, the establishment of a Bank under the existing circumstances as the only expedient for substituting a sound currency in place of the viciated one working so much mischief, I did not feel myself, as a public man, at liberty, to sacrifice all these public considerations to my private opinion.

Andrew Jackson, Veto Message on the Bank

July 10, 1832

To the Senate.

The bill "to modify and continue" the act entitled "An act to incorporate the subscribers to the Bank of the United States" was presented to me on the 4th July instant. Having considered it with that solemn regard to the principles of the Constitution which the day was calculated to inspire, and come to the conclusion that it ought not to become a law, I herewith return it to the Senate, in which it originated, with my objections.

A bank of the United States is in many respects convenient for the Government and useful to the people. Entertaining this opinion, and deeply impressed with the belief that some of the powers and privileges possessed by the existing bank are unauthorized by the Constitution, subversive of the rights of the States, and dangerous to the liberties of the people, I felt it my duty at an early period of my Administration to call the attention of Congress to the practicability of organizing an institution combining all its advantages and obviating these objections. I sincerely regret that in the act before me I can perceive none of those modifications of the bank charter which are necessary, in my opinion, to make it compatible with justice, with sound policy, or with the Constitution of our country. . . .

Every monopoly and all exclusive privileges are granted at the expense of the public, which ought to receive a fair equivalent. The many millions which this act proposes to bestow on the stockholders of the existing bank must come directly or indirectly out of the earnings of the American people. It is due to them, therefore, if their Government sell monopolies and exclusive privileges, that they should at least exact for them as much as they are worth in open market. The value of the monopoly in this case may be correctly ascertained. . . . The present value of the monopoly . . . is $17,000,000, and this the act proposes to sell for three millions . . .

It is maintained by the advocates of the bank that its constitutionality in all its features ought to be considered as settled by precedent and by the decision of the Supreme Court. To this conclusion I can not assent. Mere precedent is a dangerous source of authority, and should not be regarded as deciding questions of constitutional power except where the acquiescence of the people and the States can be considered as well settled. So far from this being the case on this subject, an argument against the bank might be based on precedent. One Congress, in 1791, decided in favor of a bank; another, in 1811, decided against it. One Congress, in 1815, decided against a bank; another, in 1816, decided in its favor. Prior to the present Congress, therefore, the precedents drawn from that source were equal. If we resort to the States, the expressions of legislative, judicial, and executive opinions against the bank have been probably to those in its favor as 4 to 1. There is nothing in precedent, therefore, which, if its authority were admitted, ought to weigh in favor of the act before me.

If the opinion of the Supreme Court covered the whole ground of this act, it ought not to control the coordinate authorities of this Government. The Congress, the Executive, and the Court must each for itself be guided by its own opinion of the Constitution. Each public officer who takes an oath to support the Constitution swears that he will support it as he understands it, and not as it is understood by others. It is as much the duty of the House of Representatives, of the Senate, and of the President to decide upon the constitutionality of any bill or resolution which may be presented to them for passage or approval as it is of the supreme judges when it may be brought before them for judicial decision. The opinion of the judges has no more authority over Congress than the opinion of Congress has over the judges, and on that point the President is independent of both. The authority of the Supreme Court must not, therefore, be permitted to control the Congress or the Executive when acting in their legislative capacities, but to have only such influence as the force of their reasoning may deserve.

But in the case relied upon the Supreme Court have not decided that all the features of this corporation are compatible with the Constitution. It is true that the court have said that the law incorporating the bank is a constitutional exercise of power by Congress; but taking into view the whole opinion of the court and the reasoning by which they have come to that conclusion, I understand them to have decided that inasmuch as a bank is an appropriate means for carrying into effect the enumerated powers of the General Government, therefore the law incorporating it is in accordance with that provision of the Constitution which declares that Congress shall have power "to make all laws which shall be necessary and proper for carrying those powers into execution." Having satisfied themselves that the word *"necessary"* in the Constitution means *needful,* "requisite," "essential," "conducive to," and that "a bank" is a convenient, a useful, and essential instrument in the prosecution of the Government's "fiscal operations," they conclude that to "use one must be within the discretion of Congress" and that "the act to incorporate the Bank of the United States is a law made in pursuance of the Constitution"; "but," say they, *"where the law is not prohibited and is really calculated to effect any of the objects intrusted to the Government, to undertake here to inquire into the degree of its necessity would be to pass the line which circumscribes the judicial department and to tread on legislative ground."*

The principle here affirmed is that the "degree of its necessity," involving all the details of a banking institution, is a question exclusively for legislative consideration. A bank is constitutional, but it is the province of the Legislature to determine whether this or that particular power, privilege, or exemption is "necessary and proper" to enable the bank to discharge its duties to the Government, and from their decision there is no appeal to the courts of justice. Under the decision of the Supreme Court, therefore, it is the exclusive province of Congress and the President to decide whether the particular features of this act are *necessary* and *proper* in order to enable the bank to perform conveniently and efficiently the public duties assigned to it as a fiscal agent, and therefore constitutional, or *unnecessary* and *improper*, and therefore unconstitutional.

Without commenting on the general principle affirmed by the Supreme Court, let us examine the details of this act in accordance with the rule of legislative action which they have laid down. It will be found that many of the powers and privileges conferred on it can not be supposed necessary for the purpose for which it is proposed to be created, and are not, therefore, means necessary to attain the end in view, and consequently not justified by the Constitution. . . .

This act authorizes and encourages transfers of its stock to foreigners and grants them an exemption from all State and national taxation. So far from being *"necessary and proper"* that the bank should possess this power to make it a safe and efficient agent of the Government in its fiscal operations, it is calculated to convert the Bank of the United States into a foreign bank, to impoverish our people in time of peace, to disseminate a foreign influence through every section of the Republic, and in war to endanger our independence. . . .

A general discussion will now take place, eliciting new light and settling important principles; and a new Congress, elected in the midst of such discussion, and furnishing an equal representation of the people according to the last census, will bear to the Capitol the verdict of public opinion, and, I doubt not, bring this important question to a satisfactory result. . . .

Nor is our Government to be maintained or our Union preserved by invasions of the rights and powers of the several States. In thus attempting to make our General Government strong we make it weak. Its true strength consists in leaving individuals and States as much as possible to themselves—in making itself felt, not in its power, but in its beneficence; not in its control, but in its protection; not in binding the States more closely to the center, but leaving each to move unobstructed in its proper orbit.

Experience should teach us wisdom. Most of the difficulties our Government now encounters and most of the dangers which impend over our Union have sprung from an abandonment of the legitimate objects of Government by our national legislation, and the adoption of such principles as are embodied in this act. Many of our rich men have not been content with equal protection and equal benefits, but have besought us to make them richer by act of Congress. By attempting to gratify their desires we have in the results of our legislation arrayed section against section, interest against interest, and man against man, in a fearful commotion which threatens to shake the foundations of our Union. It is time to pause in our career to review our principles, and if possible revive that devoted patriotism and spirit of compromise which distinguished the sages of the Revolution and the fathers of our Union. If we can not at once, in justice to interests vested under improvident legislation, make our Government what it ought to be, we can at least take a stand against all new grants of monopolies and exclusive privileges, against any prostitution of our Government to the advancement of the few at the expense of the many, and in favor of compromise and gradual reform in our code of laws and system of political economy. . . .

The Death of the Second Bank

President Jackson's veto set off a titanic struggle with the Senate. After winning re-election, President Jackson directed the secretary of the treasury to withdraw the federal government's deposits from the Bank (to destroy it). When the secretary of the treasury refused, President Jackson fired him for insubordination, appointing in his place Attorney General Roger Taney—a fiercely partisan ally whom President Jackson would later appoint to be chief justice. Taney promptly withdrew all federal deposits from the Bank, and the outraged Senate adopted a resolution censuring the president. The Bank tried to save itself by triggering a financial panic, but President Jackson succeeded in persuading the public that the panic was not his fault but the Bank's. The issue was taken to the public in the 1834 midterm elections, and the president's allies won a major victory—leading the reconstituted Senate to expunge the resolution censuring the president from its records. Although Congress twice passed bills recreating the Bank in the 1840s, President John Tyler vetoed them on the same grounds of unconstitutionality that had been cited by President Jackson.[3] No institution remotely resembling the Bank of the United States would be created until the passage of the Federal Reserve Act in 1913.

The debate over the constitutionality of the Bank eventually faded into history. Today, its main legacy is Chief Justice Marshall's opinion in *McCulloch v. Maryland* and the precedent it set of broad national power. Yet this is not how the matter seemed to be settled in the nineteenth century. President Jackson won the Bank War, killing the Bank for the next seventy years. The resolution seemed to reaffirm the Jeffersonian view of more limited national government powers.

The Bank and Constitutional Interpretation

The Bank controversy is an important early case for considering the how and who of constitutional interpretation. Consider first whether Congress had the power under the Constitution to create the Bank in light of the five types of constitutional argument (see p. 42).

What *textual* arguments do Madison, Jefferson, Hamilton, Marshall, and Jackson make? In understanding the text, should an interpreter look to how the text would be understood when it was enacted (or ratified), or rather to how it is understood today? In deciding how the text would be understood—whether then or now—what sorts of evidence should count? For example, would it make sense to look at the leading dictionary at the founding, Dr. Johnson's DICTIONARY OF THE ENGLISH LANGUAGE (6th ed. 1785)? Dr. Johnson includes among the definitions of *necessary* "1. Needful; indispensably requisite," and among the definitions of *proper* he includes "1. Peculiar; not belonging to more; not common.... 3. One's own.... 5. Fit; accommodated; adapted; suitable; qualified." Or does using dictionaries introduce too much indeterminacy and subjectivity, because the interpreter has to choose which dictionary to consult and which meaning to use?

Next consider Jefferson's argument from *historical context*: the Philadelphia Convention considered giving Congress a power to charter corporations and deliberately decided not to. Is this persuasive? Also, what was the point of the Necessary and Proper Clause? Was it to keep the national government from having all of its other powers frustrated? What is the relationship of the Necessary and Proper Clause to the background principle of incidental powers?

Now consider the following *structural* arguments:

(1)   The Necessary and Proper Clause cannot decrease the powers of Congress because it appears with the list of congressional powers in

---

[3]   Had those bills been signed by President Tyler, the Supreme Court—the membership of which had been completely transformed by Presidents Jackson and Van Buren—might well have overruled *McCulloch*. See Gerard Magliocca, ANDREW JACKSON AND THE CONSTITUTION: THE RISE AND FALL OF GENERATIONAL REGIMES (2007).

Article I, Section 8 instead of with the restraints in Article I, Section 9.

(2) "Necessary" cannot mean "absolutely necessary," because Article I, Section 10 uses the phrase "absolutely necessary."

(3) The omission of the word "expressly" in the Tenth Amendment, given its inclusion in the Articles of Confederation, indicates that Congress has implied powers under the Constitution.

(4) The clause cannot be read to justify most of what the national government does, or there would be no point in enumerating its powers.

Which of these structural arguments are persuasive? Do any lead inexorably to a conclusion about the Bank's constitutionality?

And what about *practice and precedent*? Should *McCulloch* have simply affirmed in a few sentences because of settled practice?

Finally, consider arguments from *policy*. Would a narrow reading of the Necessary and Proper Clause hobble the national government's ability to solve problems the states could not solve by themselves? Or would a broad reading risk concentrating all governmental power in the national government? And consider a policy argument about the judiciary as an institution: Once Congress and the president have determined that an institution such as the Bank is "necessary," should the courts defer to their expertise?

When you consider all five kinds of arguments, is it really possible that "necessary and proper" could be limited to laws that are absolutely necessary, The One Thing We Must Do Or The Sky Will Fall? On the other hand, is it really possible that it allows Congress to do anything "convenient" or "useful" for exercising an enumerated power? And if the answer lies somewhere between those extremes, where is it exactly? How would you express what the clause allows Congress to do?

One final question about constitutional interpretation is raised by the Bank controversy. *Who* interprets the Constitution? It is obvious that courts must interpret it. Article III gives to the Supreme Court and other federal courts "the judicial Power," and it defines the kinds of cases and controversies that the federal courts can hear, including all cases "arising under this Constitution." When deciding these cases, a federal court will often have to decide what the Constitution means and how it applies to the case at hand. But are courts the only government actors who must interpret the Constitution? How should each branch respond to the interpretations made by other branches? And when does a decision by the Supreme Court finally settle a constitutional question? The various actors in the controversy over the First and Second Banks had to answer these important questions for themselves, and they often disagreed. What do you think?

[*Assignment 25*]

B. THE POWER TO REGULATE COMMERCE AMONG THE SEVERAL STATES

Art. I, § 8: The Congress shall have Power

To regulate Commerce with foreign Nations, and among the several States, and with the Indian tribes; . . .

To make all Laws which shall be necessary and proper for carrying into Execution the foregoing Powers and all other Powers vested by this Constitution in the Government of the United States, or in any Department or Officer thereof.

The most persistent debates about the scope of national power have involved the powers enumerated in Article I, Section 8, especially the powers to "regulate Commerce . . . among the several States"; to "lay and collect Taxes, Duties, Imposts and Excises, to pay the Debts and provide for the common Defence and general Welfare of the United States"; to spend money so raised, for various purposes; and to "make all Laws which shall be necessary and proper for carrying into Execution the foregoing Powers" and all other powers vested in the national government.

This section considers the Commerce Clause and the Necessary and Proper Clause. It also touches on the Tenth Amendment's relevance to interpreting constitutional silence about federal power. The following sections consider the scope of the taxing power and spending power. We then turn to the recent landmark decision upholding the Affordable Care Act, *National Federation of Independent Business v. Sebelius*, 132 S.Ct. 2566 (2012). This case brings together all of these powers—commerce, necessary and proper, taxing, and spending—and shows the continuing relevance of the debates about their scope. Before we get there, though, we need to go back almost to *McCulloch*. Five years after that decision, the Supreme Court decided another important case interpreting the Commerce Clause and the Supremacy Clause, *Gibbons v. Ogden*:

Gibbons v. Ogden

22 U.S. (9 Wheat.) 1 (1824)

[*The New York legislature enacted a statute granting Robert Fulton and Robert Livingston the exclusive right to operate steamboats in New York waters. Its stated purpose was to encourage investment in the development of steamboat technology. Fulton and Livingston licensed Aaron Ogden to operate a ferry between New York City and Elizabethtown, New Jersey. Thomas Gibbons, once Ogden's partner, began operating a competing ferry service that, because it necessarily entered New York waters, violated the grant given to Fulton and Livingston. Ogden obtained an injunction from New York's Court of Chancery that ordered Gibbons to stop operating his vessels in New York waters. On appeal, Gibbons argued that his vessels were enrolled and licensed to be employed in carrying on the coasting trade under the act of Congress, passed on February 18, 1793. Gibbons claimed that this congressional act preempted the New York statute, and thus he was entitled to navigate the waters of New York.—Editors]*

■ MR. CHIEF JUSTICE MARSHALL delivered the opinion of the Court, and, after stating the case, proceeded as follows:

The appellant contends that . . . the [New York] laws which purport to give the exclusive privilege . . . are repugnant to the constitution and laws of the United States. They are said to be repugnant—

1st. To that clause in the constitution which authorizes Congress to regulate commerce. . . .

As preliminary to the very able discussions of the constitution, which we have heard from the bar, and as having some influence on its construction, reference has been made to the political situation of these States, anterior to its formation. It has been said, that they were sovereign, were completely independent, and were connected with each other only by a league. This is true. But, when these allied sovereigns converted their league into a government, when they converted their Congress of Ambassadors, deputed to deliberate on their common concerns, and to recommend measures of general utility, into a Legislature, empowered to enact laws on the most interesting subjects, the whole character in which the States appear, underwent a change, the extent of which must be determined by a fair consideration of the instrument by which that change was effected.

This instrument contains an enumeration of powers expressly granted by the people to their government. It has been said, that these powers ought to be construed strictly. But why ought they to be so construed? Is there one sentence in the constitution which gives countenance to this rule? In the last of the enumerated powers, that which grants, expressly, the means for carrying all others into execution, Congress is authorized 'to make all laws which shall be necessary and proper' for the purpose. But this limitation on the means which may be used, is not extended to the powers which are conferred; nor is there one sentence in the constitution, which has been pointed out by the gentlemen of the bar, or which we have been able to discern, that prescribes this rule. We do not, therefore, think ourselves justified in adopting it. What do gentlemen mean, by a strict construction? If they contend only against that enlarged construction, which would extend words beyond their natural and obvious import, we might question the application of the term, but should not controvert the principle. If they contend for that narrow construction which, in support or some theory not to be found in the constitution, would deny to the government those powers which the words of the grant, as usually understood, import, and which are consistent with the general views and objects of the instrument; for that narrow construction, which would cripple the government, and render it unequal to the object for which it is declared to be instituted, and to which the powers given, as fairly understood, render it competent; then we cannot perceive the propriety of this strict construction, nor adopt it as the rule by which the constitution is to be expounded. As men, whose intentions require no concealment, generally employ the words which most directly and aptly express the ideas they intend to convey, the enlightened patriots who framed our constitution, and the people who adopted it, must be understood to have employed words in their natural sense, and to have intended what they have said. If, from the imperfection of human language, there should be serious doubts respecting the extent of any given power, it is a well settled rule, that the objects for which it was given, especially when those objects are expressed in the instrument itself, should have great influence in the construction. We know of no reason for excluding this rule from the present case. . . .

The subject to be regulated is commerce; and our constitution being, as was aptly said at the bar, one of enumeration, and not of definition, to ascertain the extent of the power, it becomes necessary to settle the meaning of the word. The counsel for the appellee would limit it to traffic, to buying and selling, or the interchange of commodities, and do not admit that it comprehends navigation. This would restrict a general term, applicable to many objects, to one of its significations. Commerce, undoubtedly, is traffic, but it is something more: it is intercourse. It describes the commercial intercourse between nations, and parts of nations, in all its branches, and is regulated by prescribing rules for carrying on that intercourse. The mind can scarcely conceive a system for regulating commerce between nations, which shall exclude all laws concerning navigation, which shall be silent on the admission of the vessels of the one nation into the ports of the other, and be confined to prescribing rules for the conduct of individuals, in the actual employment of buying and selling, or of barter.

If commerce does not include navigation, the government of the Union has no direct power over that subject, and can make no law prescribing what shall constitute American vessels, or requiring that they shall be navigated by American seamen. Yet this power has been exercised from the commencement of the government, has been exercised with the consent of all, and has been understood by all to be a commercial regulation. All America understands, and has uniformly understood, the word "commerce," to comprehend navigation. It was so understood, and must have been so understood, when the constitution was framed. The power over commerce, including navigation, was one of the primary objects for which the people of America adopted their government, and must have been contemplated in forming it. . . .

The subject to which the power is next applied, is to commerce "among the several States." The word "among" means intermingled with. A thing which is among others, is intermingled with them. Commerce among the States, cannot stop at the external boundary line of each State, but may be introduced into the interior.

It is not intended to say that these words comprehend that commerce, which is completely internal, which is carried on between man and man in a State, or between different parts of the same State, and which does not extend to or affect other States. Such a power would be inconvenient, and is certainly unnecessary.

Comprehensive as the word "among" is, it may very properly be restricted to that commerce which concerns more States than one. The phrase is not one which would probably have been selected to indicate the completely interior traffic of a State, because it is not an apt phrase for that purpose; and the enumeration of the particular classes of commerce, to which the power was to be extended, would not have been made, had the intention been to extend the power to every description. The enumeration presupposes something not enumerated; and that something, if we regard the language or the subject of the sentence, must be the exclusively internal commerce of a State. The genius and character of the whole government seem to be, that its action is to be applied to all the external concerns of the nation, and to those internal concerns which affect the States generally; but not to those which are completely within a particular State, which do not affect other States, and with which it is not necessary to interfere, for the purpose of executing some of the general powers of the government. The completely internal commerce of a State, then, may be considered as reserved for the State itself.

But, in regulating commerce with foreign nations, the power of Congress does not stop at the jurisdictional lines of the several States. It would be a very useless power, if it could not pass those lines. The commerce of the United States with foreign nations, is that of the whole United States. Every district has a right to participate in it. The deep streams which penetrate our country in every direction, pass through the interior of almost every State in the Union, and furnish the means of exercising this right. If Congress has the power to regulate it, that power must be exercised whenever the subject exists. If it exists within the States, if a foreign voyage may commence or terminate at a port within a State, then the power of Congress may be exercised within a State.

This principle is, if possible, still more clear, when applied to commerce "among the several States." They either join each other, in which case they are separated by a mathematical line, or they are remote from each other, in which case other States lie between them. What is commerce "among" them; and how is it to be conducted? Can a trading expedition between two adjoining States, commence and terminate outside of each? And if the trading intercourse be between two States remote from each other, must it not commence in one, terminate in the other, and probably pass through a third? Commerce among the States must, of necessity, be commerce with the States. . . .

We are now arrived at the inquiry—What is this power?

It is the power to regulate; that is, to prescribe the rule by which commerce is to be governed. This power, like all others vested in Congress, is complete in itself, may be exercised to its utmost extent, and acknowledges no limitations, other than are prescribed in the constitution. These are expressed in plain terms, and do not affect the questions which arise in this case, or which have been discussed at the bar. If, as has always been understood, the sovereignty of Congress, though limited to specified objects, is plenary as to those objects, the power over commerce with foreign nations, and among the several States, is vested in Congress as absolutely as it would be in a single government, having in its constitution the same restrictions on the exercise of the power as are found in the constitution of the United States. The wisdom and the discretion of Congress, their identity with the people, and the influence which their constituents possess at elections, are, in this, as in many other instances, as that, for example, of declaring war, the sole restraints on which they have relied, to secure them from its abuse. They are the restraints on which the people must often rely solely, in all representative governments.

The power of Congress, then, comprehends navigation, within the limits of every State in the Union; so far as that navigation may be, in any manner, connected with "commerce with foreign nations, or among the several States, or with the Indian tribes." It may, of consequence, pass the jurisdictional line of New-York, and act upon the very waters to which the prohibition now under consideration applies.

But it has been urged with great earnestness, that, although the power of Congress to regulate commerce with foreign nations, and among the several States, be co-extensive with the subject itself, and have no other limits than are prescribed in the constitution, yet the States may severally exercise the same power, within their respective jurisdictions. In support of this argument, it is said, that they possessed it as an inseparable attribute of sovereignty, before the formation of the constitution, and still retain it, except so far as they have surrendered it by that instrument; that this principle results from the nature of the government, and is secured by the tenth amendment; that an affirmative grant of power is not exclusive, unless in its own nature it be such that the continued exercise of it by the former possessor is inconsistent with the grant, and that this is not of that description.

The grant of the power to lay and collect taxes is, like the power to regulate commerce, made in general terms, and has never been understood to interfere with the exercise of the same power by the State; and hence has been drawn an argument which has been applied to the question under consideration. But the two grants are not, it is conceived, similar in their terms or their nature. Although many of the powers formerly exercised by the States, are transferred to the government of the Union, yet the State governments remain, and constitute a most important part of our system. The power of taxation is indispensable to their existence, and is a power which, in its own nature, is capable of residing in, and being exercised by, different authorities at the same time. . . . [A] power in one to take what is necessary for certain purposes, is not, in its nature, incompatible with a power in another to take what is necessary for other purposes. Congress is authorized to lay and collect taxes, and to pay the debts, and provide for the common defense and general welfare of the United States. This does not interfere with the power of the States to tax for the support of their own governments; nor is the exercise of that power by the States, an exercise of any portion of the power that is granted to the United States. In imposing taxes for State purposes, they are not doing what Congress is empowered to do. Congress is not empowered to tax for those purposes which are within the exclusive province of the States. When, then, each government exercises the power of taxation, neither is exercising the power of the other. But, when a State proceeds to regulate commerce with foreign nations, or among the several States, it is exercising the very power that is granted to Congress, and is doing the very thing which Congress is authorized to do. There is no analogy, then, between the power of taxation and the power of regulating commerce. . . .

It is obvious, that the government of the Union, in the exercise of its express powers, that, for example, of regulating commerce with foreign nations and among the States, may use means that may also be employed by a State, in the exercise of its acknowledged powers; that, for example, of regulating commerce within the State. If Congress license vessels to sail from one port to another, in the same State, the act is supposed to be, necessarily, incidental to the power expressly granted to Congress, and implies no claim of a direct power to regulate the purely internal commerce of a State, or to act directly on its system of police. So, if a State, in passing laws on subjects acknowledged to be within its control, and with a view to those subjects, shall adopt a measure of the same character with one which Congress may adopt, it does not derive its authority from the particular power which has been granted, but from some other, which remains with the State, and may be executed by the same means. All experience shows, that the same measures, or measures scarcely distinguishable from each other, may flow from distinct powers; but this does not prove that the powers themselves are identical. Although the means used in their execution may sometimes approach each other so nearly as to be confounded, there are other situations in which they are sufficiently distinct to establish their individuality. . . .

Since, however, in exercising the power of regulating their own purely internal affairs, whether of trading or police, the States may sometimes enact laws, the validity of which depends on their interfering with, and being contrary to, an act of Congress passed in pursuance of the constitution, the Court will enter upon the inquiry, whether the laws of New-York, as expounded by the highest tribunal of that State, have, in their application to this case, come into collision with an act of Congress, and deprived a citizen of a right to which that act entitles him. Should this collision exist, it will be immaterial whether those laws were passed in virtue of a concurrent power "to regulate commerce with foreign nations and among the several States," or, in virtue of a power to regulate their domestic trade and police. In one case and the other, the acts of New-York must yield to the law of Congress; and the decision sustaining the privilege they confer, against a right given by a law of the Union, must be erroneous. . . .

[I]t has been contended, that if a law passed by a State, in the exercise of its acknowledged sovereignty, comes into conflict with a law passed by Congress in pursuance of the constitution, they affect the subject, and each other, like equal opposing powers.

But the framers of our constitution foresaw this state of things, and provided for it, by declaring the supremacy not only of itself, but of the laws made in pursuance of it. The nullity of any act, inconsistent with the constitution, is produced by the declaration, that the constitution is the supreme law. The appropriate application of that part of the clause which confers the same supremacy on laws and treaties, is to such acts of the State Legislatures as do not transcend their powers, but, though enacted in the execution of acknowledged State powers, interfere with, or are contrary to the laws of Congress, made in pursuance of the constitution, or some treaty made under the authority of the United States. In every such case, the act of Congress, or the treaty, is supreme; and the law of the State, though enacted in the exercise of powers not controverted, must yield to it. . . .

[*Chief Justice Marshall then found that the New York law conflicted with the federal laws licensing those engaged in the coastal trade and was thus invalid under the Supremacy Clause. The injunction against Gibbons was dissolved.—Editors*]

NOTES

1.   Chief Justice Marshall's opinion in *Gibbons* has two primary parts. The first examines the scope of Congress's power under the Commerce Clause. The second examines the issue of conflicting federal and state laws affecting commerce. In this respect, the structure of his opinion parallels *McCulloch,* which first looked to the question of *national power* to create a Bank of the United States and then to whether a *state law* affecting the exercise of that national power was unconstitutional because it conflicted with national authority.

2.   On the scope of the Commerce Clause power, Chief Justice Marshall breaks down the analysis largely according to the words of the text. First, how does he understand "commerce"? Broadly or narrowly? Second, how does he describe the meaning of "among the several states"? What are the implications? Third, what does he think is contained in the power to "regulate"? How broadly should it be construed? On each question, is he persuasive? On all three questions *Gibbons* has had an enduring influence.

3.   Then there is the question of what happens when a state law, otherwise within the states' general legislative powers, conflicts with a federal law enacted within the scope of the national government's enumerated powers. Note the resemblance with *McCulloch*. In *McCulloch*: If Congress has power to create a national bank, may states, which can generally tax any entities operating within their borders, impose a tax on this nationally chartered institution? In *Gibbons*: If Congress, exercising its power to regulate commerce among the states, grants licenses to coasting vessels, may a state grant a steamboat monopoly that conflicts with the federal licenses? *Gibbons* says *no*. Is there any reason to doubt the conclusion? (Is there a colorable argument that the federal and state laws are *not* actually in conflict?) Remember the Supremacy Clause: Where a valid federal law conflicts with a state law, the federal law prevails.

4.   *Gibbons* also introduced (albeit tentatively and in dicta) another variation on the question of federal-versus-state authority. It hints that the grant of power to Congress over commerce among the states—"commerce which concerns more states than one"— might be *exclusive*, so that states are divested of power to regulate commerce which concerns more than one state: "But, when a State proceeds to regulate commerce with foreign nations, or among the several States, it is exercising the very power that is granted to Congress, and is doing the very thing which Congress is authorized to do." Put differently, the proposition is that the grant of power to Congress to regulate interstate commerce negates, to the very same extent, the power of the states. This dictum in *Gibbons* has given rise to what has come to be known as the "dormant Commerce Clause" doctrine. This line of cases says, in essence, that states may not regulate commerce that falls within the scope of congressional power to regulate interstate commerce. Does it make sense for this question to be strictly binary—*only* state authority or *only* federal authority in any given circumstance?

The Supreme Court's Subsequent Interpretation of the Commerce and Necessary and Proper Clauses

The Commerce and Necessary and Proper Clauses have had a long history. What follows is a sketch of the Supreme Court's cases that continue, even today, to frame the interpretive issues. As you read these materials, ask yourself what the words of these two clauses mean when they are read together. And never forget that these two clauses do not exhaust the scope of national power. In particular, the national government's powers of taxing and spending often work in tandem with the commerce and necessary and proper powers.

1.   In several cases after *McCulloch* and *Gibbons* the Marshall Court considered the scope of national and state powers over commerce. The Court generally recognized that states had broad powers to regulate commerce, but if Congress chose to act, the state regulation had to give way. For example, in *Willson v. Black-Bird Creek Marsh Co.*, 27 U.S. (2 Pet.) 245 (1829), the Court unanimously upheld a Delaware statute authorizing a dam across a navigable waterway. In Chief Justice Marshall's words, "If congress had passed any act which bore upon the case; any act in execution of the power to regulate commerce, the object of which was to control state legislation over those small navigable creeks into which the tide flows, and which abound throughout the lower country of the middle and southern states; we should feel not much difficulty in saying that a state law coming in conflict with such act would be void. But congress has passed no such act."

2.   With the death of Chief Justice Marshall, it might have been expected that the Court—now dominated by appointees of President Jackson and President Van

Buren, and led by Chief Justice Roger Taney—would dramatically restrict federal power. That did not happen. While the Taney Court's precedents may have gently expanded state authority over commerce, there was nonetheless considerable continuity, and none of the Marshall Court decisions about the Commerce Clause or Necessary and Proper Clause were reversed.

Instead, most of the Commerce Clause cases in the Taney Court were (like *Willson*) about state laws, and usually about whether they impermissibly regulated interstate commerce, or instead were a permissible exercise of the state's "police power," that is, its general power as a sovereign to legislate in the interest of public health, morals, safety, and welfare. (In modern doctrine, these challenges to state laws would be called "dormant Commerce Clause" cases.) Two Taney Court cases are representative.

First, in *New York v. Miln*, 36 U.S. (11 Pet.) 102 (1837) (8–1), the Court upheld a New York statute that required any ship captain arriving in New York harbor from out of state to provide a written report, within twenty-four hours, containing the names of all passengers. The state wanted to deter indigent passengers and convicted criminals, and the Court had no trouble finding that these were police-power purposes. It did not matter that the means the state chose was a direct regulation of a person acting in interstate commerce (i.e., of the ship captain arriving from a non-New York port).

Second, in *Cooley v. Board of Wardens of the Port of Philadelphia*, 53 U.S. (12 How.) 299 (1851) (6–2), the Court upheld a Pennsylvania statute that required any ship arriving in or leaving from Philadelphia to employ a local pilot: the penalty for not doing so was a fine that had to be paid to a local pension fund administered by the Society for the Relief of Distressed and Decayed Pilots. The statute exempted ships in the Pennsylvania coal-trade. In form the statute was again a regulation of commerce by the state, and the historical context of the Commerce Clause ran strongly against the statute: these kinds of barriers to trade between the states were the reasons for the clause in the first place. But the Court emphasized that the state had a police-power purpose (raising funds for elderly pilots), and also pointed to a federal statute—enacted by the First Congress—that endorsed state regulation of pilots. In dicta, the author of the majority opinion, Justice Curtis, also made a distinction that would prove influential in later cases: "commerce" was not a single thing, but rather there were some subjects of commerce "imperatively demanding a single uniform rule" and others, "like the subject now in question, . . . imperatively demanding that diversity, which alone can meet the local necessities of navigation."

3.   After the Civil War Congress began to more broadly exercise its regulatory power under the Commerce Clause, first with the Interstate Commerce Act of 1887 and then with the Sherman Antitrust Act of 1890. In *United States v. E.C. Knight Co.*, 156 U.S. 1 (1895) (5–4), the Court adopted a restrictive interpretation of "commerce." The United States had invoked the Sherman Act when the American Sugar Refining Company acquired the stock of four other refineries—an acquisition that gave the company control of 98% of the country's sugar supply. But the Supreme Court refused to apply the Sherman Antitrust Act to defeat the monopolization of sugar *manufacturing* because "Manufacturing" was not included within the meaning of "Commerce." Chief Justice Fuller's majority opinion stated: "Doubtless the power to control the manufacture of a given thing involves in a certain sense the control of its disposition, but this is a secondary and not the primary sense; and although the

exercise of that power may result in bringing the operation of commerce into play, it does not control it, and affects it only incidentally and indirectly. Commerce succeeds to manufacture and is not a part of it."

The Court feared that the control of manufacturing would give Congress too much power under the Commerce Clause and would consequently deprive the states of all regulatory power in this area. It said: "If it be held that the [the Commerce power] includes the regulation of all such manufactures as are intended to be the subject of commercial transactions in the future [the] result would be that Congress would be invested, to the exclusion of the States, with the power to regulate, not only manufactures, but also agriculture, horticulture, stock raising, domestic fisheries, mining—in short every branch of human industry."

4.   *Champion v. Ames (The Lottery Case),* 188 U.S. 321 (1903) (5–4), leaned in the opposite direction from *E.C. Knight,* adopting an expansive interpretation of the commerce power. In this case, a man was indicted for shipping a box of Paraguayan lottery tickets from Texas to California despite the Federal Lottery Act of 1895, which prohibited importing, mailing, or interstate transporting of lottery tickets. The Court found that the transportation of lottery tickets from one state to another was "commerce." Writing for the majority, Justice Harlan held: "[T]he carrying from one state to another by independent carriers of things or commodities that are ordinary subjects of traffic, and which have in themselves a recognized value of money, constitutes interstate commerce." The Court also held that the power "to regulate" commerce included the power "to prohibit" commerce in noxious goods, like lottery tickets. The power to regulate commerce is more than the power to make it regular by eliminating trade barriers: Congress can also ban certain categories of commerce altogether.

The Court further stated: "[Congress] has not assumed to interfere with the completely internal affairs of any State, and has only legislated in respect of a matter which concerns the people of the United States. As a State may, for the purpose of guarding the morals of its own people, forbid all sales of lottery tickets within its limits, so Congress, for the purpose of guarding the people of the United States against the 'widespread pestilence of lotteries' and to protect the commerce which concerns all the States, may prohibit the carrying of lottery tickets from one State to another."

Champion has come to stand for the proposition that Congress has broad power to regulate the "channels" of interstate commerce as well as any articles moving "in" commerce, even for reasons reminiscent of the states' police power: Congress may employ its commerce power by *excluding* from interstate commerce things or conduct of which it disapproves. Is a prohibition on the shipment of a certain good a "regulation" of commerce? Must the power to regulate interstate commerce be employed for a commercial-regulatory purpose? Or is the power complete in itself, so it can be used for any purpose Congress desires?

5.   *Houston E. & W. T. Ry. Co. v. United States (The Shreveport Rate Case),* 234 U.S. 342 (1914) (7–2), also adopted an expansive interpretation of the power to regulate the "instrumentalities" of commerce—including their *intra*state activities. The Interstate Commerce Commission was regulating intrastate railroad rates because it found that several railroads were "discriminating" against shipments to and from Shreveport, Louisiana. For example, shipments by the railroads from

Dallas, Texas to Marshall, Texas, a distance of 148 miles, cost 37 cents; but the railroads' shipments from Shreveport, Louisiana to Marshall, a distance of 42 miles, cost 56 cents. The Court held that the ICC may regulate even intrastate railroad rates because Congress has the power to regulate the "instrumentalities" of commerce, even reaching intrastate activities that may injure interstate commerce.

Justice Hughes, writing the majority opinion, stated: "The fact that carriers are instruments of intrastate commerce, as well as of interstate commerce, does not derogate from the complete and paramount authority of Congress over the latter, or preclude the Federal power from being exerted to prevent the intrastate operations of such carriers from being made a means of injury to that which has been confided to Federal Care. . . . Congress in the exercise of its paramount power may prevent the common instrumentalities of interstate and intrastate commercial intercourse from being used in their intrastate operations to the injury of interstate commerce. This is not to say that Congress possesses the authority to regulate the internal commerce of a state, as such, but that it does possess the power to foster and protect interstate commerce, and to take all measures necessary or appropriate to that end, although intrastate transactions of interstate carriers may thereby be controlled."

Note Justice Hughes' reference to congressional power "to take all measures necessary and appropriate" to the protection of interstate commerce—even if in doing so intrastate commerce gets regulated. Is the Necessary and Proper Clause doing the real work here?

6.   *Caminetti v. United States*, 242 U.S. 470 (1917) (5–3), rested on a broad interpretation of the Commerce Clause power along the lines of *Champion*. In *Caminetti*, three men were convicted of violating the so-called White Slave Traffic Act of 1910. Specifically, the men were charged with "transporting and causing to be transported, and aiding and assisting in obtaining transportation for certain women in interstate commerce, for the purpose of debauchery, and for an immoral purpose." (They drove mistresses from Sacramento, California, to Reno, Nevada, and from Oklahoma City, Oklahoma, to Wichita, Kansas.) The three men argued that "the act of Congress is intended to reach only 'commercialized vice,' or the traffic in women for gain." Thus, they claimed that the statute did not apply to them because "in none of the cases was it charged or proved that the transportation was for gain or for the purpose of furnishing women for prostitution or for hire."

The Court conceded that the men did not engage in "commercial activity," but upheld the convictions. It concluded: "The transportation of passengers in interstate commerce, it has long been settled, is within the regulatory power of Congress, under the Commerce Clause of the Constitution, and the authority of Congress to keep the channels of interstate commerce free from immoral and injurious uses has been frequently sustained, and is no longer open to question."

7.   *Hammer v. Dagenhart*, 247 U.S. 251 (1918) (5–4), took a more restrictive view of the Commerce Clause power. At issue was a federal law banning the interstate shipment of goods produced in violation of certain restrictions on the use of child labor. The majority struck down the regulation, distinguishing *Champion*, *Caminetti*, and other cases upholding interstate transportation restrictions, on the ground that "[i]n each of these instances the use of interstate transportation was necessary to the accomplishment of harmful results" and that this element "is wanting in the present case." The federal law "does not regulate transportation

among the states, but aims to standardize the ages at which children may be employed in mining and manufacturing within the states. The goods shipped are themselves harmless." The majority added that "[t]he grant of power to Congress over the subject of interstate commerce was to enable it to regulate such commerce, and not to give it authority to control the states in their exercise of the police power over local trade and manufacture. . . . The grant of authority over a purely federal matter was not intended to destroy the local power always existing and carefully reserved to the states in the Tenth Amendment to the Constitution."

Was *Hammer*'s distinction of *Champion* and *Caminetti* persuasive? Should the existence of a constitutional power to regulate or prohibit items in interstate commerce depend on whether the prohibition is because Congress regards the items themselves as harmful (and therefore wishes to prohibit them) or because it regards the manner of their production or manufacture as harmful (and therefore wishes to prohibit the interstate shipment of goods so produced)? Was the Court's decision in *Hammer* influenced by its view that permitting such an exercise of the federal commerce power would impair state power? Is that reasoning sound?

Justice Holmes's dissent emphasized that "the statute in question is within the power expressly given to Congress if considered only as to its immediate effects and that if invalid it is so only upon some collateral ground." In other words, the statute clearly and directly regulated interstate commerce; Congress's purpose and motivation was irrelevant in determining whether the statute fell within the literal terms of that constitutional power. Justice Holmes also disapproved of the notion that recognizing such a federal power interfered "with anything belonging to the States. They may regulate their internal affairs and their domestic commerce as they like. But when they seek to send their products across the State line they are no longer within their rights. If there were no Constitution and no Congress their power to cross the line would depend upon their neighbors. Under the Constitution such commerce belongs not to the States but to Congress to regulate. It may carry out its views of public policy whatever indirect effect that may have upon the activities of the States." Are you persuaded by the reasoning of the majority, or by that of the dissent? (*Hammer* was overruled twenty-two years later in *United States v. Darby*, 312 U.S. 100 (1941). See p. 522.)

8. Meanwhile, on the Taxing Clause front, in *Bailey v. Drexel Furniture Co.* (*The Child Labor Tax Case*), 259 U.S. 20 (1922) (8–1), the Court considered a challenge to Congress's use of the taxing power to try to accomplish the very policy objective that the Court had held was beyond Congress's commerce-regulating power in *Hammer*. The law at issue in *Bailey* imposed an "excise tax equivalent to 10 per centum of the entire net profits received or accrued" in a year on mills, canneries, workshops, factories, or other manufacturing establishments employing child labor in violation of prescribed standards. Relying on *Hammer*, the Court struck down the tax on the ground that it operated as a regulatory law that exceeded Congress's power to regulate commerce We will return to *Bailey* when considering the scope of the taxing power. See p. 606. But for now, note that the Court's Commerce Clause jurisprudence did not develop in a silo apart from the other enumerated powers.

9. *A.L.A. Schechter Poultry Corp. v. United States*, 295 U.S. 495 (1935) (9–0), took a more restrictive approach to the Commerce Clause power. The National Industrial Recovery Act of 1933 had authorized the president to approve "codes of fair competition." President Roosevelt approved codes establishing a forty-hour work

week and a minimum wage of fifty cents an hour, applicable to the Schechters' slaughterhouse in Brooklyn. The Schechter company purchased chickens that had been shipped to New York from other states and then used the poultry for slaughter and resale to butchers within the state of New York. The Schechters were convicted for violating the wage and hour provisions of the code.

The Court struck down the regulations fixing the hours and wages of individuals employed by an intrastate business because the activity being regulated was related to interstate commerce only "indirectly": "Where the effect of intrastate transactions upon interstate commerce is merely indirect, such transactions remain within the domain of state power." The Court further stated that "[the regulations] are imposed in order to govern the details of defendants' management of their local business. The persons employed in slaughtering and selling in local trade are not employed in interstate commerce. Their hours and wages have no direct relation to interstate commerce . . . [and] if the federal government may determine the wages and hours of employees in the internal commerce of a State, because of their relation to costs and prices and their indirect effect on interstate commerce, it would seem that a similar control might be exerted over other elements of cost, also affecting prices." (This case, too, was repudiated by the rulings in *Jones & Laughlin Steel* (1937) and *Darby* (1941). See p. 522.) *Schechter Poultry* is also famous for its other holding, invalidating the act as an improper "delegation" of legislative power. See p. 94.

10. *Carter v. Carter Coal Co.*, 293 U.S. 238 (1936), was another case interpreting the scope of the Commerce Clause restrictively. The Bituminous Coal Conservation Act of 1935 regulated the maximum hours and minimum wages of coal mine workers. A stockholder in Carter Coal sued to enjoin the company from complying with the provisions of the code. The Court struck down the regulations, finding that mining (like "manufacturing") is not itself "commerce." Writing for the majority, Justice Sutherland held that "[t]he effect of the labor provisions falls upon production and not upon commerce. . . . Production is a purely local activity. It follows that none of these essential antecedents of production constitutes a transaction in or forms any part of interstate commerce." (This case, too, was effectively repudiated by *Jones & Laughlin Steel* and *Darby*.)

11. The Court's decisions invalidating New Deal legislation greatly displeased President Franklin D. Roosevelt. Buoyed by his landslide reelection in 1936, he proposed a "court-packing" plan. It would have added new justices to the Supreme Court in order to dilute the power of the existing justices. Depending on how many justices refused to retire at age seventy, the number of seats on the Supreme Court could have increased to fifteen, allowing Roosevelt to appoint six new justices. (For an excerpt from President Roosevelt's radio address defending the plan, see p. 1537.) Although the proposal was defeated, beginning in 1937 the Court's decisions upheld a broader interpretation of Congress's powers under the Commerce Clause. One of the justices formerly in the majority against a broad interpretation of Congress's powers (Justice Roberts) began voting more consistently with the justices who favored a broad interpretation, leading to the quip—not necessarily justified—that there had been a "switch in time that saved nine."

12. *National Labor Relations Board v. Jones & Laughlin Steel Corp.*, 301 U.S. 1 (1937), was a turning point. With this decision, the Court shifted to a more expansive interpretation of the Commerce Clause power of Congress—a shift that has proved enduring. The opinion was written by Chief Justice Charles Evans

Hughes, who had been the author of *The Shreveport Rate Case* (1914) twenty-three years earlier. (Chief Justice Hughes left the Court in 1916 and was the Republican nominee for president, narrowly losing to incumbent Woodrow Wilson. He later served as secretary of state before returning to the Court as chief justice in 1930.) In *Jones & Laughlin Steel*, the Court upheld the National Labor Relations Act, which comprehensively regulated labor practices and relationships. The decision rejected the "direct" versus "indirect" effects on interstate commerce approach of *Schecter Poultry*, at least where intrastate activities have "such a close and substantial relation to interstate commerce that their control is essential or appropriate to protect that commerce from burdens and obstructions." Additionally, the Court downplayed the "production" distinction of *Carter Coal Co.*, stating that "[i]t is the effect upon commerce, not the source of the injury, which is the criterion.... [T]he fact that the employees here concerned were engaged in production is not determinative." The Court held that "the National Labor Relations Act may be construed so as to operate within the sphere of constitutional authority. The grant of authority to the Board does not purport to extend to the relationship between all industrial employees and employers. Its terms do not impose collective bargaining upon all industry regardless of effects upon interstate or foreign commerce. It purports to reach only what may be deemed to burden or obstruct commerce and, thus qualified, it must be construed as contemplating the exercise of control within constitutional bounds."

Jones & Laughlin Steel was a narrowly written decision for a 5–4 majority of the Court. Within five years, however, its principles had been reaffirmed and expanded. The "New Deal Revolution" (or "restoration"?) in interpretation of the Commerce Clause was cemented by *United States v. Darby* (1941), which explicitly overruled *Hammer v. Dagenhart*. *Darby* was unanimous. It continues to be embraced by the Court today. But was it right?

United States v. Darby
312 U.S. 100 (1941)

■ MR. JUSTICE STONE delivered the opinion of the Court.

The two principal questions raised by the record in this case are, *first*, whether Congress has constitutional power to prohibit the shipment in interstate commerce of lumber manufactured by employees whose wages are less than a prescribed minimum or whose weekly hours of labor at that wage are greater than a prescribed maximum, and, *second*, whether it has power to prohibit the employment of workmen in the production of goods "for interstate commerce" at other than prescribed wages and hours....

The Fair Labor Standards Act set up a comprehensive legislative scheme for preventing the shipment in interstate commerce of certain products and commodities produced in the United States under labor conditions as respects wages and hours which fail to conform to standards set up by the Act....

Section 15 of the statute prohibits certain specified acts.... Section 15(a)(1) makes unlawful the shipment in interstate commerce of any goods "in the production of which any employee was employed in violation of section 6 or section 7," which provide, among other things, that during the first year of operation of the Act a minimum wage of 25 cents per hour shall be paid to employees "engaged in

[handwritten margin note: Should you read this as necessary & proper clause?]

(interstate) commerce or in the production of goods for (interstate) commerce," and that the maximum hours of employment for employees "engaged in commerce or in the production of goods for commerce" without increased compensation for overtime, shall be forty-four hours a week. Section 15(a)(2) makes it unlawful to violate the provisions of §§ 6 and 7 including the minimum wage and maximum hour requirements just mentioned for employees engaged in production of goods for commerce. . . .

While manufacture is not, of itself, interstate commerce, the shipment of manufactured goods interstate is such commerce, and the prohibition of such shipment by Congress is indubitably a regulation of the commerce. The power to regulate commerce is the power "to prescribe the rule by which commerce is governed." *Gibbons v. Ogden*, 22 U.S. (9 Wheat.) 1, 196 (1824). It extends not only to those regulations which aid, foster and protect the commerce, but embraces those which prohibit it. It is conceded that the power of Congress to prohibit transportation in interstate commerce includes noxious articles, stolen articles, kidnapped persons, and articles such as intoxicating liquor or convict made goods, traffic in which is forbidden or restricted by the laws of the state of destination.

But it is said that the present prohibition falls within the scope of none of these categories; that, while the prohibition is nominally a regulation of the commerce, its motive or purpose is regulation of wages and hours of persons engaged in manufacture, the control of which has been reserved to the states and upon which Georgia and some of the states of destination have placed no restriction; that the effect of the present statute is not to exclude the proscribed articles from interstate commerce in aid of state regulation, but instead, under the guise of a regulation of interstate commerce, it undertakes to regulate wages and hours within the state contrary to the policy of the state which has elected to leave them unregulated.

The power of Congress over interstate commerce "is complete in itself, may be exercised to its utmost extent, and acknowledges no limitations other than are prescribed in the Constitution." *Gibbons*, at 196. That power can neither be enlarged nor diminished by the exercise or nonexercise of state power. . . .

Such regulation is not a forbidden invasion of state power merely because either its motive or its consequence is to restrict the use of articles of commerce within the states of destination, and is not prohibited unless by other Constitutional provisions. It is no objection to the assertion of the power to regulate interstate commerce that its exercise is attended by the same incidents which attend the exercise of the police power of the states.

The motive and purpose of the present regulation are plainly to make effective the Congressional conception of public policy that interstate commerce should not be made the instrument of competition in the distribution of goods produced under substandard labor conditions, which competition is injurious to the commerce and to the states from and to which the commerce flows. The motive and purpose of a regulation of interstate commerce are matters for the legislative judgment upon the exercise of which the Constitution places no restriction, and over which the courts are given no control. . . . Whatever their motive and purpose, regulations of commerce which do not infringe some constitutional prohibition are within the plenary power conferred on Congress by the Commerce Clause. Subject only to that limitation, presently to be considered, we conclude that the prohibition of the shipment interstate of goods produced under the forbidden substandard labor conditions is within the constitutional authority of Congress.

In the more than a century which has elapsed since the decision of *Gibbons v. Ogden*, these principles of constitutional interpretation have been so long and repeatedly recognized by this Court as applicable to the Commerce Clause that there would be little occasion for repeating them now were it not for the decision of this Court twenty-two years ago in *Hammer v. Dagenhart*, 247 U.S. 251 (1918). In that case, it was held by a bare majority of the Court, over the powerful and now classic dissent of Mr. Justice Holmes setting forth the fundamental issues involved, that Congress was without power to exclude the products of child labor from interstate commerce. The reasoning and conclusion of the Court's opinion there cannot be reconciled with the conclusion which we have reached, that the power of Congress under the Commerce Clause is plenary to exclude any article from interstate commerce subject only to the specific prohibitions of the Constitution.

Hammer v. Dagenhart has not been followed. The distinction on which the decision was rested, that Congressional power to prohibit interstate commerce is limited to articles which in themselves have some harmful or deleterious property— a distinction which was novel when made and unsupported by any provision of the Constitution—has long since been abandoned. The thesis of the opinion—that the motive of the prohibition or its effect to control in some measure the use or production within the states of the article thus excluded from the commerce can operate to deprive the regulation of its constitutional authority—has long since ceased to have force. . . .

The conclusion is inescapable that *Hammer v. Dagenhart* was a departure from the principles which have prevailed in the interpretation of the Commerce Clause both before and since the decision, and that such vitality, as a precedent, as it then had, has long since been exhausted. It should be, and now is, overruled. . . .

There remains the question whether such restriction on the production of goods for commerce is a permissible exercise of the commerce power. The power of Congress over interstate commerce is not confined to the regulation of commerce among the states. It extends to those activities intrastate which so affect interstate commerce or the exercise of the power of Congress over it as to make regulation of them appropriate means to the attainment of a legitimate end, the exercise of the granted power of Congress to regulate interstate commerce. See *McCulloch v. Maryland*, 17 U.S. (4 Wheat.) 316, 421 (1819). . . .

Congress, having by the present Act adopted the policy of excluding from interstate commerce all goods produced for the commerce which do not conform to the specified labor standards, it may choose the means reasonably adapted to the attainment of the permitted end even though they involve control of intrastate activities. Such legislation has often been sustained with respect to powers other than the commerce power granted to the national government when the means chosen, although not themselves within the granted power, were nevertheless deemed appropriate aids to the accomplishment of some purpose within an admitted power of the national government. . . .

As we have said, the evils aimed at by the Act are the spread of substandard labor conditions through the use of the facilities of interstate commerce for competition by the goods so produced with those produced under the prescribed or better labor conditions, and the consequent dislocation of the commerce itself caused by the impairment or destruction of local businesses by competition made effective through interstate commerce. The Act is thus directed at the suppression of a method or kind of competition in interstate commerce which it has, in effect, condemned as "unfair," as the Clayton Act has condemned other "unfair methods of competition" made effective through interstate commerce.

Our conclusion is unaffected by the Tenth Amendment, which provides: "The powers not delegated to the United States by the Constitution, nor prohibited by it to the States, are reserved to the States respectively, or to the people." The amendment states but a truism that all is retained which has not been surrendered. There is nothing in the history of its adoption to suggest that it was more than declaratory of the relationship between the national and state governments as it had been established by the Constitution before the amendment, or that its purpose was other than to allay fears that the new national government might seek to exercise powers not granted, and that the states might not be able to exercise fully their reserved powers.

From the beginning and for many years, the amendment has been construed as not depriving the national government of authority to resort to all means for the exercise of a granted power which are appropriate and plainly adapted to the permitted end. . . .

NOTES

1.   Is the reasoning in *Darby* persuasive? Does it align with or extend *Gibbons* and *McCulloch*?

2.   Is the following passage from *Darby*—"The power of Congress over interstate commerce . . . extends to those activities intrastate which so affect interstate commerce . . . as to make regulation of them appropriate means to the attainment of a legitimate end"—an interpretation of the Commerce Clause or the Necessary and Proper Clause? What supports your answer? Does it matter?

[*Assignment 26*]

The Modern Debate

Right or wrong, the broad reading of national legislative power in *Darby* has endured. What follows are three cases about the outer boundaries of congressional power under the Commerce Clause. In two the Court upheld the challenged federal statutes, *Wickard v. Filburn* (1942) and *Heart of Atlanta Motel v. United States* (1964). In the third, *United States v. Lopez* (1995), the Court—for the first time in half a century—held that a statute exceeded Congress's power under the Commerce Clause.

Wickard v. Filburn
317 U.S. 111 (1942)

■ MR. JUSTICE JACKSON delivered the opinion of the Court.

The appellee filed his complaint against the Secretary of Agriculture of the United States, three members of the County Agricultural Conservation Committee for Montgomery County, Ohio, and a member of the State Agricultural Conservation Committee for Ohio. He sought to enjoin enforcement against himself of the marketing penalty imposed by the amendment of May 26, 1941, to the Agricultural Adjustment Act of 1938, upon that part of his 1941 wheat crop which was available for marketing in excess of the marketing quota established for his farm. He also sought a declaratory judgment that the wheat marketing quota provisions of the Act as amended and applicable to him were unconstitutional because not sustainable under the Commerce Clause or consistent with the Due Process Clause of the Fifth Amendment. . . .

The appellee for many years past has owned and operated a small farm in Montgomery County, Ohio, maintaining a herd of dairy cattle, selling milk, raising poultry, and selling poultry and eggs. It has been his practice to raise a small acreage of winter wheat, sown in the Fall and harvested in the following July; to sell a portion of the crop; to feed part to poultry and livestock on the farm, some of which is sold; to use some in making flour for home consumption; and to keep the rest for the following seeding. The intended disposition of the crop here involved has not been expressly stated.

In July of 1940, pursuant to the Agricultural Adjustment Act of 1938, as then amended, there were established for the appellee's 1941 crop a wheat acreage allotment of 11.1 acres and a normal yield of 20.1 bushels of wheat an acre. He was given notice of such allotment in July of 1940 before the Fall planting of his 1941 crop of wheat, and again in July of 1941, before it was harvested. He sowed, however, 23 acres, and harvested from his 11.9 acres of excess acreage 239 bushels, which under the terms of the Act as amended on May 26, 1941, constituted farm marketing excess, subject to a penalty of 49 cents a bushel, or $117.11 in all. The appellee has not paid the penalty and he has not postponed or avoided it by storing the excess under regulations of the Secretary of Agriculture, or by delivering it up to the Secretary. The Committee, therefore, refused him a marketing card, which was, under the terms of Regulations promulgated by the Secretary, necessary to protect a buyer from liability to the penalty and upon its protecting lien.

The general scheme of the Agricultural Adjustment Act of 1938 as related to wheat is to control the volume moving in interstate and foreign commerce in order to avoid surpluses and shortages and the consequent abnormally low or high wheat prices and obstructions to commerce. Within prescribed limits and by prescribed standards the Secretary of Agriculture is directed to ascertain and proclaim each year a national acreage allotment for the next crop of wheat, which is then apportioned to the states and their counties, and is eventually broken up into allotments for individual farms. Loans and payments to wheat farmers are authorized in stated circumstances. . . .

It is urged that under the Commerce Clause of the Constitution, Article I, § 8, clause 3, Congress does not possess the power it has in this instance sought to exercise. The question would merit little consideration since our decision in *United States v. Darby*, 312 U.S. 100 (1941), sustaining the federal power to regulate production of goods for commerce except for the fact that this Act extends federal regulation to production not intended in any part for commerce but wholly for consumption on the farm. The Act includes a definition of "market" and its derivatives so that as related to wheat in addition to its conventional meaning it also means to dispose of "by feeding (in any form) to poultry or livestock which, or the products of which, are sold, bartered, or exchanged, or to be so disposed of." Hence, marketing quotas not only embrace all that may be sold without penalty but also what may be consumed on the premises. Wheat produced on excess acreage is designated as "available for marketing" as so defined and the penalty is imposed thereon. Penalties do not depend upon whether any part of the wheat either within or without the quota is sold or intended to be sold. The sum of this is that the Federal Government fixes a quota including all that the farmer may harvest for sale or for his own farm needs, and declares that wheat produced on excess acreage may neither be disposed of nor used except upon payment of the penalty or except it is stored as required by the Act or delivered to the Secretary of Agriculture.

Appellee says that this is a regulation of production and consumption of wheat. Such activities are, he urges, beyond the reach of Congressional power under the Commerce Clause, since they are local in character, and their effects upon interstate commerce are at most "indirect." In answer the Government argues that the statute regulates neither production nor consumption, but only marketing; and, in the alternative, that if the Act does go beyond the regulation of marketing it is sustainable as a "necessary and proper" implementation of the power of Congress over interstate commerce.

The Government's concern lest the Act be held to be a regulation of production or consumption rather than of marketing is attributable to a few dicta and decisions of this Court which might be understood to lay it down that activities such as "production," "manufacturing," and "mining" are strictly "local" and, except in special circumstances which are not present here, cannot be regulated under the commerce power because their effects upon interstate commerce are, as matter of law, only "indirect." Even today, when this power has been held to have great latitude, there is no decision of this Court that such activities may be regulated where no part of the product is intended for interstate commerce or intermingled with the subjects thereof. We believe that a review of the course of decision under the Commerce Clause will make plain, however, that questions of the power of Congress are not to be decided by reference to any formula which would give controlling force to nomenclature such as "production" and "indirect" and foreclose consideration of the actual effects of the activity in question upon interstate commerce.

At the beginning Chief Justice Marshall described the Federal commerce power with a breadth never yet exceeded. *Gibbons v. Ogden*, 22 U.S. (9 Wheat.) 1, 194, 195 (1824). He made emphatic the embracing and penetrating nature of this power by warning that effective restraints on its exercise must proceed from political rather than from judicial processes. . . .

It was not until 1887 with the enactment of the Interstate Commerce Act that the interstate commerce power began to exert positive influence in American law and life. This first important federal resort to the commerce power was followed in 1890 by the Sherman Anti-Trust Act and, thereafter, mainly after 1903, by many others. These statutes ushered in new phases of adjudication, which required the Court to approach the interpretation of the Commerce Clause in the light of an actual exercise by Congress of its power thereunder. . . .

The Court's recognition of the relevance of the economic effects in the application of the Commerce Clause . . . has made the mechanical application of legal formulas no longer feasible. Once an economic measure of the reach of the power granted to Congress in the Commerce Clause is accepted, questions of federal power cannot be decided simply by finding the activity in question to be "production" nor can consideration of its economic effects be foreclosed by calling them "indirect." . . .

Whether the subject of the regulation in question was "production," "consumption," or "marketing" is, therefore, not material for purposes of deciding the question of federal power before us. That an activity is of local character may help in a doubtful case to determine whether Congress intended to reach it. The same consideration might help in determining whether in the absence of Congressional action it would be permissible for the state to exert its power on the subject matter, even though in so doing it to some degree affected interstate commerce. But even if appellee's activity be local and though it may not be regarded as commerce, it may still, whatever its nature, be reached by Congress if it exerts a substantial economic effect on interstate commerce and this irrespective of whether such effect is what might at some earlier time have been defined as "direct" or "indirect."

The parties have stipulated a summary of the economics of the wheat industry. Commerce among the states in wheat is large and important. Although wheat is raised in every state but one, production in most states is not equal to consumption. Sixteen states on average have had a surplus of wheat above their own requirements for feed, seed, and food. Thirty-two states and the District of Columbia, where production has been below consumption, have looked to these surplus-producing states for their supply as well as for wheat for export and carryover.

The wheat industry has been a problem industry for some years. Largely as a result of increased foreign production and import restrictions, annual exports of wheat and flour from the United States during the ten-year period ending in 1940 averaged less than 10 per cent of total production, while during the 1920s they averaged more than 25 per cent. The decline in the export trade has left a large surplus in production which in connection with an abnormally large supply of wheat and other grains in recent years caused congestion in a number of markets; tied up railroad cars; and caused elevators in some instances to turn away grains, and railroads to institute embargoes to prevent further congestion. . . .

The effect of consumption of homegrown wheat on interstate commerce is due to the fact that it constitutes the most variable factor in the disappearance of the wheat crop. Consumption on the farm where grown appears to vary in an amount greater than 20 per cent of average production. The total amount of wheat consumed as food varies but relatively little, and use as seed is relatively constant.

The maintenance by government regulation of a price for wheat undoubtedly can be accomplished as effectively by sustaining or increasing the demand as by limiting the supply. The effect of the statute before us is to restrict the amount which may be produced for market and the extent as well to which one may forestall resort to the market by producing to meet his own needs. That appellee's own contribution to the demand for wheat may be trivial by itself is not enough to remove him from the scope of federal regulation where, as here, his contribution, taken together with that of many others similarly situated, is far from trivial. *Darby*, at 123.

It is well established by decisions of this Court that the power to regulate commerce includes the power to regulate the prices at which commodities in that commerce are dealt in and practices affecting such prices. One of the primary purposes of the Act in question was to increase the market price of wheat and to that end to limit the volume thereof that could affect the market. It can hardly be denied that a factor of such volume and variability as home-consumed wheat would have a substantial influence on price and market conditions. This may arise because being in marketable condition such wheat overhangs the market and if induced by rising prices tends to flow into the market and check price increases. But if we assume that it is never marketed, it supplies a need of the man who grew it which would otherwise be reflected by purchases in the open market. Home-grown wheat in this sense competes with wheat in commerce. The stimulation of commerce is a use of the regulatory function quite as definitely as prohibitions or restrictions thereon. This record leaves us in no doubt that Congress may properly have considered that wheat consumed on the farm where grown if wholly outside the scheme of regulation would have a substantial effect in defeating and obstructing its purpose to stimulate trade therein at increased prices.

It is said, however, that this Act, forcing some farmers into the market to buy what they could provide for themselves, is an unfair promotion of the markets and prices of specializing wheat growers. It is of the essence of regulation that it lays a restraining hand on the self interest of the regulated and that advantages from the regulation commonly fall to others. The conflicts of economic interest between the regulated and those who advantage by it are wisely left under our system to resolution by the Congress under its more flexible and responsible legislative process. Such conflicts rarely lend themselves to judicial determination. And with the wisdom, workability, or fairness, of the plan of regulation we have nothing to do. . . .

[The Court's analysis of the due process claim is omitted.—Editors]

NOTES

1.   The doctrinal innovation of *Wickard v. Filburn* is the aggregation principle: the idea that one should look at all homegrown wheat in the country and its effect on commerce, not the wheat of this one farmer. Is the principle sound? And what power does *Wickard* rely on? Is the regulation of homegrown wheat for home consumption a regulation of "interstate commerce"? If not, is the decision wrong? Or can regulation of purely local production and consumption be "necessary and proper" for regulation of an interstate commercial market?

2.   Recall the Court's admonition in *Gibbons v. Ogden* that the Constitution's enumeration of powers "presupposes something not enumerated." In light of *Darby* and *Wickard*, is there anything Congress cannot do pursuant to its power to regulate commerce, as aided by the Necessary and Proper Clause? (Set to one side laws that would violate some specific *prohibition* on Congress's power, like the First Amendment.) Try to imagine laws that Congress lacks power to enact after *Wickard*. Can you come up with any? If not, is that a problem?

Heart of Atlanta Motel v. United States

379 U.S. 241 (1964)

■ MR. JUSTICE CLARK delivered the opinion of the Court.

. . .

1.   The Factual Background and Contentions of the Parties.

The case comes here on admissions and stipulated facts. Appellant owns and operates the Heart of Atlanta Motel which has 216 rooms available to transient guests. The motel . . . is readily accessible to interstate highways 75 and 85 and state highways 23 and 41. Appellant solicits patronage from outside the State of Georgia through various national advertising media, including magazines of national circulation; it maintains over 50 billboards and highway signs within the State, soliciting patronage for the motel; it accepts convention trade from outside Georgia and approximately 75% of its registered guests are from out of state. Prior to passage of the Act the motel had followed a practice of refusing to rent rooms to Negroes, and it alleged that it intended to continue to do so. In an effort to perpetuate that policy this suit was filed.

The appellant contends that Congress in passing this Act exceeded its power to regulate commerce under Art. I, § 8, cl. 3, of the Constitution of the United States; that the Act violates the Fifth Amendment because appellant is deprived of the right to choose its customers and operate its business as it wishes, resulting in a taking of its liberty and property without due process of law and a taking of its property without just compensation; and, finally, that by requiring appellant to rent available rooms to Negroes against its will, Congress is subjecting it to involuntary servitude in contravention of the Thirteenth Amendment. . . .

The appellees counter that the unavailability to Negroes of adequate accommodations interferes significantly with interstate travel, and that Congress, under the Commerce Clause, has power to remove such obstructions and restraints; that the Fifth Amendment does not forbid reasonable regulation and that consequential damage does not constitute a "taking" within the meaning of that amendment; that the Thirteenth Amendment claim fails because it is entirely frivolous to say that an amendment directed to the abolition of human bondage and the removal of widespread disabilities associated with slavery places discrimination in public accommodations, beyond the reach of both federal and state law. . . .

2.   Title II of the Act.

[Title II of the Civil Rights Act of 1964] is divided into seven sections beginning with § 201 (a) which provides that:

> "All persons shall be entitled to the full and equal enjoyment of the goods, services, facilities, privileges, advantages, and accommodations of any place of public accommodation, as defined in this section, without discrimination or segregation on the ground of race, color, religion, or national origin."

There are listed in § 201 (b) four classes of business establishments, each of which 'serves the public' and 'is a place of public accommodation' within the meaning of § 201 (a) "if its operations affect commerce, or if discrimination or segregation by it is supported by State action." The covered establishments are:

"(1) any inn, hotel, motel, or other establishment which provides lodging to transient guests, other than an establishment located within a building which contains not more than five rooms for rent or hire and which is actually occupied by the proprietor of such establishment as his residence;

"(2) any restaurant, cafeteria . . . [not here involved];

"(3) any motion picture house . . . [not here involved];

"(4) any establishment . . . which is physically located within the premises of any establishment otherwise covered by this subsection, or . . . within the premises of which is physically located any such covered establishment . . . [not here involved]."

Section 201 (c) defines the phrase "affect commerce" as applied to the above establishments. It first declares that "any inn, hotel, motel, or other establishment which provides lodging to transient guests" affects commerce *per se*. Restaurants, cafeterias, etc., in class two affect commerce only if they serve or offer to serve interstate travelers or if a substantial portion of the food which they serve or products which they sell have "moved in commerce." Motion picture houses and other places listed in class three affect commerce if they customarily present films, performances, etc., "which move in commerce." And the establishments listed in class four affect commerce if they are within, or include within their own premises, an establishment "the operations of which affect commerce." Private clubs are excepted under certain conditions. . . .

4. Application of Title II to Heart of Atlanta Motel.

It is admitted that the operation of the motel brings it within the provisions of § 201 (a) of the Act and that appellant refused to provide lodging for transient Negroes because of their race or color and that it intends to continue that policy unless restrained.

The sole question posed is, therefore, the constitutionality of the Civil Rights Act of 1964 as applied to these facts. The legislative history of the Act indicates that Congress based the Act on § 5 and the Equal Protection Clause of the Fourteenth Amendment as well as its power to regulate interstate commerce under Art. I, § 8, cl. 3, of the Constitution. . . . *[The Court noted that because it found the commerce power sufficient, the other possible grounds were not examined.—Editors]*

6. The Basis of Congressional Action.

While the Act as adopted carried no congressional findings the record of its passage through each house is replete with evidence of the burdens that discrimination by race or color places upon interstate commerce. This testimony included the fact that our people have become increasingly mobile with millions of people of all races traveling from State to State; that Negroes in particular have been the subject of discrimination in transient accommodations, having to travel great distances to secure the same; that often they have been unable to obtain accommodations and have had to call upon friends to put them up overnight; and that these conditions had become so acute as to require the listing of available lodging for Negroes in a special guidebook which was itself "dramatic testimony to the difficulties" Negroes encounter in travel. These exclusionary practices were found to be nationwide, the Under Secretary of Commerce testifying that there is "no question that this discrimination in the North still exists to a large degree" and in the West and Midwest as well.... [T]his uncertainty stemming from racial discrimination had the effect of discouraging travel on the part of a substantial portion of the Negro community....

7. *The Power of Congress Over Interstate Travel.*

The power of Congress to deal with these obstructions depends on the meaning of the Commerce Clause. Its meaning was first enunciated 140 years ago by the great Chief Justice John Marshall in *Gibbons v. Ogden*, 22 U.S. (9 Wheat.) 1 (1824) ... In short, the determinative test of the exercise of power by the Congress under the Commerce Clause is simply whether the activity sought to be regulated is "commerce which concerns more States than one" and has a real and substantial relation to the national interest. Let us now turn to this facet of the problem.

That the "intercourse" of which the Chief Justice spoke included the movement of persons through more States than one was settled as early as 1849.... Nor does it make any difference whether the transportation is commercial in character....

The same interest in protecting interstate commerce which led Congress to deal with segregation in interstate carriers and the white-slave traffic has prompted it to extend the exercise of its power to gambling; to criminal enterprises; to deceptive practices in the sale of products; to fraudulent security transactions; to misbranding of drugs; to wages and hours; *United States v. Darby*, 312 U.S. 100 (1941); to members of labor unions; to crop control, *Wickard v. Filburn*, 317 U.S. 111 (1942); to discrimination against shippers; to the protection of small business from injurious price cutting; to resale price maintenance; to professional football; and to racial discrimination by owners and managers of terminal restaurants.

That Congress was legislating against moral wrongs in many of these areas rendered its enactments no less valid. In framing Title II of this Act Congress was also dealing with what it considered a moral problem. But that fact does not detract from the overwhelming evidence of the disruptive effect that racial discrimination has had on commercial intercourse. It was this burden which empowered Congress to enact appropriate legislation, and, given this basis for the exercise of its power, Congress was not restricted by the fact that the particular obstruction to interstate commerce with which it was dealing was also deemed a moral and social wrong.

It is said that the operation of the motel here is of a purely local character. But, assuming this to be true, "[i]f it is interstate commerce that feels the pinch, it does not matter how local the operation which applies the squeeze." *United States v. Women's Sportswear Mfg. Ass'n*, 336 U.S. 460, 464 (1949).... Thus the power of Congress to promote interstate commerce also includes the power to regulate the local incidents thereof, including local activities in both the States of origin and destination, which might have a substantial and harmful effect upon that commerce....

We, therefore, conclude that the action of the Congress in the adoption of the Act as applied here to a motel which concededly serves interstate travelers is within the power granted it by the Commerce Clause of the Constitution, as interpreted by this Court for 140 years. It may be argued that Congress could have pursued other methods to eliminate the obstructions it found in interstate commerce caused by racial discrimination. But this is a matter of policy that rests entirely with the Congress not with the courts. How obstructions in commerce may be removed—what means are to be employed—is within the sound and exclusive discretion of the

Congress. It is subject only to one caveat—that the means chosen by it must be reasonably adapted to the end permitted by the Constitution. We cannot say that its choice here was not so adapted. The Constitution requires no more.

■ [The concurring opinions of JUSTICE BLACK, JUSTICE DOUGLAS, and JUSTICE GOLDBERG are omitted.]

NOTES

1. Which Article I powers does the Court rely on to uphold Title II of the Civil Rights Act? Only the Commerce Clause or also the Necessary and Proper Clause? Is this an easy case after *Wickard*?

2. In *Heart of Atlanta Motel's* companion case, *Katzenbach v. McClung*, 379 U.S. 294 (1964), the Court unanimously upheld the Civil Rights Act as applied to a locally-owned restaurant, Ollie's Barbecue in Birmingham, Alabama, even though there was "no claim that interstate travelers frequented the restaurant." The Court gave two reasons for its holding: (a) racial discrimination by restaurants generally had a direct and highly restrictive effect upon interstate travel and relocation by black Americans; and (b) the restaurant served meat that had once traveled in interstate commerce, though Ollie's Barbecue purchased it from a local supplier. *Katzenbach v. McClung* also introduced the rational-basis test to enumerated-powers case law: all Congress needs is a rational basis for thinking that its regulation of interstate commerce is convenient and useful to the promotion of interstate commerce.

3. In *Perez v. United States*, 402 U.S. 146 (1971), the Court upheld the constitutionality of a statute making "extortionate credit transactions" (loan sharking) a federal crime. The Court held that even when the extortion is wholly intrastate, it directly affects interstate commerce because loan sharking "provides organized crime with its second most lucrative source of revenue, exacts millions from the pockets of people, coerces its victims into the commission of crimes against property, and causes the takeover by racketeers of legitimate businesses. . . . [L]oan sharking in its national setting is one way organized interstate crime holds its guns to the heads of the poor and the rich alike and syphons funds from numerous localities to finance its national operations." The defendant was convicted even though there was no showing that his own loan sharking involved interstate commerce.

United States v. Lopez
514 U.S. 549 (1995)

■ CHIEF JUSTICE REHNQUIST delivered the opinion of the Court.

In the Gun-Free School Zones Act of 1990, Congress made it a federal offense "for any individual knowingly to possess a firearm at a place that the individual knows, or has reasonable cause to believe, is a school zone." The Act neither regulates a commercial activity nor contains a requirement that the possession be connected in any way to interstate commerce. We hold that the Act exceeds the authority of Congress "[t]o regulate Commerce . . . among the several States. . . ."

On March 10, 1992, respondent, who was then a 12th-grade student, arrived at Edison High School in San Antonio, Texas, carrying a concealed .38-caliber handgun and five bullets. Acting upon an anonymous tip, school authorities confronted respondent, who admitted that he was carrying the weapon. He was arrested and charged under Texas law with firearm possession on school premises. The next day, the state charges were dismissed after federal agents charged respondent by complaint with violating the Gun-Free School Zones Act of 1990.[1] . . .

[Lopez was convicted]. On appeal, [he] challenged his conviction based on his claim that § 922(q) exceeded Congress' power to legislate under the Commerce Clause. The Court of Appeals for the Fifth Circuit agreed and reversed respondent's conviction. . . . Because of the importance of the issue, we granted certiorari, and we now affirm.

We start with first principles. The Constitution creates a Federal Government of enumerated powers. See Art. I, § 8. As James Madison wrote: "The powers delegated by the proposed Constitution to the federal government are few and defined. Those which are to remain in the State governments are numerous and indefinite." The Federalist No. 45. This constitutionally mandated division of authority "was adopted by the Framers to ensure protection of our fundamental liberties." "Just as the separation and independence of the coordinate branches of the Federal Government serve to prevent the accumulation of excessive power in any one branch, a healthy balance of power between the States and the Federal Government will reduce the risk of tyranny and abuse from either front."

The Constitution delegates to Congress the power "[t]o regulate Commerce with foreign Nations, and among the several States, and with the Indian Tribes." Art. I, § 8, cl. 3. The Court, through Chief Justice Marshall, first defined the nature of Congress' commerce power in *Gibbons v. Ogden*, 22 U.S. (9 Wheat.) 1, 189–190 (1824):

> Commerce, undoubtedly, is traffic, but it is something more: it is intercourse. It describes the commercial intercourse between nations, and parts of nations, in all its branches, and is regulated by prescribing rules for carrying on that intercourse.

The commerce power "is the power to regulate; that is, to prescribe the rule by which commerce is to be governed. This power, like all others vested in congress, is complete in itself, may be exercised to its utmost extent, and acknowledges no limitations, other than are prescribed in the constitution." *Id.*, at 196. The *Gibbons* Court, however, acknowledged that limitations on the commerce power are inherent in the very language of the Commerce Clause.

> It is not intended to say that these words comprehend that commerce, which is completely internal, which is carried on between man and man in a State, or between different parts of the same State, and which does not extend to or affect other States. Such a power would be inconvenient, and is certainly unnecessary.

> Comprehensive as the word "among" is, it may very properly be restricted to that commerce which concerns more States than one. . . . The enumeration presupposes something not enumerated; and that something, if we regard the language, or the subject of the sentence, must be the exclusively internal commerce of a State.

For nearly a century thereafter, the Court's Commerce Clause decisions dealt but rarely with the extent of Congress' power, and almost entirely with the

---

[1] The term "school zone" is defined as "in, or on the grounds of, a public, parochial or private school" or "within a distance of 1,000 feet from the grounds of a public, parochial or private school." § 921(a)(25).

Commerce Clause as a limit on state legislation that discriminated against interstate commerce. Under this line of precedent, the Court held that certain categories of activity such as "production," "manufacturing," and "mining" were within the province of state governments, and thus were beyond the power of Congress under the Commerce Clause. . . .

[Then], in the watershed case of *NLRB v. Jones & Laughlin Steel Corp.,* 301 U.S. 1 (1937), the Court upheld the National Labor Relations Act against a Commerce Clause challenge, and in the process, departed from the distinction between "direct" and "indirect" effects on interstate commerce. *Id.,* at 36–38 ("The question [of the scope of Congress' power] is necessarily one of degree"). The Court held that intrastate activities that "have such a close and substantial relation to interstate commerce that their control is essential or appropriate to protect that commerce from burdens and obstructions" are within Congress' power to regulate. *Id.,* at 37.

In *United States v. Darby,* 312 U.S. 100 (1941), the Court upheld the Fair Labor Standards Act, stating:

> The power of Congress over interstate commerce is not confined to the regulation of commerce among the states. It extends to those activities intrastate which so affect interstate commerce or the exercise of the power of Congress over it as to make regulation of them appropriate means to the attainment of a legitimate end, the exercise of the granted power of Congress to regulate interstate commerce. . . .

In *Wickard v. Filburn,* the Court . . . explicitly rejected earlier distinctions between direct and indirect effects on interstate commerce. . . . The *Wickard* Court emphasized that although Filburn's own contribution to the demand for wheat may have been trivial by itself, that was not "enough to remove him from the scope of federal regulation where, as here, his contribution, taken together with that of many others similarly situated, is far from trivial."

Jones & Laughlin Steel, Darby, and *Wickard* ushered in an era of Commerce Clause jurisprudence that greatly expanded the previously defined authority of Congress under that clause. In part, this was a recognition of the great changes that had occurred in the way business was carried on in this country. Enterprises that had once been local or at most regional in nature had become national in scope. But the doctrinal change also reflected a view that earlier Commerce Clause cases artificially had constrained the authority of Congress to regulate interstate commerce.

But even these modern-era precedents which have expanded congressional power under the Commerce Clause confirm that this power is subject to outer limits. In *Jones & Laughlin Steel,* the Court warned that the scope of the interstate commerce power "must be considered in the light of our dual system of government and may not be extended so as to embrace effects upon interstate commerce so indirect and remote that to embrace them, in view of our complex society, would effectually obliterate the distinction between what is national and what is local and create a completely centralized government." See also *Darby,* at 119–120 (Congress may regulate intrastate activity that has a "substantial effect" on interstate commerce); *Wickard,* at 125 (Congress may regulate activity that "exerts a substantial economic effect on interstate commerce"). Since that time, the Court has heeded that warning and undertaken to decide whether a rational basis existed for concluding that a regulated activity sufficiently affected interstate commerce. . . .

[W]e have identified three broad categories of activity that Congress may regulate under its commerce power. First, Congress may regulate the use of the channels of interstate commerce. See, *e.g.*, *Darby*, at 114; *Heart of Atlanta Motel, Inc. v. United States*, 379 U.S. 241, 256 (1964) (" '[T]he authority of Congress to keep the channels of interstate commerce free from immoral and injurious uses has been frequently sustained, and is no longer open to question.' " (quoting *Caminetti v. United States*, 242 U.S. 470, 491 (1917))). Second, Congress is empowered to regulate and protect the instrumentalities of interstate commerce, or persons or things in interstate commerce, even though the threat may come only from intrastate activities. See, *e.g.*, *Shreveport Rate Cases*, 234 U.S. 342 (1914); *Southern R. Co. v. United States*, 222 U.S. 20 (1911) (upholding amendments to Safety Appliance Act as applied to vehicles used in intrastate commerce); *Perez v. United States*, 402 U.S. 146, 150 (1971) ("[F]or example, the destruction of an aircraft (18 U.S.C. § 32), or . . . thefts from interstate shipments (18 U.S.C. § 659)"). Finally, Congress' commerce authority includes the power to regulate those activities having a substantial relation to interstate commerce, *Jones & Laughlin Steel*, at 37, *i.e.*, those activities that substantially affect interstate commerce.

Within this final category, admittedly, our case law has not been clear whether an activity must "affect" or "substantially affect" interstate commerce in order to be within Congress' power to regulate it under the Commerce Clause. Compare *Preseault v. ICC*, 494 U.S. 1, 17 (1990), with *Maryland v. Wirtz*, 392 U.S. 183, 196, n.27 (1968) (the Court has never declared that "Congress may use a relatively trivial impact on commerce as an excuse for broad general regulation of state or private activities"). We conclude, consistent with the great weight of our case law, that the proper test requires an analysis of whether the regulated activity "substantially affects" interstate commerce.

We now turn to consider the power of Congress, in the light of this framework, to enact § 922(q). The first two categories of authority may be quickly disposed of: the Act is not a regulation of the use of the channels of interstate commerce, nor is it an attempt to prohibit the interstate transportation of a commodity through the channels of commerce; nor can § 922(q) be justified as a regulation by which Congress has sought to protect an instrumentality of interstate commerce or a thing in interstate commerce. Thus, if § 922(q) is to be sustained, it must be under the third category as a regulation of an activity that substantially affects interstate commerce.

First, we have upheld a wide variety of congressional Acts regulating intrastate economic activity where we have concluded that the activity substantially affected interstate commerce. Examples include the regulation of intrastate coal mining; intrastate extortionate credit transactions, restaurants utilizing substantial interstate supplies, inns and hotels catering to interstate guests, and production and consumption of homegrown wheat. These examples are by no means exhaustive, but the pattern is clear. Where economic activity substantially affects interstate commerce, legislation regulating that activity will be sustained.

Even *Wickard*, which is perhaps the most far reaching example of Commerce Clause authority over intrastate activity, involved economic activity in a way that the possession of a gun in a school zone does not. Roscoe Filburn operated a small farm in Ohio, on which, in the year involved, he raised 23 acres of wheat. It was his practice to sow winter wheat in the fall, and after harvesting it in July to sell a portion of the crop, to feed part of it to poultry and livestock on the farm, to use some in making flour for home consumption, and to keep the remainder for seeding future crops. The Secretary of Agriculture assessed a penalty against him under the Agricultural Adjustment Act of 1938 because he harvested about 12 acres more wheat than his allotment under the Act permitted. The Act was designed to regulate the volume of wheat moving in interstate and foreign commerce in order to avoid surpluses and shortages, and concomitant fluctuation in wheat prices, which had previously obtained. . . .

Section 922(q) is a criminal statute that by its terms has nothing to do with "commerce" or any sort of economic enterprise, however broadly one might define those terms. Section 922(q) is not an essential part of a larger regulation of economic activity, in which the regulatory scheme could be undercut unless the intrastate activity were regulated. It cannot, therefore, be sustained under our cases upholding regulations of activities that arise out of or are connected with a commercial transaction, which viewed in the aggregate, substantially affects interstate commerce.

[handwritten: provision of law itself that requires in order to be applied some proof of commerce]

Second, § 922(q) contains no jurisdictional element which would ensure, through case-by-case inquiry, that the firearm possession in question affects interstate commerce. For example, in *United States v. Bass,* 404 U.S. 336 (1971), the Court interpreted former 18 U.S.C. § 1202(a), which made it a crime for a felon to "receiv[e], posses[s], or transpor[t] in commerce or affecting commerce . . . any firearm." . . . Unlike the statute in *Bass,* § 922(q) has no express jurisdictional element which might limit its reach to a discrete set of firearm possessions that additionally have an explicit connection with or effect on interstate commerce.

Although as part of our independent evaluation of constitutionality under the Commerce Clause we of course consider legislative findings, and indeed even congressional committee findings, regarding effect on interstate commerce, the Government concedes that "[n]either the statute nor its legislative history contain[s] express congressional findings regarding the effects upon interstate commerce of gun possession in a school zone." We agree with the Government that Congress normally is not required to make formal findings as to the substantial burdens that an activity has on interstate commerce. But to the extent that congressional findings would enable us to evaluate the legislative judgment that the activity in question substantially affected interstate commerce, even though no such substantial effect was visible to the naked eye, they are lacking here.

The Government's essential contention, *in fine,* is that we may determine here that § 922(q) is valid because possession of a firearm in a local school zone does indeed substantially affect interstate commerce. The Government argues that possession of a firearm in a school zone may result in violent crime and that violent crime can be expected to affect the functioning of the national economy in two ways. First, the costs of violent crime are substantial, and, through the mechanism of insurance, those costs are spread throughout the population. Second, violent crime reduces the willingness of individuals to travel to areas within the country that are perceived to be unsafe. Cf. *Heart of Atlanta Motel*, at 253. The Government also argues that the presence of guns in schools poses a substantial threat to the educational process by threatening the learning environment. A handicapped educational process, in turn, will result in a less productive citizenry. That, in turn, would have an adverse effect on the Nation's economic well-being. As a result, the Government argues that Congress could rationally have concluded that § 922(q) substantially affects interstate commerce.

We pause to consider the implications of the Government's arguments. The Government admits, under its "costs of crime" reasoning, that Congress could regulate not only all violent crime, but all activities that might lead to violent crime, regardless of how tenuously they relate to interstate commerce. Tr. of Oral Arg. 8–9. Similarly, under the Government's "national productivity" reasoning, Congress could regulate any activity that it found was related to the economic productivity of individual citizens: family law (including marriage, divorce, and child custody), for example. Under the theories that the Government presents in support of § 922(q), it is difficult to perceive any limitation on federal power, even in areas such as criminal law enforcement or education where States historically have been sovereign. Thus, if we were to accept the Government's arguments, we are hard pressed to posit any activity by an individual that Congress is without power to regulate.

Although JUSTICE BREYER argues that acceptance of the Government's rationales would not authorize a general federal police power, he is unable to identify any activity that the States may regulate but Congress may not. JUSTICE BREYER posits that there might be some limitations on Congress' commerce power, such as family law or certain aspects of education. These suggested limitations, when viewed in light of the dissent's expansive analysis, are devoid of substance.

JUSTICE BREYER focuses, for the most part, on the threat that firearm possession in and near schools poses to the educational process and the potential economic consequences flowing from that threat. Specifically, the dissent reasons that (1) gun-related violence is a serious problem; (2) that problem, in turn, has an adverse effect on classroom learning; and (3) that adverse effect on classroom learning, in turn, represents a substantial threat to trade and commerce. This analysis would be equally applicable, if not more so, to subjects such as family law and direct regulation of education.

For instance, if Congress can, pursuant to its Commerce Clause power, regulate activities that adversely affect the learning environment, then, *a fortiori,* it also can regulate the educational process directly. Congress could determine that a school's curriculum has a "significant" effect on the extent of classroom learning. As a result, Congress could mandate a federal curriculum for local elementary and secondary schools because what is taught in local schools has a significant "effect on classroom learning," and that, in turn, has a substantial effect on interstate commerce.

JUSTICE BREYER rejects our reading of precedent and argues that "Congress . . . could rationally conclude that schools fall on the commercial side of the line." Again, JUSTICE BREYER's rationale lacks any real limits because, depending on the level of generality, any activity can be looked upon as commercial. Under the dissent's rationale, Congress could just as easily look at child rearing as "fall[ing] on the commercial side of the line" because it provides a "valuable service—namely, to equip [children] with the skills they need to survive in life and, more specifically, in the workplace." We do not doubt that Congress has authority under the Commerce Clause to regulate numerous commercial activities that substantially affect interstate commerce and also affect the educational process. That authority, though broad, does not include the authority to regulate each and every aspect of local schools.

Admittedly, a determination whether an intrastate activity is commercial or noncommercial may in some cases result in legal uncertainty. But, so long as Congress' authority is limited to those powers enumerated in the Constitution, and so long as those enumerated powers are interpreted as having judicially enforceable outer limits, congressional legislation under the Commerce Clause always will engender "legal uncertainty." . . . Any possible benefit from eliminating this "legal uncertainty" would be at the expense of the Constitution's system of enumerated powers.

In *Jones & Laughlin Steel*, at 37, we held that the question of congressional power under the Commerce Clause "is necessarily one of degree." To the same effect is the concurring opinion of Justice Cardozo in *A.L.A. Schechter Poultry Corp. v. United States*, 295 U.S. 495, 554 (1935):

> "There is a view of causation that would obliterate the distinction between what is national and what is local in the activities of commerce. Motion at the outer rim is communicated perceptibly, though minutely, to recording instruments at the center. A society such as ours 'is an elastic medium which transmits all tremors throughout its territory; the only question is of their size.' "

These are not precise formulations, and in the nature of things they cannot be. But we think they point the way to a correct decision of this case. The possession of a gun in a local school zone is in no sense an economic activity that might, through repetition elsewhere, substantially affect any sort of interstate commerce. Respondent was a local student at a local school; there is no indication that he had recently moved in interstate commerce, and there is no requirement that his possession of the firearm have any concrete tie to interstate commerce.

To uphold the Government's contentions here, we would have to pile inference upon inference in a manner that would bid fair to convert congressional authority under the Commerce Clause to a general police power of the sort retained by the States. Admittedly, some of our prior cases have taken long steps down that road, giving great deference to congressional action. The broad language in these opinions has suggested the possibility of additional expansion, but we decline here to proceed any further. To do so would require us to conclude that the Constitution's enumeration of powers does not presuppose something not enumerated, cf. *Gibbons*, at 195, and that there never will be a distinction between what is truly national and what is truly local, cf. *Jones & Laughlin Steel*, at 30. This we are unwilling to do.

■ JUSTICE KENNEDY, with whom JUSTICE O'CONNOR joins, concurring.

The history of the judicial struggle to interpret the Commerce Clause during the transition from the economic system the Founders knew to the single, national market still emergent in our own era counsels great restraint before the Court determines that the Clause is insufficient to support an exercise of the national power. That history gives me some pause about today's decision, but I join the Court's opinion with these observations on what I conceive to be its necessary though limited holding. . . .

The case that seems to mark the Court's definitive commitment to the practical conception of the commerce power is *Jones & Laughlin Steel Corp.*, where the Court sustained labor laws that applied to manufacturing facilities, making no real attempt to distinguish *Carter v. Carter Coal Co.*, 298 U.S. 238 (1936), and *Schechter Poultry*. The deference given to Congress has since been confirmed. *Darby* overruled *Hammer v. Dagenhart*. And in *Wickard v. Filburn*, the Court disapproved *United States v. E.C. Knight Co.*, 156 U.S. 1 (1895), and the entire line of direct-indirect and manufacture-production cases, explaining that "broader interpretations of the Commerce Clause [were] destined to supersede the earlier ones," and "[w]hatever terminology is used, the criterion is necessarily one of degree and must be so defined. This does not satisfy those who seek mathematical or rigid formulas. But such formulas are not provided by the great concepts of the Constitution." . . . These and like authorities are within the fair ambit of the Court's practical conception of commercial regulation and are not called in question by our decision today.

. . . [T]he Court as an institution and the legal system as a whole have an immense stake in the stability of our Commerce Clause jurisprudence as it has evolved to this point. *Stare decisis* operates with great force in counseling us not to call in question the essential principles now in place respecting the congressional power to regulate transactions of a commercial nature. That fundamental restraint on our power forecloses us from reverting to an understanding of commerce that would serve only an 18th-century economy, dependent then upon production and trading practices that had changed but little over the preceding centuries; it also mandates against returning to the time when congressional authority to regulate undoubted commercial activities was limited by a judicial determination that those matters had an insufficient connection to an interstate system. Congress can regulate in the commercial sphere on the assumption that we have a single market and a unified purpose to build a stable national economy. . . .

The statute before us upsets the federal balance to a degree that renders it an unconstitutional assertion of the commerce power, and our intervention is required. As THE CHIEF JUSTICE explains, unlike the earlier cases to come before the Court here neither the actors nor their conduct has a commercial character, and neither the purposes nor the design of the statute has an evident commercial nexus. The statute makes the simple possession of a gun within 1,000 feet of the grounds of the school a criminal offense. In a sense any conduct in this interdependent world of ours has an ultimate commercial origin or consequence, but we have not yet said the commerce power may reach so far. If Congress attempts that extension, then at the least we must inquire whether the exercise of national power seeks to intrude upon an area of traditional state concern. . . .

■ JUSTICE THOMAS, concurring.

The Court today properly concludes that the Commerce Clause does not grant Congress the authority to prohibit gun possession within 1,000 feet of a school, as it attempted to do in the Gun-Free School Zones Act of 1990. Although I join the majority, I write separately to observe that our case law has drifted far from the original understanding of the Commerce Clause. In a future case, we ought to temper our Commerce Clause jurisprudence in a manner that both makes sense of our more recent case law and is more faithful to the original understanding of that Clause.

We have said that Congress may regulate not only "Commerce . . . among the several States," U.S. Const., Art. I, § 8, cl. 3, but also anything that has a "substantial effect" on such commerce. This test, if taken to its logical extreme, would give

Congress a "police power" over all aspects of American life. Unfortunately, we have never come to grips with this implication of our substantial effects formula. Although we have supposedly applied the substantial effects test for the past 60 years, we *always* have rejected readings of the Commerce Clause and the scope of federal power that would permit Congress to exercise a police power; our cases are quite clear that there are real limits to federal power. . . .

While the principal dissent concedes that there are limits to federal power, the sweeping nature of our current test enables the dissent to argue that Congress can regulate gun possession. But it seems to me that the power to regulate "commerce" can by no means encompass authority over mere gun possession, any more than it empowers the Federal Government to regulate marriage, littering, or cruelty to animals, throughout the 50 States. Our Constitution quite properly leaves such matters to the individual States, notwithstanding these activities' effects on interstate commerce. Any interpretation of the Commerce Clause that even suggests that Congress could regulate such matters is in need of reexamination.

In an appropriate case, I believe that we must further reconsider our "substantial effects" test with an eye toward constructing a standard that reflects the text and history of the Commerce Clause without totally rejecting our more recent Commerce Clause jurisprudence. . . .

At the time the original Constitution was ratified, "commerce" consisted of selling, buying, and bartering, as well as transporting for these purposes. . . . In fact, when Federalists and Anti-Federalists discussed the Commerce Clause during the ratification period, they often used trade (in its selling/bartering sense) and commerce interchangeably.

As one would expect, the term "commerce" was used in contradistinction to productive activities such as manufacturing and agriculture. Alexander Hamilton, for example, repeatedly treated commerce, agriculture, and manufacturing as three separate endeavors. The same distinctions were made in the state ratification conventions. . . .

The Constitution not only uses the word "commerce" in a narrower sense than our case law might suggest, it also does not support the proposition that Congress has authority over all activities that "substantially affect" interstate commerce. The Commerce Clause does not state that Congress may "regulate matters that substantially affect commerce with foreign Nations, and among the several States, and with the Indian Tribes." In contrast, the Constitution itself temporarily prohibited amendments that would "affect" Congress' lack of authority to prohibit or restrict the slave trade or to enact unproportioned direct taxation. Art. V. Clearly, the Framers could have drafted a Constitution that contained a "substantially affects interstate commerce" Clause had that been their objective.

In addition to its powers under the Commerce Clause, Congress has the authority to enact such laws as are "necessary and proper" to carry into execution its power to regulate commerce among the several States. U.S. Const., Art. I, § 8, cl. 18. But on this Court's understanding of congressional power under these two Clauses, many of Congress' other enumerated powers under Art. I, § 8, are wholly superfluous. After all, if Congress may regulate all matters that substantially affect commerce, there is no need for the Constitution to specify that Congress may enact bankruptcy laws, or coin money and fix the standard of weights and measures, or punish counterfeiters of United States coin and securities. Likewise, Congress would not need the separate authority to establish post offices and post roads, or to grant patents and copyrights or to "punish Piracies and Felonies committed on the high Seas." It might not even need the power to raise and support an Army and Navy, for fewer people would engage in commercial shipping if they thought that a foreign power could expropriate their property with ease. Indeed, if Congress could regulate matters that substantially affect interstate commerce, there would have been no need to specify that Congress can regulate international trade and commerce with the Indians. As the Framers surely understood, these other branches of trade substantially affect interstate commerce.

Put simply, much if not all of Art. I, § 8 (including portions of the Commerce Clause itself), would be surplusage if Congress had been given authority over matters that substantially affect interstate commerce. An interpretation of cl. 3 that makes the rest of § 8 superfluous simply cannot be correct. Yet this Court's Commerce Clause jurisprudence has endorsed just such an interpretation: The power we have accorded Congress has swallowed Art. I, § 8.

Indeed, if a "substantial effects" test can be appended to the Commerce Clause, why not to every other power of the Federal Government? There is no reason for singling out the Commerce Clause for special treatment. Accordingly, Congress could regulate all matters that "substantially affect" the Army and Navy, bankruptcies, tax collection, expenditures, and so on. In that case, the Clauses of § 8 all mutually overlap, something we can assume the Founding Fathers never intended.

Our construction of the scope of congressional authority has the additional problem of coming close to turning the Tenth Amendment on its head. Our case law could be read to reserve to the United States all powers not expressly *prohibited* by the Constitution. Taken together, these fundamental textual problems should, at the very least, convince us that the "substantial effects" test should be reexamined.

The exchanges during the ratification campaign reveal the relatively limited reach of the Commerce Clause and of federal power generally. . . .

Hamilton, for instance, acknowledged that the Federal Government could not regulate agriculture and like concerns:

> "The administration of private justice between the citizens of the same State, the supervision of agriculture and of other concerns of a similar nature, all those things in short which are proper to be provided for by local legislation, can never be desirable cares of a general jurisdiction." The Federalist No. 17. . . .

Apart from its recent vintage and its corresponding lack of any grounding in the original understanding of the Constitution, the substantial effects test suffers from the further flaw that it appears to grant Congress a police power over the Nation. When asked at oral argument if there were *any* limits to the Commerce Clause, the Government was at a loss for words. Likewise, the principal dissent insists that there are limits, but it cannot muster even one example. Indeed, the dissent implicitly concedes that its reading has no limits when it criticizes the Court for "threaten[ing] legal uncertainty in an area of law that . . . seemed reasonably well settled." The one advantage of the dissent's standard is certainty: It is certain that under its analysis everything may be regulated under the guise of the Commerce Clause.

The substantial effects test suffers from this flaw, in part, because of its "aggregation principle." Under so-called "class of activities" statutes, Congress can regulate whole categories of activities that are not themselves either "interstate" or "commerce." In applying the effects test, we ask whether the class of activities *as a whole* substantially affects interstate commerce, not whether any specific activity within the class has such effects when considered in isolation.

The aggregation principle is clever, but has no stopping point. Suppose all would agree that gun possession within 1,000 feet of a school does not substantially affect commerce, but that possession of weapons generally (knives, brass knuckles, nunchakus, etc.) does. Under our substantial effects doctrine, even though Congress cannot single out gun possession, it can prohibit weapon possession generally. But one *always* can draw the circle broadly enough to cover an activity that, when taken in isolation, would not have substantial effects on commerce. Under our jurisprudence, if Congress passed an omnibus "substantially affects interstate commerce" statute, purporting to regulate every aspect of human existence, the Act apparently would be constitutional. Even though particular sections may govern only trivial activities, the statute in the aggregate regulates matters that substantially affect commerce.

This extended discussion of the original understanding and our first century and a half of case law does not necessarily require a wholesale abandonment of our more recent opinions.[8] It simply reveals that our substantial effects test is far removed from both the Constitution and from our early case law and that the Court's opinion should not be viewed as "radical" or another "wrong turn" that must be corrected in the future. The analysis also suggests that we ought to temper our Commerce Clause jurisprudence.

Unless the dissenting Justices are willing to repudiate our long-held understanding of the limited nature of federal power, I would think that they, too, must be willing to reconsider the substantial effects test in a future case. If we wish to be true to a Constitution that does not cede a police power to the Federal Government, our Commerce Clause's boundaries simply cannot be "defined" as being "commensurate with the national needs" or self-consciously intended to let the Federal Government "defend itself against economic forces that Congress decrees inimical or destructive of the national economy." Such a formulation of federal power is no test at all: It is a blank check.

At an appropriate juncture, I think we must modify our Commerce Clause jurisprudence. Today, it is easy enough to say that the Clause certainly does not empower Congress to ban gun possession within 1,000 feet of a school.

■ JUSTICE BREYER, with whom JUSTICE STEVENS, JUSTICE SOUTER, and JUSTICE GINSBURG join, dissenting.

The issue in this case is whether the Commerce Clause authorizes Congress to enact a statute that makes it a crime to possess a gun in, or near, a school. In my view, the statute falls well within the scope of the commerce power as this Court has understood that power over the last half century.

---

8   Although I might be willing to return to the original understanding, I recognize that many believe that it is too late in the day to undertake a fundamental reexamination of the past 60 years. Consideration of *stare decisis* and reliance interests may convince us that we cannot wipe the slate clean.

In reaching this conclusion, I apply three basic principles of Commerce Clause interpretation. First, the power to "regulate Commerce . . . among the several States" encompasses the power to regulate local activities insofar as they significantly affect interstate commerce. As the majority points out, the Court, in describing how much of an effect the Clause requires, sometimes has used the word "substantial" and sometimes has not. . . . I use the word "significant" because the word "substantial" implies a somewhat narrower power than recent precedent suggests. But to speak of "substantial effect" rather than "significant effect" would make no difference in this case.

Second, in determining whether a local activity will likely have a significant effect upon interstate commerce, a court must consider, not the effect of an individual act (a single instance of gun possession), but rather the cumulative effect of all similar instances (*i.e.*, the effect of all guns possessed in or near schools). See, *e.g.*, *Wickard*, at 127–128. . . .

Third, the Constitution requires us to judge the connection between a regulated activity and interstate commerce, not directly, but at one remove. Courts must give Congress a degree of leeway in determining the existence of a significant factual connection between the regulated activity and interstate commerce—both because the Constitution delegates the commerce power directly to Congress and because the determination requires an empirical judgment of a kind that a legislature is more likely than a court to make with accuracy. The traditional words "rational basis" capture this leeway. Thus, the specific question before us, as the Court recognizes, is not whether the "regulated activity sufficiently affected interstate commerce," but, rather, whether Congress could have had "*a rational basis*" for so concluding. . . .

Applying these principles to the case at hand, we must ask whether Congress could have had a *rational basis* for finding a significant (or substantial) connection between gun-related school violence and interstate commerce. Or, to put the question in the language of the *explicit* finding that Congress made when it amended this law in 1994: Could Congress rationally have found that "violent crime in school zones," through its effect on the "quality of education," significantly (or substantially) affects "interstate" or "foreign commerce"? As long as one views the commerce connection, not as a "technical legal conception," but as "a practical one," *Swift & Co. v. United States,* 196 U.S. 375, 398 (1905) (Holmes, J.), the answer to this question must be yes. Numerous reports and studies—generated both inside and outside government—make clear that Congress could reasonably have found the empirical connection that its law, implicitly or explicitly, asserts.

For one thing, reports, hearings, and other readily available literature make clear that the problem of guns in and around schools is widespread and extremely serious. These materials report, for example, that four percent of American high school students (and six percent of inner-city high school students) carry a gun to school at least occasionally; that 20 percent of those students have been threatened with guns; and that, in any 6-month period, several hundred thousand schoolchildren are victims of violent crimes in or near their schools. And, they report that this widespread violence in schools throughout the Nation significantly interferes with the quality of education in those schools. . . . Congress could therefore have found a substantial educational problem—teachers unable to teach, students unable to learn—and concluded that guns near schools contribute substantially to the size and scope of that problem.

Having found that guns in schools significantly undermine the quality of education in our Nation's classrooms, Congress could also have found, given the effect of education upon interstate and foreign commerce, that gun-related violence in and around schools is a commercial, as well as a human, problem. Education, although far more than a matter of economics, has long been inextricably intertwined with the Nation's economy. . . .

To hold this statute constitutional is not to "obliterate" the "distinction between what is national and what is local"; nor is it to hold that the Commerce Clause permits the Federal Government to "regulate any activity that it found was related to the economic productivity of individual citizens," to regulate "marriage, divorce, and child custody," or to regulate any and all aspects of education. First, this statute is aimed at curbing a particularly acute threat to the educational process—the possession (and use) of life-threatening firearms in, or near, the classroom. The empirical evidence that I have discussed above unmistakably documents the special way in which guns and education are incompatible. This Court has previously recognized the singularly disruptive potential on interstate commerce that acts of violence may have. Second, the immediacy of the connection between education and the national economic well-being is documented by scholars and accepted by society at large in a way and to a degree that may not hold true for other social institutions. It must surely be the rare case, then, that a statute strikes at conduct that (when considered in the abstract) seems so removed from commerce, but which (practically speaking) has so significant an impact upon commerce.

In sum, a holding that the particular statute before us falls within the commerce power would not expand the scope of that Clause. Rather, it simply would apply preexisting law to changing economic circumstances. It would recognize that, in today's economic world, gun-related violence near the classroom makes a significant difference to our economic, as well as our social, well-being. In accordance with well-accepted precedent, such a holding would permit Congress "to act in terms of economic . . . realities," would interpret the commerce power as "an affirmative power commensurate with the national needs," and would acknowledge that the "commerce clause does not operate so as to render the nation powerless to defend itself against economic forces that Congress decrees inimical or destructive of the national economy." *North American Co. v. SEC*, 327 U.S. 686, 705 (1946) (citing *Swift & Co.*, at 398 (Holmes, J.)).

The majority's holding—that § 922(q) falls outside the scope of the Commerce Clause—creates three serious legal problems. First, the majority's holding runs contrary to modern Supreme Court cases that have upheld congressional actions despite connections to interstate or foreign commerce that are less significant than the effect of school violence. . . .

The second legal problem the Court creates comes from its apparent belief that it can reconcile its holding with earlier cases by making a critical distinction between "commercial" and noncommercial "transaction[s]." That is to say, the Court believes the Constitution would distinguish between two local activities, each of which has an identical effect upon interstate commerce, if one, but not the other, is "commercial" in nature. As a general matter, this approach fails to heed this Court's earlier warning not to turn "questions of the power of Congress" upon "formula[s]" that would give "controlling force to nomenclature such as 'production' and 'indirect' and foreclose consideration of the actual effects of the activity in question upon interstate commerce." *Wickard,* at 120. . . .

The third legal problem created by the Court's holding is that it threatens legal uncertainty in an area of law that, until this case, seemed reasonably well settled. . . .

Upholding this legislation would do no more than simply recognize that Congress had a "rational basis" for finding a significant connection between guns in or near schools and (through their effect on education) the interstate and foreign commerce they threaten.

■ [The dissenting opinions of JUSTICE STEVENS and JUSTICE SOUTER are omitted.]

NOTES

1.   The different opinions in *Lopez* start from different premises, and they represent different views of the Court's precedents under the Commerce Clause. Which one do you find most persuasive? What is that decision's *weakest* point?

2.   Could Congress accomplish its objectives for the Gun-Free School Zone Act by including a "jurisdictional element" (or "jurisdictional hook")—a requirement of proof that the gun had some specific connection to interstate commerce? After *Lopez*, Congress did so, amending the statute to provide: "It shall be unlawful for any individual knowingly to possess a firearm *that has moved in or that otherwise affects* interstate commerce at a place that the individual knows, or has reasonable cause to believe, is a school zone." Does the italicized language save the statute?

In thinking about the amended statute, it may help to separate the alternatives— "has moved in" or "otherwise affects" commerce. For items that have moved in interstate commerce: does the fact that Congress had the power to regulate something *in the past* imply that Congress has the power to regulate it at any time in the future? For items that "otherwise affect" commerce: does this element fit the Court's limits on regulating activity that "substantially affects" interstate commerce? Several courts of appeals have upheld the amended statute, but the Supreme Court has not addressed it—yet. Cf. *Alderman v. United States*, 562 U.S. 1163, 1166–67 (2011) (Thomas, J., dissenting from denial of cert.) (arguing that this kind of jurisdictional hook "cannot be reconciled with *Lopez*," and "by trumping the *Lopez* framework, could very well remove any limit on the commerce power" because it "seems to permit Congress to regulate or ban possession of any item that has ever been offered for sale or crossed state lines").

3.   In *United States v. Morrison*, 529 U.S. 598 (2000), the Court held that the Commerce Clause did not empower Congress to enact the Violence Against Women Act, which made certain acts of domestic violence federal crimes and torts. (The decision was 5–4, with the same alignment of justices as in *Lopez*.) The *Morrison* Court held that the Commerce Clause could not be leveraged into a power to regulate purely intrastate noncommercial activity: "Gender-motivated crimes of violence are not, in any sense of the phrase, economic activity. . . . We accordingly reject the argument that Congress may regulate noneconomic, violent criminal conduct based solely on that conduct's aggregate effect on interstate commerce." In the Act, Congress made factual findings that gender-motivated violence had a substantial impact on commerce. These findings made no difference to the Court: "As we stated in *Lopez*, '[s]imply because Congress may conclude that a particular activity substantially affects interstate commerce does not necessarily make it so.'" Does *Morrison* follow *a fortiori* from *Lopez*? Is the connection-to-commerce

justification stronger in one case than the other? Was *Morrison* correct in discounting the significance of congressional findings?

4.   There has been renewed scholarly attention to the economics of federalism. E.g., Robert D. Cooter & Neil S. Siegel, *Collective Action Federalism: A General Theory of Article I, Section 8*, 63 Stan. L. Rev. 115 (2010). A central idea is that a federal system allows the states to compete with each other, making every state better off, but the national government can step in to solve collective-action problems—the kind of problems where each state by acting in its own self-interest will make all of the states collectively worse off. Was the statute in *Lopez* solving a problem that the states were unable to resolve by themselves? (Note that at the time *Lopez* was decided, more than forty states already had laws against carrying guns in or near schools.) Yet even if this particular statute did not solve a problem the states were unable to solve, do other federal restrictions on the sale and transportation of firearms more clearly respond to a state collective-action problem?

Related questions were actually considered at the Philadelphia Convention. One of the delegates, Gunning Bedford of Delaware, put forward the following resolution: "the national Legislature ought to possess the legislative rights vested in Congress by the confederation [and the right] to legislate in all cases for the general interests of the Union, and also *in those to which the States are separately incompetent*, or in which the harmony of the United States may be interrupted by the exercise of individual legislation." 2 THE RECORDS OF THE FEDERAL CONVENTION OF 1787, at 21, 27 (Max Farrand ed., 1911) (emphasis added). The Bedford Resolution was approved, and the Committee of Detail was charged with writing this outcome into the text of the Constitution. The result, however, was Article I, Section 8—the long sentence with eighteen clauses enumerating the national legislative powers. How is the approach of the Bedford Resolution similar to and different from the text that was adopted? Should a collective-action-problem concept of federalism affect the interpretation of Article I, Section 8?

[*Assignment 27*]

In Closer Focus: The Commerce and Necessary and Proper Clauses

Gonzales v. Raich
545 U.S. 1 (2005)

■ JUSTICE STEVENS delivered the opinion of the Court.

California is one of at least nine States that authorize the use of marijuana for medicinal purposes. The question presented in this case is whether the power vested in Congress by Article I, § 8, of the Constitution "[t]o make all Laws which shall be necessary and proper for carrying into Execution" its authority to "regulate Commerce with foreign Nations, and among the several States" includes the power to prohibit the local cultivation and use of marijuana in compliance with California law.

I

California has been a pioneer in the regulation of marijuana. . . . In 1996, California voters passed Proposition 215, now codified as the Compassionate Use Act of 1996. The proposition was designed to ensure that "seriously ill" residents of the State have access to marijuana for medical purposes, and to encourage Federal and State Governments to take steps towards ensuring the safe and affordable distribution of the drug to patients in need. The Act creates an exemption from criminal prosecution for physicians as well as for patients and primary caregivers who possess or cultivate marijuana for medicinal purposes with the recommendation or approval of a physician. . . .

Respondents Angel Raich and Diane Monson are California residents who suffer from a variety of serious medical conditions and have sought to avail themselves of medical marijuana pursuant to the terms of the Compassionate Use Act. . . .

On August 15, 2002, county deputy sheriffs and agents from the federal Drug Enforcement Administration (DEA) came to Monson's home. After a thorough investigation, the county officials concluded that her use of marijuana was entirely lawful as a matter of California law. Nevertheless, after a 3-hour standoff, the federal agents seized and destroyed all six of her cannabis plants.

Respondents thereafter brought this action against the Attorney General of the United States and the head of the DEA seeking injunctive and declaratory relief prohibiting the enforcement of the federal Controlled Substances Act (CSA), to the extent it prevents them from possessing, obtaining, or manufacturing cannabis for their personal medical use. . . .

II

. . . In 1970, after declaration of the national "war on drugs," federal drug policy underwent a significant transformation. . . . Prompted by a perceived need to consolidate the growing number of piecemeal drug laws and to enhance federal drug enforcement powers, Congress enacted the Comprehensive Drug Abuse Prevention and Control Act.

Title II of that Act, the [Controlled Substances Act], repealed most of the earlier antidrug laws in favor of a comprehensive regime to combat the international and interstate traffic in illicit drugs. The main objectives of the CSA were to conquer drug abuse and to control the legitimate and illegitimate traffic in controlled substances. Congress was particularly concerned with the need to prevent the diversion of drugs from legitimate to illicit channels.

To effectuate these goals, Congress devised a closed regulatory system making it unlawful to manufacture, distribute, dispense, or possess any controlled substance except in a manner authorized by the CSA. . . .

III

Respondents in this case do not dispute that passage of the CSA, as part of the Comprehensive Drug Abuse Prevention and Control Act, was well within Congress' commerce power. Nor do they contend that any provision or section of the CSA amounts to an unconstitutional exercise of congressional authority. Rather, respondents' challenge is actually quite limited; they argue that the CSA's categorical prohibition of the manufacture and possession of marijuana as applied to the intrastate manufacture and possession of marijuana for medical purposes pursuant to California law exceeds Congress' authority under the Commerce Clause. . . .

Our case law firmly establishes Congress' power to regulate purely local activities that are part of an economic "class of activities" that have a substantial effect on interstate commerce. See, *e.g., Perez v. United States,* 402 U.S. 146, 151 (1971); *Wickard v. Filburn,* 317 U.S. 111, 128–129 (1942). . . . When Congress decides that the "total incidence" of a practice poses a threat to a national market, it may regulate the entire class. . . . [W]e have reiterated that when "a general regulatory statute bears a substantial relation to commerce, the *de minimis* character of individual instances arising under that statute is of no consequence." *E.g., United States v. Lopez,* 514 U.S. 549, 558 (1995).

Our decision in *Wickard* is of particular relevance. . . . [It] establishes that Congress can regulate purely intrastate activity that is not itself "commercial," in that it is not produced for sale, if it concludes that failure to regulate that class of activity would undercut the regulation of the interstate market in that commodity.

The similarities between this case and *Wickard* are striking. Like the farmer in *Wickard,* respondents are cultivating, for home consumption, a fungible commodity for which there is an established, albeit illegal, interstate market. Just as the Agricultural Adjustment Act was designed "to control the volume [of wheat] moving in interstate and foreign commerce in order to avoid surpluses" and consequently control the market price, a primary purpose of the CSA is to control the supply and demand of controlled substances in both lawful and unlawful drug markets. In *Wickard,* we had no difficulty concluding that Congress had a rational basis for believing that, when viewed in the aggregate, leaving home-consumed wheat outside the regulatory scheme would have a substantial influence on price and market conditions. Here too, Congress had a rational basis for concluding that leaving home-consumed marijuana outside federal control would similarly affect price and market conditions.

More concretely, one concern prompting inclusion of wheat grown for home consumption in the 1938 Act was that rising market prices could draw such wheat into the interstate market, resulting in lower market prices. The parallel concern making it appropriate to include marijuana grown for home consumption in the CSA is the likelihood that the high demand in the interstate market will draw such marijuana into that market. While the diversion of homegrown wheat tended to frustrate the federal interest in stabilizing prices by regulating the volume of commercial transactions in the interstate market, the diversion of homegrown marijuana tends to frustrate the federal interest in eliminating commercial transactions in the interstate market in their entirety. In both cases, the regulation is squarely within Congress' commerce power because production of the commodity meant for home consumption, be it wheat or marijuana, has a substantial effect on supply and demand in the national market for that commodity.

Nonetheless, respondents suggest that *Wickard* differs from this case in three respects: (1) the Agricultural Adjustment Act, unlike the CSA, exempted small farming operations; (2) *Wickard* involved a "quintessential economic activity"—a commercial farm—whereas respondents do not sell marijuana; and (3) the *Wickard* record made it clear that the aggregate production of wheat for use on farms had a significant impact on market prices. Those differences, though factually accurate, do not diminish the precedential force of this Court's reasoning.

The fact that Filburn's own impact on the market was "trivial by itself" was not a sufficient reason for removing him from the scope of federal regulation. That the Secretary of Agriculture elected to exempt even smaller farms from regulation does not speak to his power to regulate all those whose aggregated production was significant, nor did that fact play any role in the Court's analysis. Moreover, even though Filburn was indeed a commercial farmer, the activity he was engaged in—the cultivation of wheat for home consumption—was not treated by the Court as part of his commercial farming operation. And while it is true that the record in the *Wickard* case itself established the causal connection between the production for local use and the national market, we have before us findings by Congress to the same effect. . . .

In assessing the scope of Congress' authority under the Commerce Clause, we stress that the task before us is a modest one. We need not determine whether respondents' activities, taken in the aggregate, substantially affect interstate commerce in fact, but only whether a "rational basis" exists for so concluding. Given the enforcement difficulties that attend distinguishing between marijuana cultivated locally and marijuana grown elsewhere, and concerns about diversion into illicit channels, we have no difficulty concluding that Congress had a rational basis for believing that failure to regulate the intrastate manufacture and possession of marijuana would leave a gaping hole in the CSA. Thus, as in *Wickard,* when it enacted comprehensive legislation to regulate the interstate market in a fungible commodity, Congress was acting well within its authority to "make all Laws which shall be necessary and proper" to "regulate Commerce . . . among the several States." U.S. Const., Art. I, § 8. That the regulation ensnares some purely intrastate activity is of no moment. As we have done many times before, we refuse to excise individual components of that larger scheme.

IV

To support their contrary submission, respondents rely heavily on two of our more recent Commerce Clause cases. . . .

Unlike those at issue in *Lopez* and *United States v. Morrison,* 529 U.S. 598 (2000), the activities regulated by the CSA are quintessentially economic. "Economics" refers to "the production, distribution, and consumption of commodities." Webster's Third New International Dictionary 720 (1966). The CSA is a statute that regulates the production, distribution, and consumption of commodities for which there is an established, and lucrative, interstate market. . . .

The Court of Appeals was able to conclude otherwise only by isolating a "separate and distinct" class of activities that it held to be beyond the reach of federal power, defined as "the intrastate, noncommercial cultivation, possession and use of marijuana for personal medical purposes on the advice of a physician and in accordance with state law." The court characterized this class as "different in kind from drug trafficking." The differences between the members of a class so defined and the principal traffickers in Schedule I substances might be sufficient to justify a policy decision exempting the narrower class from the coverage of the CSA. The question, however, is whether Congress' contrary policy judgment, *i.e.,* its decision to include this narrower "class of activities" within the larger regulatory scheme, was constitutionally deficient. We have no difficulty concluding that Congress acted rationally in determining that none of the characteristics making up the purported class, whether viewed individually or in the aggregate, compelled an exemption from the CSA; rather, the subdivided class of activities defined by the Court of Appeals was an essential part of the larger regulatory scheme. . . .

[First,] if, as the principal dissent contends, the personal cultivation, possession, and use of marijuana for medicinal purposes is beyond the " 'outer limits' of Congress'

Commerce Clause authority," it must also be true that such personal use of marijuana (or any other homegrown drug) for recreational purposes is also beyond those " 'outer limits,' " whether or not a State elects to authorize or even regulate such use. . . .

Second, limiting the activity to marijuana possession and cultivation "in accordance with state law" cannot serve to place respondents' activities beyond congressional reach. The Supremacy Clause unambiguously provides that if there is any conflict between federal and state law, federal law shall prevail. . . . Just as state acquiescence to federal regulation cannot expand the bounds of the Commerce Clause, see, e.g., *Morrison*, at 661–662, so too state action cannot circumscribe Congress' plenary commerce power. See *United States v. Darby*, 312 U.S. 100, 114 (1941) ("That power can neither be enlarged nor diminished by the exercise or non-exercise of state power").[38] . . .

V

Respondents also raise a substantive due process claim and seek to avail themselves of the medical necessity defense. These theories of relief were set forth in their complaint but were not reached by the Court of Appeals. We therefore do not address the question whether judicial relief is available to respondents on these alternative bases. We do note, however, the presence of another avenue of relief. As the Solicitor General confirmed during oral argument, the statute authorizes procedures for the reclassification of Schedule I drugs. But perhaps even more important than these legal avenues is the democratic process, in which the voices of voters allied with these respondents may one day be heard in the halls of Congress. Under the present state of the law, however, the judgment of the Court of Appeals must be vacated. . . .

■ JUSTICE SCALIA, concurring in the judgment.

I agree with the Court's holding that the Controlled Substances Act (CSA) may validly be applied to respondents' cultivation, distribution, and possession of marijuana for personal, medicinal use. I write separately because my understanding of the doctrinal foundation on which that holding rests is, if not inconsistent with that of the Court, at least more nuanced.

Since *Perez*, our cases have mechanically recited that the Commerce Clause permits congressional regulation of three categories: (1) the channels of interstate commerce; (2) the instrumentalities of interstate commerce, and persons or things in interstate commerce; and (3) activities that "substantially affect" interstate commerce. The first two categories are self-evident, since they are the ingredients of interstate commerce itself. See *Gibbons v. Ogden,* 22 U.S. (9 Wheat.) 1, 189–190

---

[38] That is so even if California's current controls (enacted eight years after the Compassionate Use Act was passed) are "effective," as the dissenters would have us blindly presume. California's decision (made 34 years after the CSA was enacted) to impose "stric[t] controls" on the "cultivation and possession of marijuana for medical purposes," cannot retroactively divest Congress of its authority under the Commerce Clause. . . .

Moreover, in addition to casting aside more than a century of this Court's Commerce Clause jurisprudence, it is noteworthy that JUSTICE THOMAS' suggestion that States possess the power to dictate the extent of Congress' commerce power would have far-reaching implications beyond the facts of this case. For example, under his reasoning, Congress would be equally powerless to regulate, let alone prohibit, the intrastate possession, cultivation, and use of marijuana for recreational purposes, an activity which all States "strictly contro[l]." . . .

(1824). The third category, however, is different in kind, and its recitation without explanation is misleading and incomplete.

It is *misleading* because, unlike the channels, instrumentalities, and agents of interstate commerce, activities that substantially affect interstate commerce are not themselves part of interstate commerce, and thus the power to regulate them cannot come from the Commerce Clause alone. Rather, as this Court has acknowledged since at least *United States v. Coombs,* 37 U.S. (12 Pet.) 72 (1838), Congress's regulatory authority over intrastate activities that are not themselves part of interstate commerce (including activities that have a substantial effect on interstate commerce) derives from the Necessary and Proper Clause. And the category of "activities that substantially affect interstate commerce," *Lopez,* at 559, is *incomplete* because the authority to enact laws necessary and proper for the regulation of interstate commerce is not limited to laws governing intrastate activities that substantially affect interstate commerce. Where necessary to make a regulation of interstate commerce effective, Congress may regulate even those intrastate activities that do not themselves substantially affect interstate commerce.

I

Our cases show that the regulation of intrastate activities may be necessary to and proper for the regulation of interstate commerce in two general circumstances. Most directly, the commerce power permits Congress not only to devise rules for the governance of commerce between States but also to facilitate interstate commerce by eliminating potential obstructions, and to restrict it by eliminating potential stimulants. See *NLRB v. Jones & Laughlin Steel Corp.,* 301 U.S. 1, 36–37 (1937). That is why the Court has repeatedly sustained congressional legislation on the ground that the regulated activities had a substantial effect on interstate commerce. . . .

This principle is not without limitation. In *Lopez* and *Morrison,* the Court—conscious of the potential of the "substantially affects" test to " 'obliterate the distinction between what is national and what is local' "—rejected the argument that Congress may regulate *noneconomic* activity based solely on the effect that it may have on interstate commerce through a remote chain of inferences. "[I]f we were to accept [such] arguments," the Court reasoned in *Lopez,* "we are hard pressed to posit any activity by an individual that Congress is without power to regulate." Thus, although Congress's authority to regulate intrastate activity that substantially affects interstate commerce is broad, it does not permit the Court to "pile inference upon inference," in order to establish that noneconomic activity has a substantial effect on interstate commerce.

As we implicitly acknowledged in *Lopez,* however, Congress's authority to enact laws necessary and proper for the regulation of interstate commerce is not limited to laws directed against economic activities that have a substantial effect on interstate commerce. Though the conduct in *Lopez* was not economic, the Court nevertheless recognized that it could be regulated as "an essential part of a larger regulation of economic activity, in which the regulatory scheme could be undercut unless the intrastate activity were regulated." This statement referred to those cases permitting the regulation of intrastate activities "which in a substantial way interfere with or obstruct the exercise of the granted power." As the Court put it in *United States v. Wrightwood Dairy Co.,* 315 U.S. 110, 118–119 (1942), where Congress has the authority to enact a regulation of interstate commerce, "it possesses every power needed to make that regulation effective."

Although this power "to make . . . regulation effective" commonly overlaps with the authority to regulate economic activities that substantially affect interstate commerce,[2] and may in some cases have been confused with that authority, the two are distinct. The regulation of an intrastate activity may be essential to a comprehensive regulation of interstate commerce even though the intrastate activity does not itself "substantially affect" interstate commerce. Moreover, as the passage from *Lopez* quoted above suggests, Congress may regulate even noneconomic local activity if that regulation is a necessary part of a more general regulation of interstate commerce. The relevant question is simply whether the means chosen are "reasonably adapted" to the attainment of a legitimate end under the commerce power. . . .

II

Today's principal dissent objects that, by permitting Congress to regulate activities necessary to effective interstate regulation, the Court reduces *Lopez* and *Morrison* to "little more than a drafting guide." I think that criticism unjustified. Unlike the power to regulate activities that have a substantial effect on interstate commerce, the power to enact laws enabling effective regulation of interstate commerce can only be exercised in conjunction with congressional regulation of an interstate market, and it extends only to those measures necessary to make the interstate regulation effective. As *Lopez* itself states, and the Court affirms today, Congress may regulate noneconomic intrastate activities only where the failure to do so "could . . . undercut" its regulation of interstate commerce. This is not a power that threatens to obliterate the line between "what is truly national and what is truly local." . . .

And there are other restraints upon the Necessary and Proper Clause authority. As Chief Justice Marshall wrote in *McCulloch v. Maryland,* 17 U.S. (4 Wheat.) 316 (1819), even when the end is constitutional and legitimate, the means must be "appropriate" and "plainly adapted" to that end. Moreover, they may not be otherwise "prohibited" and must be "consistent with the letter and spirit of the constitution." These phrases are not merely hortatory. For example, cases such as *Printz v. United States,* 521 U.S. 898 (1997) . . . affirm that a law is not " '*proper* for carrying into Execution the Commerce Clause' " "[w]hen [it] violates [a constitutional] principle of state sovereignty."

III

The application of these principles to the case before us is straightforward. In the CSA, Congress has undertaken to extinguish the interstate market in Schedule I controlled substances, including marijuana. The Commerce Clause unquestionably permits this. . . . That simple possession is a noneconomic activity is immaterial to whether it can be prohibited as a necessary part of a larger regulation. Rather, Congress's authority to enact all of these prohibitions of intrastate controlled-substance activities depends only upon whether they are appropriate means of

---

[2]   *Wickard* presented such a case. . . . [The] potential disruption of Congress's interstate regulation, and not only the effect that personal consumption of wheat had on interstate commerce, justified Congress's regulation of that conduct.

achieving the legitimate end of eradicating Schedule I substances from interstate commerce. . . .

By this measure, I think the regulation must be sustained. Not only is it impossible to distinguish "controlled substances manufactured and distributed intrastate" from "controlled substances manufactured and distributed interstate," but it hardly makes sense to speak in such terms. Drugs like marijuana are fungible commodities. As the Court explains, marijuana that is grown at home and possessed for personal use is never more than an instant from the interstate market—and this is so whether or not the possession is for medicinal use or lawful use under the laws of a particular State. . . .

■ JUSTICE O'CONNOR, with whom THE CHIEF JUSTICE and JUSTICE THOMAS join as to all but Part III, dissenting.

We enforce the "outer limits" of Congress' Commerce Clause authority not for their own sake, but to protect historic spheres of state sovereignty from excessive federal encroachment and thereby to maintain the distribution of power fundamental to our federalist system of government. One of federalism's chief virtues, of course, is that it promotes innovation by allowing for the possibility that "a single courageous State may, if its citizens choose, serve as a laboratory; and try novel social and economic experiments without risk to the rest of the country." *New State Ice Co. v. Liebmann*, 285 U.S. 262, 311 (1932) (Brandeis, J., dissenting).

This case exemplifies the role of States as laboratories. The States' core police powers have always included authority to define criminal law and to protect the health, safety, and welfare of their citizens. Exercising those powers, California (by ballot initiative and then by legislative codification) has come to its own conclusion about the difficult and sensitive question of whether marijuana should be available to relieve severe pain and suffering. . . .

The Court's decision rests on two facts about the CSA: (1) Congress chose to enact a single statute providing a comprehensive prohibition on the production, distribution, and possession of all controlled substances, and (2) Congress did not distinguish between various forms of intrastate noncommercial cultivation, possession, and use of marijuana. Today's decision suggests that the federal regulation of local activity is immune to Commerce Clause challenge because Congress chose to act with an ambitious, all-encompassing statute, rather than piecemeal. In my view, allowing Congress to set the terms of the constitutional debate in this way, *i.e.*, by packaging regulation of local activity in broader schemes, is tantamount to removing meaningful limits on the Commerce Clause. . . .

If the Court is right, then *Lopez* stands for nothing more than a drafting guide: Congress should have described the relevant crime as "transfer or possession of a firearm anywhere in the nation"—thus including commercial and noncommercial activity, and clearly encompassing some activity with assuredly substantial effect on interstate commerce. Had it done so, the majority hints, we would have sustained its authority to regulate possession of firearms in school zones. . . .

I agree with the Court that we must look beyond respondents' own activities. Otherwise, individual litigants could always exempt themselves from Commerce Clause regulation merely by pointing to the obvious—that their personal activities do not have a substantial effect on interstate commerce. The task is to identify a mode of analysis that allows Congress to regulate more than nothing (by declining to reduce each case to its litigants) and less than everything (by declining to let Congress set the terms of analysis). . . .

A number of objective markers are available to confine the scope of constitutional review here. Both federal and state legislation—including the CSA itself, the California Compassionate Use Act, and other state medical marijuana legislation—recognize that medical and nonmedical (*i.e.*, recreational) uses of drugs are realistically distinct and can be segregated, and regulate them differently. . . . To ascertain whether Congress' encroachment is constitutionally justified in this case, then, I would focus here on the personal cultivation, possession, and use of marijuana for medicinal purposes.

Having thus defined the relevant conduct, we must determine whether, under our precedents, the conduct is economic and, in the aggregate, substantially affects interstate commerce. Even if intrastate cultivation and possession of marijuana for one's own medicinal use can properly be characterized as economic, and I question whether it can, it has not been shown that such activity substantially affects interstate commerce. Similarly, it is neither self-evident nor demonstrated that regulating such activity is necessary to the interstate drug control scheme.

The Court's definition of economic activity is breathtaking. It defines as economic any activity involving the production, distribution, and consumption of commodities. . . . It will not do to say that Congress may regulate noncommercial activity simply because it may have an effect on the demand for commercial goods, or because the noncommercial endeavor can, in some sense, substitute for commercial activity. Most commercial goods or services have some sort of privately producible analogue. Home care substitutes for daycare. Charades games substitute for movie tickets. Backyard or windowsill gardening substitutes for going to the supermarket. To draw the line wherever private activity affects the demand for market goods is to draw no line at all, and to declare everything economic. We have already rejected the result that would follow—a federal police power. . . . [And] *Lopez* makes clear that possession is not itself commercial activity. . . .

Even assuming that economic activity is at issue in this case, the Government has made no showing in fact that the possession and use of homegrown marijuana for medical purposes, in California or elsewhere, has a substantial effect on interstate commerce. Similarly, the Government has not shown that regulating such activity is necessary to an interstate regulatory scheme. Whatever the specific theory of "substantial effects" at issue (*i.e.*, whether the activity substantially affects interstate commerce, whether its regulation is necessary to an interstate regulatory scheme, or both), a concern for dual sovereignty requires that Congress' excursion into the traditional domain of States be justified.

That is why characterizing this as a case about the Necessary and Proper Clause does not change the analysis significantly. Congress must exercise its authority under the Necessary and Proper Clause in a manner consistent with basic constitutional principles. . . .

There is simply no evidence that homegrown medicinal marijuana users constitute, in the aggregate, a sizable enough class to have a discernable, let alone substantial, impact on the national illicit drug market—or otherwise to threaten the CSA regime. . . . In this regard, again, this case is readily distinguishable from

Wickard. . . . [T]he Court was able to consider "actual effects" because the parties had "stipulated a summary of the economics of the wheat industry." . . .

[T]he CSA's introductory declarations are too vague and unspecific to demonstrate that the federal statutory scheme will be undermined if Congress cannot exert power over individuals like respondents. The declarations are not even specific to marijuana. (Facts about substantial effects may be developed in litigation to compensate for the inadequacy of Congress' findings; in part because this case comes to us from the grant of a preliminary injunction, there has been no such development.) . . .

The Government has not overcome empirical doubt that the number of Californians engaged in personal cultivation, possession, and use of medical marijuana, or the amount of marijuana they produce, is enough to threaten the federal regime. Nor has it shown that Compassionate Use Act marijuana users have been or are realistically likely to be responsible for the drug's seeping into the market in a significant way. The Government does cite one estimate that there were over 100,000 Compassionate Use Act users in California in 2004, but does not explain, in terms of proportions, what their presence means for the national illicit drug market. It also provides anecdotal evidence about the CSA's enforcement. . . . Piling assertion upon assertion does not, in my view, satisfy the substantiality test of *Lopez* and *Morrison.* . . .

■ JUSTICE THOMAS, dissenting.

Respondents Diane Monson and Angel Raich use marijuana that has never been bought or sold, that has never crossed state lines, and that has had no demonstrable effect on the national market for marijuana. If Congress can regulate this under the Commerce Clause, then it can regulate virtually anything—and the Federal Government is no longer one of limited and enumerated powers. . . .

[T]he Commerce Clause empowers Congress to regulate the buying and selling of goods and services trafficked across state lines. The Clause's text, structure, and history all indicate that, at the time of the founding, the term " 'commerce' consisted of selling, buying, and bartering, as well as transporting for these purposes." Commerce, or trade, stood in contrast to productive activities like manufacturing and agriculture. . . .

On this traditional understanding of "commerce," the CSA regulates a great deal of marijuana trafficking that is interstate and commercial in character. The CSA does not, however, criminalize only the interstate buying and selling of marijuana. Instead, it bans the entire market—intrastate or interstate, noncommercial or commercial—for marijuana. Respondents are correct that the CSA exceeds Congress' commerce power as applied to their conduct, which is purely intrastate and noncommercial.

More difficult, however, is whether the CSA is a valid exercise of Congress' power to enact laws that are "necessary and proper for carrying into Execution" its power to regulate interstate commerce. Art. I, § 8, cl. 18. The Necessary and Proper Clause is not a warrant to Congress to enact any law that bears some conceivable connection to the exercise of an enumerated power. Nor is it, however, a command to Congress to enact only laws that are absolutely indispensable to the exercise of an enumerated power. . . .

Congress has exercised its power over interstate commerce to criminalize trafficking in marijuana across state lines. The Government contends that banning Monson and Raich's intrastate drug activity is "necessary and proper for carrying into Execution" its regulation of interstate drug trafficking. However, in order to be "necessary," the intrastate ban must be more than "a reasonable means [of] effectuat[ing] the regulation of interstate commerce." Brief for Petitioners 14. It must be "plainly adapted" to regulating interstate marijuana trafficking—in other words, there must be an "obvious, simple, and direct relation" between the intrastate ban and the regulation of interstate commerce.

On its face, a ban on the intrastate cultivation, possession and distribution of marijuana may be plainly adapted to stopping the interstate flow of marijuana. Unregulated local growers and users could swell both the supply and the demand sides of the interstate marijuana market, making the market more difficult to regulate. But respondents do not challenge the CSA on its face. Instead, they challenge it as applied to their conduct. The question is thus whether the intrastate ban is "necessary and proper" as applied to medical marijuana users like respondents.

Respondents are not regulable simply because they belong to a large class (local growers and users of marijuana) that Congress might need to reach, if they also belong to a distinct and separable subclass (local growers and users of state-authorized, medical marijuana) that does not undermine the CSA's interstate ban. The Court of Appeals found that respondents' "limited use is distinct from the broader illicit drug market," because "th[eir] medicinal marijuana . . . is not intended for, nor does it enter, the stream of commerce." If that is generally true of individuals who grow and use marijuana for medical purposes under state law, then even assuming Congress has "obvious" and "plain" reasons why regulating intrastate cultivation and possession is necessary to regulating the interstate drug trade, none of those reasons applies to medical marijuana patients like Monson and Raich. . . .

California's Compassionate Use Act sets respondents' conduct apart from other intrastate producers and users of marijuana. . . . This class of intrastate users is therefore distinguishable from others. . . .

These controls belie the Government's assertion that placing medical marijuana outside the CSA's reach "would prevent effective enforcement of the interstate ban on drug trafficking." Enforcement of the CSA can continue as it did prior to the Compassionate Use Act. Only now, a qualified patient could avoid arrest or prosecution by presenting his identification card to law enforcement officers. In the event that a qualified patient is arrested for possession or his cannabis is seized, he could seek to prove as an affirmative defense that, in conformity with state law, he possessed or cultivated small quantities of marijuana intrastate solely for personal medical use. . . . No one argues that permitting use of these drugs under medical supervision has undermined the CSA's restrictions. . . .

In sum, neither in enacting the CSA nor in defending its application to respondents has the Government offered any obvious reason why banning medical marijuana use is necessary to stem the tide of interstate drug trafficking. Congress' goal of curtailing the interstate drug trade would not plainly be thwarted if it could not apply the CSA to patients like Monson and Raich. That is, unless Congress' aim is really to exercise police power of the sort reserved to the States in order to eliminate even the intrastate possession and use of marijuana.

Even assuming the CSA's ban on locally cultivated and consumed marijuana is "necessary," that does not mean it is also "proper." The means selected by Congress to regulate interstate commerce cannot be "prohibited" by, or inconsistent with the "letter and spirit" of, the Constitution. *McCulloch,* at 421. . . .

Even if Congress may regulate purely intrastate activity when essential to exercising some enumerated power, Congress may not use its incidental authority to subvert basic principles of federalism and dual sovereignty.

Here, Congress has encroached on States' traditional police powers to define the criminal law and to protect the health, safety, and welfare of their citizens. Further, the Government's rationale—that it may regulate the production or possession of any commodity for which there is an interstate market—threatens to remove the remaining vestiges of States' traditional police powers. This would convert the Necessary and Proper Clause into precisely what Chief Justice Marshall did not envision, a "pretext . . . for the accomplishment of objects not intrusted to the government." *McCulloch,* at 423. . . .

NOTES

1. Is *Raich* a Commerce Clause case or a Necessary and Proper Clause case? Does it matter?

2. Is *Raich* easy or hard? Is it an easy case because the Necessary and Proper Clause allows Congress to make regulations that are appropriate for its regulations of interstate commerce? Or should it have been an easy case for the other side because it raises the same concern as *Lopez*: if this can happen, there is no limit? Or is it a harder case, because the Court's precedents clearly give one answer, while the framers' attempt to strike a balance between national and state power points to a different answer?

3. If the majority is right, can Congress legislate on anything, no matter how local, as long as its scheme of regulation is very broad? Are some federal statutes too big to fail? But if the dissenters are right, does every federal statute become a patchwork, with individual exemptions for wholly in-state conduct? What about farmers who sell only in-state and want out of federal food-safety laws? Or hobbyist pilots who want to fly helicopters only in their home state, without complying with federal aviation regulations? Is it possible to have a system of federal regulation that is limited *and* uniform?

4. Should it be of any relevance that medical marijuana was allowed—and indeed, regulated and controlled—by state law? Does the Supremacy Clause imply that the answer is "no"? How, exactly, would the dissents make state law relevant?

United States v. Comstock

560 U.S. 126 (2010)

■ JUSTICE BREYER delivered the opinion of the Court.

    . . .

I

The federal statute before us allows a district court to order the civil commitment of an individual who is currently "in the custody of the [Federal] Bureau of Prisons," if that individual (1) has previously "engaged or attempted to engage in sexually violent conduct or child molestation," (2) currently "suffers from a serious mental illness, abnormality, or disorder," and (3) "as a result of" that mental illness, abnormality, or disorder is "sexually dangerous to others," in that "he would have serious difficulty in refraining from sexually violent conduct or child molestation if released."

In order to detain such a person, the Government (acting through the Department of Justice) must certify to a federal district judge that the prisoner meets the conditions just described. . . . When such a certification is filed, the statute automatically stays the individual's release from prison, thereby giving the Government an opportunity to prove its claims at a hearing through psychiatric (or other) evidence. The statute provides that the prisoner "shall be represented by counsel" and shall have "an opportunity" at the hearing "to testify, to present evidence, to subpoena witnesses on his behalf, and to confront and cross-examine" the Government's witnesses.

If the Government proves its claims by "clear and convincing evidence," the court will order the prisoner's continued commitment in "the custody of the Attorney General," who must "make all reasonable efforts to cause" the State where that person was tried, or the State where he is domiciled, to "assume responsibility for his custody, care, and treatment." If either State is willing to assume that responsibility, the Attorney General "shall release" the individual "to the appropriate official" of that State. But if, "notwithstanding such efforts, neither such State will assume such responsibility," then "the Attorney General shall place the person for treatment in a suitable [federal] facility."

Confinement in the federal facility will last until either (1) the person's mental condition improves to the point where he is no longer dangerous (with or without appropriate ongoing treatment), in which case he will be released; or (2) a State assumes responsibility for his custody, care, and treatment. . . .

[Three of the] five respondents in this case . . . had previously pleaded guilty in federal court to possession of child pornography, the fourth had pleaded guilty to sexual abuse of a minor, . . . [and] the fifth . . . had been charged in federal court with aggravated sexual abuse of a minor, but was found mentally incompetent to stand trial.

Each of the five respondents moved to dismiss the civil-commitment proceeding on constitutional grounds. *[They invoked the Double Jeopardy Clause, the Ex Post Facto Clause, the Sixth and Eighth Amendments, the Equal Protection Clause, and the Due Process Clause.—Editors]* . . . And, finally, they claimed that, in enacting the statute, Congress exceeded the powers granted to it by Art. I, § 8 of the Constitution, including those granted by the Commerce Clause and the Necessary and Proper Clause. . . .

II

The question presented is whether the Necessary and Proper Clause, Art. I, § 8, cl. 18, grants Congress authority sufficient to enact the statute before us. In resolving that question, we assume, but we do not decide, that other provisions of the Constitution—such as the Due Process Clause—do not prohibit civil commitment in these circumstances. In other words, we assume for argument's sake that the Federal Constitution would permit a State to enact this statute, and we ask solely whether the Federal Government, exercising its enumerated powers, may enact such a statute as well. On that assumption, we conclude that the Constitution grants Congress legislative power sufficient to enact § 4248. We base this conclusion on five considerations, taken together.

First, the Necessary and Proper Clause grants Congress broad authority to enact federal legislation. Nearly 200 years ago, this Court stated that the Federal "[G]overnment is acknowledged by all to be one of enumerated powers," *McCulloch v. Maryland,* 17 U.S. (4 Wheat.) 316, 405 (1819), which means that "[e]very law enacted by Congress must be based on one or more of" those powers, *United States v. Morrison,* 529 U.S. 598, 607 (2000). But, at the same time, "a government, entrusted with such" powers "must also be entrusted with ample means for their execution." *McCulloch,* at 408. Accordingly, the Necessary and Proper Clause makes clear that the Constitution's grants of specific federal legislative authority are accompanied by broad power to enact laws that are "convenient, or useful" or "conducive" to the authority's "beneficial exercise." *Id.,* at 413, 418. Chief Justice Marshall emphasized that the word "necessary" does not mean "absolutely necessary." In language that has come to define the scope of the Necessary and Proper Clause, he wrote:

> "Let the end be legitimate, let it be within the scope of the constitution, and all means which are appropriate, which are plainly adapted to that end, which are not prohibited, but consist with the letter and spirit of the constitution, are constitutional."

We have since made clear that, in determining whether the Necessary and Proper Clause grants Congress the legislative authority to enact a particular federal statute, we look to see whether the statute constitutes a means that is rationally related to the implementation of a constitutionally enumerated power.

Of course, as Chief Justice Marshall stated, a federal statute, in addition to being authorized by Art. I, § 8, must also "not [be] prohibited" by the Constitution. *McCulloch,* at 421. But as we have already stated, the present statute's validity under provisions of the Constitution other than the Necessary and Proper Clause is an issue that is not before us. Under the question presented, the relevant inquiry is simply "whether the means chosen are 'reasonably adapted' to the attainment of a legitimate end under the commerce power" or under other powers that the Constitution grants Congress the authority to implement. *Gonzales v. Raich,* 545 U.S. 1, 37 (2005) (SCALIA, J., concurring in judgment) (quoting *United States v. Darby,* 312 U.S. 100, 121 (1941)).

We have also recognized that the Constitution "addresse[s]" the "choice of means"

> "primarily . . . to the judgment of Congress. If it can be seen that the means adopted are really calculated to attain the end, the degree of their necessity, the extent to which they conduce to the end, the closeness of the relationship between the means adopted and the end to be attained, are matters for congressional determination alone." *Burroughs v. United States,* 290 U.S. 534, 547–548 (1934).

Thus, the Constitution, which nowhere speaks explicitly about the creation of federal crimes beyond those related to "counterfeiting," "treason," or "Piracies and Felonies committed on the high Seas" or "against the Law of Nations," Art. I, § 8, cls.

6, 10; Art. III, § 3, nonetheless grants Congress broad authority to create such crimes. See *McCulloch,* at 416 ("All admit that the government may, legitimately, punish any violation of its laws; and yet, this is not among the enumerated powers of Congress"); see also *United States v. Fox,* 95 U.S. 670, 672 (1878). And Congress routinely exercises its authority to enact criminal laws in furtherance of, for example, its enumerated powers to regulate interstate and foreign commerce, to enforce civil rights, to spend funds for the general welfare, to establish federal courts, to establish post offices, to regulate bankruptcy, to regulate naturalization, and so forth. Art. I, § 8, cls. 1, 3, 4, 7, 9; Amdts. 13–15. *[Here the Court cited statutes defining postal crimes, bankruptcy crimes, and immigration crimes; and cases upholding criminal prohibitions enacted in furtherance of the Commerce Clause, the spending power, the Fourteenth and Fifteenth Amendments, and the power to constitute federal tribunals.—Editors]*

Similarly, Congress, in order to help ensure the enforcement of federal criminal laws enacted in furtherance of its enumerated powers, "can cause a prison to be erected at any place within the jurisdiction of the United States, and direct that all persons sentenced to imprisonment under the laws of the United States shall be confined there." *Ex parte Karstendick*, 93 U.S. 396, 400 (1876). Moreover, Congress, having established a prison system, can enact laws that seek to ensure that system's safe and responsible administration by, for example, requiring prisoners to receive medical care and educational training, and can also ensure the safety of the prisoners, prison workers and visitors, and those in surrounding communities by, for example, creating further criminal laws governing entry, exit, and smuggling, and by employing prison guards to ensure discipline and security.

Neither Congress' power to criminalize conduct, nor its power to imprison individuals who engage in that conduct, nor its power to enact laws governing prisons and prisoners, is explicitly mentioned in the Constitution. But Congress nonetheless possesses broad authority to do each of those things in the course of "carrying into Execution" the enumerated powers "vested by" the "Constitution in the Government of the United States," Art. I, § 8, cl. 18—authority granted by the Necessary and Proper Clause.

Second, the civil-commitment statute before us constitutes a modest addition to a set of federal prison-related mental-health statutes that have existed for many decades. We recognize that even a longstanding history of related federal action does not demonstrate a statute's constitutionality. See, *e.g., Walz v. Tax Comm'n of City of New York,* 397 U.S. 664, 678 (1970) ("[N]o one acquires a vested or protected right in violation of the Constitution by long use . . . "). A history of involvement, however, can nonetheless be "helpful in reviewing the substance of a congressional statutory scheme," *Gonzales,* at 21, and, in particular, the reasonableness of the relation between the new statute and pre-existing federal interests.

Here, Congress has long been involved in the delivery of mental health care to federal prisoners, and has long provided for their civil commitment. In 1855 it established Saint Elizabeth's Hospital in the District of Columbia to provide treatment to "the insane of the army and navy . . . and of the District of Columbia." Act of Mar. 3, 1855, 10 Stat. 682; 39 Stat. 309. . . . [Over the next] three decades, Congress created a national, federal civil-commitment program under which any person who was either charged with or convicted of any federal offense in any federal court could be confined in a federal mental institution.

These statutes did not raise the question presented here, for they all provided that commitment in a federal hospital would end upon the completion of the relevant "terms" of federal "imprisonment" as set forth in the underlying criminal sentence or statute. . . .

[In the late 1940s Congress provided] for the civil commitment of individuals who are, or who become, mentally incompetent at any time after their arrest and before the expiration of their federal sentence. . . .

In 2006, Congress enacted the particular statute before us. 18 U.S.C. § 4248. It differs from earlier statutes in that it focuses directly upon persons who, due to a mental illness, are sexually dangerous. Notably, many of these individuals were likely already subject to civil commitment under § 4246, which, since 1949, has authorized the postsentence detention of federal prisoners who suffer from a mental illness and who are thereby dangerous (whether sexually or otherwise). Aside from its specific focus on sexually dangerous persons, § 4248 is similar to the provisions first enacted in 1949. In that respect, it is a modest addition to a longstanding federal statutory framework, which has been in place since 1855.

Third, Congress reasonably extended its longstanding civil-commitment system to cover mentally ill and sexually dangerous persons who are already in federal custody, even if doing so detains them beyond the termination of their criminal sentence. For one thing, the Federal Government is the custodian of its prisoners. As federal custodian, it has the constitutional power to act in order to protect nearby (and other) communities from the danger federal prisoners may pose. . . . If a federal prisoner is infected with a communicable disease that threatens others, surely it would be "necessary and proper" for the Federal Government to take action, pursuant to its role as federal custodian, to refuse (at least until the threat diminishes) to release that individual among the general public, where he might infect others (even if not threatening an interstate epidemic, cf. Art. I, § 8, cl. 3). And if confinement of such an individual is a "necessary and proper" thing to do, then how could it not be similarly "necessary and proper" to confine an individual whose mental illness threatens others to the same degree?

Moreover, § 4248 is "reasonably adapted," *Darby,* at 121, to Congress' power to act as a responsible federal custodian (a power that rests, in turn, upon federal criminal statutes that legitimately seek to implement constitutionally enumerated authority). Congress could have reasonably concluded that federal inmates who suffer from a mental illness that causes them to "have serious difficulty in refraining from sexually violent conduct," § 4247(a)(6), would pose an especially high danger to the public if released. And Congress could also have reasonably concluded (as detailed in the Judicial Conference's report) that a reasonable number of such individuals would likely *not* be detained by the States if released from federal custody, in part because the Federal Government itself severed their claim to "legal residence in any State" by incarcerating them in remote federal prisons. . . .

Fourth, the statute properly accounts for state interests. Respondents and the dissent contend that § 4248 violates the Tenth Amendment because it "invades the province of state sovereignty" in an area typically left to state control. *New York v. United States,* 505 U.S. 144, 155 (1992). See also *Jackson v. Indiana,* 406 U.S. 715, 736 (1972) ("The States have traditionally exercised broad power to commit persons found to be mentally ill"). But the Tenth Amendment's text is clear: "The powers *not delegated to the United States* by the Constitution, nor prohibited by it to the States, are reserved to the States respectively, or to the people." (Emphasis added.) The powers "delegated to the United States by the Constitution" include those specifically enumerated powers listed in Article I along with the implementation authority granted by the Necessary and Proper Clause. Virtually by definition, these powers are not powers that the Constitution "reserved to the States."

Nor does this statute invade state sovereignty or otherwise improperly limit the scope of "powers that remain with the States." *Post* (THOMAS, J., dissenting). To the contrary, it requires *accommodation* of state interests: The Attorney General must inform the State in which the federal prisoner "is domiciled or was tried" that he is detaining someone with respect to whom those States may wish to assert their authority, and he must encourage those States to assume custody of the individual. § 4248(d). . . .

Fifth, the links between § 4248 and an enumerated Article I power are not too attenuated. Neither is the statutory provision too sweeping in its scope. Invoking the cautionary instruction that we may not "pile inference upon inference" in order to sustain congressional action under Article I, *United States v. Lopez,* 514 U.S. 549, 567 (1995), respondents argue that, when legislating pursuant to the Necessary and Proper Clause, Congress' authority can be no more than one step removed from a specifically enumerated power. But this argument is irreconcilable with our precedents. [T]ake *Greenwood v. United States,* 350 U.S. 366 (1956), as an example. In that case we upheld the (likely indefinite) civil commitment of a mentally incompetent federal defendant who was accused of robbing a United States Post Office. The underlying enumerated Article I power was the power to "Establish Post Offices and Post Roads." Art. I, § 8, cl. 7. But, as Chief Justice Marshall recognized in *McCulloch,*

> "the power 'to establish post offices and post roads' . . . is executed by the single act of *making* the establishment. . . . [F]rom this has been inferred the power and duty of *carrying* the mail along the post road, from one post office to another. And, from this *implied* power, has *again* been inferred the right to *punish* those who steal letters from the post office, or rob the mail." (emphasis added).

And, as we have explained, from the implied power to punish we have *further* inferred both the power to imprison and, in *Greenwood,* the federal civil-commitment power.

Our necessary and proper jurisprudence contains multiple examples of similar reasoning. . . .

Indeed even the dissent acknowledges that Congress has the implied power to criminalize any conduct that might interfere with the exercise of an enumerated power, and also the additional power to imprison people who violate those (inferentially authorized) laws, and the additional power to provide for the safe and reasonable management of those prisons, and the additional power to regulate the prisoners' behavior even after their release. Of course, each of those powers, like the power[ ] addressed in *McCulloch,* is ultimately "derived from" an enumerated power. And, as the dissent agrees, that enumerated power is "the enumerated power that justifies the defendant's statute of conviction." Neither we nor the dissent can point to a single specific enumerated power "that justifies a criminal defendant's arrest or conviction" in *all* cases because Congress relies on different enumerated powers (often, but not exclusively, its Commerce Clause power) to enact its various federal criminal statutes. But every such statute must itself be legitimately predicated on an enumerated power. And the same enumerated power that justifies the creation of a federal criminal statute, and that justifies the additional implied federal powers that the dissent considers legitimate, justifies civil commitment under § 4248 as well. Thus, we must reject respondents' argument that the Necessary and Proper Clause permits no more than a single step between an enumerated power and an Act of Congress.

Nor need we fear that our holding today confers on Congress a general "police power, which the Founders denied the National Government and reposed in the States." *Morrison,* at 618. As the Solicitor General repeatedly confirmed at oral argument, § 4248 is narrow in scope. It has been applied to only a small fraction of federal prisoners. See Tr. of Oral Arg. 24–25 (105 individuals have been subject to § 4248 out of over 188,000 federal inmates). And its reach is limited to individuals already "in the custody of the" Federal Government. . . .

Taken together, these considerations lead us to conclude that the statute is a "necessary and proper" means of exercising the federal authority that permits Congress to create federal criminal laws, to punish their violation, to imprison violators, to provide appropriately for those imprisoned, and to maintain the security of those who are not imprisoned but who may be affected by the federal imprisonment of others. The Constitution consequently authorizes Congress to enact the statute. . . .

■ JUSTICE KENNEDY, concurring in the judgment.

The Court is correct, in my view, to hold that the challenged portions of 18 U.S.C. § 4248 are necessary and proper exercises of congressional authority.

Respondents argue that congressional authority under the Necessary and Proper Clause can be no more than one step removed from an enumerated power. This is incorrect. When the inquiry is whether a federal law has sufficient links to an enumerated power to be within the scope of federal authority, the analysis depends not on the number of links in the congressional-power chain but on the strength of the chain.

Concluding that a relation can be put into a verbal formulation that fits somewhere along a causal chain of federal powers is merely the beginning, not the end, of the constitutional inquiry. See *United States v. Lopez,* 514 U.S. 549, 566–567 (1995). The inferences must be controlled by some limitations lest, as Thomas Jefferson warned, congressional powers become completely unbounded by linking one power to another *ad infinitum* in a veritable game of " 'this is the house that Jack built.' " Letter from Thomas Jefferson to Edward Livingston (Apr. 30, 1800), 31 The Papers of Thomas Jefferson 547 (B. Oberg ed. 2004). . . .

I had thought it a basic principle that the powers reserved to the States consist of the whole, undefined residuum of power remaining after taking account of powers granted to the National Government. The Constitution delegates limited powers to the National Government and then reserves the remainder for the States (or the people), not the other way around, as the Court's analysis suggests. And the powers reserved to the States are so broad that they remain undefined. Residual power, sometimes referred to (perhaps imperfectly) as the police power, belongs to the States and the States alone.

It is correct in one sense to say that if the National Government has the power to act under the Necessary and Proper Clause then that power is not one reserved to the States. But the precepts of federalism embodied in the Constitution inform which powers are properly exercised by the National Government in the first place. See *Lopez*, at 580–581 (KENNEDY, J., concurring); see also *McCulloch*, at 421 (powers "consist[ent] with the letter and spirit of the constitution, are constitutional"). It is of fundamental importance to consider whether essential attributes of state sovereignty are compromised by the assertion of federal power under the Necessary and Proper Clause; if so, that is a factor suggesting that the power is not one properly within the reach of federal power. . . .

The federal program in question applies only to those in federal custody and thus involves little intrusion upon the ordinary processes and powers of the States. . . .

■ JUSTICE ALITO, concurring in the judgment.

. . . I entirely agree with the dissent that "[t]he Necessary and Proper Clause empowers Congress to enact only those laws that 'carr[y] into Execution' one or more of the federal powers enumerated in the Constitution," but § 4248 satisfies that requirement because it is a necessary and proper means of carrying into execution the enumerated powers that support the federal criminal statutes under which the affected prisoners were convicted. The Necessary and Proper Clause provides the constitutional authority for most federal criminal statutes. In other words, most federal criminal statutes rest upon a congressional judgment that, in order to execute one or more of the powers conferred on Congress, it is necessary and proper to criminalize certain conduct, and in order to do that it is obviously necessary and proper to provide for the operation of a federal criminal justice system and a federal prison system.

All of this has been recognized since the beginning of our country. The First Congress enacted federal criminal laws, created federal law enforcement and prosecutorial positions, established a federal court system, provided for the imprisonment of persons convicted of federal crimes, and gave United States marshals the responsibility of securing federal prisoners.

The only additional question presented here is whether, in order to carry into execution the enumerated powers on which the federal criminal laws rest, it is also necessary and proper for Congress to protect the public from dangers created by the federal criminal justice and prison systems. In my view, the answer to that question is "yes." Just as it is necessary and proper for Congress to provide for the apprehension of escaped federal prisoners, it is necessary and proper for Congress to provide for the civil commitment of dangerous federal prisoners who would otherwise escape civil commitment as a result of federal imprisonment. . . .

The Necessary and Proper Clause does not give Congress *carte blanche*. Although the term "necessary" does not mean "absolutely necessary" or indispensable, the term requires an "appropriate" link between a power conferred by the Constitution and the law enacted by Congress. See *McCulloch,* at 415. And it is an obligation of this Court to enforce compliance with that limitation. . . .

■ JUSTICE THOMAS, with whom Justice Scalia joins in all but Part III–A–1–b, dissenting.

. . . The Necessary and Proper Clause empowers Congress to enact only those laws that "carr[y] into Execution" one or more of the federal powers enumerated in the Constitution. Because § 4248 "Execut[es]" no enumerated power, I must respectfully dissent.

I

. . . *McCulloch's* summation is descriptive of the Clause itself, providing that federal legislation is a valid exercise of Congress' authority under the Clause if it satisfies a two-part test: First, the law must be directed toward a "legitimate" end, which *McCulloch* defines as one "within the scope of the [C]onstitution"—that is, the powers expressly delegated to the Federal Government by some provision in the Constitution. Second, there must be a necessary and proper fit between the "means" (the federal law) and the "end" (the enumerated power or powers) it is designed to serve. *McCulloch* accords Congress a certain amount of discretion in assessing means-end fit under this second inquiry. The means Congress selects will be deemed "necessary" if they are "appropriate" and "plainly adapted" to the exercise of an enumerated power, and "proper" if they are not otherwise "prohibited" by the Constitution and not "[in]consistent" with its "letter and spirit."

Critically, however, *McCulloch* underscores the linear relationship the Clause establishes between the two inquiries: Unless the end itself is "legitimate," the fit between means and end is irrelevant. In other words, no matter how "necessary" or "proper" an Act of Congress may be to its objective, Congress lacks authority to legislate if the objective is anything other than "carrying into Execution" one or more of the Federal Government's enumerated powers. Art. I, § 8, cl. 18.

This limitation was of utmost importance to the Framers. During the State ratification debates, Anti-Federalists expressed concern that the Necessary and Proper Clause would give Congress virtually unlimited power. See, *e.g.*, Essays of Brutus, in 2 The Complete Anti-Federalist 421 (H. Storing ed. 1981). Federalist supporters of the Constitution swiftly refuted that charge, explaining that the Clause did not grant Congress any freestanding authority, but instead made explicit what was already implicit in the grant of each enumerated power. Referring to the "powers declared in the Constitution," Alexander Hamilton noted that "it is *expressly* to execute these powers that the sweeping clause . . . authorizes the national legislature to pass all *necessary* and *proper* laws." The Federalist No. 33. James Madison echoed this view, stating that "the sweeping clause . . . only extend[s] to the enumerated powers." 3 J. Elliot, The Debates in the Several State Conventions on the Adoption of the Federal Constitution 455 (2d ed. 1854). Statements by delegates to the state ratification conventions indicate that this understanding was widely held by the founding generation.

Roughly 30 years after the Constitution's ratification, *McCulloch* firmly established this understanding in our constitutional jurisprudence. Since then, our precedents uniformly have maintained that the Necessary and Proper Clause is not an independent fount of congressional authority, but rather "a *caveat* that Congress possesses all the means necessary to carry out the specifically granted 'foregoing' powers of § 8 'and all other Powers vested by this Constitution.'" *Kinsella v. United States ex rel. Singleton*, 361 U.S. 234, 247 (1960).

II

... No enumerated power in Article I, § 8, expressly delegates to Congress the power to enact a civil-commitment regime for sexually dangerous persons, nor does any other provision in the Constitution vest Congress or the other branches of the Federal Government with such a power. Accordingly, § 4248 can be a valid exercise of congressional authority only if it is "necessary and proper for carrying into Execution" one or more of those federal powers actually enumerated in the Constitution.

Section 4248 does not fall within any of those powers. The Government identifies no specific enumerated power or powers as a constitutional predicate for § 4248, and none are readily discernable. Indeed, not even the Commerce Clause—the enumerated power this Court has interpreted most expansively, see, *e.g.*, *NLRB v. Jones & Laughlin Steel Corp.*, 301 U.S. 1, 37 (1937)—can justify federal civil detention of sex offenders. Under the Court's precedents, Congress may not regulate noneconomic activity (such as sexual violence) based solely on the effect such activity may have, in individual cases or in the aggregate, on interstate commerce. *Morrison*, at 617–618; *Lopez*, at 563–567. That limitation forecloses any claim that § 4248 carries into execution Congress' Commerce Clause power, and the Government has never argued otherwise.

This Court, moreover, consistently has recognized that the power to care for the mentally ill and, where necessary, the power "to protect the community from the dangerous tendencies of some" mentally ill persons, are among the numerous powers that remain with the States. *Addington v. Texas*, 441 U.S. 418, 426 (1979). . . .

Section 4248 closely resembles the involuntary civil-commitment laws that States have enacted under their *parens patriae* and general police powers. Indeed, it is clear, on the face of the Act and in the Government's arguments urging its constitutionality, that § 4248 is aimed at protecting society from acts of sexual violence, not toward "carrying into Execution" any enumerated power or powers of the Federal Government.

To be sure, protecting society from violent sexual offenders is certainly an important end. . . . But the Constitution does not vest in Congress the authority to protect society from every bad act that might befall it.[6]

In my view, this should decide the question. Section 4248 runs afoul of our settled understanding of Congress' power under the Necessary and Proper Clause. Congress may act under that Clause only when its legislation "carr[ies] into Execution" one of the Federal Government's enumerated powers. Art. I, § 8, cl. 18. Section 4248 does not execute *any* enumerated power. Section 4248 is therefore unconstitutional.

III

The Court perfunctorily genuflects to *McCulloch*'s framework for assessing Congress' Necessary and Proper Clause authority, and to the principle of dual sovereignty it helps to maintain, then promptly abandons both in favor of a novel

---

[6]   The absence of a constitutional delegation of general police power to Congress does not leave citizens vulnerable to the harms Congress seeks to regulate in § 4248 because, as recent legislation indicates, the States have the capacity to address the threat that sexual offenders pose. See n. 15, infra. *[Footnote fifteen, omitted below, indicates that all 50 states require registration for sex offenders and that 22 have "laws substantially similar to § 4248."—Editors]*

five-factor test supporting its conclusion that § 4248 is a " 'necessary and proper' " adjunct to a jumble of *unenumerated* "authorit[ies]." The Court's newly minted test cannot be reconciled with the Clause's plain text or with two centuries of our precedents interpreting it. It also raises more questions than it answers. Must each of the five considerations exist before the Court sustains future federal legislation as proper exercises of Congress' Necessary and Proper Clause authority? What if the facts of a given case support a finding of only four considerations? Or three? And if three or four will suffice, *which* three or four are imperative? At a minimum, this shift from the two-step *McCulloch* framework to this five-consideration approach warrants an explanation as to why *McCulloch* is no longer good enough and which of the five considerations will bear the most weight in future cases, assuming some number less than five suffices. (Or, if not, why all five are required.) The Court provides no answers to these questions.

A–1

. . . [I]nstead of asking the simple question of what enumerated power § 4248 "carr[ies] into Execution" at *McCulloch*'s first step, the Court surveys other laws Congress has enacted and concludes that, because § 4248 is related to those laws, the "links" between § 4248 and an enumerated power are not "too attenuated"; hence, § 4248 is a valid exercise of Congress' Necessary and Proper Clause authority. This unnecessarily confuses the analysis and, if followed to its logical extreme, would result in an unwarranted expansion of federal power. . . .

The Court observes that Congress has the undisputed authority to "criminalize conduct" that interferes with enumerated powers; to "imprison individuals who engage in that conduct"; to "enact laws governing [those] prisons"; and to serve as a "custodian of its prisoners." From this, the Court assumes that § 4248 must also be a valid exercise of congressional power because it is " 'reasonably adapted' " to *those* exercises of Congress' incidental—and thus unenumerated—authorities. But that is not the question. The Necessary and Proper Clause does not provide Congress with authority to enact any law simply because it furthers *other laws* Congress has enacted in the exercise of its incidental authority; the Clause plainly requires a showing that every federal statute "carr[ies] into Execution" one or more of the Federal Government's *enumerated* powers.[8]

Federal laws that criminalize conduct that interferes with enumerated powers, establish prisons for those who engage in that conduct, and set rules for the care and treatment of prisoners awaiting trial or serving a criminal sentence satisfy this test because each helps to "carr[y] into Execution" the enumerated powers that justify a criminal defendant's arrest or conviction. For example, Congress' enumerated power "[t]o establish Post Offices and post Roads," Art. I, § 8, cl. 7, would lack force or practical effect if Congress lacked the authority to enact criminal laws "to punish those who steal letters from the post office, or rob the mail." *McCulloch*, at 417. Similarly, that enumerated power would be compromised if there were no prisons to

---

[8] . . . [*McCulloch*'s dictum about mail theft] does not suggest that the relationship between Congress' implied power to punish postal crimes and its implied power to carry the mail is alone sufficient to satisfy review under the Necessary and Proper Clause. Instead, *McCulloch* directly links the constitutionality of the former to Congress' enumerated power " 'to establish post offices and post roads.' " More importantly, *McCulloch*'s holding, as well as the holdings of this Court's subsequent decisions, make plain that congressional action is valid under the Necessary and Proper Clause only if it carries into execution one or more enumerated powers.

hold persons who violate those laws, or if those prisons were so poorly managed that prisoners could escape or demand their release on the grounds that the conditions of their confinement violate their constitutional rights, at least as we have defined them. Civil detention under § 4248, on the other hand, lacks any such connection to an enumerated power.

2

After focusing on the relationship between § 4248 and several of Congress' implied powers, the Court finally concludes that the civil detention of a "sexually dangerous person" under § 4248 carries into execution the enumerated power that justified that person's arrest or conviction in the first place. In other words, the Court analogizes § 4248 to federal laws that authorize prison officials to care for federal inmates while they serve sentences or await trial. But while those laws help to "carr[y] into Execution" the enumerated power that justifies the imposition of criminal sanctions on the inmate, § 4248 does not bear that essential characteristic for three reasons.

First, the statute's definition of a "sexually dangerous person" contains no element relating to the subject's crime. . . . As a consequence, § 4248 allows a court to civilly commit an individual without finding that he was ever charged with or convicted of a federal crime involving sexual violence. That possibility is not merely hypothetical: The Government concedes that nearly 20% of individuals against whom § 4248 proceedings have been brought fit this description.

Second, § 4248 permits the term of federal civil commitment to continue beyond the date on which a convicted prisoner's sentence expires or the date on which the statute of limitations on an untried defendant's crime has run. The statute therefore authorizes federal custody over a person at a time when the Government would lack jurisdiction to detain him for violating a criminal law that executes an enumerated power. . . .

Third, . . . [the statute] authorizes civil commitment upon a showing that the person is "sexually dangerous," and presents a risk "to others." It requires no evidence that this sexually dangerous condition will manifest itself in a way that interferes with a federal law that executes an enumerated power or in a geographic location over which Congress has plenary authority.

In sum, the enumerated powers that justify a criminal defendant's arrest or conviction cannot justify his subsequent civil detention under § 4248.

B

The remaining "considerations" in the Court's five-part inquiry do not alter this conclusion . . .

[T]he Court describes § 4248 as a "modest" expansion on a statutory framework with a long historical pedigree. Yet even if the antiquity of a practice could serve as a substitute for its constitutionality—and the Court admits that it cannot—the Court overstates the relevant history.

Congress' first foray into this general area occurred in 1855, when it established St. Elizabeth's Hospital to provide treatment to "insane" persons in the military and the District of Columbia. Act of Mar. 3, 1855, 10 Stat. 682. But Congress was acting pursuant to *enumerated* powers when it took this step. See Art. I, § 8, cl. 17 (granting Congress plenary authority over the District of Columbia); Art. I, § 8, cl. 14

(authorizing Congress to "make Rules for the Government and Regulation of the land and naval Forces"). . . .

Finally, the Court offers two arguments regarding § 4248's impact on the relationship between the Federal Government and the States. First, the Court and both concurrences . . . appear to assume that, in the absence of 18 U.S.C. § 4248, a State would take no action when informed by the BOP that a sexually dangerous federal prisoner was about to be released within its jurisdiction. In light of the plethora of state laws enacted in recent decades to protect communities from sex offenders, the likelihood of such an occurrence seems quite remote. But even in the event a State made such a decision, the Constitution assigns the responsibility for that decision, and its consequences, to the state government alone.

Next, the Court submits that § 4248 does not upset the balance of federalism or invade the States' reserved powers because it "requires accommodation of state interests" by instructing the Attorney General to release a committed person to the State in which he was domiciled or tried if that State wishes to " 'assume . . . responsibility' " for him. This right of first refusal is mere window dressing. More importantly, it is an altogether hollow assurance that § 4248 preserves the principle of dual sovereignty—the "letter and spirit" of the Constitution—as the Necessary and Proper Clause requires. For once it is determined that Congress has the authority to provide for the civil detention of sexually dangerous persons, Congress "is acting within the powers granted it under the Constitution," and "may impose its will on the States." *Gregory v. Ashcroft,* 501 U.S. 452, 460 (1991); see Art. VI, cl. 2. Section 4248's right of first refusal is thus not a matter of constitutional necessity, but an act of legislative grace. . . .

* * *

Not long ago, this Court described the Necessary and Proper Clause as "the last, best hope of those who defend ultra vires congressional action." *Printz,* at 923. Regrettably, today's opinion breathes new life into that Clause, and—the Court's protestations to the contrary notwithstanding—comes perilously close to transforming the Necessary and Proper Clause into a basis for the federal police power that "we *always* have rejected," *Lopez,* at 584 (THOMAS, J., concurring). In so doing, the Court endorses the precise abuse of power Article I is designed to prevent—the use of a limited grant of authority as a "pretext . . . for the accomplishment of objects not intrusted to the government." *McCulloch,* at 423.

NOTES

1.   Which enumerated power is the statute in *Comstock* necessary and proper for carrying into execution? Does the statute satisfy the *McCulloch* test? In thinking about whether the law is "necessary and proper," does it matter that it intrudes on traditional state police powers?

2.   Review the five considerations offered by the opinion of the Court. Which ones do you think are the soundest guides to interpreting the Necessary and Proper Clause? Are any of them unsound guides? What is the majority's answer to Justice Thomas's questions about which of the five considerations are essential? Are all five required? If the five considerations are present, does it follow that a law is "necessary and proper"?

3.   Does Justice Breyer's argument depend on the assumption that "a reasonable number" of sexually dangerous prisoners "would likely not be detained by the States if

released from federal custody"? Professor Rick Hills, writing about the *Comstock* decision, called the latter assumption "a tribute to the justices' capacity to keep a straight face when engaging in legal fiction." Professor Hills asked: "Does any reader seriously believe that, upon receiving a phone call from a federal warden explaining that a 'sexually dangerous' ex-con was about to be released from a federal prison into their jurisdiction, the governor or mayor of that jurisdiction would not jump to confine such a person as tightly as the 14th Amendment would permit?" Rick Hills, *Comstock*'s Folly, Prawfsblawg (May 18, 2010) (some quotation marks omitted). What do you think?

4.   Justice Scalia joined Justice Thomas's dissent in *Comstock*, but he wrote a broad Necessary and Proper Clause concurrence in *Gonzales v. Raich*. Are Justice Scalia's votes in these two cases consistent? Is the argument for federal power stronger in *Comstock* or in *Raich*?

[*Assignment 28*]

In Closer Focus: The Necessary and Proper Clause and State Sovereignty

Garcia v. San Antonio Metropolitan Transit Authority
469 U.S. 528 (1985)

■ JUSTICE BLACKMUN delivered the opinion of the Court.

We revisit in these cases an issue raised in *National League of Cities v. Usery*, 426 U.S. 833 (1976). In that litigation, this Court, by a sharply divided vote, ruled that the Commerce Clause does not empower Congress to enforce the minimum-wage and overtime provisions of the Fair Labor Standards Act (FLSA) against the States "in areas of traditional governmental functions." Although *National League of Cities* supplied some examples of "traditional governmental functions," it did not offer a general explanation of how a "traditional" function is to be distinguished from a "nontraditional" one. Since then, federal and state courts have struggled with the task, thus imposed, of identifying a traditional function for purposes of state immunity under the Commerce Clause.

In the present cases, a Federal District Court concluded that municipal ownership and operation of a mass-transit system is a traditional governmental function and thus, under *National League of Cities,* is exempt from the obligations imposed by the FLSA. Faced with the identical question, three Federal Courts of Appeals and one state appellate court have reached the opposite conclusion.

Our examination of this "function" standard applied in these and other cases over the last eight years now persuades us that the attempt to draw the boundaries of state regulatory immunity in terms of "traditional governmental function" is not only unworkable but is also inconsistent with established principles of federalism and, indeed, with those very federalism principles on which *National League of Cities* purported to rest. That case, accordingly, is overruled.

I

[The Court traces the development of public transportation in San Antonio. The city began regulating private mass transit in 1915, and began operating a public mass

transit system in 1959. Federal subsidies were necessary for its continued operation by 1970, when it received its first federal grant under the Urban Mass Transportation Act of 1964. In 1985, federal subsidies and local sales taxes accounted for roughly 75 percent of the system's budget.

    When first enacted in 1938, the FLSA wage and overtime provisions did not apply to employees of state and local governments, including local mass-transit employees. Congress slowly expanded the coverage of the FLSA, and in 1974 amended the FLSA to cover mass-transit employees. SAMTA complied with the FLSA until 1976, when National League of Cities *"held that the FLSA could not be applied constitutionally to the 'traditional governmental functions' of state and local governments."*

    In 1979, the Department of Labor issued an opinion that the FLSA applied to SAMTA's operations. SAMTA filed suit in federal district court, seeking a declaratory judgment that National League of Cities *precluded that application of the FLSA. The court allowed Garcia, an employee of SAMTA, to intervene in support of the Secretary of Labor. The district court granted summary judgment for SAMTA. While on appeal, the Supreme Court decided* Transportation Union v. Long Island R. Co., *which ruled that a state-owned commuter rail service was not a "traditional governmental function" and thus did not enjoy immunity under* National League of Cities. *The Supreme Court vacated the district court's decision, and remanded for reconsideration in light of* Long Island. *On remand, the district court again entered judgment for SAMTA. The Supreme Court heard the case on direct appeal.—Editors]*

II

    Appellees have not argued that SAMTA is immune from regulation under the FLSA on the ground that it is a local transit system engaged in intrastate commercial activity . . . Any constitutional exemption from the requirements of the FLSA therefore must rest on SAMTA's status as a governmental entity rather than on the "local" nature of its operations.

    [U]nder *National League of Cities*, four conditions must be satisfied before a state activity may be deemed immune from a particular federal regulation under the Commerce Clause. First, it is said that the federal statute at issue must regulate "the 'States as States.'" Second, the statute must "address matters that are indisputably 'attribute[s] of state sovereignty.'" Third, state compliance with the federal obligation must "directly impair [the States'] ability 'to structure integral operations in areas of traditional governmental functions.'" Finally, the relation of state and federal interests must not be such that "the nature of the federal interest . . . justifies state submission."

    The controversy in the present cases has focused on the third . . . requirement—that the challenged federal statute trench on "traditional governmental functions." The District Court voiced a common concern: "Despite the abundance of adjectives, identifying which particular state functions are immune remains difficult." Just how troublesome the task has been is revealed by the results reached in other federal cases. Thus, courts have held that regulating ambulance services, licensing automobile drivers, operating a municipal airport, performing solid waste disposal, and operating a highway authority are functions *protected* under *National League of Cities*. At the same time, courts have held that issuance of industrial development bonds, regulation of intrastate natural gas sales, regulation of traffic on public roads, regulation of air transportation, operation of a telephone system, leasing and sale of natural gas, operation of a mental health facility, and provision of in-house domestic services for the aged and handicapped are *not* entitled to immunity. We find it difficult, if not impossible, to identify an organizing principle that places each of the cases in the first group on one side of a line and each of the cases in the second group on the other side. The constitutional distinction between licensing drivers and regulating traffic, for example, or between operating a highway authority and operating a mental health facility, is elusive at best. . . .

[None] of the alternative standards that might be employed to distinguish between protected and unprotected governmental functions appear manageable. We rejected the possibility of making immunity turn on a purely historical standard of "tradition" in *Transportation Union v. Long Island R. Co.*, 455 U.S. 678 (1982), and properly so. The most obvious defect of a historical approach to state immunity is that it prevents a court from accommodating changes in the historical functions of States, changes that have resulted in a number of once-private functions like education being assumed by the States and their subdivisions. At the same time, the only apparent virtue of a rigorous historical standard, namely, its promise of a reasonably objective measure for state immunity, is illusory. Reliance on history as an organizing principle results in line-drawing of the most arbitrary sort; the genesis of state governmental functions stretches over a historical continuum from before the Revolution to the present, and courts would have to decide by fiat precisely how longstanding a pattern of state involvement had to be for federal regulatory authority to be defeated.

A nonhistorical standard for selecting immune governmental functions is likely to be just as unworkable as is a historical standard. The goal of identifying "uniquely" governmental functions, for example, has been rejected by the Court in the field of governmental tort liability in part because the notion of a "uniquely" governmental function is unmanageable. Another possibility would be to confine immunity to "necessary" governmental services, that is, services that would be provided inadequately or not at all unless the government provided them. The set of services that fits into this category, however, may well be negligible. The fact that an unregulated market produces less of some service than a State deems desirable does not mean that the State itself must provide the service; in most if not all cases, the State can "contract out" by hiring private firms to provide the service or simply by providing subsidies to existing suppliers. It also is open to question how well equipped courts are to make this kind of determination about the workings of economic markets.

. . . [The more fundamental] problem is that neither the governmental/proprietary distinction nor any other that purports to separate out important governmental functions can be faithful to the role of federalism in a democratic society. The essence of our federal system is that within the realm of authority left open to them under the Constitution, the States must be equally free to engage in any activity that their citizens choose for the common weal, no matter how unorthodox or unnecessary anyone else—including the judiciary—deems state involvement to be. Any rule of state immunity that looks to the "traditional," "integral," or "necessary" nature of governmental functions inevitably invites an unelected federal judiciary to make decisions about which state policies it favors and which ones it dislikes. "The science of government . . . is the science of experiment," and the States cannot serve as laboratories for social and economic experiment if they must pay an added price when they meet the changing needs of their citizenry by taking up functions that an earlier day and a different society left in private hands . . .

We therefore now reject, as unsound in principle and unworkable in practice, a rule of state immunity from federal regulation that turns on a judicial appraisal of whether a particular governmental function is "integral" or "traditional." Any such rule leads to inconsistent results at the same time that it disserves principles of democratic self-governance, and it breeds inconsistency precisely because it is divorced from those principles. If there are to be limits on the Federal Government's power to interfere with state functions—as undoubtedly there are—we must look elsewhere to find them. We accordingly return to the underlying issue that confronted this Court in *National League of Cities*—the manner in which the Constitution insulates States from the reach of Congress' power under the Commerce Clause.

III

The central theme of *National League of Cities* was that the States occupy a special position in our constitutional system and that the scope of Congress' authority under the Commerce Clause must reflect that position. Of course, the Commerce Clause by its specific language does not provide any special limitation on Congress' actions with respect to the States. It is equally true, however, that the text of the Constitution provides the beginning rather than the final answer to every inquiry into questions of federalism, for "[b]ehind the words of the constitutional provisions are postulates which limit and control." *National League of Cities* reflected the general conviction that the Constitution precludes "the National Government [from] devour[ing] the essentials of state sovereignty." In order to be faithful to the underlying federal premises of the Constitution, courts must look for the "postulates which limit and control."

What has proved problematic is not the perception that the Constitution's federal structure imposes limitations on the Commerce Clause, but rather the nature and content of those limitations. One approach to defining the limits on Congress' authority to regulate the States under the Commerce Clause is to identify certain underlying elements of political sovereignty that are deemed essential to the States' "separate and independent existence." . . .

We doubt that courts ultimately can identify principled constitutional limitations on the scope of Congress' Commerce Clause powers over the States merely by relying on *a priori* definitions of state sovereignty. In part, this is because of the elusiveness of objective criteria for "fundamental" elements of state sovereignty, a problem we have witnessed in the search for "traditional governmental functions." There is, however, a more fundamental reason: the sovereignty of the States is limited by the Constitution itself. A variety of sovereign powers, for example, are withdrawn from the States by Article I, § 10. Section 8 of the same Article works an equally sharp contraction of state sovereignty by authorizing Congress to exercise a wide range of legislative powers and (in conjunction with the Supremacy Clause of Article VI) to displace contrary state legislation. By providing for final review of questions of federal law in this Court, Article III curtails the sovereign power of the States' judiciaries to make authoritative determinations of law. Finally, the developed application, through the

Fourteenth Amendment, of the greater part of the Bill of Rights to the States limits the sovereign authority that States otherwise would possess to legislate with respect to their citizens and to conduct their own affairs.

The States unquestionably do "retai[n] a significant measure of sovereign authority." They do so, however, only to the extent that the Constitution has not divested them of their original powers and transferred those powers to the Federal Government. In the words of James Madison to the Members of the First Congress: "Interference with the power of the States was no constitutional criterion of the power of Congress. If the power was not given, Congress could not exercise it; if given, they might exercise it, although it should interfere with the laws, or even the Constitution of the States." 2 Annals of Cong. 1897 (1791) . . .

In short, we have no license to employ freestanding conceptions of state sovereignty when measuring congressional authority under the Commerce Clause.

When we look for the States' "residuary and inviolable sovereignty," The Federalist No. 39 (J. Madison), in the shape of the constitutional scheme rather than in predetermined notions of sovereign power, a different measure of state sovereignty emerges. Apart from the limitation on federal authority inherent in the delegated nature of Congress' Article I powers, the principal means chosen by the Framers to ensure the role of the States in the federal system lies in the structure of the Federal Government itself. It is no novelty to observe that the composition of the Federal Government was designed in large part to protect the States from overreaching by Congress. The Framers thus gave the States a role in the selection both of the Executive and the Legislative Branches of the Federal Government. The States were vested with indirect influence over the House of Representatives and the Presidency by their control of electoral qualifications and their role in Presidential elections. U.S. Const., Art. I, § 2, and Art. II, § 1. They were given more direct influence in the Senate, where each State received equal representation and each Senator was to be selected by the legislature of his State. Art. I, § 3. The significance attached to the States' equal representation in the Senate is underscored by the prohibition of any constitutional amendment divesting a State of equal representation without the State's consent. Art. V.

The extent to which the structure of the Federal Government itself was relied on to insulate the interests of the States is evident in the views of the Framers. James Madison explained that the Federal Government "will partake sufficiently of the spirit [of the States], to be disinclined to invade the rights of the individual States, or the prerogatives of their governments." The Federalist No. 46. Similarly, James Wilson observed that "it was a favorite object in the Convention" to provide for the security of the States against federal encroachment and that the structure of the Federal Government itself served that end. 2 Debates in the Several State Conventions on the Adoption of the Federal Constitution 438–439 (J. Elliot ed. 2d ed. 1876). Madison placed particular reliance on the equal representation of the States in the Senate, which he saw as "at once a constitutional recognition of the portion of sovereignty remaining in the individual States, and an instrument for preserving that residuary sovereignty." The Federalist No. 62. He further noted that "the residuary sovereignty of the States [is] implied *and secured* by that principle of representation in one branch of the [federal] legislature" (emphasis added). The Federalist No. 43. See also *McCulloch v. Maryland,* 17 U.S. (4 Wheat.) 316, 435 (1819). In short, the Framers chose to rely on a federal system in which special restraints on federal power over the States inhered principally in the workings of the National Government itself, rather than in discrete limitations on the objects of federal authority. State sovereign interests, then, are more properly protected by procedural safeguards inherent in the structure of the federal system than by judicially created limitations on federal power.

The effectiveness of the federal political process in preserving the States' interests is apparent even today in the course of federal legislation. On the one hand, the States have been able to direct a substantial proportion of federal revenues into their own treasuries in the form of general and program-specific grants in aid . . . Moreover, at the same time that the States have exercised their influence to obtain federal support, they have been able to exempt themselves from a wide variety of obligations imposed by Congress under the Commerce Clause . . .

We realize that changes in the structure of the Federal Government have taken place since 1789, not the least of which has been the substitution of popular election of Senators by the adoption of the Seventeenth Amendment in 1913, and that these changes may work to alter the influence of the States in the federal political process. Nonetheless, against this background, we are convinced that the fundamental limitation that the constitutional scheme imposes on the Commerce Clause to protect the "States as States" is one of process rather than one of result. Any substantive restraint on the exercise of Commerce Clause powers must find its justification in the procedural nature of this basic limitation, and it must be tailored to compensate for possible failings in the national political process rather than to dictate a "sacred province of state autonomy."

Insofar as the present cases are concerned, then, we need go no further than to state that we perceive nothing in the overtime and minimum-wage requirements of the FLSA, as applied to SAMTA, that is destructive of state sovereignty or violative of any constitutional provision. SAMTA faces nothing more than the same minimum-wage and overtime obligations that hundreds of thousands of other employers, public as well as private, have to meet. . . .

IV

This analysis makes clear that Congress' action in affording SAMTA employees the protections of the wage and hour provisions of the FLSA contravened no affirmative limit on Congress' power under the Commerce Clause. The judgment of the District Court therefore must be reversed.

Of course, we continue to recognize that the States occupy a special and specific position in our constitutional system and that the scope of Congress' authority under the Commerce Clause must reflect that position. But the principal and basic limit on the federal commerce power is that inherent in all congressional action—the built-in restraints that our system provides through state participation in federal governmental action. The political process ensures that laws that unduly burden the States will not be promulgated. In the factual setting of these cases the internal safeguards of the political process have performed as intended.

These cases do not require us to identify or define what affirmative limits the constitutional structure might impose on federal action affecting the States under the Commerce Clause . . .

National League of Cities v. Usery is overruled. . . .

■ JUSTICE POWELL, with whom THE CHIEF JUSTICE, JUSTICE REHNQUIST, and JUSTICE O'CONNOR join, dissenting.

The Court today, in its 5–4 decision, overrules *National League of Cities*, a case in which we held that Congress lacked authority to impose the requirements of the Fair Labor Standards Act on state and local governments. Because I believe this decision substantially alters the federal system embodied in the Constitution, I dissent.

I

... Whatever effect the Court's decision may have in weakening the application of *stare decisis,* it is likely to be less important than what the Court has done to the Constitution itself. A unique feature of the United States is the *federal* system of government guaranteed by the Constitution and implicit in the very name of our country. Despite some genuflecting in the Court's opinion to the concept of federalism, today's decision effectively reduces the Tenth Amendment to meaningless rhetoric when Congress acts pursuant to the Commerce Clause. The Court holds that the Fair Labor Standards Act (FLSA) "contravened no affirmative limit on Congress' power under the Commerce Clause" to determine the wage rates and hours of employment of all state and local employees ... I note that it does not seem to have occurred to the Court that *it*—an unelected majority of five Justices— today rejects almost 200 years of the understanding of the constitutional status of federalism. In doing so, there is only a single passing reference to the Tenth Amendment. Nor is so much as a dictum of any court cited in support of the view that the role of the States in the federal system may depend upon the grace of elected federal officials, rather than on the Constitution as interpreted by this Court ...

II–A

Much of the Court's opinion is devoted to arguing that it is difficult to define *a priori* "traditional governmental functions." *National League of Cities* neither engaged in, nor required, such a task. The Court discusses and condemns as standards "traditional governmental functions," "purely historical" functions, " 'uniquely' governmental functions," and " 'necessary' governmental services." But nowhere does it mention that *National League of Cities* adopted a familiar type of balancing test for determining whether Commerce Clause enactments transgress constitutional limitations imposed by the federal nature of our system of government.[5] ...

In *EEOC v. Wyoming,* 460 U.S. 226 (1983), for example, the Court stated that "[t]he principle of immunity articulated in *National League of Cities* is a functional doctrine ... whose ultimate purpose is not to create a sacred province of state autonomy, but to ensure that the unique benefits of a federal system ... not be lost through undue federal interference in certain core state functions." In overruling *National League of Cities,* the Court incorrectly characterizes the mode of analysis established therein and developed in subsequent cases.

---

[5] In undertaking such balancing, we have considered, on the one hand, the strength of the federal interest in the challenged legislation and the impact of exempting the States from its reach. Central to our inquiry into the federal interest is how closely the challenged action implicates the central concerns of the Commerce Clause, viz., the promotion of a national economy and free trade among the States. Similarly, we have considered whether exempting States from federal regulation would undermine the goals of the federal program. On the other hand, we have also assessed the injury done to the States if forced to comply with federal Commerce Clause enactments.

Moreover, the statute at issue in this case, the FLSA, is the identical statute that was at issue in *National League of Cities.* Although Justice Blackmun's concurrence noted that he was "not untroubled by certain possible implications of the Court's opinion" in *National League of Cities,* it also stated that "the result with respect to the statute under challenge here [the FLSA] is *necessarily correct.*" 426 U.S., at 856 (emphasis added). His opinion for the Court today does not discuss the statute, nor identify any changed circumstances that warrant the conclusion today that *National League of Cities* is *necessarily wrong.*

B

Today's opinion does not explain how the States' role in the electoral process guarantees that particular exercises of the Commerce Clause power will not infringe on residual state sovereignty. Members of Congress are elected from the various States, but once in office they are Members of the Federal Government. Although the States participate in the Electoral College, this is hardly a reason to view the President as a representative of the States' interest against federal encroachment. . . . The fact that Congress generally does not transgress constitutional limits on its power to reach state activities does not make judicial review any less necessary to rectify the cases in which it does do so. The States' role in our system of government is a matter of constitutional law, not of legislative grace. "The powers not delegated to the United States by the Constitution, nor prohibited by it to the States, are reserved to the States, respectively, or to the people." U.S. Const., Amdt. 10.

More troubling than the logical infirmities in the Court's reasoning is the result of its holding, *i.e.,* that federal political officials, invoking the Commerce Clause, are the sole judges of the limits of their own power. This result is inconsistent with the fundamental principles of our constitutional system. See, *e.g.,* The Federalist No. 78 (Hamilton). At least since *Marbury v. Madison,* 5 U.S. (1 Cranch) 137 (1803), it has been the settled province of the federal judiciary "to say what the law is" with respect to the constitutionality of Acts of Congress. In rejecting the role of the judiciary in protecting the States from federal overreaching, the Court's opinion offers no explanation for ignoring the teaching of the most famous case in our history.

III–B

. . . The Framers had definite ideas about the nature of the Constitution's division of authority between the Federal and State Governments . . .

Madison elaborated on the content of these separate spheres of sovereignty in The Federalist No. 45:

> "The powers delegated by the proposed Constitution to the Federal Government, are few and defined. Those which are to remain in the State Governments are numerous and indefinite. The former will be exercised principally on external objects, as war, peace, negotiation, and foreign commerce . . . The powers reserved to the several States will extend to all the objects, which, in the ordinary course of affairs, concern the lives, liberties and properties of the people; and the internal order, improvement, and prosperity of the State."

Madison considered that the operations of the Federal Government would be "most extensive and important in times of war and danger; those of the State Governments in times of peace and security." *Ibid.* As a result of this division of powers, the state governments generally would be more important than the Federal Government. *Ibid.*

The Framers believed that the separate sphere of sovereignty reserved to the States would ensure that the States would serve as an effective "counterpoise" to the power of the Federal Government. The States would serve this essential role because they would attract and retain the loyalty of their citizens . . . [through] the States' involvement in the everyday concerns of the people. . . .

Thus, the harm to the States that results from federal overreaching under the Commerce Clause is not simply a matter of dollars and cents. Nor is it a matter of the wisdom or folly of certain policy choices. Rather, by usurping functions traditionally performed by the States, federal overreaching under the Commerce Clause undermines the constitutionally mandated balance of power between the States and the Federal Government, a balance designed to protect our fundamental liberties. . . .

D

In contrast, the Court today propounds a view of federalism that pays only lipservice to the role of the States. Although it says that the States "unquestionably do 'retai[n] a significant measure of sovereign authority,' " it fails to recognize the broad, yet specific areas of sovereignty that the Framers intended the States to retain. Indeed, the Court barely acknowledges that the Tenth Amendment exists. That Amendment states explicitly that "[t]he powers not delegated to the United States . . . are reserved to the States." The Court recasts this language to say that the States retain their sovereign powers "only to the extent that the Constitution has not divested them of their original powers and transferred those powers to the Federal Government." This rephrasing is not a distinction without a difference; rather, it reflects the Court's unprecedented view that Congress is free under the Commerce Clause to assume a State's traditional sovereign power, and to do so without judicial review of its action. Indeed, the Court's view of federalism appears to relegate the States to precisely the trivial role that opponents of the Constitution feared they would occupy.

In *National League of Cities,* we spoke of fire prevention, police protection, sanitation, and public health as "typical of [the services] performed by state and local governments in discharging their dual functions of administering the public law and furnishing public services." Not only are these activities remote from any normal concept of interstate commerce, they are also activities that epitomize the concerns of local, democratic self-government. In emphasizing the need to protect traditional governmental functions, we identified the kinds of activities engaged in by state and local governments that affect the everyday lives of citizens. These are services that people are in a position to understand and evaluate, and in a democracy, have the right to oversee. We recognized that "it is functions such as these which governments are created to provide . . . " and that the States and local governments are better able than the National Government to perform them.

The Court maintains that the standard approved in *National League of Cities* "disserves principles of democratic self-governance." In reaching this conclusion, the Court looks myopically only to persons elected to positions in the Federal Government. It disregards entirely the far more effective role of democratic self-government at the state and local levels. One must compare realistically the operation of the state and local governments with that of the Federal Government. Federal legislation is drafted primarily by the staffs of the congressional committees. In view of the hundreds of bills introduced at each session of Congress and the complexity of many of them, it is virtually impossible for even the most conscientious legislators to be truly familiar with many of the statutes enacted. Federal departments and agencies customarily are authorized to write regulations. Often these are more important than the text of the statutes. As is true of the original legislation, these are drafted largely by staff personnel. The administration and enforcement of federal laws and regulations necessarily are largely in the hands of staff and civil service employees. These employees may have little or no knowledge of the States and localities that will be affected by the statutes and regulations for which they are responsible. In any case, they hardly are as accessible and responsive as those who occupy analogous positions in state and local governments . . .

[The dissent argued that SAMTA "is a classic example of the type of service traditionally provided by local government" and would thus be immune from the FLSA under National League of Cities.*—Editors]*

V

. . . [In *Maryland v. Wirtz*, 392 U.S. 183, 205 (1968),] Justice Douglas, in dissent, wrote presciently that the Court's reading of the Commerce Clause would enable "the National Government [to] devour the essentials of state sovereignty, though that sovereignty is attested by the Tenth Amendment." Today's decision makes Justice Douglas' fear once again a realistic one.

As I view the Court's decision today as rejecting the basic precepts of our federal system and limiting the constitutional role of judicial review, I dissent.

■ JUSTICE O'CONNOR, with whom JUSTICE POWELL and JUSTICE REHNQUIST join, dissenting.

[Justice O'Connor begins by discussing the "emergence of an integrated and industrialized national economy" along with the "breathtaking expansion" of the Commerce Power.—Editors]

. . . It is worth recalling the cited passage in *McCulloch v. Maryland* that lies at the source of the recent expansion of the commerce power. "Let the end be legitimate, let it be within the scope of the constitution," Chief Justice Marshall said, "and all means which are appropriate, which are plainly adapted to that end, which are not prohibited, but consist with the letter *and spirit* of the constitution, are constitutional" (emphasis added). The *spirit* of the Tenth Amendment, of course, is that the States will retain their integrity in a system in which the laws of the United States are nevertheless supreme.

It is not enough that the "end be legitimate"; the means to that end chosen by Congress must not contravene the spirit of the Constitution. Thus many of this Court's decisions acknowledge that the means by which national power is exercised must take into account concerns for state autonomy. . . .

This principle requires the Court to enforce affirmative limits on federal regulation of the States to complement the judicially crafted expansion of the interstate commerce power. *National League of Cities v. Usery* represented an attempt to define such limits. The Court today rejects *National League of Cities* and washes its hands of all efforts to protect the States. In the process, the Court opines that unwarranted federal encroachments on state authority are and will remain " 'horrible possibilities that never happen in the real world.' " There is ample reason to believe to the contrary.

The last two decades have seen an unprecedented growth of federal regulatory activity, as the majority itself acknowledges. In 1954, one could still speak of a "burden of persuasion on those favoring national intervention" in asserting that "National action has . . . always been regarded as exceptional in our polity, an intrusion to be justified by some necessity, the special rather than the ordinary case." Today, as federal legislation and coercive grant programs have expanded to embrace innumerable activities that were once viewed as local, the burden of persuasion has surely shifted, and the extraordinary has become ordinary. For example, recently the Federal Government has, with this Court's blessing, undertaken to tell the States the age at which they can retire their law enforcement officers, and the regulatory standards, procedures, and even the agenda which their utilities commissions must consider and follow. The political process has not protected against these encroachments on state activities, even though they directly impinge on a State's ability to make and enforce its laws. With the abandonment of *National League of Cities,* all that stands between the remaining essentials of state sovereignty and Congress is the latter's underdeveloped capacity for self-restraint. . . .

■ [The dissenting opinion of JUSTICE REHNQUIST is omitted.]

NOTES

1.   What is the holding of *Garcia*? What, exactly, does the Court consider "the principal and basic limit" on congressional power? It is true that in our system the principal and basic safeguard for all constitutional limits—individual rights as well as federalism—comes from aspects of constitutional structure, such as the extent of the union, bicameralism, and checks and balances. (For further discussion, see *The Federalist No. 10*, p. 464.) But does that safeguard "ensure" that no unconstitutional laws will be "promulgated"? Does the *Garcia* Court mean to imply that there is no need for constitutional judicial review as a backstop? Is that consistent with *Marbury*? With *McCulloch*? How can the Court tell whether "the internal safeguards of the political process have performed as intended" in any particular case unless there are criteria for identifying those outcomes?

2.   Justice O'Connor says that the majority "washes its hands of all efforts to protect the States." Is that correct? Under the majority's holding is there *no* room for judicially-enforceable limits on federal power at the expense of the states? Some observers have suggested that, although the Court does not use the term, *Garcia* effectively holds that federalism questions are "political questions" and thus not justiciable. (On the political question doctrine, see p. 431.) Why might that be? Perhaps because there are no "judicially manageable standards" for determining the proper line. Much of the *Garcia* opinion is devoted to the proposition that neither the four-part test of *National League of Cities* nor any alternative is workable. Perhaps because there is a "textually demonstrable commitment" of these questions to a coordinate branch of government, namely Congress. Much of the *Garcia* opinion is also devoted to the claim that Congress is the true safeguard for the interests of states. Of course, the political question doctrine is understood to be jurisdictional, in the sense of affecting whether a court has jurisdiction to even decide the case; the *Garcia* holding is not jurisdictional. But is *Garcia* an exemplar of the "political question" doctrine in non-jurisdictional form? Might this be said of other

constitutional doctrines that lack judicially manageable standards, such as the non-delegation doctrine?

3.   As the opinion notes, the principal original safeguard for federalism, the representation of state governments in the Senate, was eliminated by the Seventeenth Amendment. How should that amendment be taken into consideration? Consider two conflicting approaches. First, perhaps the decision of The People to eliminate the original safeguard for federalism evinces a sovereign decision that federalism is no longer one of the key features of our constitutional structure. Second, perhaps elimination of the principal safeguard for federalism made it all the more important for the courts to be vigilant to protect the original federalism balance. Does the choice between these approaches depend on the intentions behind the Seventeenth Amendment? Was that amendment defended as a way to make our system more democratic through direct election of senators—or was it understood as an assault on federalism? Is it anachronistic to ask that question, imposing a contemporary question on quite different debates in the past? Is this an instance where the *intentions* of those advocating an amendment matter, and not just its meaning?

4.   Think about Justice Blackmun's critique of the four-part *National League of Cities* test. Is it as hopelessly vapid as he says? Does Justice Powell's defense of that test—as a balancing of interests—rehabilitate it, or is that defense really a confession that the test has no genuine substance?

5.   Justice Rehnquist's dissent, not reproduced here, was indignant about the majority's cavalier treatment of the stare decisis authority of *National League of Cities*, which he had authored and which Justice Blackmun had joined. Was *Garcia* an appropriate case for overruling a constitutional precedent? Had anything changed between *National League of Cities* and *Garcia*, other than Justice Blackmun's attitude toward federalism? This was not the only precedent that Justices Blackmun and Rehnquist would sharply disagree about. In *Planned Parenthood v. Casey*, 505 U.S. 833 (1992), Chief Justice Rehnquist argued that *Roe v. Wade* should be overruled, while Justice Blackmun, the author of the opinion, defended it on grounds of stare decisis. See p. 1576. Is sauce for the goose, sauce for the gander? And what would that imply? Overrule *National League of Cities* and *Roe*, or else overrule neither? Or is there a principled way to apply stare decisis?

Printz, Sheriff/Coroner, Ravalli County, Montana v. United States

521 U.S. 898 (1997)

■ JUSTICE SCALIA delivered the opinion of the Court.

The question presented in these cases is whether certain interim provisions of the Brady Handgun Violence Prevention Act, commanding state and local law enforcement officers to conduct background checks on prospective handgun purchasers and to perform certain related tasks, violate the Constitution.

I

The Gun Control Act of 1968 establishes a detailed federal scheme governing the distribution of firearms. . . . In 1993, Congress amended the GCA by enacting the Brady Act. The Act requires the Attorney General to establish a national instant background-check system by November 30, 1998, and immediately puts in place certain interim provisions until that system becomes operative. Under the interim provisions, a firearms dealer who proposes to transfer a handgun must first receive from the transferee a statement (the Brady Form), containing the name, address, and date of birth of the proposed transferee . . . and provide the "chief law enforcement officer" (CLEO) of the transferee's residence with notice of the contents (and a copy) of the Brady Form. With some exceptions, the dealer must then wait five business days before consummating the sale, unless the CLEO earlier notifies the dealer that he has no reason to believe the transfer would be illegal. . . .

When a CLEO receives the required notice of a proposed transfer from the firearms dealer, the CLEO must "make a reasonable effort to ascertain within 5 business days whether receipt or possession would be in violation of the law, including research in whatever State and local recordkeeping systems are available and in a national system designated by the Attorney General." The Act does not require the CLEO to take any particular action if he determines that a pending transaction would be unlawful; he may notify the firearms dealer to that effect, but is not required to do so. If, however, the CLEO notifies a gun dealer that a prospective purchaser is ineligible to receive a handgun, he must, upon request, provide the would-be purchaser with a written statement of the reasons for that determination. . . . [A]ny person who "knowingly violates [the section of the GCA amended by the Brady Act] shall be fined under this title, imprisoned for not more than 1 year, or both."

Petitioners Jay Printz and Richard Mack, the CLEOs for Ravalli County, Montana, and Graham County, Arizona, respectively, filed separate actions challenging the constitutionality of the Brady Act's interim provisions. In each case, the District Court held that the provision requiring CLEOs to perform background checks was unconstitutional. . . . A divided panel of the Court of Appeals for the Ninth Circuit reversed. . . .

II

From the description set forth above, it is apparent that the Brady Act purports to direct state law enforcement officers to participate, albeit only temporarily, in the administration of a federally enacted regulatory scheme. . . . Petitioners here object to being pressed into federal service, and contend that congressional action compelling state officers to execute federal laws is unconstitutional. Because there is no constitutional text speaking to this precise question, the answer to the CLEOs' challenge must be sought in historical understanding and practice, in the structure of the Constitution, and in the jurisprudence of this Court. We treat those three sources, in that order, in this and the next two sections of this opinion. . . .

The Government contends . . . that "the earliest Congresses enacted statutes that required the participation of state officials in the implementation of federal laws." The Government's contention demands our careful consideration, since early congressional enactments "provid[e] contemporaneous and weighty evidence of the Constitution's meaning." Indeed, such "contemporaneous legislative exposition of the Constitution . . . , acquiesced in for a long term of years, fixes the construction to be given its provisions." . . .

The Government observes that statutes enacted by the first Congresses required state courts to record applications for citizenship, to transmit abstracts of citizenship applications and other naturalization records to the Secretary of State, and to register aliens seeking naturalization and issue certificates of registry. . . . Other statutes of that era apparently or at least arguably required state courts to perform functions unrelated to naturalization, such as resolving controversies between a captain and the crew of his ship concerning the seaworthiness of the vessel, hearing the claims of slave owners who had apprehended fugitive slaves and issuing certificates authorizing the slave's forced removal to the State from which he had fled, taking proof of the claims of Canadian refugees who had assisted the United States during the Revolutionary War, and ordering the deportation of alien enemies in times of war.

These early laws establish, at most, that the Constitution was originally understood to permit imposition of an obligation on state *judges* to enforce federal prescriptions, insofar as those prescriptions related to matters appropriate for the judicial power. . . . It is understandable why courts should have been viewed distinctively in this regard; unlike legislatures and executives, they applied the law of other sovereigns all the time. The principle underlying so-called "transitory" causes of action was that laws which operated elsewhere created obligations in justice that courts of the forum State would enforce. The Constitution itself, in the Full Faith and Credit Clause, Art. IV, § 1, generally required such enforcement with respect to obligations arising in other States.

For these reasons, we do not think the early statutes imposing obligations on state courts imply a power of Congress to impress the state executive into its service. Indeed, it can be argued that the numerousness of these statutes, contrasted with the utter lack of statutes imposing obligations on the States' executive (notwithstanding the attractiveness of that course to Congress), suggests an assumed *absence* of such power. . . .

Not only do the enactments of the early Congresses, as far as we are aware, contain no evidence of an assumption that the Federal Government may command the States' executive power in the absence of a particularized constitutional authorization, they contain some indication of precisely the opposite assumption. On September 23, 1789—the day before its proposal of the Bill of Rights—the First Congress enacted a law aimed at obtaining state assistance of the most rudimentary and necessary sort for the enforcement of the new Government's laws: the holding of federal prisoners in state jails at federal expense. Significantly, the law issued not a command to the States' executive, but a recommendation to their legislatures. . . .

In addition to early legislation, the Government also appeals to other sources we have usually regarded as indicative of the original understanding of the Constitution. It points to portions of The Federalist which . . . [state] that Congress will probably "make use of the State officers and State regulations, for collecting" federal taxes, The Federalist No. 36 (A. Hamilton), and predicted that "the eventual collection [of internal revenue] under the immediate authority of the Union, will generally be made by the officers, and according to the rules, appointed by the several States," No. 45 (J. Madison). The Government also invokes The Federalist's more general observations that the Constitution would "enable the [national] government to employ the ordinary magistracy of each [State] in the execution of its laws," No. 27 (A. Hamilton), and that it was "extremely probable that in other instances, particularly in the organization of the judicial power, the officers of the States will be clothed with the correspondent authority of the Union," No. 45 (J. Madison). But none of these statements necessarily implies—what is the critical point here—that Congress could impose these responsibilities *without the consent of the States.* They appear to rest on the natural assumption that the States would consent to allowing their officials to assist the Federal Government, an assumption proved correct by the extensive mutual assistance the States and Federal Government voluntarily provided one another in the early days of the Republic. . . .

Another passage of The Federalist reads as follows:

> "It merits particular attention . . . that the laws of the Confederacy as to the enumerated and legitimate objects of its jurisdiction will become the supreme law of the land; to the observance of which all officers, legislative, executive, and judicial in each State will be bound by the sanctity of an oath. Thus, the legislatures, courts, and magistrates, of the respective members will be incorporated into the operations of the national government *as far as its just and constitutional authority extends*; and will be rendered auxiliary to the enforcement of its laws." The Federalist No. 27 (A. Hamilton) (emphasis in original).

The Government does not rely upon this passage, but JUSTICE SOUTER . . . makes it the very foundation of his position. . . . There are several obstacles to such an interpretation. First, the consequences in question ("incorporated into the operations of the national government" and "rendered auxiliary to the enforcement of its laws") are said in the quoted passage to flow automatically from the officers' oath to observe "the laws of the Confederacy as to the enumerated and legitimate objects of its jurisdiction." Thus, if the passage means that state officers must take an active role in the implementation of federal law, it means that they must do so without the necessity for a congressional directive that they implement it. But no one has ever thought, and no one asserts in the present litigation, that that is the law. The second problem with JUSTICE SOUTER's reading is that it makes state legislatures subject to federal direction. (The passage in question, after all, does not include legislatures merely incidentally, as by referring to "all state officers"; it refers to legislatures specifically and first of all.) We have held, however, that state legislatures are not subject to federal direction. *New York v. United States.* . . .[9]

To complete the historical record, we must note that there is not only an absence of executive-commandeering statutes in the early Congresses, but there is an absence of them in our later history as well, at least until very recent years. The Government points to the Act of August 3, 1882, which enlisted state officials "to take charge of the local affairs of immigration in the ports within such State, and to provide for the support and relief of such immigrants therein landing as may fall into distress or need of public aid"; to inspect arriving immigrants and exclude any person found to be a "convict, lunatic, idiot," or indigent; and to send convicts back to their country of origin "without compensation." The statute did not, however, *mandate* those duties, but merely empowered the Secretary of the Treasury "to *enter into*

---

[9]   Even if we agreed with JUSTICE SOUTER's reading of The Federalist No. 27, it would still seem to us most peculiar to give the view expressed in that one piece, not clearly confirmed by any other writer, the determinative weight he does. That would be crediting the most expansive view of federal authority ever expressed, and from the pen of the most expansive expositor of federal power. Hamilton was "from first to last the most nationalistic of all nationalists in his interpretation of the clauses of our federal Constitution." C. Rossiter, Alexander Hamilton and the Constitution 199 (1964). . . . To choose Hamilton's view, as Justice Souter would, is to turn a blind eye to the fact that it was Madison's—not Hamilton's— that prevailed, not only at the Constitutional Convention and in popular sentiment, but in the subsequent struggle to fix the meaning of the Constitution by early congressional practice.

contracts with such State . . . officers as *may be designated* for that purpose *by the governor* of any State." (Emphasis added.)

The Government [also] cites the World War I selective draft law that authorized the President "to utilize the service of any or all departments and any or all officers or agents of the United States *and of the several States,* Territories, and the District of Columbia, and subdivisions thereof, in the execution of this Act," and made any person who refused to comply with the President's directions guilty of a misdemeanor. Act of May 18, 1917 (emphasis added). However, it is far from clear that the authorization "to utilize the service" of state officers was an authorization to *compel* the service of state officers; and the misdemeanor provision surely applied only to refusal to comply with the President's *authorized* directions, which might not have included directions to officers of States whose Governors had not volunteered their services. It is interesting that in implementing the Act President Wilson did not commandeer the services of state officers, but instead requested the assistance of the States' Governors, obtained the consent of each of the Governors, and left it to the Governors to issue orders to their subordinate state officers. It is impressive that even with respect to a wartime measure the President should have been so solicitous of state independence.

The Government points to a number of federal statutes enacted within the past few decades that require the participation of state or local officials in implementing federal regulatory schemes. Some of these are connected to federal funding measures, and can perhaps be more accurately described as conditions upon the grant of federal funding than as mandates to the States; others, which require only the provision of information to the Federal Government, do not involve the precise issue before us here, which is the forced participation of the States' executive in the actual administration of a federal program. . . . Even assuming they represent assertion of the very same congressional power challenged here, they are of such recent vintage that they are no more probative than the statute before us of a constitutional tradition that lends meaning to the text. Their persuasive force is far outweighed by almost two centuries of apparent congressional avoidance of the practice. . . .

III

The constitutional practice we have examined above tends to negate the existence of the congressional power asserted here, but is not conclusive. We turn next to consideration of the structure of the Constitution, to see if we can discern among its "essential postulate[s]," *Principality of Monaco v. Mississippi,* 292 U.S. 313, 322 (1934), a principle that controls the present cases.

A

It is incontestable that the Constitution established a system of "dual sovereignty." *Gregory v. Ashcroft,* 501 U.S. 452, 457 (1991). Although the States surrendered many of their powers to the new Federal Government, they retained "a residuary and inviolable sovereignty," The Federalist No. 39 (J. Madison). This is reflected throughout the Constitution's text, including (to mention only a few examples) the prohibition on any involuntary reduction or combination of a State's territory, Art. IV, § 3; the Judicial Power Clause, Art. III, § 2, and the Privileges and Immunities Clause, Art. IV, § 2, which speak of the "Citizens" of the States; the amendment provision, Article V, which requires the votes of three-fourths of the

States to amend the Constitution; and the Guarantee Clause, Art. IV, § 4, which "presupposes the continued existence of the states and . . . those means and instrumentalities which are the creation of their sovereign and reserved rights," *Helvering v. Gerhardt,* 304 U.S. 405, 414–415 (1938). Residual state sovereignty was also implicit, of course, in the Constitution's conferral upon Congress of not all governmental powers, but only discrete, enumerated ones, Art. I, § 8, which implication was rendered express by the Tenth Amendment's assertion that "[t]he powers not delegated to the United States by the Constitution, nor prohibited by it to the States, are reserved to the States respectively, or to the people." . . .

[T]he Framers rejected the concept of a central government that would act upon and through the States, and instead designed a system in which the State and Federal Governments would exercise concurrent authority over the people—who were, in Hamilton's words, "the only proper objects of government," The Federalist No. 15. We have set forth the historical record in more detail elsewhere, see *New York v. United States,* 505 U.S. 144, 161–166 (1992), and need not repeat it here. It suffices to repeat the conclusion: "the Framers explicitly chose a Constitution that confers upon Congress the power to regulate individuals, not States." *Id.,* at 166. The great innovation of this design was that "our citizens would have two political capacities, one state and one federal, each protected from incursion by the other"— "a legal system unprecedented in form and design, establishing two orders of government, each with its own direct relationship, its own privity, its own set of mutual rights and obligations to the people who sustain it and are governed by it." *U.S. Term Limits, Inc. v. Thornton,* 514 U.S. 779, 838 (1995) (Kennedy, J., concurring). The Constitution thus contemplates that a State's government will represent and remain accountable to its own citizens. . . .

This separation of the two spheres is one of the Constitution's structural protections of liberty. "Just as the separation and independence of the coordinate branches of the Federal Government serve to prevent the accumulation of excessive power in any one branch, a healthy balance of power between the States and the Federal Government will reduce the risk of tyranny and abuse from either front." *Gregory,* at 458. . . . The power of the Federal Government would be augmented immeasurably if it were able to impress into its service—and at no cost to itself—the police officers of the 50 States.

B

. . . [F]ederal control of state officers . . . would also have an effect upon the . . . separation and equilibration of powers between the three branches of the Federal Government itself. The Constitution does not leave to speculation who is to administer the laws enacted by Congress; the President, it says, "shall take Care that the Laws be faithfully executed," Art. II, § 3, personally and through officers whom he appoints (save for such inferior officers as Congress may authorize to be appointed by the "Courts of Law" or by "the Heads of Departments" who are themselves Presidential appointees), Art. II, § 2. The Brady Act effectively transfers this responsibility to thousands of CLEOs in the 50 States, who are left to implement the program without meaningful Presidential control. . . . The insistence of the Framers upon unity in the Federal Executive—to ensure both vigor and accountability—is well known. See The Federalist No. 70 (A. Hamilton); see also Calabresi & Prakash, The President's Power to Execute the Laws, 104 Yale L.J. 541 (1994). That unity would be shattered, and the power of the President would be

[handwritten margin note: Scalia suggest sep. of. Powers Problem]

subject to reduction, if Congress could act as effectively without the President as with him, by simply requiring state officers to execute its laws. . . .

C

The dissent of course resorts to the last, best hope of those who defend ultra vires congressional action, the Necessary and Proper Clause. It reasons that the power to regulate the sale of handguns under the Commerce Clause, coupled with the power to "make all Laws which shall be necessary and proper for carrying into Execution the foregoing Powers," Art. I, § 8, conclusively establishes the Brady Act's constitutional validity, because the Tenth Amendment imposes no limitations on the exercise of delegated powers but merely prohibits the exercise of powers "not delegated to the United States." What destroys the dissent's Necessary and Proper Clause argument, however, is not the Tenth Amendment but the Necessary and Proper Clause itself. When a "La[w] . . . for carrying into Execution" the Commerce Clause violates the principle of state sovereignty reflected in the various constitutional provisions we mentioned earlier, it is not a "La[w] . . . *proper* for carrying into Execution the Commerce Clause," and is thus, in the words of The Federalist, "merely [an] ac[t] of usurpation" which "deserve[s] to be treated as such." The Federalist No. 33 (A. Hamilton). We in fact answered the dissent's Necessary and Proper Clause argument in *New York*: "[E]ven where Congress has the authority under the Constitution to pass laws requiring or prohibiting certain acts, it lacks the power directly to compel the States to require or prohibit those acts. . . . [T]he Commerce Clause, for example, authorizes Congress to regulate interstate commerce directly; it does not authorize Congress to regulate state governments' regulation of interstate commerce." 505 U.S., at 166. . . .

IV

Finally, and most conclusively in the present litigation, we turn to the prior jurisprudence of this Court. . . . [O]pinions of ours have made clear that the Federal Government may not compel the States to implement, by legislation or executive action, federal regulatory programs. In *Hodel v. Virginia Surface Mining & Reclamation Assn., Inc.,* 452 U.S. 264 (1981), and *FERC v. Mississippi,* 456 U.S. 742 (1982), we sustained statutes against constitutional challenge only after assuring ourselves that they did not require the States to enforce federal law. . . .

When we were at last confronted squarely with a federal statute that unambiguously required the States to enact or administer a federal regulatory program, our decision should have come as no surprise. At issue in *New York* were the so-called "take title" provisions of the Low-Level Radioactive Waste Policy Amendments Act of 1985, which required States either to enact legislation providing for the disposal of radioactive waste generated within their borders, or to take title to, and possession of, the waste—effectively requiring the States either to legislate pursuant to Congress's directions, or to implement an administrative solution. 505 U.S. at 175–176. We concluded that Congress could constitutionally require the States to do neither. "The Federal Government," we held, "may not compel the States to enact or administer a federal regulatory program." *Id.,* at 188.

The Government contends that *New York* is distinguishable on the following ground: Unlike the "take title" provisions invalidated there, the background-check provision of the Brady Act does not require state legislative or executive officials to make policy, but instead issues a final directive to state CLEOs. It is permissible, the Government asserts, for Congress to command state or local officials to assist in the implementation of federal law so long as "Congress itself devises a clear legislative solution that regulates private conduct" and requires state or local officers to provide only "limited, non-policymaking help in enforcing that law." "[T]he constitutional line is crossed only when Congress compels the States to make law in their sovereign capacities." Brief for United States 16.

The Government's distinction between "making" law and merely "enforcing" it, between "policymaking" and mere "implementation," is an interesting one. . . . [But e]xecutive action that has utterly no policymaking component is rare, particularly at an executive level as high as a jurisdiction's chief law enforcement officer. Is it really true that there is no policymaking involved in deciding, for example, what "reasonable efforts" shall be expended to conduct a background check? It may well satisfy the Act for a CLEO to direct that (a) no background checks will be conducted that divert personnel time from pending felony investigations, and (b) no background check will be permitted to consume more than one-half hour of an officer's time. But nothing in the Act *requires* a CLEO to be so parsimonious; diverting at least *some* felony-investigation time, and permitting at least *some* background checks beyond one-half hour would certainly not be *un*reasonable. Is this decision whether to devote maximum "reasonable efforts" or minimum "reasonable efforts" not preeminently a matter of policy? It is quite impossible, in short, to draw the Government's proposed line at "no policymaking," and we would have to fall back upon a line of "not too much policymaking." How much is too much is not likely to be answered precisely; and an imprecise barrier against federal intrusion upon state authority is not likely to be an effective one.

Even assuming, moreover, that the Brady Act leaves no "policymaking" discretion with the States, we fail to see how that improves rather than worsens the intrusion upon state sovereignty. Preservation of the States as independent and autonomous political entities is arguably less undermined by requiring them to make policy in certain fields than (as Judge Sneed aptly described it over two decades ago) by "reduc[ing] [them] to puppets of a ventriloquist Congress," *Brown v. EPA,* 521 F.2d 827, 839 (9th Cir. 1975). It is an essential attribute of the States' retained sovereignty that they remain independent and autonomous within their proper sphere of authority. It is no more compatible with this independence and autonomy that their officers be "dragooned" . . . into administering federal law, than it would be compatible with the independence and autonomy of the United States that its officers be impressed into service for the execution of state laws.

The Government purports to find support for its proffered distinction of *New York* in our decisions in *Testa v. Katt,* 330 U.S. 386 (1947). . . . We [do not find this case] relevant. *Testa* stands for the proposition that state courts cannot refuse to apply federal law—a conclusion mandated by the terms of the Supremacy Clause ("the Judges in every State shall be bound [by federal law]"). As we have suggested earlier, that says nothing about whether state executive officers must administer federal law. . . .

The Government also maintains that requiring state officers to perform discrete, ministerial tasks specified by Congress does not violate the principle of *New York* because it does not diminish the accountability of state or federal officials. This argument fails even on its own terms. By forcing state governments to absorb the financial burden of implementing a federal regulatory program, Members of

Congress can take credit for "solving" problems without having to ask their constituents to pay for the solutions with higher federal taxes. And even when the States are not forced to absorb the costs of implementing a federal program, they are still put in the position of taking the blame for its burdensomeness and for its defects. Under the present law, for example, it will be the CLEO and not some federal official who stands between the gun purchaser and immediate possession of his gun. And it will likely be the CLEO, not some federal official, who will be blamed for any error (even one in the designated federal database) that causes a purchaser to be mistakenly rejected.

The dissent makes no attempt to defend the Government's basis for distinguishing *New York,* but instead advances what seems to us an even more implausible theory. The Brady Act, the dissent asserts, is different from the "take title" provisions invalidated in *New York* because the former is addressed to individuals—namely, CLEOs—while the latter were directed to the State itself. That is certainly a difference, but it cannot be a constitutionally significant one. While the Brady Act is directed to "individuals," it is directed to them in their official capacities as state officers; it controls their actions, not as private citizens, but as the agents of the State. The distinction between judicial writs and other government action directed against individuals in their personal capacity, on the one hand, and in their official capacity, on the other hand, is an ancient one, principally because it is dictated by common sense. We have observed that "a suit against a state official in his or her official capacity is not a suit against the official but rather is a suit against the official's office. . . . As such, it is no different from a suit against the State itself." *Will v. Michigan Dept. of State Police,* 491 U.S. 58, 71 (1989). . . .

Finally, the Government puts forward a cluster of arguments that can be grouped under the heading: "The Brady Act serves very important purposes, is most efficiently administered by CLEOs during the interim period, and places a minimal and only temporary burden upon state officers." Assuming *all* the mentioned factors were true, they might be relevant if we were evaluating whether the incidental application to the States of a federal law of general applicability excessively interfered with the functioning of state governments. But where, as here, it is the whole *object* of the law to direct the functioning of the state executive, and hence to compromise the structural framework of dual sovereignty, such a "balancing" analysis is inappropriate. It is the very *principle* of separate state sovereignty that such a law offends, and no comparative assessment of the various interests can overcome that fundamental defect. We expressly rejected such an approach in *New York.* . . .

V

. . . We held in *New York* that Congress cannot compel the States to enact or enforce a federal regulatory program. Today we hold that Congress cannot circumvent that prohibition by conscripting the State's officers directly. The Federal Government may neither issue directives requiring the States to address particular problems, nor command the States' officers, or those of their political subdivisions, to administer or enforce a federal regulatory program. It matters not whether policymaking is involved, and no case-by-case weighing of the burdens or benefits is necessary; such commands are fundamentally incompatible with our constitutional system of dual sovereignty.

■ JUSTICE STEVENS, with whom JUSTICE SOUTER, JUSTICE GINSBURG, and JUSTICE BREYER join, dissenting.

When Congress exercises the powers delegated to it by the Constitution, it may impose affirmative obligations on executive and judicial officers of state and local governments as well as ordinary citizens. This conclusion is firmly supported by the text of the Constitution, the early history of the Nation, decisions of this Court, and a correct understanding of the basic structure of the Federal Government. . . .

Indeed, since the ultimate issue is one of power, we must consider its implications in times of national emergency. Matters such as the enlistment of air raid wardens, the administration of a military draft, the mass inoculation of children to forestall an epidemic, or perhaps the threat of an international terrorist, may require a national response before federal personnel can be made available to respond. If the Constitution empowers Congress and the President to make an appropriate response, is there anything in the Tenth Amendment, "in historical understanding and practice, in the structure of the Constitution, [or] in the jurisprudence of this Court," that forbids the enlistment of state officers to make that response effective? More narrowly, what basis is there in any of those sources for concluding that it is the Members of this Court, rather than the elected representatives of the people, who should determine whether the Constitution contains the unwritten rule that the Court announces today?

Perhaps today's majority would suggest that no such emergency is presented by the facts of these cases. But such a suggestion is itself an expression of a policy judgment. And Congress' view of the matter is quite different from that implied by the Court today.

The Brady Act was passed in response to what Congress described as an "epidemic of gun violence." The Act's legislative history notes that 15,377 Americans were murdered with firearms in 1992, and that 12,489 of these deaths were caused by handguns. Congress expressed special concern that "[t]he level of firearm violence in this country is, by far, the highest among developed nations." The partial solution contained in the Brady Act, a mandatory background check before a handgun may be purchased, has met with remarkable success. Between 1994 and 1996, approximately 6,600 firearm sales each month to potentially dangerous persons were prevented by Brady Act checks; over 70% of the rejected purchasers were convicted or indicted felons. See U.S. Dept. of Justice, Bureau of Justice Statistics Bulletin, A National Estimate: Presale Firearm Checks 1 (Feb. 1997). Whether or not the evaluation reflected in the enactment of the Brady Act is correct as to the extent of the danger and the efficacy of the legislation, the congressional decision surely warrants more respect than it is accorded in today's unprecedented decision.

I

The text of the Constitution provides a sufficient basis for a correct disposition of these cases.

Article I, § 8, grants Congress the power to regulate commerce among the States. Putting to one side the revisionist views expressed by Justice Thomas in his concurring opinion in *United States v. Lopez,* 514 U.S. 549, 584 (1995), there can be no question that that provision adequately supports the regulation of commerce in handguns effected by the Brady Act. Moreover, the additional grant of authority in that section of the Constitution "[t]o make all Laws which shall be necessary and proper for carrying into Execution the foregoing Powers" is surely adequate to support the temporary enlistment of local police officers in the process of identifying persons who should not be entrusted with the possession of handguns. In short, the affirmative delegation of power in Article I provides ample authority for the congressional enactment. . . .

The [Tenth] Amendment confirms the principle that the powers of the Federal Government are limited to those affirmatively granted by the Constitution, but it does not purport to limit the scope or the effectiveness of the exercise of powers that are delegated to Congress. Thus, the Amendment provides no support for a rule that immunizes local officials from obligations that might be imposed on ordinary citizens. Indeed, it would be more reasonable to infer that federal law may impose greater duties on state officials than on private citizens because another provision of the Constitution requires that "all executive and judicial Officers, both of the United States and of the several States, shall be bound by Oath or Affirmation, to support this Constitution." Art. VI, cl. 3. . . .

There is not a clause, sentence, or paragraph in the entire text of the Constitution of the United States that supports the proposition that a local police officer can ignore a command contained in a statute enacted by Congress pursuant to an express delegation of power enumerated in Article I.

II

Under the Articles of Confederation the National Government had the power to issue commands to the several sovereign States, but it had no authority to govern individuals directly. . . . That method of governing proved to be unacceptable, not because it demeaned the sovereign character of the several States, but rather because it was cumbersome and inefficient. . . . The basic change in the character of the government that the Framers conceived was designed to enhance the power of the national government, not to provide some new, unmentioned immunity for state officers. Because indirect control over individual citizens ("the only proper objects of government") was ineffective under the Articles of Confederation, Alexander Hamilton explained that "we must *extend* the authority of the Union to the persons of the citizens." The Federalist No. 15 (emphasis added).

Indeed, the historical materials strongly suggest that the founders intended to enhance the capacity of the Federal Government by empowering it—as a part of the new authority to make demands directly on individual citizens—to act through local officials. Hamilton made clear that the new Constitution, "by extending the authority of the federal head to the individual citizens of the several States, will enable the government to employ the ordinary magistracy of each in the execution of its laws." The Federalist No. 27. Hamilton's meaning was unambiguous; the Federal Government was to have the power to demand that local officials implement national policy programs. . . .

More specifically, during the debates concerning the ratification of the Constitution, it was assumed that state agents would act as tax collectors for the Federal Government. Opponents of the Constitution had repeatedly expressed fears that the new Federal Government's ability to impose taxes directly on the citizenry would result in an overbearing presence of federal tax collectors in the States. Federalists rejoined that this problem would not arise because, as Hamilton explained, "the United States . . . will make use of the State officers and State regulations for collecting" certain taxes. No. 36. . . .

Bereft of support in the history of the founding, the Court rests its conclusion on the claim that there is little evidence the National Government actually exercised such a power in the early years of the Republic. This reasoning is misguided in principle and in fact. While we have indicated that the express consideration and resolution of difficult constitutional issues by the First Congress in particular "provides contemporaneous and weighty evidence of the Constitution's meaning since many of [its] Members . . . had taken part in framing that instrument," we have never suggested that the failure of the early Congresses to address the scope of federal power in a particular area or to exercise a particular authority was an argument against its existence. That position, if correct, would undermine most of our post-New Deal Commerce Clause jurisprudence. . . .

More importantly, the fact that Congress did elect to rely on state judges and the clerks of state courts to perform a variety of executive functions is surely evidence of a contemporary understanding that their status as state officials did not immunize them from federal service. . . .

For example, statutes of the early Congresses required in mandatory terms that state judges and their clerks perform various executive duties with respect to applications for citizenship. . . . Similarly, the First Congress enacted legislation requiring state courts to serve, functionally, like contemporary regulatory agencies in certifying the seaworthiness of vessels. . . . The majority's insistence that this evidence of federal enlistment of state officials to serve executive functions is irrelevant simply because the assistance of "judges" was at issue rests on empty formalistic reasoning of the highest order.

III

The Court's "structural" arguments are not sufficient [either]. . . . As we explained in *Garcia v. San Antonio Metropolitan Transit Authority,* 469 U.S. 528 (1985): "[T]he principal means chosen by the Framers to ensure the role of the States in the federal system lies in the structure of the Federal Government itself. It is no novelty to observe that the composition of the Federal Government was designed in large part to protect the States from overreaching by Congress." *Id.,* at 550–551. Given the fact that the Members of Congress are elected by the people of the several States, with each State receiving an equivalent number of Senators in order to ensure that even the smallest States have a powerful voice in the Legislature, it is quite unrealistic to assume that they will ignore the sovereignty concerns of their constituents. It is far more reasonable to presume that their decisions to impose modest burdens on state officials from time to time reflect a considered judgment that the people in each of the States will benefit therefrom. . . .

Recent developments demonstrate that the political safeguards protecting our Federalism are effective. The majority expresses special concern that were its rule not adopted the Federal Government would be able to avail itself of the services of state government officials "at no cost to itself." But this specific problem of federal actions that have the effect of imposing so-called "unfunded mandates" on the States has been identified and meaningfully addressed by Congress in [the] Unfunded Mandates Reform Act of 1995. . . . Whatever the ultimate impact of the new legislation, its passage demonstrates that unelected judges are better off leaving the protection of federalism to the political process in all but the most extraordinary circumstances.

Perversely, the majority's rule seems more likely to damage than to preserve the safeguards against tyranny provided by the existence of vital state governments. By limiting the ability of the Federal Government to enlist state officials in the implementation of its programs, the Court creates incentives for the National Government to aggrandize itself. In the name of State's rights, the majority would have the Federal Government create vast national bureaucracies to implement its policies. This is exactly the sort of thing that the early Federalists promised would not occur, in part as a result of the National Government's ability to rely on the magistracy of the States. . . .

IV

Finally, the Court advises us that the "prior jurisprudence of this Court" is the most conclusive support for its position. That "prior jurisprudence" is *New York v. United States*. The case involved the validity of a federal statute that provided the States with three types of incentives to encourage them to dispose of radioactive wastes generated within their borders. The Court held that the first two sets of incentives were authorized by affirmative grants of power to Congress, and therefore "not inconsistent with the Tenth Amendment." . . .

The third so-called "incentive" gave the States the option either of adopting regulations dictated by Congress or of taking title to and possession of the low level radioactive waste. The Court concluded that, because Congress had no power to compel the state governments to take title to the waste, the "option" really amounted to a simple command to the States to enact and enforce a federal regulatory program. . . .

After noting that the "take title provision appears to be unique" because no other federal statute had offered "a state government no option other than that of implementing legislation enacted by Congress," the Court concluded that the provision was "inconsistent with the federal structure of our Government established by the Constitution."

Our statements, taken in context, clearly did not decide the question presented here, whether state executive officials—as opposed to state legislators—may in appropriate circumstances be enlisted to implement federal policy. The "take title" provision at issue in New York was beyond Congress' authority to enact because it was "in principle . . . no different than a congressionally compelled subsidy from state governments to radioactive waste producers," almost certainly a legislative Act.

The majority relies upon dictum in *New York* to the effect that "[t]he Federal Government may not compel the States to enact *or administer* a federal regulatory program." But that language was wholly unnecessary to the decision of the case. It is, of course, beyond dispute that we are not bound by the dicta of our prior opinions. To the extent that it has any substance at all, *New York*'s administration language may have referred to the possibility that the State might have been able to take title to and devise an elaborate scheme for the management of the radioactive waste through purely executive policymaking. But despite the majority's effort to suggest that similar activities are required by the Brady Act, it is hard to characterize the minimal requirement that CLEO's perform background checks as one involving the exercise of substantial policymaking discretion on that essentially legislative scale. . . .

Finally, the majority provides an incomplete explanation of our decision in *Testa v. Katt,* and demeans its importance. In that case the Court unanimously held that state courts of appropriate jurisdiction must occupy themselves adjudicating claims brought by private litigants under the federal Emergency Price Control Act of 1942, regardless of how otherwise crowded their dockets might be with state-law matters. . . . Even if the Court were correct in its suggestion that it was the reference to judges in the Supremacy Clause, rather than the central message of the entire Clause, that dictated the result in *Testa,* the Court's implied *expressio unius* argument that the Framers therefore did *not* intend to permit the enlistment of other state officials is implausible. Throughout our history judges, state as well as federal, have merited as much respect as executive agents. The notion that the Framers would have had no reluctance to press state judges into federal service against their will but would have regarded the imposition of a similar—indeed, far lesser—burden on town constables as an intolerable affront to principles of state sovereignty can only be considered perverse. If such a distinction had been contemplated by the learned and articulate men who fashioned the basic structure of our government, surely some of them would have said so.

The provision of the Brady Act that crosses the Court's newly defined constitutional threshold is more comparable to a statute requiring local police officers to report the identity of missing children to the Crime Control Center of the Department of Justice than to an offensive federal command to a sovereign State. If Congress believes that such a statute will benefit the people of the Nation, and serve the interests of cooperative federalism better than an enlarged federal bureaucracy, we should respect both its policy judgment and its appraisal of its constitutional power.

■ [The concurring opinions of JUSTICES O'CONNOR and THOMAS and the dissenting opinions of JUSTICES SOUTER and BREYER are omitted.]

NOTES

1. Which of the five types of constitutional argument (p. 42) does the majority opinion rely on? Which ones does the dissent rely on? Work through each one, asking yourself which opinion is more persuasive:

a. Which textual provisions does each opinion adduce? Does the text clearly resolve the case, as Justice Stevens suggests, or is it ambiguous? How much does the majority's argument depend on treating "necessary" and "proper" as separate requirements?

b. Each opinion draws on copious amounts of materials about the intentions of the founders, especially statements in *The Federalist.* Which side is most persuasive? How specifically do each of the opinions expect the founders to speak about a constitutional question? How specifically should we expect them to speak?

c. Are there inferences that can be drawn from the structure of the Constitution? If so, are these general structural inferences, or are they drawn from the interaction of specific textual provisions? What is the stopping point, or limiting principle, in applying these structural arguments?

d. *Printz* came on the heels of the Court's decision in *New York*. Are the efforts by Justice Stevens to distinguish that case persuasive? What deference, if any, is he giving to the Court's decision on the constitutional question in *New York*? What deference should he give?

e. In which direction do the policy arguments cut? Should the policy decision be left in the hands of Congress? Should the federal courts defer as long as the states speak out in support of the congressional legislation? (If most states *oppose* the constitutionality of a federal statute, should the federal courts defer to that judgment?) Who exactly is federalism supposed to protect?

2. It has long been held that Congress *does* have power to require the state courts to hear and decide issues of federal law. A modern case for this proposition is cited by the majority and Justice Stevens: *Testa v. Katt*, 330 U.S. 386 (1947). Does that proposition mean that Congress can "commandeer" state judicial branches to exercise the federal judicial power? If so, does that undermine the anti-commandeering premises of *New York v. United States* and *Printz v. United States*? Are state executive branch officials more like state judges, who can be "commandeered" (after a fashion); or more like state legislatures, which cannot be?

3. Recent historical scholarship has argued that the majority opinion in *Printz* rests on a misunderstanding. At the Founding, the argument goes, commandeering was *opposed* by those who believed in strong national power, and *supported* by those who wanted to preserve state sovereignty. Why? Because commandeering was seen as an alternative to a large central government. Commandeering meant that state governments would not be cut out of the enforcement of federal policy. On this argument, when the majority rejects Alexander Hamilton's view as "the most expansive view of federal authority ever expressed, and from the pen of the most expansive expositor of federal power," it misunderstands what is going on. Hamilton actually opposed commandeering, and he was *conceding* commandeering to the Anti-Federalists who favored it. See generally Wesley J. Campbell, *Commandeering and Constitutional Change*, 122 Yale L. J. 1104 (2013).

Suppose these historical arguments are correct. If federal commandeering of state officers was once seen as good for federalism, but today might be bad for federalism, what should the Supreme Court do? Follow the original view, and uphold commandeering, or take account of the change? More generally, should judges—especially originalist ones— change their constitutional beliefs every time new historical evidence is discovered?

4. The "non-commandeering" doctrine of *New York* and *Printz* can be seen as the Court tacking back in the other direction after *Garcia*. How is this doctrine, as elaborated by *Printz*, different from the four-part test of *National League of Cities*?

[*Assignment 29*]

C. THE POWER TO TAX

Art. I, § 2: . . . direct Taxes shall be apportioned among the several States which may be included within this Union, according to their respective Numbers, which shall be determined by adding to the whole Number of free persons, including those bound to Service for a Term of Years, and excluding Indians not taxed, three fifth of all other Persons. . . .

§ 8: The Congress shall have Power

To lay and collect Taxes, Duties, Imposts and Excises, to pay the Debts and provide for the common Defence and general Welfare of the United States; but all Duties, Imposts and Excises shall be uniform throughout the United States; . . .

§ 9: . . . No capitation, or other direct, Tax shall be laid, unless in Proportion to the Census or Enumeration herein before directed to be taken.

No Tax or Duty shall be laid on Articles exported from any State. . . .

Amend. XVI: The Congress shall have power to lay and collect taxes on incomes, from whatever source derived, without apportionment among the several States, and without regard to any census or enumeration.

Although the Commerce Clause power receives the most attention, two other national powers are also vitally important and closely linked: the power to tax and the power to spend. Any thorough account of federalism and national legislative authority must pay significant attention to these powers. This is especially true in light of the Supreme Court's reliance on these powers in *National Federation of Independent Business v. Sebelius*, 132 S.Ct. 2566 (2012). In these assignments, we first discuss the course of the Court's decisions concerning the Taxing Clause power prior to the decision in *NFIB*. We then take up the Court's decisions concerning the scope of Congress's spending power.

As Chief Justice John Marshall colorfully put it in *McCulloch v. Maryland*, "the power to tax is the power to destroy." And Congress has the power to tax. Indeed, it is the first power listed in the Article I, Section 8 enumeration of eighteen national legislative powers. What are the limits of that power?

Express Limits on the Power to Tax

Article I contains several express constraints on the taxing power, such as the ban on export taxes, and the requirement that "Duties, Imposts and Excises" be "uniform." But one of the most important, and most disputed, limits is the requirement that "direct taxes" be "apportioned" on the basis of population. This requirement is effectively listed twice in Article I, once in Section 2, and then again in Section 9.

A uniform tax has the same *rate* in every state. An apportioned tax must have the same *amount per person* in every state. Notice that the requirements of apportionment and of uniformity are mutually inconsistent. Imagine, for instance, that there is going to be a tax on whiskey stills, and that there are twice as many whiskey stills in Wisconsin as in Maryland. (The population of the two states is nearly identical.) A tax of $10 per still, across the entire United States, would be uniform. But it would not be apportioned: the amount of the tax per person in Wisconsin would be double the amount per person in Maryland, because of Wisconsin's greater number of stills. By contrast, a tax of $10 per still in Wisconsin and $20 per still in Maryland would be apportioned. But it would not be uniform. There is one exception: the apportionment and uniformity requirements could both be satisfied by a per-person tax, called a head tax or capitation tax. (Can you see why?)

All of this means that it can be very important to figure out what makes a tax "direct" in the constitutional sense, since this determines whether the apportionment requirement applies. As it happens, this question was presented by the Supreme Court's very first case directly challenging the constitutionality of an act of Congress, seven years before *Marbury v. Madison* would be decided: *Hylton v. United States*, 3 U.S. (3 Dall.) 171 (1796).

Hylton was a challenge to a congressional tax on carriages, which was not apportioned on the basis of population. The case came before the Supreme Court on the basis of stipulated facts, and with an arrangement of parties that may well have been contrived to create a test case rather than a genuinely adversarial dispute. (The United States apparently paid Hylton's attorneys, and the parties stipulated that Hylton owned 125 carriages, which was almost certainly untrue, but which just happened to add up to the minimum amount in controversy necessary for jurisdiction.) One of the attorneys arguing in favor of the tax was Alexander Hamilton.

All three of the justices who wrote seriatim opinions in *Hylton* (Chase, Paterson, and Iredell) upheld the tax as an indirect tax, not requiring apportionment but only uniformity. (At the time the Court had six members: Justice Wilson had upheld the tax while sitting as a judge on the circuit court, and while he did not write his own substantive opinion, he indicated that his views remained unchanged; Justice Cushing did not participate because he had been ill at the time of argument, and Chief Justice Ellsworth was sworn in the very morning the decision was announced.)

Hylton v. United States

3 U.S. (3 Dall.) 171 (1796)

■ Opinion of JUSTICE CHASE.

By the case stated, only one question is submitted to the opinion of this court; whether the law of Congress, of the 5th of June, 1794, entitled, "An act to lay duties upon carriages, for the conveyance of persons," is unconstitutional and void? . . .

As it was incumbent on the Plaintiff's Council in Error, so they took great pains to prove, that the tax on carriages was a direct tax; but they did not satisfy my mind. I think, at least, it may be doubted; and if I only doubted, I should affirm the judgment of the Circuit Court. The deliberate decision of the National Legislature, (who did not consider a tax on carriages a direct tax, but thought it was within the description of a duty) would determine me, if the case was doubtful, to receive the construction of the Legislature: But I am inclined to think, that a tax on carriages is not a direct tax, within the letter, or meaning, of the Constitution.

The great object of the Constitution was, to give Congress a power to lay taxes, adequate to the exigencies of government; but they were to observe two rules in imposing them, namely, the rule of uniformity, when they laid duties, imposts, or excises; and the rule of apportionment, according to the census, when they laid any direct tax.

If there are any other species of taxes that are not direct, and not included within the words duties, imposts, or excises, they may be laid by the rule of uniformity, or not; as Congress shall think proper and reasonable. If the framers of the Constitution did not contemplate other taxes than direct taxes, and duties, imposts, and excises, there is great inaccuracy in their language. If these four species of taxes were all that were meditated, the general power to lay taxes was unnecessary. If it was intended, that Congress should have authority to lay only one of the four above enumerated, to wit, direct taxes, by the rule of apportionment, and the other three by the rule of uniformity, the expressions would have run thus: "Congress shall have power to lay and collect direct taxes, and duties, imposts, and excises; the first shall be laid according to the census; and the three last shall be uniform throughout the United States." . . .

. . . The rule of apportionment is only to be adopted in such cases where it can reasonably apply; and the subject taxed, must ever determine the application of the rule.

If it is proposed to tax any specific article by the rule of apportionment, and it would evidently create great inequality and injustice, it is unreasonable to say, that the Constitution intended such tax should be laid by that rule.

It appears to me, that a tax on carriages cannot be laid by the rule of apportionment, without very great inequality and injustice. . . .

I think, an annual tax on carriages for the conveyance of persons, may be considered as within the power granted to Congress to lay duties. The term duty, is the most comprehensive next to the generical term tax; and practically in Great Britain, (whence we take our general ideas of taxes, duties, imposts, excises, customs, etc.) embraces taxes on stamps, tolls for passage, etc. etc. and is not confined to taxes on importation only. . . .

I am inclined to think, but of this I do not give a judicial opinion, that the direct taxes contemplated by the Constitution, are only two, to wit, a capitation, or poll tax, simply, without regard to property, profession, or any other circumstance; and a tax on LAND. I doubt whether a tax, by a general assessment of personal property, within the United States, is included within the term direct tax. . . .

■ Opinion of JUSTICE PATERSON.

. . . The question is, whether a tax upon carriages be a direct tax? If it be a direct tax, it is unconstitutional, because it has been laid pursuant to the rule of uniformity, and not to the rule of apportionment. In behalf of the Plaintiff in error, it has been urged, that a tax on carriages does not come within the description of a duty, impost, or excise, and therefore is a direct tax. It has, on the other hand, been contended, that as a tax on carriages is not a direct tax; it must fall within one of the classifications just enumerated, and particularly must be a duty or excise. The argument on both sides turns in a circle; it is not a duty, impost, or excise, and therefore must be a direct tax; it is not tax, and therefore must be a duty or excise. What is the natural and common, or technical and appropriate, meaning of the words, duty and excise, it is not easy to ascertain. They present no clear and precise idea to the mind. Different persons will annex different significations to the terms.

It was, however, obviously the intention of the framers of the Constitution, that Congress should possess full power over every species of taxable property, except exports. The term taxes, is generical, and was made use of to vest in Congress plenary authority in all cases of taxation. The general division of taxes is into direct and indirect. Although the latter term is not to be found in the Constitution, yet the former necessarily implies it. Indirect stands opposed to direct. There may, perhaps, be an indirect tax on a particular article, that cannot be comprehended within the description of duties, or imposts, or excises; in such case it will be comprised under the general denomination of taxes. For the term tax is the genus, and includes,

1. Direct taxes.

2. Duties, imposts, and excises.

3. All other classes of an indirect kind, and not within any of the classifications enumerated under the preceding heads. . . .

. . . I never entertained a doubt, that the principal, I will not say, the only, objects, that the framers of the Constitution contemplated as falling within the rule of apportionment, were a capitation tax and a tax on land. Local considerations, and the particular circumstances, and relative situation of the states, naturally lead to this view of the subject. The provision was made in favor of the southern States. They possessed a large number of slaves; they had extensive tracts of territory, thinly settled, and not very productive. A majority of the states had but few slaves, and several of them a limited territory, well settled, and in a high state of cultivation. The southern states, if no provision had been introduced in the Constitution, would have been wholly at the mercy of the other states. Congress in such case, might tax slaves, at discretion or arbitrarily, and land in every part of the Union after the same rate or measure: so much a head in the first instance, and so much an acre in the second. To guard them against imposition in these particulars, was the reason of introducing the clause in the Constitution, which directs that representatives and direct taxes shall be apportioned among the states, according to their respective numbers.

On the part of the Plaintiff in error, it has been contended, that the rule of apportionment is to be favored rather than the rule of uniformity; and, of course, that the instrument is to receive such a construction, as will extend the former and restrict the latter. I am not of that opinion. The Constitution has been considered as an accommodating system; it was the effect of mutual sacrifices and concessions; it was the work of compromise. The rule of apportionment is of this nature; it is radically wrong; it cannot be supported by any solid reasoning. Why should slaves, who are a species of property, be represented more than any other property? The rule, therefore, ought not to be extended by construction.

Again, numbers do not afford a just estimate or rule of wealth. It is, indeed, a very uncertain and incompetent sign of opulence. There is another reason against the extension of the principle laid down in the Constitution. . . .

. . . All taxes on expenses or consumption are indirect taxes. A tax on carriages is of this kind, and of course is not a direct tax. Indirect taxes are circuitous modes of reaching the revenue of individuals, who generally live according to their income. In many cases of this nature the individual may be said to tax himself. I shall close the discourse with reading a passage or two from Smith's Wealth of Nations.

"The impossibility of taxing people in proportion to their revenue, by any capitation, seems to have given occasion to the invention of taxes upon consumable commodities; the state not knowing how to tax directly and proportionably the revenue of its subjects, endeavours to tax it indirectly by taxing their expense, which it is supposed in most cases will be neatly in proportion to their revenue. Their expense is taxed by taxing the consumable commodities upon which it is laid out." . . .

■ Opinion of JUSTICE IREDELL.

. . . If it can be considered as a tax, neither direct within the meaning of the Constitution, nor comprehended within the term duty, impost or excise; there is no provision in the Constitution, one way or another, and then it must be left to such an operation of the power, as if the authority to lay taxes had been given generally in all instances, without saying whether they should be apportioned or uniform; and in that case, I should presume, the tax ought to be uniform; because the present Constitution was particularly intended to affect individuals, and not states, except in particular cases specified: And this is the leading distinction between the articles of Confederation and the present Constitution.

As all direct taxes must be apportioned, it is evident that the Constitution contemplated none as direct but such as could be apportioned.

If this cannot be apportioned, it is, therefore, not a direct tax in the sense of the Constitution.

That this tax cannot be apportioned is evident. Suppose 10 dollars contemplated as a tax on each chariot, or post chaise, in the United States, and the number of both in all the United States be computed at 105, the number of Representatives in Congress.

This would produce in the whole .... 1050 dollars

The share of *Virginia* being 19/105 parts, would be .... 190 dollars

The share of *Connecticut* being 7/105 parts, would be .... 70 dollars

Then suppose *Virginia* had 50 carriages, [and] Connecticut 2.

The share of *Virginia* being 190 dollars, this must of course be collected from the owners of carriages, and there would therefore be collected from each carriage[:] 3 dollars, 80 cents

The share of *Connecticut* being 70 dollars, each carriage would pay 35 dollars.

If any state had no carriages, there could be no apportionment at all. This mode is too manifestly absurd to be supported, and has not even been attempted in debate. . . .

There is no necessity, or propriety, in determining what is or is not, a direct, or indirect, tax in all cases. . . .

NOTES

1.   Consider the similarities and differences between the three opinions. How much do they agree about the definition of a direct tax? Is there a core of agreement between them? Do they use the same methods of constitutional argument to get there?

(Are you glad that now the justices usually produce a single majority opinion?) For an examination of the *Hylton* opinions, see Joel Alicea & Donald Drakeman, *The Limits of New Originalism*, 15 U. Pa. J. Const. L. 1161 (2012).

2.   What do you make of the argument that a tax should be direct only if it could reasonably be apportioned? Is that common sense, or circular? And is it consistent with the agreement among the justices that a tax on land would be a direct tax? How would a tax on land be apportioned more fairly than a tax on carriages?

3.   Are all federal taxes subject to either uniformity or apportionment? That is, are all federal taxes either "direct" taxes or else "duties, imposts, and excises"? If not, what falls in the gap between them? Why might the framers of the Constitution have wanted for some taxes to be subject to neither uniformity nor apportionment?

4.   The line between direct and indirect taxes remains elusive. There is widespread agreement that land taxes and capitation taxes are direct, and *Hylton* became an early precedent establishing broad national power to impose unapportioned taxes on commodities, consumption, and conduct.

Nonetheless, ninety-nine years later the Court reaffirmed the limits on the taxing power, and invalidated the federal income tax. In *Pollock v. Farmers' Loan & Trust*, 158 U.S. 601 (1895), in an opinion by Chief Justice Fuller, the Court concluded that "a tax upon a person's entire income—whether derived from rents or products, or otherwise, of real estate, or from bonds, stocks, or other forms of personal property" was a direct tax. The Court concluded that Alexander Hamilton had believed that "all internal taxes, except duties and excises on articles of consumption, fell into the category of direct taxes." It distinguished *Hylton*, and observed that "[t]he case is badly reported." The Court explained its own view of the purposes of the direct tax restrictions:

> The reasons for the clauses of the constitution in respect of direct taxation are not far to seek. The states, respectively, possessed plenary powers of taxation. They could tax the property of their citizens in such manner and to such extent as they saw fit. They had unrestricted powers to impose duties or imposts on imports from abroad, and excises on manufactures, consumable commodities, or otherwise. They gave up the great sources of revenue derived from commerce. They retained the concurrent power of levying excises, and duties if covering anything other than excises; but in respect of them the range of taxation was narrowed by the power granted over interstate commerce, and by the danger of being put at disadvantage in dealing with excises on manufactures. They retained the power of direct taxation, and to that they looked as their chief resource; but even in respect of that they granted the concurrent power, and, if the tax were placed by both governments on the same subject, the claim of the United States had preference. Therefore they did not grant the power of direct taxation without regard to their own condition and resources as states, but they granted the power of apportioned direct taxation,—a power just as efficacious to serve the needs of the general government, but securing to the states the opportunity to pay the amount apportioned, and to recoup from their own citizens in the most feasible way, and in harmony with their systems of local self-government. . . .

> The founders anticipated that the expenditures of the states, their counties, cities, and towns, would chiefly be met by direct taxation on accumulated property, while they expected that those of the federal government would be for the most part met by indirect taxes. And in order that the power of direct taxation by the general government should not be exercised

except on necessity, and, when the necessity arose, should be so exercised as to leave the states at liberty to discharge their respective obligations, and should not be so exercised unfairly and discriminatingly, as to particular states or otherwise, by a mere majority vote, possibly of those whose constituents were intentionally not subjected to any part of the burden, the qualified grant was made. . . .

Id. at 620–622. The Court concluded that the income tax was direct, as a matter of text and historical context:

Whatever the speculative views of political economists or revenue reformers may be, can it be properly held that the constitution, taken in its plain and obvious sense, and with due regard to the circumstances attending the formation of the government, authorizes a general unapportioned tax on the products of the farm and the rents of real estate, although imposed merely because of ownership, and with no possible means of escape from payment, as belonging to a totally different class from that which includes the property from whence the income proceeds?

There can be but one answer, unless the constitutional restriction is to be treated as utterly illusory and futile, and the object of its framers defeated. We find it impossible to hold that a fundamental requisition deemed so important as to be enforced by two provisions, one affirmative and one negative, can be refined away by forced distinctions between that which gives value to property and the property itself.

Nor can we perceive any ground why the same reasoning does not apply to capital in personalty held for the purpose of income, or ordinarily yielding income, and to the income therefrom. . . .

Id. at 627–628.

The Court's analysis was focused specifically on the income *from property*. The Court suggested that Congress might "lay excise taxes on business, privileges, employments, and vocations," but it concluded that the current income tax scheme was not severable and invalidated the whole thing. The Court said, "We are not here concerned with the question whether an income tax be or be not desirable . . . . Questions of that character belong to the controversies of political parties, and cannot be settled by judicial decision." Moreover, the Court added, speaking of the Constitution: "the instrument defines the way for its amendment. In no part of it was greater sagacity displayed."

5.   After a decade and a half of populist agitation, and with the endorsement of President William Howard Taft, Congress proposed an income tax amendment in 1909. In 1913, it was ratified as the Sixteenth Amendment:

The Congress shall have power to lay and collect taxes on incomes, from whatever source derived, without apportionment among the several States, and without regard to any census or enumeration.

U.S. Const. Amdt. XVI. It was the third time in history that the country had reversed a Supreme Court decision with a constitutional amendment, and it would not be the last.

Does the Sixteenth Amendment moot the question of which taxes are "direct"? Does it suggest that *Pollock*'s view was wrong and that *Hylton*'s was right? Or does it concede that *Pollock* had interpreted the Constitution correctly, and that was why it needed to be amended?

Implied Limits on the Power to Tax?

Note that there was no issue in *Hylton* or *Pollock* as to the bare power of Congress to impose a tax on carriages or land in the first place. The only issue was whether the tax imposed was direct as opposed to indirect and thus in need of being apportioned on the basis of population. Aside from the requirements of apportionment and uniformity, are there any other limits on the taxing power?

Consider: May Congress impose a tax on essentially anything it likes (or, perhaps, that it *doesn't* like), with the only constraints being apportionment for direct taxes and geographical uniformity for all others? The power to tax is a freestanding, independent national legislative power—indeed, it is the very first power listed in Article I, Section 8. But what is the scope of that power, and for what purposes may it be employed? May Congress impose a tax to achieve a regulatory or policy purpose apart from raising revenue—such as to express disfavor for the carriage industry or aid its competitors (or, alternatively, to protect a favored industry by imposing tariffs or excises on competing products from abroad)? May Congress impose a tax, for regulatory purposes, even where it might not have the express power to regulate that activity directly? (Would Congress otherwise have power to regulate a purely intrastate carriage business?) Is there any limitation on how large such a tax may be before it becomes in effect a regulation of something Congress lacks power to regulate, or are there no such limits because the taxing power is its own, independent power?

The Supreme Court's cases have charted an uncertain path on these questions, as the following brief survey illustrates, but generally the Court has held that the Taxing Clause power is an independent power that can be used to achieve goals not attainable under the other enumerated powers. At the same time, it has sometimes attempted to enunciate a limit to that power.

1. In the *License Tax Cases*, 72 U.S. (5 Wall.) 462 (1866), the Court upheld the Internal Revenue Act's license-and-fee requirement for selling lottery tickets and retailing liquor, even as to purely intrastate activities. The taxpayers challenging the exaction argued that Congress lacked such taxing authority as to activities carried on purely within a state. The Court agreed that Congress would have had "no power of regulation nor any direct control" over the businesses at issue. But the Court nonetheless found that Congress could impose a license requirement *as a tax*: "[T]he power of Congress to tax is a very extensive power. It is given in the Constitution, with only one exception and only two qualifications. Congress cannot tax exports, and it must impose direct taxes by the rule of apportionment, and indirect taxes by the rule of uniformity. Thus limited, and thus only, it reaches every subject, and may be exercised at discretion."

At the same, the Court also stressed that the taxing power could not be used to actually authorize businesses to sell lottery tickets or retail liquor, if forbidden by state law: "[I]t reaches only existing subjects. Congress cannot authorize a trade or business within a State in order to tax it. . . . The granting of a license, therefore, must be regarded as nothing more than a mere form of imposing a tax, and of implying nothing except that the licensee shall be subject to no penalties under national law, if he pays it."

The *License Tax Cases* are thus early authority for the proposition that Congress can tax activities that it has no authority to directly regulate under the Commerce

Clause. If so, how much can the taxing power be used to get around the limits of the other enumerated powers? What limits *can't* it circumvent?

2.   Not long after the *License Tax Cases,* in *Veazie Bank v. Fenno,* 75 U.S. (8 Wall.) 533 (1869), the Court upheld a federal tax on state bank notes against a charge that it was "excessive." That did not disable the Taxing Clause power, the Court held, but was a matter for political judgment: "[T]he judicial cannot prescribe to the legislative departments of the government limitations upon the exercise of its acknowledged powers. The power to tax may be exercised oppressively upon persons, but the responsibility of the Legislature is not to the courts, but to the people by whom its members are elected."

In dicta, however, the Court added that: "There are, indeed, certain virtual limitations, arising from the principles of the Constitution itself. It would undoubtedly be an abuse of the power if so exercised as to impair the separate existence and independent self-government of the States, or if exercised for ends inconsistent with the limited grants of power in the Constitution."

Was the Court correct in saying that the size of a tax is for legislative judgment? Is there anything in the Constitution that would supply a principled basis for distinguishing between when a tax is excessive and when it is not? What should we make of the dictum? How could a tax threaten the existence and independence of the states? What does it mean for it to be "exercised for ends inconsistent with the limited grants of power in the Constitution"? Did *The License Tax Cases* themselves violate that principle?

3.   The next notable case was *McCray v. United States,* 195 U.S. 27 (1904), which involved an excise tax on "oleomargarine," now known as margarine. Oleomargarine was a butter substitute made from other fats and oils. The tax was almost certainly enacted to benefit butter producers. The Court sustained the validity of the tax, noting that while the courts possessed the duty of upholding the Constitution, this did not include "the responsibility of correcting every possible abuse arising from the exercise by the other departments of their conceded authority." To so hold would "overthrow the entire distinction between the legislative, judicial, and executive departments of the government, upon which our system is founded, and would be a mere act of judicial usurpation." The Court disclaimed any power to invalidate a tax simply because of the policy motivations that might have prompted it:

> It is, however, argued, if a lawful power may be exerted for an unlawful purpose, and thus, by abusing the power, it may be made to accomplish a result not intended by the Constitution, all limitations of power must disappear, and the grave function lodged in the judiciary, to confine all the departments within the authority conferred by the Constitution, will be of no avail. This, when reduced to its last analysis, comes to this: that, because a particular department of the government may exert its lawful powers with the object or motive of reaching an end not justified, therefore it becomes the duty of the judiciary to restrain the exercise of a lawful power wherever it seems to the judicial mind that such lawful power has been abused. But this reduces itself to this contention that, under our constitutional system, the abuse by one department of the government of

its lawful powers is to be corrected by the abuse of its powers by another department.

The remedy for an alleged abuse of the taxing power, the Court said, "lies, not in the abuse by the judicial authority of its functions, but in the people, upon whom, after all, under our institutions, reliance must be placed for the correction of abuses committed in the exercise of a lawful power."

Is it possible to find any limits on the taxing power if one ignores the motive behind the tax? If so, how? If not, does that make *McCray* incorrect? What did the Court mean that it would be an "abuse of its powers" to review Congress's motive?

4.   This brings us to *Bailey v. Drexel Furniture Co.,* 259 U.S. 20 (1922), also known as the *Child Labor Tax Case.* As noted earlier, p. 519, *Hammer v. Dagenhart* (1918) denied that the Commerce Clause gave Congress any power to regulate the interstate shipment of goods produced by child labor. That decision was eventually overruled by *United States v. Darby* (1941). In the meantime, though, Congress tried another way around *Hammer*—it imposed a 10% tax on the profits of businesses using child labor.

More precisely, the tax required the following:

> That every person (other than a bona fide boys' or girls' canning club recognized by the Agricultural Department of a State and of the United States) operating (a) any mine or quarry situated in the United States in which children under the age of sixteen years have been employed or permitted to work during any portion of the taxable year; or (b) any mill, cannery, workshop, factory, or manufacturing establishment situated in the United States in which children under the age of fourteen years have been employed or permitted to work, or children between the ages of fourteen and sixteen have been employed or permitted to work more than eight hours in any day or more than six days in any week, or after the hour of seven o'clock post meridian, or before the hour of six o'clock ante meridian, during any portion of the taxable year, shall pay for each taxable year, in addition to all other taxes imposed by law, an excise tax equivalent to 10 per centum of the entire net profits received or accrued for such year from the sale or disposition of the product of such mine, quarry, mill, cannery, workshop, factory, or manufacturing establishment.

40 Stat. 1057, 1038 (1919).

The law also provided a defense to the tax if the employer made a reasonable mistake or relied on a government document certifying the child to be of legal age, and provided that the tax was enforceable either by the commissioner of internal revenue or the secretary of labor.

In a shift from its previous cases, the Court invalidated the law. It distinguished *Veazie* and *McCray* on the ground that they did not involve "the detailed specifications of a regulation of a state concern and business with a heavy exaction to promote the efficacy of such regulation." The Court found that "[t]he case before us . . . cannot be distinguished from that of *Hammer v. Dagenhart.*" It explained:

> Out of a proper respect for the acts of a co-ordinate branch of the government, this court has gone far to sustain taxing acts as such, even though there has been ground for suspecting, from the weight of the tax, it

was intended to destroy its subject. But in the act before us the presumption of validity cannot prevail, because the proof of the contrary is found on the very face of its provisions. Grant the validity of this law, and all that Congress would need to do, hereafter, in seeking to take over to its control any one of the great number of subjects of public interest, jurisdiction of which the states have never parted with, and which are reserved to them by the Tenth Amendment, would be to enact a detailed measure of complete regulation of the subject and enforce it by a so called tax upon departures from it. To give such magic to the word "tax" would be to break down all constitutional limitations of the powers of Congress and completely wipe out the sovereignty of the states.

The difference between a tax and a penalty is sometimes difficult to define, and yet the consequences of the distinction in the required method of their collection often are important. Where the sovereign enacting the law has power to impose both tax and penalty, the difference between revenue production and mere regulation may be immaterial, but not so when one sovereign can impose a tax only, and the power of regulation rests in another. Taxes are occasionally imposed in the discretion of the Legislature on proper subjects with the primary motive of obtaining revenue from them and with the incidental motive of discouraging them by making their continuance onerous. They do not lose their character as taxes because of the incidental motive. But there comes a time in the extension of the penalizing features of the so-called tax when it loses its character as such and becomes a mere penalty, with the characteristics of regulation and punishment. Such is the case in the law before us. Although Congress does not invalidate the contract of employment or expressly declare that the employment within the mentioned ages is illegal, it does exhibit its intent practically to achieve the latter result by adopting the criteria of wrongdoing and imposing its principal consequence on those who transgress its standard.

Is *Bailey* right that there has to be some point where something labeled as a "tax" is *really* a penalty, and therefore must be justified (if at all) by the other enumerated powers? If so, does *Bailey* actually tell us how to find that point, or it just ad hoc? Also, is *Bailey* consistent with the *License Tax Cases, Veazie,* and *McCray*? If not, which cases are correct?

5.   In *Steward Machine Company v. Davis,* 301 U.S. 548 (1937), and *Helvering v. Davis,* 301 U.S. 619 (1937), the Court tacked back again in the direction of broad national government power to impose taxes and spend money to further regulatory and social policy purposes. These decisions occurred in the same year as the Court's decisions in *NLRB v. Jones & Laughlin Steel,* the 5–4 decision adopting a broad construction of Congress's legislative commerce power, and *West Coast Hotel v. Parrish,* which repudiated earlier cases imposing substantive due process restrictions on state laws regulating economic activity, discussed at p. 1540. *Steward Machine* and *Helvering* thus coincided with the "Revolution of 1937," or the supposed "switch in time that saved nine."

Steward Machine sustained, by vote of 5–4, the unemployment compensation tax provisions of the Social Security Act of 1935, which were designed to induce states to adopt their own unemployment compensation laws—laws that the national government clearly could not directly require states to enact. Title IX of the act imposed a payroll tax on employers but provided a credit of up to 90% of the federal tax for any contributions to a state unemployment fund certified by the federal government as complying with prescribed federal standards. Though the tax and refund scheme was plainly intended to achieve social policy goals, it nonetheless was within the Taxing Clause power. Thus, the core of the challenge in *Steward Machine* was not to the tax itself, but to its supposed effect of "coercing" the states. The Court rejected that challenge: "The statute does not call for a surrender by the states of powers essential to their quasi-sovereign existence." The Court distinguished the *Child Labor Tax Case* as presenting different issues.

Steward Machine raises a variety of questions in connection with Congress's spending power: Are there principled constitutional limitations on Congress's ability to use its financial powers—the power to tax and the power to spend—to compel or induce action *by states*? Do state-autonomy concerns check what would otherwise be the scope of these congressional powers? We will return to these questions, but for now, it is sufficient to note that *Steward Machine* upheld a broad power to impose taxes in order to achieve social policy objectives, and not merely to raise revenues.

6.   Finally, in *United States v. Kahriger,* 345 U.S. 22 (1953), the Court upheld a federal tax on "persons engaged in the business of accepting wagers"—that is, "bookies." The tax was challenged as unconstitutional on the ground that "Congress, under the pretense of exercising its power to tax has attempted to penalize illegal intrastate gambling through the regulatory features of the Act . . . and has thus infringed the police power which is reserved to the states." The Court upheld the tax, citing the *License Tax Cases, Veazie, McCray,* and several other cases upholding taxes where "the intent to curtail and hinder, as well as tax," an activity was "manifest." The Court in *Kahriger* noted that it was "conceded that a federal excise tax does not cease to be valid merely because it discourages or deters the activities taxed. Nor is the tax invalid because the revenue obtained is negligible. Appellee, however, argues that the sole purpose of the statute is to penalize only illegal gambling in the states through the guise of a tax measure. As with the above excise taxes which we have held to be valid, the instant tax has a regulatory effect. But regardless of its regulatory effect, the wagering tax produces revenue."

Two justices dissented. Justice Jackson joined the Court's opinion but expressed reservations: "I concur in the judgment and opinion of the Court, but with such doubt that if the minority agreed upon an opinion which did not impair legitimate use of the taxing power I probably would join it."

What happened to the *Child Labor Tax Cases*? Can they be distinguished from *Kahriger*? Or does *Kahriger* prove that the *Child Labor Tax Cases* couldn't come up with an administrable line between taxes and penalties? And what do you make of Justice Jackson's reservations?

7.   A summary question: Based on this whirlwind tour, what do you believe is the correct understanding of the Taxing Clause power? Which cases are right, and which are wrong? May Congress impose taxes purely for policy purposes? If so, are there any limits? If not, how do you tell if a tax is a "real" tax, or instead one that impermissibly seeks to accomplish a collateral purpose? Does one look to legislative motivation? Is the distinction between a "tax" and a "penalty" sensible, or does it lack meaningful content? Should (or does) how Congress characterizes its financial

exactions matter in deciding whether an exercise of its Taxing Clause power is legitimate? Or is it the substance that counts? Must a tax actually raise some revenue to be a tax? If so, how much? Keep these questions in mind—and your preliminary answers—as we return to these issues in *National Federation of Independent Business v. Sebelius*, p. 629.

[*Assignment 30*]

D. THE POWER TO SPEND

Art. I, § 8: The Congress shall have Power

To lay and collect Taxes, Duties, Imposts and Excises, to pay the Debts and provide for the common Defence and general Welfare of the United States;
. . .

To make all Laws which shall be necessary and proper for carrying into Execution the foregoing Powers and all other Powers vested by this Constitution in the Government of the United States, or in any Department or Officer thereof.

Art. IV, § 3: The Congress shall have Power to dispose of and make all needful Rules and Regulations respecting the Territory or other Property belonging to the United States. . . .

The Spending Power

It is generally assumed that Article I, Section 8, Clause 1 empowers Congress not only to collect money through taxes but also to spend money ("for the common Defence and general Welfare"). But read it carefully. Does the clause actually say that? It reads like a limitation on the purposes for which *taxes* may be imposed. If that provision is the basis for the spending power, would it authorize Congress to spend money from sources other than taxes? For example, the federal government once gained significant revenues from the sale of western lands. Surely those revenues could be spent.

But if the "general Welfare" clause is not the source of the spending power, where does it come from? One possibility is the Necessary and Proper Clause. If that were the source, then Congress could spend money only in service of its other enumerated powers; there would be no free-standing power to spend. One scholar suggests the spending power comes from Congress's "Power to dispose of . . . Property belonging to the United States," which is in Article IV, not Article I. David Engdahl, *The Basis for the Spending Power*, 18 Seattle U. L. Rev. 215 (1995). Despite these other textual possibilities, the widespread assumption, both at the Founding and today, is that the basis for the spending power is indeed the "general Welfare" clause.

The spending power raises many questions. What is the relation between the spending power and the taxing power? And what is the relationship between the spending power and the other enumerated powers? For instance, can the spending power be used to accomplish goals otherwise outside of Congress's enumerated powers? If so, does that allow circumvention of the principles of federalism? But if not, does that make the spending power redundant?

For modern purposes, the most significant question involving the spending power is the scope of conditions that Congress can attach to appropriations. Can the federal government effectively "buy" state acquiescence, granting money on the condition that the state do (or refrain from doing) something that the federal government does not have power to require? To put it bluntly, may Congress tax the people of all fifty states, and then "give" the money back only to those states that toe the federal line? At one end of the spectrum, Congress surely may impose conditions to ensure that funds are spent for the purposes they are appropriated for. States have the power to train their own police forces, but if Congress appropriates money to train state police in proper techniques for the use of force, no one doubts the states must use the funds as Congress directs, or else not at all. But could Congress say that citizens of Arkansas will not get their Social Security checks unless the legislature repeals its religious freedom law? Or no Social Security checks for Coloradans, until the state repeals its recreational marijuana law? In particular, must the conditions attached have some relationship to the goal of the spending? Or does the fact that a state or individual is always free to refuse the money (and thus the strings attached to it) mean that Congress can impose any conditions it wants? (Remember, federal grants to states are not gifts or freebies, like money on the Free Parking square; the people of every state are coerced to pay taxes, and then get some of *their money* back in the form of federal spending.)

We first present several early debates about the spending power, which include the Assumption Controversy, the contrasting views of Madison and Hamilton, and the congressional debate over providing relief to the city of Savannah, Georgia after a fire ravaged the city in 1796. We then turn to the modern era, briefly describing the New Deal interpretation of the spending power and considering the major case of *South Dakota v. Dole*, 483 U.S. 203 (1987). The arguments made from the Founding until *Dole* are still with us, and our consideration of them will culminate in *National Federation of Independent Business v. Sebelius*, p. 629.

The Assumption Controversy

An early controversy over the scope of the new national government's power, predating by a year even the issue of the power to create a Bank of the United States, was the issue of "assumption." In 1790, Secretary of the Treasury Alexander Hamilton proposed that the national government assume (i.e., take over) the vast unpaid debts that the state governments had incurred in the Revolutionary War. The national government would then finance the debt through notes (i.e., bonds) that would be backed by revenue from national excise taxes, including taxes on coffee, tea, wine, and spirits. Hamilton argued that his plan would free the states of their debts, establish a national system of credit and public finance, and provide government notes that would circulate through the economy and function as currency. The effect, Hamilton hoped, would be to secure the economic and political supremacy of the national government.

There was resistance. (Which was unsurprising: could anyone forget another excise tax on tea, one that led to a little party in Boston Harbor?) The assumption plan, the critics said, would tend to consolidate power in the national government and subordinate the states. James Madison objected that funding the notes would reward speculators, who bought them at pennies on the dollar from impoverished veterans. Virginia, which claimed to have paid most of its debt, objected to what was in effect a bailout for the other states. And there were constitutional objections. For instance, Representative Michael Stone, of Maryland, said:

> It does not appear to me that the debts of the particular States are the debts of the United States. State debts, and debts of the United States, are hardly convertible terms; and I question very much, whether it is strictly within our constitutional power to levy taxes and collect duties, except it be to pay the debts of the United States. Will it be admitted that Congress can adopt any debts they think proper, whether they come within the idea of being debts contracted for the purposes of the Confederation or not? . . . If this is granted to be a principle of our Constitution, it may be a dangerous one. If Congress say they want money for some purpose which they conceive to be salutary to the United States, but which, at the same time, is not a constitutional object of their power, have they a right to levy duties for such a purpose? And if they have, where is the limit to which they may not go? Or where is the boundary by which they are restrained.

2 ANNALS OF CONGRESS 1314 (History of Congress edition). Representative Roger Sherman of Connecticut later responded that the issue of assumption necessarily involved two questions:

> 1st. Is Congress, by the principles of the Constitution, authorized to assume the debts?

> 2d. Supposing the power to exist, does prudence, policy, and justice, dictate the proposed measure?

>   It should be observed that Congress, by the Constitution, is authorized to levy money in all instances where, in their opinion, the expenditure shall be for the "general welfare"; an answer, therefore, to the second of these questions would depend on the decision of the first: if prudence, policy, and justice dictated the assumption of the State debts, it must be for the general welfare that they should be assumed.

2 ANNALS OF CONGRESS 1334 (History of Congress edition).

   A version of Hamilton's assumption plan was eventually enacted. At first, the House voted against it, but after an informal meeting between Hamilton, Madison, and Jefferson, a compromise was reached. Most state debts were assumed, and Virginia was promised reimbursement and the future national capital city. Cf. *The Room Where it Happens*, HAMILTON (Original Broadway Cast Recording, Atlantic Records 2015).

   Was assumption justified by Congress's spending power, and if so why? Was national assumption of (varying) state debts—and the indirect burdens this placed on other parts of the nation—consistent with the Constitution's principles of federalism? Or was the real constitutional problem with assumption the pressure it created to raise taxes, or perhaps the way those taxes were imposed? Can the taxing power and the spending power be separated?

Two Views of the Spending Power: Madison and Hamilton

   In his speech opposing the constitutionality of the Bank of the United States, p. 472, Madison had also put forth, in passing, a restricted view of the "general Welfare" clause. "No argument," he said, "could be drawn from the terms 'common defence and general welfare.' The power as to these general purposes was limited to acts laying taxes for them; and the general purposes themselves were limited and explained by the particular enumeration subjoined." Alexander Hamilton, by contrast, took a broader view of "general welfare," and hence of Congress's spending power.

Madison elaborated his view throughout his career. On the last day of his presidency, March 3, 1817, Madison vetoed the "Bonus Bill," which was designed to fund roads and canals and other "internal improvements." In his veto message he first concluded that the legislation exceeded Congress's commerce power. He then argued, in the excerpt given here, that it followed that the legislation was beyond the spending power as well. The next excerpt is from Hamilton's Report on Manufactures, written shortly after his Report on Public Credit that led to the assumption policy.

James Madison, Veto Message on the Bonus Bill
Mar. 3, 1817

To refer the power in question to the clause "to provide for the common defense and general welfare" would be contrary to the established and consistent rules of interpretation, as rendering the special and careful enumeration of powers which follow the clause nugatory and improper. Such a view of the Constitution would have the effect of giving to Congress a general power of legislation instead of the defined and limited one hitherto understood to belong to them, the terms "common defense and general welfare" embracing every object and act within the purview of a legislative trust. It would have the effect of subjecting both the Constitution and laws of the several States in all cases not specifically exempted to be superseded by laws of Congress, it being expressly declared "that the Constitution of the United States and laws made in pursuance thereof shall be the supreme law of the land, and the judges of every State shall be bound thereby, anything in the constitution or laws of any State to the contrary notwithstanding." Such a view of the Constitution, finally, would have the effect of excluding the judicial authority of the United States from its participation in guarding the boundary between the legislative powers of the General and the State Governments, inasmuch as questions relating to the general welfare, being questions of policy and expediency, are unsusceptible of judicial cognizance and decision.

A restriction of the power "to provide for the common defense and general welfare" to cases which are to be provided for by the expenditure of money would still leave within the legislative power of Congress all the great and most important measures of Government, money being the ordinary and necessary means of carrying them into execution.

Alexander Hamilton, Report on Manufactures
Dec. 5, 1791

The National Legislature has express authority "To lay and Collect taxes, duties, imposts and excises, to pay the debts and provide for the *Common defence* and *general welfare*" with no other qualifications than that "all duties, imposts and excises, shall be *uniform* throughout the United states, that no capitation or other direct tax shall be laid unless in proportion to numbers ascertained by a census or enumeration taken on the principles prescribed in the Constitution, and that "no tax or duty shall be laid on articles exported from any state." These three qualifications excepted, the power to *raise money* is *plenary*, and *indefinite*; and the objects to which it may be *appropriated* are no less comprehensive, than the payment of the public debts and the providing for the common defence and *"general Welfare."* The terms *"general Welfare"* were doubtless intended to signify more than was expressed or imported in those which Preceded; otherwise numerous exigencies incident to the affairs of a Nation would have been left without a provision. The phrase is as comprehensive as any that could have been used; because it was not fit that the constitutional authority of the Union, to appropriate its revenues shou'd have been restricted within narrower limits than the "General Welfare" and because this necessarily embraces a vast variety of particulars, which are susceptible neither of specification nor of definition.

It is therefore of necessity left to the discretion of the National Legislature, to pronounce, upon the objects, which concern the general Welfare, and for which under that description, an appropriation of money is requisite and proper. And there seems to be no room for a doubt that whatever concerns the general Interests of *learning* of *Agriculture* of *Manufactures* and of *Commerce* are within the sphere of the national Councils *as far as regards an application of Money*.

The only qualification of the generallity of the Phrase in question, which seems to be admissible, is this—That the object to which an appropriation of money is to be made be *General* and not *local*; its operation extending in fact, or by possibility, throughout the Union, and not being confined to a particular spot.

No objection ought to arise to this construction from a supposition that it would imply a power to do whatever else should appear to Congress conducive to the General Welfare. A power to appropriate money with this latitude which is granted too in *express terms* would not carry a power to do any other thing, not authorised in the constitution, either expressly or by fair implication.

NOTES

1.   Weigh the arguments given by Madison and Hamilton. Madison alludes to the "general welfare" clause of the Articles of Confederation, Article VIII, p. 1675. Is Madison right that the phrase should mean the same thing in the Constitution that it meant in the Articles? How would we find out what it meant in the Articles? Why does Hamilton say that his interpretation does "not imply a power to do whatever else should appear to Congress conducive to the General Welfare"? What are the limits to the Hamiltonian view of the spending power?

2.   The debate between the Madisonian and Hamiltonian views of the spending power was persistent, but Congress found ways to avoid answering the question.

The First Congress appropriated money to build a lighthouse on Cape Henry in Virginia. Madison justified the appropriation as an exercise of the commerce power. (Does *spending* to protect commerce fall within the authority to *regulate* commerce?) For Hamiltonians, the question of whether the spending was "general" was mooted by enactment of a broader law taking over the expense of maintaining lighthouses from Maine to Georgia. (Do you see why?)

The same Congress also rejected other spending proposals: to fund a voyage to Baffin's Bay for a better understanding of the magnetic pole; to establish a national university or subsidize existing schools; and to lend money to a struggling glass factory in Maryland. In each case the scope of the spending power was debated, but not resolved.

In 1792, many members of Congress wanted to provide a subsidy to the struggling codfish industry. Madison found a way to finesse his position to allow the federal spending. He convinced his colleagues to amend the bill and recharacterize the subsidy as relief from federal taxes the industry would otherwise have had to pay. This, he thought, would avoid any reliance on a federal spending power.

And in 1793 a number of French citizens were driven out of the colony on the island of Hispaniola (referred to at the time as "St. Domingo") and petitioned for federal financial assistance. Madison pointed out that the United States owed money to France for assistance during the Revolution, and suggested that the relief to the refugees be characterized as a partial repayment, thus allowing Congress "to relieve the sufferers" without "establishing a dangerous precedent" that would allow "a right to Congress of expending, on objects of benevolence, the money of their constituents." 4 ANNALS OF CONGRESS 170 (Jan. 10, 1794).

But these circumventions would not work in 1796, when the port city of Savannah, Georgia, was devastated by a fire. "Two hundred and twenty-nine houses were destroyed, only one hundred and seventy-nine left standing; four hundred families were left quite destitute." Mrs. Paschal N. Strong, Sr., *Glimpses of Savannah, 1780–1825*, Georgia Hist. Q. 26, 28 (1949). Congress struggled with whether it had the power to provide financial assistance. Be aware that Congress had earlier debated and refused to provide relief for the victims of a fire in a much smaller, and inland, town in Virginia.

The Savannah Fire Debate

House of Representatives, Dec. 28, 1796 (6 Annals of Cong. 1712–1727)

Mr. W. SMITH wished the House to resolve itself into a Committee of the Whole on the resolution, which he had the other day laid upon the table, proposing to afford some relief to the sufferers by the late fire at Savannah. For his part, he said, he could see no reasonable objection which could be made to so benevolent a proposition. A gentleman in the House had got a plan of the ruins of the city; it was, indeed, a most distressful scene. There had never occurred so calamitous an event of the kind in the United States, or which had so strong a claim upon the General Government for relief. He said they had granted assistance to the sufferers by fire at St. Domingo; and surely if it were justifiable to grant relief to foreigners in distress, it was at least equally so when the objects were our own citizens. If gentlemen had objections to the measure, he wished they would state them. The sum with which he should think of filling up the blank would not be such as to materially affect our finances. . . .

[Mr. MACON:] The sufferings of the people of Savannah were doubtless very great; no one could help feeling for them. But he wished gentlemen to put their finger upon that part of the Constitution which gave that House power to afford them relief. Many other towns had suffered very considerably by fire. He believed he knew one that had suffered more than Savannah in proportion to its size: he alluded to Lexington in Virginia, as every house in the place was burnt. If the United States were to become underwriters to the whole Union, where must the line be drawn when their assistance might be claimed? Was it when three-fourths or four-fifths of a town was destroyed, or what other proportion? Insurance offices were the proper securities against fire. . . .

Mr. KITCHELL was opposed to the amendment and to the resolution itself. He had doubts if even they were to give the citizens 15,000 dollars, as was proposed by the gentleman from South Carolina, whether they should not, instead of service, be doing them an injury; because, if the General Government were only to give this sum, the State Legislatures would proportion their donations accordingly, and probably give much less than they would otherwise have done, if they had not had this example before them. He had doubts as to the constitutionality of the measure; he thought the Constitution did not authorize them to make such a use of public money; however he thought it might be a very flexible instrument; it would bend to every situation, and every situation to that. He thought, in this instance, if we grant money, while we attempt to serve, we shall eventually injure. . . .

Mr. CLAIRBORNE . . . was not certain whether he could vote upon Constitutional grounds or not. It was a sharp conflict between humanity to that suffering country and the Constitution. If any case could be admissible, he thought this could; it ought to be remembered, that that part of the Union has suffered much. Georgia was a slaughter-pen during the war, besides being continually harassed by the hostile Indians. He thought 15,000 dollars would not be ill-spent, as from motives of policy it would be of more advantage to the United States from the quick return the revenue would gain. Indeed, if Constitutional, he hoped the sum would be made more than proposed. These are your fellow-citizens who are suffering, and if not speedily relieved, the whole interest will be involved. . . .

Mr. HARPER hoped the amendment would be rejected, for the same reason that he hoped all amendments which were brought forward with the same view with which it was produced, viz: to defeat the original motion, might be rejected. . . . With respect to the constitutionality of affording the relief in question, that had already been determined by the several instances which had been quoted, which were also founded upon humanity. The present case might justly be included under the head of promoting the general welfare of the country. Gentlemen who doubted the constitutionality of the present proceeding, had done the same in the instances alluded to. But, since their doubts had been so frequently overruled, he hoped they should hear no more of them. With respect to the policy of the measure, Savannah, he said, was the only considerable port except Charleston, which the United States had in that quarter. It was situated at the mouth of a river which watered a space of country containing a thousand square miles. The average revenue of this city was $76,000. Was not this an object of importance? Was it not an object to foster, to relieve the distresses of such a place? Many great statesmen had employed themselves in founding cities, and should they not hold out a helping hand to one in distress? Peter the Great founded a city upon a morass, and Louis XIV attempted to build one in the English channel. He trusted the American Government would have more wisdom than to see one of hers sink for want of a little timely assistance. . . .

Mr. BALDWIN said, he had doubted whether to make any observations on this motion; not that he was insensible to the calamitous situation which had been the cause of it, but from an apprehension that it might be thought he was too strongly affected by it. Though it might be disagreeable to one to give his judgment and urge his opinions, when his own relation to the question was different from that of others, yet some of the reflections might not be useless to those who were to determine it. He was sure it was not a want of disposition to relieve the unhappy sufferers that had or would draw forth an observation on this occasion, but merely doubts as to the powers of the Federal Government in money matters. The use of a written Constitution, and of that provision in it which declared that no money should be drawn from the Treasury but under appropriations made by law, was very manifest from the caution which it gave in the expenditure of public money and in laying burdens on the people; yet he believed it impossible to obtain absolute directions from it in every case. The objection is, that Congress is empowered to raise money only to pay the debts and to provide for the common defence, and the other purposes, exactly as specified in the 8th section. The objection has often been made, but many laws have passed not exactly specified in that section. He mentioned the private acts before alluded to, the law for establishing light-houses, to aid navigation in the improvement of harbors, beacons, buoys, and public piers, establishing trading-houses with the Indians, and some others, to show that though the Constitution was very useful in giving general directions, yet it was not capable of being administered under so rigorous and mechanical a construction as had been sometimes contended for. He begged leave to ask and to urge the question, whether there was no possible accumulation of calamity and distress that might be brought upon some part of the country which would justify the Federal Government in granting some relief? No doubt the usual pressure of private misfortune is relieved by the poor-laws and other acts of the State Governments; but, suppose a State belonging to this Union, the greater part, or, perhaps, the whole, was situated on an island, and that at once, by some of the great causes which we know operate in Nature, by tremendous convulsions and earthquakes, it was to be thrown into such a situation as some parts of the world have been, not only the whole property of the wretched survivors destroyed, but their place no longer habitable, would the Federal Government think they had no powers even to grant them some of their new land as a place of refuge? He was sensible that he had put a case so strong that the bare mention almost seemed improper, and that the mind of no gentleman could follow him to that extent. He only wished to establish the principle that there were possible instances in which it would be the duty of the Federal Government to interpose relief. Whether the present calamity was so great and the distress so pressing, that proper relief was scarcely to be expected from the State where it happened, was a question which he must leave to their determination. He was sure they could not want for inducements from the nature of the scene, or from their own dispositions. He could not wish to heighten the coloring in which it stood before them.

Mr. RUTHERFORD again rose in support of the motion. Is it not clear, he said, that it is the duty of the people at large to come forward at this time and hold up the helping hand to those poor distressed people? He presumed the rising dignity of this great Confederation demanded mutual assistance in distress. If the people are left to recover of themselves from this terrible dilemma, the nation will suffer. It is the duty and the interest of this rising nation to help the people of Georgia; it is a part of this great family, and demands assistance from every member. This idea should be conclusive. But for gentlemen to say the law is to have its full operation at this time, is saying nothing at all; it is pouring cold water upon their distresses; it is as though you were to say to a man that is drowning, stay awhile and we will come and assist you. This would be poor comfort. Policy, humanity, and justice, should prompt the House to the noble action. If one part of a system is injured the whole suffers by it. All the generous feelings of the human heart call aloud for help, and I hope we shall grant it.

Mr. NICHOLAS said, he meant to have given a silent vote upon this subject, and have left other gentlemen to follow their own inclinations in the business; but an attempt had been made to ridicule the opinion which he and others held of the sacredness of the Constitution. In reference to what had fallen from the gentleman from Georgia, he said he had never heard it said that no individual instance could occur which might be an exception to a Constitutional rule. He had never heard that our laws should be so general as to admit of no latitude, or that money should never be expended but for payment of debts or for defence. . . .

Mr. GILES said, if the present resolution passed it would make them answerable for all future losses by fire. The small sum of $15,000 was not of any consequence when compared with the establishment of a principle of that House acting upon generosity. He believed that neither the money nor humanity, but the establishment of the principle, was the thing aimed at. . . . The gentleman from Georgia had said that "affairs of men" made it necessary to depart from the strict Constitutional power. For his part, he did not think they ought to attend to what "the affairs of men" or what generosity and humanity required, but what the Constitution and their duty required. . . .

Mr. W. SMITH said, that gentlemen had spoken of a sum in contemplation; but the question was not on the sum to be granted; that would be for future consideration, and if gentlemen wished to make it commensurate with the object, they could do so. The present question was, whether any relief should be granted? He wished gentlemen would say whether no case of calamity could exist in which the United States ought to grant relief? He believed every one admitted such a case might occur. The question was, whether this was the case? He trusted it was, since it was an unexampled calamity.

The precedents which had been adduced appeared to be no more strongly warranted than this. First, with respect to the relief granted the sufferers at St. Domingo. In order to make the thing more palatable, it was said that sum should be charged to the French Republic. It was provisional, and the fact was they had not admitted it, and the United States paid it. In reference to the relief granted to the daughters of Count de Grasse: it was said to be for services. Did the daughters perform any services? No, but the father did. But did the Constitution of the United States acknowledge any hereditary claim of this sort? He believed not. This was a mere pretence. It was an act of generosity. Another case occurred to him, which had not been mentioned, viz: the recompense allowed to persons who suffered from the Western insurrection. Was this authorized by the Constitution any more than the present? He believed not. . . .

In examining different cases, Mr. S. said, he found that of the widow of Major Forsyth, and also that of the orphan children of Major Trueman. Gentlemen would perhaps say that these were cases where the husband and ancestor had rendered services to the United States; and he had no doubt that the ancestors of those sufferers at Savannah, and perhaps the sufferers themselves, had rendered services to the United States. If gentlemen pleased, therefore, the words, "in consideration of services performed," &c. might be inserted. . . .

Mr. CLAIBORNE said, the more he heard, the more he found himself in favor of the resolution. By the discussion it had undergone, he was inclined to think it was, perhaps, reconcilable with the Constitution; perhaps it was, he said, for he was not certain. The annual revenue, he said, of that place, was seventy thousand dollars to the United States, besides the great consideration of it as a frontier town. He had compared the advantages and disadvantages with respect to its relief in his own mind, and thought it would be highly consistent with policy to grant relief. It was a place which had been in great distress, and had great struggles with enemies in times past. Can it be possible to suppose that we have not power to assist in erecting that place again, and putting it upon a footing to do good to the United States by a return of her revenue? Certainly not. Would the Committee be willing that Savannah should be erased from the revenue? Are they willing to let it rest, and lose it? This is impossible. Then, surely, it becomes policy to give aid towards its re-erection. Unless the people do receive some aid, it will be a long time before seventy thousand dollars will be again produced from the revenue of that place.

For what purpose was it, Mr. C. asked, that money was spent to erect trading-houses in the back countries? He answered, for the general welfare; for the support of trade, and the increase of the revenue. So will a small sum given towards the relief of this suffering town. If there could be reason to grant money to the widows of Major Forsyth and Major Trueman, there surely must be as much to do this.

NOTES

1. At the end of the debate, the relief was defeated, 55–34. What would James Madison have said? What would Alexander Hamilton have said? (Don't forget about Hamilton's "qualification . . . [t]hat the object to which an appropriation of money is to be made be General and not local; its operation extending in fact, or by possibility, throughout the Union, and not being confined to a particular spot."). Is there any theory that justifies relief to the people of Savannah?

2. As Representative Smith pointed out, Congress had repeatedly given money to the widows or families of those who had served in the military. Why was that spending any more constitutional than relief to the people of Savannah?

3. As a general matter, Hamiltonians who supported broader spending were more plentiful in the North, and ideological opponents of federal spending were more plentiful in the South. But Savannah was a Southern city, which might have made it hard for Southern representatives to say *no*. (William Smith, who championed the relief, was from South Carolina; Abraham Baldwin, who seemed to favor it as well, was from Georgia.) Remarking on this, one scholar wrote: "One has the sense the wily Federalists were hoping to slip this one by on sympathy grounds, only to employ it mercilessly as a precedent later on." David P. Currie, THE CONSTITUTION IN CONGRESS: THE FEDERALIST PERIOD 1789–1801, at 224 (1996). Does that seem plausible?

4. What do you make of the several representatives who seemed to suggest that "humanity" might be more important than the formal requirements of the Constitution? Is that inconsistent with the congressional oath of office? Or does it reflect refreshing candor and decency? Is there ever a time when, in the words of one law professor, "you have to put aside your principles and do what's right"?

5. Recently, Congress has debated the propriety of so-called "earmarks"—the funding of specific projects to benefit one particular place. The topic of the funding can be almost anything, from turning an old railroad track into a bike path to the construction of a Speedway gas station and pizza parlor. (The Speedway earmark, secured by Rep. David Hobson (R–OH), was defended as "vitally important" for a place "with hundreds of college students and no pizza delivery or nearby fast food options.") At least for now,

Congress has voted to prohibit the practice of earmarking. Defenders note that earmarks are a miniscule part of the federal budget, and say they grease the wheels for legislative compromises. But can you see why earmarks are viewed as an abuse?

Almost no one regards earmarking as a constitutional question. But is it? On the Madisonian view, does it matter what the earmarks are for? What is the enumerated power that covers the Speedway? Commerce? On the Hamiltonian view, does it matter what the pattern is for the distribution of earmarks? What if earmarks tend to be distributed to swing districts and swing states where the party in power needs support? Would that influence your thinking about the constitutional logic of limiting spending to "general" rather than "local" concerns? And wherever the line is between "general" and "local," who should enforce it?

Spending Litigation During the New Deal

The scope of the spending power remained relatively unsettled until the New Deal, when several taxing and spending measures came before the Court. The first major case was *United States v. Butler*, 297 U.S. 1 (1936), a constitutional challenge to the Agricultural Adjustment Act of 1933, a New Deal measure designed to stabilize agricultural production and prices during the Great Depression. The Act authorized the secretary of agriculture to make contracts with farmers to reduce the production of agricultural commodities in exchange for direct benefit payments, financed by a tax on the "first domestic processing" of the particular agricultural commodity. Recall that, at the time, the Court's precedents did not let Congress rely on the Commerce Clause to directly regulate these agricultural activities. The government, therefore, did not seek to defend the program as a regulation of commerce. Rather, the question was whether the program could be sustained under Congress's taxing and spending powers, even though it was not within Congress's power to regulate interstate commerce.

Justice Owen Roberts wrote a somewhat confusing majority opinion, describing the government's argument thus:

> The argument is that Congress may appropriate and authorize the spending of moneys for the "general welfare"; that the phrase should be liberally construed to cover anything conducive to national welfare; that decision as to what will promote such welfare rests with Congress alone, and that courts may not review the determination; and finally that the appropriation under attack was in fact for the general welfare of the United States.

The Court first adopted the Hamiltonian position on the spending power and rejected the Madisonian position:

> While . . . the power to tax is not unlimited, its confines are set in the clause which confers it, and not in those of section 8 which bestow and define the legislative powers of the Congress. It results that the power of Congress to authorize expenditure of public moneys for public purposes is not limited by the direct grants of legislative power found in the Constitution.

The Court also reaffirmed Hamilton's view that "the purpose" of the spending "must be 'general, and not local.' " But, the Court went on to say:

> We are not now required to ascertain the scope of the phrase "general welfare of the United States" or to determine whether an appropriation in

> aid of agriculture falls within it. Wholly apart from that question, another principle embedded in our Constitution prohibits the enforcement of the Agricultural adjustment Act. The act invades the reserved rights of the states. It is a statutory plan to regulate and control agricultural production, a matter beyond the powers delegated to the federal government. The tax, the appropriation of the funds raised, and the direction for their disbursement, are but parts of the plan. They are but means to an unconstitutional end.

It concluded:

> Congress has no power to enforce its commands on the farmer to the ends sought by the Agricultural Adjustment Act. It must follow that it may not indirectly accomplish those ends by taxing and spending to purchase compliance. The Constitution and the entire plan of our government negative any such use of the power to tax and to spend as the act undertakes to authorize. It does not help to declare that local conditions throughout the nation have created a situation of national concern; for this is but to say that whenever there is a widespread similarity of local conditions, Congress may ignore constitutional limitations upon its own powers and usurp those reserved to the states. If, in lieu of compulsory regulation of subjects within the states' reserved jurisdiction, which is prohibited, the Congress could invoke the taxing and spending power as a means to accomplish the same end, clause 1 of section 8 of article 1 would become the instrument for total subversion of the governmental powers reserved to the individual states.

Justice Stone, joined by Justices Brandeis and Cardozo, dissented. "[C]ourts are concerned only with the power to enact statutes, not with their wisdom." The only constitutional limitation on the spending power, he argued, was "that public funds shall be spent for a defined purpose, the promotion of the general welfare." The power to spend was not limited to purposes within other grants of enumerated power, and thus could be used to achieve ends not within Congress's powers of direct regulation.

The majority opinion in *Butler* may seem self-contradictory, simultaneously claiming that the spending power was "not limited" to the enumerated powers, yet could not be used to "indirectly accomplish" anything that could not be accomplished by the enumerated powers. The broader reading of the case, however, was adopted the next year. In *Helvering v. Davis*, the Court upheld the payment of Old Age Benefits under the Social Security Act. It emphasized:

> Congress may spend money in aid of the "general welfare." U.S. Const. art. 1, § 8; *United States v. Butler*, 297 U.S. 1, 65 (1936). There have been great statesmen in our history who have stood for other views. We will not resurrect the contest. It is now settled by decision. *United States v. Butler*, supra. The conception of the spending power advocated by Hamilton and strongly reinforced by Story has prevailed over that of Madison, which has not been lacking in adherents. Yet difficulties are left when the power is conceded. The line must still be drawn between one welfare and another, between particular and general. Where this shall be placed cannot be known through a formula in advance of the event. There is a middle ground or certainly a penumbra in which discretion is at large. The discretion,

however, is not confided to the courts. The discretion belongs to Congress, unless the choice is clearly wrong, a display of arbitrary power, not an exercise of judgment. This is now familiar law.

The Court concluded that the problem targeted by the Social Security Act was "plainly national in area and dimensions," and therefore satisfied the general welfare. It did not discuss the restrictive portion of *Butler*. Thus, after *Helvering*'s affirmation of part of *Butler*, the Court had settled on a broad, Hamiltonian view of the spending power.

There remained another question, however. Even putting aside the question of what aims Congress could spend money on, what is the scope of Congress's power to attach strings to that money? The Court considered this problem in *South Dakota v. Dole*:

South Dakota v. Dole
483 U.S. 203 (1987)

■ CHIEF JUSTICE REHNQUIST delivered the opinion of the Court.

Petitioner South Dakota permits persons 19 years of age or older to purchase beer containing up to 3.2% alcohol. In 1984 Congress enacted 23 U.S.C. § 158, which directs the Secretary of Transportation to withhold a percentage of federal highway funds otherwise allocable from States "in which the purchase or public possession . . . of any alcoholic beverage by a person who is less than twenty-one years of age is lawful." The State sued in United States District Court seeking a declaratory judgment that § 158 violates the constitutional limitations on congressional exercise of the spending power and violates the Twenty-first Amendment to the United States Constitution. The District Court rejected the State's claims, and the Court of Appeals for the Eighth Circuit affirmed.

In this Court, the parties direct most of their efforts to defining the proper scope of the Twenty-first Amendment. Relying on our statement in *California Retail Liquor Dealers Assn. v. Midcal Aluminum, Inc.,* 445 U.S. 97, 110 (1980), that the "Twenty-first Amendment grants the States virtually complete control over whether to permit importation or sale of liquor and how to structure the liquor distribution system," South Dakota asserts that the setting of minimum drinking ages is clearly within the "core powers" reserved to the States under § 2 of the Amendment.[1] Section 158, petitioner claims, usurps that core power. The Secretary in response asserts that the Twenty-first Amendment is simply not implicated by § 158; the plain language of § 2 confirms the States' broad power to impose restrictions on the sale and distribution of alcoholic beverages but does not confer on them any power to *permit* sales that Congress seeks to *prohibit*. That Amendment, under this reasoning, would not prevent Congress from affirmatively enacting a national minimum drinking age more restrictive than that provided by the various state laws; and it would follow *a fortiori* that the indirect inducement involved here is compatible with the Twenty-first Amendment. . . .

---

[1] Section 2 of the Twenty-first Amendment provides: "The transportation or importation into any State, Territory, or possession of the United States for delivery or use therein of intoxicating liquors, in violation of the laws thereof, is hereby prohibited."

Despite the extended treatment of the question by the parties, however, we need not decide in this case whether that Amendment would prohibit an attempt by Congress to legislate directly a national minimum drinking age. Here, Congress has acted indirectly under its spending power to encourage uniformity in the States' drinking ages. As we explain below, we find this legislative effort within constitutional bounds even if Congress may not regulate drinking ages directly.

The Constitution empowers Congress to "lay and collect Taxes, Duties, Imposts, and Excises, to pay the Debts and provide for the common Defence and general Welfare of the United States." Art. I, § 8, cl. 1. Incident to this power, Congress may attach conditions on the receipt of federal funds, and has repeatedly employed the power "to further broad policy objectives by conditioning receipt of federal moneys upon compliance by the recipient with federal statutory and administrative directives." *Fullilove v. Klutznick,* 448 U.S. 448, 474 (1980) (opinion of Burger, C.J.). The breadth of this power was made clear in *United States v. Butler,* 297 U.S. 1, 66 (1936), where the Court, resolving a longstanding debate over the scope of the Spending Clause, determined that "the power of Congress to authorize expenditure of public moneys for public purposes is not limited by the direct grants of legislative power found in the Constitution." Thus, objectives not thought to be within Article I's "enumerated legislative fields," may nevertheless be attained through the use of the spending power and the conditional grant of federal funds.

The spending power is of course not unlimited, but is instead subject to several general restrictions articulated in our cases. The first of these limitations is derived from the language of the Constitution itself: the exercise of the spending power must be in pursuit of "the general welfare." In considering whether a particular expenditure is intended to serve general public purposes, courts should defer substantially to the judgment of Congress.[2] Second, we have required that if Congress desires to condition the States' receipt of federal funds, it "must do so unambiguously . . . , enabl[ing] the States to exercise their choice knowingly, cognizant of the consequences of their participation." *Pennhurst State School and Hospital v. Halderman,* 451 U.S. 1, 17 (1981). Third, our cases have suggested (without significant elaboration) that conditions on federal grants might be illegitimate if they are unrelated "to the federal interest in particular national projects or programs." *Massachusetts v. United States,* 435 U.S. 444, 461 (1978) (plurality opinion). Finally, we have noted that other constitutional provisions may provide an independent bar to the conditional grant of federal funds.

South Dakota does not seriously claim that § 158 is inconsistent with any of the first three restrictions mentioned above. We can readily conclude that the provision is designed to serve the general welfare, especially in light of the fact that "the concept of welfare or the opposite is shaped by Congress. . . ." *Helvering v. Davis,* 301 U.S. 619, 645 (1937). Congress found that the differing drinking ages in the States created particular incentives for young persons to combine their desire to drink with their ability to drive, and that this interstate problem required a national solution. The means it chose to address this dangerous situation were reasonably calculated to advance the general welfare. The conditions upon which States receive the funds, moreover, could not be more clearly stated by Congress. And the State itself, rather

---

[2]   The level of deference to the congressional decision is such that the Court has more recently questioned whether "general welfare" is a judicially enforceable restriction at all. See Buckley v. Valeo, 424 U.S. 1, 90–91 (1976) (*per curiam*).

than challenging the germaneness of the condition to federal purposes, admits that it "has never contended that the congressional action was . . . unrelated to a national concern in the absence of the Twenty-first Amendment." Indeed, the condition imposed by Congress is directly related to one of the main purposes for which highway funds are expended—safe interstate travel. See 23 U.S.C. § 101(b).[3]

This goal of the interstate highway system had been frustrated by varying drinking ages among the States. A Presidential commission appointed to study alcohol-related accidents and fatalities on the Nation's highways concluded that the lack of uniformity in the States' drinking ages created "an incentive to drink and drive" because "young persons commut[e] to border States where the drinking age is lower." By enacting § 158, Congress conditioned the receipt of federal funds in a way reasonably calculated to address this particular impediment to a purpose for which the funds are expended.

The remaining question about the validity of § 158—and the basic point of disagreement between the parties—is whether the Twenty-first Amendment constitutes an "independent constitutional bar" to the conditional grant of federal funds. Petitioner, relying on its view that the Twenty-first Amendment prohibits *direct* regulation of drinking ages by Congress, asserts that "Congress may not use the spending power to regulate that which it is prohibited from regulating directly under the Twenty-first Amendment." But our cases show that this "independent constitutional bar" limitation on the spending power is not of the kind petitioner suggests. *United States v. Butler*, for example, established that the constitutional limitations on Congress when exercising its spending power are less exacting than those on its authority to regulate directly.

We have also held that a perceived Tenth Amendment limitation on congressional regulation of state affairs did not concomitantly limit the range of conditions legitimately placed on federal grants. In *Oklahoma v. Civil Service Comm'n*, 330 U.S. 127 (1947), the Court considered the validity of the Hatch Act insofar as it was applied to political activities of state officials whose employment was financed in whole or in part with federal funds. *[The Hatch Act is a civil service statute that limits federal employees' political speech while using federal resources.—Editors]* The State contended that an order under this provision to withhold certain federal funds unless a state official was removed invaded its sovereignty in violation of the Tenth Amendment. Though finding that "the United States is not concerned with, and has no power to regulate, local political activities as such of state officials," the Court nevertheless held that the Federal Government "does have power to fix the terms upon which its money allotments to states shall be disbursed." *Id.*, at 143. The Court found no violation of the State's sovereignty because the State could, and did, adopt "the 'simple expedient' of not yielding to what she urges is federal coercion. The offer of benefits to a state by the United States

---

[3] Our cases have not required that we define the outer bounds of the "germaneness" or "relatedness" limitation on the imposition of conditions under the spending power. *Amici* urge that we take this occasion to establish that a condition on federal funds is legitimate only if it relates directly to the purpose of the expenditure to which it is attached. Because petitioner has not sought such a restriction, and because we find any such limitation on conditional federal grants satisfied in this case in any event, we do not address whether conditions less directly related to the particular purpose of the expenditure might be outside the bounds of the spending power.

dependent upon cooperation by the state with federal plans, assumedly for the general welfare, is not unusual." *Id.,* at 143–144.

These cases establish that the "independent constitutional bar" limitation on the spending power is not, as petitioner suggests, a prohibition on the indirect achievement of objectives which Congress is not empowered to achieve directly. Instead, we think that the language in our earlier opinions stands for the unexceptionable proposition that the power may not be used to induce the States to engage in activities that would themselves be unconstitutional. Thus, for example, a grant of federal funds conditioned on invidiously discriminatory state action or the infliction of cruel and unusual punishment would be an illegitimate exercise of the Congress' broad spending power. But no such claim can be or is made here. Were South Dakota to succumb to the blandishments offered by Congress and raise its drinking age to 21, the State's action in so doing would not violate the constitutional rights of anyone.

Our decisions have recognized that in some circumstances the financial inducement offered by Congress might be so coercive as to pass the point at which "pressure turns into compulsion." *Steward Machine Co. v. Davis,* 301 U.S. 548, 590 (1937). Here, however, Congress has directed only that a State desiring to establish a minimum drinking age lower than 21 lose a relatively small percentage of certain federal highway funds. Petitioner contends that the coercive nature of this program is evident from the degree of success it has achieved. We cannot conclude, however, that a conditional grant of federal money of this sort is unconstitutional simply by reason of its success in achieving the congressional objective.

When we consider, for a moment, that all South Dakota would lose if she adheres to her chosen course as to a suitable minimum drinking age is 5% of the funds otherwise obtainable under specified highway grant programs, the argument as to coercion is shown to be more rhetoric than fact. As we said a half century ago in *Steward Machine Co. v. Davis:*

> "[E]very rebate from a tax when conditioned upon conduct is in some measure a temptation. But to hold that motive or temptation is equivalent to coercion is to plunge the law in endless difficulties. The outcome of such a doctrine is the acceptance of a philosophical determinism by which choice becomes impossible. Till now the law has been guided by a robust common sense which assumes the freedom of the will as a working hypothesis in the solution of its problems."

Here Congress has offered relatively mild encouragement to the States to enact higher minimum drinking ages than they would otherwise choose. But the enactment of such laws remains the prerogative of the States not merely in theory but in fact. Even if Congress might lack the power to impose a national minimum drinking age directly, we conclude that encouragement to state action found in § 158 is a valid use of the spending power.

■ JUSTICE BRENNAN, dissenting.

I agree with JUSTICE O'CONNOR that regulation of the minimum age of purchasers of liquor falls squarely within the ambit of those powers reserved to the States by the Twenty-first Amendment. Since States possess this constitutional power, Congress cannot condition a federal grant in a manner that abridges this right. The Amendment, itself, strikes the proper balance between federal and state authority. I therefore dissent.

■ JUSTICE O'CONNOR, dissenting.

The Court today upholds the National Minimum Drinking Age Amendment, 23 U.S.C. § 158, as a valid exercise of the spending power conferred by Article I, § 8. But § 158 is not a condition on spending reasonably related to the expenditure of federal funds and cannot be justified on that ground. Rather, it is an attempt to regulate the sale of liquor, an attempt that lies outside Congress' power to regulate commerce because it falls within the ambit of § 2 of the Twenty-first Amendment.

My disagreement with the Court is relatively narrow on the spending power issue: it is a disagreement about the application of a principle rather than a disagreement on the principle itself. I agree with the Court that Congress may attach conditions on the receipt of federal funds to further "the federal interest in particular national projects or programs." *Massachusetts v. United States*, at 461. I also subscribe to the established proposition that the reach of the spending power "is not limited by the direct grants of legislative power found in the Constitution." *United States v. Butler*, at 66. Finally, I agree that there are four separate types of limitations on the spending power: the expenditure must be for the general welfare, the conditions imposed must be unambiguous, they must be reasonably related to the purpose of the expenditure, and the legislation may not violate any independent constitutional prohibition. Insofar as two of those limitations are concerned, the Court is clearly correct that § 158 is wholly unobjectionable. Establishment of a national minimum drinking age certainly fits within the broad concept of the general welfare and the statute is entirely unambiguous. I am also willing to assume, *arguendo,* that the Twenty-first Amendment does not constitute an "independent constitutional bar" to a spending condition.

But the Court's application of the requirement that the condition imposed be reasonably related to the purpose for which the funds are expended is cursory and unconvincing. We have repeatedly said that Congress may condition grants under the spending power only in ways reasonably related to the purpose of the federal program. *Massachusetts v. United States*, at 461; *Ivanhoe Irrigation Dist. v. McCracken,* 357 U.S. 275, 295 (1958) (the United States may impose "reasonable conditions relevant to federal interest in the project and to the over-all objectives thereof"); *Steward Machine Co. v. Davis*, at 590 ("We do not say that a tax is valid, when imposed by act of Congress, if it is laid upon the condition that a state may escape its operation through the adoption of a statute unrelated in subject matter to activities fairly within the scope of national policy and power"). In my view, establishment of a minimum drinking age of 21 is not sufficiently related to interstate highway construction to justify so conditioning funds appropriated for that purpose.

In support of its contrary conclusion, the Court relies on a supposed concession by counsel for South Dakota that the State "has never contended that the congressional action was . . . unrelated to a national concern in the absence of the Twenty-first Amendment." In the absence of the Twenty-first Amendment, however, there is a strong argument that the Congress might regulate the conditions under which liquor is sold under the commerce power, just as it regulates the sale of many other commodities that are in or affect interstate commerce. The fact that the

Twenty-first Amendment is crucial to the State's argument does not, therefore, amount to a concession that the condition imposed by § 158 is reasonably related to highway construction. The Court also relies on a portion of the argument transcript in support of its claim that South Dakota conceded the reasonable relationship point. But counsel's statements there are at best ambiguous. Counsel essentially said no more than that he was not prepared to argue the reasonable relationship question discussed at length in the Brief for the National Conference of State Legislatures et al. as *Amici Curiae*.

Aside from these "concessions" by counsel, the Court asserts the reasonableness of the relationship between the supposed purpose of the expenditure—"safe interstate travel"—and the drinking age condition. The Court reasons that Congress wishes that the roads it builds may be used safely, that drunken drivers threaten highway safety, and that young people are more likely to drive while under the influence of alcohol under existing law than would be the case if there were a uniform national drinking age of 21. It hardly needs saying, however, that if the purpose of § 158 is to deter drunken driving, it is far too over and under-inclusive. It is over-inclusive because it stops teenagers from drinking even when they are not about to drive on interstate highways. It is under-inclusive because teenagers pose only a small part of the drunken driving problem in this Nation. See, *e.g.,* 130 Cong. Rec. 18648 (1984) (remarks of Sen. Humphrey) ("Eighty-four percent of all highway fatalities involving alcohol occur among those whose ages exceed 21"); *id.,* at 18651 (remarks of Sen. McClure) ("Certainly, statistically, if you use that one set of statistics, then the mandatory drinking age ought to be raised at least to 30"); *ibid.* (remarks of Sen. Symms) ("[M]ost of the studies point out that the drivers of age 21–24 are the worst offenders").

When Congress appropriates money to build a highway, it is entitled to insist that the highway be a safe one. But it is not entitled to insist as a condition of the use of highway funds that the State impose or change regulations in other areas of the State's social and economic life because of an attenuated or tangential relationship to highway use or safety. Indeed, if the rule were otherwise, the Congress could effectively regulate almost any area of a State's social, political, or economic life on the theory that use of the interstate transportation system is somehow enhanced. If, for example, the United States were to condition highway moneys upon moving the state capital, I suppose it might argue that interstate transportation is facilitated by locating local governments in places easily accessible to interstate highways—or, conversely, that highways might become overburdened if they had to carry traffic to and from the state capital. In my mind, such a relationship is hardly more attenuated than the one which the Court finds supports § 158. Cf. Tr. of Oral Arg. 39 (counsel for the United States conceding that to condition a grant upon adoption of a unicameral legislature would violate the "germaneness" requirement).

There is a clear place at which the Court can draw the line between permissible and impermissible conditions on federal grants. It is the line identified in the Brief for the National Conference of State Legislatures et al. as *Amici Curiae:*

> "Congress has the power to *spend* for the general welfare[;] it has the power to *legislate* only for delegated purposes. . . . The appropriate inquiry, then, is whether the spending requirement or prohibition is a condition on a grant or whether it is regulation. The difference turns on whether the

requirement specifies in some way how the money should be spent, so that Congress' intent in making the grant will be effectuated. Congress has no power under the Spending Clause to impose requirements on a grant that go beyond specifying how the money should be spent. A requirement that is not such a specification is not a condition, but a regulation, which is valid only if it falls within one of Congress' delegated regulatory powers."

This approach harks back to *United States v. Butler*, the last case in which this Court struck down an Act of Congress as beyond the authority granted by the Spending Clause. There the Court wrote that "[t]here is an obvious difference between a statute stating the conditions upon which moneys shall be expended and one effective only upon assumption of a contractual obligation to submit to a regulation which otherwise could not be enforced." The *Butler* Court saw the Agricultural Adjustment Act for what it was—an exercise of regulatory, not spending, power. The error in *Butler* was not the Court's conclusion that the act was essentially regulatory, but rather its crabbed view of the extent of Congress' regulatory power under the Commerce Clause. The Agricultural Adjustment Act was regulatory but it was regulation that today would likely be considered within Congress' commerce power. See, *e.g., Katzenbach v. McClung,* 379 U.S. 294 (1964); *Wickard v. Filburn,* 317 U.S. 111 (1942).

While *Butler's* authority is questionable insofar as it assumes that Congress has no regulatory power over farm production, its discussion of the spending power and its description of both the power's breadth and its limitations remain sound. The Court's decision in *Butler* also properly recognizes the gravity of the task of appropriately limiting the spending power. If the spending power is to be limited only by Congress' notion of the general welfare, the reality, given the vast financial resources of the Federal Government, is that the Spending Clause gives "power to the Congress to tear down the barriers, to invade the states' jurisdiction, and to become a parliament of the whole people, subject to no restrictions save such as are self-imposed." *United States v. Butler*, at 78. This, of course, as *Butler* held, was not the Framers' plan and it is not the meaning of the Spending Clause.

Our later cases are consistent with the notion that, under the spending power, the Congress may only condition grants in ways that can fairly be said to be related to the expenditure of federal funds. . . .

As discussed above, a condition that a State will raise its drinking age to 21 cannot fairly be said to be reasonably related to the expenditure of funds for highway construction. The only possible connection, highway safety, has nothing to do with how the funds Congress has appropriated are expended. Rather than a condition determining how federal highway money shall be expended, it is a regulation determining who shall be able to drink liquor. As such it is not justified by the spending power.

Of the other possible sources of congressional authority for regulating the sale of liquor only the commerce power comes to mind. But in my view, the regulation of the age of the purchasers of liquor, just as the regulation of the price at which liquor may be sold, falls squarely within the scope of those powers reserved to the States by the Twenty-first Amendment. As I emphasized in *324 Liquor Corp. v. Duffy,* 479 U.S. 335, 356 (1987) (dissenting opinion):

The history of the Amendment strongly supports Justice Black's view that the Twenty-first Amendment was intended to return absolute control of the liquor trade to the States, and that the Federal Government could not use its Commerce Clause powers to interfere in any manner with the States' exercise of the power conferred by the Amendment.

Accordingly, Congress simply lacks power under the Commerce Clause to displace state regulation of this kind.

The immense size and power of the Government of the United States ought not obscure its fundamental character. It remains a Government of enumerated powers. *McCulloch v. Maryland*, 17 U.S. (4 Wheat.) 316, 405 (1819). Because 23 U.S.C. § 158 cannot be justified as an exercise of any power delegated to the Congress, it is not authorized by the Constitution. The Court errs in holding it to be the law of the land, and I respectfully dissent.

NOTES

1.   The Twenty-first Amendment discussion in this case may be a distraction from the spending power issue. For now, put it aside and assume that Congress has the power to impose a 21-year-old drinking age on its own authority. The question presented by *South Dakota v. Dole* becomes whether Congress has the power to coerce states to pass their own 21-year-old drinking ages, by denying them highway funds if they do not. Under *New York v. United States* and *United States v. Printz* (p. 582), it would be unconstitutional for Congress to pass a law requiring states to enact a 21-year-old drinking age. Can Congress achieve the same objective by means of conditions on highway appropriations?

2.   What view does the Court take of the basis for the federal spending power? What are the constraints that the majority identifies for the spending power? On which of these do the majority and the dissent agree? What is the basis for each one? Which ones are more constraining, and which ones are less?

3.   Is the question whether a spending condition is sufficiently related or germane simply another way of asking whether the condition is "necessary and proper" for carrying into effect its highway appropriation? Are such issues really Necessary and Proper Clause issues rather than matters of the scope of the spending power standing alone? Notice the different approaches and formulations of the majority and the dissent concerning this issue in *South Dakota v. Dole*. How similar or different are they from the formulations in *McCulloch v. Maryland*? Does the majority's formulation ensure that strings attached to congressional spending bills are really necessary and proper means for carrying federal spending programs into execution? Does the dissent's formulation?

4.   *South Dakota v. Dole* avoided deciding explicitly the question of how the Twenty-first Amendment—which repealed Prohibition under the Eighteenth Amendment—interacts with the Commerce Clause power, and thus did not explicitly decide whether direct regulatory power would exist to impose a nationwide 21-year-old drinking age. How would you answer that constitutional question? Section 2 of the Twenty-first Amendment says: "The transportation or importation into any State, Territory, or possession of the United States for delivery or use therein of intoxicating liquors, in violation of the laws thereof, is hereby prohibited." The Twenty-first Amendment thus gives every state an indefeasible right to be a dry state. Congress cannot force a state to allow the sale of alcohol if it does not want to allow it. But is the converse true? Does the Twenty-first Amendment stop Congress from banning alcohol in

states that want to allow it? The Twenty-first Amendment repeals the Eighteenth Amendment's ban on alcohol and its special grant of an enumerated power to prohibit alcohol, but does the Twenty-first Amendment withdraw congressional power under the Commerce and Necessary and Proper Clauses to pass nationwide regulations on the sale of alcohol?

5.   A recurring question in the taxing power and spending power cases is whether a use of these powers might be so "coercive" as to impair a state's constitutional autonomy with respect to some reserved power, prerogative, or essential attribute guaranteed by the Constitution. The difficult question is *at what point*—if any—the use of such granted powers to accomplish an objective that the national government could not command directly becomes so coercive as to be irresistible (and thus unconstitutional). Is it possible to draw a principled line? Is this a question of degree, or does it turn on the conceptual distinction between germane and non-germane conditions? This may be the real difference between the Rehnquist majority and the O'Connor dissent. The majority treats the condition as germane because highway-construction appropriations and drinking-age laws both serve the same general purpose of promoting highway safety. O'Connor treats germaneness as a more demanding requirement: a condition is not germane unless it is relevant to ensuring that the underlying program achieve *its* purposes. Highway spending promotes safety, and so does a higher drinking age. But the efficacy, the marginal impact, of the highway spending is the same whether or not there is a 21-year-old drinking age. According to O'Connor, that makes the condition non-germane. On the other hand, could Congress just redefine the purpose of its highway spending to get around O'Connor's rule?

[*Assignments 31–32*]

E.   SYNTHESIS: THE COMMERCE, TAXING, SPENDING, AND NECESSARY AND PROPER POWERS

We turn now to the Supreme Court's most recent and highly significant decision interpreting the scope of Congress's legislative powers under the Commerce Clause, the Necessary and Proper Clause, the Taxing Clause, and the conditional spending power: the controversial decision of a closely divided Court upholding in part and invalidating in part the Patient Protection and Affordable Care Act of 2010 (colloquially referred to by some as "Obamacare").

National Federation of Independent Business v. Sebelius
132 S.Ct. 2566 (2012)

■ CHIEF JUSTICE ROBERTS announced the judgment of the Court and delivered the opinion of the Court with respect to Parts I, II, and III–C, an opinion with respect to Part IV, in which JUSTICE BREYER and JUSTICE KAGAN join, and an opinion with respect to Parts III–A, III–B, and III–D.

Today we resolve constitutional challenges to two provisions of the Patient Protection and Affordable Care Act of 2010: the individual mandate, which requires individuals to purchase a health insurance policy providing a minimum level of coverage; and the Medicaid expansion, which gives funds to the States on the condition that they provide specified health care to all citizens whose income falls below a certain threshold. We do not consider whether the Act embodies sound policies. That judgment is entrusted to the Nation's elected leaders. We ask only whether Congress has the power under the Constitution to enact the challenged provisions.

In our federal system, the National Government possesses only limited powers; the States and the people retain the remainder. Nearly two centuries ago, Chief Justice Marshall observed that "the question respecting the extent of the powers actually granted" to the Federal Government "is perpetually arising, and will probably continue to arise, as long as our system shall exist." *McCulloch v. Maryland*, 17 U.S. (4 Wheat.) 316, 405 (1819). In this case we must again determine whether the Constitution grants Congress powers it now asserts, but which many States and individuals believe it does not possess. Resolving this controversy requires us to examine both the limits of the Government's power, and our own limited role in policing those boundaries.

The Federal Government "is acknowledged by all to be one of enumerated powers." *Ibid.* That is, rather than granting general authority to perform all the conceivable functions of government, the Constitution lists, or enumerates, the Federal Government's powers. . . . The enumeration of powers is also a limitation of powers, because "[t]he enumeration presupposes something not enumerated." *Gibbons v. Ogden*, 22 U.S. (9 Wheat.) 1, 195 (1824). The Constitution's express conferral of some powers makes clear that it does not grant others. And the Federal government "can exercise only the powers granted to it." *McCulloch*, at 405.

Today, the restrictions on government power foremost in many Americans' minds are likely to be affirmative prohibitions, such as contained in the Bill of Rights. These affirmative prohibitions come into play, however, only where the Government possesses authority to act in the first place. If no enumerated power authorizes Congress to pass a certain law, that law may not be enacted, even if it would not violate any of the express prohibitions in the Bill of Rights or elsewhere in the Constitution.

Indeed, the Constitution did not initially include a Bill of Rights at least partly because the Framers felt the enumeration of powers sufficed to restrain the Government. As Alexander Hamilton put it, "the Constitution is itself, in every rational sense, and to every useful purpose, A BILL OF RIGHTS." The Federalist No. 84. And when the Bill of Rights was ratified, it made express what the enumeration of powers necessarily implied: "The powers not delegated to the United States by the Constitution . . . are reserved to the States respectively, or to the people." U.S. Const., Amdt. 10. The Federal Government has expanded dramatically over the past two centuries, but it still must show that a constitutional grant of power authorizes each of its actions.

The same does not apply to the States, because the Constitution is not the source of their power. The Constitution may restrict state governments—as it does, for example, by forbidding them to deny any person the equal protection of the laws. But where such prohibitions do not apply, state governments do not need constitutional authorization to act. The States thus can and do perform many of the vital functions of modern government—punishing street crime, running public schools, and zoning property for development, to name but a few—even though the Constitution's text does not authorize any government to do so. Our cases refer to this general power of governing, possessed by the States but not by the Federal Government, as the "police power."

"State sovereignty is not just an end in itself: Rather, federalism secures to citizens the liberties that derive from the diffusion of sovereign power." *New York v. United States,* 505 U.S. 144, 181 (1992). Because the police power is controlled by 50 different States instead of one national sovereign, the facets of governing that touch on citizens' daily lives are normally administered by smaller governments closer to the governed. The Framers thus ensured that powers which "in the ordinary course of affairs, concern the lives, liberties, and properties of the people" were held by governments more local and more accountable than a distant federal bureaucracy. The Federalist No. 45 (J. Madison). The independent power of the States also serves as a check on the power of the Federal Government: "By denying any one government complete jurisdiction over all the concerns of public life, federalism protects the liberty of the individual from arbitrary power." *Bond v. United States,* 131 S.Ct. 2355, 2364 (2011).

This case concerns two powers that the Constitution does grant the Federal Government, but which must be read carefully to avoid creating a general federal authority akin to the police power. The Constitution authorizes Congress to "regulate Commerce with foreign Nations, and among the several States, and with the Indian Tribes." Art. I, § 8, cl. 3. Our precedents read that to mean that Congress may regulate "the channels of interstate commerce," "persons or things in interstate commerce," and "those activities that substantially affect interstate commerce." . . .

Congress may also "lay and collect Taxes, Duties, Imposts and Excises, to pay the Debts and provide for the common Defence and general Welfare of the United States." U.S. Const., Art. I, § 8, cl. 1. Put simply, Congress may tax and spend. This grant gives the Federal Government considerable influence even in areas where it cannot directly regulate. The Federal Government may enact a tax on an activity that it cannot authorize, forbid, or otherwise control. And in exercising its spending power, Congress may offer funds to the States, and may condition those offers on compliance with specified conditions. These offers may well induce the States to adopt policies that the Federal Government itself could not impose. See, *e.g., South Dakota v. Dole,* 483 U.S. 203, 205–206 (1987) (conditioning federal highway funds on States raising their drinking age to 21).

The reach of the Federal Government's enumerated powers is broader still because the Constitution authorizes Congress to "make all Laws which shall be necessary and proper for carrying into Execution the foregoing Powers." Art. I, § 8, cl. 18. We have long read this provision to give Congress great latitude in exercising its powers: "Let the end be legitimate, let it be within the scope of the constitution, and all means which are appropriate, which are plainly adapted to that end, which are not prohibited, but consist with the letter and spirit of the constitution, are constitutional." *McCulloch,* at 421.

Our permissive reading of these powers is explained in part by a general reticence to invalidate the acts of the Nation's elected leaders. . . . Members of this Court are vested with the authority to interpret the law; we possess neither the expertise nor the prerogative to make policy judgments. Those decisions are entrusted to our Nation's elected leaders, who can be thrown out of office if the people disagree with them. It is not our job to protect the people from the consequences of their political choices.

Our deference in matters of policy cannot, however, become abdication in matters of law. "The powers of the legislature are defined and limited; and that those limits may not be mistaken, or forgotten, the constitution is written." *Marbury v. Madison*, 5 U.S. (1 Cranch) 137, 176 (1803). Our respect for Congress's policy judgments thus can never extend so far as to disavow restraints on federal power that the Constitution carefully constructed. . . .

I

. . . The individual mandate requires most Americans to maintain "minimum essential" health insurance coverage. . . . Beginning in 2014, those who do not comply with the mandate must make a "[s]hared responsibility payment" to the Federal Government. That payment, which the Act describes as a "penalty," is calculated as a percentage of household income, subject to a floor based on a specified dollar amount and a ceiling based on the average annual premium the individual would have to pay for qualifying private health insurance. In 2016, for example, the penalty will be 2.5 percent of an individual's household income, but no less than $695 and no more than the average yearly premium for insurance that covers 60 percent of the cost of 10 specified services (*e.g.*, prescription drugs and hospitalization). The Act provides that the penalty will be paid to the Internal Revenue Service with an individual's taxes. . . .

II

[The Court first found that the individual mandate, because not denominated a "tax" in the statute, was not subject to the restrictions of the tax Anti-Injunction Act, which forbids suits for injunctive relief against tax statutes. The challenge to the constitutionality of the individual mandate was thus not barred. The Court stated that this statutory holding did not control the constitutional question of whether the mandate was a valid exercise of Congress's taxing power. That issue is considered in part IV of Chief Justice Roberts's opinion.—Editors]

III–A

The Government's first argument is that the individual mandate is a valid exercise of Congress's power under the Commerce Clause and the Necessary and Proper Clause. According to the Government, the health care market is characterized by a significant cost-shifting problem. Everyone will eventually need health care at a time and to an extent they cannot predict, but if they do not have insurance, they often will not be able to pay for it. Because state and federal laws nonetheless require hospitals to provide a certain degree of care to individuals without regard to their ability to pay, see, *e.g.*, 42 U.S.C. § 1395dd; Fla. Stat. Ann. § 395.1041, hospitals end up receiving compensation for only a portion of the services they provide. To recoup the losses, hospitals pass on the cost to insurers through higher rates, and insurers, in turn, pass on the cost to policy holders in the form of higher premiums. . . .

In the Affordable Care Act, Congress addressed the problem of those who cannot obtain insurance coverage because of preexisting conditions or other health issues. It did so through the Act's "guaranteed-issue" and "community-rating" provisions. These provisions together prohibit insurance companies from denying coverage to those with such conditions or charging unhealthy individuals higher premiums than healthy individuals.

The guaranteed-issue and community-rating reforms do not, however, address the issue of healthy individuals who choose not to purchase insurance to cover potential health care needs. In fact, the reforms sharply exacerbate that problem, by providing an incentive for individuals to delay purchasing health insurance until they become sick, relying on the promise of guaranteed and affordable coverage. The reforms also threaten to impose massive new costs on insurers, who are required to accept unhealthy individuals but prohibited from charging them rates necessary to pay for their coverage. This will lead insurers to significantly increase premiums on everyone.

The individual mandate was Congress's solution to these problems. By requiring that individuals purchase health insurance, the mandate prevents cost-shifting by those who would otherwise go without it. In addition, the mandate forces into the insurance risk pool more healthy individuals, whose premiums on average will be higher than their health care expenses. This allows insurers to subsidize the costs of covering the unhealthy individuals the reforms require them to accept. The Government claims that Congress has power under the Commerce and Necessary and Proper Clauses to enact this solution.

1

The Government contends that the individual mandate is within Congress's power because the failure to purchase insurance "has a substantial and deleterious effect on interstate commerce" by creating the cost-shifting problem. The path of our Commerce Clause decisions has not always run smooth, see *United States v. Lopez*, 514 U.S. 549, 552–559 (1995), but it is now well established that Congress has broad authority under the Clause. We have recognized, for example, that "[t]he power of Congress over interstate commerce is not confined to the regulation of commerce among the states," but extends to activities that "have a substantial effect on interstate commerce." *United States v. Darby,* 312 U.S. 100, 118–119 (1941). Congress's power, moreover, is not limited to regulation of an activity that by itself substantially affects interstate commerce, but also extends to activities that do so only when aggregated with similar activities of others. See *Wickard v. Filburn,* 317 U.S. 111, 127–128 (1942).

Given its expansive scope, it is no surprise that Congress has employed the commerce power in a wide variety of ways to address the pressing needs of the time. But Congress has never attempted to rely on that power to compel individuals not engaged in commerce to purchase an unwanted product. Legislative novelty is not necessarily fatal; there is a first time for everything. But sometimes "the most telling indication of [a] severe constitutional problem . . . is the lack of historical precedent" for Congress's action. *Free Enterprise Fund v. Public Company Accounting Oversight Bd.*, 130 S.Ct. 3138, 3159 (2010). . . .

The Constitution grants Congress the power to "*regulate* Commerce." Art. I, § 8, cl. 3 (emphasis added). The power to *regulate* commerce presupposes the existence of commercial activity to be regulated. If the power to "regulate" something included the power to create it, many of the provisions in the Constitution would be superfluous. For example, the Constitution gives Congress the power to "coin Money," in addition to the power to "regulate the Value thereof." And it gives Congress the power to "raise and support Armies" and to "provide and maintain a Navy," in addition to the power to "make Rules for the Government and Regulation of the land and naval Forces." If the power to regulate the armed forces or the value of money included the power to bring the subject of the regulation into existence, the specific grant of such powers would have been unnecessary. The language of the Constitution reflects the natural understanding that the power to regulate assumes there is already something to be regulated. See *Gibbons v. Ogden*, at 188 ("[T]he enlightened patriots who framed our constitution, and the people who adopted it, must be understood to have employed words in their natural sense, and to have intended what they have said").

Our precedent also reflects this understanding. As expansive as our cases construing the scope of the commerce power have been, they all have one thing in common: They uniformly describe the power as reaching "activity." It is nearly impossible to avoid the word when quoting them. See, *e.g., Lopez,* at 560 ("Where economic activity substantially affects interstate commerce, legislation regulating that activity will be sustained"); *Wickard,* at 125 ("[E]ven if appellee's activity be local and though it may not be regarded as commerce, it may still, whatever its nature, be reached by Congress if it exerts a substantial economic effect on interstate commerce").

The individual mandate, however, does not regulate existing commercial activity. It instead compels individuals to *become* active in commerce by purchasing a product, on the ground that their failure to do so affects interstate commerce. Construing the Commerce Clause to permit Congress to regulate individuals precisely *because* they are doing nothing would open a new and potentially vast domain to congressional authority. Every day individuals do not do an infinite number of things. In some cases they decide not to do something; in others they simply fail to do it. Allowing Congress to justify federal regulation by pointing to the effect of inaction on commerce would bring countless decisions an individual could *potentially* make within the scope of federal regulation, and—under the Government's theory—empower Congress to make those decisions for him.

Applying the Government's logic to the familiar case of *Wickard v. Filburn* shows how far that logic would carry us from the notion of a government of limited powers. In *Wickard,* the Court famously upheld a federal penalty imposed on a farmer for growing wheat for consumption on his own farm. That amount of wheat caused the farmer to exceed his quota under a program designed to support the price of wheat by limiting supply. The Court rejected the farmer's argument that growing wheat for home consumption was beyond the reach of the commerce power. It did so on the ground that the farmer's decision to grow wheat for his own use allowed him to avoid purchasing wheat in the market. That decision, when considered in the aggregate along with similar decisions of others, would have had a substantial effect on the interstate market for wheat.

Wickard has long been regarded as "perhaps the most far reaching example of Commerce Clause authority over intrastate activity," *Lopez,* at 560, but the Government's theory in this case would go much further. Under *Wickard* it is within Congress's power to regulate the market for wheat by supporting its price. But price can be supported by increasing demand as well as by decreasing supply. The aggregated decisions of some consumers not to purchase wheat have a substantial effect on the price of wheat, just as decisions not to purchase health insurance have on the price of insurance. Congress can therefore command that those not buying wheat do so, just as it argues here that it may command that those not buying health insurance do so. The farmer in *Wickard* was at least actively engaged in the production of wheat, and the Government could regulate that activity because of its effect on commerce. The Government's theory here would effectively override that limitation, by establishing that individuals may be regulated under the Commerce Clause whenever enough of them are not doing something the Government would have them do.

Indeed, the Government's logic would justify a mandatory purchase to solve almost any problem. To consider a different example in the health care market, many Americans do not eat a balanced diet. That group makes up a larger percentage of the total population than those without health insurance. The failure of that group to have a healthy diet increases health care costs, to a greater extent than the failure of the uninsured to purchase insurance. Those increased costs are borne in part by other Americans who must pay more, just as the uninsured shift costs to the insured. Congress addressed the insurance problem by ordering everyone to buy insurance. Under the Government's theory, Congress could address the diet problem by ordering everyone to buy vegetables.

People, for reasons of their own, often fail to do things that would be good for them or good for society. Those failures—joined with the similar failures of others—can readily have a substantial effect on interstate commerce. Under the Government's logic, that authorizes Congress to use its commerce power to compel citizens to act as the Government would have them act.

That is not the country the Framers of our Constitution envisioned. James Madison explained that the Commerce Clause was "an addition which few oppose and from which no apprehensions are entertained." The Federalist No. 45. . . . Congress already enjoys vast power to regulate much of what we do. Accepting the Government's theory would give Congress the same license to regulate what we do not do, fundamentally changing the relation between the citizen and the Federal Government.

To an economist, perhaps, there is no difference between activity and inactivity; both have measurable economic effects on commerce. But the distinction between doing something and doing nothing would not have been lost on the Framers. . . . As we have explained, "the framers of the Constitution were not mere visionaries, toying with speculations or theories, but practical men, dealing with the facts of political life as they understood them, putting into form the government they were creating, and prescribing in language clear and intelligible the powers that government was to take." *South Carolina v. United States,* 199 U.S. 437, 449 (1905). The Framers gave Congress the power to *regulate* commerce, not to *compel* it, and for over 200 years both our decisions and Congress's actions have reflected this understanding. There is no reason to depart from that understanding now.

The Government sees things differently. It argues that because sickness and injury are unpredictable but unavoidable, "the uninsured as a class are active in the market for health care, which they regularly seek and obtain." The individual mandate "merely regulates how individuals finance and pay for that active participation—requiring that they do so through insurance, rather than through attempted self-insurance with the back-stop of shifting costs to others."

The Government repeats the phrase "active in the market for health care" throughout its brief, but that concept has no constitutional significance. An individual who bought a car two years ago and may buy another in the future is not "active in the car market" in any pertinent sense. The phrase "active in the market" cannot obscure the fact that most of those regulated by the individual mandate are not currently engaged in any commercial activity involving health care, and that fact is fatal to the Government's effort to "regulate the uninsured as a class." Our precedents recognize Congress's power to regulate "class[es] of *activities*," not classes of *individuals,* apart from any activity in which they are engaged.

The individual mandate's regulation of the uninsured as a class is, in fact, particularly divorced from any link to existing commercial activity. The mandate primarily affects healthy, often young adults who are less likely to need significant health care and have other priorities for spending their money. It is precisely because these individuals, as an actuarial class, incur relatively low health care costs that the mandate helps counter the effect of forcing insurance companies to cover others who impose greater costs than their premiums are allowed to reflect. If the individual mandate is targeted at a class, it is a class whose commercial inactivity rather than activity is its defining feature.

The Government, however, claims that this does not matter. The Government regards it as sufficient to trigger Congress's authority that almost all those who are uninsured will, at some unknown point in the future, engage in a health care transaction. Asserting that "[t]here is no temporal limitation in the Commerce Clause," the Government argues that because "[e]veryone subject to this regulation is in or will be in the health care market," they can be "regulated in advance."

The proposition that Congress may dictate the conduct of an individual today because of prophesied future activity finds no support in our precedent. We have said that Congress can anticipate the *effects* on commerce of an economic activity. . . . Each one of our cases, including those cited by JUSTICE GINSBURG, involved preexisting economic activity. See, *e.g., Wickard,* at 127–129 (producing wheat); *Gonzales v. Raich,* 545 U.S. 1, 25 (2005) (growing marijuana).

Everyone will likely participate in the markets for food, clothing, transportation, shelter, or energy; that does not authorize Congress to direct them to purchase particular products in those or other markets today. The Commerce Clause is not a general license to regulate an individual from cradle to grave, simply because he will predictably engage in particular transactions. Any police power to regulate individuals as such, as opposed to their activities, remains vested in the States.

The Government argues that the individual mandate can be sustained as a sort of exception to this rule, because health insurance is a unique product. According to the Government, upholding the individual mandate would not justify mandatory purchases of items such as cars or broccoli because, as the Government puts it, "[h]ealth insurance is not purchased for its own sake like a car or broccoli; it is a means of financing health-care consumption and covering universal risks." But cars and broccoli are no more purchased for their "own sake" than health insurance. They are purchased to cover the need for transportation and food.

The Government says that health insurance and health care financing are "inherently integrated." But that does not mean the compelled purchase of the first is properly regarded as a regulation of the second. No matter how "inherently integrated" health insurance and health care consumption may be, they are not the same thing: They involve different transactions, entered into at different times, with

[handwritten margin note: Ginsburg says no. Just requires you to buy-in to something you will inevitably use.]

different providers. And for most of those targeted by the mandate, significant health care needs will be years, or even decades, away. The proximity and degree of connection between the mandate and the subsequent commercial activity is too lacking to justify an exception of the sort urged by the Government. The individual mandate forces individuals into commerce precisely because they elected to refrain from commercial activity. Such a law cannot be sustained under a clause authorizing Congress to "regulate Commerce."

2

The Government next contends that Congress has the power under the Necessary and Proper Clause to enact the individual mandate because the mandate is an "integral part of a comprehensive scheme of economic regulation"—the guaranteed-issue and community-rating insurance reforms. Under this argument, it is not necessary to consider the effect that an individual's inactivity may have on interstate commerce; it is enough that Congress regulate commercial activity in a way that requires regulation of inactivity to be effective.

The power to "make all Laws which shall be necessary and proper for carrying into Execution" the powers enumerated in the Constitution, Art. I, § 8, cl. 18, vests Congress with authority to enact provisions "incidental to the [enumerated] power, and conducive to its beneficial exercise," McCulloch, at 418. Although the Clause gives Congress authority to "legislate on that vast mass of incidental powers which must be involved in the constitution," it does not license the exercise of any "great substantive and independent power[s]" beyond those specifically enumerated. Id., at 411, 421. Instead, the Clause is " 'merely a declaration, for the removal of all uncertainty, that the means of carrying into execution those [powers] otherwise granted are included in the grant.' " Kinsella v. United States ex rel. Singleton, 361 U.S. 234, 247 (1960) (quoting James Madison).

As our jurisprudence under the Necessary and Proper Clause has developed, we have been very deferential to Congress's determination that a regulation is "necessary." We have thus upheld laws that are " 'convenient, or useful' or 'conducive' to the authority's 'beneficial exercise.' " United States v. Comstock, 130 S.Ct. 1949, 1965 (2010) (quoting McCulloch, at 413, 418). But we have also carried out our responsibility to declare unconstitutional those laws that undermine the structure of government established by the Constitution. Such laws, which are not "consist[ent] with the letter and spirit of the constitution," McCulloch, at 421, are not "proper [means] for carrying into Execution" Congress's enumerated powers. Rather, they are, "in the words of The Federalist, 'merely acts of usurpation' which 'deserve to be treated as such.' " Printz v. United States, 521 U.S. 898, 924 (1997) (quoting The Federalist No. 33).

Applying these principles, the individual mandate cannot be sustained under the Necessary and Proper Clause as an essential component of the insurance reforms. Each of our prior cases upholding laws under that Clause involved exercises of authority derivative of, and in service to, a granted power. For example, we have upheld provisions permitting continued confinement of those already in federal custody when they could not be safely released; criminalizing bribes involving organizations receiving federal funds; and tolling state statutes of limitations while cases are pending in federal court. The individual mandate, by contrast, vests

Congress with the extraordinary ability to create the necessary predicate to the exercise of an enumerated power.   federal
prisoners

This is in no way an authority that is "narrow in scope," *Comstock*, at 1964, or "incidental" to the exercise of the commerce power, *McCulloch*, at 418. Rather, such a conception of the Necessary and Proper Clause would work a substantial expansion of federal authority. No longer would Congress be limited to regulating under the Commerce Clause those who by some preexisting activity bring themselves within the sphere of federal regulation. Instead, Congress could reach beyond the natural limit of its authority and draw within its regulatory scope those who otherwise would be outside of it. Even if the individual mandate is "necessary" to the Act's insurance reforms, such an expansion of federal power is not a "proper" means for making those reforms effective.

The Government relies primarily on our decision in *Gonzales v. Raich*. In *Raich*, . . . Congress's attempt to regulate the interstate market for marijuana would . . . have been substantially undercut if it could not also regulate intrastate possession and consumption. Accordingly, we recognized that "Congress was acting well within its authority" under the Necessary and Proper Clause even though its "regulation ensnare[d] some purely intrastate activity." *Raich*, at 22. *Raich* thus did not involve the exercise of any "great substantive and independent power," *McCulloch*, at 411, of the sort at issue here. Instead, it concerned only the constitutionality of "individual *applications* of a concededly valid statutory scheme." *Raich*, at 23 (emphasis added).

Just as the individual mandate cannot be sustained as a law regulating the substantial effects of the failure to purchase health insurance, neither can it be upheld as a "necessary and proper" component of the insurance reforms. The commerce power thus does not authorize the mandate.

B

That is not the end of the matter. Because the Commerce Clause does not support the individual mandate, it is necessary to turn to the Government's second argument: that the mandate may be upheld as within Congress's enumerated power to "lay and collect Taxes." Art. I, § 8, cl. 1.

The Government's tax power argument asks us to view the statute differently than we did in considering its commerce power theory. In making its Commerce Clause argument, the Government defended the mandate as a regulation requiring individuals to purchase health insurance. The Government does not claim that the taxing power allows Congress to issue such a command. Instead, the Government asks us to read the mandate not as ordering individuals to buy insurance, but rather as imposing a tax on those who do not buy that product.

The text of a statute can sometimes have more than one possible meaning. . . . [I]t is well established that if a statute has two possible meanings, one of which violates the Constitution, courts should adopt the meaning that does not do so. Justice Story said that 180 years ago: "No court ought, unless the terms of an act rendered it unavoidable, to give a construction to it which should involve a violation, however unintentional, of the constitution." *Parsons v. Bedford*, 28 U.S. (3 Pet.) 433, 448–449 (1830). . . .

The most straightforward reading of the mandate is that it commands individuals to purchase insurance. After all, it states that individuals "shall" maintain health insurance. Congress thought it could enact such a command under the Commerce Clause, and the Government primarily defended the law on that basis. But, for the reasons explained above, the Commerce Clause does not give Congress that power. Under our precedent, it is therefore necessary to ask whether the Government's alternative reading of the statute—that it only imposes a tax on those without insurance—is a reasonable one.

Under the mandate, if an individual does not maintain health insurance, the only consequence is that he must make an additional payment to the IRS when he pays his taxes. . . . [I]f the mandate is in effect just a tax hike on certain taxpayers who do not have health insurance, it may be within Congress's constitutional power to tax.

The question is not whether that is the most natural interpretation of the mandate, but only whether it is a "fairly possible" one. *Crowell v. Benson,* 285 U.S. 22, 62 (1932). . . .

C

The exaction the Affordable Care Act imposes on those without health insurance looks like a tax in many respects. The "[s]hared responsibility payment," as the statute entitles it, is paid into the Treasury by "taxpayer[s]" when they file their tax returns. It does not apply to individuals who do not pay federal income taxes because their household income is less than the filing threshold in the Internal Revenue Code. For taxpayers who do owe the payment, its amount is determined by such familiar factors as taxable income, number of dependents, and joint filing status. The requirement to pay is found in the Internal Revenue Code and enforced by the IRS, which—as we previously explained—must assess and collect it "in the same manner as taxes." This process yields the essential feature of any tax: it produces at least some revenue for the Government. *United States v. Kahriger,* 345 U.S. 22, 28, n. 4 (1953). Indeed, the payment is expected to raise about $4 billion per year by 2017.

It is of course true that the Act describes the payment as a "penalty," not a "tax." But while that label is fatal to the application of the Anti-Injunction Act, it does not determine whether the payment may be viewed as an exercise of Congress's taxing power. It is up to Congress whether to apply the Anti-Injunction Act to any particular statute, so it makes sense to be guided by Congress's choice of label on that question. That choice does not, however, control whether an exaction is within Congress's constitutional power to tax. . . .

Our cases confirm this functional approach. For example, in *Bailey v. Drexel Furniture Co.,* 259 U.S. 20 (1922), we focused on three practical characteristics of the so-called tax on employing child laborers that convinced us the "tax" was actually a penalty. First, the tax imposed an exceedingly heavy burden—10 percent of a company's net income—on those who employed children, no matter how small their infraction. Second, it imposed that exaction only on those who knowingly employed underage laborers. Such scienter requirements are typical of punitive statutes, because Congress often wishes to punish only those who intentionally break the law. Third, this "tax" was enforced in part by the Department of Labor, an agency responsible for punishing violations of labor laws, not collecting revenue.

The same analysis here suggests that the shared responsibility payment may for constitutional purposes be considered a tax, not a penalty: First, for most Americans the amount due will be far less than the price of insurance, and, by statute, it can never be more. It may often be a reasonable financial decision to make the payment rather than purchase insurance, unlike the "prohibitory" financial punishment in *Drexel Furniture*. Second, the individual mandate contains no scienter requirement. Third, the payment is collected solely by the IRS through the normal means of taxation—except that the Service is *not* allowed to use those means most suggestive of a punitive sanction, such as criminal prosecution. The reasons the Court in *Drexel Furniture* held that what was called a "tax" there was a penalty support the conclusion that what is called a "penalty" here may be viewed as a tax.

None of this is to say that the payment is not intended to affect individual conduct. Although the payment will raise considerable revenue, it is plainly designed to expand health insurance coverage. But taxes that seek to influence conduct are nothing new. Some of our earliest federal taxes sought to deter the purchase of imported manufactured goods in order to foster the growth of domestic industry. Today, federal and state taxes can compose more than half the retail price of cigarettes, not just to raise more money, but to encourage people to quit smoking. And we have upheld such obviously regulatory measures as taxes on selling marijuana and sawed-off shotguns. . . .

In distinguishing penalties from taxes, this Court has explained that "if the concept of penalty means anything, it means punishment for an unlawful act or omission." *United States v. Reorganized CF & I Fabricators of Utah, Inc.*, 518 U.S. 213, 224 (1996). While the individual mandate clearly aims to induce the purchase of health insurance, it need not be read to declare that failing to do so is unlawful. Neither the Act nor any other law attaches negative legal consequences to not buying health insurance, beyond requiring payment to the IRS. . . .

Indeed, it is estimated that four million people each year will choose to pay the IRS rather than buy insurance. We would expect Congress to be troubled by that prospect if such conduct were unlawful. That Congress apparently regards such extensive failure to comply with the mandate as tolerable suggests that Congress did not think it was creating four million outlaws. It suggests instead that the shared responsibility payment merely imposes a tax citizens may lawfully choose to pay in lieu of buying health insurance.

The joint dissenters argue that we cannot uphold § 5000A as a tax because Congress did not "frame" it as such. In effect, they contend that even if the Constitution permits Congress to do exactly what we interpret this statute to do, the law must be struck down because Congress used the wrong labels. An example may help illustrate why labels should not control here. Suppose Congress enacted a statute providing that every taxpayer who owns a house without energy efficient windows must pay $50 to the IRS. The amount due is adjusted based on factors such as taxable income and joint filing status, and is paid along with the taxpayer's income tax return. Those whose income is below the filing threshold need not pay. The required payment is not called a "tax," a "penalty," or anything else. No one would doubt that this law imposed a tax, and was within Congress's power to tax. That conclusion should not change simply because Congress used the word "penalty" to describe the payment. Interpreting such a law to be a tax would hardly "[i]mpos[e] a tax through judicial legislation." Rather, it would give practical effect to the Legislature's enactment. . . .

Even if the taxing power enables Congress to impose a tax on not obtaining health insurance, any tax must still comply with other requirements in the

Constitution. Plaintiffs argue that the shared responsibility payment does not do so, citing Article I, § 9, clause 4. That clause provides: "No Capitation, or other direct, Tax shall be laid, unless in Proportion to the Census or Enumeration herein before directed to be taken." This requirement means that any "direct Tax" must be apportioned so that each State pays in proportion to its population. . . .

Even when the Direct Tax Clause was written it was unclear what else, other than a capitation (also known as a "head tax" or a "poll tax"), might be a direct tax. Soon after the framing, Congress passed a tax on ownership of carriages, over James Madison's objection that it was an unapportioned direct tax. This Court upheld the tax, in part reasoning that apportioning such a tax would make little sense, because it would have required taxing carriage owners at dramatically different rates depending on how many carriages were in their home State. See *Hylton v. United States,* 3 U.S. (3 Dall.) 171, 174 (1796) (opinion of Chase, J.). The Court was unanimous, and those Justices who wrote opinions either directly asserted or strongly suggested that only two forms of taxation were direct: capitations and land taxes. . . .

In 1895, we expanded our interpretation to include taxes on personal property and income from personal property, in the course of striking down aspects of the federal income tax. *Pollock v. Farmers' Loan & Trust Co.,* 158 U.S. 601, 618 (1895). That result was overturned by the Sixteenth Amendment, although we continued to consider taxes on personal property to be direct taxes.

A tax on going without health insurance does not fall within any recognized category of direct tax. It is not a capitation. Capitations are taxes paid by every person, "without regard to property, profession, or *any other circumstance.*" *Hylton,* at 175 (opinion of Chase, J.) (emphasis altered). The whole point of the shared responsibility payment is that it is triggered by specific circumstances—earning a certain amount of income but not obtaining health insurance. The payment is also plainly not a tax on the ownership of land or personal property. The shared responsibility payment is thus not a direct tax that must be apportioned among the several States.

There may, however, be a more fundamental objection to a tax on those who lack health insurance. Even if only a tax, the payment under § 5000A(b) remains a burden that the Federal Government imposes for an omission, not an act. If it is troubling to interpret the Commerce Clause as authorizing Congress to regulate those who abstain from commerce, perhaps it should be similarly troubling to permit Congress to impose a tax for not doing something.

Three considerations allay this concern. First, and most importantly, it is abundantly clear the Constitution does not guarantee that individuals may avoid taxation through inactivity. A capitation, after all, is a tax that everyone must pay simply for existing, and capitations are expressly contemplated by the Constitution. The Court today holds that our Constitution protects us from federal regulation under the Commerce Clause so long as we abstain from the regulated activity. But from its creation, the Constitution has made no such promise with respect to taxes. See Letter from Benjamin Franklin to M. Le Roy (Nov. 13, 1789) ("Our new Constitution is now established . . . but in this world nothing can be said to be certain, except death and taxes").

Whether the mandate can be upheld under the Commerce Clause is a question about the scope of federal authority. Its answer depends on whether Congress can exercise what all acknowledge to be the novel course of directing individuals to purchase insurance. Congress's use of the Taxing Clause to encourage buying something is, by contrast, not new. Tax incentives already promote, for example, purchasing homes and professional educations. Sustaining the mandate as a tax depends only on whether Congress *has* properly exercised its taxing power to encourage purchasing health insurance, not whether it *can*. Upholding the individual mandate under the Taxing Clause thus does not recognize any new federal power. It determines that Congress has used an existing one.

Second, Congress's ability to use its taxing power to influence conduct is not without limits. A few of our cases policed these limits aggressively, invalidating punitive exactions obviously designed to regulate behavior otherwise regarded at the time as beyond federal authority. See, *e.g., United States v. Butler,* 297 U.S. 1 (1936); Drexel Furniture. More often and more recently we have declined to closely examine the regulatory motive or effect of revenue-raising measures. We have nonetheless maintained that " 'there comes a time in the extension of the penalizing features of the so-called tax when it loses its character as such and becomes a mere penalty with the characteristics of regulation and punishment.' " *Department of Revenue of Mont. v. Kurth Ranch,* 511 U.S. 767, 779 (1994) (quoting *Drexel Furniture*, at 38). . . .

Third, although the breadth of Congress's power to tax is greater than its power to regulate commerce, the taxing power does not give Congress the same degree of control over individual behavior. . . . Congress's authority under the taxing power is limited to requiring an individual to pay money into the Federal Treasury, no more. If a tax is properly paid, the Government has no power to compel or punish individuals subject to it. We do not make light of the severe burden that taxation— especially taxation motivated by a regulatory purpose—can impose. But imposition of a tax nonetheless leaves an individual with a lawful choice to do or not do a certain act, so long as he is willing to pay a tax levied on that choice.

The Affordable Care Act's requirement that certain individuals pay a financial penalty for not obtaining health insurance may reasonably be characterized as a tax. Because the Constitution permits such a tax, it is not our role to forbid it, or to pass upon its wisdom or fairness. . . .

IV–A

The States also contend that the Medicaid expansion exceeds Congress's authority under the Spending Clause. They claim that Congress is coercing the States to adopt the changes it wants by threatening to withhold all of a State's Medicaid grants, unless the State accepts the new expanded funding and complies with the conditions that come with it. . . .

The Spending Clause grants Congress the power "to pay the Debts and provide for the . . . general Welfare of the United States." U.S. Const., Art. I, § 8, cl. 1. We have long recognized that Congress may use this power to grant federal funds to the States, and may condition such a grant upon the States' "taking certain actions that Congress could not require them to take." College Savings Bank v. *Florida Prepaid Postsecondary Ed. Expense Bd.*, 527 U.S. 666, 686 (1999). Such measures "encourage a State to regulate in a particular way, [and] influenc[e] a State's policy choices." *New York,* at 166. The conditions imposed by Congress ensure that the funds are used by the States to "provide for the . . . general Welfare" in the manner Congress intended.

At the same time, our cases have recognized limits on Congress's power under the Spending Clause to secure state compliance with federal objectives. "We have repeatedly characterized . . . Spending Clause legislation as much in the nature of a *contract." Barnes v. Gorman,* 536 U.S. 181, 186 (2002). The legitimacy of Congress's exercise of the spending power "thus rests on whether the State voluntarily and knowingly accepts the terms of the 'contract.' " *Pennhurst State School and Hospital v. Halderman,* 451 U.S. 1, 17 (1981)). Respecting this limitation is critical to ensuring that Spending Clause legislation does not undermine the status of the States as independent sovereigns in our federal system. . . . "[T]he Constitution has never been understood to confer upon Congress the ability to require the States to govern according to Congress' instructions." *New York,* at 162. . . .

That insight has led this Court to strike down federal legislation that commandeers a State's legislative or administrative apparatus for federal purposes. See, *e.g., Printz,* at 933 (striking down federal legislation compelling state law enforcement officers to perform federally mandated background checks on handgun purchasers); *New York,* at 174–175 (invalidating provisions of an Act that would compel a State to either take title to nuclear waste or enact particular state waste regulations). It has also led us to scrutinize Spending Clause legislation to ensure that Congress is not using financial inducements to exert a "power akin to undue influence." *Steward Machine Co. v. Davis,* 301 U.S. 548, 590 (1937). Congress may use its spending power to create incentives for States to act in accordance with federal policies. But when "pressure turns into compulsion," *ibid.,* the legislation runs contrary to our system of federalism. "[T]he Constitution simply does not give Congress the authority to require the States to regulate." New York, at 178. That is true whether Congress directly commands a State to regulate or indirectly coerces a State to adopt a federal regulatory system as its own. . . .

As our decision in *Steward Machine* confirms, Congress may attach appropriate conditions to federal taxing and spending programs to preserve its control over the use of federal funds. . . . The States, however, argue that the Medicaid expansion is far from the typical case. They object that Congress has "crossed the line distinguishing encouragement from coercion," *New York,* at 175, in the way it has structured the funding: Instead of simply refusing to grant the new funds to States that will not accept the new conditions, Congress has also threatened to withhold those States' existing Medicaid funds. The States claim that this threat serves no purpose other than to force unwilling States to sign up for the dramatic expansion in health care coverage effected by the Act.

Given the nature of the threat and the programs at issue here, we must agree. We have upheld Congress's authority to condition the receipt of funds on the States' complying with restrictions on the use of those funds, because that is the means by which Congress ensures that the funds are spent according to its view of the "general Welfare." Conditions that do not here govern the use of the funds, however, cannot be justified on that basis. When, for example, such conditions take the form of threats to terminate other significant independent grants, the conditions are properly viewed as a means of pressuring the States to accept policy changes.

In *South Dakota v. Dole,* we . . . asked whether "the financial inducement offered by Congress" was "so coercive as to pass the point at which 'pressure turns into compulsion.' " *Id.,* at 211 (quoting *Steward Machine,* at 590). By "financial inducement" the Court meant the threat of losing five percent of highway funds; no new money was offered to the States to raise their drinking ages. We found that the inducement was not impermissibly coercive, because Congress was offering only "relatively mild encouragement to the States." We observed that "all South Dakota would lose if she adheres to her chosen course as to a suitable minimum drinking age is 5%" of her highway funds. In fact, the federal funds at stake constituted less than half of one percent of South Dakota's budget at the time. In consequence, "we conclude[d] that [the] encouragement to state action [was] a valid use of the spending power." Whether to accept the drinking age change "remain[ed] the prerogative of the States not merely in theory but in fact."

In this case, the financial "inducement" Congress has chosen is much more than "relatively mild encouragement"—it is a gun to the head. Section 1396c of the Medicaid Act provides that if a State's Medicaid plan does not comply with the Act's requirements, the Secretary of Health and Human Services may declare that "further payments will not be made to the State." A State that opts out of the Affordable Care Act's expansion in health care coverage thus stands to lose not merely "a relatively small percentage" of its existing Medicaid funding, but *all* of it. Medicaid spending accounts for over 20 percent of the average State's total budget, with federal funds covering 50 to 83 percent of those costs. . . . It is easy to see how the *Dole* Court could conclude that the threatened loss of less than half of one percent of South Dakota's budget left that State with a "prerogative" to reject Congress's desired policy, "not merely in theory but in fact." The threatened loss of over 10 percent of a State's overall budget, in contrast, is economic dragooning that leaves the States with no real option but to acquiesce in the Medicaid expansion.

JUSTICE GINSBURG claims that *Dole* is distinguishable because here "Congress has not threatened to withhold funds earmarked for any other program." But that begs the question: The States contend that the expansion is in reality a new program and that Congress is forcing them to accept it by threatening the funds for the existing Medicaid program. We cannot agree that existing Medicaid and the expansion dictated by the Affordable Care Act are all one program simply because "Congress styled" them as such. If the expansion is not properly viewed as a modification of the existing Medicaid program, Congress's decision to so title it is irrelevant. . . .

The Court in *Steward Machine* did not attempt to "fix the outermost line" where persuasion gives way to coercion. . . . We have no need to fix a line either. It is enough for today that wherever that line may be, this statute is surely beyond it. . . .

B

Nothing in our opinion precludes Congress from offering funds under the Affordable Care Act to expand the availability of health care, and requiring that States accepting such funds comply with the conditions on their use. What Congress is not free to do is to penalize States that choose not to participate in that new program by taking away their existing Medicaid funding. . . . In light of the Court's holding, the Secretary cannot apply § 1396c to withdraw existing Medicaid funds for failure to comply with the requirements set out in the expansion. . . .

This is not to say, as the joint dissent suggests, that we are "rewriting the Medicaid Expansion." Instead, we determine, first, that § 1396c is unconstitutional when applied to withdraw existing Medicaid funds from States that decline to comply with the expansion. We then follow Congress's explicit textual instruction to leave unaffected "the remainder of the chapter, and the application of [the challenged] provision to other persons or circumstances." § 1303. When we invalidate an application of a statute because that application is unconstitutional, we are not "rewriting" the statute; we are merely enforcing the Constitution. . . .

* * *

The Affordable Care Act is constitutional in part and unconstitutional in part. The individual mandate cannot be upheld as an exercise of Congress's power under the Commerce Clause. That Clause authorizes Congress to regulate interstate commerce, not to order individuals to engage in it. In this case, however, it is reasonable to construe what Congress has done as increasing taxes on those who have a certain amount of income, but choose to go without health insurance. Such legislation is within Congress's power to tax.

As for the Medicaid expansion, that portion of the Affordable Care Act violates the Constitution by threatening existing Medicaid funding. Congress has no authority to order the States to regulate according to its instructions. Congress may offer the States grants and require the States to comply with accompanying conditions, but the States must have a genuine choice whether to accept the offer. The States are given no such choice in this case: They must either accept a basic change in the nature of Medicaid, or risk losing all Medicaid funding. The remedy for that constitutional violation is to preclude the Federal Government from imposing such a sanction. That remedy does not require striking down other portions of the Affordable Care Act.

The Framers created a Federal Government of limited powers, and assigned to this Court the duty of enforcing those limits. The Court does so today. But the Court does not express any opinion on the wisdom of the Affordable Care Act. Under the Constitution, that judgment is reserved to the people. . . .

■ JUSTICE GINSBURG, with whom JUSTICE SOTOMAYOR joins, and with whom JUSTICE BREYER and JUSTICE KAGAN join as to Parts I, II, III, and IV, concurring in part, concurring in the judgment in part, and dissenting in part.

I agree with THE CHIEF JUSTICE that the Anti-Injunction Act does not bar the Court's consideration of this case, and that the minimum coverage provision is a proper exercise of Congress' taxing power. I therefore join Parts I, II, and III–C of THE CHIEF JUSTICE's opinion. Unlike THE CHIEF JUSTICE, however, I would hold, alternatively, that the Commerce Clause authorizes Congress to enact the minimum coverage provision. I would also hold that the Spending Clause permits the Medicaid expansion exactly as Congress enacted it.

I

The provision of health care is today a concern of national dimension, just as the provision of old-age and survivors' benefits was in the 1930's. In the Social Security Act, Congress installed a federal system to provide monthly benefits to retired wage earners and, eventually, to their survivors. Beyond question, Congress could have adopted a similar scheme for health care. Congress chose, instead, to preserve a central role for private insurers and state governments. According to The Chief

Justice, the Commerce Clause does not permit that preservation. This rigid reading of the Clause makes scant sense and is stunningly retrogressive. . . .

States cannot resolve the problem of the uninsured on their own. Like Social Security benefits, a universal health-care system, if adopted by an individual State, would be "bait to the needy and dependent elsewhere, encouraging them to migrate and seek a haven of repose." *Helvering v. Davis,* 301 U.S. 619, 644 (1937). An influx of unhealthy individuals into a State with universal health care would result in increased spending on medical services. To cover the increased costs, a State would have to raise taxes, and private health-insurance companies would have to increase premiums. Higher taxes and increased insurance costs would, in turn, encourage businesses and healthy individuals to leave the State.

States that undertake health-care reforms on their own thus risk "placing themselves in a position of economic disadvantage as compared with neighbors or competitors." *Davis,* at 644. Facing that risk, individual States are unlikely to take the initiative in addressing the problem of the uninsured, even though solving that problem is in all States' best interests. Congress' intervention was needed to overcome this collective-action impasse. . . .

To ensure that individuals with medical histories have access to affordable insurance, Congress devised a three-part solution. First, Congress imposed a "guaranteed issue" requirement, which bars insurers from denying coverage to any person on account of that person's medical condition or history. Second, Congress required insurers to use "community rating" to price their insurance policies. Community rating, in effect, bars insurance companies from charging higher premiums to those with preexisting conditions. . . .

Congress comprehended that guaranteed-issue and community-rating laws alone would not work. When insurance companies are required to insure the sick at affordable prices, individuals can wait until they become ill to buy insurance. Pretty soon, those in need of immediate medical care—*i.e.,* those who cost insurers the most—become the insurance companies' main customers. This "adverse selection" problem leaves insurers with two choices: They can either raise premiums dramatically to cover their ever-increasing costs or they can exit the market. In the seven States that tried guaranteed-issue and community-rating requirements without a minimum coverage provision, that is precisely what insurance companies did. . . .

II

The Commerce Clause, it is widely acknowledged, "was the Framers' response to the central problem that gave rise to the Constitution itself." *EEOC v. Wyoming,* 460 U.S. 226, 244, 245 n.1 (1983) (Stevens, J., concurring). Under the Articles of Confederation, the Constitution's precursor, the regulation of commerce was left to the States. This scheme proved unworkable, because the individual States, understandably focused on their own economic interests, often failed to take actions critical to the success of the Nation as a whole. . . .

Consistent with the Framers' intent, we have repeatedly emphasized that Congress' authority under the Commerce Clause is dependent upon "practical" considerations, including "actual experience." *NLRB v. Jones & Laughlin Steel Corp.,* 301 U.S. 1, 41–42 (1937). We afford Congress the leeway "to undertake to solve national problems directly and realistically." *American Power & Light Co. v. SEC,* 329 U.S. 90, 103 (1946).

Until today, this Court's pragmatic approach to judging whether Congress validly exercised its commerce power was guided by two familiar principles. First, Congress has the power to regulate economic activities "that substantially affect interstate commerce." *Raich,* at 17. . . . Second, we owe a large measure of respect to Congress when it frames and enacts economic and social legislation. See *id.,* at 17. . . .

Straightforward application of these principles would require the Court to hold that the minimum coverage provision is proper Commerce Clause legislation. Beyond dispute, Congress had a rational basis for concluding that the uninsured, as a class, substantially affect interstate commerce. Those without insurance consume billions of dollars of health-care products and services each year. Those goods are produced, sold, and delivered largely by national and regional companies who routinely transact business across state lines. The uninsured also cross state lines to receive care. Some have medical emergencies while away from home. Others, when sick, go to a neighboring State that provides better care for those who have not prepaid for care.

Not only do those without insurance consume a large amount of health care each year; critically, as earlier explained, their inability to pay for a significant portion of that consumption drives up market prices, foists costs on other consumers, and reduces market efficiency and stability. Given these far-reaching effects on interstate commerce, the decision to forgo insurance is hardly inconsequential or equivalent to "doing nothing"; it is, instead, an economic decision Congress has the authority to address under the Commerce Clause. . . .

Rather than evaluating the constitutionality of the minimum coverage provision in the manner established by our precedents, THE CHIEF JUSTICE relies on a newly minted constitutional doctrine. The commerce power does not, THE CHIEF JUSTICE announces, permit Congress to "compe[l] individuals to become active in commerce by purchasing a product."

THE CHIEF JUSTICE's novel constraint on Congress' commerce power gains no force from our precedent and for that reason alone warrants disapprobation. But even assuming, for the moment, that Congress lacks authority under the Commerce Clause to "compel individuals not engaged in commerce to purchase an unwanted product," such a limitation would be inapplicable here. Everyone will, at some point, consume health-care products and services. Thus, if THE CHIEF JUSTICE is correct that an insurance-purchase requirement can be applied only to those who "actively" consume health care, the minimum coverage provision fits the bill.

THE CHIEF JUSTICE does not dispute that all U.S. residents participate in the market for health services over the course of their lives. But, THE CHIEF JUSTICE insists, the uninsured cannot be considered active in the market for health care, because "[t]he proximity and degree of connection between the [uninsured today] and [their] subsequent commercial activity is too lacking."

This argument has multiple flaws. First, more than 60% of those without insurance visit a hospital or doctor's office each year. Nearly 90% will within five years. An uninsured's consumption of health care is thus quite proximate: It is virtually certain to occur in the next five years and more likely than not to occur this year. . . .

Second, it is Congress' role, not the Court's, to delineate the boundaries of the market the Legislature seeks to regulate. . . . Congress could reasonably have viewed the market from a long-term perspective, encompassing all transactions virtually certain to occur over the next decade, not just those occurring here and now.

Third, contrary to THE CHIEF JUSTICE's contention, our precedent does indeed support "[t]he proposition that Congress may dictate the conduct of an individual today because of prophesied future activity." . . . Our decisions . . . acknowledge Congress' authority, under the Commerce Clause, to direct the conduct of an individual today (the farmer in *Wickard,* stopped from growing excess wheat; the plaintiff in *Raich,* ordered to cease cultivating marijuana) because of a prophesied future transaction (the eventual sale of that wheat or marijuana in the interstate market). Congress' actions are even more rational in this case, where the future activity (the consumption of medical care) is certain to occur, the sole uncertainty being the time the activity will take place.

Maintaining that the uninsured are not active in the health-care market, THE CHIEF JUSTICE draws an analogy to the car market. An individual "is not 'active in the car market,'" THE CHIEF JUSTICE observes, simply because he or she may someday buy a car. The analogy is inapt. The inevitable yet unpredictable need for medical care and the guarantee that emergency care will be provided when required are conditions nonexistent in other markets. That is so of the market for cars, and of the market for broccoli as well. Although an individual *might* buy a car or a crown of broccoli one day, there is no certainty she will ever do so. And if she eventually wants a car or has a craving for broccoli, she will be obliged to pay at the counter before receiving the vehicle or nourishment. She will get no free ride or food, at the expense of another consumer forced to pay an inflated price. Upholding the minimum coverage provision on the ground that all are participants or will be participants in the health-care market would therefore carry no implication that Congress may justify under the Commerce Clause a mandate to buy other products and services. . . .

THE CHIEF JUSTICE asserts, "[t]he language of the Constitution reflects the natural understanding that the power to regulate assumes there is already something to be regulated." This argument is difficult to fathom. Requiring individuals to obtain insurance unquestionably regulates the interstate health-insurance and health-care markets, both of them in existence well before the enactment of the ACA. See *Wickard,* at 128 ("The stimulation of commerce is a use of the regulatory function quite as definitely as prohibitions or restrictions thereon."). Thus, the "something to be regulated" was surely there when Congress created the minimum coverage provision. . . .

In concluding that the Commerce Clause does not permit Congress to regulate commercial "inactivity," and therefore does not allow Congress to adopt the practical solution it devised for the health-care problem, THE CHIEF JUSTICE views the Clause as a "technical legal conception," precisely what our case law tells us not to do. This Court's former endeavors to impose categorical limits on the commerce power have not fared well. . . .

These line-drawing exercises were untenable, and the Court long ago abandoned them. "[Q]uestions of the power of Congress [under the Commerce Clause]," we held in *Wickard*, "are not to be decided by reference to any formula which would give controlling force to nomenclature such as 'production' and 'indirect' and foreclose consideration of the actual effects of the activity in question upon interstate commerce." Failing to learn from this history, THE CHIEF JUSTICE plows ahead with his formalistic distinction between those who are "active in commerce," and those who are not. . . .

Underlying THE CHIEF JUSTICE's view that the Commerce Clause must be confined to the regulation of active participants in a commercial market is a fear that the commerce power would otherwise know no limits. The joint dissenters express a similar apprehension. This concern is unfounded.

First, THE CHIEF JUSTICE could certainly uphold the individual mandate without giving Congress *carte blanche* to enact any and all purchase mandates. As several times noted, the unique attributes of the health-care market render everyone active in that market and give rise to a significant free-riding problem that does not occur in other markets.

Nor would the commerce power be unbridled, absent The Chief Justice's "activity" limitation. Congress would remain unable to regulate noneconomic conduct that has only an attenuated effect on interstate commerce and is traditionally left to state law. See *Lopez*, at 567. . . .

As an example of the type of regulation he fears, THE CHIEF JUSTICE cites a Government mandate to purchase green vegetables. One could call this concern "the broccoli horrible." Congress, The Chief Justice posits, might adopt such a mandate, reasoning that an individual's failure to eat a healthy diet, like the failure to purchase health insurance, imposes costs on others.

Consider the chain of inferences the Court would have to accept to conclude that a vegetable-purchase mandate was likely to have a substantial effect on the health-care costs borne by lithe Americans. The Court would have to believe that individuals forced to buy vegetables would then eat them (instead of throwing or giving them away), would prepare the vegetables in a healthy way (steamed or raw, not deep-fried), would cut back on unhealthy foods, and would not allow other factors (such as lack of exercise or little sleep) to trump the improved diet. Such "pil[ing of] inference upon inference" is just what the Court refused to do in *Lopez* and *Morrison*.

Other provisions of the Constitution also check congressional overreaching. A mandate to purchase a particular product would be unconstitutional if, for example, the edict impermissibly abridged the freedom of speech, interfered with the free exercise of religion, or infringed on a liberty interest protected by the Due Process Clause.

Supplementing these legal restraints is a formidable check on congressional power: the democratic process. As the controversy surrounding the passage of the Affordable Care Act attests, purchase mandates are likely to engender political resistance. This prospect is borne out by the behavior of state legislators. Despite their possession of unquestioned authority to impose mandates, state governments have rarely done so.

When contemplated in its extreme, almost any power looks dangerous. The commerce power, hypothetically, would enable Congress to prohibit the purchase and home production of all meat, fish, and dairy goods, effectively compelling Americans to eat only vegetables. Yet no one would offer the "hypothetical and unreal possibilit[y]," *Pullman Co. v. Knott,* 235 U.S. 23, 26 (1914), of a vegetarian state as a credible reason to deny Congress the authority ever to ban the possession and sale of goods. THE CHIEF JUSTICE accepts just such specious logic when he cites the broccoli horrible as a reason to deny Congress the power to pass the individual mandate. Cf. R. Bork, The Tempting of America 169 (1990) ("Judges and lawyers live on the slippery slope of analogies; they are not supposed to ski it to the bottom."). . . .

III

. . . The Necessary and Proper Clause "empowers Congress to enact laws in effectuation of its [commerce] powe[r] that are not within its authority to enact in isolation." *Raich,* at 39 (SCALIA, J., concurring in judgment). Hence, "[a] complex regulatory program . . . can survive a Commerce Clause challenge without a showing that every single facet of the program is independently and directly related to a valid congressional goal." *Hodel v. Indiana,* 452 U.S. 314, 329, n. 17 (1981). . . .

Recall that one of Congress' goals in enacting the Affordable Care Act was to eliminate the insurance industry's practice of charging higher prices or denying coverage to individuals with preexisting medical conditions. The commerce power allows Congress to ban this practice, a point no one disputes.

Congress knew, however, that simply barring insurance companies from relying on an applicant's medical history would not work in practice. Without the individual mandate, Congress learned, guaranteed-issue and community-rating requirements would trigger an adverse-selection death-spiral in the health-insurance market: Insurance premiums would skyrocket, the number of uninsured would increase, and insurance companies would exit the market. When complemented by an insurance mandate, on the other hand, guaranteed issue and community rating would work as intended, increasing access to insurance and reducing uncompensated care. The minimum coverage provision is thus an "essential par[t] of a larger regulation of economic activity"; without the provision, "the regulatory scheme [w]ould be undercut." *Raich,* at 24–25. Put differently, the minimum coverage provision, together with the guaranteed-issue and community-rating requirements, is "reasonably adapted to the attainment of a legitimate end under the commerce power": the elimination of pricing and sales practices that take an applicant's medical history into account. See *id.,* at 37 (SCALIA, J., concurring in judgment).

Asserting that the Necessary and Proper Clause does not authorize the minimum coverage provision, THE CHIEF JUSTICE focuses on the word "proper." A mandate to purchase health insurance is not "proper" legislation, THE CHIEF JUSTICE urges, because the command "undermine[s] the structure of government established by the Constitution." If long on rhetoric, THE CHIEF JUSTICE's argument is short on substance.

THE CHIEF JUSTICE cites only two cases in which this Court concluded that a federal statute impermissibly transgressed the Constitution's boundary between state and federal authority: *Printz v. United States* and *New York v. United States.* The statutes at issue in both cases, however, compelled *state officials* to act on the Federal Government's behalf. . . .

The minimum coverage provision, in contrast, acts "directly upon individuals, without employing the States as intermediaries." *New York,* at 164. The provision is thus entirely consistent with the Constitution's design. See *Printz*, at 920 ("[T]he Framers explicitly chose a Constitution that confers upon Congress the power to regulate individuals, not States."). . . .

Nor does THE CHIEF JUSTICE pause to explain *why* the power to direct either the purchase of health insurance or, alternatively, the payment of a penalty collectible as a tax is more far-reaching than other implied powers this Court has found meet under the Necessary and Proper Clause. These powers include the power to enact criminal laws; the power to imprison, including civil imprisonment; and the power to create a national bank.

In failing to explain why the individual mandate threatens our constitutional order, THE CHIEF JUSTICE disserves future courts. How is a judge to decide, when ruling on the constitutionality of a federal statute, whether Congress employed an "independent power," or merely a "derivative" one. Whether the power used is "substantive," or just "incidental"? The instruction THE CHIEF JUSTICE, in effect, provides lower courts: You will know it when you see it. . . .

[Next Justice Ginsburg noted that she agreed with the holding on the Taxing Power, and therefore considered Chief Justice Roberts's discussion of the Commerce Clause unnecessary.—Editors]

V

. . . THE CHIEF JUSTICE acknowledges that Congress may "condition the receipt of [federal] funds on the States' complying with restrictions on the use of those funds," but nevertheless concludes that the 2010 expansion is unduly coercive. His conclusion rests on three premises, each of them essential to his theory. First, the Medicaid expansion is, in THE CHIEF JUSTICE's view, a new grant program, not an addition to the Medicaid program existing before the ACA's enactment. Congress, THE CHIEF JUSTICE maintains, has threatened States with the loss of funds from an old program in an effort to get them to adopt a new one. Second, the expansion was unforeseeable by the States when they first signed on to Medicaid. Third, the threatened loss of funding is so large that the States have no real choice but to participate in the Medicaid expansion. THE CHIEF JUSTICE therefore—for the first time ever—finds an exercise of Congress' spending power unconstitutionally coercive.

Medicaid, as amended by the ACA, however, is not two spending programs; it is a single program with a constant aim—to enable poor persons to receive basic health care when they need it. Given past expansions, plus express statutory warning that Congress may change the requirements participating States must meet, there can be no tenable claim that the ACA fails for lack of notice. Moreover, States have no entitlement to receive any Medicaid funds; they enjoy only the opportunity to accept funds on Congress' terms. Future Congresses are not bound by their predecessors' dispositions; they have authority to spend federal revenue as they see fit. The Federal Government, therefore, is not, as THE CHIEF JUSTICE charges, threatening States with the loss of "existing" funds from one spending program in order to induce them to opt into another program. Congress is simply requiring States to do what States have long been required to do to receive Medicaid funding: comply with the conditions Congress prescribes for participation. . . .

Congress' authority to condition the use of federal funds is not confined to spending programs as first launched. The legislature may, and often does, amend the law, imposing new conditions grant recipients henceforth must meet in order to continue receiving funds. Yes, there are federalism-based limits on the use of Congress' conditional spending power. In the leading decision in this area, *South Dakota v. Dole*, the Court identified four criteria. The conditions placed on federal grants to States must (a) promote the "general welfare," (b) "unambiguously" inform States what is demanded of them, (c) be germane "to the federal interest in particular national projects or programs," and (d) not "induce the States to engage in activities that would themselves be unconstitutional."

The Court in *Dole* mentioned, but did not adopt, a further limitation, one hypothetically raised a half-century earlier: In "some circumstances," Congress might be prohibited from offering a "financial inducement . . . so coercive as to pass the point at which 'pressure turns into compulsion.' " *Id.,* at 211 (quoting *Steward Machine*, at 590). Prior to today's decision, however, the Court has never ruled that the terms of any grant crossed the indistinct line between temptation and coercion. . . .

This case does not present the concerns that led the Court in *Dole* even to consider the prospect of coercion. In *Dole,* the condition—set 21 as the minimum drinking age—did not tell the States how to use funds Congress provided for highway construction. Further, in view of the Twenty-First Amendment, it was an open question whether Congress could directly impose a national minimum drinking age.

The ACA, in contrast, relates solely to the federally funded Medicaid program; if States choose not to comply, Congress has not threatened to withhold funds earmarked for any other program. Nor does the ACA use Medicaid funding to induce States to take action Congress itself could not undertake. The Federal Government undoubtedly could operate its own health-care program for poor persons, just as it operates Medicare for seniors' health care.

That is what makes this such a simple case, and the Court's decision so unsettling. . . .

■ JUSTICE SCALIA, JUSTICE KENNEDY, JUSTICE THOMAS, and JUSTICE ALITO, dissenting.

. . . This case is in one respect difficult: it presents two questions of first impression. The first of those is whether failure to engage in economic activity (the purchase of health insurance) is subject to regulation under the Commerce Clause. Failure to act does result in an effect on commerce, and hence might be said to come under this Court's "affecting commerce" criterion of Commerce Clause jurisprudence. But in none of its decisions has this Court extended the Clause that far. The second question is whether the congressional power to tax and spend, U.S. Const., Art. I, § 8, cl. 1, permits the conditioning of a State's continued receipt of all funds under a massive state-administered federal welfare program upon its acceptance of an expansion to that program. Several of our opinions have suggested that the power to tax and spend cannot be used to coerce state administration of a federal program, but we have never found a law enacted under the spending power to be coercive. Those questions are difficult.

The case is easy and straightforward, however, in another respect. What is absolutely clear, affirmed by the text of the 1789 Constitution, by the Tenth Amendment ratified in 1791, and by innumerable cases of ours in the 220 years since, is that there are structural limits upon federal power—upon what it can prescribe with respect to private conduct, and upon what it can impose upon the sovereign States. Whatever may be the conceptual limits upon the Commerce Clause and upon the power to tax and spend, they cannot be such as will enable the Federal Government to regulate all private conduct and to compel the States to function as administrators of federal programs.

That clear principle carries the day here. The striking case of Wickard v. Filburn, which held that the economic activity of growing wheat, even for one's own consumption, affected commerce sufficiently that it could be regulated, always has been regarded as the *ne plus ultra* of expansive Commerce Clause jurisprudence. To go beyond that, and to say the *failure* to grow wheat (which is *not* an economic activity, or any activity at all) nonetheless affects commerce and therefore can be federally regulated, is to make mere breathing in and out the basis for federal prescription and to extend federal power to virtually all human activity.

I

The Individual Mandate

[The joint dissenters agreed with Chief Justice Roberts that the individual mandate was not supported by the Commerce Clause and Necessary and Proper Clause.—Editors]

A few respectful responses to JUSTICE GINSBURG's dissent on the issue of the Mandate are in order. That dissent duly recites the test of Commerce Clause power that our opinions have applied, but disregards the premise the test contains. It is true enough that Congress needs only a "rational basis for concluding that the *regulated activity* substantially affects interstate commerce" (emphasis added). But it must be *activity* affecting commerce that is regulated, and not merely the failure to engage in commerce. And one is not now purchasing the health care covered by the insurance mandate simply because one is likely to be purchasing it in the future. Our test's premise of regulated activity is not invented out of whole cloth, but rests upon the Constitution's requirement that it be commerce which is regulated. If all inactivity affecting commerce is commerce, commerce is everything. Ultimately the dissent is driven to saying that there is really no difference between action and inaction, a proposition that has never recommended itself, neither to the law nor to common sense. To say, for example, that the inaction here consists of activity in "the self-insurance market," seems to us wordplay. By parity of reasoning the failure to buy a car can be called participation in the non-private-car-transportation market. Commerce becomes everything. . . .

The dissent's exposition of the wonderful things the Federal Government has achieved through exercise of its assigned powers, such as "the provision of old-age and survivors' benefits" in the Social Security Act, is quite beside the point. The issue here is whether the federal government can impose the Individual Mandate through the Commerce Clause. And the relevant history is not that Congress has achieved wide and wonderful results through the proper exercise of its assigned powers in the past, but that it has never before used the Commerce Clause to compel entry into commerce. The dissent treats the Constitution as though it is an enumeration of those problems that the Federal Government can address—among which, it finds, is "the Nation's course in the economic and social welfare realm," and more specifically "the problem of the uninsured." The Constitution is not that. It enumerates not federally soluble *problems,* but federally available *powers.* The Federal Government can address whatever problems it wants but can bring to their solution only those powers that the Constitution confers, among which is the power to regulate commerce. None of our cases say anything else. Article I contains no whatever-it-takes-to-solve-a-national-problem power. . . .

II

The Taxing Power

. . . The provision challenged under the Constitution is either a penalty or else a tax. Of course in many cases what was a regulatory mandate enforced by a penalty *could have been* imposed as a tax upon permissible action; or what was imposed as a tax upon permissible action *could have been* a regulatory mandate enforced by a penalty. But we know of no case, and the Government cites none, in which the imposition was, for constitutional purposes, both. . . . The issue is not whether Congress had the *power* to frame the minimum-coverage provision as a tax, but whether it *did* so. . . . In this case, there is simply no way, "without doing violence to the fair meaning of the words used," *Grenada County Supervisors v. Brogden*, 112 U.S. 261, 269 (1884), to escape what Congress enacted: a mandate that individuals maintain minimum essential coverage, enforced by a penalty.

Our cases establish a clear line between a tax and a penalty: "[A] tax is an enforced contribution to provide for the support of government; a penalty . . . is an exaction imposed by statute as punishment for an unlawful act." *Reorganized CF & I Fabricators of Utah,* at 224. In a few cases, this Court has held that a "tax" imposed upon private conduct was so onerous as to be in effect a penalty. But we have never held—*never*—that a penalty imposed for violation of the law was so trivial as to be in effect a tax. We have never held that *any* exaction imposed for violation of the law is an exercise of Congress' taxing power—even when the statute *calls* it a tax, much less when (as here) the statute repeatedly calls it a penalty. . . .

So the question is, quite simply, whether the exaction here is imposed for violation of the law. It unquestionably is. The minimum-coverage provision is found in 26 U.S.C. § 5000A, entitled *"Requirement* to maintain minimum essential coverage." (Emphasis added.) It commands that every "applicable individual *shall* . . . ensure that the individual . . . is covered under minimum essential coverage." *Ibid.* (emphasis added). And the immediately following provision states that, [i]f . . . an applicable individual . . . fails to meet the *requirement* of subsection (a) . . . there is hereby imposed . . . a *penalty*." § 5000A(b) (emphasis added). . . . Eighteen times in § 5000A itself and elsewhere throughout the Act, Congress called the exaction in § 5000A(b) a "penalty."

That § 5000A imposes not a simple tax but a mandate to which a penalty is attached is demonstrated by the fact that some are exempt from the tax who are not exempt from the mandate—a distinction that would make no sense if the mandate were not a mandate. . . .

And the nail in the coffin is that the mandate and penalty are located in Title I of the Act, its operative core, rather than where a tax would be found—in Title IX, containing the Act's "Revenue Provisions." . . . For all these reasons, to say that the Individual Mandate merely imposes a tax is not to interpret the statute but to rewrite it. . . .

Finally, we must observe that rewriting § 5000A as a tax in order to sustain its constitutionality would force us to confront a difficult constitutional question:

whether this is a direct tax that must be apportioned among the States according to their population. Art. I, § 9, cl. 4. Perhaps it is not (we have no need to address the point); but the meaning of the Direct Tax Clause is famously unclear, and its application here is a question of first impression that deserves more thoughtful consideration than the lick-and-a-promise accorded by the Government and its supporters. The Government's opening brief did not even address the question— perhaps because, until today, no federal court has accepted the implausible argument that § 5000A is an exercise of the tax power. And once respondents raised the issue, the Government devoted a mere 21 lines of its reply brief to the issue. At oral argument, the most prolonged statement about the issue was just over 50 words. One would expect this Court to demand more than fly-by-night briefing and argument before deciding a difficult constitutional question of first impression. . . .

[Next the joint dissenters agreed with Chief Justice Roberts that the Anti-Injunction Act did not apply. Then they agreed with Chief Justice Roberts that the Medicaid Expansion provisions of the ACA exceeded constitutional limitations on Congress's spending power, but not as to the appropriate remedy. They would have held both the individual mandate and the Medicaid Expansion unconstitutional, and would have held that those provisions were so central to the ACA that they required invalidation of the entire act. Most of the joint dissent's lengthy severability analysis is omitted.—Editors]

* * *

The Court today decides to save a statute Congress did not write. It rules that what the statute declares to be a requirement with a penalty is instead an option subject to a tax. And it changes the intentionally coercive sanction of a total cut-off of Medicaid funds to a supposedly noncoercive cut-off of only the incremental funds that the Act makes available.

The Court regards its strained statutory interpretation as judicial modesty. It is not. It amounts instead to a vast judicial overreaching. It creates a debilitated, inoperable version of health-care regulation that Congress did not enact and the public does not expect. It makes enactment of sensible health-care regulation more difficult, since Congress cannot start afresh but must take as its point of departure a jumble of now senseless provisions, provisions that certain interests favored under the Court's new design will struggle to retain. And it leaves the public and the States to expend vast sums of money on requirements that may or may not survive the necessary congressional revision. . . .

The values that should have determined our course today are caution, minimalism, and the understanding that the Federal Government is one of limited powers. But the Court's ruling undermines those values at every turn. In the name of restraint, it overreaches. In the name of constitutional avoidance, it creates new constitutional questions. In the name of cooperative federalism, it undermines state sovereignty.

The Constitution, though it dates from the founding of the Republic, has powerful meaning and vital relevance to our own times. The constitutional protections that this case involves are protections of structure. Structural protections—notably, the restraints imposed by federalism and separation of powers—are less romantic and have less obvious a connection to personal freedom than the provisions of the Bill of Rights or the Civil War Amendments. Hence they tend to be undervalued or even forgotten by our citizens. It should be the responsibility of the Court to teach otherwise, to remind our people that the Framers considered structural protections of freedom the most important ones, for which reason they alone were embodied in the original Constitution and not left to later amendment. The fragmentation of power produced by the structure of our Government is central to liberty, and when we destroy it, we place liberty at peril. Today's decision should have vindicated, should have taught, this truth; instead, our judgment today has disregarded it.

■ [The dissenting opinion of JUSTICE THOMAS is omitted.]

NOTES

1.   Start with the holdings and the alignment of the justices. Which parts of the Affordable Care Act were upheld and which parts were struck down?

Only one justice—Chief Justice Roberts—agreed with the entirety of the Court's reasoning and judgment. Was there in fact majority support for all of the constitutional conclusions set forth in Chief Justice Roberts's opinion? First, five justices concluded that the individual mandate was not within Congress's power under the Commerce Clause and Necessary and Proper Clause—Roberts and the four justices in the joint dissent. But why did the four dissenters not *join* those parts of Roberts's opinion? Was it because they disagreed with the ultimate disposition of the case? Or was it for some other reason? Second, was there majority support for that part of the opinion upholding the individual mandate provision on Taxing Clause grounds? Does that holding make the Commerce Clause part of Chief Justice Roberts's opinion—which *calls* itself a holding—actually dictum, because it was unnecessary to the judgment?

2.   As a matter of constitutional interpretation, what do you think of the part of Chief Justice Roberts's opinion holding that the individual mandate could be sustained, in the alternative, as an exercise of the Taxing Clause power, even if not the "most straightforward reading" of the provision? Was this a proper use of the constitutional avoidance doctrine—the idea that a Court should construe a statute, where possible, to conform to the Constitution? (It would not have been necessary to construe the mandate as a "tax" if the mandate were constitutional under the Commerce Clause and Necessary and Proper Clause.)

3.   Now consider the merits on the Commerce Clause, apart from the Necessary and Proper Clause. Which opinion is most persuasive? Which types of constitutional argument does each opinion employ? Is there any good answer to the Chief Justice's textual arguments that the power to "regulate" commerce presupposes existing commerce to regulate, and therefore does not contain a power to create or mandate commercial activity? Is there any good answer to the Chief Justice's argument that, if inactivity can be regulated because it affects commerce, *everything* can be regulated because it affects commerce? Is the Chief Justice persuasive in arguing that such a conclusion is inconsistent with the first principles of federalism? On the other hand, is there any good answer to Justice Ginsburg's argument that everyone is eventually a consumer of healthcare services, and that the individual mandate merely regulates the system of payment for these services? Is there any good answer to her argument that there is no coherent difference between regulating "activity" and "inactivity," provided that both have substantial market consequences?

Evaluate the effect of *NFIB v. Sebelius* on Commerce Clause jurisprudence: Is the rejection of the Commerce Clause rationale something hugely important and entirely new? Is it a departure from prior cases? Is it a new limitation on the scope of the Commerce Clause, but one not foreclosed by prior cases? Or is it simply an application (or extension) of principles set forth in earlier cases?

4.   Even if the individual mandate cannot be justified solely as a regulation of "commerce," might it be justified as "necessary and proper" to a regulation of commerce? The government argued that the mandate was necessary to enable the enforcement of the "guaranteed issue" and "community rating" rules, which are undoubtedly regulations of commerce. Make sure you understand the logic of that argument. What is Chief Justice Roberts's answer to it? Who has the better of the argument on this point? Is Chief Justice Roberts's line of distinction between permissible and impermissible applications of the Necessary and Proper Clause persuasive? Is it clear? Is it consistent with *McCulloch?* Or does it, as Justice Ginsburg suggests, depart from precedents interpreting the Necessary and Proper Clause broadly? If it is such a departure, is it a justified one?

a.   The Roberts opinion twice quotes *McCulloch* to the effect that the Necessary and Proper Clause does not "license the exercise of any 'great substantive and independent power[s]' beyond those specifically enumerated." The idea was that relatively minor powers could be implied as incidental to the enumerated powers, but that "great substantive and independent powers" must be granted explicitly. On the idea of incidental powers, see p. 471. On this way of interpreting the clause, see William Baude, *Rethinking the Federal Eminent Domain Power*, 122 Yale L.J. 1738, 1749–1761 (2013); *but cf.* John Harrison, *Enumerated Federal Power and the Necessary and Proper Clause*, 78 U. Chi. L. Rev. 1101, 1125–1126 (2011) ("That reasoning is fine in form . . . but filling in the substance is famously difficult."). In effect, the majority holds that the power to mandate individual action is too important and independent a power to be merely incidental. The centuries-old interpretive dilemma presented by the Necessary and Proper Clause is that the clause can be construed either to permit almost anything or else to add almost nothing to other congressional powers, but it does not seem to easily fit any in-between position. Does the "great substantive and independent powers doctrine" offer a solution, a plausible middle ground? But does it explain why the framers thought it essential to spell out such powers as taxing and spending, regulating commerce, fixing the standards of weights and measures, and establishing post roads, but not such powers as passing and enforcing criminal laws, conscripting troops, condemning land through eminent domain, making notes legal tender for private debts, or expelling aliens? Are these latter powers, which Congress has long exercised with little controversy, any less great, substantive, and independent than the power to impose an individual mandate? What about the power to compel states to pass laws or to enforce federal laws?

b.   What do you make of Chief Justice Roberts's characterization of the individual mandate as not an "essential component of the insurance reforms"? Is that factually accurate? Is that a determination reserved for Congress?

c.   What do you make of Chief Justice Roberts's emphasis on the word "proper" as embracing federalism concerns about the limited power of the national government? How does one answer the objection that, if the Necessary and Proper Clause, when allied with the Commerce Clause, permits Congress to regulate inactivity as well as activity, it is a license for the national government to regulate all activity—and that this is inconsistent with the Constitution's basic design? Does the word "proper" provide a standard for invalidating acts that would otherwise be "necessary" to carry out an enumerated power?

d.   Chief Justice Roberts observes that upholding the mandate would "vest[ ] Congress with the extraordinary ability to create the necessary predicate to the exercise of an enumerated power." Does this mean that Congress can never invoke the Necessary and Proper Clause when the necessity for a particular measure was created by Congress's own predicate acts? Are *NFIB* and *Comstock* in tension with each other on this point, or are there valid points of distinction? If inconsistent, which one states the correct principle? Is *NFIB* consistent with Justice Scalia's separate opinion in *Raich*? Is *NFIB* a landmark limitation on the scope of the Necessary and Proper Clause power?

5.   Now consider the taxing power.

a.   Who needs the Commerce Clause? If the national government can accomplish its objectives simply by imposing a tax—which it can even call a "penalty"—on the activity (or inactivity) it wishes to eliminate (or reduce), what does the Commerce Clause add? How does Chief Justice Roberts's majority opinion upholding the individual mandate on taxing power grounds respond to this objection?

What distinctions does the Court identify that make the taxing power a *different* power from the Commerce Clause power? What *limitations* does the Court identify on the taxing power? Is such a broad understanding of the taxing power any less objectionable on federalism grounds? Or is the answer to the "federalism" objection that the taxing power sometimes permits an exercise of national authority through incentives and penalties that the commerce power does not permit through direct regulation, and that this is simply part of American federalism?

Is this view troubling? Is it the Taxing Clause power, not the Commerce Clause power, that is really the ultimate national power? Is the Taxing Clause power a Trojan horse for federalism? Would Chief Justice Roberts's opinion allow a tax on people who fail to donate a kidney, or refuse to eat broccoli, or refrain from having children? Would it matter for these questions if the tax were small rather than being financially ruinous? The Court likes to say the power to tax is not the power to destroy—"while this Court sits"—but how can it be otherwise?

b.   Are you persuaded by Chief Justice Roberts's distinction between a tax and a penalty? Is the basketball rule giving the other team free throws when there has been a foul a penalty or a tax? If you were a high school basketball coach wanting to use the game to teach your players lessons about personal integrity, would you tell them it is against the rules to foul players of the other team, or would you tell them to calculate whether the benefits of committing the foul are worth the "tax" of the free throws? Is that a good analogy for the individual mandate?

c.   The joint dissenters do not argue that Congress *could not* have enacted the individual mandate as an exercise of the taxing power, but only that Congress *did not* do so. Should this matter? Is there a persuasive answer to Chief Justice Roberts's argument that, if the enactment was validly within Congress's constitutional taxing power, then it should not matter—other than perhaps for political purposes—what Congress called the provision? On the other hand, should Congress be held to its choice of characterizing the individual mandate as a "penalty" for the purpose of determining whether the mandate falls within the power to lay and collect taxes? What do you think of the dissent's argument that the majority had to twist—"rewrite"—the individual mandate provision in order to uphold it, and that this was illegitimate? What do you think of Chief Justice Roberts's argument that the Court has an obligation to construe a statute, if fairly possible, in such a manner as to sustain its constitutionality? Who has the better of the argument here?

d.   The dissent questions Chief Justice Roberts's conclusion that the mandate is an indirect tax. As noted earlier, see p. 597, indirect taxes, like import taxes and sales taxes, need only be set at a uniform level in each of the states, but direct taxes, like a capitation tax or a land tax, must be apportioned according to population. U.S. Const.,

Art. I, § 9, cl. 4. Does the dissent assert that the tax (if a tax) would be a direct tax, or does the dissent simply raise the question?

Chief Justice Roberts's opinion appears to limit the category of direct taxes to capitation taxes and property taxes and thus holds that the insurance penalty is not a direct tax. Is that a sound interpretation of the constitution? Recall the discussions of direct taxes in *Hylton*, p. 598, and *Pollock*, p. 602. The mandate is not a tax on a transaction, like a sales or excise tax, nor does it fall on a third party. The healthcare mandate falls directly on any person who does not have health insurance unless the person's income is below a certain level. Is it essentially a head tax on anyone who does not have health insurance? Can it fairly be characterized as an *income* tax, since it is imposed via the income tax system and because those below a certain income level are exempt? If so, is the tax—even if otherwise characterized as "direct"—authorized by the Sixteenth Amendment?

e. In a portion of the opinion not presented here, the Court held that the individual mandate was not a tax for purposes of applying the tax Anti-Injunction Act, a statutory provision forbidding taxpayers from bringing suits for injunctive relief from the collection of taxes. (In effect, the Anti-Injunction Act requires taxpayers to pay a disputed tax and then sue for a refund.) The Court held that Congress can designate something as not a tax for purposes of applying the Anti-Injunction Act but that this characterization does not foreclose the exaction being a "tax" within the meaning of the scope of Congress's constitutional powers to enact. Is that a contradiction? Or does it mean that Congress is the master of its own statutes, and can repeal, modify, or limit one statute by enacting another one, but that Congress cannot alter the scope of its own constitutional powers by virtue of the labels it uses?

6. Now for the spending power. A 7–2 majority found that the Medicaid Expansion provisions of the Affordable Care Act exceeded Congress's power to attach conditions to the receipt of federal funds by the states, because the states were essentially coerced to accept the funds and the conditions attached to them. Is the Court's reasoning persuasive? The majority opinion characterized the conditions imposed by the statute as "a gun to the head." What did the Court identify as the essential features of the act's new conditions that make them coercive? Is it the size of the program as a percentage of states' budgets? Is it the fact that the condition involved forfeiture of funds under the existing Medicaid program, if a state did not accept funds for the expanded Medicaid program? Is it a combination of the two? Where is the line? Can you apply the logic of Justice O'Connor's *South Carolina v. Dole* dissent to that question? Is the expansion of Medicaid to a larger cohort of people "germane" to the original Medicaid program?

The Supreme Court held that the remedy for the condition ruled unconstitutional was elimination of the power to impose the condition on the states, not the invalidation of the Medicaid expansion itself. The joint dissenters disagreed, calling this, too, a rewriting of the statute and an improper exercise of judicial power. Who is right? Why?

Is the Court's spending power holding dictated by concerns of federalism—that is, is it specific to the situation of federal spending grants made to states? Or is it a general limitation on the national government's power to spend, such that private recipients of federal government grants and expenditures could argue, based on *NFIB v. Sebelius*, that a particular grant condition was a "gun to the head" to coerce behavior the national government could not command?

[*Assignment 33*]

F. OTHER NATIONAL POWERS?

The powers enumerated in Article I were long thought to be the outer limit of federal authority. But by the second half of the nineteenth century, the United States was becoming an economic and military power. With this newfound status there came an ascendant argument—that the United States, by virtue of being a nation, must have certain inherent powers not specified in the Constitution. These powers were controversial, however, and they raise major questions of constitutional interpretation. What follows are materials on two of the most important of these powers: the power to make paper money legal tender for private debts and the power to expel aliens.

As you read these cases, consider several questions: Can the claimed power be justified under Article I, Section 8? If so, that would make unnecessary an appeal to inherent powers. If not, then the question of inherent powers must be squarely faced. If there are no inherent powers, would the government be too feeble to act in a crisis? But if there are inherent powers, how can they possibly be squared with the principle of enumerated and limited federal powers from Article I, Section 8? And who decides what the inherent powers are?

Legal Tender

> *Art. I, § 8: The Congress shall have Power . . .*
>
> *To borrow Money on the credit of the United States; . . .*
>
> *To Coin Money, regulate the Value thereof, and of foreign Coin, and fix the Standard of Weights and Measures; . . .*
>
> *§ 10: No State shall . . . coin Money; emit Bills of Credit; make any Thing but gold and silver Coin a Tender in Payment of Debts; . . . .*

At the Founding, Americans were more consumed than we are today with questions about money—the question of what counts as money and the question of who gets to decide. Indeed, the Boston Tea Party was about money: not only did the English government want to collect a customs tax on tea, but also it insisted that the tax be paid in silver, a scarce commodity in the colonies. What vexed the colonists was not just the tax but also Parliament's dictating its monetary form. Then, during the American War of Independence, the states and the Congress under the Articles of Confederation printed vast quantities of paper money. What followed was predictable but tragic: severe inflation and for many people financial ruin. That experience made some of the founders deeply suspicious of populist control over the definition of money. In establishing a new national government for the United States, many of the founders wanted a constrained freedom—a measure of government control over what counted as money, in order to ease commerce and taxpaying, while avoiding the danger that the national or state governments would try to escape their economic problems through reckless monetary choices. That danger was expressed this way by Alexander Hamilton in his Report on Public Credit to the House of Representatives: "The stamping of paper is an operation so much easier than the laying of taxes, that a government in the practice of paper emissions would rarely fail, in any such emergency, to indulge itself too far in the employment of that resource, to avoid, as much as possible, one less auspicious to present popularity." 3 THE WORKS OF ALEXANDER HAMILTON 124 (John C. Hamilton ed., 1850). In short, the Founders were trying to navigate around the shoals of too little and too much government control over the definition and supply of money.

The founding generation was familiar with three kinds of money, in the sense of something that circulates throughout the economy and is exchanged for goods and services. (To be precise, "money" must have two other attributes as well: it must be a measure for the worth of other things, and a means of storing value.)

First, there were *coins*. These were made of precious metals, such as gold, silver, and copper. The value of these coins was determined by the value of the metal, with a proxy for that value being the authority of the government that minted the coin. What made a shilling valuable was the silver in the coin, as attested by the English government.

Second, there were *notes*. These were made of paper and had a value printed on them, and crucially, they were interest-bearing. The longer the note was kept, the more interest it would accumulate. (We now call these "bonds.") They might be issued by governments, but also by private banks. Notes were a way for a government to borrow money. For example, a government might offer ten-pound notes at a certain interest rate, and anyone could give the government ten pounds and receive in return a note that promised the repayment of the ten pounds with interest. And the person who received the note could then use it as money to buy goods or services from someone else.

Third, there were *bills of credit*. Like a note, a bill of credit was a piece of paper with a value printed on it (e.g., "ten pounds"). But it was not interest-bearing. All that made a bill of credit valuable was that it could be redeemed for coins or used for paying taxes; it was like an IOU from the government. But what if the government emitted a huge quantity of bills of credit, far more than it could redeem in gold or silver and far more than it could accept as payment for taxes? That question was not hypothetical—it was exactly what the newly independent states and the Congress had done during the American War of Independence, bringing ruin on the economy.

One more distinction is critical. Each of these forms of money—coins, notes, and bills of credit—could circulate throughout the economy and be used in commerce. But there was a further step a government might wish to take, which was declaring that one or more of these kinds of currency was "legal tender"—that it had to be accepted for debts, both public and private. (If you look closely at a printed U.S. dollar, you will see that it is declared to be "Legal Tender for All Debts, Public and Private.") Imagine somebody owed you money, and you expected to be paid in gold or silver. It would be one thing for a government to emit bills of credit that you could agree to treat as money if you wanted to, but quite another thing for the government to say that you now had to accept the government's bills instead of the gold or silver you expected, especially if the government's bills were rapidly devalued due to inflationary printing.

With this background in mind, consider the allocation of monetary powers between the national and state governments. We can start with the easier questions.

Can Congress coin money? (Look at Article I, Section 8.)

Can the states coin money? (Look at Article I, Section 10.)

Can the states emit bills of credit? (Article I, Section 10.)

Can the states make some things legal tender for the payment of debts? What things? (Article I, Section 10.)

Can Congress borrow money? (Article I, Section 8.)

If Congress can borrow money, can it issue notes as a means of borrowing money? (Which clause might affirm that power?)

Now consider two harder questions. First, if Congress coins money, can it declare those coins to be legal tender for public and private debts? The Constitution never expressly says Congress can make its coins legal tender, but that power seems to have been understood and uncontroversial; perhaps it was implicit in coining *money*. Second, can the states borrow money? Again the Constitution is silent on this point. For state powers, which way should this silence be understood? (Remember the Tenth Amendment.)

Here is the scorecard so far:

Coining money: states no, federal yes

Borrowing money (including notes): states yes, federal yes

Emitting bills of credit: states no, federal?

Making gold and silver legal tender: states yes, federal yes

Making other coins legal tender: states no, federal yes

Making anything else legal tender: states no, federal?

That leaves the hardest questions for last. Can Congress emit bills of credit, and if so, can it make those bills legal tender?

Under the Articles of Confederation the first question at least was easy. Congress had the power to coin money and "to borrow money, or emit bills on the credit of the United States," though these powers could only be exercised with the agreement of nine of the thirteen state delegations. These same powers were proposed for the new national government in an early draft of the U.S. Constitution. But there was a spirited debate at the Constitutional Convention about the words "or emit bills."

One delegate said these three words were "as alarming as the mark of the beast in Revelation," and another announced that if these words were retained he would vote against the Constitution. James Wilson also objected, but in more measured tones: "It will have a most saluatary influence on the credit of the United States, to remove the possibility of paper money. This expedient can never succeed whilst its mischiefs are remembered; and as long as it can be resorted to, it will be a bar to other resources." 5 DEBATES ON THE ADOPTION OF THE FEDERAL CONSTITUTION 435 (Jonathan Elliot ed., 1845) (Aug. 18, 1787). Others argued for this national power, and Madison took the position that Congress should have the power to emit bills of credit so long as it did not make them legal tender. There was even debate about what would be the implication if the Convention removed "or emit bills." Most thought the effect would be a prohibition on Congress emitting bills of credit. (Why might that be?) But Nathaniel Gorham, of Massachusetts, argued that removing "or emit bills" would not prohibit them, because the power of emitting bills of credit was "involved in that of borrowing." In the end, by a vote of nine state delegations to two, the Convention struck out the words "or emit bills." In his notes, Madison remarked that he was "satisfied that the striking out of the words would not disable the government from the use of public notes so far as they could be safe and proper; and would only cut off the pretext for a paper currency, and particularly for making the bills a tender, either for public or private debts." *Id.* at n. *.

No bills of credit were issued by the national government until the War of 1812. The charter of the first Bank of the United States had elapsed, the second Bank had not yet been chartered, and the government's finances were dire. (On the Bank of the United States, see p. 470.) To raise money, in 1812 Congress authorized the Treasury to issue interest-bearing notes that had two features that made them function like paper money. First, they could be used to pay federal duties and taxes. (In other words, they were legal tender for public debts but not private debts.) Second, they could be transferred from one person to another as long as they were endorsed, i.e., signed by the previous holder. In 1815, Congress authorized the Treasury to go further, issuing notes that were in effect bills of credit. They were not redeemable for gold or silver. And the notes in denominations less than $100 were not interest-bearing, and to make it easier for them to circulate throughout the economy they did not need to be endorsed when transferred. After the war ended, these "notes" were retired and Congress repealed the authorization to issue them. At moments of financial crisis in the 1830s, 1840s, and 1850s, the national government would again rely on bills of credit, but they were never made legal tender for private debts.

Then came the Civil War. By 1862 the Union was desperate for money and victory was elusive. In this great crisis, Congress passed the Legal Tender Act of 1862. The statute authorized the issuance of paper dollars, called "greenbacks." These were bills of credit that could not be redeemed for gold, though there was a promise that Congress would one day allow the holder of the paper dollar to redeem it for a gold dollar. Critically, the statute made the new paper money "a legal tender in payment of all debts, public and private."

After the war ended, the Supreme Court considered a challenge to the Legal Tender Act in *Hepburn v. Griswold*, 75 U.S. (8 Wall.) 603 (1870). A Mrs. Hepburn had incurred a debt to Mr. Griswold, in 1860, of $11,250. But then, after the Legal Tender Act became law, she tried to pay that debt with the new paper dollars—which were worth much less than the gold or silver coins that were used when she incurred the debt. In fact, two years after the Legal Tender Act, the value of a paper dollar had fallen to about one-third of a gold or silver dollar (though its value subsequently rose to about five-sixths of a gold or silver dollar). By a 4–3 vote, the Court held that Congress had no constitutional power to declare that its paper money was legal tender for debts already incurred. Echoing *McCulloch v. Maryland*, Chief Justice Salmon P. Chase wrote: "We are obliged to conclude that an act making mere promises to pay dollars a legal tender in payment of debts previously contracted, is not a means appropriate, plainly adapted, really calculated to carry into effect any express power vested in Congress; that such an act is inconsistent with the spirit of the Constitution; and that it is prohibited by the Constitution." *Id.* at 625. Strikingly, Chase himself had been secretary of the Treasury under President Lincoln, and in that role he had issued the first printed dollars. In fact, the first one-dollar bills printed in 1862 bore Secretary Chase's image. But now, with the crisis past and his service in a different branch of the national government, he thought the legal-tender provision unconstitutional.

Then President Grant appointed two new justices, Joseph Bradley and William Strong, bringing the Court back up to its full complement of nine members. They wasted no time. *Hepburn* was reversed in *Knox v. Lee*, 79 U.S. (12 Wall.) 457 (1870), by a vote of 5–4.

Knox v. Lee

79 U.S. (12 Wall.) 457 (1870)

■ MR. JUSTICE STRONG delivered the opinion of the court.

The controlling questions in these cases are the following: Are the acts of Congress, known as the legal tender acts, constitutional when applied to contracts made before their passage; and, secondly, are they valid as applicable to debts contracted since their enactment? ... It would be difficult to overestimate the consequences which must follow our decision. They will affect the entire business of the country, and take hold of the possible continued existence of the government. If it be held by this court that Congress has no constitutional power, under any circumstances, or in any emergency, to make treasury notes a legal tender for the payment of all debts (a power confessedly possessed by every independent sovereignty other than the United States), the government is without those means of self-preservation which, all must admit, may, in certain contingencies, become indispensable. . . . It is also clear that if we hold the acts invalid as applicable to debts incurred, or transactions which have taken place since their enactment, our decision must cause, throughout the country, great business derangement, widespread distress, and the rankest injustice. . . . Men have bought and sold, borrowed and lent, and assumed every variety of obligations contemplating that payment might be made with such notes. Indeed, legal tender treasury notes have become the universal measure of values. . . . [T]he fundamental question, that which tests of the validity of the legislation, is, can Congress constitutionally give to treasury notes the character and qualities of money? Can such notes be constituted a legitimate circulating medium, having a defined legal value? . . .

The consequences of which we have spoken, serious as they are, must be accepted, if there is a clear incompatibility between the Constitution and the legal tender acts. But we are unwilling to precipitate them upon the country unless such an incompatibility plainly appears. A decent respect for a co-ordinate branch of the government demands that the judiciary should presume, until the contrary is clearly shown, that there has been no transgression of power by Congress—all the members of which act under the obligation of an oath of fidelity to the Constitution. . . .

Nor can it be questioned that, when investigating the nature and extent of the powers conferred by the Constitution upon Congress, it is indispensable to keep in view the objects for which those powers were granted. This is a universal rule of construction applied alike to statutes, wills, contracts, and constitutions. . . . And there are more urgent reasons for looking to the ultimate purpose in examining the powers conferred by a constitution than there are in construing a statute, a will, or a contract. We do not expect to find in a constitution minute details. It is necessarily brief and comprehensive. . . . Thus the power to levy and collect taxes, to coin money and regulate its value, to raise and support armies, or to provide for and maintain a navy, are instruments for the paramount object, which was to establish a government, sovereign within its sphere, with capability of self-preservation, thereby forming a union more perfect than that which existed under the old Confederacy.

The same may be asserted also of all the non-enumerated powers included in the authority expressly given "to make all laws which shall be necessary and proper for carrying into execution the specified powers vested in Congress, and all other powers vested by the Constitution in the government of the United States, or in any department or officer thereof." It is impossible to know what those non-enumerated powers are, and what is their nature and extent, without considering the purposes they were intended to subserve. Those purposes, it must be noted, reach beyond the mere execution of all powers definitely intrusted to Congress and mentioned in detail. They embrace the execution of all other powers vested by the Constitution in the government of the United States, or in any department or officer thereof. It certainly was intended to confer upon the government the power of self-preservation. . . . That would appear, then, to be a most unreasonable construction of the Constitution which denies to the government created by it, the right to employ freely every means, not prohibited, necessary for its preservation, and for the fulfilment of its acknowledged duties. Such a right, we hold, was given by the last clause of the eighth section of its first article *[i.e., the Necessary and Proper Clause]*. The means or instrumentalities referred to in that clause, and authorized, are not enumerated or defined. In the nature of things enumeration and specification were impossible. But they were left to the discretion of Congress, subject only to the restrictions that they be not prohibited, and be necessary and proper for carrying into execution the enumerated powers given to Congress, and all other powers vested in the government of the United States, or in any department or officer thereof.

And here it is to be observed it is not indispensable to the existence of any power claimed for the Federal government that it can be found specified in the words of the Constitution, or clearly and directly traceable to some one of the specified powers. Its existence may be deduced fairly from more than one of the substantive powers expressly defined, or from them all combined. It is allowable to group together any number of them and infer from them all that the power claimed has been conferred. Such a treatment of the Constitution is recognized by its own provisions. This is well illustrated in its language respecting the writ of habeas corpus. The power to suspend the privilege of that writ is not expressly given, nor can it be deduced from any one of the particularized grants of power. Yet it is provided that the privileges of the writ shall not be suspended except in certain defined contingencies. This is no express grant of power. It is a restriction. But it shows irresistibly that somewhere in the Constitution power to suspend the privilege of the writ was granted, either by some one or more of the specifications of power, or by them all combined. And, that important powers were understood by the people who adopted the Constitution to have been created by it, powers not enumerated, and not included incidentally in any one of those enumerated, is shown by the amendments. The first ten of these . . . tend plainly to show that, in the judgment of those who adopted the Constitution, there were powers created by it, neither expressly specified nor deducible from any one specified power, or ancillary to it alone, but which grew out of the aggregate of powers conferred upon the government, or out of the sovereignty instituted. Most of these amendments are denials of power which had not been expressly granted, and which cannot be said to have been necessary and proper for carrying into execution any other powers. Such, for example, is the prohibition of any laws respecting the establishment of religion, prohibiting the free exercise thereof, or abridging the freedom of speech or of the press.

And it is of importance to observe that Congress has often exercised, without question, powers that are not expressly given nor ancillary to any single enumerated power. Powers thus exercised are what are called by Judge Story in his Commentaries on the Constitution, resulting powers, arising from the aggregate powers of the government. He instances the right to sue and make contracts. Many others might be given. The oath required by law from officers of the government is one. So is building a capitol or a presidential mansion, and so also is the penal code. This last is worthy of brief notice. Congress is expressly authorized "to provide for the punishment of counterfeiting the securities and current coin of the United States, and to define and punish piracies and felonies committed on the high seas and offences against the laws of nations." It is also empowered to declare the punishment of treason, and provision is made for impeachments. This is the extent of power to punish crime expressly conferred. It might be argued that the expression of these limited powers implies an exclusion of all other subjects of criminal legislation. Such is the argument in the present cases. It is said because Congress is authorized to coin money and regulate its value it cannot declare anything other than gold and silver to be money or make it a legal tender. Yet Congress, by the act of April 30, 1790, entitled "An act more effectually to provide for the punishment of certain crimes against the United States," and the supplementary act of March 3d, 1825, defined and provided for the punishment of a large class of crimes other than those mentioned in the Constitution, and some of the punishments prescribed are manifestly not in aid of any single substantive power. . . .

Indeed the whole history of the government and of congressional legislation has exhibited the use of a very wide discretion, even in times of peace and in the absence of any trying emergency, in the selection of the necessary and proper means to carry into effect the great objects for which the government was framed, and this discretion has generally been unquestioned, or, if questioned, sanctioned by this court. . . . Under the power to establish post-offices and post-roads Congress has provided for carrying the mails, punishing theft of letters and mail robberies, and even for transporting the mails to foreign countries. Under the power to regulate commerce, provision has been made by law for the improvement of harbors, the establishment of observatories, the erection of lighthouses, breakwaters, and buoys, the registry, enrolment, and construction of ships, and a code has been enacted for the government of seamen. Under the same power and other powers over the revenue and the currency of the country, for the convenience of the treasury and internal commerce, a corporation known as the United States Bank was early created. . . .

This is enough to show how, from the earliest period of our existence as a nation, the powers conferred by the Constitution have been construed by Congress and by this court whenever such action by Congress has been called in question. Happily the true meaning of the clause authorizing the enactment of all laws necessary and proper for carrying into execution the express powers conferred upon Congress, and all other powers vested in the government of the United States, or in any of its departments or officers, has long since been settled.

It was . . . in *McCulloch v. Maryland*, 17 U.S. (4 Wheat.) 316 (1819), that the fullest consideration was given to this clause of the Constitution granting auxiliary powers, and a construction adopted that has ever since been accepted as determining its true meaning. . . .

Before we can hold the legal tender acts unconstitutional, we must be convinced they were not appropriate means, or means conducive to the execution of any or all of the powers of Congress, or of the government, not appropriate in any degree (for we are not judges of the degree of appropriateness), or we must hold that they were prohibited. This brings us to the inquiry whether they were, when enacted, appropriate instrumentalities for carrying into effect, or executing any of the known powers of Congress, or of any department of the government. . . .

We do not propose to dilate at length upon the circumstances in which the country was placed, when Congress attempted to make treasury notes a legal tender. They are of too recent occurrence to justify enlarged description. Suffice it to say that a civil war was then raging which seriously threatened the overthrow of the government and the destruction of the Constitution itself. It demanded the equipment and support of large armies and navies, and the employment of money to an extent beyond the capacity of all ordinary sources of supply. Meanwhile the public treasury was nearly empty, and the credit of the government, if not stretched to its utmost tension, had become nearly exhausted. Moneyed institutions had advanced largely of their means, and more could not be expected of them. They had been compelled to suspend specie payments. Taxation was inadequate to pay even the interest on the debt already incurred, and it was impossible to await the income of additional taxes. The necessity was immediate and pressing. The army was unpaid. There was then due to the soldiers in the field nearly a score of millions of dollars. The requisitions from the War and Navy Departments for supplies exceeded fifty millions, and the current expenditure was over one million per day. The entire amount of coin in the country, including that in private hands, as well as that in banking institutions, was insufficient to supply the need of the government three months, had it all been poured into the treasury. Foreign credit we had none. We say nothing of the overhanging paralysis of trade, and of business generally, which threatened loss of confidence in the ability of the government to maintain its continued existence, and therewith the complete destruction of all remaining national credit.

It was at such a time and in such circumstances that Congress was called upon to devise means for maintaining the army and navy, for securing the large supplies of money needed, and, indeed, for the preservation of the government created by the Constitution. It was at such a time and in such an emergency that the legal tender acts were passed. . . .

It is urged now, after the lapse of nine years, and when the emergency has passed, that treasury notes without the legal tender clause might have been issued, and that the necessities of the government might thus have been supplied. . . . But admitting it to be true, what does it prove? Nothing more than that Congress had the choice of means for a legitimate end, each appropriate, and adapted to that end, though, perhaps, in different degrees. What then? . . . The degree of the necessity for any congressional enactment, or the relative degree of its appropriateness, if it have any appropriateness, is for consideration in Congress, not here. Said Chief Justice Marshall, in *McCulloch v. Maryland*, . . . "When the law is not prohibited, and is really calculated to effect any of the objects entrusted to the government, to undertake here to inquire into the degree of its necessity, would be to pass the line which circumscribes the judicial department, and to tread on legislative ground." . . .

Concluding, then, that the provision which made treasury notes a legal tender for the payment of all debts other than those expressly excepted, was not an inappropriate means for carrying into execution the legitimate powers of the government, we proceed to inquire whether it was forbidden by the letter or spirit of the Constitution. It is not claimed that any express prohibition exists, but it is insisted that the spirit of the Constitution was violated by the enactment. Here those who assert the unconstitutionality of the acts mainly rest their argument. They claim that the clause which conferred upon Congress power "to coin money, regulate the value thereof, and of foreign coin," contains an implication that nothing but that which is the subject of coinage, nothing but the precious metals can ever be declared by law to be money, or to have the uses of money. If by this is meant that because certain powers over the currency are expressly given to Congress, all other powers relating to the same subject are impliedly forbidden, we need only remark that such is not the manner in which the Constitution has always been construed. On the contrary it has been ruled that power over a particular subject may be exercised as auxiliary to an express power, though there is another express power relating to the same subject, less comprehensive. There an express power to punish a certain class of crimes (the only direct reference to criminal legislation contained in the Constitution), was not regarded as an objection to deducing authority to punish other crimes from another substantive and defined grant of power. There are other decisions to the same effect. To assert, then, that the clause enabling Congress to coin money and regulate its value tacitly implies a denial of all other power over the currency of the nation, is an attempt to introduce a new rule of construction against the solemn decisions of this court. So far from its containing a lurking prohibition, many have thought it was intended to confer upon Congress that general power over the currency which has always been an acknowledged attribute of sovereignty in every other civilized nation than our own, especially when considered in connection with the other clause which denies to the States the power to coin money, emit bills of credit, or make anything but gold and silver coin a tender in payment of debts. . . . The States can no longer declare what shall be money, or regulate its value. Whatever power there is over the currency is vested in Congress. Such a construction, it might be said, would be in close analogy to the mode of construing other substantive powers granted to Congress. They have never been construed literally, and the government could not exist if they were. Thus the power to carry on war is conferred by the power to "declare war." The whole system of the transportation of the mails is built upon the power to establish post-offices and post-roads. The power to regulate commerce has also been extended far beyond the letter of the grant. Even the advocates of a strict literal construction of the phrase, "to coin money and regulate the value thereof," while insisting that it defines the material to be coined as metal, are compelled to concede to Congress large discretion in all other particulars. The Constitution does not ordain what metals may be coined, or prescribe that the legal value of the metals, when coined, shall correspond at all with their intrinsic value in the market. Nor does it even affirm that Congress may declare anything to be a legal tender for the payment of debts. . . . How then can the grant of a power to coin money and regulate its value, made in terms so liberal and unrestrained, coupled also with a denial to the States of all power over the currency, be regarded as an implied prohibition to Congress against declaring treasury notes a legal tender, if such declaration is appropriate, and adapted to carrying into execution the admitted powers of the government? . . .

But, without extending our remarks further, it will be seen that we hold the acts of Congress constitutional as applied to contracts made either before or after their passage. In so holding, we overrule so much of what was decided in *Hepburn v. Griswold*, 75 U.S. (8 Wall.) 603 (1870), as ruled the acts unwarranted by the Constitution so far as they apply to contracts made before their enactment. That case was decided by a divided court, and by a court having a less number of judges than the law then in existence provided this court shall have. These cases have been heard before a full court, and they have received our most careful consideration. The questions involved are constitutional questions of the most vital importance to the government and to the public at large. . . . [I]t is no unprecedented thing in courts of last resort, both in this country and in England, to overrule decisions previously made. We agree this should not be done inconsiderately, but in a case of such far-reaching consequences as the present, thoroughly convinced as we are that Congress has not transgressed its powers, we regard it as our duty so to decide and to affirm both these judgments.

■ JUSTICE BRADLEY, concurring.

. . . I am aware that according to the report of Mr. Madison in the original draft of the Constitution, the clause relating to the borrowing of money read, "to borrow money and emit bills on the credit of the United States," and that the words, "and emit bills," were, after some debate, struck out. But they were struck out with diverse views of members, some deeming them useless and others deeming them hurtful. The result was that they chose to adopt the Constitution as it now stands, without any words either of grant or restriction of power, and it is our duty to construe the instrument by its words, in the light of history, of the general nature of government, and the incidents of sovereignty.

The same argument was employed against the creation of a United States bank. A power to create corporations was proposed in the Convention and rejected. The power was proposed with a limited application to cases where the public good might require them and the authority of a single State might be incompetent. It was still rejected. It was then confined to the building of canals, but without effect. It was argued that such a power was unnecessary and might be dangerous. Yet Congress has not only chartered two United States banks, whose constitutionality has been sustained by this court, but several other institutions. As a means appropriate and conducive to the end of carrying into effect the other powers of the government, such as that of borrowing money with promptness and dispatch, and facilitating the fiscal operations of the government, it was deemed within the power of Congress to create such an institution under the general power given to pass all such laws as might be necessary and proper for carrying into execution the other powers granted. The views of particular members or the course of proceedings in the Convention cannot control the fair meaning and general scope of the Constitution as it was finally framed and now stands. It is a finished document, complete in itself, and to be interpreted in the light of history and of the circumstances of the period in which it was framed.

No one doubts at the present day nor has ever seriously doubted that the power of the government to emit bills exists. It has been exercised by the government without question for a large portion of its history. This being conceded, the incidental power of giving such bills the quality of legal tender follows almost as a matter of course.

I hold it to be the prerogative of every government not restrained by its Constitution to anticipate its resources by the issue of exchequer bills, bills of credit, bonds, stock, or a banking apparatus. Whether those issues shall or shall not be receivable in payment of private debts is an incidental matter in the discretion of such government unless restrained by constitutional prohibition.

This power is entirely distinct from that of coining money and regulating the value thereof. It is not only embraced in the power to make all necessary auxiliary laws, but it is incidental to the power of borrowing money. It is often a necessary means of anticipating and realizing promptly the national resources, when, perhaps, promptness is necessary to the national existence. It is not an attempt to coin money out of a valueless material, like the coinage of leather or ivory or kowrie shells. It is a pledge of the national credit. It is a promise by the government to pay dollars; it is not an attempt to make dollars. The standard of value is not changed. The government simply demands that its credit shall be accepted and received by public and private creditors during the pending exigency. Every government has a right to demand this when its existence is at stake. The interests of every citizen are bound up with the fate of the government. None can claim exemption. If they cannot trust their government in its time of trial they are not worthy to be its citizens.

But it is said, why not borrow money in the ordinary way? The answer is, the legislative department, being the nation itself, speaking by its representatives, has a choice of methods, and is the master of its own discretion. One mode of borrowing, it is true, is to issue the government bonds, and to invite capitalists to purchase them. But this is not the only mode. It is often too tardy and inefficient. . . .

No one supposes that these government certificates are never to be paid—that the day of specie payments is never to return. And it matters not in what form they are issued. The principle is still the same. Instead of certificates they may be treasury notes, or paper of any other form. And their payment may not be made directly in coin, but they may be first convertible into government bonds, or other government securities. Through whatever changes they pass, their ultimate destiny is *to be paid*. But it is the prerogative of the legislative department to determine when the fit time for payment has come. It may be long delayed, perhaps many may think it too long after the exigency has passed. But the abuse of a power, if proven, is no argument against its existence. And the courts are not responsible therefor. Questions of political expediency belong to the legislative halls, not to the judicial forum. It might subserve the present good if we should declare the legal tender act unconstitutional, and a temporary public satisfaction might be the result. But what a miserable consideration would that be for a permanent loss of one of the just and necessary powers of the government; a power which, had Congress failed to exercise it when it did, we might have had no court here to-day to consider the question, not a government or a country to make it important to do so. . . .

■ THE CHIEF JUSTICE, dissenting [joined by JUSTICE FIELD and JUSTICE CLIFFORD].

. . . A majority of the court, five of four, in the opinion which has just been read, reverses the judgment rendered by the former majority of five to three, in pursuance of an opinion formed after repeated arguments, at successive terms, and careful consideration; and declares the legal tender clause to be constitutional; that is to say, that an act of Congress making promises to pay dollars legal tender as coined dollars in payment of pre-existing debts is a means appropriate and plainly adapted to the exercise of powers expressly granted by the Constitution, and not prohibited itself by the Constitution but consistent with its letter and spirit. And this reversal, unprecedented in the history of the court, has been produced by no change in the opinions of those who concurred in the former judgment. . . .

We agree that much of what was said in the dissenting opinion in that case, which has become the opinion of a majority of the court as now constituted, was correctly said. We fully agree in all that was quoted from Chief Justice Marshall. We had indeed accepted, without reserve, the definition of implied powers in which that great judge summed up his argument, of which the language quoted formed a part. . . . We assert only that the words of the Constitution are such as admonish Congress that implied powers are not to be rashly or lightly assumed, and that they are not to be exercised at all, unless, in the words of Judge Story, they are "*bonâ fide* appropriate to the end*,*" 1 Story on the Constitution, p. 42, § 1251, or, in the words of Chief Justice Marshall, "appropriate, plainly adapted" to a constitutional and legitimate end, and "not prohibited, but consistent with the letter and spirit of the Constitution."

There appears, therefore, to have been no real difference of opinion in the court as to the rule by which the existence of an implied power is to be tested, when *Hepburn v. Griswold* was decided, though the then minority seem to have supposed there was. The difference had reference to the application of the rule rather than to the rule itself. . . .

Now it is a common error, and in our judgment it was the error of the opinion of the minority in *Hepburn v. Griswold*, and is the error of the opinion just read, that considerations pertinent to the issue of United States notes have been urged in justification of making them a legal tender. The real question is, was the making them a legal tender a necessary means to the execution of the power to borrow money? If the notes would circulate as well without as with this quality it is idle to urge the plea of such necessity. But the circulation of the notes was amply provided for by making them receivable for all national taxes, all dues to the government, and all loans. This was the provision relied upon for the purpose by the secretary when the bill was first prepared, and his reflections since have convinced him that it was sufficient. Nobody could pay a tax, or any debt, or buy a bond without using these notes. As the notes, not being immediately redeemable, would undoubtedly be cheaper than coin, they would be preferred by debtors and purchasers. They would thus, by the universal law of trade, pass into general circulation. As long as they were maintained by the government at or near par value of specie they would be accepted in payment of all dues, private as well as public. . . .

Now, does making the notes a legal tender increase their value? It is said that it does, by giving them a new use. The best political economists say that it does not. When the government compels the people to receive its notes, it virtually declares that it does not expect them to be received without compulsion. It practically represents itself insolvent. This certainly does not improve the value of its notes. It is an element of depreciation. In addition, it creates a powerful interest in the debtor class and in the purchasers of bonds to depress to the lowest point the credit of the notes. The cheaper these become, the easier the payment of debts, and the more profitable the investments in bonds bearing coin interest.

On the other hand, the higher prices become, for everything the government needs to buy, and the greater the accumulation of public as well as private debt. It is true that such a state of things is acceptable to debtors, investors in bonds, and speculators. It is their opportunity of relief or wealth. And many are persuaded by their representations that the forced circulation is not only a necessity but a benefit. But the apparent benefit is a delusion and the necessity imaginary. In their legitimate use, the notes are hurt not helped by being made a legal tender. The legal tender quality is only valuable for the purposes of dishonesty. Every honest purpose is answered as well and better without it.

We have no hesitation, therefore, in declaring our conviction that the making of these notes a legal tender, was not a necessary or proper means to the carrying on war or to the exercise of any express power of the government. . . .

[Chief Justice Chase next argued that the statute was inconsistent with the letter and spirit of the Constitution, including the Due Process Clause of the Fifth Amendment, for it "violates that fundamental principle of all just legislation that the legislature shall not take the property of A. and give it to B."—Editors]

It is unnecessary to say that we reject wholly the doctrine, advanced for the first time, we believe, in this court, by the present majority, that the legislature has any "powers under the Constitution which grow out of the aggregate of powers conferred upon the government, or out of the sovereignty instituted by it." If this proposition be admitted, and it be also admitted that the legislature is the sole judge of the necessity for the exercise of such powers, the government becomes practically absolute and unlimited. . . .

■ [The dissenting opinions of JUSTICE FIELD and JUSTICE CLIFFORD are omitted. JUSTICE NELSON also dissented.]

NOTES

1.   Does Justice Strong's opinion rest on a broad reading of the enumerated powers or on the proposition that the national government has inherent powers?

a.   Start with the enumerated powers, and think through the types of constitutional argument. Taken together, do the monetary provisions in Article I, Sections 8 and 10 suggest that the national government has the power to emit bills of credit (i.e., to print paper money)? To make those bills legal tender for private debts? What did the framers think they were doing when they struck "or emit bills" from a draft of the Constitution? How far does the practice go—supporting bills of credit but not making them legal tender for private debts? What side did precedent fall on? Does it matter that the statute was thought to be an essential measure during the Civil War? Does it matter that the war was over?

b.   Now think of the Necessary and Proper Clause, and note the Court's emphasis on *McCulloch v. Maryland*. Does the Necessary and Proper Clause make this an easy case because making paper money legal tender is useful for the specifically enumerated powers? Does that bring us back to asking which powers? And if the Necessary and Proper Clause allows the implication of a power to print money and make it legal tender, couldn't the same argument be used for coinage—why is there an enumerated power to coin money? Does the debate at the Convention suggest that emitting bills of credit would be, in *McCulloch*'s language, one of the "great substantive and independent powers"?

c.   What is the best argument for inherent powers? Is it that the U.S. government should have the powers that are exercised by the governments of other nations? Is there a reason to think the practice of other nations illuminates the meaning of the Constitution of the United States? Or is the argument founded on necessity? If you reject the argument from necessity, does that mean you would rather have the national government risk losing a war or suffering an economic depression than exercise powers it lacks under the Constitution? But if you accept the argument from necessity, what principle should be used by interpreters—whether judges, members of Congress, or the president—when deciding whether an unenumerated power is inherent in nationhood? If good presidents get to invoke inherent powers, do bad presidents, too? And is there any possible way for a principle of inherent powers to be squared with the enumerated and thus limited powers of Article I? Does the Tenth Amendment speak to that question?

2.   Thirteen years later, in *Juilliard v. Greenman*, 110 U.S. 421 (1884), the Court extended the holding of *Knox v. Lee* to statutes passed in peacetime. Given its conclusion that Congress could declare its paper bills legal tender for private debts, as necessary and proper to the execution of various enumerated powers, the Court concluded: "the question whether at any particular time, in war or in peace, the exigency is such, by reason of unusual and pressing demands on the resources of the government, or of the inadequacy of the supply of gold and silver coin to furnish the currency needed for the uses of the government and of the people, that it is, as matter of fact, wise and expedient to resort to this means, is a political question, to be determined by congress when the question of exigency arises, and not a judicial question, to be afterwards passed upon by the courts." *Id.* at 450. Justice Field again dissented. Together *Knox* and *Juilliard* are known as *The Legal Tender Cases*.

Expulsion of Aliens

Art. I, § 8: The Congress shall have Power . . .

To establish an uniform Rule of Naturalization[;] . . .

To make all Laws which shall be necessary and proper for carrying into Execution . . . all other Powers vested by this Constitution in the Government of the United States, or in any Department or Officer thereof.

No clause in the Constitution specifically gives Congress the power to exclude aliens from coming into the United States, and no clause provides the power to expel them once they are here. These powers have long been exercised, but not without controversy. The Alien Acts of 1798 granted President John Adams the power to expel aliens unilaterally, and both James Madison and Thomas Jefferson objected that the acts were unconstitutional. (On the Alien and Sedition Acts, see p. 46.) The issue of excluding or expelling aliens next became salient in the 1880s, with the immigration of Chinese laborers to California. In *Chae Chan Ping v. United States*, 130 U.S. 581 (1889), also called *The Chinese Exclusion Case*, the Supreme Court addressed whether Congress had power to *exclude* aliens from entering the country, upholding such a power. In the case that follows, the Court reviewed that decision and extended it, upholding a power to *expel* resident aliens with no more process than an order from an executive branch official.

Fong Yue Ting v. United States

149 U.S. 698 (1893)

■ MR. JUSTICE GRAY, after stating the facts, delivered the opinion of the court.

The general principles of public law which lie at the foundation of these cases are clearly established by previous judgments of this court, and by the authorities therein referred to.

In the recent case of *Nishimura Ekiu v. U.S.*, 142 U.S. 651, 659 (1892), the court, in sustaining the action of the executive department, putting in force an act of Congress for the exclusion of aliens, said "It is an accepted maxim of international law that every sovereign nation has the power, as inherent in sovereignty, and essential to self-preservation, to forbid the entrance of foreigners within its dominions, or to admit them only in such cases and upon such conditions as it may see fit to prescribe. In the United States, this power is vested in the national government, to which the Constitution has committed the entire control of international relations, in peace as well as in war. It belongs to the political department of the government, and may be exercised either through treaties made by the President and Senate, or through statutes enacted by Congress."

The same views were more fully expounded in the earlier case of *Chae Chan Ping v. U.S.*, 130 U.S. 581 (1889), in which the validity of a former act of Congress, excluding Chinese laborers from the United States, under the circumstances therein stated, was affirmed. . . .

[Next the Court noted that Justice Field, writing for the Court in Chae Chan Ping, *had relied on* Knox v. Lee *and had concluded that "The power of the government to exclude foreigners from the country, whenever, in its judgment, the public interests require such exclusion, has been asserted in repeated instances, and never denied by the executive or legislative departments."—Editors]*

The right of a nation to expel or deport foreigners, who have not been naturalized or taken any steps towards becoming citizens of the country, rests upon the same grounds, and is as absolute and unqualified as the right to prohibit and prevent their entrance into the country. . . .

In England, the only question that has ever been made in regard to the power to expel aliens has been whether it could be exercised by the King without the consent of Parliament. It was formerly exercised by the King, but in later times by Parliament, which passed several acts on the subject between 1793 and 1848. . . .

The right to exclude or to expel all aliens, or any class of aliens, absolutely or upon certain conditions, in war or in peace, being an inherent and inalienable right of every sovereign and independent nation, essential to its safety, its independence and its welfare, the question now before the court is whether the manner in which Congress has exercised this right in sections 6 and 7 of the act of 1892 is consistent with the Constitution. . . .

As long ago said by Chief Justice Marshall, and since constantly maintained by this court[:] "The sound construction of the Constitution must allow to the national legislature that discretion, with respect to the means by which the powers it confers are to be carried into execution, which will enable that body to perform the high duties assigned to it, in the manner most beneficial to the people. Let the end be legitimate, let it be within the scope of the Constitution, and all means which are appropriate, which are plainly adapted to that end, which are not prohibited, but consistent with the letter and spirit of the Constitution, are constitutional." "Where the law is not prohibited, and is really calculated to effect any of the objects intrusted to the government, to undertake here to inquire into the degree of its necessity would be to pass the line which circumscribes the judicial department, and to tread on legislative ground. This court disclaims all pretensions to such a power." *McCulloch v. Maryland*, 17 U.S. (4 Wheat.) 316, 421, 423 (1819). . . .

Congress, having the right, as it may see fit, to expel aliens of a particular class, or to permit them to remain, has undoubtedly the right to provide a system of registration and identification of the members of that class within the country, and to take all proper means to carry out the system which it provides. . . .

By the law of nations, doubtless, aliens residing in a country, with the intention of making it a permanent place of abode, acquire, in one sense, a domicil there, and, while they are permitted by the nation to retain such a residence and domicil, are subject to its laws, and may invoke its protection against other nations. This is recognized by those publicists who, as has been seen, maintain in the strongest terms the right of the nation to expel any or all aliens at its pleasure.

Chinese laborers, therefore, like all other aliens residing in the United States for a shorter or longer time, are entitled, so long as they are permitted by the government of the United States to remain in the country, to the safeguards of the Constitution, and to the protection of the laws, in regard to their rights of person and of property, and to their civil and criminal responsibility. But they continue to be aliens, having taken no steps towards becoming citizens, and incapable of becoming such under the naturalization laws, and therefore remain subject to the power of Congress to expel them, or to order them to be removed and deported from the country, whenever, in its judgment, their removal is necessary or expedient for the public interest. . . .

The question whether, and upon what conditions, these aliens shall be permitted to remain within the United States being one to be determined by the political departments of the government, the judicial department cannot properly express an opinion upon the wisdom, the policy or the justice of the measures enacted by Congress in the exercise of the powers confided to it by the Constitution over this subject. . . .

Upon careful consideration of the subject, the only conclusion which appears to us to be consistent with the principles of international law, with the Constitution and laws of the United States, and with the previous decisions of this court, is that in each of these cases the judgment of the Circuit Court, dismissing the writ of *habeas corpus*, is right, and must be affirmed.

■ MR. JUSTICE BREWER dissenting.

. . . I rest my dissent on three propositions. First, that the persons against whom the penalties of section 6 of the act of 1892 are directed are persons lawfully residing within the United States, secondly, that as such they are within the protection of the Constitution, and secured by its guaranties against oppression and wrong, and, third, that section 6 deprives them of liberty and imposes punishment without due process of law, and in disregard of constitutional guarantees, especially those found in the Fourth, Fifth, Sixth, and Eighth Articles of the Amendments. . . .

We must take judicial notice of that which is disclosed by the census, and which is also a matter of common knowledge. There are 100,000 and more of these persons living in this country, making their homes here, and striving by their labor to earn a livelihood. They are not travelers, but resident aliens. . . .

That those who have become domiciled in a country are entitled to a more distinct and larger measure of protection than those who are simply passing through, or temporarily in, it, has long been recognized by the law of nations. . . .

Indeed, there is force in the contention of counsel for appellants that these persons are "denizens," within the true meaning and spirit of that word as used in the common law. The old definition was this . . .

"A denizen is an alien born, but who has obtained *ex donatione regis* [ ] letters patent to make him an English subject[.] A denizen is in a kind of middle state between an alien and a natural-born subject, and partakes of both of them." 1 Blackstone, Commentaries 374. . . .

But whatever rights a resident alien might have in any other nation, here he is within the express protection of the Constitution, especially in respect to those guarantees which are declared in the original amendments. It has been repeated so often as to become axiomatic, that this government is one of enumerated and delegated powers, and, as declared in Article 10 of the amendments, "the powers not delegated to the United States by the Constitution, nor prohibited by it to the States, are reserved to the States respectively, or to the people."

It is said that the power here asserted is inherent in sovereignty. This doctrine of powers inherent in sovereignty is one both indefinite and dangerous. Where are the limits to such powers to be found, and by whom are they to be pronounced? Is it within legislative capacity to declare the limits? If so, then the mere assertion of an inherent power creates it, and despotism exists. May the courts establish the boundaries? Whence do they obtain the authority for this? Shall they look to the practices of other nations to ascertain the limits? The governments of other nations have elastic powers—ours is fixed and bounded by a written constitution. The expulsion of a race may be within the inherent powers of a despotism. History, before the adoption of this Constitution, was not destitute of examples of the exercise of such a power, and its framers were familiar with history, and wisely, as it seems to me, they gave to this government no general power to banish. Banishment may be resorted to as punishment for crime, but among the powers reserved to the people and not delegated to the government is that of determining whether whole classes in our midst shall, for no crime but that of their race and birthplace, be driven from our territory.

Whatever may be true as to exclusion, . . . I deny that there is any arbitrary and unrestrained power to banish residents, even resident aliens. What, it may be asked, is the reason for any difference? The answer is obvious. The Constitution has no extraterritorial effect, and those who have not come lawfully within our territory cannot claim any protection from its provisions. And it may be that the national government, having full control of all matters relating to other nations, has the power to build, as it were, a Chinese wall around our borders and absolutely forbid aliens to enter. But the Constitution has potency everywhere within the limits of our territory, and the powers which the national government may exercise within such limits are those, and only those, given to it by that instrument. Now, the power to remove resident aliens is, confessedly, not expressed. Even if it be among the powers implied, yet still it can be exercised only in subordination to the limitations and restrictions imposed by the Constitution. . . .

If the use of the word "person" in the Fourteenth Amendment protects all individuals lawfully within the State, the use of the same word "person" in the Fifth must be equally comprehensive, and secures to all persons lawfully within the territory of the United States the protection named therein, and a like conclusion must follow as to the Sixth.

I pass, therefore, to the consideration of my third proposition: Section 6 deprives of "life, liberty, and property without due process of law." It imposes punishment without a trial, and punishment cruel and severe. It places the liberty of one individual subject to the unrestrained control of another. . . .

It is true this statute is directed only against the obnoxious Chinese, but if the power exists, who shall say it will not be exercised to-morrow against other classes and other people? If the guarantees of these amendments can be thus ignored in order to get rid of this distasteful class, what security have others that a like disregard of its provisions may not be resorted to? . . .

In view of this enactment of the highest legislative body of the foremost Christian nation, may not the thoughtful Chinese disciple of Confucius fairly ask, Why do they send missionaries here?

■ MR. JUSTICE FIELD, dissenting.

[Justice Field began by noting that he was the author of the opinion in Chae Chan Ping v. United States, *130 U.S. 581 (1889).—Editors]*

. . . I still adhere to the views there expressed in all particulars, but between legislation for the exclusion of Chinese persons—that is, to prevent them from entering the country—and legislation for the deportation of those who have acquired a residence in the country under a treaty with China, there is a wide and essential difference. The power of the government to exclude foreigners from this country, that is, to prevent them from entering it, whenever the public interests in its judgment require such exclusion, has been repeatedly asserted by the legislative and executive departments of our government and never denied, but its power to deport from the country persons lawfully domiciled therein by its consent, and engaged in the ordinary pursuits of life, has never been asserted by the legislative or executive departments except for crime, or as an act of war in view of existing or anticipated hostilities, unless the alien act of June 25, 1798 can be considered as recognizing that doctrine. . . .

The passage of this act produced great excitement throughout the country and was severely denounced by many of its ablest statesmen and jurists as unconstitutional and barbarous, and among them may be mentioned the great names of Jefferson and Madison, who are throughout our country honored and revered for their lifelong devotion to principles of constitutional liberty. It was defended by its advocates as a war measure. . . .

Aliens from countries at peace with us, domiciled within our country by its consent, are entitled to all the guaranties for the protection of their persons and property which are secured to native-born citizens. The moment any human being from a country at peace with us comes within the jurisdiction of the United States, with their consent—and such consent will always be implied when not expressly withheld, and, in the case of the Chinese laborers before us was in terms given by the treaty referred to—he becomes subject to all their laws, is amenable to their punishment and entitled to their protection. Arbitrary and despotic power can no more be exercised over them with reference to their persons and property, than over the persons and property of native-born citizens. They differ only from citizens in that they cannot vote or hold any public office. As men having our common humanity, they are protected by all the guaranties of the Constitution. To hold that they are subject to any different law or are less protected in any particular than other persons, is in my judgment to ignore the teachings of our history, the practice of our government, and the language of our Constitution. Let us test this doctrine by an illustration. If a foreigner who resides in the country by its consent commits a public offence, is he subject to be cut down, maltreated, imprisoned, or put to death by violence, without accusation made, trial had, and judgment of an established tribunal following the regular forms of judicial procedure? If any rule in the administration of justice is to be omitted or discarded in his case, what rule is it to be? If one rule may lawfully be laid aside in his case, another rule may also be laid aside, and all rules may be discarded. . . .

The statement that in England the power to expel aliens has always been recognized and often exercised, and the only question that has ever been as to this power is whether it could be exercised by the King without the consent of Parliament, is, I think, not strictly accurate. The citations given by Mr. Choate in his brief show conclusively, it seems to me, that deportation from the realm has not been exercised in England since Magna Charta, except in punishment for crime, or as a measure in view of existing or anticipated hostilities. But even if that power were exercised by every government of Europe, it would have no bearing in these cases. It may be admitted that the power has been exercised by the various governments of Europe. Spain expelled the Moors; England, in the reign of Edward I., banished fifteen thousand Jews, and Louis XIV, in 1685, by revoking the Edict of Nantes, which gave religious liberty to Protestants in France, drove out the Huguenots. Nor does such severity of European governments belong only to the distant past. Within three years Russia has banished many thousands of Jews, and apparently intends the expulsion of the whole race—an act of barbarity which has aroused the indignation of all Christendom. Such was the feeling in this country that, friendly as our relations with Russia had always been, President Harrison felt compelled to call the attention of Congress to it in his message in 1891 as a fit subject for national remonstrance. Indeed, all the instances mentioned have been condemned for their barbarity and cruelty, and no power to perpetrate such barbarity is to be implied from the nature of our government, and certainly is not found in any delegated powers under the constitution.

The government of the United States is one of limited and delegated powers. It takes nothing from the usages or the former action of European governments, nor does it take any power by any supposed inherent sovereignty. There is a great deal of confusion in the use of the word "sovereignty" by law writers. Sovereignty or supreme power is in this country vested in the people, and only in the people. By them certain sovereign powers have been delegated to the government of the United States, and other sovereign powers reserved to the states or to themselves. This is not a matter of inference and argument, but is the express declaration of the Tenth

Amendment to the Constitution, passed to avoid any misinterpretation of the powers of the general government. That amendment declares that "The powers not delegated to the United States by the Constitution, nor prohibited by it to the States, are reserved to the States, respectively, or to the people." When, therefore, power is exercised by Congress, authority for it must be found in express terms in the constitution, or in the means necessary or proper for the execution of the power expressed. If it cannot be thus found, it does not exist. . . .

The decision of the court and the sanction it would give to legislation depriving resident aliens of the guaranties of the Constitution fills me with apprehensions. Those guaranties are of priceless value to every one resident in the country, whether citizen or alien. I cannot but regard the decision as a blow against constitutional liberty. . . .

What answer could the naturalized citizen in that case make to his arrest for deportation, which cannot be urged in behalf of the Chinese laborers of to-day?

■ [The dissenting opinion of CHIEF JUSTICE FULLER is omitted.]

NOTES

1.   Start with the question the justices agreed about: that the national government has the power to exclude (not expel) aliens from coming to the United States. What part of the Constitution gives the national government that power? Is it the Commerce Clause? Remember the Migration or Importation Clause in Article I, Section 9: when read with the Commerce Clause, did it imply that Congress had power to exclude slavers and slaves from coming to the United States? Did it matter whether their travel to the United States was commercial?

2.   Now consider the issue in *Fong Yue Ting*. Is the majority opinion outrageous? Or is it simply the logical consequence of Congress's power over "naturalization" as augmented by the Necessary and Proper Clause—that Congress has comprehensive power over all matters of immigration and admission of aliens into the nation? Does it matter whether expelling aliens is part of the naturalization power or is instead "necessary and proper" for its exercise? (Is it easier to see the naturalization power as exclusive to Congress, whereas the Necessary and Proper Clause does not give Congress exclusive power?)

Shorn of the questions of policy, who has the better argument as to the correct interpretation of the scope of Congress's constitutional power in this area, the majority or the dissents? What do you think of the dissenters' argument that expulsion from the country violates individual constitutional rights to due process of law and trial? Note that in some respects this case remains the law: Resident aliens remain subject to expulsion through predominately non-Article III proceedings even if they have long lived in the United States.

3.   Is expelling aliens a "great substantive and independent power"?

4.   The states once exercised broad powers over immigration. See, e.g., Gerald L. Neuman, STRANGERS TO THE CONSTITUTION: IMMIGRANTS, BORDERS, AND FUNDAMENTAL LAW (1996). Even now the relative powers of the national government and the states remain a subject of controversy. In *Arizona v. United States,* 132 S.Ct. 2492 (2012), the Court considered a constitutional challenge to several provisions of an Arizona law that made violations of federal immigration law into state law crimes and that required state law enforcement officers to determine immigration status. The Court struck down most of the challenged provisions as preempted by federal law, including a provision that made

it a crime under state law for a person to be in Arizona without valid immigration papers. Justice Kennedy emphasized federal power over immigration policy. For the majority, this power was derived from Article I Section 8—which authorizes the national government to "establish an uniform Rule of Naturalization"—and from the national government's "inherent power as a sovereign to control and conduct relations with foreign nations." In partial dissent, Justice Scalia argued that the states had never surrendered the powers they had as sovereigns to regulate immigration. He appealed to the debate over the Alien and Sedition Acts, the historical practice of state regulation of immigration, and several constitutional provisions recognizing state authority over borders.

[Assignment 34]

G. THE TREATY-EXECUTING POWER

Article II of the Constitution provides that the president may make treaties that have the force of U.S. law, where consented to by two-thirds vote of the Senate. Congress's legislative power under the Necessary and Proper Clause has long been understood to include the power to enact laws for carrying into execution America's treaty obligations. Does this mean that the president, acting with the Senate, may make a treaty that has the effect, as a practical matter, of enlarging Congress's legislative powers under the Constitution? If so, does the treaty power enable an end-run around the Constitution's principle of limited and enumerated legislative power? A related question is whether a treaty may abridge an individual right protected under the Bill of Rights. For example, could we join an international agreement to prohibit "hate speech" or "laws defaming religion," despite the protection afforded to these kinds of speech by the First Amendment? Or could we join an international agreement that allowed indefinite detention of all suspected terrorists, without trial or writ of habeas corpus, even though it would contravene the Due Process Clause of the Fifth Amendment (and the Suspension Clause in Article I)?

These questions are important ones—and increasingly so as the United States has assumed, by treaty, ever broader international legal commitments (and corresponding domestic-law obligations). The issue was addressed in the context of federalism in *Missouri v. Holland* (1920), and in the context of individual rights in *Reid v. Covert* (1957). A final case addressing this question combines federalism and the separation of powers, *Medellín v. Texas* (2008).

Missouri v. Holland
252 U.S. 416 (1920)

■ MR. JUSTICE HOLMES delivered the opinion of the Court.

This is a bill in equity brought by the State of Missouri to prevent a game warden of the United States from attempting to enforce the Migratory Bird Treaty Act of July 3, 1918, and the regulations made by the Secretary of Agriculture in pursuance of the same. The ground of the bill is that the statute is an unconstitutional interference with the rights reserved to the States by the Tenth Amendment, and that the acts of the defendant done and threatened under that authority invade the sovereign right of the State and contravene its will manifested in statutes. The State also alleges a pecuniary interest, as owner of the wild birds within its borders. . . .

On December 8, 1916, a treaty between the United States and Great Britain was proclaimed by the President. It recited that many species of birds in their annual migrations traversed many parts of the United States and of Canada, that they were of great value as a source of food and in destroying insects injurious to vegetation, but were in danger of extermination through lack of adequate protection. It therefore provided for specified closed seasons and protection in other forms, and agreed that the two powers would take or propose to their lawmaking bodies the necessary measures for carrying the treaty out. The above mentioned act of July 3, 1918, entitled an act to give effect to the convention, prohibited the killing, capturing or selling any of the migratory birds included in the terms of the treaty except as permitted by regulations compatible with those terms, to be made by the Secretary of Agriculture. . . . [T]he question raised is the general one whether the treaty and statute are void as an interference with the rights reserved to the States. . . .

It is said that a treaty cannot be valid if it infringes the Constitution, that there are limits, therefore, to the treaty-making power, and that one such limit is that what an act of Congress could not do unaided, in derogation of the powers reserved to the States, a treaty cannot do. An earlier act of Congress that attempted by itself and not in pursuance of a treaty to regulate the killing of migratory birds within the States had been held bad in the District Court. Those decisions were supported by arguments that migratory birds were owned by the States in their sovereign capacity for the benefit of their people, and that . . . this control was one that Congress had no power to displace. The same argument is supposed to apply now with equal force.

Whether the two cases cited were decided rightly or not they cannot be accepted as a test of the treaty power. Acts of Congress are the supreme law of the land only when made in pursuance of the Constitution, while treaties are declared to be so when made under the authority of the United States. It is open to question whether the authority of the United States means more than the formal acts prescribed to make the convention. We do not mean to imply that there are no qualifications to the treaty-making power; but they must be ascertained in a different way. It is obvious that there may be matters of the sharpest exigency for the national well being that an act of Congress could not deal with but that a treaty followed by such an act could, and it is not lightly to be assumed that, in matters requiring national action, "a power which must belong to and somewhere reside in every civilized government" is not to be found. *Andrews v. Andrews*, 188 U.S. 14, 33 (1903). What was said in that case with regard to the powers of the States applies with equal force to the powers of the nation in cases where the States individually are incompetent to act. We are not yet discussing the particular case before us but only are considering the validity of the test proposed. With regard to that we may add that when we are dealing with words that also are a constituent act, like the Constitution of the United States, we must realize that they have called into life a being the development of which could not have been foreseen completely by the most gifted of its begetters. It was enough for them to realize or to hope that they had created an organism; it has taken a century and has cost their successors much sweat and blood to prove that they created a nation. The case before us must be considered in the light of our whole experience and not merely in that of what was said a hundred years ago. The treaty in question does not contravene any prohibitory words to be found in the Constitution. The only question is whether it is forbidden by some invisible radiation from the general terms of the Tenth Amendment. We must consider what this country has become in deciding what that amendment has reserved.

The State as we have intimated founds its claim of exclusive authority upon an assertion of title to migratory birds, an assertion that is embodied in statute. No doubt it is true that as between a State and its inhabitants the State may regulate the killing and sale of such birds, but it does not follow that its authority is exclusive of paramount powers. To put the claim of the State upon title is to lean upon a slender reed. Wild birds are not in the possession of anyone; and possession is the beginning of ownership. The whole foundation of the State's rights is the presence within their jurisdiction of birds that yesterday had not arrived, tomorrow may be in another State and in a week a thousand miles away. . . .

Here a national interest of very nearly the first magnitude is involved. It can be protected only by national action in concert with that of another power. The subject matter is only transitorily within the State and has no permanent habitat therein. But for the treaty and the statute there soon might be no birds for any powers to deal with. We see nothing in the Constitution that compels the Government to sit by while a food supply is cut off and the protectors of our forests and our crops are destroyed. It is not sufficient to rely upon the States. The reliance is vain, and were it otherwise, the question is whether the United States is forbidden to act. We are of opinion that the treaty and statute must be upheld. . . .

Reid v. Covert
354 U.S. 1 (1957)

■ MR. JUSTICE BLACK delivered the opinion of the Court.

These cases raise basic constitutional issues of the utmost concern. They call into question the role of the military under our system of government. They involve the power of Congress to expose civilians to trial by military tribunals, under military regulations and procedures, for offenses against the United States thereby depriving them of trial in civilian courts, under civilian laws and procedures and with all the safeguards of the Bill of Rights. These cases are particularly significant because for the first time since the adoption of the Constitution wives of soldiers have been denied trial by jury in a court of law and forced to trial before courts-martial. . . .

I

At the beginning we reject the idea that when the United States acts against citizens abroad it can do so free of the Bill of Rights. The United States is entirely a creature of the Constitution. Its power and authority have no other source. It can only act in accordance with all the limitations imposed by the Constitution. When the Government reaches out to punish a citizen who is abroad, the shield which the Bill of Rights and other parts of the Constitution provide to protect his life and liberty should not be stripped away just because he happens to be in another land. . . .

II

At the time of Mrs. Covert's alleged offense, an executive agreement was in effect between the United States and Great Britain which permitted United States' military courts to exercise exclusive jurisdiction over offenses committed in Great Britain by American servicemen or their dependents. . . . Even though a court-martial does not give an accused trial by jury and other Bill of Rights protections, the Government contends that article 2(11) of [Uniform Code of Military Justice], insofar as it provides for the military trial of dependents accompanying the armed forces in Great Britain and Japan, can be sustained as legislation which is necessary and proper to carry out the United States' obligations under the international agreements made with those countries. The obvious and decisive answer to this, of course, is that no agreement with a foreign nation can confer power on the Congress, or on any other branch of Government, which is free from the restraints of the Constitution.

Article VI, the Supremacy Clause of the Constitution, declares:

> This Constitution, and the Laws of the United States which shall be made in Pursuance thereof; and all Treaties made, or which shall be made, under the Authority of the United States, shall be the supreme Law of the Land
> . . .

There is nothing in this language which intimates that treaties and laws enacted pursuant to them do not have to comply with the provisions of the Constitution. Nor is there anything in the debates which accompanied the drafting and ratification of the Constitution which even suggests such a result. These debates as well as the history that surrounds the adoption of the treaty provision in Article VI make it clear that the reason treaties were not limited to those made in "pursuance" of the Constitution was so that agreements made by the United States under the Articles of Confederation, including the important peace treaties which concluded the Revolutionary War, would remain in effect. It would be manifestly contrary to the objectives of those who created the Constitution, as well as those who were responsible for the Bill of Rights—let alone alien to our entire constitutional history and tradition—to construe Article VI as permitting the United States to exercise power under an international agreement without observing constitutional prohibitions. In effect, such construction would permit amendment of that document in a manner not sanctioned by Article V. The prohibitions of the Constitution were designed to apply to all branches of the National Government and they cannot be nullified by the Executive or by the Executive and the Senate combined.

NOTES

1.   What, precisely, is the holding of *Missouri v. Holland*? The opinion states: "We do not mean to imply that there are no qualifications to the treaty-making power; but they must be ascertained in a different way." Is that consistent with the Court's argument from the text of the Supremacy Clause? Later in the opinion, the Court comments that the treaty in question involves "a national interest of very nearly the first magnitude" on which the "the States individually are incompetent to act." Should we understand those criteria to be limitations on the treaty power? Where do those limits come from, if they are limits? Is there some natural scope or limit deriving from the nature of treaties? When the Constitution was drafted, the law of nations limited treaties to matters of clashing sovereign interests; more recently, treaties have often constrained the choices of governments vis-à-vis their own citizens. Is this modern development legitimate under our constitutional system?

Advocates of various causes, impatient with limits on federal power, have proposed that we enter into treaties to achieve their aims. They rely on *Missouri v. Holland* to say that Congress would have power under the Necessary and Proper Clause to implement the treaty. For example, treaties could supply the federal authority found lacking to enforce the Religious Freedom Restoration Act against state governments, or to enact the Violence Against Women Act, or to create protections for wholly intrastate endangered species. For critique of *Missouri v. Holland*, see Nicholas Rosenkranz, *Executing the Treaty Power,* 118 Harv. L. Rev. 1867 (2005). For a different view, emphasizing political safeguards, see Oona A. Hathaway et al., *The Treaty Power: Its History, Scope, and Limits*, 98 Cornell L. Rev. 239 (2013).

Rosenkranz's argument does not extend to self-executing treaties, about which there is also a lively academic debate. The treaty most important to the framers, the Treaty of Paris ending the Revolutionary War, contained provisions interfering with state laws regarding the debts and other property of English citizens and Tories. These provisions might be seen to fall outside the enumerated powers of Congress. Federalists nonetheless regarded them as binding on the states, though there was great disagreement about how the states could be compelled to comply with them. See John T. Perry, *Congress, the Supremacy Clause, and the Implementation of Treaties*, 32 Fordham Int'l Law J. 1209 (2009).

2.   The Court had the opportunity to reconsider *Missouri v. Holland* and the scope of the treaty power in a recent case, *Bond v. United States*, 134 S.Ct. 2077 (2014). Its facts were memorable: Carol Bond learned that her friend Myrlinda Haynes was pregnant and that the father was Ms. Bond's husband. Ms. Bond acquired highly toxic chemicals and put them on Ms. Haynes' mailbox, car door handles, and house doorknob. She was indicted for violating the Chemical Weapons Convention Implementation Act of 1998, which implemented the 1993 Chemical Weapons Convention Act, a treaty to which the United States is a party. Ms. Bond challenged her conviction on the ground that the statute violated the Tenth Amendment. (An earlier Supreme Court decision in the same case had upheld the standing of individuals to raise Tenth Amendment and enumerated-powers constitutional objections to statutes to which they were subject.) In the end, though, the Court adopted a somewhat strained reading of the statute to avoid reaching the constitutional question. *Missouri v. Holland* lives on.

3.   Think of *Missouri v. Holland* and *Reid v. Covert* together. How broad is the treaty power of the president and the Senate acting together? Could a treaty forbid the fifty states from having a death penalty if Congress lacks the enumerated power to enact such a federal law? Could a treaty reverse *Roe v. Wade*? Abrogate the First Amendment? Enact a tax without being passed by the House of Representatives? Should enumerated-powers limitations on Congress be more easily overcome than the limitations the Bill of Rights puts on the federal government? Why?

Medellín v. Texas

552 U.S. 491 (2008)

■ CHIEF JUSTICE ROBERTS delivered the opinion of the Court.

. . .

I

[Materials in this section have been reordered for clarity.—Editors]

In 1969, the United States, upon the advice and consent of the Senate, ratified the Vienna Convention on Consular Relations (Vienna Convention or Convention), and the Optional Protocol Concerning the Compulsory Settlement of Disputes to the Vienna Convention (Optional Protocol or Protocol). . . . [The Optional Protocol] provides that if a person detained by a foreign country "so requests, the competent authorities of the receiving State shall, without delay, inform the consular post of the sending State" of such detention, and "inform the [detainee] of his righ[t]" to request assistance from the consul of his own state. . . .

The Optional Protocol provides . . . for the resolution of disputes arising out of the interpretation or application of the Vienna Convention [before] International Court of Justice (ICJ). . . . In the Case Concerning Avena and Other Mexican Nationals (Mex. v. U.S.), 2004 I.C.J. 12 (Judgment of Mar. 31) (*Avena*), that tribunal considered a claim brought by Mexico against the United States. The ICJ held that, based on violations of the Vienna Convention, 51 named Mexican nationals were entitled to review and reconsideration of their state-court convictions and sentences in the United States. This was so regardless of any forfeiture of the right to raise Vienna Convention claims because of a failure to comply with generally applicable state rules governing challenges to criminal convictions. . . .

Under Article 94(1) of the U.N. Charter, "[e]ach Member of the United Nations undertakes to comply with the decision of the [ICJ] in any case to which it is a party." The ICJ's jurisdiction in any particular case, however, is dependent upon the consent of the parties. . . . By ratifying the Optional Protocol to the Vienna Convention, the United States consented to the specific jurisdiction of the ICJ with respect to claims arising out of the Vienna Convention. On March 7, 2005, subsequent to the ICJ's judgment in Avena, the United States gave notice of withdrawal from the Optional Protocol to the Vienna Convention.

Petitioner José Ernesto Medellín, a Mexican national, has lived in the United States since preschool. A member of the "Black and Whites" gang, Medellín was convicted of capital murder and sentenced to death in Texas for the gang rape and brutal murders of two Houston teenagers. . . .

Local law enforcement officers did not, however, inform Medellín of his Vienna Convention right to notify the Mexican consulate of his detention.

Medellín first raised his Vienna Convention claim in his first application for state postconviction relief. The state trial court held that the claim was procedurally defaulted because Medellín had failed to raise it at trial or on direct review. The trial court also rejected the Vienna Convention claim on the merits, finding that Medellín had "fail[ed] to show that any non-notification of the Mexican authorities impacted the validity of his conviction or punishment."

Medellín then filed a habeas petition in Federal District Court. The District Court denied relief. [After an appeal and an initial grant of certiorari by the Supreme Court] President George W. Bush issued his Memorandum for the United States Attorney General, providing:

> "I have determined, pursuant to the authority vested in me as President by the Constitution and the laws of the United States of America, that the United States will discharge its international obligations under the decision of the International Court of Justice in [Avena], by having State courts give effect to the decision in accordance with general principles of comity in cases filed by the 51 Mexican nationals addressed in that decision."

Medellín, relying on the President's Memorandum and the ICJ's decision in *Avena*, filed a second application for habeas relief in state court. . . .

The Texas Court of Criminal Appeals subsequently dismissed Medellín's second state habeas application as an abuse of the writ. In the court's view, neither the *Avena* decision nor the President's Memorandum was "binding federal law" that could displace the State's limitations on the filing of successive habeas applications. We again granted certiorari . . . *[Certiorari was granted to decide two questions. First, is the ICJ's judgment in* Avena *directly enforceable as domestic law in a state court in the United States? Second, does the President's Memorandum independently require the states to provide review and reconsideration of the claims of the 51 Mexican nationals named in* Avena *without regard to state procedural default rules?—Editors]*

II

Medellín first contends that the ICJ's judgment in *Avena* constitutes a "binding" obligation on the state and federal courts of the United States. He argues that "by virtue of the Supremacy Clause, the treaties requiring compliance with the *Avena* judgment are already the 'Law of the Land' by which all state and federal courts in this country are 'bound.' " . . .

This Court has long recognized the distinction between treaties that automatically have effect as domestic law, and those that—while they constitute international law commitments—do not by themselves function as binding federal law. The distinction was well explained by Chief Justice Marshall's opinion in *Foster v. Neilson*, 27 U.S. (2 Pet. 253), 315 (1829), overruled on other grounds, *United States v. Percheman*, 32 U.S. (7 Pet.) 51 (1833), which held that a treaty is "equivalent to an act of the legislature," and hence self-executing, when it "operates of itself without the aid of any legislative provision." *Foster*, at 314. When, in contrast, "[treaty] stipulations are not self-executing they can only be enforced pursuant to legislation to carry them into effect." *Whitney v. Robertson*, 124 U.S. 190, 194 (1888). . . .

Because none of these treaty sources creates binding federal law in the absence of implementing legislation, and because it is uncontested that no such legislation exists, we conclude that the *Avena* judgment is not automatically binding domestic law. . . .

The obligation on the part of signatory nations to comply with ICJ judgments derives not from the Optional Protocol, but rather from Article 94 of the United Nations Charter—the provision that specifically addresses the effect of ICJ decisions. Article 94(1) provides that "[e]ach Member of the United Nations undertakes to comply with the decision of the [ICJ] in any case to which it is a party." 59 Stat. 1051 (emphasis added). The Executive Branch [as Amicus Curiae] contends that the phrase "undertakes to comply" is not "an acknowledgement that an ICJ decision will have immediate legal effect in the courts of U.N. members," but rather "a commitment on the part of U.N. members to take future action through their political branches to comply with an ICJ decision."

We agree with this construction of Article 94. The Article is not a directive to domestic courts. It does not provide that the United States "shall" or "must" comply with an ICJ decision, nor indicate that the Senate that ratified the U.N. Charter intended to vest ICJ decisions with immediate legal effect in domestic courts. . . .

The remainder of Article 94 confirms that the U.N. Charter does not contemplate the automatic enforceability of ICJ decisions in domestic courts. Article 94(2)—the enforcement provision—provides the sole remedy for noncompliance:

referral to the United Nations Security Council by an aggrieved state. The U.N. Charter's provision of an express diplomatic—that is, nonjudicial—remedy is itself evidence that ICJ judgments were not meant to be enforceable in domestic courts. . . .

Our conclusion that *Avena* does not by itself constitute binding federal law is confirmed by the "postratification understanding" of signatory nations. There are currently 47 nations that are parties to the Optional Protocol and 171 nations that are parties to the Vienna Convention. Yet neither Medellín nor his amici have identified a single nation that treats ICJ judgments as binding in domestic courts. . . .

Even the dissent flinches at reading the relevant treaties to give rise to self-executing ICJ judgments in all cases. It admits that "Congress is unlikely to authorize automatic judicial enforceability of all ICJ judgments, for that could include some politically sensitive judgments and others better suited for enforcement by other branches." Our point precisely. But the lesson to draw from that insight is hardly that the judiciary should decide which judgments are politically sensitive and which are not. In short, and as we observed in *Sanchez-Llamas v. Oregon*, 548 U.S. 331 (2006), "[n]othing in the structure or purpose of the ICJ suggests that its interpretations were intended to be conclusive on our courts." Given that holding, it is difficult to see how that same structure and purpose can establish, as Medellín argues, that judgments of the ICJ nonetheless were intended to be conclusive on our courts. A judgment is binding only if there is a rule of law that makes it so. . . .

Contrary to the dissent's suggestion, neither our approach nor our cases require that a treaty provide for self-execution in so many talismanic words; that is a caricature of the Court's opinion. Our cases simply require courts to decide whether a treaty's terms reflect a determination by the President who negotiated it and the Senate that confirmed it that the treaty has domestic effect. . . .

III

Medellín next argues that the ICJ's judgment in *Avena* is binding on state courts by virtue of the President's February 28, 2005 Memorandum. The United States contends that while the *Avena* judgment does not of its own force require domestic courts to set aside ordinary rules of procedural default, that judgment became the law of the land with precisely that effect pursuant to the President's Memorandum and his power "to establish binding rules of decision that preempt contrary state law." Accordingly, we must decide whether the President's declaration alters our conclusion that the *Avena* judgment is not a rule of domestic law binding in state and federal courts.

A

The United States maintains that the President's constitutional role "uniquely qualifies" him to resolve the sensitive foreign policy decisions that bear on compliance with an ICJ decision and "to do so expeditiously." We do not question these propositions. . . . In this case, the President seeks to vindicate United States interests in ensuring the reciprocal observance of the Vienna Convention, protecting relations with foreign governments, and demonstrating commitment to the role of international law. These interests are plainly compelling.

Such considerations, however, do not allow us to set aside first principles. . . .

B–1

The United States marshals two principal arguments in favor of the President's authority "to establish binding rules of decision that preempt contrary state law." The Solicitor General first argues that the relevant treaties give the President the authority to implement the *Avena* judgment and that Congress has acquiesced in the exercise of such authority. The United States also relies upon an "independent" international dispute-resolution power wholly apart from the asserted authority based on the pertinent treaties. Medellín adds the additional argument that the President's Memorandum is a valid exercise of his power to take care that the laws be faithfully executed.

The United States maintains that the President's Memorandum is authorized by the Optional Protocol and the U.N. Charter. That is, because the relevant treaties "create an obligation to comply with *Avena*," they "implicitly give the President authority to implement that treaty-based obligation." As a result, the President's Memorandum is well grounded in the first category of the *Youngstown* framework.

We disagree. The President has an array of political and diplomatic means available to enforce international obligations, but unilaterally converting a non-self-executing treaty into a self-executing one is not among them. The responsibility for transforming an international obligation arising from a non-self-executing treaty into domestic law falls to Congress. *Foster*, at 315; *Whitney*, at 194. . . . Once a treaty is ratified without provisions clearly according it domestic effect, however, whether the treaty will ever have such effect is governed by the fundamental constitutional principle that " '[t]he power to make the necessary laws is in Congress; the power to execute in the President.' " *Hamdan v. Rumsfeld*, 548 U.S. 557, 591 (2006) (quoting *Ex parte Milligan*, 71 U.S. (4 Wall.) 2, 139 (1866) (opinion of Chase, C.J.)); see U.S. Const., Art. I, § 1 ("All legislative Powers herein granted shall be vested in a Congress of the United States"). As already noted, the terms of a non-self-executing treaty can become domestic law only in the same way as any other law—through passage of legislation by both Houses of Congress, combined with either the President's signature or a congressional override of a Presidential veto. See Art. I, § 7. Indeed, "the President's power to see that the laws are faithfully executed refutes the idea that he is to be a lawmaker." *Youngstown Sheet & Tube Co. v. Sawyer*, 343 U.S. 579, 587 (1952). . . .

The United States nonetheless maintains that the President's Memorandum should be given effect as domestic law because "this case involves a valid Presidential action in the context of Congressional 'acquiescence.' " Under the *Youngstown* tripartite framework, [however] congressional acquiescence is pertinent [only] when the President's action falls within the second category—that is, when he "acts in absence of either a congressional grant or denial of authority." 343 U.S., at 637 (Jackson, J., concurring). . . .

In any event, even if we were persuaded that congressional acquiescence could support the President's asserted authority to create domestic law pursuant to a non-self-executing treaty, such acquiescence does not exist here. The United States first locates congressional acquiescence in Congress's failure to act following the President's resolution of prior ICJ controversies. . . . [But] none of [those cases] remotely involved transforming an international obligation into domestic law and thereby displacing state law.[14]

The United States also directs us to the President's "related" statutory responsibilities and to his "established role" in litigating foreign policy concerns as support for the President's asserted authority to give the ICJ's decision in *Avena* the force of domestic law. [B]ut the authority of the President to represent the United States before such bodies speaks to the President's international responsibilities, not any unilateral authority to create domestic law. . . .

2

We thus turn to the United States' claim that—independent of the United States' treaty obligations—the Memorandum is a valid exercise of the President's foreign affairs authority to resolve claims disputes with foreign nations. The United States relies on a series of cases in which this Court has upheld the authority of the President to settle foreign claims pursuant to an executive agreement. See *American Ins. Assn. v. Garamendi*, 539 U.S. 396, 415 (2003); *Dames & Moore v. Regan*, 453 U.S. 654, 679–680 (1981); *United States v. Pink*, 315 U.S. 203, 229 (1942); *United States v. Belmont*, 301 U.S. 324, 330 (1937). In these cases this Court has explained that, if pervasive enough, a history of congressional acquiescence can be treated as a "gloss on 'Executive Power' vested in the President by § 1 of Art. II." *Dames & Moore*, at 686. . . .

The claims-settlement cases involve a narrow set of circumstances: the making of executive agreements to settle civil claims between American citizens and foreign governments or foreign nationals. See, e.g., *Belmont*, at 327. They are based on the view that "a systematic, unbroken, executive practice, long pursued to the knowledge of the Congress and never before questioned," can "raise a presumption that the [action] had been [taken] in pursuance of its consent." *Dames & Moore*, at 686. As this Court explained in *Garamendi*:

> Making executive agreements to settle claims of American nationals against foreign governments is a particularly longstanding practice. . . . Given the fact that the practice goes back over 200 years, and has received congressional acquiescence throughout its history, the conclusion that the President's control of foreign relations includes the settlement of claims is indisputable."

Even still, the limitations on this source of executive power are clearly set forth and the Court has been careful to note that "[p]ast practice does not, by itself, create power." *Dames & Moore*, at 686.

The President's Memorandum is not supported by a "particularly longstanding practice" of congressional acquiescence, but rather is what the United States itself has described as "unprecedented action[.]" Indeed, the Government has not identified a single instance in which the President has attempted (or Congress has acquiesced in) a Presidential directive issued to state courts, much less one that reaches deep

---

[14]   *[This footnote cites: (1) a presidential refusal to comply with an ICJ decision requiring reparations to Nicaragua; (2) an agency rulemaking complying with an ICJ decision regarding maritime boundaries; (3) presidential acquiescence in an ICJ decision involving the rights of U.S. citizens in Morocco, unrelated to domestic judicial proceedings; and (4) two incidents in which the State Department wrote to certain states "requesting" or "encouraging" them to comply with ICJ rulings regarding violations of the consular treaty.—Editors]*

into the heart of the State's police powers and compels state courts to reopen final criminal judgments and set aside neutrally applicable state laws. . . .

3

Medellín argues that the President's Memorandum is a valid exercise of his "take Care" power. . . . This authority allows the President to execute the laws, not make them. For the reasons we have stated, the *Avena* judgment is not domestic law; accordingly, the President cannot rely on his Take Care powers here.

■ [JUSTICE STEVENS's concurring opinion is omitted.]

■ JUSTICE BREYER, with whom JUSTICE SOUTER and JUSTICE GINSBURG join, dissenting.

The Constitution's Supremacy Clause provides that "all Treaties . . . which shall be made . . . under the Authority of the United States, shall be the supreme Law of the Land; and the Judges in every State shall be bound thereby." Art. VI, cl. 2. The Clause means that the "courts" must regard "a treaty . . . as equivalent to an act of the legislature, whenever it operates of itself without the aid of any legislative provision." *Foster*, at 314 (majority opinion of Marshall, C. J.).

I

. . . The critical question here is whether the Supremacy Clause requires Texas to follow, i.e., to enforce, this ICJ judgment. The Court says "no." And it reaches its negative answer by interpreting the labyrinth of treaty provisions as creating a legal obligation that binds the United States internationally, but which, for Supremacy Clause purposes, is not automatically enforceable as domestic law. . . .

In my view, the President has correctly determined that Congress need not enact additional legislation. The majority places too much weight upon treaty language that says little about the matter. . . . To answer [the] question we must look instead to our own domestic law, in particular, to the many treaty-related cases interpreting the Supremacy Clause. Those cases, including some written by Justices well aware of the Founders' original intent, lead to the conclusion that the ICJ judgment before us is enforceable as a matter of domestic law without further legislation. . . .

[Next Justice Breyer discussed at length early precedent.—Editors]

All of these cases make clear that self-executing treaty provisions are not uncommon or peculiar creatures of our domestic law; that they cover a wide range of subjects; [and] that the Supremacy Clause itself answers the self-execution question by applying many, but not all, treaty provisions directly to the States. . . .

The case law provides no simple magic answer to the question whether a particular treaty provision is self-executing. But the case law does make clear that, insofar as today's majority looks for language about "self-execution" in the treaty itself and insofar as it erects "clear statement" presumptions designed to help find an answer, it is misguided. . . .

Applying the approach just described, I would find the relevant treaty provisions self-executing as applied to the ICJ judgment before us (giving that judgment domestic legal effect) for the following reasons, taken together.

First, the language of the relevant treaties strongly supports direct judicial enforceability, at least of judgments of the kind at issue here. . . .

The upshot is that treaty language says that an ICJ decision is legally binding, but it leaves the implementation of that binding legal obligation to the domestic law of each signatory nation. In this Nation, the Supremacy Clause, as long and consistently interpreted, indicates that ICJ decisions rendered pursuant to provisions for binding adjudication must be domestically legally binding and enforceable in domestic courts at least sometimes. . . . *[Justice Breyer enumerated several other reasons why the ICJ decision should be judicially enforceable.—Editors]*

III

Because the majority concludes that the Nation's international legal obligation to enforce the ICJ's decision is not automatically a domestic legal obligation, it must then determine whether the President has the constitutional authority to enforce it. And the majority finds that he does not.

In my view, that second conclusion has broader implications than the majority suggests. The President here seeks to implement treaty provisions in which the United States agrees that the ICJ judgment is binding with respect to the Avena parties. Consequently, his actions draw upon his constitutional authority in the area of foreign affairs. In this case, his exercise of that power falls within that middle range of Presidential authority where Congress has neither specifically authorized nor specifically forbidden the Presidential action in question. See *Youngstown*, 343 U.S. at 637 (Jackson, J., concurring). At the same time, if the President were to have the authority he asserts here, it would require setting aside a state procedural law.

It is difficult to believe that in the exercise of his Article II powers pursuant to a ratified treaty, the President can never take action that would result in setting aside state law. Cf. *United States v. Pink*, 315 U.S. 203, 233 (1942) ("No State can rewrite our foreign policy to conform to its own domestic policies"). Suppose that the President believes it necessary that he implement a treaty provision requiring a prisoner exchange involving someone in state custody in order to avoid a proven military threat. Cf. *Ware v. Hylton*, 3 U.S. (3 Dall.) 199, 205 (1796). . . . Does the Constitution require the President in each and every such instance to obtain a special statute authorizing his action? On the other hand, the Constitution must impose significant restrictions upon the President's ability, by invoking Article II treaty-implementation authority, to circumvent ordinary legislative processes and to pre-empt state law as he does so.

Previously this Court has said little about this question. [I]t has reserved judgment as to "the scope of the President's power to preempt state law pursuant to authority delegated by . . . a ratified treaty"—a fact that helps to explain the majority's inability to find support in precedent for its own conclusions. *Barclays Bank PLC v. Franchise Tax Bd. of Cal.*, 512 U.S. 298, 329 (1994).

Given the Court's comparative lack of expertise in foreign affairs; given the importance of the Nation's foreign relations; given the difficulty of finding the proper constitutional balance among state and federal, executive and legislative, powers in such matters; and given the likely future importance of this Court's efforts to do so, I would very much hesitate before concluding that the Constitution implicitly sets forth broad prohibitions (or permissions) in this area. . . .

I would thus be content to leave the matter in the constitutional shade from which it has emerged. Given my view of this case, I need not answer the question.

And I shall not try to do so. That silence, however, cannot be taken as agreement with the majority's Part III conclusion.

IV

The majority's two holdings taken together produce practical anomalies. They unnecessarily complicate the President's foreign affairs task insofar as, for example, they increase the likelihood of Security Council *Avena* enforcement proceedings, of worsening relations with our neighbor Mexico, of precipitating actions by other nations putting at risk American citizens who have the misfortune to be arrested while traveling abroad, or of diminishing our Nation's reputation abroad as a result of our failure to follow the "rule of law" principles that we preach. The holdings also encumber Congress with a task (postratification legislation) that, in respect to many decisions of international tribunals, it may not want and which it may find difficult to execute. At the same time, insofar as today's holdings make it more difficult to enforce the judgments of international tribunals, including technical non-politically-controversial judgments, those holdings weaken that rule of law for which our Constitution stands.

These institutional considerations make it difficult to reconcile the majority's holdings with the workable Constitution that the Founders envisaged. They reinforce the importance, in practice and in principle, of asking Chief Justice Marshall's question: Does a treaty provision address the "Judicial" Branch rather than the "Political Branches" of Government. See *Foster*, at 314. And they show the wisdom of the well-established precedent that indicates that the answer to the question here is "yes." . . .

NOTES

1.   What is the basis for the Court's decision that President Bush's memorandum had no legal force—separation of powers? federalism? both?

2.   Do you think the Court's ruling was correct? Can (or should) the interpretation of a treaty by an international body override state law? If so, what is the enforcement mechanism? What is the president's role? What could Congress have done had it wished to comply with the ICJ decision? What if Congress wanted to commit us, *in advance*, to complying with any decisions of the ICJ? Does Article III permit it to do that?

3.   Suppose *Medellín* is correct and the treaty is non-self-executing. Does the president have an obligation to obey and enforce it, even if the courts will not enforce that obligation? Look at the Take Care Clause and the Supremacy Clause. How are they best read together?

[*Assignment 35*]

II. ARTICLE IV: FEDERALISM AND THE RELATIONSHIP OF THE STATES TO EACH OTHER AND TO THE NATION

Articles I, II, and III of the Constitution set forth, respectively, the powers of the legislative, executive, and judicial branches of the national government. Article IV is different: its provisions *bind the states to one another as a Union*. Article IV provides for interstate comity—each state must recognize the judgments of other states' court systems, and must to some extent recognize and apply other states' laws (the Full

Faith and Credit Clause). Article IV provides for certain reciprocal benefits and privileges for the citizens of each state (the Privileges and Immunities Clause). Article IV requires the rendition of fugitives from one state to another—both fugitives from justice (the Extradition Clause) and, originally, fugitive slaves (the Fugitive Slave Clause). It provides for the admission of new states, and for Congress's power to legislate for the territories unless and until they are admitted as new states (the Statehood Admission Clause and the Territories Clause). And Article IV establishes the Union's power, and duty, to guarantee each state a republican form of government and protect each state's security against foreign invasion or domestic insurrection (the Guarantee Clause).

Several provisions in Article IV were infected by—one was *about*—the original Constitution's protection of slavery. At the Philadelphia Convention in 1787, the opponents of slavery made a grudging decision that its abolition in North America could be accomplished only if they first set up a more powerful central government in place of the one existing under the Articles of Confederation (p. 1673). Among the concessions the framers made to slavery was the Fugitive Slave Clause, which, as noted above, obligated the free states to return fugitive slaves. This clause forced the free states to become complicit in the institution of slavery. Nothing did more to inflame Northern opinion against slavery than the efforts in the 1840s and 1850s of slave-catchers to force the extradition to the South of alleged fugitive slaves in the federal and state courts sitting in the free states. Slave-catching and extradition fueled the Abolitionist movement in the North.

The study of major nineteenth century cases involving slavery is fascinating and important in its own right, both historically and as a study of constitutional injustice. And—relevant for the consideration of these cases here—slavery was the theme in many of the early cases arising under Article IV. We turn to those cases soon, for they show how Article IV works, then and now. But first we begin with a map of the federalism provisions of Article IV.

A Map of Article IV

Art. IV, § 1: Full Faith and Credit shall be given in each State to the public Acts, Records, and judicial Proceedings of every other State. And the Congress may by general Laws prescribe the Manner in which such Acts, Records and Proceedings shall be proved, and the Effect thereof.

Article IV begins with the Full Faith and Credit Clause, which provides that the judicial decrees of each state shall be recognized by the other states. In addition, the *content* of the laws of each state are to be recognized by the other states; they do not need to be "proved" as facts in a sister state's courts (the traditional rule for introducing the content of the law of a "foreign" jurisdiction). For such purposes, the states are not "foreign" to one another. See Stephen E. Sachs, *Full Faith and Credit in the Early Congress*, 95 Va. L. Rev. 1201, 1209–1216, 1230–1231 (2009).

Beyond this obligation of giving effect to sister-state judgments and recognizing the content of sister-state laws, the Supreme Court has interpreted the Full Faith and Credit Clause as imposing only the barest minimum of constraints on states' choice-of-law principles and state choices made pursuant to those principles. A state is free to apply its own laws to any matter in its courts as long as some connection to the state means that it would not be fundamentally unfair for that state to apply its own laws. The Court has derived that standard from both the Full Faith and Credit Clause and from the Due Process Clause of the Fourteenth Amendment. See *Allstate Insurance Co. v. Hague*, 449 U.S. 302 (1981).

The Full Faith and Credit Clause also gives Congress the power to decide what "Effect" each state's laws and judgments will have in another. Congress has used this power to require that states give the same "full faith and credit" to judgments rendered by another state that the rendering state's courts would give. 28 U.S.C. § 1738.

> *Art. IV, § 2, Clause 1: The Citizens of each State shall be entitled to all Privileges and Immunities of Citizens in the several States.*

The Privileges and Immunities Clause of Article IV is a bulwark of constitutional federalism. It descends in slightly altered form from a clause in Article IV of the Articles of Confederation (see p. 1673). What are the "Privileges and Immunities of Citizens in the several States" and who is a citizen? Were free black men and women in the North "citizens" who were entitled by this Clause to exercise First and Second Amendment freedoms while travelling through the South such that they could hand out abolitionist literature and carry guns? Conversely, did Southern slave owners have a constitutional right to hold their slaves in slavery while they were travelling through free states? Did that mean that slavery could not constitutionally be abolished altogether even in the free states?

The best and most widely accepted reading of the Privileges and Immunities Clause is that it prescribes a rule forbidding states from discriminating against out-of-staters with respect to those fundamental "privileges and immunities" of citizenship or civil rights that it accords its own citizens. Rhode Island cannot treat Minnesotans differently from the way it treats Rhode Islanders. Thus, the clause is sometimes called the Comity Clause. Whatever civil rights a state gives to its own citizens, it must give the same civil rights to out-of-state citizens.

Does that mean that a state must treat out-of-staters the same as its own citizens with respect to *everything*? No—or, at least, that is what courts have consistently held. The Privileges and Immunities Clause forbids discrimination against out-of-staters only with respect to "civil rights," also called "fundamental rights." But states can discriminate against out-of-staters with respect to what are called "political rights," such as the right to vote, to stand for elective office, and to serve on juries. (That distinction is discussed more below, see p. 711, and in connection with the Reconstruction Amendments, see, e.g., p. 1267.) States may also discriminate in the use of state property. For example, a state may charge out-of-staters higher fees to use state parks or obtain fishing licenses, on the theory that in-staters might have had to pay state taxes to support some of these services.

> *Art. IV, § 2, Clause 2: A Person charged in any State with Treason, Felony, or other Crime, who shall flee from Justice, and be found in another State. . . .*

The Extradition Clause of Article IV requires, "on Demand of the executive Authority of the State from which [the person charged] fled," that the charged person "be delivered up, to be removed to the State having Jurisdiction of the Crime." This is an obvious interstate-comity provision. It deals with the federalism problem of criminals who flee the state where they committed their crime.

Art. IV, § 2, Clause 3: No Person held to Service or Labour in one State, under the Laws thereof, escaping into another, shall . . . be discharged from such Service or Labour, but shall be delivered up on Claim of the Party to whom such Service or Labour may be due.

This is the Fugitive Slave Clause of the Constitution. Like the immediately preceding Extradition Clause, it is a kind of comity clause. Two notable differences: First, it is not the "executive Authority" of the state that demands a fugitive's return. Rather, with alleged fugitive slaves, as opposed to fugitives charged with crimes, the person shall be "delivered up" *"on Claim of the Party"*—the person who says he is the master. Second, it applies only to those "held to Service or Labor," not merely those who are "charged," as in the Extradition Clause.

Does this mean that the Clause applies only if a free state first determines that the accused is indeed a fugitive slave? Or does it require a free state to deliver the accused simply on the say-so of any out-of-state person who claims to be the person's master? May a state pass laws providing due process, or jury trial rights, to guard against improper claims? May Congress pass laws specifying federal procedures, as it did with the Fugitive Slave Acts of 1793 and 1850—hotly contested, bitterly divisive pieces of legislation?

Art. IV, § 3: New States may be admitted by the Congress into this Union. . . . The Congress shall have Power to dispose of and make all needful Rules and Regulations respecting the Territory or other Property belonging to the United States. . . .

Some of the most important non-judicial constitutional controversies in our nation's early history concerned the scope (and exercise) of the power to admit new states, and the power of Congress to legislate with respect to U.S. territories that are not yet states. Note that new states entering the Union are co-equal with the thirteen original states.

Art. IV, § 4: The United States shall guarantee to every State in this Union a Republican Form of Government, and shall protect each of them against Invasion; and . . . domestic Violence.

The "Guarantee Clause" is a commitment by the Union as a whole to each state, a commitment that each state will always have a "Republican Form of Government." (This is also called the Republican Form of Government Clause.) It is combined with a pledge of the protection of each state against invasion or domestic violence. President Lincoln relied in part on this clause for his conclusion that the Constitution does not permit a state to secede from the Union, it then being impossible any longer to guarantee it a republican form of government.

The Guarantee Clause is ambiguous about which branch is primarily responsible for enforcing these "guarantees" and about exactly how far the national power created by the Guarantee Clause extends. In *Luther v. Borden*, 48 U.S. (7 How.) 1 (1849) (p. 431), the Supreme Court found these issues to be "political questions" assigned to the discretion of the political branches of the national government. During the Civil War, the Guarantee Clause was invoked by Congress as a source of *its* authority to take legislative action directed against secessionist governments. And the Guarantee Clause was invoked by President Lincoln as a source of *his* authority to take such actions. The clause's ambiguity about enforcement permitted each branch to make claims for itself. That ambiguity may have reduced tensions between the branches for a time, but those tensions would become full-blown conflict after the Civil War during Reconstruction.

What are the essentials of "Republican . . . Government"? What is the furthest that the concept can be pushed as a justification for federal power over state governments? These and similar questions have troubled the interpretation of the Guarantee Clause for over two hundred years and are, even today, not fully settled.

A. PRELUDE: SLAVERY IN THE CONSTITUTION

Was the antebellum Constitution a pro-slavery document? Some have argued that the compromises over slavery in the Constitution made it, in the words of one abolitionist, "a covenant with death" and "an agreement with Hell." Others have argued that those compromises were essential to forming a national government that would be strong enough to someday eliminate slavery entirely. (These questions are also explored in the chapter on the Reconstruction Amendments, see p. 1249, but here they are considered with an emphasis on state-state relations under the Constitution.) Although the antebellum Constitution never uses the word *slavery*, it does have some provisions that contemplate slavery, or that create powers or limitations related to it. Look again at the Constitution as it stood before the Civil War, and see for yourself what it says on the subject.

———

After you have reviewed what the Constitution says about slavery, consider the following questions that bedeviled our nation during its first century and that ultimately led to the Civil War, answering them as if you were a member of Congress in the 1790s:

(1) Did the Constitution prohibit slavery? Could any provision of the Constitution have been legitimately interpreted to require abolition? (Remember, this is before the Civil War and the Thirteenth Amendment.)

(2) Did the Constitution guarantee slavery, in the sense of providing an affirmative constitutional right of some persons to own others as slaves?

(3) To what government did the Constitution allocate the power to make decisions about whether slavery was prohibited or required? If there was any room for states to make decisions about slavery within their borders, were there any limits on those decisions?

(4) What were the powers of *Congress* with respect to slavery? In particular, consider the following questions about Congress before the Civil War, and ask yourself on which interpretive premises you are relying:

    (a) Could Congress have passed a "Fugitive Slave Act" providing a procedure for capturing slaves that escaped into states where slavery was illegal?

    (b) Could Congress have abolished the international slave trade? Could it have prohibited the slave trade between the states of the Union? Within a single state?

(c) Could Congress have prohibited slavery within the United States?

(d) Could Congress have prohibited slavery in the "territories" of the United States? Could it have required, as a condition for the entry of any new state into the union, that it prohibit slavery in its own constitution?

(e) Could Congress have prohibited slavery within the District of Columbia? Could it have permitted slavery there?

(5) Summing up: Taking into account all of the provisions in the antebellum Constitution that touch on slavery, do you think their net effect was to protect or to frustrate the institution of slavery in the United States?

As you ponder these questions, consider the story of two of the brothers who founded Brown University in Providence, Rhode Island. One brother, John, was a slave trader. The other, Moses, was a Quaker and a leading abolitionist. The brothers fought vigorously over slavery, yet remained friends. (Their story is told in Charles Rappleye, SONS OF PROVIDENCE: THE BROWN BROTHERS, THE SLAVE TRADE, AND THE AMERICAN REVOLUTION (2006).)

Moses converted to Quakerism in 1773 on the death of his beloved first wife. That autumn, he freed six household slaves. He seemingly regarded the loss of his wife as a divine punishment for his family's and his own involvement in the slave trade—which included a disastrous venture with his brother on a slave ship called *The Sally* on which 109 slaves died. Moses offered his freed slaves employment and shelter.

Moses began lobbying the Rhode Island General Assembly to curtail slavery—or at least the slave trade—to no avail. He and other New England Quakers had more success, however, with the First Continental Congress, which was meeting in Philadelphia to debate American relations with England. In 1774, "the second article of the Continental Association," as the agreement to ban the importation of slaves from England was called, said explicitly: "We will neither import nor purchase, any slave imported after the first of December next; after which time we will wholly discontinue the slave trade, and will neither be concerned in it ourselves, nor will we hire our vessels, nor sell our commodities or manufactures to those who are concerned in it." This was an astonishing step toward abolition by a "legislature" which lacked constitutional powers and even a country of its own at the time. (Evidently, some of those fighting for liberty from England in the 1770s appreciated that there was incongruity in their enslaving others.) After the adoption of this resolution, the slavery issue would not resurface in government until after peace with England was achieved in the 1780s.

The mid-1780s saw progress and setbacks for the abolitionist cause. A number of societies to promote the manumission of slaves were formed, and public opinion began to shift against slavery. Moses and other Quakers petitioned the Continental Congress in 1783 to ban the slave trade. It received the petitions but referred them to committee, where they were forgotten. Congress was too weak under the Articles of Confederation to take real action against the slave trade; it was beset by other problems.

In 1787, however, the Continental Congress was persuaded to ban slavery in the huge Northwest Territory, which eventually would become the free states of

Ohio, Indiana, Illinois, Michigan, and Wisconsin (and part of Minnesota). And in the fall of 1787, Moses persuaded the Rhode Island legislature and governor to outlaw the slave trade—a momentous step, given the importance in the slave trade of merchants from Rhode Island and other New England states. The law made it illegal for any citizen of the state to "directly or indirectly import or transport, buy or sell, or receive on board their vessel . . . any of the natives or inhabitants of any state or kingdom in that part of the world called Africa, as slaves or without their voluntary consent." The penalty was one hundred pounds for each slave imported and one thousand pounds for each ship engaged in the slave trade, with the fines to be divided between the state and the person who filed the complaint.

But 1787 also brought discouraging news for abolitionists and Quakers when the text of the proposed new Constitution drafted in Philadelphia was published. No one knew then of the impassioned debates over slavery in which the drafters had engaged, but the text of the Constitution nowhere limited slavery, and several clauses in fact condoned it. First, the Three-Fifths Clause in Article I counted slaves as three-fifths of a person for apportioning representatives in the House of Representatives, in effect providing the states with large slave populations a representation "bonus" in the new government. Second, Article I, Section 9 forbade Congress from banning the international slave trade until 1808. And, finally, Article IV included a Fugitive Slave Clause that imposed a duty on *all* federal and state governments to arrest fugitive slaves and return them to their masters. The South insisted on these provisions as a condition of agreeing to a government that gave the new nation the powers over commerce that New England's delegates desired. Southerners also wanted the greater representation in the House of Representatives—and thus also in the Electoral College—that came from counting slaves, who could not vote, as three-fifths of a person. This system led to white Southerners "voting their slaves" and gave the South a huge advantage in Congress and in presidential elections. In part due to this advantage, Southerners—and particularly Virginians—dominated the presidency from 1789 until 1861, and with domination of the presidency came Southern domination of the Supreme Court.

Would the new government created by the Constitution restrict slavery? Or would it protect slavery and enable its expansion? This became one of the most contentious issues in America's constitutional history from 1789 through the Civil War of 1861–1865. (Additional excerpts from the long-running national debate over slavery and the Constitution can be found at p. 1253.) A great many of the constitutional arguments in that seventy-five-year debate were made in 1790 when the First Congress considered two petitions for legislation.

The Quaker Anti-Slavery Petitions of 1790

In February 1790, Quaker societies presented petitions to Congress proposing abolition of the foreign slave trade and consideration of measures to abolish slavery in America. One petition was presented under the signature of Benjamin Franklin.

What follows are excerpts from the congressional debates over those petitions, which eventually led to the petitions being referred to a committee (as proposed by Representative James Madison). The committee produced a report, which was then amended by the House of Representatives as a whole. The committee version and the full House report are, in essence, constitutional interpretations concerning Congress's power with respect to slavery. Evaluate the reports. Are they right? The outcome, known as the Decision of 1790, later came to be treated by Congress as a "precedent" establishing the impropriety of any congressional action to abolish slavery in the states. See Joseph Ellis, FOUNDING BROTHERS 118 (2001).

The Petition of the Quakers of Pennsylvania, New Jersey, and Other States

Presented in the House of Representatives, Feb. 11, 1790

To the Senate and House of Representatives of the United States.

The Address of the people called Quakers, in their annual assembly convened.

Firmly believing that unfeigned righteousness in public as well as private stations, is the only sure ground of hope for the Divine blessing, whence alone rulers can derive true honor, establish sincere confidence in the hearts of the people, and feeling their minds animated with the ennobling principle of universal good-will to men, find a conscious dignity and felicity in the harmony and success attending the exercise of a solid uniform virtue, short of which the warmest pretensions to public spirit, zeal for our country, and the rights of men, are fallacious and illusive.

Under this persuasion, as professors of faith in that ever blessed all-perfect Lawgiver, whose injunctions remain of undiminished obligation on all who profess to believe in him, "whatsoever ye would that men should do unto you, do you even so unto them"; we apprehend ourselves religiously bound to request your serious Christian attention, to the deeply interesting subject whereon our religious society, in their annual assembly, on the tenth month, 1783, addressed the then Congress, who, thought the Christian rectitude of the concern was by the Delegates generally acknowledged, yet not being vested with the powers of Legislation, they declined promoting any public remedy against the gross national iniquity of trafficking in the persons of fellow-men; but divers of the Legislative bodies of the different States, on the Continent, have since manifested their sense of the public detestation due to the licentious wickedness of the African trade for slaves, and the inhuman tyranny and blood guiltiness inseparable from it: the debasing influence whereof most certainly tends to lay waste the virtue, and, of course, the happiness of the people.

Many are the enormities abhorrent to common humanity, and common honesty; which, under the Federal countenance given to this abominable commerce, are practiced in some of the United States, which we judge it not needful to particularize to a body of men, chosen as eminently distinguished for wisdom as extensive information. But we find it indispensably incumbent on us, as a religious body, assuredly believing that both the true temporal interest of nations, and eternal well-being of individuals, depend on doing justly, loving mercy, and walking humbly before God, the creator, preserver, and benefactor of men, thus to attempt to excite your attention to the affecting subject; earnestly desiring that the infinite Father of Spirits may so enrich your minds with his love and truth, and so influence your understandings, by that pure wisdom which is full of mercy and good fruits, as that a sincere and impartial inquiry may take place, whether it be not an essential part of the duty of your exalted station, to exert upright endeavors, to the full extent of your power, to remove every obstruction to public righteousness, which the influence of artifice of particular persons, governed by the narrow mistaken views of self-interest, has occasioned, and whether, notwithstanding such seeming impediments, it be not in reality within your power to exercise justice and mercy, which, if adhered to, we cannot doubt, must produce the abolition of the slave trade.

We consider this subject so essentially and extensively important, as to warrant a hope, that the liberty we now take will be understood, as it really is, a compliance with a sense of religious duty; and that your Christian endeavors to remove reproach from the land may be efficacious to sweeten the labor, and lessen the difficulties incident to the discharge of your important trust.

Signed in and on behalf of the Yearly Meeting, for Pennsylvania, New Jersey, Delaware, and the Western parts of Maryland and Virginia; held by adjournments from the twenty-eighth day of the ninth month, to the third day of the tenth month, inclusive, 1789, by NICHOLAS WALN, Clerk to the meeting this year.

The Petition of the Pennsylvania Society for Promoting the Abolition of Slavery
Presented in the House of Representatives, Feb. 12, 1790

The following memorial of the Pennsylvania Society for promoting the Abolition of Slavery, the relief of free negroes unlawfully held in bondage, and the improvement of the condition of the African race, was presented and read:

The memorial respectfully showeth,

That from a regard for the happiness of mankind, as association was formed several years since in this State, by a number of her citizens, of various religious denominations, for promoting the abolition of slavery, and for the relief of those unlawfully held in bondage. A just and acute conception of the true principles of liberty, as it spread through the land, produced accessions to their numbers, many friends to their cause, and a Legislative co-operation with their views, which, by the blessing of Divine Providence, have been successfully directed to the relieving from bondage a large number of their fellow-creatures of the African race. They have also the satisfaction to observe, that in consequence of that spirit of philanthropy and genuine liberty which is generally diffusing its beneficial influence, similar institutions are forming at home and abroad.

That mankind are all formed by the same Almighty Being, alike objects of his care, and equally designed for the enjoyment of happiness, the Christian religion teaches us to believe, and the political creed of Americans fully coincides with the position. Your memorialists, particularly engaged in attending to the distresses arising from slavery, believe it their indispensable duty to present this subject to your notice. They have observed, with real satisfaction, that many important and salutary powers are vested in you for "promoting the welfare and securing the blessings of liberty to the people of the United States"; and as they conceive that these blessings ought rightfully to be administered, without distinction of color, to all descriptions of people, so they indulge themselves in the pleasing expectation, that nothing which can be done for the relief of the unhappy objects of their care will be either omitted or delayed.

From a persuasion that equal liberty was originally the portion, and is still the birth-right of all men; and influenced by the strong ties of humanity, and the principles of their institution, your memorialists conceive themselves bound to use all justifiable endeavors to loosen the bands of slavery, and promoted a general enjoyment of the blessings of freedom. Under these impressions, they earnestly entreat you serious attention to the subject of slavery; that you will be pleased to countenance the restoration of liberty to those unhappy men, who alone, in this land of freedom are degraded into perpetual bondage, and who, amidst the general joy of surrounding free-men, are groaning in servile subjections; that you will devise means for removing this inconsistency from the character of the American people; that you will promote mercy and justice towards this distressed races, and that you will step to the very verge of the power vested in you for discouraging every species of traffic in the persons of our fellow-men.

BENJ. FRANKLIN, *President.*

Slave Trade Debates

The House of Representatives, Feb. 12, 1790

. . . Mr. TUCKER was sorry the petition had a second reading, as he conceived it contained an unconstitutional request, and from that consideration he wished it thrown aside. He feared the commitment of it would be a very alarming circumstance to the Southern States; for, if the object was to engage Congress in an unconstitutional measure, it would be considered as an interference with their rights, the people would become very uneasy under the Government, and lament that they ever put additional powers into their hands. He was surprised to see another memorial on the same subject, and that signed by a man who ought to have known the Constitution better: He thought it a mischievous attempt, as it respected the persons in whose favor it was intended. It would buoy them up with hopes, without a foundation, and as they could not reason on the subject, as more enlightened men would, they might be led to what they would be punished for, and the owners of them, in their own defence, would be compelled to exercise over them a severity they were not accustomed to. Do these men expect a general emancipation of slaves by law? This would never be submitted to by the Southern States without a civil war. Do they mean to purchase their freedom? He believed their money would fall short of the price. But how is it they are more concerned in this business than others? Are they the only persons who possess religion and morality? If the people are not so exemplary, certainly they will admit, the clergy are; why then do we not find them uniting in the body, praying us to adopt measures for the promotion of religion and piety, or any moral object? They know it would be an improper interference; and, to say the best of this memorial, it is an act of imprudence, which he hoped would receive no countenance from the house.

Mr. SENEY denied that there was any thing unconstitutional in the memorial; at least, if there was, it had escaped his attention, and he should be obliged to the gentleman to point it out. Its only object was, that Congress should exercise their constitutional authority, to abate the horrors of slavery, as far as they could; indeed, he considered that all altercation on the subject of commitment was at an end, as the house had impliedly determined yesterday that it should be committed.

Mr. BURKE saw the disposition of the House, and he feared it would be referred to a committee, maugre [*i.e., "in spite of"—Editors*] all their opposition; but he must insist, that it prayed for an unconstitutional measure; did it not desire Congress to interfere and abolish the slave trade, while the Constitution expressly stipulated that Congress should exercise no such power? He was certain the commitment would sound an alarm, and blow the trumpet of sedition in the Southern States. He was sorry to see the petitioners paid more attention to than the Constitution; however, he would do his duty, and opposed the business totally; and if it was referred to a committee, as mentioned yesterday, consisting of a member from each State, and he was appointed, he would decline serving.

Mr. SCOTT.—I cannot entertain a doubt but the memorial is strictly agreeable to the Constitution; it respects of part of the duty particularly assigned to us by that instrument, and I hope we may be inclined to take it into consideration. We can, at present, lay our hands upon a small duty of ten dollars; I would take this, and if it is all we can do, we must be content: but I am sorry that the framers of the Constitution did not go farther, and enable us to interdict the traffic entirely; for I look upon the slave trade to be one of the most abominable things on earth; and if there was neither God nor devil, I should oppose it upon the principles of humanity, and the law of nature. I cannot, for my part, conceive how any person can be said to acquire a property in another; is it by virtue of conquest? What are the rights of conquest? Some have dared to advance this monstrous principle, that the conqueror is absolute master of his conquest; that he may dispose of it as his property, and treat it as he pleases; but, enough of those who reduce man to the state of transferable goods, or use them like beasts of burthen, who deliver them up as the property or patrimony to others. Let us argue on principles countenanced by reason and becoming humanity; the petitioners view the subject in a religious light, but I do not stand in need of religious motives to induce me to reprobate the traffic in human flesh; other considerations weigh with me to support the commitment of the memorial, and to support every constitutional measure likely to bring about its total abolition. Perhaps, in our legislative capacity, we can go no further than to impose a duty of ten dollars, but I do not know how far I might go, if I was one of the Judges of the United States, and those people were to come before me and claim their emancipation; but I am sure I would go as far as I could.

Mr. JACKSON differed with the gentleman last up, and supposed the master had a qualified property in his slave. He said the contrary doctrine would go to the destruction of every species of personal service. The gentleman said, he did not stand in need of religion to induce him to reprobate slavery, but if he is guided by that evidence upon which the christian system is founded, he will find that religion is not against it. He will see, from Genesis to Revelations, the current setting strong that way. There never was a Government on the face of the earth, but what permitted slavery. The purest sons of freedom in the Grecian Republics, the citizens of Athens and Lacedaemon all held slaves. On this principle, the nations of Europe are associated; it is the basis of the feudal system. But suppose all this to have been wrong, let me ask the gentleman if it is policy to bring forward a business at this moment, likely to light up the flame of civil discord; for the people of the Southern States will resist one tyranny as soon as another? The other parts of the Continent may bear them down by force of arms, but they will never suffer themselves to be divested of their property without a struggle. The gentleman says, if he was a Federal Judge, he does not know to what length he would go in emancipating these people; but, I believe his judgment would be of short duration in Georgia, perhaps even the existence of such a Judge might be in danger.

Mr. SHERMAN could see no difficulty in committing the memorial; because it was probable the committee would understand their business, and perhaps they might bring in such a report as would be satisfactory to gentlemen on both sides of the House.

Mr. BALDWIN was sorry the subject had ever been brought before Congress, because it was of a delicate nature as it respected some of the States. Gentlemen who had been present at the formation of this Constitution could not avoid the recollection of the pain and difficulty which the subject caused in that body. The members from the Southern States were so tender upon this point, that they had well nigh broken up without coming to any determination; however, from the extreme desire of preserving the Union, and obtaining an efficient Government, they were induced mutually to concede, and the Constitution jealously guarded what they agreed to. If gentlemen look over the footsteps of that body, they will find the greatest degree of caution used to imprint them, so as not to be easily eradicated; but the moment we go to jostle on that ground, said he, I fear we shall feel it tremble under our feet. Congress have no power to interfere with the importation of slaves beyond what is in the ninth section of the 1st article of the Constitution; every thing else is interdicted to them in the strongest terms. If we examine the constitution, we shall find the expressions relative to this subject cautiously expressed, and more punctiliously guarded than any other part, "The migration or importation of such persons shall not be prohibited by Congress." But lest this should not have secured the object sufficiently, it is declared, in the same section, "That no capitation or direct tax shall be laid, unless in proportion to the census"; this was intended to prevent Congress from laying any special tax upon negro slaves, as they might, in this way, so burthen the possessors of them as to induce a general emancipation. If we go on to the fifth article, we shall find the first and fifth clauses of the ninth section of the first article restrained from being altered before the year 1808.

Gentlemen have said, that this petition does not pray for an abolition of the slave trade. I think, sir, it prays for nothing else, and therefore we have no more to do with it than if it prayed us to establish an order of nobility, or a national religion.

Mr. SYLVESTER said, that he had always been in the habit of respecting the society called Quakers; he respected them for their exertions in the cause of humanity; but he thought the present was not a time to enter into a consideration of the subject, especially as he conceived it to be a business within the province of the State Legislatures.

Mr. LAWRENCE observed, that the subject would undoubtedly come under the consideration of the House; and he thought, as it was now before them, that the present time was as proper as any; he was therefore for committing the memorial, and when the prayer of it had been properly examined, they could see how far Congress may, constitutionally, interfere; as they knew the limits of their power on this, as well as on every other occasion, there was no just apprehension to be entertained that they would go beyond it.

Mr. SMITH, of South Carolina, insisted that it was not in the power of the House to grant the prayer of the petition, which went to the total abolishment of the slave trade, and it was therefore unnecessary to commit it. He observed, that in the Southern States, difficulties had arisen on adopting the Constitution, inasmuch as it was apprehended that Congress might take measures under it for abolishing the slave trade.

Perhaps the petitioners, when they applied to this House, did not think their object unconstitutional, but now they are told that it is they will be satisfied with the answer, and press it no further. If their object had been for Congress to lay a duty of ten dollars per head on the importation of slaves, they would have said so, but that does not appear to have been the case. The commitment of the petition, on that ground, cannot be contended. If they will not be content with that, shall it be committed to investigate facts? The petition speaks of none. For what purpose, then, shall it be committed? If gentlemen can assign no good reason for the measure, they will not support it, when they are told that it will create great jealousies and alarm in the Southern States; for I can assure them that there is no point on which they are more jealous and suspicious than on a business with which they think the government has nothing to do.

When we entered into this confederacy, we did it from political, not from moral motives, and I do not think my constituents want to learn morals from the petitioners; I do not believe they want improvement in their moral system; if they do, they can get it at home.

The gentleman from Georgia has justly stated the jealousy of the Southern States. On entering into this Government, they apprehend that the other States, not knowing the necessity the citizens of the Southern States were under to hold this species of property, would, from motives of humanity and benevolence, be led to vote for a general emancipation; and had they not seen that the constitution provided against the effect of such a disposition, I may be bold to say they never would have adopted it. And, notwithstanding all the calmness with which some gentlemen have viewed the subject, they will find that the discussion alone will create great alarm. We have been told, that if this would be the case, we ought to have avoided it, by saying nothing; but it was not for that purpose that we were sent here. We look to this measure as an attack upon the palladium of the property of our country; it is therefore our duty to oppose it by every means in our power. Gentlemen should consider, that when we entered into a political connexion with other States, that this property was there; it was acquired under a former Government, conformably to the laws and constitution, therefore, any thing that will tend to deprive them of that property, must be an *ex post facto* law, and, as such, is forbidden by our political compact.

I said the States would never have entered into the Confederation, unless their property had been guaranteed to them, for such is the state of agriculture in that country, that without slaves it must be abandoned. Why will these people, then, make use of arguments to induce the slave to turn his hand against his master? We labor under difficulties enough from the ravages of the late war. A gentleman can hardly come from that country with a servant or two, either to this place or Philadelphia, but there are persons trying to seduce his servants to leave him; and, when they have done this, the poor wretches are obliged to rob their master, in order to obtain a subsistence; all those, therefore, who are concerned in this seduction, are accessaries to the robbery.

The reproaches which they cast upon the owners of negro property, is charging them with the want of humanity. I believe the proprietors have as much humanity as persons in any part of the continent, and are as conspicuous for their good morals as their neighbors. It was said yesterday, that the Quakers are a society known to the laws and the constitution, but they are no more so than other religious societies;

they stand exactly in the same situation; their memorial, therefore, relates to a matter in which they are no more interested than any other sect, and can only be considered as a piece of advice, which it is not customary to refer to a committee, but if it is supposed to pray for what they think a moral purpose, is that sufficient to induce us to commit it? What may appear a moral virtue in their eyes, may not be so in reality. I have heard of a sect of Shaking Quakers, who, I presume, suppose their tenets of a moral tendency. I am informed one of them forbids to intermarry, yet you may see them with a numerous offspring about them. Now, if these people were to petition Congress to pass a law prohibiting matrimony, would gentlemen agree to refer such a petition? I think if they would reject one of that nature, as improper, they ought also to reject this.

Mr. PAGE was in favor of the commitment. He hoped that the designs of the respectable memorialists would not be stopped at the threshold, in order to preclude a fair discussion of the prayer of the memorial. He observed, that gentlemen had founded their arguments upon a misrepresentation; for the object of the memorial is not declared to be the total abolition of the slave trade; but that Congress will consider whether it be not in reality within their power to exercise justice and mercy, which, if adhered to, they cannot doubt must produce the abolition of the slave trade. If, then, the prayer contained nothing unconstitutional, he trusted the meritorious effort would not be frustrated.

With respect to the alarm that was apprehended, he conjectured there was none; but there might be just cause if the memorial was not taken into consideration. He placed himself in the case of a slave, and said, that, on hearing that Congress had refused to listen to the decent suggestions of a respectable part of the community, he should infer that the General Government (from which was expected great good would result to every class of citizens) had shut their ears against the voice of humanity, and he should despair of any alleviation of the miseries he and his posterity had in prospect; if any thing could induce him to rebel, it must be a stroke like this, impressing on his mind all the horrors of despair. But if he was told that application was made in his behalf, and that Congress was willing to hear what could be urged in favor of discouraging the practice of importing his fellow-wretches, he would trust in their justice and humanity, and wait the decision patiently. He presumed that these unfortunate people would reason in the same way, and he, therefore, conceived the most likely way to prevent danger was to commit the petition. He lived in a State which had the misfortune of having in her bosom a great number of slaves; he held many of them himself, and was as much interested in the business, as any gentleman in South Carolina or Georgia, yet, if he was determined to hold them in eternal bondage, he should feel no uneasiness or alarm on account of the present measure, because he should rely upon the virtue of Congress that they would not exercise any unconstitutional authority.

Mr. MADISON.—The debate has taken a serious turn, and it will be owing to this alone if an alarm is created; for had the memorial been treated in the usual way, it would have been considered as a matter of course, and a report might have been made so as to have given general satisfaction.

If there was the slightest tendency by the commitment to break in upon the Constitution, he would object to it; but he did not see upon what ground such an event was to be apprehended. The petition prayed, in general terms, for the interference of Congress, so far as they were constitutionally authorized; but even if its prayer was in some degree, unconstitutional, it might be committed, as was the case on Mr. Churchman's petition, one part of which was supposed to apply for an unconstitutional interference by the General Government. He admitted, that Congress is restricted by the Constitution from taking measures to abolish the slave trade; yet there are a variety of ways by which it could countenance the abolition, and regulations might be made in relation to the introduction of them into the new States to be formed out of the Western Territory. He thought the object well worthy of consideration.

Mr. GERRY thought the interference of Congress fully compatible with the constitution, and could not help lamenting the miseries to which the natives of Africa were exposed by this inhuman commerce. He never contemplated the subject, without reflecting what his own feelings would be, in case himself, his children, or friends were placed in the same deplorable circumstances. He then adverted to the flagrant acts of cruelty which are committed in carrying on that traffic; and asked, whether it can be supposed that Congress has no power to prevent such abuses? He then referred to the Constitution, and pointed out the restrictions laid on the General Government respecting the importation of slaves. It was not, he presumed, in the contemplation of any gentleman in this House to violate that part of the Constitution; but that we have a right to regulate this business, is as clear as that we have any rights whatever; nor has the contrary been shown by any person who has spoken on the occasion. Congress can, agreeably to the Constitution, lay a duty of ten dollars on imported slaves; they may do this immediately. He made a calculation of the value of the slaves in the Southern States, and supposed they may be worth ten millions of dollars. Congress have a right, if they see proper, to make a proposal to the Southern States to purchase the whole of them, and their resources in the Western Territory might furnish them with the means: He did not intend to suggest a measure of this kind; he only instanced these particulars to show that Congress certainly has the right to intermeddle in the business. He thought that no objection had been offered of any force to prevent the commitment of the memorial.

Mr. BOUDINOT had carefully examined the petition and found nothing like what was complained of by gentlemen contained in it; he, therefore, hoped they would withdraw their opposition and suffer it to be committed.

Mr. SMITH, of South Carolina, said, that, as the petitioners had particularly prayed Congress to take measures for the annihilation of the slave trade; and as that was admitted, on all hands, to be beyond their power; and as the petitioners would not be gratified by a tax of ten dollars per head, which was all that was within their power, there was, of consequence, no occasion for committing it. . . .

Slave Trade Debates:
Report of the Special Committee
The House of Representatives, Mar. 23, 1790

The committee to whom were referred sundry memorials from the people called Quakers; and also a memorial from the Pennsylvania Society for promoting the Abolition of Slavery, submit the following report:

That from the nature of the matters contained in those memorials, they were induced to examine the powers vested in Congress, under the present constitution, relating to the abolition of slavery, and are clearly of opinion,

First. THAT the General Government is expressly restrained from prohibiting the importation of such persons "as any of the States now existing shall think proper to admit, until the year one thousand eight hundred and eight."

Secondly. THAT Congress, by a fair construction of the Constitution, are equally restrained from interfering in the emancipation of slaves, who already are, or who may, within the period mentioned, be imported into, or born within any of the said States.

Thirdly. THAT Congress have no authority to interfere in the internal regulations of particular States, relative to the instruction of slaves in the principles of morality and religion; to their comfortable cloathing, accommodations and subsistence; to the regulation of their marriages, and the prevention of the violation of the rights thereof, or to the separation of children from their parents; to a comfortable provision in cases of sickness, age or infirmity; or to the seizure, transportation or sale of free negroes; but have the fullest confidence in the wisdom and humanity of the Legislatures of the several States, that they will revise their laws from time to time, when necessary, and promote the objects mentioned in the memorials, and every other measure that may tend to the happiness of slaves.

Fourthly. THAT nevertheless Congress have authority, if they shall think it necessary, to lay at any time a tax or duty, not exceeding ten dollars for each person of any description, the importation of whom shall be by any of the States admitted as aforesaid.

Fifthly. THAT Congress have authority to interdict, or (so far as it is or may be carried on by citizens of the united States for supplying foreigners) to regulate the African trade, and to make provision for the humane treatment of slaves, in all cases while on their passage to the United States, or to foreign ports, as far as it respects the citizens of the United States.

Sixthly. THAT Congress have also authority to prohibit foreigners from fitting out vessels, in any port of the United States, for transporting persons from Africa to any foreign port.

Seventhly. THAT the memorialists be informed, that in all cases, to which the authority of Congress extends, they will exercise it for the humane objects of the memorialists, so far as they can be promoted on the principles of justice, humanity and good policy.

Slave Trade Debates: Report of the Committee of the Whole House

The House of Representatives, Mar. 23, 1790

The committee of the whole House, to whom was committed the report of the committee on the memorials of the people called Quakers, and of the Pennsylvania Society for promoting the Abolition of Slavery, report the following amendments:

STRIKE out the first clause, together with the recital thereto, and in lieu thereof insert, "That the migration or importation of such persons as any of the States now existing shall think proper to admit, cannot be prohibited by Congress, prior to the year one thousand eight hundred and eight."

Strike out the second and third clauses, and in lieu thereof insert, "That congress have no authority to interfere in the emancipation of slaves, or in the treatment of them within any of the States; it remaining with the several States alone to provide any regulations therein, which humanity and true policy may require."

Strike out the fourth and fifth clauses, and in lieu thereof insert, "That Congress have authority to restrain the citizens of the United States from carrying on the African trade, for the purpose of supplying foreigners with slaves, and of providing by proper regulations for the humane treatment, during their passage, of slaves imported by the said citizens into the states admitting such importation."

Strike out the seventh clause.

ORDERED, That the said report of the committee of the whole House do lie on the table. . . .

————

In the wake of this fiasco, the Quakers tried again to petition Congress to act to discourage slavery. They met with Representative James Madison (a slaveowner) about the question of congressional power to inhibit slavery under the new Constitution. After considering the question closely, Madison pronounced that under the Constitution "Congress has the power to suppress all immoralities." Rappleye, SONS OF PROVIDENCE at 295. The new government could, with Madison's blessing, take steps to curtail slavery. On March 22, 1794, the Senate approved a bill, already passed by the House, entitled "an Act to prohibit the carrying on of the slave trade from the United States to any foreign place or country" with substantial enforcement penalties. This bill was constitutional because it did not restrict the importation of slaves into the United States. President Washington (also a slaveowner) signed the bill into law the same day it passed Congress. And in 1807, President Jefferson (again, a slaveowner) signed into law an "Act to prohibit the importation of slaves into any port or place within the jurisdiction of the United States," which took effect at the earliest constitutionally allowed date. That same year, Parliament passed "An Act for the Abolition of the Slave Trade," and other nations of Europe soon did the same. (The slave trade continued, however, illegally.)

But the cotton gin was coming. It made slavery in the American South far more profitable than before, and the institution spread westward, eventually reaching as far as Texas. The opportunity for slavery to be checked in the early Republic had come and gone. The next chance to stop it would not come until the election of Abraham Lincoln in 1860—and the Civil War.

NOTES

1.   In 1820, Congress addressed the question of slavery in the territories with what was called the Missouri Compromise. An imaginary line was drawn across the North American continent, from the Atlantic Ocean going west along the northern edge of Maryland, the so-called Mason-Dixon Line. Slavery would be excluded from territories north of the line (except for Missouri itself, which was admitted as a slave state). This accord held until 1857 when the Supreme Court in *Dred Scott v. Sandford* said the

Missouri Compromise was unconstitutional because slave owners had a right to settle with their slaves in the Northern territories. *Dred Scott* made it impossible for the federal government to stop the spread of slavery anywhere, inflaming sectional tensions and leading to the Civil War. *Dred Scott* is presented on p. 733.

2.   Several participants in the slave trade debates were at pains to insist that the federal government had little power to ban slavery itself. Do you think they were right? Under the text and historical purpose of the Commerce Clause, the Necessary and Proper Clause, and the other enumerated powers in Article I (taxing? spending?), what could Congress do to eliminate slavery, if it wished to? What about under modern doctrine?

3.   Are these debates about slavery still relevant today? Does the fact that arguments about federalism were made to preserve slavery "taint" arguments about federalism today? Or do the Reconstruction Amendments make this moot?

4.   Consider more generally whether the original Constitution was a pro-slavery document. It was abolitionist William Lloyd Garrison who in 1844 called the Constitution "a covenant with death" and "an agreement with Hell" and publicly burned a copy of it—on the Fourth of July no less—in front of a huge crowd in Boston. (For Garrison's speech, see p. 1259.) Was Garrison right? The Constitution certainly contains compromises with the slave states that acknowledge the existence of slavery. Does it thus condone and protect slavery? Is its great moral defect its failure to eradicate slavery? The Constitution did put in place a national government of sufficient power to destroy the institution of slavery—but it also tilted the composition of that government in favor of stronger representation of the slaveholding states. Isn't it painful to see the framers' failure to do almost any of the things they could have done in the 1790s to more firmly put slavery on the road toward extinction?

5.   Many people think that the Constitution would never have been written without these compromises about slavery. If so, was it worth it?

[Assignment 36]

B.   THE FULL FAITH AND CREDIT AND PRIVILEGES AND IMMUNITIES CLAUSES

The most cited and discussed early case on Article IV is *Corfield v. Coryell*, 6 F.Cas. 546 (C.C.E.D. Pa. 1825), a Circuit Court opinion written by Supreme Court Justice Bushrod Washington. He was a nephew of the first president and the inheritor of his Mount Vernon estate, exclusive of a slave whom George Washington freed in his will.

This Article IV case is of huge importance because the framers of the Fourteenth Amendment, which has a Privileges *or* Immunities Clause, cited it repeatedly as evidence of what the fundamental civil rights (i.e., privileges and immunities) were that they meant the Fourteenth Amendment to protect from state action. Modern debates, such as the debate over whether the Constitution creates abortion rights, thus turn in part on the way Justice Washington memorialized the Privileges and Immunities Clause of Article IV. Unfortunately, for us, Justice Washington's opinion in *Corfield* is almost void for vagueness.

The facts of *Corfield* are picturesque: Some Pennsylvanians rented a boat and sailed it out of Philadelphia into the coastal waters of New Jersey, where they raked for clams in violation of a New Jersey law that restricted clam-raking in New Jersey waters to in-state residents. The penalty was $10 and forfeiture of the offenders' vessel, as well as the clams. In *Corfield*, the Philadelphia boat owner sued for trespass, seeking to get his boat back after the renters had lost it to New Jersey authorities. The plaintiff claimed (1) that the New Jersey law violated the Commerce Clause (on a dormant commerce theory); and (2) that the New Jersey law violated the Privileges and Immunities Clause. The court rejected both claims. With respect to the Privileges and Immunities Clause, Justice Washington had "no hesitation in confining these expressions to those privileges and immunities which are, in their nature, fundamental; which belong, of right, to the citizens of all free governments; and which have, at all times, been enjoyed by the citizens of the several states which compose this Union, from the time of their becoming free, independent and sovereign."

Thus, a state must accord out-of-staters only the "fundamental" privileges and immunities or civil rights of citizens. And just what are those? Justice Washington said it would be "more tedious than difficult" to list them, but then said they would fall

> under the following general heads: Protection by the government; the enjoyment of life and liberty, with the right to acquire and possess property of every kind, and to pursue and obtain happiness and safety; subject nevertheless to such restraints as the government may justly prescribe for the general good of the whole. The right of a citizen of one state to pass through, or to reside in any other state, for purposes of trade, agriculture, professional pursuits, or otherwise; to claim the benefit of the writ of habeas corpus; to institute and maintain actions of any kind in the courts of the state; to take, hold and dispose of property, either real or personal; and an exemption from higher taxes or impositions than are paid by the other citizens of the state; may be mentioned as some of the particular privileges and immunities of citizens, which are clearly embraced by the general description of privileges deemed to be fundamental: to which may be added, the elective franchise, as regulated and established by the laws or constitution of the state in which it is to be exercised. These, and many others which might be mentioned, are, strictly speaking, privileges and immunities, and the enjoyment of them by the citizens of each state, in every other state, was manifestly calculated (to use the expressions of the preamble of the corresponding provision in the old articles of confederation) "the better to secure and perpetuate mutual friendship and intercourse among the people of the different states of the Union."

What about the right to rake clams along the shore—or, at a higher level of generality, the right to share in state-owned property? Is that a "fundamental" privilege or immunity of citizenship, a civil right like the common law rights to own property and sue in contract or like civil rights under state constitutional law? Certainly not: "[W]e cannot accede to the proposition . . . [that] the citizens of the several states are permitted to participate in all the rights which belong exclusively to the citizens of any other particular state, merely upon the ground that they are enjoyed by those citizens; much less, that in regulating the use of the common property of the citizens of such state, the legislature is bound to extend to the citizens of all the other states the same advantages as are secured to their own citizens."

As noted above, *Corfield* became an influential decision decades later in our constitutional history. The Privileges and Immunities Clause (Comity Clause) of

Article IV was the model on which the Privileges *or* Immunities Clause of the Fourteenth Amendment was patterned, four decades later, after the Civil War. *Corfield* was cited by the amendment's congressional sponsors as central to their understanding of the meaning of this provision of the Fourteenth Amendment, suggesting that the meaning of the two provisions is closely related. We will return to that issue—and to *Corfield v. Coryell*—when considering the drafting of the Fourteenth Amendment (see p. 1269). You should know that *Corfield*'s iconic status to the framers of the Fourteenth Amendment is somewhat ironic because Justice Washington, like many Southern judges of his time, may have been eager to read the Privileges and Immunities Clause as narrowly as possible for fear that it might confer civil rights—such as the rights to speak, preach, and carry a firearm—on free black men and women who traveled to the South. Hence his desire to confine "Privileges and Immunities" to rights that are fundamental and that date back to 1776.

To return to the Privileges and Immunities Clause of Article IV, Section 2: Whatever the scope of the "privileges and immunities" or civil rights that a state must accord citizens of other states on the same terms as it gives such privileges to its own citizens, it is clear that out-of-staters do not carry *their* state's rights with them into another state: A Minnesota fishing license is not good in Wisconsin. Wisconsin has to accord Minnesotans only the ("fundamental") civil rights it accords Wisconsinites. The word *civil* is derived from the same Latin root as the words *citizen* and *city*. Civil rights are the rights of citizens. As noted above, they are often contrasted with the narrower category of so-called political rights like the right to vote, to run for office, or to serve on a jury. Behind the distinction is the idea that certain rights inhere not in the individual but in the polity, and can only be exercised by members of the polity and according to its customs. The Privileges and Immunities Clause was understood to bind the states to give out-of-staters equal civil rights, but not equal political rights.

A good illustration is the pre-Civil War case of *Lemmon v. The People*, presented below. The question was whether New York was required to recognize a Virginia family's Virginia-law right to own slaves, when that Virginia family traveled through New York en route to another state where slavery was permitted. The case raises questions concerning the meaning of the Full Faith and Credit Clause, the Privileges and Immunities Clause, and even the Commerce Clause.

What about the reverse of the *Lemmon* situation? A master takes his slave to "free soil" and lives there for several years. When he returns to a slave state, the slave sues for his freedom. Is the slave state obliged to apply the law of the free state? In *Scott v. Emerson*, 15 Mo. 576 (1852), the Missouri Supreme Court held that Missouri was permitted to apply Missouri law to determine the status of a Missouri resident as slave or free, in a Missouri court proceeding—at least in the absence of a judgment from a sister state awarding Scott his freedom. (In such a case, the Full Faith and Credit Clause would oblige Missouri to honor the sister-state judgment awarding Scott his freedom; and he would be entitled to return to Missouri as a free man, entitled to the privileges and immunities Missouri accorded its own citizens.) The Missouri decision in *Scott v. Emerson* was the first of two cases involving the slave Scott, eventually culminating in the Supreme Court's *Dred Scott* decision.

Lemmon v. The People

20 N.Y. 562 (1860)

[Two slaveowners, Jonathan and Juliet Lemmon, were traveling from Virginia to Texas with eight slaves. Strange as it may seem, the easiest route was to take a ship from Norfolk to New York and then take a larger ship from New York down the east coast and around to the Gulf of Mexico, to New Orleans, and proceed from there to Texas.—Editors]

On the 6th day of November, 1852, [while docked in New York harbor,] Louis Napoleon, a colored citizen of this State, made application . . . for a writ of *habeas corpus* to be directed to one Jonathan Lemmon and the keeper of house No. 3 Carlisle street, New York, requiring them to bring before said justice the bodies of eight colored persons, one man, two women and five children, who on the day preceding were confined and restrained of their liberty on board the steamer City of Richmond, in the harbor of New York, and were taken therefrom on the night of that day to No. 3 Carlisle street, and there detained under the pretence that they were slaves.

. . . Lemmon made a return to the writ under oath, in which he averred that the eight persons named were the slaves and property of Juliet Lemmon his wife, who had been the owner of such persons as slaves . . . under the Constitution and laws of Virginia: "that the said Juliet, with her said slaves, persons or property, is now *in transitu* or transit from the State of Virginia aforesaid to the State of Texas, the ultimate place of destination and another slaveholding State of the United States of America . . . that the said slaves, sailing from the port of Norfolk in the said State of Virginia, on board the steamship City of Richmond, never touched, landed nor came into the harbor or State of New York except for the mere purpose of passage and transit from the State of Virginia, aforesaid, to the State of Texas, aforesaid, and for no other purpose, intention, object or design whatever: that the said Juliet with her said slaves was compelled by necessity or accident to take passage in the steamship City of Richmond . . . for the State of Texas aforesaid, the ultimate place of destination." The return also denied any intention, on the part of Mrs. Lemmon or her husband, of selling the negroes.

To this return the relator orally interposed a general demurrer. Mr. Justice PAINE held the case under advisement until the 13th of November, 1852, when he discharged the colored Virginians. . . . *[Lemmon appealed to the intermediate appellate court, which affirmed, and then to this court.—Editors]*

■ DENIO, J.

. . . I understand the effect of these statements to be that Mrs. Lemmon, being the owner of these slaves, desired to take them from her residence in Norfolk to the State of Texas; and, as a means of effecting that purpose, she embarked . . . for New York, with a view to secure a passage from thence to her place of destination. As nothing is said of any stress of weather, and no marine casualty is mentioned, the necessity of landing, which is spoken of, refers, no doubt, to the exigency of that mode of prosecuting her journey. . . . The question to be decided is whether the bringing the slaves into this State under these circumstances entitled them to their freedom.

The intention, and the effect, of the statutes of this State bearing upon the point are very plain and unequivocal. By an act passed in 1817, it was declared that no person held as a slave should be imported, introduced or brought into this State on any pretence whatever, except [that] . . . "Any person, not being an inhabitant of this State, who shall be traveling to or from, or passing through this State, may bring with him any person lawfully held in slavery, and may take such person with him from this State; but the person so held in slavery shall not reside or continue in this State more than nine months; if such residence be continued beyond that time such person shall be free." In the year 1841, the Legislature repealed this section . . . [making freedom] absolute and unqualified. . . . [T]he meaning of the statute is as plain as though the Legislature had declared in terms that if any person should introduce a slave into this State, in the course of a journey to or from it, or in passing through it, the slave shall be free.

If, therefore, the Legislature had the constitutional power to enact this statute, the law of the State precisely meets the case of the persons who were brought before the judge on the writ of *habeas corpus*, and his order discharging them from constraint was unquestionably correct. Every sovereign State has a right to determine by its laws the condition of all persons who may at any time be within its jurisdiction; to exclude therefrom those whose introduction would contravene its policy, or to declare the conditions upon which they may be received, and what subordination or restraint may lawfully be allowed by one class or description of persons over another. Each State has, moreover, the right to enact such rules as it may see fit respecting the title to property, and to declare what subjects shall, within the State, possess the attributes of property, and what shall be incapable of a proprietary right. . . .

The power which has been mentioned as residing in the States is assumed by the Constitution itself to extend to persons held as slaves by such of the States as allow the condition of slavery. . . . The provision respecting the return of fugitives from service contains a very strong implication to that effect. It declares that no person held to service or labor in one State, under the laws thereof, escaping into another, shall in consequence of any law or regulation therein, be discharged from such service or labor, &c. . . . It was assumed by the authors of the Constitution, that the fact of a Federative Union would not of itself create a duty on the part of the States which should abolish slavery to respect the rights of the owners of slaves escaping thence from the States where it continued to exist. The apprehension was not that any of the States would establish rules or regulations looking primarily to the emancipation of fugitives from labor, but that the abolition of slavery in any State would draw after it the principle that a person held in slavery would immediately become free on arriving, in any manner, within the limits of such State.

. . . The aspect in which the case of fugitive slaves was presented to the authors of the Constitution therefore was this: A number of the States had very little interest in continuing the institution of slavery, and were likely soon to abolish it within their limits. When they should do so, the principle of the laws of England as to personal rights and the remedies for illegal imprisonment, would immediately prevail in such States. The judgment in Somerset's case and the principles announced by Lord MANSFIELD, were standing admonitions that even a temporary restraint of personal liberty by virtue of a title derived under the laws of slavery, could not be sustained where that institution did not exist by positive law. [Somerset's Case, *captioned* Somerset v. Stewart, *is presented at p. 1250.—Editors]* . . . This was not unreasonable, as the owner was free to determine whether he would voluntarily permit his slave to go within a jurisdiction which did not allow him to be held in bondage. That was within his own power, but he could not always prevent his slaves from escaping out of the State in which their servile condition was recognized. The provision was precisely suited to the exigency of the case, and it went no further.

In examining other arrangements of the Constitution, apparently inserted for purposes having no reference to slavery, we ought to bear in mind that when passing the fugitive slave provision the Convention was contemplating the future existence of States which should have abolished slavery, in a political union with other States where the institution would still remain in force. It would naturally be supposed that if there were other cases in which the rights of slave owners ought to be protected in the States which should abolish slavery, they would be adjusted in connection with the provision looking specially to that case, instead of being left to be deduced by construction from clauses intended primarily for cases to which slavery had no necessary relation. . . .

The Constitution declares that the citizens of each State shall be entitled to all privileges and immunities of citizens in the several States. (*Art.* 4, § 2.) No provision in that instrument has so strongly tended to constitute the citizens of the United States one people as this. . . . The question now to be considered is, how far the State jurisdiction . . . is restricted by the provision we are considering; or, to come at once to the precise point in controversy, whether it obliges the State governments to recognize, in any way, within their own jurisdiction, the property in slaves which the citizens of States in which slavery prevails may lawfully claim within their own States—beyond the case of fugitive slaves. The language is that they shall have the privileges and immunities of citizens in the several States. In my opinion the meaning is, that in a given State, every citizen of every other State shall have the same privileges and immunities—that is, the same rights—which the citizens of that State possess. . . . They can hold property by the same titles by which every other citizen may hold it, and by no other. . . . A citizen of Virginia, having his home in that State, and never having been within the State of New York, has the same rights under our laws which a native born citizen, domiciled elsewhere, would have, and no other rights. . . .

The position that a citizen carries with him, into every State into which he may go, the legal institutions of the one in which he was born, cannot be supported. . . .

The Legislature has declared, in effect, that no person shall bring a slave into this State, even in the course of a journey between two slaveholding States, and that if he does, the slave shall be free. Our own citizens are of course bound by this regulation. . . . [T]he [slave]owner cannot lawfully do anything which our laws do not permit to be done by one of our own citizens, and as a citizen of this State cannot bring a slave within its limits except under the condition that he shall immediately become free, the owner of these slaves could not do it without involving herself in the same consequences.

It remains to consider the effect upon this case of the provision by which power is given to Congress to regulate commerce among the several States. . . .

The act under consideration is not in any just sense a regulation of commerce. It does not suggest to me the idea that it has any connection with that subject. It would have an extensive operation altogether independent of commerce. . . . We will concede, for the purpose of the argument, that the transportation of slaves from one slaveholding State to another is an act of inter-state commerce, which may be legally protected and regulated by federal legislation. Acts have been passed to regulate the coasting trade, so that if these slaves had been *in transitu* between Virginia and Texas, in a coasting vessel, at the time the *habeas corpus* was served, they could not have been interfered with while passing through the navigable waters of a free State by the authority of a law of such State. But they were not thus in transit at that time. Congress has not passed any act to regulate commerce between the States when carried on by land, or otherwise than in coasting vessels. But conceding that, in order to facilitate commerce among the States, Congress has power to provide for precisely such a case as the present . . . the unexercised power to enact such a law, to regulate such a transit, would not affect the power of the States to deal with the *status* of all persons within their territory in the meantime, and before the existence of such a law. . . . Upon the whole case, I have come to the conclusion that there is nothing in the National Constitution or the laws of Congress to preclude the State judicial authorities from declaring these slaves thus introduced into the territory of this State, free, and setting them at liberty, according to the direction of the statute referred to. For the foregoing reasons, I am in favor of affirming the judgment of the Supreme Court.

■ WRIGHT, J., concurring.

. . . The question is one affecting the State in her sovereignty. As a sovereign State she may determine and regulate the *status* or social and civil condition of her citizens, and every description of persons within her territory. This power she possesses exclusively; and when she has declared or expressed her will in this respect, no authority or power from without can rightly interfere, except in the single instance of a slave escaping from a State of the Union into her territory; and in this, only because she has, by compact, yielded her right of sovereignty. . . .

The constitutional provision that "the citizens of each State shall be entitled to all the privileges and immunities of citizens in the several States" (*U.S. Const., art.* 4, § 2, subd. 1), is also invoked as having some bearing on the question of the appellant's right. I think this is the first occasion in the juridical history of the country that an attempt has been made to torture this provision into a guaranty of the right of a slave owner to bring his slaves into, and hold them for any purpose in, a non-slaveholding State. The provision was always understood as having but one design and meaning, viz., to secure to the citizens of every State, within every other, the privileges and immunities (whatever they might be) accorded in each to its own citizens. It was intended to guard against a State discriminating in favor of its own citizens. A citizen of Virginia coming into New York was to be entitled to all the privileges and immunities accorded to the citizens of New York. He was not to be received or treated as an alien or enemy in the particular sovereignty.

. . . The State has declared, through her Legislature, that the *status* of African slavery shall not exist, and her laws transform the slave into a freeman the instant he is brought voluntarily upon her soil. . . . She says, in effect, to the foreign slave owner, if you bring your slaves within the State, on any pretence whatever, neither by comity nor in any other way shall the municipal law let in and give place to the foreign law . . . and the persons before held as slaves shall stand upon her soil in their natural relations as men and as freemen. . . . It is the *status*, the unjust and unnatural relation, which the policy of the State aims to suppress, and her policy fails, at least in part, if the *status* be upheld at all. . . .

■ DAVIES, BACON and WELLES, JS., concurred.

■ CLERKE, J. (Dissenting.)

. . . Whether slavery is agreeable or in opposition to the law of nature; whether it is morally right or wrong; whether it is expedient or inexpedient; whether the African race are adapted, by their physical and moral organization, only to this condition; whether they can be induced to labor only by compulsion; whether the fairest and most fertile portions of the earth—those lying near and within the tropical zones—can alone be cultivated to any extent by that race, and whether, if without their labor, therefore, this large portion of the globe will, contrary to the manifest design of the Creator, continue or become a sterile waste, are questions very interesting within the domain of theology, or ethics, or political economy, but totally inappropriate to the discussion of the purely legal questions now presented for our consideration. Those questions are, 1st, whether the Legislature of this State has declared that all slaves brought by their masters into this State, under any circumstances whatever, even for a moment, shall be free; and 2d, if it has so declared, had it the constitutional power to do so.

1.   The act passed in 1817 . . . allows a person, not an inhabitant of this State, traveling to or from, or passing through this State, to bring his slave here and take him away again; but if the slave continues here more than nine months, he shall be free. These exceptions were repealed by an act passed May 25, 1841. . . . [T]he language of the acts referred to is too plain to admit of any doubt of that intent. It evidently intended to declare that all slaves voluntarily brought into this State, under any circumstances whatever, should become instantly free.

2.   But it is a question of much greater difficulty, whether the Legislature had the constitutional power to do so.

New York is a member of a confederacy of free and sovereign States, united for certain specific and limited purposes, under a solemn written covenant. And this covenant not only establishes a confederacy of States, but also, in regard to its most material functions, it gives this confederacy the character of a homogeneous national government. The Constitution is not alone federal or alone national; but, by the almost divine wisdom which presided over its formation, while its framers desired to preserve the independence and sovereignty of each State within the sphere of ordinary domestic legislation, yet they evidently designed to incorporate this people into one nation, not only in its character as a member of the great family of nations, but also in the internal, moral, social and political effect of the Union upon the people themselves. It was essential to this grand design that there should be as free and as uninterrupted an intercommunication between the inhabitants and citizens of the different States, as between the inhabitants and citizens of the same State. The people of the United States, therefore, "in order to form a more perfect union" than had existed under the old Confederacy, declare and provide, among other things in the Constitution under which we have now the privilege of living, that Congress (alone) shall have power to regulate commerce among the several States . . . that full faith or credit shall be given in each State to the public acts, records and judicial proceedings of every other State, and that citizens of each State shall be entitled to all the privileges and immunities of citizens in the several States. The people, in adopting this Constitution, declare in its very preamble that they intended to form a more perfect union than had bound them under the old Articles of Confederation. . . .

Most assuredly, the people who adopted the present Constitution did not intend that the intercourse between the people of the different States should be more limited or restricted than the States, in their corporate capacity, provided in the Articles of Confederation. . . .

Is it consistent with this purpose of perfect union, and perfect and unrestricted intercourse, that property which the citizen of one State brings into another State, for the purpose of passing through it to a State where he intends to take up his residence, shall be confiscated in the State through which he is passing, or shall be declared to be no property, and liberated from his control? . . . By the law of nations, the citizens of one government have a right of passage through the territory of another, peaceably, for business or pleasure; and the latter acquires no right over such person or his property. This privilege is yielded between foreign nations towards each other without any express compact. It is a principle of the unwritten law of nations.

Of course this principle is much more imperative on the several States than between foreign nations in their relations towards each other. For it can be clearly deduced, as we have seen, from the compact on which their union is based. Therefore, making this principle of the law of nations applicable to the compact which exists between the several States, we say, that the citizens of any one State have a right of passage through the territory of another, peaceably, for business or pleasure; and the latter acquires no right over such person or his property. . . .

The error into which the judge who decided this case in the first instance fell, consisted in supposing, because the law of nations refused to recognize slaves as property, the several States of this Union were at liberty to do the same; forgetting that the compact, by which the latter are governed in their relation towards each other, modifies the law of nations in this respect; and while each particular State is at liberty to abolish or retain slavery in reference to its own inhabitants and within its own borders, as its sense of right or expediency may dictate, it is not permitted in its dealings or intercourse with other States or their inhabitants to ignore the right to property in the labor and service of persons in transitu from those States. The Supreme Court having fallen into the same error, their order should be reversed. . . .

[Brief statements by Chief Justice Comstock and Justice Selden indicated that neither one had been able to give the case, as the chief justice put it, "the attention which its importance might justify." Nevertheless, Chief Justice Comstock joined, and Justice Selden expressed sympathy with, the dissent.—Editors]

NOTES

1.   *Lemmon* is a famous and fascinating case, widely believed to have been headed for the U.S. Supreme Court—and feared by anti-slavery advocates (including Abraham Lincoln) to be a potential "Second *Dred Scott*" decision, in which the Supreme Court might make slavery *national*, by forbidding Northern states to exclude slavery within their territorial limits. *Lemmon* was decided by the New York Court of Appeals (the state's highest court) in 1860. Lincoln was elected president later that year, and in April 1861 the South fired on Fort Sumter, launching the Civil War. *Lemmon* never reached the Supreme Court, and the question of whether it would be a "Second *Dred Scott*" was, of course, overtaken by other events.

2.   Was *Lemmon* rightly or wrongly decided, as a matter of U.S. constitutional law? The case raised three main constitutional questions: First, did the Full Faith and Credit Clause of Article IV require New York courts to apply Virginia law to the question of the legal status (slave versus free) of the slaves temporarily present in New York? Second, did the Privileges and Immunities Clause of Article IV require that New York recognize the property rights of the Lemmons in their slaves, in New York, by according them the same rights they possessed in Virginia? Third, did New York's law interfere with commerce among the states and thereby violate an implied constitutional prohibition on such a state law, resulting from the grant to Congress of the power to regulate interstate commerce (a "dormant Commerce Clause" issue)? What were the court's answers? Were they correct?

On the dormant Commerce Clause issue, Justice Wright noted the Court's decision in *Groves v. Slaughter*, 40 U.S. (15 Pet.) 449 (1841), which considered whether a Mississippi constitutional provision forbidding the importation of slaves into the state for sale interfered with interstate commerce. The majority opinion in *Groves* sidestepped the issue by construing the state constitutional provision as not self-executing. Justice McLean's concurrence found that slaves were persons, not articles of commerce—and so not subject to Congress's power over commerce. Chief Justice Taney's concurrence in *Groves* held that slavery was purely a matter of state law and that "the action of the several States upon this subject[ ] cannot be controlled by Congress, either by virtue of its power to regulate commerce, or by virtue of any other power[.]" Justice Baldwin argued that interstate trade in slavery was subject to national power and that "wherever slavery exists, by the laws of a state, slaves are property in every constitutional sense, and for every purpose" so that states could not interfere with interstate commerce in such property if their own laws recognized slaves as property. Is *Groves* relevant to the issues in *Lemmon*?

3.   Consider *Lemmon* in variation: A family brings its slaves from a slave state to a free state, but *returns to the slave state* with its slaves, without the free state having taken any legal action. Is *Virginia* bound to apply *New York* law and declare the slaves free? Or is it as free to apply its own law as New York was, in *Lemmon*, to apply its? (Wouldn't your answer be different if New York *had* rendered a decision in favor of freedom, and the family returned to Virginia with their slaves in any event?) Interestingly, this fact variation is almost *exactly* the situation presented by the *Dred Scott* case, and the Missouri Supreme Court, in the first round of that litigation (*Scott v. Emerson*), held that Missouri was not obliged to apply the law of free-state Illinois or of free-territory Minnesota, where Captain Emerson had traveled with his slave, Dred Scott.

4.   The Supreme Court has permitted states a broad berth in deciding to apply their own law, rather than another state's laws, under the Full Faith and Credit Clause and the Due Process Clause. A leading case is *Allstate Insurance Co. v. Hague*, 449 U.S. 302 (1981). A Wisconsin resident, insured by Allstate in Wisconsin, was hit and killed in Wisconsin by an uninsured Wisconsin driver. His Wisconsin widow moves to Minnesota and sues in Minnesota court. May Minnesota courts constitutionally choose to apply Minnesota law (which permitted triple the recovery on these facts) or are they required to apply Wisconsin law? The Minnesota Supreme Court held that its state's multi-factor choice-of-law rules permitted it to apply Minnesota law—with the tipping factor being that Minnesota had the "better law." Allstate appealed to the U.S. Supreme Court, arguing that this violated the Full Faith and Credit Clause. The Court ruled for the widow, a plurality holding that a state could choose to apply its own substantive law as long as there were "a significant contact or significant aggregation of contacts, creating

state interests, such that [the state's] choice of law is neither arbitrary nor unfair"—and that the widow's new residence in Minnesota was sufficient. The full Court embraced this generous constitutional standard in *Phillips Petroleum Co. v. Shutts*, 472 U.S. 797 (1985). Is this right? Is there an alternative, principled standard for applying the Full Faith and Credit Clause?

5.   Modern cases continue to apply the general principle that states may not discriminate against out-of-state citizens, except with respect to political rights and state resources which are jointly owned by in-state citizens. In *Hicklin v. Orbeck*, 437 U.S. 518 (1978), the Court struck down "Alaska Hire," a state law providing an absolute preference for Alaska residents over out-of-staters for employment in connection with "oil and gas leases, easements . . . for oil or gas pipeline purposes . . . or any renegotiation of any of the preceding to which the state is a party[.]" This law clearly gave out-of-staters different civil rights to make contracts from the civil rights enjoyed by Alaskans. Justice Brennan's opinion for the Court quoted *Paul v. Virginia*, 75 U.S. (8 Wall.) 168, 180 (1869), as aptly stating the purpose of the Privileges and Immunities Clause:

> To place the citizens of each State upon the same footing with citizens of other States, so far as the advantages resulting from citizenship in those States are concerned. It relieves them from the disabilities of alienage in other States; it inhibits discriminating legislation against them by other States; it gives them the right of free ingress into other States, and egress from them; it insures to them in other States the same freedom possessed by the citizens of those States in the acquisition and enjoyment of property and in the pursuit of happiness; and it secures to them in other States the equal protection of their laws. It has been justly said that no provision in the Constitution has tended so strongly to constitute the citizens of the United States one people as this.

Alaska contended that oil and gas were resources of the state—state property—and that the state could give preference to its own citizens with respect to benefits derived from these property resources. (Recall *Corfield v. Coryell*, with respect to New Jersey's exclusion from Pennsylvanians from clam-raking on New Jersey shores.) The Court rejected the argument: "We do not agree that the fact that a State owns a resource, of itself, completely removes a law concerning that resource from the prohibitions of the Clause." The reason was "that Alaska has little or no proprietary interest in much of the activity swept within the ambit of Alaska Hire; and the connection of the State's oil and gas with much of the covered activity is sufficiently attenuated so that it cannot justifiably be the basis for requiring private employers to discriminate against nonresidents."

Hicklin has not been the modern Court's last word in this area. In *United Building & Construction Trades Council v. Mayor and Council of Camden*, 465 U.S. 208 (1984), the Court considered a Camden, New Jersey ordinance requiring that at least 40% of the employees of contractors and subcontractors working on city construction projects be Camden residents. Justice Rehnquist's majority opinion quoted earlier cases noting that, "like many other constitutional provisions, the privileges and immunities clause is not an absolute," and that "state should have considerable leeway in analyzing local evils and in prescribing appropriate cures." But the Court found it "impossible to evaluate Camden's justification on the record as it now stands," and remanded the case for further findings. In *Supreme Court of New Hampshire v. Piper*, 470 U.S. 274 (1985), the Court struck down a New Hampshire action denying admission to the bar to a Vermont woman who lived 400 yards from the New Hampshire border as a violation of the Privileges and Immunities Clause, finding that none of the state's reasons for New Hampshire's residency requirement constituted a substantial reason justifying discrimination against nonresidents.

Finally, in the notable recent case of *Saenz v. Roe*, 526 U.S. 489 (1999), the Court relied in part on the Privileges and Immunities Clause of Article IV in support of a "right to travel"—"the right of the newly arrived citizen to the same privileges and immunities enjoyed by other citizens of the same State." The Court struck down a California statute providing lower welfare benefits to residents who had been in the state less than a year. The Court also relied on two clauses of the Fourteenth Amendment, the Citizenship Clause and the Privileges *or* Immunities Clause, as supporting a right to travel: all citizens of the United States "have the right to choose to be citizens 'of the State wherein they reside' " under Section One of the Fourteenth Amendment. "The States, however, do not have any right to select their citizens. The Fourteenth Amendment, like the Constitution itself, was, as Justice Cardozo put it, 'framed upon the theory that the peoples of the several states must sink or swim together; and that in the long run prosperity and salvation are in union and not division.' "

What is the right answer? What *are* "the privileges and immunities of citizens" of the states? Do you agree with *Corfield*'s formulation that the privileges and immunities included within the Article IV Clause are limited to "fundamental" privileges and immunities associated with "citizenship"? Does it make more sense to read the clause as protecting equal civil rights but not equal political rights or equal access to state property? What does this mean for the right of non-residents to practice law? (Technically, a state's lawyers are officers of the state courts, so maybe the right to practice law in a state is a political right, like jury service, about which a state may discriminate against out-of-staters.) What other things may a state give to in-staters but not out-of-staters, consistent with the Privileges and Immunities Clause? In answering these questions about the meaning of the clause, which types of constitutional argument are you relying on most?

C. THE FUGITIVE SLAVE AND FUGITIVE EXTRADITION CLAUSES

> *Art. IV, § 2: . . . No Person held to Service or Labour in one State, under the Laws thereof, escaping into another, shall, in Consequence of any Law or Regulation therein, be discharged from such Service or Labour, but shall be delivered up on Claim of the Party to whom such Service or Labour may be due.*

The Fugitive Slave Clause requires that any "persons held to service or labour" under the laws of one state—i.e., "slaves"—who escape to another state "shall be delivered up" on claim of the person to whom that service may be due. Does that clause, which imposes a duty on states, also give Congress legislative *power* to enforce the duty by legislation? Does that clause bar all state laws providing for due process or jury trial, or forbidding kidnapping in the recovery of alleged slaves?

Prigg v. Pennsylvania (1842) is a gut-wrenching case. Edward Prigg, a professional "slavecatcher" travelled from Maryland to Pennsylvania to capture an alleged fugitive slave woman named Margaret. Margaret had at one time been owned by Marylander John Ashmore. Ashmore had allowed several of his slaves to live freely, and Margaret had married a free black man named James Morgan and moved to Pennsylvania, seemingly with her (former?) master's consent, if not explicit act of emancipation. While living in Pennsylvania, the couple had several children. Enter Prigg, the slavecatcher, acting on behalf of Ashmore's heirs. In defiance of a

Pennsylvania law that forbade "self-help" remedies, Prigg essentially kidnapped Margaret *and her children* in the middle of the night, lied to Margaret's husband as to their intentions, and then dragged them back to Maryland, where they apparently were sold to be slaves in the deep South, from which they could not be found or recovered. Pennsylvania prosecuted Prigg (who, interestingly, was delivered to Pennsylvania pursuant to the requirements of the Fugitive *Extradition* Clause). Prigg argued that Pennsylvania's law was unconstitutional.

Prigg v. Pennsylvania
41 U.S. (16 Pet.) 539 (1842)

[Prigg was indicted by Pennsylvania for violating a state law that made it a felony to recapture an alleged fugitive slave by force. Prigg pleaded not guilty, on the ground that he was acting on behalf of the Ashmore family. The Pennsylvania court found him guilty, and he appealed to the U.S. Supreme Court.—Editors]

■ STORY, J.

Few questions which have ever come before this court involve more delicate and important considerations; and few upon which the public at large may be presumed to feel a more profound and pervading interest.

Before, however, we proceed to the points more immediately before us, it may be well, in order to clear the case of difficulty, to say, that in the exposition of this part of the constitution, we shall limit ourselves to those considerations which appropriately and exclusively belong to it, without laying down any rules of interpretation of a more general nature. It will, indeed, probably, be found, when we look to the character of the constitution itself, the objects which it seeks to attain, the powers which it confers, the duties which it enjoins, and the rights which it secures, as well as the known historical fact, that many of its provisions were matters of compromise of opposing interests and opinions, that no uniform rule of interpretation can be applied to it, which may not allow, even if it does not positively demand, many modifications, in its actual application to particular clauses. And, perhaps, the safest rule of interpretation, after all, will be found to be to look to the nature and objects of the particular powers, duties and rights, with all the lights and aids of contemporary history; and to give to the words of each just such operation and force, consistent with their legitimate meaning, as may fairly secure and attain the ends proposed.

There are two clauses in the constitution upon the subject of fugitives, which stand in juxtaposition with each other, and have been thought mutually to illustrate each other. They are both contained in the second section of the fourth article, and are in the following words: "A person charged in any state with treason, felony or other crime, who shall flee from justice, and be found in another state, shall, on demand of the executive authority of the state from which he fled, be delivered up, to be removed to the state having jurisdiction of the crime." "No person held to service or labor in one state, under the laws thereof, escaping into another, shall, in consequence of any law or regulation therein, be discharged from such service or labor; but shall be delivered up, on claim of the party to whom such service or labor may be due."

The last clause is that, the true interpretation whereof is directly in judgment before us. Historically, it is well known, that the object of this clause was to secure to the citizens of the slave-holding states the complete right and title of ownership in their slaves, as property, in every state in the Union into which they might escape from the state where they were held in servitude. The full recognition of this right and title was indispensable to the security of this species of property in all the slave-holding states; and, indeed, was so vital to the preservation of their domestic interests and institutions, that it cannot be doubted, that it constituted a fundamental article, without the adoption of which the Union could not have been formed. Its true design was, to guard against the doctrines and principles prevalent in the non-slave-holding states, by preventing them from intermeddling with, or obstructing, or abolishing the rights of the owners of slaves.

By the general law of nations, no nation is bound to recognise the state of slavery, as to foreign slaves found within its territorial dominions, when it is in opposition to its own policy and institutions, in favor of the subjects of other nations where slavery is recognised. If it does it, it is as a matter of comity, and not as a matter of international right. The state of slavery is deemed to be a mere municipal regulation, founded upon and limited to the range of the territorial laws. . . . It is manifest, from this consideration, that if the constitution had not contained this clause, every non-slave-holding state in the Union would have been at liberty to have declared free all runaway slaves coming within its limits, and to have given them entire immunity and protection against the claims of their masters; a course which would have created the most bitter animosities, and engendered perpetual strife between the different states. The clause was, therefore, of the last importance to the safety and security of the southern states, and could not have been surrendered by them, without endangering their whole property in slaves. The clause was accordingly adopted into the constitution, by the unanimous consent of the framers of it; a proof at once of its intrinsic and practical necessity.

How, then, are we to interpret the language of the clause? The true answer is, in such a manner as, consistently with the words, shall fully and completely effectuate the whole objects of it. If, by one mode of interpretation, the right must become shadowy and unsubstantial, and without any remedial power adequate to the end, and by another mode, it will attain its just end and secure its manifest purpose, it would seem, upon principles of reasoning, absolutely irresistible, that the latter ought to prevail. No court of justice can be authorized so to construe any clause of the constitution as to defeat its obvious ends, when another construction, equally accordant with the words and sense thereof, will enforce and protect them.

The clause manifestly contemplates the existence of a positive, unqualified right on the part of the owner of the slave, which no state law or regulation can in any way qualify, regulate, control or restrain. The slave is not to be discharged from service or labor, in consequence of any state law or regulation. Now, certainly, without indulging in any nicety of criticism upon words, it may fairly and reasonably be said, that any state law or state regulation, which interrupts, limits, delays or postpones the right of the owner to the immediate possession of the slave, and the immediate command of his service and labor, operates, *pro tanto*, a discharge of the slave therefrom. The question can never be, how much the slave is discharged from; but whether he is discharged from any, by the natural or necessary operation of state laws or state regulations. The question is not one of quantity or degree, but of withholding or controlling the incidents of a positive and absolute right.

. . . We have not the slightest hesitation in holding, that under and in virtue of the constitution, the owner of a slave is clothed with entire authority, in every state in the Union, to seize and recapture his slave, whenever he can do it, without any breach of the peace or any illegal violence. In this sense, and to this extent, this clause of the constitution may properly be said to execute itself, and to require no aid from legislation, state or national.

But the clause of the constitution does not stop here; nor, indeed, consistently with its professed objects, could it do so. Many cases must arise, in which, if the remedy of the owner were confined to the mere right of seizure and recaption, he would be utterly without any adequate redress. He may not be able to lay his hands upon the slave. He may not be able to enforce his rights against persons, who either secrete or conceal, or withhold the slave. He may be restricted by local legislation, as to the mode of proofs of his ownership; as to the courts in which he shall sue, and as to the actions which he may bring; or the process be may use to compel the delivery of the slave. Nay! the local legislation may be utterly inadequate to furnish the appropriate redress, . . . and this may be innocently as well as designedly done, since every state is perfectly competent, and has the exclusive right, to prescribe the remedies in its own judicial tribunals, to limit the time as well as the mode of redress, and to deny jurisdiction over cases, which its own policy and its own institutions either prohibit or discountenance. If, therefore, the clause of the constitution had stopped at the mere recognition of the right, without providing or contemplating any means by which it might be established and enforced, in cases where it did not execute itself, it is plain, that it would have been, in a great variety of cases, a delusive and empty annunciation. . . .

And this leads us to the consideration of the other part of the clause, which implies at once a guarantee and duty. It says, "but he (the slave) shall be delivered up, on claim of the party to whom such service or labor may be due." Now, we think it exceedingly difficult, if not impracticable, to read this language, and not to feel, that it contemplated some further remedial redress than that which might be administered at the hands of the owner himself. . . . If, indeed, the constitution guaranties the right, and if it requires the delivery upon the claim of the owner (as cannot well be doubted), the natural inference certainly is, that the national government is clothed with the appropriate authority and functions to enforce it. The fundamental principle, applicable to all cases of this sort, would seem to be, that where the end is required, the means are given; and where the duty is enjoined, the ability to perform it is contemplated to exist, on the part of the functionaries to whom it is intrusted. The clause is found in the national constitution, and not in that of any state. It does not point out any state functionaries, or any state action, to carry its provisions into effect. The states cannot, therefore, be compelled to enforce them; and it might well be deemed an unconstitutional exercise of the power of interpretation, to insist, that the states are bound to provide means to carry into effect the duties of the national government, nowhere delegated or intrusted to them by the constitution. On the contrary, the natural, if not the necessary, conclusion is, that the national government, in the absence of all positive provisions to the contrary, is bound, through its own proper departments, legislative, judicial or executive, as the case may require, to carry into effect all the rights and duties imposed upon it by the constitution. It is plain, then, that where a claim is made by the owner, out of possession, for the delivery of a slave, it must be made, if at all, against some other person; and inasmuch as the right is a right of property, capable of being recognized and asserted by proceedings before a court of justice, between parties adverse to each other, it constitutes, in the strictest sense, a controversy between the parties, and a case "arising under the constitution" of the United States, within the express delegation of judicial power given by that instrument. Congress, then, may call that power into activity, for the very purpose of giving effect to that right; and if so, then it may prescribe the mode and extent in which it shall be applied, and how, and under what circumstances, the proceedings shall afford a complete protection and guarantee to the right.

Congress has taken this very view of the power and duty of the national government. As early as the year 1791, the attention of congress was drawn to it (as we shall hereafter more fully see), in consequence of some practical difficulties arising under the other clause, respecting fugitives from justice escaping into other states. The result of their deliberations was the passage of the act of the 12th of February 1793, ch. 51, which, after having, in the first and second sections, provided by the case of fugitives from justice, by a demand to be made of the delivery, through the executive authority of the state where they are found, proceeds, in the third section, to provide, that when a person held to labor or service in any of the United States, shall escape into any other of the states or territories, the person to whom such labor or service may be due, his agent or attorney, is hereby empowered to seize or arrest such fugitive from labor, and take him or her before any judge of the circuit or district courts of the United States, residing or being within the state, or before any magistrate of a county, city or town corporate, wherein such seizure or arrest shall be made; and upon proof, to the satisfaction of such judge or magistrate, . . . to give a certificate thereof to such claimant, his agent or attorney, which shall be sufficient warrant for removing the said fugitive from labor, to the state or territory from which he or she fled. The fourth section provides a penalty against any person, who shall knowingly and willingly obstruct or hinder such claimant, his agent or attorney, in so seizing or arresting such fugitive from labor, or rescue such fugitive from the claimant, or his agent or attorney, when so arrested, or who shall harbor or conceal such fugitive, after notice that he is such; and it also saves to the person claiming such labor or service, his right of action for or on account of such injuries.

In a general sense, this act may be truly said to cover the whole ground of the constitution, both as to fugitives from justice, and fugitive slaves . . . because it points out fully all the modes of attaining those objects, which congress, in their discretion, have as yet deemed expedient or proper to meet the exigencies of the constitution. If this be so, then it would seem, upon just principles of construction, that the legislation of congress, if constitutional, must supersede all state legislation upon the same subject; and by necessary implication prohibit it. For, if congress have a constitutional power to regulate a particular subject, and they do actually regulate it in a given manner, and in a certain form, it cannot be, that the state legislatures have a right to interfere, . . . In such a case, the legislation of congress, in what it does prescribe, manifestly indicates, that it does not intend that there shall be any further legislation to act upon the subject-matter. Its silence as to what it does not do, is as expressive of what its intention is, as the direct provisions made by it. . . . [W]here congress have exercised a power over a particular subject given them by the constitution, it is not competent for state legislation to add to the provisions of congress upon that subject; for that the will of congress upon the whole subject is as clearly established by what it has not declared, as by what it has expressed.

But it has been argued, that the act of congress is unconstitutional, because it does not fall within the scope of any of the enumerated powers of legislation confided to that body; and therefore, it is void. Stripped of its artificial and technical structure, the argument comes to this, that although rights are exclusively secured by, or duties are exclusively imposed upon, the national government, yet, unless the power to enforce these rights or to execute these duties, can be found among the express powers of legislation enumerated in the constitution, they remain without any means of giving them effect by any act of congress; and they must operate solely *proprio vigore*, however defective may be their operation; nay! even although, in a practical sense, they may become a nullity, from the want of a proper remedy to enforce them, or to provide against their violation. If this be the true interpretation of the constitution, it must, in a great measure, fail to attain many of its avowed and positive objects, as a security of rights, and recognition of duties. Such a limited construction of the constitution has never yet been adopted as correct, either in theory or practice. No one has ever supposed that congress could, constitutionally, by its legislation, exercise powers, or enact laws, beyond the powers delegated to it by the constitution. But it has, on various occasions, exercised powers which were necessary and proper as means to carry into effect rights expressly given, and duties expressly enjoined thereby. The end being required, it has been deemed a just and necessary implication, that the means to accomplish it are given also; or, in other words, that the power flows as a necessary means to accomplish the end.

. . . [The] nature of the provision and the objects to be attained by it, require that it should be controlled by one and the same will, and act uniformly by the same system of regulations throughout the Union. If, then, the states have a right, in the absence of legislation by congress, to act upon the subject, each state is at liberty to prescribe just such regulations as suit its own policy, local convenience and local feelings. The legislation of one state may not only be different from, but utterly repugnant to and incompatible with, that of another.

It is scarcely conceivable, that the slave-holding states would have been satisfied with leaving to the legislation of the non-slave-holding states, a power of regulation, in the absence of that of congress, which would or might practically amount to a power to destroy the rights of the owner. If the argument, therefore, of a concurrent power in the states to act upon the subject-matter, in the absence of legislation by congress, be well founded; then, if congress had never acted at all, or if the act of congress should be repealed, without providing a substitute, there would be a resulting authority in each of the states to regulate the whole subject, at its pleasure, and to dole out its own remedial justice, or withhold it, at its pleasure, and according to its own views of policy and expediency. Surely, such a state of things never could have been intended, under such a solemn guarantee of right and duty. On the other hand, construe the right of legislation as exclusive in congress, and every evil and every danger vanishes. The right and the duty are then co-extensive and uniform in remedy and operation throughout the whole Union.

These are some of the reasons, but by no means all, upon which we hold the power of legislation on this subject to be exclusive in congress. To guard, however, against any possible misconstruction of our views, it is proper to state, that we are by no means to be understood, in any manner whatsoever, to doubt or to interfere with the police power belonging to the states, in virtue of their general sovereignty. That police power extends over all subjects within territorial limits of the states, and has never been conceded to the United States. It is wholly distinguishable from the right and duty secured by the provision now under consideration; which is exclusively derived from and secured by the constitution of the United States, and owes its whole efficacy thereto. We entertain no doubt whatsoever, that the states, in virtue of their general police power, possesses full jurisdiction to arrest and restrain runaway slaves, and remove them from their borders, and otherwise to secure themselves against their depredations and evil example, as they certainly may do in cases of idlers, vagabonds and paupers. The rights of the owners of fugitive slaves are in no just sense interfered with, or regulated, by such a course; and in many cases, the operations of this police power, although designed generally for other purposes, for protection, safety and peace of the state, may essentially promote and aid the interests of the owners. But such regulations can never be permitted to interfere with, or to obstruct, the just rights of the owner to reclaim his slave, derived from the constitution of the United States, or with the remedies prescribed by congress to aid and enforce the same.

Upon these grounds, we are of opinion, that the act of Pennsylvania upon which this indictment is founded, is unconstitutional and void. It purports to punish as a public offence against that state, the very act of seizing and removing a slave, by his master, which the constitution of the United States was designed to justify and uphold. The special verdict finds this fact, and the state courts have rendered judgment against the plaintiff in error upon that verdict. That judgment must, therefore, be reversed, and the cause remanded to the supreme court of Pennsylvania, with directions to carry into effect the judgment of this court rendered upon the special verdict, in favor of the plaintiff in error.

■ TANEY, CHIEF JUSTICE, concurring.

. . . The opinion of the court maintains, that the power over this subject is so exclusively vested in congress, that no state, since the adoption of the constitution, can pass any law in relation to it. In other words, according to the opinion just delivered, the state authorities are prohibited from interfering, for the purpose of protecting the right of the master, and aiding him in the recovery of his property. I think, the states are not prohibited; and that, on the contrary, it is enjoined upon them as a duty, to protect and support the owner, when he is endeavoring to obtain possession of his property found within their respective territories. The language used in the constitution does not, in my judgment, justify this construction given to it by the court. It contains no words prohibiting the several states from passing laws to enforce this right. They are, in express terms, forbidden to make any regulation that shall impair it; but there the prohibition stops. And according to the settled rules of construction for all written instruments, the prohibition being confined to laws injurious to the right, the power to pass laws to support and enforce it, is necessarily implied. And the words of the article which direct that the fugitive "shall be delivered up," seem evidently designed to impose it as a duty upon the people of the several states, to pass laws to carry into execution, in good faith, the compact into which they thus solemnly entered with each other. . . .

I dissent, therefore, upon these grounds, from that part of the opinion of the court which denies the obligation and the right of the state authorities to protect the master, when he is endeavoring to seize a fugitive from his service, in pursuance of the right given to him by the constitution of the United States; provided the state law is not in conflict with the remedy provided by congress.

■ McLean, Justice, dissenting.

As this case involves questions deeply interesting, if not vital, to the permanency of the Union of these states; and as I differ on one point from the opinion of the court, I deem it proper to state my own views on the subject.

The plaintiff, Edward Prigg, was indicted under the first section of an act of Pennsylvania, entitled "an act to give effect to the provisions of the constitution of the United States, relative to fugitives from labor, for the protection of free people of color, and to prevent kidnapping." It provides, "if any person or persons shall, from and after the passing of this act, by force and violence, take and carry away, or cause to be taken or carried away, and shall, by fraud or false pretence seduce, or cause to be seduced, or shall attempt to take, carry away or seduce, any negro or mulatto, from any part or parts of this commonwealth, to any other place or places whatsoever, out of this commonwealth, with a design and intention of selling and disposing of, or of causing to be sold, or of keeping and detaining, or of causing to be kept and detained, such negro or mulatto, as a slave or servant for life, or for any term whatsoever; every such person or persons, his or their aiders or abettors, shall, on conviction thereof, be deemed guilty of felony, and shall be fined in a sum not less than five hundred nor more than one thousand dollars, and shall be sentenced to imprisonment and hard labor not less than seven nor more than twenty-one years."

The plaintiff, being a citizen of Maryland, with others, took Margaret Morgan, a colored woman, and a slave, by force and violence, without the certificate required by the act of congress, from the state of Pennsylvania, and brought her to the state of Maryland. By an amicable arrangement between the two states, judgment was entered against the defendant, in the court where the indictment was found; and on the cause being removed to the supreme court of the state, that judgment, *pro forma*, was affirmed. And the case is now here for our examination and decision. . . .

Does the provision in regard to the reclamation of fugitive slaves, vest the power exclusively in the federal government? This must be determined from the language of the constitution, and the nature of the power. . . . The states are inhibited from passing "any law or regulation which shall discharge a fugitive slave from the service of his master"; and a positive duty is enjoined on them to deliver him up, "on claim of the party to whom his service may be due." . . . Under the confederation, the master had no legal means of enforcing his rights, in a state opposed to slavery. A disregard of rights thus asserted was deeply felt in the south; it produced great excitement, and would have led to results destructive of the Union. To avoid this, the constitutional guarantee was essential. The necessity for this provision was found in the views and feelings of the people of the states opposed to slavery; and who, under such an influence, could not be expected favorably to regard the rights of the master. . . .

It is contended, that the power to execute it rests with the states. The law was designed to protect the rights of the slave-holder against the states opposed to those rights; and yet, by this argument, the effective power is in the hands of those on whom it is to operate. This would produce a strange anomaly in the history of legislation; it would show an inexperience and folly in the venerable framers of the constitution, from which, of all public bodies that ever assembled, they were, perhaps, most exempt. . . . It is, therefore, essential to the uniform efficacy of his constitutional provision, that it should be considered exclusively a federal power. . . . The constitution provides that the fugitive from labor shall be delivered up, on claim being made by the person entitled to such labor; but it is silent as to how and on whom this claim shall be made; the act of congress provides for this defect and uncertainty, by establishing the mode of procedure.

. . . I come now to a most delicate and important inquiry in this case, and that is, whether the claimant of a fugitive from labor may seize and remove him by force, out of the state in which he may be found, in defiance of its laws. I refer not to laws which are in conflict with the constitution, or the act of 1793. Such state laws, I have already said, are void. But I have reference to those laws which regulate the police of the state, maintain the peace of its citizens, and preserve its territory and jurisdiction from acts of violence. . . . In my judgment, there is not the least foundation in the act for the right asserted in the argument, to take the fugitive by force and remove him out of the state.

Such a proceeding can receive no sanction under the act, for it is in express violation of it. The claimant having seized the fugitive, is required by the act, to take him before a federal judge within the state, or a state magistrate within the county, city or town corporate, within which the seizure was made. Now, can there be any pretence, that after the seizure under the statute, the claimant may disregard the other express provision of it, by taking the fugitive, without claim, out of the state. But it is said, the master may seize his slave wherever he finds him, if by doing so, he does not violate the public peace; that the relation of master and slave is not affected by the laws of the state, to which the slave may have fled, and where he is found. If the master has a right to seize and remove the slave, without claim, he can commit no breach of the peace, by using all the force necessary to accomplish his object. . . .

It is very clear, that no power to seize and forcibly remove the slave, without claim, is given by the act of congress. Can it be exercised under the constitution? Congress have legislated on the constitutional power, and have directed the mode in which it shall be executed. The act, it is admitted, covers the whole ground; and that it is constitutional, there seems to be no reason to doubt. Now, under such circumstances, can the provisions of the act be disregarded, and an assumed power set up under the constitution? This is believed to be wholly inadmissible by any known rule of construction. . . .

It appears, in the case under consideration, that the state magistrate before whom the fugitive was brought refused to act. In my judgment, he was bound to perform the duty required of him by a law paramount to any act, on the same subject, in his own state. But this refusal does not justify the subsequent action of the claimant; he should have taken the fugitive before a judge of the United States, two of whom resided within the state. . . .

NOTES

1.   The Fugitive Slave Clause plainly says that fugitive slaves must be "delivered up" on claim. But this leaves a few things up for grabs. On each of the following questions, what do you think is the legally right answer? And what answer is given to each question

by Justice Story's majority opinion, Chief Justice Taney's concurrence, Justice McLean's dissent?

First, does the Fugitive Slave Clause, of its own force, invalidate all state legislation, of any kind, that might affect the ability of slave owners to recapture their (alleged) fugitive slaves? Does it invalidate state laws providing for due process—for hearings as to the propriety of the claim of ownership? Does it invalidate state laws providing for jury trial of such claims? (Does it matter in this regard that local juries in some Northern states might never rule for slave owners?) Does the Fugitive Slave Clause, of its own force, invalidate anti-self-help, anti-kidnapping laws, like Pennsylvania's?

Second, does the Fugitive Slave Clause imply—it does not say—that there exists *federal legislative power* in Congress to enact federal laws for enforcing the obligation to return fugitives? Is such an inferred power supported by the Necessary and Proper Clause? (Re-read the words of that clause carefully!) Is the existence of a power to enact national fugitive slave laws impliedly *negated* by the absence of its mention *in Article IV*—and by the specific mention of legislative powers of Congress elsewhere in Article IV, with respect to other clauses (like Full Faith and Credit)?

Third, assuming that Congress possesses legislative power, is that power exclusive? That is, does federal legislative power preempt all state legislation in the area?

Fourth, even if preemption is not automatic, did Congress's enactment of the Fugitive Slave Act of 1793 preempt all state legislation concerning fugitive slave rendition, including Pennsylvania's anti-kidnapping statute?

2. Consider Justice Story's interpretive methodology (and whether he is faithful to it). Is his emphasis on the actual text of the Fugitive Slave Clause or the Necessary and Proper Clause? Or is his analysis better described as focused on the historical purpose behind those clauses? If the latter, should that purpose then be the focus of interpretation (so that whatever best fulfills that purpose is the preferred interpretation of the words)? Or is the "purpose" limited by the degree to which the words of the text actually fulfill it (so that courts cannot rightly pursue a text's supposed purpose further than the words themselves support)? Consider the question in its most extreme form: what if the words of a legal text clearly said one thing, yet evidence of the historical purpose of the text clearly said something else entirely? Which one counts? If the Necessary and Proper Clause is the source of all implied powers under the Constitution, and the Fugitive Slave Clause suggests an implied power, then isn't that reason enough to find an implied power in *Prigg*? Does the fact that Congress passed a Fugitive Slave Law in the 1790s, early in our constitutional history, matter in resolving this question, as it did with the constitutionality of the Bank of the United States?

3. Are other constitutional issues lurking, unaddressed, in *Prigg*? Could the federal government have created fugitive slave "Commissioners"—who were not Article III judges—to hear claims by slave owners? Did alleged slaves have a *federal* constitutional right to trial by jury?

4. How does the text of the Fugitive Slave Clause differ from the text of the Extradition Clause? One difference is that the Fugitive Slave Clause "applied only to those *actually* held to 'service or labour' in marked contrast to the Extradition Clause, which applied to all those 'charged' with crime. So the application of the federal rule required a determination of whether the target was a slave or not—the subject of two fugitive slave statutes and plenty of litigation." William Baude, *Beyond DOMA: Choice of State Law in Federal Statutes*, 64 Stan. L. Rev. 1371, 1425 (2012). The Extradition Clause is similar to a clause in the Articles of Confederation, and early in our history Congress passed an extradition statute carrying into execution its implied power under this clause.

The major early case under the clause was *Kentucky v. Dennison,* 65 U.S. (24 How.) 66 (1860). It involved a free black man, Willis Lago, who had violated Kentucky law by helping a slave girl escape. He fled to Ohio, where the governor refused to extradite him. Chief Justice Taney's opinion came to the astonishing conclusion that while the governor of Ohio was constitutionally obligated to extradite Lago, the Supreme Court lacked the power to issue a writ of mandamus compelling the governor to do so. The decision can be explained only by what were at that time Chief Justice Taney's expansive views of state and executive power. The Court unanimously overruled *Dennison* in *Puerto Rico v. Branstad,* 483 U.S. 219 (1987).

[Assignment 37]

D. THE TERRITORIES CLAUSE, THE NEW STATES ADMISSION CLAUSE, AND CITIZENSHIP

> *Art. I, § 3: The Congress shall have Power to dispose of and make all needful Rules and Regulations respecting the Territory or other Property belonging to the United States.*
>
> *Art. IV, § 2: The Citizens of each State shall be entitled to all Privileges and Immunities of citizens in the several States.*
>
> *§ 3: New States may be admitted . . . into this Union.*

The stakes for the interpretation of these clauses could hardly be higher: a fight over slavery in the territories led to the Civil War. But first consider two important early controversies involving these clauses—the "Louisiana Purchase" and the "Missouri Compromise." The Louisiana Purchase of 1803 was probably the most important event in American constitutional history between the ratification of the Bill of Rights (1789–1791) and the crisis of secession and the Civil War (1860–1865). President Thomas Jefferson was presented with an unexpected opportunity to purchase the entirety of the vast trans-Mississippi territory of "Louisiana" from France, when Napoleon Bonaparte offered to sell the entire territory for the bargain price of $15 million. Jefferson's envoys, Robert Livingston and James Monroe, who had been sent to negotiate the possible purchase of New Orleans only, seized the opportunity. The Purchase doubled the physical size of the United States, and the treaty committed the United States to incorporating the territory and its residents into the nation—over time, eventually accounting for fourteen new states.

Jefferson had doubts about whether it was constitutional to add to the territory of the United States beyond its initial borders. Echoing his "strict construction" position with respect to the Bank, he said it was arguably beyond the powers enumerated by the Constitution, which would mean that a constitutional amendment was needed. See Thomas Jefferson, Letter to Wilson Cary Nicholas (Sept. 7, 1803), in 41 WORKS OF THOMAS JEFFERSON (Barbara B. Oberg ed., 2014) ("I had rather ask an enlargement of power from the nation where it is found necessary, than to assume it by a construction which would make our powers boundless. our peculiar security is in the possession of a written constitution. let us not make it a blank paper by construction.").

(Do you agree or disagree that the federal government lacked enumerated power to acquire new territory? Is there any reason why new territory or property may not be added to the United States by treaty or by purchase, provided Congress appropriates the necessary funds? The president and the Senate together have the power to make treaties, and English kings had for centuries acquired and divested themselves of parts of France by treaty. Does that example establish that Jefferson could acquire the Louisiana Purchase by treaty? Could the acquisition of new territory be a "great substantive and independent power"?)

Yet Jefferson went forward with the Louisiana Purchase notwithstanding his constitutional qualms—and without seeking an amendment that might upend the bargain. As he would later write, in reply to a letter:

> "The question you propose, Whether circumstances do not sometimes occur which make it a duty in officers of high trust to assume authorities beyond the law, is easy of solution in principle, but sometimes embarrasing in practice, a strict observance of the written law is doubtless *one* of the high duties of a good citizen: but it is not *the highest*. the laws of necessity, of self-preservation, and of saving our country when in danger, are of higher obligation. to lose our country by a scrupulous adherence to written law, would be to lose the law itself, with life, liberty, property & all those who are enjoying them with us; thus absurdly sacrificing the end to the means."

To John B. Colvin (Sept. 20, 1810), in 3 THE PAPERS OF THOMAS JEFFERSON: RETIREMENT SERIES, 12 AUGUST 1810 TO 17 JUNE 1811, at 99 (J. Jefferson Looney ed., 2006). Do you agree? If Jefferson was right to be troubled about the constitutional question, was it lawless for him to forge ahead? Does the Constitution contain implied exceptions in favor of "necessity"? Cf. Michael Stokes Paulsen, *The Constitution of Necessity*, 79 Notre Dame L. Rev. 1257 (2004).

One constitutional legacy of the Louisiana Purchase was vast new territory in which slavery could expand. The Northwest Ordinance of 1787 (re-enacted by the First Congress in 1789) forever banned slavery in the regions of the old Northwest. But Jefferson and his political allies did not seek such a restriction for the new Louisiana Territory. The battle over whether slavery would be permitted in new territories—or which ones—and whether new slave states would be admitted to the Union was *the* major political-constitutional controversy of the first half of the nineteenth century, dwarfing even the Bank and Nullification controversies of the 1820s and 1830s. The question of the expansion of slavery, and the balance between slave-state and free-state power, eventually produced several tenuous compromises. Most notable among them was the "Missouri Compromise" of 1820, which admitted Maine and Missouri to statehood (one free state for one slave state) and crafted a geographical rule—a line—concerning where slavery might be allowed in the territories and (by implication) in future states carved out of those territories. North of a line of 36 degrees 30 minutes north latitude (excluding the state of Missouri itself), slavery would be prohibited; below that line, it would be permitted. The Missouri Compromise was invoked by Dred Scott's lawyers in support of his freedom—only to have the Supreme Court declare it unconstitutional in *Dred Scott v. Sandford*.

The *Dred Scott* case involves several aspects of Article IV. First, it involved the question of whether black men and women, suing for their freedom under state or federal law, were "citizens" of the states in which they claimed residence and entitled to the "privileges and immunities of citizens in the several States." The Court's holding that no black person, whether slave or free, could constitutionally be a "citizen" of the United States—and therefore could not be a citizen of any state—had a lot to do with the majority's view that it would be unthinkable for free blacks to possess the "Privileges and Immunities" or civil rights of citizens in the several states: that probably would mean they had the freedom of speech under the First Amendment and the right to bear arms under the Second Amendment, even in Southern states.

Second, the case had everything to do with Congress's power under the Territories Clause. The case came to the Court in the context of a long and bitter period of territorial expansion and battles between North and South over the admission of new states. Would newly admitted states be free states or slave states? Did Congress have the power to enforce a prohibition on slavery in new states? And did Congress have the power to prohibit slavery in some or all of the *territories,* while they were still territories and before they applied for statehood? The decision famously struck down the important "Missouri Compromise" Act of Congress of 1820, which had forbidden slavery in territories north of a designated line, as part of a compromise assuring a continued balance of slave states and free states. *Dred Scott* declared that compromise unconstitutional, saying that the federal government had no legitimate constitutional power to limit the spread of slavery to new territories and essentially ending all hopes of a political compromise to settle the long-simmering conflict between free states and slave states.

Just as significant was the Court's reason the Missouri Compromise was unconstitutional. The Court in *Dred Scott* held that slave owners had a substantive right under the Due Process Clause of the Fifth Amendment to own slaves and to carry their slave "property" into any federal territory and that the national government lacked power under the Constitution to restrict ownership of slaves in the territories. The breadth of such a claim portended that the Court might hold that *states* could not exclude slavery either. Thus, there was a very real threat that *Dred Scott* might lead to Northern states being required to allow slavery within their own borders. (Recall *Lemmon v. The People*, which it was feared might become, were it to reach the Supreme Court, in the words of Abraham Lincoln, a "Second *Dred Scott*" decision making slavery *national.*)

It would be overstating matters to say that the *Dred Scott* case caused the Civil War. But it was certainly an important link in the fateful chain of events. Lincoln's opposition to *Dred Scott* contributed to his election as president, his election led to the South's secession, and secession led to the Civil War. *Dred Scott* was hugely significant, as demonstrated by the leading historical work on the case, Don Fehrenbacher, THE DRED SCOTT CASE: ITS SIGNIFICANCE IN AMERICAN LAW AND POLITICS (1978).

To spoil the plot: Lincoln issued the Emancipation Proclamation as a war measure; the Union won the war and defeated secession; and in the aftermath of the War the Constitution was amended to abolish slavery and to overrule and repudiate the *Dred Scott* decision (the Thirteenth and Fourteenth Amendments). The case is, therefore, also hugely significant in terms of the major constitutional changes that it ultimately led to.

Something of a roadmap, and a warning, is required before one's first reading of Chief Justice Taney's opinion for the Court: Most of what Chief Justice Taney says is directed to achieving the firmest possible pro-slavery outcome on every conceivable issue. Read the opinion with a sharply critical eye. He first addresses whether there was proper jurisdiction under the Diversity Clause of the Constitution, and uses that question as a vehicle for considering whether there can ever be a black citizen of the United States. Here you will find some of the most racist rhetoric ever found in a Supreme Court opinion. Next, he considers whether the Missouri Compromise statute's prohibition of slavery in the territories could really operate to grant Dred Scott his freedom by virtue of his stay at Fort Snelling, in free federal territory. He concludes it could not have this result, because the statute was an unconstitutional deprivation of slaveholders' property "without due process of law." Finally, he concludes that, in any event, neither the Missouri Compromise law concerning slavery in federal territory, nor Illinois's law as a free state, could operate to make Dred Scott free in Missouri. Neither law had "extraterritorial" effect.

Dred Scott v. Sandford
60 U.S. (19 How.) 393 (1857)

[The facts were agreed to by the parties and are relocated here from where they appear later in the opinion of the Court.—Editors]

In the year 1834, the plaintiff was a negro slave belonging to Dr. Emerson, who was a surgeon in the army of the United States. In that year, 1834, said Dr. Emerson took the plaintiff from the State of Missouri to the military post at Rock Island, in the State of Illinois, and held him there as a slave until the month of April or May, 1836.

[Dr. Emerson took Dred Scott to Fort Snelling, in present-day Minnesota, then part of the territory known as Upper Louisiana. Slavery in that territory was banned by the Missouri Compromise federal statute of 1820, which admitted Missouri as a slave state, Maine as a free state, and prohibited slavery in the remainder of the Louisiana Purchase north of the line of thirty-six degrees and thirty minutes latitude. In 1836, Dr. Emerson acquired Harriet, a slave.—Editors]

In the year 1836, the plaintiff and said Harriet, at said Fort Snelling, with the consent of said Dr. Emerson, who then claimed to be their master and owner, intermarried. . . . Eliza and Lizzie . . . are the fruit of that marriage. Eliza is about fourteen years old, and was born on board the steamboat Gipsey, north of the north line of the State of Missouri, and upon the river Mississippi. Lizzie is about seven years old, and was born in the State of Missouri, at the military post called Jefferson Barracks.

In the year 1838, said Dr. Emerson removed the plaintiff and said Harriet and their said daughter Eliza, from said Fort Snelling to the State of Missouri, where they have ever since resided.

[The procedural history of the case is famously convoluted. To compress drastically: Dred Scott first brought suit against Dr. Emerson's widow, in Missouri state court, asserting his freedom. He won in the trial court, but the Missouri Supreme Court reversed, overruling its own prior precedents which would have treated Scott's long stay in Illinois, a free state, as sufficient to confer on him freedom. Under the earlier cases, Missouri would have applied Illinois's law to determine Scott's status, as a matter of "comity." The Missouri Supreme Court decided instead to apply Missouri law to Scott's status, and found him to be a slave under Missouri law. Before

the judgment became final (apparently), Scott was (apparently) either sold or transferred to Mrs. Emerson's brother, Mr. Sanford, a citizen of New York state. (Sanford's name was misspelled in the official Supreme Court report, giving the case the name Dred Scott v. Sandford.) *Scott's lawyers commenced a new suit in federal court, invoking federal diversity jurisdiction, which exists for cases between a citizen of one state and a citizen of another state. Sanford was a citizen of New York; if Scott was a citizen of Missouri, the federal courts would have jurisdiction under Article III of the Constitution to hear his case. But if even free black persons could not be "citizens" as the word is used in Article III, then Scott's case would have to be dismissed and he would have no remedy in federal court. Scott lost in the lower federal court, and appealed to the U.S. Supreme Court.—Editors]*

■ MR. CHIEF JUSTICE TANEY delivered the opinion of the court. . . .

There are two leading questions presented by the record:

1. Had the Circuit Court of the United States jurisdiction to hear and determine the case between these parties? And

2. If it had jurisdiction, is the judgment it has given erroneous or not?

The plaintiff in error, . . . was, with his wife and children, held as slaves by the defendant, in the State of Missouri; and he brought this action in the Circuit Court of the United States for that district, to assert the title of himself and his family to freedom. . . .

The defendant pleaded in abatement to the jurisdiction of the court, that the plaintiff was not a citizen of the State of Missouri, as alleged in his declaration, being a negro of African descent, whose ancestors were of pure African blood, and who were brought into this country and sold as slaves. . . .

The question is simply this: Can a negro, whose ancestors were imported into this country, and sold as slaves, become a member of the political community formed and brought into existence by the Constitution of the United States, and as such become entitled to all the rights, and privileges, and immunities, guaranteed by that instrument to the citizen? One of which rights is the privilege of suing in a court of the United States in the cases specified in the Constitution. . . .

The words "people of the United States" and "citizens" are synonymous terms, and mean the same thing. They both describe the political body who, according to our republican institutions, form the sovereignty, and who hold the power and conduct the Government through their representatives. They are what we familiarly call the "sovereign people," and every citizen is one of this people, and a constituent member of this sovereignty. The question before us is, whether [persons of African descent] compose a portion of this people, and are constituent members of this sovereignty? We think they are not, and that they are not included, and were not intended to be included, under the word "citizens" in the Constitution, and can therefore claim none of the rights and privileges which that instrument provides for and secures to citizens of the United States. On the contrary, they were at that time considered as a subordinate and inferior class of beings, who had been subjugated by the dominant race, and, whether emancipated or not, yet remained subject to their authority, and had no rights or privileges but such as those who held the power and the Government might choose to grant them. . . .

In discussing this question, we must not confound the rights of citizenship which a State may confer within its own limits, and the rights of citizenship as a member of the Union. It does not by any means follow, because he has all the rights and privileges of a citizen of a State, that he must be a citizen of the United States. He may have all of the rights and privileges of the citizen of a State, and yet not be entitled to the rights and privileges of a citizen in any other State. For, previous to the adoption of the Constitution of the United States, every State had the undoubted right to confer on whomsoever it pleased the character of citizen, and to endow him with all its rights. But this character of course was confined to the boundaries of the State, and gave him no rights or privileges in other States beyond those secured to him by the laws of nations and the comity of States. Nor have the several States surrendered the power of conferring these rights and privileges by adopting the Constitution of the United States. Each State may still confer them upon an alien, or any one it thinks proper, or upon any class or description of persons; yet he would not be a citizen in the sense in which that word is used in the Constitution of the United States, nor entitled to sue as such in one of its courts, nor to the privileges and immunities of a citizen in the other States. The rights which he would acquire would be restricted to the State which gave them. The Constitution has conferred on Congress the right to establish an uniform rule of naturalization, and this right is evidently exclusive, and has always been held by this court to be so. Consequently, no State, since the adoption of the Constitution, can by naturalizing an alien invest him with the rights and privileges secured to a citizen of a State under the Federal Government, although, so far as the State alone was concerned, he would undoubtedly be entitled to the rights of a citizen, and clothed with all the rights and immunities which the Constitution and laws of the State attached to that character.

It is very clear, therefore, that no State can, by any act or law of its own, passed since the adoption of the Constitution, introduce a new member into the political community created by the Constitution of the United States. It cannot make him a member of this community by making him a member of its own. And for the same reason it cannot introduce any person, or description of persons, who were not intended to be embraced in this new political family, which the Constitution brought into existence, but were intended to be excluded from it.

The question then arises, whether the provisions of the Constitution, in relation to the personal rights and privileges to which the citizen of a State should be entitled, embraced the negro African race, at that time in this country, or who might afterwards be imported, who had then or should afterwards be made free in any State; and to put it in the power of a single State to make him a citizen of the United States, and endue him with the full rights of citizenship in every other State without their consent? Does the Constitution of the United States act upon him whenever he shall be made free under the laws of a State, and raised there to the rank of a citizen, and immediately cloth him with all the privileges of a citizen in every other State, and in its own courts?

The court think the affirmative of these propositions cannot be maintained. And if it cannot, the plaintiff in error could not be a citizen of the State of Missouri, within the meaning of the Constitution of the United States, and, consequently, was not entitled to sue in its courts.

It is true, every person, and every class and description of persons, who were at the time of the adoption of the Constitution recognized as citizens in the several

States, became also citizens of this new political body; but none other; it was formed by them, and for them and their posterity, but for no one else. And the personal rights and privileges guarantied to citizens of this new sovereignty were intended to embrace those only who were then members of the several State communities, or who should afterwards by birthright or otherwise become members, according to the provisions of the Constitution and the principles on which it was founded. It was the union of those who were at that time members of distinct and separate political communities into one political family, whose power, for certain specified purposes, was to extend over the whole territory of the United States. And it gave to each citizen rights and privileges outside of his State which he did not before possess, and placed him in every other State upon a perfect equality with its own citizens as to rights of person and rights of property; it made him a citizen of the United States.

It becomes necessary, therefore, to determine who were citizens of the several States when the Constitution was adopted. And in order to do this, we must recur to the Governments and institutions of the thirteen colonies, when they separated from Great Britain and formed new sovereignties, and took their places in the family of independent nations. . . .

In the opinion of the court, the legislation and histories of the times, and the language used in the Declaration of Independence, show, that neither the class of persons who had been imported as slaves, nor their descendants, whether they had become free or not, were then acknowledged as a part of the people, nor intended to be included in the general words used in that memorable instrument.

It is difficult at this day to realize the state of public opinion in relation to that unfortunate race, which prevailed in the civilized and enlightened portions of the world at the time of the Declaration of Independence, and when the Constitution of the United States was framed and adopted. But the public history of every European nation displays it in a manner too plain to be mistaken.

They had for more than a century before been regarded as beings of an inferior order, and altogether unfit to associate with the white race, either in social or political relations; and so far inferior, that they had no rights which the white man was bound to respect; and that the negro might justly and lawfully be reduced to slavery for his benefit. He was bought and sold, and treated as an ordinary article of merchandise and traffic, whenever a profit could be made by it. This opinion was at that time fixed and universal in the civilized portion of the white race. It was regarded as an axiom in morals as well as in politics, which no one thought of disputing, or supposed to be open to dispute; and men in every grade and position in society daily and habitually acted upon it in their private pursuits, as well as in matters of public concern, without doubting for a moment the correctness of this opinion.

And in no nation was this opinion more firmly fixed or more uniformly acted upon than by the English Government and English people. They not only seized them on the coast of Africa, and sold them or held them in slavery for their own use; but they took them as ordinary articles of merchandise to every country where they could make a profit on them, and were far more extensively engaged in this commerce than any other nation in the world.

The opinion thus entertained and acted upon in England was naturally impressed upon the colonies they founded on this side of the Atlantic. And, accordingly, a negro of the African race was regarded by them as an article of property, and held, and bought and sold as such, in every one of the thirteen colonies which united in the Declaration of Independence, and afterwards formed the Constitution of the United States. The slaves were more or less numerous in the different colonies, as slave labor was found more or less profitable. But no one seems to have doubted the correctness of the prevailing opinion of the time.

The legislation of the different colonies furnishes positive and indisputable proof of this fact. *[Chief Justice Taney then proceeds to give illustrations.—Editors]* . . .

The language of the Declaration of Independence is equally conclusive: . . . "We hold these truths to be self-evident: that all men are created equal; that they are endowed by their Creator with certain unalienable rights; that among them is life, liberty, and the pursuit of happiness; that to secure these rights, Governments are instituted, deriving their just powers from the consent of the governed."

The general words above quoted would seem to embrace the whole human family, and if they were used in a similar instrument at this day would be so understood. But it is too clear for dispute, that the enslaved African race were not intended to be included, and formed no part of the people who framed and adopted this declaration; for if the language, as understood in that day, would embrace them, the conduct of the distinguished men who framed the Declaration of Independence would have been utterly and flagrantly inconsistent with the principles they asserted; and instead of the sympathy of mankind, to which they so confidently appeared, they would have deserved and received universal rebuke and reprobation.

Yet the men who framed this declaration were great men—high in literary acquirements—high in their sense of honor, and incapable of asserting principles inconsistent with those on which they were acting. They perfectly understood the meaning of the language they used, and how it would be understood by others; and they knew that it would not in any part of the civilized world be supposed to embrace the negro race, which, by common consent, had been excluded from civilized Governments and the family of nations, and doomed to slavery. They spoke and acted according to the then established doctrines and principles, and in the ordinary language of the day, no one misunderstood them. The unhappy black race were separated from the white by indelible marks, and laws long before established, and were never thought of or spoken of except as property, and when the claims of the owner or the profit of the trader were supposed to need protection. . . .

[T]here are two clauses in the Constitution which point directly and specifically to the negro race as a separate class of persons, and show clearly that they were not regarded as a portion of the people or citizens of the Government then formed.

One of these clauses reserves to each of the thirteen States the right to import slaves until the year 1808, if it thinks proper. . . . *[The other is the Fugitive Slave Clause.—Editors]* By the first above-mentioned clause, therefore, the right to purchase and hold this property is directly sanctioned and authorized for twenty years by the people who framed the Constitution. And by the second, they pledge themselves to maintain and uphold the right of the master in the manner specified, as long as the Government they then formed should endure. And these two provisions show, conclusively, that neither the description of persons therein referred to, not their descendants, were embraced in any of the other provisions of the Constitution; for certainly these two clauses were not intended to confer on them or their posterity the blessings of liberty, or any of the personal rights so carefully provided for the citizen.

No one of that race had ever migrated to the United States voluntarily; all of them had been brought here as articles of merchandise. The number that had been emancipated at that time were but few in comparison with those held in slavery; and they were identified in the public mind with the race to which they belonged, and regarded as a part of the slave population rather than the free. It is obvious that they were not even in the minds of the framers of the Constitution when they were conferring special rights and privileges upon the citizens of a State in every other part of the Union. . . .

A clause similar to the one in the Constitution, in relation to the rights and immunities of citizens of one State in the other States, was contained in the Articles of Confederation. But there is a difference of language, which is worthy of note. The provision in the Articles of Confederation was, "that the *free inhabitants* of each of the States, paupers, vagabonds, and fugitives from justice, excepted, should be entitled to all the privileges and immunities of free citizens in the several States."

. . . The term *free inhabitant*, in the generality of its terms, would certainly include one of the African race who had been manumitted. But . . . notwithstanding the generality of the words "free inhabitants," it is very clear that, according to their accepted meaning in that day, they did not include the African race, whether free or not: for the fifth section of the ninth article provides that Congress should have the power "to agree upon the number of land forces to be raised, and to make requisitions from each State for its quota in proportion to the number of *white* inhabitants in such State, which requisition should be binding."

Words could hardly have been used which more strongly mark the line of distinction between the citizen and the subject; the free and the subjugated races. . . .

The only two provisions [in the Constitution] which point to them and include them, treat them as property, and make it the duty of the Government to protect it; no other power, in relation to this race, is to be found in the Constitution; and as it is a Government of special, delegated, powers, no authority beyond these two provisions can be constitutionally exercised. The Government of the United States had no right to interfere for any other purpose but that of protecting the rights of the owner, leaving it altogether with the several States to deal with this race, whether emancipated or not, as each State may think justice, humanity, and the interests and safety of society, require. The States evidently intended to reserve this power exclusively to themselves.

No one, we presume, supposes that any change in public opinion or feeling, in relation to this unfortunate race, in the civilized nations of Europe or in this country, should induce the court to give to the words of the Constitution a more liberal construction in their favor than they were intended to bear when the instrument was framed and adopted. Such an argument would be altogether inadmissible in any tribunal called on to interpret it. If any of its provisions are deemed unjust, there is a mode prescribed in the instrument itself by which it may be amended; but while it remains unaltered, it must be construed now as it was understood at the time of its adoption. It is not only the same in words, but the same in meaning, and delegates the same powers to the Government, and reserves and secures the same rights and privileges to the citizen; and as long as it continues to exist in its present form, it speaks not only in the same words, but with the same meaning and intent with which it spoke when it came from the hands of its framers, and was voted on and adopted by the people of the United States. Any other rule of construction would abrogate the judicial character of this court, and make it the mere reflex of the popular opinion or passion of the day. This court was not created by the Constitution for such purposes. Higher and graver trusts have been confided to it, and it must not falter in the path of duty.

What the construction was at that time, we think can hardly admit of doubt. We have the language of the Declaration of Independence and of the Articles of Confederation, in addition to the plain words of the Constitution itself; we have the legislation of the different States, before, about the time, and since, the Constitution was adopted; we have the legislation of Congress, from the time of its adoption to a recent period; and we have the constant and uniform action of the Executive Department, all concurring together, and leading to the same result. And if anything in relation to the construction of the Constitution can be regarded as settled, it is that which we now give to the word "citizen" and the word "people."

And upon a full and careful consideration of the subject, the court is of opinion, that, upon the facts stated in the plea in abatement, Dred Scott was not a citizen of Missouri within the meaning of the Constitution of the United States, and not entitled as such to sue in its courts; and, consequently, that the Circuit Court had no jurisdiction of the case . . .

It is true that the result either way, by dismissal or by a judgment for the defendant, makes very little, if any, difference in a pecuniary or personal point of view to either party. But the fact that the result would be very nearly the same to the parties in either form of judgment, would not justify this court in sanctioning an error in the judgment which is patent on the record, and which, if sanctioned, might be drawn into precedent, and lead to serious mischief and injustice in some future suit.

We proceed, therefore, to inquire whether the facts relied on by the plaintiff entitled him to his freedom. *[The opinion then proceeds to lay out the facts as relocated to the beginning of this edited opinion.—Editors]* . . .

Before the commencement of this suit, said Dr. Emerson sold and conveyed the plaintiff, and Harriet, Eliza, and Lizzie, to the defendant, as slaves, and the defendant has ever since claimed to hold them, and each of them, as slaves.

In considering this part of the controversy, two questions arise: 1. Was he, together with his family, free in Missouri by reason of the stay in the territory of the United States hereinbefore mentioned? And 2. If they were not, is Scott himself free by reason of his removal to Rock Island, in the State of Illinois, as stated in the above admissions?

We proceed to examine the first question.

The act of Congress, upon which the plaintiff relies, declares that slavery and involuntary servitude, except as a punishment for crime, shall be forever prohibited in all that part of the territory ceded by France, under the name of Louisiana, which lies north of thirty-six degrees thirty minutes north latitude, and not included within the limits of Missouri. And the difficulty which meets us at the threshold of this part of the inquiry is, whether Congress was authorized to pass this law under any of the powers granted to it by the Constitution; for if the authority is not given by that instrument, it is the duty of this court to declare it void and inoperative, and incapable of conferring freedom upon any one who is held as a slave under the laws of any one of the States.

The counsel for the plaintiff has laid much stress upon that article in the Constitution which confers on Congress the power "to dispose of and make all needful rules and regulations respecting the territory or other property belonging to the United States"; but, in the judgment of the court, that provision has no bearing on the present controversy, and the power there given, whatever it may be, is confined, and was intended to be confined, to the territory which at that time belonged to, or was claimed by, the United States, and was within their boundaries as settled by the treaty with Great Britain, and can have no influence upon a territory afterwards acquired from a foreign Government. It was a special provision for a known and particular territory, and to meet a present emergency, and nothing more. . . .

The language used in the clause, the arrangement and combination of the powers, and the somewhat unusual phraseology it uses, when it speaks of the political power to be exercised in the government of the territory, all indicate the design and meaning of the clause to be such as we have mentioned. It does not speak of *any* territory, nor of *Territories*, but uses language which, according to its legitimate meaning, points to a particular thing. The power is given in relation only to *the* territory of the United States—that is, to a territory then in existence, and then known or claimed as the territory of the United States. It begins its enumeration of powers by that of disposing, in other words, making sale of the lands, or raising money from them, which, as we have already said, was the main object to the cession, and which is accordingly the first thing provided for in the article. It then gives the power which was necessarily associated with the disposition and sale of the lands—that is, the power of making needful rules and regulations respecting the territory. And whatever construction may now be given to these words, every one, we think, must admit that they are not the words usually employed by statesmen in giving supreme power of legislation. They are certainly very unlike the words used in the power granted to legislate over territory which the new Government might afterwards itself obtain by cession from a State, either for its seat of Government, of for forts, magazines, arsenals, dock yards, and other needful buildings.

And the same power of making needful rules respecting the territory is, in precisely the same language, applied to the other property belonging to the United States—associating the power over the territory in this respect with the power over movable or personal property—that is, the ships, arms, and munitions of war, which then belonged in common to the State sovereignties. And it will hardly be said, that this power, in relation to the last-mentioned objects, was deemed necessary to be thus specially given to the new Government, in order to authorize it to make needful rules and regulations respecting the ships it might itself build, or arms and munitions of war it might itself manufacture or provide for the public service.

No one, it is believed, would think a moment of deriving the power of Congress to make needful rules and regulations in relation to property of this kind from this clause of the Constitution. Nor can it, upon any fair construction, be applied to any property but that which the new Government was about to receive from the confederated States. And if this be true as to this property, it must be equally true and limited as to the territory, which is so carefully and precisely coupled with it—and like it referred to as property in the power granted. The concluding words of the clause appear to render this construction irresistible; for, after the provisions we have mentioned, it proceeds to say, "that nothing in the Constitution shall be so construed as to prejudice any claims of the United States, or of any particular State." . . .

The words "needful rules and regulations" would seem, also, to have been cautiously used for some definite object. They are not the words usually employed by statesmen, when they mean to give the powers of sovereignty, or to establish a Government, or to authorize its establishment. Thus, in the law to renew and keep alive the ordinance of 1787, and to reestablish the Government, the title of the law is: "An act to provide for the government of the territory northwest of the river Ohio." And in the Constitution, when granting the power to legislate over the territory that may be selected for the seat of Government independently of a State, it does not say Congress shall have power "to make all needful rules and regulations respecting the territory"; but it declares that "Congress shall have power to exercise exclusive legislation in all cases whatsoever over such District (not exceeding ten miles square) as may, by cession of particular States and the acceptance of Congress, become the seat of the Government of the United States.["] . . .

Whether, therefore, we take the particular clause in question, by itself, or in connection with the other provisions of the Constitution, we think it clear, that it applies only to the particular territory of which we have spoken, and cannot, by any just rule of interpretation, be extended to territory which the new Government might afterwards obtain from a foreign nation. . . .

This brings us to examine by what provision of the Constitution the present Federal Government, under its delegated and restricted powers, is authorized to acquire territory outside of the original limits of the United States, and what powers it may exercise therein over the person or property of a citizen of the United States, while it remains a Territory, and until it shall be admitted as one of the States of the Union. . . .

We do not mean, however, to question the power of Congress in this respect. The power to expand the territory of the United States by the admission of new States is plainly given; and in the construction of this power by all the departments of the Government, it has been held to authorize the acquisition of territory, not fit for admission at the time, but to be admitted as soon as its population and situation would entitle it to admission. It is acquired to become a State, and not to be held as a colony and governed by Congress with absolute authority; and as the propriety of admitting a new State is committed to the sound discretion of Congress, the power to acquire territory for that purpose, to be held by the United States until it is in a suitable condition to become a State upon an equal footing with the other States, must rest upon the same discretion. . . . [W]hatever the political department of the Government shall recognize as within the limits of the United States, the judicial department is also bound to recognize, and to administer in it the laws of the United States, . . . and to maintain in the Territory . . . the personal rights and rights of property of individual citizens, as secured by the Constitution. . . .

Taking this rule to guide us, it may be safely assumed that citizens of the United States who migrate to a Territory belonging to the people of the United States, cannot be ruled as mere colonists, dependent upon the will of the General Government, and to be governed by any laws it may think proper to impose. . . . A power . . . in the

General Government to obtain and hold colonies and dependent territories, over which they might legislate without restriction, would be inconsistent with its own existence in its present form. Whatever it acquires, it acquires for the benefit of the people of the several states who created it. It is their trustee acting for them, and charged with the duty of promoting the interests of the whole people of the Union in the exercise of the powers specifically granted.

At the time when the Territory in question was obtained by cession from France, it contained no population fit to be associated together and admitted as a State; and it therefore was absolutely necessary to hold possession of it, as a Territory belonging to the United States, until it was [settled, inhabited, and ready to be admitted as a State]. . . .

But until that time arrives, it is undoubtedly necessary that some Government should be established, in order to organize society, and to protect the inhabitants in their persons and property . . . The power to acquire necessarily carries with it the power to preserve and apply to the purposes for which it was acquired. . . . [S]ome form of civil authority would be absolutely necessary to organize and preserve civilized society, and prepare it to become a State; and what is the best form must always depend on the condition of the Territory at the time, and the choice of the mode must depend upon the exercise of a discretionary power by Congress, acting within the scope of its constitutional authority, and not infringing upon the rights of person or rights of property of the citizen who might go there to reside, or for any other lawful purpose. . . .

But the power of Congress over the person or property of a citizen can never be a mere discretionary power. . . . The powers of the Government and the rights and privileges of the citizen are regulated and plainly defined by the Constitution itself. And when the Territory becomes a part of the United States, the Federal Government enters into possession in the character impressed upon it by those who created it. It enters upon it with its powers over the citizen strictly defined, and limited by the Constitution, from which it derives its own existence, and by virtue of which alone it continues to exist and act as a Government and sovereignty. It has no power of any kind beyond it; and it cannot, when it enters a Territory of the United States, put off its character, and assume discretionary or despotic powers which the Constitution has denied to it. . . . [T]he Government and the citizen both enter it under the authority of the Constitution, with their respective rights defined and marked out; and the Federal Government can exercise no power over his person or property, beyond what that instrument confers, nor lawfully deny any right which it has reserved. . . .

For example, no one, we presume, will contend that Congress can make any law in a Territory respecting that establishment of religion, or the free exercise thereof, or abridging the freedom of speech or of the press, or the right of the people of the Territory peaceably to assemble, and to petition the Government for the redress of grievances.

Nor can Congress deny to the people the right to keep and bear arms, nor the right to trial by jury, nor compel any one to be a witness against himself in a criminal proceeding.

These powers, and others, in relation to rights of person, which it is not necessary here to enumerate, are, in express and positive terms, denied to the

General Government; and the rights of private property have been guarded with equal care. Thus the rights of property are united with the rights of person, and placed on the same ground by the Fifth Amendment to the Constitution, which provides that no person shall be deprived of life, liberty, and property, without due process of law. And an act of Congress which deprives a citizen of the United States of his liberty or property, merely because he came himself or brought his property into a particular Territory of the United States, and who had committed no offence against the laws, could hardly be dignified with the name of due process of law.

So, too, it will hardly be contended that Congress could by law quarter a soldier in a house in a Territory . . . [or] take private property for public use without just compensation.

The powers over person and property of which we speak are not only not granted to Congress, but are in express terms denied, and they are forbidden to exercise them. And this prohibition is not confined to the States, but the words are general, and extend to the whole territory over which the Constitution gives it power to legislate, including those portions of it remaining under Territorial Government, as well as that covered by States. It is a total absence of power everywhere within the dominion of the United States, and places the citizens of a Territory, so far as these rights are concerned, on the same footing with citizens of the States, and guards them as firmly and plainly against any inroads which the General Government might attempt, under the plea of implied or incidental powers. And if Congress itself cannot do this—if it is beyond the powers conferred on the Federal Government—it will be admitted, we presume, that it could not authorize a Territorial Government to exercise them. It could confer no power on any local Government, established by its authority, to violate the provisions of the Constitution.

It seems, however, to be supposed, that there is a difference between property in a slave and other property, and that different rules may be applied to it in expounding the Constitution of the United States. And the laws and usages of nations, and the writing of eminent jurists upon the relation of master and slave and their mutual rights and duties, and the powers which Governments may exercise over it, have been dwelt upon in the argument.

But in considering the question before us, it must be borne in mind that there is no law of nations standing between the people of the United States and their Government, and interfering with their relation to each other. The powers of the Government, and the rights of the citizen under it, are positive and practical regulations plainly written down. . . . And if the Constitution recognises the right of property of the master in a slave, and makes no distinction between that description of property and other property owned by a citizen, no tribunal, acting under the authority of the United States, whether it be legislative, executive, or judicial, has a right to draw such a distinction, or deny to it the benefit of the provisions and guarantees which have been provided for the protection of private property against the encroachments of the Government.

Now, as we have already said in an earlier part of this opinion, upon a different point, the right of property in a slave is distinctly and expressly affirmed in the Constitution. The right to traffic in it, like an ordinary article of merchandise and property, was guaranteed to the citizens of the United States, in every State that might desire it, for twenty years. And the Government in express terms is pledged to protect it in all future time, if the slave escapes from his owner. This is done in plain words—too plain to be misunderstood. And no word can be found in the Constitution which gives Congress a greater power over slave property, or which entitles property of that kind to less protection than property of any other description. The only power conferred is the power coupled with the duty of guarding and protecting the owner in his rights.

Upon these considerations, it is the opinion of the court that the act of Congress which prohibited a citizen from holding and owning property of this kind in the territory of the United States north of the line therein mentioned, is not warranted by the Constitution, and is therefore void; and that neither Dred Scott himself, nor any of his family, were made free by being carried into this territory; even if they had been carried there by the owner, with the intention of becoming a permanent resident. . . .

But there is another point in the case which depends on State power and State law. And it is contended, on the part of the plaintiff, that he is made free by being taken to Rock Island, in the State of Illinois, independently of his residence in the territory of the United States; and being so made free, he was not again reduced to a state of slavery by being brought back to Missouri.

Our notice of this part of the case will be very brief; for the principle on which it depends was decided . . . in the case of *Strader et al. v. Graham*, 51 U.S. (10 How.) 82 (1850). In that case, the slaves had been taken from Kentucky to Ohio, with the consent of the owner, and afterwards brought back to Kentucky. And this court held that their *status* or condition, as free or slave, depended upon the laws of Kentucky, when they were brought back into that State, and not of Ohio; and that this court had no jurisdiction to revise the judgment of a State court upon its own laws. . . .

So in this case. As Scott was a slave when taken into the State of Illinois by his owner, and was there held as such, and brought back in that character, his *status*, as free or slave, depended on the laws of Missouri, and not of Illinois.

It has, however, been urged in the argument, that by the laws of Missouri he was free on his return, and that this case, therefore, cannot be governed by the case of *Strader et al. v. Graham*, where it appeared, by the laws of Kentucky, that the plaintiffs continued to be slaves on their return from Ohio. But whatever doubts or opinions may, at one time, have been entertained upon this subject, we are satisfied, upon a careful examination of all the cases decided in the State courts of Missouri referred to, that it is now firmly settled by the decisions of the highest court in the State, that Scott and his family upon their return were not free, but were, by the laws of Missouri, the property of the defendant; and that the Circuit Court of the United States had no jurisdiction, when, by the laws of the State, the plaintiff was a slave, and not a citizen.

Moreover, the plaintiff, it appears, brought a similar action against the defendant in the State court of Missouri, claiming the freedom of himself and his family upon the same grounds and the same evidence upon which he relies in the case before the court. The case was carried before the Supreme Court of the State; was fully argued there; and that court decided that neither the plaintiff nor his family were entitled to freedom, and were still the slaves of the defendant; and reversed the judgment of the inferior State court, which had given a different decision. If the plaintiff supposed that this judgment of the Supreme Court of the

State was erroneous, and that this court had jurisdiction to revise and reverse it, the only mode by which he could legally bring it before this court was by writ of error directed to the Supreme Court of the State, requiring it to transmit the record to this court. If this had been done, it is too plain for argument that the writ must have been dismissed for want of jurisdiction in this court. The case of Strader and others v. Graham is directly in point; and, indeed, independent of any decision, the language of the 25th section of the act of 1789 is too clear and precise to admit of controversy.

But the plaintiff did not pursue the mode prescribed by law for bringing the judgment of a State court before this court for revision, but suffered the case to be remanded to the inferior State court, where it is still continued, and is, by agreement of parties, to await the judgment of this court on the point. . . .

And while the case is yet open and pending in the inferior State court, the plaintiff goes into the Circuit Court of the United States, upon the same case and the same evidence, and against the same party, and proceeds to judgment, and then brings here the same case from the Circuit Court, which the law would not have permitted him to bring directly from the State court. . . . It would ill become this court to sanction such an attempt to evade the law, or to exercise an appellate power in this circuitous way, which it is forbidden to exercise in the direct and regular and invariable forms of judicial proceedings.

Upon the whole, therefore, it is the judgment of this court, that it appears by the record before us that the plaintiff in error is not a citizen of Missouri, in the sense in which that word is used in the Constitution; and that the Circuit Court of the United States, for that reason, had no jurisdiction in the case, and could give no judgment in it. Its judgment for the defendant must, consequently, be reversed, and a mandate issued, directing the suit to be dismissed for want of jurisdiction.

■ [The concurring opinions of JUSTICES WAYNE, GRIER, DANIEL, CAMPBELL, and CATON are omitted.]

■ MR. JUSTICE NELSON [concurring].

. . . The question upon the merits, in general terms, is, whether or not the removal of the plaintiff, who was a slave, with his master, from the State of Missouri to the State of Illinois . . . works an emancipation.

As appears from an agreed statement of facts, this question has been before the highest court of the State of Missouri, and a judgment rendered that this residence in the free State has no such effect; but, on the contrary, that his original condition continued unchanged. . . .

The argument against these decisions is, that the laws of Illinois, forbidding slavery within her territory, had the effect to set the slave free while residing in that State, and to impress upon him the condition and status of a freeman; and that, by force of these laws, this status and condition accompanied him on his return to the slave State, and of consequence he could not be there held as a slave.

. . . Our opinion is, that the question is one which belongs to each State to decide for itself, either by its Legislature or courts of justice; and hence, in respect to the case before us, to the State of Missouri. . . . In other words, except in cases where the power is restrained by the Constitution of the United States, the law of the State is supreme over the subject of slavery within its jurisdiction.

As a practical illustration of the principle, we may refer to the legislation of the free States in abolishing slavery, and prohibiting its introduction into their territories. Confessedly, except as restrained by the Federal Constitution, they exercised, and rightfully, complete and absolute power over the subject. Upon what principle, then, can it be denied to the State of Missouri? The power flows from the sovereign character of the States of this Union; sovereign, not merely as respects the Federal Government—except as they have consented to its limitation—but sovereign as respects each other. Whether, therefore, the State of Missouri will recognize or give effect to the laws of Illinois within her territories on the subject of slavery, is a question for her to determine. Nor is there any constitutional power in this Government that can rightfully control her.

Every State . . . may regulate the manner and circumstances under which property is held, and the condition, capacity, and state, of all persons therein; and, also, the remedy and modes of administering justice. And it is equally true, that no State or nation can affect or bind property out of its territory, or persons not residing within it. . . . Such laws can have no inherent authority extra-territorially. This is the necessary result of the independence of distinct and separate sovereignties.

Now, it follows from these principles, that whatever force or effect the laws of one State or nation may have in the territories of another, must depend solely upon the laws and municipal regulations of the latter, upon its own jurisprudence and polity, and upon its own express or tacit consent. . . .

Nations, from convenience and comity, and from mutual interest, and a sort of moral necessity to do justice, recognize and administer the laws of other countries. But, of the nature, extent, and utility, of them, respecting property, or the state and condition of persons within her territories, each nation judges for itself; and is never bound, even upon the ground of comity, to recognize them, if prejudicial to her own interests. The recognition is purely from comity, and not from any absolute or paramount obligation. . . .

These principles fully establish, that it belongs to the sovereign State of Missouri to determine by her laws the question of slavery within her jurisdiction, subject only to such limitations as may be found in the Federal Constitution; and, further, that the laws of other States[,] . . . whether enacted by their Legislatures or expounded by their courts, can have no operation within her territory, or affect rights growing out of her own laws on the subject. This is the necessary result of the independent and sovereign character of the State. . . .

In view of these principles, let us examine a little more closely the doctrine of those who maintain that the law of Missouri is not to govern the status and condition of the plaintiff. They insist that the removal and temporary residence with his master in Illinois, where slavery is inhibited, had the effect to set him free, and that the same effect is to be given to the law of Illinois, within the State of Missouri, after his return. Why was he set free in Illinois? Because the law of Missouri, under which he was held as a slave, had no operation by its own force extra-territorially; and the State of Illinois refused to recognize its effect within her limits, upon principles of comity, as a state of slavery was inconsistent with her laws, and contrary to her policy. But, how is the case different on the return of the plaintiff to the State of Missouri? Is she bound to recognize and enforce the law of Illinois? For, unless she is, the status and condition of the slave upon his return remains the same as originally existed. Has the law of Illinois any greater force within the jurisdiction of Missouri, than the laws of the latter within that of the former? Certainly not. They stand upon an equal footing. Neither has any force extra-territorially, except what may be voluntarily conceded to them. . . .

It is perhaps not unfit to notice, in this connection, that many of the most eminent statesmen and jurists of the country entertain the opinion that . . . the act of Congress, even within the territory to which it relates, was not authorized by any power under the Constitution. The doctrine here contended for, not only upholds its validity in the territory, but claims for it effect beyond and within the limits of a sovereign State—an effect, as insisted, that displaces the laws of the State, and substitutes its own provisions in their place.

The consequences of any such construction are apparent. If Congress possesses the power, under the Constitution, to abolish slavery in a Territory, it must necessarily possess the like power to establish it. It cannot be a one-sided power, as may suit the convenience or particular views of the advocates. It is a power, if it exists at all, over the whole subject; and then, upon the process of reasoning which seeks to extend its influence beyond the Territory, and within the limits of a State, if Congress should establish, instead of abolish, slavery, we do not see but that, if a slave should be removed from the Territory into a free State, his status would accompany him, and continue, notwithstanding its laws against slavery. The laws of the free State, according to the argument, would be displaced, and the act of Congress, in its effect, be substituted in their place. We do not see how this conclusion could be avoided, if the construction against which we are contending should prevail. We are satisfied, however, it is unsound, and that the true answer to it is, that even conceding, for the purposes of the argument, that this provision of the act of Congress is valid within the Territory for which it was enacted, it can have no operation or effect beyond its limits, or within the jurisdiction of a State. It can neither displace its laws, nor change the status or condition of its inhabitants.

Our conclusion, therefore, is, upon this branch of the case, that the question involved is one depending solely upon the law of Missouri, and that the Federal court sitting in the State, and trying the case before us, was bound to follow it. . . .

■ MR. JUSTICE MCLEAN dissenting.

. . . In the great and leading case of *Prigg v. The State of Pennsylvania* (16 Peters, 594; 14 Curtis, 421,) this court say that, by the general law of nations, no nation is bound to recognize the state of slavery, as found within its territorial dominions, where it is in opposition to its own policy and institutions, in favor of the subjects of other nations where slavery is organized. If it does it, it is as a matter of comity, and not as a matter of international right. The state of slavery is deemed to be a mere municipal regulation, founded upon and limited to the range of the territorial laws. This was fully recognized in Somersett's case, which was decided before the American Revolution. . . .

No case in England appears to have been more thoroughly examined than that of Somersett. The judgment pronounced by Lord Mansfield was the judgment of the Court of King's Bench . . . :

> The state of slavery is of such a nature that it is incapable of being introduced on any reasons, moral or political, but only by positive law, which preserves its force long after the reasons, occasion, and time itself,

from whence it was created, is erased from the memory; it is of a nature that nothing can be suffered to support it but positive law. . . .

The power of Congress to establish Territorial Governments, and to prohibit the introduction of slavery therein, is the next point to be considered. . . .

[I]f it be admitted that the word territory as used means land, and nothing but land, the power of Congress to organize a temporary Government is clear. It has power to make all needful regulations respecting the public lands, and the extent of those "needful regulations" depends upon the direction of Congress, where the means are appropriate to the end, and do not conflict with any of the prohibitions of the Constitution. . . .

If Congress may establish a Territorial Government in the exercise of its discretion, it is a clear principle that a court cannot control that discretion. This being the case, I do not see on what ground the act is held to be void. It did not purport to forfeit property, or take it for public purposes. It only prohibited slavery; in doing which, it followed the ordinance of 1787. . . .

If the principle laid down in the case of *Prigg v. The State of Pennsylvania* is to be maintained, and it is certainly to be maintained until overruled, as the law of this court, there can be no difficulty on this point. In that case, the court says: "The state of slavery is deemed to be a mere municipal regulation, founded upon and limited to the range of the territorial laws." If this be so, slavery can exist nowhere except under the authority of law, founded on usage having the force of law, or by statutory recognition. And the court further says: "It is manifest, from this consideration, that if the Constitution had not contained the clause requiring the rendition of fugitives from labor, every non-slaveholding State in the Union would have been at liberty to have declared free all runaway slaves coming within its limits, and to have given them entire immunity and protection against the claims of their masters." . . .

By virtue of what law is it, that a master may take his slave into free territory, and exact from him the duties of a slave? The law of the Territory does not sanction it. No authority can be claimed under the Constitution of the United States, or any law of Congress. Will it be said that the slave is taken as property, the same as other property which the master may own? To this I answer, that colored persons are made property by the law of the State, and no such power has been given to Congress. Does the master carry with him the law of the State from which he removes into the Territory? . . .

It is said the Territories are common property of the States, and that every man has a right to go there with his property. This is not controverted. But the courts say a slave is not property beyond the operation of the local law which makes him such. . . .

The States of Missouri and Illinois are bounded by a common line. The one prohibits slavery, the other admits it. This has been done by the exercise of that sovereign power which appertains to each. We are bound to respect the institutions of each. . . . Have the people of either any right to disturb the relations of the other? . . .

Illinois has declared in the most solemn and impressive form that there shall be neither slavery nor involuntary servitude in that State, and that any slave brought into it, with a view of becoming a resident, shall be emancipated. . . . With a full knowledge of these facts, a slave is brought from Missouri to Rock Island, in the State of Illinois, and is retained there as a slave for two years, and then taken to Fort Snelling, where slavery is prohibited by the Missouri compromise act, and there he is detained two years longer in a state of slavery. Harriet, his wife, was also kept at the same place four years as a slave. . . . They were then removed to the State of Missouri, and sold as slaves, and in the action before us they are not only claimed as slaves, but a majority of my brethren have held that on their being returned to Missouri the status of slavery attached to them.

I am not able to reconcile this result with the respect due to the State of Illinois. Having the same rights of sovereignty as the State of Missouri in adopting a Constitution, I can perceive no reason why the institutions of Illinois should not receive the same consideration as those of Missouri. . . . [I]t seems to me the principle laid down will enable the people of a slave State to introduce slavery into a free State, for a longer or shorter time, as may suit their convenience; and by returning the slave to the State whence he was brought, by force or otherwise, the status of slavery attaches, and protects the rights of the master, and defies the sovereignty of the free State. There is no evidence before us that Dred Scott and his family returned to Missouri voluntarily. . . . He was removed; which shows that he was passive, as a slave, having exercised no volition on the subject. He did not resist the master by absconding or force. But that was not sufficient to bring him within Lord Stowell's decision; he must have acted voluntarily. It would be a mockery of law and an outrage on his rights to coerce his return, and then claim that it was voluntary, and on that ground that his former status of slavery attached. . . .

In every decision of a slave case prior to that of *Dred Scott v. Emerson*, the Supreme Court of Missouri considered it as turning upon the Constitution of Illinois, the ordinance of 1787, or the Missouri compromise act of 1820. The court treated these acts as in force, and held itself bound to execute them, by declaring the slave to be free who had acquired a domicile under them with the consent of his master.

The late decision reversed this whole line of adjudication, and held that neither the Constitution and laws of the States, nor acts of Congress in relation to Territories, could be judicially noticed by the Supreme Court of Missouri. This is believed to be in conflict with the decisions of all the courts in the Southern States, with some exceptions of recent cases. . . .

I now come to inquire . . . "whether the decisions of the Supreme Court of Missouri, on the question before us, are binding on this court."

While we respect the learning and high intelligence of the State courts, and consider their decisions, with others, as authority, we follow them only where they give a construction to the State statutes. . . .

For twenty-eight years, the decisions of the Supreme Court of Missouri were consistent on all the points made in this case. But this consistent course was suddenly terminated, whether by some new light suddenly springing up, or an excited public opinion, or both, it is not necessary to say. In the case of *Scott v. Emerson*, in 1852, they were overturned and repudiated. . . .

But there is another ground which I deem conclusive, and which I will re-state.

The Supreme Court of Missouri refused to notice the act of Congress or the Constitution of Illinois, under which Dred Scott, his wife and children, claimed that they are entitled to freedom.

This being rejected by the Missouri court, there was no case before it, or least it was a case with only one side. And this is the case which, in the opinion of this court, we are bound to follow. The Missouri court disregards the express provisions of an act of Congress and the Constitution of a sovereign State, both of which laws for twenty-eight years it had not only regarded, but carried into effect.

If a State court may do this, on a question involving the liberty of a human being, what protection do the laws afford? So far from this being a Missouri question, it is a question, as it would seem, within the twenty-fifth section of the judiciary act, where a right to freedom being set up under the act of Congress, and the decision being against such right, it may be brought for revision before this court, from the Supreme Court of Missouri.

■ MR. JUSTICE CURTIS dissenting.

I dissent from the opinion pronounced by the Chief Justice, and from the judgment which the majority of the court think it proper to render in this case. . . .

[U]nder the allegations contained in this plea, and admitted by the demurrer, the question is, whether any person of African descent, whose ancestors were sold as slaves in the United States, can be a citizen of the United States. If any such person can be a citizen, this plaintiff has the right to the judgment of the court that he is so; for no cause is shown by the plea why he is not so, except his descent and the slavery of his ancestors. . . .

To determine whether any free persons, descended from Africans held in slavery, were citizens of the United States under the Confederation, and consequently at the time of the adoption of the Constitution of the United States, it is only necessary to know whether any such persons were citizens of either of the States under the Confederation, at the time of the adoption of the Constitution.

Of this there can be no doubt. At the time of the ratification of the Articles of Confederation, all free native-born inhabitants of the States of New Hampshire, Massachusetts, New York, New Jersey, and North Carolina, though descended from African slaves, were not only citizens of those States, but such of them as had the other necessary qualifications possessed the franchise of electors, on equal terms with other citizens. . . .

The fourth of the fundamental articles of the Confederation was as follows: "The free inhabitants of each of these States, paupers, vagabonds, and fugitives from justice, excepted, shall be entitled to all the privileges and immunities of free citizens in the several States."

The fact that free persons of color were citizens of some of the several States, and the consequence, that this fourth article of the Confederation would have the effect to confer on such persons the privileges and immunities of general citizenship, were not only known to those who framed and adopted those articles, but the evidence is decisive, that the fourth article was intended to have that effect, and that more restricted language, which would have excluded such persons, was deliberately and purposely rejected. . . .

Did the Constitution of the United States deprive them or their descendants of citizenship? . . .

I can find nothing in the Constitution which, *proprio vigore*, deprives of their citizenship any class of persons who were citizens of the United States at the time of its adoption, or who should be native-born citizens of any State after its adoption; nor any power enabling Congress to disfranchise persons born on the soil of any State, and entitled to citizenship of such State by its Constitution and laws. And my opinion is, that, under the Constitution of the United States, every free person born on the soil of a State, who is a citizen of that State by force of its Constitution or laws, is also a citizen of the United States. . . .

The first section of the second article of the Constitution uses the language, "a natural-born citizen." It thus assumes that citizenship may be acquired by birth. Undoubtedly, this language of the Constitution was used in reference to that principle of public law, well understood in this country at the time of the adoption of the Constitution, which referred citizenship to the place of birth. . . .

That the Constitution itself has defined citizenship of the United States by declaring what persons, born within the several States, shall or shall not be citizens of the United States, will not be pretended. . . .

Has it empowered Congress to enact what free persons, born within the several States, shall or shall not be citizens of the United States? . . . Among the powers expressly granted to Congress is "the power to establish a uniform rule of naturalization." It is not doubted that this is a power to prescribe a rule for the removal of the disabilities consequent on foreign birth. To hold that it extends further than this, would do violence to the meaning of the term naturalization. . . .

It appears, then, that the only power expressly granted to Congress to legislate concerning citizenship, is confined to the removal of the disabilities of foreign birth. . . .

It has been often asserted that the Constitution was made exclusively by and for the white race. It has already been shown that in five of the thirteen original States, colored persons then possessed the elective franchise, and were among those by whom the Constitution was ordained and established. If so, it is not true, in point of fact, that the Constitution was made exclusively by the white race. And that it was made exclusively for the white race is, in my opinion, not only an assumption not warranted by anything in the Constitution, but contradicted by its opening declaration, that it was ordained and established by the people of the United States, for themselves and their posterity. And as free colored persons were then citizens of at least five States, and so in every sense part of the people of the United States, they were among those for whom and whose posterity the Constitution was ordained and established. . . .

I dissent, therefore, from that part of the opinion of the majority of the court, in which it is held that a person of African descent cannot be a citizen of the United States; and I regret I must go further, and dissent both from what I deem their assumption of authority to examine the constitutionality of the act of Congress commonly called the Missouri compromise act, and the grounds and conclusions announced in their opinion. . . .

The judgment of this court is, that the case is to be dismissed for want of jurisdiction, because the plaintiff was not a citizen of Missouri, as he alleged in his declaration. Into that judgment, according to the settled course of this court, nothing appearing after a plea to the merits can enter. A great question of constitutional law, deeply affecting the peace and welfare of the country, is not, in my opinion, a fit subject to be thus reached.

But as, in my opinion, the Circuit Court had jurisdiction, I am obliged to consider the question whether its judgment on the merits of the case should stand or be reversed. . . .

The general question may be stated to be, whether the plaintiff's *status*, as a slave, was so changed by his residence within [the Wisconsin] territory, that he was not a slave in the State of Missouri, at the time this action was brought.

In such cases, two inquiries arise, which may be confounded, but should be kept distinct.

The first is, what was the law of the Territory into which the master and slave went, respecting the relation between them?

The second is, whether the State of Missouri recognizes and allows the effect of that law of the Territory, on the *status* of the slave, on his return within its jurisdiction.

As to the first of these questions[:] . . . In the *Commonwealth v. Aves* (18 Pick., 218), Mr. Chief Justice Shaw said: "From the principle above stated, on which a slave brought here becomes free, to wit: that he becomes entitled to the protection of our laws, it would seem to follow, as a necessary conclusion, that if the slave waives the protection of those laws, and returns to the State where he is held as a slave, his condition is not changed." It was upon this ground, as is apparent from his whole reasoning, that Sir William Scott rests his opinion in the case of the slave Grace. To use one of his expressions, the effect of the law of England was to put the liberty of the slave into a parenthesis. If there had been an act of Parliament declaring that a slave coming to England with his master should thereby be deemed no longer to be a slave, it is easy to see that the learned judge could not have arrived at the same conclusion. . . .

[I]f the acts of Congress on this subject are valid, the law of the Territory of Wisconsin, within whose limits the residence of the plaintiff and his wife, and their marriage and the birth of one or both of their children, took place, . . . is a law operating directly on the *status* of the slave [setting him free and terminating the rights of the master]. By the eighth section of the act of March 6, 1820, it was enacted that, within this Territory, "slavery and involuntary servitude, otherwise than in the punishment of crimes, whereof the parties shall have been duly convicted, shall be, and is hereby, forever prohibited: *Provided, always*, that any person escaping into the same, from whom labor or service is lawfully claimed in any State or Territory of the United States, such fugitive may be lawfully reclaimed, and conveyed to the person claiming his or her labor or service, as aforesaid." . . .

It thus appears that, by these acts of Congress . . . it was positively enacted that slavery and involuntary servitude, with only one exception, specifically described, should not exist there. It is not simply that slavery is not recognized and cannot be aided by the municipal law. It is recognised for the purpose of being absolutely prohibited, and declared incapable of existing within the Territory, save in the instance of a fugitive slave. . . .

I must conclude, therefore, that it was the will of Congress that the state of involuntary servitude of a slave, coming into the Territory with his master, should cease to exist. . . .

But it is a distinct question, whether the law of Missouri recognised and allowed effect to the change wrought in the status of the plaintiff, by force of the laws of the Territory of Wisconsin.

. . . Undoubtedly, every sovereign State may refuse to recognise a change, wrought by the law of a foreign State, on the *status* of a person, while within such foreign State. . . . Its will to refuse such recognition may be manifested by what we term statute law, or by the customary law of the State. It is within the province of its judicial tribunals to inquire and adjudge whether it appears, from the statute or customary law of the State, to be the will of the State to refuse to recognise such changes of *status* by force of foreign law, as the rules of the law of nations require to be recognised. But, in my opinion, it is not within the province of any judicial tribunal to refuse such recognition from any political considerations, or any view it may take of the exterior political relations between the State and one or more foreign States, or any impressions it may have that a change of foreign opinion and action on the subject of slavery may afford a reason why the State should change its own action. To understand and give just effect to such considerations, and to change the action of the State in consequence of them, are functions of diplomatists and legislators, not of judges. . . .

[T]here are other facts stated on the record which should not be passed over. It is agreed that, in the year 1836, the plaintiff, while residing in the Territory, was married, with the consent of Dr. Emerson, to Harriet, . . . and that Eliza and Lizzie were the children of that marriage, the first named having been born on the Mississippi river, north of the line of Missouri, and the other having been born after their return to Missouri. And the inquiry is, whether . . . any other State or Country can, consistently with the settled rules of international law, refuse to recognise and treat him as a free man, when suing for the liberty of himself, his wife, and the children of that marriage. It is in reference to his [and his family's] *status*, as viewed in other States and countries, that the contract of marriage and the birth of children becomes strictly material. . . .

It is a principle of international law, settled beyond controversy in England and America, that a marriage, valid by the law of the place where it was contracted, and not in fraud of the law of any other place, is valid everywhere; and that no technical domicile at the place of the contract is necessary to make it so.

If, in Missouri, the plaintiff were held to be a slave, the validity and operation of his contract of marriage must be denied. . . .

What, then, shall we say of the consent of the master, that the slave may contract a lawful marriage, attended with all the civil rights and duties which belong to that relation; that he may enter into a relation which none but a free man can assume . . . ? In my judgment, there can be no more effectual abandonment of the legal rights of a master over his slave, than by the consent of the master that the slave should enter into a contract of marriage, in a free State, attended by all the civil rights and obligations which belong to that condition.

And any claim by Dr. Emerson, or any one claiming under him, the effect of which is to deny the validity of this marriage, and the lawful paternity of the children born from it, wherever asserted, is, in my judgment, a claim inconsistent with good faith and sound reason, as well as with the rules of international law. And I go further: in my opinion, a law of the State of Missouri, which should thus annul a marriage, lawfully contracted by these parties while resident in Wisconsin, not in fraud of any law of Missouri, or of any right of Dr. Emerson, who consented thereto, would be a law impairing the obligation of a contract, and within the prohibition of the Constitution of the United States. (See *Trustees of Dartmouth College v. Woodward*, 17 U.S. (4 Wheat.) 518, 629, 695, 696 (1819).) . . .

But it is insisted that the Supreme Court of Missouri has settled this case by its decision in *Scott v. Emerson*. . . .

To the correctness of such a decision I cannot assent. In my judgment, the opinion of the majority of the court in that case is in conflict with its previous decisions, with a great weight of judicial authority in other slaveholding States. . . .

When the decisions of the highest court of a State are directly in conflict with each other, it has been repeatedly held, here, that the last decision is not necessarily to be taken as the rule. . . .

I have thus far assumed, merely for the purpose of the argument, that the laws of the United States, respecting slavery in this Territory, were constitutionally enacted by Congress. It remains to inquire whether they are constitutional and binding laws. . . . *[Justice Curtis rejects the proposition that the Territory Clause of Article IV applies only to original territory.—Editors]*

It has been urged that the words "rules and regulations" are not appropriate terms in which to convey authority to make laws for the government of the territory.

But it must be remembered that this is a grant of power to the Congress—that it is therefore necessarily a grant of power to legislate. . . . Power granted to a Legislature to make all needful rules and regulations respecting the territory, is a power to pass all needful laws respecting it. . . .

But it is insisted, that whatever other powers Congress may have respecting the territory of the United States, the subject of negro slavery forms an exception.

The Constitution declares that Congress shall have power to make "*all* needful rules and regulations" respecting the territory belonging to the United States. . . .

There is nothing in the context which qualifies the grant of power. The regulations must be "respecting the territory." An enactment that slavery may or may not exist there, is a regulation respecting the territory. Regulations must be needful; but it is necessarily left to the legislative discretion to determine whether a law be needful. No other clause of the Constitution has been referred to at the bar, or has been seen by me, which imposes any restriction or makes any exception concerning the power of Congress to allow or prohibit slavery in the territory belonging to the United States. . . .

It appears, however, from what has taken place at the bar, that notwithstanding the language of the Constitution, and the long line of legislative and executive precedents under it, three different and opposite views are taken of the power of Congress respecting slavery in the Territories.

One is, that though Congress can make a regulation prohibiting slavery in a Territory, they cannot make a regulation allowing it; another is, that it can neither be established nor prohibited by Congress, but that the people of a Territory, when organized by Congress, can establish or prohibit slavery; while the third is, that the Constitution itself secures to every citizen who holds slaves, under the laws of any

State, the indefeasible right to carry them into any Territory, and there hold them as property.

No particular clause of the Constitution has been referred to at the bar in support of either of these views. The first seems to be rested upon general considerations concerning the social and moral evils of slavery, its relations to republican Governments, its inconsistency with the Declaration of Independence and with natural right.

The second is drawn from considerations equally general, concerning the right of self-government, and the nature of the political institutions which have been established by the people of the United States.

While the third is said to rest upon the equal right of all citizens to go with their property upon the public domain, and the inequality of a regulation which would admit the property of some and exclude the property of other citizens. . . .

With the weight of either of these considerations, when presented to Congress to influence its action, this court has no concern. One or the other may be justly entitled to guide or control the legislative judgment upon what is a needful regulation. The question here is, whether they are sufficient to authorize this court to insert into this clause of the Constitution an exception of the exclusion or allowance of slavery, not found therein, nor in any other part of that instrument. . . . To allow this to be done with the Constitution, upon reasons purely political, renders its judicial interpretation impossible—because judicial tribunals, as such, cannot decide upon political considerations. Political reasons have not the requisite certainty to afford rules of juridical interpretation. They are different in different men. They are different in the same men at different times. And when a strict interpretation of the Constitution, according to the fixed rules which govern the interpretation of laws, is abandoned, and the theoretical opinions of individuals are allowed to control its meaning, we have no longer a Constitution; we are under the government of individual men, who for the time being have power to declare what the Constitution is, according to their own views of what it ought to mean. . . .

Looking at the power of Congress over the Territories as of the extent just described, what positive prohibition exists in the Constitution, which restrained Congress from enacting [the Missouri Compromise]?

The only one suggested is that clause in the fifth article of the amendments of the Constitution which declares that no person shall be deprived of his life, liberty, or property, without due process of law. . . .

Is it conceivable that the Constitution has conferred the right on every citizen to become a resident on the territory of the United States with his slaves, and there to hold them as such, but has neither made nor provided for any municipal regulations which are essential to the existence of slavery? . . .

Nor, in my judgment, will the position, that a prohibition to bring slaves into a Territory deprives any one of his property without due process of law, bear examination.

. . . It was certainly understood by the Convention which framed the Constitution, and has been so understood ever since, that, under the power to regulate commerce, Congress could prohibit the importation of slaves; and the exercise of the power was restrained till 1808. A citizen of the United States owns slaves in Cuba, and brings them to the United States, where they are set free by the legislation of Congress. Does this legislation deprive him of his property without due process of law? If so, what becomes of the laws prohibiting the slave trade? If not, how can a similar regulation respecting a Territory violate the fifth amendment of the Constitution? . . .

For these reasons, I am of opinion that so much of the several acts of Congress as prohibited slavery and involuntary servitude within that part of the Territory of Wisconsin lying north of thirty-six degrees thirty minutes north latitude, and west of the river Mississippi, were constitutional and valid laws. . . .

NOTES

1.   In *Dred Scott* the Court seemed to go out of its way to decide as many issues as possible, in the most pro-slavery manner possible. Why? Any answer remains speculative, but it was clearly a moment of deep political division. The preceding year (1856) had seen the raids and executions of "Bleeding Kansas"; Representative Preston Brooks's brutal caning of Senator Charles Sumner on the Senate floor after an anti-slavery speech; and a contentious presidential election. It was at this moment that Chief Justice Taney tried to settle the constitutional issues concerning slavery and national expansion. There is evidence that a year earlier, before the presidential election and re-argument, the Court was prepared to rule against Dred Scott on narrower legal grounds, along the lines of Justice Nelson's concurring opinion (which apparently was originally drafted as the majority opinion of the Court). When it became clear that the dissenting justices would assert that that Dred Scott was free, on the basis of the Missouri Compromise, Taney decided to write a more comprehensive opinion. He was even urged on by President-elect Buchanan, who lobbied the Court about a matter that was *sub judice*. This case, which had begun nearly eleven years earlier as a state-court lawsuit that seemed certain to result in Scott's freedom under then-controlling Missouri law, had drawn the attention of the nation.

2.   Consider the three holdings in Taney's opinion: (a) the jurisdiction and "citizenship" holding; (b) the Territory Clause Power and Missouri Compromise holding; and (c) the state choice-of-law holding. There was and still is much debate about whether some of these were dicta, but each purports to be part of the Opinion of the Court. See Fehrenbacher, THE DRED SCOTT CASE at 322–334.

a.   The first issue is whether the district court properly had diversity-of-citizenship jurisdiction. John Sanford (Mrs. Emerson's brother) was a resident and citizen of New York state. What was Dred Scott's state citizenship for purposes of federal diversity jurisdiction under Article III's provision authorizing federal court suits between "citizens of different states"? Taney concludes that Dred Scott may not be considered a citizen of Missouri. He has *no* state citizenship—he cannot be a citizen of *any* state, Taney claims, because he cannot be a citizen of the *United States*, given his race. And, to Taney, the Declaration of Independence and the Constitution said nothing that could change that status.

How many ways is this wrong? Study Taney's argument and the rejoinder of the dissenters. Justice Curtis points out that, among other flaws, Taney's point is simply false as an historical matter: many free blacks were citizens of states at the time of the founding. What is really going on here? Apparently, Taney simply could not countenance the prospect of free blacks as citizens entitled to the "privileges and immunities" that citizens possess in other states (pursuant to Article IV's Privileges and Immunities Clause).

b.   The next question the Court decides is whether Dred Scott could be considered entitled to his freedom by virtue of his master's long sojourn in (present-day) Minnesota, in a federal territory where slavery was prohibited by the Missouri Compromise. By the time *Dred Scott* was decided, the Missouri Compromise limiting slavery in the territories was thirty-seven years old and the Northwest Ordinance banning slavery in the original federal territories was seventy years old. Isn't it astonishing that a majority of the Supreme Court would so cavalierly depart from a practice and constitutional interpretation that dated back to the founding of the Republic?

Note Taney's holding that it is not the Territory Clause that gives Congress the power to pass laws governing the territories. That clause was meant only for territory possessed by the nation *at the time the Constitution was adopted*, Taney said. (Is that reasoning is flawed? Can the text of a constitutional provision keep its meaning but be applied to new factual situations not present when it was ratified?) Nonetheless, Taney says, the power *to admit new states* gives rise to an *implied power* to legislate for the territories in the interim.

But then Taney says: Surely Congress cannot, in passing laws for the territories, pass a law that violates one of the provisions of the Bill of Rights. Surely Congress could not establish an official territorial religion. Or abolish the freedom of speech in a territory. And likewise, surely Congress could not pass a law depriving someone of their property, could it? Here Taney invoked the Due Process Clause of the Fifth Amendment: "[T]he rights of property are united with the rights of person, and placed on the same ground by the fifth amendment to the Constitution, which provides that no person shall be deprived of life, liberty, and property, without due process of law. *And an act of Congress which deprives a citizen of the United States of his liberty or property, merely because he came himself or brought his property into a particular Territory of the United States, and who had committed no offence against the laws, could hardly be dignified with the name of due process of law*" (emphasis added).

Did you catch the sleight-of-hand? The Due Process Clause does not forbid the national government from ever depriving someone of life, liberty, or property. It allows these deprivations as long as there is "due process of law." (The Due Process Clauses are considered in more detail at p. 1476.) But Taney seemingly reads those words out of the clause, changing it from a guarantee of procedural regularity into a substantive protection of property rights. And not just any property rights: a judicially invented fundamental right of (white) persons to own slaves. On this point, as with the citizenship holding, Taney's opinion illustrates how constitutional interpretation can go wrong: first picking a desired result, then distorting the Constitution's language to produce that result; reading constitutional texts to mean the opposite of what they say, either by ignoring what they plainly say, or by making up things they plainly do not say; and then predicating those readings on false claims about original intent, history, or precedent.

c.   Taney is not quite finished at this point. There remains the question of whether Dred Scott might be free by virtue of his time in the free *state* of Illinois. Taney's reasoning here is perhaps not entirely indefensible: Illinois law might have made Scott free, but Scott brought his claim in Missouri courts and Missouri might legitimately have determined that Missouri law, not Illinois law, governed Scott's status in such a suit. Illinois law might have operated to free Scott, but it had not been brought to bear in an actual adjudication. So, upon his return to Missouri, his status as a slave might validly re-attach, it never having been *legally* severed.

Recall *Lemmon*. Is Chief Justice Taney's analysis so clearly wrong on this point? Might it have been different if Illinois had *adjudicated* Scott to be free and he then *returned* to Missouri? Might Missouri then have been required to honor and enforce the

Illinois judgment under the Full Faith and Credit Clause? Indeed, would not Scott in such an instance then have been entitled, in Missouri, to the "Privileges and Immunities of citizens of the several States"—the same privileges or civil rights that Missouri provided any of its citizens?

This is the argument set forth at greater length (and with greater precision) in Justice Nelson's concurrence, which apparently had been the original draft majority opinion for the Court—a narrower argument for the result that Dred Scott remained, legally, a slave. Is this position right? If it is, wouldn't the same reasoning apply to the legal consequences of Scott's sojourn in federal territory? Perhaps the Missouri Compromise, had it been brought to bear in a suit adjudicating Scott's claim for freedom, would have made him free. But that had never happened. Unless somehow the bare act of *touching* free soil makes a slave (if not a fugitive) free, why was not Missouri permitted to apply Missouri law to determine the legal status of a Missouri domiciliary, in an action brought in courts situated in Missouri?

What is the dissenters' response to this argument? Is it that the Missouri Compromise law really was self-executing? What about the argument that allowing Dred Scott and Harriet to be married constituted an affirmative act of manumission? Do you find any of these arguments persuasive? What should have been the outcome?

3.   How would you describe Chief Justice Taney's interpretive method? Was it originalist? Many commentators have thought so, citing *Dred Scott* as an example of the perils of looking to original intent or to the original understanding of the Constitution. See, e.g., Christopher Eisgruber, *Dred Again: Originalism's Forgotten Past*, 10 Const. Comm. 37 (1993); *cf.* Mark Graber, DRED SCOTT AND THE PROBLEM OF CONSTITUTIONAL EVIL (2006). What did Justice Curtis think? Did he think the Court followed the original meaning of the Constitution too closely, or disregarded it?

4.   The Court's decision produced the strongest and most sustained backlash against the authority of the Supreme Court's decisions in our nation's history. One of the critics of *Dred Scott* was Abraham Lincoln, then a candidate for the U.S. Senate from Illinois. The debate between Lincoln and his rival, Senator Stephen Douglas, is discussed at p. 391.

5.   Does Congress have power under the Territories Clause to create non-Article III courts in the territorial governments? If Congress can create territorial courts that do not comply with Article III, as the Marshall Court held in *American Insurance Company v. Canter*, 26 U.S. (1 Pet.) 511 (1828), then why could it not violate the Bill of Rights in the territories?

[Assignment 38]

E. THE GUARANTEE CLAUSE: SECESSION, RECONSTRUCTION, AND REPRESENTATION

Art. IV, § 4: The United States shall guarantee to every State in this Union a Republican Form of Government, and shall protect each of them against Invasion; and on Application of the Legislature, or of the Executive (when the Legislature cannot be convened) against domestic Violence.

The most nationalist of the framers had high hopes for the Guarantee Clause, but it was not used until an uprising in Rhode Island in the 1840s called "Dorr's Rebellion." (Dorr's Rebellion is described in the discussion of *Luther v. Borden*, at p. 431.) In the Civil War and Reconstruction, however, this Clause became extraordinarily important. Did the eleven Confederate states have a Republican Form of Government? If not, was President Lincoln constitutionally obligated by his oath of office and the Take Care Clause to put down what he termed the War of the Rebellion, and to reconstruct these states to ensure that a Republican Form of Government was established?

We begin with President Lincoln's First Inaugural Address. It consists almost entirely of an examination of important constitutional questions, such as the Constitution's treatment of slavery, secession, judicial supremacy, and the duties and powers of the executive.

Abraham Lincoln, First Inaugural Address
Mar. 4, 1861

Fellow citizens of the United States:

In compliance with a custom as old as the Government itself, I appear before you to address you briefly and to take in your presence the oath prescribed by the Constitution of the United States to be taken by the President "before he enters on the execution of this office."

I do not consider it necessary at present for me to discuss those matters of administration about which there is no special anxiety or excitement.

Apprehension seems to exist among the people of the Southern States that by the accession of a Republican Administration their property and their peace and personal security are to be endangered. There has never been any reasonable cause for such apprehension. Indeed, the most ample evidence to the contrary has all the while existed and been open to their inspection. It is found in nearly all the published speeches of him who now addresses you. I do but quote from one of those speeches when I declare that "I have no purpose, directly or indirectly, to interfere with the institution of slavery in the States where it exists. I believe I have no lawful right to do so, and I have no inclination to do so." Those who nominated and elected me did so with full knowledge that I had made this and many similar declarations and had never recanted them; and more than this, they placed in the platform for my acceptance, and as a law to themselves and to me, the clear and emphatic resolution which I now read:

> *Resolved,* That the maintenance inviolate of the rights of the States, and especially the right of each State to order and control its own domestic institutions according to its own judgment exclusively, is essential to that balance of power on which the perfection and endurance of our political fabric depend; and we denounce the lawless invasion by armed force of the soil of any State or Territory, no matter what pretext, as among the gravest of crimes.

I now reiterate these sentiments, and in doing so I only press upon the public attention the most conclusive evidence of which the case is susceptible that the property, peace, and security of no section are to be in any wise endangered by the now incoming Administration. I add, too, that all the protection which, consistently with the Constitution and the laws, can be given will be cheerfully given to all the States when lawfully demanded, for whatever cause—as cheerfully to one section as to another.

There is much controversy about the delivering up of fugitives from service or labor. The clause I now read is as plainly written in the Constitution as any other of its provisions:

> No person held to service or labor in one State, under the laws thereof, escaping into another, shall in consequence of any law or regulation therein be discharged from such service or labor, but shall be delivered up on claim of the party to whom such service or labor may be due.

It is scarcely questioned that this provision was intended by those who made it for the reclaiming of what we call fugitive slaves; and the intention of the lawgiver is the law. All members of Congress swear their support to the whole Constitution—to this provision as much as to any other. To the proposition, then, that slaves whose cases come within the terms of this clause "shall be delivered up" their oaths are unanimous. Now, if they would make the effort in good temper, could they not with nearly equal unanimity frame and pass a law by means of which to keep good that unanimous oath?

There is some difference of opinion whether this clause should be enforced by national or by State authority, but surely that difference is not a very material one. If the slave is to be surrendered, it can be of but little consequence to him or to others by which authority it is done. And should anyone in any case be content that his oath shall go unkept on a merely unsubstantial controversy as to *how* it shall be kept?

Again, in any law upon this subject ought not all the safeguards of liberty known in civilized and humane jurisprudence to be introduced, so that a free man be not in any case surrendered as a slave? And might it not be well at the same time to provide by law for the enforcement of that clause in the Constitution which guarantees that "the citizens of each State shall be entitled to all privileges and immunities of citizens in the several States"?

I take the official oath to-day with no mental reservations and with no purpose to construe the Constitution or laws by any hypercritical rules; and while I do not choose now to specify particular acts of Congress as proper to be enforced, I do suggest that it will be much safer for all, both in official and private stations, to conform to and abide by all those acts which stand unrepealed than to violate any of them trusting to find impunity in having them held to be unconstitutional.

It is seventy-two years since the first inauguration of a President under our National Constitution. During that period fifteen different and greatly distinguished citizens have in succession administered the executive branch of the Government. They have conducted it through many perils, and generally with great success. Yet, with all this scope of precedent, I now enter upon the same task for the brief constitutional term of four years under great and peculiar difficulty. A disruption of the Federal Union, heretofore only menaced, is now formidably attempted.

I hold that in contemplation of universal law and of the Constitution the Union of these States is perpetual. Perpetuity is implied, if not expressed, in the fundamental law of all national governments. It is safe to assert that no government proper ever had a provision in its organic law for its own termination. Continue to execute all the express provisions of our National Constitution, and the Union will endure forever, it being impossible to destroy it except by some action not provided for in the instrument itself.

Again, if the United States be not a government proper, but an association of States in the nature of contract merely, can it, as a contract, be peaceably unmade by less than all the parties who made it? One party to a contract may violate it—break it, so to speak—but does it not require all to lawfully rescind it?

Descending from these general principles, we find the proposition that in legal contemplation the Union is perpetual confirmed by the history of the Union itself. The Union is much older than the Constitution. It was formed, in fact, by the Articles of Association in 1774. It was matured and continued by the Declaration of Independence in 1776. It was further matured, and the faith of all the then thirteen States expressly plighted and engaged that it should be perpetual, by the Articles of Confederation in 1778. And finally, in 1787, one of the declared objects for ordaining and establishing the Constitution was *"to form a more perfect Union."*

But if destruction of the Union by one or by a part only of the States be lawfully possible, the Union is *less* perfect than before the Constitution, having lost the vital element of perpetuity.

It follows from these views that no State upon its own mere motion can lawfully get out of the Union; that *resolves* and *ordinances* to that effect are legally void, and that acts of violence within any State or States against the authority of the United States are insurrectionary or revolutionary, according to circumstances.

I therefore consider that in view of the Constitution and the laws the Union is unbroken, and to the extent of my ability, I shall take care, as the Constitution itself expressly enjoins upon me, that the laws of the Union be faithfully executed in all the States. Doing this I deem to be only a simple duty on my part, and I shall perform it so far as practicable unless my rightful masters, the American people, shall withhold the requisite means or in some authoritative manner direct the contrary. I trust this will not be regarded as a menace, but only as the declared purpose of the Union that it *will* constitutionally defend and maintain itself.

In doing this there needs to be no bloodshed or violence, and there shall be none unless it be forced upon the national authority. The power confided to me will be used to hold, occupy, and possess the property and places belonging to the Government and to collect the duties and imposts; but beyond what may be necessary for these objects, there will be no invasion, no using of force against or among the people anywhere. Where hostility to the United States in any interior locality shall be so great and universal as to prevent competent resident citizens from holding the Federal offices, there will be no attempt to force obnoxious strangers among the people for that object. While the strict legal right may exist in the Government to enforce the exercise of these offices, the attempt to do so would be so irritating and so nearly impracticable withal that I deem it better to forego for the time the uses of such offices.

The mails, unless repelled, will continue to be furnished in all parts of the Union. So far as possible the people everywhere shall have that sense of perfect security which is most favorable to calm thought and reflection. The course here indicated will be followed unless current events and experience shall show a modification or change to be proper, and in every case and exigency my best discretion will be exercised, according to circumstances actually existing and with a view and a hope of a peaceful solution of the national troubles and the restoration of fraternal sympathies and affections.

That there are persons in one section or another who seek to destroy the Union at all events and are glad of any pretext to do it I will neither affirm nor deny; but if there be such, I need address no word to them. To those, however, who really love the Union may I not speak?

Before entering upon so grave a matter as the destruction of our national fabric, with all its benefits, its memories, and its hopes, would it not be wise to ascertain precisely why we do it? Will you hazard so desperate a step while there is any possibility that any portion of the ills you fly from have no real existence? Will you, while the certain ills you fly to are greater than all the real ones you fly from, will you risk the commission of so fearful a mistake?

All profess to be content in the Union if all constitutional rights can be maintained. Is it true, then, that any right plainly written in the Constitution has been denied? I think not. Happily, the human mind is so constituted that no party can reach to the audacity of doing this. Think, if you can, of a single instance in which a plainly written provision of the Constitution has ever been denied. If by the mere force of numbers a majority should deprive a minority of any clearly written constitutional right, it might in a moral point of view justify revolution; certainly would if such right were a vital one. But such is not our case. All the vital rights of minorities and of individuals are so plainly assured to them by affirmations and negations, guaranties and prohibitions, in the Constitution that controversies never arise concerning them. But no organic law can ever be framed with a provision specifically applicable to every question which may occur in practical administration. No foresight can anticipate nor any document of reasonable length contain express provisions for all possible questions. Shall fugitives from labor be surrendered by national or by State authority? The Constitution does not expressly say. *May* Congress prohibit slavery in the Territories? The Constitution does not expressly say. *Must* Congress protect slavery in the Territories? The Constitution does not expressly say.

From questions of this class spring all our constitutional controversies, and we divide upon them into majorities and minorities. If the minority will not acquiesce, the majority must, or the Government must cease. There is no other alternative, for continuing the Government is acquiescence on one side or the other. If a minority in such case will secede rather than acquiesce, they make a precedent which in turn will divide and ruin them, for a minority of their own will secede from them whenever a majority refuses to be controlled by such minority. For instance, why may not any portion of a new confederacy a year or two hence arbitrarily secede again, precisely as portions of the present Union now claim to secede from it? All who cherish disunion sentiments are now being educated to the exact temper of doing this. Is there such perfect identity of interests among the States to compose a new union as to produce harmony only and prevent renewed secession?

Plainly the central idea of secession is the essence of anarchy. A majority held in restraint by constitutional checks and limitations, and always changing easily with deliberate changes of popular opinions and sentiments, is the only true sovereign of a free people. Whoever rejects it does of necessity fly to anarchy or to despotism. Unanimity is impossible. The rule of a minority, as a permanent arrangement, is wholly inadmissible; so that, rejecting the majority principle, anarchy or despotism in some form is all that is left.

I do not forget the position assumed by some that constitutional questions are to be decided by the Supreme Court, nor do I deny that such decisions must be binding in any case upon the parties to a suit as to the object of that suit, while they are also entitled to very high respect and consideration in all parallel cases by all other departments of the Government. And while it is obviously possible that such decision may be erroneous in any given case, still the evil effect following it, being limited to that particular case, with the chance that it may be overruled and never become a precedent for other cases, can better be borne than could the evils of a different practice. At the same time, the candid citizen must confess that if the policy of the Government upon vital questions affecting the whole people is to be irrevocably fixed by decisions of the Supreme Court, the instant they are made in ordinary litigation between parties in personal actions the people will have ceased to be their own rulers, having to that extent practically resigned their Government into the hands of that eminent tribunal. Nor is there in this view any assault upon the court or the judges. It is a duty from which they may not shrink to decide cases properly brought before them, and it is no fault of theirs if others seek to turn their decisions to political purposes.

One section of our country believes slavery is *right* and ought to be extended, while the other believes it is *wrong* and ought not to be extended. This is the only substantial dispute. The fugitive-slave clause of the Constitution and the law for the suppression of the foreign slave trade are each as well enforced, perhaps, as any law can ever be in a community where the moral sense of the people imperfectly supports the law itself. The great body of the people abide by the dry legal obligation in both cases, and a few break over in each. This, I think, can not be perfectly cured, and it would be worse in both cases *after* the separation of the sections than before. The foreign slave trade, now imperfectly suppressed, would be ultimately revived without restriction in one section, while fugitive slaves, now only partially surrendered, would not be surrendered at all by the other.

Physically speaking, we can not separate. We can not remove our respective sections from each other nor build an impassable wall between them. A husband and wife may be divorced and go out of the presence and beyond the reach of each other, but the different parts of our country can not do this. They can not but remain face to face, and intercourse, either amicable or hostile, must continue between them. Is it possible, then, to make that intercourse more advantageous or more satisfactory *after* separation than *before?* Can aliens make treaties easier than friends can make laws? Can treaties be more faithfully enforced between aliens than laws can among friends? Suppose you go to war, you can not fight always; and when, after much loss on both sides and no gain on either, you cease fighting, the identical old questions, as to terms of intercourse, are again upon you.

This country, with its institutions, belongs to the people who inhabit it. Whenever they shall grow weary of the existing Government, they can exercise their *constitutional* right of amending it or their *revolutionary* right to dismember or overthrow it. I can not be ignorant of the fact that many worthy and patriotic citizens are desirous of having the National Constitution amended. While I make no recommendation of amendments, I fully recognize the rightful authority of the people over the whole subject, to be exercised in either of the modes prescribed in the instrument itself; and I should, under existing circumstances, favor rather than oppose a fair opportunity being afforded the people to act upon it. I will venture to add that to me the convention mode seems preferable, in that it allows amendments to originate with the people themselves, instead of only permitting them to take or reject propositions originated by others, not especially chosen for the purpose, and which might not be precisely such as they would wish to either accept or refuse. I understand a proposed amendment to the Constitution—which amendment, however, I have not seen—has passed Congress, to the effect that the Federal Government shall never interfere with the domestic institutions of the States, including that of persons held to service. To avoid misconstruction of what I have said, I depart from my purpose not to speak of particular amendments so far as to say that, holding such a provision to now be implied constitutional law, I have no objection to its being made express and irrevocable.

The Chief Magistrate derives all his authority from the people, and they have referred none upon him to fix terms for the separation of the States. The people themselves can do this if also they choose, but the Executive as such has nothing to do with it. His duty is to administer the present Government as it came to his hands and to transmit it unimpaired by him to his successor.

Why should there not be a patient confidence in the ultimate justice of the people? Is there any better or equal hope in the world? In our present differences, is either party without faith of being in the right? If the Almighty Ruler of Nations, with His eternal truth and justice, be on your side of the North, or on yours of the South, that truth and that justice will surely prevail by the judgment of this great tribunal of the American people.

By the frame of the Government under which we live this same people have wisely given their public servants but little power for mischief, and have with equal wisdom provided for the return of that little to their own hands at very short intervals. While the people retain their virtue and vigilance no Administration by any extreme of wickedness or folly can very seriously injure the Government in the short space of four years.

My countrymen, one and all, think calmly and *well* upon this whole subject. Nothing valuable can be lost by taking time. If there be an object to *hurry* any of you in hot haste to a step which you would never take *deliberately,* that object will be frustrated by taking time; but no good object can be frustrated by it. Such of you as are now dissatisfied still have the old Constitution unimpaired, and, on the sensitive point, the laws of your own framing under it; while the new Administration will have no immediate power, if it would, to change either. If it were admitted that you who are dissatisfied hold the right side in the dispute, there still is no single good reason for precipitate action. Intelligence, patriotism, Christianity, and a firm reliance on Him who has never yet forsaken this favored land are still competent to adjust in the best way all our present difficulty.

In *your* hands, my dissatisfied fellow-countrymen, and not in *mine,* is the momentous issue of civil war. The Government will not assail *you.* You can have no conflict without being yourselves the aggressors. *You* have no oath registered in heaven to destroy the Government, while I shall have the most solemn one to "preserve, protect, and defend it."

I am loath to close. We are not enemies, but friends. We must not be enemies. Though passion may have strained it must not break our bonds of affection. The mystic chords of memory, stretching from every battlefield and patriot grave to every living heart and hearthstone all over this broad land, will yet swell the chorus of the Union, when again touched, as surely they will be, by the better angels of our nature.

NOTES

1.   Lincoln's First Inaugural reviews much of the pre-Civil War constitutional law of slavery, as well as Article IV. According to Lincoln, does the Constitution create a general constitutional right to own slaves? What are the federal government's obligations and powers with respect to slavery? What do you think of Lincoln's willingness to support a constitutional amendment making permanent his understanding that the federal government lacks power to interfere with slavery in the states (the "Corwin Amendment")?

2.   Evaluate Lincoln's legal argument for the unconstitutionality of secession. Consider how he argues from text, structure, political theory, and history. How is Lincoln's argument related to the position of Madison and Jefferson in the Virginia and Kentucky resolutions (see p. 53)? Does Jefferson's support for "nullification" and "interposition" lead inexorably to an argument for the constitutionality of secession?

3.   Where does "sovereignty" reside under the U.S. Constitution? Lincoln thought that "the central idea of secession, is the essence of anarchy" and that it was inconsistent with the democratic theory of the Constitution for a minority, whenever feeling itself aggrieved, to secede rather than acquiesce. Lincoln amplified this denial of states' sovereignty in a Message to Congress on July 4, 1861 (after the states of the Upper South had seceded and the war had begun). He argued that "secession" should be called "rebellion," conveying the idea of "*violation* of law." He attacked the theory of state sovereignty as a systematic and "insidious debauching of the public mind." Referring to secessionist theorists, he said:

> They invented an ingenious sophism, which, if conceded, was followed by perfectly logical steps, through all the incidents, to the complete destruction of the Union. The sophism itself is, that any state of the Union may, *consistently* with the national Constitution, and therefore *lawfully*, and *peacefully*, withdraw from the Union, without the consent of the Union, or of any other state. The little disguise that the supposed right is to be exercised only for just cause, themselves to be the sole judge of its justice, is too thin to merit any notice. . . .
>
> This sophism derives much—perhaps the whole—of its currency, from the assumption, that there is some omnipotent, and sacred supremacy, pertaining to a *State*—to each State of our Federal Union. Our States have neither more, nor less power, than that reserved to them, in the Union, by the Constitution— no one of them ever having been a State *out* of the Union. . . . Having never been States, either in substance, or in name, *outside* of the Union, whence this magical omnipotence of "State rights," asserting a claim of power to lawfully destroy the Union itself? Much is said about the "sovereignty" of the States; but the word, even, is not in the national Constitution; nor, as is believed, in any of the State constitutions. What is a "sovereignty," in the political sense of the term? Would it be far wrong to define it "A political community, without a political superior"? Tested by this, no one of our States, except Texas, ever as a sovereignty. And even Texas gave up the character on coming into the Union; by which act, she acknowledged the Constitution of the United States, and the laws and treaties of the United States made in pursuance of the Constitution, to be, for her, the supreme law of the land. The States have their *status* IN the

Union, and they have no other *legal status*. If they break from this, they can only do so against law, and by revolution. The Union, and not themselves separately, procured their independence, and their liberty. By conquest or purchase, the Union gave each of them, whatever of independence, and liberty, it has. The Union is older than any of the States; and, in fact, it created them as States. . . . Not one of them ever had a State constitution, independent of the Union. . . .

Unquestionably the States have the powers, and rights, reserved to them in, and by the National Constitution; but among these, surely, are not included all conceivable powers, however mischievous, or destructive; but, at most, such only, as were known in the world, at the time, as governmental powers; and certainly, a power to destroy the government itself, had never been known as a governmental—as a merely administrative powers. This relative matter of National power, and State rights, as a principle, is no other than the principle of *generality*, and *locality*. Whatever concerns the whole should be confided to the whole—to the general government; while, whatever concerns *only* the State, should be left exclusively, to the State. This is all there is of original principle about it.

Do you agree with Lincoln's assessment of the nature of the Union and the location of sovereignty? Lincoln added an argument from the Guarantee Clause of Article IV:

The Constitution provides, and all the States have accepted the provision, that "The United States shall guarantee to every State in this Union a republican form of government." But, if a State may lawfully go out of the Union, having done so, it may also discard the republican form of government; so that to prevent its going out, is an indispensable *means*, to the *end*, of maintaining the guarantee mentioned.

What do you think of this constitutional argument against secession, which Lincoln would also use to justify the use of coercive national force?

4.   Even if you agree with Lincoln's argument against state sovereignty, what about the problem presented if the national government were truly to violate the Constitution, at the expense of the rights of the states? (This problem was presented, in one form, by the Alien and Sedition Acts. See p. 46.) Imagine, for example, that the rest of the Union, decided to kick a state out; the nation refused to seat its senators or representatives, to grant it protection from invasion, or to honor its citizens with the privileges and immunities of citizenship in any other state. Would the aggrieved state then have the right to secede from a Constitution from which it had been in effect expelled? Is there anything in Lincoln's refutation of the broader Southern argument of "state sovereignty" that weakens the force of this narrower argument for a right to secede for egregious, intentional, irremediable violations of the Constitution itself?

This narrower argument was almost exactly how the "moderate" Southern secessionists justified the lawfulness of secession under the Constitution. (Radical secessionists embraced the "state sovereignty" position that states could secede for whatever reason they chose. Others thought secession was perhaps literally unconstitutional, but nonetheless justifiable as an act of revolution, after the fashion of the American Revolution of 1776.) Consider the speeches of two Southern senators during the secession crisis of the winter of 1860–1861, after Lincoln's election but before his inauguration. Their argument, in a nutshell, was that Lincoln's pledged opposition to *Dred Scott was* a gross violation of the South's constitutional rights. Hear first Senator Nicholson of Tennessee:

This [Republican] party promises us, as the inducement to our repose, that our rights of property in slaves shall not be interfered with in the States, because the Constitution recognizes those rights. But they refuse to extend that promise to our rights of property in slaves outside of the States, although, upon the authority of the high judicial tribunal of the country for deciding constitutional questions, we have exactly the same rights outside of the States, within the jurisdiction of the Federal Government, as the owners of any other species of property have. They . . . [deny our rights] and, in so doing, repudiate the authoritative adjudication of the Supreme Court. . . . Although this principle has been declared by the Supreme Court to be the true intent and meaning of the Constitution, . . . the Republican party repudiated that solemn adjudication.

And hear Senator Benjamin of Louisiana, explicitly drawing the analogy equating refusal to accede to the Supreme Court's rulings to refusal to seat a state's representatives in Congress:

[T]he Constitution . . . has provided for a supreme judiciary to determine cases arising in law or equity which may involve the construction of the Constitution. . . .

For the purpose of illustrating the argument upon this subject, let us suppose a clear, palpable case of violation of the Constitution. Let us suppose that the State of South Carolina, having sent two Senators to sit upon this floor, had been met by a resolution of the majority here that, according to her just weight in the Confederacy, one was enough. . . . The Constitution says that each State shall be entitled to two Senators and each Senator shall have one vote. . . . [W]hat man will stand up in this Senate and pretend that if, under these circumstances, the State of South Carolina had declared, "I entered into a Confederacy or a compact by which I was to have my rights guarantied by the constant presence of two Senators upon your floor; you allow me but one; you refuse to repair the injustice; I withdraw," what man would dare say that that was a violation of the Constitution on the part of South Carolina? Who would say that was a revolutionary remedy? Who would deny the plain and palpable proposition that it was the exercise of a right inherent in her under the very principles of the Constitution, and necessarily so inherent for self-defense?

. . . Suppose this violation occurs under circumstances where it does not appear so plain to you, but where it does appear equally plain to South Carolina. . . . South Carolina says, "You forced me to the expenditure of my treasure, you forced me to the shedding of the blood of my people, by a majority vote, and with my aid you acquired territory; now I have a constitutional right to go into that territory with my property, and to be there secured by your laws against its loss." You say, no, she has not. Now there is this to be said: that right is not put down in the Constitution in quite so clear terms as the right to have two Senators; but it is a right which she asserts . . . in accordance with the opinion expressed by the Supreme Court of the United States.

What is the answer to this argument for the validity of secession?

5.   Why not have the Supreme Court resolve the question of the validity of secession? Lincoln, of course, had denied that the Court's decisions were binding on the policy of the nation: Thus, his famous, carefully hedged denial of judicial supremacy in the First Inaugural, culminating in the conclusion that "if the policy of the government, upon vital questions, affecting the whole people, is to be irrevocably fixed by decisions of

the Supreme Court, . . . the people will have ceased, to be their own rulers, having, to that extent, practically resigned their government, into the hands of that eminent tribunal." Lincoln's earlier draft—before advisers convinced him to soften it somewhat—had the concluding phrase read that "the people will have ceased to be their own rulers, *having turned their government over to the despotism of the few life-officers composing the Court.*" The draft original thus explicitly linked the notion of judicial supremacy to the "despotism" of a minority over a majority, in the preceding paragraph.

If Lincoln was *wrong* about judicial supremacy, was the South *right* to secede—acting lawfully, in defense of its constitutional rights, as authoritatively interpreted by the Supreme Court? What if a case presenting the lawfulness of secession had reached the Supreme Court? Imagine the following scenario. South Carolina fires on Fort Sumter, and Lincoln calls up troops to suppress the rebellion. Virginia argues that South Carolina's secession was within its constitutional rights and that national "coercion" is thus unconstitutional. Suppose Virginia brought a suit against the United States, seeking to prohibit the passage of federal armies through its territory to invade a "former" state of the Union. What result? The argument that the national government lacked power to "coerce" the states to remain in the Union was very much part of the discussion at the time. The feckless lame-duck President Buchanan had argued in his December 3, 1860 annual message to Congress that secession was unconstitutional but that the national government had no legitimate power to prevent secession by force, because that would be making war on a state. Republicans ridiculed Buchanan's position as saying, in effect, that no state could secede—unless it wants to—and that the president has a duty to enforce the laws—unless somebody opposes him. There is also evidence that Chief Justice Taney held the same view that the national government lacked power to coerce states to remain in the Union. Suppose then that the Taney Court—essentially the same Court that had decided *Dred Scott* just three years earlier—had ruled in favor of Virginia and ordered the national government to allow the states of the South to leave the Union. Would Lincoln have been required to obey the order? What if Taney had ordered the White House vacated and the Union government moved to some point north of the Mason-Dixon line. Should Lincoln have packed his bags? (And, later in the war, suppose the Supreme Court had declared the Emancipation Proclamation unconstitutional. Should Lincoln have returned freed slaves to their Southern masters?) Who was right about judicial supremacy—Lincoln, the South, or neither?

6.   On the merits, did the national government possess the power to "coerce" the seceding states to remain in the Union? Lincoln's First Inaugural lays out his view that it was his constitutional duty as President to resist what he regarded as a massive violation of the Constitution. What do you think of Lincoln's conception of presidential duty? Could he have negotiated terms for dissolving the Union, consistent with his oath?

Lincoln's theory was that secession was illegal—unconstitutional—and thus of no effect. Accordingly, the Civil War was not a "war" in the constitutional sense that Congress need declare it. It was a massive domestic insurrection, subject to the Guarantee Clause power of the national government to assure republican government and to the duty of the national government to protect each state from "domestic violence." Lincoln consistently referred to the South as "rebels" or "so-called seceding States," never as the "Confederacy" or the "Confederate States of America." Lincoln nonetheless maintained that, as the military power was in operation as a practical matter, he possessed power under the Commander in Chief Clause to employ the law of war to confiscate property and materiel within the control of an enemy force or power—thus, his claimed authority for the Emancipation Proclamation. (Is this position inconsistent?) Lincoln's theory would have other consequences, too: for the conduct of the war, for recognizing temporary or permanent "reconstructed" state governments in the South, and for the constitutional amendment process.

7.   The central constitutional question of "Reconstruction" during and after the war, in both the Lincoln and Andrew Johnson administrations, was what to do with states that had purported to secede. This question turned on whether those states had in fact left the Union. If they had, then they had ceased to exist as states of the Union. Upon defeat and surrender, the region could be treated as part of the "territory" of the United States, subject to Congress's plenary legislative power under the Territories Clause of Article IV. Similarly, "re-admission" as states would be subject to Congress's plenary legislative power with respect to statehood admissions, also under Article IV. If, however, the states had never legally left, but throughout the War remained technically part of the Union, but simply lacked lawful, loyal governments—Lincoln's theory—then Reconstruction was largely a matter of executive policy, supported by congressional legislation, as to how to restore and recognize lawful state governments, under the Guarantee Clause of Article IV.

Which view is right? Consider the creation of the State of West Virginia. Here are the facts in a nutshell: when Virginia purported to secede from the Union, a convention at Wheeling, in the northwest part of the state, declared itself the lawful (loyal) government of Virginia. The federal government recognized that government as the government of Virginia. The loyal government at Wheeling then gave Virginia's consent to the creation of a new state of West Virginia (which would include Wheeling). In short, essentially the same body gave consent to itself to partition Virginia and form a new state. Does this satisfy the Constitution? Article IV, Section 3, Clause 1 provides: "New States may be admitted by the Congress into this Union; but no new State shall be formed or erected within the Jurisdiction of any other State; nor any State be formed by the Junction of two or more States, or Parts of States, without the Consent of the Legislatures of the States concerned as well as of the Congress." (Read the clause carefully: is it permissible *at all* to carve a new state out of an existing one? Does the "consent" proviso apply only to the creation of a new state from the "junction" of two or more existing states or parts of states?) For an argument that West Virginia probably is a legal state of the Union, see Kesavan & Paulsen, *Is West Virginia Unconstitutional?* 90 Cal. L. Rev. 291 (2002).

8.   Several years after the War, a (somewhat) reconstituted Supreme Court considered a case in which the outcome turned in part on whether Texas had or had not left the Union—ceased to be a state of the United States—during the period of the Civil War when Texas purported to secede. That case, *Texas v. White*, 74 U.S. (7 Wall.) 700 (1868), advanced the legal theory of the Lincoln administration (and the Johnson administration) on secession, national authority to combat secession, and reconstruction.

Texas v. White

74 U.S. (7 Wall.) 700 (1868)

[The specific question in the case concerned the validity of certain United States bonds, issued in 1851 and payable after 1864 to the state of Texas or the bearer, as affected by the intervening legislative acts of Texas seizing such property in the rebellion. The Court began by reciting at length the history of Texas's actions.—Editors]

■ THE CHIEF JUSTICE delivered the opinion of the court.

. . . In all respects, so far as the object [of secession] could be accomplished by ordinances of the convention, by acts of the legislature, and by votes of the citizens, the relations of Texas to the Union were broken up, and new relations to a new government were established by them. . . . Did Texas, in consequence of these acts, cease to be a State? Or, if not, did the State cease to be a member of the Union?

It is needless to discuss, at length, the question whether the right of a State to withdraw from the Union for any cause, regarded by herself as sufficient, is consistent with the Constitution of the United States.

The Union of the States never was a purely artificial and arbitrary relation. It began among the Colonies, and grew out of common origin, mutual sympathies, kindred principles, similar interests, and geographical relations. It was confirmed and strengthened by the necessities of war, and received definite form, and character, and sanction from the Articles of Confederation. By these the Union was solemnly declared to "be perpetual." And when these Articles were found to be inadequate to the exigencies of the country, the Constitution was ordained "to form a more perfect Union." It is difficult to convey the idea of indissoluble unity more clearly than by these words. What can be indissoluble if a perpetual Union, made more perfect, is not?

But the perpetuity and indissolubility of the Union, by no means implies the loss of distinct and individual existence, or of the right of self-government by the States. Under the Articles of Confederation each State retained its sovereignty, freedom, and independence, and every power, jurisdiction, and right not expressly delegated to the United States. Under the Constitution, though the powers of the States were much restricted, still, all powers not delegated to the United States nor prohibited to the States, are reserved to the States respectively, or to the people. And we have already had occasion to remark at this term, that "the people of each State compose a State, having its own government, and endowed with all the functions essential to separate and independent existence," and that "without the States in union, there could be no such political body as the United States." Not only, therefore, can there be no loss of separate and independent autonomy to the States, through their union under the Constitution, but it may be not unreasonably said that the preservation of the States, and the maintenance of their governments, are as much within the design and care of the Constitution as the preservation of the Union and the maintenance of the National government. The Constitution, in all its provisions, looks to an indestructible Union, composed of indestructible States.

When, therefore, Texas became one of the United States, she entered into an indissoluble relation. All the obligations of perpetual union, and all the guaranties of republican government in the Union, attached at once to the State. The act which consummated her admission into the Union was something more than a compact; it was the incorporation of a new member into the political body. And it was final. The union between Texas and the other States was as complete, as perpetual and indissoluble as the union between the original States. There was no place for reconsideration, or revocation, except through revolution, or through consent of the States.

Considered therefore as transactions under the Constitution, the ordinance of secession, adopted by the convention and ratified by a majority of the citizens of

Texas, and all the acts of her legislature intended to give effect to that ordinance, were absolutely null. They were utterly without operation in law. The obligations of the State, as a member of the Union, and of every citizen of the State, as a citizen of the United States, remained perfect and unimpaired. It certainly follows that the States did not cease to be a State, nor her citizens to be citizens of the Union. If this were otherwise, the State must have become foreign, and her citizens foreigners. The war must have ceased to be a war for the suppression of rebellion, and must have become a war for conquest and subjugation.

Our conclusion therefore is, that Texas continued to be a State, and a State of the Union, notwithstanding the transactions to which we have referred. . . .

[I]t is by no means a logical conclusion . . . that the governmental relations of Texas to the Union remained unaltered. Obligations often remained unimpaired, while relations are greatly changed. . . . And the same must necessarily be true of the obligations and relations of States and citizens to the Union. No one has been bold enough to contend that, while Texas was controlled by a government hostile to the United States, and in affiliation with a hostile confederation, waging war upon the United States, senators chosen by her legislature, or representatives elected by her citizens, were entitled to seats in Congress; . . . All admit that, during this condition of civil war, the rights of the State as a member, and of her people as citizens of the Union, were suspended. The government and the citizens of the State, refusing to recognize their constitutional obligations, assumed the character of enemies, and incurred the consequences of rebellion.

These new relations imposed new duties upon the United States. The first was that of suppressing the rebellion. The next was that of re-establishing the broken relations of the State with the Union. The first of these duties having been performed, the next necessarily engaged the attention of the National government.

The authority for the performance of the first had been found in the power to suppress insurrection and carry on war; for the performance of the second, authority was derived from the obligation of the United States to guarantee to every State in the Union a republican form of government. The latter, indeed, in the case of a rebellion which involves the government of a State . . . seems to be a necessary complement to the former.

Of this, the case of Texas furnishes a striking illustration. . . . Slaves, in the insurgent States, with certain local exceptions, had been declared free by the Proclamation of Emancipation; and whatever questions might be made as to the effect of that act, under the Constitution, it was clear, from the beginning, that its practical operation, in connection with legislative acts of like tendency, must be complete enfranchisement. Wherever the National forces obtained control, the slaves became freemen. Support to the acts of Congress and the proclamation of the President, concerning slaves, was made a condition of amnesty by President Lincoln, in December 1863, and by President Johnson in May, 1865. And emancipation was confirmed, rather than ordained, in the insurgent States, by the amendment to the Constitution prohibiting slavery throughout the Union, which was proposed by Congress in February 1865, and ratified, before the close of the following autumn, by the requisite three-fourths of the States.

The new freemen necessarily became part of the people, and the people still constituted the State; for States, like individuals, retain their identity, though changed to some extent in their constituent elements. And it was the State, thus constituted, which was now entitled to the benefit of the constitutional guaranty.

There being then no government in Texas in constitutional relations with the Union, it became the duty of the United States to provide for the restoration of such a government. But the restoration of the government which existed before the rebellion, without a new election of officers, was obviously impossible; and before any such election could be properly held, it was necessary that the old constitution should receive such amendments as would conform its provisions to the new conditions created by emancipation, and afford adequate security to the people of the State.

In the exercise of the power conferred by the guaranty clause, as in the exercise of every other constitutional power, a discretion in the choice of means is necessary allowed. It is essential only that the means must be necessary and proper for carrying into execution the power conferred, through the restoration of the State to its constitutional relations, under a republican form of government, and that no acts be done, and no authority exerted, which is either prohibited or unsanctioned by the Constitution.

. . . [A]lmost immediately after the cessation of organized hostilities, and while the war yet smouldered in Texas, the President of the United States issued his proclamation appointing a provisional governor for the State, and providing for the assembling of a convention, with a view to the re-establishment of a republican government, under an amended constitution, and to the restoration of the State to her proper relations. A convention was accordingly assembled, the constitution amended, elections held, and a State government, acknowledging its obligations to the Union, established.

Whether the action then taken was, in all respects, warranted by the Constitution, it is not now necessary to determine. The power exercised by the President was supposed, doubtless, to be derived from his constitutional functions, as commander-in-chief; and so long as the war continued, it cannot be denied that he might institute temporary government within insurgent districts, occupied by the National forces, or take measures, in any State, for the restoration of State government faithful to the Union. . . .

But, the power to carry into effect the clause of guaranty is primarily a legislative power, and resides in Congress. . . . *[The opinion then quotes the Guarantee Clause and discusses* Luther v. Borden.—*Editors]*

The action of the President must, therefore, be considered as provisional, and, in that light, it seems to have regarded by Congress. . . . But, it is important to observe that these [Reconstruction Acts of Congress] themselves show that the governments, which had been established and had been in actual operation under executive direction, were recognized by Congress as provisional, as existing, and as capable of continuance. . . .

[Therefore,] the title of the State [to the bonds] was not divested by the act of the insurgent government in entering into this contract.

NOTES

1.   Does Article IV explicitly provide for the division of a state? Indeed, as to Texas itself, it may not be that the state as currently constituted is "indestructible." The act of

Congress admitting Texas as a state permits it to divide into as many as five states; these terms have never been expressly repealed and might still be good law today. See Vasan Kesavan & Michael Stokes Paulsen, *Let's Mess with Texas*, 82 TEX. L. REV. 1587 (2004).

2.   Article IV, Clause 3 provides a way for new states to join the Union, but it does not expressly provide for any mechanism for states to leave, whether unilaterally or with Congress's consent. Does this mean that before a state could leave the Union, the Constitution would first have to be amended to provide a way out? *Expressio unius est exclusio alterius*: the specification of a way to enter without the specification of a way to leave implies that leaving has not been authorized? Or could a state leave with Congress's consent, under the theory that the power to undo is incident to the power to do? Congress can decide to admit new states to the union, so perhaps it can decide to let them leave. Are there other answers?

3.   The Canadian Supreme Court was asked by the government in the 1990s to render an advisory opinion on whether Quebec could unilaterally secede from Canada if the people of that province voted for secession in a popular referendum (as they almost did). The Court concluded, in *Reference re Secession of Quebec*, 2 S.C.R. 217 (Supreme Court of Canada 1998), that if the people of Quebec voted for secession the central government would be obligated to enter into negotiations with it on the terms of secession, including how to apportion the national debt and where to draw the new nation's boundary lines as well as how effectively to protect the rights of English speakers in Quebec.

[Assignment 39]

Representation and Republicanism

Art. I, § 2: The House of Representatives shall be composed of Members chosen every second Year by the People of the several States, and the Electors in each State shall have the Qualifications requisite for Electors of the most numerous Branch of the State Legislature. . . .

Representatives and direct Taxes shall be apportioned among the several States which may be included within this Union, according to their respective Numbers, which shall be determined by adding to the whole Number of free Persons, including those bound to Service for a Term of Years, and excluding Indians not taxed, three fifths of all other Persons. . . .

§ 3: The Senate of the United States shall be composed of two Senators from each State, chosen by the Legislature thereof, for six Years; and each Senator shall have one Vote. . . .

§ 4: The Times, Places and Manner of holding Elections for Senators and Representatives, shall be prescribed in each State by the Legislature thereof; but the Congress may at any time by Law make or alter such Regulations, except as to the Places of chusing Senators. . . .

The Congress shall assemble at least once in every Year, and such Meeting shall be on the first Monday in December, unless they shall by Law appoint a different Day.

Art. IV, § 4: The United States shall guarantee to every State in this Union a Republican Form of Government, and shall protect each of them against

Invasion; and on Application of the Legislature, or of the Executive (when the Legislature cannot be convened) against domestic Violence.

Amend. XVII: The Senate of the United States shall be composed of two Senators from each State, elected by the people thereof, for six years . . .

Amend. XIX: The right of citizens of the United States to vote shall not be denied or abridged by the United States or by any State on account of sex. . . .

Amend. XXIV, § 1: The right of citizens of the United States to vote in any primary or other election for President or Vice President, for electors for President or Vice President, or for Senator or Representative in Congress, shall not be denied or abridged by the United States or any state by reason of failure to pay any poll tax or other tax. . . .

Amend. XXVI, § 1: The right of citizens of the United States, who are 18 years of age or older, to vote, shall not be denied or abridged by the United States or any state on account of age.

One final aspect of Article IV is its reference to a "Republican Form of Government." If you were to ask people what kind of political regime the United States has, most would answer: a democracy. As Article IV suggests, however, the founders would have been more likely to answer: a republic. Indeed, Benjamin Franklin is reported to have said that the Constitution created "A republic . . . if you can keep it." 3 THE RECORDS OF THE FEDERAL CONVENTION OF 1787, at 85 (Max Farrand ed., 1911).

By "democracy" the founders understood government directly by the people through something like town meetings or even through mobs. In *The Federalist No. 39*, James Madison defined a "republic" as "a government which derives all its powers directly or indirectly from the great body of the people, and is administered by persons holding their offices during pleasure for a limited period, or during good behavior." In other words, a republic is a government in which the people rule indirectly, through representatives—what today might be called a representative democracy.

These ideas of republicanism and representation run beyond Article IV, through much of the constitutional text. In various ways they create state and popular control of the national government, and some national limits on state democracy, so understanding them is crucial to understanding the operation of the federal structure.Members of the House of Representatives are elected by "the People" of "the several States," and (until the Seventeenth Amendment) senators were elected by the state legislatures. Art. I, Secs. 2–3. House members are allotted among the states according to population, and each state is entitled to two senators. The president is elected indirectly, by "Electors" chosen by each state "in such Manner as the Legislature thereof may direct." Art. II, Sec. 1. Each state is allotted a number of electors equal to the number of its representatives plus its senators, thus giving a slight edge to the smaller states. Nothing in the Constitution requires that electors be chosen by popular election, and for the first several decades, it was common for legislatures themselves to elect the electors. (This had a tendency to convert state legislative elections into a kind of national referendum.) Since 1824, all states have chosen electors by popular vote, usually on a state-wide basis.

The original constitutional text had little to say about the machinery of elections. Article I, Section 4 provides that "The Time, Places and Manner of holding

Elections for Senators and Representatives, shall be prescribed in each State by the Legislature thereof; but the Congress may at any time by Law make or alter such Regulations, except as to the Places of chusing Senators." This gives state legislatures the authority to determine how elections will be conducted for state offices, and allows them to control elections for Congress in the first instance. But it allows Congress, when it wishes, to override state law and make its own regulations for congressional elections. Congress has exercised this power from time to time, such as by requiring single-member districting for elections to the House.

Voting qualifications and electoral structure have predominated in subsequent amendments. Since 1789, the Constitution has been amended eighteen times, for a total of twenty-seven amendments. Twelve of those amendments pertain to selection of representatives or executive officers. Read all of the amendments, and identify those that fall in this category. Think about what they accomplish, and why. Several of the amendments expanded suffrage, including the Fifteenth Amendment (race) (p. 1662), the Nineteenth Amendment (sex) (p. 1440), the Twenty-fourth Amendment (poll taxes), and the Twenty-sixth Amendment (age). The Seventeenth Amendment provides for the election of senators by popular vote rather than by the state legislatures, thus reversing one of the major structural compromises of the Constitutional Convention. Although justified largely on the ground that popular election of senators would make government more democratic, it had the effect of eliminating the representation of states as states in the national legislature, thus removing one of the Constitution's structural safeguard for federalism. On the Seventeenth Amendment, see p. 464; on the implications of the amendment for federalism, see p. 582.

Determining who can vote is just the first step. The shape, size, and contours of electoral districts can have profound effects on the allocation of political power. For most of our history, these decisions were made by state legislatures without federal judicial oversight. In many states, legislatures failed or refused to draw new maps in response to changes in the distribution of population. This coincided with a time of relative decline in rural populations and the dramatic growth of suburbs. The effect was to preserve rural and agricultural political dominance even after these areas ceased to have a majority of the population. In *Colegrove v. Green*, 328 U.S. 549 (1946), plaintiffs challenged an Illinois congressional districting plan that was largely unchanged from that created after the census of 1900. The Supreme Court held that a suit challenging the congressional districting scheme for the State of Illinois was not justiciable in federal court. The Court stated: "To sustain this action would cut very deep into the very being of Congress. Courts ought not to enter this political thicket. The remedy for unfairness in districting is to secure State legislatures that will apportion properly, or to invoke the ample powers of Congress."

That changed in the 1960s, with *Baker v. Carr*, a challenge to state legislative districting in Tennessee. Despite a state constitutional requirement that state legislative districts be drawn according to population, which lacked any procedure for state judicial enforcement, the legislature left existing legislative boundaries in place from 1901 to 1963. As a result, the suburbs and cities were grossly underrepresented. For example, rural Moore County, Tennessee, had a single representative for 2,340 voters, whereas urban Shelby County was allotted only eight representatives for its over 312,000 voters—roughly 44,000 voters per representative. Voters in rural districts having only 40% of the voting population elected 63 of the 99 members of the state House of Representatives—almost a two-thirds majority. Districts having only 37% of the voting population elected 20 of the 33 senators—a 61% majority. Moreover, the urban and suburban majority had no peaceful political means for redressing the electoral balance. The state supreme court held that it had no power to order reapportionment, and Tennessee had no mechanism for bypassing the legislature to achieve constitutional reform. No matter how loudly the people of Nashville, Memphis, Chattanooga, and their suburbs complained, the rural legislators had no incentive to respond. They were in control. Why would they give up power when they did not have to?

Baker v. Carr
369 U.S. 186 (1962)

■ MR. JUSTICE BRENNAN delivered the opinion of the Court.

. . . The complaint, alleging that by means of a 1901 statute of Tennessee apportioning the members of the General Assembly among the State's 95 counties, "these plaintiffs and others similarly situated, are denied the equal protection of the laws accorded them by the Fourteenth Amendment to the Constitution of the United States by virtue of the debasement of their votes," was dismissed by a three-judge court convened under 28 U.S.C. § 2281 in the Middle District of Tennessee. The court held that it lacked jurisdiction of the subject matter and also that no claim was stated upon which relief could be granted. . . . We hold that the dismissal was error, and remand the cause to the District Court for trial and further proceedings consistent with this opinion.

. . . We understand the District Court to have read the cited cases as compelling the conclusion that since the appellants sought to have a legislative apportionment held unconstitutional, their suit presented a "political question" and was therefore nonjusticiable. We hold that this challenge to an apportionment presents no nonjusticiable "political question." . . .

Of course the mere fact that the suit seeks protection of a political right does not mean it presents a political question. Such an objection "is little more than a play upon words." Nixon v. Herndon, 273 U.S. 536 (1927). Rather, it is argued that apportionment cases, whatever the actual wording of the complaint, can involve no federal constitutional right except one resting on the guaranty of a republican form of government, and that complaints based on that clause have been held to present political questions which are nonjusticiable.

We hold that the claim pleaded here neither rests upon nor implicates the Guaranty Clause and that its justiciability is therefore not foreclosed by our decisions of cases involving that clause. . . . Appellants' claim that they are being denied equal protection is justiciable, and if "discrimination is sufficiently shown, the right to relief under the equal protection clause is not diminished by the fact that the discrimination relates to political rights." *Snowden v. Hughes*, 321 U.S. 1, 11 (1944). . . .

Our discussion . . . requires review of a number of political question cases . . . That review reveals that in the Guaranty Clause cases and in the other "political question" cases, it is the relationship between the judiciary and the coordinate branches of the Federal Government, and not the federal judiciary's relationship to the States, which gives rise to the "political question." . . .

Prominent on the surface of any case held to involve a political question is found a textually demonstrable constitutional commitment of the issue to a coordinate political department; or a lack of judicially discoverable and manageable standards for resolving it; or the impossibility of deciding without an initial policy determination of a kind clearly for nonjudicial discretion; or the impossibility of a court's undertaking independent resolution without expressing lack of the respect due coordinate branches of government; or an unusual need for unquestioning adherence to a political decision already made; or the potentiality of embarrassment from multifarious pronouncements by various departments on one question.

Unless one of these formulations is inextricable from the case at bar, there should be no dismissal for non-justiciability on the ground of a political question's presence. . . .

But it is argued that this case shares the characteristics of decisions that constitute a category not yet considered, cases concerning the Constitution's guaranty, in Art. IV, § 4, of a republican form of government. . . . Guaranty Clause claims involve those elements which define a "political question," and for that reason and no other, they are nonjusticiable. In particular, we shall discover that the nonjusticiability of such claims has nothing to do with their touching upon matters of state governmental organization. . . .

Clearly, several factors were thought by the Court in *Luther v. Borden*, 48 U.S. (7 How.) 1 (1849), to make the question there "political": the commitment to the other branches of the decision as to which is the lawful state government; the unambiguous action by the president, in recognizing the charter government as the lawful authority; the need for finality in the executive's decision; and the lack of criteria by which a court could determine which form of government was republican.

But the only significance that *Luther* could have for our immediate purposes is in its holding that the Guaranty Clause is not a repository of judicially manageable standards which a court could utilize independently in order to identify a State's lawful government. The Court has since refused to resort to the Guaranty Clause— which alone had been invoked for the purpose—as the source of a constitutional standard for invalidating state action.

Just as the Court has consistently held that a challenge to state action based on the Guaranty Clause presents no justiciable question so has it held, and for the same reasons, that challenges to congressional action on the ground of inconsistency with that clause present no justiciable question. . . .

We come, finally, to the ultimate inquiry whether our precedents as to what constitutes a nonjusticiable "political question" bring the case before us under the umbrella of that doctrine. A natural beginning is to note whether any of the common characteristics which we have been able to identify and label descriptively are present. We find none: The question here is the consistency of state action with the Federal Constitution. We have no question decided, or to be decided, by a political branch of government coequal with this Court. Nor do we risk embarrassment of our government abroad, or grave disturbance at home if we take issue with Tennessee as to the constitutionality of her action here challenged. Nor need the appellants, in order to succeed in this action, ask the Court to enter upon policy determinations for which judicially manageable standards are lacking. Judicial standards under the Equal Protection Clause are well developed and familiar, and it has been open to courts since the enactment of the Fourteenth Amendment to determine, if on the particular facts they must, that a discrimination reflects no policy, but simply arbitrary and capricious action.

This case does, in one sense, involve the allocation of political power within a State, and the appellants might conceivably have added a claim under the Guaranty Clause. Of course, as we have seen, any reliance on that clause would be futile. But because any reliance on the Guaranty Clause could not have succeeded it does not follow that appellants may not be heard on the equal protection claim which in fact they tender. True, it must be clear that the Fourteenth Amendment claim is not so enmeshed with those political question elements which render Guaranty Clause claims nonjusticiable as actually to present a political question itself. But we have found that not to be the case here. . . .

We conclude that the complaint's allegations of a denial of equal protection present a justiciable constitutional cause of action upon which appellants are entitled to a trial and a decision. The right asserted is within the reach of judicial protection under the Fourteenth Amendment. . . .

■ MR. JUSTICE FRANKFURTER, whom MR. JUSTICE HARLAN joins, dissenting.

The Court today reverses a uniform course of decision established by a dozen cases, including one by which the very claim now sustained was unanimously rejected only five years ago. The impressive body of rulings thus cast aside reflected the equally uniform course of our political history regarding the relationship between population and legislative representation—a wholly different matter from denial of the franchise to individuals because of race, color, religion or sex. Such a massive repudiation of the experience of our whole past in asserting destructively novel judicial power demands a detailed analysis of the role of this Court in our constitutional scheme. Disregard of inherent limits in the effective exercise of the Court's "judicial Power" not only presages the futility of judicial intervention in the essentially political conflict of forces by which the relation between population and representation has time out of mind been and now is determined. It may well impair the Court's position as the ultimate organ of "the supreme Law of the Land" in that vast range of legal problems, often strongly entangled in popular feeling, on which this Court must pronounce. The Court's authority—possessed of neither the purse nor the sword—ultimately rests on sustained public confidence in its moral sanction. Such feeling must be nourished by the Court's complete detachment, in fact and in appearance, from political entanglements and by abstention from injecting itself into the clash of political forces in political settlements. . . .

The present case involves all of the elements that have made the Guarantee Clause cases non-justiciable. It is, in effect, a Guarantee Clause claim masquerading under a different label. But it cannot make the case more fit for judicial action that appellants invoke the Fourteenth Amendment rather than Art. IV, § 4, where, in fact, the gist of their complaint is the same—unless it can be found that the Fourteenth Amendment speaks with greater particularity to their situation. . . . Of course, if a controversy falls within judicial power, it depends "on how he (the plaintiff) casts his action," whether he brings himself within a jurisdictional statute.

But where judicial competence is wanting, it cannot be created by invoking one clause of the Constitution rather than another. . . .

To find such a political conception legally enforceable in the broad and unspecific guarantee of equal protection is to rewrite the Constitution. See *Luther v. Borden.* Certainly, "equal protection" is no more secure a foundation for judicial judgment of the permissibility of varying forms of representative government than is "Republican Form." Indeed since "equal protection of the laws" can only mean an equality of persons standing in the same relation to whatever governmental action is challenged, the determination whether treatment is equal presupposes a determination concerning the nature of the relationship. This, with respect to apportionment, means an inquiry into the theoretic base of representation in an acceptably republican state. For a court could not determine the equal-protection issue without in fact first determining the Republican-Form issue, simply because what is reasonable for equal-protection purposes will depend upon what frame of government, basically, is allowed. To divorce "equal protection" from "Republican Form" is to talk about half a question.

The notion that representation proportioned to the geographic spread of population is so universally accepted as a necessary element of equality between man and man that it must be taken to be the standard of a political equality preserved by the Fourteenth Amendment—that it is, in appellants' words "the basic principle of representative government"—is, to put it bluntly, not true. However desirable and however desired by some among the great political thinkers and framers of our government, it has never been generally practiced, today or in the past. It was not the English system, it was not the colonial system, it was not the system chosen for the national government by the Constitution, it was not the system exclusively or even predominantly practiced by the States at the time of adoption of the Fourteenth Amendment, it is not predominantly practiced by the States today. . . .

Manifestly, the Equal Protection Clause supplies no clearer guide for judicial examination of apportionment methods than would the Guarantee Clause itself. Apportionment, by its character, is a subject of extraordinary complexity, involving— even after the fundamental theoretical issues concerning what is to be represented in a representative legislature have been fought out or compromised—considerations of geography, demography, electoral convenience, economic and social cohesions or divergencies among particular local groups, communications, the practical effects of political institutions like the lobby and the city machine, ancient traditions and ties of settled usage, respect for proven incumbents of long experience and senior status, mathematical mechanics, censuses compiling relevant data, and a host of others. Legislative responses throughout the country to the reapportionment demands of the 1960 Census have glaringly confirmed that these are not factors that lend themselves to evaluations of a nature that are the staple of judicial determinations or for which judges are equipped to adjudicate by legal training or experience or native wit. And this is the more so true because in every strand of this complicated, intricate web of values meet the contending forces of partisan politics. The practical significance of apportionment is that the next election results may differ because of it. Apportionment battles are overwhelmingly party or intra-party contests. It will add a virulent source of friction and tension in federal-state relations to embroil the federal judiciary in them. . . .

NOTES

1.   Note the deep similarity between *Baker* and *Luther v. Borden* (p. 431). In both cases, as a result of state electoral rules, a minority held political control over a state, and there was nothing the majority could do about it. Does this violate the Guarantee Clause? If so, how is the "guarantee" to be made effective?

2.   The Court seems to offer two grounds for distinguishing prior cases that held that apportionment issues were non-justiciable. The first was that the "political question" doctrine does not apply to cases involving state governments rather than "coordinate branches" of the federal government. Why does that matter? Does that distinguish *Luther*? Does that distinguish *Colegrove*? Is vertical comity less important than horizontal comity? If there are no "judicially manageable standards" for deciding a controversy, or if some non-judicial body has been entrusted with a constitutional decision, why does it matter that the defendant is a state? The Court's second ground is that the plaintiff proceeded under the Equal Protection Clause, not the Guarantee Clause. Why might that matter? Would a standard be any more judicially manageable if it were advanced under the heading of the Equal Protection Clause instead of the Guarantee Clause?

3.   What is Justice Frankfurter worried about? Is there really a "political thicket" here? To be sure, if the federal courts were asked to make subjective judgments about political matters like districting, they would appear to be partisan and might lose the public's confidence. But is "one person, one vote" a subjective or malleable standard? Does its application give the appearance of partisanship? Note that at the time *Baker* was decided, "one person, one vote" was only one possible approach to the merits. Many observers thought that other rational considerations could be taken into account—and many of those considerations would have had predictable partisan consequences. Did the conclusion that there were "judicially manageable standards" to decide the controversy depend, in advance, on resolution of the merits? Can a court determine that the constitutional standard applicable to a case is "judicially manageable" without first deciding, on the merits, exactly which standard is applicable?

Reynolds v. Sims
377 U.S. 533 (1964)

■ MR. CHIEF JUSTICE WARREN delivered the opinion of the Court:

. . . Legislators represent people, not trees or acres. Legislators are elected by voters, not farms or cities or economic interests. As long as ours is a representative form of government, and our legislatures are those instruments of government elected directly by and directly representative of the people, the right to elect legislators in a free and unimpaired fashion is a bedrock of our political system. It could hardly be gainsaid that a constitutional claim had been asserted by an allegation that certain otherwise qualified voters had been entirely prohibited from voting for members of their state legislature. And, if a State should provide that the votes of citizens in one part of the State should be given two times, or five times, or 10 times the weight of votes of citizens in another part of the State, it could hardly be contended that the right to vote of those residing in the disfavored areas had not been effectively diluted. . . . Weighting the votes of citizens differently, by any method or means, merely because of where they happen to reside, hardly seems justifiable. . . .

[T]he concept of equal protection has been traditionally viewed as requiring the uniform treatment of persons standing in the same relation to the governmental action questioned or challenged. With respect to the allocation of legislative representation, all voters, as citizens of a State, stand in the same relation regardless of where they live. Any suggested criteria for the differentiation of citizens are insufficient to justify any discrimination, as to the weight of their votes, unless relevant to the permissible purposes of legislative apportionment. Since the achieving of fair and effective representation for all citizens is concededly the basic aim of legislative apportionment, we conclude that the Equal Protection Clause guarantees the opportunity for equal participation by all voters in the election of state legislators. Diluting the weight of votes because of place of residence impairs basic constitutional rights under the Fourteenth Amendment just as much as invidious discriminations based upon factors such as race, or economic status. Our constitutional system amply provides for the protection of minorities by means other than giving them majority control of state legislatures. . . .

We are told that the matter of apportioning representation in a state legislature is a complex and many-faceted one. We are advised that States can rationally consider factors other than population in apportioning legislative representation. We are admonished not to restrict the power of the States to impose differing views as to political philosophy on their citizens. We are cautioned about the dangers of entering into political thickets and mathematical quagmires. Our answer is this: a denial of constitutionally protected rights demands judicial protection; our oath and our office require no less of us. . . .

We hold that, as a basic constitutional standard, the Equal Protection Clause requires that the seats in both houses of a bicameral state legislature must be apportioned on a population basis. Simply stated, an individual's right to vote for state legislators is unconstitutionally impaired when its weight is in a substantial fashion diluted when compared with votes of citizens living in other parts of the State. . . .

Since neither of the houses of the Alabama Legislature, under any of the three plans considered by the District Court, was apportioned on a population basis, we would be justified in proceeding no further. However, one of the proposed plans, that contained in the so-called 67-Senator Amendment, at least superficially resembles the scheme of legislative representation followed in the Federal Congress. . . .

Much has been written since our decision in *Baker v. Carr* about the applicability of the so-called federal analogy to state legislative apportionment arrangements. After considering the matter, the court below concluded that no conceivable analogy could be drawn between the federal scheme and the apportionment of seats in the Alabama Legislature under the proposed constitutional amendment. We agree. . . . Attempted reliance on the federal analogy appears often to be little more than an after-the-fact rationalization offered in defense of maladjusted state apportionment arrangements. The original constitutions of 36 of our States provided that representation in both houses of the state legislatures would be based completely, or predominantly, on population. And the Founding Fathers clearly had no intention of establishing a pattern or model for the apportionment of seats in state legislatures when the system of representation in the Federal Congress was adopted. Demonstrative of this is the fact that the Northwest Ordinance, adopted in the same year, 1787, as the Federal Constitution, provided for the apportionment of seats in territorial legislatures solely on the basis of population.

The system of representation in the two Houses of the Federal Congress is one ingrained in our Constitution, as part of the law of the land. It is one conceived out of compromise and concession indispensable to the establishment of our federal republic. Arising from unique historical circumstances, it is based on the consideration that in establishing our type of federalism a group of formerly independent States bound themselves together under one national government. . . . [A]t the time of the inception of the system of representation in the Federal Congress, a compromise between the larger and smaller States on this matter averted a deadlock in the Constitutional Convention which had threatened to abort the birth of our Nation. . . .

Political subdivisions of States—counties, cities, or whatever—never were and never have been considered as sovereign entities. Rather, they have been traditionally regarded as subordinate governmental instrumentalities created by the State to assist in the carrying out of state governmental functions. . . . The relationship of the States to the Federal Government could hardly be less analogous. . . .

■ [The dissent of JUSTICE HARLAN and the concurrence of JUSTICE CLARK are omitted.]

NOTES

1.   *Reynolds* involved state legislative districts. It was preceded by *Wesberry v. Sanders*, 376 U.S. 1 (1964), which involved federal congressional districts. The outcomes were analytically indistinguishable: *Reynolds* required "substantial" equality for state legislative districts; *Wesberry* required that federal congressional districts be equal "as nearly as is practicable." But they were decided under different provisions of the Constitution. *Reynolds* was an interpretation of the Equal Protection Clause, while *Wesberry* rested on the command of Article I, Section 2, Clause 1, that representatives be chosen "by the People of the several States." Is one textual basis stronger than the other? Do they have different implications?

2.   *Wesberry* and *Reynolds* were among the most transformative decisions in the history of the Supreme Court. Unlike de jure segregation, the phenomenon of unequal districts was not confined to any one region. Nearly every state was out of compliance with the new standard. In fully 37 of the 45 states entitled to more than one representative, the difference between the largest and the smallest House district exceeded 100,000 persons—making the boundaries of 398 of the 435 House districts unconstitutional. Disparities among state legislative districts were even more extreme: a dozen states had districts with five times the population of another district.

For most of its history, the United States was predominantly rural. But by the 1960s, almost two-thirds of Americans lived in metropolitan areas (cities or suburbs). Yet at the time of *Wesberry* and *Reynolds*, 214 congressional districts still had a rural majority. After the redistricting forced by these decisions, this number fell to 155 in 1968 and 130 in 1972. What policy changes would you expect to see from this shift in political power?

3.   If Article I, Section 2, Clause 1 (*Wesberry*) or the Fourteenth Amendment (*Reynolds*) required equipopulous districts, no one seemed to notice it at the time. In the first election after adoption of the original Constitution, every state with multiple single-member districts drew lines with substantial population disparities. The smallest district

in Georgia comprised 19,273 people (13,261 of whom were slaves), while the largest comprised 37,946 (including 8,801 slaves). In Massachusetts, the smallest comprised 39,594 and the largest 89,972. The largest disparity within a state was in New York. New York's First District comprised 40,784 people (5,598 of them slaves), while the Sixth District comprised 105,659 people (including 4,523 slaves). Much the same was true after ratification of the Fourteenth Amendment. For example, districts in Iowa ranged from 46,733 to 138,032. See Samuel B. Parsons et al., UNITED STATES CONGRESSIONAL DISTRICTS, 1788–1841 (1978) and UNITED STATES CONGRESSIONAL DISTRICTS, 1843–1883 (1978).

4. The degree of malapportionment in *Baker* and *Reynolds* screamed out for remedy. In these states, disparities were both systematic and self-perpetuating: a rural minority controlled state government, and there was no constitutional or peaceful mechanism for reform. What of inequality that is less dramatic, or cases where there is a democratic remedy? In *Lucas v. Forty-Fourth General Assembly of the State of Colorado*, 377 U.S. 713 (1964), decided the same day as *Reynolds*, the Court considered the constitutionality of a districting scheme for the State of Colorado. Just two years previously, in 1962, the voters of Colorado were presented with two alternative districting schemes: one based representation in both houses of the state legislature almost exclusively on population, and the other created somewhat smaller districts for sparsely populated areas of the state (leaving the metropolitan areas with a majority of the legislators, but a smaller majority than they would be entitled to as a matter of sheer population). The voters overwhelmingly chose the second plan; it carried a majority in every county. How should this case have been decided? How would you articulate the proper standard?

Unlike *Reynolds*, which was an 8–1 decision, there were three dissenters in *Lucas*. The majority held that the Colorado map violated the one person, one vote rule. Justice Stewart argued in dissent that the Equal Protection Clause "demands but two basic attributes of any plan of state legislative apportionment." First, it must be rational. Second, it "must be such as not to permit the systematic frustration of the will of a majority of the electorate of the State." How is such a standard derived from the Equal Protection Clause? Would it be more persuasively derived from the Guarantee Clause?

5. *Reynolds* and *Wesberry* seemed to allow some flexibility: "Mathematical exactness or precision is hardly a workable constitutional requirement." *Reynolds*, 377 U.S. at 577. By 1969, however, the Court held that the one person, one vote rule "permits only the limited population variances which are unavoidable despite a good-faith effort to achieve absolute equality, or for which justification is shown." *Kirkpatrick v. Preisler*, 394 U.S. 526, 531 (1969). That case involved a maximum deviation of 3.13 percent between the largest district and the mathematical ideal, and the Court rejected a number of rationales for deviations set forth by the state, including: geographical compactness; following existing county, municipal, or other jurisdictional boundaries; avoiding fragmentation of areas with distinctive economic or social interests; compensating for large numbers of persons ineligible to vote; and anticipating population shifts. Since then precise mathematical equality has become possible, but the Court has varied in how aggressively it polices minute differences in district size. Compare *Karcher v. Daggett*, 462 U.S. 725 (1983) (striking down federal congressional districting scheme on account of a deviation of 0.69%), with *Tennant v. Jefferson County Commission*, 133 S.Ct. 3 (2012) (per curiam) (upholding, for purposes of federal constitutional law, a federal congressional districting scheme in which the deviation was .79%, even though that deviation could have been completely eliminated, because of deference to state interests such as "avoiding contests between incumbents and not splitting political subdivisions").

For purposes of state legislative districting, the Court has allowed a variance of 10 percent between the largest and smallest districts. The Court grounded this distinction in part on the difference between the Equal Protection Clause and Article I, Section 2. Is that persuasive? Is it perhaps backwards? Does a rule of precise mathematical equality have any untoward consequences?

6.   How can *Reynolds* and *Wesberry* be squared with the requirement of Article I, Section 2, Clause 3, that representatives "be apportioned among the several States . . . according to their respective Numbers," which has generally been interpreted as meaning total population? See, e.g., *Evenwel v. Abbot*, 136 S.Ct. 1120 (2016) (holding that states may apportion based on total population). Total population includes people not eligible to vote, such as aliens and children, who are not evenly distributed across districts. A vote cast in a district with relatively large numbers of aliens or children thus is weighted more heavily than a vote cast in other districts. These effects can be quite large. For example, in one case, federal congressional districts of nearly equal population in a state ranged from 282,000 to 429,000 in voting age population. *Karcher*, 462 U.S. at 772 n.6 (White, J., dissenting). This disparity far exceeds what would be tolerated under one person, one vote. Does it suggest that voting power should be apportioned among districts according to some other measure, such as voting age citizen population? Does it make sense for the Court to create a standard that cannot be achieved in light of Article I, Section 2, Clause 3?

7.   Lovers of historical irony may appreciate the fact that the United States Constitution would likely not have been ratified if the one person, one vote rule had prevailed at the time of selection of delegates to the state ratifying conventions. In Virginia, the largest state, the Constitution was ratified by a slim majority of 89–79 (88–80 on a key procedural motion). At its ratifying convention, each county was authorized two delegates, regardless of population. This favored ratification, because the tidewater counties, which tended to support the Constitution, were less populous than the piedmont counties, which tended to oppose it. Jean Edward Smith, JOHN MARSHALL: DEFINER OF A NATION 119 (1996).

———

Even assuming districts are equal in population, district boundaries can have profound effects on the outcomes of elections. The process of drawing lines for the purpose of affecting outcomes is called "gerrymandering." The practice is as old as the republic. Its name derives from Elbridge Gerry, a delegate to the Constitutional Convention and later vice president under James Madison. A political cartoonist depicted a districting map devised under Gerry's governorship as looking like a salamander—hence a the word "gerrymander." As long as legislatures were free to use districts that were unequal in population, there was not as much occasion for cartographic creativity. In recent decades, however, gerrymandering has become a more prevalent, and more precise, phenomenon, for two primary reasons. First, the advent of computer districting programs has enabled mapmakers to manipulate election data with surgical precision. Second, the precise mathematical equality rule forced mapmakers to deviate substantially from traditional jurisdictional boundaries, such as counties and municipalities; adherence to these boundaries had been the main constraint against gerrymandering.

Gerrymandering comes in three flavors: partisan, incumbency protection, and racial. A partisan gerrymander seeks to maximize the number of legislative seats that will likely be won by the party that controls the districting. An incumbency-protection gerrymander protects the seats of incumbent legislators of both parties. A racial gerrymander seeks to achieve certain results along racial lines. In earlier times, this often took the form of attempts to reduce the political influence of racial minorities. Since passage of the Voting Rights Act, it has become more common for mapmakers to create districts likely to elect minority legislators. Because racial minorities have historically had lower percentages of voting-age population, and within that population a lower percentage of registered voters, it was thought necessary to have a supermajority of minority voters to assure political victory. Creating such a district reduces the numbers and influence of minority voters in other districts.

If Democrats and Republicans were evenly distributed throughout the state it would not be possible to gerrymander by party. But residential patterns are not uniform. Rural areas and suburbs tend to be more Republican, and urban areas more Democratic. The two principal techniques of gerrymandering are called "packing" and "cracking." Packing is the most effective. This involves packing the largest possible numbers of the other party into a single district. Since every vote in excess of a majority is "wasted," it serves the interest of the party in power to create districts with 70, 80, or 90 percent of voters of the other party. Cracking involves dividing voters of the other party into two or more districts, rendering them a minority in each.

What do the critics of gerrymandering say is wrong with it? It makes the legislature less responsive and accountable to the public. Changes in popular opinion are less likely to be translated into changes in political outcomes. The creation of racially or politically homogeneous districts may cause politics to become more divisive—more racially polarized or more partisan. Most fundamentally, it allows those in power at the time of districting to determine (within limits) the probable outcome of future elections. This seems undemocratic (and unrepublican): in a democratic republic, the electorate chooses its representatives, rather than having the representatives choose their electorates. And in extreme cases, gerrymandering may allow a party to cling to control even if it no longer represents the majority of voters.

In response, supporters of gerrymandering argue that the drawing of districts is an inherently political activity. It can never really be non-partisan—regardless of whether it is done by legislatures, by courts, or by citizen commissions. Given that it is a quintessentially political decision, these supporters say, there is no reason not to allow these decisions to be made by the body that makes most of our political decisions, namely the legislature.

You might ask yourself what provisions of the Constitution, if any, have purposes or values that are implicated by gerrymanders. Equal Protection? The requirement that representatives and senators be chosen by "the People"? The Guarantee Clause? Are the same constitutional values implicated by racial gerrymandering as by partisan gerrymandering or incumbency protection? What, if anything, is the judicial role in all of this?

Vieth v. Jubelirer

541 U.S. 267 (2004)

■ JUSTICE SCALIA announced the judgment of the Court and delivered an opinion, in which THE CHIEF JUSTICE, JUSTICE O'CONNOR, and JUSTICE THOMAS join. . . .

I

The facts, as alleged by the plaintiffs, are as follows. The population figures derived from the 2000 census showed that Pennsylvania was entitled to only 19 Representatives in Congress, a decrease in 2 from the Commonwealth's previous delegation. Pennsylvania's General Assembly took up the task of drawing a new districting map. At the time, the Republican Party controlled a majority of both state Houses and held the Governor's office. . . . On January 3, 2002, the General Assembly passed [a plan creating 13 seats with a Republican advantage], which was signed into law by Governor Schweiker.

Plaintiffs, registered Democrats who vote in Pennsylvania, brought suit. . . .

II

Political gerrymanders are not new to the American scene. One scholar traces them back to the Colony of Pennsylvania at the beginning of the 18th century. . . .

It is significant that the Framers provided a remedy for such practices in the Constitution. Article I, § 4, while leaving in state legislatures the initial power to draw districts for federal elections, permitted Congress to "make or alter" those districts if it wished. Many objected to the congressional oversight established by this provision. In the course of the debates in the Constitutional Convention, Charles Pinckney and John Rutledge moved to strike the relevant language. James Madison responded in defense of the provision that Congress must be given the power to check partisan manipulation of the election process by the States:

> "Whenever the State Legislatures had a favorite measure to carry, they would take care so to mould their regulations as to favor the candidates they wished to succeed. Besides, the inequality of the Representation in the Legislatures of particular States, would produce a like inequality in their representation in the Natl. Legislature, as it was presumable that the Counties having the power in the former case would secure it to themselves in the latter. What danger could there be in giving a controuling power to the Natl. Legislature?" 2 Records of the Federal Convention of 1787, pp. 240–241 (M. Farrand ed. 1911).

Although the motion of Pinckney and Rutledge failed, opposition to the "make or alter" provision of Article I, § 4 and the defense that it was needed to prevent political gerrymandering continued to be voiced in the state ratifying debates. . . .

The power bestowed on Congress to regulate elections, and in particular to restrain the practice of political gerrymandering, has not lain dormant. In the Apportionment Act of 1842, Congress provided that Representatives must be elected from single-member districts "composed of contiguous territory." Congress . . . in 1872 further required that districts "contai[n] as nearly as practicable an equal number of inhabitants." In the Apportionment Act of 1901, Congress imposed a compactness requirement. 31 Stat. 733. The requirements of contiguity, compactness, and equality of population were repeated in the 1911 apportionment legislation, but were not thereafter continued. Today, only the single-member-district-requirement remains. See 2 U.S.C. § 2c. Recent history, however, attests to Congress's awareness of the sort of districting practices appellants protest, and of its power under Article I, § 4, to control them. Since 1980, no fewer than five bills have been introduced to regulate gerrymandering in congressional districting.

Eighteen years ago, we held that the Equal Protection Clause grants judges the power—and duty—to control political gerrymandering, see *Davis v. Bandemer*, 478 U.S. 109 (1986). It is to consideration of this precedent that we now turn.

III

... Over the dissent of three Justices, the Court held in *Davis v. Bandemer* that, since it was "not persuaded that there are no judicially discernible and manageable standards by which political gerrymander cases are to be decided," such cases *were* justiciable. The clumsy shifting of the burden of proof for the premise (the Court was "not persuaded" that standards do not exist, rather than "persuaded" that they do) was necessitated by the uncomfortable fact that the six-Justice majority could not discern what the judicially discernable standards might be.... The lower courts have lived with that assurance of a standard (or more precisely, lack of assurance that there is no standard), coupled with that inability to specify a standard, for the past 18 years....

Nor can it be said that the lower courts have, over 18 years, succeeded in shaping the standard that this Court was initially unable to enunciate. They have simply applied the standard set forth in *Bandemer*'s four-Justice plurality opinion. This might be thought to prove that the four-Justice plurality standard has met the test of time—but for the fact that its application has almost invariably produced the same result (except for the incurring of attorney's fees) as would have obtained if the question were nonjusticiable: Judicial intervention has been refused.... To think that [the lower court in the one case in which relief was provided] has brought forth "judicially discernible and manageable standards" would be fantasy.

Eighteen years of judicial effort with virtually nothing to show for it justify us in revisiting the question whether the standard promised by *Bandemer* exists. As the following discussion reveals, no judicially discernible and manageable standards for adjudicating political gerrymandering claims have emerged. Lacking them, we must conclude that political gerrymandering claims are nonjusticiable and that *Bandemer* was wrongly decided.

A

We begin our review of possible standards with that proposed by Justice White's plurality opinion in *Bandemer* because, as the narrowest ground for our decision in that case, it has been the standard employed by the lower courts. The plurality concluded that a political gerrymandering claim could succeed only where plaintiffs showed "both intentional discrimination against an identifiable political group and an actual discriminatory effect on that group." As to the intent element, the plurality acknowledged that "[a]s long as redistricting is done by a legislature, it should not be very difficult to prove that the likely political consequences of the reapportionment were intended." However, the effects prong was significantly harder to satisfy. Relief could not be based merely upon the fact that a group of persons banded together for political purposes had failed to achieve representation commensurate with its numbers, or that the apportionment scheme made its winning of elections more difficult. Rather, it would have to be shown that, taking into account a variety of historic factors and projected election results, the group had been "denied its chance to effectively influence the political process" as a whole, which could be achieved even without electing a candidate. It would not be enough to establish, for example, that Democrats had been "placed in a district with a supermajority of other Democratic voters" or that the district "departs from pre-existing political boundaries." Rather, in a challenge to an individual district the inquiry would focus "on the opportunity of members of the group to participate in party deliberations in the slating and nomination of candidates, their opportunity to register and vote, and hence their chance to directly influence the election returns and to secure the attention of the winning candidate." A statewide challenge, by contrast, would involve an analysis of "the voters' direct *or indirect* influence on the elections of the state legislature as a whole." (Emphasis added.) With what has proved to be a gross understatement, the plurality acknowledged this was "of necessity a difficult inquiry." . . .

In the lower courts, the legacy of the plurality's test is one long record of puzzlement and consternation. . . . Because this standard was misguided when proposed, has not been improved in subsequent application, and is not even defended before us today by the appellants, we decline to affirm it as a constitutional requirement.

B

Appellants take a run at enunciating their own workable standard based on Article I, § 2, and the Equal Protection Clause. We consider it at length not only because it reflects the litigant's view as to the best that can be derived from 18 years of experience, but also because it shares many features with other proposed standards, so that what is said of it may be said of them as well. Appellants' proposed standard retains the two-pronged framework of the *Bandemer* plurality—intent plus effect—but modifies the type of showing sufficient to satisfy each.

To satisfy appellants' intent standard, a plaintiff must "show that the mapmakers acted with a *predominant intent* to achieve partisan advantage," which can be shown "by direct evidence or by circumstantial evidence that other neutral and legitimate redistricting criteria were subordinated to the goal of achieving partisan advantage." Brief for Appellants 19 (emphasis added). As compared with the *Bandemer* plurality's test of mere intent to disadvantage the plaintiff's group, this proposal seemingly makes the standard more difficult to meet—but only at the expense of making the standard more indeterminate.

"Predominant intent" to disadvantage the plaintiff's political group refers to the relative importance of that goal as compared with all the other goals that the map seeks to pursue—contiguity of districts, compactness of districts, observance of the lines of political subdivision, protection of incumbents of all parties, cohesion of natural racial and ethnic neighborhoods, compliance with requirements of the Voting Rights Act of 1965 regarding racial distribution, etc. Appellants contend that their intent test *must* be discernible and manageable because it has been borrowed from our racial gerrymandering cases. . . .

[A]pplying a "predominant intent" test to *racial* gerrymandering is easier and less disruptive. The Constitution clearly contemplates districting by political entities, see Article I, § 4, and unsurprisingly that turns out to be root-and-branch a matter of politics. By contrast, the purpose of segregating voters on the basis of race is not a lawful one, and is much more rarely encountered. Determining whether the shape of a particular district is so substantially affected by the presence of a rare and constitutionally suspect motive as to invalidate it is quite different from determining whether it is so substantially affected by the excess of an ordinary and lawful motive as to invalidate it. Moreover, the fact that partisan districting is a lawful and common practice means that there is almost *always* room for an election-impeding lawsuit contending that partisan advantage was the predominant motivation; not so for claims of racial gerrymandering. Finally, courts might be justified in accepting a modest degree of unmanageability to enforce a constitutional command which (like the Fourteenth Amendment obligation to refrain from racial discrimination) is clear; whereas they are not justified in inferring a judicially enforceable constitutional obligation (the obligation not to apply *too much* partisanship in districting) which is both dubious and severely unmanageable. For these reasons, to the extent that our racial gerrymandering cases represent a model of discernible and manageable standards, they provide no comfort here.

The effects prong of appellants' proposal replaces the *Bandemer* plurality's vague test of "denied its chance to effectively influence the political process," with criteria that are seemingly more specific. The requisite effect is established when "(1) the plaintiffs show that the districts systematically 'pack' and 'crack' the rival party's voters, *and* (2) the court's examination of the 'totality of circumstances' confirms that the map can thwart the plaintiffs' ability to translate a majority of votes into a majority of seats." Brief for Appellants 20. This test is loosely based on our cases applying § 2 of the Voting Rights Act of 1965, to discrimination by race. But a person's politics is rarely as readily discernible—and *never* as permanently discernible—as a person's race. Political affiliation is not an immutable characteristic, but may shift from one election to the next; and even within a given election, not all voters follow the party line. . . . These facts make it impossible to assess the effects of partisan gerrymandering, to fashion a standard for evaluating a violation, and finally to craft a remedy.

Assuming, however, that the effects of partisan gerrymandering can be determined, appellants' test would invalidate the districting only when it prevents a majority of the electorate from electing a majority of representatives. . . . [T]his standard rests upon the principle that groups (or at least political-action groups) have a right to proportional representation. But the Constitution contains no such principle. It guarantees equal protection of the law to persons, not equal representation in government to equivalently sized groups. . . .

Our one-person, one-vote cases have no bearing upon this question, neither in principle nor in practicality. Not in principle, because to say that each individual must have an equal say in the selection of representatives, and hence that a majority of individuals must have a majority say, is not at all to say that each discernible group, whether farmers or urban dwellers or political parties, must have representation equivalent to its numbers. And not in practicality, because the easily administrable standard of population equality adopted by *Wesberry* and *Reynolds* enables judges to decide whether a violation has occurred (and to remedy it) essentially on the basis of three readily determined factors where the plaintiff lives, how many voters are in his district, and how many voters are in other districts; whereas requiring judges to decide whether a districting system will produce a statewide majority for a majority party casts them forth upon a sea of imponderables, and asks them to make determinations that not even election experts can agree upon.

For these reasons, we find appellants' proposed standards neither discernible nor manageable. . . .

IV

We turn next to consideration of the standards proposed by today's dissenters. We preface it with the observation that the mere fact that these four dissenters come up with three different standards—all of them different from the two proposed in *Bandemer* and the one proposed here by appellants—goes a long way to establishing that there is no constitutionally discernible standard.

A

. . . JUSTICE STEVENS's confidence that what courts have done with racial gerrymandering can be done with political gerrymandering rests in part upon his belief that "the same standards should apply." But in fact the standards are quite different. A purpose to discriminate on the basis of race receives the strictest scrutiny under the Equal Protection Clause, while a similar purpose to discriminate on the basis of politics does not. . . .

JUSTICE STEVENS relies on *First Amendment cases* to suggest that politically discriminatory gerrymanders are subject to strict scrutiny under the *Equal Protection Clause.* It is elementary that scrutiny levels are claim specific. An action that triggers a heightened level of scrutiny for one claim may receive a very different level of scrutiny for a different claim because the underlying rights, and consequently constitutional harms, are not comparable. To say that suppression of political speech (a claimed First Amendment violation) triggers strict scrutiny is not to say that failure to give political groups equal representation (a claimed equal protection violation) triggers strict scrutiny. . . .

B

. . . Under JUSTICE SOUTER's proposed standard, in order to challenge a particular district, a plaintiff must show (1) that he is a member of a "cohesive political group"; (2) "that the district of his residence . . . paid little or no heed" to traditional districting principles; (3) that there were "specific correlations between the district's deviations from traditional districting principles and the distribution of the population of his group"; (4) that a hypothetical district exists which includes the plaintiff's residence, remedies the packing or cracking of the plaintiff's group, and deviates less from traditional districting principles; and (5) that "the defendants acted intentionally to manipulate the shape of the district in order to pack or crack his group." When those showings have been made, the burden would shift to the defendants to justify the district "by reference to objectives other than naked partisan advantage."

While this five-part test seems eminently scientific, upon analysis one finds that each of the last four steps requires a quantifying judgment that is unguided and ill suited to the development of judicial standards. . . . What is a lower court to do when, as will often be the case, the district adheres to some traditional criteria but not others? JUSTICE SOUTER's only response to this question is to evade it: "It is not necessary now to say exactly how a district court would balance a good showing on one of these indices against a poor showing on another, for that sort of detail is best worked out case by case." But the devil lurks precisely in such detail. The central problem is determining when political gerrymandering has gone too far. . . .

JUSTICE SOUTER's proposal is doomed to failure for a more basic reason: No test—yea, not even a five-part test—can possibly be successful unless one knows what he is testing *for*. In the present context, the test ought to identify deprivation of that minimal degree of representation or influence to which a political group is constitutionally entitled. . . . JUSTICE SOUTER avoids the difficulties of those formulations by never telling us what his test is looking for, other than the utterly unhelpful "extremity of unfairness." . . .

C

. . . The criterion JUSTICE BREYER proposes is nothing more precise than "the *unjustified* use of political factors to entrench a minority in power." While he invokes in passing the Equal Protection Clause, it should be clear to any reader that what constitutes *unjustified* entrenchment depends on his own theory of "effective government." . . .

JUSTICE BREYER provides no real guidance for the journey. Despite his promise to do so, he never tells us what he is testing for, beyond the unhelpful *"unjustified* entrenchment." Instead, he "set[s] forth several sets of circumstances that lay out the indicia of abuse," "along a continuum," proceeding (presumably) from the most clearly unconstitutional to the possibly unconstitutional. . . . In sum, we neither know precisely what JUSTICE BREYER is testing for, nor precisely what fails the test.

V

JUSTICE KENNEDY recognizes that we have "demonstrat[ed] the shortcomings of the other standards that have been considered to date." He acknowledges, moreover, that we "lack . . . comprehensive and neutral principles for drawing electoral boundaries"; and that there is an "absence of rules to limit and confine judicial intervention." From these premises, one might think that JUSTICE KENNEDY would reach the conclusion that political gerrymandering claims are nonjusticiable. Instead, however, he concludes that courts should continue to adjudicate such claims because a standard *may* one day be discovered. . . .

VI

We conclude that neither Article I, § 2, nor the Equal Protection Clause, nor (what appellants only fleetingly invoke) Article I, § 4, provides a judicially enforceable limit on the political considerations that the States and Congress may take into account when districting.

Considerations of *stare decisis* do not compel us to allow *Bandemer* to stand. That case involved an interpretation of the Constitution, and the claims of *stare decisis* are at their weakest in that field, where our mistakes cannot be corrected by Congress. See *Payne v. Tennessee,* 501 U.S. 808, 828 (1991). . . .

While we do not lightly overturn one of our own holdings, "when governing decisions are unworkable or are badly reasoned, this Court has never felt constrained to follow precedent." 501 U.S., at 827. Eighteen years of essentially pointless litigation have persuaded us that *Bandemer* is incapable of principled application. We would therefore overrule that case, and decline to adjudicate these political gerrymandering claims. . . .

■ JUSTICE KENNEDY, concurring in the judgment.

. . . While agreeing with the plurality that the complaint the appellants filed in the District Court must be dismissed, and while understanding that great caution is necessary when approaching this subject, I would not foreclose all possibility of judicial relief if some limited and precise rationale were found to correct an established violation of the Constitution in some redistricting cases.

When presented with a claim of injury from partisan gerrymandering, courts confront two obstacles. First is the lack of comprehensive and neutral principles for drawing electoral boundaries. No substantive definition of fairness in districting seems to command general assent. Second is the absence of rules to limit and confine judicial intervention. With uncertain limits, intervening courts—even when proceeding with best intentions—would risk assuming political, not legal, responsibility for a process that often produces ill will and distrust.

That courts can grant relief in districting cases where race is involved does not answer our need for fairness principles here. Those controversies implicate a different inquiry. They involve sorting permissible classifications in the redistricting context from impermissible ones. Race is an impermissible classification. . . . Politics is quite a different matter. . . . Because there are yet no agreed upon substantive principles of fairness in districting, we have no basis on which to define clear, manageable, and politically neutral standards for measuring the particular burden a given partisan classification imposes on representational rights. . . .

Because, in the case before us, we have no standard by which to measure the burden appellants claim has been imposed on their representational rights, appellants cannot establish that the alleged political classifications burden those same rights. . . . As a consequence, appellants' complaint alleges no impermissible use of political classifications and so states no valid claim on which relief may be granted. . . .

The plurality thinks I resolve this case with reference to no standard, but that is wrong. The Fourteenth Amendment standard governs; and there is no doubt of that. My analysis only notes that if a subsidiary standard could show how an otherwise permissible classification, as applied, burdens representational rights, we could conclude that appellants' evidence states a provable claim under the Fourteenth Amendment standard.

. . . [T]he complaint in this case also alleged a violation of First Amendment rights. The First Amendment may be the more relevant constitutional provision in future cases that allege unconstitutional partisan gerrymandering. After all, these allegations involve the First Amendment interest of not burdening or penalizing citizens because of their participation in the electoral process, their voting history, their association with a political party, or their expression of political views. See *Elrod v. Burns*, 427 U.S. 347 (1976) (plurality opinion). Under general First Amendment principles those burdens in other contexts are unconstitutional absent a compelling government interest. . . . First Amendment concerns arise where a State enacts a law that has the purpose and effect of subjecting a group of voters or their party to disfavored treatment by reason of their views. In the context of partisan gerrymandering, that means that First Amendment concerns arise where an apportionment has the purpose and effect of burdening a group of voters' representational rights.

Where it is alleged that a gerrymander had the purpose and effect of imposing burdens on a disfavored party and its voters, the First Amendment may offer a sounder and more prudential basis for intervention than does the Equal Protection Clause. The equal protection analysis puts its emphasis on the permissibility of an enactment's classifications. This works where race is involved since classifying by race is almost never permissible. It presents a more complicated question when the inquiry is whether a generally permissible classification has been used for an impermissible purpose. That question can only be answered in the affirmative by the subsidiary showing that the classification as applied imposes unlawful burdens. The First Amendment analysis concentrates on whether the legislation burdens the representational rights of the complaining party's voters for reasons of ideology, beliefs, or political association. . . .

■ JUSTICE STEVENS, dissenting.

. . . The concept of equal justice under law requires the State to govern impartially. Today's plurality opinion would exempt governing officials from that duty in the context of legislative redistricting and would give license, for the first time, to partisan gerrymanders that are devoid of any rational justification. In my view, when partisanship is the legislature's sole motivation—when any pretense of neutrality is forsaken unabashedly and all traditional districting criteria are subverted for partisan advantage—the governing body cannot be said to have acted impartially. . . .

The judicial standards applicable to gerrymandering claims are deeply rooted in decisions that long preceded *Bandemer* and have been refined in later cases. Among those well-settled principles is the understanding that a district's peculiar shape might be a symptom of an illicit purpose in the line-drawing process. . . . [Our] decisions . . . have also considered the process by which the districting schemes were enacted, looked to other evidence demonstrating that purely improper considerations motivated the decision, and included maps illustrating outlandish district shapes.

Given this clear line of precedents, I should have thought the question of justiciability in cases such as this—where a set of plaintiffs argues that a single motivation resulted in a districting scheme with discriminatory effects—to be well settled. The plurality's contrary conclusion cannot be squared with our long history of voting rights decisions. Especially perplexing is the plurality's *ipse dixit* distinction of our racial gerrymandering cases. . . .

To begin with, the plurality errs in assuming that politics is "an ordinary and lawful motive." We have squarely rejected the notion that a "purpose to discriminate on the basis of politics" is never subject to strict scrutiny. On the contrary, "political belief and association constitute the core of those activities protected by the First Amendment," Elrod, at 356 (plurality opinion), and discriminatory governmental decisions that burden fundamental First Amendment interests are subject to strict scrutiny. Thus, unless party affiliation is an appropriate requirement for the position in question, government officials may not base a decision to hire, promote, transfer, recall, discharge, or retaliate against an employee, or to terminate a contract, on the individual's partisan affiliation or speech. It follows that political affiliation is not an appropriate standard for excluding voters from a congressional district. . . .

[O]ur recent racial gerrymandering cases have examined the shape of the district and the purpose of the districting body to determine whether race, above all other criteria, predominated in the line-drawing process. . . . Under the *Shaw* cases, then, the use of race as a criterion in redistricting is not *per se* impermissible, . . . but when race is elevated to paramount status—when it is the be-all and end-all of the redistricting process—the legislature has gone too far. . . .

Just as irrational shape can serve as an objective indicator of an impermissible legislative purpose, other objective features of a districting map can save the plan from invalidation. We have explained that "traditional districting principles," which include "compactness, contiguity, and respect for political subdivisions," are "important not because they are constitutionally required . . . but because they are objective factors that may serve to defeat a claim that a district has been gerrymandered on racial lines." . . .

In my view, the same standards should apply to claims of political gerrymandering, for the essence of a gerrymander is the same regardless of whether the group is identified as political or racial. Gerrymandering always involves the drawing of district boundaries to maximize the voting strength of the dominant political faction and to minimize the strength of one or more groups of opponents. In seeking the desired result, legislators necessarily make judgments about the probability that the members of identifiable groups—whether economic, religious, ethnic, or racial—will vote in a certain way. The overriding purpose of those predictions is political. It follows that the standards that enable courts to identify and redress a racial gerrymander could also perform the same function for other species of gerrymanders. . . .

The plurality reasons that the standards for evaluating racial gerrymanders are not workable in cases such as this because partisan considerations, unlike racial ones, are perfectly legitimate. Until today, however, there has not been the slightest intimation in any opinion written by any Member of this Court that a naked purpose to disadvantage a political minority would provide a rational basis for drawing a district line. On the contrary, our opinions referring to political gerrymanders have consistently assumed that they were at least undesirable, and we always have indicated that political considerations are among those factors that may not dominate districting decisions. Purely partisan motives are "rational" in a literal sense, but there must be a limiting principle. . . . The rational basis for government decisions must satisfy a standard of legitimacy and neutrality; an acceptable rational basis can be neither purely personal nor purely partisan. . . .

In sum, in evaluating a challenge to a specific district, I would apply the standard set forth in the *Shaw* cases and ask whether the legislature allowed partisan considerations to dominate and control the lines drawn, forsaking all neutral principles. Under my analysis, if no neutral criterion can be identified to justify the lines drawn, and if the only possible explanation for a district's bizarre shape is a naked desire to increase partisan strength, then no rational basis exists to save the district from an equal protection challenge. Such a narrow test would cover only a few meritorious claims, but it would preclude extreme abuses, . . . and it would perhaps shorten the time period in which the pernicious effects of such a gerrymander are felt. This test would mitigate the current trend under which partisan considerations are becoming the be-all and end-all in apportioning representatives. . . .

■ JUSTICE SOUTER, with whom JUSTICE GINSBURG joins, dissenting.

The Constitution guarantees both formal and substantial equality among voters. For 40 years, we have recognized that lines dividing a State into voting districts must produce divisions with equal populations: one person, one vote. . . .

Creating unequally populous districts is not, however, the only way to skew political results by setting district lines. . . . However equal districts may be in population as a formal matter, the consequence of a vote cast can be minimized or maximized, and if unfairness is sufficiently demonstrable, the guarantee of equal protection condemns it as a denial of substantial equality . . .

Since this Court has created the problem no one else has been able to solve, it is up to us to make a fresh start. There are a good many voices saying it is high time that we did, for in the years since *Davis*, the increasing efficiency of partisan redistricting has damaged the democratic process to a degree that our predecessors only began to imagine. *[Lengthy citation to scholarly commentary omitted.—Editors]*

I would therefore preserve *Davis's* holding that political gerrymandering is a justiciable issue, but otherwise start anew. I would adopt a political gerrymandering test analogous to the summary judgment standard crafted in *McDonnell Douglas Corp. v. Green*, 411 U.S. 792 (1973), calling for a plaintiff to satisfy elements of a prima facie cause of action, at which point the State would have the opportunity not only to rebut the evidence supporting the plaintiff's case, but to offer an affirmative justification for the districting choices, even assuming the proof of the plaintiff's allegations. My own judgment is that we would have better luck at devising a workable prima facie case if we concentrated as much as possible on suspect characteristics of individual districts instead of statewide patterns. . . . Finally, in the same interest of threshold simplicity, I would stick to problems of single-member districts; if we could not devise a workable scheme for dealing with claims about these, we would have to forget the complications posed by multimember districts.

For a claim based on a specific single-member district, I would require the plaintiff to make out a prima facie case with five elements. First, the resident plaintiff would identify a cohesive political group to which he belonged . . .

Second, a plaintiff would need to show that the district of his residence paid little or no heed to those traditional districting principles whose disregard can be shown straightforwardly: contiguity, compactness, respect for political subdivisions, and conformity with geographic features like rivers and mountains. . . .

Indeed, although compactness is at first blush the least likely of these principles to yield precision, it can be measured quantitatively in terms of dispersion, perimeter, and population ratios, and the development of standards would thus be possible. It is not necessary now to say exactly how a district court would balance a good showing on one of these indices against a poor showing on another, for that sort of detail is best worked out case by case.

Third, the plaintiff would need to establish specific correlations between the district's deviations from traditional districting principles and the distribution of the population of his group. . . . To make their claim stick, they would need to point to specific protuberances on the Draconian shape that reach out to include Democrats, or fissures in it that squirm away from Republicans. . . . That would begin, but not complete, the plaintiff's case that the defendant had chosen either to pack the group (drawn a district in order to include a uselessly high number of the group) or to crack it (drawn it so as to include fatally few), the ordinary methods of vote dilution in single-member district systems.

Fourth, a plaintiff would need to present the court with a hypothetical district including his residence, one in which the proportion of the plaintiff's group was lower (in a packing claim) or higher (in a cracking one) and which at the same time deviated less from traditional districting principles than the actual district. . . .

Fifth, and finally, the plaintiff would have to show that the defendants acted intentionally to manipulate the shape of the district in order to pack or crack his group. I would, however, treat any showing of intent in a major-party case as too equivocal to count unless the entire legislature were controlled by the governor's party (or the dominant legislative party were vetoproof). . . .

A plaintiff who got this far would have shown that his State intentionally acted to dilute his vote, having ignored reasonable alternatives consistent with traditional districting principles. I would then shift the burden to the defendants to justify their decision by reference to objectives other than naked partisan advantage. They might show by rebuttal evidence that districting objectives could not be served by the plaintiff's hypothetical district better than by the district as drawn, or they might affirmatively establish legitimate objectives better served by the lines drawn than by the plaintiff's hypothetical. . . .

■ JUSTICE BREYER, dissenting.

. . . [Consideration of the fundamentals of democratic governance] can help identify at least one circumstance where use of purely political boundary-drawing factors can amount to a serious, and remediable, abuse, namely, the *unjustified* use of political factors to entrench a minority in power. By entrenchment I mean a situation in which a party that enjoys only minority support among the populace has nonetheless contrived to take, and hold, legislative power. By *unjustified* entrenchment I mean that the minority's hold on power is purely the result of partisan manipulation and not other factors. These "other" factors that could lead to "justified" (albeit temporary) minority entrenchment include sheer happenstance, the existence of more than two major parties, the unique constitutional requirements of certain representational bodies such as the Senate, or reliance on traditional (geographic, communities of interest, etc.) districting criteria.

The democratic harm of unjustified entrenchment is obvious. . . . Where unjustified entrenchment takes place, voters find it far more difficult to remove those responsible for a government they do not want; and these democratic values are dishonored.

. . . Unless some other justification can be found in particular circumstances, political gerrymandering that so entrenches a minority party in power violates basic democratic norms and lacks countervailing justification. For this reason, whether political gerrymandering does, or does not, violate the Constitution in other instances, gerrymandering that leads to entrenchment amounts to an abuse that violates the Constitution's Equal Protection Clause. . . .

I do not claim that the problem of identification and separation is easily solved, even in extreme instances. But courts can identify a number of strong indicia of abuse. The presence of actual entrenchment, while not always unjustified (being perhaps a chance occurrence), is such a sign, particularly when accompanied by the use of partisan boundary-drawing criteria in the way that JUSTICE STEVENS describes, *i.e.*, a use that both departs from traditional criteria and cannot be explained other than by efforts to achieve partisan advantage. . . .

In the case before us, there is a strong likelihood that the plaintiffs' complaint could be amended readily to assert circumstances consistent with those I have set forth as appropriate for judicial intervention. For that reason, I would authorize the plaintiffs to proceed; and I dissent from the majority's contrary determination.

NOTES

1.   Because Justice Kennedy dissented from the conclusion that political gerrymandering claims are non-justiciable, but concurred with the dismissal of the complaint on the ground the plaintiff had set forth no constitutional standard that had been violated, his opinion is the narrowest, and therefore the controlling opinion. What does it mean? What is the point of holding such cases justiciable if there is no available constitutional theory on which plaintiffs might succeed?

At the time of *Baker v. Carr*, the Court had not yet hit upon a judicially manageable standard for cases of unequal district size. Justices Frankfurter and Harlan, among others, thought that because there were many possible legitimate criteria for districting, the courts could not interfere without appearing partisan and political. The one person, one vote standard answered that objection: it could be applied unflinchingly in all cases, and it did not systematically favor one political party over the other. Of course, adoption of this standard came at the cost of a more nuanced system, such as that advocated by the dissenters in *Lucas*, the Colorado case. Is there a comparable standard for gerrymandering cases?

2.   The dissenters rely on different constitutional theories. Justice Souter rests on Equal Protection. Justice Stevens invokes the First Amendment. Justice Breyer does not mention the Guarantee Clause, but his concern about "minority entrenchment" sounds like a claim that the government is unrepublican. Interestingly, none of the justices invokes the provision of Article I, Section Two, Clause 1 that representatives must be chosen by "the People," even though this case involves federal congressional districts and that Clause had previously been the textual peg for challenges to congressional districting (e.g., *Wesberry*). Are these seemingly quite different constitutional principles interchangeable in the context of partisan gerrymandering cases?

3.   Why, precisely, does the plurality maintain that racial gerrymandering presents a different question from partisan gerrymandering? There are three main reasons. First, race is more discernible and immutable than political allegiance. But is it true, as the plurality asserts, that these facts "make it impossible to assess the effects of partisan gerrymandering"? Professional politicians seem capable of assessing these effects; why can't courts? Second, racial discrimination entails strict scrutiny, while discrimination on the basis of political allegiance does not (except sometimes). But Justice Stevens's argument is that discrimination on the basis of politics, at least in this context, *should* receive strict scrutiny. Is he right? The plurality says that partisan districting is "common" and "lawful." But so was unequal districting before *Baker*. Why not venture again into the political thicket? Third, the Constitution explicitly condemns discrimination on the basis of race and does not mention partisan gerrymandering. But is it so clear that the intentional creation of a majority-minority district violates this principle, assuming that the non-minority population is not deprived of its "fair share" of political influence? And the Constitution does mention, and "guarantee," a republican form of government. Why does the plurality avoid that principle?

But maybe the racial gerrymandering cases cut the other way. As we have seen, the Court set out on a path of disapproving districts that were drawn predominantly on racial lines, but it never embraced the usual constitutional principle that race is a forbidden consideration altogether. *Miller v. Johnson*, 515 U.S. 900, 928–29 (1995) (O'Connor, J., concurring). In later cases, the Court seemingly relaxed its scrutiny. E.g., *Easley v. Cromartie*, 532 U.S. 234 (2001). At this point, does the race analogy offer judicially manageable standards for partisan gerrymandering?

4.   If we think of the Equal Protection Clause, the plurality's assumption that the Constitution speaks more directly to racial gerrymandering than to partisan gerrymandering seems right. But is the same true of the Guarantee Clause? Partisan gerrymandering, at least in its extreme form (as described by Justice Breyer) allows a minority to entrench itself, which arguably goes to the heart of republicanism. Racial gerrymandering involves a decision by the majority to allow a minority to exercise a greater degree of political power. Is that unrepublican?

5.   Two means of controlling gerrymandering are computer programs and commissions. When politicians draw lines personally, no one can say what their real motives are, but computers take into account only the factors they are programmed to take into account. What would you think of a computer program that takes into account only population, compactness, contiguity, and established political boundaries? Another possibility is having a nonpartisan commission draw districting lines, as is done in about a dozen states. One question to consider is how a reliably nonpartisan commission could be selected, without effectively empowering incumbents and political insiders. Another questions is whether federal actors could require the more extensive use of such commissions. Could Congress require commission-based districting for federal elections under its Article I, Section 4, Clause 1 power to "make or alter" state regulations governing the "Times, Places, and Manner of holding Elections for Senators and Representatives"? Could Congress require commission-based districting for state elections under its Fourteenth Amendment, Section Five enforcement power? Or could a federal court require commission-based districting as a remedy for partisan gerrymandering?

CHAPTER 4

THE AMENDMENT PROCESS

[Assignment 40]

> *Art. V: The Congress, whenever two thirds of both Houses shall deem it necessary, shall propose Amendments to this Constitution, or, on the Application of the Legislatures of two thirds of the several States, shall call a Convention for proposing Amendments, which, in either Case, shall be valid to all Intents and Purposes, as Part of this Constitution, when ratified by the Legislatures of three fourths of the several States, or by Conventions in three fourths thereof, as the one or the other Mode of Ratification may be proposed by the Congress; Provided that no Amendment which may be made prior to the Year one thousand eight hundred and eight shall in any Manner affect the first and fourth Clauses in the ninth Section of the first Article; and that no State, without its Consent, shall be deprived of its equal Suffrage in the Senate.*

I. A PERFECT PROBLEM

This short but important chapter considers the process for constitutional amendment, which is set out in Article V of the Constitution. We begin with a situation that raised, directly or indirectly, nearly every issue concerning the amendment process. In 1789, as part of the originally proposed Bill of Rights, Congress put forward the following amendment: "No law, varying the compensation for the services of Senators and Representatives, shall take effect, until an election of Representatives shall have intervened." The amendment was declared ratified in *1992,* more than two centuries later, and is now listed as the Twenty-seventh Amendment to the Constitution. But is this amendment, sometimes called the Congressional Pay Amendment, really part of the Constitution? Was it proposed and ratified in accordance with the procedures specified by the Constitution for making amendments?

Here are the rules: Article V provides that amendments to the Constitution may be *proposed* in either of two ways: (1) by two-thirds majorities of both houses of Congress; or (2) by a national convention for proposing amendments, to be called by Congress upon application by two-thirds of the states. A proposed amendment must then be *ratified* by three-fourths of the states, acting either through their state legislatures or through special state ratifying conventions—whichever method Congress chooses in the particular case. (Recall from Chapter 1 that the framers provided that the original Constitution was to be ratified by state ratifying conventions—that was meant to circumvent the state legislatures, which jealously guarded their own powers.)

After being proposed by Congress in 1789, the Congressional Pay Amendment gathered only six state ratifications in the period during which the first ten amendments were ratified—well short of the three-fourths required by Article V. Ohio, which had not been a state at the time of the original proposal, ratified the amendment in 1873—still making the number far short of a three-fourths majority of the states. A large number of states ratified the amendment in the 1980s and early 1990s, with Michigan's ratification on May 7, 1992, as the thirty-eighth state (*of fifty*) putting the amendment over the three-fourths mark. Is this valid under Article V?

II. THE RIDDLES OF ARTICLE V

In assessing whether the Twenty-seventh Amendment is part of the Constitution, think about the following questions. Very few judicial opinions interpret Article V, which means this is a rare opportunity for you to engage in constitutional interpretation without the courts having given their view first.

1.   Article V does not specify a time limit for a proposed amendment to be ratified. Is it proper to read in an implicit time limit? Should adoption of a constitutional amendment require a "contemporaneous consensus" of some sort? See *Dillon v. Gloss*, 256 U.S. 368 (1921) (suggesting such a view in dicta). If so, what is that time limit? Is it a "reasonable" period of time?

2.   Could Congress, in the proposed amendment itself, specify a deadline for ratification, after which the proposal would be deemed dead? (Look at the Eighteenth, Twentieth, Twenty-first, and Twenty-second Amendments.) Could Congress specify a deadline not in the text of the proposed amendment (perhaps for stylistic reasons) but rather in the bill or resolution proposing the amendment to the states?

3.   Could Congress specify a deadline after an amendment has already been proposed? (Again, this would necessarily not be in the text of the proposed amendment.) Could Congress rescind a proposed amendment, effectively imposing a deadline of "now"? For example, could Congress have "terminated" the proposed Congressional Pay Amendment sometime before Michigan's 1992 ratification, if it thought that the proposal had lingered too long, or was just a bad idea? Instead of imposing a deadline, could Congress wait until after the scale-tipping state ratification and judge whether the ratification was timely? (Note that Congress voted 414–3 in the House and 99–0 in the Senate to "accept" the Twenty-seventh Amendment as validly ratified. What if Congress had voted not to accept it?)

4.   Could Congress judge other things about the validity of state ratifications—such as whether or not the state legislature acted properly, according to its own rules of procedure, in purporting to ratify an amendment? See *Coleman v. Miller,* 307 U.S. 433 (1939) (suggesting, without a controlling majority opinion, either that Congress possesses this power or that its acceptance of a state ratification is a "political question").

5.   Should the executive branch have a role in any of these determinations? Before Congress voted to "accept" the Twenty-seventh Amendment, Don W. Wilson, the Archivist of the United States, had already decided to "certify the adoption of the amendment," in reliance on an opinion from the Office of Legal Counsel. Sanford Levinson, *Authorizing Constitutional Text: On the Purported Twenty-Seventh Amendment*, 11 Const. Commentary 101, 107 (1994). Does the National Archives have a role in deciding what is in the text of the Constitution?

6.   How sure are you of your answers to the preceding two questions? See if they hold up—or whether you might be tempted to reconsider—when you are presented with the following question: Could Congress conclude that a state's failure

to ratify a proposed constitutional amendment was illegitimate, install a new state legislature that would be more sympathetic, and refuse to seat that state's U.S. representatives and senators in Congress until that state changed its mind and ratified the proposed amendments? This hypothetical is remarkably close to the story of the ratification of the Fourteenth Amendment—perhaps the amendment most central to modern constitutional law. Was the Fourteenth Amendment illegally adopted? (We return to this in question 15.) Note that at least Congress did not out-and-out declare the amendment *ratified* by the state legislatures when it had in fact been *rejected* by them. Congress at least felt it necessary to replace the recalcitrant state legislatures and have them vote to ratify the amendment proposal.

7.   Back to the question of the validity of the Twenty-seventh Amendment and the time limit for ratification: If Article V does not contain a time limit, and Congress did not specify one in advance as part of the enactment proposing the amendment, does a proposed constitutional amendment live forever, floating above us, waiting to be ratified (like the Congressional Pay Amendment)? Or could Congress "recall" a constitutional amendment proposal? If so, should it take the same two-thirds majority vote of both houses of Congress that it took to propose the amendment?

8.   Here are some amendments passed by two-thirds of both houses of Congress, but not ratified: First, there is the proposal (also part of the original proposed Bill of Rights) to increase the size of the House of Representatives. (There is a dispute about whether adoption of that amendment would affect anything today.) Second, there is a proposal from 1810 that would strip U.S. citizenship from anyone who accepts a title of nobility from any foreign government or who (without Congress's consent) accepts any "emolument" from a foreign nation. (This amendment would have real consequences if adopted, but would be less harmful if it were not deemed retroactive.)

Third, there is the "Corwin Amendment," a proposed amendment passed by Congress during the secession crisis of the winter of 1860–1861 that would have permanently forbidden any constitutional amendment giving Congress power over the "domestic institutions" of the states, "including that of persons held to labor or service by the laws of said State"—i.e., slavery. Had it been ratified at the time, it would have become the Thirteenth Amendment.

Query: Does the adoption of the *real* Thirteenth Amendment—abolishing slavery—extinguish this proposal? Or could the Corwin Amendment still be ratified today, and grant protection to other "domestic institutions" (like what?) from federal regulation? And what about the fact that the Thirteenth Amendment does not abolish *all* slavery? (Go reread it.)

Finally, there is the "Child Labor Amendment" of the 1920s, intended to overrule Supreme Court decisions of that era finding no power under the Commerce Clause or the Taxing Clause to regulate child labor. (Adoption of that amendment would now largely embrace the rules the Supreme Court subsequently adopted, as a matter of interpretation of those existing provisions.)

9.   May an amendment forbid future amendments, as the Corwin Amendment purported to do? If it did, couldn't a subsequent amendment simply repeal the supposedly un-repealable amendment's no-repeal provision, in the course of repealing it? But if it could, what of the other provisions of the Constitution that Article V itself makes (or purports to make) un-repealable: the prohibition (until

1808) of amendments permitting Congress to restrict the international slave trade and the prohibition of amendments depriving any state of equal representation in the Senate? Could an amendment be adopted changing Article V's no-amendment proviso with respect to the Senate without its consent? Could one *then* pass an amendment changing the representation rule for the Senate? If so, why not do both in one step, in a single amendment?

10. Is there anything in the Constitution (other than the Article V provisos) that limits what a constitutional amendment can say or do? Can there be such a thing as an *unconstitutional* constitutional amendment, or is the idea nonsensical? If there is no limit on what an amendment proposal might say, couldn't an "amendment" essentially create a whole new system of government, scrapping the Constitution? Is it then no longer an "amendment"? (But isn't that pretty much what happened with the Constitutional Convention and the adoption of the Constitution?) Push the hypothetical a step further: Are there some amendments that would be "out of keeping with" the "spirit" of the Constitution, and thus cannot be adopted? See Jeffrey Rosen, Note, *Was the Flag Burning Amendment Unconstitutional?*, 100 Yale L.J. 1073 (1991) (arguing that a proposed amendment to overturn the Court's decision finding flag-burning to be constitutionally protected by the freedom of speech would violate natural law limitations on the Article V amendment power); see also Laurence H. Tribe, *A Constitution We are Amending: In Defense of a Restrained Judicial Role*, 97 Harv. L. Rev. 433, 438–39 (1983) (suggesting that some amendments would not "fit" the Constitution). In fact, such claims were raised in, and rejected by, *Leser v. Garnett*, 258 U.S. 130 (1922).

11. Back to the question of time limits: If Congress did adopt a time limit in an amendment proposal or in the text of the amendment itself, may a later Congress change the time limit? If so, how? This was a major constitutional controversy in the 1970s and early 1980s, when the proposed Equal Rights Amendment ("ERA")—forbidding denial of equal treatment by the federal government or by any state government on the basis of sex—narrowly failed to receive the necessary number of state ratifications. Congress initially enacted a seven-year time limit for ratification, as part of the joint resolution proposing the ERA. As the deadline neared without enough states ratifying, Congress voted to extend the deadline by seven more years. Is this permissible? See Michael Stokes Paulsen, *A General Theory of Article V: The Constitutional Lessons of the Twenty-seventh Amendment*, 103 Yale L.J. 677, 726 (1993) (surveying discussion of the issue and concluding that Congress needed to enact a new amendment proposal and solicit new ratifications). As it happened, the ERA did not receive the requisite number of state ratifications, even assuming the extension was legitimate. But what is the right answer? Could Congress, by majority vote, resurrect the ERA yet again?

12. May a state legislature rescind its ratification of a proposed amendment? Certainly not after the three-fourths threshold has been crossed, right? Once the amendment has been ratified, it remains ratified; the scale-tipping ratification locks the amendment in place. (Unless, of course, the amendment is superseded by another amendment—as the Twenty-first Amendment repealed the Eighteenth Amendment, ending Prohibition.) Were it otherwise, couldn't a state "secede" from some or all of the Constitution, by withdrawing its earlier consent? (What would be wrong with that?)

Now change the situation: What about a state's rescission *before* the scale-tipping ratification that makes an amendment part of the Constitution? Is ratification like a light-switch that a state can turn on and then off again? Idaho rescinded its ratification of the ERA while the proposal was still pending, a move upheld by a federal district court before the issue became moot. See *Idaho v. Freeman*, 529 F.Supp.1107 (D. Idaho 1981), *vacated as moot sub nom. National Organization for Women v. Idaho*, 459 U.S. 809 (1982). Is that the right answer? Ohio and New Jersey rescinded their ratifications of the Fourteenth Amendment before that amendment took effect. While the issue remains disputed as a matter of history, it appears that these ratifications were not counted by the secretary of state in the three-fourths needed for ratification. (But Congress apparently wanted them counted. Does this make a difference?)

13. If, as suggested above, "the scale-tipping ratification locks the amendment in place," then what happens if we learn about an old ratification that had been forgotten? This may not be a hypothetical question. Remember (from question 8) the 1789 amendment to increase the size of the House? That amendment came close to meeting the threshold for ratification in the early years of the country, before many new states were omitted. Indeed, some people claim to have found evidence that there was a "forgotten" ratification by Connecticut in 1792, which would have been enough for the amendment to become part of the Constitution (at the time, it would have given the amendment 12 out of 15 states). This would imply that the amendment has been part of the Constitution for 224 years, and nobody has known about it! Is this absurd? Is there some point at which it becomes too late to "discover" a ratification vote? (A recent lawsuit to enforce the allegedly forgotten amendment was rejected by the federal courts on standing and political question grounds. But the court did not address the merits. See *LaVergne v. Bryson*, 497 Fed. Appx. 219 (3d Cir. 2012).)

14. May a state ratify an amendment after previously rejecting it? If your answer to the preceding question was that a state may change its ratification light-switch from on to off, surely it may turn its switch from off back to on, right? Or might ratification be a one-way street, rather than an on-off switch? That is, may a state change its mind in one direction but not the other? Does the text of Article V help you?

15. Return now to an issue mentioned in question 6. There, we were concerned with whether Congress had complete control to decide whether an amendment has been validly ratified by the states. Here, we pick up on the question of states changing their minds from "no" to "yes." Several Southern states in fact switched from "no" to "yes" on ratifying the Fourteenth Amendment during Reconstruction— after Congress either *replaced* those state governments or *required* that they ratify the Fourteenth Amendment as a condition of being re-admitted to representation in Congress. Was this permissible? Does the question turn on Article IV issues of Congress's powers of reconstruction, pursuant to the Republican Form of Government Clause, rather than on Article V? See Akhil Amar, AMERICA'S CONSTITUTION: A BIOGRAPHY 364–380 (2005) (arguing that Congress could fairly conclude that the Southern governments in question were not "republican" within the meaning of Article IV, in that they denied the vote to large numbers of their free male citizens even after slavery had been abolished by the Thirteenth Amendment). A related question involving constitutional amendments and the Civil War: in

counting state ratifications of the Thirteenth and Fourteenth Amendments, should you include in the denominator states that have purported to secede from the Union? If your theory is President Lincoln's, that a state may not lawfully leave the Union, don't you need three-fourths of all the states, including the so-called "seceded" states? Isn't that a problem if you don't have operating loyal, *Union* governments in those states? Or can you just set up such governments, provisionally, using military reconstruction powers—and have those governments ratify your proposed amendment? Compare Vasan Kesavan & Michael Stokes Paulsen, *Is West Virginia Unconstitutional?* 90 Cal. L. Rev. 291 (2002) (yes) with Bruce Ackerman, 2 WE THE PEOPLE: TRANSFORMATIONS 99–109 (1998); Bruce A. Ackerman *The Storrs Lectures: Discovering the Constitution*, 93 Yale L.J. 1013 (1984) (no). See generally John Harrison, *The Lawfulness of the Reconstruction Amendments*, 68 U. Chi. L. Rev. 375 (2001).

16.   Bruce Ackerman has argued that the Constitution can be amended through political events in the life of the nation. He concludes that the Fourteenth Amendment was not properly ratified under the rules of Article V but nonetheless is part of the Constitution: the series of dramatic Reconstruction-era events were a "constitutional moment" that could achieve a change in the Constitution without complying with Article V's prescribed process. Ackerman, 2 WE THE PEOPLE: TRANSFORMATIONS at 99–119, 207–34. Ackerman also maintains that the Constitution was illegally adopted, under the rules of the Articles of Confederation. For Ackerman, the transformative "constitutional moments" were the adoption of the Constitution, Reconstruction, and the New Deal. What do you think? May the Constitution be amended by great political events? If so, were there other constitutional moments? How should that question be answered?

17.   Akhil Amar has argued for a rather different theory of extra-Article V constitutional amendment. Unlike Ackerman's approach, Amar's concerns the adoption of an actual constitutional text. Amar proposes that Article V should not be read as the exclusive mode even for adopting textual amendments. His argument is that Congress, or a convention called pursuant to Article V, could propose that an amendment be ratified not by three-fourths of the states (whether legislatures or special ratifying conventions) but by a national referendum. After all, Amar argues, the Constitutional Convention at Philadelphia in 1787 proposed a method of ratification that departed from the rules of the document it was amending. i.e., the Articles of Confederation. It was legitimate for the Convention to do so because the framers were returning to the source of authority that made the Articles—the separate, sovereign "peoples" of each of the individual states. Now, under the Constitution, the legitimate source of authority is "We the People of the United States" taken as a whole. Why not therefore turn to that ultimate popular sovereign as the relevant ratifying authority? Akhil R. Amar, *Philadelphia Revisited: Amending the Constitution Outside Article V*, 55 U. Chi. L. Rev. 1043 (1988). Is Amar's argument sound? Why go to the bother of listing the prescribed methods of amendment if they are not *the* prescribed methods of amendment? Is it possible that Amar's argument is sound as a matter of political theory and sovereignty but not as an interpretation of Article V? Is it an act of revolution or quasi-revolution, perhaps justified as such (like the American Revolution or the adoption of the Constitution), but not justified under the Constitution itself?

18. The convention method of proposing amendments was explicitly contemplated by the framers as an alternative route to circumvent Congress if its members were too resistant to constitutional change. (Does this provide some further reason to question whether Congress is the ultimate judge of whether an amendment has been adopted?) The convention method provides that, "The Congress, . . . on the Application of the legislatures of two thirds of the several States shall call a Convention for proposing Amendments."

One problem is whether a constitutional convention could be limited in the topics that it considers for amendments. The Supreme Court has never addressed the question, and scholars are split. Charles Black suggested that Article V's spare language—"a Convention for proposing Amendments"—would seem to contemplate a convention for "proposing such amendments as that convention decides to propose." Charles L. Black, *Amending the Constitution: A Letter to a Congressman*, 82 Yale L.J. 189, 199 (1972). More recently, Michael Rappaport has argued that text and history allow a limited convention: " '[A] Convention for proposing Amendments' is broad enough to cover not merely unlimited conventions but also limited conventions," and "the evidence bearing on the original meaning of the phrase strongly suggests that a limited convention is such a 'Convention for proposing Amendments.'" Michael. B. Rappaport, *The Constitutionality of A Limited Convention: An Originalist Analysis*, 28 Const. Comment. 53, 64, 65 (2012).

What do you think? And whatever the answer, who would enforce it? (That is, who would enforce either the convention's limits or its power to proceed without limits?)

19. What do you think of Article V's procedure for amending the Constitution? The framers appear to have wanted to make it difficult to amend the Constitution, in order to assure stability and prevent frequent changes. Does Article V permit a small minority of the people to block constitutional change? In theory, all that is needed to defeat even an overwhelmingly popular constitutional amendment proposal is a blocking coalition in one house of a two-house state legislature, in one-fourth (plus one) of the smallest-population states. Isn't that unfair—just a slightly different version of the problem James Madison complained about in *The Federalist No. 43* with respect to the Articles of Confederation, which permitted tiny, obstreperous Rhode Island to block needed reform because of the rule of state unanimity? What do the number of amendments suggest about this concern?

Around the world there is huge variety in constitutional amendment processes. The U.S. Constitution is regarded as among the most difficult to amend, though some other constitutions have substantial parts that may not be amended at all. But the difficulty of the amendment procedures might not actually be as important as it seems. A recent empirical analysis of amendments around the world argues that "amendment culture" is more important than the formal amendment procedures in determining how often a constitution will be amended. See Tom Ginsburg & James Melton, *Does The Constitutional Amendment Rule Matter At All? Amendment Cultures and the Challenges of Measuring Amendment Difficulty*, 18 Int'l Journal of Constitutional Law 686 (2015). What are the conditions—whether as a matter of law, politics, or institutions—that make it desirable for constitutional amendment to be difficult or easy? Should we amend Article V's amendment process?

20. One final set of questions about the amendment process: Does the presence of Article V in the Constitution suggest any general rules for constitutional interpretation? Does the difficulty of amending the Constitution imply that courts should be active in updating it by means of constitutional interpretation? Or does the existence of Article V—by virtue of its rules for making amendments to the text—imply that the Constitution is not to be "amended" by interpretation?

PART 2

RIGHTS AGAINST THE GOVERNMENT

CHAPTER 5

THE BILL OF RIGHTS

[Assignment 41]

The Bill of Rights—the name customarily given to the first ten amendments to the Constitution—is practically a second Constitution all its own. These amendments recognize or assert important individual and collective liberties against the government. Even where the government might otherwise possess *power* in a certain area, the enumeration of *rights* overcomes that power and limits what the government may constitutionally do.

In this chapter, we explore the Bill of Rights and major judicial cases interpreting these amendments. We begin with an extended discussion of the First Amendment, especially the freedom of speech and the religion clauses (the Free Exercise Clause and the Establishment Clause). Next we consider more briefly the "Military Amendments," the Second Amendment right to keep and bear arms and the Third Amendment right against government quartering of soldiers. We then consider, also briefly, the constitutional law of criminal procedure, addressing questions of police search and seizure, the privilege against self-incrimination, and the prohibition on cruel and unusual punishments, covered by the Fourth, Fifth, Sixth, and Eighth Amendments (with a note on the Seventh Amendment). We conclude with the provisions of the Ninth and Tenth Amendments.

A Short History of the Bill of Rights

The Bill of Rights has its origins in English constitutional history. Beginning with Magna Carta in 1215 and continuing with the Petition of Right of 1628, English kings signed written documents that intertwined what we today would call "individual" and "structural" constitutional rights. Thus, the Petition of Right, which Sir Edward Coke and Parliament forced King Charles I to sign in 1628, confirmed that the king could not arrest or detain his subjects without the authority of a statute and the protection of a jury trial; that only Parliament could raise taxes; and that there were limits to the royal power of quartering soldiers in private homes. King Charles went back on his pledges, and in the English Civil War that followed he was beheaded. In 1688, his son, King James II, was driven into exile in the Glorious Revolution, and Parliament enacted the English Bill of Rights of 1689.

This English Bill of Rights was a statute codifying a Declaration of Rights that Parliament presented to James II's successors, William and Mary. Their succession to the throne was conditioned on their accepting these rights as being absolutely binding on them and their successors. It is almost a constitution, and is binding down to the present day. As you will notice, most of the English Bill of Rights found its way in some form or another into the U.S. Constitution:

The English Bill of Rights of 1689

And whereas the said late King James the Second having abdicated the government, and the throne being thereby vacant . . . the said lords spiritual and temporal, and commons . . . do in the first place (as their ancestors in like case have usually done) for the vindicating and asserting their ancient rights and liberties, declare

1. That the pretended power of suspending of laws, or the execution of laws, by regal authority, without consent of parliament, is illegal.

2. That the pretended power of dispensing with laws, or the execution of laws, by regal authority, as it hath been assumed and exercised of late, is illegal.

3. That the commission for erecting the late court of commissioners for ecclesiastical causes, and all other commissions and courts of like nature are illegal and pernicious.

4. That levying money for or to the use of the crown, by pretence of prerogative, without grant of parliament, for longer time, or in other manner than the same is or shall be granted, is illegal.

5. That it is the right of the subjects to petition the King, and all commitments and prosecutions for such petitioning are illegal.

6. That the raising or keeping a standing army within the kingdom in time of peace, unless it be with consent of parliament, is against law.

7. That the subjects which are protestants, may have arms for their defence suitable to their conditions, and as allowed by law.

8. That election of members of parliament ought to be free.

9. That the freedom of speech, and debates or proceedings in parliament, ought not to be impeached or questioned in any court or place out of parliament.

10. That excessive bail ought not to be required, nor excessive fines imposed; nor cruel and unusual punishments inflicted.

11. That jurors ought to be duly impaneled and returned, and jurors which pass upon men in trials for high treason ought to be freeholders.

12. That all grants and promises of fines and forfeitures of particular persons before conviction are illegal and void.

13. And that for redress of all grievances, and for the amending, strengthening, and preserving of the laws, parliaments ought to be held frequently.

As discussed in Chapter 1 (p. 31), the supporters of ratification of the U.S. Constitution argued that a separate Bill of Rights was unnecessary. They claimed that the proposed Constitution already accomplished the main aims of the English Bill of Rights because it (1) obligated the president to take care that the laws were faithfully executed, (2) gave the power of taxation to Congress, (3) also gave Congress the power to create new federal courts, (4) protected speech and debate in Congress, (5) provided for jury trial in criminal cases, and (6) required that Congress meet at least once a year. More importantly, the Federalists argued, the careful enumeration of national legislative powers in Article I, Section 8 did not invest the federal government with any authority to invade personal rights. It did not, for example, allow any federal regulation of the press or of religion. This argument did not prove persuasive; supporters of a Bill of Rights did not find it hard to show how virtually every grant of power in Section 8 could be abused.[4]

The absence of a Bill of Rights was the Anti-Federalists' most potent argument against the proposed Constitution, and five state conventions demanded a Bill of Rights as the price of ratification. The Anti-Federalist argument for a Bill of Rights was a states-rights argument and an individual-rights argument intertwined as one. The Anti-Federalists thought that liberty would be best protected by keeping government local and close to the people. (Note the difference between the Anti-Federalists' view and the warnings about faction in state governments in *The Federalist No. 10*, p. 464.) Such governments, they thought, would be more vigilant in protecting their rights than a distant and less accountable central government— whether in London or in the capital of the new United States. The Anti-Federalists prevailed, and they received a Bill of Rights that contained a collection of important, but largely uncontroversial, provisions.

This is illustrated by a few key facts you need to know. The Bill of Rights as it originally passed Congress consisted of *twelve* amendments. The first two were not immediately ratified. Congress's proposed First Amendment dealt with the size of the House of Representatives, and its proposed Second Amendment dealt with pay increases for members of Congress. These are issues of what would now be called structural constitutional law. The Establishment Clause in what would have been the Third (our First) Amendment was also structural. It forbade national legislation that would either establish a national church or interfere with state established churches, such as the Congregational establishment in Connecticut. Our Sixth and Seventh Amendments give rights to jury trial in criminal and civil cases. These amendments, too, can be seen as structural guarantees that empower local juries to protect citizens against government officials—national as well as state. In addition, the Bill of Rights ends with a federalism guarantee in our Tenth Amendment. Thus the original Bill of Rights of 1791 was partly a structural, even communitarian, document.

James Madison also proposed an amendment that would have secured a small set of rights—the "equal rights of conscience," the "freedom of speech, or of the press," and the "right of trial by jury in criminal cases"—against infringement by the *state* governments. But the Senate, which was then elected by state legislators, rejected this proposal. Thus, the Bill of Rights was generally regarded as applicable only to actions of the federal government. But this question is important, and it deserves further consideration.

Did the Bill of Rights Bind the States?

The Bill of Rights originally applied only to the federal government's actions This is understandable, given its origins in Anti-Federalist concerns about the national government using its powers to violate individual rights or intrude on the states. It was not until after the adoption of the Fourteenth Amendment that the Bill

---

[4]   Some have argued that the "necessary and proper" standard would forbid enactment of "improper" laws infringing rights. See Gary Lawson & Patricia B. Granger, *The "Proper" Scope of Federal Power: A Jurisdictional Interpretation of the Sweeping Clause*, 43 Duke L.J. 267 (1993). This is linguistically plausible, but is it consistent with the Necessary and Proper Clause's placement among the powers of Article I, Section 8?

of Rights would be generally understood as applying to actions taken by state governments. But even before the adoption of the Fourteenth Amendment, some argued that the Bill of Rights actually applied to state governments, too. A famous case presenting this issue, *Barron v. Baltimore*, was decided by the U.S. Supreme Court in 1833. The case is worthy of study for Chief Justice Marshall's sophisticated textual analysis and for the light it sheds on the structure of the original Constitution—the relationship between the national government and the states, and the relationship between powers and rights.

Barron provides a good occasion to consider systematically how to interpret and apply the Constitution. As you read Chief Justice Marshall's opinion, consider the types of constitutional arguments he uses. Look for arguments from text, historical context, structure, practice and precedent, and policy. (For a summary of these kinds of arguments, see p. 42.)

Barron v. Baltimore
32 U.S. (7 Pet.) 243 (1833)

■ MR. CHIEF JUSTICE MARSHALL delivered the opinion of the Court.

[John Barron owned a commercial wharf in the Baltimore harbor. His ability to make money from that wharf was impaired when the City of Baltimore took actions that made the water near the wharf too shallow for most ships. Barron sued the city in the Maryland state courts, claiming that the state and city had taken his property without just compensation, in violation of the Fifth Amendment to the U.S. Constitution, which provides, in relevant part: "nor shall private property be taken for public use, without just compensation." Barron won $4,500 in the trial court, but that judgment was reversed on appeal. He then appealed to the U.S. Supreme Court.—Editors]

. . . The plaintiff in error contends that [this case] comes within that clause in the fifth amendment to the constitution, which inhibits the taking of private property for public use, without just compensation. He insists that this amendment, being in favour of the liberty of the citizen, ought to be so construed as to restrain the legislative power of a state, as well as that of the United States. If this proposition be untrue, the court can take no jurisdiction of the cause.

The question thus presented is, we think, of great importance, but not of much difficulty.

The constitution was ordained and established by the people of the United States for themselves, for their own government, and not for the government of the individual states. Each state established a constitution for itself, and, in that constitution, provided such limitations and restrictions on the powers of its particular government as its judgment dictated. The people of the United States framed such a government for the United States as they supposed best adapted to their situation, and best calculated to promote their interests. The powers they conferred on this government were to be exercised by itself; and the limitations on power, if expressed in general terms, are naturally, and, we think, necessarily applicable to the government created by the instrument. They are limitations of power granted in the instrument itself; not of distinct governments, framed by different persons and for different purposes.

If these propositions be correct, the fifth amendment must be understood as restraining the power of the general government, not as applicable to the states. In their several constitutions they have imposed such restrictions on their respective governments as their own wisdom suggested; such as they deemed most proper for themselves. It is a subject on which they judge exclusively, and with which others interfere no farther than they are supposed to have a common interest.

The counsel for the plaintiff in error insists that the constitution was intended to secure the people of the several states against the undue exercise of power by their respective state governments; as well as against that which might be attempted by their general government. In support of this argument he relies on the inhibitions contained in the tenth section of the first article.

We think that section affords a strong if not a conclusive argument in support of the opinion already indicated by the court.

The preceding section contains restrictions which are obviously intended for the exclusive purpose of restraining the exercise of power by the departments of the general government. Some of them use language applicable only to congress: others are expressed in general terms. The third clause, for example, declares that "no bill of attainder or ex post facto law shall be passed." No language can be more general; yet the demonstration is complete that it applies solely to the government of the United States. In addition to the general arguments furnished by the instrument itself, some of which have been already suggested, the succeeding section, the avowed purpose of which is to restrain state legislation, contains in terms the very prohibition. It declares that "no state shall pass any bill of attainder or ex post facto law." This provision, then, of the ninth section, however comprehensive its language, contains no restriction on state legislation.

The ninth section having enumerated, in the nature of a bill of rights, the limitations intended to be imposed on the powers of the general government, the tenth proceeds to enumerate those which were to operate on the state legislatures. These restrictions are brought together in the same section, and are by express words applied to the states. "No state shall enter into any treaty," & c. Perceiving that in a constitution framed by the people of the United States for the government of all, no limitation of the action of government on the people would apply to the state government, unless expressed in terms; the restrictions contained in the tenth section are in direct words so applied to the states.

It is worthy of remark, too, that these inhibitions generally restrain state legislation on subjects entrusted to the general government, or in which the people of all the states feel an interest.

A state is forbidden to enter into any treaty, alliance or confederation. If these compacts are with foreign nations, they interfere with the treaty making power which is conferred entirely on the general government; if with each other, for political purposes, they can scarcely fail to interfere with the general purpose and intent of the constitution. To grant letters of marque and reprisal, would lead directly to war; the power of declaring which is expressly given to congress. To coin money is also the exercise of a power conferred on congress. It would be tedious to recapitulate the several limitations on the powers of the states which are contained in this section. They will be found, generally, to restrain state legislation on subjects entrusted to the government of the union, in which the citizens of all the states are interested. In these alone were the whole people concerned. The question of their application to states is not left to construction. It is averred in positive words.

If the original constitution, in the ninth and tenth sections of the first article, draws this plain and marked line of discrimination between the limitations it imposes on the powers of the general government, and on those of the states; if in every inhibition intended to act on state power, words are employed which directly express that intent; some strong reason must be assigned for departing from this safe and judicious course in framing the amendments, before that departure can be assumed.

We search in vain for that reason. . . . Had the people of the several states, or any of them, required changes in their constitutions; had they required additional safeguards to liberty from the apprehended encroachments of their particular governments: the remedy was in their own hands, and would have been applied by themselves. A convention would have been assembled by the discontented state, and the required improvements would have been made by itself. The unwieldy and cumbrous machinery of procuring a recommendation from two-thirds of congress, and the assent of three-fourths of their sister states, could never have occurred to any human being as a mode of doing that which might be effected by the state itself. Had the framers of these amendments intended them to be limitations on the powers of the state governments, they would have imitated the framers of the original constitution, and have expressed that intention. Had congress engaged in the extraordinary occupation of improving the constitutions of the several states by affording the people additional protection from the exercise of power by their own governments in matters which concerned themselves alone, they would have declared this purpose in plain and intelligible language.

But it is universally understood, it is a part of the history of the day, that the great revolution which established the constitution of the United States, was not effected without immense opposition. Serious fears were extensively entertained that those powers which the patriot statesmen, who then watched over the interests of our country, deemed essential to union, and to the attainment of those invaluable objects for which union was sought, might be exercised in a manner dangerous to liberty. In almost every convention by which the constitution was adopted, amendments to guard against the abuse of power were recommended. These amendments demanded security against the apprehended encroachments of the general government—not against those of the local governments.

In compliance with a sentiment thus generally expressed, to quiet fears thus extensively entertained, amendments were proposed by the required majority in congress, and adopted by the states. These amendments contain no expression indicating an intention to apply them to the state governments. This court cannot so apply them.

We are of opinion that the provision in the fifth amendment to the constitution, declaring that private property shall not be taken for public use without just compensation, is intended solely as a limitation on the exercise of power by the government of the United States, and is not applicable to the legislation of the states. We are therefore of opinion that there is no repugnancy between the several acts of the general assembly of Maryland, given in evidence by the defendants at the trial of this cause, in the court of that state, and the constitution of the United States. . . .

NOTES

1.   Which of the five types of constitutional argument (see p. 42) does Chief Justice Marshall use? He does not start with the text of the Takings Clause. After all, the text itself does not say whether it limits state governments. If anything, the passive voice might seem to limit all governments who have the power to take. Instead, Marshall starts with a kind of structural argument about which government is created and primarily empowered and restrained by the Constitution as a whole. He next turns one of Barron's own arguments around on him as a textual argument. Barron had said, in effect, "Look here, the Constitution does sometimes limit state governments—look at Article I, Section 10." What difference does Marshall point to between Article I, Section 9 and Article I, Section 10? (Marshall's reasoning would later be taken into account by the drafters of the Fourteenth Amendment: When they mimicked Article I, Section 10's prohibitions, they made clear that the Fourteenth Amendment was directed at abridgment of civil rights by the states.) Marshall also considers the historical context, arguing that part of what everyone understood about the Bill of Rights was that it was added to limit the actions of the national government, not the state governments. Largely absent from *Barron* is any argument from precedent and practice. *Barron* appears to have presented a question of first impression in 1833. But should that have been the basis for an argument—does the mere fact that no one tried to argue that the Bill of Rights bound the states during the first forty-two years of the Court suggest that it did not? And Marshall makes a policy argument: It would be cumbersome to have state officials bound by the federal Bill of Rights because the whole country would have to follow the Article V process if a state changed its mind about wanting to be bound by a right. Which of these arguments do you find most compelling? Are any unpersuasive?

2.   Are there good arguments Marshall omits?

—————

Between 1791 and the adoption of the Fourteenth Amendment in 1868, it became increasingly evident that the states—in particular, the slave states—posed as much or more of a danger to individual rights than did the distant federal government. In their defense of slavery, Southern states violated almost every one of the rights addressed by the first eight amendments. Southern states found that they could maintain slavery only by restricting the abolitionist press, punishing clergy who preached sermons against slavery, limiting access to guns, denying due process to those alleged to be fugitive slaves, censoring the mail, and restricting travel. After the Civil War, the victorious Republicans imposed the Fourteenth Amendment as the price for readmitting Southern representatives to Congress. Among other things, that amendment protects against state laws the "privileges or immunities of citizens of the United States," and one interpretation of that clause is that it "incorporated" (or applied) the Bill of Rights against the states. If so, the Supreme Court was slow to recognize the meaning. Provisions of the Bill of Rights have been applied to the states only selectively, and most of them only after 1940. In the middle of the twentieth century, when the subject of incorporation was hotly debated, the justices held a number of views regarding the Bill of Rights and the states. Three of those views are sketched here:

Total Incorporation—Nothing More, Nothing Less: Justice Hugo Black, who served on the Supreme Court from 1937 until 1971, argued that Section One of the Fourteenth Amendment, and particularly the Privileges or Immunities Clause, incorporated all of the rights in the federal Bill of Rights against the states. In other words, the privileges and immunities of national citizenship *were* the rights in the federal Bill of Rights. No other justice has ever accepted this view.

Fundamental Fairness: At the opposite end of the spectrum, Justice Felix Frankfurter, who served on the Supreme Court from 1939 to 1962, argued that the Fourteenth Amendment did not incorporate any of the Bill of Rights against the states but that it did, through the Due Process Clause, embody principles of fundamental fairness and ordered liberty. To Frankfurter, freedom of speech and of religion were fundamental, but he did not consider fundamental the criminal procedure provisions of the Bill of Rights, like the right to a jury trial and the right against self-incrimination. His view opposing incorporation while protecting fundamental fairness generally prevailed in the 1940s and 1950s, but it was rejected by the Warren Court in the 1960s.

Selective Incorporation: This approach was championed by Justice William J. Brennan, who served on the Supreme Court from 1956 to 1990, and it is the view that has carried the day. Under selective incorporation, the Supreme Court decides whether each right ought to apply against the states on a case-by-case basis. Ultimately the Court has incorporated all of the Bill of Rights against the states except the Third Amendment; the Fifth Amendment grand jury right; the Seventh Amendment right to civil jury trial; and the Eighth Amendment prohibition of excessive fines.

The selective-incorporation approach is now well established, and the Court has based it on the Due Process Clause. That is, the Due Process Clause is taken to be the textual provision that incorporates (most of) the Bill of Rights against the states. Another clause of the Fourteenth Amendment, the Privileges or Immunities Clause, is thought by many scholars to be the more apt vehicle for incorporating the Bill of Rights against the states. That clause is discussed more in the next chapter, p. 1301, as is the doctrine of incorporation, p. 1497.

The Bill of Rights decisions we are going to study below make no distinction between cases brought against the federal government under the Bill of Rights proper and those brought against the states under the Fourteenth Amendment. Should it make a difference? Should the Bill of Rights, as incorporated through the Fourteenth Amendment, be applied more rigorously to the states? The theory might be that states are less protective of minority rights, as James Madison suggested in *The Federalist No. 10*, p. 464. Or should the Bill of Rights be applied less rigorously to the states? The theory might be that the Bill of Rights applies to the national government in full force, but what the Fourteenth Amendment requires is something less rigid; this is yet another view of incorporation, one associated with the second Justice Harlan.

There is one more point to keep in mind as you read the federal and state Bill of Rights cases below. When provisions of the Bill of Rights are being applied to the national government, the relevant historical context is 1791, the year the Bill of Rights was ratified. When provisions of the Fourteenth Amendment are being applied to the states, the historical context is 1868. But what about provisions of the Bill of Rights applied to the states *through the Fourteenth Amendment?* Would 1791 or 1868 be the defining historical context for "the freedom of speech," the prohibition on "cruel and unusual punishments," and the other provisions of the Bill of Rights? Consider that question as you read the cases that follow.

[*Assignment 42*]

I. THE FIRST AMENDMENT AND FREEDOM OF SPEECH

Amend. I: Congress shall make no law respecting an establishment of religion, or prohibiting the free exercise thereof; or abridging the freedom of speech, or of the press; or the right of the people peaceably to assemble, and to petition the Government for the redress of grievances.

Read the First Amendment carefully. What does it mean? What interpretative questions does it raise?

Two quick preliminaries: First, the subject of the First Amendment is "Congress." Does that mean that executive and judicial officials may abridge the freedom of speech? The Supreme Court has never squarely addressed the question, but remember that, according to the Due Process Clause, no person may be deprived of "life, *liberty*, or property" without "due process of *law*." The freedom of speech is presumably a "liberty." The Supremacy Clause in Article VI tells us that "law" refers to statutes passed by Congress, as well as the Constitution and treaties. It follows that persons cannot be deprived of their freedom of speech, even by executive or judicial officers, except pursuant to a law. And if Congress cannot pass such a law, the freedom is thus secured against all three branches. (Is it secured against treaties? That could become an important question in future years, if the United States joins treaties reflecting international norms on matters such as hate speech or the "defamation of religion"—norms that are at odds with American notions of freedom of speech and religion.)

Second, the prohibition of the First Amendment now applies to actions of *state* government bodies, as well as those of the federal government. As discussed above, the Bill of Rights originally applied only to the actions of the national government. But the Due Process Clause of the Fourteenth Amendment has been understood to "incorporate" against the states most of the Bill of Rights, including the freedom of speech.

A Map of the First Amendment

Freedom of Speech and of the Press

When you read the Free Speech Clause of the First Amendment, four questions stand out:

What is "speech"?

What is meant by "the freedom of" speech?

What is a "law" "abridging" the freedom of speech?

What is meant by "or of the Press"?

1.   *What is "speech"?* "Speech" might be, for example, the vocal expression of messages of discernible content. The framers of the Bill of Rights did not discuss the term at length, perhaps assuming that the phrase had a commonly understood meaning in ordinary discourse. Is it confined to oral expression and its close cognates, such as sign language? The framers spoke far more often about the freedom of the press, and evidently regarded it as more important. The freedom of the press protects the publication of ideas and opinions to the general public—originally by means of

the printing press, but presumably also through other media of public communications. "Assembly" protects gatherings of individuals for expressive purposes, such as conventions, rallies, and demonstrations. As you will see, the initial controversy over the meaning of the First Amendment concerned whether it protected the right to gather in self-selected groups, or just in spontaneous public meetings. "Petition" protects communications with the officials of government. What protects written communication of a nonpublic nature, like a private letter?

And what about expressive *conduct*—actions that communicate a message or idea? Is that "speech"? The received answer is that the government may regulate conduct, including conduct of an expressive nature, if its interest in doing so is unrelated to the suppression of expression; if it has an important, substantial interest in regulating the conduct at issue; and if its regulation involves no greater incidental restriction of *expression* than is necessary to accomplish its legitimate interest in regulating the *conduct* at issue. If this (concededly imperfect) standard is satisfied, it cannot be said that the regulation at issue is a law abridging the freedom of "speech."

2.   *What is "the freedom of" speech?* Not everything that seems to be included in the term "speech" is necessarily protected by "the freedom of" speech. In contrast to the religion clauses, this part of the First Amendment does not say that "Congress shall make no law prohibiting speech," which would be more absolute, nor even that Congress shall make no law "abridging freedom of speech," which would be more abstract—perhaps referring to a philosophical notion of speech freedom. Does the use of the definite article indicate that before the First Amendment was proposed and ratified that there already existed something called "the" freedom of speech? By analogy, someone who says she goes to "university" is saying only that she is getting a college education; someone who says she goes to "the university" is likely referring to a particular local institution. Thus "the" freedom of speech can be seen as a particular and familiar instantiation of the idea of freedom of speech. That language suggests reference to legal arrangements prior to 1789, either the formal English precedent or informal American practice (which was broader). What exactly that preexisting understanding was at the time of the Founding—and the degree to which it should be controlling in constitutional law today—are hotly contested questions.

There are certain categories of speech that, the Court tells us, have never enjoyed free speech protection, such as true threats, false advertising, and words used to effectuate a criminal act (such as "your money or your life"). We will consider below what these categories are.

Standard doctrine tells us that content-neutral regulations of the time, the place, or the manner of expression do not abridge the freedom of speech, so long as the regulations are (1) "reasonable," (2) justified "without reference to the content of the regulated speech," (3) "narrowly tailored to serve a significant governmental interest," and (4) "leave open ample alternative channels for communication of the information." *Clark v. Community for Creative Non-Violence*, 468 U.S. 288, 293 (1984). Notice the very close resemblance of this test to the test for regulation of expressive conduct mixed with expression. In both instances, the government's interest must be unrelated to regulating speech *content* and must be an important or substantial one.

There are also ways in which "the freedom of" speech may be *broader* in its protections than the universe of "speech" itself. Consider two.

First: The First Amendment protects the freedom *not* to speak—a freedom not to be compelled or coerced by the government to engage in expression or promotion of views not truly one's own. This logical corollary (or flipside) to the freedom to express one's own views has been recognized in such disparate circumstances as the right of schoolchildren not to recite the Pledge of Allegiance, the right of a New Hampshire driver to cover up the "Live Free or Die" slogan on a license plate, and the right of a worker not to have to contribute toward the political advocacy of a labor union—all real cases, presented below.

Second: Since the right to freedom of speech is not limited to individuals acting alone, but also extends to groups acting for common purposes, the First Amendment protects an allied right of "expressive association," i.e., the freedom of groups of persons to band together to advance their desired messages, to control their own identity by deciding which speakers or messages represent them, and to exclude messages or speakers they do not wish to include. This corollary to the freedom of speech has produced cases upholding a political party's right to exclude voters who are not party members from its primary elections, the right of the organizers of a parade to exclude contingents they do not wish included, and the right of the Boy Scouts to exclude openly gay scoutmasters (but not a right of a law school religious group to meet on campus if it limits its leaders to Christians, or a right of civic clubs to exclude women members).

3.   *What is a law "abridging" the freedom of speech?* The verb "to abridge" means to shorten or diminish—an abridged book is a shortened version of the full text. Does the First Amendment mean that Congress cannot reduce the level of protection for speech that Americans enjoyed before the First Amendment? In other words, does the amendment embed and constitutionalize a preexisting freedom, protecting it from the future vicissitudes of politics? Note that the question is not what laws "abridge speech"—presumably any laws whatsoever that prohibit, regulate, or punish speech would fall within that term. The question is what laws abridge "the freedom of speech," meaning the legal protections for speech.

One particularly important question is whether the freedom of speech (or possibly the freedom of assembly) entails a right to use public property, such as the town square, for meetings or demonstrations. For many decades, the answer was "no." But under current doctrine certain areas—streets, sidewalks, public parks— are traditional public fora that the government may not close to all expression. In addition, where the government has *chosen* to make facilities available for a range of expressive purposes, it has created a "limited public forum" and may not then pick and choose among the speakers based on the content of their messages. But what happens when the government is acting as proprietor, educator, patron, publisher, editor, employer, speaker, or program-funder? The answers offered by current cases are not necessarily perfectly clear or consistent.

Is there a general, implied exception to the First Amendment freedom of speech—an all-purpose escape hatch—when the public interest (the *government's* interest?) in suppressing speech is so great that the seemingly absolute terms of the First Amendment ("no law abridging") simply make no sense? The illustration frequently given is Justice Holmes's aphorism about falsely shouting "Fire!" in a crowded theatre. *Schenck v. United States*, 249 U.S. 47, 52 (1919). Does anything in the text of the First Amendment permit this move? And how can the category of overriding interests be cabined so that the exception does not swallow the rule?

4.   *What is "the press"?* It is widely agreed that "the press" includes all media of communicating messages to the general public. Virtually all free speech protections apply to the press. But does the "freedom of the press" mean something quite different: a set of additional freedoms belonging not to everyone but only to professional media organizations, however defined? Most such claims have been rejected. See, e.g., *Branzburg v. Hayes*, 408 U.S. 665 (1972) (rejecting a claimed constitutional privilege for reporters to refuse to reveal their sources or provide other evidence in a criminal grand jury investigation); *Zurcher v. The Stanford Daily*, 436 U.S. 547 (1978) (rejecting a claimed *First* Amendment right of newspapers to immunity from searches, where the *Fourth* Amendment's standards for constitutionally valid searches and seizures are satisfied). Is there a workable definition of "the press" for these purposes? Do these special freedoms, not enjoyed by ordinary Americans, extend to bloggers, to authors, to freelancers, to writers of letters to the editor, to pamphleteers?

Freedoms of Assembly and Petition

The Supreme Court has almost completely collapsed assembly and petition into the freedoms of speech and association. See *McDonald v. Smith*, 472 U.S. 479, 485 (1985) (holding that the Petition Clause did not provide absolute immunity for libel contained in a letter to the president and noting that "there is no sound basis for granting greater constitutional protection to statements made in a petition to the President than other First Amendment expressions"); see generally John D. Inazu, LIBERTY'S REFUGE: THE FORGOTTEN FREEDOM OF ASSEMBLY (2012).

Restrictions on assembly are evaluated under the public forum doctrine. In *Cox v. New Hampshire*, 312 U.S. 569 (1941), the Court upheld a conviction for holding a parade without a license, because the licensing system was a reasonable time, place, and manner restriction. In *Clark v. Community for Creative Non-Violence*, 468 U.S. 288 (1984), the National Park Service denied the Community for Creative Non-Violence a permit to sleep in symbolic tent cities erected to call attention to the plight of the homeless. Camping was allowed only in designated campgrounds. The Court upheld the permit denial as a reasonable and content-neutral time, place, and manner restriction.

Freedom of Association

If you read the text of the First Amendment carefully, you noticed that freedom of association is not mentioned. Association is understood to be protected because of its expressive elements: "It is beyond debate that freedom to engage in association for advancement of beliefs and ideas is an inseparable aspect of the 'liberty' assured by the Due Process Clause of the Fourteenth Amendment, which embraces freedom of speech." *NAACP v. Alabama*, 357 U.S. 449, 460 (1958). Although freedom of association is most closely linked with freedom of speech, it protects a different set of expressive activities: the right to associate or not associate with other individuals when engaging in or planning protected public speech. Infringements of the right of association must be viewpoint neutral, justified by a compelling interest, and narrowly tailored. Some scholars say the authentic textual home for freedom of association is the Assembly Clause.

Many freedom of association cases involve the application of anti-discrimination laws to private groups. The Supreme Court has upheld the application of these laws to private groups when the discrimination was not related to the group's message and application of the law would not interfere with the group's speech. See *Board of Directors of Rotary International v. Rotary Club of Duarte*, 481 U.S. 537 (1987); *Roberts v. United States Jaycees*, 468 U.S. 609 (1984). But the Court has refused to apply anti-discrimination laws when these conditions were not met. See *Boy Scouts of America v. Dale*, 530 U.S. 640 (2000) (permitting the exclusion of gay Scout leaders); *Hurley v. Irish-American Gay, Lesbian and Bisexual Group of Boston*, Inc., 515 U.S. 557 (1995) (permitting parade organizers to exclude a group).

In the public-forum context, freedom of association may have been collapsed into freedom of speech. In *Christian Legal Society v. Martinez*, 561 U.S. 661 (2010), the Court upheld a school's "all-comers" policy that required all registered student organizations to allow any student to participate, become a member, or seek leadership positions in the organization. The plaintiffs were a Christian student group that required members and group officers to be Christians; they had been denied status as a registered student organization. The Court applied public-forum analysis, and upheld the all-comers policy as reasonable and viewpoint neutral.

The Religion Clauses

Six large questions are presented by the Religion Clauses:

What is "religion"?

What is "the free exercise of" religion?

What is a law "prohibiting" the free exercise of religion?

What is an "establishment of religion"?

What is a law "respecting" an establishment of religion?

Do Free Exercise accommodations violate the Establishment Clause?

1. *What is "religion"?* The contemporary ambiguity of the term "religion" was less pronounced at the founding, when the great majority of Americans were Protestant Christians. In the Virginia Declaration of Rights, George Mason and James Madison defined religion as "the duty which we owe to our Creator, and the manner of discharging it." This definition works well for the traditional Western monotheistic religions, but not for other religions that lack a creator god to whom duties are owed. While the Supreme Court has never directly addressed the constitutional definition of religion, in the context of statutory protections for conscientious objectors to military conscription it has defined religion broadly to include nontheistic beliefs. See *United States v. Seeger*, 380 U.S. 163 (1965).

2. *What is "the free exercise of" religion?* At the Founding, "the phrase [free exercise of religion] generally connoted various forms of free public religious action— religious speech, religious worship, religious assembly, religious publication, religious education, among others." John Witte, Jr., *The Essential Rights and Liberties of Religion in the American Constitutional Experiment*, 71 Notre Dame L. Rev. 371, 395 (1996). The phrase has been interpreted more narrowly by the Supreme Court. In *Reynolds v. United States*, 98 U.S. 145 (1879), which concerned a law criminalizing the Mormon practice at the time of plural marriage, the Court distinguished between belief and conduct. Belief is fully protected; conduct is not. To protect conduct fully, the Court said, would "make the professed doctrines of religious

belief superior to the law of the land" and "permit every citizen to become a law unto himself." *Id.*, at 166–67. In the mid-twentieth century, the Court moved away from *Reynolds*, applying strict scrutiny to neutral laws that substantially burdened religious conduct. But the Court cabined this approach in *Employment Division v. Smith*, 494 U.S. 872, 877–88 (1990). Under *Smith*, "the right of free exercise does not relieve an individual of the obligation to comply with a valid and neutral law of general applicability on the ground that the law proscribes (or prescribes) conduct that his religion prescribes (or proscribes)." *Id.* at 879. Laws that are not neutral and generally applicable, however, must still survive strict scrutiny. Recently, the Court has recognized a broader freedom for the internal decisions of religious institutions.

3.   *What is a law "prohibiting" the free exercise of religion?* Note that while the First Amendment forbids laws "abridging" the freedoms of speech, press, and assembly, it forbids laws "prohibiting" free exercise. Does this mean that the government may abridge free exercise, so long as it does not prohibit it? Or is the choice of verb a reflection of the fact that, under British law, there was no preexisting right of free exercise of religion (unlike speech or press)? Plaintiffs in free exercise cases must demonstrate a constitutionally cognizable burden on their exercise of religion. The issue of burden is often thorny. It may be clear in cases where a law criminalizes religious practice. But what if a government action makes the plaintiff's religious exercise more expensive, or more inconvenient?

4.   *What is an "establishment of religion"?* At the time of the founding, there was an established religion in England that had four primary legal features: government control over doctrine and personnel, suppression of alternative faiths, religious tests for office, and compelled church attendance and support. In the colonies, the degree and nature of establishment varied, with an exclusive Anglican establishment in the South, and localized Puritan establishments in the New England colonies.

The Supreme Court has formulated several tests for identifying an establishment of religion. The most well-known is the three-part test of *Lemon v. Kurtzman*, 403 U.S. 602 (1971). Under *Lemon*, a law must (1) have a secular purpose; (2) have a "primary effect" that "neither advances nor inhibits religion"; and (3) not foster an "excessive entanglement" between government and religion. The Court has applied the *Lemon* test in a number of contexts, including aid to religious schools, school prayer and curriculum, government symbolic displays, chaplaincy programs, and many more. Each of the prongs is ambiguous, and while the Court frequently invokes the test, it has not consistently applied it.

Another test is the endorsement test articulated by Justice Sandra Day O'Connor in *Lynch v. Donnelly*, 465 U.S. 668, 687–88 (1984) (O'Connor, J., concurring). In her view, the Establishment Clause "prohibits government from making adherence to a religion relevant in any way to a person's standing in the political community," which it may do through "excessive entanglement with religious institutions" or by "endorsement or disapproval of religion." *Id.* This is a reformulation of the *Lemon* test, where the first prong "asks whether government's actual purpose is to endorse or disapprove of religion," and the second prong, "asks whether, irrespective of government's actual purpose, the practice under review in fact conveys a message of endorsement or disapproval." *Id.* at 690. While Justice O'Connor's reformulation has had some influence on the doctrine, it has primarily been confined to cases involving public displays of religious symbols. E.g., *County of*

Allegheny v. ACLU, 492 U.S. 573 (1989) (applying the endorsement test to hold that a crèche display was unconstitutional, but not the display of a Hanukkah menorah accompanied by a decorated Christmas tree).

Justice Thomas has argued for a return to the original meaning of establishment as government coercion of religion, such as mandatory observance or mandatory payment of taxes supporting ministers. *Elk Grove Unified School Dist. v. Newdow*, 542 U.S. 1, 45–54 (2004) (Thomas, J., concurring). The Court has not adopted this approach.

5.   *What is a law "respecting" an establishment of religion?* One of the original purposes of the Establishment Clause was to limit the power of the federal government to interfere with state establishments. See 1 ANNALS OF CONG. 729–33 (1789) (Joseph Gales ed., 1834). Thus, Congress could make no law "respecting" an establishment, meaning either a law establishing religion or a law disturbing an existing state establishment. See Akhil Amar, THE BILL OF RIGHTS 36–39 (1998). It was not until the Establishment Clause was incorporated against the states through the Fourteenth Amendment, that the clause was held to limit state establishments. Some, notably Justice Thomas, have argued that the Establishment Clause is a federalism provision, rather than a provision protecting an individual right, and because it protects the states it cannot logically be incorporated against them.

6.   *Do Free Exercise accommodations violate the Establishment Clause?* The *Lemon* test, if taken literally, might seem to forbid any legislative accommodation of religious exercise. After all, won't accommodations lack a secular purpose, or have the effect of advancing religion, or entangle the government and religion? The Supreme Court upheld one of these accommodations, the Religious Land Use and Institutionalized Persons Act (RLUIPA), but did so without applying the *Lemon* test. See *Cutter v. Wilkinson*, 544 U.S. 709 (2005). Instead, the Court argued that RLUIPA "alleviates exceptional government-created burdens on private religious exercise," "take[s] adequate account of the burdens a requested accommodation may impose on non-beneficiaries," and is "administered neutrally among different faiths."

Procedural Issues in Free Speech Cases

1.   *Vagueness.* In theory, any law—especially any criminal law—can be challenged under the Due Process Clauses for vagueness. If a reasonable person can't tell what is prohibited, the "notice" essential to due process is absent. In practice, however, the vagueness doctrine has little bite outside of the First Amendment. In the context of restrictions on speech, however, the vagueness principle has particular force because the vagueness of a law serves to "chill" the exercise of constitutional rights of expression—to avoid risk of punishment, a person might refrain from engaging in entirely lawful expression. See Anthony Amsterdam, *The Void-for-Vagueness Doctrine in the Supreme Court*, 109 U. Pa. L. Rev. 67 (1960). For example, an ordinance forbidding speech that might "annoy" others in a public place is likely void for vagueness: How is a speaker supposed to guess what speech others might find annoying? See *Coates v. Cincinnati*, 402 U.S. 611 (1971). Note that what matters is whether the speaker can tell if his or her intended speech is lawful, not whether the speaker understands every ramification of the law as it might be applied to other conduct.

2.   *Overbreadth.* Ordinarily, a person has no standing to challenge laws as they apply to other people, but in the free speech context, the overbreadth doctrine allows

a speaker to challenge a law on the grounds that it would be unconstitutional as to others, even if the speech of the person bringing the challenge is not constitutionally protected. See *Gooding v. Wilson*, 405 U.S. 518 (1972). For example, if an anti-abortion protestor grabs the arm of a woman attempting to enter a clinic, that conduct (though expressive) is not protected; but if that protestor is then prosecuted under a law that attempts to ban all anti-abortion protests based on content, the protestor can nevertheless challenge the ordinance on overbreadth grounds. In recent years, recognizing its anomalous nature, the Court has narrowed the overbreadth doctrine, allowing a facial challenge only when the overbreadth is "substantial."

Overbreadth and vagueness are conceptually distinct but often travel together. In *Coates*, the Court struck down a city ordinance that made it illegal for "three or more persons to assemble" on city sidewalks and "conduct themselves in a manner annoying to persons passing by." The Court found the "annoying" standard to be no standard at all (a vagueness problem) and to interfere with too much clearly protected expression (an overbreadth problem). Another example is *Houston v. Hill*, 482 U.S. 451 (1987). Hill, seeing police officers question a friend, said to the officers, "Why don't you pick on somebody your own size?" One of the police officers then asked Hill: "Are you interrupting me in my official capacity as a Houston police officer?" When Hill answered "Yes, why don't you pick on somebody my size?" he was arrested, pursuant to a municipal law making it "unlawful for any person to assault, strike or in any manner *oppose*, molest, abuse, *or interrupt* any policeman in the execution of his duty" (emphases added). The Court found the law unconstitutionally overbroad in that it permitted police "unfettered discretion" to arrest individuals "for words or conduct that annoy or offend them." Was the law unduly vague—or was it clear enough, but too broad?

3.   *"Unfettered Discretion."* Joining "vagueness" and "overbreadth" in the lineup of First Amendment procedural doctrines is the problem of enforcement discretion. *Houston v. Hill*, in the passage just quoted, noted the problem that an overbroad law gives those enforcing it "unfettered discretion" which could be employed to abridge rights of free speech. *Board of Airport Commissioners v. Jews for Jesus*, 482 U.S. 569 (1987), involved possibly the most overbroad ordinance in the annals of American law: it purported to forbid all "First Amendment activities" in the Los Angeles airport (LAX). Think of everything that includes! The Court noted that if the airport officials did not actually enforce the rule against all violators (and how could they?), the ordinance would "give LAX officials alone the power to decide in the first instance whether a given activity is" within the purposes of the ordinance. The law would improperly "confer[ ] on police a virtually unrestrained power" to make arrests. The "opportunity for abuse, especially where a statute has received a virtually open-ended interpretation, is self-evident." Thus laws that permit government officials sweeping discretion to punish or permit speech are generally considered presumptive violations of the Free Speech Clause. See, e.g., *City of Lakewood v. Plain Dealer Publishing Co.*, 486 U.S. 750 (1988) (striking down city ordinance that vested a mayor with essentially "unbridled discretion" to decide which publishers could place newsracks on public property).

A. BACKGROUND AND DRAFTING HISTORY

The eighteenth century English understanding of First Amendment freedoms stands far removed from ours today. Speech, press, assembly, petition, and religion received considerably less protection under the English constitutional tradition, which included written texts and unwritten traditions (see p. 20). None of the rights codified in the English Bill of Rights of 1689, for example, restricted the powers of Parliament; all were restrictions on the power of the king. As James Madison put it, when discussing the need for a Bill of Rights in the United States, "their Magna Charta does not contain any one provision for the security of those rights, respecting which the people of America are most alarmed. The freedom of the press and rights of conscience, those choicest privileges of the people, are unguarded in the British constitution." 1 ANNALS OF CONG. 453 (1789) (Joseph Gales ed., 1834). Nonetheless, although providing no constitutional protection vis-à-vis Parliament, the common law in practice made England one of the freest nations on earth. And many people in England argued that their freedoms of speech, press, assembly, and petition were broader than the legal precedents might indicate. In particular, juries often declined to convict in cases involving these freedoms.

1.   *Speech.* Freedom of speech under the English constitution was a parliamentary privilege, not a right of the people against the government. The English Bill of Rights of 1689 specified that "the freedom of speech and debates or proceedings in Parliament ought not to be impeached or questioned in any court or place out of Parliament." The right protected members of Parliament against punishment by the king for their conduct in the House of Commons. But it was also used by legislators to punish public critics of Parliament. David S. Bogen, *The Origins of Freedom of Speech and Press*, 42 Md. L. Rev. 429, 431–39 (1983).

In England, sovereignty rested in Parliament, in conjunction with the king. The right of parliamentarians to deliberate among themselves without fear of punishment can be seen as part of their rights as sovereign. In America, however, the People are sovereign. Should they have the same sovereign right to deliberate among themselves? Perhaps the parliamentary freedom of speech, as applied in the different circumstances of a republic, produces a broader principle: the right of all citizens to exchange information and opinion on public matters.

2.   *Press.* In England the press operated under a licensing scheme until 1695. The Licensing Act of 1662—its longer title was "The Act for preventing abuses in printing seditious, treasonable, and unlicensed books and pamphlets, and for regulating of printing and printing-presses"—provided for the prepublication censorship of "heretical, seditious, schismatical, or offensive" works. 14 Car. II, c. 33. Every manuscript had to be approved by the licensing authority before printing. The act restricted the number and location of printers and printing presses, and it permitted the king's representatives to search for and seize unauthorized presses and publications. Raymond Astbury, *The Renewal of the Licensing Act in 1693 and its Lapse in 1695*, 33 Libr. 296 (1978). Printers resented the state-licensed monopolies and the delay involved in obtaining licenses. Changes in the religious and political bents of the licensers exposed the arbitrariness of the licensing system. After extensive debate emphasizing the value of press freedom, Parliament allowed the act to lapse in 1695. See Philip Hamburger, *The Development of the Law of Seditious Libel and the Control of the Press*, 37 Stan. L. Rev. 661, 714–25 (1985).

After the demise of the licensing system, the Crown relied on the law of seditious libel to punish producers of offensive material, and between 1702 and 1760 at least 115 such prosecutions were brought. *Id.* at 724–25. The legitimacy of these prosecutions was hotly debated.

3.   *Assembly.* Freedom of assembly was the least protected. Gatherings of three or more people were regulated by statutes and the common law as early as 1415. If three individuals gathered for a common and illegal purpose, they committed the crime of unlawful assembly. If they acted in furtherance of that purpose, they were guilty of rout or riot, depending on the private or public nature of the purpose. M. Glenn Abernathy, THE RIGHT OF ASSEMBLY AND ASSOCIATION 20–23 (2d. rev. ed. 1981). By the 1715 enactment of the Riot Act, individuals could be said to commit the crime of unlawful assembly whenever they gathered for a common purpose, lawful or unlawful, in such a manner as to create a reasonable fear of a breach of the peace. 1 William Hawkins, PLEAS OF THE CROWN 513–16 (John Curwood ed., 8th ed. 1824). Authorities used the law to suppress meetings by political opponents and religious minorities.

4.   *Petition.* The right to petition enjoyed the most secure protection, perhaps because it was convenient for the Crown to have access to the uncensored complaints of the people about the conduct of nobles and subordinate royal officials. The right to petition was first recognized in Magna Carta (1215), and later reaffirmed in the English Bill of Rights of 1689. Petitions began as "an error-correcting device for a limited set of [private] grievances," where relief would benefit the sovereign. Gregory A. Mark, *The Vestigial Constitution: The History and Significance of the Right of Petition*, 66 Fordham L. Rev. 2153, 2163 (1998). After Magna Carta, petitions developed a public dimension: through petitions, a citizen could request a policy change or the review of an administrative action. *Id.* at 2165–66. Often petitions garnered hundreds of signatures, and were (like assembly) a means of demonstrating the strength and direction of public opinion in a world before opinion polls. In the eighteenth century, though, Parliament limited petitions to relatively small numbers of signatories, just as it limited assemblies to small numbers of participants. Perhaps this is why the framers of the First Amendment specified that these rights—unlike speech, press, and religion—are rights of "the people": to make clear that petition and assembly may be exercised collectively in groups.

5.   *Religion.* England also had an array of laws restricting the exercise of religion. The Act of Supremacy of 1534 severed England's connection with the Roman Catholic Church and established the English crown as "the only supreme head on earth of the Church in England." 26 Hen. VIII c. 1. Disavowal of the act was treason, punishable by death. Treasons Act 1534, 26 Hen. VIII c. 13. Any person taking public or church office had to swear the Oath of Supremacy, which affirmed the monarch as the head of the Church of England, and declare the invalidity of the Catholic doctrine of transubstantiation. 25 Car. II. c. 2. The Act of Uniformity made the Book of Common Prayer the only legal form of worship in the Church of England. 2 & 3 Edw. VI c. 1. Various penal laws forbade worship in disfavored churches, such as (at different times) those of Puritans, Quakers, and Catholics. And the Conventicles Act forbade dissenting religious assemblies of more than five people. 16 Car. II c. 4.

6.   *A Note on Order.* The provisions of the First Amendment about the freedom of religion come before the provisions about speech, press, assembly, and petition. Originally, while the First Congress was debating the Bill of Rights, these were in

separate parts, or "Articles"—numbers Three and Four. (So much for the idea that the First Amendment is the first because it takes priority.) The materials on speech, press, assembly, and petition are presented here before the materials on religion for a practical reason: Much of free speech law applies equally to religious speech and many of the doctrines carry over. To a great extent, the religion clauses take the law of speech, press, and association and add new elements: protections for conduct (the "exercise" of religion) and restrictions on governmental support and control (the "establishment" of religion). It is, therefore, more convenient to study the non-religious parts of the amendment first. The framers of the Bill of Rights do not appear to have attached any significance to the order of these two sets of provisions.

William Blackstone on the Liberty of the Press
4 COMMENTARIES ON THE LAWS OF ENGLAND *151–53 (first published 1756)

In this, and the other instances which we have lately considered, where blasphemous, immoral, treasonable, schismatical, seditious, or scandalous libels are punished by the English law, some with a greater, others with a less degree of severity; the liberty of the press, properly understood, is by no means infringed or violated. The liberty of the press is indeed essential to the nature of a free state: but this consists in laying no previous restraints upon publications, and not in freedom from censure for criminal matter when published. Every freeman has an undoubted right to lay what sentiments he pleases before the public: to forbid this, is to destroy the freedom of the press: but if he publishes what is improper, mischievous, or illegal, he must take the consequence of his own temerity. To subject the press to the restrictive power of a licenser, as was formerly done, both before and since the revolution, is to subject all freedom of sentiment to the prejudices of one man, and make him the arbitrary and infallible judge of all controverted points in learning, religion, and government. But to punish (as the law does at present) any dangerous or offensive writings, which, when published, shall on a fair and impartial trial be adjudged of a pernicious tendency, is necessary for the preservation of peace and good order, of government and religion, the only solid foundations of civil liberty. Thus the will of individuals is still left free; the abuse only of that free will is the object of legal punishment. Neither is any restraint hereby laid upon freedom of thought or enquiry: liberty of private sentiment is still left; the disseminating, or making public, of bad sentiments, destructive of the ends of society, is the crime which society corrects. A man (says a fine writer on this subject) may be allowed to keep poisons in his closet, but not publicly to vend them as cordials. And to this we may add, that the only plausible argument heretofore used for restraining the just freedom of the press, "that it was necessary to prevent the daily abuse of it," will entirely lose its force, when it is shewn (by a seasonable exertion of the laws) that the press cannot be abused to any bad purpose, without incurring a suitable punishment: whereas it never can be used to any good one, when under the control of an inspector. So true will it be found, that to censure the licentiousness, is to maintain the liberty, of the press.

————

Contrast Blackstone's relatively narrow interpretation with that espoused by the radical Whig opposition. The Whigs were regarded as dissidents and malcontents at home in England, but their writings were widely reprinted and commanded widespread agreement and respect in the American colonies. Of all of *Cato's Letters*— political essays by John Trenchard and Thomas Gordon criticizing the political establishment— the following two essays were the most commonly reprinted in the American colonies.

Cato's Letter No. 15, "Of Freedom of Speech: That the same is inseparable from publick Liberty"
Thomas Gordon, Feb. 4, 1720

SIR,

Without freedom of thought, there can be no such thing as wisdom; and no such thing as publick liberty, without freedom of speech: Which is the right of every man, as far as by it he does not hurt and control the right of another; and this is the only check which it ought to suffer, the only bounds which it ought to know.

This sacred privilege is so essential to free government, that the security of property; and the freedom of speech, always go together; and in those wretched countries where a man can not call his tongue his own, he can scarce call any thing else his own. Whoever would overthrow the liberty of the nation, must begin by subduing the freedom of speech; a thing terrible to publick traitors.

This secret was so well known to the court of King Charles I that his wicked ministry procured a proclamation to forbid the people to talk of Parliaments, which those traitors had laid aside. To assert the undoubted right of the subject, and defend his Majesty's legal prerogative, was called disaffection, and punished as sedition. Nay, people were forbid to talk of religion in their families: For the priests had combined with the ministers to cook up tyranny, and suppress truth and the law. While the late King James, when Duke of York, went avowedly to mass; men were fined, imprisoned, and undone, for saying that he was a papist: And, that King Charles II might live more securely a papist, there was an act of Parliament made, declaring it treason to say that he was one.

That men ought to speak well of their governors, is true, while their governors deserve to be well spoken of; but to do publick mischief, without hearing of it, is only the prerogative and felicity of tyranny: A free people will be shewing that they are so, by their freedom of speech.

The administration of government is nothing else, but the attendance of the trustees of the people upon the interest and affairs of the people. And as it is the part and business of the people, for whose sake alone all publick matters are, or ought to be, transacted, to see whether they be well or ill transacted; so it is the interest, and ought to be the ambition, of all honest magistrates, to have their deeds openly examined, and publickly scanned: Only the wicked governors of men dread what is said of them. . . .

Freedom of speech is the great bulwark of liberty; they prosper and die together: And it is the terror of traitors and oppressors, and a barrier against them. It produces excellent writers, and encourages men of fine genius. Tacitus tells us, that the Roman commonwealth bred great and numerous authors, who writ with equal boldness and eloquence: But when it was enslaved, those great wits were no more. . . . The minds of men, terrified by unjust power, degenerated into all the vileness and methods of servitude: Abject sycophancy and blind submission grew the only means of preferment, and indeed of safety; men durst not open their mouths, but to flatter. . . .

All ministers, therefore, who were oppressors, or intended to be oppressors, have been loud in their complaints against freedom of speech, and the licence of the press; and always restrained, or endeavoured to restrain, both. In consequence of this, they have brow-beaten writers, punished them violently, and against law, and burnt their works. By all which they shewed how much truth alarmed them, and how much they were at enmity with truth. . . .

The best princes have ever encouraged and promoted freedom of speech; they knew that upright measures would defend themselves, and that all upright men would defend them. . . .

Cato's Letter No. 38, "The Right and Capacity of the People to Judge of Government"
Thomas Gordon, July 22, 1721

Of all the sciences that I know in the world, that of government concerns us most, and is the easiest to be known, and yet is the least understood. Most of those who manage it would make the lower world believe that there is I know not what difficulty and mystery in it, far above vulgar understandings; which proceeding of theirs is direct craft and imposture: Every ploughman knows a good government from a bad one, from the effects of it: he knows whether the fruits of his labour be his own, and whether he enjoy them in peace and security: And if he do not know the principles of government, it is for want of thinking and enquiry, for they lie open to common sense; but people are generally taught not to think of them at all, or to think wrong of them.

What is government, but a trust committed by all, or the most, to one, or a few, who are to attend upon the affairs of all, that every one may, with the more security, attend upon his own? A great and honourable trust; but too seldom honourably executed; those who possess it having it often more at heart to increase their power, than to make it useful; and to be terrible, rather than beneficent. It is therefore a trust, which ought to be bounded with many and strong restraints, because power renders men wanton, insolent to others, and fond of themselves. . . .

But some have said, It is not the business of private man to meddle with government. A bold, false, and dishonest saying; and whoever says it, either knows not what he says, or cares not, or slavishly speaks the sense of others. It is a cant now almost forgot in England, and which never prevailed but when liberty and the constitution were attacked, and never can prevail but upon the like occasion. . . .

But to the falsehood of the thing: Publick truths ought never to be kept secrets; and they who do it, are guilty of a solecism, and a contradiction: Every man ought to know what it concerns all to know. Now, nothing upon earth is of a more universal nature than government; and every private man upon earth has a concern in it, because in it is concerned, and nearly and immediately concerned, his virtue, his property, and the security of his person: And where all these are best preserved and advanced, the government is best administered; and where they are not, the government is impotent, wicked, or unfortunate; and where the government is so, the people will be so, there being always and every where a certain sympathy and analogy between the nature of the government and the nature of the people. This holds true in every instance. Public men are the patterns of private; and the virtues and vices of the governors become quickly the virtues and vices of the governed. . . .

Such is the difference between one government and another, and of such important concernment is the nature and administration of government to a people. And to say that private men have nothing to do with government, is to say that private men have nothing to do with their own happiness and misery. What is the publick, but the collective body of private men, as every private man is a member of the publick? And as the whole ought to be concerned for the preservation of every private individual, it is the duty of every individual to be concerned for the whole, in which himself is included.

One man, or a few men, have often pretended the publick, and meant themselves, and consulted their own personal interest, in instances essential to its well-being; but the whole people, by consulting their own interest, consult the publick, and act for the publick by acting for themselves: This is particularly the spirit of our constitution, in which the whole nation is represented; and our records afford instances, where the House of Commons have declined entering upon a question of importance, till they had gone into the country, and consulted their principals, the people: So far were they from thinking that private men had no right to meddle with government. In truth, our whole worldly happiness and misery (abating for accidents and diseases) are owing to the order or mismanagement of government; and he who says that private men have no concern with government, does wisely and modestly tell us, that men have no concern in that which concerns them most; it is saying that people ought not to concern themselves whether they be naked or clothed, fed or starved, deceived or instructed, and whether they be protected or destroyed: What nonsense and servitude in a free and wise nation!

For myself, who have thought pretty much of these matters, I am of opinion, that a whole nation are like to be as much attached to themselves, as one man or a few men are like to be, who may by many means be detached from the interest of a nation. It is certain that one man, and several men, may be bribed into an interest opposite to that of the publick; but it is as certain that a whole country can never find an equivalent for itself, and consequently a whole country can never be bribed. It is the eternal interest of every nation, that their government should be good; but they who direct it frequently reason a contrary way and find their own account in plunder and oppression; and while the publick voice is pretended to be declared, by one or a few, for vile and private ends, the publick know nothing of what is done, till they feel the terrible effects of it.

By the Bill of Rights, and the Act of Settlement, at the Revolution; a right is asserted to the people applying to the King and to the Parliament, by petition and address, for a redress of publick grievances and mismanagements, when such there are, of which they are left to judge; and the difference between free and enslaved countries lies principally here, that in the former, their magistrates must consult the voice and interest of the people; but in the latter, the private will, interest, and pleasure of the governors, are the sole end and motives of their administration.

NOTES

1.   Blackstone and Cato's Letters represent the two poles of pre-Independence thinking in England about freedom of speech and press. Do they have anything in common? What, precisely, are the differences between them?

2.   Which of Blackstone and Cato's Letters is the better guide for the meaning of our First Amendment? Why?

Demands for First Amendment Protections

In the final days of the Constitutional Convention, two delegates, Elbridge Gerry and George Mason proposed that a bill of rights be added to the Constitution, but their proposals failed. Because the document lacked a bill of rights, both Gerry and Mason refused to sign it. Anti-Federalist opponents of the Constitution exploited the lack of a bill of rights, arguing that one would be a bulwark of liberty against an encroaching federal government. The Constitution's Federalist supporters responded that a bill of rights would be unnecessary, because the federal government had only limited powers. The Anti-Federalist argument was effective; a handful of key states, including Virginia and New York, attached proposals for amendments to their ratification resolutions. The relevant text of these proposals for what became the First Amendment is as follows:

New Hampshire (June 21, 1788)

Congress shall make no Laws touching Religion, or to infringe the rights of Conscience.

New York (July 26, 1788)

That the People have an equal, natural and unalienable right, freely and peaceably to Exercise their Religion according to the dictates of Conscience, and that no Religious Sect or Society ought to be favoured or established by Law in preference of others. . . .

That the People have a right peaceably to assemble together to consult for their common good, or to instruct their Representatives; and that every person has a right to Petition or apply to the Legislature for redress of Grievances.—That the Freedom of the Press ought not to be violated or restrained.[5]

Virginia (July 26, 1788)[6]

That the people have a right peaceably to assemble together to consult for the common good, or to instruct their Representatives; and that every freeman has a right to petition or apply to the legislature for redress of grievances.

That the people have a right to freedom of speech, and of writing and publishing their Sentiments; but the freedom of the press is one of the greatest bulwarks of liberty and ought not to be violated.

---

[5]   New York did not propose these provisions as amendments, rather it "declar[ed] that the rights aforesaid cannot be abridged or violated, and that the Explanations aforesaid are consistent with the said Constitution. . . ."

[6]   North Carolina, which ratified the Constitution more than a year after Virginia, proposed an identical set of amendments. Rhode Island proposed a nearly identical set of amendments, but in slightly different order.

That any person religiously scrupulous of bearing arms ought to be exempted upon payment of an equivalent to employ another to bear arms in his stead.

That religion or the duty which we owe to our Creator, and the manner of discharging it can be directed only by reason and conviction, not by force or violence, and therefore all men have an equal, natural and unalienable right to the free exercise of religion according to the dictates of conscience, and that no particular religious sect or society ought to be favored or established by Law in preference to others.

––––––

Consider next the key sources in the drafting history of the First Amendment: James Madison's initial proposal, the debate in the House of Representatives, and the draft of the First Amendment sent by the House to the Senate.

James Madison's Initial Proposal for the Freedoms of Speech, Press, Assembly, and Petition

House of Representatives, June 8, 1789 (1 Annals of Cong. 434)

That in article 1st, section 9, between clauses 3 and 4, be inserted these clauses, to wit:

. . . The people shall not be deprived or abridged of their right to speak, to write, or to publish their sentiments; and the freedom of the press, as one of the great bulwarks of liberty, shall be inviolable.

The people shall not be restrained from peaceably assembling and consulting for their common good; nor from applying to the Legislature by petitions, or remonstrances, for redress of their grievances.

Debate on Speech, Press, Assembly, and Petition

House of Representatives, Aug. 15 & 21, 1789 (1 Annals of Cong. 729–33, 767–68)

The next clause of the fourth proposition was taken into consideration, and was as follows:

"The freedom of speech and of the press, and the right of the people peaceably to assemble and consult for their common good, and to apply to the Government for redress of grievances, shall not be infringed."

Mr. SEDGWICK submitted to those gentlemen who had contemplated the subject, what effect such an amendment as this would have; he feared it would tend to make them appear trifling in the eyes of their constituents; what, said he, shall we secure the freedom of speech, and think it necessary, at the same time, to allow the right of assembling? If people freely converse together, they must assemble for that purpose; it is a self-evident, unalienable right which the people possess; it is certainly a thing that never would be called in question; it is derogatory to the dignity of the House to descend to such minutiae; he therefore moved to strike out "assemble and."

Mr. BENSON. The committee who framed this report proceeded on the principle that these rights belonged to the people; they conceived them to be inherent; and all that they meant to provide against was their being infringed by the Government.

Mr. SEDGWICK replied, that if the committee were governed by that general principle, they might have gone into a very lengthy enumeration of rights; they might have declared that a man should have a right to wear his hat if he pleased; that he might get up when he pleased, and go to bed when he thought proper; but he would ask the gentleman whether he thought it necessary to enter these trifles in a declaration of rights, in a Government where none of them were intended to be infringed.

Mr. TUCKER hoped the words would not be struck out, for lie considered them of importance; besides, they were recommended by the States of Virginia and North Carolina, though he noticed that the most material part proposed by those States was omitted, which was a declaration that the people should have a right to instruct their representatives. He would move to have those words inserted as soon as the motion for striking out was decided.

Mr. GERRY was also against the words being struck out, because he conceived it to be an essential right; it was inserted in the constitutions of several States; and though it had been abused in the year 1786 in Massachusetts, yet that abuse ought not to operate as an argument against the use of it. The people ought to be secure in the peaceable enjoyment of this privilege, and that can only be done by making a declaration to that effect in the Constitution.

Mr. PAGE. The gentleman from Massachusetts, (Mr. SEDGWICK,) who made this motion, objects to the clause, because the right is of so trivial a nature. He supposes it no more essential than whether a man has a right to wear his hat or not; but let me observe to him that such rights have been opposed, and a man has been obliged to pull off his hat when lie appeared before the face of authority; people have also been prevented from assembling together on their lawful occasions, therefore it is well to guard against such stretches of authority, by inserting the privilege in the declaration of rights. If the people could be deprived of the power of assembling under any pretext whatsoever, they might be deprived of every other privilege contained in the clause.

Mr. VINING said, if the thing were harmless and it would tend to gratify the States that had proposed amendments, he should agree to it.

Mr. HARTLEY observed that it had been asserted in the convention of Pennsylvania, by the friends of the Constitution, that all the rights and powers that were not given to the Government, were retained by the States and the people thereof. This was also his own opinion; but as four or five States had required to be secured in those rights by an express declaration in the Constitution, he is disposed to gratify them; he thought every thing that was not incompatible with the general good, ought to be granted, if it would tend to obtain the confidence of the people in the Government; and, upon the whole, he thought these words were as necessary to be inserted in the declaration of rights as most in the clause.

Mr. GERRY said that his colleague contended for nothing, if he supposed that the people had a right to consult for the common good, because they could not consult unless they met for the purpose.

Mr. SEDGWICK replied, that if they were understood or implied in the word consult, they were utterly unnecessary, and upon that ground he moved to have them struck out.

The question was now put upon Mr. SEDGWICK's motion, and lost by a considerable majority.

House Draft Transmitted to the Senate
1 Senate Journal 70–71 (Sept. 4, 1789)

The freedom of speech, and of the press, and the right of the people peaceably to assemble, and consult for their common good, and to apply to the Government for redress of grievances, shall not be infringed.

B. EARLY CONTROVERSIES AND INTERPRETATION

Early controversies often cast valuable light on the meaning of the Constitution. Sometimes they set the course of constitutional interpretation for the next two centuries or more. And sometimes they offer compelling constitutional arguments, either by courts or by other constitutional interpreters. We begin here with one of the controversies about the First Amendment that broke out in the first decade of the Republic, the controversy over the Democratic-Republican Clubs. Another early controversy that is highly useful for understanding the First Amendment occurred over the Sedition Act (see p. 46). Both controversies were resolved politically, but only after extensive debate.

The Democratic-Republican Clubs Controversy

Recall that in the House debate over the First Amendment, Theodore Sedgwick objected to the Assembly Clause on the ground that it was redundant and unnecessary. "If people freely converse together, they must assemble for that purpose," he said. "[I]it is a self-evident, unalienable right which the people possess; it is certainly a thing that never would be called in question." Ironically, the nation's first major civil liberties controversy erupted over precisely that question. In the early years of President Washington's second term, political opponents—perhaps inspired by the Jacobin Clubs of France—created what were called the Democratic-Republican Societies. These were voluntary political associations where self-selected groups of like-minded citizens would gather to discuss—and criticize—policies of the federal government. See Robert M. Chesney, *Democratic-Republican Societies, Subversion, and the Limits of Legitimate Political Dissent in the Early Republic*, 82 N.C. L. Rev. 1525 (2004). In the summer of 1794, opponents of a whiskey excise tax razed the home of a local Treasury official in western Pennsylvania, and 5,000 armed men marched through Pittsburgh. *Id.* at 1556. A federal army commanded by Washington and Hamilton put down the so-called Whiskey Rebellion. Federalists accused the Democratic-Republican societies of subversive activity and blamed them for instigating the uprising.

Pay particular attention to Washington's distinction between societies that are "self-created" and "permanent," versus the right of the people "to meet occasionally" to remonstrate against acts of the Congress. Does the freedom of assembly extend to organized associations of self-selected membership, meeting in secret—or does the freedom apply only to occasional gatherings of members of the public at large?

George Washington, Letter to Burgess Ball
Sept. 25, 1794

Dear Sir:

. . . The Insurrection in the Western counties of this State . . . may be considered as the first *ripe fruit* of the Democratic Societies. I did not, I must confess; expect their labours would come to maturity so soon; though I never had a doubt, that such conduct would produce some such issue; if it did not meet the frown of those who were well disposed to order and good government, in time; for can any thing be more absurd, more arrogant, or more pernicious to the peace of Society, than for self created bodies, forming themselves into *permanent* Censors, and under the shade of Night in a conclave, resolving that acts of Congress which have undergone the most deliberate, and solemn discussion by the Representatives of the people, chosen for the express purpose, and bringing with them from the different parts of the Union the sense of their Constituents, endeavouring as far as the nature of the thing will admit, to form *that will* into Laws for the government of the whole; I say, under these circumstances, for a self created, *permanent* body, (for no one denies the right of the people to meet occasionally, to petition for, or to remonstrate against, any Act of the Legislature [etc.]) to declare that *this act* is unconstitutional, and *that* act is pregnant of mischief; and that all who vote contrary to their dogmas are actuated by selfish motives, or under foreign influence; nay in plain terms are traitors to their Country, is such a stretch of arrogant presumption as is not to be reconciled with laudable motives. . . .

In his Sixth Annual Message to Congress, President Washington denounced the Democratic-Republican Clubs, urging their censure. The Federalist-controlled Senate quickly passed a resolution praising President Washington's address and censuring the societies. 4 ANNALS OF CONG. 794–95. The Republican-controlled House debated Washington's address and the propriety of censuring the societies for five days. The following is a small sampling of the arguments.

Debate on Self-Created Societies
House of Representatives, Nov. 1794 (4 Annals of Cong. 895–949)

Monday, November 24

Mr. FITZSIMONS then rose and said, that it would seem somewhat incongruous for the House to present an Address to the PRESIDENT which omitted all notice of so very important an article in his Speech as that referring to the self-created societies. Mr. F. then read an amendment, which gave rise to a very interesting debate. The amendment was in these words:

> "As part of this subject, we cannot withhold our reprobation of the self-created societies, which have risen up in some parts of the Union, misrepresenting the conduct of the Government, and disturbing the operation of the laws, and which, by deceiving and inflaming the ignorant and the weak, may naturally be supposed to have stimulated and urged the insurrection."

These are "institutions, not strictly unlawful, yet not less fatal to good order and true liberty; and reprehensible in the degree that our system of government approaches to perfect political freedom." . . .

Mr. G[ILES] began by declaring that, when he saw, or thought he saw, the House of Representatives about to erect itself into an office of censorship, he could not sit silent.

. . . He then entered into an examination of the propriety of the expression employed by the PRESIDENT, with regard to self-created societies. Mr. G. said, that there was not an individual in America, who might not come under the charge of being a member of someone or other self-created society. Associations of this kind, religious, political, and philosophical, were to be found in every quarter of the Continent. The Baptists and Methodists, for example, might be termed self-created societies. The people called the Friends, were of the same kind. Every pulpit in the United States might be included in this vote of censure, since, from every one of them, upon occasion, instructions had been delivered, not only for the eternal welfare, but likewise for the temporal happiness of the people. . . . If the self-created societies act contrary to law, they arc unprotected, and let the law pursue them. That a man is a member of one of these societies will not protect him from an accusation for treason, if the charge is well founded. If the charge is not well founded, if the societies, in their proceedings, keep within the verge of the law, Mr. G. would be glad to learn what was to be the sequel? If the House undertake to censure particular classes of men, who can tell where they will stop? . . . Mr. G. rejected all aiming at a restraint on the opinions of private persons. . . .

Mr. [W.] S[MITH] declared that he was a friend to the freedom of the press; but would any one compare a regular town meeting where deliberations were cool and unruffled, to these societies, to the nocturnal meetings of individuals, after they have dined, where they shut their doors, pass votes in secret, and admit no members into their societies, but those of their own choosing? Mr. S., by way of illustration, observed, that this House had never done much business after dinner. . . .

Tuesday, November 25

. . . Mr. DEXTER believed that such societies were in themselves, wrong, but he was still not for making laws against them. He had, however, numerous objections to their conduct. One of these was, that they erected themselves into a model for the rest of their fellow-citizens to copy. The great principle of Republicanism was, that the minority should submit to the will of the majority. But these people have elevated themselves into tyrants. Such societies are proper in a country where Government is despotic, but it is improper that such societies should exist in a free country like the United States, and hence Mr. D. was a friend to the amendment proposed by Mr. FITZSIMONS. . . .

Wednesday, November 26

[Mr. GILES:] It had yesterday been alleged, as the very worst trait in the character of Democratic societies, that they began their business after dinner, bolted their doors, and voted in the dark. This was a very alarming and detestable species of conduct! Whether the accusation were true, or not, Mr. G. could not tell from personal knowledge, for he knew nothing about these societies, but from report. But, Mr. Chairman, (pointing to the roof of the room,) is there no other place where people bolt their doors, and vote in the dark? Is there not a branch of our Legislature which transacts its business in this way? *[This was a reference to the Senate, whose deliberations were at that time neither open to the public nor published.—Editors]* And, while things are so, does it become us to censure other people for voting in the dark?

Thursday, November 27

. . . [Mr. MADISON] conceived it to be a sound principle, that an action innocent in the eye of the law could not be the object of censure to a Legislative body. When the people have formed a Constitution, they retain those rights which they have not expressly delegated. It is a question whether what is thus retained can be legislated upon. Opinions are not the objects of legislation. You animadvert on the abuse of reserved rights: how far will this go? It may extend to the liberty of speech, and of the press. It is in vain to say that this indiscriminate censure is no punishment. If it falls on classes, or individuals, it will be a severe punishment. He wished it to be considered how extremely guarded the Constitution was in respect to cases not within its limits. Murder, or treason, cannot be noticed by the Legislature. Is not this proposition, if voted, a vote of attainder? To consider a principle, we must try its nature, and see how far it will go: in the present case, he considered the effects of the principle contended for would be pernicious. If we advert to the nature of Republican Government, we shall find that the censorial power is in the people over the Government, and not in the Government over the people. As he had confidence in the good sense and patriotism of the people, he did not anticipate any lasting evil to result from the publications of these societies; they will stand or fall by the public opinion; no line can be drawn in this case. The law is the only rule of right: what is consistent with that, is not punishable; what is not contrary to that, is innocent, or at least not censurable by the Legislative body. . . .

Mr. DEXTER rose in reply to Mr. MADISON. He said that . . . the most certain way to destroy this freedom was, to encourage an unlimited abuse of it; and the way to render a free press useless, was to prostitute it to the base purposes of party and falsehood, until, wearied with constant impositions, the public would reject all information from that source as uncertain and delusive. He said that the most successful weapon used by the enemies of civil freedom over had been, to push the ideas of liberty to such wild extremes as to render it impracticable and ridiculous, and thus to compel the sober part of the community to submit to usurpation as a less evil than utter insecurity and anarchy: he added, if America loses her liberty, this will be the instrument of her destruction. . . . Let men meet for deliberating on public matters; let them freely express their opinions in conversation or in print, but let them do this with a decent respect for the will of the majority, and for the Government and rulers which the people have appointed; let them not become a band of conspirators, to make and propagate falsehood and slander; let them not instigate to the highest crimes against society; and, sir, if any have so done, let not us encourage them in these outrages by calling them the exercise of the inviolable rights of freemen. . . .

[Mr. DEXTER] was no more inclined to infringe rights which the people had reserved than that gentleman; but he did not know any article or principle of the Constitution by which the people had reserved to themselves the precious right of vilifying and misrepresenting their own Government and laws and exciting treason and rebellion with impunity. However inestimable the right of free discussion of public matters, and of a free press, might be, (and no man valued them more highly than himself,) he thought that when they were so abused as to become hostile to liberty, and threaten her destruction, the abuses ought to be corrected; and he argued from the principle of self-preservation, that the Government of every country must have the right to do so. Unless those are more sacred than the very liberty they are designed to secure, this cannot be denied. . . .

————

The Federalist attempt to censure the societies ultimately failed by a handful of votes. The final House resolution contained only a vague reference to "combinations of men." 4 ANNALS OF CONG. 947–48. Madison wrote that Washington's attack on the clubs was the worst mistake of his career. What constitutional principles can you glean from this debate? Do Americans have the right to form permanent societies consisting of "no members, but those of their own choosing"? May they be required to be open to anyone who wishes to participate in their deliberations? May they meet in secret? May they dissent from public measures or organize opposition to laws passed by Congress? Is there anything wrong with the legislature passing statutes criticizing such groups?

[*Assignment 43*]

C. FREEDOM OF THE PRESS

New York Times Co. v. Sullivan
376 U.S. 254 (1964)

■ MR. JUSTICE BRENNAN delivered the opinion of the Court.

We are required in this case to determine for the first time the extent to which the constitutional protections for speech and press limit a State's power to award damages in a libel action brought by a public official against critics of his official conduct.

Respondent L. B. Sullivan is one of the three elected Commissioners of the City of Montgomery, Alabama. . . . He brought this civil libel action against the four individual petitioners, who are Negroes and Alabama clergymen, and against petitioner the New York Times Company, a New York corporation which publishes the New York Times, a daily newspaper. . . .

Respondent's complaint alleged that he had been libeled by statements in a full-page advertisement that was carried in the New York Times on March 29, 1960. Entitled "Heed Their Rising Voices," the advertisement [described the civil rights movement and concluded with an appeal for funds]. . . .

Of the 10 paragraphs of text in the advertisement, the third and a portion of the sixth were the basis of respondent's claim of libel. They read as follows:

> [¶ 3] In Montgomery, Alabama, after students sang "My Country, 'Tis of Thee" on the State Capitol steps, their leaders were expelled from school, and truckloads of police armed with shotguns and tear-gas ringed the Alabama State College Campus. When the entire student body protested to state authorities by refusing to re-register, their dining hall was padlocked in an attempt to starve them into submission.

[¶ 6] Again and again the Southern violators have answered Dr. King's peaceful protests with intimidation and violence. They have bombed his home almost killing his wife and child. They have assaulted his person. They have arrested him seven times—for "speeding," "loitering" and similar "offenses." And now they have charged him with "perjury"—a *felony* under which they could imprison him for *ten years*. . . .

Although neither of these statements mentions respondent by name, he contended that the word "police" in the third paragraph referred to him as the Montgomery Commissioner who supervised the Police Department, so that he was being accused of "ringing" the campus with police. He further claimed that the paragraph would be read as imputing to the police, and hence to him, the padlocking of the dining hall in order to starve the students into submission. As to the sixth paragraph, he contended that since arrests are ordinarily made by the police, the statement "They have arrested (Dr. King) seven times" would be read as referring to him. . . .

It is uncontroverted that some of the statements contained in the two paragraphs were not accurate descriptions of events which occurred in Montgomery. Although Negro students staged a demonstration on the State Capital steps, they sang the National Anthem and not "My Country, 'Tis of Thee." Although nine students were expelled by the State Board of Education, this was not for leading the demonstration at the Capitol, but for demanding service at a lunch counter in the Montgomery County Courthouse on another day. Not the entire student body, but most of it, had protested the expulsion, not by refusing to register, but by boycotting classes on a single day; virtually all the students did register for the ensuing semester. The campus dining hall was not padlocked on any occasion, and the only students who may have been barred from eating there were the few who had neither signed a preregistration application nor requested temporary meal tickets. Although the police were deployed near the campus in large numbers on three occasions, they did not at any time "ring" the campus, and they were not called to the campus in connection with the demonstration on the State Capitol steps, as the third paragraph implied. Dr. King had not been arrested seven times, but only four; and although he claimed to have been assaulted some years earlier in connection with his arrest for loitering outside a courtroom, one of the officers who made the arrest denied that there was such an assault. . . .

The cost of the advertisement was approximately $4800, and it was published by the Times upon an order from a New York advertising agency acting for the signatory Committee. The agency submitted the advertisement with a letter from A. Philip Randolph, Chairman of the Committee, certifying that the persons whose names appeared on the advertisement had given their permission. Mr. Randolph was known to the Times' Advertising Acceptability Department as a responsible person, and, in accepting the letter as sufficient proof of authorization it followed its established practice. . . . The manager of the Advertising Acceptability Department testified that he had approved the advertisement for publication because he knew nothing to cause him to believe that anything in it was false, and because it bore the endorsement of "a number of people who are well known and whose reputation" he "had no reason to question." Neither he nor anyone else at the Times made an effort to confirm the accuracy of the advertisement, either by checking it against recent Times news stories relating to some of the described events or by any other means.

Alabama law denies a public officer recovery of punitive damages in a libel action brought on account of a publication concerning his official conduct unless he first makes a written demand for a public retraction and the defendant fails or refuses to comply. Respondent served such a demand upon each of the petitioners. . . . The Times did not publish a retraction in response to the demand, but wrote respondent a letter stating, among other things, that "we . . . are somewhat puzzled as to how you think the statements in any way reflect on you," and "you might, if you desire, let us know in what respect you claim that the statements in the advertisement reflect on you." Respondent filed this suit a few days later without answering the letter. . . .

The trial judge submitted the case to the jury under instructions that the statements in the advertisement were "libelous per se" and were not privileged, so that petitioners might be held liable if the jury found that they had published the advertisement and that the statements were made "of and concerning" respondent. . . . The judge rejected petitioners' contention that his rulings abridged the freedoms of speech and of the press that are guaranteed by the First and Fourteenth Amendments.

[The jury returned a verdict for $500,000, the amount requested by the plaintiffs; the Alabama Supreme Court affirmed.—Editors]

. . . We reverse the judgment. We hold that the rule of law applied by the Alabama courts is constitutionally deficient for failure to provide the safeguards for freedom of speech and of the press that are required by the First and Fourteenth Amendments in a libel action brought by a public official against critics of his official conduct. We further hold that under the proper safeguards the evidence presented in this case is constitutionally insufficient to support the judgment for respondent.

I

[The Supreme Court held that the libel judgment was state action and was thus subject to constitutional scrutiny.—Editors]

The second contention is that the constitutional guarantees of freedom of speech and of the press are inapplicable here, at least so far as the Times is concerned, because the allegedly libelous statements were published as part of a paid, "commercial" advertisement. The argument relies on *Valentine v. Chrestensen*, 316 U.S. 52 (1942), where the Court held that a city ordinance forbidding street distribution of commercial and business advertising matter did not abridge the First Amendment freedoms, even as applied to a handbill having a commercial message on one side but a protest against certain official action on the other. The reliance is wholly misplaced. The Court in *Chrestensen* reaffirmed the constitutional protection for "the freedom of communicating information and disseminating opinion"; its holding was based upon the factual conclusions that the handbill was "purely commercial advertising" and that the protest against official action had been added only to evade the ordinance.

The publication here was not a "commercial" advertisement in the sense in which the word was used in *Chrestensen*. It communicated information, expressed opinion, recited grievances, protested claimed abuses, and sought financial support on behalf of a movement whose existence and objectives are matters of the highest public interest and concern. That the Times was paid for publishing the advertisement is as immaterial in this connection as is the fact that newspapers and books are sold. Any other conclusion would discourage newspapers from carrying "editorial advertisements" of this type, and so might shut off an important outlet for the promulgation of information and ideas by persons who do not themselves have access to publishing facilities and who wish to exercise their freedom of speech even though they are not members of the press. The effect would be to shackle the First Amendment in its attempt to secure "the widest possible dissemination of information from diverse and antagonistic sources." To avoid placing such a handicap upon the freedoms of expression, we hold that if the allegedly libelous statements would otherwise be constitutionally protected from the present judgment, they do not forfeit that protection because they were published in the form of a paid advertisement.

II

Under Alabama law as applied in this case, a publication is "libelous per se" if the words "tend to injure a person . . . in his reputation" or to "bring (him) into public contempt"; the trial court stated that the standard was met if the words are such as to "injure him in his public office, or impute misconduct to him in his office, or want of official integrity, or want of fidelity to a public trust. . . ." The jury must find that the words were published "of and concerning" the plaintiff, but where the plaintiff is a public official his place in the governmental hierarchy is sufficient evidence to support a finding that his reputation has been affected by statements that reflect upon the agency of which he is in charge. Once "libel per se" has been established, the defendant has no defense as to stated facts unless he can persuade the jury that they were true in all their particulars. His privilege of "fair comment" for expressions of opinion depends on the truth of the facts upon which the comment is based. Unless he can discharge the burden of proving truth, general damages are presumed, and may be awarded without proof of pecuniary injury. A showing of actual malice is apparently a prerequisite to recovery of punitive damages, and the defendant may in any event forestall a punitive award by a retraction meeting the statutory requirements. Good motives and belief in truth do not negate an inference of malice, but are relevant only in mitigation of punitive damages if the jury chooses to accord them weight.

The question before us is whether this rule of liability, as applied to an action brought by a public official against critics of his official conduct, abridges the freedom of speech and of the press that is guaranteed by the First and Fourteenth Amendments.

Respondent relies heavily, as did the Alabama courts, on statements of this Court to the effect that the Constitution does not protect libelous publications. Those statements do not foreclose our inquiry here. None of the cases sustained the use of libel laws to impose sanctions upon expression critical of the official conduct of public officials. . . . In deciding the question now, we are compelled by neither precedent nor policy to give any more weight to the epithet "libel" than we have to other "mere labels" of state law. Like insurrection, contempt, advocacy of unlawful acts, breach of the peace, obscenity, solicitation of legal business, and the various other formulae for the repression of expression that have been challenged in this Court, libel can claim no talismanic immunity from constitutional limitations. It must be measured by standards that satisfy the First Amendment.

The general proposition that freedom of expression upon public questions is secured by the First Amendment has long been settled by our decisions. The constitutional safeguard, we have said, "was fashioned to assure unfettered interchange of ideas for the bringing about of political and social changes desired by the people." "The maintenance of the opportunity for free political discussion to the end that government may be responsive to the will of the people and that changes may be obtained by lawful means, an opportunity essential to the security of the Republic, is a fundamental principle of our constitutional system." "[I]t is a prized American privilege to speak one's mind, although not always with perfect good taste, on all public institutions," and this opportunity is to be afforded for "vigorous advocacy" no less than "abstract discussion." The First Amendment, said Judge Learned Hand, "presupposes that right conclusions are more likely to be gathered out of a multitude of tongues, than through any kind of authoritative selection. To many this is, and always will be, folly; but we have staked upon it our all." . . .

Thus we consider this case against the background of a profound national commitment to the principle that debate on public issues should be uninhibited, robust, and wide-open, and that it may well include vehement, caustic, and sometimes unpleasantly sharp attacks on government and public officials. The present advertisement, as an expression of grievance and protest on one of the major public issues of our time, would seem clearly to qualify for the constitutional protection. The question is whether it forfeits that protection by the falsity of some of its factual statements and by its alleged defamation of respondent.

Authoritative interpretations of the First Amendment guarantees have consistently refused to recognize an exception for any test of truth—whether administered by judges, juries, or administrative officials—and especially one that puts the burden of proving truth on the speaker. The constitutional protection does not turn upon "the truth, popularity, or social utility of the ideas and beliefs which are offered." As Madison said, "Some degree of abuse is inseparable from the proper use of every thing; and in no instance is this more true than in that of the press." 4 Elliot's Debates on the Federal Constitution (1876), p. 571. In *Cantwell v. Connecticut*, 310 U.S. 296 (1940), the Court declared:

> In the realm of religious faith, and in that of political belief, sharp differences arise. In both fields the tenets of one man may seem the rankest error to his neighbor. To persuade others to his own point of view, the pleader, as we know, at times, resorts to exaggeration, to vilification of men who have been, or are, prominent in church or state, and even to false statement. But the people of this nation have ordained in the light of history, that, in spite of the probability of excesses and abuses, these liberties are, in the long view, essential to enlightened opinion and right conduct on the part of the citizens of a democracy.

[E]rroneous statement is inevitable in free debate, and . . . must be protected if the freedoms of expression are to have the "breathing space" that they "need . . . to survive." . . .

If neither factual error nor defamatory content suffices to remove the constitutional shield from criticism of official conduct, the combination of the two elements is no less inadequate. This is the lesson to be drawn from the great controversy over the Sedition Act of 1798, 1 Stat. 596, which first crystallized a national awareness of the central meaning of the First Amendment. That statute made it a crime, punishable by a $5,000 fine and five years in prison, "if any person shall write, print, utter or publish . . . any false, scandalous and malicious writing or writings against the government of the United States, or either house of the Congress . . . , or the President . . . , with intent to defame . . . or to bring them, or either of them, into contempt or disrepute; or to excite against them, or either or any of them, the hatred of the good people of the United States." The Act allowed the defendant the defense of truth, and provided that the jury were to be judges both of the law and the facts. Despite these qualifications, the Act was vigorously condemned as unconstitutional in an attack joined in by Jefferson and Madison. . . .

Madison prepared the Report in support of the protest. His premise was that the Constitution created a form of government under which "The people, not the government, possess the absolute sovereignty." The structure of the government dispersed power in reflection of the people's distrust of concentrated power, and of power itself at all levels. This form of government was "altogether different" from the British form, under which the Crown was sovereign and the people were subjects. "Is it not natural and necessary, under such different circumstances," he asked, "that a different degree of freedom in the use of the press should be contemplated?" Earlier, in a debate in the House of Representatives, Madison had said: "If we advert to the nature of Republican Government, we shall find that the censorial power is in the people over the Government, and not in the Government over the people." 4 Annals of Congress, p. 934 (1794). Of the exercise of that power by the press, his Report said: "In every state, probably, in the Union, the press has exerted a freedom in canvassing the merits and measures of public men, of every description, which has not been confined to the strict limits of the common law. On this footing the freedom of the press has stood; on this foundation it yet stands. . . ." 4 Elliot's Debates, p. 570. The right of free public discussion of the stewardship of public officials was thus, in Madison's view, a fundamental principle of the American form of government.

Although the Sedition Act was never tested in this Court, the attack upon its validity has carried the day in the court of history. Fines levied in its prosecution were repaid by Act of Congress on the ground that it was unconstitutional. Calhoun, reporting to the Senate on February 4, 1836, assumed that its invalidity was a matter "which no one now doubts." Report with Senate bill No. 122, 24th Cong., 1st Sess., p. 3. Jefferson, as President, pardoned those who had been convicted and sentenced under the Act and remitted their fines, stating: "I discharged every person under punishment or prosecution under the sedition law, because I considered, and now consider, that law to be a nullity, as absolute and as palpable as if Congress had ordered us to fall down and worship a golden image." Letter to Mrs. Adams, July 22, 1804. The invalidity of the Act has also been assumed by Justices of this Court. These views reflect a broad consensus that the Act, because of the restraint it imposed upon criticism of government and public officials, was inconsistent with the First Amendment. . . .

What a State may not constitutionally bring about by means of a criminal statute is likewise beyond the reach of its civil law of libel. The fear of damage awards under a rule such as that invoked by the Alabama courts here may be markedly more inhibiting than the fear of prosecution under a criminal statute. . . . Whether or not a newspaper can survive a succession of such judgments, the pall of fear and timidity imposed upon those who would give voice to public criticism is an atmosphere in which the First Amendment freedoms cannot survive. Plainly the Alabama law of civil libel is "a form of regulation that creates hazards to protected freedoms markedly greater than those that attend reliance upon the criminal law."

The state rule of law is not saved by its allowance of the defense of truth. . . . A rule compelling the critic of official conduct to guarantee the truth of all his factual assertions—and to do so on pain of libel judgments virtually unlimited in amount— leads to a comparable "self-censorship." Allowance of the defense of truth, with the burden of proving it on the defendant, does not mean that only false speech will be deterred. . . . Under such a rule, would-be critics of official conduct may be deterred from voicing their criticism, even though it is believed to be true and even though it is in fact true, because of doubt whether it can be proved in court or fear of the expense of having to do so. They tend to make only statements which "steer far wider of the unlawful zone." The rule thus dampens the vigor and limits the variety of public debate. It is inconsistent with the First and Fourteenth Amendments.

The constitutional guarantees require, we think, a federal rule that prohibits a public official from recovering damages for a defamatory falsehood relating to his official conduct unless he proves that the statement was made with "actual malice"— that is, with knowledge that it was false or with reckless disregard of whether it was false or not. An oft-cited statement of a like rule, which has been adopted by a number of state courts, is found in the Kansas case of *Coleman v. MacLennan*, 78 Kan. 711 (1908). . . .

We conclude that such a privilege is required by the First and Fourteenth Amendments.

III

We hold today that the Constitution delimits a State's power to award damages for libel in actions brought by public officials against critics of their official conduct. Since this is such an action,[23] the rule requiring proof of actual malice is applicable. . . .

Since respondent may seek a new trial, we deem that considerations of effective judicial administration require us to review the evidence in the present record to determine whether it could constitutionally support a judgment for respondent. . . .

Applying these standards, we consider that the proof presented to show actual malice lacks the convincing clarity which the constitutional standard demands, and hence that it would not constitutionally sustain the judgment for respondent under the proper rule of law. The case of the individual petitioners requires little discussion. Even assuming that they could constitutionally be found to have authorized the use of their names on the advertisement, there was no evidence whatever that they were aware of any erroneous statements or were in any way reckless in that regard. The judgment against them is thus without constitutional support.

---

[23] We have no occasion here to determine how far down into the lower ranks of government employees the 'public official' designation would extend for purposes of this rule, or otherwise to specify categories of persons who would or would not be included. Nor need we here determine the boundaries of the 'official conduct' concept. It is enough for the present case that respondent's position as an elected city commissioner clearly made him a public official, and that the allegations in the advertisement concerned what was allegedly his official conduct as Commissioner in charge of the Police Department.

As to the Times, we similarly conclude that the facts do not support a finding of actual malice. . . .

We think the evidence against the Times supports at most a finding of negligence in failing to discover the misstatements, and is constitutionally insufficient to show the recklessness that is required for a finding of actual malice.

We also think the evidence was constitutionally defective in another respect: it was incapable of supporting the jury's finding that the allegedly libelous statements were made "of and concerning" respondent. . . .

■ MR. JUSTICE BLACK, with whom MR. JUSTICE DOUGLAS joins (concurring).

. . . I base my vote to reverse on the belief that the First and Fourteenth Amendments not merely "delimit" a State's power to award damages to "public officials against critics of their official conduct" but completely prohibit a State from exercising such a power. The Court goes on to hold that a State can subject such critics to damages if "actual malice" can be proved against them. "Malice," even as defined by the Court, is an elusive, abstract concept, hard to prove and hard to disprove. The requirement that malice be proved provides at best an evanescent protection for the right critically to discuss public affairs and certainly does not measure up to the sturdy safeguard embodied in the First Amendment. Unlike the Court, therefore, I vote to reverse exclusively on the ground that the Times and the individual defendants had an absolute, unconditional constitutional right to publish in the Times advertisement their criticisms of the Montgomery agencies and officials. . . .

While our Court has held that some kinds of speech and writings, such as "obscenity," *Roth v. United States*, 354 U.S. 476 (1957), and "fighting words," *Chaplinsky v. New Hampshire*, 315 U.S. 568 (1942), are not expression within the protection of the First Amendment, freedom to discuss public affairs and public officials is unquestionably, as the Court today holds, the kind of speech the First Amendment was primarily designed to keep within the area of free discussion. To punish the exercise of this right to discuss public affairs or to penalize it through libel judgments is to abridge or shut off discussion of the very kind most needed. This Nation, I suspect, can live in peace without libel suits based on public discussions of public affairs and public officials. But I doubt that a country can live in freedom where its people can be made to suffer physically or financially for criticizing their government, its actions, or its officials. . . . An unconditional right to say what one pleases about public affairs is what I consider to be the minimum guarantee of the First Amendment.

I regret that the Court has stopped short of this holding indispensable to preserve our free press from destruction.

■ [JUSTICE GOLDBERG's opinion concurring in result is omitted.]

NOTES

1.   The majority relies on the opposition to the Sedition Act and its ultimate political repudiation. Why? Why was the opposition to the act by the Jeffersonians authoritative, but not support for the act by the Federalists?

2.   Note that *Sullivan* involved two different sets of petitioners, with separate petitions for certiorari: (1) The New York Times Co., a corporation in the business of

producing and distributing newspapers, which ran a paid advertisement written by others; and (2) a group of Southern clergy and civil rights leaders, not professional journalists, who wrote the ad and contributed money to secure its publication. The Supreme Court treated both as fully protected by the First Amendment, without distinguishing between them. Was that correct? Is a newspaper really "the press" insofar as what is written is not the product of professional journalism, and is published for profit? Do private citizens exercise the freedom of the press when they purchase advertising space in a newspaper? Does it matter whether they are protected under the Speech Clause or the Press Clause?

Assume that the advertisement was published within sixty days of an election, and that Sullivan was running for reelection. Consistent with the First Amendment, could the individual signatories have been prosecuted under the campaign finance laws for making an illegal campaign expenditure? Could the newspaper? Is there more protection for libels than for electioneering?

3.   Does the First Amendment preclude suits for defamatory falsehoods against private individuals? In *Rosenbloom v. Metromedia*, 403 U.S. 29 (1971), the Supreme Court produced five different answers. A three-justice plurality, led by Justice Brennan, concluded that the privilege applied when the defamation concerned a private individual's "involvement in an event of public or general interest." *Id.* at 31–32. Justice Black argued that the privilege extended to every discussion of matters of public concern, without regard to the individual's fame, and even if the statements are known to be false. *Id.* at 57. Justice White argued that, absent actual malice, the privilege applied to defamatory falsehoods about private individuals made incident to report and comment about public figures. *Id.* at 62. In dissent, Justice Harlan argued that the privilege for defamatory falsehoods about private individuals limited the jury's authority to award unreasonable punitive damages. *Id.* at 77. And Justice Marshall argued that strict liability could not be used, and punitive damages could not be imposed, for defamation of private individuals. *Id.* at 82–86. Where did these various formulations come from? In *Gertz v. Robert Welch, Inc.*, 418 U.S. 323 (1974), a 5–4 Court ruled that the actual-malice rule does not apply to non-public figures, but that strict liability for defamation was unconstitutional in all cases and that punitive damages require a finding of actual malice.

4.   That raises the question: Who is a "public figure"? In *Gertz*, the Court identified two categories of public figures. First, "an individual may achieve such pervasive fame or notoriety that he becomes a public figure for all purposes and in all contexts." 418 U.S. at 351. Second, "an individual [who] voluntarily injects himself or is drawn into a particular public controversy . . . becomes a public figure for a limited range of issues." *Id.* at 351. What do these categories include? A wealthy socialite and her divorce proceedings? *Time Inc. v. Firestone*, 424 U.S. 448 (1975) (no). A scientist's receipt of federal grants and accusations of wasteful government spending? *Hutchinson v. Proxmire*, 442 U.S. 111 (1979) (no). The president of a local teacher's union and contract negotiations? *Bartnicki v. Vopper*, 532 U.S. (2001) (Breyer, J., concurring) (yes).

5.   In your opinion, are Justices Black and Douglas right? Should we worry about the potential impact of intentional falsehoods (perhaps disseminated at the last minute before an election) on our political system? Is self-censorship all bad?

New York Times Co. v. United States
[The Pentagon Papers Case]
403 U.S. 713 (1971)

[In 1967, Defense Secretary Robert McNamara commissioned a top-secret study of the Vietnam War. It contained information indicating that successive administrations had misled the public about the war's scope, the probable casualties, and the prospects for success. Dr. Daniel Ellsberg, a Pentagon official with a top-secret security clearance, had access to the papers. After becoming convinced that the war was a mistake, he made copies of the materials (without proper authorization) and shared them with several people outside the Pentagon. He gave a copy to a New York Times reporter under a promise of confidentiality. After several months of study, and consultation with its lawyers, the newspaper started publishing portions of the Pentagon Papers on June 13, 1971. The Nixon administration quickly went to court to restrain further publication. Court orders delayed publication for fifteen days, until the Supreme Court entered the following decision on June 30.—Editors]

■ PER CURIAM.

We granted certiorari in these cases in which the United States seeks to enjoin the New York Times and the Washington Post from publishing the contents of a classified study entitled "History of U.S. Decision-Making Process on Viet Nam Policy."

"Any system of prior restraints of expression comes to this Court bearing a heavy presumption against its constitutional validity." *Bantam Books, Inc. v. Sullivan*, 372 U.S. 58, 70 (1963). The Government "thus carries a heavy burden of showing justification for the imposition of such a restraint." *Organization for a Better Austin v. Keefe*, 402 U.S. 415, 419 (1971). The District Court for the Southern District of New York in the New York Times case and the District Court for the District of Columbia and the Court of Appeals for the District of Columbia Circuit in the Washington Post case held that the Government had not met that burden. We agree. . . .

■ MR. JUSTICE BLACK, with whom MR. JUSTICE DOUGLAS joins, concurring.

I adhere to the view that the Government's case against the Washington Post should have been dismissed and that the injunction against the New York Times should have been vacated without oral argument when the cases were first presented to this Court. I believe that every moment's continuance of the injunctions against these newspapers amounts to a flagrant, indefensible, and continuing violation of the First Amendment. . . . In my view it is unfortunate that some of my Brethren are apparently willing to hold that the publication of news may sometimes be enjoined. Such a holding would make a shambles of the First Amendment. . . .

In seeking injunctions against these newspapers and in its presentation to the Court, the Executive Branch seems to have forgotten the essential purpose and history of the First Amendment. When the Constitution was adopted, many people strongly opposed it because the document contained no Bill of Rights to safeguard certain basic freedoms. They especially feared that the new powers granted to a central government might be interpreted to permit the government to curtail freedom of religion, press, assembly, and speech. In response to an overwhelming public clamor, James Madison offered a series of amendments to satisfy citizens that these great liberties would remain safe and beyond the power of government to abridge. . . . The Bill of Rights changed the original Constitution into a new charter under which no branch of government could abridge the people's freedoms of press, speech, religion, and assembly. Yet the Solicitor General argues and some members of the Court appear to agree that the general powers of the Government adopted in the original Constitution should be interpreted to limit and restrict the specific and emphatic guarantees of the Bill of Rights adopted later. I can imagine no greater perversion of history. Madison and the other Framers of the First Amendment, able men that they were, wrote in language they earnestly believed could never be misunderstood: "Congress shall make no law . . . abridging the freedom . . . of the press. . . ." Both the history and language of the First Amendment support the view that the press must be left free to publish news, whatever the source, without censorship, injunctions, or prior restraints.

In the First Amendment the Founding Fathers gave the free press the protection it must have to fulfill its essential role in our democracy. The press was to serve the governed, not the governors. The Government's power to censor the press was abolished so that the press would remain forever free to censure the Government. The press was protected so that it could bare the secrets of government and inform the people. Only a free and unrestrained press can effectively expose deception in government. And paramount among the responsibilities of a free press is the duty to prevent any part of the government from deceiving the people and sending them off to distant lands to die of foreign fevers and foreign shot and shell. In my view, far from deserving condemnation for their courageous reporting, the New York Times, the Washington Post, and other newspapers should be commended for serving the purpose that the Founding Fathers saw so clearly. In revealing the workings of government that led to the Vietnam war, the newspapers nobly did precisely that which the Founders hoped and trusted they would do.

The Government's case here is based on premises entirely different from those that guided the Framers of the First Amendment. . . . [T]he Government argues in its brief that in spite of the First Amendment, "[t]he authority of the Executive Department to protect the nation against publication of information whose disclosure would endanger the national security stems from two interrelated sources: the constitutional power of the President over the conduct of foreign affairs and his authority as Commander-in-Chief."

In other words, we are asked to hold that despite the First Amendment's emphatic command, the Executive Branch, the Congress, and the Judiciary can make laws enjoining publication of current news and abridging freedom of the press in the name of "national security." The Government does not even attempt to rely on any act of Congress. Instead it makes the bold and dangerously far-reaching contention that the courts should take it upon themselves to "make" a law abridging freedom of the press in the name of equity, presidential power and national security, even when the representatives of the people in Congress have adhered to the command of the First Amendment and refused to make such a law. To find that the President has "inherent power" to halt the publication of news by resort to the courts would wipe out the First Amendment and destroy the fundamental liberty and security of the very people the Government hopes to make "secure." No one can read the history of the adoption of the First Amendment without being convinced beyond any doubt that it was injunctions like those sought here that Madison and his collaborators intended to outlaw in this Nation for all time. . . .

■ [JUSTICE DOUGLAS's concurring opinion, joined by JUSTICE BLACK, is omitted.]

■ MR. JUSTICE BRENNAN, concurring.

I write separately in these cases only to emphasize what should be apparent: that our judgments in the present cases may not be taken to indicate the propriety, in the future, of issuing temporary stays and restraining orders to block the publication of material sought to be suppressed by the Government. So far as I can determine, never before has the United States sought to enjoin a newspaper from publishing information in its possession. The relative novelty of the questions presented, the necessary haste with which decisions were reached, the magnitude of the interests asserted, and the fact that all the parties have concentrated their arguments upon the question whether permanent restraints were proper may have justified at least some of the restraints heretofore imposed in these cases. Certainly it is difficult to fault the several courts below for seeking to assure that the issues here involved were preserved for ultimate review by this Court. But even if it be assumed that some of the interim restraints were proper in the two cases before us, that assumption has no bearing upon the propriety of similar judicial action in the future. To begin with, there has now been ample time for reflection and judgment; whatever values there may be in the preservation of novel questions for appellate review may not support any restraints in the future. More important, the First Amendment stands as an absolute bar to the imposition of judicial restraints in circumstances of the kind presented by these cases.

The error that has pervaded these cases from the outset was the granting of any injunctive relief whatsoever, interim or otherwise. The entire thrust of the Government's claim throughout these cases has been that publication of the material sought to be enjoined "could," or "might," or "may" prejudice the national interest in various ways. But the First Amendment tolerates absolutely no prior judicial restraints of the press predicated upon surmise or conjecture that untoward consequences may result. Our cases, it is true, have indicated that there is a single, extremely narrow class of cases in which the First Amendment's ban on prior judicial restraint may be overridden. Our cases have thus far indicated that such cases may arise only when the Nation "is at war," *Schenck v. United States*, 249 U.S. 47, 52 (1919), during which times "[n]o one would question but that a government might prevent actual obstruction to its recruiting service or the publication of the sailing dates of transports or the number and location of troops." *Near v. Minnesota ex rel. Olson*, 283 U.S. 697, 716 (1931). Even if the present world situation were assumed to be tantamount to a time of war, or if the power of presently available armaments would justify even in peacetime the suppression of information that would set in motion a nuclear holocaust, in neither of these actions has the Government presented or even alleged that publication of items from or based upon the material at issue would cause the happening of an event of that nature. "[T]he chief purpose of [the First Amendment's] guaranty [is] to prevent previous restraints upon publication." *Near v. Minnesota*, at 713. Thus, only governmental allegation and proof that publication must inevitably, directly, and immediately cause the occurrence of an event kindred to imperiling the safety of a transport already at sea can support even the issuance of an interim restraining order. In no event may mere conclusions be sufficient: for if the Executive Branch seeks judicial aid in preventing publication, it must inevitably submit the basis upon which that aid is sought to scrutiny by the judiciary. And therefore, every restraint issued in this case, whatever its form, has violated the First Amendment—and not less so because that restraint was justified as necessary to afford the courts an opportunity to examine the claim more thoroughly. Unless and until the Government has clearly made out its case, the First Amendment commands that no injunction may issue.

■ MR. JUSTICE STEWART, with whom MR. JUSTICE WHITE joins, concurring.

In the governmental structure created by our Constitution, the Executive is endowed with enormous power in the two related areas of national defense and international relations. This power, largely unchecked by the Legislative and Judicial branches, has been pressed to the very hilt since the advent of the nuclear missile age. For better or for worse, the simple fact is that a President of the United States possesses vastly greater constitutional independence in these two vital areas of power than does, say, a prime minister of a country with a parliamentary form of government.

In the absence of the governmental checks and balances present in other areas of our national life, the only effective restraint upon executive policy and power in the areas of national defense and international affairs may lie in an enlightened citizenry—in an informed and critical public opinion which alone can here protect the values of democratic government. For this reason, it is perhaps here that a press that is alert, aware, and free most vitally serves the basic purpose of the First Amendment. For without an informed and free press there cannot be an enlightened people.

Yet it is elementary that the successful conduct of international diplomacy and the maintenance of an effective national defense require both confidentiality and secrecy. Other nations can hardly deal with this Nation in an atmosphere of mutual trust unless they can be assured that their confidences will be kept. And within our own executive departments, the development of considered and intelligent international policies would be impossible if those charged with their formulation could not communicate with each other freely, frankly, and in confidence. In the area of basic national defense the frequent need for absolute secrecy is, of course, self-evident.

I think there can be but one answer to this dilemma, if dilemma it be. The responsibility must be where the power is. If the Constitution gives the Executive a large degree of unshared power in the conduct of foreign affairs and the maintenance of our national defense, then under the Constitution the Executive must have the largely unshared duty to determine and preserve the degree of internal security necessary to exercise that power successfully. . . . [I]t is clear to me that it is the constitutional duty of the Executive—as a matter of sovereign prerogative and not as a matter of law as the courts know law—through the promulgation and enforcement of executive regulations, to protect the confidentiality necessary to carry out its responsibilities in the fields of international relations and national defense.

This is not to say that Congress and the courts have no role to play. Undoubtedly Congress has the power to enact specific and appropriate criminal laws to protect government property and preserve government secrets. Congress has passed such laws, and several of them are of very colorable relevance to the apparent circumstances of these cases. And if a criminal prosecution is instituted, it will be the responsibility of the courts to decide the applicability of the criminal law under which the charge is brought. Moreover, if Congress should pass a specific law authorizing civil proceedings in this field, the courts would likewise have the duty to decide the constitutionality of such a law as well as its applicability to the facts proved.

But in the cases before us we are asked neither to construe specific regulations nor to apply specific laws. We are asked, instead, to perform a function that the Constitution gave to the Executive, not the Judiciary. We are asked, quite simply, to prevent the publication by two newspapers of material that the Executive Branch insists should not, in the national interest, be published. I am convinced that the Executive is correct with respect to some of the documents involved. But I cannot say that disclosure of any of them will surely result in direct, immediate, and irreparable damage to our Nation or its people. That being so, there can under the First Amendment be but one judicial resolution of the issues before us. I join the judgments of the Court.

■ MR. JUSTICE WHITE, with whom MR. JUSTICE STEWART joins, concurring.

I concur in today's judgments, but only because of the concededly extraordinary protection against prior restraints enjoyed by the press under our constitutional system. I do not say that in no circumstances would the First Amendment permit an injunction against publishing information about government plans or operations. Nor, after examining the materials the Government characterizes as the most sensitive and destructive, can I deny that revelation of these documents will do substantial damage to public interests. Indeed, I am confident that their disclosure will have that result. But I nevertheless agree that the United States has not satisfied the very heavy burden that it must meet to warrant an injunction against publication in these cases, at least in the absence of express and appropriately limited congressional authorization for prior restraints in circumstances such as these.

The Government's position is simply stated: The responsibility of the Executive for the conduct of the foreign affairs and for the security of the Nation is so basic that the President is entitled to an injunction against publication of a newspaper story whenever he can convince a court that the information to be revealed threatens "grave and irreparable" injury to the public interest; and the injunction should issue whether or not the material to be published is classified, whether or not publication would be lawful under relevant criminal statutes enacted by Congress, and regardless of the circumstances by which the newspaper came into possession of the information.

At least in the absence of legislation by Congress, based on its own investigations and findings, I am quite unable to agree that the inherent powers of the Executive and the courts reach so far as to authorize remedies having such sweeping potential for inhibiting publications by the press. . . . To sustain the Government in these cases would start the courts down a long and hazardous road that I am not willing to travel, at least without congressional guidance and direction. . . .

[T]erminating the ban on publication of the relatively few sensitive documents the Government now seeks to suppress does not mean that the law either requires or invites newspapers or others to publish them or that they will be immune from criminal action if they do. Prior restraints require an unusually heavy justification under the First Amendment; but failure by the Government to justify prior restraints does not measure its constitutional entitlement to a conviction for criminal publication. That the Government mistakenly chose to proceed by injunction does not mean that it could not successfully proceed in another way.

When the Espionage Act was under consideration in 1917, Congress eliminated from the bill a provision that would have given the President broad powers in time of war to proscribe, under threat of criminal penalty, the publication of various categories of information related to the national defense. Congress at that time was unwilling to clothe the President with such far-reaching powers to monitor the press, and those opposed to this part of the legislation assumed that a necessary concomitant of such power was the power to "filter out the news to the people through some man." 55 Cong. Rec. 2008 (remarks of Sen. Ashurst). However, these same members of Congress appeared to have little doubt that newspapers would be subject to criminal prosecution if they insisted on publishing information of the type Congress had itself determined should not be revealed. Senator Ashurst, for example, was quite sure that the editor of such a newspaper "should be punished if he did publish information as to the movements of the fleet, the troops, the aircraft, the location of powder factories, the location of defense works, and all that sort of thing."

The Criminal Code contains numerous provisions potentially relevant to these cases. Section 797 makes it a crime to publish certain photographs or drawings of military installations. Section 798, also in precise language, proscribes knowing and willful publication of any classified information concerning the cryptographic systems or communication intelligence activities of the United States as well as any information obtained from communication intelligence operations. If any of the material here at issue is of this nature, the newspapers are presumably now on full notice of the position of the United States and must face the consequences if they publish. I would have no difficulty in sustaining convictions under these sections on facts that would not justify the intervention of equity and the imposition of a prior restraint.

The same would be true under those sections of the Criminal Code casting a wider net to protect the national defense. Section 793(e) makes it a criminal act for any unauthorized possessor of a document "relating to the national defense" either (1) willfully to communicate or cause to be communicated that document to any person not entitled to receive it or (2) willfully to retain the document and fail to deliver it to an officer of the United States entitled to receive it. The subsection was added in 1950 because pre-existing law provided no penalty for the unauthorized possessor unless demand for the documents was made. "The dangers surrounding the unauthorized possession of such items are self-evident, and it is deemed advisable to require their surrender in such a case, regardless of demand, especially since their unauthorized possession may be unknown to the authorities who would otherwise make the demand." S. Rep. No. 2369, pt. 1, 81st Cong., 2d Sess., 9 (1950). . . .

It is thus clear that Congress has addressed itself to the problems of protecting the security of the country and the national defense from unauthorized disclosure of potentially damaging information. Cf. *Youngstown Sheet & Tube Co. v. Sawyer*, 343 U.S. 579, 585–586 (1952). It has not, however, authorized the injunctive remedy against threatened publication. It has apparently been satisfied to rely on criminal sanctions and their deterrent effect on the responsible as well as the irresponsible press. I am not, of course, saying that either of these newspapers has yet committed a crime or that either would commit a crime if it published all the material now in its possession. That matter must await resolution in the context of a criminal proceeding if one is instituted by the United States. In that event, the issue of guilt or innocence would be determined by procedures and standards quite different from those that have purported to govern these injunctive proceedings.

■ MR. JUSTICE MARSHALL, concurring.

The Government contends that the only issue in these cases is whether in a suit by the United States, "the First Amendment bars a court from prohibiting a newspaper from publishing material whose disclosure would pose a grave and immediate danger to the security of the United States." With all due respect, I believe the ultimate issue in this case is even more basic than the one posed by the Solicitor General. The issue is whether this Court or the Congress has the power to make law.

In these cases there is no problem concerning the President's power to classify information as "secret" or "top secret." Congress has specifically recognized Presidential authority . . . to classify documents and information. See, *e.g.*, 18 U.S.C. § 798. Nor is there any issue here regarding the President's power as Chief Executive and Commander in Chief to protect national security by disciplining employees who disclose information and by taking precautions to prevent leaks.

The problem here is whether in these particular cases the Executive Branch has authority to invoke the equity jurisdiction of the courts to protect what it believes to be the national interest. See *In re Debs*, 158 U.S. 564, 584 (1895). The Government argues that in addition to the inherent power of any government to protect itself, the President's power to conduct foreign affairs and his position as Commander in Chief give him authority to impose censorship on the press to protect his ability to deal effectively with foreign nations and to conduct the military affairs of the country. . . .

It would, however, be utterly inconsistent with the concept of separation of powers for this Court to use its power of contempt to prevent behavior that Congress has specifically declined to prohibit. There would be a similar damage to the basic concept of these co-equal branches of Government if when the Executive Branch has adequate authority granted by Congress to protect "national security" it can choose instead to invoke the contempt power of a court to enjoin the threatened conduct. The Constitution provides that Congress shall make laws, the President execute laws, and courts interpret laws. *Youngstown*. It did not provide for government by injunction in which the courts and the Executive Branch can "make law" without regard to the action of Congress. . . .

■ MR. CHIEF JUSTICE BURGER, dissenting.

So clear are the constitutional limitations on prior restraint against expression, that from the time of *Near v. Minnesota* (1931), until recently in *Organization for a Better Austin v. Keefe* (1971), we have had little occasion to be concerned with cases involving prior restraints against news reporting on matters of public interest. There is, therefore, little variation among the members of the Court in terms of resistance to prior restraints against publication. Adherence to this basic constitutional principle, however, does not make these cases simple ones. In these cases, the imperative of a free and unfettered press comes into collision with another imperative, the effective functioning of a complex modern government and specifically the effective exercise of certain constitutional powers of the Executive. Only those who view the First Amendment as an absolute in all circumstances—a view I respect, but reject—can find such cases as these to be simple or easy.

These cases are not simple for another and more immediate reason. We do not know the facts of the cases. No District Judge knew all the facts. No Court of Appeals Judge knew all the facts. No member of this Court knows all the facts.

Why are we in this posture, in which only those judges to whom the First Amendment is absolute and permits of no restraint in any circumstances or for any reason, are really in a position to act?

I suggest we are in this posture because these cases have been conducted in unseemly haste. . . . The prompt settling of these cases reflects our universal abhorrence of prior restraint. But prompt judicial action does not mean unjudicial haste.

Here, moreover, the frenetic haste is due in large part to the manner in which the Times proceeded from the date it obtained the purloined documents. It seems reasonably clear now that the haste precluded reasonable and deliberate judicial treatment of these cases and was not warranted. . . .

An issue of this importance should be tried and heard in a judicial atmosphere conducive to thoughtful, reflective deliberation, especially when haste, in terms of hours, is unwarranted in light of the long period the Times, by its own choice, deferred publication.[1]

It is not disputed that the Times has had unauthorized possession of the documents for three to four months, during which it has had its expert analysts studying them, presumably digesting them and preparing the material for publication. During all of this time, the Times, presumably in its capacity as trustee of the public's "right to know," has held up publication for purposes it considered proper and thus public knowledge was delayed. No doubt this was for a good reason; the analysis of 7,000 pages of complex material drawn from a vastly greater volume of material would inevitably take time and the writing of good news stories takes time. But why should the United States Government, from whom this information was illegally acquired by someone, along with all the counsel, trial judges, and appellate judges be placed under needless pressure? After these months of deferral, the alleged "right to know" has somehow and suddenly become a right that must be vindicated instanter.

Would it have been unreasonable, since the newspaper could anticipate the Government's objections to release of secret material, to give the Government an opportunity to review the entire collection and determine whether agreement could be reached on publication? Stolen or not, if security was not in fact jeopardized, much of the material could not doubt have been declassified, since it spans a period ending in 1968. With such an approach—one that great newspapers have in the past

---

[1]   As noted elsewhere the Times conducted its analysis of the 47 volumes of Government documents over a period of several months and did so with a degree of security that a government might envy. Such security was essential, of course, to protect the enterprise from others. Meanwhile the Times has copyrighted its material and there were strong intimations in the oral argument that the Times contemplated enjoining its use by any other publisher in violation of its copyright. Paradoxically this would afford it a protection, analogous to prior restraint, against all others—a protection the Times denies the Government of the United States.

practiced and stated editorially to be the duty of an honorable press—the newspapers and Government might well have narrowed the area of disagreement as to what was and was not publishable, leaving the remainder to be resolved in orderly litigation, if necessary. To me it is hardly believable that a newspaper long regarded as a great institution in American life would fail to perform one of the basic and simple duties of every citizen with respect to the discovery or possession of stolen property or secret government documents. That duty, I had thought—perhaps naively—was to report forthwith, to responsible public officers. This duty rests on taxi drivers, Justices, and the New York Times. . . .

I should add that I am in general agreement with much of what Mr. Justice WHITE has expressed with respect to penal sanctions concerning communication or retention of documents or information relating to the national defense. . . .

■ MR. JUSTICE HARLAN, with whom THE CHIEF JUSTICE and MR. JUSTICE BLACKMUN join, dissenting.

. . . With all respect, I consider that the Court has been almost irresponsibly feverish in dealing with these cases.

Both the Court of Appeals for the Second Circuit and the Court of Appeals for the District of Columbia Circuit rendered judgment on June 23. The New York Times' petition for certiorari, its motion for accelerated consideration thereof, and its application for interim relief were filed in this Court on June 24 at about 11 a.m. The application of the United States for interim relief in the Post case was also filed here on June 24 at about 7:15 p.m. This Court's order setting a hearing before us on June 26 at 11 a.m., a course which I joined only to avoid the possibility of even more peremptory action by the Court, was issued less than 24 hours before. The record in the Post case was filed with the Clerk shortly before 1 p.m. on June 25; the record in the Times case did not arrive until 7 or 8 o'clock that same night. The briefs of the parties were received less than two hours before argument on June 26.

This frenzied train of events took place in the name of the presumption against prior restraints created by the First Amendment. Due regard for the extraordinarily important and difficult questions involved in these litigations should have led the Court to shun such a precipitate timetable. In order to decide the merits of these cases properly, some or all of the following questions should have been faced:

1. Whether the Attorney General is authorized to bring these suits in the name of the United States. Compare *In re Debs* with *Youngstown*. This question involves as well the construction and validity of a singularly opaque statute—the Espionage Act, 18 U.S.C. § 793(e).

2. Whether the First Amendment permits the federal courts to enjoin publication of stories which would present a serious threat to national security. See *Near v. Minnesota*, at 716 (dictum).

3. Whether the threat to publish highly secret documents is of itself a sufficient implication of national security to justify an injunction on the theory that regardless of the contents of the documents harm enough results simply from the demonstration of such a breach of secrecy.

4. Whether the unauthorized disclosure of any of these particular documents would seriously impair the national security.

5.   What weight should be given to the opinion of high officers in the Executive Branch of the Government with respect to questions 3 and 4.

6.   Whether the newspapers are entitled to retain and use the documents notwithstanding the seemingly uncontested facts that the documents, or the originals of which they are duplicates, were purloined from the Government's possession and that the newspapers received them with knowledge that they had been feloniously acquired.

7.   Whether the threatened harm to the national security or the Government's possessory interest in the documents justifies the issuance of an injunction against publication in light of—

    a.   The strong First Amendment policy against prior restraints on publication;

    b.   The doctrine against enjoining conduct in violation of criminal statutes; and

    c.   The extent to which the materials at issue have apparently already been otherwise disseminated.

These are difficult questions of fact, of law, and of judgment; the potential consequences of erroneous decision are enormous. The time which has been available to us, to the lower courts, and to the parties has been wholly inadequate for giving these cases the kind of consideration they deserve. . . .

Forced as I am to reach the merits of these cases, I dissent from the opinion and judgments of the Court. Within the severe limitations imposed by the time constraints under which I have been required to operate, I can only state my reasons in telescoped form, even though in different circumstances I would have felt constrained to deal with the cases in the fuller sweep indicated above.

. . . It is plain to me that the scope of the judicial function in passing upon the activities of the Executive Branch of the Government in the field of foreign affairs is very narrowly restricted. This view is, I think, dictated by the concept of separation of powers upon which our constitutional system rests.

In a speech on the floor of the House of Representatives, Chief Justice John Marshall, then a member of that body, stated: "The President is the sole organ of the nation in its external relations, and its sole representative with foreign nations." From that time, shortly after the founding of the Nation, to this, there has been no substantial challenge to this description of the scope of executive power. See *United States v. Curtiss-Wright Export Corp.*, 299 U.S. 304, 319–321 (1936).

From this constitutional primacy in the field of foreign affairs, it seems to me that certain conclusions necessarily follow. Some of these were stated concisely by President Washington, declining the request of the House of Representatives for the papers leading up to the negotiation of the Jay Treaty:

The nature of foreign negotiations requires caution, and their success must often depend on secrecy; and even when brought to a conclusion a full disclosure of all the measures, demands, or eventual concessions which may have been proposed or contemplated would be extremely impolitic; for this might have a pernicious influence on future negotiations, or produce immediate inconveniences, perhaps danger and mischief, in relation to other powers.

J. Richardson, MESSAGES AND PAPERS OF THE PRESIDENTS 194–195 (1896).

The power to evaluate the "pernicious influence" of premature disclosure is not, however, lodged in the Executive alone. I agree that, in performance of its duty to protect the values of the First Amendment against political pressures, the judiciary must review the initial Executive determination to the point of satisfying itself that the subject matter of the dispute does lie within the proper compass of the President's foreign relations power. . . .

But in my judgment the judiciary may not properly redetermine for itself the probable impact of disclosure on the national security.

> [T]he very nature of executive decisions as to foreign policy is political, not judicial. Such decisions are wholly confided by our Constitution to the political departments of the government, Executive and Legislative. They are delicate, complex, and involve large elements of prophecy. They are and should be undertaken only by those directly responsible to the people whose welfare they advance or imperil. They are decisions of a kind for which the Judiciary has neither aptitude, facilities nor responsibility and have long been held to belong in the domain of political power not subject to judicial intrusion or inquiry.

Chicago & Southern Air Lines, Inc. v. Waterman Steamship Corp., 333 U.S. 103, 111 (1948) (Jackson, J.).

Even if there is some room for the judiciary to override the executive determination, it is plain that the scope of review must be exceedingly narrow. I can see no indication in the opinions of either the District Court or the Court of Appeals in the *Post* litigation that the conclusions of the Executive were given even the deference owing to an administrative agency, much less that owing to a co-equal branch of the Government operating within the field of its constitutional prerogative. . . .

Pending further hearings in each case conducted under the appropriate ground rules, I would continue the restraints on publication. I cannot believe that the doctrine prohibiting prior restraints reaches to the point of preventing courts from maintaining the *status quo* long enough to act responsibly in matters of such national importance as those involved here.

■ MR. JUSTICE BLACKMUN, dissenting.

. . . The First Amendment, after all, is only one part of an entire Constitution. Article II of the great document vests in the Executive Branch primary power over the conduct of foreign affairs and places in that branch the responsibility for the Nation's safety. Each provision of the Constitution is important, and I cannot subscribe to a doctrine of unlimited absolutism for the First Amendment at the cost of downgrading other provisions. . . .

I therefore would remand these cases to be developed expeditiously, of course, but on a schedule permitting the orderly presentation of evidence from both sides, with the use of discovery, if necessary, as authorized by the rules, and with the preparation of briefs, oral argument, and court opinions of a quality better than has been seen to this point. . . .

The Court, however, decides the cases today the other way. I therefore add one final comment.

I strongly urge, and sincerely hope, that these two newspapers will be fully aware of their ultimate responsibilities to the United States of America. Judge Wilkey, dissenting in the District of Columbia case, after a review of only the affidavits before his court (the basic papers had not then been made available by either party), concluded that there were a number of examples of documents that, if in the possession of the Post, and if published, "could clearly result in great harm to the nation," and he defined "harm" to mean "the death of soldiers, the destruction of alliances, the greatly increased difficulty of negotiation with our enemies, the inability of our diplomats to negotiate. . . ." I, for one, have now been able to give at least some cursory study not only to the affidavits, but to the material itself. I regret to say that from this examination I fear that Judge Wilkey's statements have possible foundation. I therefore share his concern. I hope that damage has not already been done. If, however, damage has been done, and if, with the Court's action today, these newspapers proceed to publish the critical documents and there results therefrom "the death of soldiers, the destruction of alliances, the greatly increased difficulty of negotiation with our enemies, the inability of our diplomats to negotiate," to which list I might add the factors of prolongation of the war and of further delay in the freeing of United States prisoners, then the Nation's people will know where the responsibility for these sad consequences rests.

NOTES

1.   One of the main purposes of the First Amendment was to prohibit prior restraints on speech. As you have seen, Blackstone's *Commentaries*, the leading legal treatise of the founding era, argued that freedom of the press was limited to prohibiting prior restraints. Thus, under one reading of the First Amendment, the freedoms of speech and press protects speakers against prior restraints on their speech, but not against subsequent punishment. *Patterson v. Colorado*, 205 U.S. 454, 462 (1907). This makes distinguishing between prior restraint and punishment essential. According to Justice Kennedy, "In its simple, most blatant form, a prior restraint is a law which requires submission of speech to an official who may grant or deny permission to utter or publish it based upon its contents. . . . In contrast are laws which punish speech or expression only after it has occurred and been found unlawful." *Alexander v. United States*, 509 U.S. 544, 566 (1993). One problem, however, is that "some governmental actions may have the characteristics both of punishment and prior restraint." *Id.* at 567.

While the distinction is difficult to manage, it has a theoretical justification. As the Court stated in *Southeastern Promotions, Ltd. v. Conrad*, "Behind the distinction is a theory deeply etched in our law: a free society prefers to punish the few who abuse rights of speech after they break the law than to throttle them and all others beforehand. It is always difficult to know in advance what an individual will say, and the line between legitimate and illegitimate speech is often so finely drawn that the risks of freewheeling censorship are formidable." 420 U.S. 546, 559 (1975). Perhaps more important are the institutional considerations. Subsequent punishment is put to a jury, while judges or (more commonly) executive officials administer licensing schemes.

2.   Prior restraints commonly take two forms. One is a compulsory licensing scheme, in which a speaker must obtain government approval before speaking. The other is a judicial injunction, like the one at issue in *The Pentagon Papers Case*.

The Court first reviewed a licensing law in *Lovell v. City of Griffin*. 303 U.S. 444 (1938). *Lovell* concerned a city ordinance that required pamphleteers to obtain written permission from the city manager before distributing their pamphlets. The plaintiff was a Jehovah's Witness convicted under the ordinance for distributing religious material. The Court struck the ordinance down, declaring that the law "strikes at the very foundation of the freedom of the press by subjecting it to license and censorship." *Id.* at 451. Despite this strong language, the Court has not made licensing systems unconstitutional per se. In *Freedman v. Maryland*, the Court held that certain procedural safeguards would allow a licensing system to avoid constitutional infirmity. 380 U.S. 51, 58–59 (1965) (striking down a state motion picture censorship statute). The burden of proof must be on the censor, there must be judicial review of the censor's decision to deny a license, and there must be a mechanism for a "prompt final judicial decision" to minimize the deterrent effect of a denial of a license. *Id.*

Another line of prior restraint cases involves judicial injunctions. In *Near v. Minnesota*, the Court addressed a Minnesota law that declared any "malicious, scandalous and defamatory newspaper, magazine or other periodical" to be a nuisance, and allowed county attorneys to obtain injunctions against their publication. 283 U.S. 697, 701–02 (1931). The Court considered the function of the law to be "the essence of censorship" and struck it down. *Id.* at 713. Writing for the four dissenters, Justice Butler argued that the regular publication of defamatory material was "an abuse of the right of free press" and that the law was not a prior restraint because it only enjoined further publication of defamatory material. *Id.* at 735–36 (Butler J., dissenting).

3.   The Court's brief per curiam opinion in *The Pentagon Papers Case* notes only that there is a "heavy presumption" against the validity of a prior restraint and that the government had failed to carry its burden. Prior restraints are not unconstitutional per se, and may be permissible depending on the content of the speech. Prior restraints involving imminent threats to national security, injunctions necessary to protect a defendant's right to a fair trial, or censorship of obscenity may be permissible. See *Near v. Minnesota*, 283 U.S. 697, 716 (1931). How would this case have come out if, instead of a prior restraint, the government had sought to punish the New York Times after the fact?

4.   Do the protections against prior restraints apply to everyone, or just to the institutional press? Suppose the government had become aware that Dr. Ellsberg had made copies of the Pentagon Papers, and it sought an injunction against his disseminating them to the public in any way. Would the legal analysis have been any different?

Branzburg v. Hayes
408 U.S. 665 (1972)

■ Opinion of the Court by MR. JUSTICE WHITE, announced by THE CHIEF JUSTICE.

The issue in these cases is whether requiring newsmen to appear and testify before state or federal grand juries abridges the freedom of speech and press guaranteed by the First Amendment. We hold that it does not.

I

[Paul Branzburg, a staff reporter, wrote two articles for the Courier-Journal about drug manufacturing and use in Kentucky. The first article included a photograph of hashish held in an unidentified person's hands above a laboratory

table. The second article included interviews with several marijuana users. To gain access to these sources, Branzburg promised that he would not identify those interviewed. He was subpoenaed by two grand juries but refused to identify his sources. He asserted that he was protected by a reporter's privilege in the First Amendment of the U.S. Constitution. The Supreme Court consolidated Branzburg with cases involving a reporter from the New York Times and a television news reporter, who wrote about Black Panther groups allegedly planning acts of civil disorder.—Editors]

II

Petitioners . . . press First Amendment claims that may be simply put: that to gather news it is often necessary to agree either not to identify the source of information published or to publish only part of the facts revealed, or both; that if the reporter is nevertheless forced to reveal these confidences to a grand jury, the source so identified and other confidential sources of other reporters will be measurably deterred from furnishing publishable information, all to the detriment of the free flow of information protected by the First Amendment. Although the newsmen in these cases do not claim an absolute privilege against official interrogation in all circumstances, they assert that the reporter should not be forced either to appear or to testify before a grand jury or at trial until and unless sufficient grounds are shown for believing that the reporter possesses information relevant to a crime the grand jury is investigating, that the information the reporter has is unavailable from other sources, and that the need for the information is sufficiently compelling to override the claimed invasion of First Amendment interests occasioned by the disclosure. Principally relied upon are prior cases emphasizing the importance of the First Amendment guarantees to individual development and to our system of representative government, decisions requiring that official action with adverse impact on First Amendment rights be justified by a public interest that is "compelling" or "paramount," and those precedents establishing the principle that justifiable governmental goals may not be achieved by unduly broad means having an unnecessary impact on protected rights of speech, press, or association. The heart of the claim is that the burden on news gathering resulting from compelling reporters to disclose confidential information outweighs any public interest in obtaining the information. . . .

The sole issue before us is the obligation of reporters to respond to grand jury subpoenas as other citizens do and to answer questions relevant to an investigation into the commission of crime. Citizens generally are not constitutionally immune from grand jury subpoenas; and neither the First Amendment nor any other constitutional provision protects the average citizen from disclosing to a grand jury information that he has received in confidence. The claim is, however, that reporters are exempt from these obligations because if forced to respond to subpoenas and identify their sources or disclose other confidences, their informants will refuse or be reluctant to furnish newsworthy information in the future. This asserted burden on news gathering is said to make compelled testimony from newsmen constitutionally suspect and to require a privileged position for them.

It is clear that the First Amendment does not invalidate every incidental burdening of the press that may result from the enforcement of civil or criminal statutes of general applicability. Under prior cases, otherwise valid laws serving substantial public interests may be enforced against the press as against others, despite the possible burden that may be imposed. The Court has emphasized that "the publisher of a newspaper has no special immunity from the application of general laws. He has no special privilege to invade the rights and liberties of others." *Associated Press v. NLRB*, 301 U.S. 103, 132–133 (1937). It was there held that the Associated Press, a news-gathering and disseminating organization, was not exempt from the requirements of the National Labor Relations Act. The holding was reaffirmed in *Oklahoma Press Publishing Co. v. Walling*, 327 U.S. 186, 192–193 (1946), where the Court rejected the claim that applying the Fair Labor Standards Act to a newspaper publishing business would abridge the freedom of press guaranteed by the First Amendment. *Associated Press v. United States*, 326 U.S. 1 (1945), similarly overruled assertions that the First Amendment precluded application of the Sherman Act to a newsgathering and disseminating organization. Likewise, a newspaper may be subjected to nondiscriminatory forms of general taxation. *Grosjean v. American Press Co.*, 297 U.S. 233, 250 (1936); *Murdock v. Pennsylvania*, 319 U.S. 105, 112 (1943). . . .

It has generally been held that the First Amendment does not guarantee the press a constitutional right of special access to information not available to the public generally. In *Zemel v. Rusk*, 318 U.S. 1 (1965), for example, the Court sustained the Government's refusal to validate passports to Cuba even though that restriction "render[ed] less than wholly free the flow of information concerning that country." The ban on travel was held constitutional, for "the right to speak and publish does not carry with it the unrestrained right to gather information."

Despite the fact that news gathering may be hampered, the press is regularly excluded from grand jury proceedings, our own conferences, the meetings of other official bodies gathered in executive session, and the meetings of private organizations. Newsmen have no constitutional right of access to the scenes of crime or disaster when the general public is excluded, and they may be prohibited from attending or publishing information about trials if such restrictions are necessary to assure a defendant a fair trial before an impartial tribunal. . . .

It is thus not surprising that the great weight of authority is that newsmen are not exempt from the normal duty of appearing before a grand jury and answering questions relevant to a criminal investigation. At common law, courts consistently refused to recognize the existence of any privilege authorizing a newsman to refuse to reveal confidential information to a grand jury. In 1958, a news gatherer asserted for the first time that the First Amendment exempted confidential information from public disclosure pursuant to a subpoena issued in a civil suit, *Garland v. Torre*, 259 F.2d 545 (CA2), cert. denied, 358 U.S. 910 (1958), but the claim was denied, and this argument has been almost uniformly rejected since then. . . .

A number of States have provided newsmen a statutory privilege of varying breadth, but the majority have not done so, and none has been provided by federal statute. Until now the only testimonial privilege for unofficial witnesses that is rooted in the Federal Constitution is the Fifth Amendment privilege against compelled self-incrimination. We are asked to create another by interpreting the First Amendment to grant newsmen a testimonial privilege that other citizens do not enjoy. This we decline to do. Fair and effective law enforcement aimed at providing security for the person and property of the individual is a fundamental function of government, and the grand jury plays an important, constitutionally mandated role in this process. On the records now before us, we perceive no basis for holding that the public interest in law enforcement and in ensuring effective grand jury proceedings is insufficient to override the consequential, but uncertain, burden on news gathering that is said to result from insisting that reporters, like other citizens, respond to relevant questions put to them in the course of a valid grand jury investigation or criminal trial. . . .

The argument that the flow of news will be diminished by compelling reporters to aid the grand jury in a criminal investigation is not irrational, nor are the records before us silent on the matter. But we remain unclear how often and to what extent informers are actually deterred from furnishing information when newsmen are forced to testify before a grand jury. The available data indicate that some newsmen rely a great deal on confidential sources and that some informants are particularly sensitive to the threat of exposure and may be silenced if it is held by this Court that, ordinarily, newsmen must testify pursuant to subpoenas, but the evidence fails to demonstrate that there would be a significant constriction of the flow of news to the public if this Court reaffirms the prior common-law and constitutional rule regarding the testimonial obligations of newsmen. Estimates of the inhibiting effect of such subpoenas on the willingness of informants to make disclosures to newsmen are widely divergent and to a great extent speculative. It would be difficult to canvass the views of the informants themselves; surveys of reporters on this topic are chiefly opinions of predicted informant behavior and must be viewed in the light of the professional self-interest of the interviewees. Reliance by the press on confidential informants does not mean that all such sources will in fact dry up because of the later possible appearance of the newsman before a grand jury. The reporter may never be called and if he objects to testifying, the prosecution may not insist. . . .

Accepting the fact, however, that an undetermined number of informants not themselves implicated in crime will nevertheless, for whatever reason, refuse to talk to newsmen if they fear identification by a reporter in an official investigation, we cannot accept the argument that the public interest in possible future news about crime from undisclosed, unverified sources must take precedence over the public interest in pursuing and prosecuting those crimes reported to the press by informants and in thus deterring the commission of such crimes in the future. . . .

We are admonished that refusal to provide a First Amendment reporter's privilege will undermine the freedom of the press to collect and disseminate news. But this is not the lesson history teaches us. As noted previously, the common law recognized no such privilege, and the constitutional argument was not even asserted until 1958. From the beginning of our country the press has operated without constitutional protection for press informants, and the press has flourished. The existing constitutional rules have not been a serious obstacle to either the development or retention of confidential news sources by the press. . . .

The requirements of those cases which hold that a State's interest must be "compelling" or "paramount" to justify even an indirect burden on First Amendment rights, are also met here. As we have indicated, the investigation of crime by the grand jury implements a fundamental governmental role of securing the safety of the person and property of the citizen, and it appears to us that calling reporters to give testimony in the manner and for the reasons that other citizens are called "bears a reasonable relationship to the achievement of the governmental purpose asserted as its justification." If the test is that the government "convincingly show a substantial relation between the information sought and a subject of overriding and compelling state interest," *Gibson v. Florida Legislative Investigation Committee*, 372 U.S. 539, 546 (1963), it is quite apparent (1) that the State has the necessary interest in extirpating the traffic in illegal drugs, in forestalling assassination attempts on the President, and in preventing the community from being disrupted by violent disorders endangering both persons and property; and (2) that, based on the stories [written by the petitioners], the grand jury called these reporters as they would others—because it was likely that they could supply information to help the government determine whether illegal conduct had occurred and, if it had, whether there was sufficient evidence to return an indictment.

Similar considerations dispose of the reporters' claims that preliminary to requiring their grand jury appearance, the State must show that a crime has been committed and that they possess relevant information not available from other sources, for only the grand jury itself can make this determination. The role of the grand jury as an important instrument of effective law enforcement necessarily includes an investigatory function with respect to determining whether a crime has been committed and who committed it. To this end it must call witnesses, in the manner best suited to perform its task. . . . It is only after the grand jury has examined the evidence that a determination of whether the proceeding will result in an indictment can be made. . . .

We are unwilling to embark the judiciary on a long and difficult journey to such an uncertain destination. The administration of a constitutional newsman's privilege would present practical and conceptual difficulties of a high order. Sooner or later, it would be necessary to define those categories of newsmen who qualified for the privilege, a questionable procedure in light of the traditional doctrine that liberty of the press is the right of the lonely pamphleteer who uses carbon paper or a mimeograph just as much as of the large metropolitan publisher who utilizes the latest photocomposition methods. Freedom of the press is a "fundamental personal right" which "is not confined to newspapers and periodicals. It necessarily embraces pamphlets and leaflets. . . . The press in its historic connotation comprehends every sort of publication which affords a vehicle of information and opinion." *Lovell v. Griffin*, 303 U.S. 444, 450, 452 (1938). See also *Mills v. Alabama*, 384 U.S. 214, 219 (1966); *Murdock*, at 111. The informative function asserted by representatives of the organized press in the present cases is also performed by lecturers, political pollsters, novelists, academic researchers, and dramatists. Almost any author may quite accurately assert that he is contributing to the flow of information to the public, that he relies on confidential sources of information, and that these sources will be silenced if he is forced to make disclosures before a grand jury.[40]

In each instance where a reporter is subpoenaed to testify, the courts would also be embroiled in preliminary factual and legal determinations with respect to whether the proper predicate had been laid for the reporter's appearance: Is there probable cause to believe a crime has been committed? Is it likely that the reporter has useful

---

[40] Such a privilege might be claimed by groups that set up newspapers in order to engage in criminal activity and to, therefore, be insulated from grand jury inquiry, regardless of Fifth Amendment grants of immunity. It might appear that such "sham" newspapers would be easily distinguishable, yet the First Amendment ordinarily prohibits courts from inquiring into the content of expression, except in cases of obscenity or libel, and protects speech and publications regardless of their motivation, orthodoxy, truthfulness, timeliness, or taste. By affording a privilege to some organs of communication but not to others, courts would inevitably be discriminating on the basis of content.

information gained in confidence? Could the grand jury obtain the information elsewhere? Is the official interest sufficient to outweigh the claimed privilege?

Thus, in the end, by considering whether enforcement of a particular law served a "compelling" governmental interest, the courts would be inextricably involved in distinguishing between the value of enforcing different criminal laws. By requiring testimony from a reporter in investigations involving some crimes but not in others, they would be making a value judgment that a legislature had declined to make, since in each case the criminal law involved would represent a considered legislative judgment, not constitutionally suspect, of what conduct is liable to criminal prosecution. The task of judges, like other officials outside the legislative branch, is not to make the law but to uphold it in accordance with their oaths. . . .

Finally, as we have earlier indicated, news gathering is not without its First Amendment protections, and grand jury investigations if instituted or conducted other than in good faith, would pose wholly different issues for resolution under the First Amendment. Official harassment of the press undertaken not for purposes of law enforcement but to disrupt a reporter's relationship with his news sources would have no justification. Grand juries are subject to judicial control and subpoenas to motions to quash. We do not expect courts will forget that grand juries must operate within the limits of the First Amendment as well as the Fifth. . . .

■ MR. JUSTICE STEWART, with whom MR. JUSTICE BRENNAN and MR. JUSTICE MARSHALL join, dissenting.

The Court's crabbed view of the First Amendment reflects a disturbing insensitivity to the critical role of an independent press in our society. The question whether a reporter has a constitutional right to a confidential relationship with his source is of first impression here, but the principles that should guide our decision are as basic as any to be found in the Constitution. While MR. JUSTICE POWELL's enigmatic concurring opinion gives some hope of a more flexible view in the future, the Court in these cases holds that a newsman has no First Amendment right to protect his sources when called before a grand jury. The Court thus invites state and federal authorities to undermine the historic independence of the press by attempting to annex the journalistic profession as an investigative arm of government. Not only will this decision impair performance of the press' constitutionally protected functions, but it will, I am convinced, in the long run, harm rather than help the administration of justice. . . .

■ [The concurring opinion of JUSTICE POWELL and the dissenting opinion of JUSTICE DOUGLAS are omitted.]

NOTES

1. If members of "the press" are given special protections not accorded to ordinary members of the public, it is necessary to define who comprises "the press." The Court notes that this definition "would present practical and conceptual difficulties of a high order." This has been borne out in the scholarly debate over the proper interpretation of the Press Clause. One group of scholars has argued that the institutional press receives special protection under the Press Clause. E.g., Randall P. Bezanson, *Whither Freedom of the Press?*, 97 Iowa L. Rev. 1259 (2012); David A. Anderson, *Freedom of the Press*, 80 Tex. L. Rev. 429 (2002). Another group has argued that the clause protects every person's right to use the printing press and analogous technology to disseminate a message. E.g.,

Eugene Volokh, *Freedom for the Press as an Industry, or for the Press as a Technology? From the Framing to Today*, 160 U. Pa. L. Rev. 459 (2012).

Media stalwarts like the New York Times Company clearly qualify as "the press." What about advocacy journalists? What about student journalists? What about stringers (i.e., people who write occasionally for news media without having a formal contract)? What about writers for news organizations that do not make money and that operate at a loss for purposes of advocacy? What about book authors? Novelists? Pamphleteers? Bloggers? Tweeters? Was "freedom of the press" originally meant to refer to organized news media, or did it guarantee the right of all persons to disseminate their ideas to the public? The Supreme Court has sometimes spoken of the press in broad terms. *Branzburg v. Hayes*, 408 U.S. 665, 703 (1972) ("[L]iberty of the press is the right of the lonely pamphleteer who uses carbon paper or a mimeograph just as much as of the large metropolitan publisher who utilizes the latest photocomposition methods."); *Lovell v. City of Griffin*, 303 U.S. 444, 452 (1938) ("The press in its historic connotation comprehends every sort of publication which affords a vehicle of information and opinion."). Under this view, "the freedom of the press" is not a privilege for a particular industry or profession, but for all persons to disseminate their views to the public through the various media of communications. What are the consequences of defining the press so expansively?

Justice Potter Stewart advocated for robust protections for a much narrower group— the "organized press" comprising "the daily newspapers and other established news media." Potter Stewart, *Or of the Press*, 26 Hastings L.J. 631, 631 (1975). Legislatures responded to *Branzburg* and other decisions by enacting statutes protecting various press privileges and defining the press for the purposes of the statute. Consider New Jersey's journalist's privilege statute: "Subject to [evidentiary rules governing waiver of privilege], a person engaged on, engaged in, connected with, or employed by news media for the purpose of gathering, procuring, transmitting, compiling, editing or disseminating news for the general public or on whose behalf news is so gathered, procured, transmitted, compiled, edited or disseminated has a privilege to refuse to disclose. . . ." N.J. Stat. Ann. § 2A:84A–21 (West 2012). "News media" is defined as "newspapers, magazines, press associations, news agencies, wire services, radio, television or other similar printed, photographic, mechanical or electronic means of disseminating news to the general public." *Id.* Would this protect book authors? Freelance reporters? Would it protect the civil rights leaders who wrote the advertisement at issue in *Sullivan*?

2. The Court analyzes the subpoenaing of a journalist as an "indirect" restraint on the freedom of the press—not a prohibition on publishing, but a generally applicable law that, as applied to journalists, has a restraining effect. We will encounter other indirect restraints in other First Amendment context, also involving the enforcement of generally applicable laws. Among these are the application of criminal laws to expressive conduct and the application of generally applicable laws to acts of religious exercise. When you come to these, think about *Branzburg*, and ask yourself whether the Court is applying a consistent theory.

3. You might compare the arguments for a journalist-source privilege with those for other privileges, such as doctor-patient or husband-wife. The priest-penitent privilege is now recognized as a federal constitutional right; unlike the claimed privilege in *Branzburg*, it is absolute.

[*Assignment 44*]

D. THE RISE AND FALL OF CATEGORICAL EXCEPTIONS

Chaplinsky v. New Hampshire
315 U.S. 568 (1942)

■ MR. JUSTICE MURPHY delivered the opinion of the Court.

Appellant, a member of the sect known as Jehovah's Witnesses, was convicted in the municipal court of Rochester, New Hampshire, for violation of Chapter 378, § 2, of the Public Laws of New Hampshire:

> No person shall address any offensive, derisive or annoying word to any other person who is lawfully in any street or other public place, nor call him by any offensive or derisive name, nor make any noise or exclamation in his presence and hearing with intent to deride, offend or annoy him, or to prevent him from pursuing his lawful business or occupation.

The complaint charged that appellant,

> with force and arms, in a certain public place in said city of Rochester, to-wit, on the public sidewalk on the easterly side of Wakefield Street, near unto the entrance of the City Hall, did unlawfully repeat the words following, addressed to the complainant, that is to say, "You are a God damned racketeer" and "a damned Fascist and the whole government of Rochester are Fascists or agents of Fascists," the same being offensive, derisive and annoying words and names.

Upon appeal, there was a trial *de novo* of appellant before a jury in the Superior Court. He was found guilty, and the judgment of conviction was affirmed by the Supreme Court of the State.

By motions and exceptions, appellant raised the questions that the statute was invalid under the Fourteenth Amendment of the Constitution of the United States in that it placed an unreasonable restraint on freedom of speech, freedom of the press, and freedom of worship, and because it was vague and indefinite. These contentions were overruled, and the case comes here on appeal.

There is no substantial dispute over the facts. Chaplinsky was distributing the literature of his sect on the streets of Rochester on a busy Saturday afternoon. Members of the local citizenry complained to the City Marshal, Bowering, that Chaplinsky was denouncing all religion as a "racket." Bowering told them that Chaplinsky was lawfully engaged, and then warned Chaplinsky that the crowd was getting restless. Some time later, a disturbance occurred and the traffic officer on duty at the busy intersection started with Chaplinsky for the police station, but did not inform him that he was under arrest or that he was going to be arrested. On the way, they encountered Marshal Bowering, who had been advised that a riot was under way and was, therefore, hurrying to the scene. Bowering repeated his earlier warning to Chaplinsky, who then addressed to Bowering the words set forth in the complaint. . . .

It is now clear that "Freedom of speech and freedom of the press, which are protected by the First Amendment from infringement by Congress, are among the fundamental personal rights and liberties which are protected by the Fourteenth Amendment from invasion by state action." *Lovell v. Griffin*, 303 U.S. 444, 450 (1938). Freedom of worship is similarly sheltered. *Cantwell v. Connecticut*, 310 U.S. 296, 303 (1940).

Appellant assails the statute as a violation of all three freedoms, speech, press and worship, but only an attack on the basis of free speech is warranted. The spoken, not the written, word is involved. And we cannot conceive that cursing a public officer is the exercise of religion in any sense of the term. But even if the activities of the appellant which preceded the incident could be viewed as religious in character, and therefore entitled to the protection of the Fourteenth Amendment, they would not cloak him with immunity from the legal consequences for concomitant acts committed in violation of a valid criminal statute. We turn, therefore, to an examination of the statute itself.

Allowing the broadest scope to the language and purpose of the Fourteenth Amendment, it is well understood that the right of free speech is not absolute at all times and under all circumstances. There are certain well defined and narrowly limited classes of speech, the prevention and punishment of which have never been thought to raise any Constitutional problem.[3] These include the lewd and obscene, the profane, the libelous, and the insulting or "fighting" words—those which, by their very utterance, inflict injury or tend to incite an immediate breach of the peace. It has been well observed that such utterances are no essential part of any exposition of ideas, and are of such slight social value as a step to truth that any benefit that may be derived from them is clearly outweighed by the social interest in order and morality. "Resort to epithets or personal abuse is not in any proper sense communication of information or opinion safeguarded by the Constitution, and its punishment as a criminal act would raise no question under that instrument." *Cantwell*, at 309–310. . . .

On the authority of its earlier decisions, the state court declared that the statute's purpose was to preserve the public peace, no words being "forbidden except such as have a direct tendency to cause acts of violence by the persons to whom, individually, the remark is addressed." It was further said:

> The word "offensive" is not to be defined in terms of what a particular addressee thinks. . . . The test is what men of common intelligence would understand would be words likely to cause an average addressee to fight. . . . The English language has a number of words and expressions which, by general consent, are "fighting words" when said without a disarming smile. . . . [S]uch words, as ordinary men know, are likely to cause a fight. So are threatening, profane or obscene revilings. Derisive and annoying words can be taken as coming within the purview of the statute as heretofore interpreted only when they have this characteristic of plainly tending to excite the addressee to a breach of the peace. . . . The statute, as construed, does no more than prohibit the face-to-face words plainly likely to cause a breach of the peace by the addressee, words whose speaking constitutes a breach of the peace by the speaker—including "classical

---

[3]   The protection of the First Amendment, mirrored in the Fourteenth, is not limited to the Blackstonian idea that freedom of the press means only freedom from restraint prior to publication. *Near v. Minnesota*, 283 U.S. 697, 714–715.

fighting words," words in current use less "classical" but equally likely to cause violence, and other disorderly words, including profanity, obscenity and threats.

We are unable to say that the limited scope of the statute as thus construed contravenes the Constitutional right of free expression. It is a statute narrowly drawn and limited to define and punish specific conduct lying within the domain of state power, the use in a public place of words likely to cause a breach of the peace. Cf. *Cantwell*, at 311; *Thornhill v. Alabama*, 310 U.S. 88, 105 (1940). This conclusion necessarily disposes of appellant's contention that the statute is so vague and indefinite as to render a conviction thereunder a violation of due process. A statute punishing verbal acts, carefully drawn so as not unduly to impair liberty of expression, is not too vague for a criminal law. Cf. *Fox v. Washington*, 236 U.S. 273, 277 (1915).

Nor can we say that the application of the statute to the facts disclosed by the record substantially or unreasonably impinges upon the privilege of free speech. Argument is unnecessary to demonstrate that the appellations "damned racketeer" and "damned Fascist" are epithets likely to provoke the average person to retaliation, and thereby cause a breach of the peace. . . .

NOTES

1.   Fighting words are "those which by their very utterance inflict injury or tend to incite an immediate breach of the peace." Are these two different theories, or only one? Does the doctrine authorize punishment of speech that "inflicts injury" on others by insulting or degrading them? Or does it only prohibit speech that might inspire a violent response? In thinking about these questions, consider recent episodes of high-profile criticism of Islam.

In 1988, British author Salman Rushdie published *The Satanic Verses*. The title alludes to the so-called Satanic Verses, verses that Mohammed supposedly proclaimed as revelation from God but later renounced as deception by Satan. The book also contains a dream sequence about a prophet named Mahound whose story resembles Mohammed's and several other elements offensive to Muslims. The book sparked outrage. Several bookstores that carried it were bombed and dozens were threatened. Ayatollah Khomeini, a Muslim leader, issued a fatwa calling for the death of Rushdie and his publishers. Later, Rushdie said, "I expected a few mullahs would be offended, call me names, and then I could defend myself in public . . . I honestly never expected anything like this." Hunter Davies, *The Real Life Salman Rushdie*, The Independent (Feb. 11, 1993).

In 2005, a Danish newspaper, the *Jyllands-Posten*, published cartoons that depicted Mohammad, including one of him wearing a bomb as a turban. The cartoons were republished in newspapers around the world. Death threats were made against the cartoonists and publishers. Violent demonstrations in predominantly Muslim countries resulted in over two hundred deaths. See Patricia Cohen, *Danish Cartoon Controversy*, N.Y. Times (Aug. 12, 2009).

In 2010, Terry Jones, the pastor of a small Florida church, announced he would burn two hundred Korans on the anniversary of the 9/11 attacks. Media coverage of his plan led to international outrage. Shortly before 9/11, Jones canceled his plan to burn the Korans, but protests in the Middle East and Asia had already resulted in over twenty deaths. In 2011, he held a "trial of the Koran," found the book guilty of "crimes against humanity," and burned a copy in his church's sanctuary. Afterwards, protestors in

Afghanistan attacked a United Nations mission, killing twelve people. See Enayat Najafizada and Rod Nordland, *Afghans Avenge Florida Koran Burning, Killing 12*, N.Y. Times (Apr. 1, 2012).

In 2012, an American of Egyptian Coptic descent uploaded to YouTube a fourteen-minute movie trailer entitled *Innocence of Muslims*. The film shows a Muslim mob attacking Egyptian Christians and has several scenes portraying Mohammad as a fraud. A two-minute clip was broadcast on Egyptian television. The clip sparked protests around the world, including attacks on the American embassy in Cairo. Administration officials blamed the film (incorrectly, as it turned out) for inspiring the attack on the diplomatic outpost in Benghazi, Libya, which killed five Americans including the ambassador, and the secretary of state reportedly assured the father of one of the murdered Americans that the filmmaker responsible for causing the attacks would be punished. The filmmaker was arrested and jailed for probation violations in connection with a prior fraud offense.

Does the speech in any of these episodes "inflict injury" by "its very utterance"? If the purpose of prohibiting "fighting words" is to keep the peace by preventing speech that might precipitate a violent reaction, do these episodes count? The Supreme Court's fighting words cases have all concerned face-to-face speech. But if one rationale for proscribing fighting words is a concern for public safety, why shouldn't mass communication of fighting words be proscribed? Are mass riots causing the murder of hundreds of innocent people less serious than outbreaks of "fisticuffs"? Does it matter if, as in the above episodes, the audience willingly exposed themselves to the speaker's message? Does it matter whether the audience reaction is reasonable? By whose lights? When are riots reasonable?

If inflammatory speech threatens a breach of the peace, should the police arrest the speaker or the hostile audience? Both? Won't speech on important topics often threaten a breach of the peace? Consider the following from *Terminiello v. Chicago*, 337 U.S. 1, 4–5 (1949):

> [A] function of free speech under our system of government is to invite dispute. It may indeed best serve its high purpose when it induces a condition of unrest, creates dissatisfaction with conditions as they are, or even stirs people to anger. Speech is often provocative and challenging. It may strike at prejudices and preconceptions and have profound unsettling effects as it presses for acceptance of an idea. That is why freedom of speech, though not absolute, is nevertheless protected against censorship or punishment, unless shown likely to produce a clear and present danger of a serious substantive evil that rises far above public inconvenience, annoyance, or unrest.

In each of the above episodes, dozens of people were killed. Should we censor speech that produces violent reactions? Speech that leads to deaths? What incentives does this create? Should the fighting words doctrine be overruled?

2.   Are there other ways in which such speech may injure? Jeremy Waldron has argued that offensive speech directed at minorities is a form of group libel that undermines the ability of minorities to participate in society. Jeremy Waldron, THE HARM IN HATE SPEECH (2012). In *Beauharnais v. Illinois*, the Supreme Court upheld a state law that criminalized defamation of a race or religion. 343 U.S. 250 (1952). Although it has never explicitly overruled *Beauharnais*, the Court struck down a similar statute in *R.A.V. v. City of St. Paul*, reasoning that the government could proscribe an entire category of unprotected speech but it could not pick favorites. 505 U.S. 377 (1992). Fighting words, the Court held, are not "entirely invisible to the Constitution" and cannot be "vehicles for

content discrimination unrelated to their distinctively proscribable content." *Id.* at 383–384.

Can the fighting words doctrine be stretched to cover speech that insults beliefs, or groups of people? In *Cohen v. California*, presented below, the Supreme Court reversed Cohen's conviction in part because his speech was not "a direct personal insult." 403 U.S. 15, 20 (1971) (reversing a breach of the peace conviction for wearing a jacket bearing the words, "Fuck the Draft"). But insulting someone's religion may be more hurtful or inflammatory than a personal insult. Cf. *Texas v. Johnson*, 491 U.S. 397, 409 (1989) (concluding that "[n]o reasonable onlooker would have regarded Johnson's [flag burning] as a direct personal insult"). Why should this matter?

Categorical Content-Based Exclusions from First Amendment Protection

The Court states that "[t]here are certain well defined and narrowly limited classes of speech, the prevention and punishment of which have never been thought to raise any Constitutional problem." Are these "classes" of unprotected speech defined historically, functionally, or in some other way? The Court has identified the following categories. This is not a comprehensive list. Is it possible to compose a comprehensive list?

1. *Fighting words.* As we have just seen, in *Chaplinsky*, the Court recognized an exclusion from the domain of protected expression for "fighting words"—words in the immediate presence of another that would constitute an immediate provocation to "fisticuffs." In cases subsequent to *Chaplinsky*, the decision is often cited, never overruled, but always distinguished. The fighting-words exception thus remains a recognized (though shrinking) categorical exception to "the freedom of" speech. Can you think of contexts where it should be applied? Doesn't this doctrine reward those who respond to speech with violence, by lending the support of the law to the censorship they desire?

2. *True threats.* True threats are not protected expression under the First Amendment. No one has the right to threaten another, whether for extortionate purpose or just to frighten them. But it is not always easy to distinguish between true threats and hateful (but protected) speech. Suppose a political activist tells a businessman that if he takes a certain action there is likely to be a riot at his place of business. Is that a true threat? Suppose someone says that anyone who supports gun rights should be shot. Is that really a threat? What if speech does not literally include a threat, but is reasonably perceived as threatening? "People like you do not belong in this neighborhood." Cross-burnings present a particularly thorny problem. In some contexts, the Court has treated them as protected speech, it has left open the possibility that burning a cross could, under some circumstances, be punishable as a threat. See *Virginia v. Black*, 538 U.S. 343 (2003).

3. *Defamation and false statements of fact.* False statements of fact, injurious to a person's reputation, traditionally have fallen outside the protection of the freedom of speech. Instead, they constitute the common law tort of libel (if in print) or slander (if made orally). Yet as we have seen, in order to provide "breathing space" to First Amendment freedoms, the Court limited the traditional defamation exception in cases involving criticism of public figures to false statements of fact made "knowingly" or in "reckless disregard" of whether they were true or not. Federal courts are divided on whether false statements of opinion are constitutionally

protected. See *Ollman v. Evans*, 750 F.2d 970 (D.C. Cir. 1984) (en banc). Scathing, offensive, *satirical* depictions, however, are not "false" statements of *fact*, and do not fit within any exception to the freedom of speech. Other countries have very stringent tort laws (by American standards) that restrict libelous speech. See Vikram David Amar & Mark V. Tushnet, GLOBAL PERSPECTIVES ON CONSTITUTIONAL LAW 228–239 (2009).

In many opinions, the Court seemed to say that false statements of fact in general are unprotected, but recently rejected that broad proposition. *United States v. Alvarez*, 132 S.Ct. 2537 (2012). A divided majority struck down the federal Stolen Valor Act, which made it illegal for anyone to falsely claim he had been awarded a medal of honor. The plurality opinion, by Justice Kennedy, stated that the Court's "prior decisions" had never recognized a categorical exception for false statements of fact. Under *Chaplinsky*, though, isn't that a historical inquiry? Should the Court have sought to determine whether false statements of fact historically enjoyed protection under American law? Justice Breyer, concurring, rejected categorical analysis and argued that the Court should examine "whether the statute works speech-related harm that is out of proportion to its justifications." The three dissenters pointed to "a long line of cases recognizing that the right to free speech does not protect false factual statements that inflict real harm and serve no legitimate interest." Why did that not satisfy *Chaplinsky*? Has the Court simply shut the door on any categorical exemption not already recognized?

False statements of fact about commercial products or services, in advertisements of those products or services, are not protected by the First Amendment. The boundaries of this doctrine are contested. In one famous case, Nike (the shoe manufacturer) defended itself against the charge that its production facilities abroad are sweat shops, and was sued under a California law on the ground that the defense contained inaccuracies. See *Nike, Inc. v. Kasky*, 539 U.S. 654 (2003). Was that commercial speech? May a drug company distribute copies of a scientific paper indicating an off-label use for its drug, if the FDA has not approved the drug for that purpose? If the drug company did so, and the FDA sought to impose punishment, would the government have to prove the scientific study is false?

4. *Commercial speech generally?* In 1942, the Court declared that there had never been protection for commercial speech—speech advertising a product or proposing a commercial transaction—whether or not the speech was "false." *Valentine v. Chrestensen*, 316 U.S. 52 (1942). Thus, governments could regulate advertising content as they saw fit. The historical basis for that holding is contested, and since 1942 the categorical exclusion of commercial speech from First Amendment protection has eroded considerably. Query: Can the government legalize the use of a harmful substance like alcohol, cigarettes, or marijuana but forbid the advertising of it?

5. *Obscenity and child pornography.* The Supreme Court has long held that "obscene" material—"sexually explicit material that violates fundamental notions of decency"—does not fall within the traditional understanding of "the freedom of" speech. *United States v. Williams*, 553 U.S. 285 (2008). But because it is not always clear what material falls on which side of the line, the Court has fashioned a test that provides limited protection even to patently offensive sexually explicit material that may have some serious literary, artistic, or scientific merit. See *id.* (collecting cases and discussing this test). In contrast, the Canadian Supreme Court has upheld

government power to prohibit pornography, broadly defined. See *R. v. Butler,* [1992] 1 S.C.R. 452 (Supreme Court of Canada). American law draws the line, though, at sexually explicit visual depictions of children—including virtually all nudity—which is one reason movies about teenagers commonly employ older actors. Moreover, the government may limit the sale of sexually explicit materials, even those falling far short of being "obscene," to minors.

6. *Crime-facilitating speech.* Although there are not many cases, it is undisputed that speech is not protected if it is used to carry out a crime. If a gang member shouted "The Supreme Court is Awesome" as a signal to confederates to attack another gang, this would not be protected. The government would not be punishing the speech because of its message. Similarly, the government may punish fraud, perjury, extortionate speech, and similar speech acts.

7. *Others?* Are there other exclusions from what is thought embraced by "the freedom of" speech? If not, should there be? And what, if anything, unites the above categorical exclusions? Is it simply the original understanding of the term "the freedom of speech"?

Brown v. Entertainment Merchants Association
564 U.S. 786 (2011)

■ Justice Scalia delivered the opinion of the Court.

We consider whether a California law imposing restrictions on violent video games comports with the First Amendment.

I

California Assembly Bill 1179 (2005), prohibits the sale or rental of "violent video games" to minors, and requires their packaging to be labeled "18." The Act covers games "in which the range of options available to a player includes killing, maiming, dismembering, or sexually assaulting an image of a human being, if those acts are depicted" in a manner that "[a] reasonable person, considering the game as a whole, would find appeals to a deviant or morbid interest of minors," that is "patently offensive to prevailing standards in the community as to what is suitable for minors," and that "causes the game, as a whole, to lack serious literary, artistic, political, or scientific value for minors." § 1746(d)(1)(A). Violation of the Act is punishable by a civil fine of up to $1,000. § 1746.3.

Respondents, representing the video-game and software industries, brought a preenforcement challenge to the Act in the United States District Court for the Northern District of California. That court concluded that the Act violated the First Amendment and permanently enjoined its enforcement. The Court of Appeals affirmed, and we granted certiorari.

II

California correctly acknowledges that video games qualify for First Amendment protection. The Free Speech Clause exists principally to protect discourse on public matters, but we have long recognized that it is difficult to distinguish politics from entertainment, and dangerous to try. "Everyone is familiar with instances of propaganda through fiction. What is one man's amusement, teaches another's doctrine." *Winters v. New York,* 333 U.S. 507, 510 (1948). Like the protected books, plays, and movies that preceded them, video games communicate ideas—and even social messages—through many familiar literary devices (such as characters, dialogue, plot, and music) and through features distinctive to the medium (such as the player's interaction with the virtual world). That suffices to confer First Amendment protection. . . . And whatever the challenges of applying the Constitution to ever-advancing technology, "the basic principles of freedom of speech and the press, like the First Amendment's command, do not vary" when a new and different medium for communication appears. *Joseph Burstyn, Inc. v. Wilson*, 343 U.S. 495, 503 (1952).

The most basic of those principles is this: "[A]s a general matter, . . . government has no power to restrict expression because of its message, its ideas, its subject matter, or its content." *Ashcroft v. American Civil Liberties Union*, 535 U.S. 564, 573 (2002). There are of course exceptions. "From 1791 to the present, . . . the First Amendment has permitted restrictions upon the content of speech in a few limited areas, and has never include[d] a freedom to disregard these traditional limitations." *United States v. Stevens*, 559 U.S. 460, 468 (2010). These limited areas—such as obscenity, *Roth v. United States*, 354 U S. 476, 483 (1957), incitement, *Brandenburg v. Ohio*, 395 U.S. 444, 447–449 (1969) (*per curiam*), and fighting words, *Chaplinsky v. New Hampshire*, 315 U.S. 568, 572 (1942)—represent "well-defined and narrowly limited classes of speech, the prevention and punishment of which have never been thought to raise any Constitutional problem," *id.*, at 571–572.

Last Term, in *Stevens*, we held that new categories of unprotected speech may not be added to the list by a legislature that concludes certain speech is too harmful to be tolerated. *Stevens* concerned a federal statute purporting to criminalize the creation, sale, or possession of certain depictions of animal cruelty. See 18 U.S.C. § 48 (amended 2010). The statute covered depictions "in which a living animal is intentionally maimed, mutilated, tortured, wounded, or killed" if that harm to the animal was illegal where the "the creation, sale, or possession t[ook] place," § 48(c)(1). . . . We held that statute to be an impermissible content-based restriction on speech. There was no American tradition of forbidding the *depiction of* animal cruelty—though States have long had laws against *committing* it.

The Government argued in *Stevens* that lack of a historical warrant did not matter; that it could create new categories of unprotected speech by applying a "simple balancing test" that weighs the value of a particular category of speech against its social costs and then punishes that category of speech if it fails the test. We emphatically rejected that "startling and dangerous" proposition. "Maybe there are some categories of speech that have been historically unprotected, but have not yet been specifically identified or discussed as such in our case law." But without persuasive evidence that a novel restriction on content is part of a long (if heretofore unrecognized) tradition of proscription, a legislature may not revise the "judgment [of] the American people," embodied in the First Amendment, "that the benefits of its restrictions on the Government outweigh the costs."

That holding controls this case. As in *Stevens*, California has tried to make violent-speech regulation look like obscenity regulation by appending a saving clause required for the latter. That does not suffice. Our cases have been clear that the obscenity exception to the First Amendment does not cover whatever a legislature finds shocking, but only depictions of "sexual conduct," *Miller v. California*, 413 U.S. 15, 24 (1973). . . .

Because speech about violence is not obscene, it is of no consequence that California's statute mimics the New York statute regulating obscenity-for-minors that we upheld in *Ginsberg v. New York*, 390 U.S. 629 (1968). That case approved a prohibition on the sale to minors of *sexual* material that would be obscene from the perspective of a child. We held that the legislature could "adjus[t] the definition of obscenity to social realities by permitting the appeal of this type of material to be assessed in terms of the sexual interests . . . of . . . minors." And because "obscenity is not protected expression," the New York statute could be sustained so long as the legislature's judgment that the proscribed materials were harmful to children "was not irrational." 390 U.S., at 641.

The California Act is something else entirely. It does not adjust the boundaries of an existing category of unprotected speech to ensure that a definition designed for adults is not uncritically applied to children. California does not argue that it is empowered to prohibit selling offensively violent works *to adults*—and it is wise not to, since that is but a hair's breadth from the argument rejected in *Stevens*. Instead, it wishes to create a wholly new category of content-based regulation that is permissible only for speech directed at children.

That is unprecedented and mistaken. "[M]inors are entitled to a significant measure of First Amendment protection, and only in relatively narrow and well-defined circumstances may government bar public dissemination of protected materials to them." *Erznoznik v. Jacksonville*, 422 U.S. 205, 212–213 (1975). No doubt a State possesses legitimate power to protect children from harm, *Ginsberg*, at 640–641; *Prince v. Massachusetts*, 321 U.S. 158, 165 (1944), but that does not include a free-floating power to restrict the ideas to which children may be exposed. "Speech that is neither obscene as to youths nor subject to some other legitimate proscription cannot be suppressed solely to protect the young from ideas or images that a legislative body thinks unsuitable for them." *Erznoznik*, at 213–214.

California's argument would fare better if there were a longstanding tradition in this country of specially restricting children's access to depictions of violence, but there is none. Certainly the *books* we give children to read—or read to them when they are younger—contain no shortage of gore. Grimm's Fairy Tales, for example, are grim indeed. As her just deserts for trying to poison Snow White, the wicked queen is made to dance in red hot slippers "till she fell dead on the floor, a sad example of envy and jealousy." The Complete Brothers Grimm Fairy Tales 198 (2006 ed.). Cinderella's evil stepsisters have their eyes pecked out by doves. And Hansel and Gretel (children!) kill their captor by baking her in an oven.

High-school reading lists are full of similar fare. Homer's Odysseus blinds Polyphemus the Cyclops by grinding out his eye with a heated stake. In the Inferno, Dante and Virgil watch corrupt politicians struggle to stay submerged beneath a lake of boiling pitch, lest they be skewered by devils above the surface. And Golding's Lord of the Flies recounts how a schoolboy called Piggy is savagely murdered *by other children* while marooned on an island.

This is not to say that minors' consumption of violent entertainment has never encountered resistance. In the 1800's, dime novels depicting crime and "penny dreadfuls" (named for their price and content) were blamed in some quarters for juvenile delinquency. When motion pictures came along, they became the villains instead. "The days when the police looked upon dime novels as the most dangerous of textbooks in the school for crime are drawing to a close. . . . They say that the moving picture machine . . . tends even more than did the dime novel to turn the thoughts of the easily influenced to paths which sometimes lead to prison." For a time, our Court did permit broad censorship of movies because of their capacity to be "used for evil," see *Mutual Film Corp. v. Industrial Comm'n of Ohio*, 236 U.S. 230, 242 (1915), but we eventually reversed course, *Joseph Burstyn, Inc.*, at 502; see also *Erznoznik*, at 212–214 (invalidating a drive-in movies restriction designed to protect children). Radio dramas were next, and then came comic books. Many in the late 1940's and early 1950's blamed comic books for fostering a "preoccupation with violence and horror" among the young, leading to a rising juvenile crime rate. See Note, Regulation of Comic Books, 68 Harv. L. Rev. 489, 490 (1955). But efforts to convince Congress to restrict comic books failed. And, of course, after comic books came television and music lyrics.

California claims that video games present special problems because they are "interactive," in that the player participates in the violent action on screen and determines its outcome. The latter feature is nothing new: Since at least the publication of The Adventures of You: Sugarcane Island in 1969, young readers of choose-your-own-adventure stories have been able to make decisions that determine the plot by following instructions about which page to turn to. Cf. *Interactive Digital Software Assn. v. St. Louis County*, 329 F.3d 954, 957–958 (CA8 2003). As for the argument that video games enable participation in the violent action, that seems to us more a matter of degree than of kind. As Judge Posner has observed, all literature is interactive. "[T]he better it is, the more interactive. Literature when it is successful draws the reader into the story, makes him identify with the characters, invites him to judge them and quarrel with them, to experience their joys and sufferings as the reader's own." *American Amusement Machine Assn. v. Kendrick*, 244 F.3d 572, 577 (CA7 2001) (striking down a similar restriction on violent video games).

JUSTICE ALITO has done considerable independent research to identify video games in which "the violence is astounding." "Victims are dismembered, decapitated, disemboweled, set on fire, and chopped into little pieces. . . . Blood gushes, splatters, and pools." JUSTICE ALITO recounts all these disgusting video games in order to disgust us—but disgust is not a valid basis for restricting expression. And the same is true of JUSTICE ALITO's description of those video games he has discovered that have a racial or ethnic motive for their violence—"ethnic cleansing [of] . . . African Americans, Latinos, or Jews." To what end does he relate this? Does it somehow increase the "aggressiveness" that California wishes to suppress? Who knows? But it does arouse the reader's ire, and the reader's desire to put an end to this horrible message. Thus, ironically, JUSTICE ALITO's argument highlights the precise danger posed by the California Act: that the *ideas* expressed by speech—whether it be violence, or gore, or racism—and not its objective effects, may be the real reason for governmental proscription.

III

Because the Act imposes a restriction on the content of protected speech, it is invalid unless California can demonstrate that it passes strict scrutiny—that is, unless it is justified by a compelling government interest and is narrowly drawn to serve that interest. The State must specifically identify an "actual problem" in need of solving, and the curtailment of free speech must be actually necessary to the solution. That is a demanding standard. "It is rare that a regulation restricting speech because of its content will ever be permissible." *United States v. Playboy Entertainment Group, Inc.*, 529 U.S. 803, 818 (2000).

California cannot meet that standard. . . . California relies primarily on the research of Dr. Craig Anderson and a few other research psychologists whose studies purport to show a connection between exposure to violent video games and harmful effects on children. These studies have been rejected by every court to consider them, and with good reason: They do not prove that violent video games *cause* minors to *act* aggressively (which would at least be a beginning). Instead, "[n]early all of the research is based on correlation, not evidence of causation, and most of the studies suffer from significant, admitted flaws in methodology." *Video Software Dealers Assn.*, at 964. They show at best some correlation between exposure to violent entertainment and minuscule real-world effects, such as children's feeling more aggressive or making louder noises in the few minutes after playing a violent game than after playing a nonviolent game. . . .

The Act is also seriously underinclusive in another respect—and a respect that renders irrelevant the contentions of the concurrence and the dissents that video games are qualitatively different from other portrayals of violence. The California Legislature is perfectly willing to leave this dangerous, mind-altering material in the hands of children so long as one parent (or even an aunt or uncle) says it's OK. And there are not even any requirements as to how this parental or avuncular relationship is to be verified; apparently the child's or putative parent's, aunt's, or uncle's say-so suffices. That is not how one addresses a serious social problem.

California claims that the Act is justified in aid of parental authority: By requiring that the purchase of violent video games can be made only by adults, the Act ensures that parents can decide what games are appropriate. At the outset, we note our doubts that punishing third parties for conveying protected speech to children *just in case* their parents disapprove of that speech is a proper governmental means of aiding parental authority. Accepting that position would largely vitiate the rule that "only in relatively narrow and well-defined circumstances may government bar public dissemination of protected materials to [minors]." *Erznoznik*, at 212–213.

But leaving that aside, California cannot show that the Act's restrictions meet a substantial need of parents who wish to restrict their children's access to violent video games but cannot do so. The video-game industry has in place a voluntary rating system designed to inform consumers about the content of games. . . . This system does much to ensure that minors cannot purchase seriously violent games on their own, and that parents who care about the matter can readily evaluate the games their children bring home. Filling the remaining modest gap in concerned-parents' control can hardly be a compelling state interest.

And finally, the Act's purported aid to parental authority is vastly overinclusive. Not all of the children who are forbidden to purchase violent video games on their own have parents who *care* whether they purchase violent video games. While some of the legislation's effect may indeed be in support of what some parents of the restricted children actually want, its entire effect is only in support of what the State thinks parents *ought* to want. This is not the narrow tailoring to "assisting parents" that restriction of First Amendment rights requires. . . .

■ JUSTICE ALITO, with whom THE CHIEF JUSTICE joins, concurring in the judgment.

The California statute that is before us in this case represents a pioneering effort to address what the state legislature and others regard as a potentially serious social problem: the effect of exceptionally violent video games on impressionable minors, who often spend countless hours immersed in the alternative worlds that these games create. Although the California statute is well intentioned, its terms are not framed with the precision that the Constitution demands, and I therefore agree with the Court that this particular law cannot be sustained.

I disagree, however, with the approach taken in the Court's opinion. In considering the application of unchanging constitutional principles to new and rapidly evolving technology, this Court should proceed with caution. We should make every effort to understand the new technology. We should take into account the possibility that developing technology may have important societal implications that will become apparent only with time. We should not jump to the conclusion that new technology is fundamentally the same as some older thing with which we are familiar. And we should not hastily dismiss the judgment of legislators, who may be in a better position than we are to assess the implications of new technology. The opinion of the Court exhibits none of this caution.

In the view of the Court, all those concerned about the effects of violent video games—federal and state legislators, educators, social scientists, and parents—are unduly fearful, for violent video games really present no serious problem. Spending hour upon hour controlling the actions of a character who guns down scores of innocent victims is not different in "kind" from reading a description of violence in a work of literature.

The Court is sure of this; I am not. There are reasons to suspect that the experience of playing violent video games just might be very different from reading a book, listening to the radio, or watching a movie or a television show.

I

[Justice Alito argued that the statute's definition of "violent video game" was unconstitutionally vague and that there was thus "no need to reach the broader First Amendment issues addressed by the Court."—Editors]

II

Having outlined how I would decide this case, I will now briefly elaborate on my reasons for questioning the wisdom of the Court's approach. . . .

A

The Court is wrong in saying that the holding in *Stevens* "controls this case." . . . The portion of *Stevens* on which the Court relies rejected the Government's contention that depictions of animal cruelty were categorically outside the range of *any* First Amendment protection. Going well beyond *Stevens*, the Court now holds that any law that attempts to prevent minors from purchasing violent video games must satisfy strict scrutiny instead of the more lenient standard applied in *Ginsberg*, our most closely related precedent. As a result of today's decision, a State may prohibit the sale to minors of what *Ginsberg* described as "girlie magazines," but a State must surmount a formidable (and perhaps insurmountable) obstacle if it wishes to prevent children from purchasing the most violent and depraved video games imaginable.

... *Stevens* expressly left open the possibility that a more narrowly drawn statute targeting depictions of animal cruelty might be compatible with the First Amendment. In this case, the Court's sweeping opinion will likely be read by many, both inside and outside the video-game industry, as suggesting that no regulation of minors' access to violent video games is allowed—at least without supporting evidence that may not be realistically obtainable given the nature of the phenomenon in question.

B

The Court's opinion distorts the effect of the California law. I certainly agree with the Court that the government has no "free-floating power to restrict the ideas to which children may be exposed," but the California law does not exercise such a power. If parents want their child to have a violent video game, the California law does not interfere with that parental prerogative. Instead, the California law reinforces parental decisionmaking in exactly the same way as the New York statute upheld in *Ginsberg*. Under both laws, minors are prevented from purchasing certain materials; and under both laws, parents are free to supply their children with these items if that is their wish.

Citing the video-game industry's voluntary rating system, the Court argues that the California law does not "meet a substantial need of parents who wish to restrict their children's access to violent video games but cannot do so." The Court does not mention the fact that the industry adopted this system in response to the threat of federal regulation, a threat that the Court's opinion may now be seen as largely eliminating. Nor does the Court acknowledge that compliance with this system at the time of the enactment of the California law left much to be desired—or that future enforcement may decline if the video-game industry perceives that any threat of government regulation has vanished. Nor does the Court note, as JUSTICE BREYER points out, that many parents today are simply not able to monitor their children's use of computers and gaming devices.

C

Finally, the Court is far too quick to dismiss the possibility that the experience of playing video games (and the effects on minors of playing violent video games) may be very different from anything that we have seen before. Any assessment of the experience of playing video games must take into account certain characteristics of the video games that are now on the market and those that are likely to be available in the near future.

Today's most advanced video games create realistic alternative worlds in which millions of players immerse themselves for hours on end. These games feature visual imagery and sounds that are strikingly realistic, and in the near future video-game graphics may be virtually indistinguishable from actual video footage. . . .

Persons who play video games also have an unprecedented ability to participate in the events that take place in the virtual worlds that these games create. Players can create their own video-game characters and can use photos to produce characters that closely resemble actual people. A person playing a sophisticated game can make a multitude of choices and can thereby alter the course of the action in the game. In addition, the means by which players control the action in video games now bear a closer relationship to the means by which people control action in the real world. While the action in older games was often directed with buttons or a joystick, players dictate the action in newer games by engaging in the same motions that they desire a character in the game to perform. For example, a player who wants a video-game character to swing a baseball bat—either to hit a ball or smash a skull—could bring that about by simulating the motion of actually swinging a bat.

These present-day and emerging characteristics of video games must be considered together with characteristics of the violent games that have already been marketed.

In some of these games, the violence is astounding. Victims by the dozens are killed with every imaginable implement, including machine guns, shotguns, clubs, hammers, axes, swords, and chainsaws. Victims are dismembered, decapitated, disemboweled, set on fire, and chopped into little pieces. They cry out in agony and beg for mercy. Blood gushes, splatters, and pools. Severed body parts and gobs of human remains are graphically shown. In some games, points are awarded based, not only on the number of victims killed, but on the killing technique employed.

It also appears that there is no antisocial theme too base for some in the video-game industry to exploit. There are games in which a player can take on the identity and reenact the killings carried out by the perpetrators of the murders at Columbine High School and Virginia Tech. The objective of one game is to rape a mother and her daughters; in another, the goal is to rape Native American women. There is a game in which players engage in "ethnic cleansing" and can choose to gun down African-Americans, Latinos, or Jews. In still another game, players attempt to fire a rifle shot into the head of President Kennedy as his motorcade passes by the Texas School Book Depository.

If the technological characteristics of the sophisticated games that are likely to be available in the near future are combined with the characteristics of the most violent games already marketed, the result will be games that allow troubled teens to experience in an extraordinarily personal and vivid way what it would be like to carry out unspeakable acts of violence.

The Court is untroubled by this possibility. According to the Court, the "interactive" nature of video games is "nothing new" because "all literature is interactive." Disagreeing with this assessment, the International Game Developers Association (IGDA)—a group that presumably understands the nature of video games and that supports respondents—tells us that video games are "far more concretely interactive." Brief for IGDA et al. as *Amici Curiae* 3. And on this point, the game developers are surely correct. . . .

When all of the characteristics of video games are taken into account, there is certainly a reasonable basis for thinking that the experience of playing a video game may be quite different from the experience of reading a book, listening to a radio broadcast, or viewing a movie. And if this is so, then for at least some minors, the effects of playing violent video games may also be quite different. The Court acts prematurely in dismissing this possibility out of hand. . . .

For all these reasons, I would hold only that the particular law at issue here fails to provide the clear notice that the Constitution requires. I would not squelch legislative efforts to deal with what is perceived by some to be a significant and developing social problem. If differently framed statutes are enacted by the States or by the Federal Government, we can consider the constitutionality of those laws when cases challenging them are presented to us.

■ JUSTICE THOMAS, dissenting.

The Court's decision today does not comport with the original public understanding of the First Amendment. . . . The practices and beliefs of the founding generation establish that "the freedom of speech," as originally understood, does not include a right to speak to minors (or a right of minors to access speech) without going through the minors' parents or guardians.

[Justice Thomas performed a detailed historical analysis of colonial attitudes to childrearing and concludes: "The history clearly shows a founding generation that believed parents to have complete authority over their minor children and expected parents to direct the development of those children."—Editors]

■ JUSTICE BREYER, dissenting.

. . . A facial challenge to this statute based on the First Amendment can succeed only if "a substantial number of its applications are unconstitutional, judged in relation to the statute's plainly legitimate sweep." Moreover, it is more difficult to mount a facial First Amendment attack on a statute that seeks to regulate activity that involves action as well as speech. Hence, I shall focus here upon an area within which I believe the State can legitimately apply its statute, namely sales to minors under the age of 17 (the age cutoff used by the industry's own ratings system), of highly realistic violent video games, which a reasonable game maker would know meet the Act's criteria. That area lies at the heart of the statute. I shall assume that the number of instances in which the State will enforce the statute within that area is comparatively large, and that the number outside that area (for example, sales to 17-year-olds) is comparatively small. And the activity the statute regulates combines speech with action (a virtual form of target practice).

In determining whether the statute is unconstitutional, I would apply both this Court's "vagueness" precedents and a strict form of First Amendment scrutiny. In doing so, the special First Amendment category I find relevant is not (as the Court claims) the category of "depictions of violence," but rather the category of "protection of children." This Court has held that the "power of the state to control the conduct of children reaches beyond the scope of its authority over adults." *Prince v. Massachusetts*, at 170. And the "regulatio[n] of communication addressed to [children] need not conform to the requirements of the [F]irst [A]mendment in the same way as those applicable to adults." *Ginsberg*, at 638, n. 6 (quoting Emerson, *Toward a General Theory of the First Amendment*, 72 Yale L.J. 877, 939 (1963)).

The majority's claim that the California statute, if upheld, would create a "new categor[y] of unprotected speech," is overstated. No one here argues that depictions of violence, even extreme violence, *automatically* fall outside the First Amendment's protective scope as, for example, do obscenity and depictions of child pornography. We properly speak of *categories* of expression that lack protection when, like "child pornography," the category is broad, when it applies automatically, and when the State can prohibit everyone, including adults, from obtaining access to the material within it. But where, as here, careful analysis must precede a narrower judicial conclusion (say, denying protection to a shout of "fire" in a crowded theater, or to an effort to teach a terrorist group how to peacefully petition the United Nations), we do not normally describe the result as creating a "new category of unprotected speech."

Thus, in *Stevens*, after rejecting the claim that *all* depictions of animal cruelty (a category) fall outside the First Amendment's protective scope, we went on to decide whether the particular statute at issue violates the First Amendment under traditional standards; and we held that, because the statute was overly broad, it was invalid. Similarly, here the issue is whether, applying traditional First Amendment standards, this statute does, or does not, pass muster.

II

[Justice Breyer argued that the statute was not unconstitutionally vague.—Editors]

III

Video games combine physical action with expression. Were physical activity to predominate in a game, government could appropriately intervene, say by requiring parents to accompany children when playing a game involving actual target practice, or restricting the sale of toys presenting physical dangers to children. But because video games also embody important expressive and artistic elements, I agree with the Court that the First Amendment significantly limits the State's power to regulate. And I would determine whether the State has exceeded those limits by applying a strict standard of review.

Like the majority, I believe that the California law must be "narrowly tailored" to further a "compelling interest," without there being a "less restrictive" alternative that would be "at least as effective." *Reno v. American Civil Liberties Union*, 521 U.S. 844, 874, 875, 879 (1997). I would not apply this strict standard "mechanically." Rather, in applying it, I would evaluate the degree to which the statute injures speech-related interests, the nature of the potentially-justifying "compelling interests," the degree to which the statute furthers that interest, the nature and effectiveness of possible alternatives, and, in light of this evaluation, whether, overall, "the statute works speech-related harm . . . out of proportion to the benefits that the statute seeks to provide."

First Amendment standards applied in this way are difficult but not impossible to satisfy. . . . *[Justice Breyer next described cases in which restrictions on speech were upheld under strict scrutiny.—Editors]*

B

The interest that California advances in support of the statute is compelling. As this Court has previously described that interest, it consists of both (1) the "basic" parental claim "to authority in their own household to direct the rearing of their children," which makes it proper to enact "laws designed to aid discharge of [parental] responsibility," and (2) the State's "independent interest in the well-being of its youth." *Ginsberg*, at 639–640. And where these interests work in tandem, it is not fatally "underinclusive" for a State to advance its interests in protecting children against the special harms present in an interactive video game medium through a default rule that still allows parents to provide their children with what their parents wish.

Both interests are present here. As to the need to help parents guide their children, the Court noted in 1968 that "parental control or guidance cannot always be provided." 390 U.S., at 640. Today, 5.3 million grade-school-age children of working parents are routinely home alone. . . . Thus, it has, if anything, become more important to supplement parents' authority to guide their children's development.

As to the State's independent interest, we have pointed out that juveniles are more likely to show a "lack of maturity" and are "more vulnerable or susceptible to negative influences and outside pressures," and that their "character . . . is not as well formed as that of an adult." *Roper v. Simmons*, 543 U.S. 551, 569–570 (2005). And we have therefore recognized "a compelling interest in protecting the physical and psychological well-being of minors." *Sable Communications*, at 126.

At the same time, there is considerable evidence that California's statute significantly furthers this compelling interest. That is, in part, because video games are excellent teaching tools. Learning a practical task often means developing habits, becoming accustomed to performing the task, and receiving positive reinforcement when performing that task well. Video games can help develop habits, accustom the player to performance of the task, and reward the player for performing that task well. Why else would the Armed Forces incorporate video games into its training? . . .

There are many scientific studies that support California's views. Social scientists, for example, have found *causal* evidence that playing these games results in harm. Longitudinal studies, which measure changes over time, have found that increased exposure to violent video games causes an increase in aggression over the same period. . . .

And "meta-analyses," *i.e.*, studies of all the studies, have concluded that exposure to violent video games "was positively associated with aggressive behavior, aggressive cognition, and aggressive affect," and that "playing violent video games is a *causal* risk factor for long-term harmful outcomes." . . .

Some of these studies take care to explain in a common-sense way why video games are potentially more harmful than, say, films or books or television. In essence, they say that the closer a child's behavior comes, not to watching, but to *acting* out horrific violence, the greater the potential psychological harm. . . .

Experts debate the conclusions of all these studies. Like many, perhaps most, studies of human behavior, each study has its critics, and some of those critics have produced studies of their own in which they reach different conclusions. (I list both sets of research in the appendixes.) I, like most judges, lack the social science expertise to say definitively who is right. But associations of public health professionals who do possess that expertise have reviewed many of these studies and found a significant risk that violent video games, when compared with more passive media, are particularly likely to cause children harm. . . .

Unlike the majority, I would find sufficient grounds in these studies and expert opinions for this Court to defer to an elected legislature's conclusion that the video games in question are particularly likely to harm children. This Court has always thought it owed an elected legislature some degree of deference in respect to legislative facts of this kind, particularly when they involve technical matters that are beyond our competence, and even in First Amendment cases. The majority, in reaching its own, opposite conclusion about the validity of the relevant studies, grants the legislature no deference at all. . . .

The industry also argues for an alternative technological solution, namely "filtering at the console level." But it takes only a quick search of the Internet to find guides explaining how to circumvent any such technological controls. . . .

IV

. . . I add that the majority's different conclusion creates a serious anomaly in First Amendment law. *Ginsberg* makes clear that a State can prohibit the sale to minors of depictions of nudity; today the Court makes clear that a State cannot prohibit the sale to minors of the most violent interactive video games. But what sense does it make to forbid selling to a 13-year-old boy a magazine with an image of a nude woman, while protecting a sale to that 13-year-old of an interactive video game in which he actively, but virtually, binds and gags the woman, then tortures and kills her? What kind of First Amendment would permit the government to protect children by restricting sales of that extremely violent video game *only* when the woman—bound, gagged, tortured, and killed—is also topless?

This anomaly is not compelled by the First Amendment. It disappears once one recognizes that extreme violence, where interactive, and *without literary, artistic, or similar justification*, can prove at least as, if not more, harmful to children as photographs of nudity. And the record here is more than adequate to support such a view. That is why I believe that *Ginsberg* controls the outcome here *a fortiori*. And it is why I believe California's law is constitutional on its face.

This case is ultimately less about censorship than it is about education. Our Constitution cannot succeed in securing the liberties it seeks to protect unless we can raise future generations committed cooperatively to making our system of government work. Education, however, is about choices. Sometimes, children need to learn by making choices for themselves. Other times, choices are made for children—by their parents, by their teachers, and by the people acting democratically through their governments. In my view, the First Amendment does not disable government from helping parents make such a choice here—a choice not to have their children buy extremely violent, interactive video games, which they more than reasonably fear pose only the risk of harm to those children.

NOTES

1.   Does *Brown*, together with *Stevens* (the animal cruelty-depiction case discussed in *Brown*) sound the death knell for the categorical approach? Can any "class" of speech ever be added to the list of unprotected categories? What evidence would it take? Does this mean that any new form of content-based regulation of speech will have to satisfy strict scrutiny? You should read Justice Breyer's dissent carefully to appreciate just how strictly the majority interpreted strict scrutiny.

2.   Are you persuaded by the majority's reasoning? Consider the following:

a.   What is the Court's theory about what constitutional rights fully apply to minors? Do they have the right to bear arms, to own property, to marry, to vote, to enter into contracts, to avoid coercive indoctrination (in the form of public education)? Any idea why this case is about their rights, as opposed to whether profit-making corporations have a right to direct speech *to them*? Is it true that speech directed to minors is fully protected, and subject to strict scrutiny? The Court cites *Erznoznik v. City of Jacksonville* for this proposition, but *Erznoznik* involved an ordinance, a prohibition of nudity in drive-in movies, that was directed to everyone. It is well established that the government may not censor speech for everyone on the ground that there might be minors in the audience. Moreover, the *Erznoznik* Court stated in a footnote:

> The First Amendment rights of minors are not "co-extensive with those of adults." *Tinker v. Des Moines School Dist.*, 393 U.S. 503, 515 (1969) (STEWART, J., concurring). "[A] State may permissibly determine that, at least in some precisely delineated areas, a child—like someone in a captive audience—is not possessed of that full capacity for individual choice which is the presupposition of First Amendment guarantees." *Ginsberg v. New York*, 390 U.S. 629, 649–650 (1968) (STEWART, J., concurring). In assessing whether a minor has the requisite capacity for individual choice the age of the minor is a significant factor.

Isn't that what California thought it was doing?

The Court recounts a series of attempts through American history to censor materials thought harmful to minors, from dime novels to movies, radio dramas, comic books, television, music lyrics. Obviously the majority regards these efforts as having been wrong-headed. But do they not point to a "tradition"—albeit one the majority disapproves of—"of specifically restricting children's access to materials" thought harmful?

b.   Is exposure to extreme violence any less harmful to children than exposure to depictions of nudity? In *Ginsberg*, cited in *Brown*, the Court upheld a prosecution for the sale to a 16-year-old boy of what it described as a "girlie magazine," based on the Court's judgment that it was "rational for the legislature to find that the minors' exposure to such material might be harmful." Why is exposure to extreme violence so very different? The Court cites examples of violent material, such as Snow White, the Odyssey, and the Inferno, to which minors are exposed, suggesting that the extremely violent video games are similar in kind. Presumably one could have made the same argument about nudity, pointing to Botticelli's Venus, Michelangelo's David, *Schindler's List*, and a sex education textbook. Children are often exposed to depictions of nudity, just as they are to violence— just not to particular kinds of depictions of nudity (those without redeeming social value) and particular kinds of violence. What do these examples prove?

c.   The Court is surely right that violent video games involve speech—messages disseminated by the producers of the games to the gamers. But don't they also involve significant elements of conduct by the gamer—such things as murdering people, raping women, cutting off heads, and torturing victims? Is it crazy to think that engaging in such conduct for hours on end in the fictional world of video games might habituate a young person to such conduct in reality? Should the Court have analyzed the case as one that involved pure speech, rather than speech mixed with conduct?

d.   What do you make of the disagreement between the majority and Justice Breyer over the social science evidence? How should judges—who are usually not trained in the methods of empirical social science—treat this kind of evidence?

e.   The majority observed that voluntary industry codes provide sufficient protection. But what if those codes were adopted to forestall legislation? Can the industry now repeal those codes, confident that any legislative attempt to replace them will be struck down?

3.   It is interesting to compare the two dissents, by Justices Thomas and Breyer. Thomas relies on history; Breyer relies on social science. Which offers the more persuasive reading of the Constitution?

4.   For several decades after *Chaplinsky*, the Court's principal approach to interpretation of the First Amendment was to carve out specific, content-based exclusions based on some combination of history (usually without much historical research) and intuition. That approach seems to have come to an end. Now the Court applies strict scrutiny to content-based speech regulation, and lesser scrutiny to speech regulation that is not content-based. As you read the modern cases, you should ask yourself: Is the new approach an improvement? Despite its new approach, the Court has not overruled the old categorical cases. The list has simply been frozen, like an insect in amber, leading to an odd jurisprudence where some regulation based on content is allowed with little or no scrutiny, and other regulation based on content is subject to strict (and if *Brown* is any indication, extremely strict) scrutiny. Is there any logic to this—historical, pragmatic, utilitarian, or otherwise?

5.   If "it is difficult to distinguish politics from entertainment, and dangerous to try," as the majority says, do all the doctrines extending protection to speech on "matters of public concern" now apply across the board, even to speech that is merely entertaining?

[Assignment 45]

E.   CONTENT-BASED AND CONTENT-NEUTRAL RESTRICTIONS

As we see in *Brown* and *Stevens*, the Court has slammed the door on the creation of any new content-based categorical exceptions, though it is theoretically possible the Court may recognize a historically-grounded exception that has always existed but has not featured in a Court case. Instead, the modern approach is to apply strict scrutiny to any law that restricts speech on the basis of its content (unless it falls within a recognized content-based categorical exception, such as fighting words or obscenity), and various degrees of lesser scrutiny to laws restricting speech on the basis of time, place and manner, or other content-neutral criteria. Restrictions on the basis of speaker identity are an important and unsettled example of the latter.

The classic case of content-discriminatory laws is *Police Dep't of Chicago v. Mosley*, 408 U.S. 92 (1972). It involved a Chicago ordinance forbidding picketing and demonstrations within 150 feet of a school, except in the case of a labor dispute. The exception rendered the ordinance content-discriminatory. The Court held the ordinance unconstitutional; the question was not whether the school district might have a legitimate (even compelling) basis for forbidding demonstrations close to schools, but whether it had such a basis for forbidding some demonstrations and not others. "The central problem with Chicago's ordinance," the Court explained, "is that it describes permissible picketing in terms of its subject matter." Note that content-based *underinclusion*, like that in *Mosley*, has constitutional significance in two different respects. First, the content-based character of the restriction determines the standard of review, namely strict scrutiny. Second, the government's failure to apply the restriction across the board suggests that the restriction does not serve a compelling governmental interest. If preventing noisy and distracting demonstrations outside of schools is important enough to criminalize speech, why are labor demonstrations permitted?

The *Mosley* holding is now a staple of First Amendment doctrine. See Geoffrey R. Stone, *Restrictions of Speech Because of its Content: The Peculiar Case of Subject-Matter Restrictions*, 46 U. Chi. L. Rev. 81 (1978). Recall that in *Brown*, the Court majority stated that the "most basic" of First Amendment principles is this: "[A]s a general matter, . . . government has no power to restrict expression because of its message, its ideas, its subject matter, or its content."

The Court recently synthesized its decisions on content-neutrality in *Reed v. Town of Gilbert*, 135 S.Ct. 2218 (2015). In this case, applying strict scrutiny, the Court struck down an ordinance regulating the size and duration of placement of outdoor signs, with different rules application to "temporary directional signs" and others. In doing so, the Court held that benign motives are not enough to save a content-based restriction:

> A law that is content based on its face is subject to strict scrutiny regardless of the government's benign motive, content-neutral justification, or lack of "animus toward the ideas contained" in the regulated speech. *Cincinnati v. Discovery Network, Inc.*, 507 U.S. 410, 429 (1993). We have thus made clear that "[i]llicit legislative intent is not the *sine qua non* of a violation of the First Amendment," and a party opposing the government "need adduce no evidence of an improper censorial motive." *Simon & Schuster v. Members of New York State Crime Victims Bd.*, 502 U.S. 105, 117 (1991). Although "a content-based purpose may be sufficient in certain circumstances to show that a regulation is content based, it is not necessary." *Turner Broadcasting System, Inc. v. FCC*, 512 U.S. 622, 642 (1994). In other words, an innocuous justification cannot transform a facially content-based law into one that is content neutral. . . .

> The First Amendment requires no less. Innocent motives do not eliminate the danger of censorship presented by a facially content-based statute, as future government officials may one day wield such statutes to suppress disfavored speech. That is why the First Amendment expressly targets the operation of the laws—i.e., the "abridg[ement] of speech"—rather than merely the motives of those who enacted them. U.S. Const. Amdt. 1. "The vice of content-based legislation . . . is not that it is always used for invidious, thought-control purposes, but that it lends itself to use for those purposes." *Hill v. Colorado*, 530 U.S. 703, 743 (2000) (SCALIA, J., dissenting).

135 S.Ct. at 2228–2229. One recurring question is whether this rule is overprotective. Justice Kagan concurred in the judgment, but questioned the rule that strict scrutiny necessarily must apply to all content-based restrictions:

> Countless cities and towns across America have adopted ordinances regulating the posting of signs, while exempting certain categories of signs based on their subject matter. For example, some municipalities generally prohibit illuminated signs in residential neighborhoods, but lift that ban for signs that identify the address of a home or the name of its owner or occupant. In other municipalities, safety signs such as "Blind Pedestrian Crossing" and "Hidden Driveway" can be posted without a permit, even as other permanent signs require one. Elsewhere, historic site markers—for example, "George Washington Slept Here"—are also exempt from general regulations. And similarly, the federal Highway Beautification Act limits signs along interstate highways unless, for instance, they direct travelers to "scenic and historical attractions" or advertise free coffee.

So on the majority's view, courts would have to determine that a town has a compelling interest in informing passersby where George Washington slept. And likewise, courts would have to find that a town has no other way to prevent hidden-driveway mishaps than by specially treating hidden-driveway signs. (Well-placed speed bumps? Lower speed limits? Or how about just a ban on hidden driveways?) The consequence—unless courts water down strict scrutiny to something unrecognizable—is that our communities will find themselves in an unenviable bind: They will have to either repeal the exemptions that allow for helpful signs on streets and sidewalks, or else lift their sign restrictions altogether and resign themselves to the resulting clutter.

Although the majority insists that applying strict scrutiny to all such ordinances is "essential" to protecting First Amendment freedoms, I find it challenging to understand why that is so.

Justice Kagan suggests that strict scrutiny should apply only to subject-matter regulation that has "the intent or effect of favoring some ideas over others," in other words, "when the restriction 'raises the specter that the Government may effectively drive certain ideas or viewpoints from the marketplace.' " What are the virtues and vices of that approach? Why did she join the majority in *Brown*?

Justice Breyer similarly criticized the use of strict scrutiny for all content-based restriction, but he offered a different proposal for reform:

I would use content discrimination as a supplement to a more basic analysis, which, tracking most of our First Amendment cases, asks whether the regulation at issue works harm to First Amendment interests that is disproportionate in light of the relevant regulatory objectives. Answering this question requires examining the seriousness of the harm to speech, the importance of the countervailing objectives, the extent to which the law will achieve those objectives, and whether there are other, less restrictive ways of doing so.

How does Justice Breyer's proposal differ from Justice Kagan's? Note that Justice Breyer dissented in *Brown*. How would application of Justice Breyer's balancing test by a judge differ from the sorts of policy judgments a city councilmember would make about whether to vote for the ordinance? Why should we assume that judges are best informed about whether a restriction on speech will serve "the relevant regulatory objectives"?

On the other hand, is the Court's sharp distinction between content-based and content-neutral restrictions *underprotective*? Is it so clear that restrictions based on time, on place, on manner, or on speaker cannot have the intent or effect of favoring some ideas over others? What if all speech near polling places were banned on the day of an election? What if all gatherings were banned in front of abortion clinics, churches, and military recruiting centers? What if all outsiders to a campus, or a political convention, were confined to "free speech zones"? Would "manner" restrictions like these really be neutral? And what about speaker discrimination? Could a city limit the right to speak in the public square to citizens? How about the right to contribute to a political campaign? What would Justice Kagan and Justice Breyer have to say about these questions?

Keep these views in mind, as we now turn now to two cases about protesters who were prosecuted. One of the protesters burned a draft card; the other one burned an American flag. But what is more important is the character of the law under which each was prosecuted. As you read the cases, ask yourself what is fundamentally different between the draft-card-burning law and the flag-burning law. Think about the reasons for government prosecution and their connection to the message that was conveyed.

United States v. O'Brien
391 U.S. 367 (1968)

■ MR. CHIEF JUSTICE WARREN delivered the opinion of the Court.

On the morning of March 31, 1966, David Paul O'Brien and three companions burned their Selective Service registration certificates on the steps of the South Boston Courthouse. A sizable crowd, including several agents of the Federal Bureau of Investigation, witnessed the event. Immediately after the burning, members of the crowd began attacking O'Brien and his companions. An FBI agent ushered O'Brien to safety inside the courthouse. After he was advised of his right to counsel and to silence, O'Brien stated to FBI agents that he had burned his registration certificate because of his beliefs, knowing that he was violating federal law. He produced the charred remains of the certificate, which, with his consent, were photographed.

For this act, O'Brien was indicted, tried, convicted, and sentenced in the United States District Court for the District of Massachusetts. He did not contest the fact that he had burned the certificate. He stated in argument to the jury that he burned the certificate publicly to influence others to adopt his antiwar beliefs, as he put it, "so that other people would reevaluate their positions with Selective Service, with the armed forces, and reevaluate their place in the culture of today, to hopefully consider my position."

The indictment upon which he was tried charged that he "willfully and knowingly did mutilate, destroy, and change by burning . . . [his] Registration Certificate . . . in violation of Title 50, App., United States Code, Section 462(b)" . . . of the Universal Military Training and Service Act of 1948. Section 462(b)(3) . . . was amended by Congress in 1965, 79 Stat. 586 (adding the words italicized below), so that at the time O'Brien burned his certificate an offense was committed by any person, "who *forges, alters, knowingly destroys, knowingly mutilates, or* in any manner changes any such certificate. . . ." (Italics supplied.) . . .

[T]he Court of Appeals . . . held the 1965 Amendment unconstitutional as a law abridging freedom of speech. At the time the Amendment was enacted, a regulation of the Selective Service System required registrants to keep their registration certificates in their "personal possession at all times." 32 CFR § 1617.1 (1962). Wilful violations of regulations promulgated pursuant to the Universal Military Training and Service Act were made criminal by statute. 50 U.S.C. App. § 462(b)(6). The Court of Appeals, therefore, was of the opinion that conduct punishable under the 1965 Amendment was already punishable under the nonpossession regulation, and consequently that the Amendment served no valid purpose; further, that in light of the prior regulation, the Amendment must have been "directed at public as distinguished from private destruction." On this basis, the court concluded that the 1965 Amendment ran afoul of the First Amendment by singling out persons engaged in protests for special treatment.... We hold that the 1965 Amendment is constitutional both as enacted and as applied....

I

When a male reaches the age of 18, he is required by the Universal Military Training and Service Act to register with a local draft board. He is assigned a Selective Service number, and within five days he is issued a registration certificate.... Subsequently, ... he is assigned a classification denoting his eligibility for induction, and "[a]s soon as practicable" thereafter he is issued a Notice of Classification.... Both the registration and classification certificates are small white cards, approximately 2 by 3 inches. . . .

Congress demonstrated its concern that certificates issued by the Selective Service System might be abused well before the 1965 Amendment here challenged.... By the 1965 Amendment, Congress added to § 12(b)(3) of the 1948 Act the provision here at issue, subjecting to criminal liability not only one who "forges, alters, or in any manner changes" but also one who "knowingly destroys [or] knowingly mutilates" a certificate. We note at the outset that the 1965 Amendment plainly does not abridge free speech on its face, and we do not understand O'Brien to argue otherwise. Amended § 12(b)(3) on its face deals with conduct having no connection with speech. It prohibits the knowing destruction of certificates issued by the Selective Service System, and there is nothing necessarily expressive about such conduct. The Amendment does not distinguish between public and private destruction, and it does not punish only destruction engaged in for the purpose of expressing views. Compare *Stromberg v. People of State of California*, 283 U.S. 359 (1931). A law prohibiting destruction of Selective Service certificates no more abridges free speech on its face than a motor vehicle law prohibiting the destruction of drivers' licenses, or a tax law prohibiting the destruction of books and records.

O'Brien nonetheless argues that the 1965 Amendment is unconstitutional in its application to him, and is unconstitutional as enacted because what he calls the "purpose" of Congress was "to suppress freedom of speech." We consider these arguments separately.

II

O'Brien first argues that the 1965 Amendment is unconstitutional as applied to him because his act of burning his registration certificate was protected "symbolic speech" within the First Amendment. His argument is that the freedom of expression which the First Amendment guarantees includes all modes of "communication of ideas by conduct," and that his conduct is within this definition because he did it in "demonstration against the war and against the draft."

We cannot accept the view that an apparently limitless variety of conduct can be labeled "speech" whenever the person engaging in the conduct intends thereby to express an idea. However, even on the assumption that the alleged communicative element in O'Brien's conduct is sufficient to bring into play the First Amendment, it does not necessarily follow that the destruction of a registration certificate is constitutionally protected activity. This Court has held that when "speech" and "nonspeech" elements are combined in the same course of conduct, a sufficiently important governmental interest in regulating the nonspeech element can justify incidental limitations on First Amendment freedoms. To characterize the quality of the governmental interest which must appear, the Court has employed a variety of descriptive terms: compelling; substantial; subordinating; paramount; cogent; strong. Whatever imprecision inheres in these terms, we think it clear that a government regulation is sufficiently justified if it is within the constitutional power of the Government; if it furthers an important or substantial governmental interest; if the governmental interest is unrelated to the suppression of free expression; and if the incidental restriction on alleged First Amendment freedoms is no greater than is essential to the furtherance of that interest. We find that the 1965 Amendment to § 12(b)(3) of the Universal Military Training and Service Act meets all of these requirements, and consequently that O'Brien can be constitutionally convicted for violating it.

The constitutional power of Congress to raise and support armies and to make all laws necessary and proper to that end is broad and sweeping. The power of Congress to classify and conscript manpower for military service is "beyond question." Pursuant to this power, Congress may establish a system of registration for individuals liable for training and service, and may require such individuals within reason to cooperate in the registration system. The issuance of certificates indicating the registration and eligibility classification of individuals is a legitimate and substantial administrative aid in the functioning of this system. And legislation to insure the continuing availability of issued certificates serves a legitimate and substantial purpose in the system's administration.

O'Brien's argument to the contrary is necessarily premised upon his unrealistic characterization of Selective Service certificates. He essentially adopts the position that such certificates are so many pieces of paper designed to notify registrants of their registration or classification, to be retained or tossed in the wastebasket according to the convenience or taste of the registrant.... We agree that the registration certificate contains much information of which the registrant needs no notification. This circumstance, however, does not lead to the conclusion that the certificate serves no purpose, but that, like the classification certificate, it serves purposes in addition to initial notification. Many of these purposes would be defeated by the certificates' destruction or mutilation. Among these are:

1.   The registration certificate serves as proof that the individual described thereon has registered for the draft. The classification certificate shows the eligibility classification of a named but undescribed individual. Voluntarily displaying the two certificates is an easy and painless way for a young man to dispel a question as to whether he might be delinquent in his Selective Service obligations. Correspondingly, the availability of the certificates for such display relieves the Selective Service System of the administrative burden it would otherwise have in verifying the registration and classification of all suspected delinquents. Further, since both certificates are in the nature of "receipts" attesting that the registrant has done what the law requires, it is in the interest of the just and efficient administration of the system that they be continually available, in the event, for example, of a mix-up in the registrant's file. Additionally, in a time of national crisis, reasonable availability to each registrant of the two small cards assures a rapid and uncomplicated means for determining his fitness for immediate induction, no matter how distant in our mobile society he may be from his local board.

2.   The information supplied on the certificates facilitates communication between registrants and local boards, simplifying the system and benefiting all concerned. To begin with, each certificate bears the address of the registrant's local

board, an item unlikely to be committed to memory. Further, each card bears the registrant's Selective Service number. . . . Finally, a registrant's inquiry, particularly through a local board other than his own, concerning his eligibility status is frequently answerable simply on the basis of his classification certificate; whereas, if the certificate were not reasonably available and the registrant were uncertain of his classification, the task of answering his questions would be considerably complicated.

3.   Both certificates carry continual reminders that the registrant must notify his local board of any change of address, and other specified changes in his status. . . . [T]he destruction of certificates deprives the system of a potentially useful notice device.

4.   The regulatory scheme involving Selective Service certificates includes clearly valid prohibitions against the alteration, forgery, or similar deceptive misuse of certificates. The destruction or mutilation of certificates obviously increases the difficulty of detecting and tracing abuses such as these. Further, a mutilated certificate might itself be used for deceptive purposes.

The many functions performed by Selective Service certificates establish beyond doubt that Congress has a legitimate and substantial interest in preventing their wanton and unrestrained destruction and assuring their continuing availability by punishing people who knowingly and willfully destroy or mutilate them. And we are unpersuaded that the pre-existence of the nonpossession regulations in any way negates this interest.

. . . [A] comparison of the regulations with the 1965 Amendment indicates that they protect overlapping but not identical governmental interests, and that they reach somewhat different classes of wrongdoers. The gravamen of the offense defined by the statute is the deliberate rendering of certificates unavailable for the various purposes which they may serve. Whether registrants keep their certificates in their personal possession at all times, as required by the regulations, is of no particular concern under the 1965 Amendment, as long as they do not mutilate or destroy the certificates so as to render them unavailable. . . .

We think it apparent that the continuing availability to each registrant of his Selective Service certificates substantially furthers the smooth and proper functioning of the system that Congress has established to raise armies. We think it also apparent that the Nation has a vital interest in having a system for raising armies that functions with maximum efficiency and is capable of easily and quickly responding to continually changing circumstances. For these reasons, the Government has a substantial interest in assuring the continuing availability of issued Selective Service certificates.

It is equally clear that the 1965 Amendment specifically protects this substantial governmental interest. We perceive no alternative means that would more precisely and narrowly assure the continuing availability of issued Selective Service certificates than a law which prohibits their wilful mutilation or destruction. Compare *Sherbert v. Verner*, 374 U.S. 398, 407–408 (1963), and the cases cited therein. The 1965 Amendment prohibits such conduct and does nothing more. In other words, both the governmental interest and the operation of the 1965 Amendment are limited to the noncommunicative aspect of O'Brien's conduct. The governmental interest and the scope of the 1965 Amendment are limited to preventing harm to the smooth and efficient functioning of the Selective Service System. When O'Brien deliberately rendered unavailable his registration certificate, he willfully frustrated this governmental interest. For this noncommunicative impact of his conduct, and for nothing else, he was convicted.

The case at bar is therefore unlike one where the alleged governmental interest in regulating conduct arises in some measure because the communication allegedly integral to the conduct is itself thought to be harmful. In *Stromberg*, for example, this Court struck down a statutory phrase which punished people who expressed their "opposition to organized government" by displaying "any flag, badge, banner, or device." Since the statute there was aimed at suppressing communication it could not be sustained as a regulation of noncommunicative conduct.

In conclusion, we find that because of the Government's substantial interest in assuring the continuing availability of issued Selective Service certificates, because amended § 462(b) is an appropriately narrow means of protecting this interest and condemns only the independent noncommunicative impact of conduct within its reach, and because the noncommunicative impact of O'Brien's act of burning his registration certificate frustrated the Government's interest, a sufficient governmental interest has been shown to justify O'Brien's conviction.

III

O'Brien finally argues that the 1965 Amendment is unconstitutional as enacted because what he calls the "purpose" of Congress was "to suppress freedom of speech." We reject this argument because under settled principles the purpose of Congress, as O'Brien uses that term, is not a basis for declaring this legislation unconstitutional.

It is a familiar principle of constitutional law that this Court will not strike down an otherwise constitutional statute on the basis of an alleged illicit legislative motive. As the Court long ago stated:

> The decisions of this court from the beginning lend no support whatever to the assumption that the judiciary may restrain the exercise of lawful power on the assumption that a wrongful purpose or motive has caused the power to be exerted.

McCray v. United States, 195 U.S. 27, 56 (1904). This fundamental principle of constitutional adjudication was reaffirmed and the many cases were collected by Mr. Justice Brandeis for the Court in *State of Arizona v. State of California*, 283 U.S. 423 (1931).

Inquiries into congressional motives or purposes are a hazardous matter. When the issue is simply the interpretation of legislation, the Court will look to statements by legislators for guidance as to the purpose of the legislature, because the benefit to sound decision-making in this circumstance is thought sufficient to risk the possibility of misreading Congress' purpose. It is entirely a different matter when we are asked to void a statute that is, under well-settled criteria, constitutional on its face, on the basis of what fewer than a handful of Congressmen said about it. What motivates one legislator to make a speech about a statute is not necessarily what motivates scores of others to enact it, and the stakes are sufficiently high for us to eschew guesswork. We decline to void essentially on the ground that it is unwise legislation which Congress had the undoubted power to enact and which could be reenacted in its exact form if the same or another legislator made a "wiser" speech about it. . . .

IV

Since the 1965 Amendment to § 12(b)(3) of the Universal Military Training and Service Act is constitutional as enacted and as applied, . . . [we] reinstate the judgment and sentence of the District Court. . . .

■ MR. JUSTICE HARLAN, concurring.

The crux of the Court's opinion . . . is . . . its general statement that:

> a government regulation is sufficiently justified if it is within the constitutional power of the Government; if it furthers an important or substantial governmental interest; if the governmental interest is unrelated to the suppression of free expression; and if the incidental restriction on alleged First Amendment freedoms is no greater than is essential to the furtherance of that interest.

I wish to make explicit my understanding that this passage does not foreclose consideration of First Amendment claims in those rare instances when an "incidental" restriction upon expression, imposed by a regulation which furthers an "important or substantial" governmental interest and satisfies the Court's other criteria, in practice has the effect of entirely preventing a "speaker" from reaching a significant audience with whom he could not otherwise lawfully communicate. This is not such a case, since O'Brien manifestly could have conveyed his message in many ways other than by burning his draft card.

■ MR. JUSTICE DOUGLAS, dissenting.

The Court states that the constitutional power of Congress to raise and support armies is "broad and sweeping" and that Congress' power "to classify and conscript manpower for military service is beyond question." This is undoubtedly true in times when, by declaration of Congress, the Nation is in a state of war. The underlying and basic problem in this case, however, is whether conscription is permissible in the absence of a declaration of war. That question has not been briefed nor was it presented in oral argument; but it is, I submit, a question upon which the litigants and the country are entitled to a ruling. . . .

NOTES

1. *United States v. O'Brien* illustrates a host of First Amendment issues. Does "speech" include *conduct* that has an expressive component? If so, does it include such conduct only when engaged in *for such expressive purposes*? Can it really include *any* and *all* conduct? If not, how does one tell which conduct also can be considered "speech" for First Amendment purposes? Identify the Court's answers.

2. Does the categorization of expressive conduct, either as protected or unprotected, depend on the understandings of the speaker, of the government, or of both? In other words: is conduct protected because the individual sought to convey a message through his conduct, or because the government seeks to regulate it on account of its communicative impact? Or should the outcome depend on balancing the practical impact on speech against the government's interest? Consider the following examples from real cases. (1) The government bans the street distribution of leaflets because of the litter problem they produce. (2) The government requires bands performing in a public park to

use the city's audio engineers to prevent excessive decibel levels. (3) The government bans sleeping in urban parks, thus precluding the Occupy Movement from engaging in its characteristic protests. (4) The government bans public nudity, thus preventing both political protests involving nudity and also nude dancing.

3.   Try to generalize toward a rule: What should be the test for whether government regulation of *conduct* (that has an identifiable expressive component to it) violates the First Amendment? What is the test that the Court in *O'Brien* employs for this inquiry? This is worth finding, marking, and studying, in the context of the case, for it is a much-repeated formulation in the Court's modern First Amendment law.

4.   Why does the Court refuse to consider Congress's motive in enacting the law? In 1965, Representative Mendel Rivers introduced a bill to make willful destruction of a draft card a criminal offense, championing the bill as a "clear answer to those who would make a mockery of our efforts in South Vietnam by engaging in the mass destruction of draft cards." Burning a draft card, one senator said, was "treason." See Geoffrey R. Stone, PERILOUS TIMES: FREE SPEECH IN WARTIME; FROM THE SEDITION ACT OF 1798 TO THE WAR ON TERRORISM 471–472 (2004). Isn't that the strongest possible evidence that Congress is regulating on the basis of communicative impact rather than the administrative issues involved in destruction of a draft card?

Texas v. Johnson
491 U.S. 397 (1989)

■ JUSTICE BRENNAN delivered the opinion of the Court.

After publicly burning an American flag as a means of political protest, Gregory Lee Johnson was convicted of desecrating a flag in violation of Texas law. This case presents the question whether his conviction is consistent with the First Amendment. We hold that it is not.

I

While the Republican National Convention was taking place in Dallas in 1984, respondent Johnson participated in a political demonstration dubbed the "Republican War Chest Tour." As explained in literature distributed by the demonstrators and in speeches made by them, the purpose of this event was to protest the policies of the Reagan administration and of certain Dallas-based corporations. The demonstrators marched through the Dallas streets, chanting political slogans and stopping at several corporate locations to stage "die-ins" intended to dramatize the consequences of nuclear war. On several occasions they spray-painted the walls of buildings and overturned potted plants, but Johnson himself took no part in such activities. He did, however, accept an American flag handed to him by a fellow protestor who had taken it from a flagpole outside one of the targeted buildings.

The demonstration ended in front of Dallas City Hall, where Johnson unfurled the American flag, doused it with kerosene, and set it on fire. While the flag burned, the protestors chanted: "America, the red, white, and blue, we spit on you." After the demonstrators dispersed, a witness to the flag burning collected the flag's remains and buried them in his backyard. No one was physically injured or threatened with injury, though several witnesses testified that they had been seriously offended by the flag burning.

Of the approximately 100 demonstrators, Johnson alone was charged with a crime. The only criminal offense with which he was charged was the desecration of a venerated object in violation of Tex. Penal Code Ann. § 42.09(a)(3) (1989). After a trial, he was convicted, sentenced to one year in prison, and fined $2,000. . . . [T]he Texas Court of Criminal Appeals reversed, holding that the State could not, consistent with the First Amendment, punish Johnson for burning the flag in these circumstances. . . .

II

. . . We must first determine whether Johnson's burning of the flag constituted expressive conduct, permitting him to invoke the First Amendment in challenging his conviction. See, *e.g., Spence v. Washington,* 418 U.S. 405, 409–411 (1974). If his conduct was expressive, we next decide whether the State's regulation is related to the suppression of free expression. See, *e.g., United States v. O'Brien,* 391 U.S. 367, 377 (1968). If the State's regulation is not related to expression, then the less stringent standard we announced in *O'Brien* for regulations of noncommunicative conduct controls. If it is, then we are outside of *O'Brien*'s test, and we must ask whether this interest justifies Johnson's conviction under a more demanding standard. . . .

The First Amendment literally forbids the abridgment only of "speech," but we have long recognized that its protection does not end at the spoken or written word. While we have rejected "the view that an apparently limitless variety of conduct can be labeled 'speech' whenever the person engaging in the conduct intends thereby to express an idea," [*O'Brien*], we have acknowledged that conduct may be "sufficiently imbued with elements of communication to fall within the scope of the First and Fourteenth Amendments[.]" [*Spence.*]

In deciding whether particular conduct possesses sufficient communicative elements to bring the First Amendment into play, we have asked whether "[a]n intent to convey a particularized message was present, and [whether] the likelihood was great that the message would be understood by those who viewed it." 418 U.S., at 410–411. Hence, we have recognized the expressive nature of students' wearing of black armbands to protest American military involvement in Vietnam, *Tinker v. Des Moines Independent Community School Dist.,* 393 U.S. 503, 505 (1969); of a sit-in by blacks in a "whites only" area to protest segregation, *Brown v. Louisiana,* 383 U.S. 131, 141–142 (1966); of the wearing of American military uniforms in a dramatic presentation criticizing American involvement in Vietnam, *Schacht v. United States,* 398 U.S. 58 (1970); and of picketing about a wide variety of causes, see, *e.g., Food Employees v. Logan Valley Plaza, Inc.,* 391 U.S. 308, 313–314 (1968).

Especially pertinent to this case are our decisions recognizing the communicative nature of conduct relating to flags. Attaching a peace sign to the flag, *Spence,* at 409–410; refusing to salute the flag, *West Virginia Board of Education v. Barnette,* 319 U.S. 624, 632 (1943); and displaying a red flag, *Stromberg v. California,* 283 U.S. 359, 368–369 (1931), we have held, all may find shelter under the First Amendment. See also *Smith v. Goguen,* 415 U.S. 566, 588 (1974) (WHITE, J., concurring in judgment) (treating flag "contemptuously" by wearing pants with small flag sewn into their seat is expressive conduct). That we have had little difficulty identifying an expressive element in conduct relating to flags should not be surprising. The very purpose of a national flag is to serve as a symbol of our country;

it is, one might say, "the one visible manifestation of two hundred years of nationhood." *Id.* at 603 (Rehnquist, J., dissenting). . . .

The State of Texas conceded for purposes of its oral argument in this case that Johnson's conduct was expressive conduct and this concession seems to us [prudent]. Johnson burned an American flag as part—indeed, as the culmination—of a political demonstration that coincided with the convening of the Republican Party and its renomination of Ronald Reagan for President. The expressive, overtly political nature of this conduct was both intentional and overwhelmingly apparent. . . . In these circumstances, Johnson's burning of the flag was conduct "sufficiently imbued with elements of communication," *Spence,* at 409, to implicate the First Amendment.

III

The government generally has a freer hand in restricting expressive conduct than it has in restricting the written or spoken word. It may not, however, proscribe particular conduct *because* it has expressive elements. "[W]hat might be termed the more generalized guarantee of freedom of expression makes the communicative nature of conduct an inadequate *basis* for singling out that conduct for proscription. A law *directed at* the communicative nature of conduct must, like a law directed at speech itself, be justified by the substantial showing of need that the First Amendment requires." *Community for Creative Non-Violence v. Watt,* 227 U.S. App. D.C. 19, 55–56 (1983) (Scalia, J., dissenting) (emphasis in original), rev'd *sub nom. Clark v. Community for Creative Non-Violence,* 468 U.S. 288, 293 (1984). It is, in short, not simply the verbal or nonverbal nature of the expression, but the governmental interest at stake, that helps to determine whether a restriction on that expression is valid.

Thus, although we have recognized that where "speech and nonspeech elements are combined in the same course of conduct, a sufficiently important governmental interest in regulating the nonspeech element can justify incidental limitations on First Amendment freedoms," [*O'Brien*], we have limited the applicability of *O'Brien*'s relatively lenient standard to those cases in which "the governmental interest is unrelated to the suppression of free expression." In stating, moreover, that *O'Brien*'s test "in the last analysis is little, if any, different from the standard applied to time, place, or manner restrictions," *Clark,* at 298, we have highlighted the requirement that the governmental interest in question be unconnected to expression in order to come under *O'Brien*'s less demanding rule.

In order to decide whether *O'Brien*'s test applies here, therefore, we must decide whether Texas has asserted an interest in support of Johnson's conviction that is unrelated to the suppression of expression. If we find that an interest asserted by the State is simply not implicated on the facts before us, we need not ask whether *O'Brien*'s test applies. The State offers two separate interests to justify this conviction: preventing breaches of the peace and preserving the flag as a symbol of nationhood and national unity. We hold that the first interest is not implicated on this record and that the second is related to the suppression of expression.

A

Texas claims that its interest in preventing breaches of the peace justifies Johnson's conviction for flag desecration. However, no disturbance of the peace actually occurred or threatened to occur because of Johnson's burning of the flag. Although the State stresses the disruptive behavior of the protestors during their march toward City Hall, it admits that "no actual breach of the peace occurred at the time of the flagburning or in response to the flagburning." . . . The only evidence offered by the State at trial to show the reaction to Johnson's actions was the testimony of several persons who had been seriously offended by the flag burning.

The State's position, therefore, amounts to a claim that an audience that takes serious offense at particular expression is necessarily likely to disturb the peace and that the expression may be prohibited on this basis. Our precedents do not countenance such a presumption. On the contrary, they recognize that a principal "function of free speech under our system of government is to invite dispute. It may indeed best serve its high purpose when it induces a condition of unrest, creates dissatisfaction with conditions as they are, or even stirs people to anger." *Terminiello v. Chicago*, 337 U.S. 1, 4 (1949). It would be odd indeed to conclude *both* that "if it is the speaker's opinion that gives offense, that consequence is a reason for according it constitutional protection," *FCC v. Pacifica Foundation*, 438 U.S. 726, 745 (1978), *and* that the government may ban the expression of certain disagreeable ideas on the unsupported presumption that their very disagreeableness will provoke violence.

Thus, we have not permitted the government to assume that every expression of a provocative idea will incite a riot, but have instead required careful consideration of the actual circumstances surrounding such expression, asking whether the expression "is directed to inciting or producing imminent lawless action and is likely to incite or produce such action." *Brandenburg v. Ohio*, 395 U.S. 444, 447 (1969) (reviewing circumstances surrounding rally and speeches by Ku Klux Klan). To accept Texas' arguments that it need only demonstrate "the potential for a breach of the peace," and that every flag burning necessarily possesses that potential, would be to eviscerate our holding in *Brandenburg*. This we decline to do.

Nor does Johnson's expressive conduct fall within that small class of "fighting words" that are "likely to provoke the average person to retaliation, and thereby cause a breach of the peace." *Chaplinsky v. New Hampshire*, 315 U.S. 568, 574 (1942). No reasonable onlooker would have regarded Johnson's generalized expression of dissatisfaction with the policies of the Federal Government as a direct personal insult or an invitation to exchange fisticuffs.

We thus conclude that the State's interest in maintaining order is not implicated on these facts. The State need not worry that our holding will disable it from preserving the peace. We do not suggest that the First Amendment forbids a State to prevent "imminent lawless action." *Brandenburg*, at 447. And, in fact, Texas already has a statute specifically prohibiting breaches of the peace, Tex. Penal Code Ann. § 42.01 (1989), which tends to confirm that Texas need not punish this flag desecration in order to keep the peace.

B

The State also asserts an interest in preserving the flag as a symbol of nationhood and national unity. In *Spence*, we acknowledged that the government's interest in preserving the flag's special symbolic value "is directly related to expression in the context of activity" such as affixing a peace symbol to a flag. We are equally persuaded that this interest is related to expression in the case of Johnson's burning of the flag. The State, apparently, is concerned that such conduct will lead people to believe either that the flag does not stand for nationhood and national unity, but instead reflects other, less positive concepts, or that the concepts reflected in the flag do not in fact exist, that is, that we do not enjoy unity as a Nation. These concerns blossom only when a person's treatment of the flag communicates some message, and thus are related "to the suppression of free expression" within the meaning of *O'Brien*. We are thus outside of *O'Brien*'s test altogether.

IV

It remains to consider whether the State's interest in preserving the flag as a symbol of nationhood and national unity justifies Johnson's conviction.

As in *Spence*, "[w]e are confronted with a case of prosecution for the expression of an idea through activity," and "[a]ccordingly, we must examine with particular care the interests advanced by [petitioner] to support its prosecution." Johnson was not, we add, prosecuted for the expression of just any idea; he was prosecuted for his expression of dissatisfaction with the policies of this country, expression situated at the core of our First Amendment values.

Moreover, Johnson was prosecuted because he knew that his politically charged expression would cause "serious offense." If he had burned the flag as a means of disposing of it because it was dirty or torn, he would not have been convicted of flag desecration under this Texas law: federal law designates burning as the preferred means of disposing of a flag "when it is in such condition that it is no longer a fitting emblem for display," 36 U.S.C. § 176(k), and Texas has no quarrel with this means of disposal. The Texas law is thus not aimed at protecting the physical integrity of the flag in all circumstances, but is designed instead to protect it only against impairments that would cause serious offense to others. . . .

Whether Johnson's treatment of the flag violated Texas law thus depended on the likely communicative impact of his expressive conduct. Our decision in *Boos v. Barry*, 485 U.S. 312 (1988), tells us that this restriction on Johnson's expression is content based. In *Boos*, we considered the constitutionality of a law prohibiting "the display of any sign within 500 feet of a foreign embassy if that sign tends to bring that foreign government into public odium or public disrepute." Rejecting the argument that the law was content neutral because it was justified by "our international law obligation to shield diplomats from speech that offends their dignity," we held that "[t]he emotive impact of speech on its audience is not a 'secondary effect'" unrelated to the content of the expression itself. *Id.* at 321 (plurality opinion).

According to the principles announced in *Boos*, Johnson's political expression was restricted because of the content of the message he conveyed. We must therefore subject the State's asserted interest in preserving the special symbolic character of the flag to "the most exacting scrutiny."

. . . [T]he State's claim is that it has an interest in preserving the flag as a symbol of *nationhood* and *national unity*, a symbol with a determinate range of meanings. According to Texas, if one physically treats the flag in a way that would tend to cast doubt on either the idea that nationhood and national unity are the flag's referents or that national unity actually exists, the message conveyed thereby is a harmful one and therefore may be prohibited.

If there is a bedrock principle underlying the First Amendment, it is that the government may not prohibit the expression of an idea simply because society finds the idea itself offensive or disagreeable. *[The Court then cited a long list of cases for this proposition.—Editors]*

We have not recognized an exception to this principle even where our flag has been involved. In *Street v. New York*, 394 U.S. 576 (1969), we held that a State may not criminally punish a person for uttering words critical of the flag. Rejecting the argument that the conviction could be sustained on the ground that Street had "failed to show the respect for our national symbol which may properly be demanded of every citizen," we concluded that "the constitutionally guaranteed 'freedom to be intellectually . . . diverse or even contrary,' and the 'right to differ as to things that touch the heart of the existing order,' encompass the freedom to express publicly one's opinions about our flag, including those opinions which are defiant or contemptuous." Nor may the government, we have held, compel conduct that would evince respect for the flag. "To sustain the compulsory flag salute we are required to say that a Bill of Rights which guards the individual's right to speak his own mind, left it open to public authorities to compel him to utter what is not in his mind."

In holding in *Barnette* that the Constitution did not leave this course open to the government, Justice Jackson described one of our society's defining principles in words deserving of their frequent repetition: "If there is any fixed star in our constitutional constellation, it is that no official, high or petty, can prescribe what shall be orthodox in politics, nationalism, religion, or other matters of opinion or force citizens to confess by word or act their faith therein." . . .

Texas' focus on the precise nature of Johnson's expression, moreover, misses the point of our prior decisions: their enduring lesson, that the government may not prohibit expression simply because it disagrees with its message, is not dependent on the particular mode in which one chooses to express an idea. If we were to hold that a State may forbid flag burning wherever it is likely to endanger the flag's symbolic role, but allow it wherever burning a flag promotes that role—as where, for example, a person ceremoniously burns a dirty flag—we would be saying that when it comes to impairing the flag's physical integrity, the flag itself may be used as a symbol—as a substitute for the written or spoken word or a "short cut from mind to mind"—only in one direction. We would be permitting a State to "prescribe what shall be orthodox" by saying that one may burn the flag to convey one's attitude toward it and its referents only if one does not endanger the flag's representation of nationhood and national unity.

We never before have held that the Government may ensure that a symbol be used to express only one view of that symbol or its referents. . . . To conclude that the government may permit designated symbols to be used to communicate only a limited set of messages would be to enter territory having no discernible or defensible boundaries. Could the government, on this theory, prohibit the burning of state flags? Of copies of the Presidential seal? Of the Constitution? In evaluating these choices under the First Amendment, how would we decide which symbols were sufficiently special to warrant this unique status? To do so, we would be forced to consult our own political preferences, and impose them on the citizenry, in the very way that the First Amendment forbids us to do.

There is, moreover, no indication—either in the text of the Constitution or in our cases interpreting it—that a separate juridical category exists for the American flag alone. . . . The First Amendment does not guarantee that other concepts virtually sacred to our Nation as a whole—such as the principle that discrimination on the basis of race is odious and destructive—will go unquestioned in the marketplace of ideas. See *Brandenburg*. We decline, therefore, to create for the flag an exception to the joust of principles protected by the First Amendment.

It is not the State's ends, but its means, to which we object. It cannot be gainsaid that there is a special place reserved for the flag in this Nation, and thus we do not doubt that the government has a legitimate interest in making efforts to "preserv[e] the national flag as an unalloyed symbol of our country." We reject the suggestion, urged at oral argument by counsel for Johnson, that the government lacks "any state interest whatsoever" in regulating the manner in which the flag may be displayed. Congress has, for example, enacted precatory regulations describing the proper treatment of the flag, see 36 U.S.C. §§ 173–177, and we cast no doubt on the legitimacy of its interest in making such recommendations. To say that the government has an interest in encouraging proper treatment of the flag, however, is not to say that it may criminally punish a person for burning a flag as a means of political protest. "National unity as an end which officials may foster by persuasion and example is not in question. The problem is whether under our Constitution compulsion as here employed is a permissible means for its achievement." *Barnette*, at 640.

We are fortified in today's conclusion by our conviction that forbidding criminal punishment for conduct such as Johnson's will not endanger the special role played by our flag or the feelings it inspires. To paraphrase Justice Holmes, we submit that nobody can suppose that this one gesture of an unknown man will change our Nation's attitude towards its flag. See *Abrams v. United States*, 250 U.S. 616, 628 (1919) (Holmes, J., dissenting). Indeed, Texas' argument that the burning of an American flag "is an act having a high likelihood to cause a breach of the peace," and its statute's implicit assumption that physical mistreatment of the flag will lead to "serious offense," tend to confirm that the flag's special role is not in danger; if it were, no one would riot or take offense because a flag had been burned.

We are tempted to say, in fact, that the flag's deservedly cherished place in our community will be strengthened, not weakened, by our holding today. Our decision is a reaffirmation of the principles of freedom and inclusiveness that the flag best reflects, and of the conviction that our toleration of criticism such as Johnson's is a sign and source of our strength. . . .

The way to preserve the flag's special role is not to punish those who feel differently about these matters. It is to persuade them that they are wrong. "To courageous, self-reliant men, with confidence in the power of free and fearless reasoning applied through the processes of popular government, no danger flowing from speech can be deemed clear and present, unless the incidence of the evil apprehended is so imminent that it may befall before there is opportunity for full discussion. If there be time to expose through discussion the falsehood and fallacies, to avert the evil by the processes of education, the remedy to be applied is more speech, not enforced silence." *Whitney v. California*, 274 U.S. 357, 377 (1927) (Brandeis, J., concurring). And, precisely because it is our flag that is involved, one's response to the flag burner may exploit the uniquely persuasive power of the flag itself. We can imagine no more appropriate response to burning a flag than waving one's own, no better way to counter a flag burner's message than by saluting the flag that burns, no surer means of preserving the dignity even of the flag that burned than by—as one witness here did—according its remains a respectful burial. We do not consecrate the flag by punishing its desecration, for in doing so we dilute the freedom that this cherished emblem represents.

V

Johnson was convicted for engaging in expressive conduct. The State's interest in preventing breaches of the peace does not support his conviction because Johnson's conduct did not threaten to disturb the peace. Nor does the State's interest in preserving the flag as a symbol of nationhood and national unity justify his criminal conviction for engaging in political expression.

■ [JUSTICE KENNEDY'S concurrence is omitted.]

■ CHIEF JUSTICE REHNQUIST, with whom JUSTICE WHITE and JUSTICE O'CONNOR join, dissenting.

In holding this Texas statute unconstitutional, the Court ignores Justice Holmes' familiar aphorism that "a page of history is worth a volume of logic." . . . *[The dissent gives many examples of the honor attributed to the flag in American history.—Editors]*

The American flag, then, throughout more than 200 years of our history, has come to be the visible symbol embodying our Nation. It does not represent the views of any particular political party, and it does not represent any particular political philosophy. The flag is not simply another "idea" or "point of view" competing for recognition in the marketplace of ideas. Millions and millions of Americans regard it with an almost mystical reverence regardless of what sort of social, political, or philosophical beliefs they may have. I cannot agree that the First Amendment invalidates the Act of Congress, and the laws of 48 of the 50 States, which make criminal the public burning of the flag. . . .

But the Court insists that the Texas statute prohibiting the public burning of the American flag infringes on respondent Johnson's freedom of expression. Such freedom, of course, is not absolute. See *Schenck v. United States*, 249 U.S. 47 (1919). In *Chaplinsky v. New Hampshire*, 315 U.S. 568 (1942), a unanimous Court said:

> Allowing the broadest scope to the language and purpose of the Fourteenth Amendment, it is well understood that the right of free speech is not absolute at all times and under all circumstances. There are certain well-defined and narrowly limited classes of speech, the prevention and punishment of which have never been thought to raise any Constitutional problem. These include the lewd and obscene, the profane, the libelous, and the insulting or "fighting" words—those which by their very utterance inflict injury or tend to incite an immediate breach of the peace. It has been well observed that such utterances are no essential part of any exposition of ideas, and are of such slight social value as a step to truth that any benefit that may be derived from them is clearly outweighed by the social interest in order and morality.

The Court upheld Chaplinsky's conviction under a state statute that made it unlawful to "address any offensive, derisive or annoying word to any person who is lawfully in any street or other public place." Chaplinsky had told a local marshal, "You are a God damned racketeer" and a "damned Fascist and the whole government of Rochester are Fascists or agents of Fascists."

Here it may equally well be said that the public burning of the American flag by Johnson was no essential part of any exposition of ideas, and at the same time it had a tendency to incite a breach of the peace. Johnson was free to make any verbal denunciation of the flag that he wished; indeed, he was free to burn the flag in private. He could publicly burn other symbols of the Government or effigies of political leaders. He did lead a march through the streets of Dallas, and conducted a rally in front of the Dallas City Hall. He engaged in a "die-in" to protest nuclear weapons. He shouted out various slogans during the march, including: "Reagan, Mondale which will it be? Either one means World War III"; "Ronald Reagan, killer of the hour, Perfect example of U.S. power"; and "red, white and blue, we spit on you, you stand for plunder, you will go under." Brief for Respondent 3. For none of these acts was he arrested or prosecuted; it was only when he proceeded to burn publicly an American flag stolen from its rightful owner that he violated the Texas statute.

The Court could not, and did not, say that Chaplinsky's utterances were not expressive phrases—they clearly and succinctly conveyed an extremely low opinion of the addressee. The same may be said of Johnson's public burning of the flag in this case; it obviously did convey Johnson's bitter dislike of his country. But his act, like Chaplinsky's provocative words, conveyed nothing that could not have been conveyed and was not conveyed just as forcefully in a dozen different ways. As with "fighting words," so with flag burning, for purposes of the First Amendment: It is "no essential part of any exposition of ideas, and [is] of such slight social value as a step to truth that any benefit that may be derived from [it] is clearly outweighed" by the public interest in avoiding a probable breach of the peace . . .

The result of the Texas statute is obviously to deny one in Johnson's frame of mind one of many means of "symbolic speech." Far from being a case of "one picture being worth a thousand words," flag burning is the equivalent of an inarticulate grunt or roar that, it seems fair to say, is most likely to be indulged in not to express any particular idea, but to antagonize others. . . . The Texas statute deprived Johnson of only one rather inarticulate symbolic form of protest—a form of protest that was profoundly offensive to many—and left him with a full panoply of other symbols and every conceivable form of verbal expression to express his deep disapproval of national policy. Thus, in no way can it be said that Texas is punishing him because his hearers—or any other group of people—were profoundly opposed to the message that he sought to convey. Such opposition is no proper basis for restricting speech or expression under the First Amendment. It was Johnson's use of this particular symbol, and not the idea that he sought to convey by it or by his many other expressions, for which he was punished. . . .

But the Court today will have none of this. The uniquely deep awe and respect for our flag felt by virtually all of us are bundled off under the rubric of "designated symbols" that the First Amendment prohibits the government from "establishing." But the government has not "established" this feeling; 200 years of history have done that. The government is simply recognizing as a fact the profound regard for the American flag created by that history when it enacts statutes prohibiting the disrespectful public burning of the flag. . . .

■ Justice Stevens, dissenting.

As the Court analyzes this case, it presents the question whether the State of Texas, or indeed the Federal Government, has the power to prohibit the public desecration of the American flag. The question is unique. In my judgment rules that apply to a host of other symbols, such as state flags, armbands, or various privately promoted emblems of political or commercial identity, are not necessarily controlling. Even if flag burning could be considered just another species of symbolic speech under the logical application of the rules that the Court has developed in its interpretation of the First Amendment in other contexts, this case has an intangible dimension that makes those rules inapplicable. . . .

The Court is therefore quite wrong in blandly asserting that respondent "was prosecuted for his expression of dissatisfaction with the policies of this country, expression situated at the core of our First Amendment values." Respondent was prosecuted because of the method he chose to express his dissatisfaction with those policies. Had he chosen to spray-paint—or perhaps convey with a motion picture projector—his message of dissatisfaction on the facade of the Lincoln Memorial, there would be no question about the power of the Government to prohibit his means of expression. The prohibition would be supported by the legitimate interest in preserving the quality of an important national asset. Though the asset at stake in this case is intangible, given its unique value, the same interest supports a prohibition on the desecration of the American flag. . . .

NOTES

1.   Identify the *"O'Brien* test" as used by the Court in *Texas v. Johnson.* Does Texas's criminal punishment of flag-burning fit within the set of situations described by that test—government regulation of conduct for reasons unrelated to the suppression of free expression? What is the Court's answer? Do you agree with the Court's analysis or not? Is Texas regulating conduct, and in the process only incidentally restricting the expression of ideas? What do you think of Justice Stevens's analogy, in dissent, to spray-painting the Lincoln Memorial?

2.   Even assuming that Johnson's conduct constitutes "speech" falling within the protection of the First Amendment, are there not some interests of the state, and of society, that must prevail over the individual's right to free speech? If so, what might those be? Can you formulate a general proposition from your consideration of those interests that might justify suppression of free speech—something like "The freedom of speech is absolute except. . . ." Except when?

3.   When, if ever, should government be able to suppress speech because of the offensiveness of the message being conveyed? What about the offensiveness of the *manner* in which or *means or method* by which it is being conveyed? Are there some ideas that are just so offensive and of so little or even negative value that their expression need never be permitted? Is flag-burning in some such category? Are you persuaded by the dissenters' arguments about the special circumstances of the U.S. flag? If so, are there other things that fit in a similar category?

4.   What if the offensiveness of certain speech or expressive conduct is so great that it is likely to produce a violent reaction—start a fight, trigger a riot, lead to murders? May the government regulate it in the interest of preserving public peace or saving lives or property? How does the Court in *Texas v. Johnson* deal with this problem? What do you make of the "fighting words" doctrine and precedent? In 2005, the largest circulation paper in Denmark, *Jyllands-Posten,* published a series of cartoon depictions of the Muslim prophet Mohammed. The depictions were considered so offensive that they produced violent demonstrations in response, including the burnings of Danish

embassies in Syria and Gaza. The same year, a false Newsweek report (later retracted) that U.S. interrogators had flushed a Koran down a toilet sparked riots that resulted in seventeen deaths. See Katherine Q. Seelye & Neil A. Lewis, *Newsweek Says It Is Retracting Koran Report*, N.Y. Times (May 17, 2005). Should anticipated violence in response to offensive speech permit the government to restrict such speech?

Aside from the possibility of violence, what if the offensiveness of certain speech or expressive conduct is so great that it makes other people—perhaps members of a vulnerable minority—frightened or unwelcome? Don't they have a right to move in public places without being subjected to verbal assaults?

As we noted above, other Western nations' constitutions handle these issues differently. On the one hand, they are often written more broadly, explicitly to protect "freedom of expression" rather than merely "freedom of speech and of the press." On the other hand, they sometimes explicitly say that the right of free expression must be balanced against the need to promote a democratic society, and that balancing inevitably permits more restrictions on speech considered harmful. See generally Vicki C. Jackson & Mark Tushnet, COMPARATIVE CONSTITUTIONAL LAW 1468–1637 (2d ed. 2006). Which approach do you prefer?

Reasonable, Neutral Time, Place, and Manner Regulations

One important subcategory of content-neutral restrictions on speech comprises reasonable, content-neutral, time, place, and manner regulations. Unlike laws regulating expressive conduct, these rules single out speech for particular restrictions, but (1) do not distinguish between different cases on the basis of the content of the speech, (2) do not prohibit the speech, but only confine it to certain reasonable times, places, or manners. What issues does this form of regulation raise?

1. *Some "time, place, and manner" cases.* In *Kovacs v. Cooper*, 336 U.S. 77 (1949), the Court upheld a ban on "sound trucks" (loudspeaker systems). In *Grayned v. Rockford*, 408 U.S. 104 (1972), the Court upheld (against Free Speech Clause challenge) a conviction for violating an "anti-noise" ordinance prohibiting disturbing noise adjacent to a school building when classes are in session—distinguishing situations where similar speech might occur in a public park. In *Heffron v. International Society for Krishna Consciousness (ISKCON)*, 452 U.S. 640 (1981), the Court upheld a Minnesota State Fair regulation requiring anyone wishing to sell, distribute, or promote anything to do so in a "booth"—as applied to prohibit the Hare Krishna sect's desire to walk around the fairgrounds and distribute literature to fairgoers. In *Frisby v. Schultz*, 487 U.S. 474 (1988), the Court upheld a ban on targeted residential picketing of a person's home. In *Ward v. Rock Against Racism*, 491 U.S. 781 (1989), the Court upheld New York City's regulation requiring use of city-provided sound systems and technicians to control the volume of performances in Central Park. In *City of Ladue v. Gilleo*, 512 U.S. 43 (1994), the Court unanimously struck down an ordinance banning most yard signs in residential neighborhoods (but exempting certain categories—for-sale signs, business signs). The city wanted to avoid "visual clutter." The Court thought this left too few "alternative channels" for persons to express their messages. In *Hill v. Colorado*, 530 U.S. 703 (2000), the Court upheld, 5–4, a law prohibiting persons from "knowingly" approaching within eight feet of another person, in order to present a handbill or leaflet, counsel, or protest, in front of a hospital or other medical facility. Which of these cases do you think were rightly decided?

2.   *Time*: May the government restrict public demonstrations or rallies to daylight hours? To weekend days? To between 4:00 PM and 5:00 PM on Tuesdays and Thursdays? How is the reasonableness of a "time" restriction to be evaluated?

3.   *Place*: May the government forbid demonstrations, rallies, picketing, leafleting, or personal advocacy of a point of view within one hundred feet of a school? A church? A cemetery? A hospital? An animal-research facility? A foreign embassy? A military base? In front of all public buildings? Near abortion clinics? In airport corridors? Within public-school hallways? (Many of these are real cases.) Could it do so at certain times of day (combining a time regulation and a place regulation)?

4.   *Manner*: May the government forbid the use of megaphones or other amplification devices? May it set limits on the total decibel level of speech? May it prohibit group chanting? Subliminal messages during movies? Would such restrictions be content-based or content-neutral? Reasonable? Where is the line between regulating "manner" and regulating a particular type of expressive conduct because of its emotive force (like burning a flag or draft card or sleeping in a "Reaganville" across the street from the White House)? Could you describe the violent video game regulation in *Brown* as a "manner" regulation?

Renton v. Playtime Theaters
475 U.S. 41 (1986)

■ JUSTICE REHNQUIST delivered the opinion of the Court.

This case involves a constitutional challenge to a zoning ordinance . . . that prohibits adult motion picture theaters from locating within 1,000 feet of any residential zone, single- or multiple-family dwelling, church, park, or school. Appellees [sought] a declaratory judgment that the Renton ordinance violated the First and Fourteenth Amendments and a permanent injunction against its enforcement. The District Court ruled in favor of Renton and denied the permanent injunction, but the Court of Appeals for the Ninth Circuit reversed and remanded for reconsideration. We . . . reverse the judgment of the Ninth Circuit . . .

In our view, the resolution of this case is largely dictated by our decision in *Young v. American Mini Theatres*, 427 U.S. 50 (1976). There, although five Members of the Court did not agree on a single rationale for the decision, we held that the city of Detroit's zoning ordinance, which prohibited locating an adult theater within 1,000 feet of any two other "regulated uses" or within 500 feet of any residential zone, did not violate the First and Fourteenth Amendments. The Renton ordinance, like the one in *American Mini Theatres,* does not ban adult theaters altogether, but merely provides that such theaters may not be located within 1,000 feet of any residential zone, single- or multiple-family dwelling, church, park, or school. The ordinance is therefore properly analyzed as a form of time, place, and manner regulation.

Describing the ordinance as a time, place, and manner regulation is, of course, only the first step in our inquiry. This Court has long held that regulations enacted for the purpose of restraining speech on the basis of its content presumptively violate the First Amendment. On the other hand, so-called "content-neutral" time, place, and manner regulations are acceptable so long as they are designed to serve a substantial governmental interest and do not unreasonably limit alternative avenues of communication.

At first glance, the Renton ordinance, like the ordinance in *American Mini Theatres,* does not appear to fit neatly into either the "content-based" or the "content-neutral" category. To be sure, the ordinance treats theaters that specialize in adult films differently from other kinds of theaters. Nevertheless, as the District Court concluded, the Renton ordinance is aimed not at the *content* of the films shown at "adult motion picture theatres," but rather at the *secondary effects* of such theaters on the surrounding community. The District Court found that the City Council's *"predominate* concerns" were with the secondary effects of adult theaters, and not with the content of adult films themselves. But the Court of Appeals . . . held that this was not enough to sustain the ordinance. According to the Court of Appeals, if *"a motivating factor"* in enacting the ordinance was to restrict respondents' exercise of First Amendment rights the ordinance would be invalid, apparently no matter how small a part this motivating factor may have played in the City Council's decision. This view of the law was rejected in *O'Brien.* . . . *[O'Brien had stated that "an otherwise constitutional statute" is not unconstitutional "on the basis of an alleged illicit legislative motive."—Editors]*

The District Court's finding as to "predominate" intent, left undisturbed by the Court of Appeals, is more than adequate to establish that the city's pursuit of its zoning interests here was unrelated to the suppression of free expression. The ordinance by its terms is designed to prevent crime, protect the city's retail trade, maintain property values, and generally "protec[t] and preserv[e] the quality of [the city's] neighborhoods, commercial districts, and the quality of urban life," not to suppress the expression of unpopular views. As JUSTICE POWELL observed in *American Mini Theatres,* "[i]f [the city] had been concerned with restricting the message purveyed by adult theaters, it would have tried to close them or restrict their number rather than circumscribe their choice as to location."

In short, the Renton ordinance is completely consistent with our definition of "content-neutral" speech regulations as those that "are *justified* without reference to the content of the regulated speech." The ordinance does not contravene the fundamental principle that underlies our concern about "content-based" speech regulations: that "government may not grant the use of a forum to people whose views it finds acceptable, but deny use to those wishing to express less favored or more controversial views."

It was with this understanding in mind that, in *American Mini Theatres,* a majority of this Court decided that, at least with respect to businesses that purvey sexually explicit materials, zoning ordinances designed to combat the undesirable secondary effects of such businesses are to be reviewed under the standards applicable to "content-neutral" time, place, and manner regulations. JUSTICE STEVENS, writing for the plurality, concluded that the city of Detroit was entitled to draw a distinction between adult theaters and other kinds of theaters "without violating the government's paramount obligation of neutrality in its regulation of protected communication," that "[i]t is th[e] secondary effect which these zoning ordinances attempt to avoid, not the dissemination of 'offensive' speech." JUSTICE POWELL, in concurrence, elaborated:

> "[The] dissent misconceives the issue in this case by insisting that it involves an impermissible time, place, and manner restriction based on the content of expression. It involves nothing of the kind. We have here merely a decision by the city to treat certain movie theaters differently because

they have markedly different effects upon their surroundings. . . . Moreover, even if this were a case involving a special governmental response to the content of one type of movie, it is possible that the result would be supported by a line of cases recognizing that the government can tailor its reaction to different types of speech according to the degree to which its special and overriding interests are implicated. See, *e.g., Tinker v. Des Moines School Dist.*, 393 U.S. 503 (1969).

The appropriate inquiry in this case, then, is whether the Renton ordinance is designed to serve a substantial governmental interest and allows for reasonable alternative avenues of communication. It is clear that the ordinance meets such a standard. As a majority of this Court recognized in *American Mini Theatres,* a city's "interest in attempting to preserve the quality of urban life is one that must be accorded high respect." Exactly the same vital governmental interests are at stake here.

The Court of Appeals ruled, however, that because the Renton ordinance was enacted without the benefit of studies specifically relating to "the particular problems or needs of Renton," the city's justifications for the ordinance were "conclusory and speculative." We think the Court of Appeals imposed on the city an unnecessarily rigid burden of proof. The record in this case reveals that Renton relied heavily on the experience of, and studies produced by, the city of Seattle. In Seattle, as in Renton, the adult theater zoning ordinance was aimed at preventing the secondary effects caused by the presence of even one such theater in a given neighborhood . . .

We hold that Renton was entitled to rely on the experiences of Seattle and other cities, and in particular on the "detailed findings" summarized in the Washington Supreme Court's *Northend Cinema* opinion, in enacting its adult theater zoning ordinance. The First Amendment does not require a city, before enacting such an ordinance, to conduct new studies or produce evidence independent of that already generated by other cities, so long as whatever evidence the city relies upon is reasonably believed to be relevant to the problem that the city addresses. That was the case here. Nor is our holding affected by the fact that Seattle ultimately chose a different method of adult theater zoning than that chosen by Renton, since Seattle's choice of a different remedy to combat the secondary effects of adult theaters does not call into question either Seattle's identification of those secondary effects or the relevance of Seattle's experience to Renton.

We also find no constitutional defect in the method chosen by Renton to further its substantial interests. Cities may regulate adult theaters by dispersing them, as in Detroit, or by effectively concentrating them, as in Renton. "It is not our function to appraise the wisdom of [the city's] decision to require adult theaters to be separated rather than concentrated in the same areas. . . . [T]he city must be allowed a reasonable opportunity to experiment with solutions to admittedly serious problems." *American Mini Theatres.* Moreover, the Renton ordinance is "narrowly tailored" to affect only that category of theaters shown to produce the unwanted secondary effects, thus avoiding the flaw that proved fatal to the regulations [in other cases].

Respondents contend that the Renton ordinance is "under-inclusive," in that it fails to regulate other kinds of adult businesses that are likely to produce secondary effects similar to those produced by adult theaters. On this record the contention must fail. There is no evidence that, at the time the Renton ordinance was enacted, any other adult business was located in, or was contemplating moving into, Renton. In fact, Resolution No. 2368, enacted in October 1980, states that "the City of Renton does not, at the present time, have any business whose primary purpose is the sale, rental, or showing of sexually explicit materials." That Renton chose first to address the potential problems created by one particular kind of adult business in no way suggests that the city has "singled out" adult theaters for discriminatory treatment. We simply have no basis on this record for assuming that Renton will not, in the future, amend its ordinance to include other kinds of adult businesses that have been shown to produce the same kinds of secondary effects as adult theaters. *Williamson v. Lee Optical*, 348 U.S. 483, 488–489 (1955).

Finally, turning to the question whether the Renton ordinance allows for reasonable alternative avenues of communication, we note that the ordinance leaves some 520 acres, or more than five percent of the entire land area of Renton, open to use as adult theater sites . . .

Respondents argue [that none of the available land is "commercially viable."] The Court of Appeals accepted these arguments . . . and therefore held that the Renton ordinance "would result in a substantial restriction" on speech.

We disagree with both the reasoning and the conclusion of the Court of Appeals. That respondents must fend for themselves in the real estate market, on an equal footing with other prospective purchasers and lessees, does not give rise to a First Amendment violation. . . . In our view, the First Amendment requires only that Renton refrain from effectively denying respondents a reasonable opportunity to open and operate an adult theater within the city, and the ordinance before us easily meets this requirement.

In sum, we find that the Renton ordinance represents a valid governmental response to the "admittedly serious problems" created by adult theaters. Renton has not used "the power to zone as a pretext for suppressing expression," but rather has sought to make some areas available for adult theaters and their patrons, while at the same time preserving the quality of life in the community at large by preventing those theaters from locating in other areas. This, after all, is the essence of zoning. Here, as in *American Mini Theatres,* the city has enacted a zoning ordinance that meets these goals while also satisfying the dictates of the First Amendment.

■ JUSTICE BLACKMUN concurs in the result.

■ JUSTICE BRENNAN, with whom JUSTICE MARSHALL joins, dissenting.

Renton's zoning ordinance selectively imposes limitations on the location of a movie theater based exclusively on the content of the films shown there. The constitutionality of the ordinance is therefore not correctly analyzed under standards applied to content-neutral time, place, and manner restrictions. But even assuming that the ordinance may fairly be characterized as content neutral, it is plainly unconstitutional under the standards established by the decisions of this Court. Although the Court's analysis is limited to cases involving "businesses that purvey sexually explicit materials," and thus does not affect our holdings in cases involving state regulation of other kinds of speech, I dissent.

I

"[A] constitutionally permissible time, place, or manner restriction may not be based upon either the content or subject matter of speech." The Court asserts that the ordinance is "aimed not at the *content* of the films shown at 'adult motion picture theatres,' but rather at the *secondary effects* of such theaters on the surrounding community," and thus is simply a time, place, and manner regulation.[1] This analysis is misguided.

The fact that adult movie theaters may cause harmful "secondary" land-use effects may arguably give Renton a compelling reason to regulate such establishments; it does not mean, however, that such regulations are content neutral. Because the ordinance imposes special restrictions on certain kinds of speech on the basis of *content,* I cannot simply accept, as the Court does, Renton's claim that the ordinance was not designed to suppress the content of adult movies . . . In this case, both the language of the ordinance and its dubious legislative history belie the Court's conclusion that "the city's pursuit of its zoning interests here was unrelated to the suppression of free expression."

A

The ordinance discriminates on its face against certain forms of speech based on content . . . Other [types of] motion picture theaters, and other forms of "adult entertainment," such as bars, massage parlors, and adult bookstores, are not subject to the same restrictions. This selective treatment strongly suggests that Renton was interested not in controlling the "secondary effects" associated with adult businesses, but in discriminating against adult theaters based on the content of the films they exhibit. The Court ignores this discriminatory treatment, declaring that Renton is free "to address the potential problems created by one particular kind of adult business," and to amend the ordinance in the future to include other adult enterprises. However, because of the First Amendment interests at stake here, this one-step-at-a-time analysis is wholly inappropriate.

> "This Court frequently has upheld underinclusive classifications on the sound theory that a legislature may deal with one part of a problem without addressing all of it. See *e.g., Williamson v. Lee Optical Inc.*, 348 U.S. 483 (1955). This presumption of statutory validity, however, has less force when a classification turns on the subject matter of expression. '[A]bove all else, the First Amendment means that government has no power to restrict expression because of its message, its ideas, its subject matter, or its content.'" *Erznoznik v. City of Jacksonville*, 422 U.S. 205, 215 (1975).

In this case, the city has not justified treating adult movie theaters differently from other adult entertainment businesses. The ordinance's underinclusiveness is cogent evidence that it was aimed at the *content* of the films shown in adult movie theaters.

B

Shortly *after* this lawsuit commenced, the Renton City Council amended the ordinance, adding a provision explaining that its intention in adopting the ordinance

---

[1]   The Court apparently finds comfort in the fact that the ordinance does not "deny use to those wishing to express less favored or more controversial views." However, content-based discrimination is not rendered "any less odious" because it distinguishes "among entire classes of ideas, rather than among points of view within a particular class." . . .

had been "to promote the City of Renton's great interest in protecting and preserving the quality of its neighborhoods, commercial districts, and the quality of urban life through effective land use planning." The amended ordinance also lists certain conclusory "findings" concerning adult entertainment land uses that the Council purportedly relied upon in adopting the ordinance. The city points to these provisions as evidence that the ordinance was designed to control the secondary effects associated with adult movie theaters, rather than to suppress the content of the films they exhibit. However, the "legislative history" of the ordinance strongly suggests otherwise.

Prior to the amendment, there was no indication that the ordinance was designed to address any "secondary effects" a single adult theater might create. In addition to the suspiciously coincidental timing of the amendment, many of the City Council's "findings" do not relate to legitimate land-use concerns. As the Court of Appeals observed, "[b]oth the magistrate and the district court recognized that many of the stated reasons for the ordinance were no more than expressions of dislike for the subject matter." That some residents may be offended by the *content* of the films shown at adult movie theaters cannot form the basis for state regulation of speech.

Some of the "findings" added by the City Council do relate to supposed "secondary effects" associated with adult movie theaters. However, the Court cannot, as it does, merely accept these *post hoc* statements at face value . . . *[The Court noted that the City Council "conducted no studies, and heard no expert testimony" and "never considered" less restrictive alternatives. It also did not demonstrate that the experiences of other cities "were relevant to Renton's problems."—Editors]*

Rather than speculate about Renton's motives for adopting such measures, our cases require the conclusion that the ordinance, like any other content-based restriction on speech, is constitutional "only if the [city] can show that [it] is a precisely drawn means of serving a compelling [governmental] interest." Only this strict approach can insure that cities will not use their zoning powers as a pretext for suppressing constitutionally protected expression.

Applying this standard to the facts of this case, the ordinance is patently unconstitutional. Renton has not shown that locating adult movie theaters in proximity to its churches, schools, parks, and residences will necessarily result in undesirable "secondary effects," or that these problems could not be effectively addressed by less intrusive restrictions . . .

NOTES

1.   Is there any answer to Justice Brennan's point that the "secondary effects" invoked by the city are nothing other than justifications, to be judged according to the appropriate standard of review (in his view, strict scrutiny)? Is the majority correct to say that an ordinance directed at some movies and not others is "content-neutral"?

2.   Perhaps the opinion is best understood as creating an entirely new mode of analysis, rather than as a type of "content-neutrality." Under this view, an ordinance restricting the time, place, or manner of speech is subject to lesser scrutiny if (1) it does not distinguish between types of speech on the basis of content, or (2) if the justification for the restriction is unrelated to the communicative impact of the speech. Does that principle make sense of the purposes of the First Amendment? Is it too broad? Think of

the various cases we have encountered. How many of them could be recast as "secondary effects" cases?

3. It is important to keep in mind two restrictions on the application of the secondary-effects analysis. First, it applies only to time, place, and manner regulations, and not to complete prohibitions on speech. Second, it applies only to secondary effects that are not the result of the communicative impact, or message, of the speech. In *Renton*, for example, prostitutes and crime might well be attracted to XXX-rated theaters because of the clientele these theaters attract, which is not a result of the images being conveyed. In *Boos v. Barry* (a case distinguished by the *Renton* Court), the offense to the foreign embassies entailed by hostile demonstrations was a direct result of the messages themselves. Is that a coherent distinction? Is it an important distinction, grounded in genuine First Amendment logic?

[Assignment 46]

F. INCITEMENT, SUBVERSIVE ADVOCACY, AND THREATS

As the cases in the preceding section have illustrated, a core principle of the First Amendment's Free Speech Clause is that the government may not prohibit, punish, or penalize speech because of its content or message. But what about where the speech advocates unlawful conduct? What if the speech advocates murder? Overthrow of the government by force or violence? Criminal resistance to the draft? Should the usual free speech answer—the government may not prohibit, punish, or penalize speech based on its content or viewpoint—be different where the speaker is advocating illegal conduct, or trying to "incite" violence or other illegal action? The government certainly may regulate or prohibit the underlying conduct that the speaker is advocating. When, if ever, does this mean that the government should be able to prohibit the advocacy itself?

A Historical Introduction to Incitement, Subversive Advocacy, and Speech Urging Violation of the Law

1. Section 1 of the Sedition Act of 1798, entitled "An Act for the Punishment of Certain Crimes Against the United States," made it a crime to "unlawfully combine or conspire together, with *intent to oppose any measure or measures of the government of the United States,* which are or shall be directed by proper authority, *or to impede the operation of any law of the United State.*" It further provided that "if any person or persons, *with intent as aforesaid, shall counsel, advise or attempt to procure* any insurrection, riot, unlawful assembly, or combination, . . . he or they shall be deemed guilty of a high misdemeanor." (The controversy over the Alien and Sedition Acts is further discussed at p. 46). Was Section 1 of the Sedition Act unconstitutional?

It was Section 2 of the Sedition Act that punished "false, scandalous and malicious writing" against the government of the United States and that gave rise to the prosecution of journalists, members of Congress, and others for scurrilous public criticism of the Adams administration. Was *that* part of the Sedition Act unconstitutional?

2. Long before the issue of unlawful advocacy first made its appearance in U.S. Supreme Court cases in the World War I era, there was a fascinating example in the middle of the Civil War. General Ambrose Burnside had issued "General Order

No. 38," which announced that anyone who committed "acts for the benefit of the enemies of our country," including "the habit of declaring sympathies for the enemy," would be arrested.

Former Congressman Clement Vallandigham, an irascible, racist "copperhead" (or "peace") Democratic critic of the administration, decided to test the order. He gave a contentious, anti-war speech against Lincoln and the draft within Burnside's jurisdiction. Vallandigham railed against "King Lincoln," and his "black Republican" policies like the Emancipation Proclamation and urged his fellow Ohio citizens not to cooperate with the administration. The war was "wicked, cruel, and unnecessary," a war "for the freedom of the blacks and the enslavement of the whites," Vallandigham railed. By innuendo, at least, his two-hour tirade suggested that individuals resist military service and the authority of the administration and military officers in the enforcement of the draft. On May 5, 1863, Burnside and Union soldiers arrested Vallandigham and tried him, before a military commission, for violating General Order 38. The action created a small political firestorm, including a public letter from a group of citizens in New York arguing that the action was unconstitutional.

Lincoln was presented with a difficult problem. On the one hand, it was hard to defend General Burnside's action. On the other, releasing Vallandigham and repudiating his own general would have undermined the general's authority and created a host of other problems. Lincoln, in a public letter "To Erastus Corning and Others" (June 12, 1863) made the best defense he could of the constitutional validity of the arrest of Vallandigham—and then commuted his sentence to banishment behind Confederate lines. Lincoln, a shrewd lawyer, laid out versions of arguments that would become the building blocks of Supreme Court doctrine many decades later:

> Take the particular case mentioned by the meeting. It is asserted in substance that Mr. Vallandigham was by a military commander, seized and tried "for no other reason than words addressed to a public meeting, in criticism of the course of the administration, and in condemnation of the military orders of that general." Now, if there be no mistake about this—if this assertion is the truth and the whole truth—if there was no other reason for the arrest, then I concede that the arrest was wrong. But the arrest, as I understand, was made for a very different reason. Mr. Vallandigham avows his hostility to the war on the part of the Union; and his arrest was made because he was laboring, with some effect, to prevent the raising of troops, to encourage desertions from the army, and to leave the rebellion without an adequate military force to suppress it. He was not arrested because he was damaging the political prospects of the administration, or the personal interests of the commanding general; but because he was damaging the army, upon the existence, and vigor of which, the life of the nation depends. He was warring upon the military; and this gave the military constitutional jurisdiction to lay hands upon him. If Mr. Vallandigham was not damaging the military power of the country, then his arrest was made on mistake of fact, which I would be glad to correct, on reasonably satisfactory evidence.
>
> I understand the meeting, whose resolutions I am considering, to be in favor of suppressing the rebellion by military force—by armies. Long

experience has shown that armies can not be maintained unless desertion shall be punished by the severe penalty of death. The case requires, and the law and the constitution, sanction this punishment. Must I shoot a simple-minded soldier boy who deserts, while I must not touch a hair of a wily agitator who induces him to desert? This is none the less injurious when effected by getting a father, or brother, or friend, into a public meeting, and there working upon his feeling, till he is persuaded to write the soldier boy, that he is fighting in a bad cause, for a wicked administration of a contemptible government, too weak to arrest and punish him if he shall desert. I think that in such a case, to silence the agitator, and save the boy, is not only constitutional, but, withal, a great mercy.

If I be wrong on this question of constitutional power, my error lies in believing that certain proceedings are constitutional when, in cases of rebellion or Invasion, the public Safety requires them, which would not be constitutional when, in absence of rebellion or invasion, the public Safety does not require them—in other words, that the constitution is not in its application in all respects the same, in cases of Rebellion or invasion, involving the public Safety, as it is in times of profound peace and public security. The constitution itself makes the distinction; and I can no more be persuaded that the government can constitutionally take no strong measure in time of rebellion, because it can be shown that the same could not be lawfully taken in time of peace, than I can be persuaded that a particular drug is not good medicine for a sick man, because it can be shown to not be good food for a well one. . . .

And yet, let me say that in my own discretion, I do not know whether I would have ordered the arrest of Mr. V. While I can not shift the responsibility from myself, I hold that, as a general rule, the commander in the field is the better judge of the necessity in any particular case. Of course I must practice a general directory and revisory power in the matter.

One of the resolutions expresses the opinion of the meeting that arbitrary arrests will have the effect to divide and distract those who should be united in suppressing the rebellion; and I am specifically called on to discharge Mr. Vallandigham. I regard this as, at least, a fair appeal to me, on the expediency of exercising a constitutional power which I think exists. In response to such appeal I have to say it gave me pain when I learned that Mr. V. had been arrested, that is, I was pained that there should have seemed to be a necessity for arresting him and that it will afford me great pleasure to discharge him so soon as I can, by any means, believe the public safety will not suffer by it. . . .

What do you make of Lincoln's argument that Vallandigham was arrested for "warring on the military"—for punishable *conduct*, not for his *expression of views* criticizing the government? Lincoln concedes in principle that the latter would not be a constitutional basis for suppressing speech. Is incitement to draft resistance, or even to desertion, punishable conduct or protected speech? What is the appropriate answer to Lincoln's famous rhetorical question: "Must I shoot a simple-minded soldier boy who deserts, while I must not touch a hair of a wily agitator who induces him to desert?" Lincoln also makes an argument from necessity, under the circumstances—that sometimes even the most valued liberties must yield to pressing public necessity. Do you agree?

3.   Of all the speech restrictions that have been adopted in American history on the grounds that certain speech has harmful tendencies, perhaps the most severe came during the administration of President Woodrow Wilson. During World War I, the administration pressed for adoption of the Espionage Age of 1917 and the Sedition Act of 1918, as tools for combating opposition to the war, the draft, and the administration's wartime policies. Congress gave the administration much of what it sought, and the Wilson administration gave these acts the broadest possible readings "in order to suppress a broad range of political dissent." Stone, PERILOUS TIMES at 146. Even after the war was over, the administration continued to arrest and prosecute alleged communists, radicals, and anarchists.

The Espionage Act of 1917 was largely directed at the disclosure of military secrets. But the act also created three new offenses:

> [1] Whoever, when the United States is at war, shall willfully make or convey false reports or false statements with intent to interfere with the operation or success of the military or naval forces of the United States or to promote the success of its enemies, and [2] whoever, when the United States is at war, shall willfully cause or attempt to cause insubordination, disloyalty, mutiny, or refusal of duty, in the military or naval forces of the United States, or [3] shall willfully obstruct the recruiting or enlistment service of the United States, to the injury of the service or of the United States, shall be punished by a fine of not more than $10,000 or imprisonment for not more than twenty years, or both.

There were over 2,000 convictions for violations of the act. Were these provisions constitutional? In 1919, a trio of cases reached the Supreme Court. The majority opinion in the lead case, *Schenck v. United States*, 249 U.S. 47 (1919), written by Justice Oliver Wendell Holmes, is famous for its creation of the "clear and present danger" test. The offense consisted of a printed pamphlet arguing that conscription violated the Thirteenth Amendment (prohibiting slavery), championing "your right to assert your opposition to the draft," and denying the power of the government to order troops abroad. "You must do your share to maintain, support and uphold the rights of the people of this country," the pamphlet argued.

Justice Holmes wrote: "Of course the document would not have been sent unless it had been intended to have some effect, and we do not see what effect it could be expected to have upon persons subject to the draft except to influence them to obstruct the carrying of it out. The defendants do not deny that the jury might find against them [in this respect]." As to the defendant's objection on First Amendment grounds, he said:

> We admit that in many places and in ordinary times the defendants in saying all that was said in the circular would have been within their constitutional rights. But . . . the most stringent protection of free speech would not protect a man in falsely shouting fire in a theatre and causing a panic. . . . The question in every case is whether the words used are used in such circumstances and are of such a nature as to create a clear and present danger that they will bring about the substantive evils that Congress has a right to prevent. It is a question of proximity and degree. When a nation

is at war many things that might be said in time of peace are such a hindrance to its effort that their utterance will not be endorsed so long as men fight, and that no Court could regard them as protected by any constitutional right.

The Court concluded that if such words had the actual effect of obstructing recruitment, they could be punished. It followed that if the words were spoken with intent to produce such effect, and had such a natural tendency, they could be punished whether or not they had actually obstructed recruitment.

Frohwerk v. United States, 249 U.S. 204 (1919), decided a week after *Schenck*, upheld a conviction for publishing a newspaper that allegedly attempted to cause disloyalty, mutiny, and refusal of duty in the military. There was, "so far as the language of the articles goes," no difference between them and those in *Schenck*. "The first begins by declaring it a monumental and inexcusable mistake to send our soldiers to France, says that it comes no doubt from the great trusts, and later that it appears to be outright murder without serving anything practical; speaks of the unconquerable spirit and undiminished strength of the German nation, and characterizes its own discourse as words of warning to the American people." Holmes again wrote for the Court: "[W]e find ourselves unable to say that the articles could not furnish a basis for a conviction."

But perhaps the most controversial decision of the Court concerning "seditious" speech or incitement was *Debs v. United States,* 249 U.S. 211 (1919). Eugene V. Debs was a Socialist Party presidential candidate, who at one time received over a million votes for the Presidency of the United States. Debs delivered a speech, the "main theme" of which was "Socialism, its growth, and a prophecy of its ultimate success." The Court noted: "With that we have nothing to do, but if a part or the manifest intent of the more general utterances was to encourage those present to obstruct the recruiting service and if in passages such encouragement was directly given, the immunity of the general theme may not be enough to protect the speech." In an opinion by Justice Holmes, the Supreme Court affirmed his conviction under the Espionage Act.

Most of the speech, as summarized in the opinion, consisted of praise for various "loyal comrades" in the struggle for the "working class." One of these men had been convicted of obstructing the recruiting service and attempting to cause insubordination and refusal of duty in the military forces of the United States. In the course of the trial, the defendant addressed the jury himself, and while contending that his speech did not warrant the charges said, "I have been accused of obstructing the war. I admit it. Gentlemen, I abhor war. I would oppose the war if I stood alone." The Court observed that "The statement was not necessary to warrant the jury in finding that one purpose of the speech, whether incidental or not does not matter, was to oppose not only war in general but this war, and that the opposition was so expressed that its natural and intended effect would be to obstruct recruiting. If that was intended and if, in all the circumstances, that would be its probable effect, it would not be protected by reason of its being part of a general program and expressions of a general and conscientious belief." The Court concluded that "the jury were most carefully instructed that they could not find the defendant guilty for advocacy of any of his opinions unless the words used had as their natural tendency and reasonably probable effect to obstruct the recruiting service, & c., and unless the defendant had the specific intent to do so in his mind."

Debs was sentenced to prison for ten years, which he served in a maximum security prison in Georgia. Debs ran again for president in 1920—from prison—and received nearly a million votes, approximately as many as he had received in 1912. Following the election, the lame-duck President Wilson was urged to commute Debs's sentence, because sixty-five-year-old Debs was in poor health and it was feared he might die in prison. Wilson refused. Eventually, on Christmas Day of 1921, President Warren Harding commuted Debs's sentence.

Following *Debs*, the next term, in *Abrams v. United States*, 250 U.S. 616 (1919), the Court again upheld a conviction under the statute for publishing circulars advocating a general strike and urging munitions factory workers to stop producing weapons that might be used against Russian revolutionaries. The majority applied the "clear and present danger" formulation that Justice Holmes set forth in *Schenck*. This time, however, Justice Holmes disagreed with the result, finding insufficient proof of intent to interfere with the war effort. His dissent, joined by Justice Brandeis, began by reaffirming the correctness of the *Schenck-Frohwerk-Debs* trilogy and the "clear and present danger" test he coined:

> I do not doubt for a moment that by the same reasoning that would justify punishing persuasion to murder, the United States constitutionally may punish speech that produces or is intended to produce a clear and imminent danger that it will bring about forthwith certain substantive evils that the United States constitutionally may seek to prevent. The power undoubtedly is greater in time of war than in time of peace because war opens dangers that do not exist at other times. But as against dangers peculiar to war, as against others, the principle of the right to free speech is always the same. It is only the present danger of immediate evil or an intent to bring it about that warrants Congress in setting a limit to the expression of opinion where private rights are not concerned.

But Holmes challenged the *application* of this rule to the pamphlets at issue and the charges against Abrams:

> Now nobody can suppose that the surreptitious publishing of a silly leaflet by an unknown man, without more, would present any immediate danger that its opinion would hinder the success of the government arms or have any appreciable tendency to do so. Publishing those opinions for the very purpose of obstructing, however, might indicate a greater danger and at any rate would have the quality of an attempt . . . [but] I do not see how anyone can find the intent required by the statute in any of the defendants' words.

Is Holmes's disagreement with the majority in *Abrams* simply a factual disagreement as to how dangerous one pamphlet's message is as opposed to another's? How secure is the freedom of speech of an agitator, if he must guess, at his "own peril, subject to a jury's guessing at motive, tendency and possible effect," whether his speech will be protected? Ernst Freund, *The Debs Case and Freedom of Speech*, The New Republic (May 3, 1919). Holmes's *Abrams* dissent ended with stirring words about the value of freedom of speech:

> Persecution for the expression of opinions seems to me perfectly logical. If you have no doubt of your premises or your power and want a certain result with all your heart you naturally express your wishes in law and sweep

away all opposition. To allow opposition by speech seems to indicate that you think the speech impotent, as when a man says that he has squared the circle, or that you do not care whole-heartedly for the result, or that you doubt either your power or your premises. But when men have realized that time has upset many fighting faiths, they may come to believe even more than they believe the very foundations of their own conduct that the ultimate good desired is better reached by free trade in ideas—that the best test of truth is the power of the thought to get itself accepted in the competition of the market, and that truth is the only ground upon which their wishes safely can be carried out. That at any rate is the theory of our Constitution. . . . I wholly disagree with the argument of the Government that the First Amendment left the common law as to seditious libel in force. History seems to me against the notion. I had conceived that the United States through many years had shown its repentance for the Sedition Act of 1798, by repaying fines that it imposed. Only the emergency that makes it immediately dangerous to leave the correction of evil counsels to time warrants making any exception to the sweeping command, "Congress shall make no [law] abridging the freedom of speech."

Is this consistent with Holmes's opinion affirming the conviction of Eugene Debs?

4.   Two important successors to the World War I era cases are *Gitlow v. New York*, 268 U.S. 652 (1925), and *Whitney v. California*, 274 U.S. 357 (1927). Unlike the World War I era cases, these arose under the Fourteenth Amendment. The Court upheld state convictions for "criminal anarchy" (*Gitlow*) and "criminal syndicalism" (*Whitney*) based on advocacy, or organization to engage in advocacy, of the "duty, necessity and propriety of overthrowing and overturning organized government by force, violence, and unlawful means." *Gitlow*, 268 U.S. at 654. Justices Holmes, joined by Justice Brandeis, dissented in *Gitlow*:

If what I think the correct test is applied, it is manifest that there was no present danger of an attempt to overthrow the government by force on the part of the admittedly small minority who shared the defendant's views. It is said that this manifesto was more than a theory, that it was an incitement. Every idea is an incitement. It offers itself for belief and if believed it is acted on unless some other belief outweighs it or some failure of energy stifles the movement at its birth. The only difference between the expression of an opinion and an incitement in the narrower sense is the speaker's enthusiasm for the result. Eloquence may set fire to reason. But whatever may be thought of the redundant discourse before us it had no chance of starting a present conflagration. If in the long run the beliefs expressed in proletarian dictatorship are destined to be accepted by the dominant forces of the community, the only meaning of free speech is that they should be given their chance and have their way.

If the publication of this document had been laid as an attempt to induce an uprising against government at once and not at some indefinite time in the future it would have presented a different question. The object would have been one with which the law might deal, subject to the doubt whether there was any danger that the publication could produce any result, or in other words, whether it was not futile and too remote from possible consequences.

Under the Holmes-Brandeis reasoning, is "incendiary" speech permissible—unless it is likely to be effective?

In *Whitney*, Justice Brandeis, joined by Justice Holmes, concurred in the judgment affirming the conviction. Justice Brandeis's opinion is significant for its refinement of the formulation of the "clear and present danger" test. Elements of this opinion now form part of the Supreme Court's modern doctrine, as set forth in *Brandenburg v. Ohio* (1969). But Brandeis and Holmes nonetheless voted to affirm the conviction of a "radical" for advocating "criminal syndicalism" based on her membership in the Communist Labor Party and its adopted manifesto.

5.   What if there exists an ideological group committed to engaging in acts of violence for political purposes, and organizing for such common purposes, and the government believes—or fears—that the group may have, or may in due time acquire, the means of actually carrying out its goals? May it punish such an organization as a criminal conspiracy, on the basis of the content of its message? Make the group in question the Communist Party of the United States and you have *Dennis v. United States*, 341 U.S. 494 (1951), a mammoth case involving the criminal prosecution of the leadership of the Communist Party USA during the height of Cold War fears. The Court upheld the conviction for organizing a group to teach and advocate the overthrow of the government of the United States by force and violence. A four-justice plurality, in an opinion by Chief Justice Vinson, applied a version of the "clear and present danger" test to uphold the convictions:

> [T]he words "clear and present danger" cannot mean that before the Government may act, it must wait until the putsch is about to be executed, the plans have been laid and the signal is awaited. If Government is aware that a group aiming at its overthrow is attempting to indoctrinate its members and to commit them to a course whereby they will strike when the leaders feel the circumstances permit, action by the Government is required. . . . Certainly an attempt to overthrow the Government by force, even though doomed from the outset because of inadequate numbers or power of the revolutionists, is a sufficient evil for Congress to prevent. The damage which such attempts create both physically and politically to a nation makes it impossible to measure the validity in terms of the probability of success, or the immediacy of a successful attempt. [We] must therefore reject the contention that success or probability of success is the criterion.

The plurality's analysis provoked the vigorous dissents of Justices Black and Douglas, who argued that the application of the test had severely watered down the original standard.

The majority to affirm the conviction was supplied by the separate concurrences of Justice Frankfurter and of Justice Jackson. Frankfurter's opinion eschewed absolute rules and embraced balancing of interests and deference to legislative judgments:

> [It] is not for us to decide how we would adjust the clash of interests which this case presents were the primary responsibility . . . ours. Congress has determined that the danger created by advocacy of overthrow justifies the

ensuing restriction on freedom of speech. [To] make validity of legislation depend on judicial reading of events still in the womb of time—a forecast, that is, of the outcome of forces at best appreciated only with knowledge of the topmost secrets of nations—is to charge the judiciary with duties beyond its [capacity].

Justice Jackson argued that the "clear and present danger" test was more appropriate as a "rule of reason" reserved for the types of cases in which it arose—"criminality of a hotheaded speech on a street corner, or circulation of a few incendiary pamphlets." In Jackson's view, applying the clear-and-present-danger test to organizations advocating violent overthrow would require the Court to

> appraise imponderables, including international and national phenomena which baffle the best informed foreign offices and our most experienced politicians. . . . The judicial process simply is not adequate to a trial of such far-flung issues. The answers given would reflect our own political predilections and nothing more. The authors of the clear and present danger test never applied it to a case like this, nor would I. If applied as it is proposed here, it means that the Communist plotting is protected during its period of incubation; its preliminary stages of organization and preparation are immune from the law; the Government can move only after imminent action is manifest, when it would, of course, be too late.

Dennis is a transitional case in terms of Supreme Court doctrine. No opinion commanded a majority and the clear-and-present danger test governing speech advocating violent action was changed in *Brandenburg*, which we take up next.

It is easy to unthinkingly dismiss the fears of Communist conspiracies in the United States during the Cold War. In THE LOGIC OF PERSECUTION: FREE EXPRESSION AND THE MCCARTHY ERA (2005), Martin Redish notes that former Soviet archives show that there really was a form of Communist conspiracy in the United States, involving espionage and subterfuge and including high-ranking government officers. If you were confident of those facts, would they justify the prosecution in *Dennis*? It may help to think about a more modern example.

A NOTE ON *HOLDER V. HUMANITARIAN LAW PROJECT*

Holder v. Humanitarian Law Project, 561 U.S. 1 (2010), raised a facial challenge to a law prohibiting "material support" to foreign terrorist organizations. The central question was whether the national security considerations supporting the statute were sufficiently compelling to justify prohibiting *speech* assisting such organizations—even speech that did not directly facilitate an unlawful act. The Court, 6–3, upheld the statute, as applied, in an opinion by Chief Justice Roberts.

The Court rejected the government's broader position that the law regulated only conduct for reasons unrelated to its message, and thus should be sustained under the standards of *United States v. O'Brien*: "The Government is wrong that the only thing actually at issue in this litigation is conduct, and therefore wrong to argue that *O'Brien* provides the correct standard of review. *O'Brien* does not provide the applicable standard for reviewing a content-based regulation of speech, and [the material-support statute] regulates speech on the basis of its content. Plaintiffs want to speak to the [groups identified by the government as foreign terrorist organizations] and whether they may do so under [the material-support statute] depends on what they say. If plaintiffs' speech to these groups imparts a 'specific skill' or communicates advice derived from 'specialized knowledge'—for example, training on the use of international law or advice on petitioning the United Nations—then it is barred. On the other hand, plaintiffs' speech is not barred if it imparts only general or unspecialized knowledge." Nor did the Court accept the government's argument that the *O'Brien* standard should apply because the statute "*generally* functions as a regulation of conduct." That argument, the Court said, "runs headlong into a number of our precedents, most prominently *Cohen v. California*, 403 U.S. 15 (1971)." *Cohen* involved a general breach of the peace statute; but as applied to Cohen's expression, the relevant standard was the one regulating speech because of its content.

Nevertheless, the Court sustained the statute, even as a content-based regulation of speech, because of the compelling interest in combating terrorism. "Everyone agrees that the Government's interest in combating terrorism is an urgent objective of the highest order," Chief Justice Roberts wrote. The disagreement centered on plaintiffs' contention that the ban on material support to terrorist organizations, as applied to plaintiffs' expression, was not necessary to further that interest. Plaintiffs claimed that their speech-support would advance "only the legitimate activities of the designated terrorist organizations, not their terrorism." The Court disagreed, wryly noting that, "[w]hether foreign terrorist organizations meaningfully segregate support of their legitimate activities from support of terrorism" was "an empirical question," adding that Congress had considered and appropriately rejected such a view. Material support for the ostensibly peaceable conduct of terrorist organizations "can further terrorism in multiple ways. 'Material support' is a valuable resource by definition. Such support frees up other resources within the organization that may be put to violent ends." The Court noted that "[m]oney is fungible," and, furthermore, that assistance given to certain activities of terrorist organizations may serve to "legitimize and further" their terrorist means. Moreover, such material support "furthers terrorism by straining the United States' relationships with its allies."

The Court rejected the dissent's argument that such reasoning has "no natural stopping place" because "Congress has settled on just such a natural stopping place: The statute reaches only material support coordinated with or under the direction of a designated foreign terrorist organization. Independent advocacy that might be viewed as promoting the group's legitimacy is not covered."

The Court continued: "In analyzing whether it is possible in practice to distinguish material support for a foreign terrorist group's violent activities and its nonviolent activities, we do not rely exclusively on our own inferences drawn from the record evidence." Rather, the Court found the assessments of Congress and the executive branch "entitled to deference." "This litigation implicates sensitive and weighty interests of national security and foreign affairs" on which it was vital that the judicial branch not substitute its own evaluation of evidence for the reasonable judgments of the political branches. Although this did not mean "abdication of the judicial role," the courts have a relative lack of competence in collecting and evaluating this evidence. In such matters, "respect for the Government's conclusions is appropriate."

The Court limited its holding: "All this is not to say that any future applications of the material-support statute to speech or advocacy will survive First Amendment scrutiny. It is also not to say that any other statute relating to speech and terrorism would satisfy the First Amendment. In particular, we in no way suggest that a regulation of independent speech would pass constitutional muster, even if the Government were to show that such speech benefits foreign terrorist organizations. We also do not suggest that Congress could extend the same prohibition on material support at issue here to domestic organizations. We simply hold that, in prohibiting the particular forms of support that plaintiffs seeks to provide to foreign terrorist groups, [the statute] does not violate the freedom of speech." The Court also rejected a claim that the statute unconstitutionally interfered with the freedom of association protected by the First Amendment.

Justice Breyer, joined by Justices Ginsburg and Sotomayor, dissented: "I cannot agree with the Court's conclusion that the Constitution permits the Government to prosecute the plaintiffs criminally for engaging in coordinated teaching and advocacy furthering the designated organizations' lawful political objectives." The dissent emphasized that the activities in which plaintiffs wished to engage—training on "how to use humanitarian and international law to peacefully resolve disputes," political advocacy, and teaching about how to petition representative bodies such as the United Nations—"are of a kind that the First Amendment ordinarily protects."

He acknowledged that "[t]he Government does identify a compelling countervailing interest, namely, the interest in protecting the security of the United States and its nationals from the threats that foreign terrorist organizations pose by denying those organizations financial and other fungible resources." But he added: "I do not dispute the importance of this interest. But I do dispute whether the interest can justify the statute's criminal prohibition."

Justice Breyer therefore would have construed the statute to avoid what he considered "serious doubt" as to its constitutionality: "I would "I would read the statute as criminalizing First-Amendment-protected pure speech and association only when the defendant knows or intends that those activities will assist the organization's unlawful terrorist actions. Under this reading, the Government would have to show, at a minimum, that such defendants provided support that they knew was significantly likely to help the organization pursue its unlawful terrorist aims."

Is this case in any way doctrinally different from cases involving association with the Communist Party?

Do you understand why the majority rejects the analogy to *O'Brien*, and thus applies strict scrutiny? According to the Court, the plaintiffs "want to speak" to the terrorist groups, and whether they may do so under the statute "depends on what they say." Why did the Court not apply "secondary effects" analysis? To be sure, the statute targets "what they say," just as the ordinance did in *Renton*. But might it be argued that the reason for the regulation was not based on the communicative impact of the speech? The government does not care whether anyone is persuaded by the plaintiffs' speech, but only about whether that speech helps the terrorist group. Is that covered by *Renton*? If so, does it suggest a better way to analyze the problem in *Humanitarian Law Project*? Or does it suggest that *Renton*'s "secondary effects" theory is alarmingly broad?

Brandenburg v. Ohio

395 U.S. 444 (1969)

■ PER CURIAM.

The appellant, a leader of a Ku Klux Klan group, was convicted under the Ohio Criminal Syndicalism statute for "advocat[ing] . . . the duty, necessity, or propriety of crime, sabotage, violence, or unlawful methods of terrorism as a means of accomplishing industrial or political reform' and for 'voluntarily assembl[ing] with any society, group, or assemblage of persons formed to teach or advocate the doctrines of criminal syndicalism." He was fined $1,000 and sentenced to one to 10 years' imprisonment. . . .

The record shows that a man, identified at trial as the appellant, telephoned an announcer-reporter on the staff of a Cincinnati television station and invited him to come to a Ku Klux Klan "rally" to be held at a farm in Hamilton County. With the cooperation of the organizers, the reporter and a cameraman attended the meeting and filmed the events. Portions of the films were later broadcast on the local station and on a national network.

The prosecution's case rested on the films and on testimony identifying the appellant as the person who communicated with the reporter and who spoke at the rally. The State also introduced into evidence several articles appearing in the film, including a pistol, a rifle, a shotgun, ammunition, a Bible, and a red hood worn by the speaker in the films.

One film showed 12 hooded figures, some of whom carried firearms. They were gathered around a large wooden cross, which they burned. No one was present other than the participants and the newsmen who made the film. Most of the words uttered during the scene were incomprehensible when the film was projected, but scattered phrases could be understood that were derogatory of Negroes and, in one instance, of Jews.[1] Another scene on the same film showed the appellant, in Klan regalia, making a speech. The speech, in full, was as follows:

> This is an organizers' meeting. We have had quite a few members here today which are—we have hundreds, hundreds of members throughout the State of Ohio. I can quote from a newspaper clipping from the Columbus, Ohio *Dispatch*, five weeks ago Sunday morning. The Klan has more members in the State of Ohio than does any other organization. We're not a revengent organization, but if our President, our Congress, our Supreme Court, continues to suppress the white, Caucasian race, it's possible that there might have to be some revengeance taken.
>
>   We are marching on Congress July the Fourth, four hundred thousand strong. From there we are dividing into two groups, one group to march on St. Augustine, Florida, the other group to march into Mississippi. Thank you.

The second film showed six hooded figures one of whom, later identified as the appellant, repeated a speech very similar to that recorded on the first film. The

---

[1]   The significant portions that could be understood were:
'How far is the nigger going to—yeah.'
'This is what we are going to do to the niggers.'
'A dirty nigger.'
'Send the Jews back to Israel.'
'Let's give them back to the dark garden.'
'Save America.'
'Let's go back to constitutional betterment.'
'Bury the niggers.'
'We intend to do our part.'
'Give us our state rights.'
'Freedom for the whites.'
'Nigger will have to fight for every inch he gets from now on.'

reference to the possibility of "revengeance" was omitted, and one sentence was added: "Personally, I believe the nigger should be returned to Africa, the Jew returned to Israel." Though some of the figures in the films carried weapons, the speaker did not.

The Ohio Criminal Syndicalism Statute was enacted in 1919. From 1917 to 1920, identical or quite similar laws were adopted by 20 States and two territories. E. Dowell, A History of Criminal Syndicalism Legislation in the United States 21 (1939). In 1927, this Court sustained the constitutionality of California's Criminal Syndicalism Act, the text of which is quite similar to that of the laws of Ohio. *Whitney v. California*, 274 U.S. 357 (1927). The Court upheld the statute on the ground that, without more, 'advocating' violent means to effect political and economic change involves such danger to the security of the State that the State may outlaw it. But *Whitney* has been thoroughly discredited by later decisions. See *Dennis v. United States*, 341 U.S. 494, at 507 (1951). These later decisions have fashioned the principle that the constitutional guarantees of free speech and free press do not permit a State to forbid or proscribe advocacy of the use of force or of law violation except where such advocacy is directed to inciting or producing imminent lawless action and is likely to incite or produce such action. As we said in *Noto v. United States*, 367 U.S. 290, 297–298 (1961), "the mere abstract teaching . . . of the moral propriety or even moral necessity for a resort to force and violence, is not the same as preparing a group for violent action and steeling it to such action." A statute which fails to draw this distinction impermissibly intrudes upon the freedoms guaranteed by the First and Fourteenth Amendments. It sweeps within its condemnation speech which our Constitution has immunized from governmental control.

Measured by this test, Ohio's Criminal Syndicalism Act cannot be sustained. The Act punishes persons who "advocate or teach the duty, necessity, or propriety" of violence "as a means of accomplishing industrial or political reform"; or who publish or circulate or display any book or paper containing such advocacy; or who "justify" the commission of violent acts "with intent to exemplify, spread or advocate the propriety of the doctrines of criminal syndicalism"; or who "voluntarily assemble" with a group formed "to teach or advocate the doctrines of criminal syndicalism." Neither the indictment nor the trial judge's instructions to the jury in any way refined the statute's bald definition of the crime in terms of mere advocacy not distinguished from incitement to imminent lawless action.

Accordingly, we are here confronted with a statute which, by its own words and as applied, purports to punish mere advocacy and to forbid, on pain of criminal punishment, assembly with others merely to advocate the described type of action. Such a statute falls within the condemnation of the First and Fourteenth Amendments. The contrary teaching of *Whitney v. California*, cannot be supported, and that decision is therefore overruled. . . .

■ [The concurring opinions of JUSTICE BLACK and JUSTICE DOUGLAS are omitted.]

NOTES

1.   The *Brandenburg* test combines some of the features of the old clear-and-present danger test and some of the features of Justice Brandeis's concurrence in *Whitney*. The core of the test is the following: "[T]he constitutional guarantees of free speech and free press do not permit a State to forbid or proscribe advocacy of the use of

force or of criminality except where such advocacy is directed to inciting or producing imminent lawless action and is likely to incite or produce such action." Break apart the elements:

(1) *"directed to"* (an intent-of-the-speaker element?)

(2) *"inciting or producing"* (words as triggers to action; not pure advocacy)

(3) *"imminent"* (no time for "answering speech" or intervening reflection?)

(4) *"lawless action"* (of *any* kind? No matter how *harmful* the legal violation may be?)

(5) *"**and** likely to produce such action"* (probability of the harm).

Is this a sound dissection of the test? Is *Brandenburg* a *good* test? Is it likely to be a stable, enduring test? Does it accurately capture the meaning of the First Amendment's *language* as applied to this type of problem? How does it differ from Lincoln's "test"? Holmes's? How does it decide cases like Lincoln's concerning Clement Vallandigham? Eugene Debs's speech? *Dennis?* An ISIS sleeper cell?

2.   Consider here the European Court of Human Rights' decision in *Zana v. Turkey*, 27 Eur. Ct. H.R. 667 (1997). Mr. Mehdi Zana was a Turkish national who had once served as mayor of a city in the Kurdish southeast of Turkey. Since 1985, more than 8,000 people had been killed in this part of Turkey as a result of conflict between the government and the PKK (Worker's Party of Kurdistan). Mr. Zana had long been a supporter of the Kurdish cause who was opposed to violence. While in a Turkish prison on other charges, he gave an interview to a newspaper. He said: "I support the PKK national liberation movement, on the other hand, I am not in favor of massacres. Anyone can make mistakes, and the PKK kill women and children by mistake." Mr. Zana was charged with the crime of supporting an armed organization, the PKK, whose aim was to break up Turkey's territorial integrity. Zana was accused of inciting people to disobey the law and with stirring up hatred and hostility in a way that endangered the public safety. Mr. Zana argued that his conviction under Turkish law violated Article 10 of the European Convention on Human Rights, which protects "freedom of expression," and Article 9 of the Convention, which protects freedom of thought. Turkey responded that paragraph 2 of Article 10 allows the government to suppress freedom of expression where doing so is "necessary in a democratic society, in the interest of national security, territorial integrity, or public safety, for the prevention of disorder or crime for the protection of public health and morals." The European Court of Human Rights ruled in favor of Turkey and upheld Zana's conviction under the Convention. Support given to the PKK by a former mayor could be construed as incitement to violence. In any event, the European Court said Turkey was entitled to "a margin of appreciation" such that standards of what might constitute incitement in the whole of Europe might be relaxed in Turkey given its unique history and circumstances. Eight judges dissented, at least in part. Was Zana guilty of incitement? Is the European Convention insufficiently protective of freedom of expression because of the explicit balancing language in the text of Article 10 quoted above? What do you think in this context of the idea of a margin of appreciation? Would the robust protection of freedom of speech Americans enjoy have been appropriate in West Germany in 1949—right after the defeat of Hitler and in a time of conflict with Stalin?

A NOTE ON *PLANNED PARENTHOOD OF THE COLUMBIA/WILLAMETTE, INC. V. AMERICAN COALITION OF LIFE ACTIVISTS*

Consider the case of *Planned Parenthood of the Columbia/Willamette, Inc. v. American Coalition of Life Activists*, 290 F.3d 1058 (9th Cir. 2002) (en banc). The facts in brief: Plaintiffs were abortion clinics and abortion-performing doctors. Defendants were strident anti-abortion, "pro-life" activists—individuals and an organization called "American Coalition of Life Activists" (ACLA). ACLA maintained a web site called "The Nuremburg Files." The web site identified certain abortion doctors by name, address, and photograph. It described the doctors as murderers who, while not capable of being punished under present law, perhaps could be punished one day, just as Nazi war criminals were punished in the Nuremburg trials following World War II. Where an abortion provider had been killed, the web site put a black X through his picture. Defendants also distributed printed "DEADLY DOZEN" and "WANTED" posters, identifying certain abortion doctors as criminal baby-killers.

As the Ninth Circuit's opinion describes, several abortion-performing doctors had been murdered by anti-abortion extremists—none of whom were the individual defendants in this case or part of the ACLA. The plaintiff abortion clinics and doctors brought a civil suit against defendants, seeking an injunction against the website and the distribution of the posters on the ground that they constituted "true threats" of actual violence against them or (alternatively) "incitement" to violence and murder. The suit was brought pursuant to two federal statutes, the Freedom of Access to Clinics Entrances Act and the Racketeer Influenced and Corrupt Organizations Act.

Following a jury trial, the district court awarded actual and punitive damages against the defendants totaling more than $100 million. The court also issued a permanent injunction restraining defendants from publishing or distributing the "DEADLY DOZEN" poster or other posters identifying any of the plaintiffs with intent to threaten them or from posting such materials on the "Nuremburg Files" website or any other website, or from otherwise publishing or distributing personally identifying information about the plaintiffs. A panel of the Ninth Circuit reversed, but the Ninth Circuit granted rehearing *en banc* and held for the plaintiff abortion clinics and doctors:

> Construing the facts in the light most favorable to physicians, the verdict is supported by substantial evidence. ACLA was aware that a "wanted"-type poster would likely be interpreted as a serious threat of death or bodily harm by a doctor in the reproductive health services community who was identified on one, given the previous pattern of "WANTED" posters identifying a specific physician followed by that physician's murder. The same is true of the posting about these physicians on that part of the "Nuremberg Files" where lines were drawn through the names of doctors who provided abortion services and who had been killed or wounded. We are independently satisfied that to this limited extent, ACLA's conduct amounted to a true threat and is not protected speech.

Judge Kozinski wrote for himself and four other dissenters (Berzon, Kleinfeld, O'Scannlain, and Reinhardt), emphasizing that the "true threat" exception applied only when the *speaker himself* was the one threatening to do violence to someone. There was no evidence—apart from the defendants' speech itself—from which anyone could find or infer a threat. In addition, the website and posters did not threaten violence against the plaintiffs, but in fact *disclaimed* any such intention. While the website and posters could be construed as potentially *intimidating*, that did not rob the defendants of their constitutional right to free expression; the *Brandenburg* test for incitement was not met. Judge Kozinski said:

In this case, none of the statements on which liability was premised were overtly threatening. On the contrary, the two posters and the web page, by their explicit terms, foreswore the use of violence and advocated lawful means of persuading plaintiffs to stop performing abortions or punishing them for continuing to do so. Nevertheless, because context matters, the statements could reasonably be interpreted as an effort to intimidate plaintiffs into ceasing their abortion-related activities. If that were enough to strip the speech of First Amendment protection, there would be nothing left to decide. But the Supreme Court has told us that "[s]peech does not lose its protected character . . . simply because it may embarrass others *or coerce them into action*." *NAACP v. Claiborne Hardware Co.*, 458 U.S. 886, 910 (1982) (emphasis added). In other words, some forms of intimidation enjoy constitutional protection. . . .

Even assuming that one could somehow distill a true threat from the posters themselves, the majority opinion is still fatally defective because it contradicts the central holding of *Claiborne Hardware*: Where the speaker is engaged in public political speech, the public statements themselves cannot be the sole proof that they were true threats, unless the speech directly threatens actual injury to identifiable individuals. Absent such an unmistakable, specific threat, there must be evidence *aside from the political statements themselves* showing that the public speaker would himself or in conspiracy with others inflict unlawful harm. 458 U.S. at 932–34. The majority cites not a scintilla of evidence—other than the posters themselves—that plaintiffs or someone associated with them would carry out the threatened harm.

Given this lack of evidence, the posters can be viewed, at most, as a call to arms for *other* abortion protesters to harm plaintiffs. However, the Supreme Court made it clear that under *Brandenburg*, encouragement or even advocacy of violence is protected by the First Amendment: "[M]ere *advocacy* of the use of force or violence does not remove speech from the protection of the First Amendment." *Claiborne Hardware*, 458 U.S. at 927 (citing *Brandenburg*, 395 U.S. at 447) (emphasis in the original). *Claiborne Hardware* in fact goes much farther; it cautions that where liability is premised on "politically motivated" activities, we must "examine critically the basis on which liability was imposed." *Id.* at 915. As the Court explained, "Since respondents would impose liability on the basis of a public address—which predominantly contained highly charged political rhetoric lying at the core of the First Amendment—we approach this suggested basis for liability with extreme care." *Id.* at 926–27. This is precisely what the majority does *not* do; were it to do so, it would have no choice but to reverse. . . .

The Nuremberg Files website is clearly an expression of a political point of view. The posters and the website are designed both to rally political support for the views espoused by defendants, and to intimidate plaintiffs and others like them into desisting abortion-related activities. This political agenda may not be to the liking of many people—political dissidents are often unpopular— but the speech, including the intimidating message, does not constitute a direct threat because there is no evidence other than the speech itself that the speakers intend to resort to physical violence if their threat is not heeded. . . . While today it is abortion protesters who are singled out for punitive treatment, the precedent set by this court—the broad and uncritical deference to the judgment of a jury—will haunt dissidents of all political stripes for many years to come. [T]his is contrary to the principles of the First Amendment as explicated by the Supreme Court in *Claiborne Hardware* and its long-standing jurisprudence stemming from *Brandenburg v. Ohio*.

R.A.V. v. St. Paul

505 U.S. 377 (1992)

■ JUSTICE SCALIA delivered the opinion of the Court.

In the predawn hours of June 21, 1990, petitioner and several other teenagers allegedly assembled a crudely made cross by taping together broken chair legs. They then allegedly burned the cross inside the fenced yard of a black family that lived across the street from the house where petitioner was staying. Although this conduct could have been punished under any of a number of laws,[1] one of the two provisions under which respondent city of St. Paul chose to charge petitioner (then a juvenile) was the St. Paul Bias-Motivated Crime Ordinance, St. Paul, Minn., Legis. Code § 292.02 (1990), which provides:

> Whoever places on public or private property a symbol, object, appellation, characterization or graffiti, including, but not limited to, a burning cross or Nazi swastika, which one knows or has reasonable grounds to know arouses anger, alarm or resentment in others on the basis of race, color, creed, religion or gender commits disorderly conduct and shall be guilty of a misdemeanor.

Petitioner moved to dismiss this count on the ground that the St. Paul ordinance was substantially overbroad and impermissibly content based and therefore facially invalid under the First Amendment. The trial court granted this motion, but the Minnesota Supreme Court reversed. . . .

I

In construing the St. Paul ordinance, we are bound by the construction given to it by the Minnesota court. Accordingly, we accept the Minnesota Supreme Court's authoritative statement that the ordinance reaches only those expressions that constitute "fighting words" within the meaning of *Chaplinsky v. New Hampshire*, 315 U.S. 568 (1942). Petitioner and his *amici* urge us to modify the scope of the *Chaplinsky* formulation, thereby invalidating the ordinance as "substantially overbroad." We find it unnecessary to consider this issue. Assuming, *arguendo*, that all of the expression reached by the ordinance is proscribable under the "fighting words" doctrine, we nonetheless conclude that the ordinance is facially unconstitutional in that it prohibits otherwise permitted speech solely on the basis of the subjects the speech addresses.

The First Amendment generally prevents government from proscribing speech, or even expressive conduct, see, *e.g., Texas v. Johnson*, 491 U.S. 397 (1989), because of disapproval of the ideas expressed. Content-based regulations are presumptively invalid. *Simon & Schuster, Inc. v. Members of N.Y. State Crime Victims Bd.*, 502 U.S. 105, 115 (1991); *Police Dept. of Chicago v. Mosley*, 408 U.S. 92, 95 (1972). From 1791

---

[1] The conduct might have violated Minnesota statutes carrying significant penalties. See, *e.g.,* Minn.Stat. § 609.713(1) (1987) (providing for up to five years in prison for terroristic threats); § 609.563 (arson) (providing for up to five years and a $10,000 fine, depending on the value of the property intended to be damaged); § 609.595 (Supp.1992) (criminal damage to property) (providing for up to one year and a $3,000 fine, depending upon the extent of the damage to the property).

to the present, however, our society, like other free but civilized societies, has permitted restrictions upon the content of speech in a few limited areas, which are "of such slight social value as a step to truth that any benefit that may be derived from them is clearly outweighed by the social interest in order and morality." *Chaplinsky*, at 572. We have recognized that "the freedom of speech" referred to by the First Amendment does not include a freedom to disregard these traditional limitations. See*, e.g., Roth v. United States*, 354 U.S. 476 (1957) (obscenity); Beauharnais v. Illinois, 343 U.S. 250 (1952) (defamation); *Chaplinsky* ("fighting words"). Our decisions . . . have narrowed the scope of the traditional categorical exceptions for defamation, see *New York Times Co. v. Sullivan*, 376 U.S. 254 (1964); and for obscenity, see *Miller v. California*, 413 U.S. 15 (1973), but a limited categorical approach has remained an important part of our First Amendment jurisprudence.

We have sometimes said that these categories of expression are "not within the area of constitutionally protected speech," or that the "protection of the First Amendment does not extend" to them. Such statements must be taken in context, however. What they mean is that these areas of speech can, consistently with the First Amendment, be regulated *because of their constitutionally proscribable content* (obscenity, defamation, etc.)—not that they are categories of speech entirely invisible to the Constitution, so that they may be made the vehicles for content discrimination unrelated to their distinctively proscribable content. Thus, the government may proscribe libel; but it may not make the further content discrimination of proscribing *only* libel critical of the government. . . .

The proposition that a particular instance of speech can be proscribable on the basis of one feature (*e.g.*, obscenity) but not on the basis of another (*e.g.*, opposition to the city government) is commonplace and has found application in many contexts. We have long held, for example, that nonverbal expressive activity can be banned because of the action it entails, but not because of the ideas it expresses—so that burning a flag in violation of an ordinance against outdoor fires could be punishable, whereas burning a flag in violation of an ordinance against dishonoring the flag is not. See *Johnson*, at 406–407. See also *United States v. O'Brien*, 391 U.S. 367, 376–377 (1968). Similarly, we have upheld reasonable "time, place, or manner" restrictions, but only if they are "justified without reference to the content of the regulated speech." *Ward v. Rock Against Racism*, 491 U.S. 781, 791 (1989) [upholding a noise ordinance as applied to rock concerts]; see also *Clark v. Community for Creative Non-Violence*, 468 U.S. 288, 298 (1984) (noting that the *O'Brien* test differs little from the standard applied to time, place, or manner restrictions). And just as the power to proscribe particular speech on the basis of a noncontent element (*e.g.*, noise) does not entail the power to proscribe the same speech on the basis of a content element; so also, the power to proscribe it on the basis of *one* content element (*e.g.*, obscenity) does not entail the power to proscribe it on the basis of *other* content elements. . . .

Fighting words are thus analogous to a noisy sound truck. . . . As with the sound truck, however, so also with fighting words: The government may not regulate use based on hostility—or favoritism—towards the underlying message expressed. . . .

II

Applying these principles to the St. Paul ordinance, we conclude that, even as narrowly construed by the Minnesota Supreme Court, the ordinance is facially unconstitutional. Although the phrase in the ordinance, "arouses anger, alarm or resentment in others," has been limited by the Minnesota Supreme Court's construction to reach only those symbols or displays that amount to "fighting words," the remaining, unmodified terms make clear that the ordinance applies only to "fighting words" that insult, or provoke violence, "on the basis of race, color, creed, religion or gender." Displays containing abusive invective, no matter how vicious or severe, are permissible unless they are addressed to one of the specified disfavored topics. Those who wish to use "fighting words" in connection with other ideas—to express hostility, for example, on the basis of political affiliation, union membership, or homosexuality—are not covered. The First Amendment does not permit St. Paul to impose special prohibitions on those speakers who express views on disfavored subjects. *Simon & Schuster*, at 116. In its practical operation, moreover, the ordinance goes even beyond mere content discrimination, to actual viewpoint discrimination. Displays containing some words—odious racial epithets, for example—would be prohibited to proponents of all views. But "fighting words" that do not themselves invoke race, color, creed, religion, or gender—aspersions upon a person's mother, for example—would seemingly be usable *ad libitum* in the placards of those arguing *in favor* of racial, color, etc., tolerance and equality, but could not be used by those speakers' opponents. One could hold up a sign saying, for example, that all "anti-Catholic bigots" are misbegotten; but not that all "papists" are, for that would insult and provoke violence "on the basis of religion." St. Paul has no such authority to license one side of a debate to fight freestyle, while requiring the other to follow Marquis of Queensberry rules.

What we have here, it must be emphasized, is not a prohibition of fighting words that are directed at certain persons or groups (which would be *facially* valid if it met the requirements of the Equal Protection Clause); but rather, a prohibition of fighting words that contain (as the Minnesota Supreme Court repeatedly emphasized) messages of "bias-motivated" hatred and in particular, as applied to this case, messages "based on virulent notions of racial supremacy." " *In re Welfare of R.A.V.*, 464 N.W.2d 507, 511 (Minn.1991). One must wholeheartedly agree with the Minnesota Supreme Court that "[i]t is the responsibility, even the obligation, of diverse communities to confront such notions in whatever form they appear," *id.*, at 508, but the manner of that confrontation cannot consist of selective limitations upon speech. St. Paul's brief asserts that a general "fighting words" law would not meet the city's needs because only a content-specific measure can communicate to minority groups that the "group hatred" aspect of such speech "is not condoned by the majority." The point of the First Amendment is that majority preferences must be expressed in some fashion other than silencing speech on the basis of its content. . . .

Finally, St. Paul and its *amici* defend the conclusion of the Minnesota Supreme Court that, even if the ordinance regulates expression based on hostility towards its protected ideological content, this discrimination is nonetheless justified because it is narrowly tailored to serve compelling state interests. Specifically, they assert that the ordinance helps to ensure the basic human rights of members of groups that have historically been subjected to discrimination, including the right of such group members to live in peace where they wish. We do not doubt that these interests are compelling, and that the ordinance can be said to promote them. But the "danger of censorship" presented by a facially content-based statute, requires that that weapon be employed only where it is *"necessary* to serve the asserted [compelling] interest." . . . The dispositive question in this case, therefore, is whether content discrimination is reasonably necessary to achieve St. Paul's compelling interests; it plainly is not. An ordinance not limited to the favored topics, for example, would have precisely the same beneficial effect. In fact the only interest distinctively served by the content limitation is that of displaying the city council's special hostility towards the particular biases thus singled out. That is precisely what the First Amendment forbids. The politicians of St. Paul are entitled to express that hostility—but not through the means of imposing unique limitations upon speakers who (however benightedly) disagree. . . .

Let there be no mistake about our belief that burning a cross in someone's front yard is reprehensible. But St. Paul has sufficient means at its disposal to prevent such behavior without adding the First Amendment to the fire.

■ JUSTICE WHITE, with whom JUSTICE BLACKMUN and JUSTICE O'CONNOR join, and with whom JUSTICE STEVENS joins except as to [a subpart not printed here], concurring in the judgment.

I agree with the majority that the judgment of the Minnesota Supreme Court should be reversed. However, our agreement ends there.

This case could easily be decided within the contours of established First Amendment law by holding, as petitioner argues, that the St. Paul ordinance is fatally overbroad because it criminalizes not only unprotected expression but expression protected by the First Amendment. . . .

■ [The opinions of JUSTICE BLACKMUN and JUSTICE STEVENS, both concurring in the judgment, are omitted.]

NOTES

1. *R.A.V.* (the defendant was identified by initials, because he was a minor) is a much-discussed free speech case arising under the Fourteenth Amendment. At bottom, it stands for the proposition that the government may not engage in content- or viewpoint-based regulation of expression, *even within otherwise "unprotected" categories of expression*, like defamation, obscenity, or asserted "fighting words." The result was unanimous, though the four concurring justices disagreed with the breadth of the principle as stated by the majority, and would have preferred to strike down St. Paul's bias-motivated crime ordinance on the basis of the First Amendment doctrine of "overbreadth"—that is, that the ordinance reached much constitutionally protected speech as well as unprotected expression or conduct. One apparent effect of the Court's decision in *R.A.V.* is to render invalid government laws or rules that prohibit or punish "hate speech" directed at particular groups. Government may not authoritatively pick and choose which messages are too hateful to be communicated; and even within the (increasingly narrow, but not quite dead) category of "fighting words," government may not be selective in imposing punishment only for certain viewpoints or only for certain subcategories of fighting words.

Does *R.A.V.* mean that the government may not prohibit racially discriminatory *conduct* (or other forms of discriminatory conduct)? No: Government may regulate conduct, such as racially discriminatory employment practices, even where such conduct is engaged in for assertedly expressive purposes (recall *United States v. O'Brien*). A racist employer may not discriminate on the basis of race in employment; the government may penalize such conduct. But a racist employer may not be penalized for racist speech alone. Does this distinction make sense? But press the hypotheticals one step further: Certainly a racist employer who expressed racially discriminatory views would find those words used as evidence of his possible motive for taking employment actions that an aggrieved employee might believe were taken because of discrimination on the basis of race. Is there anything wrong with this use of one's expressed views as evidence of the reason for conduct the motives of which are disputed or unclear? (Consider in this regard *Wisconsin v. Mitchell*, discussed in the next note.) One more variation: What about where the alleged discriminatory conduct consists solely or chiefly of a "hostile work environment" attributable to racially (or other) discriminatory or similarly hateful speech? For contrasting views, with excellent analysis, compare Eugene Volokh, Comment, *Freedom of Speech and Workplace Harassment*, 39 UCLA L. Rev. 1791 (1992) (hostile-environment laws constitutionally problematic) with Richard H. Fallon, Jr., *Sexual Harassment, Content-Neutrality, and the First Amendment Dog That Didn't Bark*, 1994 S.Ct. Rev. 1 (1994) (defending such laws).

2.   The very next year after *R.A.V.*, in *Wisconsin v. Mitchell*, 508 U.S. 476 (1993), the Court drew a sharp distinction between statutes regulating and punishing certain hateful *speech* (as in *R.A.V.*) and punishing certain hateful *conduct* more severely because of an assertedly aggravating mind-state of racial animus. The Court's opinion was unanimous. The facts of *Mitchell*, as set forth in the Court's opinion, were as follows:

> On the evening of October 7, 1989, a group of young black men and boys, including Mitchell, gathered at an apartment complex in Kenosha, Wisconsin. Several members of the group discussed a scene from the motion picture "Mississippi Burning," in which a white man beat a young black boy who was praying. The group moved outside and Mitchell asked them: "Do you all feel hyped up to move on some white people?" Shortly thereafter, a young white boy approached the group on the opposite side of the street where they were standing. As the boy walked by, Mitchell said: "You all want to fuck somebody up? There goes a white boy; go get him." Mitchell counted to three and pointed in the boy's direction. The group ran towards the boy, beat him severely, and stole his tennis shoes. The boy was rendered unconscious and remained in a coma for four days.

Mitchell was convicted of aggravated battery. Under Wisconsin law, the fact that Mitchell had intentionally selected his victim on the basis of the boy's race was an aggravating factor that increased his maximum sentence from two to seven years. Mitchell was sentenced to four years. Before the U.S. Supreme Court, Mitchell argued that the penalty-enhancement statute was unconstitutional under *R.A.V.* But the Court rejected the argument, concluding that it was not supported by the analysis in *R.A.V.* Motive for a crime, the Court said in *Mitchell*, is a traditional factor that affects the level of punishment in criminal law, and it

> plays the same role under the Wisconsin statute as it does under federal and state antidiscrimination laws, which we have previously upheld against constitutional challenge. Title VII of the Civil Rights Act of 1964], for example, makes it unlawful for an employer to discriminate against an employee "because of such individual's race, color, religion, sex, or national origin." . . . In *R.A.V.* we cited Title VII as an example of a permissible content-neutral regulation of conduct. . . . Whereas the ordinance struck down in *R.A.V.* was explicitly directed at expression (i.e., "speech" or "messages"), the statute in this

case is aimed at conduct unprotected by the First Amendment. Moreover, the Wisconsin statute singles out for enhancement bias-inspired conduct because this conduct is thought to inflict greater individual and societal harm.

508 U.S. at 477.

3.   The Court confronted cross-burning prosecutions again in *Virginia v. Black*, 538 U.S. 343 (2003), also a Fourteenth Amendment case dealing with free speech principles. In a somewhat convoluted split decision, a majority of the Court held that a state may, notwithstanding *R.A.V.*, "ban cross burning carried out with the intent to intimidate," on the theory that the First Amendment does not protect "true threats" of violence. That holding commanded a majority of six justices of the Court (O'Connor, Rehnquist, Stevens, Breyer, Scalia, and Thomas).

But a different majority was formed by O'Connor, Rehnquist, Stevens, and Breyer (four of the original six), together with the separate concurring opinion of Justices Souter, Kennedy, and Ginsburg, to *strike down* one aspect of Virginia's statute: the provision stating that the fact of burning a cross was itself "prima facie evidence of an intent to intimidate a person or group of persons." Justice O'Connor's plurality opinion on this point said that the prima facie evidence provision could be interpreted and applied (and had been so interpreted and applied by the trial court, in its instructions to the jury) in such a manner as to "create an unacceptable risk of the suppression of ideas": "The act of burning a cross may mean that a person is engaging in constitutionally proscribable intimidation. But that same act may mean only that the person is engaged in core political speech. [The] prima facie provision makes no effort to distinguish among these different types of cross burnings. . . . The prima facie evidence provision in this case ignores all of the contextual factors that are necessary to decide whether a particular cross burning is intended to intimidate. The First Amendment does not permit such a shortcut." Justice Souter's concurring opinion (joined by Justices Kennedy and Ginsburg) did not join in Justice O'Connor's rationale. It was more categorical, rejecting the conviction under *R.A.V.*: "I agree with the majority that the Virginia statute makes a content-based distinction within the category of punishable intimidating or threatening expression, the very type of distinction we considered in *R.A.V.* I disagree that any exception should save Virginia's law from unconstitutionality under the holding in *R.A.V.* or any acceptable variation of it."

Justice Scalia and Justice Thomas joined in the first holding, but disagreed with the (second) majority about the effect of the "prima facie evidence" provision, finding "no justification for the plurality's apparent decision to invalidate" it. Justice Thomas, the only black member of the Court at the time, filed a lone dissent that would have held that cross-burning is simply not protected expression under the First Amendment: "Although I agree with the majority's conclusion that it is constitutionally permissible to 'ban . . . cross burning carried out with intent to intimidate,' I believe that the majority errs in imputing an expressive component to the activity in question. . . . In light of my conclusion that the statute here addresses only conduct, there is no need to analyze it under any of our First Amendment tests."

Thus, a six-justice majority (all joining in the same controlling opinion) agreed that true threats can be punished, without violating the First Amendment, and that cross-burning can be a true threat. A different seven-justice majority (*not* all joining in the same reasoning) agreed that Virginia's law, by treating cross-burning itself as prima facie evidence of an intent to intimidate by threat, was unconstitutional under the First Amendment. Is the result in *Black* coherent?

Nazis in Skokie

In the late 1970s, a group of American neo-Nazis sought to march through the streets of Skokie, Illinois, wearing Nazi uniforms and displaying the swastika. Skokie, a Chicago suburb, at the time had the largest concentration of Holocaust survivors of any community in America. The efforts to resist the Nazis led to a series of noteworthy judicial decisions.

The town of Skokie first sought, and obtained from an Illinois trial court, an *injunction* prohibiting parading in the uniform of the Nazi party, displaying the swastika, and distributing pamphlets that "incite or promote hatred against persons of Jewish faith or ancestry, race or religion." The Illinois Appellate Court declined to stay the injunction, and the Illinois Supreme Court denied expedited review. The Nazi group petitioned the U.S. Supreme Court for a stay. The Court treated the stay as a petition for certiorari and reversed in a per curiam opinion, *National Socialist Party v. Skokie*, 432 U.S. 43 (1977), holding that the First Amendment required, at minimum, procedural safeguards before a judicial injunction could be issued against speech. Injunctions against speech—judicial orders—have long been considered a form of "prior restraint" against speech, an especially severe type of restriction in the Court's view. (The Court had just a few years earlier invalidated injunctions against publication by the press of leaked classified material, in *The Pentagon Papers Case*, 403 U.S. 713 (1971), presented at p. 847.) The Court in *National Socialist Party* started from the premise that such injunctions limiting speech are strongly disfavored, but its holding necessarily touched on the fact that the restriction of speech was obviously based on the content, and offensiveness, of the Nazis' message:

> [T]he outstanding injunction will deprive [petitioners] of rights protected by the First Amendment during the period of appellate review which, in the normal course, may take a year or more to complete. If a State seeks to impose a restraint of this kind, it must provide strict procedural safeguards including immediate appellate review . . . Absent such review, the State must instead allow a stay. The order of the Illinois Supreme Court constituted a denial of that right.

On remand, the Illinois courts struck down the injunction, finding it not justified by the "fighting words" doctrine. In light of cases like *Cohen*, the Illinois Supreme Court held, it was not permissible to restrict speech on the basis of the expected hostile reaction of the audience. The offensiveness of the swastika symbol was not a proper basis for banning the group's expression, either, the court said. Rather, it was up to Skokie's offended citizens to "avoid the offensive symbol if they can do so without unreasonable inconvenience." 373 N.E. 2d at 21 (Ill. 1978). In the words of the Illinois Supreme Court:

> The decisions of [the Supreme Court], particularly *Cohen v. California*, . . . in our opinion compel us to permit the demonstration as proposed, including display of the swastika. "It is firmly settled that under our Constitution the public expression of ideas may not be prohibited merely because the ideas are themselves offensive to some of their hearers" (*Bachellar v. Maryland*, 397 U.S. 564, 567 (1970)), and it is entirely clear that the wearing of distinctive clothing can be symbolic expression of a thought or philosophy. The symbolic expression of thought falls within the free speech clause of the First Amendment (*Tinker v. Des Moines*

Independent Sch. Dist., 393 U.S. 503 (1969) [upholding constitutional right of public high school and junior high school students to wear black armbands to school in protest of Vietnam War]) and the plaintiff village has the heavy burden of justifying the imposition of a prior restraint upon defendants' right to freedom of speech. . . .

Plaintiff urges, and the appellate court has held, that the exhibition of the Nazi symbol, the swastika, addresses to ordinary citizens a message which is tantamount to fighting words. Plaintiff further asks this court to extend *Chaplinsky*, which upheld a statute punishing the use of such words, and hold that the fighting-words doctrine permits a prior restraint on defendants' symbolic speech. In our judgment we are precluded from doing so. . . .

The display of the swastika, as offensive to the principles of a free nation as the memories it recalls may be, is symbolic political speech intended to convey to the public the beliefs of those who display it. It does not, in our opinion, fall within the definition of "fighting words," and that doctrine cannot be used here to overcome the heavy presumption against the constitutional validity of a prior restraint. Nor can we find that the swastika, while not representing fighting words, is nevertheless so offensive and peace threatening to the public that its display can be enjoined. We do not doubt that the sight of this symbol is abhorrent to the Jewish citizens of Skokie, and that the survivors of the Nazi persecutions, tormented by their recollections, may have strong feelings regarding its display. Yet it is entirely clear that this factor does not justify enjoining defendants' speech. . . .

In summary, as we read the controlling Supreme Court opinions, use of the swastika is a symbolic form of free speech entitled to First Amendment protections. Its display on uniforms or banners by those engaged in peaceful demonstrations cannot be totally precluded solely because that display may provoke a violent reaction by those who view it. Particularly is this true where, as here, there has been advance notice by the demonstrators of their plans so that they have become, as the complaint alleges, "common knowledge" and those to whom sight of the swastika banner or uniforms would be offensive are forewarned and need not view them. A speaker who gives prior notice of his message has not compelled a confrontation with those who voluntarily listen.

While the first case was proceeding, Skokie passed several ordinances targeting the Nazi groups' parade requests. One required $300,000 in liability insurance and $50,000 in property insurance before a group could receive a parade permit. A second prohibited "dissemination of . . . materials" in Skokie that "promotes and incites hatred against persons by reason of their race, national origin, or religion." A third prohibited public demonstrations by political groups wearing military-like uniforms. A challenge was quickly brought in federal court, and the district court and Court of Appeals for the Seventh Circuit struck down the ordinances as violating the First Amendment. *Collin v. Smith*, 578 F.2d 1197 (7th Cir. 1978).

This time Skokie sought a stay in the U.S. Supreme Court. The Court denied the stay, with two justices dissenting. The Nazis, having won the right to march, did not do so, but staged rallies in Chicago and in Evanston, another nearby suburb.

Is a Nazi swastika in Skokie, or neo-Nazis marching in uniform through the streets of a community with many Jewish Holocaust survivors, any *less* a "threat" than a Ku Klux Klan cross-burning? Is the cross-burning in *Virginia v. Black* anything other than a different instance of hateful, deeply offensive speech? Is it really possible for courts to draw principled lines among different types of "hate speech" based on social context? Is *Black* wrong? Are the Illinois Nazi cases wrong?

[*Assignment 47*]

G. OFFENSIVE AND DEGRADING SPEECH

Cohen v. California
403 U.S. 15 (1971)

■ MR. JUSTICE HARLAN delivered the opinion of the Court.

This case may seem at first blush too inconsequential to find its way into our books, but the issue it presents is of no small constitutional significance.

Appellant Paul Robert Cohen was convicted in the Los Angeles Municipal Court of violating that part of California Penal Code § 415 which prohibits "maliciously and willfully disturb(ing) the peace or quiet of any neighborhood or person . . . by . . . offensive conduct. . . ." He was given 30 days' imprisonment. The facts upon which his conviction rests . . . are as follows:

> On April 26, 1968, the defendant was observed in the Los Angeles County Courthouse in the corridor outside of division 20 of the municipal court wearing a jacket bearing the words "Fuck the Draft" which were plainly visible. There were women and children present in the corridor. The defendant was arrested. The defendant testified that he wore the jacket knowing that the words were on the jacket as a means of informing the public of the depth of his feelings against the Vietnam War and the draft.
>
> The defendant did not engage in, nor threaten to engage in, nor did anyone as the result of his conduct in fact commit or threaten to commit any act of violence. The defendant did not make any loud or unusual noise, nor was there any evidence that he uttered any sound prior to his arrest. 1 Cal. App. 3d 94, 97–98 (1969).

In affirming the conviction the Court of Appeal held that "offensive conduct" means "behavior which has a tendency to provoke *others* to acts of violence or to in turn disturb the peace," and that the State had proved this element because, on the facts of this case, "[i]t was certainly reasonably foreseeable that such conduct might cause others to rise up to commit a violent act against the person of the defendant or attempt to forceably remove his jacket." . . . We now reverse. . . .

I

In order to lay hands on the precise issue which this case involves, it is useful first to canvass various matters which this record does not present.

The conviction quite clearly rests upon the asserted offensiveness of the *words* Cohen used to convey his message to the public. The only "conduct" which the State sought to punish is the fact of communication. Thus, we deal here with a conviction resting solely upon "speech," cf. *Stromberg v. California*, 283 U.S. 359 (1931), not upon any separately identifiable conduct which allegedly was intended by Cohen to be perceived by others as expressive of particular views but which, on its face, does not necessarily convey any message and hence arguably could be regulated without effectively repressing Cohen's ability to express himself. Cf. *United States v. O'Brien*, 391 U.S. 367 (1968). Further, the State certainly lacks power to punish Cohen for the underlying content of the message the inscription conveyed. At least so long as there is no showing of an intent to incite disobedience to or disruption of the draft, Cohen could not, consistently with the First and Fourteenth Amendments, be punished for asserting the evident position on the inutility or immorality of the draft his jacket reflected. *Yates v. United States*, 354 U.S. 298 (1957).

Appellant's conviction, then, rests squarely upon his exercise of the "freedom of speech" protected from arbitrary governmental interference by the Constitution and can be justified, if at all, only as a valid regulation of the manner in which he exercised that freedom, not as a permissible prohibition on the substantive message it conveys. This does not end the inquiry, of course, for the First and Fourteenth Amendments have never been thought to give absolute protection to every individual to speak whenever or wherever he pleases or to use any form of address in any circumstances that he chooses. In this vein, too, however, we think it important to note that several issues typically associated with such problems are not presented here.

In the first place, Cohen was tried under a statute applicable throughout the entire State. Any attempt to support this conviction on the ground that the statute seeks to preserve an appropriately decorous atmosphere in the courthouse where Cohen was arrested must fail in the absence of any language in the statute that would have put appellant on notice that certain kinds of otherwise permissible speech or conduct would nevertheless, under California law, not be tolerated in certain places. No fair reading of the phrase "offensive conduct" can be said sufficiently to inform the ordinary person that distinctions between certain locations are thereby created.

In the second place, as it comes to us, this case cannot be said to fall within those relatively few categories of instances where prior decisions have established the power of government to deal more comprehensively with certain forms of individual expression simply upon a showing that such a form was employed. This is not, for example, an obscenity case. Whatever else may be necessary to give rise to the States' broader power to prohibit obscene expression, such expression must be, in some significant way, erotic. *Roth v. United States*, 354 U.S. 476 (1957). It cannot plausibly be maintained that this vulgar allusion to the Selective Service System would conjure up such psychic stimulation in anyone likely to be confronted with Cohen's crudely defaced jacket.

This Court has also held that the States are free to ban the simple use, without a demonstration of additional justifying circumstances, of so-called "fighting words," those personally abusive epithets which, when addressed to the ordinary citizen, are, as a matter of common knowledge, inherently likely to provoke violent reaction. *Chaplinsky v. New Hampshire*, 315 U.S. 568 (1942). While the four-letter word displayed by Cohen in relation to the draft is not uncommonly employed in a personally provocative fashion, in this instance it was clearly not "directed to the person of the hearer." *Cantwell v. Connecticut*, 310 U.S. 296, 309 (1940). No individual actually or likely to be present could reasonably have regarded the words on appellant's jacket as a direct personal insult. Nor do we have here an instance of the exercise of the State's police power to prevent a speaker from intentionally provoking a given group to hostile reaction. Cf. *Feiner v. New York*, 340 U.S. 315 (1951); *Terminiello v. Chicago*, 337 U.S. 1 (1949). There is, as noted above, no showing that anyone who saw Cohen was in fact violently aroused or that appellant intended such a result.

Finally, in arguments before this Court much has been made of the claim that Cohen's distasteful mode of expression was thrust upon unwilling or unsuspecting viewers, and that the State might therefore legitimately act as it did in order to protect the sensitive from otherwise unavoidable exposure to appellant's crude form of protest. Of course, the mere presumed presence of unwitting listeners or viewers does not serve automatically to justify curtailing all speech capable of giving offense. See, *e.g., Organization for a Better Austin v. Keefe*, 402 U.S. 415 (1971). While this Court has recognized that government may properly act in many situations to prohibit intrusion into the privacy of the home of unwelcome views and ideas which cannot be totally banned from the public dialogue, *e.g., Rowan v. United States Post Office Dept.*, 397 U.S. 728 (1970), we have at the same time consistently stressed that "we are often 'captives' outside the sanctuary of the home and subject to objectionable speech." *Id.*, at 738. The ability of government, consonant with the Constitution, to shut off discourse solely to protect others from hearing it is, in other words, dependent upon a showing that substantial privacy interests are being invaded in an essentially intolerable manner. Any broader view of this authority would effectively empower a majority to silence dissidents simply as a matter of personal predilections.

In this regard, persons confronted with Cohen's jacket were in a quite different posture than, say, those subjected to the raucous emissions of sound trucks blaring outside their residences. Those in the Los Angeles courthouse could effectively avoid further bombardment of their sensibilities simply by averting their eyes. And, while it may be that one has a more substantial claim to a recognizable privacy interest when walking through a courthouse corridor than, for example, strolling through Central Park, surely it is nothing like the interest in being free from unwanted expression in the confines of one's own home. Cf. *Keefe*. Given the subtlety and complexity of the factors involved, if Cohen's "speech" was otherwise entitled to constitutional protection, we do not think the fact that some unwilling "listeners" in a public building may have been briefly exposed to it can serve to justify this breach of the peace conviction where, as here, there was no evidence that persons powerless to avoid appellant's conduct did in fact object to it, and where that portion of the statute upon which Cohen's conviction rests evinces no concern, either on its face or as construed by the California courts, with the special plight of the captive auditor, but, instead, indiscriminately sweeps within its prohibitions all "offensive conduct" that disturbs "any neighborhood or person." Cf. *Edwards v. South Carolina*, 372 U.S. 229 (1963).

II

Against this background, the issue flushed by this case stands out in bold relief. It is whether California can excise, as "offensive conduct," one particular scurrilous epithet from the public discourse, either upon the theory of the court below that its use is inherently likely to cause violent reaction or upon a more general assertion that the States, acting as guardians of public morality, may properly remove this offensive word from the public vocabulary.

The rationale of the California court is plainly untenable. At most it reflects an "undifferentiated fear or apprehension of disturbance (which) is not enough to overcome the right to freedom of expression." *Tinker v. Des Moines Indep. Community School Dist.*, 393 U.S. 503, 508 (1969). We have been shown no evidence that substantial numbers of citizens are standing ready to strike out physically at whoever may assault their sensibilities with execrations like that uttered by Cohen. There may be some persons about with such lawless and violent proclivities, but that is an insufficient base upon which to erect, consistently with constitutional values, a governmental power to force persons who wish to ventilate their dissident views into avoiding particular forms of expression. The argument amounts to little more than the self-defeating proposition that to avoid physical censorship of one who has not sought to provoke such a response by a hypothetical coterie of the violent and lawless, the States may more appropriately effectuate that censorship themselves.

Admittedly, it is not so obvious that the First and Fourteenth Amendments must be taken to disable the States from punishing public utterance of this unseemly expletive in order to maintain what they regard as a suitable level of discourse within the body politic. We think, however, that examination and reflection will reveal the shortcomings of a contrary viewpoint.

At the outset, we cannot overemphasize that, in our judgment, most situations where the State has a justifiable interest in regulating speech will fall within one or more of the various established exceptions, discussed above but not applicable here, to the usual rule that governmental bodies may not prescribe the form or content of individual expression. Equally important to our conclusion is the constitutional backdrop against which our decision must be made. The constitutional right of free expression is powerful medicine in a society as diverse and populous as ours. It is designed and intended to remove governmental restraints from the arena of public discussion, putting the decision as to what views shall be voiced largely into the hands of each of us, in the hope that use of such freedom will ultimately produce a more capable citizenry and more perfect polity and in the belief that no other approach would comport with the premise of individual dignity and choice upon which our political system rests. See *Whitney v. California*, 274 U.S. 357, 375–377 (1927) (Brandeis, J., concurring).

To many, the immediate consequence of this freedom may often appear to be only verbal tumult, discord, and even offensive utterance. These are, however, within established limits, in truth necessary side effects of the broader enduring values which the process of open debate permits us to achieve. That the air may at times seem filled with verbal cacophony is, in this sense not a sign of weakness but of strength. We cannot lose sight of the fact that, in what otherwise might seem a trifling and annoying instance of individual distasteful abuse of a privilege, these fundamental societal values are truly implicated. That is why "(w)holly neutral futilities . . . come under the protection of free speech as fully as do Keats' poems or Donne's sermons," *Winters v. New York*, 333 U.S. 507, 528 (1948) (Frankfurter, J., dissenting), and why "so long as the means are peaceful, the communication need not meet standards of acceptability," *Keefe*, 402 U.S. 415.

. . . [T]he principle contended for by the State seems inherently boundless. How is one to distinguish this from any other offensive word? Surely the State has no right to cleanse public debate to the point where it is grammatically palatable to the most squeamish among us. Yet no readily ascertainable general principle exists for stopping short of that result were we to affirm the judgment below. For, while the particular four-letter word being litigated here is perhaps more distasteful than most others of its genre, it is nevertheless often true that one man's vulgarity is another's lyric. Indeed, we think it is largely because governmental officials cannot make principled distinctions in this area that the Constitution leaves matters of taste and style so largely to the individual.

Additionally, we cannot overlook the fact, because it is well illustrated by the episode involved here, that much linguistic expression serves a dual communicative function: it conveys not only ideas capable of relatively precise, detached explication, but otherwise inexpressible emotions as well. In fact, words are often chosen as much for their emotive as their cognitive force. We cannot sanction the view that the Constitution, while solicitous of the cognitive content of individual speech has little or no regard for that emotive function which practically speaking, may often be the more important element of the overall message sought to be communicated. Indeed, as Mr. Justice Frankfurter has said, "[o]ne of the prerogatives of American citizenship is the right to criticize public men and measures—and that means not only informed and responsible criticism but the freedom to speak foolishly and without moderation."

Finally, and in the same vein, we cannot indulge the facile assumption that one can forbid particular words without also running a substantial risk of suppressing ideas in the process. Indeed, governments might soon seize upon the censorship of particular words as a convenient guise for banning the expression of unpopular views. We have been able, as noted above, to discern little social benefit that might result from running the risk of opening the door to such grave results.

It is, in sum, our judgment that, absent a more particularized and compelling reason for its actions, the State may not, consistently with the First and Fourteenth Amendments, make the simple public display here involved of this single four-letter expletive a criminal offense. Because that is the only arguably sustainable rationale for the conviction here at issue, the judgment below must be reversed.

■ MR. JUSTICE BLACKMUN, with whom THE CHIEF JUSTICE and MR. JUSTICE BLACK join.

I dissent . . . Cohen's absurd and immature antic, in my view, was mainly conduct and little speech. The California Court of Appeal appears so to have described it, and I cannot characterize it otherwise. Further, the case appears to me to be well within the sphere of *Chaplinsky.* . . . As a consequence, this Court's agonizing over First Amendment values seems misplaced and unnecessary. . . .

NOTES

1.   *Cohen v. California* is a Free Speech Clause classic. Was it rightly decided, or was it a disgraceful tribute to the increasing coarseness of our discourse? Note that the United States is exceptional in its legal protection of "coarse" speech. Our northern neighbor Canada, for example, is much less protective of such speech. Why? One scholar has argued that it is because Canada was populated, after the American Revolution, by Tories who supported the monarchy and the established Church of England, rather than by those who valued dissident speech. See Seymour Martin Lipset, CONTINENTAL DIVIDE: THE VALUES AND INSTITUTIONS OF THE UNITED STATES AND CANADA (1990).

2.   Break down the First Amendment question in this Fourteenth Amendment case into some possible component parts: Was Cohen's jacket "speech" or "conduct"? If conduct, was it expressive conduct? If speech or expressive conduct, was it obscene? Did it constitute "fighting words"? What is it that might cause offense to those who see it—is it the particular word used or the message of strong anti-draft/anti-war feeling? Is that offensiveness ground for regulation? Does that provide a legitimate basis for regulating it? Could the government legitimately prohibit the use of particularly offensive words (or images) on the ground that the speaker could just as effectively communicate his message through the use of other words (or images)? Would this be just a limitation on the "manner" of the expression of the speaker's views? Or is it a limitation on its content or message in some meaningful sense?

3.   Try a different tack: Cohen's "speech" occurred in a courthouse. Many citizens are there on official business—indeed, many are *required* to be there as witnesses, government employees, or parties in a case. Are they a "captive audience" that the government has a legitimate interest in shielding from exposure to unwanted (and offensive) speech? Is there a "privacy right" of individuals to be free from exposure to the offensive speech of others, at least in public buildings? Does the government have a legitimate interest in protecting unwilling hearers—especially vulnerable or sensitive persons—from messages or words they might strongly wish not to hear? Does the First Amendment permit the government to balance this interest against Cohen's interest in expressing his particular message in a particular way? What if children are likely to be present? Does that provide a ground for regulating or prohibiting Cohen's jacket? If so, how far does that justification extend?

4.   Is it possible the decision in Cohen was affected by the obvious political character of the message? Might the Court have thought, without saying, that Cohen was singled out for his anti-war advocacy? What if he had been wearing a t-shirt with a crude but nonpolitical message? Is it really possible that the government cannot maintain some standards of public decorum in public places?

Hustler Magazine v. Falwell

485 U.S. 46 (1988)

■ CHIEF JUSTICE REHNQUIST delivered the opinion of the Court.

Petitioner Hustler Magazine, Inc., is a magazine of nationwide circulation. Respondent Jerry Falwell, a nationally known minister who has been active as a commentator on politics and public affairs, sued petitioner and its publisher, petitioner Larry Flynt, to recover damages for invasion of privacy, libel, and intentional infliction of emotional distress. . . .

The inside front cover of the November 1983 issue of Hustler Magazine featured a "parody" of an advertisement for Campari Liqueur that contained the name and picture of respondent and was entitled "Jerry Falwell talks about his first time." This parody was modeled after actual Campari ads that included interviews with various celebrities about their "first times." Although it was apparent by the end of each interview that this meant the first time they sampled Campari, the ads clearly played on the sexual double entendre of the general subject of "first times." Copying the form and layout of these Campari ads, Hustler's editors chose respondent as the featured celebrity and drafted an alleged "interview" with him in which he states that his "first time" was during a drunken incestuous rendezvous with his mother in an outhouse. The Hustler parody portrays respondent and his mother as drunk and immoral, and suggests that respondent is a hypocrite who preaches only when he is drunk. In small print at the bottom of the page, the ad contains the disclaimer, "ad parody—not to be taken seriously." The magazine's table of contents also lists the ad as "Fiction; Ad and Personality Parody."

Soon after the November issue of Hustler became available to the public, respondent brought this diversity action in the United States District Court against Hustler Magazine, Inc., Larry C. Flynt, and Flynt Distributing Co., Inc. Respondent stated in his complaint that publication of the ad parody in Hustler entitled him to recover damages for libel, invasion of privacy, and intentional infliction of emotional distress. The case proceeded to trial. At the close of the evidence, the District Court granted a directed verdict for petitioners on the invasion of privacy claim. The jury then found against respondent on the libel claim, specifically finding that the ad parody could not "reasonably be understood as describing actual facts about [respondent] or actual events in which [he] participated." The jury ruled for respondent on the intentional infliction of emotional distress claim, however, and stated that he should be awarded $100,000 in compensatory damages, as well as $50,000 each in punitive damages from petitioners. . . .

This case presents us with a novel question involving First Amendment limitations upon a State's authority to protect its citizens from the intentional infliction of emotional distress. We must decide whether a public figure may recover damages for emotional harm caused by the publication of an ad parody offensive to him, and doubtless gross and repugnant in the eyes of most. Respondent would have us find that a State's interest in protecting public figures from emotional distress is sufficient to deny First Amendment protection to speech that is patently offensive and is intended to inflict emotional injury, even when that speech could not reasonably have been interpreted as stating actual facts about the public figure involved. This we decline to do.

At the heart of the First Amendment is the recognition of the fundamental importance of the free flow of ideas and opinions on matters of public interest and concern. "[T]he freedom to speak one's mind is not only an aspect of individual liberty—and thus a good unto itself—but also is essential to the common quest for truth and the vitality of society as a whole." *Bose Corp. v. Consumers Union of United States, Inc.*, 466 U.S. 485, 503–504 (1984). We have therefore been particularly vigilant to ensure that individual expressions of ideas remain free from governmentally imposed sanctions. The First Amendment recognizes no such thing as a "false" idea. *Gertz v. Robert Welch, Inc.*, 418 U.S. 323, 339 (1974). As Justice Holmes wrote, "when men have realized that time has upset many fighting faiths, they may come to believe even more than they believe the very foundations of their own conduct that the ultimate good desired is better reached by free trade in ideas—that the best test of truth is the power of the thought to get itself accepted in the competition of the market. . . ." *Abrams v. United States*, 250 U.S. 616, 630 (1919) (dissenting opinion).

The sort of robust political debate encouraged by the First Amendment is bound to produce speech that is critical of those who hold public office or those public figures who are "intimately involved in the resolution of important public questions or, by reason of their fame, shape events in areas of concern to society at large." *Associated Press v. Walker*, decided with *Curtis Publishing Co. v. Butts*, 388 U.S. 130, 164 (1967) (Warren, C.J., concurring in result). Justice Frankfurter put it succinctly in *Baumgartner v. United States*, 322 U.S. 665, 673–674 (1944), when he said that "[o]ne of the prerogatives of American citizenship is the right to criticize public men and measures." Such criticism, inevitably, will not always be reasoned or moderate; public figures as well as public officials will be subject to "vehement, caustic, and sometimes unpleasantly sharp attacks," *New York Times Co. v. Sullivan*, 376 U.S. 254, 270 (1964). "[T]he candidate who vaunts his spotless record and sterling integrity cannot convincingly cry 'Foul!' when an opponent or an industrious reporter attempts to demonstrate the contrary." *Monitor Patriot Co. v. Roy*, 401 U.S. 265, 274 (1971).

Of course, this does not mean that any speech about a public figure is immune from sanction in the form of damages. Since *New York Times Co. v. Sullivan,* we have consistently ruled that a public figure may hold a speaker liable for the damage to reputation caused by publication of a defamatory falsehood, but only if the statement was made "with knowledge that it was false or with reckless disregard of whether it was false or not." 376 U.S., at 279–280. False statements of fact are particularly valueless; they interfere with the truth-seeking function of the marketplace of ideas, and they cause damage to an individual's reputation that cannot easily be repaired by counterspeech, however persuasive or effective. See *Gertz,* at 340, 344, n. 9. But even though falsehoods have little value in and of themselves, they are "nevertheless inevitable in free debate," *id.,* at 340, and a rule that would impose strict liability on a publisher for false factual assertions would have an undoubted "chilling" effect on speech relating to public figures that does have constitutional value. "Freedoms of expression require 'breathing space.'" *Philadelphia Newspapers, Inc. v. Hepps*, 475 U.S. 767, 772 (1986) (quoting *New York Times,* at 272). This breathing space is provided by a constitutional rule that allows public figures to recover for libel or defamation only when they can prove both that the statement was false and that the statement was made with the requisite level of culpability.

Respondent argues, however, that a different standard should apply in this case because here the State seeks to prevent not reputational damage, but the severe emotional distress suffered by the person who is the subject of an offensive publication. In respondent's view, and in the view of the Court of Appeals, so long as the utterance was intended to inflict emotional distress, was outrageous, and did in fact inflict serious emotional distress, it is of no constitutional import whether the statement was a fact or an opinion, or whether it was true or false. It is the intent to cause injury that is the gravamen of the tort, and the State's interest in preventing emotional harm simply outweighs whatever interest a speaker may have in speech of this type.

Generally speaking the law does not regard the intent to inflict emotional distress as one which should receive much solicitude, and it is quite understandable that most if not all jurisdictions have chosen to make it civilly culpable where the conduct in question is sufficiently "outrageous." But in the world of debate about public affairs, many things done with motives that are less than admirable are protected by the First Amendment. In *Garrison v. Louisiana*, 379 U.S. 64 (1964), we held that even when a speaker or writer is motivated by hatred or illwill his expression was protected by the First Amendment:

> Debate on public issues will not be uninhibited if the speaker must run the risk that it will be proved in court that he spoke out of hatred; even if he did speak out of hatred, utterances honestly believed contribute to the free interchange of ideas and the ascertainment of truth.

Thus while such a bad motive may be deemed controlling for purposes of tort liability in other areas of the law, we think the First Amendment prohibits such a result in the area of public debate about public figures.

Were we to hold otherwise, there can be little doubt that political cartoonists and satirists would be subjected to damages awards without any showing that their work falsely defamed its subject. Webster's defines a caricature as "the deliberately distorted picturing or imitating of a person, literary style, etc. by exaggerating features or mannerisms for satirical effect." The appeal of the political cartoon or caricature is often based on exploitation of unfortunate physical traits or politically embarrassing events—an exploitation often calculated to injure the feelings of the subject of the portrayal. The art of the cartoonist is often not reasoned or evenhanded, but slashing and one-sided. One cartoonist expressed the nature of the art in these words:

> The political cartoon is a weapon of attack, of scorn and ridicule and satire; it is least effective when it tries to pat some politician on the back. It is usually as welcome as a bee sting and is always controversial in some quarters.

. . . Despite their sometimes caustic nature, from the early cartoon portraying George Washington as an ass down to the present day, graphic depictions and satirical cartoons have played a prominent role in public and political debate . . . Lincoln's tall, gangling posture, Teddy Roosevelt's glasses and teeth, and Franklin D. Roosevelt's jutting jaw and cigarette holder have been memorialized by political cartoons with an effect that could not have been obtained by the photographer or the portrait artist. From the viewpoint of history it is clear that our political discourse would have been considerably poorer without them.

Respondent contends, however, that the caricature in question here was so "outrageous" as to distinguish it from more traditional political cartoons. There is no doubt that the caricature of respondent and his mother published in Hustler is at best a distant cousin of the political cartoons described above, and a rather poor relation at that. If it were possible by laying down a principled standard to separate the one from the other, public discourse would probably suffer little or no harm. But we doubt that there is any such standard, and we are quite sure that the pejorative description "outrageous" does not supply one. "Outrageousness" in the area of political and social discourse has an inherent subjectiveness about it which would allow a jury to impose liability on the basis of the jurors' tastes or views, or perhaps on the basis of their dislike of a particular expression. An "outrageousness" standard thus runs afoul of our longstanding refusal to allow damages to be awarded because the speech in question may have an adverse emotional impact on the audience. See *NAACP v. Claiborne Hardware Co.*, 458 U.S. 886, 910 (1982) ("Speech does not lose its protected character . . . simply because it may embarrass others or coerce them into action"). And, as we stated in *FCC v. Pacifica Foundation*, 438 U.S. 726 (1978):

> [T]he fact that society may find speech offensive is not a sufficient reason for suppressing it. Indeed, if it is the speaker's opinion that gives offense, that consequence is a reason for according it constitutional protection. For it is a central tenet of the First Amendment that the government must remain neutral in the marketplace of ideas.

See also *Street v. New York*, 394 U.S. 576, 592 (1969) ("It is firmly settled that . . . the public expression of ideas may not be prohibited merely because the ideas are themselves offensive to some of their hearers").

Admittedly, these oft-repeated First Amendment principles, like other principles, are subject to limitations. We recognized in *Pacifica Foundation*, that speech that is "vulgar, offensive, and shocking" is "not entitled to absolute constitutional protection under all circumstances." 438 U.S., at 747. In *Chaplinsky v. New Hampshire*, 315 U.S. 568 (1942), we held that a State could lawfully punish an individual for the use of insulting "fighting words—those which by their very utterance inflict injury or tend to incite an immediate breach of the peace." *Id.*, at 571–572. These limitations are but recognition of the observation in *Dun & Bradstreet, Inc. v. Greenmoss Builders, Inc.*, 472 U.S. 749, 758 (1985), that this Court has "long recognized that not all speech is of equal First Amendment importance." But the sort of expression involved in this case does not seem to us to be governed by any exception to the general First Amendment principles stated above.

We conclude that public figures and public officials may not recover for the tort of intentional infliction of emotional distress by reason of publications such as the one here at issue without showing in addition that the publication contains a false statement of fact which was made with "actual malice," *i.e.*, with knowledge that the statement was false or with reckless disregard as to whether or not it was true. This is not merely a "blind application" of the *New York Times* standard, see *Time, Inc. v. Hill*, 385 U.S. 374, 390 (1967), it reflects our considered judgment that such a standard is necessary to give adequate "breathing space" to the freedoms protected by the First Amendment.

Here it is clear that respondent Falwell is a "public figure" for purposes of First Amendment law. The jury found against respondent on his libel claim when it decided that the Hustler ad parody could not "reasonably be understood as describing actual facts about [respondent] or actual events in which [he] participated." The Court of Appeals interpreted the jury's finding to be that the ad parody "was not reasonably believable," 97 F.2d, at 1278, and in accordance with our custom we accept this finding. Respondent is thus relegated to his claim for damages awarded by the jury for the intentional infliction of emotional distress by "outrageous" conduct. But for reasons heretofore stated this claim cannot, consistently with the First Amendment, form a basis for the award of damages when the conduct in question is the publication of a caricature such as the ad parody involved here.

Jerry Falwell talks about his first time.*

FALWELL: My first time was in an outhouse outside Lynchburg, Virginia.

INTERVIEWER: Wasn't it a little cramped?

FALWELL: Not after I kicked the goat out.

INTERVIEWER: I see. You must tell me all about it.

FALWELL: I never *really* expected to make it with Mom, but then after she showed all the other guys in town such a good time, I figured, "What the hell!"

INTERVIEWER: But your mom? Isn't that a bit odd?

FALWELL: I don't think so. Looks don't mean that much to me in a woman.

INTERVIEWER: Go on.

FALWELL: Well, we were drunk off our God-fearing asses on Campari, ginger ale and soda—that's called a Fire and Brimstone—at the time. And Mom looked better than a Baptist whore with a $100 donation.

INTERVIEWER: Campari in the crapper with Mom . . . how interesting. Well, how was it?

FALWELL: The Campari was great, but Mom passed out before I could come.

INTERVIEWER: Did you ever try it again?

FALWELL: Sure . . .

lots of times. But not in the outhouse. Between Mom and the shit, the flies were too much to bear.

INTERVIEWER: We meant the Campari.

FALWELL: Oh, yeah. I always get sloshed before I go out to the pulpit. You don't think I could lay down all that bullshit sober, do you?

Campari, like all liquor, was made to mix you up. It's a light, 48-proof, refreshing spirit, just mild enough to make you drink too much before you know you're schnockered. For your first time, mix it with orange juice. Or maybe some white wine. Then you won't remember anything the next morning. **Campari. The mixable that smarts.**

CAMPARI You'll never forget your first time.

*AD PARODY—NOT TO BE TAKEN SERIOUSLY

NOTES

1.   Presumably no one reading the offensive parody in Hustler thought it was making a claim of fact. So why did the Court talk about "actual malice," which means knowing or reckless falsehood? Every parody meets that standard. What is the proper First Amendment test for speech that makes no claims of fact but is designed to inflict emotional distress?

2.   In *Snyder v. Phelps,* 562 U.S. 443 (2011), the Court held that the First Amendment forbade an award of damages against Fred Phelps and other members of the Westboro Baptist Church for picketing near a soldier's funeral service. As described in Chief Justice Roberts's majority opinion, "[t]he church's congregation believes that God hates and punishes the United States for its tolerance of homosexuality, particularly in America's military," and that "God kills American soldiers as punishment" for the nation's undue toleration of homosexuality. "The church frequently communicates its views by picketing, often at military funerals."

Church members picketed near the memorial service held for Marine Lance Corporal Matthew Snyder, who had been killed in Iraq in the line of duty. The picketing took place on public property, within a 10-by-25-foot plot of land adjacent to a public street. As the Court said, the picketers carried signs saying:

"God Hates the USA/Thank God for 9/11," "America is Doomed," Don't Pray for the USA," "Thank God for IEDs," "Thank God for Dead Soldiers," "Pope in Hell," "Priests Rape Boys," "God Hates Fags," "You're Going to Hell," and "God Hates You."

Snyder's father sued Phelps and other church members for, among other things, intentional infliction of emotional distress, intrusion upon seclusion, and civil conspiracy. A jury found for Snyder on these claims and awarded damages totaling (after remittitur) $5 million.

The Supreme Court rejected the tort award as inconsistent with the First Amendment, under the reasoning of *Hustler v. Falwell* and other decisions. "[T]he church members had the right to be where they were," the Court held, and "[t]he record confirms that any distress occasioned by Westboro's picketing turned on the content and viewpoint of the message conveyed, rather than any interference with the funeral itself." The Court said:

> Given that Westboro's speech was at a public place on a matter of public concern, that speech is entitled to 'special protection' under the First Amendment. Such speech cannot be restricted simply because it is upsetting or arouses contempt. "If there is a bedrock principle underlying the First Amendment, it is that the government may not prohibit the expression of an idea simply because society finds the idea itself offensive or disagreeable." *Texas v. Johnson*, 491 U.S. 397, 414 (1989). Indeed, "the point of all speech protection . . . is to shield just those choices of content that in someone's eyes are misguided, or even hurtful." *Hurley v. Irish-American Gay, Lesbian and Bisexual Group of Boston, Inc.*, 515 U.S. 557, 574 (1995).

As in *Hustler*, the Court held that "outrageousness" was a "highly malleable standard with 'an inherent subjectiveness about it which would allow a jury to impose liability on the basis of the jurors' tastes or views, or perhaps on the basis of their dislike of a particular expression'" (quoting *Hustler*). The Court noted that its holding was "narrow" and did not implicate laws imposing time, place, or manner restrictions on funeral picketing. "To the extent these laws are content neutral, they raise very different questions from the tort verdict at issue in this case. . . . [W]e have no occasion to consider how [Maryland's such law] might apply to facts such as those before us, or whether it or other similar regulations are constitutional."

The Court concluded:

> Westboro believes that America is morally flawed; many Americans might feel the same about Westboro. Westboro's funeral picketing is certainly hurtful and its contribution to public discourse may be negligible. But Westboro addressed matters of public import on public property, in a peaceful manner, in full compliance with the guidance of local officials. . . .
>
> Speech is powerful. It can stir people to action, move them to tears of both joy and sorrow, and—as it did here—inflict great pain. On the facts before us, we cannot react to that pain by punishing the speaker. As a Nation, we have chosen a different course—to protect even hurtful speech on public issues to ensure that we do not stifle public debate. That choice requires that we shield Westboro from tort liability for its picketing in this case.

Only Justice Alito dissented, stating that "[o]ur profound national commitment to free and open debate is not a license for the vicious verbal assault that occurred in this case." He emphasized that Snyder was not a "public figure," and argued that the attack was not truly expression on any issue of public concern, but a "brutal" attack on an individual. "Respondents' outrageous conduct caused petitioner great injury, and the Court now compounds that injury by depriving petitioner of a judgment that acknowledges the wrong he suffered. In order to have a society in which public issues can be openly and vigorously debated, it is not necessary to allow the brutalization of innocent victims like petitioner."

————

What if the offensive speech is degrading to a person on the basis of race, gender, religion, or sexual orientation? May speech be punished on the ground that it communicates a message of subordination? If so, should it be?

American Booksellers Association v. Hudnut

771 F.2d 323 (7th Cir. 1985), *aff'd mem.* 475 U.S. 1001 (1986)

■ EASTERBROOK, CIRCUIT JUDGE.

Indianapolis enacted an ordinance defining "pornography" as a practice that discriminates against women. "Pornography" is to be redressed through the administrative and judicial methods used for other discrimination. The City's definition of "pornography" is considerably different from "obscenity," which the Supreme Court has held is not protected by the First Amendment.

To be "obscene" under *Miller v. California*, 413 U.S. 15 (1973), "a publication must, taken as a whole, appeal to the prurient interest, must contain patently offensive depictions or descriptions of specified sexual conduct, and on the whole have no serious literary, artistic, political, or scientific value." *Brockett v. Spokane Arcades, Inc.*, 472 U.S. 491 (1985). Offensiveness must be assessed under the standards of the community. Both offensiveness and an appeal to something other than "normal, healthy sexual desires" (*Brockett*, at 498) are essential elements of "obscenity."

"Pornography" under the ordinance is "the graphic sexually explicit subordination of women, whether in pictures or in words, that also includes one or more of the following:

(1) Women are presented as sexual objects who enjoy pain or humiliation; or

(2) Women are presented as sexual objects who experience sexual pleasure in being raped; or

(3) Women are presented as sexual objects tied up or cut up or mutilated or bruised or physically hurt, or as dismembered or truncated or fragmented or severed into body parts; or

(4) Women are presented as being penetrated by objects or animals; or

(5) Women are presented in scenarios of degradation, injury, abasement, torture, shown as filthy or inferior, bleeding, bruised, or hurt in a context that makes these conditions sexual; or

(6) Women are presented as sexual objects for domination, conquest, violation, exploitation, possession, or use, or through postures or positions of servility or submission or display.

The statute provides that the "use of men, children, or transsexuals in the place of women in paragraphs (1) through (6) above shall also constitute pornography under this section." The ordinance as passed in April 1984 defined "sexually explicit" to mean actual or simulated intercourse or the uncovered exhibition of the genitals, buttocks or anus. An amendment in June 1984 deleted this provision, leaving the term undefined.

[Unlike the obscenity standard, the] Indianapolis ordinance does not refer to the prurient interest, to offensiveness, or to the standards of the community. It demands attention to particular depictions, not to the work judged as a whole. It is irrelevant under the ordinance whether the work has literary, artistic, political, or scientific value. The City and many amici point to these omissions as virtues. They maintain that pornography influences attitudes, and the statute is a way to alter the socialization of men and women rather than to vindicate community standards of offensiveness. And as one of the principal drafters of the ordinance has asserted, "if a woman is subjected, why should it matter that the work has other value?" Catharine A. MacKinnon, *Pornography, Civil Rights, and Speech*, 20 Harv.Civ.Rts.-Civ.Lib.L.Rev. 1, 21 (1985).

Civil rights groups and feminists have entered this case as amici on both sides. Those supporting the ordinance say that it will play an important role in reducing the tendency of men to view women as sexual objects, a tendency that leads to both unacceptable attitudes and discrimination in the workplace and violence away from it. Those opposing the ordinance point out that much radical feminist literature is explicit and depicts women in ways forbidden by the ordinance and that the ordinance would reopen old battles. It is unclear how Indianapolis would treat works from James Joyce's *Ulysses* to Homer's *Iliad;* both depict women as submissive objects for conquest and domination.

We do not try to balance the arguments for and against an ordinance such as this. The ordinance discriminates on the ground of the content of the speech. Speech treating women in the approved way—in sexual encounters "premised on equality"—is lawful no matter how sexually explicit. Speech treating women in the disapproved way—as submissive in matters sexual or as enjoying humiliation—is unlawful no matter how significant the literary, artistic, or political qualities of the work taken as a whole. The state may not ordain preferred viewpoints in this way. The Constitution forbids the state to declare one perspective right and silence opponents.

I

The ordinance contains four prohibitions. People may not "traffic" in pornography, "coerce" others into performing in pornographic works, or "force" pornography on anyone. Anyone injured by someone who has seen or read pornography has a right of action against the maker or seller. . . .

For purposes of all four offenses, it is generally "not . . . a defense that the respondent did not know or intend that the materials were pornography. . . ." But the ordinance provides that damages are unavailable in trafficking cases unless the complainant proves "that the respondent knew or had reason to know that the materials were pornography." . . .

The district court held the ordinance unconstitutional. The court concluded that the ordinance regulates speech rather than the conduct involved in making pornography. The regulation of speech could be justified, the court thought, only by a compelling interest in reducing sex discrimination, an interest Indianapolis had not established. . . .

II

The plaintiffs are a congeries of distributors and readers of books, magazines, and films. The American Booksellers Association comprises about 5,200 bookstores and chains. The Association for American Publishers includes most of the country's publishers. Video Shack, Inc., sells and rents video cassettes in Indianapolis. Kelly Bentley, a resident of Indianapolis, reads books and watches films. There are many more plaintiffs. Collectively the plaintiffs (or their members, whose interests they represent) make, sell, or read just about every kind of material that could be affected by the ordinance, from hard-core films to W.B. Yeats's poem "Leda and the Swan" (from the myth of Zeus in the form of a swan impregnating an apparently subordinate Leda), to the collected works of James Joyce, D.H. Lawrence, and John Cleland. . . .

III

"If there is any fixed star in our constitutional constellation, it is that no official, high or petty, can prescribe what shall be orthodox in politics, nationalism, religion, or other matters of opinion or force citizens to confess by word or act their faith therein." *West Virginia State Board of Education v. Barnette*, 319 U.S. 624, 642 (1943). Under the First Amendment the government must leave to the people the evaluation of ideas. Bald or subtle, an idea is as powerful as the audience allows it to be. A belief may be pernicious—the beliefs of Nazis led to the death of millions, those of the Klan to the repression of millions. A pernicious belief may prevail. Totalitarian governments today rule much of the planet, practicing suppression of billions and spreading dogma that may enslave others. One of the things that separates our society from theirs is our absolute right to propagate opinions that the government finds wrong or even hateful.

The ideas of the Klan may be propagated. *Brandenburg v. Ohio*, 395 U.S. 444 (1969). Communists may speak freely and run for office. *DeJonge v. Oregon*, 299 U.S. 353 (1937). The Nazi Party may march through a city with a large Jewish population. *Collin v. Smith*, 578 F.2d 1197 (7th Cir.), *cert. denied*, 439 U.S. 916 (1978). People may criticize the President by misrepresenting his positions, and they have a right to post their misrepresentations on public property. *Lebron v. Washington Metropolitan Area Transit Authority*, 749 F.2d 893 (D.C.Cir.1984) (Bork, J.). People may teach religions that others despise. People may seek to repeal laws guaranteeing equal opportunity in employment or to revoke the constitutional amendments granting the vote to blacks and women. They may do this because "above all else, the First Amendment means that government has no power to restrict expression because of its message [or] its ideas. . . ." *Police Department v. Mosley*, 408 U.S. 92, 95 (1972).

Under the ordinance graphic sexually explicit speech is "pornography" or not depending on the perspective the author adopts. Speech that "subordinates" women and also, for example, presents women as enjoying pain, humiliation, or rape, or even simply presents women in "positions of servility or submission or display" is forbidden, no matter how great the literary or political value of the work taken as a whole. Speech that portrays women in positions of equality is lawful, no matter how graphic the sexual content. This is thought control. It establishes an "approved" view of women, of how they may react to sexual encounters, of how the sexes may relate to each other. Those who espouse the approved view may use sexual images; those who do not, may not.

Indianapolis justifies the ordinance on the ground that pornography affects thoughts. Men who see women depicted as subordinate are more likely to treat them so. Pornography is an aspect of dominance. It does not persuade people so much as change them. It works by socializing, by establishing the expected and the permissible. In this view pornography is not an idea; pornography is the injury.

There is much to this perspective. Beliefs are also facts. People often act in accordance with the images and patterns they find around them. People raised in a religion tend to accept the tenets of that religion, often without independent examination. People taught from birth that black people are fit only for slavery rarely rebelled against that creed; beliefs coupled with the self-interest of the masters established a social structure that inflicted great harm while enduring for centuries. Words and images act at the level of the subconscious before they persuade at the level of the conscious. Even the truth has little chance unless a statement fits within the framework of beliefs that may never have been subjected to rational study.

Therefore we accept the premises of this legislation. Depictions of subordination tend to perpetuate subordination. The subordinate status of women in turn leads to affront and lower pay at work, insult and injury at home, battery and rape on the streets. . . .

Yet this simply demonstrates the power of pornography as speech. All of these unhappy effects depend on mental intermediation. Pornography affects how people see the world, their fellows, and social relations. If pornography is what pornography does, so is other speech. Hitler's orations affected how some Germans saw Jews. Communism is a worldview, not simply a *Manifesto* by Marx and Engels or a set of speeches. Efforts to suppress communist speech in the United States were based on the belief that the public acceptability of such ideas would increase the likelihood of totalitarian government. Religions affect socialization in the most pervasive way. . . . Many people believe that the existence of television, apart from the content of specific programs, leads to intellectual laziness, to a penchant for violence, to many other ills. The Alien and Sedition Acts passed during the administration of John Adams rested on a sincerely held belief that disrespect for the government leads to social collapse and revolution—a belief with support in the history of many nations. Most governments of the world act on this empirical regularity, suppressing critical speech. In the United States, however, the strength of the support for this belief is irrelevant. Seditious libel is protected speech unless the danger is not only grave but also imminent. See *New York Times Co. v. Sullivan*, 376 U.S. 254 (1964); cf. *Brandenburg v. Ohio; New York Times Co. v. United States*, 403 U.S. 713 (1971).

Racial bigotry, anti-semitism, violence on television, reporters' biases—these and many more influence the culture and shape our socialization. None is directly answerable by more speech, unless that speech too finds its place in the popular culture. Yet all is protected as speech, however insidious. Any other answer leaves the government in control of all of the institutions of culture, the great censor and director of which thoughts are good for us.

Sexual responses often are unthinking responses, and the association of sexual arousal with the subordination of women therefore may have a substantial effect.

But almost all cultural stimuli provoke unconscious responses. Religious ceremonies condition their participants. Teachers convey messages by selecting what not to cover; the implicit message about what is off limits or unthinkable may be more powerful than the messages for which they present rational argument. Television scripts contain unarticulated assumptions. People may be conditioned in subtle ways. If the fact that speech plays a role in a process of conditioning were enough to permit governmental regulation, that would be the end of freedom of speech.

It is possible to interpret the claim that the pornography is the harm in a different way. Indianapolis emphasizes the injury that models in pornographic films and pictures may suffer. The record contains materials depicting sexual torture, penetration of women by red-hot irons and the like. These concerns have nothing to do with written materials subject to the statute, and physical injury can occur with or without the "subordination" of women. A state may make injury in the course of producing a film unlawful independent of the viewpoint expressed in the film. . . .

Much of Indianapolis's argument rests on the belief that when speech is "unanswerable," and the metaphor that there is a "marketplace of ideas" does not apply, the First Amendment does not apply either. The metaphor is honored; Milton's *Aeropagitica* and John Stewart Mill's *On Liberty* defend freedom of speech on the ground that the truth will prevail, and many of the most important cases under the First Amendment recite this position. The Framers undoubtedly believed it. As a general matter it is true. But the Constitution does not make the dominance of truth a necessary condition of freedom of speech. To say that it does would be to confuse an outcome of free speech with a necessary condition for the application of the amendment.

A power to limit speech on the ground that truth has not yet prevailed and is not likely to prevail implies the power to declare truth. At some point the government must be able to say (as Indianapolis has said): "We know what the truth is, yet a free exchange of speech has not driven out falsity, so that we must now prohibit falsity." If the government may declare the truth, why wait for the failure of speech? Under the First Amendment, however, there is no such thing as a false idea, *Gertz v. Robert Welch, Inc.*, 418 U.S. 323, 339 (1974), so the government may not restrict speech on the ground that in a free exchange truth is not yet dominant.

At any time, some speech is ahead in the game; the more numerous speakers prevail. Supporters of minority candidates may be forever "excluded" from the political process because their candidates never win, because few people believe their positions. This does not mean that freedom of speech has failed. . . .

We come, finally, to the argument that pornography is "low value" speech, that it is enough like obscenity that Indianapolis may prohibit it. Some cases hold that speech far removed from politics and other subjects at the core of the Framers' concerns may be subjected to special regulation. These cases do not sustain statutes that select among viewpoints, however. . . .

At all events, "pornography" is not low value speech within the meaning of these cases. Indianapolis seeks to prohibit certain speech because it believes this speech influences social relations and politics on a grand scale, that it controls attitudes at home and in the legislature. This precludes a characterization of the speech as low value. . . .

Any rationale we could imagine in support of this ordinance could not be limited to sex discrimination. Free speech has been on balance an ally of those seeking change. Governments that want stasis start by restricting speech. Culture is a powerful force of continuity; Indianapolis paints pornography as part of the culture of power. Change in any complex system ultimately depends on the ability of outsiders to challenge accepted views and the reigning institutions. Without a strong guarantee of freedom of speech, there is no effective right to challenge what is. . . .

NOTES

1.   The "speech" in question in this case was not "legally obscene"—it did not fall in that category of wholly unprotected expression. We have seen, several times now, references to "obscenity" and child pornography as categories of expression excluded from First Amendment protection. Justice Scalia's opinion for the Court in *United States v. Williams*, 553 U.S. 285 (2008), provides a concise summary of the Court's doctrines in these areas:

> We have long held that obscene speech—sexually explicit material that violates fundamental notions of decency—is not protected by the First Amendment. But to protect explicit material that has social value, we have limited the scope of the obscenity exception, and have overturned convictions for the distribution of sexually graphic but nonobscene material. . . .

> Over the last 25 years, we have confronted a related and overlapping category of proscribable speech: child pornography. See *Ashcroft v. Free Speech Coalition*, 535 U.S. 234 (2002); *Osborne v. Ohio*, 495 U.S. 103 (1990); *New York v. Ferber*, 458 U.S. 747 (1982). This consists of sexually explicit visual portrayals that feature children. We have held that a statute which proscribes the distribution of all child pornography, even material that does not qualify as obscenity, does not on its face violate the First Amendment. . . . Moreover, we have held that the government may criminalize the possession of child pornography, even though it may not criminalize the mere possession of obscene material involving adults. Compare *Osborne*, at 111, with *Stanley v. Georgia*, 394 U.S. 557, 568 (1969).

2.   Judge Easterbrook's opinion is an excellent (if again painful) review and distillation of the First Amendment principle that the government may not prohibit, punish, or penalize speech because of its content. Is the First Amendment freedom of speech really worth all this? Nazis marching through Skokie, Illinois? KKK cross burnings? Porn shops? Is some speech so offensive, and of so little value to meaningful public discourse, that it should just be prohibited as out-of-bounds for a civilized society? Alternatively, can't some such "speech" be deemed "threats" or "assaults" that should be punishable as *unlawful conduct*, irrespective of whether they might flow from the communication of messages?

3.   In American law, there has never been an exception to the freedom of speech simply because of the "hateful," discriminatory, or demeaning nature of the expression—though there have been attempts to expand the "fighting words" exception to embrace such types of expression. In the 1990s, some public university campuses promulgated "speech codes" regulating what students could and could not say in public discourse—typically forbidding remarks that were offensive or derogatory on the basis of race, gender, sexual orientation, or some other category. In *R.A.V. v. City of St. Paul*, 505 U.S. 377 (1992), presented above, the Supreme Court unanimously struck down St. Paul, Minnesota's "Bias-Oriented Crime Ordinance" as a violation of the First Amendment,

overturning the petitioner's conviction for burning a cross on a black family's lawn. The City could not validly make the alarm or affront caused by a speaker's message, no matter how hateful, the basis for criminal punishment. (There were many statutes under which the City could have punished the petitioner's *conduct* on grounds *not* related to the content of his message.) It is thus reasonably clear under present doctrine that there is no general "hate speech" exception to the First Amendment freedom of speech. The Canadian Supreme Court, however, operating under a much less speech-protective constitution, has upheld laws against hate speech. See *R. v. Keegstra*, 3 S.C.R. 697 (Supreme Court of Canada 1990). The United States is exceptional in finding that hate speech laws are unconstitutional.

4.   May speech that communicates a message that members of a minority racial, gender, religious, or sexual orientation group is inferior be punished if it takes place in a workplace? A university? Or a place of public accommodation, such as a restaurant?

[*Assignment 48*]

H. COMMERCIAL SPEECH

Valentine v. Chrestensen
316 U.S. 52 (1942)

■ MR. JUSTICE ROBERTS delivered the opinion of the Court.

The respondent, a citizen of Florida, owns a former United States Navy submarine which he exhibits for profit. In 1940 he brought it to New York City and moored it at a State pier in the East River. He prepared and printed a handbill advertising the boat and soliciting visitors for a stated admission fee. On his attempting to distribute the bill in the city streets, he was advised by the petitioner, as Police Commissioner, that this activity would violate section 318 of the Sanitary Code which forbids distribution in the streets of commercial and business advertising matter, but was told that he might freely distribute handbills solely devoted to "information or a public protest."

Respondent thereupon prepared and showed to the petitioner, in proof form, a double-faced handbill. On one side was a revision of the original, altered by the removal of the statement as to admission fee but consisting only of commercial advertising. On the other side was a protest against the action of the City Dock Department in refusing the respondent wharfage facilities at a city pier for the exhibition of his submarine, but no commercial advertising. The Police Department advised that distribution of a bill containing only the protest would not violate section 318, and would not be restrained, but that distribution of the double-faced bill was prohibited. The respondent, nevertheless, proceeded with the printing of his proposed bill and started to distribute it. He was restrained by the police.

Respondent then brought this suit to enjoin the petitioner from interfering with the distribution. In his complaint he alleged diversity of citizenship; an amount in controversy in excess of $3,000; the acts and threats of the petitioner under the purported authority of section 318; asserted a consequent violation of section 1 of the Fourteenth Amendment of the Constitution; and prayed an injunction. The District Court granted an interlocutory injunction, and after trial on a stipulation from which the facts appear as above recited, granted a permanent injunction. The Circuit Court of Appeals, by a divided court, affirmed.

The question is whether the application of the ordinance to the respondent's activity was, in the circumstances, an unconstitutional abridgement of the freedom of the press and of speech.

1.   This court has unequivocally held that the streets are proper places for the exercise of the freedom of communicating information and disseminating opinion and that, though the states and municipalities may appropriately regulate the privilege in the public interest, they may not unduly burden or proscribe its employment in these public thoroughfares. We are equally clear that the Constitution imposes no such restraint on government as respects purely commercial advertising. Whether, and to what extent, one may promote or pursue a gainful occupation in the streets, to what extent such activity shall be adjudged a derogation of the public right of user, are matters for legislative judgment. The question is not whether the legislative body may interfere with the harmless pursuit of a lawful business, but whether it must permit such pursuit by what it deems an undesirable invasion of, or interference with, the full and free use of the highways by the people in fulfillment of the public use to which streets are dedicated. If the respondent was attempting to use the streets of New York by distributing commercial advertising, the prohibition of the code provision was lawfully invoked against his conduct.

2.   The respondent contends that, in truth, he was engaged in the dissemination of matter proper for public information, none the less so because there was inextricably attached to the medium of such dissemination commercial advertising matter. The court below appears to have taken this view since it adverts to the difficulty of apportioning, in a given case, the contents of the communication as between what is of public interest and what is for private profit. We need not indulge nice appraisal based upon subtle distinctions in the present instance nor assume possible cases not now presented. It is enough for the present purpose that the stipulated facts justify the conclusion that the affixing of the protest against official conduct to the advertising circular was with the intent, and for the purpose, of evading the prohibition of the ordinance. If that evasion were successful, every merchant who desires to broadcast advertising leaflets in the streets need only append a civic appeal, or a moral platitude, to achieve immunity from the law's command.

NOTES

1.   Did the Court's decision in *Valentine* depend on the content of the handbill, or on whether the distribution of the handbill was part of a business—a "gainful occupation in the streets"? Would the case have been different if he were selling newspapers? What if the respondent were in the business of distributing political leaflets for hire? What if ideological enthusiasts for a movie—leftwingers inspired by *Fahrenheit 9/11*, rightwingers by *2016: Obama's America*, or Christians by *Chariots of Fire*—circulate leaflets urging people to view these films?

2.   The Court provided no citation for the proposition that "the Constitution imposes no such restraint on government as respects purely commercial advertising." The following article, co-written by a legal scholar and a distinguished judge on the Ninth Circuit Court of Appeals, provides some historical context.

Alex Kozinski & Stuart Banner, "The Anti-History and Pre-History of Commercial Speech"

71 Texas L. Rev. 747 (1993)

In at least five cases before *Valentine*, the Court assessed the constitutionality of state regulation of advertising. The earliest was *Halter v. Nebraska*, in 1907, in which a beer bottler intent on placing the American flag on its bottles claimed that a state law barring this practice denied liberty and property without due process. Even in the heyday of substantive due process—*Lochner* had been decided only two years before—the Court wouldn't go for it. Selling beer might be part of liberty, but even "the rights inhering in personal liberty are subject . . . to such reasonable restraints as may be required for the general good," a good which wouldn't tolerate disrespect for the flag. And while the bottler had a property right in the bottle, he had no property right in the representation of the flag, "which, in itself, cannot belong, as property, to an individual.'" No speech-related claim was made in *Halter*, probably because of the murky status of the First Amendment's application to Nebraska, but probably also because the litigants didn't conceive of bottle-labeling as speech.

The following decade, still a period of uncertainty as to whether there was a freedom of speech as against a state, the Court decided three cases involving municipal ordinances banning certain outdoor advertising. *Fifth Avenue Coach Co. v. City of New York* involved an ordinance prohibiting advertising on the outside of buses—still called "stages" in 1911. The other two cases, *Thomas Cusack Co. v. City of Chicago* and *St. Louis Poster Advertising Co. v. City of St. Louis*, involved ordinances limiting the size of billboards. In all three cases, the advertiser raised substantive due process claims; the primary argument in each was that the ordinance deprived the advertiser of property and of the liberty to carry on its business. The advertiser lost in all three. No speech-related issue was raised in any of the cases, again suggesting that advertising at the time was considered to be a business, not a vehicle of expression.

The fifth pre-*Valentine* case involving state regulation of advertising was *Packer Corp. v. Utah*, decided in 1932. By then, as we have seen, it was clear that the Due Process Clause limited a state's power to abridge the freedom of speech. *Packer* involved a state statute implicating what is today one of the quintessential issues of commercial speech—the statute prohibited the advertising of cigarettes on billboards and streetcar signs. The billboard company's lawyers were not ignorant of the Constitution; they claimed that the statute violated the Equal Protection Clause because advertising in newspapers was permitted, that the statute took property without due process because it arbitrarily curtailed the liberty of contract, and that the statute burdened interstate commerce in violation of the Commerce Clause. The Court rejected all three arguments. Relevant for our purposes is a claim the billboard company did not make: despite the incorporation of the First Amendment and what seems today like an obvious limitation on the company's ability to communicate with customers, the company did not make any claim relating to the freedom of speech. While one can come up with any number of possible reasons why this might have been so, the most likely candidate is simply that the Packer Corporation's lawyers didn't think of advertising as speech.

A second group of pre-*Valentine* cases presents an even better opportunity to look at contemporary notions of what we think of today as commercial speech, because this group involved the federal government, and we thus avoid the difficulty posed by the uncertain status of the First Amendment's applicability to the states. While the federal government did little at the time that could potentially abridge speech, it did run the post office. In the late nineteenth and early twentieth centuries, the Court decided three cases involving First Amendment challenges to various aspects of the postal system.

In 1868, Congress banned advertisements for lotteries from the mail. Nine years later, in *Ex parte Jackson*, the Court reasoned that the ban didn't violate the First Amendment, provided that lottery advertisements could still be circulated by other means. "[W]e do not think," wrote Justice Field (speaking of "newspapers and pamphlets"), "that Congress possesses the power to prevent the transportation in other ways, as merchandise, of matter which it excludes from the mails." Such a complete ban on circulation would be "a fatal blow given to the freedom of the press." The petitioner had been convicted of mailing a lottery advertisement; the Court formulated its First Amendment rule by discussing only newspapers and pamphlets, with no indication in the opinion that advertisements are any different from newspapers so far as the First Amendment is concerned. Unless this is just sloppy writing, the *Jackson* Court implicitly considered advertising (or at least printed circulars advertising lotteries) to be speech entitled to the same degree of First Amendment protection as any other.

The sloppy-writing hypothesis is rendered unlikely by the Court's repetition of *Jackson*'s holding fifteen years later, in another lottery case, *In re Rapier*. Citing only *Jackson*, the Court reiterated

> that in excluding various articles from the mails the object of Congress is not to interfere with the freedom of the press or with any other rights of the people, but to refuse the facilities for the distribution of matter deemed injurious by Congress to the public morals; and that the transportation in any other way of matters excluded from the mails would not be forbidden.

The petitioner does *not* lose because lottery advertisements do not receive First Amendment protection; he loses because the First Amendment protects him only from complete bans on circulation, not the mere refusal to carry his ads in the mail.

The third postal case, *Lewis Publishing Co. v. Morgan*, reinforces the inference that advertising wasn't beyond the coverage of the First Amendment. The Post Office Appropriation Act of 1912 required newspapers and magazines, as a condition of second-class mailing privileges (i.e., cheaper postal rates), to mark all advertisements with the word "advertisement." The Act was upheld against a First Amendment challenge, not because advertising was outside the scope of the Amendment, but simply because the statute didn't concern "any general regulation of what should be published in newspapers." It concerned only "the right on behalf of the publishers to continue to enjoy great privileges and advantages at the public expense," a matter that raised no First Amendment concern. One gets the sense that the opinion could have read just the same had the statute required editorials to be marked "editorial"; the publisher lost its case, but not because the case involved advertising.

A final case from this period deserves its own category. *Mutual Film Corp. v. Industrial Commission*, decided by a unanimous Court in 1915, produced an opinion that is startling to read today. The case concerned a classic prior restraint—Ohio's establishment of a film censorship board, empowered to determine in advance of public exhibition the films that could be shown in the state. But a prior restraint on film exhibition abridges the freedom of speech only if film is speech, and the Court was quite certain that it wasn't. Justice McKenna wrote:

> The first impulse of the mind is to reject the contention. We immediately feel that the argument is wrong or strained which extends the guaranties of free opinion and speech to the multitudinous shows which are advertised on the bill-boards of our cities and towns . . . , and which seeks to bring motion pictures and other spectacles into practical and legal similitude to a free press and liberty of opinion.

Film, like the theater, the circus, and "all other shows and spectacles," was beyond the scope of the First Amendment.

In a particularly striking passage, Justice McKenna continued:

> It cannot be put out of view that the exhibition of moving pictures is a business pure and simple, originated and conducted for profit, like other spectacles, not to be regarded . . . as part of the press of the country or as organs of public opinion. They are mere representations of events, of ideas and sentiments published and known, vivid, useful and entertaining no doubt, but . . . capable of evil, having power for it, the greater because of their attractiveness and manner of exhibition.

This case is fascinating for a number of reasons, not the least of which is the jurisprudential view of the brand new medium of film and the ancient medium of theater—a view which hasn't survived. More to the point, the Court's emphasis on the fact that films are shown for a profit might be read to mean that the First Amendment doesn't protect profit-motivated speech. But this probably wouldn't be an accurate reading. The opinion suggests quite strongly that (1) the publication of the script of a play, even if for profit, would be protected by the First Amendment, even though the actual staging of the play would not; and (2) a film not produced and shown for profit would still not be entitled to the protection of the First Amendment. Despite the sentence about profit motive, it is the medium that is important, not the motive. *Mutual Film* can't plausibly be read as a blanket statement about the constitutional status of profit-motivated speech.

That brings us back to the two groups of pre-*Valentine* advertising cases discussed above. These two groups of cases present two snapshots of the contemporary legal climate that are difficult to reconcile. On one hand, when a state or local government regulated advertising on billboards and public transportation, the advertisers never thought to raise any speech-related claims. On the other hand, when the federal government regulated advertising in the mail, the advertisers did raise claims based on the First Amendment, and although the claims were unsuccessful, that apparently was not because they involved advertisements.

For our purposes, no reconciliation is necessary, as we aren't trying to discern the law—we're trying only to get a sense of what was commonly thought about advertising and the First Amendment in the late nineteenth and early twentieth centuries. And while this set of evidence is admittedly small, we think it excludes the two extreme hypotheses. First, it probably can't be said about this period that advertising was obviously within the scope of the First Amendment. If that had been so, surely one of the state-regulated advertisers would have braved the incorporation question and raised a speech-related claim. Second, it probably can't be said about the period that advertising was obviously not within the scope of the First Amendment. If that had been so, surely one of the three federal postal cases would have been decided on that ground; such a decision would have been far easier to reach and write than the elaborate theory of postal regulation set forth in *Jackson* and *Lewis*.

Eliminate the two extremes, and we're left with a picture of contemporary jurisprudence in which the status of advertising as speech protected by the First Amendment was uncertain. Certainly the Supreme Court had said nothing either way. To answer this question in a less cursory fashion than we have, research into lower court decisions and other indications of contemporary opinion is necessary. From our limited look at what the Supreme Court had to say, and at what litigants chose to present to the Court, we can tentatively conclude that the status of advertising as speech was murky in the decades before *Valentine*.

Virginia State Board of Pharmacy v. Virginia Citizens Consumer Council
425 U.S. 748 (1976)

■ MR. JUSTICE BLACKMUN delivered the opinion of the Court.

The plaintiff-appellees in this case attack, as violative of the First and Fourteenth Amendments, that portion of [the Virginia Code], which provides that a pharmacist licensed in Virginia is guilty of unprofessional conduct if he "(3) publishes, advertises or promotes, directly or indirectly, in any manner whatsoever, any amount, price, fee, premium, discount, rebate or credit terms . . . for any drugs which may be dispensed only by prescription." The three-judge District Court [enjoined the defendant-appellants from enforcing it].

. . . The present [attack] on the statute is one made not by one directly subject to its prohibition, that is, a pharmacist, but by prescription drug consumers who claim that they would greatly benefit if the prohibition were lifted and advertising freely allowed. . . . Their claim is that the First Amendment entitles the user of prescription drugs to receive information that pharmacists wish to communicate to them through advertising and other promotional means, concerning the prices of such drugs. . . .

III

The question first arises whether, even assuming that First Amendment protection attaches to the flow of drug price information, it is a protection enjoyed by the appellees as recipients of the information, and not solely, if at all, by the advertisers themselves who seek to disseminate that information.

Freedom of speech presupposes a willing speaker. But where a speaker exists, as is the case here, the protection afforded is to the communication, to its source and to its recipients both. . . . If there is a right to advertise, there is a reciprocal right to receive the advertising, and it may be asserted by these appellees.

IV

The appellants contend that the advertisement of prescription drug prices is outside the protection of the First Amendment because it is "commercial speech." There can be no question that in past decisions the Court has given some indication that commercial speech is unprotected. In *Valentine v. Chrestensen*, 316 U.S. 52 (1942), the Court upheld a New York statute that prohibited the distribution of any "handbill, circular . . . or other advertising matter whatsoever in or upon any street." The Court concluded that, although the First Amendment would forbid the banning of all communication by handbill in the public thoroughfares, it imposed "no such restraint on government as respects purely commercial advertising." Further support for a "commercial speech" exception to the First Amendment may perhaps be found in *Breard v. Alexandria*, 341 U.S. 622 (1951), where the Court upheld a conviction for violation of an ordinance prohibiting door-to-door solicitation of magazine subscriptions. The Court reasoned: "The selling . . . brings into the transaction a commercial feature," and it distinguished *Martin v. Struthers*, 319 U.S. 141 (1943), where it had reversed a conviction for door-to-door distribution of leaflets publicizing a religious meeting, as a case involving "no element of the commercial." Moreover, the Court several times has stressed that communications to which First Amendment protection was given were not "purely commercial."

Since the decision in *Breard*, however, the Court has never denied protection on the ground that the speech in issue was "commercial speech." . . . *[The Court next discusses* Pittsburgh Press Co. v. Human Relations Comm'n, *413 U.S. 376 (1973), which upheld a law banning sex-designated "help wanted" ads. The* Pittsburgh Press *Court characterized the advertisements as "classic examples of commercial speech," but upheld the law because the discriminatory hirings, and their newspaper layout, were themselves illegal.—Editors]*

Last Term, in *Bigelow v. Virginia*, 421 U.S. 809 (1975), the notion of unprotected "commercial speech" all but passed from the scene. We reversed a conviction for violation of a Virginia statute that made the circulation of any publication to encourage or promote the processing of an abortion in Virginia a misdemeanor. . . .

[T]he question whether there is a First Amendment exception for "commercial speech" is squarely before us. Our pharmacist does not wish to editorialize on any subject, cultural, philosophical, or political. He does not wish to report any particularly newsworthy fact, or to make generalized observations even about commercial matters. The "idea" he wishes to communicate is simply this: "I will sell you the X prescription drug at the Y price." Our question, then, is whether this communication is wholly outside the protection of the First Amendment.

V

We begin with several propositions that already are settled or beyond serious dispute. It is clear, for example, that speech does not lose its First Amendment protection because money is spent to project it, as in a paid advertisement of one form or another. Speech likewise is protected even though it is carried in a form that is "sold" for profit, and even though it may involve a solicitation to purchase or otherwise pay or contribute money.

If there is a kind of commercial speech that lacks all First Amendment protection, therefore, it must be distinguished by its content. Yet the speech whose content deprives it of protection cannot simply be speech on a commercial subject.

No one would contend that our pharmacist may be prevented from being heard on the subject of whether, in general, pharmaceutical prices should be regulated, or their advertisement forbidden. Nor can it be dispositive that a commercial advertisement is noneditorial, and merely reports a fact. Purely factual matter of public interest may claim protection.

Our question is whether speech which does "no more than propose a commercial transaction," is so removed from any "exposition of ideas," and from "truth, science, morality, and arts in general, in its diffusion of liberal sentiments on the administration of Government," that it lacks all protection. Our answer is that it is not.

Focusing first on the individual parties to the transaction that is proposed in the commercial advertisement, we may assume that the advertiser's interest is a purely economic one. That hardly disqualifies him from protection under the First Amendment. The interests of the contestants in a labor dispute are primarily economic, but it has long been settled that both the employee and the employer are protected by the First Amendment when they express themselves on the merits of the dispute in order to influence its outcome. We know of no requirement that, in order to avail themselves of First Amendment protection, the parties to a labor dispute need address themselves to the merits of unionism in general or to any subject beyond their immediate dispute. . . .

As to the particular consumer's interest in the free flow of commercial information, that interest may be as keen, if not keener by far, than his interest in the day's most urgent political debate. Appellees' case in this respect is a convincing one. Those whom the suppression of prescription drug price information hits the hardest are the poor, the sick, and particularly the aged. A disproportionate amount of their income tends to be spent on prescription drugs; yet they are the least able to learn, by shopping from pharmacist to pharmacist, where their scarce dollars are best spent. When drug prices vary as strikingly as they do, information as to who is charging what becomes more than a convenience. It could mean the alleviation of physical pain or the enjoyment of basic necessities.

Generalizing, society also may have a strong interest in the free flow of commercial information. Even an individual advertisement, though entirely "commercial," may be of general public interest. The facts of decided cases furnish illustrations: advertisements stating that referral services for legal abortions are available; that a manufacturer of artificial furs promotes his product as an alternative to the extinction by his competitors of fur-bearing mammals; and that a domestic producer advertises his product as an alternative to imports that tend to deprive American residents of their jobs. Obviously, not all commercial messages contain the same or even a very great public interest element. There are few to which such an element, however, could not be added. Our pharmacist, for example, could cast himself as a commentator on store-to-store disparities in drug prices, giving his own and those of a competitor as proof. We see little point in requiring him to do so, and little difference if he does not.

Moreover, there is another consideration that suggests that no line between publicly "interesting" or "important" commercial advertising and the opposite kind could ever be drawn. Advertising, however tasteless and excessive it sometimes may seem, is nonetheless dissemination of information as to who is producing and selling what product, for what reason, and at what price. So long as we preserve a predominantly free enterprise economy, the allocation of our resources in large measure will be made through numerous private economic decisions. It is a matter of public interest that those decisions, in the aggregate, be intelligent and well informed. To this end, the free flow of commercial information is indispensable. And if it is indispensable to the proper allocation of resources in a free enterprise system, it is also indispensable to the formation of intelligent opinions as to how that system ought to be regulated or altered. Therefore, even if the First Amendment were thought to be primarily an instrument to enlighten public decisionmaking in a democracy, we could not say that the free flow of information does not serve that goal.

Arrayed against these substantial individual and societal interests are a number of justifications for the advertising ban. These have to do principally with maintaining a high degree of professionalism on the part of licensed pharmacists. Indisputably, the State has a strong interest in maintaining that professionalism. It is exercised in a number of ways for the consumer's benefit. . . .

Price advertising, it is argued, will place in jeopardy the pharmacist's expertise and, with it, the customer's health. It is claimed that the aggressive price competition that will result from unlimited advertising will make it impossible for the pharmacist to supply professional services in the compounding, handling, and dispensing of prescription drugs. Such services are time consuming and expensive; if competitors who economize by eliminating them are permitted to advertise their resulting lower prices, the more painstaking and conscientious pharmacist will be forced either to follow suit or to go out of business. It is also claimed that prices might not necessarily fall as a result of advertising. If one pharmacist advertises, others must, and the resulting expense will inflate the cost of drugs. It is further claimed that advertising will lead people to shop for their prescription drugs among the various pharmacists who offer the lowest prices, and the loss of stable pharmacist-customer relationships will make individual attention and certainly the practice of monitoring impossible. Finally, it is argued that damage will be done to the professional image of the pharmacist. This image, that of a skilled and specialized craftsman, attracts talent to the profession and reinforces the better habits of those who are in it. Price advertising, it is said, will reduce the pharmacist's status to that of a mere retailer.

The strength of these proffered justifications is greatly undermined by the fact that high professional standards, to a substantial extent, are guaranteed by the close regulation to which pharmacists in Virginia are subject. And this case concerns the retail sale by the pharmacist more than it does his professional standards. Surely, any pharmacist guilty of professional dereliction that actually endangers his customer will promptly lose his license. At the same time, we cannot discount the Board's justifications entirely. The Court regarded justifications of this type sufficient to sustain the advertising bans challenged on due process and equal protection grounds[.]

The challenge now made, however, is based on the First Amendment. This casts the Board's justifications in a different light, for on close inspection it is seen that the State's protectiveness of its citizens rests in large measure on the advantages of their being kept in ignorance. The advertising ban does not directly affect professional standards one way or the other. It affects them only through the reactions it is assumed people will have to the free flow of drug price information.

There is no claim that the advertising ban in any way prevents the cutting of corners by the pharmacist who is so inclined. That pharmacist is likely to cut corners in any event. The only effect the advertising ban has on him is to insulate him from price competition and to open the way for him to make a substantial, and perhaps even excessive, profit in addition to providing an inferior service. The more painstaking pharmacist is also protected but, again, it is a protection based in large part on public ignorance.

It appears to be feared that if the pharmacist who wishes to provide low cost, and assertedly low quality, services is permitted to advertise, he will be taken up on his offer by too many unwitting customers. They will choose the low-cost, low-quality service and drive the "professional" pharmacist out of business. They will respond only to costly and excessive advertising, and end up paying the price. They will go from one pharmacist to another, following the discount, and destroy the pharmacist-customer relationship. They will lose respect for the profession because it advertises. All this is not in their best interests, and all this can be avoided if they are not permitted to know who is charging what.

There is, of course, an alternative to this highly paternalistic approach. That alternative is to assume that this information is not in itself harmful, that people will perceive their own best interests if only they are well enough informed, and that the best means to that end is to open the channels of communication rather than to close them. If they are truly open, nothing prevents the "professional" pharmacist from marketing his own assertedly superior product, and contrasting it with that of the low-cost, high-volume prescription drug retailer. But the choice among these alternative approaches is not ours to make or the Virginia General Assembly's. It is precisely this kind of choice, between the dangers of suppressing information, and the dangers of its misuse if it is freely available, that the First Amendment makes for us. Virginia is free to require whatever professional standards it wishes of its pharmacists; it may subsidize them or protect them from competition in other ways. But it may not do so by keeping the public in ignorance of the entirely lawful terms that competing pharmacists are offering. In this sense, the justifications Virginia has offered for suppressing the flow of prescription drug price information, far from persuading us that the flow is not protected by the First Amendment, have reinforced our view that it is. We so hold.

VI

In concluding that commercial speech, like other varieties, is protected, we of course do not hold that it can never be regulated in any way. Some forms of commercial speech regulation are surely permissible. We mention a few only to make clear that they are not before us and therefore are not foreclosed by this case.

There is no claim, for example, that the prohibition on prescription drug price advertising is a mere time, place, and manner restriction. We have often approved restrictions of that kind provided that they are justified without reference to the content of the regulated speech, that they serve a significant governmental interest, and that in so doing they leave open ample alternative channels for communication of the information. Whatever may be the proper bounds of time, place, and manner restrictions on commercial speech, they are plainly exceeded by this Virginia statute, which singles out speech of a particular content and seeks to prevent its dissemination completely.

Nor is there any claim that prescription drug price advertisements are forbidden because they are false or misleading in any way. Untruthful speech, commercial or otherwise, has never been protected for its own sake. Obviously, much commercial speech is not provably false, or even wholly false, but only deceptive or misleading. We foresee no obstacle to a State's dealing effectively with this problem.[24] The First Amendment, as we construe it today does not prohibit the State from insuring that the stream of commercial information flow cleanly as well as freely.

Also, there is no claim that the transactions proposed in the forbidden advertisements are themselves illegal in any way. Finally, the special problems of the electronic broadcast media are likewise not in this case.

What is at issue is whether a State may completely suppress the dissemination of concededly truthful information about entirely lawful activity, fearful of that information's effect upon its disseminators and its recipients. Reserving other questions, we conclude that the answer to this one is in the negative.

■ [The concurring opinions of CHIEF JUSTICE BURGER and JUSTICE STEWART are omitted.]

■ MR. JUSTICE REHNQUIST, dissenting.

The logical consequences of the Court's decision in this case, a decision which elevates commercial intercourse between a seller hawking his wares and a buyer seeking to strike a bargain to the same plane as has been previously reserved for the free marketplace of ideas, are far reaching indeed. Under the Court's opinion the way will be open not only for dissemination of price information but for active promotion of prescription drugs, liquor, cigarettes, and other products the use of which it has previously been thought desirable to discourage. Now, however, such promotion is protected by the First Amendment so long as it is not misleading or does not promote an illegal product or enterprise. In coming to this conclusion, the Court has overruled a legislative determination that such advertising should not be allowed and has done so on behalf of a consumer group which is not directly disadvantaged by the statute in question. This effort to reach a result which the Court obviously considers desirable is a troublesome one, for two reasons. It extends standing to raise First Amendment claims beyond the previous decisions of this Court. It also extends the protection of that Amendment to purely commercial endeavors which its most vigorous champions on this Court had thought to be beyond its pale. . . .

---

[24] In concluding that commercial speech enjoys First Amendment protection, we have not held that it is wholly undifferentiable from other forms. There are commonsense differences between speech that does "no more than propose a commercial transaction," and other varieties. Even if the differences do not justify the conclusion that commercial speech is valueless, and thus subject to complete suppression by the State, they nonetheless suggest that a different degree of protection is necessary to insure that the flow of truthful and legitimate commercial information is unimpaired. The truth of commercial speech, for example, may be more easily verifiable by its disseminator than, let us say, news reporting or political commentary, in that ordinarily the advertiser seeks to disseminate information about a specific product or service that he himself provides and presumably knows more about than anyone else. Also, commercial speech may be more durable than other kinds. Since advertising is the sine qua non of commercial profits, there is little likelihood of its being chilled by proper regulation and forgone entirely.

Attributes such as these, the greater objectivity and hardiness of commercial speech, may make it less necessary to tolerate inaccurate statements for fear of silencing the speaker. They may also make it appropriate to require that a commercial message appear in such a form, or include such additional information, warnings, and disclaimers, as are necessary to prevent its being deceptive. They may also make inapplicable the prohibition against prior restraints.

Thus the issue on the merits is not, as the Court phrases it, whether "[o]ur pharmacist" may communicate the fact that he "will sell you the X prescription drug at the Y price." No pharmacist is asserting any such claim to so communicate. The issue is rather whether appellee consumers may override the legislative determination that pharmacists should not advertise even though the pharmacists themselves do not object. In deciding that they may do so, the Court necessarily adopts a rule which cannot be limited merely to dissemination of price alone, and which cannot possibly be confined to pharmacists but must likewise extend to lawyers, doctors, and all other professions.

The Court speaks of the consumer's interest in the free flow of commercial information, particularly in the case of the poor, the sick, and the aged. It goes on to observe that "society also may have a strong interest in the free flow of commercial information." One need not disagree with either of these statements in order to feel that they should presumptively be the concern of the Virginia Legislature, which sits to balance these and other claims in the process of making laws such as the one here under attack. The Court speaks of the importance in a "predominantly free enterprise economy" of intelligent and well-informed decisions as to allocation of resources. While there is again much to be said for the Court's observation as a matter of desirable public policy, there is certainly nothing in the United States Constitution which requires the Virginia Legislature to hew to the teachings of Adam Smith in its legislative decisions regulating the pharmacy profession. . . .

There are undoubted difficulties with an effort to draw a bright line between "commercial speech" on the one hand and "protected speech" on the other, and the Court does better to face up to these difficulties than to attempt to hide them under labels. In this case, however, the Court has unfortunately substituted for the wavering line previously thought to exist between commercial speech and protected speech a no more satisfactory line of its own than between "truthful" commercial speech, on the one hand, and that which is "false and misleading" on the other. The difficulty with this line is not that it wavers, but on the contrary that it is simply too Procrustean to take into account the congeries of factors which I believe could, quite consistently with the First and Fourteenth Amendments, properly influence a legislative decision with respect to commercial advertising.

The Court insists that the rule it lays down is consistent even with the view that the First Amendment is "primarily an instrument to enlighten public decisionmaking in a democracy." I had understood this view to relate to public decisionmaking as to political, social, and other public issues, rather than the decision of a particular individual as to whether to purchase one or another kind of shampoo. It is undoubtedly arguable that many people in the country regard the choice of shampoo as just as important as who may be elected to local, state, or national political office, but that does not automatically bring information about competing shampoos within the protection of the First Amendment. It is one thing to say that the line between strictly ideological and political commentaries and other kinds of commentary is difficult to draw, and that the mere fact that the former may have in it an element of commercialism does not strip it of First Amendment protection. But it is another thing to say that because that line is difficult to draw, we will stand at the other end of the spectrum and reject out of hand the observation of so dedicated a champion of the First Amendment as Mr. Justice Black that the protections of that Amendment do not apply to a "merchant who goes from door to door selling pots." . . .

Both Congress and state legislatures have by law sharply limited the permissible dissemination of information about some commodities because of the potential harm resulting from those commodities, even though they were not thought to be sufficiently demonstrably harmful to warrant outright prohibition of their sale. Current prohibitions on television advertising of liquor and cigarettes are prominent in this category, but apparently under the Court's holding so long as the advertisements are not deceptive they may no longer be prohibited. . . .

Here the rights of the appellees seem to me to be marginal at best. There is no ideological content to the information which they seek and it is freely available to them they may even publish it if they so desire. The only persons directly affected by this statute are not parties to this lawsuit. On the other hand, the societal interest against the promotion of drug use for every ill, real or imaginary, seems to me extremely strong. I do not believe that the First Amendment mandates the Court's "open door policy" toward such commercial advertising.

NOTES

1.   Is the lower protection for commercial speech one of those categorical "traditional limitations" recognized in *Chaplinsky* and *Brown*? Does it satisfy *Brown*'s requirement of a "historical warrant" based on "persuasive evidence" of a "long tradition of proscription"? Or is it justified by weighing the value of commercial speech against its cost—an approach the *Brown* Court called "startling and dangerous"? After canvassing the Court's own precedents, from *Valentine* to *Bigelow*, and finding the question of protection for commercial speech unresolved, the Court seemed to draw its own conclusions about the dangers and benefits of restricting commercial speech. Pay careful attention to the "commonsense differences" attributable to commercial speech in footnote 24. Is regulation of commercial speech limited to the implications of these differences, or may the entire field of commercial speech be subject to a lower standard of scrutiny on account of being of lower value in a democracy? Is the latter what Justice Rehnquist suggests?

2.   Did it matter whether the speakers in this case were corporations? Note the Court's statement: "No one would contend that our pharmacist may be prevented from being heard on the subject of whether, in general, pharmaceutical prices should be regulated, or their advertisement forbidden." Is that true? Do profit-making businesses have a First Amendment right to make their opinions about public policy matters known to the public? Do they have a right to spend money to do so, by buying advertising on websites or on television? Think about these questions as you consider the question of campaign finance restrictions presented below.

3.   The plaintiffs in this case were consumers who wanted to receive information about drug prices, not pharmacies who wanted to disseminate it. Justice Blackmun's references to "our pharmacist" were therefore entirely hypothetical. Do you see why no pharmacy in Virginia chose to challenge the law? What is the economics of a ban on price advertising? Justice Rehnquist treats the fact that the directly regulated parties were not challenging the law as reason not to question its constitutionality. Does he perhaps have it backwards?

Is this aspect of the decision merely about standing to sue, or does it imply that willing listeners or readers have a constitutional right against laws that ban willing speakers or writers from communicating with them? Is there a constitutional right to hear, view, and read—as well as a constitutional right to speak, write, and publish? What are the implications of that? On the one hand, this seems intuitively correct: *Brown v. Entertainment Merchants* was concerned with the rights of teenage gamers to purchase violent video games; a prisoner presumably has free speech rights to read newspapers or religious materials; a householder may challenge postal regulations preventing the delivery of lewd magazines. But this holding could have a powerful and unsettling consequence: it may render presumptively unconstitutional any speaker-based restrictions on speech, if challenged by a person who wants access to the message. Think about this as you consider presently whether corporations can be prohibited from engaging in the same sort of speech that natural persons and groups have a right to engage in.

A NOTE ON THE *CENTRAL HUDSON* TEST

In *Central Hudson Gas & Elect. Corp. v. Public Service Comm'n*, 447 U.S. 557, 563–64 (1980), the Supreme Court announced what appeared to be a general test for the regulation of commercial speech:

> In commercial speech cases, then, a four-part analysis has developed. At the outset, we must determine whether the expression is protected by the First Amendment. For commercial speech to come within that provision, it at least must concern lawful activity and not be misleading. Next, we ask whether the asserted governmental interest is substantial. If both inquiries yield positive answers, we must determine whether the regulation directly advances the governmental interest asserted, and whether it is not more extensive than is necessary to serve that interest.

This test is familiar; it is essentially the same as other forms of "intermediate scrutiny": the government's interest need only be "substantial" (not "compelling"); it must "directly advance" that interest (as opposed to being "necessary"); and there must not be a more limited restriction that would serve that interest "as well." This approach is in tension with the idea that commercial speech is fully protected unless it falls within one of the "commonsense differences" that distinguish commercial speech from other forms of expression. Under *Central Hudson*, all governmental justifications are treated the same way and are subject to intermediate scrutiny. Under the alternative approach, only certain justifications warrant regulation. See the way this tension plays out in this subsequent case:

44 Liquormart, Inc. v. Rhode Island

517 U.S. 484 (1996)

[Rhode Island law prohibited "advertising in any manner whatsoever" the price of alcohol, except for price tags and signs inside liquor stores. The Rhode Island Supreme Court had upheld the law against multiple challenges, holding that the law reasonably furthered "the substantial state interest in the promotion of temperance" and was not "more extensive than necessary to further that interest." Two discount liquor stores sought a declaratory judgment in federal court that the advertising ban violated the First Amendment. The Rhode Island Liquor Stores Association intervened as a defendant. The district court found "as a fact that Rhode Island's off-premises liquor price advertising ban has no significant impact on levels of alcohol consumption in Rhode Island." The court of appeals reversed, noting "inherent merit"

in the state's submission that competitive price advertising would lower prices and that lower prices would produce more sales."—Editors]

■ JUSTICE STEVENS announced the judgment of the Court and delivered the opinion of the Court with respect to Parts I, II, VII, and VIII, an opinion with respect to Parts III and V, in which JUSTICE KENNEDY, JUSTICE SOUTER, and JUSTICE GINSBURG join, an opinion with respect to Part VI, in which JUSTICE KENNEDY, JUSTICE THOMAS, and JUSTICE GINSBURG join, and an opinion with respect to Part IV, in which JUSTICE KENNEDY and JUSTICE GINSBURG join.

III

Advertising has been a part of our culture throughout our history. Even in colonial days, the public relied on "commercial speech" for vital information about the market. Early newspapers displayed advertisements for goods and services on their front pages, and town criers called out prices in public squares. Indeed, commercial messages played such a central role in public life prior to the founding that Benjamin Franklin authored his early defense of a free press in support of his decision to print, of all things, an advertisement for voyages to Barbados.

In accord with the role that commercial messages have long played, the law has developed to ensure that advertising provides consumers with accurate information about the availability of goods and services. In the early years, the common law, and later, statutes, served the consumers' interest in the receipt of accurate information in the commercial market by prohibiting fraudulent and misleading advertising. It was not until the 1970's, however, that this Court held that the First Amendment protected the dissemination of truthful and nonmisleading commercial messages about lawful products and services. See generally Kozinski & Banner, The Anti-History and Pre-History of Commercial Speech, 71 Texas L. Rev. 747 (1993).

. . . At the same time, our early cases recognized that the State may regulate some types of commercial advertising more freely than other forms of protected speech. Specifically, we explained that the State may require commercial messages to "appear in such a form, or include such additional information, warnings, and disclaimers, as are necessary to prevent its being deceptive," *Virginia Bd. of Pharmacy v. Virginia Citizens Consumer Council, Inc.*, 425 U.S. 748 (1976), and that it may restrict some forms of aggressive sales practices that have the potential to exert "undue influence" over consumers, see *Bates v. State Bar of Ariz.*, 433 U.S. 350 (1977).

Virginia Bd. of Pharmacy attributed the State's authority to impose these regulations in part to certain "commonsense differences" that exist between commercial messages and other types of protected expression. Our opinion noted that the greater "objectivity" of commercial speech justifies affording the State more freedom to distinguish false commercial advertisements from true ones, and that the greater "hardiness" of commercial speech, inspired as it is by the profit motive, likely diminishes the chilling effect that may attend its regulation.

Subsequent cases explained that the State's power to regulate commercial transactions justifies its concomitant power to regulate commercial speech that is "linked inextricably" to those transactions. As one commentator has explained: "The entire commercial speech doctrine, after all, represents an accommodation between the right to speak and hear expression *about* goods and services and the right of government to regulate the sales *of* such goods and services." Nevertheless, as we explained in *Linmark Associates, Inc. v. Willingboro,* 431 U.S. 85 (1977), the State retains less regulatory authority when its commercial speech restrictions strike at "the substance of the information communicated" rather than the "commercial aspect of [it]—with offerors communicating offers to offerees."

In *Central Hudson Gas & Elec. Corp. v. Public Serv. Comm'n of N.Y.,* 447 U.S. 557 (1980), we took stock of our developing commercial speech jurisprudence. In that case, we considered a regulation "completely" banning all promotional advertising by electric utilities. Our decision acknowledged the special features of commercial speech but identified the serious First Amendment concerns that attend blanket advertising prohibitions that do not protect consumers from commercial harms.

Five Members of the Court recognized that the state interest in the conservation of energy was substantial, and that there was "an immediate connection between advertising and demand for electricity." Nevertheless, they concluded that the regulation was invalid because respondent commission had failed to make a showing that a more limited speech regulation would not have adequately served the State's interest.

In reaching its conclusion, the majority explained that although the special nature of commercial speech may require less than strict review of its regulation, special concerns arise from "regulations that entirely suppress commercial speech in order to pursue a nonspeech-related policy." In those circumstances, "a ban on speech could screen from public view the underlying governmental policy." As a result, the Court concluded that "special care" should attend the review of such blanket bans, and it pointedly remarked that "in recent years this Court has not approved a blanket ban on commercial speech unless the expression itself was flawed in some way, either because it was deceptive or related to unlawful activity."

IV

As our review of the case law reveals, Rhode Island errs in concluding that *all* commercial speech regulations are subject to a similar form of constitutional review simply because they target a similar category of expression. The mere fact that messages propose commercial transactions does not in and of itself dictate the constitutional analysis that should apply to decisions to suppress them.

When a State regulates commercial messages to protect consumers from misleading, deceptive, or aggressive sales practices, or requires the disclosure of beneficial consumer information, the purpose of its regulation is consistent with the reasons for according constitutional protection to commercial speech and therefore justifies less than strict review. However, when a State entirely prohibits the dissemination of truthful, nonmisleading commercial messages for reasons unrelated to the preservation of a fair bargaining process, there is far less reason to depart from the rigorous review that the First Amendment generally demands.

Sound reasons justify reviewing the latter type of commercial speech regulation more carefully. Most obviously, complete speech bans, unlike content-neutral restrictions on the time, place, or manner of expression, are particularly dangerous because they all but foreclose alternative means of disseminating certain information. . . .

The special dangers that attend complete bans on truthful, nonmisleading commercial speech cannot be explained away by appeals to the "commonsense distinctions" that exist between commercial and noncommercial speech. Regulations that suppress the truth are no less troubling because they target objectively verifiable information, nor are they less effective because they aim at durable messages. As a result, neither the "greater objectivity" nor the "greater hardiness" of truthful, nonmisleading commercial speech justifies reviewing its complete suppression with added deference.

It is the State's interest in protecting consumers from "commercial harms" that provides "the typical reason why commercial speech can be subject to greater governmental regulation than noncommercial speech." Yet bans that target truthful, nonmisleading commercial messages rarely protect consumers from such harms. Instead, such bans often serve only to obscure an "underlying governmental policy" that could be implemented without regulating speech. In this way, these commercial speech bans not only hinder consumer choice, but also impede debate over central issues of public policy.

Precisely because bans against truthful, nonmisleading commercial speech rarely seek to protect consumers from either deception or overreaching, they usually rest solely on the offensive assumption that the public will respond "irrationally" to the truth. The First Amendment directs us to be especially skeptical of regulations that seek to keep people in the dark for what the government perceives to be their own good. That teaching applies equally to state attempts to deprive consumers of accurate information about their chosen products: . . .

V

In this case, there is no question that Rhode Island's price advertising ban constitutes a blanket prohibition against truthful, nonmisleading speech about a lawful product. There is also no question that the ban serves an end unrelated to consumer protection. Accordingly, we must review the price advertising ban with "special care," mindful that speech prohibitions of this type rarely survive constitutional review.

The State argues that the price advertising prohibition should nevertheless be upheld because it directly advances the State's substantial interest in promoting temperance, and because it is no more extensive than necessary. Although there is some confusion as to what Rhode Island means by temperance, we assume that the State asserts an interest in reducing alcohol consumption.

In evaluating the ban's effectiveness in advancing the State's interest, we note that a commercial speech regulation "may not be sustained if it provides only ineffective or remote support for the government's purpose." *Central Hudson*, at 564. For that reason, the State bears the burden of showing not merely that its regulation will advance its interest, but also that it will do so "to a material degree." The need for the State to make such a showing is particularly great given the drastic nature of its chosen means-the wholesale suppression of truthful, nonmisleading information. Accordingly, we must determine whether the State has shown that the price advertising ban will *significantly* reduce alcohol consumption.

We can agree that common sense supports the conclusion that a prohibition against price advertising, like a collusive agreement among competitors to refrain from such advertising, will tend to mitigate competition and maintain prices at a higher level than would prevail in a completely free market. Despite the absence of proof on the point, we can even agree with the State's contention that it is reasonable to assume that demand, and hence consumption throughout the market, is somewhat lower whenever a higher, noncompetitive price level prevails. However, without any findings of fact, or indeed any evidentiary support whatsoever, we cannot agree with the assertion that the price advertising ban will significantly advance the State's interest in promoting temperance.

Although the record suggests that the price advertising ban may have some impact on the purchasing patterns of temperate drinkers of modest means, the State has presented no evidence to suggest that its speech prohibition will *significantly* reduce marketwide consumption. Indeed, the District Court's considered and uncontradicted finding on this point is directly to the contrary. Moreover, the evidence suggests that the abusive drinker will probably not be deterred by a marginal price increase, and that the true alcoholic may simply reduce his purchases of other necessities. . . .

As is evident, any conclusion that elimination of the ban would significantly increase alcohol consumption would require us to engage in the sort of "speculation or conjecture" that is an unacceptable means of demonstrating that a restriction on commercial speech directly advances the State's asserted interest. Such speculation certainly does not suffice when the State takes aim at accurate commercial information for paternalistic ends.

The State also cannot satisfy the requirement that its restriction on speech be no more extensive than necessary. It is perfectly obvious that alternative forms of regulation that would not involve any restriction on speech would be more likely to achieve the State's goal of promoting temperance. As the State's own expert conceded, higher prices can be maintained either by direct regulation or by increased taxation. Per capita purchases could be limited as is the case with prescription drugs. Even educational campaigns focused on the problems of excessive, or even moderate, drinking might prove to be more effective.

As a result, even under the less than strict standard that generally applies in commercial speech cases, the State has failed to establish a "reasonable fit" between its abridgment of speech and its temperance goal. It necessarily follows that the price advertising ban cannot survive the more stringent constitutional review that *Central Hudson* itself concluded was appropriate for the complete suppression of truthful, nonmisleading commercial speech.

VI

The State responds by arguing that it merely exercised appropriate "legislative judgment" in determining that a price advertising ban would best promote temperance. [R]hode Island first argues that, because expert opinions as to the effectiveness of the price advertising ban "go both ways," the Court of Appeals correctly concluded that the ban constituted a "reasonable choice" by the legislature. The State next contends that precedent requires us to give particular deference to that legislative choice because the State could, if it chose, ban the sale of alcoholic beverages outright. Finally, the State argues that deference is appropriate because alcoholic beverages are so-called "vice" products. We consider each of these contentions in turn.

The State's first argument fails to justify the speech prohibition at issue. Our commercial speech cases recognize some room for the exercise of legislative judgment. However, Rhode Island errs in concluding that *United States v. Edge Broadcasting Corp.*, 509 U.S. 418 (1993), and *Posadas de Puerto Rico Associates v.*

Tourism Co. of P. R., 478 U.S. 328 (1986), establish the degree of deference that its decision to impose a price advertising ban warrants.

In Edge we upheld a federal statute [that] was designed to regulate advertising about an activity that had been deemed illegal in the jurisdiction in which the broadcaster was located [lottery advertising]. Here, by contrast, the commercial speech ban targets information about entirely lawful behavior.

Posadas is more directly relevant. There, a five-Member majority held that, under the *Central Hudson* test, it was "up to the legislature" to choose to reduce gambling by suppressing in-state casino advertising rather than engaging in educational speech. Rhode Island argues that this logic demonstrates the constitutionality of its own decision to ban price advertising in lieu of raising taxes or employing some other less speech-restrictive means of promoting temperance.

The reasoning in *Posadas* does support the State's argument, but, on reflection, we are now persuaded that *Posadas* erroneously performed the First Amendment analysis. The casino advertising ban was designed to keep truthful, nonmisleading speech from members of the public for fear that they would be more likely to gamble if they received it. As a result, the advertising ban served to shield the State's antigambling policy from the public scrutiny that more direct, nonspeech regulation would draw.

Given our longstanding hostility to commercial speech regulation of this type, *Posadas* clearly erred in concluding that it was "up to the legislature" to choose suppression over a less speech-restrictive policy. The *Posadas* majority's conclusion on that point cannot be reconciled with the unbroken line of prior cases striking down similarly broad regulations on truthful, nonmisleading advertising when non-speech-related alternatives were available.

Because the 5-to-4 decision in *Posadas* marked such a sharp break from our prior precedent, and because it concerned a constitutional question about which this Court is the final arbiter, we decline to give force to its highly deferential approach. . . .

We also cannot accept the State's second contention, which is premised entirely on the "greater-includes-the-lesser" reasoning endorsed toward the end of the majority's opinion in *Posadas*. There, the majority stated that "the greater power to completely ban casino gambling necessarily includes the lesser power to ban advertising of casino gambling." It went on to state that "*because* the government could have enacted a wholesale prohibition of [casino gambling] it is permissible for the government to take the less intrusive step of allowing the conduct, but reducing the demand through restrictions on advertising."

Although we do not dispute the proposition that greater powers include lesser ones, we fail to see how that syllogism requires the conclusion that the State's power to regulate commercial *activity* is "greater" than its power to ban truthful, nonmisleading commercial *speech*. Contrary to the assumption made in *Posadas,* we think it quite clear that banning speech may sometimes prove far more intrusive than banning conduct. As a venerable proverb teaches, it may prove more injurious to prevent people from teaching others how to fish than to prevent fish from being sold. Similarly, a local ordinance banning bicycle lessons may curtail freedom far more than one that prohibits bicycle riding within city limits. In short, we reject the assumption that words are necessarily less vital to freedom than actions, or that logic somehow proves that the power to prohibit an activity is necessarily "greater" than the power to suppress speech about it.

As a matter of First Amendment doctrine, the *Posadas* syllogism is even less defensible. The text of the First Amendment makes clear that the Constitution presumes that attempts to regulate speech are more dangerous than attempts to regulate conduct. That presumption accords with the essential role that the free flow of information plays in a democratic society. As a result, the First Amendment directs that government may not suppress speech as easily as it may suppress conduct, and that speech restrictions cannot be treated as simply another means that the government may use to achieve its ends. . . .

That the State has chosen to license its liquor retailers does not change the analysis. Even though government is under no obligation to provide a person, or the public, a particular benefit, it does not follow that conferral of the benefit may be conditioned on the surrender of a constitutional right. In *Perry v. Sindermann,* 408 U.S. 593 (1972), relying on a host of cases applying that principle during the preceding quarter century, the Court explained that government "may not deny a benefit to a person on a basis that infringes his constitutionally protected interests— especially his interest in freedom of speech." That teaching clearly applies to state attempts to regulate commercial speech, as our cases striking down bans on truthful, nonmisleading speech by licensed professionals attest. . . .

Finally, we find unpersuasive the State's contention that, under *Posadas* and *Edge,* the price advertising ban should be upheld because it targets commercial speech that pertains to a "vice" activity. . . . [T]he scope of any "vice" exception to the protection afforded by the First Amendment would be difficult, if not impossible, to define. Almost any product that poses some threat to public health or public morals might reasonably be characterized by a state legislature as relating to "vice activity." Such characterization, however, is anomalous when applied to products such as alcoholic beverages, lottery tickets, or playing cards, that may be lawfully purchased on the open market. The recognition of such an exception would also have the unfortunate consequence of either allowing state legislatures to justify censorship by the simple expedient of placing the "vice" label on selected lawful activities, or requiring the federal courts to establish a federal common law of vice. For these reasons, a "vice" label that is unaccompanied by a corresponding prohibition against the commercial behavior at issue fails to provide a principled justification for the regulation of commercial speech about that activity.

VII

[The Court held that the Twenty-first Amendment "does not in any way diminish the force" of the First Amendment and thus could not save Rhode Island's ban on liquor price advertising.—Editors]

VIII

Because Rhode Island has failed to carry its heavy burden of justifying its complete ban on price advertising, we conclude that [the Rhode Island statutes] abridge speech in violation of the First Amendment as made applicable to the States by the Due Process Clause of the Fourteenth Amendment.

■ JUSTICE SCALIA, concurring in part and concurring in the judgment.

I share JUSTICE THOMAS's discomfort with the *Central Hudson* test, which seems to me to have nothing more than policy intuition to support it. I also share JUSTICE STEVENS's aversion towards paternalistic governmental policies that prevent men and women from hearing facts that might not be good for them. On the other hand, it would also be paternalism for us to prevent the people of the States from enacting laws that we consider paternalistic, unless we have good reason to believe that the Constitution itself forbids them. I will take my guidance as to what the Constitution forbids, with regard to a text as indeterminate as the First Amendment's preservation of "the freedom of speech," and where the core offense of suppressing particular political ideas is not at issue, from the long accepted practices of the American people. . . .

■ JUSTICE THOMAS, concurring in Parts I, II, VI, and VII, and concurring in the judgment.

In cases such as this, in which the government's asserted interest is to keep legal users of a product or service ignorant in order to manipulate their choices in the marketplace, the balancing test adopted in *Central Hudson*, should not be applied, in my view. Rather, such an "interest" is *per se* illegitimate and can no more justify regulation of "commercial" speech than it can justify regulation of "noncommercial" speech. . . .

II

I do not join the principal opinion's application of the *Central Hudson* balancing test because I do not believe that such a test should be applied to a restriction of "commercial" speech, at least when, as here, the asserted interest is one that is to be achieved through keeping would-be recipients of the speech in the dark. Application of the advancement-of-state-interest prong of *Central Hudson* makes little sense to me in such circumstances. Faulting the State for failing to show that its price advertising ban decreases alcohol consumption "significantly," as JUSTICE STEVENS does, seems to imply that if the State had been *more successful* at keeping consumers ignorant and thereby decreasing their consumption, then the restriction might have been upheld. This contradicts *Virginia Bd. of Pharmacy's* rationale for protecting "commercial" speech in the first instance. . . .

[Justice Thomas points out that the argument (made by Justices Stevens and O'Connor) that the restriction on price advertising is not the least restrictive means of achieving the governmental purpose "would appear to commit the courts to striking down restrictions on speech whenever a direct regulation (i.e., a regulation involving no restriction on speech regarding lawful activity at all) would be an equally effective method of dampening demand by legal users," something which is "virtually always" true.—Editors]

[R]ather than "applying" the fourth prong of *Central Hudson* to reach the inevitable result that all or most such advertising restrictions must be struck down, I would adhere to the doctrine adopted in *Virginia Bd. of Pharmacy* and in Justice Blackmun's *Central Hudson* concurrence, that all attempts to dissuade legal choices by citizens by keeping them ignorant are impermissible.

III

Although the Court took a sudden turn away from *Virginia Bd. of Pharmacy* in *Central Hudson,* it has never explained why manipulating the choices of consumers by keeping them ignorant is more legitimate when the ignorance is maintained through suppression of "commercial" speech than when the same ignorance is maintained through suppression of "noncommercial" speech. The courts, including this Court, have found the *Central Hudson* "test" to be, as a general matter, very difficult to apply with any uniformity. This may result in part from the inherently nondeterminative nature of a case-by-case balancing "test" unaccompanied by any categorical rules, and the consequent likelihood that individual judicial preferences will govern application of the test. Moreover, the second prong of *Central Hudson,* as applied to the facts of that case and to those here, apparently requires judges to delineate those situations in which citizens cannot be trusted with information, and invites judges to decide whether they themselves think that consumption of a product is harmful enough that it *should* be discouraged. In my view, the *Central Hudson* test asks the courts to weigh incommensurables—the value of knowledge versus the value of ignorance—and to apply contradictory premises—that informed adults are the best judges of their own interests, and that they are not. Rather than continuing to apply a test that makes no sense to me when the asserted state interest is of the type involved here, I would return to the reasoning and holding of *Virginia Bd. of Pharmacy.* Under that decision, these restrictions fall.

■ [The concurring opinion by JUSTICE O'CONNOR, which was joined by THE CHIEF JUSTICE and JUSTICES SOUTER and BREYER, is omitted.]

NOTES

1.   Do you agree with Justice Thomas that the *Central Hudson* test is unhelpful and should be jettisoned? Why or why not?

2.   Do you agree with the Court that it is impermissible for the government to seek to regulate behavior by suppressing speech that might encourage that behavior? Why is this not the least restrictive means? The experience of Prohibition suggests that banning the sale of alcohol may not work very well: among other things it led to an increase in violence and organized crime (though it reduced some forms of violence, such as domestic violence). Why not adopt the lesser measure of allowing the sale of alcohol but not public promotion of drinking? Agreements between regulators and the relevant industries now sharply restrict television advertising of liquor and cigarettes. Is that a bad thing? Why not allow those restrictions to be imposed legislatively?

3.   On the other hand, maybe current doctrine is too permissive about government regulation of commercial speech. Drug companies can be prohibited from disseminating reprints of scholarly articles reporting beneficial uses of their products, if the Food and Drug Administration has not approved those uses. Much of this information is entirely truthful and nonmisleading, and could be of great value to doctors and patients. In effect, the law treats claims by drug manufacturers as "misleading" because they have not been proven to the satisfaction of the regulators. Does this go too far? Who should bear the burden of proof that a claim is misleading—the government or the speaker?

A NOTE ON *CINCINNATI V. DISCOVERY NETWORK*

In *Cincinnati v. Discovery Network*, 507 U.S. 410 (1993), the Court invalidated a city ordinance barring commercial advertising supplements from using newsracks on public sidewalks. The ordinance's justification was a reduction of visual clutter. "The city argued that since a number of courts had held that a complete ban on the use of newsracks dispensing traditional newspapers would be unconstitutional, and that the 'Constitution . . . accords a lesser protection to commercial speech than to other constitutionally guaranteed expression,' *Central Hudson Gas & Electric Corp. v. Public Serv. Comm'n*, 447 U.S. 557, 563 (1980), its preferential treatment of newspapers over commercial publications was a permissible method of serving its legitimate interest in ensuring safe streets and regulating visual blight. The Court of Appeals disagreed, holding that the lesser status of commercial speech is relevant only when its regulation was designed either to prevent false or misleading advertising, or to alleviate distinctive adverse effects of the specific speech at issue." The Supreme Court affirmed, holding:

> Not only does Cincinnati's categorical ban on commercial newsracks place too much importance on the distinction between commercial and noncommercial speech, but in this case, the distinction bears no relationship whatsoever to the particular interests that the city has asserted. . . . The city has asserted an interest in esthetics, but respondent publishers' newsracks are no greater an eyesore than the newsracks permitted to remain on Cincinnati's sidewalks. Each newsrack, whether containing "newspapers" or "commercial handbills," is equally unattractive. . . . [T]he city's primary concern, as argued to us, is with the aggregate number of newsracks on its streets. On that score, however, all newsracks, regardless of whether they contain commercial or noncommercial publications, are equally at fault. In fact, the newspapers are arguably the greater culprit because of their superior number.

507 U.S. at 424–26.

Does this make sense to you? If the Supreme Court itself can apply a lower standard of scrutiny to commercial speech across the board, why can't a city similarly prefer noncommercial over commercial speech when allocating scarce resources? If it is true that the First Amendment prohibits discriminating against commercial speech except when its commercial character relates to the public policy, does that imply that *Central Hudson* is wrong and the broader approach of *Virginia Pharmacy* is restored?

In *Metromedia, Inc. v. San Diego*, 453 U.S. 490 (1981), a billboard case, the Court held that cities may not favor commercial over noncommercial speech. Does *Discovery Network* mean that the converse is also true (assuming, as is likely, that commercial and noncommercial billboards pose the same safety and aesthetic concerns)? Must billboard ordinances be absolutely neutral as the content of the messages?

[Assignment 49]

I.   CAMPAIGN FINANCE

Speech about matters of "public concern," and particularly candidates, officials, and democratic decisions, are at the core of First Amendment protections, yet advertisements in the course of political campaigns are among the most heavily regulated of all forms of speech. This is because money is involved. Does that make a difference? Should it? Almost all forms of speech involve the expenditure of money. Certainly that was true of the advertisement criticizing the police commissioner, which was the subject of *New York Times v. Sullivan*. Money is not speech. But are regulations limiting the use of money for the dissemination of speech of a particular content regulations on speech? Think about these questions as you read the following cases.

Buckley v. Valeo
424 U.S. 1 (1976)

■ PER CURIAM.

These appeals present constitutional challenges to the key provisions of the Federal Election Campaign Act of 1971 (Act), and related provisions of the Internal Revenue Code of 1954, all as amended in 1974. . . .

The statutes at issue summarized in broad terms, contain the following provisions: (a) individual political contributions are limited to $1,000 to any single candidate per election, with an overall annual limitation of $25,000 by any contributor; independent expenditures by individuals and groups "relative to a clearly identified candidate" are limited to $1,000 a year; campaign spending by candidates for various federal offices and spending for national conventions by political parties are subject to prescribed limits; (b) contributions and expenditures above certain threshold levels must be reported and publicly disclosed; (c) a system for public funding of Presidential campaign activities is established . . . ; and (d) a Federal Election Commission is established to administer and enforce the legislation. . . .

The Act's contribution and expenditure limitations operate in an area of the most fundamental First Amendment activities. Discussion of public issues and debate on the qualifications of candidates are integral to the operation of the system of government established by our Constitution. . . . Appellees contend that what the Act regulates is conduct, and that its effect on speech and association is incidental at most. Appellants respond that contributions and expenditures are at the very core of political speech, and that the Act's limitations thus constitute restraints on First Amendment liberty that are both gross and direct.

In upholding the constitutional validity of the Act's contribution and expenditure provisions on the ground that those provisions should be viewed as regulating conduct, not speech, the Court of Appeals relied upon *United States v. O'Brien*, 391 U.S. 367 (1968). . . .

We cannot share the view that the present Act's contribution and expenditure limitations are comparable to the restrictions on conduct upheld in *O'Brien*. The expenditure of money simply cannot be equated with such conduct as destruction of a draft card. Some forms of communication made possible by the giving and spending of money involve speech alone, some involve conduct primarily, and some involve a combination of the two. Yet this Court has never suggested that the dependence of a communication on the expenditure of money operates itself to introduce a nonspeech element or to reduce the exacting scrutiny required by the First Amendment. See *New York Times Co. v. Sullivan*, 376 U.S. 254 (1964).

Even if the categorization of the expenditure of money as conduct were accepted, the limitations challenged here would not meet the *O'Brien* test because the governmental interests advanced in support of the Act involve "suppressing communication." The interests served by the Act include restricting the voices of people and interest groups who have money to spend and reducing the overall scope of federal election campaigns. Although the Act does not focus on the ideas expressed by persons or groups subject to its regulations, it is aimed in part at equalizing the relative ability of all voters to affect electoral outcomes by placing a ceiling on expenditures for political expression by citizens and groups. Unlike *O'Brien*, where the Selective Service System's administrative interest in the preservation of draft cards was wholly unrelated to their use as a means of communication, it is beyond dispute that the interest in regulating the alleged "conduct" of giving or spending money "arises in some measure because the communication allegedly integral to the conduct is itself thought to be harmful.".

Nor can the Act's contribution and expenditure limitations be sustained, as some of the parties suggest, by reference to . . . the proposition that the government may adopt reasonable time, place, and manner regulations, which do not discriminate among speakers or ideas, in order to further an important governmental interest unrelated to the restriction of communication. . . . The critical difference between this case and those time, place, and manner cases is that the present Act's contribution and expenditure limitations impose direct quantity restrictions on political communication and association by persons, groups, candidates, and political parties in addition to any reasonable time, place, and manner regulations otherwise imposed.[17]

A restriction on the amount of money a person or group can spend on political communication during a campaign necessarily reduces the quantity of expression by restricting the number of issues discussed, the depth of their exploration, and the size of the audience reached. This is because virtually every means of communicating ideas in today's mass society requires the expenditure of money. The distribution of the humblest handbill or leaflet entails printing, paper, and circulation costs. Speeches and rallies generally necessitate hiring a hall and publicizing the event. The electorate's increasing dependence on television, radio, and other mass media for news and information has made these expensive modes of communication indispensable instruments of effective political speech.

By contrast with a limitation upon expenditures for political expression, a limitation upon the amount that any one person or group may contribute to a candidate or political committee entails only a marginal restriction upon the contributor's ability to engage in free communication. A contribution serves as a general expression of support for the candidate and his views, but does not communicate the underlying basis for the support. The quantity of communication by the contributor does not increase perceptibly with the size of his contribution, since the expression rests solely on the undifferentiated, symbolic act of contributing. At most, the size of the contribution provides a very rough index of the intensity of

---

[17] The nongovernmental appellees argue that just as the decibels emitted by a sound truck can be regulated consistently with the First Amendment, *Kovacs v. Cooper*, 336 U.S. 77 (1949), the Act may restrict the volume of dollars in political campaigns without impermissibly restricting freedom of speech. This comparison underscores a fundamental misconception. The decibel restriction upheld in *Kovacs* limited the *manner* of operating a soundtruck but not the extent of its proper use. By contrast, the Act's dollar ceilings restrict the *extent* of the reasonable use of virtually every means of communicating information. As the *Kovacs* Court emphasized, the nuisance ordinance only barred sound trucks from broadcasting "in a loud and raucous manner on the streets," and imposed "no restriction upon the communication of ideas or discussion of issues by the human voice, by newspapers, by pamphlets, by dodgers," or by soundtrucks operating at a reasonable volume.

the contributor's support for the candidate. A limitation on the amount of money a person may give to a candidate or campaign organization thus involves little direct restraint on his political communication, for it permits the symbolic expression of support evidenced by a contribution but does not in any way infringe the contributor's freedom to discuss candidates and issues. While contributions may result in political expression if spent by a candidate or an association to present views to the voters, the transformation of contributions into political debate involves speech by someone other than the contributor. . . .

The Act's contribution and expenditure limitations also impinge on protected associational freedoms. Making a contribution, like joining a political party, serves to affiliate a person with a candidate. In addition, it enables like-minded persons to pool their resources in furtherance of common political goals. The Act's contribution ceilings thus limit one important means of associating with a candidate or committee, but leave the contributor free to become a member of any political association and to assist personally in the association's efforts on behalf of candidates. And the Act's contribution limitations permit associations and candidates to aggregate large sums of money to promote effective advocacy. By contrast, the Act's $1,000 limitation on independent expenditures "relative to a clearly identified candidate" precludes most associations from effectively amplifying the voice of their adherents, the original basis for the recognition of First Amendment protection of the freedom of association. . . .

[Accordingly, the Court generally upheld "reasonable" restrictions on contributions to political candidates and political parties, while striking down restrictions on expenditures by those candidates and parties. The Court also struck down restrictions on "independent expenditures" by persons or groups who are not candidates or parties, in support of candidates, so long as those expenditures were not "coordinated" with the campaign. (To avoid vagueness problems, the Court construed this portion of the statute as applying only to messages that clearly identify a candidate.) The Court also struck down limits on expenditures by a candidate from his personal or family resources, on the ground that this could not possibly contribute to corruption or the appearance of it. Because of its importance, we provide some of the Court's reasoning as to why independent expenditures enjoy constitutional protection.—Editors]

We find that the governmental interest in preventing corruption and the appearance of corruption is inadequate to justify § 608(e)(1)'s ceiling on independent expenditures. First, assuming, arguendo, that large independent expenditures pose the same dangers of actual or apparent quid pro quo arrangements as do large contributions, § 608(e)(1) does not provide an answer that sufficiently relates to the elimination of those dangers. . . . *[The Court said that because groups are free to disseminate messages that benefit campaigns without clearly identifying the candidate, the restrictions are easily evaded.—Editors]*

Second, quite apart from the shortcomings of § 608(e)(1) in preventing any abuses generated by large independent expenditures, the independent advocacy restricted by the provision does not presently appear to pose dangers of real or apparent corruption comparable to those identified with large campaign contributions. The parties defending § 608(e)(1) contend that it is necessary to prevent would-be contributors from avoiding the contribution limitations by the simple expedient of paying directly for media advertisements or for other portions of the candidate's campaign activities. . . . Unlike contributions, such independent expenditures may well provide little assistance to the candidate's campaign and indeed may prove counterproductive. The absence of prearrangement and coordination of an expenditure with the candidate or his agent not only undermines the value of the expenditure to the candidate, but also alleviates the danger that expenditures will be given as a quid pro quo for improper commitments from the candidate. Rather than preventing circumvention of the contribution limitations, § 608(e)(1) severely restricts all independent advocacy despite its substantially diminished potential for abuse.

While the independent expenditure ceiling thus fails to serve any substantial governmental interest in stemming the reality or appearance of corruption in the electoral process, it heavily burdens core First Amendment expression. . . . Advocacy of the election or defeat of candidates for federal office is no less entitled to protection under the First Amendment than the discussion of political policy generally or advocacy of the passage or defeat of legislation.

It is argued, however, that the ancillary governmental interest in equalizing the relative ability of individuals and groups to influence the outcome of elections serves to justify the limitation on express advocacy of the election or defeat of candidates imposed by § 608(e)(1)'s expenditure ceiling. But the concept that government may restrict the speech of some elements of our society in order to enhance the relative voice of others is wholly foreign to the First Amendment, which was designed "to secure the widest possible dissemination of information from diverse and antagonistic sources," and "to assure unfettered interchange of ideas for the bringing about of political and social changes desired by the people." *New York Times Co. v. Sullivan*, at 266, 269. The First Amendment's protection against governmental abridgment of free expression cannot properly be made to depend on a person's financial ability to engage in public discussion. . . .

[The Court also uphold the Act's reporting and disclosure requirements, and its public financing of presidential election campaigns.—Editors]

■ MR. JUSTICE STEVENS took no part in the consideration or decision of these cases.

■ MR. CHIEF JUSTICE BURGER, concurring in part and dissenting in part.

. . . I agree fully with that part of the Court's opinion that holds unconstitutional the limitations the Act puts on campaign expenditures which "place substantial and direct restrictions on the ability of candidates, citizens, and associations to engage in protected political expression, restrictions that the First Amendment cannot tolerate." Yet when it approves similarly stringent limitations on contributions, the Court ignores the reasons it finds so persuasive in the context of expenditures. For me contributions and expenditures are two sides of the same First Amendment coin.

. . . The Court's attempt to distinguish the communication inherent in political contributions from the speech aspects of political expenditures simply "will not wash." We do little but engage in word games unless we recognize that people candidates and contributors spend money on political activity because they wish to communicate ideas, and their constitutional interest in doing so is precisely the same whether they or someone else utters the words.

. . . At any rate, the contribution limits are a far more severe restriction on First Amendment activity than the sort of "chilling" legislation for which the Court has shown such extraordinary concern in the past. See, *e.g., Cohen v. California*, 403 U.S.

15 (1971); see also cases reviewed in *Miller v. California*, 413 U.S. 15 (1973). If such restraints can be justified at all, they must be justified by the very strongest of state interests. . . .

After a bow to the "weighty interests" Congress meant to serve, the Court then forsakes this analysis in one sentence: "Congress was surely entitled to conclude that disclosure was only a partial measure, and that contribution ceilings were a necessary legislative concomitant to deal with the reality or appearance of corruption. . . ." In striking down the limitations on campaign expenditures, the Court relies in part on its conclusion that other means namely, disclosure and contribution ceilings will adequately serve the statute's aim. It is not clear why the same analysis is not also appropriate in weighing the need for contribution ceilings in addition to disclosure requirements. Congress may well be entitled to conclude that disclosure was a "partial measure," but I had not thought until today that Congress could enact its conclusions in the First Amendment area into laws immune from the most searching review by this Court.

Finally, it seems clear to me that in approving these limitations on contributions the Court must rest upon the proposition that "pooling" money is fundamentally different from other forms of associational or joint activity. I see only two possible ways in which money differs from volunteer work, endorsements, and the like. Money can be used to buy favors, because an unscrupulous politician can put it to personal use; second, giving money is a less visible form of associational activity. With respect to the first problem, the Act does not attempt to do any more than the bribery laws to combat this sort of corruption. In fact, the Act does not reach at all, and certainly the contribution limits do not reach, forms of "association" that can be fully as corrupt as a contribution intended as a quid pro quo such as the eleventh-hour endorsement by a former rival, obtained for the promise of a federal appointment. . . .

■ Mr. Justice White, concurring in part and dissenting in part.

. . . Since the contribution and expenditure limitations are neutral as to the content of speech and are not motivated by fear of the consequences of the political speech of particular candidates or of political speech in general, this case depends on whether the nonspeech interests of the Federal Government in regulating the use of money in political campaigns are sufficiently urgent to justify the incidental effects that the limitations visit upon the First Amendment interests of candidates and their supporters.

Despite its seeming struggle with the standard by which to judge this case, this is essentially the question the Court asks and answers in the affirmative with respect to the limitations on contributions which individuals and political committees are permitted to make to federal candidates. In the interest of preventing undue influence that large contributors would have or that the public might think they would have, the Court upholds the provision that an individual may not give to a candidate, or spend on his behalf if requested or authorized by the candidate to do so, more than $1,000 in any one election. This limitation is valid although it imposes a low ceiling on what individuals may deem to be their most effective means of supporting or speaking on behalf of the candidate[,] i.e., financial support given directly to the candidate. The Court thus accepts the congressional judgment that the evils of unlimited contributions are sufficiently threatening to warrant restriction regardless of the impact of the limits on the contributor's opportunity for effective speech and in turn on the total volume of the candidate's political communications by reason of his inability to accept large sums from those willing to give.

The congressional judgment, which I would also accept, was that other steps must be taken to counter the corrosive effects of money in federal election campaigns. One of these steps is § 608(e), which, aside from those funds that are given to the candidate or spent at his request or with his approval or cooperation limits what a contributor may independently spend in support or denigration of one running for federal office. Congress was plainly of the view that these expenditures also have corruptive potential; but the Court strikes down the provision, strangely enough claiming more insight as to what may improperly influence candidates than is possessed by the majority of Congress that passed this bill and the President who signed it. Those supporting the bill undeniably included many seasoned professionals who have been deeply involved in elective processes and who have viewed them at close range over many years.

It would make little sense to me, and apparently made none to Congress, to limit the amounts an individual may give to a candidate or spend with his approval but fail to limit the amounts that could be spent on his behalf. Yet the Court permits the former while striking down the latter limitation. No more than $1,000 may be given to a candidate or spent at his request or with his approval or cooperation; but otherwise, apparently, a contributor is to be constitutionally protected in spending unlimited amounts of money in support of his chosen candidate or candidates.

. . . It is also important to restore and maintain public confidence in federal elections. It is critical to obviate or dispel the impression that federal elections are purely and simply a function of money, that federal offices are bought and sold or that political races are reserved for those who have the facility and the stomach for doing whatever it takes to bring together those interests, groups, and individuals that can raise or contribute large fortunes in order to prevail at the polls.

The ceiling on candidate expenditures represents the considered judgment of Congress that elections are to be decided among candidates none of whom has overpowering advantage by reason of a huge campaign war chest. At least so long as the ceiling placed upon the candidates is not plainly too low, elections are not to turn on the difference in the amounts of money that candidates have to spend. This seems an acceptable purpose and the means chosen a common-sense way to achieve it. The Court nevertheless holds that a candidate has a constitutional right to spend unlimited amounts of money, mostly that of other people, in order to be elected. The holding perhaps is not that federal candidates have the constitutional right to purchase their election, but many will so interpret the Court's conclusion in this case. I cannot join the Court in this respect. . . .

■ [JUSTICE REHNQUIST's opinion, concurring in part and dissenting in part, is omitted.]

NOTES

1. Do you understand the Court's distinctions between contributions and independent expenditures? From the individual's point of view, according to the Court, limiting the size of a contribution "entails only a marginal restriction" on freedom of speech because the "quantity of communication by the contributor does not increase

perceptibly with the size of his contribution, since the expression rests solely on the undifferentiated, symbolic act of contributing." Is that right? Is a $50 contribution not "perceptibly" different from $500? If the purpose of making a contribution is to help persuade the public to vote for a candidate, doesn't the amount matter? Why do some people contribute multiple times? Conversely, why does the Court not apply the same reasoning to independent expenditures in support of the candidates? Why does quantity matter in one context but not the other?

From the government's point of view, according to the Court, independent expenditures are far less likely to result in actual or apparent corruption. Why?

2.   Note the practical effect of the Court's holdings. Allowing contribution limits but not independent expenditure limits has the effect of directing campaign money away from candidates and political parties, who arguably are most accountable to the public, toward advocacy groups, including "super-PACs," who can receive and spend essentially unlimited sums of money to support or oppose candidates of their choice. What good does this accomplish? What evils might it magnify? Do you imagine this was Congress's intention?

The Court also struck down limits on expenditures by a candidate from his personal or family resources, on the ground that this could not possibly contribute to corruption or the appearance of it. The logic may be sound, but the effect is to privilege wealthy candidates—so-called "self-funding candidates"—over those who have to raise money in dribs and drabs. Is this a good thing?

Congress's theory was that limiting campaign expenditures would make it unnecessary for candidate to raise so much money, thus freeing them from the need to spend so much of their time fundraising. By striking down expenditure limits while upholding contribution limits, the Court likely *increased* the amount of time needed for fundraising, relative to what it was before the statute was passed. Candidates need just as large a war chest, but it is more time-consuming to raise money in small sums than large sums. Critics also claim that this feature of the decision favors incumbents, whose name recognition and pull with interest groups makes it easier for them to raise money.

Some critics say that, as a result of the combination of holdings in *Buckley*, the campaign finance system makes no sense and pleases no one. Was the Court wrong to apply the "severability" doctrine to "save" only portions of the legislation it thought constitution, leaving the rest in place? Should the Court have struck the statute down completely, leaving it Congress to decide how to replace it? Can you think of ways to reform the campaign finance system that are consistent with the Court's constitutional holdings?

3.   *Buckley's* distinction between contributions and expenditures has few defenders on constitutional grounds and even fewer defenders on policy grounds. But it has never been repudiated and remains in force today. About half the Court believes that contribution limitations should be stuck down, and about half think that expenditure limits should be restored, producing a compromise that seemingly pleases no one. Is there a way out of this quandary?

Nixon v. Shrink Missouri Government PAC
528 U.S. 377 (2000)

[In the majority opinion, the Court upheld Missouri's $1,000 cap on campaign contributions despite the fact that this sum, though approved in Buckley, *had greatly diminished in value through inflation. The majority largely deferred to legislative judgments.—Editors]*

■ JUSTICE BREYER, with whom JUSTICE GINSBURG joins, concurring.

. . . If the dissent believes that the Court diminishes the importance of the First Amendment interests before us, it is wrong. The Court's opinion does not question the constitutional importance of political speech or that its protection lies at the heart of the First Amendment. Nor does it question the need for particularly careful, precise, and independent judicial review where, as here, that protection is at issue. But this is a case where constitutionally protected interests lie on both sides of the legal equation. For that reason there is no place for a strong presumption against constitutionality, of the sort often thought to accompany the words "strict scrutiny." Nor can we expect that mechanical application of the tests associated with "strict scrutiny"—the tests of "compelling interests" and "least restrictive means"—will properly resolve the difficult constitutional problem that campaign finance statutes pose.

On the one hand, a decision to contribute money to a campaign is a matter of First Amendment concern—not because money is speech (it is not); but because it enables speech. Through contributions the contributor associates himself with the candidate's cause, helps the candidate communicate a political message with which the contributor agrees, and helps the candidate win by attracting the votes of similarly minded voters. *Buckley v. Valeo*, 424 U.S. 1, 24–25 (1976) (*per curiam*). Both political association and political communication are at stake.

On the other hand, restrictions upon the amount any one individual can contribute to a particular candidate seek to protect the integrity of the electoral process—the means through which a free society democratically translates political speech into concrete governmental action. Moreover, by limiting the size of the largest contributions, such restrictions aim to democratize the influence that money itself may bring to bear upon the electoral process. In doing so, they seek to build public confidence in that process and broaden the base of a candidate's meaningful financial support, encouraging the public participation and open discussion that the First Amendment itself presupposes.

In service of these objectives, the statute imposes restrictions of degree. It does not deny the contributor the opportunity to associate with the candidate through a contribution, though it limits a contribution's size. Nor does it prevent the contributor from using money (alone or with others) to pay for the expression of the same views in other ways. Instead, it permits all supporters to contribute the same amount of money, in an attempt to make the process fairer and more democratic.

Under these circumstances, a presumption against constitutionality is out of place. . . . In such circumstances—where a law significantly implicates competing constitutionally protected interests in complex ways—the Court has closely scrutinized the statute's impact on those interests, but refrained from employing a simple test that effectively presumes unconstitutionality. Rather, it has balanced interests. And in practice that has meant asking whether the statute burdens any one such interest in a manner out of proportion to the statute's salutary effects upon the others (perhaps, but not necessarily, because of the existence of a clearly superior, less restrictive alternative). Where a legislature has significantly greater institutional expertise, as, for example, in the field of election regulation, the Court in practice defers to empirical legislative judgments—at least where that deference does not risk such constitutional evils as, say, permitting incumbents to insulate themselves from effective electoral challenge. . . .

Applying this approach to the present case, I would uphold the statute essentially for the reasons stated by the Court. I agree that the legislature understands the problem—the threat to electoral integrity, the need for democratization—better than do we. We should defer to its political judgment that unlimited spending threatens the integrity of the electoral process. But we should not defer in respect to whether its solution, by imposing too low a contribution limit, significantly increases the reputation-related or media-related advantages of incumbency and thereby insulates legislators from effective electoral challenge. The statutory limit here, $1,075 (or 378, 1976 dollars), is low enough to raise such a question. But given the empirical information presented—the type of election at issue; the record of adequate candidate financing postreform; and the fact that the statute indexes the amount for inflation—I agree with the Court that the statute does not work disproportionate harm. The limit may have prevented the plaintiff, Zev David Fredman, from financing his own campaign for office, for Fredman's support among potential contributors was not sufficiently widespread. But any contribution statute will narrow the field of conceivable challengers to some degree. Undue insulation is a practical matter, and it cannot be inferred automatically from the fact that the limit makes ballot access more difficult for one previously unsuccessful candidate. . . .

■ JUSTICE KENNEDY, dissenting.

. . . The justifications for the case system and stare decisis must rest upon the Court's capacity, and responsibility, to acknowledge its missteps. It is our duty to face up to adverse, unintended consequences flowing from our own prior decisions. With all respect, I submit the Court does not accept this obligation in the case before us. Instead, it perpetuates and compounds a serious distortion of the First Amendment resulting from our own intervention in *Buckley*.

The plain fact is that the compromise the Court invented in *Buckley* set the stage for a new kind of speech to enter the political system. It is covert speech. The Court has forced a substantial amount of political speech underground, as contributors and candidates devise ever more elaborate methods of avoiding contribution limits, limits which take no account of rising campaign costs. The preferred method has been to conceal the real purpose of the speech. Soft money may be contributed to political parties in unlimited amounts, see *Colorado Republican Federal Campaign Comm. v. Federal Election Comm'n*, 518 U.S. 604, 616 (1996), and is used often to fund so-called issue advocacy, advertisements that promote or attack a candidate's positions without specifically urging his or her election or defeat. Issue advocacy, like soft money, is unrestricted, while straightforward speech in the form of financial contributions paid to a candidate, speech subject to full disclosure and prompt evaluation by the public, is not. Thus has the Court's decision given us covert speech. This mocks the First Amendment. The current system would be unfortunate, and suspect under the First Amendment, had it evolved from a deliberate legislative choice; but its unhappy origins are in our earlier decree in *Buckley*, which by accepting half of what Congress did (limiting contributions) but rejecting the other (limiting expenditures) created a misshapen system, one which distorts the meaning of speech. . . .

■ JUSTICE THOMAS, with whom JUSTICE SCALIA joins, dissenting.

I begin with a proposition that ought to be unassailable: Political speech is the primary object of First Amendment protection. The Founders sought to protect the rights of individuals to engage in political speech because a self-governing people depends upon the free exchange of political information. And that free exchange should receive the most protection when it matters the most—during campaigns for elective office.

I do not start with these foundational principles because the Court openly disagrees with them—it could not, for they are solidly embedded in our precedents. Instead, I start with them because the Court today abandons them. For nearly half a century, this Court has extended First Amendment protection to a multitude of forms of "speech," such as making false defamatory statements, filing lawsuits, dancing nude, exhibiting drive-in movies with nudity, burning flags, and wearing military uniforms. Not surprisingly, the Courts of Appeals have followed our lead and concluded that the First Amendment protects, for example, begging, shouting obscenities, erecting tables on a sidewalk, and refusing to wear a necktie. In light of the many cases of this sort, today's decision is a most curious anomaly. Whatever the proper status of such activities under the First Amendment, I am confident that they are less integral to the functioning of our Republic than campaign contributions. Yet the majority today, rather than going out of its way to protect political speech, goes out of its way to avoid protecting it. As I explain below, contributions to political campaigns generate essential political speech. And contribution caps, which place a direct and substantial limit on core speech, should be met with the utmost skepticism and should receive the strictest scrutiny. . . .

To justify its decision upholding contribution limitations while striking down expenditure limitations, the Court in *Buckley* explained that expenditure limits "represent substantial rather than merely theoretical restraints on the quantity and diversity of political speech," while contribution limits "entai[l] only a marginal restriction upon the contributor's ability to engage in free communication." In drawing this distinction, the Court in *Buckley* relied on the premise that contributing to a candidate differs qualitatively from directly spending money. It noted that "[w]hile contributions may result in political expression if spent by a candidate or an association to present views to the voters, the transformation of contributions into political debate involves speech by someone other than the contributor." But this was a faulty distinction *ab initio* because it ignored the reality of how speech of all kinds is disseminated:

> "Even in the case of a direct expenditure, there is usually some go-between that facilitates the dissemination of the spender's message—for instance, an advertising agency or a television station. To call a contribution 'speech by proxy' thus does little to differentiate it from an expenditure. The only possible difference is that contributions involve an extra step in the proxy chain. But again, that is a difference in form, not substance." *Colorado*

Republican, at 638–639 (THOMAS, J., concurring in judgment and dissenting in part).

And, insofar as the speech-by-proxy argument was disconnected from the realities of political speech to begin with, it is not surprising that we have firmly rejected it since *Buckley*. In *Federal Election Comm'n v. National Conservative Political Action Comm.*, 470 U.S. 480 (1985), we cast aside the argument that a contribution does not represent the constitutionally protected speech of a contributor, recognizing "that the contributors obviously like the message they are hearing from these organizations and want to add their voices to that message; otherwise they would not part with their money." Id., at 495. Though in that case we considered limitations on expenditures made by associations, our holding that the speech-by-proxy argument fails to diminish contributors' First Amendment rights is directly applicable to this case. In both cases, donors seek to disseminate information by giving to an organization controlled by others. Through contributing, citizens see to it that their views on policy and politics are articulated.

Without the assistance of the speech-by-proxy argument, the remainder of *Buckley*'s rationales founder. Those rationales—that the "quantity of communication by the contributor does not increase perceptibly with the size of his contribution," that "the size of the contribution provides a very rough index of the intensity of the contributor's support for the candidate," and that "[a] contribution serves as a general expression of support for the candidate and his views, but does not communicate the underlying basis for the support," still rest on the proposition that speech by proxy is not fully protected. These contentions simply ignore that a contribution, by amplifying the voice of the candidate, helps to ensure the dissemination of the messages that the contributor wishes to convey. . . .

Citizens United v. Federal Election Commission
558 U.S. 310 (2010)

■ JUSTICE KENNEDY delivered the opinion of the Court.

Federal law prohibits corporations and unions from using their general treasury funds to make independent expenditures for speech defined as an "electioneering communication" or for speech expressly advocating the election or defeat of a candidate. 2 U.S.C. § 441b. Limits on electioneering communications were upheld in *McConnell v. Federal Election Comm'n*, 540 U.S. 93, 203–209 (2003). The holding of *McConnell* rested to a large extent on an earlier case, *Austin v. Michigan Chamber of Commerce*, 494 U.S. 652 (1990). *Austin* had held that political speech may be banned based on the speaker's corporate identity.

In this case we are asked to reconsider *Austin* and, in effect, *McConnell*. . . . [We] hold that *stare decisis* does not compel the continued acceptance of *Austin*. The Government may regulate corporate political speech through disclaimer and disclosure requirements, but it may not suppress that speech altogether. . . .

I–A

Citizens United is a nonprofit corporation. . . . [It] has an annual budget of about $12 million. Most of its funds are from donations by individuals; but, in addition, it accepts a small portion of its funds from for-profit corporations.

In January 2008, Citizens United released a film entitled *Hillary: The Movie*. We refer to the film as *Hillary*. It is a 90-minute documentary about then-Senator Hillary Clinton, who was a candidate in the Democratic Party's 2008 Presidential primary elections. *Hillary* mentions Senator Clinton by name and depicts interviews with political commentators and other persons, most of them quite critical of Senator Clinton. *Hillary* was released in theaters and on DVD, but Citizens United wanted to increase distribution by making it available through video-on-demand.

Video-on-demand allows digital cable subscribers to select programming from various menus, including movies, television shows, sports, news, and music. The viewer can watch the program at any time and can elect to rewind or pause the program. In December 2007, a cable company offered, for a payment of $1.2 million, to make *Hillary* available on a video-on-demand channel called "Elections '08." Some video-on-demand services require viewers to pay a small fee to view a selected program, but here the proposal was to make *Hillary* available to viewers free of charge.

To implement the proposal, Citizens United was prepared to pay for the video-on-demand; and to promote the film, it produced two 10-second ads and one 30-second ad for *Hillary*. Each ad includes a short (and, in our view, pejorative) statement about Senator Clinton, followed by the name of the movie and the movie's Website address. Citizens United desired to promote the video-on-demand offering by running advertisements on broadcast and cable television.

B

Before the Bipartisan Campaign Reform Act of 2002 (BCRA), federal law prohibited—and still does prohibit—corporations and unions from using general treasury funds to make direct contributions to candidates or independent expenditures that expressly advocate the election or defeat of a candidate, through any form of media, in connection with certain qualified federal elections. BCRA § 203 amended [the law] to prohibit any "electioneering communication" as well. An electioneering communication is defined as "any broadcast, cable, or satellite communication" that "refers to a clearly identified candidate for Federal office" and is made within 30 days of a primary or 60 days of a general election. § 434(f)(3)(A). The Federal Election Commission's (FEC) regulations further define an electioneering communication as a communication that is "publicly distributed." 11 CFR § 100.29(a)(2) (2009). "In the case of a candidate for nomination for President . . . *publicly distributed* means" that the communication "[c]an be received by 50,000 or more persons in a State where a primary election . . . is being held within 30 days." § 100.29(b)(3)(ii). Corporations and unions are barred from using their general treasury funds for express advocacy or electioneering communications. They may establish, however, a "separate segregated fund" (known as a political action committee, or PAC) for these purposes. The moneys received by the segregated fund are limited to donations from stockholders and employees of the corporation or, in the case of unions, members of the union. . . .

III

. . . The law before us is an outright ban, backed by criminal sanctions. Section 441b makes it a felony for all corporations—including nonprofit advocacy corporations—either to expressly advocate the election or defeat of candidates or to broadcast electioneering communications within 30 days of a primary election and

60 days of a general election. Thus, the following acts would all be felonies under § 441b: The Sierra Club runs an ad, within the crucial phase of 60 days before the general election, that exhorts the public to disapprove of a Congressman who favors logging in national forests; the National Rifle Association publishes a book urging the public to vote for the challenger because the incumbent U.S. Senator supports a handgun ban; and the American Civil Liberties Union creates a Web site telling the public to vote for a Presidential candidate in light of that candidate's defense of free speech. These prohibitions are classic examples of censorship.

Section 441b is a ban on corporate speech notwithstanding the fact that a PAC created by a corporation can still speak. A PAC is a separate association from the corporation. So the PAC exemption from § 441b's expenditure ban, § 441b(b)(2), does not allow corporations to speak. Even if a PAC could somehow allow a corporation to speak—and it does not—the option to form PACs does not alleviate the First Amendment problems with § 441b. PACs are burdensome alternatives; they are expensive to administer and subject to extensive regulations. For example, every PAC must appoint a treasurer, forward donations to the treasurer promptly, keep detailed records of the identities of the persons making donations, preserve receipts for three years, and file an organization statement and report changes to this information within 10 days. . . .

Speech is an essential mechanism of democracy, for it is the means to hold officials accountable to the people. The right of citizens to inquire, to hear, to speak, and to use information to reach consensus is a precondition to enlightened self-government and a necessary means to protect it. The First Amendment "has its fullest and most urgent application to speech uttered during a campaign for political office." *Eu v. San Francisco County Democratic Central Comm.*, 489 U.S. 214, 223 (1989); see *Buckley v. Valeo*, 424 U.S. 1, 14 (1976) ("Discussion of public issues and debate on the qualifications of candidates are integral to the operation of the system of government established by our Constitution").

For these reasons, political speech must prevail against laws that would suppress it, whether by design or inadvertence. Laws that burden political speech are "subject to strict scrutiny," which requires the Government to prove that the restriction "furthers a compelling interest and is narrowly tailored to achieve that interest." *Federal Election Comm'n v. Wisconsin Right to Life, Inc.*, 551 U.S. 449, 464 (2007) (opinion of ROBERTS, C.J.) [hereinafter *WRTL*]. . . .

Quite apart from the purpose or effect of regulating content, moreover, the Government may commit a constitutional wrong when by law it identifies certain preferred speakers. By taking the right to speak from some and giving it to others, the Government deprives the disadvantaged person or class of the right to use speech to strive to establish worth, standing, and respect for the speaker's voice. The Government may not by these means deprive the public of the right and privilege to determine for itself what speech and speakers are worthy of consideration. The First Amendment protects speech and speaker, and the ideas that flow from each. . . .

A–1

The Court has recognized that First Amendment protection extends to corporations. *[Extensive string cite omitted.—Editors]* . . .

Under the rationale of these precedents, political speech does not lose First Amendment protection "simply because its source is a corporation." *First Nat. Bank of Boston v. Bellotti,* 435 U.S. 765, 784 (1978); see *Pacific Gas & Elec. Co. v. Public Util. Comm'n of Cal.,* 475 U.S. 1, 8 (1986) (plurality opinion) ("The identity of the speaker is not decisive in determining whether speech is protected. Corporations and other associations, like individuals, contribute to the 'discussion, debate, and the dissemination of information and ideas' that the First Amendment seeks to foster" (quoting *Bellotti,* at 783)). The Court has thus rejected the argument that political speech of corporations or other associations should be treated differently under the First Amendment simply because such associations are not "natural persons." *Bellotti,* at 776.

At least since the latter part of the 19th century, the laws of some States and of the United States imposed a ban on corporate direct contributions to candidates. See B. Smith, Unfree Speech: The Folly of Campaign Finance Reform 23 (2001). Yet not until 1947 did Congress first prohibit independent expenditures by corporations and labor unions in § 304 of the Labor Management Relations Act 1947, 61 Stat. 159 (codified at 2 U.S.C. § 251 (1946 ed., Supp. I)). In passing this Act Congress overrode the veto of President Truman, who warned that the expenditure ban was a "dangerous intrusion on free speech." . . .

2

. . . Less than two years after *Buckley, Bellotti* reaffirmed the First Amendment principle that the Government cannot restrict political speech based on the speaker's corporate identity. *Bellotti* could not have been clearer when it struck down a state-law prohibition on corporate independent expenditures related to referenda issues:

> We thus find no support in the First . . . Amendment, or in the decisions of this Court, for the proposition that speech that otherwise would be within the protection of the First Amendment loses that protection simply because its source is a corporation that cannot prove, to the satisfaction of a court, a material effect on its business or property. . . . [That proposition] amounts to an impermissible legislative prohibition of speech based on the identity of the interests that spokesmen may represent in public debate over controversial issues and a requirement that the speaker have a sufficiently great interest in the subject to justify communication. . . .
>
> In the realm of protected speech, the legislature is constitutionally disqualified from dictating the subjects about which persons may speak and the speakers who may address a public issue.

Id. at 784–785. . . .

3

Thus the law stood until *Austin. Austin* "uph[eld] a direct restriction on the independent expenditure of funds for political speech for the first time in [this Court's] history." 494 U.S., at 695 (KENNEDY, J., dissenting). There, the Michigan Chamber of Commerce sought to use general treasury funds to run a newspaper ad supporting a specific candidate. Michigan law, however, prohibited corporate independent expenditures that supported or opposed any candidate for state office. A violation of the law was punishable as a felony. The Court sustained the speech prohibition.

. . . [T]he *Austin* Court identified a new governmental interest in limiting political speech: an antidistortion interest. *Austin* found a compelling governmental interest in preventing "the corrosive and distorting effects of immense aggregations of wealth that are accumulated with the help of the corporate form and that have little or no correlation to the public's support for the corporation's political ideas." 494 U.S., at 660.

B

. . . In its defense of the corporate-speech restrictions in § 441b, the Government notes the antidistortion rationale on which *Austin* and its progeny rest in part, yet it all but abandons reliance upon it. It argues instead that two other compelling interests support *Austin*'s holding that corporate expenditure restrictions are constitutional: an anticorruption interest, and a shareholder-protection interest. We consider the three points in turn.

1

As for *Austin*'s antidistortion rationale, the Government does little to defend it. And with good reason, for the rationale cannot support § 441b.

If the First Amendment has any force, it prohibits Congress from fining or jailing citizens, or associations of citizens, for simply engaging in political speech. If the antidistortion rationale were to be accepted, however, it would permit Government to ban political speech simply because the speaker is an association that has taken on the corporate form. The Government contends that *Austin* permits it to ban corporate expenditures for almost all forms of communication stemming from a corporation. If *Austin* were correct, the Government could prohibit a corporation from expressing political views in media beyond those presented here, such as by printing books. The Government responds "that the FEC has never applied this statute to a book," and if it did, "there would be quite [a] good as-applied challenge." Tr. of Oral Arg. 65 (Sept. 9, 2009). This troubling assertion of brooding governmental power cannot be reconciled with the confidence and stability in civic discourse that the First Amendment must secure.

. . . *Austin* sought to defend the antidistortion rationale as a means to prevent corporations from obtaining "an unfair advantage in the political marketplace" by using "resources amassed in the economic marketplace." 494 U.S., at 659. But *Buckley* rejected the premise that the Government has an interest "in equalizing the relative ability of individuals and groups to influence the outcome of elections." *Buckley* was specific in stating that "the skyrocketing cost of political campaigns" could not sustain the governmental prohibition. The First Amendment's protections do not depend on the speaker's "financial ability to engage in public discussion." *Id.*, at 49. . . .

Either as support for its antidistortion rationale or as a further argument, the *Austin* majority undertook to distinguish wealthy individuals from corporations on the ground that "[s]tate law grants corporations special advantages—such as limited liability, perpetual life, and favorable treatment of the accumulation and distribution of assets." This does not suffice, however, to allow laws prohibiting speech. "It is rudimentary that the State cannot exact as the price of those special advantages the forfeiture of First Amendment rights." *Id.*, at 680 (SCALIA, J., dissenting).

It is irrelevant for purposes of the First Amendment that corporate funds may "have little or no correlation to the public's support for the corporation's political ideas." All speakers, including individuals and the media, use money amassed from the economic marketplace to fund their speech. The First Amendment protects the resulting speech, even if it was enabled by economic transactions with persons or entities who disagree with the speaker's ideas.

Austin's antidistortion rationale would produce the dangerous, and unacceptable, consequence that Congress could ban political speech of media corporations. Media corporations are now exempt from § 441b's ban on corporate expenditures. Yet media corporations accumulate wealth with the help of the corporate form, the largest media corporations have "immense aggregations of wealth," and the views expressed by media corporations often "have little or no correlation to the public's support" for those views. Thus, under the Government's reasoning, wealthy media corporations could have their voices diminished to put them on par with other media entities. There is no precedent for permitting this under the First Amendment.

The media exemption discloses further difficulties with the law now under consideration. There is no precedent supporting laws that attempt to distinguish between corporations which are deemed to be exempt as media corporations and those which are not. "We have consistently rejected the proposition that the institutional press has any constitutional privilege beyond that of other speakers." With the advent of the Internet and the decline of print and broadcast media, moreover, the line between the media and others who wish to comment on political and social issues becomes far more blurred. . . .

There is simply no support for the view that the First Amendment, as originally understood, would permit the suppression of political speech by media corporations. The Framers may not have anticipated modern business and media corporations. Yet television networks and major newspapers owned by media corporations have become the most important means of mass communication in modern times. The First Amendment was certainly not understood to condone the suppression of political speech in society's most salient media. It was understood as a response to the repression of speech and the press that had existed in England and the heavy taxes on the press that were imposed in the colonies. The great debates between the Federalists and the Anti-Federalists over our founding document were published and expressed in the most important means of mass communication of that era— newspapers owned by individuals. At the founding, speech was open, comprehensive, and vital to society's definition of itself; there were no limits on the sources of speech and knowledge. . . .

When Government seeks to use its full power, including the criminal law, to command where a person may get his or her information or what distrusted source he or she may not hear, it uses censorship to control thought. This is unlawful. The First Amendment confirms the freedom to think for ourselves.

2

What we have said also shows the invalidity of other arguments made by the Government. For the most part relinquishing the antidistortion rationale, the Government falls back on the argument that corporate political speech can be banned in order to prevent corruption or its appearance. In *Buckley*, the Court found this interest "sufficiently important" to allow limits on contributions but did not extend that reasoning to expenditure limits. When *Buckley* examined an expenditure ban, it found "that the governmental interest in preventing corruption and the appearance of corruption [was] inadequate to justify [the ban] on independent expenditures." *Id.*, at 45. . . .

"The absence of prearrangement and coordination of an expenditure with the candidate or his agent not only undermines the value of the expenditure to the candidate, but also alleviates the danger that expenditures will be given as a *quid pro quo* for improper commitments from the candidate." *Buckley,* at 47. Limits on independent expenditures, such as § 441b, have a chilling effect extending well beyond the Government's interest in preventing *quid pro quo* corruption. The anticorruption interest is not sufficient to displace the speech here in question. Indeed, 26 States do not restrict independent expenditures by for-profit corporations. The Government does not claim that these expenditures have corrupted the political process in those States. . . .

3

The Government contends further that corporate independent expenditures can be limited because of its interest in protecting dissenting shareholders from being compelled to fund corporate political speech. . . . The First Amendment does not allow that power. There is, furthermore, little evidence of abuse that cannot be corrected by shareholders "through the procedures of corporate democracy." *Bellotti,* at 794.

Those reasons are sufficient to reject this shareholder-protection interest; and, moreover, the statute is both underinclusive and overinclusive. As to the first, if Congress had been seeking to protect dissenting shareholders, it would not have banned corporate speech in only certain media within 30 or 60 days before an election. A dissenting shareholder's interests would be implicated by speech in any media at any time. As to the second, the statute is overinclusive because it covers all corporations, including nonprofit corporations and for-profit corporations with only single shareholders. As to other corporations, the remedy is not to restrict speech but to consider and explore other regulatory mechanisms. The regulatory mechanism here, based on speech, contravenes the First Amendment.

4

We need not reach the question whether the Government has a compelling interest in preventing foreign individuals or associations from influencing our Nation's political process. Cf. 2 U.S.C. § 441e (contribution and expenditure ban applied to "foreign national[s]"). Section 441b is not limited to corporations or associations that were created in foreign countries or funded predominately by foreign shareholders. Section 441b therefore would be overbroad even if we assumed, *arguendo,* that the Government has a compelling interest in limiting foreign influence over our political process. . . .

IV–A

Citizens United next challenges BCRA's disclaimer and disclosure provisions as applied to *Hillary* and the three advertisements for the movie. . . . *[The Court upholds these provisions.—Editors]*

B

. . . Citizens United argues that disclosure requirements can chill donations to an organization by exposing donors to retaliation. Some *amici* point to recent events in which donors to certain causes were blacklisted, threatened, or otherwise targeted for retaliation. In *McConnell*, the Court recognized that § 201 would be unconstitutional as applied to an organization if there were a reasonable probability that the group's members would face threats, harassment, or reprisals if their names were disclosed. The examples cited by *amici* are cause for concern. Citizens United, however, has offered no evidence that its members may face similar threats or reprisals. To the contrary, Citizens United has been disclosing its donors for years and has identified no instance of harassment or retaliation. . . .

[M]odern technology makes disclosures rapid and informative. A campaign finance system that pairs corporate independent expenditures with effective disclosure has not existed before today. It must be noted, furthermore, that many of Congress' findings in passing BCRA were premised on a system without adequate disclosure. With the advent of the Internet, prompt disclosure of expenditures can provide shareholders and citizens with the information needed to hold corporations and elected officials accountable for their positions and supporters. Shareholders can determine whether their corporation's political speech advances the corporation's interest in making profits, and citizens can see whether elected officials are " 'in the pocket' of so-called moneyed interests." 540 U.S., at 259. The First Amendment protects political speech; and disclosure permits citizens and shareholders to react to the speech of corporate entities in a proper way. This transparency enables the electorate to make informed decisions and give proper weight to different speakers and messages. . . .

V

. . . Modern day movies, television comedies, or skits on Youtube.com might portray public officials or public policies in unflattering ways. Yet if a covered transmission during the blackout period creates the background for candidate endorsement or opposition, a felony occurs solely because a corporation, other than an exempt media corporation, has made the "purchase, payment, distribution, loan, advance, deposit, or gift of money or anything of value" in order to engage in political speech. Speech would be suppressed in the realm where its necessity is most evident: in the public dialogue preceding a real election. Governments are often hostile to speech, but under our law and our tradition it seems stranger than fiction for our Government to make this political speech a crime. Yet this is the statute's purpose and design.

Some members of the public might consider *Hillary* to be insightful and instructive; some might find it to be neither high art nor a fair discussion on how to set the Nation's course; still others simply might suspend judgment on these points but decide to think more about issues and candidates. Those choices and assessments, however, are not for the Government to make. . . .

■ CHIEF JUSTICE ROBERTS, with whom JUSTICE ALITO joins, concurring.

The Government urges us in this case to uphold a direct prohibition on political speech. It asks us to embrace a theory of the First Amendment that would allow censorship not only of television and radio broadcasts, but of pamphlets, posters, the Internet, and virtually any other medium that corporations and unions might find useful in expressing their views on matters of public concern. Its theory, if accepted, would empower the Government to prohibit newspapers from running editorials or opinion pieces supporting or opposing candidates for office, so long as the newspapers were owned by corporations—as the major ones are. First Amendment rights could be confined to individuals, subverting the vibrant public discourse that is at the foundation of our democracy.

The Court properly rejects that theory, and I join its opinion in full. . . .

■ Justice Scalia, with whom Justice Alito joins, and with whom Justice Thomas joins in part, concurring.

I join the opinion of the Court.

I write separately to address Justice Stevens' discussion of *"Original Understandings."* This section of the dissent purports to show that today's decision is not supported by the original understanding of the First Amendment. The dissent attempts this demonstration, however, in splendid isolation from the text of the First Amendment. It never shows why "the freedom of speech" that was the right of Englishmen did not include the freedom to speak in association with other individuals, including association in the corporate form. To be sure, in 1791 (as now) corporations could pursue only the objectives set forth in their charters; but the dissent provides no evidence that their speech in the pursuit of those objectives could be censored. . . .

. . . The Framers didn't like corporations, the dissent concludes, and therefore it follows (as night the day) that corporations had no rights of free speech. Of course the Framers' personal affection or disaffection for corporations is relevant only insofar as it can be thought to be reflected in the understood meaning of the text they enacted—not, as the dissent suggests, as a freestanding substitute for that text. . . .

Even if we thought it proper to apply the dissent's approach of excluding from First Amendment coverage what the Founders disliked, and even if we agreed that the Founders disliked founding-era corporations; modern corporations might not qualify for exclusion. Most of the Founders' resentment towards corporations was directed at the state-granted monopoly privileges that individually chartered corporations enjoyed. Modern corporations do not have such privileges, and would probably have been favored by most of our enterprising Founders—excluding, perhaps, Thomas Jefferson and others favoring perpetuation of an agrarian society. Moreover, if the Founders' specific intent with respect to corporations is what matters, why does the dissent ignore the Founders' views about other legal entities that have more in common with modern business corporations than the founding-era corporations? At the time of the founding, religious, educational, and literary corporations were incorporated under general incorporation statutes, much as business corporations are today. There were also small unincorporated business associations, which some have argued were the "true progenitors" of today's business corporations. Were all of these silently excluded from the protections of the First Amendment? . . .

Historical evidence relating to the textually similar clause "the freedom of . . . the press" also provides no support for the proposition that the First Amendment excludes conduct of artificial legal entities from the scope of its protection. The freedom of "the press" was widely understood to protect the publishing activities of individual editors and printers. But these individuals often acted through newspapers, which (much like corporations) had their own names, outlived the individuals who had founded them, could be bought and sold, were sometimes owned by more than one person, and were operated for profit. Their activities were not stripped of First Amendment protection simply because they were carried out under the banner of an artificial legal entity. And the notion which follows from the dissent's view, that modern newspapers, since they are incorporated, have free-speech rights only at the sufferance of Congress, boggles the mind. . . .

The dissent says that when the Framers "constitutionalized the right to free speech in the First Amendment, it was the free speech of individual Americans that they had in mind." That is no doubt true. All the provisions of the Bill of Rights set forth the rights of individual men and women—not, for example, of trees or polar bears. But the individual person's right to speak includes the right to speak *in association with other individual persons*. Surely the dissent does not believe that speech by the Republican Party or the Democratic Party can be censored because it is not the speech of "an individual American." It is the speech of many individual Americans, who have associated in a common cause, giving the leadership of the party the right to speak on their behalf. The association of individuals in a business corporation is no different—or at least it cannot be denied the right to speak on the simplistic ground that it is not "an individual American."

But to return to, and summarize, my principal point, which is the conformity of today's opinion with the original meaning of the First Amendment. The Amendment is written in terms of "speech," not speakers. Its text offers no foothold for excluding any category of speaker, from single individuals to partnerships of individuals, to unincorporated associations of individuals, to incorporated associations of individuals—and the dissent offers no evidence about the original meaning of the text to support any such exclusion. We are therefore simply left with the question whether the speech at issue in this case is "speech" covered by the First Amendment. No one says otherwise. A documentary film critical of a potential Presidential candidate is core political speech, and its nature as such does not change simply because it was funded by a corporation. Nor does the character of that funding produce any reduction whatever in the "inherent worth of the speech" and "its capacity for informing the public," Indeed, to exclude or impede corporate speech is to muzzle the principal agents of the modern free economy. We should celebrate rather than condemn the addition of this speech to the public debate.

■ JUSTICE STEVENS, with whom JUSTICE GINSBURG, JUSTICE BREYER, and JUSTICE SOTOMAYOR join, concurring in part and dissenting in part.

The real issue in this case concerns how, not if, the appellant may finance its electioneering. Citizens United is a wealthy nonprofit corporation that runs a political action committee (PAC) with millions of dollars in assets. Under the Bipartisan Campaign Reform Act of 2002 (BCRA), it could have used those assets to televise and promote *Hillary: The Movie* wherever and whenever it wanted to. It also could have spent unrestricted sums to broadcast *Hillary* at any time other than the 30 days before the last primary election. Neither Citizens United's nor any other corporation's speech has been "banned." All that the parties dispute is whether Citizens United had a right to use the funds in its general treasury to pay for broadcasts during the 30-day period. The notion that the First Amendment dictates an affirmative answer to that question is, in my judgment, profoundly misguided. Even more misguided is the notion that the Court must rewrite the law relating to campaign expenditures by *for-profit* corporations and unions to decide this case.

The basic premise underlying the Court's ruling is its iteration, and constant reiteration, of the proposition that the First Amendment bars regulatory distinctions based on a speaker's identity, including its "identity" as a corporation. While that glittering generality has rhetorical appeal, it is not a correct statement of the law. Nor does it tell us when a corporation may engage in electioneering that some of its shareholders oppose. It does not even resolve the specific question whether Citizens United may be required to finance some of its messages with the money in its PAC. The conceit that corporations must be treated identically to natural persons in the political sphere is not only inaccurate but also inadequate to justify the Court's disposition of this case.

In the context of election to public office, the distinction between corporate and human speakers is significant. Although they make enormous contributions to our society, corporations are not actually members of it. They cannot vote or run for office. Because they may be managed and controlled by nonresidents, their interests may conflict in fundamental respects with the interests of eligible voters. The financial resources, legal structure, and instrumental orientation of corporations raise legitimate concerns about their role in the electoral process. Our lawmakers have a compelling constitutional basis, if not also a democratic duty, to take measures designed to guard against the potentially deleterious effects of corporate spending in local and national races.

The majority's approach to corporate electioneering marks a dramatic break from our past. Congress has placed special limitations on campaign spending by corporations ever since the passage of the Tillman Act in 1907, ch. 420, 34 Stat. 864. We have unanimously concluded that this "reflects a permissible assessment of the dangers posed by those entities to the electoral process," *FEC v. National Right to Work Comm.*, 459 U.S. 197 (1982) (*NRWC*), and have accepted the "legislative judgment that the special characteristics of the corporate structure require particularly careful regulation," *id.*, at 209–210. The Court today rejects a century of history when it treats the distinction between corporate and individual campaign spending as an invidious novelty born of *Austin v. Michigan Chamber of Commerce.* . . .

III

Identity-Based Distinctions

The second pillar of the Court's opinion is its assertion that "the Government cannot restrict political speech based on the speaker's . . . identity." The case on which it relies for this proposition is *Bellotti*. As I shall explain, the holding in that case was far narrower than the Court implies. Like its paeans to unfettered discourse, the Court's denunciation of identity-based distinctions may have rhetorical appeal but it obscures reality.

"Our jurisprudence over the past 216 years has rejected an absolutist interpretation" of the First Amendment. *WRTL*, at 482 (opinion of ROBERTS, C.J.). The First Amendment provides that "Congress shall make no law . . . abridging the freedom of speech, or of the press." Apart perhaps from measures designed to protect the press, that text might seem to permit no distinctions of any kind. Yet in a variety of contexts, we have held that speech can be regulated differentially on account of the speaker's identity, when identity is understood in categorical or institutional terms. The Government routinely places special restrictions on the speech rights of students, prisoners, members of the Armed Forces, foreigners, and its own employees. When such restrictions are justified by a legitimate governmental interest, they do not necessarily raise constitutional problems. In contrast to the blanket rule that the majority espouses, our cases recognize that the Government's interests may be more or less compelling with respect to different classes of speakers. . . .

The election context is distinctive in many ways, and the Court, of course, is right that the First Amendment closely guards political speech. But in this context, too, the authority of legislatures to enact viewpoint-neutral regulations based on content and identity is well settled. . . .

The same logic applies to this case with additional force because it is the identity of corporations, rather than individuals, that the Legislature has taken into account. As we have unanimously observed, legislatures are entitled to decide "that the special characteristics of the corporate structure require particularly careful regulation" in an electoral context. Not only has the distinctive potential of corporations to corrupt the electoral process long been recognized, but within the area of campaign finance, corporate spending is also "furthest from the core of political expression, since corporations' First Amendment speech and association interests are derived largely from those of their members and of the public in receiving information," *Federal Election Comm'n v. Beaumont*, 539 U.S. 146, 161, n. 8 (2003). Campaign finance distinctions based on corporate identity tend to be less worrisome, in other words, because the "speakers" are not natural persons, much less members of our political community, and the governmental interests are of the highest order. Furthermore, when corporations, as a class, are distinguished from noncorporations, as a class, there is a lesser risk that regulatory distinctions will reflect invidious discrimination or political favoritism.

If taken seriously, our colleagues' assumption that the identity of a speaker has *no* relevance to the Government's ability to regulate political speech would lead to some remarkable conclusions. Such an assumption would have accorded the propaganda broadcasts to our troops by "Tokyo Rose" during World War II the same protection as speech by Allied commanders. More pertinently, it would appear to afford the same protection to multinational corporations controlled by foreigners as to individual Americans: To do otherwise, after all, could "enhance the relative voice" of some (*i.e.*, humans) over others (*i.e.*, nonhumans). Under the majority's view, I suppose it may be a First Amendment problem that corporations are not permitted to vote, given that voting is, among other things, a form of speech.

In short, the Court dramatically overstates its critique of identity-based distinctions, without ever explaining why corporate identity demands the same treatment as individual identity. Only the most wooden approach to the First Amendment could justify the unprecedented line it seeks to draw.

Our First Amendment Tradition

A third fulcrum of the Court's opinion is the idea that *Austin* and *McConnell* are radical outliers, "aberration[s]," in our First Amendment tradition. See *infra* (professing fidelity to "our law and our tradition"). The Court has it exactly backwards. It is today's holding that is the radical departure from what had been settled First Amendment law. To see why, it is useful to take a long view.

1. *Original Understandings*

Let us start from the beginning. The Court invokes "ancient First Amendment principles," and original understandings, to defend today's ruling, yet it makes only a perfunctory attempt to ground its analysis in the principles or understandings of those who drafted and ratified the Amendment. Perhaps this is because there is not a scintilla of evidence to support the notion that anyone believed it would preclude regulatory distinctions based on the corporate form. To the extent that the Framers' views are discernible and relevant to the disposition of this case, they would appear to cut strongly against the majority's position.

This is not only because the Framers and their contemporaries conceived of speech more narrowly than we now think of it, see Bork, *Neutral Principles and Some First Amendment Problems*, 47 Ind. L.J. 1, 22 (1971), but also because they held very different views about the nature of the First Amendment right and the role of corporations in society. Those few corporations that existed at the founding were authorized by grant of a special legislative charter. Corporate sponsors would petition the legislature, and the legislature, if amenable, would issue a charter that specified the corporation's powers and purposes and "authoritatively fixed the scope and content of corporate organization," including "the internal structure of the corporation." Corporations were created, supervised, and conceptualized as quasi-public entities, "designed to serve a social function for the state." It was "assumed that [they] were legally privileged organizations that had to be closely scrutinized by the legislature because their purposes had to be made consistent with public welfare."

The individualized charter mode of incorporation reflected the "cloud of disfavor under which corporations labored" in the early years of this Nation. Thomas Jefferson famously fretted that corporations would subvert the Republic. General incorporation statutes, and widespread acceptance of business corporations as socially useful actors, did not emerge until the 1800's.

The Framers thus took it as a given that corporations could be comprehensively regulated in the service of the public welfare. Unlike our colleagues, they had little trouble distinguishing corporations from human beings, and when they constitutionalized the right to free speech in the First Amendment, it was the free speech of individual Americans that they had in mind. While individuals might join together to exercise their speech rights, business corporations, at least, were plainly not seen as facilitating such associational or expressive ends. . . . In light of these background practices and understandings, it seems to me implausible that the Framers believed "the freedom of speech" would extend equally to all corporate speakers, much less that it would preclude legislatures from taking limited measures to guard against corporate capture of elections. . . .

IV

. . . The majority recognizes that *Austin* and *McConnell* may be defended on anticorruption, antidistortion, and shareholder protection rationales. It badly errs both in explaining the nature of these rationales, which overlap and complement each other, and in applying them to the case at hand.

The Anticorruption Interest

Undergirding the majority's approach to the merits is the claim that the only "sufficiently important governmental interest in preventing corruption or the appearance of corruption" is one that is "limited to quid pro quo corruption." . . . While it is true that we have not always spoken about corruption in a clear or consistent voice, the approach taken by the majority cannot be right, in my judgment.

It disregards our constitutional history and the fundamental demands of a democratic society.

On numerous occasions we have recognized Congress' legitimate interest in preventing the money that is spent on elections from exerting an "undue influence on an officeholder's judgment" and from creating "the appearance of such influence," beyond the sphere of quid pro quo relationships. Corruption can take many forms. Bribery may be the paradigm case. But the difference between selling a vote and selling access is a matter of degree, not kind. And selling access is not qualitatively different from giving special preference to those who spent money on one's behalf. Corruption operates along a spectrum, and the majority's apparent belief that quid pro quo arrangements can be neatly demarcated from other improper influences does not accord with the theory or reality of politics. It certainly does not accord with the record Congress developed in passing BCRA, a record that stands as a remarkable testament to the energy and ingenuity with which corporations, unions, lobbyists, and politicians may go about scratching each other's backs—and which amply supported Congress' determination to target a limited set of especially destructive practices.

The District Court that adjudicated the initial challenge to BCRA pored over this record. In a careful analysis, Judge Kollar-Kotelly made numerous findings about the corrupting consequences of corporate and union independent expenditures in the years preceding BCRA's passage. As summarized in her own words:

> "The factual findings of the Court illustrate that corporations and labor unions routinely notify Members of Congress as soon as they air electioneering communications relevant to the Members' elections. The record also indicates that Members express appreciation to organizations for the airing of these election-related advertisements. Indeed, Members of Congress are particularly grateful when negative issue advertisements are run by these organizations, leaving the candidates free to run positive advertisements and be seen as 'above the fray.' Political consultants testify that campaigns are quite aware of who is running advertisements on the candidate's behalf, when they are being run, and where they are being run. Likewise, a prominent lobbyist testifies that these organizations use issue advocacy as a means to influence various Members of Congress.

> "The Findings also demonstrate that Members of Congress seek to have corporations and unions run these advertisements on their behalf. The Findings show that Members suggest that corporations or individuals make donations to interest groups with the understanding that the money contributed to these groups will assist the Member in a campaign. After the election, these organizations often seek credit for their support. . . . Finally, a large majority of Americans (80%) are of the view that corporations and other organizations that engage in electioneering communications, which benefit specific elected officials, receive special consideration from those officials when matters arise that affect these corporations and organizations."

Many of the relationships of dependency found by Judge Kollar-Kotelly seemed to have a *quid pro quo* basis, but other arrangements were more subtle. Her analysis shows the great difficulty in delimiting the precise scope of the *quid pro quo* category, as well as the adverse consequences that *all* such arrangements may have. There are threats of corruption that are far more destructive to a democratic society than the odd bribe. Yet the majority's understanding of corruption would leave lawmakers impotent to address all but the most discrete abuses. . . .

Quid Pro Quo Corruption

There is no need to take my side in the debate over the scope of the anticorruption interest to see that the Court's merits holding is wrong. Even under the majority's "crabbed view of corruption," *McConnell*, at 152, the Government should not lose this case. . . .

Although the Court suggests that *Buckley* compels its conclusion, *Buckley* cannot sustain this reading. It is true that, in evaluating FECA's ceiling on independent expenditures by all persons, the *Buckley* Court found the governmental interest in preventing corruption "inadequate." But *Buckley* did not evaluate corporate expenditures specifically, nor did it rule out the possibility that a future Court might find otherwise. The opinion reasoned that an expenditure limitation covering only express advocacy (*i.e.*, magic words) would likely be ineffectual, a problem that Congress tackled in BCRA, and it concluded that "the independent advocacy restricted by [FECA § 608(e)(1)] *does not presently appear* to pose dangers of real or apparent corruption comparable to those identified with large campaign contributions." . . .

Corporations, as a class, tend to be more attuned to the complexities of the legislative process and more directly affected by tax and appropriations measures that receive little public scrutiny; they also have vastly more money with which to try to buy access and votes. See Supp. Brief for Appellee 17 (stating that the Fortune 100 companies earned revenues of $13.1 trillion during the last election cycle). Business corporations must engage the political process in instrumental terms if they are to maximize shareholder value. The unparalleled resources, professional lobbyists, and single-minded focus they bring to this effort, I believe, make *quid pro quo* corruption and its appearance inherently more likely when they (or their conduits or trade groups) spend unrestricted sums on elections.

. . . The legislative and judicial proceedings relating to BCRA generated a substantial body of evidence suggesting that, as corporations grew more and more adept at crafting "issue ads" to help or harm a particular candidate, these nominally independent expenditures began to corrupt the political process in a very direct sense. The sponsors of these ads were routinely granted special access after the campaign was over; "candidates and officials knew who their friends were." Many corporate independent expenditures, it seemed, had become essentially interchangeable with direct contributions in their capacity to generate *quid pro quo* arrangements. In an age in which money and television ads are the coin of the campaign realm, it is hardly surprising that corporations deployed these ads to curry favor with, and to gain influence over, public officials. . . .

Austin and Corporate Expenditures

1. *Antidistortion*

The fact that corporations are different from human beings might seem to need no elaboration, except that the majority opinion almost completely elides it. *Austin* set forth some of the basic differences. Unlike natural persons, corporations have "limited liability" for their owners and managers, "perpetual life," separation of ownership and control, "and favorable treatment of the accumulation and distribution of assets . . . that enhance their ability to attract capital and to deploy their resources in ways that maximize the return on their shareholders' investments." Unlike voters in U.S. elections, corporations may be foreign controlled. Unlike other interest groups, business corporations have been "effectively delegated responsibility for ensuring society's economic welfare"; they inescapably structure the life of every citizen. "[T]he resources in the treasury of a business corporation," furthermore, "are not an indication of popular support for the corporation's political ideas." "They reflect instead the economically motivated decisions of investors and customers. The availability of these resources may make a corporation a formidable political presence, even though the power of the corporation may be no reflection of the power of its ideas."

It might also be added that corporations have no consciences, no beliefs, no feelings, no thoughts, no desires. Corporations help structure and facilitate the activities of human beings, to be sure, and their "personhood" often serves as a useful legal fiction. But they are not themselves members of "We the People" by whom and for whom our Constitution was established. . . .

It is an interesting question "who" is even speaking when a business corporation places an advertisement that endorses or attacks a particular candidate. Presumably it is not the customers or employees, who typically have no say in such matters. It cannot realistically be said to be the shareholders, who tend to be far removed from the day-to-day decisions of the firm and whose political preferences may be opaque to management. Perhaps the officers or directors of the corporation have the best claim to be the ones speaking, except their fiduciary duties generally prohibit them from using corporate funds for personal ends. . . . Take away the ability to use general treasury funds for some of those ads, and no one's autonomy, dignity, or political equality has been impinged upon in the least.

Corporate expenditures are distinguishable from individual expenditures in this respect. I have taken the view that a legislature may place reasonable restrictions on individuals' electioneering expenditures in the service of the governmental interests explained above, and in recognition of the fact that such restrictions are not direct restraints on speech but rather on its financing. But those restrictions concededly present a tougher case, because the primary conduct of actual, flesh-and-blood persons is involved. Some of those individuals might feel that they need to spend large sums of money on behalf of a particular candidate to vindicate the intensity of their electoral preferences. This is obviously not the situation with business corporations, as their routine practice of giving "substantial sums to *both* major national parties" makes pellucidly clear. "[C]orporate participation" in elections, any business executive will tell you, "is more transactional than ideological." Supp. Brief for Committee for Economic Development as *Amicus Curiae* 10.

In this transactional spirit, some corporations have affirmatively urged Congress to place limits on their electioneering communications. These corporations fear that officeholders will shake them down for supportive ads, that they will have to spend increasing sums on elections in an ever-escalating arms race with their competitors, and that public trust in business will be eroded. A system that effectively forces corporations to use their shareholders' money both to maintain access to, and to avoid retribution from, elected officials may ultimately prove more harmful than beneficial to many corporations. It can impose a kind of implicit tax.

. . . Recognizing the weakness of a speaker-based critique of *Austin*, the Court places primary emphasis not on the corporation's right to electioneer, but rather on the listener's interest in hearing what every possible speaker may have to say. The Court's central argument is that laws such as § 203 have "deprived [the electorate] of information, knowledge and opinion vital to its function," and this, in turn, "interferes with the 'open marketplace' of ideas protected by the First Amendment."

There are many flaws in this argument. If the overriding concern depends on the interests of the audience, surely the public's perception of the value of corporate speech should be given important weight. . . .

In a state election such as the one at issue in *Austin*, the interests of nonresident corporations may be fundamentally adverse to the interests of local voters. Consequently, when corporations grab up the prime broadcasting slots on the eve of an election, they can flood the market with advocacy that bears "little or no correlation" to the ideas of natural persons or to any broader notion of the public good. The opinions of real people may be marginalized. "The expenditure restrictions of [2 U.S.C.] § 441b are thus meant to ensure that competition among actors in the political arena is truly competition among ideas."

In addition to this immediate drowning out of noncorporate voices, there may be deleterious effects that follow soon thereafter. Corporate "domination" of electioneering can generate the impression that corporations dominate our democracy. When citizens turn on their televisions and radios before an election and hear only corporate electioneering, they may lose faith in their capacity, as citizens, to influence public policy. A Government captured by corporate interests, they may come to believe, will be neither responsive to their needs nor willing to give their views a fair hearing. The predictable result is cynicism and disenchantment: an increased perception that large spenders "call the tune" and a reduced "willingness of voters to take part in democratic governance." . . . At the least, I stress again, a legislature is entitled to credit these concerns and to take tailored measures in response. . . .

In critiquing *Austin*'s antidistortion rationale and campaign finance regulation more generally, our colleagues place tremendous weight on the example of media corporations. Yet it is not at all clear that *Austin* would permit § 203 to be applied to them. The press plays a unique role not only in the text, history, and structure of the First Amendment but also in facilitating public discourse; as the *Austin* Court explained, "media corporations differ significantly from other corporations in that their resources are devoted to the collection of information and its dissemination to the public." Our colleagues have raised some interesting and difficult questions about Congress' authority to regulate electioneering by the press, and about how to define what constitutes the press. *But that is not the case before us.* Section 203 does not apply to media corporations, and even if it did, Citizens United is not a media corporation. . . .

2. *Shareholder Protection*

There is yet another way in which laws such as § 203 can serve First Amendment values. Interwoven with *Austin*'s concern to protect the integrity of the electoral process is a concern to protect the rights of shareholders from a kind of coerced speech: electioneering expenditures that do not "reflec[t] [their] support." When corporations use general treasury funds to praise or attack a particular candidate for office, it is the shareholders, as the residual claimants, who are effectively footing the bill. Those shareholders who disagree with the corporation's electoral message may find their financial investments being used to undermine their political convictions. . . .

I would affirm the judgment of the District Court.

■ JUSTICE THOMAS, concurring in part and dissenting in part.

I join all but Part IV of the Court's opinion. . . .

I dissent from Part IV of the Court's opinion . . . because the Court's constitutional analysis does not go far enough. The disclosure, disclaimer, and reporting requirements in BCRA §§ 201 and 311 are also unconstitutional.

Congress may not abridge the "right to anonymous speech" based on the "simple interest in providing voters with additional relevant information," *McIntyre v. Ohio Elections Comm'n*, 514 U.S. 334, 348 (1995). In continuing to hold otherwise, the Court misapprehends the import of "recent events" that some *amici* describe "in which donors to certain causes were blacklisted, threatened, or otherwise targeted for retaliation." The Court properly recognizes these events as "cause for concern," but fails to acknowledge their constitutional significance. . . .

Amici's examples relate principally to Proposition 8, a state ballot proposition that California voters narrowly passed in the 2008 general election. Proposition 8 amended California's constitution to provide that "[o]nly marriage between a man and a woman is valid or recognized in California." Cal. Const., Art. I, § 7.5. Any donor who gave more than $100 to any committee supporting or opposing Proposition 8 was required to disclose his full name, street address, occupation, employer's name (or business name, if self-employed), and the total amount of his contributions. The California Secretary of State was then required to post this information on the Internet.

Some opponents of Proposition 8 compiled this information and created Web sites with maps showing the locations of homes or businesses of Proposition 8 supporters. Many supporters (or their customers) suffered property damage, or threats of physical violence or death, as a result. They cited these incidents in a complaint they filed after the 2008 election, seeking to invalidate California's mandatory disclosure laws. Supporters recounted being told: "Consider yourself lucky. If I had a gun I would have gunned you down along with each and every other supporter," or, "we have plans for you and your friends." Proposition 8 opponents also allegedly harassed the measure's supporters by defacing or damaging their property. Two religious organizations supporting Proposition 8 reportedly received through the mail envelopes containing a white powdery substance.

Those accounts are consistent with media reports describing Proposition 8-related retaliation. The director of the nonprofit California Musical Theater gave $1,000 to support the initiative; he was forced to resign after artists complained to his employer. The director of the Los Angeles Film Festival was forced to resign after giving $1,500 because opponents threatened to boycott and picket the next festival. And a woman who had managed her popular, family-owned restaurant for 26 years was forced to resign after she gave $100, because "throngs of [angry] protesters" repeatedly arrived at the restaurant and "shout[ed] 'shame on you' at customers."

The police even had to "arriv[e] in riot gear one night to quell the angry mob" at the restaurant. Some supporters of Proposition 8 engaged in similar tactics; one real estate businessman in San Diego who had donated to a group opposing Proposition 8 "received a letter from the Prop. 8 Executive Committee threatening to publish his company's name if he didn't also donate to the 'Yes on 8' campaign."

The success of such intimidation tactics has apparently spawned a cottage industry that uses forcibly disclosed donor information to *pre-empt* citizens' exercise of their First Amendment rights. Before the 2008 Presidential election, a "newly formed nonprofit group . . . plann[ed] to confront donors to conservative groups, hoping to create a chilling effect that will dry up contributions." Luo, Group Plans Campaign Against G.O.P. Donors, N.Y. Times, Aug. 8, 2008, p. A15. Its leader, "who described his effort as 'going for the jugular,'" detailed the group's plan to send a "warning letter . . . alerting donors who might be considering giving to right-wing groups to a variety of potential dangers, including legal trouble, public exposure and watchdog groups digging through their lives."

These instances of retaliation sufficiently demonstrate why this Court should invalidate mandatory disclosure and reporting requirements. But *amici* present evidence of yet another reason to do so—the threat of retaliation from *elected officials*. As *amici*'s submissions make clear, this threat extends far beyond a single ballot proposition in California. For example, a candidate challenging an incumbent state attorney general reported that some members of the State's business community feared donating to his campaign because they did not want to cross the incumbent; in his words, "I go to so many people and hear the same thing: 'I sure hope you beat [the incumbent], but I can't afford to have my name on your records. He might come after me next.'" Strassel, Challenging Spitzerism at the Polls, Wall Street Journal, Aug. 1, 2008, p. A11. The incumbent won reelection in 2008.

My point is not to express any view on the merits of the political controversies I describe. Rather, it is to demonstrate—using real-world, recent examples—the fallacy in the Court's conclusion that "[d]isclaimer and disclosure requirements . . . impose no ceiling on campaign-related activities, and do not prevent anyone from speaking." Of course they do. Disclaimer and disclosure requirements enable private citizens and elected officials to implement political strategies *specifically calculated* to curtail campaign-related activity and prevent the lawful, peaceful exercise of First Amendment rights. . . .

[T]he Court's promise that as-applied challenges will adequately protect speech is a hollow assurance. Now more than ever, §§ 201 and 311 will chill protected speech because—as California voters can attest—"the advent of the Internet" enables "prompt disclosure of expenditures," which "provide[s]" political opponents "with the information needed" to intimidate and retaliate against their foes. Thus, "disclosure permits citizens . . . to react to the speech of [political opponents] in a proper"—or undeniably *improper*—"way" long before a plaintiff could prevail on an as-applied challenge.

I cannot endorse a view of the First Amendment that subjects citizens of this Nation to death threats, ruined careers, damaged or defaced property, or pre-emptive and threatening warning letters as the price for engaging in "core political speech, the 'primary object of First Amendment protection.'" Accordingly, I respectfully dissent from the Court's judgment upholding BCRA §§ 201 and 311.

NOTES

1.   Does either the majority or the dissent offer a coherent theory as to which constitutional rights may be exercised by entities in corporate form, and which may not? Compare these cases—

Berea College v. Kentucky, 211 U.S. 45 (1908) (upholding, against an Equal Protection Clause challenge, criminal penalties for a private religious school that taught black and white students together, on the ground that the school was a corporation);

Late Corporation of Jesus Christ of Latter-Day Saints v. United States, 136 U.S. 1 (1890) (upholding federal statute disbanding the Mormon Church and seizing most of its property, on the ground that it was a corporation);

Western & Southern Life Ins. Co. v. California Bd. of Equalization, 451 U.S. 648, 656 (1981) (holding that the Privileges and Immunities Clause of Article IV does not apply to corporations)

—with these cases—

id. (holding that the Equal Protection Clause and dormant Commerce Clause protect corporations);

Santa Clara County v. Southern Pac. R. Co., 118 U.S. 394 (holding that due process applies to corporations);

44 Liquormart, Inc. v. Rhode Island, 517 U.S. 484 (1996) (protecting the commercial speech of a corporation);

Corporation of Presiding Bishop v. Amos, 483 U.S. 327 (1987) (implicitly holding that the Free Exercise Clause protects corporations);

Upjohn Co. v. United States, 449 U.S. 383 (1981) (applying attorney-client privilege to a corporation);

Marshall v. Barlow's, Inc., 436 U.S. 307 (1978) (applying Fourth Amendment protections to corporation);

New York Times v. Sullivan, 376 U.S. 254 (1964) (applying Free Press Clause to a corporation).

Kaiser Aetna v. United States, 444 U.S. 164 (1979) (applying Takings Clause of the Fifth Amendment to corporations).

2.   Can the dissent be understood not as resting on the corporate form of the speaker, but on the belief that *Buckley* was wrong to grant free speech protection to so-called "independent expenditures"? Note that the dissent does not appear to deny free speech protection to corporations when they engage in lobbying, genuine issues ads, or other political speech outside the context of elections. Why not? And if it is true, as the dissent says, that "corporate independent expenditures [have] become essentially interchangeable with direct contributions in their capacity to generate *quid pro quo* arrangements," why isn't that equally true of non-corporate independent expenditures? Recall that the distinction between contributions and independent expenditures was drawn in *Buckley v. Valeo*. Is the dissenting position in *Citizens United* predicated on rejecting that distinction? Recall also that the dissenters in *Citizens United* scolded the majority for overturning two precedents, *Austin* and *McConnell*. What is the role for *stare decisis* in this area?

3.   What is the dissent's position on non-profit corporations, wholly-owned corporations, limited partnerships, and the like? What about unions?

4.   The majority purports not to address foreign-owned corporations. Does the logic of the opinion permit banning their election expenditures? How about election expenditures by foreign governments?

5.   The majority leaves in place the ban on corporate contributions to candidates. How, given its logic, can that be justified?

6.   The majority stresses that if corporations cannot publish their views about candidates prior to elections, this would interfere with the ability of media corporations, such as newspapers, to publish editorial endorsements, which is clearly constitutionally protected. See *Mills v. Alabama*, 384 U.S. 214 (1966) (striking down state statute forbidding a newspaper owned by a corporation from endorsing or opposing a candidate on election day). How does the dissent respond? One might respond that media corporations have special protection under the Free Press Clause, but is that so? The Court has consistently rejected the claim that media corporations have special rights under the Press Clause, holding instead that the clause protects the right of all persons, including the lonely pamphleteer, to publish their views to the public. See Eugene Volokh, *"The Freedom . . . of the Press," from 1791 to 1868 to Now—Freedom for the Press as an Industry, or the Press as a Technology?*, 160 U. Pa. L. Rev. 459 (2011). If that is an accurate statement of the law, is the dissent saying that corporations have no constitutional right to own newspapers that endorse or denounce candidates in an election campaign?

For that matter, why wasn't this case litigated under the Free Press Clause? Isn't a documentary a form of "the press"? Suppose the New York Times Company produces a broadcast or video-on-demand version of its editorial page, in which journalists discuss the reasons behind the newspaper's editorial positions, including its candidate endorsements. Could it be prohibited from airing such a program within sixty days of an election? Why is Citizens United any different? Because it is not a "media corporation"? Why isn't it? It makes documentaries. What more is needed to be a "media corporation"?

7.   The majority was much criticized for reaching out for the broadest possible holding in this case. The plaintiffs did not ask the Court to overrule *Austin* and *McConnell*. The Court on its own motion ordered reargument on the broader theory. Was that inappropriate?

8.   The majority declined to defer to Congress's findings or judgment about campaign finance because of the danger that members of Congress have an incentive to write rules to favor incumbents. The dissent says there is no basis in the record for this fear. What do you think? Do campaign finance laws in general, and the rules against electioneering communications in particular, favor incumbents? What are the obstacles to a relatively unknown challenger raising the money for a successful campaign? Do incumbents experience those obstacles to the same degree? Does this matter to the First Amendment question?

9.   Maybe it is a mistake to view campaign contributions primarily as an attempt by the contributions to influence or persuade. Maybe they are a form of extortion by officeholders. "Unless you contribute to my campaign, I will use government power to punish you." See Fred S. McChesney, MONEY FOR NOTHING: POLITICS, RENT EXTRACTION, AND POLITICAL EXTORTION (1997). If that is so, does it affect your view of the First Amendment issues?

A NOTE ON THE IMPLICATIONS OF *CITIZENS UNITED*

The Supreme Court summarily decided two cases related to campaign finance and the First Amendment during the two years after *Citizens United*. A summary decision is rendered without oral argument, and generally means that the decision was governed by clear precedent. Often these decisions are issued "per curiam" (a term that means the opinion is not attributed to any particular author), and sometimes without an opinion. If there is no opinion, the holding of the court is the narrowest one that would support the judgment.

1.   A unanimous Court summarily affirmed the decision of a three-judge district court in *Bluman v. Federal Election Commission*, 800 F.Supp.2d 281 (D.D.C. 2011), aff'd, 132 S.Ct. 1087 (2011), without an opinion. The lower court had upheld the constitutionality of 2 U.S.C. 441e(a), which prohibits foreign citizens who are not lawful permanent residents of the United States from contributing to candidates for federal political office and making independent expenditures in support of or opposition to such candidates. The lower court relied on what it called the "straightforward principle" that "[i]t is fundamental to the definition of our national political community that foreign citizens do not have a constitutional right to participate in, and thus may be excluded from, activities of democratic self-government." The court relied on precedents permitting discrimination against non-citizens when the exclusion is related to democratic self-government—such as laws excluding aliens from serving as public school teachers, police officers, or jurors. It also relied on the four-justice dissent in *Citizens United*, which invoked the prohibition on independent expenditures by foreign citizens as an argument against the majority's view that speaker-based exclusions from freedom of speech are generally unconstitutional.

Do you believe the decision in *Bluman* can be squared with the rationale of *Citizens United*? What, precisely, are the free speech rights of foreigners? The lower court stated that it did "not decide whether Congress could prohibit foreign nationals from engaging in speech other than contributions to candidates and parties, express-advocacy expenditures, and donations to outside groups to be used for contributions to candidates and parties and express-advocacy expenditures." What is the answer to that question?

2.   Over four dissents, the Court summarily reversed a decision by the Montana Supreme Court upholding a ban on corporate campaign expenditures, stating that "Montana's arguments in support of the judgment below either were already rejected in *Citizens United*, or fail to meaningfully distinguish that case." *American Tradition Partnership v. Bullock*, 132 S.Ct. 2490 (2012). The Montana court held that the state of Montana had a long history of political corruption through corporate influence, which justified the ban. Three *Citizens United* dissenters once again dissented, joined by Justice Kagan (who had taken the place on the Court of the fourth dissenter in *Citizens United*, Justice Stevens). They said that "Montana's experience, like considerable experience elsewhere since the Court's decision in *Citizens United*, casts grave doubt on the Court's supposition that independent expenditures do not corrupt or appear to do so." Was *Citizens United* based on a contrary view? Was *Buckley*?

[*Assignment 50*]

J.   PUBLIC FORUM DOCTRINE

A great deal of private speech occurs on public property: street demonstrations, sidewalk protests, prayer services in parks, speeches on the town square. Do

Americans have a right to use public property for purposes of assembly, or is this just a privilege the government is entitled to grant or deny?

Commonwealth v. Davis

162 Mass. 510 (1895)

[William Davis was convicted for delivering a sermon on the Boston Common in violation of this city ordinance: "No person shall, in or upon any of the public grounds, make any public address, discharge any cannon or firearm, expose for sale any goods, wares or merchandise, erect or maintain any booth stand, tent, or apparatus for the purposes of public amusement or show, except in accordance with a permit from the mayor."—Editors]

■ HOLMES, J.

. . . There is no evidence before us to show that the power of the legislature over the common is less than its power over any other park dedicated to the use of the public, or over public streets, the legal title to which is in a city or town. As representative of the public, it may and does exercise control over the use which the public may make of such places, and it may and does delegate more or less of such control to the city or town immediately concerned. For the legislature absolutely or conditionally to forbid public speaking in a highway or public park is no more an infringement of the rights of a member of the public than for the owner of a private house to forbid it in his house. When no proprietary rights interfere, the legislature may end the right of the public to enter upon the public place by putting an end to the dedication to public uses. So it may take the less[er] step of limiting the public use to certain purposes. . . .

It is argued that the ordinance really is directed especially against free preaching of the gospel in public places, as certain western ordinances, seemingly general, have been held to be directed against the Chinese. But we have no reason to believe, and do not believe, that this ordinance was passed for any other than its ostensible purpose, namely, as a proper regulation of the use of public grounds.

[This decision was affirmed unanimously by the U.S. Supreme Court in Davis v. Massachusetts, *167 U.S. 43 (1897).—Editors]*

Hague v. CIO

307 U.S. 496 (1939)

[The Committee for Industrial Organization, which organized workers into labor unions and informed workers of their rights under the National Labor Relations Act, sought to hold outdoor meetings on public property in Jersey City, New Jersey. City ordinances required permits for holding outdoor meetings. City officials refused to issue permits to the CIO, arguing that they were Communists who advocated the overthrow of the government. CIO members proceeded without permits and were arrested. The CIO sued, arguing that the ordinances were facially unconstitutional and that the city had enforced them in a discriminatory fashion. The district court found for the CIO, concluding that the city had no legitimate basis for refusing to issue the permits. The court of appeals affirmed.—Editors]

■ MR. JUSTICE ROBERTS delivered an opinion in which MR. JUSTICE BLACK concurred [and in which MR. CHIEF JUSTICE HUGHES concurred in pertinent part].

By their specifications of error, the petitioners . . . assert that the court erred in holding that the street meeting ordinance is unconstitutional on its face, and that it has been unconstitutionally administered . . .

[The respondents' rights were infringed by the city] unless, as petitioners contend, the city's ownership of streets and parks is as absolute as one's ownership of his home, with consequent power altogether to exclude citizens from the use thereof, or unless, though the city holds the streets in trust for public use, the absolute denial of their use to the respondents is a valid exercise of the police power.

The findings of fact negative the latter assumption. In support of the former the petitioners rely upon *Davis v. Massachusetts*, 167 U.S. 43 (1897). There it appeared that, pursuant to enabling legislation, the city of Boston adopted an ordinance prohibiting anyone from speaking, discharging fire arms, selling goods, or maintaining any booth for public amusement on any of the public grounds of the city except under a permit from the Mayor. Davis spoke on Boston Common without a permit and without applying to the Mayor for one. He was charged with a violation of the ordinance and moved to quash the complaint, inter alia, on the ground that the ordinance abridged his privileges and immunities as a citizen of the United States and denied him due process of law because it was arbitrary and unreasonable. His contentions were overruled and he was convicted. The judgment was affirmed by the Supreme Court of Massachusetts and by this court.

The decision seems to be grounded on the holding of the State court that the Common "was absolutely under the control of the legislature," and that it was thus "conclusively determined there was no right in the plaintiff in error to use the common except in such mode and subject to such regulations as the legislature, in its wisdom, may have deemed proper to prescribe." The Court added that the Fourteenth Amendment did not destroy the power of the states to enact police regulations as to a subject within their control or enable citizens to use public property in defiance of the constitution and laws of the State.

The ordinance there in question apparently had a different purpose from that of the one here challenged, for it was not directed solely at the exercise of the right of speech and assembly, but was addressed as well to other activities, not in the nature of civil rights, which doubtless might be regulated or prohibited as respects their enjoyment in parks. In the instant case the ordinance deals only with the exercise of the right of assembly for the purpose of communicating views entertained by speakers, and is not a general measure to promote the public convenience in the use of the streets or parks.

We have no occasion to determine whether, on the facts disclosed, [*Davis*] was rightly decided, but we cannot agree that it rules the instant case. Wherever the title of streets and parks may rest, they have immemorially been held in trust for the use of the public and, time out of mind, have been used for purposes of assembly, communicating thoughts between citizens, and discussing public questions. Such use of the streets and public places has, from ancient times, been a part of the privileges, immunities, rights, and liberties of citizens. The privilege of a citizen of the United States to use the streets and parks for communication of views on national questions may be regulated in the interest of all; it is not absolute, but relative, and must be exercised in subordination to the general comfort and convenience, and in consonance with peace and good order; but it must not, in the guise of regulation, be abridged or denied.

We think the court below was right in holding the ordinance quoted in Note 1 void upon its face. It does not make comfort or convenience in the use of streets or parks the standard of official action. It enables the Director of Safety to refuse a permit on his mere opinion that such refusal will prevent "riots, disturbances or disorderly assemblage." It can thus, as the record discloses, be made the instrument of arbitrary suppression of free expression of views on national affairs for the prohibition of all speaking will undoubtedly "prevent" such eventualities. But uncontrolled official suppression of the privilege cannot be made a substitute for the duty to maintain order in connection with the exercise of the right . . .

■ [Concurring opinions by CHIEF JUSTICE HUGHES and JUSTICES STONE and REED, and dissenting opinions by JUSTICES MCREYNOLDS and BUTLER, are omitted.]

NOTES

1.   What support is there for the Court's declaration that public streets and parks have been used for purposes of assembly, communication, and discussion "time out of mind"? Was this true in Britain? In light of the unanimous decision in *Davis*, was it true in the United States? Consider two possible alternative explanations for the holding. First, could the Assembly Clause of the First Amendment be understood to imply a right to assemble in public spaces? Where else could "the people" assemble? Second, there is some support for the idea that certain public property is indeed held in trust for use by the public—even if, this right did not extend to assemblies for purposes of speech. This is called "the public trust doctrine." After enactment of the First Amendment, one might argue that a law singling out speech for special prohibition is not a regulation of access to public property, but one abridging the freedom of speech.

2.   Did the *Hague* Court properly distinguish *Davis*? Or are the decisions inconsistent?

3.   In *Greer v. Spock*, 424 U.S. 828 (1976), the Court upheld a rule barring speeches and demonstrations of a partisan political nature on military bases, such as by candidates for political office. The Court held that military bases are non-public forums, and that the rule was "objectively and evenhandedly applied." In *Lehman v. City of Shaker Heights*, 418 U.S. 298 (1974), the Court upheld a rule allowing private persons to purchase advertising space on public buses, but excluding political advertisements. A four-justice plurality reasoned that the bus advertising space is not a forum for speech, and that the restriction need only be reasonable and viewpoint neutral. A fifth justice—Justice Douglas—reasoned that because bus riders are a captive audience the government had an interest in protecting the right of bus riders "to be free from forced intrusions on their privacy." In *Jones v. North Carolina Prisoners Union*, 433 U.S. 119 (1977), the Court upheld a prison policy that prohibited the solicitation of prisoners to join a labor union, as well as labor union meetings, but allowed meetings by "service organizations" such as the Jaycees, Alcoholics Anonymous, and the Boy Scouts. Then came the following case:

Perry Education Association v.
Perry Local Educators Association

460 U.S. 37 (1983)

■ JUSTICE WHITE delivered the opinion of the Court.

Perry Education Association is the duly elected exclusive bargaining representative for the teachers of the Metropolitan School District of Perry Township, Ind. A collective-bargaining agreement with the Board of Education provided that Perry Education Association, but no other union, would have access to the interschool mail system and teacher mailboxes in the Perry Township schools. The issue in this case is whether the denial of similar access to the Perry Local Educators' Association, a rival teacher group, violates the First and Fourteenth Amendments.

I

The Metropolitan School District of Perry Township, Ind., operates a public school system of 13 separate schools. Each school building contains a set of mailboxes for the teachers. Interschool delivery by school employees permits messages to be delivered rapidly to teachers in the district. The primary function of this internal mail system is to transmit official messages among the teachers and between the teachers and the school administration. In addition, teachers use the system to send personal messages and individual school building principals have allowed delivery of messages from various private organizations. Local parochial schools, church groups, YMCAs, and Cub Scout units have used the system. The record does not indicate whether any requests for use have been denied, nor does it reveal whether permission must separately be sought for every message that a group wishes delivered to the teachers.—*[Text relocated from footnote.—Editors]*

Prior to 1977, both the Perry Education Association (PEA) and the Perry Local Educators' Association (PLEA) represented teachers in the school district and apparently had equal access to the interschool mail system. In 1977, [PEA was elected as exclusive representative, as provided by state law.]

The Board permits a school district to provide access to communication facilities to the union selected for the discharge of the exclusive representative duties of representing the bargaining unit and its individual members without having to provide equal access to rival unions. Following the election, PEA and the school district [contracted for] PEA "access to teachers' mailboxes in which to insert material" and the right to use the interschool mail delivery system to the extent that the school district incurred no extra expense by such use. The labor agreement noted that these access rights were being accorded to PEA "acting as the representative of the teachers" and went on to stipulate that these access rights shall not be granted to any other "school employee organization"—a term of art defined by Indiana law to mean "any organization which has school employees as members and one of whose primary purposes is representing school employees in dealing with their employer."
. . .

The exclusive access policy applies only to use of the mailboxes and school mail system. PLEA is not prevented from using other school facilities to communicate with teachers. PLEA may post notices on school bulletin boards; may hold meetings on school property after school hours; and may, with approval of the building principals, make announcements on the public address system. Of course, PLEA also may communicate with teachers by word of mouth, telephone, or the United States mail. Moreover, under Indiana law, the preferential access of the bargaining agent may continue only while its status as exclusive representative is insulated from challenge. While a representation contest is in progress, unions must be afforded equal access to such communication facilities. . . .

III

. . . There is no question that constitutional interests are implicated by denying PLEA use of the interschool mail system. "It can hardly be argued that either students or teachers shed their constitutional rights to freedom of speech or expression at the schoolhouse gate." *Tinker v. Des Moines School District*, 393 U.S. 503, 506 (1969). The First Amendment's guarantee of free speech applies to teacher's mailboxes as surely as it does elsewhere within the school, and on sidewalks outside, *Police Department of Chicago v. Mosley*, 408 U.S. 92 (1972). But this is not to say that the First Amendment requires equivalent access to all parts of a school building in which some form of communicative activity occurs. "Nowhere [have we] suggested that students, teachers, or anyone else has an absolute constitutional right to use all parts of a school building or its immediate environs for . . . unlimited expressive purposes." *Grayned v. City of Rockford*, 408 U.S. 104, 117–118 (1972). The existence of a right of access to public property and the standard by which limitations upon such a right must be evaluated differ depending on the character of the property at issue.

A

In places which by long tradition or by government fiat have been devoted to assembly and debate, the rights of the state to limit expressive activity are sharply circumscribed. At one end of the spectrum are streets and parks which "have immemorially been held in trust for the use of the public, and, time out of mind, have been used for purposes of assembly, communicating thoughts between citizens, and discussing public questions." *Hague v. CIO*, 307 U.S. 496 (1939). In these quintessential public forums, the government may not prohibit all communicative activity. For the state to enforce a content-based exclusion it must show that its regulation is necessary to serve a compelling state interest and that it is narrowly drawn to achieve that end. The state may also enforce regulations of the time, place, and manner of expression which are content-neutral, are narrowly tailored to serve a significant government interest, and leave open ample alternative channels of communication.

A second category consists of public property which the state has opened for use by the public as a place for expressive activity. The Constitution forbids a state to enforce certain exclusions from a forum generally open to the public even if it was not required to create the forum in the first place. *Widmar v. Vincent*, 454 U.S. 263 (1981) (university meeting facilities); *City of Madison Joint School District v. Wisconsin Public Employment Relations Comm'n*, 429 U.S. 167 (1976) (school board meeting); *Southeastern Promotions, Ltd. v. Conrad*, 420 U.S. 546 (1975) (municipal theater).[7] Although a state is not required to indefinitely retain the open character of the facility, as long as it does so it is bound by the same standards as apply in a

---

[7]   A public forum may be created for a limited purpose such as use by certain groups, or for the discussion of certain subjects.

traditional public forum. Reasonable time, place and manner regulations are permissible, and a content-based prohibition must be narrowly drawn to effectuate a compelling state interest.

Public property which is not by tradition or designation a forum for public communication is governed by different standards. We have recognized that the "First Amendment does not guarantee access to property simply because it is owned or controlled by the government." In addition to time, place, and manner regulations, the state may reserve the forum for its intended purposes, communicative or otherwise, as long as the regulation on speech is reasonable and not an effort to suppress expression merely because public officials oppose the speaker's view. As we have stated on several occasions, "the State, no less than a private owner of property, has power to preserve the property under its control for the use to which it is lawfully dedicated."

The school mail facilities at issue here fall within this third category. The Court of Appeals recognized that Perry School District's interschool mail system is not a traditional public forum: "We do not hold that a school's internal mail system is a public forum in the sense that a school board may not close it to all but official business if it chooses." On this point the parties agree. Nor do the parties dispute that, as the District Court observed, the "normal and intended function [of the school mail facilities] is to facilitate internal communication of school related matters to teachers." The internal mail system, at least by policy, is not held open to the general public. It is instead PLEA's position that the school mail facilities have become a "limited public forum" from which it may not be excluded because of the periodic use of the system by private non-school connected groups, and PLEA's own unrestricted access to the system prior to PEA's certification as exclusive representative.

Neither of these arguments is persuasive. The use of the internal school mail by groups not affiliated with the schools is no doubt a relevant consideration. If by policy or by practice the Perry School District has opened its mail system for indiscriminate use by the general public, then PLEA could justifiably argue a public forum has been created. This, however, is not the case. As the case comes before us, there is no indication in the record that the school mailboxes and interschool delivery system are open for use by the general public. Permission to use the system to communicate with teachers must be secured from the individual building principal. There is no court finding or evidence in the record which demonstrates that this permission has been granted as a matter of course to all who seek to distribute material. We can only conclude that the schools do allow some outside organizations such as the YMCA, Cub Scouts, and other civic and church organizations to use the facilities. This type of selective access does not transform government property into a public forum. In *Greer v. Spock*, the fact that other civilian speaker and entertainers had sometimes been invited to appear at Fort Dix did not convert the military base into a public forum. And in *Lehman v. Shaker Heights*, 418 U.S. 298 (1974) (Opinion of Blackmun, J.), a plurality of the Court concluded that a city transit system's rental of space in its vehicles for commercial advertising did not require it to accept partisan political advertising.

Moreover, even if we assume that by granting access to the Cub Scouts, YMCAs, and parochial schools, the school district has created a "limited" public forum, the constitutional right of access would in any event extend only to other entities of similar character. While the school mail facilities thus might be a forum generally open for use by the Girl Scouts, the local boys' club and other organizations that engage in activities of interest and educational relevance to students, they would not as a consequence be open to an organization such as PLEA, which is concerned with the terms and conditions of teacher employment.

PLEA also points to its ability to use the school mailboxes and delivery system on an equal footing with PEA prior to the collective bargaining agreement signed in 1978. Its argument appears to be that the access policy in effect at that time converted the school mail facilities into a limited public forum generally open for use by employee organizations, and that once this occurred, exclusions of employee organizations thereafter must be judged by the constitutional standard applicable to public forums. The fallacy in the argument is that it is not the forum, but PLEA itself, which has changed. Prior to 1977, there was no exclusive representative for the Perry school district teachers. PEA and PLEA each represented its own members. Therefore the school district's policy of allowing both organizations to use the school mail facilities simply reflected the fact that both unions represented the teachers and had legitimate reasons for use of the system. PLEA's previous access was consistent with the school district's preservation of the facilities for school-related business, and did not constitute creation of a public forum in any broader sense.

Because the school mail system is not a public forum, the School District had no "constitutional obligation per se to let any organization use the school mail boxes." In the Court of Appeals' view, however, the access policy adopted by the Perry schools favors a particular viewpoint, that of the PEA, on labor relations, and consequently must be strictly scrutinized regardless of whether a public forum is involved. There is, however, no indication that the school board intended to discourage one viewpoint and advance another. We believe it is more accurate to characterize the access policy as based on the *status* of the respective unions rather than their views. Implicit in the concept of the nonpublic forum is the right to make distinctions in access on the basis of subject matter and speaker identity. These distinctions may be impermissible in a public forum but are inherent and inescapable in the process of limiting a nonpublic forum to activities compatible with the intended purpose of the property. The touchstone for evaluating these distinctions is whether they are reasonable in light of the purpose which the forum at issue serves.

B

The differential access provided PEA and PLEA is reasonable because it is wholly consistent with the district's legitimate interest in "preserv[ing] the property . . . for the use to which it is lawfully dedicated." Use of school mail facilities enables PEA to perform effectively its obligations as exclusive representative of *all* Perry Township teachers. Conversely, PLEA does not have any official responsibility in connection with the school district and need not be entitled to the same rights of access to school mailboxes . . . Moreover, exclusion of the rival union may reasonably be considered a means of insuring labor-peace within the schools. The policy "serves to prevent the District's schools from becoming a battlefield for inter-union squabbles."

The Court of Appeals accorded little or no weight to PEA's special responsibilities. In its view these responsibilities, while justifying PEA's access, did not justify denying equal access to PLEA. The Court of Appeals would have been correct if a public forum were involved here. But the internal mail system is not a public forum. As we have already stressed, when government property is not dedicated to open communication the government may—without further justification—restrict use to those who participate in the forum's official business.

Finally, the reasonableness of the limitations on PLEA's access to the school mail system is also supported by the substantial alternative channels that remain open for union-teacher communication to take place. These means range from bulletin boards to meeting facilities to the United States mail. During election periods, PLEA is assured of equal access to all modes of communication. There is no showing here that PLEA's ability to communicate with teachers is seriously impinged by the restricted access to the internal mail system. The variety and type of alternative modes of access present here compare favorably with those in other non-public forum cases where we have upheld restrictions on access. See, *e.g. Greer v. Spock*, 424 U.S. 828, 839 (1974) (servicemen free to attend political rallies off-base); *Pell v. Procunier*, 417 U.S. 817, 827–828 (1974) (prison inmates may communicate with media by mail and through visitors).

IV

The Court of Appeals also held that the differential access provided the rival unions constituted impermissible content discrimination in violation of the Equal Protection Clause of the Fourteenth Amendment. We have rejected this contention when cast as a First Amendment argument, and it fares no better in equal protection garb. . . .

■ JUSTICE BRENNAN, with whom JUSTICE MARSHALL, JUSTICE POWELL, and JUSTICE STEVENS join, dissenting.

The Court today holds that an incumbent teachers' union may negotiate a collective bargaining agreement with a school board that grants the incumbent access to teachers' mailboxes and to the interschool mail system and denies such access to a rival union. Because the exclusive access provision in the collective bargaining agreement amounts to viewpoint discrimination that infringes the respondents' First Amendment rights and fails to advance any substantial state interest, I dissent.

I

. . . Based on a finding that the interschool mail system is not a "public forum," the Court states that the respondents have no right of access to the system, and that the school board is free "to make distinctions in access on the basis of subject matter and speaker identity," if the distinctions are "reasonable in light of the purpose which the forum at issue serves." According to the Court, the petitioner's status as the exclusive bargaining representative provides a reasonable basis for the exclusive access policy.

The Court fundamentally misperceives the essence of the respondents' claims. . . . This case does not involve an "absolute access" claim. It involves an "equal access" claim. As such it does not turn on whether the internal school mail system is a "public forum." In focusing on the public forum issue, the Court disregards the First Amendment's central proscription against censorship, in the form of viewpoint discrimination, in any forum, public or nonpublic. . . .

Once the government permits discussion of certain subject matter, it may not impose restrictions that discriminate among viewpoints on those subjects whether a nonpublic forum is involved or not. This prohibition is implicit in the *Mosley* line of cases, in *Tinker*, and in those cases in which we have approved content-based restrictions on access to government property that is not a public forum. We have never held that government may allow discussion of a subject and then discriminate among viewpoints on that particular topic, even if the government for certain reasons may entirely exclude discussion of the subject from the forum. In this context, the greater power does not include the lesser because for First Amendment purposes exercise of the lesser power is more threatening to core values. Viewpoint discrimination is censorship in its purest form and government regulation that discriminates among viewpoints threatens the continued vitality of "free speech."

Against this background, it is clear that the Court's approach to this case is flawed. By focusing on whether the interschool mail system is a public forum, the Court disregards the independent First Amendment protection afforded by the prohibition against viewpoint discrimination. This case does not involve a claim of an absolute right of access to the forum to discuss any subject whatever. If it did, public forum analysis might be relevant. This case involves a claim of equal access to discuss a subject that the board has approved for discussion in the forum. In essence, the respondents are not asserting a right of access at all; they are asserting a right to be free from discrimination. The critical inquiry, therefore, is whether the board's grant of exclusive access to the petitioner amounts to prohibited viewpoint discrimination.

II

The Court addresses only briefly the respondents' claim that the exclusive access provision amounts to viewpoint discrimination. In rejecting this claim, the Court starts from the premise that the school mail system is not a public forum and that, as a result, the board has no obligation to grant access to the respondents. The Court then suggests that there is no indication that the board intended to discourage one viewpoint and to advance another. In the Court's view, the exclusive access policy is based on the status of the respective parties rather than on their views. The Court then states that "implicit in the concept of the nonpublic forum is the right to make distinctions in access on the basis of subject matter and speaker identity." According to the Court, "these distinctions may be impermissible in a public forum but are inherent and inescapable in the process of limiting a nonpublic forum to activities compatible with the intended purpose of the property."

As noted, whether the school mail system is a public forum or not the board is prohibited from discriminating among viewpoints on particular subjects. Moreover, whatever the right of public authorities to impose content-based restrictions on access to government property that is a nonpublic forum, once access is granted to one speaker to discuss a certain subject access may not be denied to another speaker based on his viewpoint. Regardless of the nature of the forum, the critical inquiry is whether the board has engaged in prohibited viewpoint discrimination.

The Court responds to the allegation of viewpoint discrimination by suggesting that there is no indication that the board intended to discriminate and that the exclusive access policy is based on the parties' status rather than on their views. In this case, for the reasons discussed below, the intent to discriminate can be inferred from the effect of the policy, which is to deny an effective channel of communication to the respondents, and from other facts in the case. In addition, the petitioner's status has nothing to do with whether viewpoint discrimination in fact has occurred. If anything, the petitioner's status is relevant to the question of whether the exclusive access policy can be justified, not to whether the board has discriminated among viewpoints.

Addressing the question of viewpoint discrimination directly, free of the Court's irrelevant public forum analysis, it is clear that the exclusive access policy discriminates on the basis of viewpoint. The Court of Appeals found that "the access policy adopted by the Perry schools, in form a speaker restriction, favors a particular viewpoint on labor relations in the Perry schools . . . the teachers inevitably will receive from [the petitioner] self-laudatory descriptions of its activities on their behalf and will be denied the critical perspective offered by [the respondents]." This assessment of the effect of the policy is eminently reasonable. Moreover, certain other factors strongly suggest that the policy discriminates among viewpoints.

On a practical level, the only reason for the petitioner to seek an exclusive access policy is to deny its rivals access to an effective channel of communication. No other group is explicitly denied access to the mail system. In fact, as the Court points out, many other groups have been granted access to the system. Apparently, access is denied to the respondents because of the likelihood of their expressing points of view different from the petitioner's on a range of subjects. The very argument the petitioner advances in support of the policy, the need to preserve labor peace, also indicates that the access policy is not viewpoint-neutral.

In short, the exclusive access policy discriminates against the respondents based on their viewpoint. The board has agreed to amplify the speech of the petitioner, while repressing the speech of the respondents based on the respondents' point of view. This sort of discrimination amounts to censorship and infringes the First Amendment rights of the respondents. In this light, the policy can survive only if the petitioner can justify it. . . .

[Justice Brennan's discussion of governmental justifications is omitted.—Editors]

Because the grant to the petitioner of exclusive access to the internal school mail system amounts to viewpoint discrimination that infringes the respondents' First Amendment rights and because the petitioner has failed to show that the policy furthers any substantial state interest, the policy must be invalidated as violative of the First Amendment . . .

NOTES

1.   Look carefully at footnote 7. Is it consistent with the three-part forum analysis set forth in the text? In the context of a designated public forum, must limitations based on subject matter satisfy strict scrutiny? What about limitations favoring one group over another? Does this footnote collapse designated forums into nonpublic forums?

Perhaps it would be helpful to use a different vocabulary for the third category— what the Court calls a "non-public forum." Would it be helpful to call this a "selective forum"—one in which the government allows private speech only insofar as that speech affirmatively advances the government's own purposes? A selective forum may be contrasted with a genuine public forum, in which private speakers are entitled to speak on subjects of their own choosing and for their own purposes. What should be the standard for evaluating limits on a genuine "designated public forum"? How would *Perry, Jones, Lehman,* and *Greer* come out under this analysis?

2.   Can you tell the difference between speaker-based discrimination and viewpoint-based discrimination? Are those overlapping or separate categories? Which is this?

Rosenberger v. Rector and Visitors of University of Virginia
515 U.S. 819 (1995)

■ JUSTICE KENNEDY delivered the opinion of the Court.

The University of Virginia, an instrumentality of the Commonwealth for which it is named and thus bound by the First and Fourteenth Amendments, authorizes the payment of outside contractors for the printing costs of a variety of student publications. It withheld any authorization for payments on behalf of petitioners for the sole reason that their student paper "primarily promotes or manifests a particular belie[f] in or about a deity or an ultimate reality." That the paper did promote or manifest views within the defined exclusion seems plain enough. The challenge is to the University's regulation and its denial of authorization, the case raising issues under the Speech and Establishment Clauses of the First Amendment.

I

The public corporation we refer to as the "University" is denominated by state law as "the Rector and Visitors of the University of Virginia," . . . Founded by Thomas Jefferson in 1819, and ranked by him, together with the authorship of the Declaration of Independence and of the Virginia Act for Religious Freedom, as one of his proudest achievements, the University is among the Nation's oldest and most respected seats of higher learning. It has more than 11,000 undergraduate students, and 6,000 graduate and professional students. An understanding of the case requires a somewhat detailed description of the program the University created to support extracurricular student activities on its campus.

Before a student group is eligible to submit bills from its outside contractors for payment by the fund described below, it must become a "Contracted Independent Organization" (CIO). CIO status is available to any group the majority of whose members are students, whose managing officers are fulltime students, and that complies with certain procedural requirements. A CIO must file its constitution with the University; must pledge not to discriminate in its membership; and must include in dealings with third parties and in all written materials a disclaimer, stating that the CIO is independent of the University and that the University is not responsible for the CIO. CIO's enjoy access to University facilities, including meeting rooms and computer terminals. A standard agreement signed between each CIO and the University provides that the benefits and opportunities afforded to CIO's "should not be misinterpreted as meaning that those organizations are part of or controlled by the University, that the University is responsible for the organizations' contracts or other acts or omissions, or that the University approves of the organizations' goals or activities."

All CIO's may exist and operate at the University, but some are also entitled to apply for funds from the Student Activities Fund (SAF). Established and governed by University Guidelines, the purpose of the SAF is to support a broad range of extracurricular student activities that "are related to the educational purpose of the University." The SAF is based on the University's "recogni[tion] that the availability of a wide range of opportunities" for its students "tends to enhance the University environment." The Guidelines require that it be administered "in a manner consistent with the educational purpose of the University as well as with state and federal law." The SAF receives its money from a mandatory fee of $14 per semester assessed to each full-time student. The Student Council, elected by the students, has the initial authority to disburse the funds, but its actions are subject to review by a faculty body chaired by a designee of the Vice President for Student Affairs.

Some, but not all, CIO's may submit disbursement requests to the SAF. The Guidelines recognize 11 categories of student groups that may seek payment to third-party contractors because they "are related to the educational purpose of the University of Virginia." One of these is "student news, information, opinion, entertainment, or academic communications media groups." The Guidelines also specify, however, that the costs of certain activities of CIO's that are otherwise eligible for funding will not be reimbursed by the SAF. The student activities that are excluded from SAF support are religious activities, philanthropic contributions and activities, political activities, activities that would jeopardize the University's tax-exempt status, those which involve payment of honoraria or similar fees, or social entertainment or related expenses. The prohibition on "political activities" is defined so that it is limited to electioneering and lobbying. The Guidelines provide that "[t]hese restrictions on funding political activities are not intended to preclude funding of any otherwise eligible student organization which . . . espouses particular positions or ideological viewpoints, including those that may be unpopular or are not generally accepted." A "religious activity," by contrast, is defined as any activity that "primarily promotes or manifests a particular belie[f] in or about a deity or an ultimate reality."

The Guidelines prescribe these criteria for determining the amounts of third-party disbursements that will be allowed on behalf of each eligible student organization: the size of the group, its financial self-sufficiency, and the University-wide benefit of its activities. If an organization seeks SAF support, it must submit its bills to the Student Council, which pays the organization's creditors upon determining that the expenses are appropriate. No direct payments are made to the student groups. During the 1990–1991 academic year, 343 student groups qualified as CIO's. One hundred thirty-five of them applied for support from the SAF, and 118 received funding. Fifteen of the groups were funded as "student news, information, opinion, entertainment, or academic communications media groups."

Petitioners' organization, Wide Awake Productions (WAP), qualified as a CIO. Formed by petitioner Ronald Rosenberger and other undergraduates in 1990, WAP was established "[t]o publish a magazine of philosophical and religious expression," "[t]o facilitate discussion which fosters an atmosphere of sensitivity to and tolerance of Christian viewpoints," and "[t]o provide a unifying focus for Christians of multicultural backgrounds." WAP publishes Wide Awake: A Christian Perspective at the University of Virginia. The paper's Christian viewpoint was evident from the first issue, in which its editors wrote that the journal "offers a Christian perspective on both personal and community issues, especially those relevant to college students at the University of Virginia." The editors committed the paper to a two-fold mission: "to challenge Christians to live, in word and deed, according to the faith they proclaim and to encourage students to consider what a personal relationship with Jesus Christ means." The first issue had articles about racism, crisis pregnancy, stress, prayer, C.S. Lewis' ideas about evil and free will, and reviews of religious music. In the next two issues, Wide Awake featured stories about homosexuality, Christian missionary work, and eating disorders, as well as music reviews and interviews with University professors. Each page of Wide Awake, and the end of each article or review, is marked by a cross. The advertisements carried in Wide Awake also reveal the Christian perspective of the journal. For the most part, the advertisers are churches, centers for Christian study, or Christian bookstores. By June 1992, WAP had distributed about 5,000 copies of Wide Awake to University students, free of charge.

WAP had acquired CIO status soon after it was organized. This is an important consideration in this case, for had it been a "religious organization," WAP would not have been accorded CIO status. As defined by the Guidelines, a "[r]eligious [o]rganization" is "an organization whose purpose is to practice a devotion to an acknowledged ultimate reality or deity." At no stage in this controversy has the University contended that WAP is such an organization.

A few months after being given CIO status, WAP requested the SAF to pay its printer $5,862 for the costs of printing its newspaper. The Appropriations Committee of the Student Council denied WAP's request on the ground that Wide Awake was a "religious activity" within the meaning of the Guidelines, *i.e.*, that the newspaper "promote[d] or manifest[ed] a particular belie[f] in or about a deity or an ultimate reality." It made its determination after examining the first issue. WAP appealed the denial to the full Student Council, contending that WAP met all the applicable Guidelines and that denial of SAF support on the basis of the magazine's religious perspective violated the Constitution. The appeal was denied without further comment, and WAP appealed to the next level, the Student Activities Committee. In a letter signed by the Dean of Students, the committee sustained the denial of funding.

Having no further recourse within the University structure, WAP, Wide Awake, and three of its editors and members filed suit in the United States District Court for the Western District of Virginia . . . They alleged that refusal to authorize payment of the printing costs of the publication, solely on the basis of its religious editorial viewpoint, violated their rights to freedom of speech and press, to the free exercise of religion, and to equal protection of the law. They relied also upon Article I of the Virginia Constitution and the Virginia Act for Religious Freedom, but did not pursue those theories on appeal. The suit sought damages for the costs of printing the paper, injunctive and declaratory relief, and attorney's fees.

On cross-motions for summary judgment, the District Court ruled for the University, holding that denial of SAF support was not an impermissible content or viewpoint discrimination against petitioners' speech, and that the University's Establishment Clause concern over its "religious activities" was a sufficient justification for denying payment to third-party contractors . . .

[T]he Fourth Circuit . . . held that the Guidelines did discriminate on the basis of content. It ruled that, while the State need not underwrite speech, there was a presumptive violation of the Speech Clause when viewpoint discrimination was invoked to deny third-party payment otherwise available to CIO's . . . *[Nevertheless, the court of appeals affirmed on Establishment Clause grounds.—Editors]*

II

It is axiomatic that the government may not regulate speech based on its substantive content or the message it conveys. Other principles follow from this precept. In the realm of private speech or expression, government regulation may not favor one speaker over another. Discrimination against speech because of its message is presumed to be unconstitutional. These rules informed our determination that the government offends the First Amendment when it imposes financial burdens on certain speakers based on the content of their expression. When the government targets not subject matter, but particular views taken by speakers on a subject, the violation of the First Amendment is all the more blatant. Viewpoint discrimination is thus an egregious form of content discrimination. The government must abstain from regulating speech when the specific motivating ideology or the opinion or perspective of the speaker is the rationale for the restriction.

These principles provide the framework forbidding the State to exercise viewpoint discrimination, even when the limited public forum is one of its own creation. In a case involving a school district's provision of school facilities for private uses, we declared that "[t]here is no question that the District, like the private owner of property, may legally preserve the property under its control for the use to which it is dedicated." *Lamb's Chapel v. Center Moriches Union Free School Dist.*, 508 U.S. 384, 390 (1993). The necessities of confining a forum to the limited and legitimate purposes for which it was created may justify the State in reserving it for certain groups or for the discussion of certain topics. Once it has opened a limited forum, however, the State must respect the lawful boundaries it has itself set. The State may not exclude speech where its distinction is not "reasonable in light of the purpose served by the forum," nor may it discriminate against speech on the basis of its viewpoint. Thus, in determining whether the State is acting to preserve the limits of the forum it has created so that the exclusion of a class of speech is legitimate, we have observed a distinction between, on the one hand, content discrimination, which may be permissible if it preserves the purposes of that limited forum, and, on the other hand, viewpoint discrimination, which is presumed impermissible when directed against speech otherwise within the forum's limitations.

The SAF is a forum more in a metaphysical than in a spatial or geographic sense, but the same principles are applicable. The most recent and most apposite case is our decision in *Lamb's Chapel*. There, a school district had opened school facilities for use after school hours by community groups for a wide variety of social, civic, and recreational purposes. The district, however, had enacted a formal policy against opening facilities to groups for religious purposes. Invoking its policy, the district rejected a request from a group desiring to show a film series addressing various child-rearing questions from a "Christian perspective." There was no indication in the record in *Lamb's Chapel* that the request to use the school facilities was "denied, for any reason other than the fact that the presentation would have been from a religious perspective." Our conclusion was unanimous: "[I]t discriminates on the basis of viewpoint to permit school property to be used for the presentation of all views about family issues and childrearing except those dealing with the subject matter from a religious standpoint."

The University does acknowledge (as it must in light of our precedents) that "ideologically driven attempts to suppress a particular point of view are presumptively unconstitutional in funding, as in other contexts," but insists that this case does not present that issue because the Guidelines draw lines based on content, not viewpoint. As we have noted, discrimination against one set of views or ideas is but a subset or particular instance of the more general phenomenon of content discrimination. And, it must be acknowledged, the distinction is not a precise one. It is, in a sense, something of an understatement to speak of religious thought and discussion as just a viewpoint, as distinct from a comprehensive body of thought. The nature of our origins and destiny and their dependence upon the existence of a divine being have been subjects of philosophic inquiry throughout human history. We conclude, nonetheless, that here, as in *Lamb's Chapel,* viewpoint discrimination is the proper way to interpret the University's objections to Wide Awake. By the very terms of the SAF prohibition, the University does not exclude religion as a subject matter but selects for disfavored treatment those student journalistic efforts with religious editorial viewpoints. Religion may be a vast area of inquiry, but it also provides, as it did here, a specific premise, a perspective, a standpoint from which a variety of subjects may be discussed and considered. The prohibited perspective, not the general subject matter, resulted in the refusal to make third-party payments, for the subjects discussed were otherwise within the approved category of publications.

The dissent's assertion that no viewpoint discrimination occurs because the Guidelines discriminate against an entire class of viewpoints reflects an insupportable assumption that all debate is bipolar and that antireligious speech is the only response to religious speech. Our understanding of the complex and multifaceted nature of public discourse has not embraced such a contrived description of the marketplace of ideas. If the topic of debate is, for example, racism, then exclusion of several views on that problem is just as offensive to the First Amendment as exclusion of only one. It is as objectionable to exclude both a theistic and an atheistic perspective on the debate as it is to exclude one, the other, or yet another political, economic, or social viewpoint. The dissent's declaration that debate is not skewed so long as multiple voices are silenced is simply wrong; the debate is skewed in multiple ways.

The University's denial of WAP's request for third-party payments in the present case is based upon viewpoint discrimination not unlike the discrimination the school district relied upon in *Lamb's Chapel* and that we found invalid. The church group in *Lamb's Chapel* would have been qualified as a social or civic organization, save for its religious purposes. Furthermore, just as the school district in *Lamb's Chapel* pointed to nothing but the religious views of the group as the rationale for excluding its message, so in this case the University justifies its denial of SAF participation to WAP on the ground that the contents of Wide Awake reveal an avowed religious perspective. It bears only passing mention that the dissent's attempt to distinguish *Lamb's Chapel* is entirely without support in the law. Relying on the transcript of oral argument, the dissent seems to argue that we found viewpoint discrimination in that case because the government excluded Christian, but not atheistic, viewpoints from being expressed in the forum there. The Court relied on no such distinction in holding that discriminating against religious speech was discriminating on the basis of viewpoint. There is no indication in the opinion of the Court (which, unlike an advocate's statements at oral argument, is the law) that exclusion or inclusion of other religious or antireligious voices from that forum had any bearing on its decision.

The University tries to escape the consequences of our holding in *Lamb's Chapel* by urging that this case involves the provision of funds rather than access to facilities. The University begins with the unremarkable proposition that the State must have substantial discretion in determining how to allocate scarce resources to accomplish its educational mission. Citing our decisions in *Rust v. Sullivan*, 500 U.S. 173 (1991), *Regan v. Taxation with Representation of Wash.*, 461 U.S. 540 (1983), and *Widmar v. Vincent*, 454 U.S. 263 (1981), the University argues that content-based funding decisions are both inevitable and lawful. Were the reasoning of *Lamb's Chapel* to apply to funding decisions as well as to those involving access to facilities, it is urged, its holding "would become a judicial juggernaut, constitutionalizing the ubiquitous content-based decisions that schools, colleges, and other government entities routinely make in the allocation of public funds."

To this end the University relies on our assurance in *Widmar v. Vincent*. There, in the course of striking down a public university's exclusion of religious groups from use of school facilities made available to all other student groups, we stated: "Nor do we question the right of the University to make academic judgments as to how best to allocate scarce resources." The quoted language in *Widmar* was but a proper recognition of the principle that when the State is the speaker, it may make content-based choices. When the University determines the content of the education it provides, it is the University speaking, and we have permitted the government to regulate the content of what is or is not expressed when it is the speaker or when it enlists private entities to convey its own message. In the same vein, in *Rust v. Sullivan*, we upheld the government's prohibition on abortion-related advice applicable to recipients of federal funds for family planning counseling. There, the government did not create a program to encourage private speech but instead used private speakers to transmit specific information pertaining to its own program. We recognized that when the government appropriates public funds to promote a particular policy of its own it is entitled to say what it wishes. When the government disburses public funds to private entities to convey a governmental message, it may take legitimate and appropriate steps to ensure that its message is neither garbled nor distorted by the grantee.

It does not follow, however, and we did not suggest in *Widmar,* that viewpoint-based restrictions are proper when the University does not itself speak or subsidize transmittal of a message it favors but instead expends funds to encourage a diversity of views from private speakers. A holding that the University may not discriminate based on the viewpoint of private persons whose speech it facilitates does not restrict the University's own speech, which is controlled by different principles. For that reason, the University's reliance on *Regan v. Taxation with Representation of Wash.* is inapposite as well. *Regan* involved a challenge to Congress' choice to grant tax deductions for contributions made to veterans' groups engaged in lobbying, while denying that favorable status to other charities which pursued lobbying efforts. Although acknowledging that the Government is not required to subsidize the exercise of fundamental rights, we reaffirmed the requirement of viewpoint neutrality in the Government's provision of financial benefits by observing that "[t]he case would be different if Congress were to discriminate invidiously in its subsidies in such a way as to 'ai[m] at the suppression of dangerous ideas,' " *Regan* relied on a distinction based on preferential treatment of certain speakers—veterans' organizations—and not a distinction based on the content or messages of those groups' speech. The University's regulation now before us, however, has a speech-based restriction as its sole rationale and operative principle.

The distinction between the University's own favored message and the private speech of students is evident in the case before us. The University itself has taken steps to ensure the distinction in the agreement each CIO must sign. The University declares that the student groups eligible for SAF support are not the University's agents, are not subject to its control, and are not its responsibility. Having offered to pay the third-party contractors on behalf of private speakers who convey their own messages, the University may not silence the expression of selected viewpoints.

The University urges that, from a constitutional standpoint, funding of speech differs from provision of access to facilities because money is scarce and physical facilities are not. Beyond the fact that in any given case this proposition might not be true as an empirical matter, the underlying premise that the University could discriminate based on viewpoint if demand for space exceeded its availability is wrong as well. The government cannot justify viewpoint discrimination among private speakers on the economic fact of scarcity. Had the meeting rooms in *Lamb's Chapel* been scarce, had the demand been greater than the supply, our decision would have been no different. It would have been incumbent on the State, of course, to ration or allocate the scarce resources on some acceptable neutral principle; but nothing in our decision indicated that scarcity would give the State the right to exercise viewpoint discrimination that is otherwise impermissible.

Vital First Amendment speech principles are at stake here. The first danger to liberty lies in granting the State the power to examine publications to determine whether or not they are based on some ultimate idea and, if so, for the State to classify them. The second, and corollary, danger is to speech from the chilling of individual thought and expression. That danger is especially real in the University setting, where the State acts against a background and tradition of thought and experiment that is at the center of our intellectual and philosophic tradition. In ancient Athens, and, as Europe entered into a new period of intellectual awakening, in places like Bologna, Oxford, and Paris, universities began as voluntary and spontaneous assemblages or concourses for students to speak and to write and to learn. The quality and creative power of student intellectual life to this day remains a vital measure of a school's influence and attainment. For the University, by regulation, to cast disapproval on particular viewpoints of its students risks the suppression of free speech and creative inquiry in one of the vital centers for the Nation's intellectual life, its college and university campuses.

The Guideline invoked by the University to deny third-party contractor payments on behalf of WAP effects a sweeping restriction on student thought and student inquiry in the context of University sponsored publications. The prohibition on funding on behalf of publications that "primarily promot[e] or manifes[t] a particular belie[f] in or about a deity or an ultimate reality," in its ordinary and commonsense meaning, has a vast potential reach. The term "promotes" as used here would comprehend any writing advocating a philosophic position that rests upon a belief in a deity or ultimate reality. See Webster's Third New International

Dictionary 1815 (1961) (defining "promote" as "to contribute to the growth, enlargement, or prosperity of: further, encourage"). And the term "manifests" would bring within the scope of the prohibition any writing that is explicable as resting upon a premise that presupposes the existence of a deity or ultimate reality. See *id.,* at 1375 (defining "manifest" as "to show plainly: make palpably evident or certain by showing or displaying"). Were the prohibition applied with much vigor at all, it would bar funding of essays by hypothetical student contributors named Plato, Spinoza, and Descartes. And if the regulation covers, as the University says it does, those student journalistic efforts that primarily manifest or promote a belief that there is no deity and no ultimate reality, then under-graduates named Karl Marx, Bertrand Russell, and Jean-Paul Sartre would likewise have some of their major essays excluded from student publications. If any manifestation of beliefs in first principles disqualifies the writing, as seems to be the case, it is indeed difficult to name renowned thinkers whose writings would be accepted, save perhaps for articles disclaiming all connection to their ultimate philosophy. Plato could contrive perhaps to submit an acceptable essay on making pasta or peanut butter cookies, provided he did not point out their (necessary) imperfections.

Based on the principles we have discussed, we hold that the regulation invoked to deny SAF support, both in its terms and in its application to these petitioners, is a denial of their right of free speech guaranteed by the First Amendment . . . *[The Court then concluded that the Establishment Clause did not justify the university's viewpoint discrimination.—Editors]*

■ [The concurring opinions of JUSTICES O'CONNOR and THOMAS, and the dissenting opinion of JUSTICE SOUTER, which was joined by JUSTICES STEVENS, GINSBURG, and BREYER, are omitted.]

NOTES

1.   Are you persuaded that the same principles should apply to what the Court calls a "metaphysical forum"—meaning cash subsidies—as apply to the use of public real estate? Why or why not?

2.   Do you agree that exclusion of "religious activities" is viewpoint-discriminatory? The dissenters essentially argue that a restriction is not viewpoint-discriminatory unless it discriminates *among* religions. So long as Christians, Jews, Buddhists, atheists, and Zoroastrians all are excluded, the dissenters say, there is no problem. Would they take the same position if all religious perspectives were equally *favored*?

3.   The majority seems to rely on several details about the University's program: (1) that the funds are paid to the printer rather than to the student group; (2) that the funds come from mandatory student fees rather than from taxes; and (3) that the group was excluded as a religious "activity" rather than as a religious "organization." Do these details matter? Why?

4.   The case involved not just free speech questions but also whether funding *Wide Awake* would violate the Establishment Clause. See p. 1169.

[*Assignment 51*]

K. PROTESTS AND DEMONSTRATIONS

Apart from freedom of speech, the Constitution guarantees the "right of the people peaceably to assemble, and to petition for the redress of grievances." The protection of these rights by a separate clause seems to recognize the special temptations for government control of this potent method of dissent. Yet the Court's modern cases pay little attention to the Assembly Clause, instead applying (and sometimes modifying) ordinary principles of free speech and press. Recall that in the debate in the First Congress, Representative Sedgwick moved to strike the Assembly Clause, saying that it was unnecessary in light of freedom of speech, but his motion was rejected by a large margin. Has the modern Court, in effect, done what the First Congress declined to do? In the cases that follow, think about whether and why mass public assemblies need special constitutional rules.

Thomas v. Chicago Park District

534 U.S. 316 (2002)

■ SCALIA, J., delivered the opinion for a unanimous Court.

This case presents the question whether a municipal park ordinance requiring individuals to obtain a permit before conducting large-scale events must, consistent with the First Amendment, contain the procedural safeguards described in *Freedman v. Maryland,* 380 U.S. 51 (1965).

I

Respondent, the Chicago Park District (Park District), is responsible for operating public parks and other public property in Chicago. Pursuant to its authority to "establish by ordinance all needful rules and regulations for the government and protection of parks . . . and other property under its jurisdiction," the Park District adopted an ordinance that requires a person to obtain a permit in order to "conduct a public assembly, parade, picnic, or other event involving more than fifty individuals," or engage in an activity such as "creat[ing] or emit[ting] any Amplified Sound." Chicago Park Dist. Code, ch. VII, §§ C.3.a(1), C.3.a(6). The ordinance provides that "[a]pplications for permits shall be processed in order of receipt," § C.5.a, and the Park District must decide whether to grant or deny an application within 14 days unless, by written notice to the applicant, it extends the period an additional 14 days, § C.5.c. Applications can be denied on any of 13 specified grounds. § C.5.e.[1] If the Park District denies an application, it must clearly

---

[1]   Section C.5.e of the ordinance provides in relevant part:

"To the extent permitted by law, the Park District may deny an application for permit if the applicant or the person on whose behalf the application for permit was made has on prior occasions made material misrepresentations regarding the nature or scope of an event or activity previously permitted or has violated the terms of prior permits issued to or on behalf of the applicant. The Park District may also deny an application for permit on any of the following grounds:

(1) the application for permit (including any required attachments and submissions) is not fully completed and executed;

(2) the applicant has not tendered the required application fee with the application or has not tendered the required user fee, indemnification agreement, insurance certificate, or security deposit within the times prescribed by the General Superintendent;

set forth in writing the grounds for denial and, where feasible, must propose measures to cure defects in the application. When the basis for denial is prior receipt of a competing application for the same time and place, the Park District must suggest alternative times or places. An unsuccessful applicant has seven days to file a written appeal to the General Superintendent of the Park District, who must act on the appeal within seven days. If the General Superintendent affirms a permit denial, the applicant may seek judicial review in state court by common-law certiorari.

Petitioners have applied to the Park District on several occasions for permits to hold rallies advocating the legalization of marijuana. The Park District has granted some permits and denied others. Not satisfied, petitioners filed an action pursuant to 42 U.S.C. § 1983 in the United States District Court for the Northern District of Illinois, alleging, *inter alia,* that the Park District's ordinance is unconstitutional on its face. The District Court granted summary judgment in favor of the Park District, and the United States Court of Appeals for the Seventh Circuit affirmed. We granted certiorari.

II

The First Amendment's guarantee of "the freedom of speech, or of the press" prohibits a wide assortment of government restraints upon expression, but the core abuse against which it was directed was the scheme of licensing laws implemented by the monarch and Parliament to contain the "evils" of the printing press in 16th- and 17-century England. The Printing Act of 1662 had "prescribed what could be printed, who could print, and who could sell." It punished the publication of any book or pamphlet without a license and required that all works be submitted for approval to a government official, who wielded broad authority to suppress works that he found to be "heretical, seditious, schismatical, or offensive." The English licensing system expired at the end of the 17th century, but the memory of its abuses was still vivid enough in colonial times that Blackstone warned against the "restrictive power" of such a "licenser"—an administrative official who enjoyed unconfined authority to

---

(3) the application for permit contains a material falsehood or misrepresentation;

(4) the applicant is legally incompetent to contract or to sue and be sued;

(5) the applicant or the person on whose behalf the application for permit was made has on prior occasions damaged Park District property and has not paid in full for such damage, or has other outstanding and unpaid debts to the Park District;

(6) a fully executed prior application for permit for the same time and place has been received, and a permit has been or will be granted to a prior applicant authorizing uses or activities which do not reasonably permit multiple occupancy of the particular park or part hereof;

(7) the use or activity intended by the applicant would conflict with previously planned programs organized and conducted by the Park District and previously scheduled for the same time and place;

(8) the proposed use or activity is prohibited by or inconsistent with the classifications and uses of the park or part thereof designated pursuant to this chapter;

(9) the use or activity intended by the applicant would present an unreasonable danger to the health or safety of the applicant, or other users of the park, of Park District Employees or of the public;

(10) the applicant has not complied or cannot comply with applicable licensure requirements, ordinances or regulations of the Park District concerning the sale or offering for sale of any goods or services;

(11) the use or activity intended by the applicant is prohibited by law, by this Code and ordinances of the Park District, or by the regulations of the General Superintendent. . . ."

pass judgment on the content of speech. 4 W. Blackstone, Commentaries on the Laws of England 152 (1769).

In *Freedman*, we confronted a state law that enacted a strikingly similar system of prior restraint for motion pictures. It required that every motion picture film be submitted to a Board of Censors before the film was shown anywhere in the State. The board enjoyed authority to reject films that it considered "obscene" or that "tend[ed], in the judgment of the Board, to debase or corrupt morals or incite to crimes," characteristics defined by the statute in broad terms. The statute punished the exhibition of a film not submitted to the board for advance approval, even where the film would have received a license had it been properly submitted. It was no defense that the content of the film was protected by the First Amendment.

We recognized in *Freedman* that a scheme conditioning expression on a licensing body's prior approval of content "presents peculiar dangers to constitutionally protected speech." "[T]he censor's business is to censor," and a licensing body likely will overestimate the dangers of controversial speech when determining, without regard to the film's actual effect on an audience, whether speech is likely "to incite" or to "corrupt [the] morals." In response to these grave "dangers of a censorship system," we held that a film licensing process must contain certain procedural safeguards in order to avoid constituting an invalid prior restraint: "(1) any restraint prior to judicial review can be imposed only for a specified brief period during which the status quo must be maintained; (2) expeditious judicial review of that decision must be available; and (3) the censor must bear the burden of going to court to suppress the speech and must bear the burden of proof once in court."

Petitioners contend that the Park District, like the Board of Censors in *Freedman,* must initiate litigation every time it denies a permit and that the ordinance must specify a deadline for judicial review of a challenge to a permit denial. We reject those contentions. *Freedman* is inapposite because the licensing scheme at issue here is not subject-matter censorship but content-neutral time, place, and manner regulation of the use of a public forum. The Park District's ordinance does not authorize a licensor to pass judgment on the content of speech: None of the grounds for denying a permit has anything to do with what a speaker might say. Indeed, the ordinance (unlike the classic censorship scheme) is not even directed to communicative activity as such, but rather to *all* activity conducted in a public park. The picnicker and soccer player, no less than the political activist or parade marshal, must apply for a permit if the 50-person limit is to be exceeded. And the object of the permit system (as plainly indicated by the permissible grounds for permit denial) is not to exclude communication of a particular content, but to coordinate multiple uses of limited space, to assure preservation of the park facilities, to prevent uses that are dangerous, unlawful, or impermissible under the Park District's rules, and to assure financial accountability for damage caused by the event. As the Court of Appeals well put it: "[T]o allow unregulated access to all comers could easily reduce rather than enlarge the park's utility as a forum for speech."

We have never required that a content-neutral permit scheme regulating speech in a public forum adhere to the procedural requirements set forth in *Freedman.*[2] "A licensing standard which gives an official authority to censor the content of a speech differs *toto coelo* from one limited by its terms, or by nondiscriminatory practice, to considerations of public safety and the like." *Niemotko v. Maryland,* 340 U.S. 268, 282 (1951) (Frankfurter, J., concurring in result). . . . Regulations of the use of a public forum that ensure the safety and convenience of the people are not "inconsistent with civil liberties but . . . [are] one of the means of safeguarding the good order upon which [civil liberties] ultimately depend." *Cox v. New Hampshire,* 312 U.S. 569, 574 (1941). Such a traditional exercise of authority does not raise the censorship concerns that prompted us to impose the extraordinary procedural safeguards on the film licensing process in *Freedman.*

III

Of course even content-neutral time, place, and manner restrictions can be applied in such a manner as to stifle free expression. Where the licensing official enjoys unduly broad discretion in determining whether to grant or deny a permit, there is a risk that he will favor or disfavor speech based on its content. We have thus required that a time, place, and manner regulation contain adequate standards to guide the official's decision and render it subject to effective judicial review. Petitioners contend that the Park District's ordinance fails this test.

We think not. As we have described, the Park District may deny a permit only for one or more of the reasons set forth in the ordinance. It may deny, for example, when the application is incomplete or contains a material falsehood or misrepresentation; when the applicant has damaged Park District property on prior occasions and has not paid for the damage; when a permit has been granted to an earlier applicant for the same time and place; when the intended use would present an unreasonable danger to the health or safety of park users or Park District employees; or when the applicant has violated the terms of a prior permit. Moreover, the Park District must process applications within 28 days, and must clearly explain its reasons for any denial. These grounds are reasonably specific and objective, and do not leave the decision "to the whim of the administrator." *Forsyth County v. Nationalist Movement,* 505 U.S. 123, 133 (1992). They provide "narrowly drawn, reasonable and definite standards" to guide the licensor's determination. And they are enforceable on review—first by appeal to the General Superintendent of the Park District, and then by writ of common-law certiorari in the Illinois courts, which provides essentially the same type of review as that provided by the Illinois administrative procedure act.

Petitioners contend that the criteria set forth in the ordinance are insufficiently precise because they are described as grounds on which the Park District "may" deny a permit, rather than grounds on which it *must* do so. This, they contend, allows the Park District to waive the permit requirements for some favored speakers, while insisting upon them for others. That is certainly not the intent of the ordinance, which the Park District has reasonably interpreted to permit overlooking only those inadequacies that, under the circumstances, do no harm to the policies furthered by the application requirements. Granting waivers to favored speakers (or, more

---

[2]   *FW/PBS, Inc. v. Dallas,* 493 U.S. 215, 224 (1990), which applied two of the *Freedman* requirements, involved a licensing scheme that "target[ed] businesses purveying sexually explicit speech."

precisely, denying them to disfavored speakers) would of course be unconstitutional, but we think that this abuse must be dealt with if and when a pattern of unlawful favoritism appears, rather than by insisting upon a degree of rigidity that is found in few legal arrangements. On petitioners' theory, every obscenity law, or every law placing limits upon political expenditures, contains a constitutional flaw, since it merely permits, but does not require, prosecution. The prophylaxis achieved by insisting upon a rigid, no-waiver application of the ordinance requirements would be far outweighed, we think, by the accompanying senseless prohibition of speech (and of other activity in the park) by organizations that fail to meet the technical requirements of the ordinance but for one reason or another pose no risk of the evils that those requirements are designed to avoid. On balance, we think the permissive nature of the ordinance furthers, rather than constricts, free speech. . . .

NOTES

1.   Is there a good reason why the requirement of obtaining advance permission is (almost always) impermissible for publications, but permissible for mass meetings in public parks, streets, or sidewalks? What about movies? Was *Freedman v. Maryland* rightly decided? Is showing a film more like an assembly (a gathering of people in a public place) or more like the press (dissemination of a message to the general public)? What was the purpose of the regulatory scheme in *Thomas*? What was the purpose in *Freedman*? The constitutional rules set forth in *Thomas* are similar to content-neutral "time, place, and manner regulations" in substance—especially in their requirement of content-neutrality—but are different in their procedure. Most time, place, and manner regulations are enforced after the fact, not by prior restraint. Is Assembly any different?

2.   Can the government require groups to pay the costs generated by mass events on public property? In *Forsyth County v. The Nationalist Movement*, 505 U.S. 123 (1992), the Court held that the government may not charge such fees if the amount is left to the unbridled discretion of city officials, for fear that groups with different messages might not be treated equally. More interesting is another holding in the case: groups may not be assessed the actual cost of additional police protection needed to maintain public order, where that amount may be affected by the controversial nature of their message and the prospect of counterdemonstrators who threaten public order. The case involved a proposed demonstration by a far-right racist group, to which tens of thousands of civil rights demonstrators planned to respond. In one prior incident involving this group, the police presence needed to maintain the peace between these antagonists cost $670,000.

In 2011, various Tea Party groups complained that they had paid thousands of dollars in fees to city governments for the costs of their rallies, while similar laws were not enforced against the Occupy Movement. See, e.g., Wesley Hester, *Tea party say city favoring occupiers*, Richmond Time-Dispatch, A1 (Oct. 27, 2011). Once the government fails to enforce the law against one group, is it stopped from enforcing that law against anyone else? What is the proper remedy: to give the Tea Party group its money back, or to require the city to assess Occupy the costs they incurred? What if Occupy is too amorphous to pay? Some Tea Partiers pointed to statements by city council members expressing sympathy or support for the Occupiers' objectives (even if not their methods). If true, would that indicate favoritism was in the works? How can favoritism in the exercise of law enforcement discretion be controlled?

3.   In a pair of cases in the late 1960s, the Court held that protestors prosecuted for violating an *ordinance* restricting street demonstrations may defend themselves by arguing that it is unconstitutional, *Shuttlesworth v. City of Birmingham*, 394 U.S. 147

(1969); but protestors prosecuted for contempt after violating an *injunction* restricting their demonstration may not challenge the injunction's constitutionality. *Walker v. City of Birmingham*, 388 U.S. 307 (1967). Can you understand the logic? Do you agree with it?

Clark v. Community for Creative Non-Violence
468 U.S. 288 (1984)

■ JUSTICE WHITE delivered the opinion of the Court.

The issue in this case is whether a National Park Service regulation prohibiting camping in certain parks violates the First Amendment when applied to prohibit demonstrators from sleeping in Lafayette Park and the Mall in connection with a demonstration intended to call attention to the plight of the homeless. We hold that it does not and reverse the contrary judgment of the Court of Appeals.

I

The Interior Department, through the National Park Service, is charged with responsibility for the management and maintenance of the National Parks and is authorized to promulgate rules and regulations for the use of the parks in accordance with the purposes for which they were established. The network of National parks includes the National Memorial-core parks, Lafayette Park and the Mall, which are set in the heart of Washington, D.C., and which are unique resources that the Federal Government holds in trust for the American people. Lafayette Park is a roughly 7-acre square located across Pennsylvania Avenue from the White House. . . .

Under the regulations involved in this case, camping in National Parks is permitted only in campgrounds designated for that purpose. 36 CFR § 50.27(a) (1983). No such campgrounds have ever been designated in Lafayette Park or the Mall. Camping is defined as

> the use of park land for living accommodation purposes such as sleeping activities, or making preparations to sleep (including the laying down of bedding for the purpose of sleeping), or storing personal belongings, or making any fire, or using any tents or . . . other structure . . . for sleeping or doing any digging or earth breaking or carrying on cooking activities.

These activities, the regulation provides,

> constitute camping when it reasonably appears, in light of all the circumstances, that the participants, in conducting these activities, are in fact using the area as a living accommodation regardless of the intent of the participants or the nature of any other activities in which they may also be engaging.

Demonstrations for the airing of views or grievances are permitted in [Lafayette Park and the Mall], but for the most part only by Park Service permits. 36 CFR § 50.19 (1983). Temporary structures may be erected for demonstration purposes but may not be used for camping. 36 CFR § 50.19(e)(8) (1983).

In 1982, the Park Service issued a renewable permit to respondent Community for Creative Non-Violence (CCNV) to conduct a wintertime demonstration in Lafayette Park and the Mall for the purpose of demonstrating the plight of the homeless. The permit authorized the erection of two symbolic tent cities: 20 tents in Lafayette Park that would accommodate 50 people and 40 tents in the Mall with a capacity of up to 100. The Park Service, however, relying on the above regulations, specifically denied CCNV's request that demonstrators be permitted to sleep in the symbolic tents.

CCNV and several individuals then filed an action to prevent the application of the no-camping regulations to the proposed demonstration, which, it was claimed, was not covered by the regulation. It was also submitted that the regulations were unconstitutionally vague, had been discriminatorily applied, and could not be applied to prevent sleeping in the tents without violating the First Amendment. The District Court granted summary judgment in favor of the Park Service. The Court of Appeals, sitting en banc, reversed. *Community for Creative Non-Violence v. Watt,* 703 F.2d 586 (D.C. Cir. 1983). . . . [A 6–5 majority held] that application of the regulations so as to prevent sleeping in the tents would infringe the demonstrators' First Amendment right of free expression. . . . We granted the Government's petition for certiorari, and now reverse.

II

We need not differ with the view of the Court of Appeals that overnight sleeping in connection with the demonstration is expressive conduct protected to some extent by the First Amendment. We assume for present purposes, but do not decide, that such is the case, *cf. United States v. O'Brien,* 391 U.S. 367 (1968), but this assumption only begins the inquiry. Expression, whether oral or written or symbolized by conduct, is subject to reasonable time, place, or manner restrictions. We have often noted that restrictions of this kind are valid provided that they are justified without reference to the content of the regulated speech, that they are narrowly tailored to serve a significant governmental interest, and that they leave open ample alternative channels for communication of the information.

It is also true that a message may be delivered by conduct that is intended to be communicative and that, in context, would reasonably be understood by the viewer to be communicative. *Spence v. Washington,* 418 U.S. 405 (1974); *Tinker v. Des Moines School District,* 393 U.S. 503 (1969). Symbolic expression of this kind may be forbidden or regulated if the conduct itself may constitutionally be regulated, if the regulation is narrowly drawn to further a substantial governmental interest, and if the interest is unrelated to the suppression of free speech. *United States v. O'Brien.*

Petitioners submit . . . that the regulation forbidding sleeping is defensible either as a time, place, or manner restriction or as a regulation of symbolic conduct. We agree with that assessment. The permit that was issued authorized the demonstration but required compliance with 36 CFR § 50.19 (1913), which prohibits "camping" on park lands, that is, the use of park lands for living accommodations, such as sleeping, storing personal belongings, making fires, digging, or cooking. These provisions, including the ban on sleeping, are clearly limitations on the manner in which the demonstration could be carried out. That sleeping, like the symbolic tents themselves, may be expressive and part of the message delivered by the demonstration does not make the ban any less a limitation on the manner of demonstrating, for reasonable time, place, or manner regulations normally have the purpose and direct effect of limiting expression but are nevertheless valid. Neither does the fact that sleeping, *arguendo,* may be expressive conduct, rather than oral or written expression, render the sleeping prohibition any less a time, place, or manner regulation. To the contrary, the Park Service neither attempts to ban sleeping generally nor to ban it everywhere in the parks. It has established areas for camping and forbids it elsewhere, including Lafayette Park and the Mall. Considered as such, we have very little trouble concluding that the Park Service may prohibit overnight sleeping in the parks involved here.

The requirement that the regulation be content-neutral is clearly satisfied. The courts below accepted that view, and it is not disputed here that the prohibition on camping, and on sleeping specifically, is content-neutral and is not being applied because of disagreement with the message presented. Neither was the regulation faulted, nor could it be, on the ground that without overnight sleeping the plight of the homeless could not be communicated in other ways. The regulation otherwise left the demonstration intact, with its symbolic city, signs, and the presence of those who were willing to take their turns in a day-and-night vigil. Respondents do not suggest that there was, or is, any barrier to delivering to the media, or to the public by other means, the intended message concerning the plight of the homeless.

It is also apparent to us that the regulation narrowly focuses on the Government's substantial interest in maintaining the parks in the heart of our Capital in an attractive and intact condition, readily available to the millions of people who wish to see and enjoy them by their presence. To permit camping—using these areas as living accommodations—would be totally inimical to these purposes, as would be readily understood by those who have frequented the National Parks across the country and observed the unfortunate consequences of the activities of those who refuse to confine their camping to designated areas.

It is urged by respondents, and the Court of Appeals was of this view, that if the symbolic city of tents was to be permitted and if the demonstrators did not intend to cook, dig, or engage in aspects of camping other than sleeping, the incremental benefit to the parks could not justify the ban on sleeping, which was here an expressive activity said to enhance the message concerning the plight of the poor and homeless. We cannot agree. In the first place, we seriously doubt that the First Amendment requires the Park Service to permit a demonstration in Lafayette Park and the Mall involving a 24-hour vigil and the erection of tents to accommodate 150 people. Furthermore, although we have assumed for present purposes that the sleeping banned in this case would have an expressive element, it is evident that its major value to this demonstration would be facilitative. Without a permit to sleep, it would be difficult to get the poor and homeless to participate or to be present at all. This much is apparent from the permit application filed by respondents: "Without the incentive of sleeping space or a hot meal, the homeless would not come to the site." The sleeping ban, if enforced, would thus effectively limit the nature, extent, and duration of the demonstration and to that extent ease the pressure on the parks.

Beyond this, however, it is evident from our cases that the validity of this regulation need not be judged solely by reference to the demonstration at hand. *Heffron v. International Society for Krishna Consciousness, Inc.*, 452 U.S. 640, 652–653 (1981). Absent the prohibition on sleeping, there would be other groups who would demand permission to deliver an asserted message by camping in Lafayette Park. Some of them would surely have as credible a claim in this regard as does CCNV, and the denial of permits to still others would present difficult problems for the Park Service. With the prohibition, however, as is evident in the case before us, at least some around-the-clock demonstrations lasting for days on end will not materialize, others will be limited in size and duration, and the purposes of the regulation will thus be materially served. Perhaps these purposes would be more effectively and not so clumsily achieved by preventing tents and 24-hour vigils entirely in [Lafayette Park or the Mall]. But the Park Service's decision to permit nonsleeping demonstrations does not, in our view, impugn the camping prohibition as a valuable, but perhaps imperfect, protection to the parks. If the Government has a legitimate interest in ensuring that the National Parks are adequately protected, which we think it has, and if the parks would be more exposed to harm without the sleeping prohibition than with it, the ban is safe from invalidation under the First Amendment as a reasonable regulation of the manner in which a demonstration may be carried out. . . .

We have difficulty, therefore, in understanding why the prohibition against camping, with its ban on sleeping overnight, is not a reasonable time, place, or manner regulation that withstands constitutional scrutiny. Surely the regulation is not unconstitutional on its face. None of its provisions appears unrelated to the ends that it was designed to serve. Nor is it any less valid when applied to prevent camping in [Lafayette Park and the Mall] by those who wish to demonstrate and deliver a message to the public and the central Government. Damage to the parks as well as their partial inaccessibility to other members of the public can as easily result from camping by demonstrators as by nondemonstrators. In neither case must the Government tolerate it. All those who would resort to the parks must abide by otherwise valid rules for their use, just as they must observe the traffic laws, sanitation regulations, and laws to preserve the public peace. This is no more than a reaffirmation that reasonable time, place, or manner restrictions on expression are constitutionally acceptable.

Contrary to the conclusion of the Court of Appeals, the foregoing analysis demonstrates that the Park Service regulation is sustainable under the four-factor standard of *United States v. O'Brien* for validating a regulation of expressive conduct, which, in the last analysis is little, if any, different from the standard applied to time, place, or manner restrictions. No one contends that aside from its impact on speech a rule against camping or overnight sleeping in public parks is beyond the constitutional power of the Government to enforce. And for the reasons we have discussed above, there is a substantial Government interest in conserving park property, an interest that is plainly served by, and requires for its implementation, measures such as the proscription of sleeping that are designed to limit the wear and tear on park properties. That interest is unrelated to suppression of expression.

We are unmoved by the Court of Appeals' view that the challenged regulation is unnecessary, and hence invalid, because there are less speech-restrictive alternatives that could have satisfied the Government interest in preserving park lands. There is no gainsaying that preventing overnight sleeping will avoid a measure of actual or threatened damage to Lafayette Park and the Mall. The Court of Appeals' suggestions that the Park Service minimize the possible injury by reducing the size, duration, or frequency of demonstrations would still curtail the total allowable expression in which demonstrators could engage, whether by sleeping or otherwise, and these suggestions represent no more than a disagreement with the Park Service over how much protection the . . . parks require or how an acceptable level of preservation is to be attained. We do not believe, however, that either *United*

States v. O'Brien or the time, place, or manner decisions assign to the judiciary the authority to replace the Park Service as the manager of the Nation's parks or endow the judiciary with the competence to judge how much protection of park lands is wise and how that level of conservation is to be attained.

■ [CHIEF JUSTICE BURGER's concurrence is omitted.]

■ JUSTICE MARSHALL, with whom JUSTICE BRENNAN joins, dissenting.

The Court's disposition of this case is marked by two related failings. First, the majority is either unwilling or unable to take seriously the First Amendment claims advanced by respondents. Contrary to the impression given by the majority, respondents are not supplicants seeking to wheedle an undeserved favor from the Government. They are citizens raising issues of profound public importance who have properly turned to the courts for the vindication of their constitutional rights. Second, the majority misapplies the test for ascertaining whether a restraint on speech qualifies as a reasonable time, place, and manner regulation. In determining what constitutes a sustainable regulation, the majority fails to subject the alleged interests of the Government to the degree of scrutiny required to ensure that expressive activity protected by the First Amendment remains free of unnecessary limitations.

I

The proper starting point for analysis of this case is a recognition that the activity in which respondents seek to engage—sleeping in a highly public place, outside, in the winter for the purpose of protesting homelessness—is symbolic speech protected by the First Amendment. The majority assumes, without deciding, that the respondents' conduct is entitled to constitutional protection. The problem with this assumption is that the Court thereby avoids examining closely the reality of respondents' planned expression. The majority's approach denatures respondents' asserted right and thus makes all too easy identification of a Government interest sufficient to warrant its abridgment. A realistic appraisal of the competing interests at stake in this case requires a closer look at the nature of the expressive conduct at issue and the context in which that conduct would be displayed. . . .

The primary purpose for making *sleep* an integral part of the demonstration was "to re-enact the central reality of homelessness," and to impress upon public consciousness, in as dramatic a way as possible, that homelessness is a widespread problem, often ignored, that confronts its victims with life-threatening deprivations. . . .

In a long line of cases, this Court has afforded First Amendment protection to expressive conduct that qualifies as symbolic speech. In light of the surrounding context, respondents' proposed activity meets the qualifications. The Court has previously acknowledged the importance of context in determining whether an act can properly be denominated as "speech" for First Amendment purposes and has provided guidance concerning the way in which courts should "read" a context in making this determination. . . . Here, respondents clearly intended to protest the reality of homelessness by sleeping outdoors in the winter in the near vicinity of the magisterial residence of the President of the United States. In addition to accentuating the political character of their protest by their choice of location and mode of communication, respondents also intended to underline the meaning of their protest by giving their demonstration satirical names. Respondents planned to name the demonstration on the Mall "Congressional Village," and the demonstration in Lafayette Park, "Reaganville II." . . .

II

Although sleep in the context of this case is symbolic speech protected by the First Amendment, it is nonetheless subject to reasonable time, place, and manner restrictions. I agree with the standard enunciated by the majority: "[R]estrictions of this kind are valid provided that they are justified without reference to the content of the regulated speech, that they are narrowly tailored to serve a significant governmental interest, and that they leave open ample alternative channels for communication of the information." I conclude, however, that the regulations at issue in this case, as applied to respondents, fail to satisfy this standard.

According to the majority, the significant Government interest advanced by denying respondents' request to engage in sleep-speech is the interest in "maintaining the parks in the heart of our capital in an attractive and intact condition, readily available to the millions of people who wish to see and enjoy them by their presence." That interest is indeed significant. However, neither the Government nor the majority adequately explains how prohibiting respondents' planned activity will substantially further that interest. . . .

The majority's second argument is comprised of the suggestion that, although sleeping contains an element of expression, "its major value to [respondents'] demonstration would have been facilitative." While this observation does provide a hint of the weight the Court attached to respondents' First Amendment claims, it is utterly irrelevant to whether the Government's ban on sleeping advances a substantial Government interest.

The majority's third argument is based upon two claims. The first is that the ban on sleeping relieves the Government of an administrative burden because, without the flat ban, the process of issuing and denying permits to other demonstrators asserting First Amendment rights to sleep in the parks "would present difficult problems for the Park Service." The second is that the ban on sleeping will increase the probability that "some around-the-clock demonstrations for days on end will not materialize, [that] others will be limited in size and duration, and that the purpose of the regulation will thus be materially served," that purpose being "to limit the wear and tear on park properties."

The flaw in these two contentions is that neither is supported by a factual showing that evinces a real, as opposed to a merely speculative, problem. The majority fails to offer any evidence indicating that the absence of an absolute ban on sleeping would present administrative problems to the Park Service that are substantially more difficult than those it ordinarily confronts. A mere apprehension of difficulties should not be enough to overcome the right to free expression. . . .

The Court's erroneous application of the standard for ascertaining a reasonable time, place, and manner restriction is also revealed by the majority's conclusion that a substantial governmental interest is served by the sleeping ban because it will discourage "around-the-clock demonstrations for days" and thus further the regulation's purpose "to limit wear and tear on park properties." The majority cites no evidence indicating that sleeping engaged in as symbolic speech will cause *substantial* wear and tear on park property. Furthermore, the Government's application of the sleeping ban in the circumstances of this case is strikingly underinclusive. The majority acknowledges that a proper time, place, and manner restriction must be "narrowly tailored." Here, however, the tailoring requirement is virtually forsaken inasmuch as the Government offers no justification for applying its absolute ban on sleeping yet is willing to allow respondents to engage in activities—such as feigned sleeping—that is no less burdensome.

In short, there are no substantial Government interests advanced by the Government's regulations as applied to respondents. All that the Court's decision advances are the prerogatives of a bureaucracy that over the years has shown an implacable hostility toward citizens' exercise of First Amendment rights.

III

The disposition of this case impels me to make two additional observations. First, in this case, as in some others involving time, place, and manner restrictions, the Court has dramatically lowered its scrutiny of governmental regulations once it has determined that such regulations are content-neutral. The result has been the creation of a two-tiered approach to First Amendment cases: while regulations that turn on the content of the expression are subjected to a strict form of judicial review, regulations that are aimed at matters other than expression receive only a minimal level of scrutiny. The minimal scrutiny prong of this two-tiered approach has led to an unfortunate diminution of First Amendment protection. By narrowly limiting its concern to whether a given regulation creates a content-based distinction, the Court has seemingly overlooked the fact that content-neutral restrictions are also capable of unnecessarily restricting protected expressive activity. . . .

Second, the disposition of this case reveals a mistaken assumption regarding the motives and behavior of government officials who create and administer content-neutral regulations. The Court's salutary skepticism of Governmental decisionmaking in First Amendment matters suddenly dissipates once it determines that a restriction is not content-based. The Court evidently assumes that the balance struck by officials is deserving of deference so long as it does not appear to be tainted by content discrimination. What the Court fails to recognize is that public officials have strong incentives to overregulate even in the absence of an intent to censor particular views. This incentive stems from the fact that of the two groups whose interests officials must accommodate—on the one hand, the interests of the general public and, on the other, the interests of those who seek to use a particular forum for First Amendment activity—the political power of the former is likely to be far greater than that of the latter. . . .

NOTES

1.   Is sleeping "speech"? (Several of us have known students to have engaged in what might charitably be called "expressive napping" in law-school classrooms. It unquestionably communicates a message to the professor—but is it truly "speech"?) Review the First Amendment test established by the Court's doctrine for this type of issue (the *O'Brien* test). The Court in *Clark* did not decide the case explicitly on this ground, but noted the resemblance of this test to the "time, place, and manner" test. How would you apply *O'Brien*?

2.   Is the decision in *Clark v. CCNV* correct? Is the line drawn by the Court's cases principled? Is it capable of consistent application? How would you resolve this type of issue, in a way that is faithful to the text, structure, and history of the First Amendment?

3.   As part of the Occupy Movement, mentioned above, in the summer of 2012 large numbers of demonstrators camped overnight in public squares in New York, Washington, Oakland, and many other U.S. cities. Did they have a constitutional right to do so? What were they communicating by sleeping overnight? Is there a communicative difference between the sleeping itself and the maintenance of a 24-7 demonstration? What interests were sufficient for the government to squelch the Occupations? Do other citizens have a right to use public squares to stroll about, have lunch, play chess, or walk dogs?

What if a group planning a large demonstration in Washington can make a persuasive claim that they need to be able to camp in public spaces because there are not enough hotel accommodations within their price range to accommodate all the demonstrators? Do they have a constitutional right to do so? Is their claim any different from that in *CCNV*? If the government chose not to interfere with CCNV's camping or Occupy's occupation, is it stopped from interfering with other groups with different messages, who might also find it convenient to camp in Lafayette Square?

NAACP v. Claiborne Hardware Co.

458 U.S. 886 (1982)

■ JUSTICE STEVENS delivered the opinion of the Court.

The term "concerted action" encompasses unlawful conspiracies and constitutionally protected assemblies. . . . The boycott of white merchants in Claiborne County, Miss., that gave rise to this litigation had such a character; it included elements of criminality and elements of majesty. Evidence that fear of reprisals caused some black citizens to withhold their patronage from respondents' businesses convinced the Supreme Court of Mississippi that the entire boycott was unlawful and that each of the 92 petitioners was liable for all of its economic consequences. Evidence that persuasive rhetoric, determination to remedy past injustices, and a host of voluntary decisions by free citizens were the critical factors in the boycott's success presents us with the question whether the state court's judgment is consistent with the Constitution of the United States.

I

In March 1966, black citizens of Port Gibson, Miss., and other areas of Claiborne County presented white elected officials with a list of particularized demands for racial equality and integration. The complainants did not receive a satisfactory response and, at a local National Association for the Advancement of Colored People (NAACP) meeting at the First Baptist Church, several hundred black persons voted to place a boycott on white merchants in the area. On October 31, 1969, several of the merchants filed suit in state court to recover losses caused by the boycott and to enjoin future boycott activity. . . .

The complaint was filed . . . by 17 white merchants. The merchants named two corporations and 146 individuals as defendants: the NAACP, a New York membership corporation; Mississippi Action for Progress (MAP), a Mississippi corporation that implemented the federal "Head Start" program; Aaron Henry, the President of the Mississippi State Conference of the NAACP; Charles Evers, the Field Secretary of the NAACP in Mississippi; and 144 other individuals who had participated in the boycott. The complaint sought injunctive relief and an attachment of property, as well as damages. . . .

[T]he chancellor issued an opinion and decree finding that "an overwhelming preponderance of the evidence" established the joint and several liability of 130 of the defendants on three separate conspiracy [tort] theories [malicious interference with plaintiffs' businesses; illegal "secondary boycott" in that "defendants' primary dispute was with the governing authorities of Port Gibson and Claiborne County and not with the white merchants at whom the boycott was directed"; and violation of state antitrust law]. . . .

Five of the merchants offered no evidence of business losses. The chancellor found that the remaining 12 had suffered lost business earnings and lost goodwill during a 7-year period from 1966 to 1972 amounting to $944,699. That amount, plus statutory penalties and attorney's fees, produced a final judgment of $1,250,699, plus interest. . . . As noted, the chancellor found all but 18 of the original 148 defendants jointly and severally liable for the entire judgment. The court justified imposing full liability on the national organization of the NAACP on the ground that it had failed to "repudiate" the actions of Charles Evers. . . .

In addition to imposing damages liability, the chancellor entered a broad permanent injunction. He permanently enjoined petitioners from stationing "store watchers" at the respondents' business premises; from "persuading" any person to withhold his patronage from respondents; from "using demeaning and obscene language to or about any person" because that person continued to patronize the respondents; from "picketing or patroling" the premises of any of the respondents; and from using violence against any person or inflicting damage to any real or personal property. . . .

The Mississippi Supreme Court upheld the imposition of liability . . . on the basis of the chancellor's common-law tort theory. After reviewing the chancellor's recitation of the facts, the court quoted the following finding made by the trial court:

> In carrying out the agreement and design, certain of the defendants, acting for all others, engaged in acts of physical force and violence against the persons and property of certain customers and prospective customers. Intimidation, threats, social ostracism, vilification, and traduction were some of the devices used by the defendants to achieve the desired results. Most effective, also, was the stationing of guards ("enforcers," "deacons," or "black hats") in the vicinity of white-owned businesses. Unquestionably, the evidence shows that the volition of many black persons was overcome out of sheer fear, and they were forced and compelled against their personal wills to withhold their trade and business intercourse from the complainants.

On the basis of this finding, the court concluded that the entire boycott was unlawful. "If any of these factors—force, violence, or threats—is present, then the boycott is illegal regardless of whether it is primary, secondary, economical, political, social or other." In a brief passage, the court rejected petitioners' reliance on the First Amendment:

> The agreed use of illegal force, violence, and threats against the peace to achieve a goal makes the present state of facts a conspiracy. We know of no instance, and our attention has been drawn to no decision, wherein it has been adjudicated that free speech guaranteed by the First Amendment includes in its protection the right to commit crime. . . .

II–A

The boycott of white merchants at issue in this case took many forms. The boycott was launched at a meeting of a local branch of the NAACP attended by several hundred persons. Its acknowledged purpose was to secure compliance by both civic and business leaders with a lengthy list of demands for equality and racial justice. The boycott was supported by speeches and nonviolent picketing. Participants repeatedly encouraged others to join in its cause.

Each of these elements of the boycott is a form of speech or conduct that is ordinarily entitled to protection under the First and Fourteenth Amendments. The black citizens named as defendants in this action banded together and collectively expressed their dissatisfaction with a social structure that had denied them rights to equal treatment and respect. As we so recently acknowledged in *Citizens Against Rent Control Coalition for Fair Housing v. Berkeley*, 454 U.S. 290, 294 (1981), "the practice of persons sharing common views banding together to achieve a common end is deeply embedded in the American political process." We recognized that "by collective effort individuals can make their views known, when, individually, their voices would be faint or lost." . . .

The right to associate does not lose all constitutional protection merely because some members of the group may have participated in conduct or advocated doctrine that itself is not protected. . . . Of course, the petitioners in this case did more than assemble peaceably and discuss among themselves their grievances against governmental and business policy. Other elements of the boycott, however, also involved activities ordinarily safeguarded by the First Amendment. . . . Speech itself also was used to further the aims of the boycott. Nonparticipants repeatedly were urged to join the common cause, both through public address and through personal solicitation. These elements of the boycott involve speech in its most direct form. In addition, names of boycott violators were read aloud at meetings at the First Baptist Church and published in a local black newspaper. Petitioners admittedly sought to persuade others to join the boycott through social pressure and the "threat" of social ostracism. Speech does not lose its protected character, however, simply because it may embarrass others or coerce them into action. . . .

[T]he boycott clearly involved constitutionally protected activity. . . . Through exercise of these First Amendment rights, petitioners sought to bring about political, social, and economic change. Through speech, assembly, and petition—rather than through riot or revolution—petitioners sought to change a social order that had consistently treated them as second-class citizens.

The presence of protected activity, however, does not end the relevant constitutional inquiry. . . . *[The Court cited* United States v. O'Brien *in support of the authority of government to regulate conduct for reasons aside from its expressive message.—Editors]* . . . A nonviolent and totally voluntary boycott may have a disruptive effect on local economic conditions. This Court has recognized the strong governmental interest in certain forms of economic regulation, even though such regulation may have an incidental effect on rights of speech and association. . . .

[But w]hile States have broad power to regulate economic activity, we do not find a comparable right to prohibit peaceful political activity such as that found in the boycott in this case. . . . The right of the States to regulate economic activity could not justify a complete prohibition against a nonviolent, politically motivated boycott designed to force governmental and economic change. . . .

We hold that the nonviolent elements of petitioners' activities are entitled to the protection of the First Amendment.

B

. . . The First Amendment does not protect violence. . . . Although the extent and significance of the violence in this case are vigorously disputed by the parties, there is no question that acts of violence occurred. No federal rule of law restricts a State from imposing tort liability for business losses that are caused by violence and by threats of violence. When such conduct occurs in the context of constitutionally protected activity, however, "precision of regulation" is demanded. Specifically, the presence of activity protected by the First Amendment imposes restraints on the grounds that may give rise to damages liability and on the persons who may be held accountable for those damages. . . .

The First Amendment . . . restricts the ability of the State to impose liability on an individual solely because of his association with another. . . . Civil liability may not be imposed merely because an individual belonged to a group, some members of which committed acts of violence. For liability to be imposed by reason of association alone, it is necessary to establish that the group itself possessed unlawful goals and that the individual held a specific intent to further those illegal aims. . . .

III

. . . The opinion of the Mississippi Supreme Court itself demonstrates that all business losses were not proximately caused by the violence and threats of violence found to be present. The court stated that "coercion, intimidation, and threats" formed "*part* of the boycott activity" and "*contributed* to its almost complete success." The court broadly asserted—without differentiation—that "[i]ntimidation, threats, social ostracism, vilification, and traduction" were devices used by the defendants to effectuate the boycott. The court repeated the chancellor's finding that "the volition of *many* black persons was overcome out of sheer fear." These findings are inconsistent with the court's imposition of all damages "resulting from the boycott." To the extent that the court's judgment rests on the ground that "many" black citizens were "intimidated" by "threats" of "social ostracism, vilification, and traduction," it is flatly inconsistent with the First Amendment. The ambiguous findings of the Mississippi Supreme Court are inadequate to assure the "precision of regulation" demanded by that constitutional provision. . . .

[I]n this case, the Mississippi Supreme Court has relied on isolated acts of violence during a limited period to uphold respondents' recovery of *all* business losses sustained over a 7-year span. . . . The court's judgment . . . cannot stand. *[The Court also held, in a footnote, that the permanent injunction "must be dissolved." Alternatively, "the injunction must be modified to restrain only unlawful conduct and the persons responsible for conduct of that character."—Editors] . . .*

Respondents also argue that liability may be imposed on individuals who were either "store watchers" or members of the "Black Hats." There is nothing unlawful in standing outside a store and recording names. Similarly, there is nothing unlawful in wearing black hats, although such apparel may cause apprehension in others. As established above, mere association with either group—absent a specific intent to further an unlawful aim embraced by that group—is an insufficient predicate for liability. At the same time, the evidence does support the conclusion that some members of each of these groups engaged in violence or threats of violence. Unquestionably, these individuals may be held responsible for the injuries that they caused; a judgment tailored to the consequences of their unlawful conduct may be sustained.

Respondents have sought separately to justify the judgment entered against Charles Evers and the national NAACP. . . . For the reasons set forth above, liability may not be imposed on Evers for his presence at NAACP meetings or his active participation in the boycott itself. To the extent that Evers caused respondents to suffer business losses through his organization of the boycott, his emotional and persuasive appeals for unity in the joint effort, or his "threats" of vilification or social ostracism, Evers' conduct is constitutionally protected and beyond the reach of a damages award. Respondents point to Evers' speeches, however, as justification for the chancellor's damages award. . . .

There are three separate theories that might justify holding Evers liable for the unlawful conduct of others. First, a finding that he authorized, directed, or ratified specific tortious activity would justify holding him responsible for the consequences of that activity. Second, a finding that his public speeches were likely to incite lawless action could justify holding him liable for unlawful conduct that in fact followed within a reasonable period. Third, the speeches might be taken as evidence that Evers gave other specific instructions to carry out violent acts or threats.

While many of the comments in Evers' speeches might have contemplated "discipline" in the permissible form of social ostracism, it cannot be denied that references to the possibility that necks would be broken and to the fact that the Sheriff could not sleep with boycott violators at night implicitly conveyed a sterner message. In the passionate atmosphere in which the speeches were delivered, they might have been understood as inviting an unlawful form of discipline or, at least, as intending to create a fear of violence whether or not improper discipline was specifically intended.

It is clear that "fighting words"—those that provoke immediate violence—are not protected by the First Amendment. *Chaplinsky v. New Hampshire*, 315 U.S. 568, 572 (1942). . . . This Court has made clear, however, that mere *advocacy* of the use of force or violence does not remove speech from the protection of the First Amendment. . . . *Brandenburg v. Ohio*, 395 U.S. 444 (1969). . . . The emotionally charged rhetoric of Charles Evers' speeches did not transcend the bounds of protected speech set forth in *Brandenburg*. The lengthy addresses generally contained an impassioned plea for black citizens to unify, to support and respect each other, and to realize the political and economic power available to them. In the course of those pleas, strong language was used. . . . An advocate must be free to stimulate his audience with spontaneous and emotional appeals for unity and action in a common cause. When such appeals do not incite lawless action, they must be regarded as protected speech. . . .

[W]e conclude that Evers' addresses did not exceed the bounds of protected speech. . . . [T]here is no evidence—apart from the speeches themselves—that Evers authorized, ratified, or directly threatened acts of violence. . . . The chancellor made no finding that Charles Evers or any other NAACP member had either actual or apparent authority to commit acts of violence or to threaten violent conduct. The evidence in the record suggests the contrary. . . . To impose liability without a finding that the NAACP authorized—either actually or apparently—or ratified unlawful conduct would impermissibly burden the rights of political association that are protected by the First Amendment. . . .

IV

In litigation of this kind the stakes are high. Concerted action is a powerful weapon. History teaches that special dangers are associated with conspiratorial activity. And yet one of the foundations of our society is the right of individuals to combine with other persons in pursuit of a common goal by lawful means.

At times the difference between lawful and unlawful collective action may be identified easily by reference to its purpose. In this case, however, petitioners' ultimate objectives were unquestionably legitimate. The charge of illegality—like the claim of constitutional protection—derives from the means employed by the participants to achieve those goals. The use of speeches, marches, and threats of social ostracism cannot provide the basis for a damages award. But violent conduct is beyond the pale of constitutional protection.

The taint of violence colored the conduct of some of the petitioners. They, of course, may be held liable for the consequences of their violent deeds. The burden of demonstrating that it colored the entire collective effort, however, is not satisfied by evidence that violence occurred or even that violence contributed to the success of the boycott. A massive and prolonged effort to change the social, political, and economic structure of a local environment cannot be characterized as a violent conspiracy simply by reference to the ephemeral consequences of relatively few violent acts. . . . A court must be wary of a claim that the true color of a forest is better revealed by reptiles hidden in the weeds than by the foliage of countless freestanding trees. . . .

NOTES

1. There are several notable features of the Court's landmark, unanimous decision in *Claiborne Hardware*. First, the Free Speech Clause protects *collective* advocacy—the rights of groups of like-minded persons to band together for joint action in a common cause. Second, the Court strongly reaffirms the Free Speech Clause right of groups to engage in *expressive conduct*—here, conduct that otherwise arguably constituted an economic tort—under the *O'Brien* test, requiring not only that the state's interest be strong but also requiring "precision of regulation" so as not to interfere with legitimate speech. Third, following from these principles, the Court holds that, while the Free Speech Clause does not protect violence, it forbids holding *the group* responsible for the torts of individuals that the other members of the group did not authorize, direct, or ratify. The First Amendment forbids group advocacy from being considered a "conspiracy"—otherwise, all members of the group could be liable for the wrongful acts of anyone in the group. Fourth, and for similar reasons, the Court held that an *injunction* against speech or expressive conduct by members of the group is improper, merely because some members of the group may have engaged in individual wrongful acts. Group advocacy may not be enjoined based on torts committed by some members of the group. Fifth, the Court reaffirmed, emphatically, that speech does not lose its constitutionally protected character simply on account of its "coercive," "intimidating," or "vilifying" nature. The "black hats" looking for boycott-violators; the taking down of names; the reading of names aloud in church—are all protected by the First Amendment, regardless

of the fact that they may have a coercive or intimidating effect on others. Sixth, the Court vigorously reaffirmed *Brandenburg*'s holding that a speaker may not be punished even for advocacy of violence, absent strong proof of a direct and intentional connection to immediate violence.

2.   Do you agree with the Court's holdings? Are they consistent with the terms of the First Amendment, which protects the right to "peaceably" assemble? Does this limitation have any practical application? Every assembly is peaceable until it is not.

A NOTE ON ABORTION CLINIC PROTESTS

Anti-abortion protests at abortion clinics, in the 1980s and 1990s and into the twenty-first century, have presented something like the *Claiborne Hardware* controversies of their day. Like the civil rights movement of the 1960s, anti-abortion advocates have pressed their grievances vigorously, vehemently, vociferously—and sometimes violently. (Recall some of the discussion in *Planned Parenthood of the Columbia/Willamette*.) Methods have included classic exercises of the freedom of speech, such as picketing, marching, chanting, distributing pamphlets, praying, sit-ins, and direct, face-to-face counseling, and advocacy. But such protests (again like the civil rights movement) also have involved unlawful activity, including blocking of abortion clinic entrances and driveways, and threatening conduct directed at clinic workers or women seeking abortions. Women seeking abortions, and employees of the abortion provider, have been photographed (as in *Claiborne Hardware*). Some groups, such as "Operation Rescue," have been open about their desire to shut down "abortion businesses" entirely.

As with the civil rights movement, this has led to lawsuits against protesters, seeking damages and injunctive relief on a wide variety of legal theories: asserted violation of state and federal antitrust and anti-competitive conduct statutes; common law or statutory tort theories of intentional infliction of emotional distress, outrageous conduct, false imprisonment, and assault; conspiracy laws, including federal laws forbidding conspiracies to deny civil rights, 42 U.S.C. Section 1985; and state and federal anti-racketeering and organized-crime statutes. The Supreme Court rejected the use of Section 1985 as a vehicle for suing anti-abortion groups in *Bray v. Alexandria Women's Health Clinic*, 506 U.S. 263 (1993) (finding the statute inapplicable because of absence of the element of "class-based animus"; opposition to abortion does not constitute class-based animus against women as a class), but upheld the use of federal RICO (the Racketeer Influenced and Corrupt Organization provisions of a 1970 law) in *National Organization for Women, Inc. v. Scheidler*, 510 U.S. 249 (1994).

The Court also has affirmed injunctions directed against pro-life/anti-abortion advocacy groups' activities at abortion clinics, predicated (sometimes) in part on the occurrence of tortious or other wrongful conduct by some protestors. Sometimes the injunctions run against specific persons, and sometimes against organizations. They also run against anyone "in active concert or participation with" a named person or organization. See Fed. R. Civ. P. 65(d)(2)(C). Does *Claiborne Hardware* permit injunctions against the speech activities of groups seemingly defined by their association in a common cause? Does it permit statutes directed against their speech activities?

As you think about such issues—and the Supreme Court's decisions described in the next two notes, concerning anti-abortion protests—separate your own views about abortion (and about anti-abortion protests) from the analysis of the First Amendment issues. Is the Court's approach consistent in addressing how the First Amendment applies in these two contexts? Should it be?

1.   In *Madsen v. Women's Health Center, Inc.*, 512 U.S. 753 (1994), the Court upheld (in part) a state judge's issuance of an injunction creating a 36-foot "buffer zone" prohibiting anti-abortion protestors from engaging in speech on a public street and sidewalk near an abortion clinic, citing significant government interests as justification for the exclusion zone. (The Court held certain other parts of the injunction unconstitutional.)

The state court initially had issued an injunction against blocking or interfering with access to the abortion clinic, but later expanded the injunction to include the 36-foot no-speech zone and other provisions regulating anti-abortion protestors (some of which the U.S. Supreme Court struck down). The injunction's terms ran against not only named individuals but also against anti-abortion advocacy *groups*, including "Operation Rescue, Operation Rescue America, Operation Goliath, their officers, agents, members, employees and servants" and, in addition, "all persons acting in concert or participation with them, or on their behalf." Here is the Supreme Court's description of the events leading to this injunction:

Respondents operate abortion clinics throughout central Florida. Petitioners and other groups and individuals are engaged in activities near the site of one such clinic in Melbourne, Florida. They picketed and demonstrated where the public street gives access to the clinic. In September 1992, a Florida state court permanently enjoined petitioners from blocking or interfering with public access to the clinic, and from physically abusing persons entering or leaving the clinic. Six months later, respondents sought to broaden the injunction, complaining that access to the clinic was still impeded by petitioners' activities and that such activities had also discouraged some potential patients from entering the clinic, and had deleterious physical effects on others. The trial court thereupon issued a broader injunction, which is challenged here.

The court found that, despite the initial injunction, protesters continued to impede access to the clinic by congregating on the paved portion of the street—Dixie Way—leading up to the clinic, and by marching in front of the clinic's driveways. It found that as vehicles heading toward the clinic slowed to allow the protesters to move out of the way, "sidewalk counselors" would approach and attempt to give the vehicle's occupants antiabortion literature. The number of people congregating varied from a handful to 400, and the noise varied from singing and chanting to the use of loudspeakers and bullhorns.

The protests, the court found, took their toll on the clinic's patients. A clinic doctor testified that, as a result of having to run such a gauntlet to enter the clinic, the patients "manifested a higher level of anxiety and hypertension causing those patients to need a higher level of sedation to undergo the surgical procedures, thereby increasing the risk associated with such procedures." . . . The noise produced by the protesters could be heard within the clinic, causing stress in the patients both during surgical procedures and while recuperating in the recovery rooms. And those patients who turned away because of the crowd to return at a later date, the doctor testified, increased their health risks by reason of the delay.

Doctors and clinic workers, in turn, were not immune even in their homes. Petitioners picketed in front of clinic employees' residences; shouted at passersby; rang the doorbells of neighbors and provided literature identifying the particular clinic employee as a "baby killer." Occasionally, the protesters would confront minor children of clinic employees who were home alone.

This and similar testimony led the state court to conclude that its original injunction had proved insufficient "to protect the health, safety and rights of women in Brevard and Seminole County, Florida and surrounding counties seeking access to [medical and counseling] services." ... The state court therefore amended its prior order, enjoining a broader array of activities. The amended injunction prohibits petitioners from engaging in the following acts:

(1)   At all times on all days, from entering the premises and property of the Aware Woman Center for Choice [the Melbourne clinic]. ...

(2)   At all times on all days, from blocking, impeding, inhibiting, or in any other manner obstructing or interfering with access to, ingress into and egress from any building or parking lot of the Clinic.

(3)   At all times on all days, from congregating, picketing, patrolling, demonstrating or entering that portion of public right-of-way or private property within [36] feet of the property line of the Clinic. ... An exception to the 36 foot buffer zone is the area immediately adjacent to the Clinic on the east. ... The [petitioners] ... must remain at least [5] feet from the Clinic's east line. Another exception to the 36 foot buffer zone relates to the record title owners of the property to the north and west of the Clinic ... and their invitees ...

(4)   During the hours of 7:30 a.m. through noon, on Mondays through Saturdays, during surgical procedures and recovery periods, from singing, chanting, whistling, shouting, yelling, use of bullhorns, auto horns, sound amplification equipment or other sounds or images observable to or within earshot of the patients inside the Clinic.

(5)   At all times on all days, in an area within [300] feet of the Clinic, from physically approaching any person seeking the services of the Clinic unless such person indicates a desire to communicate by approaching or by inquiring of the [petitioners] ...

(6)   At all times on all days, from approaching, congregating, picketing, patrolling, demonstrating or using bullhorns or other sound amplification equipment within [300] feet of the residence of any of the [respondents'] employees, staff, owners or agents, or blocking or attempting to block, barricade, or in any other manner, temporarily or otherwise, obstruct the entrances, exits or driveways of the residences of any of the [respondents'] employees, staff, owners or agents. The [petitioners] and those acting in concert with them are prohibited from inhibiting or impeding or attempting to impede, temporarily or otherwise, the free ingress or egress of persons to any street that provides the sole access to the street on which those residences are located.

(7)   At all times on all days, from physically abusing, grabbing, intimidating, harassing, touching, pushing, shoving, crowding or assaulting persons entering or leaving, working at or using services at the [respondents'] Clinic or trying to gain access to, or leave, any of the homes of owners, staff or patients of the Clinic ...

(8)   At all times on all days, from harassing, intimidating or physically abusing, assaulting or threatening any present or former doctor, health care professional, or other staff member, employee or volunteer who assists in providing services at the [respondents'] Clinic.

(9)   At all times on all days, from encouraging, inciting, or securing other persons to commit any of the prohibited acts listed herein.

Id. at 759–761. Before you read on: which of these provisions of the injunction, as a substantive matter, are consistent with the First Amendment? Which ones abridge the freedom of speech, or the right of the people peaceably to assemble? Under the reasoning of *Claiborne Hardware*, are all of them invalid, as applied to members of the groups named (or others "acting in concert" with them) who never committed any act of blocking or interfering with access to the abortion clinics? Under the reasoning of the *Pentagon Papers Case*, are all of them invalid simply because they are contained in an injunction, a form of prior restraint? Does the occurrence of a disruptive protest that may have involved acts of trespass or other torts provide a sufficient predicate for a judicially crafted injunction regulating such protests generally? (Is this a question of state law, or of First Amendment law?)

Here were the Court's answers: First, the majority held that the injunction was not content-based or viewpoint-based, even though it restricted only the speech of anti-abortion protestors, because "[t]o accept petitioners' claim would be to classify virtually every injunction as content or viewpoint based. An injunction, by its very nature, applies only to a particular group (or individuals) and regulates the activities, and perhaps the speech, of that group." Accordingly, the majority applied an "intermediate" standard of scrutiny for injunctions directed against speech, roughly analogous to the test traditionally applied to content-neutral "time, place, and manner" regulations.

Applying that standard, the majority then *upheld* those parts of the injunction creating the 36-foot "buffer zone" and prohibiting "singing, chanting, whistling, shouting, yelling" that could be heard inside the abortion clinic. The majority *struck down* the prohibition on display of images, however: "The only plausible reason a patient would be bothered by 'images observable' inside the clinic would be if the patient found the expression contained in such images disagreeable. But it is much easier for the clinic to pull its curtains than for a patient to stop up her ears. . . . This provision of the injunction violates the First Amendment." The majority also struck down the 300-foot "no-approach" zone as too broad.

Justice Scalia's dissent (joined by Kennedy and Thomas) addressed specifically the question of injunctions against speech (as opposed to statutes or ordinances):

But this is *not* a statute, and it *is* an injunctive order. The Court might just as logically (or illogically) have begun Part III: "If this were a content-based injunction, rather than a non-content-based injunction, its constitutionality would be assessed under the strict scrutiny standard"—and have then proceeded to discuss whether *respondents* can sustain the burden of departing from *that* presumed disposition. The question should be approached, it seems to me, without any such artificial loading of the dice. And the central element of the answer is that a restriction upon speech imposed by injunction (whether nominally content based or nominally content neutral) is *at least* as deserving of strict scrutiny as a statutory, content-based restriction.

That is so for several reasons: The danger of content-based statutory restrictions upon speech is that they may be designed and used precisely to suppress the ideas in question rather than to achieve any other proper governmental aim. But that same danger exists with injunctions. Although a speech-restricting injunction may not attack content *as content* (in the present case, as I shall discuss, even that is not true), it lends itself just as readily to the targeted suppression of particular ideas. When a judge, on the motion of an employer, enjoins picketing at the site of a labor dispute, he enjoins (and he *knows* he is enjoining) the expression of pro-union views. Such targeting of one or the other side of an ideological dispute cannot readily be achieved in speech-restricting general legislation except by making content the basis of the restriction; it is achieved in speech-restricting injunctions almost invariably. The proceedings before us here illustrate well enough what I mean. The injunction was sought against a single-issue advocacy group by persons and organizations with a business or social interest in suppressing that group's point of view.

The second reason speech-restricting injunctions are at least as deserving of strict scrutiny is obvious enough: They are the product of individual judges rather than of legislatures—and often of judges who have been chagrined by prior disobedience of their orders. The right to free speech should not lightly be placed within the control of a single man or woman. And the third reason is that the injunction is a much more powerful weapon than a statute, and so should be subjected to greater safeguards. Normally, when injunctions are enforced through contempt proceedings, only the defense of factual innocence is available. The collateral bar rule of *Walker v. Birmingham*, 388 U.S. 307 (1967), eliminates the defense that the injunction itself was unconstitutional. . . . Thus, persons subject to a speech-restricting injunction who have not the money or not the time to lodge an immediate appeal face a Hobson's choice: They must remain silent, since if they speak their First Amendment rights are no defense in subsequent contempt proceedings. This is good reason to require the strictest standard for issuance of such orders. . . .

2.   In *McCullen v. Coakley*, 134 S.Ct. 2518 (2014), anti-abortion "sidewalk counselors" challenged a recently-enacted Massachusetts law that forbade any person from knowingly entering or remain on "a public way or sidewalk adjacent to a reproductive health care facility" within 35 feet of any entrance, exit or driveway. It exempted "people entering and exiting the clinic, employees of the facilities 'acting within the scope of their employment,' law enforcement . . . , and persons using the adjacent sidewalks for the purpose of reaching a destination other than the facility." A different statute, already on the books and not challenged in the litigation, prohibited harassment and intimidation of patients and clinic staff. The Court unanimously invalidated the new law on the ground that it "burdens substantially more speech than necessary to achieve the Commonwealth's asserted interests."

Dividing 5–4, however, in an opinion by Chief Justice Roberts, the Court rejected the plaintiffs' arguments that the law was content discriminatory. The plaintiffs offered two such arguments. First, they argued that it is discriminatory to regulate speech only when it occurs in front of an abortion clinic. The Court's response:

> To begin, the Act does not draw content-based distinctions on its face. The Act would be content based if it required "enforcement authorities" to "examine the content of the message that is conveyed to determine whether" a violation has occurred. But it does not. Whether petitioners violate the Act "depends" not "on what they say," but simply on where they say it. . . .

It is true, of course, that by limiting the buffer zones to abortion clinics, the Act has the "inevitable effect" of restricting abortion-related speech more than speech on other subjects. But a facially neutral law does not become content based simply because it may disproportionately affect speech on certain topics. On the contrary, "[a] regulation that serves purposes unrelated to the content of expression is deemed neutral, even if it has an incidental effect on some speakers or messages but not others."

Does this mean it is permissible for the government to restrict access to traditional public forums at any location where annoying protests are occurring? Could cities facing anti-war protests pass a similar law restricting access to sidewalks outside military recruitment centers, or cities facing animal rights protests do the same for public sidewalks outside fur stores? Are all time, place, and manner regulations "reasonable" no matter how targeted they are at particular subjects of protest? Can the impact on speech directly related to those locations be dismissed as mere "disproportionate effects on certain topics"?

Second, the plaintiffs argued that it was content-discriminatory for the law to exempt clinic employees and agents. This is a speaker-based preference. The Court rejected the argument: "There is nothing inherently suspect about providing some kind of exemption to allow individuals who work at the clinics to enter or remain within the buffer zones. In particular, the exemption cannot be regarded as simply a carve-out for the clinic escorts; it also covers employees such as the maintenance worker shoveling a snowy sidewalk or the security guard patrolling a clinic entrance. Given the need for an exemption for clinic employees, the 'scope of their employment' qualification simply ensures that the exemption is limited to its purpose of allowing the employees to do their jobs."

Does this mean speaker-based exclusions are permissible within traditional public forums? Can the streets of a city near the Republican National Convention be restricted to Republican delegates? When speaker identity is closely linked to speaker viewpoint, isn't that a problem? As Justice Scalia wrote in a concurring opinion, "Is there any serious doubt that abortion-clinic employees or agents 'acting within the scope of their employment' near clinic entrances may—indeed, often will—speak in favor of abortion ('You are doing the right thing')? Or speak in opposition to the message of abortion opponents—saying, for example, that 'this is a safe facility' to rebut the statement that it is not? The Court's contrary assumption is simply incredible." But is excluding particular people *always* an attempt to exclude particular viewpoints? What if the government does not know (or does not care) what the speakers are going to say?

Is *McCullen* consistent with basic public forum doctrine? Streets and sidewalks like those involved in *McCullen* are "quintessential" public forums. People have a right to be there, and to speak there on topics of their own choosing. Should the government be able to close off some sidewalks and some streets, based on proximity to ideologically sensitive activities? What standard of review should apply to restrictions of this sort? (What standard did the majority apply?) And should be government be able to pick and choose among the speakers admitted to those streets and sidewalks? What standard of review should apply? (What standard did the majority apply?)

Recall that in *Reed v. Town of Gilbert*, Justice Kagan wrote that some content-based restrictions are sufficiently innocuous that strict scrutiny should not apply. (See p. 886.) She recommended that strict scrutiny should apply only to subject-matter regulation that has "the intent *or effect* of favoring some ideas over others," in other words, "when the restriction 'raises the specter that the Government may effectively drive certain ideas or viewpoints from the marketplace.'" Should that standard be applied to restrictions based on time, place, manner, or speaker identity when those restrictions have the intent or effect of favoring or disfavoring particular ideas?

3.   In general: when may the government restrict public collective speech—assembly—because of its disruptive, annoying, harassing, or intimidating nature?

Because of its interference with the privacy of others? As a prophylactic measure to guard against violence or other torts?

[*Assignment 52*]

L. COMPELLED SPEECH

Does the freedom of speech embrace the freedom *not* to speak—a freedom from government-compelled expression, a freedom of individuals and groups to control the content of their own expression?

Minersville School District v. Gobitis
310 U.S. 586 (1940)

■ MR. JUSTICE FRANKFURTER delivered the opinion of the Court.

A grave responsibility confronts this Court whenever in course of litigation it must reconcile the conflicting claims of liberty and authority. But when the liberty invoked is liberty of conscience, and the authority is authority to safeguard the nation's fellowship, judicial conscience is put to its severest test. Of such a nature is the present controversy.

Lillian Gobitis, aged twelve, and her brother William, aged ten, were expelled from the public schools of Minersville, Pennsylvania, for refusing to salute the national flag as part of a daily school exercise. The local Board of Education required both teachers and pupils to participate in this ceremony. The ceremony is a familiar one. The right hand is placed on the breast and the following pledge recited in unison: "I pledge allegiance to my flag, and to the Republic for which it stands; one nation indivisible, with liberty and justice for all." While the words are spoken, teachers and pupils extend their right hands in salute to the flag. The Gobitis family are affiliated with "Jehovah's Witnesses," for whom the Bible as the Word of God is the supreme authority. The children had been brought up conscientiously to believe that such a gesture of respect for the flag was forbidden by command of scripture.

The Gobitis children were of an age for which Pennsylvania makes school attendance compulsory. Thus they were denied a free education and their parents had to put them into private schools. To be relieved of the financial burden thereby entailed, their father, on behalf of the children and in his own behalf, brought this suit. He sought to enjoin the authorities from continuing to exact participation in the flag-salute ceremony as a condition of his children's attendance at the Minersville school. . . .

Centuries of strife over the erection of particular dogmas as exclusive or all-comprehending faiths led to the inclusion of a guarantee for religious freedom in the Bill of Rights. The First Amendment, and the Fourteenth through its absorption of the First, sought to guard against repetition of those bitter religious struggles by prohibiting the establishment of a state religion and by securing to every sect the free exercise of its faith. So pervasive is the acceptance of this precious right that its scope is brought into question, as here, only when the conscience of individuals collides with the felt necessities of society.

Certainly the affirmative pursuit of one's convictions about the ultimate mystery of the universe and man's relation to it is placed beyond the reach of law.

Government may not interfere with organized or individual expression of belief or disbelief. Propagation of belief—or even of disbelief in the supernatural—is protected, whether in church or chapel, mosque or synagogue, tabernacle or meetinghouse. Likewise the Constitution assures generous immunity to the individual from imposition of penalties for offending, in the course of his own religious activities, the religious views of others, be they a minority or those who are dominant in government. . . .

But the manifold character of man's relations may bring his conception of religious duty into conflict with the secular interests of his fellow-men. When does the constitutional guarantee compel exemption from doing what society thinks necessary for the promotion of some great common end, or from a penalty for conduct which appears dangerous to the general good? To state the problem is to recall the truth that no single principle can answer all of life's complexities. The right to freedom of religious belief, however dissident and however obnoxious to the cherished beliefs of others—even of a majority—is itself the denial of an absolute. But to affirm that the freedom to follow conscience has itself no limits in the life of a society would deny that very plurality of principles which, as a matter of history, underlies protection of religious toleration. . . . Our present task then, as so often the case with courts, is to reconcile two rights in order to prevent either from destroying the other. But, because in safeguarding conscience we are dealing with interests so subtle and so dear, every possible leeway should be given to the claims of religious faith.

In the judicial enforcement of religious freedom we are concerned with a historic concept. . . . The religious liberty which the Constitution protects has never excluded legislation of general scope not directed against doctrinal loyalties of particular sects. Judicial nullification of legislation cannot be justified by attributing to the framers of the Bill of Rights views for which there is no historic warrant. Conscientious scruples have not, in the course of the long struggle for religious toleration, relieved the individual from obedience to a general law not aimed at the promotion or restriction of religious beliefs. The mere possession of religious convictions which contradict the relevant concerns of a political society does not relieve the citizen from the discharge of political responsibilities. The necessity for this adjustment has again and again been recognized. In a number of situations the exertion of political authority has been sustained, while basic considerations of religious freedom have been left inviolate. *Reynolds v. United States*, 98 U.S. 145 (1879). In all these cases the general laws in question, upheld in their application to those who refused obedience from religious conviction, were manifestations of specific powers of government deemed by the legislature essential to secure and maintain that orderly, tranquil, and free society without which religious toleration itself is unattainable. Nor does the freedom of speech . . . move in a more absolute circle of immunity than that enjoyed by religious freedom. Even if it were assumed that freedom of speech goes beyond the historic concept of full opportunity to utter and to disseminate views, however heretical or offensive to dominant opinion, and includes freedom from conveying what may be deemed an implied but rejected affirmation, the question remains whether school children, like the Gobitis children, must be excused from conduct required of all the other children in the promotion of national cohesion. We are dealing with an interest inferior to none in the hierarchy of legal values. National unity is the basis of national security. To deny the legislature the right to select appropriate means for its attainment presents a totally different order of problem from that of the propriety of subordinating the possible ugliness of littered streets to the free expression of opinion through distribution of handbills.

Situations like the present are phases of the profoundest problem confronting a democracy—the problem which Lincoln cast in memorable dilemma: "Must a government of necessity be too strong for the liberties of its people, or too weak to maintain its own existence?" No mere textual reading or logical talisman can solve the dilemma. And when the issue demands judicial determination, it is not the personal notion of judges of what wise adjustment requires which must prevail.

Unlike the instances we have cited, the case before us is not concerned with an exertion of legislative power for the promotion of some specific need or interest of secular society—the protection of the family, the promotion of health, the common defense, the raising of public revenues to defray the cost of government. But all these specific activities of government presuppose the existence of an organized political society. The ultimate foundation of a free society is the binding tie of cohesive sentiment. Such a sentiment is fostered by all those agencies of the mind and spirit which may serve to gather up the traditions of a people, transmit them from generation to generation, and thereby create that continuity of a treasured common life which constitutes a civilization. "We live by symbols." The flag is the symbol of our national unity, transcending all internal differences, however large, within the framework of the Constitution. This Court has had occasion to say that " . . . the flag is the symbol of the nation's power,—the emblem of freedom in its truest, best sense. . . . [I]t signifies government resting on the consent of the governed; liberty regulated by law; the protection of the weak against the strong; security against the exercise of arbitrary power; and absolute safety for free institutions against foreign aggression." *Halter v. Nebraska*, 205 U.S. 34, 43 (1907). . . .

The case before us must be viewed as though the legislature of Pennsylvania had itself formally directed the flag-salute for the children of Minersville; had made no exemption for children whose parents were possessed of conscientious scruples like those of the Gobitis family; and had indicated its belief in the desirable ends to be secured by having its public school children share a common experience at those periods of development when their minds are supposedly receptive to its assimilation, by an exercise appropriate in time and place and setting, and one designed to evoke in them appreciation of the nation's hopes and dreams, its sufferings and sacrifices. The precise issue, then, for us to decide is whether the legislatures of the various states and the authorities in a thousand counties and school districts of this country are barred from determining the appropriateness of various means to evoke that unifying sentiment without which there can ultimately be no liberties, civil or religious. To stigmatize legislative judgment in providing for this universal gesture of respect for the symbol of our national life in the setting of the common school as a lawless inroad on that freedom of conscience which the Constitution protects, would amount to no less than the pronouncement of pedagogical and psychological dogma in a field where courts possess no marked and certainly no controlling competence. The influences which help toward a common feeling for the common country are manifold. Some may seem harsh and others no doubt are foolish. Surely, however, the end is legitimate. And the effective means for its attainment are still so uncertain and so unauthenticated by science as to preclude us from putting the widely prevalent belief in flag-saluting beyond the pale of legislative power. It mocks reason and denies our whole history to find in the allowance of a requirement to salute our flag on fitting occasions the seeds of sanction for obeisance to a leader.

The wisdom of training children in patriotic impulses by those compulsions which necessarily pervade so much of the educational process is not for our independent judgment. Even were we convinced of the folly of such a measure, such belief would be no proof of its unconstitutionality. For ourselves, we might be tempted to say that the deepest patriotism is best engendered by giving unfettered scope to the most crochety beliefs. . . . But the court-room is not the arena for debating issues of educational policy. It is not our province to choose among competing considerations in the subtle process of securing effective loyalty to the traditional ideals of democracy, while respecting at the same time individual idiosyncracies among a people so diversified in racial origins and religious allegiances. So to hold would in effect make us the school board for the country. That authority has not been given to this Court, nor should we assume it.

We are dealing here with the formative period in the development of citizenship. Great diversity of psychological and ethical opinion exists among us concerning the best way to train children for their place in society. Because of these differences and because of reluctance to permit a single, iron-cast system of education to be imposed upon a nation compounded of so many strains, we have held that, even though public education is one of our most cherished democratic institutions, the Bill of Rights bars a state from compelling all children to attend the public schools. *Pierce v. Society of Sisters*, 268 U.S. 510 (1927). But it is a very different thing for this Court to exercise censorship over the conviction of legislatures that a particular program or exercise will best promote in the minds of children who attend the common schools an attachment to the institutions of their country.

What the school authorities are really asserting is the right to awaken in the child's mind considerations as to the significance of the flag contrary to those implanted by the parent. In such an attempt the state is normally at a disadvantage in competing with the parent's authority, so long—and this is the vital aspect of religious toleration—as parents are unmolested in their right to counteract by their own persuasiveness the wisdom and rightness of those loyalties which the state's educational system is seeking to promote. Except where the transgression of constitutional liberty is too plain for argument, personal freedom is best maintained—so long as the remedial channels of the democratic process remain open and unobstructed—when it is ingrained in a people's habits and not enforced against popular policy by the coercion of adjudicated law. That the flag salute is an allowable portion of a school program for those who do not invoke conscientious scruples is surely not debatable. But for us to insist that, though the ceremony may be required, exceptional immunity must be given to dissidents, is to maintain that there is no basis for a legislative judgment that such an exemption might introduce elements of difficulty into the school discipline, might cast doubts in the minds of the other children which would themselves weaken the effect of the exercise.

The preciousness of the family relation, the authority and independence which give dignity to parenthood, indeed the enjoyment of all freedom, presuppose the kind of ordered society which is summarized by our flag. A society which is dedicated to the preservation of these ultimate values of civilization may in self-protection utilize the educational process for inculcating those almost unconscious feelings which bind men together in a comprehending loyalty, whatever may be their lesser differences and difficulties. That is to say, the process may be utilized so long as men's right to believe as they please, to win others to their way of belief, and their right to assemble in their chosen places of worship for the devotional ceremonies of their faith, are all fully respected. . . .

■ [The dissenting opinion of JUSTICE STONE is omitted.]

NOTES

1.   Assuming no free speech right to refrain from saluting and pledging allegiance to the flag, is *Gobitis* right on the Free Exercise Clause issue? What was the nature of Lilian Gobitis's objection to the flag salute? Is it at least open to courts to make the determination whether a particular belief really is pursuant to the exercise of one's "religion"? From the school district's perspective, was a neutral law requiring *all schoolchildren* to salute the flag really a law "prohibiting the free exercise [of religion]"? Did the school district's action really "prohibit" the Gobitis family from exercising their religion? The Gobitis family was presumably free to go elsewhere, for example to a private school—the *Pierce v. Society of Sisters* case, cited in Justice Frankfurter's opinion, held that the Constitution does not permit a state to require that parents send their children to public school The problem for the Gobitis family, of course (as is true for many families), was either that a suitable private school was not available or that the expense of choosing a private school was prohibitive, especially when compared to the availability of a free public education. Is exclusion from a free public education, unless one agrees to the flag salute, a law "*prohibiting*" the free exercise of religion?

2.   Even if requiring the Gobitis family to leave the school is otherwise thought to be a law prohibiting the free exercise of religion, does a public school district have a right to prescribe its curricular program and require all families to accept it as it is, and not make piecemeal objections?

The school district's asserted interest, and the one accepted enthusiastically by Justice Frankfurter's opinion, is the importance of instilling values of patriotism and national unity as an essential part of a school district's formation of a child's character and values over time. If a child comes from a family that rejects values of the majority of society, is it good for the majority to insist on inculcating their values, overriding the values of the nonconformist family? Is it constitutional? The Court returned to these questions only three years after *Gobitis*.

West Virginia State Board of Education v. Barnette
319 U.S. 624 (1943)

■ MR. JUSTICE JACKSON delivered the opinion of the Court.

Following the decision by this Court on June 3, 1940, in *Minersville School District v. Gobitis*, 310 U.S. 586, the West Virginia legislature amended its statutes to require all schools therein to conduct courses of instruction in history, civics, and in the Constitutions of the United States and of the State "for the purpose of teaching, fostering and perpetuating the ideals, principles and spirit of Americanism, and increasing the knowledge of the organization and machinery of the government." Appellant Board of Education was directed, with advice of the State Superintendent of Schools, to "prescribe the courses of study covering these subjects" for public schools. The Act made it the duty of private, parochial and denominational schools to prescribe courses of study "similar to those required for the public schools."

The Board of Education on January 9, 1942, adopted a resolution containing recitals taken largely from the Court's *Gobitis* opinion and ordering that the salute to the flag become "a regular part of the program of activities in the public schools," that all teachers and pupils "shall be required to participate in the salute honoring the Nation represented by the Flag; provided, however, that refusal to salute the Flag be regarded as an Act of insubordination, and shall be dealt with accordingly."

. . . What is now required is the "stiff-arm" salute, the saluter to keep the right hand raised with palm turned up while the following is repeated: "I pledge allegiance to the Flag of the United States of America and to the Republic for which it stands; one Nation, indivisible, with liberty and justice for all."

Failure to conform is "insubordination" dealt with by expulsion. Readmission is denied by statute until compliance. Meanwhile the expelled child is "unlawfully absent" and may be proceeded against as a delinquent. His parents or guardians are liable to prosecution, and if convicted are subject to fine not exceeding $50 and jail term not exceeding thirty days. . . .

This case calls upon us to reconsider a precedent decision, as the Court throughout its history often has been required to do. Before turning to the *Gobitis* case, however, it is desirable to notice certain characteristics by which this controversy is distinguished.

The freedom asserted by these appellees does not bring them into collision with rights asserted by any other individual. It is such conflicts which most frequently require intervention of the State to determine where the rights of one end and those of another begin. But the refusal of these persons to participate in the ceremony does not interfere with or deny rights of others to do so. Nor is there any question in this case that their behavior is peaceable and orderly. The sole conflict is between authority and rights of the individual. The State asserts power to condition access to public education on making a prescribed sign and profession and at the same time to coerce attendance by punishing both parent and child. The latter stand on a right of self-determination in matters that touch individual opinion and personal attitude.

As the present CHIEF JUSTICE said in dissent in the *Gobitis* case, the State may "require teaching by instruction and study of all in our history and in the structure and organization of our government, including the guaranties of civil liberty which tend to inspire patriotism and love of country." Here, however, we are dealing with a compulsion of students to declare a belief. They are not merely made acquainted with the flag salute so that they may be informed as to what it is or even what it means. . . . In the present case attendance is not optional. . . .

There is no doubt that, in connection with the pledges, the flag salute is a form of utterance. Symbolism is a primitive but effective way of communicating ideas. The use of an emblem or flag to symbolize some system, idea, institution, or personality, is a short cut from mind to mind. Causes and nations, political parties, lodges and ecclesiastical groups seek to knit the loyalty of their followings to a flag or banner, a color or design. The State announces rank, function, and authority through crowns and maces, uniforms and black robes; the church speaks through the Cross, the Crucifix, the altar and shrine, and clerical raiment. Symbols of State often convey political ideas just as religious symbols come to convey theological ones. Associated with many of these symbols are appropriate gestures of acceptance or respect: a salute, a bowed or bared head, a bended knee. A person gets from a symbol the meaning he puts into it, and what is one man's comfort and inspiration is another's jest and scorn.

Over a decade ago Chief Justice Hughes led this Court in holding that the display of a red flag as a symbol of opposition by peaceful and legal means to organized government was protected by the free speech guaranties of the Constitution. *Stromberg v. California*, 283 U.S. 359 (1931). Here it is the State that employs a flag as a symbol of adherence to government as presently organized. It requires the individual to communicate by word and sign his acceptance of the political ideas it thus bespeaks. Objection to this form of communication when coerced is an old one, well known to the framers of the Bill of Rights.[13]

It is also to be noted that the compulsory flag salute and pledge requires affirmation of a belief and an attitude of mind. . . . It is now a commonplace that censorship or suppression of expression of opinion is tolerated by our Constitution only when the expression presents a clear and present danger of action of a kind the State is empowered to prevent and punish. It would seem that involuntary affirmation could be commanded only on even more immediate and urgent grounds than silence. . . . To sustain the compulsory flag salute we are required to say that a Bill of Rights which guards the individual's right to speak his own mind, left it open to public authorities to compel him to utter what is not in his mind.

Whether the First Amendment to the Constitution will permit officials to order observance of ritual of this nature does not depend upon whether as a voluntary exercise we would think it to be good, bad or merely innocuous. . . . [V]alidity of the asserted power to force an American citizen publicly to profess any statement of belief or to engage in any ceremony of assent to one presents questions of power that must be considered independently of any idea we may have as to the utility of the ceremony in question.

Nor does the issue as we see it turn on one's possession of particular religious views or the sincerity with which they are held. While religion supplies appellees' motive for enduring the discomforts of making the issue in this case, many citizens who do not share these religious views hold such a compulsory rite to infringe constitutional liberty of the individual. It is not necessary to inquire whether non-conformist beliefs will exempt from the duty to salute unless we first find power to make the salute a legal duty.

The *Gobitis* decision, however, *assumed*, as did the argument in that case and in this, that power exists in the State to impose the flag salute discipline upon school children in general. The Court only examined and rejected a claim based on religious beliefs of immunity from an unquestioned general rule. The question which underlies the flag salute controversy is whether such a ceremony so touching matters of opinion and political attitude may be imposed upon the individual by official authority under powers committed to any political organization under our Constitution. We examine rather than assume existence of this power and, against

---

[13] Early Christians were frequently persecuted for their refusal to participate in ceremonies before the statue of the emperor or other symbol of imperial authority. The story of William Tell's sentence to shoot an apple off his son's head for refusal to salute a bailiff's hat is an ancient one. The Quakers, William Penn included, suffered punishment rather than uncover their heads in deference to any civil authority.

this broader definition of issues in this case, re-examine specific grounds assigned for the *Gobitis* decision.

1.   It was said that the flag-salute controversy confronted the Court with "the problem which Lincoln cast in memorable dilemma: 'Must a government of necessity be too *strong* for the liberties of its people, or too *weak* to maintain its own existence?' " and that the answer must be in favor of strength. . . .

It may be doubted whether Mr. Lincoln would have thought that the strength of government to maintain itself would be impressively vindicated by our confirming power of the state to expel a handful of children from school. Such oversimplification, so handy in political debate, often lacks the precision necessary to postulates of judicial reasoning. If validly applied to this problem, the utterance cited would resolve every issue of power in favor of those in authority and would require us to override every liberty thought to weaken or delay execution of their policies.

Government of limited power need not be anemic government. Assurance that rights are secure tends to diminish fear and jealousy of strong government, and by making us feel safe to live under it makes for its better support. Without promise of a limiting Bill of Rights it is doubtful if our Constitution could have mustered enough strength to enable its ratification. To enforce those rights today is not to choose weak government over strong government. It is only to adhere as a means of strength to individual freedom of mind in preference to officially disciplined uniformity for which history indicates a disappointing and disastrous end.

The subject now before us exemplifies this principle. Free public education, if faithful to the ideal of secular instruction and political neutrality, will not be partisan or enemy of any class, creed, party, or faction. If it is to impose any ideological discipline, however, each party or denomination must seek to control, or failing that, to weaken the influence of the educational system. Observance of the limitations of the Constitution will not weaken government in the field appropriate for its exercise.

2.   It was also considered in the *Gobitis* case that functions of educational officers in states, counties and school districts were such that to interfere with their authority "would in effect make us the school board for the country."

The Fourteenth Amendment, as now applied to the States, protects the citizen against the State itself and all of its creatures—Boards of Education not excepted. These have, of course, important, delicate, and highly discretionary functions, but none that they may not perform within the limits of the Bill of Rights. That they are educating the young for citizenship is reason for scrupulous protection of Constitutional freedoms of the individual, if we are not to strangle the free mind at its source and teach youth to discount important principles of our government as mere platitudes.

Such Boards are numerous and their territorial jurisdiction often small. . . . There are village tyrants as well as village Hampdens, but none who acts under color of law is beyond reach of the Constitution.

3.   The *Gobitis* opinion reasoned that this is a field "where courts possess no marked and certainly no controlling competence,' that it is committed to the legislatures as well as the courts to guard cherished liberties and that it is constitutionally appropriate to "fight out the wise use of legislative authority in the forum of public opinion and before legislative assemblies rather than to transfer such

a contest to the judicial arena," since all the "effective means of inducing political changes are left free."

The very purpose of a Bill of Rights was to withdraw certain subjects from the vicissitudes of political controversy, to place them beyond the reach of majorities and officials and to establish them as legal principles to be applied by the courts. One's right to life, liberty, and property, to free speech, a free press, freedom of worship and assembly, and other fundamental rights may not be submitted to vote; they depend on the outcome of no elections. . . . [F]reedoms of speech and of press, of assembly, and of worship . . . are susceptible of restriction only to prevent grave and immediate danger to interests which the state may lawfully protect. . . .

Nor does our duty to apply the Bill of Rights to assertions of official authority depend upon our possession of marked competence in the field where the invasion of rights occurs. . . . But we act in these matters not by authority of our competence but by force of our commissions. We cannot, because of modest estimates of our competence in such specialties as public education, withhold the judgment that history authenticates as the function of this Court when liberty is infringed.

4.   Lastly, and this is the very heart of the *Gobitis* opinion, it reasons that "National unity is the basis of national security," that the authorities have "the right to select appropriate means for its attainment," and hence reaches the conclusion that such compulsory measures toward "national unity" are constitutional. Upon the verity of this assumption depends our answer in this case.

National unity as an end which officials may foster by persuasion and example is not in question. The problem is whether under our Constitution compulsion as here employed is a permissible means for its achievement.

Struggles to coerce uniformity of sentiment in support of some end thought essential to their time and country have been waged by many good as well as by evil men. Nationalism is a relatively recent phenomenon but at other times and places the ends have been racial or territorial security, support of a dynasty or regime, and particular plans for saving souls. As first and moderate methods to attain unity have failed, those bent on its accomplishment must resort to an ever-increasing severity. As governmental pressure toward unity becomes greater, so strife becomes more bitter as to whose unity it shall be. Probably no deeper division of our people could proceed from any provocation than from finding it necessary to choose what doctrine and whose program public educational officials shall compel youth to unite in embracing. Ultimate futility of such attempts to compel coherence is the lesson of every such effort from the Roman drive to stamp out Christianity as a disturber of its pagan unity, the Inquisition, as a means to religious and dynastic unity, the Siberian exiles as a means to Russian unity, down to the fast failing efforts of our present totalitarian enemies. Those who begin coercive elimination of dissent soon find themselves exterminating dissenters. Compulsory unification of opinion achieves only the unanimity of the graveyard.

It seems trite but necessary to say that the First Amendment to our Constitution was designed to avoid these ends by avoiding these beginnings. There is no mysticism in the American concept of the State or of the nature or origin of its authority. We set up government by consent of the governed, and the Bill of Rights denies those in power any legal opportunity to coerce that consent. Authority here is to be controlled by public opinion, not public opinion by authority.

The case is made difficult not because the principles of its decision are obscure but because the flag involved is our own. Nevertheless, we apply the limitations of the Constitution with no fear that freedom to be intellectually and spiritually diverse or even contrary will disintegrate the social organization. To believe that patriotism will not flourish if patriotic ceremonies are voluntary and spontaneous instead of a compulsory routine is to make an unflattering estimate of the appeal of our institutions to free minds. We can have intellectual individualism and the rich cultural diversities that we owe to exceptional minds only at the price of occasional eccentricity and abnormal attitudes. When they are so harmless to others or to the State as those we deal with here, the price is not too great. But freedom to differ is not limited to things that do not matter much. That would be a mere shadow of freedom. The test of its substance is the right to differ as to things that touch the heart of the existing order.

If there is any fixed star in our constitutional constellation, it is that no official, high or petty, can prescribe what shall be orthodox in politics, nationalism, religion, or other matters of opinion or force citizens to confess by word or act their faith therein. If there are any circumstances which permit an exception, they do not now occur to us.

We think the action of the local authorities in compelling the flag salute and pledge transcends constitutional limitations on their power and invades the sphere of intellect and spirit which it is the purpose of the First Amendment to our Constitution to reserve from all official control.

The decision of this Court in *Minersville School District v. Gobitis* and the holdings of those few *per curiam* decisions which preceded and foreshadowed it are overruled.

■ MR. JUSTICE ROBERTS and MR. JUSTICE REED adhere to the views expressed by the Court in *Minersville School District v. Gobitis*, and are of the opinion that the judgment below should be reversed.

■ [The concurring opinions of JUSTICES BLACK, DOUGLAS, and MURPHY are omitted.]

■ MR. JUSTICE FRANKFURTER, dissenting.

One who belongs to the most vilified and persecuted minority in history is not likely to be insensible to the freedoms guaranteed by our Constitution. Were my purely personal attitude relevant I should whole-heartedly associate myself with the general libertarian views in the Court's opinion, representing as they do the thought and action of a lifetime. But as judges we are neither Jew nor Gentile, neither Catholic nor agnostic. We owe equal attachment to the Constitution and are equally bound by our judicial obligations whether we derive our citizenship from the earliest or the latest immigrants to these shores. As a member of this Court I am not justified in writing my private notions of policy into the Constitution, no matter how deeply I may cherish them or how mischievous I may deem their disregard. The duty of a judge who must decide which of two claims before the Court shall prevail, that of a State to enact and enforce laws within its general competence or that of an individual to refuse obedience because of the demands of his conscience, is not that of the ordinary person. It can never be emphasized too much that one's own opinion about the wisdom or evil of a law should be excluded altogether when one is doing one's duty on the bench. The only opinion of our own even looking in that direction that is material is our opinion whether legislators could in reason have enacted such a law.

In the light of all the circumstances, including the history of this question in this Court, it would require more daring than I possess to deny that reasonable legislators could have taken the action which is before us for review. Most unwillingly, therefore, I must differ from my brethren with regard to legislation like this. I cannot bring my mind to believe that the "liberty" secured by the Due Process Clause gives this Court authority to deny to the State of West Virginia the attainment of that which we all recognize as a legitimate legislative end, namely, the promotion of good citizenship, by employment of the means here chosen. . . .

NOTES

1.   Was *Barnette* rightly decided? Is it a fair understanding of the freedom *of* speech that it embraces more than the freedom *to* speak and includes the freedom *not to* speak? If so, what is the scope of this right, as set forth in *Barnette*?

2.   Note that *Barnette* occurs in the context of public schools, and within what the school district claimed to be a matter of its curriculum. Do students have the First Amendment right to refuse to participate in classroom instructional exercises that they regard as requiring them to articulate a view (or engage in expressive conduct) with which they disagree? If so, is there any limit to this principle? If not, what is the scope of *Barnette*'s freedom from compelled expression?

3.   Not a hypothetical: Christina Axson-Flynn was a student in the University of Utah's actor training program. She was a member of the Latter-Day Saints and objected on religious grounds to being required to use the "F" word or to "take the Lord's name in vain" in classroom training exercises. School authorities said that she could not continue in the program if she did not, in all classroom exercises, perform the scripts exactly as written. She sued, challenging her *de facto* dismissal under *Barnette* (and the Free Exercise Clause). What result? The Tenth Circuit ruled in Ms. Axson-Flynn's favor, reversing the district court's grant of summary judgment on the ground that the case presented genuine issues of material fact as to whether university officials were motivated by disagreement with Ms. Axson-Flynn's religious beliefs. See *Axson-Flynn v. Johnson*, 356 F.3d 1277 (10th Cir. 2004).

4.   Does the freedom from compelled speech include the right not to be forced by the government to make financial contributions to a private organization (like a labor union or a trade association) to support speech one does not wish to endorse or be associated with? In a series of cases, the Court has said *yes*. Thus, union members may be required to pay dues for collective-bargaining negotiations but not for a union's political or ideological advocacy. *Abood v. Detroit Bd. of Education*, 431 U.S. 209 (1977). In *United States v. United Foods, Inc.* 533 U.S. 405 (2001), the Court struck down a federal government-compelled advertising assessment imposed on fresh mushroom handlers to promote mushroom sales, distinguishing (not entirely persuasively) rather than disapproving *Glickman v. Wileman Bros.*, 521 U.S. 457 (1997), which had upheld (5–4) a California marketing order assessing California fruit growers the costs of generic advertising of certain fruit products. In *Board of Regents of the University of Wisconsin v. Southworth*, 529 U.S. 217 (2000), the Court rejected students' challenge to a compulsory student activities fee that funded student groups, so long as the University's funding decisions observed "the requirement of viewpoint neutrality in the allocation of funding support." In short, if the funding program was itself viewpoint-neutral, then compelled contributions to a fund used to support a broad range of expressive activity by recipients did not present a problem under the *Barnette* and *Abood* line of decisions. (On

the requirement of actual viewpoint-neutrality in such situations, see *Rosenberger v. Rector & Visitors of the University of Virginia*, 515 U.S. 819 (1995).)

Wooley v. Maynard
430 U.S. 705 (1977)

■ MR. CHIEF JUSTICE BURGER delivered the opinion of the Court.

The issue on appeal is whether the State of New Hampshire may constitutionally enforce criminal sanctions against persons who cover the motto "Live Free or Die" on passenger vehicle license plates because that motto is repugnant to their moral and religious beliefs.

I

Since 1969 New Hampshire has required that noncommercial vehicles bear license plates embossed with the state motto, "Live Free or Die." Another New Hampshire statute makes it a misdemeanor "knowingly [to obscure] . . . the figures or letters on any number plate." The term "letters" in this section has been interpreted by the State's highest court to include the state motto. . . .

Appellees George Maynard and his wife Maxine are followers of the Jehovah's Witnesses faith. The Maynards consider the New Hampshire State motto to be repugnant to their moral, religious, and political beliefs, and therefore assert it objectionable to disseminate this message by displaying it on their automobiles. Pursuant to these beliefs, the Maynards began early in 1974 to cover up the motto on their license plates. . . .

[Maynard was issued a first citation for violating § 262:27–c, appeared in court as his own attorney to contest it, explained his religious objections, and was fined $25, the fine suspended on condition of his "good behavior." Later that month, he was charged with another violation and again fought it in court, representing himself. He was again found guilty, fined $50, and sentenced to six months in jail and ordered to pay the $25 fine for the first offense.—Editors] Maynard informed the court that, as a matter of conscience, he refused to pay the two fines. The court thereupon sentenced him to jail for a period of 15 days. He has served the full sentence. . . .

II

. . . The District Court held that by covering up the state motto "Live Free or Die" on his automobile license plate, Mr. Maynard was engaging in symbolic speech and that "New Hampshire's interest in the enforcement of its defacement statute is not sufficient to justify the restriction on [Maynard's] constitutionally protected expression." We find it unnecessary to pass on the "symbolic speech" issue, since we find more appropriate First Amendment grounds to affirm the judgment of the District Court. We turn instead to what in our view is the essence of appellees' objection to the requirement that they display the motto "Live Free or Die" on their automobile license plates. This is succinctly summarized in the statement made by Mr. Maynard in his affidavit filed with the District Court: "I refuse to be coerced by the State into advertising a slogan which I find morally, ethically, religiously and politically abhorrent." We are thus faced with the question of whether the State may constitutionally require an individual to participate in the dissemination of an ideological message by displaying it on his private property in a manner and for the express purpose that it be observed and read by the public. We hold that the State may not do so.

A

We begin with the proposition that the right of freedom of thought protected by the First Amendment against state action includes both the right to speak freely and the right to refrain from speaking at all. See *Board of Education v. Barnette*, 319 U.S. 624, 633–634 (1943). A system which secures the right to proselytize religious, political, and ideological causes must also guarantee the concomitant right to decline to foster such concepts. The right to speak and the right to refrain from speaking are complementary components of the broader concept of "individual freedom of mind," *Id.*, at 637. This is illustrated by the recent case of *Miami Herald Publishing Co. v. Tornillo*, 418 U.S. 241 (1974), where we held unconstitutional a Florida statute placing an affirmative duty upon newspapers to publish the replies of political candidates whom they had criticized. We concluded that such a requirement deprived a newspaper of the fundamental right to decide what to print or omit:

> Faced with the penalties that would accrue to any newspaper that published news or commentary arguably within the reach of the right-of-access statute, editors might well conclude that the safe course is to avoid controversy. Therefore, under the operation of the Florida statute, political and electoral coverage would be blunted or reduced. Government-enforced right of access inescapably "dampens the vigor and limits the variety of public debate," *New York Times Co. v. Sullivan*, 376 U.S. [254,] at 279.

Id., at 257.

The Court in *Barnette* was faced with a state statute which required public school students to participate in daily public ceremonies by honoring the flag both with words and traditional salute gestures. In overruling its prior decision in *Minersville District v. Gobitis*, 310 U.S. 586 (1940), the Court held that "a ceremony so touching matters of opinion and political attitude may [not] be imposed upon the individual by official authority under powers committed to any political organization under our Constitution." Compelling the affirmative act of a flag salute involved a more serious infringement upon personal liberties than the passive act of carrying the state motto on a license plate, but the difference is essentially one of degree. Here, as in *Barnette*, we are faced with a state measure which forces an individual . . . to be an instrument for fostering public adherence to an ideological point of view he finds unacceptable. In doing so, the State "invades the sphere of intellect and spirit which it is the purpose of the First Amendment to our Constitution to reserve from all official control."

New Hampshire's statute in effect requires that appellees use their private property as a "mobile billboard" for the State's ideological message—or suffer a penalty, as Maynard already has. As a condition to driving an automobile—a virtual necessity for most Americans—the Maynards must display "Live Free or Die" to hundreds of people each day. The fact that most individuals agree with the thrust of New Hampshire's motto is not the test; most Americans also find the flag salute acceptable. The First Amendment protects the right of individuals to hold a point of view different from the majority and to refuse to foster, in the way New Hampshire commands, an idea they find morally objectionable.

B

Identifying the Maynards' interests as implicating First Amendment protections does not end our inquiry however. We must also determine whether the State's countervailing interest is sufficiently compelling to justify requiring appellees to display the state motto on their license plates. See, *e.g.*, *United States v. O'Brien*, 391 U.S. 367 (1968). The two interests advanced by the State are that display of the motto (1) facilitates the identification of passenger vehicles, and (2) promotes appreciation of history, individualism, and state pride.

[The Court rejected the first asserted state interest on the basis that it was readily satisfied by the portions of the license plate not covered up.—Editors] . . . The State's second claimed interest is not ideologically neutral. The State is seeking to communicate to others an official view as to proper appreciation of history, state pride, and individualism. Of course, the State may legitimately pursue such interests in any number of ways. However, where the State's interest is to disseminate an ideology, no matter how acceptable to some, such interest cannot outweigh an individual's First Amendment right to avoid becoming the courier for such message.

We conclude that the State of New Hampshire may not require appellees to display the state motto[15] upon their vehicle license plates.

■ [JUSTICE WHITE'S dissenting opinion is omitted.]

■ Mr. JUSTICE REHNQUIST, with whom MR. JUSTICE BLACKMUN joins, dissenting.

. . . The Court cites *Barnette* for the proposition that there is a constitutional right, in some cases, to "refrain from speaking." What the Court does not demonstrate is that there is any "speech" or "speaking" in the context of this case. . . . For First Amendment principles to be implicated, the State must place the citizen in the position of either apparently to, or actually "asserting as true" the message. This was the focus of *Barnette*, and clearly distinguishes this case from that one.

In holding that the New Hampshire statute does not run afoul of our holding in *Barnette*, the New Hampshire Supreme Court in [another case] aptly articulated why there is no required affirmation of belief in this case: "The defendants' membership in a class of persons required to display plates bearing the State motto carries no implication and is subject to no requirement that they endorse that motto or profess to adopt it as matter of belief."

As found by the New Hampshire Supreme Court . . . , there is nothing in state law which precludes appellees from displaying their disagreement with the state motto as long as the methods used do not obscure the license plates. Thus appellees could place on their bumper a conspicuous bumper sticker explaining in no uncertain terms that they do not profess the motto "Live Free or Die" and that they violently disagree with the connotations of that motto. Since any implication that they affirm the motto can be so easily displaced, I cannot agree that the state statutory system for motor vehicle identification and tourist promotion may be invalidated under the

---

[15] It has been suggested that today's holding will be read as sanctioning the obliteration of the national motto, "In God We Trust" from United States coins and currency. That question is not before us today but we note that currency, which is passed from hand to hand, differs in significant respects from an automobile, which is readily associated with its operator. Currency is generally carried in a purse or pocket and need not be displayed to the public. The bearer of currency is thus not required to publicly advertise the national motto.

fiction that appellees are unconstitutionally forced to affirm, or profess belief in, the state motto.

The logic of the Court's opinion leads to startling, and I believe totally unacceptable, results. For example, the mottoes "In God We Trust" and "E Pluribus Unum" appear on the coin and currency of the United States. I cannot imagine that the statutes proscribing defacement of United States currency impinge upon the First Amendment rights of an atheist. The fact that an atheist carries and uses United States currency does not, in any meaningful sense, convey any affirmation of belief on his part in the motto "In God We Trust." Similarly, there is no affirmation of belief involved in the display of state license tags upon the private automobiles involved here.

NOTES

1.   Is "In God We Trust" on the nation's coins and currency a violation of the principle of *Barnette* and *Wooley*?

2.   Is *Wooley* persuasive on its facts? Can the state's license plate slogan be defended on the ground that it is *the state's* speech? Compare the analysis in *Pleasant Grove City v. Summum*, 129 S.Ct. 1125 (2009). The municipality of Pleasant Grove maintained a small park in which it displayed a collection of privately donated monuments, including one of the Ten Commandments. A religious group, called Summum, argued that this was a public forum, and that it had a right to erect its own monument, commemorating its version of the Commandments, called "The Seven Aphorisms." In a unanimous decision, the Court held that the monuments in the park, though privately donated, were the government's own speech and did not create a forum. Note that this holding implied that the Establishment Clause would apply to the display. In *Capitol Square Review and Advisory Bd. v. Pinette,* 515 U.S. 753 (1995), the Court had held that signs and symbols displayed by members of the public in a city square in front of the capitol building were private, and constituted a public forum—meaning that a private group (which happened to be the Ku Klux Klan, though its identity was irrelevant to the legal analysis), had the right to erect a large cross. The cross would not be attributed to the state for purposes of the Establishment Clause. All these cases, and many more, hinge on whether the speech in question is private or governmental. Can you tell the difference? Here is an oversimplified statement of the rule: The government must be evenhanded in its regulation of private speech (including religious speech), and may not compel private persons to speak. But the government may speak in its own name and may take sides even on controversial matters without having to give private persons the same opportunity, except that it may not endorse religion.

The Right of Groups to Control Their Own Expressive Messages

Barnette stands for the proposition that the government may not compel individuals to state or affirm messages other than the ones they have chosen. The next case, *Hurley v. Irish-American Gay, Lesbian and Bisexual Group of Boston*, considers a *Barnette*-like problem as applied to a *group*'s desire to control the content of its own expressive messages by excluding messages it does not wish to have mixed with its own. Is "freedom of association" to engage in expression nothing more than the aggregation of individual free speech claims by like-minded individuals?

Hurley provides a good case for reviewing and integrating a number of First Amendment doctrines introduced already in this chapter. The case involves a

St. Patrick's Day parade. Is a parade "speech"? May the government condition a permit for a parade on certain grounds? Is the condition that the government imposed here a speech-related condition, or is it content neutral? What is the government's interest? What is the "negative free speech" interest here?

Hurley v. Irish-American Gay, Lesbian and Bisexual Group of Boston
515 U.S. 557 (1995)

■ JUSTICE SOUTER delivered the opinion of the Court.

The issue in this case is whether Massachusetts may require private citizens who organize a parade to include among the marchers a group imparting a message the organizers do not wish to convey. We hold that such a mandate violates the First Amendment.

I

March 17 is set aside for two celebrations in South Boston. As early as 1737, some people in Boston observed the feast of the apostle to Ireland, and since 1776 the day has marked the evacuation of royal troops and Loyalists from the city, prompted by the guns captured at Ticonderoga and set up on Dorchester Heights under General Washington's command. Washington himself reportedly drew on the earlier tradition in choosing "St. Patrick" as the response to "Boston," the password used in the colonial lines on evacuation day. Although the General Court of Massachusetts did not officially designate March 17 as Evacuation Day until 1938, the City Council of Boston had previously sponsored public celebrations of Evacuation Day, including notable commemorations on the centennial in 1876, and on the 125th anniversary in 1901, with its parade, salute, concert, and fireworks display.

The tradition of formal sponsorship by the city came to an end in 1947. . . . Every year since that time, the [South Boston Allied War Veterans] Council has applied for and received a permit for the parade, which at times has included as many as 20,000 marchers and drawn up to 1 million watchers. No other applicant has ever applied for that permit. Through 1992, the city allowed the Council to use the city's official seal, and provided printing services as well as direct funding.

In 1992, a number of gay, lesbian, and bisexual descendants of the Irish immigrants joined together with other supporters to form the respondent organization, GLIB, to march in the parade as a way to express pride in their Irish heritage as openly gay, lesbian, and bisexual individuals. . . . Although the Council denied GLIB's application to take part in the 1992 parade, GLIB obtained a state-court order to include its contingent, which marched "uneventfully" among that year's 10,000 participants and 750,000 spectators.

In 1993, after the Council had again refused to admit GLIB to the upcoming parade, the organization and some of its members filed this suit against the Council, the individual petitioner John J. "Wacko" Hurley, and the city of Boston, alleging violations of the State and Federal Constitutions and of the state public accommodations law, which prohibits "any distinction, discrimination or restriction on account of . . . sexual orientation . . . relative to the admission of any person to, or treatment in any place of public accommodation, resort or amusement." Mass. Gen.

Laws § 272:98 (1992). . . . [T]he state trial court ruled that the parade fell within the statutory definition of a public accommodation . . . [and] rejected the Council's contention that the parade was "private" (in the sense of being exclusive), holding instead that "the lack of genuine selectivity in choosing participants and sponsors demonstrates that the Parade is a public event." . . .

The court rejected the notion that GLIB's admission would trample on the Council's First Amendment rights since the court understood that constitutional protection of any interest in expressive association would "requir[e] focus on a specific message, theme, or group" absent from the parade. "Given the [Council's] lack of selectivity in choosing participants and failure to circumscribe the marchers' message," the court found it "impossible to discern any specific expressive purpose entitling the Parade to protection under the First Amendment." It concluded that the parade is "not an exercise of [the Council's] constitutionally protected right of expressive association," but instead "an open recreational event that is subject to the public accommodations law."

The court held that because the statute did not mandate inclusion of GLIB but only prohibited discrimination based on sexual orientation, any infringement on the Council's right to expressive association was only "incidental" and "no greater than necessary to accomplish the statute's legitimate purpose" of eradicating discrimination. App. to Pet. for Cert. (citing *Roberts v. United States Jaycees,* 468 U.S. 609, 628–629 (1984)). . . . The Supreme Judicial Court of Massachusetts affirmed . . .

We granted certiorari to determine whether the requirement to admit a parade contingent expressing a message not of the private organizers' own choosing violates the First Amendment. We hold that it does and reverse.

II

. . . *[The Court noted that GLIB did not present any constitutional claim before the Court.—Editors]* [T]heir claim for inclusion in the parade rests solely on the Massachusetts public accommodations law. . . .

III–A

If there were no reason for a group of people to march from here to there except to reach a destination, they could make the trip without expressing any message beyond the fact of the march itself. Some people might call such a procession a parade, but it would not be much of one. . . . [W]e use the word "parade" to indicate marchers who are making some sort of collective point, not just to each other but to bystanders along the way. . . . Parades are thus a form of expression, not just motion, and the inherent expressiveness of marching to make a point explains our cases involving protest marches. In *Gregory v. Chicago,* 394 U.S. 111, 112 (1969), for example, petitioners had taken part in a procession to express their grievances to the city government, and we held that such a "march, if peaceful and orderly, falls well within the sphere of conduct protected by the First Amendment." Similarly, in *Edwards v. South Carolina*, 372 U.S. 229, 235 (1963), where petitioners had joined in a march of protest and pride, carrying placards and singing The Star Spangled Banner, we held that the activities "reflect an exercise of these basic constitutional rights in their most pristine and classic form."

The protected expression that inheres in a parade is not limited to its banners and songs, however, for the Constitution looks beyond written or spoken words as mediums of expression. Noting that "[s]ymbolism is a primitive but effective way of communicating ideas," *West Virginia Bd. of Ed. v. Barnette,* 319 U.S. 624, 632 (1943), our cases have recognized that the First Amendment shields such acts as saluting a flag (and refusing to do so), wearing an armband to protest a war, *Tinker v. Des Moines Independent Community School Dist.,* 393 U.S. 503, 505–506 (1969), displaying a red flag, *Stromberg v. California,* 283 U.S. 359, 369 (1931), and even "[m]arching, walking or parading" in uniforms displaying the swastika, *National Socialist Party of America v. Skokie,* 432 U.S. 43 (1977). As some of these examples show, a narrow, succinctly articulable message is not a condition of constitutional protection. . . .

Not many marches, then, are beyond the realm of expressive parades, and the South Boston celebration is not one of them. Spectators line the streets; people march in costumes and uniforms, carrying flags and banners with all sorts of messages (*e.g.,* "England get out of Ireland," "Say no to drugs"); marching bands and pipers play; floats are pulled along; and the whole show is broadcast over Boston television. To be sure, we agree with the state courts that in spite of excluding some applicants, the Council is rather lenient in admitting participants. But a private speaker does not forfeit constitutional protection simply by combining multifarious voices, or by failing to edit their themes to isolate an exact message as the exclusive subject matter of the speech. Nor, under our precedent, does First Amendment protection require a speaker to generate, as an original matter, each item featured in the communication. . . .

Respondents' participation as a unit in the parade was equally expressive. GLIB was formed for the very purpose of marching in it, as the trial court found, in order to celebrate its members' identity as openly gay, lesbian, and bisexual descendants of the Irish immigrants, to show that there are such individuals in the community, and to support the like men and women who sought to march in the New York parade. The organization distributed a fact sheet describing the members' intentions, and the record otherwise corroborates the expressive nature of GLIB's participation. In 1993, members of GLIB marched behind a shamrock-strewn banner with the simple inscription "Irish American Gay, Lesbian and Bisexual Group of Boston." GLIB understandably seeks to communicate its ideas as part of the existing parade, rather than staging one of its own.

B

The Massachusetts public accommodations law under which respondents brought suit has a venerable history. At common law, innkeepers, smiths, and others who "made profession of a public employment," were prohibited from refusing, without good reason, to serve a customer. As one of the 19th-century English judges put it, the rule was that "[t]he innkeeper is not to select his guests[;] [h]e has no right to say to one, you shall come into my inn, and to another you shall not, as every one coming and conducting himself in a proper manner has a right to be received; and for this purpose innkeepers are a sort of public servants." . . .

As with many public accommodations statutes across the Nation, the legislature continued to broaden the scope of legislation, to the point that the law today prohibits discrimination on the basis of "race, color, religious creed, national origin, sex, sexual orientation . . . , deafness, blindness or any physical or mental disability or ancestry" in "the admission of any person to, or treatment in any place of public accommodation, resort or amusement." Provisions like these are well within the State's usual power to enact when a legislature has reason to believe that a given group is the target of discrimination, and they do not, as a general matter, violate the First or Fourteenth Amendments. Nor is this statute unusual in any obvious way, since it does not, on its face, target speech or discriminate on the basis of its content, the focal point of its prohibition being rather on the act of discriminating against individuals in the provision of publicly available goods, privileges, and services on the proscribed grounds.

C

In the case before us, however, the Massachusetts law has been applied in a peculiar way. Its enforcement does not address any dispute about the participation of openly gay, lesbian, or bisexual individuals in various units admitted to the parade. Petitioners disclaim any intent to exclude homosexuals as such, and no individual member of GLIB claims to have been excluded from parading as a member of any group that the Council has approved to march. Instead, the disagreement goes to the admission of GLIB as its own parade unit carrying its own banner. Since every participating unit affects the message conveyed by the private organizers, the state courts' application of the statute produced an order essentially requiring petitioners to alter the expressive content of their parade. Although the state courts spoke of the parade as a place of public accommodation, once the expressive character of both the parade and the marching GLIB contingent is understood, it becomes apparent that the state courts' application of the statute had the effect of declaring the sponsors' speech itself to be the public accommodation. Under this approach any contingent of protected individuals with a message would have the right to participate in petitioners' speech, so that the communication produced by the private organizers would be shaped by all those protected by the law who wished to join in with some expressive demonstration of their own. But this use of the State's power violates the fundamental rule of protection under the First Amendment, that a speaker has the autonomy to choose the content of his own message.

"Since *all* speech inherently involves choices of what to say and what to leave unsaid," *Pacific Gas & Electric Co. v. Public Utilities Comm'n of Cal.,* 475 U.S. 1, 11 (1986) (plurality opinion) (emphasis in original), one important manifestation of the principle of free speech is that one who chooses to speak may also decide "what not to say," *id.,* at 16. . . . [T]his general rule, that the speaker has the right to tailor the speech, applies not only to expressions of value, opinion, or endorsement, but equally to statements of fact the speaker would rather avoid, *McIntyre v. Ohio Elections Comm'n,* 514 U.S. 334, 341–342 (1995). . . . Nor is the rule's benefit restricted to the press, being enjoyed by business corporations generally and by ordinary people engaged in unsophisticated expression as well as by professional publishers. . . .

Petitioners' claim to the benefit of this principle of autonomy to control one's own speech is as sound as the South Boston parade is expressive. . . . [T]he Council clearly decided to exclude a message it did not like from the communication it chose to make, and that is enough to invoke its right as a private speaker to shape its expression by speaking on one subject while remaining silent on another. The message it disfavored is not difficult to identify. Although GLIB's point (like the Council's) is not wholly articulate, a contingent marching behind the organization's banner would at least bear witness to the fact that some Irish are gay, lesbian, or bisexual, and the presence of the organized marchers would suggest their view that people of their sexual orientations have as much claim to unqualified social acceptance as heterosexuals and indeed as members of parade units organized around other identifying characteristics. The parade's organizers may not believe these facts about Irish sexuality to be so, or they may object to unqualified social acceptance of gays and lesbians or have some other reason for wishing to keep GLIB's message out of the parade. But whatever the reason, it boils down to the choice of a speaker not to propound a particular point of view, and that choice is presumed to lie beyond the government's power to control.

. . . On its face, the object of the [Massachusetts] law is to ensure by statute for gays and lesbians desiring to make use of public accommodations what the old common law promised to any member of the public wanting a meal at the inn, that accepting the usual terms of service, they will not be turned away merely on the proprietor's exercise of personal preference. When the law is applied to expressive activity in the way it was done here, its apparent object is simply to require speakers to modify the content of their expression to whatever extent beneficiaries of the law choose to alter it with messages of their own. But in the absence of some further, legitimate end, this object is merely to allow exactly what the general rule of speaker's autonomy forbids.

It might, of course, have been argued that a broader objective is apparent: that the ultimate point of forbidding acts of discrimination toward certain classes is to produce a society free of the corresponding biases. Requiring access to a speaker's message would thus be not an end in itself, but a means to produce speakers free of the biases, whose expressive conduct would be at least neutral toward the particular classes, obviating any future need for correction. But if this indeed is the point of applying the state law to expressive conduct, it is a decidedly fatal objective. . . . The very idea that a noncommercial speech restriction be used to produce thoughts and statements acceptable to some groups or, indeed, all people, grates on the First Amendment, for it amounts to nothing less than a proposal to limit speech in the service of orthodox expression. The Speech Clause has no more certain antithesis. See, e.g., Barnette, at 642. While the law is free to promote all sorts of conduct in place of harmful behavior, it is not free to interfere with speech for no better reason than promoting an approved message or discouraging a disfavored one, however enlightened either purpose may strike the government. . . .

IV

Our holding today rests not on any particular view about the Council's message but on the Nation's commitment to protect freedom of speech. Disapproval of a private speaker's statement does not legitimize use of the Commonwealth's power to compel the speaker to alter the message by including one more acceptable to others. . . .

NOTES

1.   Is the question of a group's freedom to control the content of its own expression at all different from the question of an individual's freedom?

2.   *Hurley* is a unanimous ruling for the proposition that a speaker—including an organization—has the right to control the content of its own expressive messages. Does a group's First Amendment freedom to control the content of its messages also include a right to exclude members that the group feels do not share the group's views or reflect its

self-definition? That is the question presented in several cases below. Does *Hurley* have anything to say about this question?

Abood v. Detroit Board of Education
431 U.S. 209 (1977)

■ Mr. Justice Stewart delivered the opinion of the Court.

The State of Michigan has enacted legislation authorizing a system for union representation of local governmental employees. A union and a local government employer are specifically permitted to agree to an "agency shop" arrangement, whereby every employee represented by a union—even though not a union member— must pay to the union, as a condition of employment, a service fee equal in amount to union dues. The issue before us is whether this arrangement violates the constitutional rights of government employees who object to public-sector unions as such or to various union activities financed by the compulsory service fees. . . . *[The Court upheld the requirement that unwilling workers pay dues to support the collective-bargaining and grievance-resolution activities of the union, but not its political advocacy.—Editors]*

To compel employees financially to support their collective-bargaining representative has an impact upon their First Amendment interests. An employee may very well have ideological objections to a wide variety of activities undertaken by the union in its role as exclusive representative. His moral or religious views about the desirability of abortion may not square with the union's policy in negotiating a medical benefits plan. One individual might disagree with a union policy of negotiating limits on the right to strike, believing that to be the road to serfdom for the working class, while another might have economic or political objections to unionism itself. An employee might object to the union's wage policy because it violates guidelines designed to limit inflation, or might object to the union's seeking a clause in the collective-bargaining agreement proscribing racial discrimination. The examples could be multiplied. To be required to help finance the union as a collective-bargaining agent might well be thought, therefore, to interfere in some way with an employee's freedom to associate for the advancement of ideas, or to refrain from doing so, as he sees fit. But . . . such interference as exists is constitutionally justified by the legislative assessment of the important contribution of the union shop to the system of labor relations established by Congress. . . .

Our decisions establish with unmistakable clarity that the freedom of an individual to associate for the purpose of advancing beliefs and ideas is protected by the First and Fourteenth Amendments. Equally clear is the proposition that a government may not require an individual to relinquish rights guaranteed him by the First Amendment as a condition of public employment. The appellants argue that they fall within the protection of these cases because they have been prohibited, not from actively associating, but rather from refusing to associate. They specifically argue that they may constitutionally prevent the Union's spending a part of their required service fees to contribute to political candidates and to express political views unrelated to its duties as exclusive bargaining representative. We have concluded that this argument is a meritorious one.

One of the principles underlying the Court's decision in *Buckley v. Valeo*, 424 U.S. 1, was that contributing to an organization for the purpose of spreading a political message is protected by the First Amendment. . . . The fact that the appellants are compelled to make, rather than prohibited from making, contributions for political purposes works no less an infringement of their constitutional rights. For at the heart of the First Amendment is the notion that an individual should be free to believe as he will, and that in a free society one's beliefs should be shaped by his mind and his conscience rather than coerced by the State. . . .

We do not hold that a union cannot constitutionally spend funds for the expression of political views, on behalf of political candidates, or toward the advancement of other ideological causes not germane to its duties as collective-bargaining representative. Rather, the Constitution requires only that such expenditures be financed from charges, dues, or assessments paid by employees who do not object to advancing those ideas and who are not coerced into doing so against their will by the threat of loss of governmental employment. . . .

■ [The concurring opinions of JUSTICES REHNQUIST and STEVENS are omitted.]

■ MR. JUSTICE POWELL, with whom THE CHIEF JUSTICE and MR. JUSTICE BLACKMUN join, concurring in the judgment.

The Court today holds that a State cannot constitutionally compel public employees to contribute to union political activities which they oppose. . . . With this much of the Court's opinion I agree, and I therefore join the Court's judgment remanding this case for further proceedings.

But the Court's holding and judgment are but a small part of today's decision. Working from the novel premise that public employers are under no greater constitutional constraints than their counterparts in the private sector, the Court apparently rules that public employees can be compelled by the State to pay full union dues to a union with which they disagree, subject only to a possible rebate or deduction if they are willing to step forward, declare their opposition to the union, and initiate a proceeding to establish that some portion of their dues has been spent on "ideological activities unrelated to collective bargaining." Such a sweeping limitation of First Amendment rights by the Court is . . . unsupported by either precedent or reason. . . .

The initial question is whether a requirement of a school board that all of its employees contribute to a teachers' union as a condition of employment impinges upon the First Amendment interests of those who refuse to support the union, whether because they disapprove of unionization of public employees or because they object to certain union activities or positions. The Court answers this question in the affirmative. . . . I agree with the Court as far as it goes, but I would make it more explicit that compelling a government employee to give financial support to a union in the public sector—regardless of the uses to which the union puts the contribution—impinges seriously upon interests in free speech and association protected by the First Amendment.

In *Buckley v. Valeo*, 424 U.S. 1 (1976), we considered the constitutional validity of the Federal Election Campaign Act, which in one of its provisions limited the amounts that individuals could contribute to federal election campaigns. We held that these limitations on political contributions "impinge on protected associational freedoms":

> Making a contribution, like joining a political party, serves to affiliate a person with a candidate. In addition, it enables like-minded persons to pool

their resources in furtherance of common political goals. The Act's contribution ceilings thus limit one important means of associating with a candidate or committee.

Id. at 22. That *Buckley* dealt with a contribution limitation rather than a contribution requirement does not alter its importance for this case. An individual can no more be required to affiliate with a candidate by making a contribution than he can be prohibited from such affiliation. The only question after *Buckley* is whether a union in the public sector is sufficiently distinguishable from a political candidate or committee to remove the withholding of financial contributions from First Amendment protection. In my view no principled distinction exists.

The ultimate objective of a union in the public sector, like that of a political party, is to influence public decisionmaking in accordance with the views and perceived interests of its membership. Whether a teachers' union is concerned with salaries and fringe benefits, teacher qualifications and in-service training, pupil-teacher ratios, length of the school day, student discipline, or the content of the high school curriculum, its objective is to bring school board policy and decisions into harmony with its own views. Similarly, to the extent that school board expenditures and policy are guided by decisions made by the municipal, State, and Federal Governments, the union's objective is to obtain favorable decisions—and to place persons in positions of power who will be receptive to the union's viewpoint. In these respects, the public-sector union is indistinguishable from the traditional political party in this country. . . .

Nor is there any basis here for distinguishing "collective-bargaining activities" from "political activities" so far as the interests protected by the First Amendment are concerned. Collective bargaining in the public sector is "political" in any meaningful sense of the word. This is most obvious when public-sector bargaining extends—as it may in Michigan—to such matters of public policy as the educational philosophy that will inform the high school curriculum. But it is also true when public-sector bargaining focuses on such "bread and butter" issues as wages, hours, vacations, and pensions. Decisions on such issues will have a direct impact on the level of public services, priorities within state and municipal budgets, creation of bonded indebtedness, and tax rates. The cost of public education is normally the largest element of a county or municipal budget. Decisions reached through collective bargaining in the schools will affect not only the teachers and the quality of education, but also the taxpayers and the beneficiaries of other important public services. Under our democratic system of government, decisions on these critical issues of public policy have been entrusted to elected officials who ultimately are responsible to the voters.

Disassociation with a public-sector union and the expression of disagreement with its positions and objectives therefore lie at "the core of those activities protected by the First Amendment." *Elrod v. Burns*, 427 U.S. 347, 356 (1976) (plurality opinion). . . .

"Neither the right to associate nor the right to participate in political activities is absolute." *CSC v. Letter Carriers*, 413 U.S. 548, 567 (1973). This is particularly true in the field of public employment, where "the State has interests as an employer in regulating the speech of its employees that differ significantly from those it possesses in connection with regulation of the speech of the citizenry in general."

Pickering v. Board of Education, 391 U.S. 563, 568 (1968). Nevertheless, even in public employment, "a significant impairment of First Amendment rights must survive exacting scrutiny." *Elrod v. Burns*, at 362 (plurality opinion).

> The [governmental] interest advanced must be paramount, one of vital importance, and the burden is on the government to show the existence of such an interest. . . . [C]are must be taken not to confuse the interest of partisan organizations with governmental interests. Only the latter will suffice. Moreover, . . . the government must emplo[y] means closely drawn to avoid unnecessary abridgment.

Id., at 362–363 (plurality opinion). . . .

Before today it had been well established that when state law intrudes upon protected speech, the State itself must shoulder the burden of proving that its action is justified by overriding state interests. The Court, for the first time in a First Amendment case, simply reverses this principle. Under today's decision, a nonunion employee who would vindicate his First Amendment rights apparently must initiate a proceedings to prove that the union has allocated some portion of its budget to "ideological activities unrelated to collective bargaining." I would adhere to established First Amendment principles and require the State to come forward and demonstrate, as to each union expenditure for which it would exact support from minority employees, that the compelled contribution is necessary to serve overriding governmental objectives. This placement of the burden of litigation, not the Court's, gives appropriate protection to First Amendment rights without sacrificing ends of government that may be deemed important.

[Assignment 53]

M. COLLECTIVE EXPRESSION: GROUPS AND THE FREEDOM OF "EXPRESSIVE ASSOCIATION"

As we have seen, the freedom of speech includes the right to engage in *collective* speech—for groups of persons to organize, join their voices, pool their resources, and speak or publish together. Does the right to engage in collective expression include a right of a group to define itself and *exclude* persons that the rest of the group believes do not embrace the message of the group or who would make poor exemplars or representatives of the group? In many ways, the right of expressive association resembles the right identified in *Barnette* and *Hurley* for individual speakers—or a group of speakers—to control the content of their own messages, and not to be required to embrace messages they disfavor.

How far does this First Amendment principle extend? Does it matter whether the group involved is a political party or something more like a "business club" or a private law firm? What if the group is a law school? What if the group is the Boy Scouts?

Democratic Party of United States v. Wisconsin
450 U.S. 107 (1981)

■ JUSTICE STEWART delivered the opinion of the Court.

The charter of the appellant Democratic Party of the United States (National Party) provides that delegates to its National Convention shall be chosen through procedures in which only Democrats can participate. Consistently with the charter, the National Party's Delegate Selection Rules provide that only those who are willing to affiliate publicly with the Democratic Party may participate in the process of selecting delegates to the Party's National Convention. The question on this appeal is whether Wisconsin may successfully insist that its delegates to the Convention be seated, even though those delegates are chosen through a process that includes a binding state preference primary election in which voters do not declare their party affiliation. The Wisconsin Supreme Court held that the National Convention is bound by the Wisconsin primary election results, and cannot refuse to seat the delegates chosen in accord with Wisconsin law. . . .

I

The election laws of Wisconsin allow non-Democrats—including members of other parties and independents—to vote in the Democratic primary without regard to party affiliation and without requiring a public declaration of party preference. The voters in Wisconsin's "open" primary express their choice among Presidential candidates for the Democratic Party's nomination; they do not vote for delegates to the National Convention. Delegates to the National Convention are chosen separately, after the primary, at caucuses of persons who have stated their affiliation with the Party. But these delegates, under Wisconsin law, are bound to vote at the National Convention in accord with the results of the open primary election. Accordingly, while Wisconsin's open Presidential preference primary does not itself violate National Party rules, the State's mandate that the results of the primary shall determine the allocation of votes cast by the State's delegates at the National Convention does. . . .

III

The question in this case is . . . whether, once Wisconsin has opened its Democratic Presidential preference primary to voters who do not publicly declare their party affiliation, it may then bind the National Party to honor the binding primary results, even though those results were reached in a manner contrary to National Party rules. . . . [T]his issue was resolved, we believe, in *Cousins v. Wigoda*, 419 U.S. 477 (1975).

In *Cousins* the Court reviewed the decision of an Illinois court holding that state law exclusively governed the seating of a state delegation at the 1972 Democratic National Convention, and enjoining the National Party from refusing to seat delegates selected in a manner in accord with state law although contrary to National Party rules. . . . The Court reversed the state judgment, holding that "Illinois' interest in protecting the integrity of its electoral process cannot be deemed compelling in the context of the selection of delegates to the National Party Convention." That disposition controls here.

The *Cousins* Court relied upon the principle that "[t]he National Democratic Party and its adherents enjoy a constitutionally protected right of political association." This First Amendment freedom to gather in association for the purpose of advancing shared beliefs is protected by the Fourteenth Amendment from infringement by any State. And the freedom to associate for the "common advancement of political beliefs" necessarily presupposes the freedom to identify the people who constitute the association, and to limit the association to those people only. "Any interference with the freedom of a party is simultaneously an interference with the freedom of its adherents." *Sweezy v. New Hampshire*, 354 U.S. 234, 250 (1957).

Here, the members of the National Party, speaking through their rules, chose to define their associational rights by limiting those who could participate in the processes leading to the selection of delegates to their National Convention. On several occasions this Court has recognized that the inclusion of persons unaffiliated with a political party may seriously distort its collective decisions—thus impairing the party's essential functions—and that political parties may accordingly protect themselves "from intrusion by those with adverse political principles." *Ray v. Blair*, 343 U.S. 214, 221–222 (1952). . . .

A political party's choice among the various ways of determining the makeup of a State's delegation to the party's national convention is protected by the Constitution. And as is true of all expressions of First Amendment freedoms, the courts may not interfere on the ground that they view a particular expression as unwise or irrational.[27] . . .

IV

We must consider, finally, whether the State has compelling interests that justify the imposition of its will upon the appellants. . . . The State asserts a compelling interest in preserving the overall integrity of the electoral process, providing secrecy of the ballot, increasing voter participation in primaries, and preventing harassment of voters. But all those interests go to the conduct of the Presidential preference primary—not to the imposition of voting requirements upon those who, in a separate process, are eventually selected as delegates. Therefore, the interests advanced by the State do not justify its substantial intrusion into the associational freedom of members of the National Party. . . .

■ JUSTICE POWELL, with whom JUSTICE BLACKMUN and JUSTICE REHNQUIST join, dissenting.

. . . The question in this case is whether, in light of the National Party's rule that only publicly declared Democrats may have a voice in the nomination process, Wisconsin's open primary law infringes the National Party's First Amendment rights of association. Because I believe that this law does not impose a substantial burden on the associational freedom of the National Party, and actually promotes the free political activity of the citizens of Wisconsin, I dissent. . . .

NOTES

1. *Democratic Party of Wisconsin* is the leading modern case in a line of decisions standing for the proposition that a group's collective constitutional rights to free speech and association to engage in expressive activity includes the right to define who is in the

---

[27] . . . It is for the National Party—and not the Wisconsin Legislature or any court—to determine the appropriate standards for participation in the Party's candidate selection process.

group, in order for the group to be able to control the content of its own collective expression. Put in doctrinal terms, the right of "expressive association" includes a right of expressive *dis*association—the right to exclude from the group persons who do not share in the group's message, purposes, beliefs, values, or ideals. (*Hurley v. GLIB* can be seen as a case of this kind as well, in addition to illustrating the more specific problem of government compulsion for a speaker to include a message the speaker does not wish to include with its own message.)

Do you agree with this notion as a general principle? How would you formulate it? Should it extend to the right of a national political party to decide the rules by which delegates to its national convention are selected—overriding state election law procedures to the contrary? That is what the Court held in *Democratic Party of Wisconsin*. Essentially, the majority said: "It's their party; they can decide who gets to come to their party." Do you agree? How far might this principle extend? What kind of groups would or should get the benefit of it?

The First Amendment speech clause basis for the doctrine has been put this way: "if the freedom of speech can be a group freedom, that group freedom means that *the group* gets to decide *what* messages the group wishes to express, *who* is in the group that is deciding what the group 'says' *as* a group, *how* the group will operate to decide these things, and *how* and *through whom* it will communicate the messages it chooses." Michael Stokes Paulsen, *Scouts, Families, and Schools*, 85 Minn. L. Rev. 1917, 1922 (2001).

2.   Next consider two cases that test the logic and limits of this doctrine. First, may a private "business club" or "service club" (like the Jaycees, Kiwanis, Rotary, Lions Club) exclude women? In answer to this question, *Roberts v. Jaycees* said *no*, on the ground that the group was primarily commercial in character and was not really seeking to preserve any particular expressive message. Second, could the Boy Scouts of America have a national policy or practice of not allowing openly gay scout leaders, on the basis that this was not consistent with the group's mission and values? *Boy Scouts of America v. Dale* said *yes*, but the Court divided 5–4 on this question, notwithstanding its unanimous decision in *Hurley* five years earlier. (The Boy Scouts retained such a policy until 2015.)

Roberts v. United States Jaycees

468 U.S. 609 (1984)

■ JUSTICE BRENNAN delivered the opinion of the Court.

This case requires us to address a conflict between a State's efforts to eliminate gender-based discrimination against its citizens and the constitutional freedom of association asserted by members of a private organization. In the decision under review, the Court of Appeals for the Eighth Circuit concluded that, by requiring the United States Jaycees to admit women as full voting members, the Minnesota Human Rights Act violates the First and Fourteenth Amendment rights of the organization's members. We . . . reverse.

I–A

The United States Jaycees [originally the "Junior Chamber of Commerce"] . . . is a nonprofit membership corporation [devoted to]

> such educational and charitable purposes as will promote and foster the growth and development of young men's organizations in the United States, designed to inculcate in the individual membership of such organization a spirit of genuine Americanism and civic interest, and as a supplementary

education institution to provide them with opportunity for personal development and achievement and an avenue for intelligent participation by young men in the affairs of their community, state and nation, and to develop true friendship and understanding among young men of all nations.

The organization's bylaws establish seven classes of membership, including individual or regular members, associate individual members, and local chapters. Regular membership is limited to young men between the ages of 18 and 35. . . . [Women may be "associate members."] The bylaws define a local chapter as "[a]ny young men's organization of good repute existing in any community within the United States, organized for purposes similar to and consistent with those" of the national organization. . . . The national organization's executive vice president estimated at trial that women associate members make up about two percent of the Jaycees' total membership. . . .

B

In 1974 and 1975, respectively, the Minneapolis and St. Paul chapters of the Jaycees began admitting women as regular members. Currently, the memberships and boards of directors of both chapters include a substantial proportion of women. As a result, the two chapters have been in violation of the national organization's bylaws for about 10 years. The national organization has imposed a number of sanctions on the Minneapolis and St. Paul chapters. . . .

In December 1978, the president of the national organization advised both chapters that a motion to revoke their charters would be considered at a forthcoming meeting of the national board of directors in Tulsa. Shortly after receiving this notification, members of both chapters filed charges of discrimination with the Minnesota Department of Human Rights. The complaints alleged that the exclusion of women from full membership required by the national organization's bylaws violated the Minnesota Human Rights Act (Act), which provides in part:

> It is an unfair discriminatory practice:
>
> > To deny any person the full and equal enjoyment of the goods, services, facilities, privileges, advantages, and accommodations of a place of public accommodation because of race, color, creed, religion, disability, national origin or sex.

Minn. Stat. § 363.03, subd. 3 (1982). The term "place of public accommodation" is defined in the Act as "a business, accommodation, refreshment, entertainment, recreation, or transportation facility of any kind, whether licensed or not, whose goods, services, facilities, privileges, advantages or accommodations are extended, offered, sold, or otherwise made available to the public." § 363.01, subd. 18. . . .

[The procedural history is omitted. The Eighth Circuit ruled that the Jaycees possessed a First Amendment right to exclude women members.—Editors]

II

. . . An individual's freedom to speak, to worship, and to petition the government for the redress of grievances could not be vigorously protected from interference by the State unless a correlative freedom to engage in group effort toward those ends were not also guaranteed. According protection to collective effort on behalf of shared goals is especially important in preserving political and cultural diversity and in shielding dissident expression from suppression by the majority. Consequently, we have long understood as implicit in the right to engage in activities protected by the First Amendment a corresponding right to associate with others in pursuit of a wide variety of political, social, economic, educational, religious, and cultural ends. In view of the various protected activities in which the Jaycees engages, that right is plainly implicated in this case.

Government actions that may unconstitutionally infringe upon this freedom can take a number of forms. Among other things, government may seek to impose penalties or withhold benefits from individuals because of their membership in a disfavored group, *e.g.*, *Healy v. James*, 408 U.S. 169, 180–184 (1972); it may attempt to require disclosure of the fact of membership in a group seeking anonymity, *e.g.*, *Brown v. Socialist Workers '74 Campaign Committee*, 459 U.S. 87, 91–92 (1982); and it may try to interfere with the internal organization or affairs of the group, *e.g.*, *Cousins v. Wigoda*, 419 U.S. 477, 487–488 (1975). By requiring the Jaycees to admit women as full voting members, the Minnesota Act works an infringement of the last type. There can be no clearer example of an intrusion into the internal structure or affairs of an association than a regulation that forces the group to accept members it does not desire. Such a regulation may impair the ability of the original members to express only those views that brought them together. Freedom of association therefore plainly presupposes a freedom not to associate. See *Abood v. Detroit Board of Education*, 431 U.S. 209, 234–235 (1977).

The right to associate for expressive purposes is not, however, absolute. Infringements on that right may be justified by regulations adopted to serve compelling state interests, unrelated to the suppression of ideas, that cannot be achieved through means significantly less restrictive of associational freedoms. We are persuaded that Minnesota's compelling interest in eradicating discrimination against its female citizens justifies the impact that application of the statute to the Jaycees may have on the male members' associational freedoms.

On its face, the Minnesota Act does not aim at the suppression of speech, does not distinguish between prohibited and permitted activity on the basis of viewpoint, and does not license enforcement authorities to administer the statute on the basis of such constitutionally impermissible criteria. Nor does the Jaycees contend that the Act has been applied in this case for the purpose of hampering the organization's ability to express its views. Instead, as the Minnesota Supreme Court explained, the Act reflects the State's strong historical commitment to eliminating discrimination and assuring its citizens equal access to publicly available goods and services. That goal, which is unrelated to the suppression of expression, plainly serves compelling state interests of the highest order. . . .

By prohibiting gender discrimination in places of public accommodation, the Minnesota Act protects the State's citizenry from a number of serious social and personal harms. In the context of reviewing state actions under the Equal Protection Clause, this Court has frequently noted that discrimination based on archaic and overbroad assumptions about the relative needs and capacities of the sexes forces individuals to labor under stereotypical notions that often bear no relationship to their actual abilities. It thereby both deprives persons of their individual dignity and denies society the benefits of wide participation in political, economic, and cultural life. . . . That stigmatizing injury, and the denial of equal opportunities that accompanies it, is surely felt as strongly by persons suffering discrimination on the basis of their sex as by those treated differently because of their race.

Nor is the state interest in assuring equal access limited to the provision of purely tangible goods and services. . . . Thus, in explaining its conclusion that the Jaycees local chapters are "place[s] of public accommodations" within the meaning of the Act, the Minnesota court noted the various commercial programs and benefits offered to members and stated that "[l]eadership skills are 'goods,' [and] business contacts and employment promotions are 'privileges' and 'advantages'. . . ." Assuring women equal access to such goods, privileges, and advantages clearly furthers compelling state interests.

In applying the Act to the Jaycees, the State has advanced those interests through the least restrictive means of achieving its ends. Indeed, the Jaycees has failed to demonstrate that the Act imposes any serious burdens on the male members' freedom of expressive association. See *Hishon v. King & Spalding*, 467 U.S. 69, 78 (1984) (law firm "has not shown how its ability to fulfill [protected] function[s] would be inhibited by a requirement that it consider [a woman lawyer] for partnership on her merits"). . . . Over the years, the national and local levels of the organization have taken public positions on a number of diverse issues, and members of the Jaycees regularly engage in a variety of civic, charitable, lobbying, fundraising, and other activities worthy of constitutional protection under the First Amendment. There is, however, no basis in the record for concluding that admission of women as full voting members will impede the organization's ability to engage in these protected activities or to disseminate its preferred views. The Act requires no change in the Jaycees' creed of promoting the interests of young men, and it imposes no restrictions on the organization's ability to exclude individuals with ideologies or philosophies different from those of its existing members. Moreover, the Jaycees already invites women to share the group's views and philosophy and to participate in much of its training and community activities. Accordingly, any claim that admission of women as full voting members will impair a symbolic message conveyed by the very fact that women are not permitted to vote is attenuated at best.

. . . In the absence of a showing far more substantial than that attempted by the Jaycees, we decline to indulge in the sexual stereotyping that underlies appellee's contention that, by allowing women to vote, application of the Minnesota Act will change the content or impact of the organization's speech.

In any event, even if enforcement of the Act causes some incidental abridgment of the Jaycees' protected speech, that effect is no greater than is necessary to accomplish the State's legitimate purposes. . . .

■ JUSTICE REHNQUIST concurs in the judgment.

■ THE CHIEF JUSTICE and JUSTICE BLACKMUN took no part in the decision of this case. *[Chief Justice Burger had been a chapter president of the St. Paul, Minnesota Jaycees, and Justice Blackmun had been a member of the Minneapolis Jaycees.—Editors]*

■ JUSTICE O'CONNOR, concurring in part and concurring in the judgment.

. . . I part company with the Court over its First Amendment analysis. . . . I agree with the Court that application of the Minnesota law to the Jaycees does not contravene the First Amendment, but I reach that conclusion for reasons distinct from those offered by the Court. I believe the Court has adopted a test that unadvisedly casts doubt on the power of States to pursue the profoundly important goal of ensuring nondiscriminatory access to commercial opportunities in our society. At the same time, the Court has adopted an approach to the general problem presented by this case that accords insufficient protection to expressive associations and places inappropriate burdens on groups claiming the protection of the First Amendment.

I

[The Court's test is] both overprotective of activities undeserving of constitutional shelter and underprotective of important First Amendment concerns. The Court declares that the Jaycees' right of association depends on the organization's making a "substantial" showing that the admission of unwelcome members "will change the message communicated by the group's speech." I am not sure what showing the Court thinks would satisfy its requirement of proof of a membership-message connection, but whatever it means, the focus on such a connection is objectionable.

Imposing such a requirement, especially in the context of the balancing-of-interests test articulated by the Court, raises the possibility that certain commercial associations, by engaging occasionally in certain kinds of expressive activities, might improperly gain protection for discrimination. . . . Whether an association is or is not constitutionally protected in the selection of its membership should not depend on what the association says or why its members say it.

The Court's readiness to inquire into the connection between membership and message reveals a more fundamental flaw in its analysis. The Court pursues this inquiry as part of its mechanical application of a "compelling interest" test, under which the Court weighs the interests of the State of Minnesota in ending gender discrimination against the Jaycees' First Amendment right of association. The Court entirely neglects to establish at the threshold that the Jaycees is an association whose activities or purposes should engage the strong protections that the First Amendment extends to expressive associations.

On the one hand, an association engaged exclusively in protected expression enjoys First Amendment protection of both the content of its message and the choice of its members. Protection of the message itself is judged by the same standards as protection of speech by an individual. Protection of the association's right to define its membership derives from the recognition that the formation of an expressive association is the creation of a voice, and the selection of members is the definition of that voice. . . . On the other hand, there is only minimal constitutional protection of the freedom of *commercial* association. . . . The Constitution does not guarantee a right to choose employees, customers, suppliers, or those with whom one engages in simple commercial transactions, without restraint from the State. A shopkeeper has no constitutional right to deal only with persons of one sex.

The dichotomy between rights of commercial association and rights of expressive association is also found in the more limited constitutional protections accorded an association's recruitment and solicitation activities and other dealings with its members and the public. . . . Many associations cannot readily be described as purely expressive or purely commercial. . . . The standard must nevertheless give substance to the ideal of complete protection for purely expressive association, even while it readily permits state regulation of commercial affairs.

In my view, an association should be characterized as commercial, and therefore subject to rationally related state regulation of its membership and other associational activities, when, and only when, the association's activities are not predominantly of the type protected by the First Amendment. It is only when the association is predominantly engaged in protected expression that state regulation of its membership will necessarily affect, change, dilute, or silence one collective voice that would otherwise be heard. An association must choose its market. Once it enters the marketplace of commerce in any substantial degree it loses the complete control over its membership that it would otherwise enjoy if it confined its affairs to the marketplace of ideas.

Determining whether an association's activity is predominantly protected expression will often be difficult, if only because a broad range of activities can be expressive. . . .

In summary, this Court's case law recognizes radically different constitutional protections for expressive and nonexpressive associations. The First Amendment is offended by direct state control of the membership of a private organization engaged exclusively in protected expressive activity, but no First Amendment interest stands in the way of a State's rational regulation of economic transactions by or within a commercial association. The proper approach to analysis of First Amendment claims of associational freedom is, therefore, to distinguish nonexpressive from expressive associations and to recognize that the former lack the full constitutional protections possessed by the latter.

II

Minnesota's attempt to regulate the membership of the Jaycees chapters operating in that State presents a relatively easy case for application of the expressive-commercial dichotomy. . . . Notwithstanding its protected expressive activities, the Jaycees—otherwise known as the Junior Chamber of Commerce—is, first and foremost, an organization that, at both the national and local levels, promotes and practices the art of solicitation and management. The organization claims that the training it offers its members gives them an advantage in business, and business firms do indeed sometimes pay the dues of individual memberships for their employees. Jaycees members hone their solicitation and management skills, under the direction and supervision of the organization, primarily through their active recruitment of new members. . . . Recruitment and selling are commercial activities, even when conducted for training rather than for profit. . . .

Boy Scouts of America v. Dale
530 U.S. 640 (2000)

■ CHIEF JUSTICE REHNQUIST delivered the opinion of the Court.

Petitioners are the Boy Scouts of America and the Monmouth Council, a division of the Boy Scouts of America, . . . a private, not-for-profit organization engaged in instilling its system of values in young people. The Boy Scouts asserts that homosexual conduct is inconsistent with the values it seeks to instill. Respondent is James Dale, a former Eagle Scout whose adult membership in the Boy Scouts was revoked when the Boy Scouts learned that he is an avowed homosexual and gay rights activist. The New Jersey Supreme Court held that New Jersey's public accommodations law requires that the Boy Scouts readmit Dale. This case presents the question whether applying New Jersey's public accommodations law in this way violates the Boy Scouts' First Amendment right of expressive association. We hold that it does.

I

[The Court began by reciting the history of Dale's membership in the Boy Scouts, his public homosexuality, and his desire to hold a position as an assistant scoutmaster. The New Jersey courts found that the Boy Scouts' decision to exclude him from such a position violated state law concerning public accommodations and was not protected by the First Amendment right of the Boy Scouts to expressive association.—Editors]

II

In *Roberts v. United States Jaycees,* 468 U.S. 609, 622 (1984), we observed that "implicit in the right to engage in activities protected by the First Amendment" is "a corresponding right to associate with others in pursuit of a wide variety of political, social, economic, educational, religious, and cultural ends." This right is crucial in preventing the majority from imposing its views on groups that would rather express other, perhaps unpopular, ideas. Government actions that may unconstitutionally burden this freedom may take many forms, one of which is "intrusion into the internal structure or affairs of an association" like a "regulation that forces the group to accept members it does not desire." Forcing a group to accept certain members may impair the ability of the group to express those views, and only those views, that it intends to express. Thus, "[f]reedom of association . . . plainly presupposes a freedom not to associate."

The forced inclusion of an unwanted person in a group infringes the group's freedom of expressive association if the presence of that person affects in a significant way the group's ability to advocate public or private viewpoints. But the freedom of expressive association, like many freedoms, is not absolute. We have held that the freedom could be overridden "by regulations adopted to serve compelling state interests, unrelated to the suppression of ideas, that cannot be achieved through means significantly less restrictive of associational freedoms." *Id.,* at 623.

To determine whether a group is protected by the First Amendment's expressive associational right, we must determine whether the group engages in "expressive association." The First Amendment's protection of expressive association is not reserved for advocacy groups. But to come within its ambit, a group must engage in some form of expression, whether it be public or private. . . .

[T]he general mission of the Boy Scouts is clear: "[T]o instill values in young people." The Boy Scouts seeks to instill these values by having its adult leaders spend time with the youth members, instructing and engaging them in activities like camping, archery, and fishing. During the time spent with the youth members, the scoutmasters and assistant scoutmasters inculcate them with the Boy Scouts' values—both expressly and by example. It seems indisputable that an association that seeks to transmit such a system of values engages in expressive activity. See *id.,* at 636 (O'CONNOR, J., concurring) ("Even the training of outdoor survival skills or participation in community service might become expressive when the activity is intended to develop good morals, reverence, patriotism, and a desire for self-improvement"). . . . The Boy Scouts asserts that homosexual conduct is inconsistent with the values embodied in the Scout Oath and Law, particularly with the values represented by the terms "morally straight" and "clean." . . .

The New Jersey Supreme Court analyzed the Boy Scouts' beliefs and found that the "exclusion of members solely on the basis of their sexual orientation is inconsistent with Boy Scouts' commitment to a diverse and 'representative' membership . . . [and] contradicts Boy Scouts' overarching objective to reach 'all eligible youth.'" The court concluded that the exclusion of members like Dale "appears antithetical to the organization's goals and philosophy." But our cases reject this sort of inquiry; it is not the role of the courts to reject a group's expressed values because they disagree with those values or find them internally inconsistent. See *Democratic Party of United States v. Wisconsin ex rel. La Follette*, 450 U.S. 107, 124 (1981) ("[A]s is true of all expressions of First Amendment freedoms, the courts may not interfere on the ground that they view a particular expression as unwise or irrational").

The Boy Scouts asserts that it "teach[es] that homosexual conduct is not morally straight," Brief for Petitioners 39, and that it does "not want to promote homosexual conduct as a legitimate form of behavior," Reply Brief for Petitioners 5. We accept the Boy Scouts' assertion. We need not inquire further to determine the nature of the Boy Scouts' expression with respect to homosexuality . . .

Dale, by his own admission, is one of a group of gay Scouts who have "become leaders in their community and are open and honest about their sexual orientation." Dale was the co-president of a gay and lesbian organization at college and remains a gay rights activist. Dale's presence in the Boy Scouts would, at the very least, force the organization to send a message, both to the youth members and the world, that the Boy Scouts accepts homosexual conduct as a legitimate form of behavior.

Hurley is illustrative on this point. There we considered whether the application of Massachusetts' public accommodations law to require the organizers of a private St. Patrick's Day parade to include among the marchers an Irish-American gay, lesbian, and bisexual group, GLIB, violated the parade organizers' First Amendment rights. We noted that the parade organizers did not wish to exclude the GLIB members because of their sexual orientations, but because they wanted to march behind a GLIB banner. We observed:

> [A] contingent marching behind the organization's banner would at least bear witness to the fact that some Irish are gay, lesbian, or bisexual, and the presence of the organized marchers would suggest their view that people of their sexual orientations have as much claim to unqualified social acceptance as heterosexuals. . . . The parade's organizers may not believe these facts about Irish sexuality to be so, or they may object to unqualified social acceptance of gays and lesbians or have some other reason for wishing to keep GLIB's message out of the parade. But whatever the reason, it boils down to the choice of a speaker not to propound a particular point of view, and that choice is presumed to lie beyond the government's power to control.

515 U.S., at 574–575. Here, we have found that the Boy Scouts believes that homosexual conduct is inconsistent with the values it seeks to instill in its youth members. . . . As the presence of GLIB in Boston's St. Patrick's Day parade would have interfered with the parade organizers' choice not to propound a particular point

of view, the presence of Dale as an assistant scoutmaster would just as surely interfere with the Boy Scouts' choice not to propound a point of view contrary to its beliefs.

The New Jersey Supreme Court determined that the Boy Scouts' ability to disseminate its message was not significantly affected by the forced inclusion of Dale as an assistant scoutmaster because of the following findings:

> Boy Scout members do not associate for the purpose of disseminating the belief that homosexuality is immoral; Boy Scouts discourages its leaders from disseminating *any* views on sexual issues; and Boy Scouts includes sponsors and members who subscribe to different views in respect of homosexuality.

We disagree with the New Jersey Supreme Court's conclusion drawn from these findings.

First, associations do not have to associate for the "purpose" of disseminating a certain message in order to be entitled to the protections of the First Amendment. An association must merely engage in expressive activity that could be impaired in order to be entitled to protection. For example, the purpose of the St. Patrick's Day parade in *Hurley* was not to espouse any views about sexual orientation, but we held that the parade organizers had a right to exclude certain participants nonetheless.

Second, even if the Boy Scouts discourages Scout leaders from disseminating views on sexual issues—a fact that the Boy Scouts disputes with contrary evidence— the First Amendment protects the Boy Scouts' method of expression. If the Boy Scouts wishes Scout leaders to avoid questions of sexuality and teach only by example, this fact does not negate the sincerity of its belief discussed above.

Third, the First Amendment simply does not require that every member of a group agree on every issue in order for the group's policy to be "expressive association." The Boy Scouts takes an official position with respect to homosexual conduct, and that is sufficient for First Amendment purposes. In this same vein, Dale makes much of the claim that the Boy Scouts does not revoke the membership of heterosexual Scout leaders that openly disagree with the Boy Scouts' policy on sexual orientation. But if this is true, it is irrelevant. The presence of an avowed homosexual and gay rights activist in an assistant scoutmaster's uniform sends a distinctly different message from the presence of a heterosexual assistant scoutmaster who is on record as disagreeing with Boy Scouts policy. The Boy Scouts has a First Amendment right to choose to send one message but not the other. The fact that the organization does not trumpet its views from the housetops, or that it tolerates dissent within its ranks, does not mean that its views receive no First Amendment protection.

Having determined that the Boy Scouts is an expressive association and that the forced inclusion of Dale would significantly affect its expression, we inquire whether the application of New Jersey's public accommodations law to require that the Boy Scouts accept Dale as an assistant scoutmaster runs afoul of the Scouts' freedom of expressive association. We conclude that it does. . . .

JUSTICE STEVENS' dissent makes much of its observation that the public perception of homosexuality in this country has changed. Indeed, it appears that homosexuality has gained greater societal acceptance. But this is scarcely an argument for denying First Amendment protection to those who refuse to accept these views. The First Amendment protects expression, be it of the popular variety or not. See, e.g., *Texas v. Johnson*, 491 U.S. 397 (1989); *Brandenburg v. Ohio*, 395 U.S. 444 (1969). And the fact that an idea may be embraced and advocated by increasing numbers of people is all the more reason to protect the First Amendment rights of those who wish to voice a different view. . . .

■ JUSTICE STEVENS, with whom JUSTICE SOUTER, JUSTICE GINSBURG, and JUSTICE BREYER join, dissenting.

. . . [The Boy Scouts'] claim finds no support in our cases. . . . [W]e have routinely and easily rejected assertions of this right by expressive organizations with discriminatory membership policies, such as private schools, law firms, and labor organizations. In fact, until today, we have never once found a claimed right to associate in the selection of members to prevail in the face of a State's antidiscrimination law. . . .

Several principles are made perfectly clear by *Jaycees* and *Rotary Club*. First, to prevail on a claim of expressive association . . . , it is not enough simply to engage in *some kind* of expressive activity. Both the Jaycees and the Rotary Club engaged in expressive activity protected by the First Amendment, yet that fact was not dispositive. Second, it is not enough to adopt an openly avowed exclusionary membership policy. Both the Jaycees and the Rotary Club did that as well. Third, it is not sufficient merely to articulate *some* connection between the group's expressive activities and its exclusionary policy. . . .

The evidence before this Court makes it exceptionally clear that BSA has, at most, simply adopted an exclusionary membership policy and has no shared goal of disapproving of homosexuality. BSA's mission statement and federal charter say nothing on the matter; its official membership policy is silent; its Scout Oath and Law—and accompanying definitions—are devoid of any view on the topic; its guidance for Scouts and Scoutmasters on sexuality declare that such matters are "not construed to be Scouting's proper area," but are the province of a Scout's parents and pastor; and BSA's posture respecting religion tolerates a wide variety of views on the issue of homosexuality. . . . In short, Boy Scouts of America is simply silent on homosexuality. There is no shared goal or collective effort to foster a belief about homosexuality at all—let alone one that is significantly burdened by admitting homosexuals.

As in *Jaycees*, there is "no basis in the record for concluding that admission of [homosexuals] will impede the [Boy Scouts'] ability to engage in [its] protected activities or to disseminate its preferred views" and New Jersey's law "requires no change in [BSA's] creed." . . .

[The Boy Scouts] has not contended, nor does the record support, that Dale had ever advocated a view on homosexuality to his troop before his membership was revoked. . . . Though [*Hurley v. GLIB*] has a superficial similarity to the present case, a close inspection reveals a wide gulf between that case and the one before us today. First, it was critical to our analysis that GLIB was actually conveying a message by participating in the parade—otherwise, the parade organizers could hardly claim that they were being forced to include any unwanted message at all. . . . Second, we found it relevant that GLIB's message "would likely be perceived" as the parade organizers' own speech. . . . Dale's inclusion in the Boy Scouts is nothing like the case in *Hurley*. His participation sends no cognizable message to the Scouts or to the world. Unlike GLIB, Dale did not carry a banner or a sign; he did not distribute any factsheet; and he expressed no intent to send any message. If there is any kind of message being sent, then, it is by the mere act of joining the Boy Scouts. . . .

The only apparent explanation for the majority's holding, then, is that homosexuals are simply so different from the rest of society that their presence alone—unlike any other individual's—should be singled out for special First Amendment treatment. Under the majority's reasoning, an openly gay male is irreversibly affixed with the label "homosexual." That label, even though unseen, communicates a message that permits his exclusion wherever he goes. His openness is the sole and sufficient justification for his ostracism. . . .

Furthermore, it is not likely that BSA would be understood to send any message, either to Scouts or to the world, simply by admitting someone as a member. . . . The notion that an organization of that size and enormous prestige implicitly endorses the views that each of those adults may express in a non-Scouting context is simply mind boggling. . . .

Unfavorable opinions about homosexuals "have ancient roots." Like equally atavistic opinions about certain racial groups, those roots have been nourished by sectarian doctrine. . . . That such prejudices are still prevalent and that they have caused serious and tangible harm to countless members of the class New Jersey seeks to protect are established matters of fact that neither the Boy Scouts nor the Court disputes. That harm can only be aggravated by the creation of a constitutional shield for a policy that is itself the product of a habitual way of thinking about strangers. As Justice Brandeis so wisely advised, "we must be ever on our guard, lest we erect our prejudices into legal principles."

If we would guide by the light of reason, we must let our minds be bold.

■ [JUSTICE SOUTER's dissenting opinion is omitted.]

NOTES

1.   Were these cases rightly decided?

2.   What is the line separating protected freedom of expressive association and the authority of government to regulate private groups' membership practices? Is it the commercial/non-commercial distinction? Is that line sustainable? Is it principled? Aren't some *commercial* enterprises "expressive"? Aren't many *expressive associations* "commercial"? (Is a private school a commercial association or an expressive association? How about a movie studio? A community theater?) Is the line a function of the strength of the state interest in regulating the type of "discrimination" in question? Is the line a function of how "expressive" the expressive association really is? Is that a sustainable or principled standard?

3.   Why is it facially permissible for a state to apply a public accommodations nondiscrimination law to a private noncommercial expressive association? If freedom of assembly/association includes the right to form "self-selected groups" (recall the Democratic-Republican Clubs controversy), how can the state purport to regulate whom they select?

A NOTE ON *CHRISTIAN LEGAL SOCIETY V. MARTINEZ*

In *Christian Legal Society v. Martinez*, 561 U.S. 661 (2010), the Court upheld a state university policy that barred official recognition (and with it preferred access to meeting rooms, internal communications channels, and other benefits) to student groups if they restricted their leadership or voting membership to persons who adhered to their fundamental beliefs. The university insisted that all groups adhere to an "all-comers" policy, meaning that they could not exclude anyone on the basis of "status or belief." If evenhandedly applied, this would mean that a Republican club would have to accept Democratic members, and a feminist club would have to accept male chauvinists. The case involved a Christian student group that limited its leaders and voting members to those who signed a "Statement of Beliefs," which included (among many other things) a belief that sexual intimacy should be limited to married heterosexual couples.

How does the "all-comers" policy compare to the position that President Washington took, contra the Democratic-Republican clubs, that there is something wrong with "self-selected" organizations?

How should this case have come out under *Democratic Party of Wisconsin*, *Roberts*, and *Dale*? The students argued that they could not be denied access to an otherwise available public benefit on account of their exercise of the constitutional right of freedom of association. Before you read the rest of this note, try to come up with plausible doctrinal reasons to reject that argument.

The Court analyzed the case under its "limited public forum" doctrine for freedom of speech. See *Rosenberger v. Rector and Visitors of the University of Virginia*, 515 U.S. 819 (1995) (see p. 1169). Under this doctrine, the government may exclude speakers from public property that has been opened up for speech activities only if it has a reason that is both viewpoint-neutral and "reasonable in light of the purposes served by the forum." The Court held that the university's policy satisfied both of these criteria. (Can you fashion arguments by the students why that might not be so?) The Court thus treated access to the forum as "effectively a state subsidy," and distinguished *Boy Scouts* and *Roberts* as cases that "involved regulations that *compelled* a group to include unwanted members" (emphasis in original). Do you agree that equal access to a forum for speech should be categorized as a "subsidy"? Could the government insist on an all-comers policy as a condition to a group's eligibility for tax exemptions, or use of the post office or roads? If an unrecognized student group were excluded from meeting on campus, would it be "compelled"?

This answered the free speech claim. But what about the freedom of association claim? The students argued they could not be denied a generally available benefit to which they would otherwise be entitled—such as use of meeting rooms and university communications media—on account of their exercise of a constitutional right. The Court rejected the claim, explaining that

> the same considerations that have led us to apply a less restrictive level of scrutiny to speech in limited public forums as compared to other environments, apply with equal force to expressive association occurring in limited public forums. . . . When these intertwined rights arise in exactly the same context, it would be anomalous for a restriction on speech to survive constitutional review under our limited-public-forum test only to be invalidated as an impermissible infringement of expressive association.

Why would it be "anomalous" to apply different constitutional tests to different constitutional rights when they arise in the same context? The Speech Clause protects a group's message, and the viewpoint-neutrality test is relevant to that. But freedom of association protects a group's prior ability to formulate their message by meeting in groups of their own choosing. The relevant constitutional principle for that is not viewpoint-neutrality, but control over group identity. One might argue that the state has a compelling interest in preventing certain kinds of discrimination, but does the state have an interest in preventing religious groups from having leaders of their own choosing?

Critics have argued that the *Martinez* decision eliminates any separate protection for freedom of association, beyond restrictions on freedom of speech. How would other freedom of association cases fare under that approach?

[*Assignment 54*]

II. THE FIRST AMENDMENT AND FREEDOM OF RELIGION

A. BACKGROUND AND DRAFTING HISTORY

The First Amendment expressly protects religious freedom in two distinct but overlapping ways. First, the Establishment Clause which forbids government from setting up "an establishment of religion," limiting citizens' religious freedom by designating an official church or official articles of faith, coercing church attendance or membership, imposing some punishment or disability for non-attendance or non-membership, or coercing direct tax support for the official church. Initially, the ban on religious "establishment" applied only to the federal government. Many states (at first) retained established churches; indeed, part of the purpose of the Establishment Clause was to forbid the federal government from interfering with—*dis*establishing—state official churches. Today, by virtue of the Fourteenth Amendment's incorporation of the Bill of Rights as a limitation on the powers of state governments, the Establishment Clause is understood to forbid states, as well as the federal government, from coercing religious exercise or observance. As we will see, however, some modern Supreme Court decisions have interpreted the Establishment Clause to prohibit considerably more. Second, the Free Exercise Clause forbids laws "prohibiting the free exercise thereof," meaning of religion. This clause gives believers the right to determine their religious beliefs for themselves and—what is more—to "exercise" them. By its language, the clause goes beyond belief and beyond speech. But what exactly is the scope of its protection?

We begin with a petition written anonymously by James Madison, which garnered thousands of signatures from Virginians in 1785. The petition opposed a proposal by Patrick Henry to force every Virginian to pay a tax for the support of religion. Each taxpayer could direct a payment to the Christian church of the taxpayer's choice (there were no non-Christian churches in Virginia at that time), or if there was no church the taxpayer wished to support, to public "seminaries of learning." Madison's petition is widely regarded as the most powerful and well-reasoned statement of the framing period on the principles of religious freedom. The Henry proposal was voted down, and in its stead, Jefferson's Bill for Establishing Religious Freedom was enacted.

James Madison, Memorial and Remonstrance Against Religious Assessments

June 20, 1785

To the Honorable the General Assembly of the Commonwealth of Virginia A Memorial and Remonstrance

We the subscribers, citizens of the said Commonwealth, having taken into serious consideration, a Bill printed by order of the last Session of General Assembly, entitled "A Bill establishing a provision for Teachers of the Christian Religion," and conceiving that the same if finally armed with the sanctions of a law, will be a dangerous abuse of power, are bound as faithful members of a free State to remonstrate against it, and to declare the reasons by which we are determined. We remonstrate against the said Bill,

1.   Because we hold it for a fundamental and undeniable truth, "that religion or the duty which we owe to our Creator and the manner of discharging it, can be directed only by reason and conviction, not by force or violence." *[This is a quotation from the 1776 Virginia Declaration of Rights.—Editors]* The Religion then of every man must be left to the conviction and conscience of every man; and it is the right of every man to exercise it as these may dictate. This right is in its nature an unalienable right. It is unalienable, because the opinions of men, depending only on the evidence contemplated by their own minds cannot follow the dictates of other men: It is unalienable also, because what is here a right towards men, is a duty towards the Creator. It is the duty of every man to render to the Creator such homage and such only as he believes to be acceptable to him. This duty is precedent, both in order of time and in degree of obligation, to the claims of Civil Society. Before any man can be considered as a member of Civil Society, he must be considered as a subject of the Governour of the Universe: And if a member of Civil Society, do it with a saving of his allegiance to the Universal Sovereign. We maintain therefore that in matters of Religion, no man's right is abridged by the institution of Civil Society and that Religion is wholly exempt from its cognizance. True it is, that no other rule exists, by which any question which may divide a Society, can be ultimately determined, but the will of the majority; but it is also true that the majority may trespass on the rights of the minority. . . .

3.   Because it is proper to take alarm at the first experiment on our liberties. We hold this prudent jealousy to be the first duty of Citizens, and one of the noblest characteristics of the late Revolution. The free men of America did not wait till usurped power had strengthened itself by exercise, and entangled the question in precedents. They saw all the consequences in the principle, and they avoided the consequences by denying the principle. We revere this lesson too much soon to forget it. Who does not see that the same authority which can establish Christianity, in exclusion of all other Religions, may establish with the same ease any particular sect of Christians, in exclusion of all other Sects? that the same authority which can force a citizen to contribute three pence only of his property for the support of any one establishment, may force him to conform to any other establishment in all cases whatsoever?

4.   Because the Bill violates the equality which ought to be the basis of every law, and which is more indispensable, in proportion as the validity or expediency of any law is more liable to be impeached. If "all men are by nature equally free and

independent," all men are to be considered as entering into Society on equal conditions; as relinquishing no more, and therefore retaining no less, one than another, of their natural rights. Above all are they to be considered as retaining an "equal title to the free exercise of Religion according to the dictates of Conscience." Whilst we assert for ourselves a freedom to embrace, to profess and to observe the Religion which we believe to be of divine origin, we cannot deny an equal freedom to those whose minds have not yet yielded to the evidence which has convinced us. If this freedom be abused, it is an offence against God, not against man: To God, therefore, not to man, must an account of it be rendered. . . .

5.   Because the Bill implies either that the Civil Magistrate is a competent Judge of Religious Truth; or that he may employ Religion as an engine of Civil policy. The first is an arrogant pretension falsified by the contradictory opinions of Rulers in all ages, and throughout the world: the second an unhallowed perversion of the means of salvation. . . .

We the Subscribers say, that the General Assembly of this Commonwealth have no such authority: And that no effort may be omitted on our part against so dangerous an usurpation, we oppose to it, this remonstrance; earnestly praying, as we are in duty bound, that the Supreme Lawgiver of the Universe, by illuminating those to whom it is addressed, may on the one hand, turn their Councils from every act which would affront his holy prerogative, or violate the trust committed to them: and on the other, guide them into every measure which may be worthy of his blessing, may redound to their own praise, and may establish more firmly the liberties, the prosperity and the happiness of the Commonwealth.

NOTES

1.   Note the theological nature of the arguments in the Paragraph 1 of Madison's petition. Is it surprising to see arguments of this sort in support of disestablishment? It may help to know that the leading opponents of Patrick Henry's bill were the Virginia Baptists—the most fervent evangelical sect in the Commonwealth. They were not opposed to the bill because it "advanced" religion but because it invaded a province reserved to the authority of God.

2.   The Memorial and Remonstrance is commonly cited in support of disestablishment of religion. But note its implications for the free exercise of religion. If duties to the Creator are "precedent, both in order of time and in degree of obligation, to the claims of Civil Society," what does that say about rights of free exercise?

3.   Just four years after the Memorial and Remonstrance, as a congressman from Virginia, Madison led the effort to amend the Constitution to add a Bill of Rights, including protections for religious liberty. Here are the results of his efforts:

James Madison's Initial Proposal
for the Religion Clauses
House of Representatives, June 8, 1789 (1 Annals of Cong. 434)

That in article 1st, section 9, between clauses 3 and 4, be inserted these clauses, to wit: The civil rights of none shall be abridged on account of religious belief or worship, nor shall any national religion be established, nor shall the full and equal rights of conscience be in any manner, or on any pretext, infringed.

Debate on Establishment of Religion
and Rights of Conscience

House of Representatives, Aug. 15 & 20, 1789 (1 Annals of Cong. 729–33, 767–68)

Saturday, August 15

The fourth proposition being under consideration, as follows:

Article 1. Section 9. Between paragraphs two and three insert "no religion shall be established by law, nor shall the equal rights of conscience be infringed."

Mr. SYLVESTER had some doubts of the propriety of the mode of expression used in this paragraph. He apprehended that it was liable to a construction different from what had been made by the committee. He feared it might be thought to have a tendency to abolish religion altogether.

Mr. VINING suggested the propriety of transposing the two members of the sentence.

Mr. GERRY said it would read better if it was, that no religious doctrine shall be established by law.

Mr. SHERMAN thought the amendment altogether unnecessary, inasmuch as Congress had no authority whatever delegated to them by the Constitution to make religious establishments; he would, therefore, move to have it struck out.

Mr. CARROLL.—As the rights of conscience are, in their nature, of peculiar delicacy, and will little bear the gentlest touch of governmental hand; and as many sects have concurred in opinion that they are not well secured under the present Constitution. He said he was much in favor of adopting the words. He thought it would tend more towards conciliating the minds of the people to the Government than almost any other amendment he had heard proposed. He would not contend with gentlemen about the phraseology, his object was to secure the substance in such a manner as to satisfy the wishes of the honest part of the community.

Mr. MADISON said, he apprehended the meaning of the words to be, that Congress should not establish a religion, and enforce the legal observation of it by law, nor compel men to worship God in any manner contrary to their conscience. Whether the words are necessary or not, he did not mean to say, but they had been required by some of the State Conventions, who seemed to entertain an opinion that under the clause of the Constitution, which gave power to Congress to make all laws necessary and proper to carry into execution the Constitution, and the laws made under it enabled them to make laws of such a nature as might infringe the rights of conscience, and establish a national religion; to prevent these effects he presumed the amendment was intended and he thought it as well expressed as the nature of the language would admit.

Mr. HUNTINGTON said that he feared, with the gentleman first up on this subject, that the words might be taken in such latitude as to be extremely hurtful to the cause of religion. He understood the amendment to mean what had been expressed by the gentleman from Virginia; but others might find it convenient to put another construction upon it. The ministers of their congregations to the Eastward were maintained by the contributions of those who belonged to their society; the expense of building meeting-houses was contributed in the same manner. These things were regulated by by-laws. If an action was brought before a Federal Court on any of these cases, the person who had neglected to perform his engagements could not be compelled to do it; for a support of ministers or building of places of worship might be construed into a religious establishment.

By the charter of Rhode Island, no religion could be established by law; he could give a history of the effects of such a regulation; indeed the people were now enjoying the blessed fruits of it. He hoped, therefore, the amendment would be made in such a way as to secure the rights of conscience, and a free exercise of the rights of religion, but not to patronise those who professed no religion at all.

Mr. MADISON thought, if the word "national" was inserted before religion, it would satisfy the minds of honorable gentlemen. He believed that the people feared one sect might obtain a pre-eminence, or two combine together, and establish a religion to which they would compel others to conform. He thought if the word "national" was introduced, it would point the amendment directly to the object it was intended to prevent.

Mr. LIVERMORE was not satisfied with that amendment; but he did not wish them to dwell long on the subject. He thought it would be better if it were altered, and made to read in this manner, that Congress shall make no laws touching religion, or infringing the rights of conscience.

Mr. GERRY did not like the term national, proposed by the gentleman from Virginia, and he hoped it would not be adopted by the House. It brought to his mind some observations that had taken place in the conventions at the time they were considering the present Constitution. It had been insisted upon by those who were called anti-federalists, that this form of Government consolidated the Union; the honorable gentleman's motion shows that he considers it in the same light. Those who were called anti-federalists at that time, complained that they had injustice done them by the title, because they were in favor of a Federal Government, and the others were in favor of a national one; the federalists were for ratifying the Constitution as it stood, and the others not until amendments were made. Their names then ought not to have been distinguished by federalists and anti-federalists, but rats and anti-rats.

Mr. MADISON withdrew his motion, but observed that the words "no national religion shall be established by law," did not imply that the Government was a national one; the question was then taken on Mr. LIVERMORE's motion, and passed in the affirmative, thirty-one for, and twenty against it. . . .

Thursday, August 20

On motion of Mr. AMES, the fourth amendment was altered so as to read "Congress shall make no law establishing religion or to prevent the free exercise thereof; or to infringe the rights of conscience." This being adopted,

The first proposition was agreed to.

Mr. SCOTT objected to the clause in the sixth amendment, "No person religiously scrupulous shall be compelled to bear arms." He observed that if this becomes part of the Constitution, such persons can neither he called upon for their services, nor can an equivalent be demanded; it is also attended with still further difficulties, for a militia can never be depended upon. This would lead to the violation of another article in the Constitution, which secures to the people the right of keeping arms, and in this case recourse must be had to a standing army. I conceive it, said he, to be a Legislative right altogether. There are many sects I know, who are religiously scrupulous in this respect; I do not mean to deprive them of any indulgence the law affords; my design is to guard against those who are of no religion. It has been urged that religion is on the decline; if so, the argument is more strong in my favor, for when the time comes that religion shall be discarded the generality of persons will have recourse to these pretexts to get excused from bearing arms.

Mr. BOUDINOT thought the provision in the clause, or something similar to it, was necessary. Can any dependence, said he, be placed in men who are conscientious in this respect? or what justice can there be in compelling them to bear arms, when, according to their religious principles, they would rather die than use them? He adverted to several instances of oppression on this point, that occurred during the war. In forming a militia, an effectual defence ought to be calculated, and no characters of this religious description ought to be compelled to take up arms. I hope that in establishing this Government, we may show the world that proper care is taken that the Government may not interfere with the religious sentiments of any person. Now, by striking out the clause, people may be led to believe that there is an intention in the General Government to compel all its citizens to bear arms.

Some further desultory conversation arose, and it was agreed to insert the words "in person," to the end of the clause; after which, it was adopted, as was the fourth, fifth, sixth, seventh, and eighth clauses of the fourth proposition; then the fifth, sixth, and seventh propositions were agreed to, and the House adjourned.

House Draft Transmitted to the Senate
1 Senate Journal 63 (Aug. 24, 1789)

Article the Third

Congress shall make no law establishing Religion, or prohibiting the free exercise thereof, nor shall the rights of conscience be infringed.

Senate Motions
1 Senate Journal 70 (Sept. 3, 1789)

On motion, To amend Article third, and to strike out these words. "Religion or prohibiting the free Exercise thereof," and Insert, "One Religious Sect or Society in preference to others,"

It passed in the Negative.

On motion, For reconsideration,

It passed in the Affirmative.

On motion, That Article the third be striken out,

It passed in the Negative.

On motion, To adopt the following, in lieu of the third Article, "Congress shall not make any law, infringing the rights of conscience or establishing any Religious Sect or Society,"

It passed in the Negative.

On motion, To amend the third Article, to read thus—"Congress shall make no law establishing any particular denomination of religion in preference to another, or prohibiting the free exercise thereof, nor shall the rights of conscience be infringed."

It passed in the Negative.

On the question upon the third Article as it came from the House of Representatives—

It passed in the Negative.

On motion, To adopt the third Article proposed in the Resolve of the House of Representatives, amended by striking out these words—"Nor shall the rights of conscience be infringed."

It passed in the Affirmative. . . .

On motion to amend article the third, to read as follows: "Congress shall make no law establishing articles of faith or a mode of worship, or prohibiting the free exercise of religion, or abridging the freedom of speech, or the press, or the right of the people peaceable to assemble, and petition to the government for the redress of grievances."

It was passed in the affirmative.

NOTES

1.   Unfortunately, we do not have records of the debates in the Senate, because its proceedings were not open to the public or the press. (The House debates were recorded unofficially by newspaper reporters sitting in the House galleries taking notes. They are presumably not complete, and they are not official.) Keep track of what the senators were arguing about. There appear to be two main issues. First, would the clause protect the "free exercise of religion," the "rights of conscience," or both? What might be the difference(s) between these terms? What is the significance of the decision to protect the "free exercise of religion" and not the "rights of conscience"? Second, would the clause extend broadly to "establishment of religion," or more narrowly to a prohibition on government-formed "articles of faith" or "modes of worship"? The latter terms referred to English laws prescribing the Church of England's statement of doctrine (the Thirty-Nine Articles) and its liturgy (the Book of Common Prayer) and requiring all ministers to conform to them. The House of Representatives insisted on the broader term, and the Senate acceded to it. What practices are part of the "establishment of religion" that would not have been included in the Senate's version?

2.   What did the debates in the House focus on? Note that several members—conspicuously Huntington of Connecticut—feared that the draft amendment would interfere with state and local establishments of religion, such as the one in place in Connecticut. Madison responded that the purpose would be made clear if the amendment used the language "national religion," leaving state establishments to state law, but Gerry objected to the word "national." Eventually, the members settled on a clause that specified that it applied only to "Congress" and prohibited laws "respecting" an establishment, likely meaning laws either establishing a national religion or disturbing state establishments. In other words, they adopted the solution of federalism—local diversity—to the contentious question of religion. Only in the twentieth century, after incorporation of the Establishment Clause, have states been unable to decide for themselves what types of support to provide for religion.

3.   Finally, consider the debate over the exemption from compulsory militia service for persons "religiously scrupulous of bearing arms." What does it tell us about free

exercise of religion? About the legitimacy of legislative acts accommodating religious exercise? Some say such acts are an unfair form of favoring religion—effectively an establishment. Would the framers have agreed?

B. THE FREE EXERCISE CLAUSE

Amend. I: Congress shall make no law respecting an establishment of religion, or prohibiting the free exercise thereof. . . .

What does it mean to "prohibit" the "free exercise of religion"? Does this mean the government may penalize or inhibit the exercise of religion, so long as it does not "prohibit" it? Or should the term be interpreted to encompass any substantial burden on the exercise of religion, as would be the case for most constitutional freedoms? And what is the "exercise" of religion? Presumably this does not mean only belief. But at the time of adoption of the Fourteenth Amendment, many state constitutions protected only acts of "worship," not all forms of "exercise of religion."[7] Should that be understood as a gloss on the First Amendment language? If so, what would be the consequence? If not, what is the reach of the constitutional term? Does it include any action that the individual believer regards as conducive to a life in accordance with the will of God? Are there any limits? More importantly, perhaps, is the right of free exercise absolute, or may it be defeated by the superior claims of the state? May a believer assert the right to commit murder or trespass in the service of God? If not, why not? How strong must the governmental interest be to interfere with the free exercise of religion, and how may it be evaluated? Finally, what is "religion"? The Virginia Declaration of Rights, on which the First Amendment may have been modeled, defined "religion" as the "duty which we owe to our Creator, and the manner of discharging it." Is that a sound definition today? Is it too narrow? Is it too broad? If you are tempted to adopt a broad definition of "religion" for purposes of the protections of the Free Exercise Clause, ask yourself whether the same definition would work for purposes of the Establishment Clause.

We start with several cases on the Free Exercise Clause. The first is the shortest case you will ever see in a law school casebook: *Stansbury v. Marks*, a 1793 Pennsylvania Supreme Court decision decided under the Pennsylvania constitution of 1790. It can be used to illustrate just about every current issue under the First Amendment's protection of religion. The remaining cases illustrate the modern Supreme Court's approaches to these questions: *Wisconsin v. Yoder* (1972), *Employment Division v. Smith* (1990) and *Hosanna-Tabor Evangelical Lutheran Church and School v. EEOC* (2012).

---

[7]   In 1868, when the Fourteenth Amendment was ratified, all thirty-seven states protected religious freedom in one way or another in their state Bills of Rights. Steven G. Calabresi & Sarah E. Agudo, *Individual Rights Under State Constitutions when the Fourteenth Amendment Was Ratified in 1868: What Rights Are Deeply Rooted in American History and Tradition?*, 87 Tex. L. Rev. 7, 33–36 (2008). Thirty-five states protected freedom of "worship"; three states protected free "exercise" of religion. In addition, the state Bill of Rights in twenty-seven states forbade an establishment of religion. Is there any significance to the fact that state constitutions used a different formulation than the First Amendment?

Stansbury v. Marks
2 Dall. 213 (Pa. 1793)

In this cause (which was tried on *Saturday*, the 5th of *April*), the defendant offered *Jonas Phillips*, a Jew, as a witness; but he refused to be sworn, because it was his *Sabbath*. The Court, therefore, fined him £10; but the defendant, afterwards, waving the benefit of his testimony, he was discharged from the fine.

NOTES

1.   *Stansbury*'s facts are cryptic; its reasoning is cryptic. It is not at all clear that the court based its actions on any constitutional provision. The Pennsylvania Constitution of 1790, Art. IX, section 3, in effect at the time of *Stansbury v. Marks*, provided as follows:

> That all men have a natural and indefeasible right to worship Almighty God according to the dictates of their own consciences; that no man can of right be compelled to attend, erect, or support any place of worship, or maintain any ministry, against his consent; that no human authority can, in any case whatever, control or interfere with the rights of conscience; and that no preference shall ever be given, by law, to any religious establishment or modes of worship.

What legal and interpretive questions does this raise? How should the case have come out under this provision? Would the result be different under the Free Exercise Clause of the First Amendment?

2.   What is the "free exercise" of religion? Does it include freedom of *conduct*, or just freedom of belief? Was Jonas Phillips's stance one of religious "belief" or religious "conduct"—or is this a false dichotomy?

3.   What does the First Amendment mean when it bans laws "prohibiting" the free exercise of religion? Does the First Amendment forbid laws that have the *effect* of burdening religious exercise, even if cast in neutral terms? Or is the better reading of the language that it forbids only government laws and practices that are *specifically directed* at religious beliefs or practices? Put differently, is the Free Exercise Clause a substantive immunity from the usual powers of government, or a rule of government nondiscrimination on the basis of religion only?

A related question concerning the meaning of "prohibit": What constitutes a law *prohibiting* religious exercise as opposed to merely *burdening* it? What if a law made Christian worship illegal, but imposed a fine of only $1 per week? Would that "prohibit" the free exercise of religion? Did the fine at issue in *Stansbury* "prohibit" Mr. Phillips's exercise of religion? (After all, he could observe his Sabbath; he merely had to pay the fine.) Does it make a difference if the burden is imposed by a facially neutral law? What if a law imposed a general tax, but payment of that tax conflicted with the individual's, or a religious sect's, sincere beliefs (just as Saturday testimony conflicted with Mr. Phillips's Jewish faith)? Is that a law prohibiting the free exercise of religion? Compare *United States v. Lee*, 455 U.S. 252 (1982) (unanimously rejecting a claimed Free Exercise Clause right of Amish religious employers not to pay Social Security taxes/contributions for their employees on grounds of religious faith requirements to the contrary).

4.   What if the issue were conscientious objection to the draft? Should the Free Exercise Clause be understood to require religious-based conscientious objection to and exemption from military service? What about *non*-religious-based conscientious

objection? Is there a problem with religious conscience being preferred over non-religious conscience? Draft exemption led to a series of Supreme Court decisions presenting these issues. *United States v. Seeger*, 380 U.S. 163 (1965); *Welsh v. United States*, 398 U.S. 333 (1970); *Gillette v. United States*, 401 U.S. 437 (1971).

5. Assuming the state was not constitutionally required to accommodate Mr. Phillips's religious objection to testifying on his Sabbath, would the Establishment Clause forbid the state from doing so as a matter of legislative policy? Would it establish religion to *excuse* Jonas Phillips from testifying (assuming the Free Exercise Clause does not require such an exception)? Does it violate the Establishment Clause to hold court on Saturdays (thus establishing a religion that does not recognize Saturdays as the Sabbath)? Fridays? Ash Wednesday? Yom Kippur? Would a law professor at a state university violate the Establishment Clause by canceling a Constitutional Law class on Yom Kippur, to accommodate Jewish students, and rescheduling a make-up class on a different day (the regular practice of one of the casebook's authors)?

In general, does government accommodation of religion violate the Establishment Clause? What about government symbolic invocation of religion? Does that violate the Establishment Clause? Are the Free Exercise and Establishment Clauses inconsistent with each other?

This is the central dilemma of the Free Exercise Clause. Is it a mere nondiscrimination provision? (Can it really mean so little?) Or does it confer a substantive immunity from society's laws, for all whose religious beliefs conflict with such laws? See Stephen Pepper, *Taking the Free Exercise Clause Seriously*, 1986 BYU L. Rev. 299 (1986). The Supreme Court has vacillated between these two positions. Compare the decision reached in *Wisconsin v. Yoder* (1970) with that reached in *Employment Division v. Smith* (1990).

Wisconsin v. Yoder

406 U.S. 205 (1972)

■ CHIEF JUSTICE BURGER delivered the opinion of the Court.

. . . Respondents Jonas Yoder and Wallace Miller are members of the Old Order Amish religion, and respondent Adin Yutzy is a member of the Conservative Amish Mennonite Church. They and their families are residents of Green County, Wisconsin. Wisconsin's compulsory school-attendance law required them to cause their children to attend public or private school until reaching age 16 but the respondents declined to send their children, ages 14 and 15, to public school after they complete the eighth grade. The children were not enrolled in any private school, or within any recognized exception to the compulsory-attendance law, and they are conceded to be subject to the Wisconsin statute.

On complaint of the school district administrator for the public schools, respondents were charged, tried, and convicted of violating the compulsory-attendance law in Green County Court and were fined the sum of $5 each. Respondents defended on the ground that the application of the compulsory-attendance law violated their rights under the First and Fourteenth Amendments. The trial testimony showed that respondents believed, in accordance with the tenets of Old Order Amish communities generally, that their children's attendance at high school, public or private, was contrary to the Amish religion and way of life. They believed that by sending their children to high school, they would not only expose themselves to the danger of the censure of the church community, but, as found by the county court, also endanger their own salvation and that of their children. The State stipulated that respondents' religious beliefs were sincere.

[Members of the Amish faith seek] to return to the early, simple, Christian life de-emphasizing material success, rejecting the competitive spirit, and seeking to insulate themselves from the modern world. . . .

Amish objection to formal education beyond the eighth grade is firmly grounded in these central religious concepts. They object to the high school, and higher education generally, because the values they teach are in marked variance with Amish values and the Amish way of life; they view secondary school education as an impermissible exposure of their children to a "worldly" influence in conflict with their beliefs. The high school tends to emphasize intellectual and scientific accomplishments, self-distinction, competitiveness, worldly success, and social life with other students. Amish society emphasizes informal learning-through-doing; a life of "goodness," rather than a life of intellect; wisdom, rather than technical knowledge, community welfare, rather than competition; and separation from, rather than integration with, contemporary worldly society.

Formal high school education beyond the eighth grade is contrary to Amish beliefs, not only because it places Amish children in an environment hostile to Amish beliefs with increasing emphasis on competition in class work and sports and with pressure to conform to the styles, manners, and ways of the peer group, but also because it takes them away from their community, physically and emotionally, during the crucial and formative adolescent period of life. During this period, the children must acquire Amish attitudes favoring manual work and self-reliance and the specific skills needed to perform the adult role of an Amish farmer or housewife. They must learn to enjoy physical labor. Once a child has learned basic reading, writing, and elementary mathematics, these traits, skills, and attitudes admittedly fall within the category of those best learned through example and "doing" rather than in a classroom.

I

[I]n order for Wisconsin to compel school attendance beyond the eighth grade against a claim that such attendance interferes with the practice of a legitimate religious belief, it must appear either that the State does not deny the free exercise of religious belief by its requirement, or that there is a state interest of sufficient magnitude to override the interest claiming protection under the Free Exercise Clause. . . . The essence of all that has been said and written on the subject is that only those interests of the highest order and those not otherwise served can overbalance legitimate claims to the free exercise of religion. We can accept it as settled, therefore, that, however strong the State's interest in universal compulsory education, it is by no means absolute to the exclusion or subordination of all other interests.

II

We come then to the quality of the claims of the respondents concerning the alleged encroachment of Wisconsin's compulsory school-attendance statute on their rights and the rights of their children to the free exercise of the religious beliefs they and their forbears have adhered to for almost three centuries. In evaluating those claims we must be careful to determine whether the Amish religious faith and their mode of life are, as they claim, inseparable and interdependent. A way of life, however virtuous and admirable, may not be interposed as a barrier to reasonable state regulation of education if it is based on purely secular considerations; to have the protection of the Religion Clauses, the claims must be rooted in religious belief. Although a determination of what is a "religious" belief or practice entitled to constitutional protection may present a most delicate question, the very concept of ordered liberty precludes allowing every person to make his own standards on matters of conduct in which society as a whole has important interests. Thus, if the Amish asserted their claims because of their subjective evaluation and rejection of the contemporary secular values accepted by the majority, much as Thoreau rejected the social values of his time and isolated himself at Walden Pond, their claims would not rest on a religious basis. Thoreau's choice was philosophical and personal rather than religious, and such belief does not rise to the demands of the Religion Clauses.

Giving no weight to such secular considerations, however, we see that the record in this case abundantly supports the claim that the traditional way of life of the Amish is not merely a matter of personal preference, but one of deep religious conviction, shared by an organized group, and intimately related to daily living. That the Old Order Amish daily life and religious practice stem from their faith is shown by the fact that it is in response to their literal interpretation of the Biblical injunction from the Epistle of Paul to the Romans, "be not conformed to this world. . . ." This command is fundamental to the Amish faith. Moreover, for the Old Order Amish, religion is not simply a matter of theocratic belief. . . .

III

Wisconsin concedes that under the Religion Clauses religious beliefs are absolutely free from the State's control, but it argues that "actions," even though religiously grounded, are outside the protection of the First Amendment But our decisions have rejected the idea that religiously grounded conduct is always outside the protection of the Free Exercise Clause. It is true that activities of individuals, even when religiously based, are often subject to regulation by the States in the exercise of their undoubted power to promote the health, safety, and general welfare, or the Federal Government in the exercise of its delegated powers. But to agree that religiously grounded conduct must often be subject to the broad police power of the State is not to deny that there are areas of conduct protected by the Free Exercise Clause of the First Amendment and thus beyond the power of the State to control, even under regulations of general applicability. . . .

Nor can this case be disposed of on the grounds that Wisconsin's requirement for school attendance to age 16 applies uniformly to all citizens of the State and does not, on its face, discriminate against religions or a particular religion, or that it is motivated by legitimate secular concerns. A regulation neutral on its face may, in its application, nonetheless offend the constitutional requirement for governmental neutrality if it unduly burdens the free exercise of religion. The Court must not ignore the danger that an exception from a general obligation of citizenship on religious grounds may run afoul of the Establishment Clause, but that danger cannot be allowed to prevent any exception no matter how vital it may be to the protection of values promoted by the right of free exercise.

[The Court then rejected the state's argument that its interest in requiring education to age sixteen was compelling, largely on the ground that Amish children received education at home that was adequate for the state's purposes.—Editors]

■ [The concurring opinions joined by JUSTICES STEWART, BRENNAN, and WHITE are omitted.]

■ JUSTICE DOUGLAS, dissenting in part.

I agree with the Court that the religious scruples of the Amish are opposed to the education of their children beyond the grade schools, yet I disagree with the Court's conclusion that the matter is within the dispensation of parents alone. The Court's analysis assumes that the only interests at stake in the case are those of the Amish parents on the one hand, and those of the State on the other. The difficulty with this approach is that, despite the Court's claim, the parents are seeking to vindicate not only their own free exercise claims, but also those of their high-school-age children. . . .

[In cases where the high-school-age children agree with their parents, Justice Douglas was in accord with the Court that the Free Exercise Clause protects their decision not to attend school. The other justices stated that this issue was not raised in the case.—Editors]

[*Assignment 55*]

Employment Division v. Smith

494 U.S. 872 (1990)

■ JUSTICE SCALIA delivered the opinion of the Court.

This case requires us to decide whether the Free Exercise Clause of the First Amendment permits the State of Oregon to include religiously inspired peyote use within the reach of its general criminal prohibition on use of that drug, and thus permits the State to deny unemployment benefits to persons dismissed from their jobs because of such religiously inspired use.

I

Oregon law prohibits the knowing or intentional possession of a "controlled substance," [including] . . . the drug peyote, a hallucinogen derived from the plant *Lophophora williamsii Lemaire.*

Respondents Alfred Smith and Galen Black (hereinafter respondents) were fired from their jobs with a private drug rehabilitation organization because they ingested peyote for sacramental purposes at a ceremony of the Native American Church, of which both are members. When respondents applied to petitioner Employment Division (hereinafter petitioner) for unemployment compensation, they were determined to be ineligible for benefits because they had been discharged for work-related "misconduct." . . .

[T]he Oregon Supreme Court held that respondents' religiously inspired use of peyote fell within the prohibition of the Oregon statute, which "makes no exception for the sacramental use" of the drug. It then considered whether that prohibition was valid under the Free Exercise Clause, and concluded that it was not. The court therefore [held] that the State could not deny unemployment benefits to respondents for having engaged in that practice.

II

Respondents' claim for relief rests on our decisions in *Sherbert v. Verner*, 374 U.S. 398 (1963), *Thomas v. Review Bd. of Indiana Employment Security Div.*, 450 U.S. 707 (1981), and *Hobbie v. Unemployment Appeals Comm'n of Florida*, 480 U.S. 136 (1987), in which we held that a State could not condition the availability of unemployment insurance on an individual's willingness to forgo conduct required by his religion. As we observed in [an earlier appeal in this case], however, the conduct at issue in those cases was not prohibited by law. . . . Now that the Oregon Supreme Court has confirmed that Oregon does prohibit the religious use of peyote, we proceed to consider whether that prohibition is permissible under the Free Exercise Clause.

A

The Free Exercise Clause of the First Amendment, which has been made applicable to the States by incorporation into the Fourteenth Amendment, provides that "Congress shall make no law respecting an establishment of religion, or *prohibiting the free exercise thereof.*" The free exercise of religion means, first and foremost, the right to believe and profess whatever religious doctrine one desires. Thus, the First Amendment obviously excludes all "governmental regulation of religious *beliefs* as such." *Sherbert v. Verner,* at 402. The government may not compel affirmation of religious belief, punish the expression of religious doctrines it believes to be false, impose special disabilities on the basis of religious views or religious status; or lend its power to one or the other side in controversies over religious authority or dogma.

But the "exercise of religion" often involves not only belief and profession but the performance of (or abstention from) physical acts: assembling with others for a worship service, participating in sacramental use of bread and wine, proselytizing, abstaining from certain foods or certain modes of transportation. It would be true, we think (though no case of ours has involved the point), that a State would be "prohibiting the free exercise [of religion]" if it sought to ban such acts or abstentions only when they are engaged in for religious reasons, or only because of the religious belief that they display. It would doubtless be unconstitutional, for example, to ban the casting of "statues that are to be used for worship purposes," or to prohibit bowing down before a golden calf.

Respondents in the present case, however, seek to carry the meaning of "prohibiting the free exercise [of religion]" one large step further. They contend that their religious motivation for using peyote places them beyond the reach of a criminal law that is not specifically directed at their religious practice, and that is concededly constitutional as applied to those who use the drug for other reasons. They assert, in other words, that "prohibiting the free exercise [of religion]" includes requiring any individual to observe a generally applicable law that requires (or forbids) the performance of an act that his religious belief forbids (or requires). As a textual matter, we do not think the words must be given that meaning. It is no more necessary to regard the collection of a general tax, for example, as "prohibiting the free exercise [of religion]" by those citizens who believe support of organized government to be sinful, than it is to regard the same tax as "abridging the freedom . . . of the press" of those publishing companies that must pay the tax as a condition of staying in business. It is a permissible reading of the text, in the one case as in the other, to say that if prohibiting the exercise of religion (or burdening the activity of printing) is not the object of the tax but merely the incidental effect of a generally applicable and otherwise valid provision, the First Amendment has not been offended.

Our decisions reveal that the latter reading is the correct one. We have never held that an individual's religious beliefs excuse him from compliance with an otherwise valid law prohibiting conduct that the State is free to regulate. We first had occasion to assert that principle in *Reynolds v. United States,* 98 U.S. 145 (1878), where we rejected the claim that criminal laws against polygamy could not be constitutionally applied to those whose religion commanded the practice. "Laws," we said, "are made for the government of actions, and while they cannot interfere with mere religious belief and opinions, they may with practices. . . . Can a man excuse his practices to the contrary because of his religious belief? To permit this would be to make the professed doctrines of religious belief superior to the law of the land, and in effect to permit every citizen to become a law unto himself." *Id.,* at 166–167. . . .

Our most recent decision involving a neutral, generally applicable regulatory law that compelled activity forbidden by an individual's religion was *United States v. Lee,* 455 U.S. 252, at 258–261 (1982). There, an Amish employer, on behalf of himself and his employees, sought exemption from collection and payment of Social Security taxes on the ground that the Amish faith prohibited participation in governmental support programs. We rejected the claim that an exemption was constitutionally required. There would be no way, we observed, to distinguish the Amish believer's objection to Social Security taxes from the religious objections that others might have to the collection or use of other taxes. "If, for example, a religious adherent believes war is a sin, and if a certain percentage of the federal budget can be identified as devoted to war-related activities, such individuals would have a similarly valid claim to be exempt from paying that percentage of the income tax. The tax system could not function if denominations were allowed to challenge the tax system because tax payments were spent in a manner that violates their religious belief."

The only decisions in which we have held that the First Amendment bars application of a neutral, generally applicable law to religiously motivated action have involved not the Free Exercise Clause alone, but the Free Exercise Clause in conjunction with other constitutional protections, such as freedom of speech and of the press, see *Cantwell v. Connecticut,* 310 U.S. 296, 304–307 (1940) (invalidating a licensing system for religious and charitable solicitations under which the administrator had discretion to deny a license to any cause he deemed nonreligious); *Murdock v. Pennsylvania,* 319 U.S. 105 (1943) (invalidating a flat tax on solicitation as applied to the dissemination of religious ideas); *Follett v. McCormick,* 321 U.S. 573 (1944) (same); or the right of parents, acknowledged in *Pierce v. Society of Sisters,* 268 U.S. 510 (1925), to direct the education of their children, see *Wisconsin v. Yoder,* 406 U.S. 205 (1972) (invalidating compulsory school-attendance laws as applied to Amish parents who refused on religious grounds to send their children to school). Some of our cases prohibiting compelled expression, decided exclusively upon free speech grounds, have also involved freedom of religion, cf. *Wooley v. Maynard,* 430 U.S. 705 (1977); *West Virginia Bd. of Education v. Barnette,* 319 U.S. 624 (1943). And it is easy to envision a case in which a challenge on freedom of association grounds would likewise be reinforced by Free Exercise Clause concerns. *Cf. Roberts v. United States Jaycees,* 468 U.S. 609, 622 (1984) ("An individual's freedom to speak, to worship, and to petition the government for the redress of grievances could not be vigorously protected from interference by the State [if] a correlative freedom to engage in group effort toward those ends were not also guaranteed").

The present case does not present such a hybrid situation, but a free exercise claim unconnected with any communicative activity or parental right. Respondents urge us to hold, quite simply, that when otherwise prohibitable conduct is accompanied by religious convictions, not only the convictions but the conduct itself must be free from governmental regulation. We have never held that, and decline to do so now. . . .

B

Respondents argue that even though exemption from generally applicable criminal laws need not automatically be extended to religiously motivated actors, at least the claim for a religious exemption must be evaluated under the balancing test set forth in *Sherbert v. Verner.* Under the *Sherbert* test, governmental actions that substantially burden a religious practice must be justified by a compelling governmental interest. . . . We have never invalidated any governmental action on the basis of the *Sherbert* test except the denial of unemployment compensation. Although we have sometimes purported to apply the *Sherbert* test in contexts other than that, we have always found the test satisfied, see *Lee,* 455 U.S. 252 (1982); *Gillette,* 401 U.S. 437 (1971). In recent years we have abstained from applying the *Sherbert* test (outside the unemployment compensation field) at all. . . .

Even if we were inclined to breathe into *Sherbert* some life beyond the unemployment compensation field, we would not apply it to require exemptions from a generally applicable criminal law. The *Sherbert* test, it must be recalled, was developed in a context that lent itself to individualized governmental assessment of the reasons for the relevant conduct. . . .

Whether or not the decisions are that limited, they at least have nothing to do with an across-the-board criminal prohibition on a particular form of conduct. Although . . . we have sometimes used the *Sherbert* test to analyze free exercise challenges to such laws, we have never applied the test to invalidate one. We conclude today that the sounder approach, and the approach in accord with the vast majority of our precedents, is to hold the test inapplicable to such challenges. The government's ability to enforce generally applicable prohibitions of socially harmful conduct, like its ability to carry out other aspects of public policy, "cannot depend on measuring the effects of a governmental action on a religious objector's spiritual development." *Lyng v. Northwest Indian Cemetery Protective Assn.,* 485 U.S. 439, 451 (1988). To make an individual's obligation to obey such a law contingent upon the law's coincidence with his religious beliefs, except where the State's interest is "compelling"—permitting him, by virtue of his beliefs, "to become a law unto himself," *Reynolds v. United States,* at 166–167—contradicts both constitutional tradition and common sense.

The "compelling government interest" requirement seems benign, because it is familiar from other fields. But using it as the standard that must be met before the government may accord different treatment on the basis of race, . . . or before the government may regulate the content of speech, . . . is not remotely comparable to using it for the purpose asserted here. What it produces in those other fields—equality of treatment and an unrestricted flow of contending speech—are constitutional norms; what it would produce here—a private right to ignore generally applicable laws—is a constitutional anomaly.

Nor is it possible to limit the impact of respondents' proposal by requiring a "compelling state interest" only when the conduct prohibited is "central" to the individual's religion. It is no more appropriate for judges to determine the "centrality" of religious beliefs before applying a "compelling interest" test in the free exercise field, than it would be for them to determine the "importance" of ideas before applying the "compelling interest" test in the free speech field. What principle of law or logic can be brought to bear to contradict a believer's assertion that a particular act is "central" to his personal faith? . . . Repeatedly and in many different contexts, we have warned that courts must not presume to determine the place of a particular belief in a religion or the plausibility of a religious claim.

If the "compelling interest" test is to be applied at all, then, it must be applied across the board, to all actions thought to be religiously commanded. Moreover, if "compelling interest" really means what it says (and watering it down here would subvert its rigor in the other fields where it is applied), many laws will not meet the test. Any society adopting such a system would be courting anarchy, but that danger increases in direct proportion to the society's diversity of religious beliefs, and its determination to coerce or suppress none of them. Precisely because we value and protect religious divergence, we cannot afford the luxury of deeming *presumptively invalid,* as applied to the religious objector, every regulation of conduct that does not protect an interest of the highest order. The rule respondents favor would open the prospect of constitutionally required religious exemptions from civic obligations of almost every conceivable kind. . . . The First Amendment's protection of religious liberty does not require this.

Values that are protected against government interference through enshrinement in the Bill of Rights are not thereby banished from the political process. Just as a society that believes in the negative protection accorded to the press by the First Amendment is likely to enact laws that affirmatively foster the dissemination of the printed word, so also a society that believes in the negative protection accorded to religious belief can be expected to be solicitous of that value in its legislation as well. It is therefore not surprising that a number of States have made an exception to their drug laws for sacramental peyote use. But to say that a nondiscriminatory religious-practice exemption is permitted, or even that it is desirable, is not to say that it is constitutionally required, and that the appropriate occasions for its creation can be discerned by the courts. It may fairly be said that leaving accommodation to the political process will place at a relative disadvantage those religious practices that are not widely engaged in; but that unavoidable consequence of democratic government must be preferred to a system in which each conscience is a law unto itself or in which judges weigh the social importance of all laws against the centrality of all religious beliefs.

Because respondents' ingestion of peyote was prohibited under Oregon law, and because that prohibition is constitutional, Oregon may, consistent with the Free Exercise Clause, deny respondents unemployment compensation when their dismissal results from use of the drug.

■ JUSTICE O'CONNOR, with whom JUSTICE BRENNAN, JUSTICE MARSHALL, and JUSTICE BLACKMUN join as to Parts I and II, concurring in the judgment.

Although I agree with the result the Court reaches in this case, I cannot join its opinion. In my view, today's holding dramatically departs from well-settled First Amendment jurisprudence, appears unnecessary to resolve the question presented, and is incompatible with our Nation's fundamental commitment to individual religious liberty. . . .

II

The Court today . . . interprets the [Free Exercise] Clause to permit the government to prohibit, without justification, conduct mandated by an individual's religious beliefs, so long as that prohibition is generally applicable. But a law that prohibits certain conduct—conduct that happens to be an act of worship for someone—manifestly does prohibit that person's free exercise of his religion. A person who is barred from engaging in religiously motivated conduct is barred from freely exercising his religion. Moreover, that person is barred from freely exercising his religion regardless of whether the law prohibits the conduct only when engaged in for religious reasons, only by members of that religion, or by all persons. . . .

The Court responds that generally applicable laws are "one large step" removed from laws aimed at specific religious practices. The First Amendment, however, does not distinguish between laws that are generally applicable and laws that target particular religious practices. Indeed, few States would be so naive as to enact a law directly prohibiting or burdening a religious practice as such. Our free exercise cases have all concerned generally applicable laws that had the effect of significantly burdening a religious practice. If the First Amendment is to have any vitality, it ought not be construed to cover only the extreme and hypothetical situation in which a State directly targets a religious practice. . . .

To say that a person's right to free exercise has been burdened, of course, does not mean that he has an absolute right to engage in the conduct. Under our established First Amendment jurisprudence, we have recognized that the freedom to act, unlike the freedom to believe, cannot be absolute. Instead, we have respected both the First Amendment's express textual mandate and the governmental interest in regulation of conduct by requiring the government to justify any substantial burden on religiously motivated conduct by a compelling state interest and by means narrowly tailored to achieve that interest. The compelling interest test effectuates the First Amendment's command that religious liberty is an independent liberty, that it occupies a preferred position, and that the Court will not permit encroachments upon this liberty, whether direct or indirect, unless required by clear and compelling governmental interests "of the highest order," *Yoder,* at 215. . . .

The Court attempts to support its narrow reading of the Clause by claiming that "[w]e have never held that an individual's religious beliefs excuse him from compliance with an otherwise valid law prohibiting conduct that the State is free to regulate." But as the Court later notes, as it must, in cases such as *Cantwell* and *Yoder* we have in fact interpreted the Free Exercise Clause to forbid application of a generally applicable prohibition to religiously motivated conduct. Indeed, in *Yoder* we expressly rejected the interpretation the Court now adopts:

> [O]ur decisions have rejected the idea that religiously grounded conduct is always outside the protection of the Free Exercise Clause. It is true that

activities of individuals, even when religiously based, are often subject to regulation by the States in the exercise of their undoubted power to promote the health, safety, and general welfare, or the Federal Government in the exercise of its delegated powers. But to agree that religiously grounded conduct must often be subject to the broad police power of the State is not to deny that there are areas of conduct protected by the Free Exercise Clause of the First Amendment and thus beyond the power of the State to control, *even under regulations of general applicability.* . . .

A regulation neutral on its face may, in its application, nonetheless offend the constitutional requirement for government neutrality if it unduly burdens the free exercise of religion.

Id., at 219–220 (emphasis added).

The Court endeavors to escape from our decisions in *Cantwell* and *Yoder* by labeling them "hybrid" decisions, but there is no denying that both cases expressly relied on the Free Exercise Clause and that we have consistently regarded those cases as part of the mainstream of our free exercise jurisprudence. Moreover, in each of the other cases cited by the Court to support its categorical rule, we rejected the particular constitutional claims before us only after carefully weighing the competing interests. That we rejected the free exercise claims in those cases hardly calls into question the applicability of First Amendment doctrine in the first place. Indeed, it is surely unusual to judge the vitality of a constitutional doctrine by looking to the win-loss record of the plaintiffs who happen to come before us. . . .

In my view . . . the essence of a free exercise claim is relief from a burden imposed by government on religious practices or beliefs, whether the burden is imposed directly through laws that prohibit or compel specific religious practices, or indirectly through laws that, in effect, make abandonment of one's own religion or conformity to the religious beliefs of others the price of an equal place in the civil community. As we explained in *Thomas:*

Where the state conditions receipt of an important benefit upon conduct proscribed by a religious faith, or where it denies such a benefit because of conduct mandated by religious belief, thereby putting substantial pressure on an adherent to modify his behavior and to violate his beliefs, a burden upon religion exists.

A State that makes criminal an individual's religiously motivated conduct burdens that individual's free exercise of religion in the severest manner possible, for it "results in the choice to the individual of either abandoning his religious principle or facing criminal prosecution." . . .

The Court today gives no convincing reason to depart from settled First Amendment jurisprudence. There is nothing talismanic about neutral laws of general applicability or general criminal prohibitions, for laws neutral toward religion can coerce a person to violate his religious conscience or intrude upon his religious duties just as effectively as laws aimed at religion. . . . The Court's parade of horribles not only fails as a reason for discarding the compelling interest test, it instead demonstrates just the opposite: that courts have been quite capable of applying our free exercise jurisprudence to strike sensible balances between religious liberty and competing state interests.

Finally, the Court today suggests that the disfavoring of minority religions is an "unavoidable consequence" under our system of government and that accommodation of such religions must be left to the political process. In my view, however, the First Amendment was enacted precisely to protect the rights of those whose religious practices are not shared by the majority and may be viewed with hostility. The history of our free exercise doctrine amply demonstrates the harsh impact majoritarian rule has had on unpopular or emerging religious groups such as the Jehovah's Witnesses and the Amish. . . .

III

The Court's holding today not only misreads settled First Amendment precedent; it appears to be unnecessary to this case. I would reach the same result applying our established free exercise jurisprudence.

A

There is no dispute that Oregon's criminal prohibition of peyote places a severe burden on the ability of respondents to freely exercise their religion. Peyote is a sacrament of the Native American Church and is regarded as vital to respondents' ability to practice their religion. . . . [M]embers of the Native American Church must choose between carrying out the ritual embodying their religious beliefs and avoidance of criminal prosecution. That choice is, in my view, more than sufficient to trigger First Amendment scrutiny.

There is also no dispute that Oregon has a significant interest in enforcing laws that control the possession and use of controlled substances by its citizens. . . .

B

Thus, the critical question in this case is whether exempting respondents from the State's general criminal prohibition "will unduly interfere with fulfillment of the governmental interest." *Lee,* at 259. Although the question is close, I would conclude that uniform application of Oregon's criminal prohibition is "essential to accomplish," *id.,* at 257, its overriding interest in preventing the physical harm caused by the use of a Schedule I controlled substance. Oregon's criminal prohibition represents that State's judgment that the possession and use of controlled substances, even by only one person, is inherently harmful and dangerous. Because the health effects caused by the use of controlled substances exist regardless of the motivation of the user, the use of such substances, even for religious purposes, violates the very purpose of the laws that prohibit them. Moreover, in view of the societal interest in preventing trafficking in controlled substances, uniform application of the criminal prohibition at issue is essential to the effectiveness of Oregon's stated interest in preventing any possession of peyote. Cf. *Jacobson v. Massachusetts,* 197 U.S. 11 (1905) (denying exemption from small pox vaccination requirement).

For these reasons, I believe that granting a selective exemption in this case would seriously impair Oregon's compelling interest in prohibiting possession of peyote by its citizens. Under such circumstances, the Free Exercise Clause does not require the State to accommodate respondents' religiously motivated conduct. . . .

I would therefore adhere to our established free exercise jurisprudence and hold that the State in this case has a compelling interest in regulating peyote use by its citizens and that accommodating respondents' religiously motivated conduct "will unduly interfere with fulfillment of the governmental interest." *Lee,* at 259. Accordingly, I concur in the judgment of the Court.

■ JUSTICE BLACKMUN, with whom JUSTICE BRENNAN and JUSTICE MARSHALL join, dissenting.

. . . I agree with JUSTICE O'CONNOR's analysis of the applicable free exercise doctrine, and I join parts I and II of her opinion. As she points out, "the critical question in this case is whether exempting respondents from the State's general criminal prohibition will unduly interfere with fulfillment of the governmental interest." I do disagree, however, with her specific answer to that question. . . .

The State's interest in enforcing its prohibition, in order to be sufficiently compelling to outweigh a free exercise claim, cannot be merely abstract or symbolic. The State cannot plausibly assert that unbending application of a criminal prohibition is essential to fulfill any compelling interest, if it does not, in fact, attempt to enforce that prohibition. In this case, the State actually has not evinced any concrete interest in enforcing its drug laws against religious users of peyote. Oregon has never sought to prosecute respondents, and does not claim that it has made significant enforcement efforts against other religious users of peyote. The State's asserted interest thus amounts only to the symbolic preservation of an unenforced prohibition. . . .

Similarly, this Court's prior decisions have not allowed a government to rely on mere speculation about potential harms, but have demanded evidentiary support for a refusal to allow a religious exception. . . . The State proclaims an interest in protecting the health and safety of its citizens from the dangers of unlawful drugs. It offers, however, no evidence that the religious use of peyote has ever harmed anyone. . . .

The carefully circumscribed ritual context in which respondents used peyote is far removed from the irresponsible and unrestricted recreational use of unlawful drugs. The Native American Church's internal restrictions on, and supervision of, its members' use of peyote substantially obviate the State's health and safety concerns. . . .

Finally, the State argues that granting an exception for religious peyote use would erode its interest in the uniform, fair, and certain enforcement of its drug laws. The State fears that, if it grants an exemption for religious peyote use, a flood of other claims to religious exemptions will follow. It would then be placed in a dilemma, it says, between allowing a patchwork of exemptions that would hinder its law enforcement efforts, and risking a violation of the Establishment Clause by arbitrarily limiting its religious exemptions. . . .

The State's apprehension of a flood of other religious claims is purely speculative. Almost half the States, and the Federal Government, have maintained an exemption for religious peyote use for many years, and apparently have not found themselves overwhelmed by claims to other religious exemptions. Allowing an exemption for religious peyote use would not necessarily oblige the State to grant a similar exemption to other religious groups. The unusual circumstances that make the religious use of peyote compatible with the State's interests in health and safety and in preventing drug trafficking would not apply to other religious claims. . . .

NOTES

1.   What is the standard that *Smith* settles on for identifying when government action violates the clause? What exceptions does *Smith* recognize to its general rule? Why does the Court adopt those exceptions?

2.   The case raises once again important questions of methodology in interpreting and applying the Constitution: What counts in constitutional interpretation? The text alone? What if the text is ambiguous, as Justice Scalia argues in his majority opinion in *Smith*? (Is the text ambiguous?) Should an ambiguous text protecting individual freedom from government action be viewed from the perspective of the individual ("Does the government's action prohibit me from exercising my religion?") or from the perspective of the government ("Is our rule a rule that prohibits religious exercise or does it prohibit conduct, irrespective of why someone might do it?")? If the text of the Free Exercise Clause is in fact ambiguous, what other type of constitutional argument is best for resolving the ambiguity (see p. 42)? Evidence of the historical context of the provision? Comparison with how similar types of questions are addressed by other provisions of the Constitution? Past practice? Prior judicial interpretations? The policy implications of one interpretation versus another? Which of these types of argument do you think is best for the Free Exercise Clause? Why? And whatever type of argument you thought most helpful, is it the type of argument that Justice Scalia turned to?

3.   The Court says that "[o]ur decisions reveal" which of the two textually plausible readings is correct: "We have never held that an individual's religious beliefs excuse him from compliance with an otherwise valid law prohibiting conduct that the State is free to regulate." 494 U.S. at 878–879. Can you square that statement with *Wisconsin v. Yoder*? Is *Smith* faithful to precedent?

4.   Justice Scalia's majority opinion states that what a "strict scrutiny" or "compelling interest" test produces with respect to the Free Exercise Clause (as opposed to in the Free Speech Clause and racial discrimination areas) is not a way of protecting a true constitutional "norm" but is instead a "constitutional anomaly," "a private right to ignore generally applicable laws." Is the charge correct? Is it possible that the charge is correct, but that that is indeed what the Free Exercise Clause is all about—an exemption from the usual rules where they conflict with legitimate religious exercise? Put the matter concretely: Is drug use different, i.e., should it be treated differently by the law, when engaged in as a matter of sincere religious exercise as opposed to simply for the purpose of "getting high"? Does the Free Exercise Clause require a different treatment for religious-exercise drug use? Put the issue in a slightly different (but analogous) context: During Prohibition, did the Free Exercise Clause require an exception for the use of communion wine in Christian worship?

5.   As a matter of history, the Volstead Act exempted the sacramental use of wine from Prohibition—which suggests a few more questions: First, assuming such an exception was *not required* by the Free Exercise Clause, was such statutory accommodation of religion—granting religious use an exception from the rules that govern other uses—*forbidden* by the Establishment Clause? (We will return to that question presently, when we take up the Establishment Clause.) Second, does the fact that such an accommodation *was* made vindicate the majority's assurance, expressed late in the opinion, that society "can be expected to be solicitous" of religious freedom? Or— quite the reverse—is the fact that such accommodations might tend to be made for majority religions and not minority religions (like Native American ritual peyote use) suggest that the democratic process *cannot* be expected to be solicitous of religious freedom, at least not equally so? But *Smith* did prompt passage of the "American Indian

Religious Freedom Act Amendments of 1994," in which Congress found that the lack of uniformity in state protections for the ceremonial use of peyote was causing Native Americans to be stigmatized and marginalized. Congress declared that "the use, possession, or transportation of peyote by an Indian for bona fide traditional ceremonial purposes" shall not be prohibited by or in the United States. 42 U.S.C. § 1996a(a)(3), (5) (1994). Is the accommodation of Native American practitioners permitting them—but not others—to use peyote an unconstitutional establishment of religion under the Establishment Clause?

6.   How would you respond to the following not-so-hypothetical hypotheticals, drawn from actual cases?

a.   A state law requires that unemployment compensation benefits are available only to persons who make themselves available for "suitable" work. May a state exclude a Seventh-Day Adventist (a member of a denomination that observes a Saturday Sabbath) from unemployment compensation, where she declines to be available for work on Saturday? *Sherbert v. Verner*, 374 U.S. 398 (1963), held no—and *Smith* retains that case. Could a state exclude a religious person from unemployment benefits when he became unavailable for work because of religious objections to working on armaments manufacturing? *Thomas v. Review Board*, 450 U.S. 707 (1981), held the individual entitled to benefits, notwithstanding the general rule—and *Smith* retains that decision as well. Would it matter if not all members of his sect or denomination held the same conviction? *Thomas* holds that it does not matter—that free exercise is determined by individual beliefs and practices, so long as they are sincere.

b.   A particular order of Amish object on sincere religious grounds to participation in Social Security (and payment of Social Security taxes), because the community provides for its own members as a matter of religious duty and obligation. May the government nonetheless require Amish employers to participate in Social Security? *United States v. Lee*, 455 U.S. 252 (1982), said that this requirement did *not* violate the Free Exercise Clause.

c.   Does the Free Exercise Clause require accommodating religion-based conscientious objection to military service, and thus an exemption from the draft for religious believers? *Gillette v. United States,* 401 U.S. 437 (1971), said *no*, even under the pre-*Smith* "compelling interest" standard. Could the national government voluntarily accommodate religion-based conscientious objection to military service? Could it do so and not similarly permit secular-conscience exemption from such (otherwise) compulsory service?

d.   Does the Free Exercise Clause permit the government to

(1)   require claimants to provide a Social Security number in order to obtain welfare benefits, over a sincere religious objection to doing so? *Bowen v. Roy*, 476 U.S. 693 (1986), says *yes*.

(2)   forbid a Jewish military officer from wearing a yarmulke, pursuant to a uniform headgear requirement? *Goldman v. Weinberger*, 475 U.S. 503 (1986), says *yes*.

(3)   build a logging and construction road, on government land, through a traditional Native American high holy ground? *Lyng v. Northwest Indian Cemetery Protection Assn.*, 485 U.S. 439 (1988), says *yes,* on the ground that it is no longer the Native Americans' land, and that there is no burden on religious exercise (within the meaning of the language "*prohibiting* the free exercise thereof") where a religious adherent seeks to tell the government what it may or may not do, as

opposed to where the government seeks to tell the religious adherent what he or she may not do.

e. Going down the slope a little faster: Does the Free Exercise Clause require that religious adherents be excused, on the basis of religious conviction, from otherwise generally applicable (1) child neglect laws? (2) animal mistreatment laws? (3) minimum wage laws? (4) anti-discrimination laws (race, sex, sexual orientation)? (5) environmental protection or endangered species laws (e.g., exempting Native Americans on religious grounds from prohibitions on the taking of bald eagle feathers)? (6) prohibitions of polygamy?

Free Exercise After *Smith*

Just three years after *Smith*, in *Church of the Lukumi Babalu Aye v. City of Hialeah*, 508 U.S. 520 (1993), the Supreme Court unanimously held that an ordinance outlawing "animal sacrifice" was unconstitutional. The prohibited practice was defined as "unnecessarily" killing an animal in a "public or private ritual or ceremony not for the primary purpose of food consumption." The Court concluded that the ordinance was not neutral because it was directed at the practices of the Santeria religion—an Afro-Cuban syncretistic sect that practiced animal sacrifice to the horror of their neighbors—and that it was not "generally applicable" because the city permitted the killing of animals, sometimes by cruel means, for a large number of purposes, including sport, pest control, and medical experimentation. Moreover, the legal category "unnecessary" required a case-by-case evaluation of whether a particular killing had a legitimate purpose. How is a civil government to decide whether a Santerian sacrifice is "unnecessary"? Santerians do not think it is.

Lukumi suggests that *Smith*'s category of "neutral and generally applicable laws" may not be as all-encompassing as it seemed to be. Many laws, though framed in general terms, with no reference to religion, contain exemptions that shield most secular conduct, or that vest discretionary normal judgments to government officials. *Lukumi* suggests that these legal schemes may remain subject to strict scrutiny.

Moreover, the Court strongly endorsed a rule prohibiting discrimination against religion or religious activities. "At a minimum," the Court wrote, "the protections of the Free Exercise Clause pertain if the law at issue discriminates against some or all religious beliefs or regulates or prohibits conduct because it is undertaken for religious reasons." Most real-world examples of such discrimination arise from government exclusions of religious beneficiaries from otherwise neutral benefits because of concerns about separation between church and state—such as exclusion from public speech forums (forbidden in *Widmar v. Vincent*, 454 U.S. 263 (1981), and *Lamb's Chapel v. Center Moriches Union School Dist.*, 508 U.S. 384 (1993)), from unemployment benefits (forbidden in *Sherbert v. Verner*, 374 U.S. 398 (1963)), from receipt of student activities funds (forbidden in *Rosenberger v. University of Virginia*, 515 U.S. 819 (1995)), or from eligibility for government grants or contracts.

Lukumi was not the only major Free Exercise Clause development after *Smith*. In the wake of *Smith*, Congress in 1993 enacted the "Religious Freedom Restoration Act," 42 U.S.C. Section 2000bb *et seq.* ("RFRA"). In essence, RFRA enacted a federal statutory protection of religious freedom comparable to the very constitutional approach rejected in *Smith*: requiring the government to justify a burden on religious exercise by showing that imposition of the burden "on that person" was the "least restrictive means" of furthering a "compelling governmental interest." Note that the statute does not ask whether the challenged law serves a compelling interest in general, but focuses specifically on the application of the law to the particular claimant. That had not been clear in pre-*Smith* free exercise law, and is a significant change. Congress also defined "religious exercise" capaciously to include "any exercise of religion, whether or not compelled by, or central to, a system of religious belief," and it declared that this concept "shall be construed in favor of a broad protection of religious exercise, to the maximum extent permitted by the terms of this chapter and the Constitution."

In *City of Boerne v. Flores*, 521 U.S. 507 (1997), the Court held RFRA could not constitutionally be applied to actions of state and local governments: it was beyond the national government's legislative powers to enact such a measure, pursuant to Section 5 of the Fourteenth Amendment, because that power is only the power "to enforce" the Fourteenth Amendment's prohibitions of state action. RFRA was not, the Court in *Boerne* held, a measure "to enforce" the Fourteenth Amendment's incorporation of the Free Exercise Clause because it adopted a much broader protection of the free exercise of religion than the Court had held was required (in *Smith*). That decision is presented at p. 1328.

Even after *Boerne*, RFRA remains valid as Congress's self-restriction on the exercise of powers by the federal government. Moreover, in response to *Boerne*, Congress enacted a more limited law applying the RFRA standard to state and local laws regarding institutionalized persons and law use restrictions. See Religious Land Use and Institutionalized Persons Act, 42 U.S.C. § 2000cc *et seq.* ("RLUIPA). The Court unanimously upheld RLUIPA, at least as it applied to institutionalized persons, in *Cutter v. Wilkinson*, 544 U.S. 709 (2005). As a result of *Lukumi*, RFRA, and RLUIPA, there are two quite different legal regimes applicable to religious freedom claims: one that applies to state and local laws of general applicability outside the scope of RLUIPA, and another, more protective regime that applies to all federal law, all law regulating religious land use (for example, zoning or historic preservation laws) and institutionalized persons (mostly prisoners), and laws that do not employ a generally applicable rule. Over half the states have enacted state-level RFRA laws, and some state courts have interpreted the free exercise clauses of their state constitutions to similar effect.

The Supreme Court has decided three cases interpreting and enforcing the compelling interest standard of RFRA and RLUIPA, two of them unanimous and one of them a controversial 5–4 decision. In *Gonzales v. O Centro Espirita Beneficente Uniao Do Vegetal*, 546 U.S. 418 (2006), a seeming reprise of *Smith*, the Court, in a unanimous opinion, upheld an injunction forbidding the federal government from prosecuting a small religious sect for the use of a hallucinogenic sacramental tea. The government lacked a "compelling interest" in "uniform enforcement" of the Act, the Court held, and RFRA therefore required an exemption from the Controlled Substances Act for this sincere religious practice: "The Government's argument echoes the classic rejoinder of bureaucrats throughout history: If I make an exception for you, I'll have to make one for everybody, so no exceptions. But RFRA operates by mandating consideration, under the compelling interest test, of exceptions to 'rules of general applicability.' "

In *Holt v. Hobbes*, 135 S.Ct. 853 (2015), the Court rendered a unanimous decision, under RLUIPA, in favor of a Muslim prisoner who wished to maintain a one-half inch beard in accordance with his religion. The Court's opinion, written by

Justice Alito, emphasizes the "rigorous" character of the statutory test, and the need for courts to independently examine the government's justification rather than simply deferring to their expertise.

Burwell v. Hobby Lobby Stores, 134 S.Ct. 2751 (2014), was a challenge by two family-owned for-profit corporations to the requirement imposed by regulations under the Affordable Care Act that employer-provided health insurance cover certain contraceptive drugs, which the plaintiffs regarded as abortifacients, without cost to the covered employee. (For most drugs, the covered employee is required to contribute a co-payment.) The Court divided sharply. The majority held that the protections of RFRA apply at least to some for-profit corporations; the dissenters disagreed. Prior to *Hobby Lobby*, the Free Exercise Clause had been held applicable to non-profit corporations, and to for-profit businesses, but no case had been decided by the Court involving a for-profit business that also was a corporation. The majority assumed for purposes of decision that the contraceptive mandate serves a compelling governmental interest, but held that the government's own accommodation of other objecting entities proved that there is a less restrict alternative. The dissenters accused the majority of allowing the RFRA claimants to shift the burden of their religious exercise onto their employees.

Do RFRA, RLUIPA, or similar state laws violate the Establishment Clause? Once again, the question is one of permissible government accommodation of religion. The implication of *Cutter v. Wilkinson*, 544 U.S. 709 (2005), presented at p. 1141, is no. *Cutter* upheld a different, somewhat narrower federal statutory requirement that states accommodate religious exercise, passed in the wake of *City of Boerne*, against Establishment Clause challenge. While not directly presenting the issue, *O Centro Espirita* appears implicitly to assume that RFRA's requirement of accommodation does not violate the Establishment Clause. Some scholars argue, however, that it is unconstitutional under the Establishment Clause for Congress or state legislatures to accommodate religious exercise when doing so would impose harms on third parties. Is that a good argument? Is it consistent with this nation's tradition of accommodating religious dissenters?

As a legislative and political matter, RFRA-like statutes—which enjoyed overwhelming bipartisan support when enacted—have become highly controversial, mainly because of their potential application to civil rights laws, including protections for LGBT persons and same-sex marriages. Consider that issue in connection with a decision you will read next, *Hosanna-Tabor Evangelical Lutheran Church and School v. EEOC*. Also unanimous, it interpreted both the Free Exercise and the Establishment Clause to limit the reach of employment discrimination laws in the context of the employment of clergy. Ask yourself, also, whether this decision is consistent with *Smith*.

Hosanna-Tabor Evangelical Lutheran Church and School v. EEOC
132 S.Ct. 694 (2012)

■ CHIEF JUSTICE ROBERTS delivered the opinion of the Court.

Certain employment discrimination laws authorize employees who have been wrongfully terminated to sue their employers for reinstatement and damages. The question presented is whether the Establishment and Free Exercise Clauses of the First Amendment bar such an action when the employer is a religious group and the employee is one of the group's ministers.

I–A

[Hosanna-Tabor is a church and school in the Lutheran Church Missouri-Synod denomination. Cheryl Perich, a "called" teacher who was a "commissioned minister" in the denomination, took a leave of absence for narcolepsy. When she tried to return to teaching in the middle of the school year, she was told that a replacement teacher had been hired for the year. She threatened to sue, and she was then discharged by Hosanna-Tabor, which cited as grounds for termination her "insubordination and disruptive behavior" as well as the damage she had done to her "working relationship" with the school by "threatening to take legal action." The church congregation also voted to rescind Perich's call as a "commissioned minister."—Editors]

. . . The Synod classifies teachers into two categories: "called" and "lay." "Called" teachers are regarded as having been called to their vocation by God through a congregation. To be eligible to receive a call from a congregation, a teacher must satisfy certain academic Synod district, and pass an oral examination by a faculty committee. A teacher who meets these requirements may be called by a congregation. Once called, a teacher receives the formal title "Minister of Religion, Commissioned." A commissioned minister serves for an open-ended term; at Hosanna-Tabor, a call could be rescinded only for cause and by a supermajority vote of the congregation.

"Lay" or "contract" teachers, by contrast, are not required to be trained by the Synod or even to be Lutheran. At Hosanna-Tabor, they were appointed by the school board, without a vote of the congregation, to one-year renewable terms. Although teachers at the school generally performed the same duties regardless of whether they were lay or called, lay teachers were hired only when called teachers were unavailable. . . .

Perich . . . taught math, language arts, social studies, science, gym, art and music. She also taught a religion class four days a week, led the students in prayer and devotional exercises each day, and attended a weekly school-wide chapel service. Perich led the chapel service herself about twice a year.

B

Perich filed a charge with the Equal Employment Opportunity Commission, alleging that her employment had been terminated in violation of the Americans with Disabilities Act, 104 Stat. 327, 42 U.S.C. § 12101 *et seq.* (1990). The ADA prohibits an employer from discriminating against a qualified individual on the basis of disability. It also prohibits an employer from retaliating "against any individual because such individual has opposed any act or practice made unlawful by [the ADA] or because such individual made a charge, testified, assisted, or participated in any manner in an investigation, proceeding, or hearing under [the ADA]." § 12203(a).

The EEOC brought suit against Hosanna-Tabor, alleging that Perich had been fired in retaliation for threatening to file an ADA lawsuit. Perich intervened in the litigation, claiming unlawful retaliation under both the ADA and the Michigan Persons with Disabilities Civil Rights Act, Mich. Comp. Laws § 37.1602(a) (1979). The EEOC and Perich sought Perich's reinstatement to her former position (or frontpay in lieu thereof), along with backpay, compensatory and punitive damages, attorney's fees, and other injunctive relief.

Hosanna-Tabor moved for summary judgment. Invoking what is known as the "ministerial exception," the Church argued that the suit was barred by the First Amendment because the claims at issue concerned the employment relationship between a religious institution and one of its ministers. According to the Church, Perich was a minister, and she had been fired for a religious reason—namely, that her threat to sue the Church violated the Synod's belief that Christians should resolve their disputes internally.

. . . The Court of Appeals recognized the existence of a ministerial exception barring certain employment discrimination claims against religious institutions—an exception "rooted in the First Amendment's guarantees of religious freedom." The court concluded, however, that Perich did not qualify as a "minister" under the exception, noting in particular that her duties as a called teacher were identical to her duties as a lay teacher. . . .

II

The First Amendment provides, in part, that "Congress shall make no law respecting an establishment of religion, or prohibiting the free exercise thereof." We have said that these two Clauses "often exert conflicting pressures," *Cutter* v. *Wilkinson* (p. 271). . . . Not so here. Both Religion Clauses bar the government from interfering with the decision of a religious group to fire one of its ministers. . . .

[The Court reviewed the history of religious establishment not only in colonial America but also in the Church of England, including government control over the selection of ministers; occasions when James Madison, once as secretary of state and once as president, had determined that the government could not choose religious "functionaries"; the Court's property cases affirming the institutional autonomy of religious organizations; and the lower court precedents that uniformly found that in one form or another there was a "ministerial exception."—Editors]

We agree that there is . . . a ministerial exception. The members of a religious group put their faith in the hands of their ministers. Requiring a church to accept or retain an unwanted minister, or punishing a church for failing to do so, intrudes upon more than a mere employment decision. Such action interferes with the internal governance of the church, depriving the church of control over the selection of those who will personify its beliefs. By imposing an unwanted minister, the state infringes the Free Exercise Clause, which protects a religious group's right to shape its own faith and mission through its appointments. According the state the power to determine which individuals will minister to the faithful also violates the Establishment Clause, which prohibits government involvement in such ecclesiastical decisions.

The EEOC and Perich acknowledge that employment discrimination laws would be unconstitutional as applied to religious groups in certain circumstances. They grant, for example, that it would violate the First Amendment for courts to apply such laws to compel the ordination of women by the Catholic Church or by an Orthodox Jewish seminary. According to the EEOC and Perich, religious organizations could successfully defend against employment discrimination claims in those circumstances by invoking the constitutional right to freedom of association—a right "implicit" in the First Amendment. The EEOC and Perich thus see no need—and no basis—for a special rule for ministers grounded in the Religion Clauses themselves.

We find this position untenable. The right to freedom of association is a right enjoyed by religious and secular groups alike. It follows under the EEOC's and Perich's view that the First Amendment analysis should be the same, whether the association in question is the Lutheran Church, a labor union, or a social club. That result is hard to square with the text of the First Amendment itself, which gives special solicitude to the rights of religious organizations. We cannot accept the remarkable view that the Religion Clauses have nothing to say about a religious organization's freedom to select its own ministers.

The EEOC and Perich also contend that our decision in *Employment Div., Dept. of Human Resources of Ore. v. Smith*, precludes recognition of a ministerial exception. In *Smith*, two members of the Native American Church were denied state unemployment benefits after it was determined that they had been fired from their jobs for ingesting peyote, a crime under Oregon law. We held that this did not violate the Free Exercise Clause, even though the peyote had been ingested for sacramental purposes, because the "right of free exercise does not relieve an individual of the obligation to comply with a valid and neutral law of general applicability on the ground that the law proscribes (or prescribes) conduct that his religion prescribes (or proscribes)."

It is true that the ADA's prohibition on retaliation, like Oregon's prohibition on peyote use, is a valid and neutral law of general applicability. But a church's selection of its ministers is unlike an individual's ingestion of peyote. *Smith* involved government regulation of only outward physical acts. The present case, in contrast, concerns government interference with an internal church decision that affects the faith and mission of the church itself. See *id.*, at 877 (distinguishing the government's regulation of "physical acts" from its "lend[ing] its power to one or the other side in controversies over religious authority or dogma"). The contention that *Smith* forecloses recognition of a ministerial exception rooted in the Religion Clauses has no merit.

III

Having concluded that there is a ministerial exception grounded in the Religion Clauses of the First Amendment, we consider whether the exception applies in this case. We hold that it does.

Every Court of Appeals to have considered the question has concluded that the ministerial exception is not limited to the head of a religious congregation, and we agree. We are reluctant, however, to adopt a rigid formula for deciding when an employee qualifies as a minister. It is enough for us to conclude, in this our first case involving the ministerial exception, that the exception covers Perich, given all the circumstances of her employment. . . .

Because Perich was a minister within the meaning of the exception, the First Amendment requires dismissal of this employment discrimination suit against her religious employer. The EEOC and Perich originally sought an order reinstating Perich to her former position as a called teacher. By requiring the Church to accept a minister it did not want, such an order would have plainly violated the Church's freedom under the Religion Clauses to select its own ministers.

Perich no longer seeks reinstatement, having abandoned that relief before this Court. But that is immaterial. Perich continues to seek frontpay in lieu of reinstatement, backpay, compensatory and punitive damages, and attorney's fees.

An award of such relief would operate as a penalty on the Church for terminating an unwanted minister, and would be no less prohibited by the First Amendment than an order overturning the termination. Such relief would depend on a determination that Hosanna-Tabor was wrong to have relieved Perich of her position, and it is precisely such a ruling that is barred by the ministerial exception.

The EEOC and Perich suggest that Hosanna-Tabor's asserted religious reason for firing Perich—that she violated the Synod's commitment to internal dispute resolution—was pretextual. That suggestion misses the point of the ministerial exception. The purpose of the exception is not to safeguard a church's decision to fire a minister only when it is made for a religious reason. The exception instead ensures that the authority to select and control who will minister to the faithful—a matter "strictly ecclesiastical," is the church's alone.

IV

. . . The case before us is an employment discrimination suit brought on behalf of a minister, challenging her church's decision to fire her. Today we hold only that the ministerial exception bars such a suit. We express no view on whether the exception bars other types of suits, including actions by employees alleging breach of contract or tortious conduct by their religious employers. There will be time enough to address the applicability of the exception to other circumstances if and when they arise.

. . . The interest of society in the enforcement of employment discrimination statutes is undoubtedly important. But so too is the interest of religious groups in choosing who will preach their beliefs, teach their faith, and carry out their mission. When a minister who has been fired sues her church alleging that her termination was discriminatory, the First Amendment has struck the balance for us. The church must be free to choose those who will guide it on its way.

■ [The concurring opinions of JUSTICE THOMAS and JUSTICE ALITO, joined by JUSTICE KAGAN, are omitted.]

NOTES

1.   *Hosanna-Tabor* contains two holdings—one narrow and one potentially very broad. The narrow holding is that the antidiscrimination laws must contain a ministerial exception—that religious organizations have the right, free of government regulation, to choose ministers, broadly defined to include all who convey the church's religious message to members and the public. The broad holding is found in the case's distinction of *Smith*. It is that the *Smith* rule that neutral laws of general applicability do not violate the Free Exercise Clause applies only to "outward physical acts" and not to an "internal church decision that affects the faith and mission of the church itself." What does that mean? Is it a persuasive distinction of *Smith*? Does the Free Exercise Clause provide more protection for religious institutions than to religious individuals?

2.   Note that the decision rests not just on the Free Exercise Clause but also on the Establishment Clause. The Court says very little about that. What could it mean?

The Florist, the Baker, the Candlestick Maker

Recall that in *NAACP v. Claiborne Hardware*, 458 U.S. 886 (1982), p. 1038, the Court unanimously held that participation in an economic boycott of white businesses as a form of political protest is constitutionally protected—even when the boycott runs afoul of generally applicable state law economic regulation such as a prohibition on secondary boycotts, intentional interference with commercial advantage, or antitrust. This holding necessarily encompassed commercial activity, such as buying and selling goods and services. And recall that in *Hurley v. Irish-American Gay, Lesbian, and Bi-Sexual Group of Boston, Inc.*, 515 U.S. 557 (1995), p. 1065, the Court held, again unanimously, that organizers of a noncommercial expressive activity (a parade) have a First Amendment right to control their message, and thus to exclude marchers who wished to display a pro-gay rights banner.

Recently, there have been several prominent controversies regarding the refusal of the owners of small businesses (a photographer, a florist, a baker, and the owner of a pizza restaurant prominent among them) to provide their services to same-sex marriage ceremonies. Some of these business owners have been taken to court (or before civil rights commissions) and have been fined substantial sums for their refusal of service, on the theory that it was discriminatory within the terms of applicable civil rights laws, usually public accommodation laws. The leading case is *Elane Photography v. Willock*, 309 P.3d 53 (N.M. 2013), from the New Mexico Supreme Court. (The U.S. Supreme Court denied certiorari, though that does not mean that the Court necessarily endorsed the decision.) The business owners have raised various defenses under the First Amendment and state-level RFRAs, but so far they have not prevailed. Nonetheless, the claims have drawn widespread attention and have galvanized opposition to the enactment of state-level RFRA laws.

These controversies provide an opportunity to reflect on three important and interesting questions. First, what speech, association, and religion-based claims are the business owners asserting, and what are the differences between those claims? How do speech claims differ from compelled speech claims and from religious freedom claims? Second, how should those claims be resolved, bearing in mind precedents like *O'Brien*, *Claiborne Hardware*, *Hurley*, *Smith*, and *Hobby Lobby*? Third, would the courts (or you!) reach different conclusions if the ideological or cultural context were different?

Four facts about *Elane Photography* are worth noting.

1.   First, it is undisputed that the photographer regularly served gay clients. Her refusal was not based on the would-be clients' LGBT status but on her objection to same-sex marriage, which she believed to be contrary to God's law. The New Mexico Supreme Court held that the refusal nevertheless violated the public accommodations law. ("[W]e see no basis for distinguishing between discrimination based on sexual orientation and discrimination based on someone's conduct of publicly committing to a person of the same sex.") This is similar to the Massachusetts' court's holding that refusing to allow an LGBT group to carry a pro-gay rights banner amounted to discrimination against gay people in *Hurley*. Do you think these holdings were correct?

Suppose a gay caterer during California's Prop 8 debate refused to provide services to a meeting of the LDS (Mormon) Church, on the ground that the Church was raising money to support Prop 8. Would that be religious discrimination, in violation of public accommodations laws? What if the caterer pointed out that he had

Mormon clients, and that the reason he refused to cater the meeting was that he disapproved of what the meeting was for?

2.   Second, it is undisputed that the gay couple could easily have obtained alternative services of equal quality elsewhere, with little or no inconvenience. The insult was the harm. Would that matter under *O'Brien*?

3.   Third, the court did not challenge Elane Photography's claim that its services "include creative and artistic work," but concluded that public accommodations laws fully apply to creative and artistic expression. Is that correct? Why *might* artistic and creative endeavors be constitutionally entitled to choose which commissions to accept? Could a graphic designer refuse to create a logo for a presidential candidate she disapproves of? Could a Jewish muralist refuse to accept a commission to paint the scene of Jesus' crucifixion? One case involves a t-shirt producer who refused to print a pro-gay rights message on a t-shirt. Is that covered by freedom of the press? Is the converse—a t-shirt producer who refused to print an anti-gay rights message—covered by the freedom of the press? Even if artists have a constitutionally protected right to refuse commissions they disapprove of, is it too great a stretch to apply this principle to photographers, florists, bakers, and t-shirt makers?

4.   The occasion which Elane Photography refused to photograph was an expressive assembly, namely a ceremony. (It could even have been a religious service; the facts do not say.) Do people who disapprove of particular expressive assemblies or ceremonies have a right not to assist or participate in them—as an aspect of the freedom not to associate? Note that this formulation of the right would apply to purveyors of non-expressive services (like pizzas) and not just to expressive or creative services, but it would not allow a business to decline to serve a particular person, so matter how much the business owner disapproves of or dislikes that person.

If you believe that photographers are entitled to protection on this ground, what would you do about the pizza restaurant that reportedly refused to cater a same-sex wedding? Would it matter if the catering was only for a reception after the wedding ceremony?

If you believe that photographers are not entitled to protection on this ground, what would you do about other creative enterprises that might engage in discrimination? Does a director have a right to discriminate on the basis of race in casting actors for roles in movies, plays, or television shows? On the basis of gender?

Now, construct the strongest possible argument for the business owner—and the strongest possible counter-argument for the state or the LGBT couple—based on the following theories:

a.   Compelled speech. (What are the limits of *Hurley*?)

b.   Expressive conduct. (What are the limits of *O'Brien*?)

c.   Compelled association. (What are the limits of *Roberts* and *Abood*?)

d.   Right to boycott as a form of protest. (What are the limits of *Claiborne Hardware*?)

e.   First Amendment Free Exercise of Religion. (What are the limits of *Smith* and *Lukumi*?)

f.   State-level RFRA. (What are the limits of *Hobby Lobby*?)

The New Mexico Supreme Court rejected Elane Photography's state-level RFRA claim on the ground that the particular language of the New Mexico RFRA statute excludes cases brought by private parties. (The couple had filed a complaint against Elane Photography before the New Mexico Human Rights Commission, which imposed sanctions on Elane Photography.) The New Mexico RFRA provides:

A government agency shall not restrict a person's free exercise of religion unless:

A.   the restriction is in the form of a rule of general applicability and does not directly discriminate against religion or among religions; and

B.   the application of the restriction to the person is essential to further a compelling governmental interest and is the least restrictive means of furthering that compelling governmental interest.

Elane Photography argued that the statute applied because it was challenging a government agency order, namely, the N.M. Human Rights Commission's order finding Elane in violation of the public accommodation law. The court, however, treated the matter as a private suit between the complaining member of the LGBT couple and Elane Photography: "the Commission acted merely as an administrative tribunal to decide the dispute between Elane Photography and herself. The government's adjudication of disputes between private parties does not constitute government restriction of a party's free exercise rights for purposes of the NMRFRA." Under this logic, was there state action in *New York Times v. Sullivan*? Would the federal RFRA apply to a comparable dispute?

[*Assignment 56*]

C.   THE ESTABLISHMENT CLAUSE

Amend. I: Congress shall make no law respecting an establishment of religion. . . .

What does the Establishment Clause mean? Does it require "separation of church and state"? Or government neutrality toward religion? Does it forbid government coercion in religious matters? Or government sponsorship or endorsement of religion? Is government accommodation of religion and religious exercise permissible?

Engel v. Vitale
370 U.S. 421 (1962)

■ MR. JUSTICE BLACK delivered the opinion of the Court.

The respondent Board of Education of Union Free School District No. 9, New Hyde Park, New York, acting in its official capacity under state law, directed the School District's principal to cause the following prayer to be said aloud by each class in the presence of a teacher at the beginning of each school day:

Almighty God, we acknowledge our dependence upon Thee, and we beg Thy blessings upon us, our parents, our teachers and our Country.

This daily procedure was adopted on the recommendation of the State Board of Regents, a governmental agency created by the [New York] State Constitution to which the New York Legislature has granted broad supervisory, executive, and legislative powers over the State's public school system. These state officials composed the prayer which they recommended and published as a part of their "Statement on Moral and Spiritual Training in the Schools."

. . . [T]he parents of ten pupils brought this action in a New York State Court insisting that use of this official prayer in the public schools was contrary to the beliefs, religions, or religious practices of both themselves and their children. Among other things, these parents challenged the constitutionality of both the state law authorizing the School District to direct the use of prayer in public schools and the School District's regulation ordering the recitation of this particular prayer on the ground that these actions [violate the Establishment Clause of the First Amendment]. . . .

We think that by using its public school system to encourage recitation of the Regents' prayer, the State of New York has adopted a practice wholly inconsistent with the Establishment Clause. There can, of course, be no doubt that New York's program of daily classroom invocation of God's blessings as prescribed in the Regents' prayer is a religious activity. It is a solemn avowal of divine faith and supplication for the blessings of the Almighty. The nature of such a prayer has always been religious, none of the respondents has denied this and the trial court expressly so found. . . .

The petitioners contend among other things that the state laws requiring or permitting use of the Regents' prayer must be struck down as a violation of the Establishment Clause because that prayer was composed by governmental officials as a part of a governmental program to further religious beliefs. For this reason, petitioners argue, the State's use of the Regents' prayer in its public school system breaches the constitutional wall of separation between Church and State. We agree with that contention since we think that the constitutional prohibition against laws respecting an establishment of religion must at least mean that in this country it is no part of the business of government to compose official prayers for any group of the American people to recite as a part of a religious program carried on by government.

It is a matter of history that this very practice of establishing governmentally composed prayers for religious services was one of the reasons which caused many of our early colonists to leave England and seek religious freedom in America. . . .

It is an unfortunate fact of history that when some of the very groups which had most strenuously opposed the established Church of England found themselves sufficiently in control of colonial governments in this country to write their own prayers into law, they passed laws making their own religion the official religion of their respective colonies. Indeed, as late as the time of the Revolutionary War, there were established churches in at least eight of the thirteen former colonies and established religions in at least four of the other five. But the successful Revolution against English political domination was shortly followed by intense opposition to the practice of establishing religion by law. . . .

By the time of the adoption of the Constitution, our history shows that there was a widespread awareness among many Americans of the dangers of a union of Church and State. These people knew, some of them from bitter personal experience, that one of the greatest dangers to the freedom of the individual to worship in his own way lay in the Government's placing its official stamp of approval upon one particular kind of prayer or one particular form of religious services. . . . Under that Amendment's prohibition against governmental establishment of religion, as reinforced by the provisions of the Fourteenth Amendment, government in this country, be it state or federal, is without power to prescribe by law any particular form of prayer which is to be used as an official prayer in carrying on any program of governmentally sponsored religious activity.

There can be no doubt that New York's state prayer program officially establishes the religious beliefs embodied in the Regents' prayer. The respondents' argument to the contrary, which is largely based upon the contention that the Regents' prayer is "nondenominational" and the fact that the program, as modified and approved by state courts, does not require all pupils to recite the prayer but permits those who wish to do so to remain silent or be excused from the room, ignores the essential nature of the program's constitutional defects. Neither the fact that the prayer may be denominationally neutral nor the fact that its observance on the part of the students is voluntary can serve to free it from the limitations of the Establishment Clause, as it might from the Free Exercise Clause. . . . Although these two clauses may in certain instances overlap, they forbid two quite different kinds of governmental encroachment upon religious freedom. The Establishment Clause, unlike the Free Exercise Clause, does not depend upon any showing of direct governmental compulsion and is violated by the enactment of laws which establish an official religion whether those laws operate directly to coerce nonobserving individuals or not. This is not to say, of course, that laws officially prescribing a particular form of religious worship do not involve coercion of such individuals. When the power, prestige and financial support of government is placed behind a particular religious belief, the indirect coercive pressure upon religious minorities to conform to the prevailing officially approved religion is plain. But the purposes underlying the Establishment Clause go much further than that. Its first and most immediate purpose rested on the belief that a union of government and religion tends to destroy government and to degrade religion. The history of governmentally established religion, both in England and in this country, showed that whenever government had allied itself with one particular form of religion, the inevitable result had been that it had incurred the hatred, disrespect and even contempt of those who held contrary beliefs. That same history showed that many people had lost their respect for any religion that had relied upon the support for government to spread its faith. The Establishment Clause thus stands as an expression of principle on the part of the Founders of our Constitution that religion is too personal, too sacred, too holy, to permit its "unhallowed perversion" by a civil magistrate. Another purpose of the Establishment Clause rested upon an awareness of the historical fact that governmentally established religions and religious persecutions go hand in hand. . . . It was in large part to get completely away from this sort of systematic religious persecution that the Founders brought into being our Nation, our Constitution, and our Bill of Rights with its prohibition against any governmental establishment of religion. . . .

It has been argued that to apply the Constitution in such a way as to prohibit state laws respecting an establishment of religious services in public schools is to indicate a hostility toward religion or toward prayer. Nothing, or course, could be more wrong. . . .

[T]he First Amendment, which tried to put an end to governmental control of religion and of prayer, was not written to destroy either. . . . [I]t was written to quiet well-justified fears which nearly all of them felt arising out of an awareness that governments of the past had shackled men's tongues to make them speak only the religious thoughts that government wanted them to speak and to pray only to the God that government wanted them to pray to. It is neither sacrilegious nor antireligious to say that each separate government in this country should stay out of the business of writing or sanctioning official prayers and leave that purely religious function to the people themselves and to those the people choose to look to for religious guidance.[21]

■ [The concurring opinion of JUSTICE DOUGLAS has been omitted.]

■ MR. JUSTICE STEWART, dissenting.

A local school board in New York has provided that those pupils who wish to do so may join in a brief prayer at the beginning of each school day, acknowledging their dependence upon God and asking His blessing upon them and upon their parents, their teachers, and their country. The Court today decides that in permitting this brief non-denominational prayer the school board has violated the Constitution of the United States. I think this decision is wrong.

The Court does not hold, nor could it, that New York has interfered with the free exercise of anybody's religion. For the state courts have made clear that those who object to reciting the prayer must be entirely free of any compulsion to do so, including any "embarrassments and pressures." Cf. *West Virginia State Board of Education v. Barnette*, 319 U.S. 624 (1943). But the Court says that in permitting school children to say this simple prayer, the New York authorities have established "an official religion."

With all respect, I think the Court has misapplied a great constitutional principle. I cannot see how an "official religion" is established by letting those who want to say a prayer say it. On the contrary, I think that to deny the wish of these school children to join in reciting this prayer is to deny them the opportunity of sharing in the spiritual heritage of our Nation. . . .

NOTES

1. *Engel* and a subsequent case, *School Dist. of Abington Township v. Schempp*, 374 US 203 (1963), which extended *Engel* to Bible readings, were and to some extent remain among the Court's most controversial decisions—though less among lawyers and legal scholars than among ordinary citizens. The Court is often said to be a reflector of

---

[21] There is of course nothing in the decision reached here that is inconsistent with the fact that school children and others are officially encouraged to express love for our country by reciting historical documents such as the Declaration of Independence which contain references to the Deity or by singing officially espoused anthems which include the composer's professions of faith in a Supreme Being, or with the fact that there are many manifestations in our public life of belief in God. Such patriotic or ceremonial occasions bear no true resemblance to the unquestioned religious exercise that the State of New York has sponsored in this instance.

popular opinion, but in these cases upwards of three-fourths of the American people disagreed with the Court. Should that have mattered to the justices?

2.   The most important doctrinal question raised in *Engel* is the role of coercion under the Establishment Clause. The historic "church by law established" was unapologetically coercive: the government dictated doctrine and liturgy, compelled financial support and attendance, and (to different degrees at different times) punished dissent and nonconforming religious exercise. Yet the Court stated: "The Establishment Clause, unlike the Free Exercise Clause, does not depend upon any showing of direct governmental compulsion and is violated by the enactment of laws which establish an official religion whether those laws operate directly to coerce nonobserving individuals or not." The Court cites no authority for the proposition and does not explain why it is true. Is it? What does it mean?

The coercion question becomes more puzzling when we think about the Free Exercise Clause as well. According to the Court, the Establishment Clause forbids all government actions (whether or not coercive) with the primary effect of "advancing or inhibiting religion," but the Free Exercise Clause is triggered only by coercive governmental acts. Why? Should the government have greater leeway to inhibit religion than to advance it? Why not have a neutral stance, applying equally to both kinds of effect? And if the Establishment Clause itself applies (minus a coercion requirement) to state action with the primary effect of "inhibiting" religion, why don't free exercise plaintiffs simply repackage their claims as establishment claims, and get the benefit of the more expansive protection?

Do you agree that the practice of spoken prayer in a public school classroom is coercive? What if children are permitted not to join in the prayer—even to leave the room (as the plaintiffs in *Barnette* won the right to do during the Pledge of Allegiance)? Is it not plausible that children might be shamed or embarrassed into participating in the prayer, on fear of displeasing the teacher or looking like odd-balls? But if classroom prayer is in fact coercive, was *Engel* an appropriate case for pronouncing, for the first time, that coercion is not a necessary element in an Establishment Clause case? What else might be coercive? What about government actions that might make religious practice more advantageous or more costly? What about the educative effect of government action—things like public school curriculum, designation of public holidays, public parks, national monuments, and a national anthem?

3.   Much of the opinion decries the practice of the government "composing" prayers. Would it be any different if the government simply chose someone to pray and allowed that person to compose or select the prayer?

4.   The *Engel* opinion speaks in broad terms: "in this country it is no part of the business of government to compose official prayers for any group of the American people to recite as a part of a religious program carried on by government." Does this mean that no government official, acting in an official capacity, may offer a public prayer? George Washington might not have gotten the memo. He began his first inaugural address, in 1789, as follows:

> it would be peculiarly improper to omit in this first official Act, my fervent
> supplications to that Almighty Being who rules over the Universe, who presides
> in the Councils of Nations, and whose providential aids can supply every
> human defect, that his benediction may consecrate to the liberties and
> happiness of the People of the United States, a Government instituted by
> themselves for these essential purposes: and may enable every instrument
> employed in its administration to execute with success, the functions allotted

to his charge. In tendering this homage to the Great Author of every public and private good I assure myself that it expresses your sentiments not less than my own; nor those of my fellow-citizens at large, less than either.

Note that Washington referred to this address as his "first official Act." And Washington was not alone. Every inauguration since 1933 has included an invocation. The first inauguration of President Barack Obama included a prayer by the Rev. Rick Warren, which ended:

> I humbly ask this in the name of the one who changed my life, Yeshua, Isa, Jesus [Spanish pronunciation], Jesus, who taught us to pray: "Our Father, who art in heaven, hallowed be thy name. Thy kingdom come. Thy will be done on earth as it is in heaven. Give us this day our daily bread and forgive us our trespasses as we forgive those who trespass against us. And lead us not into temptation, but deliver us from evil. For thine is the kingdom and the power and the glory forever. Amen."

Many more presidents, governors, mayors, and other public officials have offered public prayers on various occasions, especially at times of public tragedy. And both houses of Congress, when they are in session, begin every day with a prayer.

Did Washington, Obama, and so many other officials choose to violate the Constitution? Or did they just misunderstand it? Or did the *Engel* Court's rhetoric outstrip its proper context? Do prayers directed at largely adult audiences, outside the inherently hierarchical context of the classroom, violate the Establishment Clause? Are they coercive?

Town of Greece v. Galloway

134 S.Ct. 1811 (2014)

■ JUSTICE KENNEDY delivered the opinion of the Court, except as to Part II–B *[which was not joined by Justices Scalia and Thomas—Editors]*.

The Court must decide whether the town of Greece, New York, imposes an impermissible establishment of religion by opening its monthly board meetings with a prayer. It must be concluded, consistent with the Court's opinion in *Marsh v. Chambers*, 463 U.S. 783 (1983), that no violation of the Constitution has been shown.

I

[In 1999, the town board of Greece replaced the moment of silence that had begun its monthly meetings with a prayer practice. Following the roll call and Pledge of Allegiance, a local clergyman, designated as "chaplain of the month," was invited to deliver an invocation.—Editors]

. . . The town followed an informal method for selecting prayer givers, all of whom were unpaid volunteers. A town employee would call the congregations listed in a local directory until she found a minister available for that month's meeting. The town eventually compiled a list of willing "board chaplains" who had accepted invitations and agreed to return in the future. The town at no point excluded or denied an opportunity to a would-be prayer giver. Its leaders maintained that a minister or layperson of any persuasion, including an atheist, could give the invocation. But nearly all of the congregations in town were Christian; and from 1999 to 2007, all of the participating ministers were too.

Greece neither reviewed the prayers in advance of the meetings nor provided guidance as to their tone or content, in the belief that exercising any degree of control over the prayers would infringe both the free exercise and speech rights of the ministers. The town instead left the guest clergy free to compose their own devotions. The resulting prayers often sounded both civic and religious themes. . . .

Some of the ministers spoke in a distinctly Christian idiom; and a minority invoked religious holidays, scripture, or doctrine, as in the following prayer:

> Lord, God of all creation, we give you thanks and praise for your presence and action in the world. We look with anticipation to the celebration of Holy Week and Easter. It is in the solemn events of next week that we find the very heart and center of our Christian faith. We acknowledge the saving sacrifice of Jesus Christ on the cross. We draw strength, vitality, and confidence from his resurrection at Easter. . . . We pray for peace in the world, an end to terrorism, violence, conflict, and war. We pray for stability, democracy, and good government in those countries in which our armed forces are now serving, especially in Iraq and Afghanistan. . . . Praise and glory be yours, O Lord, now and forever more. Amen.

Respondents Susan Galloway and Linda Stephens attended town board meetings to speak about issues of local concern, and they objected that the prayers violated their religious or philosophical views. . . . [T]he town invited a Jewish layman and the chairman of the local Baha'i temple to deliver prayers. A Wiccan priestess who had read press reports about the prayer controversy requested, and was granted, an opportunity to give the invocation.

Galloway and Stephens brought suit. . . . They requested an injunction that would limit the town to "inclusive and ecumenical" prayers that referred only to a "generic God" and would not associate the government with any one faith or belief. . . . *[The district court granted summary judgment for the town; the court of appeals reversed.—Editors]*

II

Marsh is sometimes described as "carving out an exception" to the Court's Establishment Clause jurisprudence, because it sustained legislative prayer without subjecting the practice to "any of the formal 'tests' that have traditionally structured" this inquiry. *Marsh*, at 796, 813 (Brennan, J., dissenting). The Court in *Marsh* found those tests unnecessary because history supported the conclusion that legislative invocations are compatible with the Establishment Clause. The First Congress made it an early item of business to appoint and pay official chaplains, and both the House and Senate have maintained the office virtually uninterrupted since that time. . . . Although no information has been cited by the parties to indicate how many local legislative bodies open their meetings with prayer, this practice too has historical precedent. . . .

Yet *Marsh* must not be understood as permitting a practice that would amount to a constitutional violation if not for its historical foundation. The case teaches instead that the Establishment Clause must be interpreted "by reference to historical practices and understandings." That the First Congress provided for the appointment of chaplains only days after approving language for the First Amendment demonstrates that the Framers considered legislative prayer a benign acknowledgment of religion's role in society. In the 1850's, the judiciary committees in both the House and Senate reevaluated the practice of official chaplaincies after receiving petitions to abolish the office. The committees concluded that the office posed no threat of an establishment because lawmakers were not compelled to attend the daily prayer, no faith was excluded by law, nor any favored; and the cost of the chaplain's salary imposed a vanishingly small burden on taxpayers. *Marsh* stands for the proposition that it is not necessary to define the precise boundary of the Establishment Clause where history shows that the specific practice is permitted. . . .

The Court's inquiry, then, must be to determine whether the prayer practice in the town of Greece fits within the tradition long followed in Congress and the state legislatures. Respondents assert that the town's prayer exercise falls outside that tradition and transgresses the Establishment Clause for two independent but mutually reinforcing reasons. First, they argue that *Marsh* did not approve prayers containing sectarian language or themes, such as the prayers offered in Greece that referred to the "death, resurrection, and ascension of the Savior Jesus Christ," and the "saving sacrifice of Jesus Christ on the cross." Second, they argue that the setting and conduct of the town board meetings create social pressures that force nonadherents to remain in the room or even feign participation in order to avoid offending the representatives who sponsor the prayer and will vote on matters citizens bring before the board. . . .

A

Respondents maintain that the prayer must be nonsectarian. . . .

An insistence on nonsectarian or ecumenical prayer as a single, fixed standard is not consistent with the tradition of legislative prayer outlined in the Court's cases. The Court found the prayers in *Marsh* consistent with the First Amendment not because they espoused only a generic theism but because our history and tradition have shown that prayer in this limited context could "coexis[t] with the principles of disestablishment and religious freedom." The Congress that drafted the First Amendment would have been accustomed to invocations containing explicitly religious themes of the sort respondents find objectionable. One of the Senate's first chaplains, the Rev. William White, gave prayers in a series that included the Lord's Prayer, the Collect for Ash Wednesday, prayers for peace and grace, a general thanksgiving, St. Chrysostom's Prayer, and a prayer seeking "the grace of our Lord Jesus Christ, &c." The decidedly Christian nature of these prayers must not be dismissed as the relic of a time when our Nation was less pluralistic than it is today. Congress continues to permit its appointed and visiting chaplains to express themselves in a religious idiom. It acknowledges our growing diversity not by proscribing sectarian content but by welcoming ministers of many creeds. . . .

To hold that invocations must be nonsectarian would force the legislatures that sponsor prayers and the courts that are asked to decide these cases to act as supervisors and censors of religious speech, a rule that would involve government in religious matters to a far greater degree than is the case under the town's current practice of neither editing or approving prayers in advance nor criticizing their content after the fact. Cf. *Hosanna-Tabor Evangelical Lutheran Church and School v. EEOC*, 132 S.Ct. 694, 705–706 (2012). Our Government is prohibited from prescribing prayers to be recited in our public institutions in order to promote a preferred system of belief or code of moral behavior. *Engel v. Vitale*, 370 U.S. 421, 430 (1962). It would be but a few steps removed from that prohibition for legislatures to require chaplains to redact the religious content from their message in order to make it acceptable for the public sphere. Government may not mandate a civic religion that stifles any but the most generic reference to the sacred any more than it may prescribe a religious orthodoxy. See *Lee v. Weisman*, 505 U.S. 577, 590 (1992). . . .

[E]ven seemingly general references to God or the Father might alienate nonbelievers or polytheists. . . . Once it invites prayer into the public sphere, government must permit a prayer giver to address his or her own God or gods as conscience dictates, unfettered by what an administrator or judge considers to be nonsectarian.

In rejecting the suggestion that legislative prayer must be nonsectarian, the Court does not imply that no constraints remain on its content. The relevant constraint derives from its place at the opening of legislative sessions, where it is meant to lend gravity to the occasion and reflect values long part of the Nation's heritage. . . . Prayer that reflects beliefs specific to only some creeds can still serve to solemnize the occasion, so long as the practice over time is not "exploited to proselytize or advance any one, or to disparage any other, faith or belief." *Marsh*, at 794–795.

Respondents point to other invocations that disparaged those who did not accept the town's prayer practice. One guest minister characterized objectors as a "minority" who are "ignorant of the history of our country," while another lamented that other towns did not have "God-fearing" leaders. Although these two remarks strayed from the rationale set out in *Marsh*, they do not despoil a practice that on the whole reflects and embraces our tradition. . . .

Finally, the Court disagrees with the view taken by the Court of Appeals that the town of Greece contravened the Establishment Clause by inviting a predominantly Christian set of ministers to lead the prayer. The town made reasonable efforts to identify all of the congregations located within its borders and represented that it would welcome a prayer by any minister or layman who wished to give one. That nearly all of the congregations in town turned out to be Christian does not reflect an aversion or bias on the part of town leaders against minority faiths. So long as the town maintains a policy of nondiscrimination, the Constitution does not require it to search beyond its borders for non-Christian prayer givers in an effort to achieve religious balancing. The quest to promote "a 'diversity' of religious views" would require the town "to make wholly inappropriate judgments about the number of religions [it] should sponsor and the relative frequency with which it should sponsor each," *Lee*, at 617 (Souter, J. concurring). . . .

B

Respondents further seek to distinguish the town's prayer practice from the tradition upheld in *Marsh* on the ground that it coerces participation by nonadherents. They and some *amici* contend that prayer conducted in the intimate setting of a town board meeting differs in fundamental ways from the invocations delivered in Congress and state legislatures, where the public remains segregated from legislative activity and may not address the body except by occasional invitation. Citizens attend town meetings, on the other hand, to accept awards; speak on matters of local importance; and petition the board for action that may affect their economic interests, such as the granting of permits, business licenses, and zoning variances. Respondents argue that the public may feel subtle pressure to participate in prayers that violate their beliefs in order to please the board members from whom they are about to seek a favorable ruling. . . .

It is an elemental First Amendment principle that government may not coerce its citizens "to support or participate in any religion or its exercise." *County of Allegheny v. ACLU*, 492 U.S. 573, 659 (1989) (Kennedy, J., concurring in judgment in part and dissenting in part). . . .

The prayer opportunity in this case must be evaluated against the backdrop of historical practice. As a practice that has long endured, legislative prayer has become part of our heritage and tradition, part of our expressive idiom, similar to the Pledge of Allegiance, inaugural prayer, or the recitation of "God save the United States and this honorable Court" at the opening of this Court's sessions. It is presumed that the reasonable observer is acquainted with this tradition and understands that its purposes are to lend gravity to public proceedings and to acknowledge the place religion holds in the lives of many private citizens, not to afford government an opportunity to proselytize or force truant constituents into the pews. That many appreciate these acknowledgments of the divine in our public institutions does not suggest that those who disagree are compelled to join the expression or approve its content. *West Virginia State Bd. of Ed. v. Barnette*, 319 U.S. 624, 642 (1943).

The principal audience for these invocations is not, indeed, the public but lawmakers themselves, who may find that a moment of prayer or quiet reflection sets the mind to a higher purpose and thereby eases the task of governing. . . . The prayer is an opportunity for them to show who and what they are without denying the right to dissent by those who disagree.

The analysis would be different if town board members directed the public to participate in the prayers, singled out dissidents for opprobrium, or indicated that their decisions might be influenced by a person's acquiescence in the prayer opportunity. No such thing occurred in the town of Greece. Although board members themselves stood, bowed their heads, or made the sign of the cross during the prayer, they at no point solicited similar gestures by the public. Respondents point to several occasions where audience members were asked to rise for the prayer. These requests, however, came not from town leaders but from the guest ministers, who presumably are accustomed to directing their congregations in this way and might have done so thinking the action was inclusive, not coercive. [E.g.] App. 69a ("Would you bow your heads with me as we invite the Lord's presence here tonight?"). . . .

This case can be distinguished from the conclusions and holding of *Lee v. Weisman*. There the Court found that, in the context of a graduation where school authorities maintained close supervision over the conduct of the students and the substance of the ceremony, a religious invocation was coercive as to an objecting student. Four Justices dissented in Lee, but the circumstances the Court confronted there are not present in this case and do not control its outcome. Nothing in the record suggests that members of the public are dissuaded from leaving the meeting room during the prayer, arriving late, or even, as happened here, making a later protest. In this case, as in *Marsh*, board members and constituents are. . . . mature adults, who "presumably" are "not readily susceptible to religious indoctrination or peer pressure." *Marsh*, at 792.

Ceremonial prayer is but a recognition that, since this Nation was founded and until the present day, many Americans deem that their own existence must be understood by precepts far beyond the authority of government to alter or define and that willing participation in civic affairs can be consistent with a brief acknowledgment of their belief in a higher power, always with due respect for those who adhere to other beliefs. The prayer in this case has a permissible ceremonial purpose. It is not an unconstitutional establishment of religion.

■ JUSTICE KAGAN delivered, with whom JUSTICE GINSBURG, JUSTICE BREYER, and JUSTICE SOTOMAYOR join, dissenting.

For centuries now, people have come to this country from every corner of the world to share in the blessing of religious freedom. Our Constitution promises that they may worship in their own way, without fear of penalty or danger, and that in itself is a momentous offering. Yet our Constitution makes a commitment still more remarkable—that however those individuals worship, they will count as full and equal American citizens. A Christian, a Jew, a Muslim (and so forth)—each stands in the same relationship with her country, with her state and local communities, and with every level and body of government. So that when each person performs the duties or seeks the benefits of citizenship, she does so not as an adherent to one or another religion, but simply as an American.

I respectfully dissent from the Court's opinion because I think the Town of Greece's prayer practices violate that norm of religious equality—the breathtakingly generous constitutional idea that our public institutions belong no less to the Buddhist or Hindu than to the Methodist or Episcopalian. I do not contend that principle translates here into a bright separationist line. To the contrary, I agree with the Court's decision in *Marsh*. . . . But still, the town of Greece should lose this case. The practice at issue here differs from the one sustained in *Marsh* because Greece's town meetings involve participation by ordinary citizens, and the invocations given—directly to those citizens—were predominantly sectarian in content. Still more, Greece's Board did nothing to recognize religious diversity: In arranging for clergy members to open each meeting, the Town never sought (except briefly when this suit was filed) to involve, accommodate, or in any way reach out to adherents of non-Christian religions. So month in and month out for over a decade, prayers steeped in only one faith, addressed toward members of the public, commenced meetings to discuss local affairs and distribute government benefits. . . .

[T]he not-so-implicit message of the majority's opinion—"What's the big deal, anyway?"—is mistaken. The content of Greece's prayers *is* a big deal, to Christians and non-Christians alike. A person's response to the doctrine, language, and imagery contained in those invocations reveals a core aspect of identity—who that person is and how she faces the world. . . . Contrary to the majority's apparent view, such sectarian prayers are not "part of our expressive idiom" or "part of our heritage and tradition," assuming the word "our" refers to all Americans. They express beliefs that are fundamental to some, foreign to others—and because that is so they carry the ever-present potential to both exclude and divide. The majority, I think, assesses too lightly the significance of these religious differences, and so fears too little the "religiously based divisiveness that the Establishment Clause seeks to avoid." *Van Orden v. Perry*, 545 U.S. 677, 704 (2005) (Breyer, J., concurring in judgment). I would treat more seriously the multiplicity of Americans' religious commitments, along with the challenge they can pose to the project—the distinctively American project—of creating one from the many, and governing all as united.

NOTES

1.   The Court relies heavily on *Marsh v. Chambers*, and even the dissenters say they "agree" with *Marsh*. *Marsh*, in turn, relied exclusively on the historical fact that the First Congress—the same Congress that proposed the First Amendment—voted to appoint chaplains and have daily prayer. Some have criticized *Marsh* for failing to explain what interpretation of the Establishment Clause could justify that congressional decision. It appears to be one of the rare cases in which the Court relies on historical practices divorced from any theory of constitutional meaning.

In *Town of Greece*, the majority flatly rejects the idea that *Marsh* was merely a historically grounded exception to general Establishment Clause principle. Interestingly, the Court turned for guidance to a report in the 1850s by the judiciary committees of the House and Senate (a reminder that in the early republic, Congress took more seriously its duty to interpret the Constitution). Those committees decided to approve the practice of legislative chaplains and prayers for three reasons: "lawmakers were not compelled to attend the daily prayer, no faith was excluded by law, nor any favored; and the cost of the chaplain's salary imposed a vanishingly small burden on taxpayers." Did the Court embrace that reasoning? How might it differ, if at all, from modern Court doctrine? Is this passage consistent with the no-coercion holding of *Engel*?

2.   Consider the argument that prayers at city council meetings are more coercive than prayers at state legislative sessions. Why might that be so? Why might the Court be unwilling to draw fine lines of that sort? Currently, there seems to be a pattern in the Court's decisions: prayers in official school contexts are prohibited (even at clearly voluntary events, such as football games), but prayers offered to largely adult audiences are generally permitted. What is the logic of that distinction?

3.   The lower court had held the city council prayer practice unconstitutional because some of the prayers were "sectarian" and because almost all the volunteer chaplains were Christian (in a community that itself was overwhelmingly Christian). What do you think? Assuming legislative prayer is permissible (as the Court's unanimous embrace of *Marsh* suggests) would it make things better or worse from an Establishment Clause perspective for the government to require prayers to be "non-sectarian"? What is a "non-sectarian" prayer? Would it make things better or worse for the government to depart from its facially neutral first-come-first-served approach to selecting volunteer chaplains and instead deliberately create a diverse list? How diverse?

4.   A number of Supreme Court opinions have grappled with the problem of public monuments and displays that contain religious elements: nativity scenes, Christmas trees, menorahs, crosses, Ten Commandments monuments, and the like. The results are often split, and the principles for decisionmaking are difficult to discern. In general, it appears that displays that contain a mixture of religious and secular elements are permissible, as are free-standing symbols that have both religious and secular meaning.

In *Lynch v. Donnelly*, 465 U.S. 668 (1984), a divided Court held that it was not unconstitutional for the City of Pawtucket, Rhode Island to include a nativity scene among a mishmash of other holiday-related objects in a park display sponsored by the Downtown Retail Merchants Association for the purpose of attracting people to spend money downtown. Five years later, the Court decided *County of Allegheny v. American Civil Liberties Union*, 492 U.S. 573 (1989). At issue were two seasonal displays in Pittsburgh: a Christmas nativity scene located on a landing of steps in a courthouse, and a large Hanukkah Menorah situated outside the entrance to a city-county building. Three justices (Brennan, Marshall, and Stevens) found both displays unconstitutional promotions of religion, and voted to strike them down. Four justices (Kennedy, Rehnquist, White, and Scalia), applying a "coercion" test, found both displays constitutionally proper. Two justices (Blackmun and O'Connor), applying an "endorsement" test, thought that the Christmas nativity scene impermissibly advanced Christianity but the Hanukkah Menorah did not impermissibly advance Judaism, in part because of the presence of a nearby ("secular") Christmas tree. The two-justice Blackmun-O'Connor position, combined with the three-justice position, resulted in a holding that the nativity scene was unconstitutional. But the two-justice Blackmun-O'Connor position, combined with the four-justice position, resulted in a holding that the menorah was constitutional. This resulted in a disposition of the case that *seven* justices thought was wrong—indeed, the worst possible outcome—that one religion's symbol was unconstitutional and another's was permitted.

A pair of "Ten Commandments Display" cases, decided by the Court in 2005, produced a similarly mixed set of decisions. In *McCreary County v. ACLU*, 545 U.S. 844 (2005), the Court upheld an injunction against a Ten Commandments display included as part of a display of historic legal documents in a Kentucky courthouse. The same day, in *Van Orden v. Perry*, 545 U.S. 677 (2005), the Court *rejected* a challenge to a freestanding Ten Commandments monument erected on the grounds of the Texas state capitol building. As in *Allegheny*, only two justices voted in the majority in *both* cases of this split doubleheader. One of those justices—Justice Breyer—emphasized the importance of avoiding divisiveness along religious lines and suggested that displays that had existed for long period of time without controversy were likely permissible. *McCreary County* involved a new display; *Van Orden* involved one that was decades old. Is that a practical distinction? Is it theoretically justifiable?

What should be the standard of "neutrality" in such cases? Is any religious intrusion on a pristinely secularly public sphere in principle objectionable? Should these decisions rely on longstanding custom and tradition? Would it be possible to have a principle that the government should reflect the culture as it is, rather than changing the culture in either a secular or a religious direction?

More generally, why do such displays raise a constitutional question in the first place. Is anyone coerced by a nativity scene or menorah? (Recall the discussion of coercion after *Engel*.) Why does a person who dislikes the sight of a Ten Commandments monument have standing to sue? Should psychological discomfort be enough? Should the Court's struggle on the merits, trying to develop a coherent principle for holding some displays permissible and others impermissible, affect the breadth of standing to sue? If the concern is "divisiveness along religious lines," can that be avoided when the Supreme Court says that either religious traditionalists or secularists have the Constitution on their side?

5.   What about the words "under God" in the Pledge of Allegiance? In *Elk Grove Unified School District v. Newdow*, 542 U.S. 1 (2004), the Court avoided deciding whether those words violate the Establishment Clause. (The Court held that the plaintiff lacked standing to sue.) Recall that in *West Virginia State Board of Education v. Barnette*, 319 U.S. 624 (1943), p. 1054, the Court held, as a matter of Free Speech Clause freedom-from-compelled-expression doctrine, that *no one* may be required to say the Pledge. The challenge in *Newdow* was to the presence of the words "under God" in the Pledge, when it was used as part of the public school exercise.

6.   Could the Constitution itself be unconstitutional? Does the document's declaration that the Constitutional Convention submitted the document "in the year of

our Lord" 1787 violate the Establishment Clause? Or the First Amendment, which singles out "religion" for special protection? "In God We Trust" on the coinage? The final stanza of the national anthem? The Thanksgiving holiday? President Lincoln's Second Inaugural, which was suffused with theological reflection on the Civil War? Is its inclusion, in full, on a wall of the interior of the Lincoln Memorial unconstitutional?

D. ACCOMMODATION OF RELIGION: THE INTERSECTION OF FREE EXERCISE AND NON-ESTABLISHMENT

We return now to a question introduced earlier: When may the government "accommodate" religion in ways not required by the Free Exercise Clause, without violating the Establishment Clause? To introduce this question, we turn to *Corporation of Presiding Bishop v. Amos.* Title VII of the Civil Rights Act of 1964 generally prohibits employment discrimination on the basis of religion. But the statute contains an exemption that permits religious organizations to "discriminate" (if that is the right word) on the basis of religion in their hiring decisions. In *Amos* the Court unanimously upheld that accommodation—but with some disagreement about exactly why it was permissible, and where the outer bounds lie for government accommodation of religion. As you read the case, ask yourself to what degree the exemption of religious organizations from the no-discrimination-on-the-basis-of-religion rule was required by the Free Exercise Clause. Then consider whether the non-required part (if any) violates the Establishment Clause. See if you can develop a theory of why, and when, such accommodations are permissible.

Corporation of Presiding Bishop of Church of Jesus Christ of Latter-Day Saints v. Amos
483 U.S. 327 (1987)

■ JUSTICE WHITE delivered the opinion of the Court.

Section 702 of the Civil Rights Act of 1964 exempts religious organizations from Title VII's prohibition against discrimination in employment on the basis of religion.[1] The question presented is whether applying the § 702 exemption to the secular nonprofit activities of religious organizations violates the Establishment Clause of the First Amendment. . . .

I

The Deseret Gymnasium (Gymnasium) in Salt Lake City, Utah, is a nonprofit facility, open to the public, run by the Corporation of the Presiding Bishop of The Church of Jesus Christ of Latter-day Saints (CPB), and the Corporation of the President of The Church of Jesus Christ of Latter-day Saints (COP). The CPB and the COP are religious entities associated with The Church of Jesus Christ of Latter-day Saints (Church), an unincorporated religious association sometimes called the Mormon or LDS Church.

---

[1]   Section 702 provides in relevant part:
This subchapter [i.e., Title VII of the Civil Rights Act of 1964, shall] not apply . . . to a religious corporation, association, educational institution, or society with respect to the employment of individuals of a particular religion to perform work connected with the carrying on by such corporation, association, educational institution, or society of its activities.

Appellee Mayson worked at the Gymnasium for some 16 years as an assistant building engineer and then as building engineer. He was discharged in 1981 because he failed to qualify for a temple recommend, that is, a certificate that he is a member of the Church and eligible to attend its temples.

Mayson and others purporting to represent a class of plaintiffs brought an action against the CPB and the COP alleging, among other things, discrimination on the basis of religion in violation of § 703 of the Civil Rights Act of 1964, 42 U.S.C. § 2000e–2. The defendants moved to dismiss this claim on the ground that § 702 shields them from liability. The plaintiffs contended that if construed to allow religious employers to discriminate on religious grounds in hiring for nonreligious jobs, § 702 violates the Establishment Clause.

The District Court . . . found: first, that the Gymnasium is intimately connected to the Church financially and in matters of management; second, that there is no clear connection between the primary function which the Gymnasium performs and the religious beliefs and tenets of the Mormon Church or church administration; and third, that none of Mayson's duties at the Gymnasium are "even tangentially related to any conceivable religious belief or ritual of the Mormon Church or church administration." The court concluded that Mayson's case involves nonreligious activity.

The court next considered the plaintiffs' constitutional challenge to § 702. Applying the three-part test set out in *Lemon v. Kurtzman*, 403 U.S. 602 (1971), the court first held that § 702 has the permissible secular purpose of "assuring that the government remains neutral and does not meddle in religious affairs by interfering with the decision-making process in religions. . . ." The court concluded, however, that § 702 fails the second part of the *Lemon* test because the provision has the primary effect of advancing religion.[10] Among the considerations mentioned by the court were: that § 702 singles out religious entities for a benefit, rather than benefiting a broad grouping of which religious organizations are only a part; that § 702 is not supported by long historical tradition; and that § 702 burdens the free exercise rights of employees of religious institutions who work in nonreligious jobs. Finding that § 702 impermissibly sponsors religious organizations by granting them "an exclusive authorization to engage in conduct which can directly and immediately advance religious tenets and practices," the court declared the statute unconstitutional as applied to secular activity. . . .

II

"This Court has long recognized that the government may (and sometimes must) accommodate religious practices and that it may do so without violating the Establishment Clause." *Hobbie v. Unemployment Appeals Comm'n of Fla.*, 480 U.S. 136, 144–145 (1987). It is well established, too, that "[t]he limits of permissible state accommodation to religion are by no means co-extensive with the noninterference mandated by the Free Exercise Clause." *Walz v. Tax Comm'n*, 397 U.S. 664, 673 (1970). There is ample room under the Establishment Clause for "benevolent neutrality which will permit religious exercise to exist without sponsorship and without interference." *Id.* at 669. At some point, accommodation may devolve into

---

[10]   The court rejected the defendants' arguments that § 702 is required both by the need to avoid excessive governmental entanglement with religion and by the Free Exercise Clause.

"an unlawful fostering of religion," *Hobbie, supra*, 480 U.S. at 145, but these are not such cases, in our view.

The private appellants contend that we should not apply the three-part *Lemon* approach, which is assertedly unsuited to judging the constitutionality of exemption statutes such as § 702. The argument is that an exemption statute will always have the effect of advancing religion and hence be invalid under the second (effects) part of the *Lemon* test, a result claimed to be inconsistent with cases such as *Walz v. Tax Comm'n, supra*, which upheld property tax exemptions for religious organizations. . . . [W]e need not reexamine *Lemon* as applied in this context, for the exemption involved here is in no way questionable under the *Lemon* analysis.

Lemon requires first that the law at issue serve a "secular legislative purpose." This does not mean that the law's purpose must be unrelated to religion—that would amount to a requirement "that the government show a callous indifference to religious groups," *Zorach v. Clauson*, 343 U.S. 306, 314 (1952), and the Establishment Clause has never been so interpreted. Rather, *Lemon*'s "purpose" requirement aims at preventing the relevant governmental decisionmaker—in this case, Congress—from abandoning neutrality and acting with the intent of promoting a particular point of view in religious matters.

Under the *Lemon* analysis, it is a permissible legislative purpose to alleviate significant governmental interference with the ability of religious organizations to define and carry out their religious missions. Appellees argue that there is no such purpose here because § 702 provided adequate protection for religious employers prior to the 1972 amendment, when it exempted only the religious activities of such employers from the statutory ban on religious discrimination. We may assume for the sake of argument that the pre-1972 exemption was adequate in the sense that the Free Exercise Clause required no more. Nonetheless, it is a significant burden on a religious organization to require it, on pain of substantial liability, to predict which of its activities a secular court will consider religious. The line is hardly a bright one, and an organization might understandably be concerned that a judge would not understand its religious tenets and sense of mission. Fear of potential liability might affect the way an organization carried out what it understood to be its religious mission.

. . . [T]he District Court concluded that Congress' purpose was to minimize governmental "interfer[ence] with the decision-making process in religions." We agree with the District Court that this purpose does not violate the Establishment Clause.

The second requirement under *Lemon* is that the law in question have "a principal or primary effect . . . that neither advances nor inhibits religion." Undoubtedly, religious organizations are better able now to advance their purposes than they were prior to the 1972 amendment to § 702. But religious groups have been better able to advance their purposes on account of many laws that have passed constitutional muster. . . . A law is not unconstitutional simply because it *allows* churches to advance religion, which is their very purpose. For a law to have forbidden "effects" under *Lemon,* it must be fair to say that the *government itself* has advanced religion through its own activities and influence. As the Court observed in *Walz,* "for the men who wrote the Religion Clauses of the First Amendment the 'establishment' of a religion connoted sponsorship, financial support, and active involvement of the sovereign in religious activity." 397 U.S., at 668.

The District Court appeared to fear that sustaining the exemption would permit churches with financial resources impermissibly to extend their influence and propagate their faith by entering the commercial, profit-making world. The cases before us, however, involve a nonprofit activity instituted over 75 years ago in the hope that "all who assemble here, and who come for the benefit of their health, and for physical blessings, [may] feel that they are in a house dedicated to the Lord." Dedicatory Prayer for the Gymnasium. These cases therefore do not implicate the apparent concerns of the District Court. Moreover, we find no persuasive evidence in the record before us that the Church's ability to propagate its religious doctrine through the Gymnasium is any greater now than it was prior to the passage of the Civil Rights Act in 1964. In such circumstances, we do not see how any advancement of religion achieved by the Gymnasium can be fairly attributed to the Government, as opposed to the Church.[15]

We find unpersuasive the District Court's reliance on the fact that § 702 singles out religious entities for a benefit. Although the Court has given weight to this consideration in its past decisions, it has never indicated that statutes that give special consideration to religious groups are *per se* invalid. That would run contrary to the teaching of our cases that there is ample room for accommodation of religion under the Establishment Clause. Where, as here, government acts with the proper purpose of lifting a regulation that burdens the exercise of religion, we see no reason to require that the exemption comes packaged with benefits to secular entities.

We are also unpersuaded by the District Court's reliance on the argument that § 702 is unsupported by long historical tradition. There was simply no need to consider the scope of the § 702 exemption until the 1964 Civil Rights Act was passed, and the fact that Congress concluded after eight years that the original exemption was unnecessarily narrow is a decision entitled to deference, not suspicion.

. . . It cannot be seriously contended that § 702 impermissibly entangles church and state; the statute effectuates a more complete separation of the two and avoids the kind of intrusive inquiry into religious belief that the District Court engaged in this case. The statute easily passes muster under the third part of the *Lemon* test.[17]

■ JUSTICE BRENNAN, with whom JUSTICE MARSHALL joins, concurring in the judgment.

I write separately to emphasize that my concurrence in the judgment rests on the fact that these cases involve a challenge to the application of § 702's categorical exemption to the activities of a *nonprofit* organization. I believe that the particular character of nonprofit activity makes inappropriate a case-by-case determination whether its nature is religious or secular.

These cases present a confrontation between the rights of religious organizations and those of individuals. Any exemption from Title VII's proscription on religious discrimination necessarily has the effect of burdening the religious

---

[15] Undoubtedly, Mayson's freedom of choice in religious matters was impinged upon, but it was the Church (through the COP and the CPB), and not the Government, who put him to the choice of changing his religious practices or losing his job. . . .

[17] We have no occasion to pass on the argument of the COP and the CPB that the exemption to which they are entitled under § 702 is required by the Free Exercise Clause.

liberty of prospective and current employees. An exemption says that a person may be put to the choice of either conforming to certain religious tenets or losing a job opportunity, a promotion, or, as in these cases, employment itself. The potential for coercion created by such a provision is in serious tension with our commitment to individual freedom of conscience in matters of religious belief.

At the same time, religious organizations have an interest in autonomy in ordering their internal affairs, so that they may be free to:

> select their own leaders, define their own doctrines, resolve their own disputes, and run their own institutions. Religion includes important communal elements for most believers. They exercise their religion through religious organizations, and these organizations must be protected by the [Free Exercise] [C]lause.

Laycock, Towards a General Theory of the Religion Clauses: The Case of Church Labor Relations and the Right to Church Autonomy, 81 Colum. L. Rev. 1373, 1389 (1981). For many individuals, religious activity derives meaning in large measure from participation in a larger religious community. Such a community represents an ongoing tradition of shared beliefs, an organic entity not reducible to a mere aggregation of individuals. Determining that certain activities are in furtherance of an organization's religious mission, and that only those committed to that mission should conduct them, is thus a means by which a religious community defines itself. Solicitude for a church's ability to do so reflects the idea that furtherance of the autonomy of religious organizations often furthers individual religious freedom as well.

The authority to engage in this process of self-definition inevitably involves what we normally regard as infringement on free exercise rights, since a religious organization is able to condition employment in certain activities on subscription to particular religious tenets. We are willing to countenance the imposition of such a condition because we deem it vital that, if certain activities constitute part of a religious community's practice, then a religious organization should be able to require that only members of its community perform those activities.

This rationale suggests that, ideally, religious organizations should be able to discriminate on the basis of religion *only* with respect to religious activities, so that a determination should be made in each case whether an activity is religious or secular. This is because the infringement on religious liberty that results from conditioning performance of *secular* activity upon religious belief cannot be defended as necessary for the community's self-definition. Furthermore, the authorization of discrimination in such circumstances is not an accommodation that simply enables a church to gain members by the normal means of prescribing the terms of membership for those who seek to participate in furthering the mission of the community. Rather, it puts at the disposal of religion the added advantages of economic leverage in the secular realm. As a result, the authorization of religious discrimination with respect to nonreligious activities goes beyond reasonable accommodation, and has the effect of furthering religion in violation of the Establishment Clause.

What makes the application of a religious-secular distinction difficult is that the character of an activity is not self-evident. As a result, determining whether an activity is religious or secular requires a searching case-by-case analysis. This results in considerable ongoing government entanglement in religious affairs. Furthermore, this prospect of government intrusion raises concern that a religious organization may be chilled in its free exercise activity. While a church may regard the conduct of certain functions as integral to its mission, a court may disagree. A religious organization therefore would have an incentive to characterize as religious only those activities about which there likely would be no dispute, even if it genuinely believed that religious commitment was important in performing other tasks as well. As a result, the community's process of self-definition would be shaped in part by the prospects of litigation. A case-by-case analysis for all activities therefore would both produce excessive government entanglement with religion and create the danger of chilling religious activity.

The risk of chilling religious organizations is most likely to arise with respect to *nonprofit* activities. The fact that an operation is not organized as a profit-making commercial enterprise makes colorable a claim that it is not purely secular in orientation. In contrast to a for-profit corporation, a non-profit organization must utilize its earnings to finance the continued provision of the goods or services it furnishes, and may not distribute any surplus to the owners. See generally Hansmann, *The Role of Nonprofit Enterprise*, 89 Yale L.J. 835 (1980). This makes plausible a church's contention that an entity is not operated simply in order to generate revenues for the church, but that the activities themselves are infused with a religious purpose. Furthermore, unlike for-profit corporations, nonprofits historically have been organized specifically to provide certain community services, not simply to engage in commerce. Churches often regard the provision of such services as a means of fulfilling religious duty and of providing an example of the way of life a church seeks to foster.

Nonprofit activities therefore are most likely to present cases in which characterization of the activity as religious or secular will be a close question. If there is a danger that a religious organization will be deterred from classifying as religious those activities it actually regards as religious, it is likely to be in this domain. This substantial potential for chilling religious activity makes inappropriate a case-by-case determination of the character of a nonprofit organization, and justifies a categorical exemption for nonprofit activities. . . . While not every nonprofit activity may be operated for religious purposes, the likelihood that many are makes a categorical rule a suitable means to avoid chilling the exercise of religion.

. . . Sensitivity to individual religious freedom dictates that religious discrimination be permitted only with respect to employment in religious activities. Concern for the autonomy of religious organizations demands that we avoid the entanglement and the chill on religious expression that a case-by-case determination would produce. We cannot escape the fact that these aims are in tension. Because of the nature of nonprofit activities, I believe that a categorical exemption for such enterprises appropriately balances these competing concerns. As a result, I concur in the Court's judgment that the nonprofit Deseret Gymnasium may avail itself of an automatic exemption from Title VII's proscription on religious discrimination.

■ [The concurring opinion of JUSTICE BLACKMUN is omitted.]

■ JUSTICE O'CONNOR, concurring in the judgment.

Although I agree with the judgment of the Court, I write separately to note that this action once again illustrates certain difficulties inherent in the Court's use of the test articulated in *Lemon v. Kurtzman,* . . . .

The necessary first step in evaluating an Establishment Clause challenge to a government action lifting from religious organizations a generally applicable regulatory burden is to recognize that such government action *does* have the effect of advancing religion. The necessary second step is to separate those benefits to religion that constitutionally accommodate the free exercise of religion from those that provide unjustifiable awards of assistance to religious organizations. As I have suggested in earlier opinions, the inquiry framed by the *Lemon* test should be "whether government's purpose is to endorse religion and whether the statute actually conveys a message of endorsement." To ascertain whether the statute conveys a message of endorsement, the relevant issue is how it would be perceived by an objective observer, acquainted with the text, legislative history, and implementation of the statute. . . .

The above framework, I believe, helps clarify why the amended § 702 raises different questions as it is applied to nonprofit and for-profit organizations. . . . These cases involve a Government decision to lift from a nonprofit activity of a religious organization the burden of demonstrating that the particular nonprofit activity is religious as well as the burden of refraining from discriminating on the basis of religion. Because there is a probability that a nonprofit activity of a religious organization will itself be involved in the organization's religious mission, in my view the objective observer should perceive the Government action as an accommodation of the exercise of religion rather than as a Government endorsement of religion.

It is not clear, however, that activities conducted by religious organizations solely as profit-making enterprises will be as likely to be directly involved in the religious mission of the organization. . . . I [only] emphasize that under the holding of the Court, and under my view of the appropriate Establishment Clause analysis, the question of the constitutionality of the § 702 exemption as applied to for-profit activities of religious organizations remains open.

NOTES

1.   *Amos* was unanimous as to result, but with some differences as to reasoning. All the justices agreed that it was permissible for Congress to exempt religious groups from Title VII's usual prohibition of religious discrimination in employment. The majority opinion of Justice White applied the three-part *Lemon* test we have seen from other cases. *Lemon* remains in use, but is also much-criticized. *Amos* holds that the religious-hiring accommodation does not have an impermissible purpose—that there is nothing constitutionally wrong, in principle, with government's having as its goal the accommodation of religion. But what is the "effect" of an accommodation of religion? Doesn't it (in a certain sense) "advance" religion? Justice O'Connor notes this problem in her concurrence, and instead urges a no-"endorsement" test. But doesn't a special accommodation of religion (in a sense) "endorse" religion in precisely the same way? The majority's answer is that it does not advance religion, in the sense that the Establishment Clause forbids, for government to allow religious organizations to promote their missions:

"A law is not unconstitutional simply because it allows churches to advance religion, which is their very purpose. For a law to have forbidden 'effects' under *Lemon*, it must be fair to say that the government itself has advanced religion through its own activities and influence." Does this distinction make sense?

2.   Justice Brennan's concurring opinion takes issue with this approach, contending that *Amos* is a difficult case because it presents "a confrontation between the rights of religious organizations and those of individuals" and that the church's "process of self-definition" (that is, excluding persons who are not church members in good standing from employment) "involves what we normally regard as infringement on free exercise rights, since a religious organization is able to condition employment in certain activities on subscription to particular religious tenets." Is this view right? Does government's act of accommodating a religious institution's self-definition itself impair the rights of non-religious individuals?

3.   Justice Brennan's opinion nonetheless defends the rights of religious institutions to define their mission by defining their membership. Note the very strong resemblance of his reasoning on this point to the "expressive association" line of freedom of *speech* cases—cases like *Roberts v. U.S. Jaycees*, 468 U.S. 609, 622–23 (1984):

> An individual's freedom to speak, to worship, and to petition the government for the redress of grievances could not be vigorously protected from interference by the State unless a correlative freedom to engage in group effort toward those ends were not also guaranteed. . . . Government actions that may unconstitutionally infringe upon [the freedom of expressive association] can take a number of forms . . . [including] interfer[ence] with the internal organization or affairs of the group. . . . There can be no clearer example of an intrusion into the internal structure or affairs of an association than a regulation that forces the group to accept members it does not desire.

Justice Brennan wrote the majority opinion in *Roberts*. To what extent do you think Justice Brennan thought the accommodation in this case required by Free Speech Clause principles, derived from the expressive association line of cases?

4.   The line Justice Brennan would draw is between the "religious" and the "secular" activities of a religious organization. Nonetheless, he recognizes the difficulty in drawing the line, and therefore would permit an accommodation for the "non-profit" (as opposed to "profit"-making) activities of a religious organization. Does the "religious"/"secular" distinction make sense? (Which one is a church soup kitchen or homeless shelter? Are any of a church's activities "secular"?) Does the "profit"/"non-profit" distinction make sense? (Isn't this just a function of how a business is set up?) How good a proxy is it for the religious-secular line that Brennan is trying to achieve?

5.   There have been numerous other "accommodation" decisions of the Supreme Court, tending to point in different directions. Are the results correct or incorrect as applications of the Establishment Clause?

Estate of Thornton v. Caldor, Inc., 472 U.S. 703 (1985). May a state enact a law providing that employers must allow employees who observe a weekly religious sabbath to have that one day per week off? A divided Court (in a pre-*Amos* decision) held that this attempted accommodation violated the Establishment Clause. Rightly or wrongly decided? (Could Pennsylvania in the 1790s have had a statute that excused witnesses from testifying in court on their Sabbath?) Is *Caldor* consistent with *Amos*? Title VII of the Civil Rights Act of 1964 (the statute that contains the religious-employer exemption at issue in *Amos*) also provides that all employers must make "reasonable accommodation" of the religious practices of employees. Is that statute unconstitutional? Is it distinguishable from *Caldor?*

Texas Monthly, Inc. v. Bullock, 489 U.S. 1 (1989). May a state exempt religious periodicals from a sales tax it imposes on other magazines and newspapers? A divided court (6–3) held this to violate the Establishment Clause, emphasizing the fact that the exemption was not available to similarly situated non-religious periodicals. Does this adequately distinguish the *Amos* case? There was no controlling majority opinion. Might the result be correct on Free Speech Clause grounds that the tax exemption discriminates on the basis of a publication's content? Does one need the Establishment Clause for this case?

In *Board of Educ. of Kiryas Joel Village School Dist. v. Grumet,* 512 U.S. 687 (1994). New York created a special public school district to accommodate the special education needs of children of members of the Satmar Hasidim (a Jewish religious sect) that lived in its own community. Constitutional accommodation or unconstitutional establishment of religion? The Court, 6–3, struck down the accommodation because it explicitly accommodated a particular sect and the Court was concerned that there was no assurance the state would similarly accommodate others. (New York re-passed its law in different form, designed to avoid specific reference to the religious group. That accommodation was upheld by New York's highest state court against constitutional challenge.)

The Supreme Court's most recent case concerning accommodation upheld a federal statute broadly requiring that governments accommodate religious exercise in prisons and in land-use regulation. Note carefully the Supreme Court's rationale in *Cutter v. Wilkinson.*

Cutter v. Wilkinson
544 U.S. 709 (2005)

■ JUSTICE GINSBURG delivered the opinion of the Court.

Section 3 of the Religious Land Use and Institutionalized Persons Act of 2000 (RLUIPA) provides in part: "No government shall impose a substantial burden on the religious exercise of a person residing in or confined to an institution," unless the burden furthers "a compelling governmental interest," and does so by "the least restrictive means." Plaintiffs below, petitioners here, are current and former inmates of institutions operated by the Ohio Department of Rehabilitation and Correction and assert that they are adherents of "nonmainstream" religions: the Satanist, Wicca, and Asatru religions, and the Church of Jesus Christ Christian. They complain that Ohio prison officials (respondents here), in violation of RLUIPA, have failed to accommodate their religious exercise . . .

In response, . . . prison officials have mounted a facial challenge to the institutionalized-persons provision of RLUIPA; respondents contend, *inter alia,* that the Act improperly advances religion in violation of the First Amendment's Establishment Clause. . . . "This Court has long recognized that the government may . . . accommodate religious practices . . . without violating the Establishment Clause." . . . "At some point, accommodation may devolve into 'an unlawful fostering of religion.'" *Corporation of Presiding Bishop of Church of Jesus Christ of Latter-day Saints v. Amos,* 483 U.S. 327, 334 (1987). But § 3 of RLUIPA, we hold, does not, on its face, exceed the limits of permissible government accommodation of religious practices.

. . . Responding to *Employment Division v. Smith*, 494 U.S. 872 (1990), Congress enacted the Religious Freedom Restoration Act of 1993 (RFRA). . . . In *City of Boerne v. Flores,* 521 U.S. 507 (1997), this Court invalidated RFRA as applied to States and their subdivisions, holding that the Act exceeded Congress' remedial powers under the Fourteenth Amendment. . . . Congress again responded, this time by enacting RLUIPA. Less sweeping than RFRA, and invoking federal authority under the Spending and Commerce Clauses, RLUIPA targets two areas: Section 2 of the Act concerns land-use regulation; § 3 relates to religious exercise by institutionalized persons. . . .

The Religion Clauses of the First Amendment provide: "Congress shall make no law respecting an establishment of religion, or prohibiting the free exercise thereof." The first of the two Clauses, commonly called the Establishment Clause, commands a separation of church and state. The second, the Free Exercise Clause, requires government respect for, and noninterference with, the religious beliefs and practices of our Nation's people. While the two Clauses express complementary values, they often exert conflicting pressures. See *Locke v. Davey*, 540 U.S. 712, 718 (2004).

Our decisions recognize that "there is room for play in the joints" between the Clauses, *Walz v. Tax Comm'n of City of New York*, 397 U.S. 664, 669 (1970), some space for legislative action neither compelled by the Free Exercise Clause nor prohibited by the Establishment Clause. . . . [W]e hold that § 3 of RLUIPA fits within the corridor between the Religion Clauses: On its face, the Act qualifies as a permissible legislative accommodation of religion that is not barred by the Establishment Clause.

Foremost, we find RLUIPA's institutionalized-persons provision compatible with the Establishment Clause because it alleviates exceptional government-created burdens on private religious exercise. See *Board of Ed. of Kiryas Joel Village School Dist. v. Grumet*, 512 U.S. 687 (1994) (government need not "be oblivious to impositions that legitimate exercises of state power may place on religious belief and practice"). Furthermore, the Act on its face does not founder on shoals our prior decisions have identified: Properly applying RLUIPA, courts must take adequate account of the burdens a requested accommodation may impose on nonbeneficiaries, see *Estate of Thornton v. Caldor, Inc.*, 472 U.S. 703 (1985); and they must be satisfied that the Act's prescriptions are and will be administered neutrally among different faiths, see *Kiryas Joel.*

. . . Section 3 covers state-run institutions—mental hospitals, prisons, and the like—in which the government exerts a degree of control unparalleled in civilian society and severely disabling to private religious exercise. RLUIPA thus protects institutionalized persons who are unable freely to attend to their religious needs and are therefore dependent on the government's permission and accommodation for exercise of their religion.

We note in this regard the Federal Government's accommodation of religious practice by members of the military. . . .

We do not read RLUIPA to elevate accommodation of religious observances over an institution's need to maintain order and safety. Our decisions indicate that an accommodation must be measured so that it does not override other significant interests. In *Caldor,* the Court struck down a Connecticut law that "arm[ed] Sabbath observers with an absolute and unqualified right not to work on whatever day they designate[d] as their Sabbath." 472 U.S., at 709. We held the law invalid under the Establishment Clause because it "unyielding[ly] weigh[ted]" the interests of Sabbatarians "over all other interests."

We have no cause to believe that RLUIPA would not be applied in an appropriately balanced way, with particular sensitivity to security concerns. . . .

Finally, RLUIPA does not differentiate among bona fide faiths. In *Board of Ed. of Kiryas Joel Village School District v. Grumet,* we invalidated a state law that carved out a separate school district to serve exclusively a community of highly religious Jews, the Satmar Hasidim. We held that the law violated the Establishment Clause, in part because it "single[d] out a particular religious sect for special treatment." RLUIPA presents no such defect. It confers no privileged status on any particular religious sect, and singles out no bona fide faith for disadvantageous treatment.

The Sixth Circuit misread our precedents to require invalidation of RLUIPA as "impermissibly advancing religion by giving greater protection to religious rights than to other constitutionally protected rights." Our decision in *Amos* counsels otherwise. There, we upheld against an Establishment Clause challenge a provision exempting "religious organizations from Title VII's prohibition against discrimination in employment on the basis of religion." The District Court in *Amos,* reasoning in part that the exemption improperly "single[d] out religious entities for a benefit," had "declared the statute unconstitutional as applied to secular activity." Religious accommodations, we held, need not "come packaged with benefits to secular entities." . . .

■ [The concurring opinion of JUSTICE THOMAS is omitted.]

NOTES

1.   Note that the Court does not apply the *Lemon* test. Why not? In past cases, some justices argued that accommodations of religion necessarily violated all three prongs of the *Lemon* test, and that this was a good reason to revise or abandon the test. Does *Cutter* implicitly accept that criticism?

2.   In place of *Lemon, Cutter* looks to three considerations. Each of them raises new questions. First, the Court notes that the challenged statute "alleviates exceptional government-created burdens on private religious exercise." How exceptional is "exceptional"? In prior decisions, the Court had stated that accommodations must alleviate "substantial" or "significant" burdens. Why the change in vocabulary?

Second, the Court stated that under the statute, "courts must take adequate account of the burdens a requested accommodation may impose on nonbeneficiaries." How adequate is "adequate"? Why should nonbeneficiaries be required to shoulder any part of the cost of another person's religious exercise? On the other hand, if the burden on nonbeneficiaries is not religious in nature—if it involves mere cost or inconvenience— why is that a constitutional problem? Modern social welfare regulation frequently shifts burdens from one person to another—for example, from employees to employers. Why does the Establishment Clause point to a different result?

Some scholars argue that accommodations violate the Establishment Clause whenever they shift any burdens or impose any costs onto third parties. See Symposium,

Religious Exemptions, Third-Party Harms, and the Establishment Clause, 91 Notre Dame L. Rev. 1375 (2016). The Supreme Court has not gone that far—requiring only that "adequate account" be taken of those burdens. Would a more categorical prohibition on the inflicting of third party harm be a plausible interpretation of the Establishment Clause? And what is the definition of "harm"? Does it include offense or insult? Does it include marginal increase in taxes—for example, the increased cost of providing kosher or halal meals to Jewish or Muslim prisoners?

This question has arisen in recent controversies about the "contraceptive mandate" implementing the Affordable Care Act. Suppose employers are required to provide contraceptive coverage to their employees. A small number of employers say that this violates their conscience. Is it unconstitutional to make an exception for conscience claims, because employers would be "harming" their employees by withholding government-mandated coverage? Or does the harm shifting go the other way—that employers are being harmed by being forced to provide coverage they object to?

Third, the Court states that to be constitutional the Act must be "administered neutrally among different faiths." That sounds reasonable, but exactly what does it mean? Suppose there is a law exempting kosher slaughterhouses from certain meat-packing regulations. Perhaps the same exemption must be extended to halal meatpackers. But how can specific accommodations of this sort be neutral in any global sense? Many accommodations are targeted at particular religious practices known to be at odds with the law. Is that permissible under *Cutter*?

3.   Recall the First Congress's debates over whether to exempt religious conscientious objectors from compulsory service in the militia, at p. 1091. Some thought exemptions should be constitutionalized; some thought they should be left to legislative discretion; some thought they would be fair only if those exempted paid for an equivalent. This debate seems to be powerful support for the proposition that the framers of the First Amendment did not regard accommodations as establishments of religion. Why didn't the Court invoke this history in support of its reasoning?

[Assignment 57]

In Closer Focus: Financial Aid to Religious Activities

Everson v. Board of Education
330 U.S. 1 (1947)

■ MR. JUSTICE BLACK delivered the opinion of the Court.

A New Jersey statute authorizes its local school districts to make rules and contracts for the transportation of children to and from schools. The appellee, a township board of education, acting pursuant to this statute authorized reimbursement to parents of money expended by them for the bus transportation of their children on regular busses operated by the public transportation system. Part of this money was for the payment of transportation of some children in the community to Catholic parochial schools. These church schools give their students, in addition to secular education, regular religious instruction conforming to the religious tenets and modes of worship of the Catholic Faith. The superintendent of these schools is a Catholic priest.

The appellant, in his capacity as a district taxpayer, filed suit . . .

The only contention here is that the State statute and the resolution, in so far as they authorized reimbursement to parents of children attending parochial schools, . . . forced inhabitants to pay taxes to help support and maintain schools which are dedicated to, and which regularly teach, the Catholic Faith. This is alleged to be a use of State power to support church schools contrary to the prohibition of the First Amendment which the Fourteenth Amendment made applicable to the states . . .

A large proportion of the early settlers of this country came here from Europe to escape the bondage of laws which compelled them to support and attend government favored churches . . .

These practices became so commonplace as to shock the freedom-loving colonials into a feeling of abhorrence. The imposition of taxes to pay ministers' salaries and to build and maintain churches and church property aroused their indignation. It was these feelings which found expression in the First Amendment . . . The people [in Virginia], as elsewhere, reached the conviction that individual religious liberty could be achieved best under a government which was stripped of all power to tax, to support, or otherwise to assist any or all religions, or to interfere with the beliefs of any religious individual or group.

The movement toward this end reached its dramatic climax in Virginia in 1785–86 when the Virginia legislative body was about to renew Virginia's tax levy for the support of the established church . . . Madison wrote his great Memorial and Remonstrance against the law. In it, he eloquently argued that a true religion did not need the support of law; that no person, either believer or non-believer, should be taxed to support a religious institution of any kind; that the best interest of a society required that the minds of men always be wholly free; and that cruel persecutions were the inevitable result of government-established religions. Madison's Remonstrance received strong support throughout Virginia, and the Assembly postponed consideration of the proposed tax measure until its next session. When the proposal came up for consideration at that session, it not only died in committee, but the Assembly enacted the famous "Virginia Bill for Religious Liberty" originally written by Thomas Jefferson. The preamble to that Bill stated among other things that

> Almighty God hath created the mind free; that all attempts to influence it by temporal punishments, or burthens, or by civil incapacitations, tend only to beget habits of hypocrisy and meanness, and are a departure from the plan of the Holy author of our religion who being Lord both of body and mind, yet chose not to propagate it by coercions on either . . . ; that to compel a man to furnish contributions of money for the propagation of opinions which he disbelieves, is sinful and tyrannical; that even the forcing him to support this or that teacher of his own religious persuasion, is depriving him of the comfortable liberty of giving his contributions to the particular pastor, whose morals he would make his pattern. . . .

And the statute itself enacted

> That no man shall be compelled to frequent or support any religious worship, place, or ministry whatsoever, nor shall be enforced, restrained, molested, or burthened, in his body or goods, nor shall otherwise suffer on account of his religious opinions or belief. . . .

The "establishment of religion clause of the First Amendment means at least this: Neither a state nor the Federal Government can set up a church. Neither can pass laws which aid one religion, aid all religions, or prefer one religion over another. Neither can force nor influence a person to go to or to remain away from church against his will or force him to profess a belief or disbelief in any religion. No person can be punished for entertaining or professing religious beliefs or disbeliefs, for church attendance or non-attendance. No tax in any amount, large or small, can be levied to support any religious activities or institutions, whatever they may be called, or whatever form they may adopt to teach or practice religion. Neither a state nor the Federal Government can, openly or secretly, participate in the affairs of any religious organizations or groups and vice versa. In the words of Jefferson, the clause against establishment of religion by law was intended to erect "a wall of separation between Church and State."

We must consider the New Jersey statute in accordance with the foregoing limitations imposed by the First Amendment. But we must not strike that state statute down if it is within the state's constitutional power even though it approaches the verge of that power. New Jersey cannot consistently with the "establishment of religion" clause of the First Amendment contribute tax-raised funds to the support of an institution which teaches the tenets and faith of any church. On the other hand, other language of the amendment commands that New Jersey cannot hamper its citizens in the free exercise of their own religion. Consequently, it cannot exclude individual Catholics, Lutherans, Mohammedans, Baptists, Jews, Methodists, Non-believers, Presbyterians, or the members of any other faith, because of their faith, or lack of it, from receiving the benefits of public welfare legislation. While we do not mean to intimate that a state could not provide transportation only to children attending public schools, we must be careful, in protecting the citizens of New Jersey against state-established churches, to be sure that we do not inadvertently prohibit New Jersey from extending its general State law benefits to all its citizens without regard to their religious belief.

Measured by these standards, we cannot say that the First Amendment prohibits New Jersey from spending taxraised funds to pay the bus fares of parochial school pupils as a part of a general program under which it pays the fares of pupils attending public and other schools. It is undoubtedly true that children are helped to get to church schools. There is even a possibility that some of the children might not be sent to the church schools if the parents were compelled to pay their children's bus fares out of their own pockets when transportation to a public school would have been paid for by the State. The same possibility exists where the state requires a local transit company to provide reduced fares to school children including those attending parochial schools, or where a municipally owned transportation system undertakes to carry all school children free of charge. Moreover, state-paid policemen, detailed to protect children going to and from church schools from the very real hazards of traffic, would serve much the same purpose and accomplish much the same result as state provisions intended to guarantee free transportation of a kind which the state deems to be best for the school children's welfare. And parents might refuse to risk their children to the serious danger of traffic accidents going to and from parochial schools, the approaches to which were not protected by policemen. Similarly, parents might be reluctant to permit their children to attend schools which the state had cut off from such general government services as ordinary police and fire protection, connections for sewage disposal, public highways and sidewalks. Of course, cutting off church schools from these services, so separate and so indisputably marked off from the religious function, would make it far more difficult for the schools to operate. But such is obviously not the purpose of the First Amendment. That Amendment requires the state to be a neutral in its relations with groups of religious believers and non-believers; it does not require the state to be their adversary. State power is no more to be used so as to handicap religions, than it is to favor them.

This Court has said that parents may, in the discharge of their duty under state compulsory education laws, send their children to a religious rather than a public school if the school meets the secular educational requirements which the state has power to impose. See *Pierce v. Society of Sisters*, 268 U.S. 510 (1925). It appears that these parochial schools meet New Jersey's requirements. The State contributes no money to the schools. It does not support them. Its legislation, as applied, does no more than provide a general program to help parents get their children, regardless of their religion, safely and expeditiously to and from accredited schools.

The First Amendment has erected a wall between church and state. That wall must be kept high and impregnable. We could not approve the slightest breach. New Jersey has not breached it here.

■ [The dissenting opinion of JUSTICE JACKSON is omitted.]

■ MR. JUSTICE RUTLEDGE, with whom MR. JUSTICE FRANKFURTER, MR. JUSTICE JACKSON and MR. JUSTICE BURTON agree, dissenting.

I

Not simply an established church, but any law respecting an establishment of religion is forbidden. The Amendment was broadly but not loosely phrased. It is the compact and exact summation of its author's views formed during his long struggle for religious freedom . . .

The Amendment's purpose was not to strike merely at the official establishment of a single sect, creed or religion, outlawing only a formal relation such as had prevailed in England and some of the colonies. Necessarily it was to uproot all such relationships. But the object was broader than separating church and state in this narrow sense. It was to create a complete and permanent separation of the spheres of religious activity and civil authority by comprehensively forbidding every form of public aid or support for religion . . .

"Religion" and "establishment" were not used in any formal or technical sense. The prohibition broadly forbids state support, financial or other, of religion in any guise, form or degree. It outlaws all use of public funds for religious purposes.

II

No provision of the Constitution is more closely tied to or given content by its generating history than the religious clause of the First Amendment. It is at once the refined product and the terse summation of that history. The history includes not only Madison's authorship and the proceedings before the First Congress, but also the long and intensive struggle for religious freedom in America, more especially in Virginia, of which the Amendment was the direct culmination . . .

As the Remonstrance discloses throughout, Madison opposed every form and degree of official relation between religion and civil authority. For him religion was a wholly private matter beyond the scope of civil power either to restrain or to support. . . .

In no phase was he more unrelentingly absolute than in opposing state support or aid by taxation. Not even "three pence" contribution was thus to be exacted from any citizen for such a purpose. Remonstrance, Par. 3. Tithes had been the life blood of establishment before and after other compulsions disappeared. Madison and his coworkers made no exceptions or abridgments to the complete separation they created . . . And the principle was as much to prevent "the interference of law in religion" as to restrain religious intervention in political matters. In this field the authors of our freedom would not tolerate "the first experiment on our liberties" or "wait till usurped power had strengthened itself by exercise, and entangled the question in precedents." Remonstrance, Par. 3. Nor should we.

In view of this history no further proof is needed that the Amendment forbids any appropriation, large or small, from public funds to aid or support any and all religious exercises . . .

III

Does New Jersey's action furnish support for religion by use of the taxing power? Certainly it does, if the test remains undiluted as Jefferson and Madison made it, that money taken by taxation from one is not to be used or given to support another's religious training or belief, or indeed one's own. Today as then the furnishing of "contributions of money for the propagation of opinions which he disbelieves" is the forbidden exaction; and the prohibition is absolute for whatever measure brings that consequence and whatever mount may be sought or given to that end.

The funds used here were raised by taxation. The Court does not dispute nor could it that their use does in fact give aid and encouragement to religious instruction. It only concludes that this aid is not "support" in law. But Madison and Jefferson were concerned with aid and support in fact not as a legal conclusion "entangled in precedents." Remonstrance, Par. 3. Here parents pay money to send their children to parochial schools and funds raised by taxation are used to reimburse them. This not only helps the children to get to school and the parents to send them. It aids them in a substantial way to get the very thing which they are sent to the particular school to secure, namely, religious training and teaching.

Believers of all faiths, and others who do not express their feeling toward ultimate issues of existence in any creedal form, pay the New Jersey tax . . . Each [person] thus contributes to "the propagation of opinions which he disbelieves" in so far as their religious differ, as do others who accept no creed without regard to those differences. Each thus pays taxes also to support the teaching of his own religion, an exaction equally forbidden since it denies "the comfortable liberty" of giving one's contribution to the particular agency of instruction he approves.

New Jersey's action therefore exactly fits the type of exaction and the kind of evil at which Madison and Jefferson struck. Under the test they framed it cannot be said that the cost of transportation is no part of the cost of education or of the religious instruction given. That it is a substantial and a necessary element is shown most plainly by the continuing and increasing demand for the state to assume it . . . And the very purpose of the state's contribution is to defray the cost of conveying the pupil to the place where he will receive not simply secular, but also and primarily religious, teaching and guidance . . .

Finally, transportation, where it is needed, is as essential to education as any other element . . . Without buildings, without equipment, without library, textbooks and other materials, and without transportation to bring teacher and pupil together in such an effective teaching environment, there can be not even the skeleton of what our times require. Hardly can it be maintained that transportation is the least essential of these items, or that it does not in fact aid, encourage, sustain and support, just as they do, the very process which is its purpose to accomplish . . .

For me, therefore, the feat is impossible to select so indispensable an item from the composite of total costs, and characterize it as not aiding, contributing to, promoting or sustaining the propagation of beliefs which it is the very end of all to bring about. Unless this can be maintained, and the Court does not maintain it, the aid thus given is outlawed . . . No rational line can be drawn between payment for such larger, but not more necessary, items and payment for transportation. The only line that can be so drawn is one between more dollars and less. Certainly in this realm such a line can be no valid constitutional measure . . .

IV

But we are told that the New Jersey statute is valid in its present application because the appropriation is for a public, not a private purpose, namely, the promotion of education, and the majority accept this idea in the conclusion that all we have here is "public welfare legislation." . . .

If the fact alone be determinative that religious schools are engaged in education, thus promoting the general and individual welfare, together with the legislature's decision that the payment of public moneys for their aid makes their work a public function, then I can see no possible basis, except one of dubious legislative policy, for the state's refusal to make full appropriation for support of private, religious schools, just as is done for public instruction. There could not be, on that basis, valid constitutional objection.

Of course paying the cost of transportation promotes the general cause of education and the welfare of the individual . . .

To say that New Jersey's appropriation and her use of the power of taxation for raising the funds appropriated are not for public purposes but are for private ends, is to say that they are for the support of religion and religious teaching. Conversely, to say that they are for public purposes is to say that they are not for religious ones.

This is precisely for the reason that education which includes religious training and teaching, and its support, have been made matters of private right and function not public, by the very terms of the First Amendment. That is the effect not only in its guaranty of religion's free exercise, but also in the prohibition of establishments. It was on this basis of the private character of the function of religious education that this Court held parents entitled to send their children to private, religious schools. *Pierce*. Now it declares in effect that the appropriation of public funds to defray part of the cost of attending those schools is for a public purpose. If so, I do not understand why the state cannot go father or why this case approaches the verge of its power.

In truth this view contradicts the whole purpose and effect of the First Amendment as heretofore conceived. The "public function"—"public welfare"— "social legislation" argument seeks in Madison's words, to "employ Religion (that is, here, religious education) as an engine of Civil policy." Remonstrance, Par. 5 . . .

Our constitutional policy is exactly the opposite. It does not deny the value or the necessity for religious training, teaching or observance. Rather it secures their free exercise. But to that end it does deny that the state can undertake or sustain them in any form or degree. For this reason the sphere of religious activity, as distinguished from the secular intellectual liberties, has been given the twofold protection and, as the state cannot forbid, neither can it perform or aid in performing the religious function. The dual prohibition makes that function altogether private. It cannot be made a public one by legislative act. This was the very heart of Madison's Remonstrance, as it is of the Amendment itself . . .

[The majority makes two arguments:] one that the aid extended partakes of the nature of a safety measure, the other that failure to provide it would make the state unneutral in religious matters, discriminating against or hampering such children concerning public benefits all others receive . . .

[T]his approach, if valid, supplies a ready method for nullifying the Amendment's guaranty, not only for this case and others involving small grants in aid for religious education, but equally for larger ones. The only thing needed will be for the Court again to transplant the "public welfare-public function" view from its proper nonreligious due process bearing to First Amendment application, holding that religious education is not "supported" though it may be aided by the appropriation, and that the cause of education generally is furthered by helping the pupil to secure that type of training . . .

VI

Short treatment will dispose of what remains. Whatever might be said of some other application of New Jersey's statute, the one made here has no semblance of bearing as a safety measure or, indeed, for securing expeditious conveyance. The transportation supplied is by public conveyance, subject to all the hazards and delays of the highway and the streets incurred by the public generally in going about its multifarious business.

Nor is the case comparable to one of furnishing fire or police protection, or access to public highways. These things are matters of common right, part of the general need for safety.[56] Certainly the fire department must not stand idly by while the church burns. Nor is this reason why the state should pay the expense of transportation or other items of the cost of religious education . . .

Two great drives are constantly in motion to abridge, in the name of education, the complete division of religion and civil authority which our forefathers made. One is to introduce religious education and observances into the public schools. The other, to obtain public funds for the aid and support of various private religious schools. In my opinion both avenues were closed by the Constitution. Neither should be opened by this Court . . .

---

[56] The protections are of a nature which does not require appropriations specially made from the public treasury and earmarked, as is New Jersey's here, particularly for religious institutions or uses. The First Amendment does not exclude religious property or activities from protection against disorder or the ordinary accidental incidents of community life. It forbids support, not protection from interference or destruction . . .

NOTES

1.   The majority opinion is not internally consistent. The first part proclaims the necessity of strict separation; the second part relies on neutrality. Which is it?

2.   Justice Rutledge relies heavily on the history of the Virginia assessment bill. Is that really so close an analogy? The Virginia bill required taxpayers to pay money to churches for religious uses. The New Jersey statute uses money in the general treasury to defray the costs of transportation of all students to school, no matter where they go. The Virginia statute expressly sought to support religion as such; the New Jersey statute supports education and is neutral about whether that education has a religious element. How would you deal with these issues?

3.   How far would Justice Rutledge go? Must churches be denied all benefits paid for by taxes? Police protection? Use of the mails or roads?

4.   *Pierce v. Society of Sisters*, p. 1534, cited by the majority, struck down a state statute (supported by nativists, including the Ku Klux Klan) requiring all students to attend public schools. If parents have the constitutional right to send their children to schools that educate them in the tenets of their faith, are there implications for school funding? Is the question of parental educational rights separate from the question of funding to exercise those rights? Or should the government offer each family its share of the school funds? No matter what school the family sends its children to? Or only if the children attend a school that provides a satisfactory education?

5.   How do the competing principles of no-aid separation and neutral aid apply in other contexts? In *Widmar v. Vincent*, 454 U.S. 263 (1981), a student religious group at the University of Missouri-Kansas City sought to use the state university center for its religious group meetings, on the same terms that the university permitted other student groups to use the facility. University officials said no, on the ground that the students' meetings would be religious in nature. They believed that the Establishment Clause (and parallel provisions of the Missouri Constitution) dictated that they exclude the religious student group. The U.S. Supreme Court held, 8–1, for the students. The exclusion of a religious student group from a designated public forum for student expressive activities, based on the religious content of their expression, was a presumptive violation of the Free Speech Clause, the Court held. Did the Establishment Clause require exclusion otherwise forbidden by the Free Speech Clause? The Court said no. Equal inclusion within a government forum (or other benefit) did not have the purpose or effect of advancing religion specially, but merely afforded neutral, equal treatment. Nor would equal access "entangle" government with religion; to the contrary, it would avoid entanglement by requiring equal treatment, rather than placing the government in the role of roving censor of possible religious expression by student organizations. *Widmar* was an important precedent in establishing the proposition that the Establishment Clause does not require (and the Free Speech Clause does not permit) discriminatory exclusion of religion or religious persons from benefits or fora to which they otherwise would be given access on an equal basis.

Lemon v. Kurtzman

403 U.S. 602 (1971)

■ MR. CHIEF JUSTICE BURGER delivered the opinion of the Court.

These two appeals raise questions as to Pennsylvania and Rhode Island statutes providing state aid to church-related elementary and secondary schools. Both statutes are challenged as violative of the Establishment and Free Exercise Clauses of the First Amendment and the Due Process Clause of the Fourteenth Amendment . . . We hold that both statutes are unconstitutional.

I

The Rhode Island [law] rests on the legislative finding that the quality of education available in nonpublic elementary schools has been jeopardized by the rapidly rising salaries needed to attract competent and dedicated teachers. [It] supplement[s] the salaries of teachers of secular subjects in nonpublic elementary schools by paying directly to a teacher an amount not in excess of 15% of his current annual salary. As supplemented, however, a nonpublic school teacher's salary cannot exceed the maximum paid to teachers in the State's public schools, and the recipient must be certified by the state board of education in substantially the same manner as public school teachers.

In order to be eligible for the Rhode Island salary supplement, the recipient must teach in a nonpublic school at which the average per-pupil expenditure on secular education is less than the average in the State's public schools during a specified period. . . .

The Act also requires that teachers eligible for salary supplements must teach only those subjects that are offered in the State's public schools. They must use "only teaching materials which are used in the public schools." Finally, any teacher applying for a salary supplement must first agree in writing "not to teach a course in religion for so long as or during such time as he or she receives any salary supplements" under the Act . . .

[The Court's description of the Pennsylvania statute is omitted.—Editors]

II

. . . [The First Amendment's] authors did not simply prohibit the establishment of a state church or a state religion, an area history shows they regarded as very important and fraught with great dangers. Instead they commanded that there should be "no law respecting an establishment of religion." A law may be one "respecting" the forbidden objective while falling short of its total realization. A law "respecting" the proscribed result, that is, the establishment of religion, is not always easily identifiable as one violative of the Clause. A given law might not establish a state religion but nevertheless be one "respecting" that end in the sense of being a step that could lead to such establishment and hence offend the First Amendment.

In the absence of precisely stated constitutional prohibitions, we must draw lines with reference to the three main evils against which the Establishment Clause was intended to afford protection: "sponsorship, financial support, and active involvement of the sovereign in religious activity." *Walz v. Tax Commission*, 397 U.S. 664, 668 (1970).

Every analysis in this area must begin with consideration of the cumulative criteria developed by the Court over many years. Three such tests may be gleaned from our cases. First, the statute must have a secular legislative purpose; second, its principal or primary effect must be one that neither advances nor inhibits religion, *Board of Education v. Allen*, 392 U.S. 236, 243 (1968); finally, the statute must not foster "an excessive government entanglement with religion," *Walz*, at 674.

Inquiry into the legislative purposes of the Pennsylvania and Rhode Island statutes affords no basis for a conclusion that the legislative intent was to advance religion. On the contrary, the statutes themselves clearly state that they are intended to enhance the quality of the secular education in all schools covered by the compulsory attendance laws. There is no reason to believe the legislatures meant anything else . . .

In *Allen* the Court acknowledged that secular and religious teachings were not necessarily so intertwined that secular textbooks furnished to students by the State were in fact instrumental in the teaching of religion. The legislatures of Rhode Island and Pennsylvania have concluded that secular and religious education are identifiable and separable. In the abstract we have no quarrel with this conclusion.

The two legislatures, however, have also recognized that church-related elementary and secondary schools have a significant religious mission and that a substantial portion of their activities is religiously oriented. They have therefore sought to create statutory restrictions designed to guarantee the separation between secular and religious educational functions and to ensure that State financial aid supports only the former. All these provisions are precautions taken in candid recognition that these programs approached, even if they did not intrude upon, the forbidden areas under the Religion Clauses. We need not decide whether these legislative precautions restrict the principal or primary effect of the programs to the point where they do not offend the Religion Clauses, for we conclude that the cumulative impact of the entire relationship arising under the statutes in each State involves excessive entanglement between government and religion.

III

. . . Our prior holdings do not call for total separation between church and state; total separation is not possible in an absolute sense. Some relationship between government and religious organizations is inevitable. Fire inspections, building and zoning regulations, and state requirements under compulsory school-attendance laws are examples of necessary and permissible contacts. Indeed, under the statutory exemption before us in *Walz*, the State had a continuing burden to ascertain that the exempt property was in fact being used for religious worship. Judicial caveats against entanglement must recognize that the line of separation, far from being a "wall," is blurred, indistinct, and variable barrier depending on all the circumstances of a particular relationship . . .

In order to determine whether the government entanglement with religion is excessive, we must examine the character and purposes of the institutions that are benefited, the nature of the aid that the State provides, and the resulting relationship between the government and the religious authority . . . Here we find that both statutes foster an impermissible degree of entanglement.

(a)   Rhode Island program

. . . The church schools involved in the program are located close to parish churches. This understandably permits convenient access for religious exercises since instruction in faith and morals is part of the total educational process. The school buildings contain identifying religious symbols such as crosses on the exterior and crucifixes, and religious paintings and statutes either in the classrooms or hallways. Although only approximately 30 minutes a day are devoted to direct religious instruction, there are religiously oriented extracurricular activities.

Approximately two-thirds of the teachers in these schools are nuns of various religious orders. Their dedicated efforts provide an atmosphere in which religious instruction and religious vocations are natural and proper parts of life in such schools. Indeed, as the District Court found, the role of teaching nuns in enhancing the religious atmosphere has led the parochial school authorities to attempt to maintain a one-to-one ratio between nuns and lay teachers in all schools rather than to permit some to be staffed almost entirely by lay teachers.

On the basis of these findings the District Court concluded that the parochial schools constituted "an integral part of the religious mission of the Catholic Church." The various characteristics of the schools make them "a powerful vehicle for transmitting the Catholic faith to the next generation." This process of inculcating religious doctrine is, of course, enhanced by the impressionable age of the pupils, in primary schools particularly. In short, parochial schools involve substantial religious activity and purpose.

The substantial religious character of these church-related schools gives rise to entangling church-state relationships of the kind the Religion Clauses sought to avoid. Although the District Court found that concern for religious values did not inevitably or necessarily intrude into the content of secular subjects, the considerable religious activities of these schools led the legislature to provide for careful governmental controls and surveillance by state authorities in order to ensure that state aid supports only secular education.

The dangers and corresponding entanglements are enhanced by the particular form of aid that the Rhode Island Act provides. Our decisions from *Everson v. Board of Education*, 330 U.S. 1 (1947), to *Allen* have permitted the States to provide church-related schools with secular, neutral, or nonideological services, facilities, or materials. Bus transportation, school lunches, public health services, and secular textbooks supplied in common to all students were not thought to offend the Establishment Clause. We note that the dissenters in Allen seemed chiefly concerned with the pragmatic difficulties involved in ensuring the truly secular content of the textbooks provided at state expense.

In *Allen* the Court refused to make assumptions, on a meager record, about the religious content of the textbooks that the State would be asked to provide. We cannot, however, refuse here to recognize that teachers have a substantially different ideological character from books. In terms of potential for involving some aspect of faith or morals in secular subjects, a textbook's content is ascertainable, but a teacher's handling of a subject is not. We cannot ignore the danger that a teacher under religious control and discipline poses to the separation of the religious from the purely secular aspects of precollege education. The conflict of functions inheres in the situation. . . .

[The Court notes that the Catholic schools are under the supervision of clergy appointed by the local bishop, and thus "[r]eligious authority necessarily pervades the school system." According to diocesan regulations, "[r]eligious formation is not confined to formal courses."—Editors]

Several teachers testified, however, that they did not inject religion into their secular classes. And the District Court found that religious values did not necessarily affect the content of the secular instruction. But what has been recounted suggests the potential if not actual hazards of this form of state aid. The teacher is employed by a religious organization, subject to the direction and discipline of religious authorities, and works in a system dedicated to rearing children in a particular faith. These controls are not lessened by the fact that most of the lay teachers are of the Catholic faith. Inevitably some of a teacher's responsibilities hover on the border between secular and religious orientation.

We need not and do not assume that teachers in parochial schools will be guilty of bad faith or any conscious design to evade the limitations imposed by the statute and the First Amendment. We simply recognize that a dedicated religious person, teaching in a school affiliated with his or her faith and operated to inculcate its tenets, will inevitably experience great difficulty in remaining religiously neutral. Doctrines and faith are not inculcated or advanced by neutrals. With the best of intentions such a teacher would find it hard to make a total separation between secular teaching and religious doctrine. What would appear to some to be essential to good citizenship might well for others border on or constitute instruction in religion. Further difficulties are inherent in the combination of religious discipline and the possibility of disagreement between teacher and religious authorities over the meaning of the statutory restrictions.

We do not assume, however, that parochial school teachers will be unsuccessful in their attempts to segregate their religious beliefs from their secular educational responsibilities. But the potential for impermissible fostering of religion is present . . . To ensure that no trespass occurs, the State has therefore carefully conditioned its aid with pervasive restrictions . . .

A comprehensive, discriminating, and continuing state surveillance will inevitably be required to ensure that these restrictions are obeyed and the First Amendment otherwise respected. Unlike a book, a teacher cannot be inspected once so as to determine the extent and intent of his or her personal beliefs and subjective acceptance of the limitations imposed by the First Amendment. These prophylactic contacts will involve excessive and enduring entanglement between state and church.

There is another area of entanglement in the Rhode Island program that gives concern. The statute excludes teachers employed by nonpublic schools whose average per-pupil expenditures on secular education equal or exceed the comparable figures for public schools. In the event that the total expenditures of an otherwise eligible school exceed this norm, the program requires the government to examine the school's records in order to determine how much of the total expenditures is attributable to secular education and how much to religious activity. This kind of state inspection and evaluation of the religious content of a religious organization is fraught with the sort of entanglement that the Constitution forbids. It is a relationship pregnant with dangers of excessive government direction of church schools and hence of churches. The Court noted "the hazards of government supporting churches" in *Walz*, and we cannot ignore here the danger that pervasive modern governmental power will ultimately intrude on religion and thus conflict with the Religion Clauses. . . .

[*The Court's analysis of the Pennsylvania program is similar.—Editors*]

IV

A broader base of entanglement of yet a different character is presented by the divisive political potential of these state programs. In a community where such a large number of pupils are served by church-related schools, it can be assumed that state assistance will entail considerable political activity. Partisans of parochial schools, understandably concerned with rising costs and sincerely dedicated to both the religious and secular educational missions of their schools, will inevitably champion this cause and promote political action to achieve their goals. Those who oppose state aid, whether for constitutional, religious, or fiscal reasons, will inevitably respond and employ all of the usual political campaign techniques to prevail. Candidates will be forced to declare and voters to choose. It would be unrealistic to ignore the fact that many people confronted with issues of this kind will find their votes aligned with their faith.

Ordinarily political debate and division, however vigorous or even partisan, are normal and healthy manifestations of our democratic system of government, but political division along religious lines was one of the principal evils against which the First Amendment was intended to protect. The potential divisiveness of such conflict is a threat to the normal political process . . . The history of many countries attests to the hazards of religion's intruding into the political arena or of political power intruding into the legitimate and free exercise of religious belief.

Of course, as the Court noted in *Walz*, "[a]dherents of particular faiths and individual churches frequently take strong positions on public issues." We could not expect otherwise, for religious values pervade the fabric of our national life. But [h]ere we are confronted with successive and very likely permanent annual appropriations that benefit relatively few religious groups. Political fragmentation and divisiveness on religious lines are thus likely to be intensified . . .

V

The merit and benefits of these schools, however, are not the issue before us in these cases. The sole question is whether state aid to these schools can be squared with the dictates of the Religion Clauses. Under our system the choice has been made that government is to be entirely excluded from the area of religious instruction and churches excluded from the affairs of government. The Constitution decrees that religion must be a private matter for the individual, the family, and the institutions of private choice, and that while some involvement and entanglement are inevitable, lines must be drawn . . .

■ [JUSTICE DOUGLAS's concurring opinion, joined by JUSTICE BLACK, is omitted.]

■ MR. JUSTICE WHITE, dissenting:

No one in these cases questions the constitutional right of parents to satisfy their state-imposed obligation to educate their children by sending them to private schools, sectarian or otherwise, as long as those schools meet minimum standards established for secular instruction. The States are not only permitted, but required by the Constitution, to free students attending private schools from any public school attendance obligation. The States may also furnish transportation for students, and books for teaching secular subjects to students attending parochial and other private as well as public schools; we have also upheld arrangements whereby students are released from public school classes so that they may attend religious instruction. Outside the field of education, we have upheld Sunday closing laws, state and federal laws exempting church property and church activity from taxation, and governmental grants to religious organizations for the purpose of financing improvements in the facilities of hospitals managed and controlled by religious orders.

Our prior cases have recognized the dual role of parochial schools in American society: they perform both religious and secular functions. Our cases also recognize that legislation having a secular purpose and extending governmental assistance to sectarian schools in the performance of their secular functions does not constitute "law[s] respecting an establishment of religion" forbidden by the First Amendment merely because a secular program may incidentally benefit a church in fulfilling its religious mission. That religion may indirectly benefit from governmental aid to the secular activities of churches does not convert that aid into an impermissible establishment of religion . . .

It is enough for me that the States and the Federal Government are financing a separable secular function of overriding importance in order to sustain the legislation here challenged. That religion and private interests other than education may substantially benefit does not convert these laws into impermissible establishments of religion.

It is unnecessary, therefore, to urge that the Free Exercise Clause of the First Amendment at least permits government, in some respects, to modify and mold its secular programs out of express concern for free-exercise values. The Establishment Clause, however, coexists in the First Amendment with the Free Exercise Clause, and the latter is surely relevant in cases such as these. Where a state program seeks to ensure the proper education of its young, in private as well as public schools, free exercise considerations at least counsel against refusing support for students attending parochial schools simply because, in that setting, they are also being instructed in the tenets of the faith they are constitutionally free to practice.

NOTES

1.   Think about the way in which the second and third prongs of the *Lemon* test interact. The "effects" test requires the state to be "certain" that its funds do not support religion, but the "entanglement" test renders regulatory efforts to monitor use of the funds unconstitutional. In a later case, the Court called this a "Catch-22."

2.   Who is being protected by the decision in *Lemon*? The taxpayers? Assuming the schools are of equal educational quality—and no one denies this—taxpayers are getting full value for their money. Indeed, because religious schools are less expensive than public schools, they may be saving money. The children? Their parents selected these schools, and presumably like the religious education they are getting. The schools themselves? They are the most plausible candidates for recipients of protection. The state statutes effectively provide that they can receive money if and only if they secularize a significant portion of their curriculum. Financially hard-pressed schools may find that difficult to turn down. But why do taxpayers have standing to "protect" schools if the schools do not want to be protected?

3.   On the same day as *Lemon*, the Court decided *Tilton v. Richardson*, 403 U.S. 672 (1971), involving public aid to religious colleges and universities. Most of the justices thought the same principles were involved, but they split between those who thought the aid constitutional and those who thought it unconstitutional. A minority of the justices thought that higher education was distinguishable, because it was not "pervasively sectarian." Because these recipient institutions were not "pervasively sectarian," the state could rely on their assurances that they would not use public money for religious

purposes, thus making entangling "surveillance" unnecessary. Eventually, the same rule spread to religious social welfare organizations. *Bowen v. Kendrick*, 487 U.S. 589 (1988). Although recipients could not use funds for "specifically religious activities," the burden was on plaintiffs to prove a violation—in contrast to *Lemon*, where the need for entangling surveillance was simply assumed. In practice, then, the Catch-22 of the *Lemon* test applied only to "pervasively sectarian" organizations. Only churches and elementary and secondary schools were deemed to fall in this category, which meant that public funds could flow relatively freely to religious organizations other than schools. See Stephen Monsma, WHEN SACRED AND SECULAR MIX: RELIGIOUS NONPROFIT ORGANIZATIONS AND PUBLIC MONEY (2000).

Cases After *Lemon*

1.   *Committee for Public Education v. Nyquist*, 413 U.S. 756 (1973). In 1972, New York State created three programs to provide assistance to non-public elementary and secondary schools. The first program provided direct money grants to qualifying nonpublic schools for maintenance and repair. The grants, made to schools with many low-income students, were made on a per-pupil basis but could not exceed the prior year's maintenance expenses or 50 percent of the average per-student cost for public schools. The second and third programs were for families using nonpublic schools. Through the second program, low income families could receive tuition grants of $50 or $100 per child depending on grade year, not to exceed half of the child's tuition. Through the third program, higher income families were eligible for a tuition tax credit, which diminished as their taxable income increased. Schools eligible under these programs included schools that imposed religious restrictions on admissions and faculty appointments, required student attendance at religious activities and adherence to doctrines of faith, established curricula consistent with church teaching, and sough the inculcation of religious values. By a 6–3 vote, the Court invalidated all three programs under the effects prong of the *Lemon* test.

Regarding the maintenance and repair grants, the Court noted that the program made no attempt to ensure that the funds were "used exclusively for secular purposes." For instance, the school might use the grant to pay "the salaries of employees who maintain the school chapel" or to "renovat[e] classrooms in which religion is taught." The Court distinguished *Everson*, which dealt with busing, and *Allen*, which dealt with textbooks, on the basis that those were secular functions. The Court rejected the argument that the limitation of 50 percent of per-student public school spending ensured that the program aided only secular functions. Citing *Lemon*, where the Rhode Island salary supplement was invalided even though it provided only 15 percent of a teacher's salary, the Court declared that "a mere statistical judgment will not suffice as a guarantee that state funds will not be used to finance religious education."

The Court also invalidated the tuition grants. Reasoning that the grants could not be given directly to sectarian schools without "an effective means of guaranteeing that the state aid . . . will be used exclusively for secular, neutral, and nonideological purposes," it concluded that the fact that the grants went to parents instead, was merely "one among many factors to be considered." The Court dismissed the argument that the aid to secular education was more substantial than the aid to religious education, and was thus the primary effect of the program under *Lemon*:

"We do not think that such metaphysical judgments are either possible or necessary. Our cases simply do not support the notion that a law found to have a 'primary' effect to promote some legitimate end under the State's police power is immune from further examination to ascertain whether it also has the direct and immediate effect of advancing religion." The Court also noted that the tuition grants went only to private-school families, in contrast to *Everson* and *Allen*, where both public- and private-school families benefited. The state maintained that the grants sought to ensure "comparable benefits" to all families, but the Court rejected this argument, reasoning that private-school families received the grants in addition to the right to send their children to public school, and that the state's argument, if accepted, would justify "the complete subsidization of all religious schools" in order "to equalize the position of parents who elect such schools." The Court reserved the question of whether a generally available grant program that did not consider "sectarian-nonsectarian, or public-nonpublic" distinctions would violate the Establishment Clause. The Court also rejected the argument that the grants were necessary "to promote the free exercise of religion" of low-income parents, noting that "tension inevitably exists between the Free Exercise and the Establishment Clause, and . . . it may often not be possible to promote the former without offending the latter."

The Court invalidated the tax credits for similar reasons. Additionally, the Court distinguished New York's tax credits from New York's system of exempting religious organizations from property taxes that had been upheld in *Walz v. Tax Commission*, 397 U.S. 664 (1970). According to the Court, tax exemptions enjoyed "an apparently universal approval" at the time of the adoption of the First Amendment, while tax credits for religious schooling were "a recent innovation." Furthermore, tax exemptions were "a reasonable and balanced attempt to guard against" the dangers of oppressive taxation, while tax credits were "[s]pecial tax benefits" that aided sectarian institutions and "tend to increase rather than limit [church-state] involvement." And, the *Walz* tax exemption was extended to all property "devoted to religious, educational, or charitable purposes."

2.   In *Meek v. Pittenger*, 421 U.S. 349 (1975), the Court struck down a Pennsylvania law that provided instructional materials, including periodicals, photographs, maps, charts, recordings, and films. The Court wrote:

> [A]s part of general legislation made available to all students, a State may include church-related schools in programs providing bus transportation, school lunches, and public health facilities—secular and non-ideological services unrelated to the primary, religion-oriented educational function of the sectarian school. The indirect and incidental benefits to church-related schools from those programs do not offend the constitutional prohibition against establishment of religion. But the massive aid provided the church-related nonpublic schools of Pennsylvania by Act 195 is neither indirect nor incidental.
>
> For the 1972–1973 school year, the Commonwealth authorized just under $12 million of direct aid to the predominantly church-related nonpublic schools of Pennsylvania through the loan of instructional material and equipment pursuant to Act 195. To be sure, the material and equipment that are the subjects of the loan—maps, charts, and laboratory equipment, for example—are "self-polic[ing], in that, starting as secular, nonideological and neutral, they will not change in use." But faced with the

substantial amounts of direct support authorized by Act 195, it would simply ignore reality to attempt to separate secular educational functions from the predominantly religious role performed by many of Pennsylvania's church-related elementary and secondary schools, and to then characterize Act 195 as channeling aid to the secular without providing direct aid to the sectarian. Even though earmarked for secular purposes, "when it flows to an institution in which religion is so pervasive that a substantial portion of its functions are subsumed in the religious mission," state aid has the impermissible primary effect of advancing religion.

Nevertheless, the Court distinguished and reaffirmed *Allen*, which upheld the loaning of secular textbooks to religious school students.

In *Meek*, the Court also struck down Pennsylvania's provision of "auxiliary services," like remedial and therapeutic services, and English as a second language, by public school personnel on religious school premises. According to the Court, any form of educational instruction in a religious school risked the injection of religious content into the teaching.

3.   In *Aguilar v. Felton*, 473 U.S. 402 (1985), the Court declared unconstitutional New York City's use of federal funds to pay for public school teachers to provide remedial education to low-income students in religious schools. While New York City adopted a system for monitoring the religious content of the publicly funded classes, the Court held that this system would require "comprehensive surveillance" and thus inevitably result in the excessive entanglement of church and state. *Aguilar* was later overruled by *Agostini v. Felton*, 521 U.S. 203 (1997).

Zelman v. Simmons-Harris

536 U.S. 639 (2002)

■ CHIEF JUSTICE REHNQUIST delivered the opinion of the Court.

The State of Ohio has established a pilot program designed to provide educational choices to families with children who reside in the Cleveland City School District. The question presented is whether this program offends the Establishment Clause of the United States Constitution. We hold that it does not.

There are more than 75,000 children enrolled in the Cleveland City School District. The majority of these children are from low-income and minority families. Few of these families enjoy the means to send their children to any school other than an inner-city public school. For more than a generation, however, Cleveland's public schools have been among the worst performing public schools in the Nation . . .

It is against this backdrop that Ohio enacted, among other initiatives, its Pilot Project Scholarship Program. The program provides financial assistance to families in any Ohio school district that is or has been "under federal court order requiring supervision and operational management of the district by the state superintendent." Cleveland is the only Ohio school district to fall within that category.

The program provides two basic kinds of assistance to parents of children in a covered district. First, the program provides tuition aid for students in kindergarten through third grade, expanding each year through eighth grade, to attend a participating public or private school of their parent's choosing. Second, the program provides tutorial aid for students who choose to remain enrolled in public school.

The tuition aid portion of the program is designed to provide educational choices to parents who reside in a covered district. Any private school, whether religious or nonreligious, may participate in the program and accept program students so long as the school is located within the boundaries of a covered district and meets statewide educational standards. Participating private schools must agree not to discriminate on the basis of race, religion, or ethnic background, or to "advocate or foster unlawful behavior or teach hatred of any person or group on the basis of race, ethnicity, national origin, or religion." Any public school located in a school district adjacent to the covered district may also participate in the program. Adjacent public schools are eligible to receive a $2,250 tuition grant for each program student accepted in addition to the full amount of per-pupil state funding attributable to each additional student. All participating schools, whether public or private, are required to accept students in accordance with rules and procedures established by the state superintendent.

Tuition aid is distributed to parents according to financial need. Families with incomes below 200% of the poverty line are given priority and are eligible to receive 90% of private school tuition up to $2,250. For these lowest income families, participating private schools may not charge a parental copayment greater than $250. For all other families, the program pays 75% of tuition costs, up to $1,875, with no copayment cap. These families receive tuition aid only if the number of available scholarships exceeds the number of low-income children who choose to participate. Where tuition aid is spent depends solely upon where parents who receive tuition aid choose to enroll their child. If parents choose a private school, checks are made payable to the parents who then endorse the checks over to the chosen school . . .

The program has been in operation within the Cleveland City School District since the 1996–1997 school year. In the 1999–2000 school year, 56 private schools participated in the program, 46 (or 82%) of which had a religious affiliation. None of the public schools in districts adjacent to Cleveland have elected to participate. More than 3,700 students participated in the scholarship program, most of whom (96%) enrolled in religiously affiliated schools. Sixty percent of these students were from families at or below the poverty line. In the 1998–1999 school year, approximately 1,400 Cleveland public school students received tutorial aid. This number was expected to double during the 1999–2000 school year.

The program is part of a broader undertaking by the State to enhance the educational options of Cleveland's schoolchildren in response to the 1995 takeover. That undertaking includes programs governing community and magnet schools . . . During the 1999–2000 school year, there were 10 startup community schools in the Cleveland City School District with more than 1,900 students enrolled. For each child enrolled in a community school, the school receives state funding of $4,518, twice the funding a participating program school may receive.

Magnet schools are public schools operated by a local school board that emphasize a particular subject area, teaching method, or service to students. For each student enrolled in a magnet school, the school district receives $7,746, including state funding of $4,167, the same amount received per student enrolled at a traditional public school. As of 1999, parents in Cleveland were able to choose from among 23 magnet schools, which together enrolled more than 13,000 students in kindergarten through eighth grade . . .

In July 1999, respondents [sued] on the ground that [the program] violated the Establishment Clause of the United States Constitution. . . . *[The district court granted summary judgment for the respondents, and a divided court of appeals affirmed.—Editors]* We granted certiorari, and now reverse the Court of Appeals.

The Establishment Clause of the First Amendment, applied to the States through the Fourteenth Amendment, prevents a State from enacting laws that have the "purpose" or "effect" of advancing or inhibiting religion. There is no dispute that the program challenged here was enacted for the valid secular purpose of providing educational assistance to poor children in a demonstrably failing public school system. Thus, the question presented is whether the Ohio program nonetheless has the forbidden "effect" of advancing or inhibiting religion.

To answer that question, our decisions have drawn a consistent distinction between government programs that provide aid directly to religious schools, and programs of true private choice, in which government aid reaches religious schools only as a result of the genuine and independent choices of private individuals. While our jurisprudence with respect to the constitutionality of direct aid programs has "changed significantly" over the past two decades, our jurisprudence with respect to true private choice programs has remained consistent and unbroken. Three times we have confronted Establishment Clause challenges to neutral government programs that provide aid directly to a broad class of individuals, who, in turn, direct the aid to religious schools or institutions of their own choosing. Three times we have rejected such challenges.

In *Mueller v. Allen*, 463 U.S. 388 (1983), we rejected an Establishment Clause challenge to a Minnesota program authorizing tax deductions for various educational expenses, including private school tuition costs, even though the great majority of the program's beneficiaries (96%) were parents of children in religious schools . . .

In *Witters v. Washington Dept. of Servs. For the Blind*, 474 U.S. 481 (1986), we used identical reasoning to reject an Establishment Clause challenge to a vocational scholarship program that provided tuition aid to a student studying at a religious institution to become a pastor . . .

Finally, in *Zobrest v. Catalina Foothills School Dist.*, 509 U.S. 1 (1993), we applied *Mueller* and *Witters* to reject an Establishment Clause challenge to a federal program that permitted sign-language interpreters to assist deaf children enrolled in religious schools . . .

Mueller, Witters, and *Zobrest* thus make clear that where a government aid program is neutral with respect to religion, and provides assistance directly to a broad class of citizens who, in turn, direct government aid to religious schools wholly as a result of their own genuine and independent private choice, the program is not readily subject to challenge under the Establishment Clause. A program that shares these features permits government aid to reach religious institutions only by way of the deliberate choices of numerous individual recipients. The incidental advancement of a religious mission, or the perceived endorsement of a religious message, is reasonably attributable to the individual recipient, not to the government, whose role ends with the disbursement of benefits. As a plurality of this Court recently observed:

"[I]f numerous private choices, rather than the single choice of a government, determine the distribution of aid, pursuant to neutral eligibility criteria, then a government cannot, or at least cannot easily, grant special favors that might lead to a religious establishment."

It is precisely for these reasons that we have never found a program of true private choice to offend the Establishment Clause.

We believe that the program challenged here is a program of true private choice, consistent with *Mueller, Witters,* and *Zobrest,* and thus constitutional. As was true in those cases, the Ohio program is neutral in all respects toward religion. It is part of a general and multifaceted undertaking by the State of Ohio to provide educational opportunities to the children of a failed school district. It confers educational assistance directly to a broad class of individuals defined without reference to religion, *i.e.,* any parent of a school-age child who resides in the Cleveland City School District. The program permits the participation of *all* schools within the district, religious or nonreligious. Adjacent public schools also may participate and have a financial incentive to do so. Program benefits are available to participating families on neutral terms, with no reference to religion. The only preference stated anywhere in the program is a preference for low-income families, who receive greater assistance and are given priority for admission at participating schools.

There are no "financial incentive[s]" that "ske[w]" the program toward religious schools. Such incentives "[are] not present . . . where the aid is allocated on the basis of neutral, secular criteria that neither favor nor disfavor religion, and is made available to both religious and secular beneficiaries on a nondiscriminatory basis." The program here in fact creates financial *dis*incentives for religious schools, with private schools receiving only half the government assistance given to community schools and one-third the assistance given to magnet schools. Adjacent public schools, should any choose to accept program students, are also eligible to receive two to three times the state funding of a private religious school. Families too have a financial disincentive to choose a private religious school over other schools. Parents that choose to participate in the scholarship program and then to enroll their children in a private school (religious or nonreligious) must copay a portion of the school's tuition. Families that choose a community school, magnet school, or traditional public school pay nothing. Although such features of the program are not necessary to its constitutionality, they clearly dispel the claim that the program "creates . . . financial incentive[s] for parents to choose a sectarian school."

Respondents suggest that even without a financial incentive for parents to choose a religious school, the program creates a "public perception that the State is endorsing religious practices and beliefs." But we have repeatedly recognized that no reasonable observer would think a neutral program of private choice, where state aid reaches religious schools solely as a result of the numerous independent decisions of private individuals, carries with it the *imprimatur* of government endorsement. The argument is particularly misplaced here since "the reasonable observer in the endorsement inquiry must be deemed aware" of the "history and context" underlying a challenged program. Any objective observer familiar with the full history and context of the Ohio program would reasonably view it as one aspect of a broader undertaking to assist poor children in failed schools, not as an endorsement of religious schooling in general.

There also is no evidence that the program fails to provide genuine opportunities for Cleveland parents to select secular educational options for their school-age children. Cleveland schoolchildren enjoy a range of educational choices: They may remain in public school as before, remain in public school with publicly funded tutoring aid, obtain a scholarship and choose a religious school, obtain a scholarship and choose a nonreligious private school, enroll in a community school, or enroll in a magnet school. . . .

JUSTICE SOUTER speculates that because more private religious schools currently participate in the program, the program itself must somehow discourage the participation of private nonreligious schools. But Cleveland's preponderance of religiously affiliated private schools certainly did not arise as a result of the program; it is a phenomenon common to many American cities . . . It is true that 82% of Cleveland's participating private schools are religious schools, but it is also true that 81% of private schools in Ohio are religious schools. To attribute constitutional significance to this figure, moreover, would lead to the absurd result that a neutral school-choice program might be permissible in some parts of Ohio, such as Columbus, where a lower percentage of private schools are religious schools, but not in inner-city Cleveland, where Ohio has deemed such programs most sorely needed, but where the preponderance of religious schools happens to be greater . . .

Respondents and JUSTICE SOUTER claim that even if we do not focus on the number of participating schools that are religious schools, we should attach constitutional significance to the fact that 96% of scholarship recipients have enrolled in religious schools. They claim that this alone proves parents lack genuine choice, even if no parent has ever said so . . . The constitutionality of a neutral educational aid program simply does not turn on whether and why, in a particular area, at a particular time, most private schools are run by religious organizations, or most recipients choose to use the aid at a religious school. As we said in *Mueller*, "[s]uch an approach would scarcely provide the certainty that this field stands in need of, nor can we perceive principled standards by which such statistical evidence might be evaluated." . . .

Respondents finally claim that we should look to *Committee for Public Ed. & Religious Liberty v. Nyquist*, 413 U.S. 756 (1973), to decide these cases. We disagree . . . [T]the program in *Nyquist* was quite different from the program challenged here. *Nyquist* involved a New York program that gave a package of benefits exclusively to private schools and the parents of private school enrollees. Although the program was enacted for ostensibly secular purposes, we found that its "function" was "*unmistakably* to provide desired financial support for nonpublic, sectarian institutions." Its genesis, we said, was that private religious schools faced "increasingly grave fiscal problems." The program thus provided direct money grants to religious schools. It provided tax benefits "unrelated to the amount of money actually expended by any parent on tuition," ensuring a windfall to parents of children in religious schools. It similarly provided tuition reimbursements designed explicitly to "offe[r] . . . an incentive to parents to send their children to sectarian schools." Indeed, the program flatly prohibited the participation of any public school, or parent of any public school enrollee. Ohio's program shares none of these features . . .

In sum, the Ohio program is entirely neutral with respect to religion. It provides benefits directly to a wide spectrum of individuals, defined only by financial need and residence in a particular school district. It permits such individuals to exercise genuine choice among options public and private, secular and religious. The program is therefore a program of true private choice. In keeping with an unbroken line of decisions rejecting challenges to similar programs, we hold that the program does not offend the Establishment Clause.

■ [The concurring opinions of JUSTICES O'CONNOR and THOMAS, and the dissenting opinion of JUSTICE STEVENS, are omitted.]

■ JUSTICE SOUTER, with whom JUSTICE STEVENS, JUSTICE GINSBURG, and JUSTICE BREYER join, dissenting.

    ... The majority's statements of Establishment Clause doctrine cannot be appreciated without some historical perspective on the Court's announced limitations on government aid to religious education, and its repeated repudiation of limits previously set . . .

    Viewed with the necessary generality, the cases can be categorized in three groups. In the period from 1947 to 1968, the basic principle of no aid to religion through school benefits was unquestioned. Thereafter for some 15 years, the Court termed its efforts as attempts to draw a line against aid that would be divertible to support the religious, as distinct from the secular, activity of an institutional beneficiary. Then, starting in 1983, concern with divertibility was gradually lost in favor of approving aid in amounts unlikely to afford substantial benefits to religious schools, when offered evenhandedly without regard to a recipient's religious character, and when channeled to a religious institution only by the genuinely free choice of some private individual. Now, the three stages are succeeded by a fourth, in which the substantial character of government aid is held to have no constitutional significance, and the espoused criteria of neutrality in offering aid, and private choice in directing it, are shown to be nothing but examples of verbal formalism . . .

II

    Although it has taken half a century since *Everson v. Board of Ewing*, 330 U.S. 1 (1947), to reach the majority's twin standards of neutrality and free choice, the facts show that, in the majority's hands, even these criteria cannot convincingly legitimize the Ohio scheme.

A

    Consider first the criterion of neutrality . . . In order to apply the neutrality test[,] it makes sense to focus on a category of aid that may be directed to religious as well as secular schools, and ask whether the scheme favors a religious direction. Here, one would ask whether the voucher provisions, allowing for as much as $2,250 toward private school tuition (or a grant to a public school in an adjacent district), were written in a way that skewed the scheme toward benefiting religious schools.

    This, however, is not what the majority asks. The majority looks not to the provisions for tuition vouchers, but to every provision for educational opportunity: "The program permits the participation of *all* schools within the district, [as well as public schools in adjacent districts], religious or nonreligious." The majority then finds confirmation that "participation of *all* schools" satisfies neutrality by noting that the better part of total state educational expenditure goes to public schools, thus showing there is no favor of religion.

The illogic is patent. If regular, public schools (which can get no voucher payments) "participate" in a voucher scheme with schools that can, and public expenditure is still predominantly on public schools, then the majority's reasoning would find neutrality in a scheme of vouchers available for private tuition in districts with no secular private schools at all . . .

B

The majority addresses the issue of choice the same way it addresses neutrality, by asking whether recipients or potential recipients of voucher aid have a choice of public schools among secular alternatives to religious schools. Again, however, the majority asks the wrong question and misapplies the criterion. The majority has confused choice in spending scholarships with choice from the entire menu of possible educational placements, most of them open to anyone willing to attend a public school . . . If "choice" is present whenever there is any educational alternative to the religious school to which vouchers can be endorsed, then there will always be a choice and the voucher can always be constitutional, even in a system in which there is not a single private secular school as an alternative to the religious school . . .

It is not, of course, that I think even a genuine choice criterion is up to the task of the Establishment Clause when substantial state funds go to religious teaching; the discussion in Part III, shows that it is not. The point is simply that if the majority wishes to claim that choice is a criterion, it must define choice in a way that can function as a criterion with a practical capacity to screen something out.

If, contrary to the majority, we ask the right question about genuine choice to use the vouchers, the answer shows that something is influencing choices in a way that aims the money in a religious direction: of 56 private schools in the district participating in the voucher program (only 53 of which accepted voucher students in 1999–2000), 46 of them are religious; 96.6% of all voucher recipients go to religious schools, only 3.4% to nonreligious ones . . . Evidence shows, however, that almost two out of three families using vouchers to send their children to religious schools did not embrace the religion of those schools . . .

Even [this] might be consistent with true choice if the students "chose" their religious schools over a wide array of private nonreligious options, or if it could be shown generally that Ohio's program had no effect on educational choices and thus no impermissible effect of advancing religious education. But both possibilities are contrary to fact. First, [there are few, if any, open seats at nonreligious private schools]. Second, the $2,500 cap [discourages students from attending nonreligious private schools that have higher tuition]. By comparison, the average tuition at participating Catholic schools in Cleveland in 1999–2000 was $1,592, almost $1,000 below the cap . . .

And it is entirely irrelevant that the State did not deliberately design the network of private schools for the sake of channeling money into religious institutions. The criterion is one of genuinely free choice on the part of the private individuals who choose, and a Hobson's choice is not a choice, whatever the reason for being Hobsonian.

III

I do not dissent merely because the majority has misapplied its own law, for even if I assumed *arguendo* that the majority's formal criteria were satisfied on the facts, today's conclusion would be profoundly at odds with the Constitution. Proof of this is clear on two levels. The first is circumstantial, in the now discarded symptom of violation, the substantial dimension of the aid. The second is direct, in the defiance of every objective supposed to be served by the bar against establishment.

A

The scale of the aid to religious schools approved today is unprecedented, both in the number of dollars and in the proportion of systemic school expenditure supported. Each measure has received attention in previous cases. On one hand, the sheer quantity of aid, when delivered to a class of religious primary and secondary schools, was suspect on the theory that the greater the aid, the greater its proportion to a religious school's existing expenditures, and the greater the likelihood that public money was supporting religious as well as secular instruction . . .

On the other hand, the Court has found the gross amount unhelpful for Establishment Clause analysis when the aid afforded a benefit solely to one individual, however substantial as to him, but only an incidental benefit to the religious school at which the individual chose to spend the State's money. When neither the design nor the implementation of an aid scheme channels a series of individual students' subsidies toward religious recipients, the relevant beneficiaries for establishment purposes, the Establishment Clause is unlikely to be implicated . . .

The Cleveland voucher program has cost Ohio taxpayers $33 million since its implementation in 1996 ($28 million in voucher payments, $5 million in administrative costs), and its cost was expected to exceed $8 million in the 2001–2002 school year . . .

The gross amounts of public money contributed are symptomatic of the scope of what the taxpayers' money buys for a broad class of religious-school students. In paying for practically the full amount of tuition for thousands of qualifying students, the scholarships purchase everything that tuition purchases, be it instruction in math or indoctrination in faith . . .

B

[This program threatens harms that the Establishment Clause was designed to prevent. First, it violates respect for freedom of conscience and the Jeffersonian idea enshrined in the Bill for Establishing Religious Freedom that no one "shall be compelled to . . . support any religious worship, place or ministry whatsoever." Second, it risks foisting a "corrosive secularism" upon religious schools. These harms are] already being realized. In Ohio, for example, a condition of receiving government money under the program is that participating religious schools may not "discriminate on the basis of . . . religion," which means the school may not give admission preferences to children who are members of the patron faith; children of a parish are generally consigned to the same admission lotteries as non-believers . . . Nor is the State's religious antidiscrimination restriction limited to student admission policies: by its terms, a participating religious school may well be forbidden to choose a member of its own clergy to serve as teacher or principal over a layperson of a different religion claiming equal qualification for the job. Indeed, a separate condition that "[t]he school . . . not . . . teach hatred of any person or group on the basis of . . . religion," could be understood (or subsequently broadened) to prohibit religions from teaching traditionally legitimate articles of faith as to the error, sinfulness, or ignorance of others, if they want government money for their schools . . .

■ JUSTICE BREYER, with whom JUSTICE STEVENS and JUSTICE SOUTER join, dissenting.

[The Religion] Clauses embody an understanding, reached in the 17th century after decades of religious war, that liberty and social stability demand a religious tolerance that respects the religious views of all citizens, permits those citizens to "worship God in their own way," and allows all families to "teach their children and to form their characters" as they wish. The Clauses reflect the Framers' vision of an American Nation free of the religious strife that had long plagued the nations of Europe. Whatever the Framers might have thought about particular 18th-century school funding practices, they undeniably intended an interpretation of the Religion Clauses that would implement this basic First Amendment objective.

In part for this reason, the Court's 20th-century Establishment Clause cases—both those limiting the practice of religion in public schools and those limiting the public funding of private religious education—focused directly upon social conflict, potentially created when government becomes involved in religious education . . .

[A]n earlier American society might have found a less clear-cut church/state separation compatible with social tranquility. Indeed, historians point out that during the early years of the Republic, American schools—including the first public schools—were Protestant in character . . . The 20th-century Court was fully aware, however, that immigration and growth had changed American society dramatically since its early years . . .

The Court appreciated the religious diversity of contemporary American society. It realized that the status quo favored some religions at the expense of others. And it understood the Establishment Clause to prohibit (among other things) any such favoritism. Yet *how* did the Clause achieve that objective? Did it simply require the government to give each religion an equal chance to introduce religion into the primary schools—a kind of "equal opportunity" approach to the interpretation of the Establishment Clause? Or, did that Clause avoid government favoritism of some religions by insisting upon "separation"—that the government achieve equal treatment by removing itself from the business of providing religious education for children? This interpretive choice arose in respect both to religious activities in public schools and government aid to private education.

In both areas the Court concluded that the Establishment Clause required "separation," in part because an "equal opportunity" approach was not workable . . .

With respect to government aid to private education, did not history show that efforts to obtain equivalent funding for the private education of children whose parents did not hold popular religious beliefs only exacerbated religious strife? . . .

The upshot is the development of constitutional doctrine that reads the Establishment Clause as avoiding religious strife, *not* by providing every religion with an *equal opportunity* (say, to secure state funding or to pray in the public schools), but by drawing fairly clear lines of *separation* between church and state— at least where the heartland of religious belief, such as primary religious education, is at issue. . . .

IV

I do not believe that the "parental choice" aspect of the voucher program sufficiently offsets the concerns I have mentioned. Parental choice cannot help the taxpayer who does not want to finance the religious education of children. It will not always help the parent who may see little real choice between inadequate nonsectarian public education and adequate education at a school whose religious teachings are contrary to his own. It will not satisfy religious minorities unable to participate because they are too few in number to support the creation of their own private schools. It will not satisfy groups whose religious beliefs preclude them from participating in a government-sponsored program, and who may well feel ignored as government funds primarily support the education of children in the doctrines of the dominant religions. And it does little to ameliorate the entanglement problems or the related problems of social division that Part II describes. Consequently, the fact that the parent may choose which school can cash the government's voucher check does not alleviate the Establishment Clause concerns associated with voucher programs.

NOTES

1.   The majority relies primarily on a formal understanding of neutrality: if the statute makes no distinctions between religious and secular, treating all schools alike, it does not matter for constitutional purposes what choices are actually made. But the majority also argues, seemingly in the alternative, that the Cleveland program has neutral results. The difference between the majority and the dissent on this point hinges on what the denominator is. The majority asks what proportion of the total education fund goes to religious schools. The dissent focuses on the small part of the education scheme for which religious schools are eligible, and complains that religious schools predominate in that part. Which is right?

2.   The Court has come a long way from *Lemon, Nyquist, Meek,* and *Aguilar,* to *Zelman.* Which approach best accords with the text, historical context, and purposes of the First Amendment? Under which approach do Americans enjoy the widest religious freedom—including freedom not to be religious, and not to support religion? What accounts for the shift?

[*Assignment 58*]

Rosenberger v. Rector and Visitors
of University of Virginia
515 U.S. 819 (1995)

[In another part of this opinion, presented at p. 1018, the Court held that the Free Speech Clause does not allow a public university to exclude a student group from the benefits of the student activities fund on account of the religious viewpoint the group expresses. In this part of the opinion, the Court addressed whether funding the student group was a violation of the Establishment Clause. The lower court had held that the Free Speech and Establishment Clauses led to opposite results, and that the Establishment Clause prevailed over the Free Speech Clause.—Editors]

■ JUSTICE KENNEDY delivered the opinion of the Court.

III

. . . The Court of Appeals ruled that withholding SAF support from Wide Awake contravened the Speech Clause of the First Amendment, but proceeded to hold that the University's action was justified by the necessity of avoiding a violation of the Establishment Clause, an interest it found compelling. Recognizing that this Court has regularly "sanctioned awards of direct nonmonetary benefits to religious groups where government has created open fora to which all similarly situated organizations are invited," 18 F.3d, at 286 (citing *Widmar v. Vincent,* 454 U.S. 263, 277 (1981)), the Fourth Circuit asserted that direct monetary subsidization of religious organizations and projects is "a beast of an entirely different color." The court declared that the Establishment Clause would not permit the use of public funds to support "a specifically religious activity in an otherwise substantially secular setting." It reasoned that because Wide Awake is "a journal pervasively devoted to the discussion and advancement of an avowedly Christian theological and personal philosophy," the University's provision of SAF funds for its publication would "send an unmistakably clear signal that the University of Virginia supports Christian values and wishes to promote the wide promulgation of such values." . . .

A central lesson of our decisions is that a significant factor in upholding governmental programs in the face of Establishment Clause attack is their neutrality towards religion. We have decided a series of cases addressing the receipt of government benefits where religion or religious views are implicated in some degree. The first case in our modern Establishment Clause jurisprudence was *Everson v. Board of Ed. of Ewing,* 330 U.S. 1 (1947). There we cautioned that in enforcing the prohibition against laws respecting establishment of religion, we must "be sure that we do not inadvertently prohibit [the government] from extending its general state law benefits to all its citizens without regard to their religious belief." We have held that the guarantee of neutrality is respected, not offended, when the government, following neutral criteria and evenhanded policies, extends benefits to recipients whose ideologies and viewpoints, including religious ones, are broad and diverse. [E.g.,] *Mueller v. Allen,* 463 U.S. 388, 398–399 (1983); *Widmar,* at 274–275. More than once have we rejected the position that the Establishment Clause even justifies, much less requires, a refusal to extend free speech rights to religious speakers who participate in broad-reaching government programs neutral in design.

The governmental program here is neutral toward religion. There is no suggestion that the University created it to advance religion or adopted some ingenious device with the purpose of aiding a religious cause. The object of the SAF is to open a forum for speech and to support various student enterprises, including the publication of newspapers, in recognition of the diversity and creativity of student life. The University's SAF Guidelines have a separate classification for, and do not make third-party payments on behalf of, "religious organizations," which are those "whose purpose is to practice a devotion to an acknowledged ultimate reality or deity." The category of support here is for "student news, information, opinion, entertainment, or academic communications media groups," of which Wide Awake was 1 of 15 in the 1990 school year. WAP did not seek a subsidy because of its Christian editorial viewpoint; it sought funding as a student journal, which it was.

The neutrality of the program distinguishes the student fees from a tax levied for the direct support of a church or group of churches. A tax of that sort, of course, would run contrary to Establishment Clause concerns dating from the earliest days of the Republic. The apprehensions of our predecessors involved the levying of taxes upon the public for the sole and exclusive purpose of establishing and supporting specific sects. The exaction here, by contrast, is a student activity fee designed to reflect the reality that student life in its many dimensions includes the necessity of wide-ranging speech and inquiry and that student expression is an integral part of the University's educational mission. The fee is mandatory, and we do not have before us the question whether an objecting student has the First Amendment right to demand a pro rata return to the extent the fee is expended for speech to which he or she does not subscribe. We must treat it, then, as an exaction upon the students. But the $14 paid each semester by the students is not a general tax designed to raise revenue for the University. The SAF cannot be used for unlimited purposes, much less the illegitimate purpose of supporting one religion. Much like the arrangement in *Widmar*, the money goes to a special fund from which any group of students with CIO status can draw for purposes consistent with the University's educational mission; and to the extent the student is interested in speech, withdrawal is permitted to cover the whole spectrum of speech, whether it manifests a religious view, an antireligious view, or neither. Our decision, then, cannot be read as addressing an expenditure from a general tax fund. Here, the disbursements from the fund go to private contractors for the cost of printing that which is protected under the Speech Clause of the First Amendment. This is a far cry from a general public assessment designed and effected to provide financial support for a church.

Government neutrality is apparent in the State's overall scheme in a further meaningful respect. The program respects the critical difference "between *government* speech endorsing religion, which the Establishment Clause forbids, and *private* speech endorsing religion, which the Free Speech and Free Exercise Clauses protect." In this case, "the government has not fostered or encouraged" any mistaken impression that the student newspapers speak for the University. The University has taken pains to disassociate itself from the private speech involved in this case. The Court of Appeals' apparent concern that Wide Awake's religious orientation would be attributed to the University is not a plausible fear, and there is no real likelihood that the speech in question is being either endorsed or coerced by the State.

The Court of Appeals (and the dissent) are correct to extract from our decisions the principle that we have recognized special Establishment Clause dangers where the government makes direct money payments to sectarian institutions. The error is not in identifying the principle, but in believing that it controls this case. Even assuming that WAP is no different from a church and that its speech is the same as the religious exercises conducted in *Widmar* (two points much in doubt), the Court of Appeals decided a case that was, in essence, not before it, and the dissent would have us do the same. We do not confront a case where, even under a neutral program that includes nonsectarian recipients, the government is making direct money payments to an institution or group that is engaged in religious activity. Neither the Court of Appeals nor the dissent, we believe, takes sufficient cognizance of the undisputed fact that no public funds flow directly to WAP's coffers.

It does not violate the Establishment Clause for a public university to grant access to its facilities on a religion-neutral basis to a wide spectrum of student groups, including groups that use meeting rooms for sectarian activities, accompanied by some devotional exercises. See *Widmar*, at 269; *Board of Ed. of Westside Community Schools (Dist. 66) v. Mergens*, 496 U.S. 226, 252 (1990) (plurality opinion). This is so even where the upkeep, maintenance, and repair of the facilities attributed to those uses are paid from a student activities fund to which students are required to contribute. *Widmar*, at 265. The government usually acts by spending money. Even the provision of a meeting room, as in *Mergens* and *Widmar*, involved governmental expenditure, if only in the form of electricity and heating or cooling costs. The error made by the Court of Appeals, as well as by the dissent, lies in focusing on the money that is undoubtedly expended by the government, rather than on the nature of the benefit received by the recipient. If the expenditure of governmental funds is prohibited whenever those funds pay for a service that is, pursuant to a religion-neutral program, used by a group for sectarian purposes, then *Widmar, Mergens,* and *Lamb's Chapel v. Center Moriches Union Free School Dist.*, 508 U.S. 384 (1993), would have to be overruled. Given our holdings in these cases, it follows that a public university may maintain its own computer facility and give student groups access to that facility, including the use of the printers, on a religion neutral, say first-come-first-served, basis. If a religious student organization obtained access on that religion-neutral basis and used a computer to compose or a printer or copy machine to print speech with a religious content or viewpoint, the State's action in providing the group with access would no more violate the Establishment Clause than would giving those groups access to an assembly hall. There is no difference in logic or principle, and no difference of constitutional significance, between a school using its funds to operate a facility to which students have access, and a school paying a third-party contractor to operate the facility on its behalf. The latter occurs here. The University provides printing services to a broad spectrum of student newspapers qualified as CIO's by reason of their officers and membership. Any benefit to religion is incidental to the government's provision of secular services for secular purposes on a religion-neutral basis. Printing is a routine, secular, and recurring attribute of student life.

By paying outside printers, the University in fact attains a further degree of separation from the student publication, for it avoids the duties of supervision, escapes the costs of upkeep, repair, and replacement attributable to student use, and has a clear record of costs. As a result, and as in *Widmar,* the University can charge the SAF, and not the taxpayers as a whole, for the discrete activity in question. It would be formalistic for us to say that the University must forfeit these advantages and provide the services itself in order to comply with the Establishment Clause. It is, of course, true that if the State pays a church's bills it is subsidizing it, and we must guard against this abuse. That is not a danger here, based on the considerations we have advanced and for the additional reason that the student publication is not a religious institution, at least in the usual sense of that term as used in our case law, and it is not a religious organization as used in the University's own regulations. It is instead a publication involved in a pure forum for the expression of ideas, ideas that would be both incomplete and chilled were the Constitution to be interpreted to require that state officials and courts scan the publication to ferret out views that principally manifest a belief in a divine being.

Were the dissent's view to become law, it would require the University, in order to avoid a constitutional violation, to scrutinize the content of student speech, lest the expression in question—speech otherwise protected by the Constitution—contain too great a religious content. The dissent, in fact, anticipates such censorship as "crucial" in distinguishing between "works characterized by the evangelism of Wide Awake and writing that merely happens to express views that a given religion might approve." That eventuality raises the specter of governmental censorship, to ensure that all student writings and publications meet some baseline standard of secular orthodoxy. To impose that standard on student speech at a university is to imperil the very sources of free speech and expression. As we recognized in *Widmar,* official censorship would be far more inconsistent with the Establishment Clause's dictates than would governmental provision of secular printing services on a religion-blind basis.

> "[T]he dissent fails to establish that the distinction [between 'religious' speech and speech 'about' religion] has intelligible content. There is no indication when 'singing hymns, reading scripture, and teaching biblical principles' cease to be 'singing, teaching, and reading'—all apparently forms of 'speech,' despite their religious subject matter—and become unprotected 'worship.' . . .

> "[E]ven if the distinction drew an arguably principled line, it is highly doubtful that it would lie within the judicial competence to administer. Merely to draw the distinction would require the university—and ultimately the courts—to inquire into the significance of words and practices to different religious faiths, and in varying circumstances by the same faith. Such inquiries would tend inevitably to entangle the State with religion in a manner forbidden by our cases. *E.g., Walz v. Tax Comm'n of City of New York,* 397 U.S. 664 (1970)."

To obey the Establishment Clause, it was not necessary for the University to deny eligibility to student publications because of their viewpoint. The neutrality commanded of the State by the separate Clauses of the First Amendment was compromised by the University's course of action. The viewpoint discrimination inherent in the University's regulation required public officials to scan and interpret student publications to discern their underlying philosophic assumptions respecting religious theory and belief. That course of action was a denial of the right of free speech and would risk fostering a pervasive bias or hostility to religion, which could undermine the very neutrality the Establishment Clause requires. There is no Establishment Clause violation in the University's honoring its duties under the Free Speech Clause.

■ JUSTICE O'CONNOR, concurring.

. . . The nature of the dispute does not admit of categorical answers, nor should any be inferred from the Court's decision today. Instead, certain considerations specific to the program at issue lead me to conclude that by providing the same assistance to Wide Awake that it does to other publications, the University would not be endorsing the magazine's religious perspective.

First, the student organizations, at the University's insistence, remain strictly independent of the University . . . And the agreement requires that student organizations include in every letter, contract, publication, or other written materials [a] disclaimer. . . . Any reader of Wide Awake would be on notice of the publication's independence from the University.

Second, financial assistance is distributed in a manner that ensures its use only for permissible purposes. A student organization seeking assistance must submit disbursement requests; if approved, the funds are paid directly to the third-party vendor and do not pass through the organization's coffers. This safeguard . . . ensures that the funds are used only to further the University's purpose in maintaining a free and robust marketplace of ideas, from whatever perspective. This feature also makes this case analogous to a school providing equal access to a generally available printing press (or other physical facilities) and unlike a block grant to religious organizations.

Third, assistance is provided to the religious publication in a context that makes improbable any perception of government endorsement of the religious message. Wide Awake does not exist in a vacuum. It competes with 15 other magazines and newspapers for advertising and readership. The widely divergent viewpoints of these many purveyors of opinion, all supported on an equal basis by the University, significantly diminishes the danger that the message of any one publication is perceived as endorsed by the University. Besides the general news publications, for example, the University has provided support to The Yellow Journal, a humor magazine that has targeted Christianity as a subject of satire, and Al-Salam, a publication to "promote a better understanding of Islam to the University Community." Given this wide array of nonreligious, antireligious and competing religious viewpoints in the forum supported by the University, any perception that the University endorses one particular viewpoint would be illogical. This is not the harder case where religious speech threatens to dominate the forum . . .

The Court's decision today therefore neither trumpets the supremacy of the neutrality principle nor signals the demise of the funding prohibition in Establishment Clause jurisprudence. As I observed last Term, "[e]xperience proves that the Establishment Clause, like the Free Speech Clause, cannot easily be reduced to a single test." *Board of Ed. of* Kiryas Joel *Village School Dist. v. Grumet*, 512 U.S. 687, 720 (1994) (opinion concurring in part and concurring in judgment). When bedrock principles collide, they test the limits of categorical obstinacy and expose the flaws and dangers of a Grand Unified Theory that may turn out to be neither grand nor unified. The Court today does only what courts must do in many Establishment Clause cases—focus on specific features of a particular government action to ensure that it does not violate the Constitution. By withholding from Wide Awake assistance that the University provides generally to all other student publications, the University has discriminated on the basis of the magazine's religious viewpoint in violation of the Free Speech Clause. And particular features of the University's program—such as the explicit disclaimer, the disbursement of funds directly to third-party vendors, the vigorous nature of the forum at issue, and the possibility for objecting students to opt out—convince me that providing such assistance in this case would not carry the danger of impermissible use of public funds to endorse Wide Awake's religious message.

Subject to these comments, I join the opinion of the Court.

■ [The concurring opinion of JUSTICE THOMAS is omitted.]

■ JUSTICE SOUTER, with whom JUSTICE STEVENS, JUSTICE GINSBURG, and JUSTICE BREYER join, dissenting.

The Court today, for the first time, approves direct funding of core religious activities by an arm of the State . . . I would hold that the University's refusal to support petitioners' religious activities is compelled by the Establishment Clause. . . .

The Court's difficulties will be all the more clear after a closer look at Wide Awake than the majority opinion affords. The character of the magazine is candidly disclosed on the opening page of the first issue, where the editor-in-chief announces Wide Awake's mission in a letter to the readership signed, "Love in Christ": it is "to challenge Christians to live, in word and deed, according to the faith they proclaim and to encourage students to consider what a personal relationship with Jesus Christ means." App. 45. The masthead of every issue bears St. Paul's exhortation, that "[t]he hour has come for you to awake from your slumber, because our salvation is nearer now than when we first believed. Romans 13:11."

Each issue of Wide Awake contained in the record makes good on the editor's promise and echoes the Apostle's call to accept salvation: "The only way to salvation through Him is by confessing and repenting of sin. It is the Christian's duty to make sinners aware of their need for salvation. Thus, Christians must confront and condemn sin, or else they fail in their duty of love." Mourad & Prince, A Love/Hate Relationship, Nov./Dec. 1990, p. 3 . . . " 'Go into all the world and preach the good news to all creation.' (Mark 16:15) The Great Commission is the prime-directive for our lives as Christians. . . ." Liu, Christianity and the Five-legged Stool, Sept./Oct. 1991, p. 3.

"The Spirit provides access to an intimate relationship with the Lord of the Universe, awakens our minds to comprehend spiritual truth and empowers us to serve as effective ambassadors for the Lord Jesus in our earthly lives." Buterbaugh, A Spiritual Advantage, Mar./Apr. 1991, p. 21.

There is no need to quote further from articles of like tenor, but one could examine such other examples as religious poetry, religious textual analysis and commentary, and instruction on religious practice . . .

This writing . . . is straightforward exhortation to enter into a relationship with God as revealed in Jesus Christ, and to satisfy a series of moral obligations derived from the teachings of Jesus Christ . . .

Using public funds for the direct subsidization of preaching the word is categorically forbidden under the Establishment Clause, and if the Clause was meant to accomplish nothing else, it was meant to bar this use of public money . . . Four years before the First Congress proposed the First Amendment, Madison gave his opinion on the legitimacy of using public funds for religious purposes, in the Memorial and Remonstrance Against Religious Assessments, which played the central role in ensuring the defeat of the Virginia tax assessment bill in 1786 and framed the debate upon which the Religion Clauses stand: "Who does not see that . . . the same authority which can force a citizen to contribute three pence only of his property for the support of any one establishment, may force him to conform to any other establishment in all cases whatsoever?" . . .

Why does the Court not apply this clear law to these clear facts and conclude, as I do, that the funding scheme here is a clear constitutional violation? The answer must be in part that the Court fails to confront the evidence set out in the preceding section. Throughout its opinion, the Court refers uninformatively to Wide Awake's "Christian viewpoint," or its "religious perspective[.]" . . . The Court does not quote the magazine's adoption of Saint Paul's exhortation to awaken to the nearness of salvation, or any of its articles enjoining readers to accept Jesus Christ, or the religious verses, or the religious textual analyses, or the suggested prayers. And so it is easy for the Court to lose sight of what the University students and the Court of Appeals found so obvious, and to blanch the patently and frankly evangelistic character of the magazine by unrevealing allusions to religious points of view . . . This is a flat violation of the Establishment Clause. . . .

NOTES

1.   Justice Souter attributes the majority's decision to its failure to come to grips with the magazine's "patently and frankly evangelistic character," such as its "adoption of Saint Paul's exhortation to awaken to the nearness of salvation, or any of its articles enjoining readers to accept Jesus Christ, or the religious verses, or the religious textual analyses, or the suggested prayers" (which he quotes at length). What difference would this have made? Assuming the Student Activities Fund (SAF) is a type of forum for private speech, as the Court concluded in its free speech analysis (presented at p. 1018), should it matter whether the tone is moderate and objective, or strident and evangelistic? Are other student publications funded by the SAF required to be moderate and objective with respect to their ideological commitments? How would the university police the line Justice Souter suggests between a magazine with a religious perspective and one that is "patently and frankly evangelistic"? Would the university review each issue before it was published, the way publications were reviewed in England before the Licensing Act?

In *Widmar v. Vincent*, 454 U.S. 263 (1981), on which the majority relies, the Court rejected the argument that the Establishment Clause required a public university to make sure that speech by student groups within a limited public forum not be religious in nature. The Court stated in footnote: "the University would risk greater 'entanglement' by attempting to enforce its exclusion of 'religious worship' and 'religious speech.' Initially, the University would need to determine which words and activities fall within 'religious worship and religious teaching.' This alone could prove 'an impossible task in an age where many and various beliefs meet the constitutional definition of religion.' There would also be a continuing need to monitor group meetings to ensure compliance with the rule." Does Justice Souter's approach avoid that entanglement by forbidding not all religious worship and speech, but only that of a "patently and frankly evangelistic character'?

2.   The lower court had held that the Free Speech Clause required the University to give the religious magazine equal access, but that the Establishment Clause required the opposite—and the Establishment Clause trumps the Free Speech Clause. Why might that be so? And do the Free Exercise and Press Clauses have anything to say? Cf. *Texas Monthly, Inc. v. Bullock*, 489 U.S. 1 (1989) (White, J. concurring) (Press Clause is violated by state law giving a sales tax exemption to religious periodicals and not others). One virtue of the majority's interpretation is that it makes all of the relevant First Amendment principles consistent: all are satisfied when the government operates on a content- and viewpoint- neutral basis.

3.   One important difference between physical public forums—such as parks, sidewalks, or empty classrooms for meetings—and the SAF is that decisions about physical forums are binary in nature: either the speakers are allowed access to the forum or they are not. In the SAF context, once Wide Awake is deemed (by virtue of the Supreme Court's decision) eligible for participation in the SAF, the student government will decide how much money it should receive, in competition with other publications and other student activities. Can that be done in a religiously neutral fashion? Does this question raise Establishment Clause issues not addressed by the majority? For that matter, can the distribution of funds to other ideologically fraught activities be neutral? Is that of constitutional significance?

In *University of Wisconsin v. Southworth*, 529 U.S. 217 (2000), public university students challenged compulsory payments to a student activities fund on the ground that funds were used for political and ideological positions offensive to their beliefs—relying on cases such as *Abood v. Detroit Bd. of Educ.* (p. 1070). This suggests a certain similarity between the principles of compelled speech and association and the principles of non-establishment, at least as regards the compelled support for other private speakers. How are these principles different? The Court agreed with the general proposition that "[i]t infringes on the speech and beliefs of the individual to be required, by this mandatory student activity fee program, to pay subsidies for the objectionable speech of others." But the Court upheld the SAF program on the ground that as a whole it was viewpoint-neutral. Relying on *Rosenberger*, the Court held: "When a university requires its students to pay fees to support the extracurricular speech of other students, all in the interest of open discussion, it may not prefer some viewpoints to others. There is symmetry then in our holding here and in *Rosenberger*: Viewpoint neutrality is the justification for requiring the student to pay the fee in the first instance and for ensuring the integrity of the program's operation once the funds have been collected." But what if a student government does not distribute funds neutrally? What would be the consequences, under the Establishment Clause and the compelled speech and association doctrines?

Locke v. Davey

540 U.S. 712 (2004)

■ CHIEF JUSTICE REHNQUIST delivered the opinion of the Court.

The State of Washington established the Promise Scholarship Program to assist academically gifted students with postsecondary education expenses. In accordance with the State Constitution, students may not use the scholarship at an institution where they are pursuing a degree in devotional theology. We hold that such an exclusion from an otherwise inclusive aid program does not violate the Free Exercise Clause of the First Amendment.

The Washington State Legislature found that "[s]tudents who work hard . . . and successfully complete high school with high academic marks may not have the financial ability to attend college because they cannot obtain financial aid or the financial aid is insufficient." In 1999, to assist these high-achieving students, the legislature created the Promise Scholarship Program, which provides a scholarship, renewable for one year, to eligible students for postsecondary education expenses. Students may spend their funds on any education-related expense, including room and board. The scholarships are funded through the State's general fund, and their amount varies each year depending on the annual appropriation, which is evenly prorated among the eligible students. The scholarship was worth $1,125 for academic year 1999–2000 and $1,542 for 2000–2001.

To be eligible for the scholarship, a student must meet academic, income, and enrollment requirements. A student must graduate from a Washington public or private high school and either graduate in the top 15% of his graduating class, or attain on the first attempt a cumulative score of 1,200 or better on the Scholastic Assessment Test I or a score of 27 or better on the American College Test. The student's family income must be less than 135% of the State's median. Finally, the student must enroll "at least half time in an eligible postsecondary institution in the state of Washington," and may not pursue a degree in theology at that institution while receiving the scholarship. Wash. Rev. Code §§ 250–80–020(12)(f) to (g); see also Wash. Rev.Code Ann. § 28B.10.814 (West 1997) ("No aid shall be awarded to any student who is pursuing a degree in theology"). Private institutions, including those religiously affiliated, qualify as "[e]ligible postsecondary institution[s]" if they are accredited by a nationally recognized accrediting body. A "degree in theology" is not defined in the statute, but, as both parties concede, the statute simply codifies the State's constitutional prohibition on providing funds to students to pursue degrees that are "devotional in nature or designed to induce religious faith." . . .

Respondent, Joshua Davey, was awarded a Promise Scholarship, and chose to attend Northwest College. Northwest is a private, Christian college affiliated with the Assemblies of God denomination, and is an eligible institution under the Promise Scholarship Program. Davey had "planned for many years to attend a Bible college and to prepare [himself] through that college training for a lifetime of ministry, specifically as a church pastor." To that end, when he enrolled in Northwest College, he decided to pursue a double major in pastoral ministries and business management/administration. There is no dispute that the pastoral ministries degree is devotional and therefore excluded under the Promise Scholarship Program.

At the beginning of the 1999–2000 academic year, Davey met with Northwest's director of financial aid. He learned for the first time at this meeting that he could not use his scholarship to pursue a devotional theology degree. He was informed that to receive the funds appropriated for his use, he must certify in writing that he was not pursuing such a degree at Northwest. He refused to sign the form and did not receive any scholarship funds.

Davey then [sued] . . . to enjoin the State from refusing to award the scholarship solely because a student is pursuing a devotional theology degree, and for damages. He argued the denial of his scholarship based on his decision to pursue a theology degree violated, inter alia, the Free Exercise, Establishment, and Free Speech Clauses of the First Amendment, as incorporated by the Fourteenth Amendment, and the Equal Protection Clause of the Fourteenth Amendment. . . .

The Religion Clauses of the First Amendment provide: "Congress shall make no law respecting an establishment of religion, or prohibiting the free exercise thereof." These two Clauses, the Establishment Clause and the Free Exercise Clause, are frequently in tension. Yet we have long said that "there is room for play in the joints" between them. *Walz v. Tax Comm'n of City of New York*, 397 U.S. 664, 669 (1970). In other words, there are some state actions permitted by the Establishment Clause but not required by the Free Exercise Clause.

This case involves that "play in the joints" described above. Under our Establishment Clause precedent, the link between government funds and religious training is broken by the independent and private choice of recipients. See *Zelman v. Simmons-Harris*, 536 U.S. 639, 652 (2002). As such, there is no doubt that the State could, consistent with the Federal Constitution, permit Promise Scholars to pursue a degree in devotional theology, see *Witters v. Washington Dept. of Servs. for Blind*, 474 U.S. 481, 489 (1986), and the State does not contend otherwise. The question before us, however, is whether Washington, pursuant to its own constitution,[2] which has been authoritatively interpreted as prohibiting even indirectly funding religious instruction that will prepare students for the ministry, can deny them such funding without violating the Free Exercise Clause.

Davey urges us to answer that question in the negative. He contends that under the rule we enunciated in *Church of Lukumi Babalu Aye, Inc. v. Hialeah*, 508 U.S. 520 (1993), the program is presumptively unconstitutional because it is not facially neutral with respect to religion.[3] We reject his claim of presumptive unconstitutionality, however; to do otherwise would extend the *Lukumi* line of cases well beyond not only their facts but their reasoning. In *Lukumi*, the city of Hialeah made it a crime to engage in certain kinds of animal slaughter. We found that the law sought to suppress ritualistic animal sacrifices of the Santeria religion. In the present case, the State's disfavor of religion (if it can be called that) is of a far milder kind. It imposes neither criminal nor civil sanctions on any type of religious service or rite. It does not deny to ministers the right to participate in the political affairs of the community. See *McDaniel v. Paty*, 435 U.S. 618 (1978). And it does not require students to choose between their religious beliefs and receiving a government benefit. See *Sherbert v. Verner*, 374 U.S. 398 (1963). The State has merely chosen not to fund a distinct category of instruction.

JUSTICE SCALIA argues, however, that generally available benefits are part of the "baseline against which burdens on religion are measured." Because the Promise Scholarship Program funds training for all secular professions, JUSTICE SCALIA contends the State must also fund training for religious professions. But training for religious professions and training for secular professions are not fungible. Training someone to lead a congregation is an essentially religious endeavor. Indeed, majoring in devotional theology is akin to a religious calling as well as an academic pursuit. And the subject of religion is one in which both the United States and state constitutions embody distinct views—in favor of free exercise, but opposed to establishment—that find no counterpart with respect to other callings or professions. That a State would deal differently with religious education for the ministry than

---

[2]   The relevant provision of the Washington Constitution, Art. I, § 11, states:

"Religious Freedom. Absolute freedom of conscience in all matters of religious sentiment, belief and worship, shall be guaranteed to every individual, and no one shall be molested or disturbed in person or property on account of religion; but the liberty of conscience hereby secured shall not be so construed as to excuse acts of licentiousness or justify practices inconsistent with the peace and safety of the state. No public money or property shall be appropriated for or applied to any religious worship, exercise or instruction, or the support of any religious establishment."

[3]   Davey, relying on *Rosenberger v. Rector and Visitors of Univ. of Va.*, 515 U.S. 819 (1995), contends that the Promise Scholarship Program is an unconstitutional viewpoint restriction on speech. But the Promise Scholarship Program is not a forum for speech. The purpose of the Promise Scholarship Program is to assist students from low- and middle-income families with the cost of postsecondary education, not to " 'encourage a diversity of views from private speakers.' " *United States v. American Library Assn., Inc.*, 539 U.S. 194, 206 (2003) (plurality opinion) (quoting *Rosenberger*, at 834). Our cases dealing with speech forums are simply inapplicable. . . .

with education for other callings is a product of these views, not evidence of hostility toward religion.

Even though the differently worded Washington Constitution draws a more stringent line than that drawn by the United States Constitution, the interest it seeks to further is scarcely novel. In fact, we can think of few areas in which a State's antiestablishment interests come more into play. Since the founding of our country, there have been popular uprisings against procuring taxpayer funds to support church leaders, which was one of the hallmarks of an "established" religion. See F. Lambert, The Founding Fathers and the Place of Religion in America 188 (2003) ("In defending their religious liberty against overreaching clergy, Americans in all regions found that Radical Whig ideas best framed their argument that state-supported clergy undermined liberty of conscience and should be opposed"); see also J. Madison, Memorial and Remonstrance Against Religious Assessments (noting the dangers to civil liberties from supporting clergy with public funds).

Most States that sought to avoid an establishment of religion around the time of the founding placed in their constitutions formal prohibitions against using tax funds to support the ministry. E.g., Ga. Const., Art. IV, § 5 (1789) ("All persons shall have the free exercise of religion, without being obliged to contribute to the support of any religious profession but their own"); Pa. Const., Art. II (1776) ("[N]o man ought or of right can be compelled to attend any religious worship, or erect or support any place of worship, or maintain any ministry, contrary to, or against, his own free will and consent"); N.J. Const., Art. XVIII (1776) (similar); Del. Const., Art. I, § 1 (1792) (similar); Ky. Const., Art. XII, § 3 (1792) (similar); Vt. Const., Ch. I, Art. 3 (1793) (similar); Tenn. Const., Art. XI, § 3 (1796) (similar); Ohio Const., Art. VIII, § 3 (1802) (similar). The plain text of these constitutional provisions prohibited *any* tax dollars from supporting the clergy. We have found nothing to indicate, as JUSTICE SCALIA contends, that these provisions would not have applied so long as the State equally supported other professions or if the amount at stake was *de minimis*. That early state constitutions saw no problem in explicitly excluding *only* the ministry from receiving state dollars reinforces our conclusion that religious instruction is of a different ilk.

Far from evincing the hostility toward religion which was manifest in *Lukumi*, we believe that the entirety of the Promise Scholarship Program goes a long way toward including religion in its benefits. The program permits students to attend pervasively religious schools, so long as they are accredited. As Northwest advertises, its "concept of education is distinctly Christian in the evangelical sense." It prepares *all* of its students, "through instruction, through modeling, [and] through [its] classes, to use . . . the Bible as their guide, as the truth," no matter their chosen profession. And under the Promise Scholarship Program's current guidelines, students are still eligible to take devotional theology courses. Davey notes all students at Northwest are required to take at least four devotional courses, "Exploring the Bible," "Principles of Spiritual Development," "Evangelism in the Christian Life," and "Christian Doctrine," and some students may have additional religious requirements as part of their majors.

In short, we find neither in the history or text of Article I, § 11, of the Washington Constitution, nor in the operation of the Promise Scholarship Program, anything that suggests animus toward religion. Given the historic and substantial state interest at issue, we therefore cannot conclude that the denial of funding for vocational religious instruction alone is inherently constitutionally suspect.

Without a presumption of unconstitutionality, Davey's claim must fail. The State's interest in not funding the pursuit of devotional degrees is substantial and the exclusion of such funding places a relatively minor burden on Promise Scholars. If any room exists between the two Religion Clauses, it must be here. We need not venture further into this difficult area in order to uphold the Promise Scholarship Program as currently operated by the State of Washington.

■ JUSTICE SCALIA, with whom JUSTICE THOMAS joins, dissenting.

In *Lukumi*, the majority opinion held that "[a] law burdening religious practice that is not neutral . . . must undergo the most rigorous of scrutiny," and that "the minimum requirement of neutrality is that a law not discriminate on its face." The concurrence of two Justices stated that "[w]hen a law discriminates against religion as such, . . . it automatically will fail strict scrutiny." *Lukumi*, at 579 (Blackmun, J., joined by O'CONNOR, J., concurring in judgment). And the concurrence of a third Justice endorsed the "noncontroversial principle" that "formal neutrality" is a "necessary conditio[n] for free-exercise constitutionality." *Id.*, at 563 (SOUTER, J., concurring in part and concurring in judgment). These opinions are irreconcilable with today's decision, which sustains a public benefits program that facially discriminates against religion.

I

We articulated the principle that governs this case more than 50 years ago in *Everson v. Board of Ed. of Ewing*, 330 U.S. 1 (1947):

> "New Jersey cannot hamper its citizens in the free exercise of their own religion. Consequently, it cannot exclude individual Catholics, Lutherans, Mohammedans, Baptists, Jews, Methodists, Non-believers, Presbyterians, or the members of any other faith, because of their faith, or lack of it, from receiving the benefits of public welfare legislation."

When the State makes a public benefit generally available, that benefit becomes part of the baseline against which burdens on religion are measured; and when the State withholds that benefit from some individuals solely on the basis of religion, it violates the Free Exercise Clause no less than if it had imposed a special tax.

That is precisely what the State of Washington has done here. It has created a generally available public benefit, whose receipt is conditioned only on academic performance, income, and attendance at an accredited school. It has then carved out a solitary course of study for exclusion: theology. No field of study but religion is singled out for disfavor in this fashion. Davey is not asking for a special benefit to which others are not entitled. He seeks only *equal* treatment—the right to direct his scholarship to his chosen course of study, a right every other Promise Scholar enjoys.

The Court's reference to historical "popular uprisings against procuring taxpayer funds to support church leaders" is therefore quite misplaced. That history involved not the inclusion of religious ministers in public benefits programs like the one at issue here, but laws that singled them out for financial aid. For example, the Virginia bill at which Madison's Remonstrance was directed provided: "[F]or the support of Christian teachers . . . [a] sum payable for tax on the property within this Commonwealth, is hereby assessed. . . ." A Bill Establishing a Provision for Teachers of the Christian Religion (1784). Laws supporting the clergy in other States operated in a similar fashion. One can concede the Framers' hostility to funding the clergy *specifically*, but that says nothing about whether the clergy had to be excluded from benefits the State made available to all. No one would seriously contend, for example, that the Framers would have barred ministers from using public roads on their way to church.

The Court does not dispute that the Free Exercise Clause places some constraints on public benefits programs, but finds none here, based on a principle of "play in the joints." I use the term "principle" loosely, for that is not so much a legal principle as a refusal to apply *any* principle when faced with competing constitutional directives. There is nothing anomalous about constitutional commands that abut. . . . If the Religion Clauses demand neutrality, we must enforce them, in hard cases as well as easy ones. . . .

In any case, the State already has all the play in the joints it needs. There are any number of ways it could respect both its unusually sensitive concern for the conscience of its taxpayers *and* the Federal Free Exercise Clause. It could make the scholarships redeemable only at public universities (where it sets the curriculum), or only for select courses of study. Either option would replace a program that facially discriminates against religion with one that just happens not to subsidize it. The State could also simply abandon the scholarship program altogether. If that seems a dear price to pay for freedom of conscience, it is only because the State has defined that freedom so broadly that it would be offended by a program with such an incidental, indirect religious effect.

What is the nature of the State's asserted interest here? It cannot be protecting the pocketbooks of its citizens; given the tiny fraction of Promise Scholars who would pursue theology degrees, the amount of any citizen's tax bill at stake is *de minimis*. It cannot be preventing mistaken appearance of endorsement; where a State merely declines to penalize students for selecting a religious major, "[n]o reasonable observer is likely to draw . . . an inference that the State itself is endorsing a religious practice or belief." *Witters*, at 493 (O'CONNOR, J., concurring in part and concurring in judgment). Nor can Washington's exclusion be defended as a means of assuring that the State will neither favor nor disfavor Davey in his religious calling. Davey will throughout his life contribute to the public fisc through sales taxes on personal purchases, property taxes on his home, and so on; and nothing in the Court's opinion turns on whether Davey winds up a net winner or loser in the State's tax-and-spend scheme.

No, the interest to which the Court defers is not fear of a conceivable Establishment Clause violation, budget constraints, avoidance of endorsement, or substantive neutrality—none of these. It is a pure philosophical preference: the State's opinion that it would violate taxpayers' freedom of conscience not to discriminate against candidates for the ministry. This sort of protection of "freedom of conscience" has no logical limit and can justify the singling out of religion for exclusion from public programs in virtually any context. The Court never says whether it deems this interest compelling (the opinion is devoid of any mention of standard of review) but, self-evidently, it is not.

II

The Court makes no serious attempt to defend the program's neutrality, and instead identifies two features thought to render its discrimination less offensive. The first is the lightness of Davey's burden. The Court offers no authority for approving facial discrimination against religion simply because its material consequences are not severe. I might understand such a test if we were still in the business of reviewing facially neutral laws that merely happen to burden some individual's religious exercise, but we are not. See *Employment Div., Dept. of Human Resources of Ore. v. Smith*, 494 U.S. 872, 885 (1990). Discrimination *on the face of a statute* is something else. The indignity of being singled out for special burdens on the basis of one's religious calling is so profound that the concrete harm produced can never be dismissed as insubstantial. The Court has not required proof of "substantial" concrete harm with other forms of discrimination, see, e.g., *Brown v. Board of Education*, 347 U.S. 483, 493–495 (1954); cf. *Craig v. Boren*, 429 U.S. 190 (1976), and it should not do so here.

Even if there were some threshold quantum-of-harm requirement, surely Davey has satisfied it. The First Amendment, after all, guarantees free exercise of religion, and when the State exacts a financial penalty of almost $3,000 for religious exercise—whether by tax or by forfeiture of an otherwise available benefit—religious practice is anything *but* free. . . . The Court distinguishes our precedents only by swapping the benefit to which Davey was actually entitled (a scholarship for his chosen course of study) with another, less valuable one (a scholarship for any course of study *but* his chosen one). On such reasoning, any facially discriminatory benefits program can be redeemed simply by redefining what it guarantees.

The other reason the Court thinks this particular facial discrimination less offensive is that the scholarship program was not motivated by animus toward religion. The Court does not explain why the legislature's motive matters, and I fail to see why it should. If a State deprives a citizen of trial by jury or passes an *ex post facto* law, we do not pause to investigate whether it was actually trying to accomplish the evil the Constitution prohibits. It is sufficient that the citizen's rights have been infringed. "[It does not] matter that a legislature consists entirely of the purehearted, if the law it enacts in fact singles out a religious practice for special burdens." *Lukumi*, at 559 (SCALIA, J., concurring in part and concurring in judgment). . . .

The Court has not approached other forms of discrimination this way. When we declared racial segregation unconstitutional, we did not ask whether the State had originally adopted the regime, not out of "animus" against blacks, but because of a well-meaning but misguided belief that the races would be better off apart. It was sufficient to note the current effect of segregation on racial minorities. See *Brown*, at 493–95 . . . We do sometimes look to legislative intent to smoke out more subtle instances of discrimination, but we do so as a supplement to the core guarantee of facially equal treatment, not as a replacement for it. See *Hunt v. Cromartie*, 526 U.S. 541, 546 (1999).

There is no need to rely on analogies, however, because we have rejected the Court's methodology in this very context. In *McDaniel*, we considered a Tennessee statute that disqualified clergy from participation in the state constitutional convention. That statute, like the one here, was based upon a state constitutional provision—a clause in the 1796 Tennessee Constitution that disqualified clergy from sitting in the legislature. The State defended the statute as an attempt to be faithful to its constitutional separation of church and state, and we accepted that claimed benevolent purpose as bona fide. Nonetheless, because it did not justify facial discrimination against religion, we invalidated the restriction.

It may be that Washington's original purpose in excluding the clergy from public benefits was benign, and the same might be true of its purpose in maintaining the exclusion today. But those singled out for disfavor can be forgiven for suspecting more invidious forces at work. Let there be no doubt: This case is about discrimination against a religious minority. Most citizens of this country identify themselves as professing some religious belief, but the State's policy poses no obstacle to practitioners of only a tepid, civic version of faith. Those the statutory exclusion actually affects—those whose belief in their religion is so strong that they dedicate their study and their lives to its ministry—are a far narrower set. One need not delve too far into modern popular culture to perceive a trendy disdain for deep religious conviction. In an era when the Court is so quick to come to the aid of other disfavored groups, see, e.g., *Romer v. Evans*, 517 U.S. 620, 635 (1996), its indifference in this case, which involves a form of discrimination to which the Constitution actually speaks, is exceptional.

* * *

Today's holding is limited to training the clergy, but its logic is readily extendible, and there are plenty of directions to go. What next? Will we deny priests and nuns their prescription-drug benefits on the ground that taxpayers' freedom of conscience forbids medicating the clergy at public expense? This may seem fanciful, but recall that France has proposed banning religious attire from schools, invoking interests in secularism no less benign than those the Court embraces today. When the public's freedom of conscience is invoked to justify denial of equal treatment, benevolent motives shade into indifference and ultimately into repression. Having accepted the justification in this case, the Court is less well equipped to fend it off in the future.

■ [The dissenting opinion of JUSTICE THOMAS is omitted.]

NOTES

1.   The idea of "play in the joints" between the principles of free exercise and non-establishment is familiar. But how far does it go? Does the majority opinion stand for the broad proposition that the government may explicitly discriminate against religious uses in spending programs, even though it may not single out religious acts for punishment or prohibition? Note how the majority distinguishes *Lukumi*:

> [To accept Davey's argument] would extend the *Lukumi* line of cases well beyond not only their facts but their reasoning. In *Lukumi*, the city of Hialeah made it a crime to engage in certain kinds of animal slaughter. We found that the law sought to suppress ritualistic animal sacrifices of the Santeria religion. In the present case, the State's disfavor of religion (if it can be called that) is of a far milder kind. It imposes neither criminal nor civil sanctions on any type of religious service or rite.

Is this an implicit rejection of the unconstitutional conditions doctrine as applied to the Free Exercise Clause (and thus a repudiation of *Sherbert v. Verner*, p. 1110)? Does the Free Exercise Clause protect only against criminal and civil sanctions and not against the denial of otherwise available benefits?

Or does the opinion rest on the more modest claim that denial of the Promise Scholarship to Joshua Davey was a "relatively minor burden"—leaving open the possibility that a more substantial burden, like the denial of unemployment compensation to Adele Sherbert, is on a different constitutional footing? This quantitative weighing of effects is reminiscent of Chief Justice Roberts' analysis of the coercion issue in the Medicaid expansion portion of *NFIB v. Sebelius* (p. 629), and the Court's distinguishing of *Goldberg v. Kelly* in *Mathews v. Eldridge* (p. 1490) for procedural due process. How does the Court draw intelligible lines? How minor is "relatively minor" and how can the Court tell? Is it a minor burden on a college student to lose a scholarship?

2.   How does the majority distinguish *Rosenberger*? Read footnote 3 carefully. What is the definition of a forum? Why is it permissible to discriminate on the basis of viewpoint—and remember, the Court held in *Rosenberger* that religion is a viewpoint—outside the context of a forum? Could Congress grant funds to homeless shelters but exclude those that use the shelters as a platform to advocate socialism?

3.   Justice Scalia argues that generally available benefits are part of the "baseline against which burdens on religion are measured." Thus, because the Promise Scholarship Program funds training for all secular professions, the State must also fund training for religious professions. The majority responds that "training for religious professions and training for secular professions are not fungible. Training someone to lead a congregation is an essentially religious endeavor." If that is so, why does the majority say so confidently that "there is no doubt that the State could, consistent with the Federal Constitution, permit Promise Scholars to pursue a degree in devotional theology"? Doesn't the permissibility of aid under the Establishment Clause depend on the idea that the government is simply being neutral among fungible activities? *Witters, Zelman,* and the other modern Establishment Clause cases seem to rest on the idea that if the government funds *A*, it may include religious instances of *A* along with the secular (as long as the program satisfies the requirements of neutrality and private choice). But if the religious activity is not "fungible"—if it is a different sort of thing than the secular As—then we would not say the government is merely being neutral. Is the majority opinion internally consistent?

4.   When can governments exclude religious uses from generally available benefits and when can they not? As this edition is going to press, the Court is scheduled to hear argument in *Trinity Lutheran Church v. Pauley*, No. 15–577. The State of Missouri provides grants to non-profit entities on the basis of secular, objective criteria to purchase recycled scrap rubber for the purpose of rubberizing children's playground surfaces. A daycare center operated by the church satisfied these criteria but was excluded solely because it is a church. Can that exclusion be defended under *Locke*?

In *Locke*, the Court held that the state "has merely chosen not to fund a distinct category of instruction." It seems clear that the government can fund one activity and not another: it can pay for a physics department without paying for a school of theology. But does *Trinity Lutheran* fit that model? In *Trinity Lutheran*, the state is not paying for one thing and not another; it is paying for rubberized playground surfaces (the same thing) for some entities and not for others. Is that a valid distinction?

———

Having read these cases, what is your opinion? Does the government violate the Establishment Clause when it extends aid neutrally to a broad class of beneficiaries, based on criteria unrelated to religion? Does the government violate the Free Exercise Clause when it prohibits conduct pursuant to neutral and generally applicable laws? What rules best serve the interests of religious freedom in a pluralist society? What rules best comport with the text and history of the Religion Clauses?

[*Assignment 59*]

III. THE SECOND AND THIRD AMENDMENTS

> *Amend. II: A well regulated Militia, being necessary to the security of a free State, the right of the people to keep and bear Arms, shall not be infringed.*
>
> *Amend. III: No Soldier shall, in time of peace be quartered in any house, without the consent of the Owner, nor in time of war, but in a manner to be prescribed by law.*

The Second Amendment has generated much interpretive debate but little in the way of Supreme Court decisions, apart from *United States v. Miller,* 307 U.S. 174 (1939), and more recently *District of Columbia v. Heller,* 554 U.S. 570 (2008) and *McDonald v. City of Chicago,* 561 U.S. 742 (2010).

The Third Amendment has generated essentially no interpretive debate or controversy whatsoever: its language and purpose have evidently been so clear, and its resolution of the problem to which it was directed so complete, that it is one of those provisions of the Constitution that has proved successful enough to be ignored. But there has been one major exception, during the evacuation and internment of native of the Aleutian Islands during World War II. See Tom W. Bell, *"Property" in the Constitution: The View from the Third Amendment,* 20 Wm. & Mary Bill Rts. J. 1243, 1271–1276 (2012).

The two amendments share a modest but definite connection, in that both protect rights that early Americans thought essential defenses against the dangers of national military power.

The Second Amendment presents fascinating interpretive questions. Consider the language of the amendment carefully. The Second Amendment is somewhat unusual in that it contains a "purpose" statement as a preamble of sorts to its substantive statement of the "right of the people to keep and bear arms." Does this purpose limit the substantive content of the right? Or does it merely state a reason for recognizing the right? If the former, the right to keep and bear arms might be thought limited to potential militia service. If the latter, the right to keep and bear arms is a right to keep and bear arms for any lawful purpose, including hunting and defense of home, as well as defense of the community. Is the right to "keep and bear arms" an individual right or a collective right of the states? As Professor Akhil Amar notes, the text contains some important clues, but they do not necessarily all point in the same direction:

> The states-rights reading slights the fact that the amendment's actual command language—"shall not be infringed"—appeared in the second clause, which enunciated a right of "the people" and not "the States." Surely the Tenth Amendment, which contradistinguished "the States" and "the people" made clear that these two phrases were not identical and that the Founders knew how to say "States" when they meant states. . . . But the

individual-rights reading must contend with textual embarrassments of its own. The amendment announced a right of "the people" collectively rather than of "persons" individually. Also, it used a distinctly military phrase: "bear Arms."

Akhil Reed Amar, AMERICA'S CONSTITUTION: A BIOGRAPHY 322 (2005).

For the generation that ratified the Second Amendment, two historical lessons about an armed populace were prominent. First, in seventeenth century England, the Stuart kings came to be associated in the public mind with absolutism and with standing armies. They were ultimately overthrown and executed when ordinary English citizens and nobles rose in armed revolt. After the overthrow of James II, the last Stuart king, the English Bill of Rights of 1689 explicitly forbade standing armies and it guaranteed the right to keep and bear arms of the (Protestant) citizens of the realm. Second, the need for a popular check on royal tyranny was confirmed for the framers in the victories of the Massachusetts Militia over the royal army of King George III at Lexington and Concord. Once again, the colonists told themselves, a king, this time aided eventually by Hessian mercenaries, had tried to take away their freedom only to be stopped by an armed citizenry.

But are these historical lessons still determinative for what the Constitution means today? Should the Second Amendment be considered obsolete and read out of the Constitution? If not, how should its terms apply in a world not of muskets, but of AK–47 assault rifles, hand-held rocket launchers, and nuclear weapons? What are "arms"? Even on the (contestable) assumption that the amendment originally created a right of state governments and not a right of individual citizens forming the militia, does the Fourteenth Amendment give the people of each state a right to keep and bear arms as a check against the powers of state governments as well as federal? Does the Second Amendment's purpose-preamble answer any of these questions? Suppose the First Amendment began with a preamble like the Second's: "The right of the people to express views and ideas freely being essential to republican government, Congress shall make no law . . . abridging the freedom of speech or of the press. . . ." Would that make a difference in how the First Amendment should be interpreted?

Consider these questions as you read excerpts from *The Federalist* that suggest the historical context for the Second Amendment. That amendment was not, of course, part of the Constitution that Publius was writing about, yet Hamilton and Madison appear to contemplate the right to keep and bear arms—and the potential exercise of that right—as a check against an overreaching national government with a standing army. Next is presented the Supreme Court's first thorough discussion of the language and meaning of the Second Amendment, more than two centuries after the amendment was adopted. The question before the Court was whether the Second Amendment protects an individual right to keep and bear arms for purposes that extend beyond potential militia service. Did the Court get the answer right? Consider carefully the interpretive methodology of the opinions.

The Federalist No. 28

Alexander Hamilton, Dec. 26, 1787

If the representatives of the people betray their constituents, there is then no resource left but in the exertion of that original right of self-defense which is paramount to all positive forms of government, and which against the usurpations of the national rulers may be exercised with infinitely better prospect of success than against those of the rulers of an individual state. In a single state, if the persons intrusted with supreme power become usurpers, the different parcels, subdivisions, or districts of which it consists, having no distinct government in each, can take no regular measures for defense. The citizens must rush tumultuously to arms, without concert, without system, without resource; except in their courage and despair. The usurpers, clothed with the forms of legal authority, can too often crush the opposition in embryo. The smaller the extent of the territory, the more difficult will it be for the people to form a regular or systematic plan of opposition, and the more easy will it be to defeat their early efforts. . . .

The obstacles to usurpation and the facilities of resistance increase with the increased extent of the state, provided the citizens understand their rights and are disposed to defend them. . . . But in a confederacy the people, without exaggeration, may be said to be entirely the masters of their own fate. Power being almost always the rival of power, the general government will at all times stand ready to check the usurpations of the state governments, and these will have the same disposition towards the general government. The people, by throwing themselves into either scale, will infallibly make it preponderate.

The Federalist No. 46
James Madison, Jan. 29, 1788

But ambitious encroachments of the federal government on the authority of the State governments would not excite the opposition of a single State, or of a few States only. They would be signals of general alarm. Every government would espouse the common cause. A correspondence would be opened. Plans of resistance would be concerted. One spirit would animate and conduct the whole. The same combinations, in short, would result from an apprehension of the federal, as was produced by the dread of a foreign, yoke; and unless the projected innovations should be voluntarily renounced, the same appeal to a trial of force would be made in the one case as was made in the other. . . .

The only refuge left for those who prophesy the downfall of the State governments is the visionary supposition that the federal government may previously accumulate a military force for the projects of ambition. . . . Extravagant as the supposition is, let it, however, be made. Let a regular army, fully equal to the resources of the country, be formed; and let it be entirely at the devotion of the federal government; still it would not be going too far to say that the State governments with the people on their side would be able to repel the danger. The highest number to which, according to their best computation, a standing army can be carried in any country does not exceed one hundredth part of the whole number of souls; or one twenty-fifth part of the number able to bear arms. . . . To these would be opposed a militia amounting to near half a million of citizens with arms in their hands, officered by men chosen from among themselves, fighting for their common liberties and united and conducted by governments possessing their affections and confidence. It may well be doubted whether a militia thus circumstanced could ever be conquered by such a proportion of regular troops. Those who are best acquainted with the late successful resistance of this country against the British arms will be most inclined to deny the possibility of it. Besides the advantage of being armed, which the Americans possess over the people of almost every other nation, the existence of subordinate governments, to which the people are attached and by which the militia officers are appointed, forms a barrier against the enterprises of ambition, more insurmountable than any which a simple government of any form can admit of. Notwithstanding the military establishments in the several kingdoms of Europe, . . . the governments are afraid to trust the people with arms. . . . But were the people to possess the additional advantages of local governments chosen by themselves, who could collect the national will and direct the national force, and of officers appointed out of the militia by these governments and attached both to them and to the militia, it may be affirmed with the greatest assurance that the throne of every tyranny in Europe would be speedily overturned in spite of the legions which surround it. . . .

District of Columbia v. Heller

554 U.S. 570 (2008)

■ JUSTICE SCALIA delivered the opinion of the Court.

We consider whether a District of Columbia prohibition on the possession of usable handguns in the home violates the Second Amendment to the Constitution.

I

The District of Columbia generally prohibits the possession of handguns. It is a crime to carry an unregistered firearm, and the registration of handguns is prohibited. Wholly apart from that prohibition, no person may carry a handgun without a license, but the chief of police may issue licenses for 1-year periods. District of Columbia law also requires residents to keep their lawfully owned firearms, such as registered long guns, "unloaded and dissembled or bound by a trigger lock or similar device" unless they are located in a place of business or are being used for lawful recreational activities.

Respondent Dick Heller is a D.C. special police officer authorized to carry a handgun while on duty at the Federal Judicial Center. He applied for a registration certificate for a handgun that he wished to keep at home, but the District refused. He thereafter filed a lawsuit in the Federal District Court for the District of Columbia seeking, on Second Amendment grounds, to enjoin the city from enforcing the bar on the registration of handguns, the licensing requirement insofar as it prohibits the carrying of a firearm in the home without a license, and the trigger-lock requirement insofar as it prohibits the use of "functional firearms within the home." . . .

II

We turn first to the meaning of the Second Amendment.

The Second Amendment provides: "A well regulated Militia, being necessary to the security of a free State, the right of the people to keep and bear Arms, shall not be infringed." In interpreting this text, we are guided by the principle that "[t]he Constitution was written to be understood by the voters; its words and phrases were used in their normal and ordinary as distinguished from technical meaning." *United States v. Sprague,* 282 U.S. 716, 731 (1931). Normal meaning may of course include an idiomatic meaning, but it excludes secret or technical meanings that would not have been known to ordinary citizens in the founding generation.

. . . Petitioners and today's dissenting Justices believe that [the Amendment] protects only the right to possess and carry a firearm in connection with militia service. Respondent argues that it protects an individual right to possess a firearm unconnected with service in a militia, and to use that arm for traditionally lawful purposes, such as self-defense within the home.

The Second Amendment is naturally divided into two parts: its prefatory clause and its operative clause. The former does not limit the latter grammatically, but rather announces a purpose. The Amendment could be rephrased, "Because a well regulated Militia is necessary to the security of a free State, the right of the people to keep and bear Arms shall not be infringed." Although this structure of the Second Amendment is unique in our Constitution, other legal documents of the founding era, particularly individual-rights provisions of state constitutions, commonly included a prefatory statement of purpose. See generally Volokh, *The Commonplace Second Amendment*, 73 N.Y.U. L. Rev. 793, 814–821 (1998).

Logic demands that there be a link between the stated purpose and the command. The Second Amendment would be nonsensical if it read, "A well regulated Militia, being necessary to the security of a free State, the right of the people to petition for redress of grievances shall not be infringed." That requirement of logical connection may cause a prefatory clause to resolve an ambiguity in the operative clause. . . . But apart from that clarifying function, a prefatory clause does not limit or expand the scope of the operative clause. . . . Therefore, while we will begin our textual analysis with the operative clause, we will return to the prefatory clause to ensure that our reading of the operative clause is consistent with the announced purpose.[4]

1.   Operative Clause.

a.   "Right of the People." The first salient feature of the operative clause is that it codifies a "right of the people." The unamended Constitution and the Bill of Rights use the phrase "right of the people" two other times, in the First Amendment's Assembly and Petition Clause and in the Fourth Amendment's Search and Seizure Clause. The Ninth Amendment uses very similar terminology ("The enumeration in the Constitution, of certain rights, shall not be construed to deny or disparage others retained by the people"). All three of these instances unambiguously refer to individual rights, not "collective" rights, or rights that may be exercised only through participation in some corporate body.

Three provisions of the Constitution refer to "the people" in a context other than "rights"—the famous preamble ("We the people"), § 2 of Article I (providing that "the people" will choose members of the House), and the Tenth Amendment (providing that those powers not given the Federal Government remain with "the States" or "the people"). Those provisions arguably refer to "the people" acting collectively—but they deal with the exercise or reservation of powers, not rights. Nowhere else in the

---

[4] JUSTICE STEVENS criticizes us for discussing the prologue last. But if a prologue can be used only to clarify an ambiguous operative provision, surely the first step must be to determine whether the operative provision is ambiguous. It might be argued, we suppose, that the prologue itself should be one of the factors that go into the determination of whether the operative provision is ambiguous—but that would cause the prologue to be used to produce ambiguity rather than to resolve it. In any event, even if we considered the prologue *along with* the operative provision we would reach the same result we do today, since (as we explain) our interpretation of "the right of the people to keep and bear arms" furthers the purpose of an effective militia no less than (indeed, more than) the dissent's interpretation.

Constitution does a "right" attributed to "the people" refer to anything other than an individual right.

What is more, in all six other provisions of the Constitution that mention "the people," the term unambiguously refers to all members of the political community, not an unspecified subset. As we said in *United States v. Verdugo-Urquidez,* 494 U.S. 259, 265 (1990):

> "[T]he people" seems to have been a term of art employed in select parts of the Constitution. . . . [Its uses] sugges[t] that "the people" protected by the Fourth Amendment, and by the First and Second Amendments, and to whom rights and powers are reserved in the Ninth and Tenth Amendments, refers to a class of persons who are part of a national community or who have otherwise developed sufficient connection with this country to be considered part of that community.

This contrasts markedly with the phrase "the militia" in the prefatory clause. As we will describe below, the "militia" in colonial America consisted of a subset of "the people"—those who were male, able bodied, and within a certain age range. Reading the Second Amendment as protecting only the right to "keep and bear Arms" in an organized militia therefore fits poorly with the operative clause's description of the holder of that right as "the people."

We start therefore with a strong presumption that the Second Amendment right is exercised individually and belongs to all Americans.

b. "Keep and bear Arms." We move now from the holder of the right—"the people"—to the substance of the right: "to keep and bear Arms."

Before addressing the verbs "keep" and "bear," we interpret their object: "Arms." The 18th-century meaning is no different from the meaning today. The 1773 edition of Samuel Johnson's dictionary defined "arms" as "weapons of offence, or armour of defence." 1 Dictionary of the English Language 107 (4th ed.) (hereinafter Johnson). Timothy Cunningham's important 1771 legal dictionary defined "arms" as "any thing that a man wears for his defence, or takes into his hands, or useth in wrath to cast at or strike another." 1 A New and Complete Law Dictionary (1771).

The term was applied, then as now, to weapons that were not specifically designed for military use and were not employed in a military capacity. . . . Some have made the argument, bordering on the frivolous, that only those arms in existence in the 18th century are protected by the Second Amendment. We do not interpret constitutional rights that way. Just as the First Amendment protects modern forms of communications, and the Fourth Amendment applies to modern forms of search, the Second Amendment extends, prima facie, to all instruments that constitute bearable arms, even those that were not in existence at the time of the founding. . . .

The phrase "keep arms" was not prevalent in the written documents of the founding period that we have found, but there are a few examples, all of which favor viewing the right to "keep Arms" as an individual right unconnected with militia service. . . . "Keep arms" was simply a common way of referring to possessing arms, for militiamen *and everyone else.*

At the time of the founding, as now, to "bear" meant to "carry." See Johnson 161. When used with "arms," however, the term has a meaning that refers to carrying for a particular purpose—confrontation. . . . From our review of founding-era sources, we conclude that this natural meaning was also the meaning that "bear arms" had in the 18th century. In numerous instances, "bear arms" was unambiguously used to refer to the carrying of weapons outside of an organized militia. The most prominent examples are those most relevant to the Second Amendment: Nine state constitutional provisions written in the 18th century or the first two decades of the 19th, which enshrined a right of citizens to "bear arms in defense of themselves and the state" or "bear arms in defense of himself and the state." It is clear from those formulations that "bear arms" did not refer only to carrying a weapon in an organized military unit. That was also the interpretation of those state constitutional provisions adopted by pre-Civil War state courts. . . .

The phrase "bear Arms" also had at the time of the founding an idiomatic meaning that was significantly different from its natural meaning: "to serve as a soldier, do military service, fight" or "to wage war." See Linguists' Brief 18; *post,* at 2827–2828 (STEVENS, J., dissenting). But it *unequivocally* bore that idiomatic meaning only when followed by the preposition "against," which was in turn followed by the target of the hostilities. See 2 Oxford 21. (That is how, for example, our Declaration of Independence ¶ 28, used the phrase: "He has constrained our fellow Citizens taken Captive on the high Seas to bear Arms against their Country"). . . .

In any event, the meaning of "bear arms" that petitioners and JUSTICE STEVENS propose is *not even* the (sometimes) idiomatic meaning. Rather, they manufacture a hybrid definition, whereby "bear arms" connotes the actual carrying of arms (and therefore is not really an idiom) but only in the service of an organized militia. No dictionary has ever adopted that definition, and we have been apprised of no source that indicates that it carried that meaning at the time of the founding. But it is easy to see why petitioners and the dissent are driven to the hybrid definition. . . . [Under the dissent's reading], the phrase "keep and bear Arms" would be incoherent. The word "Arms" would have two different meanings at once: "weapons" (as the object of "keep") and (as the object of "bear") one-half of an idiom. It would be rather like saying "He filled and kicked the bucket" to mean "He filled the bucket and died." Grotesque.

Petitioners justify their limitation of "bear arms" to the military context by pointing out the unremarkable fact that it was often used in that context. . . . [T]he fact that the phrase was commonly used in a particular context does not show that it is limited to that context, and, in any event, we have given many sources where the phrase was used in nonmilitary contexts. . . .

JUSTICE STEVENS places great weight on James Madison's inclusion of a conscientious-objector clause in his original draft of the Second Amendment: "but no person religiously scrupulous of bearing arms, shall be compelled to render military service in person." . . . It is always perilous to derive the meaning of an adopted provision from another provision deleted in the drafting process. In any case, what JUSTICE STEVENS would conclude from the deleted provision does not follow. . . . [T]he most natural interpretation of Madison's deleted text is that those opposed to carrying weapons for potential violent confrontation would not be "compelled to render military service," in which such carrying would be required.

Finally, JUSTICE STEVENS suggests that "keep and bear Arms" was some sort of term of art, presumably akin to "hue and cry" or "cease and desist." (This suggestion

usefully evades the problem that there is no evidence whatsoever to support a military reading of "keep arms.") JUSTICE STEVENS believes that the unitary meaning of "keep and bear Arms" is established by the Second Amendment's calling it a "right" (singular) rather than "rights" (plural). There is nothing to this. State constitutions of the founding period routinely grouped multiple (related) guarantees under a singular "right," and the First Amendment protects the "right [singular] of the people peaceably to assemble, and to petition the Government for a redress of grievances."
. . .

c.   **Meaning of the Operative Clause.** Putting all of these textual elements together, we find that they guarantee the individual right to possess and carry weapons in case of confrontation. This meaning is strongly confirmed by the historical background of the Second Amendment. We look to this because it has always been widely understood that the Second Amendment, like the First and Fourth Amendments, codified a *pre-existing* right. The very text of the Second Amendment implicitly recognizes the pre-existence of the right and declares only that it "shall not be infringed."

Between the Restoration and the Glorious Revolution, the Stuart Kings Charles II and James II succeeded in using select militias loyal to them to suppress political dissidents, in part by disarming their opponents. . . . These experiences caused Englishmen to be extremely wary of concentrated military forces run by the state and to be jealous of their arms. They accordingly obtained an assurance from William and Mary, in the Declaration of Right (which was codified as the English Bill of Rights), that Protestants would never be disarmed [.] . . . This right has long been understood to be the predecessor to our Second Amendment. It was clearly an individual right, having nothing whatever to do with service in a militia. . . .

By the time of the founding, the right to have arms had become fundamental for English subjects. Blackstone, whose works, we have said, "constituted the preeminent authority on English law for the founding generation," cited the arms provision of the Bill of Rights as one of the fundamental rights of Englishmen. See 1 Blackstone 136, 139–140 (1765). His description of it cannot possibly be thought to tie it to militia or military service. It was, he said, "the natural right of resistance and self-preservation," and "the right of having and using arms for self-preservation and defence." Other contemporary authorities concurred. Thus, the right secured in 1689 as a result of the Stuarts' abuses was by the time of the founding understood to be an individual right protecting against both public and private violence.

And, of course, what the Stuarts had tried to do to their political enemies, George III had tried to do to the colonists. In the tumultuous decades of the 1760's and 1770's, the Crown began to disarm the inhabitants of the most rebellious areas. That provoked polemical reactions by Americans invoking their rights as Englishmen to keep arms. They understood the right to enable individuals to defend themselves. As the most important early American edition of Blackstone's Commentaries (by the law professor and former Antifederalist St. George Tucker) made clear in the notes to the description of the arms right, Americans understood the "right of self-preservation" as permitting a citizen to "repe[l] force by force" when "the intervention of society in his behalf, may be too late to prevent an injury." 1 Blackstone's Commentaries 145–146, n. 42 (1803).

There seems to us no doubt, on the basis of both text and history, that the Second Amendment conferred an individual right to keep and bear arms. Of course the right was not unlimited, just as the First Amendment's right of free speech was not. Thus, we do not read the Second Amendment to protect the right of citizens to carry arms for *any* sort of confrontation, just as we do not read the First Amendment to protect the right of citizens to speak for *any purpose*. Before turning to limitations upon the individual right, however, we must determine whether the prefatory clause of the Second Amendment comports with our interpretation of the operative clause.

2. Prefatory Clause.

The prefatory clause reads: "A well regulated Militia, being necessary to the security of a free State. . . ."

a. "Well-Regulated Militia." In *United States v. Miller*, 307 U.S. 174, 179 (1939), we explained that "the Militia comprised all males physically capable of acting in concert for the common defense." That definition comports with founding-era sources.

Petitioners take a seemingly narrower view of the militia, stating that "[m]ilitias are the state- and congressionally-regulated military forces described in the Militia Clauses (art. I, § 8, cls. 15–16)." Although we agree with petitioners' interpretive assumption that "militia" means the same thing in Article I and the Second Amendment, we believe that petitioners identify the wrong thing, namely, the organized militia. Unlike armies and navies, which Congress is given the power to create . . . , the militia is assumed by Article I already to be *in existence*. . . . This is fully consistent with the ordinary definition of the militia as all able-bodied men. From that pool, Congress has plenary power to organize the units that will make up an effective fighting force. . . .

Finally, the adjective "well-regulated" implies nothing more than the imposition of proper discipline and training. *Cf.* Va. Declaration of Rights § 13 (1776), in 7 Thorpe 3812, 3814 (referring to "a well-regulated militia, composed of the body of the people, trained to arms").

b. "Security of a Free State." The phrase "security of a free state" meant "security of a free polity," not security of each of the several States as the dissent below argued. . . . It is true that the term "State" elsewhere in the Constitution refers to individual States, but the phrase "security of a free state" and close variations seem to have been terms of art in 18th-century political discourse, meaning a "free country" or free polity. Moreover, the other instances of "state" in the Constitution are typically accompanied by modifiers making clear that the reference is to the several States. . . .

There are many reasons why the militia was thought to be "necessary to the security of a free state." See 3 Story § 1890. First, of course, it is useful in repelling invasions and suppressing insurrections. Second, it renders large standing armies unnecessary—an argument that Alexander Hamilton made in favor of federal control over the militia. The Federalist No. 29. Third, when the able-bodied men of a nation are trained in arms and organized, they are better able to resist tyranny.

3. Relationship between Prefatory Clause and Operative Clause.

We reach the question, then: Does the preface fit with an operative clause that creates an individual right to keep and bear arms? It fits perfectly, once one knows the history that the founding generation knew and that we have described above. That history showed that the way tyrants had eliminated a militia consisting of all the able-bodied men was not by banning the militia but simply by taking away the people's arms, enabling a select militia or standing army to suppress political opponents. This is what had occurred in England that prompted codification of the right to have arms in the English Bill of Rights.

The debate with respect to the right to keep and bear arms, as with other guarantees in the Bill of Rights, was not over whether it was desirable (all agreed that it was) but over whether it needed to be codified in the Constitution. During the 1788 ratification debates, the fear that the federal government would disarm the people in order to impose rule through a standing army or select militia was pervasive in Antifederalist rhetoric. See, *e.g.,* Letters from The Federal Farmer III (Oct. 10, 1787), in 2 The Complete Anti-Federalist 234, 242 (H. Storing ed.1981). . . . Federalists responded that because Congress was given no power to abridge the ancient right of individuals to keep and bear arms, such a force could never oppress the people. It was understood across the political spectrum that the right helped to secure the ideal of a citizen militia, which might be necessary to oppose an oppressive military force if the constitutional order broke down.

It is therefore entirely sensible that the Second Amendment's prefatory clause announces the purpose for which the right was codified: to prevent elimination of the militia. The prefatory clause does not suggest that preserving the militia was the only reason Americans valued the ancient right; most undoubtedly thought it even more important for self-defense and hunting. But the threat that the new Federal Government would destroy the citizens' militia by taking away their arms was the reason that right—unlike some other English rights—was codified in a written Constitution. . . .

We now address how the Second Amendment was interpreted from immediately after its ratification through the end of the 19th century. Before proceeding, however, we take issue with JUSTICE STEVENS' equating of these sources with postenactment legislative history, a comparison that betrays a fundamental misunderstanding of a court's interpretive task. "Legislative history," of course, refers to the pre-enactment statements of those who drafted or voted for a law; it is considered persuasive by some, not because they reflect the general understanding of the disputed terms, but because the legislators who heard or read those statements presumably voted with that understanding. "Postenactment legislative history," a deprecatory contradiction in terms, refers to statements of those who drafted or voted for the law that are made after its enactment and hence could have had no effect on the congressional vote. It most certainly does not refer to the examination of a variety of legal and other sources to determine *the public understanding* of a legal text in the period after its enactment or ratification. That sort of inquiry is a critical tool of constitutional interpretation. As we will show, virtually all interpreters of the Second Amendment in the century after its enactment interpreted the Amendment as we do. . . .

[The majority opinion then examined post-ratification commentary, pre-Civil War case law, post-Civil War legislation, and post-Civil War commentators. Next it discussed two of the Court's Reconstruction Era precedents, United States v. Cruikshank *and* Presser v. Illinois.*—Editors]*

JUSTICE STEVENS places overwhelming reliance upon this Court's decision in *United States v. Miller*, 307 U.S. 174 (1939). "[H]undreds of judges," we are told, "have relied on the view of the Amendment we endorsed there," and "[e]ven if the textual and historical arguments on both side of the issue were evenly balanced, respect for the well-settled views of all of our predecessors on this Court, and for the rule of law itself . . . would prevent most jurists from endorsing such a dramatic upheaval in the law." And what is, according to JUSTICE STEVENS, the holding of *Miller* that demands such obeisance? That the Second Amendment "protects the right to keep and bear arms for certain military purposes, but that it does not curtail the legislature's power to regulate the nonmilitary use and ownership of weapons."

Nothing so clearly demonstrates the weakness of JUSTICE STEVENS' case. *Miller* did not hold that and cannot possibly be read to have held that. The judgment in the case upheld against a Second Amendment challenge two men's federal convictions for transporting an unregistered short-barreled shotgun in interstate commerce, in violation of the National Firearms Act. It is entirely clear that the Court's basis for saying that the Second Amendment did not apply was *not* that the defendants were "bear[ing] arms" not "for . . . military purposes" but for "nonmilitary use." Rather, it was that the *type of weapon at issue* was not eligible for Second Amendment protection: "In the absence of any evidence tending to show that the possession or use of a [short-barreled shotgun] at this time has some reasonable relationship to the preservation or efficiency of a well regulated militia, we cannot say that the Second Amendment guarantees the right to keep and bear *such an instrument*." 307 U.S., at 178 (emphasis added). "Certainly," the Court continued, "it is not within judicial notice that this weapon is any part of the ordinary military equipment or that its use could contribute to the common defense." Beyond that, the opinion provided no explanation of the content of the right.

This holding is not only consistent with, but positively suggests, that the Second Amendment confers an individual right to keep and bear arms (though only arms that "have some reasonable relationship to the preservation or efficiency of a well regulated militia"). Had the Court believed that the Second Amendment protects only those serving in the militia, it would have been odd to examine the character of the weapon rather than simply note that the two crooks were not militiamen. JUSTICE STEVENS can say again and again that *Miller* did "not turn on the difference between muskets and sawed-off shotguns, it turned, rather, on the basic difference between the military and nonmilitary use and possession of guns," but the words of the opinion prove otherwise. The most JUSTICE STEVENS can plausibly claim for *Miller* is that it declined to decide the nature of the Second Amendment right. *Miller* stands only for the proposition that the Second Amendment right, whatever its nature, extends only to certain types of weapons. It is particularly wrongheaded to read *Miller* for more than what it said, because the case did not even purport to be a thorough examination of the Second Amendment. . . .

We conclude that nothing in our precedents forecloses our adoption of the original understanding of the Second Amendment. It should be unsurprising that such a significant matter has been for so long judicially unresolved. For most of our history, the Bill of Rights was not thought applicable to the States, and the Federal Government did not significantly regulate the possession of firearms by law-abiding citizens. Other provisions of the Bill of Rights have similarly remained unilluminated for lengthy periods. This Court first held a law to violate the First

Amendment's guarantee of freedom of speech in 1931, almost 150 years after the Amendment was ratified, and it was not until after World War II that we held a law invalid under the Establishment Clause. Even a question as basic as the scope of proscribable libel was not addressed by this Court until 1964, nearly two centuries after the founding. It is demonstrably not true that, as JUSTICE STEVENS claims, "for most of our history, the invalidity of Second-Amendment-based objections to firearms regulations has been well settled and uncontroversial." For most of our history the question did not present itself.

III

Like most rights, the right secured by the Second Amendment is not unlimited. From Blackstone through the 19th-century cases, commentators and courts routinely explained that the right was not a right to keep and carry any weapon whatsoever in any manner whatsoever and for whatever purpose. . . . Although we do not undertake an exhaustive historical analysis today of the full scope of the Second Amendment, nothing in our opinion should be taken to cast doubt on longstanding prohibitions on the possession of firearms by felons and the mentally ill, or laws forbidding the carrying of firearms in sensitive places such as schools and government buildings, or laws imposing conditions and qualifications on the commercial sale of arms.

We also recognize another important limitation on the right to keep and carry arms. *Miller* said, as we have explained, that the sorts of weapons protected were those "in common use at the time." 307 U.S., at 179. We think that limitation is fairly supported by the historical tradition of prohibiting the carrying of "dangerous and unusual weapons." See 4 Blackstone 148–149 (1769); 3 B. Wilson, Works of the Honourable James Wilson 79 (1804); J. Dunlap, The New-York Justice 8 (1815); C. Humphreys, A Compendium of the Common Law in Force in Kentucky 482 (1822).

It may be objected that if weapons that are most useful in military service— M–16 rifles and the like—may be banned, then the Second Amendment right is completely detached from the prefatory clause. But as we have said, the conception of the militia at the time of the Second Amendment's ratification was the body of all citizens capable of military service, who would bring the sorts of lawful weapons that they possessed at home to militia duty. It may well be true today that a militia, to be as effective as militias in the 18th century, would require sophisticated arms that are highly unusual in society at large. Indeed, it may be true that no amount of small arms could be useful against modern-day bombers and tanks. But the fact that modern developments have limited the degree of fit between the prefatory clause and the protected right cannot change our interpretation of the right.

IV

We turn finally to the law at issue here. As we have said, the law totally bans handgun possession in the home. It also requires that any lawful firearm in the home be disassembled or bound by a trigger lock at all times, rendering it inoperable.

As the quotations earlier in this opinion demonstrate, the inherent right of self-defense has been central to the Second Amendment right. The handgun ban amounts to a prohibition of an entire class of "arms" that is overwhelmingly chosen by American society for that lawful purpose. The prohibition extends, moreover, to the home, where the need for defense of self, family, and property is most acute. Under any of the standards of scrutiny that we have applied to enumerated constitutional rights, banning from the home "the most preferred firearm in the nation to 'keep' and use for protection of one's home and family" would fail constitutional muster. . . .

It is no answer to say, as petitioners do, that it is permissible to ban the possession of handguns so long as the possession of other firearms (*i.e.,* long guns) is allowed. It is enough to note, as we have observed, that the American people have considered the handgun to be the quintessential self-defense weapon. . . . Whatever the reason, handguns are the most popular weapon chosen by Americans for self-defense in the home, and a complete prohibition of their use is invalid.

We must also address the District's requirement (as applied to respondent's handgun) that firearms in the home be rendered and kept inoperable at all times. This makes it impossible for citizens to use them for the core lawful purpose of self-defense and is hence unconstitutional. . . .

[In his dissent,] JUSTICE BREYER . . . criticizes us for declining to establish a level of scrutiny for evaluating Second Amendment restrictions. He proposes, explicitly at least, none of the traditionally expressed levels (strict scrutiny, intermediate scrutiny, rational basis), but rather a judge-empowering "interest-balancing inquiry" that "asks whether the statute burdens a protected interest in a way or to an extent that is out of proportion to the statute's salutary effects upon other important governmental interests." After an exhaustive discussion of the arguments for and against gun control, JUSTICE BREYER arrives at his interest-balanced answer: because handgun violence is a problem, because the law is limited to an urban area, and because there were somewhat similar restrictions in the founding period (a false proposition that we have already discussed), the interest-balancing inquiry results in the constitutionality of the handgun ban. QED.

We know of no other enumerated constitutional right whose core protection has been subjected to a freestanding "interest-balancing" approach. The very enumeration of the right takes out of the hands of government—even the Third Branch of Government—the power to decide on a case-by-case basis whether the right is *really worth* insisting upon. A constitutional guarantee . . . is the very *product* of an interest-balancing by the people—which JUSTICE BREYER would now conduct for them anew. And whatever else [the Second Amendment] leaves to future evaluation, it surely elevates above all other interests the right of law-abiding, responsible citizens to use arms in defense of hearth and home.

[S]ince this case represents this Court's first in-depth examination of the Second Amendment, one should not expect it to clarify the entire field. . . . In sum, we hold that the District's ban on handgun possession in the home violates the Second Amendment, as does its prohibition against rendering any lawful firearm in the home operable for the purpose of immediate self-defense. Assuming that Heller is not disqualified from the exercise of Second Amendment rights, the District must permit him to register his handgun and must issue him a license to carry it in the home. . . .

We are aware of the problem of handgun violence in this country, and we take seriously the concerns raised by the many *amici* who believe that prohibition of handgun ownership is a solution. The Constitution leaves the District of Columbia a variety of tools for combating that problem, including some measures regulating handguns. But the enshrinement of constitutional rights necessarily takes certain policy choices off the table. These include the absolute prohibition of handguns held and used for self-defense in the home. Undoubtedly some think that the Second Amendment is outmoded in a society where our standing army is the pride of our Nation, where well-trained police forces provide personal security, and where gun violence is a serious problem. That is perhaps debatable, but what is not debatable is that it is not the role of this Court to pronounce the Second Amendment extinct.

■ JUSTICE STEVENS, with whom JUSTICE SOUTER, JUSTICE GINSBURG, and JUSTICE BREYER join, dissenting.

The question presented by this case is not whether the Second Amendment protects a "collective right" or an "individual right." Surely it protects a right that can be enforced by individuals. But a conclusion that the Second Amendment protects an individual right does not tell us anything about the scope of that right. . . . The text of the Amendment, its history, and our decision in *United States v. Miller,* 307 U.S. 174 (1939), provide a clear answer to that question.

The Second Amendment was adopted to protect the right of the people of each of the several States to maintain a well-regulated militia. It was a response to concerns raised during the ratification of the Constitution that the power of Congress to disarm the state militias and create a national standing army posed an intolerable threat to the sovereignty of the several States. Neither the text of the Amendment nor the arguments advanced by its proponents evidenced the slightest interest in limiting any legislature's authority to regulate private civilian uses of firearms. Specifically, there is no indication that the Framers of the Amendment intended to enshrine the common-law right of self-defense in the Constitution.

. . . The view of the Amendment we took in *Miller*—that it protects the right to keep and bear arms for certain military purposes, but that it does not curtail the Legislature's power to regulate the nonmilitary use and ownership of weapons—is both the most natural reading of the Amendment's text and the interpretation most faithful to the history of its adoption.

Since our decision in *Miller,* hundreds of judges have relied on the view of the Amendment we endorsed there. . . . In this dissent I shall first explain why our decision in *Miller* was faithful to the text of the Second Amendment and the purposes revealed in its drafting history. I shall then comment on the postratification history of the Amendment, which makes abundantly clear that the Amendment should not be interpreted as limiting the authority of Congress to regulate the use or possession of firearms for purely civilian purposes.

I

The text of the Second Amendment is brief. It provides: "A well regulated Militia, being necessary to the security of a free State, the right of the people to keep and bear Arms, shall not be infringed."

Three portions of that text merit special focus: the introductory language defining the Amendment's purpose, the class of persons encompassed within its reach, and the unitary nature of the right that it protects.

"A well regulated Militia, being necessary
to the security of a free State"

The preamble to the Second Amendment makes three important points. It identifies the preservation of the militia as the Amendment's purpose; it explains that the militia is necessary to the security of a free State; and it recognizes that the militia must be "well regulated." . . . While the need for state militias has not been a matter of significant public interest for almost two centuries, that fact should not obscure the contemporary concerns that animated the Framers. . . .

The preamble thus both sets forth the object of the Amendment and informs the meaning of the remainder of its text. Such text should not be treated as mere surplusage, for "[i]t cannot be presumed that any clause in the constitution is intended to be without effect." *Marbury v. Madison,* 5 U.S. (1 Cranch) 137, 174 (1803).

The Court today tries to denigrate the importance of this clause of the Amendment by beginning its analysis with the Amendment's operative provision and returning to the preamble merely "to ensure that our reading of the operative clause is consistent with the announced purpose." That is not how this Court ordinarily reads such texts, and it is not how the preamble would have been viewed at the time the Amendment was adopted. While the Court makes the novel suggestion that it need only find some "logical connection" between the preamble and the operative provision, it does acknowledge that a prefatory clause may resolve an ambiguity in the text. Without identifying any language in the text that even mentions civilian uses of firearms, the Court proceeds to "find" its preferred reading in what is at best an ambiguous text, and then concludes that its reading is not foreclosed by the preamble. Perhaps the Court's approach to the text is acceptable advocacy, but it is surely an unusual approach for judges to follow.

"The right of the people"

The centerpiece of the Court's textual argument is its insistence that the words "the people" as used in the Second Amendment must have the same meaning, and protect the same class of individuals, as when they are used in the First and Fourth Amendments. . . .

The Court . . . overlooks the significance of the way the Framers used the phrase "the people" in these constitutional provisions. In the First Amendment, no words define the class of individuals entitled to speak, to publish, or to worship; in that Amendment it is only the right peaceably to assemble, and to petition the Government for a redress of grievances, that is described as a right of "the people." These rights contemplate collective action. While the right peaceably to assemble protects the individual rights of those persons participating in the assembly, its concern is with action engaged in by members of a group, rather than any single individual. Likewise, although the act of petitioning the Government is a right that can be exercised by individuals, it is primarily collective in nature. For if they are to be effective, petitions must involve groups of individuals acting in concert.

Similarly, the words "the people" in the Second Amendment refer back to the object announced in the Amendment's preamble. They remind us that it is the collective action of individuals having a duty to serve in the militia that the text directly protects and, perhaps more importantly, that the ultimate purpose of the Amendment was to protect the States' share of the divided sovereignty created by the Constitution.

As used in the Fourth Amendment, "the people" describes the class of persons protected from unreasonable searches and seizures by Government officials. It is true that the Fourth Amendment describes a right that need not be exercised in any collective sense. But that observation does not settle the meaning of the phrase "the people" when used in the Second Amendment. For, as we have seen, the phrase means something quite different in the Petition and Assembly Clauses of the First Amendment. Although the abstract definition of the phrase "the people" could carry the same meaning in the Second Amendment as in the Fourth Amendment, the preamble of the Second Amendment suggests that the uses of the phrase in the First and Second Amendments are the same in referring to a collective activity. . . .

"To keep and bear Arms"

Although the Court's discussion of these words treats them as two "phrases"— as if they read "to keep" and "to bear"—they describe a unitary right: to possess arms if needed for military purposes and to use them in conjunction with military activities. . . .

When each word in the text is given full effect, the Amendment is most naturally read to secure to the people a right to use and possess arms in conjunction with service in a well-regulated militia. So far as appears, no more than that was contemplated by its drafters or is encompassed within its terms. Even if the meaning of the text were genuinely susceptible to more than one interpretation, the burden would remain on those advocating a departure from the purpose identified in the preamble and from settled law to come forward with persuasive new arguments or evidence. The textual analysis offered by respondent and embraced by the Court falls far short of sustaining that heavy burden. . . .

Indeed, not a word in the constitutional text even arguably supports the Court's overwrought and novel description of the Second Amendment as "elevat[ing] above all other interests" "the right of law-abiding, responsible citizens to use arms in defense of hearth and home."

II

The proper allocation of military power in the new Nation was an issue of central concern for the Framers. The compromises they ultimately reached, reflected in Article I's Militia Clauses and the Second Amendment, represent quintessential examples of the Framers' "split[ting] the atom of sovereignty." . . .

Madison, charged with the task of assembling the proposals for amendments sent by the ratifying States, was the principal draftsman of the Second Amendment. . . . Madison's decision to model the Second Amendment on the distinctly military Virginia proposal is . . . revealing, since it is clear that he considered and rejected formulations that would have unambiguously protected civilian uses of firearms. When Madison prepared his first draft, and when that draft was debated and modified, it is reasonable to assume that all participants in the drafting process were fully aware of the other formulations that would have protected civilian use and possession of weapons and that their choice to craft the Amendment as they did represented a rejection of those alternative formulations. . . .

The history of the adoption of the Amendment thus describes an overriding concern about the potential threat to state sovereignty that a federal standing army would pose, and a desire to protect the States' militias as the means by which to guard against that danger. But state militias could not effectively check the prospect of a federal standing army so long as Congress retained the power to disarm them, and so a guarantee against such disarmament was needed. As we explained in *Miller:* "With obvious purpose to assure the continuation and render possible the effectiveness of such forces the declaration and guarantee of the Second Amendment were made. It must be interpreted and applied with that end in view." The evidence plainly refutes the claim that the Amendment was motivated by the Framers' fears that Congress might act to regulate any civilian uses of weapons. . . .

III

. . . The Court is simply wrong when it intones that *Miller* contained *"not a word"* about the Amendment's history. The Court plainly looked to history to construe the term "Militia," and, on the best reading of *Miller,* the entire guarantee of the Second Amendment. After noting the original Constitution's grant of power to Congress and to the States over the militia, the Court explained:

> "With obvious purpose to assure the continuation and render possible the effectiveness of such forces the declaration and guarantee of the Second Amendment were made. It must be interpreted and applied with that end in view.
>
> "The Militia which the States were expected to maintain and train is set in contrast with Troops which they were forbidden to keep without the consent of Congress. The sentiment of the time strongly disfavored standing armies; the common view was that adequate defense of country and laws could be secured through the Militia—civilians primarily, soldiers on occasion.
>
> "The signification attributed to the term Militia appears from the debates in the Convention, the history and legislation of Colonies and States, and the writings of approved commentators." *Miller,* at 178–179.

The majority cannot seriously believe that the *Miller* Court did not consider any relevant evidence; the majority simply does not approve of the conclusion the *Miller* Court reached on that evidence. Standing alone, that is insufficient reason to disregard a unanimous opinion of this Court, upon which substantial reliance has been placed by legislators and citizens for nearly 70 years.

V

The Court concludes its opinion by declaring that it is not the proper role of this Court to change the meaning of rights "enshrine[d]" in the Constitution. But the right the Court announces was not "enshrined" in the Second Amendment by the Framers; it is the product of today's law-changing decision. The majority's exegesis has utterly failed to establish that as a matter of text or history, "the right of law-abiding, responsible citizens to use arms in defense of hearth and home" is "elevate[d] above all other interests" by the Second Amendment.

Until today, it has been understood that legislatures may regulate the civilian use and misuse of firearms so long as they do not interfere with the preservation of a well-regulated militia. The Court's announcement of a new constitutional right to own and use firearms for private purposes upsets that settled understanding, but leaves for future cases the formidable task of defining the scope of permissible regulations. . . .

The Court properly disclaims any interest in evaluating the wisdom of the specific policy choice challenged in this case, but it fails to pay heed to a far more important policy choice—the choice made by the Framers themselves. The Court would have us believe that over 200 years ago, the Framers made a choice to limit the tools available to elected officials wishing to regulate civilian uses of weapons, and to authorize this Court to use the common-law process of case-by-case judicial lawmaking to define the contours of acceptable gun-control policy. Absent compelling evidence that is nowhere to be found in the Court's opinion, I could not possibly conclude that the Framers made such a choice.

■ [JUSTICE BREYER's dissenting opinion is omitted.]

NOTES

1.   What is the interpretive methodology used in each of the opinions? What weight does each opinion give to the five types of constitutional argument (p. 42)?

2.   Is the purpose for the Second Amendment laid out by the preamble or prefatory clause still relevant today? If so, how should that affect the interpretation of the rest of the amendment? If not, how does that affect the amendment's interpretation? If the constitutionally stated reason for the Second Amendment vanishes, does the amendment itself vanish? (Justice Scalia and Justice Breyer had a similar dispute, on opposite sides, about the Recess Appointments Clause in *Noel Canning v. NLRB*, p. 190).

3.   What about the Third Amendment—has it vanished from the Constitution? Does the modern situation change how it should be interpreted? Or does the fact that the Third Amendment has generated so little controversy over interpretation simply mean that that amendment has been successful in accomplishing its purposes? Would it be appropriate to *expand* the meaning of the Third Amendment in order to effectuate its broader underlying "purpose" of safeguarding the integrity of the home from government intrusion? Would that be more or less appropriate than it would be to *contract* the scope of the Second Amendment if (some of) the purposes for which it was included no longer require private, individual ownership of firearms? Are we stuck with constitutional provisions (absent an amendment) even if they are no longer necessary to serve their purposes?

4.   Back to the Second Amendment. Judge J. Harvie Wilkinson III, of the Fourth Circuit U.S. Court of Appeals, has said that *Heller* rejects the "values of textualism, self-restraint, separation of powers, and federalism" and leaves "only originalism as the foundation of conservative jurisprudence. A set of reasonable tenets each providing a separate check on judicial activism has now been replaced by a singular focus on original understanding." J. Harvie Wilkinson III, *Of Guns, Abortions, and the Unraveling Rule of Law*, 95 Va. L. Rev. 253, 256 (2009). The problem, in Judge Wilkinson's view, is that an unconstrained originalism can be "a theory no less subject to judicial subjectivity and endless argumentation as any other." Do you agree? How much should constitutional interpretation rely on the original understanding of the text (emphasized by Justice Scalia in *Heller*) and how much should it temper that understanding with norms of judicial restraint, deference to the democratic process, and policy considerations (emphasized in Judge Wilkinson's critique)?

5.   Does the Second Amendment right to keep and bear arms, as interpreted by *Heller*, apply against state governments? In *McDonald v. City of Chicago*, 561 U.S. 742 (2010), the Supreme Court, by vote of 5–4, held that the Second Amendment's individual right to keep and bear arms, recognized in *Heller*, also applied against state and local government action. *McDonald* is presented at p. 1505.

One conceptual puzzle in incorporating the Second Amendment against the states lies in its historical context. If it was understood to check government tyranny at the national level by protecting an individual right to own firearms, that right could easily be incorporated against states (since they, too, could prove tyrannical). But if the purpose was to protect the state militias, on the theory that *they* would check national power, would that be consistent with incorporating the Second Amendment against the states themselves? This is not the only place in the Bill of Rights where this sort of puzzle arises. Two other provisions are sometimes read—though each reading is contested—as taking decisionmaking authority about a question away from the national government and giving it to the states, namely the Establishment Clause and the Seventh Amendment's preservation of the right to a civil jury trial. It is even possible to read nearly all of the original Bill of Rights in this way, leading to questions about how to "reconstruct" them if applied against the states. See generally Akhil Amar, THE BILL OF RIGHTS: CREATION AND RECONSTRUCTION (1998).

[Assignment 60]

IV. CRIMINAL AND CIVIL PROCEEDINGS: THE FOURTH, FIFTH, SIXTH, SEVENTH, AND EIGHTH AMENDMENTS

At the center of the Bill of Rights stands a cluster of provisions addressing the rights of the people of America against law-enforcement officials and the rights of the accused in criminal cases to fair and reliable proceedings: The right to be free from unreasonable government searches and seizures; the right to trial by jury, following an indictment by a grand jury; the requirement that proceedings be in accordance with "due process of law"; the rights to confront witnesses and to produce one's own; the right to the assistance of counsel; and the prohibitions on cruel and unusual punishments and excessive bail or fines.

These issues form the core of many law school courses on Criminal Procedure. But they are also part of the Constitution. Here is a brief sketch of these constitutional provisions, with two cases that illustrate important questions of constitutional interpretation.

The Fourth Amendment

> *Amend. IV: The right of the people to be secure in their persons, houses, papers, and effects, against unreasonable searches and seizures, shall not be violated, and no Warrants shall issue, but upon probable cause, supported by Oath or Affirmation, and particularly describing the place to be searched, and the persons or things to be seized.*

The Fourth Amendment prohibits searches and seizures that are "unreasonable." How does one determine whether a search is reasonable or unreasonable? Is that a determination of law for a judge to make? Is it a judgment committed to a jury, much as tort law questions of reasonableness sometimes call for judgment by juries? Are there certain categorical rules? Where do they come from?

What is the relationship between the prohibition of "unreasonable" searches and the requirement that warrants be supported by "probable cause"? Is a search always *unreasonable* if it is not based on "probable cause"? Is a search always *reasonable* if it *is* supported by probable cause? Do all searches require warrants? (Read the text carefully.) Is a search necessarily unreasonable if it lacks a warrant? Is a search necessarily reasonable if the police have a warrant?

What is a "search" in the first place? What is a "seizure"? How would you apply these terms, for example, to the requirement that all commercial airline passengers pass through metal detectors, empty their pockets, and remove their jackets and shoes? Is that a search or a seizure? Is there probable cause? Is a warrant required?

Does the Fourth Amendment protect only U.S. citizens, or does it apply to non-citizens as well? To whom does "[t]he right of the people" refer? Does the Fourth Amendment apply to actions taken by government officials *abroad*? Actions directed against non-U.S. citizens abroad? Does it matter if the actions are taken for law enforcement purposes or for some other purpose (for example, the conduct of war)? Are U.S. armed forces engaged in military actions abroad limited by the provisions of the Fourth Amendment? Must a soldier have probable cause or a warrant in order to search or seize an enemy soldier? Cf. *United States v. Verdugo-Urquidez*, 494 U.S. 259 (1990) (Fourth Amendment protects the "right of the people" of the United States and does not apply to extraterritorial "searches" and "seizures" conducted abroad by U.S. officials, involving non-citizens).

What is the remedy if the Fourth Amendment's prohibitions are violated? The most widely used remedy is one that has been judicially developed. It is called the exclusionary rule—a court excludes from a criminal trial any evidence obtained by officers violating the amendment. Is this remedy consistent with the Fourth Amendment? Can Congress prescribe a different remedy, or is deciding the remedy for Fourth Amendment violations a question for the judiciary? And what should the remedy be for citizens who suffer an unreasonable search or seizure that produces no incriminating evidence whatsoever?

Kyllo v. United States

533 U.S. 27 (2001)

■ JUSTICE SCALIA delivered the opinion of the Court.

This case presents the question whether the use of a thermal-imaging device aimed at a private home from a public street to detect relative amounts of heat within the home constitutes a "search" within the meaning of the Fourth Amendment.

I

In 1991 Agent William Elliott of the United States Department of the Interior came to suspect that marijuana was being grown in the home belonging to petitioner Danny Kyllo. . . . Indoor marijuana growth typically requires high-intensity lamps. In order to determine whether an amount of heat was emanating from petitioner's home consistent with the use of such lamps, at 3:20 a.m. on January 16, 1992, Agent Elliott and Dan Haas used an Agema Thermovision 210 thermal imager to scan the triplex. Thermal imagers detect infrared radiation, which virtually all objects emit but which is not visible to the naked eye. . . . The scan of Kyllo's home took only a few minutes and was performed from the passenger seat of Agent Elliott's vehicle across the street from the front of the house and also from the street in back of the house. The scan showed that the roof over the garage and a side wall of petitioner's home were relatively hot compared to the rest of the home and substantially warmer than neighboring homes in the triplex. Agent Elliott concluded that petitioner was using halide lights to grow marijuana in his house, which indeed he was. Based on tips from informants, utility bills, and the thermal imaging, a Federal Magistrate Judge issued a warrant authorizing a search of petitioner's home, and the agents found an indoor growing operation involving more than 100 plants. Petitioner was indicted on one count of manufacturing marijuana, in violation of 21 U.S.C. § 841(a)(1). He unsuccessfully moved to suppress the evidence seized from his home and then entered a conditional guilty plea.

A divided Court of Appeals . . . affirmed. The court held that petitioner had shown no subjective expectation of privacy because he had made no attempt to conceal the heat escaping from his home, and even if he had, there was no objectively reasonable expectation of privacy because the imager "did not expose any intimate details of Kyllo's life," only "amorphous 'hot spots' on the roof and exterior wall[.]" We granted certiorari.

II

The Fourth Amendment provides that "[t]he right of the people to be secure in their persons, houses, papers, and effects, against unreasonable searches and seizures, shall not be violated." "At the very core" of the Fourth Amendment "stands the right of a man to retreat into his own home and there be free from unreasonable governmental intrusion." *Silverman v. United States*, 365 U.S. 505, 511 (1961). With few exceptions, the question whether a warrantless search of a home is reasonable and hence constitutional must be answered no.

On the other hand, the antecedent question whether or not a Fourth Amendment "search" has occurred is not so simple under our precedent. The permissibility of ordinary visual surveillance of a home used to be clear because, well into the 20th century, our Fourth Amendment jurisprudence was tied to common-law trespass. Visual surveillance was unquestionably lawful because "the eye cannot by the laws of England be guilty of a trespass." We have since decoupled violation of a person's Fourth Amendment rights from trespassory violation of his property, but the lawfulness of warrantless visual surveillance of a home has still been preserved. As we observed in *California v. Ciraolo*, 476 U.S. 207, 213 (1986), "[t]he Fourth Amendment protection of the home has never been extended to require law enforcement officers to shield their eyes when passing by a home on public thoroughfares."

One might think that the new validating rationale would be that examining the portion of a house that is in plain public view, while it is a "search"[1] despite the absence of trespass, is not an "unreasonable" one under the Fourth Amendment. But in fact we have held that visual observation is no "search" at all—perhaps in order to preserve somewhat more intact our doctrine that warrantless searches are presumptively unconstitutional. In assessing when a search is not a search, we have applied somewhat in reverse the principle first enunciated in *Katz* v. *United States,* 389 U.S. 347 (1967). *Katz* involved eavesdropping by means of an electronic listening device placed on the outside of a telephone booth—a location not within the catalog ("persons, houses, papers, and effects") that the Fourth Amendment protects against unreasonable searches. We held that the Fourth Amendment nonetheless protected Katz from the warrantless eavesdropping because he "justifiably relied" upon the privacy of the telephone booth. As Justice Harlan's oft-quoted concurrence described it, a Fourth Amendment search occurs when the government violates a subjective

---

[1]   When the Fourth Amendment was adopted, as now, to "search" meant "[t]o look over or through for the purpose of finding something; to explore; to examine by inspection; as, to *search* the house for a book; to *search* the wood for a thief." N. Webster, An American Dictionary of the English Language 66 (1828) (reprint 6th ed. 1989).

expectation of privacy that society recognizes as reasonable. See *id.,* at 361. We have subsequently applied this principle to hold that a Fourth Amendment search does *not* occur—even when the explicitly protected location of a *house* is concerned—unless "the individual manifested a subjective expectation of privacy in the object of the challenged search," and "society [is] willing to recognize that expectation as reasonable." . . .

The present case involves officers on a public street engaged in more than naked-eye surveillance of a home. We have previously reserved judgment as to how much technological enhancement of ordinary perception from such a vantage point, if any, is too much. While we upheld enhanced aerial photography of an industrial complex in *Dow Chemical Co. v. United States,* 476 U.S. 227 (1986), we noted that we found "it important that this is *not* an area immediately adjacent to a private home, where privacy expectations are most heightened."

III

It would be foolish to contend that the degree of privacy secured to citizens by the Fourth Amendment has been entirely unaffected by the advance of technology. For example, as the cases discussed above make clear, the technology enabling human flight has exposed to public view (and hence, we have said, to official observation) uncovered portions of the house and its curtilage that once were private. The question we confront today is what limits there are upon this power of technology to shrink the realm of guaranteed privacy.

The *Katz* test—whether the individual has an expectation of privacy that society is prepared to recognize as reasonable—has often been criticized as circular, and hence subjective and unpredictable. [I]n the case of the search of the interior of homes—the prototypical and hence most commonly litigated area of protected privacy—there is a ready criterion, with roots deep in the common law, of the minimal expectation of privacy that *exists,* and that is acknowledged to be *reasonable.* To withdraw protection of this minimum expectation would be to permit police technology to erode the privacy guaranteed by the Fourth Amendment. We think that obtaining by sense-enhancing technology any information regarding the interior of the home that could not otherwise have been obtained without physical "intrusion into a constitutionally protected area" constitutes a search—at least where (as here) the technology in question is not in general public use. This assures preservation of that degree of privacy against government that existed when the Fourth Amendment was adopted. On the basis of this criterion, the information obtained by the thermal imager in this case was the product of a search.

The Government maintains, however, that the thermal imaging must be upheld because it detected "only heat radiating from the external surface of the house." The dissent makes this its leading point, contending that there is a fundamental difference between what it calls "off-the-wall" observations and "through-the-wall surveillance." But just as a thermal imager captures only heat emanating from a house, so also a powerful directional microphone picks up only sound emanating from a house—and a satellite capable of scanning from many miles away would pick up only visible light emanating from a house. We rejected such a mechanical interpretation of the Fourth Amendment in *Katz,* where the eavesdropping device picked up only sound waves that reached the exterior of the phone booth. Reversing that approach would leave the homeowner at the mercy of advancing technology—including imaging technology that could discern all human activity in the home. . . .

The Government also contends that the thermal imaging was constitutional because it did not "detect private activities occurring in private areas." . . . Limiting the prohibition of thermal imaging to "intimate details" would not only be wrong in principle; it would be impractical in application, failing to provide "a workable accommodation between the needs of law enforcement and the interests protected by the Fourth Amendment," *Oliver v. United States*, 466 U.S. 170, 181 (1984). To begin with, there is no necessary connection between the sophistication of the surveillance equipment and the "intimacy" of the details that it observes—which means that one cannot say (and the police cannot be assured) that use of the relatively crude equipment at issue here will always be lawful. The Agema Thermovision 210 might disclose, for example, at what hour each night the lady of the house takes her daily sauna and bath—a detail that many would consider "intimate"; and a much more sophisticated system might detect nothing more intimate than the fact that someone left a closet light on. . . .

Where, as here, the Government uses a device that is not in general public use, to explore details of the home that would previously have been unknowable without physical intrusion, the surveillance is a "search" and is presumptively unreasonable without a warrant.

Since we hold the Thermovision imaging to have been an unlawful search, it will remain for the District Court to determine whether, without the evidence it provided, the search warrant issued in this case was supported by probable cause—and if not, whether there is any other basis for supporting admission of the evidence that the search pursuant to the warrant produced.

■ JUSTICE STEVENS, with whom THE CHIEF JUSTICE, JUSTICE O'CONNOR, and JUSTICE KENNEDY join, dissenting.

There is, in my judgment, a distinction of constitutional magnitude between "through-the-wall surveillance" that gives the observer or listener direct access to information in a private area, on the one hand, and the thought processes used to draw inferences from information in the public domain, on the other hand. . . .

I

There is no need for the Court to craft a new rule to decide this case, as it is controlled by established principles from our Fourth Amendment jurisprudence. One of those core principles, of course, is that "searches and seizures *inside a home* without a warrant are presumptively unreasonable." *Payton v. New York*, 445 U.S. 573, 586 (1980) (emphasis added). But it is equally well settled that searches and seizures of property in plain view are presumptively reasonable. Whether that property is residential or commercial, the basic principle is the same: " 'What a person knowingly exposes to the public, even in his own home or office, is not a subject of Fourth Amendment protection.' " *Ciraolo*, at 213 (quoting *Katz*, at 351). That is the principle implicated here.

While the Court "take[s] the long view" and decides this case based largely on the potential of yet-to-be-developed technology that might allow "through-the-wall surveillance," this case involves nothing more than off-the-wall surveillance by law enforcement officers to gather information exposed to the general public from the outside of petitioner's home. . . . Unlike an x-ray scan, or other possible "through-the-wall" techniques, the detection of infrared radiation emanating from the home did not accomplish "an unauthorized physical penetration into the premises," nor did it "obtain information that it could not have obtained by observation from outside the curtilage of the house."

Indeed, the ordinary use of the senses might enable a neighbor or passerby to notice the heat emanating from a building, particularly if it is vented, as was the case here. . . . Such use of the senses would not convert into an unreasonable search if, instead, an adjoining neighbor allowed an officer onto her property to verify her perceptions with a sensitive thermometer. Nor, in my view, does such observation become an unreasonable search if made from a distance with the aid of a device that merely discloses that the exterior of one house, or one area of the house, is much warmer than another. Nothing more occurred in this case.

Thus, the notion that heat emissions from the outside of a dwelling are a private matter implicating the protections of the Fourth Amendment . . . is not only unprecedented but also quite difficult to take seriously. Heat waves, like aromas that are generated in a kitchen, or in a laboratory or opium den, enter the public domain if and when they leave a building. A subjective expectation that they would remain private is not only implausible but also surely not "one that society is prepared to recognize as 'reasonable.'" *Katz,* at 361 (Harlan, J., concurring).

To be sure, the homeowner has a reasonable expectation of privacy concerning what takes place within the home, and the Fourth Amendment's protection against physical invasions of the home should apply to their functional equivalent. But the equipment in this case did not penetrate the walls of petitioner's home, and while it did pick up "details of the home" that were exposed to the public, it did not obtain "any information regarding the *interior* of the home." In the Court's own words, based on what the thermal imager "showed" regarding the outside of petitioner's home, the officers "concluded" that petitioner was engaging in illegal activity inside the home. It would be quite absurd to characterize their thought processes as "searches," regardless of whether they inferred (rightly) that petitioner was growing marijuana in his house, or (wrongly) that "the lady of the house [was taking] her daily sauna and bath." . . .

Notwithstanding the implications of today's decision, there is a strong public interest in avoiding constitutional litigation over the monitoring of emissions from homes, and over the inferences drawn from such monitoring. Just as "the police cannot reasonably be expected to avert their eyes from evidence of criminal activity that could have been observed by any member of the public," so too public officials should not have to avert their senses or their equipment from detecting emissions in the public domain such as excessive heat, traces of smoke, suspicious odors, odorless gases, airborne particulates, or radioactive emissions, any of which could identify hazards to the community. In my judgment, monitoring such emissions with "sense-enhancing technology," and drawing useful conclusions from such monitoring, is an entirely reasonable public service.

On the other hand, the countervailing privacy interest is at best trivial. . . . The interest in concealing the heat escaping from one's house pales in significance to "the chief evil against which the wording of the Fourth Amendment is directed," the "physical entry of the home," and it is hard to believe that it is an interest the Framers sought to protect in our Constitution. . . .

II

Instead of trying to answer the question whether the use of the thermal imager in this case was even arguably unreasonable, the Court has fashioned a rule that is intended to provide essential guidance for the day when "more sophisticated systems" gain the "ability to 'see' through walls and other opaque barriers." The newly minted rule encompasses "obtaining [1] by sense-enhancing technology [2] any information regarding the interior of the home [3] that could not otherwise have been obtained without physical intrusion into a constitutionally protected area . . . [4] at least where (as here) the technology in question is not in general public use." [Quoting majority opinion] In my judgment, the Court's new rule is at once too broad and too narrow, and is not justified by the Court's explanation for its adoption. As I have suggested, I would not erect a constitutional impediment to the use of sense-enhancing technology unless it provides its user with the functional equivalent of actual presence in the area being searched.

Despite the Court's attempt to draw a line that is "not only firm but also bright," the contours of its new rule are uncertain because its protection apparently dissipates as soon as the relevant technology is "in general public use[.]" Yet how much use is general public use is not even hinted at by the Court's opinion, which makes the somewhat doubtful assumption that the thermal imager used in this case does not satisfy that criterion. In any event, putting aside its lack of clarity, this criterion is somewhat perverse because it seems likely that the threat to privacy will grow, rather than recede, as the use of intrusive equipment becomes more readily available.

It is clear, however, that the category of "sense-enhancing technology" covered by the new rule is far too broad. It would, for example, embrace potential mechanical substitutes for dogs trained to react when they sniff narcotics. But in *United States v. Place*, 462 U.S. 696, 707 (1983), we held that a dog sniff that "discloses only the presence or absence of narcotics" does "not constitute a 'search' within the meaning of the Fourth Amendment," and it must follow that sense-enhancing equipment that identifies nothing but illegal activity is not a search either. Nevertheless, the use of such a device would be unconstitutional under the Court's rule, as would the use of other new devices that might detect the odor of deadly bacteria or chemicals for making a new type of high explosive, even if the devices (like the dog sniffs) are "so limited both in the manner in which" they obtain information and "in the content of the information" they reveal. . . .

The two reasons advanced by the Court as justifications for the adoption of its new rule are both unpersuasive. First, the Court suggests that its rule is compelled by our holding in *Katz*[.] . . . Yet there are critical differences between the cases. In *Katz*, the electronic listening device attached to the outside of the phone booth allowed the officers to pick up the content of the conversation inside the booth, making them the functional equivalent of intruders because they gathered information that was otherwise available only to someone inside the private area; it would be as if, in this case, the thermal imager presented a view of the heat-generating activity inside petitioner's home. . . .

Second, the Court argues that the permissibility of "through-the-wall surveillance" cannot depend on a distinction between observing "intimate details" such as "the lady of the house [taking] her daily sauna and bath," and noticing only "the nonintimate rug on the vestibule floor" or "objects no smaller than 36 by 36 inches." This entire argument assumes, of course, that the thermal imager in this case could or did perform "through-the-wall surveillance" that could identify any detail "that would previously have been unknowable without physical intrusion." . . . In fact, the device could not, and did not, enable its user to identify either the lady of the house, the rug on the vestibule floor, or anything else inside the house, whether smaller or larger than 36 by 36 inches. . . . But even if the device could reliably show extraordinary differences in the amounts of heat leaving his home, drawing the inference that there was something suspicious occurring inside the residence—a conclusion that officers far less gifted than Sherlock Holmes would readily draw— does not qualify as "through-the-wall surveillance," much less a Fourth Amendment violation. . . .

NOTES

1.   The leading modern case on Fourth Amendment searches is *Katz v. United States*, 389 U.S. 347 (1967). Government agents attached a recording device to a public telephone booth, enabling them to learn of the defendant's illegal wagering activities— all without a warrant. Is such electronic surveillance of a public area a "search" covered by the Fourth Amendment? The Court said *yes*, and its analysis has framed all subsequent discussion of the threshold question of the scope of coverage of the Fourth Amendment's protections. In his majority opinion, Justice Stewart said:

> [T]he Fourth Amendment cannot be translated into a general constitutional 'right to privacy.' That Amendment protects individual privacy against certain kinds of governmental intrusion, but its protections go further, and often have nothing to do with privacy at all. Other provisions of the Constitution [i.e., the First, Third, and Fifth Amendments] protect personal privacy from other forms of governmental invasion. But the protection of a person's *general* right to privacy—his right to be let alone by other people—is, like the protection of his property and of is very life, left largely to the law of the individual States. . . .
>
> [T]he Fourth Amendment protects people, not places. What a person knowingly exposes to the public, even in his own home or office, is not a subject of Fourth Amendment protection. But what he seeks to preserve as private, even in an area accessible to the public, may be constitutionally protected. The Government stresses the fact that the telephone booth from which the petitioner made his calls was constructed partly of glass, so that he was as visible after he entered it as he would have been if he had remained outside. But what he sought to exclude when he entered the booth was not the intruding eye—it was the uninvited ear. He did not shed his right to do so simply because he made his calls from a place where he might be seen.

In a highly influential concurring opinion, Justice Harlan said:

> I join the opinion of the Court, which I read to hold only (a) that an enclosed telephone booth is an area where, like a home, and unlike a field, a person has a constitutionally protected reasonable expectation of privacy; (b) that electronic as well as physical intrusion into a place that is in this sense private may constitute a violation of the Fourth Amendment; and (c) that the invasion of a constitutionally protected area by federal authorities is, as the Court has long held, presumptively unreasonable in the absence of a search warrant. . . .

My understanding of the rule that has emerged from prior decisions is that there is a twofold requirement, first, that a person have exhibited an actual (subjective) expectation of privacy and, second, that the expectation be one that society is prepared to recognize as "reasonable."

The *Katz* decision, especially the two-part formulation of Justice Harlan's concurrence, is central to how the Court has come to view the Fourth Amendment's requirements (but with many exceptions). Consider an example: if the police rummage through someone's garbage dumpster, is that a "search" covered by the Fourth Amendment? In *California v. Greenwood*, 486 U.S. 35 (1988), the Court held that while a person might have an actual, subjective expectation of privacy in the contents of his abandoned garbage, set outside in opaque bags for collection, it is not an expectation that society recognizes as reasonable. Accordingly, the police can rummage away without a warrant.

How do the two opinions in *Kyllo* apply *Katz*?

2.   Can the "reasonable expectations of privacy" principle sometimes provide more protection than the list in the Fourth Amendment ("persons, houses, papers, and effects")? Can it sometimes provide less protection than the Fourth Amendment list? Or is it unrelated to the list?

3.   The question in *Kyllo* is about whether there was a "search." That is the question *Katz* was answering, too. But why are "reasonable expectations of privacy" relevant for deciding whether there was a *search*, instead for deciding whether the search was *reasonable*? If you were deciding *Kyllo* without *Katz*, and were just trying to apply the Fourth Amendment directly, how would you analyze the case?

4.   As noted above, the most common remedy for a violation of the Fourth Amendment is the exclusion of the evidence that officers found by violating the Fourth Amendment. Assuming that the exclusionary rule is a proper remedy, how far should such exclusion reach? To answer this question the Court has developed the colorfully named "fruit of the poisonous tree" doctrine. The constitutional violation is the "poisonous tree," and the evidence it leads to is the "fruit." The doctrine applies to both Fourth and Fifth Amendment violations. But the Court has also developed exceptions to mitigate the harshness of excluding all of the "fruit" of a constitutional violation—exceptions having to do with whether the chain-of-causation from the initial violation was broken by some intervening event.

Consider how this doctrine would apply to a scene from the movie *Dirty Harry*, where the title character is played by Clint Eastwood. Harry is a San Francisco police detective. He climbs over a fence onto private property without a warrant, breaks into the quarters of a suspected serial killer (a caretaker's room deep inside a football stadium), finds a rifle, chases the suspect across the football field, shoots the suspect's legs out from under him, and threatens to kill the suspect, who screams for his lawyer. Harry demands to know where he has left his latest victim—a teenage girl who has been buried alive. The serial killer is coerced by torture into telling Harry where she is. But by the time the police reach the girl, she is dead. Assuming Harry has violated the suspect's Fourth and Fifth Amendment rights, what should be excluded from the evidence at trial? The rifle? The serial killer's confession? The girl's body? For more discussion, see Michael Stokes Paulsen, *Dirty Harry and the Real Constitution*, 64 U. Chi. L. Rev. 1457 (1997).

The Fifth Amendment

Amend. V: No person shall be held to answer for a capital, or otherwise infamous crime, unless on a presentment or indictment of a Grand Jury, except in cases arising in the land or naval forces, or in the Militia, when in actual service in time of War or public danger; nor shall any person be subject for the same offence to be twice put in jeopardy of life or limb; nor shall be compelled in any criminal case to be a witness against himself, nor be deprived of life, liberty, or property, without due process of law; nor shall private property be taken for public use, without just compensation.

The Fifth Amendment is most well-known (at least in popular culture) for its right against compelled self-incrimination. But as you can see from reading it, that is only a part of what the amendment is about. More broadly, the Fifth Amendment is a compendium of criminal procedural protections, including the right to the screening process of a grand jury and the prohibition against "double jeopardy." It also guarantees the right to "due process of law," and the right not to have one's private property taken for public use without just compensation. (Due process is discussed at p. 1476, and the Takings Clause at p. 1231.)

Consider the following case—one of the most famous in the history of the Supreme Court—as a case study in the interpretation of the Constitution:

Miranda v. Arizona

384 U.S. 436 (1966)

■ MR. CHIEF JUSTICE WARREN delivered the opinion of the Court.

The cases before us raise questions which go to the roots of our concepts of American criminal jurisprudence: the restraints society must observe consistent with the Federal Constitution in prosecuting individuals for crime. More specifically, we deal with the admissibility of statements obtained from an individual who is subjected to custodial police interrogation and the necessity for procedures which assure that the individual is accorded his privilege under the Fifth Amendment to the Constitution not to be compelled to incriminate himself. . . .

Our holding will be spelled out with some specificity in the pages which follow but briefly stated it is this: the prosecution may not use statements, whether exculpatory or inculpatory, stemming from custodial interrogation of the defendant unless it demonstrates the use of procedural safeguards effective to secure the privilege against self-incrimination. By custodial interrogation, we mean questioning initiated by law enforcement officers after a person has been taken into custody or otherwise deprived of his freedom of action in any significant way. As for the procedural safeguards to be employed, unless other fully effective means are devised to inform accused persons of their right of silence and to assure a continuous opportunity to exercise it, the following measures are required. Prior to any questioning, the person must be warned that he has a right to remain silent, that any statement he does make may be used as evidence against him, and that he has a right to the presence of an attorney, either retained or appointed. The defendant may waive effectuation of these rights, provided the waiver is made voluntarily, knowingly and intelligently. If, however, he indicates in any manner and at any stage of the process that he wishes to consult with an attorney before speaking there can be no questioning. Likewise, if the individual is alone and indicates in any manner that he does not wish to be interrogated, the police may not question him. The mere fact that he may have answered some questions or volunteered some statements on his own does not deprive him of the right to refrain from answering any further inquiries until he has consulted with an attorney and thereafter consents to be questioned.

I

The constitutional issue we decide in each of these cases is the admissibility of statements obtained from a defendant questioned while in custody or otherwise deprived of his freedom of action in any significant way. In each, the defendant was questioned by police officers, detectives, or a prosecuting attorney in a room in which he was cut off from the outside world. In none of these cases was the defendant given a full and effective warning of his rights at the outset of the interrogation process. In all the cases, the questioning elicited oral admissions, and in three of them, signed statements as well which were admitted at their trials. They all thus share salient features—incommunicado interrogation of individuals in a police-dominated atmosphere, resulting in self-incriminating statements without full warnings of constitutional rights.

An understanding of the nature and setting of this in-custody interrogation is essential to our decisions today. . . . [W]e stress that the modern practice of in-custody interrogation is psychologically rather than physically oriented. . . . The officers are told by the [police] manuals that the "principal psychological factor contributing to a successful interrogation is *privacy*—being alone with the person under interrogation." . . .

To highlight the isolation and unfamiliar surroundings, the manuals instruct the police to display an air of confidence in the suspect's guilt and from outward appearance to maintain only an interest in confirming certain details. The guilt of the subject is to be posited as a fact. The interrogator should direct his comments toward the reasons why the subject committed the act, rather than court failure by asking the subject whether he did it. Like other men, perhaps the subject has had a bad family life, had an unhappy childhood, had too much to drink, had an unrequited desire for women. The officers are instructed to minimize the moral seriousness of the offense, to cast blame on the victim or on society. These tactics are designed to put the subject in a psychological state where his story is but an elaboration of what the police purport to know already—that he is guilty. Explanations to the contrary are dismissed and discouraged. . . .

The interrogators sometimes are instructed to induce a confession out of trickery. The technique here is quite effective in crimes which require identification or which run in series. In the identification situation, the interrogator may take a break in his questioning to place the subject among a group of men in a line-up. "The witness or complainant (previously coached, if necessary) studies the line-up and confidently points out the subject as the guilty party." Then the questioning resumes "as though there were now no doubt about the guilt of the subject." A variation on this technique is called the "reverse line-up":

> The accused is placed in a line-up, but this time he is identified by several fictitious witnesses or victims who associated him with different offenses.

It is expected that the subject will become desperate and confess to the offense under investigation in order to escape from the false accusations.

The manuals also contain instructions for police on how to handle the individual who refuses to discuss the matter entirely, or who asks for an attorney or relatives. The examiner is to concede him the right to remain silent. "This usually has a very undermining effect. First of all, he is disappointed in his expectation of an unfavorable reaction on the part of the interrogator. Secondly, a concession of this right to remain silent impresses the subject with the apparent fairness of his interrogator." After this psychological conditioning, however, the officer is told to point out the incriminating significance of the suspect's refusal to talk:

Joe, you have a right to remain silent. That's your privilege and I'm the last person in the world who'll try to take it away from you. If that's the way you want to leave this, O.K. But let me ask you this. Suppose you were in my shoes and I were in yours and you called me in to ask me about this and I told you, "I don't want to answer any of your questions." You'd think I had something to hide, and you'd probably be right in thinking that. That's exactly what I'll have to think about you, and so will everybody else. So let's sit here and talk this whole thing over.

Few will persist in their initial refusal to talk, it is said, if this monologue is employed correctly. In the event that the subject wishes to speak to a relative or an attorney, the following advice is tendered:

[T]he interrogator should respond by suggesting that the subject first tell the truth to the interrogator himself rather than get anyone else involved in the matter. If the request is for an attorney, the interrogator may suggest that the subject save himself or his family the expense of any such professional service, particularly if he is innocent of the offense under investigation. The interrogator may also add, "Joe, I'm only looking for the truth, and if you're telling the truth, that's it. You can handle this by yourself."

From these representative samples of interrogation techniques, the setting prescribed by the manuals and observed in practice becomes clear. In essence, it is this: To be alone with the subject is essential to prevent distraction and to deprive him of any outside support. The aura of confidence in his guilt undermines his will to resist. He merely confirms the preconceived story the police seek to have him describe. Patience and persistence, at times relentless questioning, are employed. . . . The police then persuade, trick, or cajole him out of exercising his constitutional rights. . . .

In the cases before us today, given this background, we concern ourselves primarily with this interrogation atmosphere and the evils it can bring. . . . In these cases, we might not find the defendants' statements to have been involuntary in traditional terms. Our concern for adequate safeguards to protect precious Fifth Amendment rights is, of course, not lessened in the slightest. In each of the cases, the defendant was thrust into an unfamiliar atmosphere and run through menacing police interrogation procedures. The potentiality for compulsion is forcefully apparent, for example, in Miranda, where the indigent Mexican defendant was a seriously disturbed individual with pronounced sexual fantasies, and in Stewart, in which the defendant was an indigent Los Angeles Negro who had dropped out of school in the sixth grade. To be sure, the records do not evince overt physical coercion or patent psychological ploys. The fact remains that in none of these cases did the officers undertake to afford appropriate safeguards at the outset of the interrogation to insure that the statements were truly the product of free choice.

It is obvious that such an interrogation environment is created for no purpose other than to subjugate the individual to the will of his examiner. This atmosphere carries its own badge of intimidation. To be sure, this is not physical intimidation, but it is equally destructive of human dignity. . . .

II

. . . The question in these cases is whether the privilege [against self-incrimination] is fully applicable during a period of custodial interrogation. In this Court, the privilege has consistently been accorded a liberal construction. We are satisfied that all the principles embodied in the privilege apply to informal compulsion exerted by law-enforcement officers during in-custody questioning. An individual swept from familiar surroundings into police custody, surrounded by antagonistic forces, and subjected to the techniques of persuasion de-scribed above cannot be otherwise than under compulsion to speak. As a practical matter, the compulsion to speak in the isolated setting of the police station may well be greater than in courts or other official investigations, where there are often impartial observers to guard against intimidation or trickery. . . .

III

Today, then, there can be no doubt that the Fifth Amendment privilege is available outside of criminal court proceedings and serves to protect persons in all settings in which their freedom of action is curtailed in any significant way from being compelled to incriminate themselves. We have concluded that without proper safeguards the process of in-custody interrogation of persons suspected or accused of crime contains inherently compelling pressures which work to undermine the individual's will to resist and to compel him to speak where he would not otherwise do so freely. In order to combat these pressures and to permit a full opportunity to exercise the privilege against self-incrimination, the accused must be adequately and effectively apprised of his rights and the exercise of those rights must be fully honored.

It is impossible for us to foresee the potential alternatives for protecting the privilege which might be devised by Congress or the States in the exercise of their creative rule-making capacities. Therefore we cannot say that the Constitution necessarily requires adherence to any particular solution for the inherent compulsions of the interrogation process as it is presently conducted. Our decision in no way creates a constitutional straitjacket which will handicap sound efforts at reform, nor is it intended to have this effect. We encourage Congress and the States to continue their laudable search for increasingly effective ways of protecting the rights of the individual while promoting efficient enforcement of our criminal laws. However, unless we are shown other procedures which are at least as effective in apprising accused persons of their right of silence and in assuring a continuous opportunity to exercise it, the following safeguards must be observed.

At the outset, if a person in custody is to be subjected to interrogation, he must first be informed in clear and unequivocal terms that he has the right to remain silent. For those unaware of the privilege, the warning is needed simply to make them aware of it—the threshold requirement for an intelligent decision as to its exercise. More important, such a warning is an absolute prerequisite in overcoming the inherent pressures of the interrogation atmosphere. . . . Further, the warning will show the individual that his interrogators are prepared to recognize his privilege should he choose to exercise it. . . .

The warning of the right to remain silent must be accompanied by the explanation that anything said can and will be used against the individual in court. This warning is needed in order to make him aware not only of the privilege, but also of the consequences of forgoing it. It is only through an awareness of these consequences that there can be any assurance of real understanding and intelligent exercise of the privilege. . . .

[T]he right to have counsel present at the interrogation is indispensable to the protection of the Fifth Amendment privilege under the system we delineate today. Our aim is to assure that the individual's right to choose between silence and speech remains unfettered throughout the interrogation process. . . . Thus, the need for counsel to protect the Fifth Amendment privilege comprehends not merely a right to consult with counsel prior to questioning, but also to have counsel present during any questioning if the defendant so desires. . . .

Accordingly we hold that an individual held for interrogation must be clearly informed that he has the right to consult with a lawyer and to have the lawyer with him during interrogation under the system for protecting the privilege we delineate today. As with the warnings of the right to remain silent and that anything stated can be used in evidence against him, this warning is an absolute prerequisite to interrogation. . . .

In order fully to apprise a person interrogated of the extent of his rights under this system then, it is necessary to warn him not only that he has the right to consult with an attorney, but also that if he is indigent a lawyer will be appointed to represent him. . . . Once warnings have been given, the subsequent procedure is clear. If the individual indicates in any manner, at any time prior to or during questioning, that he wishes to remain silent, the interrogation must cease. . . .

If the interrogation continues without the presence of an attorney and a statement is taken, a heavy burden rests on the government to demonstrate that the defendant knowingly and intelligently waived his privilege against self-incrimination and his right to retained or appointed counsel. This Court has always set high standards of proof for the waiver of constitutional rights, and we reassert these standards as applied to in custody interrogation. . . .

An express statement that the individual is willing to make a statement and does not want an attorney followed closely by a statement could constitute a waiver. But a valid waiver will not be presumed simply from the silence of the accused after warnings are given or simply from the fact that a confession was in fact eventually obtained. . . . The requirement of warnings and waiver of rights is a fundamental with respect to the Fifth Amendment privilege and not simply a preliminary ritual to existing methods of interrogation. . . .

■ [JUSTICE CLARK's dissent is omitted.]

■ MR. JUSTICE HARLAN, whom MR. JUSTICE STEWART and MR. JUSTICE WHITE join, dissenting.

I believe the decision of the Court represents poor constitutional law and entails harmful consequences for the country at large.

At the outset, it is well to note exactly what is required by the Court's new constitutional code of rules for confessions. The foremost requirement, upon which later admissibility of a confession depends, is that a fourfold warning be given to a person in custody before he is questioned, namely, that he has a right to remain silent, that anything he says may be used against him, that he has a right to have present an attorney during the questioning, and that if indigent he has a right to a lawyer without charge. To forgo these rights, some affirmative statement of rejection is seemingly required, and threats, tricks, or cajolings to obtain this waiver are forbidden. If before or during questioning the suspect seeks to invoke his right to remain silent, interrogation must be forgone or cease; a request for counsel brings about the same result until a lawyer is procured. Finally, there are a miscellany of minor directives, for example, the burden of proof of waiver is on the State, admissions and exculpatory statements are treated just like confessions, withdrawal of a waiver is always permitted, and so forth.

While the fine points of this scheme are far less clear than the Court admits, the tenor is quite apparent. The new rules are not designed to guard against police brutality or other unmistakably banned forms of coercion. Those who use third-degree tactics and deny them in court are equally able and destined to lie as skillfully about warnings and waivers. Rather, the thrust of the new rules is to negate all pressures, to reinforce the nervous or ignorant suspect, and ultimately to discourage any confession at all. The aim in short is toward "voluntariness" in a utopian sense, or to view it from a different angle, voluntariness with a vengeance. . . .

The Court's opinion in my view reveals no adequate basis for extending the Fifth Amendment's privilege against self-incrimination to the police station. Far more important, it fails to show that the Court's new rules are well supported, let alone compelled, by Fifth Amendment precedents.

The Court's opening contention, that the Fifth Amendment governs police station confessions, is perhaps not an impermissible extension of the law but it has little to commend itself in the present circumstances. Historically, the privilege against self-incrimination did not bear at all on the use of extra-legal confessions, for which distinct standards evolved. . . .

The more important premise is that pressure on the suspect must be eliminated though it be only the subtle influence of the atmosphere and surroundings. The Fifth Amendment, however, has never been thought to forbid *all* pressure to incriminate one's self in the situations covered by it. . . . The Court appears similarly wrong in thinking that precise knowledge of one's rights is a settled prerequisite under the Fifth Amendment to the loss of its protections. . . .

How much harm this decision will inflict on law enforcement cannot fairly be predicted with accuracy. Evidence on the role of confessions is notoriously incomplete, and little is added by the Court's reference to the FBI experience and the resources believed wasted in interrogation. We do know that some crimes cannot be solved without confessions, that ample expert testimony attests to their importance in crime control, and that the Court is taking a real risk with society's welfare in imposing its new regime on the country. The social costs of crime are too great to call the new rules anything but a hazardous experimentation.

While passing over the costs and risks of its experiment, the Court portrays the evils of normal police questioning in terms which I think are exaggerated. Albeit stringently confined by the due process standards interrogation is no doubt often inconvenient and unpleasant for the suspect. However, it is no less so for a man to be arrested and jailed, to have his house searched, or to stand trial in court, yet all this may properly happen to the most innocent given probable cause, a warrant, or an indictment. Society has always paid a stiff price for law and order, and peaceful interrogation is not one of the dark moments of the law.

This brief statement of the competing considerations seems to me ample proof that the Court's preference is highly debatable at best and therefore not to be read into the Constitution. However, it may make the analysis more graphic to consider the actual facts of one of the four cases reversed by the Court. *Miranda v. Arizona* serves best, being neither the hardest nor easiest of the four under the Court's standards.

On March 3, 1963, an 18-year-old girl was kidnapped and forcibly raped near Phoenix, Arizona. Ten days later, on the morning of March 13, petitioner Miranda was arrested and taken to the police station. At this time Miranda was 23 years old, indigent, and educated to the extent of completing half the ninth grade. He had "an emotional illness" of the schizophrenic type, according to the doctor who eventually examined him; the doctor's report also stated that Miranda was "alert and oriented as to time, place, and person," intelligent within normal limits, competent to stand trial, and sane within the legal definition. At the police station, the victim picked Miranda out of a lineup, and two officers then took him into a separate room to interrogate him, starting about 11:30 a.m. Though at first denying his guilt, within a short time Miranda gave a detailed oral confession and then wrote out in his own hand and signed a brief statement admitting and describing the crime. All this was accomplished in two hours or less without any force, threats or promises and—I will assume this though the record is uncertain—without any effective warnings at all.

Miranda's oral and written confessions are now held inadmissible under the Court's new rules. One is entitled to feel astonished that the Constitution can be read to produce this result. These confessions were obtained during brief, daytime questioning conducted by two officers and unmarked by any of the traditional indicia of coercion. They assured a conviction for a brutal and unsettling crime, for which the police had and quite possibly could obtain little evidence other than the victim's identifications, evidence which is frequently unreliable. There was, in sum, a legitimate purpose, no perceptible unfairness, and certainly little risk of injustice in the interrogation. Yet the resulting confessions, and the responsible course of police practice they represent, are to be sacrificed to the Court's own finespun conception of fairness which I seriously doubt is shared by many thinking citizens in this country. . . .

In conclusion: Nothing in the letter or the spirit of the Constitution or in the precedents squares with the heavy-handed and one-sided action that is so precipitously taken by the Court in the name of fulfilling its constitutional responsibilities. The foray which the Court makes today brings to mind the wise and farsighted words of Mr. Justice Jackson in *Douglas v. Jeannette,* 319 U.S. 157, 181 (separate opinion): "This Court is forever adding new stories to the temples of constitutional law, and the temples have a way of collapsing when one story too many is added."

■ MR. JUSTICE WHITE, with whom MR. JUSTICE HARLAN and MR. JUSTICE STEWART join, dissenting.

. . . First, we may inquire what are the textual and factual bases of this new fundamental rule. To reach the result announced on the grounds it does, the Court must stay within the confines of the Fifth Amendment, which forbids self-incrimination only if *compelled.* Hence the core of the Court's opinion is that because of the "compulsion inherent in custodial surroundings, no statement obtained from (a) defendant (in custody) can truly be the product of his free choice," absent the use of adequate protective devices as described by the Court. . . . Insofar as appears from the Court's opinion, it has not examined a single transcript of any police interrogation, let alone the interrogation that took place in any one of these cases which it decides today. Judged by any of the standards for empirical investigation utilized in the social sciences the factual basis for the Court's premise is patently inadequate.

Although in the Court's view in-custody interrogation is inherently coercive, the Court says that the spontaneous product of the coercion of arrest and detention is still to be deemed voluntary. An accused, arrested on probable cause, may blurt out a confession which will be admissible despite the fact that he is alone and in custody, without any showing that he had any notion of his right to remain silent or of the consequences of his admission. Yet, under the Court's rule, if the police ask him a single question such as "Do you have anything to say?" or "Did you kill your wife?" his response, if there is one, has somehow been compelled, even if the accused has been clearly warned of his right to remain silent. Common sense informs us to the contrary. While one may say that the response was "involuntary" in the sense the question provoked or was the occasion for the response and thus the defendant was induced to speak out when he might have remained silent if not arrested and not questioned, it is patently unsound to say the response is compelled. . . .

If the rule announced today were truly based on a conclusion that all confessions resulting from custodial interrogation are coerced, then it would simply have no rational foundation. . . . [E]ven if one assumed that there was an adequate factual basis for the conclusion that all confessions obtained during in-custody interrogation are the product of compulsion, the rule propounded by the Court will still be irrational, for, apparently, it is only if the accused is also warned of his right to counsel and waives both that right and the right against self-incrimination that the inherent compulsiveness of interrogation disappears. But if the defendant may not answer without a warning a question such as "Where were you last night?" without having his answer be a compelled one, how can the Court ever accept his negative answer to the question of whether he wants to consult his retained counsel or counsel whom the court will appoint? . . .

All of this makes very little sense in terms of the compulsion which the Fifth Amendment proscribes. That amendment deals with compelling the accused himself. It is his free will that is involved. Confessions and incriminating admissions, as such, are not forbidden evidence; only those which are compelled are banned. . . .

In sum, for all the Court's expounding on the menacing atmosphere of police interrogation procedures, it has failed to supply any foundation for the conclusions it draws or the measures it adopts.

Criticism of the Court's opinion, however, cannot stop with a demonstration that the factual and textual bases for the rule it propounds are, at best, less than compelling. Equally relevant is an assessment of the rule's consequences measured against community values. . . .

The most basic function of any government is to provide for the security of the individual and of his property. *Lanzetta v. State of New Jersey*, 306 U.S. 451, 455 (1939). These ends of society are served by the criminal laws which for the most part are aimed at the prevention of crime. Without the reasonably effective performance of the task of preventing private violence and retaliation, it is idle to talk about human dignity and civilized values. . . .

In some unknown number of cases the Court's rule will return a killer, a rapist or other criminal to the streets and to the environment which produced him, to repeat his crime whenever it pleases him. As a consequence, there will not be a gain, but a loss, in human dignity. The real concern is not the unfortunate consequences of this new decision on the criminal law as an abstract, disembodied series of authoritative proscriptions, but the impact on those who rely on the public authority for protection and who without it can only engage in violent self-help with guns, knives and the help of their neighbors similarly inclined. There is, of course, a saving factor: the next victims are uncertain, unnamed and unrepresented in this case. . . .

NOTES

1.   Does the Fifth Amendment privilege against self-incrimination—"nor shall [any person] be compelled in any criminal case to be a witness against himself"—apply to compulsion in a sense other than being required, on pain of legal penalty, to testify against oneself? (That seems to be the sense in which compulsion is understood in the Sixth Amendment, which gives the accused the constitutional right "to have compulsory process for obtaining witnesses in his favor.") *Miranda* is about police interrogation—specifically "custodial" interrogation (a term that has generated its own issues of interpretation), when the suspect is not free to leave the police station or walk away from the officers. It is clear what the Court in *Miranda* was concerned about: the danger that custodial interrogation is where the true action is, and the constitutional right not to testify against oneself is of little value if one has already confessed to the police and signed a written statement of guilt.

Most scholars in this area appear to agree that the privilege was designed to spare the guilty person from the temptation to commit perjury, since a person who committed perjury was understood as evading punishment for the body but at the cost of endangering his soul. See, *e.g.*, Albert W. Alschuler, *A Peculiar Privilege in Historical Perspective: The Right to Remain Silent*, 94 Mich. L. Rev. 2625, 2641–42 (1996) ("The history of the privilege . . . is almost entirely a story of when and for what purposes people would be required to speak under oath."); Akhil Reed Amar, THE CONSTITUTION AND CRIMINAL PROCEDURE 73 (1997) ("Those who framed the Fifth Amendment . . . believed that perjury was a mortal sin, resulting in eternal damnation: better to admit murder than commit perjury under oath.").

Does such an original understanding limit today's interpretation of the Fifth Amendment? *Miranda* was clearly an innovation, based on a perceived important public policy need to control police interrogation practices, in order to protect (some of) the *interests* protected by the Fifth Amendment. Is that justified? If so, what is the limit of what the Court could prescribe in order to protect Fifth Amendment interests?

2.   Even on the narrower, historical reading, the Fifth Amendment is, at its core, a right to remain silent in court, in criminal cases—a right literally not to be compelled to be a witness against oneself in court. Of course, a defendant *may* testify. (Interestingly, for some of the same reasons the constitutional privilege was created, the common law of evidence for many years held that the accused in a criminal case *forbidden* to testify— the accused was disqualified from being a witness. Now, an individual is recognized as having a constitutional right, founded in notions of "due process of law" to testify in his or her own behalf, a right that might also be grounded in the accused's right to "compulsory process" to produce witnesses in his or her favor.) Given that the defendant may testify, if the defendant chooses not to, should the Fifth Amendment be understood to forbid the prosecution from commenting on the defendant's refusal to testify, and inviting the jury to draw what inferences it will from the defendant's choice? See *Griffin v. California*, 380 U.S. 609 (1965) (holding that the Fifth Amendment "forbids either comment by the prosecution on the accused's silence or instructions by the court that such silence is evidence of guilt").

3.   Is the decision in *Miranda* really a constitutional decision? Put another way, does it actually say that the Fifth Amendment itself requires the system of warnings devised by the Court? Or is the case merely a prophylactic rule designed to protect the ability of suspects to make meaningful use of the Fifth Amendment privilege later on down the road? If it is a prophylactic rule rather than constitutionally required one, may Congress legislate a different rule, in effect repudiating *Miranda* by statute? One step further: Does a violation of *Miranda* that is not also a violation of the Fifth Amendment— imagine a purely voluntary confession by a suspect, following a failure of the police to read the defendant his rights—require exclusion of evidence as a remedy? If so, could Congress at least provide for a different remedy for violations of *Miranda*'s prophylactic rule?

These issues were presented in *United States v. Dickerson*, 530 U.S. 428 (2000). In the majority opinion, written by Chief Justice Rehnquist, the Court said:

> In *Miranda v. Arizona*, 384 U.S. 436 (1966), we held that certain warnings must be given before a suspect's statement made during custodial interrogation could be admitted in evidence. [Two years after] that decision, Congress enacted 18 U.S.C. § 3501, which in essence laid down a rule that the admissibility of such statements should turn only on whether or not they were voluntarily made. We hold that *Miranda*, being a constitutional decision of this Court, may not be in effect overruled by an Act of Congress, and we decline to overrule *Miranda* ourselves. We therefore hold that *Miranda* and its progeny in this Court govern the admissibility of statements made during custodial interrogation in both state and federal courts. . . .
>
> Congress may not legislatively supersede our decisions interpreting and applying the Constitution. This case therefore turns on whether the *Miranda* Court announced a constitutional rule or merely exercised its supervisory authority to regulate evidence in the absence of congressional direction. . . .
>
> The *Miranda* opinion itself begins by stating that the Court granted certiorari "to explore some facets of the problems of applying the privilege against self-incrimination to in-custody interrogation, *and to give concrete constitutional guidelines for law enforcement agencies and courts to follow.*" . . .

Additional support for our conclusion that *Miranda* is constitutionally based is found in the *Miranda* Court's invitation for legislative action to protect the constitutional right against coerced self-incrimination. . . .

The dissent argues that it is judicial overreaching for this Court to hold § 3501 unconstitutional unless we hold that the *Miranda* warnings are required by the Constitution, in the sense that nothing else will suffice to satisfy constitutional requirements. But we need not go further than *Miranda* to decide this case. In *Miranda*, the Court noted that reliance on the traditional totality-of-the-circumstances test raised a risk of overlooking an involuntary custodial confession, [a] risk that the Court found unacceptably great when the confession is offered in the case in chief to prove guilt. The Court therefore concluded that something more than the totality test was necessary. . . . Section 3501 therefore cannot be sustained if *Miranda* is to remain the law.

Whether or not we would agree with *Miranda*'s reasoning and its resulting rule, were we addressing the issue in the first instance, the principles of *stare decisis* weigh heavily against overruling it now. We do not think there is such justification for overruling *Miranda*. *Miranda* has become embedded in routine police practice to the point where the warnings have become part of our national culture. While we have overruled our precedents when subsequent cases have undermined their doctrinal underpinnings, we do not believe that this has happened to the *Miranda* decision. If anything, our subsequent cases have reduced the impact of the *Miranda* rule on legitimate law enforcement while reaffirming the decision's core ruling that unwarned statements may not be used as evidence in the prosecution's case in chief. . . .

In sum, we conclude that *Miranda* announced a constitutional rule that Congress may not supersede legislatively. Following the rule of *stare decisis*, we decline to overrule *Miranda* ourselves.

Justice Scalia, joined by Justice Thomas, responded with a strongly worded dissent, including this passage:

Those to whom judicial decisions are an unconnected series of judgments that produce either favored or disfavored results will doubtless greet today's decision as a paragon of moderation, since it declines to overrule *Miranda*. Those who understand the judicial process will appreciate that today's decision is not a reaffirmation of *Miranda*, but a radical revision of the most significant element of *Miranda* (as of all cases): the rationale that gives it a permanent place in our jurisprudence. *Marbury v. Madison* held that an Act of Congress will not be enforced by the courts if what it prescribes violates the Constitution of the United States. That was the basis on which *Miranda* was decided. One will search today's opinion in vain, however, for a statement (surely simple enough to make) that what 18 U.S.C. § 3501 prescribes—the use at trial of a voluntary confession, even when a *Miranda* warning or its equivalent has failed to be given—violates the Constitution. The reason the statement does not appear is not only (and perhaps not so much) that it would be absurd, inasmuch as § 3501 excludes from trial precisely what the Constitution excludes from trial, viz., compelled confessions; but also that Justices whose votes are needed to compose today's majority are on record as believing that a violation of *Miranda* is *not* a violation of the Constitution. And so, to justify today's agreed-upon result, the Court must adopt a significant *new*, if not entirely comprehensible, principle of constitutional law. As the Court chooses to describe that principle, statutes of Congress can be disregarded, not only when what they prescribe violates the Constitution, but when what they prescribe contradicts a decision of this Court that "announced a constitutional rule". . . . [T]he only thing that can possibly mean in the context of this case is that this Court has the power, not merely to apply the Constitution but to expand it, imposing what it regards as useful "prophylactic" restrictions upon Congress and the States. That is an immense and frightening antidemocratic power, and it does not exist.

A NOTE ON OTHER FIFTH AMENDMENT RIGHTS

1.   *The Grand Jury Clause.* The institution of the grand jury was intended as a citizen-check on the exercise of civilian law-enforcement power by government officials to bring serious criminal charges against individuals. But it is a power to check, not to compel: a grand jury may indict a defendant, but it may not require the executive branch to continue the prosecution. *United States v. Cox*, 342 F.2d 167 (5th Cir. 1965) p. 230. Grand juries are typically larger than the juries that decide criminal and civil trials (called "petit juries"), which are guaranteed by the Sixth and Seventh Amendments. The right to indictment by a grand jury has never been held by the Supreme Court to apply to the states through the Fourteenth Amendment.

2.   *The Double Jeopardy Clause.* The Fifth Amendment next provides: "[N]or shall any person be subject for the same offence to be twice put in jeopardy of life or limb." The Double Jeopardy Clause might be thought of as constitutionalizing the law of judgments (i.e., claim and issue preclusion) as applied to criminal proceedings—the original meaning of the term-of-art "life or limb." The Double Jeopardy Clause thus bars a second prosecution for the same offense, following an acquittal in the first proceeding (or where the prosecution has provoked a mistrial). It also forbids a second prosecution for the same offense, following a *conviction* in the first proceeding—it thus forbids double punishment for the same crime. And it forbids retrial of any ultimate fact that was determined in the defendant's favor in a prior criminal proceeding.

But the Double Jeopardy Clause does not apply to non-penal civil proceedings or to successive criminal-civil proceedings. It thus does not bar private-party civil suits against a defendant for damages following acquittal of that person on criminal charges arising out of the same conduct. (Think of O.J. Simpson being sued for wrongful death, following his acquittal on criminal charges for murder.) Nor does the Double Jeopardy Clause bar successive prosecutions (or punishments) by two different governments (two different states, or a state and the federal government) for the same conduct, if each of them has legitimate jurisdiction over the criminal conduct in question, for the reason that they were not the same "party" that maintained the first prosecution (the "dual sovereign" doctrine). *Heath v. Alabama*, 474 U.S. 82 (1985).

Over the years, the Court has waffled over what is a criminal case covered by the Double Jeopardy Clause; fashioned tests for what constitutes the "same offense" within the meaning of the clause; and struggled with when "jeopardy" "attaches" and what the rules should be for appeals, erroneous jury verdicts, and mistrials.

3.   *The Rest of the Fifth Amendment.* Next comes the Self-Incrimination Clause, which has already been considered. It is followed by the Due Process Clause, which is considered at p. 1476, and the Takings Clause, which is considered at p. 1231.

The Sixth Amendment

Amend. VI: In all criminal prosecutions, the accused shall enjoy the right to a speedy and public trial, by an impartial jury of the State and district wherein the crime shall have been committed, which district shall have been previously ascertained by law, and to be informed of the nature and cause of the accusation; to be confronted with the witnesses against him; to have compulsory process for obtaining witnesses in his favor, and to have the Assistance of Counsel for his defense.

The Sixth Amendment protects important procedural trial rights of defendants in criminal cases: the right to trial by jury; the right to counsel; the right to confront the witnesses and evidence against the defendant; and the right to compel the attendance of witnesses supporting the defense. Each of these rights is designed to protect a criminal defendant against unjust conviction resulting from an unfair process. The right to a jury trial without delay, and within the community, was designed to protect the defendant against unjust or unfair prosecution. So too, the right to the assistance of counsel was an invaluable protection against unjust conviction as a result of unequal resources. Finally, the right of a defendant to confront the evidence and witnesses against him is rightly regarded as fundamental to the ability to defend oneself and refute unjust charges; the right of compulsory process is a corollary right to muster the evidence needed on one's own side of the case. That a defendant gets to challenge the evidence, and gets to present opposing evidence, is simply necessary to a fair process honestly directed to producing right outcomes. Uniting the Sixth Amendment's several protections is a concern for the integrity of the criminal trial process and the search for truth. Here we provide notes on the Sixth Amendment, emphasizing the right to counsel.

When does the right to counsel exist—to what cases does it apply, and at what stage of proceedings? Is it a right *not to be prevented* from hiring counsel of one's choice, or is it a right to be *given* counsel if one cannot afford to hire an attorney? And when is an attorney so deficient that the defendant is effectively deprived of "the Assistance of Counsel"? The Court has considered these questions on numerous occasions.

In *Gideon v. Wainwright*, 372 U.S. 335 (1963), a man was charged with breaking and entering a poolroom with intent to commit a misdemeanor. He could not afford legal counsel and asked the court to appoint counsel for him, but under Florida law appointed counsel was available only in capital cases. The defendant represented himself and was convicted; he petitioned for habeas relief "on the ground that the trial court's refusal to appoint counsel for him denied him rights guaranteed by the Constitution and the Bill of Rights by the United States Government." Justice Black wrote the opinion of the Court:

> The Sixth Amendment provides, "In all criminal prosecutions, the accused shall enjoy the right . . . to have the Assistance of Counsel for his defence." We have construed this to mean that in federal courts counsel must be provided for defendants unable to employ counsel unless the right is competently and intelligently waived. [One of our prior cases] argued that this right is extended to indigent defendants in state courts by the Fourteenth Amendment. In response the Court stated that, while the Sixth Amendment laid down "no rule for the conduct of the states, the question

recurs whether the constraint laid by the amendment upon the national courts expresses a rule so fundamental and essential to a fair trial, and so, to due process of law, that it is made obligatory upon the states by the Fourteenth Amendment." . . .

The right of one charged with crime to counsel may not be deemed fundamental and essential to fair trials in some countries, but it is in ours. From the very beginning, our state and national constitutions and laws have laid great emphasis on procedural and substantive safeguards designed to assure fair trials before impartial tribunals in which every defendant stands equal before the law. This noble ideal cannot be realized if the poor man charged with crime has to face his accusers without a lawyer to assist him. A defendant's need for a lawyer is nowhere better stated than in the moving words of Mr. Justice Sutherland in *Powell v. Alabama*: "The right to be heard would be, in many cases, of little avail if it did not comprehend the right to be heard by counsel. Even the intelligent and educated layman . . . requires the guiding hand of counsel at every step in the proceedings against him. Without it, though he be not guilty, he faces the danger of conviction because he does not know how to establish his innocence."

Gideon is celebrated for its fulfillment of the Sixth Amendment's guarantee of the right "to have the Assistance of Counsel." But the provision of counsel might not be enough. Are there circumstances in which a defendant has an attorney, and yet the attorney is so bad that the defendant does not really have "Assistance of Counsel"? The Supreme Court has said *yes*. In *Strickland v. Washington*, 466 U.S. 668 (1984), the Court created the two-pronged modern test for ineffective-assistance-of-counsel claims. First, the defendant must prove that the lawyer was so incompetent as to not constitute the assistance of a lawyer at all; merely substandard performance by the lawyer does not violate the Sixth Amendment, as long as it falls within the broad range of professional competence. Second, the defendant must establish causation: the lawyer's ineptitude must have resulted in a miscarriage of justice. Thus defendants have a high burden of proof to establish a Sixth Amendment ineffective-assistance-of-counsel claim, though not an insurmountable one. E.g., *Burdine v. Johnson*, 262 F.3d 336 (5th Cir. 2001) (defendant successfully argued that he was denied the assistance of counsel when his lawyer slept through portions of his trial and death sentence hearing). Is the right to the effective assistance of counsel explicit in the Sixth Amendment? Is it a prophylactic rule?

A NOTE ON OTHER SIXTH AMENDMENT RIGHTS

1.   *The Compulsory Process Clause.* Immediately preceding the Assistance of Counsel Clause is the clause that provides that the accused has the right to "compulsory process for obtaining witnesses in his favor." This right to compulsory process means also that the defendant has the power, enforced by the legal process, to subpoena and compel the attendance of witnesses. What if a witness refuses to testify—or invokes his own Fifth Amendment right against compelled self-incrimination? For a discussion of this problem, and analysis of the Supreme Court's cases concerning it, see Amar, THE CONSTITUTION AND CRIMINAL PROCEDURE: FIRST PRINCIPLES at 77–88.

2.   *The Confrontation Clause.* This clause protects the right of the accused "to be confronted with the witnesses against him." The Supreme Court, after numerous

doctrinal twists and turns, has finally settled on a reasonably straightforward reading of this provision, tied to its history: the Confrontation Clause "requires that a defendant have the opportunity to confront the witnesses who give testimony against him, except in cases where an exception to the confrontation right was recognized at the time of the founding." *Giles v. California*, 554 U.S. 353, 357 (2008). The central modern case interpreting the Confrontation Clause is *Crawford v. Washington*, 541 U.S. 36 (2004). *Crawford* painstakingly examined the language and history of the clause, and concluded that "the principal evil at which the Confrontation Clause was directed was the civil-law mode of criminal procedure, and particularly its use of *ex parte* examinations as evidence against the accused." It also concluded that "the Framers would not have allowed admission of testimonial statements of a witness who did not appear at trial unless he was unavailable to testify, and the defendant had had a prior opportunity for cross-examination." According to the Court, the Sixth Amendment did not create a balancing test or authorize courts create new exceptions to the confrontation right, but instead it "is most naturally read as a reference to the right of confrontation at common law, admitting only those exceptions established at the time of the founding."

3.   *The Sixth Amendment Right to Trial By Jury.* In a recent series of cases the Court has held that the right to trial by jury means that every fact that forms an element of the offense, or that increases the penalty for a crime beyond what is specified in the statute defining the offense, must be submitted to a jury and proved beyond a reasonable doubt. *Apprendi v. New Jersey*, 530 U.S. 466 (2000). The *Apprendi* approach has upended prior precedents and practice, especially in the area of sentencing. In *Blakely v. Washington*, 542 U.S. 296 (2004), the Court invalidated state sentencing guidelines that required judges to enhance sentences on the basis of facts determined by the judge at sentencing and not by the jury at trial. In *United States v. Booker*, 543 U.S. 220 (2005), the Court invalidated the federal sentencing guidelines for similar reasons, but adopted a complex and confusing remedy for this Sixth Amendment violation.

The Seventh Amendment

Amend. VII: In Suits at common law, where the value in controversy shall exceed twenty dollars, the right of trial by jury shall be preserved, and no fact tried by a jury, shall be otherwise re-examined in any Court of the United States, than according to the rules of the common law.

The Seventh Amendment provides the right to jury trial in *civil* proceedings. Interestingly, it was the absence of a provision for civil jury trial that caught the attention of several delegates to the Constitutional Convention and led to the late-in-the-day proposal that the Constitution include a bill of rights. The Convention rejected the idea, leading some of the delegates—including George Mason of Virginia and Elbridge Gerry of Massachusetts—to decline to sign the proposed Constitution and become leading "Anti-Federalist" opponents in the ratification struggle. (On the Anti-Federalists and their arguments, see p. 32.)

The traditional understanding of the phrase "Suits at common law" is that it refers to those types of civil lawsuits that would have been heard in the courts of "law"—rather than the courts of "equity" (especially the Court of Chancery) or "admiralty"—in the division of judicial authority practiced in England and followed in the American states at the time the Seventh Amendment was adopted in 1791. Since the right to jury trial is "preserved" in such cases, the Supreme Court's interpretation and application of the amendment has followed a historical approach, asking whether a particular lawsuit is of the type that would have been heard in

England's law courts in 1791 (even though today law and equity have merged in the federal system and most state systems). Note that the amendment applies only to suits where "the value in controversy shall exceed twenty dollars." Is the Seventh Amendment indexed to inflation? See Note, *The Twenty Dollars Clause*, 118 Harv. L. Rev. 1665, 1672 (2005) (rejecting the notion that the "value" of "twenty dollars" permits inflation-adjustment over time).

The central question for interpreting the amendment is what "shall be preserved" means. Does "preserved" mean the right to a civil jury trial includes all the incidents of trial by jury as they existed in 1791? What were those incidents? Must a jury have twelve—and exactly twelve—members? May changes in procedure change the scope of the right—or is that exactly what the Seventh Amendment bars? Or, given that the Bill of Rights was designed to limit the power of only the *national* government, does "preserved" mean that if a jury trial right would have existed on some issue *in state court* that the fact that the case might have ended up in federal court (say, by virtue of diversity jurisdiction) should not alter the existence of a right to trial by jury? In other words, does "preserved" have a *historical* law-versus-equity meaning or a *federalism* meaning? There is some evidence from the founding for both views. See Ann Woolhandler & Michael G. Collins, *The Article III Jury*, 87 Va. L. Rev. 587, 612–615 (2001). Nevertheless, early in the history of the United States, Justice Story sided with the historical understanding of the Seventh Amendment. See *United States v. Wonson*, 28 F. Cas. 745, 750 (C.C.D. Mass. 1812) (Story, J.) ("Beyond all question, the common law here alluded to is not the common law of any individual state, (for it probably differs in all), but it is the common law of England, the grand reservoir of all our jurisprudence."). That conclusion has become settled in the case law.

Finally, the Seventh Amendment contains an anti-circumvention rule forbidding courts from re-examining facts found by a jury other than in accordance with the rules of the common law (which sometimes permitted judges to take cases from the jury, by directed verdict or judgment notwithstanding the verdict). Do "the rules of the common law" evolve—and thus the meaning and scope of the no-re-examination rule potentially change? Or are they fixed by 1791 practice?

The Eighth Amendment

> *Amend. VIII: Excessive bail shall not be required, nor excessive fines imposed, nor cruel and unusual punishments inflicted.*

By its terms, the Eighth Amendment appears to embrace general standards for punishments more than bright-line rules. It speaks of "excessive" bail, "excessive" fines, and "cruel and unusual" punishments. These terms raise a number of questions. Are their contents fixed at the founding? (Or, when applied against the states, is the content of these terms fixed in 1868?) Or are they meant to vary over time, as views of what is "excessive" or "cruel and unusual" vary—what if fines once thought to be excessive, and punishments once thought to be cruel and unusual, become routinely used?

For the Cruel and Unusual Punishments Clause, a threshold question is the meaning of each term. Start with a puzzle: What sense would it make to prohibit cruel punishments if they are rare but not if they are widely used? The answer appears to lie in the use of "unusual" as a term of art at the founding. It meant "contrary to long usage" or "contrary to immemorial usage," which in the context of the Eighth Amendment would mean that it refers to punishments that are departures from traditional practice. See John F. Stinneford, *The Original Meaning of "Unusual": The Eighth Amendment as a Bar to Cruel Innovation*, 102 Nw. U. L. Rev. 1739 (2008).

And what is "cruel"? Is the best approach to look to historical practice at the time of the amendment's adoption and use that practice as a baseline for what is excessive or cruel? For example, if the death penalty, or putting someone in the stocks, or branding, was not regarded as a forbidden practice in 1791, should it be possible for such a practice later to be regarded as unconstitutional under the Eighth Amendment? Or should the question be what seemed excessive or cruel in 1868, when the Fourteenth Amendment was ratified? (Almost all so-called Eighth Amendment cases involve state laws.) If a court takes a more historical approach, how should it try to determine what was excessive or cruel in 1791 or 1868? Or should what is "cruel" be determined by the standards of present legislative enactments around the country? Should it be determined by the conscience of the individual judge? Is all punishment cruel, in a sense?

And what is the relationship of the two terms? Must a punishment be both "cruel" and "unusual" to be unconstitutional? Or should the terms be seen as a unit (technically, a *hendiadys*), meaning something like "contrary to long usage *in their cruelty*"? If the latter understanding is right, then the clause would prohibit not all new punishments, nor all cruel punishments, but rather ones that are new in their cruelty.

The relationship of the terms raises one more big question about the meaning of the clause. What kind of judicial role does it suggest? There is a way to answer the preceding questions that suggests that the Supreme Court should be a *pathfinder*, leading the country toward a more refined and more just understanding of punishment. On this view, one might determine what is "cruel and unusual" by looking to present-day enactments of legislatures. The Court could then hold unconstitutional the punishments that are practiced in only a few states. If one expects punishment practices to be ameliorated, lessening in severity over time, then the Court could use the Eighth Amendment to "modernize" punishment in the United States, bringing up the straggler jurisdictions as the whole country moves forward together. That understanding does explain many recent cases in the Supreme Court, especially cases that count the number of states that use a particular punishment and use that metric to determine whether it is constitutional. See David A. Strauss, *The Modernizing Mission of Judicial Review*, 76 U. Chi. L. Rev. 859 (2009); see also Corinna Barrett Lain, *Lessons Learned from the Evolution of "Evolving Standards*," 4 Charleston L. Rev. 661 (2010).

But an alternative understanding is also possible. One could see the judicial role under the Eighth Amendment more in terms of *pathblocking*. What if the concern behind the amendment was that society might grow more punitive and vindictive, especially in times of crisis? Indeed, there is evidence that the Anti-Federalists who called for what became our Eighth Amendment had exactly this problem in mind. For example, in the Massachusetts convention called to ratify the U.S. Constitution, Abraham Holmes warned that under the Constitution—remember it had no Bill of Rights yet—Congress would be "nowhere restrained from inventing the most cruel and unheard-of punishments, and annexing them to crimes." 2 THE DEBATES IN THE

SEVERAL STATE CONVENTIONS ON THE ADOPTION OF THE FEDERAL CONSTITUTION, 109–11 (Jonathan Elliot ed. 2d ed. 1891). On this understanding, the amendment would not be so much a way of ensuring progress, as a way of preventing regress.

How should an interpreter decide between these two ways of thinking about the clause? Have our punishment practices grown more lenient? One could say *yes*, thinking about the eradication of gory punishments like cutting off the hand of a thief. One could also say *no*, thinking about innovations in punishment adopted throughout American history—prisons, solitary confinement, travel and residence restrictions on sex offenders, exacting court costs from criminal defendants (even acquitted ones) through the use of fines, and so on. What answer(s) would be suggested by the five types of constitutional argument (p. 42)?

Only one punishment has been the focus of the last several decades of Eighth Amendment cases in the Supreme Court: the death penalty. In *Furman v. Georgia*, 409 U.S. 902 (1972), the Supreme Court determined that the death penalty, as it was then applied, was random and unpredictable and therefore amounted to cruel and unusual punishment under the Eighth Amendment—"cruel and unusual in the same way that being struck by lightning is cruel and unusual." But then, in *Gregg v. Georgia*, 428 U.S. 153 (1976), the Supreme Court retreated and lifted what had in effect been a moratorium on the death penalty. The Court upheld the use of the death penalty where the jury is required to find a statutorily prescribed aggravating factor and given guidance in the exercise of its discretion. Since *Furman* and *Gregg*, the Supreme Court has decided capital punishment cases by trying to assess "the evolving standards of decency that mark a maturing society." The Supreme Court often tallies state laws to see, for a particular category of cases, whether the death penalty is widely endorsed, and whether recent trends have been favorable or unfavorable. And it sometimes considers how the death penalty is used outside the United States. See, e.g., *Roper v. Simmons*, 543 U.S. 551 (2005) (holding, 5–4, that capital punishment for a juvenile offender is "cruel and unusual"); *Kennedy v. Louisiana*, 554 U.S. 407, 422–34 (2008), as modified (Oct. 1, 2008), opinion modified on denial of reh'g (holding, 5–4, that capital punishment for raping a child is "cruel and unusual"); *Hall v. Florida*, 134 S.Ct. 1986 (2014) (holding, 5–4, that a Florida rule, which treated criminal defendants with an IQ over 70 as being not intellectually disabled, created too great a risk that capital punishment would be applied in circumstances in which it was "cruel and unusual"); but cf. *Glossip v. Gross*, 135 S.Ct. 2726 (2015) (holding, 5–4, that prisoners challenging the use of a certain mixture of drugs for lethal injection had failed to show that it was "cruel and unusual").

The Court has also restricted the punishments of minors, invoking the Cruel and Unusual Punishments Clause. See *Graham v. Florida*, 560 U.S. 48, 80–82 (2010), as modified (July 6, 2010) (holding, 6–3, that a sentence of life in prison without parole, for a juvenile offender who did not commit murder, is "cruel and unusual"); *Miller v. Alabama*, 132 S.Ct. 2455 (2012) (holding, 5–4, that a mandatory sentence of life in prison without parole, for a juvenile offender, is "cruel and unusual").

Outside of capital punishment, with the exception of juvenile offenders, the Court has generally not found punishments to be in violation of the Eighth Amendment. See, e.g., *Ewing v. California*, 538 U.S. 11 (2003) (holding, 5–4, that the application of California's "three strikes" law, in a case in which the defendant stole golf clubs and received a sentence of between twenty-five years in prison and life in prison, was not "cruel and unusual").

Reflect on the big-picture constitutional issue: What is the proper understanding of the term "cruel and unusual punishment"? What does each term mean? How do they work together? And what conception of the judicial role is implied by the answers to these questions?

[*Assignment 61*]

V. THE TAKINGS CLAUSE

> *Amend V: . . . nor shall private property be taken for public use, without just compensation.*

The original Constitution protected property rights in a number of ways. These included structural provisions designed to ensure the rule of law, such as representative government, separation of powers, and federalism. In addition, the Contracts Clause of Article I, Section 10 provided some protection against state interference with vested contractual obligations, an important safeguard of property.

Property rights gained additional protection against federal interference with the ratification of the Bill of Rights. The first ten amendments contain several provisions that pertain to property, including the Fourth Amendment and two provisions of the Fifth Amendment: the Due Process Clause, which is considered at p. 1476; and the Takings Clause, which is addressed here.

What Is a "Taking" of Property for a Public Use?

The Fifth Amendment requires the government to pay for property it acquires for public uses, such as post offices, roads, parks, office buildings, or military bases. Often these transactions are consensual, and raise no constitutional issues at all. But when the government uses its power of eminent domain to take private property, the Fifth Amendment requires that the owner receive "just compensation." In such cases, the government files a "condemnation" action against the property holder, and the amount of compensation is determined by the fact finder, usually a jury.

In these classic cases of condemnation, the Fifth Amendment is essentially self-enforcing and rarely requires interpretation or judicial enforcement. But there are a number of contexts in which the government takes action short of condemnation that has the practical effect of converting private property to a public use. When this happens, the property owner is the one who files suit for compensation, and the case is called an "inverse condemnation" action. These cases raise the question of what is a "taking."

One scenario is for the government to permanently take over part of the property, even if it does not formally condemn it or acquire formal title. For instance, the City of New York required owners of apartment buildings to permit cable television companies to install cables on their property. In *Loretto v. Teleprompter Manhattan CATV Corp.*, 458 U.S. 419 (1982), the Court held that this was a taking because it was "a permanent physical occupation authorized by government."

Apart from permanent physical invasions, a particularly common scenario is that the government imposes legal restrictions that reduce the value of the property to its owner, even though the property is not actually occupied by the government or members of the public. These are generally called "regulatory takings." How does the Takings Clause apply to such actions? Consider the following major case.

Pennsylvania Coal Co. v. Mahon
260 U.S. 393 (1922)

■ MR. JUSTICE HOLMES delivered the opinion of the Court.

This is a bill in equity brought by the defendants in error to prevent the Pennsylvania Coal Company from mining under their property in such way as to remove the supports and cause a subsidence of the surface and of their house. The bill sets out a deed executed by the Coal Company in 1878, under which the plaintiffs claim. The deed conveys the surface but in express terms reserves the right to remove all the coal under the same and the grantee takes the premises with the risk and waives all claim for damages that may arise from mining out the coal. But the plaintiffs say that whatever may have been the Coal Company's rights, they were taken away by an Act of Pennsylvania, approved May 27, 1921 (P. L. 1198), commonly known there as the Kohler Act. . . .

The statute forbids the mining of anthracite coal in such way as to cause the subsidence of . . . any structure used as a human habitation, with certain exceptions, including among them land where the surface is owned by the owner of the underlying coal and is distant more than one hundred and fifty feet from any improved property belonging to any other person. As applied to this case the statute is admitted to destroy previously existing rights of property and contract. The question is whether the police power can be stretched so far.

Government hardly could go on if to some extent values incident to property could not be diminished without paying for every such change in the general law. As long recognized some values are enjoyed under an implied limitation and must yield to the police power. But obviously the implied limitation must have its limits or the contract and due process clauses are gone. One fact for consideration in determining such limits is the extent of the diminution. When it reaches a certain magnitude, in most if not in all cases there must be an exercise of eminent domain and compensation to sustain the act. So the question depends upon the particular facts. The greatest weight is given to the judgment of the legislature but it always is open to interested parties to contend that the legislature has gone beyond its constitutional power.

This is the case of a single private house. No doubt there is a public interest even in this, as there is in every purchase and sale and in all that happens within the commonwealth. Some existing rights may be modified even in such a case. But usually in ordinary private affairs the public interest does not warrant much of this kind of interference. A source of damage to such a house is not a public nuisance even if similar damage is inflicted on others in different places. The damage is not common or public. The extent of the public interest is shown by the statute to be limited, since the statute ordinarily does not apply to land when the surface is owned by the owner of the coal. Furthermore, it is not justified as a protection of personal safety. That could be provided for by notice. Indeed the very foundation of this bill is that the defendant gave timely notice of its intent to mine under the house. On the other hand the extent of the taking is great. It purports to abolish what is recognized in

Pennsylvania as an estate in land—a very valuable estate—and what is declared by the Court below to be a contract hitherto binding the plaintiffs. If we were called upon to deal with the plaintiffs' position alone we should think it clear that the statute does not disclose a public interest sufficient to warrant so extensive a destruction of the defendant's constitutionally protected rights. . . .

The general rule at least is that while property may be regulated to a certain extent, if regulation goes too far it will be recognized as a taking. . . . In general it is not plain that a man's misfortunes or necessities will justify his shifting the damages to his neighbor's shoulders. We are in danger of forgetting that a strong public desire to improve the public condition is not enough to warrant achieving the desire by a shorter cut than the constitutional way of paying for the change. As we already have said this is a question of degree—and therefore cannot be disposed of by general propositions. But we regard this as going beyond any of the cases decided by this Court. . . .

We assume, of course, that the statute was passed upon the conviction that an exigency existed that would warrant it, and we assume that an exigency exists that would warrant the exercise of eminent domain. But the question at bottom is upon whom the loss of the changes desired should fall. So far as private persons or communities have seen fit to take the risk of acquiring only surface rights, we cannot see that the fact that their risk has become a danger warrants the giving to them greater rights than they bought.

■ MR. JUSTICE BRANDEIS dissenting.

. . . Coal in place is land, and the right of the owner to use his land is not absolute. He may not so use it as to create a public nuisance, and uses, once harmless, may, owing to changed conditions, seriously threaten the public welfare. Whenever they do, the Legislature has power to prohibit such uses without paying compensation; and the power to prohibit extends alike to the manner, the character and the purpose of the use. Are we justified in declaring that the Legislature of Pennsylvania has, in restricting the right to mine anthracite, exercised this power so arbitrarily as to violate the Fourteenth Amendment?

Every restriction upon the use of property imposed in the exercise of the police power deprives the owner of some right theretofore enjoyed, and is, in that sense, an abridgment by the state of rights in property without making compensation. But restriction imposed to protect the public health, safety or morals from dangers threatened is not a taking. The restriction here in question is merely the prohibition of a noxious use. The property so restricted remains in the possession of its owner. The state does not appropriate it or make any use of it. The state merely prevents the owner from making a use which interferes with paramount rights of the public. Whenever the use prohibited ceases to be noxious—as it may because of further change in local or social conditions—the restriction will have to be removed and the owner will again be free to enjoy his property as heretofore. . . .

It is said that one fact for consideration in determining whether the limits of the police power have been exceeded is the extent of the resulting diminution in value, and that here the restriction destroys existing rights of property and contract. But values are relative. If we are to consider the value of the coal kept in place by the restriction, we should compare it with the value of all other parts of the land. . . . But I suppose no one would contend that by selling his interest above 100 feet from the surface he could prevent the state from limiting, by the police power, the height of structures in a city. And why should a sale of underground rights bar the state's power? For aught that appears the value of the coal kept in place by the restriction may be negligible as compared with the value of the whole property, or even as compared with that part of it which is represented by the coal remaining in place and which may be extracted despite the statute. Ordinarily a police regulation, general in operation, will not be held void as to a particular property, although proof is offered that owing to conditions peculiar to it the restriction could not reasonably be applied. But even if the particular facts are to govern, the statute should, in my opinion be upheld in this case. For the defendant has failed to adduce any evidence from which it appears that to restrict its mining operations was an unreasonable exercise of the police power. . . .

NOTES

1.   When the surface owner purchased the right to use and build upon the surface estate, the coal company explicitly reserved the right to mine all the coal, and the surface owner assumed the risk from subsidence. Why should the state now deny the purchaser the benefit of the contract? Note that the Kohler Act is not a generally applicable environmental statute; it does not apply where surface rights and mineral rights are owned by the same person. Should this be framed as a case under the Takings Clause of the Fifth Amendment or under the Contracts Clause of Article I, Section 10?

2.   What is the majority's test for when a regulation amounts to a regulatory taking? Is it when the regulation "goes too far"? In *Penn Central Transportation Co. v. City of New York*, 438 U.S. 104 (1978), the Court elaborated:

> The question of what constitutes a "taking" for purposes of the Fifth Amendment has proved to be a problem of considerable difficulty. While this Court has recognized that the "Fifth Amendment's guarantee . . . [is] designed to bar Government from forcing some people alone to bear public burdens which, in all fairness and justice, should be borne by the public as a whole," *Armstrong v. United States*, 364 U.S. 40, 49 (1960), this Court, quite simply, has been unable to develop any "set formula" for determining when "justice and fairness" require that economic injuries caused by public action be compensated by the government, rather than remain disproportionately concentrated on a few persons. Indeed, we have frequently observed that whether a particular restriction will be rendered invalid by the government's failure to pay for any losses proximately caused by it depends largely "upon the particular circumstances [in that] case." *United States v. Central Eureka Mining Co.*, 357 U.S. 155, 168 (1958).
>
> In engaging in these essentially ad hoc, factual inquiries, the Court's decisions have identified several factors that have particular significance. The economic impact of the regulation on the claimant and, particularly, the extent to which the regulation has interfered with distinct investment-backed expectations are, of course, relevant considerations. So, too, is the character of the governmental action. A "taking" may more readily be found when the interference with property can be characterized as a physical invasion by government, than when interference arises from some public program adjusting the benefits and burdens of economic life to promote the common good.

Id. at 123–24. Does this clarify when a regulatory taking exists?

In subsequent decisions, the Court has held that a regulation that deprives the owner of substantially all of the economic benefit of the property is a per se regulatory taking. Regulations depriving the owner of only a portion of the economic value, however, are subject to the deferential multi-factor test of *Penn Central*. This may appear to reduce the degree to which the inquiry is ad hoc, but it presents a daunting question: substantially all of *what*? If a property owner has a thousand-acre parcel, and the government requires him or her to maintain one hundred acres as a wetlands, should this be seen as taking "substantially" all the value of the one hundred acres, or as taking only ten percent of the entire parcel?

3.   Justice Brandeis distinguishes between governmental actions that prevent a "noxious use" of property and those that "appropriate" or "make use" of the property on behalf of the public. Is that a tenable distinction? Under the state law in *Pennsylvania Coal*, was the public protected from the "harm" of subsidence, or was the public given the "use" and benefit of support? If a city passes zoning rules to block additional development in an overcrowded area, should those rules be regarded as preventing the "harm" of future development, or seizing the "benefit" of open space for the public? Can you think of cases where the distinction is more clear-cut? For a defense of the harm-benefit distinction, see Jed Rubenfeld, *Usings*, 102 Yale L.J. 1077 (1993). Rubenfeld emphasizes that the Fifth Amendment requires compensation only for takings "for a public use" and not for actions that diminish value or prevent harm to others.

In *Lucas v. South Carolina Coastal Council*, 505 U.S. 1003 (1992), a divided Court rejected a generalized harm principle in favor of a narrower principle grounded in common law principles of nuisance. Because all property is held subject to the common law of nuisance, which prevents use of property in ways that harm others, state regulatory laws that do no more than enforce these nuisance principles (or make them explicit) do not "take" anything that the property holder ever really had. The prohibited use was "always unlawful." *Id.*, at 1027. Does this mean (should it mean?) the common law of nuisance as it existed in the nineteenth century, or as state courts may fashion it today? Why is it not true that owners hold their property subject to the possibility that the state will discover and prohibit new forms of harm? In *Mugler v. Kansas*, 123 U.S. 623 (1887), the legislature had outlawed the manufacture and sale of alcohol, substantially destroying the economic value of a brewery. Was the brewery owner entitled to compensation?

What Is a Taking of "Property" for a Public Use?

The protections of the Takings Clause apply only to property. But what is that? In most cases, this part of the clause is straightforward. "Property interests . . . are not created by the Constitution. Rather, they are created and their dimensions are defined by existing rules or understandings that stem from an independent source such as state law." *Board of Regents v. Roth*, 408 U.S. 564, 577 (1972). But is there a fundamental constitutional core, which if not respected by the state, constitutes a taking? See Thomas W. Merrill, *The Landscape of Constitutional Property*, 86 Va. L. Rev. 885 (2000).

Consider a few wrinkles: When there are competing claimants to a fund or other property, the conflict is often resolved by means of an interpleader action, in which the fund or property is deposited with the clerk of the court, and the court then determines who is the proper owner. Who owns the *interest* on the fund during the time it is deposited with the court? In *Webb's Fabulous Pharmacies v. Beckwith*, 449 U.S. 155 (1980), the state of Florida declared that the interest on interpleader accounts was "public money" because the court clerk was under no legal obligation to invest the fund while it was under court control, and if the clerk did so, "the statute takes only what it creates." The Supreme Court reversed, holding:

> Neither the Florida Legislature by statute, nor the Florida courts by judicial decree, may accomplish the result the county seeks simply by recharacterizing the principal as "public money" because it is held temporarily by the court. The earnings of a fund are incidents of ownership of the fund itself and are property just as the fund itself is property. The state statute has the practical effect of appropriating for the county the value of the use of the fund for the period in which it is held in the registry.

> To put it another way: a State, by *ipse dixit*, may not transform private property into public property without compensation, even for the limited duration of the deposit in court. This is the very kind of thing that the Taking Clause of the Fifth Amendment was meant to prevent. That Clause stands as a shield against the arbitrary use of governmental power.

What is the difference between *ipse dixit* and ordinary common law adjudication? Is the principle that "[t]he earnings of a fund are incidents of ownership of the fund itself and are property just as the fund itself is property" a constitutional principle? If so, from what is it derived?

What if the state piles sand in front of a beach-front house as part of an erosion-reversal project? May the state legislature now "recharacterize" the ownership interests in the strip between dry beach and ocean to make it public property? How would that differ from the state statute in *Webb's*? May the same recharacterizing be done not by the legislature by the state supreme court? Does the answer depend on whether the state court decision applied the law or changed it? But doesn't a common law court have authority to change the common law? These questions were raised in *Stop the Beach Renourishment, Inc. v. Florida Department of Environmental Protection*, 560 U.S. 702 (2010), though the Court chose not to decide whether a judicial decision can be a "taking" that requires the payment of compensation under the Takings Clause. (Four justices would have held that there can be judicial takings, but others did not think the question essential to the decision.)

What Is a Taking of Property for a "Public Use"?

The Fifth Amendment has been interpreted to require all takings of property to be "for a public use," even if there is compensation. What counts as a public use? Must the property be owned by the government and kept forever without being sold? If the government does not have to keep the property, then what does "public use" mean? Anything the government wants? May the government use the eminent domain power to take property from one person, for the benefit of another person or entity, presumably one that is more politically "juiced"?

Kelo v. New London
545 U.S. 469 (2005)

■ JUSTICE STEVENS delivered the opinion of the Court.

In 2000, the city of New London approved a development plan that, in the words of the Supreme Court of Connecticut, was "projected to create in excess of 1,000 jobs, to increase tax and other revenues, and to revitalize an economically distressed city, including its downtown and waterfront areas." In assembling the land needed for this project, the city's development agent has purchased property from willing sellers and proposes to use the power of eminent domain to acquire the remainder of the property from unwilling owners in exchange for just compensation. The question presented is whether the city's proposed disposition of this property qualifies as a "public use" within the meaning of the Takings Clause of the Fifth Amendment to the Constitution.

I

The city of New London (hereinafter City) sits at the junction of the Thames River and the Long Island Sound in southeastern Connecticut. Decades of economic decline led a state agency in 1990 to designate the City a "distressed municipality." . . .

These conditions prompted state and local officials to target New London, and particularly its Fort Trumbull area, for economic revitalization. To this end, respondent New London Development Corporation (NLDC), a private nonprofit entity established some years earlier to assist the City in planning economic development, was reactivated. In January 1998, the State authorized a $5.35 million bond issue to support the NLDC's planning activities and a $10 million bond issue toward the creation of a Fort Trumbull State Park. In February, the pharmaceutical company Pfizer Inc. announced that it would build a $300 million research facility on a site immediately adjacent to Fort Trumbull; local planners hoped that Pfizer would draw new business to the area, thereby serving as a catalyst to the area's rejuvenation. . . .

The Fort Trumbull area is situated on a peninsula that juts into the Thames River. The area comprises approximately 115 privately owned properties, as well as the 32 acres of land formerly occupied by the naval facility (Trumbull State Park now occupies 18 of those 32 acres). The development plan encompasses seven parcels. Parcel 1 is designated for a waterfront conference hotel at the center of a "small urban village" that will include restaurants and shopping. This parcel will also have marinas for both recreational and commercial uses. A pedestrian "riverwalk" will originate here and continue down the coast, connecting the waterfront areas of the development. Parcel 2 will be the site of approximately 80 new residences organized into an urban neighborhood and linked by public walkway to the remainder of the development, including the state park. This parcel also includes space reserved for a new U.S. Coast Guard Museum. Parcel 3, which is located immediately north of the Pfizer facility, will contain at least 90,000 square feet of research and development office space. Parcel 4A is a 2.4-acre site that will be used either to support the adjacent state park, by providing parking or retail services for visitors, or to support the nearby marina. Parcel 4B will include a renovated marina, as well as the final stretch of the riverwalk. Parcels 5, 6, and 7 will provide land for office and retail space, parking, and water-dependent commercial uses.

The NLDC intended the development plan to capitalize on the arrival of the Pfizer facility and the new commerce it was expected to attract. In addition to creating jobs, generating tax revenue, and helping to "build momentum for the revitalization of downtown New London," the plan was also designed to make the

City more attractive and to create leisure and recreational opportunities on the waterfront and in the park.

The city council approved the plan in January 2000, and designated the NLDC as its development agent in charge of implementation. The city council also authorized the NLDC to purchase property or to acquire property by exercising eminent domain in the City's name. The NLDC successfully negotiated the purchase of most of the real estate in the 90-acre area, but its negotiations with petitioners failed. As a consequence, in November 2000, the NLDC initiated the condemnation proceedings that gave rise to this case.

II

Petitioner Susette Kelo has lived in the Fort Trumbull area since 1997. She has made extensive improvements to her house, which she prizes for its water view. Petitioner Wilhelmina Dery was born in her Fort Trumbull house in 1918 and has lived there her entire life. Her husband Charles (also a petitioner) has lived in the house since they married some 60 years ago. In all, the nine petitioners own 15 properties in Fort Trumbull—4 in parcel 3 of the development plan and 11 in parcel 4A. Ten of the parcels are occupied by the owner or a family member; the other five are held as investment properties. There is no allegation that any of these properties is blighted or otherwise in poor condition; rather, they were condemned only because they happen to be located in the development area. . . .

III

Two polar propositions are perfectly clear. On the one hand, it has long been accepted that the sovereign may not take the property of *A* for the sole purpose of transferring it to another private party *B,* even though *A* is paid just compensation. On the other hand, it is equally clear that a State may transfer property from one private party to another if future "use by the public" is the purpose of the taking; the condemnation of land for a railroad with common-carrier duties is a familiar example. Neither of these propositions, however, determines the disposition of this case.

As for the first proposition, the City would no doubt be forbidden from taking petitioners' land for the purpose of conferring a private benefit on a particular private party. Nor would the City be allowed to take property under the mere pretext of a public purpose, when its actual purpose was to bestow a private benefit. The takings before us, however, would be executed pursuant to a "carefully considered" development plan. . . . [T]he City's development plan was not adopted "to benefit a particular class of identifiable individuals."

On the other hand, this is not a case in which the City is planning to open the condemned land—at least not in its entirety—to use by the general public. Nor will the private lessees of the land in any sense be required to operate like common carriers, making their services available to all comers. But although such a projected use would be sufficient to satisfy the public use requirement, this "Court long ago rejected any literal requirement that condemned property be put into use for the general public." Indeed, while many state courts in the mid-19th century endorsed "use by the public" as the proper definition of public use, that narrow view steadily eroded over time. Not only was the "use by the public" test difficult to administer (*e.g.,* what proportion of the public need have access to the property? at what price?), but it proved to be impractical given the diverse and always evolving needs of society.

Accordingly, when this Court began applying the Fifth Amendment to the States at the close of the 19th century, it embraced the broader and more natural interpretation of public use as "public purpose." . . . Without exception, our cases have defined that concept broadly, reflecting our longstanding policy of deference to legislative judgments in this field.

In *Berman v. Parker,* 348 U.S. 26 (1954), this Court upheld a redevelopment plan targeting a blighted area of Washington, D. C., in which most of the housing for the area's 5,000 inhabitants was beyond repair. . . . The owner of a department store located in the area challenged the condemnation, pointing out that his store was not itself blighted and arguing that the creation of a "better balanced, more attractive community" was not a valid public use. Writing for a unanimous Court, Justice Douglas refused to evaluate this claim in isolation, deferring instead to the legislative and agency judgment that the area "must be planned as a whole" for the plan to be successful. . . .

In *Hawaii Housing Authority v. Midkiff,* 467 U.S. 229 (1984), the Court considered a Hawaii statute whereby fee title was taken from lessors and transferred to lessees (for just compensation) in order to reduce the concentration of land ownership. We unanimously upheld the statute and rejected the Ninth Circuit's view that it was "a naked attempt on the part of the state of Hawaii to take the property of A and transfer it to B solely for B's private use and benefit." Reaffirming *Berman*'s deferential approach to legislative judgments in this field, we concluded that the State's purpose of eliminating the "social and economic evils of a land oligopoly" qualified as a valid public use. Our opinion also rejected the contention that the mere fact that the State immediately transferred the properties to private individuals upon condemnation somehow diminished the public character of the taking. "[I]t is only the taking's purpose, and not its mechanics," we explained, that matters in determining public use. . . .

Viewed as a whole, our jurisprudence has recognized that the needs of society have varied between different parts of the Nation, just as they have evolved over time in response to changed circumstances. Our earliest cases in particular embodied a strong theme of federalism, emphasizing the "great respect" that we owe to state legislatures and state courts in discerning local public needs. For more than a century, our public use jurisprudence has wisely eschewed rigid formulas and intrusive scrutiny in favor of affording legislatures broad latitude in determining what public needs justify the use of the takings power.

IV

Those who govern the City were not confronted with the need to remove blight in the Fort Trumbull area, but their determination that the area was sufficiently distressed to justify a program of economic rejuvenation is entitled to our deference. The City has carefully formulated an economic development plan that it believes will provide appreciable benefits to the community, including—but by no means limited to—new jobs and increased tax revenue. . . . Given the comprehensive character of the plan, the thorough deliberation that preceded its adoption, and the limited scope of our review, it is appropriate for us, as it was in *Berman,* to resolve the challenges of the individual owners, not on a piecemeal basis, but rather in light of the entire plan. Because that plan unquestionably serves a public purpose, the takings challenged here satisfy the public use requirement of the Fifth Amendment. . . .

In affirming the City's authority to take petitioners' properties, we do not minimize the hardship that condemnations may entail, notwithstanding the payment of just compensation. We emphasize that nothing in our opinion precludes any State from placing further restrictions on its exercise of the takings power. Indeed, many States already impose "public use" requirements that are stricter than the federal baseline. Some of these requirements have been established as a matter of state constitutional law, while others are expressed in state eminent domain statutes that carefully limit the grounds upon which takings may be exercised. As the submissions of the parties and their *amici* make clear, the necessity and wisdom of using eminent domain to promote economic development are certainly matters of legitimate public debate. This Court's authority, however, extends only to determining whether the City's proposed condemnations are for a "public use" within the meaning of the Fifth Amendment to the Federal Constitution. Because over a century of our case law interpreting that provision dictates an affirmative answer to that question, we may not grant petitioners the relief that they seek. . . .

■ JUSTICE KENNEDY, concurring.

I join the opinion for the Court and add these further observations. . . .

A court applying rational-basis review under the Public Use Clause should strike down a taking that, by a clear showing, is intended to favor a particular private party, with only incidental or pretextual public benefits, just as a court applying rational-basis review under the Equal Protection Clause must strike down a government classification that is clearly intended to injure a particular class of private parties, with only incidental or pretextual public justifications. . . .

■ JUSTICE O'CONNOR, with whom THE CHIEF JUSTICE, JUSTICE SCALIA, and JUSTICE THOMAS join, dissenting.

Over two centuries ago, just after the Bill of Rights was ratified, Justice Chase wrote:

> An ACT of the Legislature (for I cannot call it a law) contrary to the great first principles of the social compact, cannot be considered a rightful exercise of legislative authority. . . . A few instances will suffice to explain what I mean. . . . [A] law that takes property from A. and gives it to B: It is against all reason and justice, for a people to entrust a Legislature with SUCH powers; and, therefore, it cannot be presumed that they have done it.

Calder v. Bull, 3 U.S. (3 Dall.) 386, 388 (1798) (emphasis deleted). Today the Court abandons this long-held, basic limitation on government power. Under the banner of economic development, all private property is now vulnerable to being taken and transferred to another private owner, so long as it might be upgraded—*i.e.,* given to an owner who will use it in a way that the legislature deems more beneficial to the public—in the process. To reason, as the Court does, that the incidental public benefits resulting from the subsequent ordinary use of private property render economic development takings "for public use" is to wash out any distinction between private and public use of property—and thereby effectively to delete the words "for public use" from the Takings Clause of the Fifth Amendment. Accordingly I respectfully dissent. . . .

While the Takings Clause presupposes that government can take private property without the owner's consent, the just compensation requirement spreads the cost of condemnations and thus "prevents the public from loading upon one individual more than his just share of the burdens of government." *Monongahela Nav. Co. v. United States,* 148 U.S. 312, 325 (1893). The public use requirement, in turn, imposes a more basic limitation, circumscribing the very scope of the eminent domain power: Government may compel an individual to forfeit her property for the *public's* use, but not for the benefit of another private person. . . . Where is the line between "public" and "private" property use? . . .

Our cases have generally identified three categories of takings that comply with the public use requirement, though it is in the nature of things that the boundaries between these categories are not always firm. Two are relatively straightforward and uncontroversial. First, the sovereign may transfer private property to public ownership—such as for a road, a hospital, or a military base. Second, the sovereign may transfer private property to private parties, often common carriers, who make the property available for the public's use—such as with a railroad, a public utility, or a stadium. But "public ownership" and "use-by-the-public" are sometimes too constricting and impractical ways to define the scope of the Public Use Clause. Thus we have allowed that, in certain circumstances and to meet certain exigencies, takings that serve a public purpose also satisfy the Constitution even if the property is destined for subsequent private use.

This case returns us for the first time in over 20 years to the hard question of when a purportedly "public purpose" taking meets the public use requirement. It presents an issue of first impression: Are economic development takings constitutional? I would hold that they are not. . . .

Here, in contrast [to *Berman* and *Midkiff*], New London does not claim that Susette Kelo's and Wilhelmina Dery's well-maintained homes are the source of any social harm. Indeed, it could not so claim without adopting the absurd argument that any single-family home that might be razed to make way for an apartment building, or any church that might be replaced with a retail store, or any small business that might be more lucrative if it were instead part of a national franchise, is inherently harmful to society and thus within the government's power to condemn. . . .

The Court protests that it does not sanction the bare transfer from A to B for B's benefit. It suggests two limitations on what can be taken after today's decision. First, it maintains a role for courts in ferreting out takings whose sole purpose is to bestow a benefit on the private transferee—without detailing how courts are to conduct that complicated inquiry. For his part, JUSTICE KENNEDY suggests that courts may divine illicit purpose by a careful review of the record and the process by which a legislature arrived at the decision to take—without specifying what courts should look for in a case with different facts, how they will know if they have found it, and what to do if they do not. Whatever the details of JUSTICE KENNEDY's as-yet-undisclosed test, it is difficult to envision anyone but the "stupid staff[er]" failing it. The trouble with economic development takings is that private benefit and incidental public benefit are, by definition, merged and mutually reinforcing. In this case, for example, any boon for Pfizer or the plan's developer is difficult to disaggregate from the promised public gains in taxes and jobs. . . .

Any property may now be taken for the benefit of another private party, but the fallout from this decision will not be random. The beneficiaries are likely to be those citizens with disproportionate influence and power in the political process, including large corporations and development firms. As for the victims, the government now has license to transfer property from those with fewer resources to those with more. The Founders cannot have intended this perverse result. "[T]hat alone is a *just* government," wrote James Madison, "which *impartially* secures to every man, whatever is his *own*." For the National Gazette, Property (Mar. 27, 1792), reprinted in 14 Papers of James Madison 266 (R. Rutland et al. eds.1983). . . .

■ JUSTICE THOMAS, dissenting.

Long ago, William Blackstone wrote that "the law of the land . . . postpone[s] even public necessity to the sacred and inviolable rights of private property." The Framers embodied that principle in the Constitution, allowing the government to take property not for "public necessity," but instead for "public use." Defying this understanding, the Court replaces the Public Use Clause with a "[P]ublic [P]urpose" Clause, . . . a restriction that is satisfied, the Court instructs, so long as the purpose is "legitimate" and the means "not irrational,". . . .

I cannot agree. If such "economic development" takings are for a "public use," any taking is, and the Court has erased the Public Use Clause from our Constitution . . . Today's decision is simply the latest in a string of our cases construing the Public Use Clause to be a virtual nullity, without the slightest nod to its original meaning. In my view, the Public Use Clause, originally understood, is a meaningful limit on the government's eminent domain power. Our cases have strayed from the Clause's original meaning, and I would reconsider them. . . .

Though one component of the protection provided by the Takings Clause is that the government can take private property only if it provides "just compensation" for the taking, the Takings Clause also prohibits the government from taking property except "for public use." Were it otherwise, the Takings Clause would either be meaningless or empty. If the Public Use Clause served no function other than to state that the government may take property through its eminent domain power—for public or private uses—then it would be surplusage. Alternatively, . . . the Clause would require the government to compensate for takings done "for public use," leaving it free to take property for purely private uses without the payment of compensation. This would contradict a bedrock principle well established by the time of the founding: that all takings required the payment of compensation. The Public Use Clause, like the Just Compensation Clause, is therefore an express limit on the government's power of eminent domain.

The most natural reading of the Clause is that it allows the government to take property only if the government owns, or the public has a legal right to use, the property, as opposed to taking it for any public purpose or necessity whatsoever. At the time of the founding, dictionaries primarily defined the noun "use" as "[t]he act of employing any thing to any purpose." 2 S. Johnson, A Dictionary of the English Language 2194 (4th ed. 1773) (hereinafter Johnson). The term "use," moreover, "is from the Latin *utor*, which means 'to use, make use of, avail one's self of, employ, apply, enjoy, etc." J. Lewis, Law of Eminent Domain § 165, p. 224, n. 4 (1888). When the government takes property and gives it to a private individual, and the public has no right to use the property, it strains language to say that the public is "employing" the property, regardless of the incidental benefits that might accrue to the public from the private use. The term "public use," then, means that either the government or its citizens as a whole must actually "employ" the taken property. See *id.*, at 223 (reviewing founding-era dictionaries). . . .

The consequences of today's decision are not difficult to predict, and promise to be harmful. So-called "urban renewal" programs provide some compensation for the properties they take, but no compensation is possible for the subjective value of these lands to the individuals displaced and the indignity inflicted by uprooting them from their homes. Allowing the government to take property solely for public purposes is bad enough, but extending the concept of public purpose to encompass any economically beneficial goal guarantees that these losses will fall disproportionately on poor communities. Those communities are not only systematically less likely to put their lands to the highest and best social use, but are also the least politically powerful. If ever there were justification for intrusive judicial review of constitutional provisions that protect "discrete and insular minorities," *United States v. Carolene Products Co.,* 304 U.S. 144, 152, n. 4 (1938), surely that principle would apply with great force to the powerless groups and individuals the Public Use Clause protects. The deferential standard this Court has adopted for the Public Use Clause is therefore deeply perverse. It encourages "those citizens with disproportionate influence and power in the political process, including large corporations and development firms," to victimize the weak.

Those incentives have made the legacy of this Court's "public purpose" test an unhappy one. In the 1950's, no doubt emboldened in part by the expansive understanding of "public use" this Court adopted in *Berman,* cities "rushed to draw plans" for downtown development. B. Frieden & L. Sagalyn, Downtown, Inc.: How America Rebuilds Cities 17 (1989). "Of all the families displaced by urban renewal from 1949 through 1963, 63 percent of those whose race was known were nonwhite, and of these families, 56 percent of nonwhites and 38 percent of whites had incomes low enough to qualify for public housing, which, however, was seldom available to them." Public works projects in the 1950's and 1960's destroyed predominantly minority communities in St. Paul, Minnesota, and Baltimore, Maryland. In 1981, urban planners in Detroit, Michigan, uprooted the largely "lower-income and elderly" Poletown neighborhood for the benefit of the General Motors Corporation. Urban renewal projects have long been associated with the displacement of blacks; "[i]n cities across the country, urban renewal came to be known as 'Negro removal.'" Over 97 percent of the individuals forcibly removed from their homes by the "slum-clearance" project upheld by this Court in *Berman* were black. Regrettably, the predictable consequence of the Court's decision will be to exacerbate these effects.

* * *

The Court relies almost exclusively on this Court's prior cases to derive today's far-reaching, and dangerous, result. But the principles this Court should employ to dispose of this case are found in the Public Use Clause itself, not in Justice Peckham's high opinion of reclamation laws. When faced with a clash of constitutional principle and a line of unreasoned cases wholly divorced from the text, history, and structure of our founding document, we should not hesitate to resolve the tension in favor of the Constitution's original meaning. For the reasons I have given, and for the reasons given in JUSTICE O'CONNOR's dissent, the conflict of principle raised by this boundless use of the eminent domain power should be resolved in petitioners' favor.

NOTES

1.   As a matter of legal doctrine, what is the difference between the position of the majority and that of Justice Kennedy? Between Justice Kennedy and Justice O'Connor?

Between Justice O'Connor and Justice Thomas? Do any of them avoid the problem of judicial second-guessing of essentially economic issues?

2. If "public use" means "public purpose," should that mean that the courts must defer to any legislative judgment about the reasons for which private property has been taken away by the government? Is that a troubling proposition, or not necessarily so? Justify your answer. Justice Thomas says that "public use" means something like "use by the public." Is he right? Is this a constitutional principle, as opposed to a mere political preference? Does his position offer the possibility of a judicially manageable standard? In deciding what "public use" means, which types of constitutional argument (see p. 42) are most helpful?

3. None of the opinions proceeds to question the presupposition that the Fifth Amendment forbids takings of property for anything other than "public use." But is that what the clause says? In form, doesn't the clause seem to say that *when* property is taken for public use, "just compensation" must be paid? If so, where does this assumption find its roots in the law? Is the answer different for the federal government than for the states?

4. There was an intense political reaction to *Kelo*, and at least forty-three states adopted increased protections against takings, either by legislation or by ballot initiatives. Many of these were relatively small, symbolic changes, but some were significant, such as Nevada's prohibition on using eminent domain for land that would be taken from one private party and transferred to another (though with an exception for blight, which is defined broadly). For an overview, see Ilya Somin, The Grasping Hand: "Kelo v. City of New London" and the Limits of Eminent Domain (2015). Does the backlash to *Kelo* suggest that the Court's decision was wrong? Or does it suggest the opposite, that this is a question that can be resolved in the political branches?

5. In 2009, Pfizer announced its decision to begin vacating its New London campus. With Pfizer gone, "[i]t would leave behind the city's biggest office complex and an adjacent swath of barren land that was cleared of dozens of homes to make room for a hotel, stores and condominiums that were never built." Patrick McGeehan, *Pfizer to Leave City that Won Land-use Case*, N.Y. Times (Nov. 12, 2009). Where Susette Kelo's house once stood is now a wasteland.

VI. The Ninth and Tenth Amendments

Amend. IX: The enumeration in the Constitution, of certain rights, shall not be construed to deny or disparage others retained by the people.

Amend. X: The powers not delegated to the United States by the Constitution, nor prohibited by it to the States, are reserved to the States respectively, or to the people.

Completing the package of amendments that we call the Bill of Rights are two amendments that, unlike the others, do not appear to confer specific rights. Rather, the Ninth and Tenth Amendments appear to function as rules of interpretation concerning inferences *not* to be drawn from the proposal and adoption of the *other* amendments contained in the Bill of Rights. Both amendments address a problem inherent in enumeration: the Ninth Amendment addresses the fact that not all rights are enumerated in the Bill of Rights; the Tenth Amendment addresses the fact that not all possible powers are enumerated in Article One, Section Eight. The amendments adopt opposite rules of construction: the enumeration of the people's rights is not exhaustive, but the enumeration of Congress's powers is exhaustive.

The Ninth Amendment

The specification in the Constitution of certain rights—both in the original Constitution, and in the (then) newly adopted First through Eighth Amendments—does not operate to repeal or rescind ("deny or disparage") any and all other legal rights that individuals might have had by virtue of other sources of law, the Ninth Amendment proclaims. The people enjoy rights arising from longstanding custom and tradition, the common law, state constitutions, legislation, and other sources of law. The adoption of the Bill of Rights does not extinguish other legal rights or assign control over all individual liberties to the national government. Nor should adoption of the Bill of Rights—the "enumeration in the Constitution of certain rights"—"be construed" even to "disparage" arguments in favor of other types of political or civil rights, or even natural law rights, within the realm of public and political debate. The Bill of Rights is a statement that the Constitution protects these rights; it is not a statement that the corpus of the rights of humanity is deemed closed.

The Ninth Amendment thus responded to concerns—expressed first by Federalist *opponents* of the idea of adding a Bill of Rights to the Constitution—that adding a list of rights might be taken to imply that all rights not so specified had been put into the hands of the new national government, thereby unwittingly enlarging its powers.

Alexander Hamilton argued in *The Federalist No. 84* that a Bill of Rights was both unnecessary and affirmatively dangerous:

> I go further, and affirm that bills of rights, in the sense and to the extent in which they are contended for, are not only unnecessary in the proposed Constitution, but would even be dangerous. They would contain various exceptions to powers not granted; and, on this very account, would afford a colorable pretext to claim more than were granted. For why declare that things shall not be done which there is no power to do? Why, for instance, should it be said that the liberty of the press shall not be restrained, when no power is given by which restrictions may be imposed? I will not contend that such a provision would confer a regulating power; but it is evident that it would furnish, to men disposed to usurp, a plausible pretense for claiming that power. They might urge with a semblance of reason, that the Constitution ought not to be charged with the absurdity of providing against the abuse of an authority which was not given, and that the provision against restraining the liberty of the press afforded a clear implication, that a power to prescribe proper regulations concerning it was intended to be vested in the national government. This may serve as a specimen of the numerous handles which would be given to the doctrine of constructive powers, by the indulgence of an injudicious zeal for bills of rights.

James Madison, in a speech introducing his proposed Bill of Rights in the First Congress, raised this explanation for inclusion of the provision that eventually became the Ninth Amendment:

> It has been objected also against a bill of rights, that, by enumerating particular exceptions to the grant of power, it would disparage those rights which were not placed in that enumeration; and it might follow by implication, that those rights that were not placed in that enumeration,

that those rights which were not singled out, were intended to be assigned into the hands of the General Government, and were consequently insecure. This is one of the most plausible arguments I have ever heard urged against the admission of a bill of rights into this system; but, I conceive, that it may be guarded against. I have attempted it, as gentlemen may see by turning to the last clause of the fourth resolution.

1 ANNALS OF CONG. 439 (1789). Madison's original proposal for what eventually became the Ninth and Tenth Amendments was as follows: "The exceptions here or elsewhere in the Constitution, made in favor of particular rights, shall not be so construed as to diminish the just importance of other rights retained by the people, or as to enlarge the powers delegated by the Constitution; but either as actual limitations of such powers, or as inserted merely for greater caution." *Id.*, at 435.

Justice Joseph Story, in his early and influential treatise on the Constitution, noted this political history as explaining the presence of the Ninth Amendment as a rule of construction designed to prevent an improper inference:

> This clause [the Ninth Amendment] was manifestly introduced to prevent any perverse, or ingenious misapplication of the well known maxim, that an affirmation in particular cases implies a negation in all others; and, *e converso*, that a negation in particular cases implies an affirmation in all others. The maxim, rightly understood, is perfectly sound and safe; but it has often been strangely forced from its natural meaning into the support of the most dangerous political heresies. The amendment was undoubtedly suggested by the reasoning of the Federalist on the subject of a general bill of rights.

3 Joseph Story, COMMENTARIES ON THE CONSTITUTION OF THE UNITED STATES, Section 1898, at 751–52 (1833).

But what does it mean to say that the rights the people retain should not be "den[ied]" or "disparage[d]? One possible answer is that the Ninth Amendment simply serves as a rule of construction for other constitutional provisions, for example by warning us not to use the Fifth Amendment's reference to being deprived of "life" to conclude that the Eighth Amendment can never ban capital punishment as cruel and unusual. See Ryan C. Williams, *The Ninth Amendment As A Rule of Construction*, 111 Colum. L. Rev. 498, 558–560 (2011). But is that an apt example? And is that really all the Ninth Amendment accomplishes? Under this theory, what are the "other[ ]" rights "retained by the people"?

Another possible answer is through presumptions in statutory interpretation. Prior to a written constitution, natural or conventional rights were protected via a kind of Blackstonian equitable interpretation: courts assumed that legislatures were aware of and did not intend to disturb natural rights, so they narrowly construed statutes to avoid doing so, on an as-applied basis. If the legislature passed legislation evincing a specific intention to abrogate such an unwritten right, however, the courts were not empowered to override that determination. See Michael W. McConnell, *Natural Rights and the Ninth Amendment: How Does Lockean Legal Theory Assist in Interpretation?*, 5 N.Y.U. J. L. & Lib. 1 (2010). Is that too weak of an interpretation of the Ninth Amendment? Is it too strong?

A third view, notwithstanding the views of Story and others, is that the Ninth Amendment is a reference to or source of other (unspecified) federal constitutional rights. These might be traceable to the common law or might meant to be discovered in the future, whether by the People, the courts, or the legislatures. Is that a plausible reading of the amendment?

If the Ninth Amendment refers to common law rights, does it transform them into constitutional ones, or simply leave them intact, as common law? If the Ninth Amendment refers to the future, creating to-be-named-later constitutional liberties—what are they? Is the Ninth Amendment an invitation to courts to engage in natural law constitutional law-making, identifying new or evolving constitutional rights? What happens if the judicially developed right conflicts with the choices of democratically elected legislatures? What would keep a willful judge from enacting his or her own policy preferences as constitutional law? Is there a principled way to identify the content of those rights?

The suggestion that the Ninth Amendment creates additional, unspecified constitutional rights has long been a favorite of constitutional law scholars. See, e.g., THE RIGHTS RETAINED BY THE PEOPLE: THE NINTH AMENDMENT AND CONSTITUTIONAL INTERPRETATION, VOLS. I & II (Randy Barnett, ed. 1991, 1993) (collecting essays). But the suggestion has never been accepted by the Supreme Court. The closest the Court has come to relying on the Ninth Amendment is Justice Goldberg's concurring opinion in *Griswold v. Connecticut*, 381 U.S. 479, 488–492 (1965) (Goldberg, J., concurring), p. 1546.

The Tenth Amendment

The Tenth Amendment is a companion provision to the Ninth Amendment. Just as the Ninth Amendment is designed to prevent the conclusion that the addition of a Bill of Rights by negative implication placed all other rights (in Madison's words) "into the hands of the General Government," the Tenth Amendment is designed to reinforce the conclusion that the enumeration of powers in Article I, Section 8 and elsewhere left all other powers in the hands of the states or the people.

In context, then, the Tenth Amendment appears not to introduce new, substantive restrictions on national government powers. Rather, the Tenth Amendment reaffirms—and emphasizes—the Constitution's original principle that the national government was to be one of limited, delegated powers only. The Supreme Court has remarked that the Tenth Amendment thus states a "truism." *United States v. Darby*, 312 U.S. 100, 124 (1941). (See p. 522.) Indeed it does. It states that the powers not delegated to the national government are reserved to the states. But does it subtly suggest something more: that it is important not to read the enumerated powers as a blank check for federal authority? Why have a Tenth Amendment if we interpret the enumerated powers, such as the Commerce Clause, so broadly that the federal government can do anything it wishes to do? See Gary Lawson, *A Truism with Attitude: The Tenth Amendment in Constitutional Context*, 83 Notre Dame L. Rev. 469 (2008).

Those who see the Tenth Amendment as a charter for strong states' rights must grapple, however, with its history. The Articles of Confederation contained a provision almost identical to the Tenth Amendment, with the difference that the powers not "expressly" delegated to the national government were left to the states. That makes a big difference. It prohibits anything other than a strict literal construction of Section 8. But the framers of the Tenth Amendment declined to use the word "expressly." Three times in the House and the Senate, anti-nationalists moved to amend the Tenth Amendment to add the word "expressly." Madison opposed the amendment, arguing that "because it was impossible to confine a Government to the exercise of express powers; there must necessarily be admitted powers by implication, unless the Constitution descended to recount every minutia." Even Roger Sherman, a principled advocate of state power, agreed. Accordingly, the motion lost, 17–32. Without the word "expressly," how potent is the Tenth Amendment's principle of construction?

The idea that the Tenth Amendment recognizes a residual "sovereignty" of sorts in the states was part of the reasoning of the Court in *New York v. United States,* 505 U.S. 144 (1992). The Court spoke of "the province of state sovereignty reserved by the Tenth Amendment." Conceding that the Amendment is "essentially a tautology" in terms of restraining the powers of Congress, the Court nonetheless concluded—as a matter of the logical structure of federalism—that Congress could not "commandeer" the legislative processes of state governments by directly compelling them to enact and enforce a federal law mandate. Does the rule of *New York* result from the text of the Tenth Amendment? Or does it result from structural principles and national-state relationships created by the document as a whole (to which the Tenth Amendment contributes)? Which type of constitutional argument is doing the heavy lifting in such a case: Text? Historical context? Structure? Precedent and practice? Policy?

CHAPTER 6

THE RECONSTRUCTION AMENDMENTS

[*Assignment 62*]

I. FOUNDATIONS OF THE THIRTEENTH AND FOURTEENTH AMENDMENTS

The Civil War (1861–1865) and the Reconstruction of the South that followed (1865–1877) produced a dramatic transformation in the American constitutional order. The War was, at one level, a struggle between visions of the Constitution—visions of the constitutional status of slavery, the authority of the Supreme Court, the location of sovereignty, and the nature of the Union. Just what *was* the legal status of slavery before the Civil War? Did the Constitution protect a state's right to maintain the institution of slavery, immune from national interference? Did the Constitution protect the right to keep slaves in federal territories (as *Dred Scott* had held in 1857)? Did the Constitution exclude *all* black persons—slave and free—from U.S. and state citizenship and thus from the rights and privileges of citizenship (as *Dred Scott* also held)? Or did the Constitution contain powers and principles that could have been used to set slavery on the path toward abolition? Perhaps the Commerce Clause, which could empower the Union to end the interstate as well as the foreign slave trade; the Due Process Clause of the Fifth Amendment, which by its text applies to all "persons"; the Privileges and Immunities Clause of Article IV, which would seem to allow free persons of color to travel throughout the Union, speaking, writing, preaching, and bearing arms; and the Guarantee Clause of Article IV, which promised "a Republican Form of Government" that was not congruent with inheritable slavery? And what about states? Was the federal union a voluntary union of sovereign states, each of which could leave if it felt aggrieved? Or was the Union a nation with sovereign authority over the states, on matters so specified in the Constitution, and with no state entitled to defy the authority of the Union or to leave without the consent of the whole? Was the term "United States" singular or plural?

These were fundamental constitutional questions. They received their answers through what Lincoln called "this fiery trial" of civil war. The Union victory resolved these longstanding constitutional arguments by force. It also produced changes to the text of the Constitution. The Thirteenth Amendment, adopted in 1865 as the War was drawing to a close, generally abolished slavery. The Fourteenth Amendment, adopted in 1868, designated a national citizenship, extended the rights of citizenship against state governments, and forbade states to deny anyone due process or the equal protection of the laws. Moreover, it empowered Congress to effectuate these commands. The Fifteenth Amendment, adopted in 1870, forbade denial of the right to vote "on account of race, color, or previous condition of servitude."

We will begin with the legal status of slavery before the Civil War, then move to the Reconstruction Amendments, trying to understand what they say and what they were understood to accomplish.

A. SLAVERY, NATURAL LAW, AND THE ANTEBELLUM CONSTITUTION

Charles Stewart, a white Virginian, brought his black slave James Somerset on a business trip to England in 1769. In October 1771, while in London, Somerset escaped. He was recaptured and held on a vessel, the *Anne and Mary*, anchored in the Thames. Stewart intended Somerset to be taken to Jamaica, there to be resold. Anti-slavery advocates engaged counsel and petitioned the Court of King's Bench for a writ of habeas corpus on Somerset's behalf. Habeas corpus is the traditional writ used to challenge unlawful confinement. The nominal defendant in a habeas proceeding is the person holding custody of the petitioner, in this case Captain Knowles of the *Anne and Mary*.

The case came before the Chief Justice of the Court of King's Bench, William Murray, Lord Mansfield. Mansfield is now best known for modernizing the field of commercial law, but at the time he was controversial in the America colonies for reducing the discretion of juries in favor of more stable and predictable judge-dominated legal proceedings. In an initial hearing, Lord Mansfield urged Stewart to "end the question, by discharging or giving freedom to [Somerset]." Mansfield noted there were 14,000 or 15,000 slaves then present in England, with a total value of over 700,000 pounds, and that any disruption in their legal status would have serious repercussions. He commented: "But if the parties will not have it decided, we must give our opinion. Compassion will not, on the one hand, nor inconvenience on the other, be to decide; but the law."

The parties persisted, and here was the result:

Somerset v. Stewart
98 Eng. Rep. 499 (K.B. 1771)

■ LORD MANSFIELD.

On return to a writ of habeas corpus . . .

The captain of the ship on board of which the negro was taken, makes his return to the writ in terms signifying that there have been, and still are, slaves to a great number in Africa; and that the trade in them is authorized by the laws and opinions of Virginia and Jamaica; that they are goods and chattels; and, as such, saleable and sold. That James Somerset, is a negro of Africa, and long before the return of the King's writ was brought to be sold, and was sold to Charles Stewart, Esq. then in Jamaica, and has not been manumitted since; that Mr. Stewart, having occasion to transact business, came over hither, with an intention to return; and brought Somerset, to attend and abide with him, and to carry him back as soon as the business should be transacted. That such intention has been, and still continues; and that the negro did remain till the time of his departure, in the service of his master Mr. Stewart, and quitted it without his consent; and thereupon, before the return of the King's writ, the said Charles Stewart did commit the slave on board the "Ann and Mary," to save custody, to be kept till he should set sail, and then to be taken with him to Jamaica, and there sold as a slave. And this is the cause why he, Captain Knowles, who was then and now is, commander of the above vessel, then and now lying in the river of Thames, did the said negro, committed to his custody, detain; and on which he now renders him to the orders of the Court. We pay all due attention to the opinion of Sir Philip Yorke, and Lord Chief Justice Talbot, whereby they pledged themselves to the British planters, for all the legal consequences of slaves coming over to this kingdom or being baptized, recognized by Lord Hardwicke, sitting as chancellor on the 19th of October 1749, that trover would lie: that a notion had prevailed, if a negro came over, or became a Christian, he was emancipated, but no ground in law; that he and Lord Talbot, when Attorney and Solicitor-General, were of opinion, that no such claim for freedom was valid; that tho' the Statute of Tenures had abolished villains regardant to a manor, yet he did not conceive but that a man might still become a villain in gross, by confessing himself such in open Court. We are so well agreed, that we think there is no occasion of having it argued (as I intimated an intention at first,) before all the Judges, as is usual, for obvious reasons, on a return to a habeas corpus; the only question before us is, whether the cause on the return is sufficient? If it is, the negro must be remanded; if it is not, he must be discharged. Accordingly, the return states, that the slave departed and refused to serve; whereupon he was kept, to be sold abroad. So high an act of dominion must be recognized by the law of the country where it is used. The power of a master over his slave has been extremely different, in different countries. The state of slavery is of such a nature, that it is incapable of being introduced on any reasons, moral or political; but only positive law, which preserves its force long after the reasons, occasion, and time itself from whence it was created, is erased from memory: it's so odious, that nothing can be suffered to support it, but positive law. Whatever inconveniences, therefore, may follow from a decision, I cannot say this case is allowed or approved by the law of England; and therefore the black must be discharged.

NOTES

1.   What did Lord Mansfield mean when he warned the parties that if they brought the case to trial, "Compassion will not, on the one hand, nor inconvenience on the other, be to decide; but the law." Did he fulfill his promise? (Or was it a threat?) What "law" governed the case?

2.   The decision in *Somerset v. Stewart* casts light on the prevailing understanding of natural law at the time of the American Founding. Lord Mansfield stated that slavery was "so odious" (where did he get that idea?) that "nothing can be suffered to support it, but positive law." Which is superior in court: natural law or positive law? What force does natural law have in court? How does this compare to the force of common law? Note that Lord Mansfield distinguished earlier common law opinions that appeared to support the legality of slavery in England. Why was that necessary?

As you study the materials in this part of the course, think about the role of natural law in (a) the adoption of the Fourteenth Amendment, (b) the *Lochner* era of substantive due process, (c) the critique of *Lochner* by Justice Black and others, (d) modern substantive due process, in cases such as *Roe v. Wade*, and (e) the criticism of *Roe* and similar cases. What role, if any, does natural law have in U.S. constitutional law? How do the various positions compare to Lord Mansfield's view in *Somerset*?

3.   What was the legal effect of the ruling in *Somerset*? Why did it not apply in Virginia and Jamaica? Did it apply in New England?

Slavery arrived in the English colonies of North America over 150 years before *Somerset v. Stewart*, and at the time of the Revolution was lawful in all thirteen states. Nine states had full slave codes. Unlike in Britain, slavery was established by positive law; its abolition therefore required positive law. Vermont abolished slavery in its 1777 constitution. Pennsylvania enacted legislation providing for gradual emancipation, in 1780. In Massachusetts, abolition came by judicial interpretation of the "free and equal" clause of the Massachusetts Constitution of 1780. See *Quock Walker's Case* (1783), reprinted in 4 JUDICIAL CASES CONCERNING AMERICAN SLAVERY AND THE NEGRO 480–81 (Helen Tunnicliff Catterall ed., 1936).

The first census, in 1790, showed the following populations:

State	Total Population	Slave Population
Connecticut	237,655	2,648
Delaware	59,096	8,887
Georgia	82,548	29,264
Maryland	319,728	103,036
Massachusetts	378,556	0
New Hampshire	141,899	157
New Jersey	184,139	11,423
New York	340,241	21,193
North Carolina	395,005	100,783
Pennsylvania	433,611	3,707
Rhode Island	69,112	958
South Carolina	249,073	107,094
Virginia	691,737	292,627

See 1 HISTORICAL STATISTICS OF THE UNITED STATES: EARLIEST TIMES TO THE PRESENT, at 1–198ff. (Susan B. Carter et al. eds., 2006); U.S. Bureau of the Census, NEGRO POPULATION IN THE UNITED STATES, 1790–1915, at 57, table 6 (1918).

Slavery was debated intensely at the Constitutional Convention in Philadelphia, with attention focused on (1) whether slaves (or 3/5 of their number) would be counted for purposes of representation in the House and the Electoral College; (2) whether Congress could forbid or tax the importation of slaves from other countries; and (3) whether fugitive slaves escaping into another state had to be returned. It was assumed that no enumerated power of Congress would allow the federal government to abolish slavery within the states. But what powers *could* Congress exert with respect to slavery? As you ponder this question, consider a statute enacted by the Continental Congress "for the government of the territory of the United States northwest of the river Ohio," commonly called the Northwest Ordinance.

The Northwest Ordinance, Article VI

July 13, 1787

There shall be neither slavery nor involuntary servitude in the said territory, otherwise than in the punishment of crimes, whereof the party shall have been duly convicted: *Provided always,* That any person escaping into the same, from whom labor or service is lawfully claimed in any one of the original States, such fugitive may be lawfully reclaimed, and conveyed to the person claiming his or her labor or service as aforesaid. . . .

NOTES

1.   If the *Somerset* decision was good law, was the prohibition of slavery in the Northwest Ordinance necessary? Note that shortly after the Northwest Ordinance, the territories south of Kentucky and west of the Appalachians were organized for settlement. Slavery was not prohibited, and soon was widespread. How does that reflect on the authority and persuasiveness of *Somerset* in the newly independent United States?

2.   Examine the Constitution as enacted in 1787, together with the Bill of Rights. Does it (a) establish positive law protecting slavery? (b) establish principles of law inconsistent with slavery? (c) remain neutral regarding slavery? Not surprisingly, this was a major debate in the years leading up to the Civil War. Consider the following views: a speech by Alexander Stephens, vice-president of the Confederate States of America, delivered in Savannah, Georgia, on the occasion of the adoption of a constitution for the Confederacy; a speech by the abolitionist Frederick Douglass, delivered in Glasgow, Scotland; a speech by the abolitionist William Lloyd Garrison, delivered in Boston, Massachusetts; and an excerpt from the U.S. Supreme Court's decision in *Dred Scott*.

Alexander Stephens, "African Slavery: The Corner-Stone of the Southern Confederacy"

Mar. 22, 1861

. . . We are in the midst of one of the greatest epochs in our history. The last ninety days will mark one of the most memorable eras in the history of modern civilization. . . . Seven States have within the last three months thrown off an old government and formed a new. This revolution has been signally marked, up to this time, by the fact of its having been accomplished without the loss of a single drop of blood. [Applause.]

This new [Confederate] constitution, or form of government, constitutes the subject to which your attention will be partly invited. In reference to it, I make this first general remark. It amply secures all our ancient rights, franchises, and liberties. All the great principles of Magna Charta are retained in it. No citizen is deprived of life, liberty, or property, but by the judgment of his peers under the laws of the land. The great principle of religious liberty, which was the honor and pride of the old constitution, is still maintained and secured. All the essentials of the old constitution, which have endeared it to the hearts of the American people, have been preserved and perpetuated. [Applause.] Some changes have been made. Of these I shall speak presently. . . .

But not to be tedious in enumerating the numerous changes for the better, allow me to allude to one other—though last, not least. The new constitution has put at rest, *forever,* all the agitating questions relating to our peculiar institution—African slavery as it exists amongst us—the proper *status* of the negro in our form of civilization. This was the immediate cause of the late rupture and present revolution. Jefferson in his forecast, had anticipated this, as the "rock upon which the old Union would split." He was right. What was conjecture with him, is now a realized fact. But whether he fully comprehended the great truth upon which that rock *stood* and *stands,* may be doubted. The prevailing ideas entertained by him and most of the leading statesmen at the time of the formation of the old constitution, were that the enslavement of the African was in violation of the laws of nature; that it was wrong in *principle,* socially, morally, and politically. It was an evil they knew not well how to deal with, but the general opinion of the men of that day was that, somehow or other in the order of Providence, the institution would be evanescent and pass away. This idea, though not incorporated in the constitution, was the prevailing idea at that time. The constitution, it is true, secured every essential guarantee to the institution while it should last, and hence no argument can be justly urged against the constitutional guarantees thus secured, because of the common sentiment of the day. Those ideas, however, were fundamentally wrong. They rested upon the assumption of the equality of races. This was an error. It was a sandy foundation, and the government built upon it fell when the "storm came and the wind blew."

Our new government is founded upon exactly the opposite idea; its foundations are laid, its corner-stone rests upon the great truth, that the negro is not equal to the white man; that slavery—subordination to the superior race—is his natural and normal condition. [Applause.] This, our new government, is the first, in the history of the world, based upon this great physical, philosophical, and moral truth. This truth has been slow in the process of its development, like all other truths in the various departments of science. It has been so even amongst us. Many who hear me, perhaps, can recollect well, that this truth was not generally admitted, even within their day. The errors of the past generation still clung to many as late as twenty years ago. . . .

In the conflict thus far, success has been on our side, complete throughout the length and breadth of the Confederate States. It is upon this, as I have stated, our social fabric is firmly planted; and I cannot permit myself to doubt the ultimate success of a full recognition of this principle throughout the civilized and enlightened world.

As I have stated, the truth of this principle may be slow in development, as all truths are and ever have been, in the various branches of science. It was so with the principles announced by Galileo-it was so with Adam Smith and his principles of political economy. It was so with Harvey, and his theory of the circulation of the blood. It is stated that not a single one of the medical profession, living at the time of the announcement of the truths made by him, admitted them. Now, they are universally acknowledged. May we not, therefore, look with confidence to the ultimate universal acknowledgment of the truths upon which our system rests? It is the first government ever instituted upon the principles in strict conformity to nature, and the ordination of Providence, in furnishing the materials of human society. Many governments have been founded upon the principle of the subordination and serfdom of certain classes of the same race; such were and are in violation of the laws of nature. Our system commits no such violation of nature's laws. With us, all of the white race, however high or low, rich or poor, are equal in the eye of the law. Not so with the negro. Subordination is his place. He, by nature, or by the curse against Canaan, is fitted for that condition which he occupies in our system. The architect, in the construction of buildings, lays the foundation with the proper material-the granite; then comes the brick or the marble. The substratum of our society is made of the material fitted by nature for it, and by experience we know that it is best, not only for the superior, but for the inferior race, that it should be so. It is, indeed, in conformity with the ordinance of the Creator. It is not for us to inquire into the wisdom of his ordinances, or to question them. For his own purposes, he has made one race to differ from another, as he has made "one star to differ from another star in glory."

The great objects of humanity are best attained when there is conformity to his laws and decrees, in the formation of governments as well as in all things else. Our confederacy is founded upon principles in strict conformity with these laws. This stone which was rejected by the first builders "is become the chief of the corner"—the real "corner-stone"—in our new edifice. [Applause.] . . .

NOTES

1.   Alexander Stephens argued that the Confederate States of America were the "first, in the history of the world," to base a constitution on the "great physical, philosophical, and moral truth" of the inequality of the races. He analogized this "truth" to recent developments in the natural and social sciences. He even criticized Jefferson and the Founders for their misunderstanding on this point, because they thought "the enslavement of the African was in violation of the laws of nature; that it was wrong in *principle,* socially, morally, and politically." Stephens was thus anything but reverent toward the original principles of the U.S. Constitution. Rather than claim that the Confederate States were faithfully preserving the original understanding of the American Union, he defended the "new" nation on the ground that modern science had shown the error in the earlier ways.

2.   Compare Stephens's view of nature and natural law to that of Lord Mansfield. In case of disagreement, how do we know the truth about nature and natural law? Do we look to science or scientific consensus? To legal tradition? To religion? To our own consciences? To what Mansfield called "compassion" on one side, and "inconvenience" on the other? If reasonable people disagree (was Stephens a reasonable person?), can either position be treated as "natural"? As natural "law"?

3.   If the framers of the Constitution were convinced that slavery was a violation of natural law, as Stephens avers, does that view find its way into the positive law of the Constitution?

Frederick Douglass, "The Constitution of the United States: Is It Pro-Slavery or Anti-Slavery?"
Mar. 26, 1860

. . . [F]irst let me state what is not the question. It is not whether slavery existed in the United States at the time of the adoption of the Constitution; it is not whether slaveholders took part in framing the Constitution; it is not whether those slaveholders, in their hearts, intended to secure certain advantages in that instrument for slavery; it is not whether the American Government has been wielded during seventy-two years in favour of the propagation and permanence of slavery; it is not whether a pro-slavery interpretation has been put upon the Constitution by the American Courts. . . . The real and exact question . . . may be fairly stated thus:—1st, Does the United States Constitution guarantee to any class or description of people in that country the right to enslave, or hold as property, any other class or description of people in that country? 2nd, Is the dissolution of the union between the slave and free States required by fidelity to the slaves, or by the just demands of conscience? . . .

I . . . deny that the Constitution guarantees the right to hold property in man, and believe that the way to abolish slavery in America is to vote such men into power as will use their powers for the abolition of slavery. . . . I think we had better ascertain what the Constitution itself is . . . I will tell you. It is no vague, indefinite, floating, unsubstantial, ideal something, coloured according to any man's fancy, now a weasel, now a whale, and now nothing. On the contrary, it is a plainly written document, not in Hebrew or Greek, but in English. . . . The American Constitution is a written instrument full and complete in itself. No Court in America, no Congress, no President, can add a single word thereto, or take a single work therefrom. . . . [I]t should be borne in mind that the mere text, and only the text, and not any commentaries or creeds written by those who wished to give the text a meaning apart from its plain reading, was adopted as the Constitution of the United States. It should also be borne in mind that the intentions of those who framed the Constitution, be they good or bad, for slavery or against slavery, are to be respected so far, and so far only, as we find those intentions plainly stated in the Constitution. It would be the wildest of absurdities, and lead to endless confusion and mischiefs, if, instead of looking to the written paper itself, for its meaning, it were attempted to make us search it out, in the secret motives, and dishonest intentions, of some of the men who took part in writing it. It was what they said that was adopted by the people, not what they were ashamed or afraid to say, and really omitted to say. Bear in mind, also, and the fact is an important one, that the framers of the Constitution sat with closed doors, and that this was done purposefully, that nothing but the result of their labours should be seen, and that the result should be judged of by the people free from any of the bias shown in the debates. It should also be borne in mind, and the fact is still more important, that the debates in the convention that framed the Constitution, and by means of which a pro-slavery interpretation is now attempted to be forced upon that instrument, were not published till more than a quarter of a century after the presentation and the adoption of the Constitution.

. . . Common sense, and common justice, and sound rules of interpretation all drive us to the words of the law for the meaning of the law. The practice of the Government is dwelt upon with much fervour and eloquence as conclusive to the slaveholding character of the Constitution. . . . But good as this argument is, it is not conclusive. A wise man has said that few people have been found better than their laws, but many have been found worse. To this last rule America is no exception. Her laws are one thing, her practice is another. . . . After all, the fact that men go out of the Constitution to prove it pro-slavery, whether that going out is to the practice of the Government, or to the secret intentions of the writers of the paper, the fact that they do go out is very significant. It is a powerful argument on my side. It is an admission that the thing for which they are looking is not to be found where only it ought to be found, and that is in the Constitution itself. . . .

It so happens that no such words as "African slave trade," no such words as "slave representation," no such words as "fugitive slaves," no such words as "slave insurrections," are anywhere used in that instrument. . . . *[Here Douglass read several provisions of the Constitution.—Editors]* Let us look at them just as they stand, one by one. Let us grant, for sake of the argument, that the first of these provisions, referring to the basis of representation and taxation, does refer to slaves. . . . [G]iving the provisions the very worst construction, what does it amount to? I answer—It is a downright disability laid upon the slaveholding States; one which deprives those States of two-fifths of their natural basis of representation. A black man in a free State is worth just two-fifths more than a black man in a slave State, as a basis of political power under the Constitution. Therefore, instead of encouraging slavery, the Constitution encourages freedom by giving an increase of "two-fifths" of political power to free over slave States. So much for the three-fifths clause; taking it at its worst, it still leans to freedom, not to slavery; for, be it remembered that the Constitution nowhere forbids a coloured man to vote. I come to the next, that which it is said guaranteed the continuance of the African slave trade for twenty years. I will also take that for just what my opponent alleges it to have been. . . . [W]hat follows? why, this—that this part of the Constitution, so far as the slave trade is concerned, became a dead letter more than 50 years ago, and now binds no man's conscience for the continuance of any slave trade whatever. . . . But there is still more to be said about this abolition of the slave trade. Men, at that time, both in England and in America, looked upon the slave trade as the life of slavery. The abolition of the slave trade was supposed to be the certain death of slavery. . . .

American statesmen, in providing for the abolition of the slave trade, thought they were providing for the abolition of slavery. . . . All regarded slavery as an expiring and doomed system, destined to speedily disappear from the country. But, again, it should be remembered that this very provision, if made to refer to the African slave trade at all, makes the Constitution anti-slavery rather than for slavery, for it says to the slave States, the price you will have to pay for coming into the American Union is, that the slave trade, which you would carry on indefinitely out of the Union, shall be put an end to in twenty years if you come into the Union. . . . [This provision] showed that the intentions of the framers of the Constitution were good, not bad. . . . I go to the "slave insurrection" clause, though, in truth, there is no such clause. . . . But I will be generous here, as well as elsewhere, and grant that it applies to slave insurrections. Let us suppose that an anti-slavery man is President of the United States (and the day that shall see this case is not distant) and this very power of suppressing slave insurrection would put an end to slavery. The right to put down an insurrection carries with it the right to determine the means by which it shall be put down. If it should turn out that slavery is a source of insurrection, that there is no security from insurrection while slavery lasts, why, the Constitution would be best obeyed by putting an end to slavery, and an anti-slavery Congress would do that very thing. Thus, you see, the so-called slave-holding provisions of the American Constitution, which a little while ago looked so formidable, are, after all, no defence or guarantee for slavery whatever. But there is one other provision. This is called the "Fugitive Slave Provision." It is called so by those who wish to make it subserve the interest of slavery in America. . . . But it may be asked—if this clause does not apply to slaves, to whom does it apply?

I answer, that when adopted, it applies to a very large class of persons—namely, redemptioners—persons who had come to America from Holland, from Ireland, and other quarters of the globe . . . and had, for a consideration duly paid, become bound to "serve and labour" for the parties to whom their service and labour was due. It applies to indentured apprentices and others who had become bound for a consideration, under contract duly made, to serve and labour[.] To such persons this provision applies, and only to such persons. The plain reading of this provision shows that it applies, and that it can only properly and legally apply, to persons "bound to service." Its object plainly is, to secure the fulfilment of contracts for "service and labour." . . . The legal condition of the slave puts him beyond the operation of this provision. He is not described in it. He is a simple article of property. He does not owe and cannot owe service. He cannot even make a contract. . . . This provision, then, only respects persons who owe service, and they only can own service who can receive an equivalent and make a bargain. The slave cannot do that, and is therefore exempted from the operation of this fugitive provision. In all matters where laws are taught to be made the means of oppression, cruelty, and wickedness, I am for strict construction. I will concede nothing. It must be shown that it is so nominated in the bond. The pound of flesh, but not one drop of blood. The very nature of law is opposed to all such wickedness, and makes it difficult to accomplish such objects under the forms of law. Law is not merely an arbitrary enactment with regard to justice, reason, or humanity. . . . These rules [of interpretation] send us to the history of the law for its meaning. I have no objection to such a course in ordinary cases of doubt. But where human liberty and justice are at stake, the case falls under an entirely different class of rules. There must be something more than history—something more than tradition. The Supreme Court of the United States lays down this rule, and it meets the case exactly—"Where rights are infringed—where the fundamental principles of the law are overthrown—where the general system of the law is departed from, the legislative intention must be expressed with irresistible clearness." The same court says that the language of the law must be construed strictly in favour of justice and liberty. Again, there is another rule of law. It is— Where a law is susceptible of two meanings, the one making it accomplish an innocent purpose, and the other making it accomplish a wicked purpose, we must in all cases adopt that which makes it accomplish an innocent purpose. . . . I only ask you to look at the American Constitution in the light of [these rules], and you will see with me that no man is guaranteed a right of property in man, under the provisions of that instrument. If there are two ideas more distinct in their character and essence than another, those ideas are "persons" and "property," "men" and "things." Now, when it is proposed to transform persons into "property" and men into beasts of burden, I demand that the law that contemplates such a purpose shall be expressed with irresistible clearness. The thing must not be left to inference, but must be done in plain English. . . . It has been said that Negroes are not included within the benefits sought under [the Preamble of the Constitution]. This is said by the slaveholders in America . . . but it is not said by the Constitution itself. Its language is "we the people"; not we the white people, not even we the citizens, not we the privileged class, not we the high, not we the low, but we the people; . . . and, if Negroes are people, they are included in the benefits for which the Constitution of America was ordained and established. . . . This, I undertake to say, as the conclusion of the whole matter, that the constitutionality of slavery can be made out only by disregarding the plain and common-sense reading of the Constitution itself; by discrediting and casting away as worthless the most beneficent rules of legal interpretation; by ruling the Negro outside of these beneficent rules; by claiming everything for slavery; by denying everything for freedom; by assuming that the Constitution does not mean what it says, and that it says what it does not mean; by disregarding the written Constitution, and interpreting it in the light of a secret understanding. . . . The Constitution declares that no person shall be deprived of life, liberty, or property without due process of law; it secures to every man the right of trial by jury, the privilege of the writ of habeas corpus—that great writ that put an end to slavery and slave-hunting in England—it secures to every State a republican form of government. Any one of these provisions, in the hands of abolition statesmen, and backed up by a right moral sentiment, would put an end to slavery in America. The Constitution forbids the passing of a bill of attainder: that is, a law entailing upon the child the disabilities and hardships imposed upon the parent. Every slave in America might be repealed on this very ground. . . .

I am, therefore, for drawing the bond of the Union more closely, and bringing the Slave States more completely under the power of the Free States. What they most dread, that I most desire. I have much confidence in the instincts of the slaveholders. They see that the Constitution will afford slavery no protection when it shall cease to be administered by slaveholders. They see, moreover, that if there is once a will in the people of America to abolish slavery, there is no word, no syllable in the Constitution to forbid that result. . . .

NOTES

1.   What interpretive methodology does Frederick Douglass employ, and why? What is his critique of reliance on evidence of original intentions? Does the same argument apply to interpretation based on original meaning? What is his view of interpretation according to tradition, precedent, or settled practice?

2.   Do Douglass and Stephens agree about the meaning of the constitutional text? About the intentions of the framers with regard to slavery?

3.   Carefully consider each of Douglass's interpretations of individual provisions of the Constitution: the Three-fifths Clause, the Slave Trade Clause, the Fugitive Slave Clause, the Due Process Clause, the Jury Clause, the Habeas Corpus Clause, and the Guarantee Clause. Are they persuasive? Are there any relevant clauses he did not discuss?

4.   He makes a great deal of the framers' decision not to use the words "slave" or "slavery" in the Constitution. This was deliberate. According to one delegate at the Convention, William Paterson, they were "ashamed to use the term 'slaves' & had substituted a description." Douglass argues, in effect, that if the slavery advocates at the Convention were too embarrassed to use the terms, we should not do their work for them. Is that a sound principle?

5.   Note the connection between Lord Mansfield's position that only explicit positive law can trump the natural law, and Douglass's position that if the law is said to convert persons into property, "such a purpose shall be expressed with irresistible clearness. The thing must not be left to inference, but must be done in plain English."

6.   Douglass argues that slavery is contrary to the Constitution, but he does not propose going to court. He asserts that "the way to abolish slavery in America is to vote such men into power as will use their powers for the abolition of slavery." Why does he rely on politics rather than litigation? Does that mean he prefers politics to law? What is the relation between political activity and constitutional interpretation?

William Lloyd Garrison, "The American Union"

First published in *The Liberator*, vol. 15, no. 2 (Jan. 10, 1845)

. . . Tyrants! confident of its overthrow, proclaim not to your vassals, that the AMERICAN UNION is an experiment of freedom, which, if it fail, will forever demonstrate the necessity of whips for the backs, and chains for the limbs of the people. Know that its subversion is essential to the triumph of justice, the deliverance of the oppressed, the vindication of the BROTHERHOOD OF THE RACE. It was conceived in sin, and brought forth in iniquity; and its career has been marked by unparalleled hypocrisy, by high-handed tyranny, by a bold defiance of the omniscience and omnipotence of God. Freedom indignantly disowns it, and calls for its extinction; for within its borders are three millions of slaves, whose blood constitutes its cement, whose flesh forms a large and flourishing branch of its commerce, and who are ranked with four-footed beasts and creeping things. To secure the adoption of the Constitution of the United States, it was agreed, first, that the African slave-trade,—till that time a feeble, isolated, colonial traffic,—should, for at least twenty years, be prosecuted as a national interest under the American flag, and protected by the national arm;—secondly, that a slaveholding oligarchy, created by allowing three-fifths of the slave population to be represented by their taskmasters, should be allowed a permanent seat in Congress;—thirdly, that the slave system should be secured against internal revolt and external invasion, by the united physical force of the country;—fourthly, that not a foot of national territory should be granted, on which the panting fugitive from slavery might stand, and be safe from his pursuers—thus making every citizen a slave-hunter and slave-catcher. To say that this "covenant with death" shall not be annulled—that this "agreement with hell" shall continue to stand—that this "refuge of lies" shall not be swept away— is to hurl defiance at the eternal throne, and to give the lie to Him who sits thereon. It is an attempt, alike monstrous and impracticable, to blend the light of heaven with the darkness of the bottomless pit, to unite the living with the dead, to associate the Son of God with the Prince of Evil.

Accursed be the AMERICAN UNION, as a stupendous republican imposture!

Accursed be it, as the most frightful despotism, with regard to three millions of the people, ever exercised over any portion of the human family!

Accursed be it, as the most subtle and atrocious compromise ever made to gratify power and selfishness!

Accursed be it, as a libel on Democracy, and a bold assault on Christianity!

Accursed be it, stained as it is with human blood, and supported by human sacrifices!

Accursed be it, for the terrible evils it has inflicted on Africa, by burning her villages, ravaging her coast, and kidnapping her children, at an enormous expense of human life, and for a diabolical purpose!

Accursed be it, for all the crimes it has committed at home—for seeking the utter extermination of the red men of its wildernesses, and for enslaving one-sixth part of its teeming population!

Accused be it, for its hypocrisy, its falsehood, its impudence, its lust, its cruelty, its oppression!

Accursed be it, as a mighty obstacle in the way of universal freedom and equality!

Accursed be it, from the foundation of the roof, and may there soon not be left one stone upon another, that shall not be thrown down!

Henceforth, the watchword of every uncompromising abolitionist, of every friend of God and liberty, must be, both in a religious and political sense—"NO UNION WITH SLAVEHOLDERS!"

NOTES

1. How does Garrison read the Constitution? Which provisions does he cite, and how does he interpret them? Whose interpretation of the Constitution is more persuasive, his or Douglass's? Why?

2. How does Garrison determine the content of natural law? How does his understanding of the sources of natural law compare to Stephens's? In Garrison's opinion, what is the relation between natural law and positive law?

Dred Scott v. Sandford

60 U.S. (19 How.) 393 (1857)

[A much longer excerpt from the case, including the dissents, is presented at p. 733. Dred Scott, a man of African descent, with his wife and children sued for freedom after they traveled into a free state and then returned to a slave state. Among the questions decided by the Court was whether a free person of African descent (as Scott was alleged to be in the complaint) was a "citizen" entitled to sue under federal diversity jurisdiction.—Editors]

■ MR. CHIEF JUSTICE TANEY delivered the opinion of the court.

. . . The question is simply this: Can a negro, whose ancestors were imported into this country, and sold as slaves, become a member of the political community formed and brought into existence by the Constitution of the United States, and as such become entitled to all the rights, and privileges, and immunities, guarantied by that instrument to the citizen? One of which rights is the privilege of suing in a court of the United States in the cases specified in the Constitution. . . .

We think they are not, and that they are not included, and were not intended to be included, under the word "citizens" in the Constitution, and can therefore claim none of the rights and privileges which that instrument provides for and secures to citizens of the United States. On the contrary, they were at that time considered as a subordinate and inferior class of beings, who had been subjugated by the dominant race, and, whether emancipated or not, yet remained subject to their authority, and had no rights or privileges but such as those who held the power and the Government might choose to grant them.

It is not the province of the court to decide upon the justice or injustice, the policy or impolicy, of these laws. The decision of that question belonged to the political or law-making power; to those who formed the sovereignty and framed the Constitution. The duty of the court is, to interpret the instrument they have framed, with the best lights we can obtain on the subject, and to administer it as we find it, according to its true intent and meaning when it was adopted. . . .

It becomes necessary, therefore, to determine who were citizens of the several States when the Constitution was adopted. . . .

In the opinion of the court, the legislation and histories of the times, and the language used in the Declaration of Independence, show, that neither the class of persons who had been imported as slaves, nor their descendants, whether they had become free or not, were then acknowledged as a part of the people, nor intended to be included in the general words used in that memorable instrument.

It is difficult at this day to realize the state of public opinion in relation to that unfortunate race, which prevailed in the civilized and enlightened portions of the world at the time of the Declaration of Independence, and when the Constitution of the United States was framed and adopted. But the public history of every European nation displays it in a manner too plain to be mistaken.

They had for more than a century before been regarded as beings of an inferior order, and altogether unfit to associate with the white race, either in social or political relations; and so far inferior, that they had no rights which the white man was bound to respect; and that the negro might justly and lawfully be reduced to slavery for his benefit. He was bought and sold, and treated as an ordinary article of merchandise and traffic, whenever a profit could be made by it. This opinion was at that time fixed and universal in the civilized portion of the white race. It was regarded as an axiom in morals as well as in politics, which no one thought of disputing, or supposed to be open to dispute; and men in every grade and position in society daily and habitually acted upon it in their private pursuits, as well as in matters of public concern, without doubting for a moment the correctness of this opinion.

And in no nation was this opinion more firmly fixed or more uniformly acted upon than by the English Government and English people. They not only seized them on the coast of Africa, and sold them or held them in slavery for their own use; but they took them as ordinary articles of merchandise to every country where they could make a profit on them, and were far more extensively engaged in this commerce than any other nation in the world. . . .

The language of the Declaration of Independence is equally conclusive:

> . . . "We hold these truths to be self-evident: that all men are created equal; that they are endowed by their Creator with certain unalienable rights; that among them is life, liberty, and the pursuit of happiness; that to secure these rights, Governments are instituted, deriving their just powers from the consent of the governed."

The general words above quoted would seem to embrace the whole human family, and if they were used in a similar instrument at this day would be so understood. But it is too clear for dispute, that the enslaved African race were not intended to be included, and formed no part of the people who framed and adopted this declaration; for if the language, as understood in that day, would embrace them, the conduct of the distinguished men who framed the Declaration of Independence would have been utterly and flagrantly inconsistent with the principles they asserted; and instead of the sympathy of mankind, to which they so confidently appealed, they would have deserved and received universal rebuke and reprobation. . . .

This state of public opinion had undergone no change when the Constitution was adopted, as is equally evident from its provisions and language. . . .

[And] there are two clauses in the Constitution which point directly and specifically to the negro race as a separate class of persons, and show clearly that they were not regarded as a portion of the people or citizens of the Government then formed.

One of these clauses reserves to each of the thirteen States the right to import slaves until the year 1808, if it thinks proper. And the importation which it thus sanctions was unquestionably of persons of the race of which we are speaking, as the traffic in slaves in the United States had always been confined to them. And by the other provision the States pledge themselves to each other to maintain the right of property of the master, by delivering up to him any slave who may have escaped from his service, and be found within their respective territories. By the first above-mentioned clause, therefore, the right to purchase and hold this property is directly sanctioned and authorized for twenty years by the people who framed the Constitution. And by the second, they pledge themselves to maintain and uphold the right of the master in the manner specified, as long as the Government they then formed should endure. And these two provisions show, conclusively, that neither the description of persons therein referred to, nor their descendants, were embraced in any of the other provisions of the Constitution; for certainly these two clauses were not intended to confer on them or their posterity the blessings of liberty, or any of the personal rights so carefully provided for the citizen. . . .

NOTES

1.   With which of the preceding interpretations of the Constitution—that of Stephens, Douglass, or Garrison—does Chief Justice Taney most closely agree? What evidence does he supply? What is his reading of the Declaration of Independence?

2.   Justices McLean and Curtis dissented (see p. 747). In dissenting from the holding "that a person of African descent cannot be a citizen of the United States," Justice Curtis said:

> Slavery, being contrary to natural right, is created only by municipal law. This is not only plain in itself, and agreed by all writers on the subject, but is inferable from the Constitution, and has been explicitly declared by this court. The Constitution refers to slaves as "persons held to service in one State, under the laws thereof." Nothing can more clearly describe a status created by municipal law.

Justice McLean agreed, adding that the state of slavery as "a mere municipal regulation, founded upon and limited to the range of the territorial laws," was a principle "fully recognized in Somersett's case, which was decided before the American Revolution."

3.   The *Dred Scott* majority opinion contains a number of holdings. In addition to its holding that no person of African descent could be a citizen of the United States, the Court also held that the Due Process Clause of the Fifth Amendment prevents Congress from prohibiting slavery in the territories. Keep in mind *Dred Scott*'s citizenship and congressional-power holdings as we turn to the Thirteenth and Fourteenth Amendments.

B. THE THIRTEENTH AMENDMENT

Amend. XIII, § 1: Neither slavery nor involuntary servitude, except as a punishment for crime whereof the party shall have been duly convicted, shall exist within the United States, or any place subject to their jurisdiction.

§ 2: Congress shall have power to enforce this article by appropriate legislation.

The Thirteenth Amendment was passed by Congress in early 1865 and ratified that year by the three-fourths majority of state legislatures required by Article V (including by some Reconstruction state legislatures in the South). It abolishes slavery, except as punishment for a crime. Unlike other amendments to the

Constitution, it regulates not merely the powers of government but private conduct as well: no state may enforce slavery by law, and no private individual may hold another person as a slave. Slavery shall not "exist."

No sooner had slavery been constitutionally banned than states and localities in the South sought to replicate the prior subjugation, insofar as possible, by enacting "Black Codes." These restricted the rights of black citizens to own property, to engage in certain occupations, and to testify in court. They also imposed stringent labor requirements, such as a requirement that the contracts of black employees have a term of at least one year, with severe penalties for leaving employment before the contract term expired. Other crimes included "vagrancy," " 'insulting' " speech, " 'malicious mischief,' " and "preaching the Gospel without a license." Eric Foner, RECONSTRUCTION: AMERICA'S UNFINISHED REVOLUTION 1863–1877, at 200 (1988). The Black Codes suggested that a large number of Southern legislators gave " '[t]heir whole thought and time . . . to plans for getting things back as near to slavery as possible.' " Id. at 199 (quoting Benjamin F. Flanders). What would Congress do to respond to Southern intransigence? What would it do to protect the newly freed slaves?

[*Assignment 63*]

C. THE FOURTEENTH AMENDMENT

The Congressional Response

When Southern states enacted the "Black Codes" to subjugate the newly freed slaves, Congress responded with legislation. It enacted the Civil Rights Act of 1866, and it also considered—but did not enact, because of constitutional objections—the Privileges and Immunities Act of 1866. Both are presented here. As you read them, and a speech by a leading member of the House of Representatives in support of the Civil Rights Act, consider what these bills set out to accomplish and also what their constitutional basis might have been (in the Constitution as of 1866).

The Civil Rights Act of 1866
39th Cong., 14 Stat. 27 (Apr. 9, 1866)

CHAP. XXXI.—*An Act to protect all Persons in the United States in their Civil Rights, and furnish the Means of their Vindication.*

Be it enacted by the Senate and House of Representatives of the United States of America in Congress assembled, That all persons born in the United States and not subject to any foreign power, excluding Indians not taxed, are hereby declared to be citizens of the United States; and such citizens, of every race and color, without regard to any previous condition of slavery or involuntary servitude, except as a punishment for crime whereof the party shall have been duly convicted, shall have the same right, in every State and Territory in the United States, to make and enforce contracts, to sue, be parties, and give evidence, to inherit, purchase, lease, sell, hold, and convey real and personal property, and to full and equal benefit of all laws and proceedings for the security of person and property, as is enjoyed by white citizens, and shall be subject to like punishment, pains, and penalties, and to none other, any law, statute, ordinance, regulation, or custom, to the contrary notwithstanding.

William Lawrence, Speech on the Civil Rights Act of 1866

Cong. Globe, 39th Cong., 1st Session 1832–1836 (Apr. 7, 1866)

. . . It is scarcely less to the people of this country than Magna Charta was to the people of England.

It declares who are citizens.

It does not affect any political right, as that of suffrage, the right to sit on juries, hold office, &c. This it leaves to the States, to be determined by each for itself. It does not confer any civil right, but so far as there is any power in the States to limit, enlarge, or declare civil rights, all these are left to the States.

But it does provide that as to certain enumerated civil rights every citizen "shall have the same right in every State and Territory." That is whatever of certain civil rights may be enjoyed by any shall be shared by all citizens in each State, and in the Territories, and these are:

1. To make and enforce contracts.

2. To sue, to be sued, and to be parties.

3. To give evidence.

4. To inherit, purchase, lease, sell, hold, and convey real and personal property.

5. To be entitled to full and equal benefit of all laws and proceedings for the security of person and property. . . .

There is . . . a national citizenship. And citizenship implies certain rights which are to be protected, and imposes the duty of allegiance and obedience to the laws. . . .

It has never been deemed necessary to enact in any constitution or law that citizens should have the right to life or liberty or the right to acquire property. These rights are recognized by the Constitution as existing anterior to and independently of all laws and all constitutions.

Without further authority I may assume, then, that there are certain absolute rights which pertain to every citizen, which are inherent, and of which a State cannot constitutionally deprive him. But not only are these rights inherent and indestructible, but the means whereby they may be possessed and enjoyed are equally so.

We learn from Coke that—"When the law granteth anything to any one that also is granted without which the thing itself cannot be." . . .

It is idle to say that a citizen shall have the right to life, yet to deny him the right to labor, whereby alone he can live. It is a mockery to say that a citizen may have a right to live, and yet deny him the right to make a contract to secure the privilege and the rewards of labor. It is worse than mockery to say that men may be clothed by the national authority with the character of citizens, yet may be stripped by State authority of the means by which citizens may exist. . . .

Every citizen, therefore, has the absolute right to live, the right of personal security, personal liberty, and the right to acquire and enjoy property. These are rights of citizenship. As necessary incidents of these absolute rights, there are others, as the right to make and enforce contracts, to purchase, hold, and enjoy property, and to share the benefit of laws for the security of person and property.

Now, there are two ways in which a State may undertake to deprive citizens of these absolute, inherent, and inalienable rights: either by prohibitory laws, or by a failure to protect any one of them.

If the people of a State should become hostile to a large class of naturalized citizens and should enact laws to prohibit them and no other citizens from making contracts, from suing, from giving evidence, from inheriting, buying, holding, or selling property, or even from coming into the State, that would be prohibitory legislation. If the State should simply enact laws for native-born citizens and provide no law under which naturalized citizens could enjoy any one of these rights, and should deny them all protection by civil process or penal enactments, that would be a denial of justice. . . .

This bill, in that broad and comprehensive philanthropy which regards all men in their civil rights as equal before the law, is not made for any class or creed, or race or color, but in the great future that awaits us will, if it become a law, protect every citizen, including the millions of people of foreign birth who will flock to our shores to become citizens and to find here a land of liberty and law.

But there is a present necessity for this bill which I find forcibly stated thus:

"The fact that no single southern Legislature has yet recognized the right of blacks to the civil rights accorded to every white alien, suffices to prove the need of such legislation by Congress. We believe no single southern State has yet enabled blacks to sue and be sued, to give testimony and rebut testimony on equal terms with whites. . . .

"The Cincinnati Commercial has a letter from a correspondent traveling through Mississippi, who states that the barbarous vagrant law recently passed by the rebel State Legislature is rigidly enforced, and under its provisions the freed slaves are rapidly being re-enslaved. No negro is allowed to buy, rent, or lease any real estate; all minors of any value are taken from their parents and bound out to planters; and every freedman who does not contract for a year's labor is taken up as a vagrant. . . ."

Since this statement of the condition of southern law, I believe Georgia, by the act of March 17, 1866, has made provision for the enforcement of civil rights.

It is barbarous, inhuman, infamous, to turn over four million liberated slaves, always loyal to the Government, to the fury of their rebel masters, who deny them the benefit of all laws for the protection of their civil rights. . . .

[Representative Lawrence proceeded to read extensive evidence from military officers and government officials about the Southern states' denial of civil rights, both to newly freed slaves and to white supporters of the Union cause. He argued that Congress had power to enforce the Privileges and Immunities Clause of Article IV "and the equal civil rights which it recognizes or by implication affirms to exist among citizens of the same State." He then quoted various authorities on the privileges and

immunities of citizens, including Chancellor Kent, Justice Story, and Corfield v. Coryell. *(Most of the passage quoted from* Corfield *can be found at p. 709.)—Editors]*

The Constitution does not define what these privileges and immunities are; but all privileges and immunities are of two kinds, to wit, those which I have shown to be inherent in every citizen of the United States, and such others as may be conferred by local law and pertain only to the citizen of the State. . . .

NOTES

1.   The first clause of the Civil Rights Act of 1866 extends United States citizenship to all persons born in the United States (except those subject to foreign powers and Indians not taxed). Is this provision a legislative reversal of the *Dred Scott* decision, which held that persons of African ancestry, "whether emancipated or not," could not be citizens? Can Congress do that? *Dred Scott* said *no.* 60 U.S. at 417. Most members of the Thirty-ninth Congress thought *Dred Scott* was wrongly decided. But should they have waited for the Supreme Court to reverse itself before acting on this belief? Other members thought that, even if *Dred Scott* were rightly decided, it was reversed by the Thirteenth Amendment. Is that correct? Did the Thirteenth Amendment address the legal status of free persons of color?

2.   Note the logical structure of the remainder of Section 1 of the Civil Rights Act. It does not require the states to extend the listed rights to anyone, but only to refrain from racial discrimination with regard to the rights they choose to extend. Nor does the provision apply to all rights, but only to the listed set. What is the unifying theme of the listed rights? All were violated by the "Black Code" provisions in some Southern states. All are basic common law rights—in fact, the rights track the traditional first-year curriculum in law school. And all were "Privileges and Immunities" of citizens protected under Article IV, meaning that they were rights that a citizen of Massachusetts would enjoy when present in the State of Ohio.

What rights are missing? Which ones does Representative Lawrence list as "political rights" that were not affected by the bill? Political rights were ones that not all citizens enjoyed. These rights of political participation were not exercised by women or by children. Moreover, they were rights that a citizen of one state could not exercise when present in another state, notwithstanding Article IV. See p. 711. Remember this distinction between "political rights" and "civil rights"—it will come up again.

3.   Was this statute constitutional? Advocates of the Civil Rights Act of 1866 asserted three possible sources of congressional authority. First was the naturalization power—the power to make new citizens and define their rights. How aggressive a reading of the naturalization power is needed to make that even plausible?

Second was the argument that the 1866 Act was within the power of Congress under Section 2 of the Thirteenth Amendment to enact "appropriate legislation" to "enforce" the prohibition on "slavery and involuntary servitude." Is that convincing? Does the abolition of slavery logically entail an equality of civil rights? Is discrimination the same thing as slavery? Even assuming it is not, may Congress decide that legislation forbidding discrimination with respect to civil rights is an "appropriate" means of abolishing slavery, or the badges or incidents of slavery? Just how far does Congress's enforcement power under the Thirteenth Amendment go? (As we will see, this question is of continuing interest because the Fourteenth Amendment is limited to state action, while the Thirteenth Amendment extends to private action. Thus, Section 2 of the Thirteenth Amendment may be a more potent source of authority for legislation combating private discrimination, at least on the basis of race.)

A third source of authority invoked by advocates of the Civil Rights Act of 1866, including Representative Lawrence, was the Privileges and Immunities Clause of Article IV. To this there were two objections. First, the standard interpretation of this clause was that it prohibited states from discriminating against citizens of other states—not against discriminating against subsets of their own population. Does the text of the clause support that interpretation? Second, Congress was not explicitly given power to enforce the Privileges and Immunities Clause of Article IV (in contrast to the Full Faith and Credit Clause, found in the same Article). This was especially awkward for the anti-slavery members of the Thirty-ninth Congress, because many of them had been critical of the Supreme Court's decision in *Prigg v. Pennsylvania* (see p. 721), holding that Congress had an implied power to enforce the Fugitive Slave Clause, which similarly lacked an enforcement provision. For some, like Representative John Bingham, this was the principal constitutional objection to the Civil Rights Act of 1866: he believed the Act appropriately asserted the privileges and immunities of the new citizens created by emancipation, but did not think Congress had power to enact legislation enforcing those rights.

4.   Representative Lawrence refers to several terms and concepts that will come up repeatedly in the following readings, and it is good to begin thinking of them here. One word he uses repeatedly is "protect." He is drawing on a long tradition—found in Hobbes, Blackstone, the Declaration of Independence, and state constitutions—when he invokes a set of reciprocal duties: the citizen owes the state a duty of allegiance, and the state owes the citizen a duty of protection. See Christopher R. Green, *The Original Sense of the (Equal) Protection Clause: Pre-Enactment History*, 19 Geo. Mason U. Civ. Rts. L. J. 1, 35–43 (2008). How does Lawrence think a state could fail to fulfill its duty of protection?

Another concept—or perhaps a tension—is the centrality of race. Who does Lawrence think the Civil Rights Act will protect? Will it protect only persons of color in the South from those who would reenslave and oppress them? Or is its application broader? On the other hand, what is the "present necessity" that motivated the bill? How is that motivation reflected in the bill itself?

Finally, Lawrence refers to the concept of "privileges and immunities." Article IV of the Constitution requires that states grant to citizens of other states the same "privileges and immunities" they grant to their own citizens—in other words, it is a requirement of equality. But what are those privileges and immunities? Lawrence points to some as being "inherent in every citizen of the United States"—which might those be? (Does the Constitution name any privileges? Look at Article I, Section 9. What else might be a privilege or immunity?) And he points to others as "conferred by local law and pertain[ing] only to the citizen of the State," that is, they can vary from state. What are those? Here Lawrence cites a passage from a decision called *Corfield v. Coryell*. The passage is reprinted on p. 710, and you should read it now. The passage is canonical, and it will be referenced repeatedly in the pages that follow.

A Bill to Declare and Protect All the Privileges and Immunities of Citizens of the United States in the Several States

39th Cong., 1st Session, H.R. 437 (Apr. 2, 1866)

. . . That every person, being a citizen of the United State shall, in right of such citizenship, be entitled, freely and without hindrance or molestation, to go from the State, Territory, or district of his or her residence, and to pass into and through and to sojourn, remain and take permanent abode within each of the several States, Territories, and districts of the United States, and therein to acquire, own, control, enjoy and dispose of property, real, personal and mixed; and to do and transact business, and to have full and speedy redress in the courts for all rights of person and property, as fully as such rights and privileges are held and enjoyed by the other citizens of such State, Territory, or district; and, moreover, therein to have, enjoy, and demand the same immunities and exemptions from high or excessive impositions, assessments, and taxation as are enjoyed by such other citizens under the laws or usages of such State, Territory, or district, and to have, demand, and enjoy all other privileges and immunities which the citizens of the same State, Territory, or district would be entitled to under the like circumstances. . . .

[The remaining sections defined the liability of those who deprived a citizen of the United States of any of the privileges or benefits that were secured by the act, and excluded from the protection of the act all who had engaged in or aided the rebellion, unless pardoned.—Editors]

NOTES

1.   What are the rights—the "privileges and immunities"—that the proposed Privileges and Immunities Act of 1866 protected? Had the statute been enacted, would it have required that states grant those privileges and immunities? Would it have required that states grant them equally among in-staters? Or would it have required only that they be granted equally in the sense of no discrimination against out-of-staters?

2.   How would the proposed Privileges and Immunities Act have gone further than the Civil Rights Act of 1866?

Drafting a New Amendment

Doubts about the scope of Congress's powers were enough to sink the proposed Privileges and Immunities Act, but not another bill that was under consideration. On March 13, the House joined the Senate in passing the Civil Rights Act of 1866. It had the support of nearly all of the Republicans in Congress, both the "Radical Republicans" who wanted a prolonged reconstruction of the conquered South and a more robust measure of racial equality, and the "Moderate Republicans" who wanted a prompt seating of Southern senators and representatives in Congress. The president, Andrew Johnson, was a Union-supporting Democrat from Tenneseee who had served as President Lincoln's vice-president, and succeeded Lincoln after his assassination. Johnson had begun to have sharp disagreements with Congress about the military governments established in the South, but the Republicans in Congress were confident of his support for the Civil Rights Act.

But then President Johnson surprised them and vetoed the bill. In his veto message, Johnson articulated several constitutional objections, chiefly that Congress lacked power to displace state laws discriminating on the basis of race. Johnson noted that the Constitution did place limits on how states could legislate (Article I, Section 10); he also noted that the Constitution gave Congress power to "make rules and regulations" for the territories (Article IV). But he denied that Congress had any power to do the same in the states. Congress could not require "a perfect equality of the white and colored races . . . in every State of the Union over the vast field of State jurisdiction covered by these enumerated rights." Andrew Johnson, Veto Message of

March 27, 1866, in A COMPILATION OF THE MESSAGES AND PAPERS OF THE PRESIDENTS 1789–1897, at 407 (James D. Richardson ed., 1897). Johnson urged gradualism in making the freed slaves citizens: "Four millions of them have just emerged from slavery into freedom. Can it be reasonably supposed that they possess the requisite qualifications to entitle them to all the privileges and immunities of citizens of the United States?" He also questioned the wisdom of conferring national citizenship upon the newly freed slaves while the Southern states were unrepresented in Congress, and warned that "[t]he tendency of the bill must be to resuscitate the spirit of rebellion and to arrest the progress of those influences which are more closely drawing around the States the bonds of union and peace." Johnson did not, however, have the last word. Congress amended the act, removing language that could have been construed to extend to voting, and then passed it again with the two-thirds majority needed to override President Johnson's veto. For the first time, Congress had overriden a veto to enact a major law.

The confrontation between Congress and President Jackson was to have a more lasting consequence. The Republican majority in Congress wanted a solid constitutional basis for the Civil Rights Act (and perhaps also for the proposed Privileges and Immunities Act), but they knew they needed another amendment to the Constitution. The task of proposing an amendment was taken up by the Joint Committee on Reconstruction, a powerful committee that Congress had set up to address questions about how the Southern states were to again take their place in the national government.

The Joint Committee's first proposal was an amendment that would have denied all representation in Congress to any states that denied the right to vote because of race. The amendment would have forced the Southern states to choose: they could have political representation in the national government, or they could continue to disenfranchise their black citizens, but not both. The amendment was passed by the House but defeated by the Senate.

The Joint Committee's next proposal was the basis for what eventually became the Fourteenth Amendment. On behalf of the committee, Congressman John Bingham submitted it to Congress on February 26, 1866:

> The Congress shall have power to make all laws which shall be necessary and proper to secure to the citizens of each State all privileges and immunities of citizens in the several States, and to all persons in the several States equal protection in the rights of life, liberty, and property.

Cong. Globe, 39th Cong., 1st Sess. 1034 (Feb. 26, 1866). In this proposal one can see the central themes of what became Section 1 of the Fourteenth Amendment: a defense of the "privileges and immunities of citizens," and an idea of "equal protection" with respect to rights of "life, liberty, and property." But the proposal does not protect those things directly—instead it simply consists of a broad power for Congress to pass laws "necessary and proper" to achieve these protections.

The House did not adopt Bingham's bill. Instead, the Joint Committee went back to work, and it produced a revised proposal. The proposal had five sections. The first laid new duties on the states with respect to "the privileges or immunities of citizens of the United States," "due process of law," and "the equal protection of the laws." The second restricted representation in Congress for any states that denied adult black males the right to vote. The third denied supporters of the Confederacy the right to vote in the next three national elections. The fourth repudiated Confederate war debts. And the fifth gave Congress the power to enforce the provisions of the first four sections. This proposal was nearly identical to what became the Fourteenth Amendment, but one more revision was required. The third section—prohibiting Confederate supporters from voting until after the 1870 election—was a nakedly political attempt by the House Republicans to preserve their majority. The Senate forced a change to that section; it now prohibited rebel oath-breakers from holding federal offices.

On June 13, 1866, the House passed the proposed amendment on a party-line vote, sending it to the states for ratification.

The Text

Now take a close look at the text of the Fourteenth Amendment as ratified and compare it with Bingham's original proposal. Start with Sections 1 and 5:

> *Amend. XIV, § 1: All persons born or naturalized in the United States, and subject to the jurisdiction thereof, are citizens of the United States and of the State wherein they reside. No State shall make or enforce any law which shall abridge the privileges or immunities of citizens of the United States; nor shall any State deprive any person of life, liberty, or property, without due process of law; nor deny to any person within its jurisdiction the equal protection of the laws.*

> *§ 5: The Congress shall have power to enforce, by appropriate legislation, the provisions of this article.*

In its first sentence the amendment reversed *Dred Scott*'s citizenship holding. This was no moot point; Southern political leaders continued after the Civil War to invoke *Dred Scott* as establishing that the newly freed slaves could not be citizens. Although Congress had asserted the contrary in the Civil Rights Act of 1866, this sentence made that declaration of citizenship for every freed slave part of the Constitution.

The second sentence of Section 1 is expressly addressed to states: "No state shall. . . ." And what states are prohibited from doing is abridging "the privileges or immunities of citizens of the United States," failing to give "due process," and denying "the equal protection of the laws." And Section 5 gives Congress power to make laws "appropriate" (a gloss on Bingham's "necessary and proper") for enforcing these prohibitions on the states. These changes and continuities—shifting from *a power to legislate with respect to civil rights* to *a prohibition of what states may do in abridging civil rights, with a power to enforce that prohibition*—had significant consequences for American constitutional law.

What did the change from Bingham's original proposal mean in practical terms? Does Congress's legislative power under the Fourteenth Amendment directly include a power to regulate the actions of private individuals (such as discrimination by private persons, groups, or businesses)? May Congress determine that such legislation is "appropriate" to carrying into execution a prohibition on *state* action? If the answer to these questions is *No*, then the amendment is narrower in that respect than the original Bingham proposal. Indeed, that appears to have been one of the purposes of the change: moderates feared that Bingham's proposal would give

Congress too sweeping a power to legislate concerning local matters, thus upsetting the balance between the national government and the states.

Another significant consequence of the restructuring of Bingham's proposal was to make the amendment more than just a grant of power to Congress to pass civil rights laws—laws that might be repealed by a subsequent Congress. Rather, because Section 1 of the Fourteenth Amendment is a direct prohibition, the amendment *itself* constrains the states. This change entrenched the protection of civil rights in Section 1 against congressional backsliding in the future—a concern that some of the amendment's backers had about the original Bingham proposal. Representative (and future President) James Garfield expressed the concern this way:

> The civil rights bill is now a part of the law of the land. But every gentleman knows it will cease to be a part of the law whenever the sad moment arrives when that gentlemen's party comes into power. It is precisely for that reason that we propose to lift that great and good law above the reach of political strife, beyond the reach of the plots and machinations of any party, and fix it in the serene sky, in the eternal firmament of the Constitution, where no storm of passion can shake it and no cloud can obscure it.

Cong. Globe, 39th Cong., 1st Sess. 2462 (May 8, 1866). The Fourteenth Amendment as finally adopted thus allows judicial enforcement of the prohibitions contained in Section 1, with or without further implementing legislation by Congress pursuant to its powers under Section 5.

Should Congress or the courts have primacy in interpreting and enforcing the Fourteenth Amendment? The historical context suggests that Congress was expected to have the primary role. After all, one reason for the Fourteenth Amendment was the desire of members of Congress to provide a more secure constitutional basis for the civil rights legislation they had already passed, such as the Civil Rights Act of 1866. In addition, recent experience with the Supreme Court had not always instilled confidence in its ability to faithfully interpret the Constitution. The drafters remembered *Dred Scott*. Yet the Republicans in Congress also expected the courts to enforce the amendment, even as they saw themselves as the primary expositors of the amendment's broad terms. Do their expectations matter?

Sandwiched between Section 1's prohibition and Section 5's enforcement power, several provisions of the Fourteenth Amendment addressed residual questions about slavery and the Civil War while also raising new questions about voting rights:

> *§ 2: Representatives shall be apportioned among the several States according to their respective numbers, counting the whole number of persons in each State, excluding Indians not taxed. But when the right to vote at any election for the choice of electors for President and Vice President of the United States, Representatives in Congress, the Executive and Judicial officers of a State, or the members of the Legislature thereof, is denied to any of the male inhabitants of such State, being twenty-one years of age, and citizens of the United States, or in any way abridged, except for participation in rebellion, or other crime, the basis of representation therein shall be reduced in the proportion which the number of such male citizens shall bear to the whole number of male citizens twenty-one years of age in such State.*

The Thirteenth Amendment had effectively repealed the Three-fifths Clause of the original Constitution. One implication was that the Southern states—without giving the freedmen the right to vote—would have far more representation in Congress than they did before the War. (Can you see why?) Section 2 was the answer. If a state discriminated against black voters, its representation in Congress would be diminished commensurately. If a state entirely denied its black citizens the right to vote, it would receive for them *zero*-fifths representation in Congress (rather than the old three-fifths).

For the Republicans in Congress this section was a matter of political survival; they wanted to avoid being swamped by a newly empowered South. It was also a matter of constitutional principle, because they questioned whether a state had a "Republican Form of Government" (as required by Article IV) if it denied the right to vote to a huge swath of its free male citizens. Indeed, Congress would soon invoke the Guarantee Clause to refuse to seat representatives from states that initially refused to ratify the Fourteenth Amendment. (One embarrassment was that some Northern states also denied the right to vote to swathes of their male citizens, forcing the Republicans to make legalistic and sometimes awkward distinctions between the Northern and Southern governments.)

What does the existence of Section 2 of the Fourteenth Amendment imply about the scope of Section 1? Did Section 1 prohibit racial discrimination in voting requirements? If so, why would Section 2 even exist? But why would voting not be a "privilege or immunity" or a matter of "equal protection"? In thinking about that question, remember that the drafters and ratifiers of the amendment recognized— some of them with deep regret—that the established meaning of "privileges and immunities" did not include political rights such as voting, standing for election, and serving on juries. It was understood that a citizen of Massachusetts who happened to be in Ohio on election day would not be permitted to vote in Ohio. Nor was equality in voting considered a matter of equal *protection* of the laws. A final, decisive consideration is the existence of the Fifteenth Amendment. If the Fourteenth prohibited racial discrimination in voting, the Fifteenth would have been unnecessary.

But push a little further on this question. Does the text *say* that voting is not among "the privileges or immunities of citizens of the United States"? Was "privileges [and/or] immunities" a term of art? Was the term of art "privileges and immunities *of citizens*" (i.e., civil rights, the rights of citizens)? Or did the text need to be read with the background of previous judicial interpretation in mind? Or did the text need to be read in its historical context? Or in light of structural arguments from Section 2 of the Fourteenth Amendment, and from the existence of the Fifteenth Amendment? Should these other considerations and arguments inform our reading of the text? Or is that exactly backwards?

> *§ 3: No person shall be a Senator or Representative in Congress, or elector of President and Vice President, or hold any office, civil or military, under the United States, or under any State, who, having previously taken an oath, as a member of Congress, or as an officer of the United States, or as a member of any State legislature, or as an executive or judicial officer of any State, to support the Constitution of the United States, shall have engaged in insurrection or rebellion against the same, or given aid or comfort to the enemies thereof. But Congress may by a vote of two-thirds of each House, remove such disability.*

The penultimate draft of Section 3, which prohibited all Confederate supporters from voting in the next three national elections, was certain to have been the most explosive part of the entire amendment in the South. Not coincidentally, for some of the Radical Republicans, it was the most important part of the amendment. Yet even the final version of Section 3—"only" a prohibition on office-holding—could still plausibly be called the most divisive part of the amendment. Why did it matter so much to both sides?

Reconstruction Republicans feared the survival of the political order of the former Confederacy, including the prospect of former rebel leaders returning to Congress. They heard from Union military commanders and other correspondents in the South about the threats to the life, liberty, and property of the freed slaves. They knew that the Southern states could not be counted on to protect their black citizens. Whether those states had even been "reconstructed" at all seemed an open question. For these reasons, the punitive first sentence of the section was key. It prevented the Southern states from sending *en masse* to Washington the very political leaders who had taken them into secession.

The South was certain to chafe at this restriction on its choice of senators and representatives—but that prospect, to some of the Radical Republicans, was not undesirable. They thought Section 3 would prove unacceptable to the Southern states, preventing them from promptly ratifying the amendment. As long as they would not ratify the amendment, Congress would not seat their senators and representatives. And as long as the Southern members of Congress were not seated, the Radical Republicans would keep control of Congress.

Now read carefully the last sentence of Section 3. If it was a matter of constitutional principle that those who had broken their oath to support the Constitution could not return to Congress, then why allow Congress itself to forgive the transgression? Again the design was careful. Congress was giving itself a valuable bargaining chip that it could trade for Southern concessions: Section 3's last sentence "would afford the opportunity later on to offer an inducement to the Southern leaders—those proscribed by the section—in the way of amnesty as a return for aid given to the party in power." Horace Edgar Flack, THE ADOPTION OF THE FOURTEENTH AMENDMENT 133 (1908). Something like that happened: six years later, when an unexpectedly strong Democratic candidate ran for president, the Republican Congress chose conciliation with the Amnesty Act of 1872, which removed the effect of Section 3 for nearly all the former Confederates.

One concluding question about Section 3: if a Southern state sent to Congress a rebel oathbreaker, and Congress refused to seat him (before the 1872 amnesty act), would Congress be violating *Section 1*? Can you see why not? Would holding a federal office be either a "privilege or immunity" or a matter of "protection"? Would it instead be a political right? Moreover, whom does Section 1 restrict? Does it restrict Congress? The context has changed, but as you will soon see, questions like the ones you just answered remain important in constitutional law today.

> *§ 4: The validity of the public debt of the United States, authorized by law, including debts incurred for payment of pensions and bounties for services in suppressing insurrection or rebellion, shall not be questioned. But neither the United States nor any State shall assume or pay any debt or obligation incurred in aid of insurrection or rebellion against the United States, or any*

*claim for the loss or emancipation of any slave; but all such debts,
obligations and claims shall be held illegal and void.*

After a major war there is always the question of how to settle accounts. (After
the Revolutionary War, there was the Assumption Controversy, p. 610). Section 4 of
the Fourteenth Amendment is a selective guarantee and a selective repudiation. On
the one hand, the Union's Civil War debt "shall not be questioned." On the other
hand, any debt incurred "in aid of insurrection or rebellion against the United States"
was repudiated, and no slave-owner could be paid "for the loss or emancipation of
any slave."

This section was the least controversial in the amendment. No one expected
Congress to pay Confederate debts; it would only encourage secession if Congress
picked up the tab. Nor was the refusal to compensate slaveowners particularly
controversial in 1866. In England, emancipation had been accompanied by
compensation, and in the United States a number of abolitionists had supported
compensation. But that was before the War. The Republican Congress would
certainly not pay slaveowners, and so the effect of Section 4 was to block any
payments that might be made in the future by a Southern-dominated Congress, or
by more sympathetic states. (This provision might also be considered a clarification
of, or amendment to, the Takings Clause, which had sometimes been thought to
require compensation for emancipation.)

Although Section 4 might seem to be of only historical interest, notice that its
first sentence secures the validity of the public debt *permanently*, not just for the
War. It drew attention in 2011, when Congress and President Obama could not agree
on the terms of a debt-ceiling increase and it appeared possible the United States
might not have sufficient funds to make interest and principal payments on the
national debt. Some scholars argued that the president has authority under Section
4 to borrow money to prevent a default. Their argument was that a default would
violate the provision that the federal debt "shall not be questioned" and that the
president has authority under the Take Care Clause to prevent that unconstitutional
result. Others argued that having insufficient funds to pay the national debt does
not mean that its "validity" is "questioned," and that only Congress can authorize the
issuance of debt. Does either interpretation of Section 4 persuade you?

Debate and Ratification

The proposed Fourteenth Amendment was the subject of intense public debate.
Members of Congress gave myriads of speeches for it and against it around the
country. President Johnson was understood to be an opponent of the amendment,
and he toured the country speaking against the Reconstruction policy of the
Republican Congress. The nation was awash in newspaper editorials, printed
sermons, and pamphlets that variously praised or denounced the amendment. Only
a tiny sliver of the debate can be printed here, and what is given is, admittedly, not
even-handed. All four of the speakers here supported the amendment, and they all
spoke about what it would do (and sometimes spoke, with regret, about what it would
not do). The first two speeches were made by members of the Joint Committee on
Reconstruction, Representative Thaddeus Stevens and Senator Jacob Howard, when
they presented the proposed amendment in Congress. Next are two speeches from
the public debate when the amendment was being considered for ratification by the
states: one by Speaker of the House Schuyler Colfax, and the other by Benjamin

Butler, a general in the Union Army and a future governor and U.S. representative. The Colfax and Butler speeches were printed by *The Commercial*, a Republican newspaper in Cincinnati, Ohio, and widely distributed during the ratification debates. (The speeches are not censored; one speaker uses the N-word when quoting a racist charge from opponents of the amendment.)

As you read these speeches, ask yourself what the speakers see as the major defect in the existing Constitution. What do they expect the Fourteenth Amendment to accomplish? What do they expect that it will not accomplish? How central is race to their understanding of the amendment? Finally, how do they understand the great phrases of Section 1—"privileges or immunities of citizens of the United States," "equal protection of the laws," and "due process of law"?

Thaddeus Stevens, Speech Presenting the Proposed Amendment in the U.S. House

Cong. Globe, 39th Cong., 1st Sess. 2459–60 (May 8, 1866)

. . . The first section prohibits the States from abridging the privileges and immunities of citizens of the United States, or unlawfully depriving them of life, liberty, or property, or of denying to any person within their jurisdiction the "equal" protection of the laws.

I can hardly believe that any person can be found who will not admit that every one of these provisions is just. They are all asserted, in some form or other, in our Declaration or organic law. But the Constitution limits only the action of Congress, and is not a limitation on the States. This amendment supplies that defect, and allows Congress to correct the unjust legislation of the States, so far that the law which operates upon one man shall operate equally upon all. Whatever law punishes a white man for a crime shall punish the black man precisely in the same way and to the same degree. Whatever law protects the white man shall afford "equal" protection to the black man. Whatever means of redress is afforded to one shall be afforded to all. Whatever law allows the white man to testify in court shall allow the man of color to do the same. These are great advantages over their present codes. Now different degrees of punishment are inflicted, not on account of the magnitude of the crime, but according to the color of the skin. Now color disqualifies a man from testifying in courts, or being tried in the same way as white men. I need not enumerate these partial and oppressive laws. Unless the Constitution should restrain them those States will all, I fear, keep up this discrimination, and crush to death the hated freedmen. Some answer, "Your civil rights bill secures the same things." That is partly true, but a law is repealable by a majority. And I need hardly say that the first time that the South with their copperhead allies obtain the command of Congress it will be repealed. . . .

The second section I consider the most important in the article. It fixes the basis of representation in Congress. If any State shall exclude any of her adult male citizens from the elective franchise, or abridge that right, she shall forfeit her right to representation in the same proportion. The effect of this provision will be either to compel the States to grant universal suffrage or so to shear them of their power as to keep them forever in a hopeless minority in the national Government, both legislative and executive. . . .

I admit that this article is not as good as the one we sent to death in the Senate. In my judgment, we shall not approach the measure of justice until we have given every adult freedman a homestead on the land where he was born and toiled and suffered. Forty acres of land and a hut would be more valuable to him than the immediate right to vote. Unless we give them this we shall receive the censure of mankind and the curse of Heaven. That article referred to provided that if one of the injured race was excluded the State should forfeit the right to have any of them represented. That would have hastened their full enfranchisement. This section allows the States to discriminate among the same class, and receive proportionate credit in representation. This I dislike. But it is a short step forward. . . .

Jacob Howard, Presenting the Proposed Amendment to the U.S. Senate

Cong. Globe, 39th Cong., 1st Sess. 2765–66 (May 23, 1866)

One result of [the joint committee's] investigations has been the joint resolutions for the amendment of the Constitution of the United States now under consideration. After most mature deliberation and discussion, reaching through weeks and even months, they came to the conclusion that it was necessary, in order to restore peace and quiet to the country and again to impart vigor and efficiency to the laws, and especially to obtain something in the shape of a security for the future against the recurrence of the enormous evils under which the country has labored for the last four years, that the Constitution of the United States ought to be amended; and the project which they have now submitted is the result of their deliberations upon that subject.

The first section of the amendment they have submitted for the consideration of the two Houses relates to the privileges and immunities of citizens of the several States, and to the rights and privileges of all persons, whether citizens or others, under the laws of the United States. It declares that—

> No State shall make or enforce any law which shall abridge the privileges or immunities of citizens of the United States; nor shall any State deprive any person of life, liberty, or property without due process of law; nor deny to any person within its jurisdiction the equal protection of the laws.

It will be observed that this is a general prohibition upon all the States, as such, from abridging the privileges and immunities of the citizens of the United States. That is its first clause, and I regard it as very important. . . .

[It] relates to the privileges and immunities of citizens of the United States as such, and as distinguished from all other persons not citizens of the United States. It is not, perhaps, very easy to define with accuracy what is meant by the expression, "citizen of the United States," although that expression occurs twice in the Constitution, once in reference to the President of the United States, in which instance it is declared that none but a citizen of the United States shall be President, and again in reference to Senators, who are likewise to be citizens of the United States. Undoubtedly the expression is used in both those instances in the same sense in which it is employed in the amendment now before us. A citizen of the United States is held by the courts to be a person who was born within the limits of the United States and subject to their laws. . . . [T]o put the citizens of the several States on an equality with each other as to all fundamental rights, a clause was introduced in the Constitution declaring that "the citizens of each State shall be entitled to all privileges and immunities of citizens in the several States."

The effect of this clause was to constitute *ipso facto* the citizens of each one of the original States citizens of the United States. They are, by constitutional right, entitled to these privileges and immunities, and may assert this right and these privileges and immunities, and ask for their enforcement whenever they go within the limits of the several States of the Union.

It would be a curious question to solve what are the privileges and immunities of citizens of each of the States in the several States. I do not propose to go at any length into that question at this time. It would be a somewhat barren discussion. But it is certain the clause was inserted in the Constitution for some good purpose. It has in view some results beneficial to the citizens of the several States, or it would not be found there; yet I am not aware that the Supreme Court have ever undertaken to define either the nature or extent of the privileges and immunities thus guarantied. Indeed, if my recollection serves me, that court, on a certain occasion not many years since, when this question seemed to present it self to them, very modestly declined to into a definition of them, leaving questions arising under the clause to be discussed and adjudicated when they should happen practically to arise. But we may gather some intimation of what probably will be the opinion of the judiciary by referring to a case adjudged many years ago in one of the circuit courts of the United States by Judge Washington. . . . *[Senator Howard next read a passage from* Coryfield v. Coryell, *most of which is printed at p. 710.—Editors]*

Such is the character of the privileges and immunities spoken of in the second section of the fourth article of the Constitution. To these privileges and immunities, whatever they may be—for they are not and cannot be fully defined in their entire extent and precise nature—to these should be added the personal rights guarantied and secured by the first eight amendments of the Constitution; such as the freedom of speech and of the press; the right of the people peaceably to assemble and petition the Government for a redress of grievances, a right appertaining to each and all the people; the right to keep and to bear arms; the right to be exempted from the quartering of soldiers in a house without the consent of the owner; the right to be exempt from unreasonable searches and seizures, and from any search or seizure except by virtue of a warrant issued upon a formal oath or affidavit; the right of an accused person to be informed of the nature of the accusation against him, and his right to be tried by an impartial jury of the vicinage; and also the right to be secure against excessive bail and against cruel and unusual punishments.

Now, sir, here is a mass of privileges, immunities, and rights, some of them secured by the second section of the fourth article of the Constitution, which I have recited, some by the first eight amendments of the Constitution; and it is a fact well worthy of attention that the course of decision of our courts and the present settled doctrine is, that all these immunities, privileges, rights, thus guarantied by the Constitution or recognized by it, are secured to the citizen solely as a citizen of the United States and as a party in their courts. They do not operate in the slightest degree as a restraint or prohibition upon State legislation. States are not affected by them, and it has been repeatedly held that the restriction contained in the Constitution against the taking of private property for public use without just compensation is not a restriction upon State legislation, but applies only to the legislation of Congress. . . .

The great object of the first section of this amendment is, therefore, to restrain the power of the States and compel them at all times to respect these great fundamental guarantees. How will it be done under the present amendment? As I have remarked, they are not powers granted to Congress, and therefore it is necessary, if they are to be effectuated and enforced, as they assuredly ought to be, that additional power should be given to Congress to that end. This is done by the fifth section of this amendment, which declares that "the Congress shall have power to enforce by appropriate legislation the provisions of this article." Here is a direct affirmative delegation of power to Congress to carry out all the principles of all these guarantees, a power not found in the Constitution.

The last two clauses of the first section of the amendment disable a State from depriving not merely a citizen of the United States, but any person, whoever he may be, of life, liberty, or property without due process of law, or from denying to him the equal protection of the laws of the State. This abolishes all class legislation in the States and does away with the injustice of subjecting one caste of persons to a code not applicable to another. It prohibits the hanging of a black man for a crime for which the white man is not to be hanged. It protects the black man in his fundamental rights as a citizen with the same shield which it throws over the white man. Is it not time, Mr. President, that we extend to the black man, I had almost called it the poor privilege of the equal protection of the law? Ought not the time to be now passed when one measure of justice is to be meted out to a member of one caste while another and a different measure is meted out to the member of another caste, both castes being alike citizens of the United States, both bound to obey the same laws, to sustain the burdens of the same Government, and both equally responsible to justice and to God for the deeds done in the body?

But, sir, the first section of the proposed amendment does not give to either of these classes the right of voting. The right of suffrage is not, in law, one of the privileges or immunities thus secured by the Constitution. It is merely the creature of law. It has always been regarded in this country as the result of positive local law, not regarded as one of those fundamental rights lying at the basis of all society and without which a people cannot exist except as slaves, subject to a despotism. . . .

It is very true, and I am sorry to be obliged to acknowledge it, that [the second] section of the amendment does not recognize the authority of the United States over the question of suffrage in the several States at all; nor does it recognize, much less secure, the right of suffrage to the colored race. I wish to meet this question fairly and frankly. . . . But, sir, it is not the question here what will we do; it is not the question of what you, or I, or half a dozen other members of the Senate may prefer in respect to colored suffrage; it is not entirely the question of what measure we can pass through the two Houses; but the question really is, what will the Legislatures of the various States to whom these amendments are to be submitted do in the premises; what is it likely will meet the general approbation of the people who are to elect the Legislatures, three fourths of whom must ratify our propositions before they have the force of constitutional provisions? . . .

Schuyler Colfax on the Proposed Amendment

Speech in Indianapolis, Indiana (Aug. 7, 1866), reprinted in CINCINNATI COMMERCIAL, SPEECHES
OF THE CAMPAIGN OF 1866: IN THE STATES OF OHIO, INDIANA, AND KENTUCKY 14 (1866)

... The first section of this Constitutional Amendment is very much denounced by our opponents—very much misrepresented and perverted. [Mr. C. here read the first section of the proposed amendment.] I stand by every word and letter of it: it's going to be the gem of the Constitution, when it is placed there, as it will be, by this American people. [Applause.] I will tell you why I love it. It is because it is the Declaration of Independence placed immutably and forever in our Constitution [Applause.] What does the Declaration of Independence say?—that baptismal vow that our fathers took upon their lips when this Republic of ours was born into the family of nations. It says that all men are created equal, and are endowed by their Creator with certain inalienable rights, among which are life, liberty, and the pursuit of happiness; *and that to secure these rights governments were instituted among men.* That's the paramount object of government, to secure the right of all men to equality before the law. So said our fathers at the beginning of the Revolution. So say their sons to-day, in this Constitutional Amendment, the noblest clause that will be in our Constitution. It declares that every person—every man, every woman, every child, born under our flag, or naturalized under our laws, shall have a birthright in this land of ours. High or low, rich or humble, learned or unlearned, distinguished or obscure, white or black, born in a palatial residence or born in the humblest cabin in the land, this great Government says "the ægis of protection is thrown over you; you can look up to this flag and your country, and say they are yours." [Applause.]

But they shudderingly say, on the other side, "This is going to protect a nigger as a citizen." [Laughter.] Who is it that most needs protection from the law in this land? It is not the rich man; it is not the man of great intellect; it is not the influential man; but it is the weak and the obscure man; it is the down-trodden, the degraded and the oppressed; and the greatest glory of a free land is that it will stretch out its arm and protect the obscurest man under its flag. [Applause.] But they say there is negro suffrage in that. Well, they ought to know whether there is or not. They have been hunting around for many a long year. They dream of it, and their waking hours have been harassed for years with this chimera and hobgoblin of negro suffrage. The second section expressly leaves this matter to the States, but bankrupt of all legitimate argument, our opponents bring up this old, worn-out, thread-bare charge, and try to prove that under this section of the Constitution there is going to be negro suffrage. It happens they have omitted one thing in all their arguments. We passed a bill on the ninth of April last, over the President's veto, known as the Civil Rights Bill, that specifically and directly declares what the rights of a citizen of the United States are—that they may make and enforce contracts, sue and be parties, give evidence, purchase, lease and sell property, and be subject to like punishments. That is the last law upon the subject. The Democrats haven't found that out yet. They have been hunting up a new edition of Webster's dictionary to find the meaning of the word citizen. Why didn't they go a little further, and find out, in the same dictionary, what a Copperhead was? I grant that the man who votes has the right to be called a citizen, but it don't follow that every citizen has a right to vote. A ship is a vessel, but all vessels are not ships. Women and children have been citizens from the very organization of the Government. They haven't voted yet, and yet Mr. Seward, Secretary of State, will give Mrs. Amelia Smith, or whatever her name is, a passport that will entitle her to protection as an American citizen all over the world. But she don't take that passport and vote on it; if she did we would have a larger majority for the Union ticket at the coming election than we have. [Applause.] . . .

Benjamin Butler on the Proposed Amendment

Speech in Toledo, Ohio (Oct. 2, 1866), reprinted in CINCINNATI COMMERCIAL,
SPEECHES OF THE CAMPAIGN OF 1866: IN THE STATES
OF OHIO, INDIANA, AND KENTUCKY 41 (1866)

. . . Now then, Congress, after making full inquiry, and being moved by a spirit of magnanimity, such as never before was exhibited toward rebels, offered that these rebels, these camps of paroled prisoners of war, might be re-instated in the Union; might have their property back; might have a share in the Government, provided they agreed to amend the Constitution in certain important particulars. The first was that every citizen of the United States should have equal rights with every other citizen of the United States, in every State. Why was this necessary? It was because the President, in vetoing the Civil Rights Bill, said that it was unconstitutional to pass a law that every citizen of the United States should have equal rights with every other citizen in every state of the Union. To render that certain, which we all supposed up to that hour was certain, Congress said: "Well, we will put it in the Constitution so it shall be there forever." [A voice, "That's the place to have it."] Just exactly. The next thing was the subject of representation. Under the old agreement in the Constitution, the master was allowed to count three-fifths of his slaves in representation. That was one of his rights. But one of his obligations was that he was to pay three-fifths of the taxes for them. When emancipation took effect, and there were no more slaves, then the negroes stood to be counted like other citizens; and if there were no changes made in the Constitution, and these slave States were allowed to come back, then the masters would represent not only three-fifths of the negroes, but five-fifths—two-fifths more than they did before. Nay, more: the negro having become a citizen, and being counted as such, the taxes assessed must be paid by himself, and the master would shirk three-fifths of the taxation; so that if we did not make change in the Constitution the masters would gain two-fifths in representation and three-fifths in taxation. Now what is the practical effect of that? It would be to give the master in South Carolina, where there are about the proportion of 250,000 white men to 350,000 black men, from two and a fourth to two and a half more power than you of Ohio have; so that South Carolina, by going out of the Union, if she is allowed to come back under the Johnsonian plan of restoration, without any amendment to the Constitution, will have gained, by her rebellion, two and one-fourth times as much political power as she had before. . . .

What was the next thing we asked of them? That hereafter no man who had perjured himself by swearing to support the Constitution of the United States, and then abjuring it, should ever have a chance to perjure himself again. Most, if not all of us, think this is too lenient. Let us see what this means. All of you that have fought against the Union; all of you that have starved our prisoners in Belle Isle, Libby, Salisbury, may come back and take a share in the Government with us, except those who have heretofore held office. . . .

I told you that there was another portion of the constitutional amendment with which I did not agree. . . . In putting the proposition of representation, Congress said to the South *[in Section 2 of the proposed amendment—Editors]*, "If you will agree that negroes shall vote when they are fit for it, then when they do vote they shall be counted in your representation." This was a sort of bribe to allow the negro to vote. Now, I am not in favor of negro sufferage, or any other suffrage but impartial suffrage. [Applause] In order that I may be understood, allow me to state my position. . . .

Now, then, I propose rather that the qualification of suffrage must be in every State a just qualification, something which every man can attain to. In the olden time, down to 1835, in North Carolina, every black man and every white man voted equally, provided he owned fifty acres of land—and there was land enough there for every body to own fifty acres of land—and there was land enough there for every body to own fifty acres, and a great deal more, and not be very rich at that. (Laughter.) But if the States say that nobody shall vote who has not blue eyes, as every body can't have blue eyes, it may disfranchise a majority. That's a qualification to which men can not attain. If reading and writing are required, that may be very well, because every body can attain to that. . . .

Nobody pretends that Congress shall interfere with the States in the Union, but I do claim that Congress has a right to fix the rules and regulations by which the camps of paroled prisoners of war shall be governed. [Applause.] Therefore I would say to each Southern State, fix your standard where you please, provided it be a standard to which every man can attain. . . .

NOTES

1.   What is the defect in the existing Constitution that the supporters of the Fourteenth Amendment were trying to remedy? Was the defect more in the definition of the rights protected by the original Constitution, or in the inability of Congress to enforce those rights against the states?

2.   In modern case law, there are sharp distinctions between "privileges or immunities," "equal protection," and "due process." But those distinctions may not have been as sharp at the time the Fourteenth Amendment was ratified. Consider each in turn, but also consider how they might overlap.

a.   What are the "privileges or immunities of citizens of the United States"? What does Senator Howard say? What does Speaker Colfax say? What sorts of enactments or practices would abridge a privilege or immunity?

b.   What is "equal protection of the laws"? What sorts of enactments or practices does Representative Stevens say would deny an equality of protection? Is there any theme that ties together the denials that he lists?

c.   What is "due process of law"? Do the speakers define it? Note that when Representative Bingham was asked in a debate in the House what he meant by "due process of law," he said: "I reply to the gentleman, the courts have settled that long ago, and the gentleman can go and read their decisions." Cong. Globe, 39th Cong., 1st Sess. 1089 (Feb. 28, 1866). On antebellum precedents on "due process of law," see p. 1480.

3.   How close is the relationship between Section 1 of the Fourteenth Amendment and the Civil Rights Act of 1866? Was everything in Section 1 already covered by the Civil Rights Act? What does Stevens mean when he says, "That is partly true"?

4.   Why do Stevens and Colfax invoke the Declaration of Independence in support of the amendment? Was the Declaration legally binding? Were its principles already reflected in the Constitution? (All of them?)

5.   Why does Stevens consider Section 2 of the Fourteenth Amendment "the most important"? Do you agree? Why does General Butler say he disagrees with Section 2? What would he have proposed instead?

6.   What do these speeches tell you about the process of drafting a constitutional amendment? You now have a sense of some of the aims of leading Republicans in Congress—coming to the aid of the newly freed slaves; ensuring that all persons, black and white, would equally have their rights and their lives protected; wresting control of Reconstruction from President Johnson; and preserving their majority in Congress. In trying to achieve these aims, they also thought about what was politically feasible—ratification would happen only if the amendment proved satisfactory to state legislatures that were controlled not by Radical Republicans but by moderates. Keeping in mind these aims and this political constraint, try your hand at drafting a better Fourteenth Amendment. What would it say? What difficulties do you encounter?

7.   In June 1866, Congress sent the proposed Fourteenth Amendment to the states for ratification. Within five weeks, three states had ratified it: Connecticut, New Hampshire, and Tennessee (a Southern state with an unusually large number of Union supporters, which then promptly had its senators and representative seated in Congress). Northern states slowly began to ratify the amendment; the other states of the former Confederacy rejected it. But the Republicans in Congress had leverage: they refused to seat the senators and representatives of the remaining Southern states until they met several requirements, including ratification of the amendment. (Could Congress do that? See p. 800.) In the summer of 1868, five Southern states ratified it. By that point, though, Ohio and New Jersey had rescinded (or tried to rescind) their ratifications. (Could they do that? See p. 802.) Between the coercion of the South and the rescinded ratifications in the North, the question has been asked whether the Fourteenth Amendment was even validly ratified under Article V. See, e.g., 2 Bruce Ackerman, WE THE PEOPLE: TRANSFORMATIONS (1998) (answering *no*); John Harrison, *The Lawfulness of the Reconstruction Amendments*, 68 U. Chi. L. Rev. 375 (2001) (answering *yes*); see also Thomas B. Colby, *Originalism and the Ratification of the Fourteenth Amendment*, 107 N.W. U. L. Rev. 1627 (2013).

As Reconstruction continued, there were fierce conflicts between the Republicans in Congress and President Johnson, culminating in Johnson's impeachment and acquittal by a single vote. See p. 350. In Congress, the debate over the meaning of the Fourteenth Amendment did not end when it was ratified. Between 1870 and 1875, Congress considered a number of bills enforcing the Fourteenth Amendment, exercising its power under Section 5. For an account of some of the congressional debates, including their potential significance for understanding the historical context of the Fourteenth Amendment, see p. 1361.

Meanwhile, a great issue that the Radical Republicans had set aside to secure the Fourteenth Amendment—black suffrage—took on new importance. Increasingly, white Republicans supported it, sometimes for reasons of principle and sometimes for reasons of political expediency, as they saw black enfranchisement and rebel disenfranchisement as critical to their continued control of Congress. In 1869 Congress proposed the Fifteenth Amendment, prohibiting the denial or abridgment of the right to vote "on account of race, color, or previous condition of servitude." It was ratified in 1870. See p. 1662. Black suffrage combined with protection from federal troops led to the election of Reconstruction governments in the South that sought a clean break with the Confederate past. Hundreds of former slaves became legislators across the South, a majority of the state legislators in South Carolina were black, and Louisiana elected a black governor. But this "new birth of freedom" would soon be challenged. See p. 1344.

——————

No change to the U.S. Constitution has been more consequential than the Fourteenth Amendment. Most of the modern cases arising under the amendment involve Section 1's second sentence—the modified language of Bingham's original proposal. The breadth and seeming ambiguity of some of Section 1's terms have given rise to enduring controversies in constitutional law. What are the "privileges or immunities of citizens of the United States" that states may not abridge? What is meant by "due process of law"? By "the equal protection of the laws"? In Bingham's original proposal, the broad language was essentially a delegation of power to Congress. But with the transformation of Bingham's proposal into a direct constitutional prohibition on state action, is the broad language now a similarly broad delegation to the judiciary? As you will see, the Fourteenth Amendment has become the basis for much of modern constitutional law—and for much of the controversy over the appropriate role of the judiciary in interpreting the Constitution.

The rest of this chapter is arranged this way: It begins with the *Slaughter-House Cases,* a famous decision in which the Supreme Court first interpreted Section 1 of the Fourteenth Amendment. Next are several cases on the Fourteenth Amendment's structure and logic—on how it "works" in actual operation. These cases consider both the "state action" doctrine and the scope of Congress's Section 5 enforcement power. After that are the complicated and challenging modern doctrines derived from the Equal Protection Clause: racial classifications (including discussion of disparate impact and affirmative action), sex classifications, and other possibly suspect classifications of persons. Finally, there is a lengthy consideration of the Due Process Clause and the doctrine of substantive due process, including famous cases such as *Lochner, Roe,* and *Obergefell.*

[*Assignment 64*]

D. THE EARLY CASES

Slaughter-House Cases
83 U.S. (16 Wall.) 36 (1873)

■ MR. JUSTICE MILLER delivered the opinion of the court.

These cases . . . arise out of the efforts of the butchers of New Orleans to resist the Crescent City Live-Stock Landing and Slaughter-House Company in the exercise of certain powers conferred by the charter which created it, and which was granted by the legislature of that State. . . .

The statute thus assailed as unconstitutional was passed March 8th, 1869, and is entitled "An act to protect the health of the city of New Orleans, to locate the stock-landings and slaughter-houses, and to incorporate the Crescent City Live-Stock Landing and Slaughter-House Company."

The first section forbids the landing or slaughtering of animals whose flesh is intended for food, within the city of New Orleans and other parishes and boundaries named and defined, or the keeping or establishing any slaughter-houses or *abattoirs* within those limits except by the corporation thereby created. . . .

The third and fourth sections authorize the company to establish and erect within certain territorial limits, therein defined, one or more stock-yards, stock-landings, and slaughter-houses, and imposes upon it the duty of erecting . . . one grand slaughter-house of sufficient capacity for slaughtering five hundred animals per day. . . . [T]he company . . . shall have the sole and exclusive privilege of conducting and carrying on the live-stock landing and slaughter-house business within the limits and privilege granted by the act, and that all such animals shall be landed at the stock-landings and slaughtered at the slaughter-houses of the company, and nowhere else. . . .

Section five orders the closing up of all other stock-landings and slaughter-houses. . . . These are the principal features of the statute, and are all that have any bearing upon the questions to be decided by us.

This statute is denounced not only as creating a monopoly and conferring odious and exclusive privileges upon a small number of persons at the expense of the great body of the community of New Orleans, but it is asserted that it deprives a large and meritorious class of citizens—the whole of the butchers of the city—of the right to exercise their trade, the business to which they have been trained and on which they depend for the support of themselves and their families; and that the unrestricted exercise of the business of butchering is necessary to the daily subsistence of the population of the city. . . .

The wisdom of the monopoly granted by the legislature may be open to question, but it is difficult to see a justification for the assertion that the butchers are deprived of the right to labor in their occupation, or the people in their daily service in preparing food, or how this statute, with the duties and guards imposed upon the company, can be said to destroy the business of the butcher, or seriously interfere with its pursuit.

The power here exercised by the legislature of Louisiana is, in its essential nature, one which has been, up to the present period in the constitutional history of this country, always conceded to belong to the States. . . .

"Unwholesome trades, slaughter-houses, operations offensive to the senses, the deposit of powder, the application of steam power to propel cars, the building with combustible materials, and the burial of the dead, may all," says Chancellor Kent, "be interdicted by law, in the midst of dense masses of population, on the general and rational principle, that every person ought so to use his property as not to injure his neighbors; and that private interests must be made subservient to the general interests of the community." This is called the police power. . . . The regulation of the place and manner of conducting the slaughtering of animals, and the business of butchering within a city, and the inspection of the animals to be killed for meat, and of the meat afterwards, are among the most necessary and frequent exercises of this power. . . .

In *Gibbons v. Ogden*, 22 U.S. (9 Wheat.) 1 (1824), Chief Justice Marshall, speaking of inspection laws passed by the States, says: "They form a portion of that immense mass of legislation which controls everything within the territory of a State not surrendered to the General Government—all which can be most advantageously administered by the States themselves. Inspection laws, quarantine laws, health laws of every description, as well as laws for regulating the internal commerce of a State, and those which respect turnpike roads, ferries, & c., are component parts. No direct general power over these objects is granted to Congress; and consequently they remain subject to State legislation." . . .

It cannot be denied that the statute under consideration is aptly framed to remove from the more densely populated part of the city, the noxious slaughter-houses, and large and offensive collections of animals necessarily incident to the slaughtering business of a large city, and to locate them where the convenience, health, and comfort of the people require they shall be located. And it must be conceded that the means adopted by the act for this purpose are appropriate, are stringent, and effectual. . . .

It may . . . be considered as established, that the authority of the legislature of Louisiana to pass the present statute is ample, unless some restraint in the exercise of that power be found in the constitution of that State or in the amendments to the Constitution of the United States, adopted since the date of the decisions we have already cited. . . .

The plaintiffs . . . allege that the statute is a violation of the Constitution of the United States in these several particulars:

That it creates an involuntary servitude forbidden by the thirteenth article of amendment;

That it abridges the privileges and immunities of citizens of the United States;

That it denies to the plaintiffs the equal protection of the laws; and,

That it deprives them of their property without due process of law, contrary to the provisions of the first section of the fourteenth article of amendment.

This court is thus called upon for the first time to give construction to these articles.

We do not conceal from ourselves the great responsibility which this duty devolves upon us. No questions so far-reaching and pervading in their consequences, so profoundly interesting to the people of this country, and so important in their bearing upon the relations of the United States, and of the several States to each other and to the citizens of the States and of the United States, have been before this court during the official life of any of its present members. . . .

[W]ithin the last eight years three . . . articles of amendment of vast importance have been added by the voice of the people to [the Constitution].

The most cursory glance at these articles discloses a unity of purpose, when taken in connection with the history of the times, which cannot fail to have an important bearing on any question of doubt concerning their true meaning. Nor can such doubts, when any reasonably exist, be safely and rationally solved without a reference to that history; for in it is found the occasion and the necessity for recurring again to the great source of power in this country, the people of the States, for additional guarantees of human rights; additional powers to the Federal government; additional restraints upon those of the States. Fortunately that history is fresh within the memory of us all, and its leading features, as they bear upon the matter before us, free from doubt.

The institution of African slavery, as it existed in about half the States of the Union, and the contests pervading the public mind for many years, between those who desired its curtailment and ultimate extinction and those who desired additional safeguards for its security and perpetuation, culminated in the effort, on the part of most of the States in which slavery existed, to separate from the Federal government, and to resist its authority. This constituted the war of the rebellion, and whatever auxiliary causes may have contributed to bring about this war, undoubtedly the overshadowing and efficient cause was African slavery.

In that struggle slavery, as a legalized social relation, perished. It perished as a necessity of the bitterness and force of the conflict. When the armies of freedom found themselves upon the soil of slavery they could do nothing less than free the poor victims whose enforced servitude was the foundation of the quarrel. And when hard pressed in the contest these men (for they proved themselves men in that terrible crisis) offered their services and were accepted by thousands to aid in suppressing the unlawful rebellion, slavery was at an end wherever the Federal government succeeded in that purpose. The proclamation of President Lincoln expressed an accomplished fact as to a large portion of the insurrectionary districts, when he declared slavery abolished in them all. But the war being over, those who had succeeded in re-establishing the authority of the Federal government were not content to permit this great act of emancipation to rest on the actual results of the contest or the proclamation of the Executive, both of which might have been questioned in after times, and they determined to place this main and most valuable result in the Constitution of the restored Union as one of its fundamental articles. Hence the thirteenth article of amendment of that instrument. Its two short sections seem hardly to admit of construction, so vigorous is their expression and so appropriate to the purpose we have indicated.

1. Neither slavery nor involuntary servitude, except as a punishment for crime, whereof the party shall have been duly convicted, shall exist within the United States or any place subject to their jurisdiction.

2. Congress shall have power to enforce this article by appropriate legislation.

To withdraw the mind from the contemplation of this grand yet simple declaration of the personal freedom of all the human race within the jurisdiction of this government—a declaration designed to establish the freedom of four millions of slaves—and with a microscopic search endeavor to find in it a reference to servitudes, which may have been attached to property in certain localities, requires an effort, to say the least of it.

That a personal servitude was meant is proved by the use of the word "involuntary," which can only apply to human beings. The exception of servitude as a punishment for crime gives an idea of the class of servitude that is meant. The word servitude is of larger meaning than slavery, as the latter is popularly understood in this country, and the obvious purpose was to forbid all shades and conditions of African slavery. . . . And it is all that we deem necessary to say on the application of that article to the statute of Louisiana, now under consideration.

The process of restoring to their proper relations with the Federal government and with the other States those which had sided with the rebellion, undertaken under the proclamation of President Johnson in 1865, and before the assembling of

Congress, developed the fact that, notwithstanding the formal recognition by those States of the abolition of slavery, the condition of the slave race would, without further protection of the Federal government, be almost as bad as it was before. Among the first acts of legislation adopted by several of the States in the legislative bodies which claimed to be in their normal relations with the Federal government, were laws which imposed upon the colored race onerous disabilities and burdens, and curtailed their rights in the pursuit of life, liberty, and property to such an extent that their freedom was of little value, while they had lost the protection which they had received from their former owners from motives both of interest and humanity.

They were in some States forbidden to appear in the towns in any other character than menial servants. They were required to reside on and cultivate the soil without the right to purchase or own it. They were excluded from many occupations of gain, and were not permitted to give testimony in the courts in any case where a white man was a party. It was said that their lives were at the mercy of bad men, either because the laws for their protection were insufficient or were not enforced.

These circumstances, whatever of falsehood or misconception may have been mingled with their presentation, forced upon the statesmen who had conducted the Federal government in safety through the crisis of the rebellion, and who supposed that by the thirteenth article of amendment they had secured the result of their labors, the conviction that something more was necessary in the way of constitutional protection to the unfortunate race who had suffered so much. They accordingly passed through Congress the proposition for the fourteenth amendment, and they declined to treat as restored to their full participation in the government of the Union the States which had been in insurrection, until they ratified that article. . . .

Before we proceed to examine more critically the provisions of this amendment, on which the plaintiffs in error rely, let us complete and dismiss the history of the recent amendments, as that history relates to the general purpose which pervades them all. A few years' experience satisfied the thoughtful men who had been the authors of the other two amendments that, notwithstanding the restraints of those articles on the States, and the laws passed under the additional powers granted to Congress, these were inadequate for the protection of life, liberty, and property, without which freedom to the slave was no boon. They were in all those States denied the right of suffrage. The laws were administered by the white man alone. It was urged that a race of men distinctively marked as was the negro, living in the midst of another and dominant race, could never be fully secured in their person and their property without the right of suffrage.

Hence the fifteenth amendment, which declares that "the right of a citizen of the United States to vote shall not be denied or abridged by any State on account of race, color, or previous condition of servitude." The negro having, by the fourteenth amendment, been declared to be a citizen of the United States, is thus made a voter in every State of the Union.

We repeat, then, in the light of this recapitulation of events, almost too recent to be called history, but which are familiar to us all; and on the most casual examination of the language of these amendments, no one can fail to be impressed with the one pervading purpose found in them all, lying at the foundation of each, and without which none of them would have been even suggested; we mean the freedom of the slave race, the security and firm establishment of that freedom, and the protection of the newly-made freeman and citizen from the oppressions of those who had formerly exercised unlimited dominion over him. It is true that only the fifteenth amendment, in terms, mentions the negro by speaking of his color and his slavery. But it is just as true that each of the other articles was addressed to the grievances of that race, and designed to remedy them as the fifteenth.

We do not say that no one else but the negro can share in this protection. Both the language and spirit of these articles are to have their fair and just weight in any question of construction. Undoubtedly while negro slavery alone was in the mind of the Congress which proposed the thirteenth article, it forbids any other kind of slavery, now or hereafter. If Mexican peonage or the Chinese coolie labor system shall develop slavery of the Mexican or Chinese race within our territory, this amendment may safely be trusted to make it void. And so if other rights are assailed by the States which properly and necessarily fall within the protection of these articles, that protection will apply, though the party interested may not be of African descent. But what we do say, and what we wish to be understood is, that in any fair and just construction of any section or phrase of these amendments, it is necessary to look to the purpose which we have said was the pervading spirit of them all, the evil which they were designed to remedy, and the process of continued addition to the Constitution, until that purpose was supposed to be accomplished, as far as constitutional law can accomplish it.

The first section of the fourteenth article, to which our attention is more specially invited, opens with a definition of citizenship—not only citizenship of the United States, but citizenship of the States. No such definition was previously found in the Constitution, nor had any attempt been made to define it by act of Congress. It had been the occasion of much discussion in the courts, by the executive departments, and in the public journals. It had been said by eminent judges that no man was a citizen of the United States, except as he was a citizen of one of the States composing the Union. Those, therefore, who had been born and resided always in the District of Columbia or in the Territories, though within the United States, were not citizens. Whether this proposition was sound or not had never been judicially decided. But it had been held by this court, in the celebrated *Dred Scott* case, only a few years before the outbreak of the civil war, that a man of African descent, whether a slave or not, was not and could not be a citizen of a State or of the United States. This decision, while it met the condemnation of some of the ablest statesmen and constitutional lawyers of the country, had never been overruled; and if it was to be accepted as a constitutional limitation of the right of citizenship, then all the negro race who had recently been made freemen, were still, not only not citizens, but were incapable of becoming so by anything short of an amendment to the Constitution.

To remove this difficulty primarily, and to establish a clear and comprehensive definition of citizenship which should declare what should constitute citizenship of the United States, and also citizenship of a State, the first clause of the first section was framed.

"All persons born or naturalized in the United States, and subject to the jurisdiction thereof, are citizens of the United States and of the State wherein they reside."

The first observation we have to make on this clause is, that it puts at rest both the questions which . . . have been the subject of differences of opinion. It declares that persons may be citizens of the United States without regard to their citizenship of a particular State, and it overturns the Dred Scott decision by making *all persons* born within the United States and subject to its jurisdiction citizens of the United States. That its main purpose was to establish the citizenship of the negro can admit of no doubt. . . .

The next observation . . . is, that the distinction between citizenship of the United States and citizenship of a State is clearly recognized and established. Not only may a man be a citizen of the United States without being a citizen of a State, but an important element is necessary to convert the former into the latter. He must reside within the State to make him a citizen of it, but it is only necessary that he should be born or naturalized in the United States to be a citizen of the Union.

It is quite clear, then, that there is a citizenship of the United States, and a citizenship of a State, which are distinct from each other, and which depend upon different characteristics or circumstances in the individual.

We think this distinction and its explicit recognition in this amendment of great weight in this argument, because the next paragraph of this same section . . . speaks only of privileges and immunities of citizens of the United States, and does not speak of those of citizens of the several States. The argument, however, in favor of the plaintiffs rests wholly on the assumption that the citizenship is the same, and the privileges and immunities guaranteed by the clause are the same.

The language is, "No State shall make or enforce any law which shall abridge the privileges or immunities of citizens of *the United States*." It is a little remarkable, if this clause was intended as a protection to the citizen of a State against the legislative power of his own State, that the word citizen of the State should be left out when it is so carefully used, and used in contradistinction to citizens of the United States, in the very sentence which precedes it. It is too clear for argument that the change in phraseology was adopted understandingly and with a purpose.

Of the privileges and immunities of the citizen of the United States, and of the privileges and immunities of the citizen of the State, and what they respectively are, we will presently consider; but we wish to state here that it is only the former which are placed by this clause under the protection of the Federal Constitution, and that the latter, whatever they may be, are not intended to have any additional protection by this paragraph of the amendment.

If, then, there is a difference between the privileges and immunities belonging to a citizen of the United States as such, and those belonging to the citizen of the State as such the latter must rest for their security and protection where they have heretofore rested; for they are not embraced by this paragraph of the amendment.

The first occurrence of the words "privileges and immunities" in our constitutional history, is to be found in the fourth of the articles of the old Confederation. . . .

In the Constitution of the United States, which superseded the Articles of Confederation, the corresponding provision is found in section two of the fourth article, in the following words: "The citizens of each State shall be entitled to all the privileges and immunities of citizens of the several States."

There can be but little question that the purpose of both these provisions is the same, and that the privileges and immunities intended are the same in each. In the article of the Confederation we have some of these specifically mentioned, and enough perhaps to give some general idea of the class of civil rights meant by the phrase.

Fortunately we are not without judicial construction of this clause of the Constitution. The first and the leading case on the subject is that of *Corfield v. Coryell*, 6 Fed. Cas. 546, decided by Mr. Justice Washington in the Circuit Court for the District of Pennsylvania in 1825.

"The inquiry," he says, "is, what are the privileges and immunities of citizens of the several States? We feel no hesitation in confining these expressions to those privileges and immunities which are *fundamental*; which belong of right to the citizens of all free governments, and which have at all times been enjoyed by citizens of the several States which compose this Union, from the time of their becoming free, independent, and sovereign. What these fundamental principles are, it would be more tedious than difficult to enumerate. They may all, however, be comprehended under the following general heads: protection by the government, with the right to acquire and possess property of every kind, and to pursue and obtain happiness and safety, subject, nevertheless, to such restraints as the government may prescribe for the general good of the whole."

. . . The description, when taken to include others not named, but which are of the same general character, embraces nearly every civil right for the establishment and protection of which organized government is instituted. They are, in the language of Judge Washington, those rights which are fundamental. Throughout his opinion, they are spoken of as rights belonging to the individual as a citizen of a State. They are so spoken of in the constitutional provision which he was construing. And they have always been held to be the class of rights which the State governments were created to establish and secure. . . .

In the case of *Paul v. Virginia*, 75 U.S. (8 Wall.) 168 (1869), the court, in expounding [the Privileges and Immunities Clause] of the Constitution, says that "the privileges and immunities secured to citizens of each State in the several States, by the provision in question, are those privileges and immunities which are common to the citizens in the latter States under their constitution and laws by virtue of their being citizens."

The constitutional provision there alluded to did not create those rights, which it called privileges and immunities of citizens of the States. It threw around them in that clause no security for the citizen of the State in which they were claimed or exercised. Nor did it profess to control the power of the State governments over the rights of its own citizens.

Its sole purpose was to declare to the several States, that whatever those rights, as you grant or establish them to your own citizens, or as you limit or qualify, or impose restrictions on their exercise, the same, neither more nor less, shall be the measure of the rights of citizens of other States within your jurisdiction.

. . . [There are] very few express limitations which the Federal Constitution imposed on the States—such, for instance, as the prohibition against ex post facto laws, bills of attainder, and laws impairing the obligation of contracts. But with the exception of these and a few other restrictions, the entire domain of the privileges and immunities of citizens of the States, as above defined, lay within the constitutional and legislative power of the States, and without that of the Federal government. Was it the purpose of the fourteenth amendment, by the simple declaration that no State should make or enforce any law which shall abridge the privileges and immunities of *citizens of the United States*, to transfer the security and protection of all the civil rights which we have mentioned, from the States to the Federal government? And where it is declared that Congress shall have the power to enforce that article, was it intended to bring within the power of Congress the entire domain of civil rights heretofore belonging exclusively to the States?

All this and more must follow, if the proposition of the plaintiffs in error be sound. For not only are these rights subject to the control of Congress whenever in its discretion any of them are supposed to be abridged by State legislation, but that body may also pass laws in advance, limiting and restricting the exercise of legislative power by the States, in their most ordinary and usual functions, as in its judgment it may think proper on all such subjects. And still further, such a construction . . . would constitute this court a perpetual censor upon all legislation of the States, on the civil rights of their own citizens, with authority to nullify such as it did not approve as consistent with those rights, as they existed at the time of the adoption of this amendment. The argument we admit is not always the most conclusive which is drawn from the consequences urged against the adoption of a particular construction of an instrument. But when, as in the case before us, these consequences are so serious, so far-reaching and pervading, so great a departure from the structure and spirit of our institutions; when the effect is to fetter and degrade the State governments by subjecting them to the control of Congress, in the exercise of powers heretofore universally conceded to them of the most ordinary and fundamental character; when in fact it radically changes the whole theory of the relations of the State and Federal governments to each other and of both these governments to the people; the argument has a force that is irresistible, in the absence of language which expresses such a purpose too clearly to admit of doubt.

We are convinced that no such results were intended by the Congress which proposed these amendments, nor by the legislatures of the States which ratified them.

Having shown that the privileges and immunities relied on in the argument are those which belong to citizens of the States as such, and that they are left to the State governments for security and protection, and not by this article placed under the special care of the Federal government, we may hold ourselves excused from defining the privileges and immunities of citizens of the United States which no State can abridge, until some case involving those privileges may make it necessary to do so.

But lest it should be said that no such privileges and immunities are to be found if those we have been considering are excluded, we venture to suggest some which owe their existence to the Federal government, its National character, its Constitution, or its laws.

One of these is well described in the case of *Crandall v. Nevada*, 73 U.S. (6 Wall.) 35 (1867). It is said to be the right of the citizen of this great country, protected by implied guarantees of its Constitution, "to come to the seat of government to assert any claim he may have upon that government, to transact any business he may have with it, to seek its protection, to share its offices, to engage in administering its functions. He has the right of free access to its seaports, through which all operations of foreign commerce are conducted, to the sub-treasuries, land offices, and courts of justice in the several States." And quoting from the language of Chief Justice Taney in another case, it is said "that *for all the great purposes for which the Federal government* was established, we are one people, with one common country, *we are all citizens of the United States,*" and it is, as such citizens, that their rights are supported in this court in *Crandall v. Nevada*.

Another privilege of a citizen of the United States is to demand the care and protection of the Federal government over his life, liberty, and property when on the high seas or within the jurisdiction of a foreign government. . . . The right to peaceably assemble and petition for redress of grievances, the privilege of the writ of *habeas corpus*, are rights of the citizen guaranteed by the Federal Constitution. The right to use the navigable waters of the United States, however they may penetrate the territory of the several States, all rights secured to our citizens by treaties with foreign nations, are dependent upon citizenship of the United States, and not citizenship of a State. One of these privileges is conferred by the very article under consideration. It is that a citizen of the United States can, of his own volition, become a citizen of any State of the Union by a *bonâ fide* residence therein, with the same rights as other citizens of that State. To these may be added the rights secured by the thirteenth and fifteenth articles of amendment, and by the other clause of the fourteenth, next to be considered.

But it is useless to pursue this branch of the inquiry, since we are of opinion that the rights claimed by these plaintiffs in error, if they have any existence, are not privileges and immunities of citizens of the United States within the meaning of the clause of the fourteenth amendment under consideration.

"All persons born or naturalized in the United States, and subject to the jurisdiction thereof, are citizens of the United States and of the State wherein they reside. No State shall make or enforce any law which shall abridge the privileges or immunities of citizens of the United States; nor shall any State deprive any person of life, liberty, or property without due process of law, nor deny to any person within its jurisdiction the equal protection of its laws."

The argument has not been much pressed in these cases that the defendant's charter deprives the plaintiffs of their property without due process of law, or that it denies to them the equal protection of the law. The first of these paragraphs has been in the Constitution since the adoption of the fifth amendment, as a restraint upon the Federal power. It is also to be found in some form of expression in the constitutions of nearly all the States, as a restraint upon the power of the States. This law then, has [not changed], except so far as the present amendment may place the restraining power over the States in this matter in the hands of the Federal government.

We are not without judicial interpretation, therefore, both State and National, of the meaning of this clause. And it is sufficient to say that under no construction of that provision that we have ever seen, or any that we deem admissible, can the restraint imposed by the State of Louisiana upon the exercise of their trade by the butchers of New Orleans be held to be a deprivation of property within the meaning of that provision.

Nor shall any State deny to any person within its jurisdiction the equal protection of the laws.

In the light of the history of these amendments, and the pervading purpose of them, which we have already discussed, it is not difficult to give a meaning to this clause. The existence of laws in the States where the newly emancipated negroes resided, which discriminated with gross injustice and hardship against them as a class, was the evil to be remedied by this clause, and by it such laws are forbidden.

If, however, the States did not conform their laws to its requirements, then by the fifth section of the article of amendment Congress was authorized to enforce it by suitable legislation. We doubt very much whether any action of a State not directed by way of discrimination against the negroes as a class, or on account of their race, will ever be held to come within the purview of this provision. It is so clearly a provision for that race and that emergency, that a strong case would be necessary for its application to any other. But as it is a State that is to be dealt with, and not alone the validity of its laws, we may safely leave that matter until Congress shall have exercised its power, or some case of State oppression, by denial of equal justice in its courts, shall have claimed a decision at our hands. We find no such case in the one before us. . . .

In the early history of the organization of the government, its statesmen seem to have divided on the line which should separate the powers of the National government from those of the State governments, and though this line has never been very well defined in public opinion, such a division has continued from that day to this. . . .

Unquestionably [the war] has given great force to the argument, and added largely to the number of those who believe in the necessity of a strong National government.

But, however pervading this sentiment, and however it may have contributed to the adoption of the amendments we have been considering, we do not see in those amendments any purpose to destroy the main features of the general system. . . .

[W]hatever fluctuations may be seen in the history of public opinion on this subject during the period of our national existence, we think it will be found that this court, so far as its functions required, has always held with a steady and an even hand the balance between State and Federal power, and we trust that such may continue to be the history of its relation to that subject so long as it shall have duties to perform which demand of it a construction of the Constitution, or of any of its parts.

■ MR. JUSTICE FIELD, dissenting[, joined by the CHIEF JUSTICE, MR. JUSTICE SWAYNE, and MR. JUSTICE BRADLEY].

. . . The act of Louisiana presents the naked case, unaccompanied by any public considerations, where a right to pursue a lawful and necessary calling, previously enjoyed by every citizen, and in connection with which a thousand persons were daily employed, is taken away and vested exclusively for twenty-five years, for an extensive district and a large population, in a single corporation, or its exercise is for that period restricted to the establishments of the corporation, and there allowed only upon onerous conditions.

If exclusive privileges of this character can be granted to a corporation of seventeen persons, they may, in the discretion of the legislature, be equally granted to a single individual. If they may be granted for twenty-five years they may be equally granted for a century, and in perpetuity. . . . Indeed, upon the theory on which the exclusive privileges granted by the act in question are sustained, there is no monopoly, in the most odious form, which may not be upheld.

The question presented is, therefore, one of the gravest importance, not merely to the parties here, but to the whole country. It is nothing less than the question whether the recent amendments to the Federal Constitution protect the citizens of the United States against the deprivation of their common rights by State legislation. In my judgment the fourteenth amendment does afford such protection, and was so intended by the Congress which framed and the States which adopted it.

The counsel for the plaintiffs in error have contended, with great force, that the act in question is also inhibited by the thirteenth amendment.

That amendment prohibits slavery and involuntary servitude, except as a punishment for crime, but I have not supposed it was susceptible of a construction which would cover the enactment in question. I have been so accustomed to regard it as intended to meet that form of slavery which had previously prevailed in this country, and to which the recent civil war owed its existence, that I was not prepared, nor am I yet, to give to it the extent and force ascribed by counsel. Still it is evident that the language of the amendment is not used in a restrictive sense. It is not confined to African slavery alone. It is general and universal in its application. Slavery of white men as well as of black men is prohibited, and not merely slavery in the strict sense of the term, but involuntary servitude in every form.

The words "involuntary servitude" . . . include something more than slavery in the strict sense of the term; they include also serfage, vassalage, villenage, peonage, and all other forms of compulsory service for the mere benefit or pleasure of others. Nor is this the full import of the terms. The abolition of slavery and involuntary servitude was intended to make every one born in this country a freeman, and as such to give to him the right to pursue the ordinary avocations of life without other restraint than such as affects all others, and to enjoy equally with them the fruits of his labor. A prohibition to him to pursue certain callings, open to others of the same age, condition, and sex, or to reside in places where others are permitted to live, would so far deprive him of the rights of a freeman, and would place him, as respects others, in a condition of servitude. A person allowed to pursue only one trade or calling, and only in one locality of the country, would not be, in the strict sense of the term, in a condition of slavery, but probably none would deny that he would be in a condition of servitude. . . .

It is not necessary . . . to rest my objections to the act in question upon the terms and meaning of the thirteenth amendment. The provisions of the fourteenth amendment, which is properly a supplement to the thirteenth, cover, in my judgment, the case before us, and inhibit any legislation which confers special and exclusive privileges like these under consideration. The amendment was adopted to obviate objections which had been raised and pressed with great force to the validity of the Civil Rights Act, and to place the common rights of American citizens under the protection of the National government. . . .

The first clause of this amendment determines who are citizens of the United States, and how their citizenship is created. Before its enactment there was much diversity of opinion among jurists and statesmen whether there was any such citizenship independent of that of the State, and, if any existed, as to the manner in which it originated. . . .

The first clause of the fourteenth amendment changes this whole subject, and removes it from the region of discussion and doubt. It recognizes in express terms, if it does not create, citizens of the United States, and it makes their citizenship dependent upon the place of their birth, or the fact of their adoption, and not upon the constitution or laws of any State or the condition of their ancestry. . . .

The amendment does not attempt to confer any new privileges or immunities upon citizens, or to enumerate or define those already existing. It assumes that there are such privileges and immunities which belong of right to citizens as such, and ordains that they shall not be abridged by State legislation. If this inhibition . . . only refers, as held by the majority of the court in their opinion, to such privileges and immunities as were before its adoption specially designated in the Constitution or necessarily implied as belonging to citizens of the United States, it was a vain and idle enactment, which accomplished nothing, and most unnecessarily excited Congress and the people on its passage. With privileges and immunities thus designated or implied no State could ever have interfered by its laws, and no new constitutional provision was required to inhibit such interference. The supremacy of the Constitution and the laws of the United States always, controlled any State legislation of that character. But if the amendment refers to the natural and inalienable rights which belong to all citizens, the inhibition has a profound significance and consequence.

What, then, are the privileges and immunities which are secured against abridgment by State legislation?

In the first section of the Civil Rights Act Congress has given its interpretation to these terms, or at least has stated some of the rights which, in its judgment, these terms include; it has there declared that they include the right "to make and enforce contracts, to sue, be parties and give evidence, to inherit, purchase, lease, sell, hold, and convey real and personal property, and to full and equal benefit of all laws and proceedings for the security of person and property." . . .

The terms, privileges and immunities, are not new in the amendment; they were in the Constitution before the amendment was adopted. They are found in the second section of the fourth article, which declares that "the citizens of each State shall be entitled to all privileges and immunities of citizens in the several States," and they have been the subject of frequent consideration in judicial decisions. In *Corfield v. Coryell*, [the opinion of] Mr. Justice Washington . . . appears to me to be a sound construction of the clause in question. The privileges and immunities designated are those *which of right belong to the citizens of all free governments*. Clearly among these must be placed the right to pursue a lawful employment in a lawful manner, without other restraint than such as equally affects all persons. In the discussions in Congress upon the passage of the Civil Rights Act repeated reference was made to this language of Mr. Justice Washington. . . .

The privileges and immunities designated in the second section of the fourth article of the Constitution are, then, according to the decision cited, those which of right belong to the citizens of all free governments, and they can be enjoyed under that clause by the citizens of each State in the several States upon the same terms and conditions as they are enjoyed by the citizens of the latter States. No discrimination can be made by one State against the citizens of the States in their enjoyment, nor can any greater imposition be levied than such as is laid upon its own citizens. It is a clause which insures equality in the enjoyment of these rights between citizens of the several States whilst in the same State. . . .

What the clause in question did for the protection of the citizens of one State against hostile and discriminating legislation of other States, the fourteenth amendment does for the protection of every citizen of the United States against hostile and discriminating legislation against him in favor of others, whether they reside in the same or in different States. If under the fourth article of the Constitution equality of privileges and immunities is secured between citizens of different States, under the fourteenth amendment the same equality is secured between citizens of the United States.

It will not be pretended that under the fourth article of the Constitution any State could create a monopoly in any known trade or manufacture in favor of her own citizens, or any portion of them, which would exclude an equal participation in the trade or manufacture monopolized by citizens of other States. She could not confer, for example, upon any of her citizens the sole right to manufacture shoes, or boots, or silk, or the sole right to sell those articles in the State so as to exclude nonresident citizens from engaging in a similar manufacture or sale. The nonresident citizens could claim equality of privilege under the provisions of the fourth article with the citizens of the State exercising the monopoly as well as with others, and thus, as respects them, the monopoly would cease. . . .

Now, what the clause in question does for the protection of citizens of one State against the creation of monopolies in favor of citizens of other States, the fourteenth amendment does for the protection of every citizen of the United States against the creation of any monopoly whatever. The privileges and immunities of citizens of the United States, of every one of them, is secured against abridgment in any form by any State. The fourteenth amendment places them under the guardianship of the National authority. . . .

This equality of right, with exemption from all disparaging and partial enactments, in the lawful pursuits of life, throughout the whole country, is the distinguishing privilege of citizens of the United States. To them, everywhere, all pursuits, all professions, all avocations are open without other restrictions than such as are imposed equally upon all others of the same age, sex, and condition. The State may prescribe such regulations for every pursuit and calling of life as will promote the public health, secure the good order and advance the general prosperity of society, but when once prescribed, the pursuit or calling must be free to be followed by every citizen who is within the conditions designated, and will conform to the regulations. . . . The fourteenth amendment, in my judgment, makes it essential to the validity of the legislation of every State that this equality of right should be respected. How widely this equality has been departed from, how entirely rejected and trampled upon by the act of Louisiana, I have already shown. And it is to me a matter of profound regret that its validity is recognized by a majority of this court, for by it the right of free labor, one of the most sacred and imprescriptible rights of man, is violated. . . . [G]rants of exclusive privileges, such as is made by the act in question, are opposed to the whole theory of free government, and it requires no aid from any bill of rights to render them void. That only is a free government, in the American sense of the term, under which the inalienable right of every citizen to pursue his happiness is unrestrained, except by just, equal, and impartial laws.

■ MR. JUSTICE BRADLEY, also dissenting.

I concur in the opinion which has just been read by Mr. Justice Field; but desire to add a few observations for the purpose of more fully illustrating my views on the important question decided in these cases, and the special grounds on which they rest. . . .

It is contended that [the act in question] abridges the privileges and immunities of citizens of the United States, . . . and whether it does so or not is the simple question in this case. And the solution of this question depends upon the solution of two other questions, to wit:

First. Is it one of the rights and privileges of a citizen of the United States to pursue such civil employment as he may choose to adopt, subject to such reasonable regulations as may be prescribed by law?

Secondly. Is a monopoly, or exclusive right, given to one person to the exclusion of all others, to keep slaughter-houses, in a district of nearly twelve hundred square miles, for the supply of meat for a large city, a reasonable regulation of that employment which the legislature has a right to impose?

The first of these questions is one of vast importance, and lies at the very foundations of our government. . . .

If a State legislature should pass a law of caste, making all trades and professions, or certain enumerated trades and professions, hereditary, so that no one could follow any such trades or professions except that which was pursued by his father, would such a law violate the privileges and immunities of the people of that State as citizens of the United States, or only as citizens of the State? Would they have no redress but to appeal to the courts of that particular State? . . .

The people of this country brought with them to its shores the rights of Englishmen; the rights which had been wrested from English sovereigns at various periods of the nation's history. One of these fundamental rights was expressed in these words, found in Magna Charta: "No freeman shall be taken or imprisoned, or be disseized of his freehold or liberties or free customs, or be outlawed or exiled, or any otherwise destroyed; nor will we pass upon him or condemn him but by lawful judgment of his peers or by the law of the land." English constitutional writers expound this article as rendering life, liberty, and property inviolable, except by due process of law. . . .

[T]he Declaration of Independence, which was the first political act of the American people in their independent sovereign capacity, lays the foundation of our National existence upon this broad proposition: "That all men are created equal; that they are endowed by their Creator with certain inalienable rights; that among these are life, liberty, and the pursuit of happiness." Here again we have the great threefold division of the rights of freemen, asserted as the rights of man. Rights to life, liberty, and the pursuit of happiness are equivalent to the rights of life, liberty, and property. These are the fundamental rights which can only be taken away by due process of law, and which can only be interfered with, or the enjoyment of which can only be modified, by lawful regulations necessary or proper for the mutual good of all; and these rights, I contend, belong to the citizens of every free government.

For the preservation, exercise, and enjoyment of these rights the individual citizen, as a necessity, must be left free to adopt such calling, profession, or trade as may seem to him most conducive to that end. Without this right he cannot be a freeman. This right to choose one's calling is an essential part of that liberty which it is the object of government to protect; and a calling, when chosen, is a man's property and right. Liberty and property are not protected where these rights are arbitrarily assailed. . . .

[E]ven if the Constitution were silent, the fundamental privileges and immunities of citizens, as such, would be no less real and no less inviolable than they now are. It was not necessary to say in words that the citizens of the United States should have and exercise all the privileges of citizens; the privilege of buying, selling, and enjoying property; the privilege of engaging in any lawful employment for a livelihood; the privilege of resorting to the laws for redress of injuries, and the like. Their very citizenship conferred these privileges. . . . [C]itizens of the United States [may] lay claim to every one of the privileges and immunities which have been enumerated; and among these none is more essential and fundamental than the right to follow such profession or employment as each one may choose, subject only to uniform regulations equally applicable to all. . . .

If my views are correct with regard to what are the privileges and immunities of citizens, it follows conclusively that any law which establishes a sheer monopoly, depriving a large class of citizens of the privilege of pursuing a lawful employment, does abridge the privileges of those citizens. . . .

[G]reat fears are expressed that this construction of the amendment will lead to enactments by Congress interfering with the internal affairs of the States, and establishing therein civil and criminal codes of law for the government of the citizens, and thus abolishing the State governments in everything but name; or else, that it will lead the Federal courts to draw to their cognizance the supervision of State tribunals on every subject of judicial inquiry, on the plea of ascertaining whether the privileges and immunities of citizens have not been abridged.

In my judgment no such practical inconveniences would arise. Very little, if any, legislation on the part of Congress would be required to carry the amendment into effect. Like the prohibition against passing a law impairing the obligation of a contract, it would execute itself. The point would be regularly raised, in a suit at law, and settled by final reference to the Federal court. As the privileges and immunities protected are only those fundamental ones which belong to every citizen, they would soon become so far defined as to cause but a slight accumulation of business in the Federal courts. Besides, the recognized existence of the law would prevent its frequent violation. But even if the business of the National courts should be increased, Congress could easily supply the remedy by increasing their number and efficiency. The great question is, What is the true construction of the amendment? When once we find that, we shall find the means of giving it effect. The argument from inconvenience ought not to have a very controlling influence in questions of this sort. The National will and National interest are of far greater importance. . . .

■ MR. JUSTICE SWAYNE, dissenting.

. . . Life, liberty, and property are forbidden to be taken "without due process of law," and "equal protection of the laws" is guaranteed to all. . . . Property is everything which has an exchangeable value, and the right of property includes the power to dispose of it according to the will of the owner. Labor is property, and as such merits protection. The right to make it available is next in importance to the rights of life and liberty. It lies to a large extent at the foundation of most other forms of property, and of all solid individual and national prosperity. "Due process of law" is the application of the law as it exists in the fair and regular course of administrative procedure. "The equal protection of the laws" places all upon a footing of legal equality and gives the same protection to all for the preservation of life, liberty, and property, and the pursuit of happiness. . . .

The cases before us, therefore, present but two questions.

(1.) Does the act of the legislature creating the monopoly in question abridge the privileges and immunities of the plaintiffs in error as citizens of the United States?

(2.) Does it deprive them of liberty or property without due process of law, or deny them the equal protection of the laws of the State, they being *persons* "within its jurisdiction"?

. . . A more flagrant and indefensible invasion of the rights of many for the benefit of a few has not occurred in the legislative history of the country. The response to both inquiries should be in the affirmative. . . .

NOTES

1.   The plaintiffs in *Slaughter-House* invoked several provisions in support of their claim that the city's grant of a monopoly was unconstitutional. Consider first the Court's discussion of the Thirteenth Amendment. How serious is the argument that its prohibition on slavery and involuntary servitude reaches the grant of a business monopoly? If this were prohibited, what else might the Thirteenth Amendment forbid? Military conscription? Forcing parents to care for their children? Enforcement of personal service contracts? Cf. *Bailey v. State of Alabama*, 219 U.S. 219 (1911) (finding that Alabama peonage laws, which made breaking labor contracts a crime punishable by specific performance, violated the Thirteenth Amendment).

2.   What does the Court say about the claim that the city's grant of a monopoly deprived the plaintiffs of their life, liberty, or property "without due process of law"? Which of life, liberty, and property does the Court focus on? Why? Is Justice Swayne's definition of *property* persuasive? And note that the ordinance was duly enacted by the Louisiana legislature. Is that all that the Due Process Clause requires, or does it also constrain the kind of laws that may be passed?

3.   The Court describes the Equal Protection Clause as being motivated by "[t]he existence of laws in the States where the newly emancipated negroes resided, which discriminated with gross injustice and hardship against them as a class." The Court noted that the lives of the newly freed slaves "were at the mercy of bad men, either because the laws for their protection were insufficient or were not enforced." The Court thus read the clause as a remedy for a failure to protect the newly freed slaves, whether by the state legislature or state executive.

If the law at issue in *Slaughter-House* had restricted the operation of animal slaughterhouses to whites only—discriminating as to who may operate a business or engage in a trade or profession on the basis of race—would it have been unconstitutional under the Equal Protection Clause? Would that be an inequality in *protection*? Would it be *unequal*? Does the clause prohibit unequal protection only where the protected and the unprotected are different in race? Does the clause say "race"? One of the enduring questions of constitutional interpretation raised by the Fourteenth Amendment is how much its scope is determined by its broad language and how much by its historical context.

If the Equal Protection Clause transcends its historical context, how broad is its command of "the equal protection of the laws"? Does it forbid every distinction the government might make? Every law has some kind of distinction between the people or activities it applies to and the ones it does not apply to. If that would go too far, how should we decide which distinctions are permissible? What about asking if the distinction is a fair one? How would that apply to the regulation in *Slaughter-House*, which granted a monopoly to one business, essentially putting competitors out of business? Or does the idea of equal protection allow the government to make distinctions, even unfair ones, as long as it does not use race or *similar* criteria?

4.   Now the major question in *Slaughter-House*: What are "the privileges or immunities of citizens of the United States"? One piece of background is needed. The opinions discuss *Corfield v. Coryell*, 6 Fed. Cas. 546 (1825), the leading case on the Privileges and Immunities Clause of Article IV. It was decided by Justice Bushrod Washington, sitting as a circuit judge. New Jersey enacted a law prohibiting out-of-staters from raking clams or gathering oysters in its coastal waters. A Pennsylvanian's boat was seized for violation of the law, and its owner sued to get it back, arguing that New Jersey's law conflicted with the Privileges and Immunities Clause. Justice Washington rejected that argument and set forth what came to be regarded as a canonical description of "privileges and immunities." The key passage in his opinion is printed at p. 710. Note that the "privileges and immunities" protected by Article IV are not protected in an absolute sense, because they do not have to be given by states, but in a relative sense, because if they are given to in-staters they also have to be given to out-of-staters.

Some provisions of the Constitution are difficult to interpret because there is little evidence of how they were understood when ratified. That is not the problem here. The records of the Fourteenth Amendment's drafting and ratification—a small part of which you have already read, p. 1264—are voluminous, as are the antebellum debates and cases which informed the views of the drafters and ratifiers. As you read the summaries below, recognize this complexity. The Privileges or Immunities Clause might have meant different things to different people. It is even possible that it did not settle, as much as raise, the question of how broadly the national government would protect the rights of the newly freed slaves. See David R. Upham, *The Meanings of the "Privileges and Immunities of Citizens" on the Eve of the Civil War,* 91 Notre Dame L. Rev. 1117, 1165 (2016). Here, then, are three major views of the meaning of the Privileges or Immunities Clause, each of which can draw on some support in the drafting and ratification history:

a.   First, there is the *incorporation view* (or the enumerated-rights view): the Privileges or Immunities Clause "incorporated" against the states the rights guaranteed by the U.S. Constitution. That means that the Bill of Rights would apply to the states—in effect, the Privileges or Immunities Clause would be reversing the result in *Barron v. Baltimore,* 32 U.S. (7 Pet.) 243 (1833), p. 812. The other individual rights guaranteed by the U.S. Constitution against the federal government would also be "privileges or immunities" guaranteed against abridgement by the states. See Kurt T. Lash, THE

FOURTEENTH AMENDMENT AND THE PRIVILEGES AND IMMUNITIES OF AMERICAN CITIZENSHIP (2014); Michael Kent Curtis, NO STATE SHALL ABRIDGE: THE FOURTEENTH AMENDMENT AND THE BILL OF RIGHTS (1986).

b.   Second, there is the *unenumerated-rights* view (or the natural-rights view): the clause protects a set of fundamental rights that is broader than those enumerated in the U.S. Constitution. At the time of ratification these rights would have been called "natural rights," the rights that belong, in the words of *Corfield*, "to the citizens of all free governments." 6 F. Cas. at 551. These would include some rights protected by positive law, such as the freedom of speech, as well as others not protected by positive law, such as some in the *Corfield* list. (Note that the rights protected on this view are also *narrower* than the Bill of Rights, for some of its procedural protections would likely be left out.) See Randy E. Barnett, RESTORING THE LOST CONSTITUTION: THE PRESUMPTION OF LIBERTY 60–68, 194–203 (2004); see also Eric R. Claeys, *Blackstone's Commentaries and the Privileges or Immunities of United States Citizens: A Modest Tribute to Professor Siegan*, 45 San Diego L. Rev. 777 (2008).

As for how these rights would be determined, there are a variety of views. For example, they might be determined by looking to the rights protected by state constitutions in 1868. See Steven G. Calabresi & Sarah E. Agudo, *Individual Rights Under State Constitutions When the Fourteenth Amendment Was Ratified in 1868: What Rights Are Deeply Rooted in American History and Tradition?* 87 Tex. L. Rev. 7 (2008). Or they might have their content determined by future generations, either through legislative enactments or judicial decisions. See John Hart Ely, DEMOCRACY AND DISTRUST: A THEORY OF JUDICIAL REVIEW 28 (1980) ("[T]he most plausible interpretation of the Privileges or Immunities Clause is, as it must be, the one suggested by its language—that it was a delegation to future constitutional decision-makers to protect certain rights that the document neither lists, at least not exhaustively, nor even in any specific way gives directions for finding.").

c.   Third, there is the *equality* view: the clause requires non-discrimination by the states in whatever privileges or immunities they choose to extend. This view starts with the Privileges and Immunities Clause in Article IV, which forbade discrimination against out-of-staters with respect to certain rights. Some holding this view would understand the Privileges or Immunities Clause in the Fourteenth Amendment as similarly forbidding discrimination against *in-staters* with respect to those same rights. Before the Civil War there had been extensive debate about whether free black citizens had to be given the same rights as white citizens. The clause is seen as answering that question, securing for the newly emancipated black citizens all the "privileges and immunities" guaranteed under Article IV. See John Harrison, *Reconstructing the Privileges or Immunities Clause*, 101 Yale L.J. 1385 (1992).

Another version of the equality view would emphasize the Article IV context, keeping the focus on comity and equal treatment for those who travel into a state, so that white and black travelers must be treated the same by the state. See Philip Hamburger, *Privileges or Immunities*, 105 Nw. U. L. Rev. 61 (2011). In either form, the equality view is consistent with the fact that constitutional amendments were proposed in the 1870s that would have incorporated the First Amendment against the states—which is difficult to understand if the Fourteenth Amendment was widely understood as already incorporating the First Amendment against the states or protecting a natural right of free speech.

Another variation would read the clause not only to forbid state discrimination against in-state citizens regarding privileges and immunities (i.e., the view of Harrison), but also to forbid states to discriminate against their own citizens relative to the citizens of other states. The latter point would forbid state outliers with respect to certain rights and have the indirect effect of incorporating most of the Bill of Rights. See Christopher R. Green, EQUAL CITIZENSHIP, CIVIL RIGHTS, AND THE CONSTITUTION: THE ORIGINAL SENSE OF THE PRIVILEGES OF IMMUNITIES CLAUSE (2015).

d.   Would the plaintiffs challenging the New Orleans slaughter-house ordinance have succeeded on the incorporation view—does the Bill of Rights protect the right to be a butcher? Would they have succeeded on the equality view? Did they need to persuade the Court of the natural rights view? Does the Court reject any of these views? Does it accept any of them? How far does the Court go toward any of these views, and what does it leave open for future cases?

5.   In *United States v. Cruikshank*, 92 U.S. 542 (1876), the Court revisited the Privileges or Immunities Clause. A posse of armed whites had massacred dozens of blacks in Louisiana, and three of the killers were convicted under a federal statute of conspiring to deny the victims their right to keep and bear arms. The Supreme Court reversed the convictions, concluding that the Second Amendment applied only to the national government and that this right was not a privilege or immunity of federal citizenship. *Cruikshank* is discussed further in *McDonald v. City of Chicago*, p. 1505. The key point here is that *Cruikshank* closed the door on the Privileges or Immunities Clause, and nearly all litigation under the Fourteenth Amendment has shifted to the Equal Protection Clause and the Due Process Clause.

The Court's next major case interpreting the Fourteenth Amendment was *Strauder v. West Virginia*, involving that state's exclusion of black citizens from criminal juries. *Strauder* is a major early case interpreting the amendment, analyzing both the protection it requires and Congress's power under Section 5 to displace state law and procedure to ensure that protection.

Strauder v. West Virginia
100 U.S. 303 (1880)

■ MR. JUSTICE STRONG delivered the opinion of the Court.

The plaintiff in error, a colored man, was indicted for murder in the Circuit Court of Ohio County, in West Virginia, on the 20th of October, 1874, and upon trial was convicted and sentenced. The record was then removed to the Supreme Court of the State, and there the judgment of the Circuit Court was affirmed. The present case is a writ of error to that court, and it is now, in substance, averred that at the trial in the State court the defendant (now plaintiff in error) was denied rights to which he was entitled under the Constitution and laws of the United States.

In the Circuit Court of the State, before the trial of the indictment was commenced, the defendant presented his petition, verified by his oath, praying for a removal of the cause into the Circuit Court of the United States, assigning, as ground for the removal, that "by virtue of the laws of the State of West Virginia no colored man was eligible to be a member of the grand jury or to serve on a petit jury in the State; that white men are so eligible, and that by reason of his being a colored man and having been a slave, he had reason to believe, and did believe, he could not have the full and equal benefit of all laws and proceedings in the State of West Virginia for the security of his person as is enjoyed by white citizens, and that he had less chance of enforcing in the courts of the State his rights on the prosecution, as a citizen of the United States, and that the probabilities of a denial of them to him as such citizen on every trial which might take place on the indictment in the courts of the State were much more enhanced than if he was a white man." This petition was denied by the State court, and the cause was forced to trial. . . .

The law of the State . . . is as follows: "All white male persons who are twenty-one years of age and who are citizens of this State shall be liable to serve as jurors, except as herein provided." The persons excepted are State officials.

In this court, several errors have been assigned, and the controlling questions underlying them all are, first, whether, by the Constitution and laws of the United States, every citizen of the United States has a right to a trial of an indictment against him by a jury selected and impanelled without discrimination against his race or color, because of race or color; and, second, if he has such a right, and is denied its enjoyment by the State in which he is indicted, may he cause the case to be removed into the Circuit Court of the United States?

It is to be observed that the first of these questions is not whether a colored man, when an indictment has been preferred against him, has a right to a grand or a petit jury composed in whole or in part of persons of his own race or color, but it is whether, in the composition or selection of jurors by whom he is to be indicted or tried, all persons of his race or color may be excluded by law, solely because of their race or color, so that by no possibility can any colored man sit upon the jury.

The questions are important, for they demand a construction of the recent amendments of the Constitution. . . . The Fourteenth Amendment . . . is one of a series of constitutional provisions having a common purpose; namely, securing to a race recently emancipated, a race that through many generations had been held in slavery, all the civil rights that the superior race enjoy. The true spirit and meaning of the amendments, as we said in the *Slaughter-House Cases*, cannot be understood without keeping in view the history of the times when they were adopted, and the general objects they plainly sought to accomplish. At the time when they were incorporated into the Constitution, it required little knowledge of human nature to anticipate that those who had long been regarded as an inferior and subject race would, when suddenly raised to the rank of citizenship, be looked upon with jealousy and positive dislike, and that State laws might be enacted or enforced to perpetuate the distinctions that had before existed. Discriminations against them had been habitual. It was well known that in some States laws making such discriminations then existed, and others might well be expected. The colored race, as a race, was abject and ignorant, and in that condition was unfitted to command the respect of those who had superior intelligence. Their training had left them mere children, and as such they needed the protection which a wise government extends to those who are unable to protect themselves. They especially needed protection against unfriendly action in the States where they were resident. It was in view of these considerations the Fourteenth Amendment was framed and adopted. It was designed to assure to the colored race the enjoyment of all the civil rights that under the law are enjoyed by white persons, and to give to that race the protection of the general government, in that enjoyment, whenever it should be denied by the States. It not only gave citizenship and the privileges of citizenship to persons of color, but it denied to any State the power to withhold from them the equal protection of the laws, and authorized Congress to enforce its provisions by appropriate legislation. . . .

If this is the spirit and meaning of the amendment, whether it means more or not, it is to be construed liberally, to carry out the purposes of its framers. It ordains that no State shall make or enforce any laws which shall abridge the privileges or immunities of citizens of the United States (evidently referring to the newly made citizens, who, being citizens of the United States, are declared to be also citizens of the State in which they reside). It ordains that no State shall deprive any person of life, liberty, or property, without due process of law, or deny to any person within its jurisdiction the equal protection of the laws. What is this but declaring that the law in the States shall be the same for the black as for the white; that all persons, whether colored or white, shall stand equal before the laws of the States, and, in regard to the colored race, for whose protection the amendment was primarily designed, that no discrimination shall be made against them by law because of their color? The words of the amendment, it is true, are prohibitory, but they contain a necessary implication of a positive immunity, or right, most valuable to the colored race,—the right to exemption from unfriendly legislation against them distinctively as colored,—exemption from legal discriminations, implying inferiority in civil society, lessening the security of their enjoyment of the rights which others enjoy, and discriminations which are steps towards reducing them to the condition of a subject race.

That the West Virginia statute respecting juries—the statute that controlled the selection of the grand and petit jury in the case of the plaintiff in error—is such a discrimination ought not to be doubted. Nor would it be if the persons excluded by it were white men. If in those States where the colored people constitute a majority of the entire population a law should be enacted excluding all white men from jury service, thus denying to them the privilege of participating equally with the blacks in the administration of justice, we apprehend no one would be heard to claim that it would not be a denial to white men of the equal protection of the laws. Nor if a law should be passed excluding all naturalized Celtic Irishmen, would there by any doubt of its inconsistency with the spirit of the amendment. The very fact that colored people are singled out and expressly denied by a statute all right to participate in the administration of the law, as jurors, because of their color, though they are citizens, and may be in other respects fully qualified, is practically a brand upon them, affixed by the law, an assertion of their inferiority, and a stimulant to that race prejudice which is an impediment to securing to individuals of the race that equal justice which the law aims to secure to all others.

The right to a trial by jury is guaranteed to every citizen of West Virginia by the Constitution of that State, and the constitution of juries is a very essential part of the protection such a mode of trial is intended to secure. The very idea of a jury is a body of men composed of the peers or equals of the person whose rights it is selected or summoned to determine; that is, of his neighbors, fellows, associates, persons having the same legal status in society as that which he holds. Blackstone, in his Commentaries, says, "The right of trial by jury, or the country, is a trial by the peers of every Englishman, and is the grand bulwark of his liberties, and is secured to him by the Great Charter." . . . It is well known that prejudices often exist against particular classes in the community, which sway the judgment of jurors, and which, therefore, operate in some cases to deny to persons of those classes the full enjoyment of that protection which others enjoy. Prejudice in a local community is held to be a reason for a change of venue. The framers of the constitutional amendment must have known full well the existence of such prejudice and its likelihood to continue against the manumitted slaves and their race, and that knowledge was doubtless a motive that led to the amendment. By their manumission and citizenship the colored race became entitled to the equal protection of the laws of the States in which they resided; and the apprehension that through prejudice they might be denied that equal protection, that is, that there might be discrimination against them, was the inducement to bestow upon the national government the power to enforce the provision that no State shall deny to them the equal protection of the laws. Without the apprehended existence of prejudice that portion of the amendment would have been unnecessary, and it might have been left to the States to extend equality of protection.

In view of these considerations, it is hard to see why the statute of West Virginia should not be regarded as discriminating against a colored man when he is put upon trial for an alleged criminal offence against the State. It is not easy to comprehend how it can be said that while every white man is entitled to a trial by a jury selected from persons of his own race or color, or, rather, selected without discrimination against his color, and a negro is not, the latter is equally protected by the law with the former. Is not protection of life and liberty against race or color prejudice, a right, a legal right, under the constitutional amendment? And how can it be maintained that compelling a colored man to submit to a trial for his life by a jury drawn from a panel from which the State has expressly excluded every man of his race, because of color alone, however well qualified in other respects, is not a denial to him of equal legal protection?

We do not say that within the limits from which it is not excluded by the amendment a State may not prescribe the qualifications of its jurors, and in so doing make discriminations. It may confine the selection to males, to freeholders, to citizens, to persons within certain ages, or to persons having educational qualifications. We do not believe the Fourteenth Amendment was ever intended to prohibit this. Looking at its history, it is clear it had no such purpose. Its aim was against discrimination because of race or color. As we have said more than once, its design was to protect an emancipated race, and to strike down all possible legal discriminations against those who belong to it. To quote further from the *Slaughter-House Cases*, 83 U.S. (16 Wall.) 36 (1873): "In giving construction to any of these articles [amendments], it is necessary to keep the main purpose steadily in view." "It is so clearly a provision for that race and that emergency, that a strong case would be necessary for its application to any other." We are not now called upon to affirm or deny that it had other purposes.

The Fourteenth Amendment makes no attempt to enumerate the rights it designed to protect. It speaks in general terms, and those are as comprehensive as possible. Its language is prohibitory; but every prohibition implies the existence of rights and immunities, prominent among which is an immunity from inequality of legal protection, either for life, liberty, or property. Any State action that denies this immunity to a colored man is in conflict with the Constitution.

Concluding, therefore, that the statute of West Virginia, discriminating in the selection of jurors, as it does, against negroes because of their color, amounts to a denial of the equal protection of the laws to a colored man when he is put upon trial for an alleged offence against the State, it remains only to be considered whether the power of Congress to enforce the provisions of the Fourteenth Amendment by appropriate legislation is sufficient to justify the enactment of sect. 641 of the Revised Statutes.

A right or an immunity, whether created by the Constitution or only guaranteed by it, even without any express delegation of power, may be protected by Congress. *Prigg v. The Commonwealth of Pennsylvania*, 41 U.S. (16 Pet.) 539 (1842). . . . But there is express authority to protect the rights and immunities referred to in the Fourteenth Amendment, and to enforce observance of them by appropriate congressional legislation. And one very efficient and appropriate mode of extending such protection and securing to a party the enjoyment of the right or immunity, is a law providing for the removal of his case from a State court, in which the right is denied by the State law, into a Federal court, where it will be upheld. This is an ordinary mode of protecting rights and immunities conferred by the Federal Constitution and laws. Sect. 641 is such a provision. It enacts that "when any civil suit or criminal prosecution is commenced in any State court for any cause whatsoever against any person who is denied, or cannot enforce, in the judicial tribunals of the State, or in the part of the State where such prosecution is pending, any right secured to him by any law providing for the equal civil rights of citizens of the United States, or of all persons within the jurisdiction of the United States, such suit or prosecution may, upon the petition of such defendant, filed in said State court at any time before the trial, or final hearing of the case, stating the facts, and verified by oath, be removed before trial into the next Circuit Court of the United States to be held in the district where it is pending."

This act plainly has reference to sects. 1977 and 1978 of the statutes which partially enumerate the rights and immunities intended to be guaranteed by the Constitution, the first of which declares that "all persons within the jurisdiction of the United States shall have the same right in every State and Territory to make and enforce contracts, to sue, be parties, give evidence, and to the full and equal benefit of all laws and proceedings for the security of persons and property, as is enjoyed by white citizens, and shall be subject to like punishment, pains, penalties, taxes, licenses, and exactions of every kind, and to no other." This act puts in the form of a statute what had been substantially ordained by the constitutional amendment. It was a step towards enforcing the constitutional provisions. Sect. 641 was an advanced step, fully warranted, we think, by the fifth section of the Fourteenth Amendment. . . .

There was error, therefore, in proceeding to the trial of the indictment against him after his petition [for removal to federal court] was filed. . . .

■ MR. JUSTICE FIELD.

I dissent from the judgment of the court in this case, on the grounds stated in my opinion in *Ex parte Virginia*, 100 U.S. 339 (1879), and MR. JUSTICE CLIFFORD concurs with me.

[In his dissent in Ex parte Virginia, *Justice Field argued that the Reconstruction Amendments did not fundamentally alter state control of local matters. He also argued that service on a jury was unaffected by the Equal Protection Clause because it required equality only in civil rights and not in political rights: "The equality of protection intended does not require that all persons shall be permitted to participate in the government of the State and the administration of its laws, to hold its offices, or be clothed with any public trusts."—Editors]*

NOTES

1.   After *Strauder*'s proposition that "all persons . . . shall stand equal before the laws of the States" and that, for the newly freed slaves, "no discrimination shall be made against them by law on account of their color," does anything else need to be said about the Equal Protection Clause and racial discrimination by the government? Alas, even great cases have their warts: we have deliberately not edited out *Strauder*'s racist language. Regrettable as it is, that language confirms the magnificence of *Strauder*'s declaration of legal principle: even a court steeped in cultural ideas of racial inferiority embraced the legal view that the Fourteenth Amendment rejected racial discrimination.

2.   Does *Strauder* support a color-blind interpretation of the Equal Protection Clause? Is there language suggesting that the Equal Protection Clause forbids state governments from ever making distinctions on the basis of race? On other hand, is there also language suggesting the clause is asymmetric at least in its purpose, being meant to protect the newly freed slaves from discrimination? Yogi Berra once said, "When you come to a fork in the road, take it." Is that what *Strauder* does on the question of whether the Equal Protection Clause requires color-blindness or no discrimination against black citizens?

3.   What do you make of the reference to "Celtic Irishmen"? It may be easy now to read that as something like "white." But in *Strauder* the reference might have had a quite different sense. Earlier in the nineteenth century, the great Irish famine of the 1840s prompted a giant wave of immigration from Ireland to the United States. Of all the immigrants to the United States in the 1840s, roughly half came from Ireland, as did roughly a third of all immigrants in the 1850s. By 1860, a quarter of the population of Boston and New York City had been born in Ireland. Kevin Kenny, *Abraham Lincoln and the American Irish*, 10 Am. J. of Irish Studies 39, 40–41 (2013). The surge of Irish immigrants drew the ire of American nativists, who especially denounced the Irish for their religion (Catholic) and their educational choices (they tended to eschew the newly established public schools in favor of parochial schools). When *Strauder* was decided, anti-Irish nativism showed no signs of ebbing. To the contrary, there was a growing movement around the country to adopt constitutional amendments (called "Blaine Amendments") that prohibited the use of state funds for religious schools—religious schools that were overwhelmingly Catholic and, in many parts of the country, overwhelmingly Irish. Cf. Mark Edward DeForrest, *An Overview and Evaluation of State Blaine Amendments: Origins, Scope, and First Amendment Concerns*, 26 Harv. J. L. & Pub. Pol'y 551, 573 (2003) (noting that in 1889 Congress required state constitutional language about schools "free from sectarian control" as a condition for new states to be admitted to the Union). In short, "Celtic Irishmen" was not a shorthand for power and privilege, but more likely the opposite.

4.   Was Justice Field correct that jury service was a political right, not a "privilege or immunity"? Does it matter that Strauder's claim was not that *he* should serve on a jury, but that in a criminal trial he should be given the protection of a jury from which black citizens were not excluded? Did that make the Equal Protection Clause the most apt grounds for decision? Could the case have been decided under the Due Process Clause?

5.   In *Yick Wo v. Hopkins,* 118 U.S. 356 (1886), the Supreme Court held unconstitutional the detention of unlicensed Chinese laundry operators. San Francisco had passed ordinances requiring those who operated laundries in wooden buildings to obtain permits. Permits were then granted to 80 non-Chinese persons, but of the 200 Chinese applicants for permits, 199 were denied. The Court found that "the conclusion

cannot be resisted that no reason for [the discrimination] exists except hostility to the race and nationality to which the petitioners belong, and which, in the eye of the law, is not justified." In finding a violation of the Equal Protection Clause, *Yick Wo* said: "the equal protection of the laws is a pledge of the protection of equal laws." It is short sentence, but a significant one. It suggests the Court was focused less on the "protection" offered by the state and more on whether a law was discriminatory. That focus explains some of the characteristic emphases of modern equal protection doctrine: a focus on classifications, a focus on laws, and an absence of focus on the state's affirmative duties. For further discussion of *Yick Wo*, see p. 1382.

[Assignment 65]

E. CONGRESS'S POWER TO ENFORCE THE RECONSTRUCTION AMENDMENTS

Central to the Reconstruction amendments—indeed, arguably their most important feature—was the grant of sweeping new legislative powers to Congress. Congress was given power to "enforce" the ban on slavery in the Thirteenth Amendment; to "enforce" with "appropriate" legislation the guarantees of the Fourteenth Amendment; and to "enforce" the Fifteenth Amendment's prohibition of racial discrimination in voting.

As noted above, the Reconstruction Congresses passed a series of important statutes pursuant to these powers, most of which remain in force today. The Civil Rights Act of 1866—passed after the Thirteenth Amendment was adopted but before the Fourteenth Amendment was proposed—provided that all persons born in the United States were citizens of the United States and listed rights and privileges of "such citizens, of every race and color, without regard to any previous condition of slavery." The law was aimed at the Black Codes adopted by Southern states. See p. 1264. Doubts about the constitutionality of the Civil Rights Act were a substantial part of what motivated Congress to propose the Fourteenth Amendment. See p. 1267. That amendment granted power to Congress to enforce its prohibitions against the states.

Enter the Civil Rights Act of 1875, in which Congress read expansively its power under these amendments. Section 1 provided that "all persons within the jurisdiction of the United States shall be entitled to the full and equal enjoyment of the accommodations, advantages, facilities, and privileges of inns, public conveyances on land or water, theatres, and other places of public amusement; subject only to the conditions and limitations established by law and applicable alike to citizens of every race and color, regardless of any condition of servitude." Section 2 provided criminal penalties and authorized civil suits for the award of monetary penalties.

The Supreme Court considered the act in *The Civil Rights Cases* (1883), made up of five consolidated cases, four involving criminal penalties and one involving civil liability. The Court held that the Civil Rights Act of 1875 was *not* within the scope of Congress's enforcement powers under the Thirteenth and Fourteenth Amendments. The Fourteenth Amendment enforcement power is limited to state action; and Congress's enforcement powers cannot be stretched to go beyond what the amendments actually prohibit. (It was not until the 1960s that such civil rights laws were again enacted—pursuant to the Commerce Clause power, rather than the power to enforce the provisions of the Fourteenth Amendment.)

The Civil Rights Cases is the foundational Supreme Court decision for two important questions of interpretation of the Fourteenth Amendment: first, the "state action" requirement; and second, the scope of Congress's enforcement power under Section 5. All subsequent interpretation of the amendment has followed the path marked out by that decision. But was the Court right? Decide for yourself as you read *The Civil Rights Cases* and two modern cases illustrating how present doctrine carries forward the principles it established: *United States v. Morrison* (2000) (on state action) and *City of Boerne v. Flores* (1997) (on the Section 5 enforcement power).

The Civil Rights Cases
109 U.S. 3 (1883)

■ MR. JUSTICE BRADLEY delivered the opinion of the court. . . .

[T]he primary and important question in all the cases is the constitutionality of the law. . . . Its effect is to declare, that in all inns, public conveyances, and places of amusement, colored citizens, whether formerly slaves or not, and citizens of other races, shall have the same accommodations and privileges in all inns, public conveyances, and places of amusement, as are enjoyed by white citizens; and *vice versa.* The second section makes it a penal offense in any person to deny to any citizen of any race or color, regardless of previous servitude, any of the accommodations or privileges mentioned in the first section.

Has Congress constitutional power to make such a law? Of course, no one will contend that the power to pass it was contained in the Constitution before the adoption of the last three amendments. The power is sought, first, in the Fourteenth Amendment, and the views and arguments of distinguished Senators, advanced whilst the law was under consideration, claiming authority to pass it by virtue of that amendment, are the principal arguments adduced in favor of the power. We have carefully considered those arguments, as was due to the eminent ability of those who put them forward, and have felt, in all its force, the weight of authority which always invests a law that Congress deems itself competent to pass. But the responsibility of an independent judgment is now thrown upon this court; and we are bound to exercise it according to the best lights we have. . . .

It is State action of a particular character that is prohibited. Individual invasion of individual rights is not the subject-matter of the amendment. It has a deeper and broader scope. It nullifies and makes void all State legislation, and State action of every kind, which impairs the privileges and immunities of citizens of the United States, or which injures them in life, liberty, or property without due process of law, or which denies to any of them the equal protection of the laws. It not only does this, but, in order that the national will, thus declared, may not be a mere *brutum fulmen [i.e., an ineffective thunderbolt, a metaphor for an empty threat—Editors]*, the last section of the amendment invests Congress with power to enforce it by appropriate legislation. To enforce what? To enforce the prohibition. To adopt appropriate legislation for correcting the effects of such prohibited State laws and State acts, and thus to render them effectually null, void, and innocuous. This is the legislative power conferred upon Congress, and this is the whole of it. It does not invest Congress with power to legislate upon subjects which are within the domain of State legislation; but to provide modes of relief against State legislation, or State action, of the kind referred to. It does not authorize Congress to create a code of municipal law for the regulation of private rights; but to provide modes of redress against the operation of State laws, and the action of State officers, executive or judicial, when these are subversive of the fundamental rights specified in the amendment. Positive rights and privileges are undoubtedly secured by the Fourteenth Amendment; but they are secured by way of prohibition against State laws and State proceedings affecting those rights and privileges, and by power given to Congress to legislate for the purpose of carrying such prohibition into effect; and such legislation must necessarily be predicated upon such supposed State laws or State proceedings, and be directed to the correction of their operation and effect. . . .

And so in the present case, until some State law has been passed, or some State action through its officers or agents has been taken, adverse to the rights of citizens sought to be protected by the Fourteenth Amendment, no legislation of the United States under said amendment, nor any proceeding under such legislation, can be called into activity, for the prohibitions of the amendment are against State laws and acts done under State authority. Of course, legislation may and should be provided in advance to meet the exigency when it arises, but it should be adapted to the mischief and wrong which the amendment was intended to provide against; and that is, State laws or State action of some kind adverse to the rights of the citizen secured by the amendment. Such legislation cannot properly cover the whole domain of rights appertaining to life, liberty, and property, defining them and providing for their vindication. That would be to establish a code of municipal law regulative of all private rights between man and man in society. It would be to make Congress take the place of the State legislatures and to supersede them. It is absurd to affirm that, because the rights of life, liberty, and property (which include all civil rights that men have) are by the amendment sought to be protected against invasion on the part of the State without due process of law, Congress may, therefore, provide due process of law for their vindication in every case; and that, because the denial by a State to any persons of the equal protection of the laws is prohibited by the amendment, therefore Congress may establish laws for their equal protection. In fine, the legislation which Congress is authorized to adopt in this behalf is not general legislation upon the rights of the citizen, but corrective legislation; that is, such as may be necessary and proper for counteracting such laws as the States may adopt or enforce, and which by the amendment they are prohibited from making or enforcing, or such acts and proceedings as the States may commit or take, and which by the amendment they are prohibited from committing or taking. It is not necessary for us to state, if we could, what legislation would be proper for Congress to adopt. It is sufficient for us to examine whether the law in question is of that character.

An inspection of the law [the Civil Rights Act of 1875] shows that it makes no reference whatever to any supposed or apprehended violation of the Fourteenth Amendment on the part of the States. It is not predicated on any such view. It proceeds *ex directo* to declare that certain acts committed by individuals shall be deemed offenses, and shall be prosecuted and punished by proceedings in the courts of the United States. It does not profess to be corrective of any constitutional wrong committed by the States; it does not make its operation to depend upon any such wrong committed. It applies equally to cases arising in States which have the justest laws respecting the personal rights of citizens, and whose authorities are ever ready to enforce such laws as to those which arise in States that may have violated the prohibition of the amendment. In other words, it steps into the domain of local jurisprudence, and lays down rules for the conduct of individuals in society towards each other, and imposes sanctions for the enforcement of those rules, without referring in any manner to any supposed action of the State or its authorities. . . . *[The Court then contrasted provisions of the Civil Rights Act of 1875 with provisions of the Civil Rights Act of 1866.—Editors]*

[The 1866 Act,] after declaring that all persons within the jurisdiction of the United States shall have the same right in every State and Territory to make and enforce contracts, to sue, be parties, give evidence, and to the full and equal benefit of all laws and proceedings for the security of persons and property as is enjoyed by white citizens, and shall be subject to like punishment, pains, penalties, taxes, licenses, and exactions of every kind, and none other, any law, statute, ordinance, regulation, or custom to the contrary notwithstanding, proceeds to . . . [prescribe punishments for violations committed by anyone who acts under color of state law.] This law is clearly corrective in its character, intended to counteract and furnish redress against State laws and proceedings, and customs having the force of law. . . .

In this connection, it is proper to state that civil rights, such as are guarantied by the Constitution against State aggression, cannot be impaired by the wrongful acts of individuals, unsupported by State authority in the shape of laws, customs, or judicial or executive proceedings. The wrongful act of an individual, unsupported by any such authority, is simply a private wrong, or a crime of that individual; an invasion of the rights of the injured party, it is true, whether they affect his person, his property, or his reputation; but if not sanctioned in some way by the State, or not done under State authority, his rights remain in full force, and may presumably be vindicated by resort to the laws of the State for redress. An individual cannot deprive a man of his right to vote, to hold property, to buy and to sell, to sue in the courts, or to be a witness or a juror; he may, by force or fraud, interfere with the enjoyment of the right in a particular case; he may commit an assault against the person, or commit murder, or use ruffian violence at the polls, or slander the good name of a fellow-citizen; but unless protected in these wrongful acts by some shield of State law or State authority, he cannot destroy or injure the right; he will only render himself amenable to satisfaction or punishment; and amenable therefore to the laws of the State where the wrongful acts are committed. . . .

The law in question [the Civil Rights Act of 1875], without any reference to adverse State legislation on the subject, declares that all persons shall be entitled to equal accommodation and privileges of inns, public conveyances, and places of public amusement, and imposes a penalty upon any individual who shall deny to any citizen such equal accommodations and privileges. This is not corrective legislation; it is primary and direct; it takes immediate and absolute possession of the subject of the right of admission to inns, public conveyances, and places of amusement. It supersedes and displaces State legislation on the same subject, or only allows it permissive force. It ignores such legislation, and assumes that the matter is one that belongs to the domain of national regulation. Whether it would not have been a more effective protection of the rights of citizens to have clothed Congress with plenary power over the whole subject, is not now the question. What we have to decide is, whether such plenary power has been conferred upon Congress by the Fourteenth Amendment; and, in our judgment, it has not.

We have discussed the question presented by the law on the assumption that a right to enjoy equal accommodations and privileges in all inns, public conveyances, and places of public amusement, is one of the essential rights of the citizen which no State can abridge or interfere with. Whether it is such a right or not is a different question, which, in the view we have taken of the validity of the law on the ground already stated, it is not necessary to examine. . . .

But the power of congress to adopt direct and primary, as distinguished from corrective, legislation on the subject in hand, is sought, in the second place, from the Thirteenth Amendment, which abolishes slavery. This amendment declares "that neither slavery, nor involuntary servitude, except as a punishment for crime, whereof the party shall have been duly convicted, shall exist within the United States, or any place subject to their jurisdiction;" and it gives Congress power to enforce the amendment by appropriate legislation. . . .

And such legislation may be primary and direct in its character; for the amendment is not a mere prohibition of State laws establishing or upholding slavery, but an absolute declaration that slavery or involuntary servitude shall not exist in any part of the United States. . . .

[I]t is assumed that the power vested in Congress to enforce the article by appropriate legislation, clothes Congress with power to pass all laws necessary and proper for abolishing all badges and incidents of slavery in the United States; and upon this assumption it is claimed that this is sufficient authority for declaring by law that all persons shall have equal accommodations and privileges in all inns, public conveyances, and places of public amusement; the argument being that the denial of such equal accommodations and privileges is in itself a subjection to a species of servitude within the meaning of the amendment. Conceding the major proposition to be true, that Congress has a right to enact all necessary and proper laws for the obliteration and prevention of slavery, with all its badges and incidents, is the minor proposition also true, that the denial to any person of admission to the accommodations and privileges of an inn, a public conveyance, or a theater, does subject that person to any form of servitude, or tend to fasten upon him any badge of slavery? If it does not, then power to pass the law is not found in the Thirteenth Amendment. . . .

Congress, as we have seen, by the Civil Rights Bill of 1866, passed in view of the Thirteenth Amendment, before the Fourteenth was adopted, undertook to wipe out these burdens and disabilities, the necessary incidents of slavery, constituting its substance and visible form; and to secure to all citizens of every race and color, and without regard to previous servitude, those fundamental rights which are the essence of civil freedom, namely, the same right to make and enforce contracts, to sue, be parties, give evidence, and to inherit, purchase, lease, sell, and convey property, as is enjoyed by white citizens. Whether this legislation was fully authorized by the Thirteenth Amendment alone, without the support which it afterwards received from the Fourteenth Amendment, after the adoption of which it was re-enacted with some additions, it is not necessary to inquire. It is referred to for the purpose of showing that at that time (in 1866) Congress did not assume, under the authority given by the Thirteenth Amendment, to adjust what may be called the social rights of men and races in the community; but only to declare and vindicate those fundamental rights which appertain to the essence of citizenship, and the enjoyment or deprivation of which constitutes the essential distinction between freedom and slavery.

We must not forget that the province and scope of the Thirteenth and Fourteenth amendments are different: the former simply abolished slavery: the latter prohibited the States from abridging the privileges or immunities of citizens of the United States, from depriving them of life, liberty, or property without due process of law, and from denying to any the equal protection of the laws. The amendments are different, and the powers of Congress under them are different. What Congress has power to do under one, it may not have power to do under the other. Under the Thirteenth Amendment, it has only to do with slavery and its incidents. Under the Fourteenth Amendment, it has power to counteract and render nugatory all State laws and proceedings which have the effect to abridge any of the privileges or immunities of citizens of the United States, or to deprive them of life, liberty, or property without due process of law, or to deny to any of them the equal protection of the laws. Under the Thirteenth Amendment the legislation, so far as necessary or proper to eradicate all forms and incidents of slavery and involuntary servitude, may be direct and primary, operating upon the acts of individuals, whether sanctioned by State legislation or not; under the Fourteenth, as we have already shown, it must necessarily be, and can only be, corrective in its character, addressed to counteract and afford relief against State regulations or proceedings.

The only question under the present head, therefore, is, whether the refusal to any persons of the accommodations of an inn, or a public conveyance, or a place of public amusement, by an individual, and without any sanction or support from any State law or regulation, does inflict upon such persons any manner of servitude, or form of slavery, as those terms are understood in this country? Many wrongs may be obnoxious to the prohibitions of the Fourteenth Amendment which are not, in any just sense, incidents or elements of slavery. Such, for example, would be the taking of private property without due process of law; or allowing persons who have committed certain crimes (horse stealing, for example) to be seized and hung by the *posse comitatus* without regular trial; or denying to any person, or class of persons, the right to pursue any peaceful avocations allowed to others. What is called class legislation would belong to this category, and would be obnoxious to the prohibitions of the Fourteenth Amendment, but would not necessarily be so to the Thirteenth, when not involving the idea of any subjection of one man to another. The Thirteenth Amendment has respect, not to distinctions of race, or class, or color, but to slavery. The Fourteenth Amendment extends its protection to races and classes, and prohibits any state legislation which has the effect of denying to any race or class, or to any individual, the equal protection of the laws.

Now, conceding, for the sake of the argument, that the admission to an inn, a public conveyance, or a place of public amusement, on equal terms with all other citizens, is the right of every man and all classes of men, is it any more than one of those rights which the States by the Fourteenth Amendment are forbidden to deny to any person? and is the Constitution violated until the denial of the right has some State sanction or authority? Can the act of a mere individual, the owner of the inn, the public conveyance, or place of amusement, refusing the accommodation, be justly regarded as imposing any badge of slavery or servitude upon the applicant, or only as inflicting an ordinary civil injury, properly cognizable by the laws of the State, and presumably subject to redress by those laws until the contrary appears?

After giving to these questions all the consideration which their importance demands, we are forced to the conclusion that such an act of refusal has nothing to do with slavery or involuntary servitude, and that if it is violative of any right of the party, his redress is to be sought under the laws of the State; or, if those laws are adverse to his rights and do not protect him, his remedy will be found in the corrective legislation which Congress has adopted, or may adopt, for counteracting the effect of State laws, or State action, prohibited by the Fourteenth Amendment. It would be running the slavery argument into the ground to make it apply to every act of discrimination which a person may see fit to make as to the guests he will entertain, or as to the people he will take into his coach or cab or car, or admit to his concert or theater, or deal with in other matters of intercourse or business. Innkeepers and public carriers, by the laws of all the States, so far as we are aware, are bound, to the extent of their facilities, to furnish proper accommodation to all unobjectionable persons who in good faith apply for them. If the laws themselves make any unjust discrimination, amenable to the prohibitions of the Fourteenth Amendment, Congress has full power to afford a remedy under that amendment and in accordance with it.

When a man has emerged from slavery, and by the aid of beneficent legislation has shaken off the inseparable concomitants of that state, there must be some stage in the progress of his elevation when he takes the rank of a mere citizen, and ceases to be the special favorite of the laws, and when his rights as a citizen, or a man, are to be protected in the ordinary modes by which other men's rights are protected. There were thousands of free colored people in this country before the abolition of slavery, enjoying all the essential rights of life, liberty, and property the same as white citizens; yet no one, at that time, thought that it was any invasion of their personal status as freemen because they were not admitted to all the privileges enjoyed by white citizens, or because they were subjected to discriminations in the enjoyment of accommodations in inns, public conveyances, and places of amusement. Mere discriminations on account of race or color were not regarded as badges of slavery. If, since that time, the enjoyment of equal rights in all these respects has become established by constitutional enactment, it is not by force of the Thirteenth Amendment, (which merely abolishes slavery), but by force of the Fourteenth and Fifteenth Amendments.

On the whole, we are of opinion that no countenance of authority for the passage of the law in question can be found in either the Thirteenth or Fourteenth Amendment of the Constitution; and no other ground of authority for its passage being suggested, it must necessarily be declared void, at least so far as its operation in the several States is concerned.

This conclusion disposes of the cases now under consideration. In the cases of *United States v. Michael Ryan*, and of *Richard A. Robinson and Wife v. The Memphis & Charleston Railroad Company*, the judgments must be affirmed. In the other cases, the answer to be given will be, that the first and second sections of the act of congress of March 1, 1875, entitled "An Act to protect all citizens in their civil and legal rights," are unconstitutional and void, and that judgment should be rendered upon the several indictments in those cases accordingly.

■ MR. JUSTICE HARLAN, dissenting.

The opinion in these case proceeds, as it seems to me, upon grounds entirely too narrow and artificial. I cannot resist the conclusion that the substance and spirit of the recent amendments of the Constitution have been sacrificed by a subtle and ingenious verbal criticism. "It is not the words of the law but the internal sense of it that makes the law. The letter of the law is the body; the sense and reason of the law is the soul." Constitutional provisions, adopted in the interest of liberty, and for the purpose of securing, through national legislation, if need be, rights inhering in a state of freedom, and belonging to American citizenship, have been so construed as to defeat the ends the people desired to accomplish, which they attempted to accomplish, and which they supposed they had accomplished by changes in their fundamental law. By this I do not mean that the determination of these cases should have been materially controlled by considerations of mere expediency or policy. I mean only, in this form, to express an earnest conviction that the court has departed from the familiar rule requiring, in the interpretation of constitutional provisions, that full effect be given to the intent with which they were adopted. . . .

The Thirteenth Amendment, it is conceded, did something more than to prohibit slavery as an *institution*, resting upon distinctions of race, and upheld by positive law. My brethren admit that it established and decreed universal *civil freedom* throughout the United States. But did the freedom thus established involve nothing more than exemption from actual slavery? Was nothing more intended than to forbid one man from owning another as property? Was it the purpose of the nation simply to destroy the institution, and then remit the race, theretofore held in bondage, to the several States for such protection, in their civil rights, necessarily growing out of freedom, as those States, in their discretion, choose to provide? Were the States, against whose solemn protest the institution was destroyed, to be left perfectly free, so far as national interference was concerned, to make or allow discriminations against that race, as such, in the enjoyment of those fundamental rights which by universal concession, inhere in a state of freedom? . . .

That there are burdens and disabilities which constitute badges of slavery and servitude, and that the power to enforce by appropriate legislation the Thirteenth Amendment may be exerted by legislation of a direct and primary character, for the eradication, not simply of the institution, but of its badges and incidents, are propositions which ought to be deemed indisputable. They lie at the foundation of the Civil Rights Act of 1866. . . . [My brethren] admit . . . that Congress, by the act of 1866, passed in view of the Thirteenth Amendment, before the Fourteenth was adopted, undertook to remove certain burdens and disabilities, the necessary incidents of slavery, and to secure to all citizens of every race and color, and without regard to previous servitude, those fundamental rights which are the essence of civil freedom, namely, the same right to make and enforce contracts, to sue, be parties, give evidence, and to inherit, purchase, lease, sell, and convey property as is enjoyed by white citizens. . . . I do not contend that the Thirteenth Amendment invests Congress with authority, by legislation, to define and regulate the entire body of the civil rights which citizens enjoy, or may enjoy, in the several States. But I do hold that since slavery, as the court has repeatedly declared, *Slaughter-House Cases*, 83 U.S. (16 Wall.) 36 (1870); *Strauder v. West Virginia*, 100 U.S. 303 (1880), was the moving or principal cause of the adoption of that amendment, and since that institution rested wholly upon the inferiority, as a race, of those held in bondage, their freedom necessarily involved immunity from, and protection against, all discrimination against them, because of their race, in respect of such civil rights as belong to freemen of other races. Congress, therefore, under its express power to enforce that amendment, by appropriate legislation, may enact laws to protect that people against the deprivation, *on account of their race*, of any civil rights granted to other freemen in the same State; and such legislation may be of a direct and primary character, operating upon States, their officers and agents, and also, upon, at least, such individuals and corporations as exercise public functions and wield power and authority under the State. . . .

It remains now to inquire what are the legal rights of colored persons in respect of the accommodations, privileges and facilities of public conveyances, inns and places of public amusement?

First, as to public conveyances on land and water. . . . In *Olcott v. Supervisors*, 83 U.S. (16 Wall.) 694 (1873), it was ruled that railroads are public highways, established by authority of the State for the public use; that they are none the less public highways because controlled and owned by private corporations; that it is a part of the function of government to make and maintain highways for the convenience of the public; that no matter who is the agent, and what is the agency, the function performed is *that of the State*; [and] that although the owners may be private companies, they may be compelled to permit the public to use these works. . . .

Such being the relations these corporations hold to the public, it would seem that the right of a colored person to use an improved public highway, upon the terms accorded to freemen of other races, is as fundamental, in the state of freedom established in this country, as are any of the rights which my brethren concede to be so far fundamental as to be deemed the essence of civil freedom. "Personal liberty consists," says Blackstone, "in the power of locomotion, of changing situation, or removing one's person to whatever place one's own inclination may direct, without restraint, unless by due course of law." But of what value is this right of locomotion, if it may be clogged by such burdens as Congress intended by the act of 1875 to remove? They are burdens which lay at the very foundation of the institution of slavery as it once existed. . . .

Second, as to inns. The same general observations which have been made as to railroads are applicable to inns. . . . In *Rex v. Ivens*, [173 Eng. Rep. 94 (1835)], the court, speaking by Mr. Justice Coleridge, said:

> An indictment lies against an innkeeper who refuses to receive a guest, he having at the time room in his house; and either the price of the guest's entertainment being tendered to him, or such circumstances occurring as will dispense with that tender. This law is founded in good sense. The innkeeper is not to select his guests. He has no right to say to one, you shall come to my inn, and to another you shall not, as every one coming and conducting himself in a proper manner has a right to be received; and for this purpose innkeepers are a sort of public servants, they having in return a kind of privilege of entertaining travelers and supplying them with that they want.

These authorities are sufficient to show a keeper of an inn is in the exercise of a quasi public employment. The law gives him special privileges, and he is charged with certain duties and responsibilities to the public. The public nature of his employment forbids him from discriminating against any person asking admission as a guest on account of the race or color of that person.

Third. As to places of public amusement. . . . [The] places of public amusement, within the meaning of the act of 1875, are such as are established and maintained under direct license of the law. The authority to establish and maintain them comes from the public. The colored race is a part of that public. The local government granting the license represents them as well as all other races within its jurisdiction. A license from the public to establish a place of public amusement, imports, in law, equality of right, at such places, among all the members of that public. . . .

I am of the opinion that such discrimination practiced by corporations and individuals in the exercise of their public or quasi-public functions is a badge of servitude the imposition of which Congress may prevent under its power, by appropriate legislation, to enforce the Thirteenth Amendment; and consequently, without reference to its enlarged power under the Fourteenth Amendment, the act of March 1, 1875, is not, in my judgment, repugnant to the Constitution.

It remains now to consider these cases with reference to the power Congress has possessed since the adoption of the Fourteenth Amendment. . . .

The assumption that this amendment consists wholly of prohibitions upon State laws and State proceedings in hostility to its provisions, is unauthorized by its language. The first clause of the first section—"All persons born or naturalized in the United States, and subject to the jurisdiction thereof, are citizens of the United States, and of the State wherein they reside"—is of a distinctly affirmative character. . . .

It is, therefore, an essential inquiry what, if any, right, privilege or immunity was given, by the nation, to colored persons, when they were made citizens of the State in which they reside? . . . That they became entitled, upon the adoption of the Fourteenth Amendment, "to all privileges and immunities of citizens in the several States," within the meaning of section 2 of article 4 of the Constitution, no one, I suppose, will for a moment question. What are the privileges and immunities to which, by that clause of the Constitution, they became entitled? To this it may be answered, generally, upon the authority of the adjudged cases, that they are those which are fundamental in citizenship in a free republican government, such as are "common to the citizens in the latter States under their constitutions and laws by virtue of their being citizens." . . .

But what was secured to colored citizens of the United States—as between them and their respective States—by the grant to them of State citizenship? With what rights, privileges, or immunities did this grant invest them? There is one, if there be no others—exemption from race discrimination in respect of any civil right belonging to citizens of the white race in the same State. That, surely, is their constitutional privilege when within the jurisdiction of other States. And such must be their constitutional right, in their own State, unless the recent amendments be splendid baubles, thrown out to delude those who deserved fair and generous treatment at the hands of the nation. Citizenship in this country necessarily imports at least equality of civil rights among citizens of every race in the same State. . . .

If the grant to colored citizens of the United States of citizenship in their respective States, imports exemption from race discrimination, in their States, in respect of such civil rights as belong to citizenship, then, to hold that the amendment remits that right to the States for their protection, primarily, and stays the hands of the nation, until it is assailed by State laws or State proceedings, is to adjudge that the amendment, so far from enlarging the powers of Congress—as we have heretofore said it did—not only curtails them, but reverses the policy which the general government has pursued from its very organization. Such an interpretation of the amendment is a denial to Congress of the power, by appropriate legislation, to enforce one of its provisions. . . .

It was said of the case of *Dred Scott v. Sandford*, 60 U.S. (19 How.) 393 (1857), that this court, there overruled the action of two generations, virtually inserted a new clause in the Constitution, changed its character, and made a new departure in the workings of the federal government. I may be permitted to say that if the recent amendments are so construed that Congress may not, in its own discretion, and independently of the action or non-action of the States, provide, by legislation of a direct character, for the security of rights created by the national Constitution; . . . then, not only the foundations upon which the national supremacy has always securely rested will be materially disturbed, but we shall enter upon an era of constitutional law, when the rights of freedom and American citizenship cannot receive from the nation that efficient protection which heretofore was unhesitatingly accorded to slavery and the rights of the master.

But if it were conceded that the power of Congress could not be brought into activity until the rights specified in the act of 1875 had been abridged or denied by some State law or State action, I maintain that the decision of the court is erroneous. There has been adverse State action within the Fourteenth Amendment as heretofore interpreted by this court. . . .

In every material sense applicable to the practical enforcement of the Fourteenth Amendment, railroad corporations, keepers of inns, and managers of places of public amusement are agents and instrumentalities of the State, because they are charged with duties to the public, and are amenable, in respect of their duties and functions, to governmental regulation. It seems to me that, within the principle settled in *Ex parte Virginia*, 100 U.S. 313 (1880) a denial, by these instrumentalities of the State, to the citizen, because of his race, of that equality of civil rights secured to him by law, is a denial by the State, within the meaning of the Fourteenth Amendment. If it be not, then that race is left, in respect of the civil rights in question, practically at the mercy of corporations and individuals wielding power under the States.

But the court says that Congress did not, in the act of 1866, assume, under the authority given by the Thirteenth Amendment, to adjust what may be called the social rights of men and races in the community. I agree that government has nothing to do with social, as distinguished from technically legal, rights of individuals. No government ever has brought, or ever can bring, its people into social intercourse against their wishes. Whether one person will permit or maintain social relations with another is a matter with which government has no concern. I agree that if one citizen chooses not to hold social intercourse with another, he is not and cannot be made amenable to the law for his conduct in that regard; for even upon grounds of race, no legal right of a citizen is violated by the refusal of others to maintain merely social relations with him. What I affirm is that no State, nor the officers of any State, nor any corporation or individual wielding power under State authority for the public benefit or the public convenience, can, consistently either with the freedom established by the fundamental law, or with that equality of civil rights which now belongs to every citizen, discriminate against freemen or citizens, in those rights, because of their race, or because they once labored under the disabilities of slavery imposed upon them as a race. The rights which Congress, by the act of 1875, endeavored to secure and protect are legal, not social rights. The right, for instance, of a colored citizen to use the accommodations of a public highway upon the same terms as are permitted to white citizens, is no more a social right than his right, under the law, to use the public streets of a city or a town, or a turnpike road, or a public market, or a post-office, or his right to sit in a public building with others, of whatever race, for the purpose of hearing the political questions of the day discussed. . . .

The court, in its opinion, reserves the question whether Congress, in the exercise of its power to regulate commerce among the several States, might or might not pass a law regulating rights in public conveyances passing from one State to another. I beg to suggest that that precise question was substantially presented here in the only one of these cases relating to railroads—*Robinson and Wife v. Memphis & Charleston Railroad Company.* In that case it appears that Mrs. Robinson, a citizen of Mississippi, purchased a railroad ticket entitling her to be carried from Grand Junction, Tennessee, to Lynchburg, Virginia. Might not the act of 1875 be maintained in that case, as applicable at least to commerce between the States, notwithstanding it does not, upon its face, profess to have been passed in pursuance of the power given to Congress to regulate commerce? Has it ever been held that the judiciary should overturn a statute because the legislative department did not accurately recite therein the particular provision of the Constitution authorizing its enactment? . . .

My brethren say, that when a man has emerged from slavery, and by the aid of beneficient legislation has shaken off the inseparable concomitants of that state, there must be some stage in the progress of his elevation when he takes the rank of a mere citizen, and ceases to be the special favorite of the laws, and when his rights as a citizen, or a man, are to be protected in the ordinary modes by which other men's rights are protected. It is, I submit, scarcely just to say that the colored race has been the special favorite of the laws. The statute of 1875, now adjudged to be unconstitutional, is for the benefit of citizens of every race and color. What the nation, through Congress, has sought to accomplish in reference to that race is—what had already been done in every State in the Union for the white race—to secure and protect rights belonging to them as freemen and citizens; nothing more. It was not deemed enough "to help the feeble up, but to support him after." The one underlying purpose of congressional legislation has been to enable the black race to take the rank of mere citizens. The difficulty has been to compel a recognition of the legal right of the black race to take the rank of citizens, and to secure the enjoyment of privileges belonging, under the law, to them as a component part of the people for whose welfare and happiness government is ordained. . . . Today it is the colored race which is denied, by corporations and individuals wielding public authority, rights fundamental in their freedom and citizenship. At some future time, it may be that some other race will fall under the ban of race discrimination. If the constitutional amendments be enforced, according to the intent with which, as I conceive, they were adopted, there cannot be, in this republic, any class of human beings in practical subjection to another class, with power in the latter to dole out to the former just such privileges as they may choose to grant. The supreme law of the land has decreed that no authority shall be exercised in this country upon the basis of discrimination, in respect of civil rights, against freemen and citizens because of their race, color, or previous condition of servitude. To that decree—for the due enforcement of which, by appropriate legislation, Congress has been invested with express power—every one must bow, whatever may have been, or whatever now are, his individual views as to the wisdom or policy, either of the recent changes in the fundamental law, or of the legislation which has been enacted to give them effect. . . .

NOTES

1. The decision in *The Civil Rights Cases* has been foundational for subsequent interpretation of the Thirteenth and Fourteenth Amendments. But was it correct? Does the Thirteenth Amendment prohibit not only "slavery" but the "badges and incidents" of subordination, including private discrimination? Even if Section 1 does not prohibit private discrimination, can Congress legislate more broadly pursuant to its power under Section 2 to "enforce" the command that slavery no longer "exist"? Would that still be "enforc[ing" Section 1? If one does accept a broad interpretation of either Section 1 or Section 2, would that mean that Congress could adopt and enforce a code of social relations throughout the United States? This is what the majority thought was untenable—more radical than the framers of the amendment envisaged. Was it? Do the Thirteenth and Fourteenth Amendments transfer authority over civil rights from states to the national government?

A century later the Supreme Court adopted a broader view of the Thirteenth Amendment enforcement clause powers of Congress, purporting to find that view supported by *The Civil Rights Cases*. In *Jones v. Alfred H. Mayer Co.*, 392 U.S. 409 (1968), the Court construed the Civil Rights Act of 1866 (re-enacted in 1870, two years after ratification of the Fourteenth Amendment) to reach purely private racial discrimination in housing and sustained its constitutionality as an exercise of Congress's enforcement powers under the Thirteenth Amendment. Subsequent cases have also held that parts of the Civil Rights Act of 1866 reach private commercial conduct of a discriminatory nature, but nonetheless fall within Congress's enforcement power under Section 2 of the Thirteenth Amendment. E.g., *Patterson v. McLean Credit Union*, 491 U.S. 164 (1989) (racial discrimination in making and enforcing contracts); *Runyon v. McCrary*, 427 U.S. 160 (1976) (racial discrimination in private schools).

2. Was the Court's decision that the Fourteenth Amendment is limited to "state action" correct? How else would one read the "No State shall" language of the amendment? Again, even if one thinks Section 1 invalidates only actions and laws of the state, is Congress's enforcement power under Section 5 broader?

3. What do you make of Justice Harlan's dissenting argument that railroads, innkeepers, and operators of public amusements are state actors—by virtue either of performing some government function or of being licensed by government (or granted a corporate charter) to perform regulated activities? Is there "state action" in every regulated business?

The Court has often had to decide where the line is between state and private action. Consider the following cases. Is there state action if a private entity serves a "public function," as with a company town? *Marsh v. Alabama*, 326 U.S. 501 (1946) (finding state action in a company town's restrictions of free speech). What if a political party's primary performs a quasi-state function in selecting candidates for a general election to public office? The "white primary" cases found such to be state action for Fifteenth Amendment purposes. *Terry v. Adams*, 345 U.S. 461 (1953); *Smith v. Allwright*, 321 U.S. 649 (1944). What about a state-employed and state-funded public defender, who provides legal representation to indigent clients? *Polk County v. Dodson*, 454 U.S. 312 (1981), held that public defenders are *not* state actors. Is state action present in judicial enforcement of a private agreement, in particular a racially restrictive covenant? *Shelley v. Kraemer*, 334 U.S. 1 (1948) (yes). In the award of damages for torts of defamation or intentional infliction of emotional distress? *New York Times Co. v. Sullivan*, 376 U.S. 254 (1964) (yes); *Hustler Magazine v. Falwell*, 485 U.S. 46 (1988) (yes). In permitting race-based peremptory strikes in jury selection? *Edmonson v. Leesville Concrete Co.*, 500 U.S. 614 (1991) (yes). In permitting nursing homes to discharge or transfer Medicaid patients? *Blum v. Yaretsky*, 457 U.S. 991 (1982) (no). Do the operations of a private restaurant, located within an off-street municipal automobile parking facility, constitute state action? *Burton v. Wilmington Parking Authority*, 365 U.S. 715 (1961) (yes). Do the operations of a publicly regulated utility company constitute state action, even if it is given a monopoly by the state? *Jackson v. Metro. Edison Co.*, 419 U.S. 345 (1974) (no). Is there a principle running through these decisions?

4.   Why not read the Equal Protection Clause as requiring states to *protect*, on an equal basis, all persons from private violence or similar wrongful acts by others? This reading finds support in the historical context, where there was a pervasive failure by Southern states to protect the newly freed slaves from violence by private actors. If the Equal Protection Clause does impose upon the states a duty of protection, how far would that duty extend? Would it forbid states from knowingly (or recklessly?) looking the other way when harm was being done? Nevertheless, the Court has emphasized "equal" more than "protection," see p. 1308, and that emphasis has meant the Equal Protection Clause has not been read to impose duties on the state. There have been challenges to state inaction under the Due Process Clause, though they have generally not succeeded. *E.g.*, *Town of Castle Rock v. Gonzales,* 545 U.S. 748 (2005).

United States v. Morrison
529 U.S. 598 (2000)

■ CHIEF JUSTICE REHNQUIST delivered the opinion of the Court. . . .

In these cases we consider the constitutionality of 42 U.S.C. § 13981, which provides a federal civil remedy for the victims of gender-motivated violence. The United States Court of Appeals for the Fourth Circuit, sitting en banc, struck down § 13981 because it concluded that Congress lacked constitutional authority to enact the section's civil remedy. Believing that these cases are controlled by our decisions in *United States v. Lopez,* 514 U.S. 549 (1995), *United States v. Harris,* 106 U.S. 629 (1883), and the *In re Civil Rights Cases,* 109 U.S. 3 (1883), we affirm.

Petitioner Christy Brzonkala enrolled at Virginia Polytechnic Institute (Virginia Tech) in the fall of 1994. In September of that year, Brzonkala met respondents Antonio Morrison and James Crawford, who were both students at Virginia Tech and members of its varsity football team. Brzonkala alleges that, within 30 minutes of meeting Morrison and Crawford, they assaulted and repeatedly raped her. . . . Shortly after the rape Brzonkala stopped attending classes and withdrew from the university. . . . *[In a university administrative hearing, Morrison was given a two-semester suspension. This was eventually set aside on appeal within the university system.—Editors]*

In December 1995, Brzonkala sued Morrison, Crawford, and Virginia Tech. . . . Her complaint alleged that Morrison's and Crawford's attack violated § 13981 and that Virginia Tech's handling of her complaint violated Title IX of the Education

Amendments of 1972. Morrison and Crawford moved to dismiss this complaint on the grounds that it failed to state a claim and that § 13981's civil remedy is unconstitutional. The United States ... intervened to defend [the Act]'s constitutionality. ...

Section 13981 was part of the Violence Against Women Act of 1994. It states that "[a]ll persons within the United States shall have the right to be free from crimes of violence motivated by gender." To enforce that right, [it] declares:

> A person (including a person who acts under color of any statute, ordinance, regulation, custom, or usage of any State) who commits a crime of violence motivated by gender and thus deprives another of the right declared in subsection (b) of this section shall be liable to the party injured, in an action for the recovery of compensatory and punitive damages, injunctive and declaratory relief, and such other relief as a court may deem appropriate.

... Every law enacted by Congress must be based on one or more of its powers enumerated in the Constitution. "The powers of the legislature are defined and limited; and that those limits may not be mistaken, or forgotten, the constitution is written." *Marbury v. Madison*, 5 U.S. (1 Cranch) 137, 176 (1803) (Marshall, C. J.). Congress explicitly identified the sources of federal authority on which it relied in enacting § 13981. It said that a "Federal civil rights cause of action" is established "[p]ursuant to the affirmative power of Congress ... under section 5 of the Fourteenth Amendment to the Constitution, as well as under section 8 of Article I of the Constitution." ... *[The Court first held that the provision could not be supported as an exercise of Congress's power under the Commerce Clause.—Editors]*

The principles governing an analysis of congressional legislation under § 5 [of the Fourteenth Amendment] are well settled. Section 5 states that Congress may " 'enforce' by 'appropriate legislation' the constitutional guarantee that no State shall deprive any person of 'life, liberty, or property, without due process of law,' nor deny any person 'equal protection of the laws.' " *City of Boerne v. Flores*, 521 U.S. 507, 517 (1997). Section 5 is "a positive grant of legislative power," that includes authority to "prohibit conduct which is not itself unconstitutional and [to] intrud[e] into 'legislative spheres of autonomy previously reserved to the States.' " However, "[a]s broad as the congressional enforcement power is, it is not unlimited."

Petitioners' § 5 argument is founded on an assertion that there is pervasive bias in various state justice systems against victims of gender-motivated violence. This assertion is supported by a voluminous congressional record. Specifically, Congress received evidence that many participants in state justice systems are perpetuating an array of erroneous stereotypes and assumptions. Petitioners contend that this bias denies victims of gender-motivated violence the equal protection of the laws and that Congress therefore acted appropriately in enacting a private civil remedy against the perpetrators of gender-motivated violence to both remedy the States' bias and deter future instances of discrimination in the state courts.

As our cases have established, state-sponsored gender discrimination violates equal protection unless it "serves important governmental objectives and ... the discriminatory means employed are substantially related to the achievement of those objectives." However, the language and purpose of the Fourteenth Amendment place certain limitations on the manner in which Congress may attack discriminatory conduct. These limitations are necessary to prevent the Fourteenth Amendment from obliterating the Framers' carefully crafted balance of power between the States and the National Government. Foremost among these limitations is the time-honored principle that the Fourteenth Amendment, by its very terms, prohibits only state action. "[T]he principle has become firmly embedded in our constitutional law that the action inhibited by the first section of the Fourteenth Amendment is only such action as may fairly be said to be that of the States. That Amendment erects no shield against merely private conduct, however discriminatory or wrongful." *Shelley v. Kraemer*, 334 U.S. 1, 13, and n. 12 (1948).

Shortly after the Fourteenth Amendment was adopted, we decided two cases interpreting the Amendment's provisions, *United States v. Harris*, 106 U.S. 629 (1883), and the *Civil Rights Cases*, 109 U.S. 3 (1883). In *Harris*, the Court considered a challenge to Section 2 of the Civil Rights Act of 1871. That section sought to punish "private persons" for "conspiring to deprive any one of the equal protection of the laws enacted by the State." We concluded that this law exceeded Congress' Section 5 power because the law was "directed exclusively against the action of private persons, without reference to the laws of the State, or their administration by her officers." . . .

We reached a similar conclusion in the *Civil Rights Cases*. In those consolidated cases, we held that the public accommodation provisions of the Civil Rights Act of 1875, which applied to purely private conduct, were beyond the scope of the Section 5 enforcement power. 109 U.S., at 11 ("Individual invasion of individual rights is not the subject-matter of the [Fourteenth] [A]mendment"). See also, *e.g., Romer v. Evans*, 517 U.S. 620, 628 (1996) ("[I]t was settled early that the Fourteenth Amendment did not give Congress a general power to prohibit discrimination in public accommodations").

The force of the doctrine of *stare decisis* behind these decisions stems not only from the length of time they have been on the books, but also from the insight attributable to the Members of the Court at that time. Every Member had been appointed by President Lincoln, Grant, Hayes, Garfield, or Arthur—and each of their judicial appointees obviously had intimate knowledge and familiarity with the events surrounding the adoption of the Fourteenth Amendment. . . .

Petitioners . . . argue that, unlike the situation in the *Civil Rights Cases*, here there has been gender-based disparate treatment by state authorities, whereas in those cases there was no indication of such state action. There is abundant evidence, however, to show that the Congresses that enacted the Civil Rights Acts of 1871 and 1875 had a purpose similar to that of Congress in enacting § 13981: There were state laws on the books bespeaking equality of treatment, but in the administration of these laws there was discrimination against newly freed slaves. . . .

But even if that distinction were valid, we do not believe it would save § 13981's civil remedy. For the remedy is simply not "corrective in its character, adapted to counteract and redress the operation of such prohibited [s]tate laws or proceedings of [s]tate officers." *Civil Right Cases*, at 18. Or, as we have phrased it in more recent cases, prophylactic legislation under § 5 must have a "congruence and proportionality between the injury to be prevented or remedied and the means adopted to that end." Section 13981 is not aimed at proscribing discrimination by officials which the Fourteenth Amendment might not itself proscribe; it is directed not at any State or state actor, but at individuals who have committed criminal acts motivated by gender bias.

In the present cases, for example, § 13981 visits no consequence whatever on any Virginia public official involved in investigating or prosecuting Brzonkala's assault. The section is, therefore, unlike any of the § 5 remedies that we have previously upheld. For example, in *Katzenbach v. Morgan*, 384 U.S. 641 (1966), Congress prohibited New York from imposing literacy tests as a prerequisite for voting because it found that such a requirement disenfranchised thousands of Puerto Rican immigrants who had been educated in the Spanish language of their home territory. That law, which we upheld, was directed at New York officials who administered the State's election law and prohibited them from using a provision of that law. In *South Carolina v. Katzenbach*, 383 U.S. 301 (1966), Congress imposed voting rights requirements on States that, Congress found, had a history of discriminating against blacks in voting. The remedy was also directed at state officials in those States. Similarly, in *Ex parte Virginia*, 100 U.S. 339 (1879), Congress criminally punished state officials who intentionally discriminated in jury selection; again, the remedy was directed to the culpable state official.

Section 13981 is also different from these previously upheld remedies in that it applies uniformly throughout the Nation. Congress' findings indicate that the problem of discrimination against the victims of gender-motivated crimes does not exist in all States, or even most States. By contrast, the § 5 remedy upheld in *Katzenbach v. Morgan* was directed only to the State where the evil found by Congress existed, and in *South Carolina v. Katzenbach* the remedy was directed only to those States in which Congress found that there had been discrimination.

For these reasons, we conclude that Congress' power under § 5 does not extend to the enactment of § 13981.

Petitioner Brzonkala's complaint alleges that she was the victim of a brutal assault. But Congress' effort in § 13981 to provide a federal civil remedy can be sustained neither under the Commerce Clause nor under § 5 of the Fourteenth Amendment. If the allegations here are true, no civilized system of justice could fail to provide her a remedy for the conduct of respondent Morrison. But under our federal system that remedy must be provided by the Commonwealth of Virginia, and not by the United States.

■ JUSTICE SOUTER, with whom JUSTICE STEVENS, JUSTICE GINSBURG, and JUSTICE BREYER join, dissenting.

    . . . Given my conclusion [that the provision is constitutional under the Commerce Clause], I need not consider Congress' authority under Section 5 of the Fourteenth Amendment. Nonetheless, I doubt the Court's reasoning rejecting that source of authority. The Court points out that in *United States v. Harris* and the *Civil Rights Cases*, the Court held that § 5 does not authorize Congress to use the Fourteenth Amendment as a source of power to remedy the conduct of *private persons*. That is certainly so. The Federal Government's argument, however, is that Congress used § 5 to remedy the actions of *state actors*, namely, those States which, through discriminatory design or the discriminatory conduct of their officials, failed to provide adequate (or any) state remedies for women injured by gender-motivated violence—a failure that the States, and Congress, documented in depth.

Neither *Harris* nor the *Civil Rights Cases* considered this kind of claim. The Court in *Harris* specifically said that it treated the federal laws in question as "directed *exclusively* against the action of private persons, without reference to the laws of the State or their administration by her officers" (emphasis added); see also *Civil Rights Cases* at 14 (observing that the statute did "not profess to be corrective of any constitutional wrong committed by the States" and that it established "rules for the conduct of individuals in society towards each other, . . . without referring in any manner to any supposed action of the State or its authorities").

The Court responds directly to the relevant "state actor" claim by finding that the present law lacks "congruence and proportionality" to the state discrimination that it purports to remedy. That is because the law, unlike federal laws prohibiting literacy tests for voting, imposing voting rights requirements, or punishing state officials who intentionally discriminated in jury selection is not "directed . . . at any State or state actor."

But why can Congress not provide a remedy against private actors? Those private actors, of course, did not themselves violate the Constitution. But this Court has held that Congress at least sometimes can enact remedial "[l]egislation . . . [that] prohibits conduct which is not itself unconstitutional." *Flores*, at 518; see also *Katzenbach v. Morgan*, at 651; *South Carolina v. Katzenbach*, at 308. The statutory remedy does not in any sense purport to "determine what constitutes a constitutional violation." . . . It restricts private actors only by imposing liability for private conduct that is, in the main, already forbidden by state law. Why is the remedy "disproportionate"? And given the relation between remedy and violation—the creation of a federal remedy to substitute for constitutionally inadequate state remedies—where is the lack of "congruence"?

The majority adds that Congress found that the problem of inadequacy of state remedies "does not exist in all States, or even most States." But Congress had before it the task force reports of at least 21 States documenting constitutional violations. And it made its own findings about pervasive gender-based stereotypes hampering many state legal systems, sometimes unconstitutionally so. The record nowhere reveals a congressional finding that the problem "does not exist" elsewhere. Why can Congress not take the evidence before it as evidence of a national problem? . . .

Despite my doubts about the majority's § 5 reasoning, I need not, and do not, answer the § 5 question, which I would leave for more thorough analysis if necessary on another occasion. . . .

■ [The concurring opinion of JUSTICE THOMAS and dissenting opinion of JUSTICE BREYER are omitted.]

NOTES

1.   Note the majority's (wooden?) reliance on the authority of *The Civil Rights Cases* and the dissent's (strained?) attempt to distinguish that precedent. Is the real question whether Congress, pursuant to Section 5, may judge for itself that state laws do not adequately protect women against private violence and directly provide that protection as a matter of federal law? Is that question in *Morrison* different from the one presented in *The Civil Rights Cases*? Should the Court have reconsidered *The Civil Rights Cases*? Or should more than one hundred years of accepting that precedent foreclose such inquiry?

2.   The dissent in *Morrison* argued that the Violence Against Women Act's regulation of private conduct could be a way of "enforcing" the Constitution as a *remedy*. The dissent's discussion of whether such a "remedy" was a true remedy—in other words, whether it was proportional to curing an actual violation of the Constitution—referenced the Court's decision three years earlier in *City of Boerne v. Flores*, the next principal case.

The Court had previously addressed the scope of Congress's Section 5 enforcement power. Most notably, in *Katzenbach v. Morgan*, 384 U.S. 641 (1966), the Court upheld Section 4(e) of the Voting Rights Act of 1965 as a valid exercise of Congress's Section 5 enforcement power. Section 4(e) prohibited states from denying the right to vote to anyone who had successfully completed sixth grade in an accredited school in Puerto Rico because of inability to read or write English. Several years earlier the Court had unanimously held that a state requirement that voters be able to read and write English did not violate the Fourteenth Amendment. Nevertheless, *Katzenbach* upheld Section 4(e) as a valid law to "enforce" the Fourteenth Amendment's prohibitions. The Court rejected the argument "that an exercise of congressional power under" Section 5 "can only be sustained if the judicial branch determines that the state law is prohibited by the provisions of the Amendment that Congress sought to enforce," since that would give Congress only an "insignificant role." Analogizing to the Necessary and Proper Clause and *McCulloch v. Maryland* (see p. 487), the Court said the question was whether Section 4(e) was "plainly adapted" to enforce the Equal Protection Clause. The Court found that it was, because securing the right to vote for the Puerto Rican community in New York would enhance that group's political power, thereby helping it achieve "nondiscriminatory treatment in public services" and "perfect equality of civil rights and equal protection of the laws." It was enough that the Court could "perceive a basis upon which Congress might predicate a judgment" that the challenged provision either helped secure equal protection or remedied invidious discrimination.

That sweeping view of the enforcement power was tested by the Voting Rights Act Amendments of 1970. That statute abolished literacy tests for voting nationwide and provided the right to vote in federal and state elections for everyone over age 18. In *Oregon v. Mitchell*, 400 U.S. 112 (1970), the Court upheld the prohibition on literacy tests but divided over the eighteen-year-old vote requirement. Four justices would have upheld the provision under *Katzenbach*. Four justices would have struck it down as beyond Congress's powers under the Fourteenth Amendment. The decisive vote was Justice Black's. He considered the voting-age provision valid as applied to federal elections—as an exercise of Congress's Article I power to displace state law concerning the time, place, or manner of elections for federal office—but invalid as applied to elections for state office. Even under the reasoning of *Katzenbach*, he did not see the voting-age provision as enforcing the Fourteenth Amendment. (Shortly after *Mitchell* the Twenty-sixth Amendment was proposed and ratified, ensuring that no state government could abridge the right to vote on account of age for persons "eighteen years of age or older.")

It was against this legal background—the sweeping view of the Section 5 power embraced in *Katzenbach* and the limitations suggested by *Mitchell*—that the Court took up the question of Congress's power to enact the Religious Freedom Restoration Act.

City of Boerne v. Flores
521 U.S. 507 (1997)

■ JUSTICE KENNEDY delivered the opinion of the Court.

A decision by local zoning authorities to deny a church a building permit was challenged under the Religious Freedom Restoration Act of 1993. The case calls into question the authority of Congress to enact RFRA. We conclude the statute exceeds Congress' power.

I

Situated on a hill in the city of Boerne, Texas, some 28 miles northwest of San Antonio, is St. Peter Catholic Church. Built in 1923, the church's structure replicates the mission style of the region's earlier history. The church seats about 230 worshippers, a number too small for its growing parish. Some 40 to 60 parishioners cannot be accommodated at some Sunday masses. In order to meet the needs of the congregation the Archbishop of San Antonio gave permission to the parish to plan alterations to enlarge the building.

A few months later, the Boerne City Council passed an ordinance authorizing the city's Historic Landmark Commission to prepare a preservation plan with proposed historic landmarks and districts. Under the ordinance, the commission must preapprove construction affecting historic landmarks or buildings in a historic district.

Soon afterwards, the Archbishop applied for a building permit so construction to enlarge the church could proceed. City authorities, relying on the ordinance and the designation of a historic district (which, they argued, included the church), denied the application. The Archbishop brought this suit challenging the permit denial. . . . The Archbishop relied upon RFRA as one basis for relief from the refusal to issue the permit. The District Court concluded that by enacting RFRA Congress exceeded the scope of its enforcement power under § 5 of the Fourteenth Amendment. [The Fifth Circuit reversed.] . . .

II

Congress enacted RFRA in direct response to the Court's decision in *Employment Div., Dept. of Human Resources of Oregon v. Smith*, 494 U.S. 872 (1990). There we considered a Free Exercise Clause claim brought by members of the Native American Church who were denied unemployment benefits when they lost their jobs because they had used peyote. Their practice was to ingest peyote for sacramental purposes, and they challenged an Oregon statute of general applicability which made use of the drug criminal. In evaluating the claim, we declined to apply the balancing test set forth in *Sherbert v. Verner*, 374 U.S. 398 (1963), under which we would have asked whether Oregon's prohibition substantially burdened a religious practice and, if it did, whether the burden was justified by a compelling government interest. . . .

The application of the *Sherbert* test, the *Smith* decision explained, would have produced an anomaly in the law, a constitutional right to ignore neutral laws of general applicability. . . .

Four Members of the Court disagreed. They argued the law placed a substantial burden on the Native American Church members so that it could be upheld only if the law served a compelling state interest and was narrowly tailored to achieve that end. . . .

These points of constitutional interpretation were debated by Members of Congress in hearings and floor debates. Many criticized the Court's reasoning, and this disagreement resulted in the passage of RFRA. Congress announced:

(1)   [T]he framers of the Constitution, recognizing free exercise of religion as an unalienable right, secured its protection in the First Amendment to the Constitution;

(2)   laws 'neutral' toward religion may burden religious exercise as surely as laws intended to interfere with religious exercise;

(3)   governments should not substantially burden religious exercise without compelling justification;

(4)   in *Smith*, the Supreme Court virtually eliminated the requirement that the government justify burdens on religious exercise imposed by laws neutral toward religion; and

(5)   the compelling interest test as set forth in prior Federal court rulings is a workable test for striking sensible balances between religious liberty and competing prior governmental interests.

42 U.S.C. § 2000bb(a).

The Act's stated purposes are:

(1)   to restore the compelling interest test as set forth in *Sherbert v. Verner*, and *Wisconsin v. Yoder*, and to guarantee its application in all cases where free exercise of religion is substantially burdened; and

(2)   to provide a claim or defense to persons whose religious exercise is substantially burdened by government. § 2000bb(b).

RFRA prohibits "[g]overnment" from "substantially burden[ing]" a person's exercise of religion even if the burden results from a rule of general applicability unless the government can demonstrate the burden "(1) is in furtherance of a compelling governmental interest; and (2) is the least restrictive means of furthering that compelling governmental interest." The Act's mandate applies to any "branch, department, agency, instrumentality, and official (or other person acting under color of law) of the United States," as well as to any "State, or . . . subdivision of a State." The Act's universal coverage is confirmed in § 2000bb–3(a), under which RFRA "applies to all Federal and State law, and the implementation of that law, whether statutory or otherwise, and whether adopted before or after [RFRA's enactment]." In accordance with RFRA's usage of the term, we shall use "state law" to include local and municipal ordinances.

III

A

. . . Congress relied on its Fourteenth Amendment enforcement power in enacting the most far-reaching and substantial of RFRA's provisions, those which impose its requirements on the States. . . . The parties disagree over whether RFRA is a proper exercise of Congress' § 5 power "to enforce" by "appropriate legislation" the [Free Exercise Clause, as incorporated against the states by the Fourteenth Amendment.]

In defense of the Act, respondent the Archbishop contends, with support from the United States, that RFRA is permissible enforcement legislation. Congress, it is said, is only protecting by legislation one of the liberties guaranteed by the

Fourteenth Amendment's Due Process Clause, the free exercise of religion, beyond what is necessary under *Smith*. It is said the congressional decision to dispense with proof of deliberate or overt discrimination and instead concentrate on a law's effects accords with the settled understanding that § 5 includes the power to enact legislation designed to prevent, as well as remedy, constitutional violations. It is further contended that Congress' § 5 power is not limited to remedial or preventive legislation.

All must acknowledge that § 5 is "a positive grant of legislative power" to Congress, *Katzenbach v. Morgan*, 384 U.S. 641, 651 (1966). In *Ex parte Virginia*, 100 U.S. 339, 345–346 (1879), we explained the scope of Congress' § 5 power in the following broad terms:

> Whatever legislation is appropriate, that is, adapted to carry out the objects the amendments have in view, whatever tends to enforce submission to the prohibitions they contain, and to secure to all persons the enjoyment of perfect equality of civil rights and the equal protection of the laws against State denial or invasion, if not prohibited, is brought within the domain of congressional power.

Legislation which deters or remedies constitutional violations can fall within the sweep of Congress' enforcement power even if in the process it prohibits conduct which is not itself unconstitutional and intrudes into "legislative spheres of autonomy previously reserved to the States." For example, the Court upheld a suspension of literacy tests and similar voting requirements under Congress' parallel power to enforce the provisions of the Fifteenth Amendment, as a measure to combat racial discrimination in voting, *South Carolina v. Katzenbach*, 383 U.S. 301, 308 (1966), despite the facial constitutionality of the tests [at the time]. We have also concluded that other measures protecting voting rights are within Congress' power to enforce the Fourteenth and Fifteenth Amendments, despite the burdens those measures placed on the States. *South Carolina v. Katzenbach* (upholding several provisions of the Voting Rights Act of 1965); *Katzenbach v. Morgan* (upholding ban on literacy tests that prohibited certain people schooled in Puerto Rico from voting); *Oregon v. Mitchell*, 400 U.S. 112 (1970) (upholding 5-year nationwide ban on literacy tests and similar voting requirements for registering to vote).

It is also true, however, that "[a]s broad as the congressional enforcement power is, it is not unlimited." In assessing the breadth of § 5's enforcement power, we begin with its text. Congress has been given the power "to enforce" the "provisions of this article." We agree with respondent, of course, that Congress can enact legislation under § 5 enforcing the constitutional right to the free exercise of religion. . . .

Congress' power under § 5, however, extends only to "enforc[ing]" the provisions of the Fourteenth Amendment. The Court has described this power as "remedial." The design of the Amendment and the text of § 5 are inconsistent with the suggestion that Congress has the power to decree the substance of the Fourteenth Amendment's restrictions on the States. Legislation which alters the meaning of the Free Exercise Clause cannot be said to be enforcing the Clause. Congress does not enforce a constitutional right by changing what the right is. It has been given the power "to enforce," not the power to determine what constitutes a constitutional violation. Were it not so, what Congress would be enforcing would no longer be, in any meaningful sense, the "provisions of [the Fourteenth Amendment]."

While the line between measures that remedy or prevent unconstitutional actions and measures that make a substantive change in the governing law is not easy to discern, and Congress must have wide latitude in determining where it lies, the distinction exists and must be observed. There must be a congruence and proportionality between the injury to be prevented or remedied and the means adopted to that end. Lacking such a connection, legislation may become substantive in operation and effect. History and our case law support drawing the distinction, one apparent from the text of the Amendment.

1

The Fourteenth Amendment's history confirms the remedial, rather than substantive, nature of the Enforcement Clause. The Joint Committee on Reconstruction of the 39th Congress began drafting what would become the Fourteenth Amendment in January 1866. The objections to the Committee's first draft of the Amendment, and the rejection of the draft, have a direct bearing on the central issue of defining Congress' enforcement power. In February, Republican Representative John Bingham of Ohio reported the following draft Amendment to the House of Representatives on behalf of the Joint Committee:

> The Congress shall have power to make all laws which shall be necessary and proper to secure to the citizens of each State all privileges and immunities of citizens in the several States, and to all persons in the several States equal protection in the rights of life, liberty, and property.

Cong. Globe, 39th Cong., 1st Sess., 1034 (1866).

The proposal encountered immediate opposition, which continued through three days of debate. Members of Congress from across the political spectrum criticized the Amendment, and the criticisms had a common theme: The proposed Amendment gave Congress too much legislative power at the expense of the existing constitutional structure. Democrats and conservative Republicans argued that the proposed Amendment would give Congress a power to intrude into traditional areas of state responsibility, a power inconsistent with the federal design central to the Constitution. . . .

As a result of these objections having been expressed from so many different quarters, the House voted to table the proposal until April. The Amendment in its early form was not again considered. Instead, the Joint Committee began drafting a new article of Amendment, which it reported to Congress on April 30, 1866.

Section 1 of the new draft Amendment imposed self-executing limits on the States. Section 5 prescribed that "[t]he Congress shall have power to enforce, by appropriate legislation, the provisions of this article." Under the revised Amendment, Congress' power was no longer plenary but remedial. Congress was granted the power to make the substantive constitutional prohibitions against the States effective. Representative Bingham said the new draft would give Congress "the power . . . to protect by national law the privileges and immunities of all the citizens of the Republic . . . whenever the same shall be abridged or denied by the unconstitutional acts of any State." Representative Stevens described the new draft Amendment as "allow[ing] Congress to correct the unjust legislation of the States." The revised Amendment proposal did not raise the concerns expressed earlier regarding broad congressional power to prescribe uniform national laws with respect to life, liberty, and property. . . .

The significance of the defeat of the Bingham proposal was apparent even then. During the debates over the Ku Klux Klan Act only a few years after the Amendment's ratification, Representative James Garfield argued there were limits on Congress' enforcement power, saying "unless we ignore both the history and the language of these clauses we cannot, by any reasonable interpretation, give to [§ 5] . . . the force and effect of the rejected [Bingham] clause." Scholars of successive generations have agreed with this assessment.

The design of the Fourteenth Amendment has proved significant also in maintaining the traditional separation of powers between Congress and the Judiciary. The first eight Amendments to the Constitution set forth self-executing prohibitions on governmental action, and this Court has had primary authority to interpret those prohibitions. The Bingham draft, some thought, departed from that tradition by vesting in Congress primary power to interpret and elaborate on the meaning of the new Amendment through legislation. . . . As enacted, the Fourteenth Amendment confers substantive rights against the States which, like the provisions of the Bill of Rights, are self-executing. The power to interpret the Constitution in a case or controversy remains in the Judiciary.

2

The remedial and preventive nature of Congress' enforcement power, and the limitation inherent in the power, were confirmed in our earliest cases on the Fourteenth Amendment. In the *Civil Rights Cases*, 109 U.S. 3 (1883), the Court invalidated sections of the Civil Rights Act of 1875 which prescribed criminal penalties for denying to any person "the full enjoyment of" public accommodations and conveyances, on the grounds that it exceeded Congress' power by seeking to regulate private conduct. The Enforcement Clause, the Court said, did not authorize Congress to pass "general legislation upon the rights of the citizen, but corrective legislation, that is, such as may be necessary and proper for counteracting such laws as the States may adopt or enforce, and which, by the amendment, they are prohibited from making or enforcing. . . ." The power to "legislate generally upon" life, liberty, and property, as opposed to the "power to provide modes of redress" against offensive state action, was "repugnant" to the Constitution. Although the specific holdings of these early cases might have been superseded or modified, their treatment of Congress' § 5 power as corrective or preventive, not definitional, has not been questioned.

Recent cases have continued to revolve around the question whether § 5 legislation can be considered remedial. . . .

3

Any suggestion that Congress has a substantive, non-remedial power under the Fourteenth Amendment is not supported by our case law. In *Oregon v. Mitchell*, a majority of the Court concluded Congress had exceeded its enforcement powers by enacting legislation lowering the minimum age of voters from 21 to 18 in state and local elections. The five Members of the Court who reached this conclusion explained that the legislation intruded into an area reserved by the Constitution to the States. . . .

There is language in our opinion in *Katzenbach v. Morgan* which could be interpreted as acknowledging a power in Congress to enact legislation that expands the rights contained in § 1 of the Fourteenth Amendment. This is not a necessary interpretation, however, or even the best one. In *Morgan*, the Court considered the constitutionality of § 4(e) of the Voting Rights Act of 1965 . . . [and] perceived a factual basis on which Congress could have concluded that New York's literacy requirement "constituted an invidious discrimination in violation of the Equal Protection Clause." . . . As Justice Stewart explained in *Oregon v. Mitchell*, interpreting *Morgan* to give Congress the power to interpret the Constitution "would require an enormous extension of that decision's rationale."

If Congress could define its own powers by altering the Fourteenth Amendment's meaning, no longer would the Constitution be "superior paramount law, unchangeable by ordinary means." It would be "on a level with ordinary legislative acts, and, like other acts, . . . alterable when the legislature shall please to alter it." *Marbury v. Madison*, 5 U.S. (1 Cranch) 137, 177 (1803). Under this approach, it is difficult to conceive of a principle that would limit congressional power. Shifting legislative majorities could change the Constitution and effectively circumvent the difficult and detailed amendment process contained in Article V. We now turn to consider whether RFRA can be considered enforcement legislation under § 5 of the Fourteenth Amendment.

B

Respondent contends that RFRA is a proper exercise of Congress' remedial or preventive power. The Act, it is said, is a reasonable means of protecting the free exercise of religion as defined by *Smith*. It prevents and remedies laws which are enacted with the unconstitutional object of targeting religious beliefs and practices. . . .

While preventive rules are sometimes appropriate remedial measures, there must be a congruence between the means used and the ends to be achieved. The appropriateness of remedial measures must be considered in light of the evil presented. . . .

A comparison between RFRA and the Voting Rights Act is instructive. In contrast to the record which confronted Congress and the Judiciary in the voting rights cases, RFRA's legislative record lacks examples of modern instances of generally applicable laws passed because of religious bigotry. . . . [T]he emphasis of the hearings was on laws of general applicability which place incidental burdens on religion. Much of the discussion centered upon anecdotal evidence of autopsies performed on Jewish individuals and Hmong immigrants in violation of their religious beliefs, and on zoning regulations and historic preservation laws (like the one at issue here), which, as an incident of their normal operation, have adverse effects on churches and synagogues. It is difficult to maintain that they are examples of legislation enacted or enforced due to animus or hostility to the burdened religious practices or that they indicate some widespread pattern of religious discrimination in this country. Congress' concern was with the incidental burdens imposed, not the object or purpose of the legislation. . . .

Regardless of the state of the legislative record, RFRA cannot be considered remedial, preventive legislation, if those terms are to have any meaning. RFRA is so out of proportion to a supposed remedial or preventive object that it cannot be understood as responsive to, or designed to prevent, unconstitutional behavior. It appears, instead, to attempt a substantive change in constitutional protections. Preventive measures prohibiting certain types of laws may be appropriate when there is reason to believe that many of the laws affected by the congressional enactment have a significant likelihood of being unconstitutional. Remedial legislation under § 5 "should be adapted to the mischief and wrong which the [Fourteenth] amendment was intended to provide against." *Civil Rights Cases*, at 13.

RFRA is not so confined. Sweeping coverage ensures its intrusion at every level of government, displacing laws and prohibiting official actions of almost every description and regardless of subject matter. RFRA's restrictions apply to every agency and official of the Federal, State, and local Governments. RFRA applies to all federal and state law, statutory or otherwise, whether adopted before or after its enactment. . . . Any law is subject to challenge at any time by any individual who alleges a substantial burden on his or her free exercise of religion. . . .

The stringent test RFRA demands of state laws reflects a lack of proportionality or congruence between the means adopted and the legitimate end to be achieved. If an objector can show a substantial burden on his free exercise, the State must demonstrate a compelling governmental interest and show that the law is the least restrictive means of furthering its interest. . . . Laws valid under *Smith* would fall under RFRA without regard to whether they had the object of stifling or punishing free exercise. We make these observations not to reargue the position of the majority in *Smith* but to illustrate the substantive alteration of its holding attempted by RFRA. . . .

When Congress acts within its sphere of power and responsibilities, it has not just the right but the duty to make its own informed judgment on the meaning and force of the Constitution. This has been clear from the early days of the Republic. In 1789, when a Member of the House of Representatives objected to a debate on the constitutionality of legislation based on the theory that "it would be officious" to consider the constitutionality of a measure that did not affect the House, James Madison explained that "it is incontrovertibly of as much importance to this branch of the Government as to any other, that the constitution should be preserved entire. It is our duty." 1 Annals of Congress 500 (1789). Were it otherwise, we would not afford Congress the presumption of validity its enactments now enjoy.

Our national experience teaches that the Constitution is preserved best when each part of the Government respects both the Constitution and the proper actions and determinations of the other branches. When the Court has interpreted the Constitution, it has acted within the province of the Judicial Branch, which embraces the duty to say what the law is. *Marbury v. Madison.* When the political branches of the Government act against the background of a judicial interpretation of the Constitution already issued, it must be understood that in later cases and controversies the Court will treat its precedents with the respect due them under settled principles, including *stare decisis,* and contrary expectations must be disappointed. RFRA was designed to control cases and controversies, such as the one before us; but as the provisions of the federal statute here invoked are beyond congressional authority, it is this Court's precedent, not RFRA, which must control. . . .

■ JUSTICE O'CONNOR, with whom JUSTICE BREYER joins . . . , dissenting.

I dissent from the Court's disposition of this case. I agree with the Court that the issue before us is whether the Religious Freedom Restoration Act of 1993 (RFRA) is a proper exercise of Congress' power to enforce § 5 of the Fourteenth Amendment.

But as a yardstick for measuring the constitutionality of RFRA, the Court uses its holding in *Smith*, the decision that prompted Congress to enact RFRA as a means of more rigorously enforcing the Free Exercise Clause. I remain of the view that *Smith* was wrongly decided, and I would use this case to reexamine the Court's holding there. Therefore, I would direct the parties to brief the question whether *Smith* represents the correct understanding of the Free Exercise Clause and set the case for reargument. If the Court were to correct the misinterpretation of the Free Exercise Clause set forth in *Smith*, it would simultaneously put our First Amendment jurisprudence back on course and allay the legitimate concerns of a majority in Congress who believed that *Smith* improperly restricted religious liberty. We would then be in a position to review RFRA in light of a proper interpretation of the Free Exercise Clause.

■ [The concurring opinions of JUSTICES STEVENS and SCALIA, and the dissenting opinion of JUSTICE SOUTER, are omitted.]

NOTES

1.   What precisely was Congress doing when it enacted the Religious Freedom Restoration Act? Was it interpreting the Free Exercise Clause and rejecting the Court's interpretation in *Employment Division v. Smith*, p. 1100? If so, is there anything wrong with that? Is Congress always bound by the Supreme Court's interpretations of the Constitution? Or as a coordinate branch of the national government may it independently interpret the Constitution? Is there some whiff of irritation in the Court's opinion in *City of Boerne*—some "how dare you question our interpretation of the Constitution"? If so, is that attitude appropriate? Necessary to vindicate the Court's authority? Was the Court right that RFRA's enactment was inconsistent with the Court's interpretive authority under *Marbury*?

2.   Could RFRA have been sustained on the ground that, fully accepting the Court's decision in *Smith*, it was "appropriate" prophylactic legislation to prevent violations of the Free Exercise Clause as interpreted by the Court? The Court in *City of Boerne* adopted as a test whether the legislation was "congruent and proportional" to the violation asserted, and concluded that RFRA was wildly incongruent and disproportionate to *Smith*'s understanding of Free Exercise and so could not be understood as remedial or prophylactic legislation. How does this standard for judging the "appropriateness" of Congress's judgment compare with *McCulloch*'s standards for judging what laws are "proper" exercises of Congress's judgment under the Necessary and Proper Clause?

3.   In a series of subsequent decisions, the Court has continued to hold that Congress's enforcement must be "congruent and proportional" with the Fourteenth Amendment *as construed by the Court*. But the Court's results are not easy to characterize. Compare *Kimel v. Florida Board of Regents*, 528 U.S. 62 (2000) (Section 5 does not justify Age Discrimination in Employment Act); *Board of Trustees of University of Alabama v. Garrett*, 531 U.S. 356 (2001) (Section 5 does not justify employment discrimination provisions of Americans with Disabilities Act); with *Nevada Department of Human Resources v. Hibbs*, 538 U.S. 721 (2003) (Section 5 does justify Family Medical Leave Act); *Tennessee v. Lane*, 541 U.S. 509 (2004) (Section 5 does justify Americans with Disabilities Act as applied to public access to courts).

[*Assignment 66*]

II. "EQUAL PROTECTION OF THE LAWS"

A. THE SEGREGATION CASES

Does the anti-discrimination guarantee of Section 1 of the Fourteenth Amendment prohibit racial discrimination by state governments? The modern answer is an unequivocal *yes*. Today, such a prohibition is understood to be at the very core of the meaning of the Equal Protection Clause. Does legally enforced racial separation—segregation—violate this principle? Again, the modern answer is an unequivocal *yes*.

Two of the earliest Supreme Court cases interpreting the Fourteenth Amendment—*Slaughter-House Cases* (1873) and *Strauder v. West Virginia* (1880)—vigorously advanced the view that the amendment forbids any discrimination by the states against black citizens. But soon afterwards the Court began, just as vigorously, to uphold segregation, discrimination, and Jim Crow.

The history of judicial interpretation of the Equal Protection Clause is not pretty. *Strauder* stands as an early, robust interpretation of the Fourteenth Amendment, to which the Court eventually returned in the landmark 1954 case of *Brown v. Board of Education*. But in between there is plenty of bad judicial history.

Do the cases that follow suggest to you that it is inevitable for judicial decisions to be a product of the times in which the justices live—and not only inevitable but desirable? Or do they suggest quite the opposite—that courts should not allow contemporary social values to affect their interpretation of the Constitution, that doing so leads to the possibility of serious error, and that it is difficult for the legal system to work its way out of such errors without enormous strain? Or do the cases teach entirely different lessons: lessons about the strength or weakness of looking to original intent? About the relationship between the intentions of drafters and the language that was ratified? This section begins with a seemingly minor statutory interpretation case from 1873, *Railroad Company v. Brown*, then proceeds with a series of decisions upholding legal segregation in various forms, often in the name of reflecting contemporary values—*Plessy v. Ferguson* (1896), *Cumming v. Board of Education* (1899), and *Berea College v. Kentucky* (1908). Another case from this period, *Giles v. Harris* (1903), concerns the right to vote, and it is discussed below in connection with the Fifteenth Amendment, at p. 1664.

Railroad Company v. Brown

84 U.S. 445 (1873)

In the year 1854, Congress authorized the Alexandria and Washington Railroad Company . . . to extend their road *into* the District of Columbia. . . .

In 1863, the company got a further grant of power, authorizing it to extend its road northward, so as to connect itself with the Baltimore and Ohio Railroad. This grant was, however, accompanied with a provision, "that no person shall be excluded from the cars on account of color." . . .

In this condition of things, one Catharine Brown, a colored woman, on the 8th of February, 1868, anterior to the adoption of the fourteenth and fifteenth amendments to the Constitution, bought a ticket to come from Alexandria to Washington. . . . No tickets were distinguished as for white persons or colored persons, nor for any particular sort or class of cars. All were exactly alike.

When the woman went to take her place in the cars there were standing there two cars, alike comfortable; the one, however, set apart for colored persons, and the other "for white ladies, and gentlemen accompanying them;" the regulation having been that in going down from Washington to Alexandria, the first should be occupied by the former, and the last by the latter; and that in coming back the use should be simply reversed. When about to get into one of the cars, a servant of the persons managing the road, stationed near the cars to direct passengers, told the woman not to get into the car into which she was about to enter, but to get into the one before it; that he had been instructed by persons in charge of the road not to permit colored persons to ride in the car in which she was getting, but to have them go in the other. The woman, however, persisted in going into the car appropriated for white ladies, and the man put her out with force, and as she alleged, some insult. She then got into the car into which she had been directed to get—the one assigned to colored people—was carried safely into Washington and got out there.

Hereupon she sued the *Washington, Alexandria, and Georgetown Railroad Company* in the Supreme Court of the District. . . .

The counsel of the company requested the court to instruct the jury: . . . That if by a standing regulation certain cars were appropriated and designated for the use of white persons, and certain others for the use of colored, and all the cars were equally safe, clean, and comfortable, and if this sort of regulation was one in force on the principal railroads of the country, and one which unless it has been adopted on this road, the travel on it would have been seriously injured and the receipts of the road decreased, and if the establishment of such a regulation itself increased the expenses of the road considerably—then, in case no insult nor greater force than was necessary had been used, and the plaintiff after taking a seat in the car appropriated for colored persons, was carried safely into Washington and got out there—that the plaintiff could not recover. The court refused to give any one of the instructions, and a verdict having been given in $1500 for the plaintiff and judgment entered on it, the company brought the case here, assigning as three causes of error the refusals to give the charges requested.

■ MR. JUSTICE DAVIS delivered the opinion of the court.

. . . The third and last assignment of error asserts the right of the company to make the regulation separating the colored from the white passengers.

If the defendant in error had the right to retain the seat she had first taken, it is conceded the verdict of the jury should not be disturbed. . . . This leads us to consider what Congress meant in directing that no person should be excluded from the cars of the company on account of color.

The plaintiff in error contends that it has literally obeyed the direction, because it has never excluded this class of persons from the cars, but on the contrary, has always provided accommodations for them.

This is an ingenious attempt to evade a compliance with the obvious meaning of the requirement. It is true the words taken literally might bear the interpretation put upon them by the plaintiff in error, but evidently Congress did not use them in any such limited sense. . . . It was the discrimination in the use of the cars on account of color, where slavery obtained, which was the subject of discussion at the time, and not the fact that the colored race could not ride in the cars at all. Congress, in the belief that this discrimination was unjust, acted. It told this company, in substance, that it could extend its road within the District as desired, but that this discrimination must cease, and the colored and white race, in the use of the cars, be placed on an equality. This condition it had the right to impose, and in the temper of Congress at the time, it is manifest the grant could not have been made without it. It was the privilege of the company to reject it, but to do this, it must reject the whole legislation with which it was connected. It cannot accept a part and repudiate the rest. Having, therefore, constructed its road as it was authorized to do, and in this way greatly added to the value of its property, it will be held to a faithful compliance with all the terms accompanying the grant by which it was enabled to secure this pecuniary advantage.

We turn next to *Plessy v. Ferguson*, which is representative of the Court's betrayal of the principles of the Equal Protection Clause as understood by its framers and reflected in the Court's earliest decisions interpreting the clause.

Plessy v. Ferguson
163 U.S. 537 (1896)

■ MR. JUSTICE BROWN, after stating the case, delivered the opinion of the court.

. . . The constitutionality of this act is attacked upon the ground that it conflicts both with the Thirteenth Amendment of the Constitution, abolishing slavery, and the Fourteenth Amendment, which prohibits certain restrictive legislation on the part of the States.

1.   That it does not conflict with the Thirteenth Amendment, which abolished slavery and involuntary servitude, except as a punishment for crime, is too clear for argument. Slavery implies involuntary servitude—a state of bondage; the ownership of mankind as a chattel, or at least the control of the labor and services of one man for the benefit of another, and the absence of a legal right to the disposal of his own person, property and services. . . .

A statute which implies merely a legal distinction between the white and colored races—a distinction which is founded in the color of the two races, and which must always exist so long as white men are distinguished from the other race by color— has no tendency to destroy the legal equality of the two races, or re-establish a state of involuntary servitude. Indeed, we do not understand that the Thirteenth Amendment is strenuously relied upon by the plaintiff in error in this connection.

2.   . . . The object of the [Fourteenth A]mendment was undoubtedly to enforce the absolute equality of the two races before the law, but in the nature of things it could not have been intended to abolish distinctions based upon color, or to enforce social, as distinguished from political equality, or a commingling of the two races upon terms unsatisfactory to either. Laws permitting, and even requiring, their separation in places where they are liable to be brought into contact do not necessarily imply the inferiority of either race to the other, and have been generally,

if not universally, recognized as within the competency of the state legislatures in the exercise of their police power. The most common instance of this is connected with the establishment of separate schools for white and colored children, which have been held to be a valid exercise of the legislative power even by courts of States where the political rights of the colored race have been longest and most earnestly enforced. . . .

Laws forbidding the intermarriage of the two races may be said in a technical sense to interfere with the freedom of contract, and yet have been universally recognized as within the police power of the State.

The distinction between laws interfering with the political equality of the negro and those requiring the separation of the two races in schools, theatres, and railway carriages has been frequently drawn by this court. Thus, in *Strauder v. West Virginia*, 100 U.S. 303 (1880), it was held that a law of West Virginia limiting to white male persons, 21 years of age and citizens of the State, the right to sit upon juries, was a discrimination which implied a legal inferiority in civil society, which lessened the security of the right of the colored race, and was a step towards reducing them to a condition of servility. . . .

While we think the enforced separation of the races, as applied to the internal commerce of the State, neither abridges the privileges or immunities of the colored man, deprives him of his property without due process of law, nor denies him the equal protection of the laws, within the meaning of the Fourteenth Amendment, we are not prepared to say that the conductor, in assigning passengers to the coaches according to their race, does not act at his peril *[Under the act, a conductor mistakenly assigning a passenger to a coach or compartment could be fined $25 or imprisoned up to twenty days—Editors]*, or that the provision of the second section of the act, that denies to the passenger compensation in damages for a refusal to receive him into the coach in which he properly belongs, is a valid exercise of the legislative power. . . . [Here] the only issue made is as to the unconstitutionality of the act, so far as it requires the railway to provide separate accommodations, and the conductor to assign passengers according to their race.

It is claimed by the plaintiff in error that, in any mixed community, the reputation of belonging to the dominant race, in this instance the white race, is *property*, in the same sense that a right of action, or of inheritance, is property. Conceding this to be so, for the purposes of this case, we are unable to see how this statute deprives him of, or in any way affects his right to, such property. If he be a white man, and assigned to a colored coach, he may have his action for damages against the company for being deprived of his so called property. Upon the other hand, if he be a colored man and be so assigned, he has been deprived of no property, since he is not lawfully entitled to the reputation of being a white man.

In this connection, it is also suggested by the learned counsel for the plaintiff in error that the same argument that will justify the state legislature in requiring railways to provide separate accommodations for the two races will also authorize them to require separate cars to be provided for people whose hair is of a certain color, or who are aliens, or who belong to certain nationalities, or to enact laws requiring colored people to walk upon one side of the street, and white people upon the other, or requiring white men's houses to be painted white, and colored men's black, or their vehicles or business signs to be of different colors, upon the theory that one side of the street is as good as the other, or that a house or vehicle of one color is as good as one of another color. The reply to all this is that every exercise of the police power must be reasonable, and extend only to such laws as are enacted in good faith for the promotion of the public good, and not for the annoyance or oppression of a particular class. Thus, in *Yick Wo v. Hopkins*, 118 U.S. 356 (1886), it was held by this court that a municipal ordinance of the city of San Francisco, to regulate the carrying on of public laundries . . . without regard to the competency of the persons applying or the propriety of the places selected for the carrying on of the business . . . [was] a covert attempt on the part of the municipality to make an arbitrary and unjust discrimination against the Chinese race. . . .

So far, then, as a conflict with the Fourteenth Amendment is concerned, the case reduces itself to the question whether the statute of Louisiana is a reasonable regulation, and with respect to this there must necessarily be a large discretion on the part of the legislature. In determining the question of reasonableness it is at liberty to act with reference to the established usages, customs and traditions of the people, and with a view to the promotion of their comfort, and the preservation of the public peace and good order. Gauged by this standard, we cannot say that a law which authorizes or even requires the separation of the two races in public conveyances is unreasonable, or more obnoxious to the Fourteenth Amendment than the acts of Congress requiring separate schools for colored children in the District of Columbia, the constitutionality of which does not seem to have been questioned, or the corresponding acts of state legislatures.

We consider the underlying fallacy of the plaintiff's argument to consist in the assumption that the enforced separation of the two races stamps the colored race with a badge of inferiority. If this be so, it is not by reason of anything found in the act, but solely because the colored race chooses to put that construction upon it. The argument necessarily assumes that if, as has been more than once the case, and is not unlikely to be so again, the colored race should become the dominant power in the state legislature, and should enact a law in precisely similar terms, it would thereby relegate the white race to an inferior position. We imagine that the white race, at least, would not acquiesce in this assumption. The argument also assumes that social prejudices may be overcome by legislation, and that equal rights cannot be secured to the negro except by an enforced commingling of the two races. We cannot accept this proposition. If the two races are to meet upon terms of social equality, it must be the result of natural affinities, a mutual appreciation of each other's merits, and a voluntary consent of individuals. . . . Legislation is powerless to eradicate racial instincts, or to abolish distinctions based upon physical differences, and the attempt to do so can only result in accentuating the difficulties of the present situation. If the civil and political rights of both races be equal, one cannot be inferior to the other civilly or politically. If one race be inferior to the other socially, the Constitution of the United States cannot put them upon the same plane.

It is true that the question of the proportion of colored blood necessary to constitute a colored person, as distinguished from a white person, is one upon which there is a difference of opinion in the different States. . . . But these are questions to be determined under the laws of each State and are not properly put in issue in this case. Under the allegations of his petition it may undoubtedly become a question of importance whether, under the laws of Louisiana, the petitioner belongs to the white or colored race.

■ Mr. Justice Harlan dissenting.

By the Louisiana statute, the validity of which is here involved, all railway companies (other than street railroad companies) carrying passengers in that State are required to have separate but equal accommodations for white and colored persons, "by providing two or more passenger coaches for each passenger train, *or* by dividing the passenger coaches by a *partition* so as to secure separate accommodations." . . . The managers of the railroad are not allowed to exercise any discretion in the premises, but are required to assign each passenger to some coach or compartment set apart for the exclusive use of his race. . . .

Only "nurses attending children of the other race" are excepted from the operation of the statute. . . .

Thus the State regulates the use of a public highway by citizens of the United States solely upon the basis of race.

However apparent the injustice of such legislation may be, we have only to consider whether it is consistent with the Constitution of the United States. . . .

In respect of civil rights, common to all citizens, the Constitution of the United States does not, I think, permit any public authority to know the race of those entitled to be protected in the enjoyment of such rights. Every true man has pride of race, and under appropriate circumstances, when the rights of others, his equals before the law, are not to be affected, it is his privilege to express such pride and to take such action based upon it as to him seems proper. But I deny that any legislative body or judicial tribunal may have regard to the race of citizens when the civil rights of those citizens are involved. . . .

It was said in argument that the statute of Louisiana does not discriminate against either race, but prescribes a rule applicable alike to white and colored citizens. But this argument does not meet the difficulty. Every one knows that the statute in question had its origin in the purpose, not so much to exclude white persons from railroad cars occupied by blacks, as to exclude colored people from coaches occupied by or assigned to white persons. . . . The thing to accomplish was, under the guise of giving equal accommodation for whites and blacks, to compel the latter to keep to themselves while traveling in railroad passenger coaches. No one would be so wanting in candor as to assert the contrary. The fundamental objection, therefore, to the statute, is that it interferes with the personal freedom of citizens. . . . If a white man and a black man choose to occupy the same public conveyance on a public highway, it is their right to do so, and no government, proceeding alone on grounds of race, can prevent it without infringing the personal liberty of each. . . .

If a State can prescribe, as a rule of civil conduct, that whites and blacks shall not travel as passengers in the same railroad coach, why may it not so regulate the use of the streets of its cities and towns as to compel white citizens to keep on one side of a street and black citizens to keep on the other? Why may it not, upon like grounds, punish whites and blacks who ride together in street cars or in open vehicles on a public road or street? Why may it not require sheriffs to assign whites to one side of a court-room and blacks to the other? And why may it not also prohibit the commingling of the two races in the galleries of legislative halls or in public assemblages convened for the consideration of the political questions of the day? Further, if this statute of Louisiana is consistent with the personal liberty of citizens, why may not the State require the separation in railroad coaches of native and naturalized citizens of the United States, or of Protestants and Roman Catholics?

The answer given at the argument to these questions was that regulations of the kind they suggest would be unreasonable, and could not, therefore, stand before the law. Is it meant that the determination of questions of legislative power depends upon the inquiry whether the statute whose validity is questioned is, in the judgment of the courts, a reasonable one, taking all the circumstances into consideration? A statute may be unreasonable merely because a sound public policy forbade its enactment. But I do not understand that the courts have anything to do with the policy or expediency of legislation. . . . There is a dangerous tendency in these latter days to enlarge the functions of the courts, by means of judicial interference with the will of the people as expressed by the legislature. Our institutions have the distinguishing characteristic that the three departments of government are co-ordinate and separate. Each much keep within the limits defined by the Constitution. And the courts best discharge their duty by executing the will of the law-making power, constitutionally expressed, leaving the results of legislation to be dealt with by the people through their representatives. . . .

The white race deems itself to be the dominant race in this country. And so it is, in prestige, in achievements, in education, in wealth, and in power. So, I doubt not, it will continue to be for all time, if it remains true to its great heritage and holds fast to the principles of constitutional liberty. But in view of the Constitution, in the eye of the law, there is in this country no superior, dominant, ruling class of citizens. There is no caste here. Our Constitution is color-blind, and neither knows nor tolerates classes among citizens. In respect of civil rights, all citizens are equal before the law. . . .

In my opinion, the judgment this day rendered will, in time, prove to be quite as pernicious as the decision made by this tribunal in the *Dred Scott case*. It was adjudged in that case that the descendants of Africans who were imported into this country, and sold as slaves, were not included nor intended to be included under the word "citizens" in the Constitution, and could not claim any of the rights and privileges which that instrument provided for and secured to citizens of the United States; that, at time of the adoption of the Constitution, they were "considered as a subordinate and inferior class of beings, who had been subjugated by the dominant race, and, whether emancipated or not, yet remained subject to their authority, and had no rights or privileges but such as those who held the power and the government might choose to grant them." 60 U.S. (19 How.) 393, 404 (1857). The recent amendments of the Constitution, it was supposed, had eradicated these principles from our institutions. But it seems that we have yet, in some of the States, a dominant race—a superior class of citizens, which assumes to regulate the enjoyment of civil rights, common to all citizens, upon the basis of race. The present decision, it may well be apprehended, will not only stimulate aggressions, more or less brutal and irritating, upon the admitted rights of colored citizens, but will encourage the belief that it is possible, by means of state enactments, to defeat the beneficent purposes which the people of the United States had in view when they adopted the recent amendments of the Constitution, by one of which the blacks of this country were made citizens of the United States and of the States in which they respectively reside, and whose privileges and immunities, as citizens, the States are forbidden to abridge. Sixty millions of whites are in no danger from the presence here of eight millions of blacks. The destinies of the two races, in this country, are indissolubly linked together, and the interests of both require that the common government of all shall not permit the seeds of race hate to be planted under the sanction of law. What can more certainly arouse race hate, what more certainly create and perpetuate a feeling of distrust between these races, than state enactments which, in fact, proceed on the ground that colored citizens are so inferior and degraded that they cannot be allowed to sit in public coaches occupied by white citizens? That, as all will admit, is the real meaning of such legislation as was enacted in Louisiana.

The sure guarantee of the peace and security of each race is the clear, distinct, unconditional recognition by our governments, National and State, of every right that inheres in civil freedom, and of the equality before the law of all citizens of the United States, without regard to race. State enactments regulating the enjoyment of civil rights upon the basis of race, and cunningly devised to defeat legitimate results of the war, under the pretence of recognizing equality of rights, can have no other result than to render permanent peace impossible, and to keep alive a conflict of races, the continuance of which must do harm to all concerned. This question is not met by the suggestion that social equality cannot exist between the white and black races in this country. That argument, if it can be properly regarded as one, is scarcely worthy of consideration; for social equality no more exists between two races when traveling in a passenger coach or a public highway than when members of the same races sit by each other in a street car or in the jury box, or stand or sit with each other in a political assembly, or when they use in common the streets of a city or town, or when they are in the same room for the purpose of having their names placed on the registry of voters, or when they approach the ballot box in order to exercise the high privilege of voting. . . .

There is a race so different from our own that we do not permit those belonging to it to become citizens of the United States. Persons belonging to it are, with few exceptions, absolutely excluded from our country. I allude to the Chinese race. But by the statute in question, a Chinaman can ride in the same passenger coach with white citizens of the United States, while citizens of the black race in Louisiana, many of whom, perhaps, risked their lives for the preservation of the Union, who are entitled, by law, to participate in the political control of the State and nation, who are not excluded, by law or by reason of their race, from public stations of any kind, and who have all the legal rights that belong to white citizens, are yet declared to be criminals, liable to imprisonment, if they ride in a public coach occupied by citizens of the white race. It is scarcely just to say that a colored citizen should not object to occupying a public coach assigned to his own race. He does not object, nor, perhaps, would he object to separate coaches for his race if his rights under the law were recognized. But he does object, and he ought never to cease objecting to the proposition, that citizens of the white and black races can be adjudged criminals because they sit, or claim the right to sit, in the same public coach on a public highway.

The arbitrary separation of citizens, on the basis of race, while they are on a public highway, is a badge of servitude wholly inconsistent with the civil freedom and the equality before the law established by the Constitution. It cannot be justified upon any legal grounds.

If evils will result from the commingling of the two races upon public highways established for the benefit of all, they will be infinitely less than those that will surely come from state legislation regulating the enjoyment of civil rights upon the basis of race. We boast of the freedom enjoyed by our people above all other peoples. But it is difficult to reconcile that boast with a state of the law which, practically, puts the brand of servitude and degradation upon a large class of our fellow-citizens, our equals before the law. The thin disguise of "equal" accommodations for passengers in railroad coaches will not mislead any one, nor atone for the wrong this day done. . . .

NOTES

1.   *Plessy* is the infamous case upholding racial segregation by law on the theory that "separate but equal" does not violate the Fourteenth Amendment's requirement of "equal protection of the laws." This statement in *Plessy* remained "good" law for decades, and was uncontradicted by the Supreme Court for 58 years, until *Brown v. Board of Education* (1954).

In *Plessy* the Court purported not to be retreating from its prior cases. Is racial segregation consistent with *Strauder*'s view that the Fourteenth Amendment commands that "the law in the States shall be the same for the black as for the white; that all persons, whether colored or white, shall stand equal before the laws of the States, and, in regard to the colored race, for whose protection the amendment was primarily designed, that no discrimination shall be made against them by law because of their color"? If separate really were equal in a given situation—and in theory do adjacent train cars, arriving at the same time and at the same station, come about as close as possible?—would segregation *in and of itself* deprive someone of the "equal protection of the laws"?

The Court asserted that any "stigma" from segregation was a matter of one's own subjective perception, purely in the eye of the beholder. That very argument had been made by opponents of the Civil Rights Act of 1875 and soundly rejected by Congress. When the argument was revived by the Court in *Plessy*, Justice Harlan suggested it was deeply untruthful. It is hard to take seriously the majority's assertion. Yet even after one concludes that stigma is not wholly subjective, how should it be ascertained by a court? And is stigma alone a cognizable injury under the Equal Protection Clause? Is the Constitution, as Justice Harlan argues, "color blind"?

2.   To support racial segregation in law, the Court appealed to "the established usages, customs, and traditions of the people . . . with a view to the promotion of their comfort, and the preservation of the public peace and good order." But Jim Crow laws were actually of recent vintage. They came after the disputed presidential election of 1876 led to the end of Reconstruction. The Democrat Samuel Tilden won more votes in the Electoral College but not a majority, because the Electoral College votes of several Southern states were contested. The election was not resolved until a congressionally appointed Electoral Commission (consisting of five senators, five representatives, and five justices), in a series of 8–7 party line votes, recognized the electors of Republican Rutherford B. Hayes for all of the disputed states. Those electors gave Hayes a 185–184 victory in the Electoral College. To secure acquiescence to the result from Democrats, Republicans made a number of concessions in what was called the Compromise of 1877— including the withdrawal of federal troops from the South.

To give just one example of the transformation of law and society that resulted, consider the University of South Carolina. It was integrated in 1873 with the admission of a black medical student. Several faculty members resigned in protest, but the board of trustees declared themselves firmly on the side of the student: "recognizing . . . the cause of these resignations this board cannot regret that a spirit so hostile to the welfare of our

State, as well as to the dictates of justice and the claims of our common humanity, will no longer be represented in the University, which is the common property of all our citizens without distinction of race." 2 Walter L. Fleming, DOCUMENTARY HISTORY OF RECONSTRUCTION 191 (1907). By 1876, the University of South Carolina had hired black faculty and a majority of the students were black. But in 1877, as federal troops pulled out of the South and black voters were left unprotected, the political and social change was dramatic. A former Confederate general was elected governor, and the legislature enacted a law requiring the flagship university to be all-white, while also funding black state colleges. The University of South Carolina was promptly closed, and when it reopened in 1880 it admitted only white students, as it would continue to do until 1963— nine years after *Brown v. Board of Education.*

In some states the shift in political fortunes was more gradual. Not until the 1880s would "the first major wave of segregation legislation" occur throughout the South. Michael W. McConnell, *The Forgotten Constitutional Moment,* 11 Const. Comm. 115, 132 (1994).

> The first genuine Jim Crow law requiring segregation of all railroad facilities was passed by Florida in 1887, followed by Mississippi in 1888 and Texas in 1889. The Louisiana statute upheld in *Plessy v. Ferguson* was passed in 1890. By 1900, a rigid system of legally enforced segregation and subordination dominated all aspects of race relations throughout the South. The Compromise of 1877 marked not just a legal revolution, but a social revolution. It transformed the way the people of the South conducted their governments, exercised their legal rights, and lived their lives. It was accompanied by corroborating ideological shifts in science, literature, journalism, history, and religion. Far more than the Fourteenth Amendment, the Compromise of 1877 created a far-reaching and long-persisting constitutional regime: the regime of Jim Crow.

Id. at 132–133. "[T]here is no question that by the turn of the century, white public opinion had abandoned the egalitarian vision of citizenship spawned by the Civil War, and had revived definitions of American freedom and nationality based on race." Eric Foner, *The Strange Career of the Reconstruction Amendments,* 108 Yale L. J. 2003, 2008 (1999). It is difficult to discount the influence of this social, political, and cultural transformation as a factor explaining the difference between the spirit that animated the drafters of the Fourteenth Amendment, the Civil Rights Act of 1866, and the Civil Rights Act of 1875 and the spirit animating *Plessy* in 1896. *Plessy*—and the laws it upheld— represented modern politics and the new consensus among elite Southern whites.

3. We have not edited out the embarrassing features of Justice Harlan's (otherwise) celebrated dissent. Justice Harlan argues against the segregation of blacks and whites by appealing to racial prejudice against those of Chinese descent. He, too, appears to be a prisoner of the common social perceptions, the intuitions of his age. Does this affect how you think about constitutional interpretation? Should constitutional interpretation reflect the moral values of the justices—but those should just be better moral values than the ones of the majority in *Plessy*? Or is giving free play to moral intuitions just as likely to produce bad results as good ones? (Here is a question that is impossible to answer: which of your moral values are so conditioned by your social context that you do not even recognize how wrong they are?) Justice Harlan was the author of the majority opinion in the next case, decided three years after *Plessy.*

Cumming v. Board of Education

175 U.S. 528 (1899)

The plaintiffs in error, Cumming, Harper, and Ladeveze, citizens of Georgia and persons of color, suing on behalf of themselves and all others in like case joining with them, brought this action against the Board of Education of Richmond County. . . .

In the petition filed by them it was alleged . . . that they were persons of color and parents of children of school age lawfully entitled to the full benefit of any system of high schools organized or maintained by the Board; that up to the time of the said tax levy and for many years continuously prior thereto, the Board maintained a system of high schools in Richmond County in which the colored school population had the same educational advantages as the white school population, but on July 10, 1897, it withdrew from and denied to the colored school population any participation in the educational facilities of a high school system in the county, and had voted to continue to deny to that population any admission to or participation in such educational facilities; and that at the time of such withdrawal and denial the petitioners respectively had children attending the colored high school then existing, but who were now debarred from participation in the benefits of a public high school education though petitioners were being taxed therefor. . . .

■ MR. JUSTICE HARLAN, after stating the facts as above, delivered the opinion of the court.

This writ of error brings up for review a final order . . . in conformity to a judgment rendered in the Supreme Court of [Georgia]. That order, it is contended, deprived the plaintiffs in error of rights secured to them by the Fourteenth Amendment to the Constitution of the United States.

The Supreme Court of Georgia, after stating in its opinion that counsel for the petitioners did not point out in his brief what particular paragraph of the Fourteenth Amendment was violated, said: ". . . In our opinion, it is impracticable to distribute taxes equally. The appropriation of a portion of the taxes for a white girls' high school is not more discrimination against these colored plaintiffs than it is against many white people in the county. A taxpayer who has boys and no girls of a school age has as much right to complain of the unequal distribution of the taxes to a girls' high school as have these plaintiffs. The action of the Board appears to us to be more a discrimination as to sex than it does as to race. While the Board appropriates some money to assist a denominational school for white boys and girls, it has never established a high school for white boys, and, if the contention of these plaintiffs is correct, white parents who have boys old enough to attend a high school have as much right to complain as these plaintiffs, if they have not more. Without, therefore, going into an analysis of the different clauses of the Fourteenth Amendment of the Constitution of the United States, we content ourselves by saying that, in our opinion, the action of the Board did not violate any of the provisions of that amendment. It does not abridge the privileges or immunities of citizens of the United States, nor does it deprive any person of life, liberty, or property without due process of law, nor does it deny to any person within the state the equal protection of its laws."

The constitution of Georgia provides: "There shall be a thorough system of common schools for the education of children in the elementary branches of an English education only, as nearly uniform as practicable, the expenses of which shall be provided for by taxation, or otherwise. The schools shall be free to all children of the state, but separate schools shall be provided for the white and colored races." Art. 8, § 1.

It was said at the argument that the vice in the common school system of Georgia was the requirement that the white and colored children of the State be educated in separate schools. But we need not consider that question in this case. No such issue was made in the pleadings. Indeed, the plaintiffs distinctly state that they have no objection to the tax in question so far as levied for the support of primary, intermediate and grammar schools, in the management of which the rule as to the separation of races is enforced. We must dispose of the case as it is presented by the record.

The plaintiffs in error complain that the Board of Education used the funds in its hands to assist in maintaining a high school for white children without providing a similar school for colored children. The substantial relief asked is an injunction that would either impair the efficiency of the high school provided for white children or compel the Board to close it. But if that were done, the result would only be to take from white children educational privileges enjoyed by them, without giving to colored children additional opportunities for the education furnished in high schools. The colored school children of the county would not be advanced in the matter of their education by a decree compelling the defendant Board to cease giving support to a high school for white children. The Board had before it the question whether it should maintain, under its control, a high school for about sixty colored children or withhold the benefits of education in primary schools from three hundred children of the same race. It was impossible, the board believed, to give educational facilities to the three hundred colored children who were unprovided for, if it maintained a separate school for the sixty children who wished to have a high school education. Its decision was in the interest of the greater number of colored children, leaving the smaller number to obtain a high school education in existing private institutions at an expense not beyond that incurred in the high school discontinued by the Board.

We are not permitted by the evidence in the record to regard that decision as having been made with any desire or purpose on the part of the Board to discriminate against any of the colored school children of the county on account of their race. But if it be assumed that the Board erred in supposing that its duty was to provide educational facilities for the three hundred colored children who were without an opportunity in primary schools to learn the alphabet and to read and write, rather than to maintain a school for the benefit of the sixty colored children who wished to attend a high school, that was not an error which a court of equity should attempt to remedy by an injunction that would compel the board to withhold all assistance from the high school maintained for white children. If, in some appropriate proceeding instituted directly for that purpose, the plaintiffs had sought to compel the Board of Education, out of the funds in its hands or under its control, to establish and maintain a high school for colored children, and if it appeared that the Board's refusal to maintain such a school was in fact an abuse of its discretion and in hostility to the colored population because of their race, different questions might have arisen in the state court.

The state court did not deem the action of the Board of Education in suspending temporarily and for economic reasons the high school for colored children a sufficient reason why the defendant should be restrained by injunction from maintaining an existing high school for white children. It rejected the suggestion that the Board proceeded in bad faith or had abused the discretion with which it was invested by the statute under which it proceeded or had acted in hostility to the colored race. Under the circumstances disclosed, we cannot say that this action of the state court was, within the meaning of the Fourteenth Amendment, a denial by the State to the plaintiffs and to those associated with them of the equal protection of the laws or of any privileges belonging to them as citizens of the United States. We may add that while all admit that the benefits and burdens of public taxation must be shared by citizens without discrimination against any class on account of their race, the education of the people in schools maintained by state taxation is a matter belonging to the respective States, and any interference on the part of Federal authority with the management of such schools cannot be justified except in the case of a clear and unmistakable disregard of rights secured by the supreme law of the land. We have here no such case to be determined; and . . . this view disposes of the only question which this court has jurisdiction to review and decide.

NOTES

1.   Does providing a high school education to (some) white children but not to any black children violate the Equal Protection Clause? Wouldn't that even violate the separate-but-equal rule of *Plessy*? If there were actually financial constraints on the board's ability to provide schools for all, should the Court have granted an injunction shutting down the all-white girls' high school? Wouldn't that have achieved equal treatment, at least? What does the majority see as wrong with that remedy? Courts of equity have traditionally had broad discretion to fashion a remedy that is appropriate for the particular case. What remedy should the Court have given here?

2.   Does maintaining a high school for white girls but no high school for white *boys* violate the Equal Protection Clause? Imagine a different scenario: that the board had offered a high school education for all children but maintained separate-sex public high schools. Would that have violated the Equal Protection Clause? (On sex discrimination, see p. 1431.)

3.   Almost three decades after *Cumming*, the Court unanimously decided *Gong Lum v. Rice*, 275 U.S. 78 (1927), which confronted the place of Asian-Americans in the system of segregated schools. Martha Lum was the daughter of a Mississippi merchant named Gong Lum, and wanted to attend the local white high school. Her father argued that she could not be forced to attend the local "colored" school because "she is not a member of the colored race, nor is she of mixed blood, but . . . she is pure Chinese." *Id.* at 81. The Court rejected her claim, relying heavily on *Plessy* and *Cumming*. It concluded:

> Most of the cases cited arose, it is true, over the establishment of separate schools as between white pupils and black pupils; but we cannot think that the question is any different, or that any different result can be reached, assuming the cases above cited to be rightly decided, where the issue is as between white pupils and the pupils of the yellow races.

Was the Court right that Gong Lum's situation is indistinguishable from *Plessy* and *Cumming*? What are the arguments on each side?

Berea College v. Kentucky

211 U.S. 45 (1908)

On October 8, 1904, the grand jury of Madison County, Kentucky, presented in the Circuit Court of that county an indictment, charging:

"The said Berea College, being a corporation duly incorporated under the laws of the state of Kentucky, and owning, maintaining, and operating a college, school, and institution of learning, known as 'Berea College,' located in the town of Berea, Madison county, Kentucky, did unlawfully and wilfully permit and receive both the white and negro races as pupils for instruction in said college, school, and institution of learning."

This indictment was found under an act of March 22, 1904, whose first section reads:

SEC. 1. That it shall be unlawful for any person, corporation, or association of persons to maintain or operate any college, school, or institution where persons of the white and negro races are both received as pupils for instruction, and any person or corporation who shall operate or maintain any such college, school, or institution shall be fined $1,000, and any person or corporation who may be convicted of violating the provisions of this act shall be fined $100 for each day they may operate said school, college, or institution after such conviction.

On a trial the defendant was found guilty and sentenced to pay a fine of one thousand dollars. . . .

■ MR. JUSTICE BREWER, after making the foregoing statement, delivered the opinion of the court.

There is no dispute as to the facts. That the act does not violate the Constitution of Kentucky is settled by the decision of its highest court, and the single question for our consideration is whether it conflicts with the Federal Constitution. . . .

In creating a corporation a State may withhold powers which may be exercised by and cannot be denied to an individual. It is under no obligation to treat both alike. In granting corporate powers the legislature may deem that the best interests of the State would be subserved by some restriction, and the corporation may not plead that, in spite of the restriction, it has more or greater powers because the citizen has. . . .

[I]t is unnecessary for us to consider anything more than the question of its validity as applied to corporations. The statute is clearly separable and may be valid as to one class while invalid as to another. Even if it were conceded that its assertion of power over individuals cannot be sustained, still it must be upheld so far as it restrains corporations.

There is no force in the suggestion that the statute, although clearly separable, must stand or fall as an entirety on the ground the legislature would not have enacted one part unless it could reach all. That the legislature of Kentucky desired to separate the teaching of white and colored children may be conceded; but it by no means follows that it would not have enforced the separation so far as it could do so, even though it could not make it effective under all circumstances. In other words, it is not at all unreasonable to believe that the legislature, although advised beforehand of the constitutional question, might have prohibited all organizations and corporations under its control from teaching white and colored children together. . . .

[The defendant] Berea College was organized under the authority of an act for the incorporation of voluntary associations. . . .

[I]t is settled "that a power reserved to the legislature to alter, amend, or repeal a charter authorizes it to make any alteration or amendment of a charter granted subject to it, which will not defeat or substantially impair the object of the grant, or any rights vested under it, and which the legislature may deem necessary to secure either that object or any public right."

Construing the statute, the Court of Appeals held that "if the same school taught the different races at different times, though at the same place, or at different times at the same place, it would not be unlawful." Now, an amendment to the original charter, which does not destroy the power of the college to furnish education to all persons, but which simply separates them by time or place of instruction, cannot be said to "defeat or substantially impair the object of the grant." The language of the statute is not in terms an amendment, yet its effect is an amendment, and it would be resting too much on mere form to hold that a statute which in effect works a change in the terms of the charter is not to be considered as an amendment, because not so designated. The act itself, being separable, is to be read as though it, in one section, prohibited any person, in another section any corporation and, in a third, any association of persons to do the acts named. Reading the statute as containing a separate prohibition on all corporations, at least, all state corporations, it substantially declares that any authority given by previous charters to instruct the two races at the same time and in the same place is forbidden, and that prohibition, being a departure from the terms of the original charter in this case, may properly be adjudged an amendment. . . .

We need concern ourselves only with the inquiry whether the first section can be upheld as coming within the power of a State over its own corporate creatures.

We are of opinion, for reasons stated, that it does come within that power.

■ MR. JUSTICE HOLMES and MR. JUSTICE MOODY concur in the judgment.

■ MR. JUSTICE HARLAN, dissenting:

This prosecution arises under the first section of an act of the General Assembly of Kentucky, approved March 22, 1904. The purpose and scope of the act is clearly indicated by its title. It is "An act to prohibit white and colored persons from attending the same school."

It is well to give here the entire statute, as follows:

SEC. 1. That it shall be unlawful for any person, corporation, or association of persons to maintain or operate any college, school, or institution where persons of the white and negro races are both received as pupils for instruction; and any person or corporation who shall operate or maintain any such college, school, or institution shall be fined $1,000, and any person or corporation who may be convicted of violating the provisions of this act shall be fined $100 for each day they may operate said school, college, or institution after such conviction.

SEC. 2. That any instructor who shall teach in any school, college, or institution where members of said two races are received as pupils for instruction shall be guilty of operating and maintaining same and fined as provided in the 1st section hereof.

SEC. 3. It shall be unlawful for any white person to attend any school or institution where negroes are received as pupils or receive instruction, and it shall be unlawful for any negro or colored person to attend any school or institution where white persons are received as pupils or receive instruction. Any person so offending shall be fined $50 for each day he attends such institution or school: *Provided*, That the provisions of this law shall not apply to any penal institution or house of reform.

SEC. 4. Nothing in this act shall be construed to prevent any private school, college, or institution of learning from maintaining a separate and distinct branch thereof, in a different locality, not less than 25 miles distant, for the education exclusively of one race or color.

SEC. 5. This act shall not take effect, or be in operation, before the 15th day of July, 1904.

The plaintiff in error, Berea College, is an incorporation, organized under the General Laws of Kentucky in 1859. Its original articles of incorporation set forth that the object of the founders was to establish and maintain an institution of learning, "in order to promote the cause of Christ." . . .

In 1904 the college was charged in a Kentucky state court with having unlawfully and willfully received both white and negro persons as pupils for instruction. . . . [A] trial was had which resulted in a verdict of guilty and the imposition of a fine of $1,000 on the college. The trial court refused an instruction asked by the defendant, to the effect that the statute was in violation of the Fourteenth Amendment of the Constitution of the United States. . . .

The state court . . . held it to be entirely competent for the State to adopt the policy of the separation of the races, even in private schools, and concluded its opinion in these words: "The right to teach white and negro children in a private school at the same time and place is not a property right." The state court (but without any discussion whatever) added, as if merely incidental to or a make-weight in the decision of the pivotal question, in this case, these words: "Besides, appellant, as a *corporation* created by this State, has no natural right to teach at all. Its right to teach is such as the State sees fit to give to it. The State may withhold it altogether or qualify it." It concluded: "We do not think the act is in conflict with the Federal Constitution." . . .

Now, can it for a moment be doubted that the legislature intended all the sections of the statute in question to be looked at, and that the purpose was to forbid the teaching of pupils of the two races together in the same institution, at the same time, *whether the teachers represented natural persons or corporations?* Can it be said that the legislature would have prohibited such teaching by corporations, and yet consciously permitted the teaching by private individuals or unincorporated associations? Are we to attribute such folly to legislators? Who can say that the legislature would have enacted one provision without the other? If not, then, in determining the intent of the legislature, the provisions of the statute relating to the teaching of the two races together by *corporations* cannot be separated in its operation from those in the same section that forbid such teaching by individuals and unincorporated associations. Therefore the court cannot, as I think, properly forbear to consider the validity of the provisions that refer to teachers who do not represent corporations. If those provisions constitute, as, in my judgment, they, do, an essential part of the legislative scheme or policy, and are invalid, then, under the authorities cited, the whole act must fall. The provision as to corporations may be valid, and yet the other clauses may be so inseparably connected with that provision and the policy underlying it, that the validity of all the clauses necessary to effectuate the legislative intent must be considered. There is no magic in the fact of incorporation which will so transform the act of teaching the two races in the same school at the same time that such teaching can be deemed lawful when conducted by private individuals, but unlawful when conducted by the representatives of corporations.

There is another line of thought. The state court evidently regarded it as necessary to consider the entire act; for it adjudged it to be competent for the State to forbid *all* teaching of the two races together, in the same institution, at the same time, no matter by whom the teaching was done. . . . The state court upheld the authority of the State, under its general police power, to forbid the association of the two races in the same institution of learning. . . .

In my judgment the court should directly meet and decide the broad question presented by the statute. It should adjudge whether the statute, as a whole, is or is not unconstitutional, in that it makes it a crime against the State to maintain or operate a private institution of learning where white and black pupils are received, at the same time, for instruction. In the view which I have as to my duty I feel obliged to express my opinion as to the validity of the act as a whole. I am of opinion that in its essential parts the statute is an arbitrary invasion of the rights of liberty and property guaranteed by the Fourteenth Amendment against hostile state action and is, therefore, void.

The capacity to impart instruction to others is given by the Almighty for beneficent purposes and its use may not be forbidden or interfered with by Government—certainly not, unless such instruction is, in its nature, harmful to the public morals or imperils the public safety. The right to impart instruction . . . is, beyond question, part of one's liberty as guaranteed against hostile state action by the Constitution of the United States. . . . If pupils, of whatever race—certainly, if they be citizens—choose with the consent of their parents or voluntarily to sit together in a private institution of learning while receiving instruction which is not in its nature harmful or dangerous to the public, no government, whether Federal or state, can legally forbid their coming together, or being together temporarily, for such an innocent purpose. If the Commonwealth of Kentucky can make it a crime to teach white and colored children together at the same time, in a private institution of learning, it is difficult to perceive why it may not forbid the assembling of white and colored children in the same Sabbath-school, for the purpose of being instructed in the Word of God, although such teaching may be done under the authority of the church to which the school is attached as well as with the consent of the parents of the children. So, if the state court be right, white and colored children may even be forbidden to sit together in a house of worship or at a communion table in the same Christian church. In the cases supposed there would be the same association of white and colored persons as would occur when pupils of the two races sit together in a private institution of learning for the purpose of receiving instruction in purely secular matters. Will it be said that the cases supposed and the case here in hand are different in that no government, in this country, can lay unholy hands on the religious faith of the people? The answer to this suggestion is that in the eye of the law the right to enjoy one's religious belief, unmolested by any human power, is no more sacred nor more fully or distinctly recognized than is the right to impart and receive instruction not harmful to the public. The denial of either right would be an infringement of the liberty inherent in the freedom secured by the fundamental law. . . . Have we become so inoculated with prejudice of race that an American government, professedly based on the principles of freedom, and charged with the protection of all citizens alike, can make distinctions between such citizens in the matter of their voluntary meeting for innocent purposes simply because of their respective races? Further, if the lower court be right, then a State may make it a crime for white and colored persons to frequent the same market places at the same time, or appear in an assemblage of citizens convened to consider questions of a public or political nature, in which all citizens, without regard to race, are equally interested. Many other illustrations might be given to show the mischievous, not to say cruel, character of the statute in question, and how inconsistent such legislation is with the great principle of the equality of citizens before the law.

Of course, what I have said has no reference to regulations prescribed for public schools, established at the pleasure of the State and maintained at the public expense. No such question is here presented and it need not be now discussed. My observations have reference to the case before the court, and only to the provision of the statute making it a crime for any person to impart harmless instruction to white and colored pupils together, at the same time, in the same private institution of learning. That provision is, in my opinion, made an essential element in the policy of the statute, and, if regard be had to the object and purpose of this legislation, it cannot be treated as separable nor intended to be separated from the provisions relating to corporations. The whole statute should therefore be held void; otherwise, it will be taken as the law of Kentucky, to be enforced by its courts, that the teaching of white and black pupils, at the same time, even in a *private* institution, is a crime against that Commonwealth, punishable by fine and imprisonment. . . .

■ MR. JUSTICE DAY also dissents.

NOTES

1.   Take a moment to untangle the majority's rationale (and the dissent's objection) in *Berea College*: the Court upheld Kentucky's mandatory segregated-education law, as applied to private schools organized as corporations, on the ground that states may amend any corporate charters they grant. (Recall how Justice Harlan, in *The Civil Rights Cases*, considered that the grant of a corporate charter or license to operate a railroad, inn, or place of amusement made the grantee a state actor.) The *Berea College* majority purported not to address the application of the statute to individuals and "associations." In his blistering dissent, Justice Harlan thought the distinction was absurd and that, on the merits, the entire statute was unconstitutional.

2.   In Justice Harlan's view, what provision of the Constitution did Kentucky's law violate? During the *Plessy* era, the Supreme Court considered challenges to state regulation under the Due Process Clause, asking whether the law at issue impaired rights of "liberty" or "property." The leading case was *Lochner v. New York*, 198 U.S. 45

(1905), presented at p. 1521. *Berea College* (1908) was decided just three years later. One can hear echoes of *Lochner*-style substantive due process in Justice Harlan's dissent in *Berea College*. But he also appears to ground his objection in the themes of the First Amendment—the freedoms of religion, speech, and association. In 1908 the Court had not yet held that the Fourteenth Amendment made most of the provisions of the Bill of Rights applicable to state government action, and so his opinion speaks in the general "liberty" idiom of the day.

3.   Now turn the factual scenario inside out—always a good test of whether your legal argument is principled rather than result-driven. Imagine a religious college that practices not racial integration but racial *segregation* as a matter of asserted religious belief, but now the law forbids racial segregation, even by private organizations. May the government prohibit, or punish, the college's practice? Or would that violate the college's rights to free exercise of religion, freedom of speech, and freedom of association? The case is drawn from a real one: *Bob Jones University v. United States*, 461 U.S. 574 (1983). The federal government withdrew the tax-exempt status of a religious university because of its racially discriminatory practices. In the Supreme Court, the religious university lost. Is this case different in a principled way from *Berea College*?

4.   Did Kentucky's law violate the Equal Protection Clause? Whose equal protection rights were violated? The students'? Both white *and* black students? The school's? Should one party, in defense of its own legal position, have standing to raise someone else's asserted constitutional rights? See *Pierce v. Society of Sisters*, 268 U.S. 510 (1925) (allowing a private religious school to have standing to raise the asserted constitutional rights of its students and their parents, as well as its own rights). For more discussion of the doctrine of standing, see p. 413.

5.   The lower court had expressed enthusiastic support for segregation, opining that "[t]he separation of the human family into races, distinguished no less by color than by temperament and other qualities, is as certain as anything in nature. Those of us who believe that all of this was divinely ordered have no doubt that there was wisdom in the provision; albeit we are unable to say with assurance why it is so. Those who see in it only nature's work must also concede that in this order, as in all others in nature, there is an unerring justification." *Berea College v. Commonwealth*, 94 S.W. 623, 626 (Ky. 1906). It therefore upheld the statute on the specific ground that it would "prevent amalgamation of the races" and that "[n]o higher welfare of society can be thought of than the preservation of the best qualities of manhood of all its races." The Supreme Court's focus on corporations allowed it to avoid this question. Was that a good thing?

6.   The racial attitudes the justices manifested in *Plessy*, *Cumming*, and *Berea College* can also be seen in other contemporaneous doctrines. For example, in *The Insular Cases*, 182 U.S. 1 (1901), the Court held that the Constitution does not apply, in all its particulars, to U.S. territories populated "by alien races, differing from us in religion, customs, laws, methods of taxation, and modes of thought." For critique, see Gary Lawson & Guy Seidman, THE CONSTITUTION OF EMPIRE: TERRITORIAL EXPANSION AND AMERICAN LEGAL HISTORY 194–201 (2004). In *Elk v. Wilkins*, 112 U.S. 94 (1884), the Court held that the members of "Indian tribes" were not covered by the Citizenship Clause of the Fourteenth Amendment, because they were "not subject to the jurisdiction" of the United States within the meaning of that clause. (Justice Harlan dissented.) Yet only two years later the Court also held that Indian tribes were subject to the "plenary power" of Congress. *United States v. Kagama*, 118 U.S. 375 (1886). It was not until 1924 that members of Indian tribes were granted U.S. citizenship by statute.

[*Assignment 67*]

B. THE DESEGREGATION CASES

The shift from *Plessy* to *Brown* may seem sharp, but it was a long time in coming. The "separate but equal" doctrine established by *Plessy* remained the law. But it was the subject of a number of legal challenges. In one line of cases brought by the NAACP, the courts invalidated various burdens and restrictions on travel by black Americans, not as violations of the Equal Protection Clause but as burdens on interstate commerce. E.g., *Morgan v. Virginia*, 328 U.S. 373 (1946). In another line of cases, the NAACP challenged segregation in public education. Its first victory in the Supreme Court was in *Missouri ex rel Gaines v. Canada*, 305 U.S. 337 (1938), which held that Missouri violated the Equal Protection Clause when it offered a law school for white students and no law school for black students. For the state to pay for a black student to go to law school in another state was not "equal." After World War II, the NAACP's efforts were joined by the Justice Department, and in several more cases the Court found racially segregated state schools to violate the Equal Protection Clause. See, e.g., *Sweatt v. Painter*, 339 U.S. 629 (1950); *McLaurin v. Oklahoma State Regents for Higher Education*, 339 U.S. 637 (1950). In these cases the Court was willing to consider challenges to whether segregated education was "equal," but not challenges to its being "separate." Moreover, these cases were about universities and professional schools, not grade schools, middle schools, or high schools. There "separate but equal" continued.

But the ugly truth of "separate but equal" was that it was never equal. Public spending on education told the tale. To take one example, consider Atlanta. Despite white domination of the city, the black middle class had relatively more voice than elsewhere in the South. Yet the gap in per-pupil expenditures remained stark. In the 1946–1947 school year, the average expenditure per black pupil was $59.88. The average expenditure per white pupil was more than double: $139.73. Tomiko Brown-Nagin, COURAGE TO DISSENT: ATLANTA AND THE LONG HISTORY OF THE CIVIL RIGHTS MOVEMENT 445 (2011).

The NAACP's litigation, led by Thurgood Marshall, eventually led to a more decisive decision in *Brown v. Board of Education*, 347 U.S. 483 (1954). *Brown* is without doubt one of the most significant decisions of U.S. constitutional history. *Brown* did not (quite) overrule *Plessy*, but it unanimously rejected its reasoning. *Brown* did not (quite) embrace the position of Justice Harlan's dissent in *Plessy*, but it came close to adopting a flat rule that the Equal Protection Clause forbids the government from classifying, segregating, or distinguishing persons—for any purpose—on the basis of their race. *Brown* declared "separate but equal" a violation of the Equal Protection Clause in one context, public education. In its wake, courts struck down racial segregation in golf courses and in transportation, in swimming pools and in marriage. *Brown* restored the constitutional guarantee of "the equal protection of the laws" to the place it held at the close of Reconstruction (as illustrated by *Strauder*). *Brown* repudiated the betrayal of this constitutional vision exemplified by *Plessy, Cumming*, and *Berea College*.

Here you will read *Brown*, as well as a companion case addressing segregation in the District of Columbia schools, *Bolling v. Sharpe*. Next you will read the successor to *Brown* that considered the question of remedy, "*Brown II*"; and an important decision a dozen years later, *Loving v. Virginia,* which invalidated a state "anti-miscegenation" law forbidding whites to marry outside of their race. Then you will read *Yick Wo* and *Washington v. Davis,* cases which raise the question whether the amendment forbids only laws that explicitly classify on the basis of race or also ones that produce a disparate impact along racial lines. Finally, you will read *Bakke* and *Adarand,* two cases that consider affirmative action. These cases raise the question whether the Fourteenth Amendment proscribes all consideration of race by state actors, or instead prohibits only "invidious discrimination."

Together, these cases present important questions not only about the substance of constitutional rights but also about the practice of constitutional interpretation: What is the meaning of the constitutional guarantee of "the equal protection of the laws"? What was the original understanding about whether that guarantee forbade segregation in education? What place should that understanding have in constitutional interpretation? What criteria should a court use in interpreting open-ended or vague constitutional language? Does such language mean that the judiciary has more freedom to adopt what it considers the best understanding? Or does it suggest the opposite—that courts should defer to democratic choices unless the text gives a contrary rule with sufficient specificity? What place should be given in constitutional interpretation to longstanding judicial precedent and social practice? When there is a constitutional violation, what should courts consider when choosing and fashioning the remedy? And are the Supreme Court's interpretations of the Constitution supreme over those of all other political and governmental actors in our constitutional system?

Brown v. Board of Education (Brown I)
347 U.S. 483 (1954)

■ MR. CHIEF JUSTICE WARREN delivered the opinion of the Court.

These cases come to us from the States of Kansas, South Carolina, Virginia, and Delaware. They are premised on different facts and different local conditions, but a common legal question justifies their consideration together in this consolidated opinion.

In each of the cases, minors of the Negro race, through their legal representatives, seek the aid of the courts in obtaining admission to the public schools of their community on a nonsegregated basis. In each instance, they have been denied admission to schools attended by white children under laws requiring or permitting segregation according to race. This segregation was alleged to deprive the plaintiffs of the equal protection of the laws under the Fourteenth Amendment. In each of the cases other than the Delaware case, a three-judge federal district court denied relief to the plaintiffs on the so-called "separate but equal" doctrine announced by this Court in *Plessy v. Ferguson,* 163 U.S. 537 (1896). Under that doctrine, equality of treatment is accorded when the races are provided substantially equal facilities, even though these facilities be separate. In the Delaware case, the Supreme Court of Delaware adhered to that doctrine, but ordered that the plaintiffs be admitted to the white schools because of their superiority to the Negro schools.

The plaintiffs contend that segregated public schools are not "equal" and cannot be made "equal," and that hence they are deprived of the equal protection of the laws. Because of the obvious importance of the question presented, the Court took jurisdiction. Argument was heard in the 1952 Term, and reargument was heard this Term on certain questions propounded by the Court.

Reargument was largely devoted to the circumstances surrounding the adoption of the Fourteenth Amendment in 1868. It covered exhaustively consideration of the Amendment in Congress, ratification by the states, then existing practices in racial segregation, and the views of proponents and opponents of the Amendment. This discussion and our own investigation convince us that, although these sources cast some light, it is not enough to resolve the problem with which we are faced. At best, they are inconclusive. The most avid proponents of the post-War Amendments undoubtedly intended them to remove all legal distinctions among "all persons born or naturalized in the United States." Their opponents, just as certainly, were antagonistic to both the letter and the spirit of the Amendments and wished them to have the most limited effect. What others in Congress and the state legislatures had in mind cannot be determined with any degree of certainty.

An additional reason for the inconclusive nature of the Amendment's history, with respect to segregated schools, is the status of public education at that time. In the South, the movement toward free common schools, supported by general taxation, had not yet taken hold. Education of white children was largely in the hands of private groups. Education of Negroes was almost nonexistent, and practically all of the race were illiterate. In fact, any education of Negroes was forbidden by law in some states. Today, in contrast, many Negroes have achieved outstanding success in the arts and sciences as well as in the business and professional world. It is true that public school education at the time of the Amendment had advanced further in the North, but the effect of the Amendment on Northern States was generally ignored in the congressional debates. Even in the North, the conditions of public education did not approximate those existing today. The curriculum was usually rudimentary; ungraded schools were common in rural areas; the school term was but three months a year in many states; and compulsory school attendance was virtually unknown. As a consequence, it is not surprising that there should be so little in the history of the Fourteenth Amendment relating to its intended effect on public education.

In the first cases in this Court construing the Fourteenth Amendment, decided shortly after its adoption, the Court interpreted it as proscribing all state-imposed discriminations against the Negro race. *In re Slaughter-House Cases*, 83 U.S. (16 Wall.) 36, 67–72 (1873); *Strauder v. West Virginia*, 100 U.S. 303, 307–308 (1880). The doctrine of "separate but equal" did not make its appearance in this court until 1896 in the case of *Plessy v. Ferguson*, involving not education but transportation. American courts have since labored with the doctrine for over half a century. In this Court, there have been six cases involving the "separate but equal" doctrine in the field of public education. In *Cumming v. Board of Education of Richmond County*, 175 U.S. 528 (1899), the validity of the doctrine itself was not challenged. In more recent cases, all on the graduate school level, inequality was found in that specific benefits enjoyed by white students were denied to Negro students of the same educational qualifications. [E.g.,] *Sweatt v. Painter*, 339 U.S. 629 (1950). In none of these cases was it necessary to re-examine the doctrine to grant relief to the Negro plaintiff. And in *Sweatt v. Painter*, the Court expressly reserved decision on the question whether *Plessy v. Ferguson* should be held inapplicable to public education.

In the instant cases, that question is directly presented. Here, unlike *Sweatt v. Painter*, there are findings below that the Negro and white schools involved have been equalized, or are being equalized, with respect to buildings, curricula, qualifications and salaries of teachers, and other "tangible" factors. Our decision, therefore, cannot turn on merely a comparison of these tangible factors in the Negro and white schools involved in each of the cases. We must look instead to the effect of segregation itself on public education.

In approaching this problem, we cannot turn the clock back to 1868 when the Amendment was adopted, or even to 1896 when *Plessy v. Ferguson* was written. We must consider public education in the light of its full development and its present place in American life throughout the Nation. Only in this way can it be determined if segregation in public schools deprives these plaintiffs of the equal protection of the laws.

Today, education is perhaps the most important function of state and local governments. Compulsory school attendance laws and the great expenditures for education both demonstrate our recognition of the importance of education to our democratic society. It is required in the performance of our most basic public responsibilities, even service in the armed forces. It is the very foundation of good citizenship. Today it is a principal instrument in awakening the child to cultural values, in preparing him for later professional training, and in helping him to adjust normally to his environment. In these days, it is doubtful that any child may reasonably be expected to succeed in life if he is denied the opportunity of an education. Such an opportunity, where the state has undertaken to provide it, is a right which must be made available to all on equal terms.

We come then to the question presented: Does segregation of children in public schools solely on the basis of race, even though the physical facilities and other "tangible" factors may be equal, deprive the children of the minority group of equal educational opportunities? We believe that it does.

In *Sweatt v. Painter*, in finding that a segregated law school for Negroes could not provide them equal educational opportunities, this Court relied in large part on "those qualities which are incapable of objective measurement but which make for greatness in a law school." In *McLaurin v. Oklahoma State Regents*, 339 U.S. 637 (1950), the Court, in requiring that a Negro admitted to a white graduate school be treated like all other students, again resorted to intangible considerations: ". . . his ability to study, to engage in discussions and exchange views with other students, and, in general, to learn his profession." Such considerations apply with added force to children in grade and high schools. To separate them from others of similar age and qualifications solely because of their race generates a feeling of inferiority as to their status in the community that may affect their hearts and minds in a way unlikely ever to be undone. The effect of this separation on their educational opportunities was well stated by a finding in the Kansas case by a court which nevertheless felt compelled to rule against the Negro plaintiffs:

> Segregation of white and colored children in public schools has a detrimental effect upon the colored children. The impact is greater when it has the sanction of the law; for the policy of separating the races is usually interpreted as denoting the inferiority of the negro group. A sense of inferiority affects the motivation of a child to learn. Segregation with the

sanction of law, therefore, has a tendency to [retard] the educational and mental development of Negro children and to deprive them of some of the benefits they would receive in a racial[ly] integrated school system.

Whatever may have been the extent of psychological knowledge at the time of *Plessy v. Ferguson*, this finding is amply supported by modern authority.[11] Any language in *Plessy v. Ferguson* contrary to this finding is rejected.

We conclude that in the field of public education the doctrine of "separate but equal" has no place. Separate educational facilities are inherently unequal. Therefore, we hold that the plaintiffs and others similarly situated for whom the actions have been brought are, by reason of the segregation complained of, deprived of the equal protection of the laws guaranteed by the Fourteenth Amendment. This disposition makes unnecessary any discussion whether such segregation also violates the Due Process Clause of the Fourteenth Amendment.[12]

Because these are class actions, because of the wide applicability of this decision, and because of the great variety of local conditions, the formulation of decrees in these cases presents problems of considerable complexity. On reargument, the consideration of appropriate relief was necessarily subordinated to the primary question—the constitutionality of segregation in public education. We have now announced that such segregation is a denial of the equal protection of the laws. In order that we may have the full assistance of the parties in formulating decrees, the cases will be restored to the docket, and the parties are requested to present further argument on Questions 4 and 5 previously propounded by the Court for the reargument this Term.[13] The Attorney General of the United States is again invited to participate. The Attorneys General of the states requiring or permitting segregation in public education will also be permitted to appear as *amici curiae* upon request. . . .

---

[11] K. B. Clark, Effect of Prejudice and Discrimination on Personality Development (Midcentury White House Conference on Children and Youth, 1950); Witmer and Kotinsky, Personality in the Making (1952), c. VI; Deutscher and Chein, The Psychological Effects of Enforced Segregation: A Survey of Social Science Opinion, 26 J. Psychol. 259 (1948); Chein, What are the Psychological Effects of Segregation Under Conditions of Equal Facilities?, 3 Int. J. Opinion and Attitude Res. 229 (1949); Brameld, Educational Costs, in Discrimination and National Welfare (MacIver, ed., 1949), 44–48; Frazier, The Negro in the United States (1949), 674–681. And see generally Myrdal, An American Dilemma (1944).

[12] See *Bolling v. Sharpe*, 347 U.S. 497 (1954), concerning the Due Process Clause of the Fifth Amendment.

[13] "4. Assuming it is decided that segregation in public schools violates the Fourteenth Amendment

(a) would a decree necessarily follow providing that, within the limits set by normal geographic school districting, Negro children should forthwith be admitted to schools of their choice, or

(b) may this Court, in the exercise of its equity powers, permit an effective gradual adjustment to be brought about from existing segregated systems to a system not based on color distinctions?

"5. On the assumption on which questions 4(a) and (b) are based, and assuming further that this Court will exercise its equity powers to the end described in question 4 (b),

(a) should this Court formulate detailed decrees in these cases;

(b) if so, what specific issues should the decrees reach;

(c) should this Court appoint a special master to hear evidence with a view to recommending specific terms for such decrees;

(d) should this Court remand to the courts of first instance with directions to frame decrees in these cases, and if so what general directions should the decrees of this Court include and what procedures should the courts of first instance follow in arriving at the specific terms of more detailed decrees?"

NOTES

1.   *Brown* is the most revered constitutional decision in modern American history. It was exceedingly, and violently, controversial in its day. More than a hundred members of Congress signed The Southern Manifesto, a document attacking the decision, and the following decade saw "massive resistance" in much of the South. Today *Brown* is exceedingly *uncontroversial*—regarded by almost everyone as morally and legally obvious. That sense of *Brown*'s obviousness, and the immorality and inhumanity of segregation, can make it hard to think critically about the case. But it is important to try, because the lessons of *Brown* remain hotly disputed and the issues the case raises are among the most important in constitutional law.

Begin with a point on which there was disagreement in 1954 and on which there is disagreement today. How would you articulate the precise reasoning and holding of the *Brown* opinion?

Is it that racial segregation is intrinsically discriminatory, regardless of context?

Or is it that segregation was perceived as discriminatory? Is it necessarily a brand of inferiority to separate schoolchildren by age, to separate sports teams by gender, or to separate worship services by religious faith? Why is race different? Note *Brown*'s discussion of social facts and realities, and its famous footnote invoking contemporary social science on the perception and psychological effects of segregation. Does the opinion depend on this line of thinking?

Or does *Brown* depend on the historical fact that the United States was from the beginning deformed by race-based slavery, and then by race-based Jim Crow laws? Is race simply different as a matter of American constitutional history? Professor Charles Black once wrote: If "a whole race of people finds itself confined within a system which is set up and continued for the very purpose of keeping it in an inferior race, and if the question is then solemnly propounded whether such a race is being treated 'equally,' I think we ought to exercise one of the sovereign prerogatives of philosophers—that of laughter." Charles L. Black, Jr., *The Lawfulness of the Segregation Decisions*, 69 Yale L.J. 421, 424 (1960). Is that what *Brown* says?

As you ponder the reasoning and significance of this landmark decision, consider three further questions: *Brown* and the historical meaning of the Fourteenth Amendment; the significance of the social science evidence cited in *Brown*; and the authority of precedent.

2.   Calling the historical sources "at best . . . inconclusive," the *Brown* opinion declares that "we cannot turn the clock back to 1868 when the Amendment was adopted." Instead, the opinion relied on the "modern authority" of social science. The decision is therefore one of the first, and the most important, of the Supreme Court's decisions expressly not relying upon the authority of the original meaning of the Constitution.

After the first oral argument in the case, in December 1952, the Court asked for supplemental briefing and re-argument on the original understanding of the framers and ratifiers of the Fourteenth Amendment with respect to segregation. (In the interim, Chief Justice Fred Vinson had died and Chief Justice Earl Warren was appointed—inspiring Justice Frankfurter to call Vinson's death " 'the first indication I have ever had that there is a God.") The standard account in modern scholarship is that the Court did not rely on historical evidence of the framers' intent because the evidence would not support the Court's conclusion. For example, Alexander Bickel, who clerked for Justice Frankfurter when *Brown* was decided, wrote a historical sketch of the Fourteenth Amendment, published the year after the decision. Alexander Bickel, *The Original Understanding and the Segregation Decision,* 69 Harv. L. Rev. 1, 1–6 (1955). Bickel argues that the framers of the Fourteenth Amendment intended it to have the "sweep and appearance of a careful enumeration of rights" while nonetheless being sufficiently open to "permit reasonable future advances" in constitutional protections. He concluded that the 1866 Congress did not specifically contemplate desegregation, but that the *Brown* Court legitimately followed the broad original understanding of the Amendment by making a decision based on the "moral and material state of the nation" in 1954.

Bickel carefully traces the development of the Fourteenth Amendment by examining four of its antecedents. First, a bill expanding the powers of the Freedmen's Bureau, which granted protections for specific enumerated rights, including the right to make and enforce contracts, to sue, and to have the "full and equal benefit of all laws and proceeding for the security of person and estate." Bickel argues that the part of the bill extending civil rights provisions was "not seriously considered on its own merits." (The bill was vetoed by President Andrew Johnson, but a later amended version passed over his veto.) Second, the Civil Rights Act, which was also enacted over presidential veto, raised concerns that the phrase "civil rights" might "include more rights than its sponsors intended to affect," yet it was nonetheless passed over these objections. Third, the proposed constitutional amendment, or Bingham amendment, rejected the term "civil rights" and instead included a privileges and immunities clause, which Bickel argues evinces Congress's implicit rejection of the "wider implications" of the former term. Lastly, since Congress began to question the constitutionality of the Civil Rights Bill itself, a joint committee was formed to create what came to be the Fourteenth Amendment, which expressly adopted the language in the Bingham amendment as opposed to the Civil Rights Bill.

In sum, Bickel argues the Amendment "carried out the relatively narrow objectives" of the Bingham amendment and "was meant to apply neither to jury service, nor suffrage, nor antimiscegenation, nor segregation." Rather, Congress, in drafting the Fourteenth Amendment, was emulating the technique of the "original framers, who were also responsible to an electorate only partly receptive to the fullness of their principles, and who similarly avoided the explicit grant of some powers without foreclosing their future assumption." According to Bickel, there was an "awareness on the part of these framers that it was a constitution they were writing, which led to a choice of language capable of growth," and they therefore understood that "Congress acting under section 5, or the Court in the exercise of the judicial function would, in light of future conditions, have power to abolish segregation." More pointedly, Raoul Berger argued that the framers and ratifiers of the Fourteenth Amendment did not intend to outlaw school segregation, and *Brown* thus worked a "revision" of the Fourteenth Amendment. Raoul Berger, GOVERNMENT BY JUDICIARY: THE TRANSFORMATION OF THE FOURTEENTH AMENDMENT 99–133 (1977).

The evidence considered by Bickel and Berger predated the ratification of the Fourteenth Amendment in 1868. One might reach a different conclusion about the original meaning by considering the deliberations of Congress between 1870 and 1875 over legislation to enforce the new Fourteenth Amendment:

> Under section five of the amendment, Congress had authority to pass legislation to enforce the dictates of the new amendment, and thus had occasion to deliberate over its meaning. During the years immediately following ratification of the amendment, the constitutionality of segregation was the most hotly debated issue in Congress. Senator Charles Sumner of Massachusetts and Representative Benjamin Butler, chairman of the House Judiciary Committee, championed legislation that would prohibit racial

segregation of common carriers, places of public accommodation, and public schools. The debate was conducted in expressly constitutional terms, with proponents maintaining that segregation of public facilities was unconstitutional and thus that the bill was an appropriate measure to enforce section one of the amendment, and opponents maintaining the opposite. These debates provide the most direct evidence of the meaning ascribed to the Fourteenth Amendment during Reconstruction.

Opponents of the legislation defended segregation in much the same terms used [at the time of *Brown*]. Senator Orris Ferry of Connecticut argued that if the "same facilities, the same advantages, the same opportunities of education are given to the white child and the black child," it is not necessary that they "receive those equal facilities and advantages in the same school-room." Senator Joshua Hill of Georgia denounced the proposition that "if there be a hotel for the entertainment of travelers, and two classes stop at it, and there is one dining room for one class and one for another, served alike in all respects, with the same accommodations, the same attention to the guests, there is anything offensive or anything that denies the civil rights of one more than the other." Senator Augustus Merrimon of North Carolina conceded in debate that it would be "a violation of the fourteenth amendment" to exclude black children from the schools, but argued that "it is competent for the State to make a distinction on account of race or color if it shall make the same provision for the black race that it makes for the white race."

In response, supporters of the desegregation bill argued that official segregation is a form of inequality barred by the Fourteenth Amendment. Sumner declared that "any rule excluding a man on account of his color is an indignity, an insult, and a wrong." Representative John Lynch of Mississippi called racial segregation "an unjust and odious proscription." Many Republicans called segregation a form of "caste" legislation. Senator Frederick Frelinghuysen of New Jersey, floor leader for the bill after Sumner's death, called segregation by law "an enactment of personal degradation" and a form of "legalized disability or inferiority," effectively a denial of citizenship and a return to slavery. The chairman of the House Judiciary Committee stated that supporters of the bill "have all come to a conclusion on this subject . . . that these are rights guaranteed by the Constitution to every citizen, and that every citizen of the United States should have the means by which to enforce them." Senator George Edmunds of Vermont, responding to a proposal to allow separate but equal facilities, declared: "If there is anything in the fourteenth amendment it is exactly opposite to that." . . .

The constitutionality of segregation under the newly enacted Fourteenth Amendment was thus squarely at issue in the debates over the Sumner-Butler bill. Throughout these debates, supporters of the Fourteenth Amendment, with few exceptions, argued that de jure segregation of public schools is unconstitutional. On ten recorded votes in the Senate and eight recorded votes in the House of Representatives, a majority voted to prohibit de jure school segregation. Margins of victory were as high as 29–16 in the Senate and 141–72 on a procedural vote in the House. There were three recorded votes in the Senate and one in the House on motions to permit separate but equal facilities. All failed, by votes of 23–30, 21–26, and 16–28 in the Senate, and by a vote of 91–114 in the House. The only reason school desegregation legislation was not enacted is that, because of procedural problems and Democratic filibustering, a two-thirds vote was required at key junctures, and support for the measure fell just short of two-thirds.

In the end, in 1875, Congress voted to bar segregation in common carriers and places of public accommodation, and to remain silent on the issue of schools. For a variety of reasons, school desegregation was more controversial than desegregation of railroads or inns, and there were some legal doubts about whether access to the benefits of public spending (including publicly funded schools) was a matter of constitutional right. Segregation, however, was roundly rejected. A large majority, even at the end, voted against a separate-but-equal provision for schools. Despite its practical advantages to black students who often were relegated to inferior facilities, the majority believed that a separate-but-equal provision would "recognize a distinction in color which we ought not to recognize by any legislation of the Congress of the United States." James Monroe, an Ohio Republican, stated that legislation authorizing racial segregation would set a "dangerous precedent." Julius Burrows, a Michigan Republican, stated that "[i]f you cannot legislate free schools, I prefer that the bill should be altogether silent upon the question until other times and other men can do the subject justice." Black citizens, according to Monroe, "think their chances for good schools will be better under the Constitution with the protection of the courts than under a bill containing [a separate-but-equal clause]."

WHAT *BROWN V. BOARD OF EDUCATION* SHOULD HAVE SAID (Jack Balkin ed., 2001) (McConnell, J., concurring). From that evidence, one conclusion that could be drawn is "that segregated facilities were deemed inherently unequal, in violation of the Fourteenth Amendment." *Id.* at 165; see generally Michael W. McConnell, *Originalism and the Desegregation Decisions*, 81 Va. L. Rev. 947 (1995). Others, however, have criticized that conclusion, in part for its reliance on post-ratification evidence to determine original meaning. See, e.g., Michael J. Klarman, *Brown, Originalism, and Constitutional Theory: A Response to Professor McConnell*, 81 Va. L. Rev. 1881 (1995); Earl M. Maltz, *Originalism and the Desegregation Decisions—A Response to Professor McConnell*, 13 Const. Comm. 223 (1996).

There have been other arguments that *Brown* is consistent with the original meaning of the Fourteenth Amendment. *E.g.*, Steven G. Calabresi & Sarah E. Agudo, *Individual Rights Under State Constitutions When the Fourteenth Amendment Was Ratified in 1868: What Rights Are Deeply Rooted in American History and Tradition?* 87 Tex. L. Rev. 7, 108–112 (2008). For a review and critique of these arguments, see Ronald Turner, *The Problematics of the* Brown-*Is-Originalist Project*, 23 J. L. & Pol'y 591 (2015).

3.   Instead of relying on text and history, the opinion for the Court in *Brown* invoked the "modern authority" of social science. Footnote 11 cited seven articles and books purporting to show that segregated classrooms had harmful effects on the motivations and achievements of black schoolchildren. In subsequent years, much of this evidence was discredited (even by researchers supporting school desegregation). See Edmond Cahn, *Jurisprudence*, 30 N.Y.U. L. Rev. 150, 157–68 (1955); Symposium, *The Courts, Social Science, and School Desegregation*, 39 Law & Contemp. Probs. 1 (1975). For example, Kenneth Clark's study of the selection of black and white dolls, the first authority cited in the footnote, had no control group, and when replicated in jurisdictions with desegregated schools showed effects even larger than those in the segregated systems of the South. This lent weight to charges that the Court had based its decisions on the justices' own notions of policy rather than on enduring principles of constitutional law.

Justice Harlan's dissent in *Plessy* did not rest on propositions about psychology or social science. He simply stated that the Constitution does not "permit any public authority to know the race of those entitled to be protected in the enjoyment of [civil] rights." What kind of proposition was that? Could it be proved, or disproved, by social science evidence? Did the *Brown* Court embrace the *Plessy* dissent? If not, why not?

Legal historian Herbert Hovenkamp adds a further cautionary note. In *Social Science and Segregation Before* Brown, 1985 Duke L. J. 624, he shows that the overwhelming weight of social science evidence in the late nineteenth century and the first forty years of the twentieth century favored segregation. Using empirical techniques that now seem dubious or worse but were then cutting-edge, such as measuring cranial capacity by filling skulls with mustard seeds, experts from leading academic institutions openly taught that "the African race" was innately inferior and that "racial mixing" degraded the genetic capacities of both races. As Hovenkamp puts it, "the science of the day indicated that close racial mixing would impose costs far greater than the benefits to be derived therefrom." *Id.* at 651. For some, the spread of belief in Darwinian evolution only reinforced their racist thinking—providing support for the view that changes in social environment, such as education, could not affect genetically determined racial differences. In fact, Hovenkamp quotes "Brandeis briefs" filed in support of segregation in *Berea College* and *Buchanan v. Warley*, filled with citations to academic authority no less credentially impressive than that cited by the Court in *Brown*. "It is easy to assume that beginning with the Warren era the Supreme Court began studying and internalizing 'correct' social science," he writes. "Yet the history of science is more complex than that. . . . Science itself goes through rapid change, and a century from now today's science will be no more correct than the science of the Victorian Era is today."

Is Hovenkamp right? If not, why not? If so, what do you think of the Court's choice to base the *Brown* decision on the "modern authority" of social science?

4.   A reading of the briefs, arguments, and commentary on *Brown* suggests that stare decisis was seen as a bigger obstacle to reaching the result than history. Finding the right constitutional answer in *Brown* was not so difficult for the justices; what was difficult was figuring out how to extricate themselves from their own precedents. It was the Court's decision in *The Civil Rights Cases*, p. 1310, that struck down Congress's statutory effort to end segregation in common carriers. It was the Court's decision in *Plessy v. Ferguson*, p. 1338, that blessed Jim Crow and embraced the fiction of separate but equal. It was the Court that, in *Cumming v. Board of Education*, p. 1346, abandoned even the requirement that separate schools must be equal, and that, in *Berea College v. Kentucky*, p. 1349, allowed states to force even a private religious educational institution to segregate white students from black. The Court had a lot of words to eat.

By the ordinary standards of stare decisis, *Plessy* and these other Jim Crow cases were deeply entrenched. The general principles of Jim Crow, established in *Plessy*, had been affirmed and reaffirmed in dozens of cases over a period of more than half a century, often by unanimous Courts and with the support of some of the Court's most renowned figures, such as Oliver Wendell Holmes, Jr. Those principles had been acted upon and endorsed by the political branches—by Congress and, especially in the presidency of Woodrow Wilson, by the executive. The social and economic structure of a large part of the nation relied on the principles of *Plessy*; millions of dollars had been invested in separate schools, transportation systems, and public amenities. In light of the Court's repeated affirmation of the principles of *Plessy*, their democratic ratification, and the reliance interests built up around them, how much weight do you think the Court should have given *Plessy* in 1954? In your opinion, what does it take to justify overturning longstanding precedent?

Now take a close look at *Brown*'s treatment of the *Plessy* precedent. Did the Court overrule *Plessy*? What exactly was its status after *Brown*? According to the *Brown* opinion, was *Plessy* wrong *when it was decided*?

After quoting a state court opinion to the effect that school segregation has a detrimental impact on "the motivation of the child to learn," the Court stated: "Whatever may have been the extent of psychological knowledge at the time of *Plessy v. Ferguson*, this finding is amply supported by modern authority. Any language in *Plessy v. Ferguson* contrary to this finding is rejected. We conclude that in the field of public education the doctrine of 'separate but equal' has no place. Separate educational facilities are inherently unequal." What does this mean? *Plessy* was about segregation in railway cars. Any "language" in the *Plessy* opinion about education would have been dicta. Was the *holding* of *Plessy* left undisturbed? Was *Brown* limited to "the field of public education"? What about segregation in transportation, golf courses, airport coffee shops, public drinking fountains, or municipal auditoriums? Cases involving exactly these questions soon had to be decided by the lower courts, as discussed on p. 1373.

5.   Although *Brown* is widely revered for the justice of its result, even on this score it has been challenged. WHAT *BROWN V. BOARD OF EDUCATION* SHOULD HAVE SAID, a work already cited, contained various alternative opinions written by scholars and attorneys. There was an opinion for the Court, as well as opinions concurring or concurring in the judgment. But there was also a searing dissent, written by Professor Derrick Bell. He argued that "the detestable segregation in the public schools that the majority finds unconstitutional is a manifestation of the evil of racism the depths and pervasiveness of which this Court fails even to acknowledge, much less address and attempt to correct." *Id.* at 185 (Bell, J., dissenting). More specifically, he faulted *Brown* and its supporters for three things. First, the Court failed to recognize how segregation furthered the domination not only of blacks but poor whites. Second, the Court was exploiting the rights claims of black Americans, accepting them when convenient for domestic politics and international relations and discarding them when inconvenient. Finally, Bell criticized the paucity of the relief offered by the Court (a point that will be considered in more detail at p. 1370). Bell even went so far as to suggest that *Brown* erred in discarding *Plessy*: "I regret that the Court fails to see in these cases the opportunity to lay bare the simplistic hypocrisy of the 'separate but equal' standard, not by overturning *Plessy*, but by ordering its strict enforcement." *Id.* at 186. Crucial to Bell's argument was the fact—shamefully true in 1954, and shamefully true today—that the public educational system offers grossly disproportionate opportunities to white children and to children of color. Did *Brown* do more to advance racial equality in the United States than would have been done by a decision that applied *Plessy* with rigor, actually insisting on equality in white and black schools? Do you agree with Bell's conclusion? If not, why not?

6.   Now recall the five types of constitutional argument (p. 42). In which direction does each of these cut in *Brown*, and how forcefully? How much weight should be given here to each type of argument? And what do the Court's decisions about race and the Equal Protection Clause—from *Strauder* to *Plessy* to *Brown*—suggest are the strengths and limits of each type of constitutional argument?

Bolling v. Sharpe

347 U.S. 497 (1954)

■ MR. CHIEF JUSTICE WARREN delivered the opinion of the Court.

This case challenges the validity of segregation in the public schools of the District of Columbia. The petitioners, minors of the Negro race, allege that such segregation deprives them of due process of law under the Fifth Amendment. They were refused admission to a public school attended by white children solely because of their race. They sought the aid of the District Court for the District of Columbia in obtaining admission. That court dismissed their complaint. The Court granted a writ of certiorari before judgment in the Court of Appeals because of the importance of the constitutional question presented.

We have this day held that the Equal Protection Clause of the Fourteenth Amendment prohibits the states from maintaining racially segregated public schools. *Brown v. Board of Education.* The legal problem in the District of Columbia is somewhat different, however. The Fifth Amendment, which is applicable in the District of Columbia, does not contain an equal protection clause as does the Fourteenth Amendment which applies only to the states. But the concepts of equal protection and due process, both stemming from our American ideal of fairness, are not mutually exclusive. The "equal protection of the laws" is a more explicit safeguard of prohibited unfairness than "due process of law," and, therefore, we do not imply that the two are always interchangeable phrases. But, as this Court has recognized, discrimination may be so unjustifiable as to be violative of due process. *Detroit Bank v. United States*, 317 U.S. 329 (1943); *Currin v. Wallace*, 306 U.S. 1, 13–14 (1939); *Steward Machine Co. v. Davis*, 301 U.S. 548, 585 (1937).

Classifications based solely upon race must be scrutinized with particular care, since they are contrary to our traditions and hence constitutionally suspect. *Korematsu v. United States*, 323 U.S. 214, 216 (1944); *Hirabayashi v. United States*, 320 U.S. 81, 100 (1943). As long ago as 1896, this Court declared the principle "that the constitution of the United States, in its present form, forbids, so far as civil and political rights are concerned, discrimination by the general government, or by the states, against any citizen because of his race". And in *Buchanan v. Warley*, 245 U.S. 60 (1917), the Court held that a statute which limited the right of a property owner to convey his property to a person of another race was, as an unreasonable discrimination, a denial of due process of law.

Although the Court has not assumed to define "liberty" with any great precision, that term is not confined to mere freedom from bodily restraint. Liberty under law extends to the full range of conduct which the individual is free to pursue, and it cannot be restricted except for a proper governmental objective. Segregation in public education is not reasonably related to any proper governmental objective, and thus it imposes on Negro children of the District of Columbia a burden that constitutes an arbitrary deprivation of their liberty in violation of the Due Process Clause.

In view of our decision that the Constitution prohibits the states from maintaining racially segregated public schools, it would be unthinkable that the same Constitution would impose a lesser duty on the Federal Government. We hold that racial segregation in the public schools of the District of Columbia is a denial of the due process of law guaranteed by the Fifth Amendment to the Constitution.

For the reasons set out in *Brown v. Board of Education*, this case will be restored to the docket for reargument on Questions 4 and 5 previously propounded by the Court. *[For the content of these questions, see footnote 13 in* Brown v. Board of Education, *on p. 1359.—Editors]*

NOTES

1.   In *Bolling v. Sharpe*, decided the same day as *Brown*, the Court extended its ruling to schools in the District of Columbia, which is an instrumentality of the federal government. On first glance it might seem obvious that the principle in *Brown* applies to the national government. But what, exactly, is the constitutional basis for that conclusion? The Fourteenth Amendment mentions no limit on the federal government; the prohibitions of Section 1 begin: "No State shall. . . ." In fact, Section 5 *empowers* the federal government. And if the Fourteenth Amendment's Equal Protection Clause did forbid the federal government to use race-based classifications, would that raise constitutional doubts about some Reconstruction statutes that aided the newly freed slaves, such as the Freedmen's Bureau Act? (On that question, see p. 1393.) Was it really "unthinkable" that the Reconstruction amendments would reflect a greater distrust of the states, barring state segregation in education but imposing no similar limit on the federal government with respect to the District of Columbia? The question is thus more complicated than it might seem. What is the constitutional basis for the decision? Consider five possibilities.

First, there is the basis given by the Court, namely the Fifth Amendment's Due Process Clause. The idea is that "due process" in the Fifth Amendment includes the content of "equal protection" in the Fourteenth Amendment, a kind of double-reverse-ricochet-incorporation of equal protection principles. Are you persuaded? Most commenters have not been kind to this reasoning. For example, John Hart Ely said, "I would have strained sorely to side with the Chief Justice had the language of the Fifth Amendment been able to bear his construction. It's hard to see how it can." John Hart Ely, DEMOCRACY AND DISTRUST: A THEORY OF JUDICIAL REVIEW 33 (1980). Moreover, The Court's reliance on the Fifth Amendment Due Process Clause raises a puzzle. The Fifth Amendment was ratified in 1791. No one thought it forbade racial discrimination, which was common in federal law and practice. Does *Bolling* hold that the meaning of the Due Process Clause changed between 1791 and 1954? It is one thing for *interpretations* of the Constitution to change (because of changes in circumstances or otherwise). But does the Constitution mean one thing when ratified and something entirely different years later? By reading "equal protection" into "due process" in an amendment enacted in 1791, was the Court interpreting the Constitution or revising it?

Second, there is a basis the Court considered and rejected, namely a fundamental right to education. A draft of *Bolling* had relied on the "fundamental liberty" of education and not just the pure equality argument of the final opinion. It concluded: "Just as a government may not impose arbitrary restrictions on the parent's right to educate his child, the government must not impose arbitrary restraints on access to the education which the government itself provides." The draft cited, among other things, *Pierce v. Society of Sisters*, p. 1534. See Dennis J. Hutchinson, *Unanimity and Desegregation: Decisionmaking in the Supreme Court, 1948–1958*, 68 Geo. L. J. 1, 45, 94 (1979). It is suspected that the earlier, "fundamental liberty" analysis was eliminated at the insistence of Justice Black, who decried the Court's recognition of unenumerated rights, or of Justice Frankfurter, who had criticized *Pierce*. Hutchinson, at 48–50. Would recognizing or expanding a fundamental right to education have been a better way to decide *Bolling*? What provision of the Constitution would that right be traced to?

Third, consider whether a general principle of equal treatment can be deduced from various constitutional provisions. One possibility is the Citizenship Clause of the Fourteenth Amendment, which grants citizenship without specifically mentioning equality or rights. See Ryan C. Williams, *Originalism and the Other Desgregation Decision*, 99 Va. L. Rev. 493 (2013). Could this provision contains an additional equality principle? Another possibility is to look to other provisions of the original Constitution, such as the Privileges and Immunities Clause of Article IV, which requires that out-of-staters be treated like in-staters for certain purposes; the Commerce Clause, which could be used by Congress to ensure that states did not favor their own merchants over foreign ones in certain ways; and Article III's grant of diversity jurisdiction, intended to prevent partiality by state courts when the residents of a state are in litigation with out-of-staters. Cf. WHAT *BROWN V. BOARD OF EDUCATION* SHOULD HAVE SAID 141 n.10 (Jack Balkin ed., 2001) (Ely, J., concurring). But why is the principle "equal treatment," instead of something narrower, like "no discrimination in favor of D.C. residents against residents of the states"? Or broader, like "no irrational laws"? How does one decide the scope of the abstract principle deduced from such specific and relatively narrow provisions? Did this principle exist in 1791 or only later? Was the Equal Protection Clause even necessary? And if there is such an equal treatment principle, recall the critique of *Brown* by Derrick Bell (see p. 1365): would the principle require *Bolling* or separate-but-really-truly-equal?

Fourth, does it matter that Congress never actually passed legislation segregating the D.C. schools? There is a line of thought going back to Blackstone that courts should engage in "equitable interpretation" of statutes. A legislature may pass a law abridging the natural rights of the people (except where those rights are also protected by positive law, such as the Constitution). But to enact such a law the legislature must speak clearly. A legislature's garbled speech, or its silence, will not suffice to abridge the rights of the people. Here, because the segregation of the D.C. schools had never been clearly required by Congress, it lacked the requisite authority. Cf. WHAT *BROWN V. BOARD OF EDUCATION* SHOULD HAVE SAID 158, 165–168 (Jack Balkin ed., 2001) (McConnell, J., concurring). But who determines the rights of the people, if they are not the ones listed in the Constitution? Are they determined as of 1791 or now? And does it matter that this principle of interpretation from Blackstone (and before him, all the way back to Aristotle) is not mentioned in the Constitution itself?

Finally, perhaps *Bolling* should be understood on purely pragmatic grounds: Southern resistance to desegregation would have been even stronger if the federal government had been exempted from the same rules. The prediction seems valid. But if that is the rationale for the decision, what do you make of the Court's extension of all of its Equal Protection Clause holdings to the federal government, including holdings that invalidate affirmative action in government contracts and sex discrimination in social welfare programs? More generally, what would happen if this methodology were adopted elsewhere? What are the opportunities, and what are the dangers, if the Court can make constitutional decisions that rest exclusively on policy and not on text, historical context, structure, and practice and precedent? If policy-only decisions are legitimate, and a major question emerged on which you disagreed with the policy views of the justices, is there anything you could say to them to dissuade them from enacting their policy views as constitutional principles?

[*Assignment 68*]

Brown v. Board of Education (Brown II)

349 U.S. 294 (1955)

■ MR. CHIEF JUSTICE WARREN delivered the opinion of the Court.

These cases were decided on May 17, 1954. The opinions of that date, declaring the fundamental principle that racial discrimination in public education is unconstitutional, are incorporated herein by reference. All provisions of federal, state, or local law requiring or permitting such discrimination must yield to this principle. There remains for consideration the manner in which relief is to be accorded.

Because these cases arose under different local conditions and their disposition will involve a variety of local problems, we requested further argument on the question of relief. In view of the nationwide importance of the decision, we invited the Attorney General of the United States and the Attorneys General of all states requiring or permitting racial discrimination in public education to present their views on that question. The parties, the United States, and the States of Florida, North Carolina, Arkansas, Oklahoma, Maryland, and Texas filed briefs and participated in the oral argument.

These presentations were informative and helpful to the Court in its consideration of the complexities arising from the transition to a system of public education freed of racial discrimination. The presentations also demonstrated that substantial steps to eliminate racial discrimination in public schools have already been taken, not only in some of the communities in which these cases arose, but in some of the states appearing as *amici curiae*, and in other states as well.

Full implementation of these constitutional principles may require solution of varied local school problems. School authorities have the primary responsibility for elucidating, assessing, and solving these problems; courts will have to consider whether the action of school authorities constitutes good faith implementation of the governing constitutional principles. Because of their proximity to local conditions and the possible need for further hearings, the courts which originally heard these cases can best perform this judicial appraisal. Accordingly, we believe it appropriate to remand the cases to those courts.

In fashioning and effectuating the decrees, the courts will be guided by equitable principles. Traditionally, equity has been characterized by a practical flexibility in shaping its remedies and by a facility for adjusting and reconciling public and private needs. These cases call for the exercise of these traditional attributes of equity power. At stake is the personal interest of the plaintiffs in admission to public schools as soon as practicable on a nondiscriminatory basis. To effectuate this interest may call for elimination of a variety of obstacles in making the transition to school systems operated in accordance with the constitutional principles set forth in our May 17, 1954, decision. Courts of equity may properly take into account the public interest in the elimination of such obstacles in a systematic and effective manner. But it should go without saying that the vitality of these constitutional principles cannot be allowed to yield simply because of disagreement with them.

While giving weight to these public and private considerations, the courts will require that the defendants make a prompt and reasonable start toward full compliance with our May 17, 1954, ruling. Once such a start has been made, the courts may find that additional time is necessary to carry out the ruling in an effective manner. The burden rests upon the defendants to establish that such time is necessary in the public interest and is consistent with good faith compliance at the earliest practicable date. To that end, the courts may consider problems related to administration, arising from the physical condition of the school plant, the school transportation system, personnel, revision of school districts and attendance areas into compact units to achieve a system of determining admission to the public schools on a nonracial basis, and revision of local laws and regulations which may be necessary in solving the foregoing problems. They will also consider the adequacy of any plans the defendants may propose to meet these problems and to effectuate a transition to a racially nondiscriminatory school system. During this period of transition, the courts will retain jurisdiction of these cases.

The judgments below, except that in the Delaware case, are accordingly reversed and the cases are remanded to the District Courts to take such proceedings and enter such orders and decrees consistent with this opinion as are necessary and proper to admit to public schools on a racially nondiscriminatory basis with all deliberate speed the parties to these cases. The judgment in the Delaware case—ordering the immediate admission of the plaintiffs to schools previously attended only by white children—is affirmed on the basis of the principles stated in our May 17, 1954, opinion, but the case is remanded to the Supreme Court of Delaware for such further proceedings as that Court may deem necessary in light of this opinion.

NOTES

1. Whatever impact policy should have when a court is interpreting the substantive requirements of the Constitution, it is traditionally a major consideration when courts are granting and fashioning equitable remedies. E.g., *Weinberger v. Romero-Barcelo*, 456 U.S. 305, 312 (1982) (" 'The essence of equity jurisdiction has been the power of the Chancellor to do equity and to mould each decree to the necessities of the particular case. Flexibility rather than rigidity has distinguished it.' " (quoting *Hecht Co. v. Bowles*, 321 U.S. 321, 329 (1944)). Indeed, when a court of equity is deciding whether to grant an injunction, one traditional requirement—mentioned briefly in *Brown II*—is that the injunction must not disserve the public interest. After the remand in *Brown II*, what if it were clear to a lower court that forced integration would provoke massive resistance, disruption, and even violence? Would that mean the public interest would be disserved by an injunction that required immediate integration? Or would the public interest be disserved by any delay in obeying the mandate of the Constitution? Why subordinate the interest of a black child in a segregated school to the interest of a segregationist?

In *Brown II*, the Court remanded to lower courts to fashion the relief, instructing them to act with "all deliberate speed." Other remedial options might have included (1) a nationwide injunction requiring the integration of all public schools that fall; (2) a nationwide injunction with a one-year delay to allow for the massive logistics of reorganizing the nation's public schools; (3) further investigation and remedial action by the Supreme Court itself instead of a remand that put the lower courts in charge of the remedy; or (4) an injunction ordering that the plaintiffs in the particular cases before the court be allowed to attend whatever school they would be entitled to attend but for their race, while waiting to order further relief until other cases were brought by other plaintiffs. Was the Court's choice a wise accommodation of reality, or a feeble toleration of the systematic violation of constitutional rights? Consider the following critique of *Brown II*, offered by an NAACP lawyer: "In essence the Court considered the potential damage to white Americans resulting from the diminution of privilege as more critical than continued damage to the underprivileged. The Court found that public reasons—the offense to white sensibilities—existed to justify the delay in school desegregation. Worse still, it gave the primary responsibility for achieving educational equality to those who had established the segregated institutions." Lewis M. Steel, *A Critic's View of the Warren Court—Nine Men in Black Who Think White*, N.Y. Times Mag. (Oct. 13, 1968). Do you agree? If so, what remedy should the Court have given?

More broadly, think about how a court should remedy the violation of a constitutional right. Should the aim be to match the right and remedy perfectly? (What would that look like in *Brown*?) Or should the courts take into account the kinds of considerations that are traditional for equitable remedies, such as the availability of other remedies; the likely burdens on the courts, the plaintiff, and the defendant; and the public interest? Cf. *Lemon v. Kurtzman*, 411 U.S. 192, 200 (1973) (plurality opinion) ("[I]n constitutional adjudication as elsewhere, equitable remedies are a special blend of what is necessary, what is fair, and what is workable."). Should they take into account those equitable considerations even though the result will sometimes be a remedy that is broader than the plaintiff's right, and sometimes a remedy that falls short of the plaintiff's right?

2.   There was widespread resistance to *Brown* by pro-segregation elected officials in the South. In Virginia, for example, the General Assembly passed laws that closed the integrated public schools, eliminated their state funding, and provided tuition grants for use in private schools. A Virginia court struck down the legislation as a violation of the Virginia Constitution's requirement that the state provide a system of free public education. The legislature responded in April 1959 by adopting a so-called "freedom of choice" program, which included the repeal of the state's compulsory school attendance laws. Prince Edward County thereupon refused to levy school taxes for the 1959–1960 year, and its public schools did not open in the fall of 1959, even though the public schools of every other county in Virginia did. A group calling itself the Prince Edward School Foundation set up private schools exclusively for white children. And the public schools of the county remained closed for four years. In *Griffin v. County School Board of Prince Edward County*, 377 U.S. 218 (1964), the Supreme Court upheld a lower court's injunction against the Prince Edward County plan:

> [W]e agree with the District Court that, under the circumstances here, closing the Prince Edward County schools while public schools in all the other counties of Virginia were being maintained denied the petitioners and class of Negro students they represent the equal protection of the laws guaranteed by the Fourteenth Amendment. . . . [T]he record in the present case could not be clearer that Prince Edward's public schools were closed and private schools operated in their place with state and county assistance, for one reason, and one reason only: to ensure, through measures taken by the county and the State, that white and colored children in Prince Edward County would not, under any circumstances, go to the same school. Whatever nonracial grounds might support a State's allowing a county to abandon public schools, the object must be a constitutional one, and grounds of race and opposition to desegregation do not qualify as constitutional.

Id. at 225, 231. For further discussion of Southern resistance, see p. 1391.

Some segregationist officials in the South argued that *Brown* was wrong on the merits and that they were therefore not bound by it, echoing arguments of Thomas Jefferson and James Madison a century and a half earlier in the Virginia and Kentucky Resolutions. In response, in *Cooper v. Aaron*, 358 U.S. 1 (1958), the Court declared that since *Marbury* the supremacy of the judiciary has "been respected by this Court and the Country as a permanent and indispensable feature of our constitutional system." See p. 400. Yet despite the Court's pronouncement about its own role, and despite its continuing adherence to *Brown*, there are questions about how much change there was on the ground. Indeed, "[b]y the end of 1964, ten years after *Brown*, more than ninety-seven percent of all Southern black children still attended segregated schools." Julian Bond, *With All Deliberate Speed:* Brown v. Board of Education, 90 Ind. L. J. 1671, 1677 (2015). Not until the Civil Rights Act of 1964—and especially the federal regulations issued the following year that tied federal funding to desegregation—would there begin to be significant integration in previously segregated public schools.

3.   The history of resistance and judicial enforcement after *Brown* has provoked great controversy about the effectiveness of the judiciary as an instrument of social change. In a study of *Brown* and its aftermath, Gerald Rosenberg explored what actually succeeded in rooting out segregation. He had some praise for the Court, noting that until the beginning of the 1970s "the Court remained steadfast in its commitment to end public-school segregation." Gerald N. Rosenberg, THE HOLLOW HOPE: CAN COURTS BRING ABOUT SOCIAL CHANGE? 46 (2d. ed., 2008). That could not be said of the other branches of the national government: "Congressional and executive branch action in the area of public-school desegregation was virtually non-existent until the passage of the 1964 Civil Rights Act. In stark contrast to the actions of the Supreme Court in *Brown*, the other two branches of the federal government remained essentially passive." *Id.* But judicial steadfastness was not enough. Rosenberg ultimately concludes:

> The use of the courts in the civil rights movement is considered the paradigm of a successful strategy for social change. . . . Yet, a closer examination reveals that before Congress and the executive branch acted, courts had virtually no direct effect on enforcing discrimination in the key fields of education, voting, transportation, accommodations and public places, and housing. Courageous and praiseworthy decisions were rendered, and nothing changed. Only when Congress and the executive branch acted in tandem with the courts did change occur in these fields. In terms of judicial effects, then, *Brown* and its progeny stand for the proposition that courts are impotent to produce significant social reform.

Id. at 70–71 (2d. ed., 2008). An alternative account, by Michael Klarman, sees *Brown* as more consequential but only indirectly—*Brown* did not itself effect change, but it motivated the supporters and the opponents of racial integration. Michael J. Klarman, FROM JIM CROW TO CIVIL RIGHTS: THE SUPREME COURT AND THE STRUGGLE FOR RACIAL EQUALITY (2006). Less polemical, but more rich in showing how much of the civil rights movement happened outside of the courts, is Tomiko Brown-Nagin, COURAGE TO DISSENT: ATLANTA AND THE LONG HISTORY OF THE CIVIL RIGHTS MOVEMENT (2011). In her study, Brown-Nagin shows the contestation between political and legal strategies within the civil rights movement. Given these revisions of what was once the conventional Court-centric and *Brown*-centric account, how should we assess the impact of the decision? Was it a powerful force for social change? Was it a missed opportunity? Was it both? Was it neither? What lessons should we learn, if any, about the enforcement of the Constitution?

A NOTE ON *BROWDER V. GAYLE*

On its own terms, *Brown* was limited to segregation in public education. It did not directly overrule *Plessy*, other than to disapprove of it in that context. How was *Brown* extended beyond education?

In fact, the Court never wrote an opinion explaining the application of *Brown* to cases outside the field of education. Instead, the Court resolved a string of cases involving other facilities by per curiam orders and summary dispositions, without any discussion of the merits. See, e.g., *Schiro v. Bynum*, 375 U.S. 395 (1964) (per curiam) (municipal auditorium); *Turner v. City of Memphis*, 369 U.S. 350 (1962) (per curiam) (restaurant in municipal airport); *State Athletic Comm'n v. Dorsey*, 359 U.S. 533 (1959) (per curiam) (athletic contests); *New Orleans City Park Improvement Ass'n v. Detiege*, 358 U.S. 54 (1958) (per curiam) (public golf course and parks); *Gayle v. Browder*, 352 U.S. 903 (1956) (per curiam) (public transportation); *Holmes v. City of Atlanta*, 350 U.S. 879 (1955) (per curiam) (municipal golf courses); *Mayor of Baltimore City v. Dawson*, 350 U.S. 877 (1955) (per curiam) (public beaches); *Muir v. Louisville Park Theatrical Ass'n*, 347 U.S. 971 (1954) (per curiam) (municipal amphitheaters).

Finally, in *Johnson v. Virginia*, 373 U.S. 61, 62 (1963) (per curiam), a case decided eight years after *Brown* involving a segregated courtroom, the Court announced that "a State may not constitutionally require segregation of public facilities." The reason the Court gave was that this issue was "no longer open to question." Three cases were cited for this proposition: *Mayor of Baltimore City v. Dawson*, which had supplied no reasons; *Turner v. City of Memphis*, which rested solely on the precedents of *Dawson* and *Brown*, with no explanation for the extension of the holding; and *Brown* itself, which appeared to be based, in some sense, on the special character of education.

Among the questions raised by the per curiam opinions extending *Brown* is how lower courts should treat Supreme Court precedent. In non-education contexts, were the lower courts bound to adhere to *Plessy* until the Supreme Court ruled separate-but-equal unconstitutional, one context at a time? Or should the lower courts have anticipated where the Supreme Court was going? In a subsequent case, the Supreme Court insisted that lower courts must "follow the [Supreme Court] case which directly controls, leaving to this Court the prerogative of overruling its own decisions." *Rodriguez de Quijas v. Shearson/American Express, Inc.*, 490 U.S. 477, 484 (1989). If you had been a federal district judge in 1956, confronted with a challenge to *de jure* segregation of a public transportation facility—a context to which the Court had not yet extended *Brown*—would you have adhered to *Plessy*?

A case that raised that question was *Browder v. Gayle*, 142 F.Supp.707 (M.D. Ala. 1956), decided by a three-judge panel, which divided 2–1. In the majority opinion, Judge Rives noted *Plessy*'s holding, the rejection of *Plessy* in public education, and lower court decisions striking down segregation in public golf courses (decisions upheld by the Supreme Court). Judge Rives then said:

> Even a statute can be repealed by implication. A fortiori, a judicial decision, which is simply evidence of the law and not the law itself, may be so impaired by later decisions as no longer to furnish any reliable evidence.

> We cannot in good conscience perform our duty as judges by blindly following the precedent of *Plessy v. Ferguson*, when our study leaves us in complete agreement with the Fourth Circuit's opinion in *Flemming v. South Carolina Electric & Gas Co.*, 224 F.2d 752, appeal dismissed April 23, 1956, 351 U.S. 901, that the separate but equal doctrine can no longer be safely followed as a correct statement of the law. [*Flemming was a transportation case in which*

the Fourth Circuit concluded that Brown *and* Bolling, *"which relate to public schools, leave no doubt that the separate but equal doctrine approved in* Plessy v. Ferguson *has been repudiated." The appeal of the Fourth Circuit's decision was dismissed by the Supreme Court, in a per curiam opinion that consisted of four words and a citation: "The appeal is dismissed.* Slaker v. O'Connor, *278 U.S. 188 (1929)."—Editors]* In fact, we think that *Plessy v. Ferguson* has been impliedly, though not explicitly, overruled, and that, under the later decisions, there is now no rational basis upon which the separate but equal doctrine can be validly applied to public carrier transportation within the City of Montgomery and its police jurisdiction. The application of that doctrine cannot be justified as a proper execution of the state police power.

We hold that the statutes and ordinances requiring segregation of the white and colored races on the motor buses of a common carrier of passengers in the City of Montgomery and its police jurisdiction violate the due process and equal protection of the law clauses of the Fourteenth Amendment to the Constitution of the United States. . . .

Id. at 716–717.

In dissent, District Judge Lynne wrote:

For many years as a trial judge in the state and federal systems I have endeavored faithfully to understand and apply precedents established by the opinions of appellate courts. This was not a blind obedience to a legalistic formula embodied in the rule of stare decisis. It was the result of a simple belief that the laws which regulate the conduct, the affairs, and sometimes the emotions of our people should evidence not only the appearance but also the spirit of stability.

Judges of trial courts frequently find themselves in disagreement with the rationale of an old, but clearly controlling precedent. . . . But they are neither designed nor equipped to perform the legislative function of putting off the old and putting on the new. To arrogate to themselves this prerogative, in my humble opinion, would be the first, fatal step in making hollow the proud boast that ours is a "government of laws and not of men." . . .

The majority recognize, [and] it was conceded in oral arguments by counsel for plaintiffs, that *Plessy v. Ferguson*, is precisely in point, and that its holding has been repeatedly followed in later transportation cases. Its authority obviously was unaffected by the action of the Supreme Court in dismissing the appeal in *South Carolina Electric & Gas Co. v. Flemming.* The citation of *Slaker v. O'Connor* is convincing that it did not place the stamp of its approval upon the decision of the Fourth Circuit in *Flemming v. South Carolina Electric & Gas Co.*, but simply concluded that its judgment was not final and hence that the appeal did not lie. . . .

A comparatively new principle of pernicious implications has found its way into our jurisprudence. Lower courts may feel free to disregard the precise precedent of a Supreme Court opinion if they perceive a "pronounced new doctrinal trend" in its later decisions which would influence a cautious judge to prophesy that in due time and in a proper case such established precedent will be overturned explicitly.

Id. at 717–719. Who was right about what a lower-court judge should do? Why? How much weight, if any, should lower courts put on orders from the Supreme Court that might suggest the inclination of the justices without directly addressing the question?

However you answer those questions, are you willing to be consistent when applied to other lines of developing precedent, even when you disagree with the direction in which the Court seems to be leaning? For example, in the early 1990s many commentators predicted (wrongly) that the Court would reverse *Roe v. Wade*; in the 2000s, many commentators predicted (rightly) that the Court would strike down a broad swathe of restrictions on political donations and spending; in the 2010s, many commentators predicted (rightly) that the Court would hold unconstitutional state laws recognizing only opposite-sex marriages; and in the same decade many commentators predicted (wrongly) that the Court would more or less prohibit race-based affirmative action in higher education. Should lower-court judges have followed all of these apparent trends in the Supreme Court's decisions? None of the trends? Only some? Why?

————

It took the Supreme Court more than a dozen years to extend the principle of *Brown* to marriage. It did so in the landmark decision which you will read next:

Loving v. Virginia
388 U.S. 1 (1967)

■ MR. CHIEF JUSTICE WARREN delivered the opinion of the Court.

This case presents a constitutional question never addressed by this Court: whether a statutory scheme adopted by the State of Virginia to prevent marriages between persons solely on the basis of racial classifications violates the Equal Protection and Due Process Clauses of the Fourteenth Amendment. For reasons which seem to us to reflect the central meaning of those constitutional commands, we conclude that these statutes cannot stand consistently with the Fourteenth Amendment.

In June 1958, two residents of Virginia, Mildred Jeter, a Negro woman, and Richard Loving, a white man, were married in the District of Columbia pursuant to its laws. Shortly after their marriage, the Lovings returned to Virginia and established their marital abode in Caroline County. At the October Term, 1958, of the Circuit Court of Caroline County, a grand jury issued an indictment charging the Lovings with violating Virginia's ban on interracial marriages. On January 6, 1959, the Lovings pleaded guilty to the charge and were sentenced to one year in jail; however, the trial judge suspended the sentence for a period of 25 years on the condition that the Lovings leave the State and not return to Virginia together for 25 years. He stated in an opinion that:

> Almighty God created the races white, black, yellow, malay and red, and he placed them on separate continents. And but for the interference with his arrangement there would be no cause for such marriages. The fact that he separated the races shows that he did not intend for the races to mix.

After their convictions, the Lovings took up residence in the District of Columbia. On November 6, 1963, they filed a motion in the state trial court to vacate the judgment and set aside the sentence on the ground that the statutes which they had violated were repugnant to the Fourteenth Amendment. . . . [The] state trial judge denied the motion to vacate the sentences, and the Lovings perfected an appeal to the Supreme Court of Appeals of Virginia. . . . The Supreme Court of Appeals upheld the constitutionality of the antimiscegenation statutes and, after modifying the sentence, affirmed the convictions.

The two statutes under which appellants were convicted and sentenced are part of a comprehensive statutory scheme aimed at prohibiting and punishing interracial marriages. The Lovings were convicted of violating § 20–58 of the Virginia Code:

> Leaving State to evade law.—If any white person and colored person shall go out of this State, for the purpose of being married, and with the intention of returning, and be married out of it, and afterwards return to and reside in it, cohabiting as man and wife, they shall be punished as provided in § 20–59, and the marriage shall be governed by the same law as if it had been solemnized in this State. The fact of their cohabitation here as man and wife shall be evidence of their marriage.

Section 20–59, which defines the penalty for miscegenation, provides:

> Punishment for marriage.—If any white person intermarry with a colored person, or any colored person intermarry with a white person, he shall be guilty of a felony and shall be punished by confinement in the penitentiary for not less than one nor more than five years.

Virginia is now one of 16 States which prohibit and punish marriages on the basis of racial classifications. Penalties for miscegenation arose as an incident to slavery and have been common in Virginia since the colonial period. The present statutory scheme dates from the adoption of the Racial Integrity Act of 1924, passed during the period of extreme nativism which followed the end of the First World War. The central features of this Act, and current Virginia law, are the absolute prohibition of a "white person" marrying other than another "white person, a prohibition against issuing marriage licenses until the issuing official is satisfied that the applicants" statements as to their race are correct, certificates of "racial composition" to be kept by both local and state registrars, and the carrying forward of earlier prohibitions against racial intermarriage.

I

In upholding the constitutionality of these provisions in the decision below, the Supreme Court of Appeals of Virginia referred to its 1955 decision in *Naim v. Naim,* 197 Va. 80, as stating the reasons supporting the validity of these laws. In *Naim,* the state court concluded that the State's legitimate purposes were "to preserve the racial integrity of its citizens," and to prevent "the corruption of blood," "a mongrel breed of citizens," and "the obliteration of racial pride," obviously an endorsement of the doctrine of White Supremacy. The court also reasoned that marriage has traditionally been subject to state regulation without federal intervention, and, consequently, the regulation of marriage should be left to exclusive state control by the Tenth Amendment.

. . . The State argues that the meaning of the Equal Protection Clause, as illuminated by the statements of the Framers, is only that state penal laws containing an interracial element as part of the definition of the offense must apply equally to whites and Negroes in the sense that members of each race are punished to the same degree. Thus, the State contends that, because its miscegenation statutes punish equally both the white and the Negro participants in an interracial marriage, these statutes, despite their reliance on racial classifications do not constitute an invidious discrimination based upon race. The second argument advanced by the

State assumes the validity of its equal application theory. The argument is that, if the Equal Protection Clause does not outlaw miscegenation statutes because of their reliance on racial classifications, the question of constitutionality would thus become whether there was any rational basis for a State to treat interracial marriages differently from other marriages. On this question, the State argues, the scientific evidence is substantially in doubt and, consequently, this Court should defer to the wisdom of the state legislature in adopting its policy of discouraging interracial marriages.

Because we reject the notion that the mere "equal application" of a statute containing racial classifications is enough to remove the classifications from the Fourteenth Amendment's proscription of all invidious racial discriminations, we do not accept the State's contention that these statutes should be upheld if there is any possible basis for concluding that they serve a rational purpose. . . . [In] cases involving distinctions not drawn according to race, the Court has merely asked whether there is any rational foundation for the discriminations, and has deferred to the wisdom of the state legislatures. In the case at bar, however, we deal with statutes containing racial classifications, and the fact of equal application does not immunize the statute from the very heavy burden of justification which the Fourteenth Amendment has traditionally required of state statutes drawn according to race.

The State argues that statements in the Thirty-ninth Congress about the time of the passage of the Fourteenth Amendment indicate that the Framers did not intend the Amendment to make unconstitutional state miscegenation laws. Many of the statements alluded to by the State concern the debates over the Freedmen's Bureau Bill, which President Johnson vetoed, and the Civil Rights Act of 1866, enacted over his veto. While these statements have some relevance to the intention of Congress in submitting the Fourteenth Amendment, it must be understood that they pertained to the passage of specific statutes and not to the broader, organic purpose of a constitutional amendment. As for the various statements directly concerning the Fourteenth Amendment, we have said in connection with a related problem, that although these historical sources "cast some light" they are not sufficient to resolve the problem; "(a)t best, they are inconclusive. The most avid proponents of the post-War Amendments undoubtedly intended them to remove all legal distinctions among 'all persons born or naturalized in the United States.' Their opponents, just as certainly, were antagonistic to both the letter and the spirit of the Amendments and wished them to have the most limited effect." *Brown v. Board of Education*, 347 U.S. 483, 489 (1954). See also *Strauder v. State of West Virginia*, 100 U.S. 303, 310 (1880). We have rejected the proposition that the debates in the Thirty-ninth Congress or in the state legislatures which ratified the Fourteenth Amendment supported the theory advanced by the State, that the requirement of equal protection of the laws is satisfied by penal laws defining offenses based on racial classifications so long as white and Negro participants in the offense were similarly punished. *McLaughlin v. State of Florida*, 379 U.S. 184 (1964).

The State finds support for its "equal application" theory in the decision of the Court in *Pace v. State of Alabama*, 106 U.S. 583 (1883). In that case, the Court upheld a conviction under an Alabama statute forbidding adultery or fornication between a white person and a Negro which imposed a greater penalty than that of a statute proscribing similar conduct by members of the same race. The Court reasoned that the statute could not be said to discriminate against Negroes because the punishment for each participant in the offense was the same. However, as recently as the 1964 Term, in rejecting the reasoning of that case, we stated *"Pace* represents a limited view of the Equal Protection Clause which has not withstood analysis in the subsequent decisions of this Court." *McLaughlin v. Florida*, 379 U.S. at 188. As we there demonstrated, the Equal Protection Clause requires the consideration of whether the classifications drawn by any statute constitute an arbitrary and invidious discrimination. The clear and central purpose of the Fourteenth Amendment was to eliminate all official state sources of invidious racial discrimination in the States. *Slaughter-House Cases*, 83 U.S. (16 Wall.) 36, 71 (1873).

There can be no question but that Virginia's miscegenation statutes rest solely upon distinctions drawn according to race. The statutes proscribe generally accepted conduct if engaged in by members of different races. . . . At the very least, the Equal Protection Clause demands that racial classifications, especially suspect in criminal statutes, be subjected to the "most rigid scrutiny," *Korematsu v. United States*, 323 U.S. 214, 216 (1944), and, if they are ever to be upheld, they must be shown to be necessary to the accomplishment of some permissible state objective, independent of the racial discrimination which it was the object of the Fourteenth Amendment to eliminate.

There is patently no legitimate overriding purpose independent of invidious racial discrimination which justifies this classification. The fact that Virginia prohibits only interracial marriages involving white persons demonstrates that the racial classifications must stand on their own justification, as measures designed to maintain White Supremacy.[11] We have consistently denied the constitutionality of measures which restrict the rights of citizens on account of race. There can be no doubt that restricting the freedom to marry solely because of racial classifications violates the central meaning of the Equal Protection Clause.

II

These statutes also deprive the Lovings of liberty without due process of law in violation of the Due Process Clause of the Fourteenth Amendment. The freedom to marry has long been recognized as one of the vital personal rights essential to the orderly pursuit of happiness by free men.

Marriage is one of the "basic civil rights of man," fundamental to our very existence and survival. *Skinner v. State of Oklahoma*, 316 U.S. 535, 541 (1942). To deny this fundamental freedom on so unsupportable a basis as the racial classifications embodied in these statutes, classifications so directly subversive of the principle of equality at the heart of the Fourteenth Amendment, is surely to deprive all the State's citizens of liberty without due process of law. The Fourteenth Amendment requires that the freedom of choice to marry not be restricted by invidious racial discriminations. Under our Constitution, the freedom to marry or

---

[11] Appellants point out that the State's concern in these statutes, as expressed in the words of the 1924 Act's title, "An Act to Preserve Racial Integrity," extends only to the integrity of the white race. While Virginia prohibits whites from marrying any nonwhite (subject to the exception for the descendants of Pocahontas), Negroes, Orientals, and any other racial class may intermarry without statutory interference. Appellants contend that this distinction renders Virginia's miscegenation statutes arbitrary and unreasonable even assuming the constitutional validity of an official purpose to preserve "racial integrity." We need not reach this contention because we find the racial classifications in these statutes repugnant to the Fourteenth Amendment, even assuming an even-handed state purpose to protect the "integrity" of all races.

not marry, a person of another race resides with the individual and cannot be infringed by the State. These convictions must be reversed.

■ [JUSTICE STEWART's concurrence is omitted.]

NOTES

1.   The statute in *Loving* did not even treat blacks and whites the same; only whites were forbidden to marry outside their race. (See footnote 11 of the opinion.) But assume, as the Court apparently did, that the statute did treat blacks and whites according to the same rule—forbidding both from marrying outside of their race. Would there be a denial of "the *equal* protection of the laws"? If so, why? Is it because the Equal Protection Clause forbids all state classifications on the basis of race? All classifications designed to subordinate a particular race? All classifications that have the effect of subordinating a particular race? (Does it matter which race?) How would you state the combined principle of *Brown* and *Loving*?

2.   About eighty years earlier, in *Pace v. Alabama*, 106 U.S. 583 (1883), the Supreme Court upheld an Alabama law prescribing a harsher sentence for cohabitating black and white couples than the sentence for cohabiting couples of the same race. The Court reasoned that because the law against interracial cohabitation was a distinct statute from the law penalizing same-race cohabitation, the disparate punishments were not a violation of equal protection. To the *Pace* court, the harsher punishment would have been problematic only if the same statute had prescribed both penalties. Does that make sense?

Pace survived until *McLaughlin v. Florida*, 379 U.S. 184 (1964), in which the Court reversed a criminal conviction for interracial cohabitation. The Court wrote that "we deal here with a classification based upon the race of the participants, which must be viewed in light of the historical fact that the central purpose of the Fourteenth Amendment was to eliminate racial discrimination emanating from official sources in the State." The state of Florida defended the law, citing *Pace* and arguing that the law did not violate equal protection because blacks and whites were punished equally if convicted. After citing a long string of cases that had undermined *Pace*'s holding, the *McLaughlin* Court rejected Florida's arguments and overruled *Pace* directly. The equal protection question was no longer whether the statute covered members of different races equally, but whether "there is an arbitrary or invidious discrimination between those classes covered by Florida's cohabitation law and those excluded." *McLaughlin* was cited by the Court in *Loving*, and it was treated as dispositive by Justice Stewart's concurrence in that case.

3.   Although there has been scholarly debate over the historical understanding of the Fourteenth Amendment with respect to racial segregation, there is a more widespread belief that the framers of the amendment did not intend it to constitutionalize a right to marry someone of a different race. Thus one question that *Loving* poses, especially for originalists, is what to do if historical understanding diverges from other types of constitutional argument, such as text, precedent, and policy. A more general way to put the question: how much weight should an interpreter give to the drafters' expectations about how a constitutional provision would be applied? On the one hand, aren't the drafters' expected applications useful for informing our understanding of what a highly general phrase in the Fourteenth Amendment means? On the other hand, should the drafters' expectations have more weight than the text, the *Brown* precedent, and the moral policy against the statute?

But perhaps *Loving* was correct as a matter of original understanding after all. In a recent article, David Upham argues that "the Fourteenth Amendment, as understood by the citizens that proposed, ratified, and initially interpreted it, precluded the making or enforcing of state racial-endogamy laws." David R. Upham, *Interracial Marriage and the Original Understanding of the Privileges or Immunities Clause*, 42 Hastings Const. L.Q. 213, 214 (2015). He relies on four categories of evidence: "(1) that before the Amendment, most (but not all) authorities concluded that such laws abridged a pre-existing right recognized at common law, which represented a privilege of citizenship; (2) that during the adoption of the Amendment, both proponents and opponents generally (though not unanimously) declared, acknowledged, or conspicuously failed to deny, that the Amendment would invalidate such laws; (3) that . . . within five years of the Amendment's ratification, racial-endogamy laws were either non-existent or unenforced in a clear majority of the states, in large part because Republican officials—including virtually every Republican judge to face the question—concluded that African Americans' constitutional entitlement to the status and privileges of citizenship precluded the making or enforcing of such laws; and (4) that the contrary holdings were made by Democratic judges hostile to Reconstruction, whose hostility was frequently manifest in their implausible interpretations of the Amendment." *Id.* at 216. If these things are true, is that enough to satisfy you that the Fourteenth Amendment was originally understood to guarantee a right to interracial marriage?

    4.   *Palmore v. Sidoti*, 466 U.S. 429 (1984) involved a child custody battle following a divorce. The husband and the wife were white. The trial court awarded custody to the mother. But when she remarried a black man, the court awarded custody to the father as being in "the best interest" of the child. "[D]espite the strides that had been made in bettering relations between the races in this country," the court held, it was inevitable that the daughter would "suffer from social stigmatization" resulting from the marriage. The Supreme Court unanimously reversed. It was absolutely clear, the Court said, "that the outcome would have been different" if the mother had remarried a white man. In the Court's words:

> A core purpose of the [Fourteenth Amendment] was to do away with all governmentally imposed discrimination based on race. Classifying persons according to their race is more likely to reflect racial prejudice than legitimate public concerns; the race, not the person, dictates the category. Such classifications are subject to the most exacting scrutiny. . . . The question . . . is whether the reality of private biases and the possible injury they might inflict are permissible considerations for removal of an infant child from the custody of its natural mother. We have little difficulty concluding that they are not. The Constitution cannot control such prejudices but neither can it tolerate them. Private biases may be outside the reach of the law, but the law cannot, directly or indirectly, give them effect.

    What does *Palmore* imply for the practice of some state and county adoption agencies that when possible match adoptive children and parents on the basis of race? What does it imply for a state actor fulfilling the preference of a prospective adoptive parents for a child of a specific race? (Does it matter what racial preference is expressed by the prospective adoptive parents?) Do such practices share the premises that the Court rejected so emphatically in *Palmore*? Are they inconsistent with the vision of *Loving*? For analysis of the problem, see Richard Banks, *The Color of Desire: Fulfilling Adoptive Parents' Racial Preferences Through Discriminatory State Action*, 107 Yale L.J. 875 (1998).

A NOTE ON BUSING

When the Court decided *Loving*, in 1967, Southern schools had just begun to integrate on a large scale. After Congress enacted the Civil Rights Act of 1964, and after the implementing regulations were promulgated, public schools faced a loss of federal funding if they did not show significant progress on desegregation. The threat worked. In 1968, the number of black children in the South in desegregated schools was ten times the number just four years earlier. But this method of achieving integration worked only where the black and white children lived in the same neighborhoods, or where the community was too small to have multiple schools. It did not achieve integration for large communities with residential segregation. And residential segregation was increasing in the United States.

In *Swann v. Charlotte-Mecklenburg Board of Education*, 402 U.S. 1 (1971), the Court unanimously upheld the reassignment of students, shifting them from the school they would ordinarily attend to another school—usually further away—in order to achieve greater integration. The colloquial term was "busing," because some students faced increased travel time, by school bus, to achieve the reassignment. There were qualifications in the Court's opinion (e.g., the remedy could be given only where there was previous *de jure* segregation and some kind of failure to comply by school officials). But on the whole it seemed like a strong commitment to using the equitable remedial powers of the federal courts to dismantle segregation. As the Court said, "Once a right and a violation have been shown, the scope of a district court's equitable powers to remedy past wrongs is broad, for breadth and flexibility are inherent in equitable remedies."

But three years later the Court cut back. In *Milliken v. Bradley*, 418 U.S. 717 (1974), the Court considered a judicial plan to desegregate the public schools in Detroit, Michigan, and its suburbs. The key to the plan was scale: it included not only Detroit but 53 suburban school districts, which meant there were enough white and black students to be able, with busing, to achieve integration. The Court invalidated the plan, 5–4, on the grounds that the district court had included school districts in the plan that had not previously been segregated and were not adjudged to be engaging in purposeful racial discrimination. The majority and dissent disagreed sharply about the meaning of *Brown II* and the equitable remedial powers of federal courts. For the majority, the remedy was too attenuated from the underlying violation, because it swept in school districts that had not been shown to have violated the Constitution. For the dissent, the failure to sweep in those white suburban school districts made integration impossible.

In hindsight, *Milliken v. Bradley* was a hugely significant decision, and it signaled the Court's retreat from aggressive use of equitable remedies to achieve desegregation. There would be other cases, some about when school districts had made sufficient progress toward desegregation, e.g., *Board of Education of Oklahoma City Public Schools v. Dowell*, 498 U.S. 237 (1991); and some about what inducements district courts could use to achieve desegregation across school district lines, e.g., *Missouri v. Jenkins*, 515 U.S. 70 (1995). But *Milliken*, when combined with extensive residential segregation, was the decision that halted the integration of the public schools. *De jure* racial segregation was gone, but *de facto* racial segregation was not.

[*Assignment 69*]

C. DISCRIMINATORY INTENT AND DISPARATE IMPACT

In the area of race, does the Equal Protection Clause apply only to statutes that explicitly classify in racial terms? Or does it also apply to ones that have no explicit racial classifications but nevertheless affect different racial groups differently, i.e., that have a "disparate impact"? And in answering that question, if a statute has no explicit mention of race but does have a disparate impact on racial minorities, does it matter whether the legislators intended that disparate impact? These questions are central to the Court's decisions in the next two cases.

Yick Wo v. Hopkins

118 U.S. 356 (1886)

. . . The plaintiff in error, Yick Wo, on August 24, 1885, petitioned the supreme court of California for the writ of habeas corpus, alleging that he was illegally deprived of his personal liberty by the defendant as sheriff of the city and county of San Francisco. The sheriff made return to the writ that he held the petitioner in custody by virtue of a sentence of the police judge's court No. 2 of the city and county of San Francisco, whereby he was found guilty of a violation of certain ordinances of the board of supervisors of that county, and adjudged to pay a fine of $10, and, in default of payment, be imprisoned in the county jail at the rate of one day for each dollar of fine until said fine should be satisfied; and a commitment in consequence of non-payment of said fine.

The ordinances for the violation of which he had been found guilty are set out as follows:

Order No. 1,569, passed May 26, 1880, prescribing the kind of buildings in which laundries may be located[:] . . .

> "Section 1. It shall be unlawful, from and after the passage of this order, for any person or persons to establish, maintain, or carry on a laundry, within the corporate limits of the city and county of San Francisco, without having first obtained the consent of the board of supervisors, except the same be located in a building constructed either of brick or stone. . . .

> "Sec. 3. Any person who shall violate any of the provisions of this order shall be deemed guilty of a misdemeanor, and upon conviction thereof shall be punished by a fine of not more than one thousand dollars, or by imprisonment in the county jail not more than six months, or by both such fine and imprisonment." . . .

The following facts are also admitted on the record: That petitioner is a native of China, and came to California in 1861, and is still a subject of the emperor of China; that he has been engaged in the laundry business in the same premises and building for 22 years last past; that he had a license from the board of fire-wardens, dated March 3, 1884, from which it appeared "that the above-described premises have been inspected by the board of fire-wardens, and upon such inspection said board found all proper arrangements for carrying on the business; that the stoves, washing and drying apparatus, and the appliances for heating smoothing-irons, are in good condition, and that their use is not dangerous to the surrounding property from fire . . . ; that he had a certificate from the health officer that the same premises had been inspected by him, and that he found that they were properly and sufficiently drained, and that all proper arrangements for carrying on the business of a laundry, without injury to the sanitary condition of the neighborhood, had been complied with; that the city license of the petitioner was in force, and expired October

1, 1885; and that the petitioner applied to the board of supervisors, June 1, 1885, for consent of said board to maintain and carry on his laundry, but that said board, on July 1, 1885, refused said consent." It is also admitted to be true, as alleged in the petition, that on February 24, 1880, "there were about 320 laundries in the city and county of San Francisco, of which about 240 were owned and conducted by subjects of China, and of the whole number, viz., 320, about 310 were constructed of wood, the same material that constitutes ninetenths of the houses in the city of San Francisco. The capital thus invested by the subjects of China was not less than two hundred thousand dollars, and they paid annually for rent, license, taxes, gas, and water about one hundred and eighty thousand dollars." It is alleged in the petition that "your petitioner, and more than one hundred and fifty of his countrymen, have been arrested upon the charge of carrying on business without having such special consent, while those who are not subjects of China, and who are conducting eighty odd laundries under similar conditions, are left unmolested, and free to enjoy the enhanced trade and profits arising from this hurtful and unfair discrimination. The business of your petitioners, and of those of his countrymen similarly situated, is greatly impaired, and in many cases practically ruined, by this system of oppression to one kind of men, and favoritism to all others."

The statement therein contained as to the arrest, etc., is admitted to be true. . . . It is also admitted "that petitioner and 200 of his countrymen similarly situated petitioned the board of supervisors for permission to continue their business in the various houses which they had been occupying and using for laundries for more than twenty years, and such petitions were denied, and all the petitions of those who were not Chinese, with one exception of Mrs. Mary Meagles, were granted." . . .

In the other case [consolidated with this one, the prisoner] petitioned for his discharge from an alleged illegal imprisonment, upon a state of facts, shown upon the record, precisely similar to that in the *Case of Yick Wo.* In disposing of the application, the learned Circuit Judge Sawyer, in his opinion, (26 Fed. Rep. 471,) after quoting the ordinance in question, proceeded at length as follows:

". . . The necessary tendency, if not the specific purpose, of this ordinance, and of enforcing it in the manner indicated in the record, is to drive out of business all the numerous small laundries, especially those owned by Chinese, and give a monopoly of the business to the large institutions established and carried on by means of large associated Caucasian capital. If the facts appearing on the face of the ordinance, on the petition and return, and admitted in the case, and shown by the notorious public and municipal history of the times, indicate a purpose to drive out the Chinese laundrymen, and not merely to regulate the business for the public safety, does it not disclose a case of violation of the provisions of the fourteenth amendment to the national constitution, and of the treaty between the United States and China, in more than one particular? . . . If this means prohibition of the occupation, and a destruction of the business and property, of the Chinese laundrymen in San Francisco,—as it seems to us this must be the effect of executing the ordinance,—and not merely the proper regulation of the business, then there is discrimination, and a violation of other highly important rights secured by the fourteenth amendment and the treaty. That it does mean prohibition, as to the Chinese, it seems to us must be apparent to every citizen of San Francisco who has been here long enough to be familiar with the course of an active and aggressive branch of public opinion and of public notorious events. Can a court be blind to what must be necessarily known to every intelligent person in the state?"

■ MR. JUSTICE MATTHEWS delivered the opinion of the Court.

. . . [T]he determination of the question whether the proceedings under these ordinances, and in enforcement of them, are in conflict with the constitution and laws of the United States, necessarily involves the meaning of the ordinances, which, for that purpose, we are required to ascertain and adjudge.

We are consequently constrained, at the outset, to differ from the supreme court of California upon the real meaning of the ordinances in question. That court considered these ordinances as vesting in the board of supervisors a not unusual discretion in granting or withholding their assent to the use of wooden buildings as laundries, to be exercised in reference to the circumstances of each case, with a view to the protection of the public against the dangers of fire. We are not able to concur in that interpretation of the power conferred upon the supervisors. There is nothing in the ordinances which points to such a regulation of the business of keeping and conducting laundries. They seem intended to confer, and actually to confer, not a discretion to be exercised upon a consideration of the circumstances of each case, but a naked and arbitrary power to give or withhold consent, not only as to places, but as to persons; so that, if an applicant for such consent, being in every way a competent and qualified person, and having complied with every reasonable condition demanded by any public interest, should, failing to obtain the requisite consent of the supervisors to the prosecution of his business, apply for redress by the judicial process of mandamus to require the supervisors to consider and act upon his case, it would be a sufficient answer for them to say that the law had conferred upon them authority to withhold their assent, without reason and without responsibility. The power given to them is not confided to their discretion in the legal sense of that term, but is granted to their mere will. It is purely arbitrary, and acknowledges neither guidance nor restraint. . . .

The ordinance drawn in question in the present case . . . does not prescribe a rule and conditions, for the regulation of the use of property for laundry purposes, to which all similarly situated may conform. It allows, without restriction, the use for such purposes of buildings of brick or stone; but, as to wooden buildings, constituting nearly all those in previous use, it divides the owners or occupiers into two classes, not having respect to their personal character and qualifications for the business, nor the situation and nature and adaptation of the buildings themselves, but merely by an arbitrary line, on one side of which are those who are permitted to pursue their industry by the mere will and consent of the supervisors, and on the other those from whom that consent is withheld, at their mere will and pleasure. And both classes are alike only in this: that they are tenants at will, under the supervisors, of their means of living. The ordinance, therefore, also differs from the not unusual case where discretion is lodged by law in public officers or bodies to grant or withhold licenses to keep taverns, or places for the sale of spirituous liquors, and the like, when one of the conditions is that the applicant shall be a fit person for the exercise of the privilege, because in such cases the fact of fitness is submitted to the judgment of the officer, and calls for the exercise of a discretion of a judicial nature.

The rights of the petitioners, as affected by the proceedings of which they complain, are not less because they are aliens and subjects of the emperor of China. . . . The fourteenth amendment to the constitution is not confined to the protection of citizens. It says: "Nor shall any state deprive any person of life, liberty, or property without due process of law; nor deny to any person within its jurisdiction the equal protection of the laws." These provisions are universal in their application, to all persons within the territorial jurisdiction, without regard to any differences of race, of color, or of nationality; and the equal protection of the laws is a pledge of the protection of equal laws. It is accordingly enacted by section 1977 of the Revised Statutes that "all persons within the jurisdiction of the United States shall have the same right, in every state and territory, to make and enforce contracts, to sue, be parties, give evidence, and to the full and equal benefit of all laws and proceedings for the security of persons and property as is enjoyed by white citizens, and shall be subject to like punishment, pains, penalties, taxes, licenses, and exactions of every kind, and to no other." The questions we have to consider and decide in these cases, therefore, are to be treated as involving the rights of every citizen of the United States equally with those of the strangers and aliens who now invoke the jurisdiction of the court.

It is contended on the part of the petitioners that the ordinances for violations of which they are severally sentenced to imprisonment are void on their face, as being within the prohibitions of the fourteenth amendment, and, in the alternative, if not so, that they are void by reason of their administration, operating unequally, so as to punish in the present petitioners what is permitted to others as lawful, without any distinction of circumstances,—an unjust and illegal discrimination, it is claimed, which, though not made expressly by the ordinances, is made possible by them.

When we consider the nature and the theory of our institutions of government, the principles upon which they are supposed to rest, and review the history of their development, we are constrained to conclude that they do not mean to leave room for the play and action of purely personal and arbitrary power. Sovereignty itself is, of course, not subject to law, for it is the author and source of law; but in our system, while sovereign powers are delegated to the agencies of government, sovereignty itself remains with the people, by whom and for whom all government exists and acts. And the law is the definition and limitation of power. It is, indeed, quite true that there must always be lodged somewhere, and in some person or body, the authority of final decision; and in many cases of mere administration, the responsibility is purely political, no appeal lying except to the ultimate tribunal of the public judgment, exercised either in the pressure of opinion, or by means of the suffrage. But the fundamental rights to life, liberty, and the pursuit of happiness, considered as individual possessions, are secured by those maxims of constitutional law which are the monuments showing the victorious progress of the race in securing to men the blessings of civilization under the reign of just and equal laws, so that, in the famous language of the Massachusetts bill of rights, the government of the commonwealth "may be a government of laws and not of men." For the very idea that one man may be compelled to hold his life, or the means of living, or any material right essential to the enjoyment of life, at the mere will of another, seems to be intolerable in any country where freedom prevails, as being the essence of slavery itself. . . .

In the present cases, we are not obliged to reason from the probable to the actual, and pass upon the validity of the ordinances complained of, as tried merely by the opportunities which their terms afford, of unequal and unjust discrimination in their administration; for the cases present the ordinances in actual operation, and the facts shown establish an administration directed so exclusively against a particular class of persons as to warrant and require the conclusion that, whatever may have been the intent of the ordinances as adopted, they are applied by the public authorities charged with their administration, and thus representing the state itself, with a mind so unequal and oppressive as to amount to a practical denial by the state of that equal protection of the laws which is secured to the petitioners, as to all other persons, by the broad and benign provisions of the fourteenth amendment to the constitution of the United States. Though the law itself be fair on its face, and impartial in appearance, yet, if it is applied and administered by public authority with an evil eye and an unequal hand, so as practically to make unjust and illegal discriminations between persons in similar circumstances, material to their rights, the denial of equal justice is still within the prohibition of the constitution. This principle of interpretation has been sanctioned by this court.

The present cases, as shown by the facts disclosed in the record, are within this class. It appears that both petitioners have complied with every requisite deemed by the law, or by the public officers charged with its administration, necessary for the protection of neighboring property from fire, or as a precaution against injury to the public health. No reason whatever, except the will of the supervisors, is assigned why they should not be permitted to carry on, in the accustomed manner, their harmless and useful occupation, on which they depend for a livelihood; and while this consent of the supervisors is withheld from them, and from 200 others who have also petitioned, all of whom happen to be Chinese subjects, 80 others, not Chinese subjects, are permitted to carry on the same business under similar conditions. The fact of this discrimination is admitted. No reason for it is shown, and the conclusion cannot be resisted that no reason for it exists except hostility to the race and nationality to which the petitioners belong, and which, in the eye of the law, is not justified. The discrimination is therefore illegal, and the public administration which enforces it is a denial of the equal protection of the laws, and a violation of the fourteenth amendment of the constitution. The imprisonment of the petitioners is therefore illegal, and they must be discharged. . . .

NOTES

1.   Which clause of the Fourteenth Amendment did the ordinance violate? Is the problem one of "discrimination" or "arbitrary power"? Which clauses of the Fourteenth Amendment address each of those things?

2.   The U.S. Supreme Court says that it "differ[s] from the supreme court of California upon the real meaning of the ordinances in question." Wouldn't we expect a state court to have a better idea about what a state law means? Is the U.S. Supreme Court's willingness to look for the "real meaning" a general principle, or something special about discrimination cases?

3.   For modern purposes, the key holding of *Yick Wo* is that even if "the law itself be fair on its face, and impartial in appearance," it is unconstitutional "if it is applied and administered by public authority with an evil eye and an unequal hand, so as practically to make unjust and illegal discriminations between persons in similar circumstances,

material to their rights." But how are courts supposed to detect the "evil eye" and "unequal hand" in practice? Consider that question as you read the next case.

Washington v. Davis
426 U.S. 229 (1976)

■ MR. JUSTICE WHITE delivered the opinion of the Court.

This case involves the validity of a qualifying test administered to applicants for positions as police officers in the District of Columbia Metropolitan Police Department. The test was sustained by the District Court but invalidated by the Court of Appeals. We are in agreement with the District Court and hence reverse the judgment of the Court of Appeals. . . .

[The amended complaint] alleged that the promotion policies of the Department were racially discriminatory and sought a declaratory judgment and an injunction. The respondents Harley and Sellers were permitted to intervene, their amended complaint asserting that their applications to become officers in the Department had been rejected, and that the Department's recruiting procedures discriminated on the basis of race against black applicants by a series of practices including, but not limited to, a written personnel test which excluded a disproportionately high number of Negro applicants. These practices were asserted to violate respondents' rights "under the due process clause of the Fifth Amendment to the United States Constitution."

According to the findings and conclusions of the District Court, to be accepted by the Department and to enter an intensive 17-week training program, the police recruit was required to satisfy certain physical and character standards, to be a high school graduate or its equivalent, and to receive a grade of at least 40 out of 80 on "Test 21," which is "an examination that is used generally throughout the federal service," which "was developed by the Civil Service Commission, not the Police Department," and which was "designed to test verbal ability, vocabulary, reading and comprehension."

The validity of Test 21 was the sole issue before the court on the motions for summary judgment. The District Court noted that there was no claim of "an intentional discrimination or purposeful discriminatory acts" but only a claim that Test 21 bore no relationship to job performance and "has a highly discriminatory impact in screening out black candidates." Respondents' evidence, the District Court said, warranted three conclusions: "(a) The number of black police officers, while substantial, is not proportionate to the population mix of the city. (b) A higher percentage of blacks fail the Test than whites. (c) The Test has not been validated to establish its reliability for measuring subsequent job performance." This showing was deemed sufficient to shift the burden of proof to the defendants in the action, petitioners here; but the court nevertheless concluded that on the undisputed facts respondents were not entitled to relief. The District Court relied on several factors. Since August 1969, 44% of new police force recruits had been black; that figure also represented the proportion of blacks on the total force and was roughly equivalent to 20-to-29-year-old blacks in the 50-mile radius in which the recruiting efforts of the Police Department had been concentrated. It was undisputed that the Department had systematically and affirmatively sought to enroll black officers many of whom passed the test but failed to report for duty. The District Court rejected the assertion that Test 21 was culturally slanted to favor whites and was "satisfied that the undisputable facts prove the test to be reasonably and directly related to the requirements of the police recruit training program and that it is neither so designed nor operates (sic) to discriminate against otherwise qualified blacks" It was thus not necessary to show that Test 21 was not only a useful indicator of training school performance but had also been validated in terms of job performance "The lack of job performance validation does not defeat the Test, given its direct relationship to recruiting and the valid part it plays in this process." The District Court ultimately concluded that "[t]he proof is wholly lacking that a police officer qualifies on the color of his skin rather than ability" and that the Department "should not be required on this showing to lower standards or to abandon efforts to achieve excellence." . . .

The Court of Appeals [reversed, declaring] that lack of discriminatory intent in designing and administering Test 21 was irrelevant; the critical fact was rather that a far greater proportion of blacks—four times as many—failed the test than did whites. This disproportionate impact, standing alone and without regard to whether it indicated a discriminatory purpose, was held sufficient to establish a constitutional violation, absent proof by petitioners that the test was an adequate measure of job performance in addition to being an indicator of probable success in the training program. . . .

The central purpose of the Equal Protection Clause of the Fourteenth Amendment is the prevention of official conduct discriminating on the basis of race. It is also true that the Due Process Clause of the Fifth Amendment contains an equal protection component prohibiting the United States from invidiously discriminating between individuals or groups. *Bolling v. Sharpe*, 347 U.S. 497 (1954). But our cases have not embraced the proposition that a law or other official act, without regard to whether it reflects a racially discriminatory purpose, is unconstitutional solely because it has a racially disproportionate impact.

Almost 100 years ago, *Strauder v. West Virginia*, 100 U.S. 303 (1880), established that the exclusion of Negroes from grand and petit juries in criminal proceedings violated the Equal Protection Clause, but the fact that a particular jury or a series of juries does not statistically reflect the racial composition of the community does not in itself make out an invidious discrimination forbidden by the Clause.

The school desegregation cases have also adhered to the basic equal protection principle that the invidious quality of a law claimed to be racially discriminatory must ultimately be traced to a racially discriminatory purpose. That there are both predominantly black and predominantly white schools in a community is not alone violative of the Equal Protection Clause. The essential element of de jure segregation is "a current condition of segregation resulting from intentional state action." *Keyes v. School Dist. No. 1*, 413 U.S. 189, 205 (1973). The differentiating factor between de jure segregation and so-called de facto segregation . . . is purpose or intent to segregate."

This is not to say that the necessary discriminatory racial purpose must be express or appear on the face of the statute, or that a law's disproportionate impact is irrelevant in cases involving Constitution-based claims of racial discrimination. A statute, otherwise neutral on its face, must not be applied so as invidiously to discriminate on the basis of race. *Yick Wo v. Hopkins*, 118 U.S. 356 (1886). It is also clear from the cases dealing with racial discrimination in the selection of juries that the systematic exclusion of Negroes is itself such an "unequal application of the law . . . as to show intentional discrimination." *Akins v. Texas,* 325 U.S. 398, 404 (1945).

Necessarily, an invidious discriminatory purpose may often be inferred from the totality of the relevant facts, including the fact, if it is true, that the law bears more heavily on one race than another. [Nevertheless,] we have not held that a law, neutral on its face and serving ends otherwise within the power of government to pursue, is invalid under the Equal Protection Clause simply because it may affect a greater proportion of one race than of another. Disproportionate impact is not irrelevant, but it is not the sole touchstone of an invidious racial discrimination forbidden by the Constitution. Standing alone, it does not trigger the rule, *McLaughlin v. Florida,* 379 U.S. 184 (1964), that racial classifications are to be subjected to the strictest scrutiny and are justifiable only by the weightiest of considerations.

There are some indications to the contrary in our cases. In *Palmer v. Thompson,* 403 U.S. 217 (1971), the city of Jackson, Miss., following a court decree to this effect, desegregated all of its public facilities save five swimming pools which had been operated by the city and which, following the decree, were closed by ordinance pursuant to a determination by the city council that closure was necessary to preserve peace and order and that integrated pools could not be economically operated. Accepting the finding that the pools were closed to avoid violence and economic loss, this Court rejected the argument that the abandonment of this service was inconsistent with the outstanding desegregation decree and that the otherwise seemingly permissible ends served by the ordinance could be impeached by demonstrating that racially invidious motivations had prompted the city council's action. The holding was that the city was not overtly or covertly operating segregated pools and was extending identical treatment to both whites and Negroes. The opinion warned against grounding decision on legislative purpose or motivation, thereby lending support for the proposition that the operative effect of the law rather than its purpose is the paramount factor. But the holding of the case was that the legitimate purposes of the ordinance to preserve peace and avoid deficits were not open to impeachment by evidence that the councilmen were actually motivated by racial considerations. Whatever dicta the opinion may contain, the decision did not involve, much less invalidate, a statute or ordinance having neutral purposes but disproportionate racial consequences. . . .

[W]e have difficulty understanding how a law establishing a racially neutral qualification for employment is nevertheless racially discriminatory and denies "any person . . . equal protection of the laws" simply because a greater proportion of Negroes fail to qualify than members of other racial or ethnic groups. [Test 21,] which is administered generally to prospective Government employees, concededly seeks to ascertain whether those who take it have acquired a particular level of verbal skill; and it is untenable that the Constitution prevents the Government from seeking modestly to upgrade the communicative abilities of its employees rather than to be satisfied with some lower level of competence, particularly where the job requires special ability to communicate orally and in writing. Respondents, as Negroes, could no more successfully claim that the test denied them equal protection than could white applicants who also failed. The conclusion would not be different in the face of proof that more Negroes than whites had been disqualified by Test 21. That other

Negroes also failed to score well would, alone, not demonstrate that respondents individually were being denied equal protection of the laws by the application of an otherwise valid qualifying test being administered to prospective police recruits.

Nor on the facts of the case before us would the disproportionate impact of Test 21 warrant the conclusion that it is a purposeful device to discriminate against Negroes and hence an infringement of the constitutional rights of respondents as well as other black applicants. As we have said, the test is neutral on its face and rationally may be said to serve a purpose the Government is constitutionally empowered to pursue. Even agreeing with the District Court that the differential racial effect of Test 21 called for further inquiry, we think the District Court correctly held that the affirmative efforts of the Metropolitan Police Department to recruit black officers, the changing racial composition of the recruit classes and of the force in general, and the relationship of the test to the training program negated any inference that the Department discriminated on the basis of race or that "a police officer qualifies on the color of his skin rather than ability." 348 F.Supp., at 18. . . .

■ [The concurring opinion of JUSTICE STEVENS is omitted.]

■ MR. JUSTICE BRENNAN, with whom MR. JUSTICE MARSHALL joins, dissenting.

The Court holds that the job qualification examination (Test 21) given by the District of Columbia Metropolitan Police Department does not unlawfully discriminate on the basis of race under either constitutional or statutory standards. [I] would affirm the Court of Appeals because petitioners have failed to prove that Test 21 satisfies the applicable statutory standards. . . .

[The bulk of the dissent focused on the asserted violation of the Title VII statute, which prohibits employment discrimination on the basis of race.—Editors]

Sound policy considerations support the view that, at a minimum, petitioners should have been required to prove that the police training examinations either measure job-related skills or predict job performance. Where employers try to validate written qualification tests by proving a correlation with written examinations in a training course, there is a substantial danger that people who have good verbal skills will achieve high scores on both tests due to verbal ability, rather than "job-specific ability." As a result, employers could validate any entrance examination that measures only verbal ability by giving another written test that measures verbal ability at the end of a training course. Any contention that the resulting correlation between examination scores would be evidence that the initial test is "job related" is plainly erroneous. It seems to me, however, that the Court's holding in this case can be read as endorsing this dubious proposition. . . .

I would hold that petitioners have not met their burden of proof and affirm the judgment of the Court of Appeals.

NOTES

1.   Are you persuaded by the Court's reasoning? Does the Equal Protection Clause forbid state laws that have an unintended disproportionate effect on the basis of race? Is the clause about the use of racial classifications or about racial effects? Recall two cases that considered government motivation, both regarding clauses of the First Amendment: *United States v. O'Brien*, allowing the government to regulate expressive conduct but not when it does so *because* of the expressive content (see p. 888); and *Employment Division v. Smith*, reading the Free Exercise Clause as allowing many laws that have the effect of

burdening religious exercise as long as they were not adopted for that reason (see p. 1100). (These are general statements of those two cases; there are qualifications.) Is the test of *Washington v. Davis* similar to these tests? Is that a good approach for the Court to adopt in the context of racial discrimination? Why or why not?

2.   In *Gomillion v. Lightfoot,* 364 U.S. 339 (1960), the Supreme Court held that the redrawing of political boundaries to disenfranchise black voters could be challenged under the Fourteenth and Fifteenth Amendments. In 1957, the Alabama Legislature passed Local Act No. 140, which redrew the boundaries of the city of Tuskegee so as to remove "all save four or five of its 400 Negro voters while not removing a single white voter or resident." Tuskegee had been square-shaped, but the Act "transformed it into a strangely irregular twenty-eight-sided figure." When the plaintiffs—black Alabama citizens who were pushed outside of Tuskegee by the redistricting measure—challenged the Act, both the district court and court of appeals dismissed the case for failure to state a claim for which relief could be granted. Despite the plaintiffs' claims that the redistricting was racially discriminatory, the lower courts held that they had "no power to change any boundaries of municipal corporations fixed by a duly convened and elected legislative body, acting for the people in the State of Alabama." The Court rejected this conclusion, holding that while a state's authority to manage its own political subdivisions was substantial and deserved deference, it was not so absolute as to trump claims that constitutional rights had been violated. The plaintiffs had stated a valid claim and could go to trial. If the evidence "remained uncontradicted or unqualified, the conclusion would be irresistible, tantamount for all practical purposes to a mathematical demonstration, that the legislation is solely concerned with segregating white and colored voters by fencing Negro citizens out of town so as to deprive them of their preexisting municipal vote."

3.   Recall the facts in *Griffin v. County School Board of Prince Edward County,* 377 U.S. 218 (1964), p. 1371, where Prince Edward County, Virginia closed its public school system rather than integrate it. Remember that the Court laid stress on the public officials' motivation: "Whatever nonracial grounds might support a State's allowing a county to abandon public schools, the object must be a constitutional one, and grounds of race and opposition to desegregation do not qualify as constitutional." *Id.* at 225, 231.

Likewise, in *Green v. County School Board,* 391 U.S. 430 (1968), the Supreme Court held that the "freedom of choice" school integration plan adopted by New Kent County, Virginia did not comply with the requirements of *Brown II.* Like Prince Edward County, New Kent County chose its own response to *Brown* following the Virginia legislature's failed anti-integration initiative. Unlike Prince Edward County, however, New Kent County had only two schools. Before *Brown,* the schools were segregated by law—New Kent for whites and George W. Watkins for blacks. The County's new "freedom of choice" plan gave students the option of attending either school. Students in the first and eighth grades chose which school they wanted to attend and were reassigned to the same school every year unless they applied for a change. From the plan's inception in 1961 until September 1964, not a single black student in the county applied to New Kent and not a single white student applied to George W. Watkins.

In striking down the New Kent County plan, the Court stated that "[w]e do not hold that a 'freedom-of-choice' plan might of itself be unconstitutional," but rather that New Kent's plan "cannot be accepted as a sufficient step to effectuate a transition to a unitary school system." It required the school board to "formulate a new plan and . . . fashion steps which promise realistically to convert promptly to a system without a 'white' school and a 'Negro' school, but just schools."

Clearly, *Griffin* and *Green* involved policies and practices designed to accomplish an impermissible goal of effectuating or maintaining racial segregation. They involved racially disparate impact *plus* the official intent to accomplish precisely that disparate impact. In each case, the official intent to discriminate could be clearly inferred from circumstances. (What if it were not? How does *Washington v. Davis* resolve this situation?)

In another case, *Palmer v. Thompson*, 403 U.S. 217 (1971), the Supreme Court found no equal protection violation where the city of Jackson, Mississippi closed its public pools following a district court ruling declaring the city's operation of segregated parks and other public facilities illegal. After the ruling, Jackson desegregated its "public parks, auditoriums, golf courses, and the city zoo," but decided to close its five public pools. In response, the plaintiffs—a group of black citizens of Jackson—filed suit, asking that the pools be reopened and desegregated. The plaintiffs argued that the pool closings were a violation of equal protection under the Fourteenth Amendment and one of the "badges and incidents" of slavery prohibited by the Thirteenth Amendment. The district court disagreed and "found that the closing was justified to preserve peace and order and because the pools could not be operated economically on an integrated basis." The court of appeals affirmed. In a 5–4 decision written by Justice Black, the Supreme Court affirmed as well, rejecting the plaintiff's reliance upon *Griffin* as precedent for their position.

Regarding *Griffin*, Justice Black wrote, "[the] case simply treated the school program for what it was—an operation of Prince Edward County schools under a thinly disguised 'private' school system actually planned and carried out by the State and the county to maintain segregated education with public funds." The pools were different, Justice Black argued, because the evidence showed that the city closed them indefinitely and had no intentions of reopening them as segregated private pools subsidized with state dollars. Do you find this reasoning persuasive? Would the Prince Edward County program really have survived judicial review if there had been no state subsidy component and the County had simply abandoned public education altogether? On the other hand, does the Equal Protection Clause impose a duty on the government to operate swimming pools? Was everyone treated equally, not "separate-but-equal" but "nobody-gets-a-public-pool" equal?

[*Assignment 70*]

D. AFFIRMATIVE ACTION

The landmark decisions in *Brown v. Board of Education* and *Loving v. Virginia* rejected efforts by state governments to subordinate and stigmatize black Americans. From these decisions, courts and commentators have often drawn the principle that the government may not discriminate, segregate, or otherwise invidiously classify on the basis of race—at least not without an overwhelmingly "compelling" justification. Even then the government may classify on the basis of race only by "narrowly tailored" means that will precisely accomplish that justification. But does this principle apply when the government, instead of discriminating against a racial minority, is using race as an "affirmative" basis to benefit a racial minority? Or should these racial classifications be judged by a different, more lenient standard? Does it matter what the government's stated objective is? These questions are central to the debate over affirmative action, and they arise in many contexts, including state university admissions, government contracts, government employment, and the drawing of election districts.

A NOTE ON THE HISTORY OF AFFIRMATIVE ACTION

It is impossible to understand the debate over affirmative action without a brief review of its history as a response to the nation's long practice of racial segregation and discrimination. In the last months of the Civil War, Congress passed the Freedmen's Bureau Act, thus creating one of the first federal programs to benefit a racial minority. The statute authorized the seizure of "abandoned lands," and each of the "refugees and freedmen from rebel states" could receive up to forty acres. 13 Stat. 507 (1865). These lands were rented to the "refugees and freedmen" with an option to buy after a period of years, if the United States could obtain valid title. The statute also authorized the Secretary of War to give "provisions, clothing, and fuel" to "destitute and suffering refugees and freedmen and their wives and children." For several years the Freedmen's Bureau provided a considerable social welfare network, "staffed largely by Union Army officers[:] during its brief existence it distributed food to destitute blacks and whites, supervised the establishment of free-labor agriculture, and furnished much-needed financial assistance to set up schools for the ex-slaves." Peter Kolchin, AMERICAN SLAVERY 1619–1877, at 212 (2003).

The initial Freedmen's Bureau Act was set to expire one year after the conclusion of "the present war of rebellion." 13 Stat. 507 (1865). But the next year Congress passed legislation expanding the Bureau's mandate and continuing it for another two years. 14 Stat. 173 (1866). The amendment extended the Bureau's charge "to all loyal refugees and freedmen, so far as the same shall be necessary to enable them as speedily as practicable to become self-supporting citizens of the United States, and to aid them in making the freedom conferred by the proclamation of the commander-in-chief, by emancipation under the laws of States, and by constitutional amendment, available to them and beneficial to the republic." § 2, 14 Stat. 173, 174. More concretely, it expanded the Secretary of War's relief authority to include transportation and medical aid. It authorized the seizure of Confederate land and buildings to be sold for "the education of the freed people." § 12, 14 Stat. 173, 176. When the Bureau's authorization expired, the proceeds would go to "such of said so-called confederate states as shall have made provision for the education of their citizens without distinction of color." *Id.* And, perhaps most sweepingly, the legislation established military jurisdiction and rules of federal equality in places "where the ordinary course of judicial proceedings has been interrupted by the rebellion" or "whose constitutional relations to the government have been practically discontinued by the rebellion," until order was restored. § 14, 14 Stat. 173, 177–176. (President Johnson vetoed the bill largely because of this last provision, but Congress overrode his veto.) Several more bills continue to extend and modify the Bureau until it was ultimately abolished in 1872.

The legacy of the Freedmen's Bureau remains disputed. Is it a precedent for race-conscious federal decisionmaking? Its central aim was certainly to provide relief to freed slaves, who were black. Notice, though, that the Bureau's full name was the Bureau of Refugees, Freedmen, and Abandoned Lands, and the Act repeatedly used the terms "freedmen" and "refugees" rather than explicitly referring to race. Indeed, "refugees" were included in response to Democratic complaints that the Freedmen's Bureau would be "caste" legislation favoring one race only. See Eric Foner, RECONSTRUCTION: AMERICA'S UNFINISHED REVOLUTION 1863–1877, at 69 (1988) ("[A]t the last moment, Congress redefined the Bureau's responsibilities so as to include Southern white refugees as well as freedmen, a vast expansion of its authority that aimed to counteract the impression of preferential treatment for blacks."). Should those distinctions matter?

In addition to the Freedmen's Bureau, the Reconstruction Congress enacted several laws thought to have provided benefits specifically to black Americans:

> One 1866 law donated federally owned land in the District of Columbia "for the sole use of schools for colored children." A second 1866 act is said to have appropriated funds for the relief of destitute colored women and children. A third 1867 law provided for money for destitute "colored" persons within the District of Columbia. A fourth 1866 law required [that] military chaplains [be] appointed for black troops to provide them with basic educational instruction. Finally, Congress adopted special rules and procedures for the payment of "colored" servicemen in the Union Army.

Michael B. Rappaport, *Originalism and the Colorblind Constitution*, 89 Notre Dame L. Rev. 71, 102 (2013). For more details, and a debate about whether these laws were in fact race-based, see *id.* at 102–113, and Jed Rubenfeld, *Affirmative Action*, 107 Yale L. J. 427 (1997).

With the end of Reconstruction, see p. 1344, whatever interest national political leaders may have had in aiding black citizens quickly waned. Indeed, under President Woodrow Wilson, the national government threw its weight behind segregation. "Early in his first administration, he capitulated to his Postmaster General, who wanted to segregate all Post Offices by race. Soon, Jim Crow swept throughout the executive branch." Dennis J. Hutchinson, *A Century of Social Reform: The Judicial Role*, 4 Green Bag 2d 157, 161 (2001).

Eventually, Presidents Franklin Roosevelt and Harry Truman began acting to remove the structures of racial discrimination in federal employment. President Truman ordered the integration of the military in 1948. Six years later came *Brown v. Board of Education*. Almost a decade after that Congress passed the Civil Rights Act of 1964, prohibiting employment discrimination on the basis of race; and the Voting Rights Act of 1965, protecting black citizens' right to vote. Only during this "Second Reconstruction" did the structure of Jim Crow laws begin to crumble.

Two centuries of slavery and a century of Jim Crow left black Americans disadvantaged in wealth, employment, education, and political power. To correct these deficits, the Kennedy, Johnson, and Nixon administrations each experimented with programs of "affirmative action" to achieve results commensurate with the promise of equality under law. The rationale was stated by President Lyndon Johnson in a commencement address at Howard University in 1965:

> [F]reedom is not enough. You do not wipe away the scars of centuries by saying: Now you are free to go where you want, and do as you desire, and choose the leaders you please. You do not take a person who, for years, has been hobbled by chains and liberate him, bring him up to the starting line of a race and then say, "you are free to compete with all the others," and still justly believe that you have been completely fair. Thus it is not enough just to open the gates of opportunity. All our citizens must have the ability to walk through those gates. This is the next and the more profound stage of the battle for civil rights. We seek not just freedom but opportunity. We seek not just legal equity but human ability, not just equality as a right and a theory but equality as a fact and equality as a result.

In this modern form, affirmative action began as an effort to recruit minority students and employees. Over time, it evolved into more sweeping commitments to racial diversity in education and in the workplace. During the 1970s, affirmative action began to include minority "set asides" in federal contracting, in employment, and in university admissions. Some proponents of this type of affirmative action saw it as a down-payment on reparations owed by white Americans for slavery and segregation. Opponents criticized the new programs for undermining merit selection and fostering race-consciousness through quotas.

As you consider the constitutional status of affirmative action, think of several questions that flow from this brief history. First, does the Fourteenth Amendment even apply to discrimination that has benign motivations, as in affirmative-action programs? Second, does the American history of slavery, racial discrimination, and segregation justify racial preferences on a class-wide basis? Third, is there a difference between affirmative action in the form of seeking and recruiting qualified minority applicants and candidates and affirmative action in the form of giving preferences on the basis of race? Fourth, is there a difference—and should there be a difference—in how the Constitution applies to affirmative action programs undertaken by the national government and by the states?

Affirmative Action in Education: An Introductory Hypothetical (*Taxman v. Piscataway*)

Before considering the Supreme Court's cases in this area, reflect on the following hypothetical based on *Taxman v. Piscataway Township Board of Education*, 91 F.3d 1547 (3d Cir. 1996) (en banc)—a case that was almost decided by the Supreme Court. The case settled after *certiorari* was granted.

In a public school district, two teachers—one a black woman, the other a white woman—are hired to teach at the same school. They have the same prior experience. They start on the same day. For budgetary reasons, the school needs to lay off one of them. The school board formally determines that the two are absolutely equal in terms of seniority, qualifications, and all other relevant considerations of merit. (Perhaps the board took this position to duck a difficult decision, avoiding the hard feelings that might come from evaluating the teachers' comparative merit. But no matter: those are the facts in the record.) The board decides to lay off the white teacher, solely on the basis of race. Otherwise its practice is to draw lots. The board's stated justification is the school district's affirmative action policy and its desire to promote racial diversity among its faculty.

Did the school district violate the Equal Protection Clause? Should affirmative action programs be governed by the same standard as other racial classifications? Or is there a difference between a benign race-based classification and an invidious one? If so, what is that difference? And is the school district's classification benign?

What justifications might the school district offer for its action that would persuade you that it should be upheld as constitutional? Consider the following options: (1) The need to remedy past societal discrimination against racial minorities? (2) The creation of more opportunities for minorities in a particular employment sector? (3) Greater diversity, in the sense of racial balance among teachers, as an independent value pursued for its own sake? (4) Promoting racial diversity where the school has a history of racial discrimination in employment? (5) Remedying the school district's past racial discrimination against this particular teacher? (6) Providing minority role models for minority students at the school? (7) None of the above?

Would your answers be different if the situation involved not school employment but rather admission to an elite state university? Or school assignment within a public school district where parents consider some schools better than others? Would your answers be different if the situation involved the consideration of race in bidding for government contracts? If you think through these questions systematically, you will have gone a long way toward understanding the constitutional debate over affirmative action and the Equal Protection Clause in the Supreme Court's decisions.

Regents of the University of California v. Bakke
438 U.S. 265 (1978)

■ MR. JUSTICE POWELL announced the judgment of the Court.

This case presents a challenge to the special admissions program of the petitioner, the Medical School of the University of California at Davis, which is designed to assure the admission of a specified number of students from certain minority groups. The Superior Court of California sustained respondent's challenge, holding that petitioner's program violated the California Constitution, Title VI of the Civil Rights Act of 1964, and the Equal Protection Clause of the Fourteenth Amendment. . . . The Supreme Court of California affirmed those portions of the trial court's judgment declaring the special admissions program unlawful and enjoining petitioner from considering the race of any applicant. It modified that portion of the judgment denying respondent's requested injunction and directed the trial court to order his admission.

For the reasons stated in the following opinion, I believe that so much of the judgment of the California court as holds petitioner's special admissions program unlawful and directs that respondent be admitted to the Medical School must be affirmed. For the reasons expressed in a separate opinion, my Brothers THE CHIEF JUSTICE, MR. JUSTICE STEWART, MR. JUSTICE REHNQUIST and MR. JUSTICE STEVENS concur in this judgment.

I also conclude for the reasons stated in the following opinion that the portion of the court's judgment enjoining petitioner from according any consideration to race in its admissions process must be reversed. For reasons expressed in separate opinions, my Brothers MR. JUSTICE BRENNAN, MR. JUSTICE WHITE, MR. JUSTICE MARSHALL, and MR. JUSTICE BLACKMUN concur in this judgment.

I

The Medical School of the University of California at Davis opened in 1968 with an entering class of 50 students. In 1971, the size of the entering class was increased to 100 students, a level at which it remains. No admissions program for disadvantaged or minority students existed when the school opened, and the first class contained three Asians but no blacks, no Mexican-Americans, and no American Indians. Over the next two years, the faculty devised a special admissions program to increase the representation of "disadvantaged" students in each Medical School class. The special program consisted of a separate admissions system operating in coordination with the regular admissions process.

Under the regular admissions procedure, . . . [c]andidates whose overall undergraduate grade point averages fell below 2.5 on a scale of 4.0 were summarily rejected. About one out of six applicants was invited for a personal interview. . . . *[Interviewed applicants were given a "benchmark" score derived from ratings by interviewers, overall GPA, GPA in science courses, MCAT scores, letters of recommendation, extracurricular activities and other biographical data.—Editors]*

The special admissions program operated with a separate committee, a majority of whom were members of minority groups. On the 1973 application form, candidates were asked to indicate whether they wished to be considered as "economically and/or educationally disadvantaged" applicants; on the 1974 form the question was whether they wished to be considered as members of a "minority group," which the Medical School apparently viewed as "Blacks," "Chicanos," "Asians," and "American Indians." If these questions were answered affirmatively, the application was forwarded to the special admissions committee. . . . [S]pecial candidates did not have to meet the 2.5 grade point average cutoff applied to regular applicants. . . . The special committee continued to recommend special applicants until a number prescribed by faculty vote were admitted. While the overall class size was still 50, the prescribed number was 8; in 1973 and 1974, when the class size had doubled to 100, the prescribed number of special admissions also doubled, to 16.

From the year of the increase in class size—1971—through 1974, the special program resulted in the admission of 21 black students, 30 Mexican-Americans, and 12 Asians, for a total of 63 minority students. Over the same period, the regular admissions program produced 1 black, 6 Mexican-Americans, and 37 Asians, for a total of 44 minority students. . . .

Allan Bakke is a white male who applied to the Davis Medical School in both 1973 and 1974. In both years Bakke's application was considered under the general admissions program, and [rejected]. There were four special admissions slots unfilled at that time however, for which Bakke was not considered. . . . In both years, applicants were admitted under the special program with grade point averages, MCAT scores, and benchmark scores significantly lower than Bakke's. . . .

III–A

. . . Petitioner argues that the court below erred in applying strict scrutiny, as this inexact term has been applied in our cases. . . .

The guarantees of the Fourteenth Amendment extend to all persons. Its language is explicit: "No State shall . . . deny to any person within its jurisdiction the equal protection of the laws." It is settled beyond question that the "rights created by the first section of the Fourteenth Amendment are, by its terms, guaranteed to the individual. The rights established are personal rights." *Shelley v. Kraemer*, 334 U.S. 1, 22 (1948). The guarantee of equal protection cannot mean one thing when applied to one individual and something else when applied to a person of another color. If both are not accorded the same protection, then it is not equal.

Nevertheless, petitioner argues that the court below erred in applying strict scrutiny to the special admissions program because white males, such as respondent, are not a "discrete and insular minority" requiring extraordinary protection from the majoritarian political process. *United States v. Carolene Products Co.*, 304 U.S. 144, 152–153 n. 4 (1938). This rationale, however, has never been invoked in our decisions as a prerequisite to subjecting racial or ethnic distinctions to strict scrutiny. Nor has this Court held that discreteness and insularity constitute necessary preconditions to a holding that a particular classification is invidious.[28] These characteristics may be relevant in deciding whether or not to add new types of classifications to the list of "suspect" categories or whether a particular classification survives close examination. Racial and ethnic classifications, however, are subject to stringent examination without regard to these additional characteristics. . . .

B

This perception of racial and ethnic distinctions is rooted in our Nation's constitutional and demographic history. The Court's initial view of the Fourteenth Amendment was that its "one pervading purpose" was "the freedom of the slave race, the security and firm establishment of that freedom, and the protection of the newly-made freeman and citizen from the oppressions of those who had formerly exercised dominion over him." *Slaughter-House Cases*, 83 U.S. (16 Wall.) 36, 71 (1873). The Equal Protection Clause, however, was "[v]irtually strangled in infancy by post-civil-war judicial reactionism." It was relegated to decades of relative desuetude while the Due Process Clause of the Fourteenth Amendment, after a short germinal period, flourished as a cornerstone in the Court's defense of property and liberty of contract. See, e.g., *Lochner v. New York*, 198 U.S. 45 (1905). In that cause, the Fourteenth Amendment's "one pervading purpose" was displaced. See, e.g., *Plessy v. Ferguson*, 163 U.S. 537 (1896). It was only as the era of substantive due process came to a close, see, e.g., *West Coast Hotel Co. v. Parrish*, 300 U.S. 379 (1937), that the Equal Protection Clause began to attain a genuine measure of vitality.

By that time it was no longer possible to peg the guarantees of the Fourteenth Amendment to the struggle for equality of one racial minority. During the dormancy of the Equal Protection Clause, the United States had become a Nation of minorities. Each had to struggle—and to some extent struggles still—to overcome the prejudices not of a monolithic majority, but of a "majority" composed of various minority groups of whom it was said—perhaps unfairly in many cases—that a shared characteristic was a willingness to disadvantage other groups. As the Nation filled with the stock of many lands, the reach of the Clause was gradually extended to all ethnic groups seeking protection from official discrimination. See *Strauder v. West Virginia*, 100 U.S. 303, 308 (1880) (Celtic Irishmen) (dictum); *Yick Wo v. Hopkins*, 118 U.S. 356 (1886) (Chinese); *Truax v. Raich*, 239 U.S. 33, 41 (1915) (Austrian resident aliens); *Korematsu v. United States*, 323 U.S. 214 (1944) (Japanese); *Hernandez v. Texas*, 347 U.S. 475 (1954) (Mexican-Americans). The guarantees of equal protection, said the Court in *Yick Wo*, "are universal in their application, to all persons within the territorial jurisdiction, without regard to any differences of race, of color, or of nationality; and the equal protection of the laws is a pledge of the protection of equal laws."

Although many of the Framers of the Fourteenth Amendment conceived of its primary function as bridging the vast distance between members of the Negro race and the white "majority," *Slaughter-House Cases*, the Amendment itself was framed in universal terms, without reference to color, ethnic origin, or condition of prior servitude. . . . Indeed, it is not unlikely that among the Framers were many who would have applauded a reading of the Equal Protection Clause that states a

---

[28] After *Carolene Products*, the first specific reference in our decisions to the elements of "discreteness and insularity" appears in *Minersville School District v. Gobitis*, 310 U.S. 586, 606 (1940) (Stone, J., dissenting). The next does not appear until 1970. These elements have been relied upon in recognizing a suspect class in only one group of cases, those involving aliens.

principle of universal application and is responsive to the racial, ethnic, and cultural diversity of the Nation. See, e.g., Cong. Globe, 39th Cong., 1st Sess., 1056 (1866) (remarks of Rep. Niblack); id., at 2891–2892 (remarks of Sen. Conness); id., 40th Cong., 2d Sess., 883 (1868) (remarks of Sen. Howe) (Fourteenth Amendment "protect[s] classes from class legislation"). See also Bickel, *The Original Understanding and the Segregation Decision*, 69 Harv. L. Rev. 1, 60–63 (1955).

Petitioner urges us to adopt for the first time a more restrictive view of the Equal Protection Clause and hold that discrimination against members of the white "majority" cannot be suspect if its purpose can be characterized as "benign."[34] The clock of our liberties, however, cannot be turned back to 1868. *Brown v. Board of Education*, 347 U.S. 483, 492 (1954). It is far too late to argue that the guarantee of equal protection to all persons permits the recognition of special wards entitled to a degree of protection greater than that accorded others. "The Fourteenth Amendment is not directed solely against discrimination due to a 'two-class theory'—that is, based upon differences between 'white' and Negro." *Hernandez*, at 478.

Once the artificial line of a "two-class theory" of the Fourteenth Amendment is put aside, the difficulties entailed in varying the level of judicial review according to a perceived "preferred" status of a particular racial or ethnic minority are intractable. The concepts of "majority" and "minority" necessarily reflect temporary arrangements and political judgments. As observed above, the white "majority" itself is composed of various minority groups, most of which can lay claim to a history of prior discrimination at the hands of the State and private individuals. Not all of these groups can receive preferential treatment and corresponding judicial tolerance of distinctions drawn in terms of race and nationality, for then the only "majority" left would be a new minority of white Anglo-Saxon Protestants. There is no principled basis for deciding which groups would merit "heightened judicial solicitude" and which would not. Courts would be asked to evaluate the extent of the prejudice and consequent harm suffered by various minority groups. Those whose societal injury is thought to exceed some arbitrary level of tolerability then would be entitled to preferential classifications at the expense of individuals belonging to other groups. Those classifications would be free from exacting judicial scrutiny. As these preferences began to have their desired effect, and the consequences of past discrimination were undone, new judicial rankings would be necessary. The kind of variable sociological and political analysis necessary to produce such rankings

---

[34] In the view of MR. JUSTICE BRENNAN, MR. JUSTICE WHITE, MR. JUSTICE MARSHALL, and MR. JUSTICE BLACKMUN, the pliable notion of "stigma" is the crucial element in analyzing racial classifications. The Equal Protection Clause is not framed in terms of "stigma." Certainly the word has no clearly defined constitutional meaning. It reflects a subjective judgment that is standardless. *All* state-imposed classifications that rearrange burdens and benefits on the basis of race are likely to be viewed with deep resentment by the individuals burdened. The denial to innocent persons of equal rights and opportunities may outrage those so deprived and therefore may be perceived as invidious. These individuals are likely to find little comfort in the notion that the deprivation they are asked to endure is merely the price of membership in the dominant majority and that its imposition is inspired by the supposedly benign purpose of aiding others. One should not lightly dismiss the inherent unfairness of, and the perception of mistreatment that accompanies, a system of allocating benefits and privileges on the basis of skin color and ethnic origin. Moreover, MR. JUSTICE BRENNAN, MR. JUSTICE WHITE, MR. JUSTICE MARSHALL, and MR. JUSTICE BLACKMUN offer no principle for deciding whether preferential classifications reflect a benign remedial purpose or a malevolent stigmatic classification, since they are willing in this case to accept mere post hoc declarations by an isolated state entity—a medical school faculty—unadorned by particularized findings of past discrimination, to establish such a remedial purpose.

simply does not lie within the judicial competence—even if they otherwise were politically feasible and socially desirable.

Moreover, there are serious problems of justice connected with the idea of preference itself. First, it may not always be clear that a so-called preference is in fact benign. Courts may be asked to validate burdens imposed upon individual members of a particular group in order to advance the group's general interest. Nothing in the Constitution supports the notion that individuals may be asked to suffer otherwise impermissible burdens in order to enhance the societal standing of their ethnic groups. Second, preferential programs may only reinforce common stereotypes holding that certain groups are unable to achieve success without special protection based on a factor having no relationship to individual worth. Third, there is a measure of inequity in forcing innocent persons in respondent's position to bear the burdens of redressing grievances not of their making.

By hitching the meaning of the Equal Protection Clause to these transitory considerations, we would be holding, as a constitutional principle, that judicial scrutiny of classifications touching on racial and ethnic background may vary with the ebb and flow of political forces. Disparate constitutional tolerance of such classifications well may serve to exacerbates racial and ethnic antagonisms rather than alleviate them. Also, the mutability of a constitutional principle, based upon shifting political and social judgments, undermines the chances for consistent application of the Constitution from one generation to the next, a critical feature of its coherent interpretation. . . .

C

Petitioner contends that on several occasions this Court has approved preferential classifications without applying the most exacting scrutiny. Most of the cases upon which petitioner relies are drawn from three areas: school desegregation, employment discrimination, and sex discrimination. Each of the cases cited presented a situation materially different from the facts of this case.

The school desegregation cases are inapposite. Each involved remedies for clearly determined constitutional violations. E.g., *Swann v. Charlotte-Mecklenburg Board of Education*, 402 U.S. 1 (1971); *Green v. County School Board*, 391 U.S. 430 (1968). . . . Moreover, the scope of the remedies was not permitted to exceed the extent of the violations. . . .

The employment discrimination cases also do not advance petitioner's cause. For example, in *Franks v. Bowman Transportation Co.*, 424 U.S. 747 (1976), we approved a retroactive award of seniority to a class of Negro truckdrivers who had been the victims of discrimination—not just by society at large, but by the respondent in that case. . . . But we have never approved preferential classifications in the absence of proved constitutional or statutory violations.

Nor is petitioner's view as to the applicable standard supported by the fact that gender-based classifications are not subjected to this level of scrutiny. E.g., *Craig v. Boren*, 429 U.S. 190, 211 (1976) (Powell, J., concurring). Gender-based distinctions are less likely to create the analytical and practical problems present in preferential programs premised on racial or ethnic criteria. With respect to gender there are only two possible classifications. The incidence of the burdens imposed by preferential classifications is clear. There are no rival groups which can claim that they, too, are entitled to preferential treatment. Classwide questions as to the group suffering previous injury and groups which fairly can be burdened are relatively manageable for reviewing courts. The resolution of these same questions in the context of racial and ethnic preferences presents far more complex and intractable problems than gender-based classifications. More importantly, the perception of racial classifications as inherently odious stems from a lengthy and tragic history that gender-based classifications do not share. In sum, the Court has never viewed such classification as inherently suspect or as comparable to racial or ethnic classifications for the purpose of equal protection analysis. . . .

IV

We have held that in "order to justify the use of a suspect classification, a State must show that its purpose or interest is both constitutionally permissible and substantial, and that its use of the classification is 'necessary . . . to the accomplishment' of its purpose or the safeguarding of its interest." The special admissions program purports to serve the purposes of: (i) "reducing the historic deficit of traditionally disfavored minorities in medical schools and in the medical profession"; (ii) countering the effects of societal discrimination; (iii) increasing the number of physicians who will practice in communities currently underserved; and (iv) obtaining the educational benefits that flow from an ethnically diverse student body. It is necessary to decide which, if any, of these purposes is substantial enough to support the use of a suspect classification.

A

If petitioner's purpose is to assure within its student body some specified percentage of a particular group merely because of its race or ethnic origin, such a preferential purpose must be rejected not as insubstantial but as facially invalid. Preferring members of any one group for no reason other than race or ethnic origin is discrimination for its own sake. This the Constitution forbids. E.g., *Loving v. Virginia*, 388 U.S. 1, 11 (1967); *Brown v. Board of Education* (1954).

B

The State certainly has a legitimate and substantial interest in ameliorating, or eliminating where feasible, the disabling effects of identified discrimination. The line of school desegregation cases, commencing with *Brown*, attests to the importance of this state goal and the commitment of the judiciary to affirm all lawful means toward its attainment. In the school cases, the States were required by court order to redress the wrongs worked by specific instances of racial discrimination. That goal was far more focused than the remedying of the effects of "societal discrimination," an amorphous concept of injury that may be ageless in its reach into the past. . . .

Hence, the purpose of helping certain groups whom the faculty of the Davis Medical School perceived as victims of "societal discrimination" does not justify a classification that imposes disadvantages upon persons like respondent, who bear no responsibility for whatever harm the beneficiaries of the special admissions program are thought to have suffered. To hold otherwise would be to convert a remedy heretofore reserved for violations of legal rights into a privilege that all institutions throughout the Nation could grant at their pleasure to whatever groups are perceived as victims of societal discrimination. That is a step we have never approved.

C

Petitioner identifies, as another purpose of its program, improving the delivery of health-care services to communities currently underserved. It may be assumed that in some situations a State's interest in facilitating the health care of its citizens is sufficiently compelling to support the use of a suspect classification. But there is virtually no evidence in the record indicating that petitioner's special admissions program is either needed or geared to promote that goal. . . .

D

The fourth goal asserted by petitioner is the attainment of a diverse student body. This clearly is a constitutionally permissible goal for an institution of higher education. Academic freedom, though not a specifically enumerated constitutional right, long has been viewed as a special concern of the First Amendment. The freedom of a university to make its own judgments as to education includes the selection of its student body. . . .

Thus, in arguing that its universities must be accorded the right to select those students who will contribute the most to the "robust exchange of ideas," petitioner invokes a countervailing constitutional interest, that of the First Amendment. In this light, petitioner must be viewed as seeking to achieve a goal that is of paramount importance in the fulfillment of its mission. . . .

Physicians serve a heterogeneous population. An otherwise qualified medical student with a particular background—whether it be ethnic, geographic, culturally advantaged or disadvantaged—may bring to a professional school of medicine experiences, outlooks, and ideas that enrich the training of its student body and better equip its graduates to render with understanding their vital service to humanity.

. . . As the interest of diversity is compelling in the context of a university's admissions program, the question remains whether the program's racial classification is necessary to promote this interest.

V–A

It may be assumed that the reservation of a specified number of seats in each class for individuals from the preferred ethnic groups would contribute to the attainment of considerable ethnic diversity in the student body. But petitioner's argument that this is the only effective means of serving the interest of diversity is seriously flawed. In a most fundamental sense the argument misconceives the nature of the state interest that would justify consideration of race or ethnic background. It is not an interest in simple ethnic diversity, in which a specified percentage of the student body is in effect guaranteed to be members of selected ethnic groups, with the remaining percentage an undifferentiated aggregation of students. The diversity that furthers a compelling state interest encompasses a far broader array of qualifications and characteristics of which racial or ethnic origin is but a single though important element. Petitioner's special admissions program, focused solely on ethnic diversity, would hinder rather than further attainment of genuine diversity. . . .

The experience of other university admissions programs, which take race into account in achieving the educational diversity valued by the First Amendment, demonstrates that the assignment of a fixed number of places to a minority group is not a necessary means toward that end. An illuminating example is found in the Harvard College program. . . .

In such an admissions program, race or ethnic background may be deemed a "plus" in a particular applicant's file, yet it does not insulate the individual from comparison with all other candidates for the available seats. The file of a particular black applicant may be examined for his potential contribution to diversity without the factor of race being decisive when compared, for example, with that of an applicant identified as an Italian-American if the latter is thought to exhibit qualities more likely to promote beneficial educational pluralism. . . .

This kind of program treats each applicant as an individual in the admissions process. The applicant who loses out on the last available seat to another candidate receiving a "plus" on the basis of ethnic background will not have been foreclosed from all consideration for that seat simply because he was not the right color or had the wrong surname. It would mean only that his combined qualifications, which may have included similar nonobjective factors, did not outweigh those of the other applicant. His qualifications would have been weighed fairly and competitively, and he would have no basis to complain of unequal treatment under the Fourteenth Amendment.

It has been suggested that an admissions program which considers race only as one factor is simply a subtle and more sophisticated—but no less effective—means of according racial preference than the Davis program. A facial intent to discriminate, however, is evident in petitioner's preference program and not denied in this case. No such facial infirmity exists in an admissions program where race or ethnic background is simply one element—to be weighed fairly against other elements—in the selection process. . . . And a court would not assume that a university, professing to employ a facially nondiscriminatory admissions policy, would operate it as a cover for the functional equivalent of a quota system. In short, good faith would be presumed in the absence of a showing to the contrary in the manner permitted by our cases.

B

In summary, it is evident that the Davis special admissions program involves the use of an explicit racial classification never before countenanced by this Court. It tells applicants who are not Negro, Asian, or Chicano that they are totally excluded from a specific percentage of the seats in an entering class. . . .

The fatal flaw in petitioner's preferential program is its disregard of individual rights as guaranteed by the Fourteenth Amendment. Such rights are not absolute. But when a State's distribution of benefits or imposition of burdens hinges on ancestry or the color of a person's skin, that individual is entitled to a demonstration that the challenged classification is necessary to promote a substantial state interest. Petitioner has failed to carry this burden. For this reason, that portion of the California court's judgment holding petitioner's special admissions program invalid under the Fourteenth Amendment must be affirmed.

C

In enjoining petitioner from ever considering the race of any applicant, however, the courts below failed to recognize that the State has a substantial interest that legitimately may be served by a properly devised admissions program involving the competitive consideration of race and ethnic origin. For this reason, so much of the

California court's judgment as enjoins petitioner from any consideration of the race of any applicant must be reversed.

VI

With respect to respondent's entitlement to an injunction directing his admission to the Medical School, petitioner has conceded that it could not carry its burden of proving that, but for the existence of its unlawful special admissions program, respondent still would not have been admitted. Hence, respondent is entitled to the injunction, and that portion of the judgment must be affirmed.

■ Opinion of MR. JUSTICE BRENNAN, MR. JUSTICE WHITE, MR. JUSTICE MARSHALL, and MR. JUSTICE BLACKMUN, concurring in the judgment in part and dissenting in part.

. . . Our Nation was founded on the principle that "all Men are created equal." Yet candor requires acknowledgment that the Framers of our Constitution, to forge the 13 Colonies into one Nation, openly compromised this principle of equality with its antithesis: slavery. The consequences of this compromise are well known and have aptly been called our "American Dilemma." Still, it is well to recount how recent the time has been, if it has yet come, when the promise of our principles has flowered into the actuality of equal opportunity for all regardless of race or color.

The Fourteenth Amendment, the embodiment in the Constitution of our abiding belief in human equality, has been the law of our land for only slightly more than half its 200 years. And for half of that half, the Equal Protection Clause of the Amendment was largely moribund . . . Not until 1954—only 24 years ago—was this odious doctrine interred by our decision in *Brown v. Board of Education (Brown I)*, and its progeny, which proclaimed that separate schools and public facilities of all sorts were inherently unequal and forbidden under our Constitution. Even then inequality was not eliminated with "all deliberate speed." *Brown v. Board of Education*, 349 U.S. 294, 301 (1955). . . .

Against this background, claims that law must be "color-blind" or that the datum of race is no longer relevant to public policy must be seen as aspiration rather than as description of reality. This is not to denigrate aspiration; for reality rebukes us that race has too often been used by those who would stigmatize and oppress minorities. Yet we cannot—and, as we shall demonstrate, need not under our Constitution . . . —let color blindness become myopia which masks the reality that many "created equal" have been treated within our lifetimes as inferior both by the law and by their fellow citizens. . . .

III

. . . Respondent argues that racial classifications are always suspect and, consequently, that this Court should weigh the importance of the objectives served by Davis' special admissions program to see if they are compelling. In addition, he asserts that this Court must inquire whether, in its judgment, there are alternatives to racial classifications which would suit Davis' purposes. Petitioner, on the other hand, states that our proper role is simply to accept petitioner's determination that the racial classifications used by its program are reasonably related to what it tells us are its benign purposes. We reject petitioner's view, but, because our prior cases are in many respects inapposite to that before us now, we find it necessary to define with precision the meaning of that inexact term, "strict scrutiny."

Unquestionably we have held that a government practice or statute which restricts "fundamental rights" or which contains "suspect classifications" is to be subjected to "strict scrutiny" and can be justified only if it furthers a compelling government purpose and, even then, only if no less restrictive alternative is available. But no fundamental right is involved here. Nor do whites as a class have any of the "traditional indicia of suspectness: the class is not saddled with such disabilities, or subjected to such a history of purposeful unequal treatment, or relegated to such a position of political powerlessness as to command extraordinary protection from the majoritarian political process." *San Antonio Independent School District v. Rodriguez*, 411 U.S. 1, 28 (1973); see *Carolene Products*, at 152 n. 4.

Moreover, if the University's representations are credited, this is not a case where racial classifications are "irrelevant and therefore prohibited." *Hirabayashi*, at 100. Nor has anyone suggested that the University's purposes contravene the cardinal principle that racial classifications that stigmatize—because they are drawn on the presumption that one race is inferior to another or because they put the weight of government behind racial hatred and separatism—are invalid without more. See *Yick Wo*, at 374; accord, *Strauder*, at 308; *Korematsu*, at 223; *Brown I*; *Loving v. Virginia*, at 11–12.

On the other hand, the fact that this case does not fit neatly into our prior analytic framework for race cases does not mean that it should be analyzed by applying the very loose rational-basis standard of review that is the very least that is always applied in equal protection cases.34 "[T]he mere recitation of a benign, compensatory purpose is not an automatic shield which protects against any inquiry into the actual purposes underlying a statutory scheme." *Califano v. Webster*, 430 U.S. 313, 317 (1977). . . .

In sum, because of the significant risk that racial classifications established for ostensibly benign purposes can be misused, causing effects not unlike those created by invidious classifications, it is inappropriate to inquire only whether there is any conceivable basis that might sustain such a classification. Instead, to justify such a classification an important and articulated purpose for its use must be shown. In addition, any statute must be stricken that stigmatizes any group or that singles out those least well represented in the political process to bear the brunt of a benign program. Thus, our review under the Fourteenth Amendment should be strict—not "'strict' in theory and fatal in fact,"36 because it is stigma that causes fatality—but strict and searching nonetheless.

IV

. . . Properly construed, therefore, our prior cases unequivocally show that a state government may adopt race-conscious programs if the purpose of such programs is to remove the disparate racial impact its actions might otherwise have and if there is reason to believe that the disparate impact is itself the product of past discrimination, whether its own or that of society at large. There is no question that Davis' program is valid under this test.

Certainly, on the basis of the undisputed factual submissions before this Court, Davis had a sound basis for believing that the problem of underrepresentation of minorities was substantial and chronic and that the problem was attributable to

---

36 Gunther, The Supreme Court, 1971 Term—Foreword: In Search of Evolving Doctrine on a Changing Court: A Model for a Newer Equal Protection, 86 Harv.L.Rev. 1, 8 (1972).

handicaps imposed on minority applicants by past and present racial discrimination. Until at least 1973, the practice of medicine in this country was, in fact, if not in law, largely the prerogative of whites. In 1950, for example, while Negroes constituted 10% of the total population, Negro physicians constituted only 2.2% of the total number of physicians. The overwhelming majority of these, moreover, were educated in two predominantly Negro medical schools, Howard and Meharry.

Davis clearly could conclude that the serious and persistent underrepresentation of minorities in medicine depicted by these statistics is the result of handicaps under which minority applicants labor as a consequence of a background of deliberate, purposeful discrimination against minorities in education and in society generally, as well as in the medical profession. From the inception of our national life, Negroes have been subjected to unique legal disabilities impairing access to equal educational opportunity. Under slavery, penal sanctions were imposed upon anyone attempting to educate Negroes. After enactment of the Fourteenth Amendment the States continued to deny Negroes equal educational opportunity, enforcing a strict policy of segregation that itself stamped Negroes as inferior, that relegated minorities to inferior educational institutions, and that denied them intercourse in the mainstream of professional life necessary to advancement. Segregation was not limited to public facilities, moreover, but was enforced by criminal penalties against private action as well. Thus, as late as 1908, this Court enforced a state criminal conviction against a private college for teaching Negroes together with whites. *Berea College v. Kentucky*, 211 U.S. 45.

Green v. County School Board gave explicit recognition to the fact that the habit of discrimination and the cultural tradition of race prejudice cultivated by centuries of legal slavery and segregation were not immediately dissipated when *Brown I* announced the constitutional principle that equal educational opportunity and participation in all aspects of American life could not be denied on the basis of race. Rather, massive official and private resistance prevented, and to a lesser extent still prevents, attainment of equal opportunity in education at all levels and in the professions. The generation of minority students applying to Davis Medical School since it opened in 1968—most of whom were born before or about the time *Brown I* was decided—clearly have been victims of this discrimination. . . .

It is not even claimed that Davis' program in any way operates to stigmatize or single out any discrete and insular, or even any identifiable, nonminority group. Nor will harm comparable to that imposed upon racial minorities by exclusion or separation on grounds of race be the likely result of the program. It does not, for example, establish an exclusive preserve for minority students apart from and exclusive of whites. Rather, its purpose is to overcome the effects of segregation by bringing the races together. True, whites are excluded from participation in the special admissions program, but this fact only operates to reduce the number of whites to be admitted in the regular admissions program in order to permit admission of a reasonable percentage—less than their proportion of the California population—of otherwise underrepresented qualified minority applicants.

Nor was Bakke in any sense stamped as inferior by the Medical School's rejection of him. Indeed, it is conceded by all that he satisfied those criteria regarded by the school as generally relevant to academic performance better than most of the minority members who were admitted. Moreover, there is absolutely no basis for concluding that Bakke's rejection as a result of Davis' use of racial preference will affect him throughout his life in the same way as the segregation of the Negro schoolchildren in *Brown I* would have affected them. Unlike discrimination against racial minorities, the use of racial preferences for remedial purposes does not inflict a pervasive injury upon individual whites in the sense that wherever they go or whatever they do there is a significant likelihood that they will be treated as second-class citizens because of their color. This distinction does not mean that the exclusion of a white resulting from the preferential use of race is not sufficiently serious to require justification; but it does mean that the injury inflicted by such a policy is not distinguishable from disadvantages caused by a wide range of government actions, none of which has ever been thought impermissible for that reason alone.

In addition, there is simply no evidence that the Davis program discriminates intentionally or unintentionally against any minority group which it purports to benefit. The program does not establish a quota in the invidious sense of a ceiling on the number of minority applicants to be admitted. Nor can the program reasonably be regarded as stigmatizing the program's beneficiaries or their race as inferior. The Davis program does not simply advance less qualified applicants; rather, it compensates applicants, who it is uncontested are fully qualified to study medicine, for educational disadvantages which it was reasonable to conclude were a product of state-fostered discrimination. Once admitted, these students must satisfy the same degree requirements as regularly admitted students; they are taught by the same faculty in the same classes; and their performance is evaluated by the same standards by which regularly admitted students are judged. . . .

Finally, Davis' special admissions program cannot be said to violate the Constitution simply because it has set aside a predetermined number of places for qualified minority applicants rather than using minority status as a positive factor to be considered in evaluating the applications of disadvantaged minority applicants. . . . There is no sensible, and certainly no constitutional, distinction between, for example, adding a set number of points to the admissions rating of disadvantaged minority applicants as an expression of the preference with the expectation that this will result in the admission of an approximately determined number of qualified minority applicants and setting a fixed number of places for such applicants as was done here.

The "Harvard" program, as those employing it readily concede, openly and successfully employs a racial criterion for the purpose of ensuring that some of the scarce places in institutions of higher education are allocated to disadvantaged minority students. . . . [A]ny State, including California, is free to adopt it in preference to a less acceptable alternative, just as it is generally free, as far as the Constitution is concerned, to abjure granting any racial preferences in its admissions program. But there is no basis for preferring a particular preference program simply because in achieving the same goals that the Davis Medical School is pursuing, it proceeds in a manner that is not immediately apparent to the public. . . .

■ MR. JUSTICE MARSHALL.

I agree with the judgment of the Court only insofar as it permits a university to consider the race of an applicant in making admissions decisions. I do not agree that petitioner's admissions program violates the Constitution. For it must be remembered that, during most of the past 200 years, the Constitution as interpreted by this Court did not prohibit the most ingenious and pervasive forms of discrimination against the Negro. Now, when a State acts to remedy the effects of that legacy of discrimination, I cannot believe that this same Constitution stands as a barrier.

I

Three hundred and fifty years ago, the Negro was dragged to this country in chains to be sold into slavery. Uprooted from his homeland and thrust into bondage for forced labor, the slave was deprived of all legal rights. It was unlawful to teach him to read; he could be sold away from his family and friends at the whim of his master; and killing or maiming him was not a crime. The system of slavery brutalized and dehumanized both master and slave. . . .

[Justice Marshall next described the protection of slavery by the Declaration of Independence, the Constitution, and Dred Scott.*—Editors]*

The status of the Negro as property was officially erased by his emancipation at the end of the Civil War. But the long-awaited emancipation, while freeing the Negro from slavery, did not bring him citizenship or equality in any meaningful way. Slavery was replaced by a system of "laws which imposed upon the colored race onerous disabilities and burdens, and curtailed their rights in the pursuit of life, liberty, and property to such an extent that their freedom was of little value." *Slaughter-House Cases,* at 70. . . .

Congress responded to the legal disabilities being imposed in the Southern States by passing the Reconstruction Acts and the Civil Rights Acts. Congress also responded to the needs of the Negroes at the end of the Civil War by establishing the Bureau of Refugees, Freedmen, and Abandoned Lands, better known as the Freedmen's Bureau, to supply food, hospitals, land, and education to the newly freed slaves. Thus, for a time it seemed as if the Negro might be protected from the continued denial of his civil rights and might be relieved of the disabilities that prevented him from taking his place as a free and equal citizen.

That time, however, was short-lived. Reconstruction came to a close, and, with the assistance of this Court, the Negro was rapidly stripped of his new civil rights. . . .

The Court began by interpreting the Civil War Amendments in a manner that sharply curtailed their substantive protections. See, e.g., *Slaughter-House Cases; United States v. Cruikshank,* 92 U.S. 542 (1876). Then in the notorious *Civil Rights Cases,* 109 U.S. 3 (1883), the Court strangled Congress' efforts to use its power to promote racial equality. In those cases the Court invalidated sections of the Civil Rights Act of 1875 that made it a crime to deny equal access to "inns, public conveyances, theatres and other places of public amusement." According to the Court, the Fourteenth Amendment gave Congress the power to proscribe only discriminatory action by the State. The Court ruled that the Negroes who were excluded from public places suffered only an invasion of their social rights at the hands of private individuals, and Congress had no power to remedy that. "When a man has emerged from slavery, and by the aid of beneficent legislation has shaken off the inseparable concomitants of that state," the Court concluded, "there must be some stage in the progress of his elevation when he takes the rank of a mere citizen, and ceases to be the special favorite of the laws. . . ." As Mr. Justice Harlan noted in dissent, however, the Civil War Amendments and Civil Rights Acts did not make the Negroes the "special favorite" of the laws but instead "sought to accomplish in reference to that race . . . —what had already been done in every State of the Union for the white race—to secure and protect rights belonging to them as freemen and citizens; nothing more."

The Court's ultimate blow to the Civil War Amendments and to the equality of Negroes came in *Plessy v. Ferguson.* . . . In the wake of *Plessy*, many States expanded their Jim Crow laws, which had up until that time been limited primarily to passenger trains and schools. The segregation of the races was extended to residential areas, parks, hospitals, theaters, waiting rooms, and bathrooms. There were even statutes and ordinances which authorized separate phone booths for Negroes and whites, which required that textbooks used by children of one race be kept separate from those used by the other, and which required that Negro and white prostitutes be kept in separate districts. . . .

Nor were the laws restricting the rights of Negroes limited solely to the Southern States. In many of the Northern States, the Negro was denied the right to vote, prevented from serving on juries, and excluded from theaters, restaurants, hotels, and inns. Under President Wilson, the Federal Government began to require segregation in Government buildings; desks of Negro employees were curtained off; separate bathrooms and separate tables in the cafeterias were provided; and even the galleries of the Congress were segregated. When his segregationist policies were attacked, President Wilson responded that segregation was "not humiliating but a benefit" and that he was "rendering [the Negroes] more safe in their possession of office and less likely to be discriminated against."

The enforced segregation of the races continued into the middle of the 20th century. In both World Wars, Negroes were for the most part confined to separate military units; it was not until 1948 that an end to segregation in the military was ordered by President Truman. And the history of the exclusion of Negro children from white public schools is too well known and recent to require repeating here. That Negroes were deliberately excluded from public graduate and professional schools—and thereby denied the opportunity to become doctors, lawyers, engineers, and the like—is also well established. It is of course true that some of the Jim Crow laws (which the decisions of this Court had helped to foster) were struck down by this Court in a series of decisions leading up to *Brown*. Those decisions, however, did not automatically end segregation, nor did they move Negroes from a position of legal inferiority to one of equality. The legacy of years of slavery and of years of second-class citizenship in the wake of emancipation could not be so easily eliminated.

II

The position of the Negro today in America is the tragic but inevitable consequence of centuries of unequal treatment. Measured by any benchmark of comfort or achievement, meaningful equality remains a distant dream for the Negro.

A Negro child today has a life expectancy which is shorter by more than five years than that of a white child. The Negro child's mother is over three times more likely to die of complications in childbirth, and the infant mortality rate for Negroes is nearly twice that for whites. The median income of the Negro family is only 60% that of the median of a white family, and the percentage of Negroes who live in families with incomes below the poverty line is nearly four times greater than that of whites.

When the Negro child reaches working age, he finds that America offers him significantly less than it offers his white counterpart. For Negro adults, the unemployment rate is twice that of whites, and the unemployment rate for Negro teenagers is nearly three times that of white teenagers. A Negro male who completes four years of college can expect a median annual income of merely $110 more than a white male who has only a high school diploma.9 Although Negroes represent 11.5% of the population, they are only 1.2% of the lawyers, and judges, 2% of the physicians, 2.3% of the dentists, 1.1% of the engineers and 2.6% of the college and university professors.

The relationship between those figures and the history of unequal treatment afforded to the Negro cannot be denied. At every point from birth to death the impact of the past is reflected in the still disfavored position of the Negro.

In light of the sorry history of discrimination and its devastating impact on the lives of Negroes, bringing the Negro into the mainstream of American life should be a state interest of the highest order. To fail to do so is to ensure that America will forever remain a divided society.

III

I do not believe that the Fourteenth Amendment requires us to accept that fate. Neither its history nor our past cases lend any support to the conclusion that a university may not remedy the cumulative effects of society's discrimination by giving consideration to race in an effort to increase the number and percentage of Negro doctors.

This Court long ago remarked that

> "in any fair and just construction of any section or phrase of these [Civil War] amendments, it is necessary to look to the purpose which we have said was the pervading spirit of them all, the evil which they were designed to remedy. . . ." *Slaughter-House Cases*, at 72.

It is plain that the Fourteenth Amendment was not intended to prohibit measures designed to remedy the effects of the Nation's past treatment of Negroes. The Congress that passed the Fourteenth Amendment is the same Congress that passed the 1866 Freedmen's Bureau Act, an Act that provided many of its benefits only to Negroes. Although the Freedmen's Bureau legislation provided aid for refugees, thereby including white persons within some of the relief measures, the bill was regarded, to the dismay of many Congressmen, as "solely and entirely for the freedmen, and to the exclusion of all other persons. . . ." Cong. Globe, 39th Cong., 1st Sess., 544 (1866) (remarks of Rep. Taylor). Indeed, the bill was bitterly opposed on the ground that it "undertakes to make the negro in some respects . . . superior . . . and gives them favors that the poor white boy in the North cannot get." Id., at 401 (remarks of Sen. McDougall). The bill's supporters defended it—not by rebutting the claim of special treatment—but by pointing to the need for such treatment:

> "The very discrimination it makes between 'destitute and suffering' negroes, and destitute and suffering white paupers, proceeds upon the distinction that, in the omitted case, civil rights and immunities are already sufficiently protected by the possession of political power, the absence of which in the case provided for necessitates governmental protection." Id., at App. 75 (remarks of Rep. Phelps).

Despite the objection to the special treatment the bill would provide for Negroes, it was passed by Congress. President Johnson vetoed this bill and also a subsequent bill that contained some modifications; one of his principal objections to both bills was that they gave special benefits to Negroes. Rejecting the concerns of the President and the bill's opponents, Congress overrode the President's second veto.

Since the Congress that considered and rejected the objections to the 1866 Freedmen's Bureau Act concerning special relief to Negroes also proposed the Fourteenth Amendment, it is inconceivable that the Fourteenth Amendment was intended to prohibit all race-conscious relief measures. It "would be a distortion of the policy manifested in that amendment, which was adopted to prevent state legislation designed to perpetuate discrimination on the basis of race or color." *Railway Mail Assn. v. Corsi*, 326 U.S. 88, 94 (1945), to hold that it barred state action to remedy the effects of that discrimination. Such a result would pervert the intent of the Framers by substituting abstract equality for the genuine equality the Amendment was intended to achieve. . . .

IV

While I applaud the judgment of the Court that a university may consider race in its admissions process, it is more than a little ironic that, after several hundred years of class-based discrimination against Negroes, the Court is unwilling to hold that a class-based remedy for that discrimination is permissible. In declining to so hold, today's judgment ignores the fact that for several hundred years Negroes have been discriminated against, not as individuals, but rather solely because of the color of their skins. It is unnecessary in 20th-century America to have individual Negroes demonstrate that they have been victims of racial discrimination; the racism of our society has been so pervasive that none, regardless of wealth or position, has managed to escape its impact. The experience of Negroes in America has been different in kind, not just in degree, from that of other ethnic groups. It is not merely the history of slavery alone but also that a whole people were marked as inferior by the law. And that mark has endured. The dream of America as the great melting pot has not been realized for the Negro; because of his skin color he never even made it into the pot. . . .

[H]ad the Court been willing in 1896, in *Plessy v. Ferguson*, to hold that the Equal Protection Clause forbids differences in treatment based on race, we would not be faced with this dilemma in 1978. We must remember, however, that the principle that the "Constitution is color-blind" appeared only in the opinion of the lone dissenter. The majority of the Court rejected the principle of color-blindness, and for the next 58 years, from *Plessy* to *Brown v. Board of Education*, ours was a Nation where, by law, an individual could be given "special" treatment based on the color of his skin.

It is because of a legacy of unequal treatment that we now must permit the institutions of this society to give consideration to race in making decisions about who will hold the positions of influence, affluence, and prestige in America. For far too long, the doors to those positions have been shut to Negroes. If we are ever to become a fully integrated society, one in which the color of a person's skin will not determine the opportunities available to him or her, we must be willing to take steps to open those doors. I do not believe that anyone can truly look into America's past and still find that a remedy for the effects of that past is impermissible. . . .

I fear that we have come full circle. After the Civil War our Government started several "affirmative action" programs. This Court in the *Civil Rights Cases* and

Plessy v. Ferguson destroyed the movement toward complete equality. For almost a century no action was taken, and this nonaction was with the tacit approval of the courts. Then we had *Brown v. Board of Education* and the Civil Rights Acts of Congress, followed by numerous affirmative-action programs. Now, we have this Court again stepping in, this time to stop affirmative-action programs of the type used by the University of California.

■ [The opinions of JUSTICE WHITE, JUSTICE BLACKMUN, and JUSTICE STEVENS are omitted.]

NOTES

1.   *Bakke* was not the Court's first case involving racial preferences in state university admissions. In *DeFunis v. Odegaard*, 416 U.S. 312 (1974), Marco DeFunis, a white applicant who had been denied admission to the University of Washington School of Law, challenged the law school's consideration of race in admissions. The state trial court granted a preliminary injunction ordering DeFunis admitted to law school while the case was pending. By the time the case reached the U.S. Supreme Court, DeFunis was nearing graduation. The law school acknowledged that it would allow him to complete his law school education no matter what the Court decided. The Court found the case moot and vacated the decisions below. Only Justice Douglas would have reached the merits; he would have ruled in DeFunis's favor, on the ground that the Equal Protection Clause requires "consideration of each applicant in a racially neutral way."

2.   The split decision in *Bakke* produced confusion for the next quarter century. But a shifting majority in *Bakke* did embrace several propositions of law that have continued as part of the Court's jurisprudence. First, *Bakke* requires strict scrutiny of minority racial preferences: "Racial and ethnic distinctions of any sort are inherently suspect and thus call for the most exacting judicial examination." Second, *Bakke* rejected racial balancing as a state interest that would be sufficiently compelling to justify a racial classification: "Preferring members of any one group for no reason other than race or ethnic origin is discrimination for its own sake. This the Constitution forbids." Third, *Bakke* rejected general societal discrimination as too "amorphous" to be sufficiently compelling to justify racial preferences: "We have never approved a classification that aids persons perceived as members of relatively victimized groups at the expense of other innocent individuals in the absence of judicial, legislative, or administrative findings of constitutional or statutory violations." Fourth, *Bakke* found insufficient the evidence that those who benefitted from the racial preferences at issue would work in "underserved" communities—which was one theory advanced to justify them. Fifth, Justice Powell's opinion considered racial diversity in education a sufficiently compelling government interest to justify "flexible" consideration of race as a "plus," though it was not sufficiently compelling to justify a racial quota or set-aside. The four justices who thought minority race could be considered without limitation implicitly agreed that race could be considered *at least* as a "plus."

3.   Since *Bakke* the Court has decided several major cases on affirmative action in higher education. In *Grutter v. Bollinger*, 539 U.S. 306 (2003), the Court heard a challenge to a University of Michigan Law School program providing an un-quantified racial preference in admissions in order to promote diversity in the entering class. It narrowly upheld (5–4) the law school's program. But in a companion case decided the same day, *Gratz v. Bollinger*, 539 U.S. 244 (2003), the Court struck down (6–3) the University of Michigan's undergraduate admissions racial preference program. That program gave a quantified racial preference—a bonus of twenty points for racial minority

status on an applicant's admissions score. There were one hundred possible points on the admissions score. (Only two justices agreed with the outcome in both cases, while seven justices thought the two affirmative-action programs should be treated the same way.) The people of Michigan subsequently enacted a state constitutional amendment prohibiting the use of race-conscious affirmative action in public education, as well as public employment and contracting. In *Schuette v. Coalition to Defend Affirmative Action, Integration and Immigrant Rights and Fight for Equality By Any Means Necessary*, 134 S.Ct. 1623 (2014), the Court rejected (6–2) a challenge to the state constitutional amendment, holding that on questions of affirmative action "the courts may not disempower the voters from choosing which path to follow."

Two other cases involved Abigail Fisher and the University of Texas. Fisher, a white applicant, was denied admission. She challenged the use of race by the university as a violation of the Equal Protection Clause. The lower courts rejected her challenge, but in *Fisher v. University of Texas at Austin*, 133 S.Ct. 2411 (2013), the Court reversed and remanded for application of a more rigorous version of "strict scrutiny" (7–1). In the sequel, *Fisher v. University of Texas at Austin*, 136 S.Ct. 2198 (2016), the Court rejected her claim on the merits (4–3), reaffirming the use of race as a factor in public university admissions.

Throughout these cases the formal doctrine has remained fairly constant: affirmative action programs must survive strict scrutiny, the only interest found "compelling" enough to justify them is educational diversity, and the program has to be "narrowly tailored" to achieve that interest. But how the standards are applied has varied from case to case. There have been four recurring points of contention:

First, how can a court know that the interest of the university in having an affirmative action program really is educational diversity (rather than, say, racial balancing)? This debate often turns on whether the courts should defer to the judgment of educational officials—about the need for racial diversity, about what their goal actually is, about which racial minorities should receive preferences, and about how broadly or granularly a racial minority is defined. Although the formal standard is strict scrutiny, the most recent case, *Fisher II*, is quite deferential to university administrators and relies on their affidavits to establish the compelling interest.

Second, in deciding whether the university program is "narrowly tailored" to accomplish the aim, the Court asks whether a university could achieve its interest in educational diversity through race-neutral means. *Fisher II* kept this standard but applied it with latitude, casting doubt on one commonly invoked means of increasing minority admissions in universities (i.e., reliance on high school class rank).

Third, there is debate about the policy question of whether affirmative action is in fact good for minority students. The supporters unwaveringly affirm that this is the goal and effect of the programs. Critics, including Justice Thomas, argue that minority students are not well-served by such programs, which instead serve the interests of college administrators. Much of the debate concerns the "mismatch effect," a hypothesis that when students are admitted (for whatever reason) to schools better than their academic qualifications would warrant, they are more likely to struggle in school and afterwards. If there is a mismatch effect, it would suggest that whatever the benefits of affirmative action may be, they do not necessarily accrue to the students it is meant to help. Whether there is a mismatch effect is highly controversial, and the debate among social scientists has been heated. For a review of the literature, see Peter Arcidiacono & Michael Lovenheim, *Affirmative Action and the Quality-Fit Tradeoff*, 54 Journal of Econ. Lit. 3 (2016).

Fourth, there is the question of whether affirmative action is a provisional measure or is here to stay. In her opinion for the Court in *Grutter v. Bollinger*, Justice O'Connor famously announced that "We expect that 25 years from now, the use of racial preferences will no longer be necessary to further the interest approved today." 539 U.S. 306, 344 (2003). Without referring to any particular sunset, the same anxiety can be seen in Justice Kennedy's opinon for the Court in *Fisher II*, where he said the university's plan might in the future not be constitutional "without refinement," and he called for the university to continuously consider race-neutral alternatives and data about the effects of affirmative action. *Fisher II*, 136 S.Ct. at 2214–2215.

4.   In *Parents Involved in Community Schools v. Seattle School District #1*, 551 U.S. 701 (2007), the Court was faced with the question "whether a public school that had not operated legally segregated schools or has been found to be unitary may choose to classify students by race and rely upon that classification in making school assignments." In a 5–4 opinion written by Chief Justice Roberts, the Court answered *no*. The classification was not justified as a remedy for past intentional discrimination, and could not be justified on grounds of seeking racial balance for its own sake. The Court distinguished *Grutter* as addressing the interest in "diversity in higher education" and involving a program in which race was only one consideration among many, not *"the* factor." The Court found no compelling interest justifying the school districts' practices: "the school districts have not carried their burden of showing that the ends they seek justify the particular extreme means they have chosen—classifying individual students on the basis of their race and discriminating among them on that basis." *Id.* at 745. Four justices vigorously dissented, arguing that "the Equal Protection Clause permits local school boards to use race-conscious criteria to achieve positive race-related goals" and that plans like those at issue were needed to undo patterns of racial segregation and vindicate the de-segregation vision of *Brown*.

[*Assignment 71*]

Affirmative Action in Government Contracts and Licenses

Federal and state governments in the United States have used affirmative action when awarding contracts and licenses. This use of racial preferences has also been challenged.

In *City of Richmond v. J.A. Croson Company*, 488 U.S. 469 (1989) (6–3), the Supreme Court considered the constitutionality under the Equal Protection Clause of an ordinance adopted by the City Council of Richmond, Virginia. The ordinance specified that prime contractors to whom the city gave construction contracts must set aside 30% of all subcontracts for minority-owned businesses. These in turn were defined as being businesses that were at least 51% minority owned. Minority group members were defined as including "[c]itizens of the United States who are Blacks, Spanish-speaking, Orientals, Indians, Eskimos, or Aleuts." Although there was most certainly a history of discrimination against black citizens in Richmond, there was no proof of any prior discrimination against "Spanish-speakers, Orientals, Indians, Eskimos, or Aleuts." The Supreme Court held that the ordinance violated the Fourteenth Amendment. Justice O'Connor's opinion for the Court did hold out the possibility that state and local governments might in some circumstances be able to discriminate on the basis of race to ameliorate the effects of past discrimination. Justice Scalia concurred separately, endorsing a color-blindness rule like the one championed by the first Justice Harlan in his dissent in *Plessy v. Ferguson*. Justice

Marshall, whose dissent was joined by Justices Brennan and Blackmun, called the set-aside rule "a welcome symbol of racial progress [in] the former capital of the Confederacy."

The year after *Croson*, in *Metro Broadcasting, Inc. v. FCC*, 497 U.S. 547 (1990) (5–4), a sharply divided Supreme Court upheld minority preference programs in the federal government's awarding of certain broadcast licenses. The Court applied intermediate scrutiny (for the only time in this area of law) and found a sufficiently important government interest in diversity of programming, keyed to the race of station owners. In one of the dissents, Justice Kennedy announced his "regret that after a century of judicial opinions we interpret the Constitution to do no more than move us from 'separate but equal' to 'unequal but benign.'"

Which path—*Croson* or *Metro Broadcasting*—should the Court take? That question was presented in the next case.

Adarand Constructors, Inc. v. Pena
515 U.S. 200 (1995)

■ JUSTICE O'CONNOR announced the judgment of the Court and delivered an opinion with respect to Parts I, II, III–A, III–B, III–D, and IV, which is for the Court except insofar as it might be inconsistent with the views expressed in JUSTICE SCALIA's concurrence, and an opinion with respect to Part III–C in which JUSTICE KENNEDY joins.

. . .

I

In 1989, the Central Federal Lands Highway Division (CFLHD), which is part of the United States Department of Transportation (DOT), awarded the prime contract for a highway construction project in Colorado to Mountain Gravel & Construction Company. Mountain Gravel then solicited bids from subcontractors for the guardrail portion of the contract. Adarand, a Colorado-based highway construction company specializing in guardrail work, submitted the low bid. Gonzales Construction Company also submitted a bid.

The prime contract's terms provide that Mountain Gravel would receive additional compensation if it hired subcontractors certified as small businesses controlled by "socially and economically disadvantaged individuals," Gonzales is certified as such a business; Adarand is not. Mountain Gravel awarded the subcontract to Gonzales, despite Adarand's low bid, and Mountain Gravel's Chief Estimator has submitted an affidavit stating that Mountain Gravel would have accepted Adarand's bid, had it not been for the additional payment it received by hiring Gonzales instead. Federal law requires that a subcontracting clause similar to the one used here must appear in most federal agency contracts, and it also requires the clause to state that "[t]he contractor shall presume that socially and economically disadvantaged individuals include Black Americans, Hispanic Americans, Native Americans, Asian Pacific Americans, and other minorities, or any other individual found to be disadvantaged by the [Small Business] Administration pursuant to section 8(a) of the Small Business Act." 15 U.S.C. §§ 637(d)(2), (3). Adarand claims that the presumption set forth in that statute discriminates on the basis of race in violation of the Federal Government's Fifth Amendment obligation not to deny anyone equal protection of the laws. . . .

[The Court next described the relevant federal statutes and regulations. A Department of Transportation appropriations measure, the Surface Transportation and Uniform Relocation Assistance Act of 1987, required that at least ten percent of the appropriated funds go to "small business concerns owned and controlled by socially and economically disadvantaged individuals," with a presumption of such status for certain racial minority groups. The statute added that "women shall be presumed to be socially and economically disadvantaged individuals for purposes of this subsection."—Editors]

After losing the guardrail subcontract to Gonzales, Adarand filed suit against various federal officials in the United States District Court for the District of Colorado, claiming that the race-based presumptions involved in the use of subcontracting compensation clauses violate Adarand's right to equal protection. . . .

III

Respondents urge that "[t]he Subcontracting Compensation Clause program is . . . a program based on disadvantage, not on race," and thus that it is subject only to "the most relaxed judicial scrutiny." Brief for Respondents 26. To the extent that the statutes and regulations involved in this case are race neutral, we agree. Respondents concede, however, that "the race-based rebuttable presumption used in some certification determinations under the Subcontracting Compensation Clause" is subject to some heightened level of scrutiny. Id., at 27. The parties disagree as to what that level should be. (We note, incidentally, that this case concerns only classifications based explicitly on race, and presents none of the additional difficulties posed by laws that, although facially race neutral, result in racially disproportionate impact and are motivated by a racially discriminatory purpose. See generally *Arlington Heights v. Metropolitan Housing Development Corp.*, 429 U.S. 252 (1977); *Washington v. Davis*, 426 U.S. 229 (1976).)

Adarand's claim arises under the Fifth Amendment to the Constitution, which provides that "No person shall . . . be deprived of life, liberty, or property, without due process of law." Although this Court has always understood that Clause to provide some measure of protection against arbitrary treatment by the Federal Government, it is not as explicit a guarantee of equal treatment as the Fourteenth Amendment, which provides that "No State shall . . . deny to any person within its jurisdiction the equal protection of the laws" (emphasis added). Our cases have accorded varying degrees of significance to the difference in the language of those two Clauses. We think it necessary to revisit the issue here.

A

Through the 1940's, this Court had routinely taken the view in non-race-related cases that, "[u]nlike the Fourteenth Amendment, the Fifth contains no equal protection clause and it provides no guaranty against discriminatory legislation by Congress." *Detroit Bank v. United States*, 317 U.S. 329, 337 (1943); see also, e.g., *Helvering v. Lerner Stores Corp.*, 314 U.S. 463, 468 (1941); *LaBelle Iron Works v. United States*, 256 U.S. 377, 392 (1921) ("Reference is made to cases decided under the equal protection clause of the Fourteenth Amendment . . . ; but clearly they are not in point. The Fifth Amendment has no equal protection clause"). When the Court first faced a Fifth Amendment equal protection challenge to a federal racial classification, it adopted a similar approach, with most unfortunate results. In *Hirabayashi v. United States*, 320 U.S. 81 (1943), the Court considered a curfew applicable only to persons of Japanese ancestry. The Court observed—correctly— that "[d]istinctions between citizens solely because of their ancestry are by their very nature odious to a free people whose institutions are founded upon the doctrine of equality," and that "racial discriminations are in most circumstances irrelevant and therefore prohibited." But it also cited *Detroit Bank* for the proposition that the Fifth Amendment "restrains only such discriminatory legislation by Congress as amounts to a denial of due process," and upheld the curfew because "circumstances within the knowledge of those charged with the responsibility for maintaining the national defense afforded a rational basis for the decision which they made."

Eighteen months later, the Court again approved wartime measures directed at persons of Japanese ancestry. *Korematsu v. United States*, 323 U.S. 214 (1944), concerned an order that completely excluded such persons from particular areas. The Court did not address the view, expressed in cases like *Hirabayashi* and *Detroit Bank*, that the Federal Government's obligation to provide equal protection differs significantly from that of the States. Instead, it began by noting that "all legal restrictions which curtail the civil rights of a single racial group are immediately suspect . . . [and] courts must subject them to the most rigid scrutiny." 323 U.S., at 216. That promising dictum might be read to undermine the view that the Federal Government is under a lesser obligation to avoid injurious racial classifications than are the States. Cf. *id.*, at 234–235 (Murphy, J., dissenting) ("[T]he order deprives all those within its scope of the equal protection of the laws as guaranteed by the Fifth Amendment"). But in spite of the "most rigid scrutiny" standard it had just set forth, the Court then inexplicably relied on "the principles we announced in the *Hirabayashi* case" to conclude that, although "exclusion from the area in which one's home is located is a far greater deprivation than constant confinement to the home from 8 p.m. to 6 a.m.," the racially discriminatory order was nonetheless within the Federal Government's power.

In *Bolling v. Sharpe*, 347 U.S. 497 (1954), the Court for the first time explicitly questioned the existence of any difference between the obligations of the Federal Government and the States to avoid racial classifications. *Bolling* did note that "[t]he 'equal protection of the laws' is a more explicit safeguard of prohibited unfairness than 'due process of law.'" But *Bolling* then concluded that, "[i]n view of [the] decision that the Constitution prohibits the states from maintaining racially segregated public schools, it would be unthinkable that the same Constitution would impose a lesser duty on the Federal Government."

Bolling's facts concerned school desegregation, but its reasoning was not so limited. The Court's observations that "[d]istinctions between citizens solely because of their ancestry are by their very nature odious," *Hirabayashi*, at 100, and that "all legal restrictions which curtail the civil rights of a single racial group are immediately suspect," *Korematsu*, at 216, carry no less force in the context of federal action than in the context of action by the States—indeed, they first appeared in cases concerning action by the Federal Government. *Bolling* relied on those observations, and reiterated " 'that the Constitution of the United States, in its present form, forbids, so far as civil and political rights are concerned, discrimination *by the General Government, or by the States*, against any citizen because of his race,' " *id.*, at 499 (quoting *Gibson v. Mississippi*, 162 U.S. 565, 591 (1896)) (emphasis added). The Court's application of that general principle to the case before it, and the resulting imposition on the Federal Government of an obligation equivalent to that of the States, followed as a matter of course.

Later cases in contexts other than school desegregation did not distinguish between the duties of the States and the Federal Government to avoid racial classifications. . . . [As] one commentator observed[,] "[i]n case after case, fifth amendment equal protection problems are discussed on the assumption that fourteenth amendment precedents are controlling." Karst, The Fifth Amendment's Guarantee of Equal Protection, 55 N.C. L. Rev. 541, 554 (1977). *Loving v. Virginia*, 388 U.S. 1 (1967), which struck down a race-based state law, cited *Korematsu* for the proposition that "the Equal Protection Clause demands that racial classifications . . . be subjected to the most rigid scrutiny." 388 U.S., at 11. The various opinions in *Frontiero v. Richardson*, 411 U.S. 677 (1973), which concerned sex discrimination by the Federal Government, took their equal protection standard of review from *Reed v. Reed*, 404 U.S. 71 (1971), a case that invalidated sex discrimination by a State, without mentioning any possibility of a difference between the standards applicable to state and federal action. Thus, in 1975, the Court stated explicitly that "[t]his Court's approach to Fifth Amendment equal protection claims has always been precisely the same as to equal protection claims under the Fourteenth Amendment." *Weinberger v. Wiesenfeld*, 420 U.S. 636, 638, n. 2; see also *Buckley v. Valeo*, 424 U.S. 1, 93 (1976) ("Equal protection analysis in the Fifth Amendment area is the same as that under the Fourteenth Amendment"); *United States v. Paradise*, 480 U.S. 149, 166, n. 16 (1987) (plurality opinion of Brennan, J.) ("[T]he reach of the equal protection guarantee of the Fifth Amendment is coextensive with that of the Fourteenth"). We do not understand a few contrary suggestions appearing in cases in which we found special deference to the political branches of the Federal Government to be appropriate, e.g., *Hampton v. Mow Sun Wong*, 426 U.S. 88, 100, 101–102, n. 21 (1976) (federal power over immigration), to detract from this general rule.

B

Most of the cases discussed above involved classifications burdening groups that have suffered discrimination in our society. In 1978, the Court confronted the question whether race-based governmental action designed to benefit such groups should also be subject to "the most rigid scrutiny." . . .

[The Court proceeded to describe in detail three cases: Regents of Univ. of Cal. v. Bakke, *438 U.S. 265 (1978);* Fullilove v. Klutznick, *448 U.S. 448 (1980); and* Wygant v. Jackson Bd. of Ed., *476 U.S. 267 (1986). In each case an affirmative action program was challenged: in* Bakke, *a state university's medical school reserved spots in its entering class for minority students (invalidated); in* Fullilove, *Congress set aside ten percent of the funds in the Public Works Employment Act of 1977 for minority-owned businesses (upheld); and in* Wygant, *a state public school gave a preference to minority teachers when deciding which teachers to lay off (invalidated).*

Although there was no majority opinion any of these cases, in all three a majority of the justices supported strict scrutiny or something similar, even while not agreeing on what to call it. In all three cases Justice Powell was in the majority, and stressed the need for applying the same equal protection standards regardless of which racial group was disadvantaged. In all three cases there were three or four justices who called for a lenient standard of review, such as intermediate scrutiny, because the racial classification was meant to aid racial minorities. In all three cases there was no majority opinion.—Editors]

The Court's failure to produce a majority opinion in *Bakke*, *Fullilove*, and *Wygant* left unresolved the proper analysis for remedial race-based governmental action.

The Court resolved the issue, at least in part, in 1989. *Richmond v. J.A. Croson Co.*, 488 U.S. 469 (1989), concerned a city's determination that 30% of its contracting work should go to minority-owned businesses. A majority of the Court in *Croson* held that "the standard of review under the Equal Protection Clause is not dependent on the race of those burdened or benefited by a particular classification," and that the single standard of review for racial classifications should be "strict scrutiny." *Id.*, at 493–494 (opinion of O'CONNOR, J., joined by Rehnquist, C.J., and White and KENNEDY, JJ.); *id.*, at 520 (SCALIA, J., concurring in judgment) ("I agree . . . with Justice O'CONNOR's conclusion that strict scrutiny must be applied to all governmental classification by race"). As to the classification before the Court, the plurality agreed that "a state or local subdivision . . . has the authority to eradicate the effects of private discrimination within its own legislative jurisdiction," but the Court thought that the city had not acted with "a strong basis in evidence for its conclusion that remedial action was necessary." The Court also thought it "obvious that [the] program is not narrowly tailored to remedy the effects of prior discrimination."

With *Croson*, the Court finally agreed that the Fourteenth Amendment requires strict scrutiny of all race-based action by state and local governments. But *Croson* of course had no occasion to declare what standard of review the Fifth Amendment requires for such action taken by the Federal Government. *Croson* observed simply that the Court's "treatment of an exercise of congressional power in *Fullilove* cannot be dispositive here," because *Croson*'s facts did not implicate Congress' broad power under § 5 of the Fourteenth Amendment. . . . Thus, some uncertainty persisted with respect to the standard of review for federal racial classifications.

Despite lingering uncertainty in the details, however, the Court's cases through *Croson* had established three general propositions with respect to governmental racial classifications. First, skepticism: " 'Any preference based on racial or ethnic criteria must necessarily receive a most searching examination,' " *Wygant*, at 273 (plurality opinion of Powell, J.); *Fullilove*, at 491 (opinion of Burger, C.J.); see also *id.*, at 523 (Stewart, J., dissenting) ("[A]ny official action that treats a person differently on account of his race or ethnic origin is inherently suspect"); *McLaughlin v. Florida*, 379 U.S. 184, 192 (1964), ("[R]acial classifications [are] 'constitutionally suspect' "); *Hirabayashi*, at 100 ("Distinctions between citizens solely because of their ancestry are by their very nature odious to a free people"). Second, consistency: "[T]he standard of review under the Equal Protection Clause is not dependent on the race of those burdened or benefited by a particular classification," *Croson*, at 494 (plurality opinion); *id.*, at 520 (SCALIA, J., concurring in judgment); see also *Bakke*, at 289–290 (opinion of Powell, J.), i.e., all racial classifications reviewable under the Equal Protection Clause must be strictly scrutinized. And third, congruence: "Equal protection analysis in the Fifth Amendment area is the same as that under the Fourteenth Amendment," *Buckley v. Valeo*, at 93; see also *Wiesenfeld*, at 638, n. 2; *Bolling v. Sharpe*, at 500. Taken together, these three propositions lead to the conclusion that any person, of whatever race, has the right to demand that any governmental actor subject to the Constitution justify any racial classification subjecting that person to unequal treatment under the strictest judicial scrutiny. . . .

A year later, however, the Court took a surprising turn. *Metro Broadcasting, Inc. v. FCC*, 497 U.S. 547 (1990), involved a Fifth Amendment challenge to two race-based policies of the Federal Communications Commission (FCC). In *Metro Broadcasting*, the Court repudiated the long-held notion that "it would be unthinkable that the same Constitution would impose a lesser duty on the Federal Government" than it does on a State to afford equal protection of the laws, *Bolling*, at 500. It did so by holding that "benign" federal racial classifications need only satisfy intermediate scrutiny, even though *Croson* had recently concluded that such classifications enacted by a State must satisfy strict scrutiny. "[B]enign" federal racial classifications, the Court said, "—even if those measures are not 'remedial' in the sense of being designed to compensate victims of past governmental or societal discrimination—are constitutionally permissible to the extent that they serve *important* governmental objectives within the power of Congress and are *substantially related* to achievement of those objectives." *Metro Broadcasting*, at 564–565 (emphasis added). The Court did not explain how to tell whether a racial classification should be deemed "benign," other than to express "confiden[ce] that an 'examination of the legislative scheme and its history' will separate benign measures from other types of racial classifications." *Id.*, at 564, n. 12.

Applying this test, the Court first noted that the FCC policies at issue did not serve as a remedy for past discrimination. Proceeding on the assumption that the policies were nonetheless "benign," it concluded that they served the "important governmental objective" of "enhancing broadcast diversity," and that they were "substantially related" to that objective. It therefore upheld the policies.

By adopting intermediate scrutiny as the standard of review for congressionally mandated "benign" racial classifications, *Metro Broadcasting* departed from prior cases in two significant respects. First, it turned its back on *Croson*'s explanation of why strict scrutiny of all governmental racial classifications is essential:

> "Absent searching judicial inquiry into the justification for such race-based measures, there is simply no way of determining what classifications are 'benign' or 'remedial' and what classifications are in fact motivated by illegitimate notions of racial inferiority or simple racial politics. Indeed, the purpose of strict scrutiny is to 'smoke out' illegitimate uses of race by assuring that the legislative body is pursuing a goal important enough to warrant use of a highly suspect tool. The test also ensures that the means chosen 'fit' this compelling goal so closely that there is little or no possibility that the motive for the classification was illegitimate racial prejudice or stereotype." *Croson*, at 493 (plurality opinion of O'CONNOR, J.).

We adhere to that view today, despite the surface appeal of holding "benign" racial classifications to a lower standard, because "it may not always be clear that a so-called preference is in fact benign," *Bakke*, at 298 (opinion of Powell, J.). . . .

Second, *Metro Broadcasting* squarely rejected one of the three propositions established by the Court's earlier equal protection cases, namely, congruence between the standards applicable to federal and state racial classifications, and in so doing also undermined the other two—skepticism of all racial classifications and consistency of treatment irrespective of the race of the burdened or benefited group. . . .

The three propositions undermined by *Metro Broadcasting* all derive from the basic principle that the Fifth and Fourteenth Amendments to the Constitution protect persons, not groups. It follows from that principle that all governmental action based on race—a group classification long recognized as "in most circumstances irrelevant and therefore prohibited," *Hirabayashi*, at 100—should be subjected to detailed judicial inquiry to ensure that the personal right to equal protection of the laws has not been infringed. These ideas have long been central to this Court's understanding of equal protection, and holding "benign" state and federal racial classifications to different standards does not square with them. "[A] free people whose institutions are founded upon the doctrine of equality," *ibid.*, should tolerate no retreat from the principle that government may treat people differently because of their race only for the most compelling reasons. Accordingly, we hold today that all racial classifications, imposed by whatever federal, state, or local governmental actor, must be analyzed by a reviewing court under strict scrutiny. In other words, such classifications are constitutional only if they are narrowly tailored measures that further compelling governmental interests. To the extent that *Metro Broadcasting* is inconsistent with that holding, it is overruled. . . .

JUSTICE STEVENS chides us for our "supposed inability to differentiate between 'invidious' and 'benign' discrimination," because it is in his view sufficient that "people understand the difference between good intentions and bad." But . . . the point of strict scrutiny is to "differentiate between" permissible and impermissible governmental use of race. And JUSTICE STEVENS himself has already explained in his dissent in *Fullilove* why "good intentions" alone are not enough to sustain a supposedly "benign" racial classification: "[E]ven though it is not the actual predicate for this legislation, a statute of this kind inevitably is perceived by many as resting on an assumption that those who are granted this special preference are less qualified in some respect that is identified purely by their race. Because that perception—*especially when fostered by the Congress of the United States*—can only exacerbate rather than reduce racial prejudice, it will delay the time when race will become a truly irrelevant, or at least insignificant, factor. *Unless Congress clearly articulates the need and basis* for a racial classification, *and also tailors the classification to its justification*, the Court should not uphold this kind of statute." *Fullilove*, at 545 (dissenting opinion) (emphasis added); see also *id.*, at 537 ("Racial classifications are simply too pernicious to permit any but the most exact connection between justification and classification"); *Croson*, at 516–517 (STEVENS, J., concurring in part and concurring in judgment) ("Although [the legislation at issue] stigmatizes the disadvantaged class with the unproven charge of past racial discrimination, it actually imposes a greater stigma on its supposed beneficiaries"). These passages make a persuasive case for requiring strict scrutiny of congressional racial classifications.

Perhaps it is not the standard of strict scrutiny itself, but our use of the concepts of "consistency" and "congruence" in conjunction with it, that leads JUSTICE STEVENS to dissent. . . . The principle of consistency simply means that whenever the government treats any person unequally because of his or her race, that person has suffered an injury that falls squarely within the language and spirit of the Constitution's guarantee of equal protection. It says nothing about the ultimate validity of any particular law; that determination is the job of the court applying strict scrutiny. The principle of consistency explains the circumstances in which the injury requiring strict scrutiny occurs. The application of strict scrutiny, in turn, determines whether a compelling governmental interest justifies the infliction of that injury. . . .

JUSTICE STEVENS also claims that we have ignored any difference between federal and state legislatures. But requiring that Congress, like the States, enact racial classifications only when doing so is necessary to further a "compelling interest" does not contravene any principle of appropriate respect for a coequal branch of the Government. . . .

C

"Although adherence to precedent is not rigidly required in constitutional cases, any departure from the doctrine of stare decisis demands special justification." *Arizona v. Rumsey*, 467 U.S. 203, 212 (1984). In deciding whether this case presents such justification, we recall Justice Frankfurter's admonition that "stare decisis is a principle of policy and not a mechanical formula of adherence to the latest decision, however recent and questionable, when such adherence involves collision with a prior doctrine more embracing in its scope, intrinsically sounder, and verified by experience." *Helvering v. Hallock*, 309 U.S. 106, 119 (1940). Remaining true to an "intrinsically sounder" doctrine established in prior cases better serves the values of stare decisis than would following a more recently decided case inconsistent with the decisions that came before it; the latter course would simply compound the recent error and would likely make the unjustified break from previously established doctrine complete. In such a situation, "special justification" exists to depart from the recently decided case.

As we have explained, *Metro Broadcasting* undermined important principles of this Court's equal protection jurisprudence, established in a line of cases stretching back over 50 years. Those principles together stood for an "embracing" and "intrinsically soun[d]" understanding of equal protection "verified by experience," namely, that the Constitution imposes upon federal, state, and local governmental actors the same obligation to respect the personal right to equal protection of the laws. This case therefore presents precisely the situation described by Justice Frankfurter in *Helvering*: We cannot adhere to our most recent decision without colliding with an accepted and established doctrine. . . .

"The real problem," Justice Frankfurter explained, "is whether a principle shall prevail over its later misapplications." *Helvering*, at 122. *Metro Broadcasting*'s untenable distinction between state and federal racial classifications lacks support in our precedent, and undermines the fundamental principle of equal protection as a personal right. In this case, as between that principle and "its later misapplications," the principle must prevail.

D

. . . Finally, we wish to dispel the notion that strict scrutiny is "strict in theory, but fatal in fact." *Fullilove*, at 519 (Marshall, J., concurring in judgment). The unhappy persistence of both the practice and the lingering effects of racial discrimination against minority groups in this country is an unfortunate reality, and government is not disqualified from acting in response to it. As recently as 1987, for example, every Justice of this Court agreed that the Alabama Department of Public

Safety's "pervasive, systematic, and obstinate discriminatory conduct" justified a narrowly tailored race-based remedy. See *Paradise*, at 167 (plurality opinion of Brennan, J.); *id.*, at 190 (STEVENS, J., concurring in judgment); *id.*, at 196 (O'CONNOR, J., dissenting). When race-based action is necessary to further a compelling interest, such action is within constitutional constraints if it satisfies the "narrow tailoring" test this Court has set out in previous cases.

IV

Because our decision today alters the playing field in some important respects, we think it best to remand the case to the lower courts for further consideration in light of the principles we have announced. . . . The question whether any of the ways in which the Government uses subcontractor compensation clauses can survive strict scrutiny, and any relevance distinctions such as these may have to that question, should be addressed in the first instance by the lower courts.

■ JUSTICE SCALIA, concurring in part and concurring in the judgment.

I join the opinion of the Court, except Part III–C, and except insofar as it may be inconsistent with the following: In my view, government can never have a "compelling interest" in discriminating on the basis of race in order to "make up" for past racial discrimination in the opposite direction. See *Croson*, at 520 (SCALIA, J., concurring in judgment). Individuals who have been wronged by unlawful racial discrimination should be made whole; but under our Constitution there can be no such thing as either a creditor or a debtor race. That concept is alien to the Constitution's focus upon the individual, see Amdt. 14, § 1 ("[N]or shall any State . . . deny *to any person*" the equal protection of the laws) (emphasis added), and its rejection of dispositions based on race, see Amdt. 15, § 1 (prohibiting abridgment of the right to vote "on account of race"), or based on blood, see Art. III, § 3 ("[N]o Attainder of Treason shall work Corruption of Blood"); Art. I, § 9, cl. 8 ("No Title of Nobility shall be granted by the United States"). To pursue the concept of racial entitlement—even for the most admirable and benign of purposes—is to reinforce and preserve for future mischief the way of thinking that produced race slavery, race privilege and race hatred. In the eyes of government, we are just one race here. It is American.

It is unlikely, if not impossible, that the challenged program would survive under this understanding of strict scrutiny, but I am content to leave that to be decided on remand.

■ JUSTICE THOMAS, concurring in part and concurring in the judgment.

I agree with the majority's conclusion that strict scrutiny applies to all government classifications based on race. I write separately, however, to express my disagreement with the premise underlying JUSTICE STEVENS and JUSTICE GINSBURG's dissents: that there is a racial paternalism exception to the principle of equal protection. I believe that there is a "moral [and] constitutional equivalence" between laws designed to subjugate a race and those that distribute benefits on the basis of race in order to foster some current notion of equality. Government cannot make us equal; it can only recognize, respect, and protect us as equal before the law.

That these programs may have been motivated, in part, by good intentions cannot provide refuge from the principle that under our Constitution, the government may not make distinctions on the basis of race. As far as the Constitution is concerned, it is irrelevant whether a government's racial classifications are drawn by those who wish to oppress a race or by those who have a sincere desire to help those thought to be disadvantaged. There can be no doubt that the paternalism that appears to lie at the heart of this program is at war with the principle of inherent equality that underlies and infuses our Constitution. See Declaration of Independence ("We hold these truths to be self-evident, that all men are created equal, that they are endowed by their Creator with certain unalienable Rights, that among these are Life, Liberty, and the pursuit of Happiness").

These programs not only raise grave constitutional questions, they also undermine the moral basis of the equal protection principle. Purchased at the price of immeasurable human suffering, the equal protection principle reflects our Nation's understanding that such classifications ultimately have a destructive impact on the individual and our society. Unquestionably, "[i]nvidious [racial] discrimination is an engine of oppression," *post* (STEVENS, J., dissenting). It is also true that "[r]emedial" racial preferences may reflect "a desire to foster equality in society," *ibid*. But there can be no doubt that racial paternalism and its unintended consequences can be as poisonous and pernicious as any other form of discrimination. So-called "benign" discrimination teaches many that because of chronic and apparently immutable handicaps, minorities cannot compete with them without their patronizing indulgence. Inevitably, such programs engender attitudes of superiority or, alternatively, provoke resentment among those who believe that they have been wronged by the government's use of race. These programs stamp minorities with a badge of inferiority and may cause them to develop dependencies or to adopt an attitude that they are "entitled" to preferences. Indeed, JUSTICE STEVENS once recognized the real harms stemming from seemingly "benign" discrimination. See *Fullilove*, at 545 (STEVENS, J., dissenting) (noting that "remedial" race legislation "is perceived by many as resting on an assumption that those who are granted this special preference are less qualified in some respect that is identified purely by their race").

In my mind, government-sponsored racial discrimination based on benign prejudice is just as noxious as discrimination inspired by malicious prejudice.[*] In each instance, it is racial discrimination, plain and simple.

■ JUSTICE STEVENS, with whom JUSTICE GINSBURG joins, dissenting.

Instead of deciding this case in accordance with controlling precedent, the Court today delivers a disconcerting lecture about the evils of governmental racial classifications. For its text the Court has selected three propositions, represented by the bywords "skepticism," "consistency," and "congruence." I shall comment on each of these propositions, then add a few words about stare decisis, and finally explain why I believe this Court has a duty to affirm the judgment of the Court of Appeals.

I

The Court's concept of skepticism is, at least in principle, a good statement of law and of common sense. Undoubtedly, a court should be wary of a governmental decision that relies upon a racial classification. "Because racial characteristics so

---

[*]   It should be obvious that every racial classification helps, in a narrow sense, some races and hurts others. As to the races benefited, the classification could surely be called "benign." Accordingly, whether a law relying upon racial taxonomy is "benign" or "malign" either turns on " 'whose ox is gored,' " *Bakke*, at 295, n. 35 (Powell, J.) (quoting, A. Bickel, The Morality of Consent 133 (1975)), or on distinctions found only in the eye of the beholder.

seldom provide a relevant basis for disparate treatment, and because classifications based on race are potentially so harmful to the entire body politic," a reviewing court must satisfy itself that the reasons for any such classification are "clearly identified and unquestionably legitimate." *Fullilove*, at 533–535 (STEVENS, J., dissenting). . . . I welcome [this principle's] renewed endorsement by the Court today. But, as the opinions in *Fullilove* demonstrate, substantial agreement on the standard to be applied in deciding difficult cases does not necessarily lead to agreement on how those cases actually should or will be resolved. In my judgment, because uniform standards are often anything but uniform, we should evaluate the Court's comments on "consistency," "congruence," and stare decisis with the same type of skepticism that the Court advocates for the underlying issue.

II

The Court's concept of "consistency" assumes that there is no significant difference between a decision by the majority to impose a special burden on the members of a minority race and a decision by the majority to provide a benefit to certain members of that minority notwithstanding its incidental burden on some members of the majority. In my opinion that assumption is untenable. There is no moral or constitutional equivalence between a policy that is designed to perpetuate a caste system and one that seeks to eradicate racial subordination. Invidious discrimination is an engine of oppression, subjugating a disfavored group to enhance or maintain the power of the majority. Remedial race-based preferences reflect the opposite impulse: a desire to foster equality in society. No sensible conception of the Government's constitutional obligation to "govern impartially," *Hampton*, at 100, should ignore this distinction. . . .

The Court's explanation for treating dissimilar race-based decisions as though they were equally objectionable is a supposed inability to differentiate between "invidious" and "benign" discrimination. But the term "affirmative action" is common and well understood. Its presence in everyday parlance shows that people understand the difference between good intentions and bad. As with any legal concept, some cases may be difficult to classify, but our equal protection jurisprudence has identified a critical difference between state action that imposes burdens on a disfavored few and state action that benefits the few "in spite of" its adverse effects on the many. *Feeney*, at 279. . . .

As a matter of constitutional and democratic principle, a decision by representatives of the majority to discriminate against the members of a minority race is fundamentally different from those same representatives' decision to impose incidental costs on the majority of their constituents in order to provide a benefit to a disadvantaged minority. . . . By insisting on a doctrinaire notion of "consistency" in the standard applicable to all race-based governmental actions, the Court obscures this essential dichotomy.

III

The Court's concept of "congruence" assumes that there is no significant difference between a decision by the Congress of the United States to adopt an affirmative-action program and such a decision by a State or a municipality. In my opinion that assumption is untenable. It ignores important practical and legal differences between federal and state or local decisionmakers.

These differences have been identified repeatedly and consistently both in opinions of the Court and in separate opinions authored by Members of today's majority. Thus, in *Metro Broadcasting*, in which we upheld a federal program designed to foster racial diversity in broadcasting, we identified the special "institutional competence" of our National Legislature. *Id.*, at 563. "It is of overriding significance in these cases," we were careful to emphasize, "that the FCC's minority ownership programs have been specifically approved—indeed, mandated—by Congress." We recalled the several opinions in *Fullilove* that admonished this Court to " 'approach our task with appropriate deference to the Congress, a co-equal branch charged by the Constitution with the power to "provide for the . . . general Welfare of the United States" and "to enforce, by appropriate legislation," the equal protection guarantees of the Fourteenth Amendment.' " We recalled that the opinions of Chief Justice Burger and Justice Powell in *Fullilove* had "explained that deference was appropriate in light of Congress' institutional competence as the National Legislature, as well as Congress' powers under the Commerce Clause, the Spending Clause, and the Civil War Amendments."

The majority in *Metro Broadcasting* and the plurality in *Fullilove* were not alone in relying upon a critical distinction between federal and state programs. In his separate opinion in *Croson*, at 520–524, JUSTICE SCALIA discussed the basis for this distinction. He observed that "it is one thing to permit racially based conduct by the Federal Government—whose legislative powers concerning matters of race were explicitly enhanced by the Fourteenth Amendment, see U.S. Const., Amdt. 14, § 5— and quite another to permit it by the precise entities against whose conduct in matters of race that Amendment was specifically directed, see Amdt. 14, § 1." Continuing, JUSTICE SCALIA explained why a "sound distinction between federal and state (or local) action based on race rests not only upon the substance of the Civil War Amendments, but upon social reality and governmental theory"[:]

> "What the record shows, in other words, is that racial discrimination against any group finds a more ready expression at the state and local than at the federal level. To the children of the Founding Fathers, this should come as no surprise. An acute awareness of the heightened danger of oppression from political factions in small, rather than large, political units dates to the very beginning of our national history. See G. Wood, The Creation of the American Republic, 1776–1787, pp. 499–506 (1969). As James Madison observed in support of the proposed Constitution's enhancement of national powers:
>
>> " 'The smaller the society, the fewer probably will be the distinct parties and interests composing it; the fewer the distinct parties and interests, the more frequently will a majority be found of the same party; and the smaller the number of individuals composing a majority, and the smaller the compass within which they are placed, the more easily will they concert and execute their plan of oppression. Extend the sphere and you take in a greater variety of parties and interests; you make it less probable that a majority of the whole will have a common motive to invade the rights of other citizens; or if such a common motive exists, it will be more difficult for all who feel it to discover their own strength and to act in unison with each other.' The Federalist No. 10." *Id.*, at 523 (opinion concurring in judgment).

In her plurality opinion in *Croson*, JUSTICE O'CONNOR also emphasized the importance of this distinction when she responded to the city's argument that *Fullilove* was controlling. She wrote:

"What appellant ignores is that Congress, unlike any State or political subdivision, has a specific constitutional mandate to enforce the dictates of the Fourteenth Amendment. The power to 'enforce' may at times also include the power to define situations which Congress determines threaten principles of equality and to adopt prophylactic rules to deal with those situations. The Civil War Amendments themselves worked a dramatic change in the balance between congressional and state power over matters of race." 488 U.S., at 490 (joined by REHNQUIST, C.J., and White, J.).

An additional reason for giving greater deference to the National Legislature than to a local lawmaking body is that federal affirmative-action programs represent the will of our entire Nation's elected representatives, whereas a state or local program may have an impact on nonresident entities who played no part in the decision to enact it. . . .

[I]t is one thing to say (as no one seems to dispute) that the Fifth Amendment encompasses a general guarantee of equal protection as broad as that contained within the Fourteenth Amendment. It is another thing entirely to say that Congress' institutional competence and constitutional authority entitles it to no greater deference when it enacts a program designed to foster equality than the deference due a state legislature.[7] The latter is an extraordinary proposition; and, as the foregoing discussion demonstrates, our precedents have rejected it explicitly and repeatedly. . . .

IV

The Court's concept of stare decisis treats some of the language we have used in explaining our decisions as though it were more important than our actual holdings. In my opinion that treatment is incorrect.

This is the third time in the Court's entire history that it has considered the constitutionality of a federal affirmative-action program. On each of the two prior occasions, the first in 1980, *Fullilove*, and the second in 1990, *Metro Broadcasting*, the Court upheld the program. Today the Court explicitly overrules *Metro Broadcasting* (at least in part), and undermines *Fullilove* by recasting the standard on which it rested and by calling even its holding into question. By way of explanation, JUSTICE O'CONNOR advises the federal agencies and private parties that have made countless decisions in reliance on those cases that "we do not depart from the fabric of the law; we restore it." A skeptical observer might ask whether this pronouncement is a faithful application of the doctrine of stare decisis. . . .

I continue to believe that the *Fullilove* case was incorrectly decided, see 448 U.S., at 532–554 (STEVENS, J., dissenting), but neither my dissent nor that filed by Justice Stewart, *id.*, at 522–532, contained any suggestion that the issue the Court

---

[7]   Despite the majority's reliance on *Korematsu*, that case does not stand for the proposition that federal remedial programs are subject to strict scrutiny. Instead, *Korematsu* specifies that "all legal restrictions *which curtail the civil rights of a single racial group* are immediately suspect." 323 U.S., at 216 (emphasis added). The programs at issue in this case (as in most affirmative-action cases) do not "curtail the civil rights of a single racial group"; they benefit certain racial groups and impose an indirect burden on the majority.

was resolving had been decided before. As was true of *Metro Broadcasting*, the Court in *Fullilove* decided an important, novel, and difficult question. Providing a different answer to a similar question today cannot fairly be characterized as merely "restoring" previously settled law.

V

The Court's holding in *Fullilove* surely governs the result in this case. . . . If the 1977 program of race-based set-asides satisfied the strict scrutiny dictated by Justice Powell's vision of the Constitution—a vision the Court expressly endorses today—it must follow as night follows the day that the Court of Appeals' judgment upholding this more carefully crafted program should be affirmed.

VI

My skeptical scrutiny of the Court's opinion leaves me in dissent. The majority's concept of "consistency" ignores a difference, fundamental to the idea of equal protection, between oppression and assistance. The majority's concept of "congruence" ignores a difference, fundamental to our constitutional system, between the Federal Government and the States. And the majority's concept of stare decisis ignores the force of binding precedent. I would affirm the judgment of the Court of Appeals.

■ JUSTICE SOUTER, with whom JUSTICE GINSBURG and JUSTICE BREYER join, dissenting.

. . . The result in *Fullilove* was controlled by the plurality for whom Chief Justice Burger spoke in announcing the judgment. Although his opinion did not adopt any label for the standard it applied, and although it was later seen as calling for less than strict scrutiny, *Metro Broadcasting*, at 564, none other than Justice Powell joined the plurality opinion as comporting with his own view that a strict scrutiny standard should be applied to all injurious race-based classifications. *Fullilove*, at 495–496 (concurring opinion) ("Although I would place greater emphasis than THE CHIEF JUSTICE on the need to articulate judicial standards of review in conventional terms, I view his opinion announcing the judgment as substantially in accord with my views"). Chief Justice Burger's noncategorical approach is probably best seen not as more lenient than strict scrutiny but as reflecting his conviction that the treble-tiered scrutiny structure merely embroidered on a single standard of reasonableness whenever an equal protection challenge required a balancing of justification against probable harm. Indeed, the Court's very recognition today that strict scrutiny can be compatible with the survival of a classification so reviewed demonstrates that our concepts of equal protection enjoy a greater elasticity than the standard categories might suggest. . . .

Finally, I should say that I do not understand that today's decision will necessarily have any effect on the resolution of an issue that was just as pertinent under *Fullilove*'s unlabeled standard as it is under the standard of strict scrutiny now adopted by the Court. The Court has long accepted the view that constitutional authority to remedy past discrimination is not limited to the power to forbid its continuation, but extends to eliminating those effects that would otherwise persist and skew the operation of public systems even in the absence of current intent to practice any discrimination. See *Albemarle Paper Co. v. Moody*, 422 U.S. 405, 418 (1975) ("Where racial discrimination is concerned, the [district] court has not merely the power but the duty to render a decree which will so far as possible eliminate the discriminatory effects of the past as well as bar like discrimination in the future"). This is so whether the remedial authority is exercised by a court, the Congress, or some other legislature. Indeed, a majority of the Court today reiterates that there are circumstances in which Government may, consistently with the Constitution, adopt programs aimed at remedying the effects of past invidious discrimination.

When the extirpation of lingering discriminatory effects is thought to require a catch-up mechanism, like the racially preferential inducement under the statutes considered here, the result may be that some members of the historically favored race are hurt by that remedial mechanism, however innocent they may be of any personal responsibility for any discriminatory conduct. When this price is considered reasonable, it is in part because it is a price to be paid only temporarily; if the justification for the preference is eliminating the effects of a past practice, the assumption is that the effects will themselves recede into the past, becoming attenuated and finally disappearing. Thus, Justice Powell wrote in his concurring opinion in *Fullilove* that the "temporary nature of this remedy ensures that a race-conscious program will not last longer than the discriminatory effects it is designed to eliminate." 448 U.S., at 513. . . .

■ JUSTICE GINSBURG, with whom JUSTICE BREYER joins, dissenting.

. . . The divisions in this difficult case should not obscure the Court's recognition of the persistence of racial inequality and a majority's acknowledgment of Congress' authority to act affirmatively, not only to end discrimination, but also to counteract discrimination's lingering effects. Those effects, reflective of a system of racial caste only recently ended, are evident in our workplaces, markets, and neighborhoods. Job applicants with identical resumés, qualifications, and interview styles still experience different receptions, depending on their race. White and African-American consumers still encounter different deals. People of color looking for housing still face discriminatory treatment by landlords, real estate agents, and mortgage lenders. Minority entrepreneurs sometimes fail to gain contracts though they are the low bidders, and they are sometimes refused work even after winning contracts. Bias both conscious and unconscious, reflecting traditional and unexamined habits of thought, keeps up barriers that must come down if equal opportunity and nondiscrimination are ever genuinely to become this country's law and practice.

Given this history and its practical consequences, Congress surely can conclude that a carefully designed affirmative action program may help to realize, finally, the "equal protection of the laws" the Fourteenth Amendment has promised since 1868. . . .

A *Korematsu*-type classification, as I read the opinions in this case, will never again survive scrutiny: Such a classification, history and precedent instruct, properly ranks as prohibited.

For a classification made to hasten the day when "we are just one race," *ante* (SCALIA, J., concurring in part and concurring in judgment), however, the lead opinion has dispelled the notion that "strict scrutiny" is "fatal in fact." Properly, a majority of the Court calls for review that is searching, in order to ferret out classifications in reality malign, but masquerading as benign. . . .

Close review also is in order for this further reason. As JUSTICE SOUTER points out, and as this very case shows, some members of the historically favored race can be hurt by catchup mechanisms designed to cope with the lingering effects of entrenched racial subjugation. Court review can ensure that preferences are not so large as to trammel unduly upon the opportunities of others or interfere too harshly with legitimate expectations of persons in once-preferred groups.

* * *

While I would not disturb the programs challenged in this case, and would leave their improvement to the political branches, I see today's decision as one that allows our precedent to evolve, still to be informed by and responsive to changing conditions.

NOTES

1.   Which of the five types of constitutional argument (p. 42) support *Adarand's* equation of the federal and state governments? Which do not? Does *Adarand* necessarily follow from *Bolling*? Do the arguments for treating alike federal and state discrimination against racial minorities also apply to federal and state discrimination on behalf of racial minorities? None of the justices in *Adarand* questioned *Bolling*. Should they have? Is it an untouchable element of our constitutional tradition, like *Brown*?

2.   The Court has also considered challenges to legislative districts that were drawn to increase the number of districts in which the majority of voters are from a racial minority. In *Shaw v. Reno [Shaw I]*, 509 U.S. 630 (1993), the Supreme Court held that the Equal Protection Clause of the Fourteenth Amendment created a cause of action to challenge the creation of race-based election districts, though the Court did not find the challenged district "so irrational on its face that it can be understood only as an effort to segregate voters into separate voting districts because of their race." *Shaw I* is presented at p. 1668. Should the Court have the same approach to affirmative action in every context—universities and kindergartens, legislative districts and government contracts? Why or why not?

3.   The implications of cases like *Adarand* may not yet be fully clear. To take just one example, does a federal color-blindness requirement actually constrain the kind of federal anti-discrimination laws that can apply even to private employers? With various caveats, federal law bans employment practices that have a "disparate impact" on race. Justice Scalia argued that this has the practical effect of "plac[ing] a racial thumb on the scales, often requiring employers to evaluate the racial outcomes of their policies, and to make decisions based on (because of) those racial outcomes." *Ricci v. DeStefano*, 557 U.S. 557, 594 (2009) (Scalia, J., concurring).

Is that constitutional? Justice Scalia argued not:

> [I]f the Federal Government is prohibited from discriminating on the basis of race, *Bolling v. Sharpe*, 347 U.S. 497, 500 (1954), then surely it is also prohibited from enacting laws mandating that third parties—e.g., employers, whether private, State, or municipal—discriminate on the basis of race. See *Buchanan v. Warley*, 245 U.S. 60, 78–82 (1917). . . . And of course the purportedly benign motive for the disparate-impact provisions cannot save the statute. See *Adarand Constructors, Inc. v. Pena*, 515 U.S. 200, 227 (1995).

Ricci, at 594–595 (Scalia, J., concurring). Can you think of more laws that might be affected? Is this a persuasive account of what colorblindness requires? Is it a reason to put equal protection doctrine on a different path? For more analysis of this argument see Richard Primus, *The Future of Disparate Impact*, 108 Mich. L. Rev. 1341 (2010).

[*Assignment 72*]

E. SEX DISCRIMINATION

In the *Slaughter-House Cases* (1872), the Court said that the "one pervading purpose" of the Reconstruction amendments was "the freedom of the slave race, the security and firm establishment of that freedom, and the protection of the newly-made freeman and citizen from the oppressions of those who had formerly exercised unlimited dominion over him." But does the Fourteenth Amendment's command that a state not "deny to any person within its jurisdiction the equal protection of the laws" apply only to denials of equal protection on the basis of race? Or does it include other government classifications of persons?

The text of the Equal Protection Clause mentions no restriction to race. And by its own terms it protects every "person." But to say that the Equal Protection Clause does apply to more than just race only begins the inquiry. What other classifications might be included? Is sex discrimination analogous to race discrimination? In what sense? For discussion of the congressional debates over the Fourteenth Amendment and their possible implications for sex, see Steven G. Calabresi & Julia T. Rickert, *Originalism and Sex Discrimination*, 90 Tex. L. Rev. 1, 47–60 (2011).

And even if one concludes that the Fourteenth Amendment extends to sex discrimination, questions remain. Exactly how, for example, would the Equal Protection Clause apply to government classifications predicated on sex? Would the Equal Protection Clause invalidate all such legal distinctions, including "separate but equal" public restrooms? If not, why not? Are sex-based classifications exactly like race-based classifications? Is there a different Equal Protection Clause for each?

The next two assignments will present four cases confronting these questions. Two are from the nineteenth century: *Bradwell v. Illinois* (1873), a case brought under the Privileges or Immunities Clause of the Fourteenth Amendment, involved the refusal of the Illinois Supreme Court to admit a woman to the practice of law. The case that follows, *Minor v. Happersett* (1875), was an early interpretation of the Equal Protection Clause. And two are from the twentieth century. *Craig v. Boren* (1976) and *United States v. Virginia* (1996) present the court's effort to work out, and then rework, the modern standards for judicial review of sex discriminatory laws.

The cases on sex discrimination raise three broad questions. First, does the guarantee of "equal protection of the laws" forbid most government classifications on the basis of sex, and if so, why? Is it because sex is like race? In what ways? Second, when the judiciary finds a type of classification "suspect" under the Equal Protection Clause, how strictly should it examine the justification for the law? Should the same "level of scrutiny" that applies to race classifications also apply to sex classifications? Finally, how should constitutional change happen? Through the Article V amendment process? Through the courts?

The Nineteenth Century

The day after its decision in the *Slaughter-House Cases*, the Court decided another case focused on the Privileges or Immunities Clause, *Bradwell v. Illinois*. *Bradwell* can also be seen as raising (though not answering) central questions about the original meaning of the phrase "equal protection of the laws." Did it refer to the equal *protection* of the laws—a right of all to have laws enacted and enforced for their protection, even against private violence? Or did it require *equality* in all the laws made by a state, thus forbidding a state to discriminate on illegitimate grounds in the provision of legal rights, privileges, and benefits? If the latter, what grounds of distinction are permissible? Clearly, the framers of the Fourteenth Amendment wanted to prohibit state discrimination in civil rights on the basis of race, and wanted to empower Congress to legislate to achieve that aim. But the amendment is not worded in terms of race. If the Equal Protection Clause applies to more than just race discrimination, what other types of distinctions or classifications does it forbid states to make? What if it were clear that most framers of the Fourteenth Amendment were not concerned with providing equal treatment on the basis of sex— and indeed would not have intended such a result? Do their intentions and expectations control the meaning of the text? Can a text take on new implications, previously unintended by its authors and ratifiers? And are these determinations left to the judgment of Congress as it exercises its enforcement power under Section 5 of the Fourteenth Amendment? Or is the scope of the Equal Protection Clause for the courts to decide?

Bradwell v. Illinois

83 (16 Wall.) U.S. 130 (1873)

■ MR. JUSTICE MILLER delivered the opinion of the court.

The record in this case is not very perfect, but it may be fairly taken that the plaintiff asserted her right to a license on the grounds, among others, that she was a citizen of the United States. . . .

In regard to [the fourteenth] amendment counsel for the plaintiff in this court truly says that there are certain privileges and immunities which belong to a citizen of the United States as such; otherwise it would be nonsense for the fourteenth amendment to prohibit a State from abridging them, and he proceeds to argue that admission to the bar of a State of a person who possesses the requisite learning and character is one of those which a State may not deny.

In this latter proposition we are not able to concur with counsel. We agree with him that there are privileges and immunities belonging to citizens of the United States, in that relation and character, and that it is these and these alone which a State is forbidden to abridge. But the right to admission to practice in the courts of a State is not one of them. This right in no sense depends on citizenship of the United States. It has not, as far as we know, ever been made in any State, or in any case, to depend on citizenship at all. Certainly many prominent and distinguished lawyers have been admitted to practice, both in the State and Federal courts, who were not citizens of the United States or of any State. But, on whatever basis this right may be placed, so far as it can have any relation to citizenship at all, it would seem that, as to the courts of a State, it would relate to citizenship of the State, and as to Federal courts, it would relate to citizenship of the United States.

The opinion just delivered in the *Slaughter-House Cases* renders elaborate argument in the present case unnecessary; for, unless we are wholly and radically mistaken in the principles on which those cases are decided, the right to control and regulate the granting of license to practice law in the courts of a State is one of those powers which are not transferred for its protection to the Federal government, and its exercise is in no manner governed or controlled by citizenship of the United States in the party seeking such license.

It is unnecessary to repeat the argument on which the judgment in those cases is founded. It is sufficient to say they are conclusive of the present case.

■ MR. JUSTICE BRADLEY [concurring, joined by MR. JUSTICE SWAYNE and MR. JUSTICE FIELD]:

I concur in the judgment of the court in this case, by which the judgment of the Supreme Court of Illinois is affirmed, but not for the reasons specified in the opinion just read. . . .

The claim of the plaintiff, who is a married woman, to be admitted to practice as an attorney and counsellor-at-law, is based upon the supposed right of every person, man or woman, to engage in any lawful employment for a livelihood. The Supreme Court of Illinois denied the application on the ground that, by the common law, which is the basis of the laws of Illinois, only men were admitted to the bar, and the legislature had not made any change in this respect, but had simply provided that no person should be admitted to practice as attorney or counsellor without having previously obtained a license for that purpose from two justices of the Supreme Court. . . . The court . . . regarded itself as bound by [the] limitation . . . that it should not admit any persons, or class of persons, not intended by the legislature to be admitted, even though not expressly excluded by statute. In view of this latter limitation the court felt compelled to deny the application of females to be admitted as members of the bar. Being contrary to the rules of the common law and the usages of Westminster Hall from time immemorial, it could not be supposed that the legislature had intended to adopt any different rule.

The claim that, under the fourteenth amendment of the Constitution, which declares that no State shall make or enforce any law which shall abridge the privileges and immunities of citizens of the United States, the statute law of Illinois, or the common law prevailing in that State, can no longer be set up as a barrier against the right of females to pursue any lawful employment for a livelihood (the practice of law included), assumes that it is one of the privileges and immunities of women as citizens to engage in any and every profession, occupation, or employment in civil life.

It certainly cannot be affirmed, as an historical fact, that this has ever been established as one of the fundamental privileges and immunities of the sex. On the contrary, the civil law, as well as nature herself, has always recognized a wide difference in the respective spheres and destinies of man and woman. Man is, or should be, woman's protector and defender. The natural and proper timidity and delicacy which belongs to the female sex evidently unfits it for many of the occupations of civil life. The constitution of the family organization, which is founded in the divine ordinance, as well as in the nature of things, indicates the domestic sphere as that which properly belongs to the domain and functions of womanhood. The harmony, not to say identity, of interest and views which belong, or should belong, to the family institution is repugnant to the idea of a woman adopting a distinct and independent career from that of her husband. So firmly fixed was this sentiment in the founders of the common law that it became a maxim of that system of jurisprudence that a woman had no legal existence separate from her husband, who was regarded as her head and representative in the social state; and, notwithstanding some recent modifications of this civil status, many of the special rules of law flowing from and dependent upon this cardinal principle still exist in full force in most States. One of these is, that a married woman is incapable, without her husband's consent, of making contracts which shall be binding on her or him. This very incapacity was one circumstance which the Supreme Court of Illinois deemed important in rendering a married woman incompetent fully to perform the duties and trusts that belong to the office of an attorney and counsellor.

It is true that many women are unmarried and not affected by any of the duties, complications, and incapacities arising out of the married state, but these are exceptions to the general rule. The paramount destiny and mission of woman are to fulfil the noble and benign offices of wife and mother. This is the law of the Creator. And the rules of civil society must be adapted to the general constitution of things, and cannot be based upon exceptional cases.

The humane movements of modern society, which have for their object the multiplication of avenues for woman's advancement, and of occupations adapted to her condition and sex, have my heartiest concurrence. But I am not prepared to say that it is one of her fundamental rights and privileges to be admitted into every office and position, including those which require highly special qualifications and demanding special responsibilities. In the nature of things it is not every citizen of every age, sex, and condition that is qualified for every calling and position. It is the prerogative of the legislator to prescribe regulations founded on nature, reason, and experience for the due admission of qualified persons to professions and callings demanding special skill and confidence. This fairly belongs to the police power of the State; and, in my opinion, in view of the peculiar characteristics, destiny, and mission of woman, it is within the province of the legislature to ordain what offices, positions, and callings shall be filled and discharged by men, and shall receive the benefit of those energies and responsibilities, and that decision and firmness which are presumed to predominate in the sterner sex.

For these reasons I think that the laws of Illinois now complained of are not obnoxious to the charge of abridging any of the privileges and immunities of citizens of the United States.

■ THE CHIEF JUSTICE [CHASE] dissented from the judgment of the court, and from all the opinions.

Minor v. Happersett
88 (21 Wall.) U.S. 162 (1875)

■ THE CHIEF JUSTICE delivered the opinion of the court.

The question is presented in this case, whether, since the adoption of the fourteenth amendment, a woman, who is a citizen of the United States and of the State of Missouri, is a voter in that State, notwithstanding the provision of the constitution and laws of the State, which confine the right of suffrage to men alone. . . .

It is contended that the provisions of the constitution and laws of the State of Missouri which confine the right of suffrage and registration therefor to men, are in violation of the Constitution of the United States, and therefore void. The argument is, that as a woman, born or naturalized in the United States and subject to the jurisdiction thereof, is a citizen of the United States and of the State in which she resides, she has the right of suffrage as one of the privileges and immunities of her citizenship, which the State cannot by its laws or constitution abridge.

There is no doubt that women may be citizens. They are persons, and by the fourteenth amendment "all persons born or naturalized in the United States and subject to the jurisdiction thereof" are expressly declared to be "citizens of the United States and of the State wherein they reside." But, in our opinion, it did not need this amendment to give them that position. . . .

[The Court shows at length that women were citizens prior to adoption of the Fourteenth Amendment, citing among other evidence that they could sue and be sued in federal court under diversity jurisdiction as "citizens of different states."—Editors]

Other proof of like character might be found, but certainly more cannot be necessary to establish the fact that sex has never been made one of the elements of citizenship in the United States. In this respect men have never had an advantage over women. The same laws precisely apply to both. The fourteenth amendment did not affect the citizenship of women any more than it did of men. In this particular, therefore, the rights of Mrs. Minor do not depend upon the amendment. She has always been a citizen from her birth, and entitled to all the privileges and immunities of citizenship. . . .

If the right of suffrage is one of the necessary privileges of a citizen of the United States, then the constitution and laws of Missouri confining it to men are in violation of the Constitution of the United States, as amended, and consequently void. The direct question is, therefore, presented whether all citizens are necessarily voters.

The Constitution does not define the privileges and immunities of citizens. For that definition we must look elsewhere. In this case we need not determine what they are, but only whether suffrage is necessarily one of them.

It certainly is nowhere made so in express terms. The United States has no voters in the States of its own creation. The elective officers of the United States are all elected directly or indirectly by State voters. The members of the House of Representatives are to be chosen by the people of the States, and the electors in each State must have the qualifications requisite for electors of the most numerous branch of the State legislature. Senators are to be chosen by the legislatures of the States, and necessarily the members of the legislature required to make the choice are elected by the voters of the State. Each State must appoint in such manner, as the legislature thereof may direct, the electors to elect the President and Vice-President. The times, places, and manner of holding elections for Senators and Representatives are to be prescribed in each State by the legislature thereof; but Congress may at any time, by law, make or alter such regulations, except as to the place of choosing Senators. It is not necessary to inquire whether this power of supervision thus given to Congress is sufficient to authorize any interference with the State laws prescribing the qualifications of voters, for no such interference has ever been attempted. The power of the State in this particular is certainly supreme until Congress acts.

The [fourteenth] amendment did not add to the privileges and immunities of a citizen. It simply furnished an additional guaranty for the protection of such as he already had. No new voters were necessarily made by it. Indirectly it may have had that effect, because it may have increased the number of citizens entitled to suffrage under the constitution and laws of the States, but it operates for this purpose, if at all, through the States and the State laws, and not directly upon the citizen.

It is clear, therefore, we think, that the Constitution has not added the right of suffrage to the privileges and immunities of citizenship as they existed at the time it was adopted. This makes it proper to inquire whether suffrage was coextensive with the citizenship of the States at the time of its adoption. If it was, then it may with force be argued that suffrage was one of the rights which belonged to citizenship, and in the enjoyment of which every citizen must be protected. But if it was not, the contrary may with propriety be assumed.

When the Federal Constitution was adopted, all the States, with the exception of Rhode Island and Connecticut, had constitutions of their own. These two continued to act under their charters from the Crown. Upon an examination of those constitutions we find that in no State were all citizens permitted to vote. Each State determined for itself who should have that power. . . . *[The Court proceeds to quote the suffrage qualifications of each of the 13 original states.—Editors]*

In this condition of the law in respect to suffrage in the several States it cannot for a moment be doubted that if it had been intended to make all citizens of the United States voters, the framers of the Constitution would not have left it to implication. So important a change in the condition of citizenship as it actually existed, if intended, would have been expressly declared.

But if further proof is necessary to show that no such change was intended, it can easily be found both in and out of the Constitution. By Article 4, section 2, it is provided that "the citizens of each State shall be entitled to all the privileges and immunities of citizens in the several States." If suffrage is necessarily a part of citizenship, then the citizens of each State must be entitled to vote in the several States precisely as their citizens are. This is more than asserting that they may change their residence and become citizens of the State and thus be voters. It goes to the extent of insisting that while retaining their original citizenship they may vote in any State. This, we think, has never been claimed. And again, by the very terms of the amendment we have been considering [the fourteenth], "Representatives shall be apportioned among the several States according to their respective numbers, counting the whole number of persons in each State, excluding Indians not taxed. But when the right to vote at any election for the choice of electors for President and Vice-President of the United States, representatives in Congress, the executive and judicial officers of a State, or the members of the legislature thereof, is denied to any of the male inhabitants of such State, being twenty-one years of age and citizens of the United States, or in any way abridged, except for participation in the rebellion, or other crimes, the basis of representation therein shall be reduced in the proportion which the number of such male citizens shall bear to the whole number of male citizens twenty-one years of age in such State." Why this, if it was not in the power of the legislature to deny the right of suffrage to some male inhabitants? And if suffrage was necessarily one of the absolute rights of citizenship, why confine the operation of the limitation to male inhabitants? Women and children are, as we have seen, "persons." They are counted in the enumeration upon which the apportionment is to be made, but if they were necessarily voters because of their citizenship unless clearly excluded, why inflict the penalty for the exclusion of males alone? Clearly, no such form of words would have been selected to express the idea here indicated if suffrage was the absolute right of all citizens.

And still again, after the adoption of the fourteenth amendment, it was deemed necessary to adopt a fifteenth, as follows: "The right of citizens of the United States to vote shall not be denied or abridged by the United States, or by any State, on account of race, color, or previous condition of servitude." The fourteenth amendment had already provided that no State should make or enforce any law which should abridge the privileges or immunities of citizens of the United States. If suffrage was one of these privileges or immunities, why amend the Constitution to prevent its being denied on account of race, & c.? Nothing is more evident than that the greater must include the less, and if all were already protected why go through with the form of amending the Constitution to protect a part?

It is true that the United States guarantees to every State a republican form of government. It is also true that no State can pass a bill of attainder, and that no person can be deprived of life, liberty, or property without due process of law. All these several provisions of the Constitution must be construed in connection with the other parts of the instrument, and in the light of the surrounding circumstances.

The guaranty is of a republican form of government. No particular government is designated as republican, neither is the exact form to be guaranteed, in any manner especially designated. Here, as in other parts of the instrument, we are compelled to resort elsewhere to ascertain what was intended.

The guaranty necessarily implies a duty on the part of the States themselves to provide such a government. All the States had governments when the Constitution was adopted. In all the people participated to some extent, through their representatives elected in the manner specially provided. These governments the Constitution did not change. They were accepted precisely as they were, and it is, therefore, to be presumed that they were such as it was the duty of the States to provide. Thus we have unmistakable evidence of what was republican in form, within the meaning of that term as employed in the Constitution. As has been seen, all the citizens of the States were not invested with the right of suffrage. In all, save perhaps New Jersey, this right was only bestowed upon men and not upon all of them. Under these circumstances it is certainly now too late to contend that a government is not republican, within the meaning of this guaranty in the Constitution, because women are not made voters.

The same may be said of the other provisions just quoted. Women were excluded from suffrage in nearly all the States by the express provision of their constitutions and laws. If that had been equivalent to a bill of attainder, certainly its abrogation would not have been left to implication. Nothing less than express language would have been employed to effect so radical a change. . . .

We have given this case the careful consideration its importance demands. If the law is wrong, it ought to be changed; but the power for that is not with us. The arguments addressed to us bearing upon such a view of the subject may perhaps be sufficient to induce those having the power, to make the alteration, but they ought not to be permitted to influence our judgment in determining the present rights of the parties now litigating before us. No argument as to woman's need of suffrage can be considered. We can only act upon her rights as they exist. It is not for us to look at the hardship of withholding. Our duty is at an end if we find it is within the power of a State to withhold.

Being unanimously of the opinion that the Constitution of the United States does not confer the right of suffrage upon any one, and that the constitutions and laws of the several States which commit that important trust to men alone are not necessarily void, we

AFFIRM THE JUDGMENT.

NOTES

1.   Six of the justices took positions in *Bradwell* that aligned with the ones they had just taken in *Slaughter-House*, p. 1284. The five justices represented by the Opinion of the Court had been the majority in *Slaughter-House*, and for them the case was not difficult: just as there was no privilege to be a butcher in Louisiana, there was no privilege to be a lawyer in Illinois. Chief Justice Chase dissented in both cases. He supported women's professional advancement, and when he had been Lincoln's secretary of the treasury he ensured that many women were hired by the Treasury Department. In his political campaigns—he had been governor of Ohio, a U.S. senator, and a presidential candidate—one of his chief advisers was his daughter Kate. But Chase wrote no opinion in *Bradwell*, for he was in poor health, and less than a month after the decision was announced he died. But the remaining three justices—Bradley, Swayne, and Field—dissented in *Slaughter-House*, and they needed to show why this case was different. Their attempt to do that was the now infamous concurrence of Justice Bradley.

Was *Bradwell* rightly decided? If it was wrong, was it wrong only because *Slaughter-House* was wrong in its interpretation of the Privileges or Immunities Clause? Or was it wrong because of the injustice of the result? (Note how *Minor* argues, at the close of the opinion, that this should not be part of constitutional interpretation. Do you agree?)

2.   Bradwell's counsel argued only on the basis of the Privileges or Immunities Clause. At the time it was not clear that the argument would be foreclosed, for *Bradwell* was argued a few months before the Court announced its decision in *Slaughter-House*. (Bradwell's counsel, Matthew Hale Carpenter, a sitting U.S. senator and frequent advocate in the Supreme Court, was also representing the state of Louisiana in *Slaughter-House*.) Would *Bradwell* have come out differently if it had been argued under the Equal Protection Clause?

If Illinois had excluded its black citizens from the practice of law, would that have violated the Equal Protection Clause? Why? If so, why would it also violate the clause to exclude women from the practice of law? Consider two possible responses (and their broader interpretive implications). One is that the Equal Protection Clause is concerned only with race, because in its historical context it was aimed at providing a constitutional basis for the Civil Rights Act of 1866 and other legislation Congress might pass to protect persons of color in the South from state oppression. The other is that the draftsmen of the Fourteenth Amendment did not intend for the Equal Protection Clause to apply to discrimination against women. But these responses can be met with objections. The Equal Protection Clause does not use any terms that limit its scope to race—even though its drafters knew how to do this (compare the Fifteenth Amendment two years later, which did refer explicitly to race). Should the meaning of the amendment be limited by the drafters' and ratifiers' expectations about how it would be applied?

Or should *Bradwell* be considered rightly decided at the time because the social context of the day made it unthinkable that the amendment would provide equal legal status and privileges to women? Does the meaning of the language of the Constitution depend on changing social values? When courts interpret and apply the Constitution, should they take into account contemporary social norms?

3.   Myra Bradwell had "read law" (apprenticed) with her husband, an Illinois attorney, and she then took the Illinois bar exam, passing with high honors. But she was denied admission by the Illinois Supreme Court on the ground "that when the legislature gave to this court the power of granting licenses to practice law, it was with not the slightest expectation that this privilege would be extended to women." Bradwell's biographer reports that by the time her case reached the U.S. Supreme Court the Illinois legislature had already passed a statute providing that "No person shall be precluded or debarred from any occupation, profession, or employment (except military) on account of sex." Jane M. Friedman, AMERICA'S FIRST WOMAN LAWYER 28 (1993). (Should that have made the case moot?) Bradwell never reapplied for admission, even after the U.S. Supreme Court's decision, having developed a career as a prominent legal journalist in Chicago. In 1890, the Illinois Supreme Court on its own reversed its prior action and admitted Bradwell to the Illinois bar. In 1892, the U.S. Supreme Court, on motion of the attorney general, retroactively granted Bradwell admission to the bar of that court as of the date of her original application in 1869.

4.   On to *Minor*, which presents a different question: Is the right to vote in state and federal elections among the "privileges or immunities of citizens of the United States"? The Court's opinion in *Minor* was unanimous. Is there any good rebuttal to the argument that, given Section 2's language restricting representation in Congress if a state denied the right to vote on the basis of race, it would make no sense to read Section 1 as completely prohibiting denial of the right to vote on the basis of race (or, for that matter, sex)? And if voting were a "privilege or immunity of citizens," then why would the Fifteenth Amendment have been necessary?

As you try to make sense of this, remember the distinction between "civil rights" and "political rights." See p. 711. Civil rights were the *Corfield*-style list of privileges and immunities—freedom to move, make contracts, own property, and so on. Political rights included the right to vote, serve on a jury, and hold political office. (There was not complete agreement, though, about what belonged in each category.) This distinction between civil rights and political rights helps explain how the Fourteenth Amendment was understood as requiring equality in civil rights, but later amendments were still needed in order to prohibit discrimination in voting.

And yet: although the framers of the Fourteenth Amendment distinguished between the two kinds of rights, and repeatedly associated the "privileges or immunities of *citizens*" with civil rights, why should we? Is that distinction crucial for understanding the text? Is it part of historical context, and the expectations of the framers? Is it both? Is that distinction ruled out by the Fifteenth, Nineteenth, and Twenty-sixth Amendments? Or do those amendments implicitly recognize and reinforce the distinction?

5.   The modern Supreme Court has interpreted the Equal Protection Clause as prohibiting certain forms of disparate treatment with respect to the right to vote. *E.g.*, *Baker v. Carr*, 369 U.S. 186 (1962) (Equal Protection Clause held to supply a judicially enforceable basis for challenging state election and representation arrangements), p. 776; *Reynolds v. Sims*, 377 U.S. 533 (1964) (Equal Protection Clause held to create a one-person, one-vote standard for state election districts), p. 780; *Harper v. Virginia Board of Elections*, 383 U.S. 663 (1966) (Equal Protection Clause held to forbid state poll tax of $1.50); *Bush v. Gore*, 531 U.S. 98 (2000) (Equal Protection Clause held to require that state-law vote recount rules and arrangements treat each voter's ballot consistently throughout the state). These decisions have become central to our national politics.

Can these decisions be justified on constitutional grounds other than the Fourteenth Amendment? One possibility, discussed by the Court in *Minor*, is that Article IV's

Guarantee Clause might supply a principle invalidating certain state rules or statutes pertaining to voting and vote-counting. If so, would the enforcement (and interpretation) of that principle be committed to Congress or to the courts? Recall *Luther v. Borden*, 48 U.S. (7 How.) 1 (1849), p. 431, that such issues are political questions for Congress and the president to decide. Wasn't that the theory when Congress refused to seat the representatives from Southern states unless they agreed to ratify the Fourteenth Amendment—that Congress was the judge of whether a state's government was "Republican"? Is that reasoning consistent with *Minor*? Could the Reconstruction Congress could have passed legislation giving women the right to vote in all elections? Pursuant to the Fourteenth Amendment or Article IV?

[Assignment 73]

The Twentieth Century

Amend. XIX: The right of citizens of the United States to vote shall not be denied or abridged by the United States or by any State on account of sex.

Congress shall have power to enforce this article by appropriate legislation.

The first half of the twentieth century brought a dramatic change in the constitutional law of sex discrimination—the ratification in 1920 of the Nineteenth Amendment. Its adoption was the culmination of almost fifty years of political advocacy by leaders who included Elizabeth Cady Stanton and Susan B. Anthony.

1869 was the first year a women's suffrage amendment was introduced in Congress, four years after the Civil War and the same year Congress passed the Fifteenth Amendment. The text, as introduced by Representative George Washington Julian, of Indiana, read: "The Right of Suffrage in the United States shall be based on citizenship, and shall be regulated by Congress, and all citizens of the United States, whether native or naturalized shall enjoy this right equally without any distinction or discrimination whatever founded on sex." Congress did not act.

In 1890, Wyoming joined the Union as the first state after the Civil War to allow women to vote in all elections. In 1912, Theodore Roosevelt's third party, the Bull Moose Party, placed in its platform a plank calling for a women's suffrage amendment to the Constitution. By 1918, with President Woodrow Wilson's endorsement, congressional majorities supported the amendment, but in the Senate it fell just short of the two-thirds majority required by Article V. In June 1919, both houses of Congress passed the women's suffrage amendment by the required majority, and it was sent to the states for ratification. Nine states ratified the amendment that very month, and within fourteen months the three-fourths required by Article V had ratified it.

The women's suffrage movement succeeded in more than amending the Constitution. It led to fundamental debates about sex, the family, and democracy, and the social transformations reflected in the amendment should not be understated. See generally Reva B. Siegel, *She the People: The Nineteenth Amendment, Sex Equality, Federalism, and the Family*, 115 Harv. L. Rev. 947 (2002).

Only three years after the ratification of the Nineteenth Amendment, another amendment related to sex discrimination was introduced into Congress. Written by Alice Paul and announced on the 75th anniversary of the Seneca Falls Convention, it would become known as the Equal Rights Amendment. As proposed in Congress in 1923 (and annually for two decades) it read:

> Men and women shall have equal rights throughout the United States and every place subject to its jurisdiction.

In 1943, Paul rewrote the amendment to more closely resemble the Fifteenth Amendment. In its new form, the Equal Rights Amendment was annually proposed in Congress:

> Equality of rights under the law shall not be denied or abridged by the United States or by any state on account of sex.

The first support for the Equal Rights Amendment from a major party came in the 1940 platform of the Republican Party, and it was subsequently endorsed by President Eisenhower and by presidential candidate John F. Kennedy. Congress began hearings on the proposed amendment in 1970, and two years later both houses of Congress passed the amendment by the majorities required by Article V, sending it to the states for ratification. As passed, the Equal Rights Amendment had its third and final form:

> § 1. Equality of rights under the law shall not be denied or abridged by the United States or by any State on account of sex.

> § 2. The Congress shall have the power to enforce, by appropriate legislation, the provisions of this article.

> § 3. This amendment shall take effect two years after the date of ratification.

It never made it. Thirty states ratified the amendment by the following year. Five more ratified it over the next four years. But that was it. By the 1979 deadline set by Congress, the ERA was still three states shy of the necessary 38. Congress extended the deadline, in an unsuccessful attempt to secure ratification (see p. 802).

Meanwhile, however, things were happening at the Supreme Court. Up to the 1970s, the Court applied a lenient standard of review when a law discriminating on the basis of sex was challenged under the Equal Protection Clause, asking whether there was any rational basis for the law. (This was the standard the Court applied to all classifications other than racial ones.) While the ERA was being considered in the early 1970s, the Court held sex-discriminatory laws unconstitutional in two cases: *Reed v. Reed*, 404 U.S. 71 (1971), invalidated an Idaho probate law that preferred men to women in disputes over who would serve as an estate administrator; *Frontiero v. Richardson*, 411 U.S. 677 (1973), invalidated laws that allowed all men in the armed forces to automatically claim their wives as "dependents," while requiring military women to show that their husbands were in fact dependent on them. Neither case settled on a heightened standard of scrutiny for sex discrimination, though a four-justice plurality advocated one in *Frontiero*.

The Court first adopted "intermediate scrutiny" as the standard of review in *Craig v. Boren* (1976). Twenty years later, in *United States v. Virginia*, the Court interpreted that test to require an "exceedingly persuasive justification" for sex-based classifications. That formulation edged closer to the "strict scrutiny" that governs racial classifications. As you read these two cases, ask yourself how the Court sees the analogy between race and sex, what standard the Court applies (not just the words, but the actual effect), and whether it would have made a difference if the Equal Rights Amendment had been ratified.

Craig v. Boren
429 U.S. 190 (1976)

■ MR. JUSTICE BRENNAN delivered the opinion of the Court.

The interaction of two sections of an Oklahoma statute prohibits the sale of "nonintoxicating" 3.2% beer to males under the age of 21 and to females under the age of 18. The question to be decided is whether such a gender-based differential constitutes a denial to males 18–20 years of age of the equal protection of the laws in violation of the Fourteenth Amendment. . . .

II–A

Before 1972, Oklahoma defined the commencement of civil majority at age 18 for females and age 21 for males. In contrast, females were held criminally responsible as adults at age 18 and males at age 16. After the Court of Appeals for the Tenth Circuit held in 1972, on the authority of *Reed v. Reed*, 404 U.S. 71 (1971) that the age distinction was unconstitutional for purposes of establishing criminal responsibility as adults, the Oklahoma Legislature fixed age 18 as applicable to both males and females. In 1972, 18 also was established as the age of majority for males and females in civil matters, except that [sections] of the 3.2% beer statute were simultaneously codified to create an exception to the gender-free rule.

Analysis may appropriately begin with the reminder that *Reed* emphasized that statutory classifications that distinguish between males and females are "subject to scrutiny under the Equal Protection Clause." To withstand constitutional challenge, previous cases establish that classifications by gender must serve important governmental objectives and must be substantially related to achievement of those objectives. Thus, in *Reed*, the objectives of "reducing the workload on probate courts," and "avoiding intrafamily controversy," were deemed of insufficient importance to sustain use of an overt gender criterion in the appointment of administrators of intestate decedents' estates. Decisions following *Reed* similarly have rejected administrative ease and convenience as sufficiently important objectives to justify gender-based classifications. And only two Terms ago, *Stanton v. Stanton*, 421 U.S. 7 (1975), expressly stating that *Reed v. Reed* was "controlling," held that *Reed* required invalidation of a Utah differential age-of-majority statute, notwithstanding the statute's coincidence with and furtherance of the State's purpose of fostering "old notions" of role typing and preparing boys for their expected performance in the economic and political worlds.

Reed v. Reed has also provided the underpinning for decisions that have invalidated statutes employing gender as an inaccurate proxy for other, more germane bases of classification. Hence, "archaic and overbroad" generalizations concerning the financial position of servicewomen and working women could not justify use of a gender line in determining eligibility for certain governmental entitlements. Similarly, increasingly outdated misconceptions concerning the role of females in the home rather than in the "marketplace and world of ideas" were rejected as loose-fitting characterizations incapable of supporting state statutory schemes that were premised upon their accuracy. In light of the weak congruence between gender and the characteristic or trait that gender purported to represent, it was necessary that the legislatures choose either to realign their substantive laws in a gender-neutral fashion, or to adopt procedures for identifying those instances where the sex-centered generalization actually comported with fact.

In this case, too, "*Reed*, we feel is controlling . . . ," *Stanton*, at 13. We turn then to the question whether, under *Reed*, the difference between males and females with respect to the purchase of 3.2% beer warrants the differential in age drawn by the Oklahoma statute. We conclude that it does not.

B

The District Court recognized that *Reed v. Reed* was controlling. In applying the teachings of that case, the court found the requisite important governmental objective in the traffic-safety goal proffered by the Oklahoma Attorney General. It then concluded that the statistics introduced by the appellees established that the gender-based distinction was substantially related to achievement of that goal.

C

We accept for purposes of discussion the District Court's identification of the objective underlying [Sections] 241 and 245 as the enhancement of traffic safety. Clearly, the protection of public health and safety represents an important function of state and local governments. However, appellees' statistics in our view cannot support the conclusion that the gender-based distinction closely serves to achieve that objective and therefore the distinction cannot under *Reed* withstand equal protection challenge.

The appellees introduced a variety of statistical surveys. First, an analysis of arrest statistics for 1973 demonstrated that 18–20-year-old male arrests for "driving under the influence" and "drunkenness" substantially exceeded female arrests for that same age period. Similarly, youths aged 17–21 were found to be overrepresented among those killed or injured in traffic accidents, with males again numerically exceeding females in this regard. Third, a random roadside survey in Oklahoma City revealed that young males were more inclined to drive and drink beer than were their female counterparts. Fourth, Federal Bureau of Investigation nationwide statistics exhibited a notable increase in arrests for "driving under the influence." Finally, statistical evidence gathered in other jurisdictions, particularly Minnesota and Michigan, was offered to corroborate Oklahoma's experience by indicating the pervasiveness of youthful participation in motor vehicle accidents following the imbibing of alcohol. Conceding that "the case is not free from doubt," the District Court nonetheless concluded that this statistical showing substantiated "a rational basis for the legislative judgment underlying the challenged classification."

Even were this statistical evidence accepted as accurate, it nevertheless offers only a weak answer to the equal protection question presented here. The most focused and relevant of the statistical surveys, arrests of 18–20-year-olds for alcohol-related driving offenses, exemplifies the ultimate unpersuasiveness of this evidentiary record. Viewed in terms of the correlation between sex and the actual activity that Oklahoma seeks to regulate driving while under the influence of alcohol the statistics broadly establish that .18% of females and 2% of males in that age group were arrested for that offense. While such a disparity is not trivial in a statistical sense, it hardly can form the basis for employment of a gender line as a classifying device. Certainly if maleness is to serve as a proxy for drinking and driving, a correlation of 2% must be considered an unduly tenuous "fit." Indeed, prior cases have consistently rejected the use of sex as a decisionmaking factor even though the statutes in question certainly rested on far more predictive empirical relationships than this.

Moreover, the statistics exhibit a variety of other shortcomings that seriously impugn their value to equal protection analysis. Setting aside the obvious methodological problems,[14] the surveys do not adequately justify the salient features of Oklahoma's gender-based traffic-safety law. None purports to measure the use and dangerousness of 3.2% beer as opposed to alcohol generally, a detail that is of particular importance since, in light of its low alcohol level, Oklahoma apparently considers the 3.2% beverage to be "nonintoxicating." Moreover, many of the studies, while graphically documenting the unfortunate increase in driving while under the influence of alcohol, make no effort to relate their findings to age-sex differentials as involved here. Indeed, the only survey that explicitly centered its attention upon young drivers and their use of beer albeit apparently not of the diluted 3.2% variety reached results that hardly can be viewed as impressive in justifying either a gender or age classification.

There is no reason to belabor this line of analysis. It is unrealistic to expect either members of the judiciary or state officials to be well versed in the rigors of experimental or statistical technique. But this merely illustrates that proving broad sociological propositions by statistics is a dubious business, and one that inevitably is in tension with the normative philosophy that underlies the Equal Protection Clause. Suffice to say that the showing offered by the appellees does not satisfy us that sex represents a legitimate, accurate proxy for the regulation of drinking and driving. In fact, when it is further recognized that Oklahoma's statute prohibits only the selling of 3.2% beer to young males and not their drinking the beverage once acquired (even after purchase by their 18–20-year-old female companions), the relationship between gender and traffic safety becomes far too tenuous to satisfy *Reed*'s requirement that the gender-based difference be substantially related to achievement of the statutory objective.

We hold, therefore, that under *Reed*, Oklahoma's 3.2% beer statute invidiously discriminates against males 18–20 years of age. . . .

■ MR. JUSTICE POWELL, concurring.

I join the opinion of the Court as I am in general agreement with it. I do have reservations as to some of the discussion concerning the appropriate standard for equal protection analysis and the relevance of the statistical evidence. Accordingly, I add this concurring statement.

---

[14] The very social stereotypes that find reflection in age-differential laws are likely substantially to distort the accuracy of these comparative statistics. Hence "reckless" young men who drink and drive are transformed into arrest statistics, whereas their female counterparts are chivalrously escorted home. See, e.g., W. Reckless & B. Kay, *The Female Offender* 4, 7, 13, 16–17 (Report to Presidential Commission on Law Enforcement and Administration of Justice, 1967). Moreover, the Oklahoma surveys, gathered under a regime where the age-differential law in question has been in effect, are lacking in controls necessary for appraisal of the actual effectiveness of the male 3.2% beer prohibition. In this regard, the disproportionately high arrest statistics for young males and, indeed, the growing alcohol-related arrest figures for all ages and sexes simply may be taken to document the relative futility of controlling driving behavior by the 3.2% beer statute and like legislation, although we obviously have no means of estimating how many individuals, if any, actually were prevented from drinking by these laws.

With respect to the equal protection standard, I agree that *Reed v. Reed* is the most relevant precedent. But I find it unnecessary, in deciding this case, to read that decision as broadly as some of the Court's language may imply. *Reed* and subsequent cases involving gender-based classifications make clear that the Court subjects such classifications to a more critical examination than is normally applied when "fundamental" constitutional rights and "suspect classes" are not present.[*]

I view this as a relatively easy case. No one questions the legitimacy or importance of the asserted governmental objective: the promotion of highway safety. The decision of the case turns on whether the state legislature, by the classification it has chosen, had adopted a means that bears a "fair and substantial relation" to this objective. . . .

■ MR. JUSTICE STEVENS, concurring.

There is only one Equal Protection Clause. It requires every State to govern impartially. It does not direct the courts to apply one standard of review in some cases and a different standard in other cases. . . .

I am inclined to believe that what has become known as the two-tiered analysis of equal protection claims does not describe a completely logical method of deciding cases, but rather is a method the Court has employed to explain decisions that actually apply a single standard in a reasonably consistent fashion. I also suspect that a careful explanation of the reasons motivating particular decisions may contribute more to an identification of that standard than an attempt to articulate it in all-encompassing terms. It may therefore be appropriate for me to state the principal reasons which persuaded me to join the Court's opinion.

In this case, the classification is not as obnoxious as some the Court has condemned, nor as inoffensive as some the Court has accepted. It is objectionable because it is based on an accident of birth, because it is a mere remnant of the now almost universally rejected tradition of discriminating against males in this age bracket, and because, to the extent it reflects any physical difference between males and females, it is actually perverse. The question then is whether the traffic safety justification put forward by the State is sufficient to make an otherwise offensive classification acceptable.

The classification is not totally irrational. For the evidence does indicate that there are more males than females in this age bracket who drive and also more who drink. Nevertheless, there are several reasons why I regard the justification as unacceptable. It is difficult to believe that the statute was actually intended to cope with the problem of traffic safety, since it has only a minimal effect on access to a not very intoxicating beverage and does not prohibit its consumption. Moreover, the empirical data submitted by the State accentuate the unfairness of treating all 18–21-year-old males as inferior to their female counterparts. The legislation imposes a

---

[*] As is evident from our opinions, the Court has had difficulty in agreeing upon a standard of equal protection analysis that can be applied consistently to the wide variety of legislative classifications. There are valid reasons for dissatisfaction with the "two-tier" approach that has been prominent in the Court's decisions in the past decade. Although viewed by many as a result-oriented substitute for more critical analysis, that approach with its narrowly limited "upper-tier" now has substantial precedential support. As has been true of *Reed* and its progeny, our decision today will be viewed by some as a "middle-tier" approach. While I would not endorse that characterization and would not welcome a further subdividing of equal protection analysis, candor compels the recognition that the relatively deferential "rational basis" standard of review normally applied takes on a sharper focus when we address a gender-based classification. So much is clear from our recent cases.

restraint on 100% of the males in the class allegedly because about 2% of them have probably violated one or more laws relating to the consumption of alcoholic beverages. It is unlikely that this law will have a significant deterrent effect either on that 2% or on the law-abiding 98%. But even assuming some such slight benefit, it does not seem to me that an insult to all of the young men of the State can be justified by visiting the sins of the 2% on the 98%.

■ [The concurring opinion of JUSTICE BLACKMUN and dissenting opinion of CHIEF JUSTICE BURGER are omitted.]

■ MR. JUSTICE REHNQUIST, dissenting.

The Court's disposition of this case is objectionable on two grounds. First is its conclusion that men challenging a gender-based statute which treats them less favorably than women may invoke a more stringent standard of judicial review than pertains to most other types of classifications. Second is the Court's enunciation of this standard, without citation to any source, as being that "classifications by gender must serve important governmental objectives and must be substantially related to achievement of those objectives." The only redeeming feature of the Court's opinion, to my mind, is that it apparently signals a retreat by those who joined the plurality opinion in *Frontiero v. Richardson*, 411 U.S. 677, 690 (1973), from their view that sex is a "suspect" classification for purposes of equal protection analysis. I think the Oklahoma statute challenged here need pass only the "rational basis" equal protection analysis expounded in cases such as *McGowan v. Maryland*, 366 U.S. 420 (1961), and *Williamson v. Lee Optical Co.*, 348 U.S. 483 (1955), and I believe that it is constitutional under that analysis.

I

. . . Most obviously unavailable to support any kind of special scrutiny in this case, is a history or pattern of past discrimination, such as was relied on by the plurality in *Frontiero* to support its invocation of strict scrutiny. There is no suggestion in the Court's opinion that males in this age group are in any way peculiarly disadvantaged, subject to systematic discriminatory treatment, or otherwise in need of special solicitude from the courts. . . .

It is true that a number of our opinions contain broadly phrased dicta implying that the same test should be applied to all classifications based on sex, whether affecting females or males. However, before today, no decision of this Court has applied an elevated level of scrutiny to invalidate a statutory discrimination harmful to males, except where the statute impaired an important personal interest protected by the Constitution. There being no such interest here, and there being no plausible argument that this is a discrimination against females, the Court's reliance on our previous sex-discrimination cases is ill-founded. It treats gender classification as a talisman which without regard to the rights involved or the persons affected calls into effect a heavier burden of judicial review.

The Court's conclusion that a law which treats males less favorably than females "must serve important governmental objectives and must be substantially related to achievement of those objectives" apparently comes out of thin air. The Equal Protection Clause contains no such language, and none of our previous cases adopt that standard. I would think we have had enough difficulty with the two standards of review which our cases have recognized the norm of "rational basis," and the "compelling state interest" required where a "suspect classification" is involved so as to counsel weightily against the insertion of still another "standard" between those two. How is this Court to divine what objectives are important? How is it to determine whether a particular law is "substantially" related to the achievement of such objective, rather than related in some other way to its achievement? Both of the phrases used are so diaphanous and elastic as to invite subjective judicial preferences or prejudices relating to particular types of legislation, masquerading as judgments whether such legislation is directed at "important" objectives or, whether the relationship to those objectives is "substantial" enough.

I would have thought that if this Court were to leave anything to decision by the popularly elected branches of the Government, where no constitutional claim other than that of equal protection is invoked, it would be the decision as to what governmental objectives to be achieved by law are "important," and which are not. As for the second part of the Court's new test, the Judicial Branch is probably in no worse position than the Legislative or Executive Branches to determine if there is any rational relationship between a classification and the purpose which it might be thought to serve. But the introduction of the adverb "substantially" requires courts to make subjective judgments as to operational effects, for which neither their expertise nor their access to data fits them. And even if we manage to avoid both confusion and the mirroring of our own preferences in the development of this new doctrine, the thousands of judges in other courts who must interpret the Equal Protection Clause may not be so fortunate.

II

The applicable rational-basis test is one which "permits the States a wide scope of discretion in enacting laws which affect some groups of citizens differently than others. The constitutional safeguard is offended only if the classification rests on grounds wholly irrelevant to the achievement of the State's objective. State legislatures are presumed to have acted within their constitutional power despite the fact that, in practice, their laws result in some inequality. A statutory discrimination will not be set aside if any state of facts reasonably may be conceived to justify it." *McGowan*, at 425–426. . . .

I believe that a more traditional type of scrutiny is appropriate in this case, and I think that the Court would have done well here to heed its own warning that "[i]t is unrealistic to expect . . . members of the judiciary . . . to be well versed in the rigors of experimental or statistical technique." *Dandridge v. Williams*, 397 U.S. 471, 485 (1970). . . .

The Court's criticism of the statistics relied on by the District Court conveys the impression that a legislature in enacting a new law is to be subjected to the judicial equivalent of a doctoral examination in statistics. Legislatures are not held to any rules of evidence such as those which may govern courts or other administrative bodies, and are entitled to draw factual conclusions on the basis of the determination of probable cause which an arrest by a police officer normally represents. In this situation, they could reasonably infer that the incidence of drunk driving is a good deal higher than the incidence of arrest.

And while, as the Court observes, relying on a report to a Presidential Commission which it cites in a footnote, such statistics may be distorted as a result of stereotyping, the legislature is not required to prove before a court that its statistics are perfect. In any event, if stereotypes are as pervasive as the Court suggests, they may in turn influence the conduct of the men and women in question, and cause the young men to conform to the wild and reckless image which is their stereotype. . . .

Nor is it unreasonable to conclude from the expressed preference for beer by four-fifths of the age-group males that that beverage was a predominant source of their intoxication-related arrests. Taking that as the predicate, the State could reasonably bar those males from any purchases of alcoholic beer, including that of the 3.2% variety. This Court lacks the expertise or the data to evaluate the intoxicating properties of that beverage, and in that posture our only appropriate course is to defer to the reasonable inference supporting the statute that taken in sufficient quantity this beer has the same effect as any alcoholic beverage.

Quite apart from these alleged methodological deficiencies in the statistical evidence, the Court appears to hold that that evidence, on its face, fails to support the distinction drawn in the statute. The Court notes that only 2% of males (as against .18% of females) in the age group were arrested for drunk driving, and that this very low figure establishes "an unduly tenuous 'fit'" between maleness and drunk driving in the 18 to 20-year-old group. On this point the Court misconceives the nature of the equal protection inquiry.

The rationality of a statutory classification for equal protection purposes does not depend upon the statistical "fit" between the class and the trait sought to be singled out. It turns on whether there may be a sufficiently higher incidence of the trait within the included class than in the excluded class to justify different treatment. Therefore the present equal protection challenge to this gender-based discrimination poses only the question whether the incidence of drunk driving among young men is sufficiently greater than among young women to justify differential treatment. Notwithstanding the Court's critique of the statistical evidence, that evidence suggests clear differences between the drinking and driving habits of young men and women. Those differences are grounds enough for the State reasonably to conclude that young males pose by far the greater drunk-driving hazard, both in terms of sheer numbers and in terms of hazard on a per-driver basis. The gender-based difference in treatment in this case is therefore not irrational.

The Court's argument that a 2% correlation between maleness and drunk driving is constitutionally insufficient therefore does not pose an equal protection issue concerning discrimination between males and females. . . .

NOTES

1.   *Craig v. Boren* is an entertaining case but it frames serious issues. Begin by thinking carefully about the nature of the constitutional right being asserted. Is there a constitutional right to drink beer? Is there a constitutional right to drink beer if one is over eighteen years old? Peruse the Eighteenth and Twenty-first Amendments. If not, then the constitutional objection is that *women* between the ages of eighteen and twenty-one may drink 3.2% "beer" but *men* may not—thus the Equal Protection Clause claim in the case. Should men be able to invoke the clause to argue that they have been discriminated against by government on the basis of sex? Is discrimination on the basis of sex against men any different from discrimination on the basis of sex against women for legal purposes? Should they be governed by different standards? (One of the plaintiffs was a bar owner who invoked men's rights to be free of unconstitutional discrimination in order to be able to serve them beer.)

The classification in this case was explicitly based on sex. Was it based on a real difference between eighteen-year-old men and women? Was it based on differences in their patterns of behavior? Is the latter an allowable basis for state legislation—the real-world fact that young men were (at the time, in that place) more than ten times more likely to drink and drive than women? Is that kind of fact rooted in biology? Is it entirely a function of social construction? Is it a stereotype? Why or why not?

2.   As noted above, the Equal Protection Clause does not expressly limit its coverage to government discrimination on the basis of race. But surely the "equal protection of the laws" does not mean that government may never make laws that affect different people differently. All criminal laws, for instance, treat people differently based on whether or not they violate the criminal prohibition. So what sorts of differential treatment are permissible? Are a person's intrinsic, permanent characteristics the ones that government may not take into account? If so, what happens as our understandings of "intrinsic" or "permanent" change? And would the government *never* be allowed to take those characteristics into account, or would the government be able to take them into account as long it has a sufficiently good reason?

In modern legal doctrine, race is at one end of the spectrum for equal protection analysis. A racial classification treats similar things differently, and is presumptively invalid. The government can make rights and privileges, benefits and burdens, hinge on an individual's race only if it has a "compelling" justification and the racial classification is "narrowly tailored" to that justification. At the other end of the spectrum lies ordinary government regulation of conduct or behavior of various forms. Here the idea is that government is usually treating different things differently. At this end of the spectrum courts have applied a deferential "rational basis" test: a law is upheld as long as there is any conceivable basis for the distinctions and classifications that the government is drawing.

Where on this spectrum do sex-based classifications fall? How would the principle that like things must be treated alike apply—are men and women alike or different? The answer generally given by the courts is that men and women are alike for many purposes, but for some purposes they are meaningfully different. The courts have considered the task of applying "equal protection of the laws" to sex-based classifications to be a matter of sorting out the respects in which men and women are alike from the respects in which there are biological differences—and limiting the government's use of sex-based classifications to the latter set of circumstances. (Easier said than done, as you will see presently.)

As you start thinking about what sex-based classifications fall into each category, consider this statement by Sylvia Law, *Rethinking Sex and the Constitution*, 132 U. Pa. L. Rev. 955, 965 (1984):

> There are . . . important points of difference between sex- and race-based discrimination. There is no reason to believe that black and white people are inherently different in any way that should ever be allowed to matter in the law. Men and women, by contrast, are different in significant sex-specific physical ways. Most differences between men and women are like differences between blacks and whites: statistical generalizations, which are more or less true in the aggregate but untrue in relation to particular individuals. Accurate statistical differences between men and women that are false in individual cases include weight, height, longevity, mathematical aptitude, aggression, capacity for nurturance, and physical strength. There are, however, other categorical differences between men and women that are not simply statistical generalizations, but rather sex-based physical differences relating to

reproductive capacity. By categorical sex-based differences, what is meant, and *all that is meant*, is that most women and no men possess the capacity to reproduce the species.

Do you agree? Why or why not?

3.   Think back to the questions raised in Note 1 about whether in *Craig v. Boren* the state's generalization about the behavior of men and women was accurate. When may governments legislate on the basis of true generalizations? Could a government-run life insurance program have different premium rates based on the different statistical life expectancies of men and women? Could a government-run health insurance program distinguish in premium rates based on the different likelihood of different health maladies or diseases for men and women? On the basis of diseases and their occurrence rate that are specific to a particular sex (like breast cancer and testicular cancer)?

Consider activities and places where the sexes are often separated. What about separate-sex bathrooms? Do social norms concerning privacy, modesty, and separation of the sexes with respect to excretory functions reflect biological differences? Improper stereotypes? Both? Neither?

4.   What about statutes that do not classify on the basis of sex but nonetheless have a disparate impact on the basis of sex? Recall the rule of *Washington v. Davis,* 426 U.S. 229 (1976), p. 1387: for race, disparate impact alone is not sufficient to establish a violation of the Equal Protection Clause. The Court has embraced the same rule in the context of sex. For example, classifications based on pregnancy are generally not treated as classifications on the basis of sex but are instead treated as classifications that have a disparate impact on women. See, e.g., *Geduldig v. Aiello*, 417 U.S. 484, 494–97 (1974) (upholding California disability compensation law that did not include pregnancy within its coverage of medical disabilities). Congress chose to address this situation in the Pregnancy Discrimination Act (an amendment to Title VII of the Civil Rights Act of 1964), forbidding the treatment of pregnancy-related illness less favorably than other medical conditions. The statute did not alter the *constitutional* holding of *Geduldig* that the Equal Protection Clause governs classifications based on sex itself and does not apply—absent evidence of intent to discriminate—to classifications that only have a disparate impact on men and women.

United States v. Virginia

518 U.S. 515 (1996)

■ JUSTICE GINSBURG delivered the opinion of the Court.

Virginia's public institutions of higher learning include an incomparable military college, Virginia Military Institute (VMI). The United States maintains that the Constitution's equal protection guarantee precludes Virginia from reserving exclusively to men the unique educational opportunities VMI affords. We agree.

I

Founded in 1839, VMI is today the sole single-sex school among Virginia's 15 public institutions of higher learning. VMI's distinctive mission is to produce "citizen-soldiers," men prepared for leadership in civilian life and in military service. VMI pursues this mission through pervasive training of a kind not available anywhere else in Virginia. Assigning prime place to character development, VMI uses an "adversative method" modeled on English public schools and once characteristic of military instruction. VMI constantly endeavors to instill physical and mental discipline in its cadets and impart to them a strong moral code. The school's graduates leave VMI with heightened comprehension of their capacity to deal with duress and stress, and a large sense of accomplishment for completing the hazardous course. . . .

Neither the goal of producing citizen-soldiers nor VMI's implementing methodology is inherently unsuitable to women. And the school's impressive record in producing leaders has made admission desirable to some women. Nevertheless, Virginia has elected to preserve exclusively for men the advantages and opportunities a VMI education affords.

II

. . . VMI today enrolls about 1,300 men as cadets. Its academic offerings in the liberal arts, sciences, and engineering are also available at other public colleges and universities in Virginia. But VMI's mission is special. It is the mission of the school:

> to produce educated and honorable men, prepared for the varied work of civil life, imbued with love of learning, confident in the functions and attitudes of leadership, possessing a high sense of public service, advocates of the American democracy and free enterprise system, and ready as citizen-soldiers to defend their country in time of national peril.

. . . VMI produces its "citizen-soldiers" through "an adversative, or doubting, model of education" which features "[p]hysical rigor, mental stress, absolute equality of treatment, absence of privacy, minute regulation of behavior, and indoctrination in desirable values." As one Commandant of Cadets described it, the adversative method "dissects the young student," and makes him aware of his "limits and capabilities," so that he knows "how far he can go with his anger, . . . how much he can take under stress, . . . exactly what he can do when he is physically exhausted."

VMI cadets live in spartan barracks where surveillance is constant and privacy nonexistent; they wear uniforms, eat together in the mess hall, and regularly participate in drills. Entering students are incessantly exposed to the rat line, "an extreme form of the adversative model," comparable in intensity to Marine Corps boot camp. Tormenting and punishing, the rat line bonds new cadets to their fellow sufferers and, when they have completed the seven-month experience, to their former tormentors. . . .

[Responding to a complaint by a female high-school student seeking admission to VMI, the United States sued Virginia and VMI, alleging that the all-male admission policy violated the Equal Protection Clause. The district court ruled for VMI. The Fourth Circuit reversed and suggested several remedies: admit women to VMI, establish parallel institutions or programs, or abandon state support and privatize the school.—Editors]

In response to the Fourth Circuit's ruling, Virginia proposed a parallel program for women: Virginia Women's Institute for Leadership (VWIL). The four-year, state-sponsored undergraduate program would be located at Mary Baldwin College, a private liberal arts school for women . . .

Although VWIL would share VMI's mission—to produce "citizen-soldiers"—the VWIL program would differ . . . from VMI in academic offerings, methods of education, and financial resources. . . .

III

The cross-petitions in this suit present two ultimate issues. First, does Virginia's exclusion of women from the educational opportunities provided by VMI—extraordinary opportunities for military training and civilian leadership development—deny to women "capable of all of the individual activities required of VMI cadets" the equal protection of the laws guaranteed by the Fourteenth Amendment? Second, if VMI's "unique" situation—as Virginia's sole single-sex public institution of higher education—offends the Constitution's equal protection principle, what is the remedial requirement?

IV

We note, once again, the core instruction of this Court's pathmarking decisions in *J.E.B. v. Alabama*, 511 U.S. 127 (1994) and *Mississippi University for Women v. Hogan*, 458 U.S. 718 (1982): Parties who seek to defend gender-based government action must demonstrate an "exceedingly persuasive justification" for that action.

Today's skeptical scrutiny of official action denying rights or opportunities based on sex responds to volumes of history. As a plurality of this Court acknowledged a generation ago, "our Nation has had a long and unfortunate history of sex discrimination." *Frontiero v. Richardson*, 411 U.S. 677, 684 (1973). . . .

In 1971, for the first time in our Nation's history, this Court ruled in favor of a woman who complained that her State had denied her the equal protection of its laws. *Reed v. Reed*, 404 U.S. 71 (1971) (holding unconstitutional Idaho Code prescription that, among "several persons claiming and equally entitled to administer [a decedent's estate], males must be preferred to females"). Since *Reed*, the Court has repeatedly recognized that neither federal nor state government acts compatibly with the equal protection principle when a law or official policy denies to women, simply because they are women, full citizenship stature—equal opportunity to aspire, achieve, participate in and contribute to society based on their individual talents and capacities.

Without equating gender classifications, for all purposes, to classifications based on race or national origin, the Court, in post-*Reed* decisions, has carefully inspected official action that closes a door or denies opportunity to women (or to men). To summarize the Court's current directions for cases of official classification based on gender: Focusing on the differential treatment or denial of opportunity for which relief is sought, the reviewing court must determine whether the proffered justification is "exceedingly persuasive." The burden of justification is demanding and it rests entirely on the State. The State must show "at least that the [challenged] classification serves 'important governmental objectives and that the discriminatory means employed' are 'substantially related to the achievement of those objectives." *Mississippi Univ. for Women*, at 724. The justification must be genuine, not hypothesized or invented *post hoc* in response to litigation. And it must not rely on overbroad generalizations about the different talents, capacities, or preferences of males and females.

The heightened review standard our precedent establishes does not make sex a proscribed classification. Supposed "inherent differences" are no longer accepted as a ground for race or national origin classifications. Physical differences between men and women, however, are enduring: "[T]he two sexes are not fungible; a community made up exclusively of one [sex] is different from a community composed of both." *Ballard v. United States*, 329 U.S. 187, 193 (1946).

"Inherent differences" between men and women, we have come to appreciate, remain cause for celebration, but not for denigration of the members of either sex or for artificial constraints on an individual's opportunity. Sex classifications may be used to compensate women "for particular economic disabilities [they have] suffered," *Califano v. Webster*, 430 U.S. 313, 320 (1977) (*per curiam*), to advance full development of the talent and capacities of our Nation's people.[7] But such classifications may not be used, as they once were, to create or perpetuate the legal, social, and economic inferiority of women.

Measuring the record in this case against the review standard just described, we conclude that Virginia has shown no "exceedingly persuasive justification" for excluding all women from the citizen-soldier training afforded by VMI. We therefore affirm the Fourth Circuit's initial judgment, which held that Virginia had violated the Fourteenth Amendment's Equal Protection Clause. Because the remedy proffered by Virginia—the Mary Baldwin VWIL program—does not cure the constitutional violation, *i.e.,* it does not provide equal opportunity, we reverse the Fourth Circuit's final judgment in this case.

V

[Virginia advanced two justifications for VMI's exclusion of women. First, "single-sex education provides important educational benefits" and contributes to "diversity in educational approaches." Second, "the unique VMI method of character development and leadership training, the school's adversative approach, would have to be modified were VMI to admit women."—Editors]

A

Single-sex education affords pedagogical benefits to at least some students, Virginia emphasizes, and that reality is uncontested in this litigation. Similarly, it is not disputed that diversity among public educational institutions can serve the public good. But Virginia has not shown that VMI was established, or has been maintained, with a view to diversifying, by its categorical exclusion of women, educational opportunities within the Commonwealth. In cases of this genre, our precedent instructs that "benign" justifications proffered in defense of categorical exclusions will not be accepted automatically; a tenable justification must describe actual state purposes, not rationalizations for actions in fact differently grounded. . . .

Neither recent nor distant history bears out Virginia's alleged pursuit of diversity through single-sex educational options. In 1839, when the Commonwealth established VMI, a range of educational opportunities for men and women was scarcely contemplated. Higher education at the time was considered dangerous for women; reflecting widely held views about women's proper place, the Nation's first

---

[7]   Several *amici* have urged that diversity in educational opportunities is an altogether appropriate governmental pursuit and that single-sex schools can contribute importantly to such diversity. Indeed, it is the mission of some single-sex schools "to dissipate, rather than perpetuate, traditional gender classifications." See Brief for Twenty-six Private Women's Colleges as *Amici Curiae* 5. We do not question the Commonwealth's prerogative evenhandedly to support diverse educational opportunities. We address specifically and only an educational opportunity recognized by the District Court and the Court of Appeals as "unique," an opportunity available only at Virginia's premier military institute, the Commonwealth's sole single-sex public university or college.

universities and colleges—for example, Harvard in Massachusetts, William and Mary in Virginia—admitted only men. VMI was not at all novel in this respect: In admitting no women, VMI followed the lead of the Commonwealth's flagship school, the University of Virginia, founded in 1819. . . .

Ultimately, in 1970, "the most prestigious institution of higher education in Virginia," the University of Virginia, introduced coeducation and, in 1972, began to admit women on an equal basis with men. . . .

Our 1982 decision in *Mississippi Univ. for Women* prompted VMI to reexamine its male-only admission policy. A Mission Study Committee, appointed by the VMI Board of Visitors, studied the problem from October 1983 until May 1986, and in that month counseled against "change of VMI status as a single-sex college." Whatever internal purpose the Mission Study Committee served—and however well meaning the framers of the report—we can hardly extract from that effort any Commonwealth policy evenhandedly to advance diverse educational options. . . .

In sum, we find no persuasive evidence in this record that VMI's male-only admission policy "is in furtherance of a state policy of 'diversity.' " . . . However "liberally" this plan serves the Commonwealth's sons, it makes no provision whatever for her daughters. That is not *equal* protection.

B

Virginia next argues that VMI's adversative method of training provides educational benefits that cannot be made available, unmodified, to women. Alterations to accommodate women would necessarily be "radical," so "drastic," Virginia asserts, as to transform, indeed "destroy," VMI's program. Neither sex would be favored by the transformation, Virginia maintains. . . .

The District Court forecast from expert witness testimony, and the Court of Appeals accepted, that coeducation would materially affect "at least these three aspects of VMI's program—physical training, the absence of privacy, and the adversative approach." And it is uncontested that women's admission would require accommodations, primarily in arranging housing assignments and physical training programs for female cadets. It is also undisputed, however, that "the VMI methodology could be used to educate women." . . .

It may be assumed, for purposes of this decision, that most women would not choose VMI's adversative method. As Fourth Circuit Judge Motz observed, however, in her dissent from the Court of Appeals' denial of rehearing en banc, it is also probable that "many men would not want to be educated in such an environment." . . . The issue, however, is not whether "women—or men—should be forced to attend VMI"; rather, the question is whether the Commonwealth can constitutionally deny to women who have the will and capacity, the training and attendant opportunities that VMI uniquely affords.

The notion that admission of women would downgrade VMI's stature, destroy the adversative system and, with it, even the school, is a judgment hardly proved, a prediction hardly different from other "self-fulfilling prophec[ies]," see *Mississippi Univ. for Women*, at 730, once routinely used to deny rights or opportunities. When women first sought admission to the bar and access to legal education, concerns of the same order were expressed. . . .

Women's successful entry into the federal military academies, and their participation in the Nation's military forces, indicate that Virginia's fears for the future of VMI may not be solidly grounded. The Commonwealth's justification for excluding all women from "citizen-soldier" training for which some are qualified, in any event, cannot rank as "exceedingly persuasive," as we have explained and applied that standard. . . .

Virginia, in sum, "has fallen far short of establishing the 'exceedingly persuasive justification,' " Mississippi Univ. for Women, at 731, that must be the solid base for any gender-defined classification.

VI

In the second phase of the litigation, Virginia presented its remedial plan— maintain VMI as a male-only college and create VWIL as a separate program for women. . . .

Virginia chose not to eliminate, but to leave untouched, VMI's exclusionary policy. . . . VWIL affords women no opportunity to experience the rigorous military training for which VMI is famed. Instead, the VWIL program "deemphasize[s]" military education and uses a "cooperative method" of education "which reinforces self-esteem." . . .

[The Court described at length the differences between the programs. VWIL was not a "military institute," did not have the same faculty or course offerings, and did not enjoy the same long and prestigious tradition. Nor did students live together in a "military-style residence," suffer the same physical rigor and mental stress, and receive the same "adversative training."—Editors]

As earlier stated, generalizations about "the way women are," estimates of what is appropriate for *most women,* no longer justify denying opportunity to women whose talent and capacity place them outside the average description. In contrast to the generalizations about women on which Virginia rests, we note again these dispositive realities: VMI's "implementing methodology" is not "inherently unsuitable to women;" "some women . . . do well under [the] adversative model;" "some women, at least, would want to attend [VMI] if they had the opportunity;" "some women are capable of all of the individual activities required of VMI cadets," and "can meet the physical standards [VMI] now impose[s] on men." It is on behalf of these women that the United States has instituted this suit, and it is for them that a remedy must be crafted, a remedy that will end their exclusion from a state-supplied educational opportunity for which they are fit, a decree that will "bar like discrimination in the future." . . .

For the reasons stated, the initial judgment of the Court of Appeals is affirmed, the final judgment of the Court of Appeals is reversed, and the case is remanded for further proceedings consistent with this opinion.

■ CHIEF JUSTICE REHNQUIST, concurring in the judgment.

. . . Two decades ago in *Craig v. Boren*, 429 U.S. 190, 197 (1976), we announced that "[t]o withstand constitutional challenge, . . . classifications by gender must serve important governmental objectives and must be substantially related to achievement of those objectives." We have adhered to that standard of scrutiny ever since. While the majority adheres to this test today, it also says that the Commonwealth must demonstrate an "exceedingly persuasive justification" to support a gender-based classification. It is unfortunate that the Court thereby introduces an element of uncertainty respecting the appropriate test.

While terms like "important governmental objective" and "substantially related" are hardly models of precision, they have more content and specificity than does the phrase "exceedingly persuasive justification." That phrase is best confined, as it was first used, as an observation on the difficulty of meeting the applicable test, not as a formulation of the test itself. See, e.g., *Personnel Administrator of Mass. v. Feeney*, 442 U.S. 256, 273 (1979). ("[T]hese precedents dictate that any state law overtly or covertly designed to prefer males over females in public employment require an exceedingly persuasive justification"). To avoid introducing potential confusion, I would have adhered more closely to our traditional, "firmly established," *Hogan*, at 723, standard that a gender-based classification "must bear a close and substantial relationship to important governmental objectives." *Feeney*, at 273.

Our cases dealing with gender discrimination also require that the proffered purpose for the challenged law be the actual purpose. It is on this ground that the Court rejects the first of two justifications Virginia offers for VMI's single-sex admissions policy, namely, the goal of diversity among its public educational institutions. While I ultimately agree that the Commonwealth has not carried the day with this justification, I disagree with the Court's method of analyzing the issue.

VMI was founded in 1839, and, as the Court notes, admission was limited to men because under the then-prevailing view men, not women, were destined for higher education. However misguided this point of view may be by present-day standards, it surely was not unconstitutional in 1839. The adoption of the Fourteenth Amendment, with its Equal Protection Clause, was nearly 30 years in the future. The interpretation of the Equal Protection Clause to require heightened scrutiny for gender discrimination was yet another century away.

Long after the adoption of the Fourteenth Amendment, and well into this century, legal distinctions between men and women were thought to raise no question under the Equal Protection Clause. . . .

Then, in 1971, we decided *Reed v. Reed*, which the Court correctly refers to as a seminal case. But its facts have nothing to do with admissions to any sort of educational institution. . . .

Even at the time of our decision in *Reed v. Reed*, therefore, Virginia and VMI were scarcely on notice that its holding would be extended across the constitutional board. They were entitled to believe that "one swallow doesn't make a summer" and await further developments. Those developments were 11 years in coming. In *Mississippi Univ. for Women v. Hogan*, a case actually involving a single-sex admissions policy in higher education, the Court held that the exclusion of men from a nursing program violated the Equal Protection Clause. This holding did place Virginia on notice that VMI's men-only admissions policy was open to serious question. . . .

Before this Court, Virginia has sought to justify VMI's single-sex admissions policy primarily on the basis that diversity in education is desirable, and that while most of the public institutions of higher learning in the Commonwealth are coeducational, there should also be room for single-sex institutions. I agree with the Court that there is scant evidence in the record that this was the real reason that Virginia decided to maintain VMI as men only. But, unlike the majority, I would consider only evidence that postdates our decision in *Hogan*, and would draw no negative inferences from the Commonwealth's actions before that time. I think that after *Hogan*, the Commonwealth was entitled to reconsider its policy with respect to VMI, and not to have earlier justifications, or lack thereof, held against it.

Even if diversity in educational opportunity were the Commonwealth's actual objective, the Commonwealth's position would still be problematic. The difficulty with its position is that the diversity benefited only one sex; there was single-sex public education available for men at VMI, but no corresponding single-sex public education available for women. When *Hogan* placed Virginia on notice that VMI's admissions policy possibly was unconstitutional, VMI could have dealt with the problem by admitting women; but its governing body felt strongly that the admission of women would have seriously harmed the institution's educational approach. Was there something else the Commonwealth could have done to avoid an equal protection violation? Since the Commonwealth did nothing, we do not have to definitively answer that question.

I do not think, however, that the Commonwealth's options were as limited as the majority may imply. . . . [T]he Commonwealth faced a condition . . . that had been brought about, not through defiance of decisions construing gender bias under the Equal Protection Clause, but, until the decision in *Hogan*, a condition that had not appeared to offend the Constitution. Had Virginia made a genuine effort to devote comparable public resources to a facility for women, and followed through on such a plan, it might well have avoided an equal protection violation. I do not believe the Commonwealth was faced with the stark choice of either admitting women to VMI, on the one hand, or abandoning VMI and starting from scratch for both men and women, on the other.

But, as I have noted, neither the governing board of VMI nor the Commonwealth took any action after 1982. If diversity in the form of single-sex, as well as coeducational, institutions of higher learning were to be available to Virginians, that diversity had to be available to women as well as to men. . . .

Virginia offers a second justification for the single-sex admissions policy: maintenance of the adversative method. I agree with the Court that this justification does not serve an important governmental objective. A State does not have substantial interest in the adversative methodology unless it is pedagogically beneficial. While considerable evidence shows that a single-sex education is pedagogically beneficial for some students, see 766 F.Supp., at 1414, and hence a State may have a valid interest in promoting that methodology, there is no similar evidence in the record that an adversative method is pedagogically beneficial or is any more likely to produce character traits than other methodologies. . . .

In the end, the women's institution Virginia proposes, VWIL, fails as a remedy, because it is distinctly inferior to the existing men's institution and will continue to be for the foreseeable future. VWIL simply is not, in any sense, the institution that VMI is. In particular, VWIL is a program appended to a private college, not a self-standing institution; and VWIL is substantially underfunded as compared to VMI. I therefore ultimately agree with the Court that Virginia has not provided an adequate remedy.

■ JUSTICE SCALIA, dissenting.

Today the Court shuts down an institution that has served the people of the Commonwealth of Virginia with pride and distinction for over a century and a half. To achieve that desired result, it rejects (contrary to our established practice) the factual findings of two courts below, sweeps aside the precedents of this Court, and ignores the history of our people. As to facts: it explicitly rejects the finding that there exist "gender-based developmental differences" supporting Virginia's restriction of the "adversative" method to only a men's institution, and the finding that the all-male composition of the Virginia Military Institute (VMI) is essential to that institution's character. As to precedent: it drastically revises our established standards for reviewing sex-based classifications. And as to history: it counts for nothing the long tradition, enduring down to the present, of men's military colleges supported by both States and the Federal Government.

I

. . . I shall devote most of my analysis to evaluating the Court's opinion on the basis of our current equal protection jurisprudence, which regards this Court as free to evaluate everything under the sun by applying one of three tests: "rational basis" scrutiny, intermediate scrutiny, or strict scrutiny. . . .

I have no problem with a system of abstract tests such as rational basis, intermediate, and strict scrutiny (though I think we can do better than applying strict scrutiny and intermediate scrutiny whenever we feel like it). Such formulas are essential to evaluating whether the new restrictions that a changing society constantly imposes upon private conduct comport with that "equal protection" our society has always accorded in the past. But in my view the function of this Court is to *preserve* our society's values regarding (among other things) equal protection, not to *revise* them; to prevent backsliding from the degree of restriction the Constitution imposed upon democratic government, not to prescribe, on our own authority, progressively higher degrees. For that reason it is my view that, whatever abstract tests we may choose to devise, they cannot supersede—and indeed ought to be crafted *so as to reflect*—those constant and unbroken national traditions that embody the people's understanding of ambiguous constitutional texts. . . .

II

To reject the Court's disposition today, however, it is not necessary to accept my view that the Court's made-up tests cannot displace longstanding national traditions as the primary determinant of what the Constitution means. It is only necessary to apply honestly the test the Court has been applying to sex-based classifications for the past two decades. . . .

Only the amorphous "exceedingly persuasive justification" phrase, and not the standard elaboration of intermediate scrutiny, can be made to yield this conclusion that VMI's single-sex composition is unconstitutional because there exist several women (or, one would have to conclude under the Court's reasoning, a single woman) willing and able to undertake VMI's program. Intermediate scrutiny has never required a least-restrictive-means analysis, but only a "substantial relation" between the classification and the state interests that it serves. . . .

III

... It is beyond question that Virginia has an important state interest in providing effective college education for its citizens. That single-sex instruction is an approach substantially related to that interest should be evident enough from the long and continuing history in this country of men's and women's colleges. But beyond that, as the Court of Appeals here stated: "That single-gender education at the college level is beneficial to both sexes is a *fact established in this case.*" (Emphasis added.)

... But besides its single-sex constitution, VMI is different from other colleges in another way. It employs a "distinctive educational method," sometimes referred to as the "adversative, or doubting, model of education." ... A State's decision to maintain within its system one school that provides the adversative method is "substantially related" to its goal of good education. Moreover, it was uncontested that "if the state were to establish a women's VMI-type [*i.e.,* adversative] program, the program would attract an insufficient number of participants to make the program work"; and it was found by the District Court that if Virginia were to include women in VMI, the school "would eventually find it necessary to drop the adversative system altogether." Thus, Virginia's options were an adversative method that excludes women or no adversative method at all. Virginia's election to fund one public all-male institution and one on the adversative model—and to concentrate its resources in a single entity that serves both these interests in diversity—is substantially related to the Commonwealth's important educational interests....

[T]he rationale of today's decision is sweeping: for sex-based classifications, a redefinition of intermediate scrutiny that makes it indistinguishable from strict scrutiny. Indeed, the Court indicates that if any program restricted to one sex is "uniqu[e]," it must be opened to members of the opposite sex "who have the will and capacity" to participate in it. I suggest that the single-sex program that will not be capable of being characterized as "unique" is not only unique but nonexistent.[8]

In any event, regardless of whether the Court's rationale leaves some small amount of room for lawyers to argue, it ensures that single-sex public education is functionally dead. The costs of litigating the constitutionality of a single-sex education program, and the risks of ultimately losing that litigation, are simply too high to be embraced by public officials. Any person with standing to challenge any sex-based classification can haul the State into federal court and compel it to establish by evidence (presumably in the form of expert testimony) that there is an "exceedingly persuasive justification" for the classification.... No state official in his right mind will buy such a high-cost, high-risk lawsuit by commencing a single-sex program. The enemies of single-sex education have won; by persuading only seven Justices (five would have been enough) that their view of the world is enshrined in the Constitution, they have effectively imposed that view on all 50 States.

This is especially regrettable because, as the District Court here determined, educational experts in recent years have increasingly come to "suppor[t] [the] view that substantial educational benefits flow from a single-gender environment, be it

---

[8] In this regard, I note that the Court—which I concede is under no obligation to do so—provides no example of a program that *would* pass muster under its reasoning today: not even, for example, a football or wrestling program. On the Court's theory, any woman ready, willing, and physically able to participate in such a program would, *as a constitutional matter,* be entitled to do so.

male or female, that cannot be replicated in a coeducational setting." 766 F.Supp., at 1415. "The evidence in th[is] case," for example, "is virtually uncontradicted" to that effect. *Ibid.* Until quite recently, some public officials have attempted to institute new single-sex programs, at least as experiments. In 1991, for example, the Detroit Board of Education announced a program to establish three boys-only schools for inner-city youth; it was met with a lawsuit, a preliminary injunction was swiftly entered by a District Court, and the Detroit Board of Education voted to abandon the litigation and thus abandon the plan. Today's opinion assures that no such experiment will be tried again. . . .

■ JUSTICE THOMAS took no part in the consideration or decision of these cases.

NOTES

1.   What is the standard employed in *United States v. Virginia*, and is it the same as the one in *Craig v. Boren*? How is it distinguishable from "strict scrutiny"? Under the standard in *United States v. Virginia*, may a state ever have a sufficient justification for single-sex higher education? Assume that a state (or a local school district) set up a diverse public school-choice program that included single-sex education options—a history distinguishable from VMI's. Would it necessarily be unconstitutional? Would the state's interest in diversity be sufficient to justify sex-segregated public education? In answering these questions, should the courts defer to the judgment of school officials?

2.   By the time *United States v. Virginia* reached the Supreme Court, a generation of women had graduated from the federal military academies. Only two institutions, VMI and the Citadel, continued to offer single-sex collegiate military training. Thus those institutions had become outliers from a national pattern of co-educational military training. Should this have had any effect on the justices? On the one hand, the federal precedent showed that gender stereotypes about women and the military had been in fact discriminatory and misguided. On the other hand, with West Point and Annapolis now co-ed, was there less harm in letting VMI and the Citadel stay the way they were? Is there a principled way to decide when national uniformity is desirable and when it is better to have diversity?

3.   The district court found that if VMI admitted female cadets, it would inevitably drop its adversative method of education. The majority opinion rejects that finding (which is rather unusual, given that a trial court's factual findings are reversed only for clear error). Who turned out to be right?

Before *United States v. Virginia*, "Life in the barracks . . . was centered on the concept of zero privacy. Cadets showered in open bays. They used toilets without stall doors. They lived in four-man rooms . . . [and] windows spanned the upper half of the doors to these rooms, so that anyone could look inside at any time." Laura Fairchild Brodie, BREAKING OUT: VMI AND THE COMING OF WOMEN 106 (2001). After the decision, there were some architectural changes. VMI housed the female cadets in the same barracks as the male cadets, but designated a block of rooms for them, installed individual showers for them, put doors on the toilet stalls in their restrooms, and added emergency call boxes to the campus.

The training, however, was largely unchanged. VMI did not change its physical fitness tests, which counted for a substantial part of the cadets' grades. Nor did VMI change the requirement that all cadets take courses in boxing and wrestling. Nor did VMI change the initiation procedures for "rats," including Hell Week. In subsequent years there were changes. By 2002, VMI decided that the "Ratline" needed reform, and it ended the "sweat parties"—intense night-time workouts with corporals yelling at new cadets—and replaced them with positive conditioning and team competitions in soccer, flag football, ultimate Frisbee, and other sports. In 2009, VMI made the required number of pullups and the times for a 2400-meter run different for men and women. In 2011, boxing and wrestling became optional courses. But it generally remains the case that cadets today receive an adversative experience in line with VMI's traditions.

4.   Was the admission of women to an adversative program the only option? One scholar has written:

> In the specific context of VMI and VWIL, it would be both narrow-minded and short-sighted to see only two alternatives—one a traditional sameness solution of admitting women to the established masculine school and rejecting the feminine one entirely, as the United States successfully proposed in the VMI case; the other a traditional difference solution of approving the two programs in single-sex and gender configurations, as Virginia unsuccessfully proposed in opposition. Disaggregating sex and gender may help us to see that there may indeed be, as the Fourth Circuit suggested, "other more creative options or combinations." Virginia might, as at least one commentator proposed, "pull every state tax dollar out of VMI and give it to VWIL" . . . This option, sounding in sameness but built on a feminine model, calls into question the value placed on the traditionally masculine and elevates the traditionally feminine into something valuable to both sexes.

> Another option, which one might call androgynous, would open up VMI and The Citadel not only to women, but to a methodology that is less obsessively masculine and explicitly incorporates positive feminine elements. This appears to be what VMI feared would in fact happen if women were admitted, what some feminists may have hoped for from the integration of women, and what is reported to have happened at the service academies following women's admission to them. . . .

> As a final creative alternative, one might retain both sets of programs as embodiments of the opposite poles of masculine and feminine, but open each up to members of either sex who are appropriately gendered; thus both masculine men and masculine women could attend VMI or The Citadel, while VWIL and SCIL would admit those of both sexes more suited to or attracted by a more feminine approach. This proposal has the advantage of accommodating, not only a broader spectrum of women, but also the sort of men not accommodated at all by VMI and The Citadel.

> Throughout the VMI litigation, Virginia and trial judge Jackson Kiser did what feminist theorists have long criticized in both the legal system and employer hiring practices—they assumed the correctness of a masculine male standard and asked only whether women could fit it, not whether it was an appropriate standard for persons of either sex. . . . This unquestioning acceptance of a masculine standard, at least for men if not also for women, and the failure even to consider the possibility of a feminine standard applied sex-neutrally is one of the central problems of gender discrimination.

Mary Anne Case, *Two Cheers for Cheerleading: The Noisy Integration of VMI and the Quiet Success of Virginia Women in Leadership*, 1999 U. Chi. Legal F. 347, 361–364 (1999). Do you agree? Why or why not?

5.   Ohio State University has a renowned football team. Is the school obligated by *United States v. Virginia* to allow women to join the team?

6.   In her opinion for the Court, Justice Ginsburg says, " 'Inherent differences' between men and women, we have come to appreciate, remain cause for celebration." What are those differences? And why cause for celebration? One question raised by this line of the opinion, and more generally by cultural changes since *United States v. Virginia*, is how to think about gender—is it given, binary, and rooted in biological differences, or plastic, individual, and entirely a matter of social construction? What does Justice Ginsburg presuppose on this question? Since the *VMI* decision, there has been increasing acceptance in American society of the view that gender is more malleable and chosen than fixed and given. Do the implications go beyond gender? Can this view—that an aspect of human identity once thought to be fixed is instead socially constructed and a matter of individual choice—be extended to race and every other aspect of identity that might lead to heightened scrutiny under the Equal Protection Clause? Consider the following perspective from 1950:

> If this new, modern anonymity, and the freedom that accompanies it, were actually brought to fulfillment, all fixed differences in people would be dissolved. There would be no Jews, no Frenchmen, no Catholics, except insofar as individuals elected to make themselves Jews, Frenchmen, or Catholics. Even racial identifications, such as kinky hair or a long nose, would be eliminated as an insufferable obstacle to free decision. Humanity would appear as a raw material, physical and mental—from which individuals would be constantly fabricating selves according to their tastes. A fantasy? Perhaps. . . . But even those who do want a clean slate usually find that some particular form has been rather heavily, if not ineradicably, engraved upon them. . . . The new anonymity of the human being, whether as a fact or as a possibility, puts an enormous emphasis on the act of defining oneself.

Harold Rosenberg, "Jewish Identity in a Free Society," reprinted in DISCOVERING THE PRESENT: THREE DECADES IN ART, CULTURE, AND POLITICS 259, 260–261 (1973). What do you think of Rosenberg's prediction? Science fiction or ahead of its time? Utopia or dystopia? And, most importantly for our subject, what are the implications for suspect classifications, standards of scrutiny, disparate impact, and affirmative action?

[Assignment 74]

F.   RACE, SEX, AND . . . WHAT ELSE? OTHER CLASSIFICATIONS UNDER THE EQUAL PROTECTION CLAUSE

The Equal Protection Clause cases we have read so far have focused on laws that classify on the basis of race or sex. As we have seen, discrimination by state governments against black citizens was the evil against which the Fourteenth Amendment was directed. Under modern precedent, racial classifications are subject to "strict scrutiny" and treated as presumptively violating the Equal Protection Clause. Sex-based classifications were not central to the Fourteenth Amendment's historical context, but they are nonetheless sufficiently analogous that over time they have come to be treated as quasi-suspect and subject to "intermediate scrutiny." (Some find additional support for heightened scrutiny of sex-based classifications in the Nineteenth Amendment, which prohibits government discrimination in voting "on account of sex.") But not every classification receives heightened scrutiny under the Equal Protection Clause. Are there any others that should be "suspect" like race or "quasi-suspect" like sex?

Some categories that have been the subject of litigation are age, alienage, disability, illegitimacy, national origin, religion, sexual orientation, and wealth. (As you will see, some of these classifications do receive heightened scrutiny, some do not, and for some the answer is unclear.) Which would be on your list of suspect or quasi-suspect classifications? What is the principled basis for your list? And how do you get to that list from the spare words of the Equal Protection Clause? Do other constitutional provisions inform your list?

Once one has figured out what types of classifications are subject to the Equal Protection Clause, there remains the problem of how to decide when classifications actually deny persons "the equal protection of the laws." In doctrinal jargon: What should the level of judicial "scrutiny" be? Should it differ from category to category? Is there any principled standard for making judgments about levels of scrutiny?

These materials begin with a quick survey of the Court's doctrine outside the areas of race and sex, and then offer two cases for thinking about the outer bounds of the Equal Protection Clause: *Buck v. Bell*, 274 U.S. 200 (1927), on physical and mental disabilities; and *Kotch v. Board of River Port Pilot Commissioners*, 330 U.S. 552 (1947), on exclusionary nepotism.

The General Rule of "Rational Basis"

The government makes classifications all the time. It is often perfectly sensible to distinguish certain actions, persons, or situations from others. As early as *Slaughter-House*, the Court adopted the view that the Equal Protection Clause is not a roving commission for judges to scrutinize and supervise every debatable policy choice made by a state legislature. The Supreme Court has adopted the term "rational basis" to describe the minimal level of scrutiny it gives to most government classifications. (Why even require a "rational basis"? Does that invite judicial-policymaking, too?)

A classic case involving minimal scrutiny is *Railway Express Agency v. New York*, 336 U.S. 106 (1949), in which the Court upheld a New York City traffic regulation permitting delivery vehicles to display advertising so long as they were "engaged in the usual business or regular work of the owner," but prohibiting all vehicles "used merely or mainly for advertising." Plaintiffs challenged the regulation as a violation of the Equal Protection Clause. In the Court's words, the plaintiffs "point out that the regulation draws the line between advertisements of products sold by the owner of the truck and general advertisements. It is argued that unequal treatment on the basis of such a distinction is not justified by the aim and purpose of the regulation." The Court, however, rejected the argument: "We cannot say that the judgment is not an allowable one. . . . [T]he classification has relation to the purpose for which it is made and does not contain the kind of discrimination against which the Equal Protection Clause affords protection. . . . [T]he fact that New York City sees fit to eliminate from traffic this kind of distraction but does not touch what may be even greater ones in a different category, such as the vivid displays on Times Square, is immaterial. It is no requirement of equal protection that all evils of the same genus be eradicated or none at all."

Another classic case is *Williamson v. Lee Optical*, 348 U.S. 483 (1955). A group of Oklahoma opticians challenged a state law permitting only licensed optometrists and ophthalmologists to "fit lenses to a face." The Court held that treating opticians differently was permitted by the Equal Protection Clause because there was a rational basis for doing so: "The District Court held that it violated the Equal Protection Clause of the Fourteenth Amendment to subject opticians to this regulatory system and to exempt . . . all sellers of ready-to-wear glasses. The problem of legislative classification is a perennial one, admitting of no doctrinaire definition. Evils in the same field may be of different dimensions and proportions, requiring different remedies. Or so the legislature may think. . . . Or the reform may take one step at a time, addressing itself to the phase of the problem which seems most acute to the legislative mind. . . . The legislature may select one phase of one field and apply a remedy there, neglecting the others. The prohibition of the Equal Protection Clause goes no further than the invidious discrimination." (In both cases the Court also rejected challenges under the Due Process Clause. See p. 1543.)

In *Railway Express* and *Lee Optical* the plaintiffs made strong objections to the laws they challenged. Both laws were riddled with inconsistencies and protected special interests against competition in the marketplace. For example, the law in *Lee Optical* has been aptly described as a "classic rent seeking statute," because "[e]ssentially all that this statute did was to generate business for eye doctors, thereby raising the price of duplicate lenses." Mark Tushnet, *Public Choice Constitutionalism and Economic Rights*, in LIBERTY, PROPERTY, AND THE FUTURE OF CONSTITUTIONAL DEVELOPMENT 23, 37 (Ellen Frankel Paul & Howard Dickman eds., 1990). Nevertheless, the Court made clear that it was unwilling to strike down the laws under the Equal Protection Clause on these grounds. Policy was for the legislatures.

The "Heightened Scrutiny" Exceptions

As you have seen, the Court's general deference to classifications made by legislatures stops when it comes to race and sex. Racial classifications are deemed "suspect" and are presumptively unconstitutional; sex-based classifications are deemed "quasi-suspect" (with all the imprecision that term entails) and are subject to intermediate scrutiny. Each level of scrutiny comes with its own test.

Beyond race and sex, the Court has had more difficulty in identifying what types of classifications should be treated as suspect or quasi-suspect. One way courts have proceeded is by analogy—is the classification like race or sex? Think of this problem as you read the following two cases.

Buck v. Bell

274 U.S. 200 (1927)

■ MR. JUSTICE HOLMES delivered the opinion of the Court.

This is a writ of error to review a judgment of the Supreme Court of Appeals of the State of Virginia, affirming a judgment of the Circuit Court of Amherst County, by which the defendant in error, the superintendent of the State Colony for Epileptics and Feeble Minded, was ordered to perform the operation of salpingectomy upon Carrie Buck, the plaintiff in error, for the purpose of making her sterile. The case comes here upon the contention that the statute authorizing the judgment is void under the Fourteenth Amendment as denying to the plaintiff in error due process of law and the equal protection of the laws.

Carrie Buck is a feeble-minded white woman who was committed to the State Colony above mentioned in due form. She is the daughter of a feeble-minded mother in the same institution, and the mother of an illegitimate feeble-minded child. She was eighteen years old at the time of the trial of her case in the Circuit Court in the latter part of 1924. An Act of Virginia approved March 20, 1924 recites that the health of the patient and the welfare of society may be promoted in certain cases by the sterilization of mental defectives, under careful safeguard, etc.; that the sterilization may be effected in males by vasectomy and in females by salpingectomy, without serious pain or substantial danger to life; that the Commonwealth is supporting in various institutions many defective persons who if now discharged would become a menace but if incapable of procreating might be discharged with safety and become self-supporting with benefit to themselves and to society; and that experience has shown that heredity plays an important part in the transmission of insanity, imbecility, etc. The statute then enacts that whenever the superintendent of certain institutions including the above named State Colony shall be of opinion that it is for the best interest of the patients and of society that an inmate under his care should be sexually sterilized, he may have the operation performed upon any patient afflicted with hereditary forms of insanity, imbecility, etc., on complying with the very careful provisions by which the act protects the patients from possible abuse.

The superintendent first presents a petition to the special board of directors of his hospital or colony, stating the facts and the grounds for his opinion, verified by affidavit. Notice of the petition and of the time and place of the hearing in the institution is to be served upon the inmate, and also upon his guardian, and if there is no guardian the superintendent is to apply to the Circuit Court of the County to appoint one. If the inmate is a minor notice also is to be given to his parents, if any, with a copy of the petition. The board is to see to it that the inmate may attend the hearings if desired by him or his guardian. The evidence is all to be reduced to writing, and after the board has made its order for or against the operation, the superintendent, or the inmate, or his guardian, may appeal to the Circuit Court of the County. The Circuit Court may consider the record of the board and the evidence before it and such other admissible evidence as may be offered, and may affirm, revise, or reverse the order of the board and enter such order as it deems just. Finally any party may apply to the Supreme Court of Appeals, which, if it grants the appeal, is to hear the case upon the record of the trial in the Circuit Court and may enter such order as it thinks the Circuit Court should have entered. There can be no doubt that so far as procedure is concerned the rights of the patient are most carefully considered, and as every step in this case was taken in scrupulous compliance with the statute and after months of observation, there is no doubt that in that respect the plaintiff in error has had due process at law.

The attack is not upon the procedure but upon the substantive law. It seems to be contended that in no circumstances could such an order be justified. It certainly is contended that the order cannot be justified upon the existing grounds. The judgment finds the facts that have been recited and that Carrie Buck "is the probable potential parent of socially inadequate offspring, likewise afflicted, that she may be sexually sterilized without detriment to her general health and that her welfare and that of society will be promoted by her sterilization," and thereupon makes the order. In view of the general declarations of the Legislature and the specific findings of the Court obviously we cannot say as matter of law that the grounds do not exist, and if they exist they justify the result. We have seen more than once that the public welfare may call upon the best citizens for their lives. It would be strange if it could not call upon those who already sap the strength of the State for these lesser sacrifices, often not felt to be such by those concerned, in order to prevent our being swamped with incompetence. It is better for all the world, if instead of waiting to execute degenerate offspring for crime, or to let them starve for their imbecility, society can prevent those who are manifestly unfit from continuing their kind. The principle that sustains compulsory vaccination is broad enough to cover cutting the Fallopian tubes. *Jacobson v. Massachusetts*, 197 U.S. 11 (1905). Three generations of imbeciles are enough.

But, it is said, however it might be if this reasoning were applied generally, it fails when it is confined to the small number who are in the institutions named and is not applied to the multitudes outside. It is the usual last resort of constitutional arguments to point out shortcomings of this sort. But the answer is that the law does all that is needed when it does all that it can, indicates a policy, applies it to all within the lines, and seeks to bring within the lines all similarly situated so far and so fast as its means allow. Of course so far as the operations enable those who otherwise must be kept confined to be returned to the world, and thus open the asylum to others, the equality aimed at will be more nearly reached.

■ MR. JUSTICE BUTLER dissents.

NOTES

1.   *Buck* is a bracing decision for a reader today. "A mere five paragraphs long," the case has been described by Victoria Nourse as having "the highest ratio of injustice per word ever signed on to by eight Supreme Court Justices, progressive and conservative alike." Victoria Nourse, *Buck v. Bell: A Constitutional Tragedy from a Lost World*, 39 Pepp. L. Rev. 101, 102 (2011). The intellectual history and scientific opinion underlying the decision have been described this way:

> Early in the twentieth century, mainstream scientific opinion was won over by eugenics following the re-discovery of Mendel's genetic laws in 1900. . . . "More children from the fit, less from the unfit," became the motto for early twentieth century eugenicists. . . .
>
> By the 1920s, in an era when genetics was institutionalized at both state land-grant and private research universities, American geneticists enthusiastically embraced eugenics. Leading this scientific chorus, with support from the newly created Carnegie Institute of Washington, [was] the pioneering geneticist Charles Davenport. . . . America's two Nobel Prize winning geneticists of the era . . . added their support to the cause, as did the American Genetics Association and various state and regional medical societies. A larger circle of distinguished professionals, including [the presidents of Harvard University, Stanford University, and the University of Michigan, a number of leading biologists,] . . . American Museum of Natural History President Henry Fairfield Osborn, birth-control advocate Margaret Sanger, inventor Alexander Graham Bell, and the legendary California plant breeder Luther Burbank, also publicly backed eugenics. Even the era's most famous American with disabilities, Helen Keller, who became blind and deaf from a childhood illness, favored eugenic remedies for those born with severe disabilities. A wide range of American political leaders, including Presidents

Theodore Roosevelt, William Howard Taft, Woodrow Wilson, and Calvin Coolidge, endorsed eugenic measures, and it was the Justices nominated by these four presidents who decided *Buck*. Wealthy philanthropists and foundations vied to support eugenics research and lawmaking. Indeed, the Virginia eugenics sterilization law upheld in *Buck* was based on a model statute drafted by the Harriman and Carnegie funded Eugenics Record Office. Advocates supported by the New York-based Rockefeller and Russell Sage Foundations lobbied for enactment of eugenics legislation throughout the South. . . . Ultimately, by 1937, thirty-two states from California to Maine had enacted compulsory eugenic sterilization statutes and five more had sterilized citizens without passing a compulsory law. Many more states enacted measures to compel the sexual segregation of mentally ill or retarded persons.

Edward J. Larson, *Putting Buck v. Bell in Scientific and Historical Context: A Response to Victoria Nourse*, 39 Pepp. L. Rev. 119, 122–124 (2011). By the time of *Buck*, the practice of eugenic sterilization in the United States was waning, though it retained intellectual respectability. Even a decade later, when a report of the American Neurological Association "denounced the sterilization of criminals," it still "endorsed the procedure for certain mental conditions covered by Virginia's sterilization statute, such as schizophrenia, manic-depression, epilepsy, and so-called mental hereditary retardation." *Id.* at 127.

Given this context, even if the Court's decision would be wrong today, was it right in 1927? Should the tide of scientific opinion in favor of eugenics have affected how the Court interpreted the Constitution? More provocatively, is the holding in *Buck v. Bell* (outrageous rhetoric aside) actually correct as a matter of constitutional interpretation? Was the Court admirably exercising judicial restraint in the face of an ugly statute that should never have been passed but which it had no basis for invalidating? Or was the Court failing in its constitutional duty to provide "equal protection of the laws" to a group that desperately needed it?

2.   In considering Carrie Buck's claim under the Equal Protection Clause, today the starting point would be to determine the appropriate level of scrutiny. Is a disability classification like a classification on the basis of race or sex? Is there a history of discrimination against the mentally disabled? Is mental disability of the kind regulated by the statute at issue in *Buck* an immutable characteristic? Are the mentally disabled a "discrete and insular minority," excluded from the political process? Or should the inquiry be whether the state classification treated like persons differently or different persons differently? These questions are taken up in the note on *City of Cleburne v. Cleburne Living Center*, at p. 1472.

3.   Should *Buck v. Bell* be considered under some other clause of the Fourteenth Amendment? Is the problem in Buck not *who* was subjected to compulsory sterilization but that *nobody* can be subjected to compulsory sterilization? Is that principle found in the Constitution? Would that principle imply a right against compulsory vaccination?

Kotch v. Board of River Port Pilot Commissioners for Port of New Orleans

330 U.S. 552 (1947)

■ MR. JUSTICE BLACK delivered the opinion of the Court.

Louisiana statutes provide in general that all seagoing vessels moving between New Orleans and foreign ports must be navigated through the Mississippi River approaches to the port of New Orleans and within it, exclusively by pilots who are State Officers. New State pilots are appointed by the governor only upon certification of a State Board of River Pilot Commissioners, themselves pilots. Only those who have served a six month apprenticeship under incumbent pilots and who possess other specific qualifications may be certified to the governor by the board. Appellants here have had at least fifteen years experience in the river, the port, and elsewhere, as pilots of vessels whose pilotage was not governed by the State law in question. Although they possess all the statutory qualifications except that they have not served the requisite six months apprenticeship under Louisiana officer pilots, they have been denied appointment as State pilots. Seeking relief in a Louisiana state court, they alleged that the incumbent pilots, having unfettered discretion under the law in the selection of apprentices, had selected with occasional exception, only the relatives and friends of incumbents; that the selections were made by electing prosepective apprentices into the pilots' association, which the pilots have formed by authority of State law; that since "membership . . . is closed to all except those having the favor of the pilots" the result is that only their relatives and friends have and can become State pilots. The Supreme Court of Louisiana has held that the pilotage law so administered does not violate the equal protection clause of the Fourteenth Amendment. The case is here on appeal from that decision . . .

The constitutional command for a state to afford "equal protection of the laws" sets a goal not attainable by the invention and application of a precise formula. This Court has never attempted that impossible task. A law which affects the activities of some groups differently from the way in which it affects the activities of other groups is not necessarily banned by the Fourteenth Amendment. Otherwise, effective regulation in the public interest could not be provided, however essential that regulation might be. For it is axiomatic that the consequence of regulating by setting apart a classified group is that those in it will be subject to some restrictions or receive certain advantages that do not apply to other groups or to all the public. This selective application of a regulation is discrimination in the broad sense, but it may or may not deny equal protection of the laws. Clearly, it might offend that constitutional safeguard if it rested on grounds wholly irrelevant to achievement of the regulation's objectives. An example would be a law applied to deny a person a right to earn a living or hold any job because of hostility to his particular race, religion, beliefs, or because of any other reason having no rational relation to the regulated activities. See *American Sugar Refining Co. v. State of Louisiana*, 179 U.S. 89, 92 (1900).

The case of *Yick Wo v. Hopkins*, 118 U.S. 356 (1886), relied on by appellants, is an illustration of a type of discrimination which is incompatible with any fair conception of equal protection of the laws. *Yick Wo* was denied the right to engage in an occupation supposedly open to all who could conduct their business in accordance with the law's requirements. He could meet these requirements, but was denied the right to do so solely because he was Chinese. And it made no difference that under the law as written Yick Wo would have enjoyed the same protection as all others. Its unequal application to Yick Wo was enough to condemn it. But Yick Wo's case, as other cases have demonstrated, was tested by the language of the law there considered and the administration there shown. So here, we must consider the relationship of the method of appointing pilots to the broad objectives of the entire Louisiana pilotage law. In so doing we must view the appointment system in the context of the historical evolution of the laws and institution of pilotage in Louisiana and elsewhere. And an important factor in our consideration is that this case tests the right and power of a state to select its own agents and officers. *Taylor v. Beckham*, 178 U.S. 548 (1900); *Snowden v. Hughes*, 321 U.S. 1, 11–13 (1944).

Studies of the long history of pilotage reveal that it is a unique institution and must be judged as such. In order to avoid invisible hazards, vessels approaching and leaving ports must be conducted from and to open waters by persons intimately familiar with the local waters. The pilot's job generally requires that he go outside the harbor's entrance in a small boat to meet incoming ships, board them and direct their course from open waters to the port. The same service is performed for vessels leaving the port. Pilots are thus indispensable cogs in the transportation system of every maritime economy. Their work prevents traffic congestion and accidents which would impair navigation in and to the ports. It affects the safety of lives and cargo, the cost and time expended in port calls, and in some measure, the competitive attractiveness of particular ports. Thus, for the same reasons that governments of most maritime communities have subsidized, regulated, or have themselves operated docks and other harbor facilities and sought to improve the approaches to their ports, they have closely regulated and often operated their ports' pilotage system.[9]

The history and practice of pilotage demonstrate that, although inextricably geared to a complex commercial economy, it is also a highly personalized calling. A pilot does not require a formalized technical education so much as a detailed and extremely intimate, almost intuitive, knowledge of the weather, waterways and conformation of the harbor or river which he serves. This seems to be particularly true of the approaches to New Orleans through the treacherous and shifting channel of the Mississippi River. Moreover, harbor entrances where pilots can most conveniently make their homes and still be close to places where they board incoming and leave outgoing ships are usually some distance from the port cities they serve. These 'pilot towns' have begun, and generally exist today, as small communities of pilots perhaps near, but usually distinct from the port cities. In these communities young men have an opportunity to acquire special knowledge of the weather and water hazards of the locality and seem to grow up with ambitions to become pilots in the traditions of their fathers, relatives, and neighbors. We are asked, in effect, to say that Louisiana is without constitutional authority to conclude that apprenticeship under persons specially interested in a pilot's future is the best way to fit him for duty as a pilot officer in the service of the State.

The States have had full power to regulate pilotage of certain kinds of vessels since 1789 when the first Congress decided that then existing state pilot laws were satisfactory and made federal regulation unnecessary. Louisiana legislation has controlled the activities and appointment of pilots since 1805—even before the Territory was admitted as a State. The State pilotage system, as it has evolved since 1805, is typical of that which grew up in most seaboard states and in foreign countries. Since 1805 Louisiana pilots have been State officers whose work has been controlled by the State. That Act forbade all but a limited number of pilots appointed by the governor to serve in that capacity. The pilots so appointed were authorized to select their own deputies. But pilots, and through them, their deputies, were literally under the command of the master and the wardens of the port of New Orleans,

---

[9]   See *Cooley v. Board of Wardens*, 53 U.S. (12 How.) 299, 308, 312, 316, 326 (1852).

appointed by the governor. The master and wardens were authorized to make rules governing the practices of pilots, specifically empowered to order pilots to their stations, and to fine them for disobedience to orders or rules. And the pilots were required to make official bond for faithful performance of their duty. Pilots' fees were fixed; ships coming to the Mississippi were required to pay pilotage whether they took on pilots or not. The pilots were authorized to organize an association whose membership they controlled in order "to enforce the legal regulations, and add to the efficiency of the service required thereby." Moreover, efficient and adequate service was sought to be insured by requiring the Board of Pilot Commissioners to report to the governor and authorizing him simmarily to remove any pilot guilty of "neglect of duty, habitual intemperance, carelessness, incompetency, or any act of conduct . . . showing" that he "ought to be removed." La. Act. No. 113, § 20 (1857). These provisions have been carried over with some revision into the present comprehensive Louisiana pilotage law. Thus in Louisiana, as elsewhere, it seems to have been accepted at an early date that in pilotage, unlike other occupations, competition for appointment, for the opportunity to serve particular ships and for fees, adversely affects the public interest in pilotage.

It is within the framework of this longstanding pilotage regulation system that the practice has apparently existed of permitting pilots, if they choose, to select their relatives and friends as the only ones ultimately eligible for appointment as pilots by the governor. Many other states have established pilotage systems which make the selection of pilots on this basis possible. Thus it was noted thirty years ago in a Department of Commerce study of pilotage that membership of pilot associations "is limited to persons agreeable to those already members, generally relatives and friends of the pilots. Probably in pilotage more than in any other occupation in the United States the male members of a family follow the same work from generation to generation."

The practice of nepotism in appointing public servants has been a subject of controversy in this country throughout our history. Some states have adopted constitutional amendments or statutes, to prohibit it. These have reflected state policies to wipe out the practice. But Louisiana and most other states have adopted no such general policy. We can only assume that the Louisiana legislature weighed the obvious possibility of evil against whatever useful function a closely knit pilotage system may serve. Thus the advantages of early experience under friendly supervision in the locality of the pilot's training, the benefits to morale and esprit de corps which family and neighborly tradition might contribute, the close association in which pilots must work and live in their pilot communities and on the water, and the discipline and regulation which is imposed to assure the State competent pilot service after appointment, might have prompted the legislature to permit Louisiana pilot officers to select those which whom they would serve.

The number of people, as a practical matter, who can be pilots is very limited. No matter what system of selection is adopted, all but the few occasionally selected must of necessity be excluded. We are aware of no decision of this Court holding that the Constitution requires a state governor, or subordinates responsible to him and removable by him for cause, to select state public servants by competitive tests or by any other particular method of selection. The object of the entire pilotage law, as we have pointed out, is to secure for the State and others interested the safest and most efficiently operated pilotage system practicable. We cannot say that the method adopted in Louisiana for the selection of pilots is unrelated to this objective. We do not need to consider hypothetical questions concerning any similar system of selection which might conceivably be practiced in other professions or businesses regulated or operated by state governments. It is enough here that considering the entirely unique institution of pilotage in the light of its history in Louisiana, we cannot say that the practice appellants attack is the kind of discrimination which violates the equal protection clause of the Fourteenth Amendment.

■ MR. JUSTICE RUTLEDGE, dissenting.

The unique history and conditions surrounding the activities of river port pilots, shortly recounted in the Court's opinion, justify a high degree of public regulation. But I do not think they can sustain a system of entailment for the occupation. If Louisiana were to provide by statute *in haec verba [i.e., in so many words—Editors]* that only members of John Smith's family would be eligible for the public calling of pilot, I have no doubt that the statute on its face would infringe the Fourteenth Amendment. And this would be true, even though John Smith and the members of his family had been pilots for generations. It would be true also if the right were expanded to include a number of designated families.

In final analysis this is, I think, the situation presented on this record. While the statutes applicable do not purport on their face to restrict the right to become a licensed pilot to members of the families of licensed pilots, the charge is that they have been so administered. And this charge not only is borne out by the record but is accepted by the Court as having been sustained.

The result of the decision therefore is to approve as constitutional state regulation which makes admission to the ranks of pilots turn finally on consanguinity. Blood is, in effect, made the crux of selection. That, in my opinion, is forbidden by the Fourteenth Amendment's guaranty against denial of the equal protection of the laws. The door is thereby closed to all not having blood relationship to presently licensed pilots. Whether the occupation is considered as having the status of "public officer" or of highly regulated private employment, it is beyond legislative power to make entrance to it turn upon such a criterion. The Amendment makes no exception from its prohibitions against state action on account of the fact that public rather than private employment is affected by the forbidden discriminations. That fact simply makes violation all the more clear where those discriminations are shown to exist.

It is not enough to avoid the Amendment's force that a familial system may have a tendency or, as the Court puts it, a direct relationship to the end of securing an efficient pilotage system. Classification based on the purpose to be accomplished may be said abstractly to be sound. But when the test adopted and applied in fact is race or consanguinity, it cannot be used constitutionally to bar all except a group chosen by such a relationship from public employment. That is not a test; it is a wholly arbitrary exercise of power.

Conceivably the familial system would be the most effective possible scheme for training many kinds of artisans or public servans, sheerly from the viewpoint of securing the highest degree of skill and competence. Indeed, something very worth while largely disappeared from our national life when the once prevalent familial system of conducting manufacturing and mercantile enterprises went out and was replaced by the highly impersonal corporate system for doing business.

But that loss is not one to be repaired under our scheme by legislation framed or administered to perpetuate family monopolies of either private occupations or branches of the public service. It is precisely because the Amendment forbids enclosing those areas by legislative lines drawn on the basis of race, color, creed, and the like, that, in cases like this, the possibly most efficient method of securing the highest development of skills cannot be established by law. Absent any such bar, the presence of such a tendency or direct relationship would be effective for sustaining the legislation. It cannot be effective to overcome the bar itself. The discrimination here is not shown to be consciously racial in character. But I am unable to differentiate in effects one founded on blood relationship.

The case therefore falls squarely within the ruling in *Yick Wo v. Hopkins*, not only with relation to the line of discrimination employed, but also in the fact that unconstitutional administration of a statute otherwise valid on its face incurs the same condemnation as if the statute had incorporated the discrimination in terms. Appellants here are entitled, in my judgment, to the same relief as was afforded in the *Yick Wo* case.

■ MR. JUSTICE REED, MR. JUSTICE DOUGLAS and MR. JUSTICE MURPHY join in this dissent.

A NOTE ON *CITY OF CLEBURNE* AND SUSPECT CLASSIFICATIONS

In *City of Cleburne v. Cleburne Living Center*, 473 U.S. 432 (1985), the Court considered a challenge to a zoning ordinance that excluded a group home for the mentally disabled. The Court struck down the ordinance, but based its conclusion on improper motive and expressly held that no heightened scrutiny should be applied to a "mental retardation" classification.

In reaching the latter conclusion, the Court emphasized institutional competence, calling regulation in this area "a task for legislators guided by qualified professionals and not by the perhaps ill-informed opinions of the judiciary." The Court also noted the passage of federal laws prohibiting discrimination against the mentally disabled. This "legislative response, which could hardly have occurred and survived without public support, negates any claim that the mentally retarded are politically powerless in the sense that they have no ability to attract the attention of the lawmakers. Any minority can be said to be powerless to assert direct control over the legislature, but if that were a criterion for higher level scrutiny by the courts, much economic and social legislation would now be suspect." Finally, the Court emphasized its concern about the need for limiting principles: "if the large and amorphous class of the mentally retarded were deemed quasi-suspect," then "it would be difficult to find a principled way to distinguish a variety of other groups who have perhaps immutable disabilities setting them off from others, who cannot themselves mandate the desired legislative responses, and who can claim some degree of prejudice from at least part of the public at large," such as "the aging . . . and the infirm."

In partial dissent, Justice Marshall noted that "the mentally retarded have been subject to a lengthy and tragic history," as "the rising tide of Social Darwinism" and "leading medical authorities" supported a "regime of state-mandated segregation and degradation . . . [that] rivaled . . . the worst excesses of Jim Crow." Are the majority's reasons not to give heightened scrutiny persuasive? Should the history of discrimination noted by the dissent be dispositive? If the Court was willing to strike down the ordinance under rational basis review, does the standard of scrutiny actually matter?

Other Suspect Classifications?

In deciding whether a classification should receive heightened scrutiny (whether "strict" or "intermediate"), the Court emphasizes three factors: (1) whether there is a *history of invidious discrimination* against the affected class; (2) whether the affected class share an *immutable characteristic*; and (3) whether the affected class is a "discrete and insular minority" that is *excluded from the political process.* (The phrase "discrete and insular minority" comes from the footnote number four in *United States v. Carolene Products Co.*, 304 U.S. 144 (1938).) One might see the Court as proceeding by analogy, asking whether the classification is like a racial classification.

Age. The Court has held that age, like disability, is not a suspect classification. Most of the cases have involved mandatory retirement ages for public employees. E.g., *Gregory v. Ashcroft*, 501 U.S. 452 (1991); *Vance v. Bradley*, 440 U.S. 93 (1979); *Massachusetts Bd. of Retirement v. Murgia*, 427 U.S. 307 (1976). Every state draws distinctions between adults and children, which is also an age classification.

Alienage. Many statutes disadvantage aliens relative to citizens. Several times in the early 1970s the Court struck down state statutes that made distinctions on the basis of citizenship, such as by denying welfare benefits to lawful resident aliens or by requiring citizenship for civil service jobs or for the practice of law. Subsequent cases mostly went the other direction, allowing states to require citizenship for state troopers and public school teachers, though not for notaries public. In *Plyler v. Doe*, 457 U.S. 202 (1982), the Court expressly rejected the idea that aliens unlawfully present in the United States are a suspect class: "Unlike most of the classifications that we have recognized as suspect," the Court said, "entry into this class, by virtue of entry into this country, is the product of voluntary action" and not "an absolutely immutable characteristic." Nonetheless, the Court by a 5–4 vote struck down a Texas statute excluding children who were unlawfully present in the United States from the state's public schools, because the restriction "is directed against children, and imposes its discriminatory burden on the basis of a legal characteristic over which children can have little control. It is thus difficult to conceive of a rational justification for penalizing these children for their presence within the United States."

Illegitimacy. In *Levy v. Louisiana*, 391 U.S. 68 (1968), the Court held that children born to unmarried parents could not be denied the right to recover in a wrongful-death suit arising out of negligent medical care given to their mother. Because the Louisiana statute in question allowed similarly situated "legitimate" children to recover for their parents' wrongful death, the Court held that construing the statute to exclude "illegitimate" children was "invidious discrimination" in violation of the Equal Protection Clause. In the Court's words: "Legitimacy or illegitimacy of birth has no relation to the nature of the wrong allegedly inflicted on the mother. These children, though illegitimate, were dependent on her; she cared for them and nurtured them; they were indeed hers in the biological and in the spiritual sense; in her death they suffered wrong in the sense that any dependent would."

National Origin. The Court has treated national origin as analogous to race and governed by the same standard. Indeed, a case that is often understood as subjecting racial classifications to strict scrutiny is *Korematsu*, p. 328, which concerned the internment of Japanese-Americans on the basis of nationality and ancestry.

Religion. The Court has described religion as a suspect classification akin to race and ethnicity. However, the First Amendment's Free Exercise and Establishment Clause provide independent protections for religion, and the Court has suggested that any protection for religion under the Equal Protection Clause is not broader than what they provide. In *Locke v. Davey*, 540 U.S. 712 (2004), p. 1177, for instance, the Court upheld a state program against the plaintiff's free exercise challenge, and then said in a footnote: "Because we hold that the program is not a violation of the Free Exercise Clause . . . we apply rational-basis scrutiny to his equal protection claim."

Sexual Orientation. In *Romer v. Evans*, 517 U.S. 620 (1996), the Court considered an Equal Protection Clause challenge to a Colorado constitutional amendment that restricted the ability of local governments to pass ordinances preventing discrimination on the basis of sexual orientation. The Court struck down the amendment, but in doing so it declined to apply strict scrutiny as the lower court had. Instead, the Court held that the law lacked a rational basis because it "has the peculiar property of imposing a broad and undifferentiated disability on a single named group" and "its sheer breadth is so discontinuous with the reasons offered for it that the amendment seems inexplicable by anything but animus toward the class it affects." Subsequently, the Court invalidated a state criminal prohibition of homosexual sodomy, *Lawrence v. Texas*, 539 U.S. 558 (2003), p. 1617; a federal law defining marriage as the union of one man and one woman, *United States v. Windsor*, 133 S.Ct. 2675 (2013); and state laws recognizing only opposite-sex marriages, *Obergefell v. Hodges*, 135 S.Ct. 2584 (2015), p. 1633. In these cases the Court has relied on substantive due process, and sometimes federalism, but it has also suggested a basis for the decisions in the confluence of due process and equal protection. See *Obergefell*, 135 S.Ct. at 2602–2604. Nevertheless, the Court has avoided calling sexual orientation a suspect classification, and in these cases the Court has never described itself as applying heightened scrutiny.

Wealth. Several times in the 1950s and '60s the Court hinted that classifications based on wealth should receive heightened scrutiny. For example, in *Griffin v. Illinois*, 351 U.S. 12 (1956), the Court said that "[i]n criminal trials a State can no more discriminate on account of poverty than on account of religion, race, or color." But a few years later, when considering the question more directly in *San Antonio Independent School District v. Rodriguez*, 411 U.S. 1 (1973), the Court by a 5–4 vote declined to apply heightened scrutiny to wealth classifications. In that case the Court upheld a state school-financing arrangement keyed to property tax values, which gave far more school funding to rich school districts than to poor ones. In neither case did the state *facially* discriminate on the basis of wealth. The challenge was to the disproportionate *effect* on the poor. Many welfare and taxation programs facially discriminate on the basis of wealth, but they do so in favor of the poor.

A NOTE ON THE "FUNDAMENTAL INTERESTS" STRAND OF EQUAL PROTECTION DOCTRINE

When analyzing a statute under the Equal Protection Clause, the Court generally looks to the kind of the classification, or distinction, the statute makes. But there is a smaller set of cases where the Court has emphasized not the distinction in the statute but the kind of interest that is affected by that distinction. The first example of this kind of analysis, and the leading case, is *Skinner v. Oklahoma*, 316 U.S. 535 (1942). Jack Skinner had committed robbery with firearms, his third felony, and he was thus subject to Oklahoma's Habitual Criminal Sterilization Act. The Court held that applying the Act to Skinner would violate the Equal Protection Clause. The Court found a number of "inequalities" in the Act, such as the fact that it applied to larceny but not embezzlement, suggesting the statute might even lack a rational basis. But the Court also emphasized the importance of the interests in the case. After reciting with approval *Buck v. Bell* and a number of other cases calling for deference to state judgments, the Court said:

> But the instant legislation runs afoul of the equal protection clause, though we give Oklahoma that large deference which the rule of the foregoing cases requires. We are dealing here with legislation which involves one of the basic civil rights of man. Marriage and procreation are fundamental to the very existence and survival of the race. The power to sterilize, if exercised, may have subtle, farreaching and devastating effects. In evil or reckless hands it can cause races or types which are inimical to the dominant group to wither and disappear.... We mention these matters not to reexamine the scope of the police power of the States. We advert to them merely in emphasis of our view that strict scrutiny of the classification which a State makes in a sterilization law is essential, lest unwittingly or otherwise invidious discriminations are made against groups or types of individuals in violation of the constitutional guaranty of just and equal laws. The guaranty of "equal protection of the laws is a pledge of the protection of equal laws." *Yick Wo v. Hopkins*, 118 U.S. 356, 369 (1886). When the law lays an unequal hand on those who have committed intrinsically the same quality of offense and sterilizes one and not the other, it has made as an invidious a discrimination as if it had selected a particular race or nationality for oppressive treatment. Sterilization of those who have thrice committed grand larceny with immunity for those who are embezzlers is a clear, pointed, unmistakable discrimination. Oklahoma makes no attempt to say that he who commits larceny by trespass or trick or fraud has biologically inheritable traits which he who commits embezzlement lacks.... We have not the slightest basis for inferring that that line has any significance in eugenics nor that the inheritability of criminal traits follows the neat legal distinctions which the law has marked between those two offenses.

Id. at 541–542. Chief Justice Stone concurred, but found the Due Process Clause, not the Equal Protection Clause, to be the right ground for decision.

In *Skinner*, the Court did not quite say that the distinction between larceny and embezzlement was irrational. (Can you see why not?) Nor did the Court say that "larcenists" was a suspect classification. (Again, can you see why not?) Instead the Court suggested that the important interest in "[m]arriage and procreation" made the line drawn by the Act a violation of "the protection of equal laws." Are you persuaded? Does *Skinner* follow from *Yick Wo*? Why does the Court suggest that a basis in eugenics could make the law constitutional? Does *that* follow from *Yick Wo*? Bottom line—what, exactly, was the problem with the statute? Was it the interest it affected (marriage and procreation)? The distinction it drew (between larceny and embezzlement)? The consequence it imposed (sterilization as a criminal punishment)? The lack of a rational basis for it? All of the above?

In later cases the Court relied on *Skinner* to apply the Equal Protection Clause to statutes restricting marriage. For example, in *Zablocki v. Redhail*, 434 U.S. 374 (1978), the Court invalidated a Wisconsin statute that made it a criminal offense for any person, while under a judicially determined obligation to pay child support, to marry without court approval. In *Turner v. Safley*, 482 U.S. 78 (1987), the Court relied on *Zablocki* to invalidate a prison regulation that required the permission of the prison superintendent before an inmate could marry another prisoner or a civilian. In both cases the Court also cited *Loving v. Virginia* for the fundamental importance of the right to marry. E.g., *Zablocki*, at 383 (" 'Marriage is one of the "basic civil rights of man," fundamental to our very existence and survival.' " (quoting *Loving*, at 12 (quoting *Skinner*, at 541))). These cases—*Skinner, Loving, Zablocki*, and *Turner*—will appear again in *Obergefell v. Hodges*, the same-sex marriage case, which is presented at p. 1633.

In other cases where the Court considered a "fundamental interest" for purposes of equal protection analysis, the interest was an express constitutional right. An example is *Police Department of Chicago v. Mosley*, 408 U.S. 92 (1972), in which the Court treated a law containing a content-based regulation of speech as a problem "under the Equal Protection Clause, not to mention the First Amendment itself." The Court has also treated voting and political participation as a "fundamental interest" for equal protection purposes, even though no constitutional provision expressly protects the right to vote *per se*. E.g., *Bush v. Gore*, 531 U.S. 98 (2000); *Harper v. Virginia*, 383 U.S. 663 (1966); *Baker v. Carr*, 369 U.S. 186 (1962). (Note that the Fifteenth, Nineteenth, and Twenty-sixth Amendments do protect the right to vote for certain citizens, and the Guarantee Clause requires that each state have "a Republican Form of Government.") In cases where the "fundamental interest" is an express constitutional right, does equal protection add something important, or would it be more straightforward to ask whether the express constitutional right has been violated?

[Assignment 75]

III. "DUE PROCESS OF LAW"

There are two Due Process Clauses in the Constitution. Although their language is essentially identical, each has a different context and constrains a different government. The Due Process Clause of the Fifth Amendment is surrounded by criminal procedure rights, and it limits the national government. It says: "No person shall . . . be deprived of life, liberty, or property, without due process of law." The Due Process Clause of the Fourteenth Amendment, which was ratified during Reconstruction, extends that limitation to the states and is surrounded by the familiar guarantees of "the privileges or immunities of citizens" and "the equal protection of the laws." It says: "No State shall . . . deprive any person of life, liberty, or property, without due process of law."

Both clauses require something: "due process of law." But both require this only when a government is doing something—depriving someone of "life, liberty, or property." Out of these phrases come the two critical questions for interpreting and applying the Due Process Clauses. The first, threshold question is whether there was a deprivation of "life, liberty, or property." If there was, the second question is whether there was "due process of law."

Throughout the history of constitutional law in the United States, there has been great debate over whether "due process of law" imposes only a requirement of *process* or also limits in some way the substance of what the government may do. It is easy to imagine government action that takes life, liberty, or property without any process. For example, if the local sheriff, not acting pursuant to a statute or warrant or court order, went to your apartment and started taking away all of your furniture, then you would be deprived of property, not only without "due process" but without any process at all. But imagine that a duly enacted statute, passed by a legislative majority, named you and said that all of your personal property now belonged to the sheriff. If the sheriff then took away your furniture, would you have received due process? And if that would be a violation of due process, what other constraints are there on the substance of the laws that the legislature might pass? For example, what if a statute, again meeting all the ordinary procedural requirements for legislation, established criminal penalties for anyone who possesses furniture? Or established criminal penalties for anyone who possesses alcohol? Or heroin? Or anyone who works more than ten hours a day? Which, if any, of these scenarios would deny someone "due process of law"? These kinds of questions all raise the central and highly contested issue of what, exactly, is required by the Due Process Clauses.

The materials in this section begin with the historical roots of due process, and its core principles. (This kind of due process is sometimes called "procedural due process.") Next comes a discussion of "incorporation." Incorporation is the idea that the Due Process Clause of the Fourteenth Amendment takes the rights guaranteed by the Constitution against the national government and makes them apply against the state governments. Then there is a lengthy consideration of the path the Court has charted in developing the doctrine of "substantive due process." That path began with *Dred Scott*, where the Court read the Due Process Clause of the Fifth Amendment to prohibit Congress from making laws limiting a slaveholder's right to take slaves into the Territories (see p. 733). From there the path wound on to *Lochner* and other economic liberty cases in the early twentieth century, and then turned back as the Court retreated from substantive due process in the middle of that century. Then the path turned again, as the Court returned to substantive due process in cases involving contraception (*Griswold*), abortion (*Roe*), sex (*Lawrence*), and marriage (*Obergefell*).

A. DUE PROCESS AND SEPARATION OF POWERS

The Due Process Clauses in the Fifth and Fourteenth Amendments require "due process of law" before the state deprives a person of "life, liberty, or property." Consider first the threshold question of what counts as a deprivation of "life, liberty, or property." What do these terms mean?

For the founders, *liberty* was the natural freedom that everyone was born with. It included the freedom to work, the freedom to worship, and what Blackstone called the freedom to "remov[e] one's person to whatsoever place one's own inclination may direct." 1 William Blackstone, COMMENTARIES ON THE LAWS OF ENGLAND *130 (1765–1769). *Property* was widely seen as a right to control something, such as land or a ship or a patent, deciding how it would be used and who would have access to it. For most of U.S. history, including when the Fifth Amendment and the Fourteenth Amendment were ratified, a property right was protected by law when it became final, or "vested." A promise to sell land, for example, did not create a vested property right; the property would vest when the sale was final. The scope of property was not deduced from natural rights, but was defined by and subject to statutes and judicial decisions. *Life* had its everyday meaning: it was what a person was deprived of through capital punishment.

Over time, the Court has recognized liberty and property interests that go beyond these traditional common law understandings. An example of this "new property" is a claim to government benefits. In *Goldberg v. Kelly*, 397 U.S. 254 (1970), the Court concluded that the termination of welfare benefits was a deprivation of property, and that the government therefore had to provide "due process"—in the form of an evidentiary hearing—before a termination.

Subsequent cases have considered how far liberty and property extend. Modern cases have found a deprivation of liberty when a police chief put up posters identifying someone as an excessive drinker, *Wisconsin v. Constantineau*, 400 U.S. 433 (1971); and when a state prisoner was involuntarily transferred to a mental hospital, *Vitek v. Jones*, 445 U.S. 480 (1980). But other cases have emphasized limits. An untenured state university professor was not deprived of liberty or property when his contract was not renewed. *Board of Regents v. Roth*, 408 U.S. 564 (1972). Nor was an individual deprived of liberty or property when labeled an "active shoplifter" by police flyers. *Paul v. Davis*, 424 U.S. 693 (1976). A child was not deprived of liberty when Social Services failed to protect him from an abusive father. *DeShaney v. Winnebago County Department of Social Services*, 489 U.S. 189 (1989). A restraining order was not property, and so a wife was not deprived of property when a restraining order against her abusive husband went unenforced. *Town of Castle Rock v. Gonzales*, 545 U.S. 748 (2005).

These cases address the outer boundaries of "liberty" and "property," and they sometimes reach inconsistent conclusions. But the core of these concepts remains well settled. *Property* includes the control of things. *Liberty* includes freedom from physical restraint.

When the government deprives someone of life, liberty, or property, the next question is whether the deprivation was made with *due process of law*. The Due Process Clauses stand in a long tradition of English and American procedural protections. These can be traced in English constitutional history back to Magna Carta (1215), which in chapter 39 declared that the king could deprive a subject of liberty and property (and by implication life) only "by the lawful judgement of his peers or by the law of the land." MAGNA CARTA 327 (J. C. Holt trans. & ed., 1969).

The "law of the land" requirement came be to be understood as demanding a kind of procedural regularity: for a person to be deprived of a right, there had to be a trial under settled law. In English constitutional history, the "law of the land" requirement was primarily a constraint on royal power. The king could deprive a person of rights *only* pursuant to some existing law (either common law or statute) and *only* after there had been a judgment from a common law court. According to Lord Coke, the greatest of the common law judges, *Magna Carta*'s requirement of acting "by the Law of the Land" could be summed up in the phrase "due process of Law." Edward Coke, *The Second Part of the Institutes of the Lawes of England*, in 2 THE SELECTED WRITINGS AND SPEECHES OF SIR EDWARD COKE 858 (Steve Sheppard ed., 2003).

In the United States, "law of the land" and "due process" tended to be used for the most part interchangeably. Most state constitutions at the founding used "law of the land," though of course the Fifth Amendment of the U.S. Constitution used "due process." In either formulation, these constitutional provisions were understood to prohibit the government from depriving someone of life, liberty, or property without application of general law by a court, according to traditional procedures. (The "due process" formulation may have been adopted in the U.S. Constitution to prevent confusion, because Article VI refers to the "supreme Law of the Land" in a different sense, describing the supremacy of federal law over state law.)

As you read the following excerpts, ask yourself two questions. First, what counts as due process? Second, what if anything does "due process" require from each branch of the national government—the legislature, the executive, and the judiciary?

St. George Tucker on Due Process

Editor's Appendix, 1 BLACKSTONE'S COMMENTARIES 203–206 (1803)

By the amendments to the constitution, no person shall be deprived of life, liberty, or property, without due process of law.

Due process of law as described by sir Edward Coke I, is by indictment or presentment of good and lawful men, where such deeds be done in due manner, or by writ original of the common law. Due process of law must then be had before a judicial court, or a judicial magistrate. The judicial power of the United States is vested in one supreme court, and such inferior tribunals, as congress may establish, and extends to all cases in law and equity, arising under the constitution, & c. . . .

In the distribution of the powers of government, the legislative powers were vested in congress . . . the executive powers (except in the instances particularly enumerated,) in the president and senate. The judicial powers (except in the cases particularly enumerated in the first article) in the courts: the word *the*, used in defining the powers of the executive, and of the judiciary, is, with these exceptions, co-extensive in it[s] signification with the word *all*: for all the powers granted by the constitution are either legislative, and executive, or judicial; to keep them for ever separate and distinct, except in the cases positively enumerated, has been uniformly the policy, and constitutes one of the fundamental principles of the American governments. . . .

It will be urged, perhaps, that the house of representatives of the United States is, like a British house of commons, a judicial court: to which the answer is, it is neither established as such by the constitution (except in respect to its own members,) nor has it been, nor can it be so established by authority of congress; for all the courts of the United States must be composed of judges commissioned by the president of the United States, and holding their offices during good behaviour, and not by the unstable tenure of biennial elections.

Joseph Story on Due Process

3 COMMENTARIES ON THE CONSTITUTION § 1783 (1833)

The [Due Process Clause of the Fifth Amendment] is but an enlargement of the language of magna charta, *"nec super eum ibimus, nec super eum mittimus, nisi per legale judicium parium suorum, vel per legem terrae,"* neither will we pass upon him, or condemn him, but by the lawful judgment of his peers, or by the law of the land. Lord Coke says, that these latter words, *per legem terrae* (by the law of the land,) mean by due process of law, that is, without due presentment or indictment, and being brought in to answer thereto by due process of the common law. So that this clause in effect affirms the right of trial according to the process and proceedings of the common law.

————

These were highly influential sources for American judges and lawyers in the early republic, and they represent the standard view of what counted as "due process." It was not a kind of abstract procedural justice deduced from first principles of fairness or natural law. Instead, it was the established and familiar processes of the common law courts known on both sides of the Atlantic. In the United States, the requirement of due process was a natural fit with the Constitution's separation of powers. See Nathan S. Chapman & Michael W. McConnell, *Due Process as Separation of Powers*, 121 Yale L.J. 1672 (2012). Courts could violate "due process" by failing to provide the established common law procedures. The executive could violate "due process" by circumventing the courts. And the legislature could violate "due process" by enacting legislation that circumvented the courts or abrogated their common law procedures. Thus each branch of the national government could violate the Due Process Clause of the Fifth Amendment: the judiciary by *not acting like a court should,* and the other two branches by acting *as if they were courts.*

A practical example of how the due process inquiry worked under the Fifth Amendment is provided by the case of *Murray's Lessee.* In 1838 the Treasury Department audited the collector of customs for the port of New York, and found that he owed the government over $1.3 million (equivalent to more than $28 million today). Rather than using the ordinary judicial process and bringing a civil action, the solicitor of the Treasury issued a warrant for that amount, employing a summary procedure that Congress had authorized for recovering money owed to the government. By the time the case arrived in the Supreme Court, the key question was whether that summary procedure was "due process." (The threshold requirement was met: taking back $1.3 million from the customs collector was certainly a deprivation of property.) The Court noted that " 'due process of law' generally implies and includes" a number of established procedural protections that were missing in the summary procedure, such as "regular allegations, opportunity to answer, and a trial according to some settled course of judicial proceedings." And yet, the Court said, these requirements were "not universally true" under American law and "the law of England after Magna Charta." There were contexts where summary procedures had been traditionally allowed, and the Court identified one of those contexts as the recovery of money owed to the government. In reaching this conclusion the Court explored at length the procedures available in the English Court of Exchequer, as well as the text of the U.S. Constitution and subsequent practice. The bottom line was that the summary process given to the embezzling customs collector was in fact "due process," and the following excerpt shows some of the Court's analysis.

Murray's Lessee v. Hoboken
Land & Improvement Co.

59 U.S. (18 How.) 272 (1856)

■ MR. JUSTICE CURTIS delivered the opinion of the Court.

. . . No objection has been taken to the warrant on account of any defect or irregularity in the proceedings which preceded its issue. It is not denied that they were in conformity with the requirements of the act of congress. . . .

[The] objection of the plaintiff [is] that the effect of the proceedings authorized by the act in question is to deprive the party, against whom the warrant issues, of his liberty and property, "without due process of law"; and, therefore, is in conflict with the fifth article of the amendments of the constitution. . . .

The words, "due process of law" were undoubtedly intended to convey the same meaning as the words "by the law of the land," in Magna Charta. Lord Coke, in his commentary on those words (2 Inst. 50), says they mean due process of law. The Constitutions which had been adopted by the several States before the formation of the federal Constitution, following the language of the great charter more closely, generally contained the words, "but by the judgment of his peers, or the law of the land." The ordinance of Congress of July 13, 1787, for the government of the territory of the United States northwest of the River Ohio, used the same words.

The Constitution of the United States, as adopted, contained the provision, that "the trial of all crimes, except in cases of impeachment, shall be by jury." When the fifth article of amendment containing the words now in question was made, the trial by jury in criminal cases had thus already been provided for. By the sixth and seventh articles of amendment, further special provisions were separately made for that mode of trial in civil and criminal cases. To have followed, as in the state constitutions, and in the ordinance of 1787, the words of Magna Charta, and declared that no person shall be deprived of his life, liberty, or property but by the judgment of his peers or the law of the land, would have been in part superfluous and inappropriate. To have taken the clause, "law of the land," without its immediate context, might possibly have given rise to doubts, which would be effectually dispelled by using those words which the great commentator on Magna Charta had declared to be the true meaning of the phrase, "law of the land," in that instrument, and which were undoubtedly then received as their true meaning.

That the warrant now in question [in this case] is legal process is not denied. It was issued in conformity with an act of Congress. But is it "due process of law"? The Constitution contains no description of those processes which it was intended to allow or forbid. It does not even declare what principles are to be applied to ascertain whether it be due process. It is manifest that it was not left to the legislative power to enact any process which might be devised. The article is a restraint on the legislative, as well as on the executive and judicial, powers of the government, and cannot be so construed as to leave Congress free to make any process "due process of law," by its mere will. To what principles, then, are we to resort to ascertain whether this process, enacted by Congress, is due process? To this the answer must be twofold. We must examine the Constitution itself to see whether this process be in conflict with any of its provisions. If not found to be so, we must look to those settled usages and modes of proceeding existing in the common and statute law of England, before the emigration of our ancestors, and which are shown not to have been unsuited to their civil and political condition by having been acted on by them after the settlement of this country. We apprehend there has been no period, since the establishment of the English monarchy, when there has not been, by the law of the land, a summary method for the recovery of debts due to the crown, and especially those due from receivers of the revenues. . . .

This brief sketch of the modes of proceeding to ascertain and enforce payment of balances due from receivers of the revenue in England, is sufficient to show that the methods of ascertaining the existence and amount of such debts, and compelling their payment, have varied widely from the usual course of the common law on other subjects; and that, as respects such debts due from such officers, "the law of the land" authorized the employment of auditors, and an inquisition without notice, and a species of execution bearing a very close resemblance to what is termed a warrant of distress in the act of 1820, now in question.

It is certain that this diversity in "the law of the land" between public defaulters and ordinary debtors was understood in this country, and entered into the legislation of the colonies and provinces, and more especially of the States, after the declaration of independence and before the formation of the constitution of the United States. Not only was the process of distress in nearly or quite universal use for the collection of taxes, but what was generally termed a warrant of distress, running against the body, goods, and chattels of defaulting receivers of public money, was issued to some public officer, to whom was committed the power to ascertain the amount of the default, and by such warrant proceed to collect it. . . .

Congress, from an early period, and in repeated instances, has legislated in a similar manner. . . . This legislative construction of the constitution, commencing so early in the government, when the first occasion for this manner of proceeding arose, continued throughout its existence, and repeatedly acted on by the judiciary and the executive, is entitled to no inconsiderable weight upon the question whether the proceeding adopted by it was "due process of law." *Prigg v. Pennsylvania*, 41 U.S. (16 Pet.) 621 (1842).

Tested by the common and statute law of England prior to the emigration of our ancestors, and by the laws of many of the States at the time of the adoption of this amendment, the proceedings authorized by the act of 1820 cannot be denied to be due process of law, when applied to the ascertainment and recovery of balances due to the government from a collector of customs, unless there exists in the constitution some other provision which restrains congress from authorizing such proceedings. For, though "due process of law" generally implies and includes *actor, reus, judex*, regular allegations, opportunity to answer, and a trial according to some settled course of judicial proceedings, yet, this is not universally true. There may be, and we have seen that there are cases, under the law of England after Magna Charta, and as it was brought to this country and acted on here, in which process, in its nature final, issues against the body, lands, and goods of certain public debtors without any such trial. . . .

NOTES

1.   In *Murray's Lessee*, the Court identifies two principles for determining whether "due process" has been violated. The first is to see if the deprivation violates some *other*

provision of the Constitution. The second is to look to the baseline of the established common law procedures in England as they have been received in the United States.

The first principle may strike you as odd and circular. In deciding whether there is a violation of the Due Process Clause of the Fifth Amendment, why would it matter whether some other provision was violated? And if some other provision was in fact violated, wouldn't that make the Due Process Clause unnecessary? What is the Court saying? The key is to recognize the relationship between the Due Process Clause and a host of other procedural protections in the Constitution. Many provisions of the Constitution require some kind of process that was well established at common law, such as the Sixth Amendment right to a jury trial in all criminal cases. And other provisions prevent Congress or state legislatures from performing a quasi-judicial function, such as the prohibitions in Article I, Sections 9 and 10 on bills of attainder and ex post facto laws, or the requirement of just compensation in the Takings Clause. These more specific constitutional provisions overlap with the Due Process Clauses; often the very same government action could be considered both a violation of "due process" and a violation of some other provision. Not only do these more specific provisions overlap with "due process," they also offer concrete illustrations of what it means.

2.   The second principle has the effect of making the Due Process Clause not a vehicle of progress, but a blockade against regress. As the Supreme Court said in another case, in which it relied on *Murray's Lessee*:

> However desirable it is that the old forms of procedure be improved with the progress of time, it cannot rightly be said that the Fourteenth Amendment furnishes a universal and self-executing remedy. Its function is negative, not affirmative, and it carries no mandate for particular measures of reform. For instance, it does not constrain the states to accept particular modern doctrines of equity, or adopt a combined system of law and equity procedure, or dispense with all necessity for form and method in pleading, or give untrammeled liberty to make amendments.

Ownbey v. Morgan, 256 U.S. 94, 112 (1921). This blockade-against-regress view of "due process" is not, however, the only possible view, as will soon become clear.

———

In more recent decisions, the Court has offered a somewhat different approach. It continues to focus on the specific situation or context in which a due process claim arises. However, instead of looking to what the traditional common law processes were in the relevant context, as the Court did *Murray's Lessee*, this approach uses a balancing test. On one side is the government's interest in the deprivation; and on the other side is the individual's interest in not suffering the deprivation. By weighing these interests against each other, the Court decides whether the process given amounted to "due process."

The following two cases illustrate these approaches. The first, *Calder v. Bull*, required the Court to decide whether a state legislature's order of a new trial in a probate case violated the Ex Post Facto Clause of the U.S. Constitution. While considering that question, the Court discusses many of the basic principles that are common to all of the more specific constitutional provisions that inform and illustrate "due process of law." The second case, *Mathews v. Eldridge*, is the central example of the Court's more recent balancing approach. As you read these cases, ask yourself what the strengths and weaknesses are of each approach.

Calder v. Bull

3 U.S. (3 Dall.) 386 (1798)

[On May 2, 1795, the Connecticut legislature passed a law ordering a new trial in a state probate case about the validity of a will. This law set aside a probate court's decree that the estate would go to the Calders. As a result, a state trial court held a new hearing in the probate case, at the end of which it ruled that the Bulls would inherit instead. All available appeals within the Connecticut state courts were then taken, and the state courts all affirmed the judgment for the Bulls. The Calders appealed to the U.S. Supreme Court. They challenged the constitutionality of the Connecticut legislature's action, arguing its retroactive operation violated Article I, Section 10's ban on ex post facto laws.—Editors]

In error from the State of *Connecticut*. The cause was argued at the last term, (in the absence of THE CHIEF JUSTICE) and now the court delivered their opinions *seriatim*.

■ CHASE, JUSTICE.

The Council for [the Calders] contend, that the said resolution or law of the *Legislature* of *Connecticut*, granting a *new hearing*, in the above case, is *an ex post facto law*, prohibited by the *Constitution of the United States*; that any law of the Federal government, or of any of the State governments, contrary to the *Constitution of the United States*, is *void*; and that this court possesses the power to declare *such* law *void.* . . .

Whether the Legislature of any of the States can revise and correct by law, a decision of any of its Courts of Justice, although not prohibited by the Constitution of the State, is a question of very great importance, and not necessary NOW to be determined; *because the resolution or law in question does not go so far.* I cannot subscribe to the *omnipotence* of a *State Legislature*, or that it is *absolute and without controul*; although its authority should not be *expressly* restrained by the *Constitution*, or *fundamental law*, of the State. The people of the *United States* erected their Constitutions, or forms of government, to establish justice, to promote the general welfare, to secure the blessings of liberty; and to protect their *persons* and *property* from violence. The purposes for which men enter into society will determine the *nature* and *terms* of the *social* compact; and as *they* are the foundation of the *legislative* power, *they* will decide what are the *proper* objects of it: The *nature*, and *ends* of *legislative* power will limit the *exercise* of it. . . . There are acts which the *Federal*, or *State*, Legislature cannot do, *without exceeding their authority*. There are certain *vital* principles in our *free Republican governments*, which will determine and over-rule an *apparent and flagrant* abuse of *legislative* power; as to authorize *manifest injustice by positive law*; or to take away that security for *personal liberty*, or private *property*, for the protection whereof of the government was established. An ACT of the Legislature (for I cannot call it a *law*) contrary to the *great first principles* of the *social compact*, cannot be considered a *rightful exercise* of *legislative* authority. . . .

A few instances will suffice to explain what I mean. A law that punished a citizen for an *innocent* action, or, in other words, for an act, which, when done, was in violation of no *existing* law; a law that destroys, or impairs, the *lawful private* contracts of citizens; a law that makes a man a *Judge in his own cause*; or a law that takes *property* from A. and gives it to B: It is against all reason and justice, for a people to entrust a Legislature with SUCH powers; and, therefore, it cannot be presumed that they have done it. . . .

ALL the restrictions contained in the Constitution of the *United States* on the power of the *State Legislatures*, were provided in favour of the authority of the *Federal* Government. The prohibition against their making *any ex post facto laws* was introduced for *greater* caution, and very probably arose from the knowledge, that *the Parliament of Great Britain* claimed and exercised a power to pass *such laws*, under the denomination of *bills of attainder*, or *bills of pains and penalties*; the *first* inflicting *capital*, and the other *less*, punishment. *These acts were legislative judgments; and an exercise of judicial power.* Sometimes [these acts of Parliament] respected the *crime*, by declaring acts to be treason, which were *not* treason, when committed; at other times, they violated the rules of evidence (to supply a deficiency of legal proof) by admitting *one* witness, when the *existing* law required *two*; by receiving evidence without *oath*; or the oath of the *wife* against the *husband*; or other testimony, which the courts of justice would not admit; at other times they inflicted *punishments*, where the party was not, by *law*, liable to *any punishment*; and in *other* cases, they inflicted *greater* punishment, than the law annexed to the offence.—The ground for the exercise of such *legislative* power was this, that the *safety* of the kingdom depended on the death, or other punishment, of the offender: as if traitors, when *discovered*, could be so formidable, or the government so insecure! With very few exceptions, the advocates of *such* laws were stimulated by ambition, or personal resentment, and vindictive malice. To prevent such, and similar, acts of violence and injustice, I believe, the Federal and State Legislatures, were prohibited from passing any bill of *attainder*; or any *ex post facto law.*

The Constitution of the *United States*, article 1, section 9, prohibits the Legislature of the *United States* from passing any *ex post facto law;* and, in section 10, lays several restrictions on the authority of the *Legislatures* of the several *states*; and, among them, "that no state shall pass any ex post facto law." . . .

I shall endeavour to show *what law* is to be considered an *ex post facto law*, within the words and meaning of the prohibition in the *Federal* Constitution. . . . [T]he plain and obvious meaning and intention of the prohibition is this; *that the Legislatures of the several states, shall not pass laws, after a fact done by a subject, or citizen, which shall have relation to such fact, and shall punish him for having done it.* The prohibition considered in this light, is an *additional* bulwark in favour of the personal security of the subject, to protect his person from *punishment by legislative acts*, having a retrospective operation. . . .

I will state *what laws* I consider *ex post facto laws*, within the *words* and the *intent* of the prohibition. 1st. Every law that makes an action, done before the passing of the law, and which was *innocent* when done, criminal; and punishes such action. 2d. Every law that *aggravates a crime*, or makes it *greater* than it was, when committed. 3d. Every law that *changes the punishment*, and inflicts a *greater punishment*, than the law annexed to the crime, when committed. 4th. Every law that alters the *legal* rules of *evidence*, and receives less, or different, testimony, than the law required at the time of the commission of the offence, *in order to convict the offender.* All these, and similar laws, are manifestly *unjust and oppressive.* . . .

The expressions "*ex post facto laws*," are *technical*, they had been in use long before the Revolution, and had acquired an appropriate meaning, by *Legislators*,

Lawyers, and *Authors*. The celebrated and judicious *Sir William Blackstone*, in his commentaries, considers an *ex post facto law* precisely in the *same* light I have done. His opinion is confirmed by his successor, *Mr. Wooddeson*; and by the author of *the Federalist*, who I esteem superior to *both*, for his extensive and accurate knowledge of the *true principles of Government*.

I also rely greatly on the definition, or explanation of EX POST FACTO LAWS, as given by the Conventions of *Massachusetts, Maryland*, and *North Carolina*; in their several Constitutions, or forms of Government. . . .

[In the remainder of his opinion, Justice Chase argued that the Ex Post Facto Clause should be read as applying only to retroactive criminal laws, and that it should not be read in a way that would make unnecessary other provisions of the Constitution, such as the Contracts Clause of Article I, Section 10, and the Takings Clause of the Fifth Amendment. He also concluded that the action of the Connecticut legislature had not actually divested the Calders of any property, since their right to the property had not vested before the legislative action.—Editors]

■ PATERSON, JUSTICE.

The Constitution of *Connecticut* is made up of usages, and it appears that its Legislature have, from the beginning, exercised the power of granting new trials. . . . They [have twice] acted in a double capacity, as a house of legislation, with undefined authority, and also as a court of judicature in certain exigencies. . . . This usage makes up part of the Constitution of *Connecticut*, and we are bound to consider it as such, unless it be inconsistent with the Constitution of the United States. True it is, that the awarding of new trials falls properly within the province of the judiciary; but if the Legislature of Connecticut have been in the uninterrupted exercise of this authority, in certain cases, we must, in such cases, respect their decisions as flowing from a competent jurisdiction, or constitutional organ. . . . [Even] if the power, thus exercised, comes more properly within the description of a judicial than of a legislative power; . . . [if] the Legislature of that state acted in both capacities; then in the case now before us, it would be fair to consider the awarding of a new trial, as an act emanating from the judiciary side of the department. But as this view of the subject militates against [the Calders], their counsel has contended for a reversal of the judgment, on the ground, that the awarding of a new trial, was the effect of a legislative act, and that it is unconstitutional, because an *ex post facto law*. For the sake of ascertaining the meaning of these terms, I will consider the resolution of the General court of *Connecticut*, as the exercise of a legislative and not a judicial authority. The question, then, which arises on the pleadings in this cause, is, whether the resolution of the Legislature of *Connecticut*, be an *ex post facto law*, within the meaning of the Constitution of the *United States*? I am of opinion, that it is not.

The words, *ex post facto*, when applied to a law, have a technical meaning, and, in legal phraseology, refer to crimes, pains, and penalties. Judge *Blackstone's* description of the terms is clear and accurate. "There is, says he, a still more unreasonable method than this, which is called making of laws, *ex post facto*, when after an action, indifferent in itself, is committed, the Legislator, then, for the first time, declares it to have been a crime, and inflicts a punishment upon the person who has committed it. Here it is impossible, that the party could foresee that an action, innocent when it was done, should be afterwards converted to guilt by a subsequent law; he had, therefore, no cause to abstain from it; and all punishment for not abstaining, must, of consequence, be cruel and unjust." 1 *Blackstone's Commentaries* 46. Here the meaning, annexed to the terms *ex post facto laws*, unquestionably refers to crimes, and nothing else. The historic page abundantly evinces, that the power of passing such laws should be withheld from legislators; as it is a dangerous instrument in the hands of bold, unprincipled, aspiring, and party men, and has been [too] often used to effect the most detestable purposes.

On inspecting such of our state Constitutions, as take notice of laws made *ex post facto*, we shall find, that they are understood in the same sense. . . .

[E]x post facto laws have an appropriate signification; they extend to penal statutes, and no further; they are restricted in legal estimation to the creation, and, perhaps, enhancement of crimes, pains and penalties. The enhancement of a crime, or penalty, seems to come within the same mischief as the creation of a crime or penalty; and therefore they may be classed together. . . .

I had an ardent desire to have extended the provision in the Constitution to retrospective laws in general. *[Justice Paterson was a delegate to the Constitutional Convention.—Editors]* There is neither policy nor safety in such laws; and, therefore, I have always had a strong aversion against them. It may, in general, be truly observed of retrospective laws of every description, that they neither accord with sound legislation, nor the fundamental principles of the social compact. But on full consideration, I am convinced, that *ex post facto laws* must be limited in the manner already expressed; they must be taken in their technical, which is also their common and general, acceptation, and are not to be understood in their literal sense.

■ IREDELL, JUSTICE.

Though I concur in the general result of the opinions, which have been delivered, I cannot entirely adopt the reasons that are assigned upon the occasion.

From the best information to be collected, relative to the Constitution of *Connecticut*, it appears, that the Legislature of that State has been in the uniform, uninterrupted, habit of exercising a general superintending power over its courts of law, by granting new trials. It may, indeed, appear strange to some of us. . . . [Yet it is not] altogether without some sanction for a Legislature to act as a court of justice. In *England*, we know, that one branch of the Parliament, the house of Lords, not only exercises a judicial power in cases of impeachment, and for the trial of its own members, but as the court of [last] resort, takes cognizance of many suits at law, and in equity: And that in construction of law, the jurisdiction there exercised is by the King in full Parliament; which shows that, in its origin, the causes were probably heard before the whole Parliament. When *Connecticut* was settled, the right of empowering her Legislature to superintend the Courts of Justice, was, I presume, early assumed. . . . The power, however, is judicial in its nature; and whenever it is exercised, as in the present instance, it is an exercise of judicial, not of legislative, authority.

But, let us, for a moment, suppose, that the resolution, granting a new trial, was a legislative act, it will by no means follow, that it is an act affected by the constitutional prohibition, that "no State shall pass any *ex post facto* law." . . .

If, then, a government, composed of Legislative, Executive and Judicial departments, were established, by a Constitution, which imposed no limits on the legislative power, the consequence would inevitably be, that whatever the legislative power chose to enact, would be lawfully enacted, and the judicial power could never interpose to pronounce it void. It is true, that some speculative jurists have held, that a legislative act against natural justice must, in itself, be void; but I cannot think that, under such a government, any Court of Justice would possess a power to declare it so. . . .

In order, therefore, to guard against so great an evil, it has been the policy of all the *American* states, which have, individually, framed their state constitutions since the revolution, and of the people of the *United States*, when they framed the Federal Constitution, to define with precision the objects of the legislative power, and to restrain its exercise within marked and settled boundaries. If any act of Congress, or of the Legislature of a state, violates those constitutional provisions, it is unquestionably void; though, I admit, that as the authority to declare it void is of a delicate and awful nature, the Court will never resort to that authority, but in a clear and urgent case. If, on the other hand, the Legislature of the Union, or the Legislature of any member of the Union, shall pass a law, within the general scope of their constitutional power, the Court cannot pronounce it to be void, merely because it is, in their judgment, contrary to the principles of natural justice. The ideas of natural justice are regulated by no fixed standard: the ablest and the purest men have differed upon the subject; and all that the Court could properly say, in such an event, would be, that the Legislature (possessed of an equal right of opinion) had passed an act which, in the opinion of the judges, was inconsistent with the abstract principles of natural justice. There are then but two lights, in which the subject can be viewed: 1st. If the Legislature pursue the authority delegated to them, their acts are valid. 2d. If they transgress the boundaries of that authority, their acts are invalid. In the former case, they exercise the discretion vested in them by the people, to whom alone they are responsible for the faithful discharge of their trust: but in the latter case, they violate a fundamental law, which must be our guide, whenever we are called upon as judges to determine the validity of a legislative act.

Still, however, in the present instance, the act or resolution of the Legislature of *Connecticut*, cannot be regarded as an *ex post facto* law; for, the true construction of the prohibition extends to criminal, not to civil, cases. It is only in criminal cases, indeed, in which the danger to be guarded against, is greatly to be apprehended. The history of every country in *Europe* will furnish flagrant instances of tyranny exercised under the pretext of penal dispensations. Rival factions, in their efforts to crush each other, have superseded all the forms, and suppressed all the sentiments, of justice; while attainders, on the principle of retaliation and proscription, have marked all the vicissitudes of party triumph. The temptation to such abuses of power is unfortunately too alluring for human virtue; and, therefore, the framers of the *American* Constitutions have wisely denied to the respective Legislatures, Federal as well as State, the possession of the power itself: They shall not pass any *ex post facto* law; or, in other words, they shall not inflict a punishment for any act, which was innocent at the time it was committed; nor increase the degree of punishment previously denounced for any specific offence.

The policy, the reason and humanity, of the prohibition, do not, I repeat, extend to civil cases, to cases that merely affect the private property of citizens. Some of the most necessary and important acts of Legislation are, on the contrary, founded upon the principle, that private rights must yield to public exigences. Highways are run through private grounds. Fortifications, Light-houses, and other public edifices, are necessarilly sometimes built upon the soil owned by individuals. In such, and similar cases, if the owners should refuse voluntarily to accommodate the public, they must be constrained, as far as the public necessities require; and justice is done, by allowing them a reasonable equivalent. Without the possession of this power the operations of Government would often be obstructed, and society itself would be endangered. It is not sufficient to urge, that the power may be abused, for, such is the nature of all power, such is the tendency of every human institution: and, it might as fairly be said, that the power of taxation, which is only circumscribed by the discretion of the Body, in which it is vested, ought not to be granted, because the Legislature, disregarding its true objects, might, for visionary and useless projects, impose a tax to the amount of nineteen shillings in the pound. We must be content to limit power where we can, and where we cannot, consistently with its use, we must be content to repose a salutary confidence. It is our consolation that there never existed a Government, in ancient or modern times, more free from danger in this respect, than the Governments of *America*.

Upon the whole, though there cannot be a case, in which an ex post facto law in criminal matters is requisite, or justifiable (for Providence never can intend to promote the prosperity of any country by bad means) yet, in the present instance the objection does not arise: Because, 1st. if the act of the Legislature of Connecticut was a judicial act, it is not within the words of the Constitution; and 2d. even if it was a legislative act, it is not within the meaning of the prohibition.

■ CUSHING, JUSTICE.

The case appears to me to be clear of all difficulty, taken either way. If the act is a judicial act, it is not touched by the Federal Constitution: and, if it is a legislative act, it is maintained and justified by the ancient and uniform practice of the state of *Connecticut*.

NOTES

1.   Do the justices agree on the scope of the prohibition on *ex post facto* laws? What examples do the justices give of laws that would violate the Ex Post Facto Clause? Note that the Court did not consider whether the action of the Connecticut legislature violated the Due Process Clause of the Fifth Amendment, since that clause applies only to the national government (and the Fourteenth Amendment was decades in the future). But imagine exactly the same case but with one change: *Congress*, not the Connecticut legislature, had ordered a new trial in a probate case. Would that legislative action have violated the Due Process Clause of the Fifth Amendment? Would there have been a deprivation of property without due process, even though Congress was actually requiring *more* process, not less? Would there have been a lack of due process even though the statute was duly enacted and passed by majority vote? In such a case, would the problem with Congress's action be best characterized as a deficiency in "process" or "substance"? Or does that dichotomy not fully capture the problem with Congress making what is essentially a judicial decision? One more question about the hypothetical case in which Congress acts like the Connecticut legislature did in *Calder*: would that action violate any other provision of the U.S. Constitution?

2.   What is the interpretive methodology in the opinions of Justice Chase and Justice Iredell? For each justice, what counts as legal authority to decide the case? Justice Chase's opinion is often cited as authority for courts being able to strike down statutes on the basis of natural law or unenumerated rights. If read more carefully, however, his opinion appears to suggest that principles of natural liberty and secure property operate

as a background presumption, as something like a canon of construction: Without a clear expression to the contrary, the legislature will not be presumed to act in violation of these principles. Yet even this invocation of natural justice was received skeptically by Justice Iredell, who noted with understatement that people do not always agree about what natural justice requires. How, if at all, should principles of natural justice affect the interpretation of the Constitution?

Mathews v. Eldridge
424 U.S. 319 (1975)

■ MR. JUSTICE POWELL delivered the opinion of the Court.

The issue in this case is whether the Due Process Clause of the Fifth Amendment requires that prior to the termination of Social Security disability benefit payments the recipient be afforded an opportunity for an evidentiary hearing. . . .

Respondent Eldridge was first awarded benefits in June 1968. In March 1972, he received a questionnaire from the state agency charged with monitoring his medical condition. Eldridge completed the questionnaire, indicating that his condition had not improved and identifying the medical sources, including physicians, from whom he had received treatment recently. The state agency then obtained reports from his physician and a psychiatric consultant. After considering these reports and other information in his file the agency informed Eldridge by letter that it had made a tentative determination that his disability had ceased in May 1972. The letter included a statement of reasons for the proposed termination of benefits, and advised Eldridge that he might request reasonable time in which to obtain and submit additional information pertaining to his condition.

In his written response, Eldridge disputed one characterization of his medical condition and indicated that the agency already had enough evidence to establish his disability. The state agency then made its final determination that he had ceased to be disabled in May 1972. This determination was accepted by the Social Security Administration (SSA), which notified Eldridge in July that his benefits would terminate after that month. The notification also advised him of his right to seek reconsideration by the state agency of this initial determination within six months.

Instead of requesting reconsideration Eldridge commenced this action challenging the constitutional validity of the administrative procedures established by the Secretary of Health, Education, and Welfare for assessing whether there exists a continuing disability. He sought an immediate reinstatement of benefits pending a hearing on the issue of his disability. The Secretary moved to dismiss on the grounds that Eldridge's benefits had been terminated in accordance with valid administrative regulations and procedures and that he had failed to exhaust available remedies. In support of his contention that due process requires a pretermination hearing, Eldridge relied exclusively upon this Court's decision in *Goldberg v. Kelly*, 397 U.S. 254 (1970), which established a right to an "evidentiary hearing" prior to termination of welfare benefits. The Secretary contended that *Goldberg* was not controlling since eligibility for disability benefits, unlike eligibility for welfare benefits, is not based on financial need and since issues of credibility and veracity do not play a significant role in the disability entitlement decision, which turns primarily on medical evidence. . . .

Procedural due process imposes constraints on governmental decisions which deprive individuals of "liberty" or "property" interests within the meaning of the Due Process Clause of the Fifth or Fourteenth Amendment. The Secretary does not contend that procedural due process is inapplicable to terminations of Social Security disability benefits. He recognizes, as has been implicit in our prior decisions, that the interest of an individual in continued receipt of these benefits is a statutorily created "property" interest protected by the Fifth Amendment. Rather, the Secretary contends that the existing administrative procedures, detailed below, provide all the process that is constitutionally due before a recipient can be deprived of that interest.

This Court consistently has held that some form of hearing is required before an individual is finally deprived of a property interest. The "right to be heard before being condemned to suffer grievous loss of any kind, even though it may not involve the stigma and hardships of a criminal conviction, is a principle basic to our society." *Joint Anti-Fascist Comm. v. McGrath*, 341 U.S. 123, 168 (1951) (Frankfurter, J., concurring). The fundamental requirement of due process is the opportunity to be heard "at a meaningful time and in a meaningful manner." Eldridge agrees that the review procedures available to a claimant before the initial determination of ineligibility becomes final would be adequate if disability benefits were not terminated until after the evidentiary hearing stage of the administrative process. The dispute centers upon what process is due prior to the initial termination of benefits, pending review.

In recent years this Court increasingly has had occasion to consider the extent to which due process requires an evidentiary hearing prior to the deprivation of some type of property interest even if such a hearing is provided thereafter. In only one case, *Goldberg v. Kelly*, has the Court held that a hearing closely approximating a judicial trial is necessary. In other cases requiring some type of pretermination hearing as a matter of constitutional right the Court has spoken sparingly about the requisite procedures. *Sniadach v. Family Finance Corp.*, 395 U.S. 337 (1969), involving garnishment of wages, was entirely silent on the matter. In *Fuentes v. Shevin*, 407 U.S. 67 (1972), the Court said only that in a replevin suit between two private parties the initial determination required something more than an *ex parte* proceeding before a court clerk. Similarly, *Bell v. Burson*, 402 U.S. 535, 540 (1971), held, in the context of the revocation of a state-granted driver's license, that due process required only that the prerevocation hearing involve a probable-cause determination as to the fault of the licensee, noting that the hearing "need not take the form of a full adjudication of the question of liability." More recently, in *Arnett v. Kennedy*, 416 U.S. 134 (1974), we sustained the validity of procedures by which a federal employee could be dismissed for cause. They included notice of the action sought, a copy of the charge, reasonable time for filing a written response, and an opportunity for an oral appearance. Following dismissal, an evidentiary hearing was provided.

These decisions underscore the truism that "[d]ue process, unlike some legal rules, is not a technical conception with a fixed content unrelated to time, place and circumstances." *Cafeteria Workers v. McElroy*, 367 U.S. 886, 895 (1961). "[D]ue process is flexible and calls for such procedural protections as the particular situation demands." *Morrissey v. Brewer*, 408 U.S. 471, 481 (1972). Accordingly, resolution of the issue whether the administrative procedures provided here are constitutionally sufficient requires analysis of the governmental and private interests that are affected. More precisely, our prior decisions indicate that identification of the specific dictates of due process generally requires consideration of three distinct factors: First, the private interest that will be affected by the official action; second, the risk of an erroneous deprivation of such interest through the procedures used, and the probable value, if any, of additional or substitute procedural safeguards; and finally, the Government's interest, including the function involved and the fiscal and administrative burdens that the additional or substitute procedural requirement would entail. See, *e.g.*, *Goldberg*, at 263–271.

We turn first to a description of the procedures for the termination of Social Security disability benefits and thereafter consider the factors bearing upon the constitutional adequacy of these procedures.

In order to establish initial and continued entitlement to disability benefits a worker must demonstrate that he is unable "to engage in any substantial gainful activity by reason of any medically determinable physical or mental impairment. . . ." 42 U.S.C. § 423(d)(1)(A).

To satisfy this test the worker bears a continuing burden of showing, by means of "medically acceptable clinical and laboratory diagnostic techniques," § 423(d)(3), that he has a physical or mental impairment of such severity that "he is not only unable to do his previous work but cannot . . . engage in any other kind of substantial gainful work which exists in the national economy. . . ." § 423(d)(2)(A). . . .

The continuing-eligibility investigation is made by a state agency acting through a "team" consisting of a physician and a nonmedical person trained in disability evaluation. The agency periodically communicates with the disabled worker, usually by mail in which case he is sent a detailed questionnaire or by telephone, and requests information concerning his present condition, including current medical restrictions and sources of treatment, and any additional information that he considers relevant to his continued entitlement to benefits.

Information regarding the recipient's current condition is also obtained from his sources of medical treatment. If there is a conflict between the information provided by the beneficiary and that obtained from medical sources such as his physician, or between two sources of treatment, the agency may arrange for an examination by an independent consulting physician. Whenever the agency's tentative assessment of the beneficiary's condition differs from his own assessment, the beneficiary is informed that benefits may be terminated, provided a summary of the evidence upon which the proposed determination to terminate is based, and afforded an opportunity to review the medical reports and other evidence in his case file. He also may respond in writing and submit additional evidence.

The state agency then makes its final determination, which is reviewed by an examiner in the SSA Bureau of Disability Insurance. . . . Upon acceptance by the SSA, benefits are terminated effective two months after the month in which medical recovery is found to have occurred.

If the recipient seeks reconsideration by the state agency and the determination is adverse, the SSA reviews the reconsideration determination and notifies the recipient of the decision. He then has a right to an evidentiary hearing before an SSA administrative law judge. The hearing is nonadversary, and the SSA is not represented by counsel. As at all prior and subsequent stages of the administrative process, however, the claimant may be represented by counsel or other spokesmen.

If this hearing results in an adverse decision, the claimant is entitled to request discretionary review by the SSA Appeals Council, and finally may obtain judicial review.

Should it be determined at any point after termination of benefits, that the claimant's disability extended beyond the date of cessation initially established, the worker is entitled to retroactive payments. If, on the other hand, a beneficiary receives any payments to which he is later determined not to be entitled, the statute authorizes the Secretary to attempt to recoup these funds in specified circumstances.

Despite the elaborate character of the administrative procedures provided by the Secretary, the courts below held them to be constitutionally inadequate, concluding that due process requires an evidentiary hearing prior to termination. In light of the private and governmental interests at stake here and the nature of the existing procedures, we think this was error.

Since a recipient whose benefits are terminated is awarded full retroactive relief if he ultimately prevails, his sole interest is in the uninterrupted receipt of this source of income pending final administrative decision on his claim. His potential injury is thus similar in nature to that of the welfare recipient in *Goldberg*, the nonprobationary federal employee in *Arnett*, and the wage earner in *Sniadach*.

Only in *Goldberg* has the Court held that due process requires an evidentiary hearing prior to a temporary deprivation. It was emphasized there that welfare assistance is given to persons on the very margin of subsistence. . . . Eligibility for disability benefits, in contrast, is not based upon financial need. Indeed, it is wholly unrelated to the worker's income or support from many other sources, such as earnings of other family members, workmen's compensation awards, tort claims awards, savings, private insurance, public or private pensions, veterans' benefits, food stamps, public assistance, or the "many other important programs, both public and private, which contain provisions for disability payments affecting a substantial portion of the work force. . . ."

As *Goldberg* illustrates, the degree of potential deprivation that may be created by a particular decision is a factor to be considered in assessing the validity of any administrative decisionmaking process. The potential deprivation here is generally likely to be less than in *Goldberg*, although the degree of difference can be overstated. As the District Court emphasized, to remain eligible for benefits a recipient must be "unable to engage in substantial gainful activity." Thus, in contrast to the discharged federal employee in *Arnett*, there is little possibility that the terminated recipient will be able to find even temporary employment to ameliorate the interim loss.

As we recognized last Term, "the possible length of wrongful deprivation of . . . benefits [also] is an important factor in assessing the impact of official action on the private interests." The Secretary concedes that the delay between a request for a hearing before an administrative law judge and a decision on the claim is currently between 10 and 11 months. Since a terminated recipient must first obtain a reconsideration decision as a prerequisite to invoking his right to an evidentiary hearing, the delay between the actual cutoff of benefits and final decision after a hearing exceeds one year.

In view of the torpidity of this administrative review process, and the typically modest resources of the family unit of the physically disabled worker, the hardship imposed upon the erroneously terminated disability recipient may be significant.

Still, the disabled worker's need is likely to be less than that of a welfare recipient. In addition to the possibility of access to private resources, other forms of government assistance will become available where the termination of disability benefits places a worker or his family below the subsistence level. In view of these potential sources of temporary income, there is less reason here than in *Goldberg* to depart from the ordinary principle, established by our decisions, that something less than an evidentiary hearing is sufficient prior to adverse administrative action.

An additional factor to be considered here is the fairness and reliability of the existing pretermination procedures, and the probable value, if any, of additional procedural safeguards. Central to the evaluation of any administrative process is the nature of the relevant inquiry. In order to remain eligible for benefits the disabled worker must demonstrate by means of "medically acceptable clinical and laboratory diagnostic techniques," that he is unable "to engage in any substantial gainful activity by reason of any *medically determinable* physical or mental impairment. . . ." (emphasis supplied). In short, a medical assessment of the worker's physical or mental condition is required. This is a more sharply focused and easily documented decision than the typical determination of welfare entitlement. In the latter case, a wide variety of information may be deemed relevant, and issues of witness credibility and veracity often are critical to the decisionmaking process. *Goldberg* noted that in such circumstances "written submissions are a wholly unsatisfactory basis for decision."

By contrast, the decision whether to discontinue disability benefits will turn, in most cases, upon "routine, standard, and unbiased medical reports by physician specialists," concerning a subject whom they have personally examined. . . . To be sure, credibility and veracity may be a factor in the ultimate disability assessment in some cases. But procedural due process rules are shaped by the risk of error inherent in the truthfinding process as applied to the generality of cases, not the rare exceptions. The potential value of an evidentiary hearing, or even oral presentation to the decisionmaker, is substantially less in this context than in *Goldberg*.

The decision in *Goldberg* also was based on the Court's conclusion that written submissions were an inadequate substitute for oral presentation because they did not provide an effective means for the recipient to communicate his case to the decisionmaker. Written submissions were viewed as an unrealistic option, for most recipients lacked the "educational attainment necessary to write effectively" and could not afford professional assistance. In addition, such submissions would not provide the "flexibility of oral presentations" or "permit the recipient to mold his argument to the issues the decision maker appears to regard as important." In the context of the disability-benefits-entitlement assessment the administrative procedures under review here fully answer these objections. . . .

A further safeguard against mistake is the policy of allowing the disability recipient's representative full access to all information relied upon by the state agency. In addition, prior to the cutoff of benefits the agency informs the recipient of its tentative assessment, the reasons therefor, and provides a summary of the evidence that it considers most relevant. Opportunity is then afforded the recipient to submit additional evidence or arguments, enabling him to challenge directly the accuracy of information in his file as well as the correctness of the agency's tentative conclusions. These procedures, again as contrasted with those before the Court in

Goldberg, enable the recipient to "mold" his argument to respond to the precise issues which the decisionmaker regards as crucial.

Despite these carefully structured procedures, amici point to the significant reversal rate for appealed cases as clear evidence that the current process is inadequate. Depending upon the base selected and the line of analysis followed, the relevant reversal rates urged by the contending parties vary from a high of 58.6% for appealed reconsideration decisions to an overall reversal rate of only 3.3%. Bare statistics rarely provide a satisfactory measure of the fairness of a decisionmaking process. Their adequacy is especially suspect here since the administrative review system is operated on an open-file basis. A recipient may always submit new evidence, and such submissions may result in additional medical examinations. Such fresh examinations were held in approximately 30% to 40% of the appealed cases, in fiscal 1973, either at the reconsideration or evidentiary hearing stage of the administrative process. In this context, the value of reversal rate statistics as one means of evaluating the adequacy of the pretermination process is diminished. Thus, although we view such information as relevant, it is certainly not controlling in this case.

In striking the appropriate due process balance the final factor to be assessed is the public interest. This includes the administrative burden and other societal costs that would be associated with requiring, as a matter of constitutional right, an evidentiary hearing upon demand in all cases prior to the termination of disability benefits. The most visible burden would be the incremental cost resulting from the increased number of hearings and the expense of providing benefits to ineligible recipients pending decision. No one can predict the extent of the increase, but the fact that full benefits would continue until after such hearings would assure the exhaustion in most cases of this attractive option. . . . We only need say that experience with the constitutionalizing of government procedures suggests that the ultimate additional cost in terms of money and administrative burden would not be insubstantial.

Financial cost alone is not a controlling weight in determining whether due process requires a particular procedural safeguard prior to some administrative decision. But the Government's interest, and hence that of the public, in conserving scarce fiscal and administrative resources is a factor that must be weighed. At some point the benefit of an additional safeguard to the individual affected by the administrative action and to society in terms of increased assurance that the action is just, may be outweighed by the cost. Significantly, the cost of protecting those whom the preliminary administrative process has identified as likely to be found undeserving may in the end come out of the pockets of the deserving since resources available for any particular program of social welfare are not unlimited.

But more is implicated in cases of this type than ad hoc weighing of fiscal and administrative burdens against the interests of a particular category of claimants. The ultimate balance involves a determination as to when, under our constitutional system, judicial-type procedures must be imposed upon administrative action to assure fairness. We reiterate the wise admonishment of Mr. Justice Frankfurter that differences in the origin and function of administrative agencies "preclude wholesale transplantation of the rules of procedure, trial and review which have evolved from the history and experience of courts." *FCC v. Pottsville Broadcasting Co.*, 309 U.S. 134, 143 (1940). The judicial model of an evidentiary hearing is neither a required, nor even the most effective, method of decisionmaking in all circumstances. The essence of due process is the requirement that "a person in jeopardy of serious loss [be given] notice of the case against him and opportunity to meet it." McGrath, at 171–172 (Frankfurter, J., concurring). All that is necessary is that the procedures be tailored, in light of the decision to be made, to "the capacities and circumstances of those who are to be heard," *Goldberg*, at 268–269, to insure that they are given a meaningful opportunity to present their case. In assessing what process is due in this case, substantial weight must be given to the good-faith judgments of the individuals charged by Congress with the administration of social welfare programs that the procedures they have provided assure fair consideration of the entitlement claims of individuals. This is especially so where, as here, the prescribed procedures not only provide the claimant with an effective process for asserting his claim prior to any administrative action, but also assure a right to an evidentiary hearing, as well as to subsequent judicial review, before the denial of his claim becomes final.

We conclude that an evidentiary hearing is not required prior to the termination of disability benefits and that the present administrative procedures fully comport with due process.

■ MR. JUSTICE BRENNAN, with whom MR. JUSTICE MARSHALL concurs, dissenting.

For the reasons stated in my dissenting opinion in *Richardson v. Wright*, 405 U.S. 208, 212 (1972), I agree with the District Court and the Court of Appeals that, prior to termination of benefits, Eldridge must be afforded an evidentiary hearing of the type required for welfare beneficiaries under Title IV of the Social Security Act. I would add that the Court's consideration that a discontinuance of disability benefits may cause the recipient to suffer only a limited deprivation is no argument. It is speculative. Moreover, the very legislative determination to provide disability benefits, without any prerequisite determination of need in fact, presumes a need by the recipient which is not this Court's function to denigrate. Indeed, in the present case, it is indicated that because disability benefits were terminated there was a foreclosure upon the Eldridge home and the family's furniture was repossessed, forcing Eldridge, his wife, and their children to sleep in one bed. Tr. of Oral Arg. 39, 47–48. Finally, it is also no argument that a worker, who has been placed in the untenable position of having been denied disability benefits, may still seek other forms of public assistance.

■ MR. JUSTICE STEVENS took no part in the consideration or decision of this petition.

NOTES

1.   Start with the threshold question for the Due Process Clauses: did Eldridge suffer a deprivation of life, liberty, or property? Next consider the Court's method for deciding whether "due process" has been given. What are the factors? How much weight does the Court give each factor? What happens if the interests strongly conflict? Are there other considerations the Court should have included?

2.   How would *Calder v. Bull* have been decided under the *Mathews* test? How would *Mathews* have been decided using the approach outlined in *Murray's Lessee*?

3.   Since *Mathews*, the Court has extended its balancing test to many contexts. The most prominent example is *Hamdi v. Rumsfeld*, 542 U.S. 507 (2004), p. 341. Hamdi was a U.S. citizen, captured in Afghanistan and held without trial in a naval brig off the coast of South Carolina. A majority of the Court applied the *Mathews* test to decide what

"due process" required for Hamdi. The detention interfered with his "liberty interests," and "the risk of erroneous deprivation of a citizen's liberty in the absence of sufficient process here is very real." "On the other side of the scale," the Court said, "are the weighty and sensitive governmental interests in ensuring that those who have in fact fought with the enemy during a war do not return to battle against the United States." Balancing these considerations, the Court concluded that Hamdi must receive "notice of the factual basis for his classification" as an enemy combatant, as well as "a fair opportunity to rebut the Government's factual assertions before a neutral decisionmaker." But the kind of hearing the Court prescribed was very different than a traditional common law trial: the Court expressly said hearsay evidence was permissible and there could be a presumption in favor of the government. In a dissenting opinion joined by Justice Stevens, Justice Scalia rejected the application of the *Mathews* balancing test: "The gist of the Due Process Clause, as understood at the founding and since, was to force the Government to follow those common-law procedures traditionally deemed necessary before depriving a person of life, liberty, or property. When a citizen was deprived of liberty because of alleged criminal conduct, those procedures typically required committal by a magistrate followed by indictment and trial." Justice Scalia's conclusion was that unless Congress were to suspend habeas corpus, Hamdi had to be either released or given a full criminal trial, with all of the procedural protections of the Bill of Rights and the common law. Is the *Mathews* balancing test helpful in thinking through the interests involved in *Hamdi*? Given the interests it was balancing, did the Court prescribe the right process? What are the strengths and weaknesses of applying a balancing test in this case? How would the case have come out under the approach to due process found in *Murray's Lessee*?

[*Assignment 76*]

B. INCORPORATION

The antebellum due process cases were concerned with the only Due Process Clause then existing in the Constitution, the one in the Fifth Amendment. That clause formed a crucial background for the framers and ratifiers of the Due Process Clause of the Fourteenth Amendment. For example, Representative John Bingham said the meaning of "due process" had been "settled long ago" by the courts. See p. 1282.

Nevertheless, after the ratification of the Fourteenth Amendment in 1868, there were new questions about what "due process" required of the states. The first major case involving these questions was *Hurtado v. California* (1884), presented here. In retrospect, it can be seen as a case about "incorporation," which is the question whether the Fourteenth Amendment made the Bill of Rights applicable to the states. In the twentieth century, incorporation would become one of the most widely discussed and controversial questions of constitutional law. Although it is less controversial now, it remains fundamental for a huge swathe of constitutional cases. Most cases about the Bill of Rights are brought against states—and all of these cases rest on the view that the Bill of Rights was made applicable against the states by the Fourteenth Amendment. The next case presented is *McDonald v. City of Chicago* (2010), the most recent major decision on incorporation. It summarizes this line of cases and offers a range of views about two key questions: (1) which part of the Fourteenth Amendment incorporates the Bill of Rights against the states, and (2) are *all* of the provisions of the Bill of Rights incorporated against the states?

The first of these cases, *Hurtado*, was about "due process" for a man convicted of murder and sentenced to capital punishment. At common law, no one could be convicted of murder without first being indicted by a grand jury. A grand jury was made up of citizens, sitting not to decide a particular case but to decide in a range of cases whether to issue indictments. Because the grand jury was thought to be an essential check on abuse of government power, the Fifth Amendment provides that no one could be prosecuted for a "capital, or otherwise infamous crime" without the approval of a grand jury. But the Fifth Amendment applied to the national government. What applied to the states was the Fourteenth Amendment, and specifically its Due Process Clause—did that clause require the use of a grand jury before someone could be convicted of a capital crime?

In the nineteenth century, critics of the grand jury argued that it was slow and secretive, and that it allowed a few unelected citizens to thwart the prosecution of crimes. Several states moved to lessen the use of the grand jury. One was California, and its constitution and penal statutes permitted offenses to be prosecuted either by "indictment" (the grand jury procedure) or by "information," a procedure in which the prosecutor alone would decide whether to bring the case. In California, Joseph Hurtado discovered his wife's affair with another man, and killed him. Hurtado was prosecuted using the information procedure, convicted, and sentenced to death. Hurtado argued that convicting him after a prosecution by information, rather than a prosecution by indictment, deprived him of his life and liberty in violation of the Due Process Clause of the Fourteenth Amendment. When the California Supreme Court rejected this argument, the United States Supreme Court took it up.

Hurtado v. California
110 U.S. 516 (1884)

■ MATTHEWS, J.

. . . It is claimed on behalf of the prisoner that the conviction and sentence are void, on the ground that they are repugnant to that clause of the fourteenth article of amendment to the constitution of the United States, which is in these words: "Nor shall any state deprive any person of life, liberty, or property without due process of law." The proposition of law we are asked to affirm is that an indictment or presentment by a grand jury, as known to the common law of England, is essential to that "due process of law," when applied to prosecutions for felonies, which is secured and guarantied by this provision of the constitution of the United States, and which accordingly it is forbidden to the states, respectively, to dispense with in the administration of criminal law. The question is one of grave and serious import, affecting both private and public rights and interests of great magnitude, and involves a consideration of what additional restrictions upon the legislative policy of the states has been imposed by the fourteenth amendment to the constitution of the United States. The supreme court of California, in the judgment now under review, . . . cites and relies upon a decision of the supreme court of Wisconsin in the case of *Rowan v. State*, 30 Wis. 129 (1872). In that case the court, speaking of the fourteenth amendment, says: "But its design was not to confine the states to a particular mode of procedure in judicial proceedings, and prohibit them from prosecuting for felonies by information instead of by indictment, if they chose to abolish the grand jury system. And the words 'due process of law' in the amendment do not mean and have not the effect to limit the powers of state governments to prosecutions for crime by indictment; but these words do mean law in its regular course of administration, according to prescribed forms, and in accordance with the general rules for the protection of individual rights. Administration and remedial proceedings must change, from time to time, with the advancement of legal science and the progress of society; and, if the people of the state find it wise and expedient to abolish the grand jury and prosecute all crimes by information, there is nothing in our state constitution and nothing in the fourteenth amendment to the constitution of the United States which prevents them from doing so."

On the other hand, it is maintained on behalf of the plaintiff in error that the phrase "due process of law" is equivalent to "law of the land," as found in the twenty-ninth chapter of *Magna Charta*; that by immemorial usage it has acquired a fixed, definite, and technical meaning; that it refers to and includes, not only the general principles of public liberty and private right, which lie at the foundation of all free government, but the very institutions which, venerable by time and custom, have been tried by experience and found fit and necessary for the preservation of those principles, and which, having been the birthright and inheritance of every English subject, crossed the Atlantic with the colonists and were transplanted and established in the fundamental laws of the state; that, having been originally introduced into the constitution of the United States as a limitation upon the powers of the government, brought into being by that instrument, it has now been added as an additional security to the individual against oppression by the states themselves; that one of these institutions is that of the grand jury, an indictment or presentment by which against the accused in cases of alleged felonies is an essential part of due process of law, in order that he may not be harassed and destroyed by prosecutions founded only upon private malice or popular fury. . . .

[The Court first considers Lord Coke's view of the "law of the land" provision in Magna Carta and "due process."—Editors]

Chancellor KENT, (2 Comm. 13,) adopts this mode of construing the phrase. Quoting the language of *Magna Charta*, and referring to Lord COKE's comment upon it, he says: "The better and larger definition of *due process of law* is that it means law in its regular course of administration through courts of justice." This accords with what is said in *Westervelt v. Gregg*, 12 N.Y. 202 (1854), by DENIO, J., p. 212: "The provision was designed to protect the citizen against all mere acts of power, whether flowing from the legislative or executive branches of the government." The principle and true meaning of the phrase have never been more tersely or accurately stated than by Mr. Justice JOHNSON in *Bank of Columbia v. Okely*, 17 U.S. (4 Wheat.) 235, 244 (1819): "As to the words from *Magna Charta*, incorporated into the constitution of Maryland, after volumes spoken and written with a view to their exposition, the good sense of mankind has at last settled down to this: that they were intended to secure the individual from the arbitrary exercise of the powers of government, unrestrained by the established principles of private right and distributive justice." And the conclusion rightly deduced is as stated by Mr. Cooley, "The principles, then, upon which the process is based, are to determine whether it is 'due process' or not, and not any considerations of mere form. Administrative and remedial process may be changed from time to time, but only with due regard to the landmarks established for the protection of the citizen."

It is urged upon us, however, in argument, that the claim made in behalf of the plaintiff in error is supported by the decision of this court in *Murray's Lessee v. Hoboken Land & Imp. Co.*, 59 U.S. (18 How.) 272 (1855). There, Mr. Justice CURTIS, delivering the opinion of the court, after showing that due process of law must mean something more then the actual existing law of the land, for otherwise it would be no restraint upon legislative power, proceeds as follows: "To what principle, then, are we to resort to ascertain whether this process, enacted by congress, is due process? To this the answer must be twofold. We must examine the constitution itself to see whether this process be in conflict with any of its provisions. If not found to be so, we must look to those settled usages and modes of proceeding existing in the common and statute law of England before the emigration of our ancestors, and which are shown not to have been unsuited to their civil and political condition by having been acted on by them after the settlement of this country." This, it is argued, furnishes an indispensable test of what constitutes "due process of law"; that any proceeding otherwise authorized by law, which is not thus sanctioned by usage, or which supersedes and displaces one that is, cannot be regarded as due process of law. But this inference is unwarranted. The real syllabus of the passage quoted is that a process of law, which is not otherwise forbidden, must be taken to be due process of law, if it can show the sanction of settled usage both in England and in this country; but it by no means follows, that nothing else can be due process of law. The point in the case cited arose in reference to a summary proceeding, questioned on that account as not due process of law. The answer was, however exceptional it may be, as tested by definitions and principles of ordinary procedure, nevertheless, this, in substance, has been immemorially the actual law of the land, and, therefore, is due process of law. But to hold that such a characteristic is essential to due process of law, would be to deny every quality of the law but its age, and to render it incapable of progress or improvement. It would be to stamp upon our jurisprudence the unchangeableness attributed to the laws of the Medes and Persians.

This would be all the more singular and surprising, in this quick and active age, when we consider that, owing to the progressive development of legal ideas and institutions in England, the words of *Magna Charta* stood for very different things at the time of the separation of the American colonies from what they represented originally. . . . [T]he primitive grand jury heard no witnesses in support of the truth of the charges to be preferred, but presented upon their own knowledge, or indicted upon common fame and general suspicion, we shall be ready to acknowledge that it is better not to go too far back into antiquity for the best securities for our "ancient liberties." It is more consonant to the true philosophy of our historical legal institutions to say that the spirit of personal liberty and individual right, which they embodied, was preserved and developed by a progressive growth and wise adaptation to new circumstances and situations of the forms and processes found fit to give, from time to time, new expression and greater effect to modern ideas of self-government. . . .

This flexibility and capacity for growth and adaptation is the peculiar boast and excellence of the common law. . . .

The constitution of the United States was ordained, it is true, by descendants of Englishmen, who inherited the traditions of the English law and history; but it was made for an undefined and expanding future, and for a people gathered, and to be gathered, from many nations and of many tongues; and while we take just pride in the principles and institutions of the common law, we are not to forget that in lands where other systems of jurisprudence prevail, the ideas and processes of civil justice are also not unknown. Due process of law, in spite of the absolutism of continental governments, is not alien to that Code which survived the Roman empire as the foundation of modern civilization in Europe. . . .

The concessions of *Magna Charta* were wrung from the king as guaranties against the oppressions and usurpations of his prerogative. It did not enter into the minds of the barons to provide security against their own body or in favor of the commons by limiting the power of parliament; so that bills of attainder, *ex post facto* laws, laws declaring forfeitures of estates, and other arbitrary acts of legislation which occur so frequently in English history, were never regarded as inconsistent with the law of the land; for notwithstanding what was attributed to Lord COKE in *Bonham's Case*, 8 Reporter, 115, 118*a* (1610), the omnipotence of parliament over the common law was absolute, even against common right and reason. The actual and practical security for English liberty against legislative tyranny was the power of a free public opinion represented by the commons. In this country written constitutions were deemed essential to protect the rights and liberties of the people against the encroachments of power delegated to their governments, and the provisions of *Magna Charta* were incorporated into bills of rights. They were limitations upon all the powers of government, legislative as well as executive and judicial. It necessarily happened, therefore, that as these broad and general maxims of liberty and justice had in our system a different place and performed a different function from their position and office in English constitutional history and law, they would receive and justify a corresponding and more comprehensive interpretation. Applied in England only as guards against executive usurpation and tyranny, here they have become bulwarks also against arbitrary legislation; but in that application, as it would be incongruous to measure and restrict them by the ancient customary English law, they must be held to guaranty, not particular forms of procedure, but the very substance of individual rights to life, liberty, and property. . . .

We are to construe this phrase in the fourteenth amendment by the *usus loquendi [i.e., habit of speaking—Editors]* of the constitution itself. The same words are contained in the fifth amendment. That article makes specific and express provision for perpetuating the institution of the grand jury, so far as relates to prosecutions for the more aggravated crimes under the laws of the United States. . . . According to a recognized canon of interpretation, especially applicable to formal and solemn instruments of constitutional law, we are forbidden to assume, without clear reason to the contrary, that any part of this most important amendment is superfluous. The natural and obvious inference is that, in the sense of the constitution, "due process of law" was not meant or intended to include, *ex vi termini [i.e., by force of the term—Editors]*, the institution and procedure of a grand jury in any case. The conclusion is equally irresistible, that when the same phrase was employed in the fourteenth amendment to restrain the action of the states, it was used in the same sense and with no greater extent; and that if in the adoption of that amendment it had been part of its purpose to perpetuate the institution of the grand jury in all the states, it would have embodied, as did the fifth amendment, express declarations to that effect. Due process of law in the latter refers to that law of the land which derives its authority from the legislative powers conferred upon congress by the constitution of the United States, exercised within the limits therein prescribed, and interpreted according to the principles of the common law. In the fourteenth amendment, by parity of reason, it refers to that law of the land in each state which derives its authority from the inherent and reserved powers of the state, exerted within the limits of those fundamental principles of liberty and justice which lie at the base of all our civil and political institutions, and the greatest security for which resides in the right of the people to make their own laws, and alter them at their pleasure. "The fourteenth amendment," as was said by Mr. Justice BRADLEY in *Missouri v. Lewis*, 101 U.S. 22, 31 (1879), "does not profess to secure to all persons in the United States the benefit of the same laws and the same remedies. Great diversities in these respects may exist in two states separated only by an imaginary line. On one side of this line there may be a right of trial by jury, and on the other side no such right. Each state prescribes its own modes of judicial proceeding."

But it is not to be supposed that these legislative powers are absolute and despotic, and that the amendment prescribing due process of law is too vague and indefinite to operate as a practical restraint. It is not every act, legislative in form, that is law. Law is something more than mere will exerted as an act of power. It must be not a special rule for a particular person or a particular case, but, in the language of Mr. Webster, in his familiar definition, "the general law, a law which hears before it condemns, which proceeds upon inquiry, and renders judgment only after trial," so "that every citizen shall hold his life, liberty, property, and immunities under the protection of the general rules which govern society," and thus excluding, as not due process of law, acts of attainder, bills of pains and penalties, acts of confiscation, acts reversing judgments, and acts directly transferring one man's estate to another, legislative judgments and decrees, and other similar special, partial, and arbitrary exertions of power under the forms of legislation. Abritrary power, enforcing its edicts to the injury of the persons and property of its subjects, is not law, whether manifested as the decree of a personal monarch or of an impersonal multitude. And the limitations imposed by our constitutional law upon the action of the governments, both state and national, are essential to the preservation of public and private rights, notwithstanding the representative character of our political institutions. The enforcement of these limitations by judicial process is the device of self-governing communities to protect the rights of individuals and minorities, as well against the power of numbers, as against the violence of public agents transcending the limits of lawful authority, even when acting in the name and wielding the force of the government. . . .

It follows that any legal proceeding enforced by public authority, whether sanctioned by age and custom, or newly devised in the discretion of the legislative power in furtherance of the general public good, which regards and preserves these principles of liberty and justice, must be held to be due process of law. . . .

Tried by these principles, we are unable to say that the substitution for a presentment or indictment by a grand jury of the proceeding by information after examination and commitment by a magistrate, certifying to the probable guilt of the defendant, with the right on his part to the aid of counsel, and to the cross-examination of the witnesses produced for the prosecution, is not due process of law. It is, as we have seen, an ancient proceeding at common law, which might include every case of an offense of less grade than a felony, except misprision of treason; and in every circumstance of its administration, as authorized by the statute of California, it carefully considers and guards the substantial interest of the prisoner.

It is merely a preliminary proceeding, and can result in no final judgment, except as the consequence of a regular judicial trial, conducted precisely as in cases of indictments. . . .

For these reasons, finding no error therein, the judgment of the supreme court of California is affirmed.

■ HARLAN, J., dissenting.

. . . My brethren concede that there are principles of liberty and justice lying at the foundation of our civil and political institutions which no state can violate consistently with that due process of law required by the fourteenth amendment in proceedings involving life, liberty, or property. Some of these principles are enumerated in the opinion of the court. But for reasons which do not impress my mind as satisfactory, they exclude from that enumeration the exemption from prosecution, by information, for a public offense involving life. By what authority is that exclusion made? Is it justified by the settled usages and modes of proceeding existing under the common and statute law of England at the emigration of our ancestors, or at the foundation of our government? Does not the fact that the people of the original states required quired an amendment of the national constitution, securing exemption from prosecution for a capital offense, except upon the indictment or presentment of a grand jury, prove that, in their judgment, such an exemption was essential to protection against accusation and unfounded prosecution, and therefore was a fundamental principle in liberty and justice? By the side of that exemption, in the same amendment, is the declaration that no person shall be put twice in jeopardy for the same offense, nor compelled to criminate himself, nor shall private property be taken for public use without just compensation. Are not these principles fundamental in every free government established to maintain liberty and justice? If it be supposed that immunity from prosecution for a capital offense, except upon the presentment or indictment of a grand jury, was regarded at the common law any less secured by the law of the land, or any less valuable, or any less essential to due process of law, than the personal rights and immunities just enumerated, I take leave to say that no such distinction is authorized by any adjudged case, determined in England or in this country prior to the adoption of our constitution, or by any elementary writer upon the principles established by *Magna Charta* and the statutes subsequently enacted in explanation or enlargement of its provisions. . . .

It is said by the court that the constitution of the United States was made for an undefined and expanding future, and that its requirement of due process of law, in proceedings involving life, liberty, and property, must be so interpreted as not to deny to the law the capacity of progress and improvement; that the greatest security for the fundamental principles of justice resides in the right of the people to make their own laws and alter them at pleasure. It is difficult, however, to perceive anything in the system of prosecuting human beings for their lives, by information, which suggests that the state which adopts it has entered upon an era of progess and improvement in the law of criminal procedure. Even the statute of Henry VII. c. 3, allowing informations, and under which, it is said, Empson and Dudley, and an arbitrary star chamber, fashioned the proceedings of the law into a thousand tyrannical forms, expressly declared that it should not extend "to treason, murder, or felony, or to any other offense wherefor any person should lose life or member." So great, however, were the outrages perpetrated by those men that this statute was repealed by 1 Henry VIII. *c.* 6. Under the local statutes in question, even the district attorney of the county is deprived of any discretion in the premises; for if in the judgment of the magistrate before whom the accused is brought—and, generally, he is only a justice of the peace—a public offense has been committed, it becomes the duty of the district attorney to proceed against him, by information, for the offense indicated by the committing magistrate. Thus, in California nothing stands between the citizen and prosecution for his life except the judgment of a justice of the peace. . . . Anglo-Saxon liberty would, perhaps, have perished long before the adoption of our constitution had it been in the power of government to put the subject on trial for his life whenever a justice of the peace, holding his office at the will of the crown, should certify that he had committed a capital crime. That such officers are, in some of the states, elected by the people, does not add to the protection of the citizen; for one of the peculiar benefits of the grand-jury system, as it exists in this country, is that it is composed, as a general rule, of private persons *who do not hold office at the will of the government, or at the will of voters.* In most, if not all of the states, civil officers are disqualified to sit on grand juries. In the secrecy of the investigations by grand juries, the weak and helpless—proscribed, perhaps, because of their race, or pursued by an unreasoning public clamor—have found, and will continue to find, security against official oppression, the cruelty of mobs, the machinations of falsehood, and the malevolence of private persons who would use the machinery of the law to bring ruin upon their personal enemies. "The grand juries perform," says STORY, "most important public functions, and are a great security to the citizens against vindictive prosecutions, either by the government or by political partisans, or by private enemies." Story, Const. § 1785. . . .

NOTES

1.   *Murray's Lessee* considered what the Fifth Amendment's Due Process Clause required of the federal government. In deciding that question, the Court could look to the other provisions of the Bill of Rights to inform the meaning of "due process." But when the Court decided *Hurtado*, it had not yet begun to apply provisions of the Bill of Rights directly to the states, and so the question answered by the majority was about what was required by the Due Process Clause of the Fourteenth Amendment, standing alone. Unlike the federal government in *Murray's Lessee*, California in *Hurtado* had departed from established common law procedures, allowing prosecution for felonies by information rather than by indictment. So the question was flipped: established common law procedures were *sufficient* to satisfy due process, but were they *necessary*? How does the Court answer that question?

2.   In *Hurtado* the information procedure had been prescribed by the state constitution and by statute. What did the Court see as the nature of the inquiry when deciding whether a legislatively prescribed procedure afforded "due process"? No inquiry, because what the legislature prescribed just *was* due process? An inquiry into whether the act was reasonable or just? An inquiry into whether it had the generality and other features traditionally associated with due process? Or something else?

3.   On which points do the majority and dissent disagree? The majority treats the case as not being about incorporation as much as about the independent meaning of "due process," while the dissent invokes the idea of incorporation. The majority hails the information procedure as a mark of progress, while the dissent considers it a step backward. The majority suggests that the judicial process (e.g., a criminal trial) will check abusive prosecutions, while the dissent warns that the protection of the grand jury is

most needed by the vulnerable, including political enemies and racial minorities. On each point, which side do you think is right?

McDonald v. City of Chicago
561 U.S. 742 (2010)

■ JUSTICE ALITO announced the judgment of the Court and delivered the opinion of the Court with respect to Parts I, II-A, II-B, II-D, III-A, and III-B, . . . and an opinion with respect to Parts II-C, IV, and V, in which THE CHIEF JUSTICE, JUSTICE SCALIA, and JUSTICE KENNEDY join.

Two years ago, in *District of Columbia v. Heller*, 554 U.S. 570 (2008), we held that the Second Amendment protects the right to keep and bear arms for the purpose of self-defense, and we struck down a District of Columbia law that banned the possession of handguns in the home. The city of Chicago (City) and the village of Oak Park, a Chicago suburb, have laws that are similar to the District of Columbia's, but Chicago and Oak Park argue that their laws are constitutional because the Second Amendment has no application to the States. We have previously held that most of the provisions of the Bill of Rights apply with full force to both the Federal Government and the States. Applying the standard that is well established in our case law, we hold that the Second Amendment right is fully applicable to the States. . . .

II–A

Petitioners argue that the Chicago and Oak Park laws violate the right to keep and bear arms for two reasons. Petitioners' primary submission is that this right is among the "privileges or immunities of citizens of the United States" and that the narrow interpretation of the Privileges or Immunities Clause adopted in the *Slaughter-House Cases*, 83 U.S. (16 Wall.) 36 (1873), should now be rejected. As a secondary argument, petitioners contend that the Fourteenth Amendment's Due Process Clause "incorporates" the Second Amendment right. . . .

B

The Bill of Rights, including the Second Amendment, originally applied only to the Federal Government. In *Barron ex rel. Tiernan v. Mayor of Baltimore*, 32 U.S. (7 Pet.) 243 (1833), . . . the Court firmly rejected the proposition that the first eight Amendments operate as limitations on the States, holding that they apply only to the Federal Government.

The constitutional Amendments adopted in the aftermath of the Civil War fundamentally altered our country's federal system. The provision at issue in this case, § 1 of the Fourteenth Amendment, provides, among other things, that a State may not abridge "the privileges or immunities of citizens of the United States" or deprive "any person of life, liberty, or property, without due process of law."

Four years after the adoption of the Fourteenth Amendment, this Court was asked to interpret the Amendment's reference to "the privileges or immunities of citizens of the United States" [in the] *Slaughter-House Cases*. . . .

In drawing a sharp distinction between the rights of federal and state citizenship, the Court relied on two principal arguments. First, the Court emphasized that the Fourteenth Amendment's Privileges or Immunities Clause spoke of "the privileges or immunities of *citizens of the United States,*" and the Court contrasted this phrasing with the wording in the first sentence of the Fourteenth Amendment and in the Privileges and Immunities Clause of Article IV, both of which refer to *state* citizenship. (Emphasis added.) Second, the Court stated that a contrary reading would "radically chang[e] the whole theory of the relations of the State and Federal governments to each other and of both these governments to the people," and the Court refused to conclude that such a change had been made "in the absence of language which expresses such a purpose too clearly to admit of doubt." . . .

Three years after the decision in the *Slaughter-House Cases,* the Court decided *United States v. Cruikshank,* 92 U.S. 542 (1876). . . . In that case, the Court reviewed convictions stemming from the infamous Colfax Massacre in Louisiana on Easter Sunday 1873. Dozens of blacks, many unarmed, were slaughtered by a rival band of armed white men. Cruikshank himself allegedly marched unarmed African-American prisoners through the streets and then had them summarily executed. Ninety-seven men were indicted for participating in the massacre, but only nine went to trial. Six of the nine were acquitted of all charges; the remaining three were acquitted of murder but convicted under the Enforcement Act of 1870, 16 Stat. 140, for banding and conspiring together to deprive their victims of various constitutional rights, including the right to bear arms.

The Court reversed all of the convictions, including those relating to the deprivation of the victims' right to bear arms. The Court wrote that the right of bearing arms for a lawful purpose "is not a right granted by the Constitution" and is not "in any manner dependent upon that instrument for its existence." *Id.,* at 553. "The second amendment," the Court continued, "declares that it shall not be infringed; but this . . . means no more than that it shall not be infringed by Congress." *Ibid.* "Our later decisions in *Presser v. Illinois,* 116 U.S. 252, 26 (1886), and *Miller v. Texas,* 153 U.S. 535, 538 (1894), reaffirmed that the Second Amendment applies only to the Federal Government." *Heller,* at 620 n. 23.

C

. . . Petitioners argue, however, that we should overrule [*Cruikshank, Presser,* and *Miller*] and hold that the right to keep and bear arms is one of the "privileges or immunities of citizens of the United States." In petitioners' view, the Privileges or Immunities Clause protects all of the rights set out in the Bill of Rights, as well as some others, but petitioners are unable to identify the Clause's full scope. Nor is there any consensus on that question among the scholars who agree that the *Slaughter-House Cases'* interpretation is flawed.

We see no need to reconsider that interpretation here. For many decades, the question of the rights protected by the Fourteenth Amendment against state infringement has been analyzed under the Due Process Clause of that Amendment and not under the Privileges or Immunities Clause. We therefore decline to disturb the *Slaughter-House* holding.

At the same time, however, this Court's decisions in *Cruikshank, Presser,* and *Miller* do not preclude us from considering whether the Due Process Clause of the Fourteenth Amendment makes the Second Amendment right binding on the States. See *Heller,* at 620 n. 23. None of those cases "engage[d] in the sort of Fourteenth Amendment inquiry required by our later cases." *Ibid.* As explained more fully below, *Cruikshank, Presser,* and *Miller* all preceded the era in which the Court began the process of "selective incorporation" under the Due Process Clause, and we have never previously addressed the question whether the right to keep and bear arms applies to the States under that theory. . . .

D–1

In the late 19th century, the Court began to consider whether the Due Process Clause prohibits the States from infringing rights set out in the Bill of Rights. See *Hurtado v. California*, 110 U.S. 516 (1884) (due process does not require grand jury indictment). Five features of the approach taken during the ensuing era should be noted.

First, the Court viewed the due process question as entirely separate from the question whether a right was a privilege or immunity of national citizenship. See *Twining v. New Jersey*, 211 U.S. 78, 99 (1908).

Second, the Court explained that the only rights protected against state infringement by the Due Process Clause were those rights "of such a nature that they are included in the conception of due process of law." *Ibid*. While it was "possible that some of the personal rights safeguarded by the first eight Amendments against National action [might] also be safeguarded against state action," the Court stated, this was "not because those rights are enumerated in the first eight Amendments." *Ibid*.

The Court used different formulations in describing the boundaries of due process. For example, in *Twining*, the Court referred to "immutable principles of justice which inhere in the very idea of free government which no member of the Union may disregard." In *Snyder v. Massachusetts*, 291 U.S. 97, 105 (1934), the Court spoke of rights that are "so rooted in the traditions and conscience of our people as to be ranked as fundamental." And in *Palko v. Connecticut*, 302 U.S. 319, 325 (1937), the Court famously said that due process protects those rights that are "the very essence of a scheme of ordered liberty" and essential to "a fair and enlightened system of justice."

Third, in some cases decided during this era the Court "can be seen as having asked, when inquiring into whether some particular procedural safeguard was required of a State, if a civilized system could be imagined that would not accord the particular protection." *Duncan v. Louisiana*, 391 U.S. 145, 149, n. 14 (1968). . . .

Fourth, the Court during this era was not hesitant to hold that a right set out in the Bill of Rights failed to meet the test for inclusion within the protection of the Due Process Clause. The Court found that some such rights qualified. See, *e.g.*, *Gitlow v. New York*, 268 U.S. 652, 666 (1925) (freedom of speech and press); *Powell v. Alabama*, 287 U.S. 45 (1932) (assistance of counsel in capital cases); *De Jonge v. Oregon*, 299 U.S. 353, 364 (1937) (freedom of assembly); *Cantwell v. Connecticut*, 310 U.S. 296 (1940) (free exercise of religion). But others did not. See, *e.g.*, *Hurtado* (grand jury indictment requirement); *Twining* (privilege against self-incrimination).

Finally, even when a right set out in the Bill of Rights was held to fall within the conception of due process, the protection or remedies afforded against state infringement sometimes differed from the protection or remedies provided against abridgment by the Federal Government. To give one example, in *Betts v. Brady*, 316 U.S. 455, 473 (1942), the Court held that, although the Sixth Amendment required the appointment of counsel in all federal criminal cases in which the defendant was unable to retain an attorney, the Due Process Clause required appointment of counsel in state criminal proceedings only where "want of counsel in [the] particular case . . . result[ed] in a conviction lacking in . . . fundamental fairness." . . .

2

An alternative theory regarding the relationship between the Bill of Rights and § 1 of the Fourteenth Amendment was championed by Justice Black. This theory held that § 1 of the Fourteenth Amendment totally incorporated all of the provisions of the Bill of Rights. See, *e.g., Adamson v. California,* 332 U.S. 46, 71–72 (1947) (Black, J. dissenting)*; Duncan,* at 166 (Black, J., concurring). As Justice Black noted, the chief congressional proponents of the Fourteenth Amendment espoused the view that the Amendment made the Bill of Rights applicable to the States and, in so doing, overruled this Court's decision in *Barron.*[9] Nonetheless, the Court never has embraced Justice Black's "total incorporation" theory.

3

While Justice Black's theory was never adopted, the Court eventually moved in that direction by initiating what has been called a process of "selective incorporation," *i.e.,* the Court began to hold that the Due Process Clause fully incorporates particular rights contained in the first eight Amendments.

The decisions during this time abandoned three of the previously noted characteristics of the earlier period. The Court made it clear that the governing standard is not whether *any* "civilized system [can] be imagined that would not accord the particular protection." *Duncan,* at 149, n. 14. Instead, the Court inquired whether a particular Bill of Rights guarantee is fundamental to *our* scheme of ordered liberty and system of justice. *Id.,* at 149, and n. 14.

The Court also shed any reluctance to hold that rights guaranteed by the Bill of Rights met the requirements for protection under the Due Process Clause. The Court eventually incorporated almost all of the provisions of the Bill of Rights.[12] Only a handful of the Bill of Rights protections remain unincorporated.[13]

---

[9]   Senator Jacob Howard, who spoke on behalf of the Joint Committee on Reconstruction and sponsored the Amendment in the Senate, stated that the Amendment protected all of "the personal rights guarantied and secured by the first eight amendments of the Constitution." Cong. Globe, 39th Cong., 1st Sess., 2765 (1866) (hereinafter 39th Cong. Globe). Representative John Bingham, the principal author of the text of § 1, said that the Amendment would "arm the Congress . . . with the power to enforce the bill of rights as it stands in the Constitution today." *Id.,* at 1088. . . . See also M. Curtis, No State Shall Abridge: The Fourteenth Amendment and the Bill of Rights 112 (1986) (counting at least 30 statements during the debates in Congress interpreting § 1 to incorporate the Bill of Rights).

[12]   *[This footnote cites cases standing for the proposition that the following provisions of the Bill of Rights are incorporated against the states: First Amendment—Establishment Clause, Free Exercise Clause, freedom of assembly, free speech, freedom of the press; Fourth Amendment—warrant requirement, exclusionary rule, freedom from unreasonable searches and seizures; Fifth Amendment—Double Jeopardy Clause, privilege against self-incrimination, Just Compensationi Clause; Sixth Amendment—trial by jury in criminal cases, compulsory process, speedy trial, right to confront adverse witness, assistance of counsel, right to a public trial; Eighth Amendment—cruel and unusual punishment, prohibition against excessive bail.—Editors]*

[13]   In addition to the right to keep and bear arms (and the Sixth Amendment right to a unanimous jury verdict), the only rights not fully incorporated are (1) the Third Amendment's protection against quartering of soldiers; (2) the Fifth Amendment's grand jury indictment requirement; (3) the Seventh Amendment right to a jury trial in civil cases; and (4) the Eighth Amendment's prohibition on excessive fines. . . . *[The Court noted that it had not considered the incorporation of the Third Amendment or the Eighth Amendment's prohibition of excessive fines, and that its decisions on the Fifth Amendment's Grand Jury Clause and the Seventh Amendment's civil jury requirement "long predate the era of selective incorporation."—Editors]*

Finally, the Court abandoned "the notion that the Fourteenth Amendment applies to the States only a watered-down, subjective version of the individual guarantees of the Bill of Rights," stating that it would be "incongruous" to apply different standards "depending on whether the claim was asserted in a state or federal court." *Malloy v. Hogan*, 378 U.S. 1, 10–11 (1964). Instead, the Court decisively held that incorporated Bill of Rights protections "are all to be enforced against the States under the Fourteenth Amendment according to the same standards that protect those personal rights against federal encroachment." *Id*. at 10. . . .

III

With this framework in mind, we now turn directly to the question whether the Second Amendment right to keep and bear arms is incorporated in the concept of due process. In answering that question, as just explained, we must decide whether the right to keep and bear arms is fundamental to *our* scheme of ordered liberty, *Duncan*, at 149, or as we have said in a related context, whether this right is "deeply rooted in this Nation's history and tradition," *Washington v. Glucksberg*, 521 U.S. 702, 721 (1997).

Our decision in *Heller* points unmistakably to the answer. Self-defense is a basic right, recognized by many legal systems from ancient times to the present day, and in *Heller*, we held that individual self-defense is "the central component " of the Second Amendment right. . . .

Heller explored the right's origins, noting that the 1689 English Bill of Rights explicitly protected a right to keep arms for self-defense, and that by 1765, Blackstone was able to assert that the right to keep and bear arms was "one of the fundamental rights of Englishmen," 554 U.S., at 594. . . .

The right to keep and bear arms was considered no less fundamental by those who drafted and ratified the Bill of Rights. . . . Antifederalists and Federalists alike agreed that the right to bear arms was fundamental to the newly formed system of government. But those who were fearful that the new Federal Government would infringe traditional rights such as the right to keep and bear arms insisted on the adoption of the Bill of Rights as a condition for ratification of the Constitution. This is surely powerful evidence that the right was regarded as fundamental in the sense relevant here. . . .

By the 1850's, the perceived threat that had prompted the inclusion of the Second Amendment in the Bill of Rights—the fear that the National Government would disarm the universal militia—had largely faded as a popular concern, but the right to keep and bear arms was highly valued for purposes of self-defense. . . .

After the Civil War, many of the over 180,000 African-Americans who served in the Union Army returned to the States of the old Confederacy, where systematic efforts were made to disarm them and other blacks. The laws of some States formally prohibited African-Americans from possessing firearms. . . .

Throughout the South, armed parties, often consisting of ex-Confederate soldiers serving in the state militias, forcibly took firearms from newly freed slaves. In the first session of the 39th Congress, Senator Henry Wilson told his colleagues: "In Mississippi rebel State forces, men who were in the rebel armies, are traversing the State, visiting the freedmen, disarming them, perpetrating murders and outrages upon them; and the same things are done in other sections of the country." 39th Cong. Globe 40 (1865). . . .

Union Army commanders took steps to secure the right of all citizens to keep and bear arms, but the 39th Congress concluded that legislative action was necessary. Its efforts to safeguard the right to keep and bear arms demonstrate that the right was still recognized to be fundamental.

The most explicit evidence of Congress' aim appears in § 14 of the Freedmen's Bureau Act of 1866, which provided that "the right . . . to have full and equal benefit of all laws and proceedings concerning personal liberty, personal security, and the acquisition, enjoyment, and disposition of estate, real and personal, *including the constitutional right to bear arms,* shall be secured to and enjoyed by all the citizens . . . without respect to race or color, or previous condition of slavery." 14 Stat. 176–177 (emphasis added). . . .

Congress, however, ultimately deemed these legislative remedies insufficient. Southern resistance, Presidential vetoes, and this Court's pre-Civil-War precedent persuaded Congress that a constitutional amendment was necessary to provide full protection for the rights of blacks. . . .

In debating the Fourteenth Amendment, the 39th Congress referred to the right to keep and bear arms as a fundamental right deserving of protection. Senator Samuel Pomeroy described three "indispensable" "safeguards of liberty under our form of Government." 39th Cong. Globe 1182. One of these, he said, was the right to keep and bear arms:

> "Every man . . . should have the right to bear arms for the defense of himself and family and his homestead. And if the cabin door of the freedman is broken open and the intruder enters for purposes as vile as were known to slavery, then should a well-loaded musket be in the hand of the occupant to send the polluted wretch to another world, where his wretchedness will forever remain complete." . . .

The right to keep and bear arms was also widely protected by state constitutions at the time when the Fourteenth Amendment was ratified. In 1868, 22 of the 37 States in the Union had state constitutional provisions explicitly protecting the right to keep and bear arms. See Calabresi & Agudo, *Individual Rights Under State Constitutions when the Fourteenth Amendment was Ratified in 1868: What Rights Are Deeply Rooted in American History and Tradition?* 87 Texas L. Rev. 7, 50 (2008). . . .

In sum, it is clear that the Framers and ratifiers of the Fourteenth Amendment counted the right to keep and bear arms among those fundamental rights necessary to our system of ordered liberty. . . .

V

. . . As we have explained, the Court, for the past half century, has moved away from the two-track approach. If we were now to accept JUSTICE STEVENS' theory across the board, decades of decisions would be undermined. We assume that this is not what is proposed. What is urged instead, it appears, is that this theory be revived solely for the individual right that *Heller* recognized, over vigorous dissents.

The relationship between the Bill of Rights' guarantees and the States must be governed by a single, neutral principle. It is far too late to exhume what Justice

Brennan, writing for the Court 46 years ago, derided as "the notion that the Fourteenth Amendment applies to the States only a watered-down, subjective version of the individual guarantees of the Bill of Rights." *Malloy*, at 10–11. . . .

■ JUSTICE THOMAS, concurring in part and concurring in the judgment.

I agree with the Court that the Fourteenth Amendment makes the right to keep and bear arms set forth in the Second Amendment "fully applicable to the States." I write separately because I believe there is a more straightforward path to this conclusion, one that is more faithful to the Fourteenth Amendment's text and history. . . .

I cannot agree that it is enforceable against the States through a clause that speaks only to "process." Instead, the right to keep and bear arms is a privilege of American citizenship that applies to the States through the Fourteenth Amendment's Privileges or Immunities Clause.

I

. . . [In the Fourteenth Amendment, the second] sentence begins with the command that "[n]o State shall make or enforce any law which shall abridge the privileges or immunities of citizens of the United States." On its face, this appears to grant the persons just made United States citizens a certain collection of rights—*i.e.,* privileges or immunities—attributable to that status.

This Court's precedents accept that point, but define the relevant collection of rights quite narrowly. In the *Slaughter-House Cases,* decided just five years after the Fourteenth Amendment's adoption, the Court . . . arguably left open the possibility that certain individual rights enumerated in the Constitution could be considered privileges or immunities of federal citizenship. See 83 U.S. (16 Wall.), at 79 (listing "[t]he right to peaceably assemble" and "the privilege of the writ of *habeas corpus*" as rights potentially protected by the Privileges or Immunities Clause). But the Court soon rejected that proposition, interpreting the Privileges or Immunities Clause even more narrowly in its later cases.

Chief among those cases is *United States v. Cruikshank.* There, the Court held that members of a white militia who had brutally murdered as many as 165 black Louisianians congregating outside a courthouse had not deprived the victims of their privileges as American citizens to peaceably assemble or to keep and bear arms. According to the Court, the right to peaceably assemble codified in the First Amendment was not a privilege of United States citizenship because "[t]he right . . . existed long *before* the adoption of the Constitution." 92 U.S., at 551 (emphasis added). Similarly, the Court held that the right to keep and bear arms was not a privilege of United States citizenship because it was not "in any manner dependent upon that instrument for its existence." *Id.,* at 553. In other words, the reason the Framers codified the right to bear arms in the Second Amendment—its nature as an inalienable right that pre-existed the Constitution's adoption—was the very reason citizens could not enforce it against States through the Fourteenth.

That circular reasoning effectively has been the Court's last word on the Privileges or Immunities Clause. In the intervening years, the Court has held that the Clause prevents state abridgment of only a handful of rights, such as the right to travel, that are not readily described as essential to liberty.

As a consequence of this Court's marginalization of the Clause, litigants seeking federal protection of fundamental rights turned to the remainder of § 1 in search of an alternative fount of such rights. They found one in a most curious place—that section's command that every State guarantee "due process" to any person before depriving him of "life, liberty, or property." At first, litigants argued that this Due Process Clause "incorporated" certain procedural rights codified in the Bill of Rights against the States. The Court generally rejected those claims, however, on the theory that the rights in question were not sufficiently "fundamental" to warrant such treatment.

That changed with time. The Court came to conclude that certain Bill of Rights guarantees *were* sufficiently fundamental to fall within § 1's guarantee of "due process." These included not only procedural protections listed in the first eight Amendments, but substantive rights as well. In the process of incorporating these rights against the States, the Court often applied them differently against the States than against the Federal Government on the theory that only those "fundamental" aspects of the right required Due Process Clause protection. In more recent years, this Court has "abandoned the notion" that the guarantees in the Bill of Rights apply differently when incorporated against the States than they do when applied to the Federal Government. But our cases continue to adhere to the view that a right is incorporated through the Due Process Clause only if it is sufficiently "fundamental"—a term the Court has long struggled to define. . . .

II

. . . The Privileges or Immunities Clause of the Fourteenth Amendment declares that "[n]o State . . . shall abridge the privileges or immunities of citizens of the United States." In interpreting this language, it is important to recall that constitutional provisions are " 'written to be understood by the voters.' " *Heller*, 554 U.S. at 576 (quoting *United States v. Sprague*, 282 U.S. 716, 731 (1931)). Thus, the objective of this inquiry is to discern what "ordinary citizens" at the time of ratification would have understood the Privileges or Immunities Clause to mean.

A–1

At the time of Reconstruction, the terms "privileges" and "immunities" had an established meaning as synonyms for "rights." The two words, standing alone or paired together, were used interchangeably with the words "rights," "liberties," and "freedoms," and had been since the time of Blackstone. . . .

2

The group of rights-bearers to whom the Privileges or Immunities Clause applies is, of course, "citizens." By the time of Reconstruction, it had long been established that both the States and the Federal Government existed to preserve their citizens' inalienable rights, and that these rights were considered "privileges" or "immunities" of citizenship.

This tradition begins with our country's English roots. Parliament declared the basic liberties of English citizens in a series of documents ranging from the Magna Carta to the Petition of Right and the English Bill of Rights. These fundamental rights, according to the English tradition, belonged to all people but became legally enforceable only when recognized in legal texts, including acts of Parliament and the decisions of common-law judges. These rights included many that later would be set forth in our Federal Bill of Rights, such as the right to petition for redress of grievances, the right to a jury trial, and the right of "Protestants" to "have arms for their defence." English Bill of Rights (1689).

As English subjects, the colonists considered themselves to be vested with the same fundamental rights as other Englishmen. They consistently claimed the rights of English citizenship in their founding documents, repeatedly referring to these rights as "privileges" and "immunities." . . .

As tensions between England and the Colonies increased, the colonists adopted protest resolutions reasserting their claim to the inalienable rights of Englishmen. Again, they used the terms "privileges" and "immunities" to describe these rights. . . .

[Justice Thomas gave examples from the Massachusetts Resolves of 1765, invoking the "Rights, Liberties, Privileges, and Immunities" of the people of Great Britain, the similar language of the First Continental Congress in 1774, similar language in early state constitutions, and similar language used by James Madison in introducing and explaining the Bill of Rights when proposed in the first Congress.—Editors]

3

Even though the Bill of Rights did not apply to the States, other provisions of the Constitution did limit state interference with individual rights. Article IV, § 2, cl. 1 provides that "[t]he Citizens of each State shall be entitled to all Privileges and Immunities of Citizens in the several States." The text of this provision resembles the Privileges or Immunities Clause, and it can be assumed that the public's understanding of the latter was informed by its understanding of the former.

Article IV, § 2 was derived from a similar clause in the Articles of Confederation, and reflects the dual citizenship the Constitution provided to all Americans after replacing that "league" of separate sovereign States. *Gibbons v. Ogden*, 22 U.S. (9 Wheat.) 1, 187 (1824). By virtue of a person's citizenship in a particular State, he was guaranteed whatever rights and liberties that State's constitution and laws made available. Article IV, § 2 vested citizens of each State with an additional right: the assurance that they would be afforded the "privileges and immunities" of citizenship in any of the several States in the Union to which they might travel.

What were the "Privileges and Immunities of Citizens in the several States"? That question was answered perhaps most famously by Justice Bushrod Washington sitting as Circuit Justice in *Corfield v. Coryell*, 6 F.Cas. 546, 551–552 (No. 3,230) (CC ED Pa. 1825). In that case, a Pennsylvania citizen claimed that a New Jersey law prohibiting nonresidents from harvesting oysters from the State's waters violated Article IV, § 2 because it deprived him, as an out-of-state citizen, of a right New Jersey availed to its own citizens. Justice Washington rejected that argument, refusing to "accede to the proposition" that Article IV, § 2 entitled "citizens of the several states . . . to participate in *all* the rights which belong exclusively to the citizens of any other particular state." *Id.*, at 552 (emphasis added). In his view, Article IV, § 2 did not guarantee equal access to all public benefits a State might choose to make available to its citizens. See *id.*, at 552. Instead, it applied only to those rights "which are, in their nature, *fundamental*; which belong, of right, to the citizens of all free governments." *Id.*, at 551 (emphasis added). Other courts generally agreed with this principle.

When describing those "fundamental" rights, Justice Washington thought it "would perhaps be more tedious than difficult to enumerate" them all, but suggested that they could "be all comprehended under" a broad list of "general heads," such as "[p]rotection by the government," "the enjoyment of life and liberty, with the right to acquire and possess property of every kind," "the benefit of the writ of habeas corpus," and the right of access to "the courts of the state," among others.[6] *Corfield,* at 551–552.

Notably, Justice Washington did not indicate whether Article IV, § 2 *required* States to recognize these fundamental rights in their own citizens and thus in sojourning citizens alike, or whether the Clause simply prohibited the States from discriminating against sojourning citizens with respect to whatever fundamental rights state law happened to recognize. On this question, the weight of legal authorities at the time of Reconstruction indicated that Article IV, § 2 prohibited States from discriminating against sojourning citizens when recognizing fundamental rights, but did not require States to recognize those rights and did not prescribe their content. The highest courts of several States adopted this view as did several influential treatise-writers. This Court adopted the same conclusion in a unanimous opinion just one year after the Fourteenth Amendment was ratified. See *Paul v. Virginia,* 75 U.S. (8 Wall.) 168, 180 (1869).

* * *

The text examined so far demonstrates three points about the meaning of the Privileges or Immunities Clause in § 1. First, "privileges" and "immunities" were synonyms for "rights." Second, both the States and the Federal Government had long recognized the inalienable rights of their citizens. Third, Article IV, § 2 of the Constitution protected traveling citizens against state discrimination with respect to the fundamental rights of state citizenship.

Two questions still remain, both provoked by the textual similarity between § 1's Privileges or Immunities Clause and Article IV, § 2. The first involves the nature of the rights at stake: Are the privileges or immunities of "citizens of the United States" recognized by § 1 the same as the privileges and immunities of "citizens in the several States" to which Article IV, § 2 refers? The second involves the restriction imposed on the States: Does § 1, like Article IV, § 2, prohibit only discrimination with respect to certain rights *if* the State chooses to recognize them, or does it require States to recognize those rights? I address each question in turn.

B

I start with the nature of the rights that § 1's Privileges or Immunities Clause protects. Section 1 overruled *Dred Scott*'s holding that blacks were not citizens of either the United States or their own State and, thus, did not enjoy "the privileges and immunities of citizens" embodied in the Constitution. . . .

Section 1 protects the rights of citizens "of the United States" specifically. The evidence overwhelmingly demonstrates that the privileges and immunities of such citizens included individual rights enumerated in the Constitution, including the right to keep and bear arms.

---

[6] *[Justice Thomas here quoted the complete list, which is printed at p. 710.—Editors]*

1

[Justice Thomas then discussed nineteenth-century antebellum legal documents employing the terms "privileges" and "immunities" of U.S. citizens as referring to a specific corpus of substantive rights.—Editors]

2

Evidence from the political branches in the years leading to the Fourteenth Amendment's adoption demonstrates broad public understanding that the privileges and immunities of United States citizenship included rights set forth in the Constitution[.] . . . Records from the 39th Congress further support this understanding. . . .

Statements made by Members of Congress leading up to, and during, the debates on the Fourteenth Amendment point in the same direction. The record of these debates has been combed before. See *Adamson*, at 92–110 (Appendix to dissenting opinion of Black, J.) (concluding that the debates support the conclusion that § 1 was understood to incorporate the Bill of Rights against the States). Before considering that record here, it is important to clarify its relevance. When interpreting constitutional text, the goal is to discern the most likely public understanding of a particular provision at the time it was adopted. Statements by legislators can assist in this process to the extent they demonstrate the manner in which the public used or understood a particular word or phrase. They can further assist to the extent there is evidence that these statements were disseminated to the public. In other words, this evidence is useful not because it demonstrates what the draftsmen of the text may have been thinking, but only insofar as it illuminates what the public understood the words chosen by the draftsmen to mean. . . .

Three speeches stand out as particularly significant. Representative John Bingham, the principal draftsman of § 1, delivered a speech on the floor of the House in February 1866 introducing his first draft of the provision. Bingham began by discussing *Barron* and its holding that the Bill of Rights did not apply to the States. He then argued that a constitutional amendment was necessary to provide "an express grant of power in Congress to enforce by penal enactment these great canons of the supreme law, securing to all the citizens in every State all the privileges and immunities of citizens, and to all the people all the sacred rights of person." 39th Cong. Globe 1089–1090 (1866). Bingham emphasized that § 1 was designed "to arm the Congress of the United States, by the consent of the people of the United States, with the power to enforce the bill of rights as it stands in the Constitution today. It 'hath that extent—no more.' " *Id.*, at 1088.

Bingham's speech was printed in pamphlet form and broadly distributed in 1866 under the title, "One Country, One Constitution, and One People," and the subtitle, "In Support of the Proposed Amendment to Enforce the Bill of Rights." Newspapers also reported his proposal, with the New York Times providing particularly extensive coverage, including a full reproduction of Bingham's first draft of § 1 and his remarks that a constitutional amendment to "enforc[e]" the "immortal bill of rights" was "absolutely essential to American nationality." N.Y. Times, Feb. 27, 1866, p. 8.

Bingham's first draft of § 1 was different from the version ultimately adopted. Of particular importance, the first draft granted Congress the "power to make all laws . . . necessary and proper to secure" the "citizens of each State all privileges and immunities of citizens in the several States," rather than restricting state power to "abridge" the privileges or immunities of citizens of the United States. . . . *[Justice Thomas next described the press coverage and public debate regarding Bingham's proposal.—Editors]*

By the time the debates on the Fourteenth Amendment resumed, Bingham had amended his draft of § 1 to include the text of the Privileges or Immunities Clause that was ultimately adopted. Senator Jacob Howard introduced the new draft on the floor of the Senate in the third speech relevant here. Howard explained that the Constitution recognized "a mass of privileges, immunities, and rights, some of them secured by the second section of the fourth article of the Constitution, . . . some by the first eight amendments of the Constitution," and that "there is no power given in the Constitution to enforce and to carry out any of these guarantees" against the States. 39th Cong. Globe 2765. Howard then stated that "the great object" of § 1 was to "restrain the power of the States and compel them at all times to respect these great fundamental guarantees." *Id.,* at 2766. Section 1, he indicated, imposed "a general prohibition upon all the States, as such, from abridging the privileges and immunities of the citizens of the United States." *Id.,* at 2765.

In describing these rights, Howard explained that they included "the privileges and immunities spoken of" in Article IV, § 2. Although he did not catalogue the precise "nature" or "extent" of those rights, he thought "Corfield v. Coryell" provided a useful description. Howard then submitted that

"[t]o these privileges and immunities, whatever they may be— . . . should be added *the personal rights guarantied and secured by the first eight amendments of the Constitution*; such as the freedom of speech and of the press; the right of the people peaceably to assemble and petition the Government for a redress of grievances, [and] . . . *the right to keep and to bear arms.*" *Ibid.* (emphasis added).

News of Howard's speech was carried in major newspapers across the country[.] . . . As a whole, these well-circulated speeches indicate that § 1 was understood to enforce constitutionally declared rights against the States, and they provide no suggestion that any language in the section other than the Privileges or Immunities Clause would accomplish that task. . . .

[Justice Thomas next discussed legislation enacted by the Reconstruction Congress, including the Civil Rights Act of 1866 and the Freedmen's Bureau Act.—Editors]

There is much else in the legislative record. Many statements by Members of Congress corroborate the view that the Privileges or Immunities Clause enforced constitutionally enumerated rights against the States. I am not aware of any statement that directly refutes that proposition. That said, the record of the debates—like most legislative history—is less than crystal clear. In particular, much ambiguity derives from the fact that at least several Members described § 1 as protecting the privileges and immunities of citizens "in the several States," harkening back to Article IV, § 2. These statements can be read to support the view that the Privileges or Immunities Clause protects some or all the fundamental rights of "citizens" described in *Corfield*. They can also be read to support the view that the Privileges or Immunities Clause, like Article IV, § 2, prohibits only state discrimination with respect to those rights it covers, but does not deprive States of the power to deny those rights to all citizens equally.

I examine the rest of the historical record with this understanding. But for purposes of discerning what the public most likely thought the Privileges or Immunities Clause to mean, it is significant that the most widely publicized statements by the legislators who voted on § 1 . . . point unambiguously toward the conclusion that the Privileges or Immunities Clause enforces at least those fundamental rights enumerated in the Constitution against the States, including the Second Amendment right to keep and bear arms.

3

. . . This evidence plainly shows that the ratifying public understood the Privileges or Immunities Clause to protect constitutionally enumerated rights, including the right to keep and bear arms. As the Court demonstrates, there can be no doubt that § 1 was understood to enforce the Second Amendment against the States. In my view, this is because the right to keep and bear arms was understood to be a privilege of American citizenship guaranteed by the Privileges or Immunities Clause. . . .

[In the rest of his opinion Justice Thomas argued that the Privileges or Immunities Clause required more of states than non-discrimination with respect to the right to keep and bear arms. Rather, he argued, it required them to recognize the right. He also considered the Court's precedents, and especially Cruikshank, *which he argued "is not a precedent entitled to any respect."—Editors]*

■ JUSTICE STEVENS, dissenting.

. . . The question we should be answering in this case is whether the Constitution "guarantees individuals a fundamental right," enforceable against the States, "to possess a functional, personal firearm, including a handgun, within the home." Complaint ¶ 34, App. 23. That is a different—and more difficult—inquiry than asking if the Fourteenth Amendment "incorporates" the Second Amendment. The so-called incorporation question was squarely and, in my view, correctly resolved in the late 19th century. . . .

[Petitioners'] briefs marshal an impressive amount of historical evidence for their argument that the Court interpreted the Privileges or Immunities Clause too narrowly in the *Slaughter-House Cases.* But the original meaning of the Clause is not as clear as they suggest[2]—and not nearly as clear as it would need to be to dislodge 137 years of precedent. The burden is severe for those who seek radical change in such an established body of constitutional doctrine. . . .

[Justice Stevens argued that the Court's cases on the Due Process Clause of the Fourteenth Amendment expressed three primary principles, the first two of which are that the clause has substantive content and that the clause protects personal liberty.—Editors]

---

[2] Cf., *e.g.,* Currie, The Reconstruction Congress, 75 U. Chi. L. Rev. 383, 406 (2008) (finding "some support in the legislative history for no fewer than four interpretations" of the Privileges or Immunities Clause, two of which contradict petitioners' submission); Hamburger, Privileges or Immunities, 105 Nw. U. L. Rev. (forthcoming 2011) (arguing that the Clause was meant to ensure freed slaves were afforded "the Privileges and Immunities" specified in Article IV, § 2, cl. 1 of the Constitution). Although he urges its elevation in our doctrine, JUSTICE THOMAS has acknowledged that, in seeking to ascertain the original meaning of the Privileges or Immunities Clause, "[l]egal scholars agree on little beyond the conclusion that the Clause does not mean what the Court said it meant in 1873." *Saenz v. Roe,* 526 U.S. 489, 522, n. 1 (1999) (dissenting opinion).

The third precept to emerge from our case law flows from the second: The rights protected against state infringement by the Fourteenth Amendment's Due Process Clause need not be identical in shape or scope to the rights protected against Federal Government infringement by the various provisions of the Bill of Rights. As drafted, the Bill of Rights directly constrained only the Federal Government. See *Barron v. Baltimore*. Although the enactment of the Fourteenth Amendment profoundly altered our legal order, it "did not unstitch the basic federalist pattern woven into our constitutional fabric." *Williams v. Florida*, 399 U.S. 78, 133 (1970) (Harlan, J., concurring in result). Nor, for that matter, did it expressly alter the Bill of Rights. The Constitution still envisions a system of divided sovereignty, still "establishes a federal republic where local differences are to be cherished as elements of liberty" in the vast run of cases, *National Rifle Assn. of Am. Inc. v. Chicago*, 567 F.3d 856, 860 (C.A.7 2009) (Easterbrook, C. J.), still allocates a general "police power . . . to the States and the States alone," *United States v. Comstock*, 560 U.S. 126, 153 (2010) (KENNEDY, J., concurring in judgment). Elementary considerations of constitutional text and structure suggest there may be legitimate reasons to hold state governments to different standards than the Federal Government in certain areas. . . .

It is true, as well, that during the 1960's the Court decided a number of cases involving procedural rights in which it treated the Due Process Clause as if it transplanted language from the Bill of Rights into the Fourteenth Amendment. "Jot-for-jot" incorporation was the norm in this expansionary era. . . . In my judgment, this line of cases is best understood as having concluded that, to ensure a criminal trial satisfies essential standards of fairness, some procedures should be the same in state and federal courts: The need for certainty and uniformity is more pressing, and the margin for error slimmer, when criminal justice is at issue. That principle has little relevance to the question whether a non procedural rule set forth in the Bill of Rights qualifies as an aspect of the liberty protected by the Fourteenth Amendment.

Notwithstanding some overheated dicta in *Malloy*, at 10–11, it is therefore an overstatement to say that the Court has "abandoned" a "two-track approach to incorporation." . . . [I]f some 1960's opinions purported to establish a general method of incorporation, that hardly binds us in this case. The Court has not hesitated to cut back on perceived Warren Court excesses in more areas than I can count.

I do not mean to deny that there can be significant practical, as well as esthetic, benefits from treating rights symmetrically with regard to the State and Federal Governments. Jot-for-jot incorporation of a provision may entail greater protection of the right at issue and therefore greater freedom for those who hold it; jot-for-jot incorporation may also yield greater clarity about the contours of the legal rule. In a federalist system such as ours, however, this approach can carry substantial costs. When a federal court insists that state and local authorities follow its dictates on a matter not critical to personal liberty or procedural justice, the latter may be prevented from engaging in the kind of beneficent "experimentation in things social and economic" that ultimately redounds to the benefit of all Americans. *New State Ice Co. v. Liebmann*, 285 U.S. 262, 311 (1932) (Brandeis, J., dissenting). The costs of federal courts' imposing a uniform national standard may be especially high when the relevant regulatory interests vary significantly across localities, and when the ruling implicates the States' core police powers.

Furthermore, there is a real risk that, by demanding the provisions of the Bill of Rights apply identically to the States, federal courts will cause those provisions to "be watered down in the needless pursuit of uniformity." *Duncan*, at 182, n. 21 (Harlan, J., dissenting). . . . Indeed, it is far from clear that proponents of an individual right to keep and bear arms ought to celebrate today's decision.

[Justice Stevens proceeded to an analyze the case not as one about the incorporation of the Second Amendment but rather as one about substantive due process, asking whether the right to keep and bear arms is a value "implicit in the concept of ordered liberty." Palko, at 325. He concluded that it is not.—Editors]

■ [The concurring opinion of JUSTICE SCALIA and the dissenting opinion of JUSTICE BREYER are omitted.]

NOTES

1.   The opinions in *McDonald* debate both a general question and a specific one. The general question is the right *approach* to incorporation. What are the three approaches? Which one do you find most persuasive? The specific question is whether the right to keep and bear arms in particular is incorporated. What do you think?

2.   Is it possible to abstract the problem of incorporation away from one's views about a particular right? You probably guessed that Justice Stevens, who dissents in *McDonald*, dissented in *Heller*. Indeed, every justice on the Court voted the same way on the incorporation question as he or she did on the initial question in *Heller*. Does that make sense? Or can't one think that the two cases presented very different questions?

3.   Does it matter whether the enumerated rights are incorporated under the Due Process Clause or instead under the Privileges or Immunities Clause? Why?

4.   Does there come a time when it is simply too late to overturn a precedent, even if it is wrong? Has that time come for the *Slaughter-House Cases*? Should the role of precedent be stronger or weaker in interpreting the Fourteenth Amendment than it is in other parts of the Constitution?

[Assignment 77]

C. THE RISE OF SUBSTANTIVE DUE PROCESS

One of the most persistent debates in constitutional law is about whether and how "due process of law" imposes restrictions on the substantive content of laws enacted by Congress and state legislatures. As you will soon see, at times in its history the Supreme Court has embraced the notion that the Due Process Clauses allow it to weigh the substantive fairness of laws passed by Congress and state legislatures. Yet there has been persistent criticism that substantive due process is incoherent, even a contradiction in terms. As one legal scholar put it, to say "substantive due process" is like saying "green pastel redness." John Hart Ely, DEMOCRACY AND DISTRUST: A THEORY OF JUDICIAL REVIEW 18 (1980).

The historical roots of due process suggest at least one possible answer. Process is what the Due Process Clauses require. The Due Process Clauses provide no absolute guarantee of life, liberty, or property, since it is expressly contemplated that each can be taken away as long as the requisite process is given. But each constitutional actor can act in a manner inconsistent with "due process of law"— including the legislature. Even when it enacts a law that complies with all the formalities of lawmaking, it can still violate due process if it is acting quasi-judicially. The classic example of such a quasi-judicial action, one that is insufficiently general and prospective, is recited in *Calder v. Bull* and scores of other cases: when a legislature takes from A to give to B. And on this view the constitutional prohibitions on bills of attainder, ex post facto laws, laws impairing the obligation of contracts, and takings without just compensation would all be addressed to specific ways that legislatures are especially likely to overstep their bounds by enacting laws that are legislative in form but quasi-judicial in substance.

But the modern doctrine of substantive due process is quite different, and it is not grounded in common law procedures and the separation of powers. Its first invocation came in *Dred Scott*, p. 733, where the Court located a right to own slaves in the Due Process Clause of the Fifth Amendment. Two decades later, after the ratification of the Fourteenth Amendment, the Court began to suggest that that amendment's Due Process Clause might supply a basis for a wide-ranging examination of the substance of state laws. In *Munn v. Illinois*, 94 U.S. 113 (1877), the Court hinted that "in private contracts, relating to matters in which the public has no interest, what is reasonable must be ascertained judicially." Within a decade, the Court had suggested several times that the power of the state to regulate business was subject to judicial scrutiny and limits. See, e.g., *Mugler v. Kansas*, 123 U.S. 623 (1887); *The Railroad Commission Cases*, 116 U.S. 307 (1886). By 1890, in *Chicago, M. & St. P. Ry. Co. v. Minnesota*, 134 U.S. 418 (1890), the Court had located this authority in the Due Process Clause of the Fourteenth Amendment, finding that a regulation of railroad rates violated due process requirements not only for its defective procedural protections, but also because rate regulation by administrative order would "in substance and effect" constitute a deprivation of property without due process. The reasonableness of the rates was "eminently a question for judicial investigation."

In *Allgeyer v. Louisiana*, 165 U.S. 578 (1897), the Court struck down a general and prospective Louisiana statute on grounds that are clearly identifiable in terms of modern substantive due process. The statute prohibited buying insurance from any company without an office or agent physically located in the state. The Court found that the prohibition "deprives the defendants of their liberty without due process of law." The Court stated: "The liberty mentioned in that amendment means not only the right of the citizen to be free from the mere physical restraint of his person, as by incarceration, but the term is deemed to embrace the right of the citizen to be free in the enjoyment of all his faculties; to be free to use them in all lawful ways; to live and work where he will; to earn his livelihood by any lawful calling; to pursue any livelihood or avocation, and for that purpose to enter into all contracts which may be proper, necessary and essential to his carrying out to a successful conclusion the purposes above mentioned." *Id.* at 589.

In this era where the Court adopted an expansively substantive conception of the Due Process Clauses, the most famous case is *Lochner v. New York*, 198 U.S. 45 (1905). As you read it, think of how the Court is interpreting the Constitution. What are the arguments? Do you agree with them? Is *Lochner* right? Or is the general approach of *Lochner* correct, but the specific application wrong? If so, how would a court know when a legislative act should be upheld and when it should instead be struck down as an excessive infringement on liberty? Or is the entire premise that a court may invalidate legislative acts in the absence of a reasonably clear constitutional text an invitation for judicial abuse?

Lochner v. New York
198 U.S. 45 (1905)

■ MR. JUSTICE PECKHAM . . . delivered the opinion of the court:

The indictment, it will be seen, charges that the plaintiff in error violated the labor law of the State of New York, in that he wrongfully and unlawfully required and permitted an employé working for him to work more than sixty hours in one week. . . . The mandate of the statute, that "no employé shall be required or permitted to work," is the substantial equivalent of an enactment that "no employé shall contract or agree to work," more than ten hours per day, and, as there is no provision for special emergencies, the statute is mandatory in all cases. It is not an act merely fixing the number of hours which shall constitute a legal day's work, but an absolute prohibition upon the employer permitting, under any circumstances, more than ten hours' work to be done in his establishment. The employé may desire to earn the extra money which would arise from his working more than the prescribed time, but this statute forbids the employer from permitting the employé to earn it.

The statute necessarily interferes with the right of contract between the employer and employés, concerning the number of hours in which the latter may labor in the bakery of the employer. The general right to make a contract in relation to his business is part of the liberty of the individual protected by the Fourteenth Amendment of the Federal Constitution. *Allgeyer v. Louisiana*, 165 U.S. 578 (1897). Under that provision no State can deprive any person of life, liberty or property without due process of law. The right to purchase or to sell labor is part of the liberty protected by this amendment, unless there are circumstances which exclude the right. There are, however, certain powers, existing in the sovereignty of each State in the Union, somewhat vaguely termed police powers, the exact description and limitation of which have not been attempted by the courts. Those powers, broadly stated, and without, at present, any attempt at a more specific limitation, relate to the safety, health, morals and general welfare of the public. Both property and liberty are held on such reasonable conditions as may be imposed by the governing power of the State in the exercise of those powers, and with such conditions the Fourteenth Amendment was not designed to interfere.

The State, therefore, has power to prevent the individual from making certain kinds of contracts, and in regard to them the Federal Constitution offers no protection. If the contract be one which the State, in the legitimate exercise of its police power, has the right to prohibit, it is not prevented from prohibiting it by the Fourteenth Amendment. Contracts in violation of a statute, either of the Federal or state government, or a contract to let one's property for immoral purposes, or to do any other unlawful act, could obtain no protection from the Federal Constitution, as coming under the liberty of person or of free contract. Therefore, when the State, by its legislature, in the assumed exercise of its police powers, has passed an act which seriously limits the right to labor or the right of contract in regard to their means of livelihood between persons who are *sui juris* (both employer and employé), it becomes of great importance to determine which shall prevail—the right of the individual to labor for such time as he may choose, or the right of the State to prevent the individual from laboring, or from entering into any contract to labor, beyond a certain time prescribed by the State.

This court has recognized the existence and upheld the exercise of the police powers of the States in many cases which might fairly be considered as border ones, and it has, in the course of its determination of questions regarding the asserted invalidity of such statutes, on the ground of their violation of the rights secured by the Federal Constitution, been guided by rules of a very liberal nature, the application of which has resulted, in numerous instances, in upholding the validity of state statutes thus assailed. . . .

It must, of course, be conceded that there is a limit to the valued exercise of the police power by the State. There is no dispute concerning this general proposition. Otherwise the Fourteenth Amendment would have no efficacy and the legislatures of the States would have unbounded power, and it would be enough to say that any piece of legislation was enacted to conserve the morals, the health or the safety of the people; such legislation would be valid, no matter how absolutely without foundation the claim might be. The claim of the police power would be a mere pretext—become another and delusive name for the supreme sovereignty of the State to be exercised free from constitutional restraint. This is not contended for. In every case that comes before this court, therefore, where legislation of this character is concerned, and where the protection of the Federal Constitution is sought, the question necessarily arises: Is this a fair, reasonable and appropriate exercise of the police power of the State, or is it an unreasonable, unnecessary and arbitrary interference with the right of the individual to his personal liberty or to enter into those contracts in relation to labor which may seem to him appropriate or necessary for the support of himself and his family? Of course the liberty of contract relating to labor includes both parties to it. The one has as much right to purchase as the other to sell labor.

This is not a question of substituting the judgment of the court for that of the legislature. If the act be within the power of the State it is valid, although the judgment of the court might be totally opposed to the enactment of such a law. But the question would still remain, Is it within the police power of the State? and that question must be answered by the court.

The question whether this act is valid as a labor law, pure and simple, may be dismissed in a few words. There is no reasonable ground for interfering with the liberty of person or the right of free contract, by determining the hours of labor, in the occupation of a baker. There is no contention that bakers as a class are not equal in intelligence and capacity to men in other trades or manual occupations, or that they are not able to assert their rights and care for themselves without the protecting arm of the State, interfering with their independence of judgment and of action. They are in no sense wards of the State. Viewed in the light of a purely labor law, with no reference whatever to the question of health, we think that a law like the one before us involves neither the safety, the morals nor the welfare of the public, and that the interest of the public is not in the slightest degree affected by such an act. The law must be upheld, if at all, as a law pertaining to the health of the individual engaged in the occupation of a baker. It does not affect any other portion of the public than those who are engaged in that occupation. Clean and wholesome bread does not depend upon whether the baker works but ten hours per day or only sixty hours a week. The limitation of the hours of labor does not come within the police power on that ground.

It is a question of which of two powers or rights shall prevail—the power of the State to legislate or the right of the individual to liberty of person and freedom of contract. The mere assertion that the subject relates, though but in a remote degree, to the public health, does not necessarily render the enactment valid. The act must have a more direct relation, as a means to an end, and the end itself must be appropriate and legitimate, before an act can be held to be valid which interferes with the general right of an individual to be free in his person and in his power to contract in relation to his own labor. . . .

We think the limit of the police power has been reached and passed in this case. There is, in our judgment, no reasonable foundation for holding this to be necessary or appropriate as a health law to safeguard the public health, or the health of the individuals who are following the trade of a baker. If this statute be valid . . . there would seem to be no length to which legislation of this nature might not go. . . .

We think that there can be no fair doubt that the trade of a baker, in and of itself, is not an unhealthy one to that degree which would authorize the legislature to interfere with the right to labor, and with the right of free contract on the part of the individual, either as employer or employé. In looking through the statistics regarding all trades and occupations, it may be true that the trade of a baker does not appear to be as healthy as some other trades, and is also vastly more healthy than still others. . . . There must be more than the mere fact of the possible existence of some small amount of unhealthiness to warrant legislative interference with liberty. It is unfortunately true that labor, even in any department, may possibly carry with it the seeds of unhealthiness. But are we all, on that account, at the mercy of legislative majorities? A printer, a tinsmith, a locksmith, a carpenter, a cabinetmaker, a dry goods clerk, a bank's, a lawyer's or a physician's clerk, or a clerk in almost any kind of business, would all come under the power of the legislature, on this assumption. No trade, no occupation, no mode of earning one's living, could escape this all-pervading power, and the acts of the legislature in limiting the hours of labor in all employments would be valid, although such limitation might seriously cripple the ability of the laborer to support himself and his family. In our large cities there are many buildings into which the sun penetrates for but a short time in each day, and these buildings are occupied by people carrying on the business of bankers, brokers, lawyers, real estate, and many other kinds of business, aided by many clerks, messengers, and other employés. Upon the assumption of the validity of this act under review, it is not possible to say that an act, prohibiting lawyers' or bank clerks, or others, from contracting to labor for their employers more than eight hours a day would be invalid. . . .

It is also urged, pursuing the same line of argument, that it is to the interest of the State that its population should be strong and robust, and therefore any legislation which may be said to tend to make people healthy must be valid as health laws, enacted under the police power. If this be a valid argument and a justification for this kind of legislation, it follows that the protection of the Federal Constitution from undue interference with liberty of person and freedom of contract is visionary, wherever the law is sought to be justified as a valid exercise of the police power. Scarcely any law but might find shelter under such assumptions, and conduct, properly so called, as well as contract, would come under the restrictive sway of the legislature. Not only the hours of employés, but the hours of employers, could be regulated, and doctors, lawyers, scientists, all professional men, as well as athletes and artisans, could be forbidden to fatigue their brains and bodies by prolonged hours of exercise, lest the fighting strength of the State be impaired. We mention these extreme cases because the contention is extreme. We do not believe in the soundness of the views which uphold this law. On the contrary, we think that such a law as this, although passed in the assumed exercise of the police power, and as relating to the public health, or the health of the employs named, is not within that power, and is invalid. The act is not, within any fair meaning of the term, a health law, but is an illegal interference with the rights of individuals, both employers and employés, to make contracts regarding labor upon such terms as they may think best, or which they may agree upon with the other parties to such contracts. Statutes of the nature of that under review, limiting the hours in which grown and intelligent men may labor to earn their living, are mere meddlesome interferences with the rights of the individual, and they are not saved from condemnation by the claim that they are passed in the exercise of the police power and upon the subject of the health of the individual whose rights are interfered with, unless there be some fair ground, reasonable in and of itself, to say that there is material danger to the public health, or to the health of the employés, if the hours of labor are not curtailed. . . .

This interference on the part of the legislatures of the Several states with the ordinary trades and occupations of the people seems to be on the increase. . . . It is impossible for us to shut our eyes to the fact that many of the laws of this character, while passed under what is claimed to be the police power for the purpose of protecting the public health or welfare, are, in reality, passed from other motives. We are justified in saying so when, from the character of the law and the subject upon which it legislates, it is apparent that the public health or welfare bears but the most remote relation to the law. . . .

It is manifest to us that the limitation of the hours of labor as provided for in this section of the statute under which the indictment was found, and the plaintiff in error convicted, has no such direct relation to, and no such substantial effect upon, the health of the employé, as to justify us in regarding the section as really a health law. It seems to us that the real object and purpose were simply to regulate the hours of labor between the master and his employés . . . in a private business, not dangerous in any degree to morals or in any real and substantial degree, to the health of the employés. Under such circumstances the freedom of master and employé to contract with each other in relation to their employment, and in defining the same, cannot be prohibited or interfered with, without violating the Federal Constitution. . . .

■ MR. JUSTICE HARLAN, with whom MR. JUSTICE WHITE and MR. JUSTICE DAY concurred, dissenting.

While this court has not attempted to mark the precise boundaries of what is called the police power of the State, the existence of the power has been uniformly recognized, both by the Federal and state courts.

All the cases agree that this power extends at least to the protection of the lives, the health and the safety of the public against the injurious exercise by any citizen of his own rights. . . .

Speaking generally, the State, in the exercise of its powers, may not unduly interfere with the right of the citizen to enter into contracts that may be necessary and essential in the enjoyment of the inherent rights belonging to every one, among which rights is the right "to be free in the enjoyment of all his faculties, to be free to use them in all lawful ways, to live and work where he will, to earn his livelihood by any lawful calling, to pursue any livelihood or avocation." This was declared in *Allgeyer v. Louisiana*, at 589. But in the same case it was conceded that the right to contract in relation to persons and property, or to do business, within a State, may be "regulated, and sometimes prohibited, when the contracts or business conflict with the policy of the State as contained in its statutes." . . .

Granting, then, that there is a liberty of contract which cannot be violated even under the sanction of direct legislative enactment, but assuming, as according to settled law we may assume, that such liberty of contract is subject to such regulations as the State may reasonably prescribe for the common good and the well-being of society, what, then, are the conditions under which the judiciary may declare such regulations to be in excess of legislative authority and void? Upon this point there is no room for dispute, for the rule is universal that a legislative enactment, Federal or state, is never to be disregarded or held invalid unless it be, beyond question, plainly and palpably in excess of legislative power. . . . If there be doubt as to the validity of the statute, that doubt must therefore be resolved in favor of its validity, and the courts must keep their hands off, leaving the legislature to meet the responsibility for unwise legislation. If the end which the legislature seeks to accomplish be one to which its power extends, and if the means employed to that end, although not the wisest or best, are yet not plainly and palpably unauthorized by law, then the court cannot interfere. In other words, when the validity of a statute is questioned, the burden of proof, so to speak, is upon those who assert it to be unconstitutional. *McCulloch v. Maryland*, 17 U.S. (4 Wheat.) 316, 421 (1819).

Let these principles be applied to the present case. . . . It is plain that this statute was enacted in order to protect the physical well-being of those who work in bakery and confectionery establishments. . . . Whether or not this be wise legislation it is not the province of the court to inquire. Under our systems of government the courts are not concerned with the wisdom or policy of legislation. So that in determining the question of power to interfere with liberty of contract, the court may inquire whether the means devised by the State are germane to an end which may be lawfully accomplished and have a real or substantial relation to the protection of health, as involved in the daily work of the persons, male and female, engaged in bakery and confectionery establishments. But when this inquiry is entered upon I find it impossible, in view of common experience, to say that there is here no real or substantial relation between the means employed by the State and the end sought to be accomplished by its legislation. . . . Still less can I say that the statute is, beyond question, a plain, palpable invasion of rights secured by the fundamental law. Therefore I submit that this court will transcend its functions if it assumes to annul the statute of New York. . . .

Professor Hirt in his treatise on the "Diseases of the Workers" has said: "The labor of the bakers is among the hardest and most laborious imaginable, because it has to be performed under conditions injurious to the health of those engaged in it. . . ." Another writer says: "The constant inhaling of flour dust causes inflammation of the lungs and of the bronchial tubes. The eyes also suffer through this dust, which is responsible for the many cases of running eyes among the bakers. The long hours of toil to which all bakers are subjected produce rheumatism, cramps, and swollen legs. . . . The average age of a baker is below that of other workmen; they seldom live over their fiftieth year, most of them dying between the ages of forty and fifty." . . .

Statistics show that the average daily working time among workingmen in different countries is, in Australia, 8 hours; in Great Britain, 9; in the United States, 9¾; in Denmark, 9¾; in Norway, 10; Sweden, France, and Switzerland, 10½; Germany, 10¼; Belgium, Italy, and Austria, 11; and in Russia, 12 hours.

We judicially know that the question of the number of hours during which a workman should continuously labor has been, for a long period, and is yet, a subject of serious consideration among civilized peoples, and by those having special knowledge of the laws of health. Suppose the statute prohibited labor in bakery and confectionery establishments in excess of eighteen hours each day. No one, I take it, could dispute the power of the State to enact such a statute. But the statute before us does not embrace extreme or exceptional cases. It may be said to occupy a middle ground in respect of the hours of labor. What is the true ground for the State to take between legitimate protection, by legislation, of the public health and liberty of contract is not a question easily solved, nor one in respect of which there is or can be absolute certainty. . . .

I do not stop to consider whether any particular view of this economic question presents the sounder theory. . . . It is enough for the determination of this case, and it is enough for this court to know, that the question is one about which there is room for debate and for an honest difference of opinion. . . .

[T]he State is not amenable to the judiciary, in respect of its legislative enactments, unless such enactments are plainly, palpably, beyond all question, inconsistent with the Constitution of the United States. We are not to presume that the State of New York has acted in bad faith. Nor can we assume that its legislature acted without due deliberation, or that it did not determine this question upon the fullest attainable information and for the common good. We cannot say that the State has acted without reason, nor ought we to proceed upon the theory that its action is a mere sham. Our duty, I submit, is to sustain the statute as not being in conflict with the Federal Constitution, for the reason—and such is an all-sufficient reason—it is not shown to be plainly and palpably inconsistent with that instrument. Let the State alone in the management of its purely domestic affairs, so long as it does not appear beyond all question that it has violated the Federal Constitution. This view necessarily results from the principle that the health and safety of the people of a State are primarily for the State to guard and protect.

I take leave to say that the New York statute, in the particulars here involved, cannot be held to be in conflict with the Fourteenth Amendment, without enlarging the scope of the Amendment far beyond its original purpose, and without bringing under the supervision of this court matters which have been supposed to belong exclusively to the legislative departments of the several States when exerting their conceded power to guard the health and safety of their citizens by such regulations as they in their wisdom deem best. Health laws of every description constitute, said Chief Justice Marshall, a part of that mass of legislation which "embraces everything within the territory of a state, not surrendered to the general government; all which can be most advantageously exercised by the states themselves." *Gibbons v. Ogden*,

22 U.S. (9 Wheat.) 1, 203 (1824). A decision that the New York statute is void under the Fourteenth Amendment will, in my opinion, involve consequences of a far-reaching and mischievous character; for such a decision would seriously cripple the inherent power of the States to care for the lives, health and well-being of their citizens. Those are matters which can be best controlled by the States. The preservation of the just powers of the States is quite as vital as the preservation of the powers of the General Government. . . .

■ MR. JUSTICE HOLMES dissenting.

I regret sincerely that I am unable to agree with the judgment in this case, and that I think it my duty to express my dissent.

This case is decided upon an economic theory which a large part of the country does not entertain. If it were a question whether I agreed with that theory, I should desire to study it further and long before making up my mind. But I do not conceive that to be my duty, because I strongly believe that my agreement or disagreement has nothing to do with the right of a majority to embody their opinions in law. It is settled by various decisions of this court that state constitutions and state laws may regulate life in many ways which we as legislators might think as injudicious, or if you like as tyrannical, as this, and which, equally with this, interfere with the liberty to contract. Sunday laws and usury laws are ancient examples. A more modern one is the prohibition of lotteries. The liberty of the citizen to do as he likes so long as he does not interfere with the liberty of others to do the same, which has been a shibboleth for some well-known writers, is interfered with by school laws, by the Post Office, by every state or municipal institution which takes his money for purposes thought desirable, whether he likes it or not. The 14th Amendment does not enact Mr. Herbert Spencer's Social Statics. The other day we sustained the Massachusetts vaccination law. United States and state statutes and decisions cutting down the liberty to contract by way of combination are familiar to this court. Two years ago we upheld the prohibition of sales of stock on margins, or for future delivery, in the constitution of California. The decision sustaining an eight hour law for miners is still recent. Some of these laws embody convictions or prejudices which judges are likely to share. Some may not. But a constitution is not intended to embody a particular economic theory, whether of paternalism and the organic relation of the citizen to the State or of *laissez faire*. It is made for people of fundamentally differing views, and the accident of our finding certain opinions natural and familiar, or novel, and even shocking, ought not to conclude our judgment upon the question whether statutes embodying them conflict with the Constitution of the United States.

General propositions do not decide concrete cases. The decision will depend on a judgment or intuition more subtle than any articulate major premise. But I think that the proposition just stated, if it is accepted, will carry us far toward the end. Every opinion tends to become a law. I think that the word liberty in the Fourteenth Amendment is perverted when it is held to prevent the natural outcome of a dominant opinion, unless it can be said that a rational and fair man necessarily would admit that the statute proposed would infringe fundamental principles as they have been understood by the traditions of our people and our law. It does not need research to show that no such sweeping condemnation can be passed upon the statute before us. A reasonable man might think it a proper measure on the score of health. Men whom I certainly could not pronounce unreasonable would uphold it as a first instalment of a general regulation of the hours of work. Whether in the latter aspect it would be open to the charge of inequality I think it unnecessary to discuss.

NOTES

1.   *Lochner* raises the fundamental question of what the Due Process Clause requires. Does it require only process—procedural regularity and the protection that comes from having authorized courts make decisions according to settled law? Or does it also require that all state laws be reasonable? How does the Court in *Lochner* decide this question? What does the Court think the limits are on state laws?

If the due process argument for *Lochner* is weak, are there other ways to justify it? Could the result in *Lochner* be justified under the Equal Protection Clause, because the statute treated bakers differently from other workers? Or could the result be justified under the Privileges or Immunities Clause, because the statute infringes a privilege to work more than ten hours a day? Given *Slaughter-House*, how would the courts decide those questions? Or consider the Contracts Clause, found in Article I, Section 10, which forbids state laws that "impair[ ] the Obligation of Contracts." This clause prohibits states from *retroactively* impairing the vested obligations created by contracts. Should we extrapolate from the Contracts Clause and its preceding provisions (the prohibitions on bills of attainder and ex post facto laws), concluding that the Constitution contains a general principle of economic freedom? Would that kind of extrapolation justify what the Court was doing in *Lochner*? Should courts extrapolate from particular textual provisions to a general principle? If so, when?

Was there a strong policy argument in favor of the statute in *Lochner*? If most bakers died before age fifty, was that a compelling health and safety reason to limit hours? Justice Harlan makes a good case. On the other hand, what if the motivation behind the statute had more to do with economic competition between different groups of bakers? What if the owners of the large bakeries, the bread factories, already scheduled workers in shifts? What if they were concerned about "competition from small, old-fashioned bakeries, especially those that employed Italian, French, and Jewish immigrants"? David E. Bernstein, Lochner v. New York: *A Centennial Retrospective*, 83 Wash. U. L. Q. 1469, 1476–77 (2005). If that concern motivated the statute, then it was well designed to achieve its purpose: the immigrant bakers worked not in factories but in the basements of tenement buildings, and the workers "often worked far more than ten hours per day," because instead of running factory shifts "the basement bakeries often demanded that workers be on call twenty-four hours a day, with the bakers sleeping in or near the bakery during down times." *Id.* at 1477. How should courts decide between these rival explanations for the policy of the statute?

2.   The due process methodology of *Lochner* reigned for another three decades, roughly until the mid-1930s. During that time the Court struck down nearly two hundred laws and regulations on substantive due process grounds, though it also upheld many others. Every case of state regulation of business, commercial activity, labor, employment, and individual conduct seemed to present a constitutional question under *Lochner*. The Court would proceed this way. First it would consider whether the regulation interfered with "liberty" (which could be freedom of contract or some other liberty). If so, the Court would then ask whether the state's regulation was a legitimate exercise of the "police power" to regulate safety, health, morals, and general welfare of the public. Then the Court would weigh the intrusion upon liberty and the propriety of the legislature's choice. To use *Lochner*'s language: "In every case that comes before this court . . . the question necessarily arises: Is this a fair, reasonable and appropriate

exercise of the police power of the State, or is it an unreasonable, unnecessary and arbitrary interference with the right of the individual to his personal liberty or to enter into those contracts in relation to labor which may seem to him appropriate . . . ?"

Lochner thus seemed to embrace pure policy balancing by courts, reviewing legislative policy choices, upholding some and rejecting others. Here are a few of the more famous decisions applying *Lochner*'s approach:

a.   In *Adair v. United States*, 208 U.S. 161 (1908), the Court held unconstitutional a federal law that prohibited interstate railroads from imposing "yellow dog" contracts on their employees. These were contracts in which a worker agreed not to join a union. In effect, by holding the law unconstitutional, the Court allowed the railroads to fire employees whenever they joined a union. Justice Harlan wrote the opinion, holding that the law violated the "right of a person to sell his labor upon such terms as he deems proper" and the "right of the purchaser of labor to prescribe the conditions" by contract. Employer and employee "have equality of right, and any legislation that disturbs that equality is an arbitrary interference with the liberty of contract."

b.   In *Muller v. Oregon*, 208 U.S. 412 (1908), the Court upheld an Oregon law prohibiting the employment of any woman for more than ten hours a day. The Court's said the law was appropriate given the "woman's physical structure" and the need to protect women "even when like legislation is not necessary for men and could not be sustained." (The Court went out of its way to say that it was not "questioning in any respect the decision in *Lochner v. New York*.")

c.   In *Bunting v. Oregon*, 243 U.S. 426 (1917), the Court upheld an Oregon law establishing a ten-hour maximum work day for all factory workers, male and female.

d.   In *Adkins v. Children's Hospital*, 261 U.S. 525 (1923), the Court struck down a District of Columbia law establishing a minimum wage for women, on the ground that this interfered with women's liberty of contract. Legislatures could impose maximum hours, but not minimum wages. In reaching this decision, it is notable that the Court emphasized social and constitutional changes. Referring to "the ancient inequality of the sexes, otherwise than physical," that had been endorsed in *Muller*, the Court said: "In view of the great—not to say revolutionary—changes which have taken place since that utterance, in the contractual, political, and civil status of women, culminating in the Nineteenth Amendment, it is not unreasonable to say that these differences have now come almost, if not quite, to the vanishing point. In this aspect of the matter, while the physical differences must be recognized in appropriate cases, and legislation fixing hours or conditions of work may properly take them into account, we cannot accept the doctrine that women of mature age, *sui juris*, require or may be subjected to restrictions upon their liberty of contract which could not lawfully be imposed in the case of men under similar circumstances."

Do these holdings make sense? Is it possible to be consistent and principled in applying *Lochner*'s approach? If not, why not?

————

The *Lochner*-era substantive due process cases were not exclusively concerned with the freedom of contract. In two leading cases, *Meyer v. Nebraska*, 262 U.S. 390 (1923) and *Pierce v. Society of Sisters*, 268 U.S. 510 (195), the Court held that certain restrictions on religious education were inconsistent with the Due Process Clause of the Fourteenth Amendment.

Meyer v. Nebraska

262 U.S. 390 (1923)

■ MR. JUSTICE MCREYNOLDS delivered the opinion of the Court.

Plaintiff in error was tried and convicted in the District Court for Hamilton County, Nebraska, under an information which charged that, on May 25, 1920, while an instructor in Zion Parochial School, he unlawfully taught the subject of reading in the German language to Raymond Parpart, a child of ten years, who had not attained and successfully passed the eighth grade. The information is based upon "An act relating to the teaching of foreign languages in the State of Nebraska," approved April 9, 1919, which follows [Laws 1919, c. 249.]:

> Section 1. No person, individually or as a teacher, shall, in any private, denominational, parochial or public school, teach any subject to any person in any language other than the English language.
>
> Sec. 2. Languages, other than the English language, may be taught as languages only after a pupil shall have attained and successfully passed the eighth grade as evidenced by a certificate of graduation issued by the county superintendent of the county in which the child resides.
>
> Sec. 3. Any person who violates any of the provisions of this act shall be deemed guilty of a misdemeanor and upon conviction, shall be subject to a fine of not less than twenty-five dollars ($25), nor more than one hundred dollars ($100) or be confined in the county jail for any period not exceeding thirty days for each offense.
>
> Sec. 4. Whereas, an emergency exists, this act shall be in force from and after its passage and approval.

The Supreme Court of the State affirmed the judgment of conviction. It declared the offense charged and established was "the direct and intentional teaching of the German language as a distinct subject to a child who had not passed the eighth grade," in the parochial school maintained by Zion Evangelical Lutheran Congregation, a collection of Biblical stories being used therefor. And it held that the statute forbidding this did not conflict with the Fourteenth Amendment, but was a valid exercise of the police power. The following excerpts from the opinion sufficiently indicate the reasons advanced to support the conclusion.

> The salutary purpose of the statute is clear. The legislature had seen the baneful effects of permitting foreigners, who had taken residence in this country, to rear and educate their children in the language of their native land. The result of that condition was found to be inimical to our own safety. To allow the children of foreigners, who had emigrated here, to be taught from early childhood the language of the country of their parents was to rear them with that language as their mother tongue. It was to educate them so that they must always think in that language, and, as a consequence, naturally inculcate in them the ideas and sentiments foreign to the best interests of this country. The statute, therefore, was intended not only to require that the education of all children be conducted in the English language, but that, until they had grown into that language and until it had become a part of them, they should not in the schools be taught any other language. The obvious purpose of this statute was that the

English language should be and become the mother tongue of all children reared in this state. The enactment of such a statute comes reasonably within the police power of the state. *Pohl v. State,* 132 N.E. (Ohio) 20; *State v. Bartels,* 181 N.W. (Ia.) 508.

It is suggested that the law is an unwarranted restriction, in that it applies to all citizens of the state and arbitrarily interferes with the rights of citizens who are not of foreign ancestry, and prevents them, without reason, from having their children taught foreign languages in school. That argument is not well taken, for it assumes that every citizen finds himself restrained by the statute. The hours which a child is able to devote to study in the confinement of school are limited. It must have ample time for exercise or play. Its daily capacity for learning is comparatively small. A selection of subjects for its education, therefore, from among the many that might be taught, is obviously necessary. The legislature no doubt had in mind the practical operation of the law. The law affects few citizens, except those of foreign lineage. Other citizens, in their selection of studies, except perhaps in rare instances, have never deemed it of importance to teach their children foreign languages before such children have reached the eighth grade. In the legislative mind, the salutary effect of the statute no doubt outweighed the restriction upon the citizens generally, which, it appears, was a restriction of no real consequence.

The problem for our determination is whether the statute, as construed and applied, unreasonably infringes the liberty guaranteed to the plaintiff in error by the Fourteenth Amendment. "No State shall . . . deprive any person of life, liberty, or property, without due process of law."

While this Court has not attempted to define with exactness the liberty thus guaranteed, the term has received much consideration and some of the included things have been definitely stated. Without doubt, it denotes not merely freedom from bodily restraint, but also the right of the individual to contract, to engage in any of the common occupations of life, to acquire useful knowledge, to marry, establish a home and bring up children, to worship God according to the dictates of his own conscience, and generally to enjoy those privileges long recognized at common law as essential to the orderly pursuit of happiness by free men. *[The long string cite here, including the* Slaughter-House Cases *and* Lochner, *is omitted.—Editors]* The established doctrine is that this liberty may not be interfered with, under the guise of protecting the public interest, by legislative action which is arbitrary or without reasonable relation to some purpose within the competency of the State to effect. Determination by the legislature of what constitutes proper exercise of police power is not final or conclusive, but is subject to supervision by the courts. *Lawton v. Steele,* 152 U.S. 133, 137 (1894).

The American people have always regarded education and acquisition of knowledge as matters of supreme importance which should be diligently promoted. The Ordinance of 1787 declares,

> Religion, morality, and knowledge being necessary to good government and the happiness of mankind, schools and the means of education shall forever be encouraged.

Corresponding to the right of control, it is the natural duty of the parent to give his children education suitable to their station in life; and nearly all the States, including Nebraska, enforce this obligation by compulsory laws.

Practically, education of the young is only possible in schools conducted by especially qualified persons who devote themselves thereto. The calling always has been regarded as useful and honorable, essential, indeed, to the public welfare. Mere knowledge of the German language cannot reasonably be regarded as harmful. Heretofore it has been commonly looked upon as helpful and desirable. Plaintiff in error taught this language in school as part of his occupation. His right thus to teach and the right of parents to engage him so to instruct their children, we think, are within the liberty of the Amendment.

The challenged statute forbids the teaching in school of any subject except in English; also the teaching of any other language until the pupil has attained and successfully passed the eighth grade, which is not usually accomplished before the age of twelve. The Supreme Court of the State has held that "the so-called ancient or dead languages" are not "within the spirit or the purpose of the act." *Nebraska District of Evangelical Lutheran Synod v. McKelvie,* 187 N.W. 927. Latin, Greek, Hebrew are not proscribed; but German, French, Spanish, Italian and every other alien speech are within the ban. Evidently the legislature has attempted materially to interfere with the calling of modern language teachers, with the opportunities of pupils to acquire knowledge, and with the power of parents to control the education of their own.

It is said the purpose of the legislation was to promote civic development by inhibiting training and education of the immature in foreign tongues and ideals before they could learn English and acquire American ideals; and "that the English language should be and become the mother tongue of all children reared in this State." It is also affirmed that the foreign born population is very large, that certain communities commonly use foreign words, follow foreign leaders, move in a foreign atmosphere, and that the children are thereby hindered from becoming citizens of the most useful type, and the public safety is imperiled.

That the State may do much, go very far, indeed, in order to improve the quality of its citizens, physically, mentally and morally, is clear; but the individual has certain fundamental rights which must be respected. The protection of the Constitution extends to all, to those who speak other languages as well as to those born with English on the tongue. Perhaps it would be highly advantageous if all had ready understanding of our ordinary speech, but this cannot be coerced by methods which conflict with the Constitution—a desirable end cannot be promoted by prohibited means.

For the welfare of his Ideal Commonwealth, Plato suggested a law which should provide:

> That the wives of our guardians are to be common, and their children are to be common, and no parent is to know his own child, nor any child his parent. . . . The proper officers will take the offspring of the good parents to the pen or fold, and there they will deposit them with certain nurses who dwell in a separate quarter; but the offspring of the inferior, or of the better when they chance to be deformed, will be put away in some mysterious, unknown place, as they should be.

In order to submerge the individual and develop ideal citizens, Sparta assembled the males at seven into barracks and intrusted their subsequent education and training to official guardians. Although such measures have been deliberately approved by men of great genius, their ideas touching the relation between individual and State were wholly different from those upon which our institutions rest, and it hardly will be affirmed that any legislature could impose such restrictions upon the people of a State without doing violence to both letter and spirit of the Constitution.

The desire of the legislature to foster a homogeneous people with American ideals prepared readily to understand current discussions of civic matters is easy to appreciate. Unfortunate experiences during the late war and aversion toward every characteristic of truculent adversaries were certainly enough to quicken that aspiration. But the means adopted, we think, exceed the limitations upon the power of the State and conflict with rights assured to plaintiff in error. The interference is plain enough, and no adequate reason therefor in time of peace and domestic tranquility has been shown.

The power of the State to compel attendance at some school and to make reasonable regulations for all schools, including a requirement that they shall give instructions in English, is not questioned. Nor has challenge been made of the State's power to prescribe a curriculum for institutions which it supports. Those matters are not within the present controversy. Our concern is with the prohibition approved by the Supreme Court. *Adams v. Tanner*, 244 U.S. 590 (1917), pointed out that mere abuse incident to an occupation ordinarily useful is not enough to justify its abolition, although regulation may be entirely proper. No emergency has arisen which renders knowledge by a child of some language other than English so clearly harmful as to justify its inhibition with the consequent infringement of rights long freely enjoyed. We are constrained to conclude that the statute as applied is arbitrary and without reasonable relation to any end within the competency of the State.

As the statute undertakes to interfere only with teaching which involves a modern language, leaving complete freedom as to other matters, there seems no adequate foundation for the suggestion that the purpose was to protect the child's health by limiting his mental activities. It is well known that proficiency in a foreign language seldom comes to one not instructed at an early age, and experience shows that this is not injurious to the health, morals or understanding of the ordinary child.

The judgment of the court below must be reversed, and the cause remanded for further proceedings not inconsistent with this opinion.

■ MR. JUSTICE HOLMES, [joined by MR. JUSTICE SUTHERLAND,] dissenting.

We all agree, I take it, that it is desirable that all the citizens of the United States should speak a common tongue, and therefore that the end aimed at by the statute is a lawful and proper one. The only question is whether the means adopted deprive teachers of the liberty secured to them by the Fourteenth Amendment. It is with hesitation and unwillingness that I differ from my brethren with regard to a law like this but I cannot bring my mind to believe that in some circumstances, and circumstances existing it is said in Nebraska, the statute might not be regarded as a reasonable or even necessary method of reaching the desired result. The part of the act with which we are concerned deals with the teaching of young children. Youth is the time when familiarity with a language is established and if there are sections in the State where a child would hear only Polish or French or German spoken at home I am not prepared to say that it is unreasonable to provide that in his early years he shall hear and speak only English at school. But if it is reasonable it is not an undue restriction of the liberty either of teacher or scholar. No one would doubt that a teacher might be forbidden to teach many things, and the only criterion of his liberty under the Constitution that I can think of is "whether, considering the end in view, the statute passes the bounds of reason and assumes the character of a merely arbitrary fiat." *Purity Extract & Tonic Co. v. Lynch*, 226 U.S. 192, 204 (1912). I think I appreciate the objection to the law but it appears to me to present a question upon which men reasonably might differ and therefore I am unable to say that the Constitution of the United States prevents the experiment being tried. . . .

Pierce v. Society of Sisters
268 U.S. 510 (1925)

■ MR. JUSTICE MCREYNOLDS delivered the opinion of the Court.

These appeals are from decrees, based upon undenied allegations, which granted preliminary orders restraining appellants from threatening or attempting to enforce the Compulsory Education Act adopted November 7, 1922, under the initiative provision of her Constitution by the voters of Oregon. . . .

The challenged Act, effective September 1, 1926, requires every parent, guardian, or other person having control or charge or custody of a child between eight and sixteen years to send him "to a public school for the period of time a public school shall be held during the current year" in the district where the child resides; and failure so to do is declared a misdemeanor. . . . The manifest purpose is to compel general attendance at public schools by normal children, between eight and sixteen, who have not completed the eighth grade. . . .

Appellee the Society of Sisters is an Oregon corporation, organized in 1880, with power to care for orphans, educate and instruct the youth, establish and maintain academies or schools, and acquire necessary real and personal property. It has long devoted its property and effort to the secular and religious education and care of children, and has acquired the valuable good will of many parents and guardians. It conducts interdependent primary and high schools and junior colleges, and maintains orphanages for the custody and control of children between eight and sixteen. In its primary schools many children between those ages are taught the subjects usually pursued in Oregon public schools during the first eight years. Systematic religious instruction and moral training according to the tenets of the Roman Catholic Church are also regularly provided. . . . The business is remunerative—the annual income from primary schools exceeds thirty thousand dollars—and the successful conduct of this requires long time contracts with teachers and parents. The Compulsory Education Act of 1922 has already caused the withdrawal from its schools of children who would otherwise continue, and their income has steadily declined. The appellants, public officers, have proclaimed their purpose strictly to enforce the statute.

After setting out the above facts, the Society's bill alleges that the enactment conflicts with the right of parents to choose schools where their children will receive appropriate mental and religious training, the right of the child to influence the parents' choice of a school, the right of schools and teachers therein to engage in a useful business or profession, and is accordingly repugnant to the Constitution and void. And, further, that unless enforcement of the measure is enjoined the corporation's business and property will suffer irreparable injury.

Appellee Hill Military Academy is a private corporation organized in 1908 under the laws of Oregon, engaged in owning, operating, and conducting for profit an elementary, college preparatory, and military training school for boys between the ages of five and twenty-one years. The average attendance is one hundred, and the annual fees received for each student amount to some eight hundred dollars. . . . By reason of the statute and threat of enforcement appellee's business is being destroyed and its property depreciated; parents and guardians are refusing to make contracts for the future instruction of their sons, and some are being withdrawn. . . .

No question is raised concerning the power of the state reasonably to regulate all schools, to inspect, supervise and examine them, their teachers and pupils; to require that all children of proper age attend some school, that teachers shall be of good moral character and patriotic disposition, that certain studies plainly essential to good citizenship must be taught, and that nothing be taught which is manifestly inimical to the public welfare.

The inevitable practical result of enforcing the Act under consideration would be destruction of appellees' primary schools, and perhaps all other private primary schools for normal children within the state of Oregon. Appellees are engaged in a kind of undertaking not inherently harmful, but long regarded as useful and meritorious. Certainly there is nothing in the present records to indicate that they have failed to discharge their obligations to patrons, students, or the state. And there are no peculiar circumstances or present emergencies which demand extraordinary measures relative to primary education.

Under the doctrine of *Meyer v. Nebraska*, 262 U.S. 390 (1923), we think it entirely plain that the Act of 1922 unreasonably interferes with the liberty of parents and guardians to direct the upbringing and education of children under their control. As often heretofore pointed out, rights guaranteed by the Constitution may not be abridged by legislation which has no reasonable relation to some purpose within the competency of the state. The fundamental theory of liberty upon which all governments in this Union repose excludes any general power of the state to standardize its children by forcing them to accept instruction from public teachers only. The child is not the mere creature of the state; those who nurture him and direct his destiny have the right, coupled with the high duty, to recognize and prepare him for additional obligations.

Appellees are corporations and therefore, it is said, they cannot claim for themselves the liberty which the Fourteenth Amendment guarantees. Accepted in the proper sense, this is true. But they have business and property for which they claim protection. These are threatened with destruction through the unwarranted compulsion which appellants are exercising over present and prospective patrons of their schools. And this court has gone very far to protect against loss threatened by such action. . . .

NOTES

1.   What kind of case is *Meyer*? *Pierce*? Are they freedom of contract cases? Are they *Lochner*-style substantive due process cases, but extending beyond freedom of

contract? Or should one or both be seen as First Amendment cases involving freedom of speech and free exercise of religion? Does it matter what the constitutional foundation is? Note that when the Court decided *Meyer* and *Pierce* it had not yet begun the process of incorporating the specific provisions of the Bill of Rights into the Fourteenth Amendment. Instead, the Court was in the habit of resorting to the Due Process Clause and speaking of deprivations of "liberty" and "property." In later cases, including the next one you will read—*Griswold v. Connecticut*, 381 U.S. 479 (1965)—the Court characterized *Meyer* and *Pierce* in terms of the rights protected by the First Amendment.

2.   *Meyer* and *Pierce* have echoed in more recent Supreme Court decisions. For example, in *Wisconsin v. Yoder,* 406 U.S. 205 (1972), the Court held that the State of Wisconsin could not require members of the Old Order Amish to send their children to school beyond eighth grade, in violation of the Amish families' religious beliefs. The decision rested squarely on the Free Exercise Clause, but the Court noted the strongly supportive language of *Meyer* and *Pierce* concerning parents' rights to direct the upbringing and education of their children, including the choice of religious education, and the absence of a right of the state to seek to standardize children into a single mold.

3.   Dean Erwin Chemerinsky has argued that to confront pervasive inequalities in today's public schools, the federal government ought to require that "every child must attend public school through high school. There will be no private schools, no parochial schools, and no home schooling." *Separate and Unequal: American Education Today*, 52 Am. U. L. Rev. 1451, 1472 (2003). Is the aim of the proposal to reduce inequalities between public schools and other schools? Would the proposal reduce the inequalities between public schools, or might it even exacerbate them? Can the proposal be squared with *Meyer* and *Prince*? If not, should those cases be overruled? Would a universal system of educational vouchers be more consistent with *Meyer* and *Pierce*'s rejection of the "power of the state to standardize its children"?

[Assignment 78]

D. THE FALL AND RISING AGAIN OF SUBSTANTIVE DUE PROCESS

When the Court held unconstitutional the laws at issue in *Allgeyer, Lochner*, and other cases, it was restricting what states and the national government could do. That is always the case when the Court invalidates a law on constitutional grounds. But these cases were controversial because the "constitutional grounds" the Court invoked were somewhat removed from the Constitution, and the Court's reasonableness inquiry was not so much a legal determination as a policy determination undertaken by the justices. The inquiry therefore depended to an unusually large extent on whatever views the justices happened to entertain about what was good policy. These criticisms can be clearly seen in the following excerpt from President Franklin Delano Roosevelt's radio address attacking the Court for its invalidation of New Deal programs. The attack succeeded. The Court retreated in haste, and for more than two decades substantive due process seemed to be dying. Then a funny thing happened on the way to the funeral parlor—substantive due process recovered. This time the topic was different, not economic freedom but sexual freedom, but the arguments for and against this application of substantive due process would be much the same. As others have said, "History never repeats itself, but it rhymes."

Franklin Delano Roosevelt, Fireside Chat on the Reorganization of the Judiciary

Mar. 9, 1937

. . . Tonight, sitting at my desk in the White House, I make my first radio report to the people in my second term of office.

I am reminded of that evening in March, four years ago, when I made my first radio report to you. We were then in the midst of the great banking crisis.

Soon after, with the authority of the Congress, we asked the Nation to turn over all of its privately held gold, dollar for dollar, to the Government of the United States.

Today's recovery proves how right that policy was.

But when, almost two years later, it came before the Supreme Court its constitutionality was upheld only by a five-to-four vote. The change of one vote would have thrown all the affairs of this great Nation back into hopeless chaos. In effect, four Justices ruled that the right under a private contract to exact a pound of flesh was more sacred than the main objectives of the Constitution to establish an enduring Nation. . . .

I want to talk with you very simply about the need for present action in this crisis—the need to meet the unanswered challenge of one-third of a Nation ill-nourished, ill-clad, ill-housed.

Last Thursday I described the American form of Government as a three horse team provided by the Constitution to the American people so that their field might be plowed. The three horses are, of course, the three branches of government—the Congress, the Executive and the Courts. Two of the horses are pulling in unison today; the third is not. Those who have intimated that the President of the United States is trying to drive that team, overlook the simple fact that the President, as Chief Executive, is himself one of the three horses.

It is the American people themselves who are in the driver's seat.

It is the American people themselves who want the furrow plowed.

It is the American people themselves who expect the third horse to pull in unison with the other two.

I hope that you have re-read the Constitution of the United States in these past few weeks. Like the Bible, it ought to be read again and again.

It is an easy document to understand when you remember that it was called into being because the Articles of Confederation under which the original thirteen States tried to operate after the Revolution showed the need of a National Government with power enough to handle national problems. In its Preamble, the Constitution states that it was intended to form a more perfect Union and promote the general welfare; and the powers given to the Congress to carry out those purposes can be best described by saying that they were all the powers needed to meet each and every problem which then had a national character and which could not be met by merely local action.

But the framers went further. Having in mind that in succeeding generations many other problems then undreamed of would become national problems, they gave to the Congress the ample broad powers "to levy taxes . . . and provide for the common defense and general welfare of the United States."

That, my friends, is what I honestly believe to have been the clear and underlying purpose of the patriots who wrote a Federal Constitution to create a National Government with national power, intended as they said, "to form a more perfect union . . . for ourselves and our posterity."

For nearly twenty years there was no conflict between the Congress and the Court. Then Congress passed a statute which, in 1803, the Court said violated an express provision of the Constitution. The Court claimed the power to declare it unconstitutional and did so declare it. But a little later the Court itself admitted that it was an extraordinary power to exercise and through Mr. Justice Washington laid down this limitation upon it: "It is but a decent respect due to the wisdom, the integrity and the patriotism of the legislative body, by which any law is passed, to presume in favor of its validity until its violation of the Constitution is proved beyond all reasonable doubt."

But since the rise of the modern movement for social and economic progress through legislation, the Court has more and more often and more and more boldly asserted a power to veto laws passed by the Congress and State Legislatures in complete disregard of this original limitation.

In the last four years the sound rule of giving statutes the benefit of all reasonable doubt has been cast aside. The Court has been acting not as a judicial body, but as a policy-making body.

When the Congress has sought to stabilize national agriculture, to improve the conditions of labor, to safeguard business against unfair competition, to protect our national resources, and in many other ways, to serve our clearly national needs, the majority of the Court has been assuming the power to pass on the wisdom of these acts of the Congress—and to approve or disapprove the public policy written into these laws.

That is not only my accusation. It is the accusation of most distinguished justices of the present Supreme Court. I have not the time to quote to you all the language used by dissenting justices in many of these cases. But in the case holding the Railroad Retirement Act unconstitutional, for instance, Chief Justice Hughes said in a dissenting opinion that the majority opinion was "a departure from sound principles," and placed "an unwarranted limitation upon the commerce clause." And three other justices agreed with him.

In the case of holding the AAA unconstitutional, Justice Stone said of the majority opinion that it was a "tortured construction of the Constitution." And two other justices agreed with him.

In the case holding the New York minimum wage law unconstitutional, Justice Stone said that the majority were actually reading into the Constitution their own "personal economic predilections," and that if the legislative power is not left free to choose the methods of solving the problems of poverty, subsistence, and health of large numbers in the community, then "government is to be rendered impotent." And two other justices agreed with him.

In the face of these dissenting opinions, there is no basis for the claim made by some members of the Court that something in the Constitution has compelled them regretfully to thwart the will of the people.

In the face of such dissenting opinions, it is perfectly clear that, as Chief Justice Hughes has said, "We are under a Constitution, but the Constitution is what the judges say it is."

The Court in addition to the proper use of its judicial functions has improperly set itself up as a third house of the Congress—a super-legislature, as one of the justices has called it—reading into the Constitution words and implications which are not there, and which were never intended to be there.

We have, therefore, reached the point as a nation where we must take action to save the Constitution from the Court and the Court from itself. We must find a way to take an appeal from the Supreme Court to the Constitution itself. We want a Supreme Court which will do justice under the Constitution and not over it. In our courts we want a government of laws and not of men.

I want—as all Americans want—an independent judiciary as proposed by the framers of the Constitution. That means a Supreme Court that will enforce the Constitution as written, that will refuse to amend the Constitution by the arbitrary exercise of judicial power—in other words by judicial say-so. It does not mean a judiciary so independent that it can deny the existence of facts which are universally recognized.

How then could we proceed to perform the mandate given us? It was said in last year's Democratic platform, "If these problems cannot be effectively solved within the Constitution, we shall seek such clarifying amendment as will assure the power to enact those laws, adequately to regulate commerce, protect public health and safety, and safeguard economic security." In other words, we said we would seek an amendment only if every other possible means by legislation were to fail.

When I commenced to review the situation with the problem squarely before me, I came by a process of elimination to the conclusion that, short of amendments, the only method which was clearly constitutional, and would at the same time carry out other much needed reforms, was to infuse new blood into all our Courts. We must have men worthy and equipped to carry out impartial justice. But, at the same time, we must have Judges who will bring to the Courts a present-day sense of the Constitution—Judges who will retain in the Courts the judicial functions of a court, and reject the legislative powers which the courts have today assumed. . . .

What is my proposal? It is simply this: whenever a Judge or Justice of any Federal Court has reached the age of seventy and does not avail himself of the opportunity to retire on a pension, a new member shall be appointed by the President then in office, with the approval, as required by the Constitution, of the Senate of the United States.

That plan has two chief purposes. By bringing into the judicial system a steady and continuing stream of new and younger blood, I hope, first, to make the administration of all Federal justice speedier and, therefore, less costly; secondly, to bring to the decision of social and economic problems younger men who have had personal experience and contact with modern facts and circumstances under which average men have to live and work. This plan will save our national Constitution from hardening of the judicial arteries. . . .

Those opposing this plan have sought to arouse prejudice and fear by crying that I am seeking to "pack" the Supreme Court and that a baneful precedent will be established.

What do they mean by the words "packing the Court"?

Let me answer this question with a bluntness that will end all honest misunderstanding of my purposes.

If by that phrase "packing the Court" it is charged that I wish to place on the bench spineless puppets who would disregard the law and would decide specific cases as I wished them to be decided, I make this answer: that no President fit for his office would appoint, and no Senate of honorable men fit for their office would confirm, that kind of appointees to the Supreme Court.

But if by that phrase the charge is made that I would appoint and the Senate would confirm Justices worthy to sit beside present members of the Court who understand those modern conditions, that I will appoint Justices who will not undertake to override the judgment of the Congress on legislative policy, that I will appoint Justices who will act as Justices and not as legislators—if the appointment of such Justices can be called "packing the Courts," then I say that I and with me the vast majority of the American people favor doing just that thing- now. . . .

I am in favor of action through legislation:

First, because I believe that it can be passed at this session of the Congress.

Second, because it will provide a reinvigorated, liberal-minded Judiciary necessary to furnish quicker and cheaper justice from bottom to top.

Third, because it will provide a series of Federal Courts willing to enforce the Constitution as written, and unwilling to assert legislative powers by writing into it their own political and economic policies.

During the past half century the balance of power between the three great branches of the Federal Government, has been tipped out of balance by the Courts in direct contradiction of the high purposes of the framers of the Constitution. It is my purpose to restore that balance. You who know me will accept my solemn assurance that in a world in which democracy is under attack, I seek to make American democracy succeed. You and I will do our part.

A NOTE ON *WEST COAST HOTEL* AND THE INTERRING OF *LOCHNER*

Beginning in the mid-1930s, the Court retreated from and then squarely repudiated the substantive due process approach of *Lochner.* There was no magic "*Lochner* is hereby overruled" proclamation, but the accumulated force of the decisions was precisely that. One of the most important of these decisions was *West Coast Hotel Co. v. Parrish*, 300 U.S. 379 (1937), which overruled *Adkins v. Children's Hospital*, 261 U.S. 525 (1923), the *Lochner*-era case that had struck down a minimum-wage law for women. Chief Justice Hughes's opinion for the Court rejected the idea that a similar minimum-wage law was a "deprivation of freedom of contract." He contended that the Court's precedent should be reconsidered because of "[t]he importance of the question, in which many States having similar laws are concerned, the close division by which the decision in the *Adkins* case was reached, and the economic conditions which have supervened." His argument ~ceeded this way:

The constitutional provision invoked is the due process clause of the Fourteenth Amendment governing the States, as the due process clause invoked in the *Adkins* case governed Congress. In each case the violation alleged by those attacking minimum wage regulation for women is deprivation of freedom of contract. What is this freedom? The Constitution does not speak of freedom of contract. It speaks of liberty and prohibits the deprivation of liberty without due process of law. In prohibiting that deprivation the Constitution does not recognize an absolute and uncontrollable liberty. Liberty in each of its phases has its history and connotation. But the liberty safeguarded is liberty in a social organization which requires the protection of law against the evils which menace the health, safety, morals and welfare of the people. Liberty under the Constitution is thus necessarily subject to the restraints of due process, and regulation which is reasonable in relation to its subject and is adopted in the interest of the community is due process. . . .

The legislature of the State was clearly entitled to consider the situation of women in employment, the fact that they are in the class receiving the least pay, that their bargaining power is relatively weak, and that they are the ready victims of those who would take advantage of their necessitous circumstances. . . . The legislature had the right to consider that its minimum wage requirements would be an important aid in carrying out its policy of protection. The adoption of similar requirements by many States evidences a deepseated conviction both as to the presence of the evil and as to the means adapted to check it. Legislative response to that conviction cannot be regarded as arbitrary or capricious, and that is all we have to decide. Even if the wisdom of the policy be regarded as debatable and its effects uncertain, still the legislature is entitled to its judgment. . . .

Our conclusion is that the case of *Adkins v. Children's Hospital* should be, and it is, overruled.

Justice Sutherland, the author of the opinion of the Court in *Adkins*, dissented for himself and three other justices. He marshaled two main arguments. First, he argued that the proposition that the Due Process Clause of the Fourteenth Amendment "includes freedom of contract is so well settled as to be no longer open to question." In making this argument he strongly objected to one reason that Chief Justice Hughes gave for why that line of cases should be reconsidered, namely "because of 'the economic conditions which have supervened.'" In Justice Sutherland's words:

[T]he meaning of the Constitution does not change with the ebb and flow of economic events. We frequently are told in more general words that the Constitution must be construed in the light of the present. If by that it is meant that the Constitution is made up of living words that apply to every new condition which they include, the statement is quite true. But to say, if that be intended, that the words of the Constitution mean today what they did not mean when written—that is, that they do not apply to a situation now to which they would have applied then—is to rob that instrument of the essential element which continues it in force as the people have made it until they, and not their official agents, have made it otherwise. . . .

If the Constitution, intelligently and reasonably construed in the light of these principles, stands in the way of desirable legislation, the blame must rest upon that instrument, and not upon the court for enforcing it according to its terms. The remedy in that situation—and the only true remedy—is to amend the Constitution.

Second, Justice Sutherland argued that the minimum-wage statute at issue was arbitrary, for it did not have

> the slightest relation to the capacity or earning power of the employee, to the number of hours which constitute the day's work, the character of the place where the work is to be done, or the circumstances or surroundings of the employment. . . .

> [It] fixes minimum wages for adult women. Adult men and their employers are left free to bargain as they please; and it is a significant and an important fact that all state statutes to which our attention has been called are of like character. The common-law rules restricting the power of women to make contracts have, under our system, long since practically disappeared. Women today stand upon a legal and political equality with men. There is no longer any reason why they should be put in different classes in respect of their legal right to make contracts; nor should they be denied, in effect, the right to compete with men for work paying lower wages which men may be willing to accept. And it is an arbitrary exercise of the legislative power to do so. . . .

> An appeal to the principle that the legislature is free to recognize degrees of harm and confine its restrictions accordingly, is but to beg the question, which is—since the contractual rights of men and women are the same, does the legislation here involved, by restricting only the rights of women to make contracts as to wages, create an arbitrary discrimination? We think it does. Difference of sex affords no reasonable ground for making a restriction applicable to the wage contracts of all working women from which like contracts of all working men are left free. Certainly a suggestion that the bargaining ability of the average woman is not equal to that of the average man would lack substance. The ability to make a fair bargain, as everyone knows, does not depend upon sex.

What do you make of these arguments? Was Chief Justice Hughes right that the Constitution says "liberty" not "freedom of contract"? Is that sufficient to decide the case? Why do you think he led the Court's retreat from its *Lochner*-style jurisprudence? And what do you make of Justice Sutherland's argument that even though the Constitution is applied to new circumstances, its meaning does not change? If so, would that support preserving the *Lochner* line of cases, as he argued? Or does it actually cut in the opposite direction? Was he right that the statute made arbitrary distinctions? Or should he have been more deferential to the legislature's policy judgment? Would his arguments have been stronger if the case had been argued under a different clause of the Fourteenth Amendment?

After *West Coast Hotel* it was certainly no longer true that due process protection of the freedom of contract was "well settled." In a succession of cases, the Court went from questioning *Lochner* to interring it. In *United States v. Carolene Products*, 304 U.S. 144 (1938), the Court rejected a substantive due process challenge to a federal prohibition of interstate shipment of "filled milk" (skim milk mixed with non-milk fats). It said that legislative judgments must be accepted where "any state of facts either known or which could reasonably be assumed, affords support for it." Along with its rejection of substantive due process, *Carolene Products* is well known for its fourth footnote, which left open the possibility of "more exacting judicial scrutiny" where legislation restricts the political processes available for redress of grievances, violates a specific prohibition of the Constitution ("such as those of the first ten amendments, which are deemed equally specific when held to be embraced within the Fourteenth"), or targets religious or racial minorities.

In *Railway Express Agency v. New York,* 336 U.S. 106 (1949) and *Williamson v. Lee Optical,* 348 U.S. 483 (1955), two cases that were discussed under "rational basis" review for equal protection analysis (see p. 1463), the Court also rejected substantive due process claims. In *Railway Express Agency,* Justice Douglas, writing for the Court, said: "We do not sit to weigh evidence on the due process issue in order to determine whether the regulation is sound or appropriate; nor is it our function to pass judgment on its wisdom." In *Lee Optical,* again writing for the Court, Justice Douglas said: "The day is gone when this Court uses the Due Process Clause of the Fourteenth Amendment to strike down state laws, regulatory of business and industrial conditions, because they may be unwise, improvident, or out of harmony with a particular school of thought." Both decisions were unanimous in their rejection of the due process claim.

To be sure, the Court's rejection of substantive due process was never quite total. The Court did not renounce *Meyer* or *Pierce.* Recall that whatever alternative grounds might be given for those decisions, they had been decided under the Due Process Clause of the Fourteenth Amendment. And substantive due process had a complicated relationship with the doctrine of incorporation (see p. 1497). The incorporation of the Bill of Rights against the states through the Due Process Clause of the Fourteenth Amendment came after the *Lochner* series of substantive due process decisions. The timing is probably not a coincidence: thinking of "due process" as substantive (*Lochner*) made it easier to think of the substantive provisions of the Bill of Rights as being part of "due process" (incorporation). But there was never any agreement on the Court about how these different concepts fit together. Different views were held about which clause incorporated the Bill of Rights, whether that clause (whichever one it was) incorporated all of the Bill of Rights, and whether the Bill of Rights exhausted the substantive content of "due process."

Despite all that was in dispute, there could be no dispute that the Court had decisively rejected *Lochner* and the conception of the judicial role that it stood for—the idea that the Court had a broad authority to weigh the reasonableness of state laws, substituting its judgment for that of the state legislature. It was not surprising, therefore, in *Ferguson v. Skrupa,* 372 U.S. 726 (1963), that the Court upheld a Kansas law that was a naked attempt by lawyers to line their own pockets. The law prohibited anyone from engaging in "the business of debt adjusting" except as part of the practice of law. Rejecting the due process claim, the Court said Kansas "was free to decide for itself" what legislation to adopt. Writing for the Court, Justice Black noted that he and his fellow justices had categorically rejected the *Lochner* approach of using "the 'vague contours' of the Due Process Clause to nullify laws which a majority of the Court believed to be economically unwise. . . . Unquestionably, there are arguments showing that the business of debt adjusting has social utility, but such arguments are properly addressed to the legislature, not to us. We refuse to sit as a 'super legislature to weigh the wisdom of legislation.' " *Id.* at 731 (quoting *Day-Brite Lighting, Inc., v. Missouri,* 342 U.S. 421, 423 (1952).). Justice Harlan wrote that he "concur[red] in the judgment on the ground that this state measure bears a rational relation to a constitutionally permissible objective. See *Williamson v. Lee Optical Co.,* 348 U.S. 483 (1955)." But Justice Black's opinion was joined by seven other justices, and it expressed the Court's determined rejection of the *Lochner* era. Was Substantive Due Process, at long last, finally dead?

Griswold v. Connecticut

381 U.S. 479 (1965)

■ MR. JUSTICE DOUGLAS delivered the opinion of the Court.

Appellant Griswold is Executive Director of the Planned Parenthood League of Connecticut. Appellant Buxton is a licensed physician and a professor at the Yale Medical School who served as Medical Director for the League at its Center in New Haven—a center open and operating from November 1 to November 10, 1961, when appellants were arrested.

They gave information, instruction, and medical advice to *married persons* as to the means of preventing conception. They examined the wife and prescribed the best contraceptive device or material for her use. Fees were usually charged, although some couples were serviced free.

The statutes whose constitutionality is involved in this appeal provide[ ]:

Any person who uses any drug, medicinal article or instrument for the purpose of preventing conception shall be fined not less than fifty dollars or imprisoned not less than sixty days nor more than one year or be both fined and imprisoned.

Any person who assists, abets, counsels, causes, hires or commands another to commit any offense may be prosecuted and punished as if he were the principal offender.

The appellants were found guilty as accessories and fined $100 each. . . .

[W]e are met with a wide range of questions that implicate the Due Process Clause of the Fourteenth Amendment. Overtones of some arguments suggest that *Lochner v. New York*, 198 U.S. 45 (1905), should be our guide. But we decline that invitation as we did in *West Coast Hotel Co. v. Parrish*, 300 U.S. 379 (1937). We do not sit as a super-legislature to determine the wisdom, need, and propriety of laws that touch economic problems, business affairs, or social conditions. This law, however, operates directly on an intimate relation of husband and wife and their physician's role in one aspect of that relation.

The association of people is not mentioned in the Constitution nor in the Bill of Rights. The right to educate a child in a school of the parents' choice—whether public or private or parochial—is also not mentioned. Nor is the right to study any particular subject or any foreign language. Yet the First Amendment has been construed to include certain of those rights.

By *Pierce v. Society of Sisters*, 268 U.S. 510 (1925), the right to educate one's children as one chooses is made applicable to the States by the force of the First and Fourteenth Amendments. By *Meyer v. Nebraska*, 262 U.S. 390 (1923), the same dignity is given the right to study the German language in a private school. In other words, the State may not, consistently with the spirit of the First Amendment, contract the spectrum of available knowledge. The right of freedom of speech and press includes not only the right to utter or to print, but the right to distribute, the right to receive, the right to read and freedom of inquiry, freedom of thought, and freedom to teach—indeed the freedom of the entire university community. *Sweezy v. New Hampshire*, 354 U.S. 234 (1957). Without those peripheral rights the specific rights would be less secure. And so we reaffirm the principle of the *Pierce* and the *Meyer* cases.

In *NAACP v. Alabama*, 357 U.S. 449, 462 (1958), we protected the "freedom to associate and privacy in one's associations," noting that freedom of association was a peripheral First Amendment right. Disclosure of membership lists of a constitutionally valid association, we held, was invalid "as entailing the likelihood of a substantial restraint upon the exercise by petitioner's members of their right to freedom of association." In other words, the First Amendment has a penumbra where privacy is protected from governmental intrusion. In like context, we have protected forms of "association" that are not political in the customary sense but pertain to the social, legal, and economic benefit of the members. In *Schware v. Board of Bar Examiners*, 353 U.S. 232 (1957), we held it not permissible to bar a lawyer from practice, because he had once been a member of the Communist Party. The man's "association with that Party" was not shown to be "anything more than a political faith in a political party" and was not action of a kind proving bad moral character.

Those cases involved more than the "right of assembly"—a right that extends to all irrespective of their race or ideology. The right of "association," like the right of belief (*Board of Education v. Barnette*, 319 U.S. 624 (1943)), is more than the right to attend a meeting; it includes the right to express one's attitudes or philosophies by membership in a group or by affiliation with it or by other lawful means. Association in that context is a form of expression of opinion; and while it is not expressly included in the First Amendment its existence is necessary in making the express guarantees fully meaningful.

The foregoing cases suggest that specific guarantees in the Bill of Rights have penumbras, formed by emanations from those guarantees that help give them life and substance. See *Poe v. Ullman,* 367 U.S. 497, 516–522 (1961) (dissenting opinion [of MR. JUSTICE HARLAN]). Various guarantees create zones of privacy. The right of association contained in the penumbra of the First Amendment is one, as we have seen. The Third Amendment in its prohibition against the quartering of soldiers "in any house" in time of peace without the consent of the owner is another facet of that privacy. The Fourth Amendment explicitly affirms the "right of the people to be secure in their persons, houses, papers, and effects, against unreasonable searches and seizures." The Fifth Amendment in its Self-Incrimination Clause enables the citizen to create a zone of privacy which government may not force him to surrender to his detriment. The Ninth Amendment provides: "The enumeration in the Constitution, of certain rights, shall not be construed to deny or disparage others retained by the people."

The Fourth and Fifth Amendments were described in *Boyd v. United States*, 116 U.S. 616, 630 (1886), as protection against all governmental invasions "of the sanctity of a man's home and the privacies of life." We recently referred in *Mapp v. Ohio*, 367 U.S. 643, 656 (1961), to the Fourth Amendment as creating a "right to privacy, no less important than any other right carefully and particularly reserved to the people."

We have had many controversies over these penumbral rights of "privacy and repose." See, *e.g.*, *Monroe v. Pape*, 365 U.S. 167 (1961); *Skinner v. Oklahoma*, 316 U.S. 535, 541 (1942). These cases bear witness that the right of privacy which presses for recognition here is a legitimate one.

The present case, then, concerns a relationship lying within the zone of privacy created by several fundamental constitutional guarantees. And it concerns a law which, in forbidding the *use* of contraceptives rather than regulating their manufacture or sale, seeks to achieve its goals by means having a maximum destructive impact upon that relationship. Such a law cannot stand in light of the familiar principle, so often applied by this Court, that a "governmental purpose to control or prevent activities constitutionally subject to state regulation may not be achieved by means which sweep unnecessarily broadly and thereby invade the area of protected freedoms." *NAACP v. Alabama*, 377 U.S. 288, 307 (1964). Would we allow the police to search the sacred precincts of marital bedrooms for telltale signs of the use of contraceptives? The very idea is repulsive to the notions of privacy surrounding the marriage relationship.

We deal with a right of privacy older than the Bill of Rights—older than our political parties, older than our school system. Marriage is a coming together for better or for worse, hopefully enduring, and intimate to the degree of being sacred. It is an association that promotes a way of life, not causes; a harmony in living, not political faiths; a bilateral loyalty, not commercial or social projects. Yet it is an association for as noble a purpose as any involved in our prior decisions.

■ MR. JUSTICE GOLDBERG, whom THE CHIEF JUSTICE and MR. JUSTICE BRENNAN join, concurring.

I agree with the Court that Connecticut's birth-control law unconstitutionally intrudes upon the right of marital privacy. . . . [T]he concept of liberty protects those personal rights that are fundamental, and is not confined to the specific terms of the Bill of Rights. My conclusion that the concept of liberty is not so restricted and that it embraces the right of marital privacy though that right is not mentioned explicitly in the Constitution is supported both by numerous decisions of this Court, referred to in the Court's opinion, and by the language and history of the Ninth Amendment. In reaching the conclusion that the right of marital privacy is protected, as being within the protected penumbra of specific guarantees of the Bill of Rights, the Court refers to the Ninth Amendment. I add these words to emphasize the relevance of that Amendment to the Court's holding. . . .

This Court, in a series of decisions, has held that the Fourteenth Amendment absorbs and applies to the States those specifics of the first eight amendments which express fundamental personal rights. The language and history of the Ninth Amendment reveal that the Framers of the Constitution believed that there are additional fundamental rights, protected from governmental infringement, which exist alongside those fundamental rights specifically mentioned in the first eight constitutional amendments.

The Ninth Amendment reads, "The enumeration in the Constitution, of certain rights, shall not be construed to deny or disparage others retained by the people." The Amendment is almost entirely the work of James Madison. It was introduced in Congress by him and passed the House and Senate with little or no debate and virtually no change in language. It was proffered to quiet expressed fears that a bill of specifically enumerated rights[3] could not be sufficiently broad to cover all essential

---

3   Madison himself had previously pointed out the dangers of inaccuracy resulting from the fact that "no language is so copious as to supply words and phrases for every complex idea." The Federalist, No. 37.

rights and that the specific mention of certain rights would be interpreted as a denial that others were protected.[4]

In presenting the proposed Amendment, Madison said:

"It has been objected also against a bill of rights, that, by enumerating particular exceptions to the grant of power, it would disparage those rights which were not placed in that enumeration; and it might follow by implication, that those rights which were not singled out, were intended to be assigned into the hands of the General Government, and were consequently insecure. This is one of the most plausible arguments I have ever heard urged against the admission of a bill of rights into this system; but, I conceive, that it may be guarded against. I have attempted it, as gentlemen may see by turning to the last clause of the fourth resolution (the Ninth Amendment)." I Annals of Congress 439 (Gales and Seaton ed., 1834).

Mr. Justice Story wrote of this argument against a bill of rights and the meaning of the Ninth Amendment:

"In regard to . . . [a] suggestion, that the affirmance of certain rights might disparage others, or might lead to argumentative implications in favor of other powers, it might be sufficient to say that such a course of reasoning could never be sustained upon any solid basis. . . . But a conclusive answer is, that such an attempt may be interdicted (as it has been) by a positive declaration in such a bill of rights that the enumeration of certain rights shall not be construed to deny or disparage others retained by the people." II Story, Commentaries on the Constitution of the United States 626–627 (5th ed. 1891).

He further stated, referring to the Ninth Amendment:

"This clause was manifestly introduced to prevent any perverse or ingenious misapplication of the well known maxim, that an affirmation in particular cases implies a negation in all others; and, *e converso*, that a negation in particular cases implies an affirmation in all others." Id., at 651.

---

[4]   Alexander Hamilton was opposed to a bill of rights on the ground that it was unnecessary because the Federal Government was a government of delegated powers and it was not granted the power to intrude upon fundamental personal rights. The Federalist, No. 84 (Cooke ed. 1961), at 578—579. He also argued, 'I go further, and affirm that bills of rights, in the sense and in the extent in which they are contended for, are not only unnecessary in the proposed constitution, but would even be dangerous. They would contain various exceptions to powers which are not granted; and on this very account, would afford a colourable pretext to claim more than were granted. For why declare that things shall not be done which there is no power to do? Why for instance, should it be said, that the liberty of the press shall not be restrained, when no power is given by which restrictions may be imposed? I will not contend that such a provision would confer a regulating power; but it is evident that it would furnish, to men disposed to usurp, a plausible pretence for claiming that power.' Id., at 579. The Ninth Amendment and the Tenth Amendment, which provides, 'The powers not delegated to the United States by the Constitution, nor prohibited by it to the States, are reserved to the States respectively, or to the people,' were apparently also designed in part to meet the above-quoted argument of Hamilton.

These statements of Madison and Story make clear that the Framers did not intend that the first eight amendments be construed to exhaust the basic and fundamental rights which the Constitution guaranteed to the people.[5] . . .

The Ninth Amendment to the Constitution may be regarded by some as a recent discovery and may be forgotten by others, but since 1791 it has been a basic part of the Constitution which we are sworn to uphold. To hold that a right so basic and fundamental and so deep-rooted in our society as the right of privacy in marriage may be infringed because that right is not guaranteed in so many words by the first eight amendments to the Constitution is to ignore the Ninth Amendment and to give it no effect whatsoever. Moreover, a judicial construction that this fundamental right is not protected by the Constitution because it is not mentioned in explicit terms by one of the first eight amendments or elsewhere in the Constitution would violate the Ninth Amendment, which specifically states that "[t]he enumeration in the Constitution, of certain rights shall not be *construed* to deny or disparage others retained by the people." (Emphasis added.)

A dissenting opinion suggests that my interpretation of the Ninth Amendment somehow "broaden[s] the powers of this Court." With all due respect, I believe that it misses the import of what I am saying. . . . I do not mean to imply that the Ninth Amendment is applied against the States by the Fourteenth. Nor do I mean to state that the Ninth Amendment constitutes an independent source of rights protected from infringement by either the States or the Federal Government. Rather, the Ninth Amendment shows a belief of the Constitution's authors that fundamental rights exist that are not expressly enumerated in the first eight amendments and an intent that the list of rights included there not be deemed exhaustive. As any student of this Court's opinions knows, this Court has held, often unanimously, that the Fifth and Fourteenth Amendments protect certain fundamental personal liberties from abridgment by the Federal Government or the States. . . . The Ninth Amendment simply shows the intent of the Constitution's authors that other fundamental personal rights should not be denied such protection or disparaged in any other way simply because they are not specifically listed in the first eight constitutional amendments. I do not see how this broadens the authority of the Court; rather it serves to support what this Court has been doing in protecting fundamental rights.

Nor am I turning somersaults with history in arguing that the Ninth Amendment is relevant in a case dealing with a *State's* infringement of a fundamental right. While the Ninth Amendment—and indeed the entire Bill of Rights—originally concerned restrictions upon federal power, the subsequently enacted Fourteenth Amendment prohibits the States as well from abridging fundamental personal liberties. And, the Ninth Amendment, in indicating that not all such liberties are specifically mentioned in the first eight amendments, is surely relevant in showing the existence of other fundamental personal rights, now protected from state, as well as federal, infringement. In sum, the Ninth Amendment simply lends strong support to the view that the "liberty" protected by the Fifth and Fourteenth Amendments from infringement by the Federal Government or the States is not restricted to rights specifically mentioned in the first eight amendments.

---

[5]   The Tenth Amendment similarly made clear that the States and the people retained all those powers not expressly delegated to the Federal Government.

In determining which rights are fundamental, judges are not left at large to decide cases in light of their personal and private notions. Rather, they must look to the "traditions and [collective] conscience of our people" to determine whether a principle is "so rooted [there] . . . as to be ranked as fundamental." *Snyder v. Com. of Massachusetts*, 291 U.S. 97, 105 (1934). The inquiry is whether a right involved "is of such a character that it cannot be denied without violating those 'fundamental principles of liberty and justice which lie at the base of all our civil and political institutions'. . . ." *Powell v. Alabama*, 287 U.S. 45, 67 (1932). "Liberty" also "gains content from the emanations of . . . specific [constitutional] guarantees" and "from experience with the requirements of a free society." *Poe v. Ullman*, at 517 (dissenting opinion of MR. JUSTICE DOUGLAS).

I agree fully with the Court that, applying these tests, the right of privacy is a fundamental personal right, emanating "from the totality of the constitutional scheme under which we live." Id., at 521. . . .

The Connecticut statutes here involved deal with a particularly important and sensitive area of privacy—that of the marital relation and the marital home. This Court recognized in *Meyer v. Nebraska* that the right "to marry, establish a home and bring up children" was an essential part of the liberty guaranteed by the Fourteenth Amendment. In *Pierce v. Society of Sisters*, the Court held unconstitutional an Oregon Act which forbade parents from sending their children to private schools because such an act "unreasonably interferes with the liberty of parents and guardians to direct the upbringing and education of children under their control." As this Court said in *Prince v. Massachusetts*, 321 U.S. 158, 166 (1944), the *Meyer* and *Pierce* decisions "have respected the private realm of family life which the state cannot enter." . . .

The entire fabric of the Constitution and the purposes that clearly underlie its specific guarantees demonstrate that the rights to marital privacy and to marry and raise a family are of similar order and magnitude as the fundamental rights specifically protected.

Although the Constitution does not speak in so many words of the right of privacy in marriage, I cannot believe that it offers these fundamental rights no protection. The fact that no particular provision of the Constitution explicitly forbids the State from disrupting the traditional relation of the family—a relation as old and as fundamental as our entire civilization—surely does not show that the Government was meant to have the power to do so. Rather, as the Ninth Amendment expressly recognizes, there are fundamental personal rights such as this one, which are protected from abridgment by the Government though not specifically mentioned in the Constitution. . . .

The logic of the dissents would sanction federal or state legislation that seems to me even more plainly unconstitutional than the statute before us. Surely the Government, absent a showing of a compelling subordinating state interest, could not decree that all husbands and wives must be sterilized after two children have been born to them. Yet by their reasoning such an invasion of marital privacy would not be subject to constitutional challenge because, while it might be "silly," no provision of the Constitution specifically prevents the Government from curtailing the marital right to bear children and raise a family. While it may shock some of my Brethren that the Court today holds that the Constitution protects the right of marital privacy, in my view it is far more shocking to believe that the personal liberty guaranteed by the Constitution does not include protection against such totalitarian limitation of family size, which is at complete variance with our constitutional concepts. Yet, if upon a showing of a slender basis of rationality, a law outlawing voluntary birth control by married persons is valid, then, by the same reasoning, a law requiring compulsory birth control also would seem to be valid. In my view, however, both types of law would unjustifiably intrude upon rights of marital privacy which are constitutionally protected.

Although the Connecticut birth-control law obviously encroaches upon a fundamental personal liberty, the State does not show that the law serves any "subordinating [state] interest which is compelling" or that it is "necessary . . . to the accomplishment of a permissible state policy." The State, at most, argues that there is some rational relation between this statute and what is admittedly a legitimate subject of state concern—the discouraging of extra-marital relations. It says that preventing the use of birth-control devices by married persons helps prevent the indulgence by some in such extra-marital relations. The rationality of this justification is dubious, particularly in light of the admitted widespread availability to all persons in the State of Connecticut, unmarried as well as married, of birth-control devices for the prevention of disease, as distinguished from the prevention of conception. But, in any event, it is clear that the state interest in safeguarding marital fidelity can be served by a more discriminately tailored statute, which does not, like the present one, sweep unnecessarily broadly, reaching far beyond the evil sought to be dealt with and intruding upon the privacy of all married couples. . . . The State of Connecticut does have statutes, the constitutionality of which is beyond doubt, which prohibit adultery and fornication. These statutes demonstrate that means for achieving the same basic purpose of protecting marital fidelity are available to Connecticut without the need to "invade the area of protected freedoms." *NAACP v. Alabama*, 357 U.S., at 307.

Finally, it should be said of the Court's holding today that it in no way interferes with a State's proper regulation of sexual promiscuity or misconduct. As my Brother HARLAN so well stated in his dissenting opinion in *Poe v. Ullman*, at 553:

> Adultery, homosexuality and the like are sexual intimacies which the State forbids . . . but the intimacy of husband and wife is necessarily an essential and accepted feature of the institution of marriage, an institution which the State not only must allow, but which always and in every age it has fostered and protected. It is one thing when the State exerts its power either to forbid extra-marital sexuality . . . or to say who may marry, but it is quite another when, having acknowledged a marriage and the intimacies inherent in it, it undertakes to regulate by means of the criminal law the details of that intimacy.

In sum, I believe that the right of privacy in the marital relation is fundamental and basic—a personal right "retained by the people" within the meaning of the Ninth Amendment. Connecticut cannot constitutionally abridge this fundamental right, which is protected by the Fourteenth Amendment from infringement by the States. I agree with the Court that petitioners' convictions must therefore be reversed.

■ MR. JUSTICE HARLAN, concurring in the judgment.

I fully agree with the judgment of reversal, but find myself unable to join the Court's opinion. The reason is that it seems to me to evince an approach to this case very much like that taken by my Brothers BLACK and STEWART in dissent, namely: the Due Process Clause of the Fourteenth Amendment does not touch this Connecticut statute unless the enactment is found to violate some right assured by the letter or penumbra of the Bill of Rights.

In other words, what I find implicit in the Court's opinion is that the "incorporation" doctrine may be used to *restrict* the reach of Fourteenth Amendment Due Process. For me this is just as unacceptable constitutional doctrine as is the use of the "incorporation" approach to *impose* upon the States all the requirements of the Bill of Rights as found in the provisions of the first eight amendments and in the decisions of this Court interpreting them.

In my view, the proper constitutional inquiry in this case is whether this Connecticut statute infringes the Due Process Clause of the Fourteenth Amendment because the enactment violates basic values "implicit in the concept of ordered liberty," Palko v. Connecticut, 302 U.S. 319, 325 (1937). For reasons stated at length in my dissenting opinion in *Poe v. Ullman*, I believe that it does. While the relevant inquiry may be aided by resort to one or more of the provisions of the Bill of Rights, it is not dependent on them or any of their radiations. The Due Process Clause of the Fourteenth Amendment stands, in my opinion, on its own bottom. . . .

While I could not more heartily agree that judicial "self restraint" is an indispensable ingredient of sound constitutional adjudication, I do submit that the formula suggested for achieving it [by the dissent] is more hollow than real. "Specific" provisions of the Constitution, no less than "due process," lend themselves as readily to "personal" interpretations by judges whose constitutional outlook is simply to keep the Constitution in supposed "tune with the times." . . .

Judicial self-restraint will . . . be achieved in this area, as in other constitutional areas, only by continual insistence upon respect for the teachings of history, solid recognition of the basic values that underlie our society, and wise appreciation of the great roles that the doctrines of federalism and separation of powers have played in establishing and preserving American freedoms. Adherence to these principles will not, of course, obviate all constitutional differences of opinion among judges, nor should it. Their continued recognition will, however, go farther toward keeping most judges from roaming at large in the constitutional field than will the interpolation into the Constitution of an artificial and largely illusory restriction on the content of the Due Process Clause.

■ MR. JUSTICE WHITE, concurring in the judgment.

In my view this Connecticut law as applied to married couples deprives them of "liberty" without due process of law, as that concept is used in the Fourteenth Amendment. . . .

[T]his is not the first time this Court has had occasion to articulate that the liberty entitled to protection under the Fourteenth Amendment includes the right "to marry, establish a home and bring up children," *Meyer v. Nebraska*, at 399, and "the liberty . . . to direct the upbringing and education of children," *Pierce v. Society of Sisters*, at 534–535, and that these are among "the basic civil rights of man." *Skinner v. Oklahoma*, at 541. These decisions affirm that there is a "realm of family life which the state cannot enter" without substantial justification. Prince, at 166. Surely the right invoked in this case, to be free of regulation of the intimacies of the marriage relationship, "come[s] to this Court with a momentum for respect lacking when appeal is made to liberties which derive merely from shifting economic arrangements." *Kovacs v. Cooper,* 336 U.S. 77, 95 (1949) (opinion of Frankfurter, J.). . . .

The Connecticut anti-contraceptive statute deals rather substantially with this relationship. For it forbids all married persons the right to use birth-control devices, regardless of whether their use is dictated by considerations of family planning, health, or indeed even of life itself. The anti-use statute, together with the general aiding and abetting statute, prohibits doctors from affording advice to married persons on proper and effective methods of birth control. And the clear effect of these statutes, as enforced, is to deny disadvantaged citizens of Connecticut, those without either adequate knowledge or resources to obtain private counseling, access to medical assistance and up-to-date information in respect to proper methods of birth control. In my view, a statute with these effects bears a substantial burden of justification when attacked under the Fourteenth Amendment. *Yick Wo v. Hopkins,* 118 U.S. 356 (1886). . . .

[T]he statute is said to serve the State's policy against all forms of promiscuous or illicit sexual relationships, be they premarital or extramarital, concededly a permissible and legitimate legislative goal. Without taking issue with the premise that the fear of conception operates as a deterrent to such relationships in addition to the criminal proscriptions Connecticut has against such conduct, I wholly fail to see how the ban on the use of contraceptives by married couples in any way reinforces the State's ban on illicit sexual relationships. . . . A statute limiting its prohibition on use to persons engaging in [a] prohibited relationship would serve the end posited by Connecticut in the same way, and with the same effectiveness, or ineffectiveness, as the broad anti-use statute under attack in this case. I find nothing in this record justifying the sweeping scope of this statute, with its telling effect on the freedoms of married persons, and therefore conclude that it deprives such persons of liberty without due process of law.

■ MR. JUSTICE BLACK, with whom MR. JUSTICE STEWART joins, dissenting.

I agree with my Brother STEWART'S dissenting opinion. And like him I do not to any extent whatever base my view that this Connecticut law is constitutional on a belief that the law is wise or that its policy is a good one. In order that there may be no room at all to doubt why I vote as I do, I feel constrained to add that the law is every bit as offensive to me as it is my Brethren of the majority and my Brothers HARLAN, WHITE and GOLDBERG who, reciting reasons why it is offensive to them, hold it unconstitutional. There is no single one of the graphic and eloquent strictures and criticisms fired at the policy of this Connecticut law either by the Court's opinion or by those of my concurring Brethren to which I cannot subscribe—except their conclusion that the evil qualities they see in the law make it unconstitutional.

. . . The two defendants here were active participants in an organization which gave physical examinations to women, advised them what kind of contraceptive devices or medicines would most likely be satisfactory for them, and then supplied the devices themselves, all for a graduated scale of fees, based on the family income. Thus these defendants admittedly engaged with others in a planned course of conduct to help people violate the Connecticut law. Merely because some speech was used in carrying on the conduct—just as in ordinary life some speech accompanies most kinds of conduct—we are not in my view justified in holding that the First Amendment forbids the State to punish their conduct. Strongly as I desire to protect all First Amendment freedoms, I am unable to stretch the Amendment so as to afford protection to the conduct of these defendants in violating the Connecticut law. What would be the constitutional fate of the law if hereafter applied to punish nothing but speech is . . . quite another matter.

The Court talks about a constitutional "right of privacy" as though there is some constitutional provision or provisions forbidding any law ever to be passed which might abridge the "privacy" of individuals. But there is not. There are, of course, guarantees in certain specific constitutional provisions which are designed in part to protect privacy at certain times and places with respect to certain activities. Such, for example, is the Fourth Amendment's guarantee against "unreasonable searches and seizures." But I think it belittles that Amendment to talk about it as though it protects nothing but "privacy." To treat it that way is [not] to give it . . . the kind of liberal reading I think any Bill of Rights provision should be given. The average man would very likely not have his feelings soothed any more by having his property seized openly than by having it seized privately and by stealth. He simply wants his property left alone. And a person can be just as much, if not more, irritated, annoyed and injured by an unceremonious public arrest by a policeman as he is by a seizure in the privacy of his office or home.

One of the most effective ways of diluting or expanding a constitutionally guaranteed right is to substitute for the crucial word or words of a constitutional guarantee another word or words, more or less flexible and more or less restricted in meaning. This fact is well illustrated by the use of the term "right of privacy" as a comprehensive substitute for the Fourth Amendment's guarantee against "unreasonable searches and seizures." "Privacy" is a broad, abstract and ambiguous concept which can easily be shrunken in meaning but which can also, on the other hand, easily be interpreted as a constitutional ban against many things other than searches and seizures. I have expressed the view many times that First Amendment freedoms, for example, have suffered from a failure of the courts to stick to the simple language of the First Amendment in construing it, instead of invoking multitudes of words substituted for those the Framers used. For these reasons I get nowhere in this case by talk about a constitutional "right of privacy" as an emanation from one or more constitutional provisions. I like my privacy as well as the next one, but I am nevertheless compelled to admit that government has a right to invade it unless prohibited by some specific constitutional provision. For these reasons I cannot agree with the Court's judgment and the reasons it gives for holding this Connecticut law unconstitutional.

This brings me to the arguments made by my Brothers HARLAN, WHITE, and GOLDBERG for invalidating the Connecticut law. Brothers HARLAN and WHITE would invalidate it by reliance on the Due Process Clause of the Fourteenth Amendment, but Brother GOLDBERG, while agreeing with Brother HARLAN, relies also on the Ninth Amendment. . . . I think that if properly construed neither the Due Process Clause nor the Ninth Amendment, nor both together, could under any circumstances be a proper basis for invalidating the Connecticut law. I discuss the due process and Ninth Amendment arguments together because on analysis they turn out to be the same thing—merely using different words to claim for this Court and the federal judiciary power to invalidate any legislative act which the judges find irrational, unreasonable or offensive.

The due process argument which my Brothers HARLAN and WHITE adopt here is based, as their opinions indicate, on the premise that this Court is vested with power to invalidate all state laws that it consider to be arbitrary, capricious, unreasonable, or oppressive, or this Court's belief that a particular state law under scrutiny has no "rational or justifying" purpose, or is offensive to a "sense of fairness and justice." If these formulas based on "natural justice," or others which mean the same thing, are to prevail, they require judges to determine what is or is not constitutional on the basis of their own appraisal of what laws are unwise or unnecessary. The power to make such decisions is of course that of a legislative body. Surely it has to be admitted that no provision of the Constitution specifically gives such blanket power to courts to exercise such a supervisory veto over the wisdom and value of legislative policies and to hold unconstitutional those laws which they believe unwise or dangerous. . . . While I completely subscribe to the holding of *Marbury v. Madison,* 5 U.S. (1 Cranch) 137 (1803), and subsequent cases, that our Court has constitutional power to strike down statutes, state or federal, that violate commands of the Federal Constitution, I do not believe that we are granted power by the Due Process Clause or any other constitutional provision or provisions to measure constitutionality by our belief that legislation is arbitrary, capricious or unreasonable, or accomplishes no justifiable purpose, or is offensive to our own notions of "civilized standards of conduct."[5] Such an appraisal of the wisdom of legislation is an attribute of the power to make laws, not of the power to interpret them. The use by federal courts of such a formula or doctrine or whatnot to veto federal or state laws simply takes away from Congress and States the power to make laws based on their own judgment of fairness and wisdom and transfers that power to this Court for ultimate determination—a power which was specifically denied to federal courts by the convention that framed the Constitution.

Of the cases on which my Brothers WHITE and GOLDBERG rely so heavily, undoubtedly the reasoning of two of them supports their result here—as would that of a number of others which they do not bother to name, e.g., *Lochner v. New York* and *Adkins v. Children's Hospital,* 261 U.S. 525 (1923). The two they do cite and quote from, *Meyer v. Nebraska* and *Pierce v. Society of Sisters,* were both decided in opinions by Mr. Justice McReynolds which elaborated the same natural law due process philosophy found in *Lochner v. New York,* one of the cases on which he relied in *Meyer,* along with such other long-discredited decisions as, e.g., *Adkins v. Children's Hospital.* . . . Without expressing an opinion as to whether either of those cases reached a correct result in light of our later decisions applying the First Amendment to the States through the Fourteenth, I merely point out that the

---

[5]   See Learned Hand, The Bill of Rights (1958) 70:

"[J]udges are seldom content merely to annul the particular solution before them; they do not, indeed they may not, say that taking all things into consideration, the legislators' solution is too strong for the judicial stomach. On the contrary they wrap up their veto in a protective veil of adjectives such as 'arbitrary,' 'artificial,' 'normal,' 'reasonable,' 'inherent,' 'fundamental,' or 'essential,' whose office usually, though quite innocently, is to disguise what they are doing and impute to it a derivation far more impressive than their personal preferences, which are all that in fact lie behind the decision."

reasoning stated in *Meyer* and *Pierce* was the same natural law due process philosophy which many later opinions repudiated, and which I cannot accept. . . .

My Brother GOLDBERG has adopted the recent discovery that the Ninth Amendment as well as the Due Process Clause can be used by this Court as authority to strike down all state legislation which this Court thinks violates "fundamental principles of liberty and justice," or is contrary to the "traditions and [collective] conscience of our people." He also states, without proof satisfactory to me, that in making decisions on this basis judges will not consider "their personal and private notions." One may ask how they can avoid considering them. Our Court certainly has no machinery with which to take a Gallup Poll. And the scientific miracles of this age have not yet produced a gadget which the Court can use to determine what traditions are rooted in the "[collective] conscience of our people." Moreover one would certainly have to look far beyond the language of the Ninth Amendment to find that the Framers vested in this Court any such awesome veto powers over law-making, either by the States or by the Congress. Nor does anything in the history of the Amendment offer any support for such a shocking doctrine. The whole history of the adoption of the Constitution and Bill of Rights points the other way, and the very material quoted by my Brother GOLDBERG shows that the Ninth Amendment was intended to protect against the idea that "by enumerating particular exceptions to the grant of power" to the Federal Government, "those rights which were not singled out, were intended to be assigned into the hands of the General Government [the United States], and were consequently insecure." That Amendment was passed, not to broaden the powers of this Court or any other department of "the General Government," but, as every student of history knows, to assure the people that the Constitution in all its provisions was intended to limit the Federal Government to the powers granted expressly or by necessary implication. If any broad, unlimited power to hold laws unconstitutional because they offend what this Court conceives to be the "[collective] conscience of our people" is vested in this Court by the Ninth Amendment, the Fourteenth Amendment, or any other provision of the Constitution, it was not given by the Framers, but rather has been bestowed on the Court by the Court. This fact is perhaps responsible for the peculiar phenomenon that for a period of a century and a half no serious suggestion was ever made that the Ninth Amendment, enacted to protect state powers against federal invasion, could be used as a weapon of federal power to prevent state legislatures from passing laws they consider appropriate to govern local affairs. Use of any such broad, unbounded judicial authority would make of this Court's members a day-to-day constitutional convention.

I repeat so as not to be misunderstood that this Court does have power, which it should exercise, to hold laws unconstitutional where they are forbidden by the Federal Constitution. My point is that there is no provision of the Constitution which either expressly or impliedly vests power in this Court to sit as a supervisory agency over acts of duly constituted legislative bodies and set aside their laws because of the Court's belief that the legislative policies adopted are unreasonable, unwise, arbitrary, capricious or irrational. The adoption of such a loose, flexible, uncontrolled standard for holding laws unconstitutional, if ever it is finally achieved, will amount to a great unconstitutional shift of power to the courts which I believe and am constrained to say will be bad for the courts and worse for the country. Subjecting federal and state laws to such an unrestrained and unrestrainable judicial control as to the wisdom of legislative enactments would, I fear, jeopardize the separation of governmental powers that the Framers set up and at the same time threaten to take away much of the power of States to govern themselves which the Constitution plainly intended them to have.

I realize that many good and able men have eloquently spoken and written, sometimes in rhapsodical strains, about the duty of this Court to keep the Constitution in tune with the times. The idea is that the Constitution must be changed from time to time and that this Court is charged with a duty to make those changes. For myself, I must with all deference reject that philosophy. The Constitution makers knew the need for change and provided for it. Amendments suggested by the people's elected representatives can be submitted to the people or their selected agents for ratification. That method of change was good for our Fathers, and being somewhat old fashioned I must add it is good enough for me. And so, I cannot rely on the Due Process Clause or the Ninth Amendment or any mysterious and uncertain natural law concept as a reason for striking down this state law. The Due Process Clause with an "arbitrary and capricious" or "shocking to the conscience" formula was liberally used by this Court to strike down economic legislation in the early decades of this century, threatening, many people thought, the tranquility and stability of the Nation. See, e.g., *Lochner v. New York*, at 45. That formula, based on subjective considerations of "natural justice," is no less dangerous when used to enforce this Court's views about personal rights than those about economic rights. I had thought that we had laid that formula, as a means for striking down state legislation, to rest once and for all in cases like *West Coast Hotel Co. v. Parrish*, 300 U.S. 379, and many other opinions. See also *Lochner*, at 74 (Holmes, J., dissenting).

In *Ferguson v. Skrupa*, 372 U.S. 726, 730 (1963), this Court two years ago said in an opinion joined by all the Justices but one that

> The doctrine that prevailed in *Lochner, Coppage, Adkins, Burns*, and like cases—that due process authorizes courts to hold laws unconstitutional when they believe the legislature has acted unwisely—has long since been discarded. We have returned to the original constitutional proposition that courts do not substitute their social and economic beliefs for the judgment of legislative bodies, who are elected to pass laws.

... In 1798, when this Court was asked to hold another Connecticut law unconstitutional, Justice Iredell said:

> ". . . [If] the Legislature of the Union, or the Legislature of any member of the Union, shall pass a law, within the general scope of their constitutional power, the Court cannot pronounce it to be void, merely because it is, in their judgment, contrary to the principles of natural justice. The ideas of natural justice are regulated by no fixed standard: the ablest and the purest men have differed upon the subject; and all that the Court could properly say, in such an event, would be, that the Legislature (possessed of an equal right of opinion) had passed an act which, in the opinion of the judges, was inconsistent with the abstract principles of natural justice." *Calder v. Bull*, 3 U.S. (3 Dall.) 386, 399 (1798).

. . . So far as I am concerned, Connecticut's law as applied here is not forbidden by any provision of the Federal Constitution as that Constitution was written, and I would therefore affirm.

■ MR. JUSTICE STEWART, whom MR. JUSTICE BLACK joins, dissenting.

Since 1879 Connecticut has had on its books a law which forbids the use of contraceptives by anyone. I think this is an uncommonly silly law. As a practical matter, the law is obviously unenforceable, except in the oblique context of the present case. As a philosophical matter, I believe the use of contraceptives in the relationship of marriage should be left to personal and private choice, based upon each individual's moral, ethical, and religious beliefs. As a matter of social policy, I think professional counsel about methods of birth control should be available to all, so that each individual's choice can be meaningfully made. But we are not asked in this case to say whether we think this law is unwise, or even asinine. We are asked to hold that it violates the United States Constitution. And that I cannot do.

In the course of its opinion the Court refers to no less than six Amendments to the Constitution: the First, the Third, the Fourth, the Fifth, the Ninth, and the Fourteenth. But the Court does not say which of these Amendments, if any, it thinks is infringed by this Connecticut law.

We *are* told that the Due Process Clause of the Fourteenth Amendment is not, as such, the "guide" in this case. With that much I agree. There is no claim that this law, duly enacted by the Connecticut Legislature, is unconstitutionally vague. There is no claim that the appellants were denied any of the elements of procedural due process at their trial, so as to make their convictions constitutionally invalid. And, as the Court says, the day has long passed since the Due Process Clause was regarded as a proper instrument for determining "the wisdom, need, and propriety" of state laws. Compare *Lochner v. New York*, 198 U.S. 45, with *Ferguson v. Skrupa*, 372 U.S. 726. . . .

As to the First, Third, Fourth, and Fifth Amendments, I can find nothing in any of them to invalidate this Connecticut law. . . . [U]nless the solemn process of constitutional adjudication is to descend to the level of a play on words, there is not involved here any abridgment of "the freedom of speech, or of the press; or the right of the people peaceably to assemble, and to petition the Government for a redress of grievances." No soldier has been quartered in any house. There has been no search, and no seizure. Nobody has been compelled to be a witness against himself.

The Court also quotes the Ninth Amendment, and my Brother GOLDBERG'S concurring opinion relies heavily upon it. But to say that the Ninth Amendment has anything to do with this case is to turn somersaults with history. The Ninth Amendment, like its companion the Tenth, which this Court held "states but a truism that all is retained which has not been surrendered," *United States v. Darby*, 312 U.S. 100, 124, was framed by James Madison and adopted by the States simply to make clear that the adoption of the Bill of Rights did not alter the plan that the *Federal* Government was to be a government of express and limited powers, and that all rights and powers not delegated to it were retained by the people and the individual States. Until today no member of this Court has ever suggested that the Ninth Amendment meant anything else, and the idea that a federal court could ever use the Ninth Amendment to annul a law passed by the elected representatives of the people of the State of Connecticut would have caused James Madison no little wonder.

What provision of the Constitution, then, does make this state law invalid? The Court says it is the right of privacy "created by several fundamental constitutional guarantees." With all deference, I can find no such general right of privacy in the Bill of Rights, in any other part of the Constitution, or in any case ever before decided by this Court.

At the oral argument in this case we were told that the Connecticut law does not "conform to current community standards." But it is not the function of this Court to decide cases on the basis of community standards. We are here to decide cases "agreeably to the Constitution and laws of the United States." It is the essence of judicial duty to subordinate our own personal views, our own ideas of what legislation is wise and what is not. If, as I should surely hope, the law before us does not reflect the standards of the people of Connecticut, the people of Connecticut can freely exercise their true Ninth and Tenth Amendment rights to persuade their elected representatives to repeal it. That is the constitutional way to take this law off the books.[8]

NOTES

1.   What is the constitutional interpretive methodology in *Griswold?* How would you describe the Court's approach? Is it textual interpretation? Historical evidence of original meaning? Is the result supported by inferential reasoning from precedent? Is the method one of extrapolating from constitutional texts and precedents to a more abstract principle? If the liberties expressly protected by the Bill of Rights are starting points, what stopping points does the Court identify? How does the majority respond to the dissenting justices' arguments that they are merely imposing their own personal views on the legislature?

2.   The majority mentions, but does not greatly rely on, the Ninth Amendment. But Justice Goldberg makes it central to his concurrence, and he draws a stinging rebuttal from Justice Black. Which of them has the better of the argument? What is the function of the Ninth Amendment in the Bill of Rights? If it does provide the basis for striking down the Connecticut law, what other statutes should be struck down on its authority? What principles should courts use in deciding its scope? (For more discussion of the Ninth Amendment, see p. 1244).

3.   What do you think of Justice Harlan's argument that the majority's rationale is *too narrow*, and that federal courts have the duty to identify and protect, in a restrained manner, the values "implicit in the concept of ordered liberty"? Justice Harlan cites his famous dissent in *Poe v. Ullman,* 367 U.S. 497 (1961), a case in which the Court had found an earlier challenge to Connecticut's birth control law to be non-justiciable. In that dissent, Justice Harlan spoke of the Fourteenth Amendment as protecting a tradition of liberty, rooted in the past and continuing to grow:

> Were due process merely a procedural safeguard, it would fail to reach those situations where the deprivation of life, liberty or property was accomplished by legislation which by operating in the future could, given even the fairest possible procedure in application to individuals, nevertheless destroy the

---

[8]   The Connecticut House of Representatives recently passed a bill repealing the birth control law. The State Senate has apparently not yet acted on the measure, and today is relieved, of that responsibility by the Court.

enjoyment of all three. Thus the guaranties of due process, though having their roots in Magna Carta's *"per legem terrae"* and considered as procedural safeguards "against executive usurpation and tyranny," have in this country "become bulwarks also against arbitrary legislation." . . .

Due process has not been reduced to any formula; its content cannot be determined by reference to any code. The best that can be said is that, through the course of this Court's decisions, it has represented the balance which our Nation, built upon postulates of respect for the liberty of the individual, has struck between that liberty and the demands of organized society. If the supplying of content to this constitutional concept has of necessity been a rational process, it certainly has not been one where judges have felt free to roam where unguided speculation might take them. The balance of which I speak is the balance struck by this country, having regard to what history teaches are the traditions from which it developed as well as the traditions from which it broke. That tradition is a living thing. A decision of this Court which radically departs from it could not long survive, while a decision which builds on what has survived is likely to be sound. No formula could serve as a substitute, in this area, for judgment and restraint.

. . . This "liberty" is not a series of isolated points pricked out in terms of the taking of property; the freedom of speech, press, and religion; the right to keep and bear arms; the freedom from unreasonable searches and seizures; and so on. It is a rational continuum which, broadly speaking, includes a freedom from all substantial arbitrary impositions and purposeless restraints, and which also recognizes, what a reasonable and sensitive judgment must, that certain interests require particularly careful scrutiny of the state needs asserted to justify their abridgment.

Id. at 541–543 (Harlan, J., dissenting). Justice Harlan proceeded to apply this approach to the Connecticut statute. He found that our legal tradition included "the category of morality among state concerns." Accordingly, he considered it unobjectionable for a state to have "laws forbidding adultery, fornication and homosexual practices," since legal restrictions "confining sexuality to lawful marriage[ ] form a pattern so deeply pressed into the substance of our social life that any constitutional doctrine in this area must build upon that basis." Nevertheless, he contended that the Connecticut statute was different because it regulated sex within marriage. In Justice Harlan's words, which would later be quoted in *Griswold*, "It is one thing when the State exerts its power either to forbid extramarital sexuality altogether, or to say who may marry, but it is quite another when, having acknowledged a marriage and the intimacies inherent in it, it undertakes to regulate by means of the criminal law the details of that intimacy." And Justice Harlan emphasized the statute's "utter novelty," for although other state and federal laws had restricted the distribution of contraceptives, none of these had criminally punished their use.

How is Justice Harlan's approach (in his *Poe* dissent and *Griswold* concurrence) different from the approach taken by the majority in *Griswold*? Would it have provided a stronger or weaker answer to the critique of the *Griswold* dissenters? What are its strengths and vulnerabilities as an approach to interpreting the Constitution?

4.   Is the majority's reasoning limited to marriage, or can *Griswold* be understood on its own terms as recognizing a general constitutional right to "privacy" in matters of sexual conduct or contraception? (Do some of the opinions explicitly deny such a general right?) Consider, for example, whether under *Griswold* there is a constitutional right to engage in nonmarital sex. Could such rights be extrapolated from *Griswold*'s reasoning?

Or would that be performing a *Griswold* on *Griswold* itself—and is there anything wrong with that?

5.   If you think *Griswold* is a strained reading of the Constitution's text, then consider the hypothetical suggested by Justice Goldberg: A state requires sterilization after a married couple has had two children (for the stated compelling interest of population control). Or make the hypothetical worse yet: after two live births, compulsory abortion of subsequent pregnancies. Would that be constitutional? If not, why not? What provision of the Constitution invalidates it? How would Justice Black answer this parade of horribles?

6.   An exercise: If you were to write a constitutional amendment explicitly granting a constitutional right to privacy, what would it say? Try it. But be careful: would the text of your proposed amendment be capable of being interpreted as conferring a constitutional right to torture puppies in your basement? To have a meth lab in your kitchen? Would you need to make any changes to your privacy amendment to achieve the popular support needed for ratification? How closely does the language of your amendment track a provision of the current Constitution?

7.   The Court extended *Griswold* to unmarried couples in *Eisenstadt v. Baird*, 405 U.S. 438 (1972). The key passage was: "It is true that in *Griswold* the right of privacy in question inhered in the marital relationship. Yet . . . [i]f the right of privacy means anything, it is the right of the individual, married or single, to be free from unwarranted governmental intrusion into matters so fundamentally affecting a person as the decision whether to bear or beget a child." The passage made two important moves. First, it took *Griswold,* a case emphasizing the sanctity of marriage, and turned it into a right "of the individual, married or single." Second, it cast *Griswold*'s privacy right as "the decision to bear or beget a child" rather than a right to be free of criminal punishment in a private relationship. Was *Eisenstadt*'s reasoning a warranted or unwarranted extension of *Griswold*? Note that *Eisenstadt* was presented by the Court as a case under the Equal Protection Clause. But marital status has not usually been treated as a suspect classification, either before or since. It is therefore easier to see *Eisenstadt* as a transitional case for substantive due process between *Griswold* and the Court's decision the next year in *Roe v. Wade.*

[*Assignment 79*]

E. ABORTION

The next substantive due process case almost needs no introduction: *Roe v. Wade.* Does the Constitution create a right to abortion of a human fetus?

Roe v. Wade

410 U.S. 113 (1973)

■ MR. JUSTICE BLACKMUN delivered the opinion of the Court.

This Texas federal appeal and its Georgia companion, *Doe v. Bolton*, 410 U.S. 179, present constitutional challenges to state criminal abortion legislation. The Texas statutes under attack here are typical of those that have been in effect in many States for approximately a century. The Georgia statutes, in contrast, have a modern cast and are a legislative product that, to an extent at least, obviously reflects the influences of recent attitudinal change, of advancing medical knowledge and techniques, and of new thinking about an old issue.

We forthwith acknowledge our awareness of the sensitive and emotional nature of the abortion controversy, of the vigorous opposing views, even among physicians, and of the deep and seemingly absolute convictions that the subject inspires. One's philosophy, one's experiences, one's exposure to the raw edges of human existence, one's religious training, one's attitudes toward life and family and their values, and the moral standards one establishes and seeks to observe, are all likely to influence and to color one's thinking and conclusions about abortion.

In addition, population growth, pollution, poverty, and racial overtones tend to complicate and not to simplify the problem.

Our task, of course, is to resolve the issue by constitutional measurement, free of emotion and of predilection.... We bear in mind[ ] Mr. Justice Holmes' admonition in his now-vindicated dissent in *Lochner v. New York*, 198 U.S. 45, 76 (1905):

> [The Constitution] is made for people of fundamentally differing views, and the accident of our finding certain opinions natural and familiar or novel and even shocking ought not to conclude our judgment upon the question whether statutes embodying them conflict with the Constitution of the United States.

I

The Texas statutes that concern us here ... make it a crime to "procure an abortion," as therein defined, or to attempt one, except with respect to "an abortion procured or attempted by medical advice for the purpose of saving the life of the mother." Similar statutes are in existence in a majority of the States.

Texas first enacted a criminal abortion statute in 1854. This was soon modified into language that has remained substantially unchanged to the present time.....

II

Jane Roe,[4] a single woman who was residing in Dallas County, Texas, instituted this federal action in March 1970 against the District Attorney of the county. She sought a declaratory judgment that the Texas criminal abortion statutes were unconstitutional on their face, and an injunction restraining the defendant from enforcing the statutes.

Roe alleged that she was unmarried and pregnant; that she wished to terminate her pregnancy by an abortion "performed by a competent, licensed physician, under safe, clinical conditions"; that she was unable to get a "legal" abortion in Texas because her life did not appear to be threatened by the continuation of her pregnancy; and that she could not afford to travel to another jurisdiction in order to secure a legal abortion under safe conditions. She claimed that the Texas statutes were unconstitutionally vague and that they abridged her right of personal privacy, protected by the First, Fourth, Fifth, Ninth, and Fourteenth Amendments. By an amendment to her complaint Roe purported to sue "on behalf of herself and all other women similarly situated."

---

4   The name is a pseudonym.

James Hubert Hallford, a licensed physician, sought and was granted leave to intervene in Roe's action. In his complaint he alleged that he had been arrested previously for violations of the Texas abortion statutes and that two such prosecutions were pending against him. . . .

On the merits, the District Court held that the "fundamental right of single women and married persons to choose where to have children is protected by the Ninth Amendment, through the Fourteenth Amendment," and that the Texas criminal abortion statutes were void on their face because they were both unconstitutionally vague and constituted an overbroad infringement of the plaintiffs' Ninth Amendment rights. . . .

[In Parts III and IV the Court addressed the procedural posture and justiciability of the case, concluding that the case was properly before it.—Editors]

V

The principal thrust of appellant's attack on the Texas statutes is that they improperly invade a right, said to be possessed by the pregnant woman, to choose to terminate her pregnancy. Appellant would discover this right in the concept of personal "liberty" embodied in the Fourteenth Amendment's Due Process Clause; or in personal marital, familial, and sexual privacy said to be protected by the Bill of Rights or its penumbras, see *Griswold v. Connecticut*, 381 U.S. 479 (1965); *Eisenstadt v. Baird*, 405 U.S. 438 (1972); or among those rights reserved to the people by the Ninth Amendment, *Griswold v. Connecticut*, 381 U.S., at 486 (Goldberg, J., concurring). Before addressing this claim, we feel it desirable briefly to survey, in several aspects, the history of abortion, for such insight as that history may afford us, and then to examine the state purposes and interests behind the criminal abortion laws.

VI

[Here Justice Blackmun offered a legal and cultural history of abortion. He noted the abortifacients of the Persian Empire, the practices of Greece and Rome, the opinion of the ancient Ephesian gynecologist Soranos, the condemnation of abortion in the Hippocratic Oath, the views of the Pythagoreans, the status of the fetus at common law, the history of statutes restricting abortion in England and America, the position of the American Medical Association, and a recent vote of the American Bar Association's House of Delegates.—Editors]

VII

Three reasons have been advanced to explain historically the enactment of criminal abortion laws in the 19th century and to justify their continued existence.

It has been argued occasionally that these laws were the product of a Victorian social concern to discourage illicit sexual conduct. Texas, however, does not advance this justification in the present case. . . .

A second reason is concerned with abortion as a medical procedure. When most criminal abortion laws were first enacted, the procedure was a hazardous one for the woman. . . . [I]t has been argued that a State's real concern in enacting a criminal abortion law was to protect the pregnant woman, that is, to restrain her from submitting to a procedure that placed her life in serious jeopardy.

Modern medical techniques have altered this situation. . . . Consequently, any interest of the State in protecting the woman from an inherently hazardous procedure, except when it would be equally dangerous for her to forgo it, has largely disappeared. Of course, important state interests in the areas of health and medical standards do remain. The State has a legitimate interest in seeing to it that abortion, like any other medical procedure, is performed under circumstances that insure maximum safety for the patient.... [T]he risk to the woman increases as her pregnancy continues. Thus, the State retains a definite interest in protecting the woman's own health and safety when an abortion is proposed at a late stage of pregnancy.

The third reason is the State's interest—some phrase it in terms of duty—in protecting prenatal life. Some of the argument for this justification rests on the theory that a new human life is present from the moment of conception. The State's interest and general obligation to protect life then extends, it is argued, to prenatal life. Only when the life of the pregnant mother herself is at stake, balanced against the life she carries within her, should the interest of the embryo or fetus not prevail. Logically, of course, a legitimate state interest in this area need not stand or fall on acceptance of the belief that life begins at conception or at some other point prior to live birth. In assessing the State's interest, recognition may be given to the less rigid claim that as long as at least *potential* life is involved, the State may assert interests beyond the protection of the pregnant woman alone....

It is with these interests, and the weight to be attached to them, that this case is concerned.

VIII

The Constitution does not explicitly mention any right of privacy. In a line of decisions, however, going back perhaps as far as *Union Pacific R. Co. v. Botsford*, 141 U.S. 250, 251 (1891), the Court has recognized that a right of personal privacy, or a guarantee of certain areas or zones of privacy, does exist under the Constitution. In varying contexts, the Court or individual Justices have, indeed, found at least the roots of that right in the First Amendment, *Stanley v. Georgia*, 394 U.S. 557, 564 (1969); in the Fourth and Fifth Amendments, *Terry v. Ohio*, 392 U.S. 1, 8–9 (1968), *Katz v. United States*, 389 U.S. 347, 350 (1967), *Boyd v. United States*, 116 U.S. 616 (1886); in the penumbras of the Bill of Rights, *Griswold v. Connecticut*, 381 U.S., at 484–485; in the Ninth Amendment, *id.*, at 486 (Goldberg, J., concurring); or in the concept of liberty guaranteed by the first section of the Fourteenth Amendment, see *Meyer v. Nebraska*, 262 U.S. 390, 399 (1923). These decisions make it clear that only personal rights that can be deemed "fundamental" or "implicit in the concept of ordered liberty," *Palko v. Connecticut*, 302 U.S. 319, 325 (1937), are included in this guarantee of personal privacy. They also make it clear that the right has some extension to activities relating to marriage, *Loving v. Virginia*, 388 U.S. 1, 12 (1967); procreation, *Skinner v. Oklahoma*, 316 U.S. 535, 541–542 (1942); contraception, *Eisenstadt v. Baird*, 405 U.S., at 453–454; family relationships, *Prince v. Massachusetts*, 321 U.S. 158, 166 (1944); and child rearing and education, *Pierce v. Society of Sisters*, 268 U.S. 510, 535 (1925).

This right of privacy, whether it be founded in the Fourteenth Amendment's concept of personal liberty and restrictions upon state action, as we feel it is, or, as the District Court determined, in the Ninth Amendment's reservation of rights to the people, is broad enough to encompass a woman's decision whether or not to terminate her pregnancy. The detriment that the State would impose upon the pregnant woman by denying this choice altogether is apparent. Specific and direct harm medically diagnosable even in early pregnancy may be involved. Maternity, or additional offspring, may force upon the woman a distressful life and future. Psychological harm may be imminent. Mental and physical health may be taxed by child care. There is also the distress, for all concerned, associated with the unwanted child, and there is the problem of bringing a child into a family already unable, psychologically and otherwise, to care for it. In other cases, as in this one, the additional difficulties and continuing stigma of unwed motherhood may be involved. All these are factors the woman and her responsible physician necessarily will consider in consultation.

On the basis of elements such as these, appellant and some *amici* argue that the woman's right is absolute and that she is entitled to terminate her pregnancy at whatever time, in whatever way, and for whatever reason she alone chooses. With this we do not agree. Appellant's arguments that Texas either has no valid interest at all in regulating the abortion decision, or no interest strong enough to support any limitation upon the woman's sole determination, are unpersuasive. The Court's decisions recognizing a right of privacy also acknowledge that some state regulation in areas protected by that right is appropriate. As noted above, a State may properly assert important interests in safeguarding health, in maintaining medical standards, and in protecting potential life. At some point in pregnancy, these respective interests become sufficiently compelling to sustain regulation of the factors that govern the abortion decision. The privacy right involved, therefore, cannot be said to be absolute. In fact, it is not clear to us that the claim asserted by some amici that one has an unlimited right to do with one's body as one pleases bears a close relationship to the right of privacy previously articulated in the Court's decisions. The Court has refused to recognize an unlimited right of this kind in the past. *Jacobson v. Massachusetts*, 197 U.S. 11 (1905) (vaccination); *Buck v. Bell*, 274 U.S. 200 (1927) (sterilization).

We, therefore, conclude that the right of personal privacy includes the abortion decision, but that this right is not unqualified and must be considered against important state interests in regulation. . . .

Where certain "fundamental rights" are involved, the Court has held that regulation limiting these rights may be justified only by a "compelling state interest," and that legislative enactments must be narrowly drawn to express only the legitimate state interests at stake.

In the recent abortion cases, courts have recognized these principles. Those striking down state laws have generally scrutinized the State's interests in protecting health and potential life, and have concluded that neither interest justified broad limitations on the reasons for which a physician and his pregnant patient might decide that she should have an abortion in the early stages of pregnancy. Courts sustaining state laws have held that the State's determinations to protect health or prenatal life are dominant and constitutionally justifiable.

IX

The District Court held that the appellee failed to meet his burden of demonstrating that the Texas statute's infringement upon Roe's rights was necessary to support a compelling state interest, and that, although the appellee presented "several compelling justifications for state presence in the area of abortions," the statutes outstripped these justifications and swept "far beyond any areas of compelling state interest." Appellant and appellee both contest that holding. Appellant, as has been indicated, claims an absolute right that bars any state imposition of criminal penalties in the area. Appellee argues that the State's determination to recognize and protect prenatal life from and after conception constitutes a compelling state interest. As noted above, we do not agree fully with either formulation.

A. The appellee and certain *amici* argue that the fetus is a "person" within the language and meaning of the Fourteenth Amendment. In support of this, they outline at length and in detail the well-known facts of fetal development. If this suggestion of personhood is established, the appellant's case, of course, collapses, for the fetus' right to life would then be guaranteed specifically by the Amendment. . . . [Yet] no case could be cited that holds that a fetus is a person within the meaning of the Fourteenth Amendment.

The Constitution does not define "person" in so many words. Section 1 of the Fourteenth Amendment contains three references to "person." The first, in defining "citizens," speaks of "persons born or naturalized in the United States." The word also appears both in the Due Process Clause and in the Equal Protection Clause. "Person" is used in other places in the Constitution: in the listing of qualifications for Representatives and Senators, Art. I, § 2, cl. 2, and § 3, cl. 3; in the Apportionment Clause, Art. I, § 2, cl. 3; in the Migration and Importation provision, Art. I, § 9, cl. 1; in the Emolument Clause, Art. I, § 9, cl. 8; in the Electors provisions, Art. II, § 1, cl. 2, and the superseded cl. 3; in the provision outlining qualifications for the office of President, Art. II, § 1, cl. 5; in the Extradition provisions, Art. IV, § 2, cl. 2, and the superseded Fugitive Slave Clause 3; and in the Fifth, Twelfth, and Twenty-second Amendments, as well as in §§ 2 and 3 of the Fourteenth Amendment. But in nearly all these instances, the use of the word is such that it has application only postnatally. None indicates, with any assurance, that it has any possible prenatal application.[54]

All this, together with our observation that throughout the major portion of the 19th century prevailing legal abortion practices were far freer than they are today, persuades us that the word "person," as used in the Fourteenth Amendment, does not include the unborn. This is in accord with the results reached in those few cases where the issue has been squarely presented. . . .

This conclusion, however, does not of itself fully answer the contentions raised by Texas, and we pass on to other considerations.

B. The pregnant woman cannot be isolated in her privacy. She carries an embryo and, later, a fetus, if one accepts the medical definitions of the developing young in the human uterus. The situation therefore is inherently different from marital intimacy, or bedroom possession of obscene material, or marriage, or procreation, or education, with which *Eisenstadt* and *Griswold, Stanley, Loving, Skinner* and *Pierce*

---

54 When Texas urges that a fetus is entitled to Fourteenth Amendment protection as a person, it faces a dilemma. Neither in Texas nor in any other State are all abortions prohibited. Despite broad proscription, an exception always exists. The exception [in the Texas statute], for an abortion procured or attempted by medical advice for the purpose of saving the life of the mother, is typical. But if the fetus is a person who is not to be deprived of life without due process of law, and if the mother's condition is the sole determinant, does not the Texas exception appear to be out of line with the Amendment's command? . . .

and *Meyer* were respectively concerned. As we have intimated above, it is reasonable and appropriate for a State to decide that at some point in time another interest, that of health of the mother or that of potential human life, becomes significantly involved. The woman's privacy is no longer sole and any right of privacy she possesses must be measured accordingly.

Texas urges that, apart from the Fourteenth Amendment, life begins at conception and is present throughout pregnancy, and that, therefore, the State has a compelling interest in protecting that life from and after conception. We need not resolve the difficult question of when life begins. When those trained in the respective disciplines of medicine, philosophy, and theology are unable to arrive at any consensus, the judiciary, at this point in the development of man's knowledge, is not in a position to speculate as to the answer. . . .

In areas other than criminal abortion, the law has been reluctant to endorse any theory that life, as we recognize it, begins before live birth or to accord legal rights to the unborn except in narrowly defined situations and except when the rights are contingent upon live birth. For example, the traditional rule of tort law denied recovery for prenatal injuries even though the child was born alive. That rule has been changed in almost every jurisdiction. . . . In short, the unborn have never been recognized in the law as persons in the whole sense.

X

In view of all this, we do not agree that, by adopting one theory of life, Texas may override the rights of the pregnant woman that are at stake. We repeat, however, that the State does have an important and legitimate interest in preserving and protecting the health of the pregnant woman, whether she be a resident of the State or a non-resident who seeks medical consultation and treatment there, and that it has still *another* important and legitimate interest in protecting the potentiality of human life. These interests are separate and distinct. Each grows in substantiality as the woman approaches term and, at a point during pregnancy, each becomes "compelling."

With respect to the State's important and legitimate interest in the health of the mother, the "compelling" point, in the light of present medical knowledge, is at approximately the end of the first trimester. This is so because of the now-established medical fact that until the end of the first trimester mortality in abortion may be less than mortality in normal childbirth. It follows that, from and after this point, a State may regulate the abortion procedure to the extent that the regulation reasonably relates to the preservation and protection of maternal health. Examples of permissible state regulation in this area are requirements as to the qualifications of the person who is to perform the abortion; as to the licensure of that person; as to the facility in which the procedure is to be performed, that is, whether it must be a hospital or may be a clinic or some other place of less-than-hospital status; as to the licensing of the facility; and the like.

This means, on the other hand, that, for the period of pregnancy prior to this "compelling" point, the attending physician, in consultation with his patient, is free to determine, without regulation by the State, that, in his medical judgment, the patient's pregnancy should be terminated. If that decision is reached, the judgment may be effectuated by an abortion free of interference by the State.

With respect to the State's important and legitimate interest in potential life, the "compelling" point is at viability. This is so because the fetus then presumably has the capability of meaningful life outside the mother's womb. State regulation protective of fetal life after viability thus has both logical and biological justifications. If the State is interested in protecting fetal life after viability, it may go so far as to proscribe abortion during that period, except when it is necessary to preserve the life or health of the mother.

Measured against these standards, [the Texas statute], in restricting legal abortions to those "procured or attempted by medical advice for the purpose of saving the life of the mother," sweeps too broadly. The statute makes no distinction between abortions performed early in pregnancy and those performed later, and it limits to a single reason, "saving" the mother's life, the legal justification for the procedure. The statute, therefore, cannot survive the constitutional attack made upon it here. . . .

XI

To summarize and to repeat:

1.   A state criminal abortion statute of the current Texas type, that excepts from criminality only a *life-saving* procedure on behalf of the mother, without regard to pregnancy stage and without recognition of the other interests involved, is violative of the Due Process Clause of the Fourteenth Amendment.

(a)   For the stage prior to approximately the end of the first trimester, the abortion decision and its effectuation must be left to the medical judgment of the pregnant woman's attending physician.

(b)   For the stage subsequent to approximately the end of the first trimester, the State, in promoting its interest in the health of the mother, may, if it chooses, regulate the abortion procedure in ways that are reasonably related to maternal health.

(c)   For the stage subsequent to viability, the State in promoting its interest in the potentiality of human life may, if it chooses, regulate, and even proscribe, abortion except where it is necessary, in appropriate medical judgment, for the preservation of the life or health of the mother.

2.   The State may define the term "physician," as it has been employed in the preceding paragraphs of this Part XI of this opinion, to mean only a physician currently licensed by the State, and may proscribe any abortion by a person who is not a physician as so defined.

In *Doe v. Bolton*, procedural requirements contained in one of the modern abortion statutes are considered. That opinion and this one, of course, are to be read together.[67]

This holding, we feel, is consistent with the relative weights of the respective interests involved, with the lessons and examples of medical and legal history, with the lenity of the common law, and with the demands of the profound problems of the

---

[67]   Neither in this opinion nor in *Doe v. Bolton*, 410 U.S. 179, do we discuss the father's rights, if any exist in the constitutional context, in the abortion decision. No paternal right has been asserted in either of the cases, and the Texas and the Georgia statutes on their face take no cognizance of the father. We are aware that some statutes recognize the father under certain circumstances. North Carolina, for example, requires written permission for the abortion from the husband when the woman is a married minor, that is, when she is less than 18 years of age; if the woman is an unmarried minor, written permission from the parents is required. We need not now decide whether provisions of this kind are constitutional.

present day. The decision leaves the State free to place increasing restrictions on abortion as the period of pregnancy lengthens, so long as those restrictions are tailored to the recognized state interests. The decision vindicates the right of the physician to administer medical treatment according to his professional judgment up to the points where important state interests provide compelling justifications for intervention. Up to those points, the abortion decision in all its aspects is inherently, and primarily, a medical decision, and basic responsibility for it must rest with the physician. If an individual practitioner abuses the privilege of exercising proper medical judgment, the usual remedies, judicial and intra-professional, are available. . . .

▪ [Concurring opinions by CHIEF JUSTICE BURGER and JUSTICE DOUGLAS are omitted.]

▪ MR. JUSTICE STEWART, concurring.

In 1963, this Court, in *Ferguson v. Skrupa*, 372 U.S. 726, purported to sound the death knell for the doctrine of substantive due process, a doctrine under which many state laws had in the past been held to violate the Fourteenth Amendment. As Mr. Justice Black's opinion for the Court in *Skrupa* put it: "We have returned to the original constitutional proposition that courts do not substitute their social and economic beliefs for the judgment of legislative bodies, who are elected to pass laws."

Barely two years later, in Griswold v. Connecticut, the Court held a Connecticut birth control law unconstitutional. In view of what had been so recently said in *Skrupa*, the Court's opinion in *Griswold* understandably did its best to avoid reliance on the Due Process Clause of the Fourteenth Amendment as the ground for decision. Yet, the Connecticut law did not violate any provision of the Bill of Rights, nor any other specific provision of the Constitution. So it was clear to me then, and it is equally clear to me now, that the *Griswold* decision can be rationally understood only as a holding that the Connecticut statute substantively invaded the "liberty" that is protected by the Due Process Clause of the Fourteenth Amendment. As so understood, *Griswold* stands as one in a long line of pre-*Skrupa* cases decided under the doctrine of substantive due process, and I now accept it as such. . . .

The asserted state interests are protection of the health and safety of the pregnant woman, and protection of the potential future human life within her. These are legitimate objectives . . . [but] I think the Court today has thoroughly demonstrated that these state interests cannot constitutionally support the broad abridgment of personal liberty worked by the existing Texas law. Accordingly, I join the Court's opinion holding that that law is invalid under the Due Process Clause of the Fourteenth Amendment.

▪ MR. JUSTICE REHNQUIST, dissenting.

. . . I would reach a conclusion opposite to that reached by the Court. I have difficulty in concluding, as the Court does, that the right of "privacy" is involved in this case. Texas, by the statute here challenged, bars the performance of a medical abortion by a licensed physician on a plaintiff such as Roe. A transaction resulting in an operation such as this is not "private" in the ordinary usage of that word. Nor is the "privacy" that the Court finds here even a distant relative of the freedom from searches and seizures protected by the Fourth Amendment to the Constitution, which the Court has referred to as embodying a right to privacy. *Katz v. United States*, 389 U.S. 347 (1967).

If the Court means by the term "privacy" no more than that the claim of a person to be free from unwanted state regulation of consensual transactions may be a form of "liberty" protected by the Fourteenth Amendment, there is no doubt that similar claims have been upheld in our earlier decisions on the basis of that liberty. . . . The test traditionally applied in the area of social and economic legislation is whether or not a law such as that challenged has a rational relation to a valid state objective. *Williamson v. Lee Optical Co.*, 348 U.S. 483, 491 (1955). The Due Process Clause of the Fourteenth Amendment undoubtedly does place a limit, albeit a broad one, on legislative power to enact laws such as this. If the Texas statute were to prohibit an abortion even where the mother's life is in jeopardy, I have little doubt that such a statute would lack a rational relation to a valid state objective under the test stated in *Williamson*. But the Court's sweeping invalidation of any restrictions on abortion during the first trimester is impossible to justify under that standard, and the conscious weighing of competing factors that the Court's opinion apparently substitutes for the established test is far more appropriate to a legislative judgment than to a judicial one. . . .

While the Court's opinion quotes from the dissent of Mr. Justice Holmes in *Lochner v. New York,* the result it reaches is more closely attuned to the majority opinion of Mr. Justice Peckham in that case. As in *Lochner* and similar cases applying substantive due process standards to economic and social welfare legislation, the adoption of the compelling state interest standard will inevitably require this Court to examine the legislative policies and pass on the wisdom of these policies in the very process of deciding whether a particular state interest put forward may or may not be "compelling." The decision here to break pregnancy into three distinct terms and to outline the permissible restrictions the State may impose in each one, for example, partakes more of judicial legislation than it does of a determination of the intent of the drafters of the Fourteenth Amendment.

The fact that a majority of the States reflecting, after all the majority sentiment in those States, have had restrictions on abortions for at least a century is a strong indication, it seems to me, that the asserted right to an abortion is not "so rooted in the traditions and conscience of our people as to be ranked as fundamental," *Snyder v. Massachusetts*, 291 U.S. 97, 105 (1934). Even today, when society's views on abortion are changing, the very existence of the debate is evidence that the "right" to an abortion is not so universally accepted as the appellant would have us believe.

To reach its result, the Court necessarily has had to find within the scope of the Fourteenth Amendment a right that was apparently completely unknown to the drafters of the Amendment. As early as 1821, the first state law dealing directly with abortion was enacted by the Connecticut Legislature. By the time of the adoption of the Fourteenth Amendment in 1868, there were at least 36 laws enacted by state or territorial legislatures limiting abortion. While many States have amended or updated their laws, 21 of the laws on the books in 1868 remain in effect today. Indeed, the Texas statute struck down today was, as the majority notes, first enacted in 1857 and "has remained substantially unchanged to the present time."

There apparently was no question concerning the validity of this provision or of any of the other state statutes when the Fourteenth Amendment was adopted. The only conclusion possible from this history is that the drafters did not intend to have the Fourteenth Amendment withdraw from the States the power to legislate with respect to this matter. . . .

■ MR. JUSTICE WHITE, with whom MR. JUSTICE REHNQUIST joins, dissenting.

At the heart of the controversy in these cases are those recurring pregnancies that pose no danger whatsoever to the life or health of the mother but are, nevertheless, unwanted for any one or more of a variety of reasons—convenience, family planning, economics, dislike of children, the embarrassment of illegitimacy, etc. The common claim before us is that for any one of such reasons, or for no reason at all, and without asserting or claiming any threat to life or health, any woman is entitled to an abortion at her request if she is able to find a medical advisor willing to undertake the procedure. . . .

With all due respect, I dissent. I find nothing in the language or history of the Constitution to support the Court's judgments. The Court simply fashions and announces a new constitutional right for pregnant women and, with scarcely any reason or authority for its action, invests that right with sufficient substance to override most existing state abortion statutes. The upshot is that the people and the legislatures of the 50 States are constitutionally disentitled to weigh the relative importance of the continued existence and development of the fetus, on the one hand, against a spectrum of possible impacts on the mother, on the other hand. As an exercise of raw judicial power, the Court perhaps has authority to do what it does today; but in my view its judgment is an improvident and extravagant exercise of the power of judicial review that the Constitution extends to this Court.

The Court apparently values the convenience of the pregnant woman more than the continued existence and development of the life or potential life that she carries. Whether or not I might agree with that marshaling of values, I can in no event join the Court's judgment because I find no constitutional warrant for imposing such an order of priorities on the people and legislatures of the States. In a sensitive area such as this, involving as it does issues over which reasonable men may easily and heatedly differ, I cannot accept the Court's exercise of its clear power of choice by interposing a constitutional barrier to state efforts to protect human life and by investing women and doctors with the constitutionally protected right to exterminate it. This issue, for the most part, should be left with the people and to the political processes the people have devised to govern their affairs. . . .

NOTES

1. *Roe v. Wade* is, of course, one of the most controversial Supreme Court decisions of all time. The case spurs heated, emotional arguments. Start, however, with a *legal* analysis of the case. (There will be plenty of time for passionate argument once the holdings are established.)

An initial question the Court faced was whether an unborn human fetus is a "person" within the meaning of Section 1 of the Fourteenth Amendment: "[N]or shall any State deprive any *person* of life, liberty, or property, without due process of law; nor deny to any *person* within its jurisdiction the equal protection of the laws." The Court acknowledged the importance of this question, and at least one pre-*Roe* court had held that any claimed right to abortion must yield to the right to life of the unborn child and to the state's obligation to safeguard that life. *Steinberg v. Brown*, 321 F.Supp.741, 746–747 (N.D. Ohio 1970) ("Once human life has commenced"—which the court found as a matter of biology occurs at conception—"the constitutional protections found in the Fifth and Fourteenth Amendments impose upon the state the *duty* of safeguarding it.").

What is the proper interpretive method for ascertaining the meaning of the word "person" as used in the amendment? Is the question decided by the text? Is there an intrinsic meaning of the word "person"? Does it refer to all human beings—all members of the species *homo sapiens*—and if so does that include living but not yet born human fetuses? Does the answer depend on the commonplace usage of the term "person" at the time the Fourteenth Amendment was adopted? Or should the question be decided by looking to the purpose of the framers of the Fourteenth Amendment and whether they specifically intended that the term "person" embrace fetal human life? Is it relevant that, as Justice Rehnquist notes, in 1868 thirty-six state and territorial legislatures prohibited abortion in most situations? Does it matter that the framers of the amendment did not specifically address this issue? Or should the question be decided by making inferences from the Constitution's structure and other provisions? As Justice Blackmun notes, the other constitutional provisions that refer to "persons" are in contexts where a limitation to *born* persons is clearly contemplated. Is the Court free to address it in whatever way it thinks is best as a matter of policy? If so, as the justices resolve that policy question, what kinds of evidence should they consider—their own moral judgments about abortion? Their perceptions of societal norms? Their perceptions of scientific knowledge?

2.   What is the scope of the abortion right recognized in *Roe*? The Court's holding requires careful parsing. First, the Court identified a substantive due process liberty of a woman to have an abortion, based in part on earlier decisions concerning the right of privacy in marriage, procreation, contraception, and the raising of children. This "right of privacy" flowed from the Fourteenth Amendment's "concept of personal liberty," and however broad it might be, it was "broad enough to encompass a woman's decision whether or not to terminate her pregnancy."

Next, the Court divided pregnancy into three stages, based on the Court's understanding of the stages of fetal development and the ability to live independently outside of the mother's womb. The Court then crafted somewhat different rules for each trimester, based on its balancing of the mother's liberty interest against the state interest in protecting fetal human life. (That state interest, the Court held, becomes theoretically stronger, even "compelling," as pregnancy progresses.)

In the first trimester, the right to abortion is plenary and may be exercised for any reason the woman chooses.

In the second stage—which the Court identified as the end of the first trimester to the point of "viability," when the fetus could survive outside the mother's womb—the Court permits regulations designed to protect "maternal health" but not to protect the fetus. The right to abortion in this stage remains plenary.

In the third stage—after viability—the state interest in protecting fetal human life becomes "compelling," *but* the state nonetheless must permit abortion during this time for reasons related to the mother's health. Thus, the third trimester *exception* to the plenary right to abortion is itself made subject to a health exception.

3.   Is the health exception narrow—in which case most late-term abortions could be prohibited? Or broad—in which case it means that a woman could almost always have an abortion, even in the eighth or ninth month of pregnancy? The answer depends on what considerations are included in "health" and who has the discretion to decide how serious a health impairment must be in order to justify a third-trimester abortion. What if carrying a child to term would delay for six months the ability of the mother to receive radiation treatment for cancer, with increased risk of death? Most everyone would agree that this is a serious risk to health—even to life. Similarly, what if a woman is unlikely to die from the pregnancy or childbirth, but might suffer from gestational diabetes, with

potentially detrimental health effects for the rest of her life? But proceed down the slope further and it becomes increasingly less obvious that the health exception should apply: How serious must the detrimental health effects be? Would the prospect of temporary but debilitating hip pain be sufficient to permit a late-term abortion? What if having a child would be a psychological burden? What if having a child would be emotionally troubling (and what sort of things should count in this category)? What if having a child would be financially difficult? An obstacle to career plans? A social embarrassment? A hateful reminder of a now despised lover? What if one feels one already has too many children?

Which of these things fall within the health exception? In *Roe*'s companion case, *Doe v. Bolton*, 410 U.S. 179 (1973), the Court adopted a broad definition of "health" for satisfying *Roe*'s requirements and vested broad discretion in a woman and her doctor to decide whether the exception should apply. In *Doe*, the Court was considering whether Georgia's statute permitting abortions where a doctor determines that "an abortion is necessary" was too restrictive of the right to abortion recognized in *Roe*. The Court found the Georgia statute constitutional because it construed it to allow doctors to consider anything that might relate, directly or indirectly, to a woman's health: "[T]he medical judgment [of the physician] may be exercised in light of all factors—physical, emotional, psychological, familial, and the woman's age—relevant to the well-being of the patient. All these factors may relate to health." *Doe v. Bolton*, at 192. How do each of the hypotheticals in the preceding paragraph come out under the Court's standard in *Doe*? Are there some reasons for having an abortion that could never fit within the health exception? Or is the consequence of *Roe*, combined with *Doe*'s elaboration of health considerations, that the Court created a constitutional right to abortion for essentially any reason, throughout all nine months of pregnancy, up to the point of birth?

4.   Now consider the constitutional legitimacy of *Roe* by pondering two sets of questions, each of which will provoke one side in the debate:

a.   Is there any plausible textual or historical basis for the substantive due process reasoning of *Roe*? Do the substantive due process precedents, such as *Griswold* and *Eisenstadt*, even support it? Is there anything about *Roe*'s approach to constitutional law that could not, in principle, be deployed to create a constitutional right to freedom of contract (*à la Lochner*) or a constitutional right to own slaves as property (*à la Dred Scott*)? Is there any defense to the charge that this is judicial activism?

b.   If there is no substantive due process right protecting childbirth decisions, what would prevent the government from passing and enforcing a law mandating forced sterilization of women who have given birth to more than two children? From mandating abortion when prenatal tests show evidence that the child would be born with a costly medical condition or disability? If the Due Process Clauses do not confer substantive rights, what constitutional check is there on Congress and state legislatures enacting these laws?

5.   The methodology and reasoning of *Roe* have been widely criticized, both by supporters and opponents of its result. John Hart Ely famously said that *Roe* was "*not* constitutional law and gives almost no sense of an obligation to try to be," for "*before* the Court can get to the 'balancing' stage, *before* it can worry about the next case and the case after that (or even about its institutional position) it is under an obligation to trace its premises to the charter from which it derives its authority." John Hart Ely, *The Wages of Crying Wolf: A Comment on* Roe v. Wade, 82 Yale L.J. 920, 947, 949 (1973). In response to these critiques, a number of alternative grounds for the decision have been advanced. See, e.g., WHAT *ROE V. WADE* SHOULD HAVE SAID (Jack M. Balkin ed., 2005). Consider and evaluate the following:

a.   Do laws prohibiting or restricting abortion constitute discrimination on the basis of sex? Before she joined the Supreme Court, Justice Ginsburg argued that *Roe* should have included "a distinct sex discrimination theme." She said:

> Society, not anatomy, places a greater stigma on unmarried women who become pregnant than on the men who father their children. Society expects, but nature does not command, that women take the major responsibility for child care and that they will stay with their children, bearing nurture and support burdens alone, when fathers deny paternity or otherwise refuse to provide care or financial support for unwanted offsprings.

Ruth Bader Ginsburg, *Some Thoughts on Autonomy and Equality in Relation to* Roe v. Wade, 63 N.C. L. Rev. 375, 382–383 (1985). Because of this, *Roe* implicated "a woman's autonomous charge of her full life's course[,] . . . her ability to stand in relation to man, society, and the state as an independent, self-sustaining, equal citizen." *Id.* at 383. For further arguments, see Sylvia A. Law, *Rethinking Sex and the Constitution*, 132 U. Pa. L. Rev. 855, 963 (1984); Catharine A. MacKinnon, *Reflections on Sex Equality Under Law*, 100 Yale L.J. 1281, 1311 (1991). As discussed above, p. 1450, current constitutional doctrine does not treat classifications keyed to pregnancy as being on the basis of sex. *Geduldig v. Aiello*, 417 U.S. 484, 494–97 (1974). Would a sex-discrimination understanding of *Roe* require changing that doctrine? If so, should those cases be overruled—should it be sufficient to establish a violation of equal protection that a law or regulation produces a disparate impact on the basis of race or sex? And would the sex-discrimination grounds for *Roe* be vitiated if a state were to hold a referendum on abortion restrictions in which only women could vote? One more question about sex discrimination and abortion: under *Roe*, may states prohibit sex-selective abortion?

b.   Do abortion restrictions violate the Ninth Amendment? Note that the Court in *Roe* brushed aside this basis for its decision, even though the court below had invoked it. What are the strengths and vulnerabilities of grounding *Roe* in the Ninth Amendment? If the Ninth Amendment contains a right to abortion, what else does it contain? Is that basis for the decision less vulnerable to the charge that courts can reach whatever result they like?

c.   Is the right to abortion protected by the Fourteenth Amendment's Privileges or Immunities Clause? For an argument that it is a privilege of citizenship to protect one's bodily integrity and to decide whether to become a parent, see Jack Balkin, *Abortion and Original Meaning*, 24 Const. Comm. 291, 328–336 (2007). Recall that in the *Slaughter-House Cases* the Court declined to read that clause as a font of substantive rights not related to *federal* citizenship, a reading narrowed further by *Cruikshank*, p. 1303. But what if a restrictive reading of the Privileges or Immunities Clause is wrong? If the Court were to read "the privileges or immunities of citizens of the United States" at a level of generality sufficiently high to include a right to abortion, would that provide a better basis for *Roe*? Would it provide a stronger defense to the objection that there is no constraint on what the courts can decide is a constitutional right?

d.   Do abortion restrictions violate the Thirteenth Amendment by requiring the "involuntary servitude" of childbearing? For an argument in the affirmative, see Andrew Koppelman, *Forced Labor: A Thirteenth Amendment Defense of Abortion*, 84 Nw. U. L. Rev. 480 (1990). Does this stretch the language of the Thirteenth Amendment too far? Does it trivialize the Constitution's ban on true slavery? If the argument were accepted, would all legal requirements on parents be invalidated?

e.   Can a narrower form of the right to abortion—"the right to abortion even after viability but only when necessary to preserve the life or health of the mother"—be justified as a form of self-defense—"a right to defend oneself using medical care, even when this requires destroying the source of the threat"? Eugene Volokh, *Medical Self-Defense, Prohibited Experimental Therapies, and Payment for Organs*, 120 Harv. L. Rev. 1813, 1824 (2007). What would be the source of the constitutional right to self defense? In what other contexts would it allow the use of lethal force? And would the right extend even more broadly to using untested drugs or even buying organs? *Id.* at 1828–1845.

     f.   Although not an alternative ground for the result in *Roe*, an alternative approach is suggested by a draft legal opinion of the widely respected late Judge Henry Friendly of the Second Circuit in an abortion case three years before *Roe* was decided. (That case became moot before a decision on the merits.) Judge Friendly concluded that "the decision what to do about abortion is for the elected representatives of the people, not for three, or even nine, appointed judges." And he specifically rejected the plaintiffs' appeal to *Griswold*: "The type of abortion the plaintiffs particularly wish to protect against governmental sanction is the antithesis of privacy. The woman consents to intervention in the uterus by a physician, with the usual retinue of assistants, nurses, and other paramedical personnel, indeed the condition calling for such intervention may very likely have been established by clinical tests. While *Griswold* may well mean that the state cannot compel a woman to submit to an abortion, but see *Buck v. Bell*, it is exceedingly hard to read it as supporting a conclusion that the state may not prohibit other persons from committing one or even her doing so herself." The entire draft opinion is reprinted in A. Raymond Randolph, *Before* Roe v. Wade*: Judge Friendly's Draft Abortion Opinion*, 29 Harv. J.L. & Pub. Pol'y 1035 (2006). If Judge Friendly is right that *Griswold* cannot be extended to cover *Roe*, is there any constraint on what the state can require or restrict in relation to childbearing? Is he right that *Griswold* can be read to prohibit compelled abortion?

     6.   In 1975, just two years after *Roe*, the West German Constitutional Court held that a recently enacted statute *legalizing* abortion during the first twelve weeks after conception violated that nation's Basic Law. See 39 BVerfGE 1 (1975). Article 2, Paragraph 2, Sentence 1 of the Basic Law provides that "Everyone [*Jeder*] has a right to life." According to the Constitutional Court, " 'Everyone' in the sense of [this provision] is 'everyone living'; expressed in another way: every life possessing human individuality; 'everyone' also includes the yet unborn human being." The court held that the "duty of the state to protect [life] is comprehensive. It forbids not only—self-evidently—direct state attacks on the life developing itself but also requires the state to take a position protecting and promoting this life, that is to say, it must, above all, preserve it even against illegal attacks by others. . . . Human life represented, within the order of the Basic Law, an ultimate value, the particulars of which need not be established; it is the living foundation of human dignity and prerequisite for all other fundamental rights." Yet the court recognized exceptions. One exception covered the first fourteen days from conception (roughly the point prior to implantation); another was a prohibition on punishing a woman for obtaining an abortion when pregnancy presents "a danger for her life or the danger of a grave impairment of her condition of health"; and another was the court's permission for the legislature to "leave the interruption of pregnancy free of punishment" in "the cases of the eugenic, ethical (criminological), and of the social or emergency indication for abortion." The two dissenting justices did not dispute that unborn life is protected by the Basic Law, but invoked the "requirement of judicial restraint," arguing that the nature of protection to be given unborn life must be determined by the legislature. The decision of the Constitutional Court was reaffirmed following reunification of Germany in 1991, but subsequently modified to permit the legislature in certain circumstances not to prescribe punishment for first trimester

abortions—notwithstanding the Court's reaffirmation that the German constitution protected the right to life of the unborn.

What accounts for the difference between the U.S. and German decisions? The decisions occurred at about the same time. Opposition to abortion is sometimes attributed to religion, but religious practice is more pervasive in the United States than in Germany. Is the German constitutional term "everyone" more comprehensive than the U.S. constitutional term "person"? Is the unqualified "right to life" under the German Basic Law different from the right of every U.S. person against deprivation of "life . . . without due process of law" and to "the equal protection of the laws"? For a translation of the German case, see 9 J. Marshall J. Prac. & Proc. 605 (1976) (R. Jonas & J. Gorby, trans). For a fuller discussion of the case, as well as a 1988 Canadian case striking down (on procedural grounds) a national law limiting abortions, see Vicki C. Jackson & Mark Tushnet, COMPARATIVE CONSTITUTIONAL LAW 74–136 (2d. ed. 2006).

7.   *Roe* led to many more cases, some arising from state laws testing the decision's limits or seeking to have it overruled or modified. Here is a brief survey of the abortion decisions between *Roe* and the next principal case, *Planned Parenthood v. Casey*, 505 U.S. 833 (1992): The Court struck down a state law requiring the father's consent to abortion, holding that the abortion choice belongs to the woman exclusively. *Planned Parenthood of Central Missouri v. Danforth,* 428 U.S. 52 (1976). In a series of cases, the Court considered state laws providing for parental consent or notice in the case of a minor daughter's abortion. The Court struck down a flat requirement of parental consent, upheld parental consent if there is a "judicial bypass" alternative for a "mature" minor, and upheld some but not all forms of parental-notice (as opposed to consent) requirements. E.g., *Bellotti v. Baird,* 428 U.S. 132 (1976); *Planned Parenthood of Kansas City v. Ashcroft,* 462 U.S. 476 (1983). The Court has upheld state and federal actions declining to fund abortion, sustaining the government's prerogative to subsidize childbirth but not abortion with Medicaid benefits. *Maher v. Roe,* 432 U.S. 464 (1977); *Harris v. McRae,* 448 U.S. 297 (1980). The Court invalidated state laws requiring informed consent, a waiting period, the performance of certain abortions in hospitals, the use of a particular abortion technique most likely in post-viability abortions to protect the life of the fetus, and the presence of a second physician. *Akron v. Akron Center for Reproductive Health,* 462 U.S. 416 (1983); *Thornburgh v. American College of Obstetricians & Gynecologists,* 476 U.S. 747 (1986). (Note that both cases were partially overruled in *Planned Parenthood v. Casey.*)

Then, in *Webster v. Reproductive Health Services,* 492 U.S. 490 (1989), the Court upheld a Missouri law that stated in its preamble that "the life of each human being begins at conception," that forbade most abortions at state hospitals, and that required physicians to determine if an unborn child of twenty weeks' gestational age or greater might be able to live outside the mother's womb. The decision in *Webster* led many observers to speculate that the Court was on the verge of overruling *Roe.* Five justices had voted to uphold all of the provisions of the Missouri law, though without a majority opinion or controlling rationale. And after Webster, two supporters of Roe—Justice Brennan and Justice Marshall—were replaced by justices thought to oppose it, Justice Souter and Justice Thomas. As you will soon see, though, *Webster* did not augur a total reversal of the Court's jurisprudence on abortion.

———

[*Assignment 80*]

The next case, *Planned Parenthood v. Casey*, 505 U.S. 833 (1992), is one of the most significant Supreme Court decisions of all time, both practically and jurisprudentially. It explicitly reaffirmed *Roe*'s embrace of a constitutional right to abortion, at a time when most observers thought that *Roe* was destined to undergo a slow, *Lochner*-style decline. Moreover, *Casey* reaffirmed a constitutional right to abortion even though a majority of the justices appear to have thought *Roe* was wrongly decided. It embraced a dramatic view of the significance of precedent and *stare decisis* in constitutional adjudication—arguably the first full-blown theory of precedent in the Court's more than two-century history. And it collated and appeared to embrace, in some form, the Court's previous substantive due process decisions.

Planned Parenthood v. Casey
505 U.S. 833 (1992)

■ JUSTICE O'CONNOR, JUSTICE KENNEDY, and JUSTICE SOUTER announced the judgment of the Court and delivered the opinion of the Court with respect to Parts I, II, III, V–A, V–C, and VI, an opinion with respect to Part V–E, in which JUSTICE STEVENS joins, and an opinion with respect to Parts IV, V–B, and V–D.

I

Liberty finds no refuge in a jurisprudence of doubt. Yet 19 years after our holding that the Constitution protects a woman's right to terminate her pregnancy in its early stages, *Roe v. Wade*, 410 U.S. 113 (1973), that definition of liberty is still questioned. Joining the respondents as amicus curiae, the United States, as it has done in five other cases in the last decade, again asks us to overrule *Roe*.

At issue in these cases are five provisions of the Pennsylvania Abortion Control Act of 1982, as amended in 1988 and 1989. The Act requires that a woman seeking an abortion give her informed consent prior to the abortion procedure, and specifies that she be provided with certain information at least 24 hours before the abortion is performed. § 3205. For a minor to obtain an abortion, the Act requires the informed consent of one of her parents, but provides for a judicial bypass option if the minor does not wish to or cannot obtain a parent's consent. § 3206. Another provision of the Act requires that, unless certain exceptions apply, a married woman seeking an abortion must sign a statement indicating that she has notified her husband of her intended abortion. § 3209. The Act exempts compliance with these three requirements in the event of a "medical emergency". . . . In addition to the above provisions regulating the performance of abortions, the Act imposes certain reporting requirements on facilities that provide abortion services. . . .

After considering the fundamental constitutional questions resolved by *Roe*, principles of institutional integrity, and the rule of *stare decisis*, we are led to conclude this: the essential holding of *Roe v. Wade* should be retained and once again reaffirmed.

It must be stated at the outset and with clarity that *Roe*'s essential holding, the holding we reaffirm, has three parts. First is a recognition of the right of the woman to choose to have an abortion before viability and to obtain it without undue interference from the State. Before viability, the State's interests are not strong enough to support a prohibition of abortion or the imposition of a substantial obstacle to the woman's effective right to elect the procedure. Second is a confirmation of the State's power to restrict abortions after fetal viability, if the law contains exceptions for pregnancies which endanger the woman's life or health.

And third is the principle that the State has legitimate interests from the outset of the pregnancy in protecting the health of the woman and the life of the fetus that may become a child. These principles do not contradict one another; and we adhere to each.

II

Constitutional protection of the woman's decision to terminate her pregnancy derives from the Due Process Clause of the Fourteenth Amendment. It declares that no State shall "deprive any person of life, liberty, or property, without due process of law." The controlling word in the cases before us is "liberty." Although a literal reading of the Clause might suggest that it governs only the procedures by which a State may deprive persons of liberty, for at least 105 years, the Clause has been understood to contain a substantive component as well, one "barring certain government actions regardless of the fairness of the procedures used to implement them." *Daniels v. Williams*, 474 U.S. 327, 331 (1986).

It is . . . tempting . . . to suppose that the Due Process Clause protects only those practices, defined at the most specific level, that were protected against government interference by other rules of law when the Fourteenth Amendment was ratified. But such a view would be inconsistent with our law. It is a promise of the Constitution that there is a realm of personal liberty which the government may not enter. We have vindicated this principle before. Marriage is mentioned nowhere in the Bill of Rights and interracial marriage was illegal in most States in the 19th century, but the Court was no doubt correct in finding it to be an aspect of liberty protected against state interference by the substantive component of the Due Process Clause in *Loving v. Virginia*, 388 U.S. 1, 12 (1967) (relying, in an opinion for eight Justices, on the Due Process Clause).

Neither the Bill of Rights nor the specific practices of States at the time of the adoption of the Fourteenth Amendment marks the outer limits of the substantive sphere of liberty which the Fourteenth Amendment protects. See U.S. Const., Amdt. 9. As the second Justice Harlan recognized:

> [T]he full scope of the liberty guaranteed by the Due Process Clause cannot be found in or limited by the precise terms of the specific guarantees elsewhere provided in the Constitution. This 'liberty' is not a series of isolated points pricked out in terms of the taking of property; the freedom of speech, press, and religion; the right to keep and bear arms; the freedom from unreasonable searches and seizures; and so on. It is a rational continuum which, broadly speaking, includes a freedom from all substantial arbitrary impositions and purposeless restraints, . . . and which also recognizes, what a reasonable and sensitive judgment must, that certain interests require particularly careful scrutiny of the state needs asserted to justify their abridgment.

Poe v. Ullman, 367 U.S. 497, 543 (1961) (opinion dissenting from dismissal on jurisdictional grounds). . . .

The inescapable fact is that adjudication of substantive due process claims may call upon the Court in interpreting the Constitution to exercise that same capacity which by tradition courts always have exercised: reasoned judgment. Its boundaries are not susceptible of expression as a simple rule. That does not mean we are free to invalidate state policy choices with which we disagree; yet neither does it permit us to shrink from the duties of our office. . . .

Men and women of good conscience can disagree, and we suppose some always shall disagree, about the profound moral and spiritual implications of terminating a pregnancy, even in its earliest stage. Some of us as individuals find abortion offensive to our most basic principles of morality, but that cannot control our decision. Our obligation is to define the liberty of all, not to mandate our own moral code. The underlying constitutional issue is whether the State can resolve these philosophic questions in such a definitive way that a woman lacks all choice in the matter, except perhaps in those rare circumstances in which the pregnancy is itself a danger to her own life or health, or is the result of rape or incest.

It is conventional constitutional doctrine that where reasonable people disagree the government can adopt one position or the other. That theorem, however, assumes a state of affairs in which the choice does not intrude upon a protected liberty. . . .

Our law affords constitutional protection to personal decisions relating to marriage, procreation, contraception, family relationships, child rearing, and education. Our cases recognize "the right of the individual, married or single, to be free from unwarranted governmental intrusion into matters so fundamentally affecting a person as the decision whether to bear or beget a child." Our precedents "have respected the private realm of family life which the state cannot enter." These matters, involving the most intimate and personal choices a person may make in a lifetime, choices central to personal dignity and autonomy, are central to the liberty protected by the Fourteenth Amendment. At the heart of liberty is the right to define one's own concept of existence, of meaning, of the universe, and of the mystery of human life. Beliefs about these matters could not define the attributes of personhood were they formed under compulsion of the State.

These considerations begin our analysis of the woman's interest in terminating her pregnancy but cannot end it, for this reason: though the abortion decision may originate within the zone of conscience and belief, it is more than a philosophic exercise. Abortion is a unique act. It is an act fraught with consequences for others: for the woman who must live with the implications of her decision; for the persons who perform and assist in the procedure; for the spouse, family, and society which must confront the knowledge that these procedures exist, procedures some deem nothing short of an act of violence against innocent human life; and, depending on one's beliefs, for the life or potential life that is aborted. Though abortion is conduct, it does not follow that the State is entitled to proscribe it in all instances. That is because the liberty of the woman is at stake in a sense unique to the human condition and so unique to the law. The mother who carries a child to full term is subject to anxieties, to physical constraints, to pain that only she must bear. That these sacrifices have from the beginning of the human race been endured by woman with a pride that ennobles her in the eyes of others and gives to the infant a bond of love cannot alone be grounds for the State to insist she make the sacrifice. Her suffering is too intimate and personal for the State to insist, without more, upon its own vision of the woman's role, however dominant that vision has been in the course of our history and our culture. The destiny of the woman must be shaped to a large extent on her own conception of her spiritual imperatives and her place in society.

It should be recognized, moreover, that in some critical respects the abortion decision is of the same character as the decision to use contraception, to which *Griswold v. Connecticut*, 381 U.S. 479 (1965); *Eisenstadt v. Baird*, 405 U.S. 438 (1972); and *Carey v. Population Services International*, 431 U.S. 678 (1977), afford constitutional protection. We have no doubt as to the correctness of those decisions. They support the reasoning in *Roe* relating to the woman's liberty because they involve personal decisions concerning not only the meaning of procreation but also human responsibility and respect for it. . . .

It was this dimension of personal liberty that *Roe* sought to protect, and its holding invoked the reasoning and the tradition of the precedents we have discussed, granting protection to substantive liberties of the person. *Roe* was, of course, an extension of those cases and, as the decision itself indicated, the separate States could act in some degree to further their own legitimate interests in protecting prenatal life. The extent to which the legislatures of the States might act to outweigh the interests of the woman in choosing to terminate her pregnancy was a subject of debate both in *Roe* itself and in decisions following it.

While we appreciate the weight of the arguments made on behalf of the State in the cases before us, arguments which in their ultimate formulation conclude that *Roe* should be overruled, the reservations any of us may have in reaffirming the central holding of *Roe* are outweighed by the explication of individual liberty we have given combined with the force of *stare decisis*.

We turn now to that doctrine.

III–A

The obligation to follow precedent begins with necessity, and a contrary necessity marks its outer limit. With Cardozo, we recognize that no judicial system could do society's work if it eyed each issue afresh in every case that raised it. See B. Cardozo, THE NATURE OF THE JUDICIAL PROCESS 149 (1921). Indeed, the very concept of the rule of law underlying our own Constitution requires such continuity over time that a respect for precedent is, by definition, indispensable. At the other extreme, a different necessity would make itself felt if a prior judicial ruling should come to be seen so clearly as error that its enforcement was for that very reason doomed.

Even when the decision to overrule a prior case is not, as in the rare, latter instance, virtually foreordained, it is common wisdom that the rule of *stare decisis* is not an "inexorable command," and certainly it is not such in every constitutional case. Rather, when this Court reexamines a prior holding, its judgment is customarily informed by a series of prudential and pragmatic considerations designed to test the consistency of overruling a prior decision with the ideal of the rule of law, and to gauge the respective costs of reaffirming and overruling a prior case. Thus, for example, we may ask whether the rule has proven to be intolerable simply in defying practical workability; whether the rule is subject to a kind of reliance that would lend a special hardship to the consequences of overruling and add inequity to the cost of repudiation; whether related principles of law have so far developed as to have left the old rule no more than a remnant of abandoned doctrine; or whether facts have so changed, or come to be seen so differently, as to have robbed the old rule of significant application or justification.

So in this case we may enquire whether *Roe*'s central rule has been found unworkable; whether the rule's limitation on state power could be removed without serious inequity to those who have relied upon it or significant damage to the stability of the society governed by it; whether the law's growth in the intervening years has left *Roe*'s central rule a doctrinal anachronism discounted by society; and whether *Roe*'s premises of fact have so far changed in the ensuing two decades as to render its central holding somehow irrelevant or unjustifiable in dealing with the issue it addressed.

1

Although *Roe* has engendered opposition, it has in no sense proven "unworkable," representing as it does a simple limitation beyond which a state law is unenforceable. While *Roe* has, of course, required judicial assessment of state laws affecting the exercise of the choice guaranteed against government infringement, and although the need for such review will remain as a consequence of today's decision, the required determinations fall within judicial competence.

2

The inquiry into reliance counts the cost of a rule's repudiation as it would fall on those who have relied reasonably on the rule's continued application. Since the classic case for weighing reliance heavily in favor of following the earlier rule occurs in the commercial context, where advance planning of great precision is most obviously a necessity, it is no cause for surprise that some would find no reliance worthy of consideration in support of *Roe*.

While neither respondents nor their *amici* in so many words deny that the abortion right invites some reliance prior to its actual exercise, one can readily imagine an argument stressing the dissimilarity of this case to one involving property or contract. . . . This argument would be premised on the hypothesis that reproductive planning could take virtually immediate account of any sudden restoration of state authority to ban abortions.

To eliminate the issue of reliance that easily, however, one would need to limit cognizable reliance to specific instances of sexual activity. But to do this would be simply to refuse to face the fact that for two decades of economic and social developments, people have organized intimate relationships and made choices that define their views of themselves and their places in society, in reliance on the availability of abortion in the event that contraception should fail. The ability of women to participate equally in the economic and social life of the Nation has been facilitated by their ability to control their reproductive lives. The Constitution serves human values, and while the effect of reliance on *Roe* cannot be exactly measured, neither can the certain cost of overruling *Roe* for people who have ordered their thinking and living around that case be dismissed.

3

No evolution of legal principle has left *Roe*'s doctrinal footings weaker than they were in 1973. No development of constitutional law since the case was decided has implicitly or explicitly left *Roe* behind as a mere survivor of obsolete constitutional thinking.

It will be recognized, of course, that *Roe* stands at an intersection of two lines of decisions, but in whichever doctrinal category one reads the case, the result for present purposes will be the same. The *Roe* Court itself placed its holding in the succession of cases most prominently exemplified by *Griswold v. Connecticut*. When it is so seen, *Roe* is clearly in no jeopardy, since subsequent constitutional developments have neither disturbed, nor do they threaten to diminish, the scope of recognized protection accorded to the liberty relating to intimate relationships, the family, and decisions about whether or not to beget or bear a child.

Roe, however, may be seen not only as an exemplar of *Griswold* liberty but as a rule (whether or not mistaken) of personal autonomy and bodily integrity, with doctrinal affinity to cases recognizing limits on governmental power to mandate medical treatment or to bar its rejection. If so, our cases since *Roe* accord with *Roe*'s view that a State's interest in the protection of life falls short of justifying any plenary override of individual liberty claims. *Cruzan v. Director, Mo. Dept. of Health*, 497 U.S. 261, 278 (1990). . . .

4

We have seen how time has overtaken some of *Roe*'s factual assumptions: advances in maternal health care allow for abortions safe to the mother later in pregnancy than was true in 1973, and advances in neonatal care have advanced viability to a point somewhat earlier. But these facts go only to the scheme of time limits on the realization of competing interests, and the divergences from the factual premises of 1973 have no bearing on the validity of *Roe*'s central holding, that viability marks the earliest point at which the State's interest in fetal life is constitutionally adequate to justify a legislative ban on nontherapeutic abortions. The soundness or unsoundness of that constitutional judgment in no sense turns on whether viability occurs at approximately 28 weeks, as was usual at the time of *Roe*, at 23 to 24 weeks, as it sometimes does today, or at some moment even slightly earlier in pregnancy, as it may if fetal respiratory capacity can somehow be enhanced in the future. Whenever it may occur, the attainment of viability may continue to serve as the critical fact, just as it has done since *Roe* was decided; which is to say that no change in *Roe*'s factual underpinning has left its central holding obsolete, and none supports an argument for overruling it.

5

The sum of the precedential enquiry to this point shows *Roe*'s underpinnings unweakened in any way affecting its central holding. While it has engendered disapproval, it has not been unworkable. An entire generation has come of age free to assume *Roe*'s concept of liberty in defining the capacity of women to act in society, and to make reproductive decisions; no erosion of principle going to liberty or personal autonomy has left *Roe*'s central holding a doctrinal remnant; *Roe* portends no developments at odds with other precedent for the analysis of personal liberty; and no changes of fact have rendered viability more or less appropriate as the point at which the balance of interests tips. Within the bounds of normal *stare decisis* analysis, then, and subject to the considerations on which it customarily turns, the stronger argument is for affirming *Roe*'s central holding, with whatever degree of personal reluctance any of us may have, not for overruling it.

B

In a less significant case, *stare decisis* analysis could, and would, stop at the point we have reached. But the sustained and widespread debate *Roe* has provoked calls for some comparison between that case and others of comparable dimension that have responded to national controversies and taken on the impress of the controversies addressed. Only two such decisional lines from the past century present themselves for examination, and in each instance the result reached by the Court accorded with the principles we apply today.

The first example is that line of cases identified with *Lochner v. New York*, 198 U.S. 45 (1905), which imposed substantive limitations on legislation limiting economic autonomy in favor of health and welfare regulation, adopting, in Justice Holmes's view, the theory of laissez-faire. *Id.*, at 75 (dissenting opinion). The *Lochner* decisions were exemplified by *Adkins v. Children's Hospital of District of Columbia*, 261 U.S. 525 (1923), in which this Court held it to be an infringement of constitutionally protected liberty of contract to require the employers of adult women to satisfy minimum wage standards. Fourteen years later, *West Coast Hotel Co. v. Parrish*, 300 U.S. 379 (1937), signaled the demise of *Lochner* by overruling *Adkins*. . . .

The second comparison that 20th century history invites is with the cases employing the separate-but-equal rule for applying the Fourteenth Amendment's equal protection guarantee. They began with *Plessy v. Ferguson*, 163 U.S. 537 (1896), holding that legislatively mandated racial segregation in public transportation works no denial of equal protection, rejecting the argument that racial separation enforced by the legal machinery of American society treats the black race as inferior. . . . But this understanding of the facts and the rule it was stated to justify were repudiated in *Brown v. Board of Education*, 347 U.S. 483 (1954). . . .

West Coast Hotel and *Brown* each rested on facts, or an understanding of facts, changed from those which furnished the claimed justifications for the earlier constitutional resolutions. Each case was comprehensible as the Court's response to facts that the country could understand, or had come to understand already, but which the Court of an earlier day, as its own declarations disclosed, had not been able to perceive. As the decisions were thus comprehensible they were also defensible, not merely as the victories of one doctrinal school over another by dint of numbers (victories though they were), but as applications of constitutional principle to facts as they had not been seen by the Court before. In constitutional adjudication as elsewhere in life, changed circumstances may impose new obligations, and the thoughtful part of the Nation could accept each decision to overrule a prior case as a response to the Court's constitutional duty.

Because the cases before us present no such occasion it could be seen as no such response. Because neither the factual underpinnings of *Roe's* central holding nor our understanding of it has changed (and because no other indication of weakened precedent has been shown), the Court could not pretend to be reexamining the prior law with any justification beyond a present doctrinal disposition to come out differently from the Court of 1973. To overrule prior law for no other reason than that would run counter to the view repeated in our cases, that a decision to overrule should rest on some special reason over and above the belief that a prior case was wrongly decided.

C

The examination of the conditions justifying the repudiation of *Adkins* by *West Coast Hotel* and *Plessy* by *Brown* is enough to suggest the terrible price that would have been paid if the Court had not overruled as it did. In the present cases, however, as our analysis to this point makes clear, the terrible price would be paid for overruling. Our analysis would not be complete, however, without explaining why overruling *Roe*'s central holding would not only reach an unjustifiable result under principles of *stare decisis*, but would seriously weaken the Court's capacity to exercise the judicial power and to function as the Supreme Court of a Nation dedicated to the rule of law. To understand why this would be so it is necessary to understand the source of this Court's authority, the conditions necessary for its preservation, and its relationship to the country's understanding of itself as a constitutional Republic.

The root of American governmental power is revealed most clearly in the instance of the power conferred by the Constitution upon the Judiciary of the United States and specifically upon this Court. As Americans of each succeeding generation are rightly told, the Court cannot buy support for its decisions by spending money and, except to a minor degree, it cannot independently coerce obedience to its decrees. The Court's power lies, rather, in its legitimacy, a product of substance and perception that shows itself in the people's acceptance of the Judiciary as fit to determine what the Nation's law means and to declare what it demands.

. . . Where, in the performance of its judicial duties, the Court decides a case in such a way as to resolve the sort of intensely divisive controversy reflected in *Roe* and those rare, comparable cases, its decision has a dimension that the resolution of the normal case does not carry. It is the dimension present whenever the Court's interpretation of the Constitution calls the contending sides of a national controversy to end their national division by accepting a common mandate rooted in the Constitution.

The Court is not asked to do this very often, having thus addressed the Nation only twice in our lifetime, in the decisions of *Brown* and *Roe*. But when the Court does act in this way, its decision requires an equally rare precedential force to counter the inevitable efforts to overturn it and to thwart its implementation. Some of those efforts may be mere unprincipled emotional reactions; others may proceed from principles worthy of profound respect. But whatever the premises of opposition may be, only the most convincing justification under accepted standards of precedent could suffice to demonstrate that a later decision overruling the first was anything but a surrender to political pressure, and an unjustified repudiation of the principle on which the Court staked its authority in the first instance. So to overrule under fire in the absence of the most compelling reason to reexamine a watershed decision would subvert the Court's legitimacy beyond any serious question. . . .

The Court's duty in the present cases is clear. In 1973, it confronted the already-divisive issue of governmental power to limit personal choice to undergo abortion, for which it provided a new resolution based on the due process guaranteed by the Fourteenth Amendment. Whether or not a new social consensus is developing on that issue, its divisiveness is no less today than in 1973, and pressure to overrule the decision, like pressure to retain it, has grown only more intense. A decision to overrule *Roe*'s essential holding under the existing circumstances would address error, if error there was, at the cost of both profound and unnecessary damage to the Court's legitimacy, and to the Nation's commitment to the rule of law. It is therefore imperative to adhere to the essence of *Roe*'s original decision, and we do so today.

IV

From what we have said so far it follows that it is a constitutional liberty of the woman to have some freedom to terminate her pregnancy. We conclude that the basic decision in *Roe* was based on a constitutional analysis which we cannot now repudiate. The woman's liberty is not so unlimited, however, that from the outset the State cannot show its concern for the life of the unborn, and at a later point in fetal development the State's interest in life has sufficient force so that the right of the woman to terminate the pregnancy can be restricted.

That brings us, of course, to the point where much criticism has been directed at *Roe*, a criticism that always inheres when the Court draws a specific rule from what in the Constitution is but a general standard. We conclude, however, that the urgent claims of the woman to retain the ultimate control over her destiny and her body, claims implicit in the meaning of liberty, require us to perform that function. Liberty must not be extinguished for want of a line that is clear. And it falls to us to give some real substance to the woman's liberty to determine whether to carry her pregnancy to full term.

We conclude the line should be drawn at viability, so that before that time the woman has a right to choose to terminate her pregnancy. We adhere to this principle for two reasons. First, as we have said, is the doctrine of *stare decisis*. Any judicial act of line-drawing may seem somewhat arbitrary, but *Roe* was a reasoned statement, elaborated with great care. We have twice reaffirmed it in the face of great opposition. Although we must overrule those parts of *Thornburgh v. American College of Obstetricians & Gynecologists*, 476 U.S. 747 (1986), and *Akron v. Akron Center for Reproductive Health*, 462 U.S. 416 (1983) (*Akron I*), which, in our view, are inconsistent with *Roe*'s statement that the State has a legitimate interest in promoting the life or potential life of the unborn, the central premise of those cases represents an unbroken commitment by this Court to the essential holding of *Roe*. It is that premise which we reaffirm today.

The second reason is that the concept of viability, as we noted in *Roe*, is the time at which there is a realistic possibility of maintaining and nourishing a life outside the womb, so that the independent existence of the second life can in reason and all fairness be the object of state protection that now overrides the rights of the woman. Consistent with other constitutional norms, legislatures may draw lines which appear arbitrary without the necessity of offering a justification. But courts may not. We must justify the lines we draw. And there is no line other than viability which is more workable. To be sure, as we have said, there may be some medical developments that affect the precise point of viability, but this is an imprecision within tolerable limits given that the medical community and all those who must apply its discoveries will continue to explore the matter. The viability line also has, as a practical matter, an element of fairness. In some broad sense it might be said that a woman who fails to act before viability has consented to the State's intervention on behalf of the developing child.

The woman's right to terminate her pregnancy before viability is the most central principle of *Roe v. Wade*. It is a rule of law and a component of liberty we cannot renounce.

On the other side of the equation is the interest of the State in the protection of potential life. The *Roe* Court recognized the State's "important and legitimate interest in protecting the potentiality of human life." The weight to be given this state interest, not the strength of the woman's interest, was the difficult question faced in *Roe*. We do not need to say whether each of us, had we been Members of the Court when the valuation of the state interest came before it as an original matter, would have concluded, as the *Roe* Court did, that its weight is insufficient to justify a ban on abortions prior to viability even when it is subject to certain exceptions. The matter is not before us in the first instance, and coming as it does after nearly 20 years of litigation in *Roe*'s wake we are satisfied that the immediate question is not the soundness of *Roe*'s resolution of the issue, but the precedential force that must be accorded to its holding. And we have concluded that the essential holding of *Roe* should be reaffirmed.

Yet it must be remembered that *Roe v. Wade* speaks with clarity in establishing not only the woman's liberty but also the State's "important and legitimate interest in potential life." That portion of the decision in *Roe* has been given too little acknowledgment and implementation by the Court in its subsequent cases. Those cases decided that any regulation touching upon the abortion decision must survive strict scrutiny, to be sustained only if drawn in narrow terms to further a compelling state interest. See, *e.g., Akron I*, at 427. Not all of the cases decided under that formulation can be reconciled with the holding in *Roe* itself that the State has legitimate interests in the health of the woman and in protecting the potential life within her. In resolving this tension, we choose to rely upon *Roe*, as against the later cases.

Roe established a trimester framework to govern abortion regulations. Under this elaborate but rigid construct, almost no regulation at all is permitted during the first trimester of pregnancy; regulations designed to protect the woman's health, but not to further the State's interest in potential life, are permitted during the second trimester; and during the third trimester, when the fetus is viable, prohibitions are permitted provided the life or health of the mother is not at stake. Most of our cases since *Roe* have involved the application of rules derived from the trimester framework.

The trimester framework no doubt was erected to ensure that the woman's right to choose not become so subordinate to the State's interest in promoting fetal life that her choice exists in theory but not in fact. We do not agree, however, that the trimester approach is necessary to accomplish this objective. A framework of this rigidity was unnecessary and in its later interpretation sometimes contradicted the State's permissible exercise of its powers.

Though the woman has a right to choose to terminate or continue her pregnancy before viability, it does not at all follow that the State is prohibited from taking steps to ensure that this choice is thoughtful and informed. Even in the earliest stages of pregnancy, the State may enact rules and regulations designed to encourage her to know that there are philosophic and social arguments of great weight that can be brought to bear in favor of continuing the pregnancy to full term and that there are procedures and institutions to allow adoption of unwanted children as well as a certain degree of state assistance if the mother chooses to raise the child herself. "[T]he Constitution does not forbid a State or city, pursuant to democratic processes, from expressing a preference for normal childbirth." *Webster v. Reproductive Health Services*, 492 U.S. 490, 511 (1989) (opinion of the Court). It follows that States are free to enact laws to provide a reasonable framework for a woman to make a decision that has such profound and lasting meaning. This, too, we find consistent with *Roe*'s central premises, and indeed the inevitable consequence of our holding that the State has an interest in protecting the life of the unborn.

We reject the trimester framework, which we do not consider to be part of the essential holding of *Roe*. Measures aimed at ensuring that a woman's choice contemplates the consequences for the fetus do not necessarily interfere with the right recognized in *Roe*, although those measures have been found to be inconsistent with the rigid trimester framework announced in that case. A logical reading of the central holding in *Roe* itself, and a necessary reconciliation of the liberty of the woman and the interest of the State in promoting prenatal life, require, in our view, that we abandon the trimester framework as a rigid prohibition on all previability regulation aimed at the protection of fetal life. The trimester framework suffers from these basic flaws: in its formulation it misconceives the nature of the pregnant woman's interest; and in practice it undervalues the State's interest in potential life, as recognized in *Roe*.

As our jurisprudence relating to all liberties save perhaps abortion has recognized, not every law which makes a right more difficult to exercise is, *ipso facto*, an infringement of that right. . . . Numerous forms of state regulation might have the incidental effect of increasing the cost or decreasing the availability of medical care, whether for abortion or any other medical procedure. The fact that a law which serves a valid purpose, one not designed to strike at the right itself, has the incidental effect of making it more difficult or more expensive to procure an abortion cannot be enough to invalidate it. Only where state regulation imposes an undue burden on a woman's ability to make this decision does the power of the State reach into the heart of the liberty protected by the Due Process Clause. . . .

These considerations of the nature of the abortion right illustrate that it is an overstatement to describe it as a right to decide whether to have an abortion "without interference from the State." All abortion regulations interfere to some degree with a woman's ability to decide whether to terminate her pregnancy. It is, as a consequence, not surprising that despite the protestations contained in the original *Roe* opinion to the effect that the Court was not recognizing an absolute right, the Court's experience applying the trimester framework has led to the striking down of some abortion regulations which in no real sense deprived women of the ultimate decision. Those decisions went too far because the right recognized by *Roe* is a right "to be free from unwarranted governmental intrusion into matters so fundamentally affecting a person as the decision whether to bear or beget a child." Not all governmental intrusion is of necessity unwarranted; and that brings us to the other basic flaw in the trimester framework: even in *Roe*'s terms, in practice it undervalues the State's interest in the potential life within the woman.

Roe v. Wade was express in its recognition of the State's "important and legitimate interest[s] in preserving and protecting the health of the pregnant woman [and] in protecting the potentiality of human life." The trimester framework, however, does not fulfill *Roe*'s own promise that the State has an interest in protecting fetal life or potential life. *Roe* began the contradiction by using the trimester framework to forbid any regulation of abortion designed to advance that interest before viability. Before viability, *Roe* and subsequent cases treat all governmental attempts to influence a woman's decision on behalf of the potential life within her as unwarranted. This treatment is, in our judgment, incompatible with the recognition that there is a substantial state interest in potential life throughout pregnancy.

The very notion that the State has a substantial interest in potential life leads to the conclusion that not all regulations must be deemed unwarranted. Not all burdens on the right to decide whether to terminate a pregnancy will be undue. In our view, the undue burden standard is the appropriate means of reconciling the State's interest with the woman's constitutionally protected liberty. . . .

A finding of an undue burden is a shorthand for the conclusion that a state regulation has the purpose or effect of placing a substantial obstacle in the path of a woman seeking an abortion of a nonviable fetus. A statute with this purpose is invalid because the means chosen by the State to further the interest in potential life must be calculated to inform the woman's free choice, not hinder it. And a statute which, while furthering the interest in potential life or some other valid state interest, has the effect of placing a substantial obstacle in the path of a woman's choice cannot be considered a permissible means of serving its legitimate ends. To the extent that the opinions of the Court or of individual Justices use the undue burden standard in a manner that is inconsistent with this analysis, we set out what in our view should be the controlling standard. In our considered judgment, an undue burden is an unconstitutional burden. Understood another way, we answer the question . . . whether a law designed to further the State's interest in fetal life which imposes an undue burden on the woman's decision before fetal viability could be constitutional. The answer is no.

Some guiding principles should emerge. What is at stake is the woman's right to make the ultimate decision, not a right to be insulated from all others in doing so. Regulations which do no more than create a structural mechanism by which the State, or the parent or guardian of a minor, may express profound respect for the life of the unborn are permitted, if they are not a substantial obstacle to the woman's exercise of the right to choose. Unless it has that effect on her right of choice, a state measure designed to persuade her to choose childbirth over abortion will be upheld if reasonably related to that goal. Regulations designed to foster the health of a woman seeking an abortion are valid if they do not constitute an undue burden.

Even when jurists reason from shared premises, some disagreement is inevitable. That is to be expected in the application of any legal standard which must accommodate life's complexity. We do not expect it to be otherwise with respect to the undue burden standard. We give this summary:

(a) To protect the central right recognized by *Roe v. Wade* while at the same time accommodating the State's profound interest in potential life, we will employ the undue burden analysis as explained in this opinion. An undue burden exists, and therefore a provision of law is invalid, if its purpose or effect is to place a substantial obstacle in the path of a woman seeking an abortion before the fetus attains viability.

(b) We reject the rigid trimester framework of *Roe v. Wade*. To promote the State's profound interest in potential life, throughout pregnancy the State may take measures to ensure that the woman's choice is informed, and measures designed to advance this interest will not be invalidated as long as their purpose is to persuade the woman to choose childbirth over abortion. These measures must not be an undue burden on the right.

(c) As with any medical procedure, the State may enact regulations to further the health or safety of a woman seeking an abortion. Unnecessary health regulations that have the purpose or effect of presenting a substantial obstacle to a woman seeking an abortion impose an undue burden on the right.

(d) Our adoption of the undue burden analysis does not disturb the central holding of *Roe* v. Wade, and we reaffirm that holding. Regardless of whether exceptions are made for particular circumstances, a State may not prohibit any woman from making the ultimate decision to terminate her pregnancy before viability.

(e) We also reaffirm *Roe*'s holding that "subsequent to viability, the State in promoting its interest in the potentiality of human life may, if it chooses, regulate, and even proscribe, abortion except where it is necessary, in appropriate medical judgment, for the preservation of the life or health of the mother."

These principles control our assessment of the Pennsylvania statute, and we now turn to the issue of the validity of its challenged provisions.

V

The Court of Appeals applied what it believed to be the undue burden standard and upheld each of the provisions except for the husband notification requirement. We agree generally with this conclusion, but refine the undue burden analysis in accordance with the principles articulated above. We now consider the separate statutory sections at issue. . . .

A

Because it is central to the operation of various other requirements, we begin with the statute's definition of medical emergency. Under the statute, a medical emergency is "[t]hat condition which, on the basis of the physician's good faith clinical judgment, so complicates the medical condition of a pregnant woman as to necessitate the immediate abortion of her pregnancy to avert her death or for which a delay will create serious risk of substantial and irreversible impairment of a major bodily function."

Petitioners argue that the definition is too narrow, contending that it forecloses the possibility of an immediate abortion despite some significant health risks. . . .

The District Court found that there were three serious conditions which would not be covered by the statute: preeclampsia, inevitable abortion, and premature ruptured membrane. Yet, as the Court of Appeals observed, it is undisputed that under some circumstances each of these conditions could lead to an illness with substantial and irreversible consequences. While the definition could be interpreted in an unconstitutional manner, the Court of Appeals construed the phrase "serious risk" to include those circumstances. . . . [We] conclude that, as construed by the Court of Appeals, the medical emergency definition imposes no undue burden on a woman's abortion right.

B

We next consider the informed consent requirement. Except in a medical emergency, the statute requires that at least 24 hours before performing an abortion a physician inform the woman of the nature of the procedure, the health risks of the abortion and of childbirth, and the "probable gestational age of the unborn child." The physician or a qualified nonphysician must inform the woman of the availability of printed materials published by the State describing the fetus and providing information about medical assistance for childbirth, information about child support from the father, and a list of agencies which provide adoption and other services as alternatives to abortion. An abortion may not be performed unless the woman certifies in writing that she has been informed of the availability of these printed materials and has been provided them if she chooses to view them.

Our prior decisions establish that as with any medical procedure, the State may require a woman to give her written informed consent to an abortion. In this respect, the statute is unexceptional. Petitioners challenge the statute's definition of informed consent because it includes the provision of specific information by the doctor and the mandatory 24-hour waiting period. The conclusions reached by a majority of the Justices in the separate opinions filed today and the undue burden standard adopted in this opinion require us to overrule in part some of the Court's past decisions, decisions driven by the trimester framework's prohibition of all previability regulations designed to further the State's interest in fetal life.

In *Akron I*, we invalidated an ordinance which required that a woman seeking an abortion be provided by her physician with specific information "designed to influence the woman's informed choice between abortion or childbirth." As we later described the *Akron I* holding in *Thornburgh*, at 762, there were two purported flaws in the Akron ordinance: the information was designed to dissuade the woman from having an abortion and the ordinance imposed "a rigid requirement that a specific body of information be given in all cases, irrespective of the particular needs of the patient. . . ."

To the extent *Akron I* and *Thornburgh* find a constitutional violation when the government requires, as it does here, the giving of truthful, nonmisleading information about the nature of the procedure, the attendant health risks and those of childbirth, and the "probable gestational age" of the fetus, those cases go too far, are inconsistent with *Roe*'s acknowledgment of an important interest in potential life, and are overruled. This is clear even on the very terms of *Akron I* and *Thornburgh*. Those decisions, along with *Planned Parenthood of Central Missouri v. Danforth*, 428 U.S. 52 (1976), recognize a substantial government interest justifying a requirement that a woman be apprised of the health risks of abortion and childbirth. It cannot be questioned that psychological well-being is a facet of health. Nor can it be doubted that most women considering an abortion would deem the impact on the fetus relevant, if not dispositive, to the decision. In attempting to ensure that a woman apprehend the full consequences of her decision, the State furthers the legitimate purpose of reducing the risk that a woman may elect an abortion, only to discover later, with devastating psychological consequences, that her decision was not fully informed. If the information the State requires to be made available to the woman is truthful and not misleading, the requirement may be permissible.

We also see no reason why the State may not require doctors to inform a woman seeking an abortion of the availability of materials relating to the consequences to the fetus, even when those consequences have no direct relation to her health. An example illustrates the point. We would think it constitutional for the State to require that in order for there to be informed consent to a kidney transplant operation the recipient must be supplied with information about risks to the donor as well as risks to himself or herself. A requirement that the physician make available information similar to that mandated by the statute here was described in *Thornburgh* as "an outright attempt to wedge the Commonwealth's message discouraging abortion into the privacy of the informed-consent dialogue between the woman and her physician." We conclude, however, that informed choice need not be defined in such narrow terms that all considerations of the effect on the fetus are made irrelevant. As we have made clear, we depart from the holdings of *Akron I* and *Thornburgh* to the extent that we permit a State to further its legitimate goal of protecting the life of the unborn by enacting legislation aimed at ensuring a decision that is mature and informed, even when in so doing the State expresses a preference for childbirth over abortion. In short, requiring that the woman be informed of the availability of information relating to fetal development and the assistance available should she decide to carry the pregnancy to full term is a reasonable measure to ensure an informed choice, one which might cause the woman to choose childbirth over abortion. This requirement cannot be considered a substantial obstacle to obtaining an abortion, and, it follows, there is no undue burden.

Our prior cases also suggest that the "straitjacket" of particular information which must be given in each case interferes with a constitutional right of privacy between a pregnant woman and her physician. As a preliminary matter, it is worth noting that the statute now before us does not require a physician to comply with the informed consent provisions "if he or she can demonstrate by a preponderance of the evidence, that he or she reasonably believed that furnishing the information would have resulted in a severely adverse effect on the physical or mental health of the patient." In this respect, the statute does not prevent the physician from exercising his or her medical judgment.

Whatever constitutional status the doctor-patient relation may have as a general matter, in the present context it is derivative of the woman's position. The doctor-patient relation does not underlie or override the two more general rights under which the abortion right is justified: the right to make family decisions and the right to physical autonomy. On its own, the doctor-patient relation here is entitled to the same solicitude it receives in other contexts. Thus, a requirement that a doctor give a woman certain information as part of obtaining her consent to an abortion is, for constitutional purposes, no different from a requirement that a doctor give certain specific information about any medical procedure.

All that is left of petitioners' argument is an asserted First Amendment right of a physician not to provide information about the risks of abortion, and childbirth, in a manner mandated by the State. To be sure, the physician's First Amendment rights not to speak are implicated, but only as part of the practice of medicine, subject to reasonable licensing and regulation by the State. We see no constitutional infirmity in the requirement that the physician provide the information mandated by the State here.

The Pennsylvania statute also requires us to reconsider the holding in *Akron I* that the State may not require that a physician, as opposed to a qualified assistant, provide information relevant to a woman's informed consent. Since there is no evidence on this record that requiring a doctor to give the information as provided by the statute would amount in practical terms to a substantial obstacle to a woman seeking an abortion, we conclude that it is not an undue burden. . . .

Our analysis of Pennsylvania's 24-hour waiting period between the provision of the information deemed necessary to informed consent and the performance of an abortion under the undue burden standard requires us to reconsider the premise behind the decision in *Akron I* invalidating a parallel requirement. In *Akron I* we said: "Nor are we convinced that the State's legitimate concern that the woman's decision be informed is reasonably served by requiring a 24-hour delay as a matter of course." We consider that conclusion to be wrong. The idea that important decisions will be more informed and deliberate if they follow some period of reflection does not strike us as unreasonable, particularly where the statute directs that important information become part of the background of the decision. The statute, as construed by the Court of Appeals, permits avoidance of the waiting period in the event of a medical emergency and the record evidence shows that in the vast majority of cases, a 24-hour delay does not create any appreciable health risk. In theory, at least, the waiting period is a reasonable measure to implement the State's interest in protecting the life of the unborn, a measure that does not amount to an undue burden.

Whether the mandatory 24-hour waiting period is nonetheless invalid because in practice it is a substantial obstacle to a woman's choice to terminate her pregnancy is a closer question. The findings of fact by the District Court indicate that because of the distances many women must travel to reach an abortion provider, the practical effect will often be a delay of much more than a day because the waiting period requires that a woman seeking an abortion make at least two visits to the doctor. The District Court also found that in many instances this will increase the exposure of women seeking abortions to "the harassment and hostility of anti-abortion protestors demonstrating outside a clinic." As a result, the District Court found that for those women who have the fewest financial resources, those who must travel long distances, and those who have difficulty explaining their whereabouts to husbands, employers, or others, the 24-hour waiting period will be "particularly burdensome."

These findings are troubling in some respects, but they do not demonstrate that the waiting period constitutes an undue burden. We do not doubt that, as the District Court held, the waiting period has the effect of "increasing the cost and risk of delay of abortions," but the District Court did not conclude that the increased costs and potential delays amount to substantial obstacles. . . . Yet, as we have stated, under the undue burden standard a State is permitted to enact persuasive measures which favor childbirth over abortion, even if those measures do not further a health interest. And while the waiting period does limit a physician's discretion, that is not, standing alone, a reason to invalidate it. In light of the construction given the statute's definition of medical emergency by the Court of Appeals, and the District Court's findings, we cannot say that the waiting period imposes a real health risk.

We also disagree with the District Court's conclusion that the "particularly burdensome" effects of the waiting period on some women require its invalidation. A particular burden is not of necessity a substantial obstacle. Whether a burden falls on a particular group is a distinct inquiry from whether it is a substantial obstacle even as to the women in that group. And the District Court did not conclude that the waiting period is such an obstacle even for the women who are most burdened by it. Hence, on the record before us, and in the context of this facial challenge, we are not convinced that the 24-hour waiting period constitutes an undue burden.

We are left with the argument that the various aspects of the informed consent requirement are unconstitutional because they place barriers in the way of abortion on demand. Even the broadest reading of *Roe,* however, has not suggested that there is a constitutional right to abortion on demand. Rather, the right protected by *Roe* is a right to decide to terminate a pregnancy free of undue interference by the State. Because the informed consent requirement facilitates the wise exercise of that right, it cannot be classified as an interference with the right *Roe* protects. The informed consent requirement is not an undue burden on that right.

C

Section 3209 of Pennsylvania's abortion law provides, except in cases of medical emergency, that no physician shall perform an abortion on a married woman without receiving a signed statement from the woman that she has notified her spouse that she is about to undergo an abortion. The woman has the option of providing an alternative signed statement certifying that her husband is not the man who impregnated her; that her husband could not be located; that the pregnancy is the result of spousal sexual assault which she has reported; or that the woman believes that notifying her husband will cause him or someone else to inflict bodily injury upon her. A physician who performs an abortion on a married woman without receiving the appropriate signed statement will have his or her license revoked, and is liable to the husband for damages.

. . . In well-functioning marriages, spouses discuss important intimate decisions such as whether to bear a child. But there are millions of women in this country who are the victims of regular physical and psychological abuse at the hands of their husbands. Should these women become pregnant, they may have very good reasons for not wishing to inform their husbands of their decision to obtain an abortion. Many may have justifiable fears of physical abuse, but may be no less fearful of the consequences of reporting prior abuse to the Commonwealth of Pennsylvania. Many may have a reasonable fear that notifying their husbands will provoke further instances of child abuse; these women are not exempt from § 3209's notification requirement. Many may fear devastating forms of psychological abuse from their husbands, including verbal harassment, threats of future violence, the destruction of possessions, physical confinement to the home, the withdrawal of financial support, or the disclosure of the abortion to family and friends. These methods of psychological abuse may act as even more of a deterrent to notification than the possibility of physical violence, but women who are the victims of the abuse are not exempt from § 3209's notification requirement. And many women who are pregnant as a result of sexual assaults by their husbands will be unable to avail themselves of the exception for spousal sexual assault, § 3209(b)(3), because the exception requires that the woman have notified law enforcement authorities within 90 days of the assault, and her husband will be notified of her report once an investigation begins, § 3128(c). If anything in this field is certain, it is that victims of spousal sexual assault are extremely reluctant to report the abuse to the government; hence, a great many spousal rape victims will not be exempt from the notification requirement imposed by § 3209.

The spousal notification requirement is thus likely to prevent a significant number of women from obtaining an abortion. It does not merely make abortions a little more difficult or expensive to obtain; for many women, it will impose a substantial obstacle. We must not blind ourselves to the fact that the significant number of women who fear for their safety and the safety of their children are likely to be deterred from procuring an abortion as surely as if the Commonwealth had outlawed abortion in all cases.

Respondents attempt to avoid the conclusion that § 3209 is invalid by pointing out that it imposes almost no burden at all for the vast majority of women seeking abortions. They begin by noting that only about 20 percent of the women who obtain abortions are married. They then note that of these women about 95 percent notify their husbands of their own volition. Thus, respondents argue, the effects of § 3209 are felt by only one percent of the women who obtain abortions. . . . The analysis does not end with the one percent of women upon whom the statute operates; it begins there. . . . The proper focus of constitutional inquiry is the group for whom the law is a restriction, not the group for whom the law is irrelevant. . . . The unfortunate yet persisting conditions we document above will mean that in a large fraction of the cases in which § 3209 is relevant, it will operate as a substantial obstacle to a woman's choice to undergo an abortion. It is an undue burden, and therefore invalid.

This conclusion is in no way inconsistent with our decisions upholding parental notification or consent requirements. Those enactments, and our judgment that they are constitutional, are based on the quite reasonable assumption that minors will benefit from consultation with their parents and that children will often not realize that their parents have their best interests at heart. We cannot adopt a parallel assumption about adult women. . . .

Section 3209 embodies a view of marriage . . . repugnant to our present understanding of marriage and of the nature of the rights secured by the Constitution. Women do not lose their constitutionally protected liberty when they marry. The Constitution protects all individuals, male or female, married or unmarried, from the abuse of governmental power, even where that power is employed for the supposed benefit of a member of the individual's family. These considerations confirm our conclusion that § 3209 is invalid.

D

We next consider the parental consent provision. Except in a medical emergency, an unemancipated young woman under 18 may not obtain an abortion unless she and one of her parents (or guardian) provides informed consent as defined above. If neither a parent nor a guardian provides consent, a court may authorize the performance of an abortion upon a determination that the young woman is mature and capable of giving informed consent and has in fact given her informed consent, or that an abortion would be in her best interests.

We . . . reaffirm today, that a State may require a minor seeking an abortion to obtain the consent of a parent or guardian, provided that there is an adequate judicial bypass procedure. . . .

E

Under the recordkeeping and reporting requirements of the statute, every facility which performs abortions is required to file a report stating its name and address as well as the name and address of any related entity, such as a controlling or subsidiary organization. In the case of state-funded institutions, the information becomes public.

For each abortion performed, a report must be filed identifying: the physician (and the second physician where required); the facility; the referring physician or agency; the woman's age; the number of prior pregnancies and abortions she has had; gestational age; the type of abortion procedure; the date of the abortion; whether there were any pre-existing medical conditions which would complicate pregnancy;

medical complications with the abortion; where applicable, the basis for the determination that the abortion was medically necessary; the weight of the aborted fetus; and whether the woman was married, and if so, whether notice was provided or the basis for the failure to give notice. Every abortion facility must also file quarterly reports showing the number of abortions performed broken down by trimester. In all events, the identity of each woman who has had an abortion remains confidential.

In Danforth, at 80, we held that recordkeeping and reporting provisions "that are reasonably directed to the preservation of maternal health and that properly respect a patient's confidentiality and privacy are permissible." We think that under this standard, all the provisions at issue here, except that relating to spousal notice, are constitutional. Although they do not relate to the State's interest in informing the woman's choice, they do relate to health. The collection of information with respect to actual patients is a vital element of medical research, and so it cannot be said that the requirements serve no purpose other than to make abortions more difficult. Nor do we find that the requirements impose a substantial obstacle to a woman's choice. At most they might increase the cost of some abortions by a slight amount. While at some point increased cost could become a substantial obstacle, there is no such showing on the record before us. . . .

VI

Our Constitution is a covenant running from the first generation of Americans to us and then to future generations. It is a coherent succession. Each generation must learn anew that the Constitution's written terms embody ideas and aspirations that must survive more ages than one. We accept our responsibility not to retreat from interpreting the full meaning of the covenant in light of all of our precedents. We invoke it once again to define the freedom guaranteed by the Constitution's own promise, the promise of liberty. . . .

■ JUSTICE STEVENS, concurring in part and dissenting in part.

. . . The Court is unquestionably correct in concluding that the doctrine of *stare decisis* has controlling significance in a case of this kind, notwithstanding an individual Justice's concerns about the merits. The central holding of *Roe v. Wade* has been a "part of our law" for almost two decades. It was a natural sequel to the protection of individual liberty established in *Griswold v. Connecticut*. The societal costs of overruling *Roe* at this late date would be enormous. *Roe* is an integral part of a correct understanding of both the concept of liberty and the basic equality of men and women. . . .

■ JUSTICE BLACKMUN, concurring in part, concurring in the judgment in part, and dissenting in part.

. . . Three years ago, in *Webster*, four Members of this Court appeared poised to "cas[t] into darkness the hopes and visions of every woman in this country" who had come to believe that the Constitution guaranteed her the right to reproductive choice. All that remained between the promise of *Roe* and the darkness of the plurality was a single, flickering flame. Decisions since *Webster* gave little reason to hope that this flame would cast much light. But now, just when so many expected the darkness to fall, the flame has grown bright. I do not underestimate the significance of today's joint opinion. Yet I remain steadfast in my belief that the right to reproductive choice is entitled to the full protection afforded by this Court before *Webster*. And I fear for the darkness as four Justices anxiously await the single vote necessary to extinguish the light.

Make no mistake, the joint opinion of JUSTICES O'CONNOR, KENNEDY, and SOUTER is an act of personal courage and constitutional principle. . . . The Court's reaffirmation of *Roe*'s central holding is also based on the force of *stare decisis*. . . . In the 19 years since *Roe* was decided, that case has shaped more than reproductive planning—"[a]n entire generation has come of age free to assume *Roe*'s concept of liberty in defining the capacity of women to act in society, and to make reproductive decisions." The Court understands that, having "call[ed] the contending sides . . . to end their national division by accepting a common mandate rooted in the Constitution," a decision to overrule *Roe* "would seriously weaken the Court's capacity to exercise the judicial power and to function as the Supreme Court of a Nation dedicated to the rule of law." What has happened today should serve as a model for future Justices and a warning to all who have tried to turn this Court into yet another political branch. . . .

In one sense, the Court's approach is worlds apart from that of THE CHIEF JUSTICE and JUSTICE SCALIA. And yet, in another sense, the distance between the two approaches is short—the distance is but a single vote.

I am 83 years old. I cannot remain on this Court forever, and when I do step down, the confirmation process for my successor well may focus on the issue before us today. That, I regret, may be exactly where the choice between the two worlds will be made.

■ CHIEF JUSTICE REHNQUIST, with whom JUSTICE WHITE, JUSTICE SCALIA, and JUSTICE THOMAS join, concurring in the judgment in part and dissenting in part.

The joint opinion, following its newly minted variation on *stare decisis*, retains the outer shell of Roe v. Wade, but beats a wholesale retreat from the substance of that case. We believe that *Roe* was wrongly decided, and that it can and should be overruled consistently with our traditional approach to *stare decisis* in constitutional cases. We would adopt the approach of the plurality in Webster, and uphold the challenged provisions of the Pennsylvania statute in their entirety. . . .

We have held that a liberty interest protected under the Due Process Clause of the Fourteenth Amendment will be deemed fundamental if it is "implicit in the concept of ordered liberty." *Palko v. Connecticut*, 302 U.S. 319, 325 (1937). Three years earlier we referred to a "principle of justice so rooted in the traditions and conscience of our people as to be ranked as fundamental." These expressions are admittedly not precise, but our decisions implementing this notion of "fundamental" rights do not afford any more elaborate basis on which to base such a classification.

In construing the phrase "liberty" incorporated in the Due Process Clause of the Fourteenth Amendment, we have recognized that its meaning extends beyond freedom from physical restraint. In *Pierce v. Society of Sisters*, 268 U.S. 510 (1925), we held that it included a parent's right to send a child to private school; in *Meyer v. Nebraska*, 262 U.S. 390 (1923), we held that it included a right to teach a foreign language in a parochial school. Building on these cases, we have held that the term "liberty" includes a right to marry, Loving v. Virginia; a right to procreate, *Skinner v. Oklahoma ex rel. Williamson*, 316 U.S. 535 (1942); and a right to use contraceptives, *Griswold v. Connecticut*; *Eisenstadt v. Baird*, 405 U.S. 438 (1972).

But a reading of these opinions makes clear that they do not endorse any all-encompassing "right of privacy."

In *Roe v. Wade*, the Court recognized a "guarantee of personal privacy" which "is broad enough to encompass a woman's decision whether or not to terminate her pregnancy." We are now of the view that, in terming this right fundamental, the Court in *Roe* read the earlier opinions upon which it based its decision much too broadly. Unlike marriage, procreation, and contraception, abortion "involves the purposeful termination of a potential life." The abortion decision must therefore "be recognized as *sui generis*, different in kind from the others that the Court has protected under the rubric of personal or family privacy and autonomy." One cannot ignore the fact that a woman is not isolated in her pregnancy, and that the decision to abort necessarily involves the destruction of a fetus.

Nor do the historical traditions of the American people support the view that the right to terminate one's pregnancy is "fundamental." The common law which we inherited from England made abortion after "quickening" an offense. At the time of the adoption of the Fourteenth Amendment, statutory prohibitions or restrictions on abortion were commonplace; in 1868, at least 28 of the then-37 States and 8 Territories had statutes banning or limiting abortion. By the turn of the century virtually every State had a law prohibiting or restricting abortion on its books. . . . On this record, it can scarcely be said that any deeply rooted tradition of relatively unrestricted abortion in our history supported the classification of the right to abortion as "fundamental" under the Due Process Clause of the Fourteenth Amendment.

We think, therefore, both in view of this history and of our decided cases dealing with substantive liberty under the Due Process Clause, that the Court was mistaken in *Roe* when it classified a woman's decision to terminate her pregnancy as a "fundamental right" that could be abridged only in a manner which withstood "strict scrutiny." . . . The Court in *Roe* reached too far when it analogized the right to abort a fetus to the rights involved in *Pierce*, *Meyer*, *Loving*, and *Griswold*, and thereby deemed the right to abortion fundamental.

The joint opinion of JUSTICES O'CONNOR, KENNEDY, and SOUTER cannot bring itself to say that *Roe* was correct as an original matter, but the authors are of the view that "the immediate question is not the soundness of *Roe*'s resolution of the issue, but the precedential force that must be accorded to its holding." Instead of claiming that *Roe* was correct as a matter of original constitutional interpretation, the opinion therefore contains an elaborate discussion of *stare decisis*. . . . *Roe* analyzed abortion regulation under a rigid trimester framework, a framework which has guided this Court's decisionmaking for 19 years. The joint opinion rejects that framework.

Stare decisis is defined in Black's Law Dictionary as meaning "to abide by, or adhere to, decided cases." Whatever the "central holding" of *Roe* that is left after the joint opinion finishes dissecting it is surely not the result of that principle. While purporting to adhere to precedent, the joint opinion instead revises it. *Roe* continues to exist, but only in the way a storefront on a western movie set exists: a mere facade to give the illusion of reality. Decisions following *Roe*, such as *Akron* and *Thornburgh*, are frankly overruled in part under the "undue burden" standard expounded in the joint opinion.

In our view, authentic principles of *stare decisis* do not require that any portion of the reasoning in *Roe* be kept intact. "*Stare decisis* is not . . . a universal, inexorable command," especially in cases involving the interpretation of the Federal Constitution. Erroneous decisions in such constitutional cases are uniquely durable, because correction through legislative action, save for constitutional amendment, is impossible. It is therefore our duty to reconsider constitutional interpretations that "depar[t] from a proper understanding" of the Constitution. Our constitutional watch does not cease merely because we have spoken before on an issue; when it becomes clear that a prior constitutional interpretation is unsound we are obliged to reexamine the question. See, *e.g., West Virginia Bd. of Ed. v. Barnette*, 319 U.S. 624, 642 (1943); *Erie R. Co. v. Tompkins*, 304 U.S. 64, 74–78 (1938).

The joint opinion discusses several *stare decisis* factors which, it asserts, point toward retaining a portion of *Roe*. Two of these factors are that the main "factual underpinning" of *Roe* has remained the same, and that its doctrinal foundation is no weaker now than it was in 1973. Of course, what might be called the basic facts which gave rise to *Roe* have remained the same—women become pregnant, there is a point somewhere, depending on medical technology, where a fetus becomes viable, and women give birth to children. But this is only to say that the same facts which gave rise to *Roe* will continue to give rise to similar cases. It is not a reason, in and of itself, why those cases must be decided in the same incorrect manner as was the first case to deal with the question. And surely there is no requirement, in considering whether to depart from *stare decisis* in a constitutional case, that a decision be more wrong now than it was at the time it was rendered. If that were true, the most outlandish constitutional decision could survive forever, based simply on the fact that it was no more outlandish later than it was when originally rendered.

The joint opinion also points to the reliance interests involved in this context in its effort to explain why precedent must be followed for precedent's sake. . . . But, as the joint opinion apparently agrees, any traditional notion of reliance is not applicable here. The Court today cuts back on the protection afforded by *Roe,* and no one claims that this action defeats any reliance interest in the disavowed trimester framework. Similarly, reliance interests would not be diminished were the Court to go further and acknowledge the full error of *Roe,* as "reproductive planning could take virtually immediate account of" this action. . . .

In the end, having failed to put forth any evidence to prove any true reliance, the joint opinion's argument is based solely on generalized assertions about the national psyche, on a belief that the people of this country have grown accustomed to the *Roe* decision over the last 19 years and have "ordered their thinking and living around" it . . . [A]t various points in the past, the same could have been said about this Court's erroneous decisions that the Constitution allowed "separate but equal" treatment of minorities, see *Plessy v. Ferguson*, or that "liberty" under the Due Process Clause protected "freedom of contract," see *Adkins v. Children's Hospital of District of Columbia; Lochner v. New York*. The "separate but equal" doctrine lasted 58 years after *Plessy*, and *Lochner*'s protection of contractual freedom lasted 32 years. However, the simple fact that a generation or more had grown used to these major decisions did not prevent the Court from correcting its errors in those cases, nor should it prevent us from correctly interpreting the Constitution here.

Apparently realizing that conventional *stare decisis* principles do not support its position, the joint opinion advances a belief that retaining a portion of *Roe* is necessary to protect the "legitimacy" of this Court. . . . But the joint opinion goes on to state that when the Court "resolve[s] the sort of intensely divisive controversy reflected in *Roe* and those rare, comparable cases," its decision is exempt from reconsideration under established principles of *stare decisis* in constitutional cases. This is so, the joint opinion contends, because in those "intensely divisive" cases the Court has "call[ed] the contending sides of a national controversy to end their national division by accepting a common mandate rooted in the Constitution," and must therefore take special care not to be perceived as "surrender[ing] to political pressure" and continued opposition. This is a truly novel principle, one which is contrary to both the Court's historical practice and to the Court's traditional willingness to tolerate criticism of its opinions. Under this principle, when the Court has ruled on a divisive issue, it is apparently prevented from overruling that decision for the sole reason that it was incorrect, *unless opposition to the original decision has died away.*

The first difficulty with this principle lies in its assumption that cases that are "intensely divisive" can be readily distinguished from those that are not. The question of whether a particular issue is "intensely divisive" enough to qualify for special protection is entirely subjective and dependent on the individual assumptions of the Members of this Court. In addition, because the Court's duty is to ignore public opinion and criticism on issues that come before it, its Members are in perhaps the worst position to judge whether a decision divides the Nation deeply enough to justify such uncommon protection. Although many of the Court's decisions divide the populace to a large degree, we have not previously on that account shied away from applying normal rules of *stare decisis* when urged to reconsider earlier decisions. Over the past 21 years, for example, the Court has overruled in whole or in part 34 of its previous constitutional decisions.

The joint opinion picks out and discusses two prior Court rulings that it believes are of the "intensely divisive" variety, and concludes that they are of comparable dimension to *Roe.* It appears to us very odd indeed that the joint opinion chooses as benchmarks two cases in which the Court chose not to adhere to erroneous constitutional precedent, but instead enhanced its stature by acknowledging and correcting its error, apparently in violation of the joint opinion's "legitimacy" principle. See *West Coast Hotel Co. v. Parrish*; *Brown v. Board of Education.* One might also wonder how it is that the joint opinion puts these, and not others, in the "intensely divisive" category, and how it assumes that these are the only two lines of cases of comparable dimension to *Roe.* . . .

There are other reasons why the joint opinion's discussion of legitimacy is unconvincing as well. In assuming that the Court is perceived as "surrender[ing] to political pressure" when it overrules a controversial decision, the joint opinion forgets that there are two sides to any controversy. The joint opinion asserts that, in order to protect its legitimacy, the Court must refrain from overruling a controversial decision lest it be viewed as favoring those who oppose the decision. But a decision to *adhere* to prior precedent is subject to the same criticism, for in such a case one can easily argue that the Court is responding to those who have demonstrated in favor of the original decision. . . . But this perceived dilemma arises only if one assumes, as the joint opinion does, that the Court should make its decisions with a view toward speculative public perceptions. If one assumes instead, as the Court surely did in both *Brown* and *West Coast Hotel*, that the Court's legitimacy is enhanced by faithful interpretation of the Constitution irrespective of public opposition, such self-engendered difficulties may be put to one side. . . .

■ JUSTICE SCALIA, with whom THE CHIEF JUSTICE, JUSTICE WHITE, and JUSTICE THOMAS join, concurring in the judgment in part and dissenting in part.

. . . The Court's reliance upon *stare decisis* can best be described as contrived. It insists upon the necessity of adhering not to all of *Roe*, but only to what it calls the "central holding." It seems to me that *stare decisis* ought to be applied even to the doctrine of *stare decisis*, and I confess never to have heard of this new, keep-what-you-want-and-throw-away-the-rest version. . . .

The Imperial Judiciary lives. It is instructive to compare this Nietzschean vision of us unelected, life-tenured judges—leading a Volk who will be "tested by following," and whose very "belief in themselves" is mystically bound up in their "understanding" of a Court that "speak[s] before all others for their constitutional ideals"—with the somewhat more modest role envisioned for these lawyers by the Founders.

> "The judiciary . . . has . . . no direction either of the strength or of the wealth of the society, and can take no active resolution whatever. It may truly be said to have neither Force nor Will, but merely judgment. . . ." The Federalist No. 78.

. . . It is particularly difficult, in the circumstances of the present decision, to sit still for the Court's lengthy lecture upon the virtues of "constancy," of "remain[ing] steadfast," and adhering to "principle." Among the five justices who purportedly adhere to *Roe*, at most three agree upon the *principle* that constitutes adherence (the joint opinion's "undue burden" standard)—and that principle is inconsistent with *Roe*. To make matters worse, two of the three, in order thus to remain steadfast, had to abandon previously stated positions. . . . The only principle the Court "adheres" to, it seems to me, is the principle that the Court must be seen as standing by *Roe*. . . .

I cannot agree with, indeed I am appalled by, the Court's suggestion that the decision whether to stand by an erroneous constitutional decision must be strongly influenced—against overruling, no less—by the substantial and continuing public opposition the decision has generated. The Court's judgment that any other course would "subvert the Court's legitimacy" must be another consequence of reading the error-filled history book that described the deeply divided country brought together by *Roe*. In my history book, the Court was covered with dishonor and deprived of legitimacy by *Dred Scott v. Sandford*, 60 U.S. (19 How.) 393 (1857), an erroneous (and widely opposed) opinion that it did not abandon, rather than by *West Coast Hotel Co.*, which produced the famous "switch in time" from the Court's erroneous (and widely opposed) constitutional opposition to the social measures of the New Deal. (Both *Dred Scott* and one line of the cases resisting the New Deal rested upon the concept of "substantive due process" that the Court praises and employs today.) Indeed, *Dred Scott* was "very possibly the first application of substantive due process in the Supreme Court, the original precedent for *Lochner v. New York* and *Roe v. Wade*." D. Currie, The Constitution in the Supreme Court 271 (1985).

But whether it would "subvert the Court's legitimacy" or not, the notion that we would decide a case differently from the way we otherwise would have in order to show that we can stand firm against public disapproval is frightening. It is a bad enough idea, even in the head of someone like me, who believes that the text of the

Constitution, and our traditions, say what they say and there is no fiddling with them. But when it is in the mind of a Court that believes the Constitution has an evolving meaning; that the Ninth Amendment's reference to "othe[r]" rights is not a disclaimer, but a charter for action; and that the function of this Court is to "speak before all others for [the people's] constitutional ideals" unrestrained by meaningful text or tradition—then the notion that the Court must adhere to a decision for as long as the decision faces "great opposition" and the Court is "under fire" acquires a character of almost czarist arrogance. We are offended by these marchers who descend upon us, every year on the anniversary of *Roe*, to protest our saying that the Constitution requires what our society has never thought the Constitution requires. These people who refuse to be "tested by following" must be taught a lesson. We have no Cossacks, but at least we can stubbornly refuse to abandon an erroneous opinion that we might otherwise change—to show how little they intimidate us.

Of course, as THE CHIEF JUSTICE points out, we have been subjected to what the Court calls " 'political pressure' " by *both* sides of this issue. Maybe today's decision not to overrule *Roe* will be seen as buckling to pressure from that direction. Instead of engaging in the hopeless task of predicting public perception—a job not for lawyers but for political campaign managers—the Justices should do what is *legally* right by asking two questions: (1) Was *Roe* correctly decided? (2) Has *Roe* succeeded in producing a settled body of law? If the answer to both questions is no, *Roe* should undoubtedly be overruled.

In truth, I am as distressed as the Court is—and expressed my distress several years ago, see *Webster*, at 535—about the "political pressure" directed to the Court: the marches, the mail, the protests aimed at inducing us to change our opinions. How upsetting it is, that so many of our citizens (good people, not lawless ones, on both sides of this abortion issue, and on various sides of other issues as well) think that we Justices should properly take into account their views, as though we were engaged not in ascertaining an objective law but in determining some kind of social consensus. The Court would profit, I think, from giving less attention to the *fact* of this distressing phenomenon, and more attention to the *cause* of it. That cause permeates today's opinion: a new mode of constitutional adjudication that relies not upon text and traditional practice to determine the law, but upon what the Court calls "reasoned judgment," which turns out to be nothing but philosophical predilection and moral intuition. All manner of "liberties," the Court tells us, inhere in the Constitution and are enforceable by this Court—not just those mentioned in the text or established in the traditions of our society. Why even the Ninth Amendment—which says only that "[t]he enumeration in the Constitution, of certain rights, shall not be construed to deny or disparage others retained by the people"—is, despite our contrary understanding for almost 200 years, a literally boundless source of additional, unnamed, unhinted—at "rights," definable and enforceable by us, through "reasoned judgment."

What makes all this relevant to the bothersome application of "political pressure" against the Court are the twin facts that the American people love democracy and the American people are not fools. As long as this Court thought (and the people thought) that we Justices were doing essentially lawyers' work up here—reading text and discerning our society's traditional understanding of that text—the public pretty much left us alone. Texts and traditions are facts to study, not convictions to demonstrate about. But if in reality our process of constitutional adjudication consists primarily of making *value judgments*; if we can ignore a long and clear tradition clarifying an ambiguous text, as we did, for example, five days ago in declaring unconstitutional invocations and benedictions at public high school graduation ceremonies, *Lee v. Weisman*, 505 U.S. 577 (1992); if, as I say, our pronouncement of constitutional law rests primarily on value judgments, then a free and intelligent people's attitude towards us can be expected to be (*ought* to be) quite different. The people know that their value judgments are quite as good as those taught in any law school—maybe better. If, indeed, the "liberties" protected by the Constitution are, as the Court says, undefined and unbounded, then the people *should* demonstrate, to protest that we do not implement *their* values instead of *ours*. Not only that, but confirmation hearings for new Justices *should* deteriorate into question-and-answer sessions in which Senators go through a list of their constituents' most favored and most disfavored alleged constitutional rights, and seek the nominee's commitment to support or oppose them. Value judgments, after all, should be voted on, not dictated; and if our Constitution has somehow accidently committed them to the Supreme Court, at least we can have a sort of plebiscite each time a new nominee to that body is put forward. JUSTICE BLACKMUN not only regards this prospect with equanimity, he solicits it.

* * *

There is a poignant aspect to today's opinion. Its length, and what might be called its epic tone, suggest that its authors believe they are bringing to an end a troublesome era in the history of our Nation and of our Court. "It is the dimension" of authority, they say, to "cal[l] the contending sides of national controversy to end their national division by accepting a common mandate rooted in the Constitution."

There comes vividly to mind a portrait by Emanuel Leutze that hangs in the Harvard Law School: Roger Brooke Taney, painted in 1859, the 82d year of his life, the 24th of his Chief Justiceship, the second after his opinion in *Dred Scott*. He is all in black, sitting in a shadowed red armchair, left hand resting upon a pad of paper in his lap, right hand hanging limply, almost lifelessly, beside the inner arm of the chair. He sits facing the viewer and staring straight out. There seems to be on his face, and in his deep-set eyes, an expression of profound sadness and disillusionment. Perhaps he always looked that way, even when dwelling upon the happiest of thoughts. But those of us who know how the lustre of his great Chief Justiceship came to be eclipsed by *Dred Scott* cannot help believing that he had that case—its already apparent consequences for the Court and its soon-to-be-played-out consequences for the Nation—burning on his mind. I expect that two years earlier he, too, had thought himself "call[ing] the contending sides of national controversy to end their national division by accepting a common mandate rooted in the Constitution."

It is no more realistic for us in this litigation, than it was for him in that, to think that an issue of the sort they both involved—an issue involving life and death, freedom and subjugation—can be "speedily and finally settled" by the Supreme Court, as President James Buchanan in his inaugural address said the issue of slavery in the territories would be. Quite to the contrary, by foreclosing all democratic outlet for the deep passions this issue arouses, by banishing the issue from the political forum that gives all participants, even the losers, the satisfaction of a fair hearing and an honest fight, by continuing the imposition of a rigid national rule instead of allowing for regional differences, the Court merely prolongs and intensifies the anguish.

We should get out of this area, where we have no right to be, and where we do neither ourselves nor the country any good by remaining.

NOTES

1.   *Casey* is a massively important case, arguably even more significant than the case it reaffirmed, *Roe v. Wade*:

a.   *Abortion. Casey*'s reaffirming of what the Joint Opinion called the "central holding" of *Roe* was a judicial act of enormous consequence. *Roe* had been the rule for nineteen years, from 1973 to 1992. *Casey* could have overruled *Roe* but instead reaffirmed it. *Casey*, rather than *Roe*, accounts for the constitutional law of abortion since 1992. Under any view, the decision affects millions of lives every year. For supporters, the decision vindicated the freedom of millions of women, indeed of all women, to have an abortion—a right regarded by many (and by the opinion) as central to women's identity and freedom. For opponents, the decision consigned more than a million innocent unborn lives to death every year. No matter one's view of the merits, the stakes are huge.

The decision in *Casey* came as a bit of a surprise. Based on votes in earlier cases, one could have reasonably predicted that as many as seven justices might have voted to uphold all of the provisions of Pennsylvania's law, and either overrule or seriously undercut *Roe*. Nevertheless, *Casey* did not reverse *Roe*. Instead, the Joint Opinion reaffirmed it, but it also replaced its trimester framework with a new "undue burden" test.

b.   *Substantive Due Process.* Part II of the Joint Opinion, which commanded a majority of the Court, reaffirmed the judicial practice of reviewing and invalidating laws based on substantive due process (albeit less on grounds that the approach is correct than on grounds of *stare decisis*). This was a significant doctrinal development, and it has had an enduring impact not only in abortion law but also in the Court's assisted-suicide and gay-rights cases.

c.   *Stare Decisis.* Part III of the Joint Opinion sets forth a full-blown judicial theory of *stare decisis*—somewhat surprisingly, for the first time in the Court's history—and appears to make that theory the centerpiece of the decision. The Joint Opinion repeatedly implies that at least some of the justices forming the majority would not have thought *Roe* correct as an original matter, and that the outcome of *Casey* is attributable to the force of precedent. Is there any other case where the Court has reached a result in a major constitutional case contrary to what a majority thought the Constitution actually requires or permits for the stated reason of following precedent?

d.   *Judicial Supremacy.* Part of the Court's explanation for adhering to *Roe* was that overruling a case on which it had "staked its authority" would "seriously weaken the Court's capacity to exercise the judicial power and to function as the Supreme Court of a nation dedicated to the rule of law." What do you make of this? Is the Court's legitimacy a legitimate consideration? Should the justices seek to preserve their political capital as they are deciding cases? Is the Court right that it is—and needs to be perceived as—the ultimate authority in understanding the Constitution? Whatever one's answer to these questions, *Casey* is a major declaration about the role of the Supreme Court in constitutional interpretation.

2.   The Supreme Court has never said that *stare decisis* is absolute, and it has overruled hundreds of its prior constitutional decisions. The Court in *Casey* cited several

factors relevant to deciding whether to overrule or adhere to a prior decision: "workability," "reliance," whether a precedent is a mere "remnant of abandoned doctrine," whether there have been "changed facts," and public perceptions of "judicial integrity" and the maintenance of the Court's institutional prestige and power. Evaluate each consideration. Which ones are you persuaded of? Which of these considerations (if any) trump the importance of deciding a constitutional question correctly? Or are these considerations part of what it actually means to decide a constitutional question correctly? How would these criteria, faithfully applied, decide a case like *Brown*, in light of decades of contrary precedent since *Plessy*? Or *West Coast Hotel*, after the decades of *Lochner*-style substantive due process decisions? Are you persuaded by *Casey*'s explanation of why those precedents were rightly overruled? Can the *Casey* standard for adherence to precedent be squared with *Casey*'s own overruling of two prior abortion decisions (*Akron* and *Thornburgh*)? After you have considered how this standard would apply to *Brown*, *West Coast Hotel*, and *Casey* itself, think again about the criteria for when the Court should follow precedent. Can these factors be applied in a principled manner, or are they inherently subject to manipulation?

Interestingly, the Court did not assert that *stare decisis* is constitutionally required but only that it was a doctrine of judicial policy. If the doctrine is one of mere policy, can it be abrogated by Congress? Indeed, taking the reasoning one step further, if adherence to precedent is a matter of judicial policy, is it proper for the Court to reach outcomes for policy reasons that it would otherwise conclude are contrary to the Constitution? Is it proper for the other branches to depart from the Constitution for policy reasons? Or would such a departure by any of the branches be inconsistent with *Marbury*'s rule that the Constitution is supreme? If so, what makes such a policy-driven approach appropriate for the judiciary?

3.   There are other judicial views of *stare decisis* beyond those given in *Casey*. Consider three. The first is from *The License Cases*, 46 U.S. (5 How.) 504, 611–612 (1847), in an opinion of Justice Daniel:

> It has been said, that the principles here objected to have been already solemnly and fully adjudged and established, and should therefore be no longer assailed. The assertion as to the extent in which these principles have been ruled, or the solemnity with which they have been fixed and settled, may in the first place be justly questioned. It is believed that they have been directly adjudged in a single case only, and then under the qualification of an able dissent.
>
> But should this assertion be conceded in its greatest latitude, my reply to it must be firmly and unhesitatingly this,—that in matters involving the meaning and integrity of the constitution, I never can consent that the text of that instrument shall be overlaid and smothered by the glosses of essay-writers, lecturers, and commentators. Nor will I abide the decisions of judges, believed by me to be invasions of the great *lex legum [i.e., the law of laws—Editors]*. I, too, have been sworn to observe and maintain the constitution. I possess no sovereign prerogative by which I can put my conscience into commission. I must interpret exclusively as that conscience shall dictate.

The second is from *Pollock v. Farmers Loan and Trust Co.*, 157 U.S. 429, 650–652 (1895), in a dissenting opinion by then-Justice White:

> I cannot resist the conviction that [the Court's] opinion and decree in this case virtually annul its previous decisions in regard to the powers of congress on the subject of taxation, and are therefore fraught with danger to the court, to each

and every citizen, and to the republic. The conservation and orderly development of our institutions rest on our acceptance of the results of the past, and their use as lights to guide our steps in the future. Teach the lesson that settled principles may be overthrown at any time, and confusion and turmoil must ultimately result. In the discharge of its function of interpreting the constitution this court exercises an august power. It sits removed from the contentions of political parties and the animosities of factions. It seems to me that the accomplishment of its lofty mission can only be secured by the stability of its teachings and the sanctity which surrounds them. If the permanency of its conclusions is to depend upon the personal opinions of those who, from time to time, may make up its membership, it will inevitably become a theater of political strife, and its action will be without coherence or consistency. There is no great principle of our constitutional law, such as the nature and extent of the commerce power, or the currency power, or other powers of the federal government, which has not been ultimately defined by the adjudications of this court after long and earnest struggle. If we are to go back to the original sources of our political system, or are to appeal to the writings of the economists in order to unsettle all these great principles, everything is lost, and nothing saved to the people. The rights of every individual are guarantied by the safeguards which have been thrown around them by our adjudications. If these are to be assailed and overthrown, as is the settled law of income taxation by this opinion, as I understand it, the rights of property, so far as the federal constitution is concerned, are of little worth. My strong convictions forbid that I take part in a conclusion which seems to me so full of peril to the country. I am unwilling to do so, without reference to the question of what my personal opinion upon the subject might be if the question were a new one, and was thus unaffected by the action of the framers, the history of the government, and the long line of decisions by this court. The wisdom of our forefathers in adopting a written constitution has often been impeached upon the theory that the interpretation of a written instrument did not afford as complete protection to liberty as would be enjoyed under a constitution made up of the traditions of a free people. Writing, it has been said, does not insure greater stability than tradition does, while it destroys flexibility. The answer has always been that by the foresight of the fathers the construction of our written constitution was ultimately confided to this body, which, from the nature of its judicial structure, could always be relied upon to act with perfect freedom from the influence of faction, and to preserve the benefits of consistent interpretation. The fundamental conception of a judicial body is that of one hedged about by precedents which are binding on the court without regard to the personality of its members. Break down this belief in judicial continuity, and let it be felt that on great constitutional questions this court is to depart from the settled conclusions of its predecessors, and to determine them all according to the mere opinion of those who temporarily fill its bench, and our constitution will, in my judgment, be bereft of value, and become a most dangerous instrument to the rights and liberties of the people.

The third is from Justice Jones, writing for the Alabama Supreme Court in *Lorence v. Hospital Board of Morgan County*, 294 Ala. 614, 618–619 (1975):

We do not overrule old case law lightly or flippantly. But, where precedent can no longer be supported by reason and justice, we perceive it our duty to reexamine, and if need be, overrule court made law.

The quaint poetic lines of Sam Walter Foss put in perspective the philosophy of those courts which feel compelled to sacrifice their sense of reason and justice upon the altar of the Golden Calf of precedent.

One day through the primeval wood

A calf walked home, as good calves should;

But left a trail all bent askew,

A crooked trail, as all calves do.

Since then, three hundred years have fled,

And, I infer, the calf is dead.

But still he left behind this trail,

And thereby hangs my moral tale.

The trail was taken up next day

By a lone dog that passed that way;

And then a wise bell-wether sheep

Pursued the trail o'er vale and steep,

And drew the flock behind him, too,

As good bell-wethers always do.

So from that day, o'er hill and glade,

Through those old woods a path was made,

And many men wound in and out,

And bent and turned and dodged about,

And uttered words of righteous wrath,

Because 'twas such a crooked path;

But still they followed—do not laugh—

The first migrations of that calf. . . .

They followed still his crooked way,

And lost one hundred years a day;

For thus such reverence is lent

To well-established precedent. . . .

As a matter of first principles, which view of precedent seems right to you—Justice Daniel's, Justice White's, Justice Jones's, or that of the Joint Opinion in *Casey*? And should a justice choose whichever approach to precedent seems right to that justice as a matter of first principles? Or should it be relevant what approaches to precedent, or to constitutional interpretation, are adopted by the *other* justices?

4.   In what ways does *Casey* change abortion law? First, consider the replacement of *Roe*'s trimester framework with a straight pre-/post-viability line. Does this change alter the circumstances in which the state could prohibit or limit the availability of abortion? (Note that *Casey* retains the requirement of a health exception that would permit aborting even viable fetuses in some circumstances.) Are there any abortions that states may prohibit under *Casey* that they could not prohibit under *Roe*? Are there any abortions that states may prohibit under either *Roe* or *Casey*?

Next, consider *Casey*'s embrace of Justice O'Connor's preferred "undue burden" standard for pre-viability abortions. Under *Roe*, any law affecting the choice of abortion prior to viability was subject to "strict scrutiny" because it violated the fundamental right to privacy; the state needed a compelling interest to justify the restriction. Under *Casey*, only laws that impose an "undue burden" on the choice to abort (before viability) receive strict scrutiny. What is an "undue burden"? The Court spoke in terms of whether a state regulation "has the purpose or effect of placing a substantial obstacle in the path of a woman seeking an abortion of a nonviable fetus." A state must choose means "calculated to inform the woman's free choice, not hinder it." But as long as the state does not impose an undue burden it can "create a structural mechanism" that "express[es] profound respect for the life of the unborn," or adopt measures that are "designed to persuade" a woman "to choose childbirth over abortion" or "to foster [her] health." What does this mean in practice? What clues are afforded by the regulations the Court upheld (with the Joint Opinion constituting only a plurality view): twenty-four-hour waiting periods and informed consent requirements? What clues are afforded by the regulations the Court struck down: the spousal notification requirements? Under *Casey*'s "undue burden" standard, is there any type of pre-viability abortion that a state may ban entirely? Could it ban sex-selective abortions? Under *Casey*'s "undue burden" standard, may a state require that an ultrasound of the human fetus be taken and shown to the mother, along with information about the stage of fetal development? Could a state require abortion providers to give pregnant women a leaflet stating that abortion "is the killing of your baby, an independent living human being"?

In all, what do you think of the "undue burden" standard? Does it preserve the essence of *Roe*? Does it gut *Roe*? Does it have a more plausible basis in the text and history of the Constitution?

5.   Does *Casey* essentially claim in Part II that the advance of women's economic and social equality over the past generation has been attributable, at least in part, to the ready availability of abortion as a back-up method of birth control? What is your reaction to this? Is it offensive and demeaning to women? Is it descriptively accurate? Is the availability of abortion essential to women's equality? Was sex equality the unarticulated true premise of the Court's decision in *Casey* in a way that differed from the reasoning of *Roe*? Is it instructive that the one provision of the Pennsylvania law not upheld by the Joint Opinion was the one requiring spousal notification? What do you think of the Court's reasoning on that point?

6.   What do you think of Justice Blackmun's invocation of the "light" and the "darkness"? What was he alluding to? Perhaps it was J.R.R. Tolkien, who wrote for a character in *The Fellowship of the Ring*: "Torment in the dark was the danger that I feared, and it did not hold me back. But I would not have come, had I known the danger of light and joy." Or perhaps it was the first chapter of the Gospel of John: "In him was life, and the life was the light of men. The light shines in the darkness, and the darkness has not overcome it." Did Justice Blackmun, the author of *Roe*, see himself as "the light" and his opponents as forces of "darkness"? Did he see himself as a martyr for the cause of *Roe*?

7.   Chief Justice Rehnquist's dissent states that the majority has abandoned *Roe* and merely left its outer shell. What do you think? Did he miss the import of *Casey*? Is there evidence in the style and writing of the first part of his dissent that it may at one time have been a draft *majority* opinion going the other way? What is your assessment of his criticisms of the majority's reliance on *stare decisis*? In what ways do the dissent of Chief Justice Rehnquist and the dissent of Justice Scalia diverge?

8.   Since *Casey*, the Court has decided three major abortion cases: *Stenberg v. Carhart*, 530 U.S. 914 (2000) (*Carhart I*), *Gonzales v. Carhart*, 550 U.S. 124 (2007) (*Carhart II*), and *Whole Women's Health v. Hellerstedt*, 136 S.Ct. 2292 (2016).

The first two of these cases present nearly identical issues of whether government may ban a particular *manner* of late-term abortion colloquially referred to as "partial-birth" abortion but known in medical terms as "dilation and extraction" or "D & X" abortion. A warning: the clinical descriptions of the procedures in the remainder of this paragraph—and even more so in the Court's opinions in these cases—are graphic. Because of the typically late stage of pregnancy at which the procedure is performed, the fetus cannot be suctioned out of the womb whole by vacuum tube (as is typical in a "dilation and evacuation," or "D & E," abortion). Accordingly, in a D & X abortion, the doctor first dilates the woman's cervix, induces labor, and delivers the fetus, except for the head (which is too large). The doctor then punctures the skull with a scissors or another sharp surgical tool, suctions out the mostly born fetus's brain matter with a vacuum tube, collapses the skull, and proceeds to deliver the head, completing the abortion.

Nebraska prohibited this manner of abortion procedure, and in *Carhart I*, a 5–4 majority struck down the Nebraska law on the grounds that (1) the law was vague and might be construed to prohibit even (more common) D & E abortions, thus creating an "undue burden" on the choice of abortion, as that term was used in *Casey*; and (2) the law lacked a health-of-the-mother exception, as required by *Roe, Doe*, and *Casey,* and thus could not be applied even to prohibit D & X abortions after the point of viability.

In *Carhart II*, decided seven years later, the Court (again in a 5–4 ruling) upheld Congress's slightly different partial-birth prohibition, distinguishing but not overruling *Carhart I*. The difference is explained by the retirement and replacement of one of the justices in the *Carhart I* majority. The Court found the federal statute not to be vague because it was, the Court said, clearly limited only to D & X abortion procedures and could not be construed to prohibit the alternative D & E method.

Taken together, *Carhart I* and *Carhart II* stand for the proposition that the federal government may prohibit "partial-birth" or "D & X" abortions, but the states may not. (What is the enumerated power that allows a federal ban on this type of abortion?)

The third case, *Hellerstedt*, was a challenge to a Texas statute that required abortion doctors to have admitting privileges at a local hospital, and also required abortion facilities to meet the same regulatory standards as ambulatory surgical centers. By a vote of 5–3, the Court reaffirmed *Casey* and struck down the statute as an "undue burden" on women seeking an abortion. The Court laid stress on what it saw as scant benefit to women's health from the provisions, and substantial reduction in access to abortion. Indeed, although the causation is disputed, the district court found that the admitting-privileges requirement had led to the closure of roughly half of the abortion facilities in Texas, and the parties had stipulated that only seven or eight abortion facilities in the state could meet the surgical-center requirement. The dissenters argued that the Court had created special exceptions to procedural rules, including *res judicata* and severability, just to be able to decide the case.

[*Assignment 81*]

F.   LIMITING PRINCIPLES?

The next two cases raise in especially acute ways the methodology of substantive due process. As you read them, think of the following questions: If the Supreme Court is going to be in the business of invalidating laws as violations of substantive due process, what principles should it use? How should it decide which liberties to protect? Should it look primarily to the past, the present, or the future? What answers are most consistent with the powers, limits, and duties that the Constitution gives to Congress, the president, and the courts? And consider this always-useful thought experiment: How would you answer these questions if you knew that the Court was entirely composed of people who disagreed with all of your most strongly held values and beliefs?

Washington v. Glucksberg
521 U.S. 702 (1997)

■ CHIEF JUSTICE REHNQUIST delivered the opinion of the Court.

The question presented in this case is whether Washington's prohibition against "caus[ing]" or "aid[ing]" a suicide offends the Fourteenth Amendment to the United States Constitution. We hold that it does not.

It has always been a crime to assist a suicide in the State of Washington. In 1854, Washington's first Territorial Legislature outlawed "assisting another in the commission of self-murder." Today, Washington law provides: "A person is guilty of promoting a suicide attempt when he knowingly causes or aids another person to attempt suicide." "Promoting a suicide attempt" is a felony, punishable by up to five years' imprisonment and up to a $10,000 fine. At the same time, Washington's Natural Death Act, enacted in 1979, states that the "withholding or withdrawal of life-sustaining treatment" at a patient's direction "shall not, for any purpose, constitute a suicide."

Petitioners in this case are the State of Washington and its Attorney General. Respondents ... are physicians who practice in Washington. These doctors occasionally treat terminally ill, suffering patients, and declare that they would assist these patients in ending their lives if not for Washington's assisted-suicide ban[, which they argue] ... is, on its face, unconstitutional.

The plaintiffs asserted "the existence of a liberty interest protected by the Fourteenth Amendment which extends to a personal choice by a mentally competent, terminally ill adult to commit physician-assisted suicide." ...

We begin, as we do in all due process cases, by examining our Nation's history, legal traditions, and practices. See, *e.g.*, *Planned Parenthood v. Casey*, 505 U.S. 833, 849–850 (1992); *Moore v. East Cleveland*, 431 U.S. 494, 503 (1977) (plurality opinion) (noting importance of "careful 'respect for the teachings of history' "). In almost every State—indeed, in almost every western democracy—it is a crime to assist a suicide. The States' assisted-suicide bans are not innovations. Rather, they are longstanding expressions of the States' commitment to the protection and preservation of all human life. ...

More specifically, for over 700 years, the Anglo-American common-law tradition has punished or otherwise disapproved of both suicide and assisting suicide. ... Sir William Blackstone, whose Commentaries on the Laws of England not only provided a definitive summary of the common law but was also a primary legal authority for 18th- and 19th-century American lawyers, referred to suicide as "self-murder" and "the pretended heroism, but real cowardice, of the Stoic philosophers, who destroyed themselves to avoid those ills which they had not the fortitude to endure. . . ." Blackstone emphasized that "the law has . . . ranked [suicide] among the highest crimes," although, anticipating later developments, he conceded that the harsh and shameful punishments imposed for suicide "borde[r] a little upon severity."

For the most part, the early American Colonies adopted the common-law approach. . . . [For example,] Virginia . . . required ignominious burial for suicides, and their estates were forfeit to the Crown.

Over time, however, the American Colonies abolished these harsh common-law penalties. . . . [T]he movement away from the common law's harsh sanctions did not represent an acceptance of suicide; rather, . . . this change reflected the growing consensus that it was unfair to punish the suicide's family for his wrongdoing. Nonetheless, although States moved away from Blackstone's treatment of suicide, courts continued to condemn it as a grave public wrong.

That suicide remained a grievous, though nonfelonious, wrong is confirmed by the fact that colonial and early state legislatures and courts did not retreat from prohibiting assisting suicide. . . . The earliest American statute explicitly to outlaw assisting suicide was enacted in New York in 1828, and many of the new States and Territories followed New York's example. . . . By the time the Fourteenth Amendment was ratified, it was a crime in most States to assist a suicide. . . .

The Washington statute at issue in this case was enacted in 1975 as part of a revision of that State's criminal code. Four years later, Washington passed its Natural Death Act, which specifically stated that the "withholding or withdrawal of life-sustaining treatment . . . shall not, for any purpose, constitute a suicide" and that "[n]othing in this chapter shall be construed to condone, authorize, or approve mercy killing. . . ." In 1991, Washington voters rejected a ballot initiative which, had it passed, would have permitted a form of physician-assisted suicide. Washington then added a provision to the Natural Death Act expressly excluding physician-assisted suicide.

. . . [M]any proposals to legalize assisted-suicide have been and continue to be introduced in the States' legislatures, but none has been enacted. . . . [T]he States are currently engaged in serious, thoughtful examinations of physician-assisted suicide and other similar issues. . . .

Attitudes toward suicide itself have changed . . . but our laws have consistently condemned, and continue to prohibit, assisting suicide. Despite changes in medical technology and notwithstanding an increased emphasis on the importance of end-of-life decisionmaking, we have not retreated from this prohibition. Against this backdrop of history, tradition, and practice, we now turn to respondents' constitutional claim.

The Due Process Clause guarantees more than fair process, and the "liberty" it protects includes more than the absence of physical restraint. The Clause also provides heightened protection against government interference with certain fundamental rights and liberty interests. In a long line of cases, we have held that, in addition to the specific freedoms protected by the Bill of Rights, the "liberty" specially protected by the Due Process Clause includes the rights to marry; to have children; to direct the education and upbringing of one's children; to marital privacy; to use contraception; to bodily integrity; and to abortion. We have also assumed, and strongly suggested, that the Due Process Clause protects the traditional right to refuse unwanted lifesaving medical treatment.

But we "ha[ve] always been reluctant to expand the concept of substantive due process because guideposts for responsible decisionmaking in this unchartered area are scarce and open-ended." By extending constitutional protection to an asserted right or liberty interest, we, to a great extent, place the matter outside the arena of public debate and legislative action. We must therefore "exercise the utmost care whenever we are asked to break new ground in this field," lest the liberty protected by the Due Process Clause be subtly transformed into the policy preferences of the Members of this Court.

Our established method of substantive-due-process analysis has two primary features: First, we have regularly observed that the Due Process Clause specially protects those fundamental rights and liberties which are, objectively, "deeply rooted in this Nation's history and tradition," *Moore v. East Cleveland*, at 503, and "implicit in the concept of ordered liberty," such that "neither liberty nor justice would exist if they were sacrificed," *Palko v. Connecticut*, 302 U.S. 319, 325, 326 (1937). Second, we have required in substantive-due-process cases a "careful description" of the asserted fundamental liberty interest. Our Nation's history, legal traditions, and practices thus provide the crucial "guideposts for responsible decisionmaking," that direct and restrain our exposition of the Due Process Clause. . . .

Justice SOUTER, relying on Justice Harlan's dissenting opinion in *Poe v. Ullman*, 367 U.S. 497, 543 (1961), would largely abandon this restrained methodology, and instead ask "whether [Washington's] statute sets up one of those 'arbitrary impositions' or 'purposeless restraints' at odds with the Due Process Clause of the Fourteenth Amendment." In our view, however, the development of this Court's substantive-due-process jurisprudence has been a process whereby the outlines of the "liberty" specially protected by the Fourteenth Amendment—never fully clarified, to be sure, and perhaps not capable of being fully clarified—have at least been carefully refined by concrete examples involving fundamental rights found to be deeply rooted in our legal tradition. This approach tends to rein in the subjective elements that are necessarily present in due-process judicial review. In addition, by establishing a threshold requirement—that a challenged state action implicate a fundamental right before requiring more than a reasonable relation to a legitimate state interest to justify the action, it avoids the need for complex balancing of competing interests in every case.

Turning to the claim at issue here, the Court of Appeals stated that "[p]roperly analyzed, the first issue to be resolved is whether there is a liberty interest in determining the time and manner of one's death," or, in other words, "[i]s there a right to die?" Similarly, respondents assert a "liberty to choose how to die" and a right to "control of one's final days," and describe the asserted liberty as "the right to choose a humane, dignified death," and "the liberty to shape death." As noted above, we have a tradition of carefully formulating the interest at stake in substantive-due-process cases. For example, although *Cruzan v. Missouri Dep't of Health*, 497 U.S. 261 (1990), is often described as a "right to die" case, we were, in fact, more precise: We assumed that the Constitution granted competent persons a "constitutionally protected right to refuse lifesaving hydration and nutrition." The Washington statute at issue in this case prohibits "aid[ing] another person to attempt suicide," and, thus, the question before us is whether the "liberty" specially protected by the Due Process

Clause includes a right to commit suicide which itself includes a right to assistance in doing so.

We now inquire whether this asserted right has any place in our Nation's traditions. Here, as discussed, we are confronted with a consistent and almost universal tradition that has long rejected the asserted right, and continues explicitly to reject it today, even for terminally ill, mentally competent adults. To hold for respondents, we would have to reverse centuries of legal doctrine and practice, and strike down the considered policy choice of almost every State.

Respondents contend, however, that the liberty interest they assert *is* consistent with this Court's substantive-due-process line of cases, if not with this Nation's history and practice. Pointing to *Casey* and *Cruzan,* respondents read our jurisprudence in this area as reflecting a general tradition of "self-sovereignty," and as teaching that the "liberty" protected by the Due Process Clause includes "basic and intimate exercises of personal autonomy." According to respondents, our liberty jurisprudence, and the broad, individualistic principles it reflects, protects the "liberty of competent, terminally ill adults to make end-of-life decisions free of undue government interference." The question presented in this case, however, is whether the protections of the Due Process Clause include a right to commit suicide with another's assistance. With this "careful description" of respondents' claim in mind, we turn to *Casey* and *Cruzan.*

In *Cruzan,* we considered whether Nancy Beth Cruzan, who had been severely injured in an automobile accident and was in a persistive vegetative state, "ha[d] a right under the United States Constitution which would require the hospital to withdraw life-sustaining treatment" at her parents' request. . . . After reviewing a long line of relevant state cases, we concluded that "the common-law doctrine of informed consent is viewed as generally encompassing the right of a competent individual to refuse medical treatment." Next, we reviewed our own cases on the subject, and stated that "[t]he principle that a competent person has a constitutionally protected liberty interest in refusing unwanted medical treatment may be inferred from our prior decisions." Therefore, "for purposes of [that] case, we assume[d] that the United States Constitution would grant a competent person a constitutionally protected right to refuse lifesaving hydration and nutrition." We concluded that, notwithstanding this right, the Constitution permitted Missouri to require clear and convincing evidence of an incompetent patient's wishes concerning the withdrawal of life-sustaining treatment.

Respondents contend that in *Cruzan* we "acknowledged that competent, dying persons have the right to direct the removal of life-sustaining medical treatment and thus hasten death," and that "the constitutional principle behind recognizing the patient's liberty to direct the withdrawal of artificial life support applies at least as strongly to the choice to hasten impending death by consuming lethal medication."
. . .

The right assumed in *Cruzan,* however, was not simply deduced from abstract concepts of personal autonomy. Given the common-law rule that forced medication was a battery, and the long legal tradition protecting the decision to refuse unwanted medical treatment, our assumption was entirely consistent with this Nation's history and constitutional traditions. The decision to commit suicide with the assistance of another may be just as personal and profound as the decision to refuse unwanted medical treatment, but it has never enjoyed similar legal protection. Indeed, the two acts are widely and reasonably regarded as quite distinct. In *Cruzan* itself, we recognized that most States outlawed assisted suicide—and even more do today— and we certainly gave no intimation that the right to refuse unwanted medical treatment could be somehow transmuted into a right to assistance in committing suicide.

Respondents also rely on *Casey*. . . . The Court of Appeals, like the District Court, found *Casey* "highly instructive" and "almost prescriptive" for determining "what liberty interest may inhere in a terminally ill person's choice to commit suicide": "Like the decision of whether or not to have an abortion, the decision how and when to die is one of the most intimate and personal choices a person may make in a lifetime, a choice central to personal dignity and autonomy."

Similarly, respondents emphasize the statement in *Casey* that: "At the heart of liberty is the right to define one's own concept of existence, of meaning, of the universe, and of the mystery of human life. Beliefs about these matters could not define the attributes of personhood were they formed under compulsion of the State." By choosing this language, the Court's opinion in *Casey* described, in a general way and in light of our prior cases, those personal activities and decisions that this Court has identified as so deeply rooted in our history and traditions, or so fundamental to our concept of constitutionally ordered liberty, that they are protected by the Fourteenth Amendment. . . . That many of the rights and liberties protected by the Due Process Clause sound in personal autonomy does not warrant the sweeping conclusion that any and all important, intimate, and personal decisions are so protected, and *Casey* did not suggest otherwise.

The history of the law's treatment of assisted suicide in this country has been and continues to be one of the rejection of nearly all efforts to permit it. That being the case, our decisions lead us to conclude that the asserted "right" to assistance in committing suicide is not a fundamental liberty interest protected by the Due Process Clause. The Constitution also requires, however, that Washington's assisted-suicide ban be rationally related to legitimate government interests. This requirement is unquestionably met here. As the court below recognized,[20] Washington's assisted-suicide ban implicates a number of state interests. . . .

We therefore hold that [the Washington statute] does not violate the Fourteenth Amendment, either on its face or "as applied to competent, terminally ill adults who wish to hasten their deaths by obtaining medication prescribed by their doctors." . . .

Throughout the Nation, Americans are engaged in an earnest and profound debate about the morality, legality, and practicality of physician-assisted suicide. Our holding permits this debate to continue, as it should in a democratic society. The decision of the en banc Court of Appeals is reversed, and the case is remanded for further proceedings consistent with this opinion.

■ JUSTICE SOUTER, concurring in the judgment.

. . . The question is whether the statute sets up one of those "arbitrary impositions" or "purposeless restraints" at odds with the Due Process Clause of the

---

[20] The court identified and discussed six state interests: (1) preserving life; (2) preventing suicide; (3) avoiding the involvement of third parties and use of arbitrary, unfair, or undue influence; (4) protecting family members and loved ones; (5) protecting the integrity of the medical profession; and (6) avoiding future movement toward euthanasia and other abuses.

Fourteenth Amendment. *Poe v. Ullman* (Harlan, J., dissenting). I conclude that the statute's application to the doctors has not been shown to be unconstitutional, but I write separately to give my reasons for analyzing the substantive due process claims as I do, and for rejecting this one. . . .

[Here Justice Souter offered a lengthy history of due process, including Magna Carta's guarantee of "the law of the land," U.S. federal and state constitutional provisions, and the development of substantive due process in the Supreme Court. Among the Court decisions discussed are Dred Scott*; the substantive due process decisions of the Lochner era, which he called "the echo of* Dred Scott*"; and the modern substantive due process doctrine reflected in* Griswold, Roe, *and* Casey*. Justice Souter approved of the second Justice Harlan's dissent in* Poe v. Ullman *as the legitimate judicial approach to substantive due process. For more discussion of that dissent, see p. 1558.—Editors]*

This enduring tradition of American constitutional practice is, in Justice Harlan's view, nothing more than what is required by the judicial authority and obligation to construe constitutional text and review legislation for conformity to that text. Like many judges who preceded him and many who followed, he found it impossible to construe the text of due process without recognizing substantive, and not merely procedural, limitations. "Were due process merely a procedural safeguard it would fail to reach those situations where the deprivation of life, liberty or property was accomplished by legislation which by operating in the future could, given even the fairest possible procedure in application to individuals, nevertheless destroy the enjoyment of all three." The text of the Due Process Clause thus imposes nothing less than an obligation to give substantive content to the words "liberty" and "due process of law." . . .

My understanding of unenumerated rights in the wake of the *Poe* dissent and subsequent cases avoids the absolutist failing of many older cases without embracing the opposite pole of equating reasonableness with past practice described at a very specific level. See *Casey,* at 847–849. That understanding begins with a concept of "ordered liberty," *Poe,* at 549 (Harlan, J., dissenting), comprising a continuum of rights to be free from "arbitrary impositions and purposeless restraints," *id.* at 543. . . .

This approach calls for a court to assess the relative "weights" or dignities of the contending interests, and to this extent the judicial method is familiar to the common law. Common-law method is subject, however, to two important constraints in the hands of a court engaged in substantive due process review. First, such a court is bound to confine the values that it recognizes to those truly deserving constitutional stature, either to those expressed in constitutional text, or those exemplified by "the traditions from which [the Nation] developed," or revealed by contrast with "the traditions from which it broke." *Id.* at 542. . . .

The second constraint, again, simply reflects the fact that constitutional review, not judicial lawmaking, is a court's business here. The weighing or valuing of contending interests in this sphere is only the first step, forming the basis for determining whether the statute in question falls inside or outside the zone of what is reasonable in the way it resolves the conflict between the interests of state and individual. It is no justification for judicial intervention merely to identify a reasonable resolution of contending values that differs from the terms of the legislation under review. It is only when the legislation's justifying principle, critically valued, is so far from being commensurate with the individual interest as to be arbitrarily or pointlessly applied that the statute must give way. Only if this standard points against the statute can the individual claimant be said to have a constitutional right. . . .

Just as results in substantive due process cases are tied to the selections of statements of the competing interests, the acceptability of the results is a function of the good reasons for the selections made. It is here that the value of common-law method becomes apparent, for the usual thinking of the common law is suspicious of the all-or-nothing analysis that tends to produce legal petrification instead of an evolving boundary between the domains of old principles. Common-law method tends to pay respect instead to detail, seeking to understand old principles afresh by new examples and new counterexamples. The "tradition is a living thing," *id.* at 542, albeit one that moves by moderate steps carefully taken. . . . Exact analysis and characterization of any due process claim are critical to the method and to the result. . . .

In my judgment, the importance of the individual interest here, as within that class of "certain interests" demanding careful scrutiny of the State's contrary claim cannot be gainsaid. Whether that interest might in some circumstances, or at some time, be seen as "fundamental" to the degree entitled to prevail is not, however, a conclusion that I need draw here, for I am satisfied that the State's interests described in the following section are sufficiently serious to defeat the present claim that its law is arbitrary or purposeless.

The State has put forward several interests to justify the Washington law as applied to physicians treating terminally ill patients, even those competent to make responsible choices: protecting life generally, discouraging suicide even if knowing and voluntary, and protecting terminally ill patients from involuntary suicide and euthanasia, both voluntary and nonvoluntary. . . . [T]he third is dispositive for me. . . . The State claims interests in protecting patients from mistakenly and involuntarily deciding to end their lives, and in guarding against both voluntary and involuntary euthanasia. . . .

The experimentation that should be out of the question in constitutional adjudication displacing legislative judgments is entirely proper, as well as highly desirable, when the legislative power addresses an emerging issue like assisted suicide. The Court should accordingly stay its hand to allow reasonable legislative consideration. While I do not decide for all time that respondents' claim should not be recognized, I acknowledge the legislative institutional competence as the better one to deal with that claim at this time.

■ [The concurring opinion of JUSTICE O'CONNOR, and the opinions concurring in the judgment of JUSTICES STEVENS and BREYER, are omitted.]

NOTES

1.   The Supreme Court had previously addressed "right to die" questions in *Cruzan v. Missouri Department of Health*, 497 U.S. 261 (1990). In that case, the Court had assumed, but did not hold, that there may exist a "liberty interest" of the individual to refuse medical care, but it ultimately found that such an interest would not be violated by a state law requiring "clear and convincing" evidence that a comatose patient actually

would have wished to refuse treatment. In *Glucksberg* the Court returned to this contested area. Did the majority in *Glucksberg* recognize a constitutional right either to die or to refuse medical treatment? What was the holding?

2.   What is the methodology established by *Glucksberg* for adjudicating claims of new substantive due process rights? Identify the relevant passage in Chief Justice Rehnquist's opinion. Does this proposition command a majority of the Court? Contrast Justice Souter's concurring opinion. How do the positions differ? Are both positions faithful to the text of the Constitution? (Is neither one faithful to the text?) What do you make of Justice Souter's view that the adjudication of "substantive due process" claims is essentially an invitation for judges to apply a "common law" method to discovering constitutional rights?

Consider what would happen if you were to apply the *Glucksberg* test to *Lochner*, *Meyer*, *Pierce*, *Griswold*, *Roe*, and *Casey*. In each, was there a right, identified at its most specific level, that was "objectively, deeply rooted" in the nation's history and its traditions of liberty?

3.   Under the standard adopted by Chief Justice Rehnquist's majority opinion, is there any plausible argument that a claim to physician-assisted suicide is "objectively, deeply rooted" in the nation's history and traditions as an essential part of ordered liberty? Does that history and tradition preclude a claim that there is a substantive due process right to physician-assisted suicide? Have cultural norms and understandings changed—and, if so, does that mean our understanding of the Constitution should also change?

A NOTE ON *BOWERS V. HARDWICK*

In *Bowers v. Hardwick*, 478 U.S. 186 (1986), the Court considered whether the application of a Georgia criminal statute to "consensual homosexual sodomy" was a violation of the Due Process Clause of the Fourteenth Amendment, and in particular whether the right to privacy was implicated. Writing for the majority, Justice White rejected the constitutional claim. He distinguished the Court's privacy cases, finding "[n]o connection between family, marriage, or procreation on the on hand and homosexual activity on the other." In rejecting the claim to a fundamental right, Justice White said the case "calls for some judgment about the limits of the Court's role in carrying out its constitutional mandate," adding:

> Striving to assure itself and the public that announcing rights not readily identifiable in the Constitution's text involves much more than the imposition of the Justices' own choice of values on the States and the Federal Government, the Court has sought to identify the nature of the rights qualifying for heightened judicial protection. In *Palko v. Connecticut*, 302 U.S. 319, 325, 326 (1937), it was said that this category includes those fundamental liberties that are "implicit in the concept of ordered liberty," such that "neither liberty nor justice would exist if [they] were sacrificed." A different description of fundamental liberties appeared in *Moore v. East Cleveland*, 431 U.S. 494, 503 (1977) (opinion of POWELL, J.), where they are characterized as those liberties that are "deeply rooted in this Nation's history and tradition."
>
> It is obvious to us that neither of these formulations would extend a fundamental right to homosexuals to engage in acts of consensual sodomy. Proscriptions against that conduct have ancient roots. See generally *Survey on the Constitutional Right to Privacy in the Context of Homosexual Activity*, 40 U. Miami L. Rev. 521, 525 (1986). Sodomy was a criminal offense at common law

and was forbidden by the laws of the original 13 States when they ratified the Bill of Rights. In 1868, when the Fourteenth Amendment was ratified, all but 5 of the 37 States in the Union had criminal sodomy laws. In fact, until 1961, all 50 States outlawed sodomy, and today, 24 States and the District of Columbia continue to provide criminal penalties for sodomy performed in private and between consenting adults. Against this background, to claim that a right to engage in such conduct is "deeply rooted in this Nation's history and tradition" or "implicit in the concept of ordered liberty" is, at best, facetious.

Nor are we inclined to take a more expansive view of our authority to discover new fundamental rights imbedded in the Due Process Clause. The Court is most vulnerable and comes nearest to illegitimacy when it deals with judge-made constitutional law having little or no cognizable roots in the language or design of the Constitution.

Finally, after rejecting the substantive due process claim, the Court rejected a claim that the statute failed rational-basis review:

Even if the conduct at issue here is not a fundamental right, respondent asserts that there must be a rational basis for the law and that there is none in this case other than the presumed belief of a majority of the electorate in Georgia that homosexual sodomy is immoral and unacceptable. This is said to be an inadequate rationale to support the law. The law, however, is constantly based on notions of morality, and if all laws representing essentially moral choices are to be invalidated under the Due Process Clause, the courts will be very busy indeed. Even respondent makes no such claim, but insists that majority sentiments about the morality of homosexuality should be declared inadequate. We do not agree, and are unpersuaded that the sodomy laws of some 25 States should be invalidated on this basis.

In a dissenting opinion for four justices, Justice Blackmun rejected the Court's framing of the case as being about whether there is "a fundamental right to engage in homosexual sodomy." Rather, he said, "This case is no more about" such a right "than *Stanley v. Georgia*, 394 U.S. 557 (1969), was about a fundamental right to watch obscene movies, or *Katz v. United States*, 389 U.S. 347 (1967), was about a fundamental right to place interstate bets from a telephone booth. Rather, this case is about 'the most comprehensive of rights and the right most valued by civilized men,'" namely, "the right to be let alone.' *Olmstead v. United States*, 277 U.S. 438, 478 (1928) (Brandeis, J., dissenting)." *Id.* at 199 (Blackmun, J., dissenting). Justice Blackmun located the constitutional claim within the right to privacy:

The Court concludes today that none of our prior cases dealing with various decisions that individuals are entitled to make free of governmental interference "bears any resemblance to the claimed constitutional right of homosexuals to engage in acts of sodomy that is asserted in this case." While it is true that these cases may be characterized by their connection to protection of the family, the Court's conclusion that they extend no further than this boundary ignores the warning in *Moore v. East Cleveland*, at 501 (plurality opinion), against "clos[ing] our eyes to the basic reasons why certain rights associated with the family have been accorded shelter under the Fourteenth Amendment's Due Process Clause." We protect those rights not because they contribute, in some direct and material way, to the general public welfare, but because they form so central a part of an individual's life. "[T]he concept of privacy embodies 'the moral fact that a person belongs to himself and not others nor to society as a whole.'" *Thornburgh v. American College of Obstetricians &*

Gynecologists, 476 U.S. 747, 777, n. 5 (1986) (STEVENS, J., concurring), quoting Fried, Correspondence, 6 Phil. & Pub. Affairs 288–289 (1977). . . .

"The right of the people to be secure in their . . . houses," expressly guaranteed by the Fourth Amendment, is perhaps the most "textual" of the various constitutional provisions that inform our understanding of the right to privacy, and thus I cannot agree with the Court's statement that "[t]he right pressed upon us here has no . . . support in the text of the Constitution." Indeed, the right of an individual to conduct intimate relationships in the intimacy of his or her own home seems to me to be the heart of the Constitution's protection of privacy.

Justice Blackmun also rejected the majority's invocation of centuries of English and American law and millennia of moral and religious teaching as a justification for the statute:

> Essentially, petitioner argues, and the Court agrees, that the fact that the acts described in [the statute] "for hundreds of years, if not thousands, have been uniformly condemned as immoral" is a sufficient reason to permit a State to ban them today.
>
> I cannot agree that either the length of time a majority has held its convictions or the passions with which it defends them can withdraw legislation from this Court's scrutiny. See, *e.g.*, *Roe v. Wade*, 410 U.S. 113 (1973); *Loving v. Virginia*, 388 U.S. 1 (1967); *Brown v. Board of Education*, 347 U.S. 483 (1954). As Justice Jackson wrote so eloquently for the Court in *West Virginia Board of Education v. Barnette*, 319 U.S. 624, 641–642 (1943), "we apply the limitations of the Constitution with no fear that freedom to be intellectually and spiritually diverse or even contrary will disintegrate the social organization. . . . [F]reedom to differ is not limited to things that do not matter much. That would be a mere shadow of freedom. The test of its substance is the right to differ as to things that touch the heart of the existing order." It is precisely because the issue raised by this case touches the heart of what makes individuals what they are that we should be especially sensitive to the rights of those whose choices upset the majority.

Almost two decades would pass before the Court heard another challenge to a state sodomy statute, and it would then be asked to overrule *Bowers v. Hardwick*.

Lawrence v. Texas

539 U.S. 558 (2003)

■ JUSTICE KENNEDY delivered the opinion of the Court.

Liberty protects the person from unwarranted government intrusions into a dwelling or other private places. In our tradition the State is not omnipresent in the home. And there are other spheres of our lives and existence, outside the home, where the State should not be a dominant presence. Freedom extends beyond spatial bounds. Liberty presumes an autonomy of self that includes freedom of thought, belief, expression, and certain intimate conduct. The instant case involves liberty of the person both in its spatial and in its more transcendent dimensions.

I

The question before the Court is the validity of a Texas statute making it a crime for two persons of the same sex to engage in certain intimate sexual conduct.

In Houston, Texas, officers of the Harris County Police Department were dispatched to a private residence in response to a reported weapons disturbance. They entered an apartment where one of the petitioners, John Geddes Lawrence, resided. The right of the police to enter does not seem to have been questioned. The officers observed Lawrence and another man, Tyron Garner, engaging in a sexual act. The two petitioners were arrested, held in custody overnight, and charged and convicted before a Justice of the Peace.

The complaints described their crime as "deviate sexual intercourse, namely anal sex, with a member of the same sex (man)." . . . The petitioners, having entered a plea of *nolo contendere*, were each fined $200 and assessed court costs of $141.25. . . .

We granted certiorari to consider three questions:

1.   Whether petitioners' criminal convictions under the Texas "Homosexual Conduct" law—which criminalizes sexual intimacy by same-sex couples, but not identical behavior by different-sex couples—violate the Fourteenth Amendment guarantee of equal protection of the laws.

2.   Whether petitioners' criminal convictions for adult consensual sexual intimacy in the home violate their vital interests in liberty and privacy protected by the Due Process Clause of the Fourteenth Amendment.

3.   Whether *Bowers v. Hardwick*, 478 U.S. 186 (1986), should be overruled. . . .

II

We conclude the case should be resolved by determining whether the petitioners were free as adults to engage in the private conduct in the exercise of their liberty under the Due Process Clause of the Fourteenth Amendment to the Constitution. For this inquiry we deem it necessary to reconsider the Court's holding in *Bowers*.

There are broad statements of the substantive reach of liberty under the Due Process Clause in earlier cases, but the most pertinent beginning point is our decision in *Griswold v. Connecticut*, 381 U.S. 479 (1965).

In *Griswold* the Court invalidated a state law prohibiting the use of drugs or devices of contraception and counseling or aiding and abetting the use of contraceptives. The Court described the protected interest as a right to privacy and placed emphasis on the marriage relation and the protected space of the marital bedroom.

After *Griswold* it was established that the right to make certain decisions regarding sexual conduct extends beyond the marital relationship. In *Eisenstadt v. Baird*, 405 U.S. 438 (1972), the Court invalidated a law prohibiting the distribution of contraceptives to unmarried persons. The case was decided under the Equal Protection Clause; but with respect to unmarried persons, the Court went on to state the fundamental proposition that the law impaired the exercise of their personal rights. . . .

The opinions in *Griswold* and *Eisenstadt* were part of the background for the decision in *Roe v. Wade*, 410 U.S. 113 (1973). . . . *Roe* recognized the right of a woman to make certain fundamental decisions affecting her destiny and confirmed once more that the protection of liberty under the Due Process Clause has a substantive dimension of fundamental significance in defining the rights of the person. . . . [T]he holding and rationale in *Roe*[ ] confirmed that the reasoning of *Griswold* could not be confined to the protection of rights of married adults. This was the state of the law with respect to some of the most relevant cases when the Court considered *Bowers v. Hardwick.*

The facts in *Bowers* had some similarities to the instant case. A police officer, whose right to enter seems not to have been in question, observed Hardwick, in his own bedroom, engaging in intimate sexual conduct with another adult male. The conduct was in violation of a Georgia statute making it a criminal offense to engage in sodomy. One difference between the two cases is that the Georgia statute prohibited the conduct whether or not the participants were of the same sex, while the Texas statute, as we have seen, applies only to participants of the same sex. . . .

The Court began its substantive discussion in *Bowers* as follows: "The issue presented is whether the Federal Constitution confers a fundamental right upon homosexuals to engage in sodomy and hence invalidates the laws of the many States that still make such conduct illegal and have done so for a very long time." That statement, we now conclude, discloses the Court's own failure to appreciate the extent of the liberty at stake. To say that the issue in *Bowers* was simply the right to engage in certain sexual conduct demeans the claim the individual put forward, just as it would demean a married couple were it to be said marriage is simply about the right to have sexual intercourse. The laws involved in *Bowers* and here are, to be sure, statutes that purport to do no more than prohibit a particular sexual act. Their penalties and purposes, though, have more far-reaching consequences, touching upon the most private human conduct, sexual behavior, and in the most private of places, the home. The statutes do seek to control a personal relationship that, whether or not entitled to formal recognition in the law, is within the liberty of persons to choose without being punished as criminals.

This, as a general rule, should counsel against attempts by the State, or a court, to define the meaning of the relationship or to set its boundaries absent injury to a person or abuse of an institution the law protects. It suffices for us to acknowledge that adults may choose to enter upon this relationship in the confines of their homes and their own private lives and still retain their dignity as free persons. When sexuality finds overt expression in intimate conduct with another person, the conduct can be but one element in a personal bond that is more enduring. The liberty protected by the Constitution allows homosexual persons the right to make this choice.

Having misapprehended the claim of liberty there presented to it, and thus stating the claim to be whether there is a fundamental right to engage in consensual sodomy, the *Bowers* Court said: "Proscriptions against that conduct have ancient roots." . . . [T]he following considerations counsel against adopting the definitive conclusions upon which *Bowers* placed such reliance.

At the outset it should be noted that there is no longstanding history in this country of laws directed at homosexual conduct as a distinct matter. Beginning in colonial times there were prohibitions of sodomy derived from the English criminal laws passed in the first instance by the Reformation Parliament of 1533. The English prohibition was understood to include relations between men and women as well as relations between men and men. Nineteenth-century commentators similarly read American sodomy, buggery, and crime-against-nature statutes as criminalizing certain relations between men and women and between men and men. The absence of legal prohibitions focusing on homosexual conduct may be explained in part by noting that according to some scholars the concept of the homosexual as a distinct category of person did not emerge until the late 19th century. Thus early American sodomy laws were not directed at homosexuals as such but instead sought to prohibit nonprocreative sexual activity more generally. This does not suggest approval of homosexual conduct. It does tend to show that this particular form of conduct was not thought of as a separate category from like conduct between heterosexual persons.

Laws prohibiting sodomy do not seem to have been enforced against consenting adults acting in private. . . . Instead of targeting relations between consenting adults in private, 19th-century sodomy prosecutions typically involved relations between men and minor girls or minor boys, relations between adults involving force, relations between adults implicating disparity in status, or relations between men and animals. . . .

[T]he infrequency of these prosecutions . . . makes it difficult to say that society approved of a rigorous and systematic punishment of the consensual acts committed in private and by adults. The longstanding criminal prohibition of homosexual sodomy upon which the *Bowers* decision placed such reliance is as consistent with a general condemnation of nonprocreative sex as it is with an established tradition of prosecuting acts because of their homosexual character. . . .

It was not until the 1970's that any State singled out same-sex relations for criminal prosecution, and only nine States have done so. Post-*Bowers* even some of these States did not adhere to the policy of suppressing homosexual conduct. Over the course of the last decades, States with same-sex prohibitions have moved toward abolishing them.

In summary, the historical grounds relied upon in *Bowers* are more complex than the majority opinion and the concurring opinion by Chief Justice Burger indicate. Their historical premises are not without doubt and, at the very least, are overstated.

It must be acknowledged, of course, that the Court in *Bowers* was making the broader point that for centuries there have been powerful voices to condemn homosexual conduct as immoral. The condemnation has been shaped by religious beliefs, conceptions of right and acceptable behavior, and respect for the traditional family. For many persons these are not trivial concerns but profound and deep convictions accepted as ethical and moral principles to which they aspire and which thus determine the course of their lives. These considerations do not answer the question before us, however. The issue is whether the majority may use the power of the State to enforce these views on the whole society through operation of the criminal law. "Our obligation is to define the liberty of all, not to mandate our own moral code." *Planned Parenthood v. Casey*, 505 U.S. 833, 850 (1992).

. . . [W]e think that our laws and traditions in the past half century are of most relevance here. These references show an emerging awareness that liberty gives substantial protection to adult persons in deciding how to conduct their private lives in matters pertaining to sex. "[H]istory and tradition are the starting point but not in all cases the ending point of the substantive due process inquiry." *County of Sacramento v. Lewis*, 523 U.S. 833, 857 (1998) (KENNEDY, J., concurring).

This emerging recognition should have been apparent when *Bowers* was decided. In 1955 the American Law Institute promulgated the Model Penal Code and made clear that it did not recommend or provide for "criminal penalties for consensual sexual relations conducted in private." . . .

In *Bowers* the Court referred to the fact that before 1961 all 50 States had outlawed sodomy, and that at the time of the Court's decision 24 States and the District of Columbia had sodomy laws. Justice Powell pointed out that these prohibitions often were being ignored, however. Georgia, for instance, had not sought to enforce its law for decades.

The sweeping references by Chief Justice Burger to the history of Western civilization and to Judeo-Christian moral and ethical standards did not take account of other authorities pointing in an opposite direction. A committee advising the British Parliament recommended in 1957 repeal of laws punishing homosexual conduct. Parliament enacted the substance of those recommendations 10 years later.

Of even more importance, almost five years before *Bowers* was decided the European Court of Human Rights considered a case with parallels to *Bowers* and to today's case. An adult male resident in Northern Ireland alleged he was a practicing homosexual who desired to engage in consensual homosexual conduct. The laws of Northern Ireland forbade him that right. He alleged that he had been questioned, his home had been searched, and he feared criminal prosecution. The court held that the laws proscribing the conduct were invalid under the European Convention on Human Rights. Authoritative in all countries that are members of the Council of Europe (21 nations then, 45 nations now), the decision is at odds with the premise in *Bowers* that the claim put forward was insubstantial in our Western civilization.

In our own constitutional system the deficiencies in *Bowers* became even more apparent in the years following its announcement. The 25 States with laws prohibiting the relevant conduct referenced in the *Bowers* decision are reduced now to 13, of which 4 enforce their laws only against homosexual conduct. In those States where sodomy is still proscribed, whether for same-sex or heterosexual conduct, there is a pattern of nonenforcement with respect to consenting adults acting in private. The State of Texas admitted in 1994 that as of that date it had not prosecuted anyone under those circumstances.

Two principal cases decided after *Bowers* cast its holding into even more doubt. In *Planned Parenthood v. Casey*, the Court reaffirmed the substantive force of the liberty protected by the Due Process Clause. The *Casey* decision again confirmed that our laws and tradition afford constitutional protection to personal decisions relating to marriage, procreation, contraception, family relationships, child rearing, and education. In explaining the respect the Constitution demands for the autonomy of the person in making these choices, we stated as follows:

> These matters, involving the most intimate and personal choices a person may make in a lifetime, choices central to personal dignity and autonomy, are central to the liberty protected by the Fourteenth Amendment. At the heart of liberty is the right to define one's own concept of existence, of meaning, of the universe, and of the mystery of human life. Beliefs about these matters could not define the attributes of personhood were they formed under compulsion of the State.

Persons in a homosexual relationship may seek autonomy for these purposes, just as heterosexual persons do. The decision in *Bowers* would deny them this right.

The second post-*Bowers* case of principal relevance is *Romer v. Evans*, 517 U.S. 620 (1996). There the Court struck down class-based legislation directed at homosexuals as a violation of the Equal Protection Clause. *Romer* invalidated an amendment to Colorado's Constitution which named as a solitary class persons who were homosexuals, lesbians, or bisexual either by "orientation, conduct, practices or relationships," and deprived them of protection under state antidiscrimination laws. We concluded that the provision was "born of animosity toward the class of persons affected" and further that it had no rational relation to a legitimate governmental purpose.

As an alternative argument in this case, counsel for the petitioners and some *amici* contend that *Romer* provides the basis for declaring the Texas statute invalid under the Equal Protection Clause. That is a tenable argument, but we conclude the instant case requires us to address whether *Bowers* itself has continuing validity. Were we to hold the statute invalid under the Equal Protection Clause some might question whether a prohibition would be valid if drawn differently, say, to prohibit the conduct both between same-sex and different-sex participants.

Equality of treatment and the due process right to demand respect for conduct protected by the substantive guarantee of liberty are linked in important respects, and a decision on the latter point advances both interests. If protected conduct is made criminal and the law which does so remains unexamined for its substantive validity, its stigma might remain even if it were not enforceable as drawn for equal protection reasons. When homosexual conduct is made criminal by the law of the State, that declaration in and of itself is an invitation to subject homosexual persons to discrimination both in the public and in the private spheres. The central holding of *Bowers* has been brought in question by this case, and it should be addressed. Its continuance as precedent demeans the lives of homosexual persons.

The stigma this criminal statute imposes, moreover, is not trivial. The offense, to be sure, is but a class C misdemeanor, a minor offense in the Texas legal system. Still, it remains a criminal offense with all that imports for the dignity of the persons charged. The petitioners will bear on their record the history of their criminal convictions. . . .

The foundations of *Bowers* have sustained serious erosion from our recent decisions in *Casey* and *Romer*. When our precedent has been thus weakened, criticism from other sources is of greater significance. In the United States criticism of *Bowers* has been substantial and continuing, disapproving of its reasoning in all respects, not just as to its historical assumptions. See, *e.g.*, C. Fried, Order and Law: Arguing the Reagan Revolution—A First-hand Account 81–84 (1991); R. Posner, Sex and Reason 341–350 (1992). The courts of five different States have declined to follow it in interpreting provisions in their own state constitutions parallel to the Due Process Clause of the Fourteenth Amendment.

To the extent *Bowers* relied on values we share with a wider civilization, it should be noted that the reasoning and holding in *Bowers* have been rejected elsewhere. The European Court of Human Rights has [not followed] *Bowers*. . . . Other nations, too, have taken action consistent with an affirmation of the protected right of homosexual adults to engage in intimate, consensual conduct. The right the petitioners seek in this case has been accepted as an integral part of human freedom in many other countries. There has been no showing that in this country the governmental interest in circumscribing personal choice is somehow more legitimate or urgent.

The doctrine of *stare decisis* is essential to the respect accorded to the judgments of the Court and to the stability of the law. It is not, however, an inexorable command. In *Casey* we noted that when a court is asked to overrule a precedent recognizing a constitutional liberty interest, individual or societal reliance on the existence of that liberty cautions with particular strength against reversing course. The holding in *Bowers*, however, has not induced detrimental reliance comparable to some instances where recognized individual rights are involved. Indeed, there has been no individual or societal reliance on *Bowers* of the sort that could counsel against overturning its holding once there are compelling reasons to do so. *Bowers* itself causes uncertainty, for the precedents before and after its issuance contradict its central holding. . . .

Bowers was not correct when it was decided, and it is not correct today. It ought not to remain binding precedent. *Bowers v. Hardwick* should be and now is overruled.

The present case does not involve minors. It does not involve persons who might be injured or coerced or who are situated in relationships where consent might not easily be refused. It does not involve public conduct or prostitution. It does not involve whether the government must give formal recognition to any relationship that homosexual persons seek to enter. The case does involve two adults who, with full and mutual consent from each other, engaged in sexual practices common to a homosexual lifestyle. The petitioners are entitled to respect for their private lives. The State cannot demean their existence or control their destiny by making their private sexual conduct a crime. Their right to liberty under the Due Process Clause gives them the full right to engage in their conduct without intervention of the government. "It is a promise of the Constitution that there is a realm of personal liberty which the government may not enter." *Casey*, at 847. The Texas statute furthers no legitimate state interest which can justify its intrusion into the personal and private life of the individual.

Had those who drew and ratified the Due Process Clauses of the Fifth Amendment or the Fourteenth Amendment known the components of liberty in its manifold possibilities, they might have been more specific. They did not presume to have this insight. They knew times can blind us to certain truths and later generations can see that laws once thought necessary and proper in fact serve only to oppress. As the Constitution endures, persons in every generation can invoke its principles in their own search for greater freedom. . . .

■ JUSTICE O'CONNOR, concurring in the judgment.

The Court today overrules *Bowers v. Hardwick*. I joined *Bowers*, and do not join the Court in overruling it. Nevertheless, I agree with the Court that Texas' statute banning same-sex sodomy is unconstitutional. Rather than relying on the substantive component of the Fourteenth Amendment's Due Process Clause, as the Court does, I base my conclusion on the Fourteenth Amendment's Equal Protection Clause.

The Equal Protection Clause of the Fourteenth Amendment "is essentially a direction that all persons similarly situated should be treated alike." *Cleburne v.*

Cleburne Living Center, 473 U.S. 432, 439 (1985). Under our rational basis standard of review, "legislation is presumed to be valid and will be sustained if the classification drawn by the statute is rationally related to a legitimate state interest." *Id.* at 440. . . .

The statute at issue here makes sodomy a crime only if a person "engages in deviate sexual intercourse with another individual of the same sex." Sodomy between opposite-sex partners, however, is not a crime in Texas. That is, Texas treats the same conduct differently based solely on the participants. Those harmed by this law are people who have a same-sex sexual orientation and thus are more likely to engage in behavior prohibited by [the statute]. . . .

And the effect of Texas' sodomy law is not just limited to the threat of prosecution or consequence of conviction. Texas' sodomy law brands all homosexuals as criminals, thereby making it more difficult for homosexuals to be treated in the same manner as everyone else. . . .

The only question in front of the Court in *Bowers* was whether the substantive component of the Due Process Clause protected a right to engage in homosexual sodomy. *Bowers* did not hold that moral disapproval of a group is a rational basis under the Equal Protection Clause to criminalize homosexual sodomy when heterosexual sodomy is not punished.

This case raises a different issue than *Bowers*: whether, under the Equal Protection Clause, moral disapproval is a legitimate state interest to justify by itself a statute that bans homosexual sodomy, but not heterosexual sodomy. It is not. Moral disapproval of this group, like a bare desire to harm the group, is an interest that is insufficient to satisfy rational basis review under the Equal Protection Clause. See, *e.g., Romer v. Evans,* at 634–635. Indeed, we have never held that moral disapproval, without any other asserted state interest, is a sufficient rationale under the Equal Protection Clause to justify a law that discriminates among groups of persons.

Moral disapproval of a group cannot be a legitimate governmental interest under the Equal Protection Clause because legal classifications must not be "drawn for the purpose of disadvantaging the group burdened by the law." *Id.,* at 633. Texas' invocation of moral disapproval as a legitimate state interest proves nothing more than Texas' desire to criminalize homosexual sodomy. But the Equal Protection Clause prevents a State from creating "a classification of persons undertaken for its own sake." *Id.,* at 635. . . .

Texas argues, however, that the sodomy law does not discriminate against homosexual persons. Instead, the State maintains that the law discriminates only against homosexual conduct. While it is true that the law applies only to conduct, the conduct targeted by this law is conduct that is closely correlated with being homosexual. Under such circumstances, Texas' sodomy law is targeted at more than conduct. It is instead directed toward gay persons as a class. . . .

[T]he State cannot single out one identifiable class of citizens for punishment that does not apply to everyone else, with moral disapproval as the only asserted state interest for the law. . . .

Whether a sodomy law that is neutral both in effect and application, see *Yick Wo v. Hopkins,* 118 U.S. 356 (1886), would violate the substantive component of the Due Process Clause is an issue that need not be decided today. I am confident, however, that so long as the Equal Protection Clause requires a sodomy law to apply equally to the private consensual conduct of homosexuals and heterosexuals alike, such a law would not long stand in our democratic society. . . .

That this law as applied to private, consensual conduct is unconstitutional under the Equal Protection Clause does not mean that other laws distinguishing between heterosexuals and homosexuals would similarly fail under rational basis review. Texas cannot assert any legitimate state interest here, such as national security or preserving the traditional institution of marriage. Unlike the moral disapproval of same-sex relations—the asserted state interest in this case—other reasons exist to promote the institution of marriage beyond mere moral disapproval of an excluded group. . . .

■ JUSTICE SCALIA, with whom THE CHIEF JUSTICE and JUSTICE THOMAS join, dissenting.

"Liberty finds no refuge in a jurisprudence of doubt." *Planned Parenthood v. Casey*, at 844. That was the Court's sententious response, barely more than a decade ago, to those seeking to overrule *Roe v. Wade*. The Court's response today, to those who have engaged in a 17-year crusade to overrule *Bowers v. Hardwick*, is very different. The need for stability and certainty presents no barrier.

Most of the rest of today's opinion has no relevance to its actual holding—that the Texas statute "furthers no legitimate state interest which can justify" its application to petitioners under rational-basis review. Though there is discussion of "fundamental proposition[s]" and "fundamental decisions," nowhere does the Court's opinion declare that homosexual sodomy is a "fundamental right" under the Due Process Clause; nor does it subject the Texas law to the standard of review that would be appropriate (strict scrutiny) if homosexual sodomy *were* a "fundamental right." Thus, while overruling the *outcome* of *Bowers*, the Court leaves strangely untouched its central legal conclusion: "[R]espondent would have us announce . . . a fundamental right to engage in homosexual sodomy. This we are quite unwilling to do." Instead the Court simply describes petitioners' conduct as "an exercise of their liberty"—which it undoubtedly is—and proceeds to apply an unheard-of form of rational-basis review that will have far-reaching implications beyond this case.

I

I begin with the Court's surprising readiness to reconsider a decision rendered a mere 17 years ago in *Bowers v. Hardwick*. I do not myself believe in rigid adherence to *stare decisis* in constitutional cases; but I do believe that we should be consistent rather than manipulative in invoking the doctrine. Today's opinions in support of reversal do not bother to distinguish—or indeed, even bother to mention—the paean to *stare decisis* coauthored by three Members of today's majority in *Planned Parenthood v. Casey*. There, when *stare decisis* meant preservation of judicially invented abortion rights, the widespread criticism of *Roe* was strong reason to *reaffirm* it:

> Where, in the performance of its judicial duties, the Court decides a case in such a way as to resolve the sort of intensely divisive controversy reflected in *Roe*[,] . . . its decision has a dimension that the resolution of the normal case does not carry. . . . [T]o overrule under fire in the absence of the most compelling reason . . . would subvert the Court's legitimacy beyond any serious question.

505 U.S., at 866–867. Today, however, the widespread opposition to *Bowers*, a decision resolving an issue as "intensely divisive" as the issue in *Roe*, is offered as a reason in favor of *overruling* it. Gone, too, is any "enquiry" (of the sort conducted in *Casey*) into whether the decision sought to be overruled has "proven unworkable," *id.*, at 855.

Today's approach to *stare decisis* invites us to overrule an erroneously decided precedent (including an "intensely divisive" decision) *if*: (1) its foundations have been "ero[ded]" by subsequent decisions; (2) it has been subject to "substantial and continuing" criticism; and (3) it has not induced "individual or societal reliance" that counsels against overturning. The problem is that *Roe* itself—which today's majority surely has no disposition to overrule—satisfies these conditions to at least the same degree as *Bowers*.

(1) A preliminary digressive observation with regard to the first factor: The Court's claim that *Planned Parenthood v. Casey* "casts some doubt" upon the holding in *Bowers* (or any other case, for that matter) does not withstand analysis. As far as its holding is concerned, *Casey* provided a *less* expansive right to abortion than did *Roe, which was already on the books when* Bowers *was decided.* And if the Court is referring not to the holding of Casey, but to the dictum of its famed sweet-mystery-of-life passage ("At the heart of liberty is the right to define one's own concept of existence, of meaning, of the universe, and of the mystery of human life"): That "casts some doubt" upon either the totality of our jurisprudence or else (presumably the right answer) nothing at all. I have never heard of a law that attempted to restrict one's "right to define" certain concepts; and if the passage calls into question the government's power to regulate *actions based on* one's self-defined "concept of existence, etc.," it is the passage that ate the rule of law.

I do not quarrel with the Court's claim that *Romer* "eroded" the "foundations" of *Bowers*' rational-basis holding. But *Roe* and *Casey* have been equally "eroded" by *Washington v. Glucksberg*, 521 U.S. 702, 721 (1997), which held that *only* fundamental rights which are "deeply rooted in this Nation's history and tradition" qualify for anything other than rational-basis scrutiny under the doctrine of "substantive due process." . . .

(2) *Bowers*, the Court says, has been subject to "substantial and continuing [criticism], disapproving of its reasoning in all respects, not just as to its historical assumptions." . . . [T]he Court [cites] two books. See *ibid.* (citing C. Fried, Order and Law; R. Posner, Sex and Reason). Of course, *Roe* too (and by extension *Casey)* had been (and still is) subject to unrelenting criticism, including criticism from the two commentators cited by the Court today. See Fried, at 75 ("*Roe* was a prime example of twisted judging"); Posner, at 337 ("[The Court's] opinion in *Roe* . . . fails to measure up to professional expectations regarding judicial opinions"); Posner, *Judicial Opinion Writing*, 62 U. Chi. L. Rev. 1421, 1434 (1995) (describing the opinion in *Roe* as an "embarrassing performanc[e]").

(3) That leaves, to distinguish the rock-solid, unamendable disposition of *Roe* from the readily overrulable *Bowers*, only the third factor [i.e., societal reliance]. . . . It seems to me that the "societal reliance" on the principles confirmed in *Bowers* and discarded today has been overwhelming. Countless judicial decisions and legislative enactments have relied on the ancient proposition that a governing majority's belief that certain sexual behavior is "immoral and unacceptable" constitutes a rational

basis for regulation. *[Here Justice Scalia cites state and federal cases relying on Bowers to uphold restrictions on the sale of sex toys, military service by those who engage in homosexual conduct, fornication, adultery, and public indecency.—Editors]* State laws against bigamy, same-sex marriage, adult incest, prostitution, masturbation, adultery, fornication, bestiality, and obscenity are likewise sustainable only in light of *Bowers'* validation of laws based on moral choices. Every single one of these laws is called into question by today's decision; the Court makes no effort to cabin the scope of its decision to exclude them from its holding. The impossibility of distinguishing homosexuality from other traditional "morals" offenses is precisely why *Bowers* rejected the rational-basis challenge. "The law," it said, "is constantly based on notions of morality, and if all laws representing essentially moral choices are to be invalidated under the Due Process Clause, the courts will be very busy indeed."

What a massive disruption of the current social order, therefore, the overruling of *Bowers* entails. Not so the overruling of *Roe*, which would simply have restored the regime that existed for centuries before 1973, in which the permissibility of, and restrictions upon, abortion were determined legislatively State by State. . . .

To tell the truth, it does not surprise me, and should surprise no one, that the Court has chosen today to revise the standards of *stare decisis* set forth in *Casey*. It has thereby exposed *Casey's* extraordinary deference to precedent for the result-oriented expedient that it is.

II

Having decided that it need not adhere to *stare decisis*, the Court still must establish that *Bowers* was wrongly decided and that the Texas statute, as applied to petitioners, is unconstitutional.

[The Texas statute] undoubtedly imposes constraints on liberty. So do laws prohibiting prostitution, recreational use of heroin, and, for that matter, working more than 60 hours per week in a bakery. But there is no right to "liberty" under the Due Process Clause, though today's opinion repeatedly makes that claim. The Fourteenth Amendment *expressly allows* States to deprive their citizens of "liberty," *so long as "due process of law" is provided.* . . .

Our opinions applying the doctrine known as "substantive due process" hold that the Due Process Clause prohibits States from infringing *fundamental* liberty interests, unless the infringement is narrowly tailored to serve a compelling state interest. *Glucksberg*, at 721. We have held repeatedly, in cases the Court today does not overrule, that *only* fundamental rights qualify for this so-called "heightened scrutiny" protection—that is, rights which are "deeply rooted in this Nation's history and tradition." All other liberty interests may be abridged or abrogated pursuant to a validly enacted state law if that law is rationally related to a legitimate state interest.

Bowers held, first, that criminal prohibitions of homosexual sodomy are not subject to heightened scrutiny because they do not implicate a "fundamental right" under the Due Process Clause. . . .

The Court today does not overrule this holding. Not once does it describe homosexual sodomy as a "fundamental right" or a "fundamental liberty interest," nor does it subject the Texas statute to strict scrutiny. Instead, having failed to establish that the right to homosexual sodomy is "deeply rooted in this Nation's history and tradition," the Court concludes that the application of Texas's statute to petitioners' conduct fails the rational-basis test, and overrules *Bowers*' holding to the contrary. "The Texas statute furthers no legitimate state interest which can justify its intrusion into the personal and private life of the individual." . . .

[Part III reviews the Court's substantive due process and fundamental rights jurisprudence and argues that Bowers *rightly rejected the claim that homosexual conduct was a fundamental right "deeply rooted in the Nation's history and tradition," and therefore so clearly "implicit in the concept of ordered liberty" that "neither liberty nor justice would exist if it were sacrificed."—Editors]*

IV

I turn now to the ground on which the Court squarely rests its holding: the contention that there is no rational basis for the law here under attack. This proposition is so out of accord with our jurisprudence—indeed, with the jurisprudence of any society we know—that it requires little discussion.

The Texas statute undeniably seeks to further the belief of its citizens that certain forms of sexual behavior are "immoral and unacceptable," *Bowers*, at 196— the same interest furthered by criminal laws against fornication, bigamy, adultery, adult incest, bestiality, and obscenity. *Bowers* held that this *was* a legitimate state interest. The Court today reaches the opposite conclusion. The Texas statute, it says, "furthers *no legitimate state interest* which can justify its intrusion into the personal and private life of the individual" (emphasis added). The Court embraces instead JUSTICE STEVENS' declaration in his *Bowers* dissent, that "the fact that a governing majority in a State has traditionally viewed a particular practice as immoral is not a sufficient reason for upholding a law prohibiting the practice." . . . This effectively decrees the end of all morals legislation. If, as the Court asserts, the promotion of majoritarian sexual morality is not even a *legitimate* state interest, none of the above-mentioned laws can survive rational-basis review.

V

Finally, I turn to petitioners' equal-protection challenge, which no Member of the Court save JUSTICE O'CONNOR embraces: On its face [the statute] applies equally to all persons. Men and women, heterosexuals and homosexuals, are all subject to its prohibition of deviate sexual intercourse with someone of the same sex. To be sure, [it] does distinguish between the sexes insofar as concerns the partner with whom the sexual acts are performed: men can violate the law only with other men, and women only with other women. But this cannot itself be a denial of equal protection, since it is precisely the same distinction regarding partner that is drawn in state laws prohibiting marriage with someone of the same sex while permitting marriage with someone of the opposite sex.

The objection is made, however, that the antimiscegenation laws invalidated in *Loving v. Virginia*, 388 U.S. 1, 8 (1967), similarly were applicable to whites and blacks alike, and only distinguished between the races insofar as the *partner* was concerned. In *Loving*, however, we correctly applied heightened scrutiny, rather than the usual rational-basis review, because the Virginia statute was "designed to maintain White Supremacy." A racially discriminatory purpose is always sufficient to subject a law to strict scrutiny, even a facially neutral law that makes no mention of race. See *Washington v. Davis*, 426 U.S. 229, 241–242 (1976). No purpose to discriminate against men or women as a class can be gleaned from the Texas law, so rational-basis review applies. That review is readily satisfied here by the same rational basis that satisfied it in *Bowers*—society's belief that certain forms of sexual behavior are "immoral and unacceptable," 478 U.S., at 196. This is the same justification that supports many other laws regulating sexual behavior that make a distinction based upon the identity of the partner—for example, laws against adultery, fornication, and adult incest, and laws refusing to recognize homosexual marriage.

JUSTICE O'CONNOR argues that the discrimination in this law which must be justified is not its discrimination with regard to the sex of the partner but its discrimination with regard to the sexual proclivity of the principal actor. . . . Of course the same could be said of any law. A law against public nudity targets "the conduct that is closely correlated with being a nudist," and hence "is targeted at more than conduct"; it is "directed toward nudists as a class." But be that as it may. Even if the Texas law *does* deny equal protection to "homosexuals as a class," that denial *still* does not need to be justified by anything more than a rational basis, which our cases show is satisfied by the enforcement of traditional notions of sexual morality.

JUSTICE O'CONNOR simply decrees application of "a more searching form of rational basis review" to the Texas statute. The cases she cites do not recognize such a standard, and reach their conclusions only after finding, as required by conventional rational-basis analysis, that no conceivable legitimate state interest supports the classification at issue. Nor does JUSTICE O'CONNOR explain precisely what her "more searching form" of rational-basis review consists of. It must at least mean, however, that laws exhibiting "a desire to harm a politically unpopular group" are invalid *even though* there may be a conceivable rational basis to support them.

This reasoning leaves on pretty shaky grounds state laws limiting marriage to opposite-sex couples. JUSTICE O'CONNOR seeks to preserve them by the conclusory statement that "preserving the traditional institution of marriage" is a legitimate state interest. But "preserving the traditional institution of marriage" is just a kinder way of describing the State's *moral disapproval* of same-sex couples. Texas's interest in [the statute] could be recast in similarly euphemistic terms: "preserving the traditional sexual mores of our society." In the jurisprudence JUSTICE O'CONNOR has seemingly created, judges can validate laws by characterizing them as "preserving the traditions of society" (good); or invalidate them by characterizing them as "expressing moral disapproval" (bad). . . .

Let me be clear that I have nothing against homosexuals, or any other group, promoting their agenda through normal democratic means. Social perceptions of sexual and other morality change over time, and every group has the right to persuade its fellow citizens that its view of such matters is the best. That homosexuals have achieved some success in that enterprise is attested to by the fact that Texas is one of the few remaining States that criminalize private, consensual homosexual acts. But persuading one's fellow citizens is one thing, and imposing one's views in absence of democratic majority will is something else. I would no more require a State to criminalize homosexual acts—or, for that matter, display *any* moral disapprobation of them—than I would *forbid* it to do so. What Texas has chosen to do is well within the range of traditional democratic action, and its hand should not be stayed through the invention of a brand-new "constitutional right" by a Court that is impatient of democratic change. It is indeed true that "later generations can see that laws once thought necessary and proper in fact serve only to oppress"; and when that happens, later generations can repeal those laws. But it is the premise of our system that those judgments are to be made by the people, and not imposed by a governing caste that knows best.

One of the benefits of leaving regulation of this matter to the people rather than to the courts is that the people, unlike judges, need not carry things to their logical conclusion. The people may feel that their disapprobation of homosexual conduct is strong enough to disallow homosexual marriage, but not strong enough to criminalize private homosexual acts—and may legislate accordingly. The Court today pretends that it possesses a similar freedom of action, so that we need not fear judicial imposition of homosexual marriage, as has recently occurred in Canada (in a decision that the Canadian Government has chosen not to appeal). At the end of its opinion—after having laid waste the foundations of our rational-basis jurisprudence—the Court says that the present case "does not involve whether the government must give formal recognition to any relationship that homosexual persons seek to enter." Do not believe it. More illuminating than this bald, unreasoned disclaimer is the progression of thought displayed by an earlier passage in the Court's opinion, which notes the constitutional protections afforded to "personal decisions relating to *marriage*, procreation, contraception, family relationships, child rearing, and education" (emphasis added), and then declares that "[p]ersons in a homosexual relationship may seek autonomy for these purposes, just as heterosexual persons do." Today's opinion dismantles the structure of constitutional law that has permitted a distinction to be made between heterosexual and homosexual unions, insofar as formal recognition in marriage is concerned. If moral disapprobation of homosexual conduct is "no legitimate state interest" for purposes of proscribing that conduct; and if, as the Court coos (casting aside all pretense of neutrality), "[w]hen sexuality finds overt expression in intimate conduct with another person, the conduct can be but one element in a personal bond that is more enduring"; what justification could there possibly be for denying the benefits of marriage to homosexual couples exercising "[t]he liberty protected by the Constitution"? Surely not the encouragement of procreation, since the sterile and the elderly are allowed to marry. This case "does not involve" the issue of homosexual marriage only if one entertains the belief that principle and logic have nothing to do with the decisions of this Court. Many will hope that, as the Court comfortingly assures us, this is so.

The matters appropriate for this Court's resolution are only three: Texas's prohibition of sodomy neither infringes a "fundamental right" (which the Court does not dispute), nor is unsupported by a rational relation to what the Constitution considers a legitimate state interest, nor denies the equal protection of the laws. I dissent.

■ JUSTICE THOMAS, dissenting.

I join JUSTICE SCALIA'S dissenting opinion. I write separately to note that the law before the Court today "is . . . uncommonly silly." *Griswold,* at 527 (Stewart, J., dissenting). If I were a member of the Texas Legislature, I would vote to repeal it. Punishing someone for expressing his sexual preference through noncommercial consensual conduct with another adult does not appear to be a worthy way to expend valuable law enforcement resources.

Notwithstanding this, I recognize that as a Member of this Court I am not empowered to help petitioners and others similarly situated. My duty, rather, is to "decide cases agreeably to the Constitution and laws of the United States." *Id.,* at 530. And, just like Justice Stewart, I "can find [neither in the Bill of Rights nor any other part of the Constitution a] general right of privacy," *ibid.,* or as the Court terms it today, the "liberty of the person both in its spatial and more transcendent dimensions."

NOTES

1.   The majority opinion begins with a sweeping statement of principle: "Liberty presumes an autonomy of self that includes freedom of thought, belief, expression, and certain intimate conduct. The instant case involves liberty of the person both in its spatial and in its more transcendent dimensions." How does the Court connect that principle to the holding in the case? What is the methodology from *Lawrence* that the Court can use in future cases? How is it different from the methodology of Justice Souter in his *Glucksberg* concurrence? How would *Glucksberg* have been decided if the Court had instead used *Lawrence*'s methodology? How would *Lochner* have been decided?

2.   What is the difference in effect between the reasoning of the *Lawrence* majority and that of Justice O'Connor's concurrence? Is the Equal Protection Clause argument embraced by Justice O'Connor broader or narrower in its implications than the majority's Due Process Clause argument? Which argument for *Lawrence*'s result—an argument based in the Equal Protection Clause or in the Due Process Clause—is easier to ground in the line of cases beginning with *Griswold*? Which is easier to anchor in the text and history of the Constitution? Which basis would have cast more doubt on statutes that restricted marriage to heterosexual couples? Does that explain why the majority did not rest its decision on the Equal Protection Clause? For further discussion of same-sex marriage, and *Obergefell*, see p. 1632.

3.   What do you make of Justice Scalia's *stare decisis* point? What, exactly, is he dissenting from? The holding in *Lawrence*? Or is his real target the holding in *Casey*? Is he objecting to the Court's inconsistent application of *stare decisis*, or is he objecting to the doctrine itself? Is *Lawrence* consistent with the criteria for overruling precedent that *Casey* establishes? If the Court is inconsistent in its approach to *stare decisis*, what should it do—adhere more strictly to past decisions, or abandon any pretense of relying on precedent and decide each constitutional case on its own merits? Recall that Justice O'Connor had been in the majority in *Bowers*, and that she would not have overruled it in *Lawrence*. Should individual justices apply some version of the doctrine of *stare decisis* to their own past opinions and votes?

4.   Is Justice Scalia right that *Lawrence* holds that moral views cannot be a rational basis for law? Is that the only way to read the majority decision? Is it the best way? Is Justice Scalia right that there is no way to distinguish "preserving the traditions of society" from "expressing moral disapproval"? After *Lawrence*, can either of those characterizations support a statutory classification? Does it depend on the kind of interest involved? How does the Court specify and characterize the interest at stake in *Lawrence*?

[*Assignment 82*]

G. SAME-SEX MARRIAGE

For the latest iteration of Supreme Court's views of what the Due Process Clauses require, we now turn to the same-sex marriage cases. In the first case, *United States v. Windsor*, 133 S.Ct. 2675 (2013), the Court held unconstitutional a federal statute, the Defense of Marriage Act of 1996. The plaintiff, Edith Windsor, had married another woman named Thea Spyer in 2007. (Their marriage was originally celebrated in Canada but also recognized by the state of New York.) When Spyer died, Windsor claimed that she was entitled to the marital exemption to the federal estate tax, without which she owed an additional $363,053. A federal statute, the Defense of Marriage Act, defined "marriage" for purposes of federal law as "mean[ing] only a legal union between one man and one woman as husband and wife." Windsor's claim turned on the constitutionality of that Act.

In an opinion blending principles of federalism and due process, the Court invalidated the Act. It first recounted at length the tradition of state control of marriage "an area that had long been regarded as a virtually exclusive province of the States." But the Court found it "unnecessary to decide" whether the Act was unconstitutional on federalism grounds, because "the State's decision to give this class of persons the right to marry conferred upon them a dignity and status of immense import." This status was protected by the Due Process Clause, and the Act's purpose, the Court said, was to denigrate that dignity. It therefore "violate[d] basic due process and equal protection principles applicable to the Federal Government." The decision was 5–4.

Windsor is also a major case on standing, because the Obama administration had refused to defend the constitutionality of the statute, thus raising the question of whether there was still a "case" or "controversy" for the Court to hear; that part of the case can be found on p. 420.

Two terms later, in *Obergefell v. Hodges*, 135 S.Ct. 2584 (2015), the Court considered challenges to the laws of four of the states that retained the traditional definition of marriage and refused to license or recognize same-sex marriages: Michigan, Ohio, Kentucky, and Tennessee. The Court held that "same-sex couples may exercise the fundamental right to marry in all States." The Court's decision was largely based on substantive due process, though it added that the Due Process Clause and the Equal Protection Clause "may converge in the identification and definition of the right."

As you read *Obergefell*, think carefully about how the Court decides what "liberty" means in the Due Process Clauses. How does the Court answer the perennial question about substantive due process, namely how it differs from the judges' own views of what the law should be? Does the Court continue to emphasize the limiting principle of tradition? Or does it reject that limiting principle? If so, what does it offer in its place?

Obergefell v. Hodges
135 S.Ct. 2584 (2015)

■ JUSTICE KENNEDY delivered the opinion of the Court.

The Constitution promises liberty to all within its reach, a liberty that includes certain specific rights that allow persons, within a lawful realm, to define and express their identity. The petitioners in these cases seek to find that liberty by marrying someone of the same sex and having their marriages deemed lawful on the same terms and conditions as marriages between persons of the opposite sex. . . .

II–A

. . . From their beginning to their most recent page, the annals of human history reveal the transcendent importance of marriage. The lifelong union of a man and a woman always has promised nobility and dignity to all persons, without regard to their station in life. Marriage is sacred to those who live by their religions and offers unique fulfillment to those who find meaning in the secular realm. Its dynamic allows two people to find a life that could not be found alone, for a marriage becomes greater than just the two persons. Rising from the most basic human needs, marriage is essential to our most profound hopes and aspirations.

The centrality of marriage to the human condition makes it unsurprising that the institution has existed for millennia and across civilizations. Since the dawn of history, marriage has transformed strangers into relatives, binding families and societies together. Confucius taught that marriage lies at the foundation of government. This wisdom was echoed centuries later and half a world away by Cicero, who wrote, "The first bond of society is marriage; next, children; and then the family." There are untold references to the beauty of marriage in religious and philosophical texts spanning time, cultures, and faiths, as well as in art and literature in all their forms. It is fair and necessary to say these references were based on the understanding that marriage is a union between two persons of the opposite sex.

That history is the beginning of these cases. The respondents say it should be the end as well. To them, it would demean a timeless institution if the concept and lawful status of marriage were extended to two persons of the same sex. Marriage, in their view, is by its nature a gender-differentiated union of man and woman. This view long has been held—and continues to be held—in good faith by reasonable and sincere people here and throughout the world.

The petitioners acknowledge this history but contend that these cases cannot end there. Were their intent to demean the revered idea and reality of marriage, the petitioners' claims would be of a different order. But that is neither their purpose nor their submission. To the contrary, it is the enduring importance of marriage that underlies the petitioners' contentions. This, they say, is their whole point. Far from seeking to devalue marriage, the petitioners seek it for themselves because of their respect—and need—for its privileges and responsibilities. And their immutable nature dictates that same-sex marriage is their only real path to this profound commitment.

Recounting the circumstances of three of these cases illustrates the urgency of the petitioners' cause from their perspective. Petitioner James Obergefell, a plaintiff in the Ohio case, met John Arthur over two decades ago. They fell in love and started a life together, establishing a lasting, committed relation. In 2011, however, Arthur was diagnosed with amyotrophic lateral sclerosis, or ALS. This debilitating disease is progressive, with no known cure. Two years ago, Obergefell and Arthur decided to commit to one another, resolving to marry before Arthur died. To fulfill their mutual promise, they traveled from Ohio to Maryland, where same-sex marriage was legal. It was difficult for Arthur to move, and so the couple were wed inside a medical transport plane as it remained on the tarmac in Baltimore. Three months later, Arthur died. Ohio law does not permit Obergefell to be listed as the surviving spouse on Arthur's death certificate. By statute, they must remain strangers even in death, a state-imposed separation Obergefell deems "hurtful for the rest of time." He brought suit to be shown as the surviving spouse on Arthur's death certificate. *[The facts of two of the other cases are omitted.—Editors]* . . .

The cases now before the Court involve other petitioners as well, each with their own experiences. Their stories reveal that they seek not to denigrate marriage but rather to live their lives, or honor their spouses' memory, joined by its bond.

B

The ancient origins of marriage confirm its centrality, but it has not stood in isolation from developments in law and society. The history of marriage is one of both continuity and change. That institution—even as confined to opposite-sex relations—has evolved over time.

For example, marriage was once viewed as an arrangement by the couple's parents based on political, religious, and financial concerns; but by the time of the Nation's founding it was understood to be a voluntary contract between a man and a woman. As the role and status of women changed, the institution further evolved. Under the centuries-old doctrine of coverture, a married man and woman were treated by the State as a single, male-dominated legal entity. See 1 William Blackstone, Commentaries on the Laws of England 430 (1765). As women gained legal, political, and property rights, and as society began to understand that women have their own equal dignity, the law of coverture was abandoned. These and other developments in the institution of marriage over the past centuries were not mere superficial changes. Rather, they worked deep transformations in its structure, affecting aspects of marriage long viewed by many as essential.

These new insights have strengthened, not weakened, the institution of marriage. Indeed, changed understandings of marriage are characteristic of a Nation where new dimensions of freedom become apparent to new generations, often through perspectives that begin in pleas or protests and then are considered in the political sphere and the judicial process.

This dynamic can be seen in the Nation's experiences with the rights of gays and lesbians. Until the mid-20th century, same-sex intimacy long had been condemned as immoral by the state itself in most Western nations, a belief often embodied in the criminal law. For this reason, among others, many persons did not deem homosexuals to have dignity in their own distinct identity. A truthful declaration by same-sex couples of what was in their hearts had to remain unspoken. Even when a greater awareness of the humanity and integrity of homosexual persons came in the period after World War II, the argument that gays and lesbians had a just claim to dignity was in conflict with both law and widespread social conventions. Same-sex intimacy remained a crime in many States. Gays and lesbians were prohibited from most government employment, barred from military service, excluded under immigration laws, targeted by police, and burdened in their rights to associate.

For much of the 20th century, moreover, homosexuality was treated as an illness. When the American Psychiatric Association published the first Diagnostic and Statistical Manual of Mental Disorders in 1952, homosexuality was classified as a mental disorder, a position adhered to until 1973. Only in more recent years have psychiatrists and others recognized that sexual orientation is both a normal expression of human sexuality and immutable.

In the late 20th century, following substantial cultural and political developments, same-sex couples began to lead more open and public lives and to establish families. This development was followed by a quite extensive discussion of the issue in both governmental and private sectors and by a shift in public attitudes toward greater tolerance. As a result, questions about the rights of gays and lesbians soon reached the courts, where the issue could be discussed in the formal discourse of the law.

This Court first gave detailed consideration to the legal status of homosexuals in *Bowers v. Hardwick*, 478 U.S. 186 (1986). There it upheld the constitutionality of a Georgia law deemed to criminalize certain homosexual acts. Ten years later, in *Romer v. Evans*, 517 U.S. 620 (1996), the Court invalidated an amendment to Colorado's Constitution that sought to foreclose any branch or political subdivision of the State from protecting persons against discrimination based on sexual orientation. Then, in 2003, the Court overruled *Bowers*, holding that laws making same-sex intimacy a crime "demea[n] the lives of homosexual persons." *Lawrence v. Texas*, 539 U.S. 558, 575 (2003).

Against this background, the legal question of same-sex marriage arose. In 1993, the Hawaii Supreme Court held Hawaii's law restricting marriage to opposite-sex couples constituted a classification on the basis of sex and was therefore subject to strict scrutiny under the Hawaii Constitution. Baehr v. Lewin, 74 Haw. 530, 852 P.2d 44.

After years of litigation, legislation, referenda, and the discussions that attended these public acts, the States are now divided on the issue of same-sex marriage.

III

Under the Due Process Clause of the Fourteenth Amendment, no State shall "deprive any person of life, liberty, or property, without due process of law." The fundamental liberties protected by this Clause include most of the rights enumerated in the Bill of Rights. In addition these liberties extend to certain personal choices central to individual dignity and autonomy, including intimate choices that define personal identity and beliefs. See, e.g., *Eisenstadt v. Baird*, 405 U.S. 438, 453 (1972); *Griswold v. Connecticut*, 381 U.S. 479, 484–486 (1965).

The identification and protection of fundamental rights is an enduring part of the judicial duty to interpret the Constitution. That responsibility, however, "has not been reduced to any formula." *Poe v. Ullman*, 367 U.S. 497, 542 (1961) (Harlan, J., dissenting). Rather, it requires courts to exercise reasoned judgment in identifying interests of the person so fundamental that the State must accord them its respect. That process is guided by many of the same considerations relevant to analysis of other constitutional provisions that set forth broad principles rather than specific requirements. History and tradition guide and discipline this inquiry but do not set its outer boundaries. See *Lawrence*, at 572. That method respects our history and learns from it without allowing the past alone to rule the present.

The nature of injustice is that we may not always see it in our own times. The generations that wrote and ratified the Bill of Rights and the Fourteenth Amendment did not presume to know the extent of freedom in all of its dimensions, and so they entrusted to future generations a charter protecting the right of all persons to enjoy liberty as we learn its meaning. When new insight reveals discord between the Constitution's central protections and a received legal stricture, a claim to liberty must be addressed.

Applying these established tenets, the Court has long held the right to marry is protected by the Constitution. In *Loving v. Virginia*, 388 U.S. 1, 12 (1967), which invalidated bans on interracial unions, a unanimous Court held marriage is "one of the vital personal rights essential to the orderly pursuit of happiness by free men." The Court reaffirmed that holding in *Zablocki v. Redhail*, 434 U.S. 374, 384 (1978), which held the right to marry was burdened by a law prohibiting fathers who were behind on child support from marrying. The Court again applied this principle in *Turner v. Safley*, 482 U.S. 78, 95 (1987), which held the right to marry was abridged by regulations limiting the privilege of prison inmates to marry. Over time and in other contexts, the Court has reiterated that the right to marry is fundamental under the Due Process Clause. See, e.g., *Griswold*, at 486; *Meyer v. Nebraska*, 262 U.S. 390, 399 (1923).

It cannot be denied that this Court's cases describing the right to marry presumed a relationship involving opposite-sex partners. The Court, like many institutions, has made assumptions defined by the world and time of which it is a part. This was evident in *Baker v. Nelson*, 409 U.S. 810 (1972), a one-line summary decision issued in 1972, holding the exclusion of same-sex couples from marriage did not present a substantial federal question.

Still, there are other, more instructive precedents. This Court's cases have expressed constitutional principles of broader reach. In defining the right to marry these cases have identified essential attributes of that right based in history, tradition, and other constitutional liberties inherent in this intimate bond. See, e.g., *Lawrence*, at 574; *Loving*, at 12; *Griswold*, at 486. And in assessing whether the force and rationale of its cases apply to same-sex couples, the Court must respect the basic reasons why the right to marry has been long protected. See, e.g., *Eisenstadt*, at 453–454; *Poe*, at 542–553, (Harlan, J., dissenting).

This analysis compels the conclusion that same-sex couples may exercise the right to marry. The four principles and traditions to be discussed demonstrate that the reasons marriage is fundamental under the Constitution apply with equal force to same-sex couples.

A first premise of the Court's relevant precedents is that the right to personal choice regarding marriage is inherent in the concept of individual autonomy. This abiding connection between marriage and liberty is why *Loving* invalidated interracial marriage bans under the Due Process Clause. Like choices concerning contraception, family relationships, procreation, and childrearing, all of which are protected by the Constitution, decisions concerning marriage are among the most intimate that an individual can make. . . .

The nature of marriage is that, through its enduring bond, two persons together can find other freedoms, such as expression, intimacy, and spirituality. This is true for all persons, whatever their sexual orientation. There is dignity in the bond between two men or two women who seek to marry and in their autonomy to make such profound choices. Cf. *Loving*, at 12 ("[T]he freedom to marry, or not marry, a person of another race resides with the individual and cannot be infringed by the State").

A second principle in this Court's jurisprudence is that the right to marry is fundamental because it supports a two-person union unlike any other in its importance to the committed individuals. This point was central to *Griswold v. Connecticut*, which held the Constitution protects the right of married couples to use contraception. Suggesting that marriage is a right "older than the Bill of Rights," *Griswold* described marriage this way:

> "Marriage is a coming together for better or for worse, hopefully enduring, and intimate to the degree of being sacred. It is an association that promotes a way of life, not causes; a harmony in living, not political faiths; a bilateral loyalty, not commercial or social projects. Yet it is an association for as noble a purpose as any involved in our prior decisions." *Id.*, at 486.

. . . The right to marry thus dignifies couples who "wish to define themselves by their commitment to each other." *Windsor*, at 2689. Marriage responds to the universal fear that a lonely person might call out only to find no one there. It offers the hope of companionship and understanding and assurance that while both still live there will be someone to care for the other. . . .

A third basis for protecting the right to marry is that it safeguards children and families and thus draws meaning from related rights of childrearing, procreation, and education. See *Pierce v. Society of Sisters*, 268 U.S. 510 (1925); *Meyer*, at 399. The Court has recognized these connections by describing the varied rights as a unified whole: "[T]he right to 'marry, establish a home and bring up children' is a central part of the liberty protected by the Due Process Clause." *Zablocki*, at 384 (quoting *Meyer*, at 399). Under the laws of the several States, some of marriage's protections for children and families are material. But marriage also confers more profound benefits. By giving recognition and legal structure to their parents' relationship, marriage allows children "to understand the integrity and closeness of their own family and its concord with other families in their community and in their daily lives." *Windsor*, at 2694–2695. Marriage also affords the permanency and stability important to children's best interests.

As all parties agree, many same-sex couples provide loving and nurturing homes to their children, whether biological or adopted. And hundreds of thousands of children are presently being raised by such couples. Most States have allowed gays and lesbians to adopt, either as individuals or as couples, and many adopted and foster children have same-sex parents. This provides powerful confirmation from the law itself that gays and lesbians can create loving, supportive families.

Excluding same-sex couples from marriage thus conflicts with a central premise of the right to marry. Without the recognition, stability, and predictability marriage offers, their children suffer the stigma of knowing their families are somehow lesser.

They also suffer the significant material costs of being raised by unmarried parents, relegated through no fault of their own to a more difficult and uncertain family life. The marriage laws at issue here thus harm and humiliate the children of same-sex couples.

That is not to say the right to marry is less meaningful for those who do not or cannot have children. An ability, desire, or promise to procreate is not and has not been a prerequisite for a valid marriage in any State. In light of precedent protecting the right of a married couple not to procreate, it cannot be said the Court or the States have conditioned the right to marry on the capacity or commitment to procreate. The constitutional marriage right has many aspects, of which childbearing is only one.

Fourth and finally, this Court's cases and the Nation's traditions make clear that marriage is a keystone of our social order. Alexis de Tocqueville recognized this truth on his travels through the United States almost two centuries ago:

> "There is certainly no country in the world where the tie of marriage is so much respected as in America . . . [W]hen the American retires from the turmoil of public life to the bosom of his family, he finds in it the image of order and of peace. . . . [H]e afterwards carries [that image] with him into public affairs." 1 Democracy in America 309 (H. Reeve transl., rev. ed. 1990).

. . . For that reason, just as a couple vows to support each other, so does society pledge to support the couple, offering symbolic recognition and material benefits to protect and nourish the union. Indeed, while the States are in general free to vary the benefits they confer on all married couples, they have throughout our history made marriage the basis for an expanding list of governmental rights, benefits, and responsibilities. These aspects of marital status include: taxation; inheritance and property rights; rules of intestate succession; spousal privilege in the law of evidence; hospital access; medical decisionmaking authority; adoption rights; the rights and benefits of survivors; birth and death certificates; professional ethics rules; campaign finance restrictions; workers' compensation benefits; health insurance; and child custody, support, and visitation rules. Valid marriage under state law is also a significant status for over a thousand provisions of federal law. The States have contributed to the fundamental character of the marriage right by placing that institution at the center of so many facets of the legal and social order.

There is no difference between same- and opposite-sex couples with respect to this principle. Yet by virtue of their exclusion from that institution, same-sex couples are denied the constellation of benefits that the States have linked to marriage. This harm results in more than just material burdens. Same-sex couples are consigned to an instability many opposite-sex couples would deem intolerable in their own lives. As the State itself makes marriage all the more precious by the significance it attaches to it, exclusion from that status has the effect of teaching that gays and lesbians are unequal in important respects. It demeans gays and lesbians for the State to lock them out of a central institution of the Nation's society. Same-sex couples, too, may aspire to the transcendent purposes of marriage and seek fulfillment in its highest meaning.. . .

Objecting that this does not reflect an appropriate framing of the issue, the respondents refer to *Washington v. Glucksberg*, 521 U.S. 702, 721 (1997), which called for a "careful description" of fundamental rights. They assert the petitioners do not seek to exercise the right to marry but rather a new and nonexistent "right to same-sex marriage." *Glucksberg* did insist that liberty under the Due Process Clause must be defined in a most circumscribed manner, with central reference to specific historical practices. Yet while that approach may have been appropriate for the asserted right there involved (physician-assisted suicide), it is inconsistent with the approach this Court has used in discussing other fundamental rights, including marriage and intimacy. *Loving* did not ask about a "right to interracial marriage"; *Turner* did not ask about a "right of inmates to marry"; and *Zablocki* did not ask about a "right of fathers with unpaid child support duties to marry." Rather, each case inquired about the right to marry in its comprehensive sense, asking if there was a sufficient justification for excluding the relevant class from the right.

That principle applies here. If rights were defined by who exercised them in the past, then received practices could serve as their own continued justification and new groups could not invoke rights once denied. This Court has rejected that approach, both with respect to the right to marry and the rights of gays and lesbians.

The right to marry is fundamental as a matter of history and tradition, but rights come not from ancient sources alone. They rise, too, from a better informed understanding of how constitutional imperatives define a liberty that remains urgent in our own era. Many who deem same-sex marriage to be wrong reach that conclusion based on decent and honorable religious or philosophical premises, and neither they nor their beliefs are disparaged here. But when that sincere, personal opposition becomes enacted law and public policy, the necessary consequence is to put the imprimatur of the State itself on an exclusion that soon demeans or stigmatizes those whose own liberty is then denied. Under the Constitution, same-sex couples seek in marriage the same legal treatment as opposite-sex couples, and it would disparage their choices and diminish their personhood to deny them this right.

The right of same-sex couples to marry that is part of the liberty promised by the Fourteenth Amendment is derived, too, from that Amendment's guarantee of the equal protection of the laws. The Due Process Clause and the Equal Protection Clause are connected in a profound way, though they set forth independent principles. Rights implicit in liberty and rights secured by equal protection may rest on different precepts and are not always co-extensive, yet in some instances each may be instructive as to the meaning and reach of the other. In any particular case one Clause may be thought to capture the essence of the right in a more accurate and comprehensive way, even as the two Clauses may converge in the identification and definition of the right. This interrelation of the two principles furthers our understanding of what freedom is and must become.

The Court's cases touching upon the right to marry reflect this dynamic. In *Loving* the Court invalidated a prohibition on interracial marriage under both the Equal Protection Clause and the Due Process Clause. The Court first declared the prohibition invalid because of its unequal treatment of interracial couples. It stated: "There can be no doubt that restricting the freedom to marry solely because of racial classifications violates the central meaning of the Equal Protection Clause." 388 U.S., at 12. With this link to equal protection the Court proceeded to hold the prohibition offended central precepts of liberty: "To deny this fundamental freedom on so unsupportable a basis as the racial classifications embodied in these statutes, classifications so directly subversive of the principle of equality at the heart of the Fourteenth Amendment, is surely to deprive all the State's citizens of liberty without due process of law." The reasons why marriage is a fundamental right became more clear and compelling from a full awareness and understanding of the hurt that resulted from laws barring interracial unions. . . .

In *Lawrence* the Court acknowledged the interlocking nature of these constitutional safeguards in the context of the legal treatment of gays and lesbians. See 539 U.S., at 575. Although *Lawrence* elaborated its holding under the Due Process Clause, it acknowledged, and sought to remedy, the continuing inequality that resulted from laws making intimacy in the lives of gays and lesbians a crime against the State. *Lawrence* therefore drew upon principles of liberty and equality to define and protect the rights of gays and lesbians, holding the State "cannot demean their existence or control their destiny by making their private sexual conduct a crime."

This dynamic also applies to same-sex marriage. It is now clear that the challenged laws burden the liberty of same-sex couples, and it must be further acknowledged that they abridge central precepts of equality. . . .

These considerations lead to the conclusion that the right to marry is a fundamental right inherent in the liberty of the person, and under the Due Process and Equal Protection Clauses of the Fourteenth Amendment couples of the same-sex may not be deprived of that right and that liberty. The Court now holds that same-sex couples may exercise the fundamental right to marry. No longer may this liberty be denied to them. *Baker v. Nelson* must be and now is overruled, and the State laws challenged by Petitioners in these cases are now held invalid to the extent they exclude same-sex couples from civil marriage on the same terms and conditions as opposite-sex couples.

II

There may be an initial inclination in these cases to proceed with caution—to await further legislation, litigation, and debate. The respondents warn there has been insufficient democratic discourse before deciding an issue so basic as the definition of marriage. In its ruling on the cases now before this Court, the majority opinion for the Court of Appeals made a cogent argument that it would be appropriate for the respondents' States to await further public discussion and political measures before licensing same-sex marriages. See *DeBoer v. Snyder*, 772 F.3d 388, 409 (C.A. 6 2014).

Yet there has been far more deliberation than this argument acknowledges. There have been referenda, legislative debates, and grassroots campaigns, as well as countless studies, papers, books, and other popular and scholarly writings. There has been extensive litigation in state and federal courts. Judicial opinions addressing the issue have been informed by the contentions of parties and counsel, which, in turn, reflect the more general, societal discussion of same-sex marriage and its meaning that has occurred over the past decades. As more than 100 amici make clear in their filings, many of the central institutions in American life—state and local governments, the military, large and small businesses, labor unions, religious organizations, law enforcement, civic groups, professional organizations, and universities—have devoted substantial attention to the question. This has led to an enhanced understanding of the issue—an understanding reflected in the arguments now presented for resolution as a matter of constitutional law.

Of course, the Constitution contemplates that democracy is the appropriate process for change, so long as that process does not abridge fundamental rights. Last Term, a plurality of this Court reaffirmed the importance of the democratic principle in *Schuette v. BAMN*, 134 S.Ct. 1623 (2014), noting the "right of citizens to debate so they can learn and decide and then, through the political process, act in concert to try to shape the course of their own times." Indeed, it is most often through democracy that liberty is preserved and protected in our lives. But as *Schuette* also said, "[t]he freedom secured by the Constitution consists, in one of its essential dimensions, of the right of the individual not to be injured by the unlawful exercise of governmental power." Thus, when the rights of persons are violated, "the Constitution requires redress by the courts," notwithstanding the more general value of democratic decisionmaking. *Id.*, at 1637. This holds true even when protecting individual rights affects issues of the utmost importance and sensitivity.

. . . The idea of the Constitution "was to withdraw certain subjects from the vicissitudes of political controversy, to place them beyond the reach of majorities and officials and to establish them as legal principles to be applied by the courts." *West Virginia Bd. of Ed. v. Barnette*, 319 U.S. 624, 638 (1943). This is why "fundamental rights may not be submitted to a vote; they depend on the outcome of no elections." *Ibid.* It is of no moment whether advocates of same-sex marriage now enjoy or lack momentum in the democratic process. The issue before the Court here is the legal question whether the Constitution protects the right of same-sex couples to marry. . . .

Were the Court to uphold the challenged laws as constitutional, it would teach the Nation that these laws are in accord with our society's most basic compact. Were the Court to stay its hand to allow slower, case-by-case determination of the required availability of specific public benefits to same-sex couples, it still would deny gays and lesbians many rights and responsibilities intertwined with marriage.

The respondents also argue allowing same-sex couples to wed will harm marriage as an institution by leading to fewer opposite-sex marriages. This may occur, the respondents contend, because licensing same-sex marriage severs the connection between natural procreation and marriage. That argument, however, rests on a counterintuitive view of opposite-sex couple's decisionmaking processes regarding marriage and parenthood. Decisions about whether to marry and raise children are based on many personal, romantic, and practical considerations; and it is unrealistic to conclude that an opposite-sex couple would choose not to marry simply because same-sex couples may do so. See *Kitchen v. Herbert*, 755 F.3d 1193, 1223 (C.A.10 2014) ("[I]t is wholly illogical to believe that state recognition of the love and commitment between same-sex couples will alter the most intimate and personal decisions of opposite-sex couples"). The respondents have not shown a foundation for the conclusion that allowing same-sex marriage will cause the harmful outcomes they describe. Indeed, with respect to this asserted basis for excluding same-sex couples from the right to marry, it is appropriate to observe these cases involve only the rights of two consenting adults whose marriages would pose no risk of harm to themselves or third parties.

Finally, it must be emphasized that religions, and those who adhere to religious doctrines, may continue to advocate with utmost, sincere conviction that, by divine precepts, same-sex marriage should not be condoned. The First Amendment ensures that religious organizations and persons are given proper protection as they seek to teach the principles that are so fulfilling and so central to their lives and faiths, and to their own deep aspirations to continue the family structure they have long revered. The same is true of those who oppose same-sex marriage for other reasons. In turn, those who believe allowing same-sex marriage is proper or indeed essential, whether as a matter of religious conviction or secular belief, may engage those who disagree with their view in an open and searching debate. The Constitution, however, does not permit the State to bar same-sex couples from marriage on the same terms as accorded to couples of the opposite sex. . . .

■ CHIEF JUSTICE ROBERTS, with whom JUSTICE SCALIA and JUSTICE THOMAS join, dissenting.

Petitioners make strong arguments rooted in social policy and considerations of fairness. They contend that same-sex couples should be allowed to affirm their love and commitment through marriage, just like opposite-sex couples. That position has undeniable appeal; over the past six years, voters and legislators in eleven States and the District of Columbia have revised their laws to allow marriage between two people of the same sex.

But this Court is not a legislature. Whether same-sex marriage is a good idea should be of no concern to us. Under the Constitution, judges have power to say what the law is, not what it should be. The people who ratified the Constitution authorized courts to exercise "neither force nor will but merely judgment." The Federalist No. 78 (A. Hamilton).

Although the policy arguments for extending marriage to same-sex couples may be compelling, the legal arguments for requiring such an extension are not. The fundamental right to marry does not include a right to make a State change its definition of marriage. And a State's decision to maintain the meaning of marriage that has persisted in every culture throughout human history can hardly be called irrational. In short, our Constitution does not enact any one theory of marriage. The people of a State are free to expand marriage to include same-sex couples, or to retain the historic definition.

Today, however, the Court takes the extraordinary step of ordering every State to license and recognize same-sex marriage. Many people will rejoice at this decision, and I begrudge none their celebration. But for those who believe in a government of laws, not of men, the majority's approach is deeply disheartening. Supporters of same-sex marriage have achieved considerable success persuading their fellow citizens—through the democratic process—to adopt their view. That ends today. Five lawyers have closed the debate and enacted their own vision of marriage as a matter of constitutional law. Stealing this issue from the people will for many cast a cloud over same-sex marriage, making a dramatic social change that much more difficult to accept.

The majority's decision is an act of will, not legal judgment. The right it announces has no basis in the Constitution or this Court's precedent. The majority expressly disclaims judicial "caution" and omits even a pretense of humility, openly relying on its desire to remake society according to its own "new insight" into the "nature of injustice." As a result, the Court invalidates the marriage laws of more than half the States and orders the transformation of a social institution that has formed the basis of human society for millennia, for the Kalahari Bushmen and the Han Chinese, the Carthaginians and the Aztecs. Just who do we think we are?

It can be tempting for judges to confuse our own preferences with the requirements of the law. But as this Court has been reminded throughout our history, the Constitution "is made for people of fundamentally differing views." *Lochner v. New York*, 198 U.S. 45, 76 (1905) (Holmes, J., dissenting). Accordingly, "courts are not concerned with the wisdom or policy of legislation." *Id.*, at 69 (Harlan, J., dissenting). The majority today neglects that restrained conception of the judicial role. It seizes for itself a question the Constitution leaves to the people, at a time when the people are engaged in a vibrant debate on that question. And it answers that question based not on neutral principles of constitutional law, but on its own "understanding of what freedom is and must become." I have no choice but to dissent.

Understand well what this dissent is about: It is not about whether, in my judgment, the institution of marriage should be changed to include same-sex couples. It is instead about whether, in our democratic republic, that decision should rest with the people acting through their elected representatives, or with five lawyers who happen to hold commissions authorizing them to resolve legal disputes according to law. The Constitution leaves no doubt about the answer.

I

Petitioners and their amici base their arguments on the "right to marry" and the imperative of "marriage equality." There is no serious dispute that, under our precedents, the Constitution protects a right to marry and requires States to apply their marriage laws equally. The real question in these cases is what constitutes "marriage," or—more precisely—who decides what constitutes "marriage"?

The majority largely ignores these questions, relegating ages of human experience with marriage to a paragraph or two. Even if history and precedent are not "the end" of these cases, I would not "sweep away what has so long been settled" without showing greater respect for all that preceded us. *Town of Greece v. Galloway*, 134 S.Ct. 1811, 1819 (2014).

A

As the majority acknowledges, marriage "has existed for millennia and across civilizations." For all those millennia, across all those civilizations, "marriage" referred to only one relationship: the union of a man and a woman. . . .

This universal definition of marriage as the union of a man and a woman is no historical coincidence. Marriage did not come about as a result of a political movement, discovery, disease, war, religious doctrine, or any other moving force of world history—and certainly not as a result of a prehistoric decision to exclude gays and lesbians. It arose in the nature of things to meet a vital need: ensuring that children are conceived by a mother and father committed to raising them in the stable conditions of a lifelong relationship. See G. Quale, A History of Marriage Systems 2 (1988); cf. M. Cicero, De Officiis 57 (W. Miller transl. 1913) ("For since the reproductive instinct is by nature's gift the common possession of all living creatures, the first bond of union is that between husband and wife; the next, that between parents and children; then we find one home, with everything in common.").

The premises supporting this concept of marriage are so fundamental that they rarely require articulation. The human race must procreate to survive. Procreation occurs through sexual relations between a man and a woman. When sexual relations result in the conception of a child, that child's prospects are generally better if the mother and father stay together rather than going their separate ways. Therefore, for the good of children and society, sexual relations that can lead to procreation should occur only between a man and a woman committed to a lasting bond.

Society has recognized that bond as marriage. And by bestowing a respected status and material benefits on married couples, society encourages men and women to conduct sexual relations within marriage rather than without. . . .

This singular understanding of marriage has prevailed in the United States throughout our history. . . .

The Constitution itself says nothing about marriage, and the Framers thereby entrusted the States with "[t]he whole subject of the domestic relations of husband and wife." *Windsor*, at 2691 (quoting *In re Burrus*, 136 U.S. 586, 593–594 (1890)). There is no dispute that every State at the founding—and every State throughout our history until a dozen years ago—defined marriage in the traditional, biologically rooted way. The four States in these cases are typical. Their laws, before and after statehood, have treated marriage as the union of a man and a woman. Even when state laws did not specify this definition expressly, no one doubted what they meant. The meaning of "marriage" went without saying.

Of course, many did say it. In his first American dictionary, Noah Webster defined marriage as "the legal union of a man and woman for life," which served the purposes of "preventing the promiscuous intercourse of the sexes, . . . promoting domestic felicity, and . . . securing the maintenance and education of children." 1 An American Dictionary of the English Language (1828). . . . The first edition of Black's Law Dictionary defined marriage as "the civil status of one man and one woman united in law for life." Black's Law Dictionary 756 (1891) (emphasis deleted). The dictionary maintained essentially that same definition for the next century.

This Court's precedents have repeatedly described marriage in ways that are consistent only with its traditional meaning. Early cases on the subject referred to marriage as "the union for life of one man and one woman," *Murphy v. Ramsey*, 114 U.S. 15, 45 (1885), which forms "the foundation of the family and of society, without which there would be neither civilization nor progress," *Maynard*, at 211. We later described marriage as "fundamental to our very existence and survival," an understanding that necessarily implies a procreative component. *Loving*, at 12. More recent cases have directly connected the right to marry with the "right to procreate." *Zablocki*, at 386.

As the majority notes, some aspects of marriage have changed over time. Arranged marriages have largely given way to pairings based on romantic love. States have replaced coverture, the doctrine by which a married man and woman became a single legal entity, with laws that respect each participant's separate status. Racial restrictions on marriage, which "arose as an incident to slavery" to promote "White Supremacy," were repealed by many States and ultimately struck down by this Court. *Loving*, at 6–7.

The majority observes that these developments "were not mere superficial changes" in marriage, but rather "worked deep transformations in its structure."

They did not, however, work any transformation in the core structure of marriage as the union between a man and a woman. If you had asked a person on the street how marriage was defined, no one would ever have said, "Marriage is the union of a man and a woman, where the woman is subject to coverture." The majority may be right that the "history of marriage is one of both continuity and change," but the core meaning of marriage has endured.

B

Shortly after this Court struck down racial restrictions on marriage in *Loving*, a gay couple in Minnesota sought a marriage license. They argued that the Constitution required States to allow marriage between people of the same sex for the same reasons that it requires States to allow marriage between people of different races. The Minnesota Supreme Court rejected their analogy to *Loving*, and this Court summarily dismissed an appeal. *Baker v. Nelson.*

In the decades after *Baker*, greater numbers of gays and lesbians began living openly, and many expressed a desire to have their relationships recognized as marriages. Over time, more people came to see marriage in a way that could be extended to such couples. Until recently, this new view of marriage remained a minority position. . . . Over the last few years, public opinion on marriage has shifted rapidly. . . .

In all, voters and legislators in eleven States and the District of Columbia have changed their definitions of marriage to include same-sex couples. The highest courts of five States have decreed that same result under their own Constitutions. The remainder of the States retain the traditional definition of marriage. . . .

II

. . . The majority . . . resolves these cases for petitioners based almost entirely on the Due Process Clause.

The majority purports to identify four "principles and traditions" in this Court's due process precedents that support a fundamental right for same-sex couples to marry. In reality, however, the majority's approach has no basis in principle or tradition, except for the unprincipled tradition of judicial policymaking that characterized discredited decisions such as *Lochner*. Stripped of its shiny rhetorical gloss, the majority's argument is that the Due Process Clause gives same-sex couples a fundamental right to marry because it will be good for them and for society. If I were a legislator, I would certainly consider that view as a matter of social policy. But as a judge, I find the majority's position indefensible as a matter of constitutional law.

A

Petitioners' "fundamental right" claim falls into the most sensitive category of constitutional adjudication. Petitioners do not contend that their States' marriage laws violate an enumerated constitutional right, such as the freedom of speech protected by the First Amendment. There is, after all, no "Companionship and Understanding" or "Nobility and Dignity" Clause in the Constitution. They argue instead that the laws violate a right implied by the Fourteenth Amendment's requirement that "liberty" may not be deprived without "due process of law."

This Court has interpreted the Due Process Clause to include a "substantive" component that protects certain liberty interests against state deprivation "no matter what process is provided." *Reno v. Flores*, 507 U.S. 292, 302 (1993). The theory is that some liberties are "so rooted in the traditions and conscience of our people as to be ranked as fundamental," and therefore cannot be deprived without compelling justification. *Snyder v. Massachusetts*, 291 U.S. 97, 105 (1934).

Allowing unelected federal judges to select which unenumerated rights rank as "fundamental"—and to strike down state laws on the basis of that determination— raises obvious concerns about the judicial role. Our precedents have accordingly insisted that judges "exercise the utmost care" in identifying implied fundamental rights, "lest the liberty protected by the Due Process Clause be subtly transformed into the policy preferences of the Members of this Court." *Glucksberg*, at 720 (1997) (internal quotation marks omitted); see Kennedy, Unenumerated Rights and the Dictates of Judicial Restraint 13 (1986) (Address at Stanford) ("One can conclude that certain essential, or fundamental, rights should exist in any just society. It does not follow that each of those essential rights is one that we as judges can enforce under the written Constitution. The Due Process Clause is not a guarantee of every right that should inhere in an ideal system.").

The need for restraint in administering the strong medicine of substantive due process is a lesson this Court has learned the hard way. The Court first applied substantive due process to strike down a statute in *Dred Scott v. Sandford*, 60 U.S. (19 How.) 393 (1857). There the Court invalidated the Missouri Compromise on the ground that legislation restricting the institution of slavery violated the implied rights of slaveholders. The Court relied on its own conception of liberty and property in doing so. It asserted that "an act of Congress which deprives a citizen of the United States of his liberty or property, merely because he came himself or brought his property into a particular Territory of the United States . . . could hardly be dignified with the name of due process of law." In a dissent that has outlasted the majority opinion, Justice Curtis explained that when the "fixed rules which govern the interpretation of laws [are] abandoned, and the theoretical opinions of individuals are allowed to control" the Constitution's meaning, "we have no longer a Constitution; we are under the government of individual men, who for the time being have power to declare what the Constitution is, according to their own views of what it ought to mean." *Id.*, at 621.

Dred Scott's holding was overruled on the battlefields of the Civil War and by constitutional amendment after Appomattox, but its approach to the Due Process Clause reappeared. In a series of early 20th-century cases, most prominently *Lochner v. New York*, this Court invalidated state statutes that presented "meddlesome interferences with the rights of the individual," and "undue interference with liberty of person and freedom of contract." 198 U.S., at 60, 61. In *Lochner* itself, the Court struck down a New York law setting maximum hours for bakery employees, because there was "in our judgment, no reasonable foundation for holding this to be necessary or appropriate as a health law."

The dissenting Justices in *Lochner* explained that the New York law could be viewed as a reasonable response to legislative concern about the health of bakery employees, an issue on which there was at least "room for debate and for an honest difference of opinion." *Id.*, at 72 (opinion of Harlan, J.). The majority's contrary conclusion required adopting as constitutional law "an economic theory which a large part of the country does not entertain." *Id.*, at 75 (opinion of Holmes, J.). As Justice Holmes memorably put it, "The Fourteenth Amendment does not enact Mr. Herbert

Spencer's Social Statics," a leading work on the philosophy of Social Darwinism. *Ibid.* The Constitution "is not intended to embody a particular economic theory. . . . It is made for people of fundamentally differing views, and the accident of our finding certain opinions natural and familiar or novel and even shocking ought not to conclude our judgment upon the question whether statutes embodying them conflict with the Constitution." *Id.*, at 75–76.

In the decades after *Lochner*, the Court struck down nearly 200 laws as violations of individual liberty, often over strong dissents contending that "[t]he criterion of constitutionality is not whether we believe the law to be for the public good." *Adkins v. Children's Hospital of D.C.*, 261 U.S. 525, 570 (1923) (opinion of Holmes, J.). By empowering judges to elevate their own policy judgments to the status of constitutionally protected "liberty," the *Lochner* line of cases left "no alternative to regarding the court as a . . . legislative chamber." Learned Hand, The Bill of Rights 42 (1958).

Eventually, the Court recognized its error and vowed not to repeat it. "The doctrine that . . . due process authorizes courts to hold laws unconstitutional when they believe the legislature has acted unwisely," we later explained, "has long since been discarded. We have returned to the original constitutional proposition that courts do not substitute their social and economic beliefs for the judgment of legislative bodies, who are elected to pass laws." *Ferguson v. Skrupa*, 372 U.S. 726, 730 (1963). Thus, it has become an accepted rule that the Court will not hold laws unconstitutional simply because we find them "unwise, improvident, or out of harmony with a particular school of thought." *Williamson v. Lee Optical of Okla., Inc.*, 348 U.S. 483, 488 (1955).

Rejecting *Lochner* does not require disavowing the doctrine of implied fundamental rights, and this Court has not done so. But to avoid repeating *Lochner*'s error of converting personal preferences into constitutional mandates, our modern substantive due process cases have stressed the need for "judicial self-restraint." *Collins v. Harker Heights*, 503 U.S. 115, 125 (1992). Our precedents have required that implied fundamental rights be "objectively, deeply rooted in this Nation's history and tradition," and "implicit in the concept of ordered liberty, such that neither liberty nor justice would exist if they were sacrificed." *Glucksberg*, at 720–721. . . .

Proper reliance on history and tradition of course requires looking beyond the individual law being challenged, so that every restriction on liberty does not supply its own constitutional justification. The Court is right about that. But given the few "guideposts for responsible decisionmaking in this unchartered area," *Collins*, at 125 "an approach grounded in history imposes limits on the judiciary that are more meaningful than any based on [an] abstract formula," *Moore*, at 504, n. 12 (plurality opinion). Expanding a right suddenly and dramatically is likely to require tearing it up from its roots. Even a sincere profession of "discipline" in identifying fundamental rights does not provide a meaningful constraint on a judge, for "what he is really likely to be 'discovering,' whether or not he is fully aware of it, are his own values," J. Ely, Democracy and Distrust 44 (1980). . . .

B

The majority acknowledges none of this doctrinal background, and it is easy to see why: Its aggressive application of substantive due process breaks sharply with decades of precedent and returns the Court to the unprincipled approach of *Lochner*.

1

The majority's driving themes are that marriage is desirable and petitioners desire it. The opinion describes the "transcendent importance" of marriage and repeatedly insists that petitioners do not seek to "demean," "devalue," "denigrate," or "disrespect" the institution. Nobody disputes those points. Indeed, the compelling personal accounts of petitioners and others like them are likely a primary reason why many Americans have changed their minds about whether same-sex couples should be allowed to marry. As a matter of constitutional law, however, the sincerity of petitioners' wishes is not relevant.

. . . the "right to marry" cases stand for the important but limited proposition that particular restrictions on access to marriage as traditionally defined violate due process. These precedents say nothing at all about a right to make a State change its definition of marriage, which is the right petitioners actually seek here. See *Windsor*, at 2715 (ALITO, J., dissenting) ("What Windsor and the United States seek . . . is not the protection of a deeply rooted right but the recognition of a very new right."). Neither petitioners nor the majority cites a single case or other legal source providing any basis for such a constitutional right. None exists, and that is enough to foreclose their claim.

2

. . . Neither *Lawrence* nor any other precedent in the privacy line of cases supports the right that petitioners assert here. Unlike criminal laws banning contraceptives and sodomy, the marriage laws at issue here involve no government intrusion. They create no crime and impose no punishment. Same-sex couples remain free to live together, to engage in intimate conduct, and to raise their families as they see fit. No one is "condemned to live in loneliness" by the laws challenged in these cases—no one. At the same time, the laws in no way interfere with the "right to be let alone." . . .

In sum, the privacy cases provide no support for the majority's position, because petitioners do not seek privacy. Quite the opposite, they seek public recognition of their relationships, along with corresponding government benefits. Our cases have consistently refused to allow litigants to convert the shield provided by constitutional liberties into a sword to demand positive entitlements from the State. Thus, although the right to privacy recognized by our precedents certainly plays a role in protecting the intimate conduct of same-sex couples, it provides no affirmative right to redefine marriage and no basis for striking down the laws at issue here.

3

Perhaps recognizing how little support it can derive from precedent, the majority goes out of its way to jettison the "careful" approach to implied fundamental rights taken by this Court in *Glucksberg*. It is revealing that the majority's position requires it to effectively overrule *Glucksberg*, the leading modern case setting the bounds of substantive due process. At least this part of the majority opinion has the virtue of candor. Nobody could rightly accuse the majority of taking a careful approach. . . .

One immediate question invited by the majority's position is whether States may retain the definition of marriage as a union of two people. Although the majority randomly inserts the adjective "two" in various places, it offers no reason at all why the two-person element of the core definition of marriage may be preserved while the man-woman element may not. Indeed, from the standpoint of history and tradition, a leap from opposite-sex marriage to same-sex marriage is much greater than one from a two-person union to plural unions, which have deep roots in some cultures around the world. If the majority is willing to take the big leap, it is hard to see how it can say no to the shorter one.

It is striking how much of the majority's reasoning would apply with equal force to the claim of a fundamental right to plural marriage. If "[t]here is dignity in the bond between two men or two women who seek to marry and in their autonomy to make such profound choices," why would there be any less dignity in the bond between three people who, in exercising their autonomy, seek to make the profound choice to marry? If a same-sex couple has the constitutional right to marry because their children would otherwise "suffer the stigma of knowing their families are somehow lesser," why wouldn't the same reasoning apply to a family of three or more persons raising children? If not having the opportunity to marry "serves to disrespect and subordinate" gay and lesbian couples, why wouldn't the same "imposition of this disability," serve to disrespect and subordinate people who find fulfillment in polyamorous relationships? See Bennett, Polyamory: The Next Sexual Revolution? Newsweek, July 28, 2009 (estimating 500,000 polyamorous families in the United States).

I do not mean to equate marriage between same-sex couples with plural marriages in all respects. There may well be relevant differences that compel different legal analysis. But if there are, petitioners have not pointed to any. When asked about a plural marital union at oral argument, petitioners asserted that a State "doesn't have such an institution." But that is exactly the point: the States at issue here do not have an institution of same-sex marriage, either.

4

Near the end of its opinion, the majority offers perhaps the clearest insight into its decision. Expanding marriage to include same-sex couples, the majority insists, would "pose no risk of harm to themselves or third parties." This argument again echoes *Lochner*, which relied on its assessment that "we think that a law like the one before us involves neither the safety, the morals nor the welfare of the public, and that the interest of the public is not in the slightest degree affected by such an act." 198 U.S., at 57.

Then and now, this assertion of the "harm principle" sounds more in philosophy than law. The elevation of the fullest individual self-realization over the constraints that society has expressed in law may or may not be attractive moral philosophy. But a Justice's commission does not confer any special moral, philosophical, or social insight sufficient to justify imposing those perceptions on fellow citizens under the pretense of "due process." There is indeed a process due the people on issues of this sort—the democratic process. Respecting that understanding requires the Court to be guided by law, not any particular school of social thought. As Judge Henry

Friendly once put it, echoing Justice Holmes's dissent in *Lochner*, the Fourteenth Amendment does not enact John Stuart Mill's On Liberty any more than it enacts Herbert Spencer's Social Statics. See Randolph, *Before* Roe v. Wade: *Judge Friendly's Draft Abortion Opinion*, 29 Harv. J.L. & Pub. Pol'y 1035, 1036–1037, 1058 (2006). And it certainly does not enact any one concept of marriage.

The majority's understanding of due process lays out a tantalizing vision of the future for Members of this Court: If an unvarying social institution enduring over all of recorded history cannot inhibit judicial policymaking, what can? But this approach is dangerous for the rule of law. The purpose of insisting that implied fundamental rights have roots in the history and tradition of our people is to ensure that when unelected judges strike down democratically enacted laws, they do so based on something more than their own beliefs. The Court today not only overlooks our country's entire history and tradition but actively repudiates it, preferring to live only in the heady days of the here and now. I agree with the majority that the "nature of injustice is that we may not always see it in our own times." As petitioners put it, "times can blind." Tr. of Oral Arg. on Question 1, at 9, 10. But to blind yourself to history is both prideful and unwise. "The past is never dead. It's not even past." W. Faulkner, Requiem for a Nun 92 (1951).

III

In addition to their due process argument, petitioners contend that the Equal Protection Clause requires their States to license and recognize same-sex marriages. The majority does not seriously engage with this claim. Its discussion is, quite frankly, difficult to follow. The central point seems to be that there is a "synergy between" the Equal Protection Clause and the Due Process Clause, and that some precedents relying on one Clause have also relied on the other. Ante, at 2603. Absent from this portion of the opinion, however, is anything resembling our usual framework for deciding equal protection cases. It is casebook doctrine that the "modern Supreme Court's treatment of equal protection claims has used a means-ends methodology in which judges ask whether the classification the government is using is sufficiently related to the goals it is pursuing." G. Stone, L. Seidman, C. Sunstein, M. Tushnet, & P. Karlan, Constitutional Law 453 (7th ed. 2013). The majority's approach today is different. . . .

The majority goes on to assert in conclusory fashion that the Equal Protection Clause provides an alternative basis for its holding. Yet the majority fails to provide even a single sentence explaining how the Equal Protection Clause supplies independent weight for its position, nor does it attempt to justify its gratuitous violation of the canon against unnecessarily resolving constitutional questions. In any event, the marriage laws at issue here do not violate the Equal Protection Clause, because distinguishing between opposite-sex and same-sex couples is rationally related to the States' "legitimate state interest" in "preserving the traditional institution of marriage." *Lawrence*, 539 U.S., at 585 (O'Connor, J., concurring in judgment). . . .

IV

The legitimacy of this Court ultimately rests "upon the respect accorded to its judgments." *Republican Party of Minn. v. White*, 536 U.S. 765, 793 (2002) (Kennedy, J., concurring). That respect flows from the perception—and reality—that we exercise humility and restraint in deciding cases according to the Constitution and law. The role of the Court envisioned by the majority today, however, is anything but humble or restrained. Over and over, the majority exalts the role of the judiciary in delivering social change. In the majority's telling, it is the courts, not the people, who are responsible for making "new dimensions of freedom ... apparent to new generations," for providing "formal discourse" on social issues, and for ensuring "neutral discussions, without scornful or disparaging commentary."

Nowhere is the majority's extravagant conception of judicial supremacy more evident than in its description—and dismissal—of the public debate regarding same-sex marriage. Yes, the majority concedes, on one side are thousands of years of human history in every society known to have populated the planet. But on the other side, there has been "extensive litigation," "many thoughtful District Court decisions," "countless studies, papers, books, and other popular and scholarly writings," and "more than 100" amicus briefs in these cases alone. What would be the point of allowing the democratic process to go on? It is high time for the Court to decide the meaning of marriage, based on five lawyers' "better informed understanding" of "a liberty that remains urgent in our own era." The answer is surely there in one of those amicus briefs or studies.

Those who founded our country would not recognize the majority's conception of the judicial role. They after all risked their lives and fortunes for the precious right to govern themselves. They would never have imagined yielding that right on a question of social policy to unaccountable and unelected judges. . . .

The Court's accumulation of power does not occur in a vacuum. It comes at the expense of the people. And they know it. Here and abroad, people are in the midst of a serious and thoughtful public debate on the issue of same-sex marriage. They see voters carefully considering same-sex marriage, casting ballots in favor or opposed, and sometimes changing their minds. They see political leaders similarly reexamining their positions, and either reversing course or explaining adherence to old convictions confirmed anew. They see governments and businesses modifying policies and practices with respect to same-sex couples, and participating actively in the civic discourse. They see countries overseas democratically accepting profound social change, or declining to do so. This deliberative process is making people take seriously questions that they may not have even regarded as questions before.

When decisions are reached through democratic means, some people will inevitably be disappointed with the results. But those whose views do not prevail at least know that they have had their say, and accordingly are—in the tradition of our political culture—reconciled to the result of a fair and honest debate. In addition, they can gear up to raise the issue later, hoping to persuade enough on the winning side to think again. "That is exactly how our system of government is supposed to work." *Post* (SCALIA, J., dissenting).

But today the Court puts a stop to all that. By deciding this question under the Constitution, the Court removes it from the realm of democratic decision. There will be consequences to shutting down the political process on an issue of such profound public significance. Closing debate tends to close minds. People denied a voice are less likely to accept the ruling of a court on an issue that does not seem to be the sort of thing courts usually decide. As a thoughtful commentator observed about another issue, "The political process was moving . . . , not swiftly enough for advocates of quick, complete change, but majoritarian institutions were listening and acting.

Heavy-handed judicial intervention was difficult to justify and appears to have provoked, not resolved, conflict." Ginsburg, *Some Thoughts on Autonomy and Equality in Relation to* Roe v. Wade, 63 N.C. L. Rev. 375, 385–386 (1985). Indeed, however heartened the proponents of same-sex marriage might be on this day, it is worth acknowledging what they have lost, and lost forever: the opportunity to win the true acceptance that comes from persuading their fellow citizens of the justice of their cause. And they lose this just when the winds of change were freshening at their backs.

Federal courts are blunt instruments when it comes to creating rights. They have constitutional power only to resolve concrete cases or controversies; they do not have the flexibility of legislatures to address concerns of parties not before the court or to anticipate problems that may arise from the exercise of a new right. Today's decision, for example, creates serious questions about religious liberty. Many good and decent people oppose same-sex marriage as a tenet of faith, and their freedom to exercise religion is—unlike the right imagined by the majority—actually spelled out in the Constitution. Amdt. 1.

Respect for sincere religious conviction has led voters and legislators in every State that has adopted same-sex marriage democratically to include accommodations for religious practice. The majority's decision imposing same-sex marriage cannot, of course, create any such accommodations. The majority graciously suggests that religious believers may continue to "advocate" and "teach" their views of marriage. The First Amendment guarantees, however, the freedom to "exercise " religion. Ominously, that is not a word the majority uses. . . .

In the face of all this, a much different view of the Court's role is possible. That view is more modest and restrained. It is more skeptical that the legal abilities of judges also reflect insight into moral and philosophical issues. It is more sensitive to the fact that judges are unelected and unaccountable, and that the legitimacy of their power depends on confining it to the exercise of legal judgment. It is more attuned to the lessons of history, and what it has meant for the country and Court when Justices have exceeded their proper bounds. And it is less pretentious than to suppose that while people around the world have viewed an institution in a particular way for thousands of years, the present generation and the present Court are the ones chosen to burst the bonds of that history and tradition.

* * *

If you are among the many Americans—of whatever sexual orientation—who favor expanding same-sex marriage, by all means celebrate today's decision. Celebrate the achievement of a desired goal. Celebrate the opportunity for a new expression of commitment to a partner. Celebrate the availability of new benefits. But do not celebrate the Constitution. It had nothing to do with it.

■ JUSTICE SCALIA, with whom JUSTICE THOMAS joins, dissenting.

. . . [I]t is not of special importance to me what the law says about marriage. It is of overwhelming importance, however, who it is that rules me. Today's decree says that my Ruler, and the Ruler of 320 million Americans coast-to-coast, is a majority of the nine lawyers on the Supreme Court. The opinion in these cases is the furthest extension in fact—and the furthest extension one can even imagine—of the Court's claimed power to create "liberties" that the Constitution and its Amendments neglect to mention. This practice of constitutional revision by an unelected committee of nine, always accompanied (as it is today) by extravagant praise of liberty, robs the People of the most important liberty they asserted in the Declaration of Independence and won in the Revolution of 1776: the freedom to govern themselves.

I

Until the courts put a stop to it, public debate over same-sex marriage displayed American democracy at its best. Individuals on both sides of the issue passionately, but respectfully, attempted to persuade their fellow citizens to accept their views. Americans considered the arguments and put the question to a vote. The electorates of 11 States, either directly or through their representatives, chose to expand the traditional definition of marriage. Many more decided not to. Win or lose, advocates for both sides continued pressing their cases, secure in the knowledge that an electoral loss can be negated by a later electoral win. That is exactly how our system of government is supposed to work.

The Constitution places some constraints on self-rule—constraints adopted by the People themselves when they ratified the Constitution and its Amendments. Forbidden are laws "impairing the Obligation of Contracts," denying "Full Faith and Credit" to the "public Acts" of other States, prohibiting the free exercise of religion, abridging the freedom of speech, infringing the right to keep and bear arms, authorizing unreasonable searches and seizures, and so forth. Aside from these limitations, those powers "reserved to the States respectively, or to the people" can be exercised as the States or the People desire. These cases ask us to decide whether the Fourteenth Amendment contains a limitation that requires the States to license and recognize marriages between two people of the same sex. Does it remove that issue from the political process?

Of course not. . . . When the Fourteenth Amendment was ratified in 1868, every State limited marriage to one man and one woman, and no one doubted the constitutionality of doing so. That resolves these cases. When it comes to determining the meaning of a vague constitutional provision—such as "due process of law" or "equal protection of the laws"—it is unquestionable that the People who ratified that provision did not understand it to prohibit a practice that remained both universal and uncontroversial in the years after ratification. See *Town of Greece v. Galloway*, 134 S.Ct. 1811, 1818–1819 (2014). We have no basis for striking down a practice that is not expressly prohibited by the Fourteenth Amendment's text, and that bears the endorsement of a long tradition of open, widespread, and unchallenged use dating back to the Amendment's ratification. Since there is no doubt whatever that the People never decided to prohibit the limitation of marriage to opposite-sex couples, the public debate over same-sex marriage must be allowed to continue.

But the Court ends this debate, in an opinion lacking even a thin veneer of law. Buried beneath the mummeries and straining-to-be-memorable passages of the opinion is a candid and startling assertion: No matter what it was the People ratified, the Fourteenth Amendment protects those rights that the Judiciary, in its "reasoned judgment," thinks the Fourteenth Amendment ought to protect. That is so because "[t]he generations that wrote and ratified the Bill of Rights and the Fourteenth Amendment did not presume to know the extent of freedom in all of its dimensions. . . ." One would think that sentence would continue: ". . . and therefore they provided for a means by which the People could amend the Constitution," or perhaps ". . . and therefore they left the creation of additional liberties, such as the freedom to marry someone of the same sex, to the People, through the never-ending process of legislation." But no. What logically follows, in the majority's judge-empowering estimation, is: "and so they entrusted to future generations a charter protecting the right of all persons to enjoy liberty as we learn its meaning." The "we," needless to say, is the nine of us. "History and tradition guide and discipline [our] inquiry but do not set its outer boundaries." Thus, rather than focusing on the People's understanding of "liberty"—at the time of ratification or even today—the majority focuses on four "principles and traditions" that, in the majority's view, prohibit States from defining marriage as an institution consisting of one man and one woman.

This is a naked judicial claim to legislative—indeed, super-legislative—power; a claim fundamentally at odds with our system of government. Except as limited by a constitutional prohibition agreed to by the People, the States are free to adopt whatever laws they like, even those that offend the esteemed Justices' "reasoned judgment." A system of government that makes the People subordinate to a committee of nine unelected lawyers does not deserve to be called a democracy.

Judges are selected precisely for their skill as lawyers; whether they reflect the policy views of a particular constituency is not (or should not be) relevant. Not surprisingly then, the Federal Judiciary is hardly a cross-section of America. Take, for example, this Court, which consists of only nine men and women, all of them successful lawyers who studied at Harvard or Yale Law School. Four of the nine are natives of New York City. Eight of them grew up in east- and west-coast States. Only one hails from the vast expanse in-between. Not a single Southwesterner or even, to tell the truth, a genuine Westerner (California does not count). Not a single evangelical Christian (a group that comprises about one quarter of Americans), or even a Protestant of any denomination. The strikingly unrepresentative character of the body voting on today's social upheaval would be irrelevant if they were functioning as judges, answering the legal question whether the American people had ever ratified a constitutional provision that was understood to proscribe the traditional definition of marriage. But of course the Justices in today's majority are not voting on that basis; they say they are not. And to allow the policy question of same-sex marriage to be considered and resolved by a select, patrician, highly unrepresentative panel of nine is to violate a principle even more fundamental than no taxation without representation: no social transformation without representation.

II

. . . The opinion is couched in a style that is as pretentious as its content is egotistic. It is one thing for separate concurring or dissenting opinions to contain extravagances, even silly extravagances, of thought and expression; it is something else for the official opinion of the Court to do so.[22] Of course the opinion's showy profundities are often profoundly incoherent. "The nature of marriage is that, through its enduring bond, two persons together can find other freedoms, such as expression, intimacy, and spirituality." (Really? Who ever thought that intimacy and spirituality [whatever that means] were freedoms? And if intimacy is, one would

---

[22] If, even as the price to be paid for a fifth vote, I ever joined an opinion for the Court that began: "The Constitution promises liberty to all within its reach, a liberty that includes certain specific rights that allow persons, within a lawful realm, to define and express their identity," I would hide my head in a bag. The Supreme Court of the United States has descended from the disciplined legal reasoning of John Marshall and Joseph Story to the mystical aphorisms of the fortune cookie.

think Freedom of Intimacy is abridged rather than expanded by marriage. Ask the nearest hippie. Expression, sure enough, is a freedom, but anyone in a long-lasting marriage will attest that that happy state constricts, rather than expands, what one can prudently say.) Rights, we are told, can "rise . . . from a better informed understanding of how constitutional imperatives define a liberty that remains urgent in our own era." (Huh? How can a better informed understanding of how constitutional imperatives [whatever that means] define [whatever that means] an urgent liberty [never mind], give birth to a right?) And we are told that, "[i]n any particular case," either the Equal Protection or Due Process Clause "may be thought to capture the essence of [a] right in a more accurate and comprehensive way," than the other, "even as the two Clauses may converge in the identification and definition of the right." (What say? What possible "essence" does substantive due process "capture" in an "accurate and comprehensive way"? It stands for nothing whatever, except those freedoms and entitlements that this Court really likes. And the Equal Protection Clause, as employed today, identifies nothing except a difference in treatment that this Court really dislikes. Hardly a distillation of essence. If the opinion is correct that the two clauses "converge in the identification and definition of [a] right," that is only because the majority's likes and dislikes are predictably compatible.) I could go on. The world does not expect logic and precision in poetry or inspirational pop-philosophy; it demands them in the law. The stuff contained in today's opinion has to diminish this Court's reputation for clear thinking and sober analysis. . . .

With each decision of ours that takes from the People a question properly left to them—with each decision that is unabashedly based not on law, but on the "reasoned judgment" of a bare majority of this Court—we move one step closer to being reminded of our impotence.

■ JUSTICE THOMAS, with whom JUSTICE SCALIA joins, dissenting.

. . .

II

Even if the doctrine of substantive due process were somehow defensible—it is not—petitioners still would not have a claim. To invoke the protection of the Due Process Clause at all—whether under a theory of "substantive" or "procedural" due process—a party must first identify a deprivation of "life, liberty, or property." The majority claims these state laws deprive petitioners of "liberty," but the concept of "liberty" it conjures up bears no resemblance to any plausible meaning of that word as it is used in the Due Process Clauses.

A

As used in the Due Process Clauses, "liberty" most likely refers to "the power of locomotion, of changing situation, or removing one's person to whatsoever place one's own inclination may direct; without imprisonment or restraint, unless by due course of law." 1 W. Blackstone, Commentaries on the Laws of England 130 (1769) (Blackstone). That definition is drawn from the historical roots of the Clauses and is consistent with our Constitution's text and structure.

Both of the Constitution's Due Process Clauses reach back to Magna Carta. . . . The Framers drew heavily upon Blackstone's formulation, adopting provisions in early State Constitutions that replicated Magna Carta's language, but were modified to refer specifically to "life, liberty, or property." . . .

. . . When read in light of the history of that formulation, it is hard to see how the "liberty" protected by the Clause could be interpreted to include anything broader than freedom from physical restraint. That was the consistent usage of the time when "liberty" was paired with "life" and "property." And that usage avoids rendering superfluous those protections for "life" and "property."

If the Fifth Amendment uses "liberty" in this narrow sense, then the Fourteenth Amendment likely does as well. See *Hurtado v. California*, 110 U.S. 516, 534–535 (1884). Indeed, this Court has previously commented, "The conclusion is . . . irresistible, that when the same phrase was employed in the Fourteenth Amendment [as was used in the Fifth Amendment], it was used in the same sense and with no greater extent." *Ibid*. And this Court's earliest Fourteenth Amendment decisions appear to interpret the Clause as using "liberty" to mean freedom from physical restraint. In *Munn v. Illinois*, 94 U.S. 113 (1877), for example, the Court recognized the relationship between the two Due Process Clauses and Magna Carta, see id., at 123–124, and implicitly rejected the dissent's argument that " 'liberty' " encompassed "something more . . . than mere freedom from physical restraint or the bounds of a prison," *id.*, at 142 (Field, J., dissenting). That the Court appears to have lost its way in more recent years does not justify deviating from the original meaning of the Clauses.

Even assuming that the "liberty" in those Clauses encompasses something more than freedom from physical restraint, it would not include the types of rights claimed by the majority. In the American legal tradition, liberty has long been understood as individual freedom from governmental action, not as a right to a particular governmental entitlement. . . .

B

Whether we define "liberty" as locomotion or freedom from governmental action more broadly, petitioners have in no way been deprived of it.

Petitioners cannot claim, under the most plausible definition of "liberty," that they have been imprisoned or physically restrained by the States for participating in same-sex relationships. To the contrary, they have been able to cohabitate and raise their children in peace. They have been able to hold civil marriage ceremonies in States that recognize same-sex marriages and private religious ceremonies in all States. They have been able to travel freely around the country, making their homes where they please. Far from being incarcerated or physically restrained, petitioners have been left alone to order their lives as they see fit.

Nor, under the broader definition, can they claim that the States have restricted their ability to go about their daily lives as they would be able to absent governmental restrictions. Petitioners do not ask this Court to order the States to stop restricting their ability to enter same-sex relationships, to engage in intimate behavior, to make vows to their partners in public ceremonies, to engage in religious wedding ceremonies, to hold themselves òut as married, or to raise children. The States have imposed no such restrictions. Nor have the States prevented petitioners from approximating a number of incidents of marriage through private legal means, such as wills, trusts, and powers of attorney. . . .

To the extent that the Framers would have recognized a natural right to marriage that fell within the broader definition of liberty, it would not have included a right to governmental recognition and benefits. Instead, it would have included a right to engage in the very same activities that petitioners have been left free to engage in—making vows, holding religious ceremonies celebrating those vows, raising children, and otherwise enjoying the society of one's spouse—without governmental interference. At the founding, such conduct was understood to predate government, not to flow from it. As Locke had explained many years earlier, "The first society was between man and wife, which gave beginning to that between parents and children." Locke § 77, at 39; see also J. Wilson, Lectures on Law, in 2 Collected Works of James Wilson 1068 (K. Hall and M. Hall eds. 2007) (concluding "that to the institution of marriage the true origin of society must be traced"). Petitioners misunderstand the institution of marriage when they say that it would "mean little" absent governmental recognition.

Petitioners' misconception of liberty carries over into their discussion of our precedents identifying a right to marry, not one of which has expanded the concept of "liberty" beyond the concept of negative liberty. Those precedents all involved absolute prohibitions on private actions associated with marriage. *Loving*, for example, involved a couple who was criminally prosecuted for marrying in the District of Columbia and cohabiting in Virginia. They were each sentenced to a year of imprisonment, suspended for a term of 25 years on the condition that they not reenter the Commonwealth together during that time. In a similar vein, *Zablocki* involved a man who was prohibited, on pain of criminal penalty, from "marry[ing] in Wisconsin or elsewhere" because of his outstanding child-support obligations. And *Turner v. Safley*, 482 U.S. 78 (1987), involved state inmates who were prohibited from entering marriages without the permission of the superintendent of the prison, permission that could not be granted absent compelling reasons. In none of those cases were individuals denied solely governmental recognition and benefits associated with marriage.

In a concession to petitioners' misconception of liberty, the majority characterizes petitioners' suit as a quest to "find . . . liberty by marrying someone of the same sex and having their marriages deemed lawful on the same terms and conditions as marriages between persons of the opposite sex." But "liberty" is not lost, nor can it be found in the way petitioners seek. As a philosophical matter, liberty is only freedom from governmental action, not an entitlement to governmental benefits. And as a constitutional matter, it is likely even narrower than that, encompassing only freedom from physical restraint and imprisonment. The majority's "better informed understanding of how constitutional imperatives define . . . liberty"—better informed, we must assume, than that of the people who ratified the Fourteenth Amendment—runs headlong into the reality that our Constitution is a "collection of 'Thou shalt nots,'" *Reid v. Covert*, 354 U.S. 1, 9 (1957) (plurality opinion), not "Thou shalt provides."

IV

Perhaps recognizing that these cases do not actually involve liberty as it has been understood, the majority goes to great lengths to assert that its decision will advance the "dignity" of same-sex couples.[8] The flaw in that reasoning, of course, is

---

8   The majority also suggests that marriage confers "nobility" on individuals. I am unsure what that means. People may choose to marry or not to marry. The decision to do so does not make one person more "noble" than another. And the suggestion that Americans who choose not to marry are inferior to those who decide to enter such relationships is specious.

that the Constitution contains no "dignity" Clause, and even if it did, the government would be incapable of bestowing dignity.

Human dignity has long been understood in this country to be innate. When the Framers proclaimed in the Declaration of Independence that "all men are created equal" and "endowed by their Creator with certain unalienable Rights," they referred to a vision of mankind in which all humans are created in the image of God and therefore of inherent worth. That vision is the foundation upon which this Nation was built.

The corollary of that principle is that human dignity cannot be taken away by the government. Slaves did not lose their dignity (any more than they lost their humanity) because the government allowed them to be enslaved. Those held in internment camps did not lose their dignity because the government confined them. And those denied governmental benefits certainly do not lose their dignity because the government denies them those benefits. The government cannot bestow dignity, and it cannot take it away.

The majority's musings are thus deeply misguided, but at least those musings can have no effect on the dignity of the persons the majority demeans. Its mischaracterization of the arguments presented by the States and their amici can have no effect on the dignity of those litigants. Its rejection of laws preserving the traditional definition of marriage can have no effect on the dignity of the people who voted for them. Its invalidation of those laws can have no effect on the dignity of the people who continue to adhere to the traditional definition of marriage. And its disdain for the understandings of liberty and dignity upon which this Nation was founded can have no effect on the dignity of Americans who continue to believe in them.

* * *

Our Constitution—like the Declaration of Independence before it—was predicated on a simple truth: One's liberty, not to mention one's dignity, was something to be shielded from—not provided by—the State. Today's decision casts that truth aside. In its haste to reach a desired result, the majority misapplies a clause focused on "due process" to afford substantive rights, disregards the most plausible understanding of the "liberty" protected by that clause, and distorts the principles on which this Nation was founded. Its decision will have inestimable consequences for our Constitution and our society.

■ JUSTICE ALITO, with whom JUSTICE SCALIA and JUSTICE THOMAS join, dissenting.

I

. . . To prevent five unelected Justices from imposing their personal vision of liberty upon the American people, the Court has held that "liberty" under the Due Process Clause should be understood to protect only those rights that are " 'deeply rooted in this Nation's history and tradition.' " *Glucksberg*, at 720–721 (1997). And it is beyond dispute that the right to same-sex marriage is not among those rights. . . .

For today's majority, it does not matter that the right to same-sex marriage lacks deep roots or even that it is contrary to long-established tradition. The Justices in the majority claim the authority to confer constitutional protection upon that right simply because they believe that it is fundamental.

II

Attempting to circumvent the problem presented by the newness of the right found in these cases, the majority claims that the issue is the right to equal treatment. Noting that marriage is a fundamental right, the majority argues that a State has no valid reason for denying that right to same-sex couples. This reasoning is dependent upon a particular understanding of the purpose of civil marriage. Although the Court expresses the point in loftier terms, its argument is that the fundamental purpose of marriage is to promote the well-being of those who choose to marry. Marriage provides emotional fulfillment and the promise of support in times of need. And by benefiting persons who choose to wed, marriage indirectly benefits society because persons who live in stable, fulfilling, and supportive relationships make better citizens. It is for these reasons, the argument goes, that States encourage and formalize marriage, confer special benefits on married persons, and also impose some special obligations. This understanding of the States' reasons for recognizing marriage enables the majority to argue that same-sex marriage serves the States' objectives in the same way as opposite-sex marriage.

This understanding of marriage, which focuses almost entirely on the happiness of persons who choose to marry, is shared by many people today, but it is not the traditional one. For millennia, marriage was inextricably linked to the one thing that only an opposite-sex couple can do: procreate.

Adherents to different schools of philosophy use different terms to explain why society should formalize marriage and attach special benefits and obligations to persons who marry. Here, the States defending their adherence to the traditional understanding of marriage have explained their position using the pragmatic vocabulary that characterizes most American political discourse. Their basic argument is that States formalize and promote marriage, unlike other fulfilling human relationships, in order to encourage potentially procreative conduct to take place within a lasting unit that has long been thought to provide the best atmosphere for raising children. They thus argue that there are reasonable secular grounds for restricting marriage to opposite-sex couples.

If this traditional understanding of the purpose of marriage does not ring true to all ears today, that is probably because the tie between marriage and procreation has frayed. Today, for instance, more than 40% of all children in this country are born to unmarried women. This development undoubtedly is both a cause and a result of changes in our society's understanding of marriage.

While, for many, the attributes of marriage in 21st-century America have changed, those States that do not want to recognize same-sex marriage have not yet given up on the traditional understanding. They worry that by officially abandoning the older understanding, they may contribute to marriage's further decay. It is far beyond the outer reaches of this Court's authority to say that a State may not adhere to the understanding of marriage that has long prevailed, not just in this country and others with similar cultural roots, but also in a great variety of countries and cultures all around the globe.

As I wrote in *Windsor*:

"The family is an ancient and universal human institution. Family structure reflects the characteristics of a civilization, and changes in family structure and in the popular understanding of marriage and the family can have profound effects. Past changes in the understanding of marriage—for example, the gradual ascendance of the idea that romantic love is a prerequisite to marriage—have had far-reaching consequences. But the process by which such consequences come about is complex, involving the interaction of numerous factors, and tends to occur over an extended period of time.

"We can expect something similar to take place if same-sex marriage becomes widely accepted. The long-term consequences of this change are not now known and are unlikely to be ascertainable for some time to come. There are those who think that allowing same-sex marriage will seriously undermine the institution of marriage. Others think that recognition of same-sex marriage will fortify a now-shaky institution.

"At present, no one—including social scientists, philosophers, and historians—can predict with any certainty what the long-term ramifications of widespread acceptance of same-sex marriage will be. And judges are certainly not equipped to make such an assessment. The Members of this Court have the authority and the responsibility to interpret and apply the Constitution. Thus, if the Constitution contained a provision guaranteeing the right to marry a person of the same sex, it would be our duty to enforce that right. But the Constitution simply does not speak to the issue of same-sex marriage. In our system of government, ultimate sovereignty rests with the people, and the people have the right to control their own destiny. Any change on a question so fundamental should be made by the people through their elected officials." 133 S.Ct., at 2715–2716 (dissenting opinion).

III

Today's decision usurps the constitutional right of the people to decide whether to keep or alter the traditional understanding of marriage. The decision will also have other important consequences.

It will be used to vilify Americans who are unwilling to assent to the new orthodoxy. In the course of its opinion, the majority compares traditional marriage laws to laws that denied equal treatment for African-Americans and women. The implications of this analogy will be exploited by those who are determined to stamp out every vestige of dissent.

Perhaps recognizing how its reasoning may be used, the majority attempts, toward the end of its opinion, to reassure those who oppose same-sex marriage that their rights of conscience will be protected. We will soon see whether this proves to be true. I assume that those who cling to old beliefs will be able to whisper their thoughts in the recesses of their homes, but if they repeat those views in public, they will risk being labeled as bigots and treated as such by governments, employers, and schools.

The system of federalism established by our Constitution provides a way for people with different beliefs to live together in a single nation. If the issue of same-sex marriage had been left to the people of the States, it is likely that some States would recognize same-sex marriage and others would not. It is also possible that some States would tie recognition to protection for conscience rights. The majority today makes that impossible. By imposing its own views on the entire country, the majority facilitates the marginalization of the many Americans who have traditional ideas. Recalling the harsh treatment of gays and lesbians in the past, some may think that turnabout is fair play. But if that sentiment prevails, the Nation will experience bitter and lasting wounds.

Today's decision will also have a fundamental effect on this Court and its ability to uphold the rule of law. If a bare majority of Justices can invent a new right and impose that right on the rest of the country, the only real limit on what future majorities will be able to do is their own sense of what those with political power and cultural influence are willing to tolerate. Even enthusiastic supporters of same-sex marriage should worry about the scope of the power that today's majority claims.

Today's decision shows that decades of attempts to restrain this Court's abuse of its authority have failed. A lesson that some will take from today's decision is that preaching about the proper method of interpreting the Constitution or the virtues of judicial self-restraint and humility cannot compete with the temptation to achieve what is viewed as a noble end by any practicable means. I do not doubt that my colleagues in the majority sincerely see in the Constitution a vision of liberty that happens to coincide with their own. But this sincerity is cause for concern, not comfort. What it evidences is the deep and perhaps irremediable corruption of our legal culture's conception of constitutional interpretation.

Most Americans—understandably—will cheer or lament today's decision because of their views on the issue of same-sex marriage. But all Americans, whatever their thinking on that issue, should worry about what the majority's claim of power portends.

NOTES

1.   Recall the five types of constitutional argument (p. 42), and think about whether each one provides more support for the majority or the dissenters: Is there any basis for the majority's decision in the text of the Constitution? In the historical context of the Fourteenth Amendment? In the structure of the constitutional system? Now consider the other types of constitutional argument:

Which way does practice cut? And whose practice matters most? That of the president, who before the decision had announced his support of same-sex marriage? Or of Congress? Or of the states? And how far back should we look? And what about precedent? As you think about precedent, remember not only the substantive due process precedents but also the "fundamental interests" strand of equal protection case law. See p. 1474. And remember *Windsor*—which side, or sides, does it support?

What about policy? To what should the justices look to decide the policy question— their own moral judgments, their perceptions of society's moral judgments, or their perceptions of empirical evidence about whether there are differences between homosexual and heterosexual couples? Are any of these considerations out of bounds? Why? As you think about policy, remember that policy arguments can happen at multiple levels: there is the level of the specific policy (i.e., what is the best policy on this question?), and also the meta-level or institutional level (i.e., who should decide the policy on this question?).

Of these five arguments—text, historical context, structure, practice and precedent, and policy—which ones most strongly support the majority and which ones most strongly support the dissent?

2.   Justice Alito's dissent argues that a majority of the justices chose one concept of the meaning and purposes of marriage, while a majority of the states chose a different concept. How are the two concepts of marriage different? Does the Constitution lock in the traditional concept of marriage and make it the basis for government decisions in the United States? Should it be understood as requiring government actors to have one concept of marriage in 1868, and a different concept of marriage now? If so, how did the constitutional concept of marriage change? Does *Obergefell* lock in a new concept of marriage?

3.   *Obergefell* is the fourth in a series of major gay-rights cases decided by the Court, following *Romer*, *Lawrence*, and *Windsor*. All four were closely divided decisions, and in all four Justice Kennedy wrote the majority opinion. The more conservative justices weighed in with many dissenting opinions, ten in all. But surprisingly, none of the more liberal justices (i.e., Breyer, Ginsburg, Kagan, Sotomayor, Stevens, Souter) ever added a concurring opinion. Why? If they had written, what kinds of arguments might they have advanced, and how would they differ from those advanced by Justice Kennedy?

4.   Ever since *Lochner* and its repudiation by the Supreme Court, the justices have been haunted by the charge that substantive due process is nothing more than the imposition of judicial preferences about what the Constitution should say. In response, justices invoking substantive due process have developed a number of potential limiting principles. One limiting principle, developed most fully in *Glucksberg*, is the requirement that a claimed right, once narrowly defined, must be "deeply rooted in this Nation's history and tradition." Another potential limiting principle is majoritarian preferences. Yet another is a super-strict adherence to precedent, as urged in *Casey*. What position does *Obergefell* adopt on each of these potential limiting principles? Does it find same-sex marriage to be deeply rooted in tradition? Does it rest its decision on "momentum in the democratic process"? Does it manifest super-strict adherence to precedent? If the answer to each of these questions is *no*, does *Obergefell* offer another limiting principle for the scope of substantive due process?

5.   More generally, what do you take away from the substantive due process cases about how to interpret the Constitution? What is the proper method? However you answer that question, how would you justify your choice of method to someone who was critical of it? Would you advise that it be used for every constitution, or is it specific to the U.S. Constitution? What are the demands it makes on judges, in the sense of what it requires them to be good at? What are the method's strengths and weaknesses? Does it lead to any constitutional results you think are dangerous or unwise? If so, are those results a reason to reject your approach? If not—if your constitutional analysis would mirror what you think is good policy—is *that* a reason to reject your approach?

[Assignment 83]

IV. THE FIFTEENTH AMENDMENT

Amend. XV, § 1: The right of citizens of the United States to vote shall not be denied or abridged by the United States or by any State on account of race, color, or previous condition of servitude.

§ 2: The Congress shall have power to enforce this article by appropriate legislation.

In the wake of the Civil War, Congress passed three constitutional amendments, proposing them to the states for ratification. The Thirteenth Amendment abolished slavery (except as punishment for a crime), whether effected by state or private actors. The Fourteenth Amendment acted on the states, demanding that all persons, black and white, equally have their rights and their lives protected. But the rights protected by Section 1 of the Fourteenth Amendment were widely understood to be civil rights, not political rights—and voting was a political right. See p. 1439. Another provision of the Fourteenth Amendment, Section 2, diminished the representation in Congress of states that denied or abridged the right of adult males to vote. That provision was squarely aimed at Southern attempts to deny the vote to the newly freed slaves. But it only *encouraged* the enfranchisement of black males; it did not *require* it. Three years after passing the Fourteenth Amendment, Congress was ready to amend the Constitution again. The Fifteenth Amendment passed Congress in 1869, and pursuant to the requirements of Article V it was submitted to the states for ratification. The required three-fourths majority ratified the amendment in 1870.

But the commitment of the national government to racial equality that was expressed in the Fourteenth and Fifteenth Amendments would not last. After the Compromise of 1877, President Rutherford B. Hayes withdrew federal troops from the South. Abandoned by the national government, the Reconstruction state governments—which relied upon black voters, and included a substantial number of black political leaders—were replaced with governments hostile to the rights of their black citizens. In the 1880s, these new governments began to enact a wave of oppressive Jim Crow laws. See p. 1265. But black citizens in the South continued to vote in large numbers. Not until the 1890s and the first decade of the twentieth century would persons of color in the South be systematically excluded from political participation. In those two decades, states throughout the South began adopting new constitutions:

> The white-supremacy purposes of these new constitutions were not disguised (though the concomitant aim of reducing populist white political influence was). As expressed by the President of the Alabama Convention whose handiwork Jackson Giles would soon challenge, "what is it that we want to do? Why it is within the limits imposed by the Federal Constitution, to establish white supremacy in this State." The resulting 1901 constitution of Alabama offered the most elaborate suffrage requirements that have ever been in force in the United States; going on for pages, they contained almost every qualification for voting ever devised by the mind of man with the exception of a religious qualification: racially-gerrymandered criminal disfranchisement provisions, lengthy residency requirements, a cumulative poll tax of $1.50, along with temporary clauses requiring good character but with grandfather provisions for ex-soldiers and their lineal descendants. This was particularly ironic in Alabama, a state that had long had the most liberal suffrage rules in the nation: universal white manhood suffrage since its admission in 1819 (along with the secret ballot, mandatory population-based apportionment in both houses every six years, relatively easy override of gubernatorial vetoes, and similarly populist provisions) and universal manhood suffrage since 1868.
>
> The effect of these disenfranchising constitutions throughout the South, combined with statutory suffrage restrictions, was immediate and devastating. . . . In Alabama, in 1900 there were 181,471 eligible black voters, but only 3,000 were registered after the new constitutional

provisions took effect. In Virginia, there was a 100% drop—in other words, to zero—in estimated black voter turnout between the Presidential elections of 1900 and 1904. North Carolina managed the same complete elimination of black voter turnout over an eight-year period, between the Presidential elections of 1896 and 1904. This was the legal situation Giles sought to challenge in the only way left, through constitutional litigation.

Richard H. Pildes, *Democracy, Anti-Democracy, and the Canon*, 17 Const. Comm. 295, 302–304 (2000) (quotation marks and citations omitted). The challenge brought by Jackson Giles, a black citizen in Alabama, reached the Court in 1903. Seven years earlier, in *Plessy v. Ferguson* (1896), p. 1338, the Supreme Court had infamously acquiesced in the segregation of transportation facilities. But what would the Court do when confronted with a system of voter disenfranchisement so total? Would the Fifteenth Amendment, ratified within the living memory of the justices, prove to be a dead letter? The answer came in *Giles v. Harris*.

Giles v. Harris

189 U.S. 475 (1903)

■ MR. JUSTICE HOLMES delivered the opinion of the court:

This is a bill in equity brought by a colored man on behalf of himself "and on behalf of more than five thousand negroes, citizens of the county of Montgomery, Alabama, similarly situated and circumstanced as himself," against the board of registrars of that county. The prayer of the bill is in substance that the defendants may be required to enroll upon the voting lists the name of the plaintiff and of all other qualified members of his race who applied for registration before August 1, 1902, and were refused, and that certain sections of the Constitution of Alabama may be declared contrary to the 14th and 15th Amendments of the Constitution of the United States, and void.

The allegations of the bill may be summed up as follows: The plaintiff is subject to none of the disqualifications set forth in the Constitution of Alabama and is entitled to vote—entitled, as the bill plainly means, under the Constitution as it is. He applied in March, 1902, for registration as a voter, and was refused arbitrarily on the ground of his color, together with large numbers of other duly qualified negroes, while all white men were registered. The same thing was done all over the State. Under § 187 of article 8 of the Alabama Constitution, persons registered before January 1, 1903, remain electors for life unless they become disqualified by certain crimes, etc., while after that date severer tests come into play which would exclude, perhaps, a large part of the black race. Therefore by the refusal the plaintiff and the other negroes excluded were deprived, not only of their vote at an election which has taken place since the bill was filed, but of the permanent advantage incident to registration before 1903. The white men generally are registered for good under the easy test, and the black men are likely to be kept out in the future as in the past. This refusal to register the blacks was part of a general scheme to disfranchise them, to which the defendants and the State itself, according to the bill, were parties. The defendants accepted their office for the purpose of carrying out the scheme. The part taken by the State, that is, by the white population which framed the Constitution, consisted in shaping that instrument so as to give opportunity and effect to the wholesale fraud which has been practiced. . . .

By § 181, after January 1, 1903, only the following persons are entitled to register: First. Those who can read and write any article of the Constitution of the United States in the English language, and who either are physically unable to work or have been regularly engaged in some lawful business for the greater part of the last twelve months, and those who are unable to read and write solely because physically disabled. Second. Owners or husbands of owners of 40 acres of land in the state, upon which they reside, and owners or husbands of owners of real or personal estate in the state assessed for taxation at $300 or more, if the taxes have been paid, unless under contest. By § 183 only persons qualified as electors can take part in any method of party action. . . . This, in brief, is the system which the plaintiff asks to have declared void.

Perhaps it should be added to the foregoing statement that the bill was filed in September, 1902, and alleged the plaintiff's desire to vote at an election coming off in November. This election has gone by, so that it is impossible to give specific relief with regard to that. But we are not prepared to dismiss the bill or the appeal on that ground, because to be enabled to cast a vote in that election is not . . . the whole object of the bill. It is not even the principal object of the relief sought by the plaintiff. The principal object of that is to obtain the permanent advantages of registration as of a date before 1903. . . .

It seems to us impossible to grant the equitable relief which is asked. It will be observed, in the first place, that the language of [the statute giving jurisdiction over the plaintiff's claim] does not extend the sphere of equitable jurisdiction in respect of what shall be held an appropriate subject-matter for that kind of relief. The words are, "shall be liable to the party injured in an action at law, suit in equity, or other proper proceeding for redress." They allow a suit in equity only when that is the proper proceeding for redress, and they refer to existing standards to determine what is a proper proceeding. The traditional limits of proceedings in equity have not embraced a remedy for political wrongs. *Green v. Mills*, 69 F. 852 (4th Cir. 1895). But we cannot forget that we are dealing with a new and extraordinary situation, and we are unwilling to stop short of the final considerations which seem to us to dispose of the case.

The difficulties which we cannot overcome are two, and the first is this: The plaintiff alleges that the whole registration scheme of the Alabama Constitution is a fraud upon the Constitution of the United States, and asks us to declare it void. But, of course, he could not maintain a bill for a mere declaration in the air. He does not try to do so, but asks to be registered as a party qualified under the void instrument. If, then, we accept the conclusion which it is the chief purpose of the bill to maintain, how can we make the court a party to the unlawful scheme by accepting it and adding another voter to its fraudulent lists? If a white man came here on the same general allegations, admitting his sympathy with the plan, but alleging some special prejudice that had kept him off the list, we hardly should think it necessary to meet him with a reasoned answer. But the relief cannot be varied because we think that in the future the particular plaintiff is likely to try to overthrow the scheme. If we accept the plaintiff's allegations for the purposes of his case, he cannot complain. We must accept or reject them. It is impossible simply to shut our eyes, put the plaintiff on the lists, be they honest or fraudulent, and leave the determination of the fundamental question for the future. If we have an opinion that the bill is right on its face, or if we are undecided, we are not at liberty to assume it to be wrong for the purposes of decision. It seems to us that unless we are prepared to say that it is wrong, that all its principal allegations are immaterial, and that the registration plan of the Alabama Constitution is valid, we cannot order the plaintiff's name to be registered. It is not an answer to say that if all the blacks who are qualified according to the letter of the instrument were registered, the fraud would be cured. In the first place, there is no probability that any way now is open by which more than a few could be registered; but, if all could be, the difficulty would not be overcome. If the sections of the Constitution concerning registration were illegal in their inception, it would be a new doctrine in constitutional law that the original invalidity could be cured by an administration which defeated their intent. We express no opinion as to the alleged fact of their unconstitutionality beyond saying that we are not willing to assume that they are valid, in the face of the allegations and main object of the bill, for the purpose of granting the relief which it was necessary to pray in order that that object should be secured.

The other difficulty is of a different sort, and strikingly reinforces the argument that equity cannot undertake now, any more than it has in the past, to enforce political rights. . . . In determining whether a court of equity can take jurisdiction, one of the first questions is what it can do to enforce any order that it may make. This is alleged to be the conspiracy of a State, although the State is not and could not be made a party to the bill. *Hans v. Louisiana*, 134 U.S. 1 (1890). The circuit court has no constitutional power to control its action by any direct means. And if we leave the state out of consideration, the court has as little practical power to deal with the people of the state in a body. The bill imports that the great mass of the white population intends to keep the blacks from voting. To meet such an intent something more than ordering the plaintiff's name to be inscribed upon the lists of 1902 will be needed. If the conspiracy and the intent exist, a name on a piece of paper will not defeat them. Unless we are prepared to supervise the voting in that State by officers of the court, it seems to us that all that the plaintiff could get from equity would be an empty form. Apart from damages to the individual, relief from a great political wrong, if done, as alleged, by the people of a state and the state itself, must be given by them or by the legislative and political department of the government of the United States.

■ MR. JUSTICE BREWER dissenting:

I am unable to concur in either the opinion or judgment in this case. The single question is whether the circuit court of the United States had jurisdiction. Accepting the statement of facts in the opinion of the majority as sufficiently full, it appears that the plaintiff was entitled to a place on the permanent registry and was denied it by the defendants, the board of registrars in the county in which he lived. No one was allowed to vote who was not registered. He desired to vote at the coming election for representative in Congress. He was deprived of that right by the action of the defendants. Has the circuit court jurisdiction to redress such wrong? It is conceded that, because of the permanence of the registry, the appeal cannot be dismissed under *Mills v. Green*, 159 U.S. 651 (1895) *[denying an injunction against an elections supervisor because the election in which the plaintiff wanted to vote was already past—Editors]*, for, if registered on the permanent registry, the plaintiff can vote at all future elections. . . .

Neither can I assent to the proposition that the case presented by the plaintiff's bill is not strictly a legal one and entitling a party to a judicial hearing and decision.

He alleges that he is a citizen of Alabama, entitled to vote; that he desired to vote at an election for representative in Congress; that without registration he could not vote, and that registration was wrongfully denied him by the defendants. That many others were similarly treated does not destroy his rights or deprive him or relief in the courts. That such relief will be given has been again and again affirmed in both national and state courts. . . .

■ [The dissenting opinion of JUSTICE HARLAN is omitted. JUSTICE BROWN also recorded his dissent from the judgment of the Court.]

NOTES

1.   Given the procedural posture of the case, the Court in *Giles* accepts the allegations of the complaint as true. It nevertheless holds that no relief is possible two grounds: first, ordering the relief sought would merely further the alleged fraudulent overall scheme by increasing voter participation in it; and second, the Court is powerless to remedy the alleged fraud because of its size and the difficulty of fashioning relief without the courts essentially taking over the management of elections in Alabama. Was the Court abdicating the enforcement of constitutional rights? Can a fraud be "too big to fail" under the Constitution? The effect of the decision could hardly have been more momentous: "*Giles* permit[ted] the virtual elimination of black citizens from political participation in the South." Pildes, 17 Const. Comm. at 297. What should the Court have done instead? What remedy should it have been willing to grant after trial? (On equitable remedies, see p. 1370.)

2.   The author of *Giles* was Justice Oliver Wendell Holmes, Jr. Twenty-four years later, he was the author of the Court's opinion in *Nixon v. Herndon*, 273 U.S. 536 (1927), an opinion that began this way:

> This is an action against the Judges of Elections for refusing to permit the plaintiff to vote at a primary election in Texas. It lays the damages at five thousand dollars. The petition alleges that the plaintiff is a negro, a citizen of the United States and of Texas and a resident of El Paso, and in every way qualified to vote, as set forth in detail, except that the statute to be mentioned interferes with his right. . . .

In *Nixon v. Herndon*, the Court reversed a district court's dismissal of the claim, and allowed the plaintiff to continue his suit for $5,000. (Or $3,000; different filings had different amounts.) Holmes distinguished *Giles*, seemingly on the ground that it involved equitable relief and not a suit for damages. "The objection that the subject-matter of the suit is political," Holmes wrote in *Nixon v. Herndon*, "is little more than a play upon words. Of course the petition concerns political action but it alleges and seeks to recover for private damage." And what was the constitutional basis for finding that the plaintiff could not be excluded because of race from the Democratic primary? Holmes wrote: "We find it unnecessary to consider the Fifteenth Amendment, because it seems to us hard to imagine a more direct and obvious infringement of the Fourteenth. That Amendment, while it applies to all, was passed, as we know, with a special intent to protect the blacks from discrimination against them. *Slaughter House Cases*, 83 U.S. (16 Wall.) 36 (1870); *Strauder v. West Virginia*, 100 U.S. 303 (1880)."

What lessons should be taken from *Giles v. Harris* and *Nixon v. Herndon* when they are read together? Are the cases consistent, with the Court allowing claims for damages but denying claims for equitable relief because plaintiffs have an adequate remedy at law? Does that conclusion require the assumption that the *Giles* Court would have approved of damages awards for tens of thousands of disenfranchised black voters in Alabama? But what damages would Giles be likely to get from a white jury? And why did Holmes choose the Fourteenth Amendment as the basis for the decision, instead of the more directly on point Fifteenth Amendment? It was surely not because he was a Fourteenth Amendment maximalist. (Two months after *Nixon v. Herndon*, in his opinion for the Court in *Buck v. Bell*, Holmes would describe the Equal Protection Clause as "the usual last resort of constitutional arguments.") What really does explain the difference between *Giles v. Harris* and *Nixon v. Herndon*? The Constitution had not changed. Had the Court? Had the country? What are the lessons for constitutional interpretation? For contrasting assessments of Holmes's life and work, see Albert W. Alschuler, LAW WITHOUT VALUES: THE LIFE, WORK, AND LEGACY OF JUSTICE HOLMES (2002); and THE ESSENTIAL HOLMES (Richard A. Posner ed., 1997).

Shaw v. Reno

509 U.S. 630 (1993)

■ JUSTICE O'CONNOR delivered the opinion of the Court.

This case involves two of the most complex and sensitive issues this Court has faced in recent years: the meaning of the constitutional "right" to vote, and the propriety of race-based state legislation designed to benefit members of historically disadvantaged racial minority groups. As a result of the 1990 census, North Carolina . . . enacted a reapportionment plan that included one majority-black congressional district. After the Attorney General of the United States objected to the plan, the General Assembly passed new legislation creating a second majority-black district. Appellants allege that the revised plan . . . constitutes an unconstitutional racial gerrymander. The question before us is whether appellants have stated a cognizable claim.

I

The voting age population of North Carolina is approximately 78% white, 20% black, and 1% Native American; the remaining 1% is predominantly Asian. The black population is relatively dispersed; blacks constitute a majority of the general population in only 5 of the State's 100 counties. . . .

The first of the two majority-black districts contained in the revised plan, District 1, is somewhat hook shaped. . . . District 1 has been compared to a "Rorschach ink-blot test," and a "bug splattered on a windshield."

The second majority-black district, District 12, is even more unusually shaped. It is approximately 160 miles long and, for much of its length, no wider than the I– 85 corridor. It winds in snakelike fashion through tobacco country, financial centers, and manufacturing areas "until it gobbles in enough enclaves of black neighborhoods." . . . Of the 10 counties through which District 12 passes, 5 are cut into 3 different districts; even towns are divided. At one point the district remains contiguous only because it intersects at a single point with two other districts before crossing over them. . . .

Appellants contended that the General Assembly's revised reapportionment plan violated several provisions of the United States Constitution, including the Fourteenth Amendment. They alleged that the General Assembly deliberately "create[d] two Congressional Districts in which a majority of black voters was concentrated arbitrarily—without regard to any other considerations, such as compactness, contiguousness, geographical boundaries, or political subdivisions" with the purpose "to create Congressional Districts along racial lines" and to assure the election of two black representatives to Congress. . . .

The three-judge District Court . . . first took judicial notice of a fact omitted from appellants' complaint: that appellants are white. It rejected the argument that race-conscious redistricting to benefit minority voters is *per se* unconstitutional. The majority also rejected appellants' claim that North Carolina's reapportionment plan was impermissible. . . .

II

. . . Our focus is on appellants' claim that the State engaged in unconstitutional racial gerrymandering. That argument strikes a powerful historical chord: It is unsettling how closely the North Carolina plan resembles the most egregious racial gerrymanders of the past. . . .

[A]ppellants' complaint alleged that the deliberate segregation of voters into separate districts on the basis of race violated their constitutional right to participate in a "color-blind" electoral process.

. . . This Court never has held that race-conscious state decisionmaking is impermissible in *all* circumstances. What appellants object to is redistricting legislation that is so extremely irregular on its face that it rationally can be viewed only as an effort to segregate the races for purposes of voting, without regard for traditional districting principles and without sufficiently compelling justification. For the reasons that follow, we conclude that appellants have stated a claim upon which relief can be granted under the Equal Protection Clause.

III–A

The Equal Protection Clause['s] . . . central purpose is to prevent the States from purposefully discriminating between individuals on the basis of race. *Washington v. Davis*, 426 U.S. 229, 239 (1976). Laws that explicitly distinguish between individuals on racial grounds fall within the core of that prohibition. . . .

Classifications of citizens solely on the basis of race "are by their very nature odious to a free people whose institutions are founded upon the doctrine of equality." They threaten to stigmatize individuals by reason of their membership in a racial group and to incite racial hostility. Accordingly, we have held that the Fourteenth Amendment requires state legislation that expressly distinguishes among citizens because of their race to be narrowly tailored to further a compelling governmental interest.

These principles apply not only to legislation that contains explicit racial distinctions, but also to those "rare" statutes that, although race neutral, are, on their face, "unexplainable on grounds other than race." *Arlington Heights v. Metropolitan Housing Development Corp.*, 429 U.S. 252, 266 (1977). . . .

B

Appellants contend that redistricting legislation that is so bizarre on its face that it is "unexplainable on grounds other than race," *Arlington Heights*, 429 U.S., at 266, demands the same close scrutiny that we give other state laws that classify citizens by race. . . .

Put differently, we believe that reapportionment is one area in which appearances do matter. A reapportionment plan that includes in one district individuals who belong to the same race, but who are otherwise widely separated by geographical and political boundaries, and who may have little in common with one another but the color of their skin, bears an uncomfortable resemblance to political apartheid. It reinforces the perception that members of the same racial group—regardless of their age, education, economic status, or the community in which they live—think alike, share the same political interests, and will prefer the same candidates at the polls. We have rejected such perceptions elsewhere as impermissible racial stereotypes. By perpetuating such notions, a racial gerrymander may exacerbate the very patterns of racial bloc voting that majority-minority districting is sometimes said to counteract.

The message that such districting sends to elected representatives is equally pernicious. . . . [E]lected officials are more likely to believe that their primary obligation is to represent only the members of that group, rather than their constituency as a whole. This is altogether antithetical to our system of representative democracy. . . .

For these reasons, we conclude that a plaintiff challenging a reapportionment statute under the Equal Protection Clause may state a claim by alleging that the legislation, though race-neutral on its face, rationally cannot be understood as anything other than an effort to separate voters into different districts on the basis of race, and that the separation lacks sufficient justification. . . . [W]e express no view as to whether "the intentional creation of majority-minority districts, without more," always gives rise to an equal protection claim. *Post* (WHITE, J., dissenting). We hold only that, on the facts of this case, appellants have stated a claim sufficient to defeat the state appellees' motion to dismiss. . . .

■ JUSTICE WHITE, with whom JUSTICE BLACKMUN and JUSTICE STEVENS join, dissenting.

. . . The grounds for my disagreement with the majority are simply stated: Appellants have not presented a cognizable claim, because they have not alleged a cognizable injury. To date, we have held that only two types of state voting practices could give rise to a constitutional claim. The first involves direct and outright deprivation of the right to vote, for example by means of a poll tax or literacy test. Plainly, this variety is not implicated by appellants' allegations and need not detain us further. The second type of unconstitutional practice is that which "affects the political strength of various groups," *Mobile v. Bolden*, 446 U.S. 55, 83 (1980) (STEVENS, J., concurring in judgment), in violation of the Equal Protection Clause. As for this latter category, we have insisted that members of the political or racial group demonstrate that the challenged action have the intent and effect of unduly diminishing their influence on the political process. . . .

The central explanation has to do with the nature of the redistricting process. As the majority recognizes, "redistricting differs from other kinds of state decision-making in that the legislature always is *aware* of race when it draws district lines, just as it is aware of age, economic status, religious and political persuasion, and a variety of other demographic factors." . . .

Redistricting plans also reflect group interests and inevitably are conceived with partisan aims in mind. To allow judicial interference whenever this occurs would be to invite constant and unmanageable intrusion. Moreover, a group's power to affect the political process does not automatically dissipate by virtue of an electoral loss. Accordingly, we have asked that an identifiable group demonstrate more than mere lack of success at the polls to make out a successful gerrymandering claim. . . .

Because districting inevitably is the expression of interest group politics, . . . the question in gerrymandering cases is "whether a particular group has been unconstitutionally denied its chance to effectively influence the political process." . . .

To distinguish a claim that alleges that the redistricting scheme has discriminatory intent and effect from one that does not has nothing to do with dividing racial classifications between the "benign" and the malicious—an enterprise which, as the majority notes, the Court has treated with skepticism. Rather, the issue is whether the classification based on race discriminates against *anyone* by denying equal access to the political process. . . .

Racial gerrymanders come in various shades: At-large voting schemes; the fragmentation of a minority group among various districts "so that it is a majority in none," otherwise known as "cracking"; the "stacking" of "a large minority population concentration . . . with a larger white population"; and, finally, the "concentration of [minority voters] into districts where they constitute an excessive majority," also called "packing." In each instance, race is consciously utilized by the legislature for electoral purposes; in each instance, we have put the plaintiff challenging the district lines to the burden of demonstrating that the plan was meant to, and did in fact, exclude an identifiable racial group from participation in the political process.

Not so, apparently, when the districting "segregates" by drawing odd-shaped lines. In that case, we are told, such proof no longer is needed. Instead, it is the *State* that must rebut the allegation that race was taken into account, a fact that, together with the legislators' consideration of ethnic, religious, and other group characteristics, I had thought we practically took for granted . . .

The consideration of race in "segregation" cases is no different than in other race-conscious districting; from the standpoint of the affected groups, moreover, the line-drawings all act in similar fashion. A plan that "segregates" being functionally indistinguishable from any of the other varieties of gerrymandering, we should be consistent in what we require from a claimant: proof of discriminatory purpose and effect. . . .

■ JUSTICE STEVENS, dissenting.

For the reasons stated by JUSTICE WHITE, the decision of the District Court should be affirmed. I add these comments to emphasize that the two critical facts in this case are undisputed: First, the shape of District 12 is so bizarre that it must have been drawn for the purpose of either advantaging or disadvantaging a cognizable group of voters; and, second, regardless of that shape, it *was* drawn for the purpose of facilitating the election of a second black representative from North Carolina.

These unarguable facts, which the Court devotes most of its opinion to proving, give rise to three constitutional questions: Does the Constitution impose a requirement of contiguity or compactness on how the States may draw their electoral districts? Does the Equal Protection Clause prevent a State from drawing district boundaries for the purpose of facilitating the election of a member of an identifiable group of voters? And, finally, if the answer to the second question is generally "No," should it be different when the favored group is defined by race? Since I have already written at length about these questions, my negative answer to each can be briefly explained.

The first question is easy. There is no independent constitutional requirement of compactness or contiguity, and the Court's opinion does not suggest otherwise. The existence of bizarre and uncouth district boundaries is powerful evidence of an ulterior purpose. . . . Such evidence will always be useful in cases that lack other evidence of invidious intent. In this case, however, we know what the legislators' purpose was: The North Carolina Legislature drew District 12 to include a majority of African-American voters. . . . Evidence of the district's shape is therefore . . . irrelevant.

As for the second question, I believe that the Equal Protection Clause is violated when the State creates . . . uncouth district boundaries . . . for the sole purpose of making it more difficult for members of a minority group to win an election. The duty to govern impartially is abused when a group with power over the electoral process defines electoral boundaries solely to enhance its own political strength at the expense of any weaker group. That duty, however, is not violated when the majority acts to facilitate the election of a member of a group that lacks such power. . . . The difference between constitutional and unconstitutional gerrymanders has nothing to do with whether they are based on assumptions about the groups they affect, but whether their purpose is . . . to strengthen the unequal distribution of electoral power. . . .

Finally, we must ask whether otherwise permissible redistricting to benefit an underrepresented minority group becomes impermissible when the minority group is defined by its race. The Court today answers this question in the affirmative, and its answer is wrong. If it is permissible to draw boundaries to provide adequate representation for rural voters, for union members, for Hasidic Jews, for Polish Americans, or for Republicans, it necessarily follows that it is permissible to do the same thing for members of the very minority group whose history in the United States gave birth to the Equal Protection Clause. A contrary conclusion could only be described as perverse.

■ [The dissent of JUSTICE SOUTER and the dissent of JUSTICE BLACKMUN are omitted.]

NOTES

1. *Shaw*, like *Nixon v. Herndon*, was decided under the Equal Protection Clause. Is that the right constitutional provision, or should it have been the Fifteenth Amendment? Does it matter which provision it was decided under?

2. In *Giles*, the Court stood by while state legislatures disenfranchised black voters in the name of white supremacy. In *Shaw*, it intervened to *reduce* legislatively authorized black voting power, and it did so in the name of the Reconstruction Amendments. Is that a cruel irony, or the belated redemption of the promise of Reconstruction?

ARTICLES OF CONFEDERATION

Preamble

To all to whom these presents shall come,

We, the undersigned, Delegates of the States affixed to our names, send greeting:

Whereas the Delegates of the United States of America in Congress assembled, did on the fifteenth day of November, in the year of our Lord one thousand seven hundred and seventy-seven, and in the second year of the Independence of America, agree to certain Articles of Confederation and Perpetual Union between the states of New Hamp- shire, Massachusetts Bay, Rhode Island and Providence Plantations, Connecticut, New York, New Jersey, Pennsylvania, Delaware, Maryland, Virginia, North Carolina, South Carolina, and Georgia, in the words following, viz.

ARTICLES OF CONFEDERATION AND PERPETUAL UNION,

between the States of New Hampshire, Massachusetts Bay, Rhode Island and Providence Plantations, Connecticut, New York, New Jersey, Pennsylvania, Delaware, Maryland, Virginia, North Carolina, South Carolina and Georgia.

Article I

The style of this confederacy shall be, "THE UNITED STATES OF AMERICA."

Article II

Each State retains its sovereignty, freedom, and independence, and every power, jurisdiction, and right, which is not by this confederation, expressly delegated to the United States, in Congress assembled.

Article III

The said States hereby severally enter into a firm league of friendship with each other, for their common defence, the security of their liberties, and their mutual and general welfare, binding themselves to assist each other, against all force offered to, or attacks made upon them, or any of them, on account of religion, sovereignty, trade, or any other pretense whatever.

Article IV

§ 1. The better to secure and perpetuate mutual friendship and intercourse among the people of the different States in this Union, the free inhabitants of each of these States, paupers, vagabonds, and fugitives from justice excepted, shall be entitled to all privileges and immunities of free citizens in the several States; and the people of each State shall free ingress and regress to and from any other State, and shall enjoy therein all the privileges of trade and commerce, subject to the same duties, impositions, and restrictions as the inhabitants thereof respectively; provided that such restrictions shall not extend so far as to prevent the removal of property imported into any State, to any other State, of which the owner is an inhabitant; provided also that no imposition, duties or restriction shall be laid by any State, on the property of the United States, or either of them.

§ 2. If any person guilty of, or charged with, treason, felony, or other high misdemeanor in any State, shall flee from justice, and be found in any of the United States, he shall, upon demand of the governor or executive power of the State from which he fled, be delivered up, and removed to the State having jurisdiction of his offence.

§ 3. Full faith and credit shall be given, in each of these States, to the records, acts, and judicial proceedings of the courts and magistrates of every other State.

Article V

§ 1. For the more convenient management of the general interests of the United States, delegates shall be annually appointed in such manner as the legislatures of each State shall direct, to meet in Congress on the first Monday in November, in every year, with a power reserved to each State to recall its delegates, or any of them, at any time within the year, and to send others in their stead, for the remainder of the year.

§ 2. No State shall be represented in Congress by less than two, nor by more than seven members; and no person shall be capable of being a delegate for more than three years, in any term of six years; nor shall any person, being a delegate, be capable of holding any office under the United States, for which he, or another for his benefit, receives any salary, fees or emolument of any kind.

§ 3. Each State shall maintain its own delegates in a meeting of the States, and while they act as members of the committee of these States.

§ 4. In determining questions in the United States in Congress assembled, each State shall have one vote.

§ 5. Freedom of speech and debate in Congress shall not be impeached or questioned in any court or place out of Congress; and the members of Congress shall be protected in their persons from arrests or imprisonments, during the time of their going to and from, and attendance on, Congress, except for treason, felony or breach of the peace.

Article VI

§ 1. No State, without the consent of the United States, in Congress assembled, shall send any embassy to, or receive any embassy from, or enter into any conference, agreement, alliance, or treaty, with any king, prince or State; nor shall any person holding any office of profit or trust under the United States, or any of them, accept of any present, emolument, office, or title of any kind whatever, from any king, prince, or foreign State; nor shall the United States, in Congress assembled, or any of them, grant any title of nobility.

§ 2. No two or more States shall enter into any treaty, confederation, or alliance whatever, between them, without the consent of the United States, in Congress assembled, specifying accurately the purposes for which the same is to be entered into, and how long it shall continue.

§ 3. No State shall lay any imposts or duties which may interfere with any stipulations in treaties, entered into by the United States, in Congress assembled, with any king, prince, or State, in pursuance of any treaties already proposed by Congress to the courts of France and Spain.

§ 4. No vessels of war shall be kept up in time of peace, by any State, except such number only, as shall be deemed necessary by the United States, in Congress assembled, for the defence of such State, or its trade; nor shall any body of forces be kept up, by any State, in time of peace, except such number only as, in the judgment of the United States, in Congress assembled, shall be deemed requisite to garrison the forts necessary for the defence of such State; but every State shall always keep up a well-regulated and disciplined militia, sufficiently armed and accoutred, and shall provide and constantly have ready for use, in public stores, a due number of field-pieces and tents, and a proper quantity of arms, ammunition, and camp equipage.

§ 5. No State shall engage in any war without the consent of the United States, in Congress assembled, unless such State be actually invaded by enemies, or shall have received certain advice of a resolution being formed by some nation of Indians to invade such State, and the danger is so imminent as not to admit of a delay till the United States, in Congress assembled, can be consulted; nor shall any State grant commissions to any ships or vessels of war, nor letters of marque or reprisal, except it be after a declaration of war by the United States, in Congress assembled, and then only against the kingdom or State, and the subjects thereof, against which war has been so declared, and under such regulations as shall be established by the United States, in Congress assembled, unless such State be infested by pirates, in which case vessels of war may be fitted out for that occasion, and kept so long as the danger shall continue, or until the United States, in Congress assembled, shall determine otherwise.

Article VII

When land forces are raised by any State, for the common defence, all officers of, or under the rank of colonel, shall be appointed by the legislature of each State respectively by whom such forces shall be raised, or in such manner as such State shall direct, and all vacancies shall be filled up by the State which first made the appointment.

Article VIII

All charges of war, and all other expenses that shall be incurred for the common defence or general welfare, and allowed by the United States, in Congress assembled, shall be defrayed out of a common treasury, which shall be supplied by the several States, in proportion to the value of all land within each State, granted to, or surveyed for, any person, as such land and the buildings and improvements thereon shall be estimated, according to such mode as the United States, in Congress assembled, shall, from time to time, direct and appoint. The taxes for paying that proportion shall be laid and levied by the authority and direction of the legislatures of the several States, within the time agreed upon by the United States, in Congress assembled.

Article IX

§ 1. The United States, in Congress assembled, shall have the sole and exclusive right and power of determining on peace and war, except in the cases mentioned in the sixth Article, of sending and receiving ambassadors; entering into treaties and alliances, provided that no treaty of commerce shall be made, whereby the legislative power of the respective States shall be restrained from imposing such imposts and duties on foreigners, as their own people are subjected to, or from prohibiting the exportation or importation of any species of goods or commodities whatsoever; of establishing rules for deciding, in all cases, what captures on land or water shall be legal, and in what manner prizes taken by land or naval forces in the service of the United States shall be divided or appropriated; of granting letters of marque and reprisal in times of peace; appointing courts for the trial of piracies and felonies committed on the high seas; and establishing courts for receiving and determining finally appeals in all cases of captures; provided that no member of Congress shall be appointed a judge of any of the said courts.

§ 2. The United States, in Congress assembled, shall also be the last resort on appeal, in all disputes and differences now subsisting, or that hereafter may arise between two or more States concerning boundary, jurisdiction, or any other cause whatever; which authority shall always be exercised in the manner following: Whenever the legislative or executive authority, or lawful agent of any State in controversy with another, shall present a petition to Congress, stating the matter in question, and praying for a hearing, notice thereof shall be given, by order of Congress, to the legislative or executive authority of the other State in controversy, and a day assigned for the appearance of the parties by their lawful agents, who shall then be directed to appoint, by joint consent, commissioners or judges to constitute a court for hearing and determining the matter in question; but if they cannot agree, Congress shall name three persons out of each of the United States, and from the list of such persons each party shall alternately strike out one, the petitioners beginning, until the number shall be reduced to thirteen; and from that number not less than seven, nor more than nine names, as Congress shall direct, shall, in the presence of Congress, be drawn out by lot; and the persons whose names shall be so drawn, or any five of them, shall be commissioners or judges, to hear and finally determine the controversy, so always as a major part of the judges, who shall hear the cause, shall agree in the determination; and if either party shall neglect to attend at the day appointed, without showing reasons which Congress shall judge sufficient, or being present, shall refuse to strike, the Congress shall proceed to nominate three persons out of each State, and the secretary of Congress shall strike in behalf of such party absent or refusing; and the judgment and sentence of the court, to be appointed in the manner before prescribed, shall be final and conclusive; and if any of the parties shall refuse to submit to the authority of such court, or to appear or defend their claim or cause, the court shall nevertheless proceed to pronounce sentence, or judgment, which shall in like manner be final and decisive; the judgment or sentence and other proceedings being in either case transmitted to Congress, and lodged among the acts of Congress, for the security of the parties concerned; provided, that every commissioner, before he sits in judgment, shall take an oath, to be administered by one of the judges of the supreme or superior court of the State where the cause shall be tried, "well and truly to hear and determine the matter in question, according to the best of his judgment, without favour, affection, or hope of reward." Provided, also, that no State shall be deprived of territory for the benefit of the United States.

§ 3. All controversies concerning the private right of soil claimed under different grants of two or more States, whose jurisdictions, as they may respect such lands, and the States which passed such grants are adjusted, the said grants or either of them being at the same time claimed to have originated antecedent to such settlement of jurisdiction, shall, on the petition of either party to the Congress of the

United States, be finally determined, as near as may be, in the same manner as is before prescribed for deciding disputes respecting territorial jurisdiction between different States.

§ 4. The United States, in Congress assembled, shall also have the sole and exclusive right and power of regulating the alloy and value of coin struck by their own authority, or by that of the respective States; fixing the standards of weights and measures throughout the United States; regulating the trade and managing all affairs with the Indians, not members of any of the States; provided that the legislative right of any State, within its own limits, be not infringed or violated; establishing and regulating post offices from one State to another, throughout all the United States, and exacting such postage on the papers passing through the same, as may be requisite to defray the expenses of the said office; appointing all officers of the land forces in the service of the United States, excepting regimental officers; appointing all the officers of the naval forces, and commissioning all officers whatever in the service of the United States; making rules for the government and regulation of the said land and naval forces, and directing their operations.

§ 5. The United States, in Congress assembled, shall have authority to appoint a committee, to sit in the recess of Congress, to be denominated "*A Committee of the States*," and to consist of one delegate from each State; and to appoint such other committees and civil officers as may be necessary for managing the general affairs of the United States under their direction; to appoint one of their number to preside; provided that no person be allowed to serve in the office of president more than one year in any term of three years; to ascertain the necessary sums of money to be raised for the service of the United States, and to appropriate and apply the same for defraying the public expenses; to borrow money, or emit bills on the credit of the United States, transmitting every half year to the respective States an account of the sums of money so borrowed or emitted; to build and equip a navy; to agree upon the number of land forces, and to make requisitions from each State for its quota, in proportion to the number of white inhabitants in such State, which requisition shall be binding; and thereupon the legislature of each State shall appoint the regimental officers, raise the men, and clothe, arm, and equip them in a soldier-like manner, at the expense of the United States; and the officers and men so clothed, armed, and equipped, shall march to the place appointed, and within the time agreed on by the United States, in Congress assembled; but if the United States, in Congress assembled, shall, on consideration of circumstances, judge proper that any State should not raise men, or should raise a smaller number of men than its quota, such extra number shall be raised, officered, clothed, armed, and equipped in the same manner as the quota of such State, unless the Legislature of such State shall judge that such extra number cannot be safely spared out of the same, in which case they shall raise, officer, clothe, arm, and equip, as many of such extra number as they judge can be safely spared, and the officers and men so clothed, armed, and equipped, shall march to the place appointed, and within the time agreed on by the United States in Congress assembled.

§ 6. The United States, in Congress assembled, shall never engage in a war, nor grant letters of marque and reprisal in time of peace, nor enter into any treaties or alliances, nor coin money, nor regulate the value thereof, nor ascertain the sums and expenses necessary for the defence and welfare of the United States, or any of them, nor emit bills, nor borrow money on the credit of the United States, nor appropriate money, nor agree upon the number of vessels of war, to be built or purchased, or the number of land or sea forces to be raised, nor appoint a commander-in-chief of the army or navy, unless nine States assent to the same, nor shall a question on any other point, except for adjourning from day to day, be determined, unless by the votes of the majority of the United States in Congress assembled.

§ 7. The Congress of the United States shall have power to adjourn to any time within the year, and to any place within the United States, so that no period of adjournment be for a longer duration than the space of six months, and shall publish the journal of their proceedings monthly, except such parts thereof relating to treaties, alliances, or military operations, as in their judgment require secrecy; and the yeas and nays of the delegates of each State, on any question, shall be entered on the journal, when it is desired by any delegate; and delegates of a State, or any of them, at his or their request, shall be furnished with a transcript of the said journal, except such parts as are above excepted, to lay before the legislatures of the several States.

Article X

The committee of the States, or any nine of them, shall be authorized to execute, in the recess of Congress, such of the powers of Congress as the United States, in Congress assembled, by the consent of nine States, shall, from time to time, think expedient to vest them with; provided that no power be delegated to the said committee, for the exercise of which, by the articles of confederation, the voice of nine States, in the Congress of the United States assembled, is requisite.

Article XI

Canada acceding to this confederation, and joining in the measures of the United States, shall be admitted into, and entitled to all the advantages of this Union: but no other colony shall be admitted into the same, unless such admission be agreed to by nine States.

Article XII

All bills of credit emitted, moneys borrowed, and debts contracted by or under the authority of Congress, before the assembling of the United States, in pursuance of the present confederation, shall be deemed and considered as a charge against the United States, for payment and satisfaction whereof the said United States and the public faith are hereby solemnly pledged.

Article XIII

Every State shall abide by the determination of the United States, in Congress assembled, on all questions which by this confederation are submitted to them. And the Articles of this Confederation shall be inviolably observed by every State, and the Union shall be perpetual; nor shall any alteration at any time hereafter be made in any of them, unless such alteration be agreed to in a Congress of the United States, and be afterwards confirmed by the legislatures of every State.

And whereas it hath pleased the great Governor of the world to incline the hearts of the legislatures we respectively represent in Congress, to approve of, and to authorize us to ratify the said articles of confederation and perpetual union, Know ye, that we, the undersigned delegates, by virtue of the power and authority to us given for that purpose, do, by these presents, in the name and in behalf of our respective constituents, fully and entirely ratify and confirm each and every of the said articles of confederation and perpetual union, and all and singular the matters and things therein contained. And we do further solemnly plight and engage the faith of our respective constituents, that they shall abide by the determinations of the United States, in Congress assembled, on all questions which by the said confederation are submitted to them; and that the articles thereof shall be inviolably observed by the States we respectively represent, and that the Union shall be perpetual. In witness whereof, we have hereunto set our hands, in Congress.

Done at Philadelphia in the State of Pennsylvania, the 9th day of July, in the year of our Lord 1778, and in the third year of the Independence of America.

INDEX

References are to Pages